PARMA PUBLIC LIBRARY
HILTON, N.Y. 14468

NOT TO BE TAKEN FROM
THIS LIBRARY

Features

Guide to Tabular Presentation *p. x*

Telephone and Internet Contacts *p. xii*

Congressional District Profiles *p. 879*

Guide to Sources of Statistics *p. 896*

Guide to State Statistical Abstracts *p. 913*

Guide to Foreign Statistical Abstracts *p. 917*

Metropolitan and Micropolitan Area Concepts and Components *p. 919*

Index by Subject *p. 974*

Visit us on the Web at
http://www.census.gov/statab/www/

Statistical Abstract of the United States: 2003 123rd Edition

The National Data Book

Issued December 2003

U.S. Department of Commerce
Donald L. Evans,
Secretary

Economics and Statistics Administration
Kathleen B. Cooper,
Under Secretary for Economic Affairs

U.S. CENSUS BUREAU
Charles Louis Kincannon,
Director

SUGGESTED CITATION

U.S. Census Bureau,
*Statistical Abstract of the
United States: 2003*
(123rd Edition)
Washington, DC,
2003

Library of Congress
Card No. 4-18089

ECONOMICS
AND STATISTICS
ADMINISTRATION

**Economics
and Statistics
Administration**

Kathleen B. Cooper,
Under Secretary
for Economic Affairs

U.S. CENSUS BUREAU

Charles Louis Kincannon,
Director

Hermann Habermann,
Deputy Director and
Chief Operating Officer

Vacant,
Principal Associate Director
and Chief Financial Officer

Ted A. Johnson, Associate Director
for Finance and Administration

Walter C. Odom, Chief, Administrative
and Customer Services Division

Acknowledgments

Lars B. Johanson was responsible for the technical supervision and coordination of this volume under the general direction of **Glenn W. King,** Chief, Statistical Compendia Branch. Assisting in the research and analytical phases of assigned sections and in the developmental aspects of new tables were **Rosemary E. Clark, Richard P. Kersey, Stacey M. Lowe,** and **Jean F. Maloney. Catherine Lavender** provided primary editorial assistance. Other editorial assistance was rendered by **Susan Antroinen, Deena Grover, Patricia S. Lancaster, Connie Nadzadi,** and **Barbara Shugart.**

Maps were designed and produced by **Connie Beard** and **Scott Wilcox** of the Cartographic Operations Branch within the Geography Division.

Greg Carroll, Penny Heiston, Patricia Edwards, Shirley Clark, Linda Chen, and **Arlene Butler** of the Administrative and Customer Services Division, **Walter C. Odom,** Chief, provided publications and printing management, graphics design and composition, and editorial review for print and electronic media. General direction and production management were provided by **James R. Clark,** Assistant Chief, and **Susan L. Rappa,** Chief, Publications Services Branch.

The cooperation of many contributors to this volume is gratefully acknowledged. The source note below each table credits the various government and private agencies that have collaborated in furnishing information for the *Statistical Abstract*. In a few instances, contributors have requested that their data be designated as subject to copyright restrictions, as indicated in the source notes to the tables affected. Permission to use copyright material should be obtained directly from the copyright owner.

For sale by Superintendent of Documents, U.S. Government Printing Office
Internet: bookstore.gpo.gov; Phone: toll-free 1-866-512-1800;
DC area 202-512-1800; Fax: 202-512-2250; Mail Stop: SSOP
Washington, DC 20402-0001

ISBN 0-16-042824-6

Preface

The *Statistical Abstract of the United States,* published since 1878, is the standard summary of statistics on the social, political, and economic organization of the United States. It is designed to serve as a convenient volume for statistical reference and as a guide to other statistical publications and sources. The latter function is served by the introductory text to each section, the source note appearing below each table, and Appendix I, which comprises the Guide to Sources of Statistics, the Guide to State Statistical Abstracts, and the Guide to Foreign Statistical Abstracts.

This volume includes a selection of data from many statistical publications, both government and private. Publications cited as sources usually contain additional statistical detail and more comprehensive discussions of definitions and concepts than can be presented here. Data not available in publications issued by the contributing agency but obtained from unpublished records are identified in the source notes as unpublished data. More information on the subjects covered in the tables so noted may generally be obtained from the source.

Except as indicated, figures are for the United States as presently constituted. Although emphasis in the *Statistical Abstract* is primarily given to national data, many tables present data for regions and individual states and a smaller number for metropolitan areas and cities. Appendix II, Metropolitan Area Concepts and Components, presents explanatory text, a complete current listing and population data for metropolitan and micropolitan areas defined as of June 6, 2003. Statistics for the Commonwealth of Puerto Rico and for island areas of the United States are included in many state tables and are supplemented by information in Section 29. Additional information for states, cities, counties, metropolitan areas, and other small units, as well as more historical data are available in various supplements to the *Abstract* (see inside back cover).

Statistics in this edition are generally for the most recent year or period available by summer 2003. Each year over 1,400 tables and charts are reviewed and evaluated; new tables and charts of current interest are added, continuing series are updated, and less timely data are condensed or eliminated. Text notes and appendices are revised as appropriate.

USA Statistics in Brief, a pocket-size pamphlet highlighting many statistical series in the *Abstract* is available. Copies can be obtained free from U.S. Census Bureau, Customer Services, Call Center, Washington, DC 20233 (telephone 301-763-INFO(4636). We attempt to update the pamphlet several times during the year. The latest data can be found on our Web site: <http://www.census.gov/statab/www/brief.html>.

Changes in this edition—This year we have added a new section, which includes selected data for each congressional district, including population, educational attainment, and housing. Tables in Section 31 of the 2002 edition of the *Statistical Abstract,* which includes data obtained from the 2000 Census Sample, have been distributed throughout the various sections. In addition, a number of new tables have been added that contain 2000 Census Sample data. In this edition, Appendix II includes the names of new metropolitan and micropolitan areas along with 2002 population estimates.

We have introduced 72 new tables throughout our core sections. These cover a variety of topics including estimated number of unauthorized immigrants, death rates of Hispanics, people without health insurance, characteristics of missing children, public school systems with alternative schools or programs for at-risk students, characteristics of murder victims of September 11 terror attacks, employed persons using computers at work, percent of U.S. agricultural commodity output exported, as well as ratios of debt payments to family income. For a complete list of new tables see Appendix VI, p. 971.

Statistical Abstract on other media—The *Abstract* is available on the Internet and on CD-ROM. Both versions contain the same material as the book, except for a few copyrighted tables for which we did not receive permission to release in these formats. Our Internet site, <http://www.census.gov/statab/www> contains this 2003 edition plus those from 1995 to 2002 in Adobe Acrobat .pdf format. The CD-ROM version also includes spreadsheet files for each table in the book and links to the Web sites of each source. Many of the spreadsheet files on the CD-ROM contain more historical and/or detailed data than are found in the book.

Statistics for counties and cities—Extensive data for counties can be found in the *County and City Data Book: 2000*. It features 191 data items covering everything from age and agriculture to water use and wholesale trade for all states and counties with U.S. totals for comparison. Also included are 103 data items for cities with population of 25,000 or more. The primary sources are Census 2000 and the 1997 Economic Census. Two tables present 11 data items from Census 2000 for all places and minor civil divisions with a population of 2,500 or more.

This publication, as well as selected rankings, is available on our Internet site at <http://www.census.gov/statab/www/ccdb.html>. Some data items that appear in the book from private sources are not available on the Internet or CD-ROM versions, because we did not receive copyright permission to release the data items in these formats. For a database with over 5,000 county items, check out USA Counties at <http://www.census.gov/statab/www/county.html>.

Statistics for states and metropolitan areas—Extensive data for the states and metropolitan areas of the United States can be found in the *State and Metropolitan Area Data Book: 1997-98*.

This publication minus some data items, as well as selected rankings of the states and metropolitan areas, is available on our Internet site at <http://www.census.gov/statab/www/smadb.html>. The CD-ROM version is also available. See the inside back cover for more information.

Limitations of the data—The contents of this volume were taken from many sources. All data from either censuses and surveys or from administrative records are subject to error arising from a number of factors: Sampling variability (for statistics based on samples), reporting errors in the data for individual units, incomplete coverage, nonresponse, imputations, and processing error. (See also Appendix III, pp. 941.) The Census Bureau cannot accept the responsibility for the accuracy or limitations of the data presented here, other than those for which it collects. The responsibility for selection of the material and for proper presentation, however, rests with the Census Bureau.

For additional information on data presented—Please consult the source publications available in local libraries or write to the agency indicated in the source notes. Write to the Census Bureau only if it is cited as the source.

Suggestions and comments—Users of the Statistical Abstract and its supplements (see inside back cover) are urged to make their data needs known for consideration in planning future editions. Suggestions and comments for improving coverage and presentation of data should be sent to the Director, U.S. Census Bureau, Washington, DC 20233.

Contents

[Numbers following subjects are page numbers]

	Page
Guide to Tabular Presentation	x
Telephone and Internet Contacts	xii

Sec. 1. Population (Tables 1 - 82) 1
Fig. 1.1. Percent Population Change: April 2000 to July 2002 7
Fig. 1.2. Center of Population: 1970 to 2000 20
Fig. 1.3. Foreign Born by Region of Birth: 2002 53
Fig. 1.4. Population With School Education or More by Nativity and World Region of Birth: 2002 53

Immigration 9	Profiles of elderly, racial, and Hispanic-origin populations 42
Estimates by age, sex, race and Hispanic origin 13	Native and foreign-born populations .. 50
States, metro. areas, cities 21	Ancestry, languages 55
	Marital status and households 59
	Religion 68

Sec. 2. Vital Statistics (Tables 83 - 126) 69
Fig. 2.1 Infant Mortality Rates by State: 2000 71

Births 72	Life expectancy 83
	Deaths 86

Sec. 3. Health and Nutrition (Tables 127 - 216) 101

Health expenditures, insurance 103	Health measures 130
	Food consumption, nutrition 141

Sec. 4. Education (Tables 217 - 304) 145

Education projections 148	Internet access 170
Educational attainment 153	Degrees conferred 191

Sec. 5. Law Enforcement, Courts, and Prisons (Tables 305 - 358) 195
Fig. 5.1 Violent Crime Rates Per 100,000 Population by State: 2001 198

Crime arrests, and victimizations ... 206	Juveniles, child abuse 217
Courts 214	Prisoners and inmates 218

Sec. 6. Geography and Environment (Tables 359 - 395) 223

Land and water 225	Hazardous waste sites 237
Air quality 233	Climate 242

Sec. 7. Elections (Tables 396 - 430) 249
Fig. 7.1. Vote Cast for President by Major Political Party: 1992 to 2000 250
Fig. 7.2. Presidential Electoral Vote by State: 2000 253

Vote results 251	Campaign finances 273

Sec. 8. State and Local Government Finances and Employment (Tables 431 - 474) 275

Governmental units 276	Local government finances 302
State government finances 295	Employment and payroll 312

Sec. 9. Federal Government Finances and Employment (Tables 475 - 508) 319
Fig. 9.1. Federal Budget Summary: 1980 to 2003 321

Budget receipts, outlays, debt 322	Federal employment and payroll 335

Sec. 10. National Defense and Veterans Affairs (Tables 509 - 533) 341

National defense outlays 342	Military manpower 345

U.S. Census Bureau, Statistical Abstract of the United States: 2003

Sec. 11. Social Insurance and Human Services (Tables 534 - 586) 353
Government transfer payments 356
Social security 361
Public aid, federal food programs ... 371
Child care, child support 373

Sec. 12. Labor Force, Employment, and Earnings (Tables 587 - 658) 381
Labor force status 385
Multiple jobholding 396
Projections 403
Productivity 417
Minimum wage 425
Union membership 431

Sec. 13. Income, Expenditures, and Wealth (Tables 659 - 711) 433
Fig. 13.1. Consumer Expenditures Per Consumer Unit by Major Types of
Expenditures: 2001 437
Fig. 13.2. Median Income of Households by Race and Hispanic Origin, in
Constant (2001) Dollars: 1990 to 2001 437
Fig. 13.3. Percent of Children Below Poverty Level by Race and Hispanic Origin:
1990 to 2001 437
Gross domestic product 438
Consumer expenditures 451
Money income of families 458
Poverty status 465

Sec. 14. Prices (Tables 712 - 730) 471
Fig. 14.1. Annual Percent change in Consumer Price Indexes: 1990 to 2002 474
Fig. 14.2. Annual Change in Producer Price Indexes by Stage of Processing:
1990 to 2002 474
Purchasing power of the dollar 473
Cost of living index 478

Sec. 15. Business Enterprise (Tables 731 - 781) 493
Fig. 15.1. Total Industrial Production and Capacity: 1980 to 2002 518
Sole proprietors, partnerships,
corporations..................... 495
Establishments, employees, payroll.. 502
Bankruptcies, mergers, and
acquisitions 510
Patents, trademarks, copyrights 512
Investment, capital expenditures 514
Economic indicators 516
Profits............................. 520
Multinationals 521

Sec. 16. Science and Technology (Tables 782 - 804) 523
Fig. 16.1. Top 15 Universities—Federal Research and Development Obligations:
2001.. 529
Fig. 16.2. Federal Funding for Research by Field of Science: 2002 529
R&D funds, outlays 526
Space program 532

Sec. 17. Agriculture (Tables 805 - 852)... 535
Farms and farmland 537
Farm balance sheet, income 539
Foreign trade 545
Crops, livestock 549

Sec. 18. Natural Resources (Tables 853 - 892) 557
Timber, lumber 561
Fishery 564
Petroleum, gas..................... 572

Sec. 19. Energy and Utilities (Tables 893 - 930) 579
Fig. 19.1. Energy Production, Trade, and Consumption: 1980 to 2001 582
Fig. 19.2. Top Suppliers of U.S. Crude Oil Imports: 2002 582
Energy consumption, expenditures . 583
Crude oil 590
Electric utilities, nuclear 592
Gas utilities 598

Sec. 20. Construction and Housing (Tables 931 - 983) 601
Construction spending 605
Home sales........................ 612
Homeownership 622
Home remodeling 632

Sec. 21. Manufactures (Tables 984 - 1023) 635
Manufacturing summary 639
Steel 650
Machine tools 651
Computer, electronics 653

Sec. 22. Domestic Trade (Tables 1024 - 1051) 657
Retail trade 660
Wholesale merchant 673

Sec. 23. Transportation (Tables 1052 - 1118) 675
Transportation outlays .... 680 Highway mileage 691
Air transportation .... 683 Motor vehicle registrations 697

Sec. 24. Information and Communications (Tables 1119 - 1159) 715
Information technologies .... 719 Book purchasing 726
Newspapers .... 722 Telecommunications 730
                                          Internet access and use 735

Sec. 25. Banking, Finance, and Insurance (Tables 1160 - 1229) 737
Flow of funds, financial assets ...... 740 Money stock, interest rates.......... 752
Financial institutions .... 744 Stocks and bonds, equity ownership. 754
Mortgage debt, consumer credit..... 748 Mutual funds securities industry..... 761
                                          Insurance, real estate................764

Sec. 26. Arts, Entertainment, and Recreation (Tables 1230 - 1264) 767
Performing arts .... 771 NCAA sports 781
Leisure activities .... 775 Travel 784

Sec. 27. Accommodation, Food Services, and Other Services
(Tables 1265 - 1279)... 787
Fig. 27.1. Advertising Expenditures: 1990 to 2002 788
Advertising........................ 794 Administrative and support and
                                          waste management 795

Sec. 28. Foreign Commerce and Aid (Tables 1280 - 1304) 797
Fig. 28.1. U.S. International Transaction Balances: 1990 to 2002................... 800
Fig. 28.2. Top Purchasers of U.S. Exports and Suppliers of U.S. General Imports: 2001 800
International transactions .... 801 Foreign grants and credits 809
Foreign investments .... 805 Exports and imports 816

Sec. 29. Puerto Rico and the Outlying Areas (Tables 1305 - 1318) 823
Fig. 28.1. Selected Island Areas of the United States 824
Population 825

Sec. 30. Comparative International Statistics (Tables 1319 - 1383) 831
World maps .... 816 Economic measures 851
World population; vital statistics .... 841 Finance 871

Sec. 31. Congressional Districts Profiles 879

Appendix I. Guide to Sources of Statistics 896
               Guide to State Statistical Abstracts 913
               Guide to Foreign Statistical Abstracts 917

Appendix II. Metropolitan and Micropolitan Statistical Areas: Concepts,
                Components, and Population 919

Appendix III. Limitations of the Data 941

Appendix IV. Weights and Measures 966

Appendix V. Tables Deleted From the 2002 Edition of the Statistical Abstract 967

Appendix VI. New Tables 971

Index 974

Example of Table Structure

No. 327. Immigration and Naturalization Service Enforcement Activities: 1990 to 2000

[For fiscal years ending in year shown. See text, Section 8]

Item	Unit	1990	1994	1995	1996	1997	1998	1999	2000
Deportable aliens located	1,000	1,169.9	1,094.7	1,394.6	1,650.0	1,536.5	1,679.4	1,714.0	1,814.7
Border Patrol	1,000	1,103.4	1,031.7	1,324.2	1,549.9	1,413.0	1,555.8	1,579.0	1,676.4
Southwestern border	1,000	(NA)	979.1	1,271.4	1,507.0	1,368.7	1,516.7	1,537.0	1,643.7
Mexican	1,000	1,054.8	999.9	1,293.5	1,523.1	1,387.7	1,522.9	1,534.5	1,636.9
Canadian	1,000	5.7	3.4	3.5	2.7	2.9	2.3	2.7	2.2
Other	1,000	42.8	28.4	27.2	24.0	22.4	30.5	41.8	37.3
Number of seizures by									
Border Patrol	Number . . .	17,275	9,134	9,327	11,129	11,792	14,401	16,803	17,269
Value of seizures by Border Patrol .	Mil. dol. . . .	843.6	1,622.0	2,011.8	1,256.0	1,094.6	1,405.0	2,004.0	1,945.0
Narcotics	Mil. dol. . . .	797.8	1,555.7	1,965.3	1,208.8	1,046.3	1,340.0	1,919.0	1,848.0
Aliens expelled:									
Formal removals [1]	1,000	30.0	45.7	45.2	69.7	114.4	173.0	180.3	184.8
Voluntary departures [2]	1,000	1,022.5	1,029.1	1,313.8	1,573.4	1,440.7	1,570.1	1,574.5	1,675.3

NA Not available. [1] Include deportations, exclusions, and removals. [2] Includes aliens under docket control required to depart and voluntary departures not under docket control.

Source: U.S. Bureau of Citizenship and Immigration Services, *Statistical Yearbook*, annual. See also <http://www.immigration.gov/graphics/shared/aboutus/statistics/index.htm>.

Headnotes immediately below table titles provide information important for correct interpretation or evaluation of the table as a whole or for a major segment of it.

Footnotes below the bottom rule of tables give information relating to specific items or figures within the table.

Unit indicators show the *specified quantities* in which data items are presented. They are used for two primary reasons. Sometimes data are not available in absolute form and are estimates (as in the case of many surveys). In other cases we round the numbers in order to save space to show more data, as in the case above.

EXAMPLES OF UNIT INDICATOR INTERPRETATION FROM TABLE

Year	Item	Unit Indicator	Number shown	Multiplier
1990	Deportable aliens located	Thousands	1,169.9	1,000
1990	Value of seizures by Border Patrol . .	$ Millions	843.6	1,000,000

To Determine the Figure It Is Necessary to Multiply the Number Shown by the Unit Indicator:
Deportable aliens located - 1,169.9 x 1,000 = 1,169,900 (over 1 million)
Value of seizures by Border Patrol - 843.6 x $1,000,000 - $843,600,000 (over $843 million).

When a table presents data with more than one unit indicator, they are found in the headnotes and column headings (Tables 2 and 23), spanner (Table 46), stub (Table 24), or unit column (shown above). When the data in a table are shown in the same unit indicator, it is shown in boldface as the first part of the headnote (Table 2). If no unit indicator is shown, data presented are in absolute form (Table 1).

Vertical rules are used to separate independent sections of a table, (Table 1), or in tables where the stub is continued into one or more additional columns (Table 2).

Averages—An average is a single number or value that is often used to represent the "typical value" of a group of numbers. It is regarded as a measure of "location" or "central tendency" of a group of numbers.

The *arithmetic mean* is the type of average used most frequently. It is derived by summing the individual item values of a particular group and dividing the total by the number of items. The arithmetic mean is often referred to as simply the "mean" or "average."

The *median* of a group of numbers is the middle number or value when each item in the group is arranged according to size (lowest to highest or visa versa); it generally has the same number of items above it as well as below it. If there is an even number if items in the group, the median is taken to be the average of the two middle numbers.

Per capita (or per person) quantities. A per capita figure represents an average computed for every person in a specified group (or population). It is derived by taking the total for an item (such as income, taxes, or retail sales) and dividing it by the number of persons in the specified population.

x   Guide to Tabular Presentation

Index numbers—An index number is the measure of difference or change, usually expressed as a percent, relating one quantity (the variable) of a specified kind to another quantity of the same kind. Index numbers are widely used to express changes in prices over periods of time, but may also be used to express differences between related subjects for a single point in time.

To compute a price index, a base year or period is selected. The base year price (of the commodity or service) is then designated as the base or reference price to which the prices for other years or periods are related. Many price indexes use the year 1982 as the base year; in tables this is shown as "1982=100." A method of expressing the price relationship is: The price of a set of one or more items for a related year (e.g. 1990) **divided by** the price of the same set of items for the base year (e.g. 1982). The result multiplied by 100 provides the index number. When 100 is subtracted from the index number, the result equals the percent change in price from the base year.

Average annual percent change—Unless otherwise stated in the *Abstract* (as in Section 1, Population), average annual percent change is computed by use of a *compound interest formula*. This formula assumes that the rate of change is constant throughout a specified compounding period (1 year for average annual rates of change). The formula is similar to that used to compute the balance of a savings account that receives compound interest. According to this formula, at the end of a compounding period the amount of accrued change (e.g. school enrollment or bank interest) is added to the amount that existed at the beginning the period. As a result, over time (e.g., with each year or quarter), the same rate of change is applied to a larger and larger figure.

The *exponential formula,* which is based on continuous compounding, is often used to measure population change. It is preferred by population experts, because they view population and population-related subjects as changing without interruption, ever ongoing. Both exponential and compound interest formulas assume a constant rate of change. The former, however, applies the amount of change continuously to the base rather than at the end of each compounding period. When the average annual rates are small (e.g., less than 5 percent) both formulas give virtually the same results. For an explanation of these two formulas as they relate to population, see U.S. Census Bureau, *The Methods and Materials of Demography,* Vol. 2, 3d printing (rev.), 1975, pp. 372-381.

Current and constant dollars—Statistics in some tables in a number of sections are expressed in both current and constant dollars (see, for example, Table 671 in Section 13, Income, Expenditures, and Wealth). Current dollar figures reflect actual prices or costs prevailing during the specified year(s). Constant dollar figures are estimates representing an effort to remove the effects of price changes from statistical series reported in dollar terms. In general, constant dollar series are derived by dividing current dollar estimates by the appropriate price index for the appropriate period (for example, the Consumer Price Index). The result is a series as it would presumably exist if prices were the same throughout, as in the base year—in other words, as if the dollar had constant purchasing power. Any changes in this constant dollar series would reflect only changes in real volume of output, income, expenditures, or other measure.

Explanation of Symbols

The following symbols, used in the tables throughout this book, are explained in condensed form in footnotes to the tables where they appear:

- Represents zero or rounds to less than half the unit of measurement shown.

B Base figure too small to meet statistical standards for reliability of a derived figure.

D Figure withheld to avoid disclosure pertaining to a specific organization or individual.

NA Data not enumerated, tabulated, or otherwise available separately.

S Figure does not meet publication standards for reasons other than that covered by symbol B, above.

X Figure not applicable because column heading and stub line make entry impossible, absurd, or meaningless.

Z Entry would amount to less than half the unit of measurement shown.

In many tables, details will not add to the totals shown because of rounding.

Telephone and Internet Contacts

To help *Abstract* users find more data and information about statistical publications, we are issuing this list of contacts for Federal agencies with major statistical programs. The intent is to give a single, first-contact point-of-entry for users of statistics. These agencies will provide general information on their statistical programs and publications, as well as specific information on how to order their publications. We are also including the Internet (World Wide Web) addresses for many of these agencies. These URL's were current in October 2000.

Executive Office of the President
Office of Management and Budget
Administrator
Office of Information and Regulatory Affairs
Office of Management and Budget
725 17th Street, N.W.
Washington, DC 20503
Information: 202-395-3080
Internet address:
http://www.whitehouse.gov/omb

Department of Agriculture
Economic Research Service
Information Center
U.S. Department of Agriculture
1800 M St. N.W., Room 3050
Washington, DC 20036-5831
Information and Publications:
202-694-5000
Internet address:
http://www.ers.usda.gov/

National Agricultural Statistics Service
National Agricultural Statistics Service
U.S. Department of Agriculture
1400 Independence Ave., S.W.,
Room 5829
Washington, DC 20250
Information hotline: 1-800-727-9540
Internet address:
http://www.usda.gov/nass/

Department of Commerce
U.S. Census Bureau
Customer Services Branch
U.S. Census Bureau
U.S. Department of Commerce
Washington, DC 20233
Information and Publications:
301-763-4636
Internet address:
http://www.census.gov/

Department of Commerce —Con.
Bureau of Economic Analysis
Bureau of Economic Analysis
U.S. Department of Commerce
Washington, DC 20230
Information and Publications:
202-606-9900
Internet address: http://www.bea.gov/

International Trade Administration
Trade Statistics Division
Office of Trade and Economic Analysis
International Trade Administration
Room 2814 B
U.S. Department of Commerce
Washington, DC 20230
Information and Publications:
202-482-2185
Internet address:
http://www.ita.doc.gov/td/industry/otea

National Oceanic and Atmospheric Administration
National Oceanic and Atmospheric Administration Central Library
U.S. Department of Commerce
1315 East-West Highway
2nd Floor
Silver Spring MD 20910
Library: 301-713-2600
Internet address:
http://www.lib.noaa.gov/

Department of Defense
Department of Defense
Office of the Assistant Secretary of Defense, Public Affairs, (DPO)
Room 2E765
Attention: Press Operations
1400 Defense Pentagon
Washington, DC 20301-1400
Information: 703-697-5131/5132
Internet address:
http://www.defenselink.mil

Department of Education
National Library of Education
U.S. Department of Education
400 Maryland Avenue, S.W.
Washington, DC 20202-5621
Education Information and Statistics
1-800-424-1616
Education Publications 1-877-433-7827
Internet address: http://www.ed.gov/

Department of Energy
Energy Information Administration
National Energy Information Center
U.S. Department of Energy
1000 Independence Ave., SW
Room E1-30
Washington, DC 20585
Information and Publications:
202-586-8800
Internet address:
http://www.eia.doe.gov/

Department of Health and Human Services
Health Resources and Services Administration
HRSA Office of Communications
5600 Fishers Lane, Room 14-45
Rockville, MD 20857
Information Center: 301-443-3376
Internet address: http://www.hrsa.gov/

Substance Abuse and Mental Health Services Administration
U.S. Department of Health and Human Services
5600 Fishers Lane
Room 12-105
Rockville, MD 20857
Information: 301-443-4795
Publications: 1-800-729-6686
Internet address:
http://www.samhsa.gov/

Centers for Disease Control and Prevention
Office of Public Affairs
1600 Clifton Road, N.E.
Atlanta, GA 30333
Public Inquiries: 1-800-311-3435
Internet address: http://www.cdc.gov/

Centers for Medicare and Medicaid Services (CMS)
Office of Public Affairs
U.S. Department of Health and Human Services
Room 303D, Humphrey Building
200 Independence Ave., S.W.
Washington, DC 20201
Media Relations: 202-690-6145
Internet address: http://www.cms.gov/

Department of Health and Human Services —Con.
National Center for Health Statistics
U.S. Department of Health and Human Services - Centers for Disease Control and Prevention
National Center for Health Statistics
Data Dissemination Branch
3311 Toledo Road
Hyattsville, MD 20782 301-458-4636
Internet address:
http://www.cdc.gov/nchs

Department of Homeland Security
Immigration and Naturalization Service
Statistics Division
Immigration and Naturalization Service
U.S. Department of Justice
425 I St., NW, Rm. 4034
Washington, DC 20536
Information and Publications:
202-305-1613
Internet address:
http://www.ins.gov/graphics/ index.htm

U.S. Department of Housing and Urban Development
Office of the Assistant Secretary for Community Planning and Development
451 7th St., S.W.
Washington, DC 20410-0555
Information and Publications:
1-800-998-9999
Internet address: http://www.hud.gov/

Department of the Interior
U.S. Geological Survey
Earth Science Information Center
U.S. Geological Survey
U.S. Department of the Interior
507 National Center
Reston, VA 20192
Information and Publications:
1-888-275-8747
Internet address for minerals:
http://minerals.usgs.gov/
Internet address for other materials:
http://ask.usgs.gov/

Department of Justice
Bureau of Justice Statistics
Statistics Division
810 7th St., N.W. 2nd Floor
Washington, DC 20531
Information and Publications:
202-307-0765
Internet address:
http://www.ojp.usdoj.gov/bjs/

Department of Justice —Con.
National Criminal Justice Reference Service
Box 6000
Rockville, MD 20849-6000
Information and Publications:
301-519-5500
Publications: 1-800-732-3277
Internet address: http://www.ncjrs.org/

Federal Bureau of Investigation
U.S. Department of Justice
J. Edgar Hoover FBI Building
935 Pennsylvania Ave., N.W.
Washington, DC 20535-0001
202-324-3000
Information and Publications:
202-324-3691
Research and Communications Unit:
202-324-5611
Internet address: http://www.fbi.gov/

Department of Labor
Bureau of Labor Statistics
Office of Publications and Special
Studies Services
Division of Information
Bureau of Labor Statistics
2 Mass. Ave., N.E., Room 2850
Washington, DC 20212
Information and Publications:
202-691-5200
Internet address: http://www.bls.gov/

Employment and Training Administration
Office of Public Affairs
Employment and Training Administration
U.S. Department of Labor
200 Constitution Ave., N.W.,
Room N4643
Washington, DC 20210
Information and Publications:
202-693-3900
Internet address: http://www.doleta.gov/

Department of Transportation
Federal Aviation Administration
U.S. Department of Transportation
800 Independence Ave., S.W.
Washington, DC 20591
Information and Publications:
202-267-3484
Internet address: http://www.faa.gov/

Bureau of Transportation Statistics
400 7th St., S.W., Room 3103
Washington, DC 20590
Products and Statistical Information:
800-853-1351
Internet address: http://www.bts.gov/eb

Department of Transportation —Con.
Federal Highway Administration
Office of Public Affairs
Federal Highway Administration
U.S. Department of Transportation
400 7th St., S.W.
Washington, DC 20590
Information: 202-366-0660
Internet address:
http://www.fhwa.dot.gov/

National Highway Traffic Safety
Administration
Office of Public & Consumer Affairs
National Highway Traffic Safety
Administration
U.S. Department of Transportation
400 7th St., S.W.
Washington, DC 20590
Information: 202-366-4000
Publications: 202-366-8892/9550
Internet address:
http://www.nhtsa.dot.gov/

Department of the Treasury
Internal Revenue Service
Statistics of Income Division
Internal Revenue Service
P.O. Box 2608
Washington, DC 20013-2608
Information and Publications:
202-874-0410
Internet address:
http://www.irs.gov/taxstats

Department of Veterans Affairs
Office of Public Affairs
Department of Veterans Affairs
810 Vermont Ave., N.W.
Washington, DC 20420
Information: 202-273-5400
Internet address: http://www.va.gov/

Independent Agencies
Administrative Office of the U.S. Courts
Statistics Division
1 Columbus Circle, N.E.
Washington, DC 20544
Information: 202-502-1455
Internet address:
http://www.uscourts.gov/

Environmental Protection Agency
US EPA Headquarters Library, Room 3340
Environmental Protection Agency West
Building
1200 Pennsylvania Ave., N.W.
Mail Code 3404T
Washington, DC 20460-0001
Information: 202-566-0556
Internet address: http://www.epa.gov/

Independent Agencies —Con.

Federal Reserve Board
Division of Research and Statistics
Federal Reserve Board
20th & C. Street, NW
Washington, DC 20551
Information: 202-452-3301
Publications: 202-452-3245
Internet address:
  http://www.federalreserve.gov/

National Science Foundation
Office of Legislation and Public Affairs
National Science Foundation
4201 Wilson Boulevard
Arlington, Virginia 22230
Information: 703-292-8070
Publications: 703-292-8129
Internet address: http://www.nsf.gov/

Independent Agencies —Con.

Securities and Exchange Commission
Office of Public Affairs
Securities and Exchange Commission
450 5th St., N.W.
Room 2500
Mail Stop 0211
Washington, DC 20549
Information: 202-942-0020
Publications: 202-942-4040
Internet address: http://www.sec.gov/

Social Security Administration
Social Security Administration
Office of Research, Evaluation and
  Statistics
4-C-15 Operations Building
6401 Security Boulevard
Baltimore, MD 21235
Information and Publications:
  1-800-772-1213
Internet Address:
  http://www.socialsecurity.gov/

Section 1
Population

This section presents statistics on the growth, distribution, and characteristics of the U.S. population. The principal source of these data is the U.S. Census Bureau, which conducts a decennial census of population, a monthly population survey, a program of population estimates and projections, and a number of other periodic surveys relating to population characteristics. For a list of relevant publications, see the Guide to Sources of Statistics in Appendix I.

Decennial censuses—The U.S. Constitution provides for a census of the population every 10 years, primarily to establish a basis for apportionment of members of the House of Representatives among the states. For over a century after the first census in 1790, the census organization was a temporary one, created only for each decennial census. In 1902, the Census Bureau was established as a permanent federal agency, responsible for enumerating the population and also for compiling statistics on other population and housing characteristics.

Historically, the enumeration of the population has been a complete count. That is, an attempt is made to account for every person, for each person's residence, and for other characteristics (sex, age, family relationships, etc.). Since the 1940 census, in addition to the complete count information, some data have been obtained from representative samples of the population. In the 1990 and 2000 censuses, variable sampling rates were employed. For most of the country, 1 in every 6 households (about 17 percent) received the long form or sample questionnaire; in governmental units estimated to have fewer than 2,500 inhabitants, every other household (50 percent) received the sample questionnaire to enhance the reliability of sample data for small areas. Exact agreement is not to be expected between sample data and the 100-percent count. Sample data may be used with confidence where large numbers are involved and assumed to indicate trends and relationships where small numbers are involved.

Current Population Survey (CPS)—This is a monthly nationwide survey of a scientifically selected sample representing the noninstitutional civilian population. The sample is located in 754 areas with coverage in every state and the District of Columbia and is subject to sampling error. At the present time, about 60,000 occupied households are eligible for interview every month; of these between 6 and 7 percent are, for various reasons, unavailable for interview.

While the primary purpose of the CPS is to obtain monthly statistics on the labor force, it also serves as a vehicle for inquiries on other subjects. Using CPS data, the Bureau issues a series of publications under the general title of *Current Population Reports*, which cover population characteristics (P20), consumer income (P60), special studies (P23), and other topics.

Estimates of population characteristics based on the CPS will not agree with the counts from the census because the CPS and the census use different procedures for collecting and processing the data for racial groups, the Hispanic population, and other topics. Caution should also be used when comparing estimates for various years because of the periodic introduction of changes into the CPS. Beginning in January 1994, a number of changes were introduced into the CPS that effect all data comparisons with prior years. These changes include the results of a major redesign of the survey questionnaire and collection methodology and the introduction of 1990 census population controls, adjusted for the estimated undercount. Beginning with the 2001 CPS Annual Demographic Supplement the independent estimates used as control totals for the CPS are based on civilian population benchmarks consistent with Census 2000. In March 2002, the sample size of the Annual Demographic Supplement was increased to approximately

78,000. These changes in population controls had relatively little impact on derived measures such as means, medians, and percent distribution, but did have a significant impact on levels.

Population estimates and projections—Estimates of the United States population are derived by updating the resident population enumerated in Census 2000 with information on the components of population change: births, deaths, and net international migration. The April 1, 2000, population used in these estimates reflects modifications to the Census 2000 population as documented in the Count Question Resolution program.

Registered births and deaths are estimated from data supplied by the National Center for Health Statistics. The net international migration component in the population estimates includes: legal immigration to the United States, emigration of foreign born and native people from the United States, net movement between the United States and Puerto Rico, estimates of temporary migrants, and estimates of net residual foreign-born population, which include unauthorized migration.

For the first time, the estimates of the international migration component incorporated data available from the Census 2000 Supplementary Survey (C2SS) and the 2001 Supplementary Survey (SS01) along with estimates developed from the Demographic Analysis and Population Estimates (DAPE) project (See Deardorff and Blumerman, 2001, "Evaluation Components of International Migration: Estimates of the Foreign-Born Population by Migrant Status in 2000," Population Division Working Paper Series, No. 58).

Estimates for states and counties areas are based on the same components of change data and sources as the national estimates with the addition of net internal migration. School enrollment statistics from state departments of education and parochial school systems, federal income tax returns from the Internal Revenue Service, group quarters data from the Federal-State Cooperative Program, and medicare data from the Centers of Medicare and Medicaid Services are also included.

The population by age for April 1, 1990, (shown in Table 11) reflects modifications to the 1990 census data counts. The review of detailed 1990 information indicated that respondents tended to report age as of the date of completion of the questionnaire, not as of April 1, 1990. In addition, there may have been a tendency for respondents to round up their age if they were close to having a birthday. A detailed explanation of the age modification procedure appears in 1990 Census of Population and Housing, Data Paper Listing CPH-L74.

Population estimates and projections are available on the Census Bureau Internet site <http://www.census.gov>. These estimates and projections are consistent with official decennial census figures with no adjustment for estimated net census coverage. However, the categories for these estimates and projections by race have been modified and are not comparable to the census race categories (see section below under "Race"). For details on methodology, see the sources cited below the individual tables.

Immigration—Immigration (migration *to* a country) is one component of international migration; the other component is emigration (migration *from* a country). In its simplest form, international migration is defined as any movement across a national border. In the United States, federal statistics on international migration are produced primarily by the U.S. Census Bureau and the Bureau of Citizenship and Immigration Services (located in the Department of Homeland Security). The U.S. Bureau of Citizenship and Immigration Services was formerly the Immigration and Naturalization Service.

The Census Bureau collects international migration data through its decennial censuses and numerous surveys of the U.S. population. The Bureau of Citizenship and Immigration Services publishes immigration data in the *Yearbook of Immigration Statistics* and collects these data from several administrative records such as the Immigrant Visa and Alien Registration (OF-155, U.S. State Department) for new arrivals, and the Memorandum of Creation of Record of Lawful Permanent Residence (I-181, INS) for persons adjusting migrant status. Immigrants are aliens admitted for legal permanent residence in the United

States. The category, immigrant, includes persons who may have entered the United States as nonimmigrants or refugees, but who subsequently changed their status to that of a permanent resident. Nonresident aliens admitted to the United States for a temporary period are nonimmigrants. Refugees are considered nonimmigrants when initially admitted into the United States but are not included in nonimmigrant admission data. A refugee is an alien outside the United States who is unable or unwilling to return to his or her country of nationality because of persecution or a well-founded fear of persecution.

U.S. immigration law gives preferential immigration status to persons with a close family relationship with a U.S. citizen or legal permanent resident, persons with needed job skills, or persons who qualify as refugees. Immigration to the United States can be divided into two general categories: (1) those subject to the annual worldwide limitation and (2) those exempt from it. Numerical limits are imposed on visas issued and not on admissions. The maximum number of visas allowed to be issued under the preference categories in 2001 was 418,074—226,000 for family-sponsored immigrants and 192,074 for employment-based immigrants. There are nine categories among which the family-sponsored and employment-based immigrant visas are distributed, beginning in fiscal year 1992. Within the overall limitations the per-country limit for independent countries is set to 7 percent of the total family-sponsored and employment-based limits, while dependent areas are limited to 2 percent of the total. The 2001 limit allowed no more than 29,265 preference visas for any independent country and 8,361 for any dependency. Those exempt from the worldwide limitation include immediate relatives of U.S. citizens, refugees and asylees adjusting to permanent residence, and other various classes of special immigrants (see Table 6).

The Refugee Act of 1980 provides for a uniform admission procedure for refugees of all countries, based on the United Nations' definition of refugees. Authorized admission ceilings are set annually by the President in consultation with Congress. After 1 year of residence in the United States, refugees are eligible for immigrant status.

Metropolitan Areas—The United States Office of Management and Budget (OMB) defines metropolitan and micropolitan statistical areas according to published standards that are applied to Census Bureau data. The general concept of a metropolitan or micropolitan statistical area is that of a core area containing a substantial population nucleus, together with adjacent communities having a high degree of economic and social integration with that core. Currently defined metropolitan and micropolitan statistical areas are based on application of 2000 standards to 2000 decennial census data. The term "metropolitan area" (MA) was adopted in 1990 and referred collectively to metropolitan statistical areas (MSAs), consolidated metropolitan statistical areas (CMSAs), and primary metropolitan statistical areas (PMSAs). The term "core based statistical area" (CBSA) became effective in 2000 and refers collectively to metropolitan and micropolitan statistical areas.

Over time, new statistical areas are created and the components of others change. Because of historical changes in geographic definitions, users must be cautious in comparing data for these statistical areas from different dates. For some purposes, comparisons of data for areas as defined at given dates may be appropriate; for other purposes, it may be preferable to maintain consistent area definitions. For descriptive details and a listing of titles and components of metropolitan and micropolitan areas, see Appendix II.

Urban and rural—For Census 2000, the Census Bureau classified as urban all territory, population, and housing units located within urbanized areas (UAs) and urban clusters (UCs). A UA consists of densely settled territory that contains 50,000 or more people, while a UC consists of densely settled territory with at least 2,500 people but fewer than 50,000 people. (UCs are a new type of geographic entity for Census 2000.) Prior to Census 2000—from the 1950 census through the 1990 census—the urban population consisted of all people living in UAs and most places outside of UAs with a census population of 2,500 or more.

UAs and UCs encompass territory that generally consists of:

- A cluster of one or more block groups or census blocks each of which has a population density of at least 1,000 people per square mile at the time.
- Surrounding block groups and census blocks each of which has a population density of at least 500 people per square mile at the time.
- Less densely settled blocks that form enclaves or indentations, or are used to connect discontiguous areas with qualifying densities.

They also may include an airport located adjacent to qualifying densely settled area if it has an annual enplanement (aircraft boarding) of at least 10,000 people.

"Rural" for Census 2000 consists of all territory, population, and housing units located outside of UAs and UCs. Prior to Census 2000, rural consisted of all territory, population, and housing outside of UAs and outside of other places designated as "urban." For Census 2000, many more geographic entities, including metropolitan areas, counties, county subdivisions, and places, contain both urban and rural territory, population, and housing units.

Residence—In determining residence, the Census Bureau counts each person as an inhabitant of a usual place of residence (i.e., the place where one usually lives and sleeps). While this place is not necessarily a person's legal residence or voting residence, the use of these different bases of classification would produce the same results in the vast majority of cases.

Race—For the 1990 census, the Census Bureau collected and published racial statistics as outlined in Statistical Policy Directive No. 15 issued by the U.S. Office of Management and Budget (OMB). This directive provided standards on ethnic and racial categories for statistical reporting to be used by all federal agencies. According to the directive, the basic racial categories were American Indian or Alaskan Native, Asian or Pacific Islander, Black, and White. (The directive identified Hispanic origin as an ethnicity.) The question on race for Census 2000 was different from the one for the 1990 census in several ways. Most significantly, respondents were given the option of selecting one or more race categories to indicate their racial identities. Because of these changes, the Census 2000 data on race are not directly comparable with data from the 1990 census or earlier censuses. Caution must be used when interpreting changes in the racial composition of the U.S. population over time. Census 2000 adheres to the federal standards for collecting and presenting data on race and Hispanic origin as established by OMB in October 1997. Starting with Census 2000, the OMB requires federal agencies to use a minimum of five race categories: White, Black or African American, American Indian or Alaska Native, Asian, and Native Hawaiian or Other Pacific Islander. For respondents unable to identify with any of these five race categories, OMB approved and included a sixth category—"Some other race" on the Census 2000 questionnaire. The Census 2000 question on race included 15 separate response categories and three areas where respondents could write in a more specific race group. The response categories and write-in answers can be combined to create the five minimum OMB race categories plus "Some other race." People who responded to the question on race by indicating only one race are referred to as the *race alone* population, or the group that reported only one race category. Six categories make up this population: White alone, Black or African American alone, American Indian and Alaska Native alone, Asian alone, Native Hawaiian and Other Pacific Island alone, and Some other race alone. Individuals who chose more than one of the six race categories are referred to as the *Two or more races* population, or as the group that reported more than one race. Additionally, respondents who reported one race together with those who reported the same race plus one or more other races are combined to create the *race alone or in combination* categories. For example, the *White alone or in combination group* consists of those respondents who reported White combined with one or more other race groups, such as "White and Black or African American," or "White and Asian and American Indian and Alaska Native." Another way to think of the group who reported White alone or in combination is as the total number of people who identified entirely or partially as White. This

4 Population

U.S. Census Bureau, Statistical Abstract of the United States: 2003

group is also described as people who reported White, whether or not they reported any other race.

The *alone or in combination* categories are tallies of *responses* rather than *respondents*. That is, the alone or in combination categories are not mutually exclusive. Individuals who reported two races were counted in two separate and distinct alone or in combination race categories, while those who reported three races were counted in three categories, and so on. Consequently, the sum of all alone or in combination categories equals the number of races reported (i.e., responses) which exceeds the total population.

The concept of race, as used by the Census Bureau, reflects self-identification by people according to the race or races with which they most closely identify. These categories are sociopolitical constructs and should not be interpreted as being scientific or anthropological in nature. Furthermore, the race categories include both racial and national-origin groups.

Data for the population by race for April 1, 2000, (shown in Table 13) are modified counts and are not comparable to Census 2000 race categories. These numbers were computed using Census 2000 data by race that had been modified to be consistent with the 1997 Office of Management and Budget's, "Revisions to the Standards for the Classification of Federal Data on Race and Ethnicity," (Federal Register Notice, Vol. 62, No 210, October 1997). A detailed explanation of the race modification procedure appears on the Census Web page, <http://eire.census.gov/popest/data/national/tables/mod_race.php>.

In the CPS and other household sample surveys in which data are obtained through personal interview, respondents are asked to classify their race as: (1) White; (2) Black, African American or Negro; (3) American Indian or Alaska Native; (4) Asian; (5) Native Hawaiian or Other Pacific Islander. Beginning January 2003, respondents were allowed to report more than one race to indicated their mixed racial heritage.

Hispanic population—The Census Bureau collected data on the Hispanic origin population in the 2000 census by using a self-identification question. Persons of Spanish/Hispanic origin are those who classified themselves in one of the specific Hispanic origin categories listed on the questionnaire— Mexican, Puerto Rican, Cuban, as well as those who indicated that they were of Other Spanish/Hispanic origin. Persons of Other Spanish/Hispanic origin are those whose origins are from Spain, the Spanish-speaking countries of Central or South America, or the Dominican Republic.

In the CPS information on Hispanic persons is gathered by using a self-identification question. Persons classify themselves in one of the Hispanic categories in response to the question: "What is the origin or descent of each person in this household?" Hispanic persons in the CPS are persons who report themselves as Mexican-American, Chicano, Mexican, Puerto Rican, Cuban, Central or South American (Spanish countries), or other Hispanic origin.

Traditional and current data collection and classification treat race and Hispanic origin as two separate and distinct concepts in accordance with guidelines from the OMB. Race and Hispanic origin are two separate concepts in the federal statistical system. People who are Hispanic may be of any race and people in each race group may be either Hispanic or Not Hispanic. Also, each person has two attributes, their race (or races) and whether or not they are Hispanic. The overlap of race and Hispanic origin is the main comparability issue. For example, Black Hispanics (Hispanic Blacks) are included in both the number of Blacks and in the number of Hispanics. For further information, see Census Web page, <http://www.census.gov/population/www/socdemo/compraceho.html>.

Foreign-born and native populations—The Census Bureau separates the U.S. resident population into two groups based on whether or not a person was a U.S. citizen at the time of birth. Anyone born in the United States or a U.S. Island Area (such as Puerto Rico) or born abroad to a U.S. citizen parent is a U.S. citizen at the time of birth and consequently included in the *native population*. The term *foreign-born population* refers to anyone who is not a U.S. citizen at birth. This includes naturalized U.S. citizens, legal permanent resident aliens (immigrants), temporary migrants (such as students), humanitarian migrants (such as refugees), and people illegally present in the United States. The Census Bureau provides a variety of demographic, social, economic, geographic, and housing information on the foreign-born population in the United States. More information on the foreign-born population collected from censuses and surveys is available at the Foreign-Born Population page, <http://www.census.gov/population/www/socdemo/foreign.html>.

Mobility status—The U.S. population is classified according to mobility status on the basis of a comparison between the place of residence of each individual at the time of the survey or census and the place of residence at a specified earlier date. Nonmovers are all persons who were living in the same house or apartment at the end of the period as at the beginning of the period. Movers are all persons who were living in a different house or apartment at the end of the period than at the beginning of the period. Movers are further classified as to whether they were living in the same or different county, state, or region or were movers from abroad. Movers from abroad include all persons, either U.S. citizens or noncitizens, whose place of residence was outside the United States at the beginning of the period; that is, in Puerto Rico, another U.S. Island Area, or a foreign country.

Living arrangements—Living arrangements refer to residency in households or in group quarters. A "household" comprises all persons who occupy a "housing unit," that is, a house, an apartment or other group of rooms, or a single room that constitutes "separate living quarters." A household includes the related family members and all the unrelated persons, if any, such as lodgers, foster children, wards, or employees who share the housing unit. A person living alone or a group of unrelated persons sharing the same housing unit is also counted as a household. See text, Section 20, Construction and Housing, for definition of housing unit.

All persons not living in housing units are classified as living in group quarters. These individuals may be institutionalized, e.g., under care or custody in juvenile facilities, jails, correctional centers, hospitals, or nursing homes; or they may be residents in noninstitutional group quarters such as college dormitories, group homes, or military barracks.

Householder—The householder is the first adult household member listed on the questionnaire. The instructions call for listing first the person (or one of the persons) in whose name the home is owned or rented. If a home is owned or rented jointly by a married couple, either the husband or the wife may be listed first. Prior to 1980, the husband was always considered the householder in married-couple households.

Family—The term family refers to a group of two or more persons related by birth, marriage, or adoption and residing together in a household. A family includes among its members the householder.

Subfamily—A subfamily consists of a married couple and their children, if any, or one parent with one or more never-married children under 18 years old living in a household. Subfamilies are divided into "related" and "unrelated" subfamilies. A related subfamily is related to, but does not include, the householder. Members of a related subfamily are also members of the family with whom they live. The number of related subfamilies, therefore, is not included in the count of families. An unrelated subfamily may include persons such as guests, lodgers, or resident employees and their spouses and/or children; none of whom is related to the householder.

Married couple—A married couple is defined as a husband and wife living together in the same household, with or without children and other relatives.

Statistical reliability—For a discussion of statistical collection and estimation, sampling procedures, and measures of statistical reliability applicable to Census Bureau data, see Appendix III.

Figure 1.1
Percent Population Change: April 2000 to July 2002

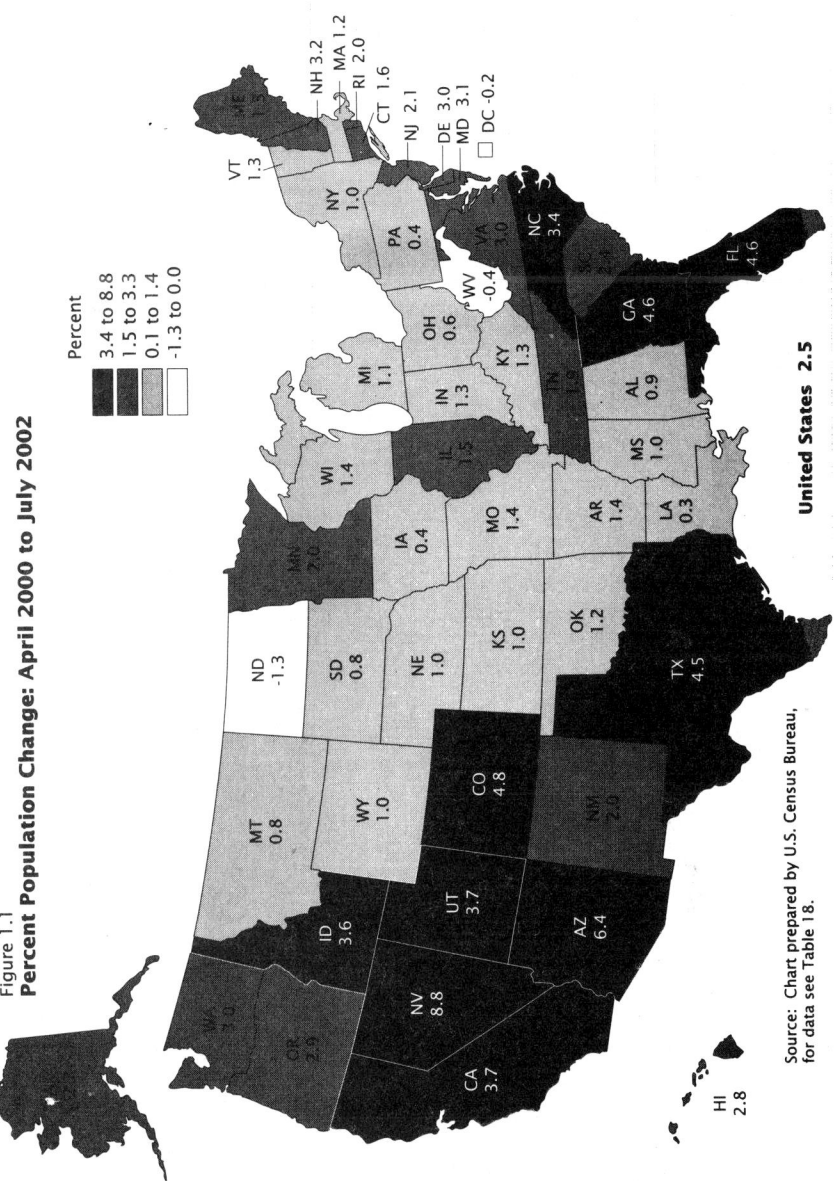

Source: Chart prepared by U.S. Census Bureau, for data see Table 18.

Population 7

No. 1. Population and Area: 1790 to 2000

[Area figures represent area on indicated date including in some cases considerable areas not then organized or settled, and not covered by the census. Total area figures for 1790 to 1970 have been recalculated on the basis of the remeasurement of states and counties for the 1980 census, but not on the basis of the 1990 census. The land and water area figures for past censuses have not been adjusted and are not strictly comparable with the total area data for comparable dates because the land areas were derived from different base data, and these values are known to have changed with the construction of reservoirs, draining of lakes, etc. Density figures are based on land area measurements as reported in earlier censuses]

Census date	Resident population				Area (square miles)		
	Number	Per square mile of land area	Increase over preceding census (Number)	Increase over preceding census (Percent)	Total	Land	Water [1]
1790 (Aug. 2)	3,929,214	4.5	(X)	(X)	891,364	864,746	24,065
1800 (Aug. 4)	5,308,483	6.1	1,379,269	35.1	891,364	864,746	24,065
1810 (Aug. 6)	7,239,881	4.3	1,931,398	36.4	1,722,685	1,681,828	34,175
1820 (Aug. 7)	9,638,453	5.5	2,398,572	33.1	1,792,552	1,749,462	38,544
1830 (June 1)	12,866,020	7.4	3,227,567	33.5	1,792,552	1,749,462	38,544
1840 (June 1)	17,069,453	9.8	4,203,433	32.7	1,792,552	1,749,462	38,544
1850 (June 1)	23,191,876	7.9	6,122,423	35.9	2,991,655	2,940,042	52,705
1860 (June 1)	31,443,321	10.6	8,251,445	35.6	3,021,295	2,969,640	52,747
1870 (June 1)	[2]39,818,449	[2]11.2	8,375,128	26.6	3,612,299	3,540,705	52,747
1880 (June 1)	50,189,209	14.2	10,370,760	26.0	3,612,299	3,540,705	52,747
1890 (June 1)	62,979,766	17.8	12,790,557	25.5	3,612,299	3,540,705	52,747
1900 (June 1)	76,212,168	21.5	13,232,402	21.0	3,618,770	3,547,314	52,553
1910 (Apr. 15)	92,228,496	26.0	16,016,328	21.0	3,618,770	3,547,045	52,822
1920 (Jan. 1)	106,021,537	29.9	13,793,041	15.0	3,618,770	3,546,931	52,936
1930 (Apr. 1)	123,202,624	34.7	17,181,087	16.2	3,618,770	3,551,608	45,259
1940 (Apr. 1)	132,164,569	37.2	8,961,945	7.3	3,618,770	3,551,608	45,259
1950 (Apr. 1)	151,325,798	42.6	19,161,229	14.5	3,618,770	3,552,206	63,005
1960 (Apr. 1)	179,323,175	50.6	27,997,377	18.5	3,618,770	3,540,911	74,212
1970 (Apr. 1)	[3]203,302,031	[3]57.5	23,978,856	13.4	3,618,770	[3]3,536,855	[3]78,444
1980 (Apr. 1)	[4]226,542,199	64.0	23,240,168	11.4	3,618,770	3,539,289	79,481
1990 (Apr. 1)	[5]248,718,302	70.3	22,176,103	9.8	[6]3,717,796	[6]3,536,278	[6]181,518
2000 (Apr. 1)	[7]281,422,509	79.6	32,704,207	13.1	3,794,083	3,537,439	256,645

X Not applicable. [1] Data for 1790 to 1980 cover inland water only. Data for 1990 comprises Great Lakes, inland, and coastal water. Data for 2000 comprises Great Lakes, inland, territorial and coastal water. [2] Revised to include adjustments for underenumeration in southern states; unrevised number is 38,558,371 (13.0 per square mile). [3] Figures corrected after 1970 final reports were issued. [4] Total population count has been revised since the 1980 census publications. Numbers by age, race, Hispanic origin, and sex have not been corrected. [5] The April 1, 1990, census count includes count question resolution corrections processed through December 1997 and does not include adjustments for census coverage errors. [6] Data reflect corrections made after publication of the results. [7] Reflects modifications to the Census 2000 population as documented in the Count Question Resolution program.

Source: U.S. Census Bureau, 1990 Census of Population and Housing, *Population and Housing Unit Counts* (CPH-2); 1990 Census of Population and Housing Listing (1990 CPH-L-157); "Table NA-EST2002-01 - National Population Estimates: April 1, 2000 to July 1, 2002"; published 31 December 2002; <http://eire.census.gov/popest/data/national/tables/NA-EST2002-01.php>. *Area data*: 2000 Census of Population and Housing, *Summary Population and Housing Characteristics*, Series PHC-1; and unpublished data from TIGER (R).

No. 2. Population: 1960 to 2002

[In thousands, except percent (180,671 represents 180,671,000). Estimates as of July 1. Total population includes Armed Forces abroad; civilian population excludes Armed Forces. For basis of estimates, see text of this section]

Year	Total Population	Percent change [1]	Resident population	Civilian population	Year	Total Population	Percent change [1]	Resident population	Civilian population
1960	180,671	1.60	179,979	178,140	1982	232,188	0.97	231,664	229,995
1961	183,691	1.67	182,992	181,143	1983	234,307	0.91	233,792	232,097
1962	186,538	1.55	185,771	183,677	1984	236,348	0.87	235,825	234,110
1963	189,242	1.45	188,483	186,493	1985	238,466	0.90	237,924	236,219
1964	191,889	1.40	191,141	189,141	1986	240,651	0.92	240,133	238,412
1965	194,303	1.26	193,526	191,605	1987	242,804	0.89	242,289	240,550
1966	196,560	1.16	195,576	193,420	1988	245,021	0.91	244,499	242,817
1967	198,712	1.09	197,457	195,264	1989	247,342	0.95	246,819	245,131
1968	200,706	1.00	199,399	197,113	1990	250,132	1.13	249,623	247,983
1969	202,677	0.98	201,385	199,145	1991	253,493	1.34	252,981	251,370
1970	205,052	1.17	203,984	201,895	1992	256,894	1.34	256,514	254,929
1971	207,661	1.27	206,827	204,866	1993	260,255	1.31	259,919	258,446
1972	209,896	1.08	209,284	207,511	1994	263,436	1.22	263,126	261,714
1973	211,909	0.96	211,357	209,600	1995	266,557	1.18	266,278	264,927
1974	213,854	0.92	213,342	211,636	1996	269,667	1.17	269,394	268,108
1975	215,973	0.99	215,465	213,789	1997	272,912	1.20	272,647	271,394
1976	218,035	0.95	217,563	215,894	1998	276,115	1.17	275,854	274,633
1977	220,239	1.01	219,760	218,106	1999	279,295	1.15	279,040	277,841
1978	222,585	1.06	222,095	220,467	2000	282,434	1.12	282,224	281,001
1979	225,055	1.11	224,567	222,969	2001	285,545	1.10	285,318	284,103
1980	227,726	1.19	227,225	225,621	2002	288,600	1.07	288,369	287,123
1981	229,966	0.98	229,466	227,818					

[1] Percent change from immediate preceding year.

Source: U.S. Census Bureau, Current Population Reports, P25-802 and P25-1095; "Table CO-EST2001-12-00 - Time Series of Intercensal State Population Estimates: April 1, 1990, to April 1, 2000"; published 11 April 2002; <http://eire.census.gov/popest/data/counties/tables/CO-EST2001-12/CO-EST2001-12-00.php>; "Table NA-2002EST-06 - Monthly National Population Estimates"; published 25 July 2003; <http://eire.census.gov/popest/data/national/tables/NA-EST2002-06.php>; and unpublished data.

No. 3. Resident Population Projections: 2003 to 2050

[290,116 represents 290,116,000. As of July 1. The projections are based on assumptions about future childbearing, mortality, and migration. The level of childbearing among women is assumed to remain close to present levels, with differences by race and Hispanic origin diminishing over time. Mortality is assumed to decline gradually with less variation by race and Hispanic origin than at present. International migration is assumed to vary over time and decrease generally relative to the size of the population]

Year	Resident population (1,000)	Percent change [1]	Year	Resident population (1,000)	Percent change [1]	Year	Resident population (1,000)	Percent change [1]
2003	290,116	0.9	2019	333,127	0.8	2035	377,886	0.8
2004	292,801	0.9	2020	335,805	0.8	2036	380,716	0.7
2005	295,507	0.9	2021	338,490	0.8	2037	383,537	0.7
2006	298,217	0.9	2022	341,195	0.8	2038	386,348	0.7
2007	300,913	0.9	2023	343,921	0.8	2039	389,151	0.7
2008	303,598	0.9	2024	346,669	0.8	2040	391,946	0.7
2009	306,272	0.9	2025	349,439	0.8	2041	394,734	0.7
2010	308,936	0.9	2026	352,229	0.8	2042	397,519	0.7
2011	311,601	0.9	2027	355,035	0.8	2043	400,301	0.7
2012	314,281	0.9	2028	357,862	0.8	2044	403,081	0.7
2013	316,971	0.9	2029	360,711	0.8	2045	405,862	0.7
2014	319,668	0.9	2030	363,584	0.8	2046	408,646	0.7
2015	322,366	0.8	2031	366,466	0.8	2047	411,435	0.7
2016	325,063	0.8	2032	369,336	0.8	2048	414,230	0.7
2017	327,756	0.8	2033	372,196	0.8	2049	417,035	0.7
2018	330,444	0.8	2034	375,046	0.8	2050	419,854	0.7

[1] Percent change from immediate preceding year. 2003, change from 2002.

Source: U.S. Census Bureau, International Data Base, Table 094; published: 10 October 2002; <http://www.census.gov/ipc/www.idbprint.html>.

No. 4. Components of Population Change: 2000 to 2002

[In thousands (281,423 represents 281,423,000), except as indicated. Resident population]

Period	Population as of beginning of period	Net increase Total	Net increase Percent [1]	Births	Deaths	Net international migration [2]	Population as of end of period
April 1, 2000, to July 1, 2000	281,423	802	0.3	989	561	374	282,224
July 1, 2000, to July 1, 2001	282,224	3,093	1.1	4,044	2,407	1,456	285,318
July 1, 2001, to July 1, 2002	285,318	3,051	1.1	4,048	2,446	1,449	288,369

[1] Percent of population at beginning of period. [2] Includes legal migration, emigration, temporary migration, net movement from Puerto Rico, and net change in the residual foreign-born population (including unauthorized migration). Includes federal civilian movement.

Source: U.S. Census Bureau, "Table NA-EST2002-03 - National Population Estimates and Population Change: 2000 to 2002"; published 31 December 2002; <http://eire.census.gov/popest/data/national/tables/NA-EST2002-03.php> and "Table NA-EST2002-05 - Components of National Population Change: 2000 to 2002"; published 31 December 2002; <http://eire.census.gov/popest/data/national/tables/NA-EST2002-05.php>.

No. 5. Immigration: 1901 to 2001

[In thousands, except rate (8,795 represents 8,795,000). For fiscal years ending in year shown; see text, Section 8. For definition of immigrants, see text of this section. Data represent immigrants admitted. Rates based on Census Bureau estimates as of July 1 for resident population through 1929 and for total population thereafter (excluding Alaska and Hawaii prior to 1959)]

Period	Number	Rate [1]	Year	Number	Rate [1]
1901 to 1910	8,795	10.4	1990	1,536	6.1
1911 to 1920	5,736	5.7	1991	1,827	7.2
1921 to 1930	4,107	3.5	1992	974	3.8
1931 to 1940	528	0.4	1993	904	3.5
1941 to 1950	1,035	0.7	1994	804	3.1
			1995	720	2.7
1951 to 1960	2,515	1.5	1996	916	3.4
1961 to 1970	3,322	1.7	1997	798	2.9
1971 to 1980	4,493	2.1	1998	654	2.4
1981 to 1990	7,338	3.1	1999	647	2.3
1991 to 2000	9,095	3.4	2000	850	3.0
			2001	1,064	3.7

[1] Annual rate per 1,000 U.S. population. Rate computed by dividing sum of annual immigration totals by sum of annual U.S. population totals for same number of years.

Source: U.S. Bureau of Citizenship and Immigration Services, *Statistical Yearbook*, annual. See also <http://www.immigration.gov/graphics/shared/aboutus/statistics/ybpage.htm>.

No. 6. Immigrants Admitted by Class of Admission: 1990 to 2001

[For fiscal year ending September 30. For definition of immigrants, see text of this section]

Class of admission	1990	1995	1998	1999	2000	2001
Immigrants, total	**1,536,483**	**720,461**	**654,451**	**646,568**	**849,807**	**1,064,318**
New arrivals	435,729	380,291	357,037	401,775	407,402	653,259
Adjustments	1,100,754	340,170	297,414	244,793	442,405	411,059
Preference immigrants, total	272,742	323,458	268,997	273,700	342,304	411,338
Family-sponsored immigrants, total	214,550	238,122	191,480	216,883	235,280	232,143
Unmarried sons/daughters of U.S. citizens and their children	15,861	15,182	17,717	22,392	27,707	27,098
Spouses, unmarried sons/daughters of alien residents, and their children	107,686	144,535	88,488	108,007	124,595	112,260
Married sons/daughters of U.S. citizens [1]	26,751	20,876	22,257	24,040	22,833	24,878
Brothers or sisters of U.S. citizens [1]	64,252	57,529	63,018	62,444	60,145	67,907
Employment-based immigrants, total	58,192	85,336	77,517	56,817	107,024	179,195
Priority workers [1]	(X)	17,339	21,408	14,898	27,706	41,801
Professionals with advanced degrees [1]	(X)	10,475	14,384	8,581	20,304	42,620
Skilled workers, professionals, unskilled workers [1]	(X)	50,245	34,317	27,966	49,736	86,058
Special immigrants [1]	4,463	6,737	6,584	5,086	9,052	8,523
Employment creation [1]	(X)	540	824	286	226	193
Professional or highly skilled immigrants [1,2]	26,546	(X)	(X)	(X)	(X)	(X)
Needed skilled or unskilled workers [1,2]	27,183	(X)	(X)	(X)	(X)	(X)
Immediate relatives	231,680	220,360	283,368	258,584	347,870	443,035
Spouses of U.S. citizens	125,426	123,238	151,172	127,988	197,525	270,545
Children of U.S. citizens	46,065	48,740	70,472	69,113	82,726	91,526
Orphans	7,088	9,384	14,867	16,037	18,120	19,087
Parents of U.S. citizens	60,189	48,382	61,724	61,483	67,619	80,964
Refugees and asylees	97,364	114,664	52,193	42,852	65,941	108,506
Refugee adjustments	92,427	106,827	44,645	39,495	59,083	97,305
Asylee adjustments	4,937	7,837	7,548	3,357	6,858	11,201
Immigration Reform and Control Act of 1986 legalization adjustments	880,372	4,267	955	8	421	263
Other immigrants	54,325	57,712	48,938	71,424	93,271	101,176
Diversity Programs [3]	29,161	47,245	45,499	47,571	50,945	42,015
Amerasians (P.L. 100-202) [4]	13,059	939	346	239	943	376
Children born abroad to alien residents	2,410	1,894	902	978	1,009	929
Legalization dependents [5]	(X)	277	21	-	55	37
Nicaraguan Adjustment and Central American Relief Sec. 202 entrants (P.L. 105-100)	(X)	(X)	1	11,267	23,641	18,926
Cancellation of removal [6]	889	3,168	428	9,032	12,349	22,506
Other	8,806	4,189	1,741	2,337	4,329	16,387

- Represents zero. X Not applicable. [1] Includes spouses and children. [2] Category was eliminated in 1992 by the Immigration Act of 1990. [3] Includes categories of immigrants admitted under three laws intended to diversify immigration: P.L. 99-603, P.L. 100-658, and P.L. 101-649. [4] Under Public Law 100-202, Amerasians are aliens born in Vietnam between January 1, 1962, and January 1, 1976, who were fathered by U.S. citizens. [5] Spouses and children of persons granted permanent resident status under provisions of the Immigration Reform and Control Act of 1986. [6] Was suspension of deportation prior to April 1, 1997.

Source: U.S. Bureau of Citizenship and Immigration Services, *Statistical Yearbook*, annual. See also <http://www.immigration.gov/graphics/shared/aboutus/statistics/ybpage.htm>.

No. 7. Estimated Unauthorized Immigrants by Selected States and Countries of Origin: 2000

[In thousands (7,000 represents 7,000,000). As of January. Unauthorized immigrants refer to foreign-born persons who entered without inspection or who violated the terms of a temporary admission and who have not acquired legal permanent resident status or gained temporary protection against removal by applying for an immigration benefit. The estimates were derived using the residual technique: the legally resident population was estimated and then subtracted from the census-based foreign-born population, leaving estimated unauthorized residents as a residual. The estimates rely primarily on data from two sources: (1) annual INS statistics (immigrants admitted, deportable aliens removed, and nonimmigrant residents admitted); and (2) data for the foreign-born population from the 2000 census. Estimates were derived separately for: (1) unauthorized residents who entered the United States in the 1990s; and (2) those who entered before 1990 and still lived here illegally in January 2000]

State	Number	Country	Number
United States, total [1]	**7,000**	**Total** [1]	**7,000**
California	2,209	Mexico	4,808
Texas	1,041	El Salvador	189
New York	489	Guatemala	144
Illinois	432	Colombia	141
Florida	337	Honduras	[2]138
Arizona	283	China	115
Georgia	228	Ecuador	108
New Jersey	221	Dominican Republic	91
North Carolina	206	Philippines	85
Colorado	144	Brazil	77
Washington	136	Haiti	76
Virginia	103	India	70
Nevada	101	Peru	61
Oregon	90	Korea	55
Massachusetts	87	Canada	47

[1] Includes other states and countries not shown separately. [2] Includes 105,000 Hondurans granted temporary protected status in December 1998.

Source: U.S. Bureau of Citizenship and Immigration Services, *Estimates of the Unauthorized Immigrant Population Residing in the United States: 1990 to 2000*, published January 2003; <http://www.immigration.gov/graphics/shared/aboutus/statistics/Ill_Report_1211.pdf>.

No. 8. Immigrants by Country of Birth: 1981 to 2001

[In thousands (7,338.1 represents 7,338,100). For fiscal years ending Sept. 30. For definition of immigrants, see text of this section]

Country of birth	1981-1990, total	1991-2000, total	2000	2001	Country of birth	1981-1990, total	1991-2000, total	2000	2001
All countries	7,338.1	9,095.4	849.8	1,064.3	Taiwan	(^{4})	106.4	9.0	12.2
Europe [1]	705.6	1,311.4	132.5	175.4	Thailand	64.4	48.4	3.8	4.3
Armenia	(X)	^{2}26.6	1.3	1.8	Turkey	20.9	26.3	2.6	3.2
Belarus	(X)	^{2}29.0	2.2	2.9	Vietnam	401.4	421.1	26.7	35.5
Bosnia and Herzegovina	(X)	^{2}39.1	11.8	23.6	Africa [1]	192.3	383.0	44.7	53.9
France	23.1	27.5	3.5	4.6	Egypt	31.4	46.7	4.5	5.2
Germany	70.1	67.7	7.6	9.9	Ethiopia	27.2	49.3	4.1	5.1
Greece	29.1	13.6	1.0	1.2	Ghana	14.9	35.6	4.3	4.0
Ireland	32.8	59.0	1.3	1.5	Nigeria	35.3	67.3	7.9	8.3
Italy	32.9	22.6	2.5	3.1	South Africa	15.7	22.6	2.8	4.1
Poland	97.4	169.6	10.1	11.8	Oceania	(NA)	48.0	5.1	6.1
Portugal	40.0	22.8	1.4	1.7	North America [1]	3,125.0	3,917.4	344.8	407.9
Romania	38.9	57.5	6.9	6.6	Canada	119.2	137.6	16.2	21.9
Russia [3]	(X)	^{2}128.0	17.1	20.4	Mexico	1,653.3	2,251.4	173.9	206.4
Soviet Union [3]	84.0	103.9	3.3	2.7	Caribbean [1]	892.7	996.1	88.2	103.5
Ukraine	(X)	^{2}141.3	15.8	21.0	Cuba	159.2	180.9	20.8	27.7
United Kingdom	142.1	135.8	13.4	18.4	Dominican Republic	251.8	340.9	17.5	21.3
Yugoslavia [3]	19.2	25.9	2.8	6.2	Haiti	140.2	181.8	22.4	27.1
Asia [1]	2,817.4	2,892.2	265.4	349.8	Jamaica	213.8	173.5	16.0	15.4
Afghanistan	26.6	17.4	1.0	1.2	Trinidad and Tobago	39.5	63.3	6.7	6.7
Bangladesh	15.2	66.0	7.2	7.2	Central America [1]	458.7	531.8	66.4	75.9
Cambodia	116.6	18.5	2.1	2.5	El Salvador	214.6	217.4	22.6	31.3
China	^{4}388.8	424.6	45.7	56.4	Guatemala	87.9	103.1	10.0	13.6
Hong Kong	63.0	74.0	5.4	8.3	Honduras	49.5	66.8	5.9	6.6
India	261.9	383.3	42.0	70.3	Nicaragua	44.1	97.7	24.0	19.9
Iran	154.8	112.6	8.5	10.5	Panama	29.0	24.0	1.8	1.9
Iraq	19.6	40.7	5.1	5.0	South America [1]	455.9	539.9	56.1	68.9
Israel	36.3	32.0	2.8	3.8	Argentina	25.7	24.3	2.3	3.3
Japan	43.2	61.5	7.1	9.6	Brazil	23.7	52.3	7.0	9.5
Jordan	32.6	39.7	3.9	4.6	Chile	23.4	16.9	1.7	1.9
Korea	338.8	171.3	15.8	20.7	Colombia	124.4	131.0	14.5	16.7
Laos	145.6	43.6	1.4	1.4	Ecuador	56.0	76.4	7.7	9.7
Lebanon	41.6	43.5	3.7	4.6	Guyana	95.4	73.9	5.7	8.3
Pakistan	61.3	124.6	14.5	16.4	Peru	64.4	105.7	9.6	11.1
Philippines	495.3	505.6	42.5	53.2	Venezuela	17.9	29.9	4.7	5.2
Syria	20.6	26.1	2.4	3.4					

NA Not available. X Not applicable. [1] Includes countries not shown separately. [2] Covers years 1992-2000. [3] Prior to 1992, data include independent republics; beginning in 1992, data are for unknown republic only. [4] Data for Taiwan included with China.

Source: U.S. Bureau of Citizenship and Immigration Services, *Statistical Yearbook*, annual. See also <http://www.immigration.gov/graphics/shared/aboutus/statistics/ybpage.htm>.

No. 9. Immigrants Admitted as Permanent Residents Under Refugee Acts by Country of Birth: 1981 to 2001

[For fiscal years ending September 30]

Country of birth	1981-1990, total	1991-2000, total	2001	Country of birth	1981-1990, total	1991-2000, total	2001
Total [1]	1,013,620	1,021,266	108,506	Asia [1]	712,092	351,347	19,992
Europe [1]	155,565	426,565	55,825	Afghanistan	22,946	9,725	257
Albania	289	3,255	114	Cambodia	114,064	6,388	75
Armenia	(X)	2,161	321	China [5]	7,928	7,608	813
Azerbaijan	(X)	^{2}12,072	476	Iran	46,773	24,313	1,364
Belarus	(X)	^{2}24,581	1,548	Iraq	7,540	22,557	3,060
Bosnia and Herzegovina	(X)	^{2}37,591	23,303	Laos	142,964	37,265	520
Croatia	(X)	1,807	2,337	Syria	2,145	2,125	327
Czechoslovakia [3]	8,204	1,255	14	Thailand	30,259	22,759	653
Georgia	(X)	^{2}2,593	178	Vietnam	324,453	206,857	10,351
Hungary	4,942	1,285	19	Africa [1]	22,149	51,649	6,906
Kazakhstan	(X)	^{2}4,269	659	Ethiopia [6]	18,542	17,865	881
Moldova	(X)	^{2}11,717	1,322	Liberia	109	3,839	976
Poland	33,889	7,500	71	Somalia	70	16,837	2,484
Romania	29,798	15,708	119	Sudan	739	5,191	593
Russia	(X)	60,404	4,758	Oceania	22	291	19
Soviet Union [4]	72,306	90,533	1,621	North America [1]	121,840	185,333	24,696
Tajikistan	(X)	^{2}2,546	100	Cuba	113,367	144,612	22,687
Ukraine	(X)	^{2}109,739	11,130	Haiti	(NA)	9,364	735
Uzbekistan	(X)	^{2}19,539	1,099	El Salvador	1,383	4,073	195
Yugoslavia [4]	324	6,274	4,190	Nicaragua	5,590	22,486	350
				South America	1,986	5,857	936

NA Not available. X Not applicable. [1] Includes other countries and unknown, not shown separately. [2] Covers years 1992-2000. [3] Prior to 1993, data include independent republics; beginning in 1993, data are for unknown republic only. [4] Prior to 1992, data include independent republics; beginning in 1992, data are for unknown republic only. [5] Includes Taiwan. [6] Prior to 1993, data include Eritrea.

Source: U.S. Bureau of Citizenship and Immigration Services, *Statistical Yearbook*, annual. See also <http://www.immigration.gov/graphics/shared/aboutus/statistics/ybpage.htm>.

No. 10. Immigrants Admitted by State and Leading Country of Birth: 2001

[For year ending September 30. For definition of immigrants, see text of this section]

State and other area	Total [1]	Mexico	India	China	Philippines	Vietnam	El Salvador	Cuba	Haiti
Total	1,064,318	206,426	70,290	56,426	53,154	35,531	31,272	27,703	27,120
Alabama	2,257	313	215	182	68	106	3	17	4
Alaska	1,401	126	11	51	366	22	19	1	4
Arizona	16,362	7,932	584	459	459	490	138	128	10
Arkansas	2,572	1,148	136	101	113	115	97	5	-
California	282,957	97,293	16,512	17,312	23,177	13,025	11,938	546	77
Colorado	12,494	4,107	786	648	229	612	123	19	28
Connecticut	12,148	177	1,001	654	339	263	74	64	409
Delaware	1,850	166	270	182	118	35	32	8	75
District of Columbia	3,043	46	53	136	88	69	752	8	26
Florida	104,715	3,596	1,782	1,113	1,933	1,178	725	21,729	17,136
Georgia	19,431	2,531	1,743	836	446	1,242	218	104	167
Hawaii	6,313	116	21	530	3,341	228	4	1	-
Idaho	2,296	942	62	108	64	59	5	9	10
Illinois	48,296	11,821	4,961	2,323	2,967	596	184	127	112
Indiana	6,010	944	575	485	306	151	57	19	18
Iowa	5,029	1,053	268	190	110	291	44	3	5
Kansas	4,030	1,195	414	230	138	354	64	12	9
Kentucky	4,548	260	289	240	114	181	14	389	7
Louisiana	3,778	247	200	210	130	519	43	107	26
Maine	1,186	9	30	71	52	46	7	4	4
Maryland	22,060	507	1,831	1,648	993	507	2,014	35	235
Massachusetts	28,965	227	2,332	2,450	313	1,405	990	92	1,822
Michigan	21,528	1,003	2,978	1,433	662	470	41	207	24
Minnesota	11,166	772	795	643	266	637	81	19	22
Mississippi	1,340	160	130	109	110	89	7	18	3
Missouri	7,616	419	543	575	270	474	38	54	28
Montana	488	30	15	36	20	7	1	-	1
Nebraska	3,850	1,370	216	121	86	246	74	25	3
Nevada	9,618	3,308	184	324	1,218	134	339	540	6
New Hampshire	2,595	35	305	157	172	105	12	-	16
New Jersey	59,920	1,098	9,154	3,262	2,905	500	2,316	1,361	1,788
New Mexico	5,207	3,575	78	129	83	116	16	117	2
New York	114,116	2,065	4,942	8,071	2,218	792	3,732	512	4,531
North Carolina	13,918	2,103	1,021	710	419	652	265	94	25
North Dakota	558	17	23	19	19	10	1	3	2
Ohio	14,725	633	1,651	1,126	452	358	48	35	31
Oklahoma	3,492	877	284	149	108	330	21	13	6
Oregon	9,638	1,985	611	557	297	704	75	123	25
Pennsylvania	21,441	1,031	2,904	1,858	518	1,159	91	109	186
Rhode Island	2,820	40	70	129	51	28	81	4	65
South Carolina	2,882	231	288	165	178	85	24	1	5
South Dakota	671	23	17	53	28	13	4	1	1
Tennessee	6,257	703	444	298	388	343	39	58	9
Texas	86,315	43,524	4,313	2,623	2,260	3,772	3,644	452	44
Utah	5,247	1,103	122	249	99	205	71	12	8
Vermont	954	4	38	71	16	50	2	2	3
Virginia	26,876	804	2,970	1,400	1,214	1,093	2,565	72	44
Washington	23,085	2,518	1,301	1,272	1,406	1,533	85	24	20
West Virginia	737	31	106	80	41	19	4	-	-
Wisconsin	8,477	2,007	645	494	247	96	31	25	9
Wyoming	308	70	23	9	22	3	3	-	-
Guam	1,722	-	9	50	1,406	9	-	-	-
Northern Mariana Islands	113	-	1	19	75	2	-	-	-
Puerto Rico	3,459	125	3	69	5	-	14	395	12
Virgin Islands	1,327	1	28	2	5	2	2	-	17
Armed Services posts	96	5	1	5	22	1	-	-	-
Unknown	15	-	1	-	4	-	-	-	-

- Represents zero. [1] Includes other countries, not shown separately.

Source: U.S. Bureau of Citizenship and Immigration Services, *Statistical Yearbook*, annual. See also <http://www.immigration.gov/graphics/shared/aboutus/statistics/ybpage.htm>.

No. 11. Resident Population by Age and Sex: 1980 to 2002

[In thousands, except as indicated (226,546 represents 226,546,000). 1980, 1990, and 2000 data are enumerated population as of April 1; data for other years are estimated population as of July 1. Excludes Armed Forces overseas. For definition of median, see Guide to Tabular Presentation]

Year and sex	Total, all years	Under 5 years	5-9 years	10-14 years	15-19 years	20-24 years	25-29 years	30-34 years	35-39 years	40-44 years	45-49 years	50-54 years	55-59 years	60-64 years	65-74 years	75-84 years	85 years and over	14-17 years	18-24 years	Median age (yr.)
1980, total [1]	226,546	16,348	16,700	18,242	21,168	21,319	19,521	17,561	13,965	11,669	11,090	11,710	11,615	10,088	15,581	7,729	2,240	16,247	30,022	30.0
Male	110,053	8,362	8,539	9,316	10,755	10,663	9,705	8,677	6,862	5,708	5,388	5,621	5,482	4,670	6,757	2,867	682	8,298	15,054	28.8
Female	116,493	7,986	8,161	8,926	10,413	10,655	9,816	8,884	7,104	5,961	5,702	6,089	6,133	5,418	8,824	4,862	1,559	7,950	14,969	31.3
1990, total [2]	248,791	18,765	18,042	17,067	17,893	19,143	21,336	21,838	19,851	17,593	13,747	11,315	10,489	10,627	18,048	10,014	3,022	13,345	26,961	32.8
Male	121,284	9,603	9,236	8,742	9,178	9,749	10,708	10,866	9,837	8,679	6,741	5,494	5,009	4,947	7,908	3,745	841	6,860	13,744	31.6
Female	127,507	9,162	8,806	8,325	8,714	9,394	10,629	10,973	10,014	8,914	7,006	5,821	5,480	5,679	10,140	6,268	2,181	6,485	13,217	34.0
1991, total	252,981	19,208	18,281	17,756	17,270	19,234	20,923	22,301	20,577	18,752	14,129	11,691	10,443	10,603	18,294	10,329	3,189	13,491	26,442	33.1
1992, total	256,514	19,528	18,431	18,246	17,246	19,188	20,503	22,494	21,184	18,792	15,413	12,135	10,521	10,477	18,486	10,555	3,315	13,775	26,137	33.4
1993, total	259,919	19,729	18,646	18,721	17,474	18,900	20,069	22,584	21,727	19,185	16,013	12,851	10,736	10,292	18,693	10,764	3,446	14,096	25,975	33.6
1994, total	263,126	19,777	19,025	19,001	17,876	18,656	19,740	22,590	22,135	19,684	16,791	13,362	11,009	10,150	18,790	10,980	3,561	14,637	25,703	33.9
1995, total	266,278	19,627	19,438	19,207	18,374	18,300	19,680	22,372	22,492	19,685	17,624	13,856	11,182	10,138	18,866	11,222	3,681	14,825	25,482	34.4
1996, total	269,394	19,408	19,861	19,435	17,876	17,877	19,864	21,945	22,786	19,684	18,300	14,189	11,481	10,109	18,824	11,524	3,795	15,013	25,275	34.4
1997, total	272,647	19,233	20,254	19,601	18,920	17,910	19,899	21,446	22,904	20,766	18,611	14,491	11,905	10,194	18,684	11,812	3,905	15,443	25,479	34.7
1998, total	275,854	19,145	20,510	19,825	19,398	18,167	19,804	20,953	22,904	21,325	19,114	16,118	12,589	10,422	18,570	12,016	4,033	15,769	26,059	34.9
1999, total	279,040	19,136	20,606	20,213	20,085	18,591	19,575	20,603	22,883	22,194	19,654	16,924	13,085	10,693	18,419	12,225	4,154	16,007	26,685	35.2
2000, total	281,422	19,176	20,550	20,528	20,220	18,964	19,381	20,510	22,707	22,442	20,092	17,586	13,469	10,805	18,391	12,361	4,240	16,093	27,143	35.3
Male	138,054	9,811	10,523	10,520	10,391	9,799	9,779	10,322	11,319	11,129	9,890	8,608	6,509	5,137	8,303	4,879	1,227	8,285	13,874	34.0
Female	143,368	9,365	10,026	10,008	9,829	9,276	9,583	10,189	11,388	11,313	10,203	8,978	6,961	5,669	10,088	7,482	3,013	7,808	13,270	36.5
2001, total	285,318	19,364	20,208	20,910	20,376	19,711	19,023	20,792	22,318	22,823	20,798	18,430	14,196	11,119	18,322	12,582	4,448	16,204	27,849	35.6
2002, total	288,369	19,609	19,901	21,136	20,376	20,214	18,972	20,956	21,915	23,002	21,302	18,782	14,991	11,611	18,274	12,735	4,593	16,365	28,342	35.7
Male	141,661	10,025	10,188	10,825	10,471	10,350	9,640	10,563	10,954	11,413	10,492	9,185	7,260	5,524	8,301	5,081	1,390	8,388	14,541	34.4
Female	146,708	9,584	9,713	10,312	9,905	9,863	9,332	10,394	10,961	11,589	10,810	9,597	7,730	6,087	9,973	7,654	3,203	7,976	13,801	37.0
Percent:																				
1980 [1]	100.0	7.2	7.4	8.1	9.3	9.4	8.6	7.8	6.2	5.2	4.9	5.2	5.1	4.5	6.9	3.4	1.0	7.2	13.3	(X)
1990 [2]	100.0	7.5	7.3	6.9	7.2	7.7	8.6	8.8	8.0	7.1	5.5	4.5	4.2	4.0	7.3	4.0	1.2	5.4	10.8	(X)
2000	100.0	6.8	7.3	7.3	7.2	6.7	6.9	7.3	8.1	8.0	7.1	6.2	4.8	3.8	6.5	4.4	1.5	5.7	9.6	(X)
2002:	100.0	6.8	6.9	7.3	7.1	7.0	6.6	7.3	7.6	8.0	7.4	6.5	5.2	4.0	6.3	4.4	1.6	5.7	9.8	(X)
Male	100.0	7.1	7.2	7.6	7.4	7.3	6.8	7.5	7.7	8.1	7.4	6.5	5.1	3.9	5.9	3.6	1.0	5.9	10.3	(X)
Female	100.0	6.5	6.6	7.0	6.8	6.7	6.4	7.1	7.5	7.9	7.4	6.5	5.3	4.1	6.8	5.2	2.2	5.4	9.4	(X)

X Not applicable. [1] Total population count has been revised since the 1980 census publications. Numbers by age, race, Hispanic origin, and sex have not been corrected. [2] The data shown has been modified from the official 1990 census counts. See text of this section for explanation. The April 1, 1990, estimates base (248,790,925) includes count resolution corrections processed through August 1997. It generally does not include adjustments for census coverage errors. However, it includes adjustments estimated for the 1995 Test Census in various localities in California, New Jersey, and Louisiana; and the 1998 census dress rehearsals in localities in California and Wisconsin. These adjustments amounted to a total of 81,052 persons.

Source: U.S. Census Bureau, Current Population Reports, P25-1095; and "Intercensal Estimates of the United States Resident Population by Age Groups and Sex, 1990-2000", published 13 September 2002; <http://eire.census.gov/popest/data/national/tables/intercensal/US-EST90INT-04.php>; and "Table NA-EST2002-ASRO-01-National Population Estimates-Characteristics", published 18 June 2003; <http://eire.census.gov/popest/data/national/tables/asro/NA-EST2002-ASRO-01.php>.

Population   13

U.S. Census Bureau, Statistical Abstract of the United States: 2003

No. 12. Resident Population Projections by Sex and Age: 2005 to 2050

[In thousands, except as indicated (295,507 represents 295,507,000). As of July. Data shown are for middle series; for assumptions, see Table 3]

Age	2005 Total	2005 Male	2005 Female	2010 Total	2010 Male	2010 Female	2015	2020	2025	2030	2035	2040	2045	2050	% 2005	% 2010	% 2015	% 2020	% 2025	% 2050
Total	295,507	145,113	150,394	308,936	151,815	157,121	322,366	335,805	349,439	363,584	377,886	391,946	405,862	419,854	100.0	100.0	100.0	100.0	100.0	100.0
Under 5 years	20,495	10,471	10,024	21,426	10,947	10,479	22,358	22,932	23,518	24,272	25,262	26,299	27,233	28,080	6.9	6.9	6.9	6.8	6.7	6.7
5 to 9 years	19,467	9,954	9,512	20,706	10,575	10,131	21,623	22,564	23,163	23,790	24,562	25,550	26,586	27,521	6.6	6.7	6.7	6.7	6.6	6.6
10 to 14 years	20,838	10,670	10,167	19,767	10,109	9,658	20,984	21,914	22,888	23,539	24,186	24,953	25,938	26,974	7.1	6.4	6.5	6.5	6.5	6.4
15 to 19 years	21,172	10,862	10,310	21,336	10,938	10,398	20,243	21,478	22,457	23,503	24,182	24,824	25,587	26,572	7.2	6.9	6.3	6.4	6.4	6.3
20 to 24 years	20,823	10,657	10,166	21,676	11,075	10,602	21,810	20,751	22,052	23,136	24,227	24,897	25,534	26,297	7.0	7.0	6.8	6.2	6.3	6.3
25 to 29 years	19,753	10,016	9,737	21,375	10,868	10,507	22,195	22,361	21,390	22,810	23,943	25,024	25,690	26,327	6.7	6.9	6.9	6.7	6.1	6.3
30 to 34 years	19,847	9,987	9,860	20,271	10,238	10,034	21,858	22,704	22,955	22,125	23,605	24,731	25,808	26,477	6.7	6.6	6.8	6.8	6.6	6.3
35 to 39 years	20,869	10,449	10,420	20,137	10,091	10,046	20,543	22,143	23,046	23,399	22,627	24,101	25,223	26,300	7.1	6.5	6.4	6.6	6.6	6.3
40 to 44 years	22,735	11,282	11,452	20,984	10,462	10,523	20,250	20,673	22,305	23,277	23,669	22,907	24,376	25,496	7.7	6.8	6.3	6.2	6.4	6.1
45 to 49 years	22,453	11,076	11,377	22,654	11,190	11,464	20,926	20,219	20,678	22,352	23,350	23,747	23,001	24,466	7.6	7.3	6.5	6.0	5.9	5.8
50 to 54 years	19,983	9,771	10,212	22,173	10,874	11,299	22,376	20,702	20,043	20,550	22,234	23,234	23,641	22,917	6.8	7.2	6.9	6.2	5.7	5.5
55 to 59 years	17,359	8,415	8,944	19,507	9,507	10,051	21,649	21,876	20,291	19,702	20,241	21,910	22,916	23,337	5.9	6.3	6.7	6.5	5.8	5.6
60 to 64 years	13,017	6,203	6,814	16,679	8,696	8,696	18,761	20,856	21,128	19,676	19,156	19,719	21,370	22,384	4.4	5.4	5.8	6.2	6.0	5.3
65 to 69 years	10,123	4,712	5,412	12,172	5,686	6,486	15,621	17,618	19,647	19,980	18,683	18,237	18,829	20,444	3.4	3.9	4.8	5.2	5.6	4.9
70 to 74 years	8,500	3,804	4,697	9,097	4,111	4,987	12,068	14,161	16,041	17,968	18,350	17,233	16,879	17,499	2.9	2.9	3.4	4.2	4.6	4.2
75 to 79 years	7,376	3,094	4,282	7,186	3,066	4,120	9,450	12,268	14,161	13,989	15,764	16,192	15,304	15,067	2.5	2.3	2.4	3.4	3.5	3.6
80 to 84 years	5,576	2,117	3,459	5,665	2,206	3,459	5,600	6,134	7,557	9,914	11,414	12,978	13,449	12,835	1.9	1.8	1.7	1.8	2.2	3.1
85 to 89 years	3,206	1,072	2,135	3,713	1,274	2,439	3,857	3,897	4,353	5,451	7,259	8,476	9,768	10,254	1.1	1.2	1.2	1.2	1.2	2.4
90 to 94 years	1,431	397	1,034	1,727	510	1,218	2,089	2,221	2,312	2,651	3,395	4,621	5,510	6,473	0.5	0.6	0.6	0.7	0.7	1.5
95 to 99 years	412	91	321	569	137	432	723	909	1,018	1,102	1,310	1,731	2,430	2,984	0.1	0.2	0.2	0.3	0.3	0.7
100 years and over	71	12	58	93	21	93	173	241	327	399	581	790	1,150	(Z)	(Z)	0.1	0.1	0.1	0.3	
5 to 13 years	35,968	18,402	17,566	36,439	18,618	17,821	38,418	40,148	41,501	42,627	43,922	45,536	47,379	49,138	12.2	11.8	11.9	12.0	11.9	11.7
14 to 17 years	17,175	8,809	8,366	16,566	8,492	8,074	16,243	17,220	18,079	18,809	19,311	19,847	20,505	21,330	5.8	5.4	5.0	5.1	5.2	5.1
18 to 24 years	29,156	14,931	14,225	30,481	15,587	14,894	30,000	29,339	30,980	32,533	33,924	34,841	35,763	36,895	9.9	9.9	9.3	8.7	8.9	8.8
16 years and over	230,335	111,774	118,561	242,936	118,082	124,854	253,361	264,085	275,339	287,281	299,051	310,182	320,974	331,940	77.9	78.6	78.6	78.6	78.8	79.1
18 years and over	221,868	107,430	114,438	234,504	113,758	120,746	245,347	255,505	266,341	277,877	289,391	300,264	310,746	321,305	75.1	75.9	76.1	76.1	76.2	76.5
16 to 64 years	193,639	96,475	97,164	202,693	101,071	101,622	206,570	209,453	211,815	215,828	222,410	230,132	238,015	245,234	65.5	65.6	64.1	62.4	60.6	58.4
55 years and over	67,072	29,916	37,156	76,429	34,450	41,980	87,201	97,363	104,944	110,831	116,039	120,132	127,245	132,427	22.7	24.7	27.1	29.0	30.0	31.5
65 years and over	36,696	15,299	21,397	40,244	17,011	23,233	46,791	54,632	63,524	71,453	76,641	80,050	82,959	86,706	12.4	13.0	14.5	16.3	18.2	20.7
75 years and over	18,072	6,783	11,289	18,974	7,214	11,761	20,183	22,852	27,835	33,506	39,609	44,579	47,251	48,763	6.1	6.1	6.3	6.3	7.6	11.6
85 years and over	5,120	1,572	3,548	6,123	1,942	4,182	6,822	7,269	8,011	9,603	12,430	15,409	18,498	20,861	1.7	2.0	2.1	2.2	2.3	5.0
Median age (years)	35.2	34.0	36.6	36.0	34.6	38.8	36.4	37.0	37.5	38.0	38.2	38.1	38.1	38.1	(X)	(X)	(X)	(X)	(X)	(X)

X Not applicable. Z Less than 0.05 percent.

Source: U.S. Census Bureau, International Data Base; published 10 October 2002; <http://www.census.gov/ipc/www/idbprint.html>.

No. 13. Resident Population by Race, Hispanic Origin, and Age: 2000 and 2002

[In thousands (281,422 represents 281,422,000); except as indicated. 2000 as of April and 2002 as of July. For definition of median, see Guide to Tabular Presentation]

Age group	Total 2000	Total 2002	White 2000	White 2002	Black 2000	Black 2002	American Indian, Alaska Native 2000	American Indian, Alaska Native 2002	Asian 2000	Asian 2002	Native Hawaiian, Other Pacific Islander 2000	Native Hawaiian, Other Pacific Islander 2002	Two or more races 2000	Two or more races 2002	Hispanic origin [1] 2000	Hispanic origin [1] 2002	Non-Hispanic White 2000	Non-Hispanic White 2002
Total	281,422	288,369	228,104	232,647	35,704	36,746	2,664	2,752	10,589	11,559	463	484	3,898	4,181	35,306	38,761	195,575	196,845
Under 5 years	19,176	19,609	14,656	14,964	2,925	2,999	233	215	708	768	41	37	613	627	3,718	3,962	11,287	11,311
5 to 9 years	20,550	19,901	15,687	15,189	3,320	3,121	258	243	716	747	44	43	524	558	3,624	3,730	12,392	11,797
10 to 14 years	20,528	21,136	15,842	16,188	3,221	3,384	264	271	715	765	42	44	443	485	3,163	3,535	12,961	12,966
15 to 19 years	20,220	20,376	15,746	15,816	3,024	3,077	251	259	776	776	44	42	380	406	3,172	3,197	12,837	12,887
20 to 24 years	18,964	20,214	14,827	15,766	2,729	2,949	218	237	848	873	46	47	297	342	3,409	3,607	11,682	12,441
25 to 29 years	19,381	18,972	15,217	14,819	2,645	2,587	204	208	1,019	1,048	42	44	254	267	3,385	3,754	12,077	11,329
30 to 34 years	20,510	20,956	16,348	16,553	2,710	2,751	202	208	980	1,150	39	42	231	251	3,125	3,578	13,451	13,228
35 to 39 years	22,707	21,915	18,371	17,537	2,910	2,855	217	213	937	1,037	38	39	233	233	2,825	3,156	15,752	14,607
40 to 44 years	22,442	23,002	18,346	18,707	2,772	2,869	202	212	870	948	33	36	219	230	2,304	2,652	16,213	16,247
45 to 49 years	20,092	21,302	16,615	17,512	2,330	2,518	169	185	770	856	27	30	183	201	1,775	2,073	14,972	15,593
50 to 54 years	17,586	18,782	14,793	15,637	1,846	2,072	135	150	641	734	21	24	149	164	1,361	1,582	13,530	14,171
55 to 59 years	13,469	14,991	11,479	12,743	1,332	1,471	95	109	443	526	15	17	106	124	960	1,138	10,581	11,683
60 to 64 years	10,805	11,611	9,214	9,897	1,082	1,137	70	79	350	398	11	13	78	88	750	837	8,511	9,113
65 to 69 years	9,534	9,581	8,238	8,204	895	931	52	57	279	314	8	9	61	66	599	657	7,675	7,587
70 to 74 years	8,857	8,693	7,799	7,608	742	738	38	42	224	247	6	7	49	51	477	524	7,348	7,114
75 to 79 years	7,416	7,420	6,634	6,589	557	576	27	30	159	182	4	5	36	39	327	375	6,325	6,235
80 to 84 years	4,945	5,314	4,466	4,779	350	378	15	19	90	110	2	3	22	25	180	224	4,296	4,567
85 to 89 years	2,790	2,943	2,525	2,662	200	203	8	10	43	54	1	1	12	14	98	112	2,432	2,556
90 to 94 years	1,113	1,250	1,007	1,125	82	93	3	4	15	21	1	1	4	6	39	50	970	1,078
95 to 99 years	287	342	254	304	27	30	1	-	4	6	-	-	-	2	11	15	243	290
100 years and over	50	59	41	49	7	7	-	-	1	1	-	-	-	1	3	3	39	46
5 to 13 years	37,025	36,921	28,381	28,206	5,923	5,864	471	461	1,288	1,357	78	78	885	955	6,186	6,611	22,753	22,189
14 to 17 years	16,093	16,365	12,522	12,667	2,426	2,505	205	209	590	611	33	34	315	339	2,438	2,552	10,290	10,335
18 to 24 years	27,143	28,342	21,199	22,086	3,944	4,163	315	340	1,178	1,192	64	64	444	497	4,744	4,906	16,829	17,568
16 years and over	217,149	223,631	178,789	183,142	25,633	26,614	1,857	1,972	8,305	9,128	328	352	2,237	2,424	24,204	26,894	156,351	158,191
18 years and over	209,128	215,474	172,545	176,811	24,430	25,378	1,755	1,868	8,003	8,823	311	335	2,084	2,260	22,964	25,637	151,244	153,010
16 to 64 years	182,157	188,029	147,825	151,822	22,773	23,658	1,713	1,808	7,490	8,195	305	326	2,051	2,220	22,470	24,933	127,022	128,719
55 years and over	59,266	62,204	51,656	53,960	5,274	5,564	310	351	1,608	1,857	48	56	371	415	3,444	3,936	48,421	50,268
65 years and over	34,992	35,602	30,964	31,320	2,860	2,956	144	163	815	934	23	26	186	203	1,734	1,961	29,329	29,472
75 years and over	16,601	17,328	14,927	15,509	1,223	1,286	55	64	312	373	8	10	77	86	657	780	14,306	14,771
85 years and over	4,240	4,593	3,827	4,140	316	332	13	15	63	81	2	2	18	22	151	180	3,685	3,969
Median age (yrs)	35.3	35.7	36.6	37.1	30.0	30.5	27.7	28.6	32.5	33.4	26.8	28.2	19.8	20.2	25.8	26.8	38.6	39.3

- Represents or rounds to zero. [1] Persons of Hispanic origin may be of any race.

Source: U.S. Census Bureau, "Table NA-EST2002-ASRO-03-National Population Estimates-Characteristics"; published 18 June 2003; <http://eire.census.gov/popest/data/national/tables/asro/NA-EST2002-ASRO-03.php>; and unpublished data.

Population 15

U.S. Census Bureau, Statistical Abstract of the United States: 2003

No. 14. Resident Population by Race, Hispanic Origin, and Single Years of Age: 2002

[In thousands, except as indicated (288,369 represents 288,369,000). As of July 1. For derivation of estimates, see text of this section]

Age	Total	Race						Hispanic origin [1]	Non-Hispanic White
		White	Black	American Indian, Alaska Native	Asian	Native Hawaiian and Other Pacific Islander	Two or more races		
Total	288,369	232,647	36,746	2,752	11,559	484	4,181	38,761	196,845
Under 5 yrs. old	19,609	14,964	2,999	215	768	37	627	3,962	11,311
Under 1 yr. old	4,034	3,074	628	39	162	6	124	834	2,290
1 yr. old	4,042	3,080	629	39	167	6	122	844	2,286
2 yrs. old	3,874	2,968	577	44	150	8	129	779	2,256
3 yrs. old	3,820	2,915	579	47	143	8	128	756	2,231
4 yrs. old	3,839	2,927	587	47	146	8	124	749	2,248
5-9 yrs. old	19,901	15,189	3,121	243	747	43	558	3,730	11,797
5 yrs. old	3,832	2,927	584	47	149	8	118	739	2,256
6 yrs. old	3,935	3,012	602	47	151	8	116	750	2,330
7 yrs. old	3,973	3,033	621	48	150	9	112	747	2,354
8 yrs. old	4,043	3,081	647	50	149	9	108	746	2,402
9 yrs. old	4,118	3,136	667	52	149	9	105	748	2,455
10-14 yrs. old	21,136	16,188	3,384	271	765	44	485	3,535	12,966
10 yrs. old	4,211	3,212	683	53	151	9	104	744	2,533
11 yrs. old	4,283	3,275	691	55	152	9	101	736	2,605
12 yrs. old	4,313	3,298	698	55	153	9	99	719	2,644
13 yrs. old	4,214	3,232	671	54	155	9	94	682	2,610
14 yrs. old	4,117	3,171	641	53	155	9	89	654	2,574
15-19 yrs. old	20,376	15,816	3,077	259	776	42	406	3,197	12,887
15 yrs. old	4,091	3,164	629	53	151	8	86	641	2,580
16 yrs. old	4,082	3,164	623	52	152	8	83	629	2,589
17 yrs. old	4,075	3,167	613	52	154	8	81	628	2,592
18 yrs. old	4,048	3,145	607	51	158	9	79	635	2,562
19 yrs. old	4,080	3,175	606	52	162	8	77	664	2,564
20-24 yrs. old	20,214	15,766	2,949	237	873	47	342	3,607	12,441
20 yrs. old	4,112	3,201	606	50	170	9	75	693	2,564
21 yrs. old	4,152	3,230	614	49	176	10	73	714	2,574
22 yrs. old	4,130	3,220	606	48	177	10	69	734	2,542
23 yrs. old	3,954	3,088	574	45	174	9	64	728	2,416
24 yrs. old	3,866	3,027	549	44	175	9	60	738	2,345
25-29 yrs. old	18,972	14,819	2,587	208	1,048	44	267	3,754	11,329
25 yrs. old	3,769	2,953	524	43	183	9	57	744	2,264
26 yrs. old	3,762	2,941	517	42	198	9	54	754	2,241
27 yrs. old	3,816	2,980	517	42	216	9	53	765	2,269
28 yrs. old	3,777	2,950	508	40	219	9	51	746	2,255
29 yrs. old	3,848	2,995	521	41	231	8	51	746	2,301
30-34 yrs. old	20,956	16,553	2,751	208	1,150	42	251	3,578	13,228
30 yrs. old	4,067	3,183	545	42	236	9	52	747	2,488
31 yrs. old	4,253	3,354	561	42	235	9	53	733	2,673
32 yrs. old	4,385	3,468	575	43	239	9	52	740	2,779
33 yrs. old	4,167	3,305	538	41	226	8	49	690	2,664
34 yrs. old	4,084	3,243	532	40	215	8	46	668	2,623
35-39 yrs. old	21,915	17,537	2,855	213	1,037	39	233	3,156	14,607
35 yrs. old	4,082	3,252	533	40	204	8	45	644	2,654
36 yrs. old	4,219	3,360	559	41	205	8	46	643	2,764
37 yrs. old	4,494	3,588	594	44	213	8	48	650	2,985
38 yrs. old	4,568	3,669	589	44	211	8	48	623	3,091
39 yrs. old	4,551	3,668	579	44	205	8	48	597	3,114
40-44 yrs. old	23,002	18,707	2,869	212	948	36	230	2,652	16,247
40 yrs. old	4,592	3,722	576	43	195	8	47	573	3,191
41 yrs. old	4,611	3,748	576	43	190	7	46	552	3,236
42 yrs. old	4,721	3,829	598	43	195	8	47	547	3,322
43 yrs. old	4,533	3,693	561	41	186	7	45	498	3,232
44 yrs. old	4,546	3,714	557	41	182	7	44	483	3,266
45-49 yrs. old	21,302	17,512	2,518	185	856	30	201	2,073	15,593
45 yrs. old	4,447	3,640	539	40	179	6	43	458	3,216
46 yrs. old	4,349	3,562	524	38	177	6	42	437	3,158
47 yrs. old	4,326	3,549	516	37	176	6	41	423	3,157
48 yrs. old	4,158	3,431	483	36	164	6	39	392	3,068
49 yrs. old	4,022	3,330	456	34	160	5	37	364	2,993

See footnotes at end of table.

No. 14. Resident Population by Race, Hispanic Origin, and Single Years of Age: 2002—Con.

[In thousands, except as indicated (288,369 represents 288,369,000). As of July 1. For derivation of estimates, see text of this section]

Age	Total	Race						Hispanic origin [1]	Non-Hispanic White
		White	Black	American Indian, Alaska Native	Asian	Native Hawaiian and Other Pacific Islander	Two or more races		
50-54 yrs. old	18,782	15,637	2,072	150	734	24	164	1,582	14,171
50 yrs. old	3,929	3,263	442	32	152	5	35	346	2,942
51 yrs. old	3,758	3,113	427	31	148	5	33	329	2,808
52 yrs. old	3,780	3,125	431	31	155	5	33	327	2,822
53 yrs. old	3,633	3,027	397	29	144	5	32	297	2,752
54 yrs. old	3,682	3,109	374	28	135	4	31	282	2,847
55-59 yrs. old	14,991	12,743	1,471	109	526	17	124	1,138	11,683
55 yrs. old	3,517	2,996	337	26	125	4	29	262	2,752
56 yrs. old	3,085	2,614	307	23	110	4	26	243	2,388
57 yrs. old	2,807	2,369	287	21	104	4	23	226	2,158
58 yrs. old	2,813	2,396	275	20	96	3	23	210	2,199
59 yrs. old	2,769	2,369	265	19	91	3	22	196	2,185
60-64 yrs. old	11,611	9,897	1,137	79	398	13	88	837	9,113
60 yrs. old	2,636	2,256	251	18	87	3	20	185	2,084
61 yrs. old	2,365	2,013	233	16	82	3	18	172	1,852
62 yrs. old	2,288	1,940	231	16	81	3	18	171	1,781
63 yrs. old	2,190	1,868	214	15	75	2	16	158	1,720
64 yrs. old	2,132	1,820	209	14	72	2	15	152	1,678
65-69 yrs. old	9,581	8,204	931	57	314	9	66	657	7,587
65 yrs. old	2,020	1,725	197	13	69	2	14	143	1,591
66 yrs. old	1,980	1,694	193	12	66	2	14	140	1,562
67 yrs. old	1,947	1,664	192	12	64	2	13	135	1,538
68 yrs. old	1,834	1,575	176	11	58	2	13	122	1,460
69 yrs. old	1,800	1,546	173	10	57	2	12	117	1,436
70-74 yrs. old	8,693	7,608	738	42	247	7	51	524	7,114
70 yrs. old	1,794	1,558	161	10	53	1	11	113	1,452
71 yrs. old	1,772	1,551	149	9	51	1	11	109	1,448
72 yrs. old	1,765	1,542	151	9	52	1	10	108	1,440
73 yrs. old	1,691	1,483	142	8	47	1	10	100	1,389
74 yrs. old	1,671	1,473	135	7	44	1	9	94	1,385
75-79 yrs. old	7,420	6,589	576	30	182	5	39	375	6,235
75 yrs. old	1,611	1,424	129	7	41	1	9	86	1,342
76 yrs. old	1,544	1,366	123	6	39	1	8	81	1,290
77 yrs. old	1,512	1,343	118	6	37	1	8	76	1,271
78 yrs. old	1,431	1,277	107	6	34	1	7	69	1,212
79 yrs. old	1,322	1,180	99	5	31	1	7	63	1,120
80-84 yrs. old	5,314	4,779	378	19	110	3	25	224	4,567
80 yrs. old	1,272	1,141	92	5	28	1	6	57	1,087
81 yrs. old	1,194	1,077	82	4	25	1	6	51	1,028
82 yrs. old	1,037	928	77	4	23	1	5	45	885
83 yrs. old	967	869	70	3	19	-	4	38	833
84 yrs. old	844	764	57	3	16	-	4	33	733
85-89 yrs. old	2,943	2,662	203	10	54	1	14	112	2,556
90-94 yrs. old	1,250	1,125	93	4	21	1	6	50	1,078
95-99 yrs. old	342	304	30	1	6	-	2	15	290
100 yrs. old and over	59	49	7	-	1	-	1	3	46
Median age (yr.)	35.7	37.1	30.5	28.6	33.4	28.2	20.2	26.8	39.3

- Represents or rounds to zero. [1] Persons of Hispanic origin may be of any race.

Source: U.S. Census Bureau, "Table NA-EST2002-ASRO-03-National Population Estimates-Characteristics"; published 18 June 2003; <http://eire.census.gov/popest/data/national/tables/asro/NA-EST2002-ASRO-03.php>; and unpublished data.

No. 15. Resident Population by Race and Hispanic Origin Status—Projections: 2005 to 2050

[In thousands, except as indicated (295,507 represents 295,507,000). As of July. Based on middle series of assumptions. See headnote, Table 3]

Year	Total	White	Black	Asian	All other races	Hispanic origin [1]	Not of Hispanic origin, White
2005	295,507	236,924	38,056	12,419	8,108	41,801	198,451
2010	308,936	244,995	40,454	14,241	9,246	47,756	201,112
2015	322,366	252,850	42,927	16,099	10,489	53,647	203,649
2020	335,805	260,629	45,365	17,988	11,822	59,756	205,936
2025	349,439	268,256	47,835	20,089	13,260	66,191	207,807
2030	363,584	275,731	50,442	22,580	14,831	73,055	209,176
2040	391,946	289,690	55,876	27,992	18,388	87,585	210,331
2050	419,854	302,626	61,361	33,430	22,437	102,560	210,283
Percent distribution:							
2005	100.0	80.2	12.9	4.2	2.7	14.1	67.2
2010	100.0	79.3	13.1	4.6	3.0	15.5	65.1
2015	100.0	78.4	13.3	5.0	3.3	16.6	63.2
2020	100.0	77.6	13.5	5.4	3.5	17.8	61.3
2025	100.0	76.8	13.7	5.7	3.8	18.9	59.5
2030	100.0	75.8	13.9	6.2	4.1	20.1	57.5
2040	100.0	73.9	14.3	7.1	4.7	22.3	53.7
2050	100.0	72.1	14.6	8.0	5.3	24.4	50.1
Percent change:							
2010-2020	8.7	6.4	12.1	26.3	27.9	25.1	2.4
2020-2030	8.3	5.8	11.2	25.5	25.4	22.3	1.6
2030-2040	7.8	5.1	10.8	24.0	24.0	19.9	0.6
2040-2050	7.1	4.5	9.8	19.4	22.0	17.1	(Z)

Z Less than 0.05 percent. [1] Persons of Hispanic origin may be of any race.

Source: U.S. Census Bureau, unpublished data.

No. 16. Resident Population by Race, Hispanic Origin Status, and Age—Projections: 2005 and 2010

[In thousands (295,507 represents 295,507,000), except as indicated. As of July. For definition of median, see Guide to Tabular Presentation. Projections are based on middle series of assumptions; see headnote, Table 3]

Age group	Total 2005	Total 2010	White 2005	White 2010	Black 2005	Black 2010	Asian 2005	Asian 2010	All other races 2005	All other races 2010	Hispanic origin[1] 2005	Hispanic origin[1] 2010	Non-Hispanic White 2005	Non-Hispanic White 2010
Total	295,507	308,936	236,924	244,995	38,056	40,454	12,419	14,241	8,108	9,246	41,801	47,756	198,451	201,112
Under 5 years	20,495	21,426	15,503	15,995	3,113	3,332	833	919	1,046	1,181	4,397	4,824	11,528	11,647
5 to 9 years	19,467	20,706	14,862	15,639	2,941	3,127	763	888	901	1,052	3,892	4,515	11,330	11,553
10 to 14 years	20,838	19,767	15,881	15,049	3,332	2,976	787	834	838	909	3,853	4,057	12,370	11,361
15 to 19 years	21,172	21,336	16,281	16,203	3,306	3,396	815	886	770	851	3,576	4,162	13,013	12,401
20 to 24 years	20,823	21,676	16,153	16,591	3,078	3,357	898	943	695	785	3,604	3,927	12,836	12,992
25 to 29 years	19,753	21,375	15,377	16,495	2,807	3,130	985	1,041	584	709	3,781	3,878	11,881	12,919
30 to 34 years	19,847	20,271	15,466	15,654	2,678	2,856	1,190	1,166	514	595	3,666	3,973	12,060	11,977
35 to 39 years	20,869	20,137	16,538	15,597	2,732	2,701	1,117	1,319	482	520	3,297	3,769	13,480	12,096
40 to 44 years	22,735	20,984	18,318	16,566	2,892	2,724	1,033	1,208	492	486	2,926	3,343	15,606	13,466
45 to 49 years	22,453	22,654	18,312	18,213	2,736	2,844	948	1,105	457	492	2,375	2,939	16,113	15,489
50 to 54 years	19,983	22,173	16,499	18,066	2,276	2,657	828	997	379	453	1,823	2,371	14,812	15,870
55 to 59 years	17,359	19,507	14,582	16,102	1,788	2,176	685	857	305	372	1,393	1,806	13,289	14,431
60 to 64 years	13,017	16,679	11,075	14,004	1,250	1,674	480	706	212	295	978	1,365	10,161	12,736
65 to 69 years	10,123	12,172	8,629	10,357	972	1,127	370	489	152	199	745	941	7,931	9,477
70 to 74 years	8,500	9,097	7,348	7,767	767	838	275	355	110	138	571	694	6,811	7,117
75 to 79 years	7,376	7,186	6,506	6,226	591	622	200	244	79	94	433	510	6,097	5,747
80 to 84 years	5,576	5,665	4,993	5,005	407	440	125	158	51	61	275	359	4,733	4,666
85 to 89 years	3,206	3,713	2,890	3,321	231	274	59	83	26	34	135	204	2,763	3,128
90 to 94 years	1,431	1,727	1,286	1,546	112	136	22	31	11	14	60	84	1,230	1,467
95 to 99 years	412	569	366	503	37	53	5	8	3	4	18	28	349	476
100 years and over	71	114	60	60	9	14	1	1	1	1	3	6	57	92
5 to 13 years	35,968	36,439	27,432	27,613	5,575	5,491	1,389	1,550	1,571	1,786	6,975	7,760	21,091	20,580
14 to 17 years	17,175	16,566	13,150	12,589	2,735	2,597	648	695	642	685	2,956	3,291	10,453	9,586
18 to 24 years	29,156	30,481	22,594	23,280	4,347	4,768	1,226	1,307	990	1,125	4,994	5,611	18,005	18,142
16 years and over	230,335	242,936	187,339	195,194	27,964	30,383	9,874	11,427	5,159	5,933	28,904	33,541	160,572	164,179
18 years and over	221,868	234,504	180,839	188,799	26,632	29,034	9,549	11,077	4,848	5,594	27,473	31,881	155,378	159,300
16 to 64 years	193,639	202,693	155,261	160,372	24,837	26,877	8,816	10,056	4,725	5,387	26,663	30,715	130,601	132,007
55 years and over	67,072	76,429	57,734	64,928	6,165	7,355	2,223	2,934	950	1,213	4,611	5,997	53,421	59,339
65 years and over	36,696	40,244	32,078	34,821	3,127	3,505	1,058	1,371	433	546	2,240	2,826	29,971	32,171
75 years and over	18,072	18,974	16,101	16,698	1,388	1,540	413	527	171	209	924	1,191	15,228	15,577
85 years and over	5,120	6,123	4,602	5,467	390	478	87	125	41	54	216	322	4,398	5,163
Median age (yrs)	35.2	36.0	36.7	37.6	29.9	30.5	33.8	35.7	22.6	23.0	26.1	27.1	39.3	40.3

[1] Persons of Hispanic origin may be of any race.

Source: U.S. Census Bureau, International Data Base, published 10 October 2002; <http://www.census.gov/ipc/www/idbprint.html>.

Figure 1.2
Center of Population: 1970 to 2000

[Prior to 1960, excludes Alaska and Hawaii. The median center is located at the intersection of two median lines, a north-south line constructed so that half of the nation's population lives east and half lives west of it, and an east-west line selected so that half of the nation's population lives north and half lives south of it. The mean center of population is that point at which an imaginary, flat, weightless, and rigid map of the United States would balance if weights of identical value were placed on it so that each weight represented the location of one person on the date of the census]

Year	Median center		Mean center		
	Latitude-N	Longitude	Latitude-N	Longitude-W	Approximate location
1790 (August 2)	(NA)	(NA)	39 16 30	76 11 12	In Kent County, MD, 23 miles E of Baltimore MD
1850 (June 1)..	(NA)	(NA)	38 59 00	81 19 00	In Wirt County, WV, 23 miles SE of Parkersburg, WV[1]
1900 (June 1)..	40 03 32	84 49 01	39 09 36	85 48 54	In Bartholomew County, IN, 6 miles SE of Columbus, IN
1950 (April 1)..	40 00 12	84 56 51	38 50 21	88 09 33	In Richland County, IL, 8 miles NNW of Olney, IL
1960 (April 1)..	39 56 25	85 16 60	38 35 58	89 12 35	In Clinton County, IL, 6.5 miles NW of Centralia, IL
1970 (April 1) .	39 47 43	85 31 43	38 27 47	89 42 22	In St. Clair County, IL, 5.3 miles ESE of Mascoutah, IL
1980 (April 1)..	39 18 60	86 08 15	38 08 13	90 34 26	In Jefferson County, MO, .25 mile W of DeSoto, MO
1990 (April 1)..	38 57 55	86 31 53	37 52 20	91 12 55	In Crawford County, MO, 10 miles SE of Steelville, MO
2000 (April 1)..	38 45 23	86 55 51	37 41 49	91 48 34	In Phelps County, MO, 3 miles E of Edgar Springs, MO

NA Not available. [1]West Virginia was set off from Virginia, Dec. 31, 1862, and admitted as a state, June 19, 1863.

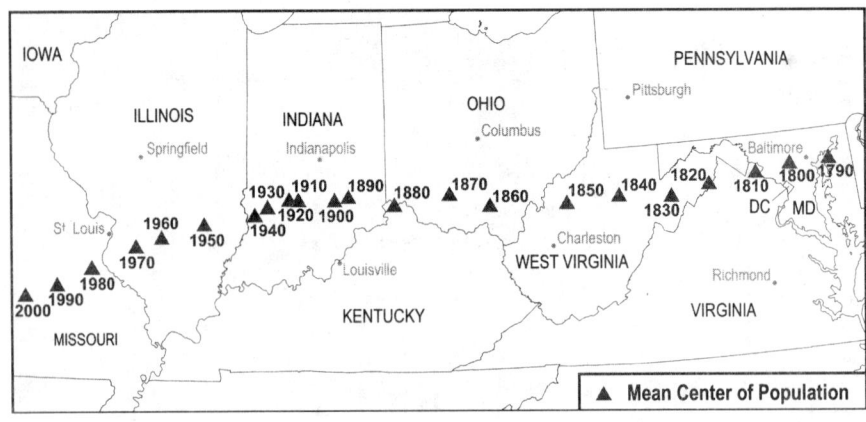

20 Population

U.S. Census Bureau, Statistical Abstract of the United States: 2003

No. 17. Resident Population—States: 1980 to 2002

[In thousands (226,546 represents 226,546,000). 1980, 1990, and 2000 data as of April 1, data for other years as of July 1. Insofar as possible, population shown for all years is that of present area of state. See Appendix III]

State	1980 [1]	1990 [2]	1995	1997	1998	1999	2000 [3]	2001	2002
United States	**226,546**	**248,791**	**266,278**	**272,647**	**275,854**	**279,040**	**281,423**	**285,318**	**288,369**
Alabama	3,894	4,040	4,297	4,368	4,405	4,430	4,447	4,469	4,487
Alaska	402	550	604	613	620	625	627	634	644
Arizona	2,718	3,665	4,432	4,737	4,883	5,024	5,131	5,307	5,456
Arkansas	2,286	2,351	2,535	2,601	2,626	2,652	2,673	2,695	2,710
California	23,668	29,811	31,697	32,486	32,988	33,499	33,872	34,600	35,116
Colorado	2,890	3,294	3,827	4,018	4,117	4,226	4,301	4,431	4,507
Connecticut	3,108	3,287	3,324	3,349	3,365	3,386	3,406	3,435	3,461
Delaware	594	666	730	751	763	775	784	797	807
District of Columbia	638	607	581	568	565	570	572	574	571
Florida	9,746	12,938	14,538	15,186	15,487	15,759	15,982	16,373	16,713
Georgia	5,463	6,478	7,328	7,685	7,864	8,046	8,186	8,406	8,560
Hawaii	965	1,108	1,197	1,212	1,215	1,210	1,212	1,227	1,245
Idaho	944	1,007	1,177	1,229	1,252	1,276	1,294	1,321	1,341
Illinois	11,427	11,431	12,008	12,186	12,272	12,359	12,419	12,520	12,601
Indiana	5,490	5,544	5,851	5,955	5,999	6,045	6,080	6,127	6,159
Iowa	2,914	2,777	2,867	2,891	2,903	2,918	2,926	2,932	2,937
Kansas	2,364	2,478	2,601	2,635	2,661	2,678	2,688	2,702	2,716
Kentucky	3,661	3,687	3,887	3,953	3,985	4,018	4,042	4,069	4,093
Louisiana	4,206	4,222	4,379	4,421	4,440	4,461	4,469	4,470	4,483
Maine	1,125	1,228	1,243	1,255	1,259	1,267	1,275	1,284	1,294
Maryland	4,217	4,781	5,070	5,157	5,204	5,255	5,296	5,386	5,458
Massachusetts	5,737	6,016	6,141	6,226	6,272	6,317	6,349	6,401	6,428
Michigan	9,262	9,295	9,676	9,809	9,848	9,897	9,938	10,006	10,050
Minnesota	4,076	4,376	4,660	4,763	4,813	4,873	4,919	4,985	5,020
Mississippi	2,521	2,575	2,723	2,777	2,805	2,828	2,845	2,860	2,872
Missouri	4,917	5,117	5,378	5,481	5,522	5,562	5,595	5,637	5,673
Montana	787	799	877	890	892	898	902	905	909
Nebraska	1,570	1,578	1,657	1,686	1,696	1,705	1,711	1,720	1,729
Nevada	800	1,202	1,582	1,764	1,853	1,935	1,998	2,098	2,173
New Hampshire	921	1,109	1,158	1,189	1,206	1,222	1,236	1,259	1,275
New Jersey	7,365	7,748	8,083	8,219	8,287	8,360	8,414	8,511	8,590
New Mexico	1,303	1,515	1,720	1,775	1,793	1,808	1,819	1,831	1,855
New York	17,558	17,991	18,524	18,657	18,756	18,883	18,976	19,084	19,158
North Carolina	5,882	6,632	7,345	7,657	7,809	7,949	8,049	8,206	8,320
North Dakota	653	639	648	650	648	644	642	637	634
Ohio	10,798	10,847	11,203	11,277	11,312	11,335	11,353	11,390	11,421
Oklahoma	3,025	3,146	3,308	3,373	3,405	3,437	3,451	3,470	3,494
Oregon	2,633	2,842	3,184	3,304	3,352	3,394	3,421	3,473	3,522
Pennsylvania	11,864	11,883	12,198	12,228	12,246	12,264	12,281	12,303	12,335
Rhode Island	947	1,003	1,017	1,025	1,031	1,040	1,048	1,060	1,070
South Carolina	3,122	3,486	3,749	3,860	3,919	3,975	4,012	4,062	4,107
South Dakota	691	696	738	744	746	750	755	758	761
Tennessee	4,591	4,877	5,327	5,499	5,570	5,639	5,689	5,749	5,797
Texas	14,229	16,986	18,959	19,740	20,158	20,558	20,852	21,371	21,780
Utah	1,461	1,723	2,014	2,120	2,166	2,203	2,233	2,279	2,316
Vermont	511	563	589	597	600	605	609	613	617
Virginia	5,347	6,189	6,671	6,829	6,901	7,000	7,078	7,197	7,294
Washington	4,132	4,867	5,481	5,675	5,770	5,843	5,894	5,993	6,069
West Virginia	1,950	1,793	1,824	1,819	1,816	1,812	1,808	1,801	1,802
Wisconsin	4,706	4,892	5,185	5,266	5,298	5,333	5,364	5,406	5,441
Wyoming	470	454	485	489	491	492	494	494	499

[1] See footnote 4, Table 1. [2] The April 1, 1990, census counts include corrections processed through August 1997, results of special censuses and test censuses, and do not include adjustments for census coverage errors. [3] Reflects modifications to the Census 2000 population as documented in the Count Question Resolution program.

Source: U.S. Census Bureau, 1990 Census of Population and Housing, *Population and Housing Unit Counts* (CPH-2); "Table CO-EST2001-12-00 — Time Series of Intercensal State Population Estimates: April 1, 1990, to April 1, 2000"; published 11 April, 2002; <http://eire.census.gov/popest/data/counties/tables/CO-EST2001-12/CO-EST2001-12-00.php>; and "Table ST-2002EST-01 — State Population Estimates: April 1, 2000, to July 1, 2002"; published 20 December 2002; <http://eire.census.gov/popest/data/states/tables/ST-2002EST-01.php>.

No. 18. State Population—Rank, Percent Change, and Population Density: 1980 to 2002

[As of April 1, except 2002 as of July 1. Insofar as possible, population shown for all years is that of present area of state. For area figures of states, see Table 359. Minus sign (-) indicates decrease. See Appendix III]

State	Rank 1980	Rank 1990	Rank 2000	Rank 2002	Percent change 1980-1990	Percent change 1990-2000	Percent change 2000-2002	Population per sq. mile of land area[1] 1980	1990	2002
United States.....	(X)	(X)	(X)	(X)	9.8	13.1	2.5	64.0	70.3	81.5
Alabama..........	22	22	23	23	3.8	10.1	0.9	76.7	79.6	88.4
Alaska	50	49	48	47	36.9	14.0	2.7	0.7	1.0	1.1
Arizona..........	29	24	20	19	34.8	40.0	6.4	23.9	32.3	48.0
Arkansas.........	33	33	33	33	2.8	13.7	1.4	43.9	45.1	52.0
California.........	1	1	1	1	26.0	13.6	3.7	151.8	191.1	225.2
Colorado.........	28	26	24	22	14.0	30.6	4.8	27.9	31.8	43.5
Connecticut.......	25	27	29	29	5.8	3.6	1.6	641.4	678.5	714.3
Delaware.........	47	46	45	45	12.1	17.6	3.0	304.2	341.0	413.3
District of Columbia...	(X)	(X)	(X)	(X)	-4.9	-5.7	-0.2	10,396.3	9,884.4	9,298.0
Florida	7	4	4	4	32.7	23.5	4.6	180.7	239.9	309.9
Georgia	13	11	10	10	18.6	26.4	4.6	94.3	111.9	147.8
Hawaii	39	41	42	42	14.9	9.3	2.8	150.2	172.6	193.8
Idaho	41	42	39	39	6.7	28.5	3.6	11.4	12.2	16.2
Illinois...........	5	6	5	5	(Z)	8.6	1.5	205.6	205.6	226.7
Indiana..........	12	14	14	14	1.0	9.7	1.3	153.1	154.6	171.7
Iowa............	27	30	30	30	-4.7	5.4	-0.4	52.2	49.7	52.6
Kansas..........	32	32	32	32	4.8	8.5	1.0	28.9	30.3	33.2
Kentucky.........	23	23	25	26	0.7	9.6	1.3	92.1	92.8	103.0
Louisiana	19	21	22	24	0.4	5.9	0.3	96.6	96.9	102.9
Maine............	38	38	40	40	9.2	3.8	1.5	36.4	39.8	41.9
Maryland.........	18	19	19	18	13.4	10.8	3.1	431.5	489.1	558.4
Massachusetts.....	11	13	13	13	4.9	5.5	1.2	731.8	767.4	819.9
Michigan.........	8	8	8	8	0.4	6.9	1.1	163.1	163.6	176.9
Minnesota........	21	20	21	21	7.4	12.4	2.0	51.2	55.0	63.1
Mississippi........	31	31	31	31	2.2	10.5	1.0	53.7	54.9	61.2
Missouri.........	15	15	17	17	4.1	9.3	1.4	71.4	74.3	82.3
Montana.........	44	44	44	44	1.6	12.9	0.8	5.4	5.5	6.2
Nebraska	35	36	38	38	0.5	8.4	1.0	20.4	20.5	22.5
Nevada..........	43	39	35	35	50.1	66.3	8.8	7.3	10.9	19.8
New Hampshire	42	40	41	41	20.5	11.4	3.2	102.7	123.7	142.2
New Jersey.......	9	9	9	9	5.2	8.6	2.1	992.9	1,044.5	1,158.1
New Mexico.......	37	37	36	36	16.3	20.1	2.0	10.7	12.5	15.3
New York	2	2	3	3	2.5	5.5	1.0	371.9	381.0	405.8
North Carolina.....	10	10	11	11	12.8	21.4	3.4	120.7	136.2	170.8
North Dakota......	46	47	47	48	-2.1	0.5	-1.3	9.5	9.3	9.2
Ohio............	6	7	7	7	0.5	4.7	0.6	263.7	264.9	278.9
Oklahoma........	26	28	27	28	4.0	9.7	1.2	44.1	45.8	50.9
Oregon..........	30	29	28	27	7.9	20.4	2.9	27.4	29.6	36.7
Pennsylvania......	4	5	6	6	0.2	3.4	0.4	264.7	265.1	275.2
Rhode Island......	40	43	43	43	5.9	4.5	2.0	906.4	960.3	1,023.7
South Carolina.....	24	25	26	25	11.7	15.1	2.4	103.7	115.8	136.4
South Dakota......	45	45	46	46	0.8	8.5	0.8	9.1	9.2	10.0
Tennessee........	17	17	16	16	6.2	16.7	1.9	111.4	118.3	140.7
Texas...........	3	3	2	2	19.4	22.8	4.5	54.4	64.9	83.2
Utah............	36	35	34	34	17.9	29.6	3.7	17.8	21.0	28.2
Vermont	48	48	49	49	10.0	8.2	1.3	55.3	60.8	66.7
Virginia..........	14	12	12	12	15.8	14.4	3.0	135.0	156.3	184.2
Washington.......	20	18	15	15	17.8	21.1	3.0	62.1	73.1	91.2
West Virginia......	34	34	37	37	-8.0	0.8	-0.4	81.0	74.5	74.8
Wisconsin	16	16	18	20	4.0	9.6	1.4	86.6	90.1	100.2
Wyoming.........	49	50	50	50	-3.4	8.9	1.0	4.8	4.7	5.1

X Not applicable.   Z Less than 0.05 percent.   [1] Persons per square mile was calculated on the basis of land area data from the 2000 census.

Source: U.S. Census Bureau, 1990 Census of Population and Housing, *Population and Housing Unit Counts* (CPH-2); "ST-99-3 — State Population Estimates: Annual Time Series, July 1, 1990, to July 1, 1999"; published 29 December 1999; <http://www.census.gov/population/estimates/state/st-99-3.txt>; *Population Change and Distribution: 1990 to 2000*, Census 2000 Brief, (C2KBR/01-2), April 2001; and "Table ST-2002EST-01 — State Population Estimates: April 1, 2000, to July 1, 2002"; published 20 December 2002; <http://eire.census.gov/popest/data/states/tables/ST-2002EST-01.php>.

No. 19. State Resident Population—Components of Change: 2000-2002

[Covers period April 1, 2000, to July 1, 2002. Minus sign (-) indicates net decrease]

State	Numeric population change [1]	Births	Deaths	Natural increase (births minus deaths)	Net internal migration	Net international migration
United States	6,946,189	9,080,744	5,413,795	3,666,949	(X)	3,279,240
Alabama	39,408	141,164	101,209	39,955	-12,940	13,344
Alaska	16,855	23,050	6,853	16,197	-3,144	3,679
Arizona	325,821	189,903	92,575	97,328	137,342	89,941
Arkansas	36,681	84,467	62,903	21,564	3,205	12,070
California	1,244,385	1,189,741	517,484	672,257	-167,775	738,015
Colorado	205,211	147,649	64,037	83,612	60,634	59,202
Connecticut	54,938	96,005	68,197	27,808	-7,438	36,270
Delaware	23,785	24,661	15,966	8,695	9,542	5,829
District of Columbia	-1,161	18,409	12,886	5,523	-16,908	10,226
Florida	730,749	467,910	375,504	92,406	356,408	276,668
Georgia	373,824	308,097	145,605	162,492	104,861	101,435
Hawaii	33,361	42,549	17,398	25,151	-6,797	15,330
Idaho	47,178	45,257	22,094	23,163	15,760	7,863
Illinois	181,324	418,059	240,356	177,703	-166,301	168,580
Indiana	78,583	192,533	125,353	67,180	-15,657	28,172
Iowa	10,433	83,324	62,976	20,348	-24,846	15,944
Kansas	27,466	86,942	56,170	30,772	-24,170	20 960
Kentucky	50,682	122,338	89,612	32,726	3,974	14,842
Louisiana	13,667	154,863	93,883	60,980	-57,826	10,787
Maine	19,541	30,046	28,113	1,933	15,640	2,316
Maryland	161,654	170,930	99,368	71,562	30,233	55,949
Massachusetts	78,704	182,496	128,614	53,882	-46,245	72,627
Michigan	112,002	303,264	196,770	106,494	-49,794	57,783
Minnesota	100,241	144,014	83,933	60,081	3,355	36,637
Mississippi	27,124	100,709	63,695	37,014	-15,862	6,060
Missouri	77,368	169,965	123,559	46,406	8,106	23,683
Montana	7,258	24,461	18,760	5,701	517	1,059
Nebraska	17,917	54,972	34,242	20,730	-14,853	12,449
Nevada	175,234	69,597	34,967	34,630	101,322	36,892
New Hampshire	39,270	32,274	22,192	10,082	24,056	5,184
New Jersey	175,950	255,719	165,004	90,715	-54,460	141,469
New Mexico	36,013	60,864	31,585	29,279	-8,016	14,817
New York	181,075	581,993	357,231	224,762	-372,929	329,727
North Carolina	270,672	271,428	160,019	111,409	73,663	85,936
North Dakota	-8,090	17,073	13,609	3,464	-13,562	1,941
Ohio	68,259	353,686	245,913	107,773	-73,720	36,893
Oklahoma	43,058	110,488	76,462	34,026	-10,551	20,268
Oregon	100,110	101,142	68,344	32,798	31,144	37,014
Pennsylvania	54,037	323,841	289,083	34,758	-26,701	50,692
Rhode Island	21,406	27,544	21,993	5,551	7,463	8,902
South Carolina	95,173	128,984	82,792	46,192	30,975	19,162
South Dakota	6,219	23,522	15,809	7,713	-3,581	2,133
Tennessee	108,012	178,486	126,612	51,874	30,371	26,490
Texas	928,081	792,093	325,428	466,665	92,712	364,562
Utah	83,087	105,187	28,654	76,533	-19,780	26,360
Vermont	7,765	14,086	11,792	2,294	3,555	2,167
Virginia	215,043	225,928	126,184	99,744	37,862	75,556
Washington	174,877	179,174	101,004	78,170	28,603	68,675
West Virginia	-6,477	42,589	45,442	-2,853	-4,896	1,631
Wisconsin	77,495	153,729	106,386	47,343	8,096	23,826
Wyoming	4,921	13,539	9,175	4,364	-647	1,223

X Not applicable.   [1] The estimated components of population change will not sum to the numerical population change due to the process of controlling to national totals.

Source: U.S. Census Bureau, "Table ST-2002EST-03 - State Population Estimates and Population Change: April 1, 2000, to July 1, 2002"; published 20 December 2002; <http://eire.census.gov/popest/data/states/tables/ST-2002EST-03.php> and "Table ST-2002EST-07 - Estimated Components of State Population Change: April 1, 2000, to July 1, 2002"; published 20 December 2002; <http://eire.census.gov/popest/data/states/tables/ST-2002EST-07.php>.

No. 20. Resident Population by Age and State: 2002

[In thousands, except percent (288,369 represents 288,369,000). As of July. Includes Armed Forces stationed in area]

State	Total	Under 5 years	5 to 17 years	18 to 24 years	25 to 34 years	35 to 44 years	45 to 54 years	55 to 64 years	65 to 74 years	75 to 84 years	85 years and over	Percent 65 years and over
U.S. . . .	288,369	19,609	53,285	28,342	39,928	44,917	40,084	26,602	18,274	12,735	4,593	12.3
AL	4,487	299	808	452	602	669	627	441	319	199	71	13.1
AK	644	49	143	59	81	108	109	56	24	12	3	6.1
AZ	5,456	420	1,057	540	777	787	684	491	374	250	78	12.9
AR	2,710	184	494	272	354	391	364	275	198	129	49	13.9
CA	35,116	2,545	6,907	3,551	5,365	5,536	4,616	2,879	1,900	1,346	471	10.6
CO	4,507	321	830	448	682	729	669	354	232	150	53	9.6
CT	3,461	224	649	287	422	571	499	336	224	178	70	13.6
DE	807	51	138	82	110	131	112	78	57	37	12	13.1
DC	571	34	78	66	107	87	76	54	35	25	9	12.0
FL	16,713	1,035	2,847	1,404	2,079	2,525	2,249	1,721	1,441	1,054	360	17.1
GA	8,560	649	1,620	869	1,330	1,393	1,152	733	448	270	96	9.5
HI	1,245	84	212	123	168	189	181	121	84	63	20	13.4
ID	1,341	100	270	149	175	191	183	121	78	54	20	11.3
IL	12,601	890	2,365	1,229	1,808	1,960	1,725	1,125	752	541	207	11.9
IN	6,159	429	1,166	629	820	936	856	566	387	272	98	12.3
IA	2,937	181	517	315	363	432	419	277	205	160	69	14.7
KS	2,716	188	509	292	352	404	378	239	171	130	54	13.1
KY	4,093	253	678	420	574	646	598	413	273	176	61	12.4
LA	4,483	323	863	496	591	664	617	409	279	180	61	11.6
ME	1,294	65	214	118	154	213	207	137	96	66	25	14.4
MD	5,458	366	1,014	489	736	925	795	516	322	221	74	11.3
MA	6,428	388	1,076	598	907	1,067	924	605	417	322	125	13.4
MI	10,050	664	1,907	970	1,329	1,563	1,449	936	629	447	156	12.3
MN	5,020	319	933	507	673	817	721	448	294	216	92	12.0
MS	2,872	209	551	323	383	416	381	263	186	116	45	12.1
MO	5,673	367	1,030	568	741	872	791	546	387	267	103	13.3
MT	909	53	164	93	103	133	146	95	62	44	17	13.5
NE	1,729	118	322	185	225	255	240	153	113	83	36	13.4
NV	2,173	161	412	187	327	338	294	215	141	78	21	11.1
NH	1,275	73	235	115	156	223	197	123	79	54	20	12.0
NJ	8,590	567	1,560	693	1,134	1,451	1,233	830	561	411	149	13.1
NM	1,855	132	368	192	233	274	260	174	121	75	26	11.9
NY	19,158	1,228	3,385	1,815	2,707	3,071	2,659	1,818	1,255	881	337	12.9
NC	8,320	585	1,484	815	1,214	1,294	1,141	789	540	343	116	12.0
ND	634	37	110	76	78	91	91	58	45	34	16	14.8
OH	11,421	765	2,115	1,098	1,482	1,738	1,636	1,073	767	555	191	13.3
OK	3,494	239	635	377	458	503	479	342	243	159	58	13.2
OR	3,522	226	629	338	487	518	533	346	216	165	63	12.6
PA	12,335	712	2,151	1,153	1,498	1,897	1,800	1,215	924	726	259	15.5
RI	1,070	60	179	114	139	173	153	100	70	60	23	14.2
SC	4,107	267	713	429	568	630	585	413	275	173	55	12.3
SD	761	51	145	83	90	110	107	67	52	39	17	14.2
TN	5,797	384	1,021	554	812	898	830	580	386	246	87	12.4
TX	21,780	1,718	4,384	2,287	3,228	3,340	2,865	1,804	1,171	727	256	9.9
UT	2,316	219	494	321	370	296	259	158	105	70	24	8.6
VT	617	32	108	62	72	100	100	64	41	28	11	12.9
VA	7,294	485	1,294	721	1,034	1,198	1,049	694	436	286	96	11.2
WA	6,069	397	1,117	594	854	968	901	561	337	248	93	11.2
WV	1,802	97	292	174	224	259	281	199	145	98	33	15.3
WI	5,441	338	1,000	557	692	864	785	500	348	255	103	13.0
WY	499	30	92	54	59	72	81	51	32	20	7	11.9

Source: U.S. Census Bureau, "State Population Estimates by Age and Sex; April 1, 2000, to July 1, 2002"; published 17 September 2003; <http://eire.census.gov/popest/data/states/ST-EST2002-ASRO-02.php>.

No. 21. Resident Population by Race and State: 2002

[In thousands (288,369 represents 288,369,000). As of July. Includes Armed Forces stationed in area]

State	Total population	One race - White	One race - Black or African American	One race - American Indian, Alaska Native	One race - Asian	One race - Native Hawaiian and Other Pacific Islander	Two or more races
U.S.	288,369	232,647	36,746	2,752	11,559	484	4,181
AL	4,487	3,207	1,181	23	36	2	38
AK	644	456	24	100	27	4	34
AZ	5,456	4,788	181	287	111	10	80
AR	2,710	2,201	434	18	24	2	31
CA	35,116	27,262	2,436	411	4,063	143	801
CO	4,507	4,072	187	51	112	6	79
CT	3,461	2,960	346	11	97	2	43
DE	807	618	157	3	20	(Z)	10
DC	571	202	342	2	17	(Z)	7
FL	16,713	13,503	2,634	66	316	12	181
GA	8,560	5,783	2,463	26	201	6	82
HI	1,245	326	28	4	536	110	241
ID	1,341	1,280	7	19	14	2	19
IL	12,601	10,026	1,921	39	482	8	125
IN	6,159	5,483	525	17	70	3	61
IA	2,937	2,789	65	10	44	1	26
KS	2,716	2,428	161	26	55	2	45
KY	4,093	3,704	306	9	35	2	36
LA	4,483	2,884	1,473	26	62	2	36
ME	1,294	1,257	8	7	11	(Z)	11
MD	5,458	3,598	1,537	17	240	3	73
MA	6,428	5,627	428	18	273	5	76
MI	10,050	8,197	1,443	60	206	4	141
MN	5,020	4,540	190	57	159	3	71
MS	2,872	1,763	1,057	12	22	1	17
MO	5,673	4,851	651	26	72	4	69
MT	909	827	3	58	5	1	15
NE	1,729	1,594	72	16	26	1	19
NV	2,173	1,830	150	31	103	10	50
NH	1,275	1,230	11	3	19	(Z)	11
NJ	8,590	6,668	1,249	26	544	6	97
NM	1,855	1,577	41	184	23	2	27
NY	19,158	14,161	3,409	104	1,207	18	259
NC	8,320	6,178	1,817	107	135	5	78
ND	634	587	5	31	4	(Z)	7
OH	11,421	9,772	1,332	26	157	4	131
OK	3,494	2,740	270	277	55	3	149
OR	3,522	3,205	62	48	115	10	82
PA	12,335	10,680	1,274	21	252	5	104
RI	1,070	957	62	6	28	1	15
SC	4,107	2,787	1,228	15	43	2	32
SD	761	676	6	63	5	(Z)	10
TN	5,797	4,695	965	17	67	3	51
TX	21,780	18,219	2,528	146	649	23	215
UT	2,316	2,168	22	33	42	18	34
VT	617	598	4	2	6	(Z)	7
VA	7,294	5,404	1,459	24	298	5	103
WA	6,069	5,201	210	100	356	27	176
WV	1,802	1,714	59	4	11	(Z)	14
WI	5,441	4,913	319	50	101	2	56
WY	499	473	4	12	3	(Z)	6

Z Less than 500.

Source: U.S. Census Bureau, "Table ST-EST2002-ASRO-03-State Characteristics Estimates"; published 18 September 2003; <http://eire.census.gov/popest/data/states/ST-EST2002-ASRO-03.php>.

No. 22. Resident Population by Hispanic or Latino Origin and State: 2000 and 2002

[In thousands, except percent (35,306 represents 35,306,000). 2000, as of April; 2002, as of July. Persons of Hispanic or Latino origin may be of any race]

State	2000 Total	Mexican	Puerto Rican	Cuban	Other Hispanic or Latino	Not Hispanic or Latino, White	2002 Total	Percent of total population	Not Hispanic or Latino, White
U.S. . . .	35,306	20,641	3,406	1,242	10,017	194,553	38,761	13.4	196,845
AL.	76	45	6	2	23	3,126	86	1.9	3,131
AK.	26	13	3	1	9	424	28	4.4	434
AZ.	1,296	1,066	18	5	207	3,274	1,476	27.1	3,390
AR.	87	61	2	1	22	2,100	97	3.6	2,111
CA.	10,967	8,456	141	72	2,298	15,817	11,936	34.0	16,030
CO	736	451	13	4	268	3,203	818	18.2	3,308
CT.	320	23	194	7	95	2,639	345	10.0	2,659
DE.	37	13	14	1	9	568	41	5.1	582
DC	45	5	2	1	36	159	52	9.2	158
FL.	2,683	364	482	833	1,004	10,459	3,020	18.1	10,664
GA	435	275	36	13	112	5,129	517	6.0	5,314
HI	88	20	30	1	37	277	91	7.3	292
ID	102	79	2	(Z)	20	1,139	114	8.5	1,173
IL	1,530	1,144	158	18	210	8,424	1,682	13.4	8,430
IN	215	153	20	3	39	5,219	237	3.8	5,263
IA	82	61	3	1	18	2,710	90	3.1	2,706
KS.	188	148	5	2	33	2,234	207	7.6	2,235
KY.	60	31	6	4	19	3,608	69	1.7	3,642
LA.	108	32	8	8	59	2,794	115	2.6	2,786
ME	9	3	2	(Z)	4	1,230	10	0.8	1,248
MD	228	40	26	7	156	3,287	257	4.7	3,368
MA	429	22	199	9	198	5,198	467	7.3	5,248
MI	324	221	27	7	69	7,807	349	3.5	7,884
MN	143	96	7	3	39	4,337	159	3.2	4,396
MS	40	22	3	2	14	1,728	43	1.5	1,727
MO	119	78	7	3	31	4,686	127	2.2	4,736
MT	18	12	1	(Z)	5	808	19	2.1	811
NE.	94	71	2	1	21	1,494	104	6.0	1,497
NV.	394	286	10	11	86	1,303	463	21.3	1,395
NH	20	5	6	1	9	1,175	23	1.8	1,210
NJ.	1,117	103	367	77	570	5,557	1,221	14.2	5,592
NM	765	330	4	3	428	813	796	42.9	817
NY.	2,868	261	1,050	63	1,494	11,761	3,072	16.0	11,695
NC	379	247	31	7	94	5,647	444	5.3	5,774
ND	8	4	1	(Z)	3	589	8	1.3	580
OH	217	91	66	5	55	9,538	229	2.0	9,572
OK	179	133	8	2	37	2,556	191	5.5	2,569
OR	275	215	5	3	52	2,858	312	8.9	2,915
PA.	394	55	229	10	100	10,322	416	3.4	10,330
RI	91	6	25	1	58	858	99	9.2	876
SC.	95	53	12	3	27	2,652	109	2.7	2,692
SD.	11	6	1	(Z)	4	665	12	1.5	667
TN.	124	77	10	4	32	4,506	140	2.4	4,568
TX.	6,670	5,072	70	26	1,502	10,933	7,315	33.6	11,133
UT.	202	136	4	1	60	1,904	224	9.7	1,956
VT.	6	1	1	(Z)	3	585	6	0.9	593
VA.	330	74	41	8	206	4,966	378	5.2	5,069
WA	442	330	16	5	91	4,652	490	8.1	4,754
WV	12	4	2	(Z)	6	1,710	13	0.7	1,703
WI	193	127	30	2	33	4,682	209	3.8	4,722
WY	32	20	1	(Z)	11	439	33	6.7	442

Z Less than 500.

Source: U.S. Census Bureau, Census 2000 Redistricting Data (P.L. 94-171) Summary File for states, Tables PL1 and PL2; and "Table ST-EST2002-ASRO-03-State Characteristics Estimates"; published 18 September 2003; <http://eire.census.gov/popest/data/states/ST-EST2002-ASRO-03.php>.

No. 23. Resident Population by Region, Race, and Hispanic Origin: 2000

[As of April (281,422 represents 281,422,000). For composition of regions, see map, inside front cover]

Race and Hispanic origin	Population (1,000) United States	North-east	Mid-west	South	West	Percent distribution United States	North-east	Mid-west	South	West
Total population	**281,422**	**53,594**	**64,393**	**100,237**	**63,198**	**100.0**	**19.0**	**22.9**	**35.6**	**22.5**
One race	274,596	52,366	63,370	98,390	60,470	100.0	19.1	23.1	35.8	22.0
White	211,461	41,534	53,834	72,819	43,274	100.0	19.6	25.5	34.4	20.5
Black or African American	34,658	6,100	6,500	18,982	3,077	100.0	17.6	18.8	54.8	8.9
American Indian and Alaska Native	2,476	163	399	726	1,188	100.0	6.6	16.1	29.3	48.0
Asian	10,243	2,119	1,198	1,922	5,004	100.0	20.7	11.7	18.8	48.8
Asian Indian	1,679	554	293	441	391	100.0	33.0	17.5	26.3	23.3
Chinese	2,433	692	212	343	1,186	100.0	28.4	8.7	14.1	48.8
Filipino	1,850	202	151	245	1,253	100.0	10.9	8.2	13.2	67.7
Japanese	797	76	63	77	580	100.0	9.6	7.9	9.7	72.8
Korean	1,077	246	132	224	474	100.0	22.9	12.3	20.8	44.0
Vietnamese	1,123	115	107	330	564	100.0	10.3	9.5	29.9	50.3
Other Asian [1]	1,285	233	239	257	556	100.0	18.2	18.6	20.0	43.2
Native Hawaiian and Other Pacific Islander	399	21	22	51	304	100.0	5.2	5.6	12.8	76.3
Native Hawaiian	141	4	6	12	118	100.0	3.2	4.1	8.9	83.8
Guamanian or Chamorro	58	5	5	15	34	100.0	7.9	7.9	25.1	59.1
Samoan	91	4	5	9	73	100.0	4.2	5.6	9.7	80.5
Other Pacific Islander [2]	109	8	7	15	79	100.0	7.3	6.4	14.0	72.2
Some other race	15,359	2,430	1,417	3,889	7,623	100.0	15.8	9.2	25.3	49.6
Two or more races	6,826	1,228	1,022	1,847	2,728	100.0	18.0	15.0	27.1	40.0
Hispanic or Latino (of any race)	35,306	5,254	3,125	11,587	15,341	100.0	14.9	8.8	32.8	43.5
Mexican	20,641	479	2,200	6,548	11,413	100.0	2.3	10.7	31.7	55.3
Puerto Rican	3,406	2,075	325	759	247	100.0	60.9	9.6	22.3	7.2
Cuban	1,242	169	45	921	106	100.0	13.6	3.6	74.2	8.5
Other Hispanic or Latino	10,017	2,531	554	3,358	3,574	100.0	25.3	5.5	33.5	35.7
Not Hispanic or Latino	246,116	48,340	61,268	88,650	47,857	100.0	19.6	24.9	36.0	19.4
White alone	194,553	39,327	52,386	65,928	36,912	100.0	20.2	26.9	33.9	19.0

[1] Other Asian alone or two or more Asian categories. [2] Other Pacific Islander alone or two or more Native Hawaiian and Other Pacific Islander categories.

Source: U.S. Census Bureau, "Demographic Profiles: Census 2000"; <http://www.census.gov/Press-Release/www/2001/demoprofile.html>.

No. 24. Population in Coastal Counties: 1970 to 2002

[Population as of April 1, except as indicated (3,536 represents 3,536,000). Areas as defined by U.S. National Oceanic and Atmospheric Agency, 1992. Covers 673 counties and equivalent areas with at least 15 percent of their land area either in a coastal watershed (drainage area) or in a coastal cataloging unit (a coastal area between watersheds). See Appendix III]

Year	Total	Counties in coastal regions Total	Atlantic	Gulf of Mexico	Great Lakes	Pacific	Balance of United States
Land area, 1990 (1,000 sq. mi.)	3,536	888	148	114	115	510	2,649
POPULATION							
1970 (mil.)	203.3	110.0	51.1	10.0	26.0	22.8	93.3
1980 (mil.)	226.5	119.8	53.7	13.1	26.0	27.0	106.7
1990 (mil.)	248.7	133.4	59.0	15.2	25.9	33.2	115.3
2000 (mil.)	281.4	148.3	65.2	18.0	27.3	37.8	133.1
2001 (July) (mil.)	285.3	150.3	66.0	18.3	27.4	38.5	135.0
2002 (July) (mil.)	288.4	151.8	66.7	18.6	27.5	39.1	136.5
1970 (percent)	100	54	25	5	13	11	46
1980 (percent)	100	53	24	6	11	12	47
1990 (percent)	100	54	24	6	10	13	46
2000 (percent)	100	53	23	6	10	13	47
2002 (July 1) (percent)	100	53	23	6	10	14	47

Source: U.S. Census Bureau, U.S. Census of Population: 1970; 1980 Census of Population, Vol. 1, Chapter A (PC80-1-A-1), U.S. Summary; 1990 Census of Population and Housing (CPH1); and unpublished data.

No. 25. Metropolitan and Nonmetropolitan Area Population by State: 1980 to 2000

[As of April (177,505 represents 177,505,000). Metropolitan refers to 258 metropolitan statistical areas and 18 consolidated metropolitan statistical areas as defined by U.S. Office of Management and Budget, June 30, 1999; nonmetropolitan is the area outside metropolitan areas; see Appendix II for county components and listing of areas according to the newest definition. Minus sign (-) indicates decrease]

State	Metropolitan population Total (1,000) 1980	1990	2000	Percent change, 1990-2000	Percent of state 1990	2000	Nonmetropolitan population Total (1,000) 1980	1990	2000	Percent change, 1990-2000	Percent of state 1990	2000
U.S.	177,505	198,407	225,982	13.9	79.8	80.3	49,037	50,311	55,440	10.2	20.2	19.7
AL	2,636	2,797	3,109	11.2	69.2	69.9	1,258	1,244	1,338	7.6	30.8	30.1
AK	174	226	260	15.0	41.1	41.5	227	324	367	13.3	58.9	58.5
AZ	2,339	3,202	4,527	41.4	87.4	88.2	378	463	604	30.4	12.6	11.8
AR	1,026	1,109	1,321	19.1	47.2	49.4	1,260	1,242	1,352	8.9	52.8	50.6
CA	22,907	28,797	32,750	13.7	96.8	96.7	760	961	1,121	16.6	3.2	3.3
CO	2,408	2,779	3,608	29.8	84.4	83.9	482	515	694	34.7	15.6	16.1
CT	2,982	3,148	3,257	3.5	95.8	95.6	126	140	149	6.5	4.2	4.4
DE	496	553	627	13.4	83.0	80.0	98	113	157	38.3	17.0	20.0
DC	638	607	572	-5.7	100.0	100.0	(X)	(X)	(X)	(X)	(X)	(X)
FL	9,039	12,024	14,837	23.4	92.9	92.8	708	915	1,145	25.2	7.1	7.2
GA	3,507	4,351	5,667	30.2	67.2	69.2	1,956	2,127	2,520	18.5	32.8	30.8
HI	763	836	876	4.8	75.5	72.3	202	272	335	23.3	24.5	27.7
ID	322	362	508	40.4	35.9	39.3	622	645	786	21.9	64.1	60.7
IL	9,461	9,574	10,542	10.1	83.8	84.9	1,967	1,857	1,878	1.1	16.2	15.1
IN	3,885	3,962	4,390	10.8	71.5	72.2	1,605	1,582	1,691	6.9	28.5	27.8
IA	1,198	1,200	1,326	10.5	43.2	45.3	1,716	1,577	1,600	1.5	56.8	54.7
KS	1,184	1,333	1,521	14.1	53.8	56.6	1,180	1,145	1,167	2.0	46.2	43.4
KY	1,735	1,780	1,973	10.9	48.3	48.8	1,925	1,907	2,069	8.5	51.7	51.2
LA	3,125	3,160	3,370	6.7	74.9	75.4	1,082	1,061	1,099	3.6	25.1	24.6
ME	405	443	467	5.4	36.1	36.6	721	785	808	2.9	63.9	63.4
MD	3,920	4,438	4,911	10.7	92.8	92.7	297	343	385	12.5	7.2	7.3
MA	5,530	5,788	6,101	5.4	96.2	96.1	207	229	248	8.4	3.8	3.9
MI	7,719	7,698	8,169	6.1	82.8	82.2	1,543	1,598	1,769	10.7	17.2	17.8
MN	2,674	3,011	3,463	15.0	68.8	70.4	1,402	1,364	1,456	6.7	31.2	29.6
MS	806	874	1,024	17.1	34.0	36.0	1,715	1,701	1,821	7.1	66.0	64.0
MO	3,314	3,491	3,795	8.7	68.2	67.8	1,603	1,626	1,800	10.7	31.8	32.2
MT	265	270	306	13.2	33.8	33.9	522	529	597	12.7	66.2	66.1
NE	728	787	900	14.3	49.9	52.6	842	791	811	2.6	50.1	47.4
NV	666	1,014	1,748	72.4	84.4	87.5	135	188	251	33.4	15.6	12.5
NH	535	659	740	12.3	59.4	59.9	386	450	496	10.1	40.6	40.1
NJ	7,365	7,730	8,414	8.9	100.0	100.0	(X)	(X)	(X)	(X)	(X)	(X)
NM	675	842	1,035	23.0	55.6	56.9	628	673	784	16.4	44.4	43.1
NY	16,144	16,516	17,473	5.8	91.8	92.1	1,414	1,475	1,503	1.9	8.2	7.9
NC	3,749	4,380	5,437	24.2	66.0	67.5	2,131	2,253	2,612	15.9	34.0	32.5
ND	234	257	284	10.3	40.3	44.2	418	381	358	-6.1	59.7	55.8
OH	8,791	8,826	9,214	4.4	81.4	81.2	2,007	2,021	2,139	5.9	18.6	18.8
OK	1,724	1,870	2,098	12.2	59.4	60.8	1,301	1,276	1,352	6.0	40.6	39.2
OR	1,867	2,056	2,502	21.7	72.3	73.1	766	787	919	16.8	27.7	26.9
PA	10,067	10,084	10,392	3.0	84.9	84.6	1,798	1,799	1,890	5.1	15.1	15.4
RI	886	938	986	5.1	93.5	94.1	61	65	62	-5.2	6.5	5.9
SC	2,114	2,422	2,807	15.9	69.5	70.0	1,006	1,064	1,205	13.2	30.5	30.0
SD	194	221	261	18.3	31.7	34.6	497	475	494	3.9	68.3	65.4
TN	3,058	3,311	3,862	16.7	67.9	67.9	1,533	1,567	1,827	16.6	32.1	32.1
TX	11,539	14,166	17,692	24.9	83.4	84.8	2,686	2,821	3,160	12.0	16.6	15.2
UT	1,132	1,341	1,708	27.4	77.8	76.5	329	382	525	37.4	22.2	23.5
VT	133	152	169	11.8	26.9	27.8	378	411	439	6.9	73.1	72.2
VA	3,966	4,775	5,528	15.8	77.2	78.1	1,381	1,414	1,550	9.6	22.8	21.9
WA	3,366	4,036	4,899	21.4	82.9	83.1	766	830	995	19.8	17.1	16.9
WV	796	748	766	2.3	41.7	42.3	1,155	1,045	1,043	-0.2	58.3	57.7
WI	3,176	3,331	3,640	9.3	68.1	67.9	1,530	1,561	1,723	10.4	31.9	32.1
WY	141	134	148	10.2	29.6	30.0	329	319	346	8.3	70.4	70.0

X Not applicable.

Source: U.S. Census Bureau, 1990 Census of Population and Housing, *Population and Housing Unit Counts* (CPH-2-1); and unpublished data.

No. 26. Large Metropolitan Statistical Areas—Population: 1990 to 2002

[1990 and 2000, as of April 1; beginning 2001 as of July 1 (658 represents 658,000). Covers metropolitan statistical areas with 250,000 and over population in 2002 as defined by the U.S. Office of Management and Budget as of June 6, 2003. For definitions and components of all metropolitan and micropolitan areas, see Appendix II. Minus sign (-) indicates decrease]

Metropolitan statistical area	Number (1,000) 1990	2000	2001	2002	Percent change 1990-2000	2000-2002	Rank, 2002
Akron, OH	658	695	698	700	5.7	0.8	67
Albany-Schenectady-Troy, NY	809	826	830	836	2.0	1.2	58
Albuquerque, NM	599	730	739	754	21.7	3.3	65
Allentown-Bethlehem-Easton, PA-NJ	687	740	749	758	7.8	2.4	63
Anchorage, AK	266	320	326	334	20.1	4.5	141
Ann Arbor, MI	283	323	329	334	14.1	3.5	140
Asheville, NC	308	369	374	379	19.9	2.5	124
Atlanta-Sandy Springs-Marietta, GA	3,069	4,248	4,418	4,529	38.4	6.6	9
Atlantic City, NJ	224	253	256	259	12.6	2.7	164
Augusta-Richmond County, GA-SC	436	500	503	507	14.7	1.5	89
Austin-Round Rock, TX	846	1,250	1,322	1,349	47.7	8.0	39
Bakersfield, CA	543	662	677	694	21.7	4.9	69
Baltimore-Towson, MD	2,382	2,553	2,580	2,602	7.2	1.9	19
Baton Rouge, LA	624	706	711	717	13.2	1.5	66
Beaumont-Port Arthur, TX	361	385	383	382	6.6	-0.7	120
Binghamton, NY	264	252	252	252	-4.6	-0.1	169
Birmingham-Hoover, AL	957	1,052	1,062	1,068	10.0	1.5	48
Boise City-Nampa, ID	320	465	485	498	45.4	7.2	93
Boston-Cambridge-Quincy, MA-NH	4,134	4,391	4,433	4,446	6.2	1.2	11
Boulder, CO [1]	225	270	277	279	19.7	3.5	156
Bridgeport-Stamford-Norwalk, CT	828	883	890	896	6.6	1.5	51
Brownsville-Harlingen, TX	260	335	345	354	28.9	5.5	133
Buffalo-Cheektowaga-Tonawanda, NY	1,189	1,170	1,165	1,163	-1.6	-0.6	45
Canton-Massillon, OH	394	407	407	407	3.3	-	112
Cape Coral-Fort Myers, FL	335	441	459	476	31.6	7.9	99
Charleston-North Charleston, SC	507	549	555	563	8.3	2.5	85
Charleston, WV	308	310	307	306	0.6	-1.1	147
Charlotte-Gastonia-Concord, NC-SC	1,025	1,330	1,376	1,410	29.8	6.0	37
Chattanooga, TN-GA	433	477	480	483	10.0	1.3	96
Chicago-Naperville-Joliet, IL-IN-WI	8,182	9,098	9,207	9,286	11.2	2.1	3
Cincinnati-Middletown, OH-KY-IN	1,845	2,010	2,028	2,041	8.9	1.5	24
Cleveland-Elyria-Mentor, OH	2,102	2,148	2,147	2,148	2.2	-	23
Colorado Springs, CO	409	537	557	565	31.3	5.2	84
Columbia, SC	548	647	656	664	18.0	2.6	71
Columbus, GA-AL	266	282	283	283	5.7	0.5	154
Columbus, OH	1,405	1,613	1,641	1,660	14.8	2.9	31
Corpus Christi, TX	368	403	402	405	9.7	0.5	113
Dallas-Fort Worth-Arlington, TX	3,989	5,162	5,355	5,484	29.4	6.2	5
Davenport-Moline-Rock Island, IA-IL	368	376	375	375	2.1	-0.2	126
Dayton, OH	844	848	846	847	0.5	-0.2	56
Deltona-Daytona Beach-Ormond Beach, FL	371	443	452	459	19.6	3.6	102
Denver-Aurora, CO [1]	1,650	2,179	2,246	2,281	32.0	4.7	22
Des Moines, IA	416	481	490	497	15.6	3.3	94
Detroit-Warren-Livonia, MI	4,249	4,453	4,474	4,484	4.8	0.7	10
Duluth, MN-WI	269	275	277	276	2.3	0.3	159
Durham, NC	345	426	438	445	23.8	4.4	104
El Paso, TX	592	680	690	698	14.9	2.6	68
Erie, PA	276	281	281	280	1.9	-0.2	155
Eugene-Springfield, OR	283	323	324	327	14.2	1.1	144
Evansville, IN-KY	325	343	343	344	5.5	0.4	136
Fayetteville-Springdale-Rogers, AR-MO	239	347	359	368	44.9	6.1	127
Fayetteville, NC	297	337	337	339	13.2	0.8	137
Flint, MI	430	436	439	441	1.3	1.2	105
Fort Collins-Loveland, CO	186	251	260	265	35.1	5.2	162
Fort Smith, AR-OK	234	273	276	278	16.7	1.9	157
Fort Wayne, IN	354	390	394	397	10.1	1.7	116
Fresno, CA	667	799	816	835	19.8	4.4	59
Grand Rapids-Wyoming, MI	646	740	751	758	14.6	2.3	64
Green Bay, WI	244	283	286	289	16.0	2.3	151
Greensboro-High Point, NC	540	643	652	658	19.1	2.3	73
Greenville, SC	472	560	569	575	18.6	2.7	83
Harrisburg-Carlisle, PA	474	509	511	515	7.3	1.1	88
Hartford-West Hartford-East Hartford, CT	1,124	1,149	1,159	1,168	2.2	1.7	44
Hickory-Morganton-Lenoir, NC	292	342	347	349	16.9	2.2	135
Honolulu, HI	836	876	884	896	4.8	2.3	52
Houston-Baytown-Sugar Land, TX	3,767	4,715	4,857	4,986	25.2	5.7	8
Huntington-Ashland, WV-KY-OH	288	289	287	286	0.2	-0.9	153
Huntsville, AL	293	342	348	354	16.8	3.3	132
Indianapolis, IN	1,294	1,525	1,554	1,575	17.8	3.3	34
Jacksonville, FL	925	1,123	1,151	1,178	21.4	4.9	43
Jackson, MS	447	497	502	506	11.2	1.7	90
Kalamazoo-Portage, MI	293	315	316	319	7.3	1.2	145
Kansas City, MO-KS	1,637	1,836	1,865	1,889	12.2	2.9	27
Killeen-Temple-Fort Hood, TX	269	331	335	338	23.0	2.2	138
Knoxville, TN	535	616	623	630	15.2	2.3	76
Lakeland-Winter Haven, FL	405	484	492	499	19.4	3.1	92
Lancaster, PA	423	471	475	479	11.3	1.7	98
Lansing-East Lansing, MI	433	448	451	454	3.5	1.3	103

See footnotes at end of table.

Population 29

U.S. Census Bureau, Statistical Abstract of the United States: 2003

No. 26. Large Metropolitan Statistical Areas—Population: 1990 to 2002—Con.

[1990 and 2000, as of April 1; beginning 2001 as of July 1 (658 represents 658,000). Covers metropolitan statistical areas with 250,000 and over population in 2002 as defined by the U.S. Office of Management and Budget as of June 6, 2003. For definitions and components of all metropolitan and micropolitan areas, see Appendix II. Minus sign (-) indicates decrease]

Metropolitan statistical area	Number (1,000) 1990	2000	2001	2002	Percent change 1990-2000	2000-2002	Rank, 2002
Las Vegas-Paradise, NV	741	1,376	1,460	1,522	85.5	10.6	35
Lexington-Fayette, KY	348	408	413	416	17.2	2.0	109
Lincoln, NE	229	267	270	274	16.5	2.8	160
Little Rock-North Little Rock, AR	535	611	617	623	14.1	2.0	77
Los Angeles-Long Beach-Santa Ana, CA	11,274	12,366	12,577	12,745	9.7	3.1	2
Louisville, KY-IN	1,056	1,162	1,174	1,183	10.0	1.8	42
Lubbock, TX	230	250	253	254	8.6	1.9	166
Madison, WI	432	502	511	520	16.1	3.6	87
Manchester-Nashua, NH	336	381	389	392	13.3	3.0	118
McAllen-Edinburg-Pharr, TX	384	569	593	614	48.5	7.9	79
Memphis, TN-MS-AR	1,067	1,205	1,218	1,231	12.9	2.1	41
Miami-Fort Lauderdale-Miami Beach, FL	4,056	5,008	5,131	5,232	23.5	4.5	6
Milwaukee-Waukesha-West Allis, WI	1,432	1,501	1,507	1,513	4.8	0.8	36
Minneapolis-St. Paul-Bloomington, MN-WI	2,539	2,969	3,025	3,055	16.9	2.9	16
Mobile, AL	379	400	401	400	5.6	0.1	115
Modesto, CA	371	447	466	482	20.6	7.9	97
Montgomery, AL	305	347	349	351	13.6	1.4	134
Naples-Marco Island, FL	152	251	265	277	65.3	10.1	158
Nashville-Davidson-Murfreesboro, TN	1,048	1,312	1,336	1,353	25.1	3.1	38
New Haven-Milford, CT	804	824	830	836	2.5	1.4	57
New Orleans-Metairie-Kenner, LA	1,264	1,317	1,313	1,315	4.1	-0.1	40
New York-Newark-Edison, NY-NJ-PA	16,846	18,323	18,496	18,603	8.8	1.5	1
Norwich-New London, CT	255	259	261	263	1.6	1.4	163
Ocala, FL	195	259	265	273	32.9	5.3	161
Ogden-Clearfield, UT	352	443	452	461	25.8	4.1	101
Oklahoma City, OK	971	1,095	1,108	1,121	12.8	2.4	47
Omaha-Council Bluffs, NE-IA	686	767	777	784	11.8	2.3	60
Orlando, FL	1,225	1,645	1,706	1,752	34.3	6.5	29
Oxnard-Thousand Oaks-Ventura, CA	669	753	770	784	12.6	4.1	61
Palm Bay-Melbourne-Titusville, FL	399	476	486	496	19.4	4.1	95
Pensacola-Ferry Pass-Brent, FL	344	412	418	424	19.7	3.0	108
Peoria, IL	359	367	365	366	2.3	-0.3	128
Philadelphia-Camden-Wilmington, PA-NJ-DE	5,435	5,687	5,718	5,752	4.6	1.1	4
Phoenix-Mesa-Scottsdale, AZ	2,238	3,252	3,389	3,500	45.3	7.6	14
Pittsburgh, PA	2,468	2,431	2,422	2,418	-1.5	-0.5	21
Port St. Lucie-Fort Pierce, FL	251	319	328	338	27.2	5.7	139
Portland-South Portland, ME	441	488	495	501	10.5	2.7	91
Portland-Vancouver-Beaverton, OR-WA	1,524	1,928	1,978	2,016	26.5	4.6	25
Poughkeepsie-Newburgh-Middletown, NY	567	622	634	645	9.6	3.7	75
Providence-New Bedford-Fall River, RI-MA	1,510	1,583	1,598	1,613	4.8	1.9	32
Provo-Orem, UT	269	377	389	396	39.9	5.2	117
Raleigh-Cary, NC	541	797	833	859	47.3	7.8	55
Reading, PA	337	374	378	382	11.0	2.3	121
Reno-Sparks, NV	257	343	355	366	33.3	6.7	129
Richmond, VA	949	1,097	1,112	1,126	15.6	2.7	46
Riverside-San Bernardino-Ontario, CA	2,589	3,255	3,391	3,515	25.7	8.0	13
Roanoke, VA	268	288	289	289	7.4	0.4	150
Rochester, NY	1,002	1,038	1,040	1,043	3.5	0.5	49
Rockford, IL	284	320	324	327	12.9	2.2	143
Sacramento-Arden-Arcade-Roseville, CA	1,481	1,797	1,869	1,930	21.3	7.4	26
Salem, OR	278	347	352	358	24.9	3.1	131
Salinas, CA	356	402	409	413	13.0	2.9	110
Salt Lake City, UT	768	969	985	997	26.1	2.9	50
San Antonio, TX	1,408	1,712	1,750	1,787	21.6	4.4	28
San Diego-Carlsbad-San Marcos, CA	2,498	2,814	2,870	2,907	12.6	3.3	17
San Francisco-Oakland-Fremont, CA	3,687	4,124	4,188	4,180	11.9	1.4	12
San Jose-Sunnyvale-Santa Clara, CA	1,534	1,736	1,751	1,739	13.1	0.2	30
San Luis Obispo-Paso Robles, CA	217	247	251	253	13.6	2.7	168
Santa Barbara-Santa Maria-Goleta, CA	370	399	401	403	8.0	0.9	114
Santa Cruz-Watsonville, CA	230	256	256	254	11.3	-0.7	167
Santa Rosa-Petaluma, CA	388	459	466	468	18.1	2.1	100
Sarasota-Bradenton-Venice, FL	489	590	606	620	20.5	5.1	78
Savannah, GA	258	293	296	300	13.5	2.3	148
Scranton-Wilkes-Barre, PA	575	561	556	553	-2.5	-1.3	86
Seattle-Tacoma-Bellevue, WA	2,559	3,044	3,097	3,126	18.9	2.7	15
Shreveport-Bossier City, LA	360	376	377	378	4.5	0.5	125
South Bend-Mishawaka, IN-MI	297	317	318	318	6.8	0.5	146
Spartanburg, SC	227	254	257	259	11.9	2.2	165
Spokane, WA	361	418	423	428	15.7	2.3	107
Springfield, MA	673	680	680	684	1.0	0.6	70
Springfield, MO	299	368	374	379	23.3	2.8	123
Stockton, CA	481	564	594	614	17.3	9.0	80

See footnotes at end of table.

No. 26. Large Metropolitan Statistical Areas—Population: 1990 to 2002—Con.

[1990 and 2000, as of April 1; beginning 2001 as of July 1 (658 represents 658,000). Covers metropolitan statistical areas with 250,000 and over population in 2002 as defined by the U.S. Office of Management and Budget as of June 6, 2003. For definitions and components of all metropolitan and micropolitan areas, see Appendix II. Minus sign (-) indicates decrease]

Metropolitan statistical area	Number (1,000)				Percent change		Rank, 2002
	1990	2000	2001	2002	1990-2000	2000-2002	
St. Louis, MO-IL	2,581	2,699	2,715	2,729	4.6	1.1	18
Syracuse, NY	660	650	652	653	-1.5	0.5	74
Tallahassee, FL	259	320	325	328	23.6	2.4	142
Tampa-St. Petersburg-Clearwater, FL	2,068	2,396	2,445	2,490	15.9	3.9	20
Toledo, OH	654	659	660	660	0.8	-	72
Trenton-Ewing, NJ	326	351	355	359	7.7	2.5	130
Tucson, AZ	667	844	863	881	26.5	4.4	53
Tulsa, OK	761	860	869	878	12.9	2.1	54
Utica-Rome, NY	317	300	299	299	-5.3	-0.4	149
Vallejo-Fairfield, CA	340	395	406	411	15.9	4.2	111
Virginia Beach-Norfolk-Newport News, VA-NC	1,449	1,576	1,592	1,613	8.8	2.3	33
Visalia-Porterville, CA	312	368	374	382	18.0	3.7	122
Washington-Arlington-Alexandria, DC-VA-MD-WV	4,123	4,796	4,933	5,026	16.3	4.8	7
Wichita, KS	511	571	576	581	11.7	1.8	82
Wilmington, NC	200	275	281	287	37.2	4.5	152
Winston-Salem, NC	361	422	429	434	16.7	2.8	106
Worcester, MA	710	751	763	770	5.8	2.6	62
York-Hanover, PA	340	382	386	389	12.4	2.0	119
Youngstown-Warren-Boardman, OH-PA	614	603	599	596	-1.7	-1.1	81

- Represents or rounds to zero. [1] Broomfield County, CO, was formed from parts of Adams, Boulder, Jefferson, and Weld Counties, CO, on November 15, 2001, and is coextensive with Broomfield city. For purposes of defining and presenting data for metropolitan statistical areas, Broomfield city is treated as if it were a county at the time of the 2000 census.

Source: U.S. Census Bureau, unpublished data.

No. 27. Metropolitan Areas With 600,000 or More Inhabitants in 2000—Selected Racial Groups: 2000

[In thousands (875.6 represents 875,600). As of April. Covers metropolitan statistical area (MSAs) and consolidated metropolitan statistical areas (CMSAs) as defined by the U.S. Office of Management and Budget as of June 30, 1999. For definitions see Appendix II. See Appendix III for comments on methodology]

Metropolitan area	Total population	One race — White	Black or African American	American Indian, Alaska Native	Asian	Native Hawaiian and Other Pacific Islander	Some other race	Two or more races
Albany-Schenectady-Troy, NY MSA	875.6	782.9	53.4	1.9	16.0	0.2	8.2	12.9
Albuquerque, NM MSA	712.7	496.4	17.8	40.0	11.9	0.7	116.4	29.6
Allentown-Bethlehem-Easton, PA MSA	638.0	572.7	18.9	1.1	10.4	0.2	24.8	9.9
Atlanta, GA MSA	4,112.2	2,589.9	1,189.2	10.3	136.0	1.7	116.6	68.6
Austin-San Marcos, TX MSA	1,249.8	906.0	99.4	7.1	44.0	0.9	159.4	33.0
Bakersfield, CA MSA	661.6	407.6	39.8	10.0	22.3	1.0	153.6	27.4
Baton Rouge, LA MSA	602.9	391.4	192.6	1.4	9.0	0.2	3.1	5.2
Birmingham, AL MSA	921.1	620.1	277.1	2.4	7.6	0.2	6.2	7.4
Boston-Worcester-Lawrence, MA-NH-ME-CT CMSA	5,819.1	4,949.8	299.0	12.9	231.6	2.2	193.8	129.8
Buffalo-Niagara Falls, NY MSA	1,170.1	980.3	137.0	7.8	15.1	0.3	14.4	15.1
Charlotte-Gastonia-Rock Hill, NC-SC MSA	1,499.3	1,103.8	307.9	5.9	28.4	0.5	34.4	18.4
Chicago-Gary-Kenosha, IL-IN-WI CMSA	9,157.5	6,121.7	1,707.6	24.4	388.8	3.8	709.0	202.2
Cincinnati-Hamilton, OH-KY-IN CMSA	1,979.2	1,688.6	231.0	3.6	24.6	0.5	9.1	21.7
Cleveland-Akron, OH CMSA	2,945.8	2,328.4	493.5	5.5	39.6	0.6	33.9	44.3
Columbus, OH MSA	1,540.2	1,251.8	206.1	4.0	36.5	0.6	12.3	28.8
Dallas-Fort Worth, TX CMSA	5,221.8	3,629.0	720.1	29.6	195.5	4.4	517.2	126.0
Dayton-Springfield, OH MSA	950.6	782.3	135.3	2.3	11.9	0.3	4.3	14.2
Denver-Boulder-Greeley, CO CMSA	2,581.5	2,079.7	119.8	22.9	73.4	2.5	208.4	74.8
Detroit-Ann Arbor-Flint, MI CMSA	5,456.4	3,986.0	1,149.3	19.6	128.3	1.3	58.3	113.6
El Paso, TX MSA	679.6	502.6	20.8	5.6	6.6	0.7	121.7	21.7
Fresno, CA MSA	922.5	510.7	47.4	16.0	65.9	1.2	237.0	44.3
Grand Rapids-Muskegon-Holland, MI MSA	1,088.5	932.6	79.3	5.8	17.0	0.5	32.6	20.8
Greensboro-Winston-Salem-High Point, NC MSA	1,251.5	931.6	252.7	4.7	16.9	0.3	30.0	15.2
Greenville-Spartanburg-Anderson, SC MSA	962.4	760.5	168.1	1.9	11.2	0.3	10.9	9.6
Harrisburg-Lebanon-Carlisle, PA MSA	629.4	552.5	49.4	0.9	9.6	0.2	8.7	8.1
Hartford, CT MSA	1,183.1	954.9	111.8	2.8	26.4	0.5	61.7	25.1
Honolulu, HI MSA	876.2	186.5	20.6	2.2	403.4	77.7	11.2	174.6
Houston-Galveston-Brazoria, TX CMSA	4,669.6	2,922.0	789.5	20.7	228.2	2.5	579.2	127.4
Indianapolis, IN MSA	1,607.5	1,319.0	224.0	3.7	19.7	0.6	20.4	20.1
Jacksonville, FL MSA	1,100.5	799.5	238.4	3.8	25.4	0.7	12.9	19.9
Kansas City, MO-KS MSA	1,776.1	1,435.4	226.5	8.4	28.7	1.8	40.4	34.8
Knoxville, TN MSA	687.2	627.7	39.7	1.9	6.8	0.2	3.4	7.6
Las Vegas, NV-AZ MSA	1,563.3	1,153.5	126.1	15.3	74.0	6.7	125.6	62.1
Los Angeles-Riverside-Orange County, CA CMSA	16,373.6	9,028.9	1,245.0	142.1	1,701.7	46.7	3,439.1	770.1
Louisville, KY-IN MSA	1,025.6	849.6	142.8	2.4	11.0	0.3	6.3	13.2
Memphis, TN-AR-MS MSA	1,135.6	600.6	492.5	2.5	15.9	0.4	12.7	11.1
Miami-Fort Lauderdale, FL CMSA	3,876.4	2,715.8	790.5	8.2	68.3	1.7	151.9	139.8
Milwaukee-Racine, WI CMSA	1,689.6	1,313.7	254.8	8.7	32.4	0.6	50.8	28.5
Minneapolis-St. Paul, MN-WI MSA	2,968.8	2,556.9	158.0	21.6	122.8	1.3	46.1	62.3
Nashville, TN MSA	1,231.3	977.9	191.9	3.6	20.0	0.6	19.7	17.7
New Orleans, LA MSA	1,337.7	766.5	502.3	5.0	28.6	0.4	16.3	18.8
New York-Northern New Jersey-Long Island, NY-NJ-CT-PA CMSA	21,199.9	13,589.3	3,638.6	70.5	1,435.9	10.5	1,733.6	721.6
Norfolk-Virginia Beach-Newport News, VA-NC MSA	1,569.5	980.5	485.4	6.2	43.0	1.3	18.5	34.7
Oklahoma City, OK MSA	1,083.3	819.6	114.4	45.4	27.2	0.8	34.3	41.7
Omaha, NE-IA MSA	717.0	611.1	59.4	3.8	10.8	0.4	19.3	12.2
Orlando, FL MSA	1,644.6	1,233.1	227.9	5.7	44.6	1.2	84.7	47.4
Philadelphia-Wilmington-Atlantic City, PA-NJ-DE-MD CMSA	6,188.5	4,489.0	1,210.8	13.4	200.9	2.2	168.7	103.3
Phoenix-Mesa, AZ MSA	3,251.9	2,502.9	119.5	70.7	67.5	4.6	392.4	94.3
Pittsburgh, PA MSA	2,358.7	2,111.3	190.5	2.6	26.1	0.5	6.2	21.5
Portland-Salem, OR-WA CMSA	2,265.2	1,909.2	54.2	22.1	93.6	6.8	104.9	74.4
Providence-Fall River-Warwick, RI-MA MSA	1,188.6	1,025.2	47.1	5.0	26.4	0.6	54.0	30.4
Raleigh-Durham-Chapel Hill, NC MSA	1,187.9	823.9	269.9	4.2	34.2	0.4	36.7	18.6
Richmond-Petersburg, VA MSA	996.5	647.2	300.5	3.7	20.5	0.5	10.9	13.3
Rochester, NY MSA	1,098.2	922.2	112.6	3.3	20.0	0.3	21.1	18.7
Sacramento-Yolo, CA CMSA	1,796.9	1,257.6	128.1	19.1	162.2	8.4	128.7	92.8
Salt Lake City-Ogden, UT MSA	1,333.9	1,168.5	14.9	10.8	29.2	12.0	66.6	32.0
San Antonio, TX MSA	1,592.4	1,124.1	105.6	12.3	23.7	1.6	269.4	55.8
San Diego, CA MSA	2,813.8	1,871.8	161.5	24.3	249.8	13.6	360.8	132.0
San Francisco-Oakland-San Jose, CA CMSA	7,039.4	4,133.6	513.6	46.0	1,298.6	36.7	665.4	345.5
Scranton-Wilkes-Barre-Hazleton, PA MSA	624.8	604.8	8.9	0.6	3.9	0.1	2.7	3.8
Seattle-Tacoma-Bremerton, WA CMSA	3,554.8	2,819.3	165.9	41.7	280.7	19.8	79.4	147.9
St. Louis, MO-IL MSA	2,603.6	2,037.4	476.7	5.9	37.1	0.7	13.5	32.4
Syracuse, NY MSA	732.1	651.0	47.9	5.1	10.8	0.2	5.6	11.6
Tampa-St. Petersburg-Clearwater, FL MSA	2,396.0	1,986.5	244.5	8.2	45.0	1.4	63.6	46.9
Toledo, OH MSA	618.2	507.7	78.9	1.6	6.9	0.1	11.2	11.7
Tucson, AZ MSA	843.7	633.4	25.6	27.2	17.2	1.1	112.2	27.1
Tulsa, OK MSA	803.2	610.2	70.9	55.8	9.9	0.3	17.2	38.9
Washington-Baltimore, DC-MD-VA-WV CMSA	7,608.1	4,795.4	1,992.3	22.6	399.8	4.2	209.2	184.7
West Palm Beach-Boca Raton, FL MSA	1,131.2	894.2	156.1	2.5	17.1	0.7	33.7	26.9

Source: U.S. Census Bureau, 2000 Census of Population and Housing, Profiles of General Demographic Characteristics. See also <http://www.census.gov/Press-Release/www/2002/demoprofiles.html>.

No. 28. Metropolitan Areas With 600,000 or More Inhabitants in 2000—Hispanic and Non-Hispanic Groups: 2000

[In thousands (875.6 represents 875,600). As of April. Covers metropolitan statistical area (MSAs) and consolidated metropolitan statistical areas (CMSAs) as defined by the U.S. Office of Management and Budget as of June 30, 1999. For definitions see Appendix II. See Appendix III for comments on methodology]

Metropolitan area	Total population	Hispanic or Latino Total	Mexican	Puerto Rican	Cuban	Other Hispanic or Latino	Not Hispanic or Latino Total	White alone
Albany-Schenectady-Troy, NY MSA	875.6	23.8	2.3	13.3	0.8	7.4	851.8	771.0
Albuquerque, NM MSA	712.7	296.4	107.0	2.5	2.0	184.9	416.4	340.3
Allentown-Bethlehem-Easton, PA MSA	638.0	50.6	3.5	33.5	0.8	12.8	587.4	552.4
Atlanta, GA MSA	4,112.2	268.9	165.1	19.4	9.2	75.2	3,843.3	2,460.7
Austin-San Marcos, TX MSA	1,249.8	327.8	248.9	4.6	2.0	72.2	922.0	758.3
Bakersfield, CA MSA	661.6	254.0	210.8	2.8	0.5	39.9	407.6	327.2
Baton Rouge, LA MSA	602.9	10.6	4.1	0.8	0.9	4.8	592.3	385.1
Birmingham, AL MSA	921.1	16.6	11.4	0.9	0.5	3.8	904.5	611.6
Boston-Worcester-Lawrence, MA-NH-ME-CT CMSA	5,819.1	358.2	22.9	137.4	8.4	189.6	5,460.9	4,802.5
Buffalo-Niagara Falls, NY MSA	1,170.1	34.0	3.1	23.0	0.8	7.2	1,136.1	965.2
Charlotte-Gastonia-Rock Hill, NC-SC MSA	1,499.3	77.1	46.6	4.9	1.9	23.7	1,422.2	1,067.6
Chicago-Gary-Kenosha, IL-IN-WI CMSA	9,157.5	1,498.5	1,121.1	164.5	17.3	195.7	7,659.0	5,435.4
Cincinnati-Hamilton, OH-KY-IN CMSA	1,979.2	22.5	10.3	2.9	1.0	8.3	1,956.7	1,676.3
Cleveland-Akron, OH CMSA	2,945.8	80.7	15.8	47.4	1.6	15.9	2,865.1	2,291.1
Columbus, OH MSA	1,540.2	28.1	13.6	4.2	1.1	9.3	1,512.0	1,238.3
Dallas-Fort Worth, TX CMSA	5,221.8	1,120.4	889.9	16.2	7.1	207.2	4,101.5	3,096.1
Dayton-Springfield, OH MSA	950.6	11.3	5.4	1.8	0.5	3.7	939.2	776.1
Denver-Boulder-Greeley, CO CMSA	2,581.5	476.6	312.6	6.9	2.6	154.5	2,104.9	1,854.4
Detroit-Ann Arbor-Flint, MI CMSA	5,456.4	155.9	103.0	17.0	3.4	32.6	5,300.5	3,904.4
El Paso, TX MSA	679.6	531.7	447.1	4.3	0.5	79.8	148.0	115.5
Fresno, CA MSA	922.5	406.2	349.1	2.1	0.6	54.3	516.4	374.9
Grand Rapids-Muskegon-Holland, MI MSA	1,088.5	68.9	46.9	5.1	1.6	15.2	1,019.6	903.8
Greensboro-Winston-Salem-High Point, NC MSA	1,251.5	62.2	45.5	3.0	1.1	12.5	1,189.3	905.0
Greenville-Spartanburg-Anderson, SC MSA	962.4	26.2	14.8	2.4	0.6	8.5	936.3	747.5
Harrisburg-Lebanon-Carlisle, PA MSA	629.4	19.6	2.6	12.2	0.6	4.1	609.8	544.1
Hartford, CT MSA	1,183.1	113.5	5.3	83.0	2.3	23.0	1,069.6	915.3
Honolulu, HI MSA	876.2	58.7	13.4	18.9	0.5	25.9	817.4	175.6
Houston-Galveston-Brazoria, TX CMSA	4,669.6	1,348.6	985.2	15.7	10.2	337.5	3,321.0	2,239.9
Indianapolis, IN MSA	1,607.5	43.0	28.7	3.0	0.9	10.4	1,564.5	1,299.3
Jacksonville, FL MSA	1,100.5	42.1	8.7	14.9	4.2	14.4	1,058.4	775.3
Kansas City, MO-KS MSA	1,776.1	92.9	71.0	2.9	1.8	17.2	1,683.2	1,391.5
Knoxville, TN MSA	687.2	8.6	4.6	0.9	0.4	2.7	678.6	623.0
Las Vegas, NV-AZ MSA	1,563.3	322.0	232.1	9.3	11.1	69.5	1,241.2	986.5
Los Angeles-Riverside-Orange County, CA CMSA	16,373.6	6,598.5	4,962.0	66.3	53.8	1,516.3	9,775.2	6,387.1
Louisville, KY-IN MSA	1,025.6	16.5	7.6	1.9	2.4	4.6	1,009.1	840.7
Memphis, TN-AR-MS MSA	1,135.6	27.5	19.1	1.4	0.9	6.2	1,108.1	588.8
Miami-Fort Lauderdale, FL CMSA	3,876.4	1,563.4	57.5	135.3	701.5	669.1	2,313.0	1,407.4
Milwaukee-Racine, WI CMSA	1,689.6	109.5	68.8	24.5	1.2	15.0	1,580.1	1,266.4
Minneapolis-St. Paul, MN-WI MSA	2,968.8	99.1	65.5	5.3	1.8	26.5	2,869.7	2,514.5
Nashville, TN MSA	1,231.9	40.1	25.2	3.0	1.2	10.7	1,191.2	960.1
New Orleans, LA MSA	1,337.7	58.5	10.2	3.7	5.8	38.9	1,279.2	731.5
New York-Northern New Jersey-Long Island, NY-NJ-CT-PA CMSA	21,199.9	3,852.1	343.1	1,325.8	135.0	2,048.3	17,347.7	11,953.7
Norfolk-Virginia Beach-Newport News, VA-NC MSA	1,569.5	49.0	13.8	17.0	1.8	16.5	1,520.6	959.4
Oklahoma City, OK MSA	1,083.3	73.0	55.6	2.5	0.7	14.1	1,010.3	789.8
Omaha, NE-IA MSA	717.0	39.7	30.6	1.3	0.4	7.4	677.3	593.9
Orlando, FL MSA	1,644.6	271.6	32.7	139.9	18.8	80.3	1,372.9	1,070.5
Philadelphia-Wilmington-Atlantic City, PA-NJ-DE-MD CMSA	6,188.5	348.1	50.0	206.8	8.6	82.7	5,840.4	4,355.5
Phoenix-Mesa, AZ MSA	3,251.9	817.0	667.7	11.8	3.7	133.8	2,434.9	2,140.2
Pittsburgh, PA MSA	2,358.7	17.1	5.7	3.3	0.9	7.1	2,341.6	2,100.5
Portland-Salem, OR-WA CMSA	2,265.2	196.6	152.5	3.7	2.7	37.8	2,068.6	1,836.0
Providence-Fall River-Warwick, RI-MA MSA	1,188.6	93.9	5.8	27.2	1.1	59.8	1,094.7	990.7
Raleigh-Durham-Chapel Hill, NC MSA	1,187.9	72.6	48.3	4.1	1.4	18.7	1,115.4	793.7
Richmond-Petersburg, VA MSA	996.5	23.3	7.2	4.6	1.0	10.5	973.2	637.8
Rochester, NY MSA	1,098.2	47.6	3.9	32.1	2.1	9.5	1,050.6	902.8
Sacramento-Yolo, CA CMSA	1,796.9	278.2	216.2	7.2	1.7	53.0	1,518.7	1,144.6
Salt Lake City-Ogden, UT MSA	1,333.9	144.6	97.6	2.9	0.7	43.5	1,189.3	1,104.5
San Antonio, TX MSA	1,592.4	816.0	572.3	10.6	1.9	231.2	776.3	627.2
San Diego, CA MSA	2,813.8	751.0	628.5	14.9	3.9	103.7	2,062.9	1,548.8
San Francisco-Oakland-San Jose, CA CMSA	7,039.4	1,383.7	981.3	34.2	9.0	359.2	5,655.7	3,559.7
Scranton-Wilkes-Barre-Hazleton, PA MSA	624.8	7.5	1.5	2.8	0.3	2.9	617.3	600.8
Seattle-Tacoma-Bremerton, WA CMSA	3,554.8	184.3	118.5	12.6	3.3	49.9	3,370.5	2,737.9
St. Louis, MO-IL MSA	2,603.6	39.7	22.3	3.4	1.3	12.7	2,563.9	2,014.8
Syracuse, NY MSA	732.1	15.1	2.0	7.9	0.9	4.3	717.0	644.0
Tampa-St. Petersburg-Clearwater, FL MSA	2,396.0	248.6	53.7	75.6	41.6	77.7	2,147.4	1,822.0
Toledo, OH MSA	618.2	27.1	20.7	1.2	0.3	5.0	591.1	495.1
Tucson, AZ MSA	843.7	247.6	205.6	3.2	1.0	37.8	596.2	518.7
Tulsa, OK MSA	803.2	38.6	27.9	1.9	0.5	8.2	764.7	593.5
Washington-Baltimore, DC-MD-VA-WV CMSA	7,608.1	484.9	75.6	41.6	11.8	355.8	7,123.2	4,572.6
West Palm Beach-Boca Raton, FL MSA	1,131.6	140.7	30.1	25.2	25.4	60.0	990.5	798.5

Source: U.S. Census Bureau, 2000 Census of Population and Housing, *Profiles of General Demographic Characteristics*. See also <http://www.census.gov/Press-Release/www/2002/demoprofiles.html>.

No. 29. Incorporated Places by Population Size: 1980 to 2002

[140.3 represents 140,300,000. See Appendix III]

Population size	Number of incorporated places				Population (mil.)				Percent of total			
	1980	1990	2000	2002	1980	1990	2000	2002	1980	1990	2000	2002
Total	19,097	19,262	19,452	19,448	140.3	152.9	173.5	177.8	100.0	100.0	100.0	100.0
1,000,000 or more	6	8	9	9	17.5	20.0	22.9	23.3	12.5	13.0	13.2	13.1
500,000 to 999,999	16	15	20	22	10.9	10.1	12.9	14.0	7.8	6.6	7.4	7.9
250,000 to 499,999	33	41	37	37	11.8	14.2	13.3	13.1	8.4	9.3	7.7	7.4
100,000 to 249,999	114	131	172	172	16.6	19.1	25.5	25.9	11.8	12.5	14.7	14.6
50,000 to 99,999	250	309	363	385	17.6	21.2	24.9	26.7	12.3	13.9	14.3	15.0
25,000 to 49,999	526	567	644	663	18.4	20.0	22.6	23.2	13.1	13.0	13.0	13.1
10,000 to 24,999	1,260	1,290	1,435	1,454	19.8	20.3	22.6	22.9	14.1	13.3	13.0	12.8
Under 10,000	16,892	16,901	16,772	16,706	28.0	28.2	28.7	28.7	20.0	18.4	16.6	16.1

Source: U.S. Census Bureau, Census of Population: 1980, Vol. I; 1990 Census of Population and Housing, *Population and Housing Unit Counts* (CPH-2-1); *County and City Data Book 2000;* and "Incorporated Place Population Estimates, Sorted Alphabetically: April 1, 2000 to July 1, 2002"; published 9 July 2003; <http://eire.census.gov/popest/data/cities/subtab07.php>.

No. 30. Urban and Rural Population by State: 2000

[In thousands, except percent (281,422 represents 281,422,000). As of April 1. Resident population]

State	Total	Urban Number	Urban Percent	Rural	State	Total	Urban Number	Urban Percent	Rural
US, total	281,422	222,361	79.0	59,061	MO	5,595	3,883	69.4	1,712
					MT	902	488	54.1	414
AL	4,447	2,466	55.4	1,981	NE	1,711	1,194	69.8	518
AK	627	411	65.6	216	NV	1,998	1,829	91.5	170
AZ	5,131	4,524	88.2	607	NH	1,236	732	59.3	503
AR	2,673	1,404	52.5	1,269					
CA	33,872	31,990	94.4	1,882	NJ	8,414	7,939	94.4	475
					NM	1,819	1,364	75.0	456
CO	4,301	3,633	84.5	668	NY	18,976	16,603	87.5	2,374
CT	3,406	2,988	87.7	418	NC	8,049	4,849	60.2	3,200
DE	784	628	80.1	156	ND	642	359	55.9	283
DC	572	572	100.0	-					
FL	15,982	14,270	89.3	1,712	OH	11,353	8,782	77.4	2,571
					OK	3,451	2,255	65.3	1,196
GA	8,186	5,864	71.6	2,322	OR	3,421	2,694	78.7	727
HI	1,212	1,108	91.5	103	PA	12,281	9,464	77.1	2,817
ID	1,294	859	66.4	434	RI	1,048	953	90.9	95
IL	12,419	10,910	87.8	1,510					
IN	6,080	4,304	70.8	1,776	SC	4,012	2,427	60.5	1,585
					SD	755	391	51.9	363
IA	2,926	1,787	61.1	1,139	TN	5,689	3,620	63.6	2,069
KS	2,688	1,921	71.4	768	TX	20,852	17,204	82.5	3,648
KY	4,042	2,254	55.8	1,788	UT	2,233	1,970	88.2	263
LA	4,469	3,246	72.6	1,223					
ME	1,275	513	40.2	762	VT	609	232	38.2	376
					VA	7,079	5,170	73.0	1,909
MD	5,296	4,559	86.1	738	WA	5,894	4,831	82.0	1,063
MA	6,349	5,801	91.4	548	WV	1,808	833	46.1	976
MI	9,938	7,419	74.7	2,519	WI	5,364	3,664	68.3	1,700
MN	4,919	3,490	70.9	1,429	WY	494	321	65.1	172
MS	2,845	1,387	48.8	1,457					

- Represents zero.

Source: U.S. Census Bureau, Census 2000 Summary File 1 Final National File, 2002.

No. 31. Incorporated Places With 100,000 or More Inhabitants in 2002— Population, 1980 to 2002, and Land Area, 2000

[Population: As of April 1 (98 represents 98,000), except 2002 as of July 1. 2002 data refer to boundaries in effect on January 1, 2002; 1990 and 2000 data, boundaries in effect on January 1, 2000; 1980 data, boundaries in effect for 1980 census. Minus sign (-) indicates decrease. See Appendix III]

Incorporated place	1980, total population (1,000)	1990, total population (1,000)	Population, 2000 Total (1,000)	Population, 2000 Percent change, 1990-2000	Population, 2002 Total (1,000)	Population, 2002 Rank	Population, 2002 Percent change, 2000-2002	Land area, 2000 (square miles)
Abilene, TX	98	107	116	8.4	115	200	-0.6	105.1
Akron, OH	237	223	217	-2.7	214	84	-1.3	62.1
Albuquerque, NM	332	387	449	15.9	464	35	3.4	180.6
Alexandria, VA	103	111	128	15.4	131	170	2.0	15.2
Allentown, PA	104	105	107	1.1	106	220	-0.5	17.7
Amarillo, TX	149	158	174	10.0	177	120	1.9	89.9
Anaheim, CA	219	267	328	23.0	333	53	1.4	48.9
Anchorage, AK	174	226	260	15.0	269	65	3.3	1,697.2
Ann Arbor, MI	108	110	114	3.5	115	201	1.0	27.0
Arlington, VA [1]	153	171	189	10.9	190	111	0.3	26.0
Arlington, TX	160	262	333	27.1	350	50	5.1	95.8

See footnotes at end of table.

No. 31. Incorporated Places With 100,000 or More Inhabitants in 2002—Population, 1980 to 2002, and Land Area, 2000—Con.

[Population: As of April 1 (98 represents 98,000), except 2002 as of July 1. 2002 data refer to boundaries in effect on January 1, 2002; 1990 and 2000 data, boundaries in effect on January 1, 2000; 1980 data, boundaries in effect for 1980 census. Minus sign (-) indicates decrease. See Appendix III]

Incorporated place	1980, total population (1,000)	1990, total population (1,000)	Population, 2000 Total (1,000)	Population, 2000 Percent change, 1990-2000	Population, 2002 Total (1,000)	Population, 2002 Rank	Population, 2002 Percent change, 2000-2002	Land area, 2000 (square miles)
Arvada, CO	85	90	102	13.8	102	233	(Z)	32.7
Athens-Clarke County, GA [2]	(NA)	87	100	15.9	103	231	2.4	117.8
Atlanta, GA	425	394	416	5.8	425	41	2.0	131.7
Augusta-Richmond County, GA [2]	(NA)	186	195	4.8	193	107	-1.1	302.1
Aurora, CO	159	222	276	24.6	286	60	3.5	142.5
Aurora, IL	81	100	143	42.6	157	134	9.8	38.5
Austin, TX	346	494	657	32.8	672	16	2.3	251.5
Bakersfield, CA	106	184	247	34.3	261	68	5.6	113.1
Baltimore, MD	787	736	651	-11.5	639	18	-1.9	80.8
Baton Rouge, LA	220	222	228	2.5	226	79	-0.9	76.8
Beaumont, TX	118	114	114	-0.5	113	208	-0.9	85.0
Bellevue, WA	74	99	110	11.1	113	207	3.0	30.7
Berkeley, CA	103	103	103	-0.1	104	225	0.9	10.5
Birmingham, AL	284	266	243	-8.7	239	72	-1.4	149.9
Boise City, ID	102	135	186	37.5	190	112	2.2	63.8
Boston, MA	563	574	589	2.6	589	20	(Z)	48.4
Bridgeport, CT	143	142	140	-1.4	140	160	0.4	16.0
Brownsville, TX	85	115	140	21.3	150	144	7.7	80.4
Buffalo, NY	358	328	293	-10.8	288	59	-1.7	40.6
Burbank, CA	87	94	100	7.1	103	230	2.6	17.3
Cambridge, MA	95	96	101	5.7	102	238	0.4	6.4
Cape Coral, FL	32	75	102	36.1	113	206	10.4	105.2
Carrollton, TX	41	83	110	32.7	115	202	5.0	36.5
Cedar Rapids, IA	110	109	121	10.9	123	188	1.5	63.1
Chandler, AZ	30	91	177	94.7	202	91	14.4	57.9
Charlotte, NC	315	427	541	26.7	581	21	7.4	242.3
Chattanooga, TN	170	153	156	1.8	155	135	-0.1	135.2
Chesapeake, VA	114	152	199	31.1	207	87	3.8	340.7
Chicago, IL	3,005	2,784	2,896	4.0	2,886	3	-0.3	227.1
Chula Vista, CA	84	135	174	28.3	194	104	11.7	48.9
Cincinnati, OH	385	365	331	-9.1	324	55	-2.2	78.0
Clarksville, TN	55	77	103	35.2	106	222	2.4	94.9
Clearwater, FL	85	97	109	11.9	108	216	-0.4	25.3
Cleveland, OH	574	505	478	-5.4	468	34	-2.2	77.6
Colorado Springs, CO	215	283	361	27.5	371	48	2.9	185.7
Columbia, SC	101	114	116	1.6	117	197	1.0	125.2
Columbus, GA	[2]169	[2]179	[2]186	4.0	186	114	-0.2	216.1
Columbus, OH	565	636	711	11.8	725	15	1.9	210.3
Concord, CA	104	111	122	9.5	125	178	2.8	30.1
Coral Springs, FL	37	79	118	48.5	126	177	6.9	23.9
Corona, CA	38	76	125	64.0	138	162	10.7	35.1
Corpus Christi, TX	232	258	277	7.4	279	62	0.4	154.6
Costa Mesa, CA	83	97	109	12.3	110	213	1.3	15.6
Dallas, TX	905	1,007	1,189	18.1	1,211	8	1.9	342.5
Daly City, CA	79	92	104	12.4	102	236	-1.7	7.6
Dayton, OH	194	182	166	-8.9	163	127	-2.1	55.8
Denver, CO	493	468	555	18.6	560	26	1.0	153.4
Des Moines, IA	191	193	199	2.8	198	95	-0.3	75.8
Detroit, MI	1,203	1,028	951	-7.5	925	10	-2.8	138.8
Downey, CA	83	91	107	17.3	110	214	2.3	12.4
Durham, NC	101	148	187	26.0	196	102	4.7	94.6
El Monte, CA	79	106	116	9.2	120	191	3.4	9.6
El Paso, TX	425	516	564	9.3	577	22	2.4	249.1
Elizabeth, NJ	106	110	121	9.5	123	185	2.2	12.2
Erie, PA	119	109	104	-4.6	102	234	-1.5	22.0
Escondido, CA	64	109	134	22.5	136	164	1.8	36.3
Eugene, OR	106	114	138	21.1	140	159	1.8	40.5
Evansville, IN	130	126	122	-3.6	119	194	-2.1	40.7
Fairfield, CA	58	79	96	22.1	102	235	6.0	37.7
Fayetteville, NC	60	113	121	7.4	124	183	2.7	58.8
Flint, MI	160	141	125	-11.6	122	190	-2.5	33.6
Fontana, CA	37	88	129	46.7	144	154	11.4	36.1
Fort Collins, CO	65	89	119	33.5	125	179	5.1	46.5
Fort Lauderdale, FL	153	149	152	2.4	158	133	3.8	31.7
Fort Wayne, IN	172	203	206	1.3	210	85	2.1	79.0
Fort Worth, TX	385	448	535	19.3	568	25	6.1	292.5
Fremont, CA	132	173	203	17.3	207	86	1.7	76.7
Fresno, CA	217	355	428	20.3	445	36	4.1	104.4
Fullerton, CA	102	113	126	11.1	129	173	2.3	22.2
Garden Grove, CA	123	144	165	15.0	167	124	1.4	18.0
Garland, TX	139	181	216	19.3	220	80	1.8	57.1
Gary, IN	152	117	103	-11.9	101	241	-1.8	50.2
Gilbert, AZ	6	30	110	265.6	135	168	23.1	43.0
Glendale, AZ	97	151	219	45.0	231	76	5.4	55.7
Glendale, CA	139	180	195	8.3	199	93	2.3	30.6
Grand Prairie, TX	71	99	127	28.1	135	167	6.2	71.4
Grand Rapids, MI	182	190	198	4.3	197	99	-0.6	44.6
Green Bay, WI	88	97	102	5.8	102	239	-0.8	43.9
Greensboro, NC	156	192	224	16.9	228	77	1.9	104.7
Hampton, VA	123	134	146	9.5	146	149	-0.4	51.8

See footnotes at end of table.

Population 35

U.S. Census Bureau, Statistical Abstract of the United States: 2003

No. 31. Incorporated Places With 100,000 or More Inhabitants in 2002—Population, 1980 to 2002, and Land Area, 2000—Con.

[Population: As of April 1 (98 represents 98,000), except 2002 as of July 1. 2002 data refer to boundaries in effect on January 1, 2002; 1990 and 2000 data, boundaries in effect on January 1, 2000; 1980 data, boundaries in effect for 1980 census. Minus sign (-) indicates decrease. See Appendix III]

Incorporated place	1980, total population (1,000)	1990, total population (1,000)	Population, 2000 Total (1,000)	Population, 2000 Percent change, 1990-2000	Population, 2002 Total (1,000)	Population, 2002 Rank	Population, 2002 Percent change, 2000-2002	Land area, 2000 (square miles)
Hartford, CT	136	137	122	-11.4	125	181	2.5	17.3
Hayward, CA	94	115	140	22.1	143	156	1.9	44.3
Henderson, NV	24	65	175	169.4	206	88	17.5	79.7
Hialeah, FL	145	188	226	20.5	228	78	0.8	19.2
Hollywood, FL	121	123	139	13.5	143	155	2.8	27.3
Honolulu, HI [1]	365	377	372	-1.4	378	45	1.7	85.7
Houston, TX	1,595	1,698	1,954	15.1	2,010	4	2.9	579.4
Huntington Beach, CA	171	183	190	3.7	194	105	2.2	26.4
Huntsville, AL	143	160	158	-1.3	163	128	2.7	174.0
Independence, MO	112	112	113	0.8	113	205	-0.2	78.3
Indianapolis, IN [2]	701	732	782	6.9	784	12	0.2	361.5
Inglewood, CA	94	110	113	1.9	115	203	2.1	9.1
Irvine, CA	62	111	143	28.4	162	129	13.3	46.2
Irving, TX	110	155	192	23.5	196	101	2.4	67.2
Jackson, MS	203	197	184	-6.3	181	117	-1.8	104.9
Jacksonville, FL	541	635	736	15.8	762	14	3.6	757.7
Jersey City, NJ	224	228	240	5.1	240	71	(Z)	14.9
Joliet, IL	78	79	106	35.2	118	196	11.5	38.1
Kansas City, KS	161	151	147	-3.0	147	147	0.1	124.3
Kansas City, MO	448	435	442	1.5	443	37	0.4	313.5
Knoxville, TN	175	173	174	0.4	174	123	-0.1	92.7
Lafayette, LA	81	103	110	7.5	111	211	0.9	47.6
Lakewood, CO	114	126	144	14.2	144	152	-0.3	41.6
Lancaster, CA	48	98	119	20.6	125	180	4.9	94.0
Lansing, MI	130	127	119	-6.1	119	195	-0.5	35.0
Laredo, TX	91	125	177	41.2	192	109	8.5	78.5
Las Vegas, NV	165	260	478	84.1	509	30	6.3	113.3
Lexington-Fayette, KY	204	225	261	15.6	264	66	1.2	284.5
Lincoln, NE	172	193	226	17.0	232	75	3.0	74.6
Little Rock, AR	159	177	183	3.4	184	115	0.5	116.2
Livonia, MI	105	101	101	-0.3	100	242	-0.2	35.7
Long Beach, CA	361	430	462	7.4	472	33	2.4	50.4
Los Angeles, CA	2,969	3,485	3,695	6.0	3,799	2	2.8	469.1
Louisville, KY	299	270	256	-5.0	251	69	-1.9	62.1
Lowell, MA	92	103	105	1.7	105	224	-0.3	13.8
Lubbock, TX	174	187	200	6.9	204	89	2.1	114.8
Madison, WI	171	191	208	9.0	215	83	3.4	68.7
Manchester, NH	91	99	107	7.9	108	215	1.3	33.0
McAllen, TX	66	86	106	24.3	114	204	7.0	46.0
Memphis, TN	646	619	650	5.0	649	17	-0.2	279.3
Mesa, AZ	152	290	396	36.6	427	40	7.7	125.0
Mesquite, TX	67	102	125	22.4	129	174	3.4	43.4
Miami, FL	347	360	362	0.7	375	47	3.4	35.7
Milwaukee, WI	636	628	597	-5.0	591	19	-1.0	96.1
Minneapolis, MN	371	368	383	3.9	376	46	-1.8	54.9
Mobile, AL	200	198	199	0.3	195	103	-2.0	117.9
Modesto, CA	107	166	189	13.5	204	90	7.8	35.8
Montgomery, AL	178	191	202	5.6	201	92	-0.1	155.4
Moreno Valley, CA	(3)	119	142	19.9	151	142	5.9	51.2
Naperville, IL	43	87	128	47.6	135	166	5.5	35.4
Nashville-Davidson, TN [2]	456	488	546	11.7	546	27	0.1	473.3
New Haven, CT	126	130	124	-5.0	124	184	0.4	18.9
New Orleans, LA	558	497	485	-2.5	474	32	-2.3	180.6
New York, NY	7,072	7,323	8,008	9.4	8,084	1	0.9	303.3
Newark, NJ	329	275	274	-0.6	277	63	1.3	23.8
Newport News, VA	145	171	180	5.1	180	118	0.1	68.3
Norfolk, VA	267	261	234	-10.3	239	73	2.0	53.7
North Las Vegas, NV	43	48	115	140.8	136	165	17.7	78.5
Norwalk, CA	85	94	103	9.7	106	221	2.7	9.7
Oakland, CA	339	400	399	-0.1	403	42	0.8	56.1
Oceanside, CA	77	129	161	25.2	166	125	3.0	40.6
Oklahoma City, OK	404	445	506	13.8	519	29	2.5	607.0
Olathe, KS	37	63	93	46.5	101	240	9.1	54.2
Omaha, NE	314	358	390	9.0	399	43	2.4	115.7
Ontario, CA	89	133	158	18.6	165	126	4.5	49.8
Orange, CA	91	111	129	16.4	132	169	2.2	23.4
Orlando, FL	128	163	186	13.8	194	106	4.2	93.5
Overland Park, KS	82	112	149	33.3	158	132	6.3	56.7
Oxnard, CA	108	142	170	19.6	178	119	4.5	25.3
Palmdale, CA	12	77	117	50.9	124	182	6.6	105.0
Pasadena, CA	118	132	134	1.7	140	161	4.3	44.2
Pasadena, TX	113	119	142	18.7	145	151	2.4	23.1
Paterson, NJ	138	158	149	-5.6	151	143	1.0	8.4
Pembroke Pines, FL	36	65	137	110.0	147	148	6.7	33.1
Peoria, AZ	12	51	108	111.8	123	186	13.7	138.2
Peoria, IL	124	114	113	-0.8	113	209	-0.2	44.4
Philadelphia, PA	1,688	1,586	1,518	-4.3	1,492	5	-1.7	135.1
Phoenix, AZ	790	989	1,321	33.6	1,372	6	3.9	474.9
Pittsburgh, PA	424	370	335	-9.6	328	54	-2.0	55.6
Plano, TX	72	129	222	72.8	238	74	7.2	71.6

See footnotes at end of table.

36 Population

U.S. Census Bureau, Statistical Abstract of the United States: 2003

No. 31. Incorporated Places With 100,000 or More Inhabitants in 2002—Population, 1980 to 2002, and Land Area, 2000—Con.

[Population: As of April 1 (98 represents 98,000), except 2002 as of July 1. 2002 data refer to boundaries in effect on January 1, 2002; 1990 and 2000 data, boundaries in effect on January 1, 2000; 1980 data, boundaries in effect for 1980 census. Minus sign (-) indicates decrease. See Appendix III]

Incorporated place	1980, total population (1,000)	1990, total population (1,000)	Population, 2000 Total (1,000)	Population, 2000 Percent change, 1990-2000	Population, 2002 Total (1,000)	Population, 2002 Rank	Population, 2002 Percent change, 2000-2002	Land area, 2000 (square miles)
Pomona, CA	93	132	149	13.0	154	137	2.7	22.8
Portland, OR	368	486	529	8.9	539	28	1.9	134.3
Providence, RI	157	160	174	8.3	176	121	1.3	18.5
Provo, UT	74	87	105	20.7	105	223	(Z)	39.6
Pueblo, CO	102	99	102	3.1	103	228	1.3	45.1
Raleigh, NC	150	220	276	25.3	307	58	11.2	114.6
Rancho Cucamonga, CA	55	101	128	26.0	144	153	12.5	37.4
Reno, NV	101	135	180	33.9	190	110	5.4	69.1
Richmond, CA	75	86	99	15.5	103	232	3.4	30.0
Richmond, VA	219	203	198	-2.4	197	97	-0.2	60.1
Riverside, CA	171	227	255	12.6	274	64	7.5	78.1
Rochester, NY	242	231	220	-4.8	217	81	-1.2	35.8
Rockford, IL	140	144	150	4.3	151	140	0.6	56.0
Sacramento, CA	276	395	407	3.0	435	38	6.9	97.2
Salem, OR	89	109	137	25.8	141	158	3.0	45.7
Salinas, CA	80	109	151	38.8	149	146	-1.5	19.0
Salt Lake City, UT	163	160	182	13.6	181	116	-0.3	109.1
San Antonio, TX	786	997	1,145	14.8	1,194	9	4.3	407.6
San Bernardino, CA	119	171	185	8.3	192	108	3.4	58.8
San Buenaventura (Ventura), CA	74	94	101	7.8	104	226	2.7	21.1
San Diego, CA	876	1,111	1,223	10.1	1,260	7	3.0	324.3
San Francisco, CA	679	724	777	7.3	764	13	-1.6	46.7
San Jose, CA	629	783	895	14.2	900	11	0.6	174.9
Santa Ana, CA	204	294	338	14.8	343	51	1.6	27.1
Santa Clara, CA	88	93	102	9.7	102	237	-0.5	18.4
Santa Clarita, CA	(3)	124	151	22.2	161	130	6.3	47.8
Santa Rosa, CA	83	120	148	22.5	153	138	4.0	40.1
Savannah, GA	142	138	132	-4.4	128	175	-2.9	74.7
Scottsdale, AZ	89	130	203	55.8	216	82	6.4	184.2
Seattle, WA	494	516	563	9.1	570	24	1.3	83.9
Shreveport, LA	206	198	200	0.9	199	94	-0.6	103.1
Simi Valley, CA	78	100	111	11.0	117	198	4.7	39.2
Sioux Falls, SD	81	101	124	22.2	130	171	5.3	56.3
South Bend, IN	110	106	108	1.6	107	219	-1.1	38.7
Spokane, WA	171	178	196	9.8	196	100	0.3	57.8
Springfield, IL	100	107	111	3.9	112	210	0.3	54.0
Springfield, MA	152	157	152	-3.1	152	139	-0.1	32.1
Springfield, MO	133	141	152	7.4	151	141	-0.4	73.2
Stamford, CT	102	108	117	8.3	120	192	2.4	37.7
Sterling Heights, MI	109	118	124	5.7	126	176	1.3	36.6
Stockton, CA	150	211	244	15.3	263	67	7.8	54.7
St. Louis, MO	453	397	348	-12.2	338	52	-2.8	61.9
St. Paul, MN	270	272	287	5.5	284	61	-1.1	52.8
St. Petersburg, FL	239	240	248	3.3	249	70	0.1	59.6
Sunnyvale, CA	107	117	132	12.3	130	172	-1.6	21.9
Syracuse, NY	170	164	147	-10.1	145	150	-1.5	25.1
Tacoma, WA	159	177	194	9.1	198	96	2.1	50.1
Tallahassee, FL	82	125	151	20.1	155	136	3.0	95.7
Tampa, FL	272	281	303	8.1	315	56	3.9	112.1
Tempe, AZ	107	142	159	11.7	160	131	0.6	40.1
Thousand Oaks, CA	77	104	117	12.5	123	187	4.9	54.9
Toledo, OH	355	333	314	-5.8	309	57	-1.4	80.6
Topeka, KS	119	121	122	1.3	122	189	-0.2	56.0
Torrance, CA	130	133	138	3.5	142	157	2.7	20.5
Tucson, AZ	331	417	487	16.7	503	31	3.4	194.7
Tulsa, OK	361	367	393	7.0	392	44	-0.3	182.6
Vallejo, CA	80	111	117	5.3	120	193	2.6	30.2
Vancouver, WA	43	105	144	37.3	150	145	4.4	42.8
Virginia Beach, VA	262	393	425	8.2	434	39	2.0	248.3
Waco, TX	101	104	114	9.4	116	199	1.8	84.2
Warren, MI	161	145	138	-4.7	138	163	-0.4	34.3
Washington, DC	638	607	572	-5.7	571	23	-0.2	61.4
Waterbury, CT	103	108	107	-0.9	108	217	0.6	28.6
West Covina, CA	80	96	105	9.6	108	218	2.5	16.1
West Valley City, UT	(3)	87	109	25.2	111	212	2.2	35.4
Westminster, CO	50	74	101	36.1	104	227	2.6	31.5
Wichita, KS	280	309	344	11.5	355	49	3.1	135.8
Wichita Falls, TX	94	97	104	7.7	103	229	-1.2	70.7
Winston-Salem, NC	132	167	186	11.1	189	113	1.7	108.9
Worcester, MA	162	170	173	1.8	175	122	1.3	37.6
Yonkers, NY	195	188	196	4.2	197	98	0.6	18.1

NA Not available. Z Less than 0.05 percent. [1] The population shown is for the census designated place (CDP).
[2] Represents the portion of a consolidated city that is not within one or more separately incorporated places. [3] Not incorporated.

Source: U.S. Census Bureau, 1990 Census of Population and Housing, *Population and Housing Unit Counts*, (CPH-2); "Population Estimates for Cities with Populations of 10,000 and Greater (Sorted Within State by 1999 Population Size): July 1, 1999 (includes April 1, 1990, Population Estimates Base)"; published 20 October 2000; <http://www.census.gov/population/estimates/metro-city/SC10K-T3.txt>; and "Incorporated Place Population Estimates, Sorted Alphabetically: April 1, 2000, to July 1, 2002"; published 9 July 2003; <http://eire.census.gov/popest/data/cities/subtab07.php>.

No. 32. Cities With 250,000 or More Inhabitants in 2000—Selected Racial Groups: 2000

[In thousands (448.6 represents 448,600). As of April. Data refer to boundaries in effect on January 1, 2000. See Appendix III]

City	Total population	One race — White	Black or African American	American Indian, Alaska Native	Asian	Native Hawaiian and Other Pacific Islander	Some other race	Two or more races
Albuquerque, NM	448.6	321.2	13.9	17.4	10.1	0.5	66.3	19.3
Anaheim, CA	328.0	179.6	8.7	3.0	39.3	1.4	79.4	16.5
Anchorage, AK	260.3	188.0	15.2	18.9	14.4	2.4	5.7	15.6
Arlington, TX	333.0	225.4	45.7	1.8	20.0	0.5	29.8	9.8
Atlanta, GA	416.5	138.4	255.7	0.8	8.0	0.2	8.3	5.2
Aurora, CO	276.4	190.3	37.1	2.2	12.1	0.5	22.5	11.7
Austin, TX	656.6	429.1	66.0	3.9	31.0	0.5	106.5	19.7
Baltimore, MD	651.2	206.0	419.0	2.1	10.0	0.5	4.4	9.6
Boston, MA	589.1	320.9	149.2	2.4	44.3	0.4	46.1	25.9
Buffalo, NY	292.6	159.3	109.0	2.3	4.1	0.1	10.8	7.2
Charlotte, NC	540.8	315.1	177.0	1.9	18.4	0.3	19.2	9.0
Chicago, IL	2,896.0	1,215.3	1,065.0	10.3	126.0	1.8	393.2	84.4
Cincinnati, OH	331.3	175.5	142.2	0.7	5.1	0.1	2.1	5.6
Cleveland, OH	478.4	198.5	243.9	1.5	6.4	0.2	17.2	10.7
Colorado Springs, CO	360.9	291.1	23.7	3.2	10.2	0.8	18.1	13.9
Columbus, OH	711.5	483.3	174.1	2.1	24.5	0.4	8.3	18.8
Corpus Christi, TX	277.5	198.7	13.0	1.8	3.6	0.2	51.6	8.7
Dallas, TX	1,188.6	604.2	308.0	6.5	32.1	0.6	204.9	32.4
Denver, CO	554.6	362.2	61.6	7.3	15.6	0.6	86.5	20.8
Detroit, MI	951.3	116.6	775.8	3.1	9.3	0.3	24.2	22.0
El Paso, TX	563.7	413.1	17.6	4.6	6.3	0.6	102.3	19.2
Fort Worth, TX	534.7	319.2	108.3	3.1	14.1	0.3	75.1	14.5
Fresno, CA	427.7	214.6	35.8	6.8	48.0	0.6	99.9	22.1
Honolulu, HI [1]	371.7	73.1	6.0	0.7	207.6	25.5	3.3	55.5
Houston, TX	1,953.6	962.6	494.5	8.6	103.7	1.2	321.6	61.5
Indianapolis, IN [2]	781.9	540.2	199.4	2.0	11.2	0.3	15.9	12.9
Jacksonville, FL	735.6	474.3	213.5	2.5	20.4	0.4	9.8	14.6
Kansas City, MO	441.5	267.9	137.9	2.1	8.2	0.5	14.2	10.8
Las Vegas, NV	478.4	334.2	49.6	3.6	22.9	2.1	46.6	19.4
Lexington-Fayette, KY	260.5	211.1	35.1	0.5	6.4	0.1	3.2	4.1
Long Beach, CA	461.5	208.4	68.6	3.9	55.6	5.6	95.1	24.3
Los Angeles, CA	3,694.8	1,734.0	415.2	29.4	369.3	5.9	949.7	191.3
Louisville, KY	256.2	161.3	84.6	0.6	3.7	0.1	1.7	4.3
Memphis, TN	650.1	223.7	399.2	1.2	9.5	0.2	9.4	6.8
Mesa, AZ	396.4	323.7	10.0	6.6	5.9	0.9	38.3	11.1
Miami, FL	362.5	241.5	80.9	0.8	2.4	0.1	19.6	17.2
Milwaukee, WI	597.0	298.4	222.9	5.2	17.6	0.3	36.4	16.2
Minneapolis, MN	382.6	249.2	68.8	8.4	23.5	0.3	15.8	16.7
Nashville-Davidson, TN [2]	545.5	359.6	146.2	1.6	13.0	0.4	13.7	11.0
New Orleans, LA	484.7	136.0	325.9	1.0	11.0	0.1	4.5	6.2
New York, NY	8,008.3	3,576.4	2,129.8	41.3	787.0	5.4	1,074.4	394.0
Newark, NJ	273.5	72.5	146.3	1.0	3.3	0.1	38.4	11.9
Oakland, CA	399.5	125.0	142.5	2.7	60.9	2.0	46.6	19.9
Oklahoma City, OK	506.1	346.2	77.8	17.7	17.6	0.4	26.7	19.7
Omaha, NE	390.0	305.7	51.9	2.6	6.8	0.2	15.3	7.5
Philadelphia, PA	1,517.6	683.3	655.8	4.1	67.7	0.7	72.4	33.6
Phoenix, AZ	1,321.0	938.9	67.4	26.7	26.4	1.8	216.6	43.3
Pittsburgh, PA	334.6	226.3	90.8	0.6	9.2	0.1	2.2	5.4
Portland, OR	529.1	412.2	35.1	5.6	33.5	2.0	18.8	22.0
Raleigh, NC	276.1	174.8	76.8	1.0	9.3	0.1	8.9	5.2
Riverside, CA	255.2	151.4	18.9	2.8	14.5	1.0	53.6	13.0
Sacramento, CA	407.0	196.5	63.0	5.3	67.6	3.9	44.6	26.1
San Antonio, TX	1,144.6	774.7	78.1	9.6	17.9	1.1	221.4	41.9
San Diego, CA	1,223.4	736.2	96.2	7.5	167.0	5.9	151.5	59.1
San Francisco, CA	776.7	385.7	60.5	3.5	239.6	3.8	50.4	33.3
San Jose, CA	894.9	425.0	31.3	6.9	240.4	3.6	142.7	45.1
Santa Ana, CA	338.0	144.4	5.7	4.0	29.8	1.2	137.4	15.5
Seattle, WA	563.4	394.9	47.5	5.7	73.9	2.8	13.4	25.1
St. Louis, MO	348.2	152.7	178.3	1.0	6.9	0.1	2.8	6.5
St. Paul, MN	287.2	192.4	33.6	3.3	35.5	0.2	11.0	11.1
Tampa, FL	303.4	194.9	79.1	1.2	6.5	0.3	12.6	8.8
Toledo, OH	313.6	220.3	73.9	1.0	3.2	0.1	7.2	8.1
Tucson, AZ	486.7	341.4	21.1	11.0	12.0	0.8	82.0	18.4
Tulsa, OK	393.0	275.5	60.8	18.6	7.2	0.2	13.6	17.3
Virginia Beach, VA	425.3	303.7	80.6	1.6	20.9	0.4	6.4	11.7
Washington, DC	572.1	176.1	343.3	1.7	15.2	0.3	22.0	13.4
Wichita, KS	344.3	258.9	39.3	4.0	13.6	0.2	17.6	10.7

[1] The population shown in this table is for the census designated place (CDP) city that is not within one or more separately incorporated places. [2] Represents the portion of a consolidated

Source: U.S. Census Bureau, 2000 Census of Population and Housing, *Profiles of General Demographic Characteristics*. See also <http://www.census.gov/Press-Release/www/2002/demoprofiles.html>.

No. 33. Cities With 250,000 or More Inhabitants in 2000—Hispanic and Non-Hispanic Groups: 2000

[In thousands, except percent (448.6 represents 448,600). As of April. Data refer to boundaries in effect on January 1, 2000. See Appendix III]

City	Total population	Hispanic or Latino Total Number	Percent of total population	Mexican	Puerto Rican	Cuban	Other Hispanic or Latino	Not Hispanic or Latino Total	White alone
Albuquerque, NM	448.6	179.1	39.9	68.5	1.7	1.7	107.1	269.5	223.9
Anaheim, CA	328.0	153.4	46.8	126.0	1.3	0.9	25.2	174.6	117.6
Anchorage, AK	260.3	14.8	5.7	7.2	1.7	0.3	5.6	245.5	182.0
Arlington, TX	333.0	60.8	18.3	46.8	2.1	0.3	11.6	272.2	198.6
Atlanta, GA	416.5	18.7	4.5	12.7	1.1	0.9	4.0	397.8	130.2
Aurora, CO	276.4	54.8	19.8	38.3	1.6	0.3	14.6	221.6	163.6
Austin, TX	656.6	200.6	30.5	153.9	2.5	1.4	42.8	456.0	347.6
Baltimore, MD	651.2	11.1	1.7	3.0	2.2	0.5	5.3	640.1	201.6
Boston, MA	589.1	85.1	14.4	4.1	27.4	2.2	51.3	504.1	291.6
Buffalo, NY	292.6	22.1	7.5	1.0	17.3	0.4	3.4	270.6	151.5
Charlotte, NC	540.8	39.8	7.4	22.2	2.4	1.1	14.1	501.0	297.8
Chicago, IL	2,896.0	753.6	26.0	530.5	113.1	8.1	102.0	2,142.4	907.2
Cincinnati, OH	331.3	4.2	1.3	1.5	0.6	0.2	1.8	327.1	173.8
Cleveland, OH	478.4	34.7	7.3	3.0	25.4	0.5	5.9	443.7	185.6
Colorado Springs, CO	360.9	43.3	12.0	23.0	2.7	0.3	17.3	317.6	271.7
Columbus, OH	711.5	17.5	2.5	8.7	2.8	0.6	5.4	694.0	475.9
Corpus Christi, TX	277.5	150.7	54.3	98.1	0.7	0.3	51.5	126.7	106.9
Dallas, TX	1,188.6	422.6	35.6	350.5	2.4	2.3	67.4	766.0	410.8
Denver, CO	554.6	175.7	31.7	120.7	1.6	0.7	52.7	378.9	288.0
Detroit, MI	951.3	47.2	5.0	33.1	6.6	0.9	6.5	904.1	99.9
El Paso, TX	563.7	431.9	76.6	359.7	3.7	0.5	68.0	131.8	103.4
Fort Worth, TX	534.7	159.4	29.8	132.9	1.9	0.6	24.0	375.3	245.0
Fresno, CA	427.7	170.5	39.9	144.8	1.1	0.3	24.4	257.1	159.5
Honolulu, HI [1]	371.7	16.2	4.4	4.0	4.6	0.2	7.4	355.4	69.5
Houston, TX	1,953.6	730.9	37.4	527.4	6.9	5.0	191.5	1,222.8	601.9
Indianapolis, IN [2]	781.9	30.6	3.9	21.1	1.9	0.5	7.2	751.2	527.7
Jacksonville, FL	735.6	30.6	4.2	6.1	11.1	3.2	10.2	705.0	457.5
Kansas City, MO	441.5	30.6	6.9	24.0	0.7	0.8	5.0	410.9	254.5
Las Vegas, NV	478.4	113.0	23.6	83.5	2.9	3.4	23.2	365.5	277.7
Lexington-Fayette, KY	260.5	8.6	3.3	6.0	0.5	0.2	1.8	252.0	206.2
Long Beach, CA	461.5	165.1	35.8	127.1	2.3	1.1	34.6	296.4	152.9
Los Angeles, CA	3,694.8	1,719.1	46.5	1,091.7	13.4	12.4	601.5	1,975.7	1,099.2
Louisville, KY	256.2	4.8	1.9	1.6	0.4	1.5	1.3	251.5	158.7
Memphis, TN	650.1	19.3	3.0	14.1	0.7	0.5	4.0	630.8	216.2
Mesa, AZ	396.4	78.3	19.7	63.5	1.5	0.4	12.9	318.1	290.2
Miami, FL	362.5	238.4	65.8	3.7	10.3	123.8	100.7	124.1	42.9
Milwaukee, WI	597.0	71.6	12.0	43.3	19.6	0.6	8.1	525.3	271.0
Minneapolis, MN	382.6	29.2	7.6	19.8	1.2	0.5	7.6	353.4	239.1
Nashville-Davidson, TN [2]	545.5	25.8	4.7	16.1	1.9	0.8	7.0	519.8	349.1
New Orleans, LA	484.7	14.8	3.1	2.6	1.0	1.6	9.6	469.8	128.9
New York, NY	8,008.3	2,160.6	27.0	186.9	789.2	41.1	1,143.4	5,847.7	2,801.3
Newark, NJ	273.5	80.6	29.5	2.3	39.7	3.0	35.7	192.9	39.0
Oakland, CA	399.5	87.5	21.9	65.1	2.3	0.6	19.5	312.0	94.0
Oklahoma City, OK	506.1	51.4	10.1	41.0	1.2	0.4	8.8	454.8	327.2
Omaha, NE	390.0	29.4	7.5	23.3	0.6	0.3	5.2	360.6	293.9
Philadelphia, PA	1,517.6	128.9	8.5	6.2	91.5	2.7	28.5	1,388.6	644.4
Phoenix, AZ	1,321.0	450.0	34.1	375.1	5.1	2.0	67.8	871.1	736.8
Pittsburgh, PA	334.6	4.4	1.3	1.2	0.8	0.3	2.1	330.1	224.0
Portland, OR	529.1	36.1	6.8	25.1	1.0	1.3	8.6	493.1	399.4
Raleigh, NC	276.1	19.3	7.0	12.2	1.3	0.4	5.4	256.8	166.4
Riverside, CA	255.2	97.3	38.1	79.0	1.6	0.6	16.1	157.9	116.3
Sacramento, CA	407.0	88.0	21.6	70.8	2.1	0.5	14.7	319.0	165.0
San Antonio, TX	1,144.6	671.4	58.7	473.4	7.8	1.5	188.7	473.3	364.4
San Diego, CA	1,223.4	310.8	25.4	259.2	5.9	1.9	43.7	912.6	603.9
San Francisco, CA	776.7	109.5	14.1	48.9	3.8	1.6	55.2	667.2	338.9
San Jose, CA	894.9	270.0	30.2	221.1	4.1	1.0	43.8	625.0	322.5
Santa Ana, CA	338.0	257.1	76.1	222.7	0.7	0.6	33.1	80.9	42.0
Seattle, WA	563.4	29.7	5.3	17.9	1.5	0.8	9.6	533.7	382.5
St. Louis, MO	348.2	7.0	2.0	4.1	0.5	0.4	2.0	341.2	149.3
St. Paul, MN	287.2	22.7	7.9	16.6	1.0	0.4	4.8	264.4	183.9
Tampa, FL	303.4	58.5	19.3	6.3	17.5	14.7	20.0	244.9	154.9
Toledo, OH	313.6	17.1	5.5	13.3	0.7	0.2	2.9	296.5	212.7
Tucson, AZ	486.7	173.9	35.7	145.2	2.1	0.6	25.9	312.8	263.7
Tulsa, OK	393.0	28.1	7.2	21.1	1.1	0.3	5.5	364.9	263.8
Virginia Beach, VA	425.3	17.8	4.2	4.9	6.3	0.6	6.0	407.5	295.4
Washington, DC	572.1	45.0	7.9	5.1	2.3	1.1	36.4	527.1	159.2
Wichita, KS	344.3	33.1	9.6	27.0	0.8	0.3	5.1	311.2	246.9

[1] The population shown in this table is for the census designated place (CDP). [2] Represents the portion of a consolidated city that is not within one or more separately incorporated places.

Source: U.S. Census Bureau, 2000 Census of Population and Housing, *Profiles of General Demographic Characteristics*. See also <http://www.census.gov/Press-Release/www/2002/demoprofiles.html>.

No. 34. Mobility Status of the Population by Selected Characteristics: 1980 to 2001

[As of March (221,641 represents 221,641,000). For persons 1 year old and over. Excludes members of the Armed Forces except those living off post or with their families on post. Based on Current Population Survey; see text, this section, and Appendix III]

Mobility period and characteristic	Total (1,000)	Non-movers	Movers (different house in United States)					Movers from abroad
			Total	Same county	Different county			
					Total	Same state	Different state	
1980-1981	221,641	83	17	10	6	3	3	1
1985-1986	232,998	82	18	11	7	4	3	1
1990-1991	244,884	83	16	10	6	3	3	1
1995-1996	260,406	84	16	10	6	3	3	1
2000-2001, total	275,611	86	14	8	6	3	3	1
1 to 4 years old	15,431	78	21	14	7	4	4	1
5 to 9 years old	20,214	83	16	10	6	3	3	1
10 to 14 years old	20,775	87	12	8	5	2	2	1
15 to 19 years old	19,926	86	13	8	5	3	2	1
20 to 24 years old	18,876	67	31	19	13	7	6	1
25 to 29 years old	18,547	70	28	16	12	6	6	2
30 to 44 years old	64,885	85	15	9	6	3	3	1
45 to 64 years old	63,392	92	7	4	3	1	2	(Z)
65 to 74 years old	18,119	96	4	2	2	1	1	(Z)
75 to 84 years old	12,064	97	3	2	1	1	1	(Z)
85 years old and over	3,383	96	4	2	2	1	1	(Z)
Northeast	52,426	89	10	6	4	2	2	1
Midwest	62,796	87	13	8	5	3	3	(Z)
South	97,946	84	15	9	6	3	3	1
West	62,442	83	16	10	6	3	3	1
Persons 16 years and over	215,157	86	13	8	6	3	3	1
Civilian labor force	143,705	84	15	9	6	3	3	1
Employed	136,995	85	15	9	6	3	3	1
Unemployed	6,710	75	24	14	10	5	5	1
Armed Forces	865	63	33	9	24	6	18	4
Not in labor force	70,587	90	9	5	4	2	2	1
Employed civilians, 16 years and over	136,995	85	15	9	6	3	3	1
Executive/administrative/managerial	20,324	86	13	7	6	3	3	(Z)
Professional specialty	21,852	85	15	8	7	3	4	1
Technical/related support	4,537	84	16	9	7	4	3	(Z)
Sales	16,336	84	16	9	7	3	3	(Z)
Admin support/clerical	19,130	86	14	8	5	3	2	(Z)
Private household service	770	77	20	13	7	4	4	2
Protective service	2,411	86	14	10	4	2	2	(Z)
Other service	15,650	81	18	11	6	3	3	1
Precision production/crafts/repair	14,934	85	14	9	5	3	2	1
Machine operator/assembler/inspector	7,113	85	14	10	5	3	2	1
Transport/material moving	5,563	85	14	9	5	3	3	(Z)
Handlers/cleaners/laborers	5,296	83	15	9	6	3	3	2
Farming/forestry/fishing	3,079	86	13	7	5	3	2	1
Tenure:								
Owner-occupied units	193,963	92	8	4	3	2	1	(Z)
Renter-occupied units	81,648	70	29	18	11	5	6	2

Z Less than 0.5 percent.
Source: U.S. Census Bureau, "Geographic Mobility: March 2000 to March 2001, Detailed Tables"; published 31 March 2003; <http://www.census.gov/population/www/socdemo/migrate/cps2001.html>.

No. 35. Mobility Status of Households by Household Income: 2000-2001

[As of March (108,220 represents 108,220,000). Covers householders 15 years old and over. Excludes members of the Armed Forces except those living off post or with their families on post. Based on Current Population Survey; see text, this section, and Appendix III]

Household income in 2000	Total (1,000)	Non-movers	Movers (different house in United States)					Movers from abroad
			Total	Same county	Different county			
					Total	Same state	Different state	
Householders, 15 years and over	**108,220**	**86**	**14**	**8**	**6**	**3**	**3**	**(Z)**
Less than $5,000	3,164	75	21	13	9	4	4	4
$5,000 to $9,999	6,495	82	17	11	6	3	3	1
$10,000 to $14,999	7,675	85	14	9	5	3	2	(Z)
$15,000 to $24,999	14,374	84	16	10	6	3	3	1
$25,000 to $34,999	13,576	83	16	10	6	3	3	(Z)
$35,000 to $49,999	16,981	85	14	9	6	3	3	(Z)
$50,000 to $74,999	16,916	87	12	7	5	3	3	(Z)
$75,000 and over	29,039	90	10	5	5	2	2	(Z)

Z Less than 0.5 percent.
Source: U.S. Census Bureau, "Geographic Mobility: March 2000 to March 2001, Detailed Tables"; published 31 March 2003; <http://www.census.gov/population/www/socdemo/migrate/cps2001.html>.

No. 36. Mobility Status of Resident Population by State: 2000

[In thousands, except percent (262,375 represents 262,375,000). **As of April 1.** Based on comparison of place of residence in 1995 and 2000. Based on sample data from the 2000 Census of Population and Housing; see text, this section, and Appendix III]

State	Population 5 years and over	Same house in 1995	Different house in United States in 1995 — Total Number	Total Percent of population 5 years and over	Same county	Different county Total	Same state	Different state	Elsewhere in 1995
U.S. ...	262,375	142,027	112,852	43.0	65,435	47,417	25,327	22,089	7,496
AL.	4,152	2,385	1,719	41.4	1,027	692	366	326	49
AK.	580	268	299	51.6	160	139	43	96	13
AZ.	4,753	2,104	2,466	51.9	1,456	1,009	213	796	183
AR.	2,492	1,327	1,131	45.4	618	513	261	252	34
CA.	31,417	15,758	14,251	45.4	9,714	4,537	3,088	1,449	1,408
CO	4,006	1,769	2,103	52.5	920	1,183	539	644	135
CT.	3,185	1,853	1,228	38.6	799	429	168	261	104
DE.	732	410	305	41.7	187	118	17	101	17
DC	540	269	240	44.5	127	113	(X)	113	30
FL.	15,044	7,352	7,039	46.8	3,866	3,173	1,312	1,861	653
GA	7,594	3,736	3,615	47.6	1,605	2,010	1,045	966	243
HI	1,134	644	444	39.1	295	149	24	125	47
ID	1,197	594	582	48.6	286	296	113	183	21
IL	11,548	6,558	4,635	40.1	3,011	1,624	959	665	354
IN	5,658	3,111	2,472	43.7	1,444	1,028	576	451	75
IA	2,738	1,558	1,142	41.7	637	504	290	215	38
KS.	2,500	1,310	1,139	45.5	606	533	256	277	51
KY.	3,776	2,112	1,618	42.8	933	686	367	319	46
LA.	4,153	2,452	1,659	39.9	1,017	642	388	254	42
ME	1,204	717	476	39.5	276	201	93	108	11
MD	4,945	2,752	2,046	41.4	1,085	960	465	495	147
MA	5,954	3,482	2,267	38.1	1,356	911	464	447	206
MI	9,269	5,307	3,802	41.0	2,324	1,478	1,010	468	160
MN	4,591	2,618	1,889	41.1	934	955	600	355	85
MS	2,641	1,545	1,071	40.6	595	476	249	227	25
MO	5,226	2,803	2,355	45.1	1,229	1,126	653	473	67
MT	847	454	386	45.6	191	195	84	112	7
NE.	1,595	872	694	43.5	373	321	167	154	28
NV.	1,854	693	1,086	58.6	567	519	53	466	75
NH	1,160	642	501	43.2	259	242	80	162	17
NJ.	7,856	4,697	2,847	36.2	1,628	1,219	684	535	312
NM	1,690	920	731	43.3	400	331	126	205	39
NY.	17,749	10,961	6,067	34.2	3,876	2,190	1,464	726	721
NC	7,513	3,980	3,337	44.4	1,679	1,658	739	919	196
ND	603	342	253	42.0	131	122	62	60	7
OH	10,600	6,096	4,384	41.4	2,793	1,591	1,002	589	121
OK	3,216	1,650	1,510	47.0	808	702	379	323	55
OR	3,199	1,497	1,619	50.6	863	756	357	399	83
PA.	11,556	7,334	4,057	35.1	2,513	1,544	875	669	165
RI	985	572	387	39.3	240	147	50	97	26
SC.	3,749	2,097	1,592	42.5	837	755	313	442	59
SD.	704	392	305	43.3	149	156	83	73	7
TN.	5,316	2,866	2,372	44.6	1,341	1,032	464	568	78
TX.	19,242	9,545	8,970	46.6	5,204	3,766	2,403	1,363	726
UT.	2,024	998	961	47.5	538	422	180	242	65
VT.	575	340	228	39.6	122	106	36	70	7
VA.	6,619	3,453	2,960	44.7	1,197	1,763	942	822	205
WA	5,501	2,676	2,650	48.2	1,511	1,139	521	618	176
WV	1,707	1,081	618	36.2	359	259	120	138	8
WI.	5,022	2,836	2,121	42.2	1,233	888	550	338	65
WY	463	238	220	47.6	111	109	36	73	5

X Not applicable.

Source: U.S. Census Bureau, 2000 Census of Population and Housing, *Profiles of General Demographic Characteristics*; <http://www.census.gov/Press-Release/www/2002/demoprofiles.html>.

No. 37. Persons 65 Years Old and Over—Characteristics by Sex: 1990 to 2002

[As of March, except as noted (29.6 represents 29,600,000). Covers civilian noninstitutional population. Excludes members of Armed Forces except those living off post or with their families on post. Data for 1990 are based on 1980 census population controls; 1995 and 2000 data based on 1990 census population controls; 2002 data based on 2000 census population controls and an expanded sample of households. Based on Current Population Survey; see text, this section, and Appendix III]

Characteristic	Total				Male				Female			
	1990	1995	2000	2002	1990	1995	2000	2002	1990	1995	2000	2002
Total (million)	29.6	31.7	32.6	33.8	12.3	13.2	13.9	14.2	17.2	18.5	18.7	19.5
PERCENT DISTRIBUTION												
Marital status:												
Never married	4.6	4.2	3.9	3.6	4.2	4.2	4.2	3.7	4.9	4.2	3.6	3.6
Married	56.1	56.9	57.2	56.7	76.5	77.0	75.2	75.7	41.4	42.5	43.8	42.9
Spouse present	54.1	54.7	54.6	54.4	74.2	74.5	72.6	73.1	39.7	40.6	41.3	40.8
Spouse absent	2.0	2.2	2.6	2.3	2.3	2.5	2.6	2.6	1.7	1.9	2.5	2.1
Widowed	34.2	33.2	32.1	32.2	14.2	13.5	14.4	13.9	48.6	47.3	45.3	45.5
Divorced	5.0	5.7	7.0	7.4	5.0	5.2	6.1	6.7	5.1	6.0	7.2	8.0
Family status:												
In families [1]	66.7	66.6	67.4	66.7	81.9	80.6	79.7	79.2	55.8	56.7	58.2	57.6
Nonfamily householders	31.9	32.4	31.1	32.1	16.6	18.4	18.2	19.3	42.8	42.4	40.7	41.5
Secondary individuals	1.4	1.0	1.5	1.2	1.5	1.0	2.1	1.5	1.4	0.9	1.1	1.0
Educational attainment:												
Less than ninth grade	28.5	21.0	16.7	15.8	30.0	22.0	17.8	16.5	27.5	20.3	15.9	15.2
Completed 9th to 12th grade, but no high school diploma	[2]16.1	15.2	13.8	14.4	[2]15.7	14.5	12.7	13.7	[2]16.4	15.6	14.7	14.9
High school graduate	[3]32.9	33.8	35.9	35.3	[3]29.0	29.2	30.4	30.2	[3]35.6	37.1	39.9	39.0
Some college or associate degree	[4]10.9	17.1	18.0	17.9	[4]10.8	17.1	17.8	17.6	[4]11.0	17.0	18.2	18.1
Bachelor's or advanced degree	[5]11.6	13.0	15.6	16.7	[5]14.5	17.2	21.4	22.0	[5]9.5	9.9	11.4	12.8
Labor force participation: [6]												
Employed	11.5	11.7	12.4	12.7	15.9	16.1	16.9	17.2	8.4	8.5	9.1	9.5
Unemployed	0.4	0.5	0.4	0.5	0.5	0.7	0.6	0.6	0.3	0.3	0.3	0.4
Not in labor force	88.1	87.9	87.2	86.8	83.6	83.2	82.5	82.1	91.3	91.2	90.6	90.2
Percent below poverty level [7]	11.4	11.7	9.7	10.1	7.8	7.2	6.9	7.0	13.9	14.9	11.8	12.4

[1] Excludes those living in unrelated subfamilies. [2] Represents those who completed 1 to 3 years of high school. [3] Represents those who completed 4 years of high school. [4] Represents those who completed 1 to 3 years of college. [5] Represents those who completed 4 years of college or more. [6] Annual averages of monthly figures. Source: U.S. Bureau of Labor Statistics, Employment and Earnings, January issues. See footnote 2, Table 587. [7] Poverty status based on income in preceding year.

Source: Except as noted, U.S. Census Bureau, Current Population Reports, P20-546, and earlier reports; P60-219; and "The Older Population in the United States: March 2002 Detailed Tables (PPL-167)"; published 20 May 2003; <http://www.census.gov/population/www/socdemo/age/ppl-167.html>.

No. 38. Persons 65 Years Old and Over—Grandparents, Disability Status, and Language Spoken at Home: 2000

[As of April 1 (5,772 represents 5,772,000). Based on the 2000 Census of Population and Housing; see text, this section, and Appendix III]

Subject	Number (1,000)	Percent
GRANDPARENTS AS CAREGIVERS		
Grandparent living in household with one or more own grandchildren under 18 years	5,772	100.0
Grandparent responsible for grandchildren	2,427	42.0
DISABILITY STATUS OF THE CIVILIAN NONINSTITUTIONALIZED POPULATION		
Population 65 years and over	33,347	100.0
With a disability [1]	13,978	41.9
Sensory disability	4,738	14.2
Physical disability	9,546	28.6
Mental disability [2]	3,593	10.8
Self-care disability [3]	3,184	9.5
Go-outside-home disability [4]	6,796	20.4
With no disability	19,369	58.1
LANGUAGE SPOKEN AT HOME		
Population 65 years and over	34,979	100.0
English only	30,564	87.4
Language other than English	4,415	12.6
Speak English less than "very well"	2,341	6.7
Spanish	1,677	4.8
Speak English less than "very well"	1,030	2.9
Other Indo-European languages	1,932	5.5
Speak English less than "very well"	774	2.2
Asian and Pacific Island languages	630	1.8
Speak English less than "very well"	456	1.3
Other languages	177	0.5
Speak English less than "very well"	81	0.2

[1] Persons with one or more disabilities. [2] Learning, remembering, or concentrating. [3] Dressing, bathing, or getting around inside the home. [4] Going outside the home alone to shop or visit a doctor's office.

Source: U.S. Census Bureau, 2000 Census of Population, Summary File 3, <http://www.census.gov/Press-Release/www/2002/sumfile3.html>.

No. 39. Social and Economic Characteristics of the White and Black Populations: 1990 to 2002

[As of March, except labor force status, annual average (134,687 represents 134,687,000). Excludes members of Armed Forces except those living off post or with their families on post. Data for 1990 are based on 1980 census population controls; 2000 data based on 1990 census population controls; 2002 data based on 2000 census population controls and an expanded sample of households. Based on Current Population Survey; see text, this section, and Appendix III]

Characteristic	Number (1,000) White 1990	2000	2002	Black 1990	2000	2002	Percent distribution White 2000	2002	Black 2000	2002
EDUCATIONAL ATTAINMENT										
Persons 25 years old and over	134,687	147,067	151,942	16,751	20,036	20,359	100.0	100.0	100.0	100.0
Elementary:										
0 to 8 years	14,131	10,035	10,377	2,701	1,417	1,433	6.8	6.8	7.1	7.0
Completed 9th to 12th grade, but no high school diploma	[1]14,080	12,153	12,761	[2]2,969	2,899	2,898	8.3	8.4	14.5	14.2
High school graduate	[2]52,449	49,105	49,131	[2]6,239	7,050	6,909	33.4	32.3	35.2	33.9
Some college or associate degree	[3]24,350	37,353	38,402	[3]2,952	5,366	5,658	25.4	25.3	26.8	27.8
Bachelor's or advanced degree	[4]29,677	38,421	41,271	[4]1,890	3,303	3,460	26.1	27.2	16.5	17.0
LABOR FORCE STATUS [5]										
Civilians 16 years old and over	160,625	176,220	179,783	21,477	24,902	25,578	100.0	100.0	100.0	100.0
Civilian labor force	107,447	118,545	120,150	13,740	16,397	16,565	67.3	66.8	65.8	64.8
Employed	102,261	114,424	114,013	12,175	15,156	14,872	64.9	63.4	60.9	58.1
Unemployed	5,186	4,121	6,137	1,565	1,241	1,693	2.3	3.4	5.0	6.6
Unemployment rate [6]	4.8	3.5	5.1	11.4	7.6	10.2	(X)	(X)	(X)	(X)
Not in labor force	53,178	57,675	59,633	7,737	8,505	9,013	32.7	33.2	34.2	35.2
FAMILY TYPE										
Total families	56,590	60,251	61,638	7,470	8,664	8,844	100.0	100.0	100.0	100.0
With own children [7]	26,718	28,107	28,537	4,378	4,782	5,065	46.6	46.3	55.2	57.3
Married couple	46,981	48,790	49,605	3,750	4,144	4,233	81.0	80.5	47.1	47.9
With own children [7]	21,579	21,809	21,978	1,972	2,093	2,148	36.2	35.7	24.2	24.3
Female householder, no spouse present	7,306	8,380	8,639	3,275	3,814	3,838	13.9	14.0	45.1	43.4
With own children [7]	4,199	4,869	5,052	2,232	2,409	2,593	8.1	8.2	27.8	29.3
Male householder, no spouse present	2,303	3,081	3,394	446	706	773	5.1	5.5	7.8	8.7
With own children [7]	939	1,429	1,507	173	280	324	2.4	2.4	3.2	3.7
FAMILY INCOME IN PREVIOUS YEAR IN CONSTANT (2001) DOLLARS										
Total families [8]	56,590	60,256	61,647	7,470	8,664	8,847	100.0	100.0	100.0	100.0
Less than $5,000	(NA)	(NA)	1,186	(NA)	(NA)	596	1.7	1.9	6.0	6.7
$5,000 to $9,999	(NA)	(NA)	1,326	(NA)	(NA)	622	2.3	2.2	7.7	7.0
$10,000 to $14,999	(NA)	(NA)	2,404	(NA)	(NA)	641	3.9	3.9	8.8	7.2
$15,000 to $24,999	(NA)	(NA)	6,489	(NA)	(NA)	1,463	10.5	10.5	15.2	16.5
$25,000 to $34,999	(NA)	(NA)	7,167	(NA)	(NA)	1,241	11.3	11.6	13.9	14.0
$35,000 to $49,999	(NA)	(NA)	9,755	(NA)	(NA)	1,343	16.1	15.8	15.0	15.2
$50,000 or more	(NA)	(NA)	33,321	(NA)	(NA)	2,941	54.2	54.1	33.5	33.3
Median income (dol.) [9]	49,595	54,411	54,067	27,860	33,755	33,598	(X)	(X)	(X)	(X)
POVERTY										
Families below poverty level [10]	4,409	4,377	4,579	2,077	1,898	1,829	7.3	7.4	21.9	20.7
Persons below poverty level [10]	20,785	21,922	22,739	9,302	8,360	8,136	9.8	9.9	23.6	22.7
HOUSING TENURE										
Total occupied units	80,163	87,671	90,682	10,486	12,849	13,315	100.0	100.0	100.0	100.0
Owner-occupied	54,094	62,077	65,149	4,445	6,055	6,414	70.8	71.8	47.1	48.2
Renter-occupied	24,685	24,253	24,211	5,862	6,563	6,699	27.7	26.7	51.1	50.3
No cash rent	1,384	1,340	1,322	178	231	202	1.5	1.5	1.8	1.5

NA Not available. X Not applicable. [1] Represents those who completed 1 to 3 years of high school. [2] Represents those who completed 4 years of high school. [3] Represents those who completed 1 to 3 years of college. [4] Represents those who completed 4 years of college or more. [5] Source: U.S. Bureau of Labor Statistics, *Employment and Earnings*, January issues. See footnote 2, Table 587. [6] Total unemployment as percent of civilian labor force. [7] Children under 18 years old. [8] Includes families in group quarters. [9] For definition of median, see Guide to Tabular Presentation. [10] For explanation of poverty level, see text, Section 13.

Source: Except as noted, U.S. Census Bureau, *Black Population in the U.S.: March 2002*, PPL-164; Current Population Reports, P20-541, P60-218, P60-219, and earlier reports; and unpublished data.

No. 40. Selected Characteristics of the White and Black Populations: 2000

[As of April 1 (143,086 represents 143,086,000). Based on a sample from the 2000 Census of Population and Housing; see text, this section, and Appendix III]

Characteristic	White alone Number (1,000)	White alone Percent	Black or African American alone Number (1,000)	Black or African American alone Percent	White alone, not Hispanic or Latino Number (1,000)	White alone, not Hispanic or Latino Percent
EDUCATIONAL ATTAINMENT						
Population 25 years and over	143,086	100.0	19,858	100.0	133,786	100.0
Less than 9th grade	8,440	5.9	1,576	7.9	6,133	4.6
9th to 12th grade, no diploma	15,059	10.5	3,932	19.8	13,327	10.0
High school graduate (includes equivalency)	42,217	29.5	5,910	29.8	40,148	30.0
Some college, no degree	30,764	21.5	4,464	22.5	29,233	21.9
Associate degree	9,316	6.5	1,145	5.8	8,885	6.6
Bachelor's degree	23,735	16.6	1,877	9.5	22,977	17.2
Graduate or professional degree	13,557	9.5	954	4.8	13,084	9.8
Percent high school graduate or higher	83.6	(X)	72.3	(X)	85.5	(X)
Percent bachelor's degree or higher	26.1	(X)	14.3	(X)	27.0	(X)
DISABILITY STATUS [1]						
Population 5 to 20 years	44,855	100.0	9,573	100.0	40,138	100.0
With a disability	3,384	7.5	957	10.0	2,966	7.4
Population 21 to 64 years	121,289	100.0	18,054	100.0	112,171	100.0
With a disability	21,012	17.3	5,005	27.7	18,753	16.7
Percent employed	58.0	(X)	51.2	(X)	58.4	(X)
No disability	100,277	82.7	13,050	72.3	93,418	83.3
Percent employed	79.4	(X)	70.7	(X)	80.3	(X)
Population 65 years and over	28,957	100.0	2,670	100.0	27,842	100.0
With a disability	11,762	40.6	1,409	52.8	11,237	40.4
RESIDENCE IN 1995						
Population 5 years and over	198,544	100.0	31,617	100.0	183,343	100.0
Same house in 1995	111,546	56.2	16,224	51.3	104,404	56.9
Different house in the U.S. in 1995	83,438	42.0	14,678	46.4	76,844	41.9
Same county	46,420	23.4	9,679	30.6	41,908	22.9
Different county	37,017	18.6	4,999	15.8	34,936	19.1
Same state	19,785	10.0	2,670	8.4	18,648	10.2
Different state	17,232	8.7	2,329	7.4	16,287	8.9
Elsewhere in 1995	3,561	1.8	715	2.3	2,095	1.1
NATIVITY AND PLACE OF BIRTH						
Total population	211,354	100.0	34,362	100.0	194,514	100.0
Native	197,978	93.7	32,262	93.9	187,674	96.5
Born in United States	195,813	92.6	31,985	93.1	186,344	95.8
State of residence	130,796	61.9	23,216	67.6	123,194	63.3
Different state	65,017	30.8	8,770	25.5	63,150	32.5
Born outside United States	2,164	1.0	276	0.8	1,330	0.7
Foreign born	13,376	6.3	2,100	6.1	6,841	3.5
Entered 1990 to March 2000	5,231	2.5	869	2.5	2,287	1.2
Naturalized citizen	5,756	2.7	934	2.7	3,729	1.9
Not a citizen	7,620	3.6	1,165	3.4	3,111	1.6
COMMUTING TO WORK						
Workers 16 years and over	101,306	100.0	12,820	100.0	94,935	100.0
Car, truck, or van — drove alone	79,815	78.8	8,442	65.9	75,704	79.7
Car, truck, or van — carpooled	10,782	10.6	2,048	16.0	9,479	10.0
Public transportation (including taxicab)	3,184	3.1	1,567	12.2	2,711	2.9
Walked	2,726	2.7	413	3.2	2,497	2.6
Other means	1,104	1.1	159	1.2	979	1.0
Worked at home	3,693	3.6	190	1.5	3,565	3.8
Mean travel time to work (minutes)	24.8	(X)	29.0	(X)	24.7	(X)
OCCUPATION						
Employed civilian population 16 yrs. and over	102,325	100.0	13,002	100.0	95,834	100.0
Management, professional, and related occupations	36,433	35.6	3,281	25.2	35,035	36.6
Service occupations	13,661	13.4	2,861	22.0	12,314	12.8
Sales and office occupations	27,667	27.0	3,545	27.3	26,101	27.2
Farming, fishing, and forestry occupations	646	0.6	49	0.4	514	0.5
Construction, extraction, and maintenance occupations	10,014	9.8	849	6.5	9,198	9.6
Production, transportation, and material moving occupations	13,903	13.6	2,417	18.6	12,673	13.2

X Not applicable. [1] Civilian noninstitutionalized population.

Source: U.S. Census Bureau, Tables DP-2: Profile of Selected Social Characteristics: 2000 and DP-3: Profile of Selected Economic Characteristics: 2000; 2000 Census of Population, Summary File 4 (SF 4); <http://www.census.gov/Press-Release/www/2003/SF4.html>.

No. 41. American Indian and Alaska Native Population by Tribe: 2000

[As of April. This table shows data for American Indian and Alaska Native tribes alone or in combination of tribes or races. Respondents who identified themselves as American Indian or Alaska Native were asked to report their enrolled or principal tribe. Therefore, data shown here reflect the written tribal entries reported on the questionnaire. Some of the entries (for example, Iroquois, Sioux, Colorado River, and Flathead) represent nations or reservations. The information on tribe is based on self-identification and includes federally- or state-recognized tribes, as well as bands and clans]

American Indian and Alaska Native tribe	Number	American Indian and Alaska Native tribe	Number
Total persons [1]	4,119,301	Osage	15,897
Apache	96,833	Ottawa	10,677
Blackfeet	85,750	Paiute	13,532
Cherokee	729,533	Pima	11,493
Cheyenne	18,204	Potawatomi	25,595
Chickasaw	38,351	Pueblo	74,085
Chippewa	149,669	Puget Sound Salish	14,631
Choctaw	158,774	Seminole	27,431
Colville	9,393	Shoshone	12,026
Comanche	19,376	Sioux	153,360
Cree	7,734	Tohono O'odham	20,087
Creek	71,310	United Houma Nation	8,713
Crow	13,394	Ute	10,385
Delaware	16,341	Yakama	10,851
Iroquois	80,822	Yaqui	22,412
Kiowa	12,242	Yuman	8,976
Latin American Indian	180,940	Alaskan Athabascan	18,838
Lumbee	57,868	Aleut	10,548
Menominee	9,840	Eskimo	54,761
Navajo	298,197	Tlingit-Haida	22,365

[1] Includes other tribes not shown separately.

Source: U.S. Census Bureau, *The American Indian and Alaska Native Population: 2000*, Census 2000 Brief (C2KBR/01-15), February 2002.

No. 42. Population Living on Selected Reservations and Trust Lands: 2000

[As of April. OTSA=Oklahoma Tribal Statistical Area; SDAISA=State Designated American Indian Statistical Area; ANRC=Alaska Native Regional Corporation]

Reservation, Trust Land, or other area	Total population	American Indian and Alaska Native population alone	American Indian and Alaska Native population alone or in combination with one or more races
Navajo Nation Reservation and Off-Reservation Trust Land, AZ-NM-UT	180,462	173,987	175,228
Cherokee OTSA, OK	462,327	76,041	104,482
Creek OTSA, OK	704,565	51,296	77,253
Lumbee SDAISA, NC	474,100	58,238	62,327
Choctaw OTSA, OK	224,472	29,521	39,984
Cook Inlet ANRC, AK	364,205	24,923	35,972
Chickasaw OTSA, OK	277,416	22,946	32,372
Calista ANRC, AK	23,032	19,617	20,353
United Houma Nation SDAISA, LA	839,880	11,019	15,305
Sealaska ANRC, AK	71,507	11,320	15,059
Pine Ridge Reservation and Off-Reservation Trust Land, SD-NE	15,521	14,304	14,484
Doyon ANRC, AK	97,190	11,182	14,128
Kiowa-Comanche-Apache-Fort Sill Apache OTSA, OK	193,260	9,675	13,045
Fort Apache Reservation, AZ	12,429	11,702	11,854
Citizen Potawatomi Nation-Absentee Shawnee OTSA, OK	106,624	6,733	10,617
Gila River Reservation, AZ	11,257	10,353	10,578
Cheyenne-Arapaho OTSA, OK	157,869	7,402	10,310
Tohono O'odham Reservation and Off-Reservation Trust Land, AZ	10,787	9,718	9,794
Osage Reservation, OK	44,437	6,410	9,209
Rosebud Reservation and Off-Reservation Trust Land, SD	10,469	9,040	9,165
San Carlos Reservation, AZ	9,385	8,921	9,065
Blackfeet Reservation and Off-Reservation Trust Land, MT	10,100	8,507	8,684
Yakama Reservation and Off-Reservation Trust Land, WA	31,799	7,411	8,193
Turtle Mountain Reservation and Off-Reservation Trust Land, MT-ND-SD	8,331	8,009	8,043
Flathead Reservation, MT	26,172	6,999	7,883
Zuni Reservation and Off-Reservation Trust Land, NM-AZ	7,758	7,426	7,466
Bering Straits ANRC, AK	9,196	6,915	7,274
Sac and Fox OTSA, OK	55,690	5,334	7,232
Eastern Cherokee Reservation, NC	8,092	6,665	6,898
Wind River Reservation and Off-Reservation Trust Land, WY	23,250	6,544	6,864
Hopi Reservation and Off-Reservation Trust Land, AZ	6,946	6,573	6,633
Fort Peck Reservation and Off-Reservation Trust Land, MT	10,321	6,391	6,577
Cheyenne River Reservation and Off-Reservation Trust Land, SD	8,470	6,249	6,346
NANA ANRC, AK	7,208	5,944	6,181
Standing Rock Reservation, SD-ND	8,250	5,964	6,054
Bristol Bay ANRC, AK	7,892	5,336	5,749
Arctic Slope ANRC, AK	7,385	5,050	5,453
Crow Reservation and Off-Reservation Trust Land, MT	6,894	5,165	5,275
Red Lake Reservation, MN	5,162	5,071	5,087

Source: U.S. Census Bureau, 2000 Census of Population and Housing, *Profiles of General Demographic Characteristics*. See also <http://factfinder.census.gov/home/aian/aian_aff2000.html>.

No. 43. Selected Characteristics of the American Indian, Alaska Native, Asian, and Native Hawaiian and Other Pacific Islander Populations: 2000

[As of April 1 (1,351 represents 1,351,000). Based on a sample from the 2000 Census of Population and Housing; see text, this section, and Appendix III]

Characteristic	American Indian and Alaska Native alone Number (1,000)	Percent	Asian alone Number (1,000)	Percent	Native Hawaiian and Other Pacific Islander alone Number (1,000)	Percent
EDUCATIONAL ATTAINMENT						
Population 25 years and over	1,351	100.0	6,641	100.0	207	100.0
Less than 9th grade	150	11.1	709	10.7	16	7.5
9th to 12th grade, no diploma	243	18.0	590	8.9	29	14.2
High school graduate (includes equivalency)	395	29.2	1,051	15.8	70	33.7
Some college, no degree	319	23.6	928	14.0	49	23.6
Associate degree	89	6.6	436	6.6	15	7.2
Bachelor's degree	103	7.6	1,772	26.7	20	9.7
Graduate or professional degree	53	3.9	1,154	17.4	8	4.1
Percent high school graduate or higher	70.9	(X)	80.4	(X)	78.3	(X)
Percent bachelor's degree or higher	11.5	(X)	44.1	(X)	13.8	(X)
DISABILITY STATUS [1]						
Population 5 to 20 years	729	100.0	2,239	100.0	112	100.0
With a disability	75	10.3	133	5.9	9	8.2
Population 21 to 64 years	1,326	100.0	6,444	100.0	208	100.0
With a disability	379	28.6	1,124	17.4	46	22.2
Percent employed	48.3	(X)	62.5	(X)	57.4	(X)
No disability	946	71.4	5,320	82.6	162	77.8
Percent employed	67.7	(X)	70.4	(X)	70.8	(X)
Population 65 years and over	132	100.0	772	100.0	18	100.0
With a disability	76	57.6	315	40.8	9	48.5
RESIDENCE IN 1995						
Population 5 years and over	2,243	100.0	9,520	100.0	347	100.0
Same house in 1995	1,132	50.5	4,374	45.9	156	44.9
Different house in the U.S. in 1995	1,070	47.7	3,790	39.8	163	47.1
Same county	595	26.5	2,136	22.4	96	27.6
Different county	475	21.2	1,653	17.4	67	19.4
Same state	279	12.4	825	8.7	30	8.7
Different state	196	8.7	829	8.7	37	10.7
Elsewhere in 1995	41	1.8	1,357	14.2	28	8.1
NATIVITY AND PLACE OF BIRTH						
Total population	2,448	100.0	10,172	100.0	379	100.0
Native	2,317	94.6	3,160	31.1	303	80.1
Born in United States	2,297	93.8	3,036	29.9	254	67.0
State of residence	1,688	69.0	2,310	22.7	176	46.6
Different state	609	24.9	726	7.1	77	20.4
Born outside United States	20	0.8	123	1.2	50	13.1
Foreign born	131	5.4	7,012	68.9	75	19.9
Entered 1990 to March 2000	60	2.5	3,050	30.0	33	8.8
Naturalized citizen	40	1.6	3,502	34.4	30	8.0
Not a citizen	91	3.7	3,510	34.5	45	11.9
COMMUTING TO WORK						
Workers 16 years and over	900	100.0	4,712	100.0	157	100.0
Car, truck, or van — drove alone	612	68.0	3,112	66.0	102	64.9
Car, truck, or van — carpooled	167	18.5	739	15.7	32	20.4
Public transportation (including taxicab)	34	3.8	480	10.2	10	6.2
Walked	41	4.6	210	4.5	6	4.0
Other means	22	2.4	57	1.2	3	2.1
Worked at home	24	2.7	113	2.4	4	2.5
Mean travel time to work (minutes)	25.1	(X)	28.2	(X)	26.1	(X)
OCCUPATION						
Employed civilian population 16 yrs and over	914	100.0	4,787	100.0	157	100.0
Management, professional, and related occupations	222	24.3	2,133	44.6	37	23.3
Service occupations	189	20.6	675	14.1	33	20.8
Sales and office occupations	219	24.0	1,149	24.0	45	28.8
Farming, fishing, and forestry occupations	12	1.3	14	0.3	1	0.9
Construction, extraction, and maintenance occupations	118	12.9	173	3.6	15	9.6
Production, transportation, and material moving occupations	154	16.8	643	13.4	26	16.5

X Not applicable.   [1] Civilian noninstitutionalized population.

Source: U.S. Census Bureau, Tables DP-2: Profile of Selected Social Characteristics: 2000 and DP-3: Profile of Selected Economic Characteristics: 2000; 2000 Census of Population, Summary File 4 (SF 4); <http://www.census.gov/Press-Release/www/2003/SF4.html>.

No. 44. Social and Economic Characteristics of the Asian and Pacific Islander Population: 1990 to 2002

[As of March (6,679 represents 6,679,000). Excludes members of Armed Forces except those living off post or with their families on post. Data for 1990 are based on 1980 census population controls; 2000 data are based on 1990 census population controls; 2002 data based on 2000 census population controls and an expanded sample of households. Based on Current Population Survey; see text, this section, and Appendix III]

Characteristic	Number (1,000)			Percent distribution		
	1990	2000	2002	1990	2000	2002
Total persons.	6,679	10,925	12,500	100.0	100.0	100.0
LABOR FORCE STATUS [1]						
Civilians 16 years old and over	4,849	8,225	9,636	100.0	100.0	100.0
Civilian labor force	3,216	5,458	6,451	66.3	66.4	66.9
Employed	3,079	5,246	6,081	63.5	63.8	63.1
Unemployed	136	212	370	2.8	2.6	3.8
Unemployment rate [2]	4.2	3.9	5.8	(X)	(X)	(X)
Not in labor force	1,634	2,767	3,185	33.7	33.6	33.1
FAMILY TYPE						
Total families	1,531	2,506	2,980	100.0	100.0	100.0
Married couple	1,257	1,996	2,378	82.1	79.6	79.8
Female householder, no spouse present	188	331	415	12.3	13.2	13.9
Male householder, no spouse present	86	179	187	5.6	7.1	6.3
HOUSING TENURE						
Total occupied units	1,988	3,337	4,071	100.0	100.0	100.0
Owner-occupied	976	1,766	2,161	49.1	52.9	53.1
Renter-occupied	982	1,526	1,861	49.4	45.7	45.7
No cash rent	30	46	49	1.5	1.4	1.2

X Not applicable. [1] See footnote 2, Table 587. [2] Total unemployment as percent of civilian labor force.

Source: U.S. Census Bureau, Current Population Reports, P20-540, and "The Asian and Pacific Islander Population in the United States: March 2002 (PPL-163)"; published 28 May 2003; <http://www.census.gov/population/www/socdemo/race/ppl-163.html>; and earlier reports.

No. 45. Selected Native Hawaiian Home Lands: 2000

[As of April 1]

Hawaiian home land	Population	Land area (sq. mi.)	Age		Race		Households
			Under 18 years old	65 years old and over	Native Hawaiian and Other Pacific Islander only	Native Hawaiian and Other Pacific Islander only or in combination	
Anahola-Kamalomalo	1,735	6.78	560	133	891	1,350	462
Auwaiolimu-Kalawahine-Kewalo-Papakolea	1,575	0.24	423	198	899	1,353	342
Hoolehua-Palaau	1,086	21.58	369	120	685	960	288
Keaukaha	1,454	2.63	432	150	792	1,281	366
Lualualei	1,826	2.50	606	123	825	1,538	444
Nanakuli	5,099	4.38	1,666	365	2,519	4,495	1,010
Waianae	1,759	0.60	612	103	825	1,534	367
Waimanalo	3,028	2.90	877	344	1,647	2,582	623

Source: U.S. Census Bureau, American FactFinder, GCT-PH1, Population, Housing Units, Area, and Density: 2000, Census Summary File 1 (SF1) 100-Percent Data and 2000 Census of Population and Housing, *Profiles of General Demographic Characteristics, Hawaii.*

No. 46. Social and Economic Characteristics of the Hispanic Population: 2002

[As of March, except labor force status, annual average (37,438 represents 37,438,000). Excludes members of the Armed Forces except those living off post or with their families on post. Based on Current Population Survey; see text, this section, and Appendix III]

Characteristic	Number (1,000)						Percent distribution					
	Hispanic, total	Mexican	Puerto Rican	Cuban	Central and South American	Other Hispanic	Hispanic, total	Mexican	Puerto Rican	Cuban	Central and South American	Other Hispanic
Total persons	37,438	25,074	3,222	1,376	5,349	2,416	100.0	100.0	100.0	100.0	100.0	100.0
Under 5 years	3,841	2,888	251	72	413	217	10.3	11.5	7.8	5.2	7.7	9.0
5 to 14 years old	7,246	5,208	579	154	829	474	19.4	20.7	18.0	11.2	15.5	19.7
15 to 44 years old	19,114	12,852	1,565	507	3,031	1,158	50.9	51.3	48.6	36.8	56.7	47.9
45 to 64 years old	5,341	3,135	611	331	849	416	14.3	12.5	19.0	24.0	15.8	17.2
65 years old and over	1,896	992	214	312	226	153	5.1	4.0	6.6	22.6	4.2	6.3
EDUCATIONAL ATTAINMENT												
Persons 25 years old and over	19,670	12,380	1,831	1,017	3,135	1,308	100.0	100.0	100.0	100.0	100.0	100.0
High school graduate or more	11,206	6,268	1,223	720	2,028	968	57.0	50.6	66.8	70.8	64.7	74.0
Bachelors degree or more	2,181	935	257	189	542	258	11.1	7.6	14.0	18.6	17.3	19.7
LABOR FORCE STATUS [1]												
Civilians 16 years old and over	25,963	16,420	2,484	1,141	4,147	1,771	100.0	100.0	100.0	100.0	100.0	100.0
Civilian labor force	17,943	11,542	1,546	635	3,024	1,196	69.1	70.3	62.2	55.6	72.9	67.5
Employed	16,590	10,673	1,401	592	2,817	1,107	63.9	65.0	56.4	51.9	67.9	62.5
Unemployed	1,353	869	145	43	208	88	5.2	5.3	5.8	3.8	5.0	5.0
Unemployment rate [2]	7.5	7.5	9.4	6.7	6.9	7.4	(X)	(X)	(X)	(X)	(X)	(X)
Male	7.2	7.1	9.4	6.5	6.7	7.5	(X)	(X)	(X)	(X)	(X)	(X)
Female	8.0	8.2	9.4	7.1	7.0	7.2	(X)	(X)	(X)	(X)	(X)	(X)
Not in labor force	8,020	4,878	938	507	1,123	574	30.9	29.7	37.8	44.4	27.1	32.4
HOUSEHOLDS												
Total	10,499	6,537	1,128	511	1,566	757	100.0	100.0	100.0	100.0	100.0	100.0
Family households	8,516	5,441	834	358	1,275	608	81.1	83.2	73.9	70.1	81.4	80.3
Married-couple families [3]	5,778	3,818	436	268	854	401	55.0	58.4	38.7	52.4	54.5	53.0
Male householder, no spouse present	817	544	79	28	119	46	7.8	8.3	7.0	5.5	7.6	6.1
Female householder, no spouse present	1,922	1,078	319	62	301	161	18.3	16.5	28.3	12.1	19.2	21.3
Nonfamily households	1,982	1,097	293	153	291	149	18.9	16.8	26.0	29.9	18.6	19.7
Male householder	1,108	636	166	67	169	71	10.6	9.7	14.7	13.1	10.8	9.4
Female householder	874	461	128	86	122	78	8.3	7.1	11.3	16.8	7.8	10.3
Size:												
One person	1,385	731	221	122	192	118	13.2	11.2	19.6	23.9	12.3	15.6
Two people	2,329	1,271	314	176	354	214	22.2	19.4	27.8	34.5	22.6	28.3
Three people	2,092	1,295	230	92	330	146	19.9	19.8	20.4	18.0	21.1	19.3
Four people	2,210	1,403	205	82	368	152	21.1	21.5	18.2	16.1	23.5	20.1
Five people	1,342	942	103	22	187	88	12.8	14.4	9.1	4.3	11.9	11.7
Six people	639	482	37	11	85	23	6.1	7.4	3.3	2.2	5.5	3.0
Seven people or more	500	413	17	5	50	15	4.8	6.3	1.5	1.0	3.2	2.0
FAMILY INCOME IN 2001												
Total families [4]	8,516	5,441	834	358	1,275	608	100.0	100.0	100.0	100.0	100.0	100.0
Less than $5,000	350	218	42	13	54	23	4.1	4.0	5.1	3.7	4.2	3.8
$5,000 to $14,999	1,080	678	157	47	130	69	12.7	12.5	18.9	13.0	10.2	11.2
$15,000 to $24,999	1,503	999	159	61	185	99	17.6	18.4	19.1	17.0	14.6	16.3
$25,000 to $34,999	1,381	932	108	58	202	81	16.2	17.1	12.9	16.1	15.9	13.4
$35,000 to $49,999	1,471	970	119	54	237	91	17.3	17.8	14.2	15.1	18.6	14.9
$50,000 to $74,999	1,427	903	126	51	231	116	16.8	16.6	15.1	14.3	18.1	19.1
$75,000 and over	1,304	742	124	75	235	129	15.3	13.6	14.8	20.9	18.4	21.2
Families below poverty level [5]	1,649	1,110	202	47	191	99	19.4	20.4	24.2	13.1	15.0	16.3
Persons below poverty level [5]	7,997	5,698	839	226	806	427	21.4	22.8	26.1	16.5	15.2	17.7
HOUSING TENURE												
Total occupied units	10,499	6,537	1,128	511	1,566	757	100.0	100.0	100.0	100.0	100.0	100.0
Owner-occupied	4,984	3,268	398	290	644	384	47.5	50.0	35.3	56.9	41.1	50.8
Renter-occupied [6]	5,514	3,269	730	220	922	373	52.5	50.0	64.7	43.1	58.9	49.2

X Not applicable. [1] Source: U.S. Bureau of Labor Statistics, *Employment and Earnings*, January 2003. [2] Total unemployment as percent of civilian labor force. [3] In married-couple families, Hispanic origin refers to the householder. [4] Includes families in group quarters. [5] For explanation of poverty level, see text, Section 13. [6] Includes no cash rent.

Source: Except as noted, U.S. Census Bureau, Current Population Reports, P20-545, and "The Hispanic Population in the United States: March 2002 Detailed Tables (PPL-165)"; published 18 June 2003; <http://www.census.gov/population/www/socdemo/hispanic/ppl-165.html>.

No. 47. Selected Characteristics of the Hispanic or Latino Populations: 2000

[In thousands, except as noted (18,270 represents 18,270,000). **As of April 1.** Persons of Hispanic origin may be of any race. Based on a sample from the 2000 Census of Population and Housing; see text, this section, and Appendix III]

Characteristic	Hispanic or Latino [1] Number	Hispanic or Latino [1] Percent	Mexican	Puerto Rican	Cuban	Central American	South American
EDUCATIONAL ATTAINMENT							
Population 25 yrs and over	18,270	100.0	10,178	1,843	935	1,082	940
Less than 9th grade	5,076	27.8	3,435	289	173	369	105
9th to 12th grade, no diploma	3,617	19.8	2,080	388	173	215	119
High school graduate (includes equivalency)	4,039	22.1	2,123	483	187	207	226
Some college, no degree	2,848	15.6	1,423	345	149	147	192
Associate degree	782	4.3	358	108	54	41	62
Bachelor's degree	1,216	6.7	513	152	108	67	137
Graduate or professional degree	692	3.8	246	78	90	36	100
Percent high school graduate or higher	52.4	(X)	45.8	63.3	62.9	46.0	76.1
Percent bachelor's degree or higher	10.4	(X)	7.5	12.5	21.2	9.5	25.2
DISABILITY STATUS [2]							
Population 5 to 20 years	10,524	100.0	6,578	1,006	202	424	299
With a disability	954	9.1	559	126	15	40	23
Population 21 to 64 years	18,857	100.0	10,883	1,825	738	1,188	958
With a disability	4,727	25.1	2,659	536	166	291	190
Percent employed	54.2	(X)	56.1	44.5	51.3	62.7	61.7
No disability	14,131	74.9	8,224	1,288	572	896	768
Percent employed	65.7	(X)	65.2	66.6	70.3	67.8	69.2
Population 65 years and over	1,660	100.0	783	181	228	54	74
With a disability	806	48.5	380	100	104	24	29
RESIDENCE IN 1995							
Population 5 years and over	31,570	100.0	18,514	3,091	1,189	1,678	1,342
Same house in 1995	14,047	44.5	8,152	1,416	595	642	512
Different house in the U.S. in 1995	14,495	45.9	8,515	1,463	486	788	567
Same county	10,030	31.8	6,082	914	340	560	360
Different county	4,465	14.1	2,433	549	146	228	208
Same state	2,454	7.8	1,389	265	78	110	104
Different state	2,011	6.4	1,044	283	69	119	104
Elsewhere in 1995	3,027	9.6	1,846	212	108	247	263
NATIVITY AND PLACE OF BIRTH							
Total population	35,238	100.0	20,900	3,404	1,250	1,812	1,420
Native	21,081	59.8	12,223	3,356	394	439	333
Born in United States	19,414	55.1	12,045	2,032	380	417	312
State of residence	15,807	44.9	10,118	1,457	275	343	225
Different state	3,607	10.2	1,927	575	105	74	87
Born outside United States	1,667	4.7	178	1,325	14	22	21
Foreign born	14,158	40.2	8,677	47	856	1,372	1,087
Entered 1990 to March 2000	6,489	18.4	4,228	20	226	612	513
Naturalized citizen	3,940	11.2	1,930	20	517	360	400
Not a citizen	10,218	29.0	6,747	27	339	1,013	688
COMMUTING TO WORK							
Workers 16 years and over	13,099	100.0	7,638	1,209	531	853	691
Car, truck, or van — drove alone	7,950	60.7	4,632	710	397	446	402
Car, truck, or van — carpooled	2,944	22.5	1,965	187	72	207	112
Public transportation (including taxicab)	1,162	8.9	451	204	29	126	115
Walked	523	4.0	279	69	14	38	33
Other means	284	2.2	189	19	7	23	11
Worked at home	236	1.8	121	20	13	15	19
Mean travel time to work (minutes)	27.2	(X)	25.9	29.5	29.0	30.3	29.8
OCCUPATION							
Employed civilian population 16 yrs. and over	13,348	100.0	7,785	1,219	543	869	705
Management, professional, and related occupations	2,411	18.1	1,164	295	172	116	195
Service occupations	2,906	21.8	1,709	241	78	245	151
Sales and office occupations	3,090	23.1	1,629	363	159	165	171
Farming, fishing, and forestry occupations	357	2.7	310	5	2	11	2
Construction, extraction, and maintenance occupations	1,755	13.1	1,171	99	53	131	63
Production, transportation, and material moving occupations	2,831	21.2	1,802	217	79	200	122

X Not applicable.   [1] Includes other Hispanic groups not shown separately.   [2] Civilian noninstitutionalized population.

Source: U.S. Census Bureau, Tables DP-2: Profile of Selected Social Characteristics: 2000 and DP-3: Profile of Selected Economic Characteristics: 2000; 2000 Census of Population, Summary File 4 (SF 4); <http://www.census.gov/Press-Release/www/2003/SF4.html>.

No. 48. Native and Foreign-Born Population by Place of Birth and State: 1980 to 2000

[In thousands, except percent (226,546 represents 226,546,000). As of April 1. Data are based on a sample from the census; for details, see text, this section, and Appendix III]

State	Total population	Native population Total	Born in United States Total	State of residence	Different state	Born outside United States [1]	Foreign-born Total Number	Percent of total population	Entered 1990 to March 2000 Number	Percent of foreign-born population
1980	226,546	212,466	210,323	144,871	65,452	2,143	14,080	6.2	(X)	(X)
1990	248,710	228,943	225,696	153,685	72,011	3,246	19,767	7.9	(X)	(X)
U.S.	281,422	250,314	246,786	168,729	78,057	3,528	31,108	11.1	13,178	42.4
AL	4,447	4,359	4,328	3,262	1,066	31	88	2.0	47	53.0
AK	627	590	580	239	341	10	37	5.9	15	39.7
AZ	5,131	4,474	4,419	1,779	2,639	56	656	12.8	317	48.4
AR	2,673	2,600	2,586	1,708	878	14	74	2.8	41	55.3
CA	33,872	25,007	24,634	17,019	7,615	374	8,864	26.2	3,271	36.9
CO	4,301	3,931	3,876	1,767	2,109	55	370	8.6	201	54.4
CT	3,406	3,036	2,922	1,941	982	114	370	10.9	144	39.0
DE	784	739	727	379	348	12	45	5.7	21	47.2
DC	572	498	491	224	267	7	74	12.9	38	51.0
FL	15,982	13,312	12,890	5,232	7,659	421	2,671	16.7	1,030	38.6
GA	8,186	7,609	7,520	4,736	2,784	90	577	7.1	345	59.7
HI	1,212	999	969	689	280	30	212	17.5	72	34.1
ID	1,294	1,230	1,219	611	608	11	64	5.0	31	47.7
IL	12,419	10,890	10,768	8,336	2,433	122	1,529	12.3	688	45.0
IN	6,080	5,894	5,862	4,216	1,646	32	187	3.1	97	52.2
IA	2,926	2,835	2,824	2,188	635	11	91	3.1	52	57.5
KS	2,688	2,554	2,533	1,600	932	21	135	5.0	74	55.1
KY	4,042	3,961	3,941	2,980	960	21	80	2.0	47	58.8
LA	4,469	4,353	4,328	3,547	781	25	116	2.6	43	37.0
ME	1,275	1,238	1,226	858	369	12	37	2.9	10	28.3
MD	5,296	4,778	4,718	2,611	2,107	60	518	9.8	228	44.1
MA	6,349	5,576	5,433	4,197	1,236	143	773	12.2	312	40.4
MI	9,938	9,415	9,358	7,490	1,868	57	524	5.3	235	44.9
MN	4,919	4,659	4,633	3,452	1,181	26	260	5.3	142	54.5
MS	2,845	2,805	2,791	2,114	677	14	40	1.4	20	49.6
MO	5,595	5,444	5,413	3,792	1,620	31	151	2.7	79	52.4
MT	902	886	879	506	373	7	16	1.8	5	29.0
NE	1,711	1,637	1,626	1,148	479	10	75	4.4	43	57.8
NV	1,998	1,682	1,655	426	1,230	26	317	15.8	139	44.0
NH	1,236	1,182	1,170	535	636	11	54	4.4	20	37.3
NJ	8,414	6,938	6,738	4,491	2,248	200	1,476	17.5	614	41.6
NM	1,819	1,669	1,651	937	714	19	150	8.2	58	39.1
NY	18,976	15,108	14,589	12,385	2,204	519	3,868	20.4	1,562	40.4
NC	8,049	7,619	7,548	5,073	2,475	71	430	5.3	268	62.4
ND	642	630	626	466	160	4	12	1.9	6	52.3
OH	11,353	11,014	10,940	8,486	2,455	73	339	3.0	143	42.2
OK	3,451	3,319	3,290	2,159	1,132	28	132	3.8	70	53.0
OR	3,421	3,132	3,102	1,549	1,553	30	290	8.5	145	50.0
PA	12,281	11,773	11,620	9,544	2,076	152	508	4.1	209	41.1
RI	1,048	929	910	644	266	19	119	11.4	41	34.8
SC	4,012	3,896	3,862	2,569	1,294	34	116	2.9	61	52.4
SD	755	741	738	514	224	4	13	1.8	7	55.0
TN	5,689	5,530	5,493	3,679	1,814	37	159	2.8	92	57.7
TX	20,852	17,952	17,727	12,970	4,757	225	2,900	13.9	1,336	46.1
UT	2,233	2,075	2,055	1,405	649	20	159	7.1	91	57.2
VT	609	586	581	331	250	5	23	3.8	8	35.3
VA	7,079	6,508	6,403	3,676	2,726	106	570	8.1	269	47.2
WA	5,894	5,280	5,196	2,781	2,414	84	614	10.4	286	46.6
WV	1,808	1,789	1,782	1,343	440	7	19	1.1	7	35.7
WI	5,364	5,170	5,137	3,939	1,198	33	194	3.6	91	46.8
WY	494	483	479	210	269	4	11	2.3	4	37.8

X Not applicable. [1] Includes Puerto Rico.

Source: U.S. Census Bureau, 1990 Census of Population Listing (1990CPH-L-121) and 2000 Census of Population and Housing, *Profiles of General Demographic Characteristics;* <http://www.census.gov/Press-Release/www/2002/demoprofiles.html>.

No. 49. Nativity and Place of Birth of Resident Population—25 Largest Metropolitan Areas: 2000

[In thousands except percent (4,112 represents 4,112,000). As of April. See headnote, Table 48. Covers metropolitan statistical area (MSAs) and consolidated metropolitan statistical areas (CMSAs) as defined by the U.S. Office of Management and Budget as of June 30, 1999. For definitions of metropolitan areas, see Appendix II]

Metropolitan area	Total population	Native population Total	Native Born in United States	Native Born outside United States	Foreign-born Number	Foreign-born Percent of total population	Entered 1990 to March 2000 Number	Entered 1990 to March 2000 Percent of foreign-born population
Atlanta, GA MSA	4,112	3,689	3,643	46	423	10.3	257	60.6
Boston-Worcester-Lawrence, MA-NH-ME-CT CMSA	5,819	5,098	4,987	111	721	12.4	301	41.8
Chicago-Gary-Kenosha, IL-IN-WI CMSA	9,158	7,691	7,581	110	1,467	16.0	653	44.5
Cincinnati-Hamilton, OH-KY-IN CMSA	1,979	1,928	1,919	9	51	2.6	25	49.5
Cleveland-Akron, OH CMSA	2,946	2,810	2,780	30	135	4.6	49	35.9
Dallas-Fort Worth, TX CMSA	5,222	4,437	4,388	49	785	15.0	431	54.9
Denver-Boulder-Greeley, CO CMSA	2,582	2,304	2,276	28	277	10.7	156	56.3
Detroit-Ann Arbor-Flint, MI CMSA	5,456	5,072	5,039	33	384	7.0	169	44.0
Houston-Galveston-Brazoria, TX CMSA	4,670	3,774	3,729	45	896	19.2	433	48.3
Kansas City, MO-KS MSA	1,776	1,696	1,683	13	81	4.5	44	54.7
Los Angeles-Riverside-Orange County, CA CMSA	16,374	11,306	11,154	152	5,068	30.9	1,775	35.0
Miami-Fort Lauderdale, FL CMSA	3,876	2,318	2,208	110	1,558	40.2	584	37.5
Minneapolis-St. Paul, MN-WI MSA	2,969	2,758	2,740	18	210	7.1	117	55.5
New York-Northern New Jersey-Long Island, NY-NJ-CT-PA CMSA	21,200	16,018	15,360	658	5,182	24.4	2,127	41.1
Philadelphia-Wilmington-Atlantic City, PA-NJ-DE-MD CMSA	6,188	5,755	5,633	122	434	7.0	183	42.1
Phoenix-Mesa, AZ MSA	3,252	2,794	2,761	33	457	14.1	245	53.6
Pittsburgh, PA MSA	2,359	2,296	2,286	11	62	2.6	25	40.0
Portland-Salem, OR-WA CMSA	2,265	2,017	1,996	21	248	11.0	132	53.1
Sacramento-Yolo, CA CMSA	1,797	1,537	1,515	21	260	14.5	113	43.6
St. Louis, MO-IL MSA	2,604	2,523	2,508	15	81	3.1	41	50.7
San Diego, CA MSA	2,814	2,208	2,162	45	606	21.5	216	35.5
San Francisco-Oakland-San Jose, CA CMSA	7,039	5,137	5,047	90	1,902	27.0	777	40.9
Seattle-Tacoma-Bremerton, WA CMSA	3,555	3,140	3,079	61	414	11.7	188	45.4
Tampa-St. Petersburg-Clearwater, FL MSA	2,396	2,162	2,102	60	234	9.8	90	38.5
Washington-Baltimore, DC-MD-VA-WV CMSA	7,608	6,627	6,516	111	981	12.9	457	46.6

Source: U.S. Census Bureau, 2000 Census of Population and Housing, *Profiles of General Demographic Characteristics*; <http://www.census.gov/Press-Release/www/2002/demoprofiles.html>.

No. 50. Nativity and Place of Birth of Resident Population—25 Largest Cities: 2000

[In thousands except percent (656 represents 656,000). As of April. See headnote, Table 48]

City	Total population	Native Total	Native Born in United States	Native Born outside United States	Foreign-born Number	Foreign-born Percent of total population	Entered 1990 to March 2000 Number	Entered 1990 to March 2000 Percent of foreign-born population
Austin, TX	656	547	537	10	109	16.6	66	60.6
Baltimore, MD	651	622	617	4	30	4.6	14	47.4
Boston, MA	589	437	418	19	152	25.8	74	48.5
Chicago, IL	2,896	2,267	2,206	61	629	21.7	292	46.4
Columbus, OH	712	664	659	5	48	6.7	30	63.7
Dallas, TX	1,188	898	888	9	290	24.4	174	60.0
Denver, CO	555	458	452	6	97	17.4	60	62.4
Detroit, MI	951	906	899	6	46	4.8	26	56.5
El Paso, TX	564	417	405	12	148	26.1	45	30.3
Houston, TX	1,955	1,439	1,420	19	516	26.4	269	52.2
Indianapolis, IN [1]	782	746	741	5	36	4.6	22	60.5
Jacksonville, FL	736	692	678	14	44	5.9	19	43.1
Los Angeles, CA	3,695	2,182	2,150	32	1,513	40.9	570	37.7
Memphis, TN	650	624	620	3	26	4.0	17	66.4
Milwaukee, WI	597	551	540	11	46	7.7	24	52.2
Nashville-Davidson, TN [1]	546	507	502	5	39	7.1	26	67.7
New York, NY	8,008	5,137	4,763	374	2,871	35.9	1,225	42.7
Philadelphia, PA	1,518	1,380	1,332	48	137	9.0	64	46.4
Phoenix, AZ	1,321	1,064	1,051	13	257	19.5	150	58.4
San Antonio, TX	1,145	1,011	989	22	134	11.7	47	35.4
San Diego, CA	1,223	909	889	20	314	25.7	118	37.4
San Francisco, CA	777	491	479	12	286	36.8	106	37.2
San Jose, CA	894	564	554	11	330	36.9	145	44.1
Seattle, WA	563	468	459	10	95	16.9	44	46.5
Washington, DC	572	498	491	7	74	12.9	38	51.0

[1] Represents the portion of a consolidated city that is not within one or more separately incorporated places.

Source: U.S. Census Bureau, 2000 Census of Population and Housing, *Profiles of General Demographic Characteristics*; <http://www.census.gov/Press-Release/www/2002/demoprofiles.html>.

No. 51. Foreign-Born Populations—Selected Characteristics by Region of Origin: 2002

[In thousands (32,453 represents 32,453,000). As of March. See headnote, Table 54. Based on Current Population Survey; see text, this section, and Appendix III]

Characteristic	Total foreign born	Europe	Asia	Latin America Total	Caribbean	Central America[1]	South America	Other areas
Total	32,453	4,548	8,281	16,943	3,102	11,819	2,022	2,680
Under 5 years old	320	41	84	165	12	139	14	30
5 to 14 years old	1,794	166	357	1,094	132	832	130	178
15 to 19 years old	1,706	148	370	1,055	153	783	120	133
20 to 29 years old	6,333	454	1,403	3,944	438	3,148	358	532
30 to 44 years old	11,004	1,157	2,860	6,089	938	4,392	760	897
45 to 54 years old	4,931	761	1,563	2,206	505	1,379	322	401
55 to 64 years old	3,054	673	875	1,248	426	640	181	258
65 to 84 years old	2,998	993	734	1,048	444	472	132	222
85 years old and over	310	154	34	92	53	34	5	30
EDUCATIONAL ATTAINMENT								
Persons 25 years old and over	25,790	3,969	6,879	12,835	2,594	8,634	1,606	2,107
Not high school graduate	8,460	634	911	6,536	820	5,409	307	379
High school grad/some college	10,500	1,957	2,605	4,915	1,346	2,707	863	1,023
Bachelor's degree	4,381	735	2,149	1,043	321	396	326	454
Advanced degree	2,448	642	1,215	341	109	122	110	251
INCOME IN 2001								
Total families	10,284	1,528	2,578	5,336	1,042	3,660	634	843
$1 to $9,999 or loss	643	65	122	413	106	270	37	43
$10,000 to $19,999	1,337	138	208	904	170	658	77	86
$20,000 to $34,999	2,182	219	363	1,457	255	1,085	116	144
$35,000 to $49,999	1,696	257	348	959	157	689	113	132
$50,000 to $74,999	1,792	299	471	855	162	550	143	166
$75,000 and over	2,634	549	1,066	748	192	409	147	271
Median income (dol.)[2]	42,447	56,906	61,229	33,706	34,174	32,168	46,595	51,116

[1] Includes Mexico. [2] For definition of median, see Guide to Tabular Presentation.
Source: U.S. Census Bureau, "Foreign-Born Population of the United States Current Population Survey - March 2002 Detailed Tables (PPL-162)"; published 10 March 2003; <http://www.census.gov/population/www/socdemo/foreign/ppl-162.html>.

No. 52. Foreign-Born Population by Place of Birth and Citizenship Status: 2001

[In thousands, except percent (31,482 represents 31,482,000). The foreign-born population includes: immigrants as well as nonimmigrants (e.g., refugees and people on student or work visas), and people residing in the United States illegally (undocumented aliens). Data based on 12 monthly samples from the 2001 Supplementary Survey and subject to sampling variability. The survey universe is limited to the household population and excludes the population living in institutions, college dormitories, and other group quarters]

Region	Foreign-born population, total	Naturalized citizen	Not U.S. citizen Number	Percent of foreign born	Region	Foreign-born population, total	Naturalized citizen	Not U.S. citizen Number	Percent of foreign born
Total	31,482	12,740	18,743	60	South America	2,015	791	1,224	61
Latin America	16,141	4,934	11,207	69	Asia	8,477	4,398	4,080	48
Caribbean	2,945	1,506	1,439	49	Europe	4,842	2,628	2,214	46
Central America	11,181	2,637	8,544	76	Africa	983	338	646	66
Mexico	9,234	2,049	7,185	78	Northern America	840	376	465	55
Other Central America	1,946	587	1,359	70	Oceania	198	66	132	67
					Born at sea	(Z)	(Z)	-	-

- Represents zero. Z Less than 500.
Source: U.S. Census Bureau, American FactFinder, 2001 Supplementary Survey Summary Tables, P039. Place of Birth by Citizenship Status for the Foreign-Born Population; (accessed: 7 August 2003).

No. 53. Foreign-Stock Population by Nativity and Parentage: 1960 to 2000

[34.1 represents 34,100,000. Information on the birthplace of parents may be used to classify the native population by parentage: native of native parentage (both parents native), native of foreign parentage (both parents foreign born), and native of mixed parentage (one parent native and one parent foreign born). The term foreign stock includes the foreign-born population and the native population of foreign or mixed parentage. For 1960 and 1970, resident population. For 2000, these data are not consistent with Census 2000 data since they are based on civilian noninstitutional population plus Armed Forces living off post or with their families on post and were adjusted based on assumptions about coverage in the 1990 census]

Nativity and parentage	Number (mil.) 1960	1970	2000	Percent of total population 1960	1970	2000
Foreign stock, total	34.1	33.6	55.9	19.0	16.5	20.4
Native population of foreign or mixed parentage	24.3	24.0	27.5	13.6	11.8	10.0
Foreign parentage	14.1	(NA)	14.8	7.9	(NA)	5.4
Mixed parentage	10.2	(NA)	12.7	5.7	(NA)	4.6
Foreign born	9.7	9.6	28.4	5.4	4.7	10.4

NA Not available.
Source: U.S. Census Bureau, Current Population Reports, P23-206.

Figure 1.3
Foreign Born by Region of Birth: 2002
(In percent)

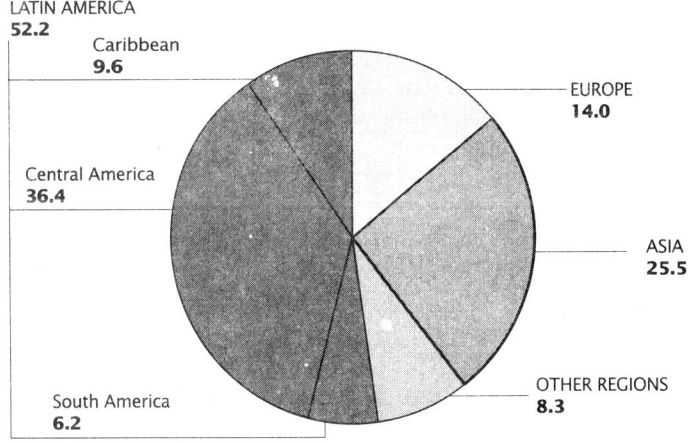

Source: Chart prepared by U.S. Census Bureau. For data, see Table 51.

Figure 1.4
Population With High School Education or More by Nativity and World Region of Birth: 2002
(In percent)[1]

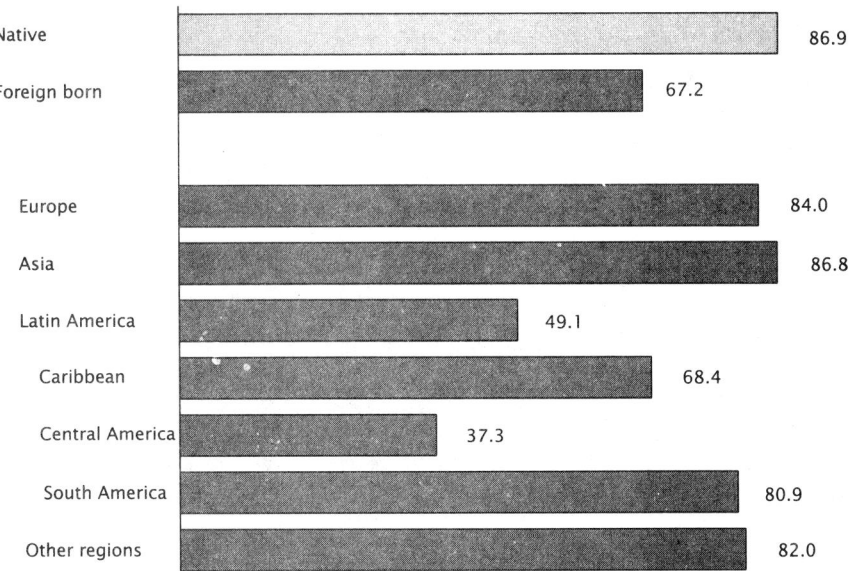

[1] Each bar represents the percent of individuals aged 25 and over, who were born in the specified area, who have at least a high school education.

Source: Chart prepared by U.S. Census Bureau. For data, see Tables 51 and 54.

No. 54. Native and Foreign-Born Populations by Selected Characteristics: 2002

[In thousands (282,082 represents 282,082,000). As of March. The foreign-born population includes anyone who is not a U.S. citizen at birth. This includes legal permanent residents (immigrants), temporary migrants (such as students), humanitarian migrants (such as refugees), and persons illegally present in the United States. Based on Current Population Survey which includes the civilian noninstitutional population plus Armed Forces living off post or with their families on post; see text, this section, and Appendix III]

Characteristic	Total population	Native population	Foreign-born population			
			Total	Naturalized citizen	Not U.S. citizen	Year of entry: 1990 to March 2002
Total.	282,082	249,629	32,453	11,962	20,491	15,781
Under 5 years old	19,428	19,107	320	55	265	320
5 to 14 years old	41,063	39,269	1,793	233	1,561	1,702
15 to 19 years old.	20,045	18,339	1,705	247	1,459	1,321
20 to 29 years old.	37,714	31,381	6,333	1,079	5,254	4,706
30 to 44 years old.	64,644	53,641	11,003	3,627	7,376	5,314
45 to 54 years old.	39,545	34,614	4,932	2,524	2,408	1,277
55 to 64 years old.	25,874	22,820	3,054	1,863	1,191	641
65 to 84 years old.	30,314	27,315	2,999	2,079	920	473
85 years old and over	3,456	3,145	310	254	56	26
Median age (years).	35.6	35.1	37.8	47.8	32.8	29.7
Male.	137,871	121,519	16,351	5,564	10,787	8,191
Female.	144,211	128,110	16,101	6,398	9,703	7,591
MARITAL STATUS						
Persons 15 years old and over	221,591	191,254	30,337	11,673	18,664	13,758
Married.	118,787	100,495	18,290	7,685	10,605	7,494
Widowed.	14,052	12,586	1,467	949	518	315
Divorced.	20,969	19,163	1,806	953	853	489
Separated	4,626	3,769	857	302	555	333
Never married	63,157	55,240	7,917	1,784	6,133	5,128
EDUCATIONAL ATTAINMENT						
Persons 25 years old and over	182,142	156,352	25,790	10,995	14,795	10,220
Not high school graduate	28,948	20,488	8,460	2,490	5,970	3,444
High school grad/some college	104,498	93,997	10,500	5,095	5,405	3,787
Bachelor's degree.	32,282	27,900	4,381	2,215	2,166	1,860
Advanced degree	16,414	13,966	2,448	1,195	1,253	1,129
EARNINGS IN 2001 [1]						
Persons 15 yrs. old and over with earnings .	100,351	85,835	14,516	5,881	8,636	6,261
$1 to $9,999 or loss	3,508	2,831	676	178	498	364
$10,000 to $19,999.	15,926	12,091	3,835	957	2,878	2,124
$20,000 to $34,999.	32,217	27,486	4,730	1,872	2,858	2,005
$35,000 to $49,999.	20,885	18,701	2,184	1,124	1,060	744
$50,000 to $74,999.	16,248	14,551	1,697	976	722	559
$75,000 and over	11,569	10,175	1,394	774	620	467
Median earnings (dol.) [2].	33,636	35,239	26,710	33,670	22,685	22,464
POVERTY STATUS IN 2001 [3]						
Persons below poverty level	32,907	27,698	5,209	1,186	4,023	3,136
Persons above poverty level	248,568	221,355	27,213	10,776	16,437	12,614
HOUSEHOLD SIZE						
Total households.	109,297	95,884	13,413	6,069	7,344	5,070
One person	28,775	26,363	2,411	1,315	1,096	813
Two persons	36,240	32,989	3,251	1,618	1,633	1,159
Three persons	17,742	15,205	2,537	1,042	1,495	1,101
Four persons.	15,794	13,251	2,543	1,035	1,508	1,042
Five persons	6,948	5,499	1,449	582	866	526
Six persons	2,438	1,761	677	277	401	249
Seven persons or more	1,360	816	545	200	345	179
INCOME IN 2001						
Total families.	74,329	64,044	10,284	4,553	5,731	3,856
$1 to $9,999 or loss	3,587	2,943	643	181	461	316
$10,000 to $19,999.	6,920	5,583	1,337	473	865	556
$20,000 to $34,999.	12,994	10,812	2,182	768	1,414	953
$35,000 to $49,999.	11,778	10,082	1,696	713	984	610
$50,000 to $74,999.	15,747	13,955	1,792	879	913	630
$75,000 and over	23,302	20,669	2,634	1,540	1,094	792
Median income (dol.) [2]	52,275	53,909	42,447	52,563	36,385	36,911
HOUSING TENURE [4]						
Owner-occupied unit	74,399	67,725	6,673	4,107	2,566	1,468
Renter-occupied unit	33,298	26,721	6,577	1,902	4,675	3,533

[1] Covers only year-round full-time workers. [2] For definition of median, see Guide to Tabular Presentation. [3] Persons for whom poverty status is determined. Excludes unrelated individuals under 15 years old. [4] Based on citizenship of householder. Excludes occupiers who paid no cash rent.

Source: U.S. Census Bureau, "Foreign-Born Population of the United States Current Population Survey - March 2002 Detailed Tables (PPL-162);" published 10 March 2003; <http://www.census.gov/population/www/socdemo/foreign/ppl-162.html>.

No. 55. Ancestry of Resident Population by State: 2000

[In thousands (281,422 represents 281,422,000). As of April. Covers single and multiple ancestries. Based on sample data from the 2000 Census of Population and Housing; see text, this section, and Appendix III]

State	Total population [1]	English	French (except Basque) [2]	German	Irish [2]	Italian	Polish	Scottish	United States or American
U.S.	281,422	24,515	8,326	42,885	30,594	15,724	8,977	4,891	20,625
AL	4,447	345	65	254	343	56	23	69	756
AK	627	60	20	104	68	18	13	16	36
AZ	5,131	532	147	800	526	225	127	103	240
AR	2,673	211	51	250	255	35	19	36	425
CA	33,872	2,521	784	3,332	2,622	1,451	491	542	1,141
CO	4,301	515	143	948	528	202	101	114	221
CT	3,406	349	214	336	566	634	284	67	111
DE	784	95	16	112	130	73	41	15	47
DC	572	25	7	27	28	13	8	7	10
FL	15,982	1,469	445	1,888	1,648	1,004	430	294	1,279
GA	8,186	665	126	571	643	163	83	141	1,102
HI	1,212	52	18	70	53	22	11	13	17
ID	1,294	234	38	244	130	35	15	41	108
IL	12,419	832	268	2,441	1,513	744	933	150	569
IN	6,080	540	149	1,378	656	141	184	100	730
IA	2,926	277	76	1,046	396	49	33	43	197
KS	2,688	290	83	695	310	51	35	50	237
KY	4,042	392	66	515	424	62	28	60	846
LA	4,469	233	546	315	315	196	19	38	450
ME	1,275	274	182	86	193	59	25	61	120
MD	5,296	476	96	834	623	268	184	90	306
MA	6,349	722	509	377	1,428	860	323	162	245
MI	9,938	989	490	2,028	1,069	451	855	225	518
MN	4,919	310	203	1,807	553	111	240	62	143
MS	2,845	174	66	129	196	40	10	35	404
MO	5,595	529	196	1,314	712	176	90	83	587
MT	902	114	38	244	134	28	18	27	46
NE	1,711	164	45	661	230	43	62	23	77
NV	1,998	201	63	282	220	133	47	38	96
NH	1,236	223	181	106	241	106	51	54	74
NJ	8,414	522	125	1,063	1,337	1,504	576	107	264
NM	1,819	138	37	179	134	43	21	29	93
NY	18,976	1,140	479	2,123	2,454	2,737	986	212	717
NC	8,049	768	128	762	596	182	88	178	1,115
ND	642	32	25	282	49	5	18	8	15
OH	11,353	1,047	272	2,867	1,448	676	433	197	982
OK	3,451	292	79	435	355	50	27	52	392
OR	3,421	453	127	701	409	111	55	109	219
PA	12,281	966	211	3,116	1,983	1,418	824	185	633
RI	1,048	125	114	56	193	199	43	20	31
SC	4,012	328	71	338	318	81	37	74	558
SD	755	53	22	307	78	8	12	8	29
TN	5,689	517	94	475	528	94	46	103	998
TX	20,852	1,463	467	2,069	1,508	363	228	290	1,554
UT	2,233	648	51	258	132	58	17	99	151
VT	609	112	88	55	100	39	20	28	50
VA	7,079	789	143	829	696	257	125	153	808
WA	5,894	707	215	1,103	673	191	103	178	316
WV	1,808	176	25	253	198	70	29	28	341
WI	5,364	348	206	2,290	583	173	498	56	189
WY	494	79	17	128	66	15	10	16	32

[1] Includes persons of other ancestries not shown separately. [2] Data represent a combination of two ancestries. French includes Alsatian. Irish includes Celtic.

Source: U.S. Census Bureau, 2000 Census of Population and Housing, *Profiles of General Demographic Characteristics*; <http://www.census.gov/Press-Release/www/2002/demoprofiles.html>.

No. 56. Language Spoken at Home by Nativity: 2000

[In thousands (262,375 represents 262,375,000), except as indicated. As of April. Based on sample data from the 2000 Census of Population and Housing; see text, this section, and Appendix III]

Ability to speak English and language spoken	Total	Native	Foreign born Number	Foreign born Percent of total
Population 5 years old and over	262,375	231,666	30,709	11.7
Speak language other than English	46,952	21,455	25,497	54.3
Speak English less than "very well"	21,320	5,648	15,673	73.5
Spanish	28,101	14,761	13,340	47.5
Other Indo-European languages	10,018	4,432	5,586	55.8
Asian and Pacific Island languages	6,960	1,448	5,512	79.2
Other languages	1,872	814	1,059	56.5

Source: U.S. Census Bureau, "Table 6. Language Spoken at Home and Ability to Speak English by Nativity for the Population 5 Years and Over by State: 2000," published 25 February 2003; <http://www.census.gov/population/cen2000/phc-t20/tab06.pdf>.

No. 57. Languages Spoken at Home by Age Group and Language: 2000

[In thousands (262,375 represents 262,375,000). As of April. Based on sample data from the 2000 Census of Population and Housing; see text, this section, and Appendix III]

Language	Total 5 years old and over	5 to 17 years old	18 years old and over	Language	Total 5 years old and over	5 to 17 years old	18 years old and over
Total	262,375	53,096	209,279	Other Indo-European languages	328	55	273
Speak only English	215,424	43,316	172,107				
Speak other language	46,952	9,780	37,172	Asian and Pacific Island languages	6,960	1,159	5,801
Spanish or Spanish Creole	28,101	6,830	21,271	Chinese	2,022	317	1,705
Other Indo-European languages	10,018	1,445	8,573	Japanese	478	56	422
French (incl Patois, Cajun)	1,644	233	1,411	Korean	894	156	738
French Creole	453	113	341	Mon-Khmer, Cambodian	182	58	124
Italian	1,008	68	940	Miao, Hmong	168	83	85
Portuguese or Portuguese Creole	565	85	479	Thai	120	14	106
German	1,383	165	1,218	Laotian	149	38	111
Yiddish	179	39	140	Vietnamese	1,010	205	805
Other West Germanic languages	251	47	205	Other Asian languages	398	53	346
Scandinavian languages	162	15	147	Tagalog	1,224	128	1,096
Greek	365	39	327	Other Pacific Island languages	314	51	263
Russian	706	118	589	Other languages	1,872	346	1,527
Polish	667	76	592	Navajo	178	43	135
Serbo-Croatian	234	41	192	Other Native North American languages	203	40	163
Other Slavic languages	301	37	264	Hungarian	118	8	110
Armenian	203	36	166	Arabic	615	124	490
Persian	312	54	258	Hebrew	195	40	155
Gujarathi	236	42	194	African languages	419	68	350
Hindi	317	41	276	Other and unspecified languages	145	23	122
Urdu	263	62	201				
Other Indic languages	439	79	360				

Source: U.S. Census Bureau, "Table 5. Detailed List of Languages Spoken at Home for the Population 5 Years and Over by State: 2000," published 25 February 2003; <http://www.census.gov/population/cen2000/phc-t20/tab05.pdf> and American FactFinder, PCT10. Age by Language Spoken At Home For The Population 5 Years and Over; Census 2000 Summary File 3 (SF 3) - Sample Data.

No. 58. Language Spoken at Home by Resident Population by State: 2000

[In thousands, except percent (262,375 represents 262,375,000). As of April. Based on sample data from the 2000 Census of Population and Housing; see text, this section, and Appendix III]

State	Population 5 years and over	English only	Language other than English, total [1] — Number	Total — Percent of population 5 yrs. and over	Total — Speak English less than "very well"	Spanish — Total	Spanish — Speak English less than "very well"	Other Indo-European languages — Total	Other Indo-European languages — Speak English less than "very well"	Asian and Pacific Island languages — Total	Asian and Pacific Island languages — Speak English less than "very well"
U.S.	262,375	215,424	46,952	17.9	21,320	28,101	13,751	10,018	3,390	6,960	3,590
AL	4,152	3,990	162	3.9	64	90	40	44	11	22	11
AK	580	497	83	14.3	31	17	6	13	4	22	12
AZ	4,753	3,523	1,229	25.9	540	927	435	102	27	62	28
AR	2,492	2,368	124	5.0	58	82	44	23	5	15	8
CA	31,417	19,015	12,402	39.5	6,278	8,106	4,304	1,335	454	2,709	1,439
CO	4,006	3,402	604	15.1	268	422	203	100	27	64	32
CT	3,185	2,601	584	18.3	235	268	117	251	90	48	23
DE	732	663	70	9.5	28	35	17	23	6	9	4
DC	540	449	90	16.8	38	49	25	24	6	9	5
FL	15,044	11,570	3,474	23.1	1,555	2,477	1,187	755	268	165	76
GA	7,594	6,843	751	9.9	374	426	246	169	53	116	63
HI	1,134	832	302	26.6	144	19	5	14	3	267	135
ID	1,197	1,085	112	9.3	47	80	36	19	5	8	4
IL	11,548	9,327	2,221	19.2	1,055	1,254	666	640	253	249	111
IN	5,658	5,296	362	6.4	143	186	84	127	38	37	18
IA	2,738	2,578	160	5.8	68	79	37	49	16	25	14
KS	2,500	2,282	219	8.7	98	137	68	41	11	33	17
KY	3,776	3,628	148	3.9	59	70	31	51	15	21	11
LA	4,153	3,771	382	9.2	117	105	39	226	54	42	22
ME	1,204	1,110	94	7.8	24	10	3	76	18	6	2
MD	4,945	4,322	623	12.6	246	231	109	199	59	136	66
MA	5,954	4,839	1,116	18.7	459	370	163	530	194	171	90
MI	9,269	8,487	781	8.4	295	247	101	303	97	104	48
MN	4,591	4,202	390	8.5	168	132	62	111	30	104	58
MS	2,641	2,546	96	3.6	36	51	21	24	6	14	6
MO	5,226	4,962	264	5.1	103	111	46	98	31	42	21
MT	847	803	44	5.2	13	13	3	18	5	3	1
NE	1,595	1,469	126	7.9	58	78	40	28	8	15	8
NV	1,854	1,426	428	23.1	208	300	162	47	12	69	29
NH	1,160	1,064	96	8.3	28	19	7	64	16	10	5
NJ	7,856	5,855	2,002	25.5	873	968	483	659	242	276	120
NM	1,690	1,073	617	36.5	201	486	159	22	5	12	5
NY	17,749	12,786	4,963	28.0	2,310	2,416	1,182	1,655	664	671	395
NC	7,513	6,910	604	8.0	298	379	219	120	32	78	39
ND	603	565	38	6.3	11	8	3	24	7	2	1
OH	10,600	9,951	648	6.1	234	213	77	297	99	85	41
OK	3,216	2,977	239	7.4	99	141	65	37	9	35	18
OR	3,199	2,811	389	12.1	189	218	117	83	28	75	40
PA	11,556	10,583	972	8.4	368	357	141	428	139	144	76
RI	985	789	197	20.0	84	79	40	91	32	20	10
SC	3,749	3,552	196	5.2	82	110	54	55	14	26	12
SD	704	658	46	6.5	16	10	4	20	8	3	2
TN	5,316	5,059	257	4.8	108	134	64	69	19	40	20
TX	19,242	13,231	6,011	31.2	2,670	5,195	2,369	358	92	374	187
UT	2,024	1,771	253	12.5	106	150	71	50	13	38	16
VT	575	541	34	5.9	9	6	1	24	6	3	2
VA	6,619	5,884	735	11.1	304	316	152	196	53	170	82
WA	5,501	4,731	771	14.0	351	321	155	177	62	243	123
WV	1,707	1,661	46	2.7	14	18	6	19	5	6	2
WI	5,022	4,653	369	7.3	149	169	77	125	37	61	32
WY	463	433	29	6.4	9	19	6	6	1	2	1

[1] Includes other language groups not shown separately.

Source: U.S. Census Bureau, 2000 Census of Population and Housing, *Profiles of General Demographic Characteristics*; <http://www.census.gov/Press-Release/www/2002/demoprofiles.html>.

No. 59. Language Spoken at Home by Resident Population—25 Largest Metropolitan Areas: 2000

[In thousands except percent (3,805 represents 3,805,000). As of April. See headnote, Table 58. Covers metropolitan statistical area (MSAs) and consolidated metropolitan statistical areas (CMSAs) as defined by the U.S. Office of Management and Budget as of June 30, 1999. For definitions of metropolitan areas, see Appendix II]

Metropolitan area	Population 5 years and over	English only	Language other than English, total [1]			Spanish	Other Indo-European languages	Asian and Pacific Island languages
			Number	Percent of population 5 years and over	Speak English less than "very well"			
Atlanta, GA MSA	3,805	3,299	507	13.3	258	263	121	88
Boston-Worcester-Lawrence, MA-NH-ME-CT CMSA	5,447	4,450	997	18.3	409	313	476	166
Chicago-Gary-Kenosha, IL-IN-WI CMSA	8,482	6,366	2,116	24.9	1,015	1,210	607	226
Cincinnati-Hamilton, OH-KY-IN CMSA	1,840	1,755	86	4.6	29	30	35	15
Cleveland-Akron, OH CMSA	2,753	2,517	236	8.6	87	71	118	24
Dallas-Fort Worth, TX CMSA	4,806	3,643	1,164	24.2	593	894	106	130
Denver-Boulder-Greeley, CO CMSA	2,399	1,989	410	17.1	198	282	66	50
Detroit-Ann Arbor-Flint, MI CMSA	5,078	4,555	523	10.3	200	120	220	73
Houston-Galveston-Brazoria, TX CMSA	4,297	2,925	1,372	31.9	665	1,074	117	148
Kansas City, MO-KS MSA	1,648	1,523	125	7.6	55	70	30	20
Los Angeles-Riverside-Orange County, CA CMSA	15,116	8,035	7,080	46.8	3,708	5,007	646	1,292
Miami-Fort Lauderdale, FL CMSA	3,629	1,759	1,870	51.5	905	1,497	313	35
Minneapolis-St. Paul, MN-WI MSA	2,757	2,477	280	10.2	127	88	71	90
New York-Northern New Jersey-Long Island, NY-NJ-CT-PA CMSA	19,775	13,154	6,622	33.5	3,076	3,271	2,159	890
Philadelphia-Wilmington-Atlantic City, PA-NJ-DE-MD CMSA	5,791	5,070	721	12.4	294	302	256	131
Phoenix-Mesa, AZ MSA	3,000	2,274	726	24.2	344	577	73	46
Pittsburgh, PA MSA	2,228	2,112	116	5.2	35	26	69	16
Portland-Salem, OR-WA CMSA	2,105	1,791	314	14.9	160	154	78	71
Sacramento-Yolo, CA CMSA	1,674	1,307	367	21.9	173	168	84	108
St. Louis, MO-IL MSA	2,430	2,301	129	5.3	49	43	55	24
San Diego, CA MSA	2,618	1,753	865	33.0	392	574	80	186
San Francisco-Oakland-San Jose, CA CMSA	6,592	4,223	2,368	35.9	1,139	995	385	931
Seattle-Tacoma-Bremerton, WA CMSA	3,325	2,838	486	14.6	212	125	124	214
Tampa-St. Petersburg-Clearwater, FL MSA	2,260	1,915	345	15.3	136	209	94	31
Washington-Baltimore, DC-MD-VA-WV CMSA	7,093	5,934	1,159	16.3	483	469	327	256

[1] Includes other language groups not shown separately.
Source: U.S. Census Bureau, 2000 Census of Population and Housing, *Profiles of General Demographic Characteristics;* <http://www.census.gov/Press-Release/www/2002/demoprofiles.html>.

No. 60. Language Spoken at Home by Resident Population—25 Largest Cities: 2000

[In thousands except percent (610 represents 610,000). As of April. See headnote, Table 58]

City	Population 5 years and over	English only	Language other than English, total [1]			Spanish	Other Indo-European languages	Asian and Pacific Island languages
			Number	Percent of population 5 years and over	Speak English less than "very well"			
Austin, TX	610	420	190	31.1	85	149	17	21
Baltimore, MD	609	562	47	7.8	18	18	18	7
Boston, MA	557	371	186	33.4	91	76	68	35
Chicago, IL	2,679	1,727	952	35.5	494	625	213	83
Columbus, OH	659	593	66	10.0	28	19	19	17
Dallas, TX	1,090	686	404	37.1	237	348	23	22
Denver, CO	517	378	139	27.0	75	109	15	11
Detroit, MI	875	795	80	9.2	38	43	18	6
El Paso, TX	517	148	369	71.3	159	357	7	4
Houston, TX	1,795	1,053	742	41.3	395	597	54	71
Indianapolis, IN [2]	725	672	53	7.3	25	30	14	6
Jacksonville, FL	682	617	65	9.5	23	28	18	14
Los Angeles, CA	3,413	1,439	1,974	57.8	1,113	1,422	225	278
Memphis, TN	600	558	42	7.0	20	23	9	7
Milwaukee, WI	550	462	87	15.9	42	55	16	13
Nashville-Davidson, TN [2]	509	458	51	10.1	25	26	13	8
New York, NY	7,476	3,921	3,555	47.6	1,769	1,832	1,046	515
Philadelphia, PA	1,420	1,168	252	17.7	114	110	79	50
Phoenix, AZ	1,207	819	388	32.2	206	326	30	17
San Antonio, TX	1,053	561	492	46.7	171	463	14	12
San Diego, CA	1,142	714	427	37.4	199	244	44	126
San Francisco, CA	746	405	341	45.7	186	90	50	195
San Jose, CA	826	403	423	51.2	222	187	49	178
Seattle, WA	538	429	108	20.2	50	22	21	56
Washington, DC	540	449	90	16.8	38	49	24	9

[1] Includes other language groups not shown separately. [2] Represents the portion of a consolidated city that is not within one or more separately incorporated places.
Source: U.S. Census Bureau, 2000 Census of Population and Housing, *Profiles of General Demographic Characteristics;* <http://www.census.gov/Press-Release/www/2002/demoprofiles.html>.

No. 61. Marital Status of the Population by Sex, Race, and Hispanic Origin: 1990 to 2002

[In millions, except percent (181.8 represents 181,800,000). As of March. Persons 18 years old and over. Excludes members of Armed Forces except those living off post or with their families on post. Beginning 2001 population controls based on Census 2000 and an expanded sample of households. Based on Current Population Survey, see text, this section, and Appendix III]

Marital status, race, and Hispanic origin	Total 1990	Total 1995	Total 2000	Total 2002	Male 1990	Male 1995	Male 2000	Male 2002	Female 1990	Female 1995	Female 2000	Female 2002
Total [1]	181.8	191.6	201.8	209.3	86.9	92.0	96.9	100.6	95.0	99.6	104.9	108.7
Never married	40.4	43.9	48.2	51.1	22.4	24.6	26.1	28.1	17.9	19.3	22.1	23.0
Married	112.6	116.7	120.1	123.2	55.8	57.7	59.6	61.2	56.7	58.9	60.4	62.0
Widowed	13.8	13.4	13.7	14.0	2.3	2.3	2.6	2.6	11.5	11.1	11.1	11.4
Divorced	15.1	17.6	19.8	20.9	6.3	7.4	8.5	8.7	8.8	10.3	11.3	12.2
Percent of total	100.0	100.0	100.0	100.0	100.0	100.0	100.0	100.0	100.0	100.0	100.0	100.0
Never married	22.2	22.9	23.9	24.4	25.8	26.8	27.0	27.9	18.9	19.4	21.1	21.2
Married	61.9	60.9	59.5	58.9	64.3	62.7	61.5	60.9	59.7	59.2	57.6	57.1
Widowed	7.6	7.0	6.8	6.7	2.7	2.5	2.7	2.6	12.1	11.1	10.5	10.5
Divorced	8.3	9.2	9.8	10.0	7.2	8.0	8.8	8.6	9.3	10.3	10.8	11.3
White, total	155.5	161.3	168.1	173.5	74.8	78.1	81.6	84.3	80.6	83.2	86.6	89.1
Never married	31.6	33.2	36.0	38.4	18.0	19.2	20.3	21.9	13.6	14.0	15.7	16.5
Married	99.5	102.0	104.1	105.9	49.5	50.6	51.8	52.9	49.9	51.3	52.2	53.1
Widowed	11.7	11.3	11.5	11.8	1.9	1.9	2.2	2.2	9.8	9.4	9.3	9.6
Divorced	12.6	14.8	16.5	17.4	5.4	6.3	7.2	7.4	7.3	8.4	9.3	9.9
Percent of total	100.0	100.0	100.0	100.0	100.0	100.0	100.0	100.0	100.0	100.0	100.0	100.0
Never married	20.3	20.6	21.4	22.1	24.1	24.6	24.9	25.9	16.9	16.9	18.1	18.5
Married	64.0	63.2	62.0	61.1	66.2	64.9	63.5	62.7	61.9	61.7	60.3	59.5
Widowed	7.5	7.0	6.8	6.8	2.6	2.5	2.7	2.6	12.2	11.3	10.8	10.8
Divorced	8.1	9.1	9.8	10.0	7.2	8.1	8.8	8.8	9.0	10.1	10.7	11.2
Black, total	20.3	22.1	24.0	24.3	9.1	9.9	10.7	10.8	11.2	12.2	13.3	13.5
Never married	7.1	8.5	9.5	9.5	3.5	4.1	4.3	4.3	3.6	4.4	5.1	5.2
Married	9.3	9.6	10.1	10.4	4.5	4.6	5.0	5.1	4.8	4.9	5.1	5.2
Widowed	1.7	1.7	1.7	1.7	0.3	0.3	0.3	0.3	1.4	1.4	1.4	1.4
Divorced	2.1	2.4	2.8	2.7	0.8	0.8	1.1	1.0	1.3	1.5	1.7	1.7
Percent of total	100.0	100.0	100.0	100.0	100.0	100.0	100.0	100.0	100.0	100.0	100.0	100.0
Never married	35.1	38.4	39.4	39.2	38.4	41.7	40.2	40.4	32.5	35.8	38.3	38.2
Married	45.8	43.2	42.1	42.8	49.2	46.7	46.7	47.7	43.0	40.4	38.3	38.9
Widowed	8.5	7.6	7.0	6.9	3.7	3.1	2.8	3.0	12.4	11.3	10.5	10.0
Divorced	10.6	10.7	11.5	11.2	8.8	8.5	10.3	8.9	12.0	12.5	12.8	12.9
Hispanic, [2] **total**	13.6	17.6	21.1	24.5	6.7	8.8	10.4	12.5	6.8	8.8	10.7	12.0
Never married	3.7	5.0	5.9	7.8	2.2	3.0	3.4	4.7	1.5	2.1	2.5	3.1
Married	8.4	10.4	12.7	14.1	4.1	5.1	6.2	6.9	4.3	5.3	6.5	7.2
Widowed	0.5	0.7	0.9	0.9	0.1	0.2	0.2	0.1	0.4	0.6	0.7	0.7
Divorced	1.0	1.4	1.6	1.7	0.4	0.6	0.7	0.7	0.6	0.8	1.0	1.0
Percent of total	100.0	100.0	100.0	100.0	100.0	100.0	100.0	100.0	100.0	100.0	100.0	100.0
Never married	27.2	28.6	28.0	31.8	32.1	33.8	32.3	37.5	22.5	23.5	23.4	25.8
Married	61.7	59.3	60.2	57.6	60.9	57.9	59.7	55.6	62.4	60.7	60.7	59.6
Widowed	4.0	4.2	4.2	3.6	1.5	1.8	1.6	1.2	6.5	6.6	6.5	6.0
Divorced	7.0	7.9	7.6	7.0	5.5	6.6	6.4	5.6	8.5	9.2	9.3	8.5

[1] Includes persons of other races, not shown separately.   [2] Hispanic persons may be of any race.

Source: U.S. Census Bureau, Current Population Reports, P20-547, and earlier reports; and unpublished data.

No. 62. Married Couples by Race and Hispanic Origin of Spouses: 1980 to 2002

[In thousands (49,714 represents 49,714,000). As of March. Persons 15 years old and over. Persons of Hispanic origin may be of any race. Based on Current Population Survey; see headnote, Table 61, and Appendix III]

Race and origin of spouses	1980	1990	1995	2000	2002
Married couples, total [1]	49,714	53,256	54,937	56,497	57,919
Interracial married couples, total [2]	651	964	1,392	1,464	1,674
Black/White	167	211	328	363	395
Black husband/White wife	122	150	206	268	279
White husband/Black wife	45	61	122	95	116
White/other race [3]	450	720	988	1,051	1,222
Black/other race [3]	34	33	76	50	57
HISPANIC ORIGIN					
Hispanic/Hispanic	1,906	3,085	3,857	4,739	5,246
Hispanic/other origin (not Hispanic)	891	1,193	1,434	1,743	1,940
All other couples (not of Hispanic origin)	46,917	48,979	49,646	50,015	50,733

[1] Includes other married couples not shown separately.   [2] Interracial married couples with at least one spouse of White or Black race.   [3] "Other race," is any race other than White or Black, such as American Indian, Japanese, Chinese, etc. This total excludes combinations of other races by other races.

Source: U.S. Census Bureau, "Table MS-3. Interracial Married Couples: 1980 to Present"; published 12 June 2003; <http://www.census.gov/population/www/socdemo/hh-fam.html>; and unpublished data.

No. 63. Marital Status of the Population by Sex and Age: 2002

[As of March (100,611 represents 100,611,000). See headnote, Table 61]

Sex and age	Number of persons (1,000)					Percent distribution				
	Total	Never married	Married	Widowed	Divorced	Total	Never married	Married	Widowed	Divorced
Male	100,611	28,107	61,212	2,632	8,659	100.0	27.9	60.9	2.6	8.6
18 to 19 years old	4,026	3,943	76	-	7	100.0	97.9	1.9	-	-
20 to 24 years old	9,670	8,261	1,350	3	56	100.0	85.4	13.9	-	0.6
25 to 29 years old	9,141	4,904	3,875	7	356	100.0	53.7	42.4	0.1	3.9
30 to 34 years old	10,079	3,429	6,012	15	623	100.0	34.0	59.7	0.1	6.2
35 to 39 years old	10,693	2,255	7,315	32	1,094	100.0	21.1	68.4	0.3	10.2
40 to 44 years old	11,109	1,852	7,909	66	1,284	100.0	16.7	71.2	0.6	11.6
45 to 54 years old	19,302	2,113	14,219	215	2,755	100.0	10.9	73.7	1.1	14.3
55 to 64 years old	12,363	818	9,688	318	1,538	100.0	6.6	78.3	2.6	12.4
65 to 74 years old	8,243	304	6,561	706	672	100.0	3.7	79.6	8.6	8.1
75 years old and over	5,984	228	4,210	1,271	275	100.0	3.8	70.4	21.2	4.6
Female	108,712	23,036	62,037	11,404	12,236	100.0	21.2	57.1	10.5	11.3
18 to 19 years old	3,880	3,640	222	2	16	100.0	93.8	5.8	-	0.4
20 to 24 years old	9,722	7,195	2,354	8	164	100.0	74.0	24.3	0.1	1.7
25 to 29 years old	9,158	3,700	4,901	33	524	100.0	40.4	53.5	0.4	5.7
30 to 34 years old	10,270	2,362	6,888	75	946	100.0	23.0	67.1	0.7	9.2
35 to 39 years old	10,947	1,613	7,831	102	1,402	100.0	14.7	71.5	0.9	12.8
40 to 44 years old	11,506	1,320	8,295	215	1,677	100.0	11.5	72.1	1.9	14.6
45 to 54 years old	20,209	1,799	14,172	672	3,566	100.0	8.9	70.1	3.3	17.6
55 to 64 years old	13,497	715	8,992	1,407	2,384	100.0	5.3	66.7	10.4	17.7
65 to 74 years old	9,876	346	5,457	3,018	1,053	100.0	3.5	55.3	30.6	10.7
75 years old and over	9,647	347	2,922	5,872	506	100.0	3.6	30.3	60.9	5.2

- Represents or rounds to zero.

No. 64. Living Arrangements of Persons 15 Years Old and Over by Selected Characteristics: 2002

[In thousands (221,459 represents 221,459,000). As of March. See headnote, Table 61]

Living arrangement	Total	15 to 19 years old	20 to 24 years old	25 to 34 years old	35 to 44 years old	45 to 54 years old	55 to 64 years old	65 to 74 years old	75 years old and over
Total [1]	221,459	20,042	19,391	38,648	44,256	39,511	25,859	18,118	15,632
Alone	28,775	137	1,155	3,923	4,103	4,744	4,248	4,279	6,187
With spouse	118,764	330	3,503	20,662	29,968	27,317	18,139	11,795	7,047
With other persons	73,920	19,575	14,733	14,063	10,185	7,450	3,472	2,044	2,398
White	182,997	15,755	15,380	30,887	36,133	32,885	22,186	15,666	14,106
Alone	23,839	111	867	3,057	3,213	3,737	3,523	3,655	5,677
With spouse	102,912	275	3,044	17,431	25,435	23,608	16,096	10,514	6,509
With other persons	56,246	15,369	11,469	10,399	7,485	5,540	2,567	1,497	1,920
Black	26,137	3,037	2,772	5,030	5,491	4,462	2,495	1,761	1,091
Alone	3,873	15	207	565	689	835	615	520	426
With spouse	9,162	40	282	1,807	2,597	2,051	1,196	859	332
With other persons	13,102	2,982	2,283	2,658	2,205	1,576	684	382	333
Hispanic origin [2]	26,332	3,122	3,557	6,902	5,432	3,393	1,939	1,175	722
Alone	1,385	14	76	283	229	223	192	189	180
With spouse	13,278	116	896	3,938	3,674	2,309	1,318	702	326
With other persons	11,669	2,992	2,585	2,771	1,529	861	429	284	216

[1] Includes other races and persons not of Hispanic origin, not shown separately. [2] Persons of Hispanic origin may be of any race.

No. 65. Households and Persons Per Household by Type of Household: 1990 to 2002

[As of March (93,347 represents 93,347,000). See headnote, Table 61]

Type of household	Households Number (1,000) 1990	2000	2002	Percent distribution 1990	2002	Persons per household 1990	2000	2002
Total households	93,347	104,705	109,297	100	100	2.63	2.62	2.58
Family households	66,090	72,025	74,329	71	68	3.22	3.24	3.21
Married couple family	52,317	55,311	56,747	56	52	3.25	3.26	3.23
Male householder, no spouse present	2,884	4,028	4,438	3	4	3.04	3.16	3.12
Female householder, no spouse present	10,890	12,687	13,143	12	12	3.10	3.17	3.14
Nonfamily households	27,257	32,680	34,969	29	32	1.22	1.25	1.25
Living alone	22,999	26,724	28,775	25	26	1.00	1.00	1.00
Male householder	11,606	14,641	15,579	12	14	1.33	1.34	1.34
Living alone	9,049	11,181	12,004	10	11	1.00	1.00	1.00
Female householder	15,651	18,039	19,390	17	18	1.14	1.17	1.17
Living alone	13,950	15,543	16,771	15	15	1.00	1.00	1.00

Source of Tables 63-65: U.S. Census Bureau, Current Population Reports, P20-547, and earlier reports; and unpublished data.

No. 66. Households, Families, Subfamilies, and Married Couples: 1980 to 2002

[In thousands, except as indicated (80,776 represents 80,776,000). As of March. Excludes members of Armed Forces except those living off post or with their families on post. Beginning 2001 population controls based on Census 2000 and an expanded sample of households. Based on Current Population Survey, see text, this section, and Appendix III. Minus sign (-) indicates decrease]

Type of unit	1980	1985	1990	1995	2000	2001	2002	Percent change 1980-1990	1990-2000	2000-2002
Households	80,776	86,789	93,347	98,990	104,705	108,209	109,297	16	12	5
Average size	2.76	2.69	2.63	2.65	2.62	2.58	2.58	(X)	(X)	(X)
Family households	59,550	62,706	66,090	69,305	72,025	73,767	74,329	11	9	3
Married couple	49,112	50,350	52,317	53,858	55,311	56,592	56,747	7	6	3
Male householder [1]	1,733	2,228	2,884	3,226	4,028	4,275	4,438	66	40	10
Female householder [1]	8,705	10,129	10,890	12,220	12,687	12,900	13,143	25	17	4
Nonfamily households	21,226	24,082	27,257	29,686	32,680	34,442	34,969	28	20	7
Male householder	8,807	10,114	11,606	13,190	14,641	15,345	15,579	32	26	6
Female householder	12,419	13,968	15,651	16,496	18,039	19,097	19,390	26	15	7
One person	18,296	20,602	22,999	24,732	26,724	28,207	28,775	26	16	8
Families	59,550	62,706	66,090	69,305	72,025	73,767	74,329	11	9	3
Average size	3.29	3.23	3.17	3.19	3.17	3.14	3.15	(X)	(X)	(X)
With own children [2]	31,022	31,112	32,289	34,296	34,605	35,355	35,705	4	7	3
Without own children [2]	28,528	31,594	33,801	35,009	37,420	38,412	38,623	18	11	3
Married couple	49,112	50,350	52,317	53,858	55,311	56,592	56,747	7	6	3
With own children [2]	24,961	24,210	24,537	25,241	25,248	25,980	25,792	-2	3	2
Without own children [2]	24,151	26,140	27,780	28,617	30,062	30,612	30,955	15	8	3
Male householder [1]	1,733	2,228	2,884	3,226	4,028	4,275	4,438	66	40	10
With own children [2]	616	896	1,153	1,440	1,786	1,836	1,903	87	55	7
Without own children [2]	1,117	1,332	1,731	1,786	2,242	2,438	2,535	55	30	13
Female householder [1]	8,705	10,129	10,890	12,220	12,687	12,900	13,143	25	17	4
With own children [2]	5,445	6,006	6,599	7,615	7,571	7,538	8,010	21	15	6
Without own children [2]	3,261	4,123	4,290	4,606	5,116	5,362	5,133	32	19	(Z)
Unrelated subfamilies	360	526	534	674	571	568	474	48	7	-17
Married couple	20	46	68	64	37	44	43	(B)	(B)	(B)
Male reference persons [1]	36	85	45	59	57	70	59	(B)	(B)	(B)
Female reference persons [1]	304	395	421	550	477	455	371	39	13	-22
Related subfamilies	1,150	2,228	2,403	2,878	2,984	3,118	2,986	109	24	(Z)
Married couple	582	719	871	1,015	1,149	1,202	1,129	50	32	-2
Father-child [1]	54	116	153	195	201	251	269	(B)	31	34
Mother-child [1]	512	1,392	1,378	1,668	1,634	1,665	1,588	169	19	-3
Married couples	49,714	51,114	53,256	54,937	56,497	57,838	57,919	7	6	3
With own household	49,112	50,350	52,317	53,858	55,311	56,592	56,747	7	6	3
Without own household	602	764	939	1,079	1,186	1,246	1,172	56	26	-1
Percent without	1.2	1.5	1.8	2.0	2.1	2.2	2.0	(X)	(X)	(X)

B Not shown; base less than 75,000.   X Not applicable.   Z Less than 0.5 percent.   [1] No spouse present: [2] Under 18 years old.

Source: U.S. Census Bureau, Current Population Reports, P20-547, and earlier reports.

No. 67. Households by Age of Householder and Size of Household: 1980 to 2002

[In millions (80.8 represents 80,800,000). As of March. Based on Current Population Survey; see headnote, Table 66]

Age of householder and size of household	1980	1990	1995	2000	2001	2002 Total [1]	White	Black	Hispanic [2]
Total	80.8	93.3	99.0	104.7	108.2	109.3	90.7	13.3	10.5
Age of householder:									
15 to 24 years old	6.6	5.1	5.4	5.9	6.4	6.4	4.9	1.1	1.0
25 to 29 years old	9.3	9.4	8.4	8.5	8.5	8.4	6.7	1.2	1.4
30 to 34 years old	9.3	11.0	11.1	10.1	10.5	10.6	8.4	1.5	1.6
35 to 44 years old	14.0	20.6	22.9	24.0	24.0	24.0	19.5	3.2	2.7
45 to 54 years old	12.7	14.5	17.6	20.9	22.0	22.2	18.3	2.7	1.7
55 to 64 years old	12.5	12.5	12.2	13.6	14.3	15.2	13.0	1.6	1.0
65 to 74 years old	10.1	11.7	11.8	11.3	11.5	11.5	9.9	1.2	0.7
75 years old and over	6.4	8.4	9.6	10.4	11.0	11.0	10.0	0.8	0.4
One person	18.3	23.0	24.7	26.7	28.2	28.8	23.8	3.9	1.4
Male	7.0	9.0	10.1	11.2	11.6	12.0	9.9	1.6	0.7
Female	11.3	14.0	14.6	15.5	16.6	16.8	14.0	2.3	0.7
Two persons	25.3	30.1	31.8	34.7	35.9	36.2	31.2	3.6	2.3
Three persons	14.1	16.1	16.8	17.2	17.4	17.7	14.2	2.4	2.1
Four persons	12.7	14.5	15.3	15.3	15.7	15.8	12.9	1.9	2.2
Five persons	6.1	6.2	6.6	7.0	7.0	6.9	5.6	0.9	1.3
Six persons	2.5	2.1	2.3	2.4	2.6	2.4	1.9	0.4	0.6
Seven persons or more	1.8	1.3	1.4	1.4	1.4	1.4	1.0	0.2	0.5

[1] Includes other races, not shown separately.   [2] Hispanic persons may be of any race.

Source: U.S. Census Bureau, Current Population Reports, P20-547, and earlier reports; and unpublished data.

No. 68. Households—States: 2000

[As of April (105,480 represents 105,480,000). For definitions of household and family, see text, this section. See Appendix III]

State	Households (1,000)									Average household size
	Family households							Nonfamily households		
	Total [1]		Married couple		Female family householder [2]			House- holder living alone	
	Total	Total	With own children under 18 years	Total	With own children under 18 years	Total	With own children under 18 years	Total		
U.S.	105,480	71,787	34,588	54,493	24,836	12,900	7,562	33,693	27,230	2.59
AL	1,737	1,216	561	907	391	246	141	521	454	2.49
AK	222	152	88	116	63	24	17	69	52	2.74
AZ	1,901	1,287	608	986	429	211	130	614	472	2.64
AR	1,043	732	335	566	237	127	77	310	267	2.49
CA	11,503	7,920	4,117	5,877	2,990	1,449	835	3,583	2,708	2.87
CO	1,658	1,084	544	859	405	159	102	574	436	2.53
CT	1,302	881	419	676	307	157	91	421	344	2.53
DE	299	205	95	153	66	39	23	94	75	2.54
DC	248	114	49	57	21	47	25	134	109	2.16
FL	6,338	4,211	1,780	3,192	1,215	759	438	2,127	1,687	2.46
GA	3,006	2,112	1,051	1,549	733	435	258	895	711	2.65
HI	403	287	129	216	97	50	24	116	88	2.92
ID	470	336	170	277	132	41	27	134	105	2.69
IL	4,592	3,106	1,515	2,354	1,114	564	316	1,486	1,230	2.63
IN	2,336	1,603	768	1,251	556	259	160	734	605	2.53
IA	1,149	770	361	633	275	98	64	380	313	2.46
KS	1,038	702	345	568	261	97	63	336	280	2.51
KY	1,591	1,104	516	858	375	188	111	486	414	2.47
LA	1,656	1,156	572	809	374	275	162	500	419	2.62
ME	518	341	157	272	113	49	32	178	140	2.39
MD	1,981	1,359	662	995	461	280	159	622	495	2.61
MA	2,444	1,577	749	1,198	548	290	164	867	684	2.51
MI	3,786	2,576	1,237	1,948	873	474	284	1,210	994	2.56
MN	1,895	1,255	626	1,018	478	169	111	640	509	2.52
MS	1,046	747	363	521	234	181	106	299	258	2.63
MO	2,195	1,477	700	1,141	497	254	157	718	600	2.48
MT	359	237	112	192	82	32	21	121	98	2.45
NE	666	443	218	361	166	60	40	223	184	2.49
NV	751	498	239	373	166	83	51	253	187	2.62
NH	475	324	158	262	120	43	27	151	116	2.53
NJ	3,065	2,155	1,026	1,638	776	387	197	910	751	2.68
NM	678	467	235	342	158	90	56	211	172	2.63
NY	7,057	4,639	2,231	3,290	1,527	1,038	573	2,417	1,983	2.61
NC	3,132	2,159	996	1,645	708	390	227	973	795	2.49
ND	257	166	80	137	62	20	14	91	75	2.41
OH	4,446	2,993	1,410	2,286	996	537	323	1,453	1,216	2.49
OK	1,342	922	435	718	312	153	94	421	359	2.49
OR	1,334	878	411	693	296	131	83	456	348	2.51
PA	4,777	3,208	1,431	2,468	1,043	555	298	1,569	1,321	2.48
RI	408	265	125	197	86	53	32	143	117	2.47
SC	1,534	1,073	495	783	334	227	131	461	383	2.53
SD	290	194	95	157	71	26	18	96	80	2.50
TN	2,233	1,548	707	1,174	499	288	166	685	576	2.48
TX	7,393	5,248	2,723	3,990	2,002	938	564	2,146	1,752	2.74
UT	701	535	300	443	246	66	40	166	125	3.13
VT	241	158	76	126	56	22	15	83	63	2.44
VA	2,699	1,848	882	1,426	646	320	187	851	677	2.54
WA	2,271	1,499	742	1,182	542	225	147	772	594	2.53
WV	736	504	213	397	157	79	42	232	200	2.40
WI	2,085	1,387	665	1,109	494	200	129	698	558	2.50
WY	194	130	63	106	47	17	12	63	51	2.48

[1] Includes male family householders with no spouse present, not shown separately. [2] No spouse present.

Source: U.S. Census Bureau, 2000 Census of Population and Housing, *Profiles of General Demographic Characteristics.*

No. 69. Unmarried-Partner Households by Sex of Partners: 2000

[As of April. See headnote, Table 68]

Item	Number
Total households	105,480,101
Unmarried-partner households	5,475,768
Male householder and male partner	301,026
Male householder and female partner	2,615,119
Female householder and female partner	293,365
Female householder and male partner	2,266,258
All other households	100,004,333

Source: U.S. Census Bureau, American FactFinder, PCT14. Unmarried-Partner Households by Sex of Partners; Census 2000 Summary File 1 (SF 1) 100-Percent Data.

No. 70. Family Groups With Children Under 18 Years Old by Race and Hispanic Origin: 1980 to 2002

[In thousands. As of March (32,150 represents 32,150,000). Family groups comprise family households, related subfamilies, and unrelated subfamilies. Excludes members of Armed Forces except those living off post or with their families on post. Beginning 2002 population controls based on Census 2000 and an expanded sample of households. Based on Current Population Survey, see text, this section, and Appendix III]

Race and Hispanic origin of householder or reference person	1980	1990	2000	2002 Total	2002 Family households	2002 Subfamilies Total	2002 Related	2002 Unrelated
All races, total [1]	32,150	34,670	37,496	38,472	35,705	2,767	2,321	446
Two-parent family groups	25,231	24,921	25,771	26,271	25,792	480	465	15
One-parent family groups	6,920	9,749	11,725	12,201	9,913	2,287	1,857	430
Maintained by mother	6,230	8,398	9,681	9,969	8,010	1,959	1,588	371
Maintained by father	690	1,351	2,044	2,232	1,903	328	269	59
White, total	27,294	28,294	30,079	30,550	28,537	2,013	1,638	375
Two-parent family groups	22,628	21,905	22,241	22,381	21,978	403	391	12
One-parent family groups	4,664	6,389	7,838	8,169	6,559	1,609	1,247	362
Maintained by mother	4,122	5,310	6,216	6,423	5,052	1,371	1,060	311
Maintained by father	542	1,079	1,622	1,746	1,507	238	187	51
Black, total	4,074	5,087	5,530	5,635	5,065	569	524	45
Two-parent family groups	1,961	2,006	2,135	2,179	2,148	31	30	1
One-parent family groups	2,114	3,081	3,396	3,456	2,917	539	495	44
Maintained by mother	1,984	2,860	3,060	3,067	2,593	474	437	37
Maintained by father	129	221	335	389	324	65	58	7
Hispanic, total [2]	2,194	3,429	5,503	6,050	5,343	707	633	74
Two-parent family groups	1,626	2,289	3,625	3,936	3,754	181	173	8
One-parent family groups	568	1,140	1,877	2,114	1,589	525	459	66
Maintained by mother	526	1,003	1,565	1,704	1,259	445	389	56
Maintained by father	42	138	313	410	330	80	70	10

[1] Includes other races, not shown separately. [2] Hispanic persons may be of any race.

Source: U.S. Census Bureau, Current Population Reports, P20-547, and earlier reports; and unpublished data.

No. 71. Families by Number of Own Children Under 18 Years Old: 1980 to 2002

[As of March (59,550 represents 59,550,000). Based on Current Population Survey; see headnote, Table 70]

Race, Hispanic origin, and year	Number of families (1,000) Total	No children	One child	Two children	Three or more children	Percent distribution Total	No children	One child	Two children	Three or more children
ALL FAMILIES [1]										
1980	59,550	28,528	12,443	11,470	7,109	100	48	21	19	12
1990	66,090	33,801	13,530	12,263	6,496	100	51	20	19	10
2000	72,025	37,420	14,311	13,215	7,080	100	52	20	18	10
2002	74,329	38,623	14,961	13,559	7,185	100	52	20	18	10
Married couple	56,747	30,955	9,832	10,440	5,519	100	55	17	18	10
Male householder [2]	4,438	2,535	1,162	538	202	100	57	26	12	5
Female householder [2]	13,143	5,133	3,967	2,580	1,463	100	39	30	20	11
WHITE FAMILIES										
1980	52,243	25,769	10,727	9,977	5,769	100	49	21	19	11
1990	56,590	29,872	11,186	10,342	5,191	100	53	20	18	9
2000	60,251	32,144	11,496	10,918	5,693	100	53	19	18	9
2002	61,638	33,101	11,754	11,106	5,677	100	54	19	18	9
Married couple	49,605	27,628	8,298	8,977	4,703	100	56	17	18	9
Male householder [2]	3,394	1,886	908	442	157	100	56	27	13	5
Female householder [2]	8,639	3,587	2,548	1,687	817	100	41	29	19	9
BLACK FAMILIES										
1980	6,184	2,364	1,449	1,235	1,136	100	38	23	20	18
1990	7,470	3,093	1,894	1,433	1,049	100	41	25	19	14
2000	8,664	3,882	2,101	1,624	1,058	100	45	24	19	12
2002	8,844	3,779	2,263	1,681	1,121	100	43	26	19	13
Married couple	4,233	2,085	829	811	507	100	49	20	19	12
Male householder [2]	773	449	205	83	36	100	58	27	11	5
Female householder [2]	3,838	1,245	1,229	787	577	100	32	32	21	15
HISPANIC FAMILIES [3]										
1980	3,029	946	680	698	706	100	31	22	23	23
1990	4,840	1,790	1,095	1,036	919	100	37	23	21	19
2000	7,561	2,747	1,791	1,693	1,330	100	36	24	22	18
2002	8,516	3,173	1,913	1,941	1,488	100	37	22	23	17
Married couple	5,778	2,023	1,190	1,461	1,104	100	35	21	25	19
Male householder [2]	817	487	191	95	43	100	60	23	12	5
Female householder [2]	1,922	663	533	385	341	100	34	28	20	18

[1] Includes other races, not shown separately. [2] No spouse present. [3] Hispanic persons may be of any race.

Source: U.S. Census Bureau, Current Population Reports, P20-547, and earlier reports; and unpublished data.

No. 72. Families by Size and Presence of Children: 1980 to 2002

[In thousands, except as indicated (59,550 represents 59,550,000). As of March. Excludes members of Armed Forces except those living off post or with their families on post. Beginning 2002 population controls based on Census 2000 and an expanded sample of households. Based on Current Population Survey, see text, this section, and Appendix III]

Characteristic	Number					Percent distribution				
	1980	1990	1995	2000	2002	1980	1990	1995	2000	2002
Total............	59,550	66,090	69,305	72,025	74,329	100	100	100	100	100
Size of family:										
Two persons.........	23,461	27,606	29,176	31,455	32,842	39	42	42	44	44
Three persons........	13,603	15,353	15,903	16,073	16,569	23	23	23	22	22
Four persons.........	12,372	14,026	14,624	14,496	14,977	21	21	21	20	20
Five persons.........	5,930	5,938	6,283	6,526	6,549	10	9	9	9	9
Six persons..........	2,461	1,997	2,106	2,226	2,194	4	3	3	3	3
Seven or more persons..	1,723	1,170	1,213	1,249	1,197	3	2	2	2	2
Average per family.....	3.29	3.17	3.19	3.17	3.15	(X)	(X)	(X)	(X)	(X)
Own children under age 18:										
None................	28,528	33,801	35,009	37,420	38,623	48	51	51	52	52
One.................	12,443	13,530	14,088	14,311	14,961	21	20	20	20	20
Two.................	11,470	12,263	13,213	13,215	13,559	19	19	19	18	18
Three...............	4,674	4,650	5,044	5,063	5,300	8	7	7	7	7
Four or more.........	2,435	1,846	1,951	2,017	1,885	4	3	3	3	3
Own children under age 6:										
None................	46,063	50,905	53,695	57,039	58,952	77	77	77	79	79
One.................	9,441	10,304	10,733	10,454	10,760	16	16	15	15	14
Two or more.........	4,047	4,882	4,876	4,533	4,617	7	7	7	6	6

X Not applicable.

Source: U.S. Census Bureau, Current Population Reports, P20-547, and earlier reports; and unpublished data.

No. 73. Families by Type, Race, and Hispanic Origin: 2002

[In thousands, except as indicated (74,329 represents 74,329,000). As of March. Excludes members of Armed Forces except those living off post or with their families on post. Population controls based on Census 2000 and an expanded sample of households. Based on Current Population Survey, see text, this section, and Appendix III]

Characteristic	All families	Married couple families				Female family householder [3]				Male family householder,[3] all races
		All races [1]	White	Black	Hispanic [2]	All races [1]	White	Black	Hispanic [2]	
All families...........	74,329	56,747	49,605	4,233	5,778	13,143	8,639	3,838	1,922	4,438
Age of householder:										
Under 25 years old........	3,618	1,535	1,314	141	353	1,359	777	498	251	724
25 to 34 years old........	13,214	9,385	8,015	769	1,662	2,854	1,691	1,029	506	976
35 to 44 years old........	18,818	14,178	12,170	1,171	1,630	3,596	2,371	1,040	539	1,045
45 to 54 years old........	16,540	13,137	11,406	970	1,046	2,530	1,753	650	322	873
55 to 64 years old........	10,500	8,922	7,970	577	590	1,188	817	315	161	389
65 to 74 years old........	6,947	5,923	5,330	432	332	807	577	179	92	217
75 years old and over.....	4,691	3,668	3,401	174	165	810	653	128	51	214
Without own children under 18..	38,623	30,955	27,628	2,085	2,023	5,133	3,587	1,245	663	2,535
With own children under 18....	35,705	25,792	21,978	2,148	3,754	8,010	5,052	2,593	1,259	1,903
One own child under 18....	14,961	9,832	8,298	829	1,190	3,967	2,548	1,229	533	1,162
Two own children under 18..	13,559	10,440	8,977	811	1,461	2,580	1,687	787	385	538
Three or more own children under 18.............	7,185	5,519	4,703	507	1,104	1,463	817	577	341	202
Average per family with own children under 18.....	1.83	1.89	1.88	2.06	2.13	1.72	1.62	1.89	1.99	1.50
Marital status of householder:										
Married, spouse present....	56,747	56,747	49,605	4,233	5,778	(X)	(X)	(X)	(X)	(X)
Married, spouse absent.....	2,583	(X)	(X)	(X)	(X)	1,995	1,291	575	479	588
Separated.............	1,880	(X)	(X)	(X)	(X)	1,515	993	443	351	365
Other.................	703	(X)	(X)	(X)	(X)	480	298	132	128	223
Widowed..............	2,575	(X)	(X)	(X)	(X)	2,147	1,616	421	224	428
Divorced..............	6,051	(X)	(X)	(X)	(X)	4,639	3,590	824	486	1,412
Never married..........	6,372	(X)	(X)	(X)	(X)	4,363	2,142	2,019	731	2,010

X Not applicable. [1] Includes other races not shown separately. [2] Persons of Hispanic origin may be of any race. [3] No spouse present.

Source: U.S. Census Bureau, Current Population Reports, P20-547.

No. 74. Family Households With Own Children Under Age 18 by Type of Family, 1990 to 2002, and by Age of Householder, 2002

[As of March (32,289 represents 32,289,000). Excludes members of Armed Forces except those living off post or with their families on post. Beginning 2001 population controls based on Census 2000 and an expanded sample of households. Based on Current Population Survey, see text, this section, and Appendix III]

Family type	1990	2000	2002 Total	15 to 24 years old	25 to 34 years old	35 to 44 years old	45 to 54 years old	55 to 64 years old	65 years old and over
NUMBER (1,000)									
Family households with children...	32,289	34,605	35,705	2,026	9,990	15,149	7,438	923	180
Married couple	24,537	25,248	25,792	887	6,795	11,385	5,839	744	141
Male householder [1]	1,153	1,786	1,903	175	569	696	381	74	10
Female householder [1]	6,599	7,571	8,010	964	2,627	3,067	1,218	105	29
HOUSEHOLDS WITH CHILDREN, AS A PERCENT OF ALL FAMILY HOUSEHOLDS BY TYPE									
Family households with children, total	49	48	48	56	76	80	45	9	2
Married couple	47	46	45	58	72	80	44	8	1
Male householder [1]	40	44	43	24	58	67	44	19	2
Female householder [1]	61	60	61	71	92	85	48	9	2

[1] No spouse present.

Source: U.S. Census Bureau, Current Population Reports, P20-547 and earlier reports.

No. 75. Nonfamily Households by Sex and Age of Householder: 2002

[In thousands (15,579 represents 15,579,000). As of March. See headnote, Table 74]

Item	Male householder Total	15 to 24 yr. old	25 to 44 yr. old	45 to 64 yr. old	65 yr. old and over	Female householder Total	15 to 24 yr. old	25 to 44 yr. old	45 to 64 yr. old	65 yr. old and over
Total	15,579	1,350	6,847	4,639	2,744	19,390	1,422	4,141	5,732	8,094
One person (living alone)	12,004	601	4,935	3,904	2,564	16,771	691	3,091	5,087	7,902
Nonrelatives present	3,575	750	1,911	734	180	2,619	731	1,050	645	193
Never married	7,881	1,318	4,778	1,401	385	5,896	1,370	2,815	1,251	459
Married [1]	1,321	21	556	515	229	1,067	30	319	466	253
Widowed	1,703	-	45	238	1,420	7,430	2	106	1,076	6,245
Divorced	4,673	11	1,468	2,485	709	4,997	20	900	2,940	1,137

- Represents or rounds to zero. [1] No spouse present.

Source: U.S. Census Bureau, Current Population Reports, P20-547.

No. 76. Persons Living Alone by Sex and Age: 1990 to 2002

[As of March (22,999 represents 22,999,000). See headnote, Table 74]

Sex and age	Number of persons (1,000) 1990	1995	2000	2001	2002	Percent distribution 1990	1995	2000	2001	2002
Both sexes	22,999	24,732	26,724	28,207	28,775	100	100	100	100	100
15 to 24 years old	1,210	1,196	1,144	1,418	1,292	5	5	4	5	4
25 to 34 years old	3,972	3,653	3,848	3,775	3,923	17	15	14	13	14
35 to 44 years old	3,138	3,663	4,109	4,175	4,103	14	15	15	15	14
45 to 64 years old	5,502	6,377	7,842	8,607	8,992	24	26	29	31	31
65 to 74 years old	4,350	4,374	4,091	4,127	4,279	19	18	15	15	15
75 years old and over	4,825	5,470	5,692	6,107	6,187	21	22	21	22	22
Male	9,049	10,140	11,181	11,648	12,004	39	41	42	41	42
15 to 24 years old	674	623	556	697	601	3	3	2	2	2
25 to 34 years old	2,395	2,213	2,279	2,180	2,322	10	9	9	8	8
35 to 44 years old	1,836	2,263	2,569	2,560	2,613	8	9	10	9	9
45 to 64 years old	2,203	2,787	3,422	3,726	3,904	10	11	13	13	14
65 to 74 years old	1,042	1,134	1,108	1,152	1,225	5	5	4	4	4
75 years old and over	901	1,120	1,247	1,332	1,339	4	5	5	5	5
Female	13,950	14,592	15,543	16,559	16,771	61	59	58	59	58
15 to 24 years old	536	572	588	722	691	2	2	2	3	2
25 to 34 years old	1,578	1,440	1,568	1,593	1,601	7	6	6	6	6
35 to 44 years old	1,303	1,399	1,540	1,614	1,490	6	6	6	6	5
45 to 64 years old	3,300	3,589	4,420	4,881	5,087	14	15	17	17	18
65 to 74 years old	3,309	3,240	2,983	2,974	3,054	14	13	11	11	11
75 years old and over	3,924	4,351	4,444	4,775	4,848	17	18	17	17	17

Source: U.S. Census Bureau, Current Population Reports, P20-547, and earlier reports; and unpublished data.

No. 77. Population in Group Quarters by Sex, Age, and Group Quarters Type: 2000

[In thousands (7,779 represents 7,779,000). As of April. For definitions of group quarters, see text, this section]

Group quarters type	Total population	Male Total	Male Under 18 years	Male 18 to 64 years	Male 65 years and over	Female Total	Female Under 18 years	Female 18 to 64 years	Female 65 years and over
Total	7,779	4,502	215	3,740	548	3,276	108	1,722	1,446
Institutionalized population	4,059	2,534	122	1,968	444	1,525	36	292	1,197
Correctional institutions	1,976	1,806	19	1,773	14	170	2	166	2
Nursing homes	1,721	488	-	88	401	1,232	-	75	1,157
Hospitals/wards and hospices for chronically ill	40	20	1	10	9	20	1	6	14
Mental (psychiatric) hospitals or wards	79	50	7	37	6	29	4	18	7
Juvenile institutions	128	101	88	13	-	27	24	2	-
Other institutions	115	68	8	47	14	47	5	25	18
Noninstitutionalized population	3,720	1,968	93	1,772	104	1,751	72	1,431	249
College dormitories [1]	2,064	958	5	952	-	1,107	5	1,101	-
Military quarters	355	307	1	306	-	48	1	47	-
Other noninstitutional group quarters	1,300	703	86	513	104	597	66	283	249

- Represents or rounds to zero. [1] Includes college quarters off campus.

Source: U.S. Census Bureau, American FactFinder, PCT17. Group Quarters Population by Sex by Age by Group Quarters Type, Census 2000 Summary File 1 (SF 1) 100-Percent Data.

No. 78. Population in Group Quarters—States: 2000

[As of April. For definitions of group quarters, see text, this section. See Appendix III]

State	Group quarters population [1]	Correctional institutions	Nursing homes	College dormitories [2]	State	Group quarters population [1]	Correctional institutions	Nursing homes	College dormitories [2]
U.S., total	7,778,633	1,976,019	1,720,500	2,064,128	MO	162,058	35,206	48,708	44,587
AL	114,720	33,542	26,697	31,086	MT	24,762	4,124	6,470	7,035
AK	19,349	3,331	803	1,748	NE	50,818	6,060	16,195	18,376
AZ	109,850	45,783	13,607	17,340	NV	33,675	15,940	4,895	2,498
AR	73,908	20,565	21,379	18,280	NH	35,539	3,468	9,316	17,574
CA	819,754	248,516	120,724	126,715	NJ	194,821	47,941	51,493	45,222
CO	102,955	30,136	18,495	23,631	NM	36,307	10,940	6,810	7,921
CT	107,939	20,023	32,223	38,051	NY	580,461	108,088	123,852	174,111
DE	24,583	5,965	4,852	9,394	NC	253,881	46,614	50,892	76,018
DC	35,562	2,838	3,759	19,322	ND	23,631	1,518	7,254	10,137
FL	388,945	139,148	88,828	54,085	OH	299,121	68,873	93,157	91,713
GA	233,822	81,773	34,812	47,910	OK	112,375	33,919	28,021	26,643
HI	35,782	3,233	2,949	4,716	OR	77,491	19,523	14,677	18,831
ID	31,496	7,401	5,735	8,006	PA	433,301	76,553	114,113	147,542
IL	321,781	67,820	91,887	90,463	RI	38,816	3,576	9,222	20,551
IN	178,154	34,676	48,745	69,147	SC	135,037	34,909	20,867	39,360
IA	104,169	11,771	33,428	41,171	SD	28,418	4,479	7,791	8,998
KS	81,950	16,703	25,248	24,492	TN	147,946	38,481	36,994	45,030
KY	114,804	28,388	29,266	31,883	TX	561,109	244,363	105,052	92,246
LA	135,965	49,854	31,521	26,959	UT	40,480	9,921	6,853	9,837
ME	34,912	2,864	9,339	13,793	VT	20,760	1,219	4,037	12,863
MD	134,056	35,698	26,716	35,371	VA	231,398	64,036	38,865	65,557
MA	221,216	23,513	55,837	103,583	WA	136,382	28,871	23,275	30,858
MI	249,889	65,330	50,113	69,854	WV	43,147	10,505	11,601	14,300
MN	135,883	16,999	40,506	44,835	WI	155,958	31,068	41,370	51,397
MS	95,414	25,778	18,382	29,238	WY	14,083	4,176	2,869	3,850

[1] Includes other group quarters types not shown separately. [2] Includes college quarters off campus.

Source: U.S. Census Bureau, 2000 Census of Population and Housing, *Profiles of General Demographic Characteristics;* and Census 2000 Summary File 1.

No. 79. Self-Described Religious Identification of Adult Population: 1990 and 2001

[In thousands (175,440 represents 175,440,000). The American Religious Identification Survey (ARIS) 2001 was based on a random digit-dialed telephone survey of 50,281 American residential households in the continental U.S.A (48 states). Respondents were asked to describe themselves in terms of religion with an open-ended question. Interviewers did not prompt or offer a suggested list of potential answers. Moreover, the self-description of respondents was not based on whether established religious bodies, institutions, churches, mosques or synagogues considered them to be members. Quite the contrary, the survey sought to determine whether the respondents themselves regarded themselves as adherents of a religious community. Subjective rather than objective standards of religious identification were tapped by the surveys]

Religious group	1990	2001	Religious group	1990	2001
Adult population, total [1]	175,440	207,980	Fundamentalist	27	61
			Salvation Army	27	25
Total Christian	151,496	159,506	Independent Christian Church	25	71
Catholic	46,004	50,873			
Baptist	33,964	33,830	Total other religions	5,853	7,740
Protestant - no denomination supplied	17,214	4,647	Jewish	3,137	2,831
Methodist/Wesleyan	14,174	14,150	Muslim/Islamic	527	1,104
Lutheran	9,110	9,580	Buddhist	401	1,082
Christian - no denomination supplied	8,073	14,150	Unitarian/Universalist	502	629
Presbyterian	4,985	5,596	Hindu	227	766
Pentecostal/Charismatic	3,191	4,407	Native American	47	103
Episcopalian/Anglican	3,042	3,451	Scientologist	45	55
Mormon/Latter-Day Saints	2,487	2,787	Baha'I	28	84
Churches of Christ	1,769	2,593	Taoist	23	40
Jehovah's Witness	1,381	1,331	New Age	20	68
Seventh-Day Adventist	668	724	Eckankar	18	26
Assemblies of God	660	1,106	Rastafarian	14	11
Holiness/Holy	610	569	Sikh	13	57
Congregational/United Church of Christ	599	1,378	Wiccan	8	134
Church of the Nazarene	549	544	Deity	6	49
Church of God	531	944	Druid	(NA)	33
Orthodox (Eastern)	502	645	Santeria	(NA)	22
Evangelical [2]	242	1,032	Pagan	(NA)	140
Mennonite	235	346	Spiritualist	(NA)	116
Christian Science	214	194	Ethical Culture	(NA)	4
Church of the Brethren	206	358	Other unclassified	837	386
Born Again [2]	204	56			
Nondenominational [2]	195	2,489	No religion specified, total	14,331	29,481
Disciples of Christ	144	492	Atheist	(NA)	902
Reformed/Dutch Reform	161	289	Agnostic	1,186	991
Apostolic/New Apostolic	117	254	Humanist	29	49
Quaker	67	217	Secular	(NA)	53
Full Gospel	51	168	No religion	13,116	27,486
Christian Reform	40	79			
Foursquare Gospel	28	70	Refused to reply to question	4,031	11,246

NA Not available. [1] Refers to the total number of adults in all 50 states. All other figures are based on projections from surveys conducted in the continental United States (48 states). [2] Because of the subjective nature of replies to open-ended question, these categories are the most unstable as they do not refer to clearly identifiable denominations as much as underlying feelings about religion. Thus they may be the most subject to fluctuation over time.

Source: 1990, Barry A. Kosmin and Seymour P. Lachman, "One Nation Under-God: Religion in Contemporary American Society," 1993; 2001 data, The Graduate Center of the City University of New York, New York, NY, Barry A. Kosmin, Egon Mayer and Ariela Keysar, American Religious Identification Survey, 2001 (copyright).

No. 80. Religious Preference, Church Membership, and Attendance: 1980 to 2002

[In percent. Covers civilian noninstitutional population, 18 years old and over. Data represent averages of the combined results of several surveys during year or period indicated. Data are subject to sampling variability, see source]

Year	Religious preference							Church/ synagogue members	Persons attending church/ synagogue [1]
	Protestant	Catholic	Jewish	Orthodox	Mormon	Other specific	None		
1980	61	28	2	(NA)	(NA)	2	7	69	40
1985	57	28	2	(NA)	(NA)	4	9	71	42
1990	56	25	2	(NA)	(NA)	6	11	65	40
1995	56	27	2	1	1	5	[2]8	69	43
1998	59	27	2	2	1	4	[2]8	70	40
1999	55	28	2	1	2	2	[2]10	70	43
2000	56	27	2	1	1	5	[2]8	68	44
2001	53	25	2	1	2	7	[2]10	66	42
2002	53	25	2	1	2	8	[2]9	65	44

NA Not available. [1] Persons who attended a church or synagogue in the last 7 days. [2] Includes those respondents who did not designate.

Source: The Gallup Organization, Princeton, NJ, <http://www.gallup.com/> (copyright).

Population 67

No. 81. Religious Bodies—Selected Data

[Membership data: 2,500 represents 2,500,000. Includes the self-reported membership of religious bodies with 650,000 or more as reported to the *Yearbook of American and Canadian Churches*. Groups may be excluded if they do not supply information. The data are not standardized so comparisons between groups are difficult. The definition of "church member" is determined by the religious body]

Religious body	Year reported	Churches reported	Membership (1,000)	Pastors serving parishes [1]
African Methodist Episcopal Church	1999	(NA)	2,500	7,741
African Methodist Episcopal Zion Church	2001	3,226	1,448	3,288
American Baptist Churches in the U.S.A.	2001	5,786	1,443	4,563
Baptist Bible Fellowship International	2002	4,500	1,200	(NA)
Christian Church (Disciples of Christ) in the United States and Canada	2001	3,717	805	3,385
Christian Churches and Churches of Christ	1988	5,579	1,072	5,525
Christian Methodist Episcopal Church	2001	3,250	850	2,980
Church Of God In Christ, The	1991	15,300	5,500	28,988
Church of God (Cleveland, Tennessee)	2001	6,605	932	4,564
Church of Jesus Christ of Latter-day Saints, The	2001	11,731	5,311	35,193
Churches of Christ	1999	15,000	1,500	14,500
Episcopal Church	2000	7,364	2,333	6,062
Evangelical Lutheran Church in America	2001	10,766	5,100	9,379
Greek Orthodox Archdiocese of America	(NA)	510	1,500	599
Jehovah's Witnesses	2001	11,706	989	(NA)
Lutheran Church—Missouri Synod (LCMS), The	2001	6,187	2,540	5,204
National Baptist Convention of America, Inc.	2000	(NA)	3,500	(NA)
National Baptist Convention, U.S.A., Inc.	(NA)	9,000	5,000	(NA)
National Missionary Baptist Convention of America	1992	(NA)	2,500	(NA)
Orthodox Church in America, The	2000	721	1,000	760
Pentecostal Assemblies of the World, Inc.	1998	1,750	1,500	4,500
Presbyterian Church (U.S.A.)	2001	11,142	3,456	9,115
Progressive National Baptist Convention, Inc.	1995	2,000	2,500	(NA)
Roman Catholic Church, The	2001	19,496	65,270	(NA)
Seventh-Day Adventist Church	2001	4,594	901	2,572
Southern Baptist Convention	2001	42,334	16,053	82,315
United Church of Christ	2001	5,888	1,359	4,304
United Methodist Church, The	2001	35,275	8,298	24,162

NA Not available. [1] Does not include retired clergy or clergy not working with congregations.

Source: National Council of Churches, New York, NY, *2003 Yearbook of American and Canadian Churches*, annual (copyright). (For more info visit <www.ncccusa.org> or call 888-870-3325.)

No. 82. Christian Church Adherents, 2000, and Jewish Population, 2002—States

[133,377 represents 133,377,000. Christian church adherents were defined as "all members, including full members, their children and the estimated number of other regular participants who are not considered as communicant, confirmed or full members." The Jewish population includes Jews who define themselves as Jewish by religion as well as those who define themselves as Jewish in cultural terms. Data on Jewish population are based primarily on a compilation of individual estimates made by local Jewish federations. Additionally, most large communities have completed Jewish demographic surveys from which the Jewish population can be determined]

State	Christian adherents, 2000 Number (1,000)	Christian adherents, 2000 Percent of population [1]	Jewish population, 2002 Number (1,000)	Jewish population, 2002 Percent of population [1]	State	Christian adherents, 2000 Number (1,000)	Christian adherents, 2000 Percent of population [1]	Jewish population, 2002 Number (1,000)	Jewish population, 2002 Percent of population [1]
U.S.	133,377	47.4	6,155	2.2	MO	2,813	50.3	62	1.1
AL	2,418	54.4	9	0.2	MT	401	44.4	1	0.1
AK	210	33.6	3	0.5	NE	995	58.2	7	0.4
AZ	1,946	37.9	82	1.6	NV	604	30.2	77	3.8
AR	1,516	56.7	2	0.1	NH	571	46.2	10	0.8
CA	14,328	42.3	999	2.9	NJ	4,262	50.7	485	5.8
CO	1,604	37.3	73	1.7	NM	1,041	57.2	11	0.6
CT	1,828	53.7	111	3.3	NY	9,569	50.4	1,657	8.7
DE	299	38.2	14	1.7	NC	3,598	44.7	26	0.3
DC	331	57.8	26	4.5	ND	468	72.9	(Z)	0.1
FL	5,904	36.9	620	3.9	OH	4,912	43.3	149	1.3
GA	3,528	43.1	94	1.1	OK	2,079	60.3	5	0.1
HI	431	35.6	7	0.6	OR	1,029	30.1	32	0.9
ID	624	48.3	1	0.1	PA	6,751	55.0	282	2.3
IL	6,457	52.0	270	2.2	RI	646	61.7	16	1.5
IN	2,578	42.4	18	0.3	SC	1,874	46.7	11	0.3
IA	1,698	58.0	6	0.2	SD	510	67.6	(Z)	(Z)
KS	1,307	48.6	14	0.5	TN	2,867	50.4	18	0.3
KY	2,141	53.0	11	0.3	TX	11,316	54.3	131	0.6
LA	2,599	58.2	16	0.4	UT	1,659	74.3	4	0.2
ME	450	35.3	9	0.7	VT	230	37.8	6	0.9
MD	2,012	38.0	213	4.0	VA	2,807	39.7	66	0.9
MA	3,725	58.7	275	4.3	WA	1,872	31.8	43	0.7
MI	3,970	39.9	110	1.1	WV	646	35.7	2	0.1
MN	2,974	60.5	42	0.9	WI	3,198	59.6	28	0.5
MS	1,549	54.5	1	0.1	WY	229	46.4	(Z)	0.1

Z Fewer than 500 or 0.05 percent. [1] Based on U.S. Census Bureau data for resident population enumerated as of April 1, 2000, and estimated as of July 1, 2002.

Source: Christian church adherents—Dale E. Jones, Sherri Doty, Clifford Grammich, James E. Horsch, Richard Houseal, John P. Marcum, Kenneth M. Sanchagrin, and Richard H. Taylor, *Religious Congregations and Membership in the United States: 2000*, Glenmary Research Center, Nashville, TN, <www.glenmary.org/grc>, 2002 (copyright); Jewish population—American Jewish Committee, New York, NY, *American Jewish Year Book, 2002* (copyright).

Section 2
Vital Statistics

This section presents vital statistics data on births, deaths, abortions, fetal deaths, fertility, life expectancy, marriages, and divorces. Vital statistics are compiled for the country as a whole by the National Center for Health Statistics (NCHS) and published in its annual report, *Vital Statistics of the United States,* in certain reports of the *Vital and Health Statistics* series, and in the *National Vital Statistics Reports* (formerly *Monthly Vital Statistics Report).* Reports in this field are also issued by the various state bureaus of vital statistics. Data on fertility, on age of persons at first marriage, and on marital status and marital history are compiled by the U.S. Census Bureau from its Current Population Survey (CPS; see text, Section 1) and published in *Current Population Reports,* P20 Series. Data on abortions are published by the Alan Guttmacher Institute, New York, NY, in selected issues of *Family Planning Perspectives.*

Registration of vital events—The registration of births, deaths, fetal deaths, and other vital events in the United States is primarily a state and local function. The civil laws of every state provide for a continuous and permanent birth- and death-registration system. Many states also provide for marriage- and divorce-registration systems. Vital events occurring to U.S. residents outside the United States are not included in the data.

Births and deaths—The live-birth, death, and fetal-death statistics prepared by NCHS are based on vital records filed in the registration offices of all states, of New York City, and of the District of Columbia. The annual collection of death statistics on a national basis began in 1900 with a national death-registration area of ten states and the District of Columbia; a similar annual collection of birth statistics for a national birth-registration area began in 1915, also with ten reporting states and the District of Columbia. Since 1933, the birth- and death-registration areas have comprised the entire United States, including Alaska (beginning 1959) and Hawaii (beginning 1960). National statistics on fetal deaths were first compiled for 1918 and annually since 1922.

Prior to 1951, birth statistics came from a complete count of records received in the Public Health Service (now received in NCHS). From 1951 through 1971, they were based on a 50-percent sample of all registered births (except for a complete count in 1955 and a 20- to 50-percent sample in 1967). Beginning in 1972, they have been based on a complete count for states participating in the Vital Statistics Cooperative Program (VSCP) (for details, see the technical appendix in *Vital Statistics of the United States*) and on a 50-percent sample of all other areas. Beginning 1986, all reporting areas participated in the VSCP. Mortality data have been based on a complete count of records for each area (except for a 50-percent sample in 1972). Beginning in 1970, births to and deaths of nonresident aliens of the United States and U.S. citizens outside the United States have been excluded from the data. Fetal deaths and deaths among Armed Forces abroad are excluded. Data based on samples are subject to sampling error; for details, see annual issues of *Vital Statistics of the United States.*

Mortality statistics by cause of death are compiled in accordance with World Health Organization regulations according to the *International Classification of Diseases* (ICD). The ICD is revised approximately every 10 years. The tenth revision of the ICD was employed beginning in 1999. Deaths for prior years were classified according to the revision of the ICD in use at the time. Each revision of the ICD introduces a number of discontinuities in mortality statistics; for a discussion of those between the ninth and tenth revisions of the ICD, see *National Vital Statistics Reports,* Vol. 49, Nos. 2 and 8. Preliminary mortality data are based on a percentage of death records weighted up to the total number of deaths reported for the given year; for a discussion of preliminary data, see *National Vital Statistics Reports*, Vol. 49, No. 3. Information on tests of statistical significance, differences between death rates, and standard errors can also be found in the reports mentioned above.

Some of the tables present age-adjusted death rates in addition to crude death rates. Age-adjusted death rates shown in this section were prepared using the direct method, in which age-specific death rates for a population of interest are applied to a standard population distributed by age. Age adjustment eliminates the differences in observed rates between points in time or among compared population groups that result from age differences in population composition.

Fertility and life expectancy—The total fertility rate, defined as the number of births that 1,000 women would have in their lifetime if, at each year of age, they experienced the birth rates occurring in the specified year, is compiled and published by NCHS. Other data relating to social and medical factors that affect fertility rates, such as contraceptive use and birth expectations, are collected and made available by both NCHS and the Census Bureau. NCHS figures are based on information in birth and fetal death certificates and on the periodic National Surveys of Family Growth; Census Bureau data are based on decennial censuses and the CPS.

Data on life expectancy, the average remaining lifetime in years for persons who attain a given age, are computed and published by NCHS. For details, see *National Vital Statistics Reports*, Vol. 50, No. 6.

Marriage and divorce—The compilation of nationwide statistics on marriages and divorces in the United States began in 1887-88, when the National Office of Vital Statistics prepared estimates for the years 1867-86. Although periodic updates took place after 1888, marriage and divorce statistics were not collected and published annually until 1944 by that office. In 1957 and 1958, respectively, the same office established marriage- and divorce-registration areas. Beginning in 1957, the marriage-registration area comprised 30 states, plus Alaska, Hawaii, Puerto Rico, and the Virgin Islands; it currently includes 42 states and the District of Columbia. The divorce-registration area, starting in 1958 with 14 states, Alaska, Hawaii, and the Virgin Islands, currently includes a total of 31 states and the Virgin Islands. Procedures for estimating the number of marriages and divorces in the registration states are discussed in *Vital Statistics of the United States*, Vol. III—Marriage and Divorce. Total counts of events for registration and nonregistration states are gathered by collecting already summarized data on marriages and divorces reported by state offices of vital statistics and by county offices of registration. The collection and publication of detailed marriage and divorce statistics (for example: by age and race) was suspended beginning in January 1996. For additional information contact the National Center for Health Statistics online at <http://www.cec.gov/nchs/releases/96facts/mardiv.htm>.

Vital statistics rates—Except as noted, vital statistics rates computed by NCHS are based on decennial census population figures as of April 1 for 1940, 1950, 1960, 1970, 1980, and 1990; and on midyear population figures for other years, as estimated by the Census Bureau (see text, Section 1).

Race—Data by race for births, deaths, marriages, and divorces from NCHS are based on information contained in the certificates of registration. The Census Bureau's Current Population Survey obtains information on race by asking respondents to classify their race as (1) White, (2) Black, (3) American Indian, Eskimo, or Aleut, or (4) Asian or Pacific Islander.

Beginning with the 1989 data year, NCHS is tabulating its birth data primarily by race of the mother. In 1988 and prior years, births were tabulated by race of the child, which was determined from the race of the parents as entered on the birth certificate.

Trend data by race shown in this section are by race of mother beginning with the 1980 data. Hispanic origin of the mother is reported and tabulated independently of race. Thus persons of Hispanic origin maybe of any race. In 1994, 91 percent of women of Hispanic origin were reported as White.

Figure 2.1
Infant Mortality Rates by State: 2001

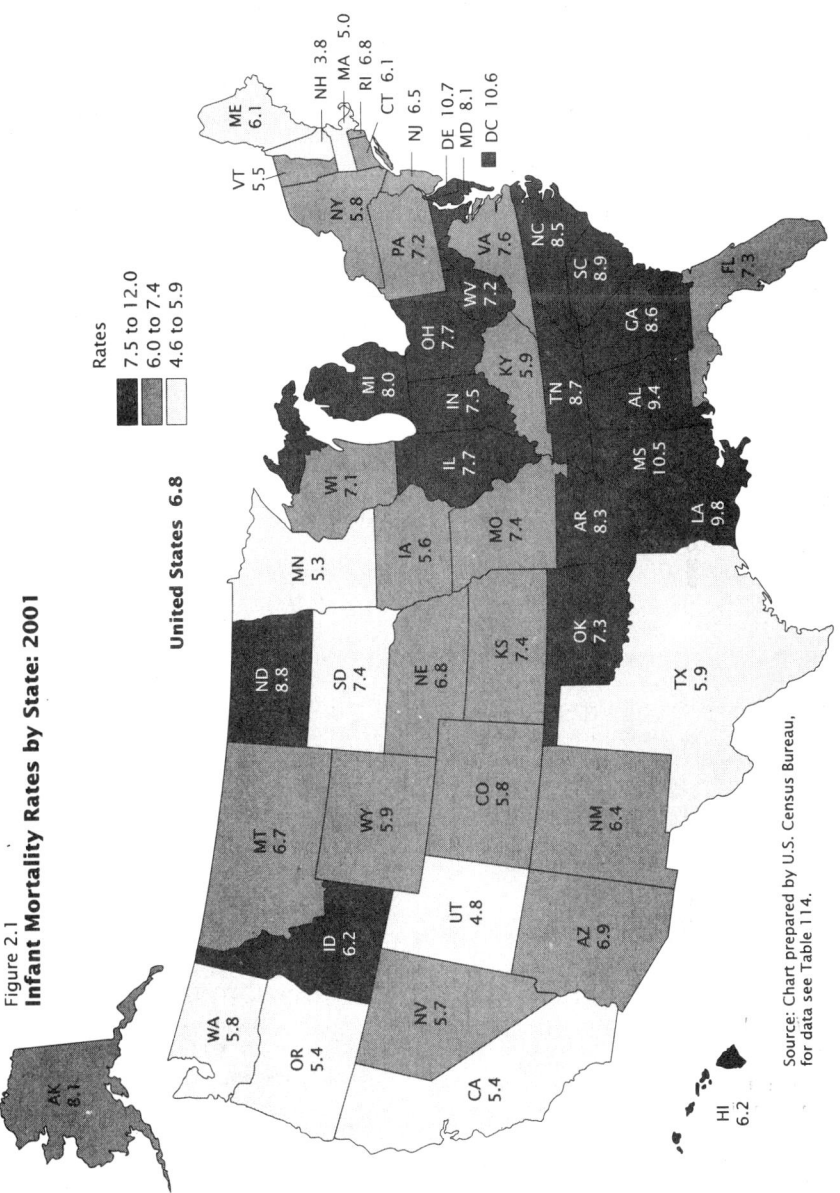

Source: Chart prepared by U.S. Census Bureau, for data see Table 114.

Vital Statistics 71

No. 83. Live Births, Deaths, Marriages, and Divorces: 1950 to 2001

[3,632 represents 3,632,000. Prior to 1960, excludes Alaska and Hawaii. Beginning 1970, excludes births to and deaths of nonresidents of the United States. See Appendix III]

Year	Number (1,000)					Rate per 1,000 population				
	Births [1]	Deaths		Marriages [3]	Divorces [4]	Births [1]	Deaths		Marriages [3]	Divorces [4]
		Total	Infant [2]				Total	Infant [2]		
1950	3,632	1,452	104	1,667	385	24.1	9.6	29.2	11.1	2.6
1955	4,097	1,529	107	1,531	377	25.0	9.3	26.4	9.3	2.3
1957	4,300	1,633	112	1,518	381	25.3	9.6	26.3	8.9	2.2
1960	4,258	1,712	111	1,523	393	23.7	9.5	26.0	8.5	2.2
1965	3,760	1,828	93	1,800	479	19.4	9.4	24.7	9.3	2.5
1970	3,731	1,921	75	2,159	708	18.4	9.5	20.0	10.6	3.5
1971	3,556	1,928	68	2,190	773	17.2	9.3	19.1	10.6	3.7
1972	3,258	1,964	60	2,282	845	15.6	9.4	18.5	10.9	4.0
1973	3,137	1,973	56	2,284	915	14.8	9.3	17.7	10.8	4.3
1974	3,160	1,934	53	2,230	977	14.8	9.1	16.7	10.5	4.6
1975	3,144	1,893	51	2,153	1,036	14.6	8.8	16.1	10.0	4.8
1976	3,168	1,909	48	2,155	1,083	14.6	8.8	15.2	9.9	5.0
1977	3,327	1,900	47	2,178	1,091	15.1	8.6	14.1	9.9	5.0
1978	3,333	1,928	46	2,282	1,130	15.0	8.7	13.8	10.3	5.1
1979	3,494	1,914	46	2,331	1,181	15.6	8.5	13.1	10.4	5.3
1980	3,612	1,990	46	2,390	1,189	15.9	8.8	12.6	10.6	5.2
1981	3,629	1,978	43	2,422	1,213	15.8	8.6	11.9	10.6	5.3
1982	3,681	1,975	42	2,456	1,170	15.9	8.5	11.5	10.6	5.1
1983	3,639	2,019	41	2,446	1,158	15.6	8.6	11.2	10.5	5.0
1984	3,669	2,039	40	2,477	1,169	15.6	8.6	10.8	10.5	5.0
1985	3,761	2,086	40	2,413	1,190	15.8	8.8	10.6	10.1	5.0
1986	3,757	2,105	39	2,407	1,178	15.6	8.8	10.4	10.0	4.9
1987	3,809	2,123	38	2,403	1,166	15.7	8.8	10.1	9.9	4.8
1988	3,910	2,168	39	2,396	1,167	16.0	8.9	10.0	9.8	4.8
1989	4,041	2,150	40	2,403	1,157	16.4	8.7	9.8	9.7	4.7
1990	4,158	2,148	38	2,443	1,182	16.7	8.6	9.2	9.8	4.7
1991	4,111	2,170	37	2,371	1,187	16.3	8.6	8.9	9.4	4.7
1992	4,065	2,176	35	2,362	1,215	15.9	8.5	8.5	9.3	4.8
1993	4,000	2,269	33	2,334	1,187	15.5	8.8	8.4	9.0	4.6
1994	3,953	2,279	31	2,362	1,191	15.2	8.8	8.0	9.1	4.6
1995	3,900	2,312	30	2,336	1,169	14.8	8.8	7.6	8.9	4.4
1996	3,891	2,315	28	2,344	1,150	14.7	8.7	7.3	8.8	4.3
1997	3,881	2,314	28	2,384	1,163	14.5	8.6	7.2	8.9	4.3
1998 [5]	3,942	2,337	28	2,244	1,135	14.6	8.6	7.2	8.3	4.2
1999 [5]	3,959	2,391	28	2,358	(NA)	14.5	8.8	7.1	8.6	4.1
2000 [5]	4,059	2,403	28	2,329	(NA)	14.4	8.7	6.9	8.5	4.2
2001 [5]	4,026	2,416	28	2,327	(NA)	14.1	8.5	6.8	8.4	4.0

NA Not available. [1] Prior to 1960, data adjusted for underregistration. [2] Infants under 1 year, excluding fetal deaths; rates per 1,000 registered live births. [3] Includes estimates for some states through 1965 and also for 1976 and 1977 and marriage licenses for some states for all years except 1973 and 1975. Beginning 1978, includes nonlicensed marriages in California. [4] Includes reported annulments and some estimated state figures for all years. [5] Divorce rate excludes data for California, Colorado, Indiana, and Louisiana; population for this rate also excludes these states.

Source: U.S. National Center for Health Statistics, *Vital Statistics of the United States*, annual; and *National Vital Statistics Reports (NVSR)* (formerly *Monthly Vital Statistics Report)*; and unpublished data. See also <http://www.cdc.gov/nchs>.

No. 84. Live Births by Race and Type of Hispanic Origin—Selected Characteristics: 1990 and 2001

[4,158 represents 4,158,000. Represents registered births. Excludes births to nonresidents of the United States. Data are based on Hispanic origin of mother and race of mother. Hispanic origin data are available from only 48 states and the District of Columbia in 1990]

Race and Hispanic origin	Number of births (1,000)		Births to teen-age mothers, percent of total		Births to unmarried mothers, per-cent of total		Prenatal care beginning first trimester		Late or no prenatal care		Percent of births with low birth weight [1]	
	1990	2001	1990	2001	1990	2001	1990	2001	1990	2001	1990	2001
Total	4,158	4,026	12.8	11.3	26.6	33.5	74.2	83.4	6.0	3.7	7.0	7.7
White	3,290	3,178	10.9	10.2	16.9	27.7	77.7	85.2	4.9	3.2	5.7	6.7
Black	684	606	23.1	18.9	66.7	68.4	60.7	74.5	10.9	6.5	13.3	13.0
American Indian, Eskimo, Aleut	39	42	19.5	19.3	53.6	59.7	57.9	69.3	12.9	8.2	6.1	7.3
Asian and Pacific Islander [2]	142	200	5.7	4.3	(NA)	14.9	(NA)	84.0	(NA)	3.4	(NA)	7.5
Filipino	26	32	6.1	5.1	15.9	20.4	77.1	85.0	4.5	3.0	7.3	8.7
Chinese	23	31	1.2	4.1	5.0	8.4	81.3	87.0	3.4	2.4	4.7	5.3
Japanese	9	9	2.9	1.7	9.6	9.2	87.0	90.1	2.9	2.0	6.2	7.3
Hawaiian	6	6	18.4	16.2	45.0	50.6	65.8	79.1	8.7	4.8	7.2	7.9
Hispanic origin [3]	595	852	16.8	15.6	36.7	42.5	60.2	75.7	12.0	5.9	6.1	6.5
Mexican	386	611	17.7	16.5	33.3	40.5	57.8	74.6	13.2	6.2	5.5	6.1
Puerto Rico	59	58	21.7	19.2	55.9	58.9	63.5	79.1	10.6	4.6	9.0	9.3
Cuban	11	14	7.7	7.5	18.2	27.2	84.8	91.8	2.8	1.3	5.7	6.5
Central and South American	83	121	9.0	9.4	41.2	44.3	61.5	77.4	10.9	5.7	5.8	6.5
Other and unknown Hispanic	56	48	(NA)	17.3	(NA)	44.2	(NA)	77.3	(NA)	5.4	(NA)	8.0

NA Not available. [1] Births less than 2,500 grams (5 lb.-8 oz.). [2] Includes other races not shown separately. [3] Hispanic persons may be of any race. Includes other types, not shown separately.

Source: U.S. National Center for Health Statistics; *Vital Statistics of the United States*, annual; *National Vital Statistics Report (NVSR)* (formerly *Monthly Vital Statistics Report)*; and unpublished data.

No. 85. Births and Birth Rates by Race, Sex, and Age: 1980 to 2001

[Births in thousands. (3,612 represents 3,612,000). Births by race of mother. Excludes births to nonresidents of the United States. For population bases used to derive these data, see text, this section, and Appendix III]

Item	1980	1985	1990	1994	1995	1996	1997	1998	1999	2000	2001
Live births [1]	3,612	3,761	4,158	3,953	3,900	3,891	3,881	3,942	3,959	4,059	4,026
White	2,936	3,038	3,290	3,121	3,099	3,093	3,073	3,119	3,134	3,194	3,178
Black	568	582	684	636	603	595	600	610	607	623	606
American Indian	29	34	39	38	37	38	39	40	41	42	42
Asian or Pacific Islander	74	105	142	158	160	166	170	173	182	201	200
Male	1,853	1,928	2,129	2,023	1,996	1,990	1,986	2,016	2,028	2,077	2,058
Female	1,760	1,833	2,029	1,930	1,903	1,901	1,895	1,925	1,934	1,982	1,968
Males per 100 females	105	105	105	105	105	105	105	105	106	105	105
Age of mother:											
Under 20 years old	562	478	533	518	512	503	493	494	485	478	454
20 to 24 years old	1,226	1,141	1,094	1,001	966	945	942	965	982	1,018	1,022
25 to 29 years old	1,108	1,201	1,277	1,089	1,064	1,071	1,069	1,083	1,078	1,088	1,058
30 to 34 years old	550	696	886	906	905	898	887	889	892	929	943
35 to 39 years old	141	214	318	372	384	400	410	425	434	452	452
40 to 44 years old	(NA)	(NA)	(NA)	(NA)	(NA)	72	76	81	83	90	93
45 to 49 years old	(NA)	(NA)	(NA)	(NA)	(NA)	3	3	4	4	4	5
Birth rate per 1,000 population	15.9	15.8	16.7	15.2	14.8	14.7	14.5	14.6	14.5	14.4	14.1
White	15.1	15.0	15.8	14.4	14.2	14.1	13.9	14.0	14.9	13.9	13.7
Black	21.3	20.4	22.4	19.5	18.2	17.8	17.7	17.7	18.4	17.0	16.3
American Indian	20.7	19.8	18.9	17.1	16.6	16.6	16.6	17.1	17.8	14.0	13.7
Asian or Pacific Islander	19.9	18.7	19.0	17.5	17.3	17.0	16.9	16.4	17.7	17.1	16.4
Plural birth ratio [2]	19.3	21.0	23.3	25.7	26.1	27.4	28.6	30.0	30.7	31.1	32.0
White	18.5	20.4	22.9	25.5	26.0	27.5	28.7	30.2	30.9	31.2	32.1
Black	24.1	25.3	27.0	29.4	28.8	29.8	30.9	32.0	32.9	34.0	34.6
Fertility rate per 1,000 women [3]	68.4	66.2	70.9	66.7	65.6	65.3	65.0	65.6	65.9	65.9	65.3
White [3]	65.6	64.1	68.3	64.9	64.4	64.3	63.9	64.6	65.1	65.3	65.0
Black [3]	84.9	78.8	86.8	76.9	72.3	70.7	70.7	71.0	70.1	70.0	67.6
American Indian [3]	82.7	78.6	76.2	70.9	69.1	68.7	69.1	70.7	70.7	58.7	58.1
Asian or Pacific Islander [3]	73.2	68.4	69.6	66.8	66.4	65.9	66.3	64.0	66.6	65.8	64.2
Age of mother:											
10 to 14 years old	1.1	1.2	1.4	1.4	1.3	1.2	1.1	1.0	1.9	0.9	0.8
15 to 19 years old	53.0	51.0	59.9	58.9	56.8	54.4	52.3	51.1	50.6	47.7	45.3
20 to 24 years old	115.1	108.3	116.5	111.1	109.8	110.4	110.4	111.2	112.0	109.7	106.2
25 to 29 years old	112.9	111.0	120.2	113.9	112.2	113.1	113.8	115.9	118.8	113.5	113.4
30 to 34 years old	61.9	69.1	80.8	81.5	82.5	83.9	85.3	87.4	90.6	91.2	91.9
35 to 39 years old	19.8	24.0	31.7	33.7	34.3	35.3	36.1	37.4	39.3	39.7	40.6
40 to 44 years old	3.9	4.0	5.5	6.4	6.6	6.8	7.1	7.3	8.4	8.0	8.1
45 to 49 years old	0.2	0.2	0.2	0.3	0.3	0.3	0.4	0.4	1.4	0.5	0.5

NA Not available. [1] Includes other races not shown separately. [2] Number of multiple births per 1,000 live births. [3] Per 1,000 women, 15 to 44 years old in specified group. The rate for age of mother 45 to 49 years old computed by relating births to mothers 45 years old and over to women 45 to 49 years old.

Source: U.S. National Center for Health Statistics, *Vital Statistics of the United States*, annual; *National Vital Statistics Report (NVSR)* (formerly *Monthly Vital Statistics Report*); and unpublished data. See also <http://www.cdc.gov/nchs.htm>.

No. 86. Teenagers—Births and Birth Rates by Race and Sex: 1990 to 2001

[Birth rates per 1,000 women in specified group, see text, this section]

Item	1990	1993	1994	1995	1996	1997	1998	1999	2000	2001
NUMBER OF BIRTHS										
All races, total [1]	521,826	501,093	505,488	499,873	494,272	489,211	484,975	476,050	468,990	445,944
15-17 years	183,327	190,535	195,169	192,508	186,762	183,324	173,252	163,588	157,209	145,324
18-19 years	338,499	310,558	310,319	307,365	307,509	305,886	311,724	312,462	311,781	300,620
White	354,482	341,817	348,081	349,635	346,509	342,029	340,894	337,888	333,013	318,563
15-17 years	114,934	121,309	126,388	127,165	124,031	121,864	116,699	111,624	106,786	99,192
18-19 years	239,548	220,508	221,693	222,470	222,477	220,164	224,195	226,264	226,227	219,371
Black	151,613	143,153	140,968	133,694	131,059	130,401	126,865	121,166	118,954	110,843
15-17 years	62,881	63,156	62,563	59,112	56,218	54,883	50,062	45,919	44,618	40,842
18-19 years	88,732	79,997	78,405	74,582	74,841	75,518	76,803	75,247	74,336	70,001
BIRTH RATE										
All races, total [1]	59.9	59.6	58.9	56.8	54.4	52.3	51.1	49.6	48.5	45.8
15-17 years	37.5	37.8	37.6	36.0	33.8	32.1	30.4	28.7	27.4	25.2
18-19 years	88.6	92.1	91.5	89.1	86.0	83.6	82.0	80.3	79.2	75.5
White	50.8	51.1	51.1	50.1	48.1	46.3	45.4	44.6	43.6	41.4
15-17 years	29.5	30.3	30.7	30.0	28.4	27.1	25.9	24.8	23.6	21.9
18-19 years	78.0	82.1	82.1	81.2	78.4	75.9	74.6	73.5	72.7	69.7
Black	112.8	108.6	104.5	96.1	91.4	88.2	85.4	81.0	79.4	73.2
15-17 years	82.3	79.8	76.3	69.7	64.7	60.8	56.8	52.0	50.4	45.6
18-19 years	152.9	151.9	148.3	137.1	132.5	130.1	126.9	122.8	121.3	113.2

[1] Includes races other than White and Black.

Source: U.S. National Center for Health Statistics, *Vital Statistics of the United States*, annual; *National Vital Statistics Report (NVSR)* (formerly *Monthly Vital Statistics Report*), and unpublished data. See also <http://www.cdc.gov/nchs.htm>.

No. 87. Live Births by State: 2001

[Number of births, except rate. Registered births. Excludes births to nonresidents of the United States. By race of mother. See Appendix III]

State	All races [1]	White Total	White Non-Hispanic	Black Total	Black Non-Hispanic	Hispanic [2]	Birth rate [3]	Fertility rate [4]
United States..	4,025,933	3,177,626	2,326,578	606,156	589,917	851,851	14.5	66.9
Alabama	60,454	40,604	38,342	19,199	19,183	2,254	13.7	62.4
Alaska	10,003	6,383	5,567	441	388	652	16.0	75.5
Arizona	85,597	75,219	38,878	2,762	2,560	36,183	17.1	84.0
Arkansas	37,010	28,836	26,082	7,435	7,422	2,649	14.3	67.5
California	527,759	428,238	167,025	33,774	32,551	261,071	15.5	69.5
Colorado	67,007	61,056	41,764	2,971	2,830	19,730	15.9	74.6
Connecticut	42,648	35,612	28,434	5,134	4,929	6,913	12.9	61.0
Delaware	10,749	7,668	6,598	2,710	2,684	1,083	13.9	61.5
Dist of Columbia	7,625	2,570	1,687	4,860	4,805	895	14.8	63.9
Florida	205,793	152,207	104,068	47,186	45,954	49,629	13.2	67.0
Georgia	133,526	85,648	69,306	43,727	43,076	15,699	16.5	71.1
Hawaii	17,072	3,815	3,119	527	495	2,237	14.5	71.4
Idaho	20,688	19,944	16,855	86	78	2,753	16.0	75.4
Illinois	184,064	142,474	101,660	33,203	32,995	40,973	15.0	69.5
Indiana	86,459	75,393	69,242	9,649	9,575	5,898	14.4	66.1
Iowa	37,619	35,324	33,068	1,266	1,237	2,232	13.0	63.4
Kansas	38,869	34,622	29,363	2,781	2,747	4,906	14.5	68.1
Kentucky	54,658	48,968	47,485	4,930	4,905	1,509	13.6	62.3
Louisiana	65,352	36,899	35,383	27,058	27,010	1,557	14.9	67.2
Maine	13,759	13,280	13,074	153	142	173	10.9	50.0
Maryland	73,218	45,068	39,798	24,252	24,046	5,301	13.9	60.9
Massachusetts	81,077	67,786	59,405	8,205	6,552	9,444	13.0	59.1
Michigan	133,427	105,235	96,346	23,613	23,399	7,335	13.4	61.0
Minnesota	67,562	57,982	53,141	4,767	4,685	4,543	13.8	63.5
Mississippi	42,282	22,808	22,073	18,817	18,809	719	15.1	67.6
Missouri	75,464	62,504	59,513	11,134	11,084	2,981	13.6	63.2
Montana	10,970	9,442	8,798	42	38	377	12.3	61.8
Nebraska	24,820	22,496	19,056	1,373	1,355	2,946	14.8	69.7
Nevada	31,382	26,284	15,323	2,518	2,414	10,855	16.1	79.4
New Hampshire	14,656	13,954	12,849	208	159	509	11.9	52.0
New Jersey	115,795	85,110	63,266	20,583	18,709	23,497	14.0	66.3
New Mexico	27,128	22,810	8,776	511	485	14,126	15.4	72.8
New York	254,026	182,191	130,637	52,190	46,709	54,544	13.9	64.4
North Carolina	118,185	85,315	70,863	28,393	28,250	14,539	15.1	70.4
North Dakota	7,629	6,625	6,299	102	101	140	12.2	59.3
Ohio	151,570	125,507	120,869	22,994	22,769	4,598	13.4	61.9
Oklahoma	50,118	39,218	34,360	4,612	4,574	4,942	14.8	70.8
Oregon	45,322	41,284	33,388	944	908	7,902	13.5	65.3
Pennsylvania	143,495	119,015	110,501	20,238	19,615	8,192	12.0	57.7
Rhode Island	12,713	10,960	7,676	1,112	994	2,196	12.7	59.2
South Carolina	55,756	35,866	32,932	18,927	18,878	2,988	14.1	62.8
South Dakota	10,483	8,475	8,254	101	97	257	14.1	67.7
Tennessee	78,340	60,216	56,363	16,603	16,568	3,905	14.0	64.3
Texas	365,410	311,979	139,104	40,750	40,221	172,354	17.6	79.9
Utah	47,959	45,440	38,682	342	325	6,543	21.8	95.0
Vermont	6,366	6,237	6,014	31	29	35	10.6	47.9
Virginia	98,884	70,946	61,871	22,272	22,082	9,143	14.0	60.9
Washington	79,570	67,437	54,468	3,334	3,219	12,140	13.6	61.9
West Virginia	20,428	19,576	19,446	704	698	83	11.4	55.6
Wisconsin	69,072	59,383	54,346	6,567	6,515	5,152	12.9	60.2
Wyoming	6,115	5,717	5,161	65	64	569	12.7	62.0
Puerto Rico	55,866	51,285	(NA)	4,564	(NA)	(NA)	14.2	61.2
Virgin Islands	1,669	367	79	1,230	1,091	385	13.7	63.4
Guam	3,564	234	209	37	37	52	22.6	113.7
American Samoa	1,655	3	(NA)	(NA)	(NA)	(NA)	24.7	113.9
Northern Marianas	1,449	19	(NA)	(NA)	(NA)	(NA)	19.4	57.5

NA Not available. [1] Includes other races not shown separately. [2] Persons of Hispanic origin may be of any race. Births by Hispanic origin of mother. [3] Per 1,000 estimated population. [4] Per 1,000 women aged 15-44 years estimated.

Source: U.S. National Center for Health Statistics, *Vital Statistics of the United States*, annual; and *National Vital Statistics Reports (NVSR)* Vol. 51, No.2. (formerly *Monthly Vital Statistics Report*). See also <http://www.cdc.gov/nchs/nvss.htm>.

No. 88. Total Fertility Rate by Race: 1970 to 2001

[Based on race of child and registered births only, thru 1979. Beginning 1980, based on race of mother. Beginning 1970, excludes births to nonresidents of United States. The *total fertility rate* is the number of births that 1,000 women would have in their lifetime if, at each year of age, they experienced the birth rates occurring in the specified year. A total fertility rate of 2,110 represents "replacement level" fertility for the total population under current mortality conditions (assuming no net immigration). See also Appendix III]

Annual average and year	Total fertility rate - Total	Total fertility rate - White	Total fertility rate - Black and other[1]	Annual average and year	Total fertility rate - Total	Total fertility rate - White	Total fertility rate - Black and other[1]
1970	2,480	2,385	3,067	1986	1,838	1,776	2,136
1971	2,267	2,161	2,920	1987	1,872	1,805	2,198
1972	2,010	1,907	2,628	1988	1,934	1,857	2,298
1973	1,879	1,783	2,443	1989	2,014	1,931	2,433
1974	1,835	1,749	2,339	1990	2,081	2,003	2,480
1975	1,774	1,686	2,276	1991	2,073	1,996	2,480
1976	1,738	1,652	2,223	1992	2,065	1,994	2,442
1977	1,790	1,703	2,279	1993	2,046	1,982	2,385
1978	1,760	1,668	2,265	1994	2,036	1,985	2,300
1979	1,808	1,716	2,310	1995	2,019	1,989	2,175
1980	1,840	1,773	2,177	1996	2,027	2,006	2,144
1981	1,812	1,748	2,118	1997	2,033	2,009	2,154
1982	1,828	1,767	2,107	1998	2,059	2,041	2,171
1983	1,799	1,741	2,066	1999	2,075	2,065	2,147
1984	1,807	1,749	2,071	2000	2,130	2,114	2,193
1985	1,844	1,787	2,109	2001	2,115	2,110	2,124

[1] Data for 1984 and earlier includes races other than Black.

Source: U.S. National Center for Health Statistics, *Vital Statistics of the United States*, annual; and unpublished data. See also <http://www.cdc.gov/nchs/>.

No. 89. Projected Fertility and Birth Rates by Race, Origin, and Age Group: 2010

[For definition of total fertility rate, see headnote, Table 88. Birth rates represent live births per 1,000 women in age group indicated. Projections are based on middle fertility assumptions. For explanations of methodology, see text, Section 1]

Age group	All races[1]	White	Black	American Indian, Eskimo, Aleut	Asian and Pacific Islanders	Hispanic[2]
Total fertility rate	2,123	2,098	2,140	2,451	2,252	2,818
Birth rates:						
10 to 14 years old	1.3	0.9	3.5	2.0	0.7	2.3
15 to 19 years old	60.2	54.3	95.6	93.6	29.6	95.7
20 to 24 years old	115.8	112.6	137.1	159.6	83.7	175.2
25 to 29 years old	115.7	118.5	95.5	118.6	134.5	146.7
30 to 34 years old	87.8	90.0	63.4	77.3	128.2	91.6
35 to 39 years old	36.7	36.6	28.9	33.7	59.0	41.9
40 to 44 years old	7.3	7.1	6.0	7.4	13.8	9.9
45 to 49 years old	0.3	0.3	0.3	0.3	0.9	0.6

[1] Includes other races not shown separately. [2] Persons of Hispanic origin may be of any race.

Source: U.S. Census Bureau, Population Division Working Paper No. 38. See also <http://www.census.gov/population/www/techpap.html>.

No. 90. Birth Rates by Live-Birth Order and Race: 1980 to 2001

[Births per 1,000 women 15 to 44 years old in specified racial group. Live-birth order refers to number of children born alive. Figures for births of order not stated are distributed. See also headnote, Table 85. See Appendix III]

Live-birth order	All races[1] 1980	1990	1995	2000	2001	White 1980	1990	1995	2000	2001	Black 1980	1990	1995	2000	2001
Total	68.4	70.9	65.6	67.5	66.9	65.6	68.3	64.4	66.5	66.3	84.9	86.8	72.3	71.7	69.5
First birth	29.5	29.0	27.3	27.1	26.6	28.8	28.4	26.9	26.8	26.4	33.7	32.4	28.7	26.9	26.1
Second birth	21.8	22.8	21.1	21.9	21.8	21.3	22.4	21.1	21.9	22.0	24.7	25.6	20.7	21.3	20.5
Third birth	10.3	11.7	10.5	11.3	11.3	9.6	11.1	10.3	11.2	11.2	14.0	15.6	12.0	12.8	12.4
Fourth birth	3.9	4.5	4.0	4.3	4.4	3.4	4.0	3.8	4.1	4.2	6.5	7.4	5.7	5.9	5.8
Fifth birth	1.5	1.7	1.5	1.6	1.6	1.3	1.4	1.3	1.4	1.4	2.9	3.2	2.6	2.6	2.5
Sixth and seventh	1.0	1.0	0.9	0.9	0.9	0.8	0.8	0.7	0.8	0.8	2.1	2.0	1.8	1.7	1.6
Eighth and over	0.4	0.3	0.3	0.3	0.3	0.3	0.2	0.2	0.3	0.3	0.9	0.5	0.6	0.6	0.5

[1] Includes other races not shown separately.

Source: U.S. National Center for Health Statistics, *Vital Statistics of the United States*, annual; and *National Vital Statistics Reports (NVSR)* (formerly *Monthly Vital Statistics Report*).

No. 91. Births to Teens, Unmarried Mothers, and Prenatal Care: 1990 to 2001

[In percent. Represents registered births. See headnote, Table 84. See Appendix III]

Characteristics	1990	1995	1997	1998	1999	2000	2001
Percent of births to teenage mothers...	**12.8**	**13.1**	**12.7**	**12.5**	**12.3**	**11.8**	**11.3**
White	10.9	11.5	11.2	11.1	10.9	10.6	10.2
Black	23.1	23.1	22.2	21.5	20.7	19.7	18.9
American Indian, Eskimo, Aleut	19.5	21.4	20.8	20.9	20.2	19.7	19.3
Asian and Pacific Islander [1]	5.7	5.6	5.2	5.4	5.1	4.5	4.3
Filipino	6.1	6.2	5.9	6.2	5.9	5.3	5.1
Chinese	1.2	0.9	0.9	0.9	0.9	0.9	1.0
Japanese	2.9	2.5	2.2	2.4	2.1	1.9	1.7
Hawaiian	18.4	19.1	18.6	18.8	18.2	17.4	16.2
Other	(NA)	6.3	5.7	5.8	5.5	4.8	4.6
Hispanic origin [2]	16.8	17.9	17.0	16.9	16.7	16.2	15.6
Mexican	17.7	18.8	17.7	17.5	17.4	17.0	16.5
Puerto Rican	21.7	23.5	22.3	21.9	21.1	20.0	19.2
Cuban	7.7	7.7	7.4	6.9	7.7	7.5	7.5
Central and South American	9.0	10.6	10.5	10.3	10.0	9.9	9.4
Other and unknown Hispanic	(NA)	20.1	19.8	20.2	19.5	18.8	17.3
Percent births to unmarried mothers...	**28.0**	**32.2**	**32.4**	**32.8**	**33.0**	**33.2**	**33.5**
White	20.4	25.3	25.8	26.3	26.8	27.1	27.7
Black	66.5	69.9	69.2	69.1	68.9	68.5	68.4
American Indian, Eskimo, Aleut	53.6	57.2	58.7	59.3	58.9	58.4	59.7
Asian and Pacific Islander [1]	13.2	16.3	15.6	15.6	15.4	14.8	14.9
Filipino	15.9	19.5	19.5	19.7	21.1	20.3	20.4
Chinese	5.0	7.9	6.5	6.4	6.9	7.6	8.4
Japanese	9.6	10.8	10.1	9.7	9.9	9.5	9.2
Hawaiian	45.0	49.0	49.1	51.1	50.4	50.0	50.6
Hispanic origin [2]	36.7	40.8	40.9	41.6	42.2	42.7	42.5
Mexican	33.3	38.1	38.9	39.6	40.1	40.7	40.8
Puerto Rican	55.9	60.0	59.4	59.5	59.6	59.6	58.9
Cuban	18.2	23.8	24.4	24.8	26.4	27.3	27.2
Central and South American	41.2	44.1	41.8	42.0	43.7	44.7	44.3
Percent of mothers beginning prenatal care 1st trimester	**74.2**	**81.3**	**82.5**	**82.8**	**83.2**	**83.2**	**83.4**
White	77.7	83.6	84.7	84.8	85.1	85.0	85.2
Black	60.7	70.4	72.3	73.3	74.1	74.3	74.5
American Indian, Eskimo, Aleut	57.9	66.7	68.1	68.8	69.5	69.3	69.3
Asian and Pacific Islander [1]	(NA)	79.9	82.1	83.1	83.7	84.0	84.0
Filipino	77.1	80.9	83.3	84.2	84.2	84.9	85.0
Chinese	81.3	85.7	87.4	88.5	88.5	87.6	87.0
Japanese	87.0	89.7	89.3	90.2	90.7	91.0	90.1
Hawaiian	65.8	75.9	78.0	78.8	79.6	79.9	79.1
Hispanic origin [2]	60.2	70.8	73.7	74.3	74.4	74.4	75.7
Mexican	57.8	69.1	72.1	72.8	73.1	72.9	74.6
Puerto Rican	63.5	74.0	76.5	76.9	77.7	78.5	79.1
Cuban	84.8	89.2	90.4	91.8	91.4	91.7	91.8
Central and South American	61.5	73.2	76.9	78.0	77.6	77.6	77.4
Percent of mothers beginning prenatal care 3d trimester or no care...	**6.0**	**4.2**	**3.9**	**3.9**	**3.8**	**3.9**	**3.7**
White	4.9	3.5	3.2	3.3	3.2	3.3	3.2
Black	10.9	7.6	7.3	7.0	6.6	6.7	6.5
American Indian, Eskimo, Aleut	12.9	9.5	8.6	8.5	8.2	8.6	8.2
Asian and Pacific Islander [1]	(NA)	4.3	3.8	3.6	3.5	3.3	3.4
Filipino	4.5	4.1	3.3	3.1	2.8	3.0	3.0
Chinese	3.4	3.0	2.4	2.2	2.0	2.2	2.4
Japanese	2.9	2.3	2.7	2.1	2.1	1.8	2.0
Hawaiian	8.7	5.1	5.4	4.7	4.0	4.2	4.8
Hispanic origin [2]	12.0	7.4	6.2	6.3	6.3	6.3	5.9
Mexican	13.2	8.1	6.7	6.8	6.7	6.9	6.2
Puerto Rican	10.6	5.5	5.4	5.1	5.0	4.5	4.6
Cuban	2.8	2.1	1.5	1.2	1.4	1.4	1.3
Central and South American	10.9	6.1	5.0	4.9	5.2	5.4	5.7
Percent of births with low birth weight [3]	**7.0**	**7.3**	**7.5**	**7.6**	**7.6**	**7.6**	**7.7**
White	5.7	6.2	6.5	6.5	6.6	6.5	6.7
Black	13.3	13.1	13.0	13.0	13.1	13.0	13.0
American Indian, Eskimo, Aleut	6.1	6.6	6.8	6.8	7.1	6.8	7.3
Asian and Pacific Islander [1]	(NA)	6.9	7.2	7.4	7.4	7.3	7.5
Filipino	7.3	7.8	8.3	8.2	8.3	8.5	8.7
Chinese	4.7	5.3	5.1	5.3	5.2	5.1	5.3
Japanese	6.2	7.3	6.8	7.5	7.9	7.1	7.3
Hawaiian	7.2	6.8	7.2	7.2	7.7	6.8	7.9
Hispanic origin [2]	6.1	6.3	6.4	6.4	6.4	6.4	6.5
Mexican	5.5	5.8	6.0	6.0	5.9	6.0	6.1
Puerto Rican	9.0	9.4	9.4	9.7	9.3	9.3	9.3
Cuban	5.7	6.5	6.8	6.5	6.8	6.5	6.5
Central and South American	5.8	6.2	6.3	6.5	6.4	6.3	6.5

NA Not available. [1] Includes other races not shown separately. [2] Hispanic persons may be of any race. Includes other types, not shown separately. [3] Births less than 2,500 grams (5 lb.-8 oz.).

Source: U.S. National Center for Health Statistics, *Vital Statistics of the United States*, annual; and *National Vital Statistics Reports (NVSR)* (formerly *Monthly Vital Statistics Report*).

No. 92. Births to Unmarried Women by Race of Child and Age of Mother: 1990 to 2001

[Excludes births to nonresidents of United States. Marital status is inferred from a comparison of the child's and parents' surnames on the birth certificate for those states that do not report on marital status. No estimates included for misstatements on birth records or failures to register births. See also Appendix III]

Race of child and age of mother	1990	1995	1999	2000	2001	Race of child and age of mother	1990	1995	1999	2000	2001
NUMBER (1,000)						30 to 34 years	10.1	10.6	9.5	9.7	10.0
Total live births [1]	1,165	1,254	1,308	1,347	1,349	35 to 39 years	(NA)	5.8	5.9	6.0	(NA)
White	647	785	840	866	880	40 years and over	(NA)	(NA)	1.1	(NA)	(NA)
Black	473	421	417	427	415	AS PERCENT OF ALL BIRTHS IN RACIAL GROUPS					
Under 15 years	11	11	9	8	7						
15 to 19 years	350	376	374	369	352						
20 to 24 years	404	432	476	504	515	Total [1]	26.6	32.2	33.0	33.2	33.5
25 to 29 years	230	229	247	255	258	White	16.9	25.3	26.8	27.1	27.7
30 to 34 years	118	133	125	130	135	Black	66.7	69.9	68.9	68.5	68.4
35 to 39 years	(NA)	60	63	65	65	BIRTH RATE [2]					
40 years and over	(NA)	13	14	16	17						
PERCENT DISTRIBUTION						Total [1,3]	43.8	45.1	44.4	45.2	45.0
						White [3]	31.8	37.5	38.1	38.9	39.2
Total [1]	100.0	100.0	100.0	100.0	100.0	Black [3]	93.9	75.9	71.5	72.5	70.1
White	55.6	62.6	64.1	64.3	65.2	15 to 19 years	42.5	44.4	40.4	39.6	37.4
Black	40.6	33.6	31.9	31.7	30.7	20 to 24 years	65.1	70.3	72.9	74.5	73.8
Under 15 years	0.9	0.9	0.7	0.6	0.6	25 to 29 years	56.0	56.1	60.2	62.2	63.7
15 to 19 years	30.0	30.0	28.6	27.4	26.1	30 to 34 years	37.6	39.6	39.3	40.7	41.9
20 to 24 years	34.7	34.5	36.4	37.4	38.2	35 to 39 years	(NA)	(NA)	19.3	20.0	20.8
25 to 29 years	19.7	18.2	18.9	18.9	19.1	40 to 44 years	(NA)	(NA)	4.6	5.0	5.3

NA Not available. [1] Includes other races not shown separately. [2] Rate per 1,000 unmarried women (never-married, widowed, and divorced) estimated as of July 1. [3] Covers women aged 15 to 44 years.

Source: U.S. National Center for Health Statistics, *Vital Statistics of the United States*, annual; and *National Vital Statistics Reports (NVSR)* (formerly *Monthly Vital Statistics Report*).

No. 93. Live Births by Plurality of Birth and Ratios and Race of Mother: 1995 to 2001

[See Appendix III]

Plurality and race of mother	1995	1997	1998	1999	2000	2001
NUMBER						
Live births, total [1]	3,899,589	3,880,894	3,941,553	3,959,417	4,058,814	4,025,933
White	3,098,885	3,072,640	3,118,727	3,132,501	3,194,005	3,177,626
Black	603,139	599,913	609,902	605,970	622,598	606,156
Live births in single deliveries [1]	3,797,880	3,770,020	3,823,258	3,837,789	3,932,573	3,897,216
White	3,018,184	2,984,532	3,024,693	3,035,757	3,094,219	3,075,683
Black	585,787	581,394	590,372	586,027	601,451	585,189
Live births in twin deliveries [1]	96,736	104,137	110,670	114,307	118,916	121,246
White	76,196	82,090	87,163	90,191	93,235	95,315
Black	17,000	17,989	19,001	19,374	20,626	20,414
Live births in higher-order multiple deliveries [1]	4,973	6,737	7,625	7,321	7,325	7,471
White	4,505	6,018	6,871	6,553	6,551	6,628
Black	352	530	529	569	521	553
RATIO PER 1,000 LIVE BIRTHS						
All multiple births [1]	26.1	28.6	30.0	30.7	31.1	32.0
White	26.0	28.7	30.2	30.9	31.2	32.1
Black	28.8	30.9	32.0	32.9	34.0	34.6
Twin births [1]	24.8	26.8	28.1	28.9	29.3	30.1
White	24.6	26.7	27.9	28.8	29.2	30.0
Black	28.2	30.0	31.2	32.0	33.1	33.7
RATIO PER 100,000 LIVE BIRTHS						
Higher-order multiple births [1]	127.5	173.6	193.5	184.9	180.5	185.6
White	145.4	195.9	220.3	209.2	205.1	208.6
Black	58.4	88.3	86.7	93.9	83.7	91.2

[1] Includes races other than White and Black.

Source: U.S. National Center for Health Statistics, *Advance Report of Final Natality Statistics*, and *National Vital Statistics Reports (NVSR)* (formerly *Monthly Vital Statistics Report*).

No. 94. Low Birth Weight and Births to Teenage Mothers and to Unmarried Women—States and Other Areas: 1990 to 2001

[Represents registered births. Excludes births to nonresidents of the United States. Based on 100 percent of births in all states and the District of Columbia. See Appendix III]

State and other area	Percent of births with low birth weight [1] 1990	1995	2001	Births to teenage mothers percent of total [2] 1990	1995	2001	Births to unmarried women percent of total 1990	1995	2001
U.S.	7.0	7.3	7.7	12.8	13.1	11.3	26.6	32.2	33.5
AL	8.4	9.0	9.6	18.2	18.5	14.9	30.1	34.5	34.4
AK	4.8	5.3	5.7	9.7	11.2	10.7	26.2	29.9	32.8
AZ	6.4	6.8	7.0	14.2	15.1	13.8	32.7	38.2	39.5
AR	8.2	8.2	8.8	19.7	19.6	16.3	29.4	32.9	36.1
CA	5.8	6.1	6.3	11.6	12.4	10.2	31.6	32.1	32.7
CO	8.0	8.4	8.5	11.3	12.1	10.9	21.2	24.9	25.0
CT	6.6	7.1	7.4	8.2	8.6	7.4	26.6	30.6	29.2
DE	7.6	8.4	9.3	11.9	13.2	12.0	29.0	34.9	39.9
DC	15.1	13.4	12.1	17.8	16.3	13.4	64.9	65.8	57.4
FL	7.4	7.7	8.2	13.9	13.7	12.0	31.7	35.8	39.0
GA	8.7	8.8	8.8	16.7	16.3	13.2	32.8	35.2	37.3
HI	7.1	7.0	8.1	10.5	10.1	9.9	24.8	29.2	33.0
ID	5.7	5.9	6.4	12.3	14.0	10.8	16.7	19.9	22.0
IL	7.6	7.9	8.0	13.1	12.9	10.9	31.7	33.8	34.5
IN	6.6	7.5	7.6	14.5	14.7	11.8	26.2	31.9	35.5
IA	5.4	6.0	6.4	10.2	11.0	9.6	21.0	25.2	28.8
KS	6.2	6.4	7.0	12.3	13.1	11.6	21.5	25.9	29.9
KY	7.1	7.6	8.3	17.5	17.2	13.2	23.6	28.5	31.7
LA	9.2	9.7	10.4	17.6	19.1	16.2	36.8	42.4	46.3
ME	5.1	6.1	6.0	10.8	10.3	8.9	22.6	27.8	31.8
MD	7.8	8.5	9.0	10.5	10.3	9.4	29.6	33.3	34.4
MA	5.9	6.3	7.2	8.0	7.5	6.2	24.7	25.6	26.7
MI	7.6	7.7	8.0	13.5	12.5	10.2	26.2	34.3	34.3
MN	5.1	5.9	6.3	8.0	8.4	7.9	20.9	23.9	26.3
MS	9.6	9.8	10.7	21.3	22.2	17.8	40.5	45.3	46.3
MO	7.1	7.6	7.6	14.4	14.4	12.5	28.6	32.1	34.8
MT	6.2	5.8	6.9	11.5	12.6	11.6	23.7	26.5	31.4
NE	5.3	6.3	6.6	9.8	10.0	9.7	20.7	24.3	27.7
NV	7.2	7.4	7.6	12.6	13.7	11.9	25.4	42.0	37.2
NH	4.9	5.5	6.5	7.2	7.6	6.3	16.9	22.2	24.2
NJ	7.0	7.6	7.9	8.4	8.2	6.8	24.3	27.6	29.2
NM	7.4	7.5	7.9	16.3	18.4	17.0	35.4	42.6	46.3
NY	7.6	7.6	7.7	9.1	9.3	8.0	33.0	37.9	35.7
NC	8.0	8.7	8.9	16.2	15.2	12.4	29.4	31.4	34.3
ND	5.5	5.3	6.2	8.6	9.6	8.9	18.4	23.5	27.9
OH	7.1	7.6	8.0	13.8	13.7	11.4	28.9	33.0	35.1
OK	6.6	7.0	7.8	16.2	17.1	15.1	25.2	30.5	35.2
OR	5.0	5.5	5.5	12.0	13.0	10.8	25.7	28.9	30.4
PA	7.1	7.4	7.9	10.9	10.8	9.6	28.6	32.4	33.8
RI	6.2	6.8	7.3	10.5	10.1	9.9	26.3	31.1	35.7
SC	8.7	9.3	9.6	17.1	17.3	14.5	32.7	37.4	40.1
SD	5.1	5.6	6.4	10.8	11.4	11.1	22.9	28.0	33.5
TN	8.2	8.7	9.2	17.6	16.9	14.1	30.2	33.1	35.7
TX	6.9	7.1	7.6	15.6	16.6	14.7	17.5	30.0	31.0
UT	5.7	6.3	6.4	10.3	10.8	8.2	13.5	15.7	17.4
VT	5.3	5.4	5.9	8.5	8.2	8.3	20.1	24.9	31.0
VA	7.2	7.7	7.9	11.7	11.4	9.7	26.0	29.3	30.3
WA	5.3	5.5	5.8	10.8	11.5	9.6	23.7	26.7	28.8
WV	7.1	7.9	8.5	17.8	17.2	13.3	25.4	30.5	32.5
WI	5.9	6.0	6.6	10.2	10.5	9.9	24.2	27.4	29.9
WY	7.4	7.4	8.3	13.6	15.2	12.9	19.8	26.4	29.6
PR	(NA)	(NA)	11.2	(NA)	(NA)	(NA)	(NA)	(NA)	51.1
VI	(NA)	(NA)	9.7	(NA)	(NA)	(NA)	(NA)	(NA)	66.8
GU	(NA)	(NA)	8.1	(NA)	(NA)	(NA)	(NA)	(NA)	55.7
AS	(NA)	(NA)	3.9	(NA)	(NA)	(NA)	(NA)	(NA)	28.3
MP	(NA)	(NA)	8.3	(NA)	(NA)	(NA)	(NA)	(NA)	57.5

NA Not available. [1] Less than 2,500 grams (5 pounds-8 ounces). [2] Defined as mothers who are 20 years of age or younger.

Source: U.S. National Center for Health Statistics, *Vital Statistics of the United States*, annual; and *National Vital Statistics Reports (NVSR)* (formerly *Monthly Vital Statistics Report*). See also <http://www.cdc.gov/nchs/>.

No. 95. Live Births by Place of Delivery, Median and Low Birth Weight, and Prenatal Care: 1990 to 2001

[Represents registered births. Excludes births to nonresidents of the United States. For total number of births, see Table 85. See Appendix III]

Item	1990	1995	1996	1997	1998	1999	2000	2001
Births attended (1,000):								
In hospital [1]	4,110	3,861	3,854	3,881	3,904	3,923	4,021	3,990
By physician, not in hospital	14	6	6	5	6	5	5	4
By midwife and other, not in hospital [2]	21	21	20	20	21	21	21	22
Median birth weight [3]	7 lb.-7 oz.	(NA)	7 lb.-7 oz.	7 lb.-7 oz.	7 lb.-7 oz.	(NA)	7 lb.-7 oz.	7 lb.-6 oz.
Percent of births with low birth weight	7.0	7.3	7.4	7.5	7.6	7.6	7.6	7.7
White	5.7	6.2	6.3	6.5	6.5	6.6	6.5	6.7
Black	13.3	13.1	13.0	13.0	13.0	13.1	13.0	13.0
Percent of births by period in which prenatal care began:								
1st trimester	74.2	81.3	81.9	82.5	82.8	83.2	83.2	83.4
3d trimester or no prenatal care	6.0	4.2	4.0	3.9	3.9	3.8	3.9	3.7

NA Not available. [1] Includes all births in hospitals or institutions and in clinics. [2] Includes births with attendant not specified. [3] Median birth weight based on race of mother; prior to 1990, based on race of child.

Source: U.S. National Center for Health Statistics, *Vital Statistics of the United States*, annual; and *National Vital Statistics Reports (NVSR)* (formerly *Monthly Vital Statistics Report*), and unpublished data. See also <http://www.cdc.gov/nchs/births.htm>.

No. 96. Method of Delivery by Race: 1990 to 2001

[In thousands (4,111 represents 4,111,000), except rate. 1990 excludes data for Oklahoma, which did not report method of delivery on the birth certificate. See Appendix III]

Age of mother	1990	2000	2001	Age of mother	1990	2000	2001
Births by method of delivery	4,111	4,059	4,026	Not stated	16	4	3
Vaginal	3,111	3,108	3,028	Hispanic births by method of delivery (1,000)	595	816	852
After previous cesarean	84	90	74	Vaginal	458	633	649
Cesarean deliveries	914	924	978	After previous cesarean	10	17	15
Primary	575	578	601	Cesarean deliveries	123	180	200
Repeat	339	346	377	Primary	76	105	114
Not stated	85	27	20	Repeat	47	75	86
White births by method of delivery	3,252	3,194	3,178	Not stated	14	3	3
Vaginal	2,454	2,449	2,395	Cesarean delivery rate [1]	22.7	22.9	24.4
After previous cesarean	67	70	58	White	23.0	22.8	24.3
Cesarean deliveries	733	723	767	Black	22.1	24.3	25.9
Primary	459	449	467	Primary [2]	16.0	16.1	16.9
Repeat	274	274	299	White	16.1	15.9	16.7
Not stated	66	22	16	Black	15.7	17.3	18.3
Black births by method of delivery	679	623	606	Rate of vaginal birth after previous cesarean [3]	19.9	20.6	16.4
Vaginal	517	468	447	White	19.7	20.4	16.2
After previous cesarean	13	14	12	Black	20.3	20.5	16.7
Cesarean deliveries	146	150	156				
Primary	93	95	97				
Repeat	53	56	59				

[1] Cesarean rates are the number of cesarean deliveries per 100 total deliveries for specified category. [2] Number of primary cesareans per 100 live births to women who have not had a previous cesarean. [3] Number of vaginal births after previous cesarean delivery per 100 live births to women with a previous cesarean delivery.

Source: U.S. National Center for Health Statistics, *Vital Statistics of the United States*, annual.

No. 97. Percent Low Birthweight by Smoking Status, Age, and Race of Mother: 2000

[Low birthweight is defined as weight of less than 2,500 grams (5 lb. 8 oz.). Excludes California, Indiana, New York State (but includes New York City), and South Dakota, which did not require reporting of tobacco use during pregnancy]

Smoking status and race of mother	All ages	Under 15 years	15-19 years Total	15-17 years	18-19 years	20-24 years	25-29 years	30-34 years	35-39 years
All races [1]	7.8	14.4	9.8	10.6	9.4	7.9	6.9	7.0	8.5
Smoker	11.9	13.3	11.4	11.9	11.1	10.5	11.2	13.2	16.9
Nonsmoker	7.2	14.3	9.5	10.3	9.0	7.3	6.4	6.5	7.6
White	6.7	12.1	8.3	8.9	8.0	6.6	6.0	6.2	7.5
Smoker	10.7	12.3	10.7	11.4	10.4	9.6	10.0	11.4	14.9
Nonsmoker	6.1	11.9	7.5	8.2	7.2	5.9	5.5	5.7	6.7
Black	13.1	16.8	13.9	14.2	13.6	12.3	12.0	13.3	15.5
Smoker	20.4	(B)	17.0	16.2	17.3	17.0	19.7	24.7	28.3
Nonsmoker	12.3	16.7	13.6	14.1	13.3	11.8	11.3	12.1	13.7

B Base figure too small to meet statistical standards for reliability of a derived figure. [1] Includes races other than White and Black.

Source: U.S. National Center for Health Statistics, *National Vital Statistics Reports (NVSR)* Vol. 50, No. 5 (formerly *Monthly Vital Report*). See also <http://www.cdc.gov/nchs/nvss.htm>.

Vital Statistics 79

No. 98. Women Who Have Had a Child in the Last Year by Age: 1980 to 2000

[3,247 represents 3,247,000. Excludes births to nonresidents of the United States. Data are by place of residence. metropolitan statistical areas (MSAs), consolidated metropolitan statistical areas (CMSAs), and New England County metropolitan areas (NECMAs) are defined by the U.S. Office of Management and Budget as of June 30, 1990. See Appendix II for definitions and components]

Age of mother	Women who had a child in last year (1,000)			Total births per 1,000 women			First births per 1,000 women		
	1980	1990	2000	1980	1990	2000	1980	1990	2000
Total	3,247	3,913	3,934	71.1	67.0	64.6	28.5	26.4	26.7
15 to 29 years old [1]	2,476	2,568	2,432	103.7	90.8	85.9	48.6	43.2	43.1
15 to 19 years old	(NA)	338	586	(NA)	39.8	59.7	(NA)	30.1	38.7
20 to 24 years old	1,396	1,038	850	96.6	113.4	91.8	(NA)	51.8	47.1
25 to 29 years old	1,081	1,192	996	114.8	112.1	107.9	(NA)	46.2	43.7
30 to 44 years old	770	1,346	1,502	35.4	44.7	46.1	6.3	10.6	12.5
30 to 34 years old	519	892	871	60.0	80.4	87.9	(NA)	21.9	27.5
35 to 39 years old	192	377	506	26.9	37.3	45.1	(NA)	6.5	9.6
40 to 44 years old	59	77	125	9.9	8.6	10.9	(NA)	1.2	2.3

NA Not available.   [1] For 1980-88, 18 to 29 years old.

Source: U.S. Census Bureau, Current Population Reports, P20-375, P20-454, and P20-543.

No. 99. Characteristics of Women Who Have Had a Child in the Last Year: 1995 and 2000

[As of June. Covers civilian noninstitutional population. Since the number of women who had a birth during the 12-month period was tabulated and not the actual numbers of births, some small underestimation of fertility for this period may exist due to the omission of: (1) Multiple births, (2) Two or more live births spaced within the 12-month period (the woman is counted only once), (3) Women who had births in the period and who did not survive to the survey date, and (4) Women who were in institutions and therefore not in the survey universe. These losses may be somewhat offset by the inclusion in the CPS of births to immigrants who did not have their children born in the United States and births to nonresident women. These births would not have been recorded in the vital registration system. Based on Current Population Survey (CPS); see text, Section 1, and Appendix III]

Characteristic	1995 Number of women (1,000)	1995 Total births per 1,000 women	1995 First births per 1,000 women	2000 Number of women (1,000)	2000 Total births per 1,000 women	2000 First births per 1,000 women
Total [1]	60,225	61.4	23.2	60,873	64.6	26.7
White	48,603	59.2	22.6	48,506	65.4	27.2
Black	8,617	70.6	26.4	8,939	63.2	21.9
Hispanic [2]	6,632	79.6	25.0	8,002	95.1	38.6
Currently married	31,616	85.5	30.3	30,497	88.8	35.5
Married, spouse present	29,202	87.2	31.4	28,215	90.8	37.0
Married, spouse absent [3]	2,414	64.5	17.4	2,282	64.5	16.6
Widowed or divorced	5,762	28.4	4.1	5,281	31.0	6.8
Never married	22,846	36.3	18.0	25,095	42.3	20.2
Educational attainment:						
Less than high school	12,629	57.3	19.6	13,006	70.7	29.5
High school, 4 years	18,404	67.4	25.5	17,205	70.0	29.5
College: 1 or more years	29,192	59.3	23.2	30,662	59.0	24.0
No degree	12,724	56.1	21.2	12,603	51.6	19.2
Associate degree	4,663	56.9	19.2	4,955	60.6	23.6
Bachelor's degree	8,884	65.3	27.0	9,926	61.7	27.7
Graduate or professional degree	2,921	59.2	26.8	3,178	77.7	32.0
Labor force status:						
Employed	39,989	46.5	20.9	41,369	47.7	20.7
Unemployed	3,287	53.5	22.8	2,493	79.4	31.1
Not in labor force	16,949	98.1	28.5	17,011	103.7	40.6
Occupation of employed women:						
Managerial-professional	11,059	46.2	22.3	12,481	52.2	22.9
Technical, sales, admin. support	16,997	48.6	21.5	16,561	44.0	20.3
Service workers	7,612	44.0	16.6	8,102	51.0	20.1
Farming, forestry, and fishing	501	41.0	27.9	473	69.6	71.8
Precision prod, craft, repair	813	56.6	37.5	880	42.3	15.1
Operators, fabricators, laborers	3,007	39.5	17.8	2,872	38.1	17.2
Family income:						
Under $10,000	6,957	91.0	32.8	4,249	86.8	32.5
$10,000 to $19,999	8,159	64.3	25.8	6,203	74.8	25.3
$20,000 to $24,999	4,542	60.6	20.3	3,439	76.2	37.3
$25,000 to $29,999	4,364	57.0	18.9	3,761	78.9	34.0
$30,000 to $34,999	4,076	60.6	24.3	3,572	62.4	27.3
$35,000 to $49,999	9,949	59.1	20.8	8,864	64.9	25.3
$50,000 to $74,999	9,720	52.5	23.3	10,646	61.2	26.8
$75,000 and over	7,088	53.1	19.2	12,506	60.1	24.3

[1] Includes women of other races and women with family income not reported, not shown separately.   [2] Persons of Hispanic origin may be of any race.   [3] Includes separated women.

Source: U.S. Census Bureau, Current Population Reports, P20-499, P20-543, and unpublished data.

No. 100. Women Who Have Had a Child in the Last Year by Age and Labor Force Status: 1980 to 2000

[3,247 represents 3,247,000. See headnote, Table 98. See Appendix III]

Year	Total, 18 to 44 years old Number (1,000)	In the labor force Number (1,000)	In the labor force Percent	18 to 29 years old Number (1,000)	In the labor force Number (1,000)	In the labor force Percent	30 to 44 years old Number (1,000)	In the labor force Number (1,000)	In the labor force Percent
1980	3,247	1,233	38	2,476	947	38	770	287	37
1981	3,381	1,411	42	2,499	1,004	40	881	407	46
1982	3,433	1,508	44	2,445	1,040	43	988	469	48
1983	3,625	1,563	43	2,682	1,138	42	942	425	45
1984	3,311	1,547	47	2,375	1,058	45	936	489	52
1985	3,497	1,691	48	2,512	1,204	48	984	488	50
1986	3,625	1,805	50	2,452	1,185	48	1,174	620	53
1987	3,701	1,881	51	2,521	1,258	50	1,180	623	53
1988	3,667	1,866	51	2,384	1,177	49	1,283	688	54
1990 [1]	3,913	2,068	53	2,568	1,275	50	1,346	793	59
1992 [1]	3,688	1,985	54	2,346	1,182	50	1,342	802	60
1994 [1]	3,890	2,066	53	2,389	1,209	51	1,501	857	57
1995 [1]	3,696	2,034	55	2,252	1,150	51	1,444	884	61
1998 [1]	3,671	2,155	59	(NA)	(NA)	(NA)	(NA)	(NA)	(NA)
2000 [1]	3,934	2,170	55	2,432	1,304	54	1,502	866	58

NA Not available. [1] Lower age limit is 15 years old.

Source: U.S. Census Bureau, Current Population Reports, P20-543; and unpublished data.

No. 101. Contraceptive Use by Women, 15 to 44 Years of Age: 1995

[60,201 represents 60,201,000. Based on samples of the female population of the United States; see source for details. See Appendix III]

Contraceptive status and method	All women [1]	Age 15-24 years	Age 25-34 years	Age 35-44 years	Non-Hispanic White	Non-Hispanic Black	Hispanic	Never married	Currently married	Formerly married
All women (1,000)	60,201	18,002	20,758	21,440	42,522	8,210	6,702	22,679	29,673	7,849
PERCENT DISTRIBUTION										
Sterile [2]	29.7	2.6	25.0	57.0	30.2	31.5	28.4	6.9	43.2	45.1
Surgically sterile	27.9	1.8	23.6	54.0	28.5	29.7	26.3	5.7	41.1	42.5
Nonsurgically sterile [3]	1.7	0.7	1.3	2.8	1.6	1.8	2.0	1.1	2.0	2.2
Pregnant, postpartum	4.6	5.9	6.9	1.3	4.3	4.5	6.3	3.1	6.4	1.9
Seeking pregnancy	4.0	2.1	6.2	3.5	3.7	4.6	4.0	1.5	6.4	2.1
Other nonusers	22.3	44.4	13.3	12.6	21.1	23.1	26.3	46.8	4.7	18.4
Never had intercourse	10.9	30.8	3.4	1.4	10.4	8.9	12.1	28.9	-	-
No intercourse in last month [4]	6.2	7.0	5.3	6.5	5.7	7.2	8.6	11.5	0.5	12.7
Had intercourse in last month [4]	5.2	6.6	4.6	4.7	5.0	7.0	5.6	6.4	4.2	5.7
Nonsurgical contraceptors	39.7	45.0	49.1	26.1	41.2	36.1	35.1	41.8	39.7	32.4
Pill	17.3	23.1	23.7	6.3	18.8	14.8	13.6	20.4	15.6	14.6
IUD	0.5	0.1	0.6	0.8	0.5	0.5	0.9	0.3	0.7	0.4
Diaphragm	1.2	0.2	1.2	2.0	1.5	0.5	0.4	0.5	1.8	0.9
Condom	13.1	13.9	15.0	10.7	13.0	12.5	12.1	13.9	13.3	10.1
Periodic abstinence	1.5	0.5	1.8	2.0	1.6	0.7	1.3	0.6	2.3	0.7
Natural family planning	0.2	-	0.3	0.3	0.3	-	0.1	-	0.4	-
Withdrawal	2.0	1.6	2.3	1.9	2.1	0.9	2.0	1.5	2.3	1.8
Other methods [5]	3.9	5.6	4.2	2.1	3.4	6.2	4.7	4.6	3.3	3.9

- Represents or rounds to zero. [1] Includes other races, not shown separately. [2] Total sterile includes male sterile for unknown reasons. [3] Persons sterile from illness, accident, or congenital conditions. [4] Data refer to no intercourse in the 3 months prior to interview. [5] Includes implants, injectables, morning-after-pill, suppository, Today™ sponge and less frequently used methods.

Source: U.S. National Center for Health Statistics, special tabulations from the 1995 National Survey of Family Growth.

No. 102. Abortions—Number, Rate, and Ratio by Race: 1972 to 1999

Year	All races Women 15-44 years old (1,000)	All races Abortions Number (1,000)	All races Rate per 1,000 women	All races Ratio per 1,000 live births [1]	White Women 15-44 years old (1,000)	White Abortions Number (1,000)	White Rate per 1,000 women	White Ratio per 1,000 live births [1]	Black and other Women 15-44 years old (1,000)	Black and other Abortions Number (1,000)	Black and other Rate per 1,000 women	Black and other Ratio per 1,000 live births [1]
1972	44,588	587	13.2	184	38,532	455	11.8	175	6,056	132	21.7	223
1975	47,606	1,034	21.7	331	40,857	701	17.2	276	6,749	333	49.3	565
1976	48,721	1,179	24.2	361	41,721	785	18.8	296	7,000	394	56.3	638
1977	49,814	1,317	26.4	400	42,567	889	20.9	333	7,247	428	59.0	679
1978	50,920	1,410	27.7	413	43,427	969	22.3	356	7,493	440	58.7	665
1979	52,016	1,498	28.8	420	44,266	1,062	24.0	373	7,750	435	56.2	625
1980	53,048	1,554	29.3	428	44,942	1,094	24.3	37	8,106	460	56.5	642
1981	53,901	1,577	29.3	430	45,494	1,108	24.3	377	8,407	470	55.9	645
1982	54,679	1,574	28.8	428	46,049	1,095	23.8	373	8,630	479	55.5	646
1983 [2]	55,340	1,575	28.5	436	46,506	1,084	23.3	376	8,834	491	55.5	670
1984	56,061	1,577	28.1	423	47,023	1,087	23.1	366	9,038	491	54.3	646
1985	56,754	1,589	28.0	422	47,512	1,076	22.6	360	9,242	513	55.5	659
1986 [2]	57,483	1,574	27.4	416	48,010	1,045	21.8	350	9,473	529	55.9	661
1987	57,964	1,559	27.1	405	48,288	1,017	21.1	338	9,676	542	56.0	648
1988	58,192	1,591	27.3	401	48,325	1,026	21.2	333	9,867	565	57.3	638
1989 [2]	58,365	1,567	26.8	380	48,104	1,006	20.9	309	10,261	561	54.7	650
1990 [2]	58,700	1,609	27.4	389	48,224	1,039	21.5	318	10,476	570	54.4	655
1991	59,305	1,557	26.2	379	48,560	982	20.2	303	10,745	574	53.5	661
1992	59,417	1,529	25.7	380	48,435	943	19.5	298	10,982	585	53.3	681
1993 [2]	59,712	1,495	25.0	376	48,497	908	18.7	290	11,215	587	52.4	698
1994 [2]	60,020	1,423	23.7	362	48,592	856	17.6	275	11,429	567	49.6	696
1995	60,368	1,359	22.5	350	48,719	817	16.8	265	11,648	542	46.6	684
1996	60,704	1,360	22.4	349	48,837	797	16.3	258	11,867	563	47.5	699
1997	61,041	1,335	21.9	341	48,942	777	15.9	251	12,099	558	46.1	684
1998	61,326	1,319	21.5	334	49,012	762	15.5	244	12,313	557	45.2	678
1999	61,475	1,315	21.4	327	48,974	743	15.2	234	12,501	572	45.8	674

[1] Live births are those which occurred from July 1 of year shown through June 30 of the following year (to match time of conception with abortions). Births are classified by race of child 1972-1988, and by race of mother after 1988. [2] Total numbers of abortions in 1983 and 1986 have been estimated by interpolation; 1989, 1990, 1993, and 1994 have been estimated using trends in CDC data.

No. 103. Abortions by Selected Characteristics: 1990 to 1999

[Number of abortions from surveys conducted by source; characteristics from the U.S. Centers for Disease Control's (CDC) annual abortion surveillance summaries, with adjustments for changes in states reporting data to the CDC each year. Total number of abortions in 1990 have been estimated using trends in CDC data]

Characteristic	Number (1,000) 1990	Number (1,000) 1995	Number (1,000) 1999	Percent distribution 1990	Percent distribution 1995	Percent distribution 1999	Abortion ratio [1] 1990	Abortion ratio [1] 1995	Abortion ratio [1] 1999
Total abortions	1,609	1,359	1,315	100	100	100	280	259	246
Age of woman:									
Less than 15 years old	13	11	9	1	1	1	515	479	497
15 to 19 years old	351	263	241	22	19	18	403	347	337
20 to 24 years old	532	441	423	33	32	32	328	317	297
25 to 29 years old	360	308	308	22	23	23	224	224	221
30 to 34 years old	216	196	188	13	14	14	196	179	171
35 to 39 years old	108	109	111	7	8	8	249	219	200
40 years old and over	29	32	36	2	2	3	354	309	283
Race of woman:									
White	1,039	817	743	65	60	56	241	209	190
Black and other	570	542	572	35	40	44	396	406	403
Marital status of woman: [2]									
Married	341	268	253	21	20	19	104	93	86
Unmarried	1,268	1,091	1,062	79	80	81	516	466	444
Number of prior live births:									
None	780	612	533	49	45	41	316	276	248
One	396	358	368	25	26	28	230	223	219
Two	280	247	259	17	18	20	292	285	279
Three	102	94	102	6	7	8	279	283	283
Four or more	50	48	54	3	4	4	223	228	243
Number of prior induced abortions:									
None	891	719	682	55	53	52	(NA)	(NA)	(NA)
One	443	382	365	28	28	28	(NA)	(NA)	(NA)
Two or more	275	259	268	17	19	20	(NA)	(NA)	(NA)
Weeks of gestation:									
Less than 9 weeks	825	726	750	51	53	57	(NA)	(NA)	(NA)
9 to 10 weeks	416	316	272	26	23	21	(NA)	(NA)	(NA)
11 to 12 weeks	195	152	139	12	11	11	(NA)	(NA)	(NA)
13 weeks or more	173	165	154	11	12	12	(NA)	(NA)	(NA)

NA Not available. [1] Number of abortions per 1,000 abortions and live births. Live births are those which occurred from July 1 of year shown through June 30 of the following year (to match time of conception with abortions). [2] Separated women included with unmarried.

Source of Tables 102 and 103: S.K. Henshaw and J. Van Vort, eds., *Abortion Factbook, 1992 Edition: Readings, Trends, and State and Local Data to 1988*, The Alan Guttmacher Institute, New York, NY, 1992 (copyright); S.K. Henshaw and J. Van Vort, Abortion Services in the United States, 1991 and 1992. *Family Planning Perspectives, 26:100, 1994*; L.B. Finer and S.K. Henshaw, Abortion Incidence and Services in the United States, 2000, *Perspectives on Sexual and Reproductive Health*, 356, 2003; and unpublished data.

No. 104. Abortions—Number and Rate by State: 1992 and 2000

[Number of abortions from surveys of hospitals, clinics, and physicians identified as providers of abortion services conducted by The Alan Guttmacher Institute. Abortion rates are computed per 1,000 women 15 to 44 years of age on July 1 of specified year]

State	Number (1,000) 1992	Number (1,000) 2000	Rate [1] 1992	Rate [1] 2000	State	Number (1,000) 1992	Number (1,000) 2000	Rate [1] 1992	Rate [1] 2000
U.S.	1,529	1,313	25.7	21.3	MO	14	8	11.5	6.6
AL	17	14	18.1	14.3	MT	3	3	18.4	13.5
AK	2	2	16.5	11.7	NE	6	4	15.6	11.6
AZ	21	18	23.5	16.5	NV	13	14	43.3	32.2
AR	7	6	13.5	9.8	NH	4	3	14.6	11.2
CA	304	236	41.8	31.2	NJ	55	66	30.4	36.3
CO	20	16	23.6	15.9	NM	6	6	17.6	14.7
CT	20	15	26.0	21.1	NY	195	165	45.6	39.1
DE	6	5	34.9	31.3	NC	36	38	22.2	21.0
DC	21	10	133.1	68.1	ND	1	1	10.7	9.9
FL	85	103	29.3	31.9	OH	50	40	19.5	16.5
GA	40	32	23.7	16.9	OK	9	7	12.5	10.1
HI	12	6	46.0	22.1	OR	16	17	23.9	23.5
ID	2	2	7.2	7.0	PA	50	37	18.6	14.3
IL	68	64	25.2	23.2	RI	7	6	29.5	24.1
IN	16	12	12.0	9.4	SC	12	8	14.2	9.3
IA	7	6	11.3	9.8	SD	1	1	6.9	5.5
KS	13	12	22.4	21.4	TN	19	19	16.1	15.2
KY	10	5	11.4	5.3	TX	97	89	23.1	18.8
LA	14	13	13.4	13.0	UT	4	4	9.2	6.6
ME	4	3	14.9	9.9	VT	3	2	21.5	12.7
MD	31	35	26.2	29.0	VA	35	29	22.6	18.1
MA	41	30	28.1	21.4	WA	33	26	27.7	20.3
MI	56	46	25.1	21.6	WV	3	3	7.8	6.8
MN	16	15	15.6	13.5	WI	15	11	13.5	9.6
MS	8	4	12.4	5.9	WY	-	-	4.4	0.9

- Represents or rounds to zero. [1] Rate per 1,000 women, 15 to 44 years old.

Source: S.K. Henshaw and J. Van Vort, *Abortion Services in the United States, 1991 and 1992*, Family Planning Perspectives, 26:100, 1994; S.K. Henshaw, *Abortion Incidence and Services in the United States, 1995-1996*, Family Planning Perspectives, 30:263, 1998; L.B. Finer and S.K. Henshaw, *Abortion Incidence and Services in the United States in 2000*, Perspectives on Sexual and Reproductive Health, 35:6, 2003; and unpublished data.

No. 105. Expectation of Life at Birth, 1970 to 2001, and Projections, 2005 and 2010

[In years. Excludes deaths of nonresidents of the United States. See Appendix III]

Year	Total Total	Total Male	Total Female	White Total	White Male	White Female	Black and other Total	Black and other Male	Black and other Female	Black Total	Black Male	Black Female
1970	70.8	67.1	74.7	71.7	68.0	75.6	65.3	61.3	69.4	64.1	60.0	68.3
1975	72.6	68.8	76.6	73.4	69.5	77.3	68.0	63.7	72.4	66.8	62.4	71.3
1980	73.7	70.0	77.4	74.4	70.7	78.1	69.5	65.3	73.6	68.1	63.8	72.5
1982	74.5	70.8	78.1	75.1	71.5	78.7	70.9	66.8	74.9	69.4	65.1	73.6
1983	74.6	71.0	78.1	75.2	71.6	78.7	70.9	67.0	74.7	69.4	65.2	73.5
1984	74.7	71.1	78.2	75.3	71.8	78.7	71.1	67.2	74.9	69.5	65.3	73.6
1985	74.7	71.1	78.2	75.3	71.8	78.7	71.0	67.0	74.8	69.3	65.0	73.4
1986	74.7	71.2	78.2	75.4	71.9	78.8	70.9	66.8	74.9	69.1	64.8	73.4
1987	74.9	71.4	78.3	75.6	72.1	78.9	71.0	66.9	75.0	69.1	64.7	73.4
1988	74.9	71.4	78.3	75.6	72.2	78.9	70.8	66.7	74.8	68.9	64.4	73.2
1989	75.1	71.7	78.5	75.9	72.5	79.2	70.9	66.7	74.9	68.8	64.3	73.3
1990	75.4	71.8	78.8	76.1	72.7	79.4	71.2	67.0	75.2	69.1	64.5	73.6
1991	75.5	72.0	78.9	76.3	72.9	79.6	71.5	67.3	75.5	69.3	64.6	73.8
1992	75.8	72.3	79.1	76.5	73.2	79.8	71.8	67.7	75.7	69.6	65.0	73.9
1993	75.5	72.2	78.8	76.3	73.1	79.5	71.5	67.3	75.5	69.2	64.6	73.7
1994	75.7	72.3	79.0	76.4	73.2	79.6	71.7	67.5	75.8	69.6	64.9	74.1
1995	75.8	72.5	78.9	76.5	73.4	79.6	71.9	67.9	75.7	69.6	65.2	73.9
1996	76.1	73.0	79.0	76.8	73.8	79.6	72.6	68.9	76.1	70.3	66.1	74.2
1997	76.5	73.6	79.4	77.1	74.3	79.9	(NA)	(NA)	(NA)	71.1	67.2	74.7
1998 [1]	76.7	73.8	79.5	77.3	74.5	80.0	(NA)	(NA)	(NA)	71.3	67.6	74.8
1999	76.7	73.9	79.4	77.3	74.6	79.9	(NA)	(NA)	(NA)	71.4	67.8	74.7
2000	77.0	74.3	79.7	77.6	74.9	80.1	(NA)	(NA)	(NA)	71.9	68.3	75.2
2001 [2]	77.2	74.4	79.8	77.7	75.0	80.2	(NA)	(NA)	(NA)	72.2	68.6	75.5
Projections: [3]												
2005	77.8	74.9	80.7	78.3	75.4	81.1	(NA)	(NA)	(NA)	73.5	69.9	76.8
2010	78.5	75.6	81.4	79.0	76.1	81.8	(NA)	(NA)	(NA)	74.5	70.9	77.8

NA Not available. [1] The 1998 life table values are based upon an 85 percent sample of deaths. [2] Preliminary data. [3] Based on middle mortality assumptions; for details, see source. Source: U.S. Census Bureau, Population Division Working Paper No. 38.

Source: Except as noted, U.S. National Center for Health Statistics, *Vital Statistics of the United States*, annual, and *National Vital Statistics Reports (NVSR)* (formerly *Monthly Vital Statistics Reports*).

No. 106. Selected Life Table Values: 1979 to 2001

[See Appendix III]

Age and sex	Total[1] 1979-1981	1985	1990	1995	1998	1999	2000	2001	White 1979-1981	1985	1990	1995	1998	1999	2000	2001	Black 1979-1981	1985	1990	1995	1998	1999	2000	2001
AVERAGE EXPECTATION OF LIVE IN YEARS																								
At birth: Male	70.1	71.1	71.8	72.5	73.8	73.9	74.3	74.4	70.8	71.8	72.7	73.4	74.5	74.6	74.9	75.0	64.1	65.0	64.5	65.4	67.6	67.8	68.3	68.6
Female	77.6	78.2	78.8	78.9	79.5	79.4	79.7	79.8	78.2	78.7	79.4	79.6	80.0	79.9	80.1	80.2	72.9	73.4	73.6	74.0	74.8	74.7	75.2	75.5
Age 20: Male	51.9	52.6	53.3	53.8	55.0	55.0	55.3	55.5	52.5	53.2	54.0	54.5	55.5	55.6	55.8	60.9	46.4	47.1	46.7	47.3	49.5	49.6	50.0	50.3
Female	59.0	59.3	59.8	59.9	60.3	60.2	60.5	60.6	59.4	59.8	60.3	60.3	60.7	60.7	60.9	60.9	54.9	55.2	55.3	55.5	56.2	56.2	56.6	56.8
Age 40: Male	33.6	34.2	35.1	35.6	36.4	36.5	36.7	37.0	34.0	34.7	35.6	36.1	36.8	36.9	37.1	37.3	29.5	29.8	30.1	30.6	31.9	31.9	32.3	32.6
Female	39.8	40.0	40.6	40.7	41.1	41.0	41.2	41.3	40.2	40.4	41.0	41.0	41.4	41.3	41.5	41.6	36.3	36.4	36.8	37.0	37.5	37.4	37.8	38.0
Age 50: Male	25.0	25.5	26.4	27.0	27.6	27.7	27.9	28.2	25.3	25.8	26.7	27.3	27.9	28.0	28.2	28.4	22.0	22.1	22.5	23.1	23.9	24.0	24.2	24.5
Female	30.7	30.8	31.3	31.4	31.8	31.7	32.0	32.1	31.1	31.1	31.7	31.7	32.0	32.0	32.2	32.3	27.8	27.8	28.2	28.5	28.8	28.7	29.1	29.4
Age 65: Male	14.2	14.5	15.1	15.6	16.0	16.1	16.2	16.4	14.3	14.5	15.2	15.7	16.1	16.1	16.3	16.5	13.3	13.0	13.2	13.7	14.3	14.3	14.2	14.4
Female	18.4	18.5	18.9	18.9	19.2	19.1	19.3	19.4	18.6	18.7	19.1	19.0	19.3	19.2	19.4	19.5	17.1	16.9	17.2	17.2	17.4	17.3	17.7	17.9
EXPECTED DEATHS PER 1,000 ALIVE AT SPECIFIED AGE[2]																								
At birth: Male	13.9	12.0	10.3	8.3	8.0	7.7	7.5	(NA)	12.3	10.6	8.6	7.0	6.5	6.4	6.2	(NA)	23.0	19.9	19.7	16.2	15.8	15.9	15.6	(NA)
Female	11.2	9.4	8.2	6.8	6.6	6.4	6.2	(NA)	9.7	8.0	6.6	5.6	5.4	5.2	5.1	(NA)	19.3	16.5	16.3	13.8	12.9	13.2	12.7	(NA)
Age 20: Male	1.8	1.5	1.6	(NA)	1.3	1.3	1.3	(NA)	1.8	1.4	1.4	(NA)	1.2	1.2	1.2	(NA)	2.2	2.7	2.7	(NA)	2.9	2.1	2.0	(NA)
Female	0.6	0.5	0.5	(NA)	0.4	0.5	0.5	(NA)	0.6	0.5	0.5	(NA)	0.4	0.4	0.4	(NA)	0.7	0.6	0.7	(NA)	0.6	0.6	0.6	(NA)
Age 40: Male	3.0	2.8	3.1	(NA)	2.5	2.6	2.5	(NA)	2.6	2.5	2.7	(NA)	2.3	2.3	2.4	(NA)	6.9	6.5	7.1	(NA)	6.0	4.8	4.6	(NA)
Female	1.6	1.4	1.4	(NA)	1.4	1.4	1.4	(NA)	1.4	1.3	1.2	(NA)	1.2	1.2	1.3	(NA)	3.2	2.9	3.1	(NA)	2.8	2.9	2.8	(NA)
Age 50: Male	7.8	6.8	6.2	(NA)	5.1	5.6	5.2	(NA)	7.1	6.2	5.6	(NA)	4.7	5.1	5.2	(NA)	14.9	13.3	12.8	(NA)	9.6	11.3	11.2	(NA)
Female	4.2	3.8	3.5	(NA)	3.1	3.2	3.1	(NA)	3.8	3.5	3.2	(NA)	2.8	2.9	2.9	(NA)	7.7	6.8	6.6	(NA)	5.5	6.0	6.0	(NA)
Age 65: Male	28.2	26.1	22.9	(NA)	16.2	20.5	15.5	(NA)	27.4	25.2	23.0	(NA)	16.0	19.8	19.2	(NA)	38.5	28.5	36.8	(NA)	19.3	30.5	29.6	(NA)
Female	14.3	14.1	13.5	(NA)	11.0	12.8	10.9	(NA)	13.6	13.5	12.8	(NA)	10.7	12.3	12.2	(NA)	21.6	21.4	21.4	(NA)	14.2	18.3	18.2	(NA)
NUMBER SURVIVING TO SPECIFIED AGE PER 1,000 BORN ALIVE																								
Age 20: Male	973	977	979	981	(NA)	984	984	(NA)	975	979	981	981	(NA)	986	986	(NA)	961	966	963	967	(NA)	971	973	(NA)
Female	982	985	986	987	(NA)	989	989	(NA)	984	986	988	987	(NA)	990	990	(NA)	972	976	976	978	(NA)	980	981	(NA)
Age 40: Male	933	941	938	940	(NA)	952	952	(NA)	940	946	946	940	(NA)	958	958	(NA)	885	897	880	885	(NA)	917	918	(NA)
Female	965	970	971	971	(NA)	974	975	(NA)	969	973	975	971	(NA)	977	978	(NA)	941	948	944	944	(NA)	954	955	(NA)
Age 50: Male	890	902	899	899	(NA)	917	917	(NA)	901	911	912	899	(NA)	926	925	(NA)	801	820	801	803	(NA)	850	855	(NA)
Female	941	948	950	950	(NA)	954	954	(NA)	947	953	957	950	(NA)	960	960	(NA)	896	908	904	902	(NA)	915	915	(NA)
Age 65: Male	706	727	741	750	(NA)	777	779	(NA)	724	744	760	750	(NA)	793	794	(NA)	551	571	571	581	(NA)	633	640	(NA)
Female	835	844	851	855	(NA)	863	863	(NA)	848	855	864	855	(NA)	874	874	(NA)	733	746	751	758	(NA)	777	780	(NA)

NA Not available. [1] Includes other races not shown separately. [2] See footnote 1, Table 107.

Source: U.S. National Center for Health Statistics, *U.S. Life Tables and Actuarial Tables, 1959-61, 1969-71, and 1979-81*; *Vital Statistics of the United States*, annual; and unpublished data.

No. 107. Expectation of Life and Expected Deaths by Race, Sex, and Age: 2000

[See Appendix III]

Age (years)	Expectation of life in years					Expected deaths per 1,000 alive at specified age [1]				
	Total	White		Black		Total	White		Black	
		Male	Female	Male	Female		Male	Female	Male	Female
At birth....	77.0	74.9	80.1	68.3	75.2	6.93	6.24	5.13	15.56	12.67
1........	76.6	74.3	79.6	68.4	75.2	0.52	0.50	0.41	1.01	0.79
2........	75.4	73.3	78.4	67.3	73.9	0.35	0.34	0.27	0.64	0.54
3........	74.5	72.3	77.4	66.4	73.0	0.24	0.26	0.18	0.43	0.33
4........	73.5	71.3	76.4	65.4	72.0	0.20	0.20	0.15	0.34	0.35
5........	72.8	70.4	75.6	64.5	71.3	0.19	0.19	0.15	0.33	0.27
6........	71.5	69.4	74.5	63.4	70.1	0.18	0.18	0.14	0.31	0.23
7........	70.5	68.4	73.5	62.5	69.1	0.17	0.18	0.13	0.28	0.21
8........	69.5	67.4	72.5	61.5	68.1	0.15	0.16	0.13	0.25	0.19
9........	68.6	66.4	71.5	60.5	67.1	0.14	0.14	0.12	0.21	0.18
10.......	67.9	65.5	70.7	59.6	66.4	0.13	0.12	0.11	0.19	0.18
11.......	66.6	64.4	69.5	58.5	65.1	0.13	0.13	0.11	0.19	0.19
12.......	65.6	63.4	68.5	57.5	64.1	0.17	0.18	0.13	0.26	0.21
13.......	64.6	62.4	67.5	56.5	63.1	0.25	0.30	0.18	0.42	0.24
14.......	63.6	61.5	66.5	55.6	62.2	0.37	0.46	0.24	0.63	0.29
15.......	62.8	60.6	65.7	54.7	61.4	0.49	0.63	0.31	0.86	0.34
16.......	61.7	59.5	64.6	53.7	60.2	0.61	0.79	0.38	1.09	0.39
17.......	60.7	58.6	63.6	52.7	59.2	0.71	0.92	0.42	1.33	0.45
18.......	59.7	57.6	62.6	51.8	58.3	0.78	1.03	0.44	1.56	0.51
19.......	58.8	56.7	61.7	50.9	57.3	0.83	1.10	0.44	1.78	0.57
20.......	58.0	55.8	60.9	50.0	56.6	0.89	1.18	0.43	2.04	0.63
21.......	56.9	54.8	59.7	49.0	55.3	0.95	1.26	0.43	2.29	0.71
22.......	55.9	53.9	58.7	48.2	54.4	0.98	1.31	0.43	2.47	0.77
23.......	55.0	52.9	57.8	47.3	53.4	1.00	1.32	0.44	2.56	0.82
24.......	54.0	52.0	56.8	46.4	52.5	0.99	1.30	0.45	2.56	0.85
25.......	53.2	51.2	56.0	45.6	51.8	0.98	1.28	0.46	2.54	0.89
26.......	52.1	50.1	54.8	44.6	50.6	0.98	1.25	0.48	2.53	0.95
27.......	51.2	49.2	53.9	43.7	49.6	0.98	1.24	0.49	2.53	1.01
28.......	50.2	48.3	52.9	42.9	48.7	0.99	1.25	0.51	2.56	1.09
29.......	49.3	47.3	51.9	42.0	47.7	1.019	1.27	0.53	2.62	1.18
30.......	48.5	46.4	51.1	41.1	47.0	1.05	1.30	0.56	2.69	1.28
31.......	47.4	45.4	50.0	40.2	45.8	1.09	1.34	0.59	2.76	1.38
32.......	46.5	44.5	49.0	39.3	44.9	1.14	1.40	0.63	2.85	1.49
33.......	45.5	43.6	48.0	38.4	44.0	1.22	1.47	0.69	2.96	1.61
34.......	44.6	42.6	47.1	37.5	43.0	1.30	1.57	0.76	3.10	1.73
35.......	43.7	41.7	46.3	36.7	42.3	1.40	1.67	0.84	3.24	1.85
36.......	42.7	40.8	45.1	35.7	41.2	1.49	1.77	0.91	3.40	1.98
37.......	41.7	39.8	44.2	34.9	40.3	1.60	1.89	1.00	3.61	2.14
38.......	40.8	38.9	43.2	34.0	39.3	1.73	2.03	1.08	3.89	2.33
39.......	39.9	38.0	42.3	33.1	38.4	1.87	2.19	1.18	4.23	2.56
40.......	39.1	37.1	41.5	32.3	37.8	2.02	2.35	1.28	4.59	2.79
41.......	38.0	36.2	40.4	31.4	36.6	2.18	2.53	1.39	4.97	3.04
42.......	37.1	35.2	39.4	30.6	35.7	2.36	2.73	1.50	5.41	3.31
43.......	36.2	34.3	38.5	29.7	34.9	2.55	2.96	1.61	5.94	3.61
44.......	35.3	33.4	37.5	28.9	34.0	2.77	3.23	1.73	6.55	3.95
45.......	34.5	32.6	36.8	28.1	33.4	3.01	3.54	1.86	7.26	4.33
46.......	33.5	31.7	35.7	27.3	32.3	3.28	3.88	2.01	8.03	4.73
47.......	32.6	30.8	34.7	26.5	31.4	3.57	4.21	2.19	8.82	5.13
48.......	31.7	29.9	33.8	25.7	30.6	3.85	4.53	2.41	9.60	5.49
49.......	30.8	29.0	32.9	25.0	29.7	4.14	4.84	2.65	10.36	5.83
50.......	30.1	28.2	32.2	24.2	29.1	4.44	5.15	2.92	11.18	6.19
51.......	29.1	27.3	31.1	23.5	28.1	4.78	5.51	3.20	12.09	6.61
52.......	28.2	26.5	30.2	22.8	27.3	5.15	5.92	3.51	13.03	7.03
53.......	27.4	25.6	29.3	22.1	26.5	5.58	6.42	3.85	13.97	7.47
54.......	26.5	24.8	28.4	21.4	25.7	6.08	7.02	4.23	14.95	7.94
55.......	25.8	24.0	27.7	20.6	25.1	6.65	7.72	4.68	16.02	8.46
56.......	24.8	23.2	26.6	20.0	24.1	7.31	8.51	5.19	17.20	9.05
57.......	24.0	22.3	25.8	19.4	23.3	8.02	9.37	5.75	18.48	9.77
58.......	23.2	21.6	24.9	18.7	22.5	8.77	10.26	6.33	19.81	10.62
59.......	22.4	20.8	24.1	18.1	21.7	9.56	11.20	6.95	21.18	11.57
60.......	21.7	20.0	23.4	17.3	21.2	10.45	12.24	7.65	22.61	12.61
61.......	20.9	19.2	22.4	16.9	20.2	11.45	13.44	8.45	24.10	13.70
62.......	20.1	18.5	21.6	16.3	19.5	12.52	14.75	9.32	25.57	14.82
63.......	19.3	17.8	20.8	15.7	18.8	13.65	16.15	10.21	26.96	15.94
64.......	18.6	17.1	20.0	15.1	18.1	14.83	17.64	11.15	28.32	17.08
65.......	18.0	16.3	19.4	14.2	17.7	16.06	19.18	12.16	29.57	18.23
70.......	14.5	13.0	15.7	11.5	14.5	24.67	30.14	19.03	41.56	27.33
75.......	11.4	10.1	12.3	9.2	11.6	37.68	45.73	30.42	60.50	41.44
80.......	8.7	7.5	9.2	7.4	9.1	58.84	71.08	50.00	85.25	61.42

[1] Based on the proportion of the cohort who are alive at the beginning of an indicated age interval who will die before reaching the end of that interval. For example, out of every 1,000 people alive and exactly 50 years old at the beginning of the period, between 4 and 5 (4.44) will die before reaching their 51st birthdays.

Source: U.S. National Center for Health Statistics, *Vital Statistics of the United States*, annual; *National Vital Statistics Report*, Vol. 51, No. 5; and unpublished data.

No. 108. Deaths and Death Rates by Sex and Race: 1970 to 2001

[1,921 represents 1,921,000. Rates are per 1,000 population for specified groups. Excludes deaths of nonresidents of the United States and fetal deaths. For explanation of age-adjustment, see text, this section. The standard population age-adjustment is the projected year 2000 population of the United States. See Appendix III]

Sex and race	1970	1975	1980	1985	1987	1988	1989	1990	1991	1992	1993	1994	1995	1996	1997	1998	1999	2000	2001
Deaths [1] (1,000)	1,921	1,893	1,990	2,086	2,123	2,168	2,150	2,148	2,170	2,176	2,269	2,279	2,312	2,315	2,314	2,337	2,391	2,403	2,416
Male [1] (1,000)	1,078	1,051	1,075	1,098	1,108	1,126	1,114	1,113	1,122	1,122	1,162	1,163	1,173	1,164	1,154	1,157	1,175	1,178	1,183
Female [1] (1,000)	843	842	915	989	1,015	1,042	1,036	1,035	1,048	1,053	1,107	1,116	1,139	1,151	1,160	1,180	1,216	1,226	1,233
White (1,000)	1,682	1,660	1,739	1,819	1,843	1,877	1,854	1,853	1,869	1,874	1,951	1,960	1,987	1,993	1,996	2,016	2,061	2,071	2,080
Male (1,000)	942	918	934	950	953	965	951	951	956	957	988	989	997	992	987	990	1,005	1,007	1,011
Female (1,000)	740	743	805	869	890	911	903	902	912	917	963	971	990	1,001	1,010	1,026	1,056	1,064	1,068
Black (1,000)	226	218	233	244	255	264	268	266	270	269	282	282	286	282	277	278	285	286	288
Male (1,000)	128	124	130	134	140	144	146	145	147	147	154	153	154	149	144	143	146	145	146
Female (1,000)	98	94	103	111	115	120	121	120	122	123	129	129	132	133	132	135	139	141	142
Death rates [1]	9.5	8.8	8.8	8.8	8.8	8.9	8.7	8.6	8.6	8.5	8.8	8.8	8.8	8.7	8.6	8.6	8.6	8.5	8.5
Male [1]	10.9	10.0	9.8	9.5	9.4	9.5	9.3	9.2	9.1	9.0	9.2	9.2	9.1	9.0	8.8	8.8	8.8	8.5	8.5
Female [1]	8.1	7.6	7.9	8.1	8.2	8.3	8.2	8.1	8.1	8.1	8.4	8.4	8.5	8.5	8.5	8.5	8.7	8.6	8.5
White	9.5	8.9	8.9	9.0	9.0	9.1	8.9	8.9	8.9	8.8	9.1	9.1	9.1	9.1	9.0	9.0	9.2	9.0	9.0
Male	10.9	10.0	9.8	9.6	9.5	9.6	9.4	9.3	9.3	9.2	9.4	9.3	9.3	9.2	9.1	9.0	9.2	8.9	8.8
Female	8.1	7.8	8.1	8.4	8.5	8.7	8.5	8.5	8.3	8.4	8.8	8.6	8.9	9.0	9.0	9.0	9.2	9.1	9.1
Black	10.0	8.8	8.8	8.5	8.7	8.9	8.9	8.8	8.6	8.5	8.8	8.6	8.6	8.4	8.1	8.1	8.2	7.8	7.7
Male	11.9	10.6	10.3	9.9	10.1	10.3	10.3	10.1	10.0	9.8	10.1	9.9	9.8	9.4	8.9	8.8	8.8	8.3	8.2
Female	8.3	7.3	7.3	7.3	7.5	7.6	7.6	7.5	7.4	7.4	7.6	7.5	7.6	7.5	7.4	7.5	7.6	7.3	7.3
Age-adjusted death rates [1]																			
Male [1]	12.2	10.9	10.4	9.9	9.7	9.8	9.5	9.4	9.3	9.1	9.3	9.2	9.2	9.0	8.9	8.8	8.8	8.7	8.5
Female [1]	15.4	14.2	13.5	12.8	12.5	12.5	12.2	12.0	11.8	11.6	11.8	11.6	11.5	11.2	10.9	10.6	10.6	10.5	10.3
	9.7	8.6	8.2	7.8	7.7	7.8	7.6	7.5	7.4	7.3	7.5	7.5	7.5	7.4	7.4	7.3	7.4	7.3	7.2
White	11.9	10.7	10.1	9.6	9.4	9.5	9.2	9.1	9.0	8.8	9.0	8.9	8.9	8.8	8.6	8.5	8.6	8.5	8.4
Male	15.1	13.9	13.2	12.5	12.1	12.2	11.8	11.7	11.5	11.3	11.4	11.2	11.1	10.9	10.6	10.4	10.4	10.3	10.1
Female	9.4	8.3	8.0	7.6	7.5	7.6	7.4	7.3	7.2	7.1	7.3	7.2	7.3	7.2	7.2	7.2	7.3	7.2	7.1
Black	15.2	13.3	13.1	12.6	12.6	12.8	12.8	12.5	12.4	12.2	12.5	12.2	12.2	11.9	11.5	11.4	11.5	11.2	11.0
Male	18.7	17.0	17.0	16.3	16.5	16.8	16.7	16.4	16.2	15.9	16.3	15.9	15.8	15.1	14.5	14.1	14.1	14.0	13.8
Female	12.3	10.4	10.3	9.9	9.9	10.1	10.0	9.8	9.7	9.5	9.8	9.7	9.6	9.6	9.4	9.4	9.6	9.3	9.1

[1] Includes other races, not shown separately.

Source: U.S. National Center for Health Statistics, *Vital Statistics of the United States*, annual; and *National Vital Statistics Reports (NVSR)* (formerly *Monthly Vital Statistics Report*).

No. 109. Death Rates by Age: 1940 to 2001

[Rates per 100,000 population. See Appendix III]

Sex, year, and race	All ages [1]	Under 1 year	1-4 years	5-14 years	15-24 years	25-34 years	35-44 years	45-54 years	55-64 years	65-74 years	75-84 years	85 years and over
MALE												
1940....	1,197.4	6,189.8	311.5	117.8	228.9	338.4	588.1	1,248.8	2,612.0	5,462.3	12,126.4	24,639.0
1950....	1,106.1	3,728.0	151.7	70.9	167.9	216.5	428.8	1,067.1	2,395.3	4,931.4	10,426.0	21,636.0
1960....	1,104.5	3,059.3	119.5	55.7	152.1	187.9	372.8	992.2	2,309.5	4,914.4	10,178.4	21,186.3
1970....	1,090.3	2,410.0	93.2	50.5	188.5	215.3	402.6	958.5	2,282.7	4,873.8	10,010.2	17,821.5
1980....	976.9	1,428.5	72.6	36.7	172.3	196.1	299.2	767.3	1,815.1	4,105.2	8,816.7	18,801.1
1990....	918.4	1,082.8	52.4	28.5	147.4	204.3	310.4	610.3	1,553.4	3,491.5	7,888.6	18,056.6
2000.,...	853.0	806.5	35.9	20.9	114.9	138.6	255.2	542.8	1,230.7	2,979.6	6,972.6	17,501.4
2001 [2] .	846.6	755.3	37.3	19.8	116.6	143.0	258.9	544.3	1,191.6	2,913.9	6,841.8	16,760.0
White:												
1980....	983.3	1,230.3	66.1	35.0	167.0	171.3	257.4	698.9	1,728.5	4,035.7	8,829.8	19,097.3
1985....	963.6	1,056.5	52.8	30.1	134.2	158.8	243.1	611.7	1,625.8	3,770.7	8,486.1	18,980.1
1990....	930.9	896.1	45.9	26.4	131.3	176.1	268.2	548.7	1,467.2	3,397.7	7,844.9	18,268.3
1995....	932.1	717.5	38.8	24.5	122.3	177.7	287.7	534.6	1,330.8	3,199.0	7,320.6	18,152.9
1997....	906.3	678.1	35.1	22.1	109.0	140.3	235.3	495.8	1,252.4	3,122.7	7,086.0	17,767.1
1998....	904.4	673.8	32.5	21.2	107.6	133.9	232.7	489.6	1,215.5	3,082.3	6,988.5	17,048.3
1999....	911.2	658.1	33.9	20.3	104.9	134.5	231.5	494.2	1,200.2	3,043.2	6,965.1	17,202.1
2000.,...	887.8	667.6	32.6	19.8	105.8	124.1	233.6	496.9	1,163.3	2,905.7	6,933.1	17,716.4
2001 [2] .	882.5	631.2	34.5	18.4	107.7	129.6	239.1	500.7	1,126.8	2,846.5	6,811.2	16,955.1
Black:												
1980....	1,034.1	2,586.7	110.5	47.4	209.1	407.3	689.8	1,479.9	2,873.0	5,131.1	9,231.6	16,098.8
1985....	989.3	2,219.9	90.1	42.3	173.6	351.9	630.2	1,292.9	2,779.8	5,172.4	9,262.3	15,774.2
1990....	1,008.0	2,112.4	85.8	41.2	252.2	430.8	699.6	1,261.0	2,618.4	4,946.1	9,129.5	16,954.9
1995....	980.7	1,590.8	77.5	40.2	249.2	416.5	721.2	1,273.0	2,437.5	4,610.5	8,778.8	16,728.7
1997....	893.9	1,671.6	67.2	34.8	215.8	308.6	523.7	1,114.1	2,320.0	4,298.3	8,296.8	16,083.5
1998....	877.7	1,717.8	69.2	35.6	194.6	282.0	483.1	1,082.6	2,269.3	4,186.0	8,311.4	15,540.9
1999....	880.0	1,694.0	66.0	34.6	185.6	268.4	473.6	1,081.9	2,244.0	4,182.8	8,352.6	16,047.8
2000.,...	834.1	1,567.6	54.5	28.2	181.4	261.0	453.0	1,017.7	2,080.1	4,253.5	8,486.0	16,791.0
2001 [2] .	822.2	1,437.2	53.1	27.7	179.9	258.6	443.4	994.5	2,019.0	4,155.4	8,343.8	16,419.5
Hispanic [3]:												
1980....	(NA)	(NA)	(NA)	(NA)	(NA)	(NA)	(NA)	(NA)	(NA)	(NA)	(NA)	(NA)
1985....	(NA)	(NA)	(NA)	(NA)	(NA)	(NA)	(NA)	(NA)	(NA)	(NA)	(NA)	(NA)
1990....	(NA)	(NA)	(NA)	(NA)	(NA)	(NA)	(NA)	(NA)	(NA)	(NA)	(NA)	(NA)
1995....	(NA)	(NA)	(NA)	(NA)	(NA)	(NA)	(NA)	(NA)	(NA)	(NA)	(NA)	(NA)
1997....	360.5	654.3	34.1	18.7	129.1	154.5	235.7	456.1	957.8	2,251.7	4,750.3	10,487.1
1998....	366.4	678.5	33.1	20.2	128.8	148.4	226.6	449.3	966.3	2,284.9	4,564.6	9,946.7
1999....	367.9	655.3	34.3	19.4	124.9	151.6	226.0	456.3	962.6	2,219.4	4,525.1	9,842.3
2000.,...	366.3	663.4	32.3	19.4	130.7	154.1	221.5	442.0	940.5	2,118.3	4,437.6	9,295.6
2001 [2] .	331.3	637.1	31.5	17.9	107.7	120.2	211.0	439.0	965.7	2,287.9	5,395.3	13,086.2
2001 [2] .	329.7	630.1	34.1	16.5	109.6	115.5	206.6	436.9	911.6	2,232.7	5,214.7	12,821.6
FEMALE												
1940....	954.6	4,774.3	267.0	89.1	181.1	274.3	452.2	860.7	1,800.4	4,222.2	10,368.6	22,759.1
1950....	823.5	2,854.6	126.7	48.9	89.1	142.7	290.3	641.5	1,404.8	3,333.2	8,399.6	19,194.7
1960....	809.2	2,321.3	98.4	37.3	61.3	106.6	229.4	526.7	1,196.4	2,871.8	7,633.1	19,008.4
1970....	807.8	1,863.7	75.4	31.8	68.1	101.6	231.1	517.2	1,098.9	2,579.7	6,677.6	15,518.0
1980....	785.3	1,141.7	54.7	24.2	57.5	75.9	159.3	412.9	934.3	2,144.7	5,440.1	14,746.9
1990....	812.0	855.7	41.0	19.3	49.0	74.2	137.9	342.7	878.8	1,991.2	4,883.1	14,274.3
2000.,...	855.0	663.4	28.7	15.0	43.1	63.5	143.2	312.5	772.2	1,921.2	4,814.7	14,719.2
2001 [2] .	851.2	620.0	29.4	14.6	42.5	65.6	147.9	316.5	753.9	1,892.3	4,764.3	14,453.4
White:												
1980....	806.1	962.5	49.3	22.9	55.5	65.4	138.2	372.7	876.2	2,066.6	5,401.7	14,979.6
1985....	840.1	799.3	40.0	19.5	48.1	59.4	121.9	341.7	869.1	2,027.1	5,111.6	14,745.4
1990....	846.9	690.0	36.1	17.9	45.9	61.5	117.4	309.3	822.7	1,923.5	4,839.1	14,400.6
1995....	891.3	571.6	31.2	16.6	44.3	64.3	125.8	294.4	788.4	1,924.5	4,831.1	14,639.1
1997....	897.8	546.0	28.0	15.6	43.8	60.0	120.9	285.0	766.3	1,900.5	4,786.3	14,681.4
1998....	903.7	563.6	27.5	15.0	41.2	58.5	122.0	278.3	740.6	1,912.9	4,792.7	14,620.4
1999....	924.1	532.6	27.4	14.9	42.2	58.4	123.3	281.8	739.1	1,916.2	4,869.7	15,053.8
2000.,...	912.3	550.5	25.5	14.1	41.1	55.1	125.7	281.4	730.9	1,868.3	4,785.3	14,890.7
2001 [2] .	909.1	516.8	26.9	13.8	40.7	58.3	130.8	286.6	712.3	1,842.7	4,744.9	14,627.6
Black:												
1980....	733.3	2,123.7	84.4	30.5	70.5	150.0	323.9	768.2	1,561.0	3,057.4	6,212.1	12,367.2
1985....	734.2	1,821.4	71.1	28.6	59.6	137.6	276.5	667.6	1,532.5	2,967.8	6,078.0	12,703.0
1990....	747.9	1,735.5	67.6	27.5	68.7	159.5	298.6	639.4	1,452.6	2,865.7	5,688.3	13,309.5
1995....	759.0	1,342.0	62.9	26.5	70.3	166.6	327.7	619.0	1,350.3	2,823.7	5,840.3	13,472.2
1997....	742.8	1,383.9	51.0	27.2	62.0	134.6	287.1	590.4	1,307.3	2,739.7	5,669.3	13,701.7
1998....	746.4	1,390.1	53.9	23.1	58.0	130.0	284.9	582.0	1,272.2	2,724.6	5,813.8	13,580.5
1999....	761.3	1,403.3	51.5	22.6	60.1	122.0	282.6	581.0	1,255.7	2,732.1	6,002.7	14,262.9
2000.,...	733.0	1,279.8	45.3	20.0	58.3	121.8	271.9	588.3	1,227.2	2,689.6	5,696.5	13,941.3
2001 [2] .	726.1	1,185.4	41.7	18.8	54.8	117.6	277.3	577.0	1,214.0	2,610.2	5,574.9	13,817.0
Hispanic [3]:												
1980....	(NA)	(NA)	(NA)	(NA)	(NA)	(NA)	(NA)	(NA)	(NA)	(NA)	(NA)	(NA)
1985....	(NA)	(NA)	(NA)	(NA)	(NA)	(NA)	(NA)	(NA)	(NA)	(NA)	(NA)	(NA)
1990....	(NA)	(NA)	(NA)	(NA)	(NA)	(NA)	(NA)	(NA)	(NA)	(NA)	(NA)	(NA)
1995....	(NA)	(NA)	(NA)	(NA)	(NA)	(NA)	(NA)	(NA)	(NA)	(NA)	(NA)	(NA)
1997....	288.0	572.3	28.4	15.6	38.3	54.6	101.1	228.5	580.3	1,381.9	3,220.5	8,708.6
1998....	283.6	568.7	27.6	14.1	34.0	51.0	96.7	225.8	543.6	1,384.3	3,140.1	8,336.3
1999....	293.7	565.9	29.8	14.4	36.4	51.8	99.9	226.7	536.0	1,366.8	3,245.6	8,838.0
2000.,...	274.6	553.6	27.5	13.4	31.7	43.4	100.5	223.8	548.4	1,423.2	3,624.5	11,202.8
2001 [2] .	277.8	528.9	26.8	12.5	33.4	44.7	95.7	225.3	538.9	1,404.5	3,562.3	11,295.8

NA Not available. [1] Figures for age not stated are included in "All ages" but not distributed among age groups. [2] Preliminary data. [3] The death rates for Hispanic origin and specified races other than White and Black should be interpreted with caution because of inconsistencies between reporting Hispanic origin and race on death certificates and censuses and surveys.

Source: U.S. National Center for Health Statistics, *Vital Statistics of the United States*, annual.

No. 110. Age-Adjusted Death Rates by Race and Sex: 1940 to 2001

[Age adjusted rates per 100,000 population; see headnote, Table 108. Populations enumerated as of April 1 for census years and estimated as of July 1 for all other years. Beginning 1970, excludes deaths of nonresidents of the United States. Data for specified races other than White and Black should be interpreted with caution because of inconsistencies reporting race on death certificates and on censuses and surveys. See Appendix III]

Sex and race	1940	1950	1960	1970	1980	1990	1995	1999	2000	2001
ALL RACES [1]										
Total	1,785.0	1,446.0	1,339.2	1,222.6	1,039.1	938.7	918.5	881.9	869.0	854.5
Male	1,976.0	1,674.2	1,609.0	1,542.1	1,348.1	1,202.8	1,150.3	1,061.8	1,053.8	1,029.1
Female	1,599.4	1,236.0	1,105.3	971.4	817.9	750.9	748.2	743.6	731.4	721.8
WHITE										
Total	1,735.3	1,410.8	1,311.3	1,193.3	1,012.7	909.8	890.0	860.7	849.8	842.9
Male	1,925.2	1,642.5	1,586.0	1,513.7	1,317.6	1,165.9	1,112.7	1,035.8	1,029.4	1,012.8
Female	1,550.4	1,198.0	1,074.4	944.0	796.1	728.8	726.6	725.7	715.3	713.5
BLACK										
Total	(NA)	(NA)	1,577.5	1,518.1	1,314.8	1,250.3	1,224.5	1,147.1	1,121.4	1,116.5
Male	(NA)	(NA)	1,811.1	1,873.9	1,697.8	1,644.5	1,582.3	1,412.5	1,403.5	1,393.7
Female	(NA)	(NA)	1,369.7	1,228.7	1,033.3	975.1	970.1	955.0	927.6	925.5
AMERICAN INDIAN [2]										
Total	(NA)	(NA)	(NA)	(NA)	867.0	716.3	716.5	716.1	709.3	688.8
Male	(NA)	(NA)	(NA)	(NA)	1,111.5	916.2	864.2	842.0	841.5	802.3
Female	(NA)	(NA)	(NA)	(NA)	662.4	561.8	592.8	608.5	604.5	595.3
ASIAN OR PACIFIC ISLANDER [3]										
Total	(NA)	(NA)	(NA)	(NA)	589.9	582.0	616.0	517.5	506.4	488.5
Male	(NA)	(NA)	(NA)	(NA)	786.5	716.4	788.1	640.6	624.2	593.2
Female	(NA)	(NA)	(NA)	(NA)	425.9	469.3	488.4	424.0	416.8	409.0

NA Not available. [1] For 1940-91 includes deaths among races not shown separately; see Other races and, race not stated, in the Technical notes for information for 1992 to present. [2] Includes Aleuts and Eskimos. [3] Includes Chinese, Filipino, Hawaiian, Japanese, and Other Asian or Pacific Islander.

Source: U.S. National Center for Health Statistics, *Vital Statistics of the United States*, annual.

No. 111. Death Rates by Hispanic Origin, Age, and Sex: 1985 to 2001

[Rates per 100,000 population. Rates are based on populations enumerated as of April 1 for census years and estimated as of July 1 for all other years. Beginning 1970, excludes deaths of nonresidents of the United States]

Year	Hispanic male [1]						Hispanic female [1]					
	1985	1990	1998	1999	2000	2001	1985	1990	1998	1999	2000	2001
Age adjusted[2]	889.2	886.4	743.7	736.0	818.1	802.5	546.1	537.1	478.2	490.1	546.0	544.2
Crude	374.6	411.6	366.4	367.9	331.3	332.9	251.9	285.4	283.6	293.7	274.6	279.0
Under 2	1,044.6	921.8	678.5	655.3	637.1	624.4	791.4	746.6	568.7	565.9	553.6	518.9
1-4 years	53.8	53.8	33.1	34.3	31.5	33.8	42.3	42.1	27.6	29.8	27.5	27.2
5-14 years	23.0	26.0	20.2	19.4	17.9	16.6	16.0	17.3	14.1	14.4	13.4	12.7
15-24 years	147.5	159.3	128.8	124.9	107.7	111.5	36.2	40.6	34.0	36.4	31.7	33.7
25-34 years	202.1	234.0	148.4	151.6	120.2	118.0	56.3	62.9	51.0	51.8	43.4	45.2
35-44 years	290.1	341.8	226.6	226.0	211.0	208.5	100.0	109.3	96.7	99.9	100.5	97.0
45-54 years	495.7	533.9	449.3	456.3	439.0	443.9	251.3	253.2	225.8	226.7	223.8	226.7
55-64 years	1,129.4	1,123.7	966.3	962.3	965.7	923.9	619.7	607.5	543.6	536.0	548.4	543.0
65-74 years	2,484.9	2,368.2	2,284.9	2,219.4	2,287.9	2,242.6	1,449.5	1,453.8	1,384.3	1,366.8	1,423.2	1,408.0
75-84 years	5,696.1	5,369.1	4,564.6	4,525.1	5,395.3	5,258.0	3,551.8	3,351.3	3,140.1	3,245.6	3,624.5	3,589.8
85 years and over	12,156.2	12,272.1	9,946.7	9,842.3	13,086.2	12,888.3	10,228.6	10,098.7	8,336.0	8,838.7	11,202.8	11,300.5

NA Not available. [1] Includes all persons of Hispanic origin of any race. [2] See headnote, Table 108.

Source: U.S. National Center for Health Statistics, *Vital Statistics of the United States*, annual.

No. 112. Deaths and Death Rates by State: 1990 to 2001

[2,148 represents 2,148,000. By state of residence. Excludes deaths of nonresidents of the United States, except as noted. Caution should be used in comparing death rates by state; rates are affected by the population composition of the area. See also Appendix III]

State	Number of deaths (1,000)							Rate per 1,000 population [1]						
	1990	1995	1997	1998	1999	2000	2001	1990	1995	1997	1998	1999	2000	2001
United States..	2,148	2,312	2,314	2,337	2,391	2,403	2,416	8.6	8.8	8.6	8.6	8.8	8.5	8.5
Alabama.........	39	42	43	44	45	45	45	9.7	10.0	10.0	10.1	10.3	10.1	10.1
Alaska..........	2	3	3	3	3	3	3	4.0	4.2	4.2	4.2	4.4	4.6	4.7
Arizona.........	29	35	37	38	40	41	41	7.9	8.4	8.1	8.2	8.4	7.9	7.7
Arkansas........	25	27	28	28	28	28	28	10.5	10.8	11.0	10.8	10.9	10.6	10.3
California.......	214	224	225	227	229	230	234	7.2	7.1	7.0	6.9	6.9	6.8	6.8
Colorado........	22	25	26	27	27	27	28	6.6	6.7	6.6	6.7	6.7	6.3	6.4
Connecticut.....	28	29	29	30	29	30	30	8.4	9.0	9.0	9.1	9.0	8.8	8.7
Delaware	6	6	7	7	7	7	7	8.7	8.8	8.9	8.8	8.8	8.8	8.9
Dist. of Columbia ...	7	7	6	6	6	6	6	12.0	12.4	11.6	11.6	11.7	10.5	10.4
Florida..........	134	153	155	158	163	164	167	10.4	10.8	10.5	10.1	10.8	10.3	10.2
Georgia	52	58	59	60	62	64	64	8.0	8.1	7.9	7.9	8.0	7.8	7.7
Hawaii	7	8	8	8	8	8	8	6.1	6.4	6.7	6.8	7.0	6.8	6.8
Idaho...........	7	9	9	9	10	10	10	7.4	7.3	7.4	7.5	7.7	7.4	7.4
Illinois	103	108	103	104	108	107	105	9.0	9.2	8.7	8.7	8.9	8.6	8.4
Indiana.........	50	53	53	53	55	55	55	8.9	9.2	9.1	9.1	9.3	9.1	9.0
Iowa	27	28	28	28	28	28	28	9.7	9.9	9.7	9.9	9.9	9.6	9.5
Kansas..........	22	24	24	24	24	25	25	9.0	9.3	9.2	9.2	9.2	9.2	9.1
Kentucky	35	37	38	38	39	40	40	9.5	9.6	9.7	9.6	9.9	9.8	9.8
Louisiana	38	40	40	40	41	41	42	8.9	9.1	9.2	9.2	9.4	9.2	9.3
Maine...........	11	12	12	12	12	12	12	9.0	9.5	9.7	9.8	9.8	9.7	9.7
Maryland	38	42	42	42	43	44	44	8.0	8.3	8.2	8.2	8.3	8.3	8.1
Massachusetts.....	53	55	55	55	56	57	57	8.8	9.1	8.9	9.0	9.0	8.9	8.9
Michigan........	79	84	83	85	87	87	86	8.5	8.8	8.5	8.7	8.8	8.7	8.6
Minnesota.......	35	38	37	37	39	38	38	7.9	8.1	7.9	7.9	8.1	7.7	7.6
Mississippi	25	27	28	28	28	29	28	9.8	10.0	10.1	10.1	10.2	10.1	9.9
Missouri	50	54	54	55	55	55	55	9.8	10.2	10.1	10.1	10.2	9.8	9.8
Montana........	7	8	8	8	8	8	8	8.6	8.8	8.8	9.1	9.2	9.0	9.1
Nebraska	15	15	15	15	16	15	15	9.4	9.3	9.2	9.1	9.4	8.8	8.8
Nevada	9	13	13	14	15	15	16	7.8	8.2	8.0	8.3	8.3	7.6	7.8
New Hampshire....	8	9	9	9	10	10	10	7.7	8.0	8.1	8.0	7.9	7.8	7.8
New Jersey......	70	74	72	72	74	75	75	9.1	9.3	9.0	8.8	9.1	8.9	8.8
New Mexico	11	13	13	13	14	13	14	7.0	7.4	7.3	7.4	7.9	7.4	7.7
New York	169	168	159	157	160	158	159	9.4	9.3	8.7	8.6	8.8	8.3	8.3
North Carolina.....	57	65	66	68	70	72	71	8.6	9.0	8.9	9.0	9.1	8.9	8.6
North Dakota.....	6	6	6	6	6	6	6	8.9	9.3	9.2	9.3	9.6	9.1	9.5
Ohio	99	106	105	106	109	108	108	9.1	9.5	9.4	9.4	9.6	9.5	9.5
Oklahoma.......	30	33	34	34	35	35	35	9.7	10.0	10.2	10.1	10.3	10.2	10.0
Oregon.........	25	28	29	29	29	30	30	8.7	9.0	8.9	9.0	8.9	8.7	8.7
Pennsylvania.....	122	128	128	127	130	131	130	10.3	10.6	10.6	10.6	10.9	10.7	10.5
Rhode Island.....	10	10	10	10	10	10	10	9.5	9.8	9.9	9.8	9.8	9.6	9.5
South Carolina.....	30	34	34	35	36	37	37	8.5	9.1	9.0	9.1	9.3	9.2	9.0
South Dakota.....	6	7	7	7	7	7	7	9.1	9.5	9.3	9.3	9.5	9.3	9.1
Tennessee	46	51	53	53	54	55	55	9.5	9.8	9.8	9.8	9.8	9.7	9.6
Texas...........	125	138	143	143	147	150	153	7.4	7.4	7.3	7.2	7.3	7.2	7.1
Utah	9	11	12	12	12	12	13	5.3	5.6	5.6	5.6	5.7	5.5	5.6
Vermont........	5	5	5	5	5	5	5	8.2	8.5	8.6	8.4	8.4	8.4	8.5
Virginia.........	48	53	54	55	55	56	56	7.8	8.0	8.0	8.0	8.0	8.0	7.8
Washington.....	37	41	41	43	44	44	45	7.6	7.5	7.4	7.5	7.6	7.5	7.4
West Virginia.....	19	20	21	21	21	21	21	10.8	11.1	11.5	11.5	11.6	11.7	11.6
Wisconsin.......	43	45	45	46	47	46	47	8.7	8.8	8.7	8.8	8.9	8.7	8.6
Wyoming	3	4	4	4	4	4	4	7.1	7.7	7.8	8.0	8.4	7.9	8.2
Puerto Rico......	26	30	29	29	28	28	29	7.3	8.1	7.6	7.7	7.4	7.2	7.6
Virgin Islands.....	(NA)	1	1	1	1	1	1	4.6	5.8	5.4	5.2	5.5	5.3	5.6
Guam	1	1	1	1	1	1	1	3.9	4.1	4.2	4.2	4.6	4.2	4.2
American Samoa ...	(NA)	(NA)	(NA)	(NA)	(NA)	(NA)	(NA)	(NA)	(NA)	4.3	3.9	3.9	3.3	4.2
Northern Marianas ..	(NA)	(NA)	(NA)	(NA)	(NA)	(NA)	(NA)	(NA)	(NA)	(NA)	2.4	2.3	1.9	2.1

NA Not available. [1] Rates based on enumerated resident population as of April 1 for 1990 and 2000; estimated resident population as of July 1 for all other years.

Source: U.S. National Center for Health Statistics, *Vital Statistics of the United States*, annual; *National Vital Statistics Reports (NVSR)* (formerly *Monthly Vital Statistics Report*).

No. 113. Infant, Maternal, and Neonatal Mortality Rates by Race: 1980 to 2001

[Deaths per 1,000 live births, except as noted. Excludes deaths of nonresidents of the United States. Beginning 1989, race for live births tabulated according to race of mother, for maternal mortality rates and mortality rates. See also Appendix III]

Item	1980	1990	1995	1997	1998	1999 [1]	2000	2001
Infant deaths [2]........	12.6	9.2	7.6	7.2	7.2	7.1	6.9	6.8
White................	10.9	7.6	6.3	6.0	6.0	5.8	5.7	5.7
Black and other.......	20.2	15.5	12.6	11.8	11.9	11.9	11.4	11.3
Black................	22.2	18.0	15.1	14.2	14.3	14.6	14.1	14.0
Maternal deaths [3].....	9.2	8.2	7.1	8.4	7.1	9.9	9.8	9.9
White................	6.7	5.4	4.2	5.8	5.1	6.8	7.5	7.2
Black and other.......	19.8	19.1	18.5	18.3	14.9	21.4	18.0	20.2
Black................	21.5	22.4	22.1	20.8	17.1	25.4	22.0	24.7
Neonatal deaths [4].....	8.5	5.8	4.9	4.8	4.8	4.7	4.6	4.5
White................	7.4	4.8	4.1	4.0	4.0	3.9	3.8	3.8
Black and other.......	13.2	9.9	8.1	7.7	7.9	7.9	7.6	7.4
Black................	14.6	11.6	9.8	9.4	9.5	9.8	9.4	9.2

[1] Beginning 1999, deaths are classified according to the tenth revision of the *International Classification of Diseases*; earlier years classified according to the revision in use at the time, see text, this section. [2] Represents deaths of infants under 1 year old, exclusive of fetal deaths. [3] Per 100,000 live births from deliveries and complications of pregnancy, childbirth, and the puerperium. Deaths are classified according to the ninth revision of the *International Classification of Diseases*; earlier years classified according to the revision in use at the time; see text, this section. [4] Represents deaths of infants under 28 days old, exclusive of fetal deaths.

Source: U.S. National Center for Health Statistics, *Vital Statistics of the United States*, annual; *National Vital Statistics Reports (NVSR)* (formerly *Monthly Vital Statistics Report*).

No. 114. Infant Mortality Rates by Race—States: 1980 to 2001

[Deaths per 1,000 live births, by place of residence. Represents deaths of infants under 1 year old, exclusive of fetal deaths. Excludes deaths of nonresidents of the United States. See Appendix III]

State	Total[1] 1980	1990	2000	2001	White 1980	1990	2000	2001	Black 1980	1990	2000	2001
United States..	12.6	9.2	6.9	6.8	10.9	7.6	5.7	5.7	22.2	18.0	14.1	14.0
Alabama.........	15.1	10.8	9.4	9.4	11.6	8.1	6.6	6.8	21.6	16.0	15.4	15.1
Alaska..........	12.3	10.5	6.8	8.1	9.4	7.6	5.8	5.8	19.5	(B)	(B)	(B)
Arizona.........	12.4	8.8	6.7	6.9	11.8	7.8	6.2	6.1	18.4	20.6	17.6	22.8
Arkansas.......	12.7	9.2	8.4	8.3	10.3	8.4	7.0	6.8	20.0	13.9	13.7	14.5
California......	11.1	7.9	5.4	5.4	10.6	7.0	5.1	5.0	18.0	16.8	12.9	12.9
Colorado........	10.1	8.8	6.2	5.8	9.8	7.8	5.6	5.5	19.1	19.4	19.5	12.8
Connecticut.....	11.2	7.9	6.6	6.1	10.2	6.3	5.6	4.7	19.1	17.6	14.4	16.9
Delaware........	13.9	10.1	9.2	10.7	9.8	9.7	7.9	8.0	27.9	20.1	14.8	19.9
District of Columbia.	25.0	20.7	12.0	10.6	17.8	0.0	(B)	(B)	26.7	24.6	16.1	15.0
Florida.........	14.6	9.6	7.0	7.3	11.8	6.7	5.4	5.5	22.8	16.8	12.6	13.5
Georgia.........	14.5	12.4	8.5	8.6	10.8	7.4	5.9	6.2	21.0	18.3	13.9	13.3
Hawaii..........	10.3	6.7	8.1	6.2	11.6	6.1	6.5	6.0	(B)	(B)	(B)	(B)
Idaho...........	10.7	8.7	7.5	6.2	10.7	8.6	7.5	6.3	(NA)	(B)	(B)	(B)
Illinois........	14.8	10.7	8.5	7.7	11.7	7.9	6.6	6.0	26.3	22.4	17.1	15.5
Indiana.........	11.9	9.6	7.8	7.5	10.5	7.9	6.9	6.8	23.4	17.4	15.8	13.7
Iowa............	11.8	8.1	6.5	5.6	11.5	7.9	6.0	5.5	27.2	21.9	21.1	(B)
Kansas..........	10.4	8.4	6.8	7.4	9.5	8.0	6.4	6.5	20.6	17.7	12.2	20.5
Kentucky........	12.9	8.5	7.2	5.9	12.0	8.2	6.7	5.6	22.0	14.3	12.7	9.7
Louisiana.......	14.3	11.1	9.0	9.8	10.5	8.1	5.9	6.5	20.6	16.7	13.3	14.4
Maine...........	9.2	6.2	4.9	6.1	9.4	6.7	4.8	5.7	(B)	(B)	(B)	(B)
Maryland........	14.0	9.5	7.6	8.1	11.6	6.8	4.8	5.5	20.4	17.1	13.2	13.7
Massachusetts...	10.5	7.0	4.6	5.0	10.1	6.1	4.0	4.6	16.8	11.9	9.9	9.6
Michigan........	12.8	10.7	8.2	8.0	10.6	7.4	6.0	6.1	24.2	21.6	18.2	17.0
Minnesota.......	10.0	7.3	5.6	5.3	9.6	6.7	4.8	4.8	20.0	23.7	14.6	9.6
Mississippi.....	17.0	12.1	10.7	10.5	11.1	7.4	6.8	7.0	23.7	16.2	15.3	14.9
Missouri........	12.4	9.4	7.2	7.4	11.1	7.9	5.9	5.9	20.7	18.2	14.7	16.5
Montana.........	12.4	9.0	6.1	6.7	11.8	6.0	5.5	6.7	(NA)	(B)	(B)	(B)
Nebraska........	11.5	8.3	7.3	6.8	10.7	6.9	6.4	6.4	25.2	18.9	20.3	(B)
Nevada..........	10.7	8.4	6.5	5.7	10.0	8.2	6.0	5.1	20.6	14.2	12.7	17.1
New Hampshire...	9.9	7.1	5.7	3.8	9.9	6.0	5.5	3.8	22.5	(B)	(B)	(B)
New Jersey......	12.5	9.0	6.3	6.5	10.3	6.4	5.0	5.1	21.9	18.4	13.6	14.2
New Mexico......	11.5	9.0	6.6	6.4	11.3	7.6	6.3	6.3	23.1	(B)	(B)	(B)
New York........	12.5	9.6	6.4	5.8	10.8	7.4	5.4	5.1	20.0	18.1	10.9	9.7
North Carolina..	14.5	10.6	8.6	8.5	12.1	8.0	6.3	6.1	20.0	16.5	15.7	15.8
North Dakota....	12.1	8.0	8.1	8.8	11.7	7.2	7.5	8.0	27.5	(B)	(B)	(B)
Ohio............	12.8	9.8	7.6	7.7	11.2	7.8	6.3	6.2	23.0	19.5	15.4	16.4
Oklahoma........	12.7	9.2	8.5	7.3	12.1	9.1	7.9	6.5	21.8	14.3	16.9	15.0
Oregon..........	12.2	8.3	5.6	5.4	12.2	7.0	5.5	5.5	15.9	(B)	(B)	(B)
Pennsylvania....	13.2	9.6	7.1	7.2	11.9	7.4	5.8	6.1	23.1	20.5	15.7	14.4
Rhode Island....	11.0	8.1	6.3	6.8	10.9	7.0	5.9	6.1	(B)	(B)	(B)	(B)
South Carolina..	15.6	11.7	8.7	8.9	10.8	8.1	5.4	5.9	22.9	17.3	14.8	15.0
South Dakota....	10.9	10.1	5.5	7.4	9.0	8.0	4.3	6.1	(NA)	(B)	(B)	(B)
Tennessee.......	13.5	10.3	9.1	8.7	11.9	7.3	6.8	6.7	19.3	17.9	18.0	16.2
Texas...........	12.2	8.1	5.7	5.9	11.2	6.7	5.1	5.2	18.8	14.7	11.4	12.0
Utah............	10.4	7.5	5.2	4.8	10.5	6.0	5.1	4.9	27.3	(B)	(B)	(B)
Vermont.........	10.7	6.4	6.0	5.5	10.7	5.9	6.1	5.6	(B)	(B)	(B)	(B)
Virginia........	13.6	10.2	6.9	7.6	11.9	7.4	5.4	5.4	19.8	19.5	12.4	15.8
Washington......	11.8	7.8	5.2	5.8	11.5	7.3	4.9	5.7	16.4	20.6	9.4	(B)
West Virginia...	11.8	9.9	7.6	7.2	11.4	8.1	7.4	7.2	21.5	(B)	(B)	(B)
Wisconsin.......	10.3	8.2	6.6	7.1	9.7	7.7	5.5	5.9	18.5	19.0	17.2	17.8
Wyoming.........	9.8	8.6	6.7	5.9	9.3	7.5	6.5	5.9	25.0	(B)	(B)	(B)

B Base figure too small to meet statistical standards for reliability.   NA Not available.   [1] Includes other races, not shown separately.

Source: U.S. National Center for Health Statistics, *Vital Statistics of the United States*, annual; and unpublished data.

No. 115. Deaths by Major Causes: 1960 to 2001

[Age-adjusted death rates per 100,000 population; see headnote, Table 108. See Appendix III]

Year	Heart disease	Cancer	Cerebro-vascular diseases	Chronic lower respiratory diseases	Accidents	Diabetes mellitus	Influenza and pneumonia	Intentional self harm (suicide)	Chronic liver disease and cirrhosis	Assault (homicide)
1960	559.0	193.9	177.9	12.5	63.1	22.5	53.7	12.5	13.3	5.2
1961	545.3	193.4	173.1	12.6	60.6	22.1	43.4	12.2	13.3	5.2
1962	556.9	193.3	174.0	14.2	62.9	22.6	47.1	12.8	13.8	5.4
1963	563.4	194.7	173.9	16.5	64.0	23.1	55.6	13.0	14.0	5.4
1964	543.3	193.6	167.0	16.3	64.1	22.5	45.4	12.7	14.2	5.7
1965	542.5	195.6	166.4	18.3	65.8	22.9	46.8	13.0	14.9	6.1
1966	541.2	196.5	165.8	19.2	67.6	23.6	47.9	12.7	15.9	6.5
1967	524.7	197.3	159.3	19.2	66.2	23.4	42.2	12.5	16.3	7.5
1968	531.0	198.8	162.5	20.7	65.5	25.3	52.8	12.4	16.9	8.1
1969	516.8	198.5	155.4	20.9	64.9	25.1	47.9	12.7	17.1	8.3
1970	492.7	198.6	147.7	21.3	62.2	24.3	41.7	13.1	17.8	9.0
1971	492.9	199.3	147.6	21.8	60.3	23.9	38.4	13.1	17.8	9.8
1972	490.2	200.3	147.3	22.8	60.2	23.7	41.3	13.3	18.0	10.0
1973	482.0	200.0	145.2	23.6	59.3	23.0	41.2	13.1	18.1	10.2
1974	458.8	201.5	136.8	23.2	52.7	22.1	35.5	13.2	17.9	10.5
1975	431.2	200.1	123.5	23.7	50.8	20.3	34.9	13.6	16.7	10.2
1976	426.9	202.5	117.4	24.9	48.7	19.5	38.8	13.2	16.4	9.2
1977	413.7	203.5	110.4	24.7	48.8	18.2	31.0	13.7	15.8	9.2
1978	409.9	204.9	103.7	26.3	48.9	18.3	34.5	12.9	15.2	9.2
1979	401.6	204.0	97.1	25.5	46.5	17.5	26.1	12.6	14.8	9.9
1980	412.1	207.9	96.4	28.3	46.4	18.1	31.4	12.2	15.1	10.5
1981	397.0	206.4	89.5	29.0	43.4	17.6	30.0	12.3	14.2	10.1
1982	389.0	208.3	84.2	29.1	40.1	17.2	26.5	12.5	13.2	9.4
1983	388.9	209.1	81.2	31.6	39.1	17.6	29.8	12.4	12.8	8.4
1984	378.8	210.8	78.7	32.4	38.8	17.2	30.6	12.6	12.7	8.1
1985	375.0	211.3	76.6	34.5	38.5	17.4	34.5	12.5	12.3	8.0
1986	365.1	211.5	73.1	34.8	38.6	17.2	34.8	13.0	11.8	8.6
1987	355.9	211.7	71.6	35.0	38.2	17.4	33.8	12.8	11.7	8.3
1988	352.5	212.5	70.6	36.5	38.9	18.0	37.3	12.5	11.6	8.5
1989	332.0	214.2	66.9	36.6	37.7	20.5	35.9	12.3	11.6	8.8
1990	321.8	216.0	65.5	37.2	36.3	20.7	36.8	12.5	11.1	9.5
1991	313.8	215.5	63.2	38.0	34.9	20.7	34.9	12.3	10.7	10.1
1992	306.1	214.3	62.0	37.9	33.4	20.8	33.1	12.1	10.5	9.6
1993	309.9	214.6	63.1	40.9	34.5	22.0	35.2	12.2	10.3	9.8
1994	299.7	213.1	63.1	40.6	34.6	22.7	33.9	12.1	10.2	9.4
1995	296.3	211.7	63.9	40.5	34.9	23.4	33.8	12.0	10.0	8.6
1996	288.3	208.7	63.2	41.0	34.9	24.0	33.2	11.7	9.8	7.8
1997	280.4	205.7	61.8	41.5	34.8	24.0	33.6	11.4	9.6	7.3
1998	272.4	202.4	59.6	42.0	35.0	24.2	34.6	11.3	9.5	6.7
1999	267.8	202.7	61.8	45.8	35.9	25.2	23.6	10.7	9.7	6.2
2000	257.6	199.6	60.9	44.2	34.9	25.0	23.7	10.4	9.5	5.9
2001	247.8	196.0	57.9	43.7	35.7	25.3	22.0	10.7	9.5	7.1

Source: U.S. National Center for Health Statistics, *Vital Statistics of the United States,* annual.

No. 116. Deaths and Death Rates by Selected Causes: 2000 and 2001

[Rates per 100,000 population. Figures for 2000 are weighted data rounded to the nearest individual, so categories may not add to total or subtotal. Excludes deaths of nonresidents of the United States, except as noted. Deaths classified according to tenth revision of *International Classification of Diseases;* See also Appendix III]

Cause of death	2000 Number	2000 Rate	2000 Age-adjusted rate[1]	2001 Number	2001 Rate	2001 Age-adjusted rate[1]
All causes	2,403,351	854.0	869.0	2,416,425	848.5	854.5
Major cardiovascular diseases	936,923	332.9	339.7	922,334	323.9	326.5
Diseases of heart	710,760	252.6	257.6	700,142	245.8	247.8
Acute rheumatic fever and chronic rheumatic heart disease	3,582	1.3	1.3	3,489	1.2	1.2
Hypertensive heart disease	23,761	8.4	8.6	24,689	8.7	8.7
Hypertensive heart and renal disease	2,785	1.0	1.0	2,826	1.0	1.0
Ischemic heart disease	515,204	183.1	186.8	502,189	176.3	177.8
Other heart diseases	165,428	58.8	60.0	166,949	58.6	59.1
Essential (primary) hypertension and hypertensive renal disease	18,073	6.4	6.5	19,250	6.8	6.8
Cerebrovascular diseases	167,661	59.6	60.9	163,538	57.4	57.9
Atherosclerosis	14,393	5.1	5.2	14,086	4.9	5.0
Other disorders of circulatory system	4,603	1.6	1.7	4,665	1.6	1.6
Malignant neoplasms	553,091	196.5	199.6	553,768	194.4	196.0
Malignant neoplasms of lip, oral cavity, and pharynx	7,492	2.7	2.7	7,702	2.7	2.7
Malignant neoplasms of colon, rectum and anus	57,477	20.4	20.8	56,887	20.0	20.1
Malignant neoplasms of trachea, bronchus and lung	155,521	56.5	56.5	156,058	54.8	55.3
Malignant neoplasm of breast	42,300	15.0	15.3	41,809	14.7	14.8
Malignant neoplasms of kidney and renal pelvis	11,736	4.2	4.2	12,078	4.2	4.3
Malignant neoplasms of lymphoid, hematopoietic and related tissue	56,518	20.1	20.4	56,341	19.8	20.0
Leukemia	21,339	7.6	7.7	21,451	7.5	7.9
Accidents (unintentional injuries)	97,900	34.8	34.9	101,537	35.7	35.7
Motor vehicle accidents	43,354	15.4	15.4	43,788	15.4	15.3
Accidental discharge of firearms	776	0.3	0.3	802	0.3	0.3
Accidental drowning and submersion	3,482	1.2	1.2	3,281	1.2	1.1
Accidental exposure to smoke, fire and flames	3,377	1.2	1.2	3,309	1.2	1.2
Accidental poisoning and exposure to noxious substances	12,757	4.5	4.5	14,078	4.9	4.9
Other acute lower respiratory infections	425	0.2	0.1	347	0.1	0.1
Chronic lower respiratory diseases	122,009	43.4	44.2	123,013	43.2	43.7
Bronchitis, chronic and unspecified	1,167	0.4	0.4	959	0.3	0.3
Emphysema	16,700	5.9	6.0	16,242	5.7	5.8
Asthma	4,487	1.6	1.6	4,269	1.5	1.5
Other chronic lower respiratory diseases	99,655	35.4	36.1	101,543	35.7	36.1
Influenza and pneumonia	65,313	23.2	23.7	62,034	21.8	22.0
Influenza	1,765	0.6	0.6	257	0.1	0.1
Pneumonia	63,548	22.6	23.1	61,777	21.7	21.9
Tuberculosis	776	0.3	0.3	764	0.3	0.3
Septicemia	31,224	11.1	11.3	32,238	11.3	11.4
Human immunodeficiency virus (HIV) disease	14,478	5.1	5.2	14,175	5.0	5.0
Anemias	4,494	1.6	1.6	4,627	1.6	1.6
Diabetes mellitus	69,301	24.6	25.0	71,372	25.1	25.3
Nutritional deficiencies	4,242	1.5	1.5	3,704	1.3	1.3
Meningitis	758	0.3	0.3	727	0.3	0.3
Parkinsons disease	15,682	5.6	5.7	16,544	5.8	5.9
Alzheimers disease	49,558	17.6	18.1	53,852	18.9	19.1
Chronic liver disease and cirrhosis	26,552	9.4	9.5	27,035	9.5	9.5
Alcoholic liver disease	12,109	4.3	4.3	12,207	4.3	4.3
Other chronic liver disease and cirrhosis	14,443	5.1	5.2	14,828	5.2	5.2
Nephritis, nephrotic syndrome and nephrosis	37,251	13.2	13.5	39,480	13.9	14.0
Renal failure	36,471	13.0	13.2	38,784	13.6	13.7
Other disorders of kidney	47	-	-	29	-	-
Infections of kidney	813	0.3	0.3	748	0.3	0.3
Pregnancy, childbirth and the puerperium	404	0.1	0.1	416	0.1	0.1
Congenital malformations, deformations and chromosomal abnormalities	10,578	3.8	3.8	10,442	3.7	3.6
All other diseases (Residual)	178,378	63.4	64.6	186,406	65.5	65.9
Intentional self-harm (suicide)	29,350	10.4	10.4	30,622	10.8	10.7
Assault (homicide)	16,765	6.0	5.9	20,308	7.1	7.1
Legal intervention	359	0.1	0.1	396	0.1	0.1
Events of undetermined intent	3,819	1.4	1.3	4,198	1.5	1.5
Operations of war and their sequelae	16	(B)	(B)	17	(Z)	(Z)
Complications of medical and surgical care	3,059	1.1	1.1	3,021	1.1	1.1
Injury by firearms [2]	28,663	10.2	10.2	28,913	10.2	10.1
Drug-induced deaths [2]	19,698	7.0	7.0	18,962	6.7	6.6
Alcohol-induced deaths [2]	19,358	6.9	6.9	19,423	6.8	6.8
Injury at work	5,430	2.5	2.5	5,431	2.4	2.4

- Represents zero. B Base figure too small to meet statistical standards for reliability; see text, this section. Z Less than 0.05. [1] See headnote, Table 108 [2] Included in selected categories.

Source: U.S. National Center for Health Statistics, *Vital Statistics of the United States,* annual; *National Vital Statistics Reports (NVSR)* (formerly *Monthly Statitics Report);* and unpublished data.

No. 117. Deaths by Selected Causes: 2000 to 2001

[Deaths in thousands (2,403 represents 2,403,000). Deaths are classified according to the Tenth Revision of the International Classification of Diseases. See Appendix III]

Cause of death	2000 All ages	Under 1 year	1-4 years	5-14 years	15-24 years	25-34 years	35-44 years	45-54 years	55-64 years	65-74 years	75-84 years	85 years over	2001 All ages	Under 1 year	1-4 years	5-14 years	15-24 years	25-34 years	35-44 years	45-54 years	55-64 years	65-74 years	75-84 years	85 years over
All causes	2,403	28	5	7	31	40	90	160	241	441	700	658	2,416	28	5	7	32	42	92	168	244	431	702	666
Tuberculosis	1	-	-	-	-	-	1	-	1	-	-	-	1	-	-	-	-	-	-	-	-	-	-	-
Viral hepatitis	5	-	-	-	-	-	1	2	1	1	-	-	6	-	-	-	-	-	1	2	1	1	1	-
Human immunodeficiency virus (HIV) disease	14	-	-	-	-	2	6	4	1	-	-	-	14	-	-	-	-	2	6	4	1	-	-	-
Malignant neoplasms	553	-	1	1	2	4	17	48	89	150	165	77	554	-	-	1	2	4	17	50	90	147	165	78
Malignant neoplasms of colon, rectum and anus	57	-	-	-	-	-	1	4	8	14	18	11	57	-	-	-	-	-	1	5	8	14	18	11
Malignant neoplasms of trachea, bronchus and lung	156	-	-	-	-	-	3	12	30	52	46	13	156	-	-	-	-	-	3	12	30	51	47	13
Malignant neoplasm of breast	42	-	-	-	-	-	3	6	8	9	10	6	42	-	-	-	-	-	3	7	8	9	10	6
Leukemia	21	-	-	-	-	-	1	1	2	5	7	4	21	-	-	-	-	1	1	1	3	5	7	4
Diabetes mellitus	69	-	-	-	-	1	2	5	9	17	22	14	71	-	-	-	-	1	2	5	10	17	23	14
Nutritional deficiencies	4	-	-	-	-	-	-	-	-	-	1	2	4	-	-	-	-	-	-	-	-	-	1	2
Alzheimers disease	50	-	-	-	-	-	-	-	-	3	17	28	54	-	-	-	-	-	-	-	-	3	19	31
Major cardiovascular diseases	937	1	-	-	1	4	17	44	77	156	296	340	922	1	-	-	1	4	17	44	76	148	292	338
Diseases of heart	711	1	-	-	1	3	13	35	63	122	220	251	700	-	-	-	1	3	13	36	62	116	217	249
Hypertensive heart disease	24	-	-	-	-	-	1	2	3	4	6	8	25	-	-	-	-	-	1	2	3	4	6	8
Ischemic heart diseases	515	-	-	-	1	1	8	25	48	93	164	177	502	-	-	-	-	1	8	25	47	87	160	174
Acute myocardial infarction	193	-	-	-	-	-	3	11	21	38	62	57	185	-	-	-	-	-	3	11	20	35	59	56
Influenza and pneumonia	65	-	-	-	-	-	1	2	3	7	20	32	62	-	-	-	-	-	1	2	3	7	19	30
Chronic lower respiratory diseases	122	-	-	-	-	-	1	3	11	31	48	27	123	-	-	-	-	-	1	3	11	31	48	28
Chronic liver disease and cirrhosis	27	-	-	-	-	-	3	7	6	5	4	1	27	-	-	-	-	-	3	7	6	5	4	1
Accidents (unintentional injuries)	98	1	2	3	14	12	15	12	8	8	12	12	102	1	2	3	14	12	16	13	8	8	13	12
Transport accidents	47	-	1	2	11	7	8	6	4	3	3	1	47	-	1	2	11	7	8	6	4	3	4	1
Motor vehicle accidents	43	-	1	2	11	7	7	5	4	3	3	1	44	-	1	2	11	7	7	6	3	3	3	1
Intentional self-harm (suicide)	29	(X)	(X)	-	4	5	7	5	3	2	2	1	31	-	-	-	4	5	7	6	3	2	2	1
Assault (homicide)	17	-	-	-	5	4	3	2	1	-	-	-	20	-	-	-	5	5	7	2	1	1	-	-
Complications of medical and surgical care	3	-	-	-	-	-	-	-	-	-	1	1	3	-	-	-	-	-	-	-	-	-	1	1

- Represents zero.   X Not applicable.

Source: U.S. National Center for Health Statistics, *Vital Statistics of the United States*, annual; *National Vital Statistics Reports (NVSR)* (formerly *Monthly Vital Statistics Report*).

No. 118. Deaths and Death Rates by Leading Causes of Death and Age: 2001

[Preliminary. Data are based on the tenth revision of the ICD. Rates per 100,000 population in specified group. Numbers are based on weighted data rounded to the nearest individual, so categories may not add to totals. See Appendix III]

Age	Number	Rate	Age	Number	Rate
ALL AGES [1]			Congenital malformations	488	1.2
All causes	2,417,798	849.0	Human immunodeficiency virus (HIV) disease	227	0.6
Diseases of heart	669,697	245.7	Cerebrovascular diseases	196	0.5
Malignant neoplasms	553,251	194.3	Influenza and pneumonia	184	0.5
Cerebrovascular diseases	163,601	57.4	Chronic lower respiratory diseases	164	0.4
Chronic lower respiratory diseases	123,974	43.5	All other causes	5,256	13.2
Accidents (unintentional injuries)	97,707	34.3			
Motor vehicle accidents	41,967	14.7	**25-44 YEARS**		
All other accidents	55,739	19.6			
Diabetes mellitus	71,252	25.0	All causes	132,553	156.6
Influenza and pneumonia	62,123	21.8	Accidents	26,138	30.9
Alzheimers disease	53,679	18.8	Motor vehicle accidents	13,471	15.9
Nephritis, nephrotic syndrome and			All other accidents	12,667	15.0
nephrosis	39,661	13.9	Malignant neoplasms	20,493	24.2
Septicemia	32,275	11.3	Diseases of heart	15,942	18.8
All other causes (Residual)	520,569	182.8	Intentional self-harm (suicide)	11,217	13.3
			Assault (homicide)	9,229	10.9
1-4 YEARS			Human immunodeficiency virus (HIV) disease	7,956	9.4
All causes	5,129	33.4	Chronic liver disease and cirrhosis	3,626	4.3
Accidents (unintentional injuries)	1,701	11.1	Cerebrovascular diseases	3,099	3.7
Motor vehicle accidents	605	3.9	Diabetes mellitus	2,511	3.0
All other accidents	1,096	7.1	Influenza and pneumonia	1,299	1.5
Congenital malformations	552	3.6	All other causes	31,043	36.7
Malignant neoplasms	413	2.7			
Assault (homicide)	394	2.6	**45-64 YEARS**		
Diseases of heart	218	1.4			
Influenza and pneumonia	111	0.7	All causes	411,545	638.1
Septicemia	107	0.7	Malignant neoplasms	139,908	216.9
Certain conditions originating in the			Diseases of heart	98,048	152.0
perinatal period	71	0.5	Accidents (unintentional injuries)	19,965	31.0
In situ neoplasms	60	0.4	Motor vehicle accidents	8,663	13.4
Cerebrovascular diseases	51	0.3	All other accidents	11,302	17.5
All other causes (Residual)	1,451	9.5	Cerebrovascular diseases	15,426	23.9
			Diabetes mellitus	14,815	23.0
5-14 YEARS			Chronic lower respiratory diseases	14,619	22.7
			Chronic liver disease and cirrhosis	12,813	19.9
All causes	7,120	17.3	Intentional self-harm (suicide)	8,823	13.7
Accidents (unintentional injuries)	2,802	6.8	Human immunodeficiency virus (HIV)		
Motor vehicle accidents	1,635	4.0	disease	5,408	8.4
All other accidents	1,168	2.8	Nephritis, nephrotic syndrome and		
Malignant neoplasms	1,002	2.4	nephrosis	5,141	8.0
Congenital malformations	366	0.9	All other causes	76,579	118.7
Assault (homicide)	322	0.8			
Intentional self-harm (suicide)	272	0.7	**65 YEARS AND OLDER**		
Diseases of heart	263	0.6			
In situ neoplasms	104	0.3	All causes	1,801,303	5,104.2
Chronic lower respiratory diseases	97	0.2	Diseases of heart	583,773	1,654.2
Influenza and pneumonia	96	0.2	Malignant neoplasms	389,657	1,104.1
Cerebrovascular diseases	78	0.2	Cerebrovascular diseases	144,626	409.8
All other causes (Residual)	1,718	4.2	Chronic lower respiratory diseases	107,787	305.4
			Influenza and pneumonia	55,668	157.7
15-24 YEARS			Diabetes mellitus	53,743	152.3
			Alzheimers disease	53,078	150.4
All causes	31,982	80.1	Nephritis, nephrotic syndrome and		
Accidents (unintentional injuries)	13,871	34.7	nephrosis	33,260	94.2
Motor vehicle accidents	10,259	25.7	Accidents (unintentional injuries)	32,214	91.3
All other accidents	3,613	9.0	Motor vehicle accidents	7,166	20.3
Assault (homicide)	5,126	12.8	All other accidents	25,048	71.0
Intentional self-harm (suicide)	3,854	9.6	Septicemia	25,420	72.0
Malignant neoplasms	1,701	4.3	All other causes	322,077	912.6
Diseases of heart	915	2.3			

[1] Includes deaths under 1 year of age.

Source: U.S. National Center for Health Statistics. *Vital Statistics of the United States*, annual; *National Vital Statistics Reports (NVSR)*, Vol. 52, No. 3.

No. 119. Death Rates for Major Causes of Death—States: 2001

[Deaths per 100,000 resident population enumerated as of July 1. By place of residence. Excludes nonresidents of the United States. Causes of death classified according to tenth revisions of International Classification of Diseases. See Appendix III]

State	Total	Heart disease	Cancer	Cerebro-vascular diseases	Acci-dents	Motor vehicle acci-dents	Chronic lower respira-tory diseases	Diabe-tes Mellitus	HIV [1]	Inten-tional self-harm (suicide)	Assault (homi-cide)
United States	848.5	245.8	194.4	57.4	35.7	15.4	43.2	25.1	5.0	10.8	7.1
AL	1,014.0	295.5	219.3	67.1	49.5	23.2	49.3	30.1	4.8	11.5	9.5
AK	469.4	95.2	108.7	24.9	54.4	16.3	23.2	12.6	(B)	16.1	6.0
AZ	773.7	199.5	172.3	46.7	46.6	19.2	47.1	19.9	2.9	14.5	9.3
AR	1,030.1	306.6	226.1	83.7	47.4	24.5	50.8	28.1	2.4	14.2	6.8
CA	676.4	197.2	155.8	52.3	23.5	11.4	37.5	18.5	4.3	8.2	6.4
CO	638.5	142.0	138.7	41.2	38.8	17.1	41.4	15.1	2.1	16.3	3.8
CT	868.4	249.9	206.5	58.3	30.7	9.2	43.3	22.1	5.6	8.2	5.0
DE	892.8	255.2	224.2	48.1	36.4	15.3	38.4	27.4	8.4	13.6	4.1
DC	1,037.1	306.9	231.3	46.2	38.9	9.4	26.1	36.4	38.9	7.0	34.3
FL	1,021.6	309.2	238.7	63.6	42.6	18.9	54.7	28.3	10.2	14.1	5.9
GA	767.2	207.9	164.4	51.3	40.4	19.4	36.8	17.5	8.6	11.1	8.1
HI	684.1	188.3	165.0	62.4	30.3	10.4	22.8	14.1	2.1	11.1	2.8
ID	738.5	188.5	158.5	59.1	43.0	19.4	44.0	24.1	(B)	15.9	3.1
IL	842.1	247.5	197.9	57.7	32.6	12.7	38.1	24.7	4.1	9.1	8.7
IN	900.9	256.0	209.4	63.3	35.7	15.8	51.2	27.4	1.9	11.7	7.1
IA	947.9	281.4	218.4	75.6	35.8	15.2	52.9	24.2	(B)	10.4	2.1
KS	912.1	248.5	201.6	68.4	42.8	19.9	53.4	26.7	1.4	10.8	5.3
KY	979.7	290.2	230.0	62.8	48.9	21.2	55.7	27.0	2.2	12.2	5.4
LA	934.1	256.7	212.9	59.0	45.4	22.1	39.4	38.8	9.0	11.0	12.1
ME	967.0	254.7	237.1	64.0	38.1	15.6	62.3	31.0	(B)	12.5	1.6
MD	813.9	228.6	191.6	53.5	24.9	13.1	35.4	27.1	10.6	8.4	10.3
MA	886.6	236.6	214.8	55.2	23.5	8.8	43.9	22.2	3.9	6.7	3.8
MI	863.7	268.8	196.8	57.0	32.9	14.3	41.5	26.5	2.5	10.5	6.9
MN	757.0	175.7	179.9	54.7	36.1	12.6	38.3	24.3	1.1	9.6	2.5
MS	988.2	316.5	208.3	67.7	54.9	28.8	46.6	23.1	7.1	11.5	11.4
MO	975.3	295.1	219.3	67.3	43.5	19.6	51.1	27.2	2.6	12.9	7.8
MT	912.9	217.6	216.0	63.8	51.7	23.4	64.4	25.3	(B)	19.3	3.5
NE	882.2	241.3	197.0	65.7	36.8	15.8	51.3	23.3	1.9	10.9	2.6
NV	776.3	209.4	181.9	43.5	35.2	15.8	54.2	15.3	3.6	18.4	8.3
NH	779.4	225.1	190.4	50.3	29.7	10.8	48.9	23.1	(B)	13.3	2.2
NJ	877.8	266.8	213.4	47.1	28.3	8.9	34.2	30.0	9.2	6.9	12.3
NM	771.7	187.0	158.4	45.0	55.7	23.5	42.3	29.4	2.1	19.8	7.1
NY	834.9	296.8	193.7	40.4	26.1	8.8	36.2	20.1	10.9	6.6	14.8
NC	864.4	229.0	195.8	65.8	41.9	20.1	42.8	26.6	5.7	12.1	7.3
ND	950.1	267.1	218.5	79.6	37.4	18.1	48.4	30.8	(B)	12.4	(B)
OH	948.5	284.9	217.8	60.5	33.9	12.9	51.6	32.9	1.8	10.7	4.6
OK	999.6	312.4	213.6	68.7	49.0	21.0	55.4	30.7	2.9	14.8	6.1
OR	868.2	203.7	203.2	74.5	37.8	14.6	49.7	29.1	1.8	14.5	2.9
PA	1,054.4	320.6	243.1	70.1	37.0	12.8	47.5	31.1	4.0	10.4	5.5
RI	945.7	290.3	226.3	57.9	27.7	9.2	48.2	25.0	2.8	8.3	3.5
SC	912.9	261.8	209.7	64.6	50.4	24.3	47.7	28.0	(B)	13.8	(B)
SD	959.2	272.9	212.7	70.2	47.1	22.7	51.2	30.4	4.8	12.4	7.9
TN	714.9	202.1	156.7	49.7	37.1	18.5	36.2	25.5	4.9	10.4	6.6
TX	555.7	127.1	101.5	38.2	28.2	13.1	23.0	22.3	(B)	14.1	3.4
UT	848.5	233.1	203.8	52.7	37.5	14.4	49.8	25.3	(B)	11.7	(B)
VT	782.0	207.2	185.4	57.4	33.8	13.4	38.1	22.4	3.8	11.1	7.1
VA	744.9	188.2	180.2	62.8	34.6	12.4	43.9	23.4	1.9	11.9	3.3
WA	1,164.2	351.2	260.1	70.6	46.3	20.7	70.7	44.5	1.6	15.9	3.8
WV	862.5	240.9	199.4	67.7	38.8	15.2	43.9	24.7	1.4	11.8	4.0
WI	816.0	199.5	186.9	52.7	55.1	28.4	54.7	24.3	(B)	16.8	(B)
WY											
PR	556.3	158.2	104.8	43.2	36.8	(B)	(B)	28.5	(B)	(B)	25.7
VI	418.7	128.8	61.3	39.2	28.4	12.6	13.9	(B)	(B)	14.5	(B)
GU	415.4	88.7	59.1	(B)	(B)	(B)	(B)	36.5	(B)	(B)	(B)
AS	205.9	32.0	37.6	(B)	(B)	(B)	(B)	(B)	(B)	(B)	(B)

B Figure does not meet standards of reliability or precision.   [1] Human immunodeficiency virus.

Source: U.S. National Center for Health Statistics, *National Vital Statistics Report (NVSR)*.

No. 120. Death Rates From Heart Disease by Sex and Age: 1990 to 2000

[Rates per 100,000 population. For explanation of age-adjustment, see headnote, Table 108. See Appendix III]

Characteristic	Male						Female					
	1990	1995	1997	1998	1999[1]	2000	1990	1995	1997	1998	1999[1]	2000
All ages, age adjusted	412.4	372.7	349.6	336.6	328.1	315.0	257.0	239.7	228.1	223.1	220.9	213.0
All ages, crude	297.6	282.7	272.2	268.0	263.8	256.1	281.8	278.8	271.1	268.3	268.0	260.2
Under 1 year	21.9	17.5	18.0	16.2	13.8	13.2	18.3	16.7	14.7	16.1	13.6	12.4
1-14 years	1.9	1.7	1.5	1.5	1.3	1.4	1.9	1.5	1.2	1.3	1.1	1.0
5-14 years	0.9	0.8	0.9	1.0	0.8	0.8	0.8	0.7	0.7	0.7	0.6	0.6
15-24 years	3.1	3.6	3.6	3.5	3.4	3.2	1.8	2.2	2.4	2.1	2.2	2.1
25-34 years	10.3	11.4	10.8	10.8	10.6	10.3	5.0	5.6	5.8	5.8	5.6	5.5
35-44 years	48.1	47.2	43.7	44.0	43.3	41.6	15.1	17.1	16.5	17.3	17.6	17.2
45-54 years	183.0	168.6	157.7	152.2	145.7	142.7	61.0	56.0	54.3	52.8	51.9	50.3
55-64 years	537.3	465.4	434.6	411.1	391.6	378.6	215.7	193.9	182.1	173.9	167.5	160.4
65-74 years	1,250.6	1,102.3	1,031.1	997.3	961.6	909.2	616.8	557.8	529.4	522.6	503.2	479.9
75-84 years	2,968.2	2,615.0	2,443.6	2,377.2	2,308.9	2,210.1	1,893.8	1,715.2	1,616.6	1,579.5	1,562.5	1,501.5
85 years and over	7,418.4	7,039.6	6,658.5	6,330.6	6,313.3	6,100.8	6,478.1	6,267.8	6,013.7	5,876.6	5,913.8	5,740.1

[1] Starting with 1999 data, cause of death is coded according to ICD-10. Discontinuity between 1998 and 1999 due to ICD-10 coding and classification changes is measured by the comparability ratio. For explanation, see text, this section.
Source: U.S. National Center for Health Statistics, *Vital Statistics of the United States*, annual; *National Vital Statistics Reports (NVSR)* (formerly *Monthly Statistics Report*); and unpublished data.

No. 121. Death Rates From Cerebrovascular Diseases by Race, Sex, and Age: 1950 to 2000

[Rates per 100,000 population. For explanation of age-adjustment, see headnote, Table 108. See Appendix III]

Characteristic	1950[1]	1960[1]	1970	1980	1985	1990	1995	1997	1998	1999[2]	2000
All ages, age adjusted	180.7	177.9	147.7	96.4	76.6	65.5	63.9	61.8	59.6	61.8	60.9
Under 1 year	5.1	4.1	5.0	4.4	3.7	3.8	5.8	7.0	7.8	2.7	3.2
1-4 years	0.9	0.8	1.0	0.5	0.3	0.3	0.4	0.4	0.4	0.3	0.3
1-14 years	0.5	0.7	0.7	0.3	0.2	0.2	0.2	0.2	0.2	0.2	0.2
15-24 years	1.6	1.8	1.6	1.0	0.8	0.6	0.5	0.5	0.5	0.5	0.5
25-34 years	4.2	4.7	4.5	2.6	2.2	2.2	1.8	1.7	1.7	1.5	1.6
35-44 years	18.7	14.7	15.6	8.5	7.2	6.5	6.5	6.3	6.0	5.7	5.8
45-54 years	70.4	49.2	41.6	25.2	21.3	18.7	17.6	16.9	16.5	15.5	16.2
55-64 years	194.2	147.3	115.8	65.2	54.8	48.0	46.1	44.4	42.6	41.3	41.5
65-74 years	554.7	469.2	384.1	219.5	172.8	144.4	137.2	134.8	130.0	132.2	130.2
75-84 years	1,499.6	1,491.3	1,254.2	788.6	601.5	499.3	481.4	462.0	455.4	472.8	463.1
86 years and over	2,990.1	3,680.5	3,014.3	2,288.9	1,865.1	1,633.9	1,636.5	1,584.6	1,500.0	1,607.7	1,568.4
Male, all ages, age adjusted	186.4	186.1	157.4	102.4	80.2	68.7	66.3	63.9	60.1	62.4	61.1
Under 1 year	6.4	5.0	5.8	5.0	4.6	4.4	6.3	7.6	9.0	3.3	3.8
1-4 years	1.1	0.9	1.2	0.4	0.4	0.3	0.4	0.5	0.3	0.3	0.3
1-14 years	0.5	0.7	0.8	0.3	0.2	0.2	0.2	0.2	0.2	0.2	0.2
15-24 years	1.8	1.9	1.8	1.1	0.7	0.7	0.5	0.6	0.6	0.5	0.5
25-34 years	4.2	4.5	4.4	2.6	2.2	2.1	1.9	1.7	1.7	1.6	1.7
35-44 years	17.5	14.6	15.7	8.7	7.4	6.8	7.1	6.5	6.2	5.6	5.8
45-54 years	67.9	52.2	44.4	27.3	23.2	20.5	19.8	19.2	18.5	17.1	17.8
55-64 years	205.2	163.8	138.7	74.7	63.5	54.4	53.4	51.4	49.5	47.6	48.1
65-74 years	589.6	530.7	449.5	259.2	201.4	166.8	155.9	153.1	145.7	149.0	146.8
75-84 years	1,543.6	1,555.9	1,361.6	868.3	661.2	552.7	517.1	488.7	474.7	494.5	482.5
86 years and over	3,048.6	3,643.1	2,895.2	2,199.2	1,730.1	1,533.2	1,537.7	1,500.7	1,347.2	1,455.5	1,408.3
Female, all ages, age adjusted	175.8	170.7	140.0	91.9	73.5	62.7	61.5	59.7	58.3	60.5	59.7
Under 1 year	3.7	3.2	4.0	3.8	2.7	3.1	5.2	6.3	6.6	2.0	2.7
1-4 years	0.7	0.7	0.7	0.5	0.3	0.3	0.3	0.3	0.4	0.3	0.4
1-14 years	0.4	0.6	0.6	0.3	0.3	0.2	0.2	0.2	0.2	0.2	0.2
15-24 years	1.5	1.6	1.4	0.8	0.8	0.6	0.4	0.5	0.4	0.5	0.5
25-34 years	4.3	4.4	4.7	2.6	2.1	2.2	1.7	1.7	1.8	1.5	1.6
35-44 years	19.9	14.8	15.6	8.4	6.9	6.1	6.0	6.2	5.7	5.6	5.8
45-54 years	72.9	46.3	39.0	23.3	19.4	17.0	15.5	14.8	14.6	14.0	14.6
55-64 years	183.1	131.8	95.3	56.9	47.2	42.2	39.4	37.9	36.3	35.5	35.6
65-74 years	522.1	415.7	333.3	189.0	150.7	126.9	122.2	120.1	117.2	118.5	116.5
75-84 years	1,462.2	1,441.1	1,183.1	741.6	566.3	467.4	458.7	444.4	442.6	458.2	450.0
86 years and over	2,949.4	3,704.4	3,081.0	2,328.2	1,918.9	1,672.7	1,675.0	1,618.4	1,563.3	1,670.6	1,637.4
White male, age adjusted	182.1	181.6	153.7	99.0	77.4	65.7	63.2	61.5	57.6	60.0	58.6
Black male, age adjusted	228.8	238.5	206.4	142.1	112.7	102.5	96.7	88.5	86.3	87.4	87.1
White female, age adjusted	169.7	165.0	135.5	89.2	70.9	60.5	59.5	57.9	56.6	58.7	57.8
Black female, age adjusted	238.4	232.5	189.3	119.8	99.4	84.0	81.0	76.1	75.3	78.1	78.1

[1] Includes deaths of persons who were not residents of the 50 states and the District of Columbia. [2] Starting with 1999 data, cause of death is coded according to ICD-10. Discontinuity between 1998 and 1999 due to ICD-10 coding and classification changes is measured by the comparability ratio. For explanation, see text, this section.

Source: U.S. National Center for Health Statistics. *Vital Statistics of the United States*, annual; *National Vital Statistics Reports (NVSR)*; and unpublished data.

No. 122. Death Rates From Malignant Neoplasms by Race, Sex, and Age: 1950 to 2000

[Rates per 100,000 population. For explanation of age-adjustment, see headnote, Table 108. See Appendix III]

Characteristic	1950 [1]	1960 [1]	1970	1980	1985	1990	1995	1997	1998	1999 [2]	2000
Total, age adjusted	193.9	193.9	198.6	207.9	211.3	216.0	211.7	205.7	202.4	202.7	199.6
Under 1 year	8.7	7.2	4.7	3.2	3.1	2.3	1.8	2.4	2.1	1.8	2.4
1-4 years	11.7	10.9	7.5	4.5	3.8	3.5	3.1	2.9	2.4	2.8	2.8
5-14 years	6.7	6.8	6.0	4.3	3.5	3.1	2.7	2.7	2.6	2.6	2.6
15-24 years	8.6	8.3	8.3	6.3	5.4	4.9	4.6	4.5	4.6	4.6	4.5
25-34 years	20.0	19.5	16.5	13.7	13.2	12.6	11.9	11.6	11.3	10.6	10.5
35-44 years	62.7	59.7	59.5	48.6	45.9	43.3	40.3	38.9	38.2	37.3	36.8
45-54 years	175.1	177.0	182.5	180.0	170.1	158.9	142.2	135.1	132.3	130.4	129.3
55-64 years	390.7	396.8	423.0	436.1	454.6	449.6	416.0	395.7	383.8	380.8	371.3
65-74 years	698.8	713.9	754.2	817.9	845.5	872.3	868.2	847.3	841.3	836.2	826.4
75-84 years	1,153.3	1,127.4	1,169.2	1,232.3	1,271.8	1,348.5	1,364.8	1,335.2	1,326.3	1,340.0	1,340.8
85 years and over	1,451.0	1,450.0	1,320.7	1,594.6	1,615.4	1,752.9	1,823.8	1,805.0	1,749.4	1,796.7	1,765.6
Male, all ages, age adjusted	208.1	225.1	247.6	271.2	274.4	280.4	268.8	258.0	252.4	251.6	247.4
Female, all ages, age adjusted	182.3	168.7	163.2	166.7	171.2	175.7	175.4	171.6	169.2	169.9	205.9
White male, all ages, age adjusted	210.0	224.7	244.8	265.1	267.1	272.2	261.8	251.9	246.9	246.5	242.5
Black male, all ages, age adjusted	178.9	227.6	291.9	353.4	373.9	397.9	372.8	354.7	343.1	340.5	333.2
White female, all ages, age adjusted	182.0	167.7	162.5	165.2	169.9	174.0	173.7	170.0	167.7	168.6	168.7
Black female, all ages, age adjusted	174.1	174.3	173.4	189.5	195.5	205.9	206.0	204.4	200.0	200.0	196.6
DEATH RATES FOR MALIGNANT NEOPLASM OF BREASTS FOR FEMALES											
All ages, age adjusted	31.9	31.7	32.1	31.9	33.0	33.3	30.8	28.6	27.9	27.0	27.1
All ages, crude	24.7	26.1	28.4	30.6	32.8	34.0	32.6	30.7	30.2	29.5	29.8
Under 25 years	(B)	(B)	(B)	(B)	-	(B)	(B)	(B)	(B)	(B)	(B)
25-34 years	3.8	3.8	3.9	3.3	3.0	2.9	2.7	2.6	2.6	2.3	2.5
35-44 years	20.8	20.2	20.4	17.9	17.5	17.8	15.0	14.0	13.4	12.1	12.5
45-54 years	46.9	51.4	52.6	48.1	47.1	45.4	41.4	37.8	35.8	33.5	33.4
55-64 years	69.9	70.8	77.6	80.5	84.2	78.6	69.8	64.4	62.2	59.9	59.7
65-74 years	95.0	90.0	93.8	101.1	107.8	111.7	103.3	94.1	93.3	89.9	89.4
75-84 years	139.8	129.9	127.4	126.4	136.2	146.3	142.0	132.2	131.4	131.3	131.2
85 years and over	195.5	191.9	157.1	169.3	178.5	196.8	203.7	198.5	194.7	202.6	206.4
DEATH RATES FOR MALIGNANT NEOPLASM OF TRACHEA, BRONCHUS, AND LUNG											
All ages, age adjusted	15.0	24.1	37.1	49.9	54.6	59.3	58.9	58.1	57.6	56.0	56.5
All ages, crude	12.2	20.3	32.1	45.8	51.5	56.8	57.5	57.3	57.2	55.8	55.6
Under 25 years	0.1	-	0.1	-	-	-	-	-	-	-	-
25-34 years	0.8	1.0	0.9	0.6	0.6	0.7	0.7	0.6	0.6	0.5	0.5
35-44 years	4.5	6.8	11.0	9.2	7.8	6.8	6.0	6.2	6.1	6.1	6.1
45-54 years	20.4	29.6	43.4	54.1	50.9	46.8	38.0	34.6	33.3	31.9	32.1
55-64 years	48.7	75.3	109.1	138.2	153.8	160.6	142.9	134.3	131.4	125.5	124.0
65-74 years	59.7	108.1	164.5	233.3	261.2	288.4	297.1	295.7	296.7	284.6	287.6
75-84 years	55.8	91.5	163.2	240.5	282.0	333.3	361.4	368.5	367.7	364.4	372.2
85 years and over	42.3	65.6	101.7	176.0	195.2	242.5	284.0	297.6	289.9	295.5	298.1

- Represents zero or rounds to less than half the unit of measurement shown.   B Base figure too small to meet statistical standards for reliability of a derived figure.   [1] Includes deaths of persons who were not residents of the 50 states and the District of Columbia.   [2] Starting with 1999 data, cause of death is coded according to ICD-10. Discontinuity between 1998 and 1999 due to ICD-10 coding and classification changes is measured by the comparability ratio. For explanation, see text, this section.

Source: U.S. National Center for Health Statistics, *Vital Statistics of the United States*, annual; *National Vital Statistics Reports (NVSR)*; and unpublished data.

No. 123. Death Rates From Suicide by Sex and Race: 1950 to 2000

[Rates per 100,000 population. For explanation of age-adjustment, see headnote, Table 108. See Appendix III]

Characteristic	1950 [1,2]	1960 [1]	1970	1980	1985	1990	1995	1997	1998	1999 [3]	2000
All ages, age adjusted	13.2	12.5	13.1	12.2	12.5	12.5	12.0	11.4	11.3	10.7	10.4
All ages, crude	11.4	10.6	11.6	11.9	12.4	12.4	11.9	11.4	11.3	10.7	10.4
Under 1 year	(X)	(X)	(X)	(X)	(X)	(X)	(X)	(X)	(X)	(X)	(X)
1-4 years	(X)	(X)	(X)	(X)	(X)	(X)	(X)	(X)	(X)	(X)	(X)
5-14 years	0.2	0.3	0.3	0.4	0.8	0.8	0.9	0.8	0.8	0.6	0.7
15-24 years	4.5	5.2	8.8	12.3	12.8	13.2	13.3	11.4	11.1	10.1	10.2
25-44 years	11.6	12.2	15.4	15.6	15.0	15.2	15.3	14.8	14.6	13.6	13.4
25-34 years	9.1	10.0	14.1	16.0	15.3	15.2	15.4	14.3	13.8	12.7	12.0
35-44 years	14.3	14.2	16.9	15.4	14.6	15.3	15.2	15.3	15.4	14.3	14.5
45-64 years	23.5	22.0	20.6	15.9	16.3	15.3	14.1	14.2	14.1	13.2	13.5
45-54 years	20.9	20.7	20.0	15.9	15.7	14.8	14.6	14.7	14.8	13.9	14.4
55-64 years	26.8	23.7	21.4	15.9	16.8	16.0	13.3	13.5	13.1	12.2	12.1
65 years and over	30.0	24.5	20.8	17.6	20.4	20.5	18.1	16.8	16.9	15.8	15.2
65-74 years	29.6	23.0	20.8	16.9	18.7	17.9	15.8	14.4	14.1	13.4	12.5
75-84 years	31.1	27.9	21.2	19.1	23.9	24.9	20.7	19.3	19.7	18.1	17.6
85 years and over	28.8	26.0	19.0	19.2	19.4	22.2	21.6	20.8	21.0	19.3	19.6
White male all ages, age adjusted	22.3	21.1	20.8	20.9	22.4	22.8	21.9	20.6	20.6	19.4	19.1
Black male, all ages, age adjusted	7.5	8.4	10.0	11.4	11.8	12.8	12.5	11.4	10.6	10.4	10.0
White female, all ages, age adjusted	6.0	5.9	7.9	6.1	5.7	5.2	4.7	4.8	4.7	4.4	4.3
Black female, all ages, age adjusted	1.8	2.0	2.9	2.4	2.3	2.4	2.1	2.0	1.8	1.6	1.8

NA Not available. X Not applicable. [1] Includes deaths of persons who were not residents of the 50 states and the District of Columbia. [2] In 1950, rate is for the age group 75 years and over. [3] Starting with 1999 data, cause of death is coded according to ICD 10.

Source: U.S. National Center for Health Statistics, *Vital Statistics of the United States*, annual; *National Vital Statistics Reports* (NVSR) (formerly *Monthly Statistics Report*); and unpublished data.

No. 124. Death Rates From Human Immunodeficiency Virus (HIV) Disease by Race, Sex, and Age: 1990 to 2000

[Rates per 100,000 population. For explanation of age-adjustment, see headnote, Table 108. See Appendix III]

Characteristic	1990	1993	1994	1995	1996	1997	1998	1999 [1]	2000
All ages, age adjusted	10.2	14.5	16.2	16.3	11.7	6.1	4.9	5.4	5.2
Under 1 year	2.7	2.2	2.5	1.5	1.1	(B)	(B)	(B)	(B)
1-4 years	0.8	1.3	1.3	1.3	0.9	0.4	0.2	0.2	(B)
5-14 years	0.2	0.4	0.5	0.5	0.5	0.3	0.1	0.2	0.1
15-24 years	1.5	1.7	1.8	1.7	1.1	0.8	0.5	0.5	0.5
25-34 years	19.7	27.0	29.3	29.1	19.9	10.1	7.5	7.2	6.5
35-44 years	27.4	39.1	44.1	44.4	31.4	16.1	12.9	13.9	13.2
45-54 years	15.2	22.6	25.6	26.3	19.3	10.4	9.0	10.9	11.1
55-64 years	6.2	8.8	10.4	11.0	8.4	4.9	4.3	4.9	5.2
65-74 years	2.0	2.9	3.1	3.6	2.7	1.8	1.6	2.2	2.2
75-84 years	0.7	0.8	0.9	0.7	0.8	0.6	0.5	0.6	0.7
85 years and over	(B)	(B)	(B)	(B)	(B)	(B)	(B)	(B)	(B)
Male, all ages, age adjusted	18.5	25.4	27.8	27.7	19.2	9.7	7.7	8.4	8.0
Under 1 year	2.4	2.1	2.1	1.7	1.1	(B)	(B)	(B)	(B)
1-4 years	0.8	1.3	1.2	1.2	0.9	0.3	(B)	(B)	(B)
5-14 years	0.3	0.4	0.5	0.5	0.5	0.3	0.1	0.2	0.1
15-24 years	2.2	2.3	2.3	2.1	1.3	0.8	0.5	0.5	0.5
25-34 years	34.5	46.0	48.5	47.1	31.4	15.1	10.7	10.2	8.6
35-44 years	50.2	68.5	76.2	75.9	51.8	25.5	20.1	21.1	19.9
45-54 years	29.1	41.7	46.3	46.9	33.6	17.4	15.2	17.9	18.1
55-64 years	12.0	16.5	19.1	19.9	14.9	8.5	7.3	8.5	8.9
65-74 years	3.7	5.4	5.8	6.4	5.1	3.4	2.9	3.9	3.8
75-84 years	1.1	1.4	1.4	1.3	1.5	1.0	0.9	1.0	1.3
85 years and over	(B)	(B)	(B)	(B)	(B)	(B)	(B)	(B)	(B)
Female, age adjusted	2.2	3.9	4.9	5.3	4.3	2.7	2.3	2.6	2.6
Under 1 year	3.0	2.4	2.9	1.2	(B)	(B)	(B)	(B)	(B)
1-4 years	0.8	1.3	1.3	1.5	1.0	0.4	(B)	(B)	(B)
5-14 years	0.2	0.4	0.5	0.5	0.4	0.2	0.2	0.2	0.1
15-24 years	0.7	1.1	1.3	1.4	1.0	0.7	0.6	0.6	0.4
25-34 years	4.9	8.0	10.1	11.1	8.5	5.1	4.4	4.3	4.4
35-45 years	5.2	10.2	12.5	13.4	11.3	6.8	5.8	6.8	6.5
45-54 years	1.9	4.4	5.8	6.7	5.7	3.8	3.1	4.2	4.5
55-64 years	1.1	1.9	2.6	2.9	2.5	1.6	1.6	1.6	1.8
65-74 years	0.8	1.0	1.0	1.4	0.8	0.5	0.6	0.8	0.8
75-84 years	0.4	0.4	0.6	0.3	0.3	0.4	0.3	0.3	0.3
85 years and over	(B)	(B)	(B)	(B)	(B)	(B)	(B)	(B)	(B)
Race, age adjusted									
White male	15.7	20.0	21.2	20.7	13.2	6.0	4.6	5.0	4.6
Black male	46.3	74.5	87.2	90.4	71.5	41.7	34.0	37.1	35.1
White female	1.1	1.9	2.3	2.5	1.9	1.0	0.8	1.0	1.0
Black female	10.1	17.8	22.6	24.7	21.1	13.9	12.2	13.4	13.2

B Base figure too small to meet statistical standards for reliability of a derived figure. [1] Starting with 1999 data, cause of death is coded according to ICD-10. Discontinuity between 1998 and 1999 due to ICD-10 coding and classification changes is measured by the comparability ratio. For explanation, see text, this section.

Source: U.S. National Center for Health Statistics. *Vital Statistics of the United States*, annual; *National Vital Statistics Reports* (NVSR); and unpublished data.

Vital Statistics

No. 125. Deaths—Life Years Lost and Mortality Costs by Age, Sex, and Cause: 1999 and 2000

[*Life years lost:* Number of years person would have lived in absence of death. Mortality cost: value of lifetime earnings lost by persons who die prematurely, discounted at 6 percent]

Characteristic	Number of deaths (1,000)	Life years lost [1] Total (1,000)	Life years lost [1] Per death	Mortality cost [2] Total (mil. dol.)	Mortality cost [2] Per death (dol.)
Total, 1999	2,391	38,383	16.1	410,022	171,483
Under 5 yrs. old	33	2,530	76.2	28,788	867,464
5 to 14 yrs. old	8	525	69.1	8,011	1,054,831
15 to 24 yrs. old	31	1,795	58.6	39,585	1,291,249
25 to 44 yrs. old	130	5,595	42.9	137,676	1,056,427
45 to 64 yrs. old	337	10,209	30.3	157,184	466,226
65 yrs old and over	1,852	17,728	9.6	38,779	20,937
Heart disease	725	9,037	12.5	70,855	97,711
Cancer	550	9,007	16.4	84,739	154,119
Cerebrovascular diseases	167	1,902	11.4	11,349	67,810
Accidents and adverse effects	98	3,262	33.4	64,910	664,012
Other	851	15,176	17.8	178,170	209,377
Male	1,175	20,148	17.1	299,386	254,757
Under 5 yrs. old	19	1,375	73.8	18,149	974,632
5 to 14 yrs. old	4	300	66.8	5,288	1,177,258
15 to 24 yrs. old	22	1,280	57.1	31,185	1,391,335
25 to 44 yrs. old	85	3,545	41.5	102,445	1,199,680
45 to 64 yrs. old	238	5,881	24.7	114,472	480,202
65 yrs. old and over	806	7,767	9.6	27,846	34,554
Heart disease	352	4,751	13.5	55,514	157,899
Cancer	286	4,367	15.3	54,112	189,318
Cerebrovascular diseases	64	759	11.8	7,345	113,908
Accidents and adverse effects	63	2,219	35.0	51,829	816,959
Other	410	8,051	19.6	130,586	318,617
Female	1,216	18,236	15.0	110,636	90,994
Under 5 yrs. old	15	1,155	79.3	10,639	730,453
5 to 14 yrs. old	3	225	72.5	2,723	877,603
15 to 24 yrs. old	8	516	62.6	8,399	1,019,066
25 to 44 yrs. old	45	2,051	45.6	35,230	784,149
45 to 64 yrs. old	99	4,329	43.8	42,712	432,491
65 yrs. old and over	1,046	9,961	9.5	10,933	10,449
Heart disease	374	4,286	11.5	15,340	41,065
Cancer	264	4,639	17.6	30,627	116,011
Cerebrovascular diseases	103	1,143	11.1	4,004	38,916
Accidents and adverse effects	34	1,043	30.4	13,081	381,230
Other	441	7,125	16.2	47,584	107,876
Total, 2000	2,403	38,843	16.2	431,992	179,772
Under 5 yrs. old	33	2,522	76.4	30,421	921,471
5 to 14 yrs. old	7	513	69.2	8,331	1,123,778
15 to 24 yrs. old	31	1,835	58.6	43,039	1,374,751
25 to 44 yrs. old	130	5,604	43.1	144,409	1,108,713
45 to 64 yrs. old	346	10,555	30.5	168,201	486,146
65 yrs old and over	1,855	17,815	9.6	37,591	20,265
Heart disease	711	8,917	12.5	72,224	101,623
Cancer	553	10,028	18.1	107,501	194,367
Cerebrovascular diseases	168	1,934	11.5	12,103	72,187
Accidents and adverse effects	98	3,303	33.8	69,429	709,801
Other	874	14,661	16.8	170,736	195,408
Male	1,177	20,415	17.3	316,850	269,135
Under 5 yrs. old	19	1,373	74.0	19,287	1,040,197
5 to 14 yrs. old	4	295	67.0	5,540	1,258,796
15 to 24 yrs. old	23	1,319	57.2	34,230	1,483,692
25 to 44 yrs. old	85	3,549	41.7	107,638	1,263,555
45 to 64 yrs. old	244	6,098	25.0	123,301	505,917
65 yrs. old and over	802	7,781	9.7	26,853	33,467
Heart disease	345	4,709	13.7	56,883	164,989
Cancer	286	5,333	18.6	75,819	265,036
Cerebrovascular diseases	65	777	12.0	7,861	121,377
Accidents and adverse effects	64	2,259	35.4	55,756	874,831
Other	418	7,336	17.6	120,531	288,386
Female	1,226	18,428	15.0	115,142	93,939
Under 5 yrs. old	14	1,149	79.4	11,134	769,356
5 to 14 yrs. old	3	218	72.4	2,791	926,495
15 to 24 yrs. old	8	516	62.6	8,809	1,069,584
25 to 44 yrs. old	45	2,054	45.6	36,770	815,994
45 to 64 yrs. old	102	4,457	43.6	44,899	439,031
65 yrs. old and over	1,053	10,034	9.5	10,738	10,201
Heart disease	366	4,208	11.5	15,341	41,923
Cancer	267	4,695	17.6	31,681	118,653
Cerebrovascular diseases	103	1,157	11.2	4,241	41,223
Accidents and adverse effects	34	1,044	30.6	13,673	401,183
Other	456	7,325	16.1	50,205	110,150

[1] Based on life expectancy at year of death.   [2] Cost estimates based on the person's age, sex, life expectancy at the time of death, labor force participation rates, annual earnings, value of homemaking services, and a 4 percent discount rate by which to convert to present worth the potential aggregate earnings lost over the years.

Source: Institute for Health and Aging, University of California, San Francisco, CA, unpublished data.

No. 126. Marriages and Divorces—Number and Rate by State: 1990 to 2001

[2,443.0 represents 2,443,000. By place of occurance. See Appendix III]

State	Marriages [1] Number (1,000) 1990	1995	2001	Rate per 1,000 population [2] 1990	1995	2001	Divorces [3] Number (1,000) 1990	1995	2001	Rate per 1,000 population [2] 1990	1995	2001
U.S. [4]	2,443.0	2,336.0	2,327.0	9.8	8.9	8.4	1,182.0	1,169.0	(NA)	4.7	4.4	4.0
Alabama	43.3	42.0	42.2	10.6	9.9	9.6	25.3	26.0	23.4	6.1	6.1	5.3
Alaska	5.7	5.5	5.1	10.2	9.0	8.2	2.9	3.0	2.6	5.5	5.0	4.1
Arizona	37.0	38.9	40.0	10.0	9.2	8.0	25.1	27.6	21.1	6.9	6.6	4.2
Arkansas	35.7	36.6	38.4	15.3	14.7	14.8	16.8	16.0	17.1	6.9	6.5	6.6
California [5]	236.7	199.6	224.2	7.9	6.3	6.6	128.0	(NA)	(NA)	4.3	(NA)	(NA)
Colorado	31.5	34.3	36.5	9.8	9.2	8.7	18.4	(NA)	(NA)	5.5	(NA)	(NA)
Connecticut	27.8	22.6	18.6	7.9	6.7	5.6	10.3	10.6	9.7	3.2	2.9	2.9
Delaware	5.6	5.4	5.2	8.4	7.5	6.7	3.0	3.7	3.1	4.4	5.1	4.0
Dist. of Columbia	4.7	3.5	3.5	8.2	6.4	6.8	2.7	1.9	1.2	4.5	3.4	2.3
Florida	142.3	144.3	151.3	10.9	10.2	9.7	81.7	79.5	84.6	6.3	5.6	5.4
Georgia	64.4	61.5	51.3	10.3	8.5	6.3	35.7	37.2	30.6	5.5	5.2	3.8
Hawaii	18.1	18.8	24.0	16.4	15.8	20.4	5.2	5.5	4.5	4.6	4.6	3.8
Idaho	15.0	15.5	14.7	13.9	13.3	11.4	6.6	6.8	7.2	6.5	5.8	5.6
Illinois	97.1	83.2	89.8	8.8	7.0	7.3	44.3	38.8	39.7	3.8	3.3	3.2
Indiana	54.3	50.4	34.1	9.6	8.7	5.7	(NA)	(NA)	(NA)	(NA)	(NA)	(NA)
Iowa	24.8	22.0	20.9	9.0	7.8	7.2	11.1	10.5	9.3	3.9	3.7	3.2
Kansas	23.4	22.1	20.3	9.2	8.6	7.6	12.6	10.7	8.7	5.0	4.2	3.2
Kentucky	51.3	47.6	36.6	13.5	12.3	9.1	21.8	22.9	22.0	5.8	5.9	5.5
Louisiana	41.2	40.8	37.5	9.6	9.4	8.6	(NA)	(NA)	(NA)	(NA)	(NA)	(NA)
Maine	11.8	10.8	11.4	9.7	8.7	9.0	5.3	5.5	4.9	4.3	4.4	3.9
Maryland	46.1	42.8	37.5	9.7	8.5	7.1	16.1	15.0	15.9	3.4	3.0	3.0
Massachusetts	47.8	43.6	40.0	7.9	7.2	6.4	16.8	13.5	14.8	2.8	2.2	2.4
Michigan	76.1	71.0	66.5	8.2	7.4	6.7	40.2	39.9	38.9	4.3	4.2	3.9
Minnesota	33.7	32.8	33.0	7.7	7.1	6.8	15.4	15.8	16.0	3.5	3.4	3.3
Mississippi	24.3	21.5	18.7	9.4	8.0	6.7	14.4	13.1	15.1	5.5	4.8	5.4
Missouri	49.3	44.9	42.2	9.6	8.4	7.6	26.4	26.8	23.8	5.1	5.0	4.3
Montana	7.0	6.6	6.4	8.6	7.6	7.2	4.1	4.2	2.3	5.1	4.8	2.6
Nebraska	12.5	12.1	13.6	8.0	7.4	8.1	6.5	6.3	6.2	4.0	3.8	3.7
Nevada	123.4	134.8	146.1	99.0	88.1	75.0	13.3	12.4	13.2	11.4	8.1	6.8
New Hampshire	10.6	9.6	10.6	9.5	8.4	8.6	5.3	4.9	6.1	4.7	4.2	5.0
New Jersey	58.0	52.4	54.1	7.6	6.7	6.6	23.6	24.3	28.5	3.0	3.1	3.5
New Mexico	13.2	15.1	13.9	8.8	9.0	7.9	7.7	11.3	9.0	4.9	6.7	5.1
New York	169.3	147.4	145.5	8.6	8.1	7.9	57.9	56.0	54.1	3.2	3.1	3.0
North Carolina	52.1	61.6	61.1	7.8	8.6	7.8	34.0	37.0	34.9	5.1	5.1	4.5
North Dakota	4.8	4.6	4.1	7.5	7.2	6.6	2.3	2.2	1.7	3.6	3.4	2.7
Ohio	95.8	90.1	82.3	9.0	8.1	7.3	51.0	48.7	45.6	4.7	4.4	4.0
Oklahoma	33.2	28.5	16.6	10.6	8.7	4.9	24.9	21.8	11.5	7.7	6.7	3.4
Oregon	25.2	25.7	26.0	8.9	8.2	7.7	15.9	15.0	16.5	5.5	4.8	4.9
Pennsylvania	86.8	75.8	71.4	7.1	6.3	6.0	40.1	39.4	38.0	3.3	3.3	3.2
Rhode Island	8.1	7.4	8.6	8.1	7.5	8.6	3.8	3.7	3.3	3.7	3.7	3.3
South Carolina	55.8	44.6	36.8	15.9	12.1	9.3	16.1	14.8	13.8	4.5	4.0	3.5
South Dakota	7.7	7.3	6.7	11.1	10.0	9.1	2.6	2.9	2.5	3.7	4.0	3.4
Tennessee	66.6	82.3	77.7	13.9	15.7	13.9	32.3	33.1	28.8	6.5	6.3	5.2
Texas	182.8	188.5	194.9	10.5	10.1	9.4	94.0	99.9	85.4	5.5	5.3	4.1
Utah	19.0	21.6	23.2	11.2	11.1	10.6	8.8	8.9	9.7	5.1	4.6	4.4
Vermont	6.1	6.1	6.0	10.9	10.3	9.9	2.6	2.8	2.4	4.5	4.8	4.0
Virginia	71.3	67.9	63.4	11.4	10.3	9.0	27.3	28.9	30.2	4.4	4.4	4.3
Washington	48.6	42.0	42.2	9.5	7.7	7.2	28.8	29.7	26.3	5.9	5.5	4.5
West Virginia	13.2	11.2	14.2	7.2	6.1	7.9	9.7	9.4	9.3	5.3	5.1	5.2
Wisconsin	41.2	36.3	34.9	7.9	7.1	6.5	17.8	17.5	17.3	3.6	3.4	3.2
Wyoming	4.8	5.2	5.0	10.7	10.7	10.3	3.1	3.2	2.9	6.6	6.7	6.1

NA Not available. [1] Data are counts of marriages performed, except as noted. [2] Based on total population residing in area; population enumerated as of April 1 for 1990; estimated as of July 1 for all other years. [3] Includes annulments. [4] U.S. totals for the number of divorces is an estimate which includes states not reporting (CA, CO, IN, and LA). [5] Marriage data include nonlicensed marriages registered.

Source: U.S. National Center for Health Statistics, *Vital Statistics of the United States*, annual; *National Vital Statistics Reports* (NVSR) (formerly *Monthly Vital Statistical Report*).

Section 3
Health and Nutrition

This section presents statistics on health expenditures and insurance coverage, including medicare and medicaid, medical personnel, hospitals, nursing homes and other care facilities, injuries, diseases, disability status, nutritional intake of the population, and food consumption. Summary statistics showing recent trends on health care and discussions of selected health issues are published annually by the U.S. National Center for Health Statistics (NCHS) in *Health, United States*. Data on national health expenditures, medical costs, and insurance coverage are compiled by the U.S. Centers for Medicare & Medicaid Services (CMS) (formerly Health Care Financing Administration), and appear on the CMS Web site at <http://www.cms.hhs.gov/statistics/nhe> and in the annual *Medicare and Medicaid Statistical Supplement* to the *Health Care Financing Review*. Statistics on health insurance are also collected by NCHS and are published in Series 10 of *Vital and Health Statistics*. U.S. Census Bureau also publishes data on utilization of insurance coverage. Statistics on hospitals are published annually by the Health Forum, L.L.C., an American Hospital Association Company, in *Hospital Statistics*. Primary sources for data on nutrition is the annual *Food Consumption, Prices, and Expenditures*, issued by the U.S. Department of Agriculture. NCHS also conducts periodic surveys of nutrient levels in the population, including estimates of food and nutrient intake, overweight and obesity, hypercholesterolemia, hypertension, and clinical signs of malnutrition.

National health expenditures—CMS compiles estimates of national health expenditures (NHE) to measure spending for health care in the United States. The NHE accounts are structured to show spending by type of expenditure (i.e., hospital care, physician and clinical care, dental care, and other professional care; home health care; retail sales of prescription drugs; other medical nondurables; vision products and other medical durables; nursing home care and other personal health expenditures; plus nonpersonal health expenditures for such items as public health, research, construction of medical facilities, administration, and the net cost of private health insurance) and by source of funding (e.g., private health insurance, out-of-pocket payments, and a range of public programs including medicare, medicaid, and those operated by the Department of Veterans Affairs (VA)).

Data used to estimate health expenditures come from existing sources, which are tabulated for other purposes. The type of expenditure estimates rely upon statistics produced by such groups as the American Hospital Association, the Census Bureau, and the Department of Health and Human Services (HHS). Source of funding estimates are constructed using administrative and statistical records from the medicare and medicaid programs, the Department of Defense and VA medical programs, the Social Security Administration, Census Bureau's *Governmental Finances*, state and local governments, other HHS agencies, and other nongovernment sources. More information and detailed descriptions of sources and methods are available on the CMS home page at <http://cms.hhs.gov/statistics/nhe/default.asp>.

Medicare and medicaid—Since July 1966, the federal medicare program has provided two coordinated plans for nearly all people age 65 and over: (1) A hospital insurance plan, which covers hospital and related services and (2) a voluntary supplementary medical insurance plan, financed partially by monthly premiums paid by participants, which partly covers physicians' and related medical services. Such insurance also applies, since July 1973, to disabled beneficiaries of any age after 24 months of entitlement to cash benefits under the social security or railroad retirement programs and to persons with end stage renal disease.

Medicaid is a health insurance program for certain low-income people. These include: certain low-income families with children; aged, blind, or disabled people on supplemental security income; certain low-income pregnant women and children; and people who have very high medical bills. Medicaid is funded and administered through a state-federal partnership. Although there are broad federal requirements for medicaid, states have a wide degree of flexibility to design their program. States have authority to establish eligibility standards, determine what benefits and services to cover, and set payment rates. All states, however, must cover these basic services: inpatient and outpatient hospital services, laboratory and X-ray services, skilled nursing and home health services, doctor's services, family planning, and periodic health checkups, diagnosis and treatment for children.

Health resources—Hospital statistics based on data from the American Hospital Association's yearly survey are published annually in *Hospital Statistics* and cover all hospitals accepted for registration by the Association. To be accepted for registration, a hospital must meet certain requirements relating to number of beds, construction, equipment, medical and nursing staff, patient care, clinical records, surgical and obstetrical facilities, diagnostic and treatment facilities, laboratory services, etc. Data obtained from NCHS cover all U.S. hospitals that meet certain criteria for inclusion. The criteria are published in *Vital and Health Statistics* reports, Series 13. NCHS defines a hospital as a nonfederal short-term general or special facility with six or more inpatient beds with an average stay of less than 60 days.

Statistics on the demographic characteristics of persons employed in the health occupations are compiled by the U.S. Bureau of Labor Statistics and reported in *Employment and Earnings* (monthly) (see Table 615, Section 12, Labor Force, Employment, and Earnings). Data based on surveys of health personnel and utilization of health facilities providing long-term care, ambulatory care, and hospital care are presented in NCHS Series 13, *Data on Health Resources Utilization and Advance Data from Vital and Health Statistics*. Statistics on patient visits to health care providers, as reported in health interviews, appear in NCHS Series 10, *National Health Interview Survey Data*.

The CMS's *Health Care Financing Review* and its annual *Medicare and Medicaid Statistical Supplement* present data for hospitals and nursing homes as well as extended care facilities and home health agencies. These data are based on records of the medicare program and differ from those of other sources because they are limited to facilities meeting federal eligibility standards for participation in medicare.

Disability and illness—General health statistics, including morbidity, disability, injuries, preventive care, and findings from physiological testing are collected by NCHS in its National Health Interview Survey and its National Health and Nutrition Examination Surveys and appear in *Vital and Health Statistics,* Series 10 and 11, respectively. The Department of Labor compiles statistics on occupational injuries (see Section 12, Labor Force, Employment, and Wealth). Annual incidence data on notifiable diseases are compiled by the Public Health Service (PHS) at its Centers for Disease Control and Prevention in Atlanta, Georgia, and are published as a supplement to its *Morbidity and Mortality Weekly Report*. The list of diseases is revised annually and includes those which, by mutual agreement of the states and PHS, are communicable diseases of national importance.

Nutrition—Statistics on annual per capita consumption of food and its nutrient value are estimated by the U.S. Department of Agriculture and published quarterly in *National Food Review*. Historical data can be found in *Food Consumption, Prices, and Expenditures*, and online at <http://www.ers.usda.gov/data/foodconsumption>. Statistics on food insufficiency and food and nutrient intake are collected by NCHS to estimate the diet of the nation's population. NCHS also collects physical examination data to assess the population's nutritional status, including growth, overweight/obesity, nutritional deficiencies, and prevalence of nutrition-related conditions, such as hypertension, hypercholesterolemia, and diabetes.

Statistical reliability—For discussion of statistical collection, estimation, and sampling procedures and measures of reliability applicable to data from NCHS and CMS, see Appendix III.

No. 127. National Health Expenditures—Summary, 1960 to 2001, and Projections, 2002 to 2012

[In billions of dollars (27 represents $27,000,000,000). Includes Puerto Rico and island areas]

Year	Total expenditures [1]	Private expenditures Total [2]	Out-of-pocket	Insurance	Public expenditures Total	Federal	State and local	Health services and supplies Total [3]	Hospital care	Physician and clinical services	Prescription drugs	Nursing home care
1960	27	20	13	6	7	3	4	25	9	5	3	1
1961	29	21	13	7	7	3	4	27	10	6	3	1
1962	31	23	14	7	8	4	4	29	11	6	3	1
1963	34	25	15	8	9	4	5	31	12	7	3	1
1964	38	28	17	9	9	4	5	34	13	8	3	1
1965	41	31	18	10	10	5	6	37	14	8	4	2
1966	45	32	19	10	14	7	6	41	16	9	4	2
1967	51	32	19	11	19	12	7	47	18	10	4	2
1968	58	36	21	12	22	14	8	53	21	11	5	3
1969	65	40	23	13	24	16	9	59	24	12	5	4
1970	73	45	25	16	28	18	10	67	28	14	6	4
1971	81	50	26	18	31	20	11	75	31	16	6	5
1972	91	56	29	21	35	23	12	84	34	17	6	6
1973	101	61	32	23	39	25	14	93	39	19	7	6
1974	114	67	35	26	46	30	16	106	45	22	7	7
1975	130	75	37	30	55	36	19	121	52	25	8	9
1976	149	87	41	37	62	43	20	139	60	28	9	10
1977	169	99	45	45	70	47	23	160	68	33	9	12
1978	189	110	48	52	80	54	26	179	76	35	10	13
1979	214	124	53	60	90	61	29	203	87	41	11	15
1980	246	141	58	68	105	71	34	234	102	47	12	18
1981	285	164	66	81	121	83	39	271	119	55	13	20
1982	321	187	72	94	134	92	42	305	135	61	15	23
1983	354	206	79	104	148	102	46	336	146	68	17	26
1984	390	229	86	118	161	113	48	372	156	77	20	28
1985	427	252	96	130	175	122	52	409	167	90	22	31
1986	457	267	103	135	190	132	59	439	178	100	24	34
1987	498	289	109	148	209	143	66	478	192	112	27	36
1988	558	332	119	175	226	154	72	535	209	127	31	41
1989	623	371	126	205	252	172	79	599	229	142	35	46
1990	696	414	137	234	283	193	90	670	254	158	40	53
1991	762	441	142	254	321	222	99	735	280	175	45	58
1992	827	469	146	274	359	251	107	797	302	190	48	62
1993	888	498	147	298	390	274	116	856	320	201	51	66
1994	937	510	144	312	427	299	129	905	332	211	55	68
1995	990	533	146	329	458	324	134	958	344	221	61	75
1996	1,039	558	152	344	482	344	138	1,005	355	229	67	80
1997	1,093	589	162	360	504	360	143	1,056	368	241	76	85
1998	1,150	628	175	382	522	369	153	1,112	378	257	87	89
1999	1,220	670	184	412	550	386	164	1,179	394	270	104	90
2000	1,310	719	195	449	591	415	176	1,262	417	289	122	94
2001	1,425	778	206	496	647	455	192	1,373	451	314	141	99
2002, proj	1,548	849	218	551	699	489	210	1,493	485	334	161	104
2003, proj	1,661	918	231	603	742	517	225	1,603	511	357	182	108
2004, proj	1,779	987	246	653	792	550	243	1,717	542	381	205	113
2005, proj	1,907	1,058	262	702	850	588	262	1,841	576	407	229	120
2006, proj	2,044	1,132	279	753	913	630	283	1,973	612	436	254	127
2007, proj	2,194	1,213	297	811	981	676	305	2,118	649	467	281	134
2008, proj	2,355	1,299	315	873	1,056	727	329	2,273	688	500	310	142
2009, proj	2,525	1,389	334	938	1,136	781	355	2,438	729	535	341	150
2010, proj	2,702	1,481	353	1,006	1,221	838	383	2,609	771	571	373	159
2011, proj	2,887	1,575	374	1,072	1,311	899	412	2,788	814	608	408	169
2012, proj	3,080	1,670	396	1,138	1,410	966	444	2,975	860	646	446	179

[1] Includes medical research and medical facilities construction, not shown separately.   [2] Includes other private expenditures, not shown separately.   [3] Includes other objects of expenditure, not shown separately.

Source: U. S. Centers for Medicare and Medicaid Services, "Health Accounts," <http://cms.hhs.gov/statistics/nhe/default.asp>.

No. 128. National Health Expenditures by Type: 1990 to 2001

[In billions of dollars (696.0 represents $696,000,000,000), except percent. Includes Puerto Rico and island areas]

Type of expenditure	1990	1995	1996	1997	1998	1999	2000	2001
Total	696.0	990.1	1,039.4	1,092.7	1,150.0	1,219.7	1,310.0	1,424.5
Annual percent change [1]	11.8	5.7	5.0	5.1	5.2	6.1	7.4	8.7
Percent of gross domestic product	12.0	13.4	13.3	13.1	13.1	13.2	13.3	14.1
Private expenditures	413.5	532.5	557.5	589.2	628.4	669.7	718.7	777.9
Health services and supplies	401.9	520.0	544.2	574.2	612.8	654.3	701.1	759.4
Out-of-pocket payments	137.3	146.2	152.0	162.2	175.2	184.4	194.7	205.5
Insurance premiums [2]	233.5	329.1	344.1	359.9	382.0	412.1	449.0	496.1
Other	31.1	44.8	48.1	52.1	55.6	57.8	57.4	57.8
Medical research	1.0	1.4	1.6	1.6	2.0	2.1	3.4	3.6
Medical facilities construction	10.7	11.1	11.6	13.3	13.6	13.3	14.2	14.9
Public expenditures	282.5	457.7	481.9	503.6	521.6	550.0	591.3	646.7
Percent federal of public	68.2	70.7	71.4	71.5	70.7	70.2	70.2	70.3
Health services and supplies	267.7	437.6	460.9	481.2	498.9	524.4	561.2	613.1
Medicare [3]	110.2	184.2	197.7	209.6	210.6	213.6	224.4	241.9
Public assistance medical payments [4]	78.7	149.5	157.6	164.7	176.6	191.6	209.4	232.9
Temporary disability insurance [5]	0.1	0.1	0.1	0.1	0.1	-	0.1	0.1
Workers' compensation (medical) [5]	17.5	21.9	21.9	20.5	20.7	23.0	24.8	27.2
Defense Dept. hospital, medical	10.4	12.1	12.0	12.1	12.2	12.7	13.7	15.5
Maternal, child health programs	1.8	2.2	2.3	2.3	2.4	2.5	2.7	2.7
Public health activities	20.2	31.4	32.9	35.4	38.0	40.9	44.1	46.4
Veterans' hospital, medical care	11.3	15.4	16.3	16.3	16.9	17.7	19.1	21.7
Medical vocational rehabilitation	0.5	0.7	0.7	0.7	0.8	0.8	0.8	0.8
State and local hospitals [6]	13.1	14.1	13.6	13.3	13.8	13.8	13.7	13.8
Other [7]	3.8	6.0	6.0	6.1	6.9	7.8	8.7	10
Medical research	11.7	15.7	16.2	17.1	18.5	21.4	25.7	29.2
Medical facilities construction	3.1	4.4	4.8	5.2	4.2	4.3	4.4	4.3

- Represents or rounds to zero. [1] Change from immediate prior year. For explanation of average annual percent change, see Guide to Tabular Presentation. [2] Covers insurance benefits and amount retained by insurance companies for expenses, additions to reserves, and profits (net cost of insurance). [3] Represents expenditures for benefits and administrative cost from federal hospital and medical insurance trust funds under old-age, survivors, disability, and health insurance programs; see text, of this section. [4] Payments made directly to suppliers of medical care (primarily medicaid). [5] Includes medical benefits paid under public law by private insurance carriers, state governments, and self-insurers. [6] Expenditures not offset by other revenues. [7] Covers expenditures for Substance Abuse and Mental Health Services Administration, Indian Health Service; school health and other programs.

Source: U. S. Centers for Medicare and Medicaid Services, "Health Accounts," <http://cms.hhs.gov/statistics/nhe/default.asp>.

No. 129. National Health Expenditures by Object, 1990 to 2001, and Projections, 2002

[In billions of dollars (696.0 represents $696,000,000,000). Includes Puerto Rico and outlying areas]

Object of expenditure	1990	1995	1996	1997	1998	1999	2000	2001	2002, proj.
Total	696.0	990.1	1,039.4	1,092.7	1,150.0	1,219.7	1,310.0	1,424.5	1,547.6
Spent by—									
Consumers	370.8	475.2	496.2	522.1	557.2	596.5	643.7	701.6	769.0
Out-of-pocket	137.3	146.2	152.0	162.2	175.2	184.4	194.7	205.5	218.0
Private insurance	233.5	329.1	344.1	359.9	382.0	412.1	449.0	496.1	551.0
Public	282.5	457.7	481.9	503.6	521.6	550.0	591.3	646.7	698.9
Other [1]	42.8	57.2	61.3	67.0	71.2	73.2	75.0	76.3	79.7
Spent for—									
Health services and supplies	669.6	957.5	1,005.1	1,055.5	1,111.8	1,178.7	1,262.3	1,372.6	1,492.9
Personal health care expenses	609.4	865.7	911.2	959.2	1,009.4	1,064.6	1,137.6	1,236.4	1,331.4
Hospital care	253.9	343.6	355.2	367.6	378.4	393.7	416.5	451.2	484.6
Physician and clinical services	157.5	220.5	229.4	241.0	256.8	270.2	288.8	313.6	334.0
Dental services	31.5	44.5	46.8	50.2	53.2	56.4	60.7	65.6	70.1
Other professional services [2]	18.2	28.5	30.9	33.4	35.5	36.7	38.8	42.3	44.8
Home health care	12.6	30.5	33.6	34.5	33.6	32.3	31.7	33.2	36.2
Prescription drugs	40.3	60.8	67.2	75.7	87.3	104.4	121.5	140.6	160.7
Other nondurable medical products	22.5	25.6	27.1	27.9	28.6	30.4	31.2	31.8	32.6
Durable medical equipment [3]	10.6	14.2	15.3	16.2	16.9	17.3	17.8	18.4	19.3
Nursing home care	52.7	74.6	79.9	85.1	89.1	89.6	93.8	98.9	103.7
Other personal health care	9.6	22.9	25.8	27.7	30.2	33.6	36.7	40.9	45.5
Public administration and net cost of private health insurance [4]	40.0	60.4	61.1	60.8	64.3	73.2	80.7	89.7	110.9
Public health activities	20.2	31.4	32.9	35.4	38.0	40.9	44.1	46.4	50.6
Medical research [5]	12.7	17.1	17.8	18.7	20.5	23.5	29.1	32.8	34.7
Medical facilities construction	13.7	15.5	16.4	18.5	17.7	17.6	18.6	19.2	20.1

[1] Includes nonpatient revenues, privately funded construction, and industrial inplant. [2] Includes services of registered and practical nurses in private duty, podiatrists, optometrists, physical therapists, clinical psychologists, chiropractors, naturopaths, and Christian Science practitioners. [3] Includes expenditures for eyeglasses, hearing aids, orthopedic appliances, artificial limbs, crutches, wheelchairs, etc. [4] Includes administrative expenses of federally financed health programs. [5] Research and development expenditures of drug companies and other manufacturers and providers of medical equipment and supplies are excluded from research expenditures, but are included in the expenditure class in which the product falls.

Source: U. S. Centers for Medicare and Medicaid Services, "Health Accounts," <http://cms.hhs.gov/statistics/nhe/default.asp>.

No. 130. Health Services and Supplies—Per Capita Consumer Expenditures by Object: 1990 to 2001

[In dollars, except percent. Based on Social Security Administration estimates of total U.S. population as of July 1, including Armed Forces and federal employees abroad and civilian population of outlying areas. Excludes research and construction]

Object of expenditure	1990	1995	1996	1997	1998	1999	2000	2001
Total, national	**2,635**	**3,576**	**3,721**	**3,870**	**4,039**	**4,244**	**4,502**	**4,851**
Annual percent change [1]	10.6	4.8	4.0	4.0	4.4	5.1	6.1	7.8
Hospital care	999	1,283	1,315	1,348	1,375	1,418	1,486	1,595
Physician and clinical services	620	824	849	884	933	973	1,030	1,109
Dental services	124	166	173	184	193	203	217	232
Other professional services [2]	72	107	114	122	129	132	138	150
Home health care	49	114	124	127	122	116	113	117
Prescription drugs	159	227	249	278	317	376	434	497
Other nondurable medical products	88	96	100	102	104	109	112	114
Durable medical equipment [2]	42	53	57	59	61	62	63	65
Nursing home care	207	279	296	312	324	323	335	350
Other personal health care	38	86	96	102	110	121	131	144
Public administration and net cost of private health insurance	157	226	226	223	234	263	288	317
Public health activities	80	117	122	130	138	147	157	164
Total, private consumer [3]	**1,459**	**1,775**	**1,837**	**1,914**	**2,024**	**2,148**	**2,296**	**2,480**
Hospital care	426	454	455	461	482	509	544	587
Physician and clinical services	386	498	510	532	558	572	610	657
Dental services	120	158	165	175	184	193	205	218
Other professional services [2]	47	69	75	83	88	91	94	102
Home health care	20	36	43	50	54	53	50	47
Prescription drugs	132	181	198	220	250	296	338	388
Other nondurable medical products	86	91	96	98	100	105	108	109
Durable medical equipment [2]	33	38	41	42	44	44	44	45
Nursing home care	90	95	100	106	117	119	119	122
Net cost of private health insurance	117	153	154	150	148	167	185	208

[1] Change from immediate prior year. [2] See footnotes for corresponding objects in Table 128. [3] Represents out-of-pocket payments and private health insurance.

No. 131. Government Expenditures for Health Services and Supplies: 2001

[In millions of dollars (613,124 represents $613,124,000,000). Includes Puerto Rico and island areas. Excludes medical research and construction]

Type of service	Total [1]	Federal	State and local	Medicare [2] (OASDHI)	Public assistance [3]	Veterans	Defense Dept. [4]	Workers' compensation [5]
Total [1]	**613,124**	**429,002**	**184,122**	**241,884**	**232,899**	**21,747**	**15,543**	**27,177**
Hospital care	263,107	209,366	53,742	134,953	80,151	16,326	9,782	9,432
Physician and clinical services	105,437	86,972	18,466	63,913	22,863	1,297	3,291	8,622
Prescription drugs	30,846	17,608	13,238	2,418	26,440	42	898	883
Nursing home care	60,853	41,807	19,046	11,588	47,165	2,099	-	-
Public administration	29,728	17,108	12,620	7,364	16,329	95	450	5,152
Public health activities	46,393	5,337	41,056	-	-	-	-	-

- Represents zero. [1] Includes other items not shown separately. [2] Covers hospital and medical insurance payments and administrative costs under old-age, survivors, disability, and health insurance program. [3] Covers medicaid and other medical public assistance. Excludes funds paid into medicare trust fund by states to cover premiums for public assistance recipients and medically indigent persons. [4] Includes care for retirees and military dependents. [5] Medical benefits.

No. 132. Personal Health Care—Third Party Payments and Private Consumer Expenditures, 1990 to 2001, and Projections, 2002

[In billions of dollars (609.4 represents $609,400,000,000), except percent. See headnote, Table 133]

Item	1990	1995	1996	1997	1998	1999	2000	2001	2002, proj.
Personal health care expenditures	609.4	865.7	911.2	959.2	1,009.4	1,064.6	1,137.6	1,236.4	1,331.4
Third party payments, total	**472.1**	**719.5**	**759.1**	**797.0**	**834.2**	**880.2**	**942.9**	**1,030.9**	**1,113.3**
Percent of personal health care	77.5	83.1	83.3	83.1	82.6	82.7	82.9	83.4	83.6
Private insurance payments	203.6	288.2	302.5	319.0	341.3	365.8	397.1	437.2	474.0
Public expenditures	237.9	387.2	409.2	426.6	438.2	457.6	489.5	537.0	580.2
Other [1]	30.6	44.1	47.4	51.4	54.8	56.8	56.3	56.7	59.1
Private consumer expenditures [2]	**340.9**	**434.4**	**454.6**	**481.3**	**516.5**	**550.2**	**591.8**	**642.7**	**692.0**
Percent met by private insurance	59.7	66.3	66.6	66.3	66.1	66.5	67.1	68.0	68.5
Hospital care	108.4	121.6	122.8	125.8	132.7	141.3	152.4	166.0	178.6
Percent met by private insurance	89.6	91.4	91.4	91.2	91.0	91.1	91.4	91.7	91.7
Physician and clinical services	98.1	133.4	137.8	145.0	153.4	158.9	171.0	185.9	199.4
Percent met by private insurance	69.0	80.3	80.5	80.2	80.0	80.2	80.4	81.2	81.5
Prescription drugs	33.6	48.5	53.3	60.0	68.8	82.2	94.8	109.7	125.8
Percent met by private insurance	29.2	46.5	50.3	53.6	55.7	58.2	59.8	60.7	61.6

[1] Includes nonpatient revenues and industrial inplant health services. [2] Includes expenditures not shown separately. Represents out-of-pocket payments and private health insurance benefits. Excludes net cost of insurance.

Source of Tables 130-132: U. S. Centers for Medicare and Medicaid Services, "Health Accounts," <http://cms.hhs.gov/statistics/nhe/default.asp>.

Health and Nutrition   105

No. 133. Personal Health Care Expenditures by Object and Source of Payment: 2001

[In millions of dollars (1,236,422 represents $1,236,422,000,000), except as indicated. Includes Puerto Rico and island areas. Covers all expenditures for health services and supplies, except net cost of insurance and administration, government public health activities, and expenditures of philanthropic agencies for fund raising activities]

Object of expenditure	Total	Private payments Total	Consumer Total	Out of pocket payments	Private health insurance	Other [1]	Government	Third party payments [2]
Total	1,236,422	699,420	642,671	205,497	437,174	56,749	537,002	1,030,925
Hospital care	451,220	188,113	165,976	13,828	152,148	22,137	263,107	437,393
Physician and clinical services	313,649	208,212	185,934	34,987	150,947	22,278	105,437	278,662
Dental services	65,568	61,849	61,721	28,471	33,250	128	3,720	37,097
Other professional services [3]	42,333	31,667	28,713	12,344	16,370	2,954	10,666	29,989
Home health care	33,168	14,446	13,247	6,258	6,988	1,199	18,722	26,910
Prescription drugs	140,574	109,729	109,729	43,126	66,602	-	30,846	97,448
Other nondurable medical products	31,758	30,312	30,312	30,312	-	-	1,446	1,446
Durable medical equipment	18,379	12,652	12,652	9,306	3,346	-	5,727	9,074
Nursing home care	98,911	38,058	34,389	26,866	7,523	3,670	60,853	72,046
Other personal health care	40,861	4,383	-	-	-	4,383	36,478	40,861

- Represents zero. [1] Includes nonpatient revenues and industrial plant. [2] Covers private health insurance, other private payments, and government. [3] See footnotes for corresponding items on Table 129.

Source: U. S. Centers for Medicare and Medicaid Services, "Health Accounts," <http://cms.hhs.gov/statistics/nhe/default.asp>.

No. 134. Hospital Care and Physician and Clinical Service Expenditures by Source of Payment: 1990 to 2001

[In billions of dollars (253.9 represents $253,900,000,000)]

Source of payment	Hospital care 1990	1995	1999	2000	2001	Physician and clinical services 1990	1995	1999	2000	2001
Total	253.9	343.6	393.7	416.5	451.2	157.5	220.5	270.2	288.8	313.6
Out-of-pocket payments	11.2	10.5	12.5	13.1	13.8	30.4	26.3	31.5	33.4	35.0
Third-party payments	242.7	333.1	381.2	403.4	437.4	127.1	194.3	238.8	255.4	278.7
Private health insurance	97.1	111.1	128.7	139.3	152.1	67.7	107.1	127.5	137.5	150.9
Other private funds	10.3	14.6	20.6	22.0	22.1	11.3	17.6	22.9	21.5	22.3
Government	135.2	207.3	231.8	242.1	263.1	48.2	69.6	88.4	96.3	105.4
Federal	102.7	167.2	185.3	193.0	209.4	38.7	56.2	73.4	79.8	87.0
State and local	32.4	40.2	46.6	49.1	53.7	9.4	13.3	15.0	16.5	18.5
Medicare [1]	67.8	108.0	122.0	125.9	135.0	30.2	41.7	55.2	59.6	63.9
Medicaid [2]	27.6	54.5	66.0	69.9	77.1	7.0	14.8	17.6	19.0	21.4

[1] Medicare expenditures come from federal funds. [2] Medicaid expenditures come from federal and state and local funds.

Source: U. S. Centers for Medicare and Medicaid Services, "Health Accounts," <http://cms.hhs.gov/statistics/nhe/default.asp>.

No. 135. Retail Prescription Drug Sales: 1995 to 2002

[2,125 represents 2,125,000,000]

Sales outlet	Number of prescriptions (millions) 1995	1999	2000	2001	2002	Retail sales (bil. dol.) 1995	1999	2000	2001	2002
Total	2,125	2,707	2,865	3,009	3,138	72.2	125.8	145.6	164.1	182.7
Traditional chain	914	1,246	1,344	1,415	1,474	28.8	53.8	61.2	67.7	73.4
Independent	666	680	689	700	707	21.1	28.9	31.4	33.9	36.7
Mass merchant	238	289	293	314	339	7.7	11.8	13.5	15.2	17.4
Supermarkets	221	357	394	418	444	7.4	13.8	17.4	19.8	21.8
Mail order	86	134	146	161	174	7.4	17.4	22.1	27.6	33.5

Source: National Association of Chain Drug Stores, Alexandria, VA, *The Chain Pharmacy Industry Profile, 2003* (copyright). <http://www.nacds.org>.

No. 136. Personal Health Care Expenditures by State, 1990 to 1998, and by Selected Object, 1998

[In millions of dollars (612,245 represents $612,245,000,000). This series of state health expenditures (SHE) uses the same definitions and, to the extent possible, the same data sources as does the national health expenditures series. For health services, this structure clusters spending according to the establishment providing those services. For retail purchases of medical products, it groups spending according to product classification. Thus, SHE is establishment-based, grouping services together according to place of service or of product sale rather than according to type of service. Establishment-based expenditures are those in which spending is located in the state of the provider rather than in the beneficiary's state of residence. Because people are able to cross state borders to receive health care services, health care spending by provider location is not necessarily an accurate reflection of spending on behalf of persons residing in that state]

State	1990	1995	1996	1997	1998 Total [1]	Hospital care	Physician and other professional services	Prescription drugs	Nursing home care
U.S.	612,245	876,212	920,970	965,701	1,016,383	380,050	296,102	90,648	87,826
AL	9,163	13,654	14,537	15,519	16,056	6,618	4,609	1,552	1,064
AK	1,347	1,921	2,042	2,133	2,299	986	568	133	42
AZ	8,562	12,352	13,146	13,834	14,782	4,977	5,135	1,397	839
AR	4,925	7,149	7,539	8,033	8,463	3,324	2,225	903	776
CA	74,369	99,215	102,378	105,790	110,057	34,948	44,239	7,537	5,626
CO	7,740	11,395	12,004	12,776	13,669	4,850	4,314	970	904
CT	10,013	13,662	13,952	14,600	15,221	4,686	4,292	1,354	2,264
DE	1,728	2,619	2,698	2,915	3,106	1,166	792	300	290
DC	3,564	4,184	4,223	4,205	4,258	2,585	781	180	245
FL	35,789	51,328	54,404	56,754	59,724	19,742	18,985	6,204	4,880
GA	15,303	23,096	24,489	25,940	27,219	10,396	8,510	2,460	1,545
HI	2,745	4,168	4,427	4,452	4,658	1,775	1,594	311	204
ID	1,697	2,758	2,994	3,194	3,397	1,236	935	334	264
IL	27,618	39,000	40,738	42,267	44,305	17,996	11,975	3,964	3,924
IN	12,692	18,388	18,727	20,207	21,259	8,515	5,613	2,058	2,337
IA	6,067	8,513	9,073	9,496	10,198	4,084	2,457	945	1,186
KS	5,540	7,989	8,417	8,890	9,394	3,580	2,538	854	920
KY	7,820	11,790	12,651	13,592	14,414	5,731	3,785	1,564	1,283
LA	9,975	14,673	15,272	15,946	16,500	7,139	4,249	1,507	1,248
ME	2,695	3,908	4,242	4,554	4,925	1,846	1,219	456	476
MD	11,755	16,838	17,824	18,596	19,646	7,313	5,978	1,678	1,695
MA	19,027	25,997	27,033	28,471	30,039	11,305	8,322	2,172	3,568
MI	22,133	31,089	32,888	34,435	35,647	14,641	9,186	3,885	2,459
MN	11,462	16,826	17,776	18,858	20,313	6,540	7,183	1,491	1,964
MS	4,729	7,447	7,997	8,431	8,882	3,848	2,212	962	687
MO	12,690	18,024	18,900	19,783	20,911	8,828	5,310	1,814	2,002
MT	1,628	2,445	2,496	2,680	2,838	1,224	695	234	222
NE	3,531	5,091	5,500	5,721	6,095	2,597	1,367	626	697
NV	2,806	4,471	4,795	5,170	5,606	1,865	1,918	478	164
NH	2,558	3,779	4,033	4,333	4,658	1,559	1,405	391	425
NJ	20,169	29,504	30,865	31,580	32,695	11,191	9,506	3,545	3,233
NM	2,917	4,430	4,839	5,075	5,344	2,317	1,415	402	257
NY	53,926	75,183	78,503	81,100	85,785	32,636	20,103	7,122	10,586
NC	13,748	21,966	23,773	25,584	27,327	10,987	7,106	2,566	2,347
ND	1,639	2,373	2,461	2,542	2,680	1,282	612	192	287
OH	26,896	37,246	39,470	40,552	42,581	16,763	11,024	3,898	4,978
OK	6,357	9,454	10,095	10,419	10,988	4,218	2,978	1,056	954
OR	6,247	9,182	9,637	10,259	10,840	3,545	3,285	918	838
PA	32,635	45,050	46,398	48,853	51,322	20,213	13,434	5,035	5,883
RI	2,728	3,783	3,900	4,149	4,515	1,702	1,095	400	468
SC	6,806	10,616	11,199	12,363	13,204	5,597	3,254	1,315	907
SD	1,513	2,301	2,479	2,635	2,842	1,257	747	201	286
TN	12,213	18,820	20,026	21,154	22,021	8,276	6,719	2,129	2,001
TX	37,682	56,504	60,410	64,245	67,750	25,322	20,071	6,023	4,346
UT	3,233	4,807	5,229	5,622	5,944	2,290	1,648	564	300
VT	1,172	1,762	1,821	1,933	2,066	712	563	183	177
VA	13,252	18,712	19,899	21,103	22,261	8,689	6,265	2,130	1,546
WA	11,276	16,810	17,461	18,214	19,292	6,362	5,908	1,603	1,492
WV	3,930	6,024	6,314	6,692	7,037	2,955	1,793	776	515
WI	11,441	16,739	17,738	18,738	19,945	7,252	5,844	1,745	2,110
WY	793	1,179	1,260	1,313	1,407	582	343	133	113

[1] Includes other expenditures not shown separately.

Source: U. S. Centers for Medicare and Medicaid Services, "Health Accounts," <http://cms.hhs.gov/statistics/nhe/default.asp>.

No. 137. Consumer Price Indexes of Medical Care Prices: 1980 to 2002

[1982-1984=100. Indexes are annual averages of monthly data based on components of consumer price index for all urban consumers; for explanation, see text, Section 14. See Appendix III]

Year	Medical care, total	Medical care services Total [1]	Professional services Total [1]	Physicians	Dental	Hospital and related services	Medical care commodities Total [2]	Prescription drugs and medical supplies	Annual percent change [3] Medical care, total	Medical care services	Medical care commodities
1980....	74.9	74.8	77.9	76.5	78.9	69.2	75.4	72.5	11.0	11.3	9.3
1985....	113.5	113.2	113.5	113.3	114.2	116.1	115.2	120.1	6.3	6.1	7.2
1990....	162.8	162.7	156.1	160.8	155.8	178.0	163.4	181.7	9.0	9.3	8.4
1995....	220.5	224.2	201.0	208.8	206.8	257.8	204.5	235.0	4.5	5.1	1.9
1996....	228.2	232.4	208.3	216.4	216.5	269.5	210.4	242.9	3.5	3.7	2.9
1997....	234.6	239.1	215.4	222.9	226.6	278.4	215.3	249.3	2.8	2.9	2.3
1998....	242.1	246.8	222.2	229.5	236.2	287.5	221.8	258.6	3.2	3.2	3.0
1999....	250.6	255.1	229.2	236.0	247.2	299.5	230.7	273.4	3.5	3.4	4.0
2000....	260.8	266.0	237.7	244.7	258.5	317.3	238.1	285.4	4.1	4.3	3.2
2001....	272.8	278.8	246.5	253.6	269.0	338.3	247.6	300.9	4.6	4.8	4.0
2002....	285.6	292.9	253.9	260.6	281.0	367.8	256.4	316.5	4.7	5.1	3.6

[1] Includes other services not shown separately. [2] Includes other commodities not shown separately. [3] Percent change from the immediate prior year.

Source: U.S. Bureau of Labor Statistics, *CPI Detailed Report*, January 2003.

No. 138. Average Annual Expenditures Per Consumer Unit for Health Care: 1990 to 2001

[In dollars, except percent. See text, Section 13, and headnote, Table 678. For composition of regions, see map, inside front cover]

Item	Health care, total Amount	Percent of total expenditures	Health insurance	Medical services	Drugs and medical supplies [1]	Percent distribution Health insurance	Medical services	Drugs and medical supplies [1]
1990	1,480	5.2	581	562	337	39.3	38.0	22.8
1995	1,732	5.4	860	512	360	49.7	29.6	20.8
1997	1,841	5.3	881	531	428	47.9	28.8	23.2
1998	1,903	5.4	913	542	448	48.0	28.5	23.5
1999	1,959	5.3	923	558	479	47.1	28.5	24.5
2000	2,066	5.4	983	568	515	47.6	27.5	24.9
2001	2,182	5.5	1,061	573	549	48.6	26.3	25.2
Age of reference person:								
Under 25 years old	530	2.3	251	135	144	47.4	25.5	27.2
25 to 34 years old.....	1,286	3.3	695	354	237	54.0	27.5	18.4
35 to 44 years old.....	1,879	4.0	925	573	381	49.2	30.5	20.3
45 to 54 years old.....	2,265	4.7	1,038	676	551	45.8	29.8	24.3
55 to 64 years old.....	2,703	6.5	1,189	769	745	44.0	28.4	27.6
65 to 74 years old.....	3,583	11.2	1,759	866	959	49.1	24.2	26.8
75 years old and over ..	3,397	14.7	1,792	507	1,098	52.8	14.9	32.3
Race of reference person:								
White and other	2,307	5.6	1,115	622	570	48.3	27.0	24.7
Black	1,264	4.4	663	214	386	52.5	16.9	30.5
Origin of reference person:								
Hispanic	1,343	3.9	652	354	338	48.5	26.4	25.2
Non-Hispanic..........	2,262	5.7	1,100	594	568	48.6	26.3	25.1
Region of residence:								
Northeast	2,084	5.1	1,045	551	488	50.1	26.4	23.4
Midwest	2,292	5.6	1,126	570	596	49.1	24.9	26.0
South	2,194	6.0	1,086	529	578	49.5	24.1	26.3
West.................	2,129	4.9	964	864	501	45.3	40.6	23.5
Size of consumer unit:								
One person	1,441	6.1	688	331	421	47.7	23.0	29.2
Two or more persons...	2,494	5.4	1,218	675	601	48.8	27.1	24.1
Two persons...........	2,827	7.0	1,366	714	746	48.3	25.3	26.4
Three persons	2,265	5.0	1,135	600	531	50.1	26.5	23.4
Four persons	2,253	4.1	1,110	680	464	49.3	30.2	20.6
Five persons or more...	2,150	4.0	1,042	656	453	48.5	30.5	21.1
Income before taxes:								
Complete income reporters [2]...	2,222	5.4	1,058	583	552	47.6	26.2	24.8
Quintiles of income:								
Lowest 20 percent	1,422	7.5	679	274	469	47.7	19.3	33.0
Second 20 percent.....	2,074	7.8	999	441	633	48.2	21.3	30.5
Third 20 percent	2,199	6.2	1,102	536	561	50.1	24.4	25.5
Fourth 20 percent......	2,494	5.1	1,192	748	553	47.8	30.0	22.2
Highest 20 percent.....	2,921	3.8	1,318	967	636	45.1	33.1	21.8
Incomplete reporters of income .	2,037	6.2	1,070	487	481	52.5	23.9	23.6

[1] Includes prescription and nonprescription drugs. [2] A complete reporter is a consumer unit providing values for at least one of the major sources of income.

Source: Bureau of Labor Statistics, *Consumer Expenditure Survey*, annual. <http://www.bls.gov/cex/>.

No. 139. Medicare Enrollees: 1980 to 2002

[In millions (28.4 represents 28,400,000). As of July 1. Includes Puerto Rico and island areas and enrollees in foreign countries and unknown place of residence]

Item	1980	1985	1990	1995	1999	2000	2001	2002
Total	28.4	31.1	34.3	37.6	39.1	39.6	40.1	40.4
Aged	25.5	28.1	31.0	33.2	33.9	34.1	34.4	34.6
Disabled	3.0	2.9	3.3	4.4	5.2	5.4	5.7	5.8
Hospital insurance	28.0	30.6	33.7	37.2	38.7	39.2	39.7	40.0
Aged	25.0	27.7	30.5	32.7	33.5	33.7	34.0	34.2
Disabled	3.0	2.9	3.3	4.4	5.2	5.4	5.7	5.8
Supplementary medical insurance	27.3	29.9	32.6	35.6	37.0	37.3	37.7	38.0
Aged	24.6	27.2	29.6	31.7	32.4	32.6	32.7	32.9
Disabled	2.7	2.7	2.9	3.9	4.6	4.8	5.0	5.2

Source: U.S. Centers for Medicare and Medicaid Services, Office of the Actuary, "Medicare Enrollment Selected Years"; published September 2002; <http://www.cms.hhs.gov/researchers/pubs/datacompendium>.

No. 140. Medicare Disbursements by Type of Beneficiary: 1990 to 2001

[In millions of dollars (109,709 represents $109,709,000,000). For years ending Sept. 30. Distribution of benefits by type is estimated and subject to change]

Type of beneficiary	1990	1995	1996	1997	1998	1999	2000	2001
Total disbursements	109,709	180,096	194,263	210,342	213,412	211,959	219,275	241,175
Hospital insurance disbursements	66,687	114,883	125,317	137,789	137,140	131,441	130,284	141,723
Benefits	65,721	113,394	123,908	136,007	134,321	129,107	125,992	135,979
Aged	58,503	100,107	109,287	120,091	118,412	113,339	110,251	118,700
Disabled	7,218	13,288	14,621	15,916	15,909	15,768	15,741	17,279
Disabled	6,467	12,300	13,548	14,755	14,793	14,733	14,707	16,120
ESRD [1]	751	988	1,073	1,161	1,116	1,035	1,034	1,158
Home health transfer [2]	-	-	-	-	978	179	1,706	3,103
Peer review activity	191	189	180	168	188	177	236	274
Administrative expenses [3]	774	1,300	1,229	1,614	1,653	1,978	2,350	2,368
Supplementary medical insurance disbursements	43,022	65,213	68,946	72,553	76,272	80,518	88,991	99,452
Benefits	41,498	63,490	67,165	71,117	75,782	79,151	88,876	100,514
Aged	36,837	54,830	57,807	60,988	65,115	67,989	76,404	86,100
Disabled	4,661	8,660	9,358	10,129	10,666	11,161	12,472	14,413
Disabled	3,758	7,363	7,976	8,654	9,247	9,790	10,956	12,614
ESRD [1]	903	1,297	1,382	1,475	1,419	1,371	1,516	1,799
Home health transfer [2]	-	-	-	-	-978	-179	-1,706	-3,103
Peer review activity	-	2	11	16	33	36	43	55
Administrative expenses	1,524	1,722	1,771	1,420	1,435	1,510	1,779	1,986

- Represents zero. [1] Represents persons entitled because of End Stage Renal Disease only. Benefits for those who have ESRD but would be entitled due to their aged or disabled status are included in aged and disabled benefits. [2] Beginning 1998 home health agency transfers are excluded from total supplementary medical insurance disbursements and included in total hospital insurance disbursements. [3] Includes costs of experiments and demonstration projects. Includes costs of the health care fraud and abuse control program.

Source: U.S. Centers for Medicare and Medicaid Services, unpublished data.

No. 141. Medicare Benefits by Type of Provider: 1990 to 2001

[In millions of dollars (65,721 represents $65,271,000,000). For years ending Sept. 30. Distribution of benefits by type is estimated and subject to change]

Type of provider	1990	1995	1996	1997	1998	1999	2000	2001
Hospital insurance benefits, total	65,721	113,395	123,908	136,007	134,321	129,107	125,992	135,979
Inpatient hospital	57,012	81,095	84,614	88,991	87,451	86,524	86,844	93,338
Skilled nursing facility	2,761	8,684	10,377	12,104	13,213	11,683	10,353	12,539
Home health agency	3,295	15,715	17,095	17,771	13,770	7,971	4,513	3,801
Hospice	318	1,854	1,969	2,082	2,080	2,494	2,818	3,464
Managed care	2,335	6,047	9,853	15,059	17,807	20,435	21,463	22,837
Supplementary medical insurance benefits, total	41,498	63,490	67,165	71,117	75,782	79,151	88,876	100,514
Physician fee schedule	(NA)	31,110	31,569	31,958	32,339	33,389	35,957	40,436
Durable medical equipment	(NA)	3,576	3,785	4,112	4,103	4,270	4,578	5,228
Carrier lab [1]	(NA)	2,819	2,654	2,414	2,166	2,086	2,196	2,365
Other carrier [2]	(NA)	4,513	4,883	5,452	5,854	6,398	7,153	8,398
Hospital [3]	(NA)	8,448	8,669	9,208	8,926	8,456	8,520	11,070
Home health [4]	(NA)	223	236	244	184	340	4,282	4,151
Intermediary lab [4]	(NA)	1,437	1,352	1,464	1,533	1,597	1,746	2,008
Other intermediary [5]	(NA)	5,110	5,664	6,373	6,545	5,645	6,096	7,610
Managed care	(NA)	6,253	8,353	9,893	14,132	16,970	18,348	19,249

NA Not available. [1] Lab services paid under the lab fee schedule performed in a physician's office lab or an independent lab. [2] Includes free-standing ambulatory surgical centers facility costs, ambulance, and supplies. [3] Includes the hospital facility costs for Medicare Part B services which are predominantly in the outpatient department. The physician reimbursement associated with these services is included on the "Physician Fee Schedule" line. [4] Lab fee services paid under the lab fee schedule performed in a hospital outpatient department. [5] Includes ESRD free-standing dialysis facility payments and payments to rural health clinics, outpatient rehabilitation facilities, psychiatric hospitals, and federally qualified health centers.

Source: U.S. Centers for Medicare and Medicaid Services, unpublished data.

No. 142. Medicare—Enrollment by State and Other Areas: 1995 to 2001

[Hospital and/or medical insurance enrollment as July 1 (37,535 represents 37,535,000)]

State and area	1995	1999	2000	2001	State and area	1995	1999	2000	2001
All areas	37,535	39,140	39,620	40,026	MO	833	854	861	867
U.S.	36,758	38,299	38,762	39,149	MT	130	135	137	138
					NE	249	252	254	255
AL	642	677	685	695	NV	194	229	240	251
AK	34	40	42	44	NH	156	167	170	173
AZ	602	658	675	691	NJ	1,168	1,195	1,203	1,208
AR	423	436	439	442	NM	211	229	234	238
CA	3,633	3,837	3,901	3,955	NY	2,630	2,694	2,715	2,729
CO	421	458	467	476	NC	1,027	1,111	1,133	1,155
CT	502	512	515	516	ND	103	103	103	103
DE	101	110	112	114	OH	1,666	1,692	1,701	1,705
DC	78	76	75	75	OK	488	504	508	511
FL	2,628	2,771	2,804	2,838	OR	469	484	489	496
GA	833	898	916	933	PA	2,071	2,088	2,095	2,095
HI	149	162	165	168	RI	168	170	172	172
ID	150	161	165	169	SC	509	555	568	580
IL	1,617	1,629	1,635	1,640	SD	117	119	119	120
IN	823	845	852	858	TN	771	815	829	842
IA	474	476	477	478	TX	2,080	2,223	2,265	2,300
KS	383	389	390	391	UT	187	201	206	210
KY	586	615	623	630	VT	83	88	89	90
LA	581	597	602	605	VA	818	876	893	910
ME	201	213	216	219	WA	688	725	736	746
MD	602	635	645	655	WV	330	336	338	340
MA	933	954	961	961	WI	762	777	783	787
MI	1,347	1,389	1,403	1,414	WY	60	64	65	66
MN	631	648	654	660	PR	477	525	537	550
MS	397	414	419	423	Other areas	300	316	321	327

Source: U.S. Centers for Medicare and Medicaid Services, "Medicare Beneficiaries Enrolled as of July 1 of Each Year. Years 1995-1998," published 29 July 1999. "Medicare Beneficiaries Enrolled by State as of July 1, 1999-2001"; published September 2002. <http://www.cms.hhs.gov/statistics>.

No. 143. Medicare—Estimated Benefit Payments by State: 2001

[For the year ending September 30. In billions of dollars (236.5 represents $236,500,000,000). Medicare fee for service payments are based on the state of the provider. Managed care organization payments are distributed based on the state of the plan. Both types of payments are on a paid basis. This distribution may differ from similar tables based on the state of the beneficiary]

State and area	Estimated[1] payments, total	Fee for service	Managed care	State and area	Estimated[1] payments, total	Fee for service	Managed care
All areas	236.5	194.4	42.1	Missouri	4.8	3.8	1.0
				Montana	0.7	0.7	-
U.S.	235.0	192.9	42.1	Nebraska	1.4	1.3	0.1
Alabama	4.3	3.9	0.4	Nevada	1.3	0.7	0.6
Alaska	0.2	0.2	-	New Hampshire	0.7	0.7	-
Arizona	3.3	1.8	1.5	New Jersey	6.9	5.9	1.0
Arkansas	2.4	2.3	0.1	New Mexico	0.9	0.7	0.2
California	24.9	13.7	11.2	New York	20.4	17.1	3.4
Colorado	2.7	1.8	0.9	North Carolina	6.8	6.5	0.3
Connecticut	3.1	2.6	0.5	North Dakota	0.6	0.6	-
Delaware	0.5	0.5	-	Ohio	10.7	9.1	1.6
District of Columbia	0.8	0.6	0.2	Oklahoma	2.3	2.1	0.3
Florida	21.6	16.3	5.3	Oregon	2.2	1.2	1.0
Georgia	4.4	4.1	0.3	Pennsylvania	15.1	11.4	3.7
Hawaii	0.7	0.4	0.3	Rhode Island	1.1	0.8	0.4
Idaho	0.7	0.7	-	South Carolina	3.4	3.4	-
Illinois	8.0	7.0	1.0	South Dakota	0.6	0.6	-
Indiana	5.0	4.9	0.1	Tennessee	5.5	5.3	0.2
Iowa	1.6	1.6	-	Texas	16.3	14.6	1.7
Kansas	2.1	2.1	0.1	Utah	1.1	1.1	-
Kentucky	3.6	3.5	0.1	Vermont	0.4	0.4	-
Louisiana	4.9	4.2	0.7	Virginia	3.9	3.9	-
Maine	0.9	0.9	-	Washington	3.2	2.3	0.9
Maryland	4.6	4.3	0.3	West Virginia	1.8	1.8	-
Massachusetts	6.0	4.4	1.6	Wisconsin	4.0	3.8	0.2
Michigan	7.0	6.5	0.6	Wyoming	0.3	0.3	-
Minnesota	3.1	2.8	0.4	Puerto Rico	1.5	1.5	-
Mississippi	2.1	2.1	-	Island areas	0.1	0.1	-

- Represents zero. [1] Medicare fee for service estimated benefit payments are based on the state of the provider.

Source: U.S. Centers for Medicare and Medicaid Services, "Medicare Estimated Benefit Payments by State." <www.cms.hhs.gov/researchers/statsdata/feeforservice/default.asp/>.

No. 144. Medicare Trust Funds: 1990 to 2002

[In billions of dollars (72.2 represents $72,200,000,000)]

Type of trust fund	1990	1995	1996	1997	1998	1999	2000	2001	2002
HOSPITAL INSURANCE (HI)									
Net contribution income [1]	72.2	103.3	115.9	119.5	130.7	140.3	154.5	160.9	162.7
Interest received [2]	8.5	10.8	10.2	9.6	9.3	10.1	11.7	14.0	15.1
Benefit payments [3]	66.2	116.4	128.6	137.8	134.0	128.8	128.5	141.2	149.9
Assets, end of year	98.9	130.3	124.9	115.6	120.4	141.4	177.5	208.7	234.8
SUPPLEMENTARY MEDICAL INSURANCE (SMI)									
Net premium income	11.3	19.7	18.8	19.3	[4]20.9	[4]19.0	20.6	22.8	25.1
Transfers from general revenue	33.0	39.0	65.0	60.2	[4]64.1	[4]59.1	65.9	72.8	78.3
Interest received [2]	1.6	1.6	1.8	2.5	2.7	2.8	3.5	3.1	2.8
Benefit payments [3]	42.5	65.0	68.6	72.8	76.1	80.7	88.9	99.7	111.0
Assets, end of year	15.5	13.1	28.3	36.1	46.2	44.8	44.0	41.3	34.3

[1] Includes income from taxation of benefits beginning in 1994. Includes premiums from aged ineligibles enrolled in HI. [2] Includes recoveries of amounts reimbursed from the trust fund. [3] Beginning 1998 monies transferred to the SMI trust fund for home health agency costs, as provided for by P.L. 105-33, are included in HI benefit payments but excluded from SMI benefit payments. [4] Premiums withheld from check and associated general revenue contributions that were to occur on Jan. 3, 1999, actually occurred on December 31, 1998. These amounts are therefore excluded from 1999 data.

Source: U.S. Centers for Medicare and Medicaid Services, *Annual Report of the Board of Trustees of the Federal Hospital Insurance Trust Fund* and *Annual Report of the Board of Trustees of the Federal Supplementary Medical Insurance Trust Fund.*

No. 145. Medicaid—Selected Characteristics of Persons Covered: 2001

[In thousands, except percent (31,375 represents 31,375,000). Represents number of persons as of March of following year who were enrolled at any time in year shown. Excludes unrelated individuals under age 15. Person did not have to receive medical care paid for by medicaid in order to be counted. See headnote, Table 565]

Poverty status	Total [1]	White	Black	Hispanic [2]	Under 18 years old	18-44 years old	45-64 years old	65 years old and over
Persons covered, total	31,375	21,400	7,927	7,026	16,276	7,950	3,878	3,270
Below poverty level	13,313	8,273	4,244	3,171	7,219	3,434	1,634	1,026
Above poverty level	18,063	13,127	3,683	3,855	9,057	4,516	2,245	2,244
Percent of population covered	11.1	9.3	22.1	18.8	22.6	7.2	5.9	9.7
Below poverty level	40.5	36.4	52.2	39.7	61.5	27.4	31.2	30.1
Above poverty level	7.3	6.3	13.3	13.2	15.0	4.6	3.7	7.4

[1] Includes other races not shown separately. [2] Persons of Hispanic origin may be of any race.

Source: U.S. Census Bureau, Current Population Reports, P60-219, earlier reports; "Table 24. Health Insurance Coverage Status and Type of Coverage by Selected Characteristics for All People in Poverty Universe: 2001"; <http://ferret.bls.census.gov/macro/032002/pov/new24001.htm>.

No. 146. Medicaid—Recipients and Payments: 1990 to 2000

[For year ending September 30 (25,255 represents 25,255,000). Includes Puerto Rico and island areas. Medical vendor payments are those made directly to suppliers of medical care]

Basis of eligibility and type of service	Recipients (1,000) 1990	1995	1998	1999	2000	Payments (mil. dol.) 1990	1995	1998	1999	2000
Total [1]	25,255	36,282	40,649	40,184	42,763	64,859	120,141	142,318	153,479	168,307
Age 65 and over	3,202	4,119	3,964	3,774	3,731	21,508	36,527	40,602	42,521	44,503
Blindness	83	92	(NA)	(NA)	(NA)	434	848	(NA)	(NA)	(NA)
Disabled [2]	3,635	5,767	6,638	6,697	6,889	23,969	48,570	60,375	65,850	72,742
AFDC [3] program	17,230	24,767	26,872	26,348	28,473	17,690	31,487	37,639	39,952	44,537
Other and unknown	1,105	1,537	3,176	3,365	3,671	1,257	2,708	3,702	5,156	6,525
Inpatient services in—										
General hospital	4,593	5,561	4,273	4,497	4,933	16,674	26,331	21,499	22,231	24,266
Mental hospital	92	84	135	97	99	1,714	2,511	2,801	1,758	1,768
Intermediate care facilities, mentally retarded	147	151	126	122	118	7,354	10,383	9,482	9,332	9,375
Nursing facility services [4]	1,461	1,667	1,646	1,617	1,703	17,693	29,052	31,892	33,251	34,432
Physicians	17,078	23,789	18,555	18,373	19,104	4,018	7,360	6,070	6,556	6,806
Dental	4,552	6,383	4,965	5,622	5,892	593	1,019	901	1,204	1,404
Other practitioner	3,873	5,528	4,342	3,986	4,735	372	986	587	470	658
Outpatient hospital	12,370	16,712	12,158	12,417	13,226	3,324	6,627	5,759	6,094	7,053
Clinic	2,804	5,322	5,285	6,746	7,667	1,688	4,280	3,921	5,801	6,174
Laboratory [5]	8,959	13,064	9,381	10,194	11,396	721	1,180	939	1,158	1,288
Home health [6]	719	1,639	1,225	814	995	3,404	9,406	2,702	2,906	3,119
Prescribed drugs	17,294	23,723	19,338	19,855	20,517	4,420	9,791	13,522	16,612	20,014
Family planning	1,752	2,501	2,011	(NA)	(NA)	265	514	449	(NA)	(NA)
Prepaid health care	(NA)	20,203	20,687	21,261	(NA)	(NA)	19,296	21,514	24,413

NA Not available. [1] Recipient data do not add due to small number of recipients that are reported in more than one category. Includes recipients of, and payments for, other care not shown separately. [2] Permanently and totally. Beginning 1998, includes blind. [3] Aid to families with dependent children. From 1997 onwards Temporary Assistance to Needy Families which includes children, adults, and foster care children. [4] Nursing facility services includes skilled nursing facility services and intermediate care facility services for all other than the mentally retarded. [5] Includes radiological services. [6] Data for 2000 not comparable with earlier years.

Source: Centers for Medicare and Medicaid Services, OIS/EDG/DQCDD 1990 through 1998 Medicaid Statistical Report HCFA-2082; Beginning from 1999, Medicaid Statistical Information System, MSIS <http://www.cms.hhs.gov/medicaid/datasources.asp>.

Health and Nutrition

No. 147. Medicaid—Summary by State and Other Areas: 1995 and 2000

[For year ending September 30 (36,282 represents 36,282,000). Data for 2000 includes managed care recipients and capitation payments]

State and area	Recipients[1] (1,000) 1995	Recipients[1] (1,000) 2000	Payments[2] (mil. dol.) 1995	Payments[2] (mil. dol.) 2000	State and area	Recipients[1] (1,000) 1995	Recipients[1] (1,000) 2000	Payments[2] (mil. dol.) 1995	Payments[2] (mil. dol.) 2000
All areas	36,282	(NA)	120,141	(NA)	MO	695	890	2,039	3,270
U.S.	35,210	42,763	119,885	168,307	MT	99	104	326	433
					NE	168	229	608	958
AL	539	619	1,455	2,391	NV	105	138	350	515
AK	68	96	252	470	NH	97	97	473	651
AZ	494	681	218	2,112	NJ	790	822	3,813	4,707
AR	353	489	1,376	1,510	NM	287	376	714	1,249
CA	5,017	7,915	10,521	17,060	NY	3,035	3,420	22,086	26,148
CO	294	381	1,063	1,809	NC	1,084	1,209	3,175	4,830
CT	380	420	2,125	2,839	ND	61	61	297	356
DE	79	115	324	528	OH	1,533	1,305	5,585	7,090
DC	138	139	532	793	OK	394	507	1,055	1,604
FL	1,735	2,360	4,802	7,350	OR	452	542	1,327	1,700
GA	1,147	1,290	3,076	3,578	PA	1,230	1,492	4,633	6,366
HI	52	204	258	535	RI	135	179	673	1,070
ID	115	131	360	594	SC	496	685	1,438	2,672
IL	1,552	1,516	5,600	7,807	SD	74	102	305	401
IN	559	705	1,878	2,976	TN	1,466	1,568	2,772	3,491
IA	304	314	1,036	1,476	TX	2,562	2,603	6,565	9,075
KS	256	263	831	1,226	UT	160	224	464	959
KY	641	771	1,945	2,913	VT	100	139	320	479
LA	785	761	2,708	2,631	VA	681	627	1,833	2,484
ME	153	192	760	1,307	WA	639	895	1,461	2,432
MD	414	665	2,019	3,586	WV	389	335	1,169	1,392
MA	728	1,047	3,972	5,397	WI	460	577	1,894	2,906
MI	1,168	1,352	3,409	4,881	WY	51	46	171	214
MN	473	559	2,550	3,277	PR	1,055	(NA)	244	(NA)
MS	520	605	1,266	1,807	VI	17	(NA)	12	(NA)

NA Not available. [1] Persons who had payments made on their behalf at any time during the fiscal year. [2] Payments are for fiscal year and reflect federal and state contribution payments. Data exclude disproportionate hospital share payments. Disproportionate share hospitals receive higher medicaid reimbursement than other hospitals because they treat a disproportionate share of medicaid patients.

Source: U.S. Centers for Medicare and Medicaid Services, OIS/EDG/DQCDD data before 1999 Medicaid Statistical Report HCFA 2082, 1999 data and onwards Medicaid Statistical Information System, MSIS <http://www.cms.hhs.gov/medicaid/datasources.asp>.

No. 148. State Children's Health Insurance Program (SCHIP)-Enrollment and Expenditures by State: 2000 and 2002

[3,334 represents 3,334,000. For year ending September 30. This program provides health benefits coverage to children living in families whose incomes exceed the eligibility limits for medicaid. Although it is generally targeted to families with incomes at or below 200 percent of the federal poverty level, each state may set its own income eligibility limits, within certain guidelines. States have three options: they may expand their medicaid programs, develop a separate child health program that functions independently of medicaid, or do a combination of both]

State	Enrollment[1] (1,000) 2000	Enrollment[1] (1,000) 2002	Expenditures[2] (mil. dol.) 2000	Expenditures[2] (mil. dol.) 2002	State	Enrollment[1] (1,000) 2000	Enrollment[1] (1,000) 2002	Expenditures[2] (mil. dol.) 2000	Expenditures[2] (mil. dol.) 2002
US	3,334	5,315	[3]1,928.8	[3]3,776.2	MO	74	112	41.2	62.2
AL	38	83	31.9	55.0	MT	8	14	4.3	12.1
AK	13	22	18.1	21.0	NE	11	16	6.1	11.8
AZ	61	93	29.4	126.8	NV	16	38	9.0	20.4
AR	2	2	1.5	1.5	NH	4	8	1.6	3.9
CA	478	857	187.3	454.2	NJ	89	117	46.9	252.5
CO	35	52	13.9	31.2	NM	6	20	3.4	13.9
CT	19	21	12.8	16.2	NY	769	807	401.0	371.6
DE	4	10	1.5	2.6	NC	104	120	65.5	86.0
DC	2	5	5.8	5.5	ND	3	4	1.8	3.8
FL	227	368	125.7	270.0	OH	111	183	53.1	129.0
GA	121	221	48.7	105.9	OK	58	84	51.3	30.2
HI	2	8	0.4	3.9	OR	37	43	12.5	16.3
ID	12	17	7.5	14.3	PA	120	149	70.7	104.0
IL	63	68	32.7	36.3	RI	12	20	10.4	34.5
IN	44	66	53.7	60.4	SC	60	69	46.6	41.6
IA	20	35	15.5	28.7	SD	6	11	3.1	8.7
KS	26	41	12.8	35.9	TN	15	(NA)	41.7	4.0
KY	56	94	60.0	71.9	TX	131	727	41.4	535.7
LA	50	88	25.3	65.1	UT	25	34	12.8	25.8
ME	23	23	11.4	17.8	VT	4	6	1.4	2.6
MD	93	125	92.2	119.2	VA	38	68	18.6	39.7
MA	113	117	44.2	59.9	WA	3	9	0.6	8.0
MI	37	72	36.2	39.6	WV	22	36	9.7	26.9
MN	(Z)	(NA)	(Z)	64.7	WI	47	62	21.4	80.3
MS	20	65	21.1	69.7	WY	3	5	1.0	3.2

NA Not available. Z Less than 500 or $50,000. [1] Number of children ever enrolled in SCHIP. [2] Expenditures for which states are entitled to federal reimbursement under Title XXI and which reconciles any advance of Title XXI federal funds made on the basis of estimates. [3] U.S. expenditures totals include Puerto Rico and island areas.

Source: U.S. Centers for Medicare & Medicaid Services, *The State Children's Health Insurance Program, Annual Enrollment Report* and the Statement of Expenditures for the SCHIP Program (CMS-21) <www.cms.gov/schip/>.

No. 149. Medicaid Managed Care Enrollment by State and Other Areas: 1995 to 2001

[For year ending June 30. (33,373 represents 33,373,000)]

State and area	Total medicaid (1,000)	Managed care enrollment Number (1,000)	Managed care enrollment Percent of total	State and area	Total medicaid (1,000)	Managed care enrollment Number (1,000)	Managed care enrollment Percent of total	State and area	Total medicaid (1,000)	Managed care enrollment Number (1,000)	Managed care enrollment Percent of total
1995	33,373	9,800	29.4	IL	1,456	136	9.4	NC	959	674	70.3
1999	31,940	17,757	55.6	IN	617	433	70.2	ND	44	26	58.3
2000	33,690	18,786	55.8	IA	233	207	88.6	OH	1,293	278	21.5
2001,				KS	205	118	57.6	OK	442	299	67.7
total	36,563	20,774	56.8	KY	608	490	80.6	OR	413	361	87.4
U.S.	35,496	19,876	54.4	LA	826	57	6.9	PA	1,369	1,037	75.8
AL	652	350	53.7	ME	222	96	43.2	RI	163	112	68.5
AK	116	-	-	MD	617	421	68.3	SC	644	42	6.5
AZ	549	528	96.1	MA	955	616	64.5	SD	82	80	97.4
AR	444	258	58.1	MI	1,138	1,023	90.0	TN	1,427	1,427	100.0
CA	5,487	2,871	52.3	MN	502	323	64.3	TX	1,822	754	41.4
CO	269	247	92.0	MS	586	298	50.8	UT	139	129	93.0
CT	331	240	72.4	MO	840	379	45.1	VT	129	78	60.8
DE	102	83	81.8	MT	73	47	64.2	VA	476	292	61.3
DC	124	80	64.4	NE	202	151	74.8	WA	766	766	100.0
FL	1,923	1,185	61.6	NV	124	48	38.2	WV	264	122	46.3
GA	1,041	878	84.4	NH	79	6	7.9	WI	515	267	51.8
HI	163	128	78.3	NJ	759	459	60.5	WY	40	-	-
ID	134	38	28.4	NM	332	212	64.0	PR	1,049	898	85.6
				NY	2,803	729	26.0	VI	18	-	-

- Represents zero. [1] The enrollment figures include individuals enrolled in state health care reform programs that expand eligibility beyond traditional medicaid eligibility standards.

Source: U.S. Centers for Medicare and Medicaid Services, "Medicaid Managed Care"; <http://www.cms.hhs.gov/medicaid/managedcare/enrolstats.asp>.

No. 150. Health Maintenance Organizations (HMOs): 1990 to 2002

[As of January 1, (33.0 represents 33,000,000). An HMO is a prepaid health plan delivering comprehensive care to members through designated providers, having a fixed periodic payment for health care services, and requiring members to be in a plan for a specified period of time (usually 1 year). A group HMO delivers health services through a physician group that is controlled by the HMO unit or contracts with one or more independent group practices to provide health services. An individual practice association (IPA) HMO contracts directly with physicians in independent practice, and/or contracts with one or more associations of physicians in independent practice, and/or contracts with one or more multispecialty group practices. Data are based on a census of HMOs]

Model type	Number of plans 1990	1995	1999	2000	2001	2002	Enrollment [1] (mil.) 1990	1995	1999	2000	2001	2002
Total	572	550	643	568	541	500	33.0	46.2	81.3	80.9	79.5	76.1
IPA	360	323	309	278	257	229	13.7	17.4	33.4	33.4	33.1	31.6
Group	212	107	126	102	104	100	19.3	12.9	15.9	15.2	15.6	14.9
Mixed	(NA)	120	208	188	180	171	(NA)	15.9	32.6	32.3	30.8	29.5

NA Not available. [1] 1990-1995 exclude enrollees participating in open-ended plans; beginning 1999 includes open-ended enrollment.

No. 151. Persons Enrolled in Health Maintenance Organizations (HMOs) by State: 2001 and 2002

[76,121 represents 76,121,000. Data are based on a census of health maintenance organizations. Pure and open-ended enrollment as of January 1]

State	Number 2002 (1,000)	Percent of population 2001	Percent of population 2002	State	Number 2002 (1,000)	Percent of population 2001	Percent of population 2002	State	Number 2002 (1,000)	Percent of population 2001	Percent of population 2002
U.S. [1]	76,121	27.9	26.4	KS	356	16.1	13.2	ND	2	1.3	0.4
				KY	1,294	30.4	31.8	OH	2,461	23.4	21.6
AL	209	6.5	4.7	LA	627	15.6	14.0	OK	513	13.9	14.8
AK	-	-	-	ME	308	27.9	23.9	OR	1,046	35.5	30.1
AZ	1,367	32.4	25.8	MD	1,865	38.4	34.7	PA	3,838	33.4	31.2
AR	208	10.5	7.7	MA	2,702	44.3	42.4	RI	369	35.0	34.8
CA	17,420	53.4	50.5	MI	2,551	26.7	25.5	SC	324	9.5	8.0
CO	1,455	36.4	32.9	MN	1,336	28.2	26.9	SD	87	9.7	11.5
CT	1,311	39.7	38.3	MS	40	0.9	1.4	TN	1,066	33.0	18.6
DE	183	22.8	23.0	MO	1,758	31.0	31.2	TX	3,180	17.5	14.9
DC	178	31.0	31.2	MT	52	7.7	5.8	UT	726	35.5	32.0
FL	4,886	29.8	29.8	NE	149	9.9	8.7	VT	64	4.2	10.5
GA	1,275	15.9	15.2	NV	472	20.4	22.4	VA	1,142	16.2	15.9
HI	402	31.8	32.8	NH	381	39.3	30.3	WA	1,042	15.3	17.4
ID	39	4.3	2.9	NJ	2,622	31.7	30.9	WV	180	10.9	10.0
IL	2,246	19.2	18.0	NM	531	27.9	29.0	WI	1,585	29.6	29.3
IN	654	11.7	10.7	NY	6,390	35.0	33.6	WY	10	1.7	2.0
IA	150	6.5	5.1	NC	1,210	16.3	14.8				

- Represents zero. [1] Includes Guam and Puerto Rico.

Source of Tables 150 and 151: InterStudy Publications, St. Paul, MN, The InterStudy Competitive Edge, annual (copyright).

Health and Nutrition 113

U.S. Census Bureau, Statistical Abstract of the United States: 2003

No. 152. Health Insurance Coverage Status by Selected Characteristics: 1990 to 2001

[Persons as of following year for coverage in the year shown (**248.9 represents 248,900,000**). Government health insurance includes medicare, medicaid, and military plans. Based on Current Population Survey; see text, Section 1, and Appendix III]

Characteristic	Total persons	Number (mil.) Covered by private or government health insurance Total [1]	Private Total	Private Group health [2]	Government Medi-care	Government Medi-caid [3]	Not covered by health insurance	Percent Covered by private or government health insurance Total [1]	Private	Medi-caid [3]	Not covered by health insurance
1990	248.9	214.2	182.1	150.2	32.3	24.3	34.7	86.1	73.2	9.7	13.9
1995 [4]	264.3	223.7	185.9	161.5	34.7	31.9	40.6	84.6	70.3	12.1	15.4
2000 [4,5]	276.5	237.9	200.2	177.3	37.0	28.6	40.7	86.0	72.4	10.4	14.0
2000 [5,6]	279.5	239.7	201.1	177.8	37.7	29.5	39.8	85.8	71.9	10.6	14.2
2001, total [5,6]	282.1	240.9	199.9	176.6	38.0	31.6	41.2	85.4	70.9	11.2	14.6
Age:											
Under 18 years	72.6	64.1	49.6	46.4	0.4	16.5	8.5	88.3	68.4	22.7	11.7
Under 6 years	23.4	20.9	15.1	14.3	0.2	6.5	2.5	89.3	64.4	28.0	10.7
6 to 11 years	24.6	21.9	16.9	16.1	0.1	5.7	2.8	88.8	68.6	23.1	11.3
12 to 17 years	24.6	21.4	17.7	16.1	0.1	4.3	3.2	86.9	71.9	17.4	13.1
18 to 24 years	27.3	19.6	17.0	13.8	0.2	2.8	7.7	71.9	62.3	10.4	28.1
25 to 34 years	38.7	29.6	26.9	25.3	0.5	2.6	9.1	76.6	69.6	6.7	23.4
35 to 44 years	44.3	37.2	34.3	32.4	0.9	2.5	7.1	83.9	77.5	5.7	16.1
45 to 54 years	39.5	34.4	31.6	29.5	1.3	2.1	5.2	86.9	80.0	5.2	13.1
55 to 64 years	25.9	22.5	19.6	17.5	2.3	1.8	3.4	86.9	75.7	7.0	13.1
65 years and over	33.8	33.5	20.8	11.6	32.5	3.3	0.3	99.2	61.5	9.7	0.8
Sex: Male	137.9	116.1	98.2	88.0	16.4	13.8	21.7	84.2	71.2	10.0	15.8
Female	144.2	124.7	101.7	88.6	21.7	17.8	19.5	86.5	70.5	12.4	13.5
Race: White	230.1	198.9	169.2	148.4	33.0	21.5	31.2	86.4	73.5	9.4	13.6
Black	36.0	29.2	20.4	19.0	3.8	8.0	6.8	81.0	56.5	22.2	19.0
Asian and Pacific Islander	12.5	10.2	8.6	7.7	0.9	1.3	2.3	81.8	69.2	10.1	18.2
Hispanic origin [7]	37.4	25.0	17.3	16.0	2.3	7.1	12.4	66.8	46.3	18.9	33.2
Household income:											
Less than $25,000	62.2	47.7	24.3	16.0	17.9	18.1	14.5	76.7	39.0	29.1	23.3
$25,000-$49,999	76.2	62.7	51.7	45.0	11.5	8.6	13.5	82.3	67.9	11.3	17.7
$50,000-$74,999	58.1	51.5	47.9	44.2	4.2	2.8	6.6	88.7	82.4	4.9	11.4
$75,000 or more	85.5	78.9	76.0	71.4	4.4	2.1	6.6	92.3	88.9	2.4	7.7
Persons below poverty	32.9	22.8	8.4	5.5	4.8	13.3	10.1	69.3	25.6	40.5	30.7

[1] Includes other government insurance, not shown separately. Persons with coverage counted only once in total, even though they may have been covered by more than one type of policy. [2] Related to employment of self or other family members. [3] Beginning 1997 persons with no coverage other than access to Indian Health Service are no longer considered covered by health insurance; instead they are considered to be uninsured. The effect of this change on the overall estimates of health insurance coverage is negligible; however, the decrease in the number of people covered by medicaid may be partially due to this change. [4] Data based on 1990 census adjusted population controls. [5] Estimates reflect results of follow-up verification questions. [6] Implementation of Census 2000 based population controls, Sample expanded by 28,000 households. [7] Persons of Hispanic origin may be of any race.

No. 153. Persons With and Without Health Insurance Coverage by State: 2001

[**240,875 represents 240,875,000**. Based on the Current Population Survey and subject to sampling error; see text, Section 1, and Appendix III]

State	Total persons covered (1,000)	Total persons not covered Number (1,000)	Total persons not covered Percent of total	Children not covered Number (1,000)	Children not covered Percent of total	State	Total persons covered (1,000)	Total persons not covered Number (1,000)	Total persons not covered Percent of total	Children not covered Number (1,000)	Children not covered Percent of total
U.S.	240,875	41,207	14.6	8,509	11.7	MO	4,960	565	10.2	66	4.7
AL	3,815	573	13.1	101	8.9	MT	771	121	13.6	27	12.2
AK	534	100	15.7	20	10.4	NE	1,523	160	9.5	32	7.3
AZ	4,365	950	17.9	273	17.8	NV	1,791	344	16.1	83	14.2
AR	2,229	428	16.1	82	11.9	NH	1,139	119	9.4	21	7.2
CA	27,770	6,718	19.5	1,489	15.1	NJ	7,361	1,109	13.1	215	11.5
CO	3,723	687	15.6	155	13.0	NM	1,431	373	20.7	75	15.0
CT	3,047	346	10.2	63	7.7	NY	15,911	2,916	15.5	425	9.3
DE	719	73	9.2	17	8.6	NC	6,932	1,167	14.4	236	11.2
DC	484	70	12.7	10	8.6	ND	561	60	9.6	10	7.9
FL	13,491	2,856	17.5	624	15.9	OH	9,943	1,248	11.2	201	7.5
GA	6,912	1,376	16.6	349	15.0	OK	2,762	620	18.3	136	15.6
HI	1,096	117	9.6	29	9.3	OR	3,018	443	12.8	97	11.0
ID	1,105	210	16.0	45	11.9	PA	10,983	1,119	9.2	220	8.0
IL	10,655	1,676	13.6	318	10.3	RI	963	80	7.7	11	4.5
IN	5,322	714	11.8	164	11.2	SC	3,517	493	12.3	101	10.0
IA	2,645	216	7.5	34	4.7	SD	670	69	9.3	14	7.6
KS	2,341	301	11.4	49	7.6	TN	5,042	640	11.3	88	6.2
KY	3,505	492	12.3	97	9.7	TX	16,105	4,960	23.5	1,320	21.3
LA	3,544	845	19.3	157	12.7	UT	1,927	335	14.8	84	11.5
ME	1,147	132	10.3	16	6.2	VT	549	58	9.6	4	3.3
MD	4,673	653	12.3	129	9.1	VA	6,331	774	10.9	142	7.6
MA	5,802	520	8.2	74	5.3	WA	5,151	780	13.1	170	11.3
MI	8,864	1,028	10.4	196	8.1	WV	1,539	234	13.2	29	7.5
MN	4,530	392	8.0	65	5.6	WI	4,927	409	7.7	54	4.2
MS	2,341	459	16.4	82	10.4	WY	411	78	15.9	14	11.7

Source of Tables 152 and 153: U.S. Census Bureau; Current Population Reports, P60-220, and unpublished data.

No. 154. People Without Health Insurance for the Entire Year by Selected Characteristics: 2000 and 2001

[In thousands, except as noted (279,517 represents 279,517,000). Based on the Current Population Survey, Annual Demographic Supplement, and subject to sampling error; see text, Section 1, and Appendix III]

Characteristic	2000 Total persons	2000 Uninsured persons Number	2000 Percent distribution	2001 Total persons	2001 Uninsured persons Number	2001 Percent distribution
Total [1]	279,517	39,804	100.0	282,082	41,207	100.0
Under 18 years	72,314	8,617	21.6	72,628	8,509	20.6
18 to 24 years	26,815	7,406	18.6	27,312	7,673	18.6
25 to 34 years	38,865	8,507	21.4	38,670	9,051	22.0
35 to 44 years	44,566	6,898	17.3	44,284	7,131	17.3
45 to 64 years	63,391	8,124	20.4	65,419	8,571	20.8
65 years and over	33,566	251	0.6	33,769	272	0.7
Male	136,559	20,791	52.2	137,871	21,722	52.7
Female	142,958	19,013	47.8	144,211	19,485	47.3
White	228,208	30,075	75.6	230,071	31,193	75.7
Non-Hispanic	193,931	18,683	46.9	194,822	19,409	47.1
Black	35,597	6,683	16.8	36,023	6,833	16.6
Asian and Pacific Islander	12,693	2,287	5.7	12,500	2,278	5.5
Hispanic [2]	36,093	11,883	29.9	37,438	12,417	30.1

[1] Includes other races not shown separately.   [2] Persons of Hispanic origin may be of any race.

Source: U.S. Census Bureau, Current Population Survey, 2001 and 2002 Annual Demographic Supplements.

No. 155. Percent of Workers Participating in Health Care Benefit Programs and Percent of Participants Required to Contribute: 2000

[Based on National Compensation Survey, a sample survey of 1,436 private industry establishments of all sizes, representing over 107 million workers; see Appendix III. See also Table 648]

Characteristic	Percent of workers participating— Medical care	Percent of workers participating— Dental care	Percent of workers participating— Vision care	Single coverage medical care Employee contributions not required (percent)	Single coverage medical care Employee contributions required (percent)	Single coverage medical care Average monthly contribution [1] (dol.)	Family coverage medical care Employee contributions not required (percent)	Family coverage medical care Employee contributions required (percent)	Family coverage medical care Average monthly contribution [1] (dol.)
Total	52	29	17	32	68	54.40	19	81	179.75
Professional, technical, and related employees	64	42	24	25	75	54.32	15	85	183.51
Clerical and sales employees	50	30	17	28	72	54.14	16	84	187.07
Blue-collar and service employees	47	24	15	38	62	54.63	23	77	172.69
Full time [2]	61	35	21	31	69	53.93	19	81	180.16
Part time [2]	13	6	4	(NA)	(NA)	(NA)	(NA)	(NA)	(NA)
Union [3]	75	53	41	(NA)	(NA)	(NA)	(NA)	(NA)	(NA)
Nonunion [3]	49	27	15	27	73	55.63	13	87	185.79

NA Not available.   [1] The average is presented for all covered workers and excludes workers without the plan provision. Averages are for plans stating a flat monthly cost.   [2] Employees are classified as working either a full-time or part-time schedule based on the definition used by each establishment.   [3] Union workers are those whose wages are determined through collective bargaining.

Source: U.S. Bureau of Labor Statistics, National Compensation Survey: Employee Benefits in Private Industry in the United States, 2000, <www.bls.gov/ncs>; (accessed 19 August 2003).

No. 156. Outpatient Prescription Drug Benefits—Selected Features: 2000

[In percent except as indicated. (50,464 represents 50,464,000). Covers only drug benefits for full-time employees. Based on National Compensation Survey, a sample survey of 1,436 private industry establishments of all sizes, representing over 107 million workers; see Appendix III. See also Table 648]

Characteristic	Full-time employees, total	Professional, technical, and related	Clerical and sales	Blue-collar and service
Number with coverage (1,000)	50,464	13,380	14,112	22,972
Percent with—				
Coverage for brand name drugs	99	99	99	99
Higher reimbursement for generic drugs	78	78	84	74
Coverage for mail order drugs [1]	64	64	64	65
Higher reimbursement for prescriptions filled at selected pharmacies	42	45	39	42

[1] Programs that provide drugs for maintenance purposes, that is, drugs required on a continuous basis.

Source: U.S. Bureau of Labor Statistics, U. S. Department of Labor Bulletin 2555, January 2003; <www.bls.gov/ncs/ebs/>.

No. 157. Medical Care Benefits of Workers by Type and Amount of Employee Contribution: 2000

[In percent except as indicated (37,961 represents 37,961,000). See headnote, Table 155]

Type and amount of contribution	Individual coverage				Type and amount of contribution	Family coverage			
	All employees	Professional, technical, and related	Clerical and sales	Blue-collar and service		All employees	Professional, technical, and related	Clerical and sales	Blue-collar and service
Number with contributory coverage (1,000)	37,961	10,913	11,306	15,742	Number with contributory coverage (1,000)	44,822	12,276	13,207	19,338
Total with contributory coverage	100	100	100	100	Total with contributory coverage	100	100	100	100
Flat monthly amount	79	76	77	81	Flat monthly amount	81	79	80	84
Less than $5.00	-	-	1	-	Less than $40.00	5	5	4	6
$5.00-$9.99	2	3	1	1	$40.00-$49.99	2	3	1	2
$10.00-$14.99	3	3	4	3	$50.00-$59.99	4	3	3	5
$15.00-$19.99	6	7	5	7	$60.00-$69.99	3	3	2	3
$20.00-$29.99	11	10	9	12	$70.00-$79.99	4	4	3	4
$30.00-$39.99	13	12	13	15	$80.00-$89.99	5	5	4	4
$40.00-$49.99	12	15	11	12	$90.00-$99.99	3	3	3	3
$50.00-$59.99	6	6	9	4	$100.00-$124.99	9	10	10	8
$60.00-$69.99	5	3	5	6	$125.00-$149.99	5	6	7	4
$70.00-$79.99	5	3	5	6	$150.00-$174.99	10	8	10	12
$80.00-$89.99	4	3	4	4	$175.00-$199.99	5	3	4	6
$90.00-$99.99	1	-	1	1	$200.00-$224.99	4	5	3	4
$100.00-$124.99	3	2	3	4	$225.00-$249.99	3	2	4	3
$125.00 or more	7	10	5	7	$250.00-$299.99	8	4	10	8
Dollar amount unspecified	-	-	-	-	$300 or more	13	15	13	11
Composite rate [1]	2	3	2	3	Composite rate [1]	2	2	1	2
Varies [2]	5	5	5	4	Varies [2]	4	5	5	4
Other	(Z)	(Z)	(Z)	(Z)	Other	(Z)	(Z)	(Z)	(Z)
Flexible benefits [3]	8	12	7	7	Flexible benefits [3]	7	11	6	6
Percent of earnings	-	-	-	-	Percent of earnings	-	-	-	-
Exists, but unknown	6	4	9	5	Exists, but unknown	5	3	8	4

- Represents zero. Z Less than 0.5 percent. [1] A composite rate is a set contribution covering more than one benefit area; for example, health care and life insurance. Cost data for individual plans cannot be determined. [2] Based on worker attributes. For example, employee contributions may vary based on earnings, length of service, or age. [3] Amount varies by options selected under a "cafeteria plan" or employer-sponsored reimbursement account.

Source: U.S. Bureau of Labor Statistics, News, USDL 02-389, July 16, 2002.

No. 158. Annual Receipts/Revenue for Health Care Industries: 1999 to 2001

[In millions of dollars (417,228 represents $417,228,000,000). Based on the 1997 North American Industry Classification System, (NAICS), see text, Section 15. All firms in NAICS 6211, 6212, 6213, and 6215 are defined as taxable. Estimates for the nonemployer portion are derived from administrative records data provided by other federal agencies. These data are available only at the total revenue level. Estimates for tax-exempt firms are derived only from a sample of employer firms. See Appendix III]

Kind of business	NAICS code	Total, all firms [1]			Employer firms		
		1999	2000	2001	1999	2000	2001
Ambulatory health care services	621	417,228	443,040	480,191	391,157	416,182	450,633
Offices of physicians	6211	201,386	215,221	232,146	190,049	202,913	219,492
Offices of dentists	6212	56,389	60,774	65,586	54,592	58,812	63,556
Offices of other health practitioners [2]	6213	39,224	41,580	44,963	30,902	32,512	35,309
Offices of chiropractors	62131	8,324	8,661	9,619	7,291	7,576	8,433
Offices of optometrists	62132	7,932	8,612	8,950	7,318	7,941	8,256
Offices of PT/OT/speech therapy & audiology [3]	62134	9,788	9,807	11,003	8,574	8,531	9,503
Outpatient care centers	6214	56,589	58,929	65,347	55,975	59,731	64,593
Medical & diagnostic laboratories	6215	20,385	23,196	26,487	19,546	22,215	25,541
Home health care services	6216	30,649	29,977	31,763	29,148	28,431	29,978
Other ambulatory health care services	6219	12,605	13,363	13,899	10,945	11,568	12,165
Hospitals	622	413,035	430,329	462,215	413,035	430,329	462,215
General medical & surgical hospitals	6221	(NA)	(NA)	(NA)	385,480	402,578	432,749
Psychiatric & substance abuse hospitals	6222	(NA)	(NA)	(NA)	15,379	14,944	15,287
Other specialty hospitals	6223	(NA)	(NA)	(NA)	12,176	12,807	14,179
Nursing and residential care facilities	623	102,336	108,607	116,066	101,049	107,174	114,472
Nursing care facilities	6231	(NA)	(NA)	(NA)	63,128	65,774	69,270
Residential mental retardation/health facilities [2]	6232	(NA)	(NA)	(NA)	13,113	14,353	15,542
Residential mental retardation facilities	62321	(NA)	(NA)	(NA)	8,609	9,301	9,985
Community care facilities for the elderly	6233	(NA)	(NA)	(NA)	19,346	21,257	23,434

NA Not available. [1] Includes taxable nonemployer firms, not shown separately. [2] Includes other kinds of business not shown separately. [3] Offices of physical, occupational and speech therapists, and audiologists.

Source: U.S. Census Bureau, Service Annual Survey, 2001.

No. 159. Receipts for Selected Health Service Industries by Source of Revenue: 2000 and 2001

[In millions of dollars (202,913 represents $202,913,000,000). Based on the 1997 North American Industry Classification System (NAICS), see text, Section 15. Based on a sample of employer firms only and does not include nonemployer revenue. See Appendix III]

Source of revenue	Offices of physicians (NAICS 6211) 2000	2001	Offices of dentists (NAICS 6212) 2000	2001	Hospitals (NAICS 622) 2000	2001	Nursing and residential care facilities (NAICS 623) 2000	2001
Total	202,913	219,492	58,812	63,556	430,329	462,215	107,174	114,472
Medicare	48,370	52,649	(S)	(S)	138,843	147,841	12,699	14,857
Medicaid	13,896	15,109	1,416	1,790	52,305	56,193	43,834	45,875
Other government [1]	2,025	2,347	(S)	(S)	22,687	24,745	7,157	8,227
Worker's compensation	7,419	8,050	(S)	(S)	4,720	5,117	(S)	(S)
Private insurance	97,193	105,846	30,232	33,201	155,206	169,885	6,231	6,617
Patient (out-of-pocket)	22,865	23,617	25,747	27,174	22,928	23,844	[2]27,019	[2]28,930
Other patient care sources, n.e.c [3]	7,299	8,128	(S)	434	10,622	11,453	3,300	3,223
Nonpatient care revenue	3,846	3,746	(S)	(S)	23,019	23,138	6,910	6,717

S Figure does not meet publication standards. [1] Veterans, National Institute of Health, Indian Affairs, etc. [2] Represents payment from patients and their families plus patients' assigned social security benefits. [3] N.e.c. represents not elsewhere classified.

Source: U.S. Census Bureau, *Service Annual Survey: 2001.*

No. 160. Employment in the Health Service Industries: 1990 to 2002

[In thousands (2,842 represents 2,842,000). See headnote Table 631]

Industry	NAICS code [1]	1990	1995	1999	2000	2001	2002
Ambulatory health care services[2]	621	2,842	3,768	4,227	4,320	4,462	4,633
Offices of physicians	6211	1,278	1,540	1,787	1,840	1,911	1,983
Offices of dentists	6212	513	592	667	688	705	726
Offices of other health practitioners	6213	276	395	439	438	457	482
Medical and diagnostic laboratories	6215	129	146	156	162	170	174
Home health care services	6216	288	622	630	633	639	675
Hospitals	622	3,513	3,734	3,936	3,954	4,051	4,153
General medical and surgical hospitals	6221	3,305	3,520	3,727	3,745	3,833	3,926
Psychiatric and substance abuse hospitals	6222	113	101	88	86	87	90
Other hospitals	6223	95	112	121	123	132	138
Nursing and residential care facilities	623	1,856	2,308	2,529	2,583	2,676	2,743
Nursing care facilities	6231	1,170	1,413	1,501	1,514	1,547	1,574

[1] Based on the North American Industry Classification System 2002 code; see text, Section 12. [2] Includes other industries not shown separately.

Source: U.S. Bureau of Labor Statistics, *Employment and Earnings*, monthly, June 2003 issue.

No. 161. Registered Nurses by Employment Status: 1996 and 2000

[As of March (2,559 represents 2,559,000). Based on a sample and subject to sampling variability; see source for details]

Age, race and Hispanic origin status	Total (1,000)	Employed in nursing Number (1,000)	Percent distribution	Not employed in nursing (1,000)
1996	2,559	2,116	100.0	443
2000	2,697	2,202	100.0	495
Less than 25 years	66	65	2.9	2
25 to 29 years	177	166	7.5	11
30 to 34 years	248	225	10.2	24
35 to 39 years	360	316	14.4	44
40 to 44 years	464	409	18.6	55
45 to 49 years	465	406	18.5	58
50 to 54 years	342	288	13.1	55
55 to 59 years	238	180	8.2	58
60 to 64 years	156	87	4.0	69
65 years and over	154	41	1.9	113
Unknown age	25	19	0.8	6
White non-Hispanic	2,334	1,891	85.9	443
Black non-Hispanic	133	113	5.1	20
Asian non-Hispanic	93	83	3.8	11
Native Hawaiian/Pacific Islander	6	6	0.3	1
American Indian/Alaska Native	13	11	0.5	2
Hispanic [1]	55	48	2.2	7
Two or more races non-Hispanic	33	27	1.2	6
Unknown race/ethnic	29	23	1.1	6

[1] Persons of Hispanic origin may be of any race.

Source: U.S. Dept. of Health and Human Services, Health Resources and Services Administration, *The Registered Nurse Population, March 2000*, September 2001.

Health and Nutrition

No. 162. Physicians by Selected Activity: 1980 to 2001

[In thousands (467.7 represents 467,700). As of Dec. 31, except 1990 as of Jan. 1, and as noted. Includes Puerto Rico and island areas]

Activity	1980	1990	1995	1998	1999	2000	2001
Doctors of medicine, total........	467.7	615.4	720.3	777.9	797.6	813.8	836.2
Professionally active................	435.5	560.0	646.0	707.0	720.9	737.5	751.7
Place of medical education:							
U.S. medical graduates	343.6	437.2	492.2	533.4	542.2	554.2	562.3
Foreign medical graduates [1]	91.8	122.8	153.8	173.7	178.7	183.4	189.4
Sex: Male......................	386.7	463.9	505.9	538.9	544.1	551.7	556.6
Female....................	48.7	96.1	140.1	168.1	176.7	185.8	195.1
Active nonfederal.................	417.7	539.5	624.9	688.0	702.8	718.1	731.7
Patient care...................	361.9	487.8	564.1	606.4	610.7	631.4	652.3
Office-based practice............	271.3	359.9	427.3	468.8	473.2	490.4	514.0
General and family practice	47.8	57.6	59.9	64.6	66.2	67.5	70.0
Cardiovascular diseases	6.7	10.7	13.7	15.1	15.6	16.3	17.0
Dermatology.................	4.4	6.0	7.0	7.6	7.8	8.0	8.2
Gastroenterology..............	2.7	5.2	7.3	7.9	8.2	8.5	8.9
Internal medicine.............	40.5	57.8	72.6	83.3	84.6	88.7	94.7
Pediatrics....................	17.4	26.5	33.9	38.7	40.5	42.2	44.8
Pulmonary diseases	2.0	3.7	5.0	4.9	5.7	6.1	6.6
General surgery...............	22.4	24.5	24.1	27.5	26.8	24.5	25.6
Obstetrics and gynecology.......	19.5	25.5	29.1	31.2	31.1	31.7	32.6
Ophthalmology	10.6	13.1	14.6	15.6	15.2	15.6	16.0
Orthopedic surgery............	10.7	14.2	17.1	18.5	17.0	17.4	17.8
Otolaryngology...............	5.3	6.4	7.1	7.5	7.3	7.6	7.9
Plastic surgery................	2.4	3.8	4.6	5.3	5.1	5.3	5.5
Urological surgery	6.2	7.4	8.0	8.4	8.2	8.5	8.6
Anesthesiology	11.3	17.8	23.8	26.2	26.6	27.6	28.9
Diagnostic radiology	4.2	9.8	12.8	14.2	14.3	14.6	15.6
Emergency medicine	(NA)	8.4	11.7	13.3	13.9	14.5	15.8
Neurology...................	3.2	5.6	7.6	8.5	8.1	8.6	9.2
Pathology, anatomical/clinical	6.0	7.3	9.0	10.0	10.1	10.3	10.6
Psychiatry...................	15.9	20.0	23.3	25.0	24.4	25.0	25.7
Other specialty	31.9	28.8	35.0	35.9	36.4	42.0	44.1
Hospital-based practice...........	90.6	127.9	136.8	137.6	137.2	141.0	138.3
Residents and interns [2].........	59.6	89.9	93.7	92.3	92.5	95.1	92.9
Full-time hospital staff.........	31.0	38.0	43.1	45.3	44.8	45.9	45.4
Other professional activity [3]	35.2	39.0	40.3	41.6	41.2	41.6	41.0
Not classified...................	20.6	12.7	20.6	40.0	50.9	45.1	38.3
Federal.........................	17.8	20.5	21.1	19.0	18.1	19.4	20.0
Patient care...................	14.6	16.1	18.1	15.3	14.7	16.0	16.6
Other professional activity [3]	3.2	4.4	3.0	3.7	3.4	3.4	3.4
Inactive/unknown address	32.1	55.4	74.3	70.8	76.8	76.3	84.5
Doctors of osteopathy [4]	18.8	30.9	35.7	40.8	43.5	44.9	47.0

NA Not available. [1] Foreign medical graduates received their medical education in schools outside the United States and Canada. [2] Includes clinical fellows. [3] Includes medical teaching, administration, research, and other. [4] As of June 1. Total DOs. Data from American Osteopathic Association, Chicago, IL.
Source: Except as noted, American Medical Association, Chicago, IL, *Physician Characteristics and Distribution in the U.S.*, annual (copyright).

No. 163. Active Nonfederal Physicians, 2001, and Nurses, 2000 by State

[As of December. Excludes doctors of osteopathy, federally-employed persons, and physicians with addresses unknown. Includes all physicians not classified according to activity status]

State	Physicians Total	Rate [1]	Nurses Total	Rate [1]	State	Physicians Total	Rate [1]	Nurses Total	Rate [1]
United States..	721,034	253	2,249,440	797	Missouri.........	13,041	231	52,590	938
Alabama.........	8,975	201	35,430	796	Montana.........	1,901	210	7,600	841
Alaska..........	1,174	185	5,030	801	Nebraska	3,887	226	15,770	920
Arizona.........	10,325	195	34,660	671	Nevada	3,659	174	10,770	533
Arkansas	5,124	190	19,470	727	New Hampshire....	3,086	245	11,140	898
California.......	85,752	248	185,500	545	New Jersey......	25,761	303	72,150	856
Colorado........	10,386	234	33,430	773	New Mexico	3,901	213	11,430	627
Connecticut......	12,234	356	33,490	982	New York	72,666	381	164,490	866
Delaware	1,896	238	7,240	921	North Carolina....	19,248	235	70,870	877
District of Columbia .	3,862	673	8,690	1,520	North Dakota......	1,403	220	6,380	995
Florida..........	38,397	235	129,210	805	Ohio	27,515	242	103,180	908
Georgia.........	17,260	205	58,420	709	Oklahoma........	5,655	163	22,520	652
Hawaii..........	3,343	272	8,570	707	Oregon..........	8,169	235	25,780	751
Idaho...........	2,064	156	8,340	642	Pennsylvania......	35,710	290	133,780	1,089
Illinois...........	32,798	262	104,790	842	Rhode Island......	3,553	335	11,160	1,062
Indiana..........	12,388	202	49,650	815	South Carolina.....	8,791	216	27,670	688
Iowa	5,182	177	29,870	1,020	South Dakota.....	1,481	195	8,310	1,100
Kansas..........	5,594	207	24,440	908	Tennessee	14,035	244	48,360	848
Kentucky	8,647	213	34,090	842	Texas...........	43,094	202	127,680	609
Louisiana	11,339	254	35,680	798	Utah	4,537	199	13,480	601
Maine...........	3,156	246	13,270	1,039	Vermont.........	2,055	335	5,800	951
Maryland	20,181	375	43,260	814	Virginia..........	17,840	248	55,110	776
Massachusetts.....	26,820	419	75,750	1,191	Washington......	14,684	245	45,130	763
Michigan........	23,064	230	83,370	837	West Virginia.....	3,946	219	15,550	860
Minnesota.......	13,072	262	46,530	943	Wisconsin........	12,721	235	49,200	915
Mississippi	4,806	168	21,670	761	Wyoming	856	173	3,750	759

[1] Per 100,000 resident population. Based on U.S. Census Bureau estimates as of July 1.
Source: Physicians: American Medical Association, Chicago, IL, *Physician Characteristics and Distribution in the U.S.*, annual (copyright); Nurses: U.S. Dept. of Health and Human Services, Health Resources and Services Administration, unpublished data.

No. 164. Health Professions—Practitioners and Schools: 1990 to 2001

[573 **represents** 573,000. Data on the number of schools and total enrollment are reported as of the beginning of the academic year; all other school data are reported as of the end of the academic year. Data are based on reporting by health professions schools]

Year	Medi- cine	Oste- opathy	Registered nursing Total	Bacca- laure- ate	Associ- ate degree	Diploma	Licensed practical nursing	Den- tistry [1]	Optom- etry	Phar- macy
ACTIVE PERSONNEL (1,000)										
1990	573	28	1,790	[2]682	[3]1,107	([3])	441	148	26	168
1995	646	36	2,116	[2]881	[3]1,235	([3])	399	159	29	181
1999	721	43	2,202	[2]965	[3]1,237	([3])	357	165	32	193
2000	738	45	2,249	[2]983	[3]1,267	([3])	374	168	32	196
NUMBER OF SCHOOLS [4]										
1990	126	15	1,470	489	829	152	1,154	56	17	74
1995	125	16	1,516	521	876	119	1,210	54	17	75
1999	125	19	1,513	550	885	78	1,138	55	17	81
2000	125	19	(NA)	(NA)	(NA)	(NA)	(NA)	55	17	82
2001	125	(NA)	(NA)	(NA)	(NA)	(NA)	(NA)	(NA)	(NA)	(NA)
TOTAL ENROLLMENT										
1990	65,016	6,615	201,458	74,865	106,175	20,418	46,720	16,412	4,723	23,013
1995	66,788	8,146	268,350	112,659	135,895	19,796	59,428	16,353	5,201	27,667
1999	66,539	9,882	211,694	93,763	109,423	8,508	52,221	17,033	5,313	28,568
2000	66,377	10,388	192,202	89,508	95,598	7,096	(NA)	17,242	5,464	29,586
2001	66,160	10,817	(NA)	(NA)	(NA)	(NA)	(NA)	17,349	5,428	30,301
GRADUATES										
1990	15,398	1,529	66,088	18,571	42,318	5,199	35,417	4,233	1,115	6,956
1995	15,883	1,843	97,052	31,254	58,749	7,049	44,234	3,908	1,219	7,837
1999	16,008	2,169	67,169	23,942	40,828	2,399	(NA)	4,095	1,316	7,141
2000	15,712	2,279	(NA)	(NA)	(NA)	(NA)	(NA)	4,171	1,315	7,260
2001	15,778	2,597	(NA)	(NA)	(NA)	(NA)	(NA)	(NA)	(NA)	(NA)

NA Not available. [1] Personnel data exclude dentists in military service, U.S. Public Health Service, and U.S. Dept. of Veterans Affairs. [2] Includes nurses with advanced degrees. [3] Diploma nurses included with associate degree nurses. [4] Some nursing schools offer more than one type of program. Numbers shown for nursing are number of nursing programs.

Source: U.S. Dept. of Health and Human Services, Bureau of Health Professions, unpublished data; American Medical Association, Chicago, IL, *Physician Characteristics and Distribution in the U.S.*, annual; and American Association of Colleges of Osteopathic Medicine, Rockville, MD, *Annual Statistical Report.*

No. 165. Percent Distribution of Number of Visits to Health Care Professionals by Selected Characteristics: 2000 and 2001

[Covers ambulatory visits to doctor's offices and emergency departments, and home health care visits during a 12-month period. Based on the redesigned National Health Interview Survey, a sample survey of the civilian noninstitutionalized population. See Appendix III]

Characteristic	None 2000	None 2001	1-3 visits 2000	1-3 visits 2001	4-9 visits 2000	4-9 visits 2001	10 or more visits 2000	10 or more visits 2001
All persons [1]	16.6	16.5	45.4	45.8	24.7	24.4	13.3	13.3
Age:								
Under 6 years	6.3	5.5	44.3	45.8	38.3	37.9	11.2	10.8
6-17 years	15.1	14.6	58.2	58.9	20.7	20.5	6.0	6.1
18-44 years	23.2	23.3	45.3	46.1	19.2	18.9	12.2	11.8
45-64 years	15.0	15.6	43.4	42.9	25.7	25.7	15.8	15.9
65-74 years	9.0	8.1	34.5	35.8	34.4	33.5	22.1	22.6
75 years and over	5.8	5.8	29.3	28.2	39.3	38.1	25.6	27.9
Sex: [1]								
Male	21.5	21.3	46.0	46.5	22.4	21.6	10.1	10.7
Female	11.9	11.9	44.8	45.1	27.0	27.1	16.4	15.9
Race: [1,2]								
White only	16.0	15.9	45.1	45.7	25.3	24.8	13.7	13.5
Black or African American only	17.3	16.4	46.7	46.4	23.4	24.0	12.6	13.2
American Indian or Alaska Native	21.2	21.4	42.9	36.4	20.0	25.4	15.8	16.9
Asian only	20.2	20.8	49.2	48.3	20.9	22.3	9.7	8.6
Two or more races	12.1	18.0	41.6	41.2	28.3	23.5	17.9	17.3
Race and Hispanic origin: [1]								
Hispanic	26.5	27.0	41.8	40.2	20.0	20.7	11.7	12.0
White, non-Hispanic	14.5	14.3	45.4	46.4	26.0	25.4	14.1	13.9
Black, non-Hispanic	17.2	16.4	46.9	46.4	23.4	24.0	12.6	13.1

[1] Estimates are age adjusted to the year 2000 standard using six age groups: Under 18 years, 18-44 years, 45-54 years, 55-64 years, 65-74 years, and 75 years and over. [2] Estimates by race and Hispanic origin are tabulated using the 1997 standards for federal data on race and ethnicity. Estimates for specific race groups are shown when they meet requirements for statistical reliability and confidentiality. The categories "White only," "Black or African American only," "American Indian and Alaska Native (AI/AN) only," and "Asian only" include persons who reported only one racial group; and the category "2 or more races" includes persons who reported more than one of the five racial groups in the 1997 standards or one of the five racial groups and "Some other race."

Source: U.S. National Center for Health Statistics, *Health, United States, 2003.*

No. 166. Medical Practice Characteristics by Selected Specialty: 1990 to 2001

[Dollar figures in thousands (164.3 represents $164,300). Based on a sample telephone survey of nonfederal office and hospital based patient care physicians, excluding residents. Survey not conducted for 2000. For details see source. For definition of mean, see Guide to Tabular Presentation]

Specialty	1990	1995	1996	1997	1998	1999	2001
MEAN PATIENT VISITS PER WEEK							
All physicians [1]	120.9	107.6	109.4	110.6	105.0	106.7	107.2
General/Family practice	146.0	133.7	133.1	130.1	125.0	122.9	126.6
Internal medicine	112.0	99.7	104.7	106.4	102.8	103.0	102.7
Surgery	107.6	97.1	95.1	99.3	93.5	95.8	97.7
Pediatrics	134.0	125.9	121.1	125.5	110.9	120.5	111.0
Obstetrics/Gynecology	120.0	94.0	104.2	103.8	99.3	101.8	101.2
MEAN HOURS IN PATIENT CARE PER WEEK							
All physicians [1]	53.3	51.3	53.4	53.2	51.7	51.6	52.8
General/Family practice	55.0	52.9	53.5	53.1	51.3	50.6	50.7
Internal medicine	55.7	53.9	57.2	56.0	54.3	54.2	56.2
Surgery	53.1	53.2	54.2	55.0	51.7	53.3	53.1
Pediatrics	52.4	50.4	51.0	51.6	48.6	49.5	49.4
Obstetrics/Gynecology	60.4	54.6	60.5	59.9	59.9	59.0	59.3
MEAN NET INCOME							
All physicians [1]	164.3	195.5	199.0	199.6	194.4	(NA)	205.7
General/Family practice	102.7	131.2	139.1	140.9	142.5	(NA)	144.7
Internal medicine	152.5	185.7	185.7	193.9	182.1	(NA)	196.1
Surgery	236.4	269.4	275.2	261.4	268.2	(NA)	274.7
Pediatrics	106.5	140.5	140.6	143.5	139.6	(NA)	137.8
Obstetrics/Gynecology	207.3	244.3	231.0	228.7	214.4	(NA)	227.0
MEAN LIABILITY PREMIUM							
All physicians [1]	14.5	15.0	14.1	14.2	16.8	(NA)	18.4
General/Family practice	7.8	9.0	8.4	12.0	10.9	(NA)	13.8
Internal medicine	9.2	9.4	8.9	9.4	16.5	(NA)	13.7
Surgery	22.8	23.3	21.7	19.7	22.8	(NA)	23.6
Pediatrics	7.8	7.9	8.3	12.3	9.0	(NA)	11.6
Obstetrics/Gynecology	34.3	38.6	35.2	33.0	35.8	(NA)	39.2

NA Not available. [1] Includes other specialties not shown separately.
Source: American Medical Association, Chicago IL, *Physician Socioeconomic Statistics, Periodic* (copyright)

No. 167. Ambulatory Care Visits to Physicians' Offices and Hospital Outpatient and Emergency Departments: 2001

[1,017.1 represents 1,017,100,000. Based on the annual National Ambulatory Medical Care Survey and National Hospital Ambulatory Medical Care Survey and subject to sampling error; see source for details. For composition of regions, see map inside front cover]

Characteristic	Number of visits (mil.) Total	Physician offices	Outpatient dept.	Emergency dept.	Visits per 100 persons Total	Physician offices	Outpatient dept.	Emergency dept.
Total	1,071.7	880.5	83.7	107.5	383	314	30	38
Age:								
Under 15 years old	187.2	146.7	18.3	22.2	310	243	30	37
15 to 24 years old	92.8	65.6	9.8	17.4	239	169	25	45
25 to 44 years old	253.9	200.6	20.6	32.7	306	242	25	40
45 to 64 years old	280.0	239.1	21.6	19.3	437	373	34	30
65 to 74 years old	126.8	113.0	7.3	6.6	702	625	40	36
75 years old and over	130.9	115.5	6.1	9.3	837	739	39	60
Sex:								
Male	443.9	360.4	33.2	50.3	325	264	24	37
Female	627.8	520.1	50.5	57.2	437	362	35	40
Race:								
White	922.8	777.5	63.2	82.0	407	343	28	36
Black/African-American	105.4	66.1	17.0	22.2	302	189	49	64
Asian/Native Hawaiian/Other Pacific Islander	34.0	29.2	2.7	2.1	307	264	24	19
American Indian/Alaska Native	2.8	1.9	0.3	[1]0.6	104	72	10	[1]23
More than one race reported	3.0	2.8	[1]0.1	0.1	76	69	[1]3	4
Region:								
Northeast	238.2	195.8	21.6	20.8	449	369	41	39
Midwest	233.7	185.2	21.8	26.7	366	290	34	42
South	355.2	287.2	27.5	40.5	357	288	28	41
West	244.5	212.3	12.8	19.5	385	334	20	31
Primary source of payment:								
Private insurance	591.5	517.4	30.9	43.2	(X)	(X)	(X)	(X)
Medicare	221.5	192.1	13.5	15.9	(X)	(X)	(X)	(X)
Medicaid	102.7	63.6	20.3	18.8	(X)	(X)	(X)	(X)
Worker's compensation	18.5	14.9	1.0	2.7	(X)	(X)	(X)	(X)
Self pay	57.4	35.3	6.2	15.9	(X)	(X)	(X)	(X)
No charge	7.4	3.1	[1]3.3	[1]1.0	(X)	(X)	(X)	(X)
Other	22.0	16.4	3.3	2.3	(X)	(X)	(X)	(X)
Unknown	50.7	37.6	5.3	7.7	(X)	(X)	(X)	(X)

X Not applicable. [1] Figures do not meet standard of reliability or precision.
Source: U.S. National Center for Health Statistics, Advance Data, Nos. 335, 337, and 338; June 4, 2003; August 11, 2003; and August 5, 2003.

No. 168. Visits to Office-Based Physicians and Hospital Outpatient Departments by Diagnosis: 2000 and 2001

[369.0 represents 369,000,000. See headnote, Table 167]

Leading diagnoses [1]	Number (mil.) 2000	Number (mil.) 2001	Rate per 1,000 persons [2] 2000	Rate per 1,000 persons [2] 2001	Leading diagnoses [1]	Number (mil.) 2000	Number (mil.) 2001	Rate per 1,000 persons [2] 2000	Rate per 1,000 persons [2] 2001
MALE					**FEMALE**				
All ages	369.0	393.6	2,760	2,883	All ages	537.8	570.6	3,829	3,975
Under 15 years old [3]	85.3	86.7	2,765	2,803	Under 15 years old [3]	75.4	78.3	2,556	2,654
Routine infant or child health check	17.9	19.9	580	642	Routine infant or child health check	17.5	18.0	593	610
Acute respiratory infections [4]	8.5	7.5	276	243	Acute respiratory infections [4]	8.1	7.0	276	239
Otitis media [5]	7.1	5.8	231	188	Otitis media [5]	6.6	6.4	222	216
Asthma	3.1	3.0	101	96	Acute pharyngitis	2.3	2.4	78	81
Attention deficit disorder	3.4	2.8	110	89	Asthma	1.2	1.6	40	54
15 to 44 years old [3]	98.9	102.5	1,660	1,697	15 to 44 years old [3]	194.8	194.2	3,199	3,159
Acute respiratory infections [4]	3.6	4.2	60	70	Normal pregnancy	24.5	20.1	402	327
General medical examination	3.9	3.8	66	63	Gynecological examination	6.1	6.1	100	99
Spinal disorders	4.4	3.7	74	62	Acute respiratory infections [4]	6.0	6.0	99	97
Rheumatism, excluding back	1.9	3.5	32	59	General medical examination	6.6	5.0	108	81
Essential hypertension	2.7	3.2	46	53	Rheumatism, excluding back	2.3	4.6	37	75
45 to 64 years old [3]	96.5	105.0	3,294	3,384	45 to 64 years old [3]	141.0	155.7	4,511	4,714
Essential hypertension	6.8	7.5	233	243	Essential hypertension	8.3	8.1	264	246
Diabetes mellitus	5.8	6.4	199	206	Arthropathies and related disorders	6.6	8.1	211	245
Spinal disorders	4.1	4.5	139	145	Diabetes mellitus	5.6	5.7	181	173
Arthropathies and related disorders	2.9	3.1	99	100	Spinal disorders	5.7	5.5	182	166
Rheumatism, excluding back	1.4	3.1	49	99	Rheumatism, excluding back	3.0	5.4	94	162
65 years old and over [3]	88.2	93.4	6,340	7,010	65 years old and over [3]	126.6	142.5	6,736	7,291
Essential hypertension	6.6	6.3	478	444	Essential hypertension	11.8	10.8	628	555
Heart disease, excluding ischemic	4.1	5.2	296	365	Diabetes mellitus	6.0	8.0	318	412
Diabetes mellitus	4.8	5.1	344	361	Arthropathies and related disorders	6.3	7.5	335	384
Ischemic heart disease	4.9	5.1	349	359	Heart disease, excluding ischemic	3.6	5.9	194	300
Malignant neoplasms	7.1	4.5	507	319	Cataract	4.0	5.0	212	258

[1] Based on the International Classification of Diseases, 9th Revision, Clinical Modification, (ICD-9-CM). [2] Based on U.S. Census Bureau estimated civilian population as of July 1. [3] Includes other first-listed diagnoses, not shown separately. [4] Excluding pharyngitis. [5] Includes Eustachian tube disorders.
Source: U.S. National Center for Health Statistics, Advance Data, Nos. 335 and 337, June 4, 2003, and August 11, 2003.

No. 169. Visits to Hospital Emergency Departments by Diagnosis: 2001

[50,321 represents 50,321,000. See headnote, Table 167]

Leading diagnoses [1]	Number (1,000)	Rate per 1,000 persons [2]	Leading diagnoses [1]	Number (1,000)	Rate per 1,000 persons [2]
MALE			**FEMALE**		
All ages	50,321	369	All ages	57,169	398
Under 15 years old [3]	12,148	393	Under 15 years old [3]	10,096	342
Otitis media and Eustachian tube disorders	1,094	35	Acute respiratory infections [4]	1,096	37
Acute upper respiratory infections [4]	1,071	35	Otitis media and Eustachian tube disorders	813	28
Open wound of head	750	24	Contusions with intact skin surfaces	467	16
Contusions with intact skin surfaces	689	22	Open wound of head	416	14
Fractures, excluding lower limb	499	16	Pyrexia of unknown origin	354	12
15 to 44 years old [3]	22,864	379	15 to 44 years old [3]	27,239	443
Open wound, excluding head	1,577	26	Abdominal pain	1,525	25
Contusions with intact skin surfaces	1,357	22	Complications of pregnancy, childbirth, and the puerperium	1,352	22
Strains and sprains of neck and back	855	14	Contusions with intact skin surfaces	1,148	19
Spinal disorders	843	14	Sprains and strains of neck and back	978	16
Fractures, excluding lower limb	716	12	Acute upper respiratory infections [4]	975	16
45 to 64 years old [3]	8,813	284	45 to 64 years old [3]	10,447	316
Chest pain	620	20	Chest pain	674	20
Open wound, excluding head	444	14	Abdominal pain	455	14
Spinal disorders	311	10	Spinal disorders	403	12
Contusions with intact skin surfaces	311	10	Contusions with intact skin surfaces	344	10
Abdominal pain	269	9	Rheumatism, excluding back	301	9
65 years old and over [3]	6,496	458	65 years old and over [3]	9,387	480
Chest pain	386	27	Heart disease, excluding ischemic	562	29
Heart disease, excluding ischemic	377	27	Chest pain	493	25
Open wound, excluding head	238	17	Contusions with intact skin surfaces	434	22
Schemic heart disease	222	16	Cerebrovascular disease	307	16
Pneumonia	214	15	Fractures, excluding lower limb	289	15

[1] Based on the International Classification of Diseases, 9th Revision, Clinical Modification, (ICD-9-CM). [2] Based on U.S. Census Bureau estimated civilian population as of July 1. [3] Includes other first-listed diagnoses, not shown separately. [4] Excluding pharyngitis.
Source: U.S. National Center for Health Statistics, Advance Data, No. 338, August 5, 2003.

No. 170. Hospitals—Summary Characteristics: 1980 to 2001

[For beds, 1,365 represents 1,365,000. Covers hospitals accepted for registration by the American Hospital Association; see text, this section. Short-term hospitals have an average patient stay of less than 30 days; long-term, an average stay of longer duration. Special hospitals include obstetrics and gynecology; eye, ear, nose, and throat; rehabilitation; orthopedic; and chronic and other special hospitals except psychiatric, tuberculosis, alcoholism, and chemical dependency hospitals]

Item	1980	1990	1995	1996	1997	1998	1999	2000	2001
Number:									
All hospitals	6,965	6,649	6,291	6,201	6,097	6,021	5,890	5,810	5,801
With 100 beds or more	3,755	3,620	3,376	3,347	3,267	3,216	3,140	3,102	3,084
Nonfederal [1]	6,606	6,312	5,992	5,911	5,812	5,746	5,626	5,565	5,558
Community hospitals [2]	5,830	5,384	5,194	5,134	5,057	5,015	4,956	4,915	4,908
Nongovernmental nonprofit	3,322	3,191	3,092	3,045	3,000	3,026	3,012	3,003	2,998
For profit	730	749	752	759	797	771	747	749	754
State and local government	1,778	1,444	1,350	1,330	1,260	1,218	1,197	1,163	1,156
Long-term general and special	157	131	112	112	125	125	129	131	136
Psychiatric	534	757	657	636	601	579	516	496	491
Tuberculosis	11	4	3	3	4	3	4	4	4
Federal	359	337	299	290	285	275	264	245	243
Beds (1,000): [3]									
All hospitals	1,365	1,213	1,081	1,062	1,035	1,013	994	984	987
Rate per 1,000 population [4]	6.0	4.9	4.1	3.9	3.8	3.7	3.6	3.5	3.5
Beds per hospital	196	182	172	171	170	168	169	169	170
Nonfederal [1]	1,248	1,113	1,004	989	973	956	939	931	936
Community hospitals [2]	988	927	873	862	853	840	830	824	826
Rate per 1,000 population [4]	4.3	3.7	3.3	3.2	3.1	3.0	3.0	2.9	2.9
Nongovernmental nonprofit	692	657	610	598	591	588	587	583	585
For profit	87	102	106	109	115	113	107	110	109
State and local government	209	169	157	155	148	139	136	131	132
Long-term general and special	39	25	19	19	17	18	20	18	19
Psychiatric	215	158	110	106	100	95	87	87	89
Tuberculosis	2	(Z)	(Z)	(Z)	(Z)	(Z)	(Z)	(Z)	(Z)
Federal	117	98	78	73	62	57	55	53	53
Average daily census (1,000):									
All hospitals	1,060	844	710	685	673	662	657	650	658
Community hospitals [2]	747	619	548	531	528	525	526	526	533
Nongovernmental nonprofit	542	455	393	379	376	377	381	382	385
For profit	57	54	55	56	60	60	58	61	63
State and local government	149	111	100	96	92	87	86	83	85
Expenses (bil. dol.): [5]									
All hospitals	91.9	234.9	320.3	330.5	342.3	355.5	372.9	395.4	426.8
Nonfederal [1]	84.0	219.6	300.0	308.3	319.6	332.9	349.2	371.5	399.3
Community hospitals [2]	76.9	203.7	285.6	293.8	305.8	318.8	335.2	356.6	383.7
Nongovernmental nonprofit	55.8	150.7	209.6	216.0	225.3	238.0	251.5	267.1	287.3
For profit	5.8	18.8	26.7	28.4	31.2	31.7	31.2	35.0	37.3
State and local government	15.2	34.2	49.3	49.4	49.3	49.1	52.5	54.5	59.1
Long-term general and special	1.2	2.7	2.2	2.3	2.5	2.6	2.8	2.8	3.3
Psychiatric	5.8	12.9	11.7	12.0	11.0	11.2	11.0	11.9	13.2
Tuberculosis	0.1	0.1	0.4	(Z)	0.1	(Z)	(Z)	(Z)	(Z)
Federal	7.9	15.2	20.2	22.3	22.7	22.6	23.7	23.9	27.5
Personnel (1,000): [6]									
All hospitals	3,492	4,063	4,273	4,276	4,333	4,407	4,369	4,454	4,535
Nonfederal [1]	3,213	3,760	3,971	3,981	4,036	4,071	4,074	4,157	4,236
Community hospitals [2]	2,873	3,420	3,714	3,725	3,790	3,831	3,838	3,911	3,987
Nongovernmental nonprofit	2,086	2,533	2,702	2,711	2,765	2,834	2,862	2,919	2,971
For profit	189	273	343	359	385	383	362	378	379
State and local government	598	614	670	654	640	614	614	614	637
Long-term general and special	56	55	38	40	37	37	42	41	44
Psychiatric	275	280	215	212	204	198	191	200	201
Tuberculosis	3	1	1	1	1	1	1	1	1
Federal	279	303	301	295	296	336	295	297	299
Outpatient visits (mil.)	263.0	368.2	483.2	505.5	520.6	545.5	573.5	592.7	612.0
Emergency	82.0	92.8	99.9	97.6	97.4	99.0	103.8	106.9	109.8

Z Less than 500 beds or $50 million.   [1] Includes hospital units of institutions.   [2] Short term (average length of stay less than 30 days) general and special (e.g., obstetrics and gynecology; eye, ear, nose and throat; rehabilitation etc. except psychiatric, tuberculosis, alcoholism and chemical dependency). Excludes hospital units of institutions.   [3] Beginning 1990, number of beds at end of reporting period; prior years, average number in 12 month period.   [4] Based on Census Bureau estimated resident population as of July 1. Estimates reflect revisions based on the 2000 Census of Population.   [5] Excludes new construction.   [6] Includes full-time equivalents of part-time personnel.

Source: Health Forum, An American Hospital Association Company, Chicago, IL, *Hospital Statistics 2003 Edition*, and prior years (copyright). <http://www.healthforum.com/>.

No. 171. Average Cost to Community Hospitals Per Patient: 1980 to 2001

[In dollars, except percent. Covers nonfederal short-term general or special hospitals (excluding psychiatric or tuberculosis hospitals and hospital units of institutions). Total cost per patient based on total hospital expenses (payroll, employee benefits, professional fees, supplies, etc.). Data have been adjusted for outpatient visits]

Type of expense and hospital	1980	1990	1994	1995	1996	1997	1998	1999	2000	2001
Average cost per day, total	245	687	931	968	1,006	1,033	1,067	1,103	1,149	1,217
Annual percent change [1]	12.9	7.8	5.7	4.0	4.0	2.6	3.3	3.3	4.2	5.9
Nongovernmental nonprofit	246	692	950	994	1,042	1,074	1,111	1,140	1,182	1,255
For profit	257	752	924	947	946	962	968	999	1,057	1,121
State and local government	239	635	859	878	903	914	949	1,007	1,064	1,114
Average cost per stay, total	1,851	4,947	6,230	6,216	6,225	6,262	6,386	6,512	6,649	6,980
Nongovernmental nonprofit	1,902	5,001	6,257	6,279	6,344	6,393	6,526	6,608	6,717	7,052
For profit	1,676	4,727	5,529	5,425	5,207	5,219	5,262	5,350	5,642	5,972
State and local government	1,750	4,838	6,513	6,445	6,419	6,475	6,612	6,923	7,106	7,400

[1] Change from immediate prior year.

No. 172. Community Hospitals—States: 1990 to 2001

[For beds, 928.1 represents 928,100. For definition of community hospitals see footnote 2, Table 170]

State	Number of hospitals 1990	2000	2001	Beds (1,000) 1990	2000	2001	Patients admitted (1,000) 2000	2001	Average daily census [1] (1,000) 2000	2001	Outpatient visits (mil.) 2000	2001
United States	5,384	4,915	4,908	928.1	823.6	826.0	33,089	33,813	525.7	532.0	521.4	538.5
Alabama	120	108	107	18.6	16.4	16.6	680	684	9.8	9.8	8.0	7.8
Alaska	16	18	19	1.2	1.4	1.4	47	49	0.8	0.8	1.3	1.4
Arizona	61	61	61	9.9	10.9	10.7	539	562	6.8	6.9	5.3	5.1
Arkansas	86	83	83	10.9	9.8	9.5	368	371	5.7	5.6	4.4	4.5
California	445	389	384	80.5	72.7	73.2	3,315	3,332	47.8	48.7	44.9	48.5
Colorado	69	69	66	10.4	9.4	9.4	397	413	5.4	5.8	6.7	6.9
Connecticut	35	35	35	9.6	7.7	8.0	349	360	5.8	6.0	6.7	6.5
Delaware	8	5	5	2.0	1.8	1.9	83	83	1.4	1.4	1.5	1.5
District of Columbia	11	11	10	4.5	3.3	3.4	129	131	2.5	2.5	1.3	1.4
Florida	224	202	202	50.7	51.2	51.8	2,119	2,207	31.0	31.5	21.8	20.8
Georgia	163	151	147	25.7	23.9	24.1	863	903	15.0	15.0	11.2	12.0
Hawaii	18	21	23	2.9	3.1	3.2	100	108	2.3	2.4	2.5	3.2
Idaho	43	42	40	3.2	3.5	3.4	123	122	1.8	1.9	2.2	2.6
Illinois	210	196	192	45.8	37.3	36.8	1,531	1,559	22.4	22.4	25.1	25.3
Indiana	113	109	110	21.8	19.2	19.0	700	718	10.8	10.8	14.1	14.4
Iowa	124	115	116	14.3	11.8	11.5	360	370	6.8	6.8	9.2	9.4
Kansas	138	129	133	11.8	10.8	11.2	310	322	5.7	5.9	5.3	5.4
Kentucky	107	105	103	15.9	14.8	15.0	582	595	9.1	9.1	8.7	8.7
Louisiana	140	123	125	19.1	17.5	18.0	654	683	9.8	10.2	10.0	10.1
Maine	39	37	37	4.5	3.7	3.8	147	149	2.4	2.5	3.2	3.5
Maryland	52	49	49	13.6	11.2	11.2	587	608	8.2	8.1	6.0	6.3
Massachusetts	101	80	80	21.7	16.6	16.5	740	767	11.7	12.0	16.7	18.8
Michigan	176	146	145	33.9	26.1	25.6	1,106	1,122	16.9	16.7	24.9	26.0
Minnesota	152	135	133	19.4	16.7	16.5	571	586	11.2	11.2	7.3	8.6
Mississippi	103	95	96	12.9	13.6	13.7	425	436	8.0	8.2	3.7	4.1
Missouri	135	119	117	24.3	20.1	19.3	773	801	11.7	11.5	14.8	14.2
Montana	55	52	53	4.6	4.3	4.5	99	103	2.9	2.9	2.6	2.6
Nebraska	90	85	84	8.5	8.2	8.3	209	207	4.8	5.0	3.4	3.4
Nevada	21	22	24	3.4	3.8	4.1	199	208	2.7	2.8	2.2	2.1
New Hampshire	27	28	28	3.5	2.9	2.9	111	116	1.7	1.7	2.8	2.9
New Jersey	95	80	78	28.9	25.3	24.6	1,074	1,084	17.3	16.8	16.3	18.4
New Mexico	37	35	35	4.2	3.5	3.6	174	164	2.0	2.1	3.1	3.4
New York	235	215	212	74.7	66.4	67.3	2,416	2,411	52.1	52.0	46.4	45.6
North Carolina	120	113	111	22.0	23.1	23.8	971	973	16.0	16.3	12.4	13.4
North Dakota	50	42	40	4.4	3.9	3.7	89	92	2.3	2.2	1.7	1.9
Ohio	190	163	166	43.1	33.8	33.3	1,404	1,439	20.6	20.4	26.9	28.4
Oklahoma	111	108	108	12.4	11.1	11.2	429	435	6.2	6.5	4.7	4.6
Oregon	70	59	60	8.1	6.6	6.7	330	335	3.9	4.0	7.3	7.7
Pennsylvania	238	207	205	52.6	42.3	42.1	1,796	1,809	28.8	28.4	31.8	32.1
Rhode Island	12	11	11	3.2	2.4	2.4	119	121	1.7	1.7	2.1	2.2
South Carolina	69	63	62	11.3	11.5	11.3	495	505	8.0	8.0	7.8	7.6
South Dakota	53	48	50	4.2	4.3	4.5	99	104	2.8	2.9	1.7	1.8
Tennessee	134	121	123	23.6	20.6	20.6	737	751	11.5	11.3	10.3	9.5
Texas	428	403	411	59.2	55.9	56.3	2,367	2,461	33.1	34.6	29.4	31.5
Utah	42	42	42	4.4	4.3	4.4	194	203	2.4	2.5	4.5	4.4
Vermont	15	14	14	1.7	1.7	1.7	52	55	1.1	1.1	1.2	1.3
Virginia	97	88	87	20.0	16.9	16.8	727	744	11.4	11.6	9.5	9.7
Washington	91	84	84	12.0	11.1	11.3	505	523	6.6	6.8	9.6	9.4
West Virginia	59	57	57	8.4	8.0	7.9	288	297	4.8	4.9	5.2	5.8
Wisconsin	129	118	121	18.6	15.3	15.6	558	579	9.1	9.4	10.9	11.0
Wyoming	27	24	24	2.2	1.9	1.9	48	48	1.1	1.0	0.9	0.8

[1] Inpatients receiving treatment each day; excludes newborn.

Source of Tables 171 and 172: Health Forum, An American Hospital Association Company, Chicago, IL, *Hospital Statistics 2003 Edition*, and prior years (copyright). <http://www.healthforum.com/>

No. 173. Hospital Use Rates by Type of Hospital: 1980 to 2001

Type of hospital	1980	1990	1995	1997	1998	1999	2000	2001
Community hospitals:[1]								
Admissions per 1,000 population[2]	159	125	116	116	115	116	117	118
Admissions per bed	37	34	35	37	38	39	40	40
Average length of stay[3] (days)	7.6	7.2	6.5	6.1	6.0	5.9	5.8	5.7
Outpatient visits per admission	5.6	9.7	13.4	14.3	14.9	15.3	15.8	15.9
Outpatient visits per 1,000 population[2]	890	1,207	1,556	1,681	1,754	1,816	1,852	1,890
Surgical operations (million)[4]	18.8	21.9	23.2	24.2	25.3	26.3	26.1	26.5
Number per admission	0.5	0.7	0.7	0.8	0.8	0.8	0.8	0.8
Nonfederal psychiatric:								
Admissions per 1,000 population[2]	2.5	2.9	2.7	2.7	2.7	2.4	2.4	2.6
Days in hospital per 1,000 population[2]	295	190	122	107	101	94	93	94

[1] For definition of community hospitals, see footnote 2, Table 170. [2] Based on U.S. Census Bureau estimated resident population as of July 1. Estimates reflect revisions based on the 2000 Census of Population. [3] Number of inpatient days divided by number of admissions. [4] 18.8 represents 18,800,000.

Source: Health Forum, An American Hospital Association Company, Chicago, IL, *Hospital Statistics 2003 Edition*, and prior years (copyright).

No. 174. Hospital Utilization Rates: 1990 to 2001

[30,788 represents 30,788,000. Represents estimates of inpatients discharged from noninstitutional, short-stay hospitals, exclusive of federal hospitals. Excludes newborn infants. Based on sample data collected from the National Hospital Discharge Survey, a sample survey of hospital records of patients discharged in year shown; subject to sampling variability]

Item and sex	1990	1994	1995	1996	1997	1998	1999	2000	2001
Patients discharged (1,000)	30,788	30,843	30,722	30,545	30,914	31,827	32,132	31,706	32,653
Patients discharged per 1,000 persons, total[1]	122	117	116	114	114	117	117	114	115
Male	100	96	94	92	93	93	95	92	93
Female	143	138	136	135	135	139	138	135	137
Days of care per 1,000 persons, total[1]	784	674	620	597	582	589	581	560	562
Male	694	599	551	533	508	517	510	491	490
Female	869	745	686	657	653	658	649	627	631
Average stay (days)	6.4	5.7	5.4	5.2	5.1	5.1	5.0	4.9	4.9
Male	6.9	6.2	5.8	5.8	5.5	5.5	5.4	5.3	5.3
Female	6.1	5.4	5.0	4.9	4.8	4.7	4.7	4.6	4.6

[1] Based on U.S. Census Bureau estimated civilian population as of July 1. Beginning with 1997 data, rates are based on the U.S. Census Bureau estimates of the civilian population that have been adjusted for net underenumeration in the 1990 census. Population estimates for the 2000 census were first used to calculate rates in 2001. The 2000 population estimates were based on the 1990 census.

Source: U.S. National Center for Health Statistics, *Vital and Health Statistics*, Series 13; and unpublished data.

No. 175. Hospital Discharges and Days of Care: 1995 and 2001

[30,722 represents 30,722,000. See headnote, Table 174. For composition of regions, see map, inside front cover]

Age, race, and region	Discharges Number (1,000) 1995	2001	Per 1,000 persons[1] 1995	2001	Days of care per 1,000 persons[1] 1995	2001	Average stay (days) 1995	2001
Total	30,722	32,653	116	115	620	562	5.4	4.9
Age:								
Under 1 year old	790	850	198	211	1,083	1,168	5.5	5.5
1 to 4 years old	744	731	46	48	153	157	3.3	3.3
5 to 14 years old	872	978	22	24	99	106	4.5	4.4
15 to 24 years old	2,943	2,968	80	76	271	265	3.4	3.5
25 to 34 years old	4,201	3,815	102	97	354	324	3.5	3.3
35 to 44 years old	3,449	3,560	81	80	381	345	4.7	4.3
45 to 64 years old	6,168	7,224	119	112	657	565	5.5	5.0
65 to 74 years old	4,832	4,692	260	256	1,685	1,450	6.5	5.7
75 years old and over	6,724	7,834	459	461	3,248	2,734	7.1	5.9
Race:								
White	19,951	20,330	91	89	491	431	5.4	4.9
Black	3,887	3,900	113	108	658	593	5.8	5.5
Asian/Pacific Islander	486	438	51	40	278	210	5.4	5.2
American Indian/Eskimo/Aleut	107	161	46	59	240	282	5.2	4.8
Region:								
Northeast	7,051	7,026	136	(NA)	858	(NA)	6.3	5.6
Midwest	6,994	7,429	113	(NA)	586	(NA)	5.2	4.3
South	11,373	12,744	122	(NA)	643	(NA)	5.3	4.9
West	5,303	5,453	91	(NA)	410	(NA)	4.5	4.5

NA Not available. [1] Based on Census Bureau estimated civilian population.

Source: U.S. National Center for Health Statistics, *Vital and Health Statistics*, Series 13; and unpublished data.

No. 176. Hospital Discharges and Days of Care by Sex: 2001

[12,852 represents 12,852,000. Represents estimates of inpatients discharged from noninstitutional, short-stay hospitals, exclusive of federal hospitals. Diagnostic categories are based on the International Classification of Diseases, Ninth Revision, Clinical Modification. See headnote, Table 174]

Age and first-listed diagnosis	Discharges Number (1,000)	Discharges Per 1,000 persons [1]	Days of care per 1,000 persons [1]	Average stay (days)	Age and first-listed diagnosis	Discharges Number (1,000)	Discharges Per 1,000 persons [1]	Days of care per 1,000 persons [1]	Average stay (days)
MALE					**FEMALE**				
All ages [2]	12,852	100.2	535.7	5.3	All ages [2]	19,801	130.9	592.9	4.5
Under 18 years [3]	1,629	43.8	200.7	4.6	Under 18 years [3]	1,523	43.0	184.3	4.3
Pneumonia	229	6.2	21.2	3.4	Pneumonia	176	5.0	17.1	3.5
Injuries and poisoning	192	5.2	21.3	4.1	Injuries and poisoning	120	3.4	[5]12.1	[5]3.6
Asthma	76	2.0	4.8	2.3	Asthma	45	1.3	2.8	2.2
18 to 44 years [3]	2,573	46.2	225.9	4.9	18 to 44 years [3]	7,178	129.1	421.5	3.3
Injuries and poisoning	412	7.4	35.7	4.8	Delivery	3,685	66.3	167.0	2.5
Serious mental illness [4]	[5]338	[5]6.1	[5]47.7	[5]7.9	Serious mental illness [4]	[5]338	[5]6.1	[5]45.4	[5]7.5
Alcohol and drug [6]	225	4.0	20.4	5.1	Injuries and poisoning	267	4.8	18.7	3.9
Diseases of heart	150	2.7	10.0	3.7					
45 to 64 years [3]	3,519	112.2	578.0	5.2	45 to 64 years [3]	3,705	111.9	551.6	4.9
Diseases of heart	768	24.5	98.4	4.0	Diseases of heart	497	15.0	64.5	4.3
Injuries and poisoning	307	9.8	50.0	5.1	Injuries and poisoning	280	8.5	45.9	5.4
Malignant neoplasms	199	6.3	48.5	7.7	Malignant neoplasms	203	6.1	37.6	6.1
Serious mental illness [4]	[5]148	[5]4.7	[5]43.9	[5]9.3	Serious mental illness [4]	184	5.6	58.1	10.4
Diabetes	107	3.4	18.7	5.5					
Cerebrovascular diseases	102	3.3	18.5	5.7	65 to 74 years [3]	2,527	252.3	1,431.5	5.7
					Diseases of heart	489	48.8	237.9	4.9
65 to 74 years [3]	2,165	260.9	1,473.0	5.6	Injuries and poisoning	189	18.9	117.9	6.2
Diseases of heart	566	68.2	315.0	4.6	Malignant neoplasms	147	14.7	106.7	7.3
Malignant neoplasms	149	18.0	136.2	7.6	Cerebrovascular diseases	118	11.7	61.8	5.3
Injuries and poisoning	143	17.3	127.5	7.4	Pneumonia	115	11.5	74.7	6.5
75 years old and older [3]	2,966	471.9	2,801.1	5.9	75 years old and older [3]	4,867	455.2	2,694.5	5.9
Diseases of heart	727	115.6	584.8	5.1	Diseases of heart	1,010	94.4	476.7	5.0
Pneumonia	248	39.5	254.5	6.4	Injuries and poisoning	503	47.1	284.9	6.1
Injuries and poisoning	199	31.6	206.2	6.5	Cerebrovascular diseases	301	28.2	146.9	5.2
Malignant neoplasms	156	24.8	171.7	6.9	Pneumonia	286	26.7	180.8	6.8
Cerebrovascular diseases	157	24.9	129.4	5.2	Malignant neoplasms	192	18.0	136.2	7.6

[1] Based on Census Bureau estimated civilian population as of July 1 Population figures are adjusted for net underenumeration using the 1990 National Population Adjustment Matrix from the U.S. Census Bureau. [2] Average length of stay and rates per 1,000 population are age-adjusted to the year 2000 standard using five age groups; Under 18 years, 18-44 years, 45-64 years, 65-74 years, and 75 years and over. [3] Includes other first-listed diagnoses not shown separately. [4] Excludes discharges from other types of facilities such as the Dept. of Veterans Affairs or long-term hospitals. [5] Estimates are considered unreliable. [6] Includes abuse, dependence, and withdrawal. Excludes discharges from other types of facilities such as the Dept. of Veterans Affairs or day treatment programs.

Source: U.S. National Center for Health Statistics, Health, United States 2003.

No. 177. Organ Transplants and Grafts: 1990 to 2002

[As of end of year. Based on reports of procurement programs and transplant centers in the United States, except as noted]

Procedure	Number of procedures 1990	1995	1999	2000	2001	2002	Number of centers 1990	2002	Number of people waiting, 2002	1-year patient survival rates, 2001 (percent)
Transplant: [1]										
Heart	2,095	2,342	2,159	2,172	2,202	2,153	148	140	3,751	85.9
Heart-lung	52	69	49	47	27	33	79	78	195	73.9
Lung	203	869	884	955	1,054	1,042	70	75	3,913	77.1
Liver	2,631	3,818	4,594	4,816	5,177	5,326	85	123	17,620	85.7
Kidney	9,358	10,957	12,455	13,258	14,152	14,741	232	248	54,933	(NA)
Kidney-pancreas	459	915	933	910	884	903	(NA)	(NA)	2,400	94.0
Pancreas	60	103	350	420	468	546	84	139	1,420	93.9
Intestine	1	21	37	29	112	107	(NA)	38	177	70.1
Multi-organ	71	124	169	213	228	309	(NA)	(NA)	(NA)	(NA)
Cornea grafts	[2]40,631	44,652	45,765	46,949	46,532	[3]46,625	[4]107	[4]93	(NA)	(NA)
Bone grafts	350,000	450,000	650,000	800,000	875,000	(NA)	30	(NA)	(X)	(NA)
Skin grafts [5]	5,500	5,500	10,000	15,000	20,000	(NA)	25	(NA)	(X)	(NA)

NA Not available. X Not applicable. [1] Kidney-pancreas and heart-lung transplants are each counted as one organ. All other multi-organ transplants, excluding kidney-pancreas and heart-lung, are included in the multi-organ row. The data and analyses reported in the 2002 Annual Report of the U.S. Organ Procurement and Transplantation Network and the Scientific Registry of Transplant Receipients have been supplied by UNOS under contract with HHS. The authors alone are responsible for the reporting and interpretation of these data. Data subject to change based on future data submission or correction. [2] 1990, number of procedures and eye banks include Canada. [3] Number of procedures does not include Canada. [4] Eye banks. [5] Procedure data are shown in terms of square feet.

Source: Based on the Organ Procurement and Transplant Network (OPTN) data as of June 6, 2003. U.S. Department of Health and Human Services, Health Resources and Services Administration, Office of Special Programs, Division of Transplantation, Rockville, MD; United Network for Organ Sharing, Richmond, VA; University Renal Research and Education Association, Ann Arbor, MI; American Association of Tissue Banks, McLean, VA; and Eye Bank Association of America, Washington, DC; and unpublished data.

Health and Nutrition 125

No. 178. Procedures for Inpatients Discharged From Short-Stay Hospitals: 1990 to 2001

[23,051 represents 23,051,000. Excludes newborn infants and discharges from federal hospitals. See headnote, Table 174]

Sex and type of procedure	Number of procedures (1,000)				Rate per 1,000 population [1]			
	1990	1995	2000	2001	1990	1995	2000	2001
Surgical procedures, total [2][3]	23,051	22,530	23,244	24,114	92.4	86.2	83.6	85.0
Cardiac catheterization	995	1,068	1,221	1,208	4.0	4.1	4.4	4.3
Removal of coronary artery obstruction [3]	285	434	1,025	1,051	1.2	1.7	3.7	3.7
Reduction of fracture [4]	609	577	628	638	2.4	2.2	2.3	2.3
Coronary artery bypass graft	392	573	519	516	1.6	2.2	1.9	1.8
Male, total [2]	8,538	8,388	8,689	9,032	70.6	65.9	63.9	65.1
Cardiac catheterization	620	660	732	710	5.1	5.2	5.4	5.1
Removal of coronary artery obstruction [3]	200	285	655	689	1.7	2.2	4.8	5.0
Coronary artery bypass graft	286	423	371	365	2.4	3.3	2.7	2.6
Female, total [2]	14,513	14,142	14,556	15,082	113.0	105.3	102.4	104.2
Repair of current obstetric laceration	795	964	1,136	1,185	6.2	7.2	8.0	8.2
Cesarean section	945	785	855	973	7.4	5.8	6.0	6.7
Hysterectomy	591	583	633	649	4.6	4.3	4.5	4.5
Diagnostic and other nonsurgical procedures [5]	17,455	17,278	16,737	16,925	70.0	66.1	60.2	59.7
Angiocardiography and arteriography [6]	1,735	1,834	2,005	1,936	7.0	7.0	7.2	6.8
Respiratory therapy	1,164	1,127	991	1,013	4.7	4.3	3.6	3.6
Diagnostic ultrasound	1,608	1,181	886	825	6.4	4.5	3.2	2.9
CAT scan [7]	1,506	967	754	763	6.0	3.7	2.7	2.7
Male, total [5]	7,378	7,261	6,965	6,973	61.0	57.1	51.2	50.2
Angiocardiography and arteriography [6]	1,051	1,076	1,157	1,051	8.7	8.5	8.5	7.6
Respiratory therapy	586	572	507	519	4.9	4.5	3.7	3.7
CAT scan [7]	736	473	345	357	6.1	3.7	2.5	2.6
Female, total [5]	10,077	10,016	9,772	9,952	78.5	74.6	68.8	68.7
Manual assisted delivery	750	866	898	941	5.9	6.5	6.3	6.5
Fetal EKG and fetal monitoring	1,377	935	750	772	10.8	7.0	5.5	5.3
Diagnostic ultrasound	941	682	501	461	7.3	5.1	3.5	3.2

[1] Based on Census Bureau estimated civilian population as of July 1. Population estimates for the 1980s do not reflect revised estimates based on the 1990 Census of Population. Beginning in 1997 population figures are adjusted for net underenumeration in the 1990 census using the 1990 National Population Adjustment Matrix from the Census Bureau. Population estimates for the 2000 census were first used to calculate rates for the 2001 data. The 2000 population estimates were based on the 1990 census.
[2] Includes other types of surgical procedures not shown separately. [3] Beginning 1999 includes separately coded "insertion of stent." [4] Excluding skull, nose, and jaw. [5] Includes other nonsurgical procedures not shown separately. [6] Using contrast material. [7] Computerized axial tomography.

Source: U.S. National Center for Health Statistics, *Vital and Health Statistics*, Series 13; and unpublished data.

No. 179. Hospital Utilization Measures for HIV Patients: 1985 to 2001

[HIV represents human immunodeficiency virus. See headnote, Table 174]

Measure of utilization	Unit	1985	1990	1995	1999	2000	2001
Number of patients discharged [1]	1,000	23	146	249	180	173	185
Rate of patient discharges [2]	Rate	1.0	5.8	9.4	6.5	6.2	6.5
Number of days of care	1,000	387	2,188	2,326	1,310	1,257	1,435
Rate of days of care [2]	Rate	16.3	86.9	87.6	47.5	45.2	50.6
Average length of stay [3]	Days	17.1	14.9	9.3	7.3	7.3	7.8

[1] Comparisons beginning 1990 with data for earlier years should be made with caution as estimates of change may reflect improvements in the 1988 sample design rather than true changes in hospital use. [2] Per 10,000 population. Based on Census Bureau estimated civilian population as of July 1. Population estimates for the 1980's do not reflect revised estimates based on the 1990 Census of Population. Beginning 1998, rates are based on civilian population estimates that have been adjusted for net underenumeration in the 1990 census. Population estimates for the 2000 census were first used to calculate rates in 2001. The 2000 population estimates were based on the 1990 census. [3] For similar data on all patients, see Table 174.

Source: National Center for Health Statistics, *Vital and Health Statistics*, Series 13; and unpublished data.

No. 180. Skilled Nursing Facilities: 1980 to 2001

[448 represents 448,000. Covers facilities and beds certified for participation under medicare as of midyear. Includes facilities which have transfer agreements with one or more participating hospitals, and are engaged primarily in providing skilled nursing care and related services for the rehabilitation of injured, disabled, or sick persons]

Item	Unit	1980	1990	1995	1998	1999	2000	2001
Skilled nursing facilities	Number	5,155	9,008	13,281	15,037	14,913	14,841	14,755
Beds	1,000	448	512	657	723	837	939	1,050
Per 1,000 medicare enrollees [1]	Rate	16.0	15.2	17.7	18.8	21.6	24.0	28.5

[1] Based on total number of beneficiaries enrolled in the medicare hospital insurance program as of July 1 of year stated.

Source: U.S. Centers for Medicare and Medicaid Services, Providers and Suppliers of Health Services, 1980; and unpublished data.

No. 181. Home Health and Hospice Care Agencies by Selected Characteristics: 2000

[In percent, except as indicated (11.4 represents 11,400). Based on the National Home and Hospice Care Survey. Home health care is provided to individuals and families in their place of residence. Hospice care is available in both the home and inpatient settings. See source for details. For composition of regions, see map, inside front cover]

Agency characteristic	Agencies, total	Current patients [1] Total	Current patients [1] Home health care	Current patients [1] Hospice care	Discharges [2] Total	Discharges [2] Home health care	Discharges [2] Hospice care
Total (1,000)	11.4	1,460.8	1,355.3	105.5	7,800.1	7,179.0	621.1
PERCENT DISTRIBUTION							
Ownership:							
Proprietary	44.7	33.2	34.1	22.3	24.2	25.0	15.8
Voluntary nonprofit	42.5	57.8	56.6	73.2	66.9	65.8	80.0
Government and other	12.8	9.0	9.3	4.4	8.9	9.3	4.2
Region:							
Northeast	15.9	31.2	31.9	22.0	39.3	41.0	20.1
Midwest	26.1	20.6	20.7	19.5	18.4	17.8	25.7
South	42.7	37.3	37.3	37.7	29.8	29.5	33.7
West	15.3	10.9	10.1	20.8	12.5	11.7	20.6

[1] Patients on the rolls of the agency as of midnight the day prior to the survey. [2] Patients removed from the rolls of the agency during the 12 months prior to the day of the survey. A patient could be included more than once if the individual had more than one episode of care during the year.

Source: U.S. National Center for Health Statistics, unpublished data.

No. 182. Home Health and Hospice Care Patients by Selected Characteristics: 2000

[In percent, except as indicated (1,460.8 represents 1,460,800). See headnote, Table 181]

Item	Current patients [1] Total	Current patients [1] Home health care	Current patients [1] Hospice care	Discharges [2] Total	Discharges [2] Home health care	Discharges [2] Hospice care
Total (1,000)	1,460.8	1,355.3	105.5	7,800.1	7,179.0	621.1
PERCENT DISTRIBUTION						
Age: [3]						
Under 45 years old	13.2	13.9	4.5	13.7	14.5	3.9
45-54 years old	6.5	6.7	5.1	6.2	6.3	5.0
55-64 years old	8.9	8.9	8.9	10.2	10.0	11.5
65 years old and over	71.3	70.5	81.4	70.0	69.1	79.6
65-69 years old	7.1	7.1	7.3	9.4	9.4	10.1
70-74 years old	10.2	10.2	9.9	11.1	10.8	14.5
75-79 years old	17.1	16.8	20.9	15.5	15.8	12.5
80-84 years old	14.6	14.5	16.1	16.2	16.2	15.9
85 years old and over	22.3	21.9	27.2	17.8	17.0	26.5
Sex:						
Male	35.8	35.2	42.6	37.3	36.2	49.8
Female	64.2	64.8	57.4	62.7	63.8	50.2
Race:						
White	76.3	76.0	82.8	79.5	79.1	84.1
Black and other [4]	14.6	14.8	12.3	12.2	12.4	10.3
Black	12.4	12.6	10.6	9.8	10.0	8.1
Unknown	9.0	9.4	5.0	8.3	8.5	5.5
Marital status: [3]						
Married	32.7	31.9	42.7	40.9	40.3	47.2
Widowed	34.9	34.8	36.7	29.9	29.6	33.2
Divorced or separated	5.5	5.5	6.3	5.3	5.2	5.7
Never married	17.4	18.0	9.2	14.7	15.3	7.7
Unknown	9.5	9.9	5.0	9.3	9.5	6.2
Primary admission diagnosis:						
Neoplasms	8.6	5.1	52.6	9.7	5.5	58.4
Endocrine, nutritional and metabolic and immunity disorders	8.8	9.5	0.3	5.8	6.2	0.3
Diseases of the nervous system and sense organs	2.3	2.4	0.4	0.7	0.7	0.2
Diseases of the circulatory system	23.0	23.6	15.6	21.4	22.3	11.7
Diseases of the respiratory system	6.8	6.8	6.5	9.2	9.4	6.9
Diseases of the musculoskeletal system and connective tissue	9.1	9.8	0.1	11.2	12.1	1.0
Injuries and poisoning	9.6	10.2	0.9	11.3	12.3	0.5

[1] Patients on the rolls of the agency as of midnight the day prior to the survey. [2] Patients removed from the rolls of the agency during the 12 months prior to the day of the survey. A patient could be included more than once if the individual had more than one episode of care during the year. [3] For current patients, current age or marital status; for discharged patients, age or marital status at time of discharge. [4] Patients with multiple races are coded in the "other" category.

Source: U.S. National Center for Health Statistics, *Health, United States, 2002*

No. 183. Elderly Home Health Patients: 2000

[1,041 represents 1,041,000. Covers the civilian population 65 years old and over who are home health care patients. Age of patient is based on age at the time of interview. Home health care is provided to individuals and families in their place of residence. Based on the 2000 National Home and Hospice Care Survey]

Item	Current patients [1] Number (1,000)	Current patients [1] Percent	Discharges [2] Number (1,000)	Discharges [2] Percent	Item	Current patients [1] Number (1,000)	Current patients [1] Percent	Discharges [2] Number (1,000)	Discharges [2] Percent
Total 65 yrs. old & over	**1,041**	**100.0**	**5,456**	**100.0**	Own income	61	5.9	85	1.6
Received help with—					Medicare	705	67.8	4,867	89.2
Bathing or showering	544	52.3	2,172	39.8	Medicaid	141	13.5	150	2.8
Dressing	480	46.1	1,900	34.8					
Eating	166	15.9	537	9.9	Services rendered: [5]				
Transferring in/out of					Nursing services	782	75.1	4,672	85.6
a bed or chair	373	35.9	1,737	31.8	Social services	138	13.3	977	17.9
Using the toilet room	289	27.8	1,092	20.0	Counseling	37	3.6	255	4.7
Doing light housework	379	36.4	1,031	18.9	Medications	106	10.2	599	11.0
Managing money	17	1.6	[3]30	[3]0.5	Physical therapy	285	27.4	2,216	40.6
Shopping for groceries or clothes	127	12.2	261	4.8	Homemaker-household services	289	27.8	691	12.7
Using the telephone	31	3.0	113	2.1	Nutrition services	53	5.1	204	3.7
Preparing meals	227	21.8	549	10.1	Physician services	48	4.6	307	5.6
Taking medications	216	20.7	1,017	18.6	Occupational therapy	83	8.0	543	10.0
Primary source of payment: [4] Private insurance	44	4.2	251	4.6	Speech therapy/audiology	19	1.8	102	1.9

[1] Patients on the rolls of the agency as of midnight the day prior to the survey. [2] Patients removed from the rolls of the agency during the 12 months prior to the day of the survey. A patient could be included more than once if the individual had more than one episode of care during the year. [3] Figure does not meet standard of reliability or precision. [4] For current patients, the expected source; for discharges the actual source for the entire episode. [5] For current patients, services currently being provided; for discharges services provided during the 30 days prior to discharge.

Source: U.S. National Center for Health Statistics, unpublished data.

No. 184. Nursing Homes—Selected Characteristics: 1985 to 1999

[Beds: 1,624 represents 1,624,000. Covers licensed and/or certified nursing homes in the conterminous United States that had three or more beds. Based on the 1999 National Nursing Home Survey, a two-stage survey sample of nursing homes and their residents. Subject to sampling variability. For composition of regions, see map, inside front cover]

Characteristic	Nursing homes	Beds Number (1,000)	Beds Per nursing home	Current residents Number (1,000)	Occupancy rate [1]	Admin., medical, therapeutic Number (1,000)	Admin., medical, therapeutic Rate per 100 beds	Nursing Number (1,000)	Nursing Rate per 100 beds
1985	19,100	1,624	85	1,491	91.8	89.4	5.5	704	43.4
1995	16,700	1,771	106	1,549	87.4	90.5	5.1	916	51.7
1997	17,000	1,821	107	1,609	88.4	100.0	5.5	950	52.2
1999, total	**18,000**	**1,965**	**109**	**1,627**	**82.8**	**96.6**	**4.9**	**961**	**48.9**
Ownership:									
Proprietary	12,000	1,291	108	1,048	81.2	60.2	4.6	597	46.2
Voluntary nonprofit	4,800	523	109	446	85.3	29.1	5.6	280	53.5
Government and other	1,200	151	126	133	88.1	7.4	4.7	84	55.6
Certification:									
Medicare and medicaid certified	14,700	1,698	116	1,414	83.3	83.2	4.9	842	49.6
Medicare only	[2]600	49	82	37	75.5	2.8	5.7	26	53.1
Medicaid only	2,100	177	89	143	80.8	9.0	5.1	75	42.4
Not certified	[2]500	40	80	33	82.5	1.6	4.0	18	45.0
Bed size:									
Less than 50 beds	2,000	72	36	59	81.9	7.1	9.9	43	59.7
50-99 beds	7,000	503	72	414	82.3	28.8	5.7	252	50.1
100-199 beds	7,500	998	133	826	82.8	45.0	4.5	476	47.7
200 beds or more	1,400	392	280	328	83.7	15.7	4.0	190	48.5
Region:									
Northeast	3,200	443	138	382	86.2	21.7	4.9	244	55.1
Midwest	6,000	619	103	498	80.4	28.3	4.6	272	43.9
South	6,000	652	109	531	81.6	30.5	4.7	311	47.7
West	2,800	251	90	215	85.7	16.1	6.4	133	53.0
Affiliation: [3]									
Chain	10,800	1,179	109	977	82.9	58.7	5.0	556	47.2
Independent	7,200	781	108	646	82.7	37.7	4.8	404	51.7

[1] Number of residents divided by number of available beds multiplied by 100. [2] Figure does not meet standards of reliability or precision. [3] Excludes a small number of homes, beds, and residents with unknown affiliation.

Source: U.S. National Center for Health Statistics, *Vital and Health Statistics*, Series 13, No. 152.

No. 185. Nursing Home Residents 65 Years Old and Over by Selected Characteristics: 1999

[1,470 represents 1,470,000. Covers licensed and/or certified nursing homes in the conterminous United States that had three or more beds. Based on the National Nursing Home Survey, a two-stage sample survey of nursing homes and their residents. Subject to sampling variability]

Characteristic [1]	Number (1,000)	Percent distribution	Item	Percent of elderly residents	Functional status	Percent of elderly residents receiving assistance
Total [2]	1,470	100.0	Type of aids used:		ADLs: [6]	
			Wheelchair	62.6	Bathing, showering	94.7
Male	378	25.7	Walker	26.1	Dressing	87.5
Female	1,092	74.3			Eating	47.1
					Transferring in or	
65 to 74 years	195	13.3	Vision impaired	28.5	out of beds or chair	30.2
75 to 84 years	518	35.2	Hearing impaired	22.8	Using toilet room	57.6
85 years and over	757	51.5				
Living quarters before admission:			Primary source of payment: [3]		IADLs: [7] Care of personal	
Private residence	447	30.4	Private sources [4]	26.3	possessions	74.3
Retirement home	23	1.6	Medicare	32.8	Managing money	70.7
Board and care, assisted living, and/or residential facility	81	5.5	Medicaid Other [5]	37.5 3.4	Securing personal items	72.9
Nursing home	164	11.1			Using telephone	62.2
Hospital	679	46.2				
Other health facility	76	5.2				

[1] At time of survey. [2] Includes other and/or unknown, not shown separately. [3] At admission. [4] Includes private insurance, own income, family support, social security benefits, and retirement funds. [5] Includes supplemental security income, other government assistance or welfare, religious organizations, foundations, agencies, Veterans Administration contract, pensions, or other compensation, payment source not yet determined, and other and unknown sources. [6] Activities of daily living. [7] Instrumental activities of daily living.

Source: U.S. National Center for Health Statistics, *Vital and Health Statistics*, Series 13, No. 152.

No. 186. Mental Health Facilities—Summary by Type of Facility: 1998

[Beds: 267.7 represents 267,700. Facilities, beds and inpatients as of year-end; excludes private psychiatric office practice and psychiatric service modes of all types in hospitals or outpatient clinics of federal agencies other than U.S. Dept. of Veterans Affairs. Excludes data from Puerto Rico, Virgin Islands, Guam, and other territories]

Type of facility	Number of facilities	Inpatient beds Total (1,000)	Rate [1]	Inpatients Total (1,000)	Rate [1]	Inpatient care episodes [2] (1,000)
Total	3,729	267.7	99.5	221.2	80.3	2,600
Mental hospitals:						
State and county	229	68.9	25.6	63.8	21.2	269
Private [3]	809	65.3	24.3	49.9	19.3	658
General hospitals [4]	1,593	54.4	20.2	37.0	13.8	1,195
Veterans Administration [5]	123	17.0	6.3	14.3	4.0	242
Other [6]	975	62.1	23.1	56.2	22.0	236

[1] Rate per 100,000 population. Based on Census Bureau estimated civilian population as of July 1. [2] "Inpatient care episodes" is defined as the number of residents in inpatient facilities at the beginning of the year plus the total additions to inpatient facilities during the year. [3] Includes residential treatment centers for emotionally disturbed children. [4] Nonfederal hospitals with separate psychiatric services. [5] Includes U.S. Department of Veterans Affairs (VA) neuropsychiatric hospitals, VA general hospitals with separate psychiatric settings and VA freestanding psychiatric outpatient clinics. [6] Includes other multiservice mental health facilities with two or more settings, which are not elsewhere classified, as well as freestanding partial care facilities which only provide psychiatric partial care services. Number of facilities, expenditures, and staff data also include freestanding psychiatric partial care facilities.

Source: U.S. Substance Abuse and Mental Health Services Administration, Center for Mental Health Services, unpublished data.

No. 187. Injury and Poisoning Episodes and Conditions by Age and Sex: 2001

[24,551 represents 24,551,000. Covers all medically attended injuries and poisonings occurring during the 3-month period prior to the survey interview. Users are strongly cautioned that national prevalence estimates derived from the 2001 NHIS injury and poisoning episode data may be underestimated. For further information go to <ftp://ftp.cdc.gov/pub/HealthStatistics/NCHS/DatasetDocumentation/NHIS/2001/srvydesc.pdf.> There may be more than one condition per episode. Based on the redesigned National Health Interview Survey, a sample survey of the civilian noninstitutionalized population; see Appendix III]

External cause and nature of injury	Both sexes							Male, total	Female, total
	Total	Total, age-adjusted[1]	Under 12 yrs. old	12 to 21 yrs. old	22 to 44 yrs. old	45 to 64 yrs. old	65 yrs. old and over		
EPISODES									
Number (1,000)	24,551	(X)	3,835	4,706	8,199	5,119	2,691	12,966	11,585
Annual rate per 1,000 population, total [2]	88.8	87.1	79.4	117.2	88.5	81.9	81.9	96.1	81.8
Fall	28.8	28.5	31.9	27.6	19.9	28.5	50.9	26.5	31.0
Struck by or against a person or an object	11.3	10.1	12.9	28.3	8.9	6.2	4.1	15.1	7.6
Transportation[3]	12.5	12.5	5.7	16.8	16.9	12.4	5.2	13.0	12.0
Overexertion	11.7	11.8	1.6	[4]13.6	15.8	15.0	6.3	12.7	10.8
Cutting, piercing instruments	7.0	6.8	6.6	9.9	7.5	7.0	2.5	[4]9.0	5.1
Poisoning	3.2	3.1	6.6	3.1	[4]2.8	1.3	[4]2.8	[4]2.6	3.7
CONDITIONS[5]									
Annual rate per 1,000 population, total [2]	110.4	109.0	85.4	138.7	115.0	111.1	98.5	116.4	104.7
Sprains/strains	20.9	20.7	4.8	31.7	28.1	19.9	12.9	19.3	22.0
Open wounds	14.5	14.1	22.2	19.0	12.4	11.0	10.3	18.5	10.7
Fractures	17.8	17.3	17.5	21.9	13.7	19.4	21.7	19.1	16.5
Contusions	8.0	7.8	4.2	10.2	7.5	8.5	11.0	7.2	8.8

X Not applicable. [1] Data were age-adjusted by the direct method to the 2000 standard population. [2] Includes other items not shown separately. [3] Includes the categories "Motor vehicle traffic"; "Pedal cycle, other"; "Pedestrian, other"; and "Transport, other." [4] Figure does not meet standard of reliability or precision. [5] Poisoning episodes are assumed to have a single condition resulting from the episode.
Source: U.S. National Center for Health Statistics, *Vital and Health Statistics*, unpublished data.

No. 188. Injuries Associated With Consumer Products: 2000

[For products associated with more than 20,000 injuries in 2000. Estimates calculated from a representative sample of hospitals with emergency treatment departments in the United States. Data are estimates of the number of emergency room treated cases nationwide associated with various products. Product involvement does not necessarily mean the product caused the accident. Products were selected from the U.S. Consumer Product Safety Commission's National Electronic Injury Surveillance System]

Product	Number	Product	Number
Home workshop equipment:		Other doors (excl. garage)	346,288
Saws (hand or power)	95,875	Ceilings and walls	290,830
Hammers	40,707	Household cabinets, racks, and shelves	253,186
Household packaging and containers:		Nails, screws, tacks, or bolts	158,982
Household containers and packaging	204,422	Windows	141,031
Bottles and jars	80,186		
Housewares:		Home entertainment equipment:	
Knives	459,898	Televisions	41,462
Tableware and flatware	109,146	Personal use items:	
Drinking glasses	98,924	Footwear	109,681
Home furnishing		Wheelchairs	95,877
Beds	466,464	Jewelry	72,300
Tables[1]	311,208	Yard and garden equipment:	
Chairs	298,894	Lawn mowers	81,888
Bathtubs and showers	201,465	Sports and recreation equipment:	
Ladders	161,627	Trampolines	100,303
Sofas, couches, davenports, etc.	130,540	Skateboards	86,781
Carpets, rugs	122,249	All-terrain vehicles	84,900
Home structures, construction:		Playground climbing equipment	81,060
Stairs or steps	1,048,257	Swimming pools	80,110
Floors or flooring materials	1,033,938	Toys, n.e.c.[2]	78,370

[1] Includes accessories. [2] n.e.c. = not elsewhere classified.

No. 189. Costs of Unintentional Injuries: 2001

[516.9 represents $516,900,000,000. Covers costs of deaths or disabling injuries together with vehicle accidents and fires]

Cost	Amount (bil. dol.)					Percent distribution				
	Total[1]	Motor vehicle	Work	Home	Other	Total[1]	Motor vehicle	Work	Home	Other
Total	516.9	199.6	132.1	118.1	82.1	100.0	100.0	100.0	100.0	100.0
Wage and productivity losses[2]	266.8	73.2	69.2	75.5	52.7	51.6	36.7	52.4	63.9	64.2
Medical expense	95.2	24.9	24.6	26.9	20.2	18.4	12.5	18.6	22.8	24.6
Administrative expenses[3]	74.1	50.4	21.7	5.4	4.0	14.3	25.3	16.4	4.6	4.9
Motor vehicle damage	49.2	49.2	2.0	(NA)	(NA)	9.5	24.6	1.5	(NA)	(NA)
Employer cost[4]	21.4	1.9	11.8	4.5	3.6	4.1	1.0	8.9	3.8	4.4
Fire loss	10.2	(NA)	2.8	5.8	1.6	2.0	(NA)	2.1	4.9	1.9

NA Not available. [1] Excludes duplication between work and motor vehicle ($15.0 billion in 2001). [2] Actual loss of wages and household production, and the present value of future earnings lost. [3] Home and other costs may include costs of administering medical treatment claims for some motor-vehicle injuries filed through health insurance plans. [4] Estimate of the uninsured costs incurred by employers, representing the money value of time lost by noninjured workers.
Source of Tables 188 and 189: National Safety Council, Itasca, IL, *Injury Facts, 2002 Edition* (copyright).

No. 190. Specified Reportable Diseases—Cases Reported: 1980 to 2001

[190.9 represents 190,900. Figures should be interpreted with caution. Although reporting of some of these diseases is incomplete, the figures are of value in indicating trends of disease incidence. Includes cases imported from outside the United States]

Disease	1980	1985	1990	1995	1997	1998	1999	2000	2001
AIDS [1]	([2])	8,249	41,595	71,547	58,492	46,521	45,104	40,758	41,868
Botulism [3]	89	122	92	97	132	116	154	138	155
Brucellosis (undulant fever)	183	153	85	98	98	79	82	87	136
Chickenpox(Varicella) [4] (1,000)	190.9	178.2	173.1	120.6	98.7	82.5	46.0	27.4	22.5
Cholera	9	4	6	23	6	17	6	5	3
Cryptosporidiosis	([2])	([2])	([2])	(NA)	2,566	3,793	2,361	3,128	3,785
Diphtheria	3	3	4	-	4	1	1	1	2
Escherichia coli O157:H7	([2])	([2])	([2])	2,139	2,555	3,161	4,513	4,528	3,287
Haemophilus influenza	([2])	([2])	([2])	1,180	1,162	1,194	1,309	1,398	1,597
Hansen disease (Leprosy)	223	361	198	144	122	108	108	91	79
Hepatitis: B (serum) (1,000)	19.0	26.6	21.1	10.8	10.4	10.3	7.7	8.0	7.8
A (infectious) (1,000)	29.1	23.2	31.4	31.6	30.0	23.2	17.0	13.4	10.6
C/Non-A, non-B (1,000) [5]	([2])	4.2	2.6	4.6	3.8	3.5	3.1	3.2	4.0
Legionellosis	([2])	830	1,370	1,241	1,163	1,355	1,108	1,127	1,168
Lyme disease	([2])	([2])	([2])	11,700	12,801	16,801	16,273	17,730	17,029
Malaria	2,062	1,049	1,292	1,419	2,001	1,611	1,666	1,560	1,544
Measles (1,000)	13.5	2.8	27.8	0.3	0.1	0.1	0.1	0.1	0.1
Meningococcal infections	2,840	2,479	2,451	3,243	3,308	2,725	2,501	2,256	2,333
Mumps (1,000)	8.6	3.0	5.3	0.9	0.7	0.7	0.4	0.3	0.3
Pertussis [6] (1,000)	1.7	3.6	4.6	5.1	6.6	7.4	7.3	7.9	7.6
Plague	18	17	2	9	4	9	9	6	2
Poliomyelitis, acute [7]	9	7	6	7	5	1	-	-	-
Psittacosis	124	119	113	64	33	47	16	17	25
Rabies, animal	6,421	5,565	4,826	7,811	8,105	7,259	6,730	6,934	7,150
Rabies, human	-	-	1	5	2	1	-	4	1
Rocky Mountain spotted fever	1,163	714	651	590	409	365	579	495	695
Rubella [8]	3,904	630	1,125	128	181	364	267	176	23
Salmonellosis [9] (1,000)	33.7	65.3	48.6	46.0	41.9	43.7	40.6	39.6	40.5
Shigellosis [10] (1,000)	19.0	17.1	27.1	32.1	23.1	23.6	17.5	22.9	20.2
Tetanus	95	83	64	41	50	41	40	35	37
Toxic-shock syndrome	([2])	384	322	191	157	138	113	135	127
Trichinosis	131	61	129	29	13	19	12	16	22
Tuberculosis [11] (1,000)	27.7	22.2	25.7	22.9	19.9	18.4	17.5	16.4	16.0
Typhoid fever	510	402	552	369	365	375	346	377	368
Sexually transmitted diseases:									
Gonorrhea (1,000)	1,004	911	690	393	325	356	360	359	362
Syphilis (1,000)	69	68	134	69	47	38	36	32	32
Chlamydia (1,000)	([2])	([2])	([2])	478	527	604	657	702	783
Chancroid	788	2,067	4,212	606	243	189	143	78	38

- Represents zero. NA Not available. [1] Acquired immunodeficiency syndrome was not a notifiable disease until 1984. Figures are shown for years in which cases were reported to the CDC. Beginning 1995, based on revised classification system and expanded surveillance case definition. [2] Disease was not notifiable. [3] Includes foodborne, infant, wound, and unspecified cases. [4] Chickenpox was taken off the nationally notifiable list in 1991, but many states continue to report. [5] Includes some persons positive for antibody to hepatitis C virus who do not have hepatitis. [6] Whooping cough. [7] Revised. Data subject to annual revisions. [8] German measles. Excludes rubella, congenital syndrome. [9] Excludes typhoid fever. [10] Bacillary dysentery. [11] Newly reported active cases.

Source: U.S. Centers for Disease Control and Prevention, Atlanta, GA, *Summary of Notifiable Diseases, United States, 2001, Morbidity and Mortality Weekly Report*, Vol. 50, No. 53, May 2, 2003.

No. 191. Children Immunized Against Specified Diseases: 1995 to 2001

[In percent. Covers civilian noninstitutionalized population ages 19 months to 35 months. Based on estimates from the National Immunization Survey. The health care providers of the children are contacted to verify and/or complete vaccination information. Results are based on race/ethnic status of the child]

Vaccination	1995, total	2000, total	2001 Total	White non-Hispanic [1]	Hispanic	Black non-Hispanic [1]	American Indian/Alaskan Native [1]	Asian/Pacific Islander [1]
Diphtheria-tetanus-pertussis (DTP)/ diphtheria-tetanus:								
3+ doses	95	94	94	95	95	92	93	96
4+ doses	79	82	82	84	83	76	77	84
Polio: 3+ doses	88	90	89	90	91	85	88	90
Hib:[2] 3+ doses	92	93	93	94	93	90	91	92
Measles, mumps, rubella vaccine	90	91	91	92	92	89	94	90
Hepatitis B: 3+ doses	68	90	89	90	90	85	86	90
Varicella [3]	(NA)	68	76	75	80	75	69	82
4+ DTP/3+ polio/1+ MCV [4]	76	78	79	80	79	73	76	80
4+ DTP/3+ polio/1+ MCV/3+ hiB [4]	74	76	77	79	77	71	76	77

NA Not available. [1] Non-Hispanic. [2] Haemophilus B. [3] Data collection for varicella (chicken pox) began in July 1996. [4] MCV=Measles containing vaccine.

Source: U.S. Centers for Disease Control and Prevention, Atlanta, GA, *Morbidity and Mortality Weekly Report*, Vol. 51, No. 30, August 2, 2002; and "Immunization Coverage in the U.S."; <http://www.cdc.gov/nip/coverage/default.htm>.

Health and Nutrition

No. 192. AIDS Cases Reported by Patient Characteristic: 1981 to 2001

[Provisional. For cases reported in the year shown. Includes Puerto Rico, Virgin Islands, Guam, and U.S. Pacific Islands. Acquired immunodeficiency syndrome (AIDS) is a specific group of diseases or conditions which are indicative of severe immunosuppression related to infection with the human immunodeficiency virus (HIV). Data are subject to retrospective changes and may differ from those data in Table 190]

Characteristic	1981-2001, total	2001	Characteristic	1981-2001, total	2001
Total [1]	816,149	43,158	Transmission category:		
Age:			Males, 13 years and over	666,026	31,901
Under 5 years old	6,975	(NA)	Men who have sex with men	368,971	13,265
5 to 12 years old	2,099	(NA)	Injecting drug use	145,750	5,261
13 to 19 years old	4,428	(NA)	Men who have sex with men and injecting drug use	51,293	1,502
20 to 29 years old	133,725	(NA)	Hemophilia/coagulation disorder	5,000	97
30 to 39 years old	362,021	(NA)	Heterosexual contact [2]	22,914	2,213
40 to 49 years old	216,387	(NA)	Heterosexual contact with injecting drug user	9,821	549
50 to 59 years old	66,060	(NA)	Transfusion [3]	5,057	105
60 years old and over	24,453	(NA)	Undetermined [4]	57,220	8,909
Sex:			Females, 13 years and over	141,048	11,082
Male	670,687	31,994	Injecting drug use	55,576	2,212
Female	145,461	11,164	Hemophilia/coagulation disorder	292	9
Race/ethnic group:			Heterosexual contact [2]	35,660	3,205
Non-Hispanic White	343,889	13,237	Heterosexual contact with injecting drug user	21,736	937
Non-Hispanic Black	313,180	21,031	Transfusion [3]	3,914	113
Hispanic	149,752	8,209	Undetermined [4]	23,870	4,606
Asian/Pacific Islander	6,157	430			
American Indian/Alaska Native	2,537	194			

NA Not available. [1] Includes persons with characteristics unknown. [2] Includes persons who have had heterosexual contact with a bisexual male, a person with hemophilia, a transfusion recipient with human immunodeficiency virus (HIV) infection, or an HIV-infected person, risk not specified. [3] Receipt of blood transfusion, blood components, or tissue. [4] Includes persons for whom risk information is incomplete (because of death, refusal to be interviewed, or loss to followup), persons still under investigation, men reported only to have had heterosexual contact with prostitutes, and interviewed persons for whom no specific risk is identified.

Source: U.S. Centers for Disease Control and Prevention, Atlanta, GA, *HIV/AIDS Surveillance Report*, Volume 13, No. 2.

No. 193. Estimated Persons Living With Acquired Immunodeficiency Syndrome (AIDS) by Selected Characteristics: 1995 to 2001

[These numbers do not represent actual cases of persons living with AIDS. Rather, these numbers are point estimates of persons living with AIDS derived by subtracting the estimated cumulative number of deaths in persons with AIDS from the estimated cumulative number of persons with AIDS diagnosed. Estimated AIDS incidence and estimated deaths are adjusted for reporting delays, but not for incomplete reporting]

Characteristic	1995	1997	1998	1999	2000	2001
Total	214,711	265,464	289,709	312,804	337,017	362,827
RACE/ETHNICITY						
White, not Hispanic	90,984	106,508	113,822	120,731	127,690	134,879
Black, not Hispanic	80,771	104,575	116,178	127,169	138,939	151,717
Hispanic	40,397	51,126	56,126	60,953	66,004	71,360
Asian/Pacific Islander	1,617	2,085	2,312	2,574	2,853	3,193
American Indian/Alaska Native	727	903	981	1,063	1,191	1,304
Other	215	267	290	315	340	374
MALE ADULT/ADOLESCENT EXPOSURE CATEGORY						
Male total	173,117	210,607	228,618	245,934	263,484	282,250
Men who have sex with men	100,131	120,951	131,184	141,080	151,212	162,151
Injecting drug use	43,635	52,599	56,450	60,075	63,756	67,366
Men who have sex with men and inject drugs	16,007	18,227	19,265	20,107	20,756	21,520
Hemophilia/coagulation disorder	1,710	1,771	1,803	1,830	([1])	([1])
Heterosexual contact	9,812	15,021	17,725	20,500	23,412	26,660
Receipt of blood transfusion, blood components, or tissue	922	1,070	1,176	1,281	([1])	([1])
Risk not reported or identified	900	968	1,015	1,061	[1]4,348	[1]4,553
FEMALE ADULT/ADOLESCENT EXPOSURE CATEGORY						
Female total	38,152	51,224	57,346	63,072	69,689	76,696
Injecting drug use	18,311	22,557	24,307	25,737	27,395	29,145
Hemophilia/coagulation disorder	133	196	224	243	([1])	([1])
Heterosexual contact	18,498	27,016	31,225	35,366	40,111	45,128
Receipt of blood transfusion, blood components, or tissue	843	1,010	1,107	1,206	([1])	([1])
Risk not reported or identified	367	445	483	520	[1]2,183	[1]2,423
Pediatric [2] exposure category	3,440	3,632	3,745	3,798	3,845	3,881

[1] Statistical estimates for AIDS prevalence in 2000 among persons exposed to HIV through hemophilia/coagulation disorder or receipt of blood transfusion, blood components, or tissue are not presented, but are included in the exposure category "other." The relatively small number of AIDS cases in these categories in recent years does not provide information that results in reliable annual estimates of prevalence. [2] Less than 13 years old.

Source: U.S. Centers for Disease Control and Prevention, Atlanta, GA, unpublished data; <http://www.cdc.gov/hiv/stats /hasrlink.htm>.

No. 194. AIDS, Syphilis, and Tuberculosis Cases Reported by State: 2001

State	AIDS	Syphilis	Tuberculosis	State	AIDS	Syphilis	Tuberculosis	State	AIDS	Syphilis	Tuberculosis
U.S.	[1]41,868	32,221	15,989	KS	98	88	63	ND	3	2	6
				KY	333	191	152	OH	581	297	306
AL	438	720	265	LA	861	793	294	OK	243	288	194
AK	18	9	54	ME	48	16	20	OR	259	48	123
AZ	540	1,147	289	MD	1,860	937	262	PA	1,840	726	350
AR	199	239	162	MA	765	446	270	RI	103	39	60
CA	4,315	3,050	3,332	MI	548	1,147	330	SC	729	913	263
CO	288	149	138	MN	157	132	239	SD	25	1	13
CT	584	165	121	MS	418	653	154	TN	602	1,478	313
DE	248	79	33	MO	445	174	157	TX	2,892	3,660	1,643
DC	870	459	74	MT	15	-	20	UT	124	25	35
FL	5,138	2,914	1,145	NE	74	16	40	VT	25	8	7
GA	1,745	1,985	575	NV	252	62	96	VA	951	524	306
HI	124	41	151	NH	40	20	20	WA	532	174	261
ID	19	11	9	NJ	1,756	1,040	530	WV	100	7	32
IL	1,323	1,541	707	NM	143	73	54	WI	193	131	86
IN	378	529	115	NY	7,476	3,604	1,676	WY	5	4	3
IA	90	44	43	NC	942	1,422	398				

- Represents zero. [1] Includes cases among persons with unknown state of residence.

Source: U.S. Centers for Disease Control and Prevention, Atlanta, GA,

No. 195. Persons With Limitation of Activity Caused by Chronic Conditions: 2000 and 2001

[In percent. Limitation of activity is assessed by asking respondents a series of questions about limitations in their ability to perform activities usual for their age group because of a physical, mental, or emotional problem. Respondents are asked about limitations in activities of daily living, instrumental activities of daily living, play, school, work, difficulty walking or remembering, and any other activity limitations. For reported limitations the causal health conditions are determined and respondents are considered limited if one or more of these conditions is chronic. Based on the National Health Interview Survey, a sample survey of the civilian noninstitutionalized population; see Appendix III]

Characteristic	2000	2001	Characteristic	2000	2001
Total [1][2]	11.7	12.1	Male [2]	11.7	12.2
Under 18 years	6.0	6.7	Female [2]	11.5	11.9
18 to 44 years	5.8	6.1			
45 to 54 years	12.4	13.1	White, non-Hispanic [2]	11.5	11.8
55 to 64 years	19.7	20.7	Black, non-Hispanic [2]	14.3	15.6
65 to 74 years	26.1	26.0	Hispanic [2][3]	10.3	10.6
75 years and over	45.1	44.7	Mexican	10.4	10.3

[1] Includes all other races not shown separately. [2] Estimates for all persons are age adjusted to the year 2000 standard using six age groups: Under 18 years, 18-44 years, 45-54 years, 55-64 years, 65-74 years, and 75 years and over. [3] Persons of Hispanic origin may be of any race.

Source: U.S. National Center for Health Statistics, *Health, United States, 2003.*

No. 196. Persons 65 Years Old and Over With Limitation of Activity Caused by Chronic Conditions: 1999 to 2001

[In percent. Covers noninstitutionalized persons 65 years old and over. To determine activities of daily living (ADL) limitations respondents were asked "Because of a physical, mental, or emotional problem, does (this person) need the help of other persons with personal care needs, such as eating, bathing, dressing, or getting around inside this home?" Instrumental activities of daily living (IADL) were determined by asking respondents "Because of a physical, mental, or emotional problem, does (this person) need the help of other persons in handling routine needs, such as everyday household chores, doing necessary business, shopping, or getting around for other purposes?" See also headnote, Table 195]

Characteristic	Percent with ADL limitation			Percent with IADL limitation		
	1999	2000	2001	1999	2000	2001
Total [1][2]	6.3	6.3	6.4	12.4	12.7	12.6
65 to 74 years	3.1	3.3	3.4	6.2	6.6	6.7
75 years and over	9.9	9.5	9.6	19.1	19.3	18.9
Male [2]	4.9	5.1	6.1	8.4	9.2	9.6
Female [2]	7.2	7.0	6.6	15.1	15.1	14.6
White, non-Hispanic [2]	8.6	8.6	11.2	14.1	13.4	17.0
Black, non-Hispanic [2]	8.9	9.4	10.6	15.6	16.3	17.0
Hispanic [2][3]	6.2	6.1	6.1	12.3	12.6	12.3
Mexican [2][3]	5.7	5.7	5.5	11.5	12.1	11.6

[1] Includes other races not shown separately. [2] Estimates are age adjusted to the year 2000 standard using two age groups: 65-74 years and 75 years and over. [3] Persons of Hispanic origin may be of any race.

Source: U.S. National Center for Health Statistics, *Health, United States, 2003.*

No. 197. Disability Status of Population by State: 2000

[In thousands except percent (64,689 represents 64,689,000). **As of April.** Covers civilian noninstitutionalized population. A disability is a long-lasting physical, mental, or emotional condition. This condition can make it difficult for a person to do activities such as walking, climbing stairs, dressing, bathing, learning, or remembering. This condition can also impede a person from being able to go outside the home alone or to work at a job or business. Based on sample data from the 2000 Census of Population and Housing; see text, Section 1, and Appendix III]

State	Population 5 to 20 years Total	With a disability Number	Percent of total	Population 21 to 64 years Total	With a disability Number	Percent of total	Population 65 years and over Total	With a disability Number	Percent of total
U.S.	**64,689**	**5,214**	**8.1**	**159,132**	**30,554**	**19.2**	**33,347**	**13,978**	**41.9**
AL	1,018	91	9.0	2,498	579	23.2	555	275	49.5
AK	166	11	6.9	358	56	15.6	34	16	46.2
AZ	1,200	96	8.0	2,813	547	19.4	654	260	39.7
AR	613	58	9.4	1,474	345	23.4	355	173	48.9
CA	8,172	609	7.5	19,211	3,848	20.0	3,470	1,466	42.2
CO	977	73	7.4	2,550	407	15.9	399	159	40.0
CT	736	56	7.6	1,945	328	16.8	440	163	37.0
DE	177	16	8.9	443	80	18.0	97	37	37.7
DC	113	11	10.0	350	76	21.9	66	28	42.5
FL	3,264	285	8.7	8,746	1,915	21.9	2,720	1,076	39.5
GA	1,915	158	8.2	4,733	940	19.9	755	359	47.5
HI	260	17	6.6	670	119	17.7	158	64	40.6
ID	332	24	7.2	702	117	16.7	141	60	42.5
IL	2,881	222	7.7	7,053	1,204	17.1	1,416	574	40.5
IN	1,422	118	8.3	3,434	636	18.5	707	302	42.6
IA	681	50	7.3	1,602	244	15.2	404	153	37.8
KS	645	47	7.2	1,465	246	16.8	331	137	41.5
KY	897	81	9.0	2,322	558	24.0	477	235	49.3
LA	1,111	104	9.3	2,446	541	22.1	490	235	48.1
ME	279	25	9.0	733	141	19.2	175	72	41.1
MD	1,194	97	8.1	3,076	530	17.2	573	228	39.8
MA	1,356	116	8.6	3,698	663	17.9	807	305	37.8
MI	2,336	198	8.5	5,631	1,018	18.1	1,171	496	42.3
MN	1,168	83	7.1	2,804	392	14.0	554	204	36.9
MS	707	61	8.6	1,542	378	24.5	326	168	51.7
MO	1,289	103	8.0	3,121	567	18.2	711	303	42.6
MT	213	15	7.1	505	85	16.9	114	45	39.6
NE	409	27	6.7	936	143	15.2	217	80	37.1
NV	436	33	7.7	1,173	256	21.8	214	87	40.6
NH	282	24	8.4	725	117	16.1	139	54	38.5
NJ	1,807	134	7.4	4,864	845	17.4	1,064	411	38.6
NM	457	37	8.1	997	209	21.0	206	92	44.8
NY	4,198	371	8.8	10,933	2,295	21.0	2,334	941	40.3
NC	1,750	148	8.5	4,643	970	20.9	924	423	45.7
ND	154	11	7.2	345	53	15.4	87	34	38.5
OH	2,601	206	7.9	6,395	1,121	17.5	1,422	583	41.0
OK	810	70	8.7	1,886	405	21.5	430	201	46.7
OR	762	63	8.2	1,973	355	18.0	423	176	41.5
PA	2,690	202	7.5	6,837	1,197	17.5	1,809	713	39.4
RI	234	22	9.3	590	116	19.7	144	58	40.3
SC	917	82	9.0	2,270	515	22.7	466	213	45.8
SD	186	13	6.8	400	62	15.6	101	40	39.5
TN	1,256	110	8.8	3,291	720	21.9	668	320	47.8
TX	5,183	410	7.9	11,612	2,315	19.9	1,966	880	44.8
UT	639	44	6.9	1,176	181	15.4	184	73	39.9
VT	141	12	8.3	354	57	16.2	73	28	38.6
VA	1,550	126	8.1	4,074	712	17.5	754	317	42.1
WA	1,356	104	7.7	3,400	607	17.8	640	270	42.3
WV	377	34	9.1	1,039	247	23.8	266	129	48.6
WI	1,258	99	7.9	3,019	450	14.9	663	242	36.5
WY	119	9	7.7	277	46	16.8	55	21	39.3

Source: U.S. Census Bureau, "2000 Census of Population and Housing, Profiles of General Demographic Characteristics"; <http://www.census.gov/Press-Release/www/2002/demoprofiles.html>.

No. 198. Disability Status of Population—25 Largest Metropolitan Areas: 2000

[In thousands except percent (944 represents 944,000). As of April. Covers civilian noninstitutionalized population. See headnote, Table 197. Covers metropolitan statistical area (MSAs) and consolidated metropolitan statistical areas (CMSAs) as defined by the U.S. Office of Management and Budget as of June 30, 1999. For definitions of metropolitan areas, see Appendix II]

Metropolitan area	Population 5 to 20 years Total	With a disability Number	Percent of total	Population 21 to 64 years Total	With a disability Number	Percent of total	Population 65 years and over Total	With a disability Number	Percent of total
Atlanta, GA MSA	944	72	7.6	2,520	427	16.9	301	132	44.0
Boston-Worcester-Lawrence, MA-NH-ME-CT CMSA	1,245	103	8.3	3,435	590	17.2	688	261	38.0
Chicago-Gary-Kenosha, IL-IN-WI CMSA	2,139	164	7.7	5,293	916	17.3	949	387	40.7
Cincinnati-Hamilton, OH-KY-IN CMSA	467	38	8.1	1,129	194	17.1	218	88	40.4
Cleveland-Akron, OH CMSA	657	51	7.8	1,661	282	17.0	399	162	40.5
Dallas-Fort Worth, TX CMSA	1,257	101	8.0	3,095	570	18.4	397	169	42.6
Denver-Boulder-Greeley, CO CMSA	581	44	7.6	1,574	247	15.7	221	87	39.3
Detroit-Ann Arbor-Flint, MI CMSA	1,261	105	8.3	3,149	579	18.4	617	266	43.0
Houston-Galveston-Brazoria, TX CMSA	1,172	90	7.7	2,727	531	19.5	344	150	43.6
Kansas City, MO-KS MSA	406	30	7.5	1,026	173	16.8	190	78	41.0
Los Angeles-Riverside-Orange County, CA CMSA	4,092	305	7.5	9,277	1,933	20.8	1,569	676	43.1
Miami-Fort Lauderdale, FL CMSA	828	65	7.9	2,210	482	21.8	546	237	43.4
Minneapolis-St. Paul, MN-WI MSA	696	49	7.0	1,764	232	13.1	268	97	36.2
New York-Northern New Jersey-Long Island, NY-NJ-CT-PA CMSA	4,558	374	8.2	12,410	2,513	20.2	2,569	1,028	40.0
Philadelphia-Wilmington-Atlantic City, PA-NJ-DE-MD CMSA	1,406	111	7.9	3,486	642	18.4	790	311	39.4
Phoenix-Mesa, AZ MSA	754	60	7.9	1,822	335	18.4	380	146	38.4
Pittsburgh, PA MSA	480	33	6.8	1,317	216	16.4	398	156	39.3
Portland-Salem, OR-WA CMSA	511	41	8.0	1,336	227	17.0	234	97	41.4
Sacramento-Yolo, CA CMSA	437	34	7.7	1,021	199	19.5	196	81	41.5
St. Louis, MO-IL MSA	610	50	8.2	1,467	244	16.6	317	128	40.4
San Diego, CA MSA	640	45	7.1	1,562	279	17.9	304	124	40.8
San Francisco-Oakland-San Jose, CA CMSA	1,465	102	7.0	4,291	739	17.2	755	303	40.2
Seattle-Tacoma-Bremerton, WA CMSA	780	59	7.5	2,117	355	16.8	354	146	41.3
Tampa-St. Petersburg-Clearwater, FL MSA	463	42	9.0	1,318	302	22.9	446	181	40.7
Washington-Baltimore, DC-MD-VA-WV CMSA	1,671	132	7.9	4,540	737	16.2	737	288	39.1

Source: U.S. Census Bureau, "2000 Census of Population and Housing, Profiles of General Demographic Characteristics"; <http://www.census.gov/Press-Release/www/2002/demoprofiles.html>.

No. 199. Disability Status of Population—25 Largest Cities: 2000

[In thousands except percent (143 represents 143,000). As of April. Covers civilian noninstitutionalized population. See headnote, Table 197]

City	Population 5 to 20 years Total	With a disability Number	Percent of total	Population 21 to 64 years Total	With a disability Number	Percent of total	Population 65 years and over Total	With a disability Number	Percent of total
Austin, TX	143	12	8.3	418	64	15.3	42	18	42.7
Baltimore, MD	151	18	11.7	363	102	28.1	82	42	51.2
Boston, MA	123	13	10.7	369	81	21.9	57	26	45.7
Chicago, IL	665	66	10.0	1,697	401	23.6	289	137	47.6
Columbus, OH	158	14	9.2	436	79	18.0	59	26	43.5
Dallas, TX	268	27	9.9	710	165	23.2	97	42	43.8
Denver, CO	105	11	10.1	346	70	20.3	60	25	41.7
Detroit, MI	258	29	11.4	510	164	32.1	96	52	54.0
El Paso, TX	153	11	7.3	297	64	21.5	59	28	47.8
Houston, TX	460	40	8.6	1,157	255	22.0	158	70	44.3
Indianapolis, IN [1]	173	16	9.1	459	94	20.4	81	35	43.9
Jacksonville, FL	171	15	8.9	417	93	22.3	72	33	46.2
Los Angeles, CA	860	72	8.4	2,175	504	23.2	345	158	45.7
Memphis, TN	159	16	9.8	361	91	25.1	67	33	48.5
Milwaukee, WI	155	17	11.2	327	77	23.6	61	27	43.2
Nashville-Davidson, TN [1]	112	11	9.7	330	64	19.5	57	27	46.4
New York, NY	1,717	172	10.0	4,780	1,226	25.6	902	417	46.2
Philadelphia, PA	358	34	9.6	835	223	26.7	205	97	47.4
Phoenix, AZ	327	29	8.9	761	153	20.1	105	46	43.5
San Antonio, TX	285	26	9.0	628	142	22.6	114	54	46.9
San Diego, CA	266	19	7.1	708	124	17.5	124	51	41.3
San Francisco, CA	103	8	8.1	533	96	17.9	105	46	44.1
San Jose, CA	204	14	7.1	547	107	19.6	71	30	42.8
Seattle, WA	87	6	7.4	377	57	15.1	66	28	42.0
Washington, DC	113	11	10.0	350	76	21.9	66	28	42.5

[1] Represents the portion of a consolidated city that is not within one or more separately incorporated places.

Source: U.S. Census Bureau, "2000 Census of Population and Housing, Profiles of General Demographic Characteristics"; <http://www.census.gov/Press-Release/www/2002/demoprofiles.html>.

No. 200. Substance Abuse Treatment Facilities and Clients: 1995 to 2002

[As of October 1. Based on the Uniform Facility Data Set (UFDS) survey, a census of all known facilities that provide substance abuse treatment in the United States and associated jurisdictions. Selected missing data for responding facilities were imputed]

Primary focus	Number	Primary focus	Number	Type of care and type of problem	Number
FACILITIES		CLIENTS		Total clients [1]	1,142,080
1995	10,746	1995	1,009,127	Outpatient rehab	1,007,142
1996	10,641	1996	940,141	Outpatient detoxification	18,430
1997	10,860	1997	929,086	24-hour rehab	101,749
1998	13,455	1998	1,038,378	24-hour detoxification	14,759
1999	15,239	2000	1,000,896		
2000	13,428				
2002 total	13,926	2002 total	1,142,080	Drug only	351,575
Substance abuse treatment services	8,391	Substance abuse treatment services	772,742	Alcohol only	241,454
Mental health services	1,152	Mental health services	46,410	Both alcohol & drug	549,051
General health care	464	General health care	33,470	Total with a drug problem [2]	900,626
Both substance abuse and mental health	3,510	Both substance abuse and mental health	261,040	Total with an alcohol problem [3]	790,505
Other	409	Other	28,418		

[1] Includes clients at facilities that did not provide data on type of substance abuse problem treated. [2] The sum of clients with a drug problem and clients with both diagnoses. [3] The sum of clients with a alcohol problem and clients with both diagnoses.

Source: U.S. Substance Abuse and Mental Health Services Administration, *Uniform Facility Data Set (UFDS): Annual surveys for 1995 - 1999* and *National Survey of Substance Abuse Treatment Services (N-SSATS) 2000 and 2002.*

No. 201. Drug Use by Type of Drug and Age Group: 2000 and 2001

[In percent. Current users are those who used drugs at least once within month prior to this study. Based on a representative sample of the U.S. population age 12 and older, including persons living in households and in some group quarters such as dormitories and homeless shelters. Estimates are based on computer-assisted interviews of about 72,000 respondents. Subject to sampling variability; see source]

Age of user and type of drug	Ever used 2000	Ever used 2001	Current user 2000	Current user 2001	Age of user and type of drug	Ever used 2000	Ever used 2001	Current user 2000	Current user 2001
12 YEARS OLD AND OVER					**18 TO 25 YEARS OLD**				
Any illicit drug	38.9	41.7	6.3	7.1	Any illicit drug	51.2	55.6	15.9	18.8
Marijuana and hashish	34.2	36.9	4.8	5.4	Marijuana and hashish	45.7	50.0	13.6	16.0
Cocaine	11.2	12.3	0.5	0.7	Cocaine	10.9	13.0	1.4	1.9
Crack	2.4	2.8	0.1	0.2	Hallucinogens	19.3	22.1	1.8	2.7
Heroin	1.2	1.4	0.1	0.1	Inhalants	12.8	13.4	0.6	0.6
Hallucinogens	11.7	12.5	0.4	0.6	Any psychotherapeutic [1]	19.5	23.3	3.6	4.8
LSD	8.8	9.0	0.2	0.1	Alcohol	84.0	85.0	56.8	58.8
PCP	2.6	2.7	-	-	"Binge" alcohol use [2]	(NA)	(NA)	37.8	38.7
Inhalants	7.5	8.1	0.3	0.2	Cigarettes	67.3	69.0	38.3	39.1
Any psychotherapeutic [1]	14.5	16.0	1.7	2.1	Smokeless tobacco	23.6	23.7	5.0	5.4
Pain relievers [1]	8.6	9.8	1.2	1.6	Cigars	42.3	43.8	10.4	10.4
Tranquilizers [1]	5.8	6.2	0.4	0.6					
Stimulants [1]	6.6	7.1	0.4	0.5	**26 TO 34 YEARS OLD**				
Methamphetamine [1]	4.0	4.3	0.2	0.3	Any illicit drug	50.9	53.3	7.8	8.8
Sedatives [1]	3.2	3.3	0.1	0.1	Marijuana and hashish	46.0	47.9	5.9	6.8
Alcohol	81.0	81.7	46.6	48.3	Cocaine	15.1	15.9	0.8	1.1
"Binge" alcohol use [2]	(NA)	(NA)	20.6	20.5	Hallucinogens	15.8	17.5	0.4	0.4
Cigarettes	66.5	67.2	24.9	24.9	Inhalants	11.0	12.0	0.2	0.2
Smokeless tobacco	18.5	19.1	3.4	3.2	Any psychotherapeutic [1]	16.9	18.0	2.1	2.4
Cigars	34.2	35.4	4.8	5.4					
Pipes	16.4	17.0	1.0	1.0	**35 YEARS OLD AND OVER**				
					Any illicit drug	35.5	38.4	3.3	3.5
12 To 17 YEARS OLD					Marijuana and hashish	31.6	34.5	2.3	2.4
Any illicit drug	26.9	28.4	9.7	10.8	Cocaine	11.8	13.0	0.3	0.5
Marijuana and hashish	18.3	19.7	7.2	8.0	Hallucinogens	10.1	10.5	-	-
Cocaine	2.4	2.3	0.6	0.4	Inhalants	5.3	5.9	0.1	-
Hallucinogens	5.8	5.7	1.2	1.2	Any psychotherapeutic [1]	13.5	14.7	1.0	1.3
Inhalants	8.9	8.6	1.0	1.0					
Any psychotherapeutic [1]	10.9	11.6	3.0	3.2	**26 YEARS OLD AND OVER**				
Alcohol	41.7	42.9	16.4	17.3	Alcohol	85.8	86.5	49.0	50.8
"Binge" alcohol use [2]	(NA)	(NA)	10.4	10.6	"Binge" alcohol use [2]	(NA)	(NA)	19.1	18.8
Cigarettes	34.6	33.6	13.4	13.0	Cigarettes	70.7	71.5	24.2	24.2
Smokeless tobacco	8.6	8.3	2.1	2.1	Smokeless tobacco	19.1	19.8	3.3	3.0
Cigars	17.1	16.4	4.5	4.3	Cigars	35.2	36.6	3.9	4.7

- Represents or rounds to zero. NA Not available. [1] Nonmedical use of any prescription-type pain reliever, tranquilizer, stimulant, or sedative; does not include over-the-counter drugs. [2] Binge use is defined as drinking five or more drinks on the same occasion on at least 1 day in the past 30 days.

Source: U.S. Substance Abuse and Mental Health Services Administration, *Summary of Findings From the 2001 National Household Survey on Drug Abuse.*

No. 202. Estimated Use of Selected Drugs by State: 2000-2001

[15,026 represents 15,026,000. Current users are those persons 12 years old and over who used drugs at least once within month prior to this study. Based on national sample of respondents (see also headnote, Table 201). The state estimates were produced by combining the prevalence rate based on the state sample data and the prevalence rate based on a national regression model applied to local-area county and census block group/tract-level estimates from the state. The parameters of the regression model are estimated from the entire national sample. Data in this table covers a 2-year period. For comparison purposes, the data shown here display estimates for all 50 states and the District of Columbia utilizing the modeled estimates for all 51 areas]

State	Estimated current users (1,000)					Current users as percent of population				
	Any illicit drug [1]	Mari- juana	Any illicit drug other than mari- juana [1]	Ciga- rettes	Binge alcohol [2]	Any illicit drug [1]	Mari- juana	Any illicit drug other than mari- juana [1]	Ciga- rettes	Binge alcohol [2]
U.S.	15,026	11,433	6,405	55,991	46,201	6.7	5.1	2.9	24.9	20.6
AL	210	152	98	907	665	5.8	4.2	2.7	25.0	18.3
AK	45	34	14	117	98	9.2	7.1	3.0	24.1	20.2
AZ	262	179	135	904	843	6.7	4.6	3.4	23.1	21.5
AR	143	106	68	599	410	6.7	5.0	3.2	28.0	19.2
CA	2,159	1,578	918	5,637	5,067	8.2	6.0	3.5	21.3	19.1
CO	316	254	117	827	752	9.2	7.4	3.4	24.2	22.0
CT	204	170	78	681	605	7.5	6.3	2.9	25.1	22.3
DE	48	40	19	161	136	7.6	6.4	2.9	25.5	21.5
DC	34	25	15	107	93	8.1	5.9	3.5	25.2	22.0
FL	771	600	312	3,126	2,401	6.0	4.7	2.4	24.4	18.8
GA	394	296	174	1,587	1,272	6.1	4.6	2.7	24.7	19.8
HI	71	55	26	198	178	7.5	5.8	2.7	20.7	18.7
ID	57	46	23	244	208	5.4	4.4	2.2	23.0	19.6
IL	704	551	284	2,623	2,364	7.2	5.6	2.9	26.7	24.1
IN	258	193	126	1,349	936	5.2	3.9	2.6	27.4	19.0
IA	106	83	49	591	522	4.5	3.5	2.1	24.8	21.9
KS	132	101	63	538	431	6.1	4.7	2.9	24.9	19.9
KY	220	163	93	1,069	601	6.7	5.0	2.8	32.5	18.3
LA	236	135	126	1,050	788	6.7	3.8	3.6	29.7	22.3
ME	89	76	31	278	240	8.4	7.1	2.9	26.2	22.7
MD	266	202	113	1,048	839	6.2	4.7	2.6	24.4	19.5
MA	552	456	183	1,184	1,333	10.7	8.9	3.6	23.0	25.9
MI	602	484	220	2,179	1,766	7.5	6.0	2.7	27.1	21.9
MN	262	212	107	981	956	6.6	5.3	2.7	24.7	24.1
MS	128	87	61	599	413	5.7	3.8	2.7	26.5	18.3
MO	257	200	103	1,252	905	5.7	4.4	2.3	27.7	20.0
MT	47	39	20	174	176	6.3	5.1	2.7	23.0	23.2
NE	63	51	28	334	312	4.6	3.7	2.1	24.4	22.8
NV	113	80	50	446	369	7.3	5.2	3.2	28.6	23.8
NH	82	71	34	263	222	8.0	7.0	3.3	25.8	21.9
NJ	390	299	166	1,560	1,438	5.8	4.4	2.5	23.1	21.3
NM	108	87	40	373	329	7.5	6.0	2.8	25.7	22.7
NY	1,010	784	416	3,448	2,927	6.8	5.3	2.8	23.2	19.7
NC	500	368	183	1,750	1,078	7.9	5.8	2.9	27.6	17.0
ND	22	17	11	134	152	4.1	3.3	2.2	25.5	29.0
OH	550	428	233	2,708	2,017	5.9	4.6	2.5	29.2	21.7
OK	148	97	82	737	503	5.4	3.6	3.0	26.9	18.3
OR	246	203	89	653	510	8.7	7.2	3.2	23.2	18.1
PA	596	479	274	2,642	2,244	5.9	4.8	2.7	26.3	22.3
RI	67	56	25	222	199	8.2	6.8	3.0	27.0	24.2
SC	182	131	86	835	627	5.7	4.1	2.7	26.2	19.7
SD	27	23	13	161	149	4.5	3.7	2.1	26.4	24.5
TN	286	221	136	1,313	741	6.2	4.8	2.9	28.4	16.0
TX	861	588	441	3,832	3,489	5.3	3.6	2.7	23.7	21.5
UT	85	60	47	285	242	5.0	3.5	2.8	16.8	14.2
VT	54	46	18	126	119	10.5	9.1	3.6	24.6	23.2
VA	314	243	146	1,415	1,008	5.5	4.3	2.6	25.0	17.8
WA	370	285	141	1,120	903	7.7	6.0	2.9	23.4	18.9
WV	77	61	41	452	280	5.0	4.0	2.7	29.4	18.2
WI	277	218	120	1,062	1,242	6.3	5.0	2.7	24.2	28.3
WY	23	18	11	112	99	5.7	4.4	2.6	27.2	24.1

[1] Any illicit drug indicates use at least once of marijuana/hashish, cocaine (including crack), inhalants, hallucinogens (including PCP and LSD), heroin, or any prescription-type psychotherapeutic used nonmedically. Any illicit drug other than marijuana indicates use at least once of any of these listed drugs, regardless of marijuana/hashish use; marijuana/hashish users who also have used any of the other listed drugs are included. [2] Binge use is defined as drinking five or more drinks on the same occasion on at least 1 day in the past 30 days. By "occasion" is meant at the same time or within a couple hours of each other.

Source: U.S. Substance Abuse and Mental Health Services Administration, *National Household Survey on Drug Abuse*, Annual. <http://www.samhsa.gov/>.

No. 203. Current Cigarette Smoking: 1990 to 2001

[In percent. Prior to 1995, a current smoker is a person who has smoked at least 100 cigarettes and who now smokes. Beginning 1995, definition includes persons who smoke only "some days." Excludes unknown smoking status. Based on the National Health Interview Survey; for details, see Appendix III]

Sex, age, and race	1990	1995	2000	2001	Sex, age, and race	1990	1995	2000	2001
Total smokers, age-adjusted [1]	25.3	24.6	23.1	22.7	Black, total	32.5	28.5	26.1	27.6
					18 to 24 years	21.3	[2]14.6	20.8	21.6
					25 to 34 years	33.8	25.1	23.3	23.8
Male	28.0	26.5	25.2	24.7	35 to 44 years	42.0	36.3	30.8	29.9
Female	22.9	22.7	21.1	20.8	45 to 64 years	36.7	33.9	32.2	34.3
					65 years and over	21.5	28.5	14.2	21.1
White male	27.6	26.2	25.5	24.9					
Black male	32.8	29.4	25.7	27.6	Female, total	22.8	22.6	21.0	20.7
					18 to 24 years	22.5	21.8	25.1	23.4
White female	23.5	23.4	22.0	22.1	25 to 34 years	28.2	26.4	22.5	23.0
Black female	20.8	23.5	20.7	17.9	35 to 44 years	24.8	27.1	26.2	25.7
					45 to 64 years	24.8	24.0	21.6	21.4
Total smokers	25.5	24.7	23.3	22.8	65 years and over	11.5	11.5	9.3	9.2
Male, total	28.4	27.0	25.7	25.2					
18 to 24 years	26.6	27.8	28.5	30.4	White, total	23.4	23.1	21.6	21.7
25 to 34 years	31.6	29.5	29.0	27.2	18 to 24 years	25.4	24.9	28.7	27.2
35 to 44 years	34.5	31.5	30.2	27.4	25 to 34 years	28.5	27.3	25.1	25.5
45 to 64 years	29.3	27.1	26.4	26.4	35 to 44 years	25.0	27.0	26.6	27.0
65 years and over	14.6	14.9	10.2	11.5	45 to 64 years	25.4	24.3	21.4	21.6
					65 years and over	11.5	11.7	9.1	9.4
White, total	28.0	26.6	25.8	25.1	Black, total	21.2	23.5	20.8	18.0
18 to 24 years	27.4	28.4	30.9	32.5	18 to 24 years	10.0	[2]8.8	14.2	17.0
25 to 34 years	31.6	29.9	29.9	29.0	25 to 34 years	29.1	26.7	15.5	16.8
35 to 44 years	33.5	31.2	30.6	27.8	35 to 44 years	25.5	31.9	30.2	24.0
45 to 64 years	28.7	26.3	25.8	25.1	45 to 64 years	22.6	27.5	25.6	22.6
65 years and over	13.7	14.1	9.8	10.7	65 years and over	11.1	13.3	10.2	9.3

[1] Estimates are age adjusted to the year 2000 standard using five age groups: 18-24 years, 25-34 years, 35-44 years, 45-64 years, 65 years and over. [2] Data have a relative standard error of 20-30 percent.

Source: U.S. National Center for Health Statistics, Health, United States, annual.

No. 204. Current Cigarette Smoking by Sex and State: 2001

[In percent. Current cigarette smoking is defined as persons who reported having smoked 100 or more cigarettes during their lifetime and who currently smoke every day or some days. Based on the Behavioral Risk Factor Surveillance System, a telephone survey of health behaviors of the civilian, noninstitutionalized U.S. population, 18 years old and over; for details, see source]

State	Total	Male	Female	State	Total	Male	Female	State	Total	Male	Female
U.S. [1]	23.4	25.5	21.5	KS	22.2	22.5	21.9	ND	22.1	24.6	19.6
				KY	30.9	31.7	30.1	OH	27.7	29.0	26.5
AL	23.9	25.8	22.1	LA	24.8	28.7	21.2	OK	28.8	31.2	26.6
AK	26.1	26.2	25.9	ME	24.0	27.1	21.1	OR	20.5	21.4	19.7
AZ	21.5	23.1	20.0	MD	21.3	24.8	18.1	PA	24.6	26.4	22.9
AR	25.6	27.4	23.9	MA	19.7	20.5	18.9	RI	24.0	25.9	22.2
CA	17.2	20.6	14.0	MI	25.7	26.7	24.7	SC	26.2	28.1	24.4
CO	22.4	23.8	21.1	MN	22.2	24.9	19.6	SD	22.4	23.3	21.5
CT	20.8	21.3	20.3	MS	25.4	29.4	21.9	TN	24.4	26.1	22.8
DE	25.1	28.2	22.3	MO	25.9	27.5	24.4	TX	22.5	25.2	19.9
DC	20.8	24.9	17.3	MT	21.9	21.6	22.2	UT	13.3	14.6	12.1
FL	22.5	25.7	19.5	NE	20.4	20.8	20.0	VT	22.4	24.5	20.6
GA	23.7	25.8	21.8	NV	27.0	27.9	26.0	VA	22.5	23.4	21.8
HI	20.6	24.7	16.4	NH	24.1	25.5	22.8	WA	22.6	24.6	20.6
ID	19.7	21.1	18.3	NJ	21.3	21.7	20.9	WV	28.2	28.9	27.6
IL	23.6	26.6	21.0	NM	23.9	27.9	20.1	WI	23.6	25.4	21.9
IN	27.5	29.7	25.4	NY	23.4	26.2	20.9	WY	22.2	22.5	21.9
IA	22.2	24.2	20.4	NC	25.9	28.6	23.3				

[1] Represents median value among the states and DC. For definition of median, see Guide to Tabular Presentations

Source: U.S. Centers for Disease Control and Prevention, Atlanta, GA, Morbidity and Mortality Weekly Report, Vol. 52, No. 14, April 11, 2003.

No. 205. Use of Mammography for Women 40 Years Old and Over by Patient Characteristics: 1990 to 2000

[Percent of women having a mammogram within the past 2 years. Covers civilian noninstitutional population. Based on National Health Interview Survey; see Appendix III]

Characteristic	1990	1994	2000	Characteristic	1990	1994	2000
Total [1]	51.4	60.9	70.3	Years of school completed:			
40 to 49 years old	55.1	61.3	64.2	Less than 12 years	36.4	48.2	57.7
50 years old and over	49.7	60.6	73.6	12 years	52.7	61.0	69.6
50 to 64 years old	56.0	66.5	78.6	13 years or more	62.8	69.7	76.1
65 years old and over	43.4	55.0	68.0				
White, non-Hispanic	52.7	61.3	72.1	Poverty status: [3]			
Black, non-Hispanic	46.0	64.4	67.9	Below poverty	28.7	44.4	55.2
Hispanic origin [2]	45.2	51.9	61.4	At or above poverty	54.8	64.8	72.2

[1] Includes all other races not shown separately and unknown education level and poverty status. [2] Persons of Hispanic origin may be of any race. [3] For explanation of poverty level, see text, Section 13.

Source: U.S. National Center for Health Statistics, Health, United States, annual.

No. 206. Cancer—Estimated New Cases, 2003, and Survival Rates, 1980-82 to 1992-99

[1,334 represents 1,334,000. The 5-year relative survival rate, which is derived by adjusting the observed survival rate for expected mortality, represents the likelihood that a person will not die from causes directly related to their cancer within 5 years. Survival data shown are based on those patients diagnosed while residents of an area listed below during the time periods shown. Data are based on information collected as part of the National Cancer Institute's Surveillance, Epidemiology and End Results (SEER) program, a collection of population-based registries in Connecticut, New Mexico, Utah, Iowa, Hawaii, Atlanta, Detroit, Seattle-Puget Sound, and San Francisco-Oakland]

Site	Estimated new cases,[1] 2003 (1,000) Total	Male	Female	5-year relative survival rates (percent) White 1980-82	1986-88	1989-91	1992-99	Black 1980-82	1986-88	1989-91	1992-99
All sites [2]	1,334	675	659	52.1	56.8	60.3	64.4	39.8	42.7	46.2	53.3
Lung	172	92	80	13.5	13.5	14.3	15.1	12.1	11.9	10.8	12.4
Breast [3]	213	1	211	77.1	83.9	86.1	87.9	65.8	69.2	71.1	73.5
Colon and rectum	148	73	75	54.9	60.9	62.3	63.0	46.6	52.5	54.0	53.4
Colon	106	49	57	55.7	61.6	63.1	63.0	49.3	53.0	53.9	53.2
Rectum	42	24	18	53.1	59.2	60.5	63.0	38.1	51.1	54.3	53.8
Prostate	221	221	(X)	74.5	82.7	91.9	98.4	64.8	69.2	80.7	93.4
Bladder	57	42	15	78.9	80.7	82.2	82.6	58.3	62.8	61.7	64.0
Corpus uteri	40	(X)	40	82.8	84.5	85.6	86.3	55.1	57.2	57.7	60.0
Non-Hodgkin's lymphoma [4]	53	28	25	51.9	52.9	52.0	57.2	50.2	50.2	43.5	47.1
Oral cavity and pharynx	28	18	10	55.7	55.4	55.5	59.7	31.1	34.7	32.8	36.1
Leukemia [4]	31	18	13	39.5	44.2	46.1	47.6	32.9	38.1	34.4	39.2
Melanoma of skin	54	30	24	83.2	88.0	88.8	89.8	60.9	69.1	79.1	64.4
Pancreas	31	15	16	2.8	3.2	4.1	4.4	4.5	6.2	4.0	3.6
Kidney	32	20	12	51.1	57.5	60.8	62.9	56.0	53.6	58.0	60.7
Stomach	22	13	9	16.5	19.1	18.4	21.4	19.1	19.3	24.8	20.5
Ovary	25	(X)	25	38.7	41.9	49.7	52.4	39.1	39.0	41.9	51.5
Cervix uteri [5]	12	(X)	12	68.2	71.8	72.4	72.9	61.4	55.6	62.6	61.0

X Not applicable. [1] Estimates provided by American Cancer Society are based on rates from the National Cancer Institute's SEER program. [2] Includes other sites not shown separately. [3] Survival rates for female only. [4] All types combined. [5] Invasive cancer only.

Source: U.S. National Institutes of Health, National Cancer Institute, *Cancer Statistics Review*, annual. <http://www.seer.cancer.gov/csr>.

No. 207. Cancer—Estimated New Cases and Deaths by State: 2003

[In thousands (1,334.1 represents 1,334,100). Excludes basal and squamous cell skin cancers and in situ carcinomas except urinary bladder]

State	New cases [1] Total [2]	Lung	Female breast	Deaths Total [2]	Lung	Female breast	State	New cases [1] Total [2]	Lung	Female breast	Deaths Total [2]	Lung	Female breast
U.S.	1,334.1	171.9	211.3	556.5	157.2	39.8							
							MO	29.5	4.2	4.1	12.3	3.9	0.8
AL	23.6	3.3	3.4	9.8	3.0	0.6	MT	4.6	0.6	0.6	1.9	0.5	0.1
AK	1.8	0.2	0.3	0.7	0.2	0.1	NE	8.1	1.0	1.1	3.4	0.9	0.2
AZ	23.3	3.0	3.9	9.7	2.7	0.7	NV	10.3	1.5	1.4	4.3	1.3	0.3
AR	14.7	2.2	2.0	6.1	2.0	0.4	NH	6.0	0.8	0.8	2.5	0.7	0.2
CA	125.0	14.4	21.1	52.2	13.2	4.0							
							NJ	42.3	5.0	7.4	17.6	4.5	1.4
CO	15.2	1.6	2.5	6.3	1.5	0.5	NM	7.4	0.8	1.3	3.1	0.7	0.2
CT	16.6	2.0	2.6	6.9	1.8	0.5	NY	85.9	10.0	14.8	35.8	9.2	2.8
DE	4.1	0.6	0.7	1.7	0.5	0.1	NC	39.6	5.6	6.0	16.5	5.1	1.1
DC	2.7	0.3	0.5	1.1	0.3	0.1	ND	3.1	0.3	0.5	1.3	0.3	0.1
FL	96.1	13.2	13.5	40.1	12.1	2.5							
							OH	60.3	8.0	9.9	25.2	7.4	1.9
GA	33.4	4.6	5.4	13.9	4.2	1.0	OK	17.7	2.6	2.7	7.4	2.4	0.5
HI	4.9	0.6	0.7	2.0	0.5	0.1	OR	17.3	2.3	2.6	7.2	2.1	0.5
ID	5.5	0.6	1.0	2.3	0.6	0.2	PA	70.8	8.7	11.1	29.6	8.0	2.1
IL	59.9	7.4	10.2	25.0	6.8	1.9	RI	5.8	0.8	0.8	2.4	0.7	0.2
IN	31.2	4.4	4.7	13.0	4.0	0.9							
							SC	20.6	2.8	3.4	8.6	2.5	0.6
IA	15.3	1.9	2.3	6.4	1.7	0.4	SD	3.9	0.4	0.6	1.6	0.4	0.1
KS	12.6	1.7	2.1	5.2	1.5	0.4	TN	30.5	4.5	4.5	12.7	4.1	0.9
KY	22.1	3.5	3.2	9.2	3.2	0.6	TX	83.4	10.9	13.7	34.8	9.9	2.6
LA	22.6	3.0	3.8	9.4	2.7	0.7	UT	6.2	0.5	1.1	2.6	0.4	0.2
ME	7.3	1.0	1.0	3.0	0.9	0.2							
							VT	3.1	0.4	0.5	1.3	0.4	0.1
MD	24.4	3.2	4.2	10.2	2.9	0.8	VA	32.8	4.3	5.4	13.7	3.9	1.0
MA	32.7	4.1	4.7	13.6	3.7	0.9	WA	26.7	3.5	3.8	11.2	3.2	0.7
MI	47.4	6.1	7.5	19.8	5.6	1.4	WV	11.3	1.7	1.6	4.7	1.6	0.3
MN	21.9	2.5	3.4	9.1	2.3	0.6	WI	25.8	3.0	3.9	10.8	2.8	0.7
MS	14.9	2.2	2.5	6.2	2.0	0.5	WY	2.3	0.3	0.3	0.9	0.3	0.1

[1] Estimates are offered as a rough guide and should be interpreted with caution. They are calculated according to the distribution of estimated 2003 cancer deaths by state. [2] Includes other types of cancer, not shown separately.

Source: American Cancer Society, Inc., Atlanta, Georgia, *Cancer Facts and Figures—2003* (copyright). <http://www.cancer.org>.

No. 208. Cumulative Percent Distribution of Population by Height and Sex: 1988-94

[Height was measured without shoes. Based on sample and subject to sampling variability; see source]

Height	Males 20-29 years	30-39 years	40-49 years	50-59 years	60-69 years	70-79 years	Females 20-29 years	30-39 years	40-49 years	50-59 years	60-69 years	70-79 years
Percent under—												
4'8"	-	-	-	-	-	-	0.6	0.1	-	-	0.2	1.7
4'9"	-	-	-	-	-	-	0.7	0.2	0.3	0.1	0.7	3.3
4'10"	-	-	-	-	0.1	-	1.2	0.7	0.7	1.9	1.7	4.9
4'11"	-	-	-	-	0.1	0.1	3.1	2.6	1.7	3.1	4.4	9.8
5'	0.1	-	0.2	-	0.4	0.1	6.0	5.5	5.3	6.6	9.9	15.4
5'1"	0.1	-	0.4	0.1	0.5	0.6	11.5	10.4	9.9	11.9	19.0	28.9
5'2"	0.5	0.8	0.7	0.2	0.7	1.9	21.8	18.5	18.8	24.4	34.3	45.6
5'3"	1.3	1.4	0.9	1.0	2.2	2.7	34.3	30.7	31.9	38.6	48.3	61.2
5'4"	3.4	2.2	1.7	2.5	5.8	7.8	48.9	42.9	49.2	52.6	65.5	74.5
5'5"	6.9	5.1	5.6	6.0	9.4	16.5	62.7	59.1	64.3	69.9	76.5	85.9
5'6"	11.7	10.1	12.1	11.7	15.8	27.3	74.0	71.8	77.0	81.6	87.8	93.9
5'7"	20.8	18.9	19.6	20.5	27.4	39.5	84.7	84.1	87.0	89.3	92.5	97.3
5'8"	32.0	28.3	28.0	32.6	38.6	53.4	92.4	91.6	94.5	95.6	96.7	99.2
5'9"	46.3	44.3	42.1	43.9	55.1	68.7	96.2	95.6	97.3	99.0	99.3	99.9
5'10"	58.7	58.0	58.1	60.6	68.8	79.5	98.6	98.1	98.9	99.6	99.8	100.0
5'11"	70.1	70.4	71.1	75.2	81.4	89.2	99.5	99.5	99.4	100.0	100.0	100.0
6'	81.2	79.7	81.5	85.4	90.0	94.1	100.0	100.0	100.0	100.0	100.0	100.0
6'1"	87.4	86.2	89.0	92.4	95.2	97.2	100.0	100.0	100.0	100.0	100.0	100.0
6'2"	94.7	92.4	94.4	96.4	98.2	99.3	100.0	100.0	100.0	100.0	100.0	100.0
6'3"	97.9	98.1	97.2	98.2	99.5	99.9	100.0	100.0	100.0	100.0	100.0	100.0

- Represents or rounds to zero.

Source: U.S. National Center for Health Statistics, unpublished data.

No. 209. Percent of U.S. Adults Who Were Overweight and Percent Who Were Obese: 2001

[Percent who are overweight includes those who are obese and represent those who have a body mass index (BMI) equal to or above 25. Percent who are obese represent those who have a BMI equal to or above 30. BMI is a measure that adjusts body weight for height. It is calculated as weight in kilograms divided by height in meters squared. These estimates are based on definitions provided in the Dietary Guidelines for Americans, published by the U.S. Dept. of Agriculture and the U.S. Dept. of Health and Human Services. Based on the National Health Interview Survey; for details, see Appendix III]

Characteristic	Both sexes Overweight	Obese	Males Overweight	Obese	Females Overweight	Obese
All ages (age-adjusted) [1]	58.1	22.5	66.5	22.6	49.9	22.3
All ages (unadjusted) [1]	58.0	22.5	66.5	22.7	50.0	22.3
18-24 years old	38.7	13.9	45.1	14.0	32.2	13.7
25-44 years old	58.2	22.4	69.0	23.2	47.4	21.6
45-64 years old	66.0	27.6	73.8	27.4	58.3	27.8
65 years old and over	58.5	20.0	63.7	19.2	54.5	20.7
Hispanic	66.5	24.3	71.5	21.9	61.3	26.4
White, non-Hispanic	56.3	21.2	66.7	22.4	46.1	20.0
Black, non-Hispanic	67.8	32.6	66.6	28.0	68.5	36.4
Asian/Other Pacific Islander, Non-Hispanic	32.6	6.4	38.9	6.6	26.1	6.1
Educational attainment:						
Fewer than 9 grades	66.0	25.0	69.4	23.3	62.3	26.6
Grades 9 - 11	62.7	28.9	65.3	26.6	60.2	31.4
General equivalency degree	65.2	26.8	68.8	23.3	61.4	30.8
High school graduate	60.0	24.0	68.3	25.1	52.3	23.0
Some college - no degree	58.6	24.3	69.3	26.0	48.9	22.8
Associate of Arts - Technical	62.1	25.3	69.5	24.0	55.0	26.4
Associate of Arts - Academic	57.2	21.0	66.0	19.2	50.4	22.1
Bachelor of Arts or Science	52.1	15.3	63.7	15.4	40.2	15.3
Graduate degree	46.7	15.2	58.2	15.6	34.0	14.0

[1] Age-specific rates are unadjusted; all other estimates were adjusted to the 2000 projected population.

Source: U.S. National Center for Health Statistics, unpublished data, <http://www.cdc.gov/nchs/>.

No. 210. Percentage of Adults Engaging in Leisure-Time Physical Activity: 2001

[In percent. Covers persons 18 years old and over. Based on responses to questions about physical activity in prior month from the Behavioral Risk Factor Surveillance System. Estimates are age-adjusted to the year 2000 standard population. Based on a survey sample of approximately 203,000 persons in 50 states and the District of Columbia in 2001]

Characteristic	Persons who meet recommended activity [1]	Persons not meeting recommended activity [2]	Persons who are physically inactive [3]	Characteristic	Persons who meet recommended activity [1]	Persons not meeting recommended activity [2]	Persons who are physically inactive [3]
Total.	45.4	54.6	25.9	30 to 44 years old	46.5	53.5	25.9
				45 to 64 years old	40.7	59.3	28.7
Male.	47.9	52.1	23.4	65 to 74 years old	36.1	63.9	32.5
Female.	43.0	57.0	28.2	75 years old and over . . .	26.9	73.1	42.7
White, non-Hispanic	48.2	51.8	22.4				
Black, non-Hispanic.	35.3	64.7	34.6	School years completed:			
Hispanic	38.3	61.7	37.9	Less than 12 years	34.5	65.5	46.2
Other	42.2	57.8	27.8	12 years	43.0	57.0	32.3
Males:				Some college (13-15 yrs) .	47.0	53.0	22.2
18 to 29 years old	57.8	42.2	18.0	College (16 or more yrs). . .	50.9	49.1	14.2
30 to 44 years old	48.3	51.7	21.6				
45 to 64 years old	43.4	56.6	25.8	Household income:			
65 to 74 years old	45.7	54.3	27.4	Less than $10,000.	35.4	64.6	44.2
75 years old and over . . .	38.4	61.6	32.8	$10,000 to $19,999	36.8	63.2	39.7
Females:				$20,000 to $34,999	42.7	57.3	30.8
18 to 29 years old	49.8	50.2	24.1	$35,000 to $49,999	47.7	52.3	23.1
				$50,000 and over	52.0	48.0	15.3

[1] Recommended activity is physical activity at least 5 times/week x 30 minutes/time or vigorous physical activity for 20 minutes at a time at least 3 times/week. [2] Persons whose reported physical activity does not meet recommended level or report no leisure-time, transporation-related, or household-related physical activity. [3] Persons with no reported physical activity.

Source: U.S. National Center for Chronic Disease Prevention and Health Promotion, "Nutrition and Physical Activity"; <http://www.cdc.gov/nccdphp/dnpa>; (accessed: 21 June 2002) and unpublished data.

No. 211. Households and Persons Having Problems With Access to Food: 1995 to 2001

[100,445 represents 100,445,000. Food secure means that a household had access at all times to enough food for an active healthy life, with no need for recourse to emergency food sources or other extraordinary coping behaviors to meet their basic food needs. A food insecure household did not have this same access to enough food to fully meet basic needs at all times. Food insecure households with hunger were those with one or more household members who were hungry at least sometime during the period due to inadequate resources for food. The omission of homeless persons may be a cause of underreporting. The federal food security measure was developed through a collaborative process between private nongovernment experts, academic researchers, and a federal interagency working group, with leadership from the U.S. Dept. of Agriculture and the U.S. Dept. of Health and Human Services. The severity of food insecurity and hunger in households is measured through a series of questions about experiences and behaviors known to characterize households that are having difficulty meeting basic food needs. These experiences and behaviors generally occur in an ordered sequence as the severity of food insecurity increases. As resources become more constrained, adults in typical households first worry about having enough food, then they stretch household resources and juggle other necessities, then decrease the quality and variety of household members' diets, then decrease the frequency and quantity of adults' food intake, and finally decrease the frequency and quantity of children's food intake. All questions refer to the previous 12 months and include a qualifying phrase reminding respondents to report only those occurrences that resulted from inadequate financial resources. Restrictions to food intake due to dieting or busy schedules are excluded. Data are from the Food Security Supplement to the Current Population Survey (CPS); for details about the CPS, see text, Section 1, and Appendix III]

Household food security level	Number (1,000) 1995	1998 [1]	1998 [2]	2001	Percent distribution 1995	1998 [1]	1998 [2]	2001
Households, total.	100,445	103,480	103,309	107,824	100.0	100.0	100.0	100.0
Food secure	90,097	92,972	91,121	96,303	89.7	89.8	88.2	89.3
Food insecure	10,348	10,509	12,188	11,521	10.3	10.2	11.8	10.7
Without hunger.	6,402	6,820	8,353	8,010	6.4	6.6	8.1	7.4
With hunger.	3,946	3,689	3,835	3,511	3.9	3.6	3.7	3.3
With hunger among children [3] . .	415	321	331	211	1.1	0.8	0.9	0.6
Adult members	191,063	197,423	197,084	204,340	100.0	100.0	100.0	100.0
Food secure	172,862	178,631	174,964	183,398	90.5	90.5	88.8	89.8
Food insecure	18,200	18,792	22,120	20,942	9.5	9.5	11.2	10.2
Without hunger.	11,611	12,657	15,632	14,879	6.1	6.4	7.9	7.3
With hunger.	6,589	6,135	6,488	6,063	3.4	3.1	3.3	3.0
Child members	70,279	71,463	71,282	72,321	100.0	100.0	100.0	100.0
Food secure	58,048	59,090	57,255	59,620	82.6	82.7	80.3	82.4
Food insecure	12,231	12,373	14,027	12,701	17.4	17.3	19.7	17.6
Without hunger.	11,344	11,682	13,311	12,234	16.1	16.3	18.7	16.9
With hunger among children [3] . .	887	691	716	467	1.3	1.0	1.0	0.6

[1] Adjusted data. These data are comparable to those of earlier years. [2] Data as collected. These data are comparable to those for 2001. [3] One or more children in these households was hungry because of the household's food insecurity. Percent distribution of households with hunger among children excludes households with no child from the denominator.

Source: U.S. Dept. of Agriculture, Economic Research Service, *Household Food Security in the United States, 2001, Food Assistance and Nutrition Research Report No. 29*; October 2002.

Health and Nutrition 141

No. 212. Nutrition—Nutrients in Foods Available for Civilian Consumption Per Capita Per Day: 1970 to 2000

[Computed by the Center for Nutrition Policy and Promotion (CNPP). Based on Economic Research Service (ERS) estimates of per capita quantities of food available for consumption from "Food Consumption, Prices, and Expenditures," on imputed consumption data for foods no longer reported by ERS, and on CNPP estimates of quantities of produce from home gardens. Food supply estimates do not reflect loss of food or nutrients from further marketing or home processing. Enrichment and fortification levels of iron, zinc, thiamin, riboflavin, niacin, vitamin A, vitamin B_6, vitamin B_{12}, and ascorbic acid are included]

Nutrient	Unit	1970-79	1980-89	1990-99	1995	2000
Food energy	Calories	3,300	3,400	3,700	3,700	3,900
Carbohydrate	Grams	396	420	489	492	505
Dietary fiber	Grams	19	21	24	24	25
Protein	Grams	95	99	108	108	112
Total fat [1]	Grams	149	156	158	156	171
Saturated	Grams	51	52	50	50	54
Monounsaturated	Grams	60	63	67	66	72
Polyunsaturated	Grams	28	31	33	33	37
Cholesterol	Milligrams	440	420	410	400	430
Vitamin A	Micrograms RE [2]	1,220	1,160	1,200	1,200	1,200
Carotenes	Micrograms RE [2]	550	590	720	720	720
Vitamin E	Milligrams α-TE [3]	13.9	15.6	17.2	16.9	19.2
Vitamin C	Milligrams	110	117	126	126	126
Thiamin	Milligrams	2.2	2.6	3.0	3.0	3.0
Riboflavin	Milligrams	2.5	2.7	2.9	2.9	2.9
Niacin	Milligrams	25.0	28.0	32.0	31.0	33.0
Vitamin B_6	Milligrams	2.0	2.2	2.4	2.4	2.5
Total Folate	Micrograms	318	348	447	380	711
Folate (DFE) [4]	Micrograms	292	305	449	326	936
Vitamin B_{12}	Micrograms	8.9	8.2	7.9	8.0	8.3
Calcium	Milligrams	920	920	970	960	970
Phosphorus	Milligrams	1,490	1,540	1,680	1,670	1,700
Magnesium	Milligrams	330	350	390	380	390
Iron	Milligrams	16.4	19.7	23.2	23.0	23.7
Zinc	Milligrams	12.9	13.9	15.1	15.0	15.2
Copper	Milligrams	1.6	1.7	1.9	1.9	1.9
Potassium	Milligrams	3,440	3,480	3,720	3,690	3,770
Selenium	Milligrams	132	142	165	161	181
Sodium [5]	Milligrams	1,360	1,350	1,360	1,360	1,340

[1] Includes other types of fat not shown separately. [2] Retinol equivalents. [3] Alpha-Tocopherol equivalents. [4] Reflects new terminology from Institute of Medicine's Dietary Reference Intakes reports. [5] Does not include amount from processed foods; underestimates actual availability.

Source: U.S. Dept. of Agriculture, Center for Nutrition Policy and Promotion, *Nutrient Content of the U.S. Food Supply, 1909-2000*, 2001. Data also published by Economic Research Service in *Food Consumption, Prices, and Expenditures*, annual. <http://www.usda.gov/cnpp/>.

No. 213. Sources of Calcium, Iron, and Cholesterol in the U.S. Food Supply: 1970 and 2000

[In percent. See headnote, Table 212]

Commodity group	Calcium 1970	Calcium 2000	Commodity group	Iron 1970	Iron 2000	Commodity group	Cholesterol 1970	Cholesterol 2000
Total	100	100	Total	100	100	Total	100	100
Whole milk	35	11	Grains and breakfast cereals	37	53	Meat, poultry, fish [1]	39	44
Low-fat and skim milk	11	21	Meat, poultry, fish [1]	23	15	Eggs	40	35
Cheese	11	25	Eggs	4	2	Whole milk	8	3
Other dairy	19	15	Vegetables	14	10	Low-fat and skim milk	1	2
Vegetables	7	7	Fruits	3	2	Cheese	3	7
Other foods	17	21	Dairy products	2	2	Other dairy	3	4
			Other foods	17	16	Other foods	6	5

[1] Includes meat alternatives.

Source: U.S. Dept. of Agriculture, Center for Nutrition Policy and Promotion, *Nutrient Content of the U.S. Food Supply, 1909-2000*, 2002. <http://www.usda.gov/cnpp/>.

No. 214. Per Capita Consumption of Major Food Commodities: 1980 to 2001

[In pounds, retail weight, except as indicated. Consumption represents the residual after exports, nonfood use and ending stocks are subtracted from the sum of beginning stocks, domestic production, and imports. Based on Census Bureau estimated population]

Commodity	Unit	1980	1985	1990	1995	1999	2000	2001
Red meat, total (boneless, trimmed weight) [1][2]	Pounds	126.4	124.9	112.2	113.6	115.1	113.7	111.3
Beef	Pounds	72.1	74.6	63.9	63.5	64.3	64.5	63.1
Veal	Pounds	1.3	1.5	0.9	0.8	0.6	0.5	0.5
Lamb and mutton	Pounds	1.0	1.1	1.0	0.9	0.8	0.8	0.8
Pork	Pounds	52.1	47.7	46.4	48.4	49.3	47.8	46.9
Poultry (boneless, trimmed weight) [2]	Pounds	40.8	45.5	56.2	62.1	66.7	66.9	66.2
Chicken	Pounds	32.7	36.4	42.4	48.2	52.8	53.2	52.4
Turkey	Pounds	8.1	9.1	13.8	13.9	13.8	13.7	13.8
Fish and shellfish (boneless, trimmed weight)	Pounds	12.4	15.0	14.9	14.8	14.8	15.2	14.7
Eggs	Number	271	255	234	232	249	250	251
Shell	Number	236	217	186	172	177	177	179
Processed	Number	35	39	48	59	72	73	73
Dairy products, total [3]	Pounds	543.2	593.7	568.0	576.2	584.6	592.8	587.2
Fluid milk products [4]	Gallons	27.9	27.1	26.2	24.5	23.6	23.2	22.8
Beverage milks	Gallons	27.6	26.7	25.7	23.9	22.9	22.5	22.0
Plain whole milk	Gallons	16.5	13.9	10.2	8.3	7.8	7.7	7.4
Plain reduced-fat milk (2%)	Gallons	6.3	7.9	9.1	8.0	7.3	7.1	7.0
Plain light and skim milks	Gallons	3.1	3.2	4.9	6.1	6.2	6.1	5.9
Flavored whole milk	Gallons	0.6	0.4	0.3	0.3	0.4	0.4	0.4
Flavored milks other than whole	Gallons	0.6	0.7	0.8	0.8	1.0	1.0	1.0
Buttermilk	Gallons	0.5	0.5	0.4	0.3	0.3	0.3	0.2
Yogurt (excl. frozen)	1/2 pints	4.6	7.3	7.4	9.2	11.4	12.0	12.9
Fluid cream products [5]	1/2 pints	10.5	13.5	14.3	15.6	17.8	18.4	20.0
Cream [6]	1/2 pints	6.3	8.2	8.7	9.4	11.4	11.7	12.8
Sour cream and dips	1/2 pints	3.4	4.3	4.7	5.4	5.7	6.1	6.5
Condensed and evaporated milks	Pounds	7.0	7.5	7.9	6.8	6.5	5.8	5.4
Whole milk	Pounds	3.8	3.6	3.2	2.3	2.1	2.0	2.0
Skim milk	Pounds	3.3	3.8	4.8	4.5	4.4	3.8	3.4
Cheese [7]	Pounds	17.5	22.5	24.6	26.9	29.0	29.8	30.0
American [8]	Pounds	9.6	12.2	11.1	11.7	12.6	12.7	12.8
Cheddar	Pounds	6.9	9.8	9.0	9.0	9.8	9.7	9.9
Italian [8]	Pounds	4.4	6.5	9.0	10.3	11.6	12.0	12.3
Mozzarella	Pounds	3.0	4.6	6.9	8.0	9.0	9.3	9.7
Other [8]	Pounds	3.4	3.9	4.5	5.0	4.9	5.1	4.9
Swiss	Pounds	1.3	1.3	1.4	1.1	1.1	1.0	1.2
Cream and Neufchatel	Pounds	1.0	1.2	1.7	2.0	2.3	2.4	2.3
Cottage cheese, total	Pounds	4.5	4.1	3.4	2.7	2.6	2.6	2.6
Lowfat	Pounds	0.8	1.0	1.2	1.2	1.3	1.3	1.3
Frozen dairy products	Pounds	26.4	27.9	28.4	29.0	28.6	28.0	26.9
Ice cream	Pounds	17.5	18.1	15.8	15.5	16.7	16.6	16.3
Lowfat ice cream	Pounds	7.1	6.9	7.7	7.4	7.5	7.3	7.3
Sherbet	Pounds	1.2	1.3	1.2	1.3	1.3	1.2	1.1
Frozen yogurt	Pounds	(NA)	(NA)	2.8	3.4	1.9	2.0	1.5
Fats and oils:								
Total, fat content only	Pounds	56.9	64.1	63.0	65.4	67.0	74.5	(NA)
Butter (product weight)	Pounds	4.5	4.9	4.4	4.4	4.4	4.6	(NA)
Margarine (product weight)	Pounds	11.3	10.8	10.9	9.1	7.9	8.2	(NA)
Lard (direct use)	Pounds	2.3	1.6	1.6	1.6	2.0	2.0	(NA)
Edible beef tallow (direct use)	Pounds	1.1	2.0	0.6	2.7	3.6	4.0	(NA)
Shortening	Pounds	18.2	22.9	22.2	22.2	21.1	23.1	(NA)
Salad and cooking oils	Pounds	21.2	23.5	25.2	26.5	28.8	33.7	(NA)
Other edible fats and oils	Pounds	1.5	1.6	1.2	1.6	1.5	1.5	(NA)
Flour and cereal products [9]	Pounds	144.7	156.5	180.9	190.2	195.5	199.8	195.7
Wheat flour	Pounds	116.9	124.6	135.9	140.0	142.6	146.3	140.9
Rice, milled	Pounds	9.4	9.1	15.8	18.6	19.5	19.6	20.2
Corn products	Pounds	12.9	17.2	21.4	24.9	27.8	28.4	28.9
Oat products	Pounds	3.9	4.0	6.5	5.4	4.4	4.3	4.4
Caloric sweeteners, total [10]	Pounds	123.0	128.8	132.4	143.8	151.3	148.9	147.1
Sugar, refined cane and beet	Pounds	83.6	62.7	64.4	64.7	66.3	65.6	64.4
Corn sweeteners [11]	Pounds	38.2	64.8	66.8	77.9	83.5	81.9	81.4
High-fructose corn syrup	Pounds	19.0	45.2	49.6	57.6	63.7	62.7	62.5
Other:								
Cocoa beans	Pounds	3.4	4.6	5.4	4.5	5.6	5.9	5.6
Coffee (green beans)	Pounds	10.3	10.5	10.3	7.9	9.8	10.3	9.4
Peanuts (shelled)	Pounds	4.8	6.3	6.0	5.6	6.0	5.8	(NA)
Tree nuts (shelled)	Pounds	1.8	2.5	2.4	1.9	2.5	2.5	2.9

NA Not available. [1] Excludes edible offals. [2] Excludes shipments to Puerto Rico and the other U.S. possessions. [3] Milk-equivalent, milkfat basis. Includes butter. [4] Fluid milk figures are aggregates of commercial sales and milk produced and consumed on farms. [5] Includes eggnog, not shown separately. [6] Heavy cream, light cream, and half and half. [7] Excludes full-skim American, cottage, pot, and baker's cheese. [8] Includes other cheeses not shown separately. [9] Includes rye flour and barley products not shown separately. Excludes quantities used in alcoholic beverages. [10] Dry weight. Includes edible syrups (maple, molasses, etc.) and honey not shown separately. [11] Includes glucose and dextrose not shown separately.

Source: U.S. Department of Agriculture, Economic Research Service, *Food Consumption, Prices, and Expenditures, 1970-2000;* online at <http://www.ers.usda.gov/data/consumption>.

No. 215. Per Capita Utilization of Commercially Produced Fruits and Vegetables: 1980 to 2001

[In pounds, farm weight. Domestic food use of fresh fruits and vegetables reflects the fresh-market share of commodity production plus imports and minus exports]

Commodity	1980	1985	1990	1995	1997	1998	1999	2000	2001
Fruits and vegetables, total [1]	608.0	629.3	659.2	690.0	707.6	698.8	698.3	705.4	688.7
Fruits, total	270.5	270.0	272.1	281.8	289.5	283.9	284.6	280.3	275.7
Fresh fruits	104.8	110.6	116.2	122.5	129.4	128.8	129.6	127.2	125.8
Noncitrus	78.7	89.1	94.9	98.7	102.9	102.3	109.3	103.8	101.5
Apples	19.2	17.3	19.6	18.7	18.1	19.0	18.5	17.5	15.6
Bananas	20.8	23.5	24.3	27.1	27.1	28.0	30.7	28.5	26.6
Cantaloupes	5.8	8.5	9.2	9.0	10.5	10.7	11.5	10.8	11.2
Grapes	4.0	6.8	7.9	7.4	7.9	7.1	8.0	7.3	7.6
Peaches and nectarines	7.1	5.5	5.5	5.3	5.5	4.8	5.4	5.4	5.2
Pears	2.6	2.8	3.2	3.4	3.4	3.3	3.3	3.2	3.1
Pineapples	1.5	1.5	2.0	1.9	2.3	2.8	3.0	3.2	3.2
Plums and prunes	1.5	1.4	1.5	0.9	1.5	1.2	1.3	1.2	1.3
Strawberries	2.0	3.0	3.2	4.1	4.1	3.9	4.9	4.9	4.2
Watermelons	10.7	13.5	13.3	15.2	15.5	14.3	15.4	13.9	15.1
Other [2]	3.5	5.3	5.2	5.7	7.0	7.2	7.3	8.0	8.4
Fresh citrus	26.1	21.5	21.4	23.8	26.5	26.6	20.3	23.4	24.3
Oranges	14.3	11.6	12.4	11.8	13.9	14.6	8.4	11.7	12.4
Grapefruit	7.3	5.5	4.4	6.0	6.2	5.9	5.7	5.1	4.8
Other [3]	4.5	4.4	4.6	6.0	6.4	6.1	6.2	6.6	7.1
Processed fruits [4]	165.7	159.5	155.8	159.3	160.1	155.1	154.9	153.2	150.0
Frozen fruits [4]	3.1	3.3	3.8	4.1	3.6	4.1	4.4	3.1	5.9
Dried fruits [5]	11.2	12.8	12.1	12.6	10.6	12.1	10.1	10.4	10.2
Canned fruits [6]	24.6	20.9	21.0	17.3	20.1	17.0	19.2	17.5	17.7
Fruit juices [7]	126.1	122.2	118.7	124.9	125.1	121.5	120.8	121.6	115.8
Vegetables, total	337.5	359.2	387.1	408.2	418.1	414.9	413.7	425.1	412.9
Fresh vegetables	150.4	157.4	170.8	180.8	190.1	186.3	191.3	200.4	196.6
Asparagus (all uses)	0.3	0.5	0.6	0.6	0.7	0.7	0.9	1.0	0.9
Broccoli	1.4	2.6	3.4	4.3	5.0	5.1	6.5	6.1	5.6
Cabbage	8.1	8.8	8.8	8.2	9.2	8.5	7.6	9.0	9.0
Carrots	6.2	6.5	8.3	11.2	14.1	12.7	10.9	10.4	10.6
Cauliflower	1.1	1.8	2.2	1.6	1.8	1.5	1.9	2.0	1.6
Celery (all uses)	7.4	6.9	7.2	6.9	6.5	6.5	6.6	6.4	6.6
Corn	6.5	6.4	6.7	7.8	8.3	9.3	9.1	9.0	9.4
Cucumbers	3.9	4.4	4.7	5.6	6.4	6.5	6.8	6.4	6.4
Head lettuce	25.6	23.7	27.7	22.2	23.9	21.6	23.9	23.4	23.5
Mushrooms	1.2	1.8	2.0	2.0	2.3	2.5	2.5	2.6	2.6
Onions	11.4	13.6	15.1	17.8	18.8	18.3	18.1	18.3	17.8
Snap beans	1.3	1.3	1.1	1.6	1.3	1.7	1.9	2.0	2.2
Bell peppers (all uses)	2.9	3.8	4.5	6.2	6.4	6.4	6.7	7.0	6.7
Potatoes	51.1	46.3	46.7	49.2	48.5	47.0	48.0	47.3	46.2
Sweetpotatoes (all uses)	4.4	5.4	4.6	4.4	4.4	4.0	3.7	4.2	4.4
Tomatoes	12.8	14.9	15.5	16.8	16.8	17.5	17.8	17.6	17.4
Other fresh vegetables [8]	4.8	8.7	11.7	14.4	15.7	16.5	18.4	27.5	25.7
Processed vegetables	187.1	201.8	216.3	227.4	228.0	228.6	222.4	224.7	216.3
Selected vegetables for freezing	51.5	64.5	66.8	78.8	81.5	80.4	80.9	79.7	78.2
Selected vegetables for canning	102.8	99.2	111.5	109.3	105.9	107.0	102.8	103.0	97.1
Vegetables for dehydrating [9]	10.5	12.8	14.6	14.5	16.8	17.7	14.7	17.7	15.7
Potatoes for chips	16.5	17.6	16.4	16.4	15.9	14.8	15.9	16.0	17.6
Pulses [10]	5.8	7.6	7.1	8.3	7.9	8.7	8.1	8.4	7.8

[1] Excludes wine grapes. [2] Apricots, avocados, cherries, cranberries, kiwifruit, mangoes, papayas, and honeydew melons. [3] Lemons, limes, tangerines, and tangelos. [4] Apples, apricots, blackberries, blueberries, boysenberries, cherries, loganberries, peaches, plums, prunes, raspberries, and strawberries. [5] Apples, apricots, dates, figs, peaches, pears, prunes, and raisins. [6] Apples, apricots, cherries, olives, peaches, pears, pineapples, plums, and prunes. [7] Apple, cranberry, grape, grapefruit, lemon, lime, orange, pineapple, and prunes. [8] Artichokes, brussels sprouts, eggplant, escarole, endive, garlic, romaine, leaf lettuce, radishes, spinach, and squash. Beginning 2000 includes collard greens, kale, mustard greens, okra, pumpkin, and turnip greens. [9] Onions and potatoes. [10] Dry peas, lentils, and dry edible beans.

No. 216. Per Capita Consumption of Selected Beverages by Type: 1980 to 2001

[In gallons. See headnote, Table 214]

Commodity	1980	1985	1990	1995	1997	1998	1999	2000	2001
Nonalcoholic	(NA)	(NA)	128.1	127.9	131.5	136.2	140.8	(NA)	(NA)
Milk (plain and flavored)	27.6	26.7	25.7	23.9	23.4	23.0	22.9	22.5	22.0
Whole	17.0	14.3	10.5	8.6	8.3	8.1	8.2	8.1	7.8
Reduced-fat, light, and skim	10.5	12.3	15.2	15.3	15.2	14.9	14.8	14.4	14.2
Tea	7.3	7.1	6.9	7.9	7.2	8.3	8.2	7.8	8.2
Coffee	26.7	27.4	26.8	20.2	23.3	23.9	25.1	26.3	24.2
Bottled water	2.4	4.5	8.0	11.5	12.9	15.7	17.7	(NA)	(NA)
Carbonated soft drinks	35.1	35.7	46.2	47.4	46.8	47.9	49.7	49.3	(NA)
Diet	5.1	7.1	10.7	10.9	10.6	11.0	11.4	11.6	(NA)
Regular	29.9	28.7	35.6	36.5	36.2	36.8	38.2	37.7	(NA)
Fruit juices	7.4	7.8	7.8	8.3	8.7	8.5	8.5	8.7	8.3
Fruit drinks, cocktails, and ades	(NA)	(NA)	6.3	7.7	8.2	7.7	7.7	(NA)	(NA)
Canned iced tea	(NA)	(NA)	0.1	0.7	0.8	0.7	0.7	(NA)	(NA)
Vegetable juices	(NA)	(NA)	0.3	0.3	0.3	0.3	0.3	(NA)	(NA)
Alcoholic	28.3	28.0	27.5	24.7	24.7	24.8	25.0	24.9	25.0
Beer	24.3	23.8	23.9	21.8	21.6	21.7	21.8	21.7	21.7
Wine [1]	2.1	2.4	2.0	1.7	1.9	1.9	2.0	2.0	2.0
Distilled spirits	2.0	1.8	1.5	1.2	1.2	1.2	1.2	1.3	1.3

NA Not available. [1] Beginning 1985, includes wine coolers.

Source of Tables 215 and 216: U.S. Dept. of Agriculture, Economic Research Service, *Food Consumption, Prices, and Expenditures,* annual; online at <http://www.ers.usda.gov/data/consumption>.

Section 4
Education

This section presents data primarily concerning formal education as a whole, at various levels, and for public and private schools. Data shown relate to the school-age population and school enrollment, educational attainment, education personnel, and financial aspects of education. In addition, data are shown for charter schools, computer usage in schools, distance education, and adult education. The chief sources are the decennial census of population and the Current Population Survey (CPS), both conducted by the U.S. Census Bureau (see text, Section 1, Population); annual, biennial, and other periodic surveys conducted by the National Center for Education Statistics (NCES), a part of the U.S. Department of Education; and surveys conducted by the National Education Association.

The censuses of population have included data on school enrollment since 1840 and on educational attainment since 1940. The CPS has reported on school enrollment annually since 1945 and on educational attainment periodically since 1947.

The NCES is continuing the pattern of statistical studies and surveys conducted by the U.S. Office of Education since 1870. The annual *Digest of Education Statistics* provides summary data on pupils, staff, finances, including government expenditures, and organization at the elementary, secondary, and higher education levels. It is also a primary source for detailed information on federal funds for education, projections of enrollment, graduates, and teachers. *The Condition of Education*, issued annually, presents a summary of information on education of particular interest to policymakers. NCES also conducts special studies periodically.

The census of governments, conducted by the Census Bureau every 5 years (for the years ending in "2" and "7"), provides data on school district finances and state and local government expenditures for education. Reports published by the Bureau of Labor Statistics contain data relating civilian labor force experience to educational attainment (see also Tables 591, 618, and 626 in Section 12, Labor Force, Employment, and Earnings).

Types and sources of data—The statistics in this section are of two general types. One type, exemplified by data from the Census Bureau, is based on direct interviews with individuals to obtain information about their own and their family members' education. Data of this type relate to school enrollment and level of education attained, classified by age, sex, and other characteristics of the population. The school enrollment statistics reflect attendance or enrollment in any regular school within a given period; educational attainment statistics reflect the highest grade completed by an individual, or beginning 1992, the highest diploma or degree received.

Beginning in 2001, the CPS used Census 2000 population controls. From 1994 to 2000, the CPS used 1990 census population controls plus adjustment for undercount. Also the survey changed from paper to computer assisted technology. For years 1981 through 1993, 1980 census population controls were used; 1971 through 1980, 1970 census population controls had been used. These changes had little impact on summary measures (e.g., medians) and proportional measures (e.g., enrollment rates); however, use of the controls may have significant impact on absolute numbers.

The second type, generally exemplified by data from the NCES and the National Education Association, is based on reports from administrators of educational institutions and of state and local agencies having jurisdiction over education. Data of this type relate to enrollment, attendance, staff, and finances for the nation, individual states, and local areas.

Unlike the NCES, the Census Bureau does not regularly include specialized vocational, trade, business, or correspondence schools in its surveys. The NCES includes nursery schools and kindergartens that are part of regular grade schools in their enrollment figures. The Census Bureau includes all nursery schools and kindergartens. At the higher education level, the statistics of both agencies are concerned with institutions granting degrees or offering work acceptable for degree-credit, such as junior colleges.

School attendance—All states require that children attend school. While state laws vary as to the ages and circumstances of compulsory attendance, generally they require that formal schooling begin by age 6 and continue to age 16.

Schools—The NCES defines a school as "a division of the school system consisting of students composing one or more grade groups or other identifiable groups, organized as one unit with one or more teachers to give instruction of a defined type, and housed in a school plant of one or more buildings. More than one school may be housed in one school plant, as is the case when the elementary and secondary programs are housed in the same school plant."

Regular schools are those which advance a person toward a diploma or degree. They include public and private nursery schools, kindergartens, graded schools, colleges, universities, and professional schools.

Public schools are schools controlled and supported by local, state, or federal governmental agencies; private schools are those controlled and supported mainly by religious organizations or by private persons or organizations.

The Census Bureau defines *elementary* schools as including grades 1 through 8; *high* schools as including grades 9 through 12; and *colleges* as including junior or community colleges, regular 4-year colleges, and universities and graduate or professional schools. Statistics reported by the NCES and the National Education Association by type of organization, such as elementary level and secondary level, may not be strictly comparable with those from the Census Bureau because the grades included at the two levels vary, depending on the level assigned to the middle or junior high school by the local school systems.

School year—Except as otherwise indicated in the tables, data refer to the school year which, for elementary and secondary schools, generally begins in September of the preceding year and ends in June of the year stated. For the most part, statistics concerning school finances are for a 12-month period, usually July 1 to June 30. Enrollment data generally refer to a specific point in time, such as fall, as indicated in the tables.

Statistical reliability—For a discussion of statistical collection, estimation, and sampling procedures and measures of statistical reliability applicable to the Census Bureau and the NCES data, see Appendix III.

No. 217. School Enrollment: 1965 to 2012

[In thousands (54,394 represents 54,394,000). As of fall]

Year	Total	All levels Public	All levels Private	K through grade 8 Public	K through grade 8 Private	Grades 9 through 12 Public	Grades 9 through 12 Private	College[1] Public	College[1] Private
1965	54,394	46,143	8,251	30,563	4,900	11,610	1,400	3,970	1,951
1970	59,838	52,322	7,516	32,558	4,052	13,336	1,311	6,428	2,153
1975	61,004	53,654	7,350	30,515	3,700	14,304	1,300	8,835	2,350
1980	58,305	50,335	7,971	27,647	3,992	13,231	1,339	9,457	2,640
1981	57,916	49,691	8,225	27,280	4,100	12,764	1,400	9,647	2,725
1982	57,591	49,262	8,330	27,161	4,200	12,405	1,400	9,696	2,730
1983	57,432	48,935	8,497	26,981	4,315	12,271	1,400	9,683	2,782
1984	57,150	48,686	8,465	26,905	4,300	12,304	1,400	9,477	2,765
1985	57,226	48,901	8,325	27,034	4,195	12,388	1,362	9,479	2,768
1986	57,709	49,467	8,242	27,420	4,116	12,333	1,336	9,714	2,790
1987	58,253	49,982	8,272	27,933	4,232	12,076	1,247	9,973	2,793
1988	58,485	50,349	8,136	28,501	4,036	11,687	1,206	10,161	2,894
1989	59,279	51,120	8,159	29,152	4,035	11,390	1,163	10,578	2,961
1990	60,269	52,061	8,208	29,878	4,084	11,338	1,150	10,845	2,974
1991	61,681	53,357	8,324	30,506	4,113	11,541	1,162	11,310	3,049
1992	62,633	54,208	8,425	31,088	4,175	11,735	1,147	11,385	3,103
1993	63,118	54,654	8,464	31,504	4,215	11,961	1,132	11,189	3,116
1994	63,888	55,245	8,643	31,898	4,335	12,213	1,163	11,134	3,145
1995	64,764	55,933	8,831	32,341	4,465	12,500	1,197	11,092	3,169
1996	65,743	56,732	9,011	32,764	4,551	12,847	1,213	11,120	3,247
1997	66,470	57,323	9,147	33,073	4,623	13,054	1,218	11,196	3,306
1998	66,983	57,676	9,306	33,346	4,702	13,193	1,235	11,138	3,369
1999	67,666	58,167	9,500	33,488	4,765	13,369	1,254	11,309	3,482
2000	68,479	58,976	9,504	33,709	4,678	13,514	1,266	11,753	3,560
2001, proj.	68,962	59,440	9,522	33,854	4,668	13,722	1,276	11,864	3,578
2002, proj.	69,174	59,599	9,575	33,756	4,660	13,857	1,292	11,986	3,622
2003, proj.	69,456	59,847	9,609	33,677	4,644	14,069	1,310	12,101	3,655
2004, proj.	69,747	60,093	9,653	33,500	4,620	14,346	1,334	12,247	3,699
2005, proj.	70,001	60,300	9,700	33,315	4,603	14,597	1,351	12,388	3,746
2006, proj.	70,183	60,441	9,743	33,174	4,592	14,739	1,358	12,528	3,793
2007, proj.	70,292	60,511	9,782	33,078	4,588	14,768	1,355	12,665	3,839
2008, proj.	70,390	60,560	9,829	33,069	4,592	14,649	1,341	12,842	3,896
2009, proj.	70,516	60,630	9,886	33,122	4,604	14,485	1,327	13,023	3,955
2010, proj.	70,683	60,740	9,945	33,244	4,625	14,317	1,313	13,179	4,007
2011, proj.	70,956	60,937	10,020	33,389	4,649	14,197	1,303	13,351	4,068
2012, proj.	71,365	61,252	10,113	33,578	4,680	14,137	1,297	13,537	4,136

[1] Data beginning 1996 based on new classification system. See footnote 1, Table 277.

Source: U.S. National Center for Education Statistics, *Digest of Education Statistics*, annual, and *Projections of Education Statistics*, annual.

No. 218. School Expenditures by Type of Control and Level of Instruction in Constant (2001-2002) Dollars: 1960 to 2002

[In billions of dollars (144.7 represents $144,700,000,000). For school years ending in year shown. Total expenditures for public elementary and secondary schools include current expenditures, interest on school debt and capital outlay. Data deflated by the Consumer Price Index, wage earners, and clerical workers through 1975; thereafter, all urban consumers, on a school year basis (supplied by the National Center for Education Statistics). See also Appendix III]

Year	Total	Elementary and secondary schools Total	Elementary and secondary schools Public	Elementary and secondary schools Private[1]	Colleges and universities[2] Total	Colleges and universities[2] Public	Colleges and universities[2] Private
1960	144.7	101.4	94.7	6.7	43.3	23.7	19.7
1970	322.9	203.7	191.9	11.8	119.2	76.6	42.7
1975	373.9	236.9	223.1	13.8	137.0	92.8	44.2
1980	380.2	236.8	220.3	16.5	143.4	95.1	48.3
1985	417.2	251.7	230.8	20.9	165.5	107.3	58.2
1986	441.3	265.0	243.3	21.6	176.3	114.7	61.6
1987	467.7	280.7	257.8	22.9	187.1	119.4	67.6
1988	482.0	289.2	265.7	23.5	192.9	122.8	70.0
1989	510.0	307.9	283.7	24.1	202.2	128.1	74.1
1990	535.4	324.1	298.6	25.5	211.3	135.3	76.0
1991	549.1	331.2	305.3	25.9	217.8	139.0	78.9
1992	558.3	336.8	310.8	26.0	221.4	140.1	81.3
1993	570.2	343.0	316.2	26.8	227.2	144.0	83.2
1994	581.6	350.4	323.3	27.1	231.2	145.7	85.5
1995	597.0	358.3	330.5	27.7	238.8	151.2	87.6
1996	610.8	367.0	338.7	28.4	243.8	153.1	90.6
1997	631.2	380.3	351.2	29.2	250.9	156.6	94.3
1998	658.3	398.2	368.3	29.9	260.2	162.0	98.2
1999	686.1	415.9	385.4	30.5	270.2	168.2	102.0
2000	714.1	433.1	401.8	31.3	281.0	176.5	104.5
2001	725.4	436.6	405.6	31.0	288.8	181.7	107.2
2002	745.2	454.1	422.1	32.0	291.1	182.5	108.6

[1] Estimated. [2] Data beginning 1996 based on new classification system. See footnote 1, Table 277.

Source: U.S. National Center for Education Statistics, *Digest of Education Statistics*, annual.

No. 219. School Enrollment, Faculty, Graduates, and Finances With Projections: 1999 to 2005

[As of fall, except as indicated (52,875 represents 52,875,000)]

Item	Unit	1999	2000, proj.	2001, proj.	2002, proj.	2003, proj.	2004, proj.	2005, proj.
ELEMENTARY AND SECONDARY SCHOOLS								
School enrollment, total[1]	1,000	52,875	53,167	53,520	53,565	53,700	53,800	53,866
Kindergarten through grade 8	1,000	38,253	38,387	38,522	38,416	38,321	38,120	37,918
Grades 9 through 12	1,000	14,623	14,780	14,998	15,149	15,379	15,680	15,948
Public[1]	1,000	46,857	47,223	47,576	47,613	47,746	47,846	47,912
Kindergarten through grade 8	1,000	33,488	33,709	33,854	33,756	33,677	33,500	33,315
Grades 9 through 12	1,000	13,369	13,514	13,722	13,857	14,069	14,346	14,597
Private[1]	1,000	6,018	5,944	5,944	5,953	5,954	5,954	5,954
Kindergarten through grade 8	1,000	4,765	4,678	4,668	4,660	4,644	4,620	4,603
Grades 9 through 12	1,000	1,254	1,266	1,276	1,292	1,310	1,334	1,351
Enrollment rate:[1]								
5 and 6 year olds	Percent	96.0	95.6	95.3	(NA)	(NA)	(NA)	(NA)
7 to 13 year olds	Percent	98.7	98.2	98.3	(NA)	(NA)	(NA)	(NA)
14 to 17 year olds	Percent	95.8	95.7	95.8	(NA)	(NA)	(NA)	(NA)
Classroom teachers, total[2]	1,000	3,306	3,343	3,379	3,502	3,523	3,546	3,533
Public	1,000	2,911	2,953	2,988	3,111	3,132	3,155	3,142
Private	1,000	395	390	390	391	391	391	391
High school graduates, total[3]	1,000	2,824	2,839	2,869	2,920	2,942	2,965	3,021
Public	1,000	2,546	2,561	2,589	2,636	2,657	2,677	2,726
Public schools:[3]								
Current dollars:								
Teachers' average salary[4]	Dol	41,754	43,335	44,604	(NA)	(NA)	(NA)	(NA)
Current school expenditure[4]	Bil. dol.	323.8	337.9	358.0	(NA)	(NA)	(NA)	(NA)
Per pupil in ADA[4]	Dol	7,392	7,654	8,048	(NA)	(NA)	(NA)	(NA)
Constant (2001-2002) dollars:								
Teachers' average salary[4]	Dol	43,949	44,102	44,604	(NA)	(NA)	(NA)	(NA)
Current school expenditure[4]	Bil. dol.	340.8	343.9	358.0	(NA)	(NA)	(NA)	(NA)
Per pupil in ADA[4]	Dol	7,780	7,789	8,048	(NA)	(NA)	(NA)	(NA)
HIGHER EDUCATION								
Enrollment, total	1,000	14,791	15,312	15,442	15,608	15,756	15,947	16,135
Male	1,000	6,491	6,722	6,772	6,817	6,860	6,919	6,985
Full time	1,000	4,026	4,111	4,220	4,258	4,278	4,313	4,361
Part time	1,000	2,465	2,611	2,552	2,559	2,582	2,606	2,624
Female	1,000	8,301	8,591	8,670	8,791	8,896	9,027	9,150
Full time	1,000	4,761	4,899	4,922	5,023	5,079	5,168	5,254
Part time	1,000	3,540	3,692	3,748	3,768	3,816	3,859	3,896
Public	1,000	11,309	11,753	11,864	11,986	12,101	12,247	12,388
Four-year institutions	1,000	5,970	6,055	6,206	6,287	6,347	6,426	6,509
Two-year institutions	1,000	5,339	5,697	5,657	5,699	5,754	5,821	5,879
Private	1,000	3,482	3,560	3,578	3,622	3,655	3,699	3,746
Four-year institutions	1,000	3,229	3,308	3,319	3,360	3,390	3,430	3,474
Two-year institutions	1,000	253	251	259	263	265	269	273
Undergraduate	1,000	12,681	13,155	13,278	13,432	13,566	13,736	13,901
Graduate	1,000	1,807	1,851	1,852	1,865	1,878	1,897	1,917
First-time professional	1,000	303	307	312	312	312	314	317
Full-time equivalent	1,000	10,944	11,267	11,402	11,552	11,654	11,802	11,956
Public	1,000	8,020	8,267	8,399	8,509	8,586	8,695	8,808
Private	1,000	2,924	3,000	3,004	3,043	3,068	3,106	3,148
Faculty, total	1,000	1,028	1,063	1,072	(NA)	(NA)	(NA)	(NA)
Public	1,000	713	741	748	(NA)	(NA)	(NA)	(NA)
Private	1,000	315	322	324	(NA)	(NA)	(NA)	(NA)
Degrees conferred, total[3]	1,000	2,385	2,416	2,495	2,527	2,548	2,561	2,582
Associate's	1,000	565	579	619	633	632	637	638
Bachelor's	1,000	1,238	1,244	1,282	1,301	1,322	1,327	1,343
Master's	1,000	457	468	468	468	467	470	473
Doctorate's	1,000	45	45	45	45	45	45	45
First-professional	1,000	80	80	81	80	82	82	82

NA Not available. [1] 2000 and 2001 are estimates. [2] Full-time equivalents. [3] For school year ending June the following year. [4] Limited financial projections are shown due to the uncertain behavior of inflation over the long term.

Source: U.S. National Center for Education Statistics, *Digest of Education Statistics*, annual, and *Projections of Educational Statistics*, annual.

No. 220. Federal Funds for Education and Related Programs: 2000 to 2002

[In millions of dollars (85,944.2 represents $85,944,200,000), except percent. For fiscal years ending in September. Figures represent on-budget funds]

Level, agency, and program	2000	2001	2002[1]	Level, agency, and program	2000	2001	2002[1]
Total, all programs	**85,944.2**	**94,505.6**	**109,468.6**	Professional development education	308.3	324.4	352.9
Percent of federal budget outlays	4.8	5.1	5.4	Department of Health and Human Services[2]	954.2	1,360.6	1,524.0
Elementary/secondary education programs	**43,790.8**	**48,530.1**	**54,624.1**	Health professions training programs	340.4	681.1	771.8
Department of Education[2]	20,039.6	22,862.4	26,535.8	National Health Service Corps scholarships	16.0	43.0	49.0
Grants for the disadvantaged	8,529.1	8,647.2	9,398.2	National Institutes of Health training grants[7]	550.2	589.7	654.5
School improvement programs	2,550.0	2,925.2	4,700.5	Department of the Interior	187.2	149.4	199.0
Indian education	65.3	77.8	4,113.0	Shared revenues, Mineral Leasing Act and other receipts—estimated education share	98.7	58.6	104.5
Special education	4,949.0	5,809.0	6,924.6	Indian programs	88.4	90.8	94.5
Vocational and adult education	1,463.0	2,262.2	1,995.0	Department of State	319.0	316.8	291.0
Education reform—Goals 2000	1,243.5	1,737.9	1,792.7	Department of Transportation	60.3	80.5	82.2
Department of Agriculture[2]	10,051.3	10,140.5	10,894.0	Department of Veterans Affairs[2]	1,132.3	1,314.9	1,790.9
Child nutrition programs	9,554.0	9,561.0	[3]10,324.0	Post-Vietnam veterans	4.0	4.0	3.4
Agricultural Marketing Service— commodities[4]	400.0	400.0	400.0	All-volunteer-force educational assistance	984.1	1,129.3	1,596.1
Special milk program	[3]	[3]	[3]	Other agencies and programs[2]	446.2	489.8	469.8
Department of Defense[2]	1,485.6	1,475.0	1,484.9	National Endowment for the Humanities	28.4	30.6	30.0
Overseas dependents schools	210.4	906.0	889.9	National Science Foundation	389.0	432.0	413.0
Section VI schools[5]	370.4	351.9	360.2	**Other education programs[2]**	**5,484.6**	**5,880.0**	**6,399.8**
Department of Health and Human Services	6,011.0	6,958.0	7,315.9	Department of Education[2]	3,223.4	3,293.4	3,606.1
Head Start	5,267.0	6,199.8	6,537.6	Administration	458.1	551.7	561.4
Social security student benefits	729.0	754.2	774.3	Rehabilitative services and handicapped research	2,755.5	2,730.3	3,026.1
Department of the Interior[2]	725.4	890.5	941.4	Department of Agriculture	444.5	454.6	460.5
Mineral Leasing Act and other funds	78.1	91.7	127.0	Department of Health and Human Services	214.0	243.0	282.0
Indian Education	645.3	797.8	813.4	Department of Justice	34.7	29.1	26.4
Department of Justice	224.8	380.6	406.4	Department of State	69.3	73.3	96.6
Inmate programs	223.8	378.6	404.4	Department of the Treasury[2]	83.0	88.0	139.0
Department of Labor	4,683.2	5,189.0	6,351.0	Other agencies and programs[2]	1,415.7	1,698.7	1,789.2
Job Corps	1,256.0	1,369.0	1,431.0	Agency for International Development	299.0	452.0	431.0
Department of Veterans Affairs	445.1	487.4	510.4	Library of Congress	299.0	315.0	359.0
Vocational rehab for disabled veterans	438.6	479.8	501.8	National Endowment for the Arts	4.0	4.6	5.1
Other agencies and programs	124.8	146.5	184.2	National Endowment for the Humanities	70.8	74.1	72.0
Higher education programs[2]	**15,008.7**	**14,893.5**	**22,586.7**	**Research programs at universities and related institutions[2]**	**21,660.1**	**25,202.0**	**25,857.9**
Department of Education	10,727.3	9,840.7	16,808.7	Department of Agriculture	553.6	677.6	500.9
Student financial assistance	9,060.3	10,161.0	11,992.5	Department of Defense	1,891.9	2,507.0	1,888.0
Federal Family Education Loans	2,707.5	-2,404.8	2,651.6	Department of Energy	3,577.0	3,746.2	3,625.1
Department of Agriculture	30.7	37.7	40.7	Department of Health and Human Services	10,491.6	12,167.2	13,736.5
Department of Commerce	3.8	4.0	4.2	National Aeronautics and Space Administration	2,071.0	2,195.2	2,060.3
Department of Defense	1,147.8	1,299.2	1,376.3	National Science Foundation	2,566.2	2,865.6	2,817.8
Tuition assistance for military personnel	263.3	346.5	342.5				
Service academies	212.7	241.2	241.6				
Senior ROTC	363.5	387.1	439.3				

[1] Estimated. [2] Includes other programs and agencies, not shown separately. [3] The Special Milk Program is included in the Child Nutrition Program. [4] Purchased under Section 32 of the Act of August 1935 for use in child nutrition programs. [5] Program provides for the education of dependents of federal employees residing on federal property where free public education is unavailable in the nearby community. [6] Instructional costs only including academics, audiovisual, academic computer center, faculty training, military training, physical education, and libraries. [7] Includes alcohol, drug abuse, and mental health training programs.

Source: U.S. National Center for Education Statistics, *Digest of Education Statistics*, annual.

Education 149

No. 221. School Enrollment by Age: 1970 to 2001

[As of October (60,357 represents 60,357,000). Covers civilian noninstitutional population enrolled in nursery school and above. Based on Current Population Survey, see text, Section 1]

Age	1970	1980	1985	1990	1995	1997	1998	1999	2000	2001
ENROLLMENT (1,000)										
Total 3 to 34 years old	60,357	57,348	58,013	60,588	66,939	69,041	69,277	69,601	69,560	70,271
3 and 4 years old	1,461	2,280	2,801	3,292	4,042	4,194	4,164	4,273	4,097	4,030
5 and 6 years old	7,000	5,853	6,697	7,207	7,901	7,964	7,902	7,774	7,648	7,526
7 to 13 years old	28,943	23,751	22,849	25,016	27,003	27,616	27,846	28,209	28,296	28,570
14 and 15 years old	7,869	7,282	7,362	6,555	7,651	7,744	7,653	7,741	7,885	7,914
16 and 17 years old	6,927	7,129	6,654	6,098	6,997	7,538	7,456	7,611	7,341	7,483
18 and 19 years old	3,322	3,788	3,716	4,044	4,274	4,618	4,914	4,840	4,926	4,871
20 and 21 years old	1,949	2,515	2,708	2,852	3,025	3,231	3,197	3,256	3,314	3,570
22 to 24 years old	1,410	1,931	2,068	2,231	2,545	2,754	2,607	2,664	2,731	2,798
25 to 29 years old	1,011	1,714	1,942	2,013	2,216	2,223	2,216	2,018	2,030	2,140
30 to 34 years old	466	1,105	1,218	1,281	1,284	1,159	1,322	1,215	1,292	1,370
35 years old and over	(NA)	1,290	1,766	2,439	2,830	2,989	2,831	2,794	2,653	2,852
ENROLLMENT RATE										
Total 3 to 34 years old	56.4	49.7	48.3	50.2	53.7	55.6	55.8	56.0	55.8	55.7
3 and 4 years old	20.5	36.7	38.9	44.4	48.7	52.6	52.1	54.2	52.1	52.2
5 and 6 years old	89.5	95.7	96.1	96.5	96.0	96.6	95.6	96.0	95.6	95.3
7 to 13 years old	99.2	99.3	99.2	99.6	98.9	99.1	98.9	98.7	98.2	98.3
14 and 15 years old	98.1	98.2	98.1	99.0	98.9	98.9	98.4	98.2	98.7	98.1
16 and 17 years old	90.0	89.0	91.7	92.5	93.6	94.3	93.9	93.6	92.8	93.4
18 and 19 years old	47.7	46.4	51.6	57.3	59.4	61.5	62.2	60.6	61.2	61.0
20 and 21 years old	31.9	31.0	35.3	39.7	44.9	45.9	44.8	45.3	44.1	45.5
22 to 24 years old	14.9	16.3	16.9	21.0	23.2	26.4	24.9	24.5	24.6	25.1
25 to 29 years old	7.5	9.3	9.2	9.7	11.6	11.8	11.9	11.1	11.4	11.7
30 to 34 years old	4.2	6.4	6.1	5.8	6.0	5.7	6.6	6.2	6.7	6.8
35 years old and over	(NA)	1.4	1.6	2.1	2.2	2.3	2.1	1.8	1.9	2.0

NA Not available.

Source: U.S. Census Bureau, Current Population Reports, PPL-148; and earlier PPL and P-20 reports. See Internet site <http://www.census.gov/population/www/socdemo/school.html>.

No. 222. School Enrollment by Race, Hispanic Origin, and Age: 1980 to 2001

[47,673 represents 47,673,000. See headnote, Table 221]

Age	White 1980	White 1990	White 2001	Black 1980	Black 1990	Black 2001	Hispanic origin[1] 1980	Hispanic origin[1] 1990	Hispanic origin[1] 2001
ENROLLMENT (1,000)									
Total 3 to 34 years old	47,673	48,899	54,447	8,251	8,854	11,141	4,263	6,073	10,852
3 and 4 years old	1,844	2,700	3,073	371	452	753	172	249	585
5 and 6 years old	4,781	5,750	5,786	904	1,129	1,201	491	835	1,414
7 to 13 years old	19,585	20,076	22,229	3,598	3,832	4,697	2,009	2,794	4,910
14 and 15 years old	6,038	5,265	6,216	1,088	1,023	1,230	568	739	1,200
16 and 17 years old	5,937	4,858	5,912	1,047	962	1,103	454	592	987
18 and 19 years old	3,199	3,271	3,777	494	596	743	226	329	633
20 and 21 years old	2,206	2,402	2,863	242	305	426	111	213	384
22 to 24 years old	1,669	1,781	2,067	196	274	397	93	121	330
25 to 29 years old	1,473	1,706	1,556	187	162	295	84	130	265
30 to 34 years old	942	1,090	969	124	119	295	54	72	144
35 years old and over	1,104	2,096	2,202	186	238	489	(NA)	145	311
ENROLLMENT RATE									
Total 3 to 34 years old	48.9	49.5	54.8	53.9	51.9	59.5	49.8	47.4	49.5
3 and 4 years old	36.3	44.9	51.7	38.2	41.6	58.8	28.5	29.8	39.7
5 and 6 years old	95.8	96.5	94.8	95.4	96.3	96.0	94.5	94.8	93.6
7 to 13 years old	99.2	99.6	98.5	99.4	99.8	97.4	99.2	99.4	97.9
14 and 15 years old	98.3	99.1	98.2	97.9	99.2	97.6	94.3	99.0	97.8
16 and 17 years old	88.6	92.5	93.5	90.6	91.7	92.1	81.8	85.4	88.2
18 and 19 years old	46.3	57.1	60.4	45.7	55.2	59.6	37.8	44.1	45.5
20 and 21 years old	31.9	41.0	45.9	23.4	28.4	37.2	19.5	27.2	27.9
22 to 24 years old	16.4	20.2	23.3	13.6	20.0	26.0	11.7	9.9	15.5
25 to 29 years old	9.2	9.9	10.7	8.8	6.1	12.2	6.9	6.3	7.7
30 to 34 years old	6.3	5.9	6.0	6.8	4.4	11.5	5.1	3.6	4.4
35 years old and over	1.3	2.1	1.8	1.8	2.1	3.2	(NA)	2.1	2.5

NA Not available. [1] Persons of Hispanic origin may be of any race.

Source: U.S. Census Bureau, Current Population Reports, PPL-148; and earlier PPL and P-20 reports. See Internet site <http://www.census.gov/population/www/socdemo/school.html>.

No. 223. Enrollment in Public and Private Schools: 1960 to 2001

[In millions (39.0 represents 39,000,000), except percent. As of October. For civilian noninstitutional population. For **1960**, 5 to 34 years old; for **1970 to 1985**, 3 to 34 years old; beginning **1986**, for 3 years old and over]

Year	Public Total	Nursery	Kindergarten	Elementary	High School	College	Private Total	Nursery	Kindergarten	Elementary	High School	College
1960	39.0	(NA)	([1])	27.5	9.2	2.3	7.2	(NA)	([1])	4.9	1.0	1.3
1970	52.2	0.3	2.6	30.0	13.5	5.7	8.1	0.8	0.5	3.9	1.2	1.7
1975	52.8	0.6	2.9	27.2	14.5	7.7	8.2	1.2	0.5	3.3	1.2	2.0
1980	(NA)	0.6	2.7	24.4	(NA)	(NA)	(NA)	1.4	0.5	3.1	(NA)	(NA)
1983	48.7	0.8	2.7	24.2	12.8	8.2	9.0	1.5	0.7	3.0	1.2	2.6
1984	49.0	0.8	3.0	24.1	12.7	8.5	8.3	1.6	0.5	2.7	1.1	2.4
1985	49.0	0.9	3.2	23.8	12.8	8.4	9.0	1.6	0.6	3.1	1.2	2.5
1986 [2]	51.2	0.8	3.4	24.2	13.0	9.8	9.4	1.7	0.6	3.0	1.2	2.9
1987 [2]	51.7	0.8	3.4	24.8	12.7	10.0	8.9	1.7	0.6	2.8	1.1	2.8
1988 [2]	52.2	0.9	3.4	25.5	12.2	10.3	8.9	1.8	0.5	2.8	1.0	2.8
1989 [2]	52.5	0.9	3.3	25.9	12.1	10.3	8.9	1.9	0.6	2.7	0.8	2.9
1990 [2]	53.8	1.2	3.3	26.6	11.9	10.7	9.2	2.2	0.6	2.7	0.9	2.9
1991 [2]	54.5	1.1	3.5	26.6	12.2	11.1	9.4	1.8	0.6	3.0	1.0	3.0
1992 [2]	55.0	1.1	3.5	27.1	12.3	11.1	9.4	1.8	0.6	3.1	1.0	3.0
1993 [2]	56.0	1.2	3.5	27.7	12.6	10.9	9.4	1.8	0.7	2.9	1.0	3.0
1994 [2]	58.6	1.9	3.3	28.1	13.5	11.7	10.7	2.3	0.6	3.4	1.1	3.3
1995 [2]	58.7	2.0	3.2	28.4	13.7	11.4	11.1	2.4	0.7	3.4	1.2	3.3
1996 [2]	59.5	1.9	3.4	28.1	14.1	12.0	10.8	2.3	0.7	3.4	1.2	3.2
1997 [2]	61.6	2.3	3.3	29.3	14.6	12.1	10.5	2.2	0.7	3.1	1.2	3.3
1998 [2]	60.8	2.3	3.1	29.1	14.3	12.0	11.3	2.3	0.7	3.4	1.2	3.6
1999 [2]	60.8	2.3	3.2	29.2	14.4	11.7	11.4	2.3	0.7	3.6	1.3	3.5
2000 [2]	61.2	2.2	3.2	29.4	14.4	12.0	11.0	2.2	0.7	3.5	1.3	3.3
2001 [2]	62.4	2.2	3.1	29.8	14.8	12.4	10.8	2.1	0.6	3.4	1.2	3.5
Percent White:												
1960	85.7	(NA)	([1])	84.3	88.2	92.2	95.7	(NA)	([1])	95.3	96.7	96.3
1970	84.5	59.5	84.4	83.1	85.6	90.7	93.4	91.1	88.2	94.1	96.1	92.8
1980	(NA)	68.2	80.7	80.9	(NA)	(NA)	(NA)	89.0	87.0	90.7	(NA)	(NA)
1990	79.8	71.7	78.3	78.9	79.2	84.1	87.4	89.6	83.2	88.2	89.4	85.0
1995	78.0	71.3	76.9	77.5	76.9	81.9	85.0	88.7	84.1	86.1	86.0	81.1
1999	77.2	69.2	76.5	77.1	77.7	78.8	84.3	87.4	81.2	85.2	87.0	80.9
2000	77.0	69.4	77.3	76.7	78.0	78.0	83.5	84.9	82.8	85.9	84.6	79.8
2001	76.5	68.7	76.1	76.7	77.4	76.5	83.1	84.3	84.4	85.6	86.7	78.4

NA Not available. [1] Included in elementary school. [2] See Table 280 for college enrollment 35 years old and over. Also data beginning 1986 based on a revised edit and tabulation package.

Source: U.S. Census Bureau, Current Population Reports, PPL-148; and earlier PPL and P-20 reports. See Internet site <http://www.census.gov/population/www/socdemo/school.html>.

No. 224. School Enrollment by Sex and Level: 1960 to 2001

[In millions (46.3 represents 46,300,000). As of Oct. For the civilian noninstitutional population. For **1960**, persons 5 to 34 years old; **1970-1979**, 3 to 34 years old; beginning **1980**, 3 years old and over. Elementary includes kindergarten and grades 1-8; high school, grades 9-12; and college, 2-year and 4-year colleges, universities, and graduate and professional schools. Data for college represent degree-credit enrollment]

Year	All levels [1] Total	Male	Female	Elementary Total	Male	Female	High school Total	Male	Female	College Total	Male	Female
1960	46.3	24.2	22.0	32.4	16.7	15.7	10.2	5.2	5.1	3.6	2.3	1.2
1970	60.4	31.4	28.9	37.1	19.0	18.1	14.7	7.4	7.3	7.4	4.4	3.0
1975	61.0	31.6	29.4	33.8	17.3	16.5	15.7	8.0	7.7	9.7	5.3	4.4
1980	58.6	29.6	29.1	30.6	15.8	14.9	14.6	7.3	7.3	11.4	5.4	6.0
1982	59.4	30.0	29.4	30.7	15.8	14.9	14.2	7.2	7.0	12.3	5.9	6.4
1983	59.3	30.1	29.2	30.6	15.7	14.8	14.1	7.1	7.0	12.4	6.0	6.3
1984	58.9	29.9	29.0	30.3	15.6	14.7	13.9	7.1	6.8	12.3	6.0	6.3
1985	59.8	30.0	29.7	30.7	15.7	15.0	14.1	7.2	6.9	12.5	5.9	6.6
1986 [2]	60.5	30.6	30.0	31.1	16.1	15.0	14.2	7.2	7.0	12.7	6.0	6.7
1987	60.6	30.7	29.9	31.6	16.3	15.3	13.8	7.0	6.8	12.7	6.0	6.7
1988	61.1	30.7	30.5	32.2	16.6	15.6	13.2	6.7	6.4	13.1	5.9	7.2
1989	61.5	30.8	30.7	32.5	16.7	15.8	12.9	6.6	6.3	13.2	6.0	7.2
1990	63.0	31.5	31.5	33.2	17.1	16.0	12.8	6.5	6.4	13.6	6.2	7.4
1991	63.9	32.1	31.8	33.8	17.3	16.4	13.1	6.8	6.4	14.1	6.4	7.6
1992	64.6	32.2	32.3	34.3	17.7	16.6	13.3	6.8	6.5	14.0	6.2	7.8
1993	65.4	32.9	32.5	34.8	17.9	16.9	13.6	7.0	6.6	13.9	6.3	7.6
1994	69.3	34.6	34.6	35.4	18.2	17.2	14.6	7.4	7.2	15.0	6.8	8.2
1995	69.8	35.0	34.8	35.7	18.3	17.4	15.0	7.7	7.3	14.7	6.7	8.0
1996	70.3	35.1	35.2	35.5	18.3	17.3	15.3	7.9	7.4	15.2	6.8	8.4
1997	72.0	35.9	36.2	36.3	18.7	17.6	15.8	8.0	7.7	15.4	6.8	8.6
1998	72.1	36.0	36.1	36.4	18.7	17.7	15.6	7.9	7.6	15.5	6.9	8.6
1999	72.4	36.3	36.1	36.7	18.8	17.9	15.9	8.2	7.7	15.2	7.0	8.2
2000	72.2	35.8	36.4	36.7	18.9	17.9	15.8	8.1	7.7	15.3	6.7	8.6
2001	73.1	36.3	36.9	36.9	19.0	17.9	16.1	8.2	7.8	15.9	6.9	9.0

[1] Beginning 1970, includes nursery schools, not shown separately. [2] Revised. Data beginning 1986, based on a revised edit and tabulation package.

Source: U.S. Census Bureau, Current Population Reports, PPL-148; and earlier PPL and P-20 reports. See Internet site <http://www.census.gov/population/www/socdemo/school.html>.

No. 225. School Enrollment by Control and Level: 1980 to 2000

[In thousands (58,305 represents 58,305,000). As of fall. Data are for regular day schools and exclude independent nursery schools and kindergartens, residential schools for exceptional children, subcollegiate departments of colleges, federal schools for Indians, and federally operated schools on federal installations. College data include degree-credit and nondegree-credit enrollment. For projections, see Table 217]

Control of school and level	1980	1990	1993	1994	1995	1996	1997	1998	1999	2000
Total............	58,305	60,269	63,118	63,888	64,764	65,743	66,470	66,983	67,666	68,479
Public.............	50,335	52,061	54,654	55,245	55,933	56,732	57,323	57,676	58,167	58,976
Private............	7,971	8,208	8,464	8,643	8,831	9,011	9,147	9,306	9,500	9,504
Kindergarten through 8..	31,639	33,962	35,719	36,233	36,806	37,316	37,696	38,048	38,253	38,387
Public............	27,647	29,878	31,504	31,898	32,341	32,764	33,073	33,346	33,488	33,709
Private...........	3,992	4,084	4,215	4,335	4,465	4,551	4,623	4,702	4,765	4,678
Grades 9 through 12....	14,570	12,488	13,093	13,376	13,697	14,060	14,272	14,427	14,623	14,780
Public...........	13,231	11,338	11,961	12,213	12,500	12,847	13,054	13,193	13,369	13,514
Private...........	1,339	1,150	1,132	1,163	1,197	1,213	1,218	1,235	1,254	1,266
College [1]............	12,097	13,819	14,305	14,279	14,262	14,368	14,502	14,507	14,791	15,312
Public...........	9,457	10,845	11,189	11,134	11,092	11,120	11,196	11,138	11,309	11,753
Private...........	2,640	2,974	3,116	3,145	3,169	3,247	3,306	3,369	3,482	3,560

[1] Data beginning 1996 reflects new classification system. See footnote 1, Table 277.

Source: U.S. National Center for Education Statistics, Digest of Education Statistics, annual.

No. 226. Students Who Are Foreign Born or Who Have Foreign-Born Parents: 2001

[In thousands (49,225 represents 49,225,000), except percent. As of October. Covers civilian noninstitutional population enrolled in elementary school and above. Based on Current Population Survey, see text, Section 1, and Appendix III]

| Characteristic | All students | Students with at least one foreign-born parent ||||||
| | | Total || Foreign-born student || Native student ||
		Number	Percent	Number	Percent	Number	Percent
ELEMENTARY AND HIGH SCHOOL							
Total [1].....................	49,225	10,154	20.6	2,452	5.0	7,703	15.6
White.......................	38,270	7,237	18.9	1,576	4.1	5,661	14.8
White, non-Hispanic.............	30,579	2,237	7.3	400	1.3	1,837	6.0
Black.......................	8,008	932	11.6	248	3.1	683	8.5
Asian and Pacific Islander.........	2,180	1,850	84.9	609	27.9	1,241	56.9
Hispanic [2].....................	8,142	5,255	64.5	1,228	15.1	4,027	49.5
COLLEGE, 1 TO 4 YEARS							
Total [1].....................	12,552	2,692	21.4	1,339	10.7	1,353	10.8
White.......................	9,742	1,564	16.1	636	6.5	928	9.5
White, non-Hispanic.............	8,355	750	9.0	270	3.2	481	5.8
Black.......................	1,822	332	18.2	210	11.5	123	6.8
Asian and Pacific Islander.........	858	781	91.0	489	57.0	292	34.0
Hispanic [2].....................	1,479	876	59.2	395	26.7	482	32.6
GRADUATE SCHOOL							
Total [1].....................	3,321	995	30.0	685	20.6	310	9.3
White.......................	2,466	478	19.4	242	9.8	237	9.6
White, non-Hispanic.............	2,248	330	14.7	159	7.1	171	7.6
Black.......................	408	103	25.2	89	21.8	14	3.4
Asian and Pacific Islander.........	423	408	96.5	348	82.3	60	14.2
Hispanic [2].....................	221	148	67.0	83	37.6	65	29.4

[1] Includes other races, not shown separately. [2] Persons of Hispanic origin may be of any race.

Source: U.S. Census Bureau, Current Population Reports, PPL-148; and earlier PPL and P-20 reports. See Internet site <http://www.census.gov/population/www/socdemo/school.html>.

No. 227. Educational Attainment by Race and Hispanic Origin: 1960 to 2002

[In percent. For persons 25 years old and over. 1960, 1970, and 1980 as of April 1 and based on sample data from the censuses of population. Other years as of March and based on the Current Population Survey; see text, Section 1, and Appendix III. See Table 228 for data by sex]

Year	Total [1]	White	Black	Asian and Pacific Islander	Hispanic [2] Total [3]	Mexican	Puerto Rican	Cuban
HIGH SCHOOL GRADUATE OR MORE [4]								
1960	41.1	43.2	20.1	(NA)	(NA)	(NA)	(NA)	(NA)
1970	52.3	54.5	31.4	(NA)	32.1	24.2	23.4	43.9
1980	66.5	68.8	51.2	(NA)	44.0	37.6	40.1	55.3
1990	77.6	79.1	66.2	80.4	50.8	44.1	55.5	63.5
1995	81.7	83.0	73.8	(NA)	53.4	46.5	61.3	64.7
1997	82.1	83.0	74.9	84.9	54.7	48.6	61.1	65.2
1998	82.8	83.7	76.0	(NA)	55.5	48.3	63.8	67.8
1999	83.4	84.3	77.0	84.7	56.1	49.7	63.9	70.3
2000	84.1	84.9	78.5	85.7	57.0	51.0	64.3	73.0
2001	84.1	84.8	78.8	87.6	56.8	50.7	64.6	72.2
2002	84.1	84.8	78.7	87.4	57.0	50.6	66.8	70.8
COLLEGE GRADUATE OR MORE [4]								
1960	7.7	8.1	3.1	(NA)	(NA)	(NA)	(NA)	(NA)
1970	10.7	11.3	4.4	(NA)	4.5	2.5	2.2	11.1
1980	16.2	17.1	8.4	(NA)	7.6	4.9	5.6	16.2
1990	21.3	22.0	11.3	39.9	9.2	5.4	9.7	20.2
1995	23.0	24.0	13.2	(NA)	9.3	6.5	10.7	19.4
1997	23.9	24.6	13.3	42.2	10.3	7.5	10.7	19.7
1998	24.4	25.0	14.7	(NA)	11.0	7.5	11.9	22.2
1999	25.2	25.9	15.4	42.4	10.9	7.1	11.1	24.8
2000	25.6	26.1	16.5	43.9	10.6	6.9	13.0	23.0
2001	26.2	26.6	15.7	47.5	11.1	7.8	12.9	19.3
2002	26.7	27.2	17.0	47.2	11.1	7.6	14.0	18.6

NA Not available. [1] Includes other races, not shown separately. [2] Persons of Hispanic origin may be of any race. [3] Includes persons of other Hispanic origin, not shown separately. [4] Through 1990, completed 4 years of high school or more and 4 years of college or more.

Source: U.S. Census Bureau, U.S. Census of Population, *U.S. Summary*, PC80-1-C1 and Current Population Report, P20-536, PPL-169 and PPL-157; earlier reports, and unpublished data. See Internet site <http://www.census.gov/population/www/socdemo/educ-attn.html>.

No. 228. Educational Attainment by Race, Hispanic Origin, and Sex: 1960 to 2002

[In percent. See Table 227 for headnote and totals for both sexes]

Year	All races [1] Male	Female	White Male	Female	Black Male	Female	Asian and Pacific Islander Male	Female	Hispanic [2] Male	Female
HIGH SCHOOL GRADUATE OR MORE [3]										
1960	39.5	42.5	41.6	44.7	18.2	21.8	(NA)	(NA)	(NA)	(NA)
1970	51.9	52.8	54.0	55.0	30.1	32.5	(NA)	(NA)	37.9	34.2
1980	67.3	65.8	69.6	68.1	50.8	51.5	(NA)	(NA)	67.3	65.8
1990	77.7	77.5	79.1	79.0	65.8	66.5	84.0	77.2	50.3	51.3
1995	81.7	81.6	83.0	83.0	73.4	74.1	(NA)	(NA)	52.9	53.8
1997	82.0	82.2	82.9	83.2	73.5	76.0	(NA)	(NA)	54.9	54.6
1998	82.8	82.9	83.6	83.8	75.2	76.7	(NA)	(NA)	55.7	55.3
1999	83.4	83.4	84.2	84.3	76.7	77.2	86.9	82.8	56.0	56.3
2000	84.2	84.0	84.8	85.0	78.7	78.3	88.2	83.4	56.6	57.5
2001	84.1	84.2	84.4	85.1	79.2	78.5	90.3	85.1	55.5	58.0
2002	83.8	84.4	84.3	85.2	78.5	78.9	89.5	85.5	56.1	57.9
COLLEGE GRADUATE OR MORE [3]										
1960	9.7	5.8	10.3	6.0	2.8	3.3	(NA)	(NA)	(NA)	(NA)
1970	13.5	8.1	14.4	8.4	4.2	4.6	(NA)	(NA)	7.8	4.3
1980	20.1	12.8	21.3	13.3	8.4	8.3	(NA)	(NA)	9.4	6.0
1990	24.4	18.4	25.3	19.0	11.9	10.8	44.9	35.4	9.8	8.7
1995	26.0	20.2	27.2	21.0	13.6	12.9	(NA)	(NA)	10.1	8.4
1997	26.2	21.7	27.0	22.3	12.5	13.9	(NA)	(NA)	10.6	10.1
1998	26.5	22.4	27.3	22.8	13.9	15.4	(NA)	(NA)	11.1	10.9
1999	27.5	23.1	28.5	23.5	14.2	16.4	46.2	39.0	10.7	11.0
2000	27.8	23.6	28.5	23.9	16.3	16.7	47.6	40.7	10.7	10.6
2001	28.2	24.3	28.7	24.0	15.3	16.1	52.3	43.2	10.8	11.4
2002	28.5	25.1	29.1	25.4	16.4	17.5	50.9	43.8	11.0	11.2

NA Not available. [1] Includes other races, not shown separately. [2] Persons of Hispanic origin may be of any race. [3] Through 1990, completed 4 years of high school or more and 4 years of college or more.

Source: U.S. Census Bureau, U.S. Census of Population, 1960, 1970, and 1980, Vol. 1; and Current Population Reports, P20-536; PPL-169 and PPL-157; earlier reports, and unpublished data. See Internet site <http://www.census.gov/population/www/socdemo/educ-attn.html>.

No. 229. Educational Attainment by Selected Characteristic: 2002

[For persons 25 years old and over (182,142 represents 182,142,000). As of March. Based on the Current Population Survey; see text, Section 1, and Appendix III. For composition of regions, see map inside front cover]

Characteristic	Population (1,000)	Percent of population—highest level					
		Not a high school graduate	High school graduate	Some college, but no degree	Associate's degree [1]	Bachelor's degree	Advanced degree
Total persons	182,142	15.9	32.1	17.0	8.3	17.7	9.0
Age:							
25 to 34 years old	38,670	13.1	28.4	19.1	8.7	23.2	7.4
35 to 44 years old	44,284	11.6	32.3	17.5	10.0	19.6	8.9
45 to 54 years old	39,545	10.9	31.4	18.0	9.7	18.4	11.6
55 to 64 years old	25,874	16.4	34.0	16.3	7.1	14.9	11.2
65 to 74 years old	18,123	26.5	36.2	13.8	4.8	11.5	7.1
75 years old or over	15,647	34.3	34.2	12.8	4.3	9.0	5.4
Sex:							
Male	86,996	16.2	31.0	16.9	7.4	18.3	10.2
Female	95,146	15.6	33.1	17.2	9.0	17.2	7.9
Race:							
White	151,942	15.2	32.3	16.9	8.4	17.9	9.2
Black	20,359	21.3	33.9	19.8	8.0	11.8	5.2
Other	9,841	15.0	24.6	13.0	7.2	26.6	13.7
Hispanic origin:							
Hispanic	19,670	43.0	27.9	12.7	5.3	8.1	3.0
Non-Hispanic	162,472	12.6	32.6	17.5	8.6	18.9	9.7
Region:							
Northeast	36,080	14.6	34.7	13.3	8.1	18.6	10.9
Midwest	42,185	12.7	35.4	17.7	8.7	17.1	8.4
South	64,295	18.5	31.8	16.7	7.6	17.1	8.3
West	39,583	16.3	26.7	20.2	9.1	18.6	9.1
Marital status:							
Never married	28,156	15.9	29.6	17.4	7.6	21.0	8.5
Married spouse present	112,246	13.3	31.7	16.7	8.6	19.3	10.5
Married spouse absent [2]	2,703	29.8	29.2	14.6	6.8	13.5	6.1
Separated	4,339	25.6	34.7	17.5	7.9	9.9	4.4
Widowed	14,032	33.4	36.5	12.9	5.6	7.8	3.9
Divorced	20,666	14.4	34.6	20.9	9.7	13.6	6.7
Civilian labor force status:							
Employed	116,132	9.9	30.4	18.0	9.6	21.0	11.1
Unemployed	6,075	20.7	37.1	17.7	7.0	13.2	4.4
Not in the labor force	59,935	27.0	34.9	15.1	5.8	11.8	5.4

[1] Includes vocational degrees. [2] Excludes those separated.

Source: U.S. Census Bureau, Current Population Reports, PPL-169; and unpublished data. See Internet site <http://www.census.gov/population/www/socdemo/educ-attn.html>.

No. 230. Mean Earnings by Highest Degree Earned: 2001

[In dollars. For persons 18 years old and over with earnings. Persons as of March the following year. Based on Current Population Survey; see text, Section 1, and Appendix III. For definition of mean, see Guide to Tabular Presentation]

Characteristic	Total persons	Level of highest degree							
		Not a high school graduate	High school graduate only	Some college, no degree	Associate's	Bachelor's	Master's	Professional	Doctorate
All persons [1]	35,805	18,793	26,795	29,095	34,744	50,623	63,592	101,375	85,675
Age:									
25 to 34 years old	32,374	21,024	24,876	28,625	31,640	43,000	48,949	63,122	54,583
35 to 44 years old	41,618	21,725	30,045	35,944	37,179	58,209	71,044	110,560	89,558
45 to 54 years old	44,522	22,149	31,894	38,368	37,727	58,612	68,110	121,487	104,847
55 to 64 years old	41,905	21,969	29,249	38,608	40,305	54,809	69,284	109,567	77,999
65 years old and over	27,487	17,423	22,474	28,563	23,393	35,354	30,857	62,214	75,301
Sex:									
Male	43,648	21,508	32,363	35,268	42,891	63,354	79,034	120,125	95,928
Female	26,962	14,524	20,489	22,776	27,531	36,913	43,689	63,378	62,200
White	36,844	19,120	27,700	29,898	35,086	51,631	64,602	104,271	87,966
Male	45,071	22,006	33,545	36,605	43,121	65,046	80,793	122,560	98,158
Female	27,240	14,197	20,866	22,831	27,696	36,698	48,089	64,668	63,787
Black	27,031	17,248	21,743	25,418	31,133	40,165	51,366	79,265	61,969
Male	30,502	18,543	25,037	28,802	38,714	46,511	63,489	(B)	(B)
Female	24,036	15,912	18,683	22,456	26,157	35,448	44,328	(B)	(B)
Hispanic [2]	24,786	18,334	22,866	26,266	31,195	40,586	54,013	85,422	(B)
Male	27,964	20,614	26,745	31,059	37,148	45,445	65,273	(B)	(B)
Female	20,330	13,976	17,786	21,224	25,117	35,142	43,891	(B)	(B)

B Base figure too small to meet statistical standards for reliability of a derived figure. [1] Includes other races, not shown separately. [2] Persons of Hispanic origin may be of any race.

Source: U.S. Census Bureau, Current Population Reports, PPL-169. See Internet site <http://www.census.gov/population/www/socdemo/educ-attn.html>.

No. 231. Educational Attainment by State: 1990 to 2002

[In percent. As of March, except 1990 as of April. For persons 25 years old and over. Based on the 1990 Census of Population and the Current Population Survey; see text, Section 1, and Appendix III]

State	1990 High school graduate or more	1990 Bachelor's degree or more	1998 High school graduate or more	1998 Bachelor's degree or more	2000 High school graduate or more	2000 Bachelor's degree or more	2002 High school graduate or more	2002 Bachelor's degree or more
United States.....	75.2	20.3	82.8	24.4	84.1	25.6	84.1	26.7
Alabama............	66.9	15.7	78.8	20.6	77.5	20.4	78.9	22.7
Alaska.............	86.6	23.0	90.6	24.2	90.4	28.1	92.2	25.6
Arizona............	78.7	20.3	81.9	21.9	85.1	24.6	84.6	26.3
Arkansas...........	66.3	13.3	76.8	16.2	81.7	18.4	81.0	18.3
California..........	76.2	23.4	80.1	26.4	81.2	27.5	80.2	27.9
Colorado...........	84.4	27.0	89.6	34.0	89.7	34.6	87.6	35.7
Connecticut........	79.2	27.2	83.7	31.4	88.2	31.6	88.0	32.6
Delaware...........	77.5	21.4	85.2	25.1	86.1	24.0	88.5	29.5
District of Columbia	73.1	33.3	83.8	36.5	83.2	38.3	83.5	44.4
Florida.............	74.4	18.3	81.9	22.5	84.0	22.8	83.3	25.7
Georgia............	70.9	19.3	80.0	20.7	82.6	23.1	82.9	25.0
Hawaii.............	80.1	22.9	84.6	24.0	87.4	26.3	87.9	26.8
Idaho..............	79.7	17.7	82.7	20.3	86.2	20.0	86.8	20.9
Illinois.............	76.2	21.0	84.2	25.8	85.5	27.1	85.9	27.3
Indiana............	75.6	15.6	83.5	17.7	84.6	17.1	85.3	23.7
Iowa...............	80.1	16.9	87.7	20.3	89.7	25.5	88.3	23.1
Kansas.............	81.3	21.1	89.2	28.5	88.1	27.3	87.5	29.1
Kentucky...........	64.6	13.6	77.9	20.1	78.7	20.5	80.8	21.6
Louisiana..........	68.3	16.1	78.6	19.5	80.8	22.5	78.8	22.1
Maine..............	78.8	18.8	86.7	19.2	89.3	24.1	87.4	23.8
Maryland...........	78.4	26.5	84.7	31.8	85.7	32.3	87.5	37.6
Massachusetts......	80.0	27.2	85.6	31.0	85.1	32.7	86.5	34.3
Michigan...........	76.8	17.4	85.4	22.1	86.2	23.0	86.5	22.5
Minnesota..........	82.4	21.8	89.4	31.0	90.8	31.2	92.2	30.5
Mississippi.........	64.3	14.7	77.3	19.5	80.3	18.7	79.1	20.9
Missouri............	73.9	17.8	82.9	22.4	86.6	26.2	88.1	26.7
Montana............	81.0	19.8	89.1	23.9	89.6	23.8	89.7	23.6
Nebraska...........	81.8	18.9	87.7	20.9	90.4	24.6	89.8	27.1
Nevada............	78.8	15.3	89.1	20.6	82.8	19.3	85.8	22.1
New Hampshire.....	82.2	24.4	84.0	26.6	88.1	30.1	90.2	30.1
New Jersey.........	76.7	24.9	86.5	30.1	87.3	30.1	85.9	31.4
New Mexico........	75.1	20.4	79.6	23.1	82.2	23.6	81.6	25.4
New York...........	74.8	23.1	81.5	26.8	82.5	28.7	83.7	28.8
North Carolina......	70.0	17.4	81.4	23.3	79.2	23.2	80.1	22.4
North Dakota.......	76.7	18.1	84.3	22.5	85.5	22.6	89.0	25.3
Ohio...............	75.7	17.0	86.2	21.5	87.0	24.0	87.3	24.5
Oklahoma..........	74.6	17.8	84.6	20.5	86.1	22.5	85.1	20.4
Oregon.............	81.5	20.6	85.5	27.7	88.1	27.2	87.7	27.1
Pennsylvania.......	74.7	17.9	84.1	22.1	85.7	24.3	86.1	26.1
Rhode Island.......	72.0	21.3	80.7	27.8	81.3	26.4	80.1	30.1
South Carolina.....	68.3	16.6	78.6	21.3	83.0	19.0	80.2	23.3
South Dakota......	77.1	17.2	86.3	21.8	91.8	25.7	89.2	23.6
Tennessee.........	67.1	16.0	76.9	16.9	79.9	22.0	80.1	21.5
Texas..............	72.1	20.3	78.3	23.3	79.2	23.9	78.1	26.2
Utah...............	85.1	22.3	89.3	27.6	90.7	26.4	91.0	26.8
Vermont............	80.8	24.3	86.7	27.1	90.0	28.8	87.4	30.8
Virginia.............	75.2	24.5	82.6	30.3	86.6	31.9	86.7	34.6
Washington........	83.8	22.9	92.0	28.1	91.8	28.6	90.4	28.3
West Virginia.......	66.0	12.3	76.4	16.3	77.1	15.3	78.5	15.9
Wisconsin..........	78.6	17.7	88.0	22.3	86.7	23.8	86.8	24.7
Wyoming...........	83.0	18.8	90.0	19.8	90.0	20.6	91.6	19.6

Source: U.S. Census Bureau, 1990 Census of Population, CPH-L-96, and Current Population Reports, P20-513, P20-536, and PPL-169. See Internet site <http://www.census.gov/population/www/socdemo/educ-attn.html>.

No. 232. Nonfatal Crimes Against Students: 1999 and 2000

[For students aged 12 through 18 (2,489.7 represents 2,489,700). For crimes occurring at school or going to or from school. Based on the National Crime Victimization Survey; see Appendix III]

Student characteristic	1999 Total	1999 Theft	1999 Violent Total	1999 Violent Serious [1]	2000 Total	2000 Theft	2000 Violent Total	2000 Violent Serious [1]
Total (1,000)	2,489.7	1,605.5	884.1	185.6	1,946.4	1,246.6	699.8	128.4
RATE PER 1,000 STUDENTS								
Total [2]	92	59	33	7	72	46	26	5
Sex:								
Male	98	62	37	8	80	47	33	7
Female	85	57	28	6	62	45	18	[3]2
Age:								
12 to 14 years old	120	74	46	11	80	48	32	5
15 to 18 years old	70	48	23	4	65	45	21	5
Race/ethnicity:								
White, non-Hispanic	98	64	34	6	75	49	26	3
Black, non-Hispanic	106	63	43	14	72	46	26	[3]5
Hispanic	62	40	21	6	63	34	29	11
Other, non-Hispanic	77	52	26	[3]5	40	32	[3]8	[3]2
Urbanicity: [4]								
Urban	93	63	29	9	68	46	22	7
Suburban	94	58	36	8	74	47	28	4
Rural	86	58	28	[3]2	70	44	26	[3]3
Household income:								
Less than $7,500	86	38	48	[3]15	61	32	[3]28	[3]6
$7,500 to $14,999	70	42	29	[3]4	57	31	26	[3]5
$15,000 to $24,999	90	58	32	[3]9	81	55	27	[3]5
$25,000 to $34,999	77	51	26	[3]2	69	40	30	[3]6
$35,000 to $49,999	108	66	42	[3]6	81	49	33	[3]6
$50,000 to $74,999	100	61	39	12	86	58	27	[3]6
$75,000 and over	108	85	23	[3]6	74	54	21	[3]4

[1] Includes rape, sexual assault, robbery, and aggravated assault. [2] Includes those whose race/ethnicity or incomes are unknown. [3] Estimate based on fewer than ten cases. [4] Urban: The largest city (or groupings of cities) of an MSA; Suburban: those portions of metro areas outside central cities; Rural: places outside MSAs.

Source: U.S. National Center for Education Statistics and U.S. Bureau of Justice Statistics, *Indicators of School Crime and Safety 2002*, November 2002, NCES 2003-009; and earlier issues.

No. 233. Students Reporting Being Threatened or Injured With a Weapon on School Property: 1993 to 2001

[In percent. For students in grades 9 through 12 reporting incident in the prior 12 months. Based on the Youth Risk Behavior Surveillance System. See source for details. See also <http://www.cdc.gov/nccdphp/dash/yrbs/index.htm>]

Student characteristic	1993	1995	1997	1999	2001
Total	7.3	8.4	7.4	7.7	8.9
Sex:					
Male	9.2	10.9	10.2	9.5	11.5
Female	5.4	5.8	4.0	5.8	6.5
Race/ethnicity:					
White	(NA)	(NA)	(NA)	6.6	8.5
Black or African American	(NA)	(NA)	(NA)	7.6	9.3
Hispanic or Latino	(NA)	(NA)	(NA)	9.8	8.6
Asian	(NA)	(NA)	(NA)	7.7	11.3
American Indian or Alaska Native	(NA)	(NA)	(NA)	13.2	15.2
Native Hawaiian or other Pacific Islander	(NA)	(NA)	(NA)	15.6	24.8
Multiple	(NA)	(NA)	(NA)	9.3	10.3
Grade:					
9th	9.4	9.6	10.1	10.5	12.7
10th	7.3	9.6	7.9	8.2	9.1
11th	7.3	7.7	5.9	6.1	6.9
12th	5.5	6.7	5.8	5.1	5.3

NA Not available.

Source: U.S. National Center for Education Statistics and U.S. Department of Justice, Bureau of Justice Statistics, *Indicators of School Crime and Safety 2002*, November 2002, NCES 2003-009.

No. 234. Children Whose Parents Are Involved in School Activities: 1999

[In percent, except as indicated (23,355 represents 23,355,000). Based on the Parent and Family Involvement Survey of the National Household Education Survey Program; see source and Appendix III for details. See also Tables 235 and 238]

Parental involvement	Students in grades K to 5					Students in grades 6 to 8				
	Total	Two-parent families	One-parent families			Total	Two-parent families	One-parent families		
			Total	Mother	Father			Total	Mother	Father
Total students (1,000)	23,355	15,841	7,514	6,634	880	11,252	7,747	3,506	3,010	496
Any adult attending a meeting	84.9	88.6	77.1	77.3	75.7	81.1	85.3	72.0	71.2	77.0
Only mother attended	39.4	25.7	68.2	77.3	(X)	38.7	28.5	61.2	71.2	(X)
Only father attended	5.7	4.1	8.9	(X)	75.7	6.9	5.1	10.9	(X)	77.0
Both attended	39.8	58.7	(X)	(X)	(X)	35.6	51.7	(X)	(X)	(X)
Any adult attending a conference	87.7	89.4	84.1	85.1	76.7	71.1	72.3	68.5	68.1	70.8
Only mother attended	52.0	41.0	75.1	85.1	(X)	41.0	33.1	58.8	68.1	(X)
Only father attended	6.4	5.1	9.0	(X)	76.7	7.1	5.8	10.0	(X)	70.8
Both attended	29.4	43.3	(X)	(X)	(X)	23.0	33.4	(X)	(X)	(X)
Any adult attending a class event	70.8	74.0	64.1	63.1	71.2	67.8	72.6	57.3	55.9	66.1
Only mother attended	31.5	20.0	55.7	63.1	(X)	24.6	14.1	48.0	55.9	(X)
Only father attended	5.1	3.6	8.3	(X)	71.2	5.3	3.5	9.3	(X)	66.1
Both attended	34.2	50.4	(X)	(X)	(X)	37.9	55.0	(X)	(X)	(X)
Any adult acted as a volunteer	48.9	55.5	34.8	36.3	23.1	31.7	36.1	21.9	22.1	20.6
Only mother attended	37.0	39.3	32.1	36.3	(X)	21.8	23.0	19.0	22.1	(X)
Only father attended	3.2	3.4	2.7	(X)	23.1	3.1	3.1	2.9	(X)	20.6
Both attended	8.6	12.7	(X)	(X)	(X)	6.8	9.9	(X)	(X)	(X)
Number of activities at least one parent participated in:										
None	3.5	2.2	6.5	6.2	8.3	7.3	4.4	13.7	14.1	11.2
One	7.4	5.7	11.0	11.1	10.3	11.7	11.0	13.4	13.9	10.8
Two	19.7	17.6	24.3	24.2	25.0	25.8	24.8	27.9	28.0	27.3
Three	32.0	31.7	32.5	31.7	39.0	32.2	33.5	29.2	28.5	33.5
Four	37.4	42.9	25.7	26.8	17.4	23.0	26.2	15.7	15.5	17.2
Number of activities both parents participated in:										
None	24.0	24.0	(X)	(X)	(X)	27.0	27.0	(X)	(X)	(X)
One	21.7	21.7	(X)	(X)	(X)	24.8	24.8	(X)	(X)	(X)
Two	26.0	26.0	(X)	(X)	(X)	24.2	24.2	(X)	(X)	(X)
Three	21.5	21.5	(X)	(X)	(X)	19.5	19.5	(X)	(X)	(X)
Four	6.7	6.7	(X)	(X)	(X)	4.5	4.5	(X)	(X)	(X)

X Not applicable.
Source: U.S. National Center for Education Statistics, *National Household Education Survey*, 1999. See Internet site <http://nces.ed.gov/pubsearch/getpubcats.asp?sid=004>.

No. 235. Children's Involvement in Home Literacy Activities: 1993 and 2001

[In percent, except number of children (8,579 represents 8,579,000). For children 3 to 5 years old not yet enrolled in kindergarten who participated in activities with a family member. Based on the School Readiness Survey of the National Education Household Survey Program; see source and Appendix III. See also Tables 234 and 238]

Characteristic	Children (1,000)		Read to [1]		Told a story [1]		Taught letters, words, or numbers [1]		Visited a library [2]	
	1993	2001	1993	2001	1993	2001	1993	2001	1993	2001
Total	8,579	8,551	78	84	43	54	58	74	38	36
Age:										
3 years old	3,889	3,795	79	84	46	54	57	71	34	35
4 years old	3,713	3,861	78	85	41	55	58	77	41	37
5 years old	976	896	76	81	36	52	58	75	38	37
Race/ethnicity:										
White, non-Hispanic	5,902	5,313	85	89	44	58	58	75	42	39
Black, non-Hispanic	1,271	1,251	66	77	39	51	63	78	29	31
Hispanic	1,026	1,506	58	71	38	42	54	68	26	30
Other	381	482	73	87	50	60	59	78	43	38
Mother's home language: [3]										
English	7,805	7,368	81	88	44	56	58	76	39	38
Not English	603	984	42	60	36	38	52	61	26	25
Mother's highest education: [3]										
Less than high school	1,036	996	60	69	37	43	56	67	22	21
High school	3,268	2,712	76	81	41	53	56	73	31	30
Vocational ed or some college	2,624	2,406	83	86	45	53	60	76	44	39
College degree	912	1,418	90	93	48	59	56	75	55	45
Graduate/professional training or degree	569	820	90	96	50	63	60	80	59	55
Family type:										
Two parents	6,226	6,416	81	87	44	55	57	74	41	38
None or one parent	2,353	2,135	71	76	41	51	59	73	30	30
Poverty status:										
Above threshold	6,323	6,499	82	87	44	55	57	75	41	39
Below threshold	2,256	2,053	68	74	39	51	59	72	28	27

[1] Three or more times in the past week. [2] At least once in the past month. [3] Excludes children with no mother in the household and no female guardian.
Source: U.S. National Center for Education Statistics, *Statistical Brief*, NCES 2000-026, November 1999; and unpublished data. See Internet site <http://nces.ed.gov/pubsearch/getpubcats.asp?sid=004>.

Education 157

No. 236. Children Who Speak a Language Other Than English at Home: 1979 to 1999

[In percent, except total. For children 5 to 17 years old (3.8 represents 3,800,000). For children reported to speak English less than "very well." Based on the Current Population Survey; see text Section 1, and Appendix III]

Characteristic	1979	1989	1992	1995 [1]	1999 [1]
Children who speak another language at home (mil.)	3.8	5.3	6.4	6.7	8.8
Percent of children 5 to 17 years old	8.5	12.6	14.2	14.1	16.7
Race and Hispanic origin:					
White, non-Hispanic	3.2	3.5	3.7	3.6	3.9
Black, non-Hispanic	1.3	2.4	4.2	3.0	4.5
Hispanic [2]	75.1	71.2	76.6	73.9	70.9
Other, non-Hispanic [3]	44.1	53.4	58.3	45.5	51.0
Region: [4]					
Northeast	10.5	13.5	16.2	15.1	17.7
Midwest	3.7	4.9	5.6	5.9	7.5
South	6.8	10.7	11.1	11.7	14.3
West	17.0	24.2	27.2	26.4	28.8
Children who speak another language at home and have difficulty speaking English (mil.)	1.3	1.9	2.2	2.4	2.6
Percent of children 5 to 17 years old	2.8	4.4	4.9	5.1	5.0
Race and Hispanic origin:					
White, non-Hispanic	0.5	0.8	0.6	0.7	1.0
Black, non-Hispanic	0.3	0.5	1.3	0.9	1.0
Hispanic [2]	28.7	27.4	29.9	31.0	23.4
Other, non-Hispanic [3]	19.8	20.4	21.0	14.1	11.7
Region: [4]					
Northeast	2.9	4.8	5.3	5.0	4.4
Midwest	1.1	1.3	1.6	2.3	2.0
South	2.2	3.8	3.5	3.4	3.6
West	6.5	8.8	10.4	11.4	10.5

[1] Reflects revised interviewing techniques and/or change in population controls to the 1990 census-based estimates. [2] Persons of Hispanic origin may be of any race. [3] Includes mostly Asian/Pacific Islanders, but also American Indian/Alaska Native children. [4] For composition of regions, see map, inside front cover.

Source: Federal Interagency Forum on Child and Family Statistics, *America's Children: Key National Indicators of Well-Being*, 2001. See Internet site <http://www.childstats.gov/americaschildren/>.

No. 237. Preprimary School Enrollment—Summary: 1970 to 2001

[As of October. Civilian noninstitutional population (10,949 represents 10,949,000). Includes public and nonpublic nursery school and kindergarten programs. Excludes 5 year olds enrolled in elementary school. Based on Current Population Survey; see text, Section 1, and Appendix III]

Item	1970	1975	1980	1985	1990	1995	1999	2000	2001
NUMBER OF CHILDREN (1,000)									
Population, 3 to 5 years old	10,949	10,183	9,284	10,733	11,207	12,518	11,920	11,858	11,653
Total enrolled [1]	4,104	4,954	4,878	5,865	6,659	7,739	7,844	7,592	7,441
Nursery	1,094	1,745	1,981	2,477	3,378	4,331	4,506	4,326	4,250
Public	332	570	628	846	1,202	1,950	2,209	2,146	2,126
Private	762	1,174	1,353	1,631	2,177	2,381	2,298	2,180	2,124
Kindergarten	3,010	3,211	2,897	3,388	3,281	3,408	3,338	3,266	3,191
Public	2,498	2,682	2,438	2,847	2,767	2,799	2,777	2,701	2,690
Private	511	528	459	541	513	608	560	565	501
White	3,443	4,105	3,994	4,757	5,389	6,144	6,093	5,861	5,677
Black	586	731	725	919	964	1,236	1,264	1,265	1,323
Hispanic [2]	(NA)	(NA)	370	496	642	1,040	1,189	1,155	1,218
3 years old	454	683	857	1,035	1,205	1,489	1,505	1,540	1,504
4 years old	1,007	1,418	1,423	1,765	2,086	2,553	2,768	2,556	2,526
5 years old	2,643	2,852	2,598	3,065	3,367	3,697	3,571	3,496	3,411
ENROLLMENT RATE									
Total enrolled [1]	37.5	48.6	52.5	54.6	59.4	61.8	65.8	64.0	63.9
White	37.8	48.6	52.7	54.7	59.7	63.0	65.3	63.2	63.2
Black	34.9	48.1	51.8	55.8	57.8	58.9	67.9	68.5	69.2
Hispanic [2]	(NA)	(NA)	43.3	43.3	49.0	51.1	53.2	52.6	53.9
3 years old	12.9	21.5	27.3	28.8	32.6	35.9	39.0	39.2	38.4
4 years old	27.8	40.5	46.3	49.1	56.0	61.6	68.8	64.9	66.4
5 years old	69.3	81.3	84.7	86.5	88.8	87.5	88.5	87.6	86.7

NA Not available. [1] Includes races not shown separately. [2] Persons of Hispanic origin may be of any race. The method of identifying Hispanic children was changed in 1980 from allocation based on status of mother to status reported for each child. The number of Hispanic children using the new method is larger.

Source: U.S. Census Bureau, Current Population Reports, PPL-148; and earlier PPL and P-20 reports. See Internet site <http://www.census.gov/population/www/socdemo/school.html>.

No. 238. Children's School Readiness Skills: 1993 and 2001

[In percent. For children 3 to 5 years old not yet enrolled in kindergarden. Based on the School Readiness Survey of the National Education Household Survey Program; see source and Appendix III for details. See also Tables 234 and 235]

Characteristic	Recognizes all letters 1993	2001	Counts to 20 or higher 1993	2001	Writes name 1993	2001	Reads or pretends to read storybooks 1993	2001	Has 3-4 skills 1993	2001
Total	21	23	52	57	50	53	72	71	35	39
Age:										
3 years old	11	12	37	39	22	23	66	64	15	16
4 years old	28	29	62	68	70	73	75	76	49	53
5 years old	36	38	78	82	84	89	81	80	65	71
Sex:										
Male	19	19	49	52	47	47	68	68	32	34
Female	23	27	56	61	53	58	76	74	39	43
Race/ethnicity:										
White, non-Hispanic	23	24	56	61	52	55	76	78	39	43
Black, non-Hispanic	18	23	53	57	45	52	63	64	31	35
Hispanic	10	14	32	39	42	43	59	52	22	22
Other	22	35	49	61	52	57	70	64	36	48
Mother's employment status:										
Employed	23	23	57	60	52	56	75	74	39	42
Unemployed	17	17	41	47	46	47	67	55	29	28
Not in the labor force	18	22	49	52	47	48	68	67	32	34
Family type:										
Two parents	22	24	54	58	51	54	74	74	37	41
None or one parent	18	17	49	51	47	48	65	61	31	31
Poverty status:										
Above threshold	24	25	57	61	53	55	74	75	40	44
Below threshold	12	14	41	43	41	45	64	57	23	23

Source: U.S. National Center for Education Statistics, *Home Literacy Activities and Signs of Children's Emerging Literacy, 1993 and 1999*, NCES 2000-026, November 1999; and unpublished data. See Internet site <http://nces.ed.gov/pubsearch/getputcats.asp?sid=004>.

No. 239. Public Charter and Traditional Schools—Selected Characteristics: 1999-2000

[A public charter school is a public school that, in accordance with an enabling state statue, has been granted a charter exempting it from selected state and local rules and regulations. All schools open as public charter schools during 1998-99 and still open in the 1999-2000 school year were surveyed. Based in the School and Staffing Survey; see source for details]

Characteristic	All schools Traditional	Public charter	Elementary Traditional	Public charter	Secondary Traditional	Public charter	Combined Traditional	Public charter
Number of schools	83,725	1,010	59,900	586	20,651	235	3,174	190
Enrollment (1,000)	45,100	267	29,050	159	15,201	58	848	50
PERCENT DISTRIBUTION OF STUDENTS								
Race/ethnicity	100.0	100.0	100.0	100.0	100.0	100.0	100.0	100.0
White	63.2	46.4	61.4	44.7	66.4	42.0	68.6	57.0
Black	16.9	27.3	18.0	31.0	14.9	23.4	17.1	19.9
Hispanic	14.9	20.8	15.8	19.5	13.6	28.9	9.1	15.5
Asian/Pacific Islander	3.7	3.2	3.6	3.3	4.1	2.8	1.7	3.5
American Indian/Alaskan Native	1.2	2.3	1.2	1.5	1.1	3.0	3.4	4.1
PERCENT DISTRIBUTION OF SCHOOLS								
Size of enrollment	100.0	100.0	100.0	100.0	100.0	100.0	100.0	100.0
Less than 300	28.5	72.2	25.5	69.3	31.1	80.2	69.9	71.4
300 to 599	39.4	16.5	46.4	18.6	22.6	10.9	16.5	16.9
600 to 999	21.8	8.4	23.4	9.9	19.2	3.9	10.3	9.2
1,000 or more	10.2	2.9	4.8	2.1	27.1	4.9	3.4	2.5
Percent minority enrollment	100.0	100.0	100.0	100.0	100.0	100.0	100.0	100.0
Less than 10.0	38.2	17.8	36.8	18.5	43.3	14.3	32.0	20.1
10.0 to 24.9	17.4	19.5	17.1	19.0	19.0	18.2	12.2	22.9
25.0 to 49.9	16.5	14.6	16.9	13.7	15.5	14.3	15.4	17.5
50.0 to 74.9	11.6	13.0	12.1	11.9	9.9	17.8	15.0	10.4
75.0 or more	16.3	35.1	17.1	36.9	12.4	35.3	25.4	29.1
Percent of students eligible for free or reduced-price lunch	100.0	100.0	100.0	100.0	100.0	100.0	100.0	100.0
Less than 15.0	23.4	29.8	20.4	30.2	32.9	28.4	17.4	30.3
15.0 to 29.9	19.7	11.4	19.2	11.6	23.0	11.9	8.4	10.5
30.0 to 49.9	21.5	16.7	22.0	16.7	19.7	17.1	23.6	16.5
50.0 to 74.9	18.6	16.7	20.2	14.8	14.1	19.8	19.4	19.0
75.0 or more	16.7	25.3	18.2	26.8	10.3	22.8	31.3	23.7

Source: U.S. National Center for Education Statistics, *Digest Education Statistics*, 2002.

No. 240. Public Elementary and Secondary Schools—Summary: 1980 to 2002

[For school year ending in year shown, except as indicated (48,041 represents 48,041,000). Data are estimates]

Item	Unit	1980	1985	1990	1995	2000	2001	2002
School districts, total	Number	16,044	15,812	15,552	14,947	15,248	15,364	15,490
ENROLLMENT								
Population 5-17 years old [1]	1,000	48,041	44,787	44,949	48,855	52,811	53,118	53,253
Percent of resident population	Percent	21.4	19.0	18.2	18.6	18.9	18.9	18.7
Fall enrollment [2]	1,000	41,778	39,354	40,527	43,898	46,578	46,937	47,370
Percent of population 5-17 years old	Percent	87.0	87.9	90.2	89.9	90.8	88.4	89.0
Elementary [3]	1,000	24,397	23,830	26,253	28,148	29,551	29,723	29,877
Secondary [4]	1,000	17,381	15,524	14,274	15,750	17,027	17,214	17,493
Average daily attendance (ADA)	1,000	38,411	36,530	37,573	40,792	43,393	43,755	44,210
High school graduates	1,000	2,762	2,424	2,327	2,282	2,535	2,553	2,612
INSTRUCTIONAL STAFF								
Total [5]	1,000	2,521	2,473	2,685	2,919	3,269	3,330	3,388
Classroom teachers	1,000	2,211	2,175	2,362	2,565	2,881	2,931	2,978
Average salaries:								
Instructional staff	Dollar	16,715	24,666	32,638	38,349	43,740	45,383	46,706
Classroom teachers	Dollar	15,970	23,600	31,367	36,675	41,827	43,400	44,683
REVENUES								
Revenue receipts	Mil. dol	97,635	141,013	208,656	273,255	366,577	394,790	407,740
Federal	Mil. dol	9,020	9,533	13,184	18,764	25,886	27,935	30,441
State	Mil. dol	47,929	69,107	100,787	129,958	183,384	198,806	202,494
Local	Mil. dol	40,686	62,373	94,685	124,533	157,308	168,049	174,805
Percent of total:								
Federal	Percent	9.2	6.8	6.3	6.9	7.1	7.1	7.5
State	Percent	49.1	49.0	48.3	47.6	50.0	50.4	49.7
Local	Percent	41.7	44.2	45.4	45.6	42.9	42.6	42.9
EXPENDITURES								
Total	Mil. dol	96,105	139,382	209,698	276,584	372,138	398,882	414,708
Current expenditures (day schools)	Mil. dol	85,661	127,230	186,583	242,995	319,496	342,461	357,535
Other current expenditures [6]	Mil. dol	1,859	2,109	3,341	5,564	6,611	7,207	7,518
Capital outlay	Mil. dol	6,504	7,529	16,012	21,646	36,366	38,986	38,627
Interest on school debt	Mil. dol	2,081	2,514	3,762	6,379	9,666	10,228	11,029
Percent of total:								
Current expenditures (day schools)	Percent	89.1	91.3	89.0	87.9	85.9	85.9	86.2
Other current expenditures [6]	Percent	1.9	1.5	1.6	2.0	1.8	1.8	1.8
Capital outlay	Percent	6.8	5.4	7.6	7.8	9.8	9.8	9.3
Interest on school debt	Percent	2.2	1.8	1.8	2.3	2.6	2.6	2.7
In current dollars:								
Revenue receipts per pupil enrolled	Dollar	2,337	3,583	5,149	6,225	7,870	8,411	8,608
Current expenditures per pupil enrolled	Dollar	2,050	3,033	4,604	5,535	6,859	7,296	7,548
In constant (2002) dollars: [7]								
Revenue receipts per pupil enrolled	Dollar	5,367	6,035	7,224	7,375	8,284	8,560	8,608
Current expenditures per pupil enrolled	Dollar	4,708	5,445	6,460	6,559	7,220	7,425	7,548

[1] Estimated resident population as of July 1 of the previous year, except 1980, 1990, and 2000 population enumerated as of April 1. Estimates reflect revisions based on the 2000 Census of Population. [2] Fall enrollment of the previous year. [3] Kindergarten through grade 6. [4] Grades 7 through 12. [5] Full-time equivalent. [6] Current expenses for summer schools, adult education, post-high school vocational education, personnel retraining, etc., when operated by local school districts and not part of regular public elementary and secondary day-school program. [7] Compiled by U.S. Census Bureau. Deflated by the Consumer Price Index, all urban consumers (for school year) supplied by U.S. National Center for Education Statistics.

Source: Except as noted. National Education Association, Washington, DC, Estimates of School Statistics Database (copyright).

No. 241. Public Elementary and Secondary Schools and Enrollment—States: 2000-2001

[For schools with membership. Based on the Common Core of Data program; see source for details]

State	Total number of schools with member-ship	Total number of students (1,000)	Regular Number of schools	Regular Percent of students	Special education [1] Number of schools	Special education [1] Percent of students	Vocational education [2] Number of schools	Vocational education [2] Percent of students	Alternative education [3] Number of schools	Alternative education [3] Percent of students
Total	90,640	47,223	84,596	98.2	1,654	0.4	345	0.4	4,045	1.0
Alabama	1,380	740	1,337	99.7	16	0.1	2	(Z)	25	0.2
Alaska	502	133	469	97.8	2	0.2	1	(Z)	30	2.0
Arizona	1,633	878	1,556	98.0	10	(Z)	4	0.5	63	1.5
Arkansas	1,130	450	1,125	99.9	-	-	-	-	5	0.1
California	8,757	6,142	7,544	96.6	124	0.5	-	-	1,089	2.9
Colorado	1,590	725	1,503	98.7	10	0.1	2	(Z)	75	1.2
Connecticut	1,073	562	987	96.4	24	0.6	17	1.9	45	1.1
Delaware	191	115	164	92.8	14	1.1	5	4.7	8	1.3
Dist. Columbia	165	69	150	94.7	10	4.0	-	-	5	1.3
Florida	3,231	2,435	2,931	98.5	126	0.6	32	0.1	142	0.7
Georgia	1,946	1,445	1,917	99.5	1	(Z)	-	-	28	0.4
Hawaii	261	184	257	99.9	3	(Z)	-	-	1	0.1
Idaho	653	245	590	98.4	9	0.1	-	-	54	1.5
Illinois	4,282	2,049	3,910	98.0	250	1.2	-	-	122	0.9
Indiana	1,882	989	1,830	99.6	8	0.1	1	(Z)	43	0.3
Iowa	1,529	495	1,482	98.8	9	0.2	-	-	38	1.0
Kansas	1,426	471	1,426	100.0	-	-	-	-	-	-
Kentucky	1,376	666	1,300	99.5	9	0.1	1	(Z)	66	0.4
Louisiana	1,508	743	1,384	98.0	28	0.2	4	0.1	92	1.6
Maine	686	207	684	100.0	2	(Z)	-	-	-	-
Maryland	1,342	853	1,241	97.5	50	0.9	12	1.1	39	0.6
Massachusetts	1,898	975	1,817	95.9	1	(Z)	45	3.5	35	0.6
Michigan	3,743	1,743	3,589	99.0	93	0.6	6	(Z)	55	0.3
Minnesota	2,105	854	1,608	96.9	191	1.2	1	(Z)	305	1.9
Mississippi	884	498	884	100.0	-	-	-	-	-	-
Missouri	2,266	913	2,146	98.7	54	0.7	5	0.3	61	0.3
Montana	878	155	872	99.9	2	(Z)	-	-	4	0.1
Nebraska	1,296	286	1,240	99.4	56	0.6	-	-	-	-
Nevada	500	341	454	98.4	13	0.3	1	0.5	32	0.8
New Hampshire	524	208	524	100.0	-	-	-	-	-	-
New Jersey	2,407	1,308	2,249	96.7	86	0.7	50	1.5	22	1.1
New Mexico	763	320	707	97.8	16	0.6	-	-	40	1.7
New York	4,292	2,882	4,157	97.6	26	0.1	25	1.1	84	1.1
North Carolina	2,192	1,294	2,109	99.3	24	0.3	2	(Z)	57	0.4
North Dakota	539	109	539	100.0	-	-	-	-	-	-
Ohio	3,827	1,835	3,696	96.7	27	0.1	72	3.0	32	0.2
Oklahoma	1,811	623	1,811	100.0	-	-	-	-	-	-
Oregon	1,263	546	1,180	98.5	12	0.1	-	-	71	1.4
Pennsylvania	3,183	1,814	3,143	98.3	12	1.0	15	0.6	13	0.1
Rhode Island	320	157	306	98.2	4	0.4	4	0.7	6	0.7
South Carolina	1,067	677	1,044	99.6	8	0.1	-	-	15	0.3
South Dakota	756	129	732	98.9	3	0.1	-	-	21	1.0
Tennessee	1,575	909	1,547	99.6	12	0.1	4	0.2	12	0.1
Texas	7,519	4,060	6,656	98.8	140	0.1	19	(Z)	704	1.1
Utah	793	482	716	98.1	21	0.4	-	-	56	1.5
Vermont	353	102	315	98.8	36	1.2	-	-	2	(Z)
Virginia	1,841	1,145	1,777	99.2	18	0.1	-	-	46	0.6
Washington	2,141	1,005	1,819	96.6	74	0.3	11	0.1	237	2.9
West Virginia	794	286	765	99.6	7	0.1	3	(Z)	19	0.3
Wisconsin	2,180	879	2,041	98.3	12	0.1	1	(Z)	126	1.5
Wyoming	387	90	366	97.7	1	(Z)	-	-	20	2.2

- Represents zero. Z Less than 0.05 percent. [1] Focuses on special education with materials and instructional approaches adapted to meet the students' needs. [2] Focuses on vocational, technical, or career education and provides education and training in at least one semiskilled or technical occupation. [3] Addresses the needs of students that typically cannot be met in the regular school setting, and provides nontraditional education.

Source: U.S. National Center for Education Statistics, *Overview of Public Elementary and Secondary Schools and Districts School Year 2000-01*, NCES2002-356, May 2002.

No. 242. Public Elementary and Secondary Schools by Type and Size of School: 2000-2001

[Enrollment in thousands (47,061 represents 47,061,000). Data reported by schools, rather than school districts]

Enrollment size of school	Number of schools					Enrollment [1]				
	Total	Elementary [2]	Secondary [3]	Combined [4]	Other [5]	Total	Elementary [2]	Secondary [3]	Combined [4]	Other [5]
Total	93,273	64,601	21,994	5,096	1,582	47,061	30,673	15,038	1,267	82
PERCENT										
Total	100.0	100.0	100.0	100.0	100.0	100.0	100.0	100.0	100.0	100.0
Under 100 students	10.7	6.2	15.4	44.8	58.6	0.9	0.6	1.0	6.2	18.2
100 to 199 students	9.7	8.7	10.8	15.9	22.7	2.8	2.8	2.2	8.5	23.6
200 to 299 students	11.4	12.6	8.4	8.7	8.0	5.6	6.7	2.9	7.8	14.1
300 to 399 students	13.2	15.5	7.8	6.9	5.8	8.9	11.4	3.8	8.7	14.6
400 to 499 students	13.3	16.1	6.7	5.4	2.7	11.5	15.1	4.2	8.8	8.7
500 to 599 students	11.0	13.1	6.4	4.6	0.5	11.6	15.1	4.9	9.1	2.0
600 to 699 students	8.2	9.5	5.5	3.9	0.3	10.2	12.9	5.0	9.1	1.6
700 to 799 students	6.0	6.7	4.9	2.4	0.2	8.6	10.4	5.2	6.5	1.0
800 to 999 students	6.9	6.8	8.3	3.1	0.3	11.8	12.6	10.4	10.0	2.0
1,000 to 1,499 students	6.0	4.1	12.7	3.0	0.5	13.9	10.0	21.9	12.9	4.5
1,500 to 1,999 students	2.1	0.5	7.3	0.9	-	7.0	1.9	17.6	5.4	-
2,000 to 2,999 students	1.2	0.1	4.9	0.4	0.3	5.6	0.5	16.2	3.9	5.1
3,000 or more students	0.2	(Z)	1.0	0.2	0.2	1.7	0.1	4.9	3.2	4.8
Average enrollment	(X)	(X)	(X)	(X)	(X)	519	477	714	274	136

- Represents zero.   X Not applicable.   Z Less than 0.05 percent.   [1] Data for those schools reporting enrollment.
[2] Includes schools beginning with grade 6 or below and with no grade higher than 8.   [3] Includes schools with no grade lower than 7.   [4] Includes schools with both elementary and secondary grades.   [5] Includes special education, alternative, and other schools not classified by grade span.

Source: U.S. National Center for Education Statistics, *Digest of Education Statistics*, annual.

No. 243. Students Who Are Homeschooled by Selected Characteristics: 1999

[As of spring. (50,188 represents 50,188,000). For students 5 to 17 with a grade equivalent of K-12. Homeschoolers are students whose parents reported them to be schooled at home instead of a public or private school. Excludes students who were enrolled in school for more than 25 hours a week or were homeschooled due to a temporary illness. Based on the Parent Survey of the National Household Education Surveys Program; see source and Appendix III for details]

Characteristic	Number of students			Percent distribution		
	Total (1,000)	Homeschooled (1,000)	Percent homeschooled	All students	Homeschooled	Non-homeschooled
Total	50,188	850	1.7	100.0	100.0	100.0
Grade equivalent: [1]						
K-5	24,428	428	1.8	48.7	50.4	48.7
Kindergarten	3,790	92	2.4	7.6	10.8	7.5
Grades 1 to 3	12,692	199	1.6	25.3	23.5	25.3
Grades 4 to 5	7,946	136	1.7	15.8	16.0	15.8
Grades 6 to 8	11,788	186	1.6	23.5	21.9	23.5
Grades 9 to 12	13,954	235	1.7	27.8	27.7	27.8
Sex:						
Male	25,515	417	1.6	50.8	49.0	50.9
Female	24,673	434	1.8	49.2	51.0	49.1
Race/ethnicity:						
White, non-Hispanic	32,474	640	2.0	64.7	75.3	64.5
Black, non-Hispanic	8,047	84	1.0	16.0	9.9	16.1
Hispanic	7,043	77	1.1	14.0	9.1	14.1
Other	2,623	49	1.9	5.2	5.8	5.2
Number of children in the household:						
One child	8,226	120	1.5	16.4	14.1	16.4
Two children	19,883	207	1.0	39.6	24.4	39.9
Three or more children	22,078	523	2.4	44.0	61.6	43.7
Number of parents in the household:						
Two parents	33,007	683	2.1	65.8	80.4	65.5
One parent	15,454	142	0.9	30.8	16.7	31.0
Nonparental guardians	1,727	25	1.4	3.4	2.9	3.5
Parents' participation in the labor force:						
Two parents—one in labor force	9,628	444	4.6	19.2	52.2	18.6
Two parents—both in labor force	22,880	237	1.0	45.6	27.9	45.9
One parent in labor force	13,907	98	0.7	27.7	11.6	28.0
No parent in labor force	3,773	71	1.9	7.5	8.3	7.5
Household income:						
$25,000 or less	16,776	262	1.6	33.4	30.9	33.5
25,001 to 50,000	15,220	278	1.8	30.3	32.7	30.3
50,001 to 75,000	8,576	162	1.9	17.1	19.1	17.1
75,001 or more	9,615	148	1.5	19.2	17.4	19.2
Parents' highest educational attainment:						
High school diploma or less	18,334	160	0.9	36.5	18.9	36.8
Voc/tech degree or some college	15,177	287	1.9	30.2	33.7	30.2
Bachelor's degree	8,269	213	2.6	16.5	25.1	16.3
Graduate/professional school	8,407	190	2.3	16.8	22.3	16.7

[1] Excludes those ungraded.

Source: U.S. National Center for Education Statistics, *Homeschooling in the United States: 1999*, NCES 2001-033, July 2001.

No. 244. Public Elementary and Secondary School Enrollment by State: 1980 to 2000

[In thousands (27,647 represents 27,647,000), except rate. As of fall. Includes unclassified students]

State	K through grade 8 [1] 1980	1990	1999	2000, prel.	Grades 9 through 12 1980	1990	1999	2000, prel.	Enrollment rate [2] 1980	1990	1999	2000, prel.
United States...	27,647	29,878	33,488	33,709	13,231	11,338	13,369	13,514	86.2	91.2	91.4	88.9
Alabama.........	528	527	539	539	231	195	202	201	87.6	93.2	95.5	89.5
Alaska..........	60	85	96	94	26	29	39	39	94.0	97.4	91.4	93.2
Arizona.........	357	479	624	641	157	161	229	237	88.9	93.3	89.9	89.1
Arkansas........	310	314	318	318	138	123	133	132	90.3	95.8	93.5	90.2
California.......	2,730	3,615	4,337	4,409	1,347	1,336	1,702	1,733	87.1	92.6	94.0	90.8
Colorado........	374	420	507	517	172	154	202	208	92.2	94.6	91.1	90.2
Connecticut.....	364	347	404	406	168	122	150	156	83.3	90.2	90.8	90.9
Delaware........	62	73	80	81	37	27	33	34	79.5	87.2	85.3	80.2
District of Columbia.	71	61	60	54	29	19	17	15	91.8	100.6	113.5	83.6
Florida..........	1,042	1,370	1,725	1,760	468	492	656	675	84.4	92.6	91.0	90.2
Georgia.........	742	849	1,044	1,060	327	303	379	385	86.8	93.7	96.3	91.8
Hawaii..........	110	123	133	132	55	49	53	52	83.4	87.4	88.9	84.7
Idaho...........	144	160	169	170	59	61	76	75	95.4	96.9	95.2	90.3
Illinois..........	1,335	1,310	1,462	1,474	649	512	565	575	82.6	86.9	88.0	86.5
Indiana..........	708	676	699	703	347	279	289	286	88.0	90.4	88.6	85.9
Iowa............	351	345	336	334	183	139	161	161	88.4	92.1	92.6	90.8
Kansas..........	283	320	326	323	133	117	146	147	88.7	92.5	91.8	89.8
Kentucky........	464	459	459	472	206	177	189	194	83.7	90.5	91.8	91.3
Louisiana........	544	586	548	547	234	199	209	197	80.2	88.1	86.4	82.3
Maine...........	153	155	149	146	70	60	60	61	91.6	96.5	93.7	89.8
Maryland........	493	527	607	609	258	188	239	244	83.9	89.1	87.9	85.1
Massachusetts....	676	604	706	703	346	230	265	273	88.6	88.8	90.3	88.4
Michigan.........	1,227	1,145	1,245	1,256	570	440	481	488	86.9	90.3	90.5	90.6
Minnesota.......	482	546	580	578	272	211	274	277	87.2	91.3	89.9	89.2
Mississippi......	330	372	365	364	147	131	135	134	79.6	91.3	91.0	87.2
Missouri.........	567	588	649	645	277	228	265	268	83.8	86.5	88.2	86.3
Montana.........	106	111	107	105	50	42	50	50	92.9	94.1	92.3	88.4
Nebraska........	189	198	197	195	91	76	91	91	86.6	88.7	87.6	85.9
Nevada.........	101	150	240	251	49	51	86	90	93.4	98.6	93.4	93.1
New Hampshire....	112	126	147	147	55	46	60	61	85.3	89.1	89.7	89.1
New Jersey......	820	784	954	953	426	306	335	355	81.5	85.9	88.3	85.8
New Mexico......	186	208	229	225	85	94	96	95	89.5	94.4	89.1	84.7
New York........	1,838	1,828	2,034	2,029	1,033	770	854	853	80.8	86.6	89.5	83.5
North Carolina....	786	783	935	945	343	304	341	348	90.1	94.8	90.7	90.8
North Dakota.....	77	85	75	72	40	33	38	37	85.9	92.6	93.3	89.9
Ohio............	1,312	1,258	1,296	1,294	645	514	540	541	84.8	88.0	87.3	86.0
Oklahoma........	399	425	447	445	179	154	180	178	92.9	95.1	96.5	95.0
Oregon..........	319	340	378	379	145	132	167	167	88.5	90.6	89.7	87.6
Pennsylvania.....	1,231	1,172	1,262	1,258	678	496	555	556	80.4	83.5	84.9	82.7
Rhode Island.....	98	102	114	114	51	37	43	44	80.1	87.5	87.3	85.5
South Carolina....	426	452	484	493	193	170	183	184	88.1	93.9	94.9	90.9
South Dakota.....	86	95	90	88	42	34	41	41	87.4	89.9	88.4	84.8
Tennessee.......	602	598	664	668	252	226	252	241	87.8	93.5	94.1	88.8
Texas...........	2,049	2,511	2,896	2,943	851	872	1,096	1,117	92.4	98.4	97.8	95.2
Utah............	250	325	329	333	93	122	151	148	98.2	97.8	96.6	94.6
Vermont.........	66	71	72	70	29	25	32	32	87.9	94.3	97.4	89.9
Virginia..........	703	728	817	816	307	270	317	329	90.7	94.2	93.4	89.7
Washington......	515	613	695	694	242	227	309	310	91.7	94.1	91.5	89.7
West Virginia.....	270	224	203	201	113	98	88	85	92.6	95.7	96.4	95.3
Wisconsin........	528	566	596	595	303	232	281	285	82.1	86.1	86.4	85.7
Wyoming........	70	71	62	60	28	27	30	30	97.3	97.7	95.5	91.8

[1] Data include a small number of prekindergarten students. [2] Percent of persons 5-17 years old. Based on enumerated resident population as of April 1, 1980, 1990, and 2000, and estimated resident population as of July 1 for other years. Data not adjusted for revisions based on the 1990 Census of Population.

Source: U.S. National Center for Education Statistics, *Digest of Education Statistics*, annual.

No. 245. Public School Districts With Alternative Schools or Programs for at-Risk Students: 2000-2001

[For the school year. Alternative schools and programs are designed to address the needs of students that typically cannot be met in regular schools. The schools and programs in data shown here serve students who are typically at risk for educational failure (as indicated by poor grades or truancy, for example). Alternative schools are usually housed in a separate facility where students are removed from regular schools. Alternative programs are usually housed within regular schools. Based on the Fast Response Survey System; see source for details]

District characteristic	Percent of districts with schools or programs	Percent distribution of districts with schools or programs by—							
		Number of schools or programs			Percent of district students enrolled			
		One	Two	Three or more	Less than 1 percent	1 to 1.99 percent	2 to 2.99 percent	3 percent or more
Total	39	65	18	17	43	27	14	16
Metropolitan status:[1]								
Urban	66	33	15	52	36	30	17	16
Suburban	41	63	19	18	49	26	12	13
Rural	35	74	17	8	38	28	16	18
Enrollment size:								
Less that 2,500	26	82	11	7	39	26	15	20
2,500 to 9,999	69	58	26	16	46	29	13	12
10,000 or more	95	27	17	56	46	25	17	12
Percent minority enrollment:								
5 percent or less	26	75	15	10	49	26	11	14
6 to 20 percent	43	63	20	17	48	22	14	16
21 to 50 percent	51	63	16	22	38	32	18	12
More than 50 percent	62	58	20	22	34	28	16	22
Poverty concentration:								
10 percent or less	31	68	15	16	56	24	10	10
11 to 20 percent	43	59	22	20	40	27	17	16
More than 20 percent	45	71	15	14	38	29	15	18

[1] Urban: Primarily serves the central city of a etropolitan statistical areas (MSA); suburban: serves an MSA, but not primarily the central city; rural: does not serve an MSA.

Source: U.S. National Center for Education Statistics, *Public School Alternative Schools and Programs for Students At Risk of Education Failure 2000-01*, September 2002, NCES 2002-004.

No. 246. Public Elementary and Secondary School Enrollment by Grade: 1980 to 2000

[In thousands (40,877 represents 40,877,000). As of fall of year. Kindergarten includes nursery schools]

Grade	1980	1985	1990	1992	1993	1994	1995	1996	1997	1998	1999	2000, prel.
Pupils enrolled	40,877	39,422	41,217	42,823	43,465	44,111	44,840	45,611	46,127	46,539	46,857	47,223
Kindergarten and grades 1 to 8	27,647	27,034	29,878	31,088	31,504	31,898	32,341	32,764	33,073	33,346	33,488	33,709
Kindergarten	2,689	3,192	3,610	3,817	3,922	4,047	4,173	4,202	4,198	4,172	4,148	4,178
First	2,894	3,239	3,499	3,542	3,529	3,593	3,671	3,770	3,755	3,727	3,684	3,635
Second	2,800	2,941	3,327	3,431	3,429	3,440	3,507	3,600	3,689	3,681	3,656	3,633
Third	2,893	2,895	3,297	3,361	3,437	3,439	3,445	3,524	3,597	3,696	3,691	3,673
Fourth	3,107	2,771	3,248	3,342	3,361	3,426	3,431	3,454	3,507	3,592	3,686	3,708
Fifth	3,130	2,776	3,197	3,325	3,350	3,372	3,438	3,453	3,458	3,520	3,604	3,703
Sixth	3,038	2,789	3,110	3,303	3,356	3,381	3,395	3,494	3,492	3,497	3,564	3,658
Seventh	3,085	2,938	3,067	3,299	3,355	3,404	3,422	3,464	3,520	3,530	3,541	3,624
Eighth	3,086	2,982	2,979	3,129	3,249	3,302	3,356	3,403	3,415	3,480	3,497	3,532
Unclassified[1]	924	511	543	539	515	494	502	401	442	451	417	366
Grades 9 to 12	13,231	12,388	11,338	11,735	11,961	12,213	12,500	12,847	13,054	13,193	13,369	13,514
Ninth	3,377	3,439	3,169	3,352	3,487	3,604	3,704	3,801	3,819	3,856	3,935	3,958
Tenth	3,368	3,230	2,896	3,027	3,050	3,131	3,237	3,323	3,376	3,382	3,415	3,487
Eleventh	3,195	2,866	2,612	2,656	2,751	2,748	2,826	2,930	2,972	3,021	3,034	3,080
Twelfth	2,925	2,550	2,381	2,431	2,424	2,488	2,487	2,586	2,673	2,722	2,782	2,799
Unclassified[1]	366	303	282	269	248	242	245	206	214	212	203	189

[1] Includes ungraded and special education.

Source: U.S. National Center for Education Statistics, *Digest of Education Statistics*, annual.

No. 247. School Enrollment Below Postseconday—Summary by Sex, Race, and Hispanic Origin: 2001

[In thousands (57,251 represents 57,251,000), except percent and rate. As of October. Covers civilian noninstitutional population enrolled in nursery school through high school. Based on Current Population Survey, see text, Section 1, and Appendix III]

Characteristic	Total [1]	Sex Male	Sex Female	White Total	White Non-Hispanic	Black	Asian and Pacific Islander	Hispanic [2]
All students	57,251	29,396	27,855	44,441	35,507	9,401	2,522	9,463
Nursery	4,289	2,173	2,115	3,278	2,725	787	161	593
Full day	1,951	998	953	1,325	1,040	517	71	308
Part day	2,338	1,176	1,162	1,953	1,686	270	90	285
Kindergarten	3,737	1,975	1,762	2,893	2,203	605	181	728
Elementary	33,166	17,024	16,142	25,729	20,298	5,478	1,409	5,779
High school	16,059	8,224	7,836	12,540	10,281	2,531	771	2,363
Students in public schools	49,936	25,676	24,260	38,199	29,859	8,645	2,251	8,817
Nursery	2,161	1,102	1,059	1,484	1,054	537	91	452
Full day	998	517	481	612	404	317	41	219
Part day	1,163	585	578	872	651	220	51	233
Kindergarten	3,145	1,687	1,459	2,394	1,781	536	161	641
Elementary	29,800	15,288	14,512	22,848	17,693	5,160	1,263	5,478
High school	14,830	7,599	7,230	11,473	9,331	2,412	736	2,246
Population 15 to 17 years old: Percent below modal grade [3]	30	34	25	29	28	36	21	35
Students, 10th to 12th grade: Annual dropout rate	5	5	4	5	4	6	2	8
Population 18 to 24 years old	26,965	13,434	13,531	21,372	16,721	3,916	1,312	4,892
Dropouts	3,519	2,028	1,491	2,865	1,390	540	47	1,548
High school graduates	21,836	10,461	11,375	17,348	14,480	3,016	1,197	3,031
Enrolled in college	9,629	4,437	5,192	7,548	6,565	1,206	794	1,035

[1] Includes other races, not shown separately. [2] Persons of Hispanic origin may be of any race. [3] The modal grade is the grade most common for a given age.

Source: U.S. Census Bureau, Current Population Reports, PPL-148; and earlier PPL and P-20 reports. See Internet site <http://www.census.gov/population/www/socdemo/school.html>

No. 248. Elementary and Secondary Schools—Teachers, Enrollment, and Pupil-Teacher Ratio: 1960 to 2001

[In thousands (1,600 represents 1,600,000), except ratios. As of fall. Data are for full-time equivalent teachers]

Item	Teachers Total	Teachers Public	Teachers Private	Enrollment Total	Enrollment Public	Enrollment Private	Pupil-teacher ratio Total	Pupil-teacher ratio Public	Pupil-teacher ratio Private
1960	1,600	1,408	192	42,181	36,281	5,900	26.4	25.8	30.7
1965	1,933	1,710	223	48,473	42,173	6,300	25.1	24.7	28.3
1970	2,292	2,059	233	51,257	45,894	6,363	22.4	22.3	23.0
1975	2,453	2,198	255	49,819	44,819	5,000	20.3	20.4	19.6
1976	2,457	2,189	268	49,478	44,311	5,167	20.1	20.2	19.3
1977	2,488	2,209	279	48,717	43,577	5,140	19.6	19.7	18.4
1978	2,479	2,207	272	47,635	42,550	5,085	19.2	19.3	18.7
1979	2,461	2,185	276	46,651	41,651	5,000	19.0	19.1	18.1
1980	2,485	2,184	301	46,208	40,877	5,331	18.6	18.7	17.7
1981	2,440	2,127	313	45,544	40,044	5,500	18.7	18.8	17.6
1982	2,458	2,133	325	45,165	39,566	5,600	18.4	18.6	17.2
1983	2,476	2,139	337	44,967	39,252	5,715	18.2	18.4	17.0
1984	2,508	2,168	340	44,908	39,208	5,700	17.9	18.1	16.8
1985	2,549	2,206	343	44,979	39,422	5,557	17.6	17.9	16.2
1986	2,592	2,244	348	45,205	39,753	5,452	17.4	17.7	15.7
1987	2,631	2,279	352	45,487	40,008	5,479	17.3	17.6	15.6
1988	2,668	2,323	345	45,430	40,189	5,242	17.0	17.3	15.2
1989	2,734	2,357	377	45,741	40,543	5,198	16.7	17.2	13.8
1990	2,753	2,398	355	46,451	41,217	5,234	16.9	17.2	14.7
1991	2,787	2,432	355	47,322	42,047	5,275	17.0	17.3	14.9
1992	2,822	2,459	363	48,145	42,823	5,322	17.1	17.4	14.7
1993	2,870	2,504	366	48,813	43,465	5,348	17.0	17.4	14.6
1994	2,926	2,552	374	49,609	44,111	5,498	17.0	17.3	14.7
1995	2,978	2,598	380	50,502	44,840	5,662	17.0	17.3	14.9
1996	3,054	2,667	387	51,375	45,611	5,764	16.8	17.1	14.9
1997	3,134	2,746	388	51,968	46,127	5,841	16.6	16.8	15.1
1998	3,221	2,830	391	52,476	46,539	5,937	16.3	16.4	15.2
1999	3,306	2,911	395	52,875	46,857	6,018	16.0	16.1	15.2
2000	3,343	2,953	390	53,167	47,223	5,944	15.9	16.0	15.2
2001, est.	3,379	2,988	390	53,520	47,576	5,944	15.8	15.9	15.2

Source: U.S. National Center for Education Statistics, *Digest of Education Statistics*, annual.

Education 165

No. 249. Public Elementary and Secondary School Teachers—Selected Characteristics: 1999-2000

[For school year. (509 represents 509,000) Based on School and Staffing Survey and subject to sampling error; for details, see source Web site at <http://nces.ed.gov/surveys/sass/>. Excludes prekindergarten teachers. See Table 263 for similar data on private school teachers]

Characteristic	Unit	Under 30 years old	30 to 39 years old	40 to 49 years old	Over 50 years old	Male	Female	White [1]	Black [1]	Hispanic
Total teachers [2]	1,000	509	661	953	879	754	2,248	2,532	228	169
Highest degree held:										
Bachelor's	Percent	77.9	56.7	46.8	39.0	49.7	52.8	51.2	51.1	65.5
Master's	Percent	20.4	38.5	46.9	51.4	42.7	41.6	43.0	40.3	28.5
Education specialist	Percent	1.2	3.8	4.9	7.3	4.7	4.8	4.6	6.2	4.1
Doctorate	Percent	(Z)	0.4	0.7	1.5	1.4	0.5	0.6	1.6	1.2
Full-time teaching experience:										
Less than 3 years	Percent	46.1	11.5	5.9	2.3	13.0	12.9	12.2	15.2	18.7
3 to 9 years	Percent	53.9	51.5	19.3	7.5	28.1	29.1	28.1	27.6	39.1
10 to 20 years	Percent	(X)	37.0	41.4	24.5	23.4	30.2	29.1	24.5	24.6
20 years or more	Percent	(X)	(X)	33.4	65.7	35.6	27.9	30.6	32.7	17.7
Full-time teachers	1,000	475	600	863	805	700	2,042	2303	214	157
Earned income	Dol.	33,583	38,468	44,375	50,278	46,891	41,596	43,032	43,150	41,241
Salary	Dol.	30,386	35,502	41,407	47,138	41,104	39,475	40,022	39,377	38,488

X Not applicable. Z Less than 0.05 percent. [1] Non-Hispanic. [2] Includes teachers with no degrees and associates degrees, not shown separately.

Source: U.S. National Center for Education Statistics, *Digest of Education Statistics, 2002.*

No. 250. Public Elementary and Secondary Schools—Number and Average Salary of Classroom Teachers, 1980 to 2002, and by State, 2002

[Estimates for school year ending in June of year shown (2,211 represents 2,211,000). Schools classified by type of organization rather than by grade-group; elementary includes kindergarten]

Year and state	Teachers [1] (1,000) Total	Elementary	Secondary	Avg. salary ($1,000) All teachers	Elementary	Secondary	Year and state	Teachers [1] (1,000) Total	Elementary	Secondary	Avg. salary ($1,000) All teachers	Elementary	Secondary
1980	2,211	1,206	1,005	16.0	15.6	16.5	LA	49.9	34.9	15.0	36.3	36.3	36.3
1985	2,175	1,212	963	23.6	23.2	24.2	ME	15.9	10.9	5.0	37.3	37.1	37.7
1990	2,362	1,390	972	31.4	30.8	32.0	MD	53.9	32.3	21.6	48.3	47.5	49.0
1991	2,409	1,436	974	33.1	32.5	33.9	MA	54.5	26.3	28.2	50.3	50.3	50.3
1992	2,429	1,466	963	34.1	33.5	34.8	MI	99.6	51.7	48.0	52.7	52.7	52.7
1993	2,466	1,496	970	35.0	34.4	35.9	MN	52.9	27.2	25.6	42.2	42.6	41.7
1994	2,512	1,517	995	35.7	35.2	36.6	MS	29.3	17.7	11.5	33.3	32.7	34.2
1995	2,565	1,517	1,048	36.7	36.1	37.5	MO	65.7	33.5	32.1	38.0	37.5	38.6
1996	2,605	1,543	1,062	37.6	37.1	38.4	MT	10.4	7.0	3.4	34.4	34.4	34.4
1997	2,671	1,586	1,086	38.4	38.0	39.2	NE	20.7	12.4	8.3	36.2	36.2	36.2
1998	2,729	1,626	1,103	39.4	39.0	39.9	NV	18.8	11.3	7.5	40.8	40.6	41.1
1999	2,803	1,649	1,155	40.6	40.1	41.3	NH	14.7	10.3	4.4	39.9	39.9	39.9
2000	2,881	1,696	1,186	41.8	41.3	42.6	NJ	102.9	38.8	64.1	53.2	51.7	54.1
2001	2,931	1,726	1,205	43.4	42.9	44.0	NM	21.0	14.9	6.1	36.4	36.1	37.2
2002, U.S.	2,978	1,745	1,232	44.7	44.3	45.2	NY	224.6	112.0	112.6	52.0	50.8	52.8
AL	46.3	27.0	19.3	37.2	37.2	37.2	NC	83.9	52.7	31.2	42.7	42.7	42.7
AK	8.0	5.1	2.8	49.4	49.4	49.4	ND	7.7	5.2	2.5	32.3	32.5	31.8
AZ	43.5	31.6	12.0	40.0	40.0	40.0	OH	119.6	79.9	39.8	44.0	43.8	44.6
AR	31.4	15.4	16.0	37.0	35.9	38.0	OK	41.6	21.6	19.9	34.7	34.5	35.0
CA	294.8	216.6	78.2	54.3	54.2	57.2	OR	29.3	19.9	9.3	46.1	45.7	46.5
CO	44.2	22.3	21.9	40.7	40.4	40.8	PA	118.5	62.0	56.5	50.6	50.6	50.6
CT	41.7	29.6	12.1	53.6	53.0	54.9	RI	13.0	7.8	5.2	49.8	49.5	49.8
DE	7.6	3.8	3.8	48.4	48.3	48.4	SC	44.3	31.6	12.7	39.9	38.0	38.7
DC	4.9	3.5	1.4	47.0	46.5	49.6	SD	9.2	6.4	2.8	31.3	31.3	31.2
FL	136.9	68.9	68.0	39.3	39.3	39.3	TN	57.4	41.6	15.7	38.5	38.3	38.9
GA	92.8	53.7	39.1	44.1	43.4	45.0	TX	282.6	144.1	138.5	39.2	38.8	39.7
HI	11.2	6.1	5.1	42.6	42.6	42.6	UT	22.7	12.4	10.3	37.4	37.4	37.4
ID	13.8	7.1	6.8	38.6	39.3	39.0	VT	8.7	4.6	4.1	39.2	39.4	39.1
IL	131.3	89.0	42.3	49.4	47.0	54.5	VA	91.9	55.2	36.8	41.7	41.7	41.7
IN	59.7	32.0	27.7	44.2	44.3	44.1	WA	52.6	29.5	23.0	43.5	43.4	43.5
IA	34.7	16.4	18.3	38.2	37.3	39.1	WV	20.0	13.7	6.3	36.8	36.5	37.3
KS	33.1	16.9	16.2	37.1	37.1	37.1	WI	59.2	40.8	18.4	42.2	42.0	42.8
KY	38.2	27.0	11.2	38.0	37.5	38.4	WY	6.7	3.2	3.4	37.8	37.9	37.8

[1] Full-time equivalent.

Source: National Education Association, Washington, DC, Estimates of School Statistics Database (copyright).

No. 251. Average Salary and Wages Paid in Public School Systems: 1980 to 2002

[In dollars. For school year ending in year shown. Data reported by a stratified sample of school systems enrolling 300 or more pupils. Data represent unweighted means of average salaries paid school personnel reported by each school system]

Position	1980	1985	1990	1995	1998	1999	2000	2001	2002
ANNUAL SALARY									
Central-office administrators:									
Superintendent (contract salary)	39,344	56,954	75,425	90,198	101,519	106,122	112,158	118,496	121,794
Deputy/assoc. superintendent	37,440	52,877	69,623	81,266	90,226	92,936	97,251	104,048	107,458
Assistant superintendent	33,452	48,003	62,698	75,236	82,339	86,005	88,913	94,137	96,627
Administrators for—									
Finance and business	27,147	40,344	52,354	61,323	67,724	71,387	73,499	77,768	80,132
Instructional services	29,790	43,452	56,359	66,767	73,058	75,680	79,023	82,725	82,418
Public relations/information	24,021	35,287	44,926	53,263	57,224	59,214	60,655	65,505	67,170
Staff personnel services	29,623	44,182	56,344	65,819	71,073	73,850	76,608	80,969	83,035
Technology	(X)	(X)	(X)	(X)	(X)	(X)	(X)	(X)	72,962
Subject area supervisors	23,974	34,422	45,929	54,534	60,359	61,083	63,103	64,659	66,351
School building administrators:									
Principals:									
Elementary	25,165	36,452	48,431	58,589	64,653	67,348	69,407	72,587	73,114
Junior high/middle	27,625	39,650	52,163	62,311	68,740	71,499	73,877	77,382	78,176
Senior high	29,207	42,094	55,722	66,596	74,380	76,768	79,839	83,367	83,944
Assistant principals:									
Elementary	20,708	30,496	40,916	48,491	53,206	54,306	56,419	59,080	60,672
Junior high/middle	23,507	33,793	44,570	52,942	57,768	59,238	60,842	63,709	64,375
Senior high	24,816	35,491	46,486	55,556	60,999	62,691	64,811	67,593	67,822
Classroom teachers	15,913	23,587	31,278	37,264	40,133	41,351	42,213	43,658	43,802
Auxiliary professional personnel:									
Counselors	18,847	27,593	35,979	42,486	46,162	47,287	48,195	50,003	50,022
Librarians	16,764	24,981	33,469	40,418	44,310	45,680	46,732	49,007	48,741
School nurses	13,788	19,944	26,090	31,066	34,619	35,520	35,540	37,188	38,221
Secretarial/clerical personnel:									
Central office:									
Secretaries	10,331	15,343	20,238	23,935	26,316	27,540	28,405	29,514	30,039
Accounting/payroll clerks	10,479	15,421	20,088	24,042	26,249	27,630	28,498	29,898	30,551
Typists/data entry clerks	8,359	12,481	16,125	18,674	21,633	22,474	22,853	24,232	24,840
School building level:									
Secretaries	8,348	12,504	16,184	19,170	21,215	21,831	22,630	23,630	24,041
Library clerks	6,778	9,911	12,152	14,381	15,742	16,033	16,509	17,052	18,104
HOURLY WAGE RATE									
Other support personnel:									
Teacher aides:									
Instructional	4.06	5.89	7.43	8.77	9.46	9.80	10.00	10.41	10.68
Noninstructional	3.89	5.60	7.08	8.29	8.82	9.31	9.77	10.15	10.42
Custodians	4.88	6.90	8.54	10.05	10.79	11.22	11.35	11.85	11.96
Cafeteria workers	3.78	5.42	6.77	7.89	8.56	8.82	9.02	9.41	9.71
Bus drivers	5.21	7.27	9.21	10.69	11.55	12.04	12.48	12.99	13.49

X Not applicable.

Source: Educational Research Service, Arlington, VA, *National Survey of Salaries and Wages in Public Schools*, annual, (All rights reserved. Copyright.)

No. 252. Public School Employment: 1982 and 1999

[In thousands (3,082 represents 3,082,000). Covers full-time employment. Excludes Hawaii. 1982 also excludes District of Columbia and New Jersey. 1982 based on sample survey of school districts with 250 or more students. 1999 based on sample survey of school districts with 100 or more employees; see source for sampling variability]

Occupation	1982 Total	Male	Female	White [1]	Black [1]	1999 Total	Male	Female	White [1]	Black [1]
All occupations	3,082	1,063	2,019	2,498	432	3,890	1,040	2,850	3,028	515
Officials, administrators	41	31	10	36	3	50	27	23	42	5
Principals and assistant principals	90	72	19	76	11	105	53	52	81	16
Classroom teachers [2]	1,680	534	1,146	1,435	186	2,157	544	1,613	1,805	208
Elementary schools	798	129	669	667	98	1,079	151	928	895	103
Secondary schools	706	363	343	619	67	795	331	464	677	73
Other professional staff	235	91	144	193	35	277	61	216	228	32
Teachers aides [3]	215	14	200	146	45	389	43	346	257	78
Clerical, secretarial staff	210	4	206	177	19	266	11	255	203	29
Service workers [4]	611	316	295	434	132	646	301	345	411	147

[1] Excludes individuals of Hispanic origin. [2] Includes other classroom teachers, not shown separately. [3] Includes technicians. [4] Includes craftworkers and laborers.

Source: U.S. Equal Employment Opportunity Commission, *Elementary-Secondary Staff Information (EEO-5)*, biennial.

No. 253. Public Elementary and Secondary School Price Indexes: 1975 to 2001

[1983=100. For years ending June 30. Reflects prices paid by public elementary-secondary schools. For explanation of average annual percent change, see Guide to Tabular Presentation]

Year	Index, total	Personnel compensation				Contracted services, supplies and equipment					
		Total	Professional salaries	Nonprofessional salaries	Fringe benefits	Total	Services	Supplies and materials	Equipment replacement	Library materials and textbooks	Utilities	Fixed costs
1975 ..	52.7	53.4	56.0	55.6	40.9	50.4	55.7	58.0	53.7	53.8	34.5	45.2
1980 ..	76.6	75.9	76.7	77.8	71.0	79.2	77.4	85.9	79.6	82.1	71.1	77.9
1985 ..	112.1	113.7	113.4	111.3	117.1	106.0	112.4	103.2	107.2	111.0	96.1	110.8
1986 ..	118.5	121.1	121.4	117.6	123.3	108.3	117.4	103.0	109.3	120.8	93.7	116.2
1987 ..	123.3	127.4	128.4	121.9	128.8	107.5	123.7	101.5	112.9	126.5	75.3	122.7
1988 ..	129.8	134.5	135.5	127.5	137.0	111.7	126.1	105.9	113.4	140.0	78.1	128.4
1989 ..	136.3	141.6	142.2	133.3	147.0	116.1	131.8	112.0	116.0	149.4	75.1	134.6
1990 ..	144.5	150.0	150.1	139.4	159.3	123.5	137.7	119.2	121.2	171.7	82.1	140.3
1991 ..	152.3	158.3	158.1	146.5	169.8	129.6	142.5	122.7	125.7	189.5	92.6	144.9
1992 ..	158.5	165.5	165.9	152.4	175.8	131.9	148.0	122.5	128.5	199.8	90.8	148.9
1993 ..	162.2	169.6	169.3	155.1	184.5	133.9	151.5	121.9	131.8	205.6	90.4	153.8
1994 ..	167.1	175.2	175.1	159.3	190.2	136.5	154.0	122.7	135.4	218.6	90.6	158.8
1995 ..	170.9	179.2	178.9	163.7	194.9	139.3	157.2	124.4	138.7	230.4	89.7	163.9
1996 ..	177.5	185.6	185.7	169.2	200.3	146.6	161.8	138.1	143.2	243.0	91.0	169.1
1997 ..	182.0	190.2	190.2	174.5	204.2	150.8	165.2	137.2	145.2	263.7	100.1	172.9
1998 ..	184.9	193.3	193.3	177.9	207.6	152.7	168.0	137.6	144.2	278.7	98.1	177.0
1999 ..	189.5	199.2	199.1	184.5	213.4	152.3	172.1	135.2	145.6	295.8	87.5	178.3
2000 ..	194.2	204.1	203.5	189.3	220.2	156.1	175.5	136.4	147.9	312.5	92.6	182.1
2001 ..	201.8	211.4	210.8	197.6	226.3	165.6	177.4	143.2	149.4	334.0	118.4	186.7

Source: Research Associates of Washington, Arlington, VA, *Inflation Measures for Schools, Colleges, and Libraries*, periodic (copyright).

No. 254. Finances of Public Elementary and Secondary School Systems by Enrollment-Size Group: 2000-2001

[In millions of dollars (402,385 represents $402,385,000,000), except as indicated. Data are based on annual survey. For details, see source. See also Appendix III]

Item	All school systems	School systems with enrollment of—						
		50,000 or more	25,000 to 49,999	15,000 to 24,999	7,500 to 14,999	5,000 to 7,499	3,000 to 4,999	Under 3,000
Fall enrollment (1,000)	47,223	9,679	5,436	4,736	6,821	4,346	5,561	10,643
General revenue	402,385	82,872	43,932	37,739	57,042	37,382	48,231	95,187
From federal sources	28,625	7,131	3,225	2,671	3,463	2,107	2,824	7,204
Through state	25,983	6,672	2,960	2,340	3,182	1,927	2,580	6,322
Child nutrition programs	6,599	1,819	847	649	861	515	669	1,240
Direct	2,642	459	265	332	281	181	244	881
From state sources [1]	200,834	39,977	22,946	20,661	28,976	17,588	22,567	48,119
General formula assistance	135,938	24,889	15,076	14,471	20,044	12,174	15,640	33,644
Compensatory programs	3,720	439	753	506	648	347	365	661
Handicapped programs	12,530	3,124	1,420	938	1,575	978	1,468	3,026
From local sources	172,926	35,765	17,760	14,407	24,603	17,686	22,840	39,864
Taxes	113,103	18,456	11,855	9,547	17,184	12,560	15,862	27,637
Contributions from parent government	29,727	12,394	2,641	2,009	3,277	2,289	3,422	3,695
From other local governments	3,983	405	427	368	382	325	571	1,506
Current charges	10,215	1,595	1,071	982	1,496	945	1,266	2,860
School lunch	5,777	850	613	586	919	606	794	1,410
Other	15,898	2,915	1,767	1,501	2,263	1,566	1,720	4,167
General expenditure	410,565	86,019	44,522	38,006	57,894	38,125	48,749	97,249
Current spending	350,628	72,706	37,909	32,558	49,455	32,506	41,818	83,677
By function:								
Instruction	212,747	45,031	22,868	19,819	30,288	19,986	25,519	49,236
Support services	118,679	23,396	12,894	10,888	16,481	10,894	14,139	29,987
Other current spending	19,202	4,278	2,147	1,851	2,686	1,626	2,160	4,453
By object:								
Total salaries and wages	224,652	46,691	24,910	21,293	32,305	21,119	26,907	51,427
Total employee benefits	58,211	12,010	6,247	5,491	8,633	5,569	7,050	13,211
Other	67,765	14,005	6,752	5,774	8,517	5,818	7,860	19,039
Capital outlay	48,927	11,313	5,443	4,460	6,797	4,441	5,463	11,011
Interest on debt	9,550	1,920	1,041	892	1,368	958	1,277	2,095
Payments to other governments	1,460	81	129	97	274	220	191	467
Debt outstanding	201,617	41,310	21,273	18,036	29,181	20,280	27,494	44,043
Long-term	195,748	40,779	20,968	17,790	28,271	19,591	26,588	41,760
Short-term	5,869	531	305	245	911	688	905	2,283
Long-term debt issued	33,797	6,356	3,952	3,080	4,766	3,371	4,485	7,786
Long-term debt retired	14,379	1,914	1,622	1,236	2,316	1,397	2,164	3,729

[1] Includes other sources, not shown separately.

Source: U.S. Census Bureau, *Public Education Finances, 2001*; Internet site <http://www.census.gov/govs/school/01fullreport.pdf> (published March 2003).

No. 255. Public Elementary and Secondary Estimated Finances, 1980 to 2002, and by State, 2002

[In millions of dollars (101,724 represents $101,724,000,000), except as noted. For school years ending in June of year shown]

Year and state	Receipts Total	Revenue receipts Total	Federal	State	Local	Non-revenue receipts [1]	Expenditures Total [2]	Per capita [3] (dol.)	Current expenditures Elementary and secondary day schools	Average per pupil in ADA [4] Amount (dol.)	Rank
1980	101,724	97,635	9,020	47,929	40,686	4,089	96,105	427	85,661	2,230	(X)
1985	146,976	141,013	9,533	69,107	62,373	5,963	139,382	591	127,230	3,483	(X)
1990	218,126	208,656	13,184	100,787	94,685	9,469	209,698	850	186,583	4,966	(X)
1995	288,501	273,255	18,764	129,958	124,533	15,246	276,584	1,051	242,995	5,957	(X)
1996	306,189	286,600	19,319	137,488	129,793	19,588	292,378	1,098	254,483	6,137	(X)
1997	325,007	303,400	19,965	148,184	135,251	21,607	310,719	1,153	269,824	6,401	(X)
1998	349,787	324,429	21,668	159,596	143,164	25,359	330,952	1,214	285,213	6,666	(X)
1999	370,735	345,901	23,583	170,606	151,711	24,835	350,539	1,271	301,380	7,005	(X)
2000	388,210	366,577	25,886	183,384	157,308	21,633	372,138	1,334	319,496	7,363	(X)
2001	424,004	394,790	27,935	198,806	168,049	29,213	398,882	1,417	342,461	7,827	(X)
2002, total	435,468	407,728	30,441	202,494	174,805	27,728	414,708	1,453	357,535	8,087	(X)
Alabama	5,541	4,524	470	2,853	1,016	1,016	4,668	1,045	3,784	5,419	47
Alaska	1,397	1,245	156	791	298	152	1,372	2,165	1,269	11,103	4
Arizona	6,515	6,328	526	3,118	2,684	186	5,802	1,093	4,669	5,353	48
Arkansas	3,121	2,840	233	1,773	833	281	3,046	1,130	2,533	6,025	45
California	53,587	51,587	5,152	30,457	15,978	2,000	50,723	1,466	43,327	7,324	34
Colorado	6,101	5,740	317	2,317	3,106	361	6,238	1,408	5,130	7,453	28
Connecticut	6,889	6,878	338	2,872	3,668	11	6,889	2,006	6,165	11,431	3
Delaware	1,343	1,223	99	822	302	120	1,254	1,574	1,118	10,166	7
Dist. Columbia	774	774	113	-	661	-	1,140	1,987	958	15,281	(X)
Florida	19,570	18,036	1,780	8,137	8,120	1,534	19,431	1,187	15,334	6,592	42
Georgia	13,939	13,061	932	6,247	5,882	878	13,224	1,573	11,506	8,395	19
Hawaii	1,890	1,883	171	1,681	31	7	1,482	1,208	1,357	7,969	23
Idaho	1,721	1,629	141	996	493	92	1,768	1,339	1,594	6,884	39
Illinois	21,143	19,400	1,654	6,144	11,602	1,743	21,904	1,750	18,424	9,788	9
Indiana	9,417	9,155	512	4,844	3,798	262	9,554	1,559	7,835	8,555	17
Iowa	4,270	3,954	233	1,963	1,758	316	3,870	1,320	3,313	7,212	35
Kansas	4,511	3,737	280	2,250	1,207	774	3,839	1,421	3,458	8,262	20
Kentucky	4,769	4,762	490	2,884	1,388	7	4,862	1,195	4,471	7,763	26
Louisiana	5,891	5,296	665	2,598	2,033	595	5,555	1,243	4,791	7,055	36
Maine	1,996	1,893	128	825	939	104	1,996	1,554	1,816	9,529	11
Maryland	8,130	7,883	409	2,825	4,649	247	7,653	1,425	6,591	8,164	21
Massachusetts	10,490	10,488	562	4,864	5,062	2	10,548	1,648	9,916	11,079	5
Michigan	13,751	13,441	716	10,446	2,279	310	15,398	1,539	14,355	8,987	14
Minnesota	8,954	7,864	437	4,824	2,604	1,090	8,351	1,675	6,442	8,139	22
Mississippi	3,241	3,090	472	1,670	947	152	3,044	1,064	2,692	5,828	46
Missouri	8,096	7,429	576	2,632	4,221	667	7,209	1,279	6,017	7,395	30
Montana	1,211	1,186	137	564	485	25	1,150	1,270	1,083	7,901	24
Nebraska	2,079	2,053	125	854	1,073	26	2,172	1,263	1,933	7,336	33
Nevada	3,430	2,614	141	746	1,727	816	2,963	1,413	2,074	6,507	43
New Hampshire	2,013	1,844	86	937	821	169	1,825	1,449	1,623	8,432	18
New Jersey	14,836	14,707	387	5,297	9,024	129	15,195	1,785	14,581	11,458	2
New Mexico	2,585	2,466	320	1,828	317	119	2,396	1,309	2,146	7,450	29
New York	36,008	35,025	1,525	16,500	17,000	983	35,531	1,862	31,300	11,472	1
North Carolina	10,233	9,541	734	6,814	1,993	692	9,903	1,207	8,411	6,970	37
North Dakota	758	718	90	302	327	40	541	850	485	4,851	50
Ohio	18,590	16,700	1,000	7,200	8,500	1,890	15,140	1,329	13,000	7,881	25
Oklahoma	4,297	4,046	482	2,212	1,352	250	4,043	1,165	3,881	6,681	41
Oregon	4,949	4,707	388	2,687	1,632	241	4,812	1,386	4,304	8,910	15
Pennsylvania	17,439	17,437	891	7,006	9,540	2	15,472	1,258	14,701	8,771	16
Rhode Island	1,385	1,385	52	518	815	-	1,552	1,465	1,484	10,118	8
South Carolina	6,519	5,727	453	3,073	2,202	792	5,846	1,439	4,696	7,381	31
South Dakota	975	918	130	330	458	57	976	1,287	821	6,911	38
Tennessee	5,721	5,430	572	2,599	2,260	290	5,703	992	5,398	6,367	44
Texas	37,864	32,587	2,948	13,213	16,426	5,276	35,235	1,649	28,405	7,374	32
Utah	2,865	2,864	215	1,670	979	1	2,698	1,184	2,233	4,989	49
Vermont	1,089	1,072	68	765	239	18	1,077	1,758	943	10,531	6
Virginia	11,366	10,682	606	4,769	5,306	684	8,357	1,161	7,378	6,792	40
Washington	9,277	8,206	711	5,234	2,261	1,071	8,804	1,469	7,072	7,501	27
West Virginia	2,337	2,254	274	1,519	461	83	2,605	1,447	2,378	9,056	13
Wisconsin	9,677	8,535	473	4,580	3,481	1,142	9,001	1,665	7,566	9,539	10
Wyoming	919	894	74	440	380	25	869	1,760	775	9,478	12

- Represents or rounds to zero. X Not applicable. [1] Amount received by local education agencies from the sales of bonds and real property and equipment, loans, and proceeds from insurance adjustments. [2] Includes interest on school debt and other current expenditures not shown separately. [3] Based on U.S. Census Bureau estimated resident population, as of July 1, the previous year, except 1980, 1990, and 2000 population enumerated as of April 1. [4] Average daily attendance.

Source: National Education Association, Washington, DC, Estimates of School Statistics Database (copyright).

No. 256. Public Schools With Internet Access: 1995 to 2001

[In percent. As of fall. Excludes special education, vocational education, and alternative schools. Based on sample and subject to sampling error; see source for details]

School characteristic	Percent of schools with Internet access				Percent of instructional classrooms with Internet access				Students per instructional computer with Internet access, 2001	Schools with Internet available to students outside of regular school hours, 2001
	1995	1999	2000	2001	1995	1999	2000	2001		
Total [1]	50	95	98	99	8	64	77	87	5	51
Instructional level:										
Elementary	46	94	97	99	8	62	76	86	6	42
Secondary	65	98	100	100	8	67	79	88	4	78
Size of enrollment:										
Less than 300	39	96	96	99	9	71	83	87	4	47
300 to 999	52	94	98	99	8	64	78	87	6	47
1,000 or more	69	96	99	100	4	58	70	86	5	82
Percent minority enrollment:										
Less than 6 percent	52	95	98	99	9	74	85	88	5	50
6 to 20 percent	58	97	100	100	10	78	83	90	5	45
21 to 49 percent	55	96	98	100	9	64	79	89	6	52
50 percent or more	39	92	96	98	3	43	64	81	6	56
Percent of students eligible for free or reduced-price lunch:										
Less than 35 percent	60	95	99	99	9	73	82	90	5	52
35 to 49 percent	48	98	99	100	6	69	81	89	5	50
50 to 74 percent	41	96	97	99	6	61	77	87	6	50
75 percent or more	31	89	94	97	3	38	60	79	7	49

[1] Includes combined schools.

Source: U.S. National Center for Education Statistics, *Internet Access in U.S. Public Schools and Classrooms: 1994-2001*, NCES 2002-018, September 2002.

No. 257. Advanced Telecommunications in Private Schools: 1995 and 1999

[For fall 1995 and school year 1998-99. Based on the Fast Response Survey System; for details, see source]

Characteristic	Number of students per computer		Internet access (percent)						Percent of schools without access that plan to have access in the future, 1999	Percent of teachers using computers for teaching, 1999 [1]
			Schools with access		Instructional rooms with access		Students enrolled in schools with access			
	1995	1999	1995	1999	1995	1999	1995	1999		
All private schools	9	6	25	67	5	25	41	81	46	45
Affiliation:										
Catholic	10	7	35	83	4	27	43	86	74	48
Other religious	9	7	16	54	2	18	30	72	41	41
Nonsectarian	6	4	32	66	13	41	59	84	38	49
Instructional level:										
Elementary	9	7	23	64	3	21	32	77	46	45
Secondary	7	5	57	90	6	32	70	97	31	47
Combined	8	5	19	64	8	28	41	80	46	44
Size of enrollment:										
Less than 150	7	5	13	48	2	16	16	60	38	41
150 to 299	9	7	27	77	3	17	28	77	60	43
300 or more	9	6	50	85	8	34	56	87	77	47
Minority enrollment:										
Less than 6 percent	9	7	24	59	3	28	38	83	13	41
6 to 20 percent	7	6	29	75	9	27	51	86	71	46
21 to 49 percent	8	6	29	76	3	32	44	85	59	45
50 percent or more	11	8	18	52	2	10	24	59	59	47

[1] Percent of teachers using computers or advanced telecommunications (e.g. networked computers and interactive television) for teaching.

Source: U.S. National Center for Education Statistics, *Advanced Telecommunications in U.S. Private Schools, Fall 1995* and *1998-99*, NCES 97-394 and 2001-037.

No. 258. Computers for Student Instruction in Elementary and Secondary Schools: 2002-2003

[53,957 represents 53,957,000. Market Data Retrieval collects student use computer information in elementary and secondary schools nationwide through a comprehensive annual technology survey that utilizes both mail, telephone, and Internet data methods]

Level	Total schools	Total enrollment (1,000)	Number of computers[1] (1,000)	Students per computer	Schools with a wireless network (percent)	Schools with distance learning programs (percent)[2] For students	Schools with distance learning programs (percent)[2] For teachers	Schools with laptop computers[3]	Schools with high speed Internet access (percent)[4]
U.S. total, 2002-03...	113,637	53,957	13,196	4.1	22.6	18.7	21.5	38.8	73.9
Public schools, total......	90,524	48,557	12,174	4.0	27.3	22.9	25.8	42.6	80.0
Elementary..........	52,922	23,799	5,297	4.5	23.3	15.7	20.5	37.2	75.9
Middle/junior high......	13,959	9,227	2,319	4.0	32.7	20.9	25.4	47.8	85.8
Senior high..........	16,488	13,148	3,901	3.4	35.7	39.5	37.8	52.5	88.2
K-12/other	7,155	2,383	656	3.6	26.9	40.7	37.7	48.4	77.9
Catholic schools, total	8,060	2,623	479	5.5	14.8	3.6	6.3	30.5	56.2
Elementary..........	6,689	1,932	330	5.9	12.8	2.2	5.9	27.5	52.0
Secondary	1,209	630	132	4.8	25.1	10.9	8.2	47.0	77.8
K-12/other	162	61	18	3.4	27.1	5.7	10.0	37.1	71.0
Other private schools, total .	15,053	2,776	543	5.1	11.7	5.3	6.6	21.2	46.1
Elementary..........	7,366	1,165	206	5.6	11.0	1.8	4.8	20.7	44.4
Secondary	1,236	254	76	3.3	21.1	16.6	9.4	35.1	48.6
K-12/other	6,451	1,357	261	5.2	10.9	8.3	8.7	19.4	45.4

[1] Includes estimates for schools not reporting number of computers. [2] Distance learning programs as determined by respondents. [3] For student instruction. [4] Statistics based on responses to those indicating type of Internet connection. High speed includes Internet connection types: T1, T3, cable modem, digital satellite.

Source: Market Data Retrieval, Shelton, CT, unpublished data (copyright).

No. 259. Public School Teachers Using Computers or the Internet for Classroom Instruction During Class Time: 1999

[In percent. Based on the Fast Survey Response System conducted in the spring of 1999 and subject to sampling error; see source]

Characteristic	Teachers using computers or Internet for classroom instruction[1]	Computer applications[2]	Practice drills	Research using the Internet	Solve problems and analyze data	Research using CD-ROM	Produce multimedia reports/ projects	Graphical presentation of materials	Demonstration/ simulations
Teachers with access to computers or the Internet at schools..	53	41	31	30	27	27	24	19	17
School instructional level:									
Elementary school	56	41	39	25	31	27	22	17	15
Secondary school.....	44	42	12	41	20	27	27	23	21
Percent of students in school eligible for free or reduced-price school lunch:									
Less than 11 percent...	61	55	26	39	25	32	29	26	22
11 to 30 percent......	52	45	29	35	29	27	23	18	16
31 to 49 percent......	53	39	33	29	26	30	23	16	17
50 to 70 percent......	47	33	33	25	27	24	25	19	13
71 percent or more....	50	31	35	18	27	19	22	19	16
Hours of professional development:									
0 hours.............	30	21	19	20	14	16	16	10	8
1-8 hours	46	36	26	28	24	24	20	16	13
9-32 hours	61	47	35	32	30	31	26	21	19
More than 32 hours ...	71	55	43	42	41	34	37	31	29

[1] Includes corresponding with others (e.g. authors, experts) via e-mail or Internet, not shown separately. [2] For example, word processing or spreadsheets.

Source: U.S. National Center for Education Statistics, Fast Response Survey System, *Teacher Use of Computers and the Internet in Public Schools*, NCES 2000-090, April 2000.

No. 260. Children's Access to Home Computer and Use of the Internet at Home: 2000

[As of August. For children 3 to 17 years old. (60,635 represents 60,635,000). Based on the Current Population Survey and subject to sampling error; see source for details]

Characteristic	Children (1,000)	Home computer access Number (1,000)	Percent	Use of the Internet at home Number (1,000)	Percent
Total	60,635	39,430	65.0	18,437	30.4
Age:					
3 to 5 years	11,915	6,905	58.0	864	7.3
6 to 11 years	24,837	15,924	64.1	6,135	24.7
12 to 17 years	23,884	16,600	69.5	11,439	47.9
Sex:					
Male	31,055	20,273	65.3	9,392	30.2
Female	29,530	19,156	64.8	9,045	30.6
Race and Hispanic origin:					
White	47,433	33,062	69.7	15,940	33.6
White non-Hispanic	38,438	29,731	77.3	14,773	38.4
Black	9,779	4,161	42.5	1,441	14.7
Asian and Pacific Islander	2,581	1,855	71.9	909	35.2
Hispanic [1]	9,568	3,546	37.1	1,229	12.8
Householder's educational attainment:					
Less than high school diploma	10,159	3,060	30.1	1,126	11.1
High school diploma/GED	18,915	10,559	55.8	4,600	24.3
Some college	16,994	12,712	74.8	5,926	34.9
Bachelor's degree or more	14,567	13,098	89.9	6,786	46.6
Household type:					
Family households	60,012	39,119	65.2	18,284	30.5
Married-couple household	42,936	31,593	73.6	15,050	35.1
Male householder	3,092	1,508	48.8	740	23.9
Female householder	13,984	6,017	43.0	2,493	17.8
Nonfamily household	620	310	50.0	154	24.8
Family income:					
Total children in families	59,288	38,729	65.3	18,139	30.6
Under $15,000	7,480	2,041	27.3	578	7.7
15,000 to 19,999	2,896	1,044	36.0	373	12.9
20,000 to 24,999	3,596	1,507	41.9	547	15.2
25,000 to 34,999	6,967	3,755	53.9	1,463	21.0
35,000 to 49,999	8,463	6,044	71.4	2,694	31.8
50,000 to 74,999	10,374	8,574	82.6	4,142	39.9
75,000 and over	12,115	11,294	93.2	6,263	51.7
Not reported	7,395	4,470	60.4	2,079	28.1

[1] Persons of Hispanic origin may be of any race.

Source: U.S. Census Bureau, Current Population Reports, Home Computer and Internet Use in the United States: August 2000. See Internet site <http://www.census.gov/prod/2001pubs/P23-207.pdf> (issued September 2001).

No. 261. Children and Youth With Disabilities Served by Selected Programs: 1991 to 2000

[For school year ending in year shown (4,361.8 represents 4,361,800). Excludes outlying areas. Through 1994, includes children with disabilities served under Chapter 1 of of ESEA (Elementary and Secondary Education Act), SOP (State Operated Programs); beginning 1995, Individuals with Disabilities ACT (IDEA), Parts B and C]

Item	1991	1994	1995	1996	1997	1998	1999	2000
NUMBER (1,000)								
Total	4,361.8	4,779.4	4,907.5	5,079.0	5,230.8	5,397.0	5,539.9	5,683.7
Specific learning disabilities	2,144.0	2,427.7	2,510.2	2,601.9	2,674.4	2,754.5	2,815.7	2,872.0
Speech impairments	987.8	1,018.0	1,020.3	1,026.9	1,048.7	1,063.6	1,074.2	1,090.0
Mental retardation	551.5	553.8	570.5	585.6	593.6	603.3	610.7	614.4
Emotional disturbance	390.8	415.0	428.0	439.2	446.3	454.4	462.8	470.1
Multiple disabilities	97.6	109.7	89.6	94.5	99.4	107.3	107.8	113.0
Hearing impairments	59.2	64.7	65.2	68.0	68.8	69.7	70.9	71.7
Orthopedically impairments	49.3	56.9	60.5	63.2	66.3	67.4	69.4	71.4
Other health impairments	56.3	83.1	107.1	134.2	161.4	191.1	221.8	254.1
Visually impaired	23.7	24.8	24.7	25.5	25.8	26.0	26.1	26.6
Autism	(NA)	19.1	22.7	29.1	34.ˈ	42.5	54.1	65.4
Deaf-blind	1.5	1.4	1.3	1.4	1.2	1.4	1.6	1.8
Traumatic brain injury [1]	(NA)	5.4	7.3	9.6	10.5	11.9	13.0	13.9
Developmental delay [1]	(NA)	(NA)	(NA)	(NA)	(NA)	3.8	11.9	19.3

NA Not available. [1] For children 3 to 9 years old.

Source: U.S. Department of Education, Office of Special Education Programs, Data Analysis System (DANS).

No. 262. Private Schools: 1999-2000

[5,163 represents 5,163,000. Based on the Private School Survey, conducted every 2 years; see source for details. For composition of regions, see map, inside front cover]

Characteristic	Schools Number	Schools Elementary	Schools Secondary	Schools Combined	Students (1,000) Number	Students Elementary	Students Secondary	Students Combined	Teachers (1,000)[1] Number	Teachers Elementary	Teachers Secondary	Teachers Combined
Total	27,223	16,530	2,538	8,155	5,163	2,831	807	1,525	395	188	63	145
School type:												
Catholic	8,102	6,707	1,114	282	2,511	1,815	608	89	150	101	41	8
Parochial	4,607	4,352	193	63	1,307	1,209	80	18	72	66	6	1
Diocesan	2,598	2,053	481	64	835	543	274	19	49	30	18	1
Private	897	302	440	155	368	63	254	52	28	5	18	5
Other religious	13,232	6,843	718	5,672	1,844	750	112	981	153	58	11	84
Conservative Christian	4,989	1,789	225	2,975	773	230	29	514	60	17	2	41
Affiliated	3,531	2,200	287	1,044	554	275	52	226	47	23	5	19
Unaffiliated	4,712	2,853	206	1,653	517	245	31	240	45	18	3	23
Nonsectarian	5,889	2,981	707	2,201	808	267	87	455	93	29	11	53
Regular	2,494	1,396	262	837	547	163	56	328	58	16	7	35
Special emphasis	2,131	1,387	257	487	175	92	22	61	20	11	2	7
Special education	1,264	198	188	878	86	11	9	66	15	2	1	11
Program emphasis:												
Regular elem/sec	22,263	14,278	1,963	6,021	4,752	2,674	751	1,327	346	170	57	119
Montessori	1,190	1,045	(B)	139	77	63	(B)	13	8	7	(B)	1
Special program emphasis	606	280	111	216	111	36	21	54	11	4	2	5
Special education	1,409	232	202	975	95	13	10	72	16	2	2	12
Vocational/tech	(B)	(B)	(B)	(B)	(B)	(B)	(B)	(B)	(B)	(B)	(B)	(B)
Alternative	1,617	579	254	784	120	39	23	58	13	4	2	6
Early childhood	133	116	-	(B)	6	5	-	(B)	1	(B)	-	(B)
Size:												
Less than 150	15,303	8,961	1,103	5,240	912	557	63	293	98	53	8	37
150 to 299	6,571	4,811	429	1,332	1,424	1,042	94	288	102	67	9	27
300 to 499	3,219	2,019	419	782	1,229	768	164	297	84	45	13	26
500 to 749	1,352	629	285	440	805	366	173	267	54	18	12	24
750 or more	778	110	305	362	792	99	314	380	57	5	20	32
Region:												
Northeast	6,452	4,049	776	1,628	1,295	750	264	281	104	49	22	32
Midwest	6,991	5,001	622	1,367	1,345	892	244	210	91	55	17	19
South	8,240	4,131	594	3,515	1,576	652	159	764	131	49	13	70
West	5,540	3,349	546	1,645	947	537	140	269	69	35	10	24

- Represents zero. B Does not meet standard of reliability or precision. [1] Full time equivalents.

Source: U.S. National Center for Education Statistics, *Private School Universe Survey*, NCES 2001-330, August 2001. See Internet site <http://nces.ed.gov/surveys/pss/>.

No. 263. Private Elementary and Secondary School Teachers—Selected Characteristics: 1999-2000

[For school year (87 represents 87,000). Based on School and Staffing Survey and subject to sampling error; for details, see source Web site at <http://nces.ed.gov/surveys/sass/>. Data revised since originally published. See Table 249 for similar data on public school teachers]

Characteristic	Unit	Age Under 30 years old	Age 30 to 39 years old	Age 40 to 49 years old	Age Over 50 years old	Sex Male	Sex Female	Race/ethnicity White[1]	Race/ethnicity Black[1]	Race/ethnicity Hispanic
Total teachers[2]	1,000	87	101	131	131	107	342	402	17	21
Highest degree held:										
Bachelor's	Percent	75.7	58.9	56.0	45.8	48.2	60.4	57.8	58.9	54.6
Master's	Percent	13.9	28.0	32.4	40.9	38.5	27.8	31.0	18.4	26.4
Education specialist	Percent	0.6	2.2	3.4	5.1	3.7	2.9	3.0	2.5	3.9
Doctorate	Percent	0.3	1.6	1.3	3.4	4.9	0.8	1.8	0.7	1.5
Full-time teaching experience:										
Less than 3 years	Percent	57.6	24.4	17.3	8.1	25.3	23.5	23.2	32.3	29.7
3 to 9 years	Percent	42.1	46.5	30.6	12.3	28.2	31.9	31.0	30.1	33.0
10 to 20 years	Percent	(NA)	29.2	36.7	34.1	22.7	28.6	27.4	22.5	28.7
20 years or more	Percent	(NA)	(NA)	15.4	46.2	23.8	15.9	18.5	15.1	8.7
Full-time teachers	1,000	76	81	104	105	86	280	327	14	17
Earned income	Dol.	25,289	29,841	29,638	33,278	36,524	27,771	29,942	27,593	29,508
Salary	Dol.	22,379	26,828	27,229	31,063	31,438	25,922	27,340	24,374	27,162

NA Not available. [1] Non-Hispanic. [2] Includes teachers with no degrees and associates degrees, not shown separately.

Source: U.S. National Center for Education Statistics, *Digest of Education Statistics, 2002*; and unpublished data.

Education 173

No. 264. Scholastic Assessment Test (SAT) Scores and Characteristics of College-Bound Seniors: 1967 to 2002

[For school year ending in year shown. Data are for the SAT I: Reasoning Tests. SAT I: Reasoning Test replaced the SAT in March 1994. Scores between the two tests have been equated to the same 200-800 scale and are thus comparable. Scores for 1995 and prior years have been recentered and revised]

Type of test and characteristic	Unit	1967	1970	1975	1980	1985	1990	1995	2000	2001	2002
AVERAGE TEST SCORES [1]											
Verbal, total [2]	Point	543	537	512	502	509	500	504	505	506	504
Male	Point	540	536	515	506	514	505	505	507	509	507
Female	Point	545	538	509	498	503	496	502	504	502	502
Math, total [2]	Point	516	512	498	492	500	501	506	514	514	516
Male	Point	535	531	518	515	522	521	525	533	533	534
Female	Point	495	493	479	473	480	483	490	498	498	500
PARTICIPANTS											
Total [3]	1,000	(NA)	(NA)	996	922	977	1,026	1,068	1,260	1,276	1,328
Male	Percent	(NA)	(NA)	49.9	48.2	48.3	47.8	46.4	46.2	46.4	46.4
White	Percent	(NA)	(NA)	86.0	82.1	81.0	73.0	69.2	66.4	66.0	65.0
Black	Percent	(NA)	(NA)	7.9	9.1	7.5	10.0	10.7	11.2	11.3	11.4
Obtaining scores [1] of—											
600 or above:											
Verbal	Percent	(NA)	(NA)	(NA)	(NA)	(NA)	20.3	21.9	21.1	21.3	21.2
Math	Percent	(NA)	(NA)	(NA)	(NA)	(NA)	20.4	23.4	24.2	24.5	25.3
Below 400:											
Verbal	Percent	(NA)	(NA)	(NA)	(NA)	(NA)	17.3	16.4	15.9	15.8	16.3
Math	Percent	(NA)	(NA)	(NA)	(NA)	(NA)	15.8	16.0	14.7	14.7	14.4
Selected intended area of study:											
Business and commerce	Percent	(NA)	(NA)	11.5	18.6	21.0	20.9	13.3	13.6	13.7	13.7
Engineering	Percent	(NA)	(NA)	6.7	11.1	11.7	10.2	8.8	8.5	8.6	8.9
Social science	Percent	(NA)	(NA)	7.7	7.8	7.5	12.6	11.6	10.6	10.2	10.1
Education	Percent	(NA)	(NA)	9.1	6.1	4.7	7.5	8.1	8.8	8.7	8.6

NA Not available. [1] Minimum score 200; maximum score, 800. [2] 1967 and 1970 are estimates based on total number of persons taking SAT. [3] 996 represents 996,000.
Source: College Entrance Examination Board, New York, NY, *College-Bound Seniors*, annual (copyright).

No. 265. ACT Program Scores and Characteristics of College-Bound Students: 1970 to 2002

[For academic year ending in year shown. Except as indicated, test scores and characteristics of college-bound students. Through 1980, data based on 10 percent sample; thereafter, based on all ACT tested graduating seniors]

Type of test and characteristic	Unit	1970	1975	1980	1985	1990 [1]	1995 [1]	1999 [1]	2000 [1]	2001 [1]	2002 [1]
TEST SCORES [2]											
Composite	Point	19.9	18.6	18.5	18.6	20.6	20.8	21.0	21.0	21.0	20.8
Male	Point	20.3	19.5	19.3	19.4	21.0	21.0	21.1	21.2	21.1	20.9
Female	Point	19.4	17.8	17.9	17.9	20.3	20.7	20.9	20.9	20.9	20.7
English	Point	18.5	17.7	17.9	18.1	20.5	20.2	20.5	20.5	20.5	20.2
Male	Point	17.6	17.1	17.3	17.6	20.1	19.8	20.0	20.0	20.0	19.7
Female	Point	19.4	18.3	18.3	18.6	20.9	20.6	20.9	20.9	20.8	20.6
Math	Point	20.0	17.6	17.4	17.2	19.9	20.2	20.7	20.7	20.7	20.6
Male	Point	21.1	19.3	18.9	18.6	20.7	20.9	21.4	21.4	21.4	21.2
Female	Point	18.8	16.2	16.2	16.0	19.3	19.7	20.2	20.2	20.2	20.4
Reading [3]	Point	19.7	17.4	17.2	17.4	(NA)	21.3	21.4	21.4	21.3	21.1
Male	Point	20.3	18.7	18.2	18.3	(NA)	21.1	21.1	21.2	21.1	20.9
Female	Point	19.0	16.4	16.4	16.6	(NA)	21.4	21.6	21.5	21.5	21.3
Science reasoning [4]	Point	20.8	21.1	21.1	21.2	(NA)	21.0	21.0	21.0	21.0	20.8
Male	Point	21.6	22.4	22.4	22.6	(NA)	21.6	21.5	21.6	21.6	21.3
Female	Point	20.0	20.0	20.0	20.0	(NA)	20.5	20.6	20.6	20.6	20.4
PARTICIPANTS [5]											
Total [6]	1,000	788	714	822	739	817	945	1,019	1,065	1,070	1,116
Male	Percent	52	46	45	46	46	44	43	43	43	44
White	Percent	(NA)	77	83	82	79	75	76	76	75	74
Black	Percent	4	7	8	8	9	10	11	11	11	12
Obtaining composite scores of— [7]											
27 or above	Percent	14	14	13	14	12	13	14	14	14	13
18 or below	Percent	21	33	33	32	35	34	33	32	33	35
Planned educational major:											
Business [8]	Percent	18	21	20	21	20	14	11	11	11	11
Engineering	Percent	8	6	8	9	9	9	7	6	6	6
Social science [9]	Percent	10	9	6	7	10	9	9	8	9	9
Education	Percent	16	12	9	6	8	9	10	9	9	9

NA Not available. [1] Beginning 1990, not comparable with previous years because a new version of the ACT was introduced. Estimated average composite scores for prior years: 1989, 20.6; 1988, 1987, and 1986, 20.8. [2] Minimum score, 1; maximum score, 36. [3] Prior to 1990, social studies; data not comparable with previous years. [4] Prior to 1990, natural sciences; data not comparable with previous years. [5] Beginning 1985, data are for seniors who graduated in year shown and had taken the ACT in their junior or senior years. Data by race are for those responding to the race question. [6] 788 represents 788,000. [7] Prior to 1990, 26 or above and 15 or below. [8] Includes political and persuasive (e.g. sales) fields through 1975; 1980 and 1985 business and commerce; thereafter, business and management and business and office. [9] Includes religion through 1975.
Source: ACT, Inc., Iowa City, IA, *High School Profile Report*, annual.

No. 266. Proficiency Test Scores for Selected Subjects by Characteristic: 1977 to 2001

[Based on The National Assessment of Educational Progress Tests which are administered to a representative sample of students in public and private schools. Test scores can range from 0 to 500, except as indicated. For details, see source]

Test and year	Total	Sex Male	Sex Female	Race White [1]	Race Black [1]	Hispanic origin	Less than high school	High school	More than high school Total	More than high school Some college	More than high school College graduate
READING											
9 year olds:											
1979-80	215	210	220	221	189	190	194	213	226	(NA)	(NA)
1987-88	212	208	216	218	189	194	193	211	220	(NA)	(NA)
1998-99	212	209	215	221	186	193	199	206	220	(NA)	(NA)
13 year olds:											
1979-80	259	254	263	264	233	237	239	254	271	(NA)	(NA)
1987-88	258	252	263	261	243	240	247	253	265	(NA)	(NA)
1998-99	259	254	265	267	238	244	238	251	270	(NA)	(NA)
17 year olds:											
1979-80	286	282	289	293	243	261	262	278	299	(NA)	(NA)
1987-88	290	286	294	295	274	271	267	282	300	(NA)	(NA)
1998-99	288	282	295	295	264	271	265	274	298	(NA)	(NA)
WRITING [2]											
4th graders:											
1983-84	204	201	208	211	182	189	179	192	217	208	218
1987-88	206	199	213	215	173	190	194	199	212	211	212
1995-96	207	200	214	216	182	191	190	203	(NA)	205	214
8th graders:											
1983-84	267	258	276	272	247	247	258	261	276	271	278
1987-88	264	254	274	269	246	250	254	258	271	275	271
1995-96	264	251	276	271	242	246	245	258	(NA)	270	274
11th graders:											
1983-84	290	281	299	297	270	259	274	284	299	298	300
1987-88	291	282	299	296	275	274	276	285	298	296	299
1995-96	283	275	292	289	267	269	260	275	(NA)	287	291
MATHEMATICS											
9 year olds:											
1977-78	219	217	220	224	192	203	200	219	231	230	231
1985-86	222	222	222	227	202	205	201	218	231	229	231
1998-99	232	233	231	239	211	213	214	224	(NA)	237	240
13 year olds:											
1977-78	264	264	265	272	230	238	245	263	280	273	284
1985-86	269	270	268	274	249	254	252	263	278	274	280
1998-99	276	277	275	283	251	259	256	264	(NA)	279	286
17 year olds:											
1977-78	300	304	297	306	268	276	280	294	313	305	317
1985-86	302	305	299	308	279	283	279	293	310	305	314
1998-99	308	310	307	315	283	293	289	299	(NA)	308	317
SCIENCE											
9 year olds:											
1976-77	220	222	218	230	175	192	199	223	233	237	232
1985-86	224	227	221	232	196	199	204	220	235	236	235
1998-99	229	231	228	240	199	206	213	218	(NA)	234	237
13 year olds:											
1976-77	247	251	244	256	208	213	224	245	264	260	266
1985-86	251	256	247	259	222	226	229	245	262	258	264
1998-99	256	259	253	266	227	227	229	243	(NA)	261	268
17 year olds:											
1976-77	290	297	282	298	240	262	265	284	304	296	309
1985-86	289	295	282	298	253	259	258	277	300	295	304
1998-99	295	300	291	306	254	276	264	281	(NA)	297	307
HISTORY, 2001											
4th graders	209	209	209	220	188	186	177	197	(NA)	214	216
8th graders	262	264	261	271	243	243	241	251	(NA)	264	270
12th graders	287	288	286	292	269	274	263	276	(NA)	287	296
GEOGRAPHY, 2001											
4th graders	209	212	207	222	181	184	186	197	(NA)	216	216
8th graders	262	264	260	273	234	240	238	250	(NA)	265	272
12th graders	285	287	282	291	260	270	263	274	(NA)	286	294
CIVICS, 1997-98 [3]											
4th graders	150	149	151	159	132	126	124	153	(NA)	150	153
8th graders	150	148	152	159	133	127	123	144	(NA)	143	160
12th graders	150	148	152	158	131	130	124	140	(NA)	145	160

NA Not available. [1] Non-Hispanic. [2] Writing scores revised from previous years; previous writing scores were recorded on a 0 to 400 rather than 0 to 500 scale. [3] Civics uses a scale of 0 to 300.

Source: U.S. National Center for Education Statistics, *Digest of Education Statistics*, annual, and *NAEP 1998 Civics Report Card for the Nation*; and *NAEP 2001 Geography* and *History Report Card for the Nation*.

No. 267. Advanced Placement Program—Summary: 2001 and 2002

[Includes exams taken by candidates abroad. In 2002, this represents 36,517 examinations taken by 24,700 students in 734 schools abroad. Minus sign indicates decrease]

Item	Schools represented, 2002	Exams taken 2001	Exams taken 2002	Percent change, 2001-02	10th grade	11th grade	12th grade	Male	Female
Exams taken, total [1]	(X)	1,414,387	1,585,516	12	102,079	557,241	877,083	723,583	861,933
By subject area:									
Art History	977	11,047	12,728	15	1,148	3,649	7,629	4,317	8,411
Biology	6,921	92,254	97,762	6	7,947	36,512	50,368	40,089	57,673
Calculus AB	10,296	146,771	157,524	7	1,562	23,105	129,376	82,328	75,196
Calculus BC	3,559	38,134	41,785	10	767	7,964	32,186	25,439	16,346
Chemistry	5,448	55,406	61,584	11	3,204	31,735	25,273	33,647	27,937
Computer Science—A	2,216	15,827	15,660	-1	2,044	6,066	7,094	13,079	2,581
Computer Science—AB	1,404	7,595	7,799	3	760	2,874	3,894	7,015	784
Economics-Macro	2,020	28,200	32,184	14	421	3,645	27,321	17,893	14,291
Economics-Micro	1,728	18,696	23,108	24	362	2,940	19,173	13,270	9,838
English Language/Composition	6,253	135,428	156,193	15	1,605	116,521	34,335	57,919	98,274
English Literature/Composition	10,671	201,288	215,313	7	304	13,923	196,515	77,847	137,466
Environmental Science	1,388	18,880	24,376	29	770	7,303	15,497	10,669	13,707
European History	3,550	65,776	68,876	5	33,645	10,247	23,185	32,588	36,288
French Language	3,095	16,533	17,372	5	877	4,679	11,151	5,192	12,180
French Literature	405	1,668	1,697	2	54	352	1,248	460	1,237
German Language	1,193	4,116	4,171	1	260	927	2,791	2,063	2,108
Government and Politics—Comparative	956	9,188	10,461	14	843	1,426	7,950	5,671	4,790
Government and Politics—U.S.	4,622	77,467	90,937	17	3,037	8,742	77,048	43,376	47,561
Human Geography	402	3,272	5,286	62	1,136	1,290	1,806	2,514	2,772
International English Language	83	7,635	7,104	-7	23	72	81	2,660	4,444
Latin—Literature	446	2,419	2,857	18	136	1,189	1,473	1,366	1,491
Latin—Vergil	624	3,767	3,740	-1	281	1,652	1,725	1,934	1,806
Music Theory	1,550	6,135	6,859	12	514	2,046	4,049	3,561	3,298
Physics B	3,370	34,001	37,447	10	732	12,756	23,085	24,477	12,970
Physics—Electricity and Magnetism	1,317	8,362	9,439	13	69	870	8,302	7,388	2,051
Physics—Mechanics	2,186	17,397	19,252	11	144	2,320	16,369	14,183	5,069
Psychology	2,442	42,978	51,831	21	932	14,594	35,098	17,761	34,070
Spanish Language	5,351	70,949	74,240	5	7,338	26,013	36,698	26,111	48,129
Spanish Literature	1,142	9,992	10,895	9	763	3,374	6,301	3,386	7,509
Statistics	3,049	41,609	49,824	20	1,770	9,920	37,087	24,961	24,863
Studio Art, Drawing	2,209	5,660	9,972	76	171	1,869	7,651	3,425	6,547
Studio Art, 2D Design	1,683	9,696	7,170	-26	95	1,184	5,702	2,392	4,778
Studio Art, 3D Design	649	-	1,358	(X)	21	201	1,087	509	849
U.S. History	8,901	206,241	227,757	10	13,741	192,066	16,560	104,455	123,302
World History	998	-	20,955	(X)	14,583	3,215	1,975	9,638	11,317
Candidates taking exams [1]	(X)	844,741	937,951	11	91,634	358,774	451,701	413,453	524,498

- Represents zero.   X Not applicable.   [1] Includes candidates and exams taken in other grades not shown separately.

Source: The College Entrance Examination Board, New York, NY, Advanced Placement Program, *National Summary Report*, 2002 (copyright). See Internet site <http://collegeboard.com>.

No. 268. Foreign Language Enrollment in Public High Schools: 1970 to 2000

[In thousands (13,301.9 represents 13,301,900), except percent. As of fall, for grades 9 through 12]

Language	1970	1974	1978	1982	1985	1990	1994	2000
Total enrollment	13,301.9	13,648.9	13,941.4	12,879.3	12,466.5	11,099.6	11,847.5	13,457.8
Enrolled in all foreign languages	3,779.3	3,294.5	3,200.1	2,909.8	4,028.9	4,256.9	5,001.9	5,899.4
Percent of all students	28.4	24.1	23.0	22.6	32.3	38.4	42.2	43.8
Enrolled in modern foreign languages [1]	3,514.1	3,127.3	3,048.3	2,740.2	3,852.0	4,093.0	4,813.0	5,721.9
Spanish	1,810.8	1,678.1	1,631.4	1,562.8	2,334.4	2,611.4	3,219.8	4,057.6
French	1,230.7	977.9	856.0	858.0	1,133.7	1,089.4	1,105.9	1,075.4
German	410.5	393.0	330.6	266.9	312.2	295.4	326.0	283.3
Italian	27.3	40.2	45.5	44.1	47.3	40.4	43.8	64.1
Japanese	(NA)	(NA)	(NA)	6.2	8.6	25.1	42.3	50.9
Russian	20.2	15.1	8.8	5.7	6.4	16.5	16.4	10.6
Percent of all students [1]	26.4	22.9	21.9	21.3	30.9	36.9	40.6	42.5
Spanish	13.6	12.3	11.7	12.1	18.7	23.5	27.2	30.2
French	9.3	7.2	6.1	6.7	9.1	9.8	9.3	8.0
German	3.1	2.9	2.4	2.1	2.5	2.7	2.8	2.1
Italian	0.2	0.3	0.3	0.3	0.4	0.4	0.4	0.5
Japanese	(NA)	(NA)	(NA)	0.1	0.1	0.2	0.4	0.4
Russian	0.2	0.1	0.1	(Z)	0.1	0.2	0.1	0.1

NA Not available.   Z Less than 0.05 percent.   [1] Includes other foreign languages, not shown separately.

Source: The American Council on the Teaching of Foreign Languages, Yonkers, NY, *Foreign Language Enrollments in Public Secondary Schools*, fall 1994 and fall 2000.

No. 269. Public High School Graduates by State: 1980 to 2002

[In thousands (2,747.7 represents 2,747,700). For school year ending in year shown]

State	1980	1990	1995	2002, est.	State	1980	1990	1995	2002, est.
United States	2,747.7	2,320.3	2,273.5	2,608.7	Missouri	62.3	49.0	48.9	53.7
Alabama	45.2	40.5	36.3	38.2	Montana	12.1	9.4	10.1	10.6
Alaska	5.2	5.4	5.8	6.8	Nebraska	22.4	17.7	18.0	20.1
Arizona	28.6	32.1	31.0	41.0	Nevada	8.5	9.5	10.0	15.8
Arkansas	29.1	26.5	24.6	27.0	New Hampshire	11.7	10.8	10.1	12.8
California	249.2	236.3	255.2	323.6					
Colorado	36.8	33.0	32.4	36.1	New Jersey	94.6	69.8	67.4	76.7
Connecticut	37.7	27.9	26.4	32.1	New Mexico	18.4	14.9	14.9	18.2
Delaware	7.6	5.6	5.2	6.5	New York	204.1	143.3	132.4	142.8
District of Columbia	5.0	3.6	3.0	2.7	North Carolina	70.9	64.8	59.5	65.6
Florida	87.3	88.9	89.8	112.9	North Dakota	9.9	7.7	7.8	8.1
					Ohio	144.2	114.5	109.4	114.8
Georgia	61.6	56.6	56.7	70.6	Oklahoma	39.3	35.6	33.3	37.2
Hawaii	11.5	10.3	9.4	10.4	Oregon	29.9	25.5	26.7	30.4
Idaho	13.2	12.0	14.2	16.0	Pennsylvania	146.5	110.5	104.1	114.4
Illinois	135.6	108.1	105.2	109.0	Rhode Island	10.9	7.8	7.8	8.7
Indiana	73.1	60.0	56.1	55.8					
					South Carolina	38.7	32.5	30.7	32.5
Iowa	43.4	31.8	31.3	33.6	South Dakota	10.7	7.7	8.4	8.8
Kansas	30.9	25.4	26.1	29.9	Tennessee	49.8	46.1	43.6	42.2
Kentucky	41.2	38.0	37.6	35.6	Texas	171.4	172.5	170.3	219.8
Louisiana	46.3	36.1	36.5	38.0	Utah	20.0	21.2	27.7	30.6
Maine	15.4	13.8	11.5	12.4					
					Vermont	6.7	6.1	5.9	6.6
Maryland	54.3	41.6	41.4	51.3	Virginia	66.6	60.6	58.3	67.2
Massachusetts	73.8	55.9	47.7	56.0	Washington	50.4	45.9	49.3	58.3
Michigan	124.3	93.8	84.6	101.3	West Virginia	23.4	21.9	20.1	17.4
Minnesota	64.9	49.1	49.4	56.1	Wisconsin	69.3	52.0	51.7	63.4
Mississippi	27.6	25.2	23.8	23.6	Wyoming	6.1	5.8	5.9	6.0

Source: U.S. National Center for Education Statistics, *Digest of Education Statistics*, annual.

No. 270. High School Dropouts by Race and Hispanic Origin: 1975 to 2001

[In percent. As of October]

Item	1975	1980	1985	1990 [1]	1994	1995	1996	1997	1998	1999	2000	2001
EVENT DROPOUTS [2]												
Total [3]	5.8	6.0	5.2	4.0	5.0	5.4	4.7	4.3	4.4	4.7	4.5	4.7
White	5.4	5.6	4.8	3.8	4.7	5.1	4.5	4.2	4.4	4.4	4.3	4.6
Male	5.0	6.4	4.9	4.1	4.6	5.4	4.8	4.9	4.4	4.1	4.7	5.3
Female	5.8	4.9	4.7	3.5	4.9	4.8	4.1	3.5	4.4	4.7	4.0	3.8
Black	8.7	8.3	7.7	5.1	6.2	6.1	6.3	4.8	5.0	6.0	5.6	5.7
Male	8.3	8.0	8.3	4.1	6.5	7.9	4.6	4.1	4.6	5.2	7.6	6.1
Female	9.0	8.5	7.2	6.0	5.7	4.4	7.8	5.7	5.5	6.8	3.8	5.4
Hispanic [4]	10.9	11.5	9.7	8.0	9.2	11.6	8.4	8.6	8.4	7.1	6.8	8.1
Male	10.1	16.9	9.3	8.7	8.4	10.9	9.2	10.4	8.6	6.9	7.1	7.6
Female	11.6	6.9	9.8	7.2	10.1	12.5	7.6	6.7	8.2	7.3	6.5	8.7
STATUS DROPOUTS [5]												
Total [3]	15.6	15.6	13.9	13.6	13.3	13.9	12.8	13.0	13.9	13.1	12.4	13.0
White	13.9	14.4	13.5	13.5	12.7	13.6	12.5	12.4	13.7	12.8	12.2	13.4
Male	13.5	15.7	14.7	14.2	13.6	14.3	12.9	13.8	15.7	13.9	13.5	15.3
Female	14.2	13.2	12.3	12.8	11.7	13.0	12.1	10.9	11.7	11.8	10.9	11.4
Black	27.3	23.5	17.6	15.1	15.5	14.4	16.0	16.7	17.1	16.0	15.3	13.8
Male	27.8	26.0	18.8	13.6	17.5	14.2	17.4	17.5	20.5	16.3	17.4	16.9
Female	26.9	21.5	16.6	16.2	13.7	14.6	14.7	16.1	14.3	15.7	13.5	11.0
Hispanic [4]	34.9	40.3	31.5	37.3	34.7	34.7	34.5	30.6	34.4	33.9	32.3	31.7
Male	32.6	42.6	35.8	39.8	36.1	34.2	36.2	33.2	39.7	36.4	36.8	37.1
Female	36.3	38.1	27.0	34.5	33.1	35.4	32.7	27.6	28.6	31.1	27.3	25.5

[1] Beginning 1990 reflects new editing procedures for cases with missing data on school enrollment. [2] Percent of students who drop out in a single year without completing high school. For grades 10 to 12. [3] Includes other races, not shown separately. [4] Persons of Hispanic origin may be of any race. [5] Percent of the population who have not completed high school and are not enrolled, regardless of when they dropped out. For persons 18 to 24 years old.

Source: U.S. Census Bureau, Current Population Reports, PPL-148; and earlier PPL and P-20 reports. See Internet site <http://www.census.gov/population/www/socdemo/school.html>.

No. 271. High School Dropouts by Age, Race, and Hispanic Origin: 1980 to 2001

[As of October (5,212 represents 5,212,000). For persons 14 to 24 years old. See Table 273 for definition of dropouts]

Age and race	Number of dropouts (1,000)					Percent of population				
	1980	1990	1995	2000	2001	1980	1990	1995	2000	2001
Total dropouts [1][2]....	5,212	3,854	3,963	3,883	4,038	12.0	10.1	9.9	9.1	9.4
16 to 17 years	709	418	406	460	399	8.8	6.3	5.4	5.8	5.0
18 to 21 years	2,578	1,921	1,980	2,005	2,067	15.8	13.4	14.2	12.9	13.0
22 to 24 years	1,798	1,458	1,491	1,310	1,452	15.2	13.8	13.6	11.8	13.1
White [2]	4,169	3,127	3,098	3,065	3,278	11.3	10.1	9.7	9.1	9.6
16 to 17 years	619	334	314	366	323	9.2	6.4	5.4	5.8	5.1
18 to 21 years	2,032	1,516	1,530	1,558	1,651	14.7	13.1	13.8	12.6	13.2
22 to 24 years	1,416	1,235	1,181	1,040	1,213	14.0	14.0	13.4	11.7	13.7
Black [2]	934	611	605	705	618	16.0	10.9	10.0	10.9	9.7
16 to 17 years	80	73	70	84	55	6.9	6.9	5.8	7.0	4.6
18 to 21 years	486	345	328	383	331	23.0	16.0	15.8	16.0	13.8
22 to 24 years	346	185	194	232	209	24.0	13.5	12.5	14.3	13.7
Hispanic [2][3]	919	1,122	1,355	1,499	1,684	29.5	26.8	24.7	23.5	23.3
16 to 17 years	92	89	94	121	113	16.6	12.9	10.7	11.0	10.1
18 to 21 years	470	502	652	733	823	40.3	32.9	29.9	30.0	29.7
22 to 24 years	323	523	598	602	726	40.6	42.8	37.4	35.5	34.2

[1] Includes other groups not shown separately. [2] Includes persons 14 to 15 years, not shown separately. [3] Persons of Hispanic origin may be of any race.

Source: U.S. Census Bureau, Current Population Reports, PPL-148; and earlier PPL and P-20 reports. See Internet site <http://www.census.gov/population/www/socdemo/school.html>.

No. 272. Enrollment Status by Race, Hispanic Origin, and Sex: 1975 and 2001

[As of October (15,693 represents 15,693,000). For persons 18 to 21 years old. For the civilian noninstitutional population. Based on the Current Population Survey; see text, Section 1, and Appendix III]

Characteristic	Total persons 18 to 21 years old (1,000)		Percent distribution							
			Enrolled in high school		High school graduates				Not high school graduates	
					Total		In college			
	1975	2001	1975	2001	1975	2001	1975	2001	1975	2001
Total [1]	15,693	15,839	5.7	9.7	78.0	77.2	33.5	43.6	16.3	13.0
White	13,448	12,498	4.7	8.9	80.6	77.9	34.6	44.2	14.7	13.2
Black	1,997	2,392	12.5	14.1	60.4	71.8	24.9	34.6	27.0	13.8
Hispanic [2]	899	2,770	12.0	10.4	57.2	59.9	24.4	26.3	30.8	29.7
Male [1]	7,584	7,866	7.4	11.4	76.6	73.5	35.4	40.0	15.9	14.9
White	6,545	6,325	6.2	10.1	79.7	74.9	36.9	40.8	14.1	14.9
Black	911	1,098	15.9	19.0	55.0	63.5	23.9	28.8	29.0	17.1
Hispanic [2]	416	1,421	17.3	11.5	54.6	52.6	25.2	20.6	27.9	35.9
Female [1]	8,109	7,973	4.2	7.9	79.2	80.8	31.8	47.0	16.6	11.2
White	6,903	6,173	3.2	7.6	81.4	80.9	32.4	47.8	15.3	11.5
Black	1,085	1,294	9.7	9.9	65.0	78.9	25.8	39.4	25.4	11.0
Hispanic [2]	484	1,349	7.6	9.3	59.3	67.6	23.6	32.3	33.1	23.1

[1] Includes other races not shown separately. [2] Persons of Hispanic origin may be of any race.

Source: U.S. Census Bureau, Current Population Reports, PPL-148; and earlier PPL and P-20 reports. See Internet site <http://www.census.gov/population/www/socdemo/school.html>.

No. 273. Employment Status of High School Graduates and School Dropouts: 1980 to 2002

[In thousands (11,622 represents 11,622,000), except percent. As of October. For civilian noninstitutional population 16 to 24 years old. Based on Current Population Survey; see text, Section 1, and Appendix III]

Employment status, sex, and race	Graduates [1]				Dropouts [3]			
	1980	1990	1995 [2]	2002 [2]	1980	1990	1995 [2]	2002 [2]
Civilian population	11,622	8,370	6,627	7,338	5,254	3,800	3,876	3,721
In labor force	9,795	7,107	5,530	5,992	3,549	2,506	2,443	2,632
Percent of population	84.3	84.9	83.4	81.7	67.5	66.0	63.0	70.8
Employed	8,567	6,279	4,863	5,222	2,651	1,993	1,894	2,136
Percent of labor force	87.5	88.3	87.9	87.1	74.7	79.5	77.5	81.2
Unemployed	1,228	828	667	769	898	513	549	496
Unemployment rate, total [4]	12.5	11.7	12.1	12.8	25.3	20.5	22.5	18.8
Male	13.5	11.1	11.7	12.2	23.5	18.8	19.2	15.8
Female	11.5	12.3	12.5	13.7	28.7	23.5	28.8	24.7
White	10.8	9.0	10.5	10.3	21.6	17.0	19.1	15.8
Black	26.1	26.0	20.3	27.2	43.9	43.3	48.0	34.8
Not in labor force	1,827	1,262	1,097	1,346	1,705	1,294	1,433	1,088
Percent of population	15.7	15.1	16.6	18.3	32.5	34.1	37.0	29.2

[1] For persons not enrolled in college who have completed 4 years of high school only. [2] Data not strictly comparable with data for earlier years. See text, this section, and February 2000 and February 2003 issues of Employment and Earnings. [3] For persons not in regular school and who have not completed the 12th grade nor received a general equivalency degree. [4] Includes other races not shown separately.

Source: U.S. Bureau of Labor Statistics, Bulletin 2307; News, USDL 03-330, June 25, 2003; and unpublished data. See Internet site <http://www.bls.gov/news.release/hsgec.nr0.htm>.

No. 274. General Educational Development (GED) Credentials Issued: 1974 to 2001

[GEDs issued in thousands (294 represents 294,000). For the 50 states and DC]

Year	GEDs issued	Percent distribution by age of test taker				
		19 years old or under	20 to 24 years old	25 to 29 years old	30 to 34 years old	35 years old and over
1974	294	35	27	13	9	17
1975	340	33	26	14	9	18
1980	479	37	27	13	8	15
1985	413	32	26	15	10	16
1990	410	36	25	13	10	15
1995	504	38	25	13	9	15
1997	460	43	24	12	8	13
1998	481	44	24	11	7	13
1999	498	44	25	11	7	13
2000	487	45	25	11	7	13
2001	648	41	26	11	8	14

Source: U.S. National Center for Education Statistics, *Digest of Education Statistics*, 2002.

No. 275. College Enrollment of Recent High School Graduates: 1960 to 2001

[High school graduates in thousands (1,679 represents 1,679,000). For persons 16 to 24 who graduated from high school in the preceeding 12 months. Includes persons receiving GEDs. Based on surveys and subject to sampling error]

Year	Number of high school graduates				Percent enrolled in college [2]			
	Total [1]	Male	Female	White	Black	Total [1]	Male	Female	White	Black
1960	1,679	756	923	1,565	(NA)	45.1	54.0	37.9	45.8	(NA)
1965	2,659	1,254	1,405	2,417	(NA)	50.9	57.3	45.3	51.7	(NA)
1970	2,758	1,343	1,415	2,461	(NA)	51.7	55.2	48.5	52.0	(NA)
1975	3,185	1,513	1,672	2,701	302	50.7	52.6	49.0	51.1	41.7
1980	3,088	1,498	1,589	2,554	350	49.3	46.7	51.8	49.8	42.7
1984	3,012	1,429	1,584	2,331	433	55.2	56.0	54.5	59.0	39.8
1985	2,668	1,287	1,381	2,104	332	57.7	58.6	56.8	60.1	42.2
1986	2,786	1,332	1,454	2,146	378	53.8	55.8	51.9	56.8	36.9
1987	2,647	1,278	1,369	2,040	333	56.8	58.3	55.3	58.6	52.2
1988	2,673	1,334	1,339	2,013	378	58.9	57.1	60.7	61.1	44.4
1989	2,450	1,204	1,246	1,889	332	59.6	57.6	61.6	60.7	53.4
1990	2,362	1,173	1,189	1,819	331	60.1	58.0	62.2	63.0	46.8
1991	2,276	1,140	1,136	1,727	310	62.5	57.9	67.1	65.4	46.4
1992	2,397	1,216	1,180	1,724	354	61.9	60.0	63.8	64.3	48.2
1993	2,342	1,120	1,223	1,719	304	62.6	59.9	65.2	62.9	55.6
1994	2,517	1,244	1,273	1,915	316	61.9	60.6	63.2	64.5	50.8
1995	2,599	1,238	1,361	1,861	349	61.9	62.6	61.3	64.3	51.2
1996	2,660	1,297	1,363	1,875	406	65.0	60.1	69.7	67.4	56.0
1997	2,769	1,354	1,415	1,909	384	67.0	63.6	70.3	68.2	58.5
1998	2,810	1,452	1,358	1,980	386	65.6	62.4	69.1	68.5	61.9
1999	2,897	1,474	1,423	1,978	436	62.9	61.4	64.4	66.3	58.9
2000	2,756	1,251	1,505	1,938	393	63.3	59.9	66.2	65.7	54.9
2001	2,545	1,275	1,270	1,832	379	61.7	59.7	63.6	64.2	54.6

NA Not available. [1] Includes other races, not shown separately. [2] As of October.
Source: U.S. National Center for Education Statistics, *Digest of Education Statistics*, annual.

No. 276. College Enrollment by Sex and Attendance Status: 1983 to 2000

[As of fall. In thousands (12,465 represents 12,465,000)]

Sex and age	1983		1988		1993		1998 [1]		2000 [1]	
	Total	Part time	Total	Part time	Total	Part time	Total	Part time	Total	Part time
Total	12,465	5,204	13,055	5,619	14,305	6,177	14,507	5,944	15,313	6,303
Male	6,024	2,264	6,002	2,340	6,427	2,537	6,369	2,436	6,722	2,611
14 to 17 years old	102	16	55	5	83	10	45	5	63	11
18 to 19 years old	1,256	158	1,290	132	1,224	138	1,535	296	1,583	333
20 to 21 years old	1,241	205	1,243	216	1,294	209	1,374	245	1,382	276
22 to 24 years old	1,158	382	1,106	378	1,260	392	1,127	350	1,293	454
25 to 29 years old	1,115	624	875	485	950	564	908	485	862	447
30 to 34 years old	570	384	617	456	661	484	463	322	527	332
35 years old and over	583	494	816	668	955	739	917	733	1,012	757
Female	6,441	2,940	7,053	3,278	7,877	3,640	8,138	3,508	8,591	3,692
14 to 17 years old	142	16	115	17	93	6	74	21	82	9
18 to 19 years old	1,496	179	1,536	195	1,416	172	1,847	292	1,948	266
20 to 21 years old	1,125	204	1,278	218	1,414	279	1,437	295	1,663	368
22 to 24 years old	884	378	932	403	1,263	493	1,250	463	1,324	510
25 to 29 years old	947	658	932	633	1,058	689	1,083	617	1,099	636
30 to 34 years old	721	553	698	499	811	575	732	506	738	511
35 years old and over	1,126	953	1,563	1,313	1,824	1,427	1,715	1,315	1,736	1,393

[1] In this table, data beginning in 1998 reflect the new classification of institutions. See footnote 1, Table 277.
Source: U.S. National Center for Education Statistics, *Digest of Education Statistics*, annual.

No. 277. Higher Education—Summary: 1980 to 2000

[Institutions, staff, and enrollment as of fall (686 represents 686,000). Finances for fiscal year ending in the following year. Covers universities, colleges, professional schools, junior and teachers colleges, both publicly and privately controlled, regular session. Includes estimates for institutions not reporting. See also Appendix III]

Item	Unit	1980	1985	1990	1995	1996	1997	1998	1999	2000
ALL INSTITUTIONS										
Number of institutions [1]	Number	3,231	3,340	3,559	3,706	4,009	4,064	4,048	4,084	4,182
4-year	Number	1,957	2,029	2,141	2,244	2,267	2,309	2,335	2,363	2,450
2-year	Number	1,274	1,311	1,418	1,462	1,742	1,755	1,713	1,721	1,732
Instructional staff—										
(Lecturer or above) [2]	1,000	686	715	817	932	932	990	999	1,028	(NA)
Percent full-time	Percent	66	64	61	59	59	57	(NA)	57.5	(NA)
Total enrollment [3][4]	1,000	12,097	12,247	13,819	14,262	1 ,368	14,502	14,507	14,791	15,312
Male	1,000	5,874	5,818	6,284	6,343	6,353	6,396	6,369	6,491	6,722
Female	1,000	6,223	6,429	7,535	7,919	8,015	8,106	8,138	8,301	8,591
4-year institutions	1,000	7,571	7,716	8,579	8,769	8,804	8,897	9,018	9,199	9,364
2-year institutions	1,000	4,526	4,531	5,240	5,493	5,563	5,606	5,489	5,593	5,948
Full-time	1,000	7,098	7,075	7,821	8,129	8,303	8,438	8,563	8,786	9,010
Part-time	1,000	4,999	5,172	5,998	6,133	6,065	6,064	5,944	6,005	6,303
Public	1,000	9,457	9,479	10,845	11,092	11,120	11,196	11,138	11,309	11,753
Private	1,000	2,640	2,768	2,974	3,169	3,247	3,306	3,369	3,482	3,560
Undergraduate [4]	1,000	10,475	10,597	11,959	12,232	12,327	12,451	12,437	12,681	13,155
Men	1,000	5,000	4,962	5,380	5,401	5,421	5,469	5,446	5,559	5,778
Women	1,000	5,475	5,635	6,579	6,831	6,906	6,982	6,991	7,122	7,377
First-time freshmen	1,000	2,588	2,292	2,257	2,169	2,274	2,219	2,213	2,352	2,428
First professional	1,000	278	274	273	298	298	298	302	303	307
Men	1,000	199	180	167	174	173	170	169	165	164
Women	1,000	78	94	107	124	126	129	134	138	143
Graduate [4]	1,000	1,343	1,376	1,586	1,732	1,742	1,753	1,768	1,807	1,850
Men	1,000	675	677	737	768	759	758	754	766	780
Women	1,000	670	700	849	965	983	996	1,013	1,041	1,071
Public institutions:										
Current funds revenues [5]	Mil. dol	43,196	65,005	94,905	123,501	129,505	137,571	144,970	157,314	(NA)
Tuition and fees	Mil. dol	5,570	9,439	15,258	23,257	24,631	26,058	27,428	29,126	(NA)
Federal government	Mil. dol	5,540	6,852	9,763	13,672	14,189	14,544	15,554	16,952	(NA)
State government	Mil. dol	19,676	29,221	38,240	44,243	46,114	49,115	52,132	56,370	(NA)
Auxiliary enterprises	Mil. dol	4,615	6,685	9,059	11,595	12,281	13,070	13,776	15,174	(NA)
Public institutions:										
Current funds expenditures [5]	Mil. dol	42,280	63,194	92,961	119,525	125,429	132,846	140,539	152,325	(NA)
Educational and general	Mil. dol	34,173	50,873	74,395	96,086	101,027	106,741	113,594	122,709	(NA)
Auxiliary enterprises	Mil. dol	4,658	6,830	9,050	11,309	12,032	12,819	13,567	14,448	(NA)
2-YEAR INSTITUTIONS										
Number of institutions [1][6]	Number	1,274	1,311	1,418	1,462	1,742	1,755	1,713	1,721	1,732
Public	Number	945	932	972	1,047	1,088	1,092	1,069	1,068	1,076
Private	Number	329	379	446	415	654	663	644	653	656
Instructional staff—										
(Lecturer or above) [2]	1,000	192	211	(NA)	285	285	307	(NA)	314	(NA)
Enrollment [3][4]	1,000	4,526	4,531	5,240	5,493	5,563	5,606	5,489	5,593	5,948
Public	1,000	4,329	4,270	4,996	5,278	5,314	5,361	5,246	5,339	5,697
Private	1,000	198	261	244	215	249	245	243	253	251
Male	1,000	2,047	2,002	2,233	2,329	2,359	2,390	2,333	2,387	2,559
Female	1,000	2,479	2,529	3,007	3,164	3,204	3,216	3,156	3,205	3,390

NA Not available. [1] Number of institutions includes count of branch campuses. Due to revised survey procedures, data beginning 1990 are not comparable with previous years. Beginning 1996 data reflect a new classification of institutions; this classification includes some additional, primarily 2-year, colleges than before and excludes a few institutions that did not award degrees. Includes institutions that were eligible to participate in Title IV federal financial aid programs. [2] Due to revised survey methods, data beginning 1990 not comparable with previous years. [3] Branch campuses counted according to actual status, e.g., 2-year branch in 2-year category. [4] Includes unclassified students. (Students taking courses for credit, but are not candidates for degrees.) [5] Includes items not shown separately. [6] Includes schools accredited by the National Association of Trade and Technical Schools. See footnote 1 for information pertaining to data beginning 1996.

Source: U.S. National Center for Education Statistics, *Digest of Education Statistics*, annual; *Projections of Education Statistics*, annual; and unpublished data.

No. 278. College Enrollment by Selected Characteristics: 1990 to 2000

[In thousands (13,818.6 represents 13,818,600). As of fall. Nonresident alien students are not distributed among racial/ethnic groups]

Characteristic	1990	1994	1995	1996 [1]	1997 [1]	1998 [1]	1999 [1]	2000 [1]
Total	**13,818.6**	**14,278.8**	**14,261.8**	**14,367.5**	**14,502.3**	**14,507.0**	**14,791.2**	**15,312.3**
Male	6,283.9	6,371.9	6,342.5	6,352.8	6,396.0	6,369.3	6,490.6	6,721.8
Female	7,534.7	7,906.9	7,919.2	8,014.7	8,106.3	8,137.7	8,300.6	8,590.5
Public	10,844.7	11,133.7	11,092.4	11,120.5	11,196.1	11,137.8	11,309.4	11,752.8
Private	2,973.9	3,145.1	3,169.4	3,247.0	3,306.2	3,369.2	3,481.8	3,559.5
2-year	5,240.1	5,529.7	5,492.5	5,563.3	5,605.6	5,489.3	5,592.7	5,948.4
4-year	8,578.6	8,749.1	8,769.3	8,804.2	8,896.8	9,017.7	9,198.5	9,363.9
Undergraduate	11,959.2	12,262.6	12,232.0	12,326.9	12,450.6	12,436.9	12,681.2	13,155.4
Graduate	1,586.2	1,721.5	1,732.0	1,742.3	1,753.5	1,767.6	1,806.8	1,850.3
First professional	273.4	294.7	297.6	298.3	298.3	302.5	303.2	306.6
White [2]	10,722.5	10,427.0	10,311.2	10,263.9	10,266.1	10,178.8	10,282.1	10,462.1
Male	4,861.0	4,650.7	4,594.1	4,552.2	4,548.8	4,499.4	4,551.1	4,634.6
Female	5,861.5	5,776.3	5,717.2	5,711.7	5,717.4	5,679.4	5,731.0	5,827.5
Public	8,385.4	8,056.3	7,945.4	7,871.9	7,857.8	7,750.6	7,803.2	7,963.4
Private	2,337.0	2,370.6	2,365.9	2,392.0	2,408.3	2,428.3	2,478.8	2,498.7
2-year	3,954.3	3,861.7	3,794.0	3,780.8	3,770.0	3,641.3	3,672.0	3,804.1
4-year	6,768.1	6,565.3	6,517.2	6,483.1	6,496.1	6,537.5	6,610.1	6,658.0
Undergraduate	9,272.6	8,916.0	8,805.6	8,769.5	8,783.9	8,703.6	8,805.7	8,983.5
Graduate	1,228.4	1,286.8	1,282.3	1,282.6	1,261.8	1,254.3	1,256.5	1,258.5
First professional	221.5	224.2	223.3	221.7	220.4	220.9	219.9	220.1
Black [2]	1,247.0	1,448.6	1,473.7	1,505.6	1,551.0	1,582.9	1,643.2	1,730.3
Male	484.7	549.7	555.9	564.1	579.8	584.0	604.2	635.3
Female	762.3	898.9	917.8	941.4	971.3	999.0	1,038.9	1,095.0
Public	976.4	1,144.6	1,160.6	1,177.4	1,205.3	1,218.8	1,253.4	1,319.2
Private	270.6	304.1	313.0	328.1	345.8	364.2	389.8	411.1
2-year	524.3	615.0	621.5	636.0	654.6	655.4	679.1	734.9
4-year	722.8	833.6	852.2	869.6	896.4	927.6	964.1	995.4
Undergraduate	1,147.2	1,317.3	1,333.6	1,358.6	1,398.1	1,421.7	1,471.9	1,548.9
Graduate	83.9	110.6	118.6	125.5	131.6	138.7	148.7	157.9
First professional	15.9	20.7	21.4	21.5	21.4	22.5	22.5	23.5
Hispanic	782.4	1,045.6	1,093.8	1,166.1	1,218.5	1,257.1	1,319.1	1,461.8
Male	353.9	464.0	480.2	506.6	525.8	538.6	563.6	627.1
Female	428.5	581.6	613.7	659.5	692.7	718.5	755.5	834.7
Public	671.4	898.7	937.1	990.7	1,031.6	1,057.8	1,099.1	1,229.3
Private	111.0	146.8	156.8	175.4	186.9	199.3	220.0	232.5
2-year	424.2	582.9	608.4	657.3	688.5	704.2	735.7	843.9
4-year	358.2	462.7	485.5	508.8	530.0	552.9	583.4	617.9
Undergraduate	724.6	968.3	1,012.0	1,079.4	1,125.9	1,159.8	1,214.0	1,351.0
Graduate	47.2	63.9	68.0	72.8	78.7	82.9	90.4	95.4
First professional	10.7	13.4	13.8	13.9	13.9	14.4	14.7	15.4
American Indian/ Alaska Native [2]	102.8	127.4	131.3	137.6	142.5	144.2	145.5	151.2
Male	43.1	53.0	54.8	57.2	59.0	59.0	58.6	61.4
Female	59.7	74.4	76.5	80.4	83.4	85.1	86.8	89.7
Public	90.4	110.7	113.8	118.8	123.6	122.6	124.2	127.3
Private	12.4	16.6	17.5	18.8	18.8	21.5	21.3	23.9
2-year	54.9	66.2	65.6	70.2	71.0	71.5	72.1	74.7
4-year	47.9	61.2	65.7	67.3	71.5	72.6	73.4	76.5
Undergraduate	95.5	117.4	120.7	126.5	130.8	132.2	133.4	138.5
Graduate	6.2	8.1	8.5	8.9	9.4	9.8	10.0	10.3
First professional	1.1	1.8	2.1	2.2	2.3	2.2	2.1	2.3
Asian/Pacific Islander [2]	572.4	774.4	797.4	828.2	859.2	900.5	913.0	978.2
Male	294.9	385.0	393.3	405.5	417.7	433.6	437.1	465.9
Female	277.5	389.3	404.1	422.6	441.5	466.9	475.8	512.3
Public	461.0	622.1	638.0	657.9	680.4	713.2	716.1	770.5
Private	111.5	152.2	159.4	170.3	178.8	187.3	196.9	207.7
2-year	215.2	312.5	314.9	327.0	340.7	361.9	356.2	401.9
4-year	357.2	461.8	482.4	501.1	518.5	538.5	556.8	576.3
Undergraduate	500.5	674.1	692.2	717.6	743.7	778.3	786.0	845.5
Graduate	53.2	72.6	75.6	79.1	82.6	87.0	90.7	95.8
First professional	18.7	27.6	29.6	31.4	32.9	35.1	36.3	36.8
Nonresident alien	391.5	455.9	454.4	466.3	465.0	443.5	488.5	528.7
Male	246.3	269.5	264.3	267.2	264.9	254.6	276.0	297.3
Female	145.2	186.4	190.1	199.0	200.1	188.9	212.4	231.4
Public	260.0	301.2	297.5	303.8	297.3	274.9	313.3	343.1
Private	131.4	154.7	156.9	162.5	167.7	168.7	175.1	185.6
2-year	67.1	91.4	88.1	92.0	80.7	55.0	77.6	89.0
4-year	324.3	364.5	366.2	374.3	384.3	388.5	410.8	439.7
Undergraduate	218.7	269.4	267.6	275.3	268.2	241.3	270.3	288.0
Graduate	167.3	179.5	179.5	183.3	189.4	194.8	210.6	232.3
First professional	5.4	7.0	7.3	7.6	7.5	7.4	7.6	8.4

[1] Beginning 1996 data reflect a new classification of institutions; this classification includes some additional, primarily 2-year, colleges than before and excludes a few institutions that did not award degrees. [2] Non-Hispanic.

Source: U.S. National Center for Education Statistics, *Digest of Education Statistics*, annual.

No. 279. Degree-Granting Institutions, Number and Enrollment by State: 2000

[15,314 represents 15,314,000. Number of institutions beginning in academic year. Opening fall enrollment of resident and extension students attending full time or part time. Excludes students taking courses for credit by mail, radio, or TV, and students in branches of U.S. institutions operated in foreign countries. See Appendix III]

State	Number of institutions [1]	Total	Male	Female	Public	Private	Full time	White [2]	Minority Total [3]	Minority Black [2]	Minority Hispanic	Non-resident alien
United States..	4,182	15,314	6,722	8,591	11,753	3,560	9,010	10,462	4,323	1,730	1,462	529
Alabama	76	234	100	134	207	27	155	157	72	62	4	6
Alaska	9	28	11	17	27	1	11	21	6	1	1	1
Arizona	75	343	156	187	285	58	163	237	96	14	56	10
Arkansas	47	115	48	67	102	13	78	90	22	18	1	3
California	419	2,257	1,010	1,247	1,928	329	1,054	1,052	1,133	170	528	72
Colorado	74	264	121	143	218	46	145	207	51	10	27	6
Connecticut	46	161	70	92	101	60	93	123	32	14	10	6
Delaware	10	44	17	26	34	10	28	33	10	7	1	1
District of Columbia	17	73	31	42	5	67	51	35	29	21	3	8
Florida	164	708	304	404	557	151	365	429	252	113	112	27
Georgia	125	346	147	199	272	74	224	220	116	97	7	10
Hawaii	21	60	26	34	45	16	37	15	39	2	2	6
Idaho	14	66	29	36	54	12	44	59	5	-	2	1
Illinois	181	744	326	417	534	210	398	495	226	98	80	23
Indiana	98	314	145	169	240	74	213	265	37	23	8	12
Iowa	64	189	86	103	135	54	132	167	14	5	4	8
Kansas	59	180	80	100	160	20	102	151	24	10	7	6
Kentucky	69	188	78	110	152	36	126	164	21	16	2	4
Louisiana	85	224	94	130	189	35	160	143	75	63	6	6
Maine	33	58	23	35	41	18	34	54	3	1	1	1
Maryland	57	274	113	161	224	50	141	166	95	68	9	12
Massachusetts	117	421	182	239	183	238	273	313	80	28	22	28
Michigan	108	568	247	321	468	100	308	444	101	65	13	23
Minnesota	113	293	134	160	219	75	183	254	30	12	4	9
Mississippi	42	137	56	81	125	12	101	85	50	48	1	2
Missouri	116	321	140	181	202	120	188	263	49	32	7	9
Montana	24	42	20	23	37	5	32	36	5	-	1	1
Nebraska	38	112	51	62	89	24	71	99	10	4	3	3
Nevada	15	88	38	49	83	5	33	61	24	6	9	2
New Hampshire	25	62	26	35	36	26	40	56	4	1	1	2
New Jersey	58	336	146	190	267	69	194	212	110	44	39	14
New Mexico	44	111	46	65	101	9	59	48	61	3	45	2
New York	325	1,044	441	602	583	460	698	660	329	141	108	54
North Carolina	120	405	170	234	329	75	252	286	110	89	7	9
North Dakota	21	40	20	20	36	4	32	36	3	-	-	1
Ohio	175	550	242	308	411	138	356	453	79	56	9	18
Oklahoma	50	178	81	97	154	24	114	130	41	14	6	8
Oregon	56	183	83	100	155	28	102	151	26	4	8	6
Pennsylvania	263	610	272	337	339	270	435	496	92	53	14	22
Rhode Island	13	75	33	42	38	37	50	61	12	4	4	3
South Carolina	62	186	77	109	156	30	120	129	53	47	2	4
South Dakota	25	43	19	24	35	8	30	38	4	-	-	1
Tennessee	87	264	113	151	203	61	179	200	58	49	4	6
Texas	201	1,034	465	569	897	137	579	584	414	113	244	36
Utah	24	164	83	81	123	41	102	147	12	1	5	5
Vermont	25	35	16	20	20	15	25	33	2	-	1	1
Virginia	96	382	164	218	314	68	220	268	102	69	11	12
Washington	79	321	143	178	274	47	192	249	62	13	14	10
West Virginia	36	88	39	49	76	12	64	80	6	4	1	2
Wisconsin	68	307	135	172	250	57	192	270	30	13	7	7
Wyoming	9	30	13	17	29	1	17	27	2	-	1	-
U.S. military [4]	4	13	11	2	13	-	13	11	2	1	1	(Z)

- Represents zero.   Z Fewer than 500.   [1] Branch campuses counted as separate institutions.   [2] Non-Hispanic.
[3] Includes other races not shown separately.   [4] Service schools.

Source: U.S. National Center for Education Statistics, *Digest of Education Statistics*, annual.

No. 280. College Enrollment by Sex, Age, Race, and Hispanic Origin: 1980 to 2001

[In thousands (11,387 represents 11,387,000). As of October for the civilian noninstitutional population, 14 years old and over. Based on the Current Population Survey; see text, Section 1, and Appendix III]

Characteristic	1980	1985	1990[1]	1994	1995	1996	1997	1998	1999	2000	2001
Total[2]	11,387	12,524	13,621	15,022	14,715	15,226	15,436	15,546	15,203	15,314	15,873
Male[3]	5,430	5,906	6,192	6,764	6,703	6,820	6,843	6,905	6,956	6,682	6,875
18 to 24 years	3,604	3,749	3,922	4,152	4,089	4,187	4,374	4,403	4,397	4,342	4,437
25 to 34 years	1,325	1,464	1,412	1,589	1,561	1,523	1,509	1,500	1,458	1,361	1,476
35 years old and over	405	561	772	958	985	1,013	899	953	1,024	918	908
Female[3]	5,957	6,618	7,429	8,258	8,013	8,406	8,593	8,641	8,247	8,631	8,998
18 to 24 years	3,625	3,788	4,042	4,576	4,452	4,582	4,829	4,919	4,863	5,109	5,192
25 to 34 years	1,378	1,599	1,749	1,830	1,788	1,920	1,760	1,915	1,637	1,846	1,946
35 years old and over	802	1,100	1,546	1,766	1,684	1,765	1,892	1,732	1,675	1,589	1,776
White[3]	9,925	10,781	11,488	12,222	12,021	12,189	12,442	12,401	12,053	11,999	12,208
18 to 24 years	6,334	6,500	6,635	7,118	7,011	7,123	7,495	7,541	7,446	7,566	7,548
25 to 34 years	2,328	2,604	2,698	2,735	2,686	2,644	2,522	2,568	2,345	2,339	2,469
35 years old and over	1,051	1,448	2,023	2,267	2,208	2,254	2,297	2,199	2,174	1,978	2,103
Male	4,804	5,103	5,235	5,524	5,535	5,453	5,552	5,602	5,562	5,311	5,383
Female	5,121	5,679	6,253	6,698	6,486	6,735	6,890	6,799	6,491	6,689	6,826
Black[3]	1,163	1,263	1,393	1,800	1,772	1,901	1,903	2,016	1,998	2,164	2,230
18 to 24 years	688	734	894	1,001	988	983	1,085	1,115	1,146	1,216	1,206
25 to 34 years	289	295	258	440	426	519	423	539	453	567	562
35 years old and over	156	213	207	323	334	354	372	340	354	361	429
Male	476	552	587	745	710	764	723	770	833	815	781
Female	686	712	807	1,054	1,062	1,136	1,180	1,247	1,164	1,349	1,449
Hispanic origin[3,4]	443	580	748	1,187	1,207	1,223	1,260	1,363	1,307	1,426	1,700
18 to 24 years	315	375	435	662	745	706	806	820	740	899	1,035
25 to 34 years	118	189	168	312	250	310	254	336	334	309	392
35 years old and over	(NA)	(NA)	130	205	193	184	151	198	226	195	260
Male	222	279	364	529	568	529	555	550	568	619	731
Female	221	299	384	659	639	693	704	814	739	807	969

NA Not available. [1] Beginning 1990, based on a revised edit and tabulation package. [2] Includes other races not shown separately. [3] Includes persons 14 to 17 years old, not shown separately. [4] Persons of Hispanic origin may be of any race.

Source: U.S. Census Bureau, Current Population Reports, PPL-148; and earlier PPL and P-20 reports. See Internet site <http://www.census.gov/population/www/socdemo/school.html>.

No. 281. Foreign (Nonimmigrant) Student Enrollment in College: 1976 to 2002

[In thousands. For fall of the previous year. (179 represents 179,000)]

Region of origin	1976	1980	1985	1990	1992	1993	1994	1995	1996	1997	1998	1999	2000	2001	2002
All regions	179	286	342	387	420	439	449	453	454	458	481	491	515	548	583
Africa	25	36	40	25	22	21	21	21	21	22	23	26	30	34	38
Nigeria	11	16	18	4	3	2	2	2	2	2	2	3	4	4	4
Asia[1]	97	165	200	245	277	291	294	292	290	291	308	308	315	339	363
China: Taiwan	11	18	23	31	36	37	37	36	33	30	31	31	29	29	29
Hong Kong	12	10	10	11	13	14	14	13	12	11	10	9	8	8	8
India	10	9	15	26	23	36	35	34	32	31	34	37	42	55	67
Indonesia	1	2	7	9	10	11	11	12	13	12	13	12	11	12	12
Iran	20	51	17	7	5	4	4	3	3	2	2	2	2	2	2
Japan	7	12	13	30	42	43	44	45	46	46	47	46	47	46	47
Malaysia	2	4	22	14	13	13	14	14	14	15	15	12	9	8	7
Saudi Arabia	3	10	8	4	4	4	4	4	4	4	5	5	5	5	6
South Korea	3	5	16	22	26	29	31	34	36	37	43	39	41	46	49
Thailand	7	7	7	7	8	9	9	11	12	13	15	12	11	11	12
Europe	14	23	33	46	54	58	62	65	67	68	72	74	78	81	82
Latin America[2]	30	42	49	48	43	43	45	47	47	50	51	55	62	64	68
Mexico	5	6	6	7	7	8	8	9	9	9	10	10	11	11	13
Venezuela	5	10	10	3	3	4	4	4	4	5	5	5	5	5	6
North America	10	16	16	19	20	22	23	24	24	23	23	23	24	26	27
Canada	10	15	15	18	19	21	22	23	23	22	23	23	24	25	27
Oceania	3	4	4	4	4	4	4	4	4	4	4	4	5	5	5

[1] Includes countries not shown separately. [2] Includes Central America, Caribbean, and South America.

Source: Institute of International Education, New York, NY, Open Doors, annual (copyright).

No. 282. College Enrollment—Summary by Sex, Race, and Hispanic Origin: 2001

[In thousands (15,873 represents 15,873,000), except percent. As of October. Covers civilian noninstitutional population 15 years old and over enrolled in colleges and graduate schools. Based on Current Population Survey, see text, Section 1, and Appendix III]

Characteristic	Total [1]	Sex Male	Sex Female	White Total	White Non-Hispanic	Black	Asian and Pacific Islander	Hispanic [2]
Total enrollment	15,873	6,875	8,998	12,208	10,602	2,230	1,280	1,700
15 to 17 years old	138	54	84	88	74	33	17	14
18 to 19 years old	3,478	1,570	1,907	2,755	2,383	444	247	387
20 to 21 years old	3,421	1,579	1,841	2,774	2,450	383	245	342
22 to 24 years old	2,731	1,287	1,444	2,019	1,732	379	302	306
25 to 29 years old	2,084	917	1,167	1,514	1,283	283	265	255
30 to 34 years old	1,337	559	778	956	827	279	90	136
35 years old and over	2,685	908	1,776	2,103	1,854	429	115	260
Type of school:								
2-year	4,159	1,802	2,357	3,201	2,595	607	279	648
15 to 19 years old	1,200	548	652	958	778	135	96	187
20 to 24 years old	1,381	665	716	1,038	833	191	125	219
25 years old and over	1,578	590	989	1,204	983	281	58	241
4-year	8,393	3,720	4,673	6,541	5,760	1,215	579	832
15 to 19 years old	2,368	1,058	1,310	1,852	1,656	332	161	205
20 to 24 years old	4,084	1,892	2,192	3,276	2,893	495	299	405
25 years old and over	1,941	769	1,172	1,412	1,210	387	119	222
Graduate school	3,321	1,353	1,968	2,466	2,248	408	423	221
15 to 24 years old	734	328	406	511	478	85	131	33
25 to 34 years old	1,442	644	798	1,021	921	185	226	102
35 years old and over	1,145	381	764	934	849	137	66	86
Public	12,421	5,373	7,048	9,503	8,133	1,766	1,026	1,445
2-year	3,749	1,633	2,117	2,909	2,365	523	249	581
4-year	6,439	2,863	3,575	4,962	4,300	950	484	700
Graduate	2,233	877	1,356	1,632	1,468	293	294	163
Percent of students:								
Employed full-time	33.0	34.4	32.0	33.4	32.2	38.6	19.9	41.0
Employed part-time	28.6	25.1	31.2	30.3	31.4	19.0	29.6	24.1

[1] Includes other races, not shown separately. [2] Persons of Hispanic origin may be of any race.

Source: U.S. Census Bureau, Current Population Reports, PPL-148. See Internet site <http://www.census.gov/population/www/socdemo/school.html>.

No. 283. Higher Education Registrations in Foreign Languages: 1970 to 1998

[As of fall (1,111.5 represents 1,111,500)]

Item	1970	1974	1977	1980	1983	1986	1990	1995	1998
Registrations [1] (1,000)	1,111.5	946.6	933.5	924.8	966.0	1,003.2	1,184.1	1,138.8	1,193.8
Index (1960=100)	171.8	146.3	144.3	142.9	149.3	155.0	183.0	176.0	184.5
By selected language (1,000):									
Spanish	389.2	362.2	376.7	379.4	386.2	411.3	533.9	606.3	656.6
French	359.3	253.1	246.1	248.4	270.1	275.3	272.5	205.4	199.1
German	202.6	152.1	135.4	126.9	128.2	121.0	133.3	96.3	89.0
Italian	34.2	33.0	33.3	34.8	38.7	40.9	49.7	43.8	49.3
Japanese	6.6	9.6	10.7	11.5	16.1	23.5	45.7	44.7	43.1
Chinese	6.2	10.7	9.8	11.4	13.2	16.9	19.5	26.5	28.5
Latin	27.6	25.2	24.4	25.0	24.2	25.0	28.2	25.9	26.1
Russian	36.2	32.5	27.8	24.0	30.4	34.0	44.6	24.7	23.8
Ancient Greek	16.7	24.4	25.8	22.1	19.4	17.6	16.4	16.3	16.4
Hebrew	16.6	22.4	19.4	19.4	18.2	15.6	13.0	13.1	15.8
American Sign Language	(X)	(X)	(X)	(X)	(X)	1.6	4.3	11.4	
Portuguese	5.1	5.1	5.0	4.9	4.4	5.1	6.2	6.5	6.9
Arabic	1.3	2.0	3.1	3.5	3.4	3.4	3.5	4.4	5.5

X Not applicable. [1] Includes other foreign languages, not shown separately.

Source: Association of Departments of Foreign Languages, New York, NY, ADFL Bulletin, Vol. 31, No. 2, and earlier issues (copyright).

No. 284. College Freshmen—Summary Characteristics: 1970 to 2001

[In percent, except as indicated (12.8 represents $12,800). As of fall for first-time full-time freshmen in 4-year colleges and universities. Based on sample survey and subject to sampling error; see source]

Characteristic	1970	1980	1985	1990	1995	1998	1999	2000	2001
Sex:									
Male	52.1	48.8	48.9	46.9	45.6	45.5	45.3	45.2	44.9
Female	47.9	51.2	51.1	53.1	54.4	54.5	54.7	54.8	55.1
Applied to three or more colleges	(NA)	31.5	35.4	42.9	44.4	46.2	47.7	50.5	51.3
Average grade in high school:									
A- to A+	19.6	26.6	28.7	29.4	36.1	39.8	42.7	42.9	44.1
B- to B+	62.5	58.2	57.1	57.0	54.2	52.3	50.7	50.5	49.5
C to C+	17.7	14.9	14.0	13.4	9.6	7.7	6.5	6.5	6.2
D	0.3	0.2	0.2	0.2	0.1	0.1	0.1	0.1	0.1
Political orientation:									
Liberal	35.7	21.0	22.4	24.6	22.9	23.3	23.6	24.8	26.9
Middle of the road	43.4	57.0	53.1	51.7	51.3	53.1	53.4	51.9	49.5
Conservative	17.3	19.0	21.3	20.6	21.8	19.9	19.3	18.9	19.1
Probable field of study:									
Arts and humanities	(NA)	10.5	10.1	10.5	11.2	11.8	11.3	12.1	12.6
Biological sciences	(NA)	4.5	4.5	4.9	8.3	7.0	7.2	6.6	6.9
Business	(NA)	21.2	24.6	21.1	15.4	16.4	16.4	16.7	16.6
Education	(NA)	8.4	6.9	10.3	10.1	11.1	10.6	11.0	10.1
Engineering	(NA)	11.2	11.0	9.7	8.1	8.2	9.0	8.7	9.1
Physical science	(NA)	3.2	3.2	2.8	3.1	2.4	2.3	2.6	2.6
Social science	(NA)	8.2	9.4	11.0	9.9	9.5	9.7	10.0	10.3
Professional	(NA)	15.5	13.1	13.0	16.5	14.5	13.1	11.6	12.0
Technical	(NA)	3.1	2.4	1.1	1.2	1.8	1.9	2.1	2.2
Data processing/computer programming	(NA)	1.7	1.7	0.7	0.8	1.2	1.4	1.5	1.4
Other [1]	(NA)	14.0	15.1	15.8	16.0	17.3	18.0	17.9	17.5
Communications	(NA)	2.4	2.8	2.9	1.8	2.2	2.4	2.7	2.6
Computer science	(NA)	2.6	2.4	1.7	2.2	3.4	3.7	3.7	3.3
Personal objectives—very important or essential:									
Being very well off financially	36.2	62.5	69.2	72.3	72.8	72.9	72.1	73.4	73.6
Developing a meaningful philosophy of life	79.1	62.5	46.9	45.9	45.4	44.1	43.0	42.4	43.1
Keeping up to date with political affairs	57.2	45.2	(NA)	46.6	32.3	30.2	28.6	28.1	31.4
Attitudes—agree or strongly agree:									
Capital punishment should be abolished	59.4	34.8	27.6	23.1	22.0	24.1	26.7	31.2	32.2
Legalize marijuana	40.6	37.1	21.4	18.8	33.4	32.7	32.4	34.2	36.5
There is too much concern for the rights of criminals	50.7	65.0	(NA)	65.1	73.2	72.3	71.2	66.5	64.4
Abortion should be legalized	85.7	53.7	56.4	65.5	59.9	54.3	53.2	53.9	55.0
Median family income ($1,000)	12.8	24.5	37.3	46.6	54.8	58.9	61.6	64.4	67.2

NA Not available. [1] Includes other fields, not shown separately.
Source: The Higher Education Research Institute, University of California, Los Angeles, CA, *The American Freshman: National Norms*, annual.

No. 285. Undergraduates Reported Disability Status by Selected Characteristic: 1999-2000

[In percent. Based on the 1999-2000 National Postsecondary Student Aid Survey; see source for details. See also Appendix III]

Student characteristic	Any disability or difficulty reported [1]	None reported	Consider self with disability	Don't consider self with disability
Total	9.3	90.7	3.6	96.4
PERCENT DISTRIBUTION				
Total	100.0	100.0	100.0	100.0
Age: [1]				
18 years or younger	5.8	9.9	3.1	9.8
19 to 23 years old	36.3	49.3	24.5	49.1
24 to 29 years old	15.5	16.1	15.3	16.1
30 to 39 years old	19.2	13.5	23.7	13.7
40 years or older	23.3	11.1	33.4	11.5
Sex:				
Male	39.6	42.4	46.2	42.0
Female	60.4	57.6	53.8	58.0
Race:				
White, non-Hispanic	70.8	66.7	70.8	67.1
Black, non-Hispanic	10.9	11.8	13.0	11.7
Hispanic	9.9	11.6	8.0	11.4
Asian	2.1	4.9	1.1	4.8
American Indian/Alaska Native	1.9	0.7	2.5	0.8
Native Hawaiian/Other Pacific Islander	0.8	0.8	1.4	0.7
Other race	1.4	1.5	0.8	1.6
More than one race	2.3	1.9	2.5	1.9
Parents' highest education level:				
High school or less	40.7	36.4	45.1	36.4
Some postsecondary education	24.1	22.8	21.6	23.0
Bachelor's degree or equivalent	35.2	40.9	33.3	40.7

[1] Those who indicated they had a long lasting condition, such as blindness or deafness; or a condition substantially limiting a basic physical activity, such as walking or lifting; or a physical, emotional, or mental condition lasting 6 months or more which made it difficult to do any one of the following: get to school, get around campus, learn, dress, or work at a job.
Source: U.S. National Center for Education Statistics, *Profile of Undergraduates in U.S. Postsecondary Education Institutions, 1999-2000*, NCES 2002-168, July 2002.

No. 286. Undergraduates in Postsecondary Institutions Taking Any Distance Education Courses: 1999-2000

[16,539 represents 16,539,000. Distance education courses are courses taken for credit and exclude correspondence courses. Based on the 1999-2000 Postsecondary Student Aid Survey and subject to sampling error; see source for details. See also Appendix III]

Characteristic	Total undergraduates (1,000)	Percent taking courses	Mode of delivery of course(s) (percent) Live interactive	Internet	Prerecorded
Total	16,539	8.4	37.0	59.0	39.1
Age: [1]					
18 years or younger	1,567	4.3	41.2	65.1	32.3
19 to 23 years old	7,895	6.9	40.2	56.9	41.8
24 to 29 years old	2,806	10.1	35.2	56.1	42.7
30 to 39 years old	2,300	12.5	32.6	63.0	35.7
40 years or older	1,971	10.2	36.1	60.9	34.2
Sex:					
Male	7,231	7.3	34.5	60.8	40.1
Female	9,308	9.2	38.6	57.9	38.5
Race:					
One race:					
White	11,975	8.6	34.6	58.2	37.6
Black or African American	2,129	8.3	46.9	60.8	37.1
Asian	927	6.8	40.4	69.7	36.3
American Indian/Alaska Native	177	10.9	52.2	44.9	41.1
Native Hawaiian/Other Pacific Islander	142	9.7	(B)	(B)	(B)
Other race	905	6.2	41.9	63.1	56.0
More than one race	284	9.3	27.7	63.6	46.9
Hispanic or Latino (any race):					
Not Hispanic or Latino	14,555	8.6	36.6	59.2	38.1
Hispanic or Latino	1,984	6.8	41.3	56.8	50.0
Institution type:					
Public	12,258	8.6	38.1	57.4	39.2
Private not-for-profit	2,447	6.6	28.2	69.3	37.1
Private for-profit	809	4.5	27.9	69.8	25.4
More than one institution	1,025	12.3	40.9	57.2	44.5

B Base too small to meet statistical standards for reliability of a derived figure. [1] As of December 31, 1999.

Source: U.S. National Center for Education Statistics, *Profile of Undergraduates in U.S. Postsecondary Education Institutions, 1999-2000*, NCES 2002-168, July 2002.

No. 287. Average Total Price of Attendance of Undergraduate Education: 1999-2000

[In dollars. Excludes students attending more than one institution. Price of attendance includes tuition and fees, books and supplies, room and board, transportation, and personal and other expenses allowed for federal cost of attendance budgets. Based on the 1999-2000 National Postsecondary Student-Aid Study; see source for details. See also Appendix III]

Student characteristic	Total [1]	Public 2-year	Public 4-year Non-doctorate	Doctorate	Private not-for-profit 4-year Non-doctorate	Doctorate	Private for-profit
Total	9,283	4,997	8,839	10,915	16,242	22,212	14,294
Age: [2]							
18 years or younger	11,077	5,674	9,127	12,006	19,170	25,991	14,289
19 to 23 years	11,150	5,688	9,461	11,563	19,551	24,529	14,112
24 to 29 years	7,962	5,038	8,397	9,571	12,474	14,190	14,517
30 to 39 years	6,696	4,555	7,817	8,624	10,327	11,050	14,452
40 years or older	5,341	3,667	6,691	7,117	9,641	9,597	14,068
Sex:							
Male	9,298	4,943	8,852	10,895	16,288	22,196	14,972
Female	9,271	5,039	8,829	10,933	16,209	22,225	13,846
Race:							
One race:							
White	9,410	4,940	8,834	10,878	16,855	22,361	14,585
Black or African American	8,559	5,041	8,826	10,655	13,647	19,489	13,270
Asian	10,132	5,200	9,166	11,890	18,513	25,991	15,688
American Indian/Alaska Native	7,369	5,132	7,381	9,381	12,225	(B)	12,292
Native Hawaiian or other Pacific Islander	8,345	5,431	9,698	9,645	(B)	(B)	13,691
Other race	8,897	5,309	8,505	10,825	12,827	20,746	14,310
More than one race	9,488	4,919	9,545	11,436	12,792	20,921	13,308
Hispanic or Latino (any race):							
Not Hispanic or Latino	9,428	5,001	8,961	10,989	17,053	22,678	14,468
Hispanic or Latino	8,235	4,974	7,922	10,119	11,090	18,279	13,639
Attendance pattern:							
Full-time, full-year	14,710	9,083	11,238	13,278	21,131	26,790	18,360
Full-time, part-year	7,991	4,978	6,537	7,394	11,584	14,865	12,875
Part-time, full-year	8,109	6,209	8,605	10,089	12,725	15,431	14,076
Part-time, part-year	2,968	2,325	3,414	4,323	5,492	5,691	7,842

B Base too small to meet statistical standards for reliability of a derived figure. [1] Includes public less-than-2-year and private not-for-profit less-than-4-year. [2] As of December 31, 1999.

Source: U.S. National Center for Education Statistics, *Student Financing of Undergraduate Education 1999-2000*, July 2002, NCES 2002-167.

No. 288. Higher Education Price Indexes: 1970 to 2001

[1983=100. For years ending June 30. Reflects prices paid by colleges and universities]

Year	Index, total	Personnel compensation				Contracted services, supplies, and equipment				
		Total	Professional salaries	Nonprofessional salaries	Fringe benefits	Total	Services	Supplies and materials	Equipment	Library acquisitions	Utilities
1970..	39.5	42.1	47.7	38.8	24.7	31.9	42.8	37.6	41.9	25.7	16.3
1975..	54.3	56.3	60.3	54.6	42.9	48.5	56.8	58.0	58.3	46.7	31.8
1977..	61.5	63.5	66.4	63.1	52.8	55.7	62.6	63.8	64.8	56.8	40.5
1978..	65.7	67.6	69.9	68.1	58.4	60.2	66.6	66.6	69.3	63.2	45.9
1979..	70.5	72.4	74.1	73.4	64.5	65.1	71.2	71.7	74.7	70.0	50.3
1980..	77.5	78.4	79.4	80.2	72.6	75.0	77.0	84.6	81.6	77.8	64.1
1981..	85.8	85.8	86.3	87.7	81.8	85.9	85.2	95.6	89.6	85.9	79.7
1982..	93.9	93.5	93.7	94.6	91.5	94.9	94.2	100.4	96.4	93.5	92.4
1983..	100.0	100.0	100.0	100.0	100.0	100.0	100.0	100.0	100.0	100.0	100.0
1984..	104.8	105.4	104.7	105.1	108.3	103.0	104.9	99.7	102.3	105.3	102.5
1985..	110.8	112.0	111.4	109.2	117.7	107.1	110.8	103.0	104.8	111.3	105.3
1986..	116.3	118.8	118.2	112.8	127.7	109.0	115.1	102.6	107.2	121.2	103.1
1987..	120.9	125.4	125.0	116.3	137.4	107.4	119.7	99.0	108.9	132.9	91.0
1988..	126.2	131.7	130.9	120.6	147.2	109.8	123.0	101.1	120.5	140.5	87.7
1989..	132.8	139.6	138.8	125.3	158.8	112.8	128.8	108.3	115.1	153.5	85.3
1990..	140.8	148.3	147.6	130.3	171.4	118.7	134.0	114.3	119.6	167.0	90.1
1991..	148.2	156.5	155.6	135.4	184.3	123.3	139.8	116.4	123.3	179.8	92.4
1992..	153.5	162.4	160.8	140.2	194.3	126.9	145.7	115.2	126.3	193.9	93.3
1993..	158.0	167.6	165.0	144.2	204.3	129.4	149.5	113.2	128.6	203.4	94.7
1994..	163.3	173.3	170.3	148.2	213.6	133.6	154.8	114.3	130.8	213.6	98.7
1995..	168.1	179.1	176.1	152.5	221.4	135.3	158.0	115.7	133.5	220.2	96.8
1996..	173.0	184.1	181.7	157.3	224.5	139.9	163.8	130.1	137.0	230.9	93.3
1997..	178.4	189.0	187.2	162.1	226.7	147.2	167.3	128.6	139.3	253.4	106.1
1998..	184.7	195.8	193.5	168.0	236.7	151.6	172.8	126.2	141.3	266.5	111.1
1999..	189.1	202.0	200.7	174.1	239.2	150.8	177.0	123.2	143.3	282.1	100.5
2000..	196.9	210.8	208.4	180.4	254.8	155.8	182.9	123.1	145.0	298.6	104.9
2001..	206.4	218.1	215.8	187.9	261.7	171.5	189.2	130.5	147.3	317.4	138.5

Source: Research Associates of Washington, Arlington, VA, *Inflation Measures for Schools, Colleges, and Libraries,* periodic (copyright).

No. 289. Federal Student Financial Assistance: 1995 to 2003

[For award years July 1 of year shown to the following June 30 (35,477 represents $35,477,000,000). Funds utilized exclude operating costs, etc., and represent funds given to students]

Award year impact data	1995	1998	1999	2000	2001	2002	2003, est.
FUNDS UTILIZED (mil. dol.)							
Total	35,477	43,072	40,162	44,007	48,582	55,296	59,346
Federal Pell Grants	5,472	7,233	7,209	7,956	9,975	11,600	11,646
Federal Supplemental Educational Opportunity Grant	764	855	875	907	1,007	918	918
Federal Work-Study	764	913	917	939	1,032	1,218	1,218
Federal Perkins Loan	1,029	1,070	1,101	1,144	1,239	1,265	1,265
Federal Direct Student Loan (FDSL)	8,296	10,933	9,953	10,348	10,635	11,689	12,763
Federal Family Education Loans (FFEL)	19,152	22,068	20,107	22,712	24,694	28,606	31,536
NUMBER OF AWARDS (1,000)							
Total	13,667	15,187	14,566	15,043	16,154	17,963	18,858
Federal Pell Grants	3,612	3,855	3,764	3,899	4,341	4,812	4,884
Federal Supplemental Educational Opportunity Grant	1,083	1,163	1,170	1,175	1,295	1,189	1,189
Federal Work-Study	702	744	733	713	740	1,073	1,073
Federal Perkins Loan	688	669	655	639	660	707	707
Federal Direct Student Loan (FDSL)	2,339	3,017	2,891	2,739	2,763	2,908	3,086
Federal Family Education Loans (FFEL)	5,243	5,739	5,354	5,878	6,355	7,274	7,919
AVERAGE AWARD (dol.)							
Total	2,596	2,836	2,757	2,925	3,007	3,078	3,147
Federal Pell Grants	1,515	1,876	1,915	2,041	2,298	2,411	2,384
Federal Supplemental Educational Opportunity Grant	705	735	748	772	778	772	772
Federal Work-Study	1,088	1,227	1,252	1,318	1,395	1,135	1,135
Federal Perkins Loan	1,496	1,599	1,681	1,790	1,877	1,789	1,790
Federal Direct Student Loan (FDSL)	3,547	3,624	3,443	3,778	3,849	4,020	4,135
Federal Family Education Loans (FFEL)	3,653	3,845	3,756	3,864	3,886	3,933	3,982
COHORT DEFAULT RATE [1]							
Federal Perkins Loan	12.6	11.5	10.61	9.9	9.51	(NA)	(NA)
FFEL/FDSL Combined Rates	10.4	6.9	5.6	5.0	(NA)	(NA)	(NA)

NA Not available. [1] As of June 30. Represents the percent of borrowers entering repayment status in year shown who defaulted in the following year.

Source: U.S. Dept. of Education, Office of Postsecondary Education, unpublished data.

No. 290. State Appropriations for Public Colleges: 2001

[For academic year ending in year shown (8,831.1 represents 8,831,100). Data for the 50 states]

State	FTE enrollment[1] (1,000)	Instructional appropriations per FTE [2] (dol.)	Higher ed. appropriations as a percent of state and local tax revenue [3]	State	FTE enrollment[1] (1,000)	Instructional appropriations per FTE [2] (dol.)	Higher ed. appropriations as a percent of state and local tax revenue [3]
Total...	8,831.1	6,264	7.4	MO.....	139.1	7,564	7.6
				MT.....	33.7	3,859	6.8
AL.....	169.5	4,737	11.5	NE.....	65.4	5,278	10.2
AK.....	16.4	10,746	8.3	NV.....	48.1	6,020	5.4
AZ.....	185.7	5,517	8.7	NH.....	29.1	3,552	3.3
AR.....	88.4	5,143	10.1	NJ.....	161.1	8,371	4.9
CA.....	1,486.6	6,298	8.7	NM.....	68.6	6,257	11.0
CO.....	141.5	4,501	5.6	NY.....	451.9	8,392	4.7
CT.....	61.0	9,418	4.4	NC.....	268.6	7,351	11.2
DE.....	26.7	6,399	7.1	ND.....	31.0	4,706	10.5
FL.....	421.0	5,600	6.4	OH.....	337.4	5,711	6.6
GA.....	176.7	8,329	7.7	OK.....	121.1	5,876	10.4
HI.....	31.8	6,995	6.9	OR.....	111.0	5,716	7.8
ID.....	43.4	6,639	9.7	PA.....	288.3	6,181	5.1
IL.....	340.3	7,452	7.4	RI.....	25.9	6,293	4.8
IN.....	192.8	5,510	7.5	SC.....	133.1	5,014	9.3
IA.....	105.5	6,691	10.3	SD.....	22.1	4,405	7.0
KS.....	100.5	6,447	10.8	TN.....	159.8	5,092	8.3
KY.....	119.5	7,000	9.8	TX.....	674.1	5,510	9.8
LA.....	168.5	3,827	8.0	UT.....	92.0	5,382	9.4
ME.....	29.3	7,123	5.2	VT.....	15.7	3,582	3.5
MD.....	175.1	6,805	7.2	VA.....	235.8	5,955	7.4
MA.....	119.7	8,685	4.5	WA.....	210.3	5,629	7.0
MI.....	333.6	6,682	7.8	WV.....	62.9	4,585	9.4
MN.....	167.2	6,783	7.2	WI.....	194.8	6,564	7.7
MS.....	126.4	4,514	12.9	WY.....	22.8	5,967	10.3

[1] Full-time equivalent. Credit and noncredit enrollment, including summer session. Excludes medical enrollments. [2] State and local appropriations. Includes aid to students attending in-state public institutions. Excludes sums for research, agriculture statistics, and cooperative extension, and hospitals and medical schools. [3] Includes state and local appropriations (including sums for research, agriculture statistics and cooperative extension, and hospitals and medical schools). Tax data from U.S. Census Bureau.

Source: State Higher Education Executive Officers, Denver, CO, (copyright). See Internet site <http://www.sheeo.org>.

No. 291. Average Amount of Aid Received by Undergraduates Receiving Aid: 1999-2000

[**Average amount in dollars.** Based on the Student Postsecondary Aid Study and subject to sampling error; see source for details. See also Appendix III]

Characteristic	Total aid [1] Percent receiving aid	Total aid [1] Average amount	Total grants Percent receiving grants	Total grants Average amount	Total loans [2] Percent receiving loans	Total loans [2] Average amount
Total..............	55.3	6,206	44.4	3,476	28.8	5,131
Attendance pattern:						
Full-time, full-year..........	72.5	8,474	58.7	4,949	45.4	5,437
Part-time or part-year.......	44.6	3,902	35.4	1,952	18.4	4,660
Institution type: [3]						
Public 2-year.............	37.8	2,311	32.7	1,571	7.4	3,319
Public 4-year.............	62.1	6,188	46.3	3,203	39.6	4,834
Private not-for-profit 4-year....	76.1	11,577	66.4	7,008	49.8	6,226
Private for-profit...........	84.9	7,218	59.7	2,654	66.5	5,772
Price of attendance: [3]						
Less than $4,000.........	24.8	763	22.1	673	1.4	1,635
$4,000 to 7,999...........	50.6	2,581	42.1	1,843	14.8	2,762
$8,000 to 11,999...........	64.2	4,948	49.7	2,692	35.4	4,268
$12,000 or more..........	78.4	11,035	62.1	6,145	59.5	6,222
Dependency status: [4]						
Dependent.............	58.9	7,367	46.1	4,574	34.9	4,612
Independent.............	51.9	4,932	42.7	2,331	23.0	5,893
Dependent 1998 income: [5]						
Low (under $30,000)........	74.8	7,005	71.4	4,383	38.1	4,427
Middle ($30,000-80,000).....	57.4	7,508	42.5	4,648	37.3	4,575
High (over $80,000)........	47.7	7,561	30.6	4,777	27.8	4,922
Independent 1998 income: [6]						
Low (under $12,000)........	72.6	6,226	67.9	2,979	38.6	5,704
Middle ($12,000-45,000).....	51.8	4,753	40.5	2,116	23.5	5,895
High (over $45,000)........	34.3	3,051	24.9	1,410	8.9	6,583

[1] Includes other aid not shown separately. [2] Includes only loans to students. [3] Excludes students attending more than one institution. [4] Dependent or independent for federal aid purposes. [5] Dependent student parent's income. [6] Independent student's income (including spouse).

Source: U.S. National Center for Education Statistics, *Student Financing of Undergraduate Education 1999-2000*, July 2002, NCES 2002-167.

No. 292. Institutions of Higher Education—Charges: 1985 to 2002

[In dollars. Estimated. For the entire academic year ending in year shown. Figures are average charges per full-time equivalent student. Room and board are based on full-time students]

Academic control and year	Tuition and required fees [1] All institutions	2-yr. colleges	4-yr. colleges	Other 4-yr. schools	Board rates [2] All institutions	2-yr. colleges	4-yr. colleges	Other 4-yr. schools	Dormitory charges All institutions	2-yr. colleges	4-yr. colleges	Other 4-yr. schools
Public:												
1985	971	584	1,386	1,117	1,241	1,302	1,276	1,201	1,196	921	1,237	1,200
1990	1,356	756	2,035	1,608	1,635	1,581	1,728	1,561	1,513	962	1,561	1,554
1995	2,057	1,192	2,977	2,499	1,949	1,712	2,108	1,866	1,959	1,232	1,992	2,044
1997	2,271	1,276	3,323	2,778	2,111	1,789	2,282	2,025	2,148	1,339	2,187	2,232
1998	2,360	1,314	3,486	2,877	2,228	1,795	2,438	2,130	2,225	1,401	2,285	2,312
1999	2,430	1,327	3,640	2,974	2,347	1,828	2,576	2,247	2,330	1,450	2,408	2,410
2000	2,506	1,338	3,768	3,091	2,364	1,834	2,628	2,239	2,440	1,549	2,516	2,521
2001	2,562	1,333	3,979	3,208	2,455	1,906	2,686	2,358	2,569	1,600	2,657	2,652
2002	2,727	1,379	4,281	3,419	2,597	2,036	2,835	2,498	2,721	1,722	2,837	2,793
Private:												
1985	5,315	3,485	6,843	5,135	1,462	1,294	1,647	1,405	1,426	1,424	1,753	1,309
1990	8,174	5,196	10,348	7,778	1,948	1,811	2,339	1,823	1,923	1,663	2,411	1,774
1995	11,111	6,914	14,537	10,653	2,509	2,023	3,035	2,362	2,587	2,233	3,469	2,347
1997	12,498	7,236	16,552	11,871	2,663	2,181	3,142	2,520	2,878	2,537	3,826	2,602
1998	12,801	7,464	17,229	12,338	2,762	2,785	3,132	2,648	2,954	2,672	3,756	2,731
1999	13,428	7,854	18,340	12,815	2,865	2,884	3,188	2,765	3,075	2,581	3,914	2,850
2000	14,081	8,235	19,307	13,361	2,882	2,922	3,157	2,790	3,224	2,808	4,070	2,976
2001	15,000	9,067	20,106	14,233	2,993	3,000	3,300	2,893	3,374	2,722	4,270	3,121
2002	15,851	10,010	21,183	14,995	3,106	2,664	3,465	2,996	3,564	3,204	4,471	3,294

[1] For in-state students. [2] Beginning 1990, rates reflect 20 meals per week, rather than meals served 7 days a week.

Source: U.S. National Center for Education Statistics, *Digest of Education Statistics,* annual.

No. 293. Voluntary Financial Support of Higher Education: 1990 to 2002

[For school years ending in years shown (9,800 represents $9,800,000,000); enrollment as of fall of preceding year. Voluntary support, as defined in Gift Reporting Standards, excludes income from endowment and other invested funds as well as all support received from federal, state, and local governments and their agencies and contract research]

Item	Unit	1990	1995	1997	1998	1999	2000	2001	2002
Estimated support, total	Mil. dol	9,800	12,750	16,000	18,400	20,400	23,200	24,200	23,900
Individuals	Mil. dol	4,770	6,540	8,500	10,000	10,740	12,220	12,030	11,300
Alumni	Mil. dol	2,540	3,600	4,650	5,500	5,930	6,800	6,830	5,900
Business corporations	Mil. dol	2,170	2,560	3,050	3,250	3,610	4,150	4,350	4,370
Foundations	Mil. dol	1,920	2,460	3,200	3,800	4,530	5,080	6,000	6,300
Fundraising consortia and other organizations	Mil. dol	700	940	1,000	1,050	1,190	1,380	1,450	1,570
Religious organizations	Mil. dol	240	250	250	300	330	370	370	360
Current operations	Mil. dol	5,440	7,230	8,500	9,000	9,900	11,270	12,200	12,400
Capital purposes	Mil. dol	4,360	5,520	7,500	9,400	10,500	11,930	12,000	11,500
Enrollment, higher education [1]	1,000	13,605	14,021	14,264	14,217	14,465	15,007	15,133	15,296
Support per student	Dollars	720	909	1,122	1,294	1,407	1,546	1,599	1,563
In 2001-2002 dollars	Dollars	989	1,070	1,254	1,424	1,515	1,611	1,620	1,563
Expenditures, higher education	Bil. dol	150.56	201.53	223.30	235.50	249.40	264.70	277	294
Expenditures per student	Dollars	11,066	14,373	15,654	16,565	17,206	17,639	18,304	19,220
In 2001-2002 dollars	Dollars	15,190	16,920	17,498	18,231	18,528	18,376	18,542	19,220
Institutions reporting support	Number	1,056	1,086	1,061	1,034	938	945	960	955
Total support reported	Mil. dol	8,214	10,992	13,801	15,771	17,229	19,419	20,569	19,824
Private 4-year institutions	Mil. dol	5,072	6,500	8,023	9,118	9,848	11,047	11,391	10,953
Public 4-year institutions	Mil. dol	3,056	4,382	5,654	6,556	7,252	8,254	9,026	8,754
2-year colleges	Mil. dol	85	110	124	98	129	117	152	117

[1] Excludes proprietary schools.

Source: Council for Aid to Education, New York, NY, *Voluntary Support of Education,* annual.

No. 294. Average Salaries for College Faculty Members: 2001 to 2003

[In thousands of dollars (58.8 represents $58,800). For academic year ending in year shown. Figures are for 9 months teaching for full-time faculty members in 4-year institutions. Fringe benefits averaged in 2001, $14,300 in public institutions and $18,000 in private institutions; in 2002, $14,926 in public institutions and $18,356 in private institutions; and in 2003, $16,208 in public institutions and $19,261 in private institutions]

Type of control and academic rank	2001	2002	2003	Type of control and academic rank	2001	2002	2003
Public:				**Private:** [1]			
All ranks	58.8	62.0	64.0	All ranks	69.9	71.5	74.4
Professor	76.1	81.3	84.1	Professor	93.2	96.1	101.2
Associate professor	57.1	59.4	61.5	Associate professor	62.2	63.4	66.3
Assistant professor	47.2	49.6	51.5	Assistant professor	51.7	53.2	55.6
Instructor	35.0	36.2	37.2	Instructor	39.3	40.1	41.1

[1] Excludes church-related colleges and universities.

Source: American Association of University Professors, Washington, DC, *AAUP Annual Report on the Economic Status of the Profession.*

No. 295. Employees in Higher Education Institutions by Sex and Occupation: 1976 to 1999

[In thousands (1,863.8 represents 1,863,800). As of fall. Based on survey and subject to sampling error; see source]

Year and status	Total	Professional staff Total	Executive, administrative, and managerial Male	Executive, administrative, and managerial Female	Faculty [1] Male	Faculty [1] Female	Research/ instruction assistants Male	Research/ instruction assistants Female	Other Male	Other Female	Nonpro- fessional staff, total
1976, total	1,863.8	1,073.1	74.6	26.6	460.6	172.7	106.5	53.6	87.5	91.0	790.7
Full time	1,339.9	709.4	72.0	25.0	326.8	107.2	18.6	9.4	76.2	74.1	630.5
Part time	523.9	363.7	2.6	1.7	133.7	65.4	87.9	44.2	11.3	16.9	160.2
1991, total	2,545.2	1,595.5	85.4	59.3	525.6	300.7	119.1	78.6	165.4	261.3	949.8
Full time	1,812.9	1,031.8	82.9	56.2	366.2	169.4	(NA)	(NA)	142.2	214.8	781.1
Part time	732.3	563.7	2.5	3.1	159.4	131.2	119.1	78.6	23.2	46.4	168.7
1999, total [2]	2,883.2	1,950.9	83.9	76.0	602.5	425.4	132.6	107.1	207.9	315.5	932.3
Full time	1,918.7	1,180.2	81.3	72.5	371.0	219.9	-	-	175.8	259.7	738.5
Part time	964.5	770.7	2.6	3.5	231.4	205.5	132.6	107.1	32.2	55.7	193.8

- Represents zero. NA Not available. [1] Instruction and research. [2] In this table, 1999 data reflect the new classification of institutions. See footnote 1, Table 277.

Source: U.S. National Center for Education Statistics, *Fall Staff in Postsecondary Institutions, 1995* March 1998, and *Digest of Education Statistics*, 2001.

No. 296. Faculty in Institutions of Higher Education: 1970 to 1999

[In thousands (474 represents 474,000), except percent. As of fall. Based on survey and subject to sampling error; see source]

Year	Employment status Total	Employment status Full time	Employment status Part time	Control Public	Control Private	Level 4-year	Level 2-year	Percent Part time	Percent Public	Percent 2-year
1970	474	369	104	314	160	382	92	22	66	19
1975	628	440	188	443	185	467	161	30	71	26
1980	686	450	236	495	191	494	192	34	72	28
1985	715	459	256	503	212	504	211	36	70	30
1989 [1]	824	524	300	577	247	584	241	36	70	29
1991	826	536	291	581	245	591	235	35	70	28
1993	915	546	370	650	265	626	289	40	71	32
1995	932	551	381	657	275	647	285	41	70	31
1997 [2]	990	569	421	695	295	683	307	43	70	31
1999 [2]	1,028	591	437	713	315	714	314	43	69	31

[1] Data beginning 1989 not comparable to prior years. [2] In this table, data beginning in 1997 reflect the new classification of institutions. See footnote 1, Table 277.

Source: U.S. National Center for Education Statistics, *Fall Staff in Postsecondary Institutions, 1995* and *1997*, March 1998 and January 2000 and *Digest of Education Statistics*, 2001.

No. 297. Salary Offers to Candidates for Degrees: 2000 to 2002

[In dollars. Data are average beginning salaries based on offers made by business, industrial, government, nonprofit, and educational employers to graduating students. Data from representative colleges throughout the United States]

Field of study	Bachelor's 2000	Bachelor's 2001	Bachelor's 2002	Master's [1] 2000	Master's [1] 2001	Master's [1] 2002	Doctor's 2000	Doctor's 2001	Doctor's 2002
Accounting	36,710	39,720	39,494	39,839	43,196	43,625	(NA)	(NA)	(NA)
Business administration/ management [2]	36,357	37,844	36,378	50,276	50,679	52,241	[3]65,865	[3]82,167	[3]81,357
Marketing	33,373	35,194	33,690	[3]45,593	[3]48,833	[3]56,000	(NA)	(NA)	(NA)
Engineering:									
Civil	37,932	40,979	41,193	44,587	44,234	47,756	[3]54,588	[3]61,606	[3]56,228
Chemical	48,890	51,255	51,137	[3]54,473	57,317	[3]55,812	68,161	74,153	75,552
Computer	50,182	53,653	51,135	[3]57,087	60,974	[3]64,268	[3]77,700	[3]71,720	[3]59,211
Electrical	48,613	52,092	50,391	60,828	64,188	62,194	74,423	79,383	77,316
Mechanical	45,952	48,588	48,282	53,581	56,565	55,013	[3]69,830	70,124	63,161
Nuclear [4]	[3]47,070	[3]47,914	[3]48,583	[3]64,986	[3]55,496	[3]51,500	(NA)	(NA)	(NA)
Petroleum	50,367	54,761	56,622	[3]50,369	[3]58,500	(NA)	(NA)	(NA)	(NA)
Engineering technology	40,110	45,458	45,059	(NA)	(NA)	(NA)	(NA)	(NA)	(NA)
Chemistry	35,942	38,744	34,566	[3]46,389	[3]51,467	[3]59,836	62,901	62,067	63,168
Mathematics	41,761	44,277	41,543	[3]46,453	[3]55,482	[3]82,000	[3]60,237	[3]58,555	[3]54,219
Physics	42,455	48,458	[3]47,471	[3]32,722	[3]61,000	[3]41,333	[3]46,500	[3]63,220	[3]51,936
Humanities	33,117	30,653	[3]31,087	(NA)	[3]32,650	[3]29,944	(NA)	(NA)	[3]41,750
Social sciences [5]	30,933	31,634	28,835	(NA)	[3]31,508	[3]38,109	(NA)	(NA)	[3]47,434
Computer science	49,055	52,473	49,413	61,377	62,312	65,001	[3]71,846	[3]84,033	[3]74,453

NA Not available. [1] Candidates with 1 year or less of full-time nonmilitary employment. [2] For master's degree, offers are after nontechnical undergraduate degree. [3] Fewer than 50 offers reported. [4] Includes engineering physics. [5] Excludes economics.

Source: National Association of Colleges and Employers, Bethlehem, PA, *Salary Survey, A Study of Beginning Offers*, annual (copyright).

190 Education

No. 298. Earned Degrees Conferred by Level and Sex: 1960 to 2001

[In thousands (477 represents 477,000), except percent. For the 50 states and DC]

Year ending	All degrees Total	Percent male	Associate's Male	Associate's Female	Bachelor's Male	Bachelor's Female	Master's Male	Master's Female	First professional Male	First professional Female	Doctor's Male	Doctor's Female
1960 [1]	477	65.8	(NA)	(NA)	254	138	51	24	(NA)	(NA)	9	1
1965	660	61.5	(NA)	(NA)	282	212	81	40	27	1	15	2
1970	1,271	59.2	117	89	451	341	126	83	33	2	26	4
1975	1,666	56.0	191	169	505	418	162	131	49	7	27	7
1980	1,731	51.1	184	217	474	456	151	147	53	17	23	10
1984	1,819	49.6	203	250	482	492	144	141	51	23	22	11
1985	1,828	49.3	203	252	483	497	143	143	50	25	22	11
1986	1,830	49.0	196	250	486	502	144	145	49	25	22	12
1987	1,823	48.4	191	245	481	510	141	148	47	25	22	12
1988	1,835	48.0	190	245	477	518	145	154	45	25	23	12
1989	1,873	47.3	186	250	483	535	149	161	45	26	23	13
1990	1,940	46.6	191	264	492	560	154	171	44	27	24	14
1991	2,025	45.8	199	283	504	590	156	181	44	28	25	15
1992	2,108	45.6	207	297	521	616	162	191	45	29	26	15
1993	2,167	45.5	212	303	533	632	169	200	45	30	26	16
1994	2,206	45.1	215	315	532	637	176	211	45	31	27	17
1995	2,218	44.9	218	321	526	634	179	219	45	31	27	18
1996 [2]	2,248	44.2	220	336	522	642	179	227	45	32	27	18
1997 [2]	2,288	43.6	224	347	521	652	181	238	46	33	27	19
1998 [2]	2,298	43.2	218	341	520	664	184	246	45	34	27	19
1999 [2]	2,323	42.7	218	342	519	682	186	254	44	34	25	19
2000 [2]	2,385	42.6	225	340	530	708	192	265	44	36	25	20
2001 [2]	2,416	42.4	232	347	532	712	194	274	43	37	25	20

NA Not available. [1] First-professional degrees are included with bachelor's degrees. [2] Data beginning in 1996 reflect the new classification of institutions. See footnote 1, Table 277.

Source: U.S. National Center for Education Statistics, *Digest of Education Statistics*, annual.

No. 299. Degrees Earned by Level and Race/Ethnicity: 1981 to 2001

[For school year ending in year shown]

Level of degree and race/ethnicity	1981 [1]	1985 [1]	1990	1995	2000 [2]	2001 [2]	Percent distribution 1981	Percent distribution 2001 [2]
Associate's degrees, total	410,174	429,815	455,102	539,691	564,933	578,865	100.0	100.0
White, non-Hispanic	339,167	355,343	376,816	420,656	408,772	411,075	82.7	71.0
Black, non-Hispanic	35,330	35,791	34,326	47,067	60,221	63,855	8.6	11.0
Hispanic	17,800	19,407	21,504	35,962	51,573	57,288	4.3	9.9
Asian or Pacific Islander	8,650	9,914	13,066	20,677	27,782	28,463	2.1	4.9
American Indian/Alaskan Native	2,584	2,953	3,430	5,482	6,497	6,623	0.6	1.1
Nonresident alien	6,643	6,407	5,960	9,847	10,088	11,561	1.6	2.0
Bachelor's degrees, total	934,800	968,311	1,051,344	1,160,134	1,237,875	1,244,171	100.0	100.0
White, non-Hispanic	807,319	826,106	887,151	914,610	929,106	927,357	86.4	74.5
Black, non-Hispanic	60,673	57,473	61,046	87,236	108,013	111,307	6.5	8.9
Hispanic	21,832	25,874	32,829	54,230	75,059	77,745	2.3	6.2
Asian or Pacific Islander	18,794	25,395	39,230	60,502	77,912	78,902	2.0	6.3
American Indian/Alaskan Native	3,593	4,246	4,390	6,610	8,719	9,049	0.4	0.7
Nonresident alien	22,589	29,217	26,698	36,946	39,066	39,811	2.4	3.2
Master's degrees, total	294,183	280,421	324,301	397,629	457,056	468,476	100.0	100.0
White, non-Hispanic	241,216	223,628	254,299	293,345	320,485	320,480	82.0	68.4
Black, non-Hispanic	17,133	13,939	15,336	24,166	35,874	38,265	5.8	8.2
Hispanic	6,461	6,864	7,892	12,905	19,253	21,543	2.2	4.6
Asian or Pacific Islander	6,282	7,782	10,439	16,847	23,218	24,283	2.1	5.2
American Indian/Alaskan Native	1,034	1,256	1,090	1,621	2,246	2,481	0.4	0.5
Nonresident alien	22,057	26,952	35,245	48,745	55,980	61,424	7.5	13.1
Doctor's degrees, total	32,839	32,307	38,371	44,446	44,808	44,904	100.0	100.0
White, non-Hispanic	25,908	23,934	26,221	27,846	27,843	27,454	78.9	61.1
Black, non-Hispanic	1,265	1,154	1,149	1,667	2,246	2,207	3.9	4.9
Hispanic	456	677	780	984	1,305	1,516	1.4	3.4
Asian or Pacific Islander	877	1,106	1,225	2,689	2,420	2,587	2.7	5.8
American Indian/Alaskan Native	130	119	98	130	160	177	0.4	0.4
Nonresident alien	4,203	5,317	8,898	11,130	10,834	10,963	12.8	24.4
First-professional degrees, total	71,340	71,057	70,988	75,800	80,057	79,707	100.0	100.0
White, non-Hispanic	64,551	63,219	60,487	59,402	59,637	58,598	90.5	73.5
Black, non-Hispanic	2,931	3,029	3,409	4,747	5,555	5,416	4.1	6.8
Hispanic	1,541	1,884	2,425	3,231	3,865	3,806	2.2	4.8
Asian or Pacific Islander	1,456	1,816	3,362	6,396	8,584	9,261	2.0	11.6
American Indian/Alaskan Native	192	248	257	407	564	543	0.3	0.7
Nonresident alien	669	861	1,048	1,611	1,852	2,083	0.9	2.6

[1] Excludes some persons whose race/ethnicity was unknown and are slight undercounts of degrees awarded. [2] In this table, data beginning in 2000 reflect the new classification of institutions. See footnote 1, Table 277.

Source: U.S. National Center for Education Statistics, *Digest of Education Statistics*, annual.

No. 300. Degrees and Awards Earned Below Bachelor's by Field: 2001

[Covers associate degrees and other awards based on postsecondary curriculums of less than 4 years in institutions of higher education]

Field of study	Less than 1-year awards Total	Less than 1-year awards Women	1- to less than 4-year awards Total	1- to less than 4-year awards Women	Associate degrees Total	Associate degrees Women
Total	146,404	77,215	141,897	77,330	578,865	347,220
Agriculture and natural resources	2,751	753	1,987	615	6,649	2,367
Architecture and related programs	16	15	114	104	417	299
Area, ethnic, and cultural studies	192	155	101	78	307	263
Biological/life sciences	122	48	28	10	1,444	988
Business management and administrative services [1]	27,433	18,483	24,501	18,266	98,389	68,406
Communications and communications technologies	903	343	689	275	4,932	2,266
Computer and information sciences	9,470	3,530	7,991	3,029	26,339	10,667
Construction trades	3,164	188	5,712	263	2,682	150
Consumer and personal services	4,600	3,608	7,143	5,441	10,429	4,639
Education	2,082	1,543	577	517	9,219	7,209
Engineering and engineering technologies	4,744	923	6,073	803	36,292	5,092
English language and literature/letters	216	149	18	13	877	555
Foreign languages and literatures	255	181	31	26	529	287
Health professions and related sciences	40,206	31,281	41,219	35,554	82,184	71,059
Home economics and vocational home economics	7,504	5,561	4,243	3,891	8,630	7,918
Law and legal studies	889	779	1,268	1,065	6,854	5,956
Liberal/general studies and humanities	263	194	1,929	1,201	196,843	123,828
Library science	236	228	45	36	103	94
Mathematics	-	-	2	1	695	246
Mechanics and repairers	7,838	856	17,122	912	12,650	797
Multi/interdisciplinary studies	375	195	197	158	10,438	5,780
Parks, recreation, leisure, and fitness	353	150	130	68	841	354
Physical sciences	139	45	207	59	2,337	1,071
Precision production trades	4,617	760	9,004	1,327	11,493	2,636
Protective services	12,927	3,139	6,556	1,139	16,425	5,995
Psychology	54	49	23	19	1,554	1,194
Public administration and services	376	312	410	340	3,333	2,856
R.O.T.C. and military technologies	66	16	-	-	120	24
Social sciences and history	155	48	32	24	5,132	3,415
Theological studies, religion and philosophy	142	76	493	266	641	307
Transportation and material moving	12,340	2,623	751	52	1,068	149
Visual and performing arts	1,517	742	3,155	1,697	18,435	10,135
Undistributed and unclassified	459	242	146	81	584	218

- Represents zero. [1] Includes marketing.

Source: U.S. National Center for Education Statistics, *Digest of Education Statistics*, annual.

No. 301. Bachelor's Degrees Earned by Field: 1971 to 2001

Field of study	1971	1980	1990	1995	2001 [1]	Percent female 1971	Percent female 2001 [1]
Total	839,730	929,417	1,051,344	1,160,134	1,244,171	43.4	57.3
Agriculture and natural resources	12,672	22,802	12,900	19,841	23,382	4.2	45.1
Architecture and environmental design	5,570	9,132	9,364	8,756	8,480	11.9	40.0
Area, ethnic and cultural studies	2,582	2,840	4,613	5,706	6,317	52.4	69.7
Biological sciences/life sciences	35,743	46,370	37,204	55,984	60,553	29.1	59.5
Business and management	114,729	184,867	248,698	234,323	265,746	9.1	49.6
Communications [2]	10,802	28,616	51,308	48,803	59,063	35.3	62.0
Computer and information sciences	2,388	11,154	27,257	24,404	41,954	13.6	27.7
Education	176,307	118,038	105,112	106,079	105,566	74.5	76.7
Engineering [2]	50,046	68,893	81,322	78,154	72,287	0.8	18.2
English language and literature/letters	64,342	32,541	47,519	51,901	51,419	65.6	68.4
Foreign languages and literatures	20,536	12,089	12,386	13,775	15,146	74.0	70.9
Health sciences	25,226	63,920	58,302	79,855	73,490	77.1	83.8
Home economics	11,167	18,411	14,491	15,345	17,777	97.3	87.6
Law and legal studies	545	683	1,592	2,032	1,958	5.0	72.9
Liberal/general studies	7,481	23,196	27,985	33,356	37,962	33.6	66.9
Library and archival sciences	1,013	398	77	50	52	92.0	86.5
Mathematics	24,937	11,872	15,176	13,723	11,674	37.9	47.7
Multi/interdisciplinary studies	6,286	11,277	16,267	26,033	25,999	22.8	67.6
Parks and recreation	1,621	5,753	4,582	12,889	19,565	34.7	52.3
Philosophy, religion, and theology	11,890	13,276	12,068	12,854	15,527	25.5	34.7
Physical sciences [2]	21,412	23,410	16,066	19,177	17,979	13.8	41.2
Protective services	2,045	15,015	15,354	24,157	25,211	9.2	45.4
Psychology	38,187	42,093	53,952	72,083	73,534	44.4	77.5
Public administration and services	5,466	16,644	13,908	18,586	19,447	68.4	81.1
R.O.T.C. and military technologies	357	38	196	27	21	0.3	4.8
Social sciences [3]	155,324	103,662	118,083	128,154	128,036	36.8	51.8
Visual and performing arts	30,394	40,892	39,934	48,690	61,148	59.7	59.2
Unclassified [4]	662	1,535	5,628	5,397	4,878	0.9	20.8

[1] In this table, data for 2001 reflect the new classification of institutions. See footnote 1, Table 277. [2] Includes technologies. [3] Includes history. [4] Includes precision production trades and transportation and materials moving.

Source: U.S. National Center for Education Statistics, *Digest of Education Statistics*, annual.

No. 302. Master's and Doctorate's Degrees Earned by Field: 1971 to 2001

Level and field of study	1971	1980	1990	1995	2001 [1]	Percent female 1971	Percent female 2001 [1]
MASTER'S DEGREES							
Total	230,509	298,081	324,301	397,629	468,476	40.1	58.5
Agriculture and natural resources	2,457	3,976	3,382	4,252	4,281	5.9	47.3
Architecture and related programs	1,705	3,139	3,499	3,923	4,302	13.8	41.5
Area, ethnic and cultural studies	1,032	852	1,212	1,639	1,601	38.3	61.1
Biological sciences/life sciences	5,728	6,510	4,869	5,393	6,344	33.6	57.6
Business management and administrative services	25,977	54,484	76,676	93,809	116,475	3.9	40.7
Communications and technologies	1,856	3,082	4,362	5,609	5,751	34.6	65.2
Computer and information sciences	1,588	3,647	9,677	10,326	16,038	10.3	33.9
Education	87,666	101,819	84,881	101,242	129,066	56.2	76.6
Engineering and engineering technologies	16,443	16,243	24,772	29,670	27,108	1.1	21.4
English language and literature/letters	10,686	6,189	6,567	7,845	6,941	60.6	67.9
Foreign languages	5,217	2,854	2,760	3,136	2,801	64.2	68.8
Health sciences	5,749	15,704	20,321	31,243	43,617	55.3	77.4
Home economics	1,452	2,690	2,100	2,864	2,801	93.9	85.1
Law and legal studies	955	1,817	1,888	2,511	3,829	4.8	41.8
Liberal arts and sciences, general studies and humanities	885	2,646	1,999	2,565	3,193	44.6	64.4
Library science	7,001	5,374	4,341	5,057	4,727	81.3	79.5
Mathematics	5,695	3,382	4,146	4,181	3,373	27.1	41.8
Multi/interdisciplinary studies	821	2,306	2,834	2,457	2,960	25.0	60.8
Parks and recreation	218	647	529	1,755	2,487	29.8	51.9
Philosophy, religion, and theology	4,036	5,126	6,265	6,620	6,240	27.1	39.5
Physical sciences and science technologies	6,367	5,219	5,449	5,753	5,082	13.3	36.5
Protective services	194	1,805	1,151	1,706	2,514	10.3	43.2
Psychology	5,717	9,938	10,730	13,921	15,196	40.6	76.2
Public administration and services	7,785	17,560	17,399	23,501	25,268	50.0	74.1
R.O.T.C. and military technologies	2	46	-	124	-	-	-
Social sciences [2]	16,539	12,176	11,634	14,845	13,791	28.5	50.6
Visual and performing arts	6,675	8,708	8,481	10,277	11,404	47.4	58.0
Unclassified [3]	63	142	2,377	1,405	1,286	-	35.3
DOCTORATE'S DEGREES							
Total	32,107	32,615	38,371	44,446	44,904	14.3	44.9
Agriculture and natural resources	1,086	991	1,295	1,264	1,139	2.9	34.2
Architecture and related programs	36	79	103	141	153	8.3	45.8
Area, ethnic and cultural studies	144	151	131	186	220	16.7	60.9
Biological sciences/life sciences	3,645	3,636	3,844	4,645	4,600	16.3	44.1
Business management and administrative services	757	753	1,093	1,394	1,180	2.8	33.6
Communications and technologies	145	193	273	321	370	13.1	48.6
Computer and information sciences	128	240	627	884	768	2.3	17.7
Education	6,041	7,314	6,502	6,905	6,716	21.0	64.9
Engineering and engineering technology	3,638	2,507	4,981	6,128	5,577	0.6	16.5
English language and literature/letters	1,650	1,294	1,078	1,561	1,506	28.8	60.3
Foreign languages	988	755	724	905	894	34.6	61.1
Health sciences	466	786	1,536	2,069	2,855	16.5	60.9
Home economics	123	192	301	388	388	61.0	72.7
Law and legal studies	20	40	111	88	286	-	48.6
Liberal arts and sciences, general studies and humanities	32	192	63	90	102	31.3	51.0
Library science	39	73	42	55	58	28.2	65.5
Mathematics	1,249	763	966	1,226	1,024	7.6	28.8
Multi/interdisciplinary studies	59	209	272	238	413	6.8	49.4
Parks and recreation	2	21	35	149	177	50.0	45.2
Philosophy, religion, and theology	866	1,693	1,756	2,098	2,065	5.8	21.7
Physical sciences and science technologies	4,390	3,089	4,164	4,483	3,976	5.6	26.8
Protective services	1	18	38	26	44	-	36.4
Psychology	2,144	3,395	3,811	3,822	4,659	24.0	68.3
Public administration and services	174	342	508	556	574	24.1	54.2
Social sciences [2]	3,660	3,230	3,010	3,725	3,930	13.9	41.4
Visual and performing arts	621	655	849	1,080	1,167	22.2	51.3
Unclassified [3]	3	4	258	19	63	-	46.0

- Represents zero. [1] Data for 2001 reflect the new classification of institutions. See footnote 1, Table 277. [2] Includes history. [3] Includes precision production trades and transportation and materials moving.

Source: U.S. National Center for Education Statistics, *Digest of Education Statistics*, annual.

Education 193

U.S. Census Bureau, Statistical Abstract of the United States: 2003

No. 303. First Professional Degrees Earned in Selected Professions: 1970 to 2001

[First professional degrees include degrees which require at least 6 years of college work for completion (including at least 2 years of preprofessional training). See Appendix III]

Type of degree and sex of recipient	1970	1975	1980	1985	1990	1995	1998	1999	2000	2001
Medicine (M.D.):										
Institutions conferring degrees	86	104	112	120	124	119	117	118	118	118
Degrees conferred, total	8,314	12,447	14,902	16,041	15,075	15,537	15,424	15,562	15,286	15,403
Percent to women	8.4	13.1	23.4	30.4	34.2	38.8	41.6	42.5	42.7	43.3
Dentistry (D.D.S. or D.M.D.):										
Institutions conferring degrees	48	52	58	59	57	53	53	53	54	54
Degrees conferred, total	3,718	4,773	5,258	5,339	4,100	3,897	4,032	4,144	4,250	4,391
Percent to women	0.9	3.1	13.3	20.7	30.9	36.4	38.2	35.5	40.1	38.6
Law (LL.B. or J.D.):										
Institutions conferring degrees	145	154	179	181	182	183	185	188	190	192
Degrees conferred, total	14,916	29,296	35,647	37,491	36,485	39,349	39,331	39,167	38,152	37,904
Percent to women	5.4	15.1	30.2	38.5	42.2	42.6	44.4	44.8	45.9	47.3
Theological (B.D., M.Div., M.H.L.):										
Institutions conferring degrees	(NA)	(NA)	(NA)	(NA)	(NA)	192	190	193	198	191
Degrees conferred, total	5,298	5,095	7,115	7,221	5,851	5,978	5,873	5,558	6,129	5,026
Percent to women	2.3	6.8	13.8	18.5	24.8	25.7	26.1	28.3	29.2	32.0

NA Not available.

Source: U.S. National Center for Education Statistics, *Digest of Education Statistics*, annual.

No. 304. Participation in Adult Education: 1994-95 and 1998-99

[In thousands (189,543 represents 189,543,000), except percent. For the civilian noninstitutional population 17 years old and over not enrolled full time in elementary or secondary school at the time of the survey. Adult education is considered any enrollment in any educational activity at any time in the prior 12 months, except full-time enrollment in a higher education credential program. Based on the Adult Education Survey of the National Household Education Survey Program and subject to sampling error; see source and Appendix III for details]

Characteristic	Adult population (1,000)	Number taking adult ed. courses (1,000)	Percent of total	Personal/ social	Advance on the job	Train for a new job	Complete degree or diploma
Total, 1995	189,543	76,261	40	44	54	11	10
Total, 1999	194,434	88,809	46	43	54	12	11
Age:							
17 to 24 years old	25,276	13,029	52	34	32	20	23
25 to 34 years old	34,880	19,431	56	38	56	16	11
35 to 44 years old	45,258	23,047	51	41	62	13	9
45 to 54 years old	37,153	18,972	51	44	65	6	7
55 to 64 years old	24,309	9,003	37	49	56	7	9
65 years old and over	27,559	5,328	19	76	22	-	4
Sex:							
Male	92,946	40,204	43	34	59	11	13
Female	101,488	48,605	48	50	50	12	9
Race/ethnicity:							
White, non-Hispanic	143,679	65,547	46	45	56	11	10
Black, non-Hispanic	22,129	10,803	49	42	52	15	13
Hispanic	19,491	7,981	41	35	45	14	11
Other non-Hispanic races	9,135	4,478	49	35	49	14	19
Marital status:							
Never married	41,530	20,773	50	34	45	17	18
Currently married	118,568	55,966	47	46	58	10	9
Other	34,337	12,070	35	45	55	11	8
Children under 18 in household:							
Yes	83,365	43,060	52	41	55	12	12
No	111,070	45,749	41	44	53	11	10
Educational attainment:							
Up to 8th grade	11,078	1,527	14	41	39	3	21
9th to 12th grade	21,375	5,578	26	35	28	15	21
High school diploma or GED	53,488	19,693	37	39	52	12	7
Vocational school after high school	6,319	2,629	42	44	57	11	5
Some college	35,147	18,220	52	48	46	14	15
Associate's degree	11,377	6,735	59	38	60	15	14
Bachelor's or higher	55,651	34,426	62	45	63	9	8
Labor force status:							
Employed	132,227	70,849	54	37	63	12	11
Unemployed	7,963	3,433	43	39	23	32	22
Not in the labor force	54,244	14,527	27	72	17	7	10

- Represents or rounds to zero. [1] Reason for taking at least one course. Includes duplication. Excludes other reasons, not shown separately.

Source: U.S. National Center for Education Statistics, *1995* and *1999 National Household Education Surveys*.

Section 5
Law Enforcement, Courts, and Prisons

This section presents data on crimes committed, victims of crimes, arrests, and data related to criminal violations and the criminal justice system. The major sources of these data are the Bureau of Justice Statistics (BJS), the Federal Bureau of Investigation (FBI), and the Administrative Office of the U.S. Courts. BJS issues several reports, including *Sourcebook of Criminal Justice Statistics, Criminal Victimization in the United States, Prisoners in State and Federal Institutions, Census of State Correctional Facilities and Survey of Prison Inmates, Census of Jails and Survey of Jail Inmates, Parole in the United States, Capital Punishment*, and the annual *Expenditure and Employment Data for the Criminal Justice System*. The Federal Bureau of Investigation's major annual reports are *Crime in the United States, Law Enforcement Officers Killed and Assaulted*, annual, and *Hate Crimes*, annual. which presents data on reported crimes as gathered from state and local law enforcement agencies.

Legal jurisdiction and law enforcement—Law enforcement is, for the most part, a function of state and local officers and agencies. The U.S. Constitution reserves general police powers to the states. By act of Congress, federal offenses include only offenses against the U.S. government and against or by its employees while engaged in their official duties and offenses which involve the crossing of state lines or an interference with interstate commerce. Excluding the military, there are 52 separate criminal law jurisdictions in the United States: 1 in each of the 50 states, 1 in the District of Columbia, and the federal jurisdiction. Each of these has its own criminal law and procedure and its own law enforcement agencies. While the systems of law enforcement are quite similar among the states, there are often substantial differences in the penalties for like offenses.

Law enforcement can be divided into three parts: Investigation of crimes and arrests of persons suspected of committing them; prosecution of those charged with crime; and the punishment or treatment of persons convicted of crime.

Crime—There are two major approaches taken in determining the extent of crime. One perspective is provided by the FBI through its Uniform Crime Reporting Program (UCR). The FBI receives monthly and annual reports from law enforcement agencies throughout the country, currently representing 94 percent of the national population. Each month, city police, sheriffs, and state police file reports on the number of index offenses, hate crimes and law enforcement assaults that become known to them. Additionally, data are collected for officers killed in the line of duty.

The FBI Crime Index offenses are as follows: *Murder and nonnegligent manslaughter* is based on police investigations, as opposed to the determination of a medical examiner or judicial body, includes willful felonious homicides and excludes attempts and assaults to kill, suicides, accidental deaths, justifiable homicides, and deaths caused by negligence; *forcible rape* includes forcible rapes and attempts; *robbery* includes stealing or taking anything of value by force or violence or threat of force or violence and includes attempted robbery; *aggravated assault* includes assault with intent to kill; *burglary* includes any unlawful entry to commit a felony or a theft and includes attempted burglary and burglary followed by larceny; *larceny* includes theft of property or articles of value without use of force and violence or fraud and excludes embezzlement, "con games," forgery, etc.; *motor vehicle theft* includes all cases where vehicles are driven away and abandoned but excludes vehicles taken for temporary use and returned by the taker. Arson was added as the eighth Index offense in April 1979 following a Congressional mandate. *Arson* includes any willful or malicious burning or attempt to burn, with or without intent to defraud, a dwelling house, public building, motor vehicle or aircraft, personal property of another, etc.

The monthly Uniform Crime Reports also contain data on crimes cleared by arrest and on characteristics of persons arrested for all criminal offenses. In summarizing and publishing crime data, the FBI depends primarily on the adherence to the established standards of reporting for statistical accuracy, presenting the data as information useful to persons concerned with the problem of crime and criminal law enforcement.

National Crime Victimization Survey (NCVS)—A second perspective on crime is provided by this survey of the Bureau of Justice Statistics. Details about the crimes come directly from the victims. No attempt is made to validate the information against police records or any other source.

The NCVS measures rape, robbery, assault, household and personal larceny, burglary, and motor vehicle theft. The NCVS includes offenses reported to the police, as well as those not reported.

Police reporting rates (percent of victimizations) varied by type of crime. In 1994, for instance, 32 percent of the rapes/sexual assaults were reported; 55 percent of the robberies; 40 percent of assaults; 33 percent of personal thefts; 51 percent of the household burglaries; and 78 percent of motor vehicle thefts.

Murder and kidnaping are not covered. Commercial burglary and robbery were dropped from the program during 1977. The so-called victimless crimes, such as drunkenness, drug abuse, and prostitution, also are excluded, as are crimes for which it is difficult to identify knowledgeable respondents or to locate data records.

Crimes of which the victim may not be aware also cannot be measured effectively. Buying stolen property may fall into this category, as may some instances of embezzlement. Attempted crimes of many types probably are under recorded for this reason. Events in which the victim has shown a willingness to participate in illegal activity also are excluded.

In any encounter involving a personal crime, more than one criminal act can be committed against an individual. For example, a rape may be associated with a robbery or a household offense, such as a burglary, can escalate into something more serious in the event of a personal confrontation. In classifying the survey-measured crimes, each criminal incident has been counted only once—by the most serious act that took place during the incident and ranked in accordance with the seriousness classification system used by the Federal Bureau of Investigation. The order of seriousness for crimes against persons is as follows: Rape, robbery, assault, and larceny. Personal crimes take precedence over household offenses.

A *victimization,* basic measure of the occurrence of crime, is a specific criminal act as it affects a single victim. The number of victimizations is determined by the number of victims of such acts. Victimization counts serve as key elements in computing rates of victimization. For crimes against persons, the rates are based on the total number of individuals age 12 and over or on a portion of that population sharing a particular characteristic or set of traits. As general indicators of the danger of having been victimized during the reference period, the rates are not sufficiently refined to represent true measures of risk for specific individuals or households.

An *incident* is a specific criminal act involving one or more victims; therefore the number of incidents of personal crimes is lower than that of victimizations.

Courts—Statistics on criminal offenses and the outcome of prosecutions are incomplete for the country as a whole, although data are available for many states individually. The only national compilations of such statistics were made by the Census Bureau for 1932 to 1945 covering a maximum of 32 states and by the Bureau of Justice Statistics for 1986, 1988, 1990, and 1992 based on a nationally representative sample survey.

The bulk of civil and criminal litigation in the country is commenced and determined in the various state courts. Only when the U.S. Constitution and acts of Congress specifically confer jurisdiction upon the federal courts may civil or criminal litigation be heard and decided by them. Generally, the federal courts have jurisdiction over the following types of cases: Suits or proceedings by or against the United States; civil actions between private parties arising under the Constitution, laws, or treaties of the United States; civil actions between private litigants who are citizens of different states; civil cases involving admiralty, maritime, or prize jurisdiction; and all matters in bankruptcy. The Administrative Office of the United States Courts has compiled statistics on the caseload of the federal courts annually since 1940.

There are several types of courts with varying degrees of legal jurisdiction. These jurisdictions include original, appellate, general, and limited or special. A court of original jurisdiction is one having the authority initially to try a case and pass judgment on the law and the facts; a court of appellate jurisdiction is one with the legal authority to review cases and hear appeals; a court of general jurisdiction is a trial court of unlimited original jurisdiction in civil and/or criminal cases, also called a "major trial court"; a court of limited or special jurisdiction is a trial court with legal authority over only a particular class of cases, such as probate, juvenile, or traffic cases.

The 94 federal courts of original jurisdiction are known as the U.S. district courts. One or more of these courts is established in every state and one each in the District of Columbia, Puerto Rico, the Virgin Islands, the Northern Mariana Islands, and Guam. Appeals from the district courts are taken to intermediate appellate courts of which there are 13, known as U.S. courts of appeals and the United States Court of Appeals for the Federal Circuit. The Supreme Court of the United States is the final and highest appellate court in the federal system of courts.

Juvenile offenders—For statistical purposes, the FBI and most states classify as juvenile offenders persons under the age of 18 years who have committed a crime or crimes.

Delinquency cases are all cases of youths referred to a juvenile court for violation of a law or ordinance or for seriously "antisocial" conduct. Several types of facilities are available for those adjudicated delinquent, ranging from the short-term physically unrestricted environment to the long-term very restrictive atmosphere.

Prisoners—Data on prisoners in federal and state prisons and reformatories were collected annually by the Census Bureau until 1950, by the Federal Bureau of Prisons until 1971, transferred then to the Law Enforcement Assistance Administration, and, in 1979, to the Bureau of Justice Statistics. Adults convicted of criminal activity may be given a prison or jail sentence. A *prison* is a confinement facility having custodial authority over adults sentenced to confinement of more than 1 year. A *jail* is a facility, usually operated by a local law enforcement agency, holding persons detained pending adjudication and/or persons committed after adjudication to 1 year or less. Nearly every state publishes annual data either for its whole prison system or for each separate state institution.

Statistical reliability—For discussion of statistical collection, estimation and sampling procedures, and measures of statistical reliability pertaining to the National Crime Victimization Survey and Uniform Crime Reporting Program, see Appendix III.

Figure 5.1
Violent Crime Rates Per 100,000 Population by State: 2001

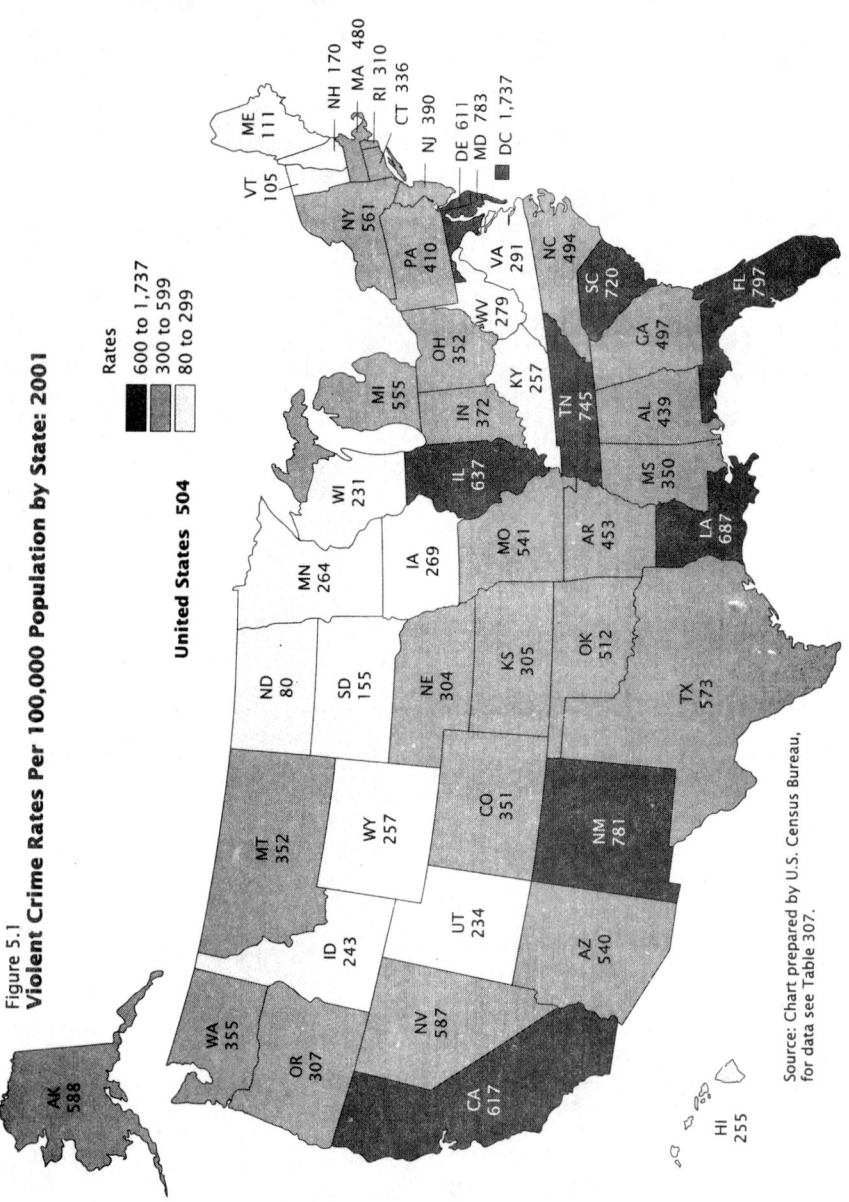

Source: Chart prepared by U.S. Census Bureau, for data see Table 307.

No. 305. Crimes and Crime Rates by Type of Offense: 1980 to 2001

[13,408 represents 13,408,000. Data refer to offenses known to the police. Rates are based on Census Bureau estimated resident population as of July 1; 1980, 1990, and 2000, enumerated as of April 1. See source for details. For definitions of crimes, see text, this section]

Item and year	Violent crime					Property crime			
	Total	Total	Murder [1,2]	Forcible rape	Robbery	Aggravated assault	Total	Burglary	Larceny/ theft	Motor vehicle theft
Number of offenses (1,000):										
1980	13,408	1,345	23	83	566	673	12,064	3,795	7,137	1,132
1985	12,430	1,328	19	88	498	723	11,103	3,073	6,926	1,103
1986	13,212	1,489	21	91	543	834	11,723	3,241	7,257	1,224
1987	13,509	1,484	20	91	518	855	12,025	3,236	7,500	1,289
1988	13,923	1,566	21	92	543	910	12,357	3,218	7,706	1,433
1989	14,251	1,646	22	95	578	952	12,605	3,168	7,872	1,565
1990	14,476	1,820	23	103	639	1,055	12,655	3,074	7,946	1,636
1991	14,873	1,912	25	107	688	1,093	12,961	3,157	8,142	1,662
1992	14,438	1,932	24	109	672	1,127	12,506	2,980	7,915	1,611
1993	14,145	1,926	25	106	660	1,136	12,219	2,835	7,821	1,563
1994	13,990	1,858	23	102	619	1,113	12,132	2,713	7,880	1,539
1995	13,863	1,799	22	97	581	1,099	12,064	2,594	7,998	1,472
1996	13,494	1,689	20	96	536	1,037	11,805	2,506	7,905	1,394
1997	13,195	1,636	18	96	499	1,023	11,558	2,461	7,744	1,354
1998	12,486	1,534	17	93	447	977	10,952	2,333	7,376	1,243
1999	11,634	1,426	16	89	409	912	10,208	2,101	6,956	1,152
2000	11,608	1,425	16	90	408	912	10,183	2,051	6,972	1,160
2001	11,849	1,437	16	90	423	907	10,412	2,110	7,076	1,226
Rate per 100,000 population:										
1980	5,950.0	596.6	10.2	36.8	251.1	298.5	5,353.3	1,684.1	3,167.0	502.2
1985	5,224.5	558.1	8.0	36.8	209.3	304.0	4,666.4	1,291.7	2,911.2	463.5
1986	5,501.9	620.1	8.6	38.1	226.0	347.4	4,881.8	1,349.8	3,022.1	509.8
1987	5,575.5	612.5	8.3	37.6	213.7	352.9	4,963.0	1,335.7	3,095.4	531.9
1988	5,694.5	640.6	8.5	37.8	222.1	372.2	5,054.0	1,316.2	3,151.7	586.1
1989	5,774.0	666.9	8.7	38.3	234.3	385.6	5,107.1	1,283.6	3,189.6	634.0
1990	5,802.7	729.6	9.4	41.1	256.3	422.9	5,073.1	1,232.2	3,185.1	655.8
1991	5,898.4	758.2	9.8	42.3	272.7	433.4	5,140.2	1,252.1	3,229.1	659.0
1992	5,661.4	757.7	9.3	42.8	263.7	441.9	4,903.7	1,168.4	3,103.6	631.6
1993	5,487.1	747.1	9.5	41.1	256.0	440.5	4,740.0	1,099.7	3,033.9	606.3
1994	5,373.8	713.6	9.0	39.3	237.8	427.6	4,660.2	1,042.1	3,026.9	591.3
1995	5,275.9	684.5	8.2	37.1	220.9	418.3	4,590.5	987.0	3,043.2	560.3
1996	5,086.6	636.6	7.4	36.3	201.9	391.0	4,451.0	945.0	2,980.3	525.7
1997	4,930.0	611.0	6.8	35.9	186.2	382.1	4,316.3	918.8	2,891.8	505.7
1998	4,619.3	567.6	6.3	34.5	165.5	361.4	4,052.5	863.2	2,729.5	459.9
1999	4,266.5	523.0	5.7	32.8	150.1	334.3	3,743.6	770.4	2,550.7	422.5
2000	4,124.8	506.5	5.5	32.0	145.0	324.0	3,618.3	728.8	2,477.3	412.2
2001	4,160.5	504.4	5.6	31.8	148.5	318.5	3,656.0	740.8	2,484.6	430.6

[1] Includes nonnegligent manslaughter. [2] The murder and non-negligent homicides that occurred as a result of the events of September 11,2001, were not included in this table.

Source: U.S. Federal Bureau of Investigation, *Crime in the United States*, annual. See also <http://www.fbi.gov/ucr/cius01/01crime.pdf> (released 28 October 2002).

No. 306. Crimes and Crime Rates by Type and Area: 2001

[In thousands (11,849 represents 11,849,000), except rate. Rate per 100,000 population; see headnote, Table 305. Estimated totals based on reports from city and rural law enforcement agencies representing 96 percent of the national population. For definitions of crimes, see text, this section]

Type of crime	United States		Metropolitan areas [1]		Other cities		Rural areas	
	Total	Rate	Total	Rate	Total	Rate	Total	Rate
Total	11,849	4,161	9,414	4,475	862	4,450	573	1,892
Violent crime	1,437	504	1,172	560	78	393	65	211
Murder and nonnegligent manslaughter [2]	16	6	13	6	1	4	1	4
Forcible rape	90	32	69	33	7	35	6	22
Robbery	423	149	372	177	12	60	5	17
Aggravated assault	907	319	718	344	59	295	57	168
Property crime	10,412	3,656	8,242	3,915	785	4,058	508	1,681
Burglary	2,110	741	1,626	769	149	764	163	540
Larceny-theft	7,076	2,485	5,549	2,647	595	3,088	307	1,014
Motor vehicle theft	1,226	431	1,066	499	40	206	38	127

[1] For definition, see Appendix II. [2] The murder and non-negligent manslaugher that occurred as a result of the events of September 11, 2001, were not included in this table.

Source: U.S. Federal Bureau of Investigation, *Crime in the United States*, annual. See also <http://www.fbi.gov/ucr/cius01/01crime.pdf> (released 28 October 2002).

No. 307. Crime Rates by State, 1999 to 2001, and by Type, 2001

[**Offenses known to the police per 100,000 population.** Based on Census Bureau estimated resident population as of July 1; 2000 enumerated as of April 1. For definitions of crimes, see text, this section]

State	1999, total	2000, total	2001 Total	Violent crime Total	Murder [1]	Forcible rape	Robbery	Aggravated assault	Property crime Total	Burglary	Larceny/theft	Motor vehicle theft
United States	4,267	4,125	4,161	504	6	32	149	319	3,656	741	2,485	431
Alabama	4,413	4,546	4,319	439	9	31	125	274	3,881	910	2,688	283
Alaska	4,360	4,249	4,236	588	6	79	81	422	3,648	606	2,630	412
Arizona	5,896	5,830	6,077	540	8	29	167	337	5,537	1,033	3,521	984
Arkansas	4,042	4,115	4,134	453	6	33	81	333	3,681	825	2,585	272
California	3,805	3,740	3,903	617	6	29	187	395	3,286	672	2,022	591
Colorado	4,063	3,983	4,219	351	4	44	81	223	3,868	646	2,747	475
Connecticut	3,389	3,233	3,118	336	3	19	122	192	2,782	501	1,920	361
Delaware [2]	4,838	4,478	4,053	611	3	53	145	411	3,441	646	2,446	349
District of Columbia [3]	8,067	7,277	7,710	1,737	41	33	690	974	5,973	876	3,755	1,341
Florida	6,205	5,695	5,570	797	5	41	201	551	4,773	1,074	3,150	548
Georgia	5,148	4,751	4,646	497	7	26	172	292	4,149	856	2,845	448
Hawaii	4,835	5,199	5,386	255	3	33	93	125	5,132	912	3,669	551
Idaho	3,150	3,186	3,133	243	2	32	19	190	2,890	568	2,141	181
Illinois [4]	4,515	4,239	4,098	637	8	32	199	398	3,461	632	2,438	391
Indiana	3,766	3,752	3,831	372	7	28	117	220	3,460	699	2,409	352
Iowa	3,224	3,234	3,301	269	2	22	40	206	3,032	578	2,266	188
Kansas [4]	4,439	4,409	4,321	405	3	35	90	276	3,917	761	2,859	296
Kentucky [4]	2,953	2,960	2,938	257	5	28	81	144	2,681	652	1,799	230
Louisiana	5,747	5,423	5,338	687	11	31	176	468	4,651	1,040	3,125	486
Maine [4]	2,875	2,620	2,688	112	1	25	21	64	2,577	536	1,911	130
Maryland	4,920	4,816	4,867	783	8	27	252	496	4,084	773	2,715	596
Massachusetts	3,262	3,026	3,099	480	2	29	102	347	2,619	508	1,675	436
Michigan	4,325	4,110	4,082	555	7	53	130	366	3,527	721	2,269	537
Minnesota	3,598	3,488	3,584	264	2	45	76	141	3,319	513	2,504	302
Mississippi	4,270	4,004	4,185	350	10	40	115	185	3,835	1,043	2,460	332
Missouri	4,578	4,528	4,776	541	7	25	138	372	4,235	763	2,974	498
Montana [4]	3,534	3,880	3,689	352	4	21	25	302	3,336	406	2,729	201
Nebraska	4,108	4,096	4,330	304	3	25	66	211	4,025	570	3,077	379
Nevada	4,653	4,269	4,266	587	9	42	234	302	3,679	841	2,140	698
New Hampshire	2,282	2,433	2,322	170	1	36	35	97	2,151	388	1,593	170
New Jersey	3,400	3,161	3,225	390	4	15	166	205	2,835	552	1,839	444
New Mexico	5,963	5,519	5,324	781	5	47	147	582	4,543	1,069	3,084	390
New York	3,279	3,100	2,925	516	5	19	192	300	2,409	423	1,732	254
North Carolina	5,176	4,919	4,938	494	6	25	163	300	4,444	1,245	2,898	301
North Dakota	2,394	2,288	2,418	80	1	26	10	43	2,338	341	1,826	171
Ohio	3,997	4,042	4,178	352	4	39	151	157	3,826	852	2,602	371
Oklahoma	4,684	4,559	4,607	512	5	43	79	385	4,095	999	2,732	363
Oregon	5,002	4,845	5,044	307	2	34	79	191	4,737	767	3,543	427
Pennsylvania	3,114	2,995	2,961	410	5	28	142	235	2,551	442	1,818	291
Rhode Island	3,583	3,476	3,685	310	4	39	93	174	3,375	644	2,255	476
South Carolina	5,325	5,347	4,753	720	6	34	131	549	4,032	907	2,763	363
South Dakota	2,644	2,320	2,332	155	1	46	14	94	2,177	408	1,662	108
Tennessee	4,694	4,890	5,153	745	7	38	178	522	4,408	1,040	2,875	493
Texas	5,032	4,956	5,153	573	6	38	166	363	4,580	958	3,140	481
Utah	4,977	4,476	4,243	234	3	40	53	139	4,009	608	3,114	287
Vermont	2,819	2,987	2,769	105	1	18	18	69	2,664	514	2,027	124
Virginia	3,374	3,028	3,178	291	5	25	95	166	2,887	440	2,185	262
Washington	5,255	5,106	5,152	355	3	43	99	210	4,797	886	3,259	653
West Virginia	2,721	2,603	2,560	279	2	18	39	220	2,280	533	1,569	179
Wisconsin	3,296	3,209	3,321	231	4	21	82	124	3,090	499	2,319	273
Wyoming	3,458	3,298	3,518	257	2	31	17	208	3,260	502	2,618	141

[1] Includes nonnegligent manslaughter. [2] Forcible rape figures furnished by the state-level uniform crime reporting (UCR) program administered by the Delaware State Bureau of Investigation were not in accordance with the national UCR guidelines; therefore, it was necessary that the forcible rape count be estimated. [3] Includes offenses reported by the police at the National Zoo. [4] Complete data were not available; therefore, it was necessary for the crime counts to be estimated for Illinois, Kansas, Kentucky, and Montana for all years shown, for Maine in 1999.

Source: U.S. Federal Bureau of Investigation, *Crime in the United States*, annual. See also <http://www.fbi.gov/ucr/cius01/01crime.pdf>. (released 28 October 2002).

No. 308. Crime Rates by Type—Selected Large Cities: 2001

[Offenses known to the police per 100,000 population. Based on U.S. Census Bureau estimated resident population enumerated as of July 1. For definitions of crimes, see text, this section]

City ranked by population size, 2001	Crime index, total	Violent crime Total	Murder	Forcible rape	Robbery	Aggravated assault	Property crime Total	Burglary	Larceny-theft	Motor vehicle theft
New York, NY	3,286.7	850.1	8.2	19.1	351.5	471.3	2,436.6	393.4	1,669.4	373.8
Los Angeles, CA	5,029.3	1,388.2	15.6	37.4	456.1	879.0	3,641.2	682.7	2,113.0	845.5
Chicago, IL [1]	(NA)	(NA)	22.9	(NA)	633.3	877.2	5,193.1	892.1	3,349.6	951.5
Houston, TX	7,106.6	1,172.1	13.4	47.3	496.6	614.9	5,934.4	1,256.7	3,472.1	1,205.7
Philadelphia, PA	6,183.1	1,409.7	20.4	66.8	632.5	690.0	4,773.4	765.9	2,984.8	1,022.7
Phoenix, AZ	7,681.8	770.7	15.3	29.3	338.7	387.4	6,911.1	1,220.1	4,038.7	1,652.3
San Diego, CA	4,048.0	594.2	4.0	27.4	138.7	424.0	3,453.8	579.3	2,010.2	864.3
Dallas, TX	9,132.1	1,462.4	19.7	54.3	685.3	703.1	7,669.8	1,697.6	4,410.4	1,561.8
San Antonio, TX	8,243.3	815.5	8.5	42.0	183.3	581.6	7,427.8	1,197.5	5,697.3	533.0
Las Vegas MPD Jurisidiction, NV	4,524.2	675.4	11.9	40.0	328.1	295.4	3,848.8	902.1	2,003.5	943.3
Detroit, MI	9,431.6	2,190.5	41.3	68.2	742.0	1,338.9	7,241.2	1,578.6	3,096.7	2,565.9
San Jose, CA	2,754.5	609.1	2.4	36.0	77.9	492.7	2,145.5	321.7	1,485.1	338.6
Honolulu, HI	5,469.9	277.0	2.3	33.1	112.8	128.8	5,192.9	828.8	3,732.1	632.0
Indianapolis, IN	5,143.5	930.5	14.0	55.4	349.1	512.0	4,213.0	1,132.9	2,283.0	797.1
San Francisco, CA	5,592.1	857.5	7.8	28.6	481.3	339.8	4,734.6	831.7	3,085.8	817.1
Jacksonville, FL	6,791.0	979.0	9.9	38.0	290.9	640.1	5,812.0	1,312.2	3,819.8	680.0
Columbus, OH	9,617.3	897.4	11.4	84.5	472.0	329.6	8,719.9	2,208.4	5,448.6	1,062.9
Austin, TX	6,470.8	473.7	3.9	40.8	176.2	252.9	5,997.1	1,112.6	4,384.8	499.7
Baltimore, MD	9,607.4	2,239.5	38.7	44.8	869.7	1,286.3	7,367.9	1,649.3	4,481.5	1,237.1
Memphis, TN	10,016.2	1,662.8	24.2	74.6	662.1	901.8	8,353.4	2,426.9	4,468.8	1,457.7
Charlotte-Mecklenburg, NC	7,817.8	1,221.6	10.4	46.0	470.7	694.5	6,596.2	1,616.0	4,287.9	692.3
Milwaukee, WI	7,609.1	908.6	21.1	49.1	484.5	353.9	6,700.4	1,111.1	4,276.6	1,312.8
Boston, MA	6,315.6	1,243.5	11.0	61.0	426.2	745.3	5,072.1	713.2	2,974.6	1,384.3
El Paso, TX	5,345.4	760.9	3.5	35.2	134.4	587.7	4,584.6	442.9	3,823.2	318.5
Seattle, WA	8,053.0	725.1	4.4	28.7	278.5	413.6	7,327.9	1,167.8	4,630.4	1,529.7
Washington, DC	7,761.7	1,607.5	40.4	31.7	660.5	874.9	6,154.2	865.1	3,895.3	1,393.8
Denver, CO	5,314.1	539.6	7.9	55.6	219.4	256.6	4,774.5	990.4	2,566.7	1,217.4
Nashville, TN	9,034.0	1,632.1	11.0	74.4	451.1	1,095.6	7,401.9	1,412.8	5,018.9	970.2
Fort Worth, TX	7,400.1	706.6	12.3	60.7	254.0	379.6	6,693.5	1,457.7	4,512.4	723.4
Portland, OR	8,040.3	848.3	3.9	56.8	235.9	551.7	7,192.0	1,041.2	5,280.0	870.8
Oklahoma City, OK	9,039.1	824.2	8.9	79.8	214.8	520.8	8,214.9	1,656.1	5,866.0	692.8
Tucson, AZ	9,883.0	958.0	8.3	63.8	337.3	548.6	8,925.0	1,301.6	6,200.5	1,423.0
New Orleans, LA	7,445.3	1,213.5	44.0	43.2	573.6	552.8	6,231:8	1,086.5	3,342.4	1,802.8
Cleveland, OH	6,899.1	1,340.4	16.1	130.2	688.1	506.0	5,558.7	1,656.1	2,696.8	1,205.8
Long Beach, CA	3,928.3	726.0	10.4	26.6	301.4	387.6	3,202.3	687.5	1,675.4	839.4
Albuquerque, NM	8,765.5	1,165.8	7.5	48.5	356.9	752.8	7,599.7	1,459.8	5,217.3	922.6
Kansas City, MO	11,245.3	1,593.9	23.2	71.8	532.8	966.1	9,651.4	1,677.8	6,105.8	1,867.8
Fresno, CA	7,961.7	940.3	9.2	46.4	312.7	572.1	7,021.3	1,194.4	4,223.6	1,603.3
Virginia Beach, VA	3,749.0	194.1	2.8	25.7	84.8	80.8	3,555.0	530.1	2,808.6	216.3
Atlanta, GA	12,237.4	2,533.8	33.5	86.0	1,017.8	1,396.4	9,703.6	2,047.1	6,030.6	1,626.0
Sacramento, CA	7,402.9	798.2	9.6	40.8	347.3	400.4	6,604.7	1,222.4	3,853.8	1,528.5
Mesa, AZ	6,708.8	613.6	4.1	25.9	110.2	473.4	6,095.2	1,051.9	3,931.7	1,111.6
Oakland, CA	6,789.5	1,309.9	20.6	72.5	522.2	694.5	5,479.6	908.3	3,214.7	1,356.6
Tulsa, OK	7,447.9	1,153.7	8.6	65.0	196.9	883.2	6,294.2	1,487.6	3,884.0	922.5
Omaha, NE	7,557.1	693.6	6.4	40.2	223.3	424.6	6,863.5	795.7	4,963.9	1,103.8
Minneapolis, MN	6,935.1	1,060.4	11.1	103.2	502.4	443.7	5,874.7	1,058.1	3,761.8	1,054.8
Miami, FL	9,490.3	1,938.9	17.7	31.7	731.2	1,158.2	7,551.4	1,672.1	4,473.4	1,405.9
Colorado Springs, CO	5,034.8	485.6	3.8	61.5	117.6	302.7	4,549.2	809.4	3,378.6	361.2
Saint Louis, MO	15,024.1	2,187.6	42.2	34.3	896.3	1,214.8	12,836.5	2,320.1	7,992.3	2,524.1
Wichita, KS	6,827.7	707.9	4.9	53.0	215.0	435.0	6,119.7	1,281.4	4,333.2	505.1
Santa Ana, CA	3,504.9	535.6	7.0	16.0	273.6	239.1	2,969.3	405.5	1,819.3	744.5
Pittsburgh, PA	5,772.5	868.2	16.1	39.2	405.4	407.4	4,904.3	950.8	3,153.4	800.2
Arlington, TX	7,209.7	625.2	4.4	42.6	201.7	376.5	6,584.5	1,043.1	4,799.9	741.5
Anaheim, CA	3,359.7	393.9	2.4	27.2	144.9	219.4	2,965.8	538.1	1,894.0	533.7
Cincinnati. OH	8,262.9	1,207.4	16.9	97.3	631.3	461.9	7,055.6	1,880.5	4,201.5	973.5
Toledo, OH	8,627.1	970.8	5.7	78.9	417.6	488.6	7,656.4	2,004.9	4,457.9	1,193.6
Tampa, FL	11,194.0	2,125.2	10.9	68.1	757.8	1,288.4	9,068.8	1,958.2	5,006.6	2,104.0
Buffalo, NY	6,785.4	1,265.1	21.8	78.1	545.7	619.4	5,520.4	1,352.4	3,297.9	870.1
Saint Paul, MN	6,562.3	770.4	3.1	76.1	234.3	456.9	5,791.9	1,036.7	3,947.5	807.6
Aurora, CO	5,953.7	567.5	6.0	68.7	166.3	326.6	5,386.2	642.5	3,698.4	1,045.2
Corpus Christi, TX	7,941.5	868.7	6.7	78.9	205.1	578.0	7,072.8	1,409.3	5,129.5	533.9
Raleigh, NC	6,618.8	778.9	3.6	32.4	286.3	456.6	5,839.9	1,418.5	3,948.5	472.9
Newark, NJ	6,797.1	1,391.1	32.6	33.0	666.0	659.5	5,406.0	925.2	2,292.8	2,188.0
Anchorage, AK	5,013.1	663.2	3.8	79.7	145.7	434.0	4,350.0	609.3	3,280.9	459.8
Lexington, KY	4,973.2	604.1	9.2	45.8	275.1	274.0	4,369.1	960.1	3,112.1	296.9
Riverside, CA	5,585.8	830.7	7.7	36.6	239.3	547.1	4,755.1	856.1	3,038.0	861.1
Louisville, KY	6,081.0	743.0	9.7	30.3	383.7	319.3	5,338.0	1,315.3	3,078.3	944.4
Mobile, AL	7,777.3	598.3	16.4	37.2	328.7	216.0	7,179.0	1,820.8	4,806.9	551.4
Saint Petersburg, FL	8,063.2	1,718.3	8.2	58.5	450.4	1,201.2	6,344.8	1,443.3	4,090.9	809.7

NA Not available. [1] The rates for forcible rape, violent crime, and crime index are not shown because the forcible rape figures were not in accordance with national Uniform Crime Reporting guidelines.

Source: U.S. Federal Bureau of Investigation, *Crime in the United States,* annual. See also <http://www.fbi.gov/ucr/Cius01/01crime.pdf> (released 28 October 2002).

No. 309. Murder Victims—Circumstances and Weapons Used or Cause of Death: 1990 to 2001

[Based solely on police investigation. For definition of murder, see text, this section]

Characteristic	1990	1995	2000	2001	Characteristic	1990	1995	2000	2001
Murders, total (1,000)	20,273	20,232	13,230	14,080	Other motives	19.4	21.6	20.2	20.4
Percent distribution	100.0	100.0	100.0	100.0	Unknown	24.8	28.9	30.8	32.3
CIRCUMSTANCES					TYPE OF WEAPON OR CAUSE OF DEATH				
Felonies, total	20.8	17.7	16.8	16.8					
Robbery	9.2	9.3	8.1	7.7	Guns	64.3	68.2	65.5	63.2
Narcotics	6.7	5.1	4.5	4.1	Handguns	49.8	55.8	51.2	49.3
Sex offenses	1.1	0.2	0.6	0.5	Cutting or stabbing	17.4	12.6	13.5	13.0
Other felonies	3.7	3.2	3.7	4.5	Blunt objects [1]	5.4	4.5	4.7	4.8
Suspected felonies	0.7	0.6	0.5	0.5	Personal weapons [2]	5.5	5.9	7.0	6.8
Argument, total	34.4	31.2	31.8	29.9	Strangulations,				
Property or money	2.5	1.7	1.6	1.4	asphyxiations	2.0	1.8	2.0	1.1
Romantic triangle	2.0	1.4	0.9	0.8	Fire	1.4	0.8	1.0	0.8
Other arguments	29.8	28.2	29.3	27.7	All other [3]	4.0	6.1	6.4	10.2

[1] Refers to club, hammer, etc. [2] Hands, fists, feet, etc. [3] Includes poison, drowning, explosives, narcotics, and unknown.

Source: U.S. Federal Bureau of Investigation, *Crime in the United States*, annual. See also <http://www.fbi.gov/ucr/cius01/01crime.pdf> (released 28 October 2002).

No. 310. Murder Victims by Age, Sex, and Race: 2001

Age	Total	Sex			Race			
		Male	Female	Unknown	White	Black	Other	Unknown
Total	14,080	10,739	3,314	27	6,892	6,604	370	182
Percent of total	100.0	76.3	23.5	0.2	48.9	46.9	2.6	1.3
Under 18 yrs. old	1,440	958	479	3	742	637	46	15
18 yrs. old and over	12,349	9,580	2,765	4	6,024	5,871	320	102
Infant (under 1 yr. old)	228	128	99	1	129	86	8	5
1 to 4 yrs. old	335	180	154	1	182	142	6	5
5 to 8 yrs. old	99	55	44	-	69	28	2	-
9 to 12 yrs. old	92	47	45	-	51	35	4	2
13 to 16 yrs. old	396	298	98	-	111	187	16	2
17 to 19 yrs. old	1,248	1,077	170	1	527	679	33	7
20 to 24 yrs. old	2,705	2,342	363	-	1,125	1,506	57	17
25 to 29 yrs. old	2,064	1,713	351	-	865	1,141	33	25
30 to 34 yrs. old	1,550	1,203	347	-	712	780	49	9
35 to 39 yrs. old	1,376	971	405	-	703	630	33	10
40 to 44 yrs. old	1,111	765	344	2	586	483	34	8
45 to 49 yrs. old	805	582	221	2	462	302	32	9
50 to 54 yrs. old	561	420	141	-	333	200	21	7
55 to 59 yrs. old	337	237	100	-	272	100	13	2
60 to 64 yrs. old	255	172	83	-	172	67	10	6
65 to 69 yrs. old	192	126	66	-	139	42	9	2
70 to 74 yrs. old	155	88	67	-	114	38	3	-
75 yrs. old and over	280	134	146	-	214	62	3	1
Age unknown	291	201	70	20	126	96	4	65

- Represents zero.
Source: U.S. Federal Bureau of Investigation, *Crime in the United States*, annual. See also <http://www.fbi.gov/ucr/Cius01/01crime.pdf> (released 28 October 2002).

No. 311. Murder Victims of September 11, 2001, Terrorist Attacks by Race, Sex, and Location

Race	Total	Sex			Race	Total	Sex		
		Male	Female	Unknown			Male	Female	Unknown
ALL LOCATIONS					PENTAGON				
Total	3,047	2,303	739	5	Total	184	108	71	5
White	2,435	1,908	527	-	White	120	79	41	-
Black	286	170	116	-	Black	49	21	28	-
Other	187	127	60	-	Other	2	2	-	-
Unknown	139	98	36	5	Unknown	13	6	2	5
WORLD TRADE CENTER					SOMERSET COUNTY, PA				
Total	2,823	2,175	648	-	Total	40	20	20	-
White	2,279	1,811	468	-	White	36	18	18	-
Black	234	148	86	-	Black	3	1	2	-
Other	184	124	60	-	Other	1	1	-	-
Unknown	126	92	34	-	Unknown	-	-	-	-

- Represents zero.
Source: U.S. Federal Bureau of Investigation, *Crime in the United States*, annual. See also <http://www.fbi.gov/ucr/cius01/01crime.pdf> (released 28 October 2002).

No. 312. Homicide Trends: 1976 to 2000

[Rate per 100,000 inhabitants. Not all agencies which report offence information to the FBI also submit supplemental data on homicides. To account for the total number of homicide victims, the data was weighted to match national and state estimates prepared by the FBI; hence, columns may not equal total.]

Year	Rate per 100,000	Estimated number of victims	Homicide rate by gender of victim Male	Homicide rate by gender of victim Female	Estimated number of homicide victims Male	Estimated number of homicide victims Female	Homicide rate by race of victim White	Homicide rate by race of victim Black	Homicide rate by race of victim Other	Estimated number of homicide victims White	Estimated number of homicide victims Black	Estimated number of homicide victims Other
1976	8.8	18,780	13.6	4.2	14,171	4,590	5.1	37.1	7.9	9,585	8,745	387
1977	8.8	19,120	13.7	4.2	14,397	4,710	5.4	36.2	7.6	10,041	8,669	377
1978	9.0	19,560	14.0	4.1	14,895	4,642	5.6	35.1	7.1	10,568	8,572	367
1979	9.7	21,460	15.4	4.4	16,428	5,017	6.1	37.5	8.9	11,625	9,311	470
1980	10.2	23,040	16.2	4.5	17,788	5,232	6.3	37.7	5.7	12,275	9,767	327
1981	9.8	22,520	15.6	4.3	17,405	5,096	6.2	36.4	6.1	12,163	9,862	348
1982	9.1	21,010	14.1	4.3	15,902	5,093	5.9	32.3	6.5	11,643	8,880	399
1983	8.3	19,310	12.8	3.9	14,588	4,703	5.3	29.4	6.4	10,604	8,200	417
1984	7.9	18,690	12.1	3.9	13,910	4,741	5.2	27.2	5.4	10,490	7,678	377
1985	7.9	18,980	12.1	4.0	14,079	4,881	5.2	27.5	5.4	10,589	7,891	399
1986	8.6	20,610	13.2	4.1	15,471	5,109	5.3	31.3	6.2	10,916	9,107	484
1987	8.3	20,100	12.5	4.2	14,811	5,268	5.1	30.6	5.2	10,526	9,000	424
1988	8.4	20,680	12.9	4.2	15,414	5,238	4.9	33.3	4.0	10,184	9,959	344
1989	8.7	21,500	13.6	4.3	16,407	5,085	4.9	34.9	4.2	10,325	10,566	390
1990	9.4	23,440	15.1	4.0	18,304	5,115	5.4	37.7	4.2	11,279	11,488	400
1991	9.8	24,700	15.7	4.2	19,270	5,394	5.5	39.3	6.0	11,661	12,226	608
1992	9.3	23,760	14.9	4.0	18,513	5,217	5.3	37.2	5.4	11,229	11,777	573
1993	9.5	24,530	15.0	4.2	18,937	5,550	5.3	38.7	5.5	11,278	12,435	601
1994	9.0	23,330	14.4	3.8	18,294	5,007	5.0	36.4	4.6	10,773	11,856	526
1995	8.2	21,610	12.9	3.7	16,551	5,023	4.8	31.6	4.9	10,371	10,444	585
1996	7.4	19,650	11.7	3.3	15,152	4,470	4.3	28.3	4.1	9,482	9,477	512
1997	6.8	18,210	10.7	3.0	14,057	4,124	3.9	26.1	4.1	8,619	8,842	524
1998	6.3	16,910	9.7	3.0	12,753	4,139	3.8	23.0	2.9	8,389	7,931	393
1999	5.7	15,533	8.8	2.7	11,704	3,800	3.5	20.5	3.3	7,777	7,139	458
2000	5.5	15,517	8.5	2.6	11,766	3,717	3.3	20.5	2.7	7,526	7,393	398

Source: U.S. Bureau of Justice Statistics, *Homicide Trends in the United States, 1976-2000*. See also <http://www.ojp.usdoj.gov/bjs/pub/pdf/htius.pdf>.

No. 313. Homicide Victims by Race and Sex: 1980 to 2000

[Rates per 100,000 resident population in specified group. Excludes deaths to nonresidents of United States. Begining 1991, deaths classified according to the tenth revision of the *International Classification of Diseases*; see text, Section 2 and footnote 3]

Year	Homicide victims Total [1]	White Male	White Female	Black Male	Black Female	Homicide rate [2] Total [1]	White Male	White Female	Black Male	Black Female
1980	24,278	10,381	3,177	8,385	1,898	10.7	10.9	3.2	66.6	13.5
1985	19,893	8,122	3,041	6,616	1,666	8.3	8.2	2.9	48.4	11.0
1987	21,103	7,979	3,149	7,518	1,969	8.7	7.9	3.0	53.3	12.6
1988	22,032	7,994	3,072	8,314	2,089	9.0	7.9	2.9	58.0	13.2
1989	22,909	8,337	2,971	8,888	2,074	9.2	8.2	2.8	61.1	12.9
1990	24,932	9,147	3,006	9,981	2,163	10.0	9.0	2.8	69.2	13.5
1991	26,513	9,581	3,201	10,628	2,330	10.5	9.3	3.0	72.0	14.2
1992	25,488	9,456	3,012	10,131	2,187	10.0	9.1	2.8	67.5	13.1
1993	26,009	9,054	3,232	10,640	2,297	10.1	8.6	3.0	69.7	13.6
1994	24,926	9,055	2,921	10,083	2,124	9.6	8.5	2.6	65.1	12.4
1995	22,895	8,336	3,028	8,847	1,936	8.7	7.8	2.7	56.3	11.1
1996	20,971	7,570	2,747	8,183	1,800	7.9	7.0	2.5	51.5	10.2
1997	19,846	7,343	2,570	7,601	1,652	7.4	6.7	2.3	47.1	9.3
1998	18,272	6,707	2,534	6,873	1,547	6.8	6.1	2.2	42.1	8.6
1999 [3]	16,889	6,162	2,466	6,214	1,434	6.2	5.6	2.2	37.5	7.8
2000	16,765	5,925	2,414	6,482	1,385	6.0	5.3	2.1	38.6	7.5

[1] Includes races not shown separately. [2] Rate based on enumerated population figures as of April 1 for 1980, 1990 and 2000; July 1 estimates for other years. [3] Effective with data for 1999, causes of death are classified by The Tenth Revision International Classification of Diseases (ICD-10), replacing the Ninth Revision (ICD-9) used for 1979-98 data. Breaks in the comparability of some cause of death statistics result from changes in category titles, changes in the structure and content of the classification, and changes in coding rules used to select the underlying cause of death. In ICD-9, the category homicide also includes death as a result of legal intervention. ICD-10 has two separate categories for these two causes of death. Some caution should be used in comparing data between 1998 and 1999.

Source: U.S. National Center for Health Statistics, *Vital Statistics of the United States*, annual; and *National Vital Statistics Reports (NVSR)* (formerly *Monthly Vital Statistics Report*); and unpublished data.

No. 314. Forcible Rape—Number and Rate: 1980 to 2001

[For definition of rape, see text, this section]

Item	1980	1990	1994	1995	1996	1997	1998	1999	2000	2001
NUMBER										
Total	82,990	102,560	102,220	97,460	96,250	96,153	93,144	89,411	90,186	90,491
By force	63,599	86,541	89,297	85,249	84,053	84,931	82,823	79,697	81,111	81,478
Attempt	19,391	16,019	12,923	12,211	12,197	11,222	10,321	9,714	9,075	9,013
RATE										
Per 100,000 population	36.8	41.1	39.3	37.1	36.3	35.9	34.5	32.8	32.0	32.0
Per 100,000 females	71.6	80.5	76.7	72.5	71.0	70.4	67.4	64.1	62.7	62.2
Per 100,000 females 12 years old and over	86.3	96.6	92.0	87.1	85.3	84.4	80.7	71.1	(NA)	(NA)
AVERAGE ANNUAL PERCENT CHANGE IN RATE [1]										
Per 100,000 population	6.1	8.1	-4.4	-5.6	-2.2	-1.0	-4.1	-5.2	-2.4	-1.4
Per 100,000 females 12 years old and over	6.0	8.2	-4.6	-5.3	-2.1	-1.0	-4.5	-5.3	(NA)	(NA)

NA Not available. [1] Represents annual average from prior year shown except for 1980, from 1979, for 1990, from 1989 and 1994 from 1993.

Source: U.S. Federal Bureau of Investigation, *Population-at-Risk Rates and Selected Crime Indicators*, annual.

No. 315. Reporting Rape and Sexual Assault to Police and Medical Attention: 1992 to 2000

[Rate per 100,000 inhabitants]

Characteristic	Completed rape Number	Completed rape Percent	Attempted rape Number	Attempted rape Percent	Sexual assault Number	Sexual assault Percent
Injury from victimization:						
Total victimizations	131,950	100	98,970	100	135,550	100
Not injured	-	-	60,010	61	112,520	83
Injured	131,950	100	38,960	39	23,020	17
Serious injury	7,180	5	(B)	(B)	(B)	(B)
Minor injury	42,630	33	25,450	26	12,390	9
Undetermined injury	81,140	61	10,730	11	8,590	6
Reporting of victimizations to police:						
Total victimizations	131,950	100	98,970	100	135,550	100
Reported to police	47,960	36	33,560	34	34,830	26
By victim	23,890	18	24,040	24	21,560	16
By other household member	10,080	8	(B)	(B)	4,970	4
By someone else	13,990	11	6,010	6	8,310	6
Not reported	83,700	63	64,600	65	99,840	74
Medical treatment received:						
Total injured	131,950	100	38,960	100	23,020	100
Treated	42,230	32	12,490	32	6,250	27

- Represents zero. B Base figure too small to meet statistical standards for reliablity of a derived figure.
Source: U.S. Bureau of Justice Statistics, *Rape and Sexual Assault: Reporting to Police and Medical Attention, 1992-2000*, Series NCJ 194530, August 2002.

No. 316. Violence by Intimate Partners by Sex, 1993 to 2001, and by Type of Crime, 2001

[Violent acts covered include murder, rape, sexual assault, robbery, and aggravated and simple assault. Intimate partners involve current spouses, former spouses, current boy/girlfriends, and former boy/girlfriends. Based on the National Criminal Victimization Survey; see text, this section, and Appendix III. See Appendix III]

Year and type of crime	All persons Number	All persons Rate per 100,000 [1]	Females Number	Females Rate per 100,000 [1]	Males Number	Males Rate per 100,000 [1]
1993	1,228,760	580.9	1,072,090	982.0	156,670	153.1
1994	1,148,210	537.2	1,003,190	908.9	145,020	140.3
1995	1,063,520	493.0	953,700	855.8	109,820	105.3
1996	1,008,860	462.8	879,290	781.7	129,570	122.8
1997	953,780	432.7	848,480	747.3	105,300	98.5
1998	1,054,260	475.7	896,030	780.9	158,230	146.7
1999	783,120	347.7	672,330	578.1	110,790	101.6
2000	630,530	277.2	547,310	466.5	83,220	75.5
2001, total	691,710	293.6	588,490	496.7	103,220	77.8
Murder	(NA)	(NA)	(NA)	(NA)	(NA)	(NA)
Rape or sexual assault	41,740	18.2	41,740	35.2	(B)	(B)
Robbery	60,630	26.4	44,060	37.2	16,570	14.9
Aggravated assault	117,480	51.1	81,140	68.5	36,350	32.6
Simple assault	471,860	205.2	421,550	355.8	50,310	45.1

B Base figure too small to meet statistical standards for reliability of derived figure. In this case, 10 or fewer sample cases.
NA Not available. [1] Rates are the number of victimizations per 100,000 persons.
Source: U.S. Bureau of Justice Statistics, *Intimate Partner Violence*, Series NCJ 197838, February 2003.

No. 317. Violent Victimizations Reported to the Police: 1992 to 2000

[In percent. Offender characteristics are based on victim's perception. See source for details. For definitions of crimes, see text, this section]

Characteristic of offender	Percent reported to the police					
	Violent crimes					Serious violent crime [1]
	All	Forcible rape	Robbery	Aggravated assault	Simple assault	
Total	43	31	57	55	38	53
Gender:						
Male	43	32	56	54	38	52
Female	40	[2]13	55	55	37	53
Both	63	[2]59	74	75	56	74
Race:						
White	42	29	55	54	38	50
Black	47	39	59	59	38	58
Number of offenders:						
One	42	31	55	53	38	50
Two	55	44	65	64	44	64
Three or more	51	28	57	62	42	59
Relationship to victim:						
Nonstranger	41	27	59	55	37	51
Intimate	54	24	72	63	53	55
Other relative	50	48	53	61	47	57
Friend/acquaintance	36	27	55	52	31	48
Stranger	45	41	56	55	39	55
Don't know relationship	43	[2]39	62	53	32	55
Drug/alcohol use:						
Using drugs/alcohol	51	32	58	60	48	55
Not using drugs/alcohol	33	23	50	47	30	43
Don't know	45	39	58	55	37	55

[1] Includes rape, sexual assault, robbery and aggravated assault. [2] Based on 10 or fewer sample cases.
Source: U.S. Bureau of Justice Statistics, *Reporting Crime to the Police: 1992-2000*, Series NCJ 195710, March 2003.

No. 318. Robbery and Property Crimes by Type and Selected Characteristic: 1990 to 2001

[For definition of crime, see text, this section]

Characteristic of offenses	Number of offenses (1,000)				Rate per 100,000 inhabitants				Average value lost (dol.)	
	1990	1995	2000	2001	1990	1995	2000	2001	2000	2001
Robbery, total [1]	639	581	408	423	256.3	220.9	144.9	148.5	1,127	1,212
Type of crime:										
Street or highway	359	315	188	187	144.2	120.0	66.7	65.7	858	917
Commercial house	73	71	57	61	29.5	27.2	20.1	21.4	1,685	1,903
Gas station	18	13	12	12	7.1	5.1	4.1	4.2	679	716
Convenience store	39	30	26	28	15.6	11.4	9.3	9.8	566	622
Residence	62	63	50	53	25.1	24.0	17.7	18.6	1,243	1,296
Bank	9	9	9	10	3.8	3.5	3.1	3.5	4,379	4,077
Weapon used:										
Firearm	234	238	161	178	94.1	90.6	57.0	62.5	(NA)	(NA)
Knife or cutting instrument	76	53	36	37	30.7	20.1	12.8	13.0	(NA)	(NA)
Other dangerous weapon	61	53	53	44	24.5	20.2	18.9	15.4	(NA)	(NA)
Strongarm	268	236	159	165	107.7	90.0	56.4	57.9	(NA)	(NA)
Burglary, total	3,074	2,594	2,050	2,110	1,232.2	987.0	728.4	740.9	1,458	1,536
Forcible entry	2,150	1,737	1,297	1,336	864.5	661.2	460.7	469.1	(NA)	(NA)
Unlawful entry	678	657	615	636	272.8	250.1	218.7	223.3	(NA)	(NA)
Attempted forcible entry	245	201	138	138	98.7	76.4	49.0	48.5	(NA)	(NA)
Residence	2,033	1,736	1,335	1,376	817.4	660.6	474.3	483.2	1,378	1,467
Nonresidence	1,041	859	715	734	418.5	327.0	254.1	257.7	1,610	1,666
Occurred during the night	1,135	905	699	718	456.4	344.4	248.3	252.1	(NA)	(NA)
Occurred during the day	1,151	1,000	836	864	462.8	380.5	297.2	303.4	(NA)	(NA)
Larceny-theft, total	7,946	7,998	6,972	7,076	3,185.1	3,043.2	2,477.3	2,484.6	727	781
Pocket picking	81	51	36	33	32.4	19.4	12.7	11.6	437	453
Purse snatching	82	51	37	38	32.8	19.5	13.2	13.3	387	352
Shoplifting	1,291	1,205	959	977	519.1	458.4	340.7	343.1	185	183
From motor vehicles	1,744	1,940	1,754	1,829	701.3	738.5	623.3	642.2	692	706
Motor vehicle accessories	1,185	964	677	722	476.3	367.0	240.6	253.5	451	433
Bicycles	443	501	312	291	178.2	190.5	110.9	102.2	273	317
From buildings	1,118	1,004	914	941	449.4	382.1	324.6	330.4	1,184	1,043
From coin-operated machines	63	50	46	52	25.4	18.9	16.2	18.3	272	291
Other	1,940	2,235	2,232	2,193	780.0	850.5	793.0	770.0	957	1,198
Motor vehicles, total [2]	1,636	1,472	1,160	1,226	655.8	560.3	412.2	430.5	6,581	6,622
Automobiles	1,304	1,154	877	904	524.3	439.2	311.5	317.4	(NA)	(NA)
Trucks and buses	238	240	209	232	95.5	91.2	74.1	81.5	(NA)	(NA)

NA Not available. [1] Includes other crimes not shown separately. [2] Includes other types of motor vehicles not shown separately.
Source: U.S. Federal Bureau of Investigation, *Population-at-Risk Rates and Selected Crime Indicators*, annual.

Law Enforcement, Courts, and Prisons

No. 319. Hate Crimes—Number of Incidents, Offenses, Victims, and Known Offenders by Bias Motivation: 2001

[The FBI collected statistics on hate crimes from 12,054 law enforcement agencies representing over 244 million inhabitants in 2001. Hate crime offenses cover incidents motivated by race, religion, sexual orientation, ethnicity/national origin, and disability]

Bias motivation	Incidents reported	Offenses	Victims [1]	Known offenders [2]
Total	9,878	11,628	12,218	9,442
Race, total	4,447	5,384	5,651	4,603
Anti-White	914	1,060	1,092	1,180
Anti-Black	2,951	3,593	3,775	2,889
Anti-American Indian/Alaskan native	81	97	102	104
Anti-Asian/Pacific Islander	282	351	365	273
Anti-multiracial group	219	283	317	157
Ethnicity/national origin, total	2,109	2,524	2,652	2,208
Anti-Hispanic	603	764	822	949
Anti-other ethnicity/national origin	1,506	1,760	1,830	1,259
Religion, total	1,864	2,047	2,165	957
Anti-Jewish	1,054	1,129	1,211	400
Anti-Catholic	38	38	40	12
Anti-Protestant	35	36	36	45
Anti-Islamic	498	565	574	353
Anti-other religious group	188	222	246	112
Anti-multireligious group	46	52	53	28
Anti-atheism/agnosticism/etc	5	5	5	7
Sexual orientation, total	1,412	1,614	1,690	1,617
Anti-male homosexual	993	1,117	1,168	1,227
Anti-female homosexual	207	247	259	171
Anti-homosexual	176	212	224	183
Anti-heterosexual	19	21	22	18
Anti-bisexual	17	17	17	18
Disability, total	38	40	40	44
Anti-physical	14	14	14	18
Anti-mental	24	26	26	26
Multiple bias	8	19	20	13

[1] The term "victim" may refer to a person, business, institution, or a society as a whole. [2] The term "known offender" does not imply that the identity of the suspect is known, but only that an attribute of the suspect is identified which distinguishes him/her from an unknown offender.

Source: U.S. Federal Bureau of Investigation, *Hate Crime Statistics*, annual; and <http://www.fbi.gov/ucr/01hate.pdf> (released October 2002) and subsequent updates because of late data submissions.

No. 320. Hate Crimes Reported by State: 2000

[See headnote, Table 319]

State	Number of participating agencies	Population covered (1,000)	Agencies submitting incidents	Incidents reported	State	Number of participating agencies	Population covered (1,000)	Agencies submitting incidents	Incidents reported
United States	11,720	237,663	1,929	8,224	Missouri	186	3,843	26	70
					Montana	102	901	8	19
Alabama	([1])	([1])	([1])	([1])	Nebraska	202	1,361	6	17
Alaska	1	261	1	4	Nevada	36	1,997	8	85
Arizona	88	4,607	22	281	New Hampshire	110	658	20	32
Arkansas	4	77	3	3	New Jersey	564	8,414	241	652
California	722	33,964	259	1,943	New Mexico	44	1,084	3	15
Colorado	234	4,299	34	102					
Connecticut	97	3,316	58	152	New York	540	18,983	36	608
Delaware	52	784	9	34	North Carolina	223	4,794	15	39
District of Columbia	2	572	2	6	North Dakota	80	580	5	5
Florida	491	15,955	107	240	Ohio	347	7,471	50	255
					Oklahoma	297	3,444	24	80
Georgia	80	1,077	4	35	Oregon	171	3,411	29	142
Hawaii	([1])	([1])	([1])	([1])	Pennsylvania	933	11,449	32	141
Idaho	114	1,274	26	46	Rhode Island	48	1,048	10	48
Illinois	46	4,463	45	183	South Carolina	352	4,009	19	36
Indiana	167	4,416	31	106					
Iowa	220	2,807	15	34	South Dakota	120	752	4	8
Kansas	24	794	24	75	Tennessee	421	5,676	73	237
Kentucky	315	3,287	38	77	Texas	941	20,609	72	287
Louisiana	173	3,828	8	12	Utah	127	2,226	29	75
Maine	181	1,270	9	28	Vermont	43	508	14	19
Maryland	146	5,294	33	218	Virginia	294	6,981	59	336
Massachusetts	341	6,278	100	470	Washington	236	5,352	57	242
Michigan	620	9,819	156	425	West Virginia	271	1,679	25	75
Minnesota	311	4,914	55	169	Wisconsin	368	5,361	22	47
Mississippi	78	1,220	1	2	Wyoming	67	493	2	9

[1] Did not report.

Source: U.S. Federal Bureau of Investigation, *Hate Crime Statistics*, annual; and <http://www.fbi.gov/ucr/cius00/hate00.pdf> (released 15 October 2001) and subsequent updates because of late data submissions.

No. 321. Criminal Victimizations and Victimization Rates: 1995 to 2001

[Based on National Crime Victimization Survey; see text, this section, and Appendix III]

Type of crime	Number of victimizations (1,000) 1995	1999	2000	2001	Victimization rates [1] 1995	1999	2000	2001
All crimes, total	39,926	28,780	25,893	24,216	(X)	(X)	(X)	(X)
Personal crimes [2]	10,436	7,565	6,597	5,932	46.2	33.7	29.1	25.9
Crimes of violence	10,022	7,357	6,323	5,744	44.5	32.8	27.9	25.1
Completed violence	2,960	2,278	2,044	1,828	12.9	10.1	9.0	8.0
Attempted/threatened violence	7,061	5,079	4,279	3,916	31.6	22.6	18.9	17.1
Rape/sexual assault	363	383	261	248	1.6	1.7	1.2	1.1
Rape/attempted rape	252	201	147	146	1.1	0.9	0.6	0.6
Rape	153	141	92	84	0.7	0.6	0.4	0.4
Attempted rape	99	60	55	63	0.4	0.3	0.2	0.3
Sexual assault	112	182	114	102	0.5	0.8	0.5	0.4
Robbery	1,171	810	732	631	5.3	3.6	3.2	2.8
Completed/property taken	753	530	520	427	3.5	2.4	2.3	1.9
With injury	224	189	160	174	1.0	0.8	0.7	0.8
Without injury	529	341	360	253	2.4	1.5	1.6	1.1
Attempted to take property	418	280	212	204	1.8	1.2	0.9	0.9
With injury	84	78	66	68	0.4	0.3	0.3	0.3
Without injury	335	202	146	136	1.4	0.9	0.6	0.6
Assault	8,487	6,164	5,330	4,865	37.6	27.4	23.5	21.2
Aggravated	2,050	1,503	1,293	1,222	8.8	6.7	5.7	5.3
With injury	533	449	346	392	2.4	2.0	1.5	1.7
Threatened with weapon	1,517	1,054	946	831	6.4	4.7	4.2	3.6
Simple	6,437	4,660	4,038	3,643	28.9	20.8	17.8	15.9
With minor injury	1,426	998	989	845	6.0	4.4	4.4	3.7
Without injury	5,012	3,662	3,048	2,798	22.9	16.3	13.4	12.2
Personal theft [3]	414	208	274	188	1.7	0.9	1.2	0.8
Property crimes	29,490	21,215	19,297	18,284	279.5	198.0	178.1	166.9
Household burglary	5,004	3,652	3,444	3,140	47.4	34.1	31.8	28.7
Completed	4,232	3,064	2,909	2,687	40.0	28.6	26.9	24.5
Attempted forcible entry	773	587	534	453	7.4	5.5	4.9	4.1
Motor vehicle theft	1,717	1,068	937	1,009	16.2	10.0	8.6	9.2
Completed	1,163	808	642	724	10.8	7.5	5.9	6.6
Attempted	554	260	295	285	5.5	2.4	2.7	2.6
Theft [4]	22,769	16,495	14,916	14,135	215.9	153.9	137.7	129.0
Completed	21,857	15,964	14,300	13,672	207.6	149.0	132.0	124.8
Attempted	911	532	616	463	8.4	5.0	5.7	4.2

X Not applicable. [1] Per 1,000 persons age 12 or older or per 1,000 households. [2] The victimization survey cannot measure murder because of the inability to question the victim. [3] Includes pocket picking, purse snatching, and attempted purse snatching. [4] Includes thefts in which the amount taken was not ascertained.

Source: U.S. Bureau of Justice Statistics, *Criminal Victimization*, annual; and *Criminal Victimization 2001, Changes 2000-01 with Trends 1993-2001*, Series NCJ-194610. See also <http://www.ojp.usdoj.gov/bjs/pub/pdf/cv01.pdf>.

No. 322. Victimization Rates by Type of Violent Crime and Characteristic of the Victim: 2001

[Rate per 1,000 persons age 12 years or older. Based on National Crime Victimization Survey; see text, this section, and Appendix III]

Characteristic of the victim	All crime	Crimes of violence Total	Rape/ sexual assault	Robbery	Assault Total	Aggra- vated	Simple	Personal theft
Total	25.9	25.1	1.1	2.8	21.2	5.3	15.9	0.8
Male	28.0	27.3	[1]0.2	3.8	23.2	6.5	16.7	0.8
Female	23.9	23.0	1.9	1.7	19.4	4.2	15.1	0.9
12 to 15 yrs. old	55.6	55.1	[1]1.7	5.2	48.3	8.7	39.6	[1]0.5
16 to 19 yrs. old	58.8	55.8	3.4	6.4	46.1	12.3	33.8	3.0
20 to 24 yrs. old	46.5	44.7	2.4	4.2	38.1	10.7	27.4	1.8
25 to 34 yrs. old	30.3	29.3	1.1	3.6	24.6	6.5	18.1	1.0
35 to 49 yrs. old	23.2	22.9	1.0	2.1	19.7	5.2	14.5	[1]0.4
50 to 64 yrs. old	9.9	9.5	[1]0.2	1.2	8.2	2.0	6.2	[1]0.3
65 yrs. old and over	3.8	3.2	[1]0.1	1.3	1.8	0.4	1.4	[1]0.7
White	25.3	24.5	1.0	2.6	20.8	5.1	15.7	0.8
Black	32.0	31.2	1.1	3.6	26.4	8.1	18.3	[1]0.8
Other	19.9	18.2	[1]1.6	[1]2.4	14.2	2.6	11.6	[1]1.7
Hispanic	30.2	29.5	[1]1.1	5.3	23.1	6.6	16.6	[1]0.7
Non-Hispanic	25.3	24.5	1.1	2.4	21.0	5.2	15.8	0.8
Household income:								
Less than $7,500	47.6	46.6	3.7	4.7	38.2	16.1	22.1	[1]1.0
$7,500-$14,999	37.7	36.9	[1]1.6	4.4	31.0	8.9	22.1	[1]0.8
$15,000-$24,999	32.6	31.8	2.0	4.3	25.5	7.8	17.6	[1]0.9
$25,000-$34,999	30.0	29.1	1.3	2.2	25.6	4.5	21.0	[1]1.0
$35,000-$49,999	26.9	26.3	1.1	2.4	22.9	6.0	16.8	[1]0.6
$50,000-$74,999	21.5	21.0	0.8	2.3	17.9	3.7	14.1	[1]0.6
$75,000 or more	19.1	18.5	[1]0.6	1.6	16.3	3.1	13.1	0.6

[1] Based on 10 or fewer sample cases.

Source: U.S. Bureau of Justice Statistics, *Criminal Victimization*, annual; and *Criminal Victimization 2001, Changes 2000-01 with Trends 1993-2001*, Series NCJ-194610. See also <http://www.ojp.usdoj.gov/bjs/pub/pdf/cv01.pdf>.

No. 323. Victim-Offender Relationship in Crimes of Violence, by Characteristics of the Criminal Incident: 2001

[In percent. Covers only crimes of violence. Based on National Crime Victimization Survey; see text, this section, and Appendix III]

Characteristics of incident	Total	Rape/ sexual assault	Robbery	Assault Total	Aggravated[1]	Simple
Total	100	100	100	100	100	100
Victim/offender relationship:[2]						
Relatives	12	4	9	13	11	13
Well-known	25	34	11	26	23	27
Casual acquaintance	17	30	4	18	14	19
Stranger	46	32	76	44	52	41
Time of day:[3]						
6 a.m. to 6 p.m.	55	38	47	57	46	60
6 p.m. to midnight	37	36	36	33	41	31
Midnight to 6 a.m.	11	26	17	10	13	9
Location of crime:						
At or near victim's home or lodging	28	34	30	28	28	28
Friend's/relative's/neighbor's home	8	17	3	8	11	8
Commercial places	14	19	5	15	15	15
Parking lots/garages	8	2	9	8	10	7
School	14	5	6	15	8	17
Streets other than near victim's home	18	9	36	16	19	15
Other[4]	10	14	12	10	8	11
Victim's activity:[5]						
At work or traveling to or from work	21	16	12	22	20	23
School	13	5	11	14	9	15
Activities at home	21	22	16	22	20	22
Shopping/errands	4	-	10	4	5	3
Leisure activities away from home	21	34	16	21	24	21
Traveling	9	4	20	8	11	7
Other[6]	21	22	16	22	20	22
Distance from victim's home:[7]						
Inside home or lodging	16	31	21	15	13	16
Near victim's home	15	13	11	15	18	15
1 mile or less	19	11	28	18	20	18
5 miles or less	25	16	22	26	24	26
50 miles or less	22	21	15	23	21	24
More than 50 miles	3	8	2	2	4	2
Weapons:						
No weapons present	73	92	40	76	6	100
Weapons present	27	8	60	24	94	-
Firearm	10	3	34	7	27	-
Other type of weapon[8]	18	6	27	17	67	-

- Represents zero. [1] An aggravated assault is any assault in which an offender possesses or uses a weapon or inflicts serious injury. [2] Excludes "don't know" relationships. [3] Excludes "not known and not available" time of day. [4] Includes areas on public transportation or inside station, in apartment yard, park, field, playground, or other areas. [5] Excludes "don't know" and "not available" victim activity. [6] Includes sleeping. [7] Excludes "don't know" and "not available" distance from victim's home. [8] Includes knives, other sharp objects, blunt objects, and other types of weapons.

Source: U.S. Bureau of Justice Statistics, *Criminal Victimization*, annual; and *Criminal Victimization 2001, Changes 2000-01 with Trends 1993-2001*, Series NCJ-194610, September 2002. See also <http://www.ojp.usdoj.gov/bjs/pub/pdf/cv01.pdf>.

No. 324. Property Victimization Rates by Selected Household Characteristic: 2001

[Victimizations per 1,000 households. Based on National Crime Victimization Survey; see text, this section, and Appendix III]

Characteristic	Total	Burglary	Motor vehicle theft	Theft
Total	166.9	28.7	9.2	129.0
Race:				
White	164.1	26.6	8.2	130.3
Black	179.7	42.8	16.1	120.8
Other	163.6	27.6	8.4	127.6
Ethnicity:				
Hispanic	224.1	33.0	19.8	171.4
Non-Hispanic	161.3	28.3	8.2	124.9
Household income:				
Less than $7,500	184.6	58.0	8.4	118.3
$7,500-$14,999	181.6	37.1	11.5	133.0
$15,000-$24,999	179.2	36.2	10.3	132.8
$25,000-$34,999	170.4	33.3	9.8	127.4
$35,000-$49,999	176.4	23.0	10.6	142.8
$50,000-$74,999	178.8	20.2	7.8	150.8
$75,000 or more	180.0	22.7	7.4	149.9
Residence:				
Urban	212.8	37.3	15.1	160.4
Suburban	156.7	24.3	8.5	123.9
Rural	131.9	26.7	3.6	101.6
Form of tenure:				
Home owned	146.3	23.8	7.3	115.2
Home rented	209.6	38.8	13.1	157.8

Source: U.S. Bureau of Justice Statistics, *Criminal Victimization*, annual; and *Criminal Victimization 2001, Changes 2000-01 With Trends 1993-01*, Series NCJ-194610. See also <http://www.ojp.usdoj.gov/bjs/pub/pdf/cv01.pdf>.

No. 325. Persons Arrested by Charge and Selected Characteristics: 2001

[10,762.3 represents 10,762,300. Represents arrests (not charges) reported by approximately 10,280 agencies with a total 2001 population of approximately 215 million as estimated by FBI. Age and sex data is mandatory, while race data is optional and not always reported with arrest data; hence, two different total number of arrests]

Offense charged	Total arrests (1,000)							
	Total	Male	Female	Total	White	Black	American Indian or Alaskan Native	Asian or Pacific Islander
Total	10,762.3	8,405.2	2,357.1	10,740.7	7,235.0	3,258.6	125.8	121.3
Serious crimes [1]:								
Murder and nonnegligent manslaughter	11.3	9.9	1.3	11.3	5.2	5.8	0.1	0.2
Forcible rape	21.1	20.9	0.3	21.1	12.7	7.8	0.2	0.3
Robbery	94.9	85.4	9.5	94.8	40.0	53.1	0.5	1.2
Aggravated assault	370.7	295.3	75.4	370.1	228.9	132.4	3.8	5.0
Burglary	216.2	187.4	28.8	216.0	147.5	63.9	2.1	2.5
Larceny/theft	881.5	560.3	321.2	879.8	573.9	281.4	10.6	13.9
Motor vehicle theft	111.3	93.4	17.9	111.1	62.7	45.4	1.0	2.0
Arson	12.8	10.8	2.0	12.8	9.7	2.9	0.1	0.1
All other nonserious crimes:								
Other assaults	999.9	766.5	233.4	998.1	644.0	329.6	13.0	11.6
Forgery and counterfeiting	90.6	56.5	34.1	90.4	58.8	29.2	0.5	1.9
Fraud	266.0	150.1	115.9	265.0	173.7	87.3	1.4	2.6
Embezzlement	15.6	7.9	7.7	15.5	10.1	5.1	0.1	0.2
Stolen property—buying, receiving, possessing	95.4	78.6	16.9	95.2	53.5	40.0	0.6	1.1
Vandalism	206.5	173.1	33.4	206.1	151.8	49.4	2.6	2.3
Weapons; carrying, possessing, etc.	131.4	120.2	11.2	131.2	76.3	52.5	0.9	1.5
Prostitution and commercialized vice	69.3	23.8	45.5	69.3	39.0	28.1	0.4	1.8
Sex offenses (except forcible rape and prostitution)	71.2	65.8	5.4	71.1	50.7	18.6	0.7	1.1
Drug abuse violations	1,266.2	1,046.6	219.6	1,264.7	783.8	464.9	6.6	9.4
Gambling	13.7	12.2	1.5	13.7	5.5	7.8	-	0.4
Offenses against family and children	101.2	78.1	23.2	100.8	67.2	30.8	1.1	1.6
Driving under the influence	970.3	808.3	162.0	967.8	848.5	96.8	13.3	9.2
Liquor laws	602.4	481.9	120.4	600.4	458.2	126.4	12.0	3.8
Drunkenness	446.1	384.9	61.2	445.2	372.2	60.8	10.0	2.2
Disorderly conduct	513.0	393.1	119.9	511.9	320.2	181.6	6.5	3.6
Vagrancy	26.7	19.9	6.8	26.7	15.4	10.7	0.5	0.1
Suspicion	2.7	2.0	0.7	2.7	1.7	1.0	-	-
Curfew and loitering law violations	103.1	71.1	32.0	102.9	72.8	27.6	0.9	1.6
Runaways	96.5	39.3	57.2	96.3	73.0	18.0	1.2	4.2
All other offenses (except traffic)	2,954.8	2,361.9	592.9	2,948.7	1,878.0	999.6	35.1	36.0

- Represents zero or rounds to zero.   [1] Includes arson.

Source: U.S. Federal Bureau of Investigation, *Crime in the United States*, annual. See also <http://www.fbi.gov/ucr/Cius01/01crime.pdf> (released 28 October 2002).

No. 326. Juvenile Arrests for Selected Offenses: 1980 to 2001

[169,439 represents 169,439,000. Juveniles are persons under 18 years of age]

Offense	1980	1990	1994	1995	1996	1997	1998	1999	2000	2001
Number of contributing agencies	8,178	10,765	10,693	10,037	10,026	9,472	9,589	9,502	9,904	10,281
Population covered (1,000)	169,439	204,543	208,035	206,762	195,805	194,925	194,612	195,324	204,965	215,380
NUMBER										
Violent crime, total	77,220	97,103	125,141	123,131	104,455	100,273	90,201	81,715	78,450	78,443
Murder	1,475	2,661	3,114	2,812	2,184	1,887	1,587	1,131	1,027	1,069
Forcible rape	3,668	4,971	4,873	4,556	4,228	4,127	3,988	3,544	3,402	3,504
Robbery	38,529	34,944	47,046	47,240	39,788	36,419	29,989	26,125	24,206	23,408
Aggravated assault	33,548	54,527	70,108	68,523	58,255	57,840	54,637	50,915	49,815	50,462
Weapon law violations	21,203	33,123	52,278	46,506	40,145	39,358	34,122	31,307	28,514	29,290
Drug abuse, total	86,685	66,300	124,931	149,236	148,783	155,444	148,066	138,774	146,594	146,758
Sale and manufacturing	13,004	24,575	32,746	34,077	32,558	30,761	29,312	26,134	26,432	24,649
Heroin/cocaine	1,318	17,511	20,327	19,187	17,465	15,855	15,094	12,686	11,000	10,535
Marijuana	8,876	4,372	8,812	10,682	11,489	11,200	10,808	10,770	11,792	10,552
Synthetic narcotics	465	346	465	701	614	671	813	722	945	911
Dangerous nonnarcotic drugs	2,345	2,346	3,142	3,507	2,990	3,027	2,597	1,956	2,695	2,651
Possession	73,681	41,725	92,185	115,159	116,225	124,683	118,754	112,640	120,162	122,109
Heroin/cocaine	2,614	15,194	21,004	21,253	17,560	18,328	16,278	13,445	12,586	11,734
Marijuana	64,465	20,940	61,003	82,015	87,712	94,046	91,467	89,523	95,962	97,088
Synthetic narcotics	1,524	1,155	1,227	2,047	1,713	1,987	1,916	1,581	2,052	2,237
Dangerous nonnarcotic drugs	5,078	4,436	8,951	9,844	9,240	10,322	9,093	8,091	9,832	11,050

Source: U.S. Federal Bureau of Investigation, *Crime in the United States*, annual. See also <http://www.fbi.gov/ucr/Cius01/01crime.pdf> (released 28 October 2002).

Law Enforcement, Courts, and Prisons

No. 327. Immigration and Naturalization Service Enforcement Activities: 1990 to 2000

[For fiscal years ending in year shown. See text, Section 8]

Item	Unit	1990	1994	1995	1996	1997	1998	1999	2000
Deportable aliens located.	1,000	1,169.9	1,094.7	1,394.6	1,650.0	1,536.5	1,679.4	1,714.0	1,814.7
Border Patrol	1,000	1,103.4	1,031.7	1,324.2	1,549.9	1,413.0	1,555.8	1,579.0	1,676.4
Southwestern border	1,000	(NA)	979.1	1,271.4	1,507.0	1,368.7	1,516.7	1,537.0	1,643.7
Mexican	1,000	1,054.8	999.9	1,293.5	1,523.1	1,387.7	1,522.9	1,534.5	1,636.9
Canadian	1,000	5.7	3.4	3.5	2.7	2.9	2.3	2.7	2.2
Other	1,000	42.8	28.4	27.2	24.0	22.4	30.5	41.8	37.3
Number of seizures by Border Patrol	Number	17,275	9,134	9,327	11,129	11,792	14,401	16,803	17,269
Value of seizures by Border Patrol	Mil. dol.	843.6	1,622.0	2,011.8	1,256.0	1,094.6	1,405.0	2,004.0	1,945.0
Narcotics	Mil. dol.	797.8	1,555.7	1,965.3	1,208.8	1,046.3	1,340.0	1,919.0	1,848.0
Aliens expelled:									
Formal removals [1]	1,000	30.0	45.7	45.2	69.7	114.4	173.0	180.3	184.8
Voluntary departures [2]	1,000	1,022.5	1,029.1	1,313.8	1,573.4	1,440.7	1,570.1	1,574.5	1,675.3

NA Not available. [1] Include deportations, exclusions, and removals. [2] Includes aliens under docket control required to depart and voluntary departures not under docket control.
Source: U.S. Bureau of Citizenship and Immigration Services, *Statistical Yearbook*, annual. See also <http://www.immigration.gov/graphics/shared/aboutus/statistics/index.htm>.

No. 328. Drug Use by Arrestees in Major U.S. Cities by Type of Drug and Sex: 2002

[Percent testing positive. Based on data from the Arrestee Drug Abuse Monitoring Program]

City	Male Any drug[1]	Male Marijuana	Male Cocaine	Male Opiates	Female Any drug[1]	Female Marijuana	Female Cocaine	Female Opiates
Albuquerque, NM	67.2	34.2	37.5	9.8	71.8	26.7	48.7	16.4
Atlanta, GA	71.3	35.2	49.4	3.4	(NA)	(NA)	(NA)	(NA)
Chicago, IL	85.3	49.4	47.9	26.0	(NA)	(NA)	(NA)	(NA)
Cleveland, OH	73.2	51.1	34.6	5.5	67.9	26.2	42.9	6.2
Dallas, TX	59.2	35.3	30.7	6.1	(NA)	(NA)	(NA)	(NA)
Denver, CO	67.4	40.3	32.7	4.0	69.8	33.3	44.6	5.4
Indianapolis, IN	67.9	46.7	34.9	4.8	78.4	38.8	55.2	8.2
Las Vegas, NV	66.5	34.7	24.2	5.6	(NA)	(NA)	(NA)	(NA)
Los Angeles, CA	62.3	36.4	32.1	5.8	(NA)	(NA)	(NA)	(NA)
New Orleans, LA	73.4	46.9	42.4	17.4	60.0	26.0	42.2	9.2
New York, NY	82.7	44.3	49.0	15.0	63.9	30.6	38.9	13.9
Oklahoma City, OK	74.1	54.1	25.5	3.3	60.0	28.0	30.0	2.0
Philadelphia, PA	76.8	47.7	38.7	15.9	(NA)	(NA)	(NA)	(NA)
Phoenix, AZ	73.5	41.5	27.1	5.0	73.3	29.4	26.2	5.2
Portland, OR	68.7	37.5	22.3	10.5	70.5	21.6	28.4	18.2
Sacramento, CA	80.1	50.9	20.9	6.2	(NA)	(NA)	(NA)	(NA)
San Antonio, TX	64.4	42.0	32.5	11.0	(NA)	(NA)	(NA)	(NA)
San Diego, CA	66.1	37.8	12.7	5.6	72.2	33.3	21.2	5.8
San Jose, CA	60.2	34.0	13.0	3.4	69.0	26.9	12.4	1.4
Seattle, WA	71.0	38.5	38.1	10.0	(NA)	(NA)	(NA)	(NA)
Tucson, AZ	74.6	47.2	42.5	6.5	72.9	25.1	45.4	9.2
Washington, DC	64.0	40.7	27.5	9.5	74.4	33.3	38.5	17.9

NA Not available. [1] Includes other drugs not shown separately.
Source: U.S. National Institute of Justice, *2002 Annual Report on Drug Use Among Adult and Juvenile Arrestees*, June 2003.

No. 329. Drug Arrest Rates for Drug Abuse Violations, 1990 to 2001, and by Region, 2001

[Rate per 100,000 inhabitants. Based on Census Bureau estimated resident population as of July 1, except 1990 and 2000, enumerated as of April 1. For composition of regions, see map, inside front cover]

Offense	1990	1995	2000	2001 Total	Northeast	Midwest	South	West
Drug arrest rate, total	435.3	564.7	587.1	553.9	667.1	377.9	534.2	607.2
Sale and/or manufacture	139.0	140.7	122.7	114.8	177.9	87.4	102.1	100.5
Heroin or cocaine [1]	93.7	83.7	60.8	58.5	124.0	19.7	56.1	37.7
Marijuana	26.4	32.7	34.2	29.3	40.0	26.6	26.3	26.5
Synthetic or manufactured drugs	2.7	3.9	6.4	6.7	4.0	4.3	11.1	5.1
Other dangerous nonnarcotic drugs	16.2	20.3	21.3	20.3	9.9	36.8	8.5	31.2
Possession	296.3	423.9	464.4	439.1	489.3	290.5	432.1	506.7
Heroin or cocaine [1]	144.4	157.4	138.7	125.6	165.3	46.2	123.2	150.7
Marijuana	104.9	192.7	244.4	227.9	291.6	185.3	256.6	175.1
Synthetic or manufactured drugs	6.6	8.5	12.0	13.2	7.3	9.0	17.7	14.9
Other dangerous nonnarcotic drugs	40.4	65.4	69.4	72.4	25.0	50.0	34.6	166.0

[1] Includes other derivatives such as morphine, heroin, and codeine.
Source: U.S. Federal Bureau of Investigation, *Crime in the United States*, annual. See also <http://www.fbi.gov/ucr/cius01/01crime.pdf> (released 28 October 2002).

210 Law Enforcement, Courts, and Prisons

U.S. Census Bureau, Statistical Abstract of the United States: 2003

No. 330. Federal Drug Seizures by Type of Drug: 1990 to 2002

[In pounds. For fiscal years ending in year shown. Reflects the combined drug seizure effort of the Drug Enforcement Administration, the Federal Bureau of Investigation, the U.S. Customs Services, and beginning October 1993 the U.S. Border Patrol within the jurisdiction of the United States as well as maritime seizures by the U.S. Coast Guard. Based on reports to the federal-wide Drug Seizure System, which eliminates duplicate reporting of a seizure involving more than one federal agency]

Drug	1990	1995	1996	1997	1998	1999	2000	2001	2002
Total	745,002	1,662,562	1,737,647	1,762,806	2,084,882	2,665,709	2,986,772	2,920,326	5,065,661
Heroin	1,515	3,407	3,014	3,592	3,214	2,538	3,357	4,394	6,841
Cocaine	211,828	244,888	283,490	221,375	259,895	291,144	248,938	240,002	226,879
Cannabis	531,660	1,414,267	1,451,142	1,537,839	1,821,773	2,372,027	2,639,002	2,678,046	2,415,970
Marijuana	514,723	1,382,366	1,397,976	1,536,170	1,821,241	2,370,269	2,615,015	2,677,613	2,415,777
Hashish	16,937	31,902	53,167	1,669	532	1,758	23,987	433	193

Source: U.S. Drug Enforcement Administration, unpublished data from federal-wide Drug Seizure System.

No. 331. Authorized Intercepts of Communication—Summary: 1980 to 2002

[Data for jurisdictions with statutes authorizing or approving interception of wire or oral communication]

Item	1980	1985	1990	1994	1995	1996	1997	1998	1999	2000	2001	2002
Jurisdictions: [1]												
With wiretap statutes	28	32	40	41	41	46	45	45	45	45	46	47
Reporting interceptions	22	22	25	18	19	24	24	26	28	26	25	20
Intercept applications authorized	564	784	872	1,154	1,058	1,149	1,186	1,329	1,350	1,190	1,491	1,358
Intercept installations	524	722	812	1,100	1,024	1,035	1,094	1,245	1,277	1,139	1,405	1,273
Federal	79	235	321	549	527	574	563	562	595	472	481	490
State	445	487	491	551	497	461	531	683	682	667	924	783
Intercepted communications, average [2]	1,058	1,320	1,487	2,139	2,028	1,969	2,081	1,858	1,921	1,769	1,565	1,708
Incriminating	315	275	321	373	459	422	418	350	390	402	333	403
Persons arrested [3]	1,871	2,469	2,057	2,852	2,577	2,464	3,086	3,450	4,372	3,411	3,683	3,060
Convictions [3]	259	660	420	772	494	502	542	911	654	736	732	493
Major offense specified:												
Gambling	199	206	116	86	95	114	98	93	60	49	82	82
Drugs	282	434	520	876	732	821	870	955	978	894	1,167	1,052
Homicide and assault	13	25	21	19	30	41	31	55	62	72	52	58
Other	70	119	215	173	201	173	187	228	250	175	190	166

[1] Jurisdictions include federal government, states, and District of Columbia. [2] Average per authorized installation. [3] Based on information received from intercepts installed in year shown; additional arrests/convictions will occur in subsequent years but are not shown here.

Source: Administrative Office of the U.S. Courts, *Report on Applications for Orders Authorizing or Approving the Interception of Wire, Oral or Electronic Communications* (Wiretap Report), annual. See also <http://www.uscourts.gov/wiretap02/2002wttxt.pdf> (issued April 2003).

No. 332. Background Checks for Firearm Transfers: 1994 to 2001

[In thousands (37,911 represents 37,911,000), except rates. For "Interim period" of 1994 to November 29, 1998, covered handgun purchases from licensed firearm dealers; beginning November 29, 1998 (effective date for the Brady Handgun Violence Prevention Act, P.L. 103-159,1993) covers the transfer of both handguns and long guns from a federal firearms licensee, as well as purchases from pawnshops and retail gun shops]

Inquiries and rejections	1994-2001, period [1]	Interim period 1994	1995	1996	1997	1998 [2]	Permanent Brady 1999	2000	2001
Applications and rejections:									
Applications received	37,911	2,483	2,706	2,593	2,574	3,277	8,621	7,699	7,958
Applications rejected	840	62	41	70	69	90	204	153	151
Rejection rate	2.2	2.5	1.5	2.7	2.7	2.9	2.4	2.0	1.9

[1] Represents from the Inception of the Brady Act on March 1, 1994 to 2001. [2] For period January 1 to November 29, 1998. Counts are from the National Instant Criminal Background Check System and may include multiple transactions for the same application.

Source: U.S. Bureau of Justice Statistics, *Background Checks for Firearm Transfers, 2001*, Series NCJ 195235, September 2002.

Law Enforcement, Courts, and Prisons

No. 333. Firearm Use by Offenders: 1997

[In percent. Based on the Survey of Inmates in State and Federal Correctional Facilities]

Characteristic	Percent of prison inmates State	Percent of prison inmates Federal	Characteristic	Percent of prison inmates State	Percent of prison inmates Federal	Characteristic	Percent of prison inmates State	Percent of prison inmates Federal
TYPE OF FIREARM[1]			Property	3.1	2.9	Criminal history:		
Total	18.4	14.8	Drug	8.1	8.7	First-time offender	22.3	9.5
Handgun	15.3	12.8	Public order	19.1	27.3	Recidivist	17.2	18.4
Rifle	1.3	1.3	Gender:					
Shotgun	2.4	2.0	Male	19.1	15.5	Use of firearm [2]	100	100
			Female	7.3	6.2	Fired	49.1	12.8
INMATES WHO CARRIED FIREARMS			Age:			Killed/injured victim	22.8	5.0
			24 or younger	29.4	19.1	Other	26.3	7.8
Offense:			25 to 34	16.5	15.5	Brandished to	73.2	46.2
Violent	30.2	35.4	35 or older	14.8	13.6	Scare someone	48.6	29.3
						Defend self	41.1	24.9

[1] Percents of subtotals may not add to totals because inmates may have had more than one firearm. [2] Percents of subtotals may not add to totals because inmates may have used a firearm in more than one way.

Source: U.S. Bureau of Justice Statistics, *Firearm Use by Offenders*, Series NCJ 189369, November 2001. See also <http://www.ojp.usdoj.gov/bjs/pub/pdf/fuo.pdf>.

No. 334. General Purpose Law Enforcement Agencies—Number and Employment: 2000

[Includes both full-time and part-time employees. State police data are based on the 49 primary law enforcement agencies; Excludes agencies that perform primarily court-related duties]

Type of agency	Number of agencies [1]	Full-time Total	Full-time Sworn	Full-time Civilian	Part-time Total	Part-time Sworn	Part-time Civilian
2000, total	15,785	946,766	661,979	284,787	86,039	37,872	48,174
Local police	12,666	565,915	440,920	124,995	62,197	27,351	34,853
Sheriff	3,070	293,823	164,711	129,112	23,025	10,426	12,599
State police	49	87,028	56,348	30,680	817	95	722

[1] The number of agencies reported here is the result of a weighted sample and not an exact enumeration.

Source: U.S. Bureau of Justice Statistics, *Law Enforcement Management and Administrative Statistics, 2000*, Series NCJ 184481, November 2001.

No. 335. Casework Loads in DNA Laboratories: 1997 and 2000

[Based on the National Study of DNA (deoxyribonucleic acid) Laboratories' Survey which obtained data from 110 of the approximately 120 known public forensic DNA laboratories.

Case status	1997	2000	Percent change	Case status	1997	2000	Percent change
Work received				Backlog of work			
Casework [1]	20,793	31,394	51	Casework	6,800	15,981	135
Convicted offender [2]	115,681	177,184	53	Convicted offender	286,819	265,329	-7
Work analyzed				Full-time employees	672	893	33
Casework	14,289	24,790	73				
Convicted offender	44,810	148,347	231				

[1] Casework refers to cases received by forensic crime laboratories which involve a criminal incident under investigation. [2] Convicted offender samples are DNA samples collected from persons convicted of a crime, normally a violent crime or felony. The samples are to be analyzed, and the results are to be included in a DNA database.

Source: U.S. Bureau of Justice Statistics, *Survey of DNA Crime Laboratories, 2001*, Series NCJ 191191, January 2002.

No. 336. Law Enforcement Officers Killed and Assaulted: 1990 to 2001

[Covers officers killed feloniously and accidentally in line of duty; includes federal officers. For composition of regions, see map, inside front cover]

Item	1990	1994	1995	1996	1997	1998	1999	2000	2001 [1]
OFFICERS KILLED									
Total killed	133	141	133	112	132	142	107	135	220
Northeast	13	17	16	17	14	6	11	13	79
Midwest	20	30	19	21	25	19	17	33	27
South	69	54	63	46	55	70	56	67	69
West	23	31	32	18	31	36	22	19	38
Puerto Rico	8	9	2	10	7	9	1	3	7
Outlying areas, foreign countries	-	-	1	-	-	2	-	-	-
Feloniously killed	66	79	74	61	70	61	42	51	142
Firearms	57	78	62	57	67	58	41	47	61
Handgun	48	66	43	50	49	40	25	33	46
Rifle	8	8	14	6	12	17	11	10	11
Shotgun	1	4	5	1	6	1	5	4	4
Knife	3	-	2	1	2	1	-	1	-
Bomb	-	-	8	-	-	1	-	-	-
Personal weapons	2	-	-	1	1	-	-	-	1
Other	4	1	2	2	-	1	1	3	80
Accidentally killed	67	62	59	51	62	81	65	84	78
ASSAULTS									
Population (1,000) [2]	197,426	215,501	191,759	165,264	184,825	193,098	196,315	204,599	212,019
Number of—									
Agencies represented	9,343	10,246	8,503	7,803	8,120	8,153	8,174	8,940	9,688
Police officers	410,131	469,426	428,379	371,964	411,015	452,361	470,145	452,531	464,515
Total assaulted	72,091	64,967	57,762	46,608	52,149	60,673	55,026	58,398	56,666
Firearm	3,651	3,174	2,354	1,878	2,110	2,126	1,783	1,749	1,837
Knife or cutting instrument	1,647	1,510	1,356	871	971	1,098	990	1,015	1,176
Other dangerous weapon	7,423	7,197	6,414	5,069	5,800	7,415	7,392	8,132	8,190
Hands, fists, feet, etc	59,370	53,086	47,638	38,790	43,268	50,034	44,861	47,502	45,463

- Represents zero. [1] The 72 officers feloniously slain during the events of September 11, 2001, are included in data for 2001. [2] Represents the number of persons covered by agencies shown.

Source: U.S. Federal Bureau of Investigation, *Law Enforcement Officers Killed and Assaulted*, annual.

No. 337. U.S. Supreme Court—Cases Filed and Disposition: 1980 to 2001

[Statutory term of court begins first Monday in **October**]

Action	1980	1990	1995	1996	1997	1998	1999	2000	2001
Total cases on docket	5,144	6,316	7,565	7,602	7,692	8,083	8,445	8,965	9,176
Appellate cases on docket	2,749	2,351	2,456	2,430	2,432	2,387	2,413	2,305	2,210
From prior term	527	365	361	375	347	326	321	351	324
Docketed during present term	2,222	1,986	2,095	2,055	2,085	2,061	2,092	1,954	1,886
Cases acted upon [1]	2,324	2,042	2,130	2,124	2,142	2,092	2,096	2,024	1,932
Granted review	167	114	92	74	75	72	78	85	82
Denied, dismissed, or withdrawn	1,999	1,802	1,945	1,955	1,990	1,940	1,958	1,842	1,751
Summarily decided	90	81	62	66	36	44	34	63	57
Cases not acted upon	425	309	326	306	290	295	317	281	278
Pauper cases on docket	2,371	3,951	5,098	5,165	5,253	5,689	6,024	6,651	6,958
Cases acted upon	2,027	3,436	4,514	4,613	4,616	4,951	5,273	5,736	6,139
Granted review	17	27	13	13	14	9	14	14	6
Denied, dismissed, or withdrawn	1,968	3,369	4,439	4,582	4,581	4,926	5,239	5,658	6,114
Summarily decided	32	28	55	15	14	11	16	61	13
Cases not acted upon	344	515	584	552	637	738	751	915	819
Original cases on docket	24	14	11	7	7	7	8	9	8
Cases disposed of during term	7	3	5	2	1	2	-	2	1
Total cases available for argument	264	201	145	140	138	124	124	138	137
Cases disposed of	162	131	93	92	97	94	87	89	90
Cases argued	154	125	90	90	96	90	83	86	88
Cases dismissed or remanded without argument	8	6	3	2	1	4	4	3	2
Cases remaining	102	70	52	48	41	30	37	49	47
Cases decided by signed opinion	144	121	87	87	93	84	79	83	85
Cases decided by per curiam opinion	8	4	3	3	1	4	2	4	3
Number of signed opinions	123	112	75	80	91	75	74	77	76

- Represents zero. [1] Includes cases granted review and carried over to next term, not shown separately.

Source: Office of the Clerk, Supreme Court of the United States, unpublished data.

No. 338. U.S. District Courts—Civil Cases Commenced and Pending: 1999 to 2002

[For years ending June 30]

Type of case	Cases commenced					Cases pending			
	1999	2000	2001	2002	1999	2000	2001	2002
Cases total [1]	251,511	263,049	253,354	268,071	246,920	249,692	251,335	270,667
Contract actions [1]	46,721	54,494	45,438	36,845	35,415	38,262	35,685	33,237
Recovery of overpayments [2]	18,822	25,636	16,116	6,737	9,733	12,107	8,987	5,342
Real property actions	5,787	6,481	7,296	7,731	3,931	4,249	5,458	6,485
Tort actions	39,785	40,877	34,071	56,565	63,683	63,116	60,320	76,907
Personal injury	35,962	36,867	30,194	52,654	59,899	59,232	56,459	72,962
Personal injury product liability [1]	17,196	15,349	12,569	35,074	31,927	31,772	29,953	46,264
Asbestos	7,413	7,893	5,656	24,844	1,686	4,949	6,247	21,045
Other personal injury	18,766	21,518	17,625	17,580	27,972	27,460	26,506	26,698
Personal property damage	3,823	4,010	3,877	3,911	3,784	3,884	3,861	3,945
Actions under statutes [1]	159,205	161,187	166,535	166,920	158,163	144,053	149,862	154,027
Civil rights [1]	41,453	41,226	40,979	40,172	45,348	44,259	43,703	43,589
Employment	22,948	21,404	21,121	20,881	26,043	24,456	23,803	23,778
Bankruptcy suits	3,875	3,378	3,012	3,792	2,597	2,555	2,216	2,921
Commerce (ICC rates, etc.)	650	1,007	554	578	486	444	459	453
Environmental matters	882	894	1,794	848	1,406	1,355	2,264	2,134
Prisoner petitions	56,037	57,706	59,159	55,596	42,302	43,560	46,157	44,210
Forfeiture and penalty	2,207	2,246	2,143	2,062	1,787	1,772	1,694	1,787
Labor laws	14,325	14,229	14,880	17,706	11,265	11,267	11,484	14,084
Protected property rights [3]	8,082	8,745	8,143	8,500	7,344	7,858	7,491	8,094
Securities commodities and exchanges	2,684	2,500	3,152	3,559	3,538	3,578	4,187	4,659
Social security laws	14,511	14,365	17,530	17,868	14,407	13,667	16,182	17,489
Tax suits	1,280	938	961	1,147	1,254	1,068	971	1,115
Freedom of information	350	335	350	284	386	380	371	348

[1] Includes other types not shown separately. [2] Includes enforcement of judgments in student loan cases, and overpayments of veterans benefits. [3] Includes copyright, patent, and trademark rights.

Source: Administrative Office of the U.S. Courts, *Statistical Tables for the Federal Judiciary*, annual.

No. 339. U.S. District Courts—Offenders Convicted and Sentenced to Prison and Length of Sentence: 2000

Most serious offense of conviction	Offenders convicted	Convicted offenders sentenced to prison	Mean length of sentence (mo.)	Most serious offense of conviction	Offenders convicted	Convicted offenders sentenced to prison	Mean length of sentence (mo.)
Total [1]	68,156	50,451	56.7	Possession	1,931	1,719	80.8
Violent offenses	2,557	2,360	86.5	Trafficking and manufacturing	22,275	20,633	75.1
Property offenses	12,454	7,462	24.2	Public-order offenses	19,906	16,896	45.8
Fraudulent offenses [2]	10,396	6,272	22.5	Regulatory offenses	1,376	647	28.4
Embezzlement	917	506	14.8	Other offenses	18,530	16,249	46.5
Fraud [3]	8,177	5,008	23.5	Weapons	4,196	3,834	91.4
Forgery	86	41	19.1	Immigration	11,125	10,073	29.5
Other offenses [2]	2,058	1,190	33.2	Tax law violations [4]	655	355	18.5
Larceny	1,394	689	27.3	Misdemeanors	8,961	1,356	10.4
Drug offenses [2]	24,206	22,352	75.5				

[1] Total may include offenders for whom offense category could not be determined. [2] Includes offenses not shown separately. [3] Excludes tax fraud. [4] Includes tax fraud.

Source: U.S. Bureau of Justice Statistics, *Compendium of Federal Justice Statistics, 2000*, Series NCJ 194067, August 2002.

No. 340. Federal Prosecutions of Public Corruption: 1980 to 2001

[As of Dec. 31. Prosecution of persons who have corrupted public office in violation of Federal Criminal Statutes]

Prosecution status	1980	1985	1990	1993	1994	1995	1996	1997	1998	1999	2000	2001
Total: [1] Indicted	727	1,157	1,176	1,371	1,165	1,051	984	1,057	1,174	1,134	1,000	1,087
Convicted	602	997	1,084	1,362	969	878	902	853	1,014	1,065	938	920
Awaiting trial	213	256	300	403	332	323	244	327	340	329	327	437
Federal officials: Indicted	123	563	615	627	571	527	456	459	442	480	441	502
Convicted	131	470	583	595	488	438	459	392	414	460	422	414
Awaiting trial	16	90	103	133	124	120	64	83	85	101	92	131
State officials: Indicted	72	79	96	113	99	61	109	51	91	115	92	95
Convicted	51	66	79	133	97	61	83	49	58	80	91	61
Awaiting trial	28	20	28	39	17	23	40	20	37	44	37	75
Local officials: Indicted	247	248	257	309	248	236	219	255	277	237	211	224
Convicted	168	221	225	272	202	191	190	169	264	219	183	184
Awaiting trial	82	49	98	132	96	89	60	118	90	95	89	110

[1] Includes individuals who are neither public officials nor employees but who were involved with public officials or employees in violating the law, not shown separately.

Source: U.S. Department of Justice, *Federal Prosecutions of Corrupt Public Officials, 1970-1980* and *Report to Congress on the Activities and Operations of the Public Integrity Section*, annual.

No. 341. Per Capita Justice Expenditure and Employment of State and Local Governments by State: 1999

[State and local expenditure and employment data per 10,000 population estimated as of July 1]

State	Expenditure per capita (dollars)				Full-time equivalent justice employment per 10,000 population [1]			
	Total justice system	Police protection	Judicial and legal	Corrections	Total justice system	Police protection	Judicial and legal	Corrections
United States	442.1	189.8	89.9	162.4	67.4	30.2	13.3	23.9
Alabama	295.0	145.3	57.9	91.7	55.2	28.1	11.1	15.9
Alaska	724.9	283.4	195.1	246.4	70.1	26.9	20.9	22.3
Arizona	472.4	201.8	105.0	165.6	73.0	30.8	17.7	24.6
Arkansas	279.7	126.2	48.4	105.1	54.9	28.5	6.8	19.5
California	602.9	240.9	169.2	192.8	65.1	28.0	14.7	22.4
Colorado	438.3	180.9	74.3	183.1	61.2	28.4	12.5	20.4
Connecticut	455.0	193.6	107.8	153.6	68.4	30.7	12.0	25.7
Delaware	561.1	194.0	109.8	257.3	79.7	29.8	20.1	29.8
District of Columbia	1,212.3	592.1	66.8	553.4	139.6	78.8	6.5	54.3
Florida	503.1	224.2	84.0	194.9	79.0	33.3	17.2	28.5
Georgia	364.8	144.6	63.1	157.2	70.7	28.2	10.9	31.5
Hawaii	429.7	182.5	136.4	110.8	70.6	28.9	22.8	18.9
Idaho	384.2	149.1	75.7	159.3	55.9	25.2	10.7	20.0
Illinois	418.2	224.4	70.6	123.3	69.7	36.4	13.2	20.1
Indiana	283.2	124.5	50.0	108.7	53.6	26.7	9.5	17.4
Iowa	314.7	135.8	82.7	96.2	48.6	23.7	10.9	14.1
Kansas	355.0	161.6	74.4	119.0	67.8	33.0	13.4	21.5
Kentucky	302.8	109.6	69.2	124.0	53.5	24.1	14.2	15.2
Louisiana	410.7	183.3	76.3	151.2	76.7	34.3	15.1	27.3
Maine	257.4	122.5	50.9	84.0	46.2	25.6	6.6	14.0
Maryland	451.1	191.2	87.8	172.1	73.3	33.2	13.1	27.0
Massachusetts	464.8	218.7	99.8	146.3	66.1	35.7	11.0	19.4
Michigan	439.3	172.3	83.2	183.7	59.6	24.9	11.5	23.2
Minnesota	363.6	166.8	85.2	111.6	48.5	21.5	11.5	15.6
Mississippi	281.7	135.7	53.6	92.5	59.7	30.0	10.2	19.4
Missouri	324.5	153.9	56.2	114.4	68.3	30.7	13.0	24.6
Montana	339.5	134.5	71.0	134.0	52.0	24.2	11.0	16.8
Nebraska	284.0	128.8	54.3	100.9	53.6	25.9	10.4	17.2
Nevada	542.7	231.7	107.8	203.2	70.4	30.7	16.2	23.5
New Hampshire	299.0	141.8	69.7	87.4	49.1	26.4	9.2	13.5
New Jersey	518.4	236.6	113.9	167.9	82.5	39.3	24.4	18.8
New Mexico	440.6	194.1	85.2	161.3	75.4	29.3	15.9	30.2
New York	630.1	292.4	113.4	224.2	92.6	44.7	15.6	32.4
North Carolina	350.9	155.4	58.1	137.5	64.4	27.6	8.2	28.5
North Dakota	243.3	102.9	66.2	74.3	46.2	22.3	11.6	12.3
Ohio	424.2	179.4	95.6	149.3	68.3	28.0	17.6	22.6
Oklahoma	301.6	119.9	51.1	130.6	63.1	31.6	11.1	20.4
Oregon	463.5	184.3	74.6	204.6	60.9	24.6	13.6	22.8
Pennsylvania	424.4	171.2	79.6	173.7	60.2	25.0	14.2	20.9
Rhode Island	408.1	179.2	94.7	134.2	58.1	29.2	11.8	17.2
South Carolina	330.9	147.0	43.9	140.0	69.4	33.3	8.8	27.3
South Dakota	268.0	115.3	49.2	103.5	49.4	22.1	9.8	17.5
Tennessee	323.3	151.0	70.2	102.1	58.9	29.6	9.6	19.8
Texas	387.6	148.5	60.0	179.2	71.1	27.8	10.5	32.8
Utah	400.4	161.4	80.7	158.4	53.3	24.2	11.7	17.5
Vermont	248.1	102.8	81.2	64.2	47.3	21.8	10.3	15.1
Virginia	388.3	156.6	67.9	163.8	66.1	25.4	9.6	31.0
Washington	418.3	162.0	83.8	172.5	55.8	23.3	12.5	20.0
West Virginia	228.0	87.3	55.7	85.0	40.0	20.2	11.3	8.5
Wisconsin	448.6	196.6	79.3	172.8	60.2	28.6	10.2	21.4
Wyoming	482.6	189.2	100.9	192.5	69.0	34.0	14.1	21.0

[1] Population based on Census Bureau, Current Population Reports, Series P-25, No. 1045, as of March 1999.

Source: U.S. Bureau of Justice Statistics, *Justice Expenditure and Employment in the United States, 1999*, Series NCJ 191746, February 2002. See also <http://www.ojp.usdoj.gov/bjs/pub/pdf/jeeus99.pdf>.

No. 342. Delinquency Cases Disposed by Juvenile Courts by Reason for Referral: 1990 to 2000

[In thousands (1,317 represents 1,317,000), except rate. A delinquency offense is an act committed by a juvenile for which an adult could be prosecuted in a criminal court. Disposition of a case involves taking a definite action such as waiving the case to criminal court, dismissing the case, placing the youth on probation, placing the youth in a facility for delinquents, or such actions as fines, restitution, and community service]

Reason for referral	1990	1991	1992	1993	1994	1995	1996	1997	1998	1999	2000
All delinquency offenses	1,317	1,414	1,482	1,522	1,666	1,768	1,796	1,811	1,743	1,667	1,612
Case rate [1]	51.4	54.0	55.2	55.3	59.4	61.9	62.0	61.7	58.8	55.5	52.5
Violent offenses	94	106	114	118	132	137	128	109	100	86	81
Criminal homicide	2	2	2	3	3	3	3	2	2	2	2
Forcible rape	5	6	6	7	7	7	6	6	5	4	5
Robbery	28	32	33	35	38	40	38	34	29	25	22
Aggravated assault	59	66	72	73	84	87	81	67	64	55	52
Property offenses	773	849	862	834	868	888	874	846	779	703	661
Burglary	564	615	619	594	609	630	621	601	539	481	452
Larceny	145	155	160	151	146	142	145	142	131	113	109
Motor vehicle theft	341	382	382	372	392	424	413	398	355	321	299
Arson	70	71	70	62	62	54	54	52	45	38	37
Delinquency offenses	660	692	749	810	925	1,001	1,048	1,101	1,103	1,100	1,079
Simple assault	132	143	162	177	198	219	223	248	254	255	248
Vandalism	99	113	119	119	130	127	123	118	117	111	107
Drug law violations	71	65	73	92	131	166	185	194	194	191	193
Obstruction of justice	80	74	78	94	110	122	150	166	169	172	179
Other [2]	278	297	317	328	356	368	367	375	370	371	352

[1] Number of cases disposed per 1,000 youth (ages 10 to 17) at risk.   [2] Includes such offenses as stolen property offenses, trespassing, weapons offenses, other sex offenses, liquor law violations, disorderly conduct, and miscellaneous offenses.

Source: National Center for Juvenile Justice, Pittsburgh, PA, *Juvenile Court Statistics*, annual. See also <http://www.ojjdp.ncjrs.org/ojstatbb/index.html>.

No. 343. Delinquency Cases and Case Rates by Sex and Race: 1992 to 2000

[A delinquency offense is an act committed by a juvenile for which an adult could be prosecuted in a criminal court. Disposition of a case involves taking a definite action such as waiving the case to criminal court, dismissing the case, placing the youth on probation, placing the youth in a facility for delinquents, or such actions as fines, restitution, and community service. Offenses may not add to total sex and race categories due to rounding]

Sex, race, and offense	Number of cases disposed 1992	1999	2000	Case rate [1] 1992	1999	2000
Male, total	1,195,200	1,270,000	1,216,500	86.6	82.4	77.2
Person	243,800	281,600	267,700	17.7	18.3	17.0
Property	694,500	535,400	499,400	50.3	34.8	31.7
Drugs	64,000	160,900	160,700	4.6	10.4	10.2
Public order	193,000	292,100	288,700	14.0	19.0	18.3
Female, total	286,900	397,100	396,000	21.9	27.2	26.5
Person	64,900	103,800	101,300	5.0	7.1	6.8
Property	167,800	167,700	162,000	12.8	11.5	10.8
Drugs	8,700	30,400	32,400	0.7	2.1	2.2
Public order	45,600	95,300	100,300	3.5	6.5	6.7
White, total	975,600	1,137,400	1,111,100	45.3	47.9	46.0
Person	177,300	241,700	229,500	8.2	10.2	9.5
Property	607,000	492,800	462,700	28.2	20.8	19.2
Drugs	37,500	135,600	145,800	1.7	5.7	6.0
Public order	153,800	267,300	273,200	7.1	11.3	11.3
Black, total	453,500	473,600	445,000	112.1	102.2	92.5
Person	121,700	132,400	128,100	30.1	28.6	26.6
Property	221,300	181,400	171,200	54.7	39.2	35.6
Drugs	33,500	51,300	42,600	8.3	11.1	8.9
Public order	77,100	108,500	103,100	19.1	23.4	21.4
Other races, total	53,000	56,100	56,400	40.5	33.9	32.3
Person	9,700	11,200	11,500	7.4	6.8	6.6
Property	34,000	28,900	27,500	26.0	17.4	15.8
Drugs	1,600	4,400	4,800	1.2	2.6	2.7
Public order	7,600	11,600	12,700	5.8	7.0	7.3

[1] Cases per 1,000 youth (ages 10 to 17) at risk.

Source: National Center for Juvenile Justice, Pittsburgh, PA, *Juvenile Court Statistics*, annual. See also <http://www/ojjdp.ncjrs.org/ojstatbb/index.html>.

No. 344. Child Abuse and Neglect Cases Substantiated and Indicated—Victim Characteristics: 1990 to 2001

[Based on reports alleging child abuse and neglect that were referred for investigation/assessment by the respective child protective services agency in each state. The reporting period may be either calendar or fiscal year. Children are counted each time they were subjects of an investigation report. In 2000, the data are from 49 states. Victims are children whose alleged maltreatments have been substantiated, indicated, or assesed as maltreatments. A substantiated case represents a type of investigation disposition that determines that there is sufficient evidence under state law to conclude that maltreatment occurred or that the child is at risk of maltreatment. An indicated case represents a type of disposition that concludes that there was a reason to suspect maltreatment had occurred. An alternative response-victim case represents a type of disposition that identifies child as a victim within the alternative response system]

Item	1990 Number	1990 Percent	1999 Number	1999 Percent	2000 Number	2000 Percent	2001 Number	2001 Percent
TYPES OF SUBSTANTIATED MALTREATMENT								
Victims, total [1]	690,658	(X)	783,632	(X)	862,922	(X)	903,141	(X)
Neglect	338,770	49.1	439,094	56.0	515,621	59.8	516,646	57.2
Physical abuse	186,801	27.0	167,703	21.4	167,307	19.4	168,284	18.6
Sexual abuse	119,506	17.3	88,801	11.3	87,567	10.2	86,834	9.6
Emotional maltreatment	45,621	6.6	59,842	7.6	66,968	7.8	61,779	6.8
Medical neglect	(NA)	(NA)	18,809	2.4	25,486	3.0	17,664	2.0
SEX OF VICTIM								
Victims, total	742,519	100.0	779,787	100.0	862,922	100.0	903,141	100.0
Male	323,339	43.5	371,588	47.7	412,373	47.8	433,108	48.0
Female	369,919	49.8	402,051	51.6	444,977	51.6	465,433	51.5
AGE OF VICTIM								
Victims, total	731,282	100.0	780,145	100.0	862,922	100.0	903,141	100.0
1 year and younger	97,101	13.3	109,597	14.1	132,791	15.4	140,786	15.6
2 to 5 years old	172,791	23.6	186,178	23.9	205,301	23.8	215,745	23.9
6 to 9 years old	157,681	21.6	196,639	25.2	211,644	24.5	217,803	24.1
10 to 13 years old	135,130	18.5	157,879	20.2	175,681	20.4	189,262	21.0
14 to 17 years old	103,383	14.1	117,436	15.1	125,946	14.6	134,099	14.9
18 and over	4,880	0.7	4,101	0.5	992	0.1	1,556	0.2

NA Not available.   X Not applicable.   [1] A child may be a victim of more than one maltreatment. Therefore, the total for this item adds up to more than 100 percent.

No. 345. Child Abuse and Neglect Cases Reported and Investigated by State: 2001

[See headnote, Table 344]

State	Population under 18 years old	Number of reports [1]	Number of children subject of an investigation [2]	Number of child victims [3]	State	Population under 18 years old	Number of reports [1]	Number of children subject of an investigation [2]	Number of child victims [3]
U.S. [4]	72,941,000	1,789,324	3,058,253	903,141	MO	1,431,000	51,752	80,743	9,237
					MT	230,000	9,281	15,032	1,935
AL	1,123,000	20,325	29,911	9,229	NE	450,000	6,602	10,707	3,314
AK	193,000	18,422	18,422	15,947	NV	538,000	12,516	22,529	4,939
AZ	1,410,000	33,789	54,166	5,389	NH	314,000	8,426	12,132	1,102
AR	683,000	18,504	25,655	6,927	NJ	2,095,000	39,373	70,733	8,514
CA	9,397,000	247,282	485,911	128,251					
CO	1,128,000	21,169	30,983	4,837	NM	511,000	13,889	23,314	6,929
CT	843,000	31,224	47,378	12,120	NY	4,677,000	149,892	251,164	77,860
DE	197,000	5,478	8,437	1,666	NC	1,991,000	60,888	122,354	36,601
DC	114,000	4,513	7,332	2,908	ND	159,000	4,028	6,963	1,359
FL	3,732,000	151,039	266,502	124,134	OH	2,882,000	70,079	113,720	51,031
GA	2,217,000	63,488	114,653	36,744	OK	893,000	36,566	63,520	13,698
					OR	856,000	16,647	25,618	9,011
HI	298,000	3,788	7,334	3,982	PA	2,912,000	23,012	23,012	4,784
ID	375,000	7,076	9,959	3,557	RI	249,000	7,451	11,369	3,319
IL	3,251,000	59,139	142,967	27,557	SC	1,018,000	18,884	36,836	11,199
IN	1,577,000	35,698	53,503	21,128					
IA	731,000	25,112	37,704	12,792	SD	203,000	8,311	9,984	3,707
KS	714,000	4,935	(NA)	7,308	TN	1,406,000	35,097	50,870	9,571
KY	997,000	37,080	56,478	16,544	TX	6,009,000	120,370	197,838	44,623
LA	1,217,000	23,320	38,085	11,158	UT	730,000	18,159	28,485	10,200
ME	303,000	4,955	9,163	4,355	VT	148,000	2,872	3,558	1,139
MD	1,372,000	18,248	(NA)	19,750	VA	1,759,000	20,950	37,988	9,873
					WA	1,532,000	22,709	35,491	6,010
MA	1,501,000	37,030	61,329	33,218	WV	399,000	16,467	26,812	7,907
MI	2,598,000	66,914	172,281	28,475	WI	1,373,000	40,216	40,216	11,917
MN	1,298,000	16,384	23,842	9,840	WY	129,000	2,705	4,184	990
MS	778,000	17,270	31,086	4,556					

NA Not available.   [1] The number of investigations includes assessments. The number of investigations is based on the total number of investigations that received a disposition in 2001.   [2] The number of children subject of an investigation of assessment is based on the total number of children for whom an alleged maltreatment was substantiated, indicated, or assesed to have occurred or the child was at risk of occurrence.   [3] Victims are defined as children subject of a substantiated, indicated, or alternative response-victim maltreatment.   [4] Includes estimates for states that did not report.

Source of Tables 344 and 345: U.S. Department of Health and Human Services, Administration on Children, Youth, and Families. *Child Maltreatment, 2001* (Washington, DC: U.S. Government Printing Office, 2003).

No. 346. Characteristics of Missing Children: 1999

Characteristic	Estimated number of children	Percent	Characteristic	Estimated number of children	Percent
RUNAWAY CHILDREN			FAMILY ABDUCTED CHILDREN		
Characteristic of episode:					
Season:			Characteristic of child:		
Winter	335,400	20	Age:		
Spring	333,600	20	0 to 3 years old	43,400	21
Summer	655,100	39	3 to 6 years old	47,100	23
Fall	343,300	20	6 to 12 years old	71,000	35
Number of miles traveled from home:			12 to 15 years old	35,200	17
			15 to 18 years old	7,200	4
2 or less	139,900	8			
3 to 10	503,100	30			
12 to 50	521,900	31	Sex:		
52 to 100	160,100	10	Male	100,300	49
More than 101	210,600	13	Female	103,500	51
No information	147,300	9			
Child left the state:			Race/ethnicity:		
Yes	147,600	9	White	119,400	59
No	1,393,000	83	Black	23,900	12
No information	142,300	8	Hispanic	40,600	20
Duration			Other	16,200	8
8 hours to 23 hours	307,400	18			
25 hours to 6 days	975,700	58	Family structure:		
2 week to less than 1 month	248,000	15	Single parent	85,500	42
			One parent and partner	35,300	17
Episode outcome:			Relative or foster parent	30,300	15
Child returned	1,676,200	99			

Source: Office of Justice Programs, Office of Juvenile Justice and Delinquency Prevention, *National Incidence Studies of Missing, Abducted, Runaway, and Thrownaway Children*, October 2002.

No. 347. Jail Inmates by Sex, Race, and Hispanic Origin: 1990 to 2001

[As of June 30. Excludes federal and state prisons or other correctional institutions; institutions exclusively for juveniles; state-operated jails in Alaska, Connecticut, Delaware, Hawaii, Rhode Island, and Vermont; and other facilities which retain persons for less than 48 hours. Data based on the Annual Survey of Jails, which is a sample survey and subject to sampling variability. Due to rounding, inmates may not add to total]

Characteristic	1990	1995	1996	1997	1998	1999	2000	2001
Total inmates	405,320	507,044	518,492	567,079	592,462	605,943	621,149	631,240
Male	365,821	448,000	454,700	498,678	520,581	528,998	543,120	551,007
Female	37,198	51,300	55,700	59,296	63,791	67,487	70,414	72,621
Juveniles	2,301	7,800	8,100	9,105	8,090	9,458	7,615	7,613
White non-Hispanic	169,600	203,300	215,700	230,300	244,900	249,900	260,500	271,700
Black non-Hispanic	172,300	220,600	213,100	237,900	244,000	251,800	256,300	256,200
Hispanic	58,100	74,400	80,900	88,900	91,800	93,800	94,100	93,000
Other [1]	5,400	8,800	8,800	10,000	11,800	10,400	10,200	10,300

[1] Includes American Indians, Alaska Natives, Asians, and Pacific Islanders.
Source: U.S. Bureau of Justice Statistics, through 1994, *Jail Inmates*, annual; beginning 1995, *Prison and Jail Inmates at Midyear*, annual.

No. 348. State and Federal Correctional Facilities—Inmates and Staff: 1990 to 2000

[Covers all state and federal correctional institutions or places of confinement such as prisons, prison farms, boot camps, and community based halfway houses and work release centers. Excludes jails and other regional detention centers, private facilities, facilities for the military, Immigration and Naturalization Service, Bureau of Indian Affairs, U.S. Marshal Service, and correctional hospital wards not operated by correctional authorities]

Characteristic	1990	1995	2000	Characteristic	1990	1995	2000
FACILITIES				INMATES			
Total	1,287	1,500	1,668	Total	715,649	1,023,572	1,305,253
Type of facility:				Male	675,624	961,210	1,219,225
Confinement	1,037	1,196	1,280	Female	40,025	62,362	86,028
Community	250	304	388	Type of facility:			
Federal	80	125	84	Confinement	698,570	992,333	1,256,398
State	1,207	1,375	1,584	Community	17,079	31,239	48,855
Size of facility:				Federal	56,821	81,930	110,974
Fewer than 500	816	854	861	State	658,828	941,642	1,194,279
500-999	260	286	305	Custody level:			
1,000-2,499	185	306	437	Maximum/close/high	150,205	202,174	244,797
2,500 or more	26	54	65	Medium	292,372	415,688	509,558
Age of facility:				Minimum/low	219,907	366,227	474,353
Less than 10 years	314	497	444	Not classified	53,165	39,483	76,545
10-19 years old	163	273	398	STAFF			
20-49 years old	373	366	380				
50-99 years old	379	310	290	Total	264,201	347,320	430,033
100 years old or more	58	45	81	Federal	18,451	25,379	32,700
Not reported	-	9	75	State	245,750	321,941	397,333

- Represents zero.
Source: U.S. Bureau of Justice Statistics, *Census of State and Federal Correctional Facilities, 2000*.

No. 349. Prisoners Under Jurisdiction of State and Federal Correctional Authorities—Summary by State: 1980 to 2001

[For years ending December 31]

State	1980	1990	2000	2001, advance Total	Percent change, 2000-2001	State	1980	1990	2000	2001, advance Total	Percent change, 2000-2001
U.S.[1]	329,821	773,919	1,391,261	1,406,519	1.1	MO	5,726	14,943	27,543	28,757	4.4
						MT	739	1,425	3,105	3,328	7.2
AL	6,543	15,665	26,332	26,741	1.6	NE	1,446	2,403	3,895	3,937	1.1
AK[2]	822	2,622	4,173	4,571	9.5	NV	1,839	5,322	10,063	10,233	1.7
AZ[3]	4,372	14,261	26,510	27,710	4.5	NH	326	1,342	2,257	2,392	6.0
AR	2,911	7,322	11,915	12,594	5.7	NJ	5,884	21,128	29,784	28,142	-5.5
CA	24,569	97,309	163,001	159,444	-2.2	NM	1,279	3,187	5,342	5,668	6.1
CO	2,629	7,671	16,833	17,448	3.7	NY	21,815	54,895	70,199	67,533	-3.8
CT[2]	4,308	10,500	18,355	19,196	4.6	NC	15,513	18,411	31,266	31,979	2.3
DE[2]	1,474	3,471	6,921	7,003	1.2	ND	253	483	1,076	1,120	4.1
DC[2 5]	3,145	9,947	7,456	2,692	-63.9	OH	13,489	31,822	45,833	45,281	-1.2
FL[3]	20,735	44,387	71,319	72,404	1.5	OK[4]	4,796	12,285	23,181	22,780	-1.7
GA[3]	12,178	22,411	44,232	45,937	3.9	OR	3,177	6,492	10,580	11,410	7.8
HI[2]	985	2,533	5,053	5,431	7.5	PA	8,171	22,290	36,847	38,062	3.3
ID[3]	817	1,961	5,535	6,006	8.5	RI[2]	813	2,392	3,286	3,241	-1.4
IL[3]	11,899	27,516	45,281	44,348	-2.1	SC	7,862	17,319	21,778	22,576	3.7
IN[3]	6,683	12,736	20,125	20,966	4.2	SD	635	1,341	2,616	2,790	6.7
IA[3]	2,481	3,967	7,955	7,962	0.1	TN	7,022	10,388	22,166	23,671	6.8
KS	2,494	5,775	8,344	8,577	2.8	TX	29,892	50,042	166,719	162,070	-2.8
KY	3,588	9,023	14,919	15,424	3.4	UT	932	2,496	5,637	5,339	-5.3
LA	8,889	18,599	35,207	35,810	1.7	VT[2]	480	1,049	1,697	1,741	2.6
ME	814	1,523	1,679	1,704	1.5	VA	8,920	17,593	30,168	31,662	5.0
MD	7,731	17,848	23,538	23,752	0.9	WA	4,399	7,995	14,915	15,159	1.6
MA[3 4]	3,185	8,345	10,722	10,588	-1.2	WV	1,257	1,565	3,856	4,215	9.3
MI[3 4]	15,124	34,267	47,718	48,849	2.4	WI	3,980	7,465	20,754	21,533	3.8
MN	2,001	3,176	6,238	6,606	5.9	WY	534	1,110	1,680	1,684	0.2
MS	3,902	8,375	20,241	21,460	6.0						

[1] State-level data excludes federal inmates. [2] Includes both jail and prison inmates (state has combined jail and prison system). [3] Numbers are for custody rather than jurisdiction counts. [4] 1980 and 1990, data are for custody counts; thereafter, jurisdiction counts are reported. [5] The transfer of responsibility for sentenced felons from the District of Columbia to the Federal system was completed by year end 2001. Since June 30, 2000, the inmate population in the District of Columbia has dropped by 5,825 inmates. Approximately 58 percent of the growth in the Federal system in the last 6 months of 2001 was the result of this transfer of responsibility.

Source: U.S. Bureau of Justice Statistics, Prisoners in 2001, Series NCJ 195189; and earlier reports.

No. 350. Adults on Probation, in Jail or Prison, or on Parole: 1980 to 2001

[As of December 31, except jail counts as of June 30]

Year	Total[1]	Percent of adult population	Probation	Jail	Prison	Parole	Male	Female
1980	1,840,400	(NA)	1,118,097	[2]182,288	319,598	220,438	(NA)	(NA)
1981	2,006,600	(NA)	1,225,934	[2]195,085	360,029	225,539	(NA)	(NA)
1982	2,192,600	(NA)	1,357,264	207,853	402,914	224,604	(NA)	(NA)
1983	2,475,100	(NA)	1,582,947	221,815	423,898	246,440	(NA)	(NA)
1984	2,689,200	(NA)	1,740,948	233,018	448,264	266,992	(NA)	(NA)
1985	3,011,400	1.7	1,968,712	254,986	487,593	300,203	2,606,000	405,500
1986	3,239,400	1.8	2,114,621	272,735	526,436	325,638	2,829,100	410,300
1987	3,459,600	1.9	2,247,158	294,092	562,814	355,505	3,021,000	438,600
1988	3,714,100	2.0	2,356,483	341,893	607,766	407,977	3,223,000	491,100
1989	4,055,600	2.2	2,522,125	393,303	683,367	456,803	3,501,600	554,000
1990	4,348,000	2.3	2,670,234	403,019	743,382	531,407	3,746,300	601,700
1991	4,535,600	2.4	2,728,472	424,129	792,535	590,442	3,913,000	622,600
1992	4,762,600	2.5	2,811,611	441,781	850,566	658,601	4,050,300	712,300
1993	4,944,000	2.6	2,903,061	455,500	909,381	676,100	4,215,800	728,200
1994	5,141,300	2.7	2,981,022	479,800	990,147	690,371	4,377,400	763,900
1995	5,335,100	2.8	3,077,861	499,300	1,078,542	679,421	4,513,000	822,100
1996	5,482,700	2.8	3,164,996	510,400	1,127,528	679,733	4,629,900	852,800
1997	5,725,800	2.9	3,296,513	557,974	1,176,564	694,787	4,825,300	900,500
1998	6,126,100	3.1	3,670,441	584,372	1,224,469	696,385	(NA)	(NA)
1999	6,331,300	3.1	3,779,922	596,485	1,287,172	714,457	(NA)	(NA)
2000	6,437,500	3.1	3,826,209	613,534	1,316,333	723,898	(NA)	(NA)
2001, advance	6,585,200	3.1	3,932,751	623,628	1,330,980	731,147	(NA)	(NA)

NA Not available. [1] Totals may not add due to individuals having multiple correctional statuses. [2] Estimated.

Source: U.S. Bureau of Justice Statistics, Correctional Populations in the United States, annual.

No. 351. Federal and State Prisoners by Sex: 1980 to 2001

[Prisoners, as of December 31. Includes all persons under jurisdiction of federal and state authorities rather than those in the custody of such authorities. Represents inmates sentenced to maximum term of more than a year]

Year	Total	Rate [1]	State	Male	Female	Year	Total	Rate [1]	State	Male	Female
1980..	315,974	139	295,363	303,643	12,331	1991..	789,610	313	732,914	745,808	43,802
1981..	353,673	154	331,504	339,375	14,298	1992..	846,277	332	780,571	799,776	46,501
1982..	395,516	171	371,864	379,075	16,441	1993..	932,074	359	857,675	878,037	54,037
1983..	419,346	179	393,015	401,870	17,476	1994..	1,016,691	389	936,896	956,566	60,125
1984..	443,398	188	415,796	424,193	19,205	1995..	1,085,022	411	1,001,359	1,021,059	63,963
1985..	480,568	202	447,873	459,223	21,345	1996..	1,137,722	427	1,048,907	1,068,123	69,599
1986..	522,084	217	485,553	497,540	24,544	1997..	1,195,498	445	1,100,511	1,121,663	73,835
1987..	560,812	231	521,289	533,990	26,822	1998..	1,245,402	461	1,141,720	1,167,802	77,600
1988..	603,732	247	560,994	573,587	30,145	1999..	1,304,074	476	1,189,799	1,221,611	82,463
1989..	680,907	276	633,739	643,643	37,264	2000..	1,331,278	[2]470	1,204,323	1,246,234	85,044
1990..	739,980	297	689,577	699,416	40,564	2001..	1,345,842	474	1,209,273	1,260,603	85,239

[1] Rate per 100,000 estimated population. Based on U.S. Census Bureau estimated resident population. [2] Decrease in incarceration rate from 1999 to 2000 due to use of new Census numbers to calculate.

Source: U.S. Bureau of Justice Statistics, *Prisoners in State and Federal Institutions on December 31*, annual.

No. 352. Prisoners Under Sentence of Death by Characteristic: 1980 to 2000

[As of December 31. Excludes prisoners under sentence of death who remained within local correctional systems pending exhaustion of appellate process or who had not been committed to prison]

Characteristic	1980	1990	1991	1992	1993	1994	1995	1996	1997	1998	1999	2000
Total [1] [2]	688	2,346	2,466	2,575	2,727	2,905	3,064	3,242	3,328	3,465	3,540	3,593
White	418	1,368	1,450	1,508	1,575	1,653	1,732	1,833	1,864	1,917	1,960	1,990
Black and other	270	978	1,016	1,067	1,152	1,252	1,332	1,409	1,464	1,548	1,515	1,603
Under 20 years	11	8	14	12	13	19	20	17	16	16	16	11
20 to 24 years	173	168	179	188	211	231	264	288	275	273	251	237
25 to 34 years	334	1,110	1,087	1,078	1,066	1,088	1,068	1,088	1,077	1,108	1,108	1,103
35 to 54 years	186	1,006	1,129	1,212	1,330	1,449	1,583	1,711	1,809	1,897	1,958	2,019
55 years and over	10	64	73	85	96	103	119	138	151	171	194	223
Years of school completed:												
7 years or less	68	178	173	181	185	186	191	196	205	208	201	214
8 years	74	186	181	180	183	198	195	201	206	218	221	233
9 to 11 years	204	775	810	836	885	930	979	1,040	1,069	1,122	1,142	1,157
12 years	162	729	783	831	887	939	995	1,037	1,084	1,128	1,157	1,184
More than 12 years	43	209	222	232	244	255	272	282	288	301	307	315
Unknown	163	279	313	315	332	382	422	486	476	488	499	490
Marital status:												
Never married	268	998	1,071	1,132	1,222	1,320	1,412	1,507	1,555	1,645	1,689	1,749
Married	229	632	663	663	671	707	718	739	740	752	731	739
Divorced [3]	217	726	746	780	823	863	924	996	1,033	1,068	1,107	1,105
Time elapsed since sentencing:												
Less than 12 months	185	231	252	265	262	280	287	306	262	293	259	208
12 to 47 months	389	753	718	720	716	755	784	816	844	816	800	786
48 to 71 months	102	438	441	444	422	379	423	447	456	482	499	507
72 months and over	38	934	1,071	1,146	1,316	1,476	1,560	1,673	1,766	1,874	1,969	2,092
Legal status at arrest:												
Not under sentence	384	1,345	1,415	1,476	1,562	1,662	1,764	1,881	1,957	2,036	2,088	2,202
Parole or probation [4]	115	578	615	702	754	800	866	894	880	879	886	921
Prison or escaped	45	128	102	101	102	103	110	112	116	127	125	126
Unknown	170	305	321	296	298	325	314	355	375	423	428	344

[1] Revisions to the total number of prisoners were not carried to the characteristics except for race. [2] Includes races not shown separately. [3] Includes persons married but separated, widows, widowers, and unknown. [4] Includes prisoners on mandatory conditional release, work release, leave, AWOL, or bail. Covers 28 prisoners in 1990, and 29 in 1991 and 1992, 33 in 1993 and 1995, 31 in 1994 and 1996, 30 in 1997, 26 in 1998, and 21 in 1999 and 2000.

Source: U.S. Bureau of Justice Statistics, *Capital Punishment*, annual. See also <http://www.ojp.usdoj.gov/bjs/pub/pdf/cp00.pdf> (released December 2001).

No. 353. Movement of Prisoners Under Sentence of Death: 1980 to 2001

[Prisoners reported under sentence of death by civil authorities. The term "under sentence of death" begins when the court pronounces the first sentence of death for a capital offense]

Status	1980	1990	1992	1993	1994	1995	1996	1997	1998	1999	2000	2001
Under sentence of death, Jan. 1 [1] [2]	595	2,243	2,465	2,580	2,727	2,905	3,064	3,242	3,328	3,465	3,540	3,593
Received death sentence [1] [2]	203	244	265	282	306	310	299	256	285	272	214	155
White	125	147	147	146	162	168	174	146	145	157	122	89
Black	77	94	114	130	136	138	119	106	132	104	86	61
Dispositions other than executions	101	108	124	108	112	105	99	89	93	112	76	109
Executions	-	23	31	38	31	56	45	74	68	98	85	66
Under sentence of death, Dec. 31 [1] [2]	688	2,346	2,575	2,727	2,890	3,054	3,242	3,335	3,452	3,527	3,593	3,581
White	425	1,368	1,508	1,575	1,645	1,730	1,833	1,876	1,906	1,948	1,990	1,969
Black	268	940	1,029	1,111	1,197	1,275	1,406	1,406	1,486	1,514	1,535	1,538

- Represents zero. [1] Includes races other than White or Black. [2] Revisions to total number of prisoners under death sentence not carried to this category.
Source: U.S. Bureau of Justice Statistics, Capital Punishment, annual. See also <http://www.ojp.usdoj.gov/bjs/pub/pdf/cpoo.pdf>.

No. 354. Prisoners Executed Under Civil Authority by Sex and Race: 1930 to 2002

[Excludes executions by military authorities. The Army (including the Air Force) carried out 160 (148 between 1942 and 1950; 3 each in 1954, 1955, and 1957; and 1 each in 1958, 1959, and 1961). Of the total, 106 were executed for murder (including 21 involving rape), 53 for rape, and 1 for desertion. The Navy carried out no executions during the period]

Year or period	Total [1]	Male	Female	White	Black	Executed for murder Total [1]	White	Black
All years, 1930-2000	4,679	4,637	42	2,274	2,350	3,692	1,884	1,770
1930 to 1939	1,667	1,656	11	827	816	1,514	803	687
1940 to 1949 [2]	1,284	1,272	12	490	781	1,064	458	595
1950 to 1959 [2]	717	709	8	336	376	601	316	280
1960 to 1967	191	190	1	98	93	155	87	68
1968 to 1976	-	-	-	-	-	-	-	-
1977 to 2000	820	810	10	523	84	820	523	289
1985	18	18	-	11	7	18	11	7
1986	18	18	-	11	7	18	11	7
1987	25	25	-	13	12	25	13	12
1988	11	11	-	6	5	11	6	5
1989	16	16	-	8	8	16	8	8
1990	23	23	-	16	7	23	16	7
1991	14	14	-	7	7	14	7	7
1992	31	31	-	19	11	31	19	11
1993	38	38	-	23	14	38	23	14
1994	31	31	-	20	11	31	20	11
1995	56	56	-	33	22	56	33	22
1996	45	45	-	31	14	45	31	14
1997	74	74	-	45	27	74	45	27
1998	68	66	2	48	18	68	48	18
1999	98	98	-	61	33	98	61	33
2000	85	83	2	48	36	85	48	36
2001	66	63	3	48	17	66	48	17
2002	71	69	2	53	18	71	53	18

- Represents zero. [1] Includes races other than White or Black. [2] Includes 25 armed robbery, 20 kidnapping, 11 burglary, 8 espionage (6 in 1942 and 2 in 1953), and 6 aggravated assault.
Source: Through 1978, U.S. Law Enforcement Assistance Administration; thereafter, U.S. Bureau of Justice Statistics, Correctional Populations in the United States, annual; and Capital Punishment, annual.

No. 355. Prisoners Under Sentence of Death and Executed Under Civil Authority by State: 1977 to 2002

[Alaska, District of Columbia, Hawaii, Iowa, Maine, Massachusetts, Michigan, Minnesota, New York, North Dakota, Rhode Island, Vermont, West Virginia, and Wisconsin are jurisdictions without a death penalty]

State	1977 to 2001	1999	2000	2001	2002	State	1977 to 2001	1999	2000	2001	2002	State	1977 to 2001	1999	2000	2001	2002
U.S.	749	98	85	66	71	IL	12	1	-	-	-	OK	48	6	11	18	7
						IN	9	1	-	2	-	OR	2	-	-	-	-
AL	23	2	4	-	2	KY	2	1	-	-	-	PA	3	1	-	-	-
AZ	22	7	3	-	-	LA	26	1	1	-	1	SC	25	4	1	-	3
AR	24	4	2	1	1	MD	3	-	-	-	-	TN	1	-	1	-	-
CA	9	2	1	1	-	MS	4	-	-	-	-	TX	256	35	40	17	33
DE	13	2	1	-	-	MO	53	9	5	7	6	UT	6	1	-	-	-
FL	51	1	6	1	3	NE	3	-	-	-	-	VA	83	14	8	2	4
GA	27	-	-	4	4	NV	9	1	-	-	-	WA	4	-	-	1	-
ID	1	-	-	-	-	NC	21	4	1	5	2	WY	1	-	-	-	-

- Represents zero.
Source: Through 1978, U.S. Law Enforcement Assistance Administration; thereafter, U.S. Bureau of Justice Statistics, Capital Punishment, annual.

No. 356. Fire Losses—Total and Percent Change: 1980 to 2000

[5,579 represents 5,579,000,000. Includes allowance for uninsured and unreported losses but excludes losses to government property and forests. Represents incurred losses]

Year	Total (mil. dol.)	Per capita (dol.)[1]	Year	Total (mil. dol.)	Per capita (dol.)[1]	Year	Total (mil. dol.)	Per capita (dol.)[1]
1980	5,579	24.56	1987	8,504	34.96	1994	12,778	49.08
1981	5,625	24.53	1988	9,626	39.11	1995	11,887	45.23
1982	5,894	25.61	1989	9,514	38.33	1996	12,544	47.29
1983	6,320	27.20	1990	9,495	38.07	1997	12,940	48.32
1984	7,602	32.35	1991	11,302	44.82	1998	11,510	45.59
1985	7,753	32.70	1992	13,588	53.28	1999	12,428	45.58
1986	8,488	35.21	1993	11,331	43.96	2000	12,659	45.86

[1] Based on U.S. Census Bureau resident population as of July 1.

Source: Insurance Information Institute, New York, NY, *The Fact Book, Property/Casualty Insurance Facts*, annual (copyright).

No. 357. Fires—Number and Loss, by Type and Property Use: 1998 to 2001

[Number of 1,755 represents 1,755,000 and property loss of 8,629 represents $8,629,000,000. Based on annual sample survey of fire departments. No adjustments were made for unreported fires and losses. Property loss includes direct property loss only]

Type and property use	Number (1,000) 1998	1999	2000	2001	Property loss (mil. dol.) 1998	1999	2000	2001
Fires, total	1,755	1,823	1,708	1,734	8,629	10,024	[1]11,207	[7]44,023
Structure	517	523	506	521	6,717	8,490	8,501	[7]42,314
Outside of structure[2]	62	64	69	75	497	123	214	86
Brush and rubbish	653	724	670	623	-	-	-	-
Vehicle	381	369	349	351	1,337	1,324	1,381	1,512
Other	142	143	114	164	78	87	111	111
Structure by property use:								
Public assembly	16	16	15	15	354	412	365	336
Educational	8	8	7	7	84	71	108	170
Institutional	9	8	7	7	23	23	20	27
Stores and offices	25	29	24	26	462	659	587	[7]34,155
Residential	381	383	380	396	4,391	5,092	5,674	5,643
1-2 family units[3]	283	283	284	295	3,642	4,123	4,639	4,652
Apartments	86	88	85	88	631	842	886	864
Other residential[4]	12	12	11	13	118	127	149	127
Storage[5]	36	36	33	34	687	[6]1,375	694	930
Industry, utility, defense[5]	16	18	15	13	496	671	778	858
Special structures	26	25	25	23	220	187	275	195

- Represents zero. [1] Includes $1 billion in property damage in the Cerro Grande, New Mexico Wildland Fire. Property loss by specific property type was not available. [2] Includes outside storage, crops, timber, etc. 1998 property loss data include $390 million loss in timber from Florida wildfires. [3] Includes mobile homes. [4] Includes hotels and motels, college dormitories, boarding houses, etc. [5] Data underreported as some incidents were handled by private fire brigades or fixed suppression systems which do not report. [6] Includes estimated losses of $515 million due to two power plant fires. [7] Includes $33.4 billion in property loss that occurred due to the events of September 11, 2001.

Source: National Fire Protection Association, Quincy, MA, "2001 U.S. Fire Loss," *NFPA Journal*, November 2002, and prior issues (copyright 2002).

No. 358. Fires and Property Loss for Incendiary and Suspicious Fires and Civilian Fire Deaths and Injuries by Selected Property Type: 1998 to 2001

[517 represents 517,000. Based on sample survey of fire departments]

Characteristic	1998	1999	2000	2001	Characteristic	1998	1999	2000	2001
NUMBER (1,000)					**CIVILIAN FIRE DEATHS**				
Structure fires, total	517	523	506	521	Deaths, total[2]	4,035	3,570	4,045	[4]6,196
Structure fires of incendiary or suspicious origin	76	72	75	-	Residential property	3,250	2,920	3,445	3,140
Fires of incendiary origin	47	44	46	46	One- and two-family dwellings	2,775	2,375	2,920	2,650
Fires of suspicious origin	29	28	29	-	Apartments	445	520	500	460
					Vehicles	575	470	465	485
PROPERTY LOSS[1] (mil. dol.)					**CIVILIAN FIRE INJURIES**				
Structure fires, total	6,717	8,490	8,501	[3]42,314	Injuries, total[2]	23,100	21,875	22,350	21,100
Structure fires of incendiary or suspicious origin	1,249	1,281	1,340	-	Residential property	17,175	16,425	17,400	15,575
Fires of incendiary origin	816	828	792	34,452	One- and two-family dwellings	11,800	11,550	12,575	11,400
Fires of suspicious origin	433	453	548	-	Apartments	5,000	4,500	4,400	3,800
					Vehicles	2,225	1,850	1,600	1,875

- Represents zero. [1] Direct property loss only. [2] Includes other not shown separately. [3] Includes 33.44 billion in property loss due to the events of September 11, 2001. [4] Includes 2,451 civilian deaths due to the events of September 11, 2001. [5] Includes 800 civilian injuries due to the events of September 11, 2201.

Source: National Fire Protection Association, Quincy, MA, "2001 U.S. Fire Loss," *NFPA Journal*, November 2002, and prior issues (copyright 2001).

Section 6
Geography and Environment

This section presents a variety of information on the physical environment of the United States, starting with basic area measurement data and ending with climatic data for selected weather stations around the country. The subjects covered between those points are mostly concerned with environmental trends but include related subjects such as land use, water consumption, air pollutant emissions, toxic releases, oil spills, hazardous waste sites, municipal waste and recycling, threatened and endangered wildlife, and the environmental industry.

The information in this section is selected from a wide range of federal agencies that compile the data for various administrative or regulatory purposes, such as the Environmental Protection Agency, U.S. Geological Survey, National Oceanic and Atmospheric Administration (NOAA), Natural Resources Conservation Service, and General Services Administration. New information on pollution abatement expenditures may be found in Tables 382 and 383 produced by the U.S. Census Bureau.

Area—For the 2000 census, area measurements were calculated by computer based on the information contained in a single, consistent geographic database, the TIGER® database, rather than relying on historical, local, and manually calculated information. Information from the 2000 census may be found in Table 359.

Geography—The U.S. Geological Survey conducts investigations, surveys, and research in the fields of geography, geology, topography, geographic information systems, mineralogy, hydrology, and geothermal energy resources as well as natural hazards. The U.S. Geological Survey provides United States cartographic data through the Earth Sciences Information Center, water resources data through the National Water Data Exchange (NAWDEX),

and a variety of research and Open-File reports which are announced monthly in *New Publications of the U.S. Geological Survey.*

In a joint project with the U.S. Census Bureau, during the 1980s, the U.S. Geological Survey provided the basic information on geographic features for input into a national geographic and cartographic database prepared by the Census Bureau, called the TIGER® (Topologically Integrated Geographic Encoding and Referencing) database. Since then, using a variety of sources, the Census Bureau has updated these features and their related attributes (names, descriptions, etc.) and inserted current information on the boundaries, names, and codes of legal and statistical geographic entities; very few of these updates added aerial water features, however. Maps prepared by the Census Bureau using the TIGER database show the names and boundaries of entites and are available on a current basis.

The Census Bureau maintains a current inventory of governmental units and their legal boundaries primary through its Boundary and Annexation Survey. The information is available to the public in the several files, all available on line: TIGER/Line®, there are also several series of maps for Census 2000: P.L. County Block Maps, Census Tract Outline Maps, and Voting District/ State Legislative District Outline Maps. These maps can be obtained online via the American Fact-Finder.

An inventory of the nation's land resources by type of use/cover was conducted by the National Resources Inventory Conservation Service (formerly the Soil Conservation Service) every 5 years beginning in 1977. The most recent survey results, which were published in the 1997 National Resources Inventory, cover all nonfederal land in Puerto Rico, the Virgin Islands, and the United States except Alaska. Tables 361 and 362 provide results from the survey. Beginning with the release of 2001 estimates (tentatively scheduled for fall 2003), this program will shift to become an annual release of land use data.

Environment—The principal federal agency responsible for pollution abatement and control activities is the Environmental Protection Agency (EPA). It is responsible for establishing and monitoring national air quality standards, water quality activities, solid and hazardous waste disposal, and control of toxic substances. Many of these series now appear in the Envirofats portion of the EPA Web site at <http://www.epa.gov/enviro/>. EPA released in 2003 a major compilation of environmental indicators, entitled *Draft Report on the Environment: 2003*, found at <http://www.epa.gov indicators/>.

National Ambient Air Quality Standards (NAAQS) for suspended particulate matter, sulfur dioxide, photochemical oxidants, carbon monoxide, and nitrogen dioxide were originally set by the EPA in April 1971. Every 5 years, each of the NAAQS is reviewed and revised if new health or welfare data indicates that a change is necessary. The standard for photochemical oxidants, now called ozone, was revised in February 1979. Also, a new NAAQS for lead was promulgated in October 1978 and for suspended particulate matter in 1987. Table 371 gives some of the health-related standards for the six air pollutants having NAAQS. Data gathered from state networks are periodically submitted to EPA's National Aerometric Information Retrieval System (AIRS) for summarization in annual reports on the nationwide status and trends in air quality; for details, see *National Air Quality and Emissions Trends Report*. More current information on emissions may be found on the EPA Web site at <http://www.epa.gov/ttn /chief/trends>.

The Toxics Release Inventory (TRI), published by the U.S. EPA, is a valuable source of information regarding toxic chemicals that are being used, manufactured, treated, transported, or released into the environment. Two rules, Section 313 of the Emergency Planning and Community Right-To-Know Act (EPCRA) and Section 6607 of the Pollution Prevention Act (PPA), mandate that a publicly accessible toxic chemical database be developed and maintained by U.S. EPA. This database, known as the TRI, contains information concerning waste management activities and the release of toxic chemicals by facilities that manufacture, process, or otherwise use said materials.

Data on the release of these chemicals are collected from manufacturing facilities and facilities added in 1998 that have the equivalent of 10 or more full-time employees and meet the established thresholds for manufacturing, processing, or "otherwise use" of listed chemicals. Facilities must report their releases and other waste management quantities. Federal facilities have been required to report since 1994, regardless of industry classification. In May 1997, EPA added seven new industry sectors that reported to the TRI for the first time in July 1999 for the 1998 reporting year.

Climate—NOAA, through the National Weather Service and the National Environmental Satellite, Data, and Information Service, is responsible for data on climate. NOAA maintains about 11,600 weather stations, of which over 3,000 produce autographic precipitation records, about 600 take hourly readings of a series of weather elements, and the remainder record data once a day. These data are reported monthly in the *Climatological Data* and *Storm Data*, published monthly, and annually in the *Local Climatological Data* (published by location for major cities).

The normal climatological temperatures, precipitation, and degree days listed in this publication are derived for comparative purposes and are averages for the 30-year period, 1971-2000. For stations that did not have continuous records for the entire 30 years from the same instrument site, the normals have been adjusted to provide representative values for the current location. The information in all other tables is based on data from the beginning of the record at that location through 2001.

No. 359. Land and Water Area of States and Other Entities: 2000

[One square mile=2.59 square kilometers. Area is calculated from the specific boundary recorded for each entity in the U.S. Census Bureau's geographic TIGER database]

State and other area	Total area Sq. mi.	Total area Sq. km.	Land area Sq. mi.	Land area Sq. km.	Water area Total Sq. mi.	Water area Total Sq. km.	Inland (sq. mi.)	Coastal (sq. mi.)	Great Lakes (sq. mi.)	Territorial (sq. mi.)
Total	3,800,286	9,842,696	3,540,999	9,171,146	259,287	671,550	79,018	42,241	60,251	77,777
United States	3,794,083	9,826,630	3,537,439	9,161,923	256,645	664,707	78,797	42,225	60,251	75,372
Alabama	52,419	135,765	50,744	131,426	1,675	4,338	956	519	-	200
Alaska	663,267	1,717,854	571,951	1,481,347	91,316	236,507	17,243	27,049	-	47,024
Arizona	113,998	295,254	113,635	294,312	364	942	364	-	-	-
Arkansas	53,179	137,732	52,068	134,856	1,110	2,876	1,110	-	-	-
California	163,696	423,970	155,959	403,933	7,736	20,037	2,674	222	-	4,841
Colorado	104,094	269,601	103,718	268,627	376	974	376	-	-	-
Connecticut	5,543	14,357	4,845	12,548	699	1,809	161	538	-	93
Delaware	2,489	6,447	1,954	5,060	536	1,388	72	371	-	93
District of Columbia	68	177	61	159	7	18	7	-	-	-
Florida	65,755	170,304	53,927	139,670	11,828	30,634	4,672	1,311	-	5,845
Georgia	59,425	153,909	57,906	149,976	1,519	3,933	1,016	48	-	455
Hawaii	10,931	28,311	6,423	16,635	4,508	11,677	38	-	-	4,470
Idaho	83,570	216,446	82,747	214,314	823	2,131	823	-	-	-
Illinois	57,914	149,998	55,584	143,961	2,331	6,037	756	-	1,575	-
Indiana	36,418	94,321	35,867	92,895	551	1,427	316	-	235	-
Iowa	56,272	145,743	55,869	144,701	402	1,042	402	-	-	-
Kansas	82,277	213,096	81,815	211,900	462	1,197	462	-	-	-
Kentucky	40,409	104,659	39,728	102,896	681	1,763	681	-	-	-
Louisiana	51,840	134,264	43,562	112,825	8,278	21,440	4,154	1,935	-	2,189
Maine	35,385	91,646	30,862	79,931	4,523	11,715	2,264	613	-	1,647
Maryland	12,407	32,133	9,774	25,314	2,633	6,819	680	1,843	-	110
Massachusetts	10,555	27,336	7,840	20,306	2,715	7,031	423	977	-	1,314
Michigan	96,716	250,494	56,804	147,121	39,912	103,372	1,611	-	38,301	-
Minnesota	86,939	225,171	79,610	206,189	7,329	18,982	4,783	-	2,546	-
Mississippi	48,430	125,434	46,907	121,489	1,523	3,945	785	590	-	148
Missouri	69,704	180,533	68,886	178,414	818	2,120	818	-	-	-
Montana	147,042	380,838	145,552	376,979	1,490	3,859	1,490	-	-	-
Nebraska	77,354	200,345	76,872	199,099	481	1,247	481	-	-	-
Nevada	110,561	286,351	109,826	284,448	735	1,903	735	-	-	-
New Hampshire	9,350	24,216	8,968	23,227	382	989	314	-	-	68
New Jersey	8,721	22,588	7,417	19,211	1,304	3,377	396	401	-	507
New Mexico	121,590	314,915	121,356	314,309	234	606	234	-	-	-
New York	54,556	141,299	47,214	122,283	7,342	19,016	1,895	981	3,988	479
North Carolina	53,819	139,389	48,711	126,161	5,108	13,229	3,960	-	-	1,148
North Dakota	70,700	183,112	68,976	178,647	1,724	4,465	1,724	-	-	-
Ohio	44,825	116,096	40,948	106,056	3,877	10,040	378	-	3,499	-
Oklahoma	69,898	181,036	68,667	177,847	1,231	3,189	1,231	-	-	-
Oregon	98,381	254,805	95,997	248,631	2,384	6,174	1,050	80	-	1,254
Pennsylvania	46,055	119,283	44,817	116,075	1,239	3,208	490	-	749	-
Rhode Island	1,545	4,002	1,045	2,706	500	1,295	178	9	-	314
South Carolina	32,020	82,932	30,110	77,983	1,911	4,949	1,008	72	-	831
South Dakota	77,117	199,731	75,885	196,540	1,232	3,191	1,232	-	-	-
Tennessee	42,143	109,151	41,217	106,752	926	2,399	926	-	-	-
Texas	268,581	695,621	261,797	678,051	6,784	17,570	5,056	404	-	1,324
Utah	84,899	219,887	82,144	212,751	2,755	7,136	2,755	-	-	-
Vermont	9,614	24,901	9,250	23,956	365	945	365	-	-	-
Virginia	42,774	110,785	39,594	102,548	3,180	8,237	1,006	1,728	-	446
Washington	71,300	184,665	66,544	172,348	4,756	12,317	1,553	2,537	-	666
West Virginia	24,230	62,755	24,078	62,361	152	394	152	-	-	-
Wisconsin	65,498	169,639	54,310	140,663	11,188	28,976	1,830	-	9,358	-
Wyoming	97,814	253,336	97,100	251,489	713	1,847	713	-	-	-
Other areas: Puerto Rico	5,325	13,790	3,425	8,870	1,900	4,921	67	16	-	1,817
U.S. Minor Outlying Islands	141	365	3	7	138	359	138	-	-	-
Virgin Islands of the U.S.	737	1,910	134	346	604	1,564	16	-	-	588

- Represents or rounds to zero.

Source: U.S. Census Bureau, 2000 Census of Population and Housing, *Summary Population and Housing Characteristics*, Series PHC-1.

Geography and Environment   225

U.S. Census Bureau, Statistical Abstract of the United States: 2003

No. 360. Total and Federally Owned Land by State: 2002

[As of end of fiscal year; see text, Section 8. Total land area figures are not comparable with those in Table 359]

State	Total (1,000 acres)	Not owned by federal government (1,000 acres)	Owned by federal government [1] Acres (1,000)	Per-cent	State	Total (1,000 acres)	Not owned by federal government (1,000 acres)	Owned by federal government [1] Acres (1,000)	Per-cent
United States...	2,271,343	1,597,076	674,267	29.7	Missouri	44,248	41,989	2,260	5.1
Alabama	32,678	31,472	1,206	3.7	Montana	93,271	64,033	29,238	31.3
Alaska	365,482	118,175	247,307	67.7	Nebraska	49,032	47,560	1,471	3.0
Arizona	72,688	36,277	36,411	50.1	Nevada	70,264	5,809	64,456	91.7
Arkansas	33,599	29,580	4,019	12.0	New Hampshire	5,769	4,938	831	14.4
California	100,207	53,129	47,078	47.0	New Jersey	4,813	4,627	187	3.9
Colorado	66,486	43,291	23,195	34.9	New Mexico	77,766	51,173	26,593	34.2
Connecticut	3,135	3,120	15	0.5	New York	30,681	30,353	328	1.1
Delaware	1,266	1,229	37	2.9	North Carolina	31,403	27,905	3,498	11.1
District of Columbia	39	28	12	29.5	North Dakota	44,452	43,110	1,343	3.0
Florida	34,721	30,108	4,614	13.3	Ohio	26,222	25,770	452	1.7
Georgia	37,295	34,987	2,308	6.2	Oklahoma	44,088	42,751	1,337	3.0
Hawaii	4,106	3,433	673	16.4	Oregon	61,599	30,955	30,644	49.7
Idaho	52,933	18,518	34,415	65.0	Pennsylvania	28,804	28,072	732	2.5
Illinois	35,795	35,129	666	1.9	Rhode Island	677	672	5	0.8
Indiana	23,158	22,624	534	2.3	South Carolina	19,374	18,140	1,235	6.4
Iowa	35,860	35,554	307	0.9	South Dakota	48,882	46,515	2,367	4.8
Kansas	52,511	51,916	595	1.1	Tennessee	26,728	24,772	1,955	7.3
Kentucky	25,512	23,839	1,673	6.6	Texas	168,218	165,018	3,200	1.9
Louisiana	28,868	27,368	1,500	5.2	Utah	52,697	17,672	35,025	66.5
Maine	19,848	19,685	163	0.8	Vermont	5,937	5,486	450	7.6
Maryland	6,319	6,111	208	3.3	Virginia	25,496	22,947	2,550	10.0
Massachusetts	5,035	4,930	105	2.1	Washington	42,694	29,537	13,156	30.8
Michigan	36,492	32,853	3,639	10.0	West Virginia	15,411	14,182	1,229	8.0
Minnesota	51,206	47,660	3,546	6.9	Wisconsin	35,011	33,025	1,986	5.7
Mississippi	30,223	28,241	1,982	6.6	Wyoming	62,343	30,812	31,531	50.6

[1] Excludes trust properties.

Source: U.S. General Services Administration, Federal Real Property Profile, annual. See also <http://www.gsa.gov/cmattachments/GSAPUBLICATIONS/AnnualReport26R2AV1-z-c0Z5RDZ-i34K-pR.pdf> (released 11 March 2003).

No. 361. Nonfederal Developed Land Use by State and Other Area: 1997

[In thousands of acres (1,944,130 represents 1,944,130,000), except percent. Excludes Alaska and District of Columbia. Developed land includes large urban and built-up areas, small built-up areas, and rural transportation land categories of use]

State and other area	Total surface area	Developed land Total	Percent of total	Change, 1992-97	State and other area	Total surface area	Developed land Total	Percent of total	Change, 1992-97
Total	1,944,130	98,252	5.0	11,217	Montana	94,110	1,032	1.1	76
					Nebraska	49,510	1,206	2.5	55
United States	1,941,823	97,745	5.0	11,105	Nevada	70,763	381	0.6	27
Alabama	33,424	2,252	6.8	315	New Hampshire	5,941	589	10.0	63
Arizona	72,964	1,491	2.1	114	New Jersey	5,216	1,778	34.1	214
Arkansas	34,037	1,409	4.2	169	New Mexico	77,823	1,153	1.5	217
California	101,510	5,456	5.4	553	New York	31,361	3,184	10.2	318
Colorado	66,625	1,652	2.5	113	North Carolina	33,709	3,856	11.5	507
Connecticut	3,195	874	27.4	39	North Dakota	45,251	992	2.2	33
Delaware	1,534	226	14.8	23	Ohio	26,445	3,611	13.7	365
Florida	37,534	5,185	13.9	825	Oklahoma	44,738	1,926	4.4	177
Georgia	37,741	3,957	10.5	852	Oregon	62,161	1,222	2.0	104
Hawaii	4,158	180	4.4	7	Pennsylvania	28,995	3,983	13.8	545
Idaho	53,488	755	1.5	92	Rhode Island	813	201	24.7	7
Illinois	36,059	3,181	8.9	247	South Carolina	19,939	2,097	10.6	362
Indiana	23,158	2,260	9.8	195	South Dakota	49,358	960	2.0	58
Iowa	36,017	1,702	4.8	69	Tennessee	26,974	2,371	8.8	402
Kansas	52,661	1,940	3.7	97	Texas	171,052	8,567	5.1	894
Kentucky	25,863	1,738	6.8	237	Utah	54,339	662	1.3	81
Louisiana	31,377	1,624	5.2	134	Vermont	6,154	318	5.2	12
Maine	20,966	712	3.4	111	Virginia	27,087	2,626	9.7	344
Maryland	7,870	1,236	15.8	178	Washington	44,035	2,065	4.7	241
Massachusetts	5,339	1,479	27.8	212	West Virginia	15,508	874	5.7	177
Michigan	37,349	3,546	9.5	364	Wisconsin	35,920	2,418	6.8	188
Minnesota	54,010	2,186	4.1	232	Wyoming	62,603	644	1.1	34
Mississippi	30,527	1,474	4.9	206					
Missouri	44,614	2,517	5.7	224	Caribbean	2,307	507	22.0	112

Source: U.S. Department of Agriculture, Natural Resources and Conservation Service, and Iowa State University, Statistical Laboratory, Summary Report, 1997 National Resources Inventory, revised December 2000. See also <http://www.NRCS.usda.gov/technical/NRI/1997/summary-report> (revised December 2000).

No. 362. Land Cover/Use by State: 1997

[In thousands of acres (1,944,130 represents 1,944,130,000), except percent. Excludes Alaska and District of Columbia]

State	Total surface area	Rural land, total	Percent of total	Crop- land	CRP land [1]	Pasture land	Range- land	Forest land	Other rural land
Total........	1,944,130	1,393,760	71.7	376,998	32,696	119,992	405,977	406,955	51,142
United States ...	1,941,823	1,392,098	71.7	376,630	32,696	119,549	405,832	406,315	51,077
Alabama.........	33,424	28,950	86.6	2,954	522	3,528	74	21,261	612
Arizona.........	72,964	40,858	56.0	1,212	-	73	32,323	4,216	3,035
Arkansas........	34,037	28,638	84.1	7,625	230	5,351	38	15,011	384
California.......	101,510	47,555	46.8	9,635	173	1,049	18,269	13,936	4,494
Colorado.........	66,625	40,850	61.3	8,770	1,890	1,211	24,574	3,442	964
Connecticut......	3,195	2,178	68.2	204	-	112	-	1,759	103
Delaware	1,534	988	64.4	485	1	24	-	352	128
Florida..........	37,534	25,498	67.9	2,752	120	4,231	3,229	12,536	2,630
Georgia	37,741	30,648	81.2	4,757	595	2,865	-	21,560	872
Hawaii..........	4,158	3,565	85.7	246	-	36	1,009	1,635	639
Idaho...........	53,488	18,618	34.8	5,517	785	1,315	6,501	3,948	553
Illinois..........	36,059	31,675	87.8	24,011	726	2,502	-	3,784	652
Indiana..........	23,158	20,069	86.7	13,407	378	1,830	-	3,781	674
Iowa	36,017	33,673	93.5	25,310	1,739	3,572	-	2,182	870
Kansas..........	52,661	49,685	94.3	26,524	2,849	2,322	15,728	1,546	716
Kentucky	25,863	22,327	86.3	5,178	332	5,686	-	10,667	465
Louisiana	31,377	24,664	78.6	5,659	140	2,385	277	13,226	2,976
Maine...........	20,966	18,794	89.6	413	30	123	-	17,691	537
Maryland	7,870	4,808	61.1	1,616	19	478	-	2,373	321
Massachusetts.....	5,339	3,394	63.6	277	-	119	-	2,744	254
Michigan.........	37,349	29,426	78.8	8,540	321	2,032	-	16,354	2,178
Minnesota........	54,010	45,356	84.0	21,414	1,544	3,434	-	16,248	2,716
Mississippi	30,527	26,429	86.6	5,352	799	3,679	-	16,209	389
Missouri.........	44,614	39,358	88.2	13,751	1,606	10,849	88	12,431	634
Montana.........	94,110	64,958	69.0	15,171	2,721	3,443	36,751	5,431	1,443
Nebraska........	49,510	47,187	95.3	19,469	1,245	1,801	23,089	826	757
Nevada	70,763	10,079	14.2	701	2	279	8,372	305	420
New Hampshire....	5,941	4,353	73.3	134	-	94	-	3,932	193
New Jersey.......	5,216	2,766	53.0	589	1	111	-	1,698	367
New Mexico	77,823	50,071	64.3	1,875	467	231	39,990	5,467	2,041
New York	31,361	26,702	85.1	5,417	54	2,722	-	17,702	808
North Carolina.....	33,709	24,592	73.0	5,639	131	2,039	-	15,959	824
North Dakota......	45,251	41,442	91.6	25,004	2,802	1,129	10,689	454	1,363
Ohio	26,445	22,070	83.5	11,627	324	2,006	-	7,081	1,032
Oklahoma........	44,738	40,610	90.8	9,737	1,138	7,963	14,033	7,281	459
Oregon..........	62,161	28,858	46.4	3,762	483	1,961	9,286	12,643	724
Pennsylvania......	28,995	23,816	82.1	5,471	90	1,845	-	15,478	932
Rhode Island......	813	458	56.3	22	-	25	-	387	24
South Carolina.....	19,939	16,018	80.3	2,574	263	1,197	-	11,188	797
South Dakota	49,358	44,411	90.0	16,738	1,686	2,108	21,876	518	1,484
Tennessee	26,974	22,597	83.8	4,644	374	4,990	-	12,042	547
Texas............	171,052	155,530	90.9	26,938	3,906	15,914	95,745	10,816	2,211
Utah	54,339	17,599	32.4	1,679	216	695	10,733	1,883	2,392
Vermont	6,154	5,183	84.2	607	-	338	-	4,150	88
Virginia..........	27,087	19,886	73.4	2,918	71	2,995	-	13,316	587
Washington.......	44,035	28,508	64.7	6,656	1,017	1,193	5,857	12,835	951
West Virginia.....	15,508	13,252	85.5	864	-	1,527	-	10,582	279
Wisconsin........	35,920	30,374	84.6	10,613	661	2,994	-	14,448	1,658
Wyoming	62,603	32,773	52.4	2,174	247	1,146	27,302	1,004	900
Caribbean........	2,307	1,662	72.0	368	-	443	145	640	65

- Represents or rounds to zero. [1] Conservation Reserve Program (CRP). A federal program established under the Food Security Act of 1985 to assist private landowners to convert highly erodible cropland to vegetative cover for 10 years.

Source: U.S. Department of Agriculture, Natural Resources and Conservation Service, and Iowa State University, Statistical Laboratory, *Summary Report, 1997 National Resources Inventory*, revised December 2000. See also <http://www.nhq.nrcs.usda.gov/NRI/1997/summaryreport/report.pdf>.

No. 363. Extreme and Mean Elevations by State and Other Area

[One foot=.305 meter]

State and other area	Highest point			Lowest point			Approximate mean elevation	
	Name	Elevation Feet	Elevation Meters	Name	Elevation Feet	Elevation Meters	Feet	Meters
U.S.	Mt. McKinley (AK)	20,320	6,198	Death Valley (CA)	-282	-86	2,500	763
AL	Cheaha Mountain	2,405	733	Gulf of Mexico	([1])	([1])	500	153
AK	Mount McKinley	20,320	6,198	Pacific Ocean	([1])	([1])	1,900	580
AZ	Humphreys Peak	12,633	3,853	Colorado River	70	21	4,100	1,251
AR	Magazine Mountain	2,753	840	Ouachita River	55	17	650	198
CA	Mount Whitney	14,494	4,419	Death Valley	-282	-86	2,900	885
CO	Mt. Elbert	14,433	4,402	Arkansas River	3,350	1,022	6,800	2,074
CT	Mt. Frissell on South slope	2,380	726	Long Island Sound	([1])	([1])	500	153
DE	Ebright Road,[2] New Castle County	448	137	Atlantic Ocean	([1])	([1])	60	18
DC	Tenleytown at Reno Reservoir	410	125	Potomac River	1	(Z)	150	46
FL	Sec. 30, T6N, R20W, Walton County	345	105	Atlantic Ocean	([1])	([1])	100	31
GA	Brasstown Bald	4,784	1,459	Atlantic Ocean	([1])	([1])	600	183
HI	Puu Wekiu	13,796	4,208	Pacific Ocean	([1])	([1])	3,030	924
ID	Borah Peak	12,662	3,862	Snake River	710	217	5,000	1,525
IL	Charles Mound	1,235	377	Mississippi River	279	85	600	183
IN	Franklin Twp., Wayne Co.	1,257	383	Ohio River	320	98	700	214
IA	Sec. 29, T100N, R41W, Osceola County[3]	1,670	509	Mississippi River	480	146	1,100	336
KS	Mount Sunflower	4,039	1,232	Verdigris River	679	207	2,000	610
KY	Black Mountain	4,139	2,162	Mississippi River	257	78	750	229
LA	Driskill Mountain	535	163	New Orleans	-8	-2	100	31
ME	Mount Katahdin	5,267	1,606	Atlantic Ocean	([1])	([1])	600	183
MD	Backbone Mountain	3,360	1,025	Atlantic Ocean	([1])	([1])	350	107
MA	Mount Greylock	3,487	1,064	Atlantic Ocean	([1])	([1])	500	153
MI	Mount Arvon	1,979	604	Lake Erie	571	174	900	275
MN	Eagle Mountain, Cook Co.	2,301	702	Lake Superior	601	183	1,200	366
MS	Woodall Mountain	806	246	Gulf of Mexico	([1])	([1])	300	92
MO	Taum Sauk Mountain	1,772	540	St. Francis River	230	70	800	244
MT	Granite Peak	12,799	3,904	Kootenai River	1,800	549	3,400	1,037
NE	Johnson Twp., Kimball Co.	5,424	1,654	Missouri River	840	256	2,600	793
NV	Boundary Peak	13,140	4,007	Colorado River	479	146	5,500	1,678
NH	Mount Washington	6,288	1,918	Atlantic Ocean	([1])	([1])	1,000	305
NJ	High Point	1,803	550	Atlantic Ocean	([1])	([1])	250	76
NM	Wheeler Peak	13,161	4,014	Red Bluff Reservoir	2,842	867	5,700	1,739
NY	Mount Marcy	5,344	1,630	Atlantic Ocean	([1])	([1])	1,000	305
NC	Mount Mitchell	6,684	2,039	Atlantic Ocean	([1])	([1])	700	214
ND	White Butte, Slope Co.	3,506	1,069	Red River	750	229	1,900	580
OH	Campbell Hill	1,549	472	Ohio River	455	139	850	259
OK	Black Mesa	4,973	1,517	Little River	289	88	1,300	397
OR	Mount Hood	11,239	3,428	Pacific Ocean	([1])	([1])	3,300	1,007
PA	Mount Davis	3,213	980	Delaware River	([1])	([1])	1,100	336
RI	Jerimoth Hill	812	248	Atlantic Ocean	([1])	([1])	200	61
SC	Sassafras Mountain	3,560	1,086	Atlantic Ocean	([1])	([1])	350	107
SD	Harney Peak	7,242	2,209	Big Stone Lake	966	295	2,200	671
TN	Clingmans Dome	6,643	2,026	Mississippi River	178	54	900	275
TX	Guadalupe Peak	8,749	2,668	Gulf of Mexico	([1])	([1])	1,700	519
UT	Kings Peak	13,528	4,126	Beaver Dam Wash	2,000	610	6,100	1,861
VT	Mount Mansfield	4,393	1,340	Lake Champlain	95	29	1,000	305
VA	Mount Rogers	5,729	1,747	Atlantic Ocean	([1])	([1])	950	290
WA	Mount Rainier	14,410	4,395	Pacific Ocean	([1])	([1])	1,700	519
WV	Spruce Knob	4,861	1,483	Potomac River	240	73	1,500	458
WI	Timms Hill	1,951	595	Lake Michigan	579	177	1,050	320
WY	Gannett Peak	13,804	4,210	Belle Fourche River	3,099	945	6,700	2,044
Other areas:								
Puerto Rico	Cerro de Punta	4,390	1,339	Atlantic Ocean	([1])	([1])	1,800	549
American Samoa	Lata Mountain	3,160	964	Pacific Ocean	([1])	([1])	1,300	397
Guam	Mount Lamlam	1,332	406	Pacific Ocean	([1])	([1])	330	101
Virgin Is.	Crown Mountain	1,556	475	Atlantic Ocean	([1])	([1])	750	229

Z Less than 0.5 meter. [1] Sea level. [2] At DE-PA state line. [3] "Sec." denotes section; "T," township; "R," range; "N," north; and "W," west.

Source: U.S. Geological Survey, for highest and lowest points, *Elevations and Distances in the United States, 1990*; for mean elevations, 1983 edition.

No. 364. U.S. Wetland Resources and Deepwater Habitats by Type: 1986 and 1997

[In thousands of acres (144,673.3 represents 144,677,300). Wetlands and deepwater habitats are defined separately because the term wetland does not include permanent water bodies. Deepwater habitats are permanently flooded land lying below the deepwater boundary of wetlands. Deepwater habitats include environments where surface water is permanent and often deep, so that water, rather than air, is the principal medium within which the dominant organisms live, whether or not they are attached to the substrate. As in wetlands, the dominant plants are hydrophytes; however, the substrates are In general terms, wetlands are lands where saturation with water is the dominant factor determining the nature of soil development and the types of plant and animal communities living in the soil and on its surface. The single feature that most wetlands share is soil or substrate that is at least periodically saturated with or covered by water. Wetlands are lands transitional between terrestrial and aquatic systems where the water table is usually at or near the surface or the land is covered by shallow water]

Wetland or deepwater category	1986	1997	Change, 1986 to 1997
All wetlands and deepwater habitats, total	144,673.3	144,136.8	-536.5
All deepwater habitats, total	38,537.6	38,645.1	107.5
Lacustrine [1]	14,608.9	14,725.3	116.4
Riverine [2]	6,291.1	6,255.9	-35.2
Estuarine subtidal [3]	17,637.6	17,663.9	26.3
All wetlands, total	106,135.7	105,491.7	-644
Intertidal wetlands [4]	5,336.6	5,326.2	-10.4
Marine intertidal	133.1	130.9	-2.2
Estuarine intertidal nonvegetated	580.4	580.1	-0.3
Estuarine intertidal vegetated	4,623.1	4,615.2	-7.9
Freshwater wetlands	100,799.1	100,165.5	-633.6
Freshwater nonvegetated	5,251.0	5,914.3	663.3
Freshwater vegetated	95,548.1	94,251.2	-1,296.9
Freshwater emergent [5]	26,383.3	25,157.1	-1,226.2
Freshwater forested [6]	51,929.6	50,728.5	-1,201.1
Freshwater shrub [7]	17,235.2	18,365.6	1,130.4

[1] The lacustrine system includes deepwater habitats with all of the following characteristics: (1) situated in a topographic depression or a dammed river channel; (2) lacking trees, shrubs, persistent emergents, emergent mosses or lichens with greater than 30 percent coverage; (3) total area exceeds 20 acres. [2] The riverine system includes deepwater habitats contained within a channel, with the exception of habitats with water containing ocean derived salts in excess of 0.5 parts per thousand. [3] The estuarine system consists of deepwater tidal habitats and adjacent tidal wetland that are usually semi-enclosed by land but have open, partly obstructed, or sporadic access to the open ocean, and in which ocean water is at least occasionally diluted by freshwater runoff from the land. Subtidal is where the substrate is continuously submerged by marine or estuarine waters. [4] Intertidal is where the substrate is exposed and flooded by tides. Intertidal includes the splash zone of coastal waters. [5] Emergent wetlands are characterized by erect, rooted, herbaceous hydrophytes, excluding mosses and lichens. This vegetation is present for most of the growing season in most years. These wetlands are usually dominated by perennial plants. [6] Forested wetlands are characterized by woody vegetation that is 20 feet tall or taller. [7] Shrub wetlands include areas dominated by woody vegetation less than 20 feet tall. The species include true shrubs, young trees, and trees or shrubs that are small or stunted because of environmental conditions.

Source: U.S. Fish and Wildlife Service, *Status and Trends of Wetlands in the Conterminous United States, 1986 to 1997*, January 2001. See also <ftp://wetlands.fws.gov/status-trends/SandT2000Reportlowres.pdf>.

No. 365. Water Areas for Selected Major Bodies of Water: 2000

[Includes only that portion of body of water under the jurisdiction of the United States, excluding Hawaii. One square mile=2.59 square kilometers]

Body of water and state	Area Sq. mi.	Area Sq. km.	Body of water and state	Area Sq. mi.	Area Sq. km.
Atlantic Coast water bodies:			Willapa Bay (WA)	125	325
Chesapeake Bay (MD-VA)	2,747	7,115	Hood Canal (WA)	117	303
Pamlico Sound (NC)	1,622	4,200			
Long Island Sound (CT-NY)	914	2,368	Interior water bodies:		
Delaware Bay (DE-NJ)	614	1,591	Lake Michigan (IL-IN-MI-WI)	22,342	57,866
Cape Cod Bay (MA)	598	1,548	Lake Superior (MI-MN-WI) [1]	20,557	53,243
Albemarle Sound (NC)	492	1,274	Lake Huron (MI) [1]	8,800	22,792
Biscayne Bay (FL)	218	565	Lake Erie (MI-NY-OH-PA) [1]	5,033	13,036
Buzzards Bay (MA)	215	558	Lake Ontario (NY) [1]	3,446	8,926
Tangier Sound (MD-VA)	172	445	Great Salt Lake (UT)	1,836	4,756
Currituck Sound (NC)	116	301	Green Bay (MI-WI)	1,396	3,617
Pocomoke Sound (MD-VA)	111	286	Lake Okeechobee (FL)	663	1,717
Chincoteague Bay (MD-VA)	105	272	Lake Sakakawea (ND)	563	1,459
			Lake Oahe (ND-SD)	538	1,394
Gulf Coast water bodies:			Lake of the Woods (MN) [1]	462	1,196
Mississippi Sound (AL-LA-MS)	813	2,105	Lake Champlain (NY-VT) [1]	414	1,072
Laguna Madre (TX)	733	1,897			
Lake Pontchartrain (LA)	631	1,635	Alaska water bodies:		
Florida Bay (FL)	616	1,596	Chatham Strait	1,559	4,039
Breton Sound (LA)	511	1,323	Prince William Sound	1,382	3,579
Mobile Bay (AL)	310	802	Clarence Strait	1,199	3,107
Lake Borgne (LA-MS)	271	702	Iliamna Lake	1,022	2,646
Matagorda Bay (TX)	253	656	Frederick Sound	792	2,051
Atchafalaya Bay (LA)	245	635	Sumner Strait	791	2,048
Galveston Bay (TX)	236	611	Stephens Passage	702	1,819
Tampa Bay (FL)	212	549	Kvichak Bay	640	1,659
			Montague Strait	463	1,198
Pacific Coast water bodies:			Becharof Lake	447	1,158
Puget Sound (WA)	808	2,092	Icy Strait	436	1,130
San Francisco Bay (CA)	264	684			

[1] Area measurements for Lake Champlain, Lake Erie, Lake Huron, Lake Ontario, Lake St. Clair, Lake Superior, and Lake of the Woods include only those portions under the jurisdiction of the United States.

Source: U. S. Census Bureau, unpublished data from the Census TIGER ™ database.

Geography and Environment

No. 366. Flows of Largest U.S. Rivers—Length, Discharge, and Drainage Area

River	Location of mouth	Source stream (name and location)	Length (miles)[1]	Average discharge at mouth (1,000 cubic ft. per second)	Drainage area (1,000 sq. mi.)
Missouri	Missouri	Red Rock Creek, MT	2,540	76.2	[2]529
Mississippi	Louisiana	Mississippi River, MN	[3]2,340	[4]593	[2,5]1,150
Yukon	Alaska	McNeil River, Canada	1,980	225	[2]328
St. Lawrence	Canada	North River, MN	1,900	348	[2]396
Rio Grande	Mexico-Texas	Rio Grande, CO	1,900	-	336
Arkansas	Arkansas	East Fork Arkansas River, CO	1,460	41	161
Colorado	Mexico	Colorado River, CO	1,450	-	246
Atchafalaya [6]	Louisiana	Tierra Blanca Creek, NM	1,420	58	95.1
Ohio	Illinois-Kentucky	Allegheny River, PA	1,310	281	203
Red	Louisiana	Tierra Blanca Creek, NM	1,290	56	93.2
Brazos	Texas	Blackwater Draw, NM	1,280	-	45.6
Columbia	Oregon-Washington	Columbia River, Canada	1,240	265	[2]258
Snake	Washington	Snake River, WY	1,040	56.9	108
Platte	Nebraska	Grizzly Creek, CO	990	-	84.9
Pecos	Texas	Pecos River, NM	926	-	44.3
Canadian	Oklahoma	Canadian River, CO	906	-	46.9
Tennessee	Kentucky	Courthouse Creek, NC	886	68	40.9
Colorado (of Texas)	Texas	Colorado River, TX	862	-	42.3
North Canadian	Oklahoma	Corrumpa Creek, NM	800	-	17.6
Mobile	Alabama	Tickanetley Creek, GA	774	67.2	44.6
Kansas	Kansas	Arikaree River, CO	743	-	59.5
Kuskokwim	Alaska	South Fork Kuskokwim River, AK	724	67	48
Yellowstone	North Dakota	North Folk Yellowstone River, WY	692	-	70
Tanana	Alaska	Nabesna River, AK	659	41	44.5
Gila	Arizona	Middle Fork Gila River, NM	649	-	58.2
Porcupine	Alaska	Porcupine River, Canada	569	23	45.1
Susquehanna	Maryland	Hayden Creek, NY	447	38.2	27.2

- Represents zero.   [1] From source to mouth.   [2] Drainage area includes both the United States and Canada.   [3] The length from the source of the Missouri River to the Mississippi River and thence to the Gulf of Mexico is about 3,710 miles.   [4] Includes about 167,000 cubic ft. per second diverted from the Mississippi into the Atchafalaya River but excludes the flow of the Red River.   [5] Excludes the drainage areas of the Red and Atchafalaya Rivers.   [6] In east-central Louisiana, the Red River flows into the Atchafalaya River, a distributary of the Mississippi River. Data on average discharge, length, and drainage area include the Red River, but exclude all water diverted into the Atchafalaya from the Mississippi River.

Source: U.S. Geological Survey, *Largest Rivers in the United States*, Open File Report 87-242, May 1990.

No. 367. U.S. Water Withdrawals and Consumptive Use Per Day by End Use: 1940 to 1995

[Includes Puerto Rico. Withdrawal signifies water physically withdrawn from a source. Includes fresh and saline water; excludes water used for hydroelectric power]

Year	Total (bil. gal.)	Per capita[1] (gal.)	Irrigation (bil. gal.)	Public supply[2] Total (bil. gal.)	Per capita[3] (gal.)	Rural[4] (bil. gal.)	Industrial and misc.[5] (bil. gal.)	Steam electric utilities (bil. gal.)
WITHDRAWALS								
1940	140	1,027	71	10	75	3.1	29	23
1950	180	1,185	89	14	145	3.6	37	40
1955	240	1,454	110	17	148	3.6	39	72
1960	270	1,500	110	21	151	3.6	38	100
1965	310	1,602	120	24	155	4.0	46	130
1970	370	1,815	130	27	166	4.5	47	170
1975	420	1,972	140	29	168	4.9	45	200
1980	440	1,953	150	34	183	5.6	45	210
1985	399	1,650	137	38	189	7.8	31	187
1990	408	1,620	137	41	195	7.9	30	195
1995	402	1,500	134	40	192	8.9	29	190
CONSUMPTIVE USE								
1960	61	339	52	3.5	25	2.8	3.0	0.2
1965	77	403	66	5.2	34	3.2	3.4	0.4
1970	87	427	73	5.9	36	3.4	4.1	0.8
1975	96	451	80	6.7	38	3.4	4.2	1.9
1980	100	440	83	7.1	38	3.9	5.0	3.2
1985	92	380	74	[6]	[6]	9.2	6.1	6.2
1990	94	370	76	[6]	[6]	8.9	6.7	4.0
1995	100	374	81	[6]	[6]	9.9	4.8	3.7

[1] Based on U.S. Census Bureau resident population as of July 1.   [2] Includes commercial water withdrawals.   [3] Based on population served.   [4] Rural farm and nonfarm household and garden use, and water for farm stock and dairies.   [5] For 1940 to 1960, includes manufacturing and mineral industries, rural commercial industries, air-conditioning, resorts, hotels, motels, military and other state and Federal agencies, and miscellaneous; thereafter, includes manufacturing, mining and mineral processing, ordnance, construction, and miscellaneous.   [6] Public supply consumptive use included in end-use categories.

Source: 1940-1960, U.S. Bureau of Domestic Business Development, based principally on committee prints, *Water Resources Activities in the United States*, for the Senate Committee on National Water Resources, U.S. Senate, thereafter, U.S. Geological Survey, *Estimated Use of Water in the United States in 1995*, circular 1200, and previous quinquennial issues. Next update expected in 2003 will include data for 2000.

230   Geography and Environment

No. 368. Water Withdrawals and Consumptive Use—State and Other Areas: 1995

[In millions of gallons per day (401,500 represents 401,500,000,000), except as noted. Figures may not add due to rounding. Withdrawal signifies water physically withdrawn from a source. Includes fresh and saline water]

State and other area	Total	Per capita (gal. per day) fresh	Ground water	Surface water	Irrigation	Public supply	Industrial	Thermo-electric	Consumptive use,[1] fresh water
U.S.[2]	401,500	1,280	77,500	324,000	134,000	43,600	26,200	190,000	100,000
Alabama	7,100	1,670	445	6,650	139	875	753	5,200	532
Alaska	329	350	132	196	0.6	90	197	30	25
Arizona	6,830	1,620	2,840	3,990	5,670	846	197	62	3,830
Arkansas	8,800	3,540	5,460	3,340	5,940	419	187	1,780	4,140
California	45,900	1,130	14,700	31,300	28,900	5,740	802	9,630	25,500
Colorado	13,800	3,690	2,270	11,600	12,700	732	191	115	5,230
Connecticut	4,450	389	166	4,290	28	448	11	3,940	97
Delaware	1,500	1,050	110	1,390	48	101	64	1,270	71
District of Columbia	10	18	1	10	-	-	1	10	15
Florida	18,200	509	4,340	13,800	3,470	2,360	649	11,600	2,780
Georgia	5,820	799	1,190	4,630	722	1,250	676	3,070	1,170
Hawaii	1,930	853	531	1,400	652	218	20	970	542
Idaho	15,100	13,000	2,830	12,300	13,000	254	76	-	4,360
Illinois	19,900	1,680	953	19,000	180	1,950	527	17,100	857
Indiana	9,140	1,570	709	8,430	116	784	2,410	5,690	505
Iowa	3,030	1,070	528	2,510	39	418	301	2,130	290
Kansas	5,240	2,040	3,510	1,720	3,380	384	77	1,260	3,620
Kentucky	4,420	1,150	226	4,190	12	521	375	3,450	318
Louisiana	9,850	2,270	1,350	8,500	769	677	2,580	5,480	1,930
Maine	326	178	80	246	27	135	16	136	48
Maryland	7,730	289	246	7,480	57	907	331	6,360	150
Massachusetts	5,510	189	351	5,160	82	759	88	4,570	180
Michigan	12,100	1,260	862	11,200	227	1,490	1,910	8,370	667
Minnesota	3,390	736	714	2,680	157	573	438	2,090	417
Mississippi	3,200	1,140	2,590	614	1,740	377	294	375	1,570
Missouri	7,030	1,320	891	6,140	567	757	63	5,550	692
Montana	8,860	10,200	217	8,640	8,550	161	80	22	1,960
Nebraska	10,500	6,440	6,200	4,350	7,550	328	175	2,350	7,020
Nevada	2,300	1,480	896	1,400	1,640	479	95	27	1,340
New Hampshire	1,320	388	81	1,240	6.3	130	50	1,110	35
New Jersey	6,110	269	580	5,530	125	1,120	486	4,360	210
New Mexico	3,510	2,080	1,700	1,800	2,990	337	69	55	1,980
New York	16,800	567	1,010	15,800	30	3,140	321	13,100	469
North Carolina	9,290	1,070	535	8,750	239	939	385	7,420	713
North Dakota	1,120	1,750	122	1,000	117	85	17	819	181
Ohio	10,500	944	905	9,620	27	1,560	650	8,190	791
Oklahoma	2,040	543	1,220	822	864	597	285	124	716
Oregon	7,910	2,520	1,050	6,860	6,170	572	379	9.0	3,210
Pennsylvania	9,680	802	860	8,820	16	1,730	1,930	5,930	565
Rhode Island	411	138	27	383	2	121	7	275	19
South Carolina	6,200	1,690	322	5,880	53	614	703	4,810	321
South Dakota	460	631	187	273	269	97	32	5	249
Tennessee	10,100	1,920	435	9,640	24	831	868	8,300	233
Texas	29,600	1,300	8,780	20,800	9,450	3,420	2,920	13,500	10,500
Utah	4,460	2,200	790	3,670	3,530	506	253	48	2,200
Vermont	565	967	50	515	3.9	66	12	452	24
Virginia	8,260	826	358	7,900	30	911	622	6,620	218
Washington	8,860	1,620	1,760	7,100	6,470	1,300	652	376	3,080
West Virginia	4,620	2,530	146	4,470	-	217	1,330	3,010	352
Wisconsin	7,250	1,420	759	6,490	169	692	453	5,820	443
Wyoming	7,060	14,700	335	6,720	6,590	100	118	220	2,800
Puerto Rico	2,840	154	135	2,680	107	443	15	2,260	187
Virgin Islands	202	113	0.7	201	-	7.8	20	173	1.9

- Represents zero. [1] Water that has been evaporated, transpired, or incorporated into products, plant or animal tissue; and therefore, is not available for immediate reuse. [2] Includes Puerto Rico and Virgin Islands.

Source: U.S. Geological Survey, *Estimated Use of Water in the United States in 1995*, circular 1200. Next update expected in 2003 will include data for 2000.

No. 369. U.S. Water Quality Conditions by Type of Waterbody: 2000

[Section 305(b) of the Clean Water Act requires states and other jurisdictions to assess the health of their waters and the extent to which their waters support water quality standards. Section 305(b) requires that states submit reports describing water quality conditions to the Environmental Protection Agency every 2 years. Water quality standards have three elements (designated uses, criteria developed to protect each use, and an antidegradation policy. For information on survey methodology and assessment criteria, see report]

Item	Rivers and streams (miles)	Lakes, reservoirs, and ponds (acres)	Estuaries (sq. miles)	Great Lakes shoreline (miles)	Ocean shoreline (miles)
Total size	3,692,830	40,603,893	87,369	5,521	58,618
Amount accessed [1]	699,946	17,339,080	31,072	5,066	3,221
Percent of total size	19	43	36	92	6
Amount accessed as—					
Good [2]	463,441	8,026,988	13,850	-	2,176
Good but threatened [3]	85,544	1,343,903	1,023	1,095	193
Polluted [4]	291,264	7,702,370	15,676	3,955	434
Percent of accessed as—					
Good [2]	53	47	45	-	79
Good but threatened [3]	8	8	4	22	7
Polluted [4]	39	45	51	78	14
Amount impaired by leading sources of pollution: [5]					
Agriculture	128,859	3,158,393	2,811	75	(NA)
Atmospheric deposition	(NA)	983,936	3,692	71	(NA)
Construction	(NA)	(NA)	(NA)	(NA)	29
Contaminated sediments	(NA)	(NA)	(NA)	519	(NA)
Forestry	28,156	(NA)	(NA)	(NA)	(NA)
Habitat modification	37,654	(NA)	(NA)	62	(NA)
Hydrologic modification	53,850	1,413,624	2,171	(NA)	(NA)
Industrial discharges/point sources	(NA)	(NA)	4,116	(NA)	76
Land disposal of wastes	(NA)	856,586	(NA)	61	123
Municipal point sources	27,988	943,715	5,779	(NA)	89
Nonpoint sources	(NA)	1,045,036	(NA)	(NA)	142
Resource extraction	27,695	(NA)	1,913	(NA)	(NA)
Septic tanks	(NA)	(NA)	(NA)	61	103
Urban runoff and storm sewers	34,871	13,699,327	5,045	152	241

- Represents zero. NA Not available. [1] Includes waterbodies accessed as not attainable for one or more uses. Most states do not assess all their waterbodies during the 2-year reporting cycle, but use a "rotating basin approach" whereby all waters are monitored over a set period of time. [2] Based on assessment of available data, water quality supports all designated uses. Water quality meets narrative and/or numeric criteria adopted to protect and support a designated use. [3] Although all assessed uses are currently met, data show a declining trend in water quality. Projections based on this trend indicate water quality will be impaired in the future, unless action is taken to prevent further degradation. [4] Impaired or not attainable. The reporting state or jurisdiction has performed a "use-attainability analysis" and demonstrated that support of one or more designated beneficial uses is not attainable due to specific biological, chemical, physical, or economic/social conditions. [5] Excludes unknown and natural sources.

Source: U.S. Environmental Protection Agency, *National Water Quality Inventory: 2000 Report*, EPA-841-R-02-001, August 2002. See also <http://www.epa.gov/305b/2000report>.

No. 370. Oil Spills in U.S. Water—Number and Volume: 1997 to 2000

[Based on reported discharges into U.S. navigable waters, including territorial waters (extending 3 to 12 miles from the coastline), tributaries, the contiguous zone, onto shoreline, or into other waters that threaten the marine environment. Data found in Marine Safety Management System]

Spill characteristic	Number of spills 1997	1998	1999	2000	Spill volume (gallons) 1997	1998	1999	2000
Total	8,624	8,315	8,539	8,354	942,574	885,303	1,172,449	1,431,370
Size of spill (gallons):								
1-100	8,299	7,962	8,212	8,058	39,082	38,093	39,119	39,355
101-1,000	243	259	240	219	81,895	86,606	86,530	78,779
1,001-3,000	40	54	42	37	78,117	96,743	74,582	67,529
3,001-5,000	14	15	18	12	58,016	64,609	73,798	45,512
5,001-10,000	15	15	10	16	109,288	108,148	66,274	112,415
10,001-50,000	11	8	12	6	282,176	216,335	301,510	108,400
50,001-100,000	1	-	4	4	84,000	-	245,406	266,380
100,000-1,000,000	1	2	1	2	210,000	274,769	285,230	713,000
1,000,000 and over	-	-	-	-	-	-	-	-
Waterbody:								
Atlantic ocean	87	109	148	150	40,857	6,674	29,440	135,010
Pacific ocean	505	644	758	623	32,841	192,775	150,694	36,301
Gulf of Mexico	2,341	2,190	1,756	1,838	105,462	181,372	45,786	112,069
Great Lakes	156	119	129	96	4,311	3,006	906	4,535
Lakes	29	25	31	32	210,270	63	624	349
Rivers and canals	1,821	1,944	1,924	1,816	182,676	280,651	504,264	663,404
Bays and sounds	811	891	1,299	1,248	46,450	24,234	136,650	49,783
Harbors	858	790	907	801	45,932	97,223	105,213	273,095
Other	2,016	1,603	1,587	1,750	273,775	99,305	198,872	156,824
Source:								
Tankship	124	104	92	111	22,429	56,673	8,414	608,176
Tankbarge	252	220	227	229	165,649	248,089	158,977	133,540
All other vessels	4,971	4,848	5,361	5,220	192,801	316,473	409,084	291,927
Facilities	838	937	1,019	1,054	204,935	166,269	367,537	311,604
Pipelines	32	45	25	25	224,122	47,863	36,140	17,021
All other nonvessels	486	571	571	566	72,208	32,584	147,704	45,136
Unknown	1,921	1,590	1,244	1,149	60,430	17,352	44,593	23,966

- Represents or rounds to zero.
Source: U.S. Coast Guard, <http://www.uscg.mil/hq/g-m/nmc/response/stats/Summary.htm> (accessed 05 December 2001).

232 Geography and Environment

U.S. Census Bureau, Statistical Abstract of the United States: 2003

No. 371. National Ambient Air Pollutant Concentrations: 1992 to 2001

[Data represent annual composite averages of pollutant based on daily 24-hour averages of monitoring stations, except carbon monoxide is based on the second-highest, nonoverlapping, 8-hour average; ozone, the second-highest daily maximum 1-hour value or the fourth-highest maximum 8-hour value; and lead, the maximum quarterly average of ambient lead levels. Based on data from the Air Quality System. µg/m³=micrograms of pollutant per cubic meter of air; ppm=parts per million]

Pollutant	Unit	Monitoring stations, number	Air quality standard [1]	1992	1995	1997	1998	1999	2000	2001
Carbon monoxide...	ppm....	387	[2]9	5.2	4.6	4.1	3.8	3.7	3.3	3.2
Ozone	ppm....	785	[3]0.12	0.104	0.111	0.104	0.110	0.107	0.1	0.101
Ozone	ppm....	785	[4]0.08	0.081	0.087	0.082	0.087	0.086	0.08	0.081
Sulfur dioxide	ppm....	449	0.03	0.0075	0.0057	0.0055	0.0055	0.0053	0.0051	0.0049
Particulates (PM-10).	µg/m³..	770	[5]50	27.7	25.7	24.6	24.3	24.8	24.4	23.9
Nitrogen dioxide....	ppm....	250	0.053	0.019	0.018	0.017	0.018	0.018	0.017	0.017
Lead	µg/m³..	96	[6]1.5	0.08	0.06	0.05	0.05	0.05	0.05	0.06

[1] Refers to the primary National Ambient Air Quality Standard that protects the public health. [2] Based on 8-hour standard of 9 ppm. [3] Based on 1-hour standard of 0.12 ppm. [4] Based on 8-hour standard of 0.08 ppm. [5] The particulates (PM-10) standard replaced the previous standard for total suspended particulates in 1987. [6] Based on 3-month standard of 1.5 µg/m³.

No. 372. National Air Pollutant Emissions: 1970 to 2001

[In thousands of tons, except as indicated. PM-10=Particulate matter of less than ten microns; PM-2.5=particulate matter of less than 2.5 microns effective diameter. Methodologies to estimate data for 1970 to 1980 period and 1985 to present emissions differ. Beginning with 1985, the methodology for more recent years is described in the document available at <http://www.epa.gov/ttn/chief/trends/trends99/neiproc99.pdf>]

Year	PM-10	PM-10, fugitive dust[1]	PM-2.5	Sulfur dioxide	Nitrogen dioxides	Volatile organic compounds	Carbon monoxide	Lead[2] (tons)
1970	13,042	(NA)	(NA)	31,161	20,928	30,982	129,444	220,869
1975	7,671	(NA)	(NA)	28,011	22,632	26,079	116,757	159,659
1980	7,013	(NA)	(NA)	25,925	27,079	31,106	185,407	74,153
1985	11,590	29,734	(NA)	23,307	25,757	27,404	176,844	22,890
1990	9,690	18,068	7,561	23,078	25,530	24,116	154,189	4,975
1991	9,270	18,075	7,320	22,375	25,179	23,577	147,128	4,169
1992	8,927	18,170	7,198	22,082	25,260	23,066	140,896	3,810
1993	8,411	18,953	7,150	21,772	25,357	22,730	135,901	3,916
1994	8,888	19,722	7,541	21,346	25,349	22,569	133,559	4,047
1995	8,807	17,012	6,929	18,619	24,956	22,041	126,777	3,929
1996	9,017	13,845	6,726	18,387	24,790	20,870	128,860	2,627
1997	8,396	14,516	6,257	18,841	24,712	19,554	117,913	(NA)
1998	8,345	14,555	6,263	18,947	24,349	18,783	115,382	(NA)
1999	9,185	12,447	6,813	17,651	23,671	19,378	117,229	(NA)
2000	10,385	14,314	8,175	16,317	23,199	19,704	123,568	(NA)
2001	9,442	14,662	7,380	15,790	22,349	17,963	120,759	(NA)

NA Not available, and wind erosion. [1] Sources such as agricultural tilling, construction, mining and quarrying, paved roads, unpaved roads, and wind erosion. [2] Beginning 1996, lead and lead compounds are inventoried through the hazardous air pollutants (HAPs) portion of the National Emission Inventory (NEI) every 3 years; data for 1997 forward are currently not available.

No. 373. Air Pollutant Emissions by Pollutant and Source: 2001

[In thousands of tons, except as indicated. See headnote, Table 372]

Source	PM-10 [1]	PM-2.5	Sulfur dioxide	Nitrogen dioxides	Volatile organic compounds	Carbon monoxide
Total emissions	**24,104**	**7,379**	**15,790**	**22,349**	**17,963**	**120,760**
Fuel combustion, stationary sources	1,504	1,319	13,632	8,599	1,184	4,592
Electric utilities	663	568	10,821	4,891	63	492
Industrial	330	258	2,262	2,640	168	1,181
Other fuel combustion	511	493	549	1,068	953	2,919
Residential	423	419	164	674	925	2,759
Industrial processes	667	483	1,405	847	1,249	2,519
Chemical and allied product manufacturing ...	54	46	329	117	305	381
Metals processing	172	143	358	96	72	1,356
Petroleum and related industries	39	26	310	129	394	169
Other	402	268	408	505	478	613
Solvent utilization	5	-	1	4	5,053	50
Storage and transport	86	41	6	11	1,150	174
Waste disposal and recycling	504	475	35	169	541	3,229
Highway vehicles	219	162	261	8,249	4,874	74,826
Light-duty gas vehicles and motorcycles	51	27	103	2,386	2,620	41,231
Light-duty trucks	31	17	71	1,503	1,805	29,333
Heavy-duty gas vehicles	10	7	14	456	224	3,133
Diesels	127	111	73	3,904	225	1,129
Off highway [2]	316	290	440	4,156	2,622	24,677
Miscellaneous [3]	20,803	4,609	10	314	1,290	10,693

- Represents or rounds to zero. [1] Represents both PM-10 and PM-10 fugitive dust; see Table 372. [2] Includes emissions from farm tractors and other farm machinery, construction equipment, industrial machinery, recreational marine vessels, and small general utility engines such as lawn mowers. [3] Includes emissions such as from forest fires and other kinds of burning, various agricultural activities, fugitive dust from paved and unpaved roads, and other construction and mining activities, and natural sources.

Source of Tables 371-373: U.S. Environmental Protection Agency, *Latest Findings on National Air Quality, 2001 Status and Trends*, EPA 454/K-02-001, September 2002. See also <http://www.epa.gov/ttn/chief/trends/index.html#tables>.

Geography and Environment 233

No. 374. Emissions of Greenhouse Gases by Type and Source: 1990 to 2001

[1,682.5 represents 1,682,500,000 tons. Emission estimates were mandated by Congress through Section 1605(a) of the Energy Policy Act of 1992 (Title XVI). Gases that contain carbon can be measured either in terms of the full molecular weight of the gas or just in terms of their carbon content. Both measures are utilized below]

Type and source	Unit	1990	1995	1998	1999	2000	2001
CARBON EQUIVALENT							
Total emissions tons	Mil. metric tons	1,682.5	1,774.9	1,842.4	1,861.0	1,907.1	1,883.4
Carbon dioxide, total	Mil. metric tons	1,364.4	1,451.2	1,526.3	1,547.1	1,596.8	1,578.7
Energy sources	Mil. metric tons	1,359.5	1,434.1	1,512.3	1,530.1	1,578.3	1,558.7
C02 in natural gas	Mil. metric tons	3.8	4.6	4.9	4.8	4.9	5.0
Cement production	Mil. metric tons	9.1	10.1	10.7	10.9	11.3	11.4
Gas flaring	Mil. metric tons	2.5	4.7	1.7	1.8	1.7	1.7
Other industrial	Mil. metric tons	7.3	7.6	8.1	8.0	8.0	7.4
Waste combustion	Mil. metric tons	4.8	6.3	6.9	7.1	6.1	6.1
Other, adjustments	Mil. metric tons	-22.6	-16.1	-18.3	-15.6	-13.4	-11.7
Methane	Mil. metric tons	199	195	182	180	178	176
Nitrous oxide	Mil. metric tons	94	102	99	100	98	97
HFCs, PFCs, and SF_6	Mil. metric tons	25	27	35	34	34	31
NATIVE GAS							
Carbon dioxide	Mil. metric tons	5,002.8	5,320.9	5,596.4	5,672.8	5,855.1	5,788.5
Methane, total	Mil. metric tons	31.68	31.13	29.03	28.74	28.33	28.02
Energy sources	Mil. metric tons	11.94	11.62	11.05	11.02	11.06	10.58
Waste management	Mil. metric tons	11.36	10.33	8.86	8.59	8.02	8.13
Agricultural sources	Mil. metric tons	8.26	9.05	8.99	9.00	9.13	9.19
Industrial sources	Mil. metric tons	0.12	0.13	0.13	0.13	0.13	0.11
Nitrous oxide, total [1]	1,000 metric tons	1,170	1,259	1,223	1,238	1,219	1,207
Agriculture	1,000 metric tons	846	861	875	870	859	852
Energy sources	1,000 metric tons	211	269	271	293	285	284
Waste management	1,000 metric tons	17	18	18	19	20	20
Industrial sources	1,000 metric tons	96	111	58	57	56	51
Hydrofluorocarbons (HFCs):							
HFC-23	1,000 metric tons	3.0	2.3	3.5	2.7	2.6	1.8
HFC-125	1,000 metric tons	-	0.5	1.1	1.3	1.6	1.9
HFC-134a	1,000 metric tons	0.6	12.2	23.1	26.1	28.9	31.6
HFC-143a	1,000 metric tons	-	0.1	0.5	0.7	0.9	1.1
Perfluorocarbons (PFCs):							
CF_4	1,000 metric tons	3	2	2	2	1	1
C_2F_6	1,000 metric tons	(Z)	(Z)	1	1	1	1
C_4F_{10}	1,000 metric tons	(Z)	(Z)	(Z)	(Z)	(Z)	(Z)
Sulfur hexafluoride (SF_6)	1,000 metric tons	2	1	1	1	1	1

- Represents zero.   Z Less than 50 or 500 metric tons.   [1] Includes sources not shown separately.

Source: U.S. Energy Information Administration, *Emissions of Greenhouse Gases in the United States*, Series DOE/EIA-0573(2001), annual. See also <ftp://ftp.eia.doe.gov/pub/oiaf/1605/cdrom/pdf/ggrpt/057301.pdf> (issued 20 December 2002).

No. 375. Municipal Solid Waste Generation, Recovery, and Disposal: 1980 to 2001

[In millions of tons (151.6 represents 151,600,000), except as indicated. Covers post-consumer residential and commercial solid wastes which comprise the major portion of typical municipal collections. Excludes mining, agricultural and industrial processing, demolition and construction wastes, sewage sludge, and junked autos and obsolete equipment wastes. Based on material-flows estimating procedure and wet weight as generated]

Item and material	1980	1990	1995	1998	1999	2000	2001
Waste generated	151.6	205.2	211.4	223.4	231.0	232.0	229.2
Per person per day (lb.)	3.7	4.5	4.4	4.5	4.6	4.5	4.4
Materials recovered	14.5	33.2	54.9	61.1	64.8	67.7	68.0
Per person per day (lb.)	0.35	0.7	1.1	1.2	1.3	1.3	1.3
Combustion for energy recovery	2.7	31.9	35.5	34.4	34.0	33.7	33.6
Per person per day (lb.)	0.06	0.7	0.7	0.7	0.7	0.7	0.7
Combustion without energy recovery	11.0	([1])	([1])	([1])	([1])	([1])	([1])
Per person per day (lb.)	0.27	([1])	([1])	([1])	([1])	([1])	([1])
Landfill, other disposal	123.4	140.1	120.9	127.1	132.1	130.6	127.6
Per person per day (lb.)	3.0	3.1	2.5	2.6	2.7	2.5	2.5
Percent distribution of generation:							
Paper and paperboard	36.4	35.4	38.6	37.7	38.2	37.4	35.7
Glass	10.0	6.4	6.1	5.7	5.6	5.4	5.5
Metals	10.2	8.1	7.5	7.5	7.7	7.8	7.9
Plastics	4.5	8.3	8.9	10.0	10.4	10.7	11.1
Rubber and leather	2.8	2.8	2.9	3.1	2.7	2.7	2.8
Textiles	1.7	2.8	3.5	3.9	3.9	4.0	4.3
Wood	4.6	6.0	4.9	5.4	5.4	5.6	5.7
Food wastes	8.6	10.1	10.3	11.2	10.9	11.2	11.4
Yard wastes	18.1	17.1	14.0	12.4	12.0	12.0	12.2
Other wastes	3.2	3.0	3.3	3.2	3.2	3.2	3.4

[1] Combustion without energy recovery is no longer available separately.

Source: Franklin Associates, a Division of ERG, Prairie Village, KS, *Municipal Solid Waste in the United States: 2001 Facts and Figures*. Prepared for the U.S. Environmental Protection Agency.

No. 376. Generation and Recovery of Selected Materials in Municipal Solid Waste: 1980 to 2001

[In millions of tons (151.6 represents 151,600,000), except as indicated. Covers postconsumer residential and commercial solid wastes which comprise the major portion of typical municipal collections. Excludes mining, agricultural and industrial processing, demolition and construction wastes, sewage sludge, and junked autos and obsolete equipment wastes. Based on material-flows estimating procedure and wet weight as generated]

Item and material	1980	1990	1995	1998	1999	2000	2001
Waste generated, total	**151.6**	**205.2**	**211.4**	**223.4**	**230.9**	**232.0**	**229.2**
Paper and paperboard	55.2	72.7	81.7	84.2	88.3	86.8	81.9
Ferrous metals	12.6	12.6	11.6	12.4	13.3	13.5	13.5
Aluminum	1.7	2.8	3.0	3.1	3.1	3.2	3.2
Other nonferrous metals	1.2	1.1	1.3	1.4	1.4	1.4	1.4
Glass	15.1	13.1	12.8	12.6	12.9	12.6	12.6
Plastics	6.8	17.1	18.9	22.4	24.1	24.7	25.4
Yard waste	27.5	35.0	29.7	27.7	27.7	27.7	28.0
Other wastes	31.5	50.7	52.4	59.6	60.1	62.1	63.3
Materials recovered, total	**14.5**	**33.2**	**54.9**	**61.1**	**64.8**	**67.7**	**68.0**
Paper and paperboard	11.9	20.2	32.7	34.4	36.1	36.7	36.7
Ferrous metals	0.4	2.2	4.1	4.3	4.5	4.6	4.6
Aluminum	0.3	1.0	0.9	0.9	0.9	0.9	0.8
Other nonferrous metals	0.5	0.7	0.8	0.9	0.9	0.9	0.9
Glass	0.8	2.6	3.1	2.9	3.0	2.7	2.4
Plastics	-	0.4	1.0	1.2	1.3	1.3	1.4
Yard waste	-	4.2	9.0	12.6	14.2	15.8	15.8
Other wastes	0.6	1.8	3.2	3.9	3.9	4.8	5.4
Percent of generation recovered, total	**9.6**	**16.2**	**26.0**	**27.4**	**28.1**	**29.2**	**29.7**
Paper and paperboard	21.6	27.8	40.0	40.9	40.9	42.3	44.9
Ferrous metals	3.2	17.5	35.3	34.7	33.8	34.0	33.8
Aluminum	17.6	35.7	30.0	29.0	29.0	27.4	24.5
Other nonferrous metals	41.7	63.6	61.5	64.3	64.3	66.9	64.8
Glass	5.3	19.8	24.2	23.0	23.3	21.1	19.1
Plastics	-	2.3	5.3	5.4	5.4	5.4	5.5
Yard waste	-	12.0	30.3	45.5	51.3	56.9	56.5
Other wastes	1.9	3.6	6.1	6.5	6.5	7.8	8.5

- Represents zero.

Source: Franklin Associates, a Division of ERG, Prairie Village, KS, *Municipal Solid Waste in the United States: 2001 Facts and Figures*. Prepared for the U.S. Environmental Protection Agency.

No. 377. Curbside Recycling Programs—Number and Population Served by Region: 1995 to 2001

[For composition of regions, see map, inside front cover]

Region	Number of programs					Population served [1] (1,000)				
	1995	1997	1999	2000	2001	1995	1997	1999	2000	2001
Total	7,375	8,969	9,349	9,247	9,704	121,335	136,229	139,826	133,165	139,366
Northeast	2,210	3,406	3,414	3,459	3,421	37,256	43,200	43,162	43,482	43,981
South	1,281	1,344	1,581	1,427	1,677	31,521	36,952	37,914	37,510	26,496
Midwest	2,985	3,357	3,477	3,582	3,572	25,487	26,970	30,106	22,618	25,851
West	899	862	877	779	1,034	27,071	29,107	28,644	29,555	43,038

[1] Calculated using population of states reporting data.

Source: Franklin Associates, a Division of ERG, Prairie Village, KS, *Municipal Solid Waste in the United States: 2001 Facts and Figures*. Prepared for the U.S. Environmental Protection Agency. Also in *Biocycle Magazine*.

No. 378. Toxic Chemical Releases and Transfers by Media: 1988 to 2001

[In millions of pounds (3,153.7 represents 3,153,700,000), except as indicated. Based on reports filed as required by Section 313 of the Emergency Planning and Community Right-to-Know Act (EPCRA, or Title III of the Superfund Amendments and Reauthorization Act of 1986), Public Law 99-499. Owners and operators of facilities that are classified within Standard Classification Code groups 20 through 39, have 10 or more full-time employees, and that manufacture, process, or otherwise uses any listed toxic chemical in quantities greater than the established threshold in the course of a calendar year are covered and required to report]

Media	Core chemicals [1]				
	1988	1998	1999	2000	2001
Total facilities reporting	19,610	19,294	18,881	18,692	17,773
Total releases	**3,153.7**	**1,873.0**	**1,709.8**	**1,639.0**	**1,435.7**
On-site releases	2,760.5	1,481.8	1,307.2	1,212.7	995.8
Air emissions	2,177.8	1,017.5	863.2	802.5	649.5
Surface water	41.7	18.5	15.5	15.4	14.6
Underground injection	161.9	114.4	109.1	111.1	94.9
Releases to land	379.1	331.4	319.3	283.6	236.7
Off-site releases	393.2	391.2	402.6	426.4	439.9
Total transfers off-site for further waste management	598.0	2,482.8	2,605.6	2,613.6	2,401.4
Transfers to recycling	(NA)	1,684.2	1,796.3	1,794.2	1,624.1
Transfers to energy recovery	(NA)	437.0	472.2	485.3	447.1
Transfers to treatment	323.8	212.9	193.8	187.8	196.9
Transfers to POTWs [2]	231.6	148.1	143.2	145.5	131.8
Other off-site transfers	42.6	0.7	0.1	0.9	1.5
Total production-related waste managed	(NA)	17,043.4	17,557.1	21,999.7	16,316.6
Recycled on-site	(NA)	5,820.3	5,672.6	6,643.9	5,676.7
Recycled off-site	(NA)	1,746.8	1,845.0	1,849.3	1,642.4
Energy recovery on-site	(NA)	2,467.5	2,476.2	2,521.9	2,317.6
Energy recovery off-site	(NA)	447.8	469.9	489.5	445.2
Treated on-site	(NA)	4,431.5	5,068.7	8,566.2	4,499.4
Treated off-site	(NA)	383.7	348.1	346.3	342.5
Quantity released on- and off-site	(NA)	1,745.8	1,676.5	1,582.5	1,392.9

NA Not available. [1] Chemicals covered for all reporting years. Excludes chemicals removed from the list, those added in 1990, 1994, and 1995, and aluminum oxide, ammonia, hydrochloric acid, PBT chemicals, sulfuric acid, vanadium and vanadium compounds. [2] POTW (Publicly Owned Treatment Work) is a wastewater treatment facility that is owned by a state or municipality.

No. 379. Toxic Chemical Releases by Industry: 2001

[In millions of pounds (6,158.0 represents 6,158,000,000), except as indicated. "Original Industries" include owners and operators Covers facilities that are classified within Standard Classification Code groups 20 through 39,10,12,49, 5169, 5171, and 4953/7169 that have 10 or more full-time employees, and that manufacture, process, or otherwise uses any listed toxic chemical in quantities greater than the established threshold in the course of a calendar year are covered and required to report]

Industry	1987 SIC[1] code	Total facilities (number)	Total on and off-site releases	On-site release				Off-site releases/transfers to disposal
				Total	Air emissions	Surface water discharges	Other [2]	
Total [3]	(X)	24,896	6,158.0	5,580.3	1,679.4	220.8	3,680.1	577.7
Metal mining	10	89	2,782.6	2,782.0	2.9	0.4	2,778.7	0.5
Coal mining	12	88	16.1	16.1	0.8	0.8	14.6	-
Food and kindred products	20	1,688	125.1	118.9	56.1	55.2	7.6	6.2
Tobacco products	21	31	3.6	3.2	2.5	0.5	0.2	0.3
Textile mill products	22	289	7.0	6.2	5.7	0.2	0.3	0.7
Apparel and other textile products	23	16	0.4	0.3	0.3	-	-	0.1
Lumber and wood products	24	1,006	31.4	30.9	30.5	-	0.4	0.5
Furniture and fixtures	25	282	8.0	7.8	7.8	-	-	0.2
Paper and allied products	26	507	195.7	189.9	157.2	16.5	16.2	5.8
Printing and publishing	27	231	19.7	19.3	19.3	-	-	0.4
Chemical and allied products	28	3,618	582.6	501.3	227.8	57.6	215.9	81.3
Petroleum and coal products	29	542	71.4	68.1	48.2	17.1	2.8	3.3
Rubber and misc. plastic products	30	1,822	88.5	78.1	77.1	0.1	0.9	10.5
Leather and leather products	31	60	2.6	1.3	1.2	0.1	-	1.3
Stone, clay, glass products	32	1,027	40.5	35.4	31.3	0.2	4.0	5.1
Primary metal industries	33	1,941	558.6	286.8	57.6	44.7	184.5	271.8
Fabricated metals products	34	2,959	64.0	42.8	40.4	1.7	0.6	21.2
Industrial machinery and equipment	35	1,143	15.4	10.7	8.3	-	2.5	4.6
Electronic, electric equipment	36	1,831	23.9	16.4	12.7	2.9	0.7	7.6
Transportation equipment	37	1,348	80.6	67.7	66.7	0.2	0.8	13.0
Instruments and related products	38	375	9.4	8.6	7.2	1.4	-	0.8
Miscellaneous	39	312	8.4	6.8	6.8	-	-	1.6
Electric utilities	49	732	1,062.2	989.2	717.6	3.5	268.1	73.1
Chemical wholesalers	5169	475	1.5	1.3	1.3	-	-	0.2
Petroleum bulk terminals	5171	596	21.3	21.2	21.2	-	-	0.2
RCRA/solvent recovery	4953/7169	223	219.9	168.4	1.0	-	167.4	51.4

- Represents or rounds to zero. X Not applicable. [1] Standard Industrial Classification, see text, Section 12. [2] Includes underground injection for Class I and Class II to V wells and land releases. [3] Includes industries with no specific industry identified, not shown separately.

Source of Tables 378 and 379: U.S. Environmental Protection Agency, Toxics Release Inventory, annual.

No. 380. Toxic Chemical Releases by State: 1988 to 2001

[In millions of pounds (3,153.7 represents 3,153,700,000). Excludes delisted chemicals, chemicals added in 1990, 1994, and 1995, and aluminum oxide, ammonia, hydorchloric acid, PBT chemicals, sulfuric acid, vanadium, and vanadium compounds. See headnote, Table 378]

State and outlying area	1988	1998	1999	2000	2001	State and outlying area	1988	1998	1999	2000	2001
Total	3,153.7	1,873.0	1,709.8	1,639.0	1,435.7	NE	16.7	9.9	8.6	10.3	12.2
U.S. total	3,138.3	1,865.5	1,704.2	1,633.3	1,430.1	NV	2.3	3.7	5.4	4.1	3.2
						NH	13.8	2.3	2.4	2.3	1.2
AL	109.5	75.9	73.6	66.7	61.0	NJ	46.7	11.3	11.3	11.3	26.8
AK	3.7	0.3	0.2	0.3	0.5	NM	29.3	23.3	19.6	0.5	0.6
AZ	61.5	50.9	47.7	38.7	52.7	NY	98.5	21.7	18.8	17.5	13.6
AR	40.8	38.6	38.8	44.8	33.5	NC	124.0	49.2	46.7	40.8	35.8
CA	107.9	23.9	23.2	23.4	16.7	ND	1.2	1.2	1.1	0.8	0.9
CO	15.4	3.1	3.0	2.8	2.5	OH	200.2	125.8	116.1	108.4	90.5
CT	37.9	6.0	4.5	4.5	3.6	OK	30.5	13.9	13.6	13.6	12.3
DE	8.7	5.8	5.2	5.6	5.2	OR	21.2	27.3	24.9	24.0	21.9
DC	-	(Z)	(Z)	(Z)		PA	133.7	82.6	81.3	88.0	97.5
FL	32.7	30.5	29.5	31.8	26.3	RI	7.8	1.6	1.2	1.1	0.9
GA	85.2	47.5	46.4	44.8	35.3	SC	65.8	50.2	55.8	51.6	52.0
HI	0.8	0.3	0.3	0.4	0.4	SD	2.4	1.4	1.1	1.2	1.1
ID	7.3	12.7	14.6	13.0	8.6	TN	126.0	84.8	88.5	81.2	62.8
IL	137.6	82.4	79.3	77.2	67.8	TX	317.8	172.8	169.0	150.9	130.2
IN	181.0	190.8	109.7	104.0	106.5	UT	122.2	93.3	77.2	101.5	48.4
IA	42.3	24.4	25.0	24.8	19.2	VT	1.7	0.2	0.2	0.1	0.1
KS	30.2	17.5	20.1	16.8	12.8	VA	112.2	39.6	39.4	34.6	31.6
KY	64.7	31.1	31.1	27.8	28.6	WA	30.5	24.1	17.3	16.6	11.7
LA	128.7	91.6	78.9	80.0	70.3	WV	39.3	16.3	11.8	10.2	9.0
ME	15.5	6.6	5.9	6.3	5.0	WI	61.1	33.7	31.7	29.0	25.5
MD	19.6	8.7	9.2	10.6	7.7	WY	2.0	1.2	1.3	1.2	0.8
MA	32.1	6.5	4.9	4.8	4.5						
MI	139.2	73.0	63.6	52.4	59.9	American					
MN	55.3	14.6	14.3	15.3	13.5	Samoa	-	-	-	-	-
MS	58.5	42.7	41.5	43.1	36.3	Guam	-	-	-	-	-
MO	82.2	44.3	43.4	46.0	43.0	Puerto Rico	12.9	6.6	5.2	5.3	4.8
MT	33.5	44.2	45.7	46.6	18.2	Virgin Island	2.6	0.9	0.5	0.4	0.8

- Represents zero.   Z Less than 50,000.

Source: U.S. Environmental Protection Agency, *Toxics Release Inventory*, annual.

No. 381. Hazardous Waste Sites on the National Priority List by State and Outlying Area: 2002

[As of December 31. Includes both proposed and final sites listed on the National Priorities List for the Superfund program as authorized by the Comprehensive Environmental Response, Compensation, and Liability Act of 1980 and the Superfund Amendments and Reauthorization Act of 1986]

State and outlying area	Total sites	Rank	Percent distribution	Federal	Non-Federal	State and outlying area	Total sites	Rank	Percent distribution	Federal	Non-Federal
Total	1,291	(X)	(X)	164	1,127	Montana	15	24	1.2	-	15
United States	1,278	(X)	100.0	163	1,115	Nebraska	11	38	0.9	1	10
						Nevada	1	49	0.1	-	1
Alabama	15	24	1.2	3	12	New Hampshire	19	20	1.5	1	18
Alaska	6	44	0.5	5	1	New Jersey	115	1	9.0	8	107
Arizona	9	41	0.7	2	7	New Mexico	12	32	0.9	1	11
Arkansas	12	32	0.9	-	12	New York	91	4	7.1	4	87
California	98	2	7.7	24	74	North Carolina	28	15	2.2	2	26
Colorado	17	22	1.3	3	14	North Dakota	-	50	-	-	-
Connecticut	16	23	1.3	1	15	Ohio	33	11	2.6	5	28
Delaware	15	24	1.2	1	14	Oklahoma	11	38	0.9	1	10
District of Columbia	1	(X)	0.1	1	-	Oregon	12	32	0.9	2	10
Florida	52	6	4.1	6	46	Pennsylvania	96	3	7.5	6	90
Georgia	15	24	1.2	2	13	Rhode Island	12	32	0.9	2	10
Hawaii	3	46	0.2	2	1	South Carolina	25	16	2.0	2	23
Idaho	10	40	0.8	2	8	South Dakota	2	47	0.2	1	1
Illinois	45	8	3.5	5	40	Tennessee	13	31	1.0	4	9
Indiana	29	14	2.3	-	29	Texas	43	9	3.4	4	39
Iowa	14	29	1.1	1	13	Utah	21	19	1.6	4	17
Kansas	12	32	0.9	2	10	Vermont	9	41	0.7	-	9
Kentucky	14	29	1.1	1	13	Virginia	30	13	2.3	11	19
Louisiana	15	24	1.2	1	14	Washington	47	7	3.7	14	33
Maine	12	32	0.9	3	9	West Virginia	9	41	0.7	2	7
Maryland	19	20	1.5	9	10	Wisconsin	40	10	3.1	-	40
Massachusetts	32	12	2.5	7	25	Wyoming	2	47	0.2	1	1
Michigan	69	5	5.4	1	68						
Minnesota	24	17	1.9	2	22	Guam	2	(X)	(X)	1	1
Mississippi	4	45	0.3	-	4	Puerto Rico	9	(X)	(X)	-	9
Missouri	23	18	1.8	3	20	Virgin Islands	2	(X)	(X)	-	2

- Represents zero.   X Not applicable.

Source: U.S. Environmental Protection Agency, *Supplementary Materials: National Priorities List, Proposed Rule*, December 2002.

No. 382. Pollution Abatement Capital Expenditures and Operating Costs by Media and Industry: 1999

[In millions of dollars. Based on probability sample of about 21,000 manufacturing, mining, and electric utility plants. Pollution abatement is the reduction of elimination of pollution that is created by the production process and has the potential to produce undesirable environmental and/or health effects. Capital expenditures include installation and retrofit that occurred for separately identifiable methods, techniques, or process technologies installed exclusively for the purpose of removing pollutants. Operating costs include all costs for operating and maintaining all pollution abatement technology]

Industry	NAICS code [1]	Pollution abatement capital expenditures			Pollution abatement operating costs		
		Total [2]	Air	Water	Solid waste	Total [2]	Air	Water	Solid waste
All industries	(X)	5,809.9	3,463.7	1,801.9	361.9	11,864.4	5,069.1	4,586.5	2,013.3
Mining	21	277.3	79.0	157.8	36.9	458.9	180.7	208.8	67.1
Oil & gas extraction	211	116.2	20.6	63.5	32.1	146.9	58.2	72.1	16.0
Mining (except oil & gas)	212	159.5	57.6	93.6	4.7	305.1	121.8	131.5	50.2
Support activities for mining	213	1.6	0.8	0.7	0.1	6.9	0.7	5.3	0.8
Electric power generation	22111	1,145.1	1,071.1	55.1	17.1	1,163.8	910.1	99.9	127.1
Manufacturing	31-33	4,387.3	2,313.4	1,588.9	307.9	10,240.3	3,977.5	4,277.4	1,818.8
Food	311	369.9	70.1	281.0	18.5	924.3	105.2	699.3	113.9
Beverage and tobacco product	312	17.1	4.4	9.0	3.5	66.1	12.2	47.4	(D)
Textile mills	313	37.1	21.3	7.5	8.2	105.0	18.6	72.4	13.6
Textile product mills	314	7.2	(D)	(D)	(D)	4.9	(D)	2.4	(D)
Apparel	315	(Z)	(D)	(D)	(D)	1.8	(D)	1.3	(D)
Leather and allied product	316	7.3	(D)	(D)	6.4	19.6	(D)	14.5	3.5
Wood product	321	82.1	65.6	12.3	3.9	134.9	86.3	26.2	19.7
Paper	322	611.9	252.8	261.3	25.5	945.6	264.4	462.0	190.6
Printing and related support activities . .	323	35.2	31.4	2.4	1.3	80.3	56.0	8.2	15.2
Petroleum and coal products	324	488.1	349.0	104.1	23.8	1,697.9	1,206.2	344.1	136.1
Chemicals	325	990.9	488.2	335.4	133.9	2,808.0	829.3	1,289.7	633.2
Plastics and rubber products	326	102.6	92.0	5.7	4.7	164.7	86.0	30.3	46.8
Nonmetallic mineral product	327	232.6	195.1	16.2	20.1	281.5	154.6	50.2	61.7
Primary metal	331	605.7	481.2	93.6	22.8	1,543.9	755.5	571.8	205.0
Fabricated metal product	332	283.3	38.2	232.4	9.7	405.3	89.2	167.2	137.0
Machinery	333	163.3	26.3	92.5	3.0	97.7	25.6	41.2	28.8
Computer and electronic product . .	334	138.0	58.5	67.5	11.7	325.4	59.5	208.6	50.6
Elect. equip., appliance, & component .	335	33.7	20.8	10.6	2.2	97.0	40.7	32.2	22.7
Transportation equipment	336	134.7	74.8	46.4	11.0	454.4	152.0	190.6	104.1
Furniture and related product	337	35.0	31.3	(D)	1.8	39.1	17.7	7.0	13.6
Miscellaneous	339	11.5	5.5	3.9	1.4	42.8	16.5	10.8	13.6

D Withheld to avoid disclosing data for individual companies. X Not applicable. Z Less than $50,000. [1] North American Industry Classification System, 1997; see text, Section 15. [2] Includes expenditures for multimedia, not shown separately.

No. 383. Pollution Abatement Capital Expenditures and Operating Costs by Media and State: 1999

[Based on probability sample of about 21,000 manufacturing, mining, and electric utility plants. Pollution abatement is the reduction of elimination of pollution that is created by the production process and has the potential to produce undesirable environmental and/or health effects. Capital expenditures include installation and retrofit that occurred for separately identifiable methods, techniques, or process technologies installed exclusively for the purpose of removing pollutants. Operating costs include all costs for operating and maintaining all pollution abatement technology]

State	Pollution abatement capital expenditures			Pollution abatement operating costs		State	Pollution abatement capital expenditures			Pollution abatement operating costs	
	Expenditures, total (mil. dol.)	Percent for air pollutants	Percent for hazardous materials	Expenditures, total (mil. dol.)	Percent for air pollutants		Expenditures, total (mil. dol.)	Percent for air pollutants	Percent for hazardous materials	Expenditures, total (mil. dol.)	Percent for air pollutants
U.S. [1]	5,809.9	59.6	22.6	11,864.4	42.7	MO	89.4	78.7	6.0	118.5	31.5
						MT	58.4	66.1	45.2	267.7	32.4
AL	45.7	50.5	54.3	53.0	18.5	NE	382.7	92.7	6.3	224.9	38.3
AK	30.2	8.6	0.7	59.2	22.0	NV	114.1	51.5	8.9	318.5	46.0
AZ	63.6	54.4	52.5	133.4	23.8	NH	107.9	76.8	26.4	205.6	28.6
AR	204.6	0.4	0.3	35.6	21.6	NJ	166.0	66.4	25.1	263.0	36.6
CA	3.1	22.6	74.2	9.4	(D)	NM	145.5	69.5	33.8	259.8	40.9
CO	28.5	54.7	22.5	10.9	(D)	NY	71.9	43.4	6.0	151.1	46.9
CT	57.0	78.4	24.6	165.1	32.1	NC	156.6	63.5	11.0	331.6	30.4
DE	160.6	76.6	78.3	310.0	51.3	ND	91.9	31.1	12.3	183.8	36.5
FL	422.2	87.1	7.2	534.0	39.6	OH	228.8	43.6	29.9	522.7	39.7
GA	172.2	43.5	19.0	511.5	36.1	OK	34.0	90.6	44.1	78.8	42.3
HA	128.5	76.3	44.6	638.4	43.6	OR	617.6	58.0	38.3	1,679.2	45.9
ID	160.1	62.3	23.2	394.0	35.0	PA	58.4	67.8	68.0	70.9	61.4
IL	271.5	57.2	11.6	947.9	57.2	RI	19.9	37.2	21.6	49.9	33.3
IN	163.1	18.4	5.5	196.0	18.8	SC	16.9	36.1	17.8	54.4	28.5
IA	42.5	46.8	3.1	138.0	26.7	SD	4.6	87.0	-	21.3	55.4
KS	40.8	54.2	36.5	145.7	9.7	TN	11.0	57.-	52.7	44.9	47.9
KY	120.4	41.8	14.4	293.6	44.2	TX	29.4	44.2	25.5	100.7	60.3
LA	209.4	84.5	54.7	180.0	45.1	UT	21.0	79.0	19.5	55.5	48.5
ME	18.5	53.0	20.0	39.5	17.2	VT	60.8	98.2	-	41.6	66.8
MD	17.2	79.7	1.2	64.4	70.0	VA	63.7	17.4	0.2	34.4	37.8
MA	3.0	36.7	3.3	8.0	27.5	WA	253.5	46.2	16.8	830.1	55.8
MI	87.0	96.6	5.6	88.8	58.8	WV	12.5	16.0	-	5.0	28.0
MN	127.0	29.8	15.0	410.2	58.8	WI	61.3	45.2	8.6	80.0	44.3
MS	210.8	46.7	26.9	241.0	31.2	WY	144.5	71.5	13.4	254.9	42.4

- Represents zero. D Withheld to avoid disclosing data for individual companies. [1] Includes offshore, not shown separately.

Source of Tables 382 and 383: U.S. Census Bureau, Current Industrial Reports, *Pollution Abatement Costs and Expenditures: 1999*, Series MA200(99).

No. 384. Environmental Industry—Revenues and Employment, by Industry Segment: 1990 to 2002

[152.2 represents $152,200,000,000. . Covers approximately 59,000 private and public companies engaged in environmental activities]

Industry segment	Revenue (bil. dol.)				Employment (1,000)			
	1990	1995	2000	2002	1990	1995	2000	2002
Industry total	152.2	182.9	208.7	221.3	1,223.8	1,374.7	1,452.9	1,510.0
Analytical services [1]	1.5	1.3	1.3	1.3	18.0	15.6	14.9	15.0
Wastewater treatment works [2]	19.8	23.4	27.8	30.2	88.8	101.5	114.8	123.7
Solid waste management [3]	26.1	32.5	39.4	42.7	205.5	243.4	266.3	284.4
Hazardous waste management [4]	6.3	6.2	5.1	4.7	53.8	52.5	41.8	38.6
Remediation/industrial services	11.1	11.1	11.2	11.1	133.3	125.9	110.7	105.9
Consulting & engineering	12.5	15.5	17.4	18.7	147.1	180.3	184.0	193.7
Water equipment & chemicals	13.5	16.5	19.8	20.8	92.7	110.3	130.5	135.3
Instrument manufacturing	2.0	3.0	3.6	3.9	18.0	26.2	29.4	30.9
Air pollution control equipment [5]	13.1	14.8	17.6	18.6	96.4	105.9	119.7	126.0
Waste management equipment [6]	8.7	9.8	9.9	9.9	69.6	75.5	74.6	74.1
Process & prevention technology	0.4	0.8	1.2	1.4	9.3	19.5	29.0	30.9
Water utilities [7]	19.8	25.3	29.9	32.3	98.5	118.2	130.0	139.1
Resource recovery [8]	13.1	16.9	16.0	14.1	142.9	136.0	127.2	110.1
Clean energy systems & power	4.3	5.6	8.6	11.5	49.9	63.9	80.0	102.3

[1] Covers environmental laboratory testing and services. [2] Mostly revenues collected by municipal entities. [3] Covers such activities as collection, transportation, transfer stations, disposal, landfill ownership and management for solid waste. [4] Transportation and disposal of hazardous, medical and nuclear waste. [5] Includes stationery and mobile sources. [6] Includes vehicles, containers, liners, processing and remediation equipment. [7] Revenues generated from the sale of water. [8] Revenues generated from the sale of recovered metals, paper, plastic, etc.

Source: Environmental Business International, Inc., San Diego, CA, *Environmental Business Journal*, monthly (copyright).

No. 385. Threatened and Endangered Wildlife and Plant Species—Number: 2003

[As of April. Endangered species: One in danger of becoming extinct throughout all or a significant part of its natural range. Threatened species: One likely to become endangered in the foreseeable future]

Item	Mammals	Birds	Reptiles	Amphibians	Fishes	Snails	Clams	Crustaceans	Insects	Arachnids	Plants
Total listings	342	273	115	30	126	33	72	21	48	12	749
Endangered species, total	316	253	78	20	82	22	64	18	39	12	600
United States	65	78	14	12	71	21	62	18	35	12	599
Foreign	251	175	64	8	11	1	2	-	4	-	1
Threatened species, total	26	20	37	10	44	11	8	3	9	-	149
United States	9	14	22	9	44	11	8	3	9	-	147
Foreign	17	6	15	1	-	-	-	-	-	-	2

- Represents zero.

Source: U.S. Fish and Wildlife Service, *Endangered Species Bulletin*, bimonthly; and <http://ecos.fws.gov/tess/html/boxscore.html> (accessed 05 May 2003).

No. 386. Tornadoes, Floods, Tropical Storms, and Lightning: 1992 to 2002

Weather type	1992	1993	1994	1995	1996	1997	1998	1999	2000	2001	2002
Tornadoes:[1]											
Lives lost	39	33	69	30	26	67	130	94	41	40	55
Injuries	(NA)	(NA)	(NA)	650	705	1,033	1,868	1,842	882	743	968
Property loss (mil. dol.)	(NA)	(NA)	(NA)	410.8	719.6	730.7	1,714.2	1,989.9	423.6	630.1	801.3
Floods and flash floods:											
Lives lost	62	103	91	80	131	118	136	68	38	48	49
Injuries	(NA)	(NA)	(NA)	57	95	525	6,440	301	47	277	88
Property loss (mil. dol.)	(NA)	(NA)	(NA)	1,250.5	2,120.7	6,910.6	2,324.8	1,420.7	1,255.1	1,220.3	655.0
North Atlantic tropical storms and hurricanes [2]	7	8	7	19	13	7	14	12	15	15	12
Number of hurricanes reaching U.S. mainland	1	1	-	2	2	1	3	3	-	-	1
Direct deaths on U.S. mainland	27	2	9	17	37	1	9	19	-	24	53
Property loss in U.S. (mil. dol.)	26,500	57	973	5,932	1,436	668	3,547	4,190	8	5,188	1,104
Lightning:											
Deaths	41	43	69	85	52	42	44	46	51	44	51
Injuries	292	295	577	433	309	306	283	243	364	371	256

- Represents zero. NA Not available. [1] Source: U.S. National Weather Service, Internet site <http://www.spc.noaa.gov/climo/torn/monthlytornstats.html> (accessed 20 May 2003). A violent, rotating column of air descending from a cumulonimbus cloud in the form of a tubular- or funnel-shaped cloud, usually characterized by movements along a narrow path and wind speeds from 100 to over 300 miles per hour. Also known as a "twister" or "waterspout." [2] Source: National Hurricane Center (NHC), Coral Gables, FL, unpublished data. For data on individual hurricanes, see the NHC Web site at <http://www.nhc.noaa.gov/>. Tropical storms have maximum winds of 39 to 73 miles per hour; hurricanes have maximum winds of 74 miles per hour or higher.

Source: Except as noted, U.S. National Oceanic and Atmospheric Administration (NOAA), *Storm Data*, monthly. See also NOAA Web site at <http://www.nws.noaa.gov/om/hazstats.shtml>.

No. 387. Major U.S. Weather Disasters: 1985 to 2002

[5.0 represents $5,000,000,000. Covers only weather related disasters costing $1 billion or more]

Event	Description	Time period	Estimated cost (bil. dol.)	Deaths
Widespread drought	Moderate to extreme drought over large portions of 30 states.	Spring to fall 2002	over $10	-
Western fire season	Major fires over 11 western states from Rockies to west coast.	Spring to fall 2002	over $2	21
Tropical Storm Allison	Tropical storm produced rainfall and severe flooding in coastal portions of TX & LA and damage in MS, FL, VA, & PA	June 2001	5.0	43
Midwest and Ohio Valley hail and tornadoes	Storms, tornadoes, and hail in TX, OK, KS, NE, IA, MO, IL, IN, WI, MI, OH, KY, and PA.	April 2001	1.7	3
Southern drought/heat wave	Severe drought and heat over south-central and southeastern states cause significant losses in agriculture and related industries.	Spring-summer 2000	over 4.0	140
Western fire season	Severe fire season in western states.	Spring-summer 2000	over 2.0	-
Hurricane Floyd	Category 2 hurricane in NC, causing severe flooding in NC and some flooding in SC, VA, MD, PA, NY, NJ, DE, RI, CT, MA, and VT.	September 1999	6.0	75
Drought/heat wave	Drought/heatwave over eastern U.S.	Summer 1999	1.0	256
Oklahoma-Kansas tornados	Category F4-F5 tornados hit OK, KS, TX, and TN	May 1999	1.0	55
Arkansas-Tennessee tornados	Two outbreaks of tornadoes in 6-day period	January 1999	1.3	31
Texas flooding	Severe flooding in southeast Texas from 2 heavy rain events with 10-20 in. totals.	Oct.-Nov. 1998	1.0	31
Hurricane Georges	Category 2 hurricane in Puerto Rico, Florida Keys, and Gulf coasts of LA, MS, AL, and FL.	September 1998	3-4	16
Hurricane Bonnie	Category 3 hurricane in eastern NC and VA.	August 1998	1.0	2
Southern drought/heat wave	Severe drought and heat wave from TX/OK to the Carolinas.	Summer 1998	6.0	200
Minnesota severe storms/hail	Very damaging severe thunderstorms with large hail over wide areas of Minnesota.	May 1998	1.5	1
Southeast severe weather	Tornadoes and flooding related to strong El Nino in the southeast	Winter/Spring 1998	1.0	over 130
Northeast ice storm	Intense ice storm hits ME, NH, VT, and NY.	January 1998	1.4	16
Northern plains flooding	Severe flooding in Dakotas and Minnesota due to heavy spring snowmelt.	April-May 1997	2.0	11
MS and OH valleys flooding and tornadoes	Tornadoes and severe flooding hit the states of AR, MO, MS, TN, IL, IN, KY, OH, and WV.	March 1997	1.0	67
West Coast flooding	Flooding from rains and snowmelt in CA, WA, OR, ID, NV, & MT	Dec. 1996-Jan. 1999	2-3	36
Hurricane Fran	Category 3 hurricane in NC and VA.	Sept. 1996	5.0	37
Southern Plains severe drought	Drought in agricultural areas of TX & OK	Fall 1995-summer 1996	Over 4	(NA)
Pacific Northwest severe flooding	Flooding from heavy rain & snowmelt in OR, WA, ID, and MT.	Feb. 1996	1.0	9
Blizzard of '96 followed by flooding	Heavy snowstorm followed by severe flooding in Appalachians, Mid-Atlantic, and Northeast.	Jan. 1996	3.0	187
Hurricane Opal	Category 3 hurricane in FL, AL, parts of GA, TN, & Carolinas.	Oct. 1995	Over 3	27
Hurricane Marilyn	Category 2 hurricane in Virgin Islands	Sept. 1995	2.1	13
TX/OK/LA/MS severe weather and flooding	Flooding, hail, & tornadoes across TX, OK, parts of LA, MS, Dallas & New Orleans hardest hit	May 1995	5-6	32
California flooding	Flooding from frequent winter storms across much of CA	Jan.-Mar. 1995	3.0	27
Western fire season	Severe fire season in western states due to dry weather.	Summer-Fall 1994	1.0	(NA)
Texas flooding	Flooding from torrential rain & thunderstorms across southeast TX	Oct. 1994	1.0	19
Tropical Storm Alberto	Flooding due to 10 to 25 inch rain across GA, AL, part of FL.	July 1994	1.0	32
Southeast ice storm	Intense ice storm in pts of TX, OK, AR, LA, MS, AL, TN, GA, SC, NC, & VA.	Feb. 1994	3.0	9
California wildfires	Out-of-control wildfires over southern CA	Fall 1993	1.0	4
Midwest flooding	Extreme flooding across central U.S.	Summer 1993	15-20	48
Drought/heat wave	Extreme drought/heatwave across southeastern U.S.	Summer 1993	1.0	(NA)
Storm/blizzard	"Storm of the Century" hits entire eastern seaboard	Mar. 1993	3-6	270
Nor'easter of 1992	Slow-moving storm batters northeast U.S. coast, New England	Dec. 1992	1-2	19
Hurricane Iniki	Category 4 hurricane hit Hawaiian island of Kauai	Sept. 1992	1.8	7
Hurricane Andrew	Category 4 hurricane hit FL & LA	Aug. 1992	27.0	58
Oakland Firestorm	Oakland, CA firestorm due to low humidity & high winds	Oct. 1991	1.5	25
Hurricane Bob	Category 2 hurricane—mainly coastal NC, Long Island, & New England	Aug. 1991	1.5	18
TX/OK/LA/AR Flooding	Torrential rains cause flooding along Trinity, Red, and Arkansas rivers	May 1990	1.0	13
Hurricane Hugo	Category 4 hurricane hit Puerto Rico & Virgin Islands, devastated NC & SC.	Sept. 1989	Over 9	86
Drought/Heat Wave	Drought/heatwave over central & eastern U.S.	Summer 1988	40.0	5,000-10,000
Hurricane Juan	Category 1 hurricane, flooding most severe problem, hit LA and southeast U.S.	Oct.-Nov. 1985	1.5	63
Hurricane Elena	Category 3 hurricane across FL to LA	Aug.-Sept. 1985	1.3	4
Florida Freeze	Severe freeze central/northern FL, damage to citrus industry.	Jan. 1985	1.2	-

- Represents zero. NA Not available or not reported.

Source: U.S. National Oceanic and Atmospheric Administration, National Climatic Data Center, "Billion Dollar U.S. Weather Disasters, 1980-2002" (release date: Jan. 1, 2003). See also <http://www.ncdc.noaa.gov/oa/pub/data/special/billionz-2002.pdf> (released 02 January 2003).

No. 388. Highest and Lowest Temperatures by State Through 2000

State	Highest temperatures Station	Temperature (F)	Date	Lowest temperatures Station	Temperature (F)	Date
U.S.	Greenland Ranch, CA	134	Jul. 10, 1913	Prospect Creek, AK	-80	Jan. 23, 1971
AL	Centerville	112	Sep. 5, 1925	New Market	-27	Jan. 30, 1966
AK	Fort Yukon	100	[1]Jun. 27, 1915	Prospect Creek Camp	-80	Jan. 23, 1971
AZ	Lake Havasu City	128	Jun. 29, 1994	Hawley Lake	-40	Jan. 7, 1971
AR	Ozark	120	Aug. 10, 1936	Pond	-29	Feb. 13, 1905
CA	Greenland Ranch	134	Jul. 10, 1913	Boca	-45	Jan. 20, 1937
CO	Bennett	118	Jul. 11, 1888	Maybell	-61	Feb. 1, 1985
CT	Danbury	106	Jul. 15, 1995	Falls Village	-32	Feb. 16, 1943
DE	Millsboro	110	Jul. 21, 1930	Millsboro	-17	Jan. 17, 1893
FL	Monticello	109	Jun. 29, 1931	Tallahassee	-2	Feb. 13, 1899
GA	Greenville	112	Aug. 20, 1983	CCC Camp F-16	-17	[1]Jan. 27, 1940
HI	Pahala	100	Apr. 27, 1931	Mauna Kea Obs. 111.2	12	May 17, 1979
ID	Orofino	118	Jul. 28, 1934	Island Park Dam	-60	Jan. 18, 1943
IL	East St. Louis	117	Jul. 14, 1954	Congerville	-36	Jan. 5, 1999
IN	Collegeville	116	Jul. 14, 1936	New Whiteland	-36	Jan. 19, 1994
IA	Keokuk	118	Jul. 20, 1934	Elkader	-47	[2]Feb. 3, 1996
KS	Alton (near)	121	[2]Jul. 24, 1936	Lebanon	-40	Feb. 13, 1905
KY	Greensburg	114	Jul. 28, 1930	Shelbyville	-37	Jan. 19, 1994
LA	Plain Dealing	114	Aug. 10, 1936	Minden	-16	Feb. 13, 1899
ME	North Bridgton	105	[2]Jul. 10, 1911	Van Buren	-48	Jan. 19, 1925
MD	Cumberland & Frederick	109	[2]Jul. 10, 1936	Oakland	-40	Jan. 13, 1912
MA	New Bedford & Chester	107	Aug. 2, 1975	Chester	-35	Jan. 12, 1981
MI	Mio	112	Jul. 13, 1936	Vanderbilt	-51	Feb. 9, 1934
MN	Moorhead	114	[2]Jul. 6, 1936	Tower	-60	Feb. 2, 1996
MS	Holly Springs	115	Jul. 29, 1930	Corinth	-19	Jan. 30, 1966
MO	Warsaw & Union	118	[2]Jul. 14, 1954	Warsaw	-40	Feb. 13, 1905
MT	Medicine Lake	117	Jul. 5, 1937	Rogers Pass	-70	Jan. 20, 1954
NE	Minden	118	[2]Jul. 24, 1936	Camp Clarke	-47	Feb. 12, 1899
NV	Laughlin	125	Jun. 29, 1994	San Jacinto	-50	Jan. 8, 1937
NH	Nashua	106	Jul. 4, 1911	Mt. Washington	-47	Jan. 29, 1934
NJ	Runyon	110	Jul. 10, 1936	River Vale	-34	Jan. 5, 1904
NM	Waste Isolat Pilot Plt	122	Jun. 27, 1994	Gavilan	-50	[2]Feb. 1, 1951
NY	Troy	108	Jul. 22, 1926	Old Forge	-52	[2]Feb. 18, 1979
NC	Fayetteville	110	Aug. 21, 1983	Mt. Mitchell	-34	Jan. 21, 1985
ND	Steele	121	Jul. 6, 1936	Parshall	-60	Feb. 15, 1936
OH	Gallipolis (near)	113	[2]Jul. 21, 1934	Milligan	-39	Feb. 10, 1899
OK	Tipton	120	[2]Jun. 27, 1994	Watts	-27	Jan. 18, 1930
OR	Pendleton	119	Aug. 10, 1898	Seneca	-54	[2]Feb. 10, 1933
PA	Phoenixville	111	[2]Jul. 10, 1936	Smethport	-42	[1]Jan. 5, 1904
RI	Providence	104	Aug. 2, 1975	Kingston	-23	Jan. 11, 1942
SC	Camden	111	[2]Jun. 28, 1954	Caesars Head	-19	Jan. 21, 1985
SD	Gannvalley	120	Jul. 5, 1936	McIntosh	-58	Feb. 17, 1936
TN	Perryville	113	[2]Aug. 9, 1930	Mountain City	-32	Dec. 30, 1917
TX	Seymour	120	Aug. 12, 1936	Seminole	-23	[2]Feb. 8, 1933
UT	Saint George	117	Jul. 5, 1985	Peter's Sink	-69	Feb. 1, 1985
VT	Vernon	105	Jul. 4, 1911	Bloomfield	-50	Dec. 30, 1933
VA	Balcony Falls	110	Jul. 15, 1954	Mtn. Lake Bio. Stn.	-30	Jan. 22, 1985
WA	Ice Harbor Dam	118	[2]Aug. 5, 1961	Mazama & Winthrop	-48	Dec. 30, 1968
WV	Martinsburg	112	[2]Jul. 10, 1936	Lewisburg	-37	Dec. 30, 1917
WI	Wisconsin Dells	114	Jul. 13, 1936	Couderay	-55	Feb. 4, 1996
WY	Basin	114	Jul. 12, 1900	Riverside R.S.	-66	Feb. 9, 1933

[1] Estimated. [2] Also on earlier dates at the same or other places.

Source: U.S. National Oceanic and Atmospheric Administration, <http://www.lwf.ncdc.noaa.gov/oa/climate/severeweather/temperatures.html> (released 25 April 2002).

No. 389. Normal Daily Mean, Maximum, and Minimum Temperatures—Selected Cities

[In Fahrenheit degrees. Airport data except as noted. Based on standard 30-year period, 1971 through 2000]

State	Station	Daily mean temperature Jan.	Daily mean temperature July	Daily mean temperature Annual average	Daily maximum temperature Jan.	Daily maximum temperature July	Daily maximum temperature Annual average	Daily minimum temperature Jan.	Daily minimum temperature July	Daily minimum temperature Annual average
AL	Mobile.........	50.1	81.5	66.8	60.7	91.2	77.4	39.5	71.8	56.2
AK	Juneau	25.7	56.8	41.5	30.6	64.3	47.6	20.7	49.2	35.3
AZ	Phoenix.........	54.2	92.8	72.9	65.0	104.2	84.5	43.4	81.4	61.1
AR	Little Rock	40.1	82.4	62.1	49.5	92.8	72.7	30.8	72.0	51.5
CA	Los Angeles	57.1	69.3	63.3	65.6	75.3	70.6	48.6	63.3	56.1
	Sacramento	46.3	75.4	61.1	53.8	92.4	73.7	38.8	58.3	48.4
	San Diego	57.8	70.9	64.4	65.8	75.8	70.8	49.7	65.9	58.1
	San Francisco	49.4	62.8	57.3	55.9	71.1	65.1	42.9	54.5	49.6
CO	Denver	29.2	73.4	50.1	43.2	88.0	64.2	15.2	58.7	35.8
CT	Hartford.........	25.7	73.7	50.2	34.1	84.9	60.5	17.2	62.4	40.0
DE	Wilmington.......	31.5	76.6	54.4	39.3	86.0	63.6	23.7	67.3	45.1
DC	Washington	34.9	79.2	57.5	42.5	88.3	66.4	27.3	70.1	48.6
FL	Jacksonville	53.1	81.6	68.0	64.2	90.8	78.4	41.9	72.4	57.6
	Miami	68.1	83.7	76.7	76.5	90.9	84.2	59.6	76.5	69.1
GA	Atlanta	42.7	80.0	62.2	51.9	89.4	72.0	33.5	70.6	52.3
HI	Honolulu	73.0	80.8	77.5	80.4	87.8	84.7	65.7	73.8	70.2
ID	Boise	30.2	74.7	52.0	36.7	89.2	62.6	23.6	60.3	41.3
IL	Chicago.........	22.0	73.3	49.1	29.6	83.5	58.3	14.3	63.2	39.8
	Peoria..........	22.5	75.1	50.8	30.7	85.7	60.7	14.3	64.6	40.9
IN	Indianapolis	26.5	75.4	52.5	34.5	85.6	62.3	18.5	65.2	42.7
IA	Des Moines	20.4	76.1	50.0	29.1	86.0	59.8	11.7	66.1	40.2
KS	Wichita	30.2	81.0	56.4	40.1	92.9	67.4	20.3	69.1	45.2
KY	Louisville	33.0	78.4	57.0	41.0	87.0	66.0	24.9	69.8	47.9
LA	New Orleans	52.6	82.7	68.8	61.8	91.1	78.0	43.4	74.2	59.6
ME	Portland	21.7	68.7	45.8	30.9	78.8	55.2	12.5	58.6	36.3
MD	Baltimore........	32.3	76.5	54.6	41.2	87.2	65.1	23.5	65.8	44.2
MA	Boston	29.3	73.9	51.6	36.5	82.2	59.3	22.1	65.5	43.9
MI	Detroit..........	24.5	73.5	49.8	31.1	83.4	58.4	17.8	63.6	41.0
	Sault Ste. Marie ..	13.2	63.9	40.1	21.5	75.7	49.6	4.9	52.0	30.5
MN	Duluth..........	8.4	65.5	39.1	17.9	76.3	48.7	-1.2	54.6	29.3
	Minneapolis-St. Paul.	13.1	73.2	45.4	21.9	83.3	54.7	4.3	63.0	35.9
MS	Jackson.........	45.0	81.4	64.1	55.1	91.4	75.0	35.0	71.4	53.2
MO	Kansas City	26.9	78.5	54.2	36.0	88.8	64.3	17.8	68.2	44.0
	St. Louis	29.6	80.2	56.3	37.9	89.8	65.7	21.2	70.6	46.9
MT	Great Falls.......	21.7	66.2	43.8	32.1	82.0	56.4	11.3	50.4	31.1
NE	Omaha	21.7	76.7	50.7	31.7	87.4	61.5	11.6	65.9	39.8
NV	Reno	33.6	71.3	51.3	45.5	91.2	67.4	21.8	51.4	35.2
NH	Concord	20.1	70.0	45.9	30.6	82.9	57.7	9.7	57.1	34.1
NJ	Atlantic City	32.1	75.3	53.5	41.4	85.1	63.6	22.8	65.4	43.3
NM	Albuquerque......	35.7	78.5	56.8	47.6	92.3	70.4	23.8	64.7	43.2
NY	Albany	22.2	71.1	47.6	31.1	82.2	57.6	13.3	60.0	37.5
	Buffalo	24.5	70.8	48.0	31.1	79.6	55.9	17.8	62.1	39.9
	New York [1]......	32.1	76.5	54.6	38.0	84.2	61.7	26.2	68.8	47.5
NC	Charlotte........	41.7	80.3	61.4	51.3	90.1	71.7	32.1	70.6	51.0
	Raleigh	39.7	78.8	59.6	49.8	89.1	70.6	29.6	68.5	48.6
ND	Bismarck........	10.2	70.4	42.3	21.1	84.5	54.5	-0.6	56.4	30.1
OH	Cincinnati........	29.7	76.3	54.2	38.0	86.4	64.0	21.3	66.1	44.3
	Cleveland	25.7	71.9	49.7	32.6	81.4	58.1	18.8	62.3	41.2
	Columbus	28.3	75.1	52.9	36.2	85.3	62.6	20.3	64.9	43.2
OK	Oklahoma City ...	36.7	82.0	60.1	47.1	93.1	71.1	26.2	70.8	49.2
OR	Portland	39.9	68.1	53.5	45.6	79.3	62.1	34.2	56.9	44.8
PA	Philadelphia......	32.3	77.6	55.3	39.0	85.5	63.2	25.5	69.7	47.4
	Pittsburgh	27.5	72.6	51.0	35.1	82.7	60.4	19.9	62.4	41.5
RI	Providence.......	28.7	73.3	51.1	37.1	82.6	60.2	20.3	64.1	42.0
SC	Columbia........	44.6	82.0	63.6	55.1	92.1	74.8	34.0	71.8	52.5
SD	Sioux Falls.......	14.0	73.0	45.1	25.2	85.6	57.2	2.9	60.3	33.0
TN	Memphis	39.9	82.5	62.4	48.6	92.1	72.1	31.3	72.9	52.5
	Nashville	36.8	79.1	58.9	45.6	88.7	69.0	27.9	69.5	48.8
TX	Dallas-Fort Worth ..	44.1	85.0	65.5	54.1	95.4	75.8	34.0	74.6	55.1
	El Paso	45.1	83.3	64.7	57.2	94.5	77.1	32.9	72.0	52.1
	Houston	51.8	83.6	68.8	62.3	93.6	79.4	41.2	73.5	58.2
UT	Salt Lake City.....	29.2	77.0	52.0	37.0	90.6	62.9	21.3	63.4	41.2
VT	Burlington	18.0	70.6	45.2	26.7	81.4	54.5	9.3	59.8	35.8
VA	Norfolk	40.1	79.1	59.6	47.8	86.8	67.8	32.3	71.4	51.4
	Richmond	36.4	77.9	57.6	45.3	87.5	67.8	27.6	68.3	47.4
WA	Seattle-Tacoma....	40.9	65.3	52.3	45.8	75.3	59.8	35.9	55.3	44.8
	Spokane	27.3	68.6	47.3	32.8	82.5	57.4	21.7	54.6	37.2
WV	Charleston.......	33.4	73.9	54.5	42.6	84.9	65.4	24.2	62.9	43.5
WI	Milwaukee	20.7	72.0	47.5	28.0	81.1	55.9	13.4	62.9	39.2
WY	Cheyenne	25.9	67.7	45.0	37.1	81.9	57.6	14.8	53.4	32.3
PR	San Juan........	76.6	82.2	79.9	82.4	87.4	85.5	70.8	76.9	74.2

[1] City office data.

Source: U.S. National Oceanic and Atmospheric Administration, *Climatography of the United States*, No. 81.

No. 390. Highest Temperature of Record—Selected Cities

[In Fahrenheit degrees. Airport data, except as noted. For period of record through 2001]

State	Station	Length of record (yr.)	Jan.	Feb.	Mar.	Apr.	May	June	July	Aug.	Sept.	Oct.	Nov.	Dec.	Annual
AL	Mobile	60	84	82	90	94	100	102	104	105	99	93	87	81	105
AK	Juneau	57	57	57	61	72	82	86	90	83	73	61	56	54	90
AZ	Phoenix	64	88	92	100	105	113	122	121	116	118	107	95	88	122
AR	Little Rock	60	83	85	91	95	98	105	112	109	106	97	86	80	112
CA	Los Angeles	66	88	92	95	102	97	104	97	98	110	106	101	94	110
	Sacramento	51	70	76	88	95	105	115	114	110	108	104	87	72	115
	San Diego	61	88	90	93	98	96	101	95	98	111	107	97	88	111
	San Francisco	74	72	78	85	92	97	106	105	100	103	99	85	75	106
CO	Denver	61	73	76	84	90	96	104	104	101	97	89	79	75	104
CT	Hartford	47	65	73	89	96	99	100	102	102	99	91	81	76	102
DE	Wilmington	54	75	78	86	94	96	100	102	101	100	91	85	75	102
DC	Washington	60	79	82	89	95	99	101	104	105	101	94	86	79	105
FL	Jacksonville	60	85	88	91	95	100	103	105	102	100	96	88	84	105
	Miami	59	88	89	92	96	96	98	98	98	97	95	89	87	98
GA	Atlanta	53	79	80	89	93	95	101	105	102	98	95	84	79	105
HI	Honolulu	32	88	88	88	91	93	92	94	93	95	94	93	89	95
ID	Boise	62	63	71	81	92	98	109	111	110	102	94	78	65	111
IL	Chicago	43	65	72	88	91	93	104	104	101	99	91	78	71	104
	Peoria	62	70	72	86	92	93	105	103	103	100	90	81	71	105
IN	Indianapolis	62	71	76	85	89	93	102	104	102	100	90	81	74	104
IA	Des Moines	62	65	73	91	93	98	103	105	108	101	95	81	69	108
KS	Wichita	49	75	87	89	96	100	110	113	110	108	95	85	83	113
KY	Louisville	54	77	77	86	91	95	102	106	101	104	92	84	76	106
LA	New Orleans	55	83	85	89	92	96	100	101	102	101	94	87	84	102
ME	Portland	61	64	64	88	85	94	98	99	103	95	88	74	71	103
MD	Baltimore	51	75	79	89	94	98	101	104	105	100	92	83	77	105
MA	Boston	50	66	70	89	94	95	100	102	102	100	90	79	76	102
MI	Detroit	43	62	70	81	89	93	104	102	100	98	91	77	69	104
	Sault Ste. Marie	61	45	49	75	85	89	93	97	98	95	80	67	62	98
MN	Duluth	60	52	55	78	88	90	94	97	97	95	86	71	55	97
	Minneapolis-St. Paul	63	58	61	83	95	96	102	105	102	98	90	77	68	105
MS	Jackson	38	82	85	89	94	99	105	106	107	104	95	88	84	107
MO	Kansas City	29	69	77	86	93	95	105	107	109	106	92	82	74	109
	St. Louis	44	76	85	89	93	94	102	107	107	104	94	85	76	107
MT	Great Falls	64	67	70	78	89	93	101	105	106	98	91	76	69	106
NE	Omaha	65	69	78	89	97	99	105	114	110	104	96	83	72	114
NV	Reno	60	70	75	83	89	96	103	104	105	101	91	77	70	105
NH	Concord	60	68	67	89	95	97	98	102	101	98	90	80	73	102
NJ	Atlantic City	58	78	75	87	94	99	106	104	103	99	90	84	77	106
NM	Albuquerque	62	69	76	85	89	98	107	105	101	100	91	77	72	107
NY	Albany	55	65	68	89	92	94	99	100	99	100	89	82	71	100
	Buffalo	58	72	71	81	94	90	96	97	99	98	87	80	74	99
	New York [1]	133	72	75	86	96	99	101	106	104	102	94	84	75	106
NC	Charlotte	62	78	81	90	93	100	103	103	103	104	98	85	78	104
	Raleigh	57	79	84	92	95	97	104	105	105	104	98	88	80	105
ND	Bismarck	62	62	69	81	93	98	107	109	109	105	95	79	65	109
OH	Cincinnati	40	69	75	84	89	93	102	103	102	98	88	81	75	103
	Cleveland	60	73	74	83	88	92	104	103	102	101	90	82	77	104
	Columbus	62	74	75	85	89	94	102	100	101	100	90	80	76	102
OK	Oklahoma City	48	80	92	93	100	104	105	110	110	108	96	87	86	110
OR	Portland	61	63	71	80	90	100	100	107	107	105	92	73	65	107
PA	Philadelphia	60	74	74	87	94	97	100	104	101	100	96	81	73	104
	Pittsburgh	49	69	76	82	89	91	98	103	100	97	87	82	74	103
RI	Providence	48	69	72	85	98	95	97	102	104	100	86	78	77	104
SC	Columbia	54	84	84	91	94	101	107	107	107	101	101	90	83	107
SD	Sioux Falls	56	66	70	87	94	100	110	108	108	104	94	81	63	110
TN	Memphis	60	78	81	85	94	99	104	108	107	103	95	86	81	108
	Nashville	62	78	84	86	91	97	106	107	104	105	94	84	79	107
TX	Dallas-Fort Worth	48	88	95	96	95	103	113	110	108	111	102	89	88	113
	El Paso	62	80	83	89	98	104	114	112	108	104	96	87	80	114
	Houston	32	84	91	91	95	99	103	104	107	109	96	89	85	109
UT	Salt Lake City	73	62	69	78	86	95	104	107	106	100	89	75	69	107
VT	Burlington	58	66	62	84	91	93	100	100	101	94	85	75	67	101
VA	Norfolk	53	78	82	88	97	100	101	103	104	99	95	86	80	104
	Richmond	72	80	83	93	96	100	104	105	102	103	99	86	81	105
WA	Seattle-Tacoma	57	64	70	75	85	93	96	100	99	98	89	74	64	100
	Spokane	54	59	63	71	90	96	101	103	108	98	86	67	56	108
WV	Charleston	54	79	79	89	94	93	98	104	101	102	92	85	80	104
WI	Milwaukee	61	62	68	82	91	93	101	103	103	98	89	77	68	103
WY	Cheyenne	66	66	71	74	83	91	100	100	96	95	83	75	69	100
PR	San Juan	47	92	96	96	97	96	97	95	97	97	98	96	94	98

[1] City office data.

Source: U.S. National Oceanic and Atmospheric Administration, *Comparative Climatic Data*, annual.

No. 391. Lowest Temperature of Record—Selected Cities

[In Fahrenheit degrees. Airport data, except as noted. For period of record through 2001]

State	Station	Length of record (yr.)	Jan.	Feb.	Mar.	Apr.	May	June	July	Aug.	Sept.	Oct.	Nov.	Dec.	Annual
AL	Mobile	60	3	11	21	32	43	49	60	59	42	30	22	8	3
AK	Juneau	57	-22	-22	-15	6	25	31	36	27	23	11	-5	-21	-22
AZ	Phoenix	64	17	22	25	32	40	50	61	60	47	34	25	22	17
AR	Little Rock	60	-4	-5	11	28	40	46	54	52	37	29	17	-1	-5
CA	Los Angeles	66	23	32	34	39	43	48	49	51	47	41	34	32	23
	Sacramento	51	23	23	26	31	36	41	48	49	43	36	26	18	18
	San Diego	61	29	36	39	41	48	51	55	57	51	43	38	34	29
	San Francisco	74	24	25	30	31	36	41	43	42	38	34	25	20	20
CO	Denver [1]	61	-25	-30	-11	-2	22	30	43	41	17	3	-8	-25	-30
CT	Hartford	47	-26	-21	-6	9	28	37	44	36	30	17	1	-14	-26
DE	Wilmington	54	-14	-6	2	18	30	41	48	43	36	24	14	-7	-14
DC	Washington	60	-5	4	11	24	34	47	54	49	39	29	16	1	-5
FL	Jacksonville	60	7	19	23	34	45	47	61	59	48	36	21	11	7
	Miami	59	30	32	32	46	53	60	69	68	68	51	39	30	30
GA	Atlanta	53	-8	5	10	26	37	46	53	55	36	28	3	-	-8
HI	Honolulu	32	53	53	55	57	60	65	66	67	66	61	57	54	53
ID	Boise	62	-17	-15	6	19	22	31	35	34	23	11	-3	-25	-25
IL	Chicago	43	-27	-19	-8	7	24	36	40	41	28	17	1	-25	-27
	Peoria	62	-25	-19	-10	14	25	39	47	41	26	19	-2	-23	-25
IN	Indianapolis	62	-27	-21	-7	16	28	37	44	41	28	17	-2	-23	-27
IA	Des Moines	62	-24	-26	-22	9	30	38	47	40	26	14	-4	-22	-26
KS	Wichita	49	-12	-21	-2	15	31	43	51	48	31	18	1	-16	-21
KY	Louisville	54	-22	-19	-1	22	31	42	50	46	33	23	-1	-15	-22
LA	New Orleans	55	14	16	25	32	41	50	60	60	42	35	24	11	11
ME	Portland	61	-26	-39	-21	8	23	33	40	33	23	15	3	-21	-39
MD	Baltimore	51	-7	-3	6	20	32	40	50	45	35	25	13	-	-7
MA	Boston	50	-12	-4	6	16	34	45	50	47	38	28	15	-7	-12
MI	Detroit	43	-21	-15	-4	10	25	36	41	38	29	17	9	-10	-21
	Sault Ste. Marie	61	-36	-35	-24	-2	18	26	36	29	25	16	-10	-31	-36
MN	Duluth	60	-39	-39	-29	-5	17	27	35	32	22	8	-23	-34	-39
	Minneapolis-St. Paul	63	-34	-32	-32	2	18	34	43	39	26	13	-17	-29	-34
MS	Jackson	38	2	10	15	27	38	47	51	55	35	26	17	4	2
MO	Kansas City	29	-17	-19	-10	12	30	42	51	43	31	17	1	-23	-23
	St. Louis	44	-18	-12	-5	22	31	43	51	47	36	23	1	-16	-18
MT	Great Falls	64	-37	-35	-29	-6	15	31	36	30	16	-11	-25	-43	-43
NE	Omaha	65	-23	-21	-16	5	27	38	44	43	25	13	-9	-23	-23
NV	Reno	60	-16	-16	-2	13	18	25	33	24	20	8	1	-16	-16
NH	Concord	60	-33	-37	-16	8	21	30	35	29	21	10	-5	-22	-37
NJ	Atlantic City	58	-10	-11	5	12	25	37	42	40	32	20	10	-7	-11
NM	Albuquerque	62	-17	-5	8	19	28	40	52	50	37	21	-7	-7	-17
NY	Albany	55	-28	-21	-21	10	26	36	40	34	24	16	5	-22	-28
	Buffalo	58	-16	-20	-7	12	26	35	43	38	32	20	9	-10	-20
	New York [2]	133	-6	-15	3	12	32	44	52	50	39	28	5	-13	-15
NC	Charlotte	62	-5	5	4	24	32	45	53	53	39	24	11	2	-5
	Raleigh	57	-9	-	11	23	31	38	48	46	37	19	11	4	-9
ND	Bismarck	62	-44	-43	-31	-12	15	30	35	33	11	-10	-30	-43	-44
OH	Cincinnati	40	-25	-11	-11	15	27	39	47	43	31	16	1	-20	-25
	Cleveland	60	-20	-15	-5	10	25	31	41	38	32	19	3	-15	-20
	Columbus	62	-22	-13	-6	14	25	35	43	39	31	20	5	-17	-22
OK	Oklahoma City	48	-4	-3	3	20	37	47	53	51	36	16	11	-8	-8
OR	Portland	61	-2	-3	19	29	29	39	43	44	34	26	13	6	-3
PA	Philadelphia	60	-7	-4	7	19	28	44	51	44	35	25	15	1	-7
	Pittsburgh	49	-22	-12	-1	14	26	34	42	39	31	16	-1	-12	-22
RI	Providence	48	-13	-7	1	14	29	41	48	40	33	20	6	-10	-13
SC	Columbia	54	-1	5	4	26	34	44	54	53	40	23	12	4	-1
SD	Sioux Falls	56	-36	-31	-23	5	17	33	38	34	22	9	-17	-28	-36
TN	Memphis	60	-4	-11	12	29	38	48	52	48	36	25	9	-13	-13
	Nashville	62	-17	-13	2	23	34	42	51	47	36	26	-1	-10	-17
TX	Dallas-Fort Worth	48	4	7	15	29	41	51	59	56	43	29	20	-1	-1
	El Paso	62	-8	8	-14	23	31	46	57	56	41	25	1	5	-8
	Houston	32	12	20	22	31	44	52	62	60	48	29	19	7	7
UT	Salt Lake City	73	-22	-30	2	14	25	35	40	37	27	16	-14	-21	-30
VT	Burlington	58	-30	-30	-20	2	24	33	39	35	25	15	-2	-26	-30
VA	Norfolk	53	-3	8	18	28	36	45	54	49	45	27	20	7	-3
	Richmond	72	-12	-10	11	23	31	40	51	46	35	21	10	-1	-12
WA	Seattle-Tacoma	57	-	1	11	29	28	38	43	44	35	28	6	6	-
	Spokane	54	-22	-24	-7	17	24	33	37	35	22	10	-21	-25	-25
WV	Charleston	54	-16	-12	-	19	26	33	46	41	34	17	6	-12	-16
WI	Milwaukee	61	-26	-26	-10	12	21	33	40	44	28	18	-5	-20	-26
WY	Cheyenne	66	-29	-34	-21	-8	16	25	38	36	8	-1	-16	-28	-34
PR	San Juan	47	61	62	60	64	66	69	69	70	69	46	66	63	46

- Represents zero. [1] Period of record through 2000. [2] City office data.

Source: U.S. National Oceanic and Atmospheric Administration, *Comparative Climatic Data*, annual.

No. 392. Normal Monthly and Annual Precipitation—Selected Cities

[In inches. Airport data, except as noted. Based on standard 30-year period, 1971 through 2000]

State	Station	Jan.	Feb.	Mar.	Apr.	May	June	July	Aug.	Sept.	Oct.	Nov.	Dec.	Annual
AL	Mobile	5.75	5.10	7.20	5.06	6.10	5.01	6.54	6.20	6.01	3.25	5.41	4.66	66.29
AK	Juneau	4.81	4.02	3.51	2.96	3.48	3.36	4.14	5.37	7.54	8.30	5.43	5.41	58.33
AZ	Phoenix	0.83	0.77	1.07	0.25	0.16	0.09	0.99	0.94	0.75	0.79	0.73	0.92	8.29
AR	Little Rock	3.61	3.33	4.88	5.47	5.05	3.95	3.31	2.93	3.71	4.25	5.73	4.71	50.93
CA	Los Angeles	2.98	3.11	2.40	0.63	0.24	0.08	0.03	0.14	0.26	0.36	1.13	1.79	13.15
	Sacramento	3.84	3.54	2.80	1.02	0.53	0.20	0.05	0.06	0.36	0.89	2.19	2.45	17.93
	San Diego	2.28	2.04	2.26	0.75	0.20	0.09	0.03	0.09	0.21	0.44	1.07	1.31	10.77
	San Francisco	4.45	4.01	3.26	1.17	0.38	0.11	0.03	0.07	0.20	1.04	2.49	2.89	20.11
CO	Denver	0.51	0.49	1.28	1.93	2.32	1.56	2.16	1.82	1.14	0.99	0.98	0.63	15.81
CT	Hartford	3.84	2.96	3.88	3.86	4.39	3.85	3.67	3.98	4.13	3.94	4.06	3.60	46.16
DE	Wilmington	3.43	2.81	3.97	3.39	4.15	3.59	4.28	3.51	4.01	3.08	3.19	3.40	42.81
DC	Washington	3.21	2.63	3.60	2.77	3.82	3.13	3.66	3.44	3.79	3.22	3.03	3.05	39.35
FL	Jacksonville	3.69	3.15	3.93	3.14	3.48	5.37	5.97	6.87	7.90	3.86	2.34	2.64	52.34
	Miami	1.88	2.07	2.56	3.36	5.52	8.54	5.79	8.63	8.38	6.19	3.43	2.18	58.53
GA	Atlanta	5.02	4.68	5.38	3.62	3.95	3.63	5.12	3.67	4.09	3.11	4.10	3.82	50.20
HI	Honolulu	2.73	2.35	1.89	1.11	0.78	0.43	0.50	0.46	0.74	2.18	2.26	2.85	18.29
ID	Boise	1.39	1.14	1.41	1.27	1.27	0.74	0.39	0.30	0.76	0.76	1.38	1.38	12.19
IL	Chicago	1.75	1.63	2.65	3.68	3.38	3.63	3.51	4.62	3.27	2.71	3.01	2.43	36.27
	Peoria	1.50	1.67	2.83	3.56	4.17	3.84	4.02	3.16	3.12	2.76	2.99	2.40	36.03
IN	Indianapolis	2.48	2.41	3.44	3.61	4.35	4.13	4.42	3.82	2.88	2.76	3.61	3.03	40.95
IA	Des Moines	1.03	1.19	2.21	3.58	4.25	4.57	4.18	4.51	3.15	2.62	2.10	1.33	34.72
KS	Wichita	0.84	1.02	2.71	2.57	4.16	4.25	3.31	2.94	2.96	2.45	1.82	1.35	30.38
KY	Louisville	3.28	3.25	4.41	3.91	4.88	3.76	4.30	3.41	3.05	2.79	3.80	3.69	44.54
LA	New Orleans	5.87	5.47	5.24	5.02	4.62	6.83	6.20	6.15	5.55	3.05	5.09	5.07	64.16
ME	Portland	4.09	3.14	4.14	4.26	3.82	3.28	3.32	3.05	3.37	4.40	4.72	4.24	45.83
MD	Baltimore	3.47	3.02	3.93	3.00	3.89	3.43	3.85	3.74	3.98	3.16	3.12	3.35	41.94
MA	Boston	3.92	3.30	3.85	3.60	3.24	3.22	3.06	3.37	3.47	3.79	3.98	3.73	42.53
MI	Detroit	1.91	1.88	2.52	3.05	3.05	3.55	3.16	3.10	3.27	2.23	2.66	2.51	32.89
	Sault Ste. Marie	2.64	1.60	2.41	2.57	2.50	3.00	3.14	3.47	3.71	3.32	3.40	2.91	34.67
MN	Duluth	1.12	0.83	1.69	2.09	2.95	4.25	4.20	4.22	4.13	2.46	2.12	0.94	31.00
	Minneapolis-St. Paul	1.04	0.79	1.86	2.31	3.24	4.34	4.04	4.05	2.69	2.11	1.94	1.00	29.41
MS	Jackson	5.67	4.50	5.74	5.98	4.86	3.82	4.69	3.66	3.23	3.42	5.04	5.34	55.95
MO	Kansas City	1.15	1.31	2.44	3.38	5.39	4.44	4.42	3.54	4.64	3.33	2.30	1.64	37.98
	St. Louis	2.14	2.28	3.60	3.69	4.11	3.76	3.90	2.98	2.96	2.76	3.71	2.86	38.75
MT	Great Falls	0.68	0.51	1.01	1.40	2.53	2.24	1.45	1.65	1.23	0.93	0.59	0.67	14.89
NE	Omaha	0.77	0.80	2.13	2.94	4.44	3.95	3.86	3.21	3.17	2.21	1.82	0.92	30.22
NV	Reno	1.06	1.06	0.86	0.35	0.62	0.47	0.24	0.27	0.45	0.42	0.80	0.88	7.48
NH	Concord	2.97	2.36	3.04	3.07	3.33	3.10	3.37	3.21	3.16	3.46	3.57	2.96	37.60
NJ	Atlantic City	3.60	2.85	4.06	3.45	3.38	2.66	3.86	4.32	3.14	2.86	3.26	3.15	40.59
NM	Albuquerque	0.49	0.44	0.61	0.50	0.60	0.65	1.27	1.73	1.07	1.00	0.62	0.49	9.47
NY	Albany	2.71	2.27	3.17	3.25	3.67	3.74	3.50	3.68	3.31	3.23	3.31	2.76	38.60
	Buffalo	3.16	2.42	2.99	3.04	3.35	3.82	3.14	3.87	3.84	3.19	3.92	3.80	40.54
	New York [1]	4.13	3.15	4.37	4.28	4.69	3.84	4.62	4.22	4.23	3.85	4.36	3.95	49.69
NC	Charlotte	4.00	3.55	4.39	2.95	3.66	3.42	3.79	3.72	3.83	3.66	3.36	3.18	43.51
	Raleigh	4.02	3.47	4.03	2.80	3.79	3.42	4.29	3.78	4.26	3.18	2.97	3.04	43.05
ND	Bismarck	0.45	0.51	0.85	1.46	2.22	2.59	2.58	2.15	1.61	1.28	0.70	0.44	16.84
OH	Cincinnati	2.92	2.75	3.90	3.96	4.59	4.42	3.75	3.79	2.82	2.96	3.46	3.28	42.60
	Cleveland	2.48	2.29	2.94	3.37	3.50	3.89	3.52	3.69	3.77	2.73	3.38	3.14	38.71
	Columbus	2.53	2.20	2.89	3.25	3.88	4.07	4.61	3.72	2.92	2.31	3.19	2.93	38.52
OK	Oklahoma City	1.28	1.56	2.90	3.00	5.44	4.63	2.94	2.48	3.98	3.64	2.11	1.89	35.85
OR	Portland	5.07	4.18	3.71	2.64	2.38	1.59	0.72	0.93	1.65	2.88	5.61	5.71	37.07
PA	Philadelphia	3.52	2.74	3.81	3.49	3.88	3.29	4.39	3.82	3.88	2.75	3.16	3.31	42.05
	Pittsburgh	2.70	2.37	3.17	3.01	3.80	4.12	3.96	3.38	3.21	2.25	3.02	2.86	37.85
RI	Providence	4.37	3.45	4.43	4.16	3.66	3.38	3.17	3.90	3.70	3.69	4.40	4.14	46.45
SC	Columbia	4.66	3.84	4.59	2.98	3.17	4.99	5.54	5.41	3.94	2.89	2.88	3.38	48.27
SD	Sioux Falls	0.51	0.51	1.81	2.65	3.39	3.49	2.93	3.01	2.58	1.93	1.36	0.52	24.69
TN	Memphis	4.24	4.31	5.58	5.79	5.15	4.30	4.22	3.00	3.31	3.31	5.76	5.68	54.65
	Nashville	3.97	3.69	4.87	3.93	5.07	4.08	3.77	3.28	3.59	2.87	4.45	4.54	48.11
TX	Dallas-Fort Worth	1.90	2.37	3.06	3.20	5.15	3.23	2.12	2.03	2.42	4.11	2.57	2.57	34.73
	El Paso	0.45	0.39	0.26	0.23	0.38	0.87	1.49	1.75	1.61	0.81	0.42	0.77	9.43
	Houston	3.68	2.98	3.36	3.60	5.15	5.35	3.18	3.83	4.33	4.50	4.19	3.69	47.84
UT	Salt Lake City	1.37	1.33	1.91	2.02	2.09	0.77	0.72	0.76	1.33	1.57	1.40	1.23	16.50
VT	Burlington	2.22	1.67	2.32	2.88	3.32	3.43	3.97	4.01	3.83	3.12	3.06	2.22	36.05
VA	Norfolk	3.93	3.34	4.08	3.38	3.74	3.77	5.17	4.79	4.06	3.47	2.98	3.03	45.74
	Richmond	3.55	2.98	4.09	3.18	3.95	3.54	4.67	4.18	3.98	3.60	3.06	3.12	43.91
WA	Seattle-Tacoma	5.13	4.18	3.75	2.59	1.77	1.49	0.79	1.02	1.63	3.19	5.90	5.62	37.07
	Spokane	1.82	1.51	1.53	1.28	1.60	1.18	0.76	0.68	0.76	1.06	2.24	2.25	16.67
WV	Charleston	3.25	3.19	3.90	3.25	4.30	4.09	4.86	4.11	3.45	2.67	3.66	3.32	44.05
WI	Milwaukee	1.85	1.65	2.59	3.78	3.06	3.56	3.58	4.03	3.30	2.49	2.70	2.22	34.81
WY	Cheyenne	0.45	0.44	1.05	1.55	2.48	2.12	2.26	1.82	1.43	0.75	0.64	0.46	15.45
PR	San Juan	3.02	2.30	2.14	3.71	5.29	3.52	4.16	5.22	5.60	5.06	6.17	4.57	50.76

[1] City office data.

Source: U.S. National Oceanic and Atmospheric Administration, *Climatography of the United States*, No. 81.

No. 393. Average Number of Days With Precipitation of 0.01 Inch or More—Selected Cities

[Airport data, except as noted. For period of record through 2001]

State	Station	Length of record (yr.)	Jan.	Feb.	Mar.	Apr.	May	June	July	Aug.	Sept.	Oct.	Nov.	Dec.	Annual
AL	Mobile	60	11	9	10	7	8	11	16	14	10	6	8	10	121
AK	Juneau	57	18	17	18	17	17	15	17	18	21	24	20	21	224
AZ	Phoenix	62	4	4	4	2	1	1	4	5	3	3	3	4	36
AR	Little Rock	59	10	9	10	10	10	8	8	7	7	7	8	9	104
CA	Los Angeles	66	6	6	6	3	1	1	1	(Z)	1	2	3	5	35
	Sacramento	62	10	9	9	5	3	1	(Z)	(Z)	1	3	7	9	58
	San Diego	61	7	6	7	4	2	1	(Z)	-	1	2	4	6	42
	San Francisco	74	11	10	10	6	3	1	(Z)	(Z)	1	4	7	10	63
CO	Denver [1]	61	6	6	9	9	11	9	9	9	6	5	6	5	89
CT	Hartford	47	11	10	12	11	12	11	10	10	9	9	11	12	127
DE	Wilmington	54	11	10	11	11	11	10	9	9	8	8	9	10	117
DC	Washington	60	10	9	11	10	11	10	10	9	8	7	8	9	112
FL	Jacksonville	60	8	8	8	6	8	13	14	15	13	8	6	8	116
	Miami	59	7	6	6	6	10	15	16	18	17	14	8	7	131
GA	Atlanta	67	12	10	11	9	9	10	12	9	8	6	8	10	115
HI	Honolulu	52	9	9	9	9	7	6	7	6	7	8	9	10	97
ID	Boise	62	12	10	10	8	8	6	2	2	4	6	10	11	90
IL	Chicago	43	11	9	12	13	11	10	10	9	9	9	11	11	125
	Peoria	62	9	8	11	12	12	10	9	8	9	8	9	10	114
IN	Indianapolis	62	12	10	13	12	12	10	10	9	8	8	10	12	126
IA	Des Moines	62	7	7	10	11	12	11	9	9	9	8	7	8	108
KS	Wichita	48	5	5	8	8	11	9	8	7	8	6	5	6	86
KY	Louisville	54	11	10	13	12	12	10	10	8	8	7	10	11	124
LA	New Orleans	53	10	9	9	7	8	11	14	13	10	6	7	10	114
ME	Portland	61	11	10	11	12	12	11	10	9	9	9	11	11	129
MD	Baltimore	51	10	9	11	11	11	9	9	8	7	7	9	9	114
MA	Boston	50	12	10	12	11	12	10	9	10	9	9	11	11	126
MI	Detroit	43	13	11	13	13	11	10	10	10	10	10	12	14	135
	Sault Ste. Marie	60	19	14	13	11	11	11	10	11	13	14	17	19	165
MN	Duluth	60	12	10	11	11	12	13	12	11	12	10	11	11	134
	Minneapolis-St. Paul	63	9	7	10	10	11	12	10	10	9	8	9	9	116
MS	Jackson	38	11	9	10	8	9	9	11	10	8	6	9	10	109
MO	Kansas City	29	7	7	10	11	12	10	9	9	8	7	8	7	105
	St. Louis	44	9	8	11	11	11	10	9	8	8	8	9	9	111
MT	Great Falls	64	9	8	9	9	11	12	8	8	7	6	7	7	100
NE	Omaha	65	6	7	8	10	12	11	9	9	8	6	6	6	99
NV	Reno	59	6	6	6	4	4	3	2	2	3	3	5	6	51
NH	Concord	60	11	9	11	11	12	11	10	10	9	9	11	11	126
NJ	Atlantic City	58	11	10	11	11	10	9	9	9	8	7	9	10	113
NM	Albuquerque	62	4	4	5	3	4	4	9	10	6	5	4	4	61
NY	Albany	55	13	11	12	12	13	11	10	10	9	9	12	12	135
	Buffalo	58	20	17	16	14	13	11	10	10	11	12	16	19	168
	New York [2]	132	11	10	11	11	11	10	11	10	8	8	9	10	121
NC	Charlotte	62	10	10	11	9	9	10	11	10	7	7	8	10	111
	Raleigh	57	10	10	10	9	10	10	11	10	8	7	8	9	113
ND	Bismarck	62	8	7	8	8	10	12	9	8	7	6	6	7	96
OH	Cincinnati	54	12	11	13	13	12	11	10	9	8	8	11	12	131
	Cleveland	60	16	14	15	14	13	11	10	10	10	11	14	16	155
	Columbus	62	13	12	13	13	13	11	11	9	8	9	11	13	137
OK	Oklahoma City	62	5	6	7	8	10	9	6	6	7	7	5	6	83
OR	Portland	61	18	16	17	15	12	9	4	5	7	12	18	19	153
PA	Philadelphia	61	11	9	11	11	11	10	9	9	8	8	9	10	117
	Pittsburgh	49	16	14	15	14	13	12	11	10	10	10	13	16	152
RI	Providence	48	11	10	12	11	11	11	9	10	9	9	10	12	124
SC	Columbia	54	10	9	10	8	9	10	12	11	8	6	7	9	109
SD	Sioux Falls	56	6	7	9	10	11	11	10	9	8	6	7	6	99
TN	Memphis	51	10	9	11	10	9	9	9	7	7	6	9	10	106
	Nashville	60	11	10	12	11	11	10	10	9	8	7	9	11	119
TX	Dallas-Fort Worth	48	7	7	8	8	9	7	5	5	7	6	6	7	79
	El Paso	62	4	3	2	2	2	3	8	8	5	4	3	4	49
	Houston	32	11	8	9	7	8	10	9	9	9	8	8	9	105
UT	Salt Lake City	73	10	9	10	10	8	5	4	6	5	6	8	9	91
VT	Burlington	58	14	12	13	12	14	12	12	13	12	12	14	15	154
VA	Norfolk	53	11	10	11	10	10	9	11	10	8	7	8	9	115
	Richmond	64	10	9	11	9	11	9	11	9	8	7	8	9	113
WA	Seattle-Tacoma	57	19	16	17	14	11	9	5	6	9	13	18	19	155
	Spokane	54	14	11	11	9	9	8	5	5	6	8	13	14	113
WV	Charleston	54	15	14	15	14	13	12	13	11	9	9	12	14	151
WI	Milwaukee	61	11	10	12	12	12	11	10	9	9	9	10	11	126
WY	Cheyenne	66	6	6	9	10	12	11	11	10	8	6	6	6	101
PR	San Juan	46	17	13	12	13	16	15	19	19	18	17	19	19	197

- Represents zero.   Z Less than 1/2 day.   [1] Period of record through 2000.   [2] City office data.

Source: U.S. National Oceanic and Atmospheric Administration, *Comparative Climatic Data*, annual.

No. 394. Snow and Ice Pellets—Selected Cities

[**In inches.** Airport data, except as noted. For period of record through 2001. T denotes trace]

State	Station	Length of record (yr)	Jan.	Feb.	Mar.	Apr.	May	June	July	Aug.	Sept.	Oct.	Nov.	Dec.	Annual
AL	Mobile	59	0.1	0.1	0.1	T	T	-	T	-	-	-	T	0.1	0.4
AK	Juneau	57	25.7	18.9	14.8	3.3	T	T	-	-	T	1.0	12.0	22.0	97.7
AZ	Phoenix	62	T	-	T	T	T	T	-	-	-	T	-	T	T
AR	Little Rock	56	2.4	1.5	0.5	T	T	T	-	-	-	T	0.2	0.6	5.2
CA	Los Angeles	62	T	T	T	-	-	-	-	-	-	-	-	T	T
	Sacramento	50	T	T	T	-	T	-	-	-	-	-	-	T	T
	San Diego	60	T	-	T	T	-	-	-	-	-	-	T	T	T
	San Francisco	69	-	T	T	-	-	-	-	-	-	-	-	-	T
CO	Denver	61	8.1	7.5	12.5	8.9	1.6	-	T	T	1.6	3.7	9.1	7.3	60.3
CT	Hartford	44	12.9	12.2	10.1	1.5	-	T	-	-	-	0.1	2.1	10.0	48.9
DE	Wilmington	51	6.8	6.1	3.2	0.2	T	T	T	-	-	0.1	0.9	3.2	20.5
DC	Washington	58	5.5	5.2	2.3	T	T	T	T	T	-	-	0.8	2.8	16.6
FL	Jacksonville	60	T	-	-	T	-	T	T	-	-	-	-	-	T
	Miami	59	-	-	-	-	T	-	-	-	-	-	-	-	T
GA	Atlanta	64	0.9	0.5	0.4	T	-	-	T	-	-	T	T	0.2	2
HI	Honolulu	52	-	-	-	-	-	-	-	-	-	-	-	-	-
ID	Boise	62	6.4	3.7	1.7	0.6	0.1	T	T	T	T	0.1	2.3	5.8	20.7
IL	Chicago	42	11.1	8.0	6.8	1.6	0.1	T	T	T	T	0.4	1.9	8.4	38.3
	Peoria	58	6.8	5.1	4.1	0.8	T	T	T	-	T	0.1	2	6.1	25.0
IN	Indianapolis	70	6.8	5.4	3.5	0.5	T	T	T	-	T	0.2	1.9	5.2	23.5
IA	Des Moines	58	8.3	7.2	6.0	1.8	-	T	T	-	T	0.3	3.1	6.6	33.3
KS	Wichita	48	4.3	4.0	2.8	0.2	T	T	T	T	T	T	1.3	3.1	15.7
KY	Louisville	54	5.4	4.4	3.2	0.1	T	T	T	T	T	0.1	1	2.3	16.5
LA	New Orleans	51	T	0.1	T	T	T	-	-	-	-	-	T	0.1	0.2
ME	Portland	61	19.4	16.8	13.5	2.9	0.2	-	-	-	T	0.2	3.3	14.5	70.8
MD	Baltimore	51	6.4	6.5	3.8	0.1	T	-	T	-	-	-	1	3.0	20.8
MA	Boston	64	12.9	11.7	8.2	0.9	-	-	-	T	-	T	1.3	7.5	42.5
MI	Detroit	43	10.5	9.1	6.9	1.7	T	-	-	-	T	0.2	2.7	9.9	41.0
	Sault Ste. Marie	57	29.2	18.2	14.6	5.8	0.5	T	T	T	T	0.1	2.4	15.6	31.0	117.4
MN	Duluth	58	17.8	11.9	13.5	6.7	0.7	T	T	T	T	0.1	1.5	13	15.4	80.6
	Minneapolis-St. Paul	62	10.7	8.1	10.5	2.8	0.1	T	T	T	T	0.5	7.8	9.4	49.9
MS	Jackson	38	0.5	0.2	0.2	T	-	-	-	-	T	-	T	0.1	1.0
MO	Kansas City	67	5.6	4.4	3.4	0.8	T	T	T	T	T	0.1	1.2	4.5	20.0
	St. Louis	65	5.4	4.4	3.9	0.5	-	T	T	-	-	T	1.4	3.9	19.5
MT	Great Falls	64	9.5	8.5	10.5	7.1	1.8	0.3	T	0.1	1.5	3.4	7.3	8.1	58.1
NE	Omaha	66	7.2	6.8	6.2	1.0	0.1	T	T	-	T	0.3	2.6	5.7	29.9
NV	Reno	54	5.8	5.2	4.3	1.2	0.8	T	T	-	-	0.3	2.4	4.3	24.3
NH	Concord	60	17.9	14.3	11.6	2.5	0.1	T	T	-	T	0.1	3.9	13.6	64.0
NJ	Atlantic City	52	4.9	5.4	2.5	0.3	T	T	T	-	-	T	0.4	2.2	15.7
NM	Albuquerque	62	2.5	2.1	1.8	0.6	T	T	T	T	T	0.1	1.2	2.7	11.0
NY	Albany	55	16.6	13.9	11.7	2.7	0.1	T	T	-	T	0.2	4.2	14.3	63.7
	Buffalo	58	24.2	17.7	12.4	3.2	0.2	T	T	T	T	0.3	11.4	24.1	93.5
	New York [1]	133	7.5	8.5	5.1	0.9	T	-	T	-	-	T	0.9	5.5	28.4
NC	Charlotte	62	2.1	1.6	1.2	T	T	T	-	-	-	T	0.1	0.5	5.5
	Raleigh	57	2.7	2.5	1.3	T	T	T	T	-	-	-	0.1	0.8	7.4
ND	Bismarck	62	7.8	7.1	8.4	4.1	0.9	T	-	T	0.2	1.8	7.1	6.9	44.3
OH	Cincinnati	54	7.2	5.5	4.4	0.5	-	T	T	T	-	0.3	2.0	3.7	23.6
	Cleveland	60	13.6	11.9	10.8	2.4	0.1	T	T	-	T	0.6	5.3	11.9	56.6
	Columbus	54	8.9	6.0	4.5	0.9	T	T	T	T	T	0.1	2.2	5.4	28.0
OK	Oklahoma City	62	3.2	2.4	1.5	T	T	T	T	T	T	T	0.5	1.9	9.5
OR	Portland	55	3.2	1.1	0.4	T	-	T	T	-	T	-	0.4	1.4	6.5
PA	Philadelphia	59	6.1	6.6	3.5	0.3	T	T	-	-	-	-	0.7	3.2	20.4
	Pittsburgh	49	11.8	9.0	8.6	1.7	0.1	T	T	T	T	0.4	3.5	8.0	43.1
RI	Providence	48	9.7	9.8	7.4	0.7	0.2	-	-	-	-	0.1	1.1	6.7	35.7
SC	Columbia	54	0.5	0.8	0.2	T	T	-	-	T	-	-	T	0.3	1.8
SD	Sioux Falls	56	7.0	8.1	9.2	2.9	T	T	T	T	T	0.8	6.2	7.1	41.3
TN	Memphis	49	2.2	1.4	0.8	T	T	T	-	-	-	T	0.1	0.6	5.1
	Nashville	57	3.7	3.0	1.5	-	-	T	-	T	-	-	0.4	1.4	10.0
TX	Dallas-Fort Worth	43	1.1	0.9	0.2	T	T	-	-	-	-	-	T	0.1	0.2	2.5
	El Paso	57	1.3	0.8	0.4	0.3	T	T	T	-	T	-	0.9	1.6	5.3
	Houston	67	0.2	0.2	T	T	T	T	-	-	-	-	T	T	0.4
UT	Salt Lake City	73	13.6	9.9	9.2	5	0.6	T	T	T	0.1	1.3	7.1	11.9	58.7
VT	Burlington	58	19.3	16.6	13.9	4.3	0.2	-	T	-	0.2	6.6	17.9	79.0
VA	Norfolk	51	2.9	3.0	1.0	-	-	T	T	-	-	-	-	0.9	7.8
	Richmond	62	4.9	3.9	2.4	0.1	T	-	T	-	-	T	0.4	2.0	13.7
WA	Seattle-Tacoma	52	4.9	1.6	1.3	0.1	T	-	T	-	-	-	1.1	2.4	11.4
	Spokane	54	15.5	7.6	3.8	0.6	0.1	T	-	-	T	0.4	6.4	14.6	49.0
WV	Charleston	49	11.1	8.7	5.4	0.9	-	T	T	T	T	0.2	2.4	5.3	34.0
WI	Milwaukee	61	13.9	9.4	8.2	1.9	0.1	T	T	T	T	0.2	3.0	10.7	47.4
WY	Cheyenne	66	6.5	6.3	11.8	9.4	3.4	0.2	T	T	1.1	3.7	7.1	6.2	55.7
PR	San Juan	46	-	-	-	-	-	-	-	-	-	-	-	-	-

- Represents zero or rounds to zero.   [1] City office data.

Source: U.S. National Oceanic and Atmospheric Administration, *Comparative Climatic Data*, annual.

No. 395. Sunshine, Average Wind Speed, Heating and Cooling Degree Days, and Average Relative Humidity—Selected Cities

[Airport data, except as noted. For period of record through 2000, except heating and cooling normals for period 1971-2000. M=morning. A=afternoon]

State	Station	Average percentage of possible sunshine [1] Length of record (yr.)	Average percentage of possible sunshine [1] Annual	Average wind speed (m.p.h.) Length of record (yr.)	Average wind speed (m.p.h.) Annual	Average wind speed (m.p.h.) Jan.	Average wind speed (m.p.h.) July	Heating degree days	Cooling degree days	Length of record (yr.)	Annual M	Annual A	Jan. M	Jan. A	July M	July A
AL	Mobile	47	60	52	8.8	10.1	6.9	1,667	2,548	38	87	61	82	64	90	64
AK	Juneau	47	23	55	8.2	8.0	7.5	8,574	-	34	80	69	77	74	78	66
AZ	Phoenix	57	81	55	6.2	5.3	7.1	1,040	4,355	40	50	23	65	32	43	20
AR	Little Rock	35	60	58	7.8	8.4	6.7	3,084	2,086	36	83	58	80	63	86	57
CA	Los Angeles	60	72	52	7.5	6.7	7.9	1,286	682	41	79	65	71	61	86	68
	Sacramento	49	73	50	7.8	7.2	8.9	2,666	1,248	14	83	46	91	71	77	29
	San Diego	55	72	60	7.0	6.0	7.5	1,063	866	40	77	63	72	58	82	67
	San Francisco	68	71	73	10.6	7.2	13.6	2,862	142	41	84	62	86	68	86	60
CO	Denver	61	67	47	8.6	8.6	8.3	6,128	695	35	67	40	63	49	68	34
CT	Hartford	41	52	46	8.4	9.0	7.3	6,104	759	41	77	52	72	56	79	51
DE	Wilmington	47	55	52	9.0	9.8	7.8	4,887	1,125	53	78	55	75	60	79	54
DC	Washington	48	55	52	9.4	10.0	8.3	3,999	1,560	40	75	54	70	56	76	53
FL	Jacksonville	47	61	51	7.9	8.1	7.0	1,353	2,636	64	89	56	87	58	89	59
	Miami	46	68	51	9.2	9.5	7.9	155	4,383	36	83	61	84	60	83	63
GA	Atlanta	61	59	62	9.1	10.4	7.7	2,827	1,810	40	82	56	79	60	88	59
HI	Honolulu	47	74	51	11.3	9.4	13.1	-	4,561	31	72	56	81	61	68	52
ID	Boise	56	58	61	8.7	8.0	8.4	5,809	769	61	69	43	80	70	54	22
IL	Chicago	37	52	42	10.4	11.7	8.4	6,493	835	42	80	62	78	69	82	59
	Peoria	52	53	57	9.9	11.0	7.8	6,095	998	41	83	64	80	71	87	62
IN	Indianapolis	64	51	52	9.6	10.9	7.5	5,521	1,042	41	84	62	81	71	87	60
IA	Des Moines	46	55	51	10.7	11.4	8.9	6,432	1,052	39	80	62	77	69	83	60
KS	Wichita	39	62	47	12.2	12.0	11.3	4,765	1,658	47	80	57	79	64	79	52
KY	Louisville	47	53	53	8.3	9.5	6.8	4,352	1,443	40	81	59	77	65	85	58
LA	New Orleans	47	60	52	8.2	9.3	6.1	1,417	2,776	52	87	65	85	68	91	67
ME	Portland	54	55	60	8.7	9.1	7.6	7,325	347	60	79	59	76	61	80	59
MD	Baltimore	45	58	50	8.9	9.6	7.6	4,634	1,220	47	77	54	73	57	80	53
MA	Boston	60	55	43	12.4	13.8	11.0	5,630	777	36	73	58	68	58	74	57
MI	Detroit	37	49	42	10.3	12.0	8.5	6,449	727	42	81	60	80	70	82	54
	Sault Ste. Marie	54	43	59	9.2	9.6	7.8	9,230	145	59	85	66	81	74	89	62
MN	Duluth	47	49	51	11.0	11.6	9.4	9,742	189	39	81	65	77	71	85	62
	Minneapolis-St. Paul	57	54	62	10.5	10.5	9.4	7,882	699	41	79	62	75	68	81	58
MS	Jackson	30	59	37	7.0	8.3	5.4	2,368	2,290	37	90	61	86	67	93	62
MO	Kansas City	23	59	28	10.6	11.2	9.2	5,249	1,325	28	81	63	77	66	85	62
	St. Louis	47	55	51	9.7	10.6	8.0	4,757	1,561	40	82	61	81	68	84	59
MT	Great Falls	57	51	59	12.6	14.9	10.0	7,675	326	39	68	46	67	61	68	31
NE	Omaha	49	59	64	10.5	10.9	8.8	6,312	1,095	36	81	62	79	67	85	62
NV	Reno	53	69	58	6.6	5.6	7.2	5,601	493	37	69	31	79	50	60	18
NH	Concord	54	55	58	6.7	7.3	5.7	7,485	442	35	81	53	76	59	84	51
NJ	Atlantic City	37	56	42	9.8	10.9	8.3	5,113	935	36	82	56	78	59	83	57
NM	Albuquerque	56	76	61	8.9	8.0	8.9	4,281	1,290	40	59	29	68	39	59	27
NY	Albany	57	49	62	8.9	9.8	7.5	6,861	544	35	80	58	78	64	81	55
	Buffalo	52	43	61	11.8	14.0	10.2	6,693	548	40	80	63	79	73	79	55
	New York [2]	42	64	63	9.3	10.7	7.6	4,744	1,160	66	72	56	68	60	75	55
NC	Charlotte	49	59	51	7.4	7.8	6.6	3,208	1,644	40	82	53	78	56	86	56
	Raleigh	47	59	51	7.6	8.4	6.7	3,465	1,521	36	85	54	79	55	89	58
ND	Bismarck	56	55	61	10.2	10.0	9.2	8,809	471	41	81	59	76	70	84	51
OH	Cincinnati	44	49	53	9.0	10.5	7.2	5,200	1,053	38	82	60	80	69	86	58
	Cleveland	54	45	59	10.5	12.2	8.6	6,097	712	40	80	62	79	70	82	57
	Columbus	46	48	51	8.3	9.8	6.5	5,546	925	41	81	59	78	68	84	56
OK	Oklahoma City	44	64	52	12.3	12.6	10.9	3,663	1,907	35	80	57	78	61	80	53
OR	Portland	47	39	52	7.9	9.9	7.6	4,366	398	60	85	59	85	75	82	45
PA	Philadelphia	55	56	60	9.5	10.3	8.2	4,759	1,235	41	76	55	73	59	79	54
	Pittsburgh	43	44	48	9.0	10.5	7.3	5,829	726	40	79	57	77	66	83	54
RI	Providence	42	55	47	10.4	11.1	9.4	5,754	714	37	75	55	71	57	77	56
SC	Columbia	48	60	52	6.8	7.2	6.3	2,595	2,063	34	87	51	83	55	88	54
SD	Sioux Falls	50	57	52	11.0	10.9	9.8	7,746	757	37	82	63	78	71	84	58
TN	Memphis	43	59	52	8.8	10.0	7.5	3,033	2,190	61	81	58	76	64	84	59
	Nashville	54	57	59	8.0	9.1	6.5	3,658	1,656	35	83	60	79	65	88	60
TX	Dallas-Fort Worth	42	64	47	10.7	11.0	9.8	2,370	2,571	37	81	58	80	62	80	52
	El Paso	53	80	58	8.8	8.3	8.3	2,604	2,165	40	56	28	65	34	61	29
	Houston	26	56	31	7.7	8.2	6.8	1,525	2,893	31	90	63	85	67	92	61
UT	Salt Lake City	69	62	71	8.8	7.5	9.5	5,607	1,089	41	67	43	79	69	52	22
VT	Burlington	52	44	57	9.0	9.8	8.0	7,665	489	35	77	59	73	64	79	53
VA	Norfolk	47	58	52	10.5	11.5	8.9	3,342	1,630	52	78	57	75	59	82	59
	Richmond	50	56	52	7.7	8.1	6.9	3,878	1,466	66	83	53	80	57	85	56
WA	Seattle-Tacoma [3]	51	38	52	8.9	9.6	8.2	4,797	173	41	83	62	82	74	82	49
	Spokane	48	48	53	8.9	8.8	8.6	6,820	394	41	78	52	78	76	65	28
WV	Charleston	47	48	53	5.9	7.1	4.8	4,589	1,064	53	83	56	78	63	90	60
WI	Milwaukee	55	52	60	11.5	12.6	9.7	7,096	616	40	80	65	76	70	82	63
WY	Cheyenne	60	64	43	12.9	15.3	10.4	7,289	280	41	66	45	58	51	70	38
PR	San Juan	40	76	45	8.4	8.4	9.7	-	5,426	45	79	65	82	64	79	67

- Represents zero. [1] Percent of days that are either clear or partly cloudy. [2] Airport data for sunshine. [3] Does not represent airport data.

Source: U.S. National Oceanic and Atmospheric Administration, *Comparative Climatic Data*, annual.

Section 7

Elections

This section relates primarily to presidential, congressional, and gubernatorial elections. Also presented are summary tables on congressional legislation; state legislatures; Black, Hispanic, and female officeholders; population of voting age; voter participation; and campaign finances.

Official statistics on federal elections, collected by the Clerk of the House, are published biennially in *Statistics of the Presidential and Congressional Election* and *Statistics of the Congressional Election*. Federal and state elections data appear also in *America Votes*, a biennial volume published by Congressional Quarterly, Inc., Washington, DC. Federal elections data also appear in the U.S. Congress, *Congressional Directory*, and in official state documents. Data on reported registration and voting for social and economic groups are obtained by the U.S. Census Bureau as part of the Current Population Survey (CPS) and are published in Current Population Reports, Series P20 (see text, Section 1).

Almost all federal, state, and local governmental units in the United States conduct elections for political offices and other purposes. The conduct of elections is regulated by state laws or, in some cities and counties, by local charter. An exception is that the U.S. Constitution prescribes the basis of representation in Congress and the manner of electing the President and grants to Congress the right to regulate the times, places, and manner of electing federal officers. Amendments to the Constitution have prescribed national criteria for voting eligibility. The 15th Amendment, adopted in 1870, gave all citizens the right to vote regardless of race, color, or previous condition of servitude. The 19th Amendment, adopted in 1919, further extended the right to vote to all citizens regardless of sex. The payment of poll taxes as a prerequisite to voting in federal elections was banned by the 24th Amendment in 1964. In 1971, as a result of the 26th Amendment, eligibility to vote in national elections was extended to all citizens, 18 years old and over.

Presidential election—The Constitution specifies how the President and Vice President are selected. Each state elects, by popular vote, a group of electors equal in number to its total of members of Congress. The 23d Amendment, adopted in 1961, grants the District of Columbia three presidential electors, a number equal to that of the least populous state. Subsequent to the election, the electors meet in their respective states to vote for President and Vice President. Usually, each elector votes for the candidate receiving the most popular votes in his or her state. A majority vote of all electors is necessary to elect the President and Vice President. If no candidate receives a majority, the House of Representatives, with each state having one vote, is empowered to elect the President and Vice President, again, with a majority of votes required.

The 22d Amendment to the Constitution, adopted in 1951, limits presidential tenure to two elective terms of 4 years each or to one elective term for any person who, upon succession to the Presidency, has held the office or acted as President for more than 2 years.

Congressional election—The Constitution provides that Representatives be apportioned among the states according to their population, that a census of population be taken every 10 years as a basis for apportionment, and that each state have at least one Representative. At the time of each apportionment, Congress decides what the total number of Representatives will be. Since 1912, the total has been 435, except during 1960 to 1962 when it increased to 437, adding one Representative each for Alaska and Hawaii. The total reverted to 435 after reapportionment following the 1960 census. Members are elected for 2-year terms, all terms covering the same period. The District of Columbia, American Samoa, Guam, and the Virgin Islands each elect one nonvoting Delegate, and Puerto Rico elects a nonvoting Resident Commissioner.

The Senate is composed of 100 members, 2 from each state, who are elected to serve for a term of 6 years. One-third of the Senate is elected every 2 years. Senators were originally chosen by the state legislatures. The 17th Amendment to the Constitution, adopted in 1913, prescribed that Senators be elected by popular vote.

Voter eligibility and participation—The Census Bureau publishes estimates of the population of voting age and the percent casting votes in each state for Presidential and congressional election years. These voting-age estimates include a number of persons who meet the age requirement but are not eligible to vote, (e.g. aliens and some institutionalized persons). In addition, since 1964, voter participation and voter characteristics data have been collected during November of election years as part of the CPS. These survey data include noncitizens in the voting age population estimates but exclude members of the Armed Forces and the institutional population.

Statistical reliability—For a discussion of statistical collection and estimation, sampling procedures, and measures of statistical reliability applicable to Census Bureau data, see Appendix III.

Figure 7.1
Vote Cast for President by Major Political Party: 1992 to 2000

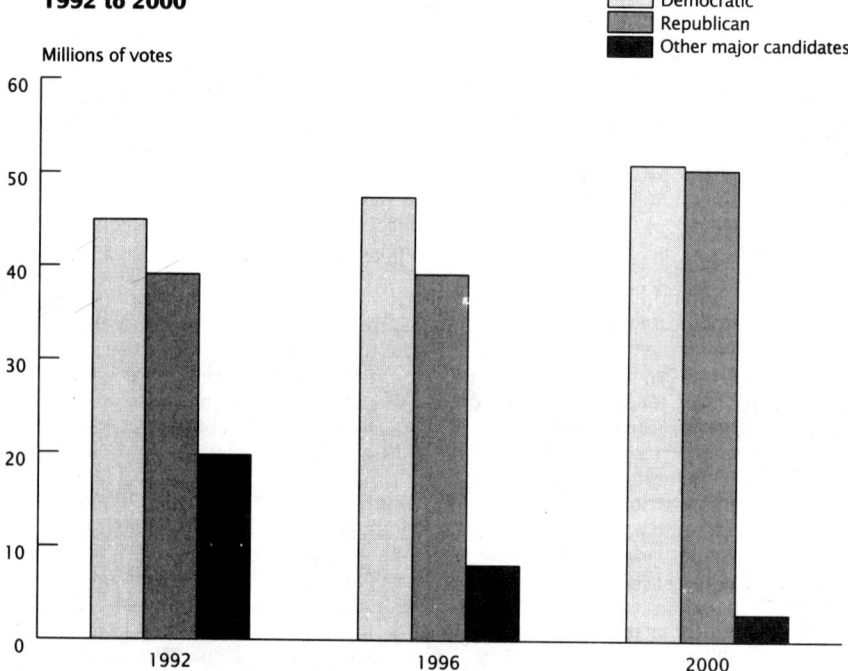

[1] Candidates with 1 million or more votes: 1992 - Independent, Ross Perot; 1996 - Reform, Ross Perot; 2000 - Green, Ralph Nader.

Source: Chart prepared by U.S. Census Bureau. For data, see Tables 396 and 397.

No. 396. Vote Cast for President by Major Political Party: 1940 to 2000

[49,900 represents 49,900,000. Prior to 1960, excludes Alaska and Hawaii; prior to 1964, excludes DC. Vote cast for major party candidates include the votes of minor parties cast for those candidates]

Year	Candidates for President (Democratic)	Candidates for President (Republican)	Total popular vote [1] (1,000)	Democratic Number (1,000)	Democratic Per-cent	Electoral vote	Republican Number (1,000)	Republican Per-cent	Electoral vote
1940	F. D. Roosevelt	Willkie	49,900	27,313	54.7	449	22,348	44.8	82
1944	F. D. Roosevelt	Dewey	47,977	25,613	53.4	432	22,018	45.9	99
1948	Truman	Dewey	48,794	24,179	49.6	303	21,991	45.1	189
1952	Stevenson	Eisenhower	61,551	27,315	44.4	89	33,936	55.1	442
1956	Stevenson	Eisenhower	62,027	26,023	42.0	73	35,590	57.4	457
1960	Kennedy	Nixon	68,838	34,227	49.7	303	34,108	49.5	219
1964	Johnson	Goldwater	70,645	43,130	61.1	486	27,178	38.5	52
1968	Humphrey	Nixon	73,212	31,275	42.7	191	31,785	43.4	301
1972	McGovern	Nixon	77,719	29,170	37.5	17	47,170	60.7	520
1976	Carter	Ford	81,556	40,831	50.1	297	39,148	48.0	240
1980	Carter	Reagan	86,515	35,484	41.0	49	43,904	50.7	489
1984	Mondale	Reagan	92,653	37,577	40.6	13	54,455	58.8	525
1988	Dukakis	Bush	91,595	41,809	45.6	111	48,886	53.4	426
1992	Clinton	Bush	104,425	44,909	43.0	370	39,104	37.4	168
1996	Clinton	Dole	96,278	47,402	49.2	379	39,199	40.7	159
2000	Gore	Bush	105,397	50,992	48.4	266	50,455	47.9	271

[1] Include votes for minor party candidates, independents, unpledged electors, and scattered write-in votes.
Source: Congressional Quarterly, Inc., Washington, DC, *America at the Polls 2*, 1965, and *America Votes*, biennial, (copyright).

No. 397. Vote Cast for Leading Minority Party Candidates for President: 1940 to 2000

[116 represents 116,000. See headnote, Table 396]

Year	Candidate	Party	Popular vote (1,000)	Candidate	Party	Popular vote (1,000)
1940	Norman Thomas	Socialist	116	Roger Babson	Prohibition	59
1944	Norman Thomas	Socialist	79	Claude Watson	Prohibition	75
1948	Strom Thurmond	States' Rights	1,176	Henry Wallace	Progressive	1,157
1952	Vincent Hallinan	Progressive	140	Stuart Hamblen	Prohibition	73
1956	T. Coleman Andrews	States' Rights	111	Eric Hass	Socialist Labor	44
1960	Eric Hass	Socialist Labor	48	Rutherford Decker	Prohibition	46
1964	Eric Hass	Socialist Labor	45	Clifton DeBerry	Socialist Workers	33
1968	George Wallace	American Independent	9,906	Henning Blomen	Socialist Labor	53
1972	John Schmitz	American	1,099	Benjamin Spock	People's	79
1976	Eugene McCarthy	Independent	757	Roger McBride	Libertarian	173
1980	John Anderson	Independent	5,720	Ed Clark	Libertarian	921
1984	David Bergland	Libertarian	228	Lyndon H. LaRouche	Independent	79
1988	Ron Paul	Libertarian	432	Lenora B. Fulani	New Alliance	217
1992	H. Ross Perot	Independent	19,742	Andre Marrou	Libertarian	292
1996	H. Ross Perot	Reform Party	8,085	Ralph Nader	Green	685
2000	Ralph Nader	Green	2,883	Pat Buchanan	Reform	449

Source: Congressional Quarterly, Inc., Washington, DC, *America at the Polls, 1920-1996*, 1997; and *America Votes*, biennial (copyright).

No. 398. Democratic and Republican Percentages of Two-Party Presidential Vote by Selected Characteristics of Voters: 1996 and 2000

[In percent. Covers citizens of voting age living in private housing units in the contiguous United States. Percentages for Democratic Presidential vote are computed by subtracting the percentage Republican vote from 100 percent; third-party or independent votes are not included as valid data. Data are from the National Election Studies and are based on a sample and subject to sampling variability; for details, see source]

Characteristic	1996 Democratic	1996 Republican	2000 Democratic	2000 Republican	Characteristic	1996 Democratic	1996 Republican	2000 Democratic	2000 Republican
Total [1]	58	42	52	48	Race:				
Year of birth:					White	51	49	46	54
1975 or later	61	39	63	37	Black	99	1	92	8
1959 to 1974	58	42	46	54					
1943 to 1958	58	42	53	47	Education:				
1927 to 1942	56	44	48	52	Grade school	88	12	74	26
1911 to 1926	64	36	64	36	High school	64	36	54	46
1895 to 1910	57	43	-	100	College	49	51	50	50
Sex:									
Male	51	49	47	53	Union household	75	25	61	39
Female	65	35	56	44	Nonunion household	54	46	50	50

- Represents zero. [1] Includes other characteristics, not shown separately.
Source: Center for Political Studies, University of Michigan, Ann Arbor, MI, National Election Studies (NES); "The NES Guide to Public Opinion and Electoral Behavior"; accessed 26 April 2003; <http://www.umich.edu/nex/nesguide/gd-index.htm#9> (copyright).

No. 399. Electoral Vote Cast for President by Major Political Party—States: 1960 to 2000

[D=Democratic, R=Republican. For composition of regions, see map, inside front cover]

State	1960 [1]	1964	1968 [2]	1972 [3]	1976 [4]	1980	1984	1988 [5]	1992	1996	2000 [6]
Democratic	303	486	191	17	297	49	13	111	370	379	266
Republican	219	52	301	520	240	489	525	426	168	159	271
Northeast:											
Democratic	121	126	102	14	86	4	-	53	106	106	102
Republican	12	-	24	108	36	118	113	60	-	-	4
Midwest:											
Democratic	71	149	31	-	58	10	10	29	100	100	68
Republican	82	-	118	145	87	135	127	108	29	29	61
South:											
Democratic	101	121	45	3	149	31	3	8	68	80	15
Republican	50	47	77	165	20	138	174	168	116	104	168
West:											
Democratic	10	90	13	-	4	4	-	21	96	93	81
Republican	75	5	82	102	97	98	111	90	23	26	38
AL	[1]D-5	R-10	([2])	R-9	D-9	R-9	R-9	R-9	R-9	R-9	R-9
AK	R-3	D-3	R-3	R-3	R-3	R-3	R-3	R-3	R-3	R-3	R-3
AZ	R-4	R-5	R-5	R-6	R-6	R-6	R-7	R-7	R-8	R-8	R-8
AR	D-8	D-6	([2])	R-6	D-6	R-6	R-6	R-6	D-6	D-6	R-6
CA	R-32	D-40	R-40	R-45	D-45	R-45	R-47	R-47	D-54	D-54	D-54
CO	R-6	D-6	R-6	R-7	R-7	R-7	R-8	R-8	D-8	R-8	R-8
CT	D-8	D-8	D-8	R-8	R-8	R-8	R-8	R-8	D-8	D-8	D-8
DE	D-3	D-3	R-3	R-3	D-3	R-3	R-3	R-3	D-3	D-3	D-3
DC	(X)	D-3	D-3	D-3	D-3	D-3	D-3	D-3	D-3	D-3	[6]D-2
FL	R-10	D-14	R-14	R-17	D-17	R-17	R-21	R-21	R-25	D-25	R-25
GA	D-12	R-12	([2])	R-12	D-12	D-12	R-12	R-12	D-13	R-13	R-13
HI	D-3	D-4	D-4	R-4	D-4	D-4	R-4	D-4	D-4	D-4	D-4
ID	R-4	R-4	R-4	R-4	R-4	R-4	R-4	R-4	R-4	R-4	R-4
IL	D-27	D-26	R-26	R-26	R-26	R-26	R-24	R-24	D-22	D-22	D-22
IN	R-13	D-13	R-13	R-13	R-13	R-13	R-12	R-12	R-12	R-12	R-12
IA	R-10	D-9	R-9	R-8	R-8	R-8	R-8	D-8	D-7	D-7	D-7
KS	R-8	D-7	R-7	R-7	R-7	R-7	R-7	R-7	R-6	R-6	R-6
KY	R-10	D-9	R-9	R-9	D-9	R-9	R-9	R-9	D-8	D-8	R-8
LA	D-10	R-10	([2])	R-10	D-10	R-10	R-10	R-10	D-9	D-9	R-9
ME	R-5	D-4	D-4	R-4	R-4	R-4	R-4	R-4	D-4	D-4	D-4
MD	D-9	D-10	D-10	R-10	D-10	R-10	R-10	R-10	D-10	D-10	D-10
MA	D-16	D-14	D-14	D-14	D-14	R-14	R-13	D-13	D-12	D-12	D-12
MI	D-20	D-21	D-21	R-21	R-21	R-21	R-20	R-20	D-18	D-18	D-18
MN	D-11	D-10	D-10	R-10	D-10	D-10	D-10	D-10	D-10	D-10	D-10
MS	([1])	R-7	([2])	R-7	D-7	R-7	R-7	R-7	R-7	R-7	R-7
MO	D-13	D-12	R-12	R-12	D-12	R-12	R-11	R-11	D-11	D-11	R-11
MT	R-4	D-4	R-4	R-4	R-4	R-4	R-4	R-4	D-3	R-3	R-3
NE	R-6	D-5	R-5	R-5	R-5	R-5	R-5	R-5	R-5	R-5	R-5
NV	D-3	D-3	R-3	R-3	R-3	R-3	R-4	R-4	D-4	D-4	R-4
NH	R-4	D-4	R-4	R-4	R-4	R-4	R-4	R-4	D-4	D-4	R-4
NJ	D-16	D-17	R-17	R-17	R-17	R-17	R-16	R-16	D-15	D-15	D-15
NM	D-4	D-4	R-4	R-4	R-4	R-4	R-5	R-5	D-5	D-5	D-5
NY	D-45	D-43	D-43	R-41	D-41	R-41	R-36	D-36	D-33	D-33	D-33
NC	D-14	D-13	[2]R-12	R-13	D-13	R-13	R-13	R-13	R-14	R-14	R-14
ND	R-4	D-4	R-4	R-3	R-3	R-3	R-3	R-3	R-3	R-3	R-3
OH	R-25	D-26	R-26	R-25	D-25	R-25	R-23	R-23	D-21	D-21	R-21
OK	[1]R-7	D-8	R-8	R-8	R-8	R-8	R-8	R-8	R-8	R-8	R-8
OR	R-6	D-6	R-6	R-6	R-6	R-6	R-7	D-7	D-7	D-7	D-7
PA	D-32	D-29	D-29	R-27	D-27	R-27	R-25	R-25	D-23	D-23	D-23
RI	D-4	D-4	D-4	D-4	D-4	D-4	R-4	D-4	D-4	D-4	D-4
SC	D-8	R-8	R-8	R-8	D-8	R-8	R-8	R-8	R-8	R-8	R-8
SD	R-4	D-4	R-4	R-4	R-4	R-4	R-3	R-3	R-3	R-3	R-3
TN	R-11	D-11	R-11	R-10	D-10	R-10	R-11	R-11	D-11	D-11	R-11
TX	D-24	D-25	D-25	R-26	D-26	R-26	R-29	R-29	R-32	R-32	R-32
UT	R-4	D-4	R-4	R-4	R-4	R-4	R-5	R-5	R-5	R-5	R-5
VT	R-3	D-3	R-3	R-3	R-3	R-3	R-3	R-3	D-3	D-3	R-3
VA	R-12	D-12	R-12	[3]R-11	R-12	R-12	R-12	R-12	R-13	R-13	R-13
WA	R-9	D-9	D-9	R-9	[4]R-8	R-9	R-10	D-10	D-11	D-11	D-11
WV	D-8	D-7	D-7	R-6	D-6	D-6	R-6	[5]D-5	D-5	D-5	R-5
WI	R-12	D-12	R-12	R-11	D-11	R-11	R-11	D-11	D-11	D-11	D-11
WY	R-3	D-3	R-3	R-3	R-3	R-3	R-3	R-3	R-3	R-3	R-3

- Represents zero.   X Not applicable.   [1] Excludes 15 electoral votes cast for Harry F. Byrd as follows: AL 6, MS 8, and OK 1.   [2] Excludes 46 electoral votes cast for American Independent George C. Wallace as follows: AL 10, AR 6, GA 12, LA 10, MS 7, and NC 1.   [3] Excludes one electoral vote cast for Libertarian John Hospers in Virginia.   [4] Excludes one electoral vote cast for Ronald Reagan in Washington.   [5] Excludes one electoral vote cast for Lloyd Bentsen for President in West Virginia.   [6] Excludes one electoral vote left blank by a Democratic elector in the District of Columbia.

Source: 1960-72, U.S. Congress, Clerk of the House, *Statistics of the Presidential and Congressional Election*, quadrennial; 1976-2000, Congressional Quarterly, Inc., Washington DC, *America Votes*, biennial (copyright).

Figure 7.2
Presidential Electoral Vote by State: 2000

*Excludes one electoral vote left blank by a Democratic elector in the District of Columbia.
Source: Chart prepared by U.S. Census Bureau, for data, see Table 399.

Elections 253

No. 400. Popular Vote Cast for President by Political Party—States: 1996 and 2000

[In thousands (96,278 represents 96,278,000), except percent]

State	1996 Total [1]	1996 Democratic Party	1996 Republican Party	1996 Perot (Reform Party)	2000 Total [1]	2000 Democratic Party	2000 Republican Party	2000 Percent Democratic	2000 Percent Republican
United States..	96,278	47,402	39,199	8,085	105,397	50,992	50,455	48.4	47.9
Alabama.........	1,534	662	769	92	1,666	693	941	41.6	56.5
Alaska..........	242	80	123	26	286	79	167	27.7	58.6
Arizona.........	1,404	653	622	112	1,532	685	782	44.7	51.0
Arkansas........	884	475	325	70	922	423	473	45.9	51.3
California.......	10,019	5,120	3,828	698	10,966	5,861	4,567	53.4	41.7
Colorado........	1,511	671	692	100	1,741	738	884	42.4	50.8
Connecticut.....	1,393	736	483	140	1,460	816	561	55.9	38.4
Delaware........	271	140	99	29	328	180	137	55.0	41.9
District of Columbia.	186	158	17	4	202	172	18	85.2	9.0
Florida..........	5,304	2,547	2,245	484	5,963	2,912	2,913	48.8	48.8
Georgia.........	2,299	1,054	1,081	146	2,597	1,116	1,420	43.0	54.7
Hawaii..........	360	205	114	27	368	205	138	55.8	37.5
Idaho............	492	165	257	63	502	139	337	27.6	67.2
Illinois..........	4,311	2,342	1,587	346	4,742	2,589	2,019	54.6	42.6
Indiana..........	2,136	887	1,007	224	2,199	902	1,246	41.0	56.6
Iowa............	1,234	620	493	105	1,316	639	634	48.5	48.2
Kansas..........	1,074	388	583	93	1,072	399	622	37.2	58.0
Kentucky........	1,389	637	623	120	1,544	639	872	41.4	56.5
Louisiana.......	1,784	928	713	123	1,766	792	928	44.9	52.6
Maine...........	606	313	186	86	652	320	287	49.1	44.0
Maryland........	1,781	966	682	116	2,020	1,141	814	56.5	40.3
Massachusetts...	2,557	1,572	718	227	2,703	1,616	879	59.8	32.5
Michigan........	3,849	1,990	1,481	337	4,233	2,170	1,953	51.3	46.1
Minnesota.......	2,193	1,120	766	258	2,439	1,168	1,110	47.9	45.5
Mississippi......	894	394	440	52	994	405	573	40.7	57.6
Missouri........	2,158	1,026	890	217	2,360	1,111	1,190	47.1	50.4
Montana........	407	168	180	55	411	137	240	33.4	58.4
Nebraska.......	677	237	363	71	697	232	434	33.3	62.2
Nevada.........	464	204	199	44	609	280	302	46.0	49.5
New Hampshire..	499	246	196	48	569	266	274	46.8	48.1
New Jersey.....	3,076	1,652	1,103	262	3,187	1,789	1,284	56.1	40.3
New Mexico.....	556	273	233	32	599	287	286	47.9	47.8
New York.......	6,316	3,756	1,933	503	6,822	4,108	2,403	60.2	35.2
North Carolina...	2,516	1,108	1,226	168	2,911	1,258	1,631	43.2	56.0
North Dakota....	266	107	125	33	288	95	175	33.1	60.7
Ohio............	4,534	2,148	1,860	483	4,702	2,184	2,350	46.4	50.0
Oklahoma.......	1,207	488	582	131	1,234	474	744	38.4	60.3
Oregon..........	1,378	650	538	121	1,534	720	714	47.0	46.5
Pennsylvania....	4,506	2,216	1,801	431	4,913	2,486	2,281	50.6	46.4
Rhode Island....	390	233	105	44	409	250	131	61.0	31.9
South Carolina...	1,152	506	573	64	1,383	566	786	40.9	56.8
South Dakota....	324	139	151	31	316	119	191	37.6	60.3
Tennessee......	1,894	909	864	106	2,076	982	1,062	47.3	51.1
Texas...........	5,612	2,460	2,736	379	6,408	2,434	3,800	38.0	59.3
Utah............	666	222	362	66	771	203	515	26.3	66.8
Vermont.........	258	138	80	31	294	149	120	50.6	40.7
Virginia.........	2,417	1,091	1,138	160	2,739	1,217	1,437	44.4	52.5
Washington.....	2,254	1,123	841	201	2,487	1,248	1,109	50.2	44.6
West Virginia....	636	328	234	72	648	295	336	45.6	51.9
Wisconsin.......	2,196	1,072	845	227	2,599	1,243	1,237	47.8	47.6
Wyoming........	212	78	105	26	218	60	148	27.7	67.8

[1] Includes other parties.

Source: Congressional Quarterly, Inc., Washington, DC, *America Votes*, biennial (copyright).

No. 401. Vote Cast for United States Senators, 2000 and 2002, and Incumbent Senators, 2002—States

[1,397 represents 1,397,000. D=Democrat; R=Republican]

State	2000 Total (1,000)[1]	2000 Percent for leading party	2002 Total (1,000)[1]	2002 Percent for leading party	Incumbent senators Name, party, and year	Incumbent senators Name, party, and year
Alabama	(X)	(X)	1,353	R-58.6	Jeff Sessions (R) 2009	Richard C. Shelby (R) 2005
Alaska	(X)	(X)	230	R-78.2	Lisa Murkowski (R) 2005	Ted Stevens (R) 2009
Arizona	1,397	R-79.3	(X)	(X)	John McCain (R) 2005	Jon Kyl (R) 2007
Arkansas	(X)	(X)	804	D-53.9	Blanche Lincoln (D) 2005	Mark Pryor (D) 2009
California	10,624	D-55.8	(X)	(X)	Barbara Boxer (D) 2005	Dianne Feinstein (D) 2007
Colorado	(X)	(X)	1,416	R-50.7	Ben N. Campbell (R) 2005	Wayne Allard (R) 2009
Connecticut	1,311	D-63.2	(X)	(X)	Christopher J. Dodd (D) 2007	Joseph I. Lieberman (D) 2007
Delaware	327	D-55.5	232	D-58.2	Joseph R. Biden Jr. (D) 2009	Thomas R. Carper (D) 2007
Florida	5,857	D-51.0	(X)	(X)	Bob Graham (D) 2005	Bill Nelson (D) 2007
Georgia	2,429	D-58.2	2,032	R-52.7	Saxby Chambliss (R) 2009	Zell Miller (D) 2005
Hawaii	346	D-72.7	(X)	(X)	Daniel K. Akaka (D) 2007	Daniel K. Inouye (D) 2005
Idaho	(X)	(X)	409	R-65.2	Larry E. Craig (R) 2009	Michael D. Crapo (R) 2005
Illinois	(X)	(X)	3,487	D-60.3	Peter Fitzgerald (R) 2005	Richard J. Durbin (D) 2009
Indiana	2,145	R-66.6	(X)	(X)	Evan Bayh (D) 2005	Richard G. Lugar (R) 2007
Iowa	(X)	(X)	1,023	D-54.2	Tom Harkin (D) 2009	Charles E. Grassley (R) 2005
Kansas	(X)	(X)	767	R-83.6	Sam Brownback (R) 2005	Pat Roberts (R) 2009
Kentucky	(X)	(X)	1,131	R-64.7	Jim Bunning (R) 2005	Mitch McConnell (R) 2009
Louisiana [2]	(X)	(X)	2,482	D-49.8	John B. Breaux (D) 2005	Mary Landrieu (D) 2009
Maine	635	R-68.9	505	R-58.4	Susan Collins (R) 2009	Olympia J. Snowe (R) 2007
Maryland	1,947	D-63.2	(X)	(X)	Barbara A. Mikulski (D) 2005	Paul S. Sarbanes (D) 2007
Massachusetts	2,599	D-72.7	2,007	D-80.0	Edward M. Kennedy (D) 2007	John F. Kerry (D) 2009
Michigan	4,168	D-49.5	3,129	D-60.6	Carl Levin (D) 2009	Debbie Stabenow (D) 2007
Minnesota	2,420	D-48.8	2,255	R-49.5	Norm Coleman (R) 2009	Mark Dayton (D) 2007
Mississippi	994	R-65.9	630	R-84.6	Thad Cochran (R) 2009	Trent Lott (R) 2007
Missouri	2,362	D-50.5	1,878	R-49.8	Christopher S. Bond (R) 2005	James Talent (R) 2007
Montana	412	R-50.6	327	D-62.7	Max Baucus (D) 2009	Conrad Burns (R) 2007
Nebraska	692	D-51.0	480	R-82.8	Chuck Hagel (R) 2009	Ben Nelson (D) 2007
Nevada	600	R-55.1	(X)	(X)	Harry Reid (D) 2005	John Ensign (R) 2007
New Hampshire	(X)	(X)	447	R-50.8	Judd Gregg (R) 2005	John Sununu (R) 2009
New Jersey	3,016	D-50.1	2,113	D-53.9	Frank Lautenberg (D) 2009	Jon Corzine (D) 2007
New Mexico	590	D-61.7	483	R-65.0	Jeff Bingaman (D) 2009	Pete V. Domenici (R) 2007
New York	6,780	D-55.3	(X)	(X)	Hillary Rodham Clinton (D) 2007	Charles E. Schumer (D) 2005
North Carolina	(X)	(X)	2,331	R-53.6	John Edwards (D) 2005	Elizabeth Dole (R) 2009
North Dakota	288	D-61.4	(X)	(X)	Byron L. Dorgan (D) 2007	Kent Conrad (D) 2007
Ohio	4,449	R-59.9	(X)	(X)	George V. Voinovich (R) 2005	Mike DeWine (R) 2007
Oklahoma	(X)	(X)	1,018	R-57.3	James Inhofe (R) 2009	Don Nickles (R) 2005
Oregon	(X)	(X)	1,267	R-56.2	Gordon Smith (R) 2009	Ron Wyden (D) 2005
Pennsylvania	4,736	R-52.4	(X)	(X)	Rick Santorum (R) 2007	Arlen Specter (R) 2005
Rhode Island	392	R-56.8	324	D-78.4	Jack Reed (D) 2009	Lincoln Chafee (R) 2007
South Carolina	(X)	(X)	1,103	R-54.4	Ernest F. Hollings (D) 2005	Lindsey Graham (R) 2009
South Dakota	(X)	(X)	338	D-49.6	Thomas A. Daschle (D) 2005	Tim Johnson (D) 2009
Tennessee	1,929	R-65.1	1,642	R-54.3	Lamar Alexander (R) 2009	Bill Frist (R) 2007
Texas	6,277	R-65.0	4,514	R-55.3	Kay Bailey Hutchison (R) 2007	John Corny (R) 2009
Utah	770	R-65.6	(X)	(X)	Robert F. Bennett (R) 2005	Orrin G. Hatch (R) 2007
Vermont [3]	289	R-65.6	(X)	(X)	Patrick J. Leahy (D) 2005	[3]James M. Jeffords (I) 2007
Virginia	2,718	R-52.3	1,489	R-82.6	George F. Allen (R) 2007	John W. Warner (R) 2009
Washington	2,461	D-48.7	(X)	(X)	Patty Murray (D) 2005	Maria Cantwell (D) 2007
West Virginia	603	D-77.8	436	D-63.1	Robert C. Byrd (D) 2007	John D. Rockefeller IV (D) 2009
Wisconsin	2,540	D-61.5	(X)	(X)	Herb Kohl (D) 2007	Russell Feingold (D) 2005
Wyoming	214	R-73.8	183	R-73.0	Mike Enzi (R) 2009	Craig Thomas (R) 2007

X Not applicable. [1] Includes vote cast for minor parties. [2] Louisiana holds an open-primary election with candidates from all parties running on the same ballot. Any candidate who receives a majority is elected. [3] Jeffords was re-elected in Vermont in 2000 as a Republican, but subsequently switched to Independent status in June 2001.

Source: Congressional Quarterly, Inc., Washington, DC, *America Votes*, biennial (copyright).

No. 402. Apportionment of Membership in House of Representatives by State: 1790 to 2000

[Total membership includes Representatives assigned to newly admitted states after the apportionment acts. Population figures used for apportionment purposes are those determined for states by each decennial census. No reapportionment based on 1920 population census. For method of calculating apportionment and a short history of apportionment, see House Report 91-1314, 91st Congress, 2d session, the decennial population census, and Congressional Apportionment]

State	\multicolumn{20}{c}{Membership based on census of—}
	1790	1800	1810	1820	1830	1840	1850	1860	1870	1880	1890	1900	1910	1930	1940	1950	1960	1970	1980	1990	2000
U.S.	106	142	186	213	242	232	237	243	293	332	357	391	435	435	435	437	435	435	435	435	435
AL	(X)	(X)	[1]1	3	5	7	7	6	8	8	9	9	10	9	9	9	8	7	7	7	7
AK	(X)	(X)	(X)	(X)	(X)	(X)	(X)	(X)	(X)	(X)	(X)	(X)	(X)	(X)	(X)	[1]1	1	1	1	1	1
AZ	(X)	(X)	(X)	(X)	(X)	(X)	(X)	(X)	(X)	(X)	(X)	(X)	[2]1	1	2	2	3	4	5	6	8
AR	(X)	(X)	(X)	(X)	[1]1	1	2	3	4	5	6	7	7	7	7	6	4	4	4	4	4
CA	(X)	(X)	(X)	(X)	(X)	[1]2	2	3	4	6	7	8	11	20	23	30	38	43	45	52	53
CO	(X)	(X)	(X)	(X)	(X)	(X)	(X)	(X)	[1]1	1	2	3	4	4	4	4	4	5	6	6	7
CT	7	7	7	6	6	4	4	4	4	4	4	5	5	6	6	6	6	6	6	6	5
DE	1	1	2	1	1	1	1	1	1	1	1	1	1	1	1	1	1	1	1	1	1
FL	(X)	(X)	(X)	(X)	(X)	[1]1	1	1	2	2	2	3	4	5	6	8	12	15	19	23	25
GA	2	4	6	7	9	8	8	7	9	10	11	11	12	10	10	10	10	10	10	11	13
HI	(X)	(X)	(X)	(X)	(X)	(X)	(X)	(X)	(X)	(X)	(X)	(X)	(X)	(X)	(X)	[1]1	2	2	2	2	2
ID	(X)	(X)	(X)	(X)	(X)	(X)	(X)	(X)	(X)	(X)	[1]1	1	2	2	2	2	2	2	2	2	2
IL	(X)	(X)	[1]1	1	3	7	9	14	19	20	22	25	27	27	26	25	24	24	22	20	19
IN	(X)	(X)	[1]1	3	7	10	11	11	13	13	13	13	13	12	11	11	11	11	10	10	9
IA	(X)	(X)	(X)	(X)	(X)	[1]2	2	6	9	11	11	11	11	9	8	8	7	6	6	5	5
KS	(X)	(X)	(X)	(X)	(X)	(X)	(X)	1	3	7	8	8	8	7	6	6	5	5	5	4	4
KY	2	6	10	12	13	10	10	9	10	11	11	11	11	9	9	8	7	7	7	6	6
LA	(X)	(X)	[1]1	3	3	4	4	5	6	6	6	7	8	8	8	8	8	8	8	7	7
ME	(X)	(X)	(X)	7	8	7	6	5	5	4	4	4	4	3	3	3	2	2	2	2	2
MD	8	9	9	9	8	6	6	5	6	6	6	6	6	6	6	7	8	8	8	8	8
MA	14	17	20	13	12	10	11	10	11	12	13	14	16	15	14	14	12	12	11	10	10
MI	(X)	(X)	(X)	(X)	[1]1	3	4	6	9	11	12	12	13	17	17	18	19	19	18	16	15
MN	(X)	(X)	(X)	(X)	(X)	(X)	[1]2	2	3	5	7	9	10	9	9	9	8	8	8	8	8
MS	(X)	(X)	[1]1	1	2	4	5	5	6	7	7	8	8	7	7	6	5	5	5	5	4
MO	(X)	(X)	(X)	1	2	5	7	9	13	14	15	16	16	13	13	11	10	10	9	9	9
MT	(X)	(X)	(X)	(X)	(X)	(X)	(X)	(X)	(X)	(X)	[1]1	1	2	2	2	2	2	2	2	1	1
NE	(X)	(X)	(X)	(X)	(X)	(X)	(X)	(X)	[1]1	3	6	6	6	5	4	4	3	3	3	3	3
NV	(X)	(X)	(X)	(X)	(X)	(X)	(X)	[1]1	1	1	1	1	1	1	1	1	1	1	2	2	3
NH	4	5	6	6	5	4	3	3	3	2	2	2	2	2	2	2	2	2	2	2	2
NJ	5	6	6	6	6	5	5	5	7	7	8	10	12	14	14	14	15	15	14	13	13
NM	(X)	(X)	(X)	(X)	(X)	(X)	(X)	(X)	(X)	(X)	(X)	(X)	[2]1	1	2	2	2	2	3	3	3
NY	10	17	27	34	40	34	33	31	33	34	34	37	43	45	45	43	41	39	34	31	29
NC	10	12	13	13	13	9	8	7	8	9	9	10	10	11	12	12	11	11	11	12	13
ND	(X)	(X)	(X)	(X)	(X)	(X)	(X)	(X)	(X)	[1]1	1	2	3	2	2	2	2	1	1	1	1
OH	(X)	[1]1	6	14	19	21	21	19	20	21	21	21	22	24	23	23	24	23	21	19	18
OK	(X)	(X)	(X)	(X)	(X)	(X)	(X)	(X)	(X)	(X)	(X)	[1]5	8	9	8	6	6	6	6	6	5
OR	(X)	(X)	(X)	(X)	(X)	(X)	[1]1	1	1	1	2	2	3	3	4	4	4	4	5	5	5
PA	13	18	23	26	28	24	25	24	27	28	30	32	36	34	33	30	27	25	23	21	19
RI	2	2	2	2	2	2	2	2	2	2	2	2	3	2	2	2	2	2	2	2	2
SC	6	8	9	9	9	7	6	4	5	7	7	7	7	6	6	6	6	6	6	6	6
SD	(X)	(X)	(X)	(X)	(X)	(X)	(X)	(X)	(X)	[1]2	2	2	3	2	2	2	2	2	1	1	1
TN	1	3	6	9	13	11	10	8	10	10	10	10	10	9	10	9	9	8	9	9	9
TX	(X)	(X)	(X)	(X)	(X)	[1]2	2	4	6	11	13	16	18	21	21	22	23	24	27	30	32
UT	(X)	(X)	(X)	(X)	(X)	(X)	(X)	(X)	(X)	(X)	[1]1	1	2	2	2	2	2	2	3	3	3
VT	2	4	6	5	5	4	3	3	3	2	2	2	2	1	1	1	1	1	1	1	1
VA	19	22	23	22	21	15	13	11	9	10	10	10	10	9	9	10	10	10	10	11	11
WA	(X)	(X)	(X)	(X)	(X)	(X)	(X)	(X)	(X)	[1]1	2	3	5	6	6	7	7	7	8	9	9
WV	(X)	(X)	(X)	(X)	(X)	(X)	(X)	(X)	3	4	4	5	6	6	6	6	5	4	4	3	3
WI	(X)	(X)	(X)	(X)	(X)	[1]2	3	6	8	9	10	11	11	10	10	10	10	9	9	9	8
WY	(X)	(X)	(X)	(X)	(X)	(X)	(X)	(X)	(X)	(X)	[1]1	1	1	1	1	1	1	1	1	1	1

X Not applicable.   [1] Assigned after apportionment.   [2] Included in apportionment in anticipation of statehood.

Source: U.S. Census Bureau, *Congressional Apportionment, Census 2000 Brief*, Series C2KBR/01-7, issued July 2001; and see also <http://www.census.gov/population/www/censusdata/apportionment.html>.

No. 403. Vote Cast for United States Representatives by Major Political Party—States: 1998 to 2002

[In thousands (65,897 represents 65,897,000), except percent. R=Republican, D=Democrat, and I=Independent. In each state, totals represent the sum of votes cast in each Congressional District or votes cast for Representative at Large in states where only one member is elected. In all years there are numerous districts within the state where either the Republican or Democratic party had no candidate. In some states the Republican and Democratic vote includes votes cast for the party candidate by endorsing parties]

State	1998 Total[1]	1998 Democratic	1998 Republican	1998 Percent for leading party	2000 Total[1]	2000 Democratic	2000 Republican	2000 Percent for leading party	2002 Total[1]	2002 Democratic	2002 Republican	2002 Percent for leading party
U.S.	65,897	31,482	32,255	R-48.9	97,226	46,521	46,954	R-48.3	73,845	33,865	37,290	R-50.5
AL	1,215	545	666	R-54.8	1,439	486	849	R-59.0	1,269	507	695	R-54.7
AK	223	77	140	R-62.6	274	45	191	R-69.6	228	39	170	R-74.5
AZ	1,004	407	574	R-57.1	1,466	558	855	R-58.3	1,194	472	682	R-57.1
AR[2]	525	169	320	R-60.9	633	355	277	D-56.2	688	392	284	D-57.0
CA	7,990	4,040	3,510	D-50.6	10,438	5,407	4,446	D-51.8	7,258	3,731	3,226	D-51.4
CO	1,274	533	716	R-56.2	1,624	496	969	R-59.7	1,397	589	753	R-53.9
CT	954	496	442	D-51.9	1,313	699	595	D-53.2	989	509	466	D-51.5
DE	181	57	120	R-66.4	313	96	212	R-67.6	228	61	165	R-72.1
FL[2]	1,213	581	558	R-47.9	5,011	1,976	2,852	R-56.9	3,767	1,537	2,161	R-57.4
GA	1,632	592	1,040	R-63.7	2,417	918	1,498	R-62.0	1,919	814	1,105	R-57.6
HI	397	261	119	D-65.7	340	221	111	D-65.0	360	232	117	D-64.5
ID	379	169	205	R-54.0	493	142	333	R-67.5	405	138	256	R-63.3
IL	3,215	1,566	1,625	R-50.5	4,393	2,454	1,907	D-55.8	3,429	1,741	1,657	D-50.8
IN	1,576	673	862	R-54.7	2,157	953	1,141	R-52.9	1,521	641	841	R-55.3
IA	901	338	552	R-61.3	1,276	532	717	R-56.2	1,013	454	546	R-54.0
KS	727	272	450	R-61.9	1,038	328	658	R-63.4	830	260	536	R-64.6
KY	1,099	456	637	R-58.0	1,435	562	825	R-57.5	1,094	351	694	R-63.4
LA	310	213	97	D-68.7	1,202	360	747	R-62.1	1,325	448	794	R-59.9
ME	415	281	125	D-67.7	638	423	203	D-66.2	495	290	206	D-58.5
MD	1,482	792	690	D-53.5	1,927	1,061	856	D-55.1	1,662	904	753	D-54.4
MA	1,742	1,306	413	D-75.0	2,347	1,968	343	D-83.8	1,841	1,529	290	D-83.0
MI	2,985	1,469	1,438	D-49.2	4,070	2,178	1,787	D-53.5	3,056	1,507	1,474	D-49.3
MN	2,040	1,090	863	D-53.5	2,364	1,234	993	D-52.2	2,202	1,098	1,030	D-49.9
MS	551	263	232	D-47.7	986	496	468	D-50.3	678	320	339	R-50.0
MO	1,572	788	748	D-50.1	2,326	1,136	1,136	D-48.8	1,854	829	986	R-53.2
MT	332	147	176	R-53.0	411	190	211	R-51.5	331	108	214	R-64.6
NE	526	105	393	R-74.7	683	178	487	R-71.2	474	47	387	R-81.6
NV	410	79	275	R-67.1	585	225	331	R-56.5	500	171	301	R-60.2
NH	318	124	190	R-59.8	556	239	303	R-54.5	443	176	255	R-57.5
NJ	1,815	902	858	D-49.7	2,988	1,532	1,384	D-51.3	2,006	1,030	934	D-51.4
NM	498	228	246	R-49.5	588	300	274	D-51.0	438	262	175	D-59.9
NY	4,267	2,278	1,858	D-53.4	5,824	3,190	2,466	D-54.8	3,822	1,771	1,527	D-46.3
NC	1,904	827	1,014	R-53.3	2,780	1,194	1,515	R-54.5	2,244	971	1,209	R-53.9
ND	213	120	88	D-56.2	286	151	127	D-52.9	231	121	110	D-52.4
OH	3,375	1,594	1,752	R-51.9	4,518	2,067	2,203	R-48.8	3,158	1,332	1,776	R-56.2
OK	859	314	538	R-62.7	1,088	337	702	R-64.5	1,002	392	547	R-54.9
OR	1,090	631	402	D-57.9	1,440	790	607	D-54.9	1,240	677	529	D-54.6
PA	2,896	1,381	1,472	R-50.8	4,554	2,279	2,229	D-50.0	3,310	1,349	1,859	R-56.2
RI	293	204	77	D-69.5	384	247	89	D-64.4	329	225	97	D-68.3
SC	974	370	580	R-59.6	1,321	525	730	R-55.2	985	346	570	R-57.8
SD	259	64	194	R-75.1	315	78	231	R-73.4	337	154	180	R-53.4
TN	914	412	470	R-51.4	1,854	819	992	R-53.5	1,529	708	771	R-50.4
TX	3,462	1,531	1,787	R-51.6	5,986	2,799	2,932	R-49.0	4,295	1,885	2,291	R-53.3
UT	471	127	304	R-64.6	759	305	427	R-56.2	557	221	322	R-57.8
VT	215	(X)	71	I-67.1	283	15	52	I-76.4	225	(X)	73	I-67.7
VA	1,149	514	542	R-47.2	2,422	1,060	1,132	R-46.7	1,516	440	1,008	R-66.5
WA	1,858	980	819	D-52.8	2,382	1,246	998	D-52.3	1,739	907	779	D-52.2
WV	351	283	29	D-80.6	580	421	109	D-72.6	400	264	136	D-66.0
WI	1,673	762	880	R-52.6	2,506	1,188	1,311	R-52.3	1,638	677	889	R-54.3
WY	174	67	101	R-57.8	212	61	142	R-66.8	182	66	110	R-60.5

X Not applicable. [1] Includes vote cast for minor parties. [2] State law does not require tabulation of votes for unopposed candidates.

Source: Congressional Quarterly, Inc., Washington, DC, *America Votes*, biennial (copyright). See also <http://www.cq.com/>.

No. 404. Vote Cast for United States Representatives by Major Political Party—Congressional Districts: 2002

[In some states the Democratic and Republican vote includes votes cast for the party candidate by endorsing parties]

State and district	Democratic candidate Name	Percent of total	Republican candidate Name	Percent of total	State and district	Democratic candidate Name	Percent of total	Republican candidate Name	Percent of total
AL	(X)	(X)	(X)	(X)	47th	Sanchez	60.56	Chavez	34.69
1st	Belk	37.78	Bonner	60.50	48th	Graham	28.44	Cox	68.44
2d	Woods	29.52	Everett	68.75	49th	(¹)	(¹)	Issa	77.22
3d	Turnham	48.20	Rogers	50.30	50th	Stewart	32.34	Cunningham	64.33
4th	(¹)	(¹)	Aderholt	86.72	51st	Filner	57.93	Garcia	39.33
5th	Cramer	73.28	Engel	24.71	52d	Moore-			
6th	(¹)	(¹)	Bachus	89.83		Kochlacs	25.75	Hunter	70.15
7th	Davis	92.44	(¹)	(¹)	53d	Davis	62.19	VanDeWeghe	37.78
AK	Greene	17.28	Young	74.51	**CO**	(X)	(X)	(X)	(X)
AZ	(X)	(X)	(X)	(X)	1st	DeGette	66.28	Chlouber	29.59
1st	Cordova	45.64	Renzi	49.21	2d	Udall	60.09	Hume	36.77
2d	Camacho	36.55	Franks	59.92	3d	Berckefeldt	31.27	McInnis	65.80
3d	Hill	30.29	Shadegg	67.32	4th	Matsunaka	41.68	Musgrave	54.94
4th	Pastor	67.38	Barnert	27.82	5th	Imrie	24.68	Hefley	69.37
5th	Columbus	36.25	Hayworth	61.17	6th	Wright	30.03	Tancredo	66.88
6th	Thomas	31.57	Flake	65.94	7th	Feeley	47.24	Beauprez	47.31
7th	Grijalva	59.00	Hieb	37.06	**CT**	(X)	(X)	(X)	(X)
8th	Ryan	33.59	Kolbe	63.33	1st	Larson	66.79	Steele	33.20
AR	(X)	(X)	(X)	(X)	2d	Courtney	45.91	Simmons	54.09
1st	Berry	66.84	Robinson	33.16	3d	DeLauro	65.58	Elser	29.54
2d	Snyder	92.92	(¹)	(¹)	4th	Sanchez	35.57	Shays	64.43
3d	(¹)	(¹)	Boozman	98.90	5th	Maloney	43.26	Johnson	54.25
4th	Ross	60.56	Dickey	39.44	**DE**	Miller	26.71	Castle	72.07
CA	(X)	(X)	(X)	(X)	**FL**	(X)	(X)	(X)	(X)
1st	Thompson	64.07	Wiesner	32.40	1st	Oram	25.40	Miller	74.59
2d	Johnson	29.31	Herger	65.79	2d	Boyd	66.90	McGurk	33.10
3d	Beeman	34.44	Ose	62.45	3d	Brown	59.29	Carroll	40.71
4th	Norberg	31.89	Doolittle	64.77	4th	(¹)	(¹)	Crenshaw	99.70
5th	Matsui	70.47	Frankhuizen	26.41	5th	Thurman	46.24	Brown-Waite	47.90
6th	Woolsey	66.69	Erickson	29.61	6th	Bruderly	34.64	Stearns	65.36
7th	Miller	70.71	Hargrave	26.44	7th	Hogan	40.42	Mica	59.58
8th	Pelosi	79.58	German	12.50	8th	Diaz	34.86	Keller	65.14
9th	Lee	81.41	Udinsky	15.18	9th	Kalogianis	28.53	Bilirakis	71.46
10th	Tauscher	75.59	(¹)	(¹)	10th	(¹)	(¹)	Young	(¹)
11th	Shaw	39.69	Pombo	60.31	11th	Davis	(¹)	(¹)	(¹)
12th	Lantos	68.13	Moloney	24.76	12th	(¹)	(¹)	Putnam	(¹)
13th	Stark	71.06	Mahmood	22.06	13th	Schneider	45.21	Harris	54.78
14th	Eshoo	68.18	Nixon	28.16	14th	(¹)	(¹)	Goss	(¹)
15th	Honda	65.77	Hermann	31.01	15th	Tso	36.85	Weldon	63.15
16th	Lofgren	67.02	McNea	29.80	16th	(¹)	(¹)	Foley	78.88
17th	Farr	68.07	Engler	27.02	17th	Meek	99.94	(¹)	(¹)
18th	Cardoza	51.26	Monteith	43.37	18th	Chote	28.61	Ros-Lehtinen	69.11
19th	Veen	30.04	Radanovich	67.31	19th	Wexler	72.16	Merkl	27.84
20th	Dooley	63.70	Minuth	34.28	20th	Deutsch	(¹)	(¹)	(¹)
21st	LaPere	26.24	Nunes	70.49	21st	(¹)	(¹)	Diaz-Balart	(¹)
22d	Corvera	23.73	Thomas	73.33	22d	Roberts	38.35	Shaw	60.77
23d	Capps	59.03	Rogers	38.59	23d	Hastings	77.49	Laurie	22.51
24th	Rudin	31.76	Gallegly	65.18	24th	Jacobs	38.16	Feeney	61.84
25th	Conaway	31.10	McKeon	64.97	25th	Betancourt	35.35	Diaz-Balart	64.65
26th	Mikels	33.49	Dreier	63.77	**GA**	(X)	(X)	(X)	(X)
27th	Sherman	61.96	Levy	38.04	1st	Smart	27.86	Kingston	72.14
28th	Berman	71.40	Hernandez	23.16	2d	Bishop	100.00	(¹)	(¹)
29th	Schiff	62.56	Scileppi	33.42	3d	Marshall	50.51	Clay	49.49
30th	Waxman	70.37	Goss	29.63	4th	Majette	77.03	Van Auken	22.97
31st	Becerra	81.15	Vega	18.85	5th	Lewis	100.00	(¹)	(¹)
32d	Solis	68.79	Fischbeck	27.46	6th	Weisberger	20.13	Isakson	79.87
33d	Watson	82.55	Kim	14.10	7th	Berlon	21.08	Linder	78.92
34th	Roybal-Allard	74.04	Miller	25.96	8th	Petrakopou-			
35th	Waters	77.51	Moen	19.37		los	21.67	Collins	78.33
36th	Harman	61.35	Johnson	35.01	9th	Irwin	27.16	Norwood	72.84
37th	Millender-				10th	(¹)	(¹)	Deal	100.00
	McDonald	72.92	Velasco	23.16	11th	Kahn	48.36	Gingrey	51.64
38th	Napolitano	71.11	Burrola	26.27	12th	Walker	44.81	Burns	55.19
39th	Sanchez	54.81	Escobar	40.82	13th	Scott	59.63	Cox	40.37
40th	Avalos	29.47	Royce	67.64	**HI**	(X)	(X)	(X)	(X)
41st	Johnson	29.63	Lewis	67.38	1st	Abercrombie	72.85	Terry	24.92
42d	Waldron	28.98	Miller	67.80	2d	Mink	56.16	McDermott	39.98
43d	Baca	66.39	Neighbor	30.47	**ID**	(X)	(X)	(X)	(X)
44th	Vandenberg	31.56	Calvert	63.66	1st	Richardson	38.94	Otter	58.57
45th	Kurpiewski	32.72	Bono	65.23	2d	Kinghorn	29.05	Simpson	68.18
46th	Schipske	34.54	Rohrabacher	61.73					

See footnotes at end of table.

No. 404. Vote Cast for United States Representatives by Major Political Party—Congressional Districts: 2002—Con.

[See headnote, p. 258]

State and district	Democratic candidate Name	Percent of total	Republican candidate Name	Percent of total	State and district	Democratic candidate Name	Percent of total	Republican candidate Name	Percent of total
IL....	(X)	(X)	(X)	(X)	4th...	Frank....	98.99	(^{1})	(^{1})
1st...	Rush....	81.17	Wardingly..	16.21	5th...	Meehan...	60.15	McCarthy..	34.03
2d...	Jackson...	82.30	Nelson....	17.70	6th...	Tierney....	68.27	Smith.....	31.63
3d...	Lipinski...	100.00	(^{1})	(^{1})	7th...	Markey....	98.24	(^{1})	(^{1})
4th...	Gutierrez..	79.68	Lopez-Cisneros...	15.12	8th...	Capuano..	99.56	(^{1})	(^{1})
5th...	Emanuel..	66.81	Augusti....	28.86	9th...	Lynch.....	99.45	(^{1})	(^{1})
6th...	Berry.....	34.91	Hyde......	65.09	10th...	Delahunt..	69.20	(^{1})	(^{1})
7th...	Davis.....	83.21	Tunney....	15.25	MI....	(X)	(X)	(X)	(X)
8th...	Bean......	42.56	Crane.....	57.42	1st...	Stupak....	67.67	Hooper....	31.10
9th...	Schakowsky...	70.27	Duric......	26.83	2d...	Wrisley....	27.70	Hoekstra...	70.40
10th...	Perritt....	31.19	Kirk.......	68.81	3d...	Lynnes....	28.32	Ehlers.....	69.97
11th...	Van Duyne.	35.68	Weller.....	64.32	4th...	Hollenbeck.	30.17	Camp.....	68.21
12th...	Costello...	69.25	Sadler.....	30.75	5th...	Kildee.....	91.56	(^{1})	(^{1})
13th...	Mason.....	29.74	Biggert....	70.26	6th...	Giguere....	29.31	Upton.....	69.17
14th...	Quick.....	25.86	Hastert....	74.14	7th...	Simpson...	38.61	Smith.....	59.66
15th...	Hartke.....	31.04	Johnson...	65.17	8th...	McAlpine..	30.75	Rogers....	67.88
16th...	Kutsch....	29.39	Manzullo...	70.61	9th...	Fink.......	39.88	Knollenberg.	58.10
17th...	Evans.....	62.42	Calderone..	37.58	10th...	Marlinga...	35.52	Miller.....	63.31
18th...	(^{1})	(^{1})	LaHood....	100.00	11th...	Kelley.....	39.66	McCotter...	57.19
19th...	Phelps....	45.21	Shimkus...	54.79	12th...	Levin......	68.26	Dean......	29.78
IN....	(X)	(X)	(X)	(X)	13th...	Kilpatrick..	91.61	(^{1})	(^{1})
1st...	Visclosky..	66.94	Leyva.....	31.02	14th...	Conyers....	83.21	Stone.....	15.20
2d...	Thompson.	45.77	Chocola...	50.45	15th...	Dingell.....	72.21	Kaltenbach.	25.72
3d...	Rigdon....	34.45	Souder....	63.14	MN....	(X)	(X)	(X)	(X)
4th...	Abbott....	26.15	Buyer.....	71.36	1st...	Andreasen.	34.65	Gutknecht..	61.50
5th...	Carr......	25.18	Burton.....	71.97	2d...	Luther.....	42.22	Kline......	53.33
6th...	Fox.......	34.40	Pence.....	63.79	3d...	Stanton....	27.88	Ramstad...	72.02
7th...	Carson....	53.13	McVey.....	44.14	4th...	McCollum..	62.22	Billington...	33.91
8th...	Hartke....	46.02	Hostettler..	51.31	5th...	Sabo......	67.03	Mathias....	25.89
9th...	Hill.......	51.15	Sodrel.....	46.13	6th...	Robert.....	35.06	Kennedy...	57.34
IA....	(X)	(X)	(X)	(X)	7th...	Peterson...	65.27	Stevens....	34.64
1st...	Hutchinson.	42.65	Nussle.....	57.15	8th...	Oberstar...	68.65	Lemen.....	31.23
2d...	Thomas...	45.74	Leach.....	52.19	MS....	(X)	(X)	(X)	(X)
3d...	Boswell....	53.41	Thompson..	45.04	1st...	Weathers...	24.20	Wicker....	71.43
4th...	Norris.....	43.07	Latham....	54.76	2d...	Thompson..	55.14	LeSueur...	42.75
5th...	Shomshor..	37.78	King......	62.15	3d...	Shows.....	34.76	Pickering...	63.58
KS....	(X)	(X)	(X)	(X)	4th...	Taylor.....	75.21	Mertz.....	21.24
1st...	(^{1})	(^{1})	Moran.....	91.09	MO....	(X)	(X)	(X)	(X)
2d...	Lykins.....	37.52	Ryun......	60.42	1st...	Clay......	70.11	Schwadron..	27.09
3d...	Moore.....	50.18	Taff.......	46.89	2d...	Hogan.....	31.03	Akin......	67.14
4th...	Nolla......	37.00	Tiahrt.....	60.58	3d...	Gephardt...	59.06	Enz.......	38.94
KY....	(X)	(X)	(X)	(X)	4th...	Skelton....	67.64	Noland....	30.66
1st...	Alexander..	34.75	Whitfield...	65.25	5th...	McCarthy...	65.88	Gordon....	32.36
2d...	Williams...	29.17	Lewis.....	69.64	6th...	Rinehart...	35.18	Graves....	63.03
3d...	Conway....	48.39	Northup....	51.61	7th...	Lapham....	23.00	Blunt......	74.81
4th...	Lucas.....	51.11	Davis......	47.54	8th...	Curtis.....	26.91	Emerson...	71.76
5th...	Bailey.....	21.71	Rogers....	78.29	9th...	Deichman..	28.55	Hulshof....	68.20
6th...	(^{1})	(^{1})	Fletcher....	71.95	MT....	Kelly......	32.67	Rehberg...	64.62
LA.... $^{2\,3}$	(X)	(X)	(X)	(X)	NE....	(X)	(X)	(X)	(X)
1st...	(^{1})	(^{1})	Vitter......	81.47	1st...	(^{1})	(^{1})	Bereuter...	85.35
2d...	Jefferson..	63.53	Sullivan....	10.86	2d...	Simon.....	32.98	Terry......	63.32
3d...	(^{1})	(^{1})	Tauzin.....	86.68	3d...	(^{1})	(^{1})	Osborne...	93.17
4th...	Milkovich..	26.45	McCrery....	71.61	NV....	(X)	(X)	(X)	(X)
5th...	Alexander.	28.68	Fletcher....	24.52	1st...	Berkley....	53.72	Boggs-McDonald	42.73
6th...	(^{1})	(^{1})	Baker.....	84.04	2d...	Souza.....	19.97	Gibbons...	74.34
7th...	John......	86.82	(^{1})	(^{1})	3d...	Herrera....	37.24	Porter.....	56.08
ME....	(X)	(X)	(X)	(X)	NH....	(X)	(X)	(X)	(X)
1st...	Allen......	63.81	Joyce.....	36.19	1st...	Clark......	38.48	Bradley....	58.11
2d...	Michaud...	52.01	Raye......	47.99	2d...	Swett.....	40.86	Bass......	56.81
MD....	(X)	(X)	(X)	(X)	NJ....	(X)	(X)	(X)	(X)
1st...	Tamlyn....	23.16	Gilchrest...	76.67	1st...	Andrews...	92.74	(^{1})	(^{1})
2d...	Ruppersberger....	54.16	Bentley....	45.57	2d...	Farkas.....	28.28	LoBiondo...	69.21
3d...	Cardin.....	65.72	Conwell....	34.18	3d...	Strada.....	33.92	Saxton....	65.02
4th...	Wynn.....	78.57	Kimble.....	20.82	4th...	Brennan...	32.11	Smith.....	66.15
5th...	Hoyer.....	69.27	Crawford...	30.52	5th...	Sumers....	38.28	Garrett....	59.48
6th...	DeArmon..	33.80	Bartlett....	66.11	6th...	Pallone....	66.46	Medrow....	30.89
7th...	Cummings.	73.53	Ward......	26.38	7th...	Carden....	40.92	Ferguson...	57.95
8th...	Van Hollen.	51.71	Morella....	47.49	8th...	Pascrell....	66.83	Silverman...	30.59
MA....	(X)	(X)	(X)	(X)	9th...	Rothman...	69.76	Glass.....	30.24
1st...	Olver......	67.56	Kinnaman..	32.38	10th...	Payne.....	84.45	Wirtz.....	15.55
2d...	Neal......	99.13	(^{1})	(^{1})	11th...	Pawar.....	26.39	Frelinghuysen....	72.38
3d...	McGovern.	98.83	(^{1})	(^{1})	12th...	Holt.......	61.04	Soaries....	36.65
					13th...	Menendez.	78.30	Geron.....	18.17

See footnotes at end of table.

No. 404. Vote Cast for United States Representatives by Major Political Party—Congressional Districts: 2002—Con.

[See headnote, p. 258]

State and district	Democratic candidate Name	Percent of total	Republican candidate Name	Percent of total	State and district	Democratic candidate Name	Percent of total	Republican candidate Name	Percent of total
NM....	(X)	(X)	(X)	(X)	11th..	Jones.....	76.33	Pappano...	23.67
1st...	Romero....	44.66	Wilson....	55.34	12th...	Brown.....	35.61	Tiberi.....	64.39
2d...	Smith.....	43.72	Pearce...	56.23	13th...	Brown.....	68.97	Oliveros...	31.03
3d...	Udall......	100.00	(¹)	(¹)	14th...	Blanchard..	27.82	LaTourette.	72.12
NY....	(X)	(X)	(X)	(X)	15th...	Brown.....	33.41	Pryce.....	66.59
1st...	Bishop....	50.23	Grucci.....	48.59	16th...	Rice......	31.13	Regula....	68.87
2d...	Israel.....	58.48	Finley.....	40.46	17th...	Ryan......	51.14	Benjamin..	33.67
3d...	Finz......	27.22	King......	71.88	18th...	(¹)	(¹)	Ney......	100.00
4th...	McCarthy..	56.25	O'Grady...	43.24	OK....	(X)	(X)	(X)	(X)
5th...	Ackerman..	92.32	(¹)	(¹)	1st...	Dodd.....	42.17	Sullivan...	55.62
6th...	Meeks.....	96.51	(¹)	(¹)	2d...	Carson....	74.12	Pharaoh...	25.88
7th...	Crowley...	73.29	Brawley...	26.71	3d...	(¹)	(¹)	Lucas.....	75.58
8th...	Nadler....	76.07	Farrin.....	18.48	4th...	Roberts....	46.17	Cole......	53.83
9th...	Weiner....	65.71	Donohue..	34.29	5th...	Barlow....	32.41	Istook.....	62.23
10th..	Towns.....	97.83	(¹)	(¹)	OR....	(X)	(X)	(X)	(X)
11th..	Owens....	86.56	Cleary.....	12.55	1st...	Wu.......	62.69	Greenfield..	33.99
12th..	Valazquez..	95.81	(¹)	(¹)	2d...	Buckley....	25.76	Walden....	71.86
13th..	Mattsson...	28.32	Fossella....	69.63	3d...	Blumenauer.	66.75	Seale.....	26.73
14th..	Maloney...	75.25	Srdanovic..	24.75	4th...	DeFazio....	63.82	VanLeeuwen	34.36
15th..	Rangel....	88.46	Fields.....	11.54					
16th..	Serrano...	92.07	Dellavalle...	7.93	5th...	Hooley....	54.75	Boquist....	45.10
17th..	Engel......	62.61	Vanderhoef.....	34.43	PA....	(X)	(X)	(X)	(X)
					1st...	Brady.....	86.43	Delany....	12.45
18th..	Lowey.....	92.04	(¹)	(¹)	2d...	Fattah.....	87.77	Dougherty..	12.23
19th..	Selendy...	25.98	Kelly......	69.97	3d...	(¹)	(¹)	English....	77.67
20th..	Stoppenbach......	23.98	Sweeney...	73.32	4th...	Drobac....	35.44	Hart......	64.55
					5th...	(¹)	(¹)	Peterson...	87.24
21st..	McNulty...	75.09	Rosenstein..	24.91	6th...	Wofford....	48.63	Gerlach....	51.36
22d...	Hinchey...	64.19	Hall......	32.87	7th...	Lennon....	33.91	Weldon....	66.09
23d...	(¹)	(¹)	McHugh...	100.00				Greenwood....	62.58
24th..	Boehlert...	70.70	(¹)	(¹)	8th...	Reece.....	37.40		
25th..	Aldersley...	26.64	Walsh.....	72.29	9th...	Henry.....	28.92	Shuster....	71.02
26th..	Nariman...	22.42	Reynolds...	73.63	10th...	(¹)	(¹)	Sherwood..	92.60
27th..	Crotty.....	27.49	Quinn.....	69.06	11th...	Kanjorski...	55.60	Barletta....	42.43
28th..	Slaughter..	62.46	Wojtaszek..	37.54	12th...	Murtha....	73.48	Choby.....	26.52
29th..	Peters.....	21.26	Houghton...	73.10	13th...	Hoeffel....	50.95	Brown.....	47.34
NC....	(X)	(X)	(X)	(X)	14th...	Doyle.....	99.93	(¹)	(¹)
1st...	Ballance...	63.74	Dority.....	34.83	15th...	O'Brien....	42.64	Toomey....	57.36
2d...	Etheridge..	65.36	Ellen......	33.27	16th...	(¹)	(¹)	Pitts......	88.45
3d...	(¹)	(¹)	Jones.....	90.70	17th...	Holden....	51.41	Gekas.....	48.59
4th...	Price......	61.18	Nguyen....	36.15	18th...	Machek....	39.86	Murphy....	60.14
5th...	Crawford...	29.81	Burr......	70.19	19th...	(¹)	(¹)	Platts.....	91.06
6th...	(¹)	(¹)	Coble.....	90.41	RI....	(X)	(X)	(X)	(X)
7th...	McIntyre...	71.13	Adams....	27.32	1st...	Kennedy...	59.88	Rogers....	37.31
8th...	Kouri.....	44.62	Hayes.....	53.63	2d...	Langevin...	76.29	Matson....	22.27
9th...	McGuire...	25.83	Myrick.....	72.42	SC....	(X)	(X)	(X)	(X)
10th..	Daugherty..	37.85	Ballenger...	59.30	1st...	(¹)	(¹)	Brown.....	89.56
11th..	Neill......	42.85	Taylor.....	55.54	2d...	(¹)	(¹)	Wilson.....	84.12
12th..	Watt......	65.34	Kish......	32.79	3d...	Brightharp..	31.28	Barrett.....	67.14
13th..	Miller.....	54.72	Grant.....	42.39	4th...	Ashy......	29.67	DeMint....	69.00
ND....	Pomeroy...	52.41	Clayburgh..	47.59	5th...	Spratt.....	85.87	(¹)	(¹)
OH....	(X)	(X)	(X)	(X)	6th...	Clyburn....	66.98	McLeod....	32.03
1st...	Harris.....	35.20	Chabot....	64.80	SD....	Herseth....	45.62	Janklow....	53.45
2d...	Sanders...	25.95	Portman...	74.05	TN....	(X)	(X)	(X)	(X)
3d...	Carne.....	41.22	Turner.....	58.77	1st...	(¹)	(¹)	Jenkins....	98.77
4th...	Clark......	32.48	Oxley.....	67.52	2d...	Greene....	19.91	Duncan....	78.98
5th...	Anderson..	27.55	Gillmor....	67.08	3d...	Wolfe.....	33.82	Wamp.....	64.54
6th...	Strickland..	59.48	Halleck....	40.52	4th...	Davis.....	52.08	Bowling....	46.49
7th...	Anastasio..	27.18	Hobson....	67.56	5th...	Cooper....	63.73	Duval!.....	33.25
8th...	Hardenbrook.....	29.19	Boehner...	70.81	6th...	Gordon....	65.92	Garrison...	32.33
					7th...	Barron....	26.48	Blackburn..	70.73
9th...	Kaptur.....	73.99	Emery.....	26.01	8th...	Tanner....	70.14	McClain....	27.30
10th..	Kucinich...	74.06	Heben.....	23.80	9th...	Ford......	83.81	(¹)	(¹)

See footnotes at end of table.

No. 404. Vote Cast for United States Representatives by Major Political Party—Congressional Districts: 2002—Con.

[See headnote, p. 258]

State and district	Democratic candidate Name	Percent of total	Republican candidate Name	Percent of total	State and district	Democratic candidate Name	Percent of total	Republican candidate Name	Percent of total
TX....	(X)	(X)	(X)	(X)	VA....	(X)	(X)	(X)	(X)
1st...	Sandlin....	56.45	Lawrence..	43.55	1st...	([1])	([1])	Davis....	95.91
2d...	Turner....	60.85	Brookshire.	38.19	2d...	([1])	([1])	Schrock...	83.15
3d...	Molera....	24.33	Johnson..	73.95	3d...	Scott.....	96.10	([1])	([1])
4th...	Hall......	57.82	Graves....	40.37	4th...	Lucas.....	([5])	Forbes...	97.92
5th...	Chapman..	40.26	Hensarling.	58.21	5th...	Richards...	36.48	Goode....	63.47
6th...	Alvarado...	27.68	Barton....	70.35	6th...	([1])	([1])	Goodlatte..	97.06
7th...	([1])	([1])	Culberson.	89.19	7th...	Jones.....	30.46	Cantor....	69.45
8th...	([1])	([1])	Brady.....	93.14	8th...	Moran.....	59.81	Tate.....	37.32
9th...	Lampson...	58.60	Williams...	40.31	9th...	Boucher...	65.76	Katzen...	34.22
10th..	Doggett....	84.37	([1])	([1])	10th..	Stevens...	28.13	Wolf.....	71.72
11th..	Edwards...	51.55	Farley.....	47.11	11th..	([1])	([1])	Davis....	82.90
12th..	([1])	([1])	Granger...	91.87	WA....	(X)	(X)	(X)	(X)
13th..	Reese.....	20.73	Thornberry.	79.27	1st...	Inslee.....	55.64	Marine....	41.31
14th..	Windham..	31.91	Paul......	68.09	2d...	Larsen....	50.07	Smith....	45.77
15th..	Hinojosa...	100.00	([1])	([1])	3d...	Baird.....	61.69	Zarelli....	38.31
16th..	Reyes.....	100.00	([1])	([1])	4th...	Mason....	33.10	Hastings..	66.90
17th..	Stenholm..	51.36	Beckham..	47.39	5th...	Haggin....	32.21	Nethercutt.	62.66
18th..	Lee.......	76.91	Abbott....	21.70	6th...	Dicks.....	64.20	Lawrence..	31.35
19th..	([1])	([1])	Combest...	91.64	7th...	McDermott.	74.07	Cassady..	21.92
20th..	Gonzalez..	100.00	([1])	([1])	8th...	Behrens-Benedict...	37.34	Dunn....	59.82
21st..	Courage...	25.31	Smith.....	72.87	9th...	Smith.....	58.52	Casada...	38.57
22d...	Riley......	35.02	DeLay.....	63.17	WV....	(X)	(X)	(X)	(X)
23d...	Cuellar....	47.20	Bonilla....	51.53	1st...	Mollohan...	99.71	([1])	([1])
24th..	Frost.....	64.66	Ortega....	33.95	2d...	Humphreys.	39.96	Capito....	60.04
25th..	Bell.......	54.76	Reiser.....	43.09	3d...	Rahall.....	70.22	Chapman..	29.78
26th..	LeBon.....	22.76	Burgess...	74.81	WI....	(X)	(X)	(X)	(X)
27th..	Ortiz......	61.10	Ahumada..	36.54	1st...	Thomas...	30.63	Ryan.....	67.19
28th..	Rodriguez..	71.09	Perales....	26.86	2d...	Baldwin....	66.01	Greer....	33.83
29th..	Green.....	95.16	([1])	([1])	3d...	Kind......	62.82	Arndt....	33.54
30th..	Johnson...	74.26	Bush......	24.19	4th...	Kleczka....	86.32	([1])	([1])
31st..	Bagley.....	27.36	Carter.....	69.08	5th...	([1])	([1])	Sensenbrenner...	86.13
32d...	Dixon.....	30.35	Sessions..	67.77	6th...	([1])	([1])	Petri.....	99.22
UT....	(X)	(X)	(X)	(X)	7th...	Obey.....	64.21	Rothbauer..	35.76
1st...	Thomas...	36.84	Bishop....	60.90	8th...	Becker....	23.89	Green....	72.58
2d...	Matheson..	49.43	Swallow...	48.69	WY....	Akin......	36.21	Cubin....	60.51
3d...	Woodside..	28.98	Cannon....	67.43					
VT[4]....	([1])	([1])	Meub.....	32.29					

X Not applicable. [1] No candidate. [2] According to state law, it is not required to tabulate votes for unopposed candidates. [3] Louisiana holds an open-primary election with candidates from all parties running on the same ballot. Any candidate who receives a majority is elected; if no candidate receives 50 percent, there is a run off election in November between the top two finishers. [4] Sanders, an Independent, was elected with 64.26 percent of the vote. [5] Lucas withdrew after the primary election. Republican candidate, Forbes, took office in her place.

Source: Congressional Quarterly Inc., *Congressional Quarterly Weekly Report* (copyright).

No. 405. Composition of Congress by Political Party: 1973 to 2003

[D=Democratic, R=Republican. Data for beginning of first session of each Congress (as of January 3), except as noted. Excludes vacancies at beginning of session]

Year	Party and President	Congress	House Majority party	House Minority party	House Other	Senate Majority party	Senate Minority party	Senate Other
1973 [1][2]	R (Nixon)........	93d..........	D-239	R-192	1	D-56	R-42	2
1975 [3]	R (Ford).........	94th.........	D-291	R-144	-	D-60	R-37	2
1977	D (Carter).......	95th.........	D-292	R-143	-	D-61	R-38	1
1979 [4]	D (Carter).......	96th.........	D-276	R-157	-	D-58	R-41	1
1981 [4]	R (Reagan)......	97th.........	D-243	R-192	-	R-53	D-46	1
1983	R (Reagan)......	98th.........	D-269	R-165	-	R-54	D-46	-
1985	R (Reagan)......	99th.........	D-252	R-182	-	R-53	D-47	-
1987	R (Reagan)......	100th........	D-258	R-177	-	D-55	R-45	-
1989	R (Bush)........	101st........	D-259	R-174	-	D-55	R-45	-
1991 [5]	R (Bush)........	102d.........	D-267	R-167	1	D-56	R-44	-
1993 [5]	D (Clinton)......	103d.........	D-258	R-176	1	D-57	R-43	-
1995 [5]	D (Clinton)......	104th........	R-230	D-204	1	R-52	D-48	-
1997 [6]	D (Clinton)......	105th........	R-226	D-207	2	R-55	D-45	-
1999 [5]	D (Clinton)......	106th........	R-222	D-212	1	R-55	D-45	-
2001 [6]	R (Bush)........	107th........	R-221	D-211	2	D-50	R-50	-
2003 [7][8]	R (Bush)........	108th........	R-229	D-205	1	R-51	D-48	1

- Represents zero. [1] Senate had one Independent and one Conservative-Republican. [2] House had one Independent-Democrat. [3] Senate had one Independent, one Conservative-Republican, and one undecided (New Hampshire). [4] Senate had one Independent. [5] House had one Independent-Socialist. [6] House had one Independent-Socialist and one Independent. [7] House and Senate each had one Independent. [8] As of August 1, 2003.

Source: U.S. Congress, Joint Committee on Printing, *Congressional Directory*, annual; beginning 1977, biennial. Also see <http://thomas.loc.gov>.

Elections 261

No. 406. Composition of Congress by Political Party Affiliation—States: 1997 to 2003

[Figures are for the beginning of the first session (as of January 3), except as noted. Dem.=Democratic; Rep.=Republican]

State	105th Cong., 1997 [1,2] Dem.	Rep.	106th Cong., 1999 [1] Dem.	Rep.	107th Cong., 2001 [1,3] [4] Dem.	Rep.	108th Cong., 2003 [1] Dem.	Rep.	105th Cong., 1997 Dem.	Rep.	106th Cong., 1999 Dem.	Rep.	107th Cong., 2001 [5,6] Dem.	Rep.	108th Cong., 2003 [6] Dem.	Rep.
U.S.	207	226	212	222	211	221	205	229	45	55	45	55	50	50	48	51
AL	2	5	2	5	2	5	2	5	-	2	-	2	-	2	-	2
AK	-	1	-	1	-	1	-	1	-	2	-	2	-	2	-	2
AZ	1	5	1	5	1	5	2	6	-	2	-	2	-	2	-	2
AR	2	2	2	2	3	1	3	1	1	1	1	1	1	1	2	-
CA	29	23	28	24	31	20	33	20	2	-	2	-	2	-	2	-
CO	2	4	2	4	2	4	2	5	-	2	-	2	-	2	-	2
CT	4	2	4	2	3	3	2	3	2	-	2	-	2	-	2	-
DE	-	1	-	1	-	1	-	1	1	1	1	1	2	-	2	-
FL	8	15	8	15	8	15	7	18	1	1	1	1	2	-	2	-
GA	3	8	3	8	3	8	5	8	1	1	1	1	2	-	1	1
HI	2	-	2	-	2	-	2	-	2	-	2	-	2	-	2	-
ID	-	2	-	2	-	2	-	2	-	2	-	2	-	2	-	2
IL	10	10	10	10	10	10	9	10	2	-	1	1	1	1	1	1
IN	4	6	4	6	4	6	3	6	-	2	1	1	1	1	1	1
IA	1	4	1	4	1	4	1	4	1	1	1	1	1	1	1	1
KS	-	4	1	3	1	3	1	3	-	2	-	2	-	2	-	2
KY	1	5	1	5	1	5	1	5	1	1	-	2	-	2	-	2
LA	2	5	2	5	2	5	3	4	2	-	2	-	2	-	2	-
ME	2	-	2	-	2	-	2	-	-	2	-	2	-	2	-	2
MD	4	4	4	4	4	4	6	2	2	-	2	-	2	-	2	-
MA	10	-	10	-	10	-	10	-	2	-	2	-	2	-	2	-
MI	10	6	10	6	9	7	6	9	1	1	1	1	2	-	2	-
MN	6	2	6	2	5	3	4	4	1	1	1	1	2	-	1	1
MS	2	3	3	2	3	2	2	2	-	2	-	2	-	2	-	2
MO	5	3	5	4	4	5	4	5	-	2	-	2	1	1	-	2
MT	-	1	-	1	-	1	-	1	1	1	1	1	1	1	1	1
NE	-	3	-	3	-	3	-	3	1	1	1	1	1	1	1	1
NV	-	2	1	1	1	1	1	2	2	-	2	-	1	1	1	1
NH	-	2	-	2	-	2	-	2	-	2	-	2	-	2	-	2
NJ	6	7	7	6	7	6	7	6	2	-	2	-	2	-	2	-
NM	1	2	1	2	1	2	1	2	1	1	1	1	1	1	1	1
NY	18	13	19	12	19	12	19	10	1	1	2	-	2	-	2	-
NC	6	6	5	7	5	7	6	7	-	2	1	1	1	1	1	1
ND	1	-	1	-	1	-	1	-	2	-	2	-	2	-	2	-
OH	8	11	8	11	8	11	6	12	1	1	-	2	-	2	-	2
OK	-	6	-	6	1	5	1	4	-	2	-	2	-	2	-	2
OR	4	1	4	1	4	1	4	1	1	1	1	1	1	1	1	1
PA	11	10	11	10	10	11	7	12	-	2	-	2	-	2	-	2
RI	2	-	2	-	2	-	2	-	1	1	1	1	1	1	1	1
SC	2	4	2	4	2	4	2	4	1	1	1	1	1	1	1	1
SD	-	1	-	1	-	1	-	1	2	-	2	-	2	-	2	-
TN	4	5	4	5	4	5	5	4	-	2	-	2	-	2	-	2
TX	17	13	17	13	17	13	17	15	-	2	-	2	-	2	-	2
UT	-	3	-	3	1	2	1	2	-	2	-	2	-	2	-	2
VT	-	-	-	-	-	-	-	-	1	1	1	1	1	1	1	-
VA	6	5	6	5	4	6	3	8	1	1	1	1	-	2	-	2
WA	3	6	5	4	6	3	6	3	1	1	1	1	2	-	2	-
WV	3	-	3	-	2	1	2	1	2	-	2	-	2	-	2	-
WI	5	4	5	4	5	4	4	4	2	-	2	-	2	-	2	-
WY	-	1	-	1	-	1	-	1	-	2	-	2	-	2	-	2

- Represents zero. [1] Vermont had one Independent Representative. [2] Missouri had one Independent. [3] As of beginning of second session. [4] Virginia had one Independent Representative. [5] California had one vacancy. [6] Vermont had one Independent Senator.

Source: U.S. Congress, Joint Committee on Printing, *Congressional Directory*, biennial; and unpublished data.

No. 407. Members of Congress—Incumbents Re-elected: 1964 to 2000

	Representatives						Senators					
		Incumbent candidates						Incumbent candidates				
			Re-elected		Defeated in—				Re-elected		Defeated in—	
Year	Retire-ments [1]	Total	Number	Percent of candidates	Primary	General election	Retire-ments [1]	Total	Number	Percent of candidates	Primary	General election
PRESIDENTIAL-YEAR ELECTIONS												
1964	33	397	344	86.6	8	45	2	33	28	84.8	1	4
1968	23	409	396	96.8	4	9	6	28	20	71.4	4	4
1972	40	390	365	93.6	12	13	6	27	20	74.1	2	5
1976	47	384	368	95.8	3	13	8	25	16	64.0	-	9
1980	34	398	361	90.7	6	31	5	29	16	55.2	4	9
1984	22	411	392	95.4	3	16	4	29	26	89.7	-	3
1988	23	409	402	98.3	1	6	6	27	23	85.2	-	4
1992	65	368	325	88.3	[2]19	[3]24	7	28	23	82.1	1	4
1996	50	384	361	94.0	2	21	13	21	19	90.5	1	1
2000	32	403	394	97.8	3	6	5	29	23	79.3	-	6
MIDTERM ELECTIONS												
1966	22	411	362	88.1	8	41	3	32	28	87.5	3	1
1970	29	401	379	94.5	10	12	4	31	24	77.4	1	6
1974	43	391	343	87.7	8	40	7	27	23	85.2	2	2
1978	49	382	358	93.7	5	19	10	25	15	60.0	3	7
1982	40	393	354	90.1	[2]10	29	3	30	28	93.3	-	2
1986	40	394	385	97.7	3	6	6	28	21	75.0	-	7
1990	27	406	390	96.1	1	15	3	32	31	96.9	-	1
1994	48	387	349	90.2	4	34	9	26	24	92.3	-	2
1998	23	404	395	97.8	1	6	5	29	26	89.7	-	3

- Represents zero. [1] Does not include persons who died or resigned before the election. [2] Number of incumbents defeated in primaries by other incumbents due to redistricting: six in 1982 and four in 1992. [3] Five incumbents defeated in general election by other incumbents due to redistricting.

Source: Ornstein, Norman J., Thomas E. Mann, and Michael J. Malbin, *Vital Statistics on Congress, 1993-1994*, Beginning 1995, Congressional Quarterly, Inc., Washington, DC, *America Votes*, biennial (copyright).

No. 408. Members of Congress—Selected Characteristics: 1983 to 2001

[As of beginning of first session of each Congress, (January 3). Figures for Representatives exclude vacancies]

Members of congress and year	Male	Female	Black [1]	API [2]	Hispanic [3]	Age [4] (in years)					Seniority [5][6]				
						Under 40	40 to 49	50 to 59	60 to 69	70 and over	Less than 2 yrs.	2 to 9 yrs.	10 to 19 yrs.	20 to 29 yrs.	30 or more
REPRESENTATIVES															
98th Cong., 1983	413	21	[7]21	3	8	86	145	132	57	14	83	224	88	28	11
99th Cong., 1985	412	22	[7]21	3	10	71	154	131	59	19	49	237	104	34	10
100th Cong., 1987	412	23	[7]23	4	11	63	153	137	56	26	51	221	114	37	12
101st Cong., 1989	408	25	[7]24	5	10	41	163	133	74	22	39	207	139	35	13
102d Cong., 1991	407	28	[7]26	3	11	39	152	134	86	24	55	178	147	44	11
103d Cong., 1993 [8]	388	47	[7]38	4	17	47	151	128	89	15	118	141	132	32	12
104th Cong., 1995	388	47	[9]40	4	17	53	155	135	79	13	92	188	110	36	9
105th Cong., 1997	379	56	[9]39	(NA)	19	25	116	173	87	35	41	236	104	46	7
106th Cong., 1999															
107th Cong., 2001	381	62	[9]39	(NA)	19	14	97	167	117	35	44	155	158	63	14
SENATORS															
98th Cong., 1983	98	2	-	2	-	7	28	39	20	6	5	61	21	10	3
99th Cong., 1985	98	2	-	2	-	4	27	38	25	6	8	56	27	7	2
100th Cong., 1987	98	2	-	2	-	5	30	36	22	7	14	41	36	7	2
101st Cong., 1989	98	2	-	2	-	-	30	40	22	8	23	22	43	10	2
102d Cong., 1991	98	2	-	2	-	-	23	46	24	7	5	34	47	10	4
103d Cong., 1993 [8]	93	7	1	2	-	1	16	48	22	12	15	30	39	11	5
104th Cong., 1995	92	8	1	2	-	1	14	41	27	17	12	38	30	15	5
106th Cong., 1999	91	9	-	(NA)	-	-	14	38	35	13	8	39	33	14	6
107th Cong., 2001	87	13	-	(NA)	-	-	8	39	33	18	11	34	30	14	9

- Represents zero. NA Not available. [1] Source: Joint Center for Political and Economic Studies, Washington, DC, *Black Elected Officials: Statistical Summary*, annual (copyright). [2] Asian and Pacific Islanders. Source: Library of Congress, Congressional Research Service, "Asian Pacific Americans in the United States Congress," Report 94-767 GOV. [3] Source: National Association of Latino Elected and Appointed Officials, Washington, DC, *National Roster of Hispanic Elected Officials*, annual. [4] Some members do not provide date of birth. [5] Represents consecutive years of service. [6] Some members do not provide years of service. [7] Includes District of Columbia delegate but not Virgin Islands delegate. [8] Includes members elected to fill vacant seats through June 14, 1993. [9] Includes District of Columbia and Virgin Islands delegate.

Source: Except as noted, compiled by U.S. Census Bureau from data published in *Congressional Directory*, biennial.

Elections 263

U.S. Census Bureau, Statistical Abstract of the United States: 2003

No. 409. U.S. Congress—Measures Introduced and Enacted and Time in Session: 1985 to 2002

[Excludes simple and concurrent resolutions]

Item	99th Cong., 1985-86	100th Cong., 1987-88	101st Cong., 1989-90	102d Cong., 1991-92	103d Cong., 1993-94	104th Cong., 1995-96	105th Cong., 1997-98	106th Cong., 1999-00	107th Cong., 2001-02
Measures introduced	9,885	9,588	6,664	6,775	8,544	6,808	7,732	9,158	9,130
Bills	8,697	8,515	5,977	6,212	7,883	6,545	7,532	8,968	8,953
Joint resolutions	1,188	1,073	687	563	661	263	200	190	177
Measures enacted	483	761	666	609	473	337	404	604	337
Public	466	713	650	589	465	333	394	580	331
Private	17	48	16	20	8	4	10	24	6
HOUSE OF REPRESENTATIVES									
Number of days	281	298	281	280	265	290	251	272	265
Number of hours	1,794	1,659	1,688	1,796	1,887	2,445	2,001	2,179	1,694
Number of hours per day	6.4	5.6	6.0	6.4	7.1	8.4	8.0	8.0	6.4
SENATE									
Number of days	313	307	274	287	291	343	296	303	322
Number of hours	2,531	2,341	2,254	2,292	2,514	2,876	2,188	2,200	2,279
Number of hours per day	8.1	7.6	8.2	8.0	8.6	8.4	7.4	7.3	7.1

Source: U.S. Congress, *Congressional Record* and *Daily Calendar*, selected issues. Also see <http://thomas.loc.gov/home/resume>.

No. 410. Congressional Bills Vetoed: 1961 to 2003

Period	President	Total vetoes	Regular vetoes	Pocket vetoes	Vetoes sustained	Bills passed over veto
1961-63	John F. Kennedy	21	12	9	21	-
1963-69	Lyndon B. Johnson	30	16	14	30	-
1969-74	Richard M. Nixon	43	26	17	36	7
1974-77	Gerald R. Ford	66	48	18	54	12
1977-81	Jimmy Carter	31	13	18	29	2
1981-89	Ronald W. Reagan	78	39	39	69	9
1989-93	George Bush	44	29	15	43	1
1993-2001	William J. Clinton	38	37	1	36	2
2001-2003 [1]	George W. Bush	-	-	-	-	-

- Represents zero. [1] Through February 28, 2003.

Source: U.S. Congress, Senate Library, *Presidential Vetoes ... 1789-1968*; U.S. Congress, *Calendars of the U.S. House of Representatives and History of Legislation*, annual. See also <http://clerkweb.house.gov/histrecs/househis/lists/vetoes>.

No. 411. Number of Governors by Political Party Affiliation: 1975 to 2003

[Reflects figures after inaugurations for each year]

Year	Democratic	Republican	Independent/other	Year	Democratic	Republican	Independent/other	Year	Democratic	Republican	Independent/other
1975	36	13	1	1992	28	20	2	1998	17	32	1
1980	31	19	-	1993	30	18	2	1999	17	31	2
1985	34	16	-	1994	29	19	2	2000	17	31	2
1989	28	22	-	1995	19	30	1	2001	21	27	2
1990	29	21	-	1996	18	31	1	2002	21	27	2
1991 [1]	29	19	2	1997	17	32	1	2003	24	26	-

- Represents zero. [1] Reflects result of runoff election in Arizona in February 1991.

Source: National Governors Association, Washington, DC, 1970-87 and 1991-2003, *Directory of Governors of the American States, Commonwealths & Territories*, annual; and 1988-90, *Directory of Governors*, annual. (copyright).

No. 412. Vote Cast for and Governor Elected by State: 1990 to 2001

[In thousands (1,216 represents 1,216,000), except percent. D=Democratic, R=Republican, I=Independent]

State	1990 Total vote[1]	1990 Percent leading party	1996 Total vote[1]	1996 Percent leading party	1998 Total vote[1]	1998 Percent leading party	2000 Total vote[1]	2000 Percent leading party	Candidate elected at most recent election
AL	1,216	R-52.1	(X)	(X)	1,318	D-57.7	(X)	(X)	Donald Siegelman
AK	195	I-38.9	(X)	(X)	220	D-51.3	(X)	(X)	Tony Knowles
AZ	[2]941	[2]R-52.4	(X)	(X)	1,018	R-60.9	(X)	(X)	Jane Dee Hull
AR	696	D-57.5	(X)	(X)	706	R-59.8	(X)	(X)	Mike Huckabee
CA	7,699	R-49.2	(X)	(X)	8,385	D-58.0	(X)	(X)	Gray Davis
CO	1,011	D-61.9	(X)	(X)	1,321	R-49.1	(X)	(X)	Bill Owens
CT	1,141	I-40.4	(X)	(X)	1,000	R-62.9	(X)	(X)	John G. Rowland
DE	(X)	(X)	271	D-69.5	(X)	(X)	324	D-59.2	Ruth Ann Minner
FL	3,531	D-56.5	(X)	(X)	3,964	R-55.3	(X)	(X)	Jeb Bush
GA	1,450	D-52.9	(X)	(X)	1,793	D-52.5	(X)	(X)	Roy Barnes
HI	340	D-59.8	(X)	(X)	408	D-50.1	(X)	(X)	Benjamin J. Cayetano
ID	321	D-68.2	(X)	(X)	381	R-67.7	(X)	(X)	Dirk Kempthorne
IL	3,257	R-50.7	(X)	(X)	3,359	R-51.0	(X)	(X)	George Ryan
IN	(X)	(X)	2,110	D-51.5	(X)	(X)	2,179	D-56.6	Frank L. O'Bannon
IA	976	R-60.6	(X)	(X)	956	D-52.3	(X)	(X)	Tom Vilsack
KS	783	D-48.6	(X)	(X)	743	R-73.4	(X)	(X)	Bill Graves
KY[2]	(X)	(X)	984	D-50.9	(X)	(X)	580	D-60.7	Paul E. Patton
LA	(X)	(X)	1,550	R-63.5	(X)	(X)	1,295	R-62.2	Mike Foster
ME	522	R-46.7	(X)	(X)	421	R-18.9	(X)	(X)	Angus King
MD	1,111	D-59.8	(X)	(X)	1,536	D-55.1	(X)	(X)	Parris N. Glendening
MA	2,343	R-50.2	(X)	(X)	1,903	R-50.8	(X)	(X)	Argeo Paul Cellucci
MI	2,565	R-49.8	(X)	(X)	3,027	R-62.2	(X)	(X)	John Engler
MN	1,807	R-49.6	(X)	(X)	2,091	R-34.3	(X)	(X)	Jesse Ventura
MS[2]	(X)	(X)	819	R-55.6	(X)	(X)	764	D-49.6	Ronnie Musgrove
MO	(X)	(X)	2,143	D-57.2	(X)	(X)	2,347	D-49.1	Bob Holden
MT	(X)	(X)	405	R-79.2	(X)	(X)	410	R-51.0	Judy Martz
NE	587	D-49.9	(X)	(X)	545	R-53.9	(X)	(X)	Mike Johanns
NV	321	D-64.8	(X)	(X)	434	R-51.6	(X)	(X)	Kenny Guinn
NH	295	R-60.3	497	D-57.2	319	D-66.1	565	D-48.7	Jeanne Shaheen
NJ[3]	2,254	D-61.2	(X)	(X)	2,418	R-46.9	2,227	D-56.4	James E. McGreevey
NM	411	D-54.6	(X)	(X)	499	R-54.5	(X)	(X)	Gary E. Johnson
NY	4,057	D-53.2	(X)	(X)	4,735	R-54.3	(X)	(X)	George E. Pataki
NC	(X)	(X)	2,566	D-56.0	(X)	(X)	2,942	D-52.0	Mike Easley
ND	(X)	(X)	264	R-66.2	(X)	(X)	289	R-55.0	John Hoeven
OH	3,478	R-55.7	(X)	(X)	3,354	R-50.0	(X)	(X)	Bob Taft
OK	911	D-57.4	(X)	(X)	874	R-57.9	(X)	(X)	Frank Keating
OR	1,113	D-45.7	(X)	(X)	1,113	D-64.4	(X)	(X)	John Kitzhaber
PA	3,053	D-67.7	(X)	(X)	3,025	R-57.4	(X)	(X)	Tom Ridge
RI	357	D-74.1	(X)	(X)	306	R-51.0	(X)	(X)	Lincoln C. Almond
SC	761	R-69.5	(X)	(X)	1,071	D-53.2	(X)	(X)	Jim Hodges
SD	257	R-58.9	(X)	(X)	260	R-64.0	(X)	(X)	William J. Janklow
TN	790	D-60.8	(X)	(X)	976	R-68.6	(X)	(X)	Don Sundquist
TX	3,893	D-49.5	(X)	(X)	3,738	R-68.2	(X)	(X)	George W. Bush
UT	(X)	(X)	672	R-75.0	(X)	(X)	762	R-55.8	Michael O. Leavitt
VT	211	R-51.8	255	D-70.5	218	D-55.7	293	D-50.5	Howard Dean
VA[3]	1,789	D-50.1	(X)	(X)	1,736	R-55.8	1,887	D-52.2	Mark Warner
WA	(X)	(X)	2,237	D-58.0	(X)	(X)	2,470	D-58.4	Gary Locke
WV	(X)	(X)	629	R-51.6	(X)	(X)	648	D-50.1	Bob Wise
WI	1,380	R-58.2	(X)	(X)	1,756	R-59.7	(X)	(X)	Tommy G. Thompson
WY	160	D-65.4	(X)	(X)	175	R-55.6	(X)	(X)	Jim Geringer

X Not applicable.   [1] Includes minor party and scattered votes.   [2] Voting years 1995 and 1999.   [3] Voting years 1993, 1997, and 2001.

Source: Congressional Quarterly Inc., Washington, DC, *America Votes*, biennial; and unpublished data (copyright).

No. 413. Composition of State Legislatures by Political Party Affiliation: 2001 and 2002

[Data reflect election results in year shown for most states; and except as noted, results in previous year for other states. Figures reflect immediate results of elections, including holdover members in state houses which do not have all of their members running for re-election. Dem.=Democrat, Rep.=Republican, Vac.=Vacancies. In general, Lower House refers to body consisting of state Representatives; Upper House, of state Senators]

State	Lower House 2001 Dem.	Rep.	Other	Vac.	Lower House 2002 Dem.	Rep.	Other	Vac.	Upper House 2001 Dem.	Rep.	Other	Vac.	Upper House 2002 Dem.	Rep.	Other	Vac.
U.S.	2,809	2,604	14	-	2,694	2,687	22	8	990	932	2	11	939	974	51	7
AL [1]	67	38	-	-	64	41	-	-	24	11	-	-	25	10	-	-
AK [2]	13	27	-	-	13	27	-	-	6	14	-	-	8	12	-	-
AZ [3]	24	36	-	-	21	39	-	-	15	15	-	-	13	17	-	-
AR [2]	70	30	-	-	72	28	-	-	27	8	-	-	27	8	-	-
CA [2]	50	30	-	-	48	32	-	-	26	14	-	-	25	15	-	-
CO [2]	28	37	-	-	28	37	-	-	18	17	-	-	17	18	-	-
CT [3]	100	51	-	-	94	57	-	-	21	15	-	-	21	15	-	-
DE [2]	15	26	-	-	12	29	-	-	13	8	-	-	13	8	-	-
FL [2]	43	77	-	-	39	81	-	-	15	25	-	-	14	25	-	1
GA [3]	105	74	-	-	107	72	1	-	32	24	-	-	26	30	-	-
HI [2]	32	19	-	-	36	15	-	-	22	3	-	-	20	5	-	-
ID [3]	9	61	-	-	16	54	-	-	3	31	-	1	7	28	-	-
IL [4]	62	56	-	-	66	52	-	-	27	32	-	-	26	32	1	-
IN [2]	52	46	-	-	51	49	-	-	18	32	-	-	18	32	-	-
IA [2]	44	56	-	-	45	54	-	1	20	30	-	-	21	29	-	-
KS [2]	46	79	-	-	45	80	-	-	10	30	-	-	10	30	-	-
KY [2]	66	34	-	-	65	35	-	-	18	20	-	-	16	22	-	-
LA [1]	70	34	-	-	70	34	1	-	25	14	-	-	23	15	-	1
ME [3]	81	69	3	-	80	67	4	-	17	16	-	1	18	17	-	-
MD [1]	106	35	-	-	98	43	-	-	33	14	-	-	33	14	-	-
MA [3]	136	22	-	-	135	23	1	1	32	6	-	2	34	6	-	-
MI [2]	52	57	-	-	62	47	-	1	15	23	-	-	16	22	-	-
MN [2]	64	70	-	-	53	80	-	1	37	27	2	2	35	31	1	-
MS [1]	86	33	3	-	81	38	3	-	34	18	-	-	31	21	-	-
MO [2]	87	76	-	-	73	90	-	-	14	18	-	2	14	20	-	-
MT [2]	42	58	-	-	47	53	-	-	19	31	-	-	21	29	-	-
NE [5]	([5])	([5])	([5])	([5])	([5])	([5])	([5])	([5])	([5])	([5])	([5])	([5])	([5])	([5])	49	-
NV [2]	27	15	-	-	23	19	-	-	9	12	-	-	8	13	-	-
NH [3]	142	255	1	-	117	282	-	1	11	13	-	-	6	18	-	-
NJ [2]	44	36	-	-	43	35	1	1	20	20	-	-	20	20	-	-
NM [2]	42	28	-	-	42	28	-	-	24	18	-	-	24	18	-	-
NY [3]	99	51	-	-	103	47	-	-	25	36	-	-	25	37	-	-
NC [3]	62	58	-	-	60	60	-	-	35	15	-	-	28	22	-	-
ND [6]	29	69	-	-	28	66	-	-	17	32	-	-	16	31	-	-
OH [2]	39	59	-	-	38	61	-	-	11	21	-	1	11	22	-	-
OK [2]	52	48	-	-	53	48	-	-	30	18	-	-	27	20	-	1
OR [2]	28	32	-	-	25	35	-	-	14	16	-	-	15	15	-	-
PA [2]	98	104	-	-	94	108	-	1	21	29	-	-	21	28	-	1
RI [3]	87	13	-	-	63	11	1	-	43	7	-	-	32	6	-	-
SC [2]	53	71	-	-	50	73	-	1	21	25	-	-	21	24	-	1
SD [3]	20	50	-	-	21	49	-	-	11	24	-	-	9	26	-	-
TN [2]	57	41	-	-	54	45	-	-	18	15	-	-	18	15	-	-
TX [2]	78	71	-	-	62	88	-	-	15	15	-	1	12	19	-	-
UT [2]	24	51	-	-	19	56	-	-	9	20	-	-	7	22	-	-
VT [3]	62	82	5	-	69	74	7	-	16	13	-	1	19	11	-	-
VA [2]	34	64	2	-	34	64	2	-	18	22	-	-	17	23	-	-
WA [2]	50	48	-	-	52	46	-	-	25	24	-	-	24	25	-	-
WV [2]	75	25	-	-	68	32	-	-	28	6	-	-	24	10	-	-
WI [2]	43	56	-	-	40	58	1	-	18	15	-	-	13	18	-	2
WY [2]	14	46	-	-	15	45	-	-	10	20	-	-	10	20	-	-

- Represents zero. [1] Members of both houses serve 4-year terms. [2] Upper House members serve 4-year terms and Lower House members serve 2-year terms. [3] Members of both houses serve 2-year terms. [4] Illinois—4- and 2-year term depending on district. [5] Nebraska—4-year term and only state to have a nonpartisan legislature since 1972. [6] North Dakota—Starting in 2001, members of both houses serve 4-year terms.

Source: The Council of State Governments, Lexington, KY, *The Book of States 2003*, biennial (copyright).

No. 414. Political Party Control of State Legislatures by Party: 1979 to 2003

[As of beginning of year. Until 1972 there were two nonpartisan legislatures in Minnesota and Nebraska. Since then only Nebraska has had a nonpartisan legislature]

Year	Democratic control	Split control or tie	Republican control	Year	Democratic control	Split control or tie	Republican control	Year	Democratic control	Split control or tie	Republican control
1979...	30	7	12	1990...	29	11	9	1997...	20	11	18
1981...	28	6	15	1992...	29	14	6	1999...	20	12	17
1983[1]...	34	4	11	1993...	25	16	8	2000...	16	15	18
1985...	27	11	11	1994...	24	17	8	2001...	16	15	18
1987...	28	12	9	1995...	18	12	19	2002...	17	15	17
1989[2]...	28	13	8	1996...	16	15	18	2003...	16	12	21

[1] Two 1984 midterm recall elections resulted in a change in control of the Michigan State Senate. At the time of the 1984 election, therefore, Democrats controlled 33 legislatures. [2] A party change during the year by a Democratic representative broke the tie in the Indiana House of Representatives, giving the Republicans control of both chambers.

Source: National Conference of State Legislatures, Denver, CO, *State Legislatures*, periodic.

No. 415. Women Holding State Public Offices by Office and State: 2002

[As of January. For data on women in U.S. Congress, see Table 408]

State	State-wide elective executive office[1]	State legislature	State	State-wide elective executive office[1]	State legislature	State	State-wide elective executive office[1]	State legislature
United States	**88**	**1,682**	Kentucky......	-	15	North Dakota...	2	25
Alabama......	3	11	Louisiana......	2	22	Ohio.........	2	29
Alaska........	1	11	Maine.........	-	55	Oklahoma......	4	15
Arizona.......	4	32	Maryland......	1	59	Oregon........	-	31
Arkansas.....	2	19	Massachusetts..	2	51	Pennsylvania...	1	36
California.....	2	34	Michigan......	2	33	Rhode Island...	-	34
Colorado......	1	34	Minnesota.....	4	59	South Carolina..	1	18
Connecticut...	4	57	Mississippi.....	1	22	South Dakota...	3	17
Delaware.....	3	16	Missouri.......	2	46	Tennessee.....	-	21
Florida........	-	38	Montana......	2	36	Texas.........	2	35
Georgia.......	3	50	Nebraska......	3	10	Utah..........	1	24
Hawaii........	1	19	Nevada.......	3	22	Vermont.......	2	51
Idaho.........	1	29	New Hampshire..	1	124	Virginia.......	-	22
Illinois........	2	47	New Jersey....	-	19	Washington....	2	57
Indiana.......	3	26	New Mexico....	2	34	West Virginia...	-	25
Iowa..........	2	33	New York......	1	47	Wisconsin......	2	31
Kansas.......	2	53	North Carolina...	4	34	Wyoming......	2	14

- Represents zero. [1] Excludes women elected to the judiciary, women appointed to state cabinet-level positions, women elected to executive posts by the legislature, and elected members of university Board of Trustees or Board of Education.

Source: Center for the American Woman and Politics, Eagleton Institute of Politics, Rutgers University, New Brunswick, NJ, information releases, copyright.

No. 416. Public Confidence Levels in Selected Public and Private Institutions: 2001

[Based on a sample survey of 4,216 persons 21 years old and over conducted during the spring and subject to sampling variability; see source]

Institution	A lot	Some	None	Don't know
Organized labor....................................	9.9	46.3	39.6	4.2
Media (e.g. newspapers, TV, radio)...................	5.1	48.2	45.3	1.4
Major corporations..................................	6.2	49.2	41.9	2.8
State government...................................	9.2	58.0	31.0	1.7
Political organizations, parties........................	2.8	36.7	58.6	1.9
Local government..................................	12.6	58.7	27.1	1.6
Congress..	4.0	44.0	49.7	2.3

Source: Toppe, Chris, Arthur Kirsch, and Westat, Inc., *Giving and Volunteering in the United States: 2001 Edition*. (Copyright and published by INDEPENDENT SECTOR, Washington, 2002.)

No. 417. Black Elected Officials by Office, 1970 to 2001, and State, 2001

[As of January 2001, no Black elected officials had been identified in Hawaii, Montana, North Dakota, or South Dakota]

State	Total	U.S. and state legisla- tures [1]	City and county offices [2]	Law enforce- ment [3]	Educa- tion [4]	State	Total	U.S. and state legisla- tures [1]	City and county offices [2]	Law enforce- ment [3]	Educa- tion [4]
1970 (Feb.)	1,469	179	715	213	362	MD	175	40	93	33	9
1980 (July)	4,890	326	2,832	526	1,206	MA	60	6	44	2	8
1990 (Jan.)	7,335	436	4,485	769	1,645	MI	346	25	147	55	119
1995 (Jan.)	8,385	604	4,954	987	1,840	MN	20	2	4	9	5
1998 (Jan.)	8,830	614	5,210	998	2,008	MS	892	46	607	109	130
1999 (Jan.)	8,896	618	5,354	997	1,927	MO	201	19	142	16	24
2000 (Jan.)	9,001	621	5,420	1,037	1,923	NE	8	1	4	-	3
2001 (Jan.)	9,061	633	5,456	1,044	1,928	NV	14	5	5	2	2
						NH	5	5	-	-	-
AL	756	36	569	57	94	NJ	249	16	139	1	93
AK	3	1	2	-	-	NM	4	1	-	2	1
AZ	12	1	1	5	5	NY	325	34	83	83	125
AR	502	15	298	67	122	NC	491	28	349	29	85
CA	224	10	70	67	77	OH	313	20	217	28	48
CO	18	4	4	9	1	OK	105	6	75	3	21
CT	72	14	47	3	8	OR	6	3	1	2	-
DE	24	4	16	1	3	PA	185	19	74	65	27
DC	176	[5]2	171	-	3	RI	8	7	1	-	-
FL	243	25	163	39	16	SC	534	32	335	9	158
GA	611	53	395	43	120	TN	180	18	108	27	27
ID	2	-	2	-	-	TX	460	19	302	44	95
IL	624	28	318	55	223	UT	5	1	3	1	-
IN	86	13	52	13	8	VT	1	1	-	-	-
IA	13	1	8	1	3	VA	246	16	130	15	85
KS	17	7	4	3	3	WA	26	2	12	11	1
KY	60	5	44	5	6	WV	19	2	13	3	1
LA	705	32	388	122	163	WI	33	8	15	5	5
ME	1	-	-	-	1	WY	1	-	1	-	-

- Represents zero. [1] Includes elected state administrators. [2] County commissioners and councilmen, mayors, vice mayors, aldermen, regional officials, and other. [3] Judges, magistrates, constables, marshals, sheriffs, justices of the peace, and other. [4] Members of state education agencies, college boards, school boards, and other. [5] Includes one shadow representative.

Source: Joint Center for Political and Economic Studies, Washington, DC, *Black Elected Officials: A Statistical Summary*, annual (copyright) and <http://www.jointcenter.org/databank/graphs/99beo.pdf> (accessed 17 April 2003).

No. 418. Hispanic Public Elected Officials by Office, 1985 to 2002, and State, 2002

[As of September, For states not shown, no Hispanic public officials had been identified]

State	Total	State execu- tives and legisla- tors [1]	County and munici- pal offi- cials	Judicial and law enforce- ment	Educa- tion and school boards	State	Total	State execu- tives and legisla- tors [1]	County and munici- pal offi- cials	Judicial and law enforce- ment	Educa- tion and school boards
1985 (Sept.)	3,147	129	1,316	517	1,185	LA	3	-	1	2	-
1988 (Sept.)	3,360	135	1,425	574	1,226	MD	4	4	-	-	-
1989 (Sept.)	3,783	143	1,724	575	1,341	MA	17	4	9	-	4
1990 (Sept.)	4,004	144	1,819	583	1,458	MI	16	1	6	3	6
1991 (Sept.)	4,202	151	1,867	596	1,588	MN	4	1	1	1	1
1992 (Sept.)	4,994	150	1,908	628	2,308	MO	1	-	1	-	-
1993 (Sept.)	5,170	182	2,023	633	2,332	MT	1	-	-	1	-
1994 (Sept.)	5,459	199	2,197	651	2,412	NE	3	1	2	-	-
2000 (Sept.)	5,205	223	1,846	454	2,682	NV	8	3	2	1	2
2001 (Sept.)	5,205	223	1,846	454	2,682	NH	2	1	-	-	1
2002	4,432	230	1,958	549	1,694	NJ	74	7	45	-	22
AZ	346	15	133	37	161	NM	602	49	309	86	158
CA	936	28	362	36	510	NY	85	15	24	8	38
CO	135	9	91	6	29	NC	4	2	2	-	-
CT	25	5	16	-	4	OH	8	-	6	2	-
DE	2	1	1	-	-	OR	13	1	6	5	1
FL	87	16	57	9	5	PA	14	1	9	3	1
GA	6	3	2	1	-	RI	5	3	2	-	-
HI	1	1	-	-	-	TX	1,913	38	801	338	736
ID	3	1	2	-	-	UT	2	-	2	-	-
IL	65	11	42	5	7	VA	2	-	1	-	1
IN	10	1	7	1	1	WA	8	3	3	-	2
IA	1	-	1	-	-	WI	13	1	4	4	4
KS	8	3	5	-	-	WY	3	1	2	-	-

- Represents zero. [1] Includes U.S. Representatives, not shown separately.

Source: National Association of Latino Elected and Appointed Officials, Washington, DC, *National Roster of Hispanic Elected Officials*, annual.

No. 419. Voting-Age Population, Percent Reporting Registered, and Voted: 1980 to 2000

[157,1 represents 157,100,000. As of November. Covers civilian noninstitutional population 18 years old and over. Includes aliens. Figures are based on Current Population Survey (see text, Section 1, and Appendix III) and differ from those in Table 421 based on population estimates and official vote counts]

Characteristic	Voting-age population (mil.)									Percent reporting they registered									Percent reporting they voted								
	1980	1988	1990	1994	1996	1998	2000			Presidential election years				Congressional election years				Presidential election years				Congressional election years			
										1980	1992	1996	2000	1986	1990	1994	1998	1980	1992	1996	2000	1986	1990	1994	1998
Total[1]	**157.1**	**178.1**	**182.1**	**190.3**	**193.7**	**198.2**	**202.6**			**66.9**	**68.2**	**65.9**	**63.9**	**64.3**	**62.2**	**62.0**	**62.1**	**59.2**	**61.3**	**54.2**	**54.7**	**46.0**	**45.0**	**44.6**	**41.9**
18 to 20 years old	12.3	10.7	10.8	10.3	10.8	11.4	11.9			44.7	48.3	45.6	40.5	35.4	35.4	37.2	32.1	35.7	38.5	31.2	28.4	18.6	18.4	16.5	13.5
21 to 24 years old	15.9	14.8	14.0	14.9	13.9	14.1	14.9			52.7	55.3	51.2	49.3	46.6	43.3	45.5	35.0	43.1	45.7	33.4	35.4	24.2	22.0	22.3	19.2
25 to 34 years old	35.7	42.7	42.7	41.1	40.1	38.6	37.3			62.0	60.6	56.9	54.7	55.8	52.0	51.5	52.4	54.6	53.2	43.1	43.7	35.1	33.8	32.2	28.0
35 to 44 years old	25.6	35.2	37.9	41.9	43.3	44.4	44.5			70.6	69.2	66.5	63.8	67.9	65.5	63.3	62.4	64.4	63.6	54.9	55.0	49.3	48.4	46.0	40.7
45 to 64 years old	43.6	45.9	46.9	50.9	53.7	57.4	61.4			75.8	75.3	73.5	71.2	74.8	71.4	71.0	71.1	69.3	70.0	64.4	64.1	58.7	55.8	56.0	53.6
65 years old and over	24.1	28.8	29.9	31.1	31.9	32.3	32.8			74.6	78.0	77.0	76.1	76.9	76.5	75.6	75.4	65.1	70.1	67.0	67.6	60.9	60.3	60.7	59.5
Male	74.1	84.5	86.6	91.0	92.6	95.2	97.1			66.6	66.9	64.4	62.2	63.4	61.2	60.8	60.6	59.1	60.2	52.8	53.1	45.8	44.6	44.4	41.4
Female	83.0	93.6	95.5	99.3	101.0	103.0	105.5			67.1	69.3	67.3	65.6	65.0	63.1	63.2	63.5	59.4	62.3	55.5	56.2	46.1	45.4	44.9	42.4
White	137.7	152.9	155.6	160.3	162.8	165.8	168.7			68.4	70.1	67.7	65.6	65.3	63.8	64.2	63.9	60.9	63.6	56.0	56.4	47.0	46.7	46.9	43.3
Black	16.4	19.7	20.4	21.8	22.5	23.3	24.1			60.0	63.9	63.5	63.6	64.0	58.8	58.3	60.2	50.5	54.0	50.6	53.5	43.2	39.2	37.0	39.6
Hispanic[2]	8.2	12.9	13.8	17.5	18.4	20.3	21.6			36.3	35.0	35.7	34.9	35.9	32.3	30.0	33.7	29.9	28.9	26.7	27.5	24.2	21.0	19.1	20.0
Region:[3]																									
Northeast	35.5	37.9	38.1	38.4	38.3	38.5	38.9			64.8	67.0	64.7	63.7	62.0	61.0	60.9	60.8	58.5	61.2	54.5	55.2	44.4	45.2	45.2	41.2
Midwest	41.5	43.3	43.9	44.5	45.2	45.9	46.4			73.8	74.6	71.6	70.2	70.7	68.2	68.7	68.2	65.8	67.2	59.3	60.9	49.5	48.6	48.8	47.3
South	50.9	60.7	62.4	66.4	65.7	67.4	71.8			64.8	67.2	65.9	64.5	63.0	61.3	60.7	62.7	55.6	59.0	52.2	53.5	43.0	42.4	40.5	38.6
West	29.5	36.2	37.7	41.0	42.1	43.7	45.5			63.3	63.6	60.8	56.9	60.8	57.7	58.1	56.0	57.2	58.5	51.8	49.9	48.4	45.0	46.4	42.3
School years completed:																									
8 years or less	22.7	19.1	17.7	14.7	14.1	13.3	12.9			53.0	43.9	40.7	36.1	50.5	44.0	40.1	40.2	42.6	35.1	28.1	26.8	32.7	27.7	23.2	24.6
High school:																									
1 to 3 years[4]	22.5	21.1	21.0	[4]20.7	21.0	21.0	20.1			54.6	50.4	47.9	45.9	52.4	47.9	44.7	43.4	45.6	41.2	33.8	33.6	33.8	30.9	27.0	25.0
4 years[5]	61.2	70.0	71.5	564.9	65.2	65.6	66.3			66.4	64.9	62.2	60.1	62.9	60.0	58.9	58.6	58.9	57.5	49.1	49.4	44.1	42.2	40.5	37.1
College:																									
1 to 3 years[6]	26.7	34.3	36.3	[6]50.4	50.9	52.9	55.3			74.4	75.4	72.9	70.0	70.0	68.7	68.4	68.3	67.2	68.7	60.5	60.3	49.9	50.0	49.1	46.2
4 years or more[7]	24.0	33.6	35.6	739.4	42.5	45.4	48.0			84.3	84.8	80.4	77.3	77.8	77.3	76.3	75.1	79.9	81.0	73.0	72.0	62.5	62.5	63.1	57.2
Employed	95.0	113.8	115.5	122.6	125.6	130.5	133.4			68.7	69.9	67.0	64.7	64.4	62.6	62.9	62.6	61.8	63.8	55.2	55.5	45.7	45.1	45.2	41.2
Unemployed	6.9	5.8	6.7	6.5	6.4	5.2	4.9			50.3	53.7	52.5	46.1	50.6	44.6	46.4	48.5	41.2	46.2	37.2	35.1	31.2	27.9	28.3	28.4
Not in labor force	55.2	58.5	59.9	61.2	61.6	62.5	64.2			65.8	66.8	65.1	63.8	65.4	63.4	61.9	62.1	57.0	58.7	54.1	54.5	48.2	46.7	45.3	44.5

[1] Includes other races not shown separately. [2] Hispanic persons may be of any race. [3] For composition of regions, see map, inside cover. [4] Beginning 1992, represents those who completed 9th to 12th grade, but have no high school diploma. [5] Beginning 1992, high school graduate. [6] Beginning 1992, some college or associate degree. [7] Beginning 1992, bachelor's or advanced degree.

Source: U.S. Census Bureau, Current Population Reports, P20-542, and earlier reports.

No. 420. Persons Reported Registered and Voted by State: 2000

[202,609 represents 202,609,000. See headnote, Table 419]

State	Voting-age population (1,000)	Percent of voting-age population — Registered	Voted	State	Voting-age population (1,000)	Percent of voting-age population — Registered	Voted
U.S.	202,609	63.9	54.7	MO	4,066	74.3	65.4
AL	3,278	73.6	59.6	MT	658	70.0	62.2
AK	412	72.5	65.5	NE	1,205	71.8	58.9
AZ	3,524	53.3	46.7	NV	1,377	52.3	46.5
AR	1,893	59.4	49.4	NH	902	69.6	63.3
CA	24,749	52.8	46.4	NJ	6,109	63.2	55.2
CO	3,049	64.1	53.6	NM	1,261	59.5	51.3
CT	2,415	62.5	55.2	NY	13,725	58.6	51.0
DE	567	67.9	62.2	NC	5,629	66.1	53.2
DC	407	72.4	65.6	ND	449	91.1	69.8
FL	11,633	60.5	51.6	OH	8,301	67.0	58.1
GA	5,775	61.1	49.0	OK	2,457	68.3	58.3
HI	855	47.0	39.7	OR	2,515	68.2	60.8
ID	927	61.4	53.9	PA	8,950	65.3	55.7
IL	8,859	66.7	56.8	RI	729	69.7	60.1
IN	4,380	68.5	58.5	SC	2,929	68.0	58.9
IA	2,110	72.2	64.1	SD	530	70.9	58.7
KS	1,908	67.7	60.2	TN	4,173	62.1	52.3
KY	2,996	69.7	54.9	TX	14,533	61.4	48.2
LA	3,143	75.4	64.6	UT	1,472	64.7	56.3
ME	979	80.3	69.2	VT	458	72.0	63.3
MD	3,812	65.6	57.1	VA	5,177	64.1	57.2
MA	4,614	70.3	60.1	WA	4,314	66.1	58.6
MI	7,231	69.1	60.1	WV	1,405	63.1	52.1
MN	3,506	76.7	67.8	WI	3,884	76.5	67.8
MS	2,029	72.2	59.8	WY	350	68.6	62.5

Source: U.S. Census Bureau, Current Population Reports, P20-466. Also see <http://www.census.gov/population/www/socdemo/voting.html>.

No. 421. Participation in Elections for President and U.S. Representatives: 1932 to 2000

[75,768 represents 75,768,000. As of November. Estimated resident population 21 years old and over, 1932-70, except as noted, and 18 years old and over thereafter; includes Armed Forces. Prior to 1960, excludes Alaska and Hawaii. District of Columbia is included in votes cast for President beginning 1964 and in votes cast for Representative from 1972 to 1994]

Year	Resident population (incl. aliens) of voting age [1] (1,000)	For President [2] (1,000)	Percent of voting-age population	For U.S. Representatives (1,000)	Percent of voting-age population	Year	Resident population (incl. aliens) of voting age [1] (1,000)	For President [2] (1,000)	Percent of voting-age population	For U.S. Representatives (1,000)	Percent of voting-age population
1932	75,768	39,758	52.5	37,657	49.7	1968	120,285	73,212	60.9	66,288	55.1
1934	77,997	(X)	(X)	32,256	41.4	1970	124,498	(X)	(X)	54,173	43.5
1936	80,174	45,654	56.9	42,886	53.5	1972	140,777	77,719	55.2	71,430	50.7
1938	82,354	(X)	(X)	36,236	44.0	1974	146,338	(X)	(X)	52,495	35.9
1940	84,728	49,900	58.9	46,951	55.4	1976	152,308	81,556	53.5	74,422	48.9
1942	86,465	(X)	(X)	28,074	32.5	1978	158,369	(X)	(X)	55,332	34.9
1944	85,654	47,977	56.0	45,103	52.7	1980	163,945	86,515	52.8	77,995	47.6
1946	92,659	(X)	(X)	34,398	37.1	1982	169,643	(X)	(X)	64,514	38.0
1948	95,573	48,794	51.1	45,933	48.1	1984	173,995	92,653	53.3	83,231	47.8
1950	98,134	(X)	(X)	40,342	41.1	1986	177,922	(X)	(X)	59,619	33.5
1952	99,929	61,551	61.6	57,571	57.6	1988	181,956	91,595	50.3	81,786	44.9
1954	102,075	(X)	(X)	42,580	41.7	1990	185,812	(X)	(X)	61,513	33.1
1956	104,515	62,027	59.3	58,426	55.9	1992	189,493	104,425	55.1	96,239	50.8
1958	106,447	(X)	(X)	45,818	43.0	1994	193,010	(X)	(X)	70,781	36.7
1960	109,672	68,838	62.8	64,133	58.5	1996	196,789	96,278	48.9	89,863	45.7
1962	112,952	(X)	(X)	51,267	45.4	1998	201,270	(X)	(X)	65,897	32.7
1964	114,090	70,645	61.9	65,895	57.8	2000 [3]	205,813	105,397	51.2	97,226	47.2
1966	116,638	(X)	(X)	52,908	45.4						

X Not applicable. [1] Population 18 and over in Georgia, 1944-70, and in Kentucky, 1956-70; 19 and over in Alaska and 20 and over in Hawaii, 1960-70. Source: U.S. Census Bureau, Current Population Reports, P25-1085; also see <http://www.census.gov/population/socdemo/voting/proj00/tab03.txt> (released July 31, 2000). [2] Source: 1932-58, U.S. Congress, Clerk of the House, *Statistics of the Presidential and Congressional Election*, biennial. [3] Projection.

Source: Except as noted, Congressional Quarterly Inc., Washington, DC, *America Votes*, annual (copyright).

No. 422. Resident Population of Voting Age and Percent Casting Votes—States: 1994 to 2000

[193,010 represents 193,010,000. As of November. Estimated population, 18 years old and over. Includes Armed Forces stationed in each state, aliens, and institutional population]

State	Voting-age population							Percent casting votes for—				
				2000 (1,000)				Presidential electors		U.S. Representatives		
	1994 (1,000)	1996 (1,000)	1998 (1,000)	Total	Female	Black	Hispanic[1]	1996	2000	1996	1998	2000
U.S.	193,010	196,789	201,270	205,813	106,865	24,635	21,305	48.9	51.2	45.8	32.8	47.3
AL	3,172	3,221	3,280	3,333	1,768	800	34	47.6	50.0	45.6	37.0	43.2
AK	413	419	425	430	203	17	16	57.7	66.4	55.8	52.5	63.8
AZ	3,059	3,245	3,421	3,625	1,853	137	700	43.3	42.3	41.8	29.3	40.4
AR	1,814	1,852	1,891	1,929	1,017	276	38	47.7	47.8	46.6	27.8	32.8
CA	22,653	23,002	23,902	24,873	12,566	1,853	6,995	43.6	44.1	41.2	33.4	42.0
CO	2,715	2,837	2,946	3,067	1,564	132	391	53.3	56.8	51.5	43.3	52.9
CT	2,476	2,475	2,489	2,499	1,307	221	182	56.3	58.4	52.3	38.3	52.6
DE	536	552	566	582	303	108	19	49.1	56.3	48.4	31.9	53.8
DC	447	428	421	411	222	230	29	43.4	49.1	(NA)	(NA)	(NA)
FL	10,721	11,078	11,398	11,774	6,155	1,600	1,784	47.9	50.6	42.4	10.6	42.6
GA	5,198	5,420	5,647	5,893	3,075	1,577	168	42.4	44.1	39.9	28.9	41.0
HI	875	886	902	909	460	27	67	40.6	40.5	39.8	44.1	37.5
ID	802	845	883	921	467	7	58	58.2	54.5	58.5	42.9	53.5
IL	8,717	8,787	8,894	8,983	4,675	1,249	837	49.1	52.8	47.0	36.2	48.9
IN	4,276	4,340	4,399	4,448	2,321	353	110	49.2	49.4	48.5	35.8	48.5
IA	2,109	2,126	2,148	2,165	1,127	45	42	58.0	60.8	56.5	41.9	58.9
KS	1,877	1,902	1,940	1,983	1,022	112	97	56.5	54.1	55.2	37.5	52.4
KY	2,864	2,918	2,959	2,993	1,568	207	25	47.6	51.6	42.4	37.1	48.0
LA	3,085	3,129	3,195	3,255	1,723	956	91	57.0	54.2	21.1	9.7	36.9
ME	930	941	955	968	503	7	7	64.4	67.3	63.8	43.4	66.0
MD	3,737	3,799	3,862	3,925	2,050	1,058	150	46.9	51.5	43.1	38.4	49.1
MA	4,616	4,652	4,701	4,749	2,500	270	255	55.0	56.9	51.8	37.1	49.4
MI	7,091	7,207	7,294	7,358	3,839	977	187	53.4	57.5	51.3	40.9	55.3
MN	3,343	3,415	3,480	3,547	1,823	106	62	64.2	68.8	62.7	58.6	66.6
MS	1,917	1,960	2,005	2,047	1,089	675	18	45.6	48.6	46.1	27.5	48.2
MO	3,932	3,984	4,046	4,105	2,155	425	68	54.2	57.5	53.1	38.9	56.7
MT	625	648	659	668	340	4	11	62.8	61.5	62.3	50.3	61.5
NE	1,186	1,208	1,222	1,234	641	49	52	56.1	56.5	54.8	43.0	55.4
NV	1,097	1,199	1,285	1,390	685	105	214	38.7	43.8	37.5	31.9	42.1
NH	846	869	889	911	468	9	14	57.4	62.5	56.5	35.7	61.1
NJ	5,979	6,042	6,144	6,245	3,272	856	750	50.9	51.0	46.7	29.5	47.9
NM	1,171	1,214	1,241	1,263	652	37	473	45.8	47.4	45.1	40.1	46.5
NY	13,633	13,606	13,721	13,805	7,294	2,309	1,833	46.4	49.4	40.8	31.1	42.2
NC	5,331	5,501	5,645	5,797	3,036	1,173	121	45.7	50.2	45.7	33.7	48.0
ND	470	476	477	477	242	4	4	56.0	60.4	55.3	44.6	59.9
OH	8,265	8,332	8,394	8,433	4,436	895	130	54.4	55.8	52.7	40.2	53.6
OK	2,384	2,427	2,477	2,531	1,316	185	91	49.7	48.8	48.6	34.7	43.0
OR	2,315	2,404	2,466	2,530	1,295	51	138	57.3	60.6	55.5	44.2	56.9
PA	9,148	9,153	9,163	9,155	4,839	820	221	49.2	53.7	47.2	31.6	49.7
RI	755	751	752	753	398	36	46	52.0	54.3	47.9	39.0	51.0
SC	2,733	2,802	2,889	2,977	1,569	816	41	41.1	46.4	37.7	33.7	44.4
SD	525	535	540	542	279	5	6	60.5	58.4	60.4	47.9	58.1
TN	3,885	4,007	4,114	4,221	2,224	635	51	47.3	49.2	44.5	22.2	43.9
TX	13,153	13,643	14,223	14,850	7,630	1,800	4,012	41.1	43.1	38.3	24.3	40.3
UT	1,285	1,350	1,411	1,465	748	16	99	49.3	52.6	49.2	33.4	51.8
VT	433	442	451	460	237	4	4	58.5	64.0	57.7	47.7	61.6
VA	4,956	5,066	5,168	5,263	2,734	1,005	197	47.7	52.1	43.4	22.2	46.0
WA	3,962	4,109	4,237	4,368	2,221	154	242	54.9	56.9	52.9	43.9	54.5
WV	1,392	1,400	1,411	1,416	746	45	9	45.5	45.8	37.3	24.9	41.0
WI	3,766	3,838	3,888	3,930	2,026	193	96	57.2	66.1	56.0	43.0	63.8
WY	340	347	354	358	180	4	19	61.0	61.0	60.5	49.2	59.3

NA Not available. [1] Persons of Hispanic origin may be of any race.

Source: Compiled by U.S. Census Bureau. Population data from U.S. Census Bureau, Current Population Reports, P25-1132, <http://www.census.gov/population/socdemo/voting/proj00/>; votes cast from Elections Research Center, Chevy Chase, MD, *America Votes*, annual, (copyright); and Congressional Quarterly Inc., Washington, DC, (copyright).

No. 423. Political Party Financial Activity by Major Political Party: 1981 to 2000

[In millions of dollars (39.3 represents $39,300,000). Covers financial activity during 2-year calendar period indicated. Some political party financial activities, such as building funds and state and local election spending, are not reported to the source. Also excludes contributions earmarked to federal candidates through the party organizations, since some of those funds never passed through the committees' accounts]

Year and type of committee	Democratic				Republican			
	Receipts, net [1]	Disbursements, net [1]	Contributions to candidates	Monies spent on behalf of party's nominees [2]	Receipts, net [1]	Disbursements, net [1]	Contributions to candidates	Monies spent on behalf of party's nominees [2]
1981-82	39.3	40.1	1.7	3.3	215.0	214.0	5.6	14.3
1983-84	98.5	97.4	2.6	9.0	297.9	300.8	4.9	20.1
1985-86	64.8	65.9	1.7	9.0	255.2	258.9	3.4	14.3
1987-88	125.7	119.6	1.8	17.9	257.5	251.4	3.4	22.7
1989-90	85.8	90.9	1.5	8.7	206.3	213.5	2.9	10.7
1991-92	187.5	180.5	1.9	28.1	267.3	256.1	3.0	33.9
1993-94, total	151.1	149.9	2.2	21.2	254.4	243.7	3.0	20.6
1995-96, total	221.6	214.3	2.2	22.6	416.5	408.5	3.7	31.0
1997-98, total	160.0	155.3	1.2	18.6	285.0	275.9	2.6	15.7
1999-00, total [3]	275.2	265.8	1.4	21.0	465.8	427.0	2.3	29.6
National committee	124.0	122.0	-	13.5	212.8	187.4	0.4	23.7
Senatorial committee	40.5	41.5	0.3	0.1	51.5	50.7	0.4	-
Congressional committee	48.4	49.3	0.6	2.6	97.3	95.4	0.7	3.7
State and local	149.3	140.0	0.5	4.7	176.6	165.9	0.8	2.2

- Represents zero. [1] Total receipts and disbursements do not include monies transferred among the listed committees. [2] Monies spent in the general election. [3] Excludes "Other national" activity.

Source: U.S. Federal Election Commission, *FEC Reports on Financial Activity, Final Report, Party and Non-Party Political Committees*, biennial; also see <http://fecweb1.fec.gov/press/051501partyfund/tables/>.

No. 424. National Party Nonfederal Activity: 1996 to 2000

[In dollars. During the 2000 election cycle, both major parties raised record amounts of *nonfederal* or "soft money." Soft money is used to pay a portion of the overhead expenses of party organizations, as well as other shared expenses that benefit both federal and nonfederal elections. In addition, it is used for issue advocacy, as well as generic party advertising. It may also be transferred from national committees to state and local party committees as well as being used to support construction and maintenance of party headquarters]

Year and type of committee	Democratic		Republican	
	Receipts	Disbursements	Receipts	Disbursements
1996				
Total	123,877,924	121,826,562	138,199,706	149,658,099
National	101,905,186	100,483,977	113,127,010	114,401,973
Senatorial	14,176,392	14,061,273	29,395,329	29,362,653
Congressional	12,340,824	11,822,790	18,530,773	28,746,879
1998				
Total	92,811,927	92,987,711	131,615,116	127,730,744
National	56,966,353	57,411,879	74,805,286	74,325,722
Senatorial	25,880,538	25,858,673	37,866,845	37,283,103
Congressional	16,865,410	16,617,533	26,914,059	24,092,993
2000				
Total	245,202,519	244,848,838	249,861,645	252,785,565
National	136,563,419	135,332,105	166,207,843	163,521,510
Senatorial	63,717,982	63,300,415	44,652,709	44,633,117
Congressional	56,702,023	57,997,220	47,295,736	52,925,581

Source: U.S. Federal Election Commission, press release of May 31, 2001, and unpublished data.

No. 425. Political Action Committees—Number by Committee Type: 1980 to 2002

[As of December 31]

Committee type	1980	1985	1990	1995	1998	1999	2000	2001	2002
Total	2,551	3,992	4,172	4,016	3,798	3,835	3,706	3,907	4,027
Corporate	1,206	1,710	1,795	1,674	1,567	1,548	1,523	1,545	1,528
Labor	297	388	346	334	321	318	316	317	320
Trade/membership/health	576	695	774	815	821	844	812	860	975
Nonconnected	374	1,003	1,062	1,020	935	972	902	1,026	1,055
Cooperative	42	54	59	44	39	38	39	41	39
Corporation without stock	56	142	136	129	115	115	114	118	110

Source: U.S. Federal Election Commission, press release of January 2003.

No. 426. Political Action Committees—Financial Activity Summary by Committee Type: 1997 to 2002

[In millions of dollars (502.6 represents $502,600,000). Covers financial activity during 2-year calendar period indicated]

Committee type	Receipts 1997-98	Receipts 1999-00	Receipts 2001-02	Disbursements [1] 1997-98	Disbursements [1] 1999-00	Disbursements [1] 2001-02	Contributions to candidates 1997-98	Contributions to candidates 1999-00	Contributions to candidates 2001-02
Total	502.6	604.9	685.3	470.8	579.4	656.5	219.9	259.8	282.0
Corporate	144.1	164.5	191.7	137.6	158.3	178.1	78.0	91.5	99.6
Labor	111.3	136.0	167.8	98.2	128.7	158.0	44.6	51.6	53.9
Trade/membership/health	119.6	142.9	166.7	114.4	137.2	165.7	62.3	71.8	46.3
Nonconnected	114.3	144.3	145.8	107.8	139.7	141.3	28.2	37.3	75.1
Cooperative	4.5	3.7	3.7	4.3	3.3	3.6	2.4	2.4	2.7
Corporation without stock	8.8	13.6	9.7	8.5	12.2	9.6	4.4	5.3	4.4

[1] Comprises contributions to candidates, independent expenditures, and other disbursements.

Source: U.S. Federal Election Commission, *FED Reports on Financial Activity, Final Report, Party and Nonparty Political Committees,* biennial.

No. 427. Presidential Campaign Finances—Federal Funds for General Election: 1980 to 2000

[In millions of dollars (62.7 represents $62,700,000). Based on FEC certifications, audit reports, and Dept. of Treasury reports]

1980 Candidate	Amount	1992 Candidate	Amount	1996 Candidate	Amount	2000 Candidate	Amount
Total	62.7	Total	110.4	Total	152.6	Total	147.7
Anderson [1]	4.2	Bush	55.2	Clinton	61.8	Bush	67.6
Carter	29.4	Clinton	55.2	Dole	61.8	Gore	67.6
Reagan	29.2	Perot	-	Perot	29.0	Buchanan	12.6

- Represents zero.   [1] John Anderson, as the candidate of a new party, was permitted to raise funds privately. Total receipts for the Anderson campaign, including federal funds, were $17.6 million, and total expenditures were $15.6 million.

Source: U.S. Federal Election Commission, periodic press releases.

No. 428. Presidential Campaign Finances—Primary Campaign Receipts and Disbursements: 1991 to 2000

[In millions of dollars (125.2 represents $125,200,000). Covers campaign finance activity during 2-year calendar period indicated. Covers candidates who received federal matching funds or who had significant financial activity]

Item	Total [1] 1991-92	Total [1] 1995-96	Total [1] 1999-00	Democratic 1991-92	Democratic 1995-96	Democratic 1999-00	Republican 1991-92	Republican 1995-96	Republican 1999-00
Receipts, total [2]	125.2	243.9	351.6	70.0	46.2	96.6	49.7	187.0	236.7
Individual contributions	82.4	126.4	238.2	44.7	31.3	66.7	34.4	93.1	159.1
Federal matching funds	41.5	56.0	61.6	24.4	14.0	29.3	15.0	41.6	26.5
Disbursements	118.7	234.1	343.5	64.4	41.8	92.2	48.8	182.1	233.2

[1] Includes other parties, not shown separately.   [2] Includes other types of receipts, not shown separately.

Source: U.S. Federal Election Commission, *FEC Reports on Financial Activity, Final Report, Presidential Pre-Nomination Campaigns,* quadrennial.

No. 429. Congressional Campaign Finances—Receipts and Disbursements: 1995 to 2000

[505.4 represents 505,400,000. Covers all campaign finance activity during 2-year calendar period indicated for primary, general, run-off, and special elections, for 1999-2000 relates to 2,083 House of Representatives candidates and 333 Senate candidates. Data have been adjusted to eliminate transfers between all committees within a campaign. For further information on legal limits of contributions, see Federal Election Campaign Act of 1971, as amended]

Item	House of representatives						Senate					
	Amount (mil. dol.)			Percent distribution			Amount (mil. dol.)			Percent distribution		
	1995-96	1997-98	1999-00	1995-96	1997-98	1999-00	1995-96	1997-98	1999-00	1995-96	1997-98	1999-00
Total receipts [1]	505.4	493.7	610.4	100	100	100	285.1	287.5	437.0	100	100	100
Individual contributions	272.9	253.2	315.6	55	52	52	166.9	166.5	252.1	59	58	58
Other committees	155.0	158.5	193.4	31	32	32	45.6	48.1	52.0	16	17	12
Candidate loans	42.0	46.8	61.9	8	10	10	40.3	52.2	89.0	14	18	20
Candidate contributions	7.0	5.3	6.3	1	1	1	16.4	1.3	18.7	6	(Z)	4
Democrats	233.1	233.4	286.7	46	47	47	126.5	134.1	230.4	44	47	53
Republicans	266.9	255.8	317.7	53	52	52	157.7	153.0	203.8	55	53	47
Others	5.4	4.5	6.0	1	1	1	0.9	0.4	2.8	(Z)	(Z)	1
Incumbents	279.8	293.6	361.8	56	60	59	81.8	135.5	130.6	29	47	30
Challengers [2]	119.1	92.8	127.4	24	19	21	79.2	113.9	99.6	28	40	23
Open seats [2]	101.1	102.7	121.1	14	21	20	124.1	37.7	206.7	44	13	47
Total disbursements	477.8	452.5	572.3	95	100	100	287.4	287.9	434.7	100	100	100
Democrats	221.1	211.1	266.8	44	47	47	127.4	134.6	226.3	44	47	52
Republicans	251.4	237.2	299.7	50	52	52	159.1	152.9	205.7	55	53	47
Others	5.3	4.2	5.7	1	1	1	0.9	0.4	2.7	(Z)	(Z)	1
Incumbents	258.1	257.2	327.0	51	57	57	85.4	137.3	130.2	30	48	30
Challengers [2]	119.6	94.7	125.6	24	21	22	78.9	112.5	99.3	27	39	23
Open seats [2]	100.2	100.6	119.7	20	22	21	123.1	38.1	205.1	43	13	47

Z Less than $50,000 or 0.5 percent. [1] Includes other types of receipts, not shown separately. [2] Elections in which an incumbent did not seek re-election.

Source: U.S. Federal Election Commission, *FEC Reports on Financial Activity, Final Report, U.S. Senate and House Campaigns*, biennial.

No. 430. Contributions to Congressional Campaigns by Political Action Committees (PAC) by Type of Committee: 1993 to 2002

[In millions of dollars (132.4 represents 132,400,000). Covers amounts given to candidates in primary, general, run-off, and special elections during the 2-year calendar period indicated. For number of political action committees, see Table 425]

Type of committee	Total [1]	Democrats	Republicans	Incumbents	Challengers	Open seats [2]
HOUSE OF REPRESENTATIVES						
1993-94	132.4	88.2	43.9	101.4	12.7	18.3
1995-96	155.8	77.3	77.7	113.9	21.4	20.5
1997-98	158.7	77.6	80.9	124.0	14.9	19.8
1999-00	193.4	98.2	94.7	150.5	19.9	23.0
2001-02, total [3]	206.9	102.6	104.2	161.0	13.8	32.1
Corporate	68.2	23.6	44.6	59.7	1.6	6.9
Trade association [4]	57.2	23.0	34.2	47.1	2.1	8.0
Labor	44.4	39.9	4.3	31.5	5.2	7.7
Nonconnected [5]	32.2	14.0	18.1	18.5	4.8	8.9
SENATE						
1993-94	47.2	24.0	23.2	26.3	5.7	15.1
1995-96	45.6	16.6	29.0	19.4	6.9	19.3
1997-98	48.1	20.7	27.3	34.3	6.6	7.2
1999-00	51.9	18.7	33.2	33.5	7.1	11.3
2001-02, total [3]	59.2	25.4	33.8	37.0	14.2	8.1
Corporate	23.4	7.0	16.4	15.8	4.3	3.4
Trade association [4]	14.3	4.9	9.3	9.5	3.1	1.7
Labor	7.5	7.0	0.5	4.1	2.4	1.1
Nonconnected [5]	12.5	5.8	6.6	6.6	4.1	1.8

[1] Includes other parties, not shown separately. [2] Elections in which an incumbent did not seek re-election. [3] Includes other types of political action committees not shown separately. [4] Includes membership organizations and health organizations. [5] Represents "ideological" groups as well as other issue groups not necessarily ideological in nature.

Source: U.S. Federal Election Commission, *FEC Reports on Financial Activity, Party and Non-Party Political Committees, Final Report*, biennial.

Section 8
State and Local Government Finances and Employment

This section presents data on revenues, expenditures, debt, and employment of state and local governments. Nationwide statistics relating to state and local governments, their numbers, finances, and employment are compiled primarily by the U.S. Census Bureau through a program of censuses and surveys. Every fifth year (for years ending in "2" and "7") the Census Bureau conducts a census of governments involving collection of data for all governmental units in the United States. In addition, the Census Bureau conducts annual surveys which cover all the state governments and a sample of local governments.

Annually, the Census Bureau releases information on the Internet which presents financial data for the federal government, nationwide totals for state and local governments, and state-local data by states. Also released annually is a series on state, city, county, and school finances and on state and local public employment. There is also a series of quarterly data releases covering tax revenue and finances of major public employee retirement systems.

Basic information for Census Bureau statistics on governments is obtained by mail canvass from state and local officials; however, financial data for each of the state governments and for many of the large local governments are compiled from their official records and reports by Census Bureau personnel. In over two-thirds of the states, all or part of local government financial data are obtained through central collection arrangements with state governments. Financial data on the federal government are primarily based on the *Budget* published by the Office of Management and Budget (see text, Section 9, Federal Government Finances and Employment).

Governmental units—The governmental structure of the United States includes, in addition to the federal government and the states, thousands of local governments—counties, municipalities, townships, school districts, and numerous kinds of "special districts." In 2002, 87,525 local governments were identified by the census of governments (see Tables 431-433). As defined by the census, governmental units include all agencies or bodies having an organized existence, governmental character, and substantial autonomy. While most of these governments can impose taxes, many of the special districts—such as independent public housing authorities and numerous local irrigation, power, and other types of districts—are financed from rentals, charges for services, benefit assessments, grants from other governments, and other nontax sources. The count of governments excludes semi-autonomous agencies through which states, cities, and counties sometimes provide for certain functions—for example, "dependent" school systems, state institutions of higher education, and certain other "authorities" and special agencies which are under the administrative or fiscal control of an established governmental unit.

Finances—The financial statistics relate to government fiscal years ending June 30 or at some date within the 12 previous months. The following governments are exceptions and are included as though they were part of the June 30 group; ending September 30, the state governments of Alabama and Michigan, the District of Columbia, and Alabama school districts; and ending August 31, the state government of Texas and Texas school districts. New York State ends its fiscal year on March 31. The federal government ended the fiscal year June 30 until 1976 when its fiscal year, by an act of Congress, was revised to extend from Oct. 1 to Sept. 30. A 3-month quarter (July 1 to Sept. 30, 1976) bridged the transition.

Nationwide government finance statistics have been classified and presented in terms of uniform concepts and categories, rather than according to the highly diverse terminology, organization, and fund structure utilized by individual governments.

Statistics on governmental finances distinguish among general government, utilities, liquor stores, and insurance trusts. *General government* comprises all activities except utilities, liquor stores, and insurance trusts. Utilities include government water supply, electric light and power, gas supply, and transit systems. Liquor stores are operated by 17 states and by local governments in 6 states. Insurance trusts relate to employee retirement, unemployment compensation, and other social insurance systems administered by the federal, state, and local governments.

Data for cities or counties relate only to municipal or county and their dependent agencies and do not include amounts for other local governments in the same geographic location. Therefore, expenditure figures for "education" do not include spending by the separate school districts which administer public schools within most municipal or county areas. Variations in the assignment of governmental responsibility for public assistance, health, hospitals, public housing, and other functions to a lesser degree also have an important effect upon reported amounts of city or county expenditure, revenue, and debt.

Employment and payrolls—These data are based mainly on mail canvassing of state and local governments. Payroll includes all salaries, wages, and individual fee payments for the month specified, and employment relates to all persons on governmental payrolls during a pay period of the month covered—including paid officials, temporary help, and (unless otherwise specified) part-time as well as full-time personnel. Beginning 1986, statistics for full-time equivalent employment have been computed with a formula using hours worked by part-time employees. A payroll based formula was used prior to 1985. Full-time equivalent employment statistics were not computed for 1985. Figures shown for individual governments cover major dependent agencies such as institutions of higher education, as well as the basic central departments and agencies of the government.

Statistical reliability—For a discussion of statistical collection and estimation, sampling procedures, and measures of statistical reliability applicable to Census Bureau data, see Appendix III.

No. 431. Number of Governmental Units by Type: 1952 to 2002

Type of government	1952 [1]	1962	1967	1972	1977	1982	1987	1992	1997	2002
Total units	116,807	91,237	81,299	78,269	79,913	81,831	83,237	85,006	87,504	87,576
U.S. government	1	1	1	1	1	1	1	1	1	1
State government	50	50	50	50	50	50	50	50	50	50
Local governments	116,756	91,186	81,248	78,218	79,862	81,780	83,186	84,955	87,453	87,525
County	3,052	3,043	3,049	3,044	3,042	3,041	3,042	3,043	3,043	3,034
Municipal	16,807	18,000	18,048	18,517	18,862	19,076	19,200	19,279	19,372	19,429
Township and town	17,202	17,142	17,105	16,991	16,822	16,734	16,691	16,656	16,629	16,504
School district	67,355	34,678	21,782	15,781	15,174	14,851	14,721	14,422	13,726	13,506
Special district	12,340	18,323	21,264	23,885	25,962	28,078	29,532	31,555	34,683	35,052

[1] Adjusted to include units in Alaska and Hawaii which adopted statehood in 1959.

Source: U.S. Census Bureau, 2002 Census of Governments, Volume 1, Number 1, *Government Organization*, Series GC02(1)-1. See also <http://www.census.gov/prod/2003pubs/gc021x1.pdf> (issued December 2002).

No. 432. Number of Local Governments by Type—States: 2002

State	All governmental units [1]	County	Municipal	Township [1]	School district	Special district [2] Total [3]	Natural resources	Fire protection	Housing & community development
United States	87,525	3,034	19,429	16,504	13,506	35,052	6,979	5,725	3,399
Alabama	1,171	67	451	-	128	525	68	12	152
Alaska	175	12	149	-	-	14	-	-	13
Arizona	638	15	87	-	231	305	83	151	-
Arkansas	1,588	75	499	-	310	704	258	80	122
California	4,409	57	475	-	1,047	2,830	484	368	71
Colorado	1,928	62	270	-	182	1,414	178	250	91
Connecticut	580	-	30	149	17	384	1	64	93
Delaware	339	3	57	-	19	260	239	-	3
District of Columbia	2	-	1	-	-	1	-	-	-
Florida	1,191	66	404	-	95	626	124	57	105
Georgia	1,448	156	531	-	180	581	38	2	201
Hawaii	19	3	1	-	-	15	14	-	-
Idaho	1,158	44	200	-	116	798	176	142	10
Illinois	6,903	102	1,291	1,431	934	3,145	979	823	112
Indiana	3,085	91	567	1,008	294	1,125	141	1	63
Iowa	1,975	99	948	-	386	542	251	67	23
Kansas	3,887	104	627	1,299	324	1,533	261	-	199
Kentucky	1,439	119	424	-	176	720	166	163	17
Louisiana	473	60	302	-	66	45	4	-	-
Maine	826	16	22	467	99	222	15	-	23
Maryland	265	23	157	-	-	85	44	-	21
Massachusetts	841	5	45	306	82	403	16	16	250
Michigan	2,804	83	533	1,242	580	366	80	4	-
Minnesota	3,482	87	854	1,793	345	403	114	-	167
Mississippi	1,000	82	296	-	164	458	242	34	57
Missouri	3,422	114	946	312	536	1,514	183	317	136
Montana	1,127	54	129	-	352	592	125	155	12
Nebraska	2,791	93	531	446	575	1,146	80	421	125
Nevada	210	16	19	-	17	158	33	19	5
New Hampshire	559	10	13	221	167	148	10	14	21
New Jersey	1,412	21	324	242	549	276	16	196	2
New Mexico	858	33	101	-	96	628	583	-	6
New York	3,420	57	616	929	683	1,135	3	911	-
North Carolina	960	100	541	-	-	319	155	-	91
North Dakota	2,735	53	360	1,332	226	764	79	281	39
Ohio	3,636	88	942	1,308	667	631	98	73	77
Oklahoma	1,798	77	590	-	571	560	97	26	105
Oregon	1,439	36	240	-	236	927	179	256	20
Pennsylvania	5,031	66	1,018	1,546	516	1,885	7	-	90
Rhode Island	118	-	8	31	4	75	3	34	25
South Carolina	701	46	269	-	85	301	48	86	46
South Dakota	1,866	66	308	940	176	376	102	72	40
Tennessee	930	92	349	-	14	475	108	-	98
Texas	4,784	254	1,196	-	1,089	2,245	442	141	398
Utah	605	29	236	-	40	300	81	19	16
Vermont	733	14	47	237	283	152	14	19	10
Virginia	521	95	229	-	1	196	47	-	-
Washington	1,787	39	279	-	296	1,173	170	387	41
West Virginia	686	55	234	-	55	342	15	-	39
Wisconsin	3,048	72	585	1,265	442	684	191	-	164
Wyoming	722	23	98	-	55	546	134	64	-

- Represents zero. [1] Includes "town" governments in the six New England States and in Minnesota, New York, and Wisconsin. [2] Single function districts. [3] Includes other special districts not shown separately.

No. 433. County, Municipal, and Township Governments by Population Size: 2002

[Number of governments as of January 2002. Population enumerated as of April 1, 2000. (252,051 represents 252,051,000). Consolidated city-county governments are classified as municipal rather than county governments. Township governments include "towns" in the six New England States, Minnesota, New York, and Wisconsin. See Appendix III]

Population-size group	County governments Number, 2002	Number (1,000)	Percent	Municipal governments Number, 2002	Number (1,000)	Percent	Township governments Number, 2002	Number (1,000)	Percent
Total	3,034	252,051	100	19,429	174,882	100	16,504	57,365	100
300,000 or more	161	131,575	52	58	47,768	27	3	1,527	3
200,000 to 299,999	84	20,606	8	30	7,163	4	3	728	1
100,000 to 199,999	228	31,576	13	153	21,076	12	30	3,974	7
50,000 to 99,999	383	27,160	11	364	24,960	14	97	6,588	11
25,000 to 49,999	638	22,913	9	643	22,576	13	273	9,275	16
10,000 to 24,999	869	14,488	6	1,436	22,589	13	773	12,067	21
5,000 to 9,999	385	2,911	1	1,637	11,644	7	1,085	7,560	13
2,500 to 4,999	173	643	-	2,070	7,352	4	1,909	6,732	12
1,000 to 2,499	84	158	-	3,677	5,951	3	3,679	5,905	10
Less than 1,000	29	21	-	9,361	3,803	2	8,652	3,008	5

- Represents or rounds to zero.
Source of Tables 432 and 433: U.S. Census Bureau, Census of Governments, *Government Organization*, Series (GC02(1)-1), quinquennial. <http://www.census.gov/prod/www/abs/govern.html> (accessed 16 June 2003).

No. 434. Government Current Receipts and Expenditures by Type: 1990 to 2002

[In billions of dollars (1,607.7 represents $1,607,700,000,000). For explanation of national income, see text, Section 13]

Item	1990	1995	1997	1998	1999	2000	2001	2002
Current receipts	1,607.7	2,117.1	2,440.0	2,613.8	2,780.3	3,000.6	2,992.3	2,872.1
Personal tax and nontax receipts	609.6	778.3	968.8	1,070.4	1,159.1	1,286.4	1,292.1	1,111.9
Corporate profits tax accruals	140.6	211.0	237.2	238.8	247.8	259.4	199.3	213.3
Indirect business tax and nontax accruals	447.3	594.6	646.2	681.3	712.9	753.6	774.8	800.4
Contributions for social insurance	410.1	533.2	587.8	623.3	660.4	701.3	726.1	746.5
Current expenditures	1,778.0	2,293.7	2,462.4	2,529.3	2,630.1	2,775.8	2,951.6	3,126.2
Consumption expenditures	965.7	1,133.9	1,223.3	1,261.4	1,336.3	1,431.2	1,522.2	1,621.0
Transfer payments (net)	583.1	869.9	945.0	965.9	998.5	1,050.8	1,146.6	1,267.3
To persons	573.1	860.1	934.4	955.0	987.2	1,037.3	1,137.0	1,252.9
To the rest of the world (net)	10.0	9.8	10.6	11.0	11.4	13.6	9.6	14.4
Net interest paid	204.3	268.0	275.3	278.8	263.1	260.1	236.0	205.8
Interest paid	297.8	357.5	371.2	372.2	360.0	363.6	341.1	314.1
To persons and business	257.1	300.1	283.2	281.1	285.4	280.6	260.4	241.0
To the rest of the world	40.8	57.4	88.1	91.1	74.5	83.0	80.7	73.0
Less: Interest received by government	93.6	89.5	96.0	93.4	96.9	103.5	105.1	108.2
Less: Dividends received by government	0.2	0.3	0.3	0.4	0.4	0.4	0.4	0.5
Subsidies less current surplus of government enterprises	25.3	22.2	19.1	23.5	32.5	34.1	47.3	32.5
Subsidies	26.8	33.2	33.0	35.4	44.0	44.1	55.3	46.2
Less: Current surplus of government enterprises	1.5	11.1	13.9	11.8	11.5	10.1	8.0	13.7
Less: Wage accruals less disbursements	0.1	-	-	-	-	-	-	-
Current surplus or deficit (-)	-170.3	-176.7	-22.3	84.5	150.2	224.8	40.7	-254.1
Social insurance funds	46.9	23.9	31.6	58.6	96.8	118.4	93.2	51.9

- Represents zero.

Source: U.S. Bureau of Economic Analysis, *National Income and Product Accounts, 1929-97*; and Survey of Current Business, May 2003. See also <http://www.bea.doc.gov/bea/dn/nipaweb/selecttable.asp?selected=N>; (released as 30 May 2003).

No. 435. Government Consumption Expenditures and Gross Investment by Level of Government and Type: 1990 to 2002

[In billions of dollars (1,181.4 represents $1,181,400,000,000). For explanation of national income, see text, Section 13]

Level of government and type	1990	1995	1997	1998	1999	2000	2001	2002
Consumption expenditures & gross investment, total	1,181.4	1,372.0	1,487.9	1,538.5	1,641.0	1,751.0	1,858.0	1,972.9
Federal	508.4	521.5	538.2	539.2	565.0	589.2	628.1	693.7
National defense	374.9	350.6	352.6	349.1	364.3	374.9	399.9	447.4
Consumption expenditures	308.9	297.5	304.2	299.7	312.0	321.4	344.5	386.6
Durable goods [1]	30.9	21.0	21.1	21.1	22.4	22.5	24.2	25.3
Nondurable goods	11.0	6.3	7.5	6.9	8.1	10.4	10.5	11.5
Services	267.0	270.2	275.6	271.7	281.5	288.5	309.8	349.9
Gross investment	65.9	53.1	48.4	49.4	52.3	53.5	55.5	60.8
Structures	6.1	6.3	5.7	5.4	5.3	5.3	5.4	5.3
Equipment and software	59.8	46.9	42.7	44.0	47.4	48.2	50.0	55.5
Nondefense	133.6	170.9	185.6	190.1	200.7	214.3	228.2	246.3
Consumption expenditures	111.0	141.8	152.7	153.4	159.6	171.9	184.0	199.9
Durable goods [1]	-0.1	0.9	1.2	-0.4	1.0	1.2	1.3	1.4
Nondurable goods	4.6	6.5	7.9	8.1	6.3	6.4	8.7	9.4
Services	106.4	134.3	143.6	145.6	152.3	164.4	174.0	189.1
Gross investment	22.6	29.2	32.9	36.7	41.1	42.4	44.2	46.4
Structures	8.0	10.8	9.7	11.2	11.6	10.8	10.4	12.3
Equipment and software	14.6	18.4	23.2	25.5	29.4	31.6	33.8	34.1
State and local	673.0	850.5	949.7	999.3	1,076.0	1,161.8	1,229.9	1,279.2
Consumption expenditures	545.8	694.7	766.4	808.3	864.7	937.9	993.7	1,034.5
Durable goods [1]	10.6	12.7	13.8	14.8	15.9	17.1	18.3	19.4
Nondurable goods	53.6	72.9	81.7	83.4	94.0	114.0	118.7	121.1
Services	481.5	609.0	670.9	710.1	754.7	806.8	856.7	894.0
Gross investment	127.2	155.8	183.3	191.0	211.3	223.9	236.2	244.7
Structures	98.5	117.3	139.3	142.4	158.3	167.4	177.6	188.2
Equipment and software	28.7	38.6	44.0	48.6	53.0	56.5	58.6	56.5

[1] Consumption expenditures for durable goods excludes expenditures classified as investment, except for goods transferred to foreign countries by the federal government.

Source: U.S. Bureau of Economic Analysis, *National Income and Product Accounts, 1929-97*; and Survey of Current Business, May 2003. See also <http://www.bea.doc.gov/bea/dn/nipaweb/selecttable.asp?selected=N>; (released as 30 May 2003).

No. 436. Real Government Consumption and Expenditures and Gross Investment in Chained (1996) Dollars by Level of Government and Type: 1990 to 2002

[In billions dollars (1,387.3 represents $1,387,300,000,000). For explanation of national income, see text, Section 13]

Item	1990	1995	1997	1998	1999	2000	2001	2002
Government consumption expenditures and gross investment, total [1]	1,387.3	1,406.4	1,455.4	1,483.3	1,540.6	1,582.5	1,640.4	1,712.8
Federal	606.8	536.5	529.6	525.4	537.7	544.4	570.6	613.3
National defense	443.2	361.9	347.7	341.6	348.8	348.7	366.0	400.0
Consumption expenditures	369.7	308.7	298.5	290.6	295.3	294.1	308.9	337.0
Durable goods [2]	33.4	21.1	21.2	21.3	22.7	22.7	24.3	25.3
Nondurable goods	10.7	6.9	7.7	8.0	8.9	9.4	9.9	11.4
Services	325.0	280.7	269.6	261.4	264.0	262.4	275.1	300.6
Compensation of general government employees, except own-account investment [3]	172.9	139.0	128.3	124.3	120.9	120.5	121.2	123.4
Consumption of general government fixed capital [4]	61.2	63.4	62.7	62.4	62.4	62.5	62.4	62.6
Other services	91.6	78.5	78.7	74.8	80.8	79.6	91.7	114.9
Gross investment	73.2	53.2	49.1	51.0	53.7	54.8	57.3	63.3
Structures	7.7	6.5	5.5	5.1	4.8	4.6	4.6	4.4
Equipment and software	65.4	46.8	43.6	45.9	49.0	50.4	53.0	59.5
Nondefense	163.0	174.6	181.8	183.8	188.8	195.6	204.4	213.3
Consumption expenditures	140.1	145.7	148.6	146.5	147.6	153.7	161.1	167.8
Durable goods [2]	-0.7	0.8	1.3	-0.2	1.2	1.4	1.5	1.7
Nondurable goods	4.6	6.4	7.9	8.3	6.4	6.8	8.9	8.5
Commodity Credit Corporation inventory change	-2.5	-0.4	-0.1	0.3	0.3	1.6	1.7	-0.1
Other nondurables	7.1	6.8	8.0	8.1	6.0	5.2	7.2	8.6
Services	135.6	138.5	139.4	138.5	140.2	146.3	151.6	157.7
Compensation of general government employees, except own-account investment [3]	83.2	78.5	75.9	76.7	77.0	79.4	79.0	80.7
Consumption of general government fixed capital [4]	13.3	16.7	19.6	21.4	23.8	26.1	28.0	30.1
Other services	39.9	43.3	44.0	40.4	39.7	41.2	45.4	48.0
Gross investment	23.5	29.0	33.3	37.5	41.6	42.3	43.6	45.9
Structures	9.3	11.1	9.4	10.6	10.7	9.5	8.9	10.4
Equipment and software	14.2	17.9	23.9	27.0	31.2	33.3	35.4	36.0
State and local	781.1	869.9	925.8	957.7	1,002.4	1,037.4	1,069.4	1,099.7
Consumption expenditures	638.9	711.3	745.7	771.9	801.2	831.1	856.8	881.1
Durable goods [2]	10.9	12.7	13.9	15.0	16.1	17.2	18.3	19.3
Nondurable goods	57.8	75.6	82.3	88.4	96.2	103.0	108.7	113.0
Services	570.3	623.1	649.5	668.8	689.8	712.0	731.1	750.5
Compensation of general government employees, except own-account investment [3]	507.1	536.5	550.9	559.9	566.4	577.6	589.6	601.7
Consumption of general government fixed capital [4]	52.7	65.3	71.7	75.7	80.2	84.6	88.7	92.6
Other services	13.6	21.3	26.8	33.0	43.1	49.9	53.2	56.8
Gross investment	142.2	158.6	180.2	185.8	201.4	206.5	212.8	218.6
Structures	114.5	120.9	134.7	134.0	143.8	145.2	148.6	154.9
Equipment and software	28.4	37.8	45.4	52.3	58.4	62.7	65.9	64.6
Residual	-4.4	-0.6	-	-1.1	-3.0	-5.1	-6.8	-7.0
Addenda:								
Compensation of general government employees [3]	769.2	761.3	763.4	769.4	773.2	786.2	800.5	817.0
Federal	258.4	219.0	205.7	202.6	199.4	201.4	201.6	205.7
State and local	512.4	542.4	557.7	566.8	573.8	584.9	598.9	611.3

- Represents zero   [1] Gross government investment consists of general government and government enterprise expenditures for fixed assets; inventory investment is included in government consumption expenditures.   [2] Consumption expenditures for durable goods excludes expenditures classified as investment, except for goods transferred to foreign countries by the federal government.   [3] Compensation of government employees engaged in new own-account investment and related expenditures for goods and services are classified as investment in structures and in software. The compensation of all general government employees is shown in the addenda.   [4] Consumption of fixed capital, or depreciation, is included in government consumption expenditures as a partial measure of the value of the services of general government fixed assets; use of depreciation assumes a zero net return.

Source: U.S. Bureau of Economic Analysis, *National Income and Product Accounts, 1929-97*; and Survey of Current Business, May 2003. See also <http://www.bea.doc.gov/bea/dn/nipaweb/selecttable.asp?selected=N>; (released as 30 May 2003).

No. 437. Federal Grants-in-Aid to State and Local Governments: 1980 to 2003

[91,385 represents $91,385,000,000, except as indicated. For fiscal year ending in year shown; see text, this section. Minus sign (-) indicates decrease]

Year	Current dollars							Constant (1996) dollars	
	Grants, total (mil. dol.)	Annual percent change [1]	Grants to individuals		Grants as percent of—			Total grants (bil. dol.)	Annual percent change [1]
			Total (mil. dol.)	Percent of total grants	State/local govt. expenditures [2]	Federal outlays	Gross domestic product		
1980	91,385	9.6	32,619	35.7	39.9	15.5	3.3	168.5	-1.3
1985	105,852	8.5	50,059	47.3	29.6	11.2	2.6	147.0	4.9
1990	135,325	11.0	77,264	57.1	25.2	10.8	2.4	157.9	6.6
1992	178,065	15.2	112,522	63.2	28.7	12.9	2.9	195.4	12.6
1993	193,612	8.7	124,155	64.1	29.6	13.7	3.0	207.3	6.1
1994	210,596	8.8	134,153	63.7	30.9	14.4	3.0	220.7	6.5
1995	224,991	6.8	144,427	64.2	31.5	14.8	3.1	229.8	4.1
1996	227,811	1.3	146,493	64.3	30.8	14.6	3.0	227.8	-0.9
1997	234,160	2.8	148,236	63.3	30.2	14.6	2.9	229.2	0.6
1998	246,128	5.1	160,305	65.1	30.3	14.9	2.8	237.6	3.7
1999	267,081	8.5	172,384	64.5	31.2	15.7	2.9	253.4	6.6
2000	284,659	6.6	182,592	64.1	30.6	15.9	2.9	262.5	3.6
2001	317,211	11.4	203,920	64.3	31.7	17.0	3.2	284.9	8.5
2002	351,550	10.8	227,373	64.7	33.8	17.5	3.4	312.2	9.6
2003, est	384,245	9.3	247,182	64.3	(NA)	18.0	3.6	333.7	6.9

NA Not available. [1] Average annual percent change from prior year shown. For explanation, see Guide to Tabular Presentation. For 1980, change from 1979, for 1985, from 1984, and 1990, from 1989. [2] Expenditures from own sources as defined in the national income and product accounts.

Source: U.S. Office of Management and Budget, based on *Historical Tables* and *Analytical Prospectives, Budget of the United States Government*, annual.

No. 438. Federal Aid to State and Local Governments: 1980 to 2003

[In millions of dollars (91,385 represents $91,385,000,000). For fiscal year ending in year shown; See text, this section. Includes trust funds. Minus sign (-) indicates previously disbursed funds returned to the federal government]

Program	1980	1990	1995	1999	2000	2001	2002	2003 est.
Grant-in-aid shared revenue [1]	91,385	135,325	224,991	267,081	284,659	317,211	351,550	384,245
National defense	93	241	68	1	2	47	91	71
Energy	499	461	492	462	433	492	528	607
Natural resources and environment	5,363	3,745	4,148	4,103	4,595	4,882	5,085	5,946
Environmental Protection Agency [2]	4,603	2,874	2,912	2,960	3,490	3,750	3,588	3,999
Agriculture	569	1,285	780	659	724	755	750	827
Commerce and Housing Credit	3	-	5	5	3	3	6	10
Transportation [1]	13,022	19,174	25,787	28,904	32,222	36,647	40,998	39,928
Airports [3]	590	1,220	1,826	1,565	1,624	2,017	2,860	3,244
Highways [3]	9,208	14,171	19,475	22,590	24,711	27,075	29,833	27,882
Urban mass transit [2]	3,129	3,730	4,353	4,188	5,262	6,963	7,462	6,972
Community and regional development [1]	6,486	4,965	7,230	9,332	8,665	9,485	10,501	15,178
Appalachian regional development	335	124	182	136	125	86	101	87
Community development block grants	3,902	2,818	4,333	4,804	4,955	4,939	5,429	6,650
Education, employment, training, social services [1]	21,862	23,359	34,125	38,217	42,125	40,133	44,827	54,450
Compensatory education for the disadvantaged	3,370	4,437	6,785	7,534	8,511	8,616	9,211	11,872
School improvement programs	523	1,080	1,288	1,255	2,394	2,721	3,401	7,530
Federally affected areas impact aid	622	799	803	1,076	875	1,021	1,116	1,182
Vocational and adult education	854	1,287	1,449	1,338	1,448	1,651	1,742	1,861
Social services-block grants to states	2,763	2,749	2,797	1,993	1,827	1,852	1,780	1,792
Children and family services programs	1,548	2,618	4,463	5,421	5,843	6,614	7,749	8,091
Training and employment assistance	6,191	3,042	3,620	3,436	2,957	3,132	4,206	4,100
Office of libraries	158	127	109	129	152	189	202	161
Health [1]	15,758	43,890	93,587	113,969	124,843	139,295	158,677	175,602
Alcohol, drug abuse, and mental health [4]	679	1,241	2,444	2,214	1,931	2,094	2,193	2,292
Grants to states for Medicaid [4]	13,957	41,103	89,070	108,042	117,921	129,434	147,650	162,668
Income security [1]	18,495	35,189	55,122	64,178	63,200	76,064	81,506	84,907
Food stamps-administration	412	2,130	2,740	3,362	3,508	3,664	3,949	4,149
Child nutrition and special milk programs [4]	3,388	4,871	7,387	8,740	9,060	9,416	10,100	11,249
Veterans benefits and services [4]	90	134	253	317	434	405	360	423
Administration of justice	529	574	1,222	4,793	5,120	6,612	5,736	4,026
General government [5]	8,616	2,309	2,172	2,141	2,287	2,388	2,488	2,886

- Represents or rounds to zero. [1] Includes items not shown separately. [2] Grants includes trust funds. [3] Trust funds. [4] Includes grants for payments to individuals. [5] Includes general purpose fiscal assistance.

Source: U.S. Office of Management and Budget, *Historical Tables, Budget of the United States Government*, annual.

No. 439. Federal Aid to State and Local Governments—Selected Programs by State: 2002

[In millions of dollars (362,389 represents $362,389,000,000). For fiscal year ending September 30]

State and island area	Federal aid total [1]	Department of Agriculture — Food and nutrition service					Department of Education				
		Total	Child nutrition programs [2]	Food stamp program [3]	Special supplemental food program (WIC)	Other	Total	Adult education for the disadvantaged	Office of Special Education and Rehabilitative Services		
									Special education	Rehabilitation services & disability research	Other
Total	362,389	21,487	10,161	3,859	4,376	3,090	32,739	1,356	8,532	2,652	20,962
United States	355,690	19,669	9,949	2,487	4,206	3,028	32,032	1,335	8,439	2,554	20,458
Alabama	5,557	363	196	32	71	64	528	27	136	55	326
Alaska	2,250	117	29	8	20	61	274	9	27	11	235
Arizona	6,314	392	203	35	98	56	730	35	130	49	544
Arkansas	3,559	228	119	18	45	46	338	20	82	35	213
California	41,627	2,653	1,301	357	757	238	3,980	344	883	261	2,758
Colorado	3,951	209	97	27	43	41	407	24	112	27	262
Connecticut	4,492	158	79	25	36	18	337	9	100	20	210
Delaware	958	52	28	4	9	11	99	2	25	9	63
District of Columbia	4,025	57	28	10	11	8	140	2	22	12	104
Florida	15,044	981	560	92	248	81	1,553	96	456	119	942
Georgia	9,300	650	394	62	125	69	894	27	232	74	572
Hawaii	1,460	100	42	11	25	22	194	3	34	11	146
Idaho	1,560	111	41	10	17	43	150	9	40	15	94
Illinois	13,296	769	408	99	169	93	1,315	60	378	100	812
Indiana	5,997	334	164	44	72	52	562	14	190	61	301
Iowa	3,391	196	84	21	34	57	294	6	93	31	165
Kansas	2,889	176	101	9	33	34	344	18	89	27	223
Kentucky	5,719	336	172	30	67	67	484	16	127	48	285
Louisiana	6,820	451	260	39	78	73	573	13	136	46	381
Maine	2,049	81	35	10	10	26	156	8	44	15	94
Maryland	5,660	284	146	43	53	43	497	9	150	39	298
Massachusetts	9,202	312	170	40	65	37	686	29	214	48	410
Michigan	11,185	586	257	99	119	111	1,143	60	291	92	742
Minnesota	5,776	329	166	44	57	62	468	9	151	44	266
Mississippi	4,605	351	179	33	57	83	403	9	87	40	268
Missouri	7,137	370	184	52	67	68	564	12	170	58	325
Montana	1,654	106	32	11	13	49	186	3	31	13	141
Nebraska	2,028	128	65	11	22	30	201	8	59	17	123
Nevada	1,646	90	47	10	23	10	165	3	48	13	100
New Hampshire	1,326	59	20	7	10	23	111	2	38	11	60
New Jersey	10,239	390	199	84	76	32	807	17	269	51	469
New Mexico	3,418	203	114	18	35	35	467	16	154	23	290
New York	38,637	1,353	714	236	280	124	2,468	64	576	138	1,708
North Carolina	9,510	581	325	59	111	85	803	20	238	79	470
North Dakota	1,189	65	25	8	10	22	131	2	20	11	99
Ohio	13,262	633	288	126	139	79	1,085	22	321	111	631
Oklahoma	4,510	332	162	38	64	68	506	9	109	42	347
Oregon	4,457	416	107	54	59	196	377	20	111	37	224
Pennsylvania	15,603	639	293	129	132	85	1,186	61	315	115	730
Rhode Island	1,794	62	32	7	13	10	122	2	34	10	75
South Carolina	4,883	312	171	32	59	50	474	9	130	45	290
South Dakota	1,350	86	30	11	13	32	164	3	24	11	127
Tennessee	7,374	427	215	39	95	78	540	10	172	60	294
Texas	21,955	1,690	1,036	164	361	129	2,544	111	675	185	1,644
Utah	2,208	158	81	20	32	26	267	9	83	24	157
Vermont	1,087	60	16	11	10	23	94	3	20	11	62
Virginia	6,233	342	142	72	76	52	703	11	212	61	417
Washington	7,103	405	166	39	93	108	644	40	164	50	421
West Virginia	3,034	157	76	11	29	40	235	4	58	25	147
Wisconsin	6,173	287	133	34	58	63	542	10	159	53	321
Wyoming	1,192	44	15	4	7	17	96	2	21	8	66
Island areas:	5,683	1,801	213	1,373	170	45	682	21	93	72	504
American Samoa	113	23	12	4	6	1	1	-	-	1	-
Micronesia	114	2	-	-	-	2	8	-	4	-	4
Guam	212	19	5	3	6	4	5	-	1	2	2
Marshall Islands	53	-	-	-	-	-	1	-	-	1	-
Northern Marianas	66	13	4	7	-	2	-	-	-	-	-
Palau	38	-	-	-	-	-	-	-	-	-	-
Puerto Rico	4,793	1,712	177	1,351	153	31	650	21	78	67	493
Virgin Islands	294	32	15	8	5	5	16	-	10	2	4
Undistributed amounts	1,015	17	-	-	-	17	26	-	-	26	-

See footnote at end of table.

No. 439. Federal Aid to State and Local Governments—Selected Programs by State: 2002—Con.

[In millions of dollars (3,406 represents $3,406,000,000). For fiscal year ending September 30]

State and island area	FEMA total [4]	Department of Housing and Urban Development							Department of Labor		
		Community development block grants	Public housing programs						State unemployment insurance and employment service	Workforce investment
			Total	Low rent housing assistance	Neighborhood revitalization	Housing certificate program	Capital program	Other	Total		
Total	3,406	36,965	5,437	3,709	467	18,499	3,767	4,761	8,376	3,607	3,431
United States [4]	3,194	36,213	5,318	3,590	465	17,909	3,596	5,019	8,067	3,572	3,173
Alabama	27	509	68	113	2	183	86	47	130	45	59
Alaska	7	174	17	12	-	31	1	113	58	30	19
Arizona	14	489	75	30	6	157	12	205	139	48	60
Arkansas	21	236	32	27	1	121	29	25	69	31	27
California	546	4,203	685	121	25	2,690	134	534	1,207	517	564
Colorado	20	415	52	18	7	261	22	51	94	53	25
Connecticut	3	599	52	58	7	352	48	78	103	62	25
Delaware	3	104	9	10	3	54	8	19	24	11	8
District of Columbia	3	686	91	51	15	165	264	92	161	69	38
Florida	178	1,324	208	96	43	412	83	470	285	118	112
Georgia	31	884	130	123	11	412	127	71	167	76	63
Hawaii	4	144	18	11	-	87	6	21	53	18	20
Idaho	3	74	12	1	-	45	2	14	50	24	17
Illinois	16	2,016	236	266	19	1,020	250	201	388	171	169
Indiana	10	538	91	40	2	298	44	60	125	61	40
Iowa	15	215	48	6	-	124	9	28	61	31	16
Kansas	44	189	43	16	-	87	15	26	54	27	15
Kentucky	21	492	68	53	10	232	76	50	104	40	27
Louisiana	22	569	108	68	13	225	80	68	120	37	76
Maine	5	179	23	9	-	115	7	25	51	19	20
Maryland	10	701	85	77	24	377	41	90	152	71	54
Massachusetts	19	1,506	154	106	9	990	82	156	173	92	59
Michigan	7	912	170	51	1	471	65	149	307	148	99
Minnesota	43	571	85	42	-	314	56	70	151	66	42
Mississippi	23	288	52	28	1	144	29	30	106	36	58
Missouri	60	589	111	45	8	274	58	89	127	62	44
Montana	20	108	14	4	-	41	3	44	35	15	16
Nebraska	6	149	31	10	-	66	19	21	39	21	11
Nevada	2	187	20	16	-	106	15	29	57	34	16
New Hampshire	5	137	19	7	-	89	8	14	32	14	13
New Jersey	82	1,381	136	155	41	768	146	120	226	125	80
New Mexico	5	180	30	9	-	79	11	49	68	19	43
New York	1,232	5,196	769	924	16	2,011	888	542	544	244	231
North Carolina	123	757	78	101	31	374	72	91	216	88	64
North Dakota	37	86	10	3	-	39	3	30	27	14	7
Ohio	11	1,473	241	161	10	739	124	183	280	114	131
Oklahoma	122	457	56	25	3	176	21	169	69	31	29
Oregon	15	359	37	15	-	227	15	62	155	62	70
Pennsylvania	16	1,808	304	240	44	775	248	177	372	179	129
Rhode Island	2	242	27	21	-	142	16	33	34	18	8
South Carolina	7	352	58	30	5	189	26	39	97	44	37
South Dakota	7	108	15	3	-	45	3	40	26	11	8
Tennessee	18	628	67	101	33	281	78	58	118	52	20
Texas	184	1,732	317	119	40	925	134	182	504	191	249
Utah	8	135	31	4	-	77	4	18	57	37	11
Vermont	4	93	19	4	-	55	3	12	18	10	7
Virginia	28	697	84	91	15	366	50	84	134	60	45
Washington	25	611	75	36	8	333	36	118	235	107	98
West Virginia	49	234	56	16	4	103	15	38	77	21	47
Wisconsin	28	462	91	19	8	244	22	75	166	85	46
Wyoming	5	36	7	1	-	18	2	8	21	11	7
Island areas:	70	752	120	118	2	292	171	159	309	34	258
American Samoa	-	-	-	-	-	-	-	-	2	-	1
Micronesia	-	-	-	-	-	-	-	-	2	-	2
Guam	25	25	1	2	-	18	2	2	15	2	11
Marshall Islands	-	-	-	-	-	-	-	-	1	-	1
Northern Marianas	1	-	-	-	-	-	-	-	1	-	1
Palau	-	-	-	-	-	-	-	-	-	-	-
Puerto Rico	32	674	116	98	1	260	155	37	280	28	240
Virgin Islands	12	53	2	18	1	14	14	2	8	3	2
Undistributed amounts	141	-	-	-	-	-	-	-	-	-	-

See footnote at end of table.

No. 439. Federal Aid to State and Local Governments—Selected Programs by State: 2002—Con.

[In millions of dollars (204,197 represents $204,197,000,000). For fiscal year ending September 30]

State and outlying area	Total	Department of Health and Human Services					Department of Transportation				Other federal aid
		Administration for children									
		Temporary assistance to needy families	Children & family services (Head Start)	Foster care and adoption assistance	Centers for Medicare and Medicaid Services	Other	Total	Highway trust fund	Federal transit administration	Other	
Total	204,197	18,538	7,749	5,881	150,640	21,388	38,719	29,444	5,223	4,052	16,500
United States	203,343	18,471	7,494	5,881	150,351	21,146	37,618	28,539	5,024	4,055	15,554
Alabama	2,931	130	125	34	2,300	342	840	673	25	141	230
Alaska	780	75	50	16	519	120	509	328	12	168	332
Arizona	3,476	297	166	62	2,597	354	639	481	61	97	435
Arkansas	2,090	60	84	44	1,721	180	476	395	10	71	102
California	23,482	3,416	936	1,318	15,503	2,308	3,975	2,628	1,008	339	1,581
Colorado	1,976	232	125	62	1,238	318	537	342	91	103	293
Connecticut	2,576	278	64	86	1,878	270	589	493	79	17	126
Delaware	489	30	18	13	361	67	131	120	3	8	57
District of Columbia	1,339	154	85	38	763	299	416	150	260	7	1,222
Florida	8,355	735	286	184	6,076	1,074	1,811	1,496	135	180	557
Georgia	5,349	449	192	111	4,078	519	1,052	873	96	82	274
Hawaii	687	70	34	29	461	94	176	122	33	21	102
Idaho	786	38	41	8	601	97	262	206	7	49	125
Illinois	7,064	600	341	389	4,783	952	1,324	889	259	177	404
Indiana	3,593	258	113	66	2,798	357	646	560	29	56	190
Iowa	2,080	118	65	40	1,667	189	404	333	22	50	128
Kansas	1,582	104	77	43	1,187	171	399	360	18	21	101
Kentucky	3,440	159	134	64	2,792	290	616	524	22	71	226
Louisiana	4,367	221	161	67	3,596	322	541	448	36	57	177
Maine	1,271	80	35	40	1,011	104	187	162	8	17	118
Maryland	3,034	306	99	158	2,023	448	727	572	105	50	255
Massachusetts	5,531	507	141	96	4,258	528	673	505	131	37	302
Michigan	6,871	926	275	242	4,649	779	1,014	823	89	102	345
Minnesota	3,375	334	109	104	2,419	409	595	384	108	104	243
Mississippi	2,803	149	179	18	2,243	214	459	385	5	69	173
Missouri	4,315	195	147	81	3,495	396	862	727	36	100	249
Montana	654	69	40	13	440	91	342	295	5	42	203
Nebraska	1,152	53	47	35	866	152	233	193	10	29	120
Nevada	736	57	31	22	485	142	234	161	16	56	176
New Hampshire	678	39	20	13	519	87	195	141	8	45	110
New Jersey	6,031	740	156	82	4,384	669	1,039	710	291	38	282
New Mexico	1,743	110	69	25	1,375	164	334	302	8	24	417
New York	24,769	2,783	515	652	19,187	1,632	2,173	1,274	773	126	901
North Carolina	5,615	361	192	84	4,395	584	1,087	959	42	86	329
North Dakota	479	29	33	15	340	61	244	216	4	24	119
Ohio	8,274	773	296	361	5,931	913	1,167	901	137	129	340
Oklahoma	2,347	150	123	44	1,751	279	432	347	20	65	246
Oregon	2,235	175	111	53	1,661	234	595	272	122	200	305
Pennsylvania	9,449	711	265	395	7,127	952	1,741	1,345	269	127	392
Rhode Island	1,027	90	32	18	796	92	221	171	26	24	85
South Carolina	2,988	131	103	51	2,415	289	482	411	14	58	170
South Dakota	539	22	44	7	391	75	241	199	5	37	178
Tennessee	4,651	248	138	39	3,813	413	617	521	39	57	375
Texas	11,949	555	589	193	9,196	1,417	2,722	2,209	271	243	631
Utah	1,063	91	52	26	749	146	321	239	55	27	198
Vermont	605	51	21	20	452	60	146	134	3	9	68
Virginia	3,002	178	181	93	2,138	412	1,036	882	66	87	290
Washington	3,988	491	155	77	2,785	480	775	548	106	121	420
West Virginia	1,686	182	57	34	1,248	165	437	318	8	111	159
Wisconsin	3,764	444	125	111	2,694	390	681	587	36	58	241
Wyoming	277	14	19	3	192	49	262	224	2	36	451
Island areas:	844	67	250	-	290	237	322	67	180	75	905
American Samoa	17	-	6	-	4	6	28	-	-	28	43
Micronesia	1	-	-	-	-	1	-	-	-	-	-
Guam	27	3	5	-	8	11	21	20	-	1	76
Marshall Islands	-	-	-	-	-	-	-	-	-	-	-
Northern Marianas	7	-	-	-	3	3	15	2	-	13	28
Palau	-	-	-	-	-	-	-	-	-	-	-
Puerto Rico	752	61	231	-	265	195	231	40	179	12	462
Virgin Islands	40	3	9	-	8	20	26	5	1	20	105
Undistributed amounts	10	-	5	-	-	5	780	828	20	-68	42

- Represents or rounds to zero. [1] Includes programs not shown separately. [2] Includes "special milk program." [3] For Puerto Rico, amount shown is for nutritional assistance grant program, all other amounts are grant payments for food stamp administration. [4] FEMA = Federal Emergency Management Agency.

Source: U.S. Census Bureau, *Federal Aid to States For Fiscal Year 2002* (Issued May 2003). See also <http://www.census.gov/prod/2003pubs/fas02.pdf>.

No. 440. State and Local Government Receipts and Current Expenditures in the National Income and Product Accounts: 1980 to 2002

[In billions of dollars (316.6 represents $316,600,000,000). For explanation of national income, see text, Section 13]

Item	1980	1990	1994	1995	1996	1997	1998	1999	2000	2001	2002
Current receipts	316.6	663.4	873.8	917.9	960.4	1,011.3	1,074.4	1,144.1	1,214.2	1,261.3	1,304.9
Personal tax and nontax receipts	53.9	136.0	174.8	186.5	199.6	216.9	235.5	255.8	277.5	281.2	266.6
Income taxes	42.6	107.7	133.4	142.5	152.9	167.6	182.7	199.7	218.1	218.7	200.7
Nontaxes	5.0	15.6	25.0	27.1	29.2	31.1	33.7	36.1	39.0	41.9	45.1
Other	6.3	12.8	16.4	17.0	17.5	18.2	19.2	20.0	20.4	20.6	20.7
Corporate profits tax accruals	14.5	22.5	30.0	31.7	33.0	34.2	34.6	34.8	35.6	29.1	33.5
Indirect business tax and nontax accruals [1]	172.3	383.4	480.1	501.6	524.9	552.5	583.9	612.7	644.5	664.4	689.8
Sales taxes	82.9	183.2	230.9	243.6	255.6	269.3	284.2	300.6	314.3	321.2	333.5
Property taxes	68.8	161.1	197.6	203.5	211.4	220.3	230.3	239.2	248.1	257.4	267.8
Contributions for social insurance	3.6	10.0	14.5	13.6	12.5	10.8	10.1	9.7	9.2	9.2	9.4
Federal grants-in-aid	72.3	111.4	174.5	184.5	190.4	196.8	210.3	231.0	247.5	277.4	305.7
Current expenditures	307.8	660.8	865.2	902.5	939.0	980.3	1,033.7	1,105.8	1,196.2	1,292.6	1,356.4
Consumption expenditures	260.5	545.8	662.6	694.7	726.5	766.4	808.3	864.7	937.9	993.7	1034.5
Transfer payments to persons	51.2	127.8	206.9	217.8	224.3	227.5	235.3	252.7	271.3	304.4	335.6
Net interest paid	-5.4	-6.3	4.4	0.5	0.9	-0.9	0.4	-0.7	-2.8	-2.1	-2.0
Interest received by government	24.7	66.7	61.3	67.3	69.5	73.5	75.0	79.4	84.2	85.4	87.1
Less: Dividends received	0.1	0.2	0.2	0.3	0.3	0.3	0.3	0.4	0.4	0.4	0.5
Subsidies	0.4	0.4	0.3	0.3	0.3	0.4	0.4	0.4	0.4	7.8	0.8
Less: Current surplus of government enterprises	-1.2	6.7	8.8	10.5	12.8	12.8	10.3	10.9	10.2	10.9	12.0
Current surplus or deficit	8.8	2.6	8.6	15.3	21.4	31.0	40.7	38.3	18.0	-31.3	-51.5
Social insurance funds	1.3	2.0	4.6	4.0	2.7	1.1	0.6	0.9	0.1	-0.1	-0.1
Other	7.5	0.7	4.0	11.4	18.7	29.9	40.0	37.4	17.8	-31.2	-51.4

[1] Includes other items not shown separately.

Source: U.S. Bureau of Economic Analysis, *National Income and Product Accounts, 1929-97;* and Survey of Current Business, May 2003 <http://www.bea.gov/bea/dn/nipaweb/selecttable.asp?selected=N> (accessed 30 May 2003).

No. 441. State and Local Government Consumption Expenditures and Transfers in the National Income and Product Accounts: 1980 to 2002

[In billions of dollars (324.4 represents $324,400,000,000). For explanation of national income, see text, Section 13]

Expenditure	1980	1990	1995	1996	1997	1998	1999	2000	2001	2002
Consumption expenditures and gross investment [1]	324.4	673.0	850.5	890.4	949.7	999.3	1,076.0	1,161.8	1,229.9	1,279.2
Consumption expenditures	260.5	545.8	694.7	726.5	766.4	808.3	864.7	937.9	993.7	1034.5
Durable goods [2]	4.7	10.6	12.7	13.1	13.8	14.8	15.9	17.1	18.3	19.4
Nondurable goods	28.3	53.6	72.9	79.9	81.7	83.4	94.0	114.0	118.7	121.1
Services	227.5	481.5	609.0	633.6	670.9	710.1	754.7	806.8	856.7	894.0
Gross investment	64.0	127.2	155.8	163.8	183.3	191.0	211.3	223.9	236.2	244.7
Structures	55.1	98.5	117.3	122.5	139.3	142.4	158.3	167.4	177.6	188.2
Equipment	8.9	28.7	38.6	41.3	44.0	48.6	53.0	56.5	58.6	56.5
Transfers	51.2	127.8	217.8	224.3	227.5	235.3	252.7	271.3	304.4	335.6
Benefits from social insurance funds	2.8	9.2	10.7	10.9	10.7	10.4	10.6	11.0	11.3	(NA)
Temporary disability insurance	0.8	2.2	2.1	2.0	2.0	2.1	2.2	2.3	2.4	(NA)
Public assistance	44.0	111.1	195.8	201.9	205.0	212.1	228.6	245.7	277.3	(NA)
Medical care	24.9	78.2	155.0	163.6	168.3	175.0	189.7	205.4	234.7	(NA)
Medicaid	23.9	73.1	149.6	158.2	163.1	170.0	184.6	199.6	227.3	(NA)
Family assistance [3]	12.5	19.2	22.6	20.3	17.7	17.0	17.7	18.3	19.2	(NA)
Supplemental security income	2.0	3.8	3.8	3.6	3.7	3.9	4.2	4.4	4.5	(NA)
General assistance	1.4	2.9	3.5	3.3	3.3	3.5	3.6	3.7	3.3	(NA)
Energy assistance	1.3	1.6	1.5	1.3	1.4	1.3	1.4	1.7	2.5	(NA)
Other [4]	1.7	5.4	9.4	9.7	10.6	11.4	11.9	12.3	13.1	(NA)
Education	2.4	5.3	8.7	9.1	9.1	9.8	10.5	11.3	12.2	(NA)
Employment and training	1.7	0.9	1.1	0.9	1.0	1.1	1.0	1.2	1.4	(NA)
Other [5]	0.3	1.2	1.5	1.6	1.6	1.8	2.0	2.2	2.2	(NA)

NA Not available. [1] Gross government investment consists of general government and government enterprise expenditures for fixed assets; inventory investment is included in government consumption expenditures. [2] Consumption expenditures for durable goods excludes expenditures classified as investment, except for goods transferred to foreign countries by the Federal Government. [3] Consists of aid to families with dependent children. Beginning with 1996, assistance programs operating under the Personal Responsibility and work opportunity Act of 1996. [4] Consists of expenditures for food under the supplemental program for women, infants, and children, foster care adoption assistance; and payments to nonprofit payments paid on behalf of indigents. [5] Consists largely of veterans benefits, Alaska dividends, and crime-victim payments.

Source: U.S. Bureau of Economic Analysis, *National Income and Product Accounts, 1929-97;* and Survey of Current Business, May 2003 <http://www.bea.gov/bea/dn/nipaweb/selecttable.asp?selected=N> (accessed 30 May 2003).

No. 442. State and Local Governments—Summary of Finances: 1980 to 2000

[In millions of dollars (451,537 represents $451,537,000,000), except as indicated. For fiscal year ending in year shown; see text, this section. Local government amounts are estimates subject to sampling variation; see Appendix III and source]

Item	Total (mil. dol.) 1980	1990	1999	2000	Per capita [1] (dol.) 1980	1990	1999	2000
Revenue [2]	451,537	1,032,115	1,794,557	1,942,328	1,993	4,150	6,581	6,902
From federal government	83,029	136,802	270,628	291,950	367	550	992	1,037
Public welfare	24,921	59,961	136,571	148,549	110	241	501	528
Highways	8,980	14,368	21,492	24,414	40	58	79	87
Education	14,435	23,233	42,051	45,873	64	93	154	163
Health and hospitals	2,513	5,904	14,516	15,611	11	24	53	55
Housing and community development	3,905	9,655	18,044	17,690	17	39	66	63
Other and unallocable	28,275	23,683	37,954	39,812	125	95	139	141
From state and local sources	368,509	895,313	1,523,929	1,650,379	1,627	3,600	5,588	5,864
General, net intergovernmental	299,293	712,700	1,163,836	1,249,373	1,321	2,865	4,268	4,439
Taxes	223,463	501,619	815,777	872,351	986	2,017	2,992	3,100
Property	68,499	155,613	240,107	249,178	302	626	881	885
Sales and gross receipts	79,927	177,885	290,993	309,290	353	715	1,067	1,099
Individual income	42,080	105,640	189,309	211,661	186	425	694	752
Corporation income	13,321	23,566	33,922	36,059	59	95	124	128
Other	19,636	38,915	61,446	66,164	87	156	225	235
Charges and miscellaneous	75,830	211,081	348,060	377,022	335	849	1,276	1,340
Utility and liquor stores	25,560	58,642	86,125	89,546	113	236	316	318
Water supply system	6,766	17,674	29,039	30,515	30	71	106	108
Electric power system	11,387	29,268	40,890	42,436	50	118	150	151
Gas supply system	2,397	5,216	7,708	8,049	8	12	16	14
Transit system	1,809	3,043	4,244	3,954	11	21	28	29
Liquor stores	3,201	3,441	4,245	4,592	14	14	16	16
Insurance trust revenue [3]	43,656	123,970	273,968	311,460	193	498	1,005	1,107
Employee retirement	25,441	94,268	236,527	273,881	112	379	867	973
Unemployment compensation	13,529	18,441	22,234	23,366	60	74	82	83
Direct expenditure	432,328	972,695	1,622,103	1,742,914	1,908	3,911	5,949	6,193
By function:								
Direct general expenditure [3]	367,340	831,573	1,398,533	1,502,768	1,622	3,356	5,129	5,340
Education [3]	133,211	288,148	483,259	521,612	588	1,159	1,772	1,853
Elementary and secondary	92,930	202,009	339,871	365,181	410	812	1,246	1,298
Higher education	33,919	73,418	122,716	134,352	150	295	450	477
Highways	33,311	61,057	93,018	101,336	147	245	341	360
Public welfare	45,552	107,287	215,190	233,350	201	444	789	829
Health	8,387	24,223	47,628	51,366	37	97	175	183
Hospitals	23,787	50,412	71,733	75,976	105	203	263	270
Police protection	13,494	30,577	53,367	56,798	60	123	196	202
Fire protection	5,718	13,186	21,262	23,102	25	53	78	82
Correction	6,448	24,635	45,598	48,805	28	100	167	173
Natural resources	5,509	12,330	18,232	20,235	24	50	67	72
Sanitation and sewerage	13,214	28,453	43,047	45,261	58	114	158	161
Housing and community development	6,062	15,479	25,234	26,590	27	62	93	94
Parks and recreation	6,520	14,326	23,417	25,038	29	58	86	89
Financial administration	6,719	16,217	27,593	29,300	30	65	101	104
Interest on general debt [4]	14,747	49,739	67,294	69,814	65	200	247	248
Utility and liquor stores [4]	36,191	77,801	108,398	114,916	160	313	398	408
Water supply system	9,228	22,101	34,089	35,789	41	89	125	127
Electric power system	15,016	30,997	38,132	39,719	66	125	140	141
Transit system	7,641	2,989	4,108	3,724	34	76	105	113
Gas supply system	1,715	18,788	28,522	31,883	8	12	15	13
Liquor stores	2,591	2,926	3,547	3,801	11	12	13	14
Insurance trust expenditure [3]	28,797	63,321	115,172	125,230	127	255	422	445
Employee retirement	14,008	38,355	85,318	95,679	56	154	313	340
Unemployment compensation	12,070	16,499	19,223	18,648	53	66	70	66
By character and object:								
Current operation	307,811	700,131	1,199,494	1,288,746	1,359	2,815	4,399	4,579
Capital outlay	62,894	123,102	198,483	217,063	278	495	728	771
Construction	51,492	89,144	147,181	161,694	227	358	540	575
Equipment, land, and existing structures	11,402	33,958	51,302	55,369	50	137	188	197
Assistance and subsidies	15,222	27,227	31,494	31,375	67	109	115	111
Interest on debt (general and utility)	17,604	58,914	77,459	80,499	78	237	284	286
Insurance benefits and repayments	28,797	63,321	115,172	125,230	127	255	422	445
Expenditure for salaries and wages [5]	163,896	340,654	522,528	548,796	723	1,372	1,916	1,950
Debt outstanding, year	335,603	858,006	1,369,253	1,451,815	1,481	3,460	5,021	5,159
Long-term	322,456	838,700	1,351,408	1,427,524	1,423	3,382	4,956	5,073
Short-term	13,147	19,306	17,844	24,291	58	78	65	86
Long-term debt:								
Issued	42,364	108,468	229,374	184,831	187	436	841	657
Retired	17,404	64,831	153,100	121,897	77	261	561	433

[1] 1980, 1990, and 2000 based on enumerated resident population as of April 1. Other years based on estimated resident population as of July 1; see Table 17. [2] Aggregates exclude duplicative transactions between state and local governments; see source. [3] Includes amounts not shown separately. [4] Interest on utility debt included in "utility expenditure." For total interest on debt, see "Interest on debt (general and utility)." [5] Included in items above.

Source: U.S. Census Bureau, "Government Finances: 1999-2000." See also "Government Finances," annual. See also <http:// www.census.gov/govs/estimate/00allpub.pdf> (issued January 2003).

State and Local Government Finances and Employment 285

No. 443. State and Local Governments—Revenue and Expenditures by Function: 2000

[In millions of dollars (1,942,328 represents $1,942,328,000,000) except as indicated. For fiscal year ending in year shown; see text, this section. Local government amounts are estimates subject to sampling variation; see Appendix III and source]

Item	Amount (mil. dol.) State and local	State	Local	Per capita [1] (dol.) State and local	State	Local
Revenue [2]	1,942,328	1,260,829	1,013,825	6,902	4,489	3,603
Intergovernmental revenue	291,950	274,382	349,894	1,037	977	1,243
Total revenue from own sources	1,650,379	986,448	663,931	5,864	3,512	2,359
General revenue from own sources	1,249,373	710,402	538,971	4,439	2,529	1,915
Taxes [3]	872,351	539,655	332,696	3,100	1,922	1,182
Property	249,178	10,996	238,182	885	39	846
Individual income	211,661	194,573	17,088	752	693	61
Corporation income	36,059	32,522	3,537	128	116	13
Sales and gross receipts	309,290	252,147	57,143	1,099	898	203
General	215,112	174,461	40,651	764	621	144
Selective [3]	94,177	77,685	16,492	335	277	59
Motor fuel	30,939	29,968	971	110	107	3
Alcoholic beverages	4,393	4,104	289	16	15	1
Tobacco products	8,585	8,391	193	31	30	1
Public utilities	17,831	9,231	8,600	63	33	31
Motor vehicle and operators' licenses	17,749	16,445	1,303	63	59	5
Death and gift	8,034	7,998	36	29	28	-
Charges and miscellaneous [3]	377,022	170,747	206,275	1,340	608	733
Current charges [3]	223,480	86,467	137,013	794	308	487
Education [3]	65,562	49,932	15,630	233	178	56
School lunch sales	5,450	16	5,434	19	-	19
Higher education	55,292	49,384	5,908	196	176	21
Natural resources	2,967	1,801	1,167	11	6	4
Hospitals	54,619	18,584	36,036	194	66	128
Sewerage	24,311	39	24,273	86	-	86
Solid waste management	10,225	388	9,837	36	1	35
Parks and recreation	6,274	1,132	5,142	22	4	18
Housing and community development	4,207	437	3,770	15	2	13
Airports	11,083	852	10,231	39	3	36
Sea and inland port facilities	2,507	693	1,813	9	2	6
Highways	7,392	4,660	2,732	26	17	10
Interest earnings	70,490	35,008	35,482	250	125	126
Special assessments	3,815	81	3,734	14	-	13
Sale of property	2,021	476	1,545	7	2	5
Utility and liquor store revenue	89,546	8,407	81,138	318	30	288
Insurance trust revenue	311,460	267,639	43,822	1,107	953	156
Expenditure	1,746,943	1,084,097	996,267	6,208	3,860	3,540
Intergovernmental expenditure	4,029	327,070	10,380	14	1,165	37
Direct expenditure	1,742,914	757,027	985,886	6,193	2,695	3,503
General expenditure [3]	1,502,768	637,653	865,114	5,340	2,270	3,074
Education [3]	521,612	138,330	383,282	1,853	493	1,362
Elementary and secondary education	365,181	3,381	361,800	1,298	12	1,286
Higher education	134,352	112,869	21,483	477	402	76
Public welfare	233,350	198,684	34,666	829	707	123
Hospitals	75,976	32,154	43,822	270	114	156
Health	51,366	27,375	23,991	183	97	85
Highways	101,336	61,942	39,394	360	221	140
Police protection	56,798	8,581	48,217	202	31	171
Fire protection	23,102	-	23,102	82	-	82
Corrections	48,805	33,040	15,766	173	118	56
Natural resources	20,235	15,001	5,234	72	53	19
Sewerage	28,052	955	27,098	100	3	96
Solid waste management	17,208	2,347	14,861	61	8	53
Housing and community development	26,590	3,163	23,427	94	11	83
Governmental administration	81,659	34,500	47,160	290	123	168
Parks and recreation	25,038	4,049	20,989	89	14	75
Interest on general debt	69,814	29,187	40,626	248	104	144
Utility	111,115	10,723	100,393	395	38	357
Liquor store expenditure	3,801	3,195	606	14	11	2
Insurance trust expenditure	125,230	105,456	19,774	445	375	70
By character and object:						
Current operation	1,288,746	523,114	765,633	4,579	1,863	2,721
Capital outlay	217,063	76,233	140,830	771	271	500
Construction	161,694	59,681	102,013	575	213	362
Equip., land, and existing structures	55,369	16,552	38,817	197	59	138
Assistance and subsidies	31,375	22,136	9,239	111	79	33
Interest on debt (general and utility)	80,499	30,089	50,410	286	107	179
Insurance benefits and repayments	125,230	105,456	19,774	445	375	70
Expenditure for salaries and wages [4]	548,796	154,504	394,292	1,950	550	1,401

- Represents or rounds to zero. [1] 1980, 1990, and 2000 based on enumerated resident population as of April 1. Other years based on estimated resident population as of July 1; see Table 17. [2] Aggregates exclude duplicative transactions between levels of government; see source. [3] Includes amounts not shown separately. [4] Included in items shown above.

Source: U.S. Census Bureau, "Governmental Finances: 1999-2000," at Internet site <http://www.census.gov/govs/estimate/00allpub.pdf> (released January 2003).

No. 444. State and Local Governments—Capital Outlays: 1985 to 2000

[In millions of dollars (79,898 represents $79,898,000,000), except percent. For fiscal year ending in year shown; see text, this section. Local government amounts are subject to sampling variation; see Appendix III and source]

Level and function	1985	1990	1995	1996	1997	1998	1999	2000
State & local governments: Total	79,898	123,102	151,440	158,911	171,414	181,871	198,483	217,063
Annual percent change [1]	13.1	4.9	1.2	10.1	4.9	6.1	9.1	9.4
Direct expenditure	656,188	972,695	1,347,763	1,393,714	1,456,698	1,525,762	1,622,103	1,742,914
Percent of direct expenditure	12.2	12.7	11.2	11.4	11.8	11.9	12.2	12.5
By function: Education [2]	13,477	25,997	35,708	40,302	44,077	49,332	54,418	60,968
Higher education	4,629	18,057	24,808	28,868	32,210	36,198	13,114	15,257
Elementary and secondary	8,358	7,441	10,461	11,006	11,279	12,590	40,768	45,150
Highways	23,900	33,867	42,561	43,453	44,962	48,067	51,906	56,439
Health and hospitals	2,709	3,848	4,883	5,166	5,065	5,692	5,699	5,502
Natural resources	1,736	2,545	2,891	3,042	3,041	3,206	3,359	4,347
Housing [3]	3,217	3,997	4,527	4,704	5,490	5,544	5,615	6,184
Air transportation	1,875	3,434	3,802	3,814	4,877	5,004	6,666	6,717
Water transportation [4]	717	924	1,101	1,246	1,376	1,252	1,487	1,618
Sewerage	5,926	8,356	8,894	9,326	9,589	9,061	9,718	10,093
Parks and recreation	2,196	3,877	4,085	4,869	5,577	6,154	6,486	6,916
Utilities	13,435	16,601	19,028	18,755	20,107	20,357	21,861	24,847
Water	4,160	6,873	7,466	7,381	8,721	8,644	10,325	10,542
Electric	5,247	3,976	3,715	3,522	3,459	3,026	3,613	4,177
Transit	3,830	310	340	318	399	986	7,533	9,728
Gas	198	5,443	7,507	7,533	7,528	7,701	389	400
Other	10,711	19,657	23,961	24,233	27,254	28,202	31,268	33,431
State governments: Total	30,657	45,524	57,829	58,927	59,599	64,441	68,509	76,233
Annual percent change [1]	16.3	5.6	5.5	9.3	1.9	8.1	6.3	11.3
Direct expenditure	269,171	397,291	596,325	607,594	629,049	651,098	693,432	757,027
Percent of direct expenditure	11.4	11.5	9.7	9.7	9.5	9.9	9.9	10.1
By function: Education [2]	4,711	7,253	10,042	10,445	10,915	11,970	12,294	14,077
Highways	17,827	24,850	31,687	32,198	32,726	35,008	37,986	41,651
Health and hospitals	1,038	1,531	2,402	2,375	2,253	2,274	2,276	2,228
Natural resources	1,076	1,593	1,956	2,044	2,058	2,199	2,349	2,758
Housing [3]	38	119	187	263	225	202	202	860
Air transportation	280	339	356	356	446	339	536	561
Water transportation [4]	274	202	223	305	269	305	270	310
Sewerage	187	333	853	913	474	639	627	403
Parks and recreation	351	601	650	706	938	1,293	1,023	1,044
Utilities	1,825	2,605	2,226	2,607	2,361	2,758	3,034	4,232
Other	3,051	6,098	7,246	6,716	6,934	7,454	7,912	8,108
Local governments: Total	49,241	77,578	93,611	99,984	111,814	117,430	129,974	140,830
Annual percent change [1]	16.2	4.5	10.6	6.8	11.8	5.0	10.7	8.4
Direct expenditure	386,753	575,404	751,438	786,120	827,648	874,664	928,671	985,886
Percent of direct expenditure	12.7	13.5	12.5	12.7	13.5	13.4	14.0	14.3
By function: Education [2]	8,766	18,744	25,667	29,858	33,162	37,362	42,124	46,890
Highways	6,073	9,017	10,874	11,255	12,235	13,059	13,920	14,789
Health and hospitals	1,671	2,316	2,481	2,790	2,811	3,418	3,423	3,274
Natural resources	660	952	935	998	983	1,007	1,010	1,589
Housing [3]	3,179	3,878	4,340	4,441	5,265	5,342	5,413	5,324
Air transportation	1,595	3,095	3,446	3,458	4,431	4,665	6,129	6,156
Water transportation [4]	443	722	877	941	1,107	947	1,217	1,308
Sewerage	5,738	8,023	8,040	8,413	9,116	8,422	9,091	9,690
Parks and recreation	1,845	3,276	3,435	4,163	4,639	4,861	5,463	5,872
Utilities	11,610	13,996	16,801	16,149	17,746	17,599	18,827	20,615
Other	7,660	13,559	16,715	17,518	20,320	20,748	23,356	25,323

[1] Change from prior year shown. [2] Includes other education. [3] Includes community development. [4] Includes terminals.
Source: U.S. Census Bureau; 1980-92 *Historical Statistics on Governmental Finances and Employment*; and *Government Finances*, Series GF, No. 5, annual; thereafter, <http://www.census.gov/govs/estimates/00allpub.pdf>; (accessed 16 June 2003).

No. 445. State and Local Governments—Expenditure for Public Works: 1990 to 2000

[In millions of dollars (161,359 represents $161,359,000,000) except percent. Public works include expenditures on highways, airports, water transport terminals, and sewerage, solid waste management, water supply, and mass transit systems. Represents direct expenditures excluding intergovernmental grants]

Item	Total	Highways	Airport transportation	Water transport and terminals	Sewerage	Solid waste management	Water supply	Mass transit
1990, total	161,359	68,370	9,290	2,168	22,785	12,829	24,621	21,296
State	50,206	42,056	915	572	1,097	1,304	188	4,074
Local	111,153	26,314	8,375	1,596	21,688	11,525	24,433	17,222
Capital expenditures (percent)	41.4	54.1	58.3	45.9	45.0	11.4	26.4	24.7
1995, total	180,148	77,109	8,397	2,309	23,583	14,990	28,041	25,719
State	56,392	46,893	783	604	1,462	1,658	178	4,814
Local	123,756	30,216	7,614	1,706	22,121	13,331	27,863	20,904
Capital expenditures (percent)	40.7	55.2	45.3	47.7	37.7	13.2	26.6	29.2
1999, total	214,378	93,018	12,632	3,070	26,980	16,067	34,089	28,522
State	67,392	56,242	1,013	798	1,128	1,958	164	6,089
Local	146,986	36,776	11,619	2,273	25,852	14,110	33,924	22,433
Capital expenditures (percent)	41.5	55.8	52.8	48.4	36.0	8.5	30.3	26.4
2000, total	230,569	101,336	13,160	3,141	28,052	17,208	35,789	31,883
State	74,974	61,942	1,106	863	955	2,347	354	7,407
Local	155,595	39,394	12,054	2,277	27,098	14,861	35,435	24,476
Capital expenditures (percent)	41.9	55.7	51.0	51.5	36.0	8.9	29.5	30.5

Source: U.S. Census Bureau; 1990-92, "Government Finances, Series GF, No. 5, annual; thereafter, <http://www.census.gov/govs/estimate/00allpub.pdf>; (accessed 16 June 2003), *State and Local Government Finance Estimates by State*, annual, and unpublished data.

State and Local Government Finances and Employment

No. 446. State and Local Governments—Revenue by State: 2000

[In millions of dollars (1,942,328 represents $1,942,328,000,000). For fiscal year ending in year shown; see text, this section]

State	Total revenue [1]	General revenue Total	Intergovernmental from federal government	General revenue own sources	Taxes Total [1]	Property	Sales and gross receipts	Income [2]	Motor vehicle	Other taxes
United States ...	1,942,328	1,541,322	291,950	1,249,372	872,351	249,178	309,290	247,720	16,401	49,763
Alabama.........	25,726	21,012	5,087	15,925	9,415	1,340	4,586	2,402	213	874
Alaska..........	10,525	9,042	1,411	7,631	2,312	761	284	438	46	782
Arizona.........	27,778	22,863	4,475	18,388	13,334	3,906	6,070	2,815	153	389
Arkansas........	13,833	11,582	2,823	8,759	5,961	966	2,947	1,707	118	224
California.......	270,380	208,373	38,476	169,897	120,068	26,235	39,695	46,213	1,764	6,160
Colorado.........	29,603	23,436	3,711	19,725	13,216	3,680	4,848	3,972	209	508
Connecticut......	25,828	23,108	3,674	19,434	15,651	5,407	5,054	4,400	233	556
Delaware........	6,224	5,203	830	4,373	2,619	382	298	1,015	33	891
District of Columbia.	6,383	5,732	1,748	3,984	3,216	693	1,000	1,339	17	168
Florida..........	92,402	75,865	11,718	64,147	41,937	14,098	22,264	1,183	955	3,436
Georgia.........	49,310	39,690	7,070	32,620	23,254	5,932	9,298	7,077	236	711
Hawaii..........	8,488	7,092	1,294	5,798	4,102	603	2,141	1,140	127	91
Idaho...........	7,590	6,077	1,150	4,927	3,294	867	1,070	1,091	113	153
Illinois..........	80,695	64,420	10,791	53,629	40,256	14,511	13,376	9,898	1,115	1,355
Indiana..........	32,716	29,749	5,169	24,580	16,363	5,552	5,113	5,193	161	345
Iowa............	17,220	15,134	2,885	12,249	8,091	2,599	2,698	2,143	349	302
Kansas..........	16,235	13,391	2,482	10,909	7,616	2,173	2,886	2,134	146	277
Kentucky........	25,200	19,423	4,595	14,828	10,172	1,722	3,686	3,755	208	801
Louisiana........	27,109	22,342	5,070	17,272	10,887	1,742	6,227	1,804	114	1,001
Maine...........	8,554	7,440	1,630	5,810	4,262	1,598	1,195	1,227	81	161
Maryland........	33,949	29,076	4,609	24,467	18,290	4,809	4,622	7,586	179	1,094
Massachusetts.....	46,103	38,295	6,439	31,856	24,042	7,643	5,156	10,348	228	667
Michigan........	70,112	56,415	10,331	46,084	31,474	9,499	9,906	10,112	817	1,141
Minnesota.......	38,785	30,957	4,769	26,188	18,173	4,565	5,909	6,351	646	702
Mississippi......	16,672	13,590	3,528	10,062	6,299	1,462	3,202	1,234	113	288
Missouri.........	31,635	25,905	5,628	20,277	14,314	3,405	5,833	4,115	252	709
Montana.........	5,643	4,856	1,306	3,550	2,132	908	346	616	68	194
Nebraska........	11,650	9,021	1,710	7,311	4,973	1,549	1,690	1,314	103	317
Nevada..........	11,885	9,592	1,233	8,359	5,825	1,437	3,586	-	114	688
New Hampshire....	6,948	5,755	1,062	4,693	2,028	1,028	556	378	65	252
New Jersey......	62,331	51,504	7,883	43,621	32,838	14,449	8,229	8,585	353	1,222
New Mexico......	13,073	10,062	2,398	7,664	4,801	620	2,434	1,040	142	564
New York........	188,907	143,901	29,249	114,652	86,868	25,202	22,465	34,687	784	3,731
North Carolina....	50,542	41,131	9,051	32,080	21,440	4,607	7,201	8,407	410	815
North Dakota.....	4,495	3,914	1,126	2,788	1,768	527	714	277	44	206
Ohio............	80,074	59,017	10,933	48,084	34,239	9,544	10,353	12,082	714	1,545
Oklahoma........	18,760	15,698	3,181	12,517	8,251	1,303	3,234	2,329	635	751
Oregon..........	28,644	20,969	5,233	15,736	9,412	2,789	912	4,505	375	832
Pennsylvania.....	80,546	64,615	12,498	52,117	36,581	10,067	10,837	10,981	791	3,905
Rhode Island.....	7,427	5,748	1,196	4,552	3,412	1,360	1,004	904	51	93
South Carolina....	23,467	19,727	4,377	15,350	9,543	2,680	3,480	2,673	124	587
South Dakota.....	4,277	3,491	869	2,622	1,736	632	874	45	58	127
Tennessee.......	33,625	24,824	6,321	18,503	12,431	2,887	7,316	794	330	1,104
Texas...........	120,666	95,539	18,576	76,963	52,227	19,817	26,579	-	1,200	4,630
Utah............	14,954	11,208	2,172	9,036	5,873	1,303	2,430	1,825	80	234
Vermont.........	4,019	3,497	903	2,594	1,876	782	485	476	35	97
Virginia..........	44,175	35,434	5,010	30,424	21,083	5,986	5,970	7,395	431	1,301
Washington......	46,372	33,426	5,828	27,598	18,734	5,493	11,481	-	416	1,344
West Virginia.....	10,760	9,055	2,489	6,566	4,362	855	1,836	1,184	88	399
Wisconsin........	43,003	30,572	5,059	25,513	18,547	5,689	5,331	6,530	304	691
Wyoming........	7,030	3,554	891	2,663	1,505	513	583	-	62	347

See footnotes at end of table.

No. 446. State and Local Governments—Revenue by State: 2000—Con.

[In millions of dollars (377,022 represents $377,022,000,000). For fiscal year ending in year shown; see text, this section]

State	General revenue								Utility and liquor stores	Insurance trust revenue
		Current charges and miscellaneous revenue								
		Current charges				Miscellaneous revenue				
	Total	Total [1]	Education	Hospitals	Sewerage	Total [1]	Interest earnings	Special assessment		
United States	377,022	223,480	65,562	54,619	24,311	153,542	70,490	3,815	89,546	311,460
Alabama	6,510	4,836	1,294	2,535	232	1,674	805	9	1,895	2,819
Alaska	5,320	725	136	52	47	4,595	2,275	3	230	1,254
Arizona	5,054	2,618	1,063	219	294	2,436	1,161	62	2,656	2,259
Arkansas	2,798	1,757	574	645	152	1,041	490	11	535	1,716
California	49,830	30,900	6,855	6,408	3,143	18,930	8,741	967	13,846	48,161
Colorado	6,508	3,989	1,431	602	399	2,519	1,205	66	1,424	4,744
Connecticut	3,784	1,610	544	231	191	2,174	902	28	497	2,223
Delaware	1,754	835	346	38	108	919	347	-	156	865
District of Columbia	769	331	21	53	101	438	196	1	448	202
Florida	22,209	12,871	2,414	2,926	1,458	9,338	3,491	950	5,062	11,476
Georgia	9,367	5,609	1,310	2,060	621	3,758	1,500	19	2,826	6,794
Hawaii	1,696	1,125	223	162	138	571	315	20	185	1,212
Idaho	1,632	1,073	266	349	86	559	301	11	190	1,323
Illinois	13,373	6,974	2,438	754	703	6,399	3,371	89	2,682	13,593
Indiana	8,217	5,289	2,280	1,711	495	2,928	1,216	19	1,307	1,660
Iowa	4,159	2,864	1,121	1,110	229	1,295	534	18	727	1,359
Kansas	3,292	1,898	718	426	179	1,394	698	75	802	2,042
Kentucky	4,656	2,529	1,015	466	251	2,127	1,459	3	962	4,815
Louisiana	6,385	4,235	1,029	2,191	200	2,150	1,038	9	724	4,043
Maine	1,547	724	266	54	114	823	336	3	171	943
Maryland	6,176	3,454	1,477	92	542	2,722	1,044	108	652	4,222
Massachusetts	7,814	3,437	1,139	178	636	4,377	1,907	64	2,006	5,802
Michigan	14,610	8,650	3,876	1,368	1,239	5,960	2,598	94	1,981	11,716
Minnesota	8,015	4,241	1,320	833	581	3,774	1,470	252	1,383	6,445
Mississippi	3,763	2,707	633	1,521	135	1,056	458	5	702	2,381
Missouri	5,963	3,706	1,332	1,076	385	2,257	1,299	20	1,273	4,457
Montana	1,418	666	287	57	55	752	313	42	121	666
Nebraska	2,337	1,332	539	312	108	1,005	435	31	2,019	611
Nevada	2,534	1,725	320	485	209	809	471	40	514	1,780
New Hampshire	1,414	746	352	5	74	668	413	1	366	827
New Jersey	10,784	6,002	1,751	570	1,033	4,782	1,787	14	1,212	9,615
New Mexico	2,863	1,310	478	429	97	1,553	760	9	328	2,683
New York	27,784	16,806	2,363	4,725	1,304	10,978	4,659	72	8,429	36,576
North Carolina	10,640	7,659	1,873	3,385	855	2,981	1,763	12	2,768	6,642
North Dakota	1,020	624	252	7	28	396	169	33	70	512
Ohio	13,846	8,368	3,395	1,493	1,399	5,478	2,184	106	2,366	18,691
Oklahoma	4,265	2,844	1,097	810	199	1,421	650	5	951	2,111
Oregon	6,324	3,696	985	751	432	2,628	1,153	71	989	6,686
Pennsylvania	15,536	8,848	3,034	1,935	991	6,688	3,488	95	2,702	13,228
Rhode Island	1,139	487	229	4	54	652	319	3	115	1,565
South Carolina	5,807	4,270	1,018	2,144	216	1,537	884	19	1,901	1,839
South Dakota	885	430	168	28	44	455	234	6	145	642
Tennessee	6,072	4,277	1,122	1,662	398	1,795	694	5	5,241	3,560
Texas	24,737	14,453	4,565	3,665	1,791	10,284	5,215	87	6,212	18,915
Utah	3,162	1,887	755	365	150	1,275	550	3	1,332	2,414
Vermont	719	393	264	-	32	326	154	5	182	340
Virginia	9,341	5,725	1,843	1,311	681	3,616	1,687	42	1,442	7,299
Washington	8,865	5,827	1,634	1,163	843	3,038	1,258	93	3,648	9,297
West Virginia	2,203	1,224	415	299	118	979	469	3	179	1,526
Wisconsin	6,967	4,309	1,578	615	513	2,658	1,199	106	863	11,568
Wyoming	1,159	584	124	338	31	575	424	8	133	3,343

- Represents or rounds to zero. [1] Includes items not shown separately. [2] Includes individual and corporate income taxes.

Source: U.S. Census Bureau; "Government Finances: 1999-2000"; issued January 2003, <http://www.census.gov/govs/estimate/00allpub.pdf>; (accessed 16 June 2003).

No. 447. State and Local Governments—Expenditures and Debt by State: 2000

[In millions of dollars (1,746,943 represents $1,746,943,000,000), except as indicated. For fiscal year ending in year shown; see text, this section]

State	Total expenditure [1]	Total Amount	Per capita [2] (dol.)	Direct general expenditures, total	Education	Public welfare	Health and hospitals	Highways	Police protection	Fire protection	Corrections
United States...	1,746,943	1,506,797	5,354	1,502,768	521,612	233,350	127,342	101,336	56,798	23,102	48,805
Alabama	25,319	22,062	4,961	22,062	7,768	3,525	3,635	1,492	656	252	404
Alaska	8,628	7,712	12,302	7,600	1,761	810	235	827	177	66	175
Arizona	27,293	23,262	4,534	23,262	7,871	2,945	1,374	1,959	1,096	682	955
Arkansas	12,245	11,059	4,137	11,057	4,198	1,999	970	870	352	122	328
California	236,645	198,296	5,854	195,767	63,559	29,214	18,055	8,604	8,704	3,588	7,170
Colorado	26,173	22,531	5,238	22,527	7,904	2,731	1,341	1,743	830	327	820
Connecticut	24,011	21,420	6,290	21,420	6,722	3,116	1,596	1,187	682	373	554
Delaware	5,153	4,692	5,987	4,691	1,715	548	279	427	166	19	228
District of Columbia	6,527	5,152	9,006	5,152	969	1,254	633	38	330	113	305
Florida	84,301	75,290	4,711	75,290	22,826	9,506	7,307	5,175	3,738	1,630	3,273
Georgia	43,517	38,078	4,651	38,078	14,768	5,568	3,554	2,496	1,279	553	1,375
Hawaii	8,254	7,306	6,030	7,291	1,854	1,040	600	353	222	101	155
Idaho	6,404	5,828	4,504	5,828	2,132	790	512	561	207	77	191
Illinois	74,727	64,406	5,186	64,403	22,728	8,853	4,382	4,077	3,053	1,300	1,763
Indiana	31,250	28,744	4,727	28,740	11,450	4,264	2,603	1,965	843	395	727
Iowa	17,275	15,599	5,330	15,563	5,964	2,259	1,678	1,836	427	127	298
Kansas	14,419	12,885	4,793	12,884	4,884	1,354	934	1,714	430	175	349
Kentucky	21,473	19,020	4,705	19,020	6,374	4,096	1,097	1,754	488	257	611
Louisiana	25,018	22,277	4,985	22,277	7,185	3,071	3,375	1,652	829	283	780
Maine	7,652	6,964	5,462	6,955	2,228	1,586	397	572	164	78	123
Maryland	30,598	27,446	5,182	27,446	10,055	4,009	1,295	1,487	1,120	475	1,104
Massachusetts	44,362	37,951	5,977	37,770	11,445	6,309	2,245	3,235	1,479	774	795
Michigan	61,506	54,812	5,515	54,750	22,484	8,242	4,179	3,085	1,793	616	1,853
Minnesota	35,424	31,166	6,335	31,166	10,283	5,970	1,826	2,388	874	256	591
Mississippi	15,379	13,932	4,898	13,932	4,818	2,320	2,113	1,231	404	155	292
Missouri	27,953	24,821	4,436	24,818	9,224	4,041	2,166	2,147	885	394	672
Montana	4,983	4,523	5,013	4,523	1,641	555	343	518	136	41	125
Nebraska	10,831	8,417	4,919	8,406	3,267	1,425	521	880	235	107	231
Nevada	11,230	9,762	4,885	9,755	3,020	886	737	1,127	539	223	471
New Hampshire	6,222	5,664	4,583	5,664	2,059	1,113	170	469	187	100	115
New Jersey	54,590	47,309	5,622	47,231	18,788	5,823	2,332	2,341	2,231	630	1,480
New Mexico	11,195	10,099	5,552	10,099	3,696	1,515	812	1,064	382	129	315
New York	171,858	140,646	7,412	140,020	40,630	29,185	11,568	6,835	5,717	2,200	4,392
North Carolina	46,135	40,434	5,023	40,434	14,164	6,299	5,536	2,637	1,381	480	1,159
North Dakota	4,041	3,674	5,720	3,674	1,255	580	91	450	68	45	40
Ohio	68,418	57,650	5,078	57,649	20,612	9,567	4,963	3,951	2,125	1,014	1,937
Oklahoma	15,962	13,808	4,002	13,767	5,836	885	1,324	1,404	518	266	511
Oregon	24,086	20,161	5,893	20,161	6,448	3,070	1,951	1,246	696	313	747
Pennsylvania	75,624	66,028	5,376	65,871	23,256	13,318	3,945	4,123	2,221	434	2,222
Rhode Island	6,432	5,586	5,329	5,560	1,857	1,144	278	286	211	152	139
South Carolina	23,436	20,260	5,050	20,260	7,126	3,458	3,016	1,328	653	190	559
South Dakota	3,760	3,444	4,562	3,444	1,218	488	150	540	88	29	81
Tennessee	32,010	25,272	4,442	25,272	8,369	4,872	2,739	1,839	940	400	604
Texas	109,634	95,762	4,593	95,762	39,217	11,460	8,854	7,201	3,204	1,373	3,756
Utah	13,044	11,013	4,932	11,013	4,233	1,473	741	1,033	381	127	351
Vermont	3,766	3,456	5,676	3,446	1,330	701	79	327	78	25	66
Virginia	38,092	34,728	4,906	34,727	13,132	4,487	2,634	2,627	1,176	549	1,246
Washington	41,794	33,483	5,681	33,475	11,565	5,100	3,317	2,212	1,007	551	1,053
West Virginia	9,990	8,711	4,817	8,711	3,171	1,763	552	888	171	55	184
Wisconsin	34,559	30,864	5,754	30,762	11,427	4,470	1,839	2,711	1,124	458	1,030
Wyoming	3,743	3,331	6,746	3,330	1,125	291	464	426	99	23	98

See footnote at end of table.

No. 447. State and Local Governments—Expenditures and Debt by State: 2000—Con.

[See page 290]

State	General expenditure — Environment and housing — Sewerage	Solid waste management	Parks and recreation	Housing[3]	Governmental administration	Interest on general debt	Other general expenditures	Utility and liquor store expenditures	Employee retirement expenditures	Debt outstanding
United States..	28,052	17,208	25,038	26,590	81,659	69,814	142,061	114,916	95,679	1,451,815
Alabama	452	221	278	304	908	768	1,399	1,861	1,209	16,799
Alaska	79	55	79	185	504	418	2,229	327	473	7,257
Arizona	389	269	469	354	1,522	1,026	2,351	2,674	1,062	23,599
Arkansas	147	122	137	128	552	351	782	545	474	7,829
California	3,743	2,370	3,095	4,547	13,471	7,549	22,100	18,805	14,233	177,920
Colorado	408	111	732	377	1,262	1,165	2,776	2,000	1,473	23,199
Connecticut	272	390	231	481	1,352	1,345	3,119	679	1,476	23,495
Delaware	94	30	68	79	376	283	380	189	206	4,585
District of Columbia	303	37	172	58	320	236	383	1,303	7	5,062
Florida	1,563	1,530	1,478	934	4,446	3,836	8,048	5,880	2,378	78,495
Georgia	865	478	540	602	2,076	1,056	2,867	3,461	1,627	29,948
Hawaii	124	134	217	266	456	587	1,182	319	519	7,909
Idaho	129	76	91	25	379	179	478	163	248	3,430
Illinois	1,105	409	1,965	1,483	3,716	3,644	5,927	4,041	5,146	67,573
Indiana	558	210	556	478	1,554	968	2,168	1,309	984	19,869
Iowa	250	128	246	132	734	357	1,127	805	680	7,310
Kansas	147	112	189	113	953	473	1,056	741	638	10,440
Kentucky	348	197	237	143	850	1,293	1,274	943	1,152	23,420
Louisiana	298	231	395	302	1,103	954	1,818	853	1,733	17,980
Maine	119	95	55	113	355	321	749	144	470	5,845
Maryland	560	430	681	632	1,568	1,442	2,587	983	1,684	23,830
Massachusetts	924	351	295	1,210	1,711	2,545	4,452	3,060	2,540	55,163
Michigan	1,694	410	740	275	2,761	2,143	4,476	2,435	3,426	47,195
Minnesota	622	258	714	591	1,572	1,356	3,865	1,622	2,201	27,409
Mississippi	126	118	139	134	630	455	997	656	686	8,519
Missouri	412	144	432	301	1,149	968	1,881	1,421	1,398	19,286
Montana	45	49	50	62	303	215	440	100	250	3,798
Nebraska	117	65	126	112	351	212	756	2,095	270	6,648
Nevada	108	14	370	147	742	505	867	835	438	13,235
New Hampshire	69	81	55	91	320	377	457	325	206	7,041
New Jersey	981	961	692	752	2,561	2,196	5,464	2,535	3,234	50,315
New Mexico	127	104	207	91	568	375	713	381	643	7,652
New York	1,786	2,152	1,783	2,979	6,466	9,259	15,067	15,133	12,988	177,550
North Carolina	598	559	605	603	1,574	1,259	3,581	3,310	1,953	29,114
North Dakota	19	30	124	92	171	146	562	73	112	2,781
Ohio	1,488	416	1,182	981	3,574	2,098	3,740	2,518	6,017	42,087
Oklahoma	226	138	272	148	748	508	982	919	996	11,409
Oregon	584	122	321	469	1,381	855	1,957	1,388	1,564	15,607
Pennsylvania	1,274	551	816	1,256	3,174	3,916	5,366	3,796	4,340	73,325
Rhode Island	94	71	46	128	340	335	481	152	429	6,878
South Carolina	245	239	270	202	906	734	1,334	1,928	963	18,671
South Dakota	44	21	91	31	186	165	311	134	168	3,289
Tennessee	466	309	449	461	1,152	785	1,888	5,418	1,013	18,377
Texas	1,591	891	1,215	1,809	4,058	4,594	6,540	7,344	5,510	100,175
Utah	182	102	238	115	780	384	873	1,483	374	12,394
Vermont	36	34	19	81	188	149	331	186	83	2,839
Virginia	752	488	592	615	2,033	1,732	2,664	1,600	1,598	31,546
Washington	722	462	633	647	1,596	1,398	3,213	4,539	1,732	38,697
West Virginia	120	50	102	104	536	608	3,049	1,093	416	7,094
Wisconsin	611	354	497	351	1,479	1,363	348	167	2,115	25,563
Wyoming	38	31	51	12	194	129	348	167	145	2,368

[1] Includes items not shown separately. [2] 1980, 1990, and 2000 based on enumerated resident population as of April 1; other years based on estimated resident population as of July 1; see Table 17. [3] Includes community development.

Source: U.S. Census Bureau, <http://www.census.gov/govs/estimate/00allpub.pdf> (released January 2003).

No. 448. State and Local Governments—Summary of Finances by State: 2000

[In millions of dollars (1,942,328 represents $1,942,328,000,000), except as indicated. For fiscal year ending in year shown; see text, this section]

State	All revenue Total	All revenue Per capita [2] (dol.)	General revenue Total	General revenue Per capita [2] (dol.)	Taxes Total	Taxes Per capita [2] (dol.)	Direct general expenditures	Direct general Per capita [2] (dol.)	Debt outstanding Total	Debt outstanding Per capita [2] (dol.)
United States	1,942,328	6,902	1,541,322	5,477	872,351	3,100	1,502,768	5,340	1,451,815	5,159
Alabama	25,726	5,785	21,012	4,725	9,415	2,117	22,062	4,961	16,799	3,778
Alaska	10,525	16,787	9,042	14,421	2,312	3,687	7,600	12,121	7,257	11,573
Arizona	27,778	5,414	22,863	4,456	13,334	2,599	23,262	4,534	23,599	4,599
Arkansas	13,833	5,175	11,582	4,333	5,961	2,230	11,057	4,137	7,829	2,929
California	270,380	7,982	208,373	6,152	120,068	3,545	195,767	5,780	177,920	5,253
Colorado	29,603	6,883	23,436	5,449	13,216	3,073	22,527	5,238	23,199	5,394
Connecticut	25,828	7,583	23,108	6,785	15,651	4,596	21,420	6,289	23,495	6,898
Delaware	6,224	7,938	5,203	6,637	2,619	3,342	4,691	5,983	4,585	5,848
District of Columbia	6,383	11,159	5,732	10,022	3,216	5,621	5,152	9,007	5,062	8,850
Florida	92,402	5,782	75,865	4,747	41,937	2,624	75,290	4,711	78,495	4,911
Georgia	49,310	6,024	39,690	4,849	23,254	2,840	38,078	4,652	29,948	3,658
Hawaii	8,488	7,004	7,092	5,851	4,102	3,385	7,291	6,016	7,909	6,526
Idaho	7,590	5,866	6,077	4,696	3,294	2,546	5,828	4,504	3,430	2,650
Illinois	80,695	6,498	64,420	5,187	40,256	3,241	64,403	5,186	67,573	5,441
Indiana	32,716	5,381	29,749	4,893	16,363	2,691	28,740	4,727	19,869	3,268
Iowa	17,220	5,885	15,134	5,172	8,091	2,765	15,563	5,319	7,310	2,498
Kansas	16,235	6,040	13,391	4,982	7,616	2,833	12,884	4,793	10,440	3,884
Kentucky	25,200	6,235	19,423	4,805	10,172	2,517	19,020	4,706	23,420	5,794
Louisiana	27,109	6,066	22,342	4,999	10,887	2,436	22,277	4,985	17,980	4,023
Maine	8,554	6,709	7,440	5,835	4,262	3,343	6,955	5,455	5,845	4,585
Maryland	33,949	6,410	29,076	5,490	18,290	3,453	27,446	5,182	23,830	4,500
Massachusetts	46,103	7,261	38,295	6,032	24,042	3,787	37,770	5,949	55,163	8,689
Michigan	70,112	7,055	56,415	5,677	31,474	3,167	54,750	5,509	47,195	4,749
Minnesota	38,785	7,885	30,957	6,293	18,173	3,694	31,166	6,336	27,409	5,572
Mississippi	16,672	5,860	13,590	4,777	6,299	2,214	13,932	4,897	8,519	2,994
Missouri	31,635	5,654	25,905	4,630	14,314	2,558	24,818	4,436	19,286	3,447
Montana	5,643	6,256	4,856	5,384	2,132	2,363	4,523	5,014	3,798	4,210
Nebraska	11,650	6,809	9,021	5,272	4,973	2,906	8,406	4,913	6,648	3,885
Nevada	11,885	5,948	9,592	4,801	5,825	2,915	9,755	4,883	13,235	6,624
New Hampshire	6,948	5,621	5,755	4,656	3,278	2,653	5,664	4,582	7,041	5,696
New Jersey	62,331	7,408	51,504	6,121	32,838	3,903	47,231	5,613	50,315	5,980
New Mexico	13,073	7,187	10,062	5,532	4,801	2,639	10,099	5,552	7,652	4,207
New York	188,907	9,955	143,901	7,583	86,868	4,578	140,020	7,379	177,550	9,357
North Carolina	50,542	6,279	41,131	5,110	21,440	2,664	40,434	5,024	29,114	3,617
North Dakota	4,495	7,002	3,914	6,096	1,768	2,753	3,674	5,722	2,781	4,331
Ohio	80,074	7,053	59,017	5,198	34,239	3,016	57,649	5,078	42,087	3,707
Oklahoma	18,760	5,436	15,698	4,549	8,251	2,391	13,767	3,989	11,409	3,306
Oregon	28,644	8,373	20,969	6,130	9,412	2,751	20,161	5,893	15,607	4,562
Pennsylvania	80,546	6,559	64,615	5,261	36,581	2,979	65,871	5,364	73,325	5,971
Rhode Island	7,427	7,087	5,748	5,484	3,412	3,255	5,560	5,305	6,878	6,563
South Carolina	23,467	5,849	19,727	4,917	9,543	2,379	20,260	5,050	18,671	4,654
South Dakota	4,277	5,666	3,491	4,623	1,736	2,299	3,444	4,561	3,289	4,356
Tennessee	33,625	5,910	24,824	4,363	12,431	2,185	25,272	4,442	18,377	3,230
Texas	120,666	5,787	95,539	4,582	52,227	2,505	95,762	4,592	100,175	4,804
Utah	14,954	6,697	11,208	5,019	5,873	2,630	11,013	4,932	12,394	5,551
Vermont	4,019	6,599	3,497	5,742	1,876	3,081	3,446	5,659	2,839	4,662
Virginia	44,175	6,240	35,434	5,005	21,083	2,978	34,727	4,906	31,546	4,456
Washington	46,372	7,868	33,426	5,671	18,734	3,178	33,475	5,680	38,697	6,566
West Virginia	10,760	5,951	9,055	5,008	4,362	2,412	8,711	4,818	7,094	3,924
Wisconsin	43,003	8,017	30,572	5,699	18,547	3,458	30,762	5,735	25,563	4,766
Wyoming	7,030	14,231	3,554	7,195	1,505	3,047	3,330	6,740	2,368	4,793

[1] Includes items not shown separately. [2] 1980, 1990, and 2000 based on enumerated resident population as of April 1; other years based on estimated resident population as of July 1; see Table 17.

Source: U.S. Census Bureau; "Government Finances: 1999-2000"; issued January 2003, <http://www.census.gov/govs/estimate/00allpub.pdf>; (accessed 16 June 2003).

No. 449. State and Local Governments—Indebtedness: 1980 to 2000

[In billions of dollars (335.6 represents $335,600,000,000), except per capita. For fiscal year ending in year shown; see text, this section. Local government amounts are estimates subject to sampling variation; see Appendix III and source]

Item	Debt outstanding							Long term		
	Total	Per capita[1] (dol.)	Long term				Short-term	Net long term	Debt issued	Debt retired
			Local schools[2]	Utilities	All other					
1980: Total	335.6	1,481	32.3	55.2	235.0	13.1	262.9	42.4	17.4
State	122.0	540	3.8	4.6	111.5	2.1	79.8	16.4	5.7
Local	213.6	943	28.5	50.6	123.5	11.0	183.1	25.9	11.7
1985: Total	568.6	2,390	43.8	90.8	414.5	19.6	430.5	101.2	43.5
State	211.9	893	6.7	8.6	193.8	2.8	110.4	41.7	16.4
Local	356.7	1,499	37.1	82.2	220.6	16.8	320.1	59.5	27.2
1990: Total	858.0	3,449	60.4	134.8	643.5	19.3	474.4	108.5	64.8
State	318.3	1,282	4.4	12.3	298.7	2.8	125.5	43.5	22.9
Local	539.8	2,169	56.0	122.4	344.8	16.5	348.9	65.0	42.0
1995: Total	1,115.4	4,244	118.2	163.9	806.2	27.0	697.3	129.3	95.1
State	427.2	1,629	11.3	17.0	392.8	6.1	205.3	52.6	37.5
Local	688.1	2,618	107.0	146.9	413.4	20.9	491.9	76.8	57.6
1997: Total	1,224.5	4,573	139.0	179.1	889.8	16.6	797.7	151.3	109.3
State	456.7	1,709	11.7	16.0	426.8	2.1	222.7	54.4	41.1
Local	767.9	2,867	127.3	163.1	463.0	14.5	575.1	96.8	68.2
1998: Total	1,283.6	4,750	159.2	182.8	925.4	17.3	842.6	204.4	144.6
State	483.1	1,791	13.6	16.7	450.6	2.2	237.2	83.4	58.1
Local	800.4	2,962	145.5	166.1	473.8	15.1	605.4	120.9	86.5
1999: Total	1,369.3	5,021	180.7	194.9	975.7	17.8	907.3	229.4	153.1
State	510.5	1,876	15.4	16.7	475.8	2.7	249.4	83.2	55.6
Local	858.8	3,149	165.3	178.3	500.0	15.2	657.9	146.2	97.5
2000: Total	1,451.8	5,159	197.7	200.1	1,029.8	24.3	959.6	184.8	121.9
State	547.9	1,951	18.7	17.9	505.0	6.4	266.9	75.0	44.4
Local	903.9	3,212	179.0	182.2	524.8	17.9	692.7	109.8	77.5

[1] 1980, 1990, and 2000 based on enumerated resident population as of April 1; other years based on estimated resident population as of July 1; see Table 2. [2] Includes debt for education activities other than higher education.

Source: U.S. Census Bureau, 1980-90, State and Local Government Finance Estimates, annual; thereafter, <http://www.census.gov/govs/www/estimate.html>; (accessed 22 May 2003).

No. 450. Long-Term Municipal New Issues for State and Local Governments: 1980 to 2002

[In billions of dollars (45.6 represents $45,600,000,000)]

Item	1980	1985	1990	1995	1997	1998	1999	2000	2001	2002
Long-term municipal new issues [1]	45.6	202.4	125.9	156.2	214.3	279.7	219.2	194.3	283.5	355.8
General obligation	13.7	39.6	40.2	60.2	72.2	92.6	69.8	65.2	101.3	125.6
Revenue	31.9	162.8	85.7	96.0	142.1	187.1	149.4	129.1	182.2	230.2
Competitive	19.3	27.8	30.2	41.0	47.8	65.2	52.8	48.7	63.1	71.9
Negotiated	26.4	174.6	95.9	115.4	166.5	214.5	166.4	145.6	220.4	283.9
States with largest issuance: [2]										
New York	2.9	12.7	16.9	18.8	27.4	36.3	19.8	19.1	22.5	48.7
California	3.6	25.3	15.7	20.2	27.7	33.9	26.5	22.9	31.7	48.5
Texas	3.8	21.2	6.5	10.4	15.3	18.1	17.7	14.7	24.6	26.6
Florida	2.2	13.2	5.9	9.1	10.5	14.7	10.8	10.1	14.1	18.7
Illinois	2.3	9.2	6.3	6.6	9.6	10.1	12.4	8.9	14.1	14.7
All others	30.8	120.8	74.6	91.1	123.8	166.6	132.0	118.6	176.5	198.5
Type of issuer: [3]										
City, town, or village	8.5	36.5	22.7	27.9	34.8	44.3	33.0	29.3	45.6	46.9
College or university	0.2	2.9	1.5	2.9	3.3	4.6	4.1	3.8	5.6	7.1
County/parish	4.6	15.8	10.0	13.3	15.5	21.2	17.1	12.7	19.0	23.5
Direct issuer	-	0.4	0.2	0.4	0.8	2.1	2.0	2.6	3.1	4.9
District	3.9	15.6	15.2	22.4	33.7	43.6	34.1	27.8	47.9	54.4
Indian tribe	(NA)	(NA)	(NA)	(NA)	(NA)	(NA)	(NA)	(NA)	0.2	0.2
Local authority	9.2	51.1	20.7	27.9	41.5	53.9	43.2	33.1	53.1	59.8
State authority	14.1	68.1	40.6	47.2	66.0	85.2	68.1	64.2	78.9	125.0
State	5.1	12.1	15.0	14.6	18.7	24.7	17.6	20.8	30.2	34.0
General use of proceeds:										
Airports	0.4	3.0	5.2	4.7	6.4	10.2	5.5	7.4	12.3	10.0
Combined utilities	0.3	2.4	1.0	0.7	1.5	1.8	1.0	0.3	1.3	2.2
Economic development	0.2	2.5	2.1	2.5	2.9	3.5	3.6	2.9	3.9	4.4
Education	4.0	20.4	20.5	28.5	42.7	56.5	47.6	39.9	64.5	76.4
Health care	3.1	30.0	12.6	11.5	22.1	33.4	22.0	14.4	20.1	22.4
Industrial development	1.0	2.9	1.9	3.2	3.5	3.6	3.5	3.4	2.9	2.3
Multifamily housing	2.5	20.2	3.1	6.1	5.4	6.4	6.1	6.2	7.3	10.1
Nursing homes/life care retirement	0.3	1.2	1.6	1.9	3.6	4.8	4.9	1.8	3.0	3.7
Other miscellaneous	11.1	37.3	36.2	44.2	57.0	71.5	58.4	52.8	81.2	102.4
Pollution control	2.3	10.0	2.5	5.0	5.6	9.7	8.9	4.8	4.5	5.5
Electric & public power	4.4	23.2	5.2	4.8	6.5	15.6	4.9	5.7	11.5	23.1
Single family housing	10.6	16.4	12.5	10.0	13.6	12.9	12.6	12.0	14.0	12.4
Solid waste/resource recovery	0.4	3.8	3.0	3.3	3.6	2.4	1.2	0.5	2.1	1.9
Student loans	0.2	4.0	0.4	4.4	3.9	4.9	5.3	7.6	8.2	11.7
Transportation	1.3	11.0	7.6	11.3	16.6	20.5	16.0	15.9	18.6	33.8
Water, sewer, and gas facilities	3.1	13.4	9.3	13.2	18.2	20.9	16.4	11.3	27.1	32.2
Waterfront/seaports	0.5	1.5	0.5	0.8	1.2	0.9	1.2	1.1	1.1	1.0

- Represents or rounds to zero. NA Not available. [1] Excludes issues with a final maturity of less than 13 months, private placements, and not-for-profit cooperative utilities. [2] Ranked by 1997 Long-term Municipal New Issue Volume. [3] Includes island areas.

Source: Thomson Financial Securities Data Company, Newark, NJ, Municipal New Issues Database (copyright).

No. 451. Bond Ratings for State Governments by State: 2002

[As of fourth quarter. Key to investment grade ratings are in declining order of quality. The ratings from AA to CCC may be modified by the addition of a plus or minus sign to show relative standing within the major rating categories. *S&P:* AAA, AA, A, BBB, BB, B, CCC, CC, C; *Moody's:* Aaa, Aa, A, Baa, Ba, B, Caa, Ca, C; Numerical modifiers 1, 2, and 3 are added to letter rating. *Fitch:* AAA, AA, A, BBB, BB, B, CCC, CC, C]

State	Standard & Poor's	Moody's	Fitch	State	Standard & Poor's	Moody's	Fitch
Alabama	AA	Aa3	AA	Montana	AA-	Aa3	(NA)
Alaska	(¹)	Aa2	AA	Nebraska	(¹)	(¹)	(NA)
Arizona	AA-	(¹)	(NA)	Nevada	AA	Aa2	AA+
Arkansas	AA	Aa2	(NA)	New Hampshire	AA+	Aa2	AA+
California	A	A1	²A	New Jersey	AA	Aa2	AA
Colorado	AA-	(¹)	(NA)	New Mexico	AA+	Aa1	(NA)
Connecticut	AA	Aa2	AA	New York	AA	A2	AA
Delaware	AAA	Aaa	AAA	North Carolina	AAA	Aa1	AAA
Florida	AA+	Aa2	AA	North Dakota	AA-	Aa3	(NA)
Georgia	AAA	Aaa	AAA	Ohio	AA+	Aa1	AA+
Hawaii	AA-	Aa3	AA-	Oklahoma	AA	Aa3	AA
Idaho	(¹)	Aa3	(NA)	Oregon	AA	Aa2	AA
Illinois	AA	Aa2	AA+	Pennsylvania	AA	Aa2	AA
Indiana	AA+	Aa1	(NA)	Rhode Island	AA-	Aa3	AA
Iowa	AA+	Aa1	³AA	South Carolina	AAA	Aaa	AAA
Kansas	AA+	Aa1	(NA)	South Dakota	(¹)	(¹)	(NA)
Kentucky	AA-	Aa2	(NA)	Tennessee	AA	Aa2	AA
Louisiana	A	A2	A	Texas	AA	Aa1	AA+
Maine	AA+	Aa2	AA+	Utah	AAA	Aaa	AAA
Maryland	AAA	Aaa	AAA	Vermont	AA+	Aa1	AA+
Massachusetts	AA-	Aa2	AA-	Virginia	AAA	Aaa	AAA
Michigan	AAA	Aaa	AA+	Washington	AA+	Aa1	AA
Minnesota	AAA	Aaa	AAA	West Virginia	AA-	Aa3	AA-
Mississippi	AA	Aa3	AA	Wisconsin	AA-	Aa3	AA
Missouri	AAA	Aaa	AAA	Wyoming	AA	(¹)	(NA)

NA Not available. ¹ Not reviewed. ² Rating watch negative. ³ Implied.

Sources: Standard & Poor's, New York, NY; Moody's Investors Service, New York, NY (copyright); and Fitch Ratings, New York, NY (copyright).

No. 452. Bond Ratings for City Governments by Largest Cities: 2002

[As of fourth quarter. See headnote in Table 451]

Cities ranked by 2000 population	Standard & Poor's	Moody's	Fitch	Cities ranked by 2000 population	Standard & Poor's	Moody's	Fitch
New York, NY	A	A2	A+	Oakland, CA	A+	A1	A+
Los Angeles, CA	AA	Aa2	AA	Mesa, AZ	AA-	A1	(¹)
Chicago, IL	A+	A1	AA-	Tulsa, OK	AA	Aa2	(¹)
Houston, TX	AA-	Aa3	AA	Omaha, NE	AAA	Aaa	(¹)
Philadelphia, PA	BBB	Baa1	A-	Minneapolis, MN	AAA	Aa1	AAA
Phoenix, AZ	AA+	Aa1	(¹)	Honolulu, HI	AA-	Aaa	AA
San Diego, CA	AA	Aa1	AAA	Miami, FL	BBB+	Baa1	BBB+
Dallas, TX	AAA	Aaa	(¹)	Colorado Springs, CO	AA	Aa3	(¹)
San Antonio, TX	AA+	Aa2	AA+	St. Louis, MO	A-	A3	A-
Detroit, MI	A-	Baa1	A	Wichita, KS	AA	Aa2	(¹)
San Jose, CA	AA+	Aa1	AA+	Santa Ana, CA	(¹)	(¹)	(¹)
Indianapolis, IN	AAA	Aaa	(¹)	Pittsburgh, PA	A-	A3	A-
San Francisco, CA	AA	Aa3	AA	Arlington, TX	AA	²Aa2	(¹)
Jacksonville, FL	(¹)	Aa2	(¹)	Cincinnati, OH	AA+	Aa1	(¹)
Columbus, OH	AAA	Aaa	(¹)	Anaheim, CA	AA	Aa2	(¹)
Austin, TX	AA+	Aa2	AA+	Toledo, OH	A	A3	(¹)
Baltimore, MD	A+	A1	(¹)	Tampa, FL	(¹)	Baa1	(¹)
Memphis, TN	AA	Aa2	AA	Buffalo, NY	BBB	Baa2	(¹)
Milwaukee, WI	AA	Aa2	AA+	St. Paul, MN	AAA	Aa2	AA+
Boston, MA	AA-	Aa2	AA-	Corpus Christi, TX	A+	A2	AA-
Washington, DC	BBB+	Baa1	BBB+	Aurora, CO	AA	Aa2	(¹)
El Paso, TX	AA	Aa3	(¹)	Raleigh, NC	AAA	Aaa	AAA
Seattle, WA	AAA	Aaa	AAA	Newark, NJ	AA-	Baa1	(¹)
Denver, CO	AA+	Aa1	AA+	Lexington-Fayette, KY	AA+	(¹)	(¹)
Nashville-Davidson, TN	AA	Aa2	AA+	Anchorage, AK	(¹)	Aa3	(¹)
Charlotte, NC	AAA	Aaa	AAA	Louisville, KY	AA-	Aa3	(¹)
Fort Worth, TX	AA+	Aa1	(¹)	Riverside, CA	AA-	(¹)	(¹)
Portland, OR	(¹)	(¹)	(¹)	St Petersburg, FL	(¹)	(¹)	(¹)
Oklahoma City, OK	AA	Aa2	(¹)	Bakersfield, CA	(¹)	(¹)	(¹)
Tucson, AZ	AA	Aa2	(¹)	Stockton CA	A+	(¹)	(¹)
New Orleans, LA	BBB+	Baa1	(¹)	Birmingham, AL	AA	Aa3	AA-
Las Vegas, NV	AA-	Aa3	(¹)	Jersey City, NJ	BBB	Baa3	BBB
Cleveland, OH	A+	A1	A+	Norfolk, VA	AA	A1	AA
Long Beach, CA	AA-	Aa3	(¹)	Baton Rouge, LA	(¹)	(¹)	(¹)
Albuquerque, NM	AA	Aa3	AA	Hialeah, FL	(¹)	(¹)	(¹)
Kansas City, MO	AA	Aa3	AAA	Lincoln, NE	AAA	Aa1	(¹)
Fresno, CA	AA-	A2	(¹)	Greensboro, NC	AAA	Aa1	AAA
Virginia Beach, VA	AA+	Aa1	AA+	Plano, TX	AAA	Aaa	AAA
Atlanta, GA	AA-	Aa3	AA-	Rochester, NY	AA	A2	(¹)
Sacramento, CA	AA	(¹)	(¹)				

¹ Not reviewed. ² Issuer rating.

Sources: Standard & Poor's, New York, NY; Moody's Investors Service, New York, NY (copyright); and Fitch Ratings, New York, NY (copyright).

No. 453. State Resources, Expenditures, and Balances: 2001 and 2002

[In millions of dollars (1,044,078 represents $1,044,078,000,000). For fiscal year ending in year shown; see text; this section. *General funds* exclude special funds earmarked for particular purposes, such as highway trust funds and federal funds; they support most on-going broad-based state services and are available for appropriation to support any governmental activity. Minus sign (-) indicates deficit]

State	Expenditures by fund source				State general fund					
	Total, 2001	2002 [1]			Resources [3,4]		Expenditures [4]		Balance [5]	
		Total [2]	General fund	Federal funds	2001	2002 [1]	2001	2002 [1]	2001	2002 [1]
Total........	1,044,078	1,098,610	508,726	296,922	(NA)	(NA)	(NA)	(NA)	(NA)	(NA)
United States....	1,024,439	1,077,932	501,260	292,514	498,427	527,793	477,462	513,479	17,487	14,013
Alabama.........	15,390	18,835	5,322	6,347	5,268	5,347	5,248	5,362	20	25
Alaska..........	(NA)	(NA)	(NA)	(NA)	2,290	(NA)	2,290	(NA)	[6]-	(NA)
Arizona.........	17,351	16,759	6,328	4,276	6,572	6,330	6,467	6,329	104	2
Arkansas........	11,133	12,133	3,248	3,560	3,261	3,250	3,261	3,250	-	-
California.......	137,655	149,426	78,380	46,516	86,266	79,865	79,708	78,380	[6]6,557	1,486
Colorado........	12,703	13,617	6,087	2,785	7,218	6,705	6,682	6,711	[6]537	57
Connecticut.....	18,953	18,583	11,899	3,304	11,914	11,686	11,413	11,899	501	-123
Delaware........	5,417	5,579	2,524	835	2,569	2,844	2,467	2,524	102	[6]320
Florida..........	52,390	47,540	19,232	12,672	20,465	19,736	20,465	19,267	-	469
Georgia.........	24,889	27,763	13,722	10,930	17,279	17,300	14,770	16,074	[6]1,128	1,226
Hawaii..........	7,277	7,189	3,624	1,088	3,716	3,834	3,385	3,624	330	210
Idaho...........	3,984	4,536	2,002	1,485	2,024	2,002	1,844	2,002	180	-
Illinois..........	37,657	39,702	18,356	8,273	25,747	25,476	24,547	24,826	1,200	650
Indiana.........	17,767	16,856	9,579	4,650	10,570	9,594	9,742	9,579	392	16
Iowa............	12,288	12,689	4,682	3,073	4,877	4,603	4,869	4,600	8	3
Kansas.........	8,850	9,483	4,528	2,502	4,864	4,702	4,434	4,528	430	174
Kentucky........	16,849	17,817	7,415	5,277	7,124	7,429	7,124	7,251	-	24
Louisiana........	15,961	17,494	6,426	5,792	6,216	6,476	6,227	6,426	[6]-	50
Maine...........	5,269	6,453	2,760	2,003	2,662	2,507	2,648	2,593	19	-86
Maryland........	20,481	21,959	10,677	4,914	10,590	11,132	10,215	10,677	375	456
Massachusetts...	30,107	31,425	21,019	6,888	20,700	24,621	20,596	22,831	104	1,790
Michigan........	37,952	38,281	9,307	10,325	9,831	9,290	9,831	9,290	-	-
Minnesota.......	20,832	21,911	13,451	4,510	14,239	14,142	13,131	12,755	[6]1,108	1,387
Mississippi......	9,726	10,400	3,401	3,361	3,634	3,422	3,633	3,584	1	5
Missouri.........	16,653	19,247	7,849	5,664	7,921	7,830	7,812	7,734	109	96
Montana........	3,104	3,629	1,330	1,548	1,371	1,503	1,264	1,339	104	165
Nebraska........	6,058	6,554	2,715	1,756	2,787	2,821	2,462	2,593	204	121
Nevada..........	4,780	5,084	1,807	1,289	1,918	1,946	1,875	1,847	106	138
New Hampshire..	3,425	3,690	1,160	1,070	1,081	1,138	1,081	1,150	-	-12
New Jersey......	32,267	33,736	21,785	7,797	22,338	21,730	21,057	21,207	[6]-	500
New Mexico......	10,794	11,082	3,937	3,188	3,855	4,400	3,718	3,988	[6]1,098	[6]2,077
New York........	79,753	85,044	38,324	26,306	40,800	43,532	39,702	41,455	-	1
North Carolina...	26,958	27,036	15,002	7,066	13,720	14,713	13,720	14,530	-	-
North Dakota....	2,297	2,518	865	994	864	887	826	847	38	40
Ohio............	42,296	49,010	21,782	6,965	21,128	21,830	20,739	21,778	190	153
Oklahoma.......	11,979	13,238	5,019	4,007	5,077	5,181	4,819	5,136	259	45
Oregon.........	17,033	18,453	5,538	3,741	5,381	5,140	4,920	5,074	461	66
Pennsylvania....	40,694	45,228	20,770	13,919	20,260	20,736	19,979	20,770	313	300
Rhode Island....	4,873	5,355	2,625	1,592	2,585	2,642	2,472	2,625	113	17
South Carolina...	14,450	15,363	5,552	4,828	5,794	5,409	5,644	5,348	[6]150	62
South Dakota....	2,353	2,509	851	995	823	864	805	853	6	-
Tennessee.......	17,434	18,818	7,929	7,057	7,244	7,610	7,231	7,568	-	-
Texas...........	52,356	54,583	30,571	15,309	(NA)	32,510	(NA)	30,572	(NA)	1,421
Utah............	6,977	7,467	3,810	1,649	3,792	3,805	3,792	3,805	-	-
Vermont.........	2,665	2,889	881	960	899	894	897	872	-	-
Virginia.........	24,218	25,084	11,176	4,445	12,652	12,241	12,339	12,131	314	109
Washington.....	23,061	22,870	11,220	6,399	11,273	11,228	10,788	11,217	486	10
West Virginia....	7,442	8,197	2,881	2,846	2,870	2,994	2,864	2,976	-	2
Wisconsin.......	28,092	23,244	11,534	5,481	11,324	11,259	11,030	11,074	[6]293	151
Wyoming........	1,546	1,574	378	277	777	659	630	630	[6]147	10
Puerto Rico.....	19,639	20,678	7,466	4,408	(NA)	(NA)	(NA)	(NA)	(NA)	(NA)

- Represents zero. NA Not available. [1] Estimated. [2] Includes bonds and other state funds not shown separately. [3] Includes funds budgeted, adjustments, and balances from previous year. [4] May or may not include budget stabilization fund transfers, depending on state accounting practices. [5] Resources less expenditures. [6] Ending balance includes the balance in a budget stabilization fund.

Source: Expenditures by fund from National Association of State Budget Officers, Washington, DC, *2001 State Expenditure Report*, and state general fund from National Governors' Association and NASBO Fiscal Survey of the States, semi-annual (copyright).

No. 454. State Governments—Summary of Finances: 1990 to 2000

[In millions of dollars (673,119 represents $673,119,000,000), except where indicated. For fiscal year ending in year shown; see text; this section]

Item	Total (mil. dol.) 1990	1998	1999	2000	Per capita [1] (dollars) 1990	1998	1999	2000
Borrowing and revenue	673,119	1,177,223	1,228,816	1,336,798	2,712	4,364	4,515	4,760
Borrowing	40,948	73,984	75,946	75,968	165	274	279	270
Revenue	632,172	1,103,239	1,152,870	1,260,829	2,547	4,090	4,236	4,489
General revenue	517,429	863,523	906,076	984,783	2,085	3,201	3,329	3,506
Taxes	300,489	473,051	499,943	539,655	1,211	1,754	1,837	1,922
Sales and gross receipts	147,069	226,643	239,367	252,147	593	840	879	898
General	99,702	155,272	164,378	174,461	402	576	604	621
Motor fuels	19,379	28,345	29,169	29,968	78	105	107	107
Alcoholic beverages	3,191	3,765	3,900	4,104	13	14	14	15
Tobacco products	5,541	7,748	8,170	8,391	22	29	30	30
Other	19,256	31,513	33,751	35,222	78	117	124	125
Licenses	18,842	29,655	30,440	32,598	76	110	112	116
Motor vehicles	9,848	13,662	14,083	15,099	40	51	52	54
Corporations in general	3,099	6,129	6,359	6,460	12	23	23	23
Other	5,895	9,864	9,998	11,039	24	37	37	39
Individual income	96,076	160,115	172,764	194,573	387	594	635	693
Corporation net income	21,751	31,089	30,766	32,522	88	115	113	116
Property	5,848	10,659	11,654	10,996	24	40	43	39
Other	10,902	14,891	14,952	16,819	44	55	55	60
Charges and miscellaneous	90,612	149,682	152,441	170,747	365	555	560	608
Intergovernmental revenue	126,329	240,789	253,692	274,382	509	893	932	977
From Federal Government	118,353	224,444	238,941	259,114	477	832	878	923
Public welfare	59,397	127,356	135,274	147,150	239	472	497	524
Education	21,271	36,138	38,738	42,086	86	134	142	150
Highways	13,931	19,659	20,874	23,790	56	73	77	85
Health and hospitals	5,475	12,579	13,205	14,223	22	47	49	51
Other	18,279	28,712	30,849	31,865	74	106	113	113
From local governments	7,976	16,345	14,751	15,268	32	61	54	54
Utility revenue	3,305	4,205	4,356	4,513	13	16	16	16
Liquor store revenue	2,907	3,483	3,599	3,895	12	13	13	14
Insurance trust revenue [2]	108,530	232,029	238,838	267,639	437	860	878	953
Employee retirement	78,898	195,603	201,500	230,166	318	725	740	820
Unemployment compensation	18,370	23,051	22,131	23,260	74	85	81	83
Expenditure and debt redemption	592,213	979,303	1,046,234	1,125,828	2,386	3,631	3,844	4,009
Expenditure	572,318	929,952	998,365	1,084,097	2,306	3,448	3,668	3,860
General expenditure	508,284	827,654	889,475	964,723	2,048	3,068	3,268	3,435
Education	184,935	294,814	318,602	346,465	745	1,093	1,171	1,234
Public welfare	104,971	207,926	221,167	238,890	423	771	813	851
Health	20,029	35,067	38,008	42,066	81	130	140	150
Hospitals	22,637	28,928	29,994	32,578	91	107	110	116
Highways	44,249	63,620	68,317	74,415	178	236	251	265
Police protection	5,166	8,038	8,794	9,788	21	30	32	35
Correction	17,266	30,601	32,843	35,129	70	113	121	125
Natural resources	9,909	13,541	14,482	15,967	40	50	53	57
Housing and community development	2,856	3,982	4,000	4,726	12	15	15	17
Other and unallocable	96,267	141,137	153,269	164,698	388	523	563	586
Utility expenditure	7,131	8,365	8,779	10,723	29	31	32	38
Liquor store expenditure	2,452	2,820	2,967	3,195	10	10	11	11
Insurance trust expenditure [2]	54,452	91,113	97,144	105,456	219	338	357	375
Employee retirement	29,562	63,002	67,353	75,971	119	234	247	271
Unemployment compensation	16,423	17,712	19,160	18,583	66	66	70	66
By character and object:								
Intergovernmental expenditure	175,028	278,853	304,933	327,070	705	1,034	1,120	1,165
Direct expenditure	397,291	651,098	693,432	757,027	1,601	2,414	2,548	2,695
Current operation	258,046	446,440	476,968	523,114	1,040	1,655	1,752	1,863
Capital outlay	45,524	64,441	68,509	76,233	183	239	252	271
Construction	34,803	50,542	53,857	59,681	140	187	198	213
Land and existing structure	3,471	3,638	3,953	4,681	14	13	15	17
Equipment	7,250	10,261	10,699	11,871	29	38	39	42
Assistance and subsidies	16,902	21,515	22,229	22,136	68	80	82	79
Interest on debt	22,367	27,590	28,582	30,089	90	102	105	107
Insurance benefits [3]	54,452	91,113	97,144	105,456	219	338	357	375
Debt redemption	19,895	49,351	47,869	41,730	80	183	176	149
Debt outstanding	318,254	483,117	510,486	547,876	1,282	1,791	1,876	1,951
Long-term	315,490	480,948	507,819	541,497	1,271	1,783	1,866	1,928
Full-faith and credit	74,972	124,653	129,326	138,525	302	462	475	493
Nonguaranteed	240,518	356,294	378,493	402,972	969	1,321	1,391	1,435
Short-term	2,764	2,169	2,667	6,379	11	8	10	23
Net long-term [4]	125,524	237,216	249,432	266,870	506	879	916	950
Full-faith and credit only	63,481	114,890	119,511	128,384	256	426	439	457

[1] 1980, 1990, and 2000 based on enumerated resident population as of April 1; other years based on estimated resident population as of July 1. [2] Includes other items not shown separately. [3] Includes repayments. [4] Less cash and investment assets specifically held for redemption of long-term debt.

Source: U.S. Census Bureau, 1990, *State Government Finances*, Series GF, No. 3, thereafter, <http://www.census.gov/govs/www/state00.html> (revised September 2002).

No. 455. State Governments—Revenue by State: 2000

[In millions of dollars (1,260,829 represents $1,260,829,000,000), except as noted. For fiscal year ending in year shown; see text, this section. Includes local shares of state imposed taxes. N.e.c. = Not elsewhere classified]

State	Total revenue [1]	General revenue Total	Per capita [2] Total (dol.)	Per capita [2] Rank	Intergovernmental revenue Total	From federal government	Charges and miscellaneous Total	Current charges	Miscellaneous general revenue	Insurance trust revenue
United States..	1,260,829	984,783	3,506	(X)	274,382	259,114	170,747	86,467	84,279	267,639
Alabama	16,857	14,117	3,174	37	4,781	4,745	2,897	2,099	798	2,588
Alaska	8,584	7,330	11,691	1	1,202	1,197	4,706	327	4,378	1,229
Arizona	16,315	14,259	2,779	47	4,120	3,840	2,038	833	1,205	2,035
Arkansas	10,789	9,118	3,411	25	2,735	2,706	1,513	895	618	1,671
California	172,481	135,782	4,009	14	36,125	33,655	15,849	9,429	6,420	36,476
Colorado	17,060	12,925	3,005	43	3,301	3,280	2,549	1,341	1,208	4,135
Connecticut	18,007	16,232	4,766	5	3,395	3,387	2,667	962	1,704	1,752
Delaware	5,162	4,333	5,526	2	827	789	1,374	591	783	820
Florida	51,621	41,665	2,607	50	10,271	9,905	6,577	2,365	4,212	9,949
Georgia	29,630	23,395	2,858	45	6,459	6,411	3,425	1,633	1,791	6,234
Hawaii	6,941	5,729	4,727	6	1,128	1,124	1,266	845	421	1,212
Idaho	5,576	4,202	3,248	33	1,074	1,070	751	364	387	1,321
Illinois	48,524	38,759	3,121	40	10,214	9,275	5,756	2,242	3,514	9,766
Indiana	20,456	18,857	3,101	41	4,952	4,792	3,801	2,281	1,520	1,600
Iowa	11,340	9,892	3,381	29	2,731	2,632	1,976	1,239	737	1,340
Kansas	10,394	8,561	3,185	36	2,401	2,365	1,312	645	666	1,833
Kentucky	19,451	14,648	3,624	21	4,341	4,319	2,613	1,529	1,084	4,802
Louisiana	18,788	14,872	3,328	31	4,785	4,730	3,575	2,259	1,316	3,912
Maine	6,294	5,274	4,136	12	1,555	1,547	1,057	367	691	943
Maryland	21,366	17,956	3,391	27	4,164	4,022	3,437	1,686	1,751	3,308
Massachusetts	32,011	27,418	4,319	10	5,787	5,428	5,479	1,756	3,723	4,497
Michigan	49,511	39,491	3,974	15	9,370	9,168	7,364	4,183	3,181	9,454
Minnesota	26,889	20,971	4,263	11	4,451	4,381	3,182	1,332	1,851	5,917
Mississippi	12,181	9,636	3,387	28	3,470	3,349	1,455	906	548	2,381
Missouri	20,309	16,486	2,946	44	5,256	5,205	2,658	1,351	1,307	3,824
Montana	4,204	3,496	3,876	19	1,206	1,187	880	337	542	666
Nebraska	6,185	5,706	3,335	30	1,568	1,541	1,156	533	623	479
Nevada	7,285	5,473	2,739	48	1,057	998	699	379	320	1,780
New Hampshire	4,993	3,876	3,136	38	1,157	994	1,023	453	570	826
New Jersey	42,340	32,237	3,831	20	7,743	7,310	6,346	3,208	3,138	9,604
New Mexico	10,570	7,888	4,336	9	2,187	2,132	1,957	759	1,198	2,683
New York	111,397	84,765	4,467	7	32,521	26,206	10,509	4,571	5,938	24,271
North Carolina	34,361	27,762	3,449	23	8,591	8,055	3,856	2,385	1,471	6,599
North Dakota	3,295	2,798	4,358	8	1,002	974	623	429	194	498
Ohio	55,274	36,166	3,186	35	10,074	9,842	6,416	3,602	2,813	18,628
Oklahoma	13,116	10,783	3,125	39	3,047	2,962	1,896	1,125	771	2,046
Oregon	21,011	14,099	4,121	13	4,685	4,625	3,468	1,787	1,681	6,684
Pennsylvania	54,517	41,700	3,395	26	10,584	10,504	8,649	4,962	3,687	11,952
Rhode Island	5,589	4,106	3,918	17	1,163	1,091	908	334	574	1,472
South Carolina	15,966	13,317	3,319	32	4,379	4,055	2,557	1,741	815	1,834
South Dakota	2,901	2,282	3,022	42	793	781	562	213	348	619
Tennessee	18,970	15,928	2,800	46	6,121	5,966	2,068	1,368	701	3,041
Texas	72,323	55,312	2,653	49	17,151	16,562	10,737	5,102	5,635	17,010
Utah	10,227	7,697	3,447	24	1,889	1,878	1,829	1,150	679	2,414
Vermont	3,292	2,943	4,833	3	918	877	542	295	248	320
Virginia	29,409	22,715	3,209	34	4,466	4,314	5,601	3,216	2,385	6,395
Washington	30,616	21,254	3,606	22	5,190	5,095	3,496	2,146	1,350	9,035
West Virginia	8,591	7,032	3,889	18	2,406	2,365	1,282	648	635	1,510
Wisconsin	32,119	21,183	3,949	16	4,734	4,633	3,873	2,164	1,710	10,936
Wyoming	5,740	2,357	4,770	4	855	843	538	99	438	3,339

See footnote at end of table.

No. 455. State Governments—Revenue by State: 2000—Con.

[See headnote, page 297]

State	All taxes Total [3]	Per capita [2] Total (dol.)	Rank	Property taxes	Sales and gross receipts taxes Total [3]	General sales taxes, total	Selective sales taxes [3] Total [3]	Alcoholic beverages and tobacco sales	Insurance premiums	Motor fuels sales	Public utilities
United States..	539,655	1,922	(X)	10,996	252,147	174,461	77,685	12,495	9,750	29,968	9,231
Alabama.......	6,438	1,448	46	180	3,228	1,702	1,527	190	191	505	483
Alaska.........	1,423	2,270	10	45	138	-	138	61	29	42	3
Arizona........	8,101	1,579	41	297	4,644	3,633	1,011	214	165	593	37
Arkansas......	4,871	1,822	27	482	2,363	1,707	656	122	95	389	-
California......	83,808	2,474	6	3,331	29,620	23,457	6,163	1,499	1,300	3,041	219
Colorado......	7,075	1,645	39	-	2,709	1,849	860	95	131	544	8
Connecticut ...	10,171	2,986	1	-	5,054	3,420	1,634	174	184	543	198
Delaware......	2,132	2,720	3	-	289	-	289	38	53	104	28
Florida.........	24,817	1,553	43	763	19,131	15,011	4,120	1,018	356	1,608	666
Georgia........	13,511	1,651	38	48	5,746	4,630	1,116	227	257	632	-
Hawaii.........	3,335	2,751	2	-	2,052	1,536	516	81	70	74	120
Idaho..........	2,377	1,837	23	-	1,055	747	308	35	56	209	3
Illinois.........	22,789	1,835	24	54	10,859	6,393	4,466	595	220	1,356	1,467
Indiana........	10,104	1,662	36	4	5,037	3,579	1,457	120	163	700	6
Iowa...........	5,185	1,772	31	-	2,479	1,723	756	109	120	346	-
Kansas........	4,848	1,804	28	49	2,304	1,741	563	126	70	356	1
Kentucky......	7,695	1,904	19	389	3,512	2,172	1,341	85	227	440	-
Louisiana......	6,512	1,457	45	25	3,719	2,061	1,658	145	239	549	12
Maine..........	2,661	2,087	14	31	1,191	847	344	109	47	181	2
Maryland......	10,354	1,955	16	256	4,362	2,498	1,863	234	173	652	154
Massachusetts ...	16,153	2,544	5	-	5,060	3,565	1,495	344	335	653	-
Michigan.......	22,756	2,290	9	1,703	9,785	7,666	2,118	737	192	1,075	12
Minnesota.....	13,339	2,712	4	9	5,775	3,724	2,052	248	172	608	-
Mississippi....	4,712	1,656	37	1	3,147	2,333	814	96	115	419	1
Missouri.......	8,572	1,532	44	18	4,032	2,788	1,244	137	210	696	1
Montana.......	1,411	1,564	42	219	344	-	344	31	43	188	20
Nebraska......	2,981	1,742	32	4	1,445	1,028	417	64	39	279	3
Nevada........	3,717	1,860	21	93	3,154	1,942	1,212	51	129	262	10
New Hampshire ..	1,696	1,372	47	474	1,152	-	556	106	54	117	58
New Jersey.....	18,148	2,157	12	3	8,200	5,508	2,692	478	282	506	854
New Mexico.....	3,743	2,058	15	35	2,007	1,502	505	61	65	233	7
New York.......	41,736	2,199	11	-	13,307	8,563	4,744	851	659	522	1,606
North Carolina ..	15,315	1,903	20	-	5,941	3,375	2,567	235	279	1,067	387
North Dakota	1,172	1,826	26	2	655	330	325	28	22	111	28
Ohio............	19,676	1,733	34	23	9,059	6,263	2,795	373	359	1,405	642
Oklahoma......	5,840	1,692	35	-	2,181	1,442	739	136	161	402	15
Oregon........	5,946	1,738	33	-	728	-	728	201	44	474	7
Pennsylvania...	22,467	1,829	25	117	10,460	7,057	3,403	504	440	764	678
Rhode Island ...	2,035	1,942	18	1	1,003	621	382	69	31	131	73
South Carolina ..	6,381	1,591	40	13	3,241	2,458	783	159	85	370	41
South Dakota ...	927	1,228	50	-	732	488	244	30	40	125	2
Tennessee.....	7,740	1,360	48	-	5,805	4,446	1,359	159	287	788	5
Texas..........	27,424	1,315	49	-	22,213	14,012	8,201	1,047	739	2,689	508
Utah............	3,979	1,782	30	-	1,924	1,423	501	72	83	330	-
Vermont	1,483	2,435	7	405	484	215	268	40	20	61	10
Virginia........	12,648	1,787	29	34	4,352	2,472	1,880	139	251	815	102
Washington....	12,567	2,132	13	1,698	9,684	7,739	1,945	440	261	775	290
West Virginia ...	3,343	1,849	22	4	1,800	917	883	41	101	240	183
Wisconsin......	12,575	2,344	8	87	5,106	3,507	1,599	302	96	916	278
Wyoming.......	964	1,951	17	101	477	369	108	12	12	81	2

See footnote at end of table.

No. 455. State Governments—Revenue by State: 2000—Con.

[See headnote, page 297]

State	License taxes					Income			Other taxes	
	Total [3]	Corporation license	Hunting and fishing license	Motor vehicle and operators license	Occupancy and business license, n.e.c. [4]	Total	Individual income	Corporation net income	Total [3]	Death and gift
United States...	32,598	6,460	1,110	16,445	7,193	227,095	194,573	32,522	16,819	7,998
Alabama	542	179	14	207	129	2,315	2,071	243	174	67
Alaska	92	2	19	36	34	438	-	438	711	2
Arizona	260	6	16	168	58	2,815	2,292	523	85	85
Arkansas	259	9	20	133	77	1,707	1,470	237	59	24
California	3,691	37	75	1,917	1,538	46,213	39,575	6,639	953	928
Colorado	300	5	53	190	45	3,972	3,637	335	94	62
Connecticut	365	13	3	262	75	4,400	3,974	427	352	238
Delaware	777	541	2	33	180	974	733	240	92	41
Florida	1,505	121	14	1,040	253	1,183	-	1,183	2,236	739
Georgia	467	40	24	269	64	7,077	6,365	712	173	148
Hawaii	111	3	-	77	21	1,140	1,064	75	32	23
Idaho	217	1	27	115	41	1,091	965	126	14	11
Illinois	1,571	144	28	1,087	301	9,898	7,637	2,261	406	348
Indiana	245	5	13	160	53	4,678	3,753	925	141	140
Iowa	493	33	18	350	70	2,105	1,890	215	109	99
Kansas	237	27	16	157	29	2,134	1,862	272	125	63
Kentucky	537	193	18	202	107	3,008	2,702	306	248	74
Louisiana	490	274	22	118	73	1,804	1,582	222	474	96
Maine	134	3	11	78	36	1,227	1,077	150	78	59
Maryland	379	13	11	197	155	5,044	4,613	431	313	157
Massachusetts	451	23	6	288	75	10,348	9,042	1,306	294	167
Michigan	1,208	13	48	863	213	9,573	7,190	2,382	488	186
Minnesota	977	4	54	673	224	6,351	5,547	803	226	83
Mississippi	279	68	11	135	53	1,234	1,007	228	50	22
Missouri	576	90	29	258	154	3,816	3,550	265	130	130
Montana	123	1	30	59	25	616	516	100	109	19
Nebraska	190	6	12	93	59	1,314	1,174	140	28	19
Nevada	362	23	6	126	113	-	-	-	108	76
New Hampshire	143	4	6	73	49	378	66	312	146	61
New Jersey	790	151	12	384	176	8,553	7,205	1,347	602	486
New Mexico	206	2	17	152	30	1,040	881	159	455	16
New York	970	67	32	710	106	25,966	23,194	2,772	1,493	1,055
North Carolina	743	158	15	452	109	8,407	7,210	1,197	225	188
North Dakota	87	-	4	47	36	277	199	78	151	6
Ohio	1,559	353	30	646	498	8,872	8,241	631	164	155
Oklahoma	829	43	14	645	115	2,329	2,135	194	501	88
Oregon	605	6	28	387	169	4,505	4,097	407	108	44
Pennsylvania	2,273	990	52	848	309	8,467	6,771	1,697	1,148	801
Rhode Island	91	13	2	52	23	904	829	75	36	34
South Carolina	375	42	14	124	111	2,673	2,446	227	80	43
South Dakota	118	2	15	41	53	45	-	45	31	28
Tennessee	899	494	25	274	94	794	180	614	242	92
Texas	3,813	2,099	63	1,043	526	-	-	-	1,398	278
Utah	138	1	23	88	22	1,825	1,651	174	91	65
Vermont	68	1	6	39	19	476	432	44	50	14
Virginia	514	30	20	339	112	7,395	6,829	566	353	150
Washington	608	14	29	324	183	-	-	-	577	83
West Virginia	174	8	16	92	30	1,184	966	218	182	21
Wisconsin	669	95	62	339	161	6,530	5,952	578	183	133
Wyoming	89	6	23	55	4	-	-	-	296	51

- Represents or rounds to zero.   X Not applicable.   [1] Duplicate intergovernmental transactions are excluded.   [2] Based on population as of April 1.   [3] Includes categories not shown separately.   [4] N.e.c. means not elsewhere classified.

Source: U.S. Census Bureau, <http://www.census.gov/govs/www/state00.html> (revised September 2002).

State and Local Government Finances and Employment

No. 456. State Governments—Expenditures and Debt by State: 2000

[In millions of dollars (1,084,097 represents $1,084,097,000,000) except as indicated. For fiscal year ending in year shown; see text, this section]

State	Total expenditure [1]	General expenditure – Total Amount	Per capita [2] (dol.)	Inter-govern-mental	Direct expenditures Total	Educa-tion	Public welfare	Health and hospitals	High-ways	Police protec-tion
United States...	1,084,097	964,723	3,435	327,070	637,653	138,330	198,684	59,529	61,942	8,581
Alabama	15,873	14,400	3,238	3,908	10,491	2,807	3,485	1,605	887	92
Alaska	6,611	5,972	9,525	1,027	4,945	646	803	120	630	50
Arizona	16,316	15,025	2,928	5,941	9,085	2,027	2,480	830	1,312	145
Arkansas	9,589	8,967	3,354	2,725	6,241	1,600	1,987	672	614	73
California	149,772	134,204	3,962	65,389	68,815	15,017	18,510	6,957	4,231	1,051
Colorado	13,930	12,485	2,903	3,703	8,782	2,617	2,211	420	963	77
Connecticut	16,723	14,856	4,362	3,363	11,493	1,504	3,020	1,473	751	140
Delaware	4,211	3,913	4,991	856	3,057	710	547	265	324	63
Florida	45,208	42,486	2,658	14,073	28,412	4,154	9,067	3,272	3,543	367
Georgia	24,813	23,092	2,821	7,180	15,912	4,173	5,469	1,011	1,578	193
Hawaii	6,605	5,975	4,930	158	5,818	1,854	1,019	572	226	4
Idaho	4,493	4,039	3,121	1,278	2,761	651	762	130	356	37
Illinois	41,183	36,895	2,971	12,050	24,845	4,651	8,466	2,814	1,829	336
Indiana	20,289	19,188	3,156	6,736	12,452	4,098	3,806	655	1,254	198
Iowa	11,453	10,520	3,595	3,212	7,309	1,862	2,153	768	1,017	80
Kansas	9,124	8,376	3,116	2,853	5,523	1,356	1,314	368	1,197	53
Kentucky	15,682	14,197	3,512	3,280	10,917	2,426	4,051	698	1,416	161
Louisiana	16,554	14,783	3,308	3,722	11,061	2,462	3,014	1,849	1,056	195
Maine	5,448	4,850	3,804	912	3,938	567	1,553	322	391	45
Maryland	19,370	17,281	3,263	4,356	12,925	2,654	3,922	1,055	878	234
Massachusetts	29,478	26,821	4,225	6,241	20,581	2,722	6,247	1,935	2,609	391
Michigan	42,749	39,004	3,925	17,201	21,803	6,284	7,606	1,735	1,259	284
Minnesota	23,326	20,975	4,264	7,610	13,364	3,119	4,777	560	953	123
Mississippi	10,972	10,049	3,532	3,248	6,801	1,468	2,295	849	776	67
Missouri	17,293	15,837	2,831	4,529	11,309	2,283	3,912	1,154	1,259	125
Montana	3,718	3,325	3,686	761	2,564	585	530	244	419	25
Nebraska	5,772	5,537	3,236	1,586	3,951	1,008	1,382	247	554	49
Nevada	6,047	5,369	2,687	2,250	3,119	711	791	194	526	58
New Hampshire	4,366	3,884	3,143	1,053	2,831	532	977	151	328	38
New Jersey	34,783	28,160	3,347	8,639	19,521	4,478	4,698	1,805	1,368	402
New Mexico	8,701	7,985	4,390	2,447	5,538	1,374	1,463	660	856	78
New York	96,925	80,617	4,248	31,273	49,344	6,225	20,698	4,519	3,147	422
North Carolina	29,615	27,242	3,384	9,301	17,941	4,203	5,158	1,732	2,256	351
North Dakota	2,856	2,569	4,001	590	1,979	512	544	73	294	12
Ohio	44,631	36,144	3,184	12,932	23,212	5,715	7,659	2,064	2,134	225
Oklahoma	10,630	9,146	2,650	3,089	6,057	2,043	864	462	977	75
Oregon	15,776	13,155	3,845	3,920	9,235	1,615	2,981	1,112	651	130
Pennsylvania	47,682	41,937	3,415	11,370	30,567	6,407	11,441	2,001	3,015	776
Rhode Island	4,648	3,987	3,805	678	3,310	569	1,135	274	220	36
South Carolina	16,237	14,195	3,538	3,806	10,389	2,404	3,441	1,330	1,116	203
South Dakota	2,403	2,228	2,951	448	1,780	321	477	107	340	18
Tennessee	16,853	15,822	2,781	4,364	11,458	2,670	4,766	999	1,184	112
Texas	60,425	54,452	2,611	16,231	38,221	8,882	11,204	3,956	4,768	338
Utah	8,592	7,956	3,563	1,978	5,979	1,819	1,452	578	765	74
Vermont	3,219	3,068	5,037	932	2,136	449	700	75	204	37
Virginia	24,314	22,608	3,194	7,132	15,476	3,943	3,540	1,871	2,142	210
Washington	25,902	21,951	3,724	6,371	15,580	4,058	5,058	1,796	1,096	153
West Virginia	7,552	6,490	3,590	1,360	5,131	1,016	1,762	237	838	52
Wisconsin	22,833	20,452	3,813	8,171	12,282	2,818	3,204	865	1,099	99
Wyoming	2,553	2,254	4,563	838	1,416	261	285	85	335	19

See footnote at end of table.

No. 456. State Governments—Expenditures and Debt by State: 2000—Con.

[See headnote, page 300]

State	General expenditure—Con. Direct expenditures—Con.					Liquor stores expenditures	Insurance trust expenditures	Cash and security holdings	Debt outstanding	
	Corrections	Natural resources	Parks and recreation	Governmental administration	Interest on general debt	Utility expenditures				Total	Per capita [2] (dol.)

State	Corrections	Natural resources	Parks and recreation	Gov. admin.	Interest on general debt	Utility exp.	Liquor stores exp.	Insurance trust exp.	Cash and security holdings	Total	Per capita [2] (dol.)
United States	33,040	15,001	4,049	34,500	29,187	10,723	3,195	105,456	2,518,936	547,876	1,951
Alabama	273	194	11	345	276	-	151	1,322	25,954	5,292	1,190
Alaska	174	249	9	336	248	65	-	574	47,024	4,150	6,619
Arizona	660	158	37	430	160	26	-	1,265	35,190	3,101	604
Arkansas	266	192	75	324	121	-	-	623	17,720	2,746	1,027
California	4,118	2,117	286	5,261	2,613	114	-	15,454	336,589	57,170	1,688
Colorado	599	174	59	366	251	10	-	1,434	30,811	4,431	1,030
Connecticut	554	101	41	892	1,089	205	-	1,662	29,080	18,456	5,419
Delaware	228	65	48	288	218	51	-	247	10,747	3,261	4,159
Florida	2,217	1,412	144	1,871	1,076	55	-	2,667	89,554	18,181	1,137
Georgia	969	496	128	566	387	-	-	1,721	49,499	7,086	866
Hawaii	155	80	46	312	483	-	-	629	12,773	5,592	4,614
Idaho	149	135	21	204	125	-	42	412	11,782	2,279	1,761
Illinois	1,277	375	141	1,160	1,825	-	-	4,288	86,684	28,828	2,321
Indiana	537	212	61	600	373	-	-	1,102	34,108	7,894	1,298
Iowa	224	236	18	410	131	-	74	859	24,551	2,362	807
Kansas	273	167	8	536	47	-	-	748	12,029	1,912	711
Kentucky	394	266	112	529	360	-	-	1,486	32,029	7,753	1,918
Louisiana	397	373	168	460	411	3	-	1,768	35,791	7,770	1,739
Maine	92	135	10	210	226	-	53	545	12,346	4,060	3,184
Maryland	894	430	173	798	801	384	-	1,705	47,984	11,365	2,146
Massachusetts	605	202	127	1,058	2,128	306	-	2,351	59,248	38,961	6,137
Michigan	1,483	386	125	792	920	-	465	3,281	77,922	19,445	1,957
Minnesota	293	436	99	664	349	-	-	2,351	53,967	5,602	1,139
Mississippi	242	228	50	223	182	-	133	790	21,915	3,222	1,132
Missouri	514	269	38	463	543	-	-	1,456	47,592	9,820	1,755
Montana	104	153	14	187	143	-	33	360	10,184	2,557	2,835
Nebraska	173	134	25	139	106	-	-	236	10,987	1,680	982
Nevada	218	76	18	152	120	45	-	633	18,562	2,990	1,496
New Hampshire	85	41	7	169	310	-	249	233	9,407	5,499	4,450
New Jersey	1,050	240	317	1,199	1,153	1,886	-	4,737	82,747	28,938	3,439
New Mexico	217	136	43	327	179	-	-	715	32,209	3,625	1,993
New York	2,298	366	495	3,469	3,663	6,378	-	9,930	211,314	78,616	4,143
North Carolina	906	559	152	724	585	-	-	2,373	73,229	9,336	1,160
North Dakota	29	75	9	80	77	-	-	287	6,842	1,520	2,367
Ohio	1,487	337	132	1,138	998	-	305	8,181	147,209	18,087	1,593
Oklahoma	462	183	61	388	236	278	-	1,205	24,404	5,663	1,641
Oregon	468	270	41	797	461	3	137	2,481	33,586	6,235	1,822
Pennsylvania	1,414	612	140	1,282	1,268	-	801	4,944	110,454	18,595	1,514
Rhode Island	139	41	13	256	277	59	-	602	11,458	5,681	5,422
South Carolina	436	246	56	325	259	797	-	1,245	24,872	7,057	1,759
South Dakota	62	71	22	98	120	-	-	175	8,539	2,305	3,053
Tennessee	351	225	116	429	190	4	-	1,027	29,018	3,292	579
Texas	2,677	653	56	1,367	1,032	-	-	5,973	188,148	19,228	922
Utah	245	141	30	408	185	-	87	548	17,492	3,885	1,740
Vermont	66	90	7	138	124	3	29	120	4,534	2,165	3,554
Virginia	859	181	76	818	792	5	264	1,436	58,387	12,011	1,697
Washington	731	502	64	504	607	-	290	3,644	66,541	11,734	1,991
West Virginia	156	149	55	330	207	9	43	1,010	9,636	3,730	2,063
Wisconsin	746	330	54	601	687	-	-	2,381	77,051	11,454	2,135
Wyoming	73	99	11	78	64	-	38	242	9,239	1,250	2,531

- Represents or rounds to zero. [1] Includes amounts not shown separately. [2] Based on estimated resident population as of April 1.

Source: U.S. Census Bureau, <http://www.census.gov/govs/www/state00.html> (accessed 21 July 2003).

No. 457. Local Governments—Revenue by State: 2000

[In millions of dollars (1,013,825 represents $1,013,825,000,000), except as noted. For fiscal year ending in year shown; see text, this section]

State	Total revenue [1]	General revenue Total	Per capita [2] (dol.)	Intergovernmental revenue Total	From federal government	From state governments	Taxes Total [1]	Property	Sales and gross receipts	Income	Motor licenses
United States..	1,013,825	888,865	3,158	349,894	32,836	317,058	332,696	238,182	57,143	20,625	1,302
Alabama	13,046	11,071	2,490	4,482	343	4,139	2,977	1,160	1,358	88	21
Alaska	2,835	2,606	4,156	1,103	213	890	889	717	146	-	11
Arizona	17,365	14,507	2,827	6,257	635	5,622	5,233	3,609	1,427	-	-
Arkansas	5,718	5,138	1,922	2,763	116	2,647	1,091	484	584	-	-
California	160,439	135,131	3,989	64,891	4,821	60,070	36,260	22,904	10,075	-	-
Colorado	15,789	13,756	3,198	3,656	431	3,224	6,141	3,680	2,139	-	34
Connecticut	11,190	10,245	3,008	3,648	286	3,361	5,480	5,407	-	-	-
Delaware	1,921	1,729	2,206	863	42	821	486	382	8	41	-
District of Columbia	6,383	5,732	10,022	1,748	1,748	-	3,216	693	1,000	1,339	17
Florida	55,505	48,923	3,061	16,171	1,813	14,358	17,119	13,336	3,133	-	28
Georgia	27,036	23,651	2,889	7,967	659	7,307	9,742	5,884	3,552	-	-
Hawaii	1,703	1,519	1,253	322	170	152	767	603	89	-	51
Idaho	3,294	3,155	2,438	1,357	80	1,276	917	867	15	-	4
Illinois	45,243	38,734	3,119	13,649	1,516	12,134	17,467	14,457	2,517	-	95
Indiana	18,046	16,679	2,743	6,004	377	5,627	6,259	5,548	76	515	2
Iowa	9,053	8,414	2,876	3,327	254	3,073	2,905	2,599	219	38	13
Kansas	8,705	7,694	2,862	2,945	117	2,828	2,768	2,125	582	-	2
Kentucky	8,723	7,749	1,917	3,229	276	2,953	2,478	1,333	174	747	17
Louisiana	12,153	11,302	2,529	4,117	340	3,776	4,375	1,717	2,508	-	4
Maine	3,197	3,103	2,433	1,011	83	928	1,601	1,568	4	-	13
Maryland	16,866	15,401	2,908	4,727	587	4,140	7,935	4,553	261	2,541	-
Massachusetts	21,422	18,206	2,868	7,982	1,011	6,971	7,889	7,642	96	-	-
Michigan	36,411	32,736	3,294	16,772	1,163	15,609	8,718	7,796	121	539	1
Minnesota	19,251	17,340	3,525	7,673	389	7,285	4,834	4,556	133	-	4
Mississippi	7,401	6,864	2,413	2,968	179	2,790	1,588	1,461	55	-	-
Missouri	15,641	13,734	2,455	4,687	423	4,264	5,742	3,386	1,801	299	12
Montana	2,132	2,054	2,277	794	119	674	721	689	2	-	13
Nebraska	6,877	4,726	2,762	1,553	169	1,384	1,992	1,545	245	-	19
Nevada	7,113	6,631	3,319	2,688	234	2,454	2,108	1,345	432	-	-
New Hampshire	3,205	3,129	2,531	1,155	68	1,087	1,582	1,554	-	-	-
New Jersey	29,133	28,409	3,376	9,281	572	8,709	14,690	14,446	30	33	-
New Mexico	5,011	4,683	2,575	2,720	266	2,454	1,057	586	427	-	-
New York	115,278	96,904	5,107	34,497	3,043	31,454	45,132	25,202	9,158	8,721	151
North Carolina	26,160	23,349	2,901	10,440	996	9,444	6,125	4,607	1,260	-	17
North Dakota	1,791	1,707	2,659	714	152	562	596	525	59	-	-
Ohio	37,394	35,444	3,122	13,452	1,091	12,362	14,562	9,522	1,294	3,210	107
Oklahoma	8,524	7,795	2,259	3,014	219	2,795	2,411	1,303	1,054	-	2
Oregon	11,786	11,024	3,222	4,702	608	4,094	3,466	2,789	185	-	8
Pennsylvania	38,472	35,359	2,879	14,358	1,993	12,364	14,114	9,949	376	2,514	-
Rhode Island	2,486	2,290	2,185	681	106	575	1,377	1,359	2	-	-
South Carolina	10,948	9,857	2,457	3,444	322	3,122	3,162	2,667	239	-	16
South Dakota	1,821	1,653	2,189	520	88	432	808	632	141	-	18
Tennessee	18,778	13,018	2,288	4,323	355	3,968	4,692	2,887	1,511	-	94
Texas	65,510	57,393	2,752	18,591	2,014	16,578	24,802	19,817	4,366	-	275
Utah	6,633	5,418	2,426	2,190	294	1,895	1,894	1,303	506	-	-
Vermont	1,580	1,406	2,309	838	26	812	392	377	1	-	-
Virginia	21,172	19,125	2,702	6,950	696	6,254	8,435	5,952	1,618	-	121
Washington	22,703	19,119	3,244	7,584	733	6,851	6,166	3,795	1,797	-	121
West Virginia	3,777	3,631	2,008	1,692	124	1,568	1,019	852	36	-	-
Wisconsin	19,137	17,642	3,289	8,578	426	8,152	5,971	5,602	226	-	1
Wyoming	2,070	1,979	4,005	817	47	769	541	411	107	-	9

See footnote at end of table.

No. 457. Local Governments—Revenue by State: 2000—Con.

[See headnote, page 302]

State	Current charges & miscellaneous general revenue	General revenue - Current charges Total [1]	Education	Hospital	Sewerage	Miscellaneous general revenue Total [1]	Interest earnings	Special assessment	Utility revenue	Liquor store revenue	Insurance trust revenue
United States..	206,275	137,013	15,630	36,036	24,273	69,262	35,482	3,734	80,441	697	43,822
Alabama	3,612	2,736	265	1,669	232	876	443	9	1,744	-	231
Alaska	614	398	37	52	47	216	155	3	204	-	25
Arizona	3,017	1,785	355	219	294	1,232	686	62	2,634	-	224
Arkansas	1,284	862	135	313	152	422	241	11	535	-	45
California	33,981	21,471	1,565	4,173	3,143	12,510	5,727	937	13,623	-	11,685
Colorado	3,959	2,648	286	570	399	1,311	657	66	1,424	-	609
Connecticut	1,117	648	77	15	191	469	235	28	474	-	471
Delaware	381	245	13	-	108	136	74	-	147	-	45
District of Columbia	769	331	21	53	101	438	196	-	448	-	202
Florida	15,632	10,506	1,255	2,806	1,458	5,126	2,639	950	5,056	-	1,526
Georgia	5,942	3,976	224	1,805	621	1,966	1,025	19	2,826	-	559
Hawaii	430	280	-	-	138	150	78	14	185	-	-
Idaho	881	709	52	336	86	172	76	11	137	-	3
Illinois	7,617	4,732	886	486	703	2,885	1,580	89	2,682	-	3,828
Indiana	4,416	3,008	287	1,705	495	1,408	480	19	1,307	-	60
Iowa	2,183	1,625	438	631	229	558	269	18	620	-	19
Kansas	1,981	1,253	230	413	179	728	455	62	802	-	210
Kentucky	2,042	1,000	104	141	250	1,042	883	3	962	-	13
Louisiana	2,810	1,975	66	1,199	200	835	565	9	720	-	131
Maine	490	358	42	51	114	132	66	3	94	-	-
Maryland	2,739	1,768	471	-	540	971	481	108	409	142	913
Massachusetts	2,335	1,681	192	159	636	654	310	64	1,911	-	1,305
Michigan	7,247	4,467	747	568	1,239	2,780	1,087	94	1,414	-	2,262
Minnesota	4,832	2,909	226	766	581	1,923	845	252	1,181	202	528
Mississippi	2,308	1,801	201	1,237	135	507	245	5	537	-	-
Missouri	3,305	2,355	428	758	385	950	535	20	1,273	-	634
Montana	539	329	53	52	55	210	103	42	78	-	-
Nebraska	1,181	799	164	229	108	382	202	31	2,019	-	132
Nevada	1,835	1,346	83	478	209	489	305	29	482	-	-
New Hampshire	391	293	37	-	74	98	53	1	75	-	1
New Jersey	4,437	2,793	527	210	1,005	1,644	620	14	713	-	11
New Mexico	906	551	73	127	97	355	222	9	328	-	-
New York	17,275	12,235	726	3,052	1,301	5,040	2,133	72	6,069	-	12,305
North Carolina	6,784	5,274	461	2,677	855	1,510	840	12	2,425	343	43
North Dakota	397	195	40	-	28	202	76	33	70	-	14
Ohio	7,430	4,765	907	789	1,396	2,665	1,438	106	1,886	-	63
Oklahoma	2,369	1,719	243	772	199	650	341	5	664	-	65
Oregon	2,856	1,909	332	304	432	947	447	71	761	-	1
Pennsylvania	6,888	3,886	549	20	990	3,002	2,055	95	1,837	-	1,276
Rhode Island	231	153	18	-	52	78	38	3	103	-	93
South Carolina	3,251	2,529	192	1,470	216	722	467	19	1,087	-	4
South Dakota	324	217	40	26	44	107	64	6	135	10	23
Tennessee	4,004	2,910	182	1,541	398	1,094	485	5	5,241	-	518
Texas	13,999	9,350	1,372	2,376	1,791	4,649	3,084	87	6,212	-	1,905
Utah	1,334	738	66	36	150	596	270	3	1,216	-	-
Vermont	176	98	16	-	32	78	25	5	153	-	20
Virginia	3,741	2,509	255	251	681	1,232	707	42	1,143	-	904
Washington	5,369	3,681	251	807	843	1,688	663	93	3,321	-	263
West Virginia	921	577	35	244	118	344	248	3	129	-	16
Wisconsin	3,093	2,145	363	116	513	948	473	87	863	-	632
Wyoming	621	484	44	334	31	137	91	8	87	-	4

- Represents or rounds to zero. [1] Includes items not shown separately. [2] Based on enumerated resident population as of April 1.

Source: U.S. Census Bureau; "Government Finances 1999-2000"; issued January 2003, <http://www.census.gov/govs/estimate/00allpub.pdf>; (accessed 16 June 2003).

State and Local Government Finances and Employment

No. 458. Local Governments—Expenditures and Debt by State: 2000

[In millions of dollars, (996,267 represents $996,267,000,000), except as indicated. For fiscal year ending in year shown; see text, this section]

State	Total expenditure [1]	General expenditure Total amount	Per capita [2] (dol.)	Direct general expenditures	Education	Public welfare	Health	Hospitals	Highways	Police protection	Fire protection
United States..	996,267	875,495	3,540	865,114	383,282	34,666	23,991	43,822	39,394	48,217	23,102
Alabama	13,357	11,574	3,004	11,571	4,961	41	268	1,762	605	564	252
Alaska	2,931	2,655	4,675	2,655	1,115	7	58	58	197	127	66
Arizona	17,092	14,351	3,331	14,177	5,844	465	175	369	647	951	682
Arkansas	5,381	4,818	2,013	4,816	2,598	13	28	270	255	279	122
California	150,813	128,033	4,452	126,953	48,542	10,704	5,275	5,823	4,373	7,653	3,588
Colorado	15,943	13,745	3,707	13,745	5,287	520	200	721	780	753	327
Connecticut	10,660	9,935	3,130	9,926	5,218	96	104	20	436	542	373
Delaware	1,800	1,637	2,296	1,634	1,005	1	13	-	103	103	19
District of Columbia	6,527	5,152	11,411	5,152	969	1,254	274	359	38	330	113
Florida	53,358	47,070	3,339	46,878	18,672	440	476	3,560	1,632	3,371	1,630
Georgia	25,931	22,214	3,168	22,166	10,595	99	717	1,826	918	1,086	553
Hawaii	1,792	1,474	1,479	1,474	-	21	28	-	127	218	101
Idaho	3,192	3,070	2,467	3,067	1,481	29	52	330	204	170	77
Illinois	45,624	39,590	3,674	39,558	18,078	387	454	1,114	2,248	2,718	1,300
Indiana	17,753	16,349	2,920	16,288	7,352	459	156	1,792	711	644	395
Iowa	9,082	8,338	3,104	8,254	4,102	106	261	649	819	346	127
Kansas	8,158	7,371	3,035	7,361	3,528	39	142	425	518	377	175
Kentucky	9,074	8,106	2,245	8,104	3,948	45	266	133	338	327	257
Louisiana	12,187	11,227	2,727	11,216	4,724	57	79	1,447	596	635	283
Maine	3,108	3,017	2,438	3,017	1,661	32	14	61	181	118	78
Maryland	15,743	14,680	2,973	14,521	7,401	88	239	-	609	886	475
Massachusetts	21,572	17,818	3,398	17,189	8,722	62	97	213	626	1,087	774
Michigan	36,046	33,098	3,627	32,948	16,200	636	1,881	563	1,826	1,509	616
Minnesota	19,799	17,893	4,025	17,802	7,164	1,193	378	888	1,435	750	256
Mississippi	7,656	7,133	2,691	7,131	3,350	26	48	1,216	455	337	155
Missouri	15,188	13,511	2,715	13,510	6,941	129	228	784	889	761	394
Montana	2,029	1,962	2,249	1,959	1,056	25	46	53	100	111	41
Nebraska	6,640	4,461	3,881	4,455	2,259	44	33	241	326	187	107
Nevada	7,430	6,640	3,719	6,637	2,309	95	69	474	601	481	223
New Hampshire	2,967	2,890	2,400	2,833	1,528	136	18	-	141	149	100
New Jersey	28,660	28,001	3,406	27,710	14,310	1,124	284	243	973	1,829	630
New Mexico	4,963	4,582	2,729	4,561	2,322	52	26	126	208	305	129
New York	111,562	96,658	5,879	90,676	34,406	8,487	2,171	4,878	3,688	5,295	2,200
North Carolina	26,145	22,818	3,248	22,494	9,960	1,141	1,229	2,576	381	1,030	480
North Dakota	1,786	1,706	2,782	1,695	742	35	18	-	156	56	45
Ohio	36,946	34,664	3,254	34,437	14,898	1,908	1,919	979	1,817	1,900	1,014
Oklahoma	8,381	7,711	2,428	7,710	3,793	22	100	762	427	443	266
Oregon	12,233	10,929	3,576	10,926	4,833	89	510	328	595	566	313
Pennsylvania	39,166	35,316	3,189	35,304	16,848	1,877	1,790	154	1,108	1,445	434
Rhode Island	2,438	2,252	2,326	2,250	1,287	9	4	-	65	175	152
South Carolina	11,024	9,889	2,748	9,871	4,722	17	275	1,411	212	450	190
South Dakota	1,806	1,665	2,392	1,664	897	11	15	28	200	70	29
Tennessee	19,561	13,855	3,438	13,815	5,699	105	209	1,531	655	828	400
Texas	65,970	58,071	3,164	57,541	30,335	255	1,300	3,597	2,433	2,866	1,373
Utah	6,438	5,042	2,883	5,034	2,414	21	131	32	268	307	127
Vermont	1,470	1,312	2,413	1,310	882	1	4	-	123	41	25
Virginia	20,932	19,273	2,957	19,251	9,189	948	494	269	485	965	549
Washington	22,293	17,933	3,782	17,895	7,506	42	588	933	1,115	854	551
West Virginia	3,804	3,587	2,104	3,581	2,156	1	60	254	51	119	55
Wisconsin	19,829	18,515	3,697	18,480	8,609	1,266	756	219	1,612	1,025	458
Wyoming	2,029	1,915	4,107	1,914	864	6	31	348	91	80	23

See footnote at end of table.

No. 458. Local Governments—Expenditures and Debt by State: 2000—Con.

[See headnote, page 304]

State	General expenditure—Con. Selected functions (direct expenditures)—Con.								Utility expenditures	Insurance trust expenditures	Debt outstanding
	Corrections	Parks and recreation	Housing[3]	Sewerage	Solid waste	Governmental administration	Interest on general debt	Other			
United States...	15,766	20,989	23,427	27,098	14,861	47,160	40,626	78,713	100,393	19,774	903,939
Alabama	131	267	301	452	217	563	492	696	1,710	74	11,507
Alaska	1	70	134	79	55	169	170	349	262	14	3,106
Arizona	295	432	352	389	235	1,092	866	1,383	2,648	93	20,498
Arkansas	61	62	124	136	110	227	231	300	545	18	5,083
California	3,052	2,809	4,402	3,627	1,638	8,209	4,936	12,321	18,691	4,088	120,750
Colorado	221	673	330	408	85	896	914	1,629	1,989	209	18,768
Connecticut	-	189	426	272	218	461	256	1,316	474	251	5,039
Delaware	-	20	41	94	10	88	65	73	138	25	1,324
District of Columbia	305	172	58	303	37	320	236	383	1,303	72	5,062
Florida	1,056	1,333	845	1,563	1,518	2,575	2,760	5,448	5,824	464	60,314
Georgia	407	412	592	865	456	1,511	669	1,461	3,461	256	22,862
Hawaii	-	171	76	122	134	144	104	227	319	-	2,317
Idaho	42	70	21	103	76	175	54	182	121	1	1,150
Illinois	485	1,824	1,430	1,080	374	2,556	1,819	3,692	4,041	1,993	38,745
Indiana	190	495	418	555	170	953	596	1,401	1,309	95	11,974
Iowa	73	228	128	250	124	323	226	491	731	12	4,948
Kansas	76	182	113	147	112	418	427	683	741	46	8,528
Kentucky	216	125	124	331	124	321	932	614	943	24	15,668
Louisiana	383	227	277	298	211	643	543	813	851	120	10,210
Maine	31	45	83	118	84	145	95	269	91	-	1,785
Maryland	210	508	536	510	412	771	641	1,235	476	464	12,464
Massachusetts	189	168	958	574	318	652	417	2,331	2,754	1,000	16,202
Michigan	370	615	234	1,694	352	1,969	1,224	3,260	1,970	978	27,750
Minnesota	298	615	561	622	229	908	1,006	1,497	1,445	284	21,806
Mississippi	50	90	130	126	118	407	273	352	523	-	5,297
Missouri	158	393	233	412	111	686	425	965	1,421	256	9,466
Montana	21	36	32	45	48	116	73	156	67	-	1,240
Nebraska	59	101	110	117	65	213	106	489	2,095	84	4,967
Nevada	254	352	135	108	8	589	385	554	790	-	10,245
New Hampshire	30	48	42	65	71	151	67	287	76	1	1,542
New Jersey	430	375	554	962	846	1,362	1,043	2,746	649	9	21,376
New Mexico	99	164	82	117	102	241	196	391	381	-	4,027
New York	2,094	1,289	2,804	1,766	1,969	2,997	5,596	11,037	8,755	6,149	98,934
North Carolina	253	452	551	597	544	849	674	1,775	3,013	17	19,778
North Dakota	12	115	81	19	30	91	69	225	73	7	1,261
Ohio	451	1,050	853	1,302	391	2,437	1,100	2,420	2,213	69	24,000
Oklahoma	49	211	141	226	136	360	272	503	641	29	5,745
Oregon	279	281	391	584	95	584	394	1,084	1,248	56	9,372
Pennsylvania	808	676	1,230	1,273	455	1,892	2,648	2,665	2,995	855	54,730
Rhode Island	-	33	113	58	29	84	58	184	93	92	1,197
South Carolina	122	215	168	245	235	581	475	553	1,131	3	11,613
South Dakota	19	68	20	44	21	88	45	108	125	7	984
Tennessee	253	332	451	466	289	723	594	1,279	5,414	292	15,085
Texas	1,078	1,159	1,166	1,591	703	2,691	3,562	3,431	7,344	555	80,947
Utah	106	208	99	182	90	372	199	479	1,396	-	8,509
Vermont	-	13	26	36	26	50	25	59	154	4	674
Virginia	387	517	513	678	451	1,215	940	1,651	1,330	329	19,535
Washington	322	569	501	722	405	1,092	791	1,905	4,232	127	26,963
West Virginia	28	48	91	120	46	205	200	147	193	25	3,364
Wisconsin	284	443	333	611	249	878	676	1,062	1,093	221	14,109
Wyoming	25	40	8	38	30	116	65	150	111	3	1,118

-Represents or rounds to zero. [1] Duplicate intergovernmental transactions are excluded. [2] Based on enumerated population as of April 1. [3] Includes community development.

Source: U.S. Census Bureau, Governmental Finances, annual. See also <http://www.census.gov/govs/estimate/00allpub.pdf> (released September 2003).

No. 459. Estimated State and Local Taxes Paid by a Family of Four in Selected Cities: 2001

[Data based on average family of four (two wage earners and two school age children) owning their own home and living in a city where taxes apply. Comprises state and local sales, income, auto, and real estate taxes. For definition of median, see Guide to Tabular Presentation]

City	Total taxes paid by gross family income level (dollars)					Total taxes paid as percent of income				
	$25,000	$50,000	$75,000	$100,000	$150,000	$25,000	$50,000	$75,000	$100,000	$150,000
Albuquerque, NM	1,592	3,901	6,613	9,293	14,803	6.4	7.8	8.8	9.3	9.9
Atlanta, GA	1,982	5,049	8,359	11,436	17,466	7.9	10.1	11.1	11.4	11.6
Baltimore, MD	1,713	5,549	8,658	11,526	17,166	6.9	11.1	11.5	11.5	11.4
Boston, MA	1,621	4,328	6,857	9,175	13,798	6.5	8.7	9.1	9.2	9.2
Charlotte, NC	1,820	4,449	7,258	10,195	15,557	7.3	8.9	9.7	10.2	10.4
Chicago, IL	2,183	4,816	7,570	9,934	14,621	8.7	9.6	10.1	9.9	9.7
Columbus, OH	2,076	4,594	7,462	10,339	16,322	8.3	9.2	9.9	10.3	10.9
Denver, CO	1,083	2,793	4,705	6,967	10,459	4.3	5.6	6.3	7.0	7.0
Detroit, MI	2,602	5,619	8,866	12,078	17,850	10.4	11.2	11.8	12.1	11.9
Honolulu, HI	1,759	4,107	6,767	9,246	14,338	7.0	8.2	9.0	9.2	9.6
Houston, TX	1,537	3,020	4,698	6,038	8,568	6.1	6.0	6.3	6.0	5.7
Indianapolis, IN	1,828	3,826	5,928	7,844	11,683	7.3	7.7	7.9	7.8	7.8
Jacksonville, FL	970	2,216	3,606	4,723	6,927	3.9	4.4	4.8	4.7	4.6
Kansas City, MO	1,904	4,334	6,674	9,079	13,937	7.6	8.7	8.9	9.1	9.3
Las Vegas, NV	1,332	2,404	3,616	4,619	6,582	5.3	4.8	4.8	4.6	4.4
Los Angeles, CA	2,127	4,240	7,736	11,364	18,740	8.5	8.5	10.3	11.4	12.5
Memphis, TN	1,661	3,044	4,627	5,925	8,540	6.6	6.1	6.2	5.9	5.7
Milwaukee, WI	1,896	5,188	8,520	11,481	17,247	7.6	10.4	11.4	11.5	11.5
Minneapolis, MN	2,125	5,564	8,957	12,158	18,605	8.5	11.1	11.9	12.2	12.4
New Orleans, LA	1,082	3,480	6,030	8,175	12,862	4.3	7.0	8.0	8.2	8.6
New York City, NY	1,793	5,170	9,058	12,734	20,335	7.2	10.3	12.1	12.7	13.6
Oklahoma City, OK	1,824	4,115	6,766	8,868	13,900	7.3	8.2	9.0	8.9	9.3
Omaha, NE	1,795	4,190	7,039	9,694	15,477	7.2	8.4	9.4	9.7	10.3
Philadelphia, PA	2,765	6,623	9,826	12,773	18,642	11.1	13.2	13.1	12.8	12.4
Phoenix, AZ	1,656	3,837	5,775	8,690	13,757	6.6	7.7	7.7	8.7	9.2
Portland, OR	2,275	5,071	8,298	11,209	16,923	9.1	10.1	11.1	11.2	11.3
Seattle, WA	1,869	3,460	5,233	6,670	9,497	7.5	6.9	7.0	6.7	6.3
Virginia Beach, VA	1,737	3,879	6,213	8,389	12,620	6.9	7.8	8.3	8.4	8.4
Washington, DC	1,761	4,933	8,177	11,220	17,215	7.0	9.9	10.9	11.2	11.5
Wichita, KS	1,167	3,224	5,708	8,174	12,916	4.7	6.4	7.6	8.2	8.6
Average [1]	1,859	4,299	6,978	9,507	14,507	7.4	8.6	9.3	9.5	9.7
Median [1]	1,779	4,185	6,767	9,289	14,338	7.1	8.4	9.0	9.3	9.6

[1] Based on selected cities and District of Columbia. For complete list of cities, see Table 460.

Source: Government of the District of Columbia, Department of Finance and Revenue, *Tax Rates and Tax Burdens in the District of Columbia: A Nationwide Comparison*, annual. <http://www.cfo.dc.gov/main.asp>.

No. 460. Residential Property Tax Rates for Largest City in Each State: 2001

[Effective tax rate is amount each jurisdiction considers based upon assessment level used. Assessment level is ratio of assessed value to assumed market value. Nominal rate is announced rates it levied at taxable value of house]

City	Effective tax rate per $100		Assessment level (percent)	Nominal rate per $100	City	Effective tax rate per $100		Assessment level (percent)	Nominal rate per $100
	Rank	Rate				Rank	Rate		
Bridgeport, CT	1	4.55	70.0	6.50	Portland, OR	28	1.47	85.0	1.73
Providence, RI	2	4.00	90.0	4.44	Salt Lake City, UT	29	1.45	79.0	1.83
Newark, NJ	3	3.59	100.0	3.59	Boston, MA	30	1.44	99.0	1.46
Manchester, NH	4	3.12	11.8	26.40	Louisville, KY	31	1.38	20.0	6.90
Milwaukee, WI	5	3.07	100.0	3.07	Wilmington, DE	32	1.31	54.8	2.38
Philadelphia, PA	6	2.65	93.4	2.84	Wichita, KS	33	1.25	33.3	3.76
Houston, TX	7	2.64	32.0	8.26	Little Rock, AR	34	1.18	86.4	1.37
Des Moines, IA	8	2.62	100.0	2.62	Minneapolis, MN	35	1.17	100.0	1.17
Baltimore, MD	9	2.40	100.0	2.40	Oklahoma City, OK	36	1.15	88.1	1.31
Portland, ME	10	2.33	100.0	2.33	Albuquerque, NM	37	1.14	19.0	6.00
Fargo, ND	11	2.23	34.5	6.46	Charlotte, NC	38	1.12	92.1	1.22
Burlington, VT	12	2.06	4.2	49.14	Virginia Beach, VA	39	1.11	11.0	10.10
Jacksonville, FL	13	2.00	82.9	2.41	Seattle, WA	40	1.11	100.0	1.11
Indianapolis, IN	14	1.97	100.0	1.97	Los Angeles, CA	41	1.07	100.0	1.07
Atlanta, GA	15	1.91	95.0	2.01	Las Vegas, NV	42	1.07	91.7	1.17
Detroit, MI	16	1.86	22.2	8.35	Phoenix, AZ	43	1.06	89.4	1.19
Omaha, NE	17	1.82	10.0	18.20	Washington, DC	44	1.06	35.0	3.03
Boise City, ID	18	1.76	25.0	7.02	Chicago, IL	45	0.91	60.0	1.52
New Orleans, LA	19	1.72	40.0	4.30	Charleston, WV	46	0.86	89.8	0.96
Anchorage, AK	20	1.70	10.0	17.00	New York City, NY	47	0.77	6.9	11.18
Jackson, MS	21	1.69	10.0	16.91	Denver, CO	48	0.70	9.5	7.33
Columbus, OH	22	1.65	95.6	1.73	Cheyenne, WY	49	0.70	10.0	6.95
Memphis, TN	23	1.63	90.8	1.80	Birmingham, AL	50	0.52	9.2	5.68
Sioux Falls, SD	24	1.59	30.6	5.19	Honolulu, HI	51	0.37	100.0	0.37
Billings, MT	25	1.52	4.0	37.93					
Columbia, SC	26	1.50	15.0	10.00	Unweighted average	(X)	1.69	59.0	6.58
Kansas City, MO	27	1.50	72.1	2.07	Median	(X)	1.50	(X)	(X)

X Not applicable.

Source: Government of the District of Columbia, Department of Finance and Revenue, *Tax Rates and Tax Burdens in the District of Columbia: A Nationwide Comparison*, annual. <http://www.cfo.dc.gov/main.asp>.

No. 461. Gross Revenue From Parimutuel and Amusement Taxes and Lotteries by State: 2000

[In millions of dollars (38,993 represents $38,993,000,000). For fiscal years; see text, this section]

State	Gross revenue (mil. dol.)	Amusement taxes [1]	Parimutuel taxes	Lottery revenue Total [2] (mil. dol.)	Prizes	Admini- stration	Proceeds available from ticket sales
United States...	38,993	3,638	338	35,018	20,701	2,235	12,092
Alabama	4	-	4	(X)	(X)	(X)	(X)
Alaska	2	2	(X)	(X)	(X)	(X)	(X)
Arizona	276	1	3	272	140	26	107
Arkansas	7	-	7	(X)	(X)	(X)	(X)
California	2,465	(X)	46	2,419	1,369	164	886
Colorado	425	75	7	343	224	31	88
Connecticut	1,171	319	11	840	502	80	257
Delaware	329	(X)	-	329	51	7	271
Florida	2,181	(X)	49	2,131	1,107	125	899
Georgia	2,060	(X)	(X)	2,060	1,260	122	677
Hawaii	(X)	(X)	(X)	(X)	(X)	(X)	(X)
Idaho	87	(X)	(X)	87	51	18	18
Illinois	1,881	488	24	1,369	799	62	508
Indiana	983	448	4	531	337	32	162
Iowa	338	177	3	158	98	23	37
Kansas	181	1	4	176	104	21	51
Kentucky	596	-	21	575	411	6	158
Louisiana	681	421	6	254	139	18	97
Maine	148	(X)	4	143	84	16	43
Maryland	1,185	10	2	1,173	657	109	408
Massachusetts	3,505	6	8	3,491	2,584	68	839
Michigan	1,683	53	13	1,616	921	81	614
Minnesota	434	62	1	370	242	71	57
Mississippi	177	177	(X)	(X)	(X)	(X)	(X)
Missouri	658	182	(X)	476	281	38	157
Montana	70	41	-	28	16	6	7
Nebraska	76	7	1	68	36	16	16
Nevada	708	708	(X)	(X)	(X)	(X)	(X)
New Hampshire	199	2	4	193	126	6	60
New Jersey	2,079	340	(X)	1,738	973	53	713
New Mexico	131	20	1	111	62	23	25
New York	3,352	2	36	3,314	1,768	100	1,446
North Carolina	11	11	(X)	(X)	(X)	(X)	(X)
North Dakota	13	13	(X)	(X)	(X)	(X)	(X)
Ohio	2,172	(X)	17	2,156	1,275	95	785
Oklahoma	12	8	4	(X)	(X)	(X)	(X)
Oregon	1,345	-	1	1,343	842	234	267
Pennsylvania	1,615	1	26	1,589	829	57	704
Rhode Island	749	(X)	5	744	591	7	147
South Carolina	38	38	(X)	(X)	(X)	(X)	(X)
South Dakota	123	-	1	122	13	8	101
Tennessee	(X)	(X)	(X)	(X)	(X)	(X)	(X)
Texas	2,691	23	12	2,657	1,509	271	878
Utah	(X)	(X)	(X)	(X)	(X)	(X)	(X)
Vermont	75	(X)	(X)	75	47	9	19
Virginia	981	(X)	(X)	981	638	117	227
Washington	455	(X)	2	453	290	62	101
West Virginia	261	(X)	8	253	95	22	136
Wisconsin	383	-	3	380	232	32	115
Wyoming	-	(X)	-	(X)	(X)	(X)	(X)

- Represents or rounds to zero.   X Not applicable.   [1] Represents nonlicense taxes.   [2] Excludes commissions.

Source: U.S. Census Bureau, unpublished data.

No. 462. Lottery Sales—Type of Game: 1980 to 2002

[In millions of dollars (2,393 represents $2,393,000,000). For fiscal years]

Game	1980	1985	1990	1995	1999	2000	2001	2002
Total ticket sales	2,393	9,035	20,017	31,931	35,966	37,201	38,441	41,979
Instant [1]	527	1,296	5,204	11,511	13,933	15,459	16,420	18,509
Three-digit [2]	1,554	3,376	4,572	5,737	5,237	5,341	5,245	5,356
Four-digit [2]	55	693	1,302	1,941	2,655	2,711	2,776	2,916
Lotto [3]	52	3,583	8,563	10,594	9,794	9,160	8,865	9,564
Other [4]	206	88	376	2,148	4,347	4,530	5,134	5,633
State proceeds (net income) [5]	978	3,735	7,703	11,100	11,255	11,404	11,916	12,478

[1] Player scratches a latex section on ticket which reveals instantly whether ticket is a winner.   [2] Players choose and bet on three or four digits, depending on game, with various payoffs for different straight order or mixed combination bets.   [3] Players typically select six digits out of a large field of numbers. Varying prizes are offered for matching three through six numbers drawn by lottery.   [4] Includes break-open tickets, spiel, keno, video lottery, etc.   [5] Sales minus prizes and expenses equal net government income.

Source: TLF Publications, Inc., Boyds, MD, *2002 World Lottery Almanac* annual; *LaFleur's Fiscal 2001 Lottery Report*; (copyright).

No. 463. City Governments—Revenue for Largest Cities: 2000

[In millions of dollars (63,471 represents $63,471,000,000). For fiscal years ending in year shown; see text, this section. Cities ranked by size of 2000 based on enumerated resident population as of April 1. Data reflect inclusion of fiscal activity of dependent school systems where applicable. Regarding intercity comparisons, see text, this section. See Appendix III]

Cities ranked by 2000 population	Total revenue	General revenue Total	Intergovernmental Total	From federal government	From state/local government	From local government	General revenue from own sources Total	Taxes Total	Property	Sales and gross receipts Total	General sales	Public utilities	Current charges Total	Parks and recreation	Sewerage[1]	Miscellaneous Total	Interest earnings	Utility revenue[2]	Employee retirement revenue
New York, NY	63,471	48,435	18,789	2,493	16,186	110	29,646	22,547	7,921	4,559	3,526	354	4,977	48	940	2,122	784	2,731	12,305
Los Angeles, CA	10,781	5,308	809	327	406	76	4,500	2,300	698	1,045	442	492	1,690	74	473	510	228	2,910	2,563
Chicago, IL	5,785	4,472	1,133	365	767	-	3,339	1,910	643	1,073	182	456	864	-	127	566	285	297	1,015
Houston, TX	2,892	1,970	153	111	39	-	1,816	1,072	538	504	314	147	575	25	279	169	109	285	637
Philadelphia, PA[2]	5,397	4,399	1,790	435	1,239	116	2,609	1,919	357	176	104	-	506	13	204	184	137	591	408
Phoenix, AZ	2,055	1,799	600	190	377	33	1,200	618	162	413	279	84	449	26	150	132	80	192	64
San Diego, CA	2,607	1,906	357	138	124	95	1,550	856	206	583	373	40	299	44	175	395	141	251	449
Dallas, TX	2,270	1,648	93	49	44	-	1,555	725	372	336	217	82	630	38	206	200	140	200	422
San Antonio, TX	2,276	912	151	45	97	9	761	384	183	185	124	21	238	26	142	139	84	1,134	230
Detroit, MI	4,860	3,750	2,244	331	1,870	43	1,506	903	392	108	-	55	299	11	221	304	87	221	889
San Jose, CA	1,425	1,193	159	34	78	46	1,034	559	191	245	140	84	298	21	155	177	87	16	217
Honolulu, HI[3]	1,172	1,042	193	126	66	-	849	516	399	62	-	21	227	17	184	106	56	130	-
Indianapolis, IN[3]	1,907	1,536	377	60	310	-	1,160	645	514	37	-	19	370	22	55	145	65	341	30
San Francisco, CA[3]	6,054	4,317	1,517	291	1,215	11	2,801	1,512	577	527	270	71	985	41	161	304	185	323	1,414
Jacksonville, FL[3]	2,246	1,065	164	49	115	-	901	497	271	211	114	78	218	-	115	186	158	857	323
Columbus, OH	1,039	901	130	44	77	-	771	474	29	11	-	-	211	9	129	87	42	138	-
Austin, TX	1,878	763	67	47	19	-	696	344	169	151	107	20	281	24	140	71	46	792	323
Baltimore, MD[3]	2,451	2,234	1,224	76	1,068	80	1,010	744	479	56	-	25	139	-	79	127	52	71	146
Memphis, TN	2,858	1,444	981	16	502	463	463	278	223	42	-	16	123	46	58	62	32	1,094	320
Milwaukee, WI	1,343	748	404	71	323	-	344	182	173	-	-	-	100	-	42	63	25	55	540
Boston, MA	2,711	2,371	1,139	209	929	-	1,233	937	873	32	-	-	181	-	104	115	38	94	246
Washington, DC	5,637	5,374	1,488	1,439	-	49	3,886	3,216	693	1,000	640	181	331	23	101	339	104	766	96
Nashville, TN[3]	2,384	1,489	309	-	302	-	1,180	800	456	272	237	-	213	11	88	166	119	61	129
El Paso, TX	565	413	53	36	11	-	360	203	106	90	67	21	106	-	56	51	26	-	92
Seattle, WA	1,776	1,122	146	49	91	-	976	598	198	251	128	87	281	43	210	97	21	458	196
Denver, CO[3]	2,075	1,725	176	14	162	-	1,549	650	169	413	361	20	665	25	67	234	133	134	216
Charlotte, NC	982	900	231	44	65	122	669	271	207	28	-	-	220	27	101	178	80	49	34
Ft Worth, TX	740	509	32	-	32	-	478	300	148	117	117	-	96	-	72	82	47	121	109
Portland, OR	805	736	117	40	34	43	620	360	231	50	-	37	169	12	117	90	48	67	-
Oklahoma City, OK	706	624	78	39	29	9	546	272	35	229	204	23	174	10	68	99	38	59	24
Tucson, AZ	678	558	209	61	137	11	349	222	37	173	148	17	98	12	10	28	11	98	22
New Orleans, LA	817	717	116	39	78	-	601	359	141	192	133	37	163	-	61	79	41	55	45
Las Vegas, NV	503	503	206	11	165	30	297	132	64	33	-	28	109	-	-	56	17	-	-
Cleveland, OH	1,216	887	183	56	127	-	705	387	63	26	-	-	144	-	59	174	45	329	-
Long Beach, CA	980	842	146	59	74	13	696	197	62	116	37	66	394	-	73	104	55	138	-

- Represents zero. [1] Includes solid waste management. [2] Includes water, electric, and transit. [3] Represents, in effect, city-county consolidated government.

Source: U.S. Census Bureau; "Government Finances: 1999-2000"; issued January 2003, <http://www.census.gov/govs/estimate/00allpub.pdf>; (accessed 16 June 2003).

No. 464. City Governments—Expenditures and Debt for Largest Cities: 2000

[In millions of dollars (59,181 represents $59,181,000,000). For fiscal year ending in year shown; see headnote, Table 463]

Cities ranked by 2000 population	Total expenditure	Total direct expenditure	Total	Education	Housing and community development	Public welfare	Health and hospitals	Police protection	Fire protection	Correction	Highways	Parks and recreation	Sewerage	Solid waste management	Governmental administration[1]	Interest on general debt	Utility expenditure[2]	Employee retirement expenditure	Debt outstanding
								General expenditure											
New York, NY	59,181	55,239	47,822	12,199	2,424	7,931	4,688	3,225	1,155	1,301	1,193	557	1,036	932	994	3,847	5,210	6,149	54,833
Los Angeles, CA	8,683	8,640	5,245	-	173	-	36	993	366	-	255	252	208	132	594	292	2,443	995	11,846
Chicago, IL	6,022	5,962	4,865	1	187	132	139	1,105	310	-	572	76	133	172	151	505	318	839	10,282
Houston, TX	2,558	2,541	2,102	-	59	-	88	403	219	28	214	114	259	56	88	211	322	134	6,509
Philadelphia, PA[3]	5,442	5,366	4,266	19	163	373	886	460	145	247	111	90	206	87	316	143	727	448	4,435
Phoenix, AZ	2,137	2,129	1,770	15	86	-	-	265	162	-	101	170	136	79	125	143	315	52	3,498
San Diego, CA	2,199	2,198	1,752	-	116	-	4	272	108	8	57	174	330	81	57	168	350	97	2,326
Dallas, TX	1,889	1,878	1,561	-	46	-	24	208	113	9	92	153	120	46	47	269	180	149	4,415
San Antonio, TX	2,201	2,196	1,075	36	17	36	37	174	109	6	108	137	134	40	31	61	1,077	49	4,634
Detroit, MI	4,853	4,782	3,806	1,561	142	-	115	307	105	1	140	112	381	105	238	107	606	441	3,721
San Jose, CA	1,277	1,251	1,164	-	172	-	3	166	82	2	80	116	126	63	69	116	24	89	2,083
Honolulu, HI[3]	1,278	1,278	1,025	-	46	-	17	153	67	-	80	128	101	112	168	81	253	-	1,835
Indianapolis, IN[3]	2,005	1,994	1,638	-	152	63	308	131	48	39	80	206	106	33	64	164	327	40	2,921
San Francisco, CA[3]	5,549	5,415	4,568	92	81	442	827	327	181	92	80	255	81	21	294	330	617	364	7,013
Jacksonville, FL	2,095	2,035	1,198	-	11	34	38	131	79	44	219	40	185	52	59	140	812	85	5,140
Columbus, OH	1,151	1,131	1,002	-	18	-	35	180	114	12	62	80	122	38	67	103	149	-	1,656
Austin, TX	1,607	1,607	879	-	20	-	80	98	68	-	94	62	47	27	50	89	657	71	4,203
Baltimore, MD	2,304	2,258	2,019	877	9	-	66	223	108	-	25	44	98	56	121	75	93	193	1,395
Memphis, TN	2,769	2,759	1,518	779	3	-	3	191	103	-	129	83	38	43	24	37	1,122	129	1,069
Milwaukee, WI	980	952	779	-	69	-	-	148	75	-	68	5	76	27	42	44	62	139	564
Boston, MA	2,630	2,398	2,331	756	23	-	33	234	121	-	57	22	110	43	75	52	62	237	1,492
Washington, DC[3]	5,644	5,483	5,313	969	102	95	68	330	113	86	78	172	303	37	262	236	259	7	4,803
Nashville, TN[3]	2,437	2,437	1,494	515	179	1,254	634	103	69	305	38	50	62	37	81	131	840	102	3,044
El Paso, TX	498	498	367	-	58	24	133	73	34	46	33	22	48	13	32	27	93	39	672
Seattle, WA	1,915	1,798	1,209	-	16	-	22	158	92	-	21	149	146	87	91	32	621	84	2,548
Denver, CO[3]	1,657	1,635	1,436	-	93	155	16	138	64	13	124	91	49	24	125	288	160	61	4,755
Charlotte, NC	891	888	656	-	41	-	36	118	50	52	74	43	37	35	17	75	222	13	1,783
Ft Worth, TX	736	736	509	-	34	-	4	105	54	-	65	78	64	21	30	31	174	54	1,037
Portland, OR	890	881	759	-	9	-	6	106	58	-	78	83	122	2	60	62	76	56	1,677
Oklahoma City, OK	660	660	581	-	64	3	-	103	57	-	114	99	44	22	38	41	70	9	860
Tucson, AZ	690	685	503	-	31	-	-	90	38	3	54	48	-	28	82	28	169	18	704
New Orleans, LA	814	814	696	-	51	2	12	97	58	29	68	99	76	26	70	69	70	48	1,106
Las Vegas, NV	441	362	440	-	86	1	2	79	54	17	39	48	26	3	53	16	1	-	292
Cleveland, OH	1,199	1,195	891	-	61	2	31	157	72	6	48	41	17	27	76	45	308	-	2,009
Long Beach, CA	1,060	1,057	842	-	95	-	29	133	56	-	70	27	15	58	57	108	215	2	1,525

- Represents or rounds to zero. [1] Excludes public buildings. [2] Includes water, electric, and transit. [3] Represents, in effect, city-county consolidated government.

Source: U.S. Census Bureau; "Government Finances 1999-2000"; issued January 2003, <http://www.census.gov/govs/estimate/00allpub.pdf>; (accessed 16 June 2003).

No. 465. County Governments—Revenue for Largest Counties: 2000

[In millions of dollars (17,782 represents $17,782,000,000). For fiscal year ending in year shown; see text, this section. See Appendix III]

Counties ranked by 2000 population	Total revenue [1]	Intergovernmental Total	From federal government Total	Hous- ing [2]	From state government Total [1]	Public welfare	Health and hospi- tals	From local govern- ment	General revenue Total	Taxes Total [1]	Prop- erty	Sales and gross receipts Total	General sales	Current charges Total [1]	Parks and recre- ation	Sewer- age [3]	Hospi- tals	Miscellaneous general revenue Total	Interest earnings
Los Angeles, CA	17,782	15,217	10,013	425	196	9,260	4,174	1,679	328	5,204	2,150	1,935	123	64	1,944	70	37	507	1,110	309
Cook, IL	2,939	2,271	459	36	33	421	159	-	-	1,811	1,310	784	512	317	375	41	-	187	126	78
Harris, TX	2,115	2,115	519	57	13	410	225	124	52	1,596	935	871	26	-	382	1	-	71	280	206
Maricopa, AZ	1,909	1,909	985	46	7	912	402	21	27	924	505	385	98	98	241	3	-	188	179	138
Orange, CA	2,998	2,596	1,355	29	11	1,248	379	183	79	1,240	356	295	52	49	398	17	94	-	486	199
San Diego, CA	3,118	2,543	1,847	74	62	1,660	633	345	113	696	416	351	22	16	132	3	16	-	147	49
Dade, FL	4,777	4,528	947	438	172	509	-	-	-	3,581	1,269	849	352	88	1,797	23	447	-	514	298
Dallas, TX	1,182	1,164	220	2	-	194	73	56	24	945	412	370	3	-	424	-	-	669	108	52
Wayne, MI	2,111	1,914	1,050	111	5	771	165	376	168	864	295	282	8	-	316	4	56	345	252	82
King, WA	1,825	1,745	468	121	15	236	-	138	111	1,277	842	347	377	304	356	12	260	-	79	51
San Bernardino, CA	2,631	2,118	1,448	134	19	1,225	553	167	89	730	211	177	18	13	408	5	33	284	110	55
Santa Clara, CA	2,383	2,383	1,445	36	9	1,358	724	122	52	938	607	401	167	165	208	3	12	124	123	79
Broward, FL	1,616	1,576	272	55	4	186	-	7	32	1,303	642	518	86	-	408	17	136	-	254	140
Riverside, CA	1,809	1,809	1,262	95	10	1,085	549	72	81	547	264	228	23	19	148	3	40	34	136	60
Tarrant, TX	711	711	187	18	12	152	54	60	17	523	302	274	10	-	100	-	-	72	122	89
Alameda, CA	2,395	1,824	1,127	19	2	1,041	666	211	67	698	402	244	132	125	136	8	-	65	159	65
Suffolk, NY	1,970	1,861	476	16	5	453	202	55	6	1,385	1,159	408	732	729	122	-	17	-	103	53
Cuyahoga, OH	1,500	1,500	627	17	16	606	321	154	5	873	454	250	167	151	290	8	3	260	129	104
Bexar, TX	735	733	154	-	3	134	-	51	15	579	271	248	7	-	230	-	-	208	78	67
Clark, NV	2,468	2,193	552	63	15	414	-	6	75	1,641	780	341	287	106	716	12	69	338	145	104
Nassau, NY	2,501	2,501	625	39	27	585	307	64	-	1,877	1,403	631	761	758	346	15	9	205	128	67
Allegheny, PA	1,403	1,216	718	42	30	672	170	322	-	498	274	229	44	36	184	4	-	-	40	50
Sacramento, CA	2,474	1,947	1,081	5	-	1,034	521	132	4	866	326	166	116	93	367	11	174	-	173	21
Oakland, MI	866	739	486	22	6	325	110	83	42	253	179	169	2	-	39	7	7	3	35	84
Palm Beach, FL	1,206	1,165	156	32	-	124	5	-	139	1,009	522	386	121	-	332	5	158	-	155	25
Hennepin, MN	1,333	1,333	520	35	5	470	295	61	15	812	421	417	-	-	334	-	49	234	58	57
Franklin, OH	889	887	445	4	4	410	133	176	27	443	344	244	87	78	48	6	3	-	50	18
St Louis, MO	540	508	50	15	1	32	-	-	4	457	385	89	288	250	43	2	-	-	29	42
Hillsborough, FL	1,289	1,170	254	41	21	211	36	20	1	916	483	364	108	144	267	1	62	-	165	16
Fairfax, VA	3,394	2,773	535	56	30	473	26	30	6	2,239	1,732	1,340	233	14	303	22	183	-	203	75
Erie, NY	1,409	1,363	344	7	-	327	200	93	10	1,019	593	242	340	335	356	1	4	267	70	139
Contra Costa, CA	1,564	1,333	602	28	6	560	236	116	14	731	236	197	19	11	408	-	17	232	86	24
Milwaukee, WI	1,165	1,036	573	99	-	464	196	63	11	463	231	173	56	56	205	44	11	58	27	39
Westchester, NY	1,868	1,860	441	11	-	416	244	75	17	1,419	758	471	285	276	626	23	-	267	35	8
Pinellas, FL	786	730	110	24	15	84	-	-	2	620	352	251	91	58	169	1	97	461	99	17

- Represents or rounds to zero. [1] Includes revenue sources not shown separately. [2] Includes urban development. [3] Includes solid waste management.

Source: U.S. Census Bureau, Government Finances, 1999-2000. See also <http://www.census.gov/govs/estimate/00allpub.pdf> (issued January 2003).

No. 466. County Governments—Expenditures and Debt for Largest Counties: 2000

[In millions of dollars (14,365 represents $14,365,000,000). For fiscal year ending in year shown; see text, this section. See headnote, Table 465. See Appendix III]

Counties ranked by 2000 population	Total expenditure	Total direct expenditure	Total[1]	Education	Housing[2]	Public welfare	Health	Hospitals	Police protection	Correction	Governmental administration	Highways	Parks and recreation	Natural resources	Sewerage and solid waste management	Interest on general debt	Utility expenditure[3]	Employee retirement expenditure	Debt outstanding
Los Angeles, CA	14,365	13,320	13,247	543	239	4,123	1,614	1,603	814	843	1,335	316	234	193	47	450	52	1,065	6,265
Cook, IL	2,521	2,502	2,322	-	19	9	40	817	80	324	507	83	103	-	-	109	-	199	2,080
Harris, TX	2,254	2,254	2,254	-	29	16	114	557	133	191	241	251	59	96	-	368	-	-	4,636
Maricopa, AZ	1,740	1,524	1,740	12	7	485	133	206	45	202	287	107	6	82	5	91	-	147	1,479
Orange, CA	2,563	2,325	2,416	194	21	558	288	-	168	195	352	42	50	38	71	209	12	144	3,209
San Diego, CA	2,656	2,493	2,500	258	62	618	348	-	143	214	408	70	22	9	23	69	427	-	753
Dade, FL	4,896	4,890	4,470	-	222	80	52	942	371	194	269	39	171	20	402	449	-	-	7,668
Dallas, TX	1,112	1,107	1,091	-	27	9	97	521	29	140	122	30	-	-	2	39	-	21	591
Wayne, MI	2,167	2,052	2,076	-	5	181	387	59	23	170	217	39	143	102	107	112	-	92	2,171
King, WA	1,927	1,892	1,434	-	21	7	259	45	77	78	171	143	62	42	233	159	494	-	2,503
San Bernardino, CA	2,283	2,175	2,167	244	9	672	152	308	151	124	162	96	13	27	55	60	5	110	1,381
Santa Clara, CA	2,438	2,172	2,438	202	7	530	220	369	62	200	394	30	32	-	24	25	127	-	710
Broward, FL	1,416	1,379	1,290	-	17	33	90	-	172	119	131	125	59	16	120	145	-	-	2,561
Riverside, CA	1,912	1,711	1,912	194	49	464	126	150	135	154	230	48	8	98	42	79	-	-	1,076
Tarrant, TX	691	687	691	2	13	5	84	261	18	78	92	60	-	-	-	83	-	119	1,463
Alameda, CA	2,031	1,906	1,912	30	19	542	119	290	59	166	228	16	26	94	40	51	143	-	1,248
Suffolk, NY	2,066	1,701	1,923	234	6	349	142	-	23	88	102	54	-	7	14	56	-	-	1,950
Cuyahoga, OH	1,553	1,532	1,553	-	19	357	253	419	339	85	202	31	-	-	-	90	-	-	2,098
Bexar, TX	714	658	711	-	-	55	39	353	23	62	77	33	2	8	-	58	-	2	830
Clark, NV	2,488	2,474	2,207	-	14	59	37	338	22	163	170	16	141	-	27	164	281	-	4,379
Nassau, NY	2,615	2,264	2,590	208	27	493	119	315	262	155	121	408	82	114	94	150	25	-	3,665
Allegheny, PA	1,267	1,175	1,222	30	34	234	279	23	498	64	89	71	54	2	-	89	-	45	1,461
Sacramento, CA	2,218	2,149	2,096	85	-	637	183	-	28	188	282	22	21	-	-	108	22	100	1,944
Oakland, MI	753	731	725	9	8	6	210	14	47	70	99	124	13	24	199	15	6	22	1,273
Palm Beach, FL	1,114	1,088	1,033	-	15	245	24	-	148	64	150	87	52	21	62	91	81	-	1,577
Hennepin, MN	1,308	1,308	1,308	-	6	213	199	324	53	107	119	83	-	5	103	24	-	-	769
Franklin, OH	855	831	854	-	6	14	276	-	20	49	95	41	-	-	47	31	-	-	594
St Louis, MO	470	331	456	-	15	46	36	-	48	17	49	42	39	8	3	27	-	14	448
Hillsborough, FL	1,178	1,164	1,049	-	29	154	24	-	101	63	88	86	19	43	76	127	129	172	2,404
Fairfax, VA	3,175	3,103	2,892	1,483	52	492	122	226	121	23	84	35	108	3	194	131	111	-	2,614
Erie, NY	1,389	1,069	1,357	110	3	245	50	372	32	57	40	53	16	-	22	44	32	-	949
Contra Costa, CA	1,512	1,462	1,410	87	6	245	128	-	57	74	117	48	-	17	19	49	-	45	782
Milwaukee, WI	1,101	1,101	917	-	13	236	77	126	36	61	89	47	106	2	-	27	103	101	495
Westchester, NY	1,921	1,691	1,890	75	-	381	176	446	23	107	66	27	38	-	119	31	31	82	813
Pinellas, FL	812	774	750	-	13	36	61	-	76	64	88	58	29	25	141	48	62	-	727

- Represents or rounds to zero. [1] Includes expenditure categories not shown separately. [2] Includes community development. [3] Includes water, electric, and transit.

Source: U.S. Census Bureau, *Government Finances, 1999-2000*. See also <http://www.census.gov/govs/estimate/00allpub.pdf> (issued January 2003).

State and Local Government Finances and Employment   311

No. 467. Governmental Employment and Payrolls: 1980 to 2001

[Employees in thousands (16,213 represents 16,213,000), payroll in millions of dollars (19,935 represents $19,935,000,000). For 1980 to 1995 as of October; later years as of March. 1996 data are not available. Covers both full-time and part-time employees. Local government data are estimates subject to sampling variation; see Appendix III and source]

Type of government	1980	1985	1990	1994	1995	1997	1998	1999	2000	2001
EMPLOYEES (1,000)										
Total	16,213	16,690	18,369	19,420	19,521	19,540	19,854	20,306	20,876	20,970
Federal (civilian)[1]	2,898	3,021	3,105	2,952	2,895	2,807	2,765	2,799	2,899	2,698
State and local	13,315	13,669	15,263	16,468	16,626	16,733	17,089	17,506	17,976	18,272
Percent of total	82	82	83	85	85	86	86	86	86	87
State	3,753	3,984	4,503	4,694	4,719	4,733	4,758	4,818	4,877	4,985
Local	9,562	9,685	10,760	11,775	11,906	12,000	12,271	12,689	13,099	13,288
Counties	1,853	1,891	2,167	(NA)	(NA)	2,425	(NA)	(NA)	(NA)	(NA)
Municipalities	2,561	2,467	2,642	(NA)	(NA)	2,755	(NA)	(NA)	(NA)	(NA)
School districts	4,270	4,416	4,950	(NA)	(NA)	455	(NA)	(NA)	(NA)	(NA)
Townships	394	392	418	(NA)	(NA)	5,675	(NA)	(NA)	(NA)	(NA)
Special districts	484	519	585	(NA)	(NA)	691	(NA)	(NA)	(NA)	(NA)
PAYROLLS (mil. dol.)										
Total	19,935	28,945	39,228	(NA)	(NA)	49,156	51,568	54,363	58,166	60,632
Federal (civilian)[1]	5,205	7,580	8,999	(NA)	(NA)	9,744	10,115	10,748	11,485	11,370
State and local	14,730	21,365	30,229	36,545	37,714	39,412	41,453	43,886	46,681	49,262
Percent of total	74	74	77	(NA)	(NA)	80	80	81	80	81
State	4,285	6,329	9,083	10,666	10,927	11,413	11,845	12,565	13,279	14,136
Local	10,445	15,036	21,146	25,878	26,787	27,999	29,608	31,321	33,402	35,126
Counties	1,936	2,819	4,192	(NA)	(NA)	5,750	(NA)	(NA)	(NA)	(NA)
Municipalities	2,951	4,191	5,564	(NA)	(NA)	7,146	(NA)	(NA)	(NA)	(NA)
School districts	4,683	6,746	9,551	(NA)	(NA)	869	(NA)	(NA)	(NA)	(NA)
Townships	330	446	642	(NA)	(NA)	12,579	(NA)	(NA)	(NA)	(NA)
Special districts	546	834	1,197	(NA)	(NA)	1,654	(NA)	(NA)	(NA)	(NA)

NA Not available. [1] Includes employees outside the United States.

Source: U.S. Census Bureau; "Government Employment, March 2001"; issued October 2002, <http://www.census.gov/govs/apes/01emppub.pdf>; (accessed 13 June 2003).

No. 468. All Governments—Employment and Payroll by Function: 2001

[Employees in thousands (20,970 represents 20,970,000), payroll in millions of dollars (60,632 represents $60,632,000,000). See headnote, Table 467]

Function	Employees (1,000) Total	Federal (civilian)[1]	State and local Total	State	Local	Payrolls (mil. dol.) Total	Federal (civilian)[1]	State and local Total	State	Local
Total	20,970	2,698	18,272	4,985	13,288	60,632	11,370	49,262	14,136	35,126
National defense[2]	682	682	(X)	(X)	(X)	2,542	2,542	(X)	(X)	(X)
Postal Service	860	860	(X)	(X)	(X)	3,107	3,107	(X)	(X)	(X)
Space research and technology	19	19	(X)	(X)	(X)	120	120	(X)	(X)	(X)
Elem and secondary educ	7,116	(X)	7,116	58	7,058	18,428	(X)	18,428	155	18,273
Higher education	2,679	(X)	2,679	2,156	523	6,156	(X)	6,156	5,125	1,031
Other education	126	11	115	115	(X)	395	54	341	341	(X)
Health	603	133	470	179	291	1,985	674	1,311	572	739
Hospitals	1,147	148	999	433	565	3,497	653	2,844	1,276	1,568
Public welfare	555	9	546	242	304	1,549	50	1,499	708	791
Social insurance administration	155	66	89	89	(X)	589	300	289	289	(X)
Police protection	1,060	106	954	105	849	4,004	581	3,423	407	3,017
Fire protection	411	(X)	411	(X)	411	1,236	(X)	1,236	(X)	1,236
Correction	747	33	714	473	241	2,349	137	2,212	1,468	744
Streets & highways	578	3	575	254	321	1,743	17	1,725	838	887
Air transportation	93	49	44	3	41	550	393	157	13	144
Water transport/terminals	18	5	13	5	9	63	14	49	17	32
Solid waste management	123	(X)	123	2	121	337	(X)	337	8	329
Sewerage	134	(X)	134	1	133	427	(X)	427	6	421
Parks & recreation	396	25	371	42	329	738	97	641	94	547
Natural resources	400	185	215	169	46	1,435	838	597	487	110
Housing & community dev	140	17	124	-	124	461	85	376	-	376
Water supply	176	-	176	1	175	521	-	521	3	517
Electric power	79	-	79	4	75	340	-	340	20	321
Gas supply	12	-	12	-	12	35	-	35	-	35
Transit	223	(X)	223	30	193	837	(X)	837	133	704
Libraries	185	4	181	1	180	326	22	304	1	303
State liquor stores	9	(X)	9	9	(X)	18	(X)	18	18	(X)
Financial administration	564	137	427	172	255	1,783	565	1,217	552	666
Other government administration	514	22	492	62	430	995	94	901	196	705
Judicial and legal	488	58	430	163	267	1,798	318	1,480	639	841
Other & unallocable	676	126	549	216	333	2,272	709	1,563	772	790

- Represents or rounds to zero. X Not applicable. [1] Includes employees outside the United States. [2] Includes international relations.

Source: U.S. Census Bureau; "Government Employment, March 2001"; issued October 2002, <http://www.census.gov/govs/apes/01emppub.pdf>; (accessed 13 June 2003).

No. 469. State and Local Government—Employer Costs Per Hour Worked: 2002

[In dollars. As of March. Based on a sample; see source for details. For additional data, see Table 648]

Occupation and industry	Total compensation	Wages and salaries	Benefits Total	Paid leave	Supplemental pay	Insurance	Retirement and savings	Legally required benefits	Other [1]
Total workers	31.89	22.40	9.49	2.49	0.28	2.96	1.81	1.89	0.06
Occupational group:									
White-collar occupations	35.43	25.55	9.88	2.58	0.16	3.12	1.94	2.01	0.07
Professional specialty and technical	41.45	30.74	10.71	2.55	0.17	3.28	2.31	2.30	0.09
Professional specialty	42.85	31.91	10.93	2.56	0.15	3.38	2.40	2.35	0.10
Teachers	45.48	34.36	11.11	2.39	0.08	3.49	2.64	2.41	0.11
Technical	27.15	18.69	8.46	2.44	0.45	2.31	1.39	1.81	0.05
Executive, admin., & managerial	39.81	27.71	12.10	4.02	0.18	3.36	2.23	2.27	0.04
Admin. support including clerical	20.72	13.73	6.98	1.87	0.13	2.64	1.01	1.30	0.04
Blue-collar occupations	25.30	16.53	8.78	2.35	0.41	2.89	1.32	1.76	0.04
Service occupations	24.26	15.63	8.62	2.26	0.60	2.50	1.65	1.57	0.06
Industry group:									
Services	33.46	24.29	9.17	2.27	0.18	2.97	1.77	1.92	0.07
Health services	26.56	17.80	8.76	2.65	0.71	2.38	1.14	1.85	0.04
Hospitals	27.35	18.40	8.95	2.74	0.69	2.38	1.19	1.91	0.04
Educational services	35.00	25.76	9.24	2.19	0.11	3.04	1.90	1.92	0.07
Elementary and secondary education	34.17	25.34	8.83	1.93	0.08	3.17	1.73	1.83	0.10
Higher education	37.59	27.39	10.20	2.82	0.17	2.80	2.27	2.14	(Z)
Public administration	29.27	19.30	9.97	2.87	0.44	2.90	1.91	1.79	0.06

Z Cost per hour worked is less than 1 cent.   [1] Includes severance pay and supplemental unemployment benefits.

Source: U.S. Bureau of Labor Statistics, *Compensation and Working Conditions*, Fall 2002.

No. 470. State and Local Governments—Full-Time Employment and Salary by Sex and Race/Ethnic Group: 1980 to 2001

[As of June 30. (2,350 represents 2,350,000). Excludes school systems and educational institutions. Based on reports from state governments (47 in 1983; 42 in 1980; 49 in 1981 and 1984 through 1987; and 50 in 1989 through 1991) and a sample of county, municipal, township, and special district jurisdictions employing 15 or more nonelected, nonappointed full-time employees. Beginning 1993, only for state and local governments with 100 or more employees. Data for 1992, 1994, 1996, 1998, and 2000 are not available. For definition of median, see Guide to Tabular Presentation]

Year and occupation	Employment (1,000) Male	Female	White [1]	Minority Total [2]	Black [1]	Hispanic [3]	Median annual salary ($1,000) Male	Female	White [1]	Minority Total [2]	Black [1]	Hispanic [3]
1980	2,350	1,637	3,146	842	619	163	15.2	11.4	13.8	11.8	11.5	12.3
1981	2,740	1,925	3,591	1,074	780	205	17.7	13.1	16.1	13.5	13.3	14.7
1983	2,674	1,818	3,423	1,069	768	219	20.1	15.3	18.5	15.9	15.6	17.3
1984	2,700	1,880	3,458	1,121	799	233	21.4	16.2	19.6	17.4	16.5	18.4
1985	2,789	1,952	3,563	1,179	835	248	22.3	17.3	20.6	18.4	17.5	19.2
1986	2,797	1,982	3,549	1,230	865	259	23.4	18.1	21.5	19.6	18.7	20.2
1987	2,818	2,031	3,600	1,249	872	268	24.2	18.9	22.4	20.9	19.3	21.1
1989	3,030	2,227	3,863	1,394	961	308	26.1	20.6	24.1	22.1	20.7	22.7
1990	3,071	2,302	3,918	1,456	994	327	27.3	21.8	25.2	23.3	22.0	23.8
1991	3,110	2,349	3,965	1,494	1,011	340	28.4	22.7	26.4	23.8	22.7	24.5
1993	2,820	2,204	3,588	1,436	948	341	30.6	24.3	28.5	25.9	24.2	26.8
1995	2,960	2,355	3,781	1,534	993	379	33.5	27.0	31.4	26.3	26.8	28.6
1997	2,898	2,307	3,676	1,529	973	392	34.6	27.9	32.2	30.2	27.4	29.5
1999	2,939	2,393	3,723	1,609	1,012	417	37.0	29.9	34.8	31.1	29.6	31.2
2001, total	3,080	2,554	3,888	1,746	1,077	471	39.8	32.1	37.5	34.0	31.5	33.8
Officials/administrators	212	118	271	60	37	15	63.2	54.8	60.8	58.2	57.7	59.5
Professionals	649	790	1,052	387	222	89	49.2	41.7	45.6	43.2	40.5	42.3
Technicians	269	197	337	128	71	37	39.9	32.1	37.2	34.5	32.7	35.5
Protective service	889	196	770	315	198	96	40.5	32.9	39.8	37.1	35.0	42.1
Paraprofessionals	106	297	234	169	120	36	29.1	26.3	28.1	26.2	24.2	28.1
Admin. support	126	803	610	318	189	97	29.1	27.3	27.4	27.3	27.2	27.5
Skilled craft	397	23	308	112	65	35	36.2	30.4	36.1	34.5	33.6	35.3
Service/maintenance	432	130	306	256	175	66	29.3	22.9	28.5	27.2	26.3	28.1

[1] Non-Hispanic.   [2] Includes other minority groups not shown separately.   [3] Persons of Hispanic origin may be of any race.

Source: U.S. Equal Employment Opportunity Commission, 1980-1991, *State and Local Government Information Report*, annual; beginning 1993, biennial.

No. 471. State and Local Government Full-Time Equivalent Employment by Selected Function and State: 2000

[In thousands (1,614.7 represents 1,614,700). For March. Local government amounts are estimates subject to sampling variation; see Appendix III and source]

State	Education Total State[1]	Education Total Local	Elem. & secondary State	Elem. & secondary Local	Higher education State	Higher education Local	Public welfare State	Public welfare Local	Health State	Health Local	Hospitals State	Hospitals Local
United States	1,614.7	6,402.0	47.1	6,097.0	1,464.8	305.0	238.9	280.2	172.4	251.4	410.5	511.9
Alabama	40.7	96.3	-	96.3	38.0	-	3.8	1.9	5.1	4.3	10.8	23.8
Alaska	8.4	15.8	3.4	15.6	4.7	0.1	1.7	0.1	0.7	0.4	0.3	0.2
Arizona	28.1	107.8	-	96.7	25.1	11.1	5.6	2.0	2.2	2.9	0.7	4.0
Arkansas	21.3	64.7	-	64.7	18.5	-	2.2	0.1	4.8	0.3	4.2	3.6
California	133.6	721.9	-	645.0	128.7	76.9	3.7	63.3	12.1	40.1	36.3	66.7
Colorado	39.7	86.4	-	84.9	38.4	1.5	2.0	5.3	1.1	3.7	3.6	9.1
Connecticut	22.3	76.6	3.5	76.6	15.9	-	4.7	1.8	2.2	1.8	10.4	-
Delaware	7.8	15.5	-	15.5	7.4	-	1.8	-	1.8	0.2	2.3	-
District of Columbia	-	12.0	-	11.1	-	0.9	-	1.2	-	1.2	-	3.7
Florida	53.4	328.1	-	304.6	50.0	23.5	13.8	5.9	20.5	5.8	5.7	33.1
Georgia	48.7	201.4	-	201.1	40.6	0.3	9.6	1.0	3.9	12.2	9.7	17.1
Hawaii	33.7	-	25.4	-	8.1	-	0.8	0.1	2.4	0.2	3.7	-
Idaho	9.2	31.2	-	30.0	8.6	1.3	1.8	0.2	1.0	0.9	1.0	4.5
Illinois	46.4	273.3	-	252.5	43.8	20.8	15.2	8.4	3.2	7.6	9.7	13.3
Indiana	49.8	133.9	-	133.9	48.6	-	5.0	1.3	1.8	3.3	4.8	24.0
Iowa	25.2	74.6	-	68.5	24.0	6.0	2.9	1.5	0.4	2.1	7.4	11.0
Kansas	19.4	77.1	-	70.0	18.8	7.1	2.9	0.9	1.0	3.2	2.7	7.6
Kentucky	31.1	99.9	-	99.9	26.7	-	6.9	0.9	2.2	4.6	5.4	4.6
Louisiana	32.5	104.2	-	104.2	29.1	-	5.4	0.5	4.8	1.5	20.0	17.2
Maine	7.5	35.1	0.1	35.1	7.1	-	2.1	0.4	1.2	0.8	0.6	0.8
Maryland	28.7	117.6	-	108.3	26.5	9.3	7.3	3.0	6.6	4.1	5.7	-
Massachusetts	26.6	147.0	-	146.9	25.5	-	7.6	2.2	8.1	5.9	7.8	0.7
Michigan	67.5	223.2	0.9	210.3	66.2	12.9	13.5	2.4	1.8	10.5	12.7	10.7
Minnesota	41.2	117.2	-	117.2	36.5	-	2.7	12.0	2.2	4.4	4.7	9.6
Mississippi	19.9	81.0	-	75.0	18.4	6.0	3.1	0.9	3.0	0.2	11.5	18.6
Missouri	30.2	130.9	-	125.0	28.0	5.9	8.3	2.5	3.5	4.0	13.1	8.9
Montana	7.9	21.6	-	21.5	7.2	0.1	1.6	0.5	0.9	0.9	0.6	0.5
Nebraska	12.7	44.8	-	42.1	12.1	2.8	2.8	1.2	0.8	0.5	5.0	4.7
Nevada	7.5	30.7	-	30.7	7.4	-	1.1	0.5	1.0	1.0	1.0	4.1
New Hampshire	6.9	30.4	-	30.4	6.6	-	1.5	2.3	0.9	0.2	0.7	-
New Jersey	46.3	194.7	13.4	184.7	29.1	9.9	6.3	11.0	2.8	3.9	15.4	2.0
New Mexico	19.1	46.4	-	43.3	18.2	3.2	1.4	1.0	2.6	0.4	8.0	0.7
New York	50.1	473.6	-	451.7	45.3	21.9	6.8	50.2	9.7	17.4	47.3	50.0
North Carolina	48.5	190.8	-	174.4	45.1	16.4	1.9	14.5	2.7	20.1	17.6	24.6
North Dakota	7.0	14.1	-	14.1	6.7	-	0.4	1.0	1.2	0.5	1.0	-
Ohio	68.8	246.1	-	239.7	66.4	6.4	2.1	26.0	3.7	17.1	11.9	12.4
Oklahoma	28.2	83.2	-	83.2	26.0	-	6.4	0.2	4.0	1.2	2.5	9.6
Oregon	14.9	71.7	-	63.4	13.8	8.3	6.1	1.0	2.5	4.5	5.0	2.4
Pennsylvania	56.5	221.7	-	215.0	53.1	6.7	12.3	21.6	1.5	5.4	13.6	-
Rhode Island	6.7	24.4	0.5	24.4	5.6	-	1.6	0.2	1.4	0.1	1.2	-
South Carolina	30.8	91.8	-	91.8	28.0	-	5.1	0.3	7.7	2.1	8.7	17.1
South Dakota	5.2	18.1	-	17.6	4.8	0.5	1.0	0.2	0.5	0.2	1.0	0.5
Tennessee	37.9	114.4	-	114.4	35.8	-	5.1	3.0	3.0	3.5	9.4	20.3
Texas	97.4	599.3	-	566.3	92.7	33.0	21.4	2.9	12.0	27.5	30.6	47.3
Utah	27.7	46.2	-	46.2	26.2	-	3.2	0.5	1.9	1.3	5.8	0.4
Vermont	5.4	18.0	-	18.0	4.9	-	1.1	-	0.6	-	0.2	-
Virginia	55.3	169.1	-	167.8	52.3	1.3	2.1	7.5	5.0	6.1	13.4	3.5
Washington	50.8	90.9	-	90.9	47.0	-	8.0	1.3	5.2	3.8	8.9	10.1
West Virginia	12.8	41.6	-	41.6	11.4	-	3.1	-	0.8	1.3	1.7	2.2
Wisconsin	34.3	128.6	-	119.5	33.1	9.1	1.4	13.6	2.0	6.0	3.9	1.8
Wyoming	3.3	17.1	-	15.4	3.1	1.7	0.8	-	0.6	0.2	1.0	4.7

See footnote at end of table.

No. 471. State and Local Government Full-Time Equivalent Employment by Selected Function and State: 2000—Con.

[In thousands. For March. Local government amounts are estimates subject to sampling variation; see Appendix III and source]

State	Highways State	Highways Local	Police protection State	Police protection Local	Fire protection State	Fire protection Local	Corrections State	Corrections Local	Parks and recreation State	Parks and recreation Local	Government administration State	Government administration Local
United States ...	249.9	301.8	103.1	781.5	(X)	299.7	468.4	232.3	36.1	217.6	381.1	671.3
Alabama	3.8	7.1	1.3	11.5	(X)	5.0	4.6	2.8	0.6	3.8	6.6	8.7
Alaska	2.8	0.7	0.5	1.2	(X)	0.6	1.7	0.1	0.1	0.6	2.8	1.9
Arizona	3.0	4.4	1.9	14.7	(X)	5.5	9.6	4.1	0.4	4.4	5.7	17.6
Arkansas	3.5	3.6	1.2	6.7	(X)	2.3	4.2	1.6	0.7	0.9	3.7	5.8
California	23.0	22.8	13.0	87.1	(X)	29.9	48.9	31.4	3.5	34.6	29.7	97.9
Colorado	3.1	5.6	1.2	11.2	(X)	4.6	6.5	3.2	0.2	6.3	6.3	10.1
Connecticut	3.6	4.1	1.8	8.9	(X)	4.6	8.7	-	0.1	2.5	8.2	5.5
Delaware	1.7	0.5	0.9	1.5	(X)	0.2	2.5	-	0.2	0.2	2.5	1.0
District of Columbia	-	0.4	-	4.3	(X)	1.9	-	2.0	-	0.7	-	2.4
Florida	9.8	13.8	4.2	53.4	(X)	21.7	28.0	15.5	1.4	17.8	26.9	40.6
Georgia	6.1	7.7	2.3	23.1	(X)	9.8	20.0	6.9	3.1	4.5	6.0	20.6
Hawaii	0.9	0.8	-	3.6	(X)	1.7	2.5	-	0.2	1.8	3.5	2.5
Idaho	1.7	1.9	0.5	3.3	(X)	1.0	1.7	1.1	0.2	0.9	2.2	3.9
Illinois	8.2	13.0	4.3	39.9	(X)	15.2	15.8	9.7	0.8	14.6	11.7	32.5
Indiana	4.3	6.9	2.1	14.6	(X)	6.7	8.3	5.1	0.1	3.6	4.5	14.7
Iowa	2.9	5.5	1.0	6.2	(X)	1.7	3.4	1.1	0.1	1.9	4.6	6.0
Kansas	3.6	5.3	1.1	7.8	(X)	2.8	3.6	2.2	0.5	2.1	4.7	6.9
Kentucky	5.5	3.5	2.2	8.0	(X)	5.5	3.8	3.0	1.7	1.4	9.2	6.4
Louisiana	5.4	5.1	1.5	14.8	(X)	4.4	7.9	6.1	1.2	3.0	5.9	12.5
Maine	2.7	2.1	0.5	2.9	(X)	1.7	1.2	0.6	0.1	0.7	2.4	3.3
Maryland	4.7	4.9	2.4	14.5	(X)	5.7	11.8	2.8	0.6	6.3	9.3	8.5
Massachusetts	4.3	7.0	5.7	18.8	(X)	13.1	7.2	2.7	1.0	1.9	17.1	9.9
Michigan	3.2	10.3	3.3	22.9	(X)	8.7	19.0	5.5	0.3	5.1	6.5	25.3
Minnesota	5.2	7.6	0.9	10.2	(X)	2.3	3.7	4.3	0.6	4.3	6.4	13.6
Mississippi	3.3	5.3	1.3	7.5	(X)	3.2	4.3	2.1	0.4	1.3	2.4	7.4
Missouri	6.6	6.4	2.4	15.0	(X)	6.2	11.6	2.1	0.7	4.3	7.8	11.0
Montana	2.1	1.3	0.4	1.9	(X)	0.6	1.1	0.6	0.1	0.4	1.6	2.3
Nebraska	2.2	3.0	0.7	3.9	(X)	1.3	2.0	1.0	0.3	1.1	1.6	4.1
Nevada	1.6	1.6	0.7	5.9	(X)	2.3	3.2	2.1	0.2	2.7	3.0	5.9
New Hampshire	1.9	2.1	0.4	3.4	(X)	1.5	1.3	0.5	0.2	0.4	1.7	2.6
New Jersey	7.6	10.7	3.9	31.1	(X)	7.7	9.8	6.5	1.8	5.1	20.8	19.5
New Mexico	2.4	1.8	0.6	5.0	(X)	1.9	3.9	1.6	0.7	2.0	5.2	4.2
New York	13.4	26.6	6.0	80.5	(X)	24.4	36.5	25.9	2.9	10.6	37.8	39.3
North Carolina	11.9	4.4	3.3	20.1	(X)	6.6	20.4	3.9	0.9	5.6	10.7	11.8
North Dakota	0.9	1.1	0.2	1.3	(X)	0.3	0.6	0.2	0.1	0.7	1.4	1.4
Ohio	7.0	14.6	2.7	31.4	(X)	16.2	18.6	8.7	0.8	8.1	12.0	35.1
Oklahoma	2.9	6.4	1.8	9.2	(X)	4.4	5.9	1.0	1.1	2.1	5.4	6.4
Oregon	3.5	4.2	1.4	7.3	(X)	3.7	4.9	3.7	0.4	2.5	8.7	7.8
Pennsylvania	13.6	10.9	5.7	26.2	(X)	6.1	15.8	12.3	1.5	4.3	14.1	32.9
Rhode Island	0.9	0.9	0.3	3.2	(X)	2.7	1.9	-	0.1	0.6	2.7	1.5
South Carolina	4.9	2.4	3.4	10.4	(X)	3.8	9.1	2.1	0.7	2.8	3.6	8.5
South Dakota	1.0	1.6	0.3	1.4	(X)	0.4	0.9	0.5	0.1	0.5	1.2	1.7
Tennessee	4.5	7.2	1.9	16.8	(X)	6.6	6.6	4.6	1.1	4.5	5.4	11.8
Texas	15.5	20.0	3.7	55.9	(X)	20.7	46.8	23.0	1.1	13.8	17.0	44.7
Utah	1.8	1.6	0.8	4.8	(X)	1.7	3.1	1.5	0.3	2.5	3.5	4.3
Vermont	1.0	1.2	0.5	0.8	(X)	0.3	1.0	-	0.1	0.2	1.8	1.0
Virginia	10.5	4.2	2.7	16.5	(X)	7.6	15.6	7.0	0.9	7.2	8.5	15.0
Washington	6.7	6.8	2.2	12.0	(X)	6.7	7.7	4.2	0.6	5.6	5.8	16.2
West Virginia	5.3	0.9	1.0	2.7	(X)	0.9	1.3	0.3	0.6	0.8	3.9	3.9
Wisconsin	2.1	9.4	0.9	14.8	(X)	4.9	9.1	4.3	0.2	3.6	6.2	11.8
Wyoming	1.8	0.7	0.2	1.5	(X)	0.3	0.9	0.4	0.1	0.7	1.0	1.4

- Represents or rounds to zero.   X Not applicable.   [1] Totals includes other education amounts which are not shown.

Source: U.S. Census Bureau, <http://www.census.gov/pub/govs/www/apesstl01.html>; (accessed 08 July 2003).

No. 472. State and Local Government Employment and Average Earnings by State: 1990 and 2001

[3,840 represents 3,840,000. 1990 as of October; 2001 as of March]

State	Full-time equivalent employment (1,000) State 1990	2001	Local[1] 1990	2001	Full-time equivalent employment per 10,000 population[2] State 1990	2001	Local[1] 1990	2001	Average earnings[3] (dol.) State 1990	2001	Local[1] 1990	2001
United States..	3,840	4,173	9,239	11,206	154	147	371	393	2,472	3,521	2,364	3,258
Alabama.........	79	84	148	184	196	189	367	412	2,196	3,133	1,749	2,542
Alaska..........	22	24	21	26	401	377	385	403	3,543	3,871	3,491	3,939
Arizona.........	50	65	136	187	137	123	370	352	2,334	3,198	2,540	3,031
Arkansas........	43	51	78	100	182	190	330	371	1,922	2,905	1,545	2,242
California.......	325	373	1,091	1,362	109	108	367	395	3,209	4,740	3,073	4,253
Colorado........	54	67	130	167	165	152	395	377	2,765	3,892	2,292	3,192
Connecticut.....	58	66	98	116	178	193	299	339	3,018	4,130	2,854	3,828
Delaware	21	24	17	21	314	306	250	269	2,245	3,408	2,458	3,207
District of Columbia..	(X)	(X)	57	45	(X)	(X)	939	778	(X)	(X)	3,024	3,989
Florida	160	188	497	616	123	114	384	375	2,095	3,102	2,247	2,914
Georgia	112	121	270	338	173	145	418	403	2,037	3,028	1,872	2,690
Hawaii	49	55	13	14	445	448	120	117	2,317	2,948	2,536	3,350
Idaho..........	19	23	37	53	186	176	372	400	2,100	3,128	1,772	2,581
Illinois.........	145	130	416	486	127	104	364	390	2,520	3,646	2,463	3,471
Indiana.........	89	87	196	238	161	142	354	389	2,496	3,147	2,036	2,788
Iowa	57	55	107	121	207	187	387	415	2,936	3,792	2,024	2,758
Kansas.........	50	44	104	127	200	163	421	470	2,077	3,141	1,979	2,669
Kentucky	75	77	114	151	204	189	310	371	2,141	3,147	1,823	2,388
Louisiana	85	94	155	186	200	210	368	417	2,047	2,876	1,713	2,357
Maine..........	22	22	42	53	179	167	345	413	2,352	3,225	1,978	2,628
Maryland	89	91	159	188	186	170	333	349	2,609	3,649	2,776	3,683
Massachusetts...	93	95	196	237	155	149	325	372	2,541	3,900	2,554	3,517
Michigan........	144	141	316	358	155	142	340	358	2,858	4,042	2,646	3,586
Minnesota......	70	76	163	205	160	152	374	412	2,936	4,151	2,552	3,429
Mississippi	47	57	105	136	183	199	407	476	1,824	2,794	1,543	2,124
Missouri........	74	93	171	213	145	164	334	379	1,965	2,793	2,052	2,728
Montana........	17	19	35	34	211	214	434	375	2,072	2,926	1,959	2,615
Nebraska.......	29	33	68	79	186	191	430	463	2,075	2,940	2,089	2,842
Nevada	19	23	42	64	160	110	348	304	2,502	3,553	2,574	3,931
New Hampshire..	16	19	33	47	145	150	301	371	2,352	3,225	2,215	2,904
New Jersey.....	112	137	304	322	145	161	393	380	2,859	4,236	2,698	4,181
New Mexico	40	48	57	73	262	262	379	397	2,100	2,800	1,783	2,531
New York	285	252	866	926	158	133	482	487	2,997	4,088	2,795	4,028
North Carolina...	107	130	244	334	161	158	368	408	2,372	3,077	2,065	2,759
North Dakota....	15	16	20	22	234	251	314	352	2,057	2,875	2,138	2,864
Ohio	139	139	385	468	128	123	355	412	2,510	3,477	2,236	3,176
Oklahoma.......	65	65	116	135	208	187	369	391	1,975	2,925	1,761	2,387
Oregon.........	52	54	100	125	184	156	353	360	2,302	3,366	2,322	3,424
Pennsylvania....	127	154	361	387	107	125	304	315	2,437	3,586	2,403	3,382
Rhode Island....	21	20	27	37	205	190	266	348	2,586	3,822	2,656	3,718
South Carolina...	79	81	116	156	227	200	333	384	1,956	2,872	1,848	2,543
South Dakota ...	13	13	24	27	192	175	349	363	1,979	2,910	1,733	2,399
Tennessee	79	83	175	223	163	144	358	388	2,055	2,923	1,883	2,640
Texas..........	223	269	706	941	131	126	415	441	2,192	3,137	1,952	2,686
Utah	37	52	51	74	216	229	294	327	2,000	3,022	2,092	2,950
Vermont........	13	14	18	23	233	223	312	380	2,302	3,304	2,090	2,647
Virginia.........	117	124	221	274	188	172	356	381	2,267	3,368	2,248	2,978
Washington.....	91	111	164	196	187	186	336	327	2,459	3,685	2,515	3,947
West Virginia....	34	35	59	61	188	196	326	340	1,919	2,763	1,862	2,581
Wisconsin.......	67	69	183	219	136	129	375	405	2,503	3,967	2,372	3,279
Wyoming	11	11	24	29	239	226	539	593	2,045	2,837	2,110	2,744

X Not applicable. [1] Estimates subject to sampling variation; see Appendix III and source. [2] 1990 based on enumerated resident population as of April 1. Other years based on estimated resident population as of July 1. [3] For full-time employees.

Source: U.S. Census Bureau, 1990, *Public Employment*, Series GE, No. 1, annual; 2001, *Government Employment*, March 2001. See also <http://www.census.gov/govs/apes/01emppub.pdf> (issued October 2002).

No. 473. City Government Employment and Payroll—Largest Cities: 1990 and 2001

[2001 for March; 1990 for October. In thousands, (456.2 represents 456,200). See footnote 3, Table 463, for those areas representing city-county consolidated governments]

Cities ranked by 2000 population	Total employment (1,000) 1990	Total employment (1,000) 2001	Full-time equivalent employment [1] Total (1,000) 1990	Full-time equivalent employment [1] Total (1,000) 2001	Per 10,000 population [1] 1990	Per 10,000 population [1] 2001	Payroll (mil. dol.) 1990	Payroll (mil. dol.) 2001	Average earnings for full-time employees (dol.) 1990	Average earnings for full-time employees (dol.) 2001
New York City, NY [2][3]	456.2	446.8	394.6	415.6	539	519	1,091.7	1712.7	2,783	4,277
Los Angeles, CA	51.3	52.1	50.8	50.9	146	138	176.5	252.1	3,488	4,990
Chicago, IL	41.6	40.7	41.6	40.2	149	139	124.9	176.2	3,002	4,423
Houston, TX	19.6	25.6	19.6	25.4	120	130	40.4	77.9	2,061	3,087
Philadelphia, PA	32.4	31.3	31.9	30.3	201	200	89.1	116.1	2,843	3,838
Phoenix, AZ	11.9	13.4	11.4	13.0	116	99	31.7	54.0	2,876	4,215
San Diego, CA	10.4	12.7	9.8	11.8	88	96	28.8	50.8	3,019	4,426
Dallas, TX	14.9	15.4	14.5	15.1	144	127	28.2	56.3	1,945	3,749
San Antonio, TX	13.4	17.3	12.8	16.0	134	140	28.4	52.1	2,227	3,339
Detroit, MI	22.1	40.6	21.2	35.9	206	377	49.8	138.9	2,390	3,908
San Jose, CA	5.9	8.0	4.9	7.2	62	80	16.0	39.0	3,453	5,720
Honolulu, HI	9.9	9.8	9.2	9.1	110	104	23.7	30.7	2,600	3,409
Indianapolis, IN	12.8	13.0	12.5	12.3	171	155	23.1	39.5	1,910	3,240
San Francisco, CA	25.8	29.3	25.7	29.3	356	377	93.8	153.7	3,648	5,247
Jacksonville, FL	10.8	10.6	9.8	10.4	154	142	23.8	37.5	2,582	3,740
Columbus, OH	7.7	9.1	7.5	8.8	118	123	17.8	31.5	2,416	3,652
Austin, TX	10.0	11.2	9.6	10.6	203	162	20.9	34.6	2,186	3,293
Baltimore, MD [2]	29.7	30.0	29.1	29.0	395	446	73.2	97.9	2,540	3,512
Memphis, TN [2]	21.7	25.9	21.1	25.1	341	386	47.6	82.3	2,287	3,332
Milwaukee, WI	9.0	8.0	8.6	7.9	137	132	20.6	29.8	2,431	3,786
Boston, MA [2]	20.9	24.0	20.9	23.0	363	390	49.8	86.2	2,391	3,860
Washington, DC [2][3]	49.6	37.7	47.9	35.8	789	626	138.7	135.7	2,930	3,846
Nashville-Davidson, TN [2]	17.9	20.8	16.9	19.8	347	348	41.8	63.2	2,510	3,275
El Paso, TX	4.9	6.0	4.8	5.9	94	105	9.5	16.4	1,973	2,815
Seattle, WA	11.2	11.7	10.2	10.7	198	190	32.3	50.8	3,274	4,890
Denver, CO	13.0	13.4	11.9	12.8	254	230	31.1	48.6	2,649	3,915
Charlotte, NC	5.0	5.5	4.8	5.4	115	99	11.5	18.7	2,399	3,465
Ft Worth, TX	5.5	6.1	5.2	5.8	117	108	11.1	20.2	2,171	3,586
Portland, OR	4.8	6.3	4.5	5.5	97	105	14.6	24.5	3,305	4,532
Oklahoma City, OK	4.8	5.1	4.5	4.9	101	97	10.5	16.6	2,430	3,496
Tucson, AZ	5.0	7.2	4.7	6.0	114	124	11.5	16.5	2,528	2,782
New Orleans, LA	9.8	9.8	9.6	9.4	194	194	15.5	24.1	1,623	2,592
Las Vegas, NV	1.9	2.7	2.0	2.6	77	54	4.9	12.1	2,563	4,827
Cleveland, OH	8.9	10.4	8.2	9.7	163	202	20.6	29.7	2,521	3,094
Long Beach, CA	5.7	6.2	5.4	5.8	126	125	17.7	26.0	3,413	4,803
Albuquerque, NM	6.9	7.1	6.2	6.8	161	151	12.2	21.2	2,040	3,238
Kansas City, MO	6.4	6.9	6.3	6.7	145	152	14.9	22.5	2,390	3,371
Fresno, CA	2.9	3.4	2.7	3.3	77	78	7.9	13.8	2,944	4,185
Virginia Beach, VA [2]	14.4	20.2	13.1	18.0	334	423	28.4	45.1	2,232	2,655
Atlanta, GA	8.3	8.6	8.1	8.3	205	200	18.4	25.8	2,286	3,111
Sacramento, CA	4.2	4.6	3.9	4.3	105	105	11.3	18.4	3,021	4,519
Oakland, CA	4.6	4.5	4.1	4.5	111	112	15.3	26.9	3,948	6,022
Mesa, AZ	2.3	3.8	2.3	3.6	81	92	6.8	15.1	2,898	4,260
Tulsa, OK	4.4	4.5	4.2	4.4	115	112	10.5	14.7	2,555	3,372
Omaha, NE	2.9	3.6	2.7	3.0	79	78	7.9	11.3	3,051	3,966
Baton Rouge, LA	6.0	7.2	5.0	6.4	132	164	11.0	16.7	2,255	2,755
Minneapolis, MN	6.4	6.3	5.7	5.8	154	152	15.2	22.8	2,815	4,010
Miami, FL	4.3	4.0	4.0	3.8	113	106	14.6	16.6	3,771	4,496
Colorado Springs, CO	5.9	7.5	5.3	7.0	188	194	13.3	26.6	2,618	3,871
St Louis, MO	7.8	8.4	7.4	7.8	186	225	17.0	25.7	2,363	3,300
Wichita, KS	2.7	3.5	2.6	3.2	87	93	5.4	10.0	2,083	3,151
Santa Ana, CA	2.0	2.6	1.7	2.3	58	68	6.8	10.9	4,144	5,763
Pittsburgh, PA	5.9	4.5	5.6	4.3	152	127	12.3	15.3	2,240	3,635
Arlington, TX	1.8	3.2	1.8	2.6	68	77	4.5	7.9	2,538	3,251
Cincinnati, OH	7.0	6.8	6.3	6.6	173	200	16.1	23.0	2,634	3,636
Anaheim, CA	3.7	3.2	2.6	2.7	99	82	8.6	12.7	3,728	5,713
Toledo, OH	3.0	3.0	3.0	3.0	91	95	8.6	11.3	2,847	3,790
Tampa, FL	4.3	4.4	4.2	4.3	151	140	10.5	14.6	2,505	3,459
Buffalo, NY [2]	13.1	12.5	12.4	11.8	379	404	31.3	43.8	2,596	3,785
St Paul, MN	3.6	3.3	3.4	3.0	124	105	10.5	12.9	3,265	4,426
Corpus Christi, TX	3.2	3.2	3.0	3.0	116	106	5.9	8.2	2,009	2,816
Aurora, CO	1.9	2.4	1.9	2.4	84	88	4.8	8.3	2,586	3,418
Raleigh, NC	3.0	3.6	3.0	3.3	141	119	5.0	9.3	2,297	2,953
Newark, NJ	5.1	5.8	4.9	5.5	177	202	8.3	24.3	1,698	4,526
Lexington-Fayette, KY	3.0	4.1	3.0	3.8	133	146	6.0	11.1	1,929	2,991
Anchorage, AK	8.8	9.9	7.9	8.8	351	338	28.4	35.8	3,706	4,165
Louisville, KY	4.5	4.8	4.3	4.4	159	173	9.1	12.5	2,180	2,832
Riverside, CA	2.0	2.1	2.0	1.9	88	75	7.0	8.9	3,459	5,054
St Petersburg, FL	3.0	3.4	3.0	3.1	125	126	7.0	10.8	2,412	3,507
Bakersfield, CA	1.0	1.3	1.0	1.2	57	51	3.0	5.5	3,112	4,570
Stockton, CA	2.0	2.5	1.0	2.0	47	83	5.0	7.7	3,554	4,166
Birmingham, AL	3.9	4.2	3.8	4.0	142	166	8.4	14.8	2,243	3,739
Jersey City, NJ	4.0	4.3	3.0	3.8	131	158	10.0	16.4	3,172	4,578
Norfolk, VA [2]	10.5	13.2	9.8	10.7	376	457	21.9	32.0	2,268	3,032
Hialeah, FL	2.0	1.6	2.0	1.5	106	66	5.0	4.9	2,241	3,490
Lincoln, NE	4.0	2.8	3.0	2.6	156	114	7.0	9.0	2,367	3,611
Greensboro, NC	(NA)	4.6	(NA)	3.9	(NA)	172	(NA)	12.6	(NA)	3,829

NA Not available. [1] 1990 based on enumerated resident population as of April 1. Other years based on estimated resident population as of July 1. [2] Includes city-operated elementary and secondary schools. [3] Includes city-operated university or college.

Source: U.S. Census Bureau; "Government Employment, March 2001"; issued October 2002, <http://www.census.gov/govs/apes/01emppub.pdf>; (accessed 13 June 2003).

No. 474. County Government Employment and Payroll—Largest Counties: 2001

[For March. See text, this section]

Counties ranked by 2000 population	Total employment (1,000)	Per 10,000 population [1]	Payroll (mil. dol.)	Avg. earnings [2] (dol.)	Counties ranked by 2000 population	Total employment (1,000)	Per 10,000 population [1]	Payroll (mil. dol.)	Avg. earnings [2] (dol.)
Los Angeles, CA	98.7	104	425.7	4,566	Hidalgo, TX	1.9	34	4.2	2,203
Cook, IL	28.4	53	108.7	3,839	San Joaquin, CA	7.7	137	23.5	3,590
Harris, TX	20.3	60	63.2	3,204	Tulsa, OK	1.5	26	3.5	2,470
Maricopa, AZ	15.3	50	43.8	2,931	Montgomery, OH	4.9	88	14.9	3,202
Orange, CA	24.9	87	88.3	3,833	Bernalillo, NM	1.7	30	4.2	2,796
San Diego, CA	20.0	71	71.6	3,793	Delaware, PA	3.4	61	7.8	2,306
Dade, FL	36.9	164	135.6	3,873	Summit, OH	4.1	75	10.6	2,650
Dallas, TX	13.5	61	43.6	3,387	Bristol, MA	0.9	16	2.8	3,299
Wayne, MI	6.8	33	26.4	3,987	Jefferson, CO	2.7	52	9.0	3,602
King, WA	16.0	92	56.7	4,089	Union, NJ	4.6	88	12.7	3,560
San Bernardino, CA	21.6	127	73.3	3,744	El Paso, CO	2.2	42	6.4	3,189
Santa Clara, CA	16.5	98	77.3	4,934	Ramsey, MN	4.0	77	14.2	4,041
Broward, FL	11.2	69	38.4	3,565	Ocean, NJ	3.8	74	11.3	3,722
Riverside, CA	17.7	114	67.0	4,073	Camden, NJ	4.8	94	16.1	3,816
Tarrant, TX	8.4	58	23.5	2,944	Will, IL	1.9	38	6.0	3,314
Alameda, CA	11.7	81	50.5	4,678	New Castle, DE	1.8	37	5.2	3,406
Suffolk, NY	12.3	87	54.1	4,798	Collin, TX	1.2	25	3.8	3,099
Cuyahoga, OH	16.3	117	51.8	3,180	Anne Arundel, MD	14.9	304	52.3	4,123
Bexar, TX	9.5	68	23.2	2,580	Passaic, NJ	4.0	83	15.8	4,561
Clark, NV	16.2	118	63.6	4,368	Arapahoe, CO	1.9	40	6.8	3,677
Nassau, NY	19.4	145	76.4	4,521	Lake, IN	2.3	47	4.4	2,329
Allegheny, PA	7.0	55	18.0	2,645	Polk, FL	4.3	88	11.0	2,747
Sacramento, CA	13.1	107	49.6	4,102	Brevard, FL	3.9	82	10.0	2,809
Oakland, MI	4.7	39	16.7	3,830	Plymouth, MA	0.6	14	2.3	3,857
Palm Beach, FL	8.7	77	28.1	3,345	Lancaster, PA	2.4	51	5.5	2,780
Hennepin, MN	12.4	111	44.4	3,996	Morris, NJ	4.0	84	10.9	3,474
Franklin, OH	6.7	63	19.6	3,102	Douglas, NE	1.9	41	5.4	3,006
St Louis, MO	4.3	42	13.3	3,253	Sonoma, CA	6.4	140	26.0	4,874
Hillsborough, FL	16.5	165	35.3	2,961	Onondaga, NY	6.0	130	16.3	3,057
Fairfax, VA	36.3	374	121.8	3,746	Jefferson, LA	10.6	232	28.3	2,954
Erie, NY	11.1	117	35.6	3,734	Lucas, OH	4.2	93	12.1	2,979
Contra Costa, CA	11.0	116	48.9	5,067	Sedgwick, KS	2.5	56	7.3	3,012
Milwaukee, WI	8.8	94	27.4	3,255	Johnson, KS	3.5	78	9.8	3,329
Westchester, NY	6.7	72	27.6	4,499	Stanislaus, CA	5.8	130	19.9	3,933
Pinellas, FL	6.5	71	20.5	3,220	Washington, OR	1.6	37	5.9	3,718
Du Page, IL	3.9	43	13.2	3,703	Volusia, FL	3.5	78	7.9	2,906
Salt Lake, UT	6.2	69	15.4	3,685	Lee, FL	3.4	78	10.0	3,037
Shelby, TN	13.9	155	38.5	2,896	Genesee, MI	2.7	61	7.3	3,371
Orange, FL	9.7	109	29.6	3,262	Chester, PA	2.4	56	6.6	3,083
Bergen, NJ	6.4	73	18.4	4,131	Denton, TX	1.7	39	4.3	2,626
Montgomery, MD	39.4	451	138.9	4,922	Dane, WI	2.8	66	7.8	3,026
Hamilton, OH	6.2	73	16.6	2,773	Burlington, NJ	3.7	87	9.7	3,216
Pima, AZ	7.8	93	21.2	3,012	Guilford, NC	13.4	318	33.6	2,910
Fulton, GA	8.1	100	25.9	3,410	Spokane, WA	1.8	42	5.7	3,202
Travis, TX	4.2	51	13.0	3,185	Kane, IL	1.3	32	3.6	2,903
Prince Georges, MD	30.5	380	94.3	3,659	Monterey, CA	5.6	140	19.2	3,767
Fresno, CA	9.3	116	29.6	3,420	Mobile, AL	2.1	53	4.3	2,076
Essex, NJ	5.8	74	21.7	4,315	Santa Barbara, CA	5.7	142	21.8	4,351
Macomb, MI	3.0	38	9.3	3,410	Solano, CA	3.2	80	10.9	3,862
Baltimore, MD	23.8	316	65.7	3,318	Knox, TN	9.7	254	21.6	2,522
Ventura, CA	8.6	114	34.8	4,198	York, PA	2.2	57	4.8	2,233
Middlesex, NJ	4.4	58	15.0	4,159	Hillsborough, NH	0.8	21	1.8	3,013
Montgomery, PA	3.7	49	9.8	2,855	Greenville, SC	2.1	56	5.1	2,733
Monroe, NY	7.0	95	21.5	3,597	Stark, OH	3.0	79	7.1	2,455
San Mateo, CA	6.6	93	28.5	4,936	Polk, IA	2.2	58	7.2	3,563
Pierce, WA	3.6	51	14.4	4,348	Berks, PA	2.5	68	5.7	2,253
Mecklenburg, NC	23.3	334	58.6	2,911	Westmoreland, PA	2.0	53	4.5	2,386
Jefferson, KY	3.6	52	9.7	2,780	Utah, UT	0.8	23	2.2	2,980
El Paso, TX	4.4	65	12.0	2,849	Tulare, CA	4.9	133	14.8	3,190
Dekalb, GA	6.6	99	21.8	3,463	Seminole, FL	2.7	73	7.5	3,079
Jefferson, AL	4.9	74	15.5	3,238	Adams, CO	1.6	45	5.2	3,329
Kern, CA	9.8	148	36.5	4,007	Pulaski, AR	1.3	36	3.0	2,471
Multnomah, OR	6.6	100	17.9	3,596	Waukesha, WI	1.6	44	4.6	3,159
Oklahoma, OK	2.2	33	4.5	2,252	Dakota, MN	1.8	51	6.1	3,902
Jackson, MO	2.2	33	5.3	2,619	Ft Bend, TX	1.1	31	2.7	2,702
Norfolk, MA	0.6	9	2.0	3,446	Mercer, NJ	3.8	108	11.3	3,925
Lake, IL	3.0	46	10.1	3,672	Clark, WA	1.4	41	5.1	3,538
Wake, NC	18.5	294	48.2	2,990	Pasco, FL	2.7	77	6.8	2,640
Monmouth, NJ	6.0	97	19.3	3,821	Orange, NY	3.4	99	10.3	3,238
Hudson, NJ	4.0	66	11.4	3,349	Washoe, NV	3.4	99	11.4	4,002
Cobb, GA	4.4	73	7.3	1,836	Clackamas, OR	2.3	68	7.4	3,900
Snohomish, WA	2.5	42	9.9	3,993	Cameron, TX	1.6	46	3.2	2,187
Bucks, PA	2.6	43	7.7	3,258	Butler, OH	2.3	69	5.9	2,700
Gwinnett, GA	3.9	67	12.4	3,411	Allen, IN	1.7	52	4.0	2,577
Kent, MI	2.4	42	7.8	3,473	Sarasota, FL	3.3	103	9.8	3,054

[1] 2001 based on enumerated resident population as of April 1, 2000. [2] Per full-time employee.

Source: U.S. Census Bureau; "Government Employment, March 2001"; issued October 2002, <http://www.census.gov/govs/apes/01emppub.pdf>; (accessed 13 June 2003).

Section 9
Federal Government Finances and Employment

This section presents statistics relating to the financial structure and the civilian employment of the federal government. The fiscal data cover taxes, other receipts, outlays, and debt. The principal sources of fiscal data are the *Budget of the United States Government* and related documents, published annually by the Office of Management and Budget (OMB), and the Department of the Treasury's *United States Government Annual Report* and its *Appendix*. Detailed data on tax returns and collections are published annually by the Internal Revenue Service. The personnel data relate to staffing and payrolls. They are published by the Office of Personnel Management and the Bureau of Labor Statistics. The primary source for data on public lands is *Public Land Statistics*, published annually by the Bureau of Land Management, Department of the Interior. Data on federally owned land and real property are collected by the General Services Administration and presented in its annual *Inventory Report on Real Property Owned by the United States Throughout the World*.

Budget concept—Under the unified budget concept, all federal monies are included in one comprehensive budget. These monies comprise both federal funds and trust funds. Federal funds are derived mainly from taxes and borrowing and are not restricted by law to any specific government purpose. Trust funds, such as the Unemployment Trust Fund, collect certain taxes and other receipts for use in carrying out specific purposes or programs in accordance with the terms of the trust agreement or statute. Fund balances include both cash balances with Treasury and investments in U.S. securities. Part of the balance is obligated, part unobligated. Prior to 1985, the budget totals, under provisions of law, excluded some federal activities—including the Federal Financing Bank, the Postal Service, the Synthetic Fuels Corporation, and the lending activities of the Rural Electrification Administration. The Balanced Budget and Emergency Deficit Control Act of 1985 (P.L.99-177) repealed the off-budget status of these entities and placed social security (federal old-age and survivors insurance and the federal disability insurance trust funds) off-budget. Though social security is now off-budget and, by law, excluded from coverage of the congressional budget resolutions, it continues to be a federal program.

Receipts arising from the government's sovereign powers are reported as governmental receipts; all other receipts; i.e., from business-type or market-oriented activities, are offset against outlays. Outlays are reported on a checks-issued (net) basis (i.e., outlays are recorded at the time the checks to pay bills are issued).

Debt concept—For most of U.S. history, the total debt consisted of debt borrowed by the Treasury (i.e., public debt). The present debt series, includes both public debt and agency debt. The *gross federal debt* includes money borrowed by the Treasury and by various federal agencies; it is the broadest generally used measure of the federal debt. *Total public debt* is covered by a statutory debt limitation and includes only borrowing by the Treasury.

Treasury receipts and outlays—All receipts of the government, with a few exceptions, are deposited to the credit of the U.S. Treasury regardless of ultimate disposition. Under the Constitution, no money may be withdrawn from the Treasury unless appropriated by the Congress.

The day-to-day cash operations of the federal government clearing through the accounts of the U.S. Treasury are reported in the *Daily Treasury Statement*. Extensive detail on the public debt is published in the *Monthly Statement of the Public Debt of the United States*.

Budget receipts such as taxes, customs duties, and miscellaneous receipts, which are collected by government agencies, and outlays represented by checks issued and cash payments made by disbursing officers as well as government agencies are reported in the *Daily Treasury Statement of Receipts and Outlays of the United States Government* and in the Treasury's *United States Government Annual Report* and its *Appendix*. These deposits in and payments from accounts maintained by government agencies are on the same basis as the unified budget.

The quarterly *Treasury Bulletin* contains data on fiscal operations and related Treasury activities, including financial statements of government corporations and other business-type activities.

Income tax returns and tax collections—Tax data are compiled by the Internal Revenue Service of the Treasury Department. The annual *Internal Revenue Service Data Book* gives a detailed account of tax collections by kind of tax and by regions, districts, and states. The agency's annual *Statistics of Income* reports present detailed data from individual income tax returns and corporation income tax returns. The quarterly *Statistics of Income Bulletin* has, in general, replaced the supplemental *Statistics of Income* publications which presented data on such diverse subjects as tax-exempt organizations, unincorporated businesses, fiduciary income tax and estate tax returns, sales of capital assets by individuals, international income and taxes reported by corporations and individuals, and estate tax wealth.

Employment and payrolls—The Office of Personnel Management collects employment and payroll data from all departments and agencies of the federal government, except the Central Intelligence Agency, the National Security Agency, and the Defense Intelligence Agency. Employment figures represent the number of persons who occupied civilian positions at the end of the report month shown and who are paid for personal services rendered for the federal government, regardless of the nature of appointment or method of payment. Federal payrolls include all payments for personal services rendered during the report month and payments for accumulated annual leave of employees who separate from the service. Since most federal employees are paid on a biweekly basis, the calendar month earnings are partially estimated on the basis of the number of work days in each month where payroll periods overlap.

Federal employment and payroll figures are published by the Office of Personnel Management in its *Federal Civilian Workforce Statistics—Employment and Trends*. It also publishes biennial employment data for minority groups, data on occupations of white- and blue-collar workers, and data on employment by geographic area; reports on salary and wage distribution of federal employees are published annually. General schedule is primarily white-collar; wage system primarily blue-collar. Data on federal employment are also issued by the Bureau of Labor Statistics in its *Monthly Labor Review* and in Employment and Earnings and by the U.S. Census Bureau in its annual *Public Employment*.

Public lands—The data on applications, entries, selections, patents, and certifications refer to transactions that involve the disposal, under the public land laws (including the homestead laws), of federal public lands to nonfederal owners. In general, original entries and selections are applications to secure title to public lands thar have been accepted as properly filed (i.e., allowed). Some types of applications, however, are not reported until issuance of the final certificate, which passes equitable title to the land to the applicant.

Figure 9.1
Federal Budget Summary: 1980 to 2003

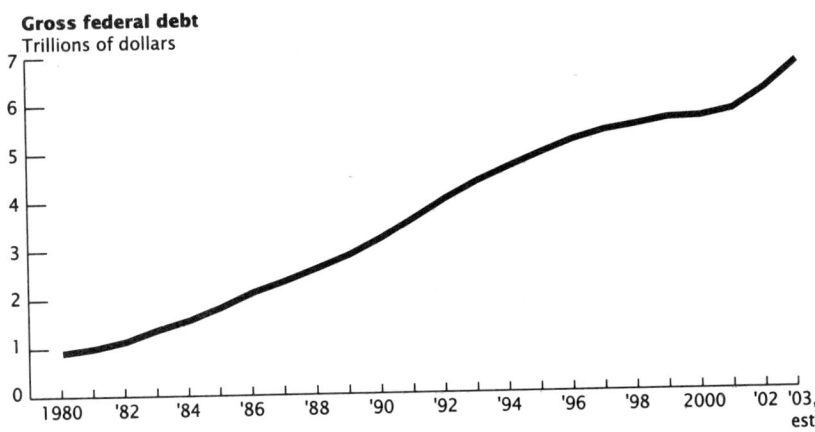

Source: Charts prepared by U.S. Census Bureau. For data, see Table 475.

Federal Government Finances and Employment

No. 475. Federal Budget—Receipts, Outlays, and Debt: 1960 to 2003

[In billions of dollars (92.5 represents $92,500,000,000), except percent. For fiscal years ending in year shown; see text, Section 8. The Balanced Budget and Emergency Deficit Control Act of 1985 put all the previously off-budget federal entities into the budget and moved social security off-budget. Minus sign (-) indicates deficit or decrease]

Year	Receipts	Outlays	Surplus or deficit(-)	Outlays as percent of GDP [1]	Gross federal debt [2] Total	Held by the public Federal gov't account	Held by the public Total	Held by the public Federal Reserve System	As percent of GDP [1]
1960	92.5	92.2	0.3	17.8	290.5	53.7	236.8	26.5	56.0
1965	116.8	118.2	-1.4	17.2	322.3	61.5	260.8	39.1	46.9
1970	192.8	195.6	-2.8	19.3	380.9	97.7	283.2	57.7	37.6
1975	279.1	332.3	-53.2	21.3	541.9	147.2	394.7	85.0	34.7
1976	298.1	371.8	-73.7	21.4	629.0	151.6	477.4	94.7	36.2
TQ [3]	81.2	96.0	-14.7	21.1	643.6	148.1	495.5	96.7	35.4
1977	355.6	409.2	-53.7	20.8	706.4	157.3	549.1	105.0	35.8
1978	399.6	458.7	-59.2	20.7	776.6	169.5	607.1	115.5	35.0
1979	463.3	504.0	-40.7	20.1	829.5	189.2	640.3	115.6	33.1
1980	517.1	590.9	-73.8	21.6	909.0	197.1	711.9	120.8	33.3
1981	599.3	678.2	-79.0	22.2	994.8	205.4	789.4	124.5	32.5
1982	617.8	745.7	-128.0	23.1	1,137.3	212.7	924.6	134.5	35.2
1983	600.6	808.4	-207.8	23.5	1,371.7	234.4	1,137.3	155.5	39.9
1984	666.5	851.9	-185.4	22.2	1,564.6	257.6	1,307.0	155.1	40.8
1985	734.1	946.4	-212.3	22.9	1,817.4	310.2	1,507.3	169.8	43.9
1986	769.2	990.4	-221.2	22.5	2,120.5	379.9	1,740.6	190.9	48.2
1987	854.4	1,004.1	-149.7	21.6	2,346.0	456.2	1,889.8	212.0	50.5
1988	909.3	1,064.5	-155.2	21.2	2,601.1	549.5	2,051.6	229.2	51.9
1989	991.2	1,143.6	-152.5	21.2	2,867.8	677.1	2,190.7	220.1	53.1
1990	1,032.0	1,253.2	-221.2	21.8	3,206.3	794.7	2,411.6	234.4	55.9
1991	1,055.0	1,324.4	-269.3	22.3	3,598.2	909.2	2,689.0	258.6	60.7
1992	1,091.3	1,381.7	-290.4	22.2	4,001.8	1,002.1	2,999.7	296.4	64.4
1993	1,154.4	1,409.5	-255.1	21.5	4,351.0	1,102.6	3,248.4	325.7	66.3
1994	1,258.6	1,461.9	-203.3	21.1	4,643.3	1,210.2	3,433.1	355.2	66.9
1995	1,351.8	1,515.8	-164.0	20.7	4,920.6	1,316.2	3,604.4	374.1	67.2
1996	1,453.1	1,560.5	-107.5	20.3	5,181.5	1,447.4	3,734.1	390.9	67.3
1997	1,579.3	1,601.3	-22.0	19.6	5,369.2	1,596.9	3,772.3	424.5	65.6
1998	1,721.8	1,652.6	69.2	19.1	5,478.2	1,757.1	3,721.1	458.2	63.2
1999	1,827.5	1,701.9	125.6	18.6	5,605.5	1,973.2	3,632.4	496.6	61.3
2000	2,025.2	1,788.8	236.4	18.4	5,628.7	2,218.9	3,409.8	511.4	57.9
2001	1,991.2	1,863.9	127.3	18.6	5,769.9	2,450.3	3,319.6	534.1	57.6
2002	1,853.2	2,011.0	-157.8	19.5	6,198.4	2,658.0	3,540.4	604.2	60.0
2003, est.	1,836.2	2,140.4	-304.2	19.9	6,752.0	2,873.6	3,878.4	(NA)	62.8

NA Not available. [1] Gross domestic product as of fiscal year; for calendar year GDP, see Section 13. [2] See text, this section, for discussion of debt concept. [3] Prior to fiscal year 1977 the federal fiscal years began on July 1 and ended on June 30. In calendar year 1976 the July-September period was a separate accounting period (known as the transition quarter or TQ) to bridge the period required to shift to the new fiscal year.

Source: U.S. Office of Management and Budget, *Budget of the United States Government, Historical Tables*, annual. See also <http://w3.access.gpo.gov/usbudget/fy2004/pdf/hist.pdf>.

No. 476. Federal Budget Outlays—Defense, Human and Physical Resources, and Net Interest Payments: 1980 to 2003

[In billions of dollars (590.9 represents $590,900,000,000). For fiscal year ending in year shown. Minus sign (-) indicates offsets]

Outlays	1980	1990	1995	1999	2000	2001	2002	2003, est.
Federal outlays, total	590.9	1,253.2	1,515.8	1,701.9	1,788.8	1,863.9	2,011.0	2,140.4
National defense	134.0	299.3	272.1	274.9	294.5	305.5	348.6	376.3
Human resources	313.4	619.3	923.8	1,057.7	1,115.5	1,194.4	1,317.9	1,419.6
Education, training, employment and social services	31.8	37.2	51.0	50.6	53.8	57.1	70.5	86.3
Health	23.2	57.7	115.4	141.1	154.5	172.3	196.5	223.1
Medicare	32.1	98.1	159.9	190.4	197.1	217.4	230.9	244.7
Income security	86.6	148.7	223.7	242.4	253.6	269.6	312.5	330.1
Social security	118.5	248.6	335.8	390.0	409.4	433.0	456.4	478.5
Veterans benefits and services	21.2	29.1	37.9	43.2	47.1	45.0	51.0	57.1
Physical resources	66.0	126.0	59.1	81.9	84.7	97.9	104.4	115.2
Energy	10.2	3.3	4.9	0.9	-1.1	-	0.5	0.7
Natural resources and environment	13.9	17.1	21.9	24.0	25.0	25.6	29.5	30.6
Commerce and housing credit	9.4	67.6	-17.8	2.6	3.2	5.9	-0.4	1.3
Transportation	21.3	29.5	39.4	42.5	46.9	54.4	61.9	64.2
Community and regional development	11.3	8.5	10.7	11.9	10.6	11.9	13.0	18.5
Net interest	52.5	184.4	232.1	229.8	223.0	206.2	171.0	161.4
International affairs	12.7	13.8	16.4	15.2	17.2	16.5	22.4	20.7
Agriculture	8.8	12.0	9.8	23.0	36.6	26.4	22.2	20.8
Administration of justice	4.6	10.0	16.2	26.1	28.0	29.7	34.3	36.1
General government	13.0	10.6	14.0	15.6	13.3	14.6	17.4	19.0
Undistributed offsetting receipts	-19.9	-36.6	-44.5	-40.4	-42.6	-47.0	-47.8	-50.3

- Represents zero.

Source: U.S. Office of Management and Budget, *Budget of the United States Government, Historical Tables*, annual. See also <http://w3.access.gpo.gov/usbudget/fy2004/pdf/hist.pdf>.

No. 477. Federal Budget Outlays in Constant (1996) Dollars: 1980 to 2003

[In billions of dollars (1,092.5 represents $1,092,500,000,000). For fiscal year ending in year shown; see text, Section 8. Given the inherent imprecision in deflating outlays, the data shown in constant dollars present a reasonable perspective—not precision. The deflators and the categories that are deflated are as comparable over time as feasible. Minus sign (-) indicates offset]

Type	1980	1990	1995	1999	2000	2001	2002	2003, est.
Constant (1996) dollar outlays, total	1,092.5	1,483.6	1,551.5	1,620.7	1,660.6	1,692.3	1,797.9	1,877.9
National defense [1]	245.3	354.7	282.0	260.7	270.9	275.9	307.6	327.4
Nondefense, total	847.3	1,128.8	1,269.5	1,360.1	1,389.8	1,416.5	1,490.3	1,550.4
Payments for individuals	514.1	688.5	895.7	955.7	982.3	1,027.6	1,118.7	1,185.5
Direct payments [2]	453.8	596.1	743.6	787.9	808.3	838.2	910.5	964.4
Grants to state and local gov'ts	60.3	92.5	152.1	167.8	174.0	189.5	208.3	221.2
All other grants	108.1	65.2	77.6	85.7	88.6	95.6	103.9	112.7
Net Interest [2]	93.8	214.3	236.8	219.3	208.8	188.5	154.3	143.9
All other [2]	173.4	209.2	106.3	136.6	147.9	145.6	153.0	149.6
Undistributed offsetting receipts [2]	-42.1	-48.4	-46.8	-37.3	-37.8	-40.8	-39.7	-41.2
Total nondefense	847.3	1,128.8	1,269.5	1,360.1	1,389.8	1,416.5	1,490.3	1,550.4
Total outlays as percent of GDP [3]	21.6	21.8	20.7	18.6	18.4	18.6	19.5	19.9
National defense [1]	4.9	5.2	3.7	3.0	3.0	3.0	3.4	3.5
Nondefense, total	16.7	16.6	17.0	15.6	15.4	15.6	16.1	16.4
Payments for individuals	10.2	10.2	12.0	11.0	10.8	11.3	12.0	12.5
Direct payments [2]	9.0	8.8	9.9	9.0	8.9	9.2	9.8	10.2
Grants to state and local governments	1.2	1.4	2.0	1.9	1.9	2.1	2.2	2.3
All other grants	2.1	1.0	1.0	1.0	1.0	1.1	1.2	1.2
Net Interest [2]	1.9	3.2	3.2	2.5	2.3	2.1	1.7	1.5
All other [2]	3.2	2.9	1.4	1.6	1.7	1.6	1.7	1.6
Total nondefense	16.7	16.6	17.0	15.6	15.4	15.6	16.1	16.4
Percent of outlays, total	100.0	100.0	100.0	100.0	100.0	100.0	100.0	100.0
National defense [1]	22.7	23.9	17.9	16.2	16.5	16.4	17.3	17.6
Payments for individuals	47.1	46.7	57.9	58.8	58.9	60.5	61.8	62.9
Direct payments [2]	41.6	40.5	48.1	48.5	48.5	49.4	50.3	51.2
Grants to state and local governments	5.5	6.3	9.8	10.3	10.4	11.2	11.5	11.7
All other grants	9.9	4.5	5.0	5.4	5.5	5.9	6.0	6.2
Net Interest [2]	8.9	14.7	15.3	13.5	12.5	11.1	8.5	7.5
All other [2]	14.8	13.1	6.8	8.5	9.0	8.7	8.7	8.1
Undistributed offsetting receipts [2]	-3.4	-2.9	-2.9	-2.4	-2.4	-2.5	-2.4	-2.3

[1] Includes a small amount of grants to state and local governments and direct payments for individuals. [2] Includes some off-budget amounts; most of the off-budget amounts are direct payments for individuals (social security benefits). [3] Gross domestic product in chained (1996) dollars.

Source: U.S. Office of Management and Budget, *Budget of the United States Government, Historical Tables*, annual. See also <http://w3.access.gpo.gov/usbudget/fy2004/pdf/hist.pdf>.

No. 478. Federal Outlays by Agency: 1980 to 2003

[In billions of dollars (590.9 represents $590,900,000,000). See headnote, Table 475]

Department or other unit	1980	1990	1995	2000	2001	2002	2003, est.
Outlays, total [1]	590.9	1,253.2	1,515.8	1,788.8	1,863.9	2,011.0	2,140.4
Legislative Branch	1.2	2.2	2.6	2.9	3.0	3.2	4.0
Judiciary Branch	0.6	1.6	2.9	4.1	4.4	4.8	5.4
Agriculture	34.8	46.0	56.7	75.7	68.1	68.7	72.8
Commerce	3.1	3.7	3.4	7.8	5.0	5.3	5.8
Defense-Military	130.9	289.8	259.6	281.2	291.0	332.0	358.2
Education	14.6	23.0	31.2	33.9	35.7	46.3	59.5
Energy	7.3	12.1	17.6	15.0	16.4	17.7	19.8
Health and Human Services	68.3	175.5	303.1	382.6	426.4	465.8	502.0
Housing and Urban Development	12.7	20.2	29.0	30.8	33.9	31.9	38.0
Interior	4.5	5.8	7.5	8.0	8.0	9.7	10.4
Justice	2.6	6.5	11.1	20.1	21.4	21.1	22.2
Labor	29.5	25.2	32.8	31.9	39.8	64.7	70.7
State	2.4	4.8	6.3	6.9	7.4	9.5	11.0
Transportation	19.8	28.7	38.8	46.0	54.1	56.1	52.3
Treasury	76.6	255.2	348.2	390.7	389.3	370.6	368.8
Veterans Affairs	21.1	29.0	37.8	47.1	45.1	50.9	56.9
Corps of Engineers	3.2	3.3	3.7	4.3	4.7	4.8	4.1
Other Defense-Civil Programs	12.0	21.7	28.0	32.9	34.2	35.2	40.1
Environmental Protection Agency	5.6	5.1	6.4	7.2	7.4	7.5	8.0
Executive Office of the President	0.1	0.2	215.0	0.3	0.2	0.5	0.3
Federal Emergency Management Administration	1.2	2.2	3.1	3.1	4.4	-	-
General Services Administration	-	-	831	-	-	-1	-
International Assistance Programs	7.7	10.1	11.1	12.1	11.8	13.3	13.0
National Aeronautics and Space Administration	5.0	12.4	13.4	13.4	14.1	14.4	14.6
National Science Foundation	0.9	1.8	2.8	3.5	3.7	4.2	4.9
Office of Personnel Management	15.1	31.9	41.3	48.7	50.9	52.5	55.8
Social Security Administration (on-budget)	8.1	18.1	31.0	45.1	40.0	45.8	44.5
Social Security Administration (off-budget)	117.9	245.0	330.4	396.2	421.3	442.4	465.4
Undistributed offsetting receipts	-32	-99	-138	-173	-191	-201	-208

- Represents zero. [1] Includes agencies and allowances not shown separately.

Source: U.S. Office of Management and Budget, *Budget of the United States Government, Historical Tables*, annual. See also <http://w3.access.gpo.gov/usbudget/fy2004/pdf/hist.pdf>.

No. 479. Federal Outlays by Detailed Function: 1980 to 2003

[In billions of dollars (590.9 represents $590,900,000,000). For fiscal years ending in year shown; see text, Section 8]

Superfunction and function	1980	1990	1995	1999	2000	2001	2002	2003, est.
Outlays, total..........................	590.9	1,253.2	1,515.8	1,701.9	1,788.8	1,863.9	2,011.0	2,140.4
National defense.........................	134.0	299.3	272.1	274.9	294.5	305.5	348.6	376.3
Department of Defense-Military..............	130.9	289.8	259.4	261.4	281.2	291.0	332.0	358.2
Military personnel......................	40.9	75.6	70.8	69.5	76.0	74.0	86.8	92.7
Operation and maintenance................	44.8	88.3	91.1	96.4	105.9	112.0	130.0	136.3
Procurement..........................	29.0	81.0	55.0	48.8	51.7	55.0	62.5	63.2
Research, development, test, and evaluation.....	13.1	37.5	34.6	37.4	37.6	40.5	44.4	52.8
Military construction.....................	2.5	5.1	6.8	5.5	5.1	5.0	5.1	6.0
Family housing........................	1.7	3.5	3.6	3.7	3.4	3.5	3.7	4.2
Atomic energy defense activities.............	2.9	9.0	11.8	12.4	12.2	13.0	14.9	16.3
International affairs.......................	12.7	13.8	16.4	15.2	17.2	16.5	22.4	20.7
International development and humanitarian assist...	3.6	5.5	7.6	5.7	6.5	7.2	7.8	8.7
International security assistance...............	4.8	8.7	5.3	5.5	6.4	6.6	7.9	6.8
Conduct of foreign affairs..................	1.4	3.1	4.2	4.2	4.7	5.1	7.1	8.1
Foreign information and exchange activities......	0.5	1.1	1.4	1.2	0.8	0.8	0.9	0.9
International financial programs..............	2.4	-4.5	-2.0	-1.3	-1.2	-3.1	-1.3	-3.7
General science, space and technology............	5.8	14.4	16.7	18.1	18.6	19.8	20.8	21.7
General science and basic research............	1.4	2.8	4.1	5.7	6.2	6.6	7.3	8.1
Space flight, research, and supporting activities....	4.5	11.6	12.6	12.4	12.4	13.2	13.5	13.6
Energy..............................	10.2	3.3	4.9	0.9	-1.1	-	0.5	0.7
Energy supply........................	8.4	2.0	3.6	-0.1	-2.1	-1.1	-0.8	-0.6
Energy conservation....................	0.6	0.4	0.7	0.6	0.7	0.8	0.9	0.8
Emergency energy preparedness............	0.3	0.4	0.2	0.2	0.2	0.2	0.2	0.2
Energy information, policy, and regulation.......	0.9	0.6	0.5	0.2	0.2	0.2	0.2	0.3
Natural resources and environment [1]............	13.9	17.1	21.9	24.0	25.0	25.6	29.5	30.6
Water resources......................	4.2	4.4	4.6	4.7	5.1	5.2	5.6	5.3
Conservation and land management..........	1.3	4.0	6.0	6.4	6.8	7.1	9.8	9.9
Recreational resources..................	1.4	1.4	2.0	2.7	2.6	2.3	2.8	3.1
Pollution control and abatement............	5.5	5.2	6.5	6.9	7.4	7.6	7.6	8.1
Agriculture...........................	8.8	12.0	9.8	23.0	36.6	26.4	22.2	20.8
Farm income stabilization................	7.4	9.8	7.0	20.0	33.5	22.7	18.4	16.3
Agricultural research and services...........	1.4	2.2	2.8	3.0	3.2	3.7	3.8	4.5
Commerce and housing credit [1]...............	9.4	67.6	-17.8	2.6	3.2	5.9	-0.4	1.3
Mortgage credit.......................	5.9	3.8	-1.0	0.4	-3.3	-1.2	-7.0	-4.3
Postal Service........................	1.2	2.1	-1.8	1.1	2.1	2.4	0.2	-4.2
Deposit insurance.....................	-0.3	57.9	-17.8	-5.3	-3.1	-1.4	-1.0	0.1
Transportation [1].......................	21.3	29.5	39.4	42.5	46.9	54.4	61.9	64.2
Ground transportation...................	15.3	19.0	25.3	28.1	31.7	35.8	40.2	37.8
Air transportation......................	3.7	7.2	10.0	10.7	10.6	14.0	16.5	20.3
Water transportation...................	2.2	3.2	3.7	3.5	4.4	4.4	5.1	5.7
Community and regional development...........	11.3	8.5	10.7	11.9	10.6	11.9	13.0	18.5
Community development.................	4.9	3.5	4.7	5.1	5.5	5.3	6.0	7.6
Area and regional development.............	4.3	2.9	2.7	2.3	2.5	2.8	2.6	2.8
Disaster relief and insurance..............	2.0	2.1	3.3	4.4	2.6	3.8	4.4	8.0
Educ./training/employment/& soc. services [1]......	31.8	37.2	51.0	50.6	53.8	57.1	70.5	86.3
Elementary, secondary, and vocational education...	6.9	9.9	14.7	17.6	20.6	22.9	25.9	32.8
Higher education......................	6.7	11.1	14.2	10.7	10.1	9.6	17.0	22.9
Research and general education aids..........	1.2	1.6	2.1	2.3	2.5	2.8	2.9	3.1
Training and employment.................	10.3	5.6	7.4	6.8	6.8	7.2	8.3	9.9
Other labor services....................	0.6	0.8	1.0	1.1	1.2	1.3	1.4	1.6
Social services.......................	6.1	8.1	11.6	12.2	12.6	13.5	14.9	16.0
Health..............................	23.2	57.7	115.4	141.1	154.5	172.3	196.5	223.1
Health care services...................	18.0	47.6	101.9	124.5	136.2	151.9	172.6	196.1
Health research and training..............	4.2	8.6	11.6	14.4	16.0	17.9	21.4	24.1
Consumer and occupational health and safety....	1.0	1.5	1.9	2.2	2.3	2.4	2.6	2.9
Medicare............................	32.1	98.1	159.9	190.4	197.1	217.4	230.9	244.7
Income security [1].......................	86.6	148.7	223.7	242.4	253.6	269.6	312.5	330.1
Gen. retirement & disability ins. (exc. soc. sec.)...	5.1	5.1	5.1	1.9	5.2	5.8	5.7	6.6
Federal employee retirement and disability......	26.6	52.0	65.9	75.1	77.2	81.0	83.4	86.3
Unemployment compensation.............	18.1	18.9	23.6	23.6	23.0	30.2	53.0	56.3
Housing assistance....................	5.6	15.9	27.5	27.7	28.8	30.1	33.1	34.2
Food and nutrition assistance.............	14.0	24.0	37.6	33.1	32.5	34.1	38.2	43.0
Social security.........................	118.5	248.6	335.8	390.0	409.4	433.0	456.4	478.5
Veterans benefits and services [1].............	21.2	29.1	37.9	43.2	47.1	45.0	51.0	57.1
Income security for veterans..............	11.7	15.2	19.4	22.7	24.5	23.2	27.4	30.3
Veterans education, training and rehabilitation.....	2.3	0.3	1.3	1.4	1.4	1.4	1.9	2.5
Hospital and medical care for veterans........	6.5	12.1	16.4	18.1	19.5	20.9	22.2	23.4
Veterans housing.....................	-0.0	0.5	0.4	0.6	0.4	-0.9	-1.0	0.3
Administration of justice..................	4.6	10.0	16.2	26.1	28.0	29.7	34.3	36.1
General government.....................	13.0	10.6	14.0	15.6	13.3	14.6	17.4	19.0
Net interest [1]..........................	52.5	184.4	232.1	229.8	223.0	206.2	171.0	161.4
Interest on Treasury debt securities (gross).....	74.8	264.7	332.4	353.5	361.9	359.5	332.5	328.3
Interest received by on-budget trust funds......	-9.7	-46.3	-59.9	-66.5	-69.3	-75.3	-76.5	-73.9
Interest received by off-budget trust funds......	-2.3	-16.0	-33.3	-52.1	-59.8	-68.8	-76.8	-83.6
Undistributed offsetting receipts.............	-19.9	-36.6	-44.5	-40.4	-42.6	-47.0	-47.8	-50.3

- Represents zero. [1] Includes functions not shown separately.

Source: U.S. Office of Management and Budget, *Budget of the United States Government, Historical Tables,* annual. See also <http://w3.access.gpo.gov/usbudget/fy2004/pdf/hist.pdf>.

No. 480. Department of Homeland Security—Budget: 2002 to 2004

[In millions of dollars (16,779 represents $16,779,000,000). For years ending Sept. 30.]

Funded program	2002 Actual	2002 Supplemental	2003, est.	2004, est.
Discretionary Budget Authority, total	16,779	14,272	27,884	29,185
Border and Transportation Security, total	7,829	4,150	16,886	16,653
Customs and Border Protection	4,063	870	5,466	5,649
Immigration and Customs Enforcement	2,127	179	2,375	2,488
Transportation Security Administration [1]	1,242	2,435	5,338	4,812
Federal Law Enforcement Training Center	137	31	143	146
Office for Domestic Preparedness	260	635	3,564	3,558
U.S. Coast Guard	4,129	464	5,149	5,634
Emergency Preparedness and Response	3,098	9,403	3,425	3,287
Science and Technology	90	77	561	803
Information Analysis and Infrastructure Protection	117	36	177	829
Other Department of Homeland Security (DHS)	1,516	142	1,686	1,979
Mandatory spending:				
Total, mandatory budget authority	5,342	-	5,801	6,993
Total, mandatory outlays	4,322	-	5,151	5,850
Border and Transportation Security:				
Budget authority	1,267	-	1,449	1,398
Outlays	1,094	-	1,181	1,176
U.S. Coast Guard:				
Budget authority	1,050	-	1,025	1,155
Outlays	970	-	1,016	1,136
Emergency Preparedness and Response:				
Budget authority	1,458	-	1,700	2,676
Outlays	872	-	1,462	2,046
Other DHS:				
Budget authority	1,567	-	1,627	1,764
Outlays	1,386	-	1,492	1,492
Credit activity:				
Direct loan disbursements:				
Disaster assistance	11	-	19	25

- Represents zero. [1] Includes discretionary fee-funded airport security activities.

Source: U.S. Office of Management and Budget, *Budget of the United States Government, Fiscal Year 2004.* See also <http://www.whitehouse.gov/omb/budget/fy2004/budget/homeland.pdf> (released 04 February 2003).

No. 481. Federal Receipts by Source: 1980 to 2003

[In billions of dollars (517.1 represents $517,100,000,000). For fiscal years ending in year shown; see text, Section 8. Receipts reflect collections. Covers both federal funds and trust funds; see text, this section. Excludes government-sponsored but privately-owned corporations, Federal Reserve System, District of Columbia government, and money held in suspense as deposit funds]

Source	1980	1990	1995	1999	2000	2001	2002	2003, est.
Total federal receipts [1]	517.1	1,032.0	1,351.8	1,827.5	2,025.2	1,991.0	1,853.2	1,836.2
Individual income taxes	244.1	466.9	590.2	879.5	1,004.5	994.3	858.3	849.1
Corporation income taxes	64.6	93.5	157.0	184.7	207.3	151.1	148.0	143.2
Social insurance and retirement receipts	157.8	380.0	484.5	611.8	652.9	694.0	700.8	726.6
Excise taxes	24.3	35.3	57.5	70.4	68.9	66.1	67.0	68.4
Social Insurance and retirement receipts [1]	157.8	380.0	484.5	611.8	652.9	694.0	700.8	726.6
Employment and general retirement	138.7	353.9	451.0	580.9	620.5	661.4	668.5	687.8
Old-age & survivors ins. (off-budget)	96.6	255.0	284.1	383.6	411.7	434.1	440.5	454.4
Disability insurance (off-budget)	16.6	26.6	67.0	60.9	68.9	73.5	74.8	77.2
Hospital insurance	23.2	68.6	96.0	132.3	135.5	149.7	149.0	152.3
Railroad retirement/pension fund	2.3	2.3	2.4	2.6	2.7	2.7	2.5	2.3
Unemployment insurance	15.3	21.6	28.9	26.5	27.6	27.8	27.6	34.2
Other retirement	3.7	4.5	4.6	4.5	4.8	4.7	4.6	4.5
Federal employees retirement-employee share	3.7	4.4	4.5	4.4	4.7	4.6	4.5	4.5
Excise taxes, total [1]	24.3	35.3	57.5	70.4	68.9	66.1	67.0	68.4
Federal funds	15.6	15.6	26.9	19.3	22.7	24.1	24.0	24.9
Alcohol	5.6	5.7	7.2	7.4	8.1	7.6	7.8	7.8
Tobacco	2.4	4.1	5.9	5.4	7.2	7.4	8.3	8.2
Telephone	-	3.0	3.8	5.2	5.7	5.8	(X)	(X)
Ozone depleting chemicals/products	-	0.4	0.6	0.1	0.1	(Z)	(X)	(X)
Transportation fuels	-	-	8.5	0.8	0.8	1.2	0.8	0.9
Trust funds	8.8	19.8	30.5	51.1	46.2	41.9	43.0	43.5
Highway	6.6	13.9	22.6	39.3	35.0	31.5	32.6	32.8
Airport and airway	1.9	3.7	5.5	10.4	9.7	9.2	9.0	9.4
Black lung disability	0.3	0.7	0.6	0.6	0.5	0.5	0.6	0.6
Inland waterway	(X)	0.1	0.1	0.1	0.1	0.1	0.1	0.1
Hazardous substance superfund	(X)	0.8	0.9	(Z)	(Z)	-	(X)	(X)
Oil spill liability	(X)	0.1	0.2	-	0.2	-	(X)	(X)
Aquatic resources	(X)	0.2	0.3	0.4	0.3	0.4	0.4	0.4
Vaccine injury compensation	(X)	0.2	0.1	0.1	0.1	0.1	0.1	0.1

- Represents zero. X Not applicable. Z $50 million or less. [1] Totals reflect interfund and intragovernmental transactions and/or other functions, not shown separately.

Source: U.S. Office of Management and Budget, *Budget of the United States Government, Historical Tables,* annual. See also <http://w3.access.gpo.gov/usbudget/fy2004/pdf/hist.pdf>.

No. 482. Tax Expenditures Estimates Relating to Individual and Corporate Income Taxes by Selected Function: 2002 to 2004

[In millions of dollars (2,190 represents $2,190,000,000). For years ending Sept. 30. Tax expenditures are defined as *revenue losses* attributable to provisions of the federal tax laws which allow a special exclusion, exemption, or deduction from gross income or which provide a special credit, a preferential rate of tax, or a deferral of liability]

Function and provision	2002	2003	2004	2004, rank
National defense:				
Exclusion of benefits and allowances to armed forces personnel	2,190	2,210	2,240	42
International affairs:				
Exclusion of income earned abroad by U.S. citizens	2,740	2,620	2,680	40
Exclusion of certain allowances for Federal employees abroad	760	800	840	57
Extraterritorial income exclusion	4,820	5,150	5,510	23
Inventory property sales source rules exception	1,470	1,540	1,620	49
Deferral of income from controlled foreign corporations (normal tax method)	7,000	7,450	7,900	17
Deferred taxes for financial firms on certain income earned overseas	1,950	2050	2130	44
General science, space, and technology:				
Expensing of research and experimentation expenditures (normal tax method)	1,660	2,200	2,760	39
Credit for increasing research activities	6,870	5,640	4,990	25
Agriculture:				
Capital gains treatment of certain income	1,010	1,060	1,120	54
Commerce and housing:				
Financial institutions and insurance:				
Exemption of credit union income	1,020	1,090	1,160	53
Exclusion of interest on life insurance savings	17,690	19,130	20,740	14
Housing:				
Exclusion of interest on owner-occupied mortgage subsidy bonds	870	960	1,050	56
Deductibility of mortgage interest on owner-occupied homes	63,590	65,540	68,440	2
Deductibility of state and local property tax on owner-occupied homes	21,760	22,320	22,160	11
Deferral of income from post 1987 installment sales	1,050	1,080	1,100	55
Capital gains exclusion on home sales	19,670	20,260	20,860	13
Exception from passive loss rules for $25,000 of rental loss	5,690	5,270	4,920	26
Credit for low-income housing investments	3,290	3,450	3,640	31
Accelerated depreciation on rental housing (normal tax method)	1,590	1,080	310	82
Commerce:				
Capital gains (except agriculture, timber, iron ore, and coal) [1]	56,060	55,010	53,930	5
Step-up basis of capital gains at death	26,890	27,390	28,500	8
Accelerated depreciation of buildings other than rental housing [1]	-1,800	-2,530	-1,980	136
Accelerated depreciation of machinery and equipment [1]	47,770	31,110	16,670	16
Expensing of certain small investments [1]	-360	-110	370	80
Graduated corporation income tax rate [1]	4,870	5,380	5,700	22
Transportation:				
Exclusion of reimbursed employee parking expenses	2,070	2,180	2,290	41
Community and regional development:				
Empowerment zones, Enterprise communities, and renewal communities	730	1,130	1,170	52
Education, training, employment, and social services:				
Education:				
Exclusion of scholarship and fellowship income [1]	1,270	1,260	1,260	51
HOPE tax credit	4,110	3,520	2,880	37
Lifetime learning tax credit	2,180	2,250	2,980	36
Deduction for higher education expenses	420	2,230	2,880	38
Parental personal exemption for students age 19 or over	2,480	3,310	3,230	34
Deductibility of charitable contributions (education)	4,020	4,140	4,350	28
Training, employment, and social services:				
Exclusion of employee meals and lodging (other than military)	740	780	810	59
Child credit	22,170	21,440	21,310	12
Credit for child and dependent care expenses	2,750	2,910	3,230	35
Deductibility of charitable contributions, other than education and health	30,860	32,100	33,990	7
Health:				
Exclusion of employer contributions for medical insurance premiums [2]	99,060	108,500	120,160	1
Self-employed medical insurance premiums	1,760	2,500	3,690	30
Workers compensation insurance premiums	5,280	5,770	6,190	21
Deductibility of medical expenses	5,710	6,060	6,340	20
Exclusion of interest on hospital construction bonds	1,200	1,320	1,440	50
Deductibility of charitable contributions (health)	4,240	4,360	4,580	27
Income security:				
Exclusion of workers compensation benefits	5,750	6,100	6,460	19
Net exclusion of pension contributions and earnings:				
Employer plans	51,260	63,480	67,870	3
401(k) plans	50,830	52,920	55,290	4
Individual Retirement Accounts	19,080	20,840	23,130	10
Low and moderate income savers credit	850	2,050	1,860	46
Keogh plans	7,000	7,282	7,616	18
Exclusion of other employee benefits:				
Premiums on group term life insurance	1,780	1,800	1,830	47
Special ESOP rules	1,630	1,710	1,790	48
Additional deduction for the elderly	1,890	1,950	2,050	45
Earned income tax credit	4,450	4,930	5,090	24
Social Security:				
Exclusion of social security benefits:				
Social security benefits for retired workers	18,340	18,560	18,930	15
Social security benefits for disabled	2,910	3,210	3,570	32
Social security benefits for dependents and survivors	3,730	3,910	4,140	29
Veterans benefits and services:				
Exclusion of veterans death benefits and disability compensation	3,160	3,230	3,400	33
General purpose fiscal assistance:				
Exclusion of interest on public purpose state and local bonds	25,250	26,780	27,310	9
Deductibility of nonbusiness state and local taxes other than on owner-occupied	47,430	50,520	50,910	6
Tax credit for corporations receiving income from doing business in U.S. possessions	2,240	2,240	2,240	43

[1] Normal tax method. [2] Includes premiums and medial care.

Source: U.S. Office of Management and Budget, *Budget of the United States Government, Analytical Perspectives, Fiscal Year 2004*. See also <http://www.whitehouse.gov/omb/budget/fy2004/pdf/spec.pdf> (released 04 February 2003).

No. 483. United States Government Ledger Balance Sheet—Assets and Liabilities: 1995 to 2002

[In millions of dollars (89,349 represents $89,349,000,000). For fiscal year ending in year shown]

Item	1995	2000	2001	2002
Assets, total	89,349	181,729	214,966	265,983
Cash and monetary assets, total	84,080	98,401	106,931	141,093
U.S. Treasury operating cash:				
Federal Reserve account	8,620	8,459	9,796	7,879
Tax and loan note accounts	29,329	44,199	34,423	53,007
Special drawing rights (SDR):				
Total holdings	11,035	10,316	10,919	11,710
SDR's certificates issued to Federal Reserve banks	-10,168	-3,200	-2,200	-2,200
Monetary assets with IMF [1]	14,682	13,690	18,407	20,864
Other cash and monetary assets:				
Cash and other assets held outside the Treasury Account	29,697	24,937	35,586	49,834
U.S. Treasury monetary assets	356	-	-	1
U.S. Treasury time deposits	528	5,977	13,352	27,369
Loan financing accounts:				
Guaranteed loans	-12,714	-22,013	-17,801	-16,293
Direct loans	19,732	105,459	124,518	139,306
Miscellaneous asset accounts	-1,748	-119	1,318	376
Total assets and excess of liabilities over assets	3,674,266	3,467,448	3,383,302	3,594,788
Excess of liabilities over assets at beginning of fiscal year	3,421,723	3,519,430	3,286,182	3,168,337
Add: Total deficit for fiscal year	163,916	-246,917	-127,276	3,864,259
Subtotal	3,585,639	3,283,464	3,158,906	7,032,595
Deduct: Other transactions not applied to surplus or deficit	722	-3,207	-9,430	-2,802
Excess of liabilities over assets at close of fiscal year	3,584,917	3,285,720	3,186,337	3,328,804
Liabilities, total	3,674,266	3,467,448	3,380,867	3,594,788
Federal securities, total	4,920,944	5,629,009	5,769,579	6,198,129
Treasury debt securities, total	4,893,989	5,601,336	5,743,238	6,170,959
Agency securities outstanding	26,955	27,672	27,011	27,170
Deduct: Net Federal securities held as investments by government accounts	1,317,645	2,218,896	2,468,757	2,675,648
Equals: Borrowing from the public, total	3,603,299	3,410,113	3,319,312	3,540,155
Accrued interest payable	50,611	44,211	39,483	32,869
Special drawing rights allocated by IMF [1]	7,380	6,359	6,316	6,481
Deposit fund liabilities	8,186	2,625	6,785	7,186
Miscellaneous liability accounts (checks outstanding, etc.)	4,790	4,140	8,301	8,098

-Represents zero. [1] IMF = International Monetary Funds.

Source: U.S. Dept. of Treasury, 1995-2002, *United States Government Annual Report*; and beginning 2000, *Combined Statement of Receipts, Outlays, and Balances of the United States 2002*. See also <http://www.fms.treas.gov/annualreport/cs2002/sc1.pdf> (released 16 December 2002).

No. 484. Government-Sponsored Enterprise Participation in the Credit Market: 1980 to 2002

[In billions of dollars (336.9 represents $336,900,000,000), except percents. Government-sponsored enterprises (GSEs) are financial intermediaries. GSE borrowing (lending) is nevertheless compared with total credit market borrowing (lending) by nonfinancial sectors, because GSE borrowing (lending) is a proxy for the borrowing (lending) by nonfinancial sectors that the GSEs assist through intermediation. The GSEs assist the ultimate nonfinancial borrower by purchasing its loans from the initial, direct lender or by other methods, which they finance by issuing securities themselves in the credit market. Borrowing and lending include mortgage-backed securities, because the GSEs assist nonfinancial borrowers through this type of intermediation as well as by types of intermediation that involve financial instruments recognized on the GSEs balance sheets. The data for this table are adjusted, with some degree of approximation, to remove double counting in making a comparison with other Federal and federally guaranteed transactions. GSE borrowing and lending are calculated net of transactions between components of GSEs and transactions in guaranteed loans; GSE borrowing is also calculated net of borrowing from other GSEs and purchases of federal debt securities]

Item	1980	1990	1995	1998	1999	2000	2001	2002
Total, net lending in credit market	336.9	705.2	702.4	981.3	1,076.2	902.8	1,012.5	1,268.3
Government-sponsored enterprise loans [1]	21.4	115.4	125.7	293.1	284.0	245.6	466.1	434.9
Government-sponsored enterprise lending participation rate (percent)	6.4	16.4	17.9	29.9	26.4	27.2	46.0	34.3
Total, net borrowing in credit market	336.9	705.2	702.4	981.3	1,076.2	902.8	1,012.5	1,268.3
Government-sponsored enterprise borrowing [1]	24.1	90.0	68.2	276.2	346.8	277.9	415.3	479.3
Government-sponsored enterprise borrowing participation rate (percent)	7.2	12.8	9.7	28.1	32.2	30.8	41.0	37.8

[1] Total net borrowing (or lending) in credit market by domestic nonfinancial sectors, excluding equities. Credit market borrowing (lending) is the acquisition (loan) of funds other than equities through formal credit channels. Financial sectors are omitted from the series used in this table to avoid double counting, since financial intermediaries borrow in the credit market primarily in order to finance lending in the credit market. Equities, trade credit, security credit, and other sources of funds are also excluded from this series. Source: Federal Reserve Board flow of funds accounts. Estimates for 2003 and 2004 are not available.

Source: U.S. Office of Management and Budget, *Budget of the United States Government, Analytical Perspectives*, annual.

No. 485. Federal Government Debt by Type and Maturity: 1990 to 2002

[In millions of dollars (3,266,073 represents $3,266,073,000,000). As of end of fiscal year]

Item	1990	1995	2000	2001	2002
Debt outstanding, total	**3,266,073**	**5,000,945**	**5,701,851**	**5,834,475**	**6,255,406**
Public debt securities	3,233,313	4,973,983	5,674,179	5,807,464	6,228,236
Agency securities	32,758	26,962	27,672	27,011	27,170
Securities held by—					
Government accounts, total	795,907	1,320,800	2,235,763	2,468,757	2,675,648
Public debt securities	795,762	1,320,784	2,235,712	2,468,757	2,675,648
Agency securities	145	16	51	-	-
The public, total	2,470,166	3,680,145	3,466,088	3,365,718	3,579,758
Public debt securities	2,437,551	3,653,199	3,438,467	3,338,707	3,552,589
Agency securities	32,613	26,946	27,621	27,011	27,170
MATURITY DISTRIBUTION					
Amount outstanding, privately held	**1,841,903**	**2,870,781**	**2,469,152**	**2,328,302**	**2,492,821**
Maturity class:					
Within 1 year	626,297	1,002,875	858,903	900,178	939,986
1-5 years	630,144	1,157,492	791,540	650,522	802,032
5-10 years	267,573	290,111	355,382	329,247	311,176
10-20 years	82,713	87,297	167,082	174,653	203,816
20 years and over	235,176	333,006	296,246	273,702	235,811

- Represents or rounds to zero.

Source: U.S. Department of the Treasury, *Treasury Bulletin*, quarterly.

No. 486. U.S. Savings Bonds: 1990 to 2002

[In billions of dollars (122.5 represents $122,500,000,000), except percent. As of end of fiscal year, see text, Section 8]

Item	1990	1993	1994	1995	1996	1997	1998	1999	2000	2001	2002
Amounts outstanding, total [1]	122.5	167.4	176.8	181.5	184.4	182.6	180.7	166.5	177.7	179.5	185.5
Sales	7.8	17.3	9.5	7.2	5.9	5.3	4.8	6.5	5.6	8.0	12.5
Accrued discounts	8.0	9.3	9.4	9.5	9.8	9.1	9.1	8.4	6.9	8.4	7.7
Redemptions [2]	7.5	7.8	9.4	11.8	2.5	2.1	14.3	16.6	14.5	13.8	12.5
Percent of total outstanding	6.1	4.7	5.3	6.5	1.4	1.1	7.9	10.0	8.2	7.7	6.7

[1] Interest-bearing debt only for amounts end of year. [2] Matured and unmatured bonds.

Source: U.S. Department of the Treasury, *Treasury Bulletin*, quarterly.

No. 487. Federal Funds—Summary Distribution by State and Outlying Area: 2002

[In millions of dollars (1,917,637 represents $1,917,637,000,000), except as indicated. For year ending Sept. 30. Data for grants, salaries and wages and direct payments to individuals are on an expenditures basis; procurement is on obligation basis]

State and outlying area	Federal funds Total	Per capita [1] (dol.)	Defense	Non-defense	Direct payments	Procurement	Grants	Salaries and wages
United States [2]	1,917,637	6,527	277,900	1,639,737	422,239	270,965	412,371	199,066
Alabama	34,291	7,643	7,026	27,265	7,086	6,035	6,344	3,109
Alaska	7,562	11,746	1,975	5,586	560	1,396	3,127	1,499
Arizona	34,761	6,371	8,605	26,157	6,193	7,291	6,664	3,142
Arkansas	18,372	6,779	1,682	16,690	5,202	1,095	4,047	1,251
California	206,401	5,878	36,152	170,250	45,166	34,753	48,084	19,143
Colorado	26,229	5,820	5,243	20,986	4,753	4,526	4,740	4,138
Connecticut	25,387	7,336	6,240	19,147	5,088	6,216	5,279	1,456
Delaware	4,766	5,903	518	4,248	1,121	207	1,121	465
District of Columbia	33,533	58,738	3,454	30,080	2,130	10,875	4,832	13,821
Florida	104,814	6,271	14,277	90,536	25,961	9,757	16,350	9,038
Georgia	51,336	5,997	10,991	40,345	10,160	7,364	10,500	7,366
Hawaii	10,474	8,414	3,964	6,510	1,435	1,621	1,835	2,684
Idaho	8,378	6,247	602	7,776	1,690	1,357	1,837	781
Illinois	70,275	5,577	4,324	65,951	20,223	4,664	14,975	6,344
Indiana	34,200	5,553	2,846	31,354	9,345	2,802	6,969	2,208
Iowa	18,839	6,415	914	17,926	6,169	955	4,060	1,084
Kansas	17,496	6,442	2,330	15,166	4,614	1,653	3,272	1,984
Kentucky	28,880	7,056	4,015	24,864	5,906	3,978	6,346	2,854
Louisiana	29,988	6,690	3,210	26,778	8,092	2,773	7,437	2,461
Maine	9,205	7,111	1,687	7,518	1,580	1,240	2,270	848
Maryland	49,537	9,076	10,220	39,318	7,285	13,488	6,312	9,664
Massachusetts	47,480	7,387	5,854	41,626	11,537	6,793	12,339	3,376
Michigan	55,909	5,563	3,134	52,775	14,564	3,539	13,279	3,286
Minnesota	27,056	5,390	1,971	25,084	7,089	2,228	6,492	2,022
Mississippi	21,308	7,420	3,658	17,651	5,000	2,734	5,046	1,840
Missouri	42,347	7,465	7,139	35,208	9,916	7,313	8,429	3,637
Montana	6,974	7,663	459	6,515	1,752	350	1,912	760
Nebraska	11,583	6,698	1,039	10,544	3,767	591	2,342	1,109
Nevada	10,737	4,940	1,244	9,493	2,126	1,250	1,840	1,096
New Hampshire	6,937	5,441	910	6,027	1,216	788	1,632	574
New Jersey	50,673	5,899	4,765	45,908	13,131	4,840	10,822	3,974
New Mexico	17,478	9,422	1,910	15,568	2,154	5,393	3,954	1,802
New York	128,994	6,733	6,288	122,707	31,389	7,417	42,461	8,526
North Carolina	48,180	5,791	6,546	41,633	10,369	2,923	10,939	5,978
North Dakota	6,437	10,151	627	5,810	2,643	329	1,425	655
Ohio	65,976	5,777	5,746	60,230	16,181	5,243	14,844	5,109
Oklahoma	24,355	6,971	3,897	20,459	5,187	2,515	5,108	3,152
Oregon	19,839	5,634	1,001	18,838	4,652	994	4,814	1,692
Pennsylvania	85,601	6,940	6,827	78,773	22,917	7,415	18,017	6,058
Rhode Island	7,503	7,014	916	6,587	1,650	495	2,094	786
South Carolina	26,103	6,355	3,765	22,339	5,063	3,105	5,592	2,636
South Dakota	6,315	8,297	471	5,844	2,099	378	1,506	631
Tennessee	39,276	6,775	2,551	36,724	8,309	5,912	8,658	3,200
Texas	123,431	5,667	22,267	101,164	27,648	20,581	24,858	13,019
Utah	12,302	5,311	2,508	9,794	1,869	2,084	2,697	1,929
Vermont	4,111	6,667	465	3,645	736	431	1,281	359
Virginia	74,537	10,220	29,632	44,904	8,515	26,170	7,714	13,504
Washington	40,218	6,627	6,500	33,717	7,994	5,586	8,296	5,278
West Virginia	13,361	7,415	474	12,887	2,780	602	3,298	1,221
Wisconsin	28,844	5,301	1,621	27,222	6,830	1,888	7,255	1,713
Wyoming	3,666	7,351	331	3,335	553	319	1,234	465
Outlying areas:								
American Samoa	154	2,691	6	148	2	13	93	6
Federated States of Micronesia	140	1,326	-	140	13	1	126	-
Guam	1,114	7,195	562	552	78	308	251	279
Marshall Islands	203	3,590	143	59	-	144	58	-
Northern Marianas	102	1,474	7	95	3	9	66	3
Palau	42	2,146	1	42	-	-	41	-
Puerto Rico	14,062	3,644	603	13,459	2,658	365	4,828	930
Virgin Islands	573	5,271	29	544	90	29	266	50
Undistributed	18,996	(X)	11,759	7,237	-	15,844	65	3,071

- Represents zero. X Not applicable. [1] Based on U.S. Census Bureau estimated resident population as of July 1. [2] Includes outlying areas and undistributed.

Source: U.S. Census Bureau, *Consolidated Federal Funds Report, 2002*. See also <http://www.census.gov/prod/2003pubs/cffr02.pdf> (issued May 2003).

No. 488. Tax Returns Filed—Examination Coverage: 1990 to 2002

[In thousands (109,868 represents 109,868,000, except as indicated). Return classification as Schedule C or C-EZ (nonfarm sole proprietorships) or Schedule F (farm proprietorships) for audit examination purposes was based on the largest source of income on the return and certain other characteristics. Therefore, some returns with business activity are reflected in the nonbusiness individual income tax return statistics in the table below (and vise versa), so that the statistics for the number of returns with Schedule C is not comparable to the number of nonfarm sole proprietorship returns in Table 734]

Year and type of return	Returns filed [1]	Returns examined Total	Percent coverage	By— Revenue agents	By— Tax auditors	By— Service centers [2]	Average tax and penalty per return (dollars) Revenue agents [3]	Tax auditors	Service centers
INDIVIDUAL RETURNS									
1990	109,868	1,145	1.04	202	517	426	309,566	1,962	2,432
1991	112,305	1,313	1.17	200	500	613	664,440	2,398	2,738
1992	113,829	1,206	1.06	210	537	459	1,365,896	2,280	2,539
1993	114,719	1,059	0.92	251	506	303	103,250	2,625	2,974
1994	113,754	1,226	1.08	364	456	406	246,785	3,113	1,963
1995	114,683	1,919	1.67	339	459	1,122	204,616	3,497	1,404
1996	116,060	1,942	1.67	252	509	1,180	818,753	3,051	1,714
1997	118,363	1,519	1.28	210	506	804	802,549	3,460	2,963
1998	120,342	1,193	0.99	168	383	625	177,830	3,372	2,760
1999	122,547	1,100	0.90	124	236	716	322,230	3,265	2,085
2000	124,887	618	0.49	92	146	367	123,337	3,337	2,602
2001	127,097	732	0.58	78	116	529	99,990	3,396	2,517
2002	129,445	744	0.57	89	112	539	1,597,215	3,910	2,589
ALL RETURNS, 2002 [4]									
Individual, total	129,445	744	0.57	89	112	539	1,597,215	3,910	2,589
1040A, TPI under $25,000 [5]	40,561	289	0.71	8	15	265	7,504	2,874	2,682
Non 1040, TPI under $25,000 [5]	14,106	91	0.64	5	7	78	10,822	3,210	3,134
TPI $25,000 under $50,000 [5]	30,720	72	0.23	12	20	39	5,369	2,290	1,593
TPI $50,000 under $100,000 [5]	24,703	70	0.28	13	22	34	62,228	2,639	1,548
TPI $100,000 and over [5]	10,693	80	0.75	23	17	40	1,027,708	5,742	3,975
Sch C—TGR under $25,000 [6]	2,542	68	2.67	2	9	56	10,874	2,807	2,040
Sch C—TGR $25,000 under $100,000 [6]	3,426	41	1.18	7	14	19	45,897	5,338	1,567
Sch C—TGR $100,000 and over [6]	2,059	30	1.45	16	7	6	5,004,846	9,673	2,820
Sch F—TGR under $100,000 [6]	367	2	0.47	0.3	0.5	1	9,224	1,268	882
Sch F—TGR $100,000 and over [6]	268	2	0.72	1	0.2	0.9	976,404	3,551	4,324
Corporation (except S Corporation)	2,412	23	0.97	21	(NA)	2	4,905,766	(NA)	8,375
Fiduciary	3,919	7	0.18	5	(NA)	2	26,349	(NA)	4,166
Estate	122	7	5.84	7	(NA)	0.001	200,229	(NA)	449,766
Gift	304	2	0.63	2	(NA)	0.001	213,369	(NA)	72,363
Employment	28,936	17	0.06	13	0.5	0.3	141,735	6,930	2,275
Excise	815	8	1.03	8	0.002	(NA)	40,617	5,775	(NA)
Windfall profit	(NA)	(NA)	(NA)	(NA)	(NA)	(NA)	(NA)	(NA)	(NA)
Misc. taxable	(NA)	0.5	(NA)	0.5	(NA)	0.05	674,007	(NA)	3,594
Partnerships	2,165	6	0.26	4	(NA)	1	(NA)	(NA)	(NA)
S Corporations (nontaxable)	3,023	12	0.39	11	(NA)	0.6	(NA)	(NA)	(NA)
Miscellaneous nontaxable [7]	(NA)	0.02	(NA)	0.002	(NA)	(NA)	(NA)	(NA)	(NA)

NA Not available. [1] Returns filed in previous calendar year. [2] Includes taxpayer contacts by correspondence. [3] Mostly reflects coordinated examination of large corporations and related returns. [4] Includes activities to protect release of funds in Treasury in response to taxpayer efforts to recoup tax previously assessed and paid with penalty. [5] Total positive income, i.e., excludes losses. [6] TGR= Total gross receipts. [7] Includes Domestic International Sales Corporations, Interest Charge Domestic International Sales Corporations, Real Estate Investment Mortgage Conduits, and other.

Source: U.S. Internal Revenue Service, *IRS Data Book*, annual, Publication 55B.

No. 489. Internal Revenue Gross Collections by Source: 1990 to 2002

[1,078 represents $1,078,000,000,000. For fiscal year ending in year shown; see text, Section 8]

Source of revenue	Collections (bil. dol.) 1990	1995	2000	2001	2002	Percent of total 1990	1995	2000	2001	2002
All taxes	1,078	1,389	2,097	2,129	2,017	100.0	100.0	100.0	100.0	100.0
Individual income taxes	540	676	1,137	1,178	1,038	50.1	48.7	54.2	55.3	51.5
Withheld by employers	388	534	781	795	751	36.0	38.4	37.2	37.3	37.2
Employment taxes [1]	367	465	640	682	688	34.0	33.5	30.5	32.0	34.1
Old-age and disability insurance	358	455	628	670	677	33.2	32.8	29.9	31.5	33.6
Unemployment insurance	6	6	7	7	7	0.6	0.4	0.3	0.3	0.3
Corporation income taxes	110	174	236	187	211	10.2	12.5	11.2	8.8	10.5
Estate and gift taxes	12	15	30	29	27	1.1	1.1	1.4	1.4	1.4
Excise taxes	49	59	55	52	52	4.5	4.2	2.6	2.5	2.6

[1] Includes railroad retirement, not shown separately.

Source: U.S. Internal Revenue Service, *IRS Data Book*, annual. For most recent report, see <http://www.irs.gov/pub/irs-soi/02databk.pdf>.

No. 490. Federal Individual Income Tax Returns With Adjusted Gross Income (AGI)—Summary: 1999 and 2000

[Includes Puerto Rico and Virgin Islands. Includes returns of resident aliens, based on a sample of unaudited returns as filed. Data are not comparable for all years because of tax changes and other changes, as indicated. See *Statistics of Income, Individual Income Tax Returns* publications for a detailed explanation. See Appendix III]

Item	Number of returns (1,000) 1999	Number of returns (1,000) 2000	Amount (mil. dol.) 1999	Amount (mil. dol.) 2000	Average amount (dollars) 1999	Average amount (dollars) 2000
Total returns	127,075	129,374	5,855,468	6,365,377	46,079	49,202
Adjusted gross income (AGI)	127,075	129,374	5,855,468	6,365,377	46,079	49,202
Salaries and wages	108,184	110,169	4,132,473	4,456,167	38,199	40,449
Taxable interest received	67,219	68,046	175,675	199,322	2,613	2,929
Tax-exempt interest	4,802	4,658	52,513	53,952	10,936	11,582
Dividends in AGI	32,226	34,141	132,466	146,988	4,111	4,305
Business or profession net income	13,165	13,313	233,746	244,598	17,755	18,373
Business or profession net loss	4,147	4,287	25,332	30,733	6,109	7,168
Net capital gain in AGI	22,498	22,646	552,605	644,285	24,562	28,451
Net capital loss in AGI	5,203	6,875	9,847	13,742	1,893	1,999
Sales of property other than capital assets, net gain	835	827	6,558	7,445	7,854	8,997
Sales of property other than capital assets, net loss	898	873	8,270	8,364	9,209	9,586
Pensions and annuities in AGI	21,344	21,765	304,311	325,828	14,257	14,970
Unemployment compensation in AGI	6,776	6,478	17,531	16,913	2,587	2,611
Social security benefits in AGI	9,459	10,609	75,079	89,964	7,937	8,480
Rent net income	4,356	4,201	43,460	45,099	9,977	10,736
Rent net loss	4,617	4,520	28,342	30,309	6,139	6,705
Royalty net income	1,117	1,104	6,482	7,998	5,803	7,245
Royalty net loss	47	36	132	101	2,809	2,800
Partnerships and S Corporations net income [1]	4,155	4,180	269,758	285,425	64,924	68,291
Partnerships and S Corporations net loss [1]	2,122	2,121	58,686	72,511	27,656	34,191
Estate or trust net income	516	557	10,976	12,134	21,271	21,803
Estate or trust net loss	40	39	1,092	1,128	27,300	28,900
Farm net income	726	703	9,201	8,270	12,674	11,763
Farm net loss	1,321	1,359	15,444	17,305	11,691	12,736
Statutory adjustments, total	22,660	23,197	56,699	58,610	2,502	2,527
Individual Retirement Arrangements	3,687	3,505	7,883	7,477	2,138	2,133
Student loan interest deduction	4,137	4,478	2,255	2,639	545	589
Medical savings accounts	50	65	82	120	1,627	1,839
Self-employed retirement plans	986	957	2,231	2,138	2,262	2,235
Deduction for self-employment tax	14,030	14,300	16,690	17,393	1,190	1,216
Self-employment health insurance	3,492	3,565	6,755	7,569	1,935	2,123
Exemptions, total [2]	248,657	252,332	669,241	690,109	2,691	2,735
Deductions, total	126,000	128,205	1,205,337	1,293,181	9,566	10,087
Standard deductions	85,755	85,671	449,696	470,821	5,244	5,496
Returns with additional standard deductions for age 65 or older or for blindness	11,200	11,331	14,264	14,736	1,274	1,301
Itemized deductions, total [3]	40,244	42,534	741,377	822,361	18,422	19,334
Medical and dental expenses	5,884	6,513	35,376	39,251	6,012	6,026
Taxes paid	39,564	41,824	265,365	294,712	6,707	7,047
Interest paid	33,706	35,405	291,553	322,932	8,650	9,121
Home mortgage interest paid	33,268	34,914	272,149	299,963	8,181	8,591
Charitable contributions	35,523	37,525	125,799	140,682	3,541	3,749
Taxable income	102,846	105,259	4,136,120	4,544,242	40,217	43,172
Income tax before credits	102,834	105,278	906,812	1,018,219	8,818	9,672
Tax credits, total [2]	36,622	37,736	35,892	37,722	980	1,000
Child care credit	6,182	6,368	2,675	2,794	433	439
Elderly and disabled credit	182	156	34	33	187	209
Child tax credit	26,016	26,405	19,399	19,689	746	746
Education credit	6,437	6,815	4,772	4,851	741	712
Foreign tax credit	3,267	3,936	4,941	5,990	1,512	1,522
General business credit	288	275	784	764	2,722	2,778
Income tax after credits	94,512	96,816	870,919	980,497	9,215	10,127
Income tax, total [4]	94,546	96,818	877,401	980,645	9,280	10,129
Alternative minimum tax	1,018	1,304	6,478	9,601	6,363	7,361
Earned income credit	19,259	19,277	31,901	32,296	1,656	1,675
Used to offset income tax before credits	5,352	5,416	1,918	1,969	358	363
Used to offset other taxes	3,137	3,148	2,379	2,524	758	802
Excess earned income credit (refundable)	16,050	16,126	27,604	27,804	1,720	1,724
Tax payments, total	119,809	122,244	981,100	1,084,868	8,189	8,875
Income tax withheld	111,194	113,733	695,527	763,901	6,255	6,717
Excess social security tax withheld	1,378	1,641	1,713	2,185	1,243	1,332
Estimated tax payments	13,169	13,327	196,916	221,622	14,953	16,630
Payments with requests for extension of filing time	1,510	1,611	53,984	63,397	35,751	39,354
Taxes due at time of filing	29,201	30,624	119,092	134,904	4,078	4,406
Tax overpayments, total	94,827	95,921	182,049	196,199	1,920	2,045
Overpayment refunds	91,601	93,000	155,514	167,577	1,698	1,802

[1] S Corporations are certain small corporations with up to 35 shareholders. [2] Includes items not shown separately. [3] Beginning 1998, total exemptions amount is after limitation. Beginning 1998, total itemized deductions are after limitation. [4] Includes minimum tax or alternative minimum tax.

Source: U.S. Internal Revenue Service, *Statistics of Income Bulletin*, and *Statistics of Income, Individual Income Tax Returns*, annual.

No. 491. Individual Income Tax Returns—Number, Income Tax, and Average Tax by Size of Adjusted Gross Income: 1999 and 2000

[In billions of dollars (5,855.5 represents $5,855,500,000,000), except as indicated. See Appendix III]

Size of adjusted gross income	Number of returns (1,000) 1999	2000	Adjusted gross income (AGI) 1999	2000	Income tax total [1] 1999	2000	Tax as percent of AGI [2] 1999	2000	Average tax[2] 1999	2000
Total	127,075	129,374	5,855.5	6,365.4	877.4	980.6	15.7	16.1	8,531	10,129
Less than $1,000 [3]	2,880	2,966	-52.8	-57.5	0.1	0.1	1.9	2.3	518	648
$1,000 to $2,999	5,922	5,385	11.9	10.8	0.1	0.1	7.0	6.9	132	134
$3,000 to $4,999	5,614	5,599	22.4	22.3	0.2	0.2	4.0	4.2	171	179
$5,000 to $6,999	5,220	5,183	31.3	31.1	0.5	0.5	5.1	5.0	301	297
$7,000 to $8,999	5,102	4,972	40.8	39.6	0.8	0.8	3.7	4.1	250	331
$9,000 to $10,999	5,069	5,089	50.5	50.8	1.4	1.3	5.0	4.7	464	470
$11,000 to $12,999	4,957	4,859	59.5	58.3	2.0	1.9	6.0	5.9	599	704
$13,000 to $14,999	4,907	4,810	68.7	67.4	2.6	2.6	6.2	6.3	680	883
$15,000 to $16,999	5,023	4,785	80.3	76.5	3.5	3.2	6.6	6.6	781	1,052
$17,000 to $18,999	4,609	4,633	82.9	83.4	3.9	3.9	7.2	7.1	923	1,279
$19,000 to $21,999	6,245	6,502	127.8	133.2	6.9	7.1	7.5	7.6	1,154	1,565
$22,000 to $24,999	5,873	5,735	137.8	134.9	8.7	8.2	7.8	7.7	1,513	1,815
$25,000 to $29,999	8,393	8,369	229.8	229.4	16.9	16.4	8.3	8.2	2,049	2,248
$30,000 to $39,999	13,288	13,548	461.8	470.9	39.7	40.2	8.9	8.9	3,007	3,094
$40,000 to $49,999	9,870	10,412	441.5	465.6	43.5	45.7	10.0	10.0	4,418	4,462
$50,000 to $74,999	16,756	17,076	1,023.7	1,044.7	113.2	115.7	11.1	11.2	6,770	6,824
$75,000 to $99,999	7,812	8,597	671.2	737.5	91.8	99.8	13.7	13.6	11,760	11,631
$100,000 to $199,999	7,105	8,083	934.8	1,066.3	162.2	184.0	17.4	17.3	22,858	22,783
$200,000 to $499,999	1,877	2,136	542.4	613.8	130.3	146.5	24.0	23.9	69,479	68,628
$500,000 to $999,999	348	396	235.7	269.0	67.0	76.0	28.4	28.3	192,428	192,092
$1,000,000 or more	205	240	653.2	817.4	182.3	226.3	27.9	27.7	889,234	945,172

[1] Consists of income after credits, and alternative minimum tax. [2] Computed using taxable returns only. [3] In addition to low income taxpayers, this size class (and others) includes taxpayers with "tax preferences," not reflected in adjusted gross income or taxable income which are subject to the "alternative minimum tax" (included in total income tax).
Source: U.S. Internal Revenue Service, Statistics of Income Bulletin, quarterly and Statistics of Income, Individual Income Tax Returns, annual.

No. 492. Individual Income Tax Returns—Itemized Deductions and Statutory Adjustments by Size of Adjusted Gross Income: 2000

[Preliminary. See Appendix III]

Item	Unit	Total	Under $10,000	$10,000 to $19,999	$20,000 to $29,999	$30,000 to $39,999	$40,000 to $49,999	$50,000 to $99,999	$100,000 and over
Returns with itemized deductions:									
Number of returns [1]	1,000	42,534	653	2,056	3,341	4,345	4,637	17,677	9,825
Amount	Mil. dol.	822,361	7,391	23,189	37,418	50,901	58,045	277,009	368,408
Medical and dental expenses:									
Returns	1,000	6,513	371	1,144	1,157	1,092	822	1,615	312
Amount	Mil. dol.	39,251	2,496	7,297	6,019	5,146	3,797	9,950	4,546
Taxes paid:									
Returns, total	1,000	41,824	577	1,896	3,208	4,253	4,576	17,534	9,778
Amount, total	Mil. dol.	294,712	1,200	3,754	7,189	11,563	15,193	86,304	169,508
State, local income taxes:									
Returns	1,000	35,423	304	1,259	2,547	3,526	3,927	15,253	8,608
Amount	Mil. dol.	191,767	271	871	2,466	5,104	7,446	48,660	126,948
Real estate taxes:									
Returns	1,000	37,111	464	1,548	2,553	3,536	3,935	15,943	9,130
Amount	Mil. dol.	93,299	855	2,626	4,199	5,692	6,912	33,965	39,050
Interest paid:									
Returns	1,000	35,405	423	1,305	2,460	3,475	3,883	15,467	8,392
Amount	Mil. dol.	322,932	2,903	7,835	15,171	21,998	25,569	122,165	127,291
Home mortgages interest:									
Returns	1,000	34,914	413	1,279	2,442	3,455	3,864	15,351	8,111
Amount	Mil. dol.	299,963	2,834	7,645	15,034	21,689	25,304	120,293	107,159
Charitable contributions:									
Returns	1,000	37,525	419	1,591	2,647	3,598	3,922	16,019	9,329
Amount	Mil. dol.	140,682	473	2,433	4,612	6,646	7,673	37,674	81,170
Returns with statutory adjustments:[2]									
Number of returns [2]	1,000	23,197	3,019	3,174	3,071	2,804	2,289	5,626	3,214
Amount of adjustments	Mil. dol.	58,610	2,468	3,644	4,567	4,390	4,208	13,964	25,367
Payments to IRAs:[3] Returns	1,000	3,505	160	283	484	513	435	1,073	557
Amount	Mil. dol.	7,477	269	518	956	939	970	2,318	1,506
Student loan interest deduction	1,000	4,478	208	621	928	979	683	1,059	-
Amount	Mil. dol.	2,639	116	317	575	659	439	533	-
Medical Savings Account deduction	1,000	65	3	6	7	9	6	12	23
Amount	Mil. dol.	120	2	11	14	8	25	52
Moving expenses	1,000	957	33	101	145	124	112	285	156
Amount	Mil. dol.	2,138	63	131	239	219	250	724	511
Payments to Keogh plans	1,000	1,288	17	27	47	45	85	388	678
Amount	Mil. dol.	12,475	33	95	142	164	346	2,103	9,592
Alimony paid	1,000	657	29	43	62	66	62	216	179
Amount	Mil. dol.	7,460	370	280	418	381	377	1,756	3,879

- Represents zero. [1] After limitations. [2] Includes disability income exclusion, employee business expenses, moving expenses, forfeited interest penalty, alimony paid, deduction for expense of living abroad, and other data not shown separately. [3] Individual Retirement Account.
Source: U.S. Internal Revenue Service, Statistics of Income, Individual Income Tax Returns, annual.

No. 493. Federal Individual Income Tax Returns—Adjusted Gross Income (AGI) by Source of Income and Income Class for Taxable Returns: 2000

[In millions of dollars (6,083,504 represents $6,083,504,000,000), except as indicated. Minus sign (-) indicates net loss was greater than net income. See headnote, Table 490. See Appendix III]

Item	Total [1]	Under $10,000	$10,000 to $19,999	$20,000 to $29,999	$30,000 to $39,999	$40,000 to $49,999	$50,000 to $99,999	$100,000 and over
Number of taxable returns (1,000)	96,822	7,837	14,478	14,863	13,004	10,250	25,542	10,847
Source of income:								
Adjusted gross income (AGI)	6,083,504	44,334	219,071	370,902	452,498	458,466	1,774,029	2,764,203
Salaries and wages	4,173,099	38,014	157,810	297,559	369,099	374,216	1,406,890	1,529,512
Percent of AGI for taxable returns	68.6	85.7	72.0	80.2	81.6	81.6	79.3	55.3
Interest received	186,464	3,223	12,025	11,486	11,719	10,827	42,425	94,759
Dividends in AGI	140,942	1,833	4,462	4,650	5,031	6,087	26,723	92,155
Business; profession, net profit less loss	191,177	1,107	6,139	9,251	11,391	11,534	47,796	103,959
Sales of property,[2] net gain less loss	621,730	5,054	4,255	5,491	6,485	7,993	45,949	546,502
Pensions and annuities in AGI	308,693	2,349	27,516	32,604	33,628	29,643	109,058	73,896
Rents and royalties, net income less loss	29,763	153	815	375	378	-20	2,547	25,514
Other sources,[3] net	431,636	-7,399	6,049	9,486	14,767	18,186	92,641	297,906
Percent of all returns:[4]								
Number of returns	74.8	6.1	11.2	11.5	10.1	7.9	19.7	8.4
Adjusted gross income (AGI)	95.6	0.7	3.4	5.8	7.1	7.2	27.9	43.4
Salaries and wages	93.6	0.9	3.5	6.7	8.3	8.4	31.6	34.3
Interest received	93.5	1.6	6.0	5.8	5.9	5.4	21.3	47.5
Dividends in AGI	95.9	1.2	3.0	3.2	3.4	4.1	18.2	62.7
Business; profession, net profit less loss	89.4	0.5	2.9	4.3	5.3	5.4	22.3	48.6
Sales of property,[2] net gain less loss	98.7	0.8	0.7	0.9	1.0	1.3	7.3	86.8
Pensions and annuities in AGI	94.7	0.7	8.4	10.0	10.3	9.1	33.5	22.7
Rents and royalties, net income less loss	105.7	0.5	2.9	1.3	1.3	-	9.0	90.6

- Represents zero. [1] Includes a small number of taxable returns with no adjusted gross income. [2] Includes sales of capital assets and other property; net gain less loss. [3] Excludes rental passive losses disallowed in the computation of AGI; net income less loss. [4] Without regard to taxability.

Source: U.S. Internal Revenue Service, *Statistics of Income, Individual Income Tax Returns*, annual.

No. 494. Federal Individual Income Tax Returns by State: 2000

[See Appendix III]

State	Number of returns[1] (1,000)	Adjusted gross income (AGI)[2] (mil. dol.)	Income tax Total[3] (mil. dol.)	Income tax Per capita[4] (dol.)	State	Number of returns[1] (1,000)	Adjusted gross income (AGI)[2] (mil. dol.)	Income tax Total[3] (mil. dol.)	Income tax Per capita[4] (dol.)
U.S.	130,122	6,307,009	980,064	3,483	MT	424	14,523	1,766	1,958
AL	1,904	72,591	9,476	2,131	NE	809	33,605	4,561	2,666
AK	329	13,964	2,064	3,291	NV	954	48,858	7,845	3,927
AZ	2,153	98,821	14,165	2,761	NH	629	34,469	5,673	4,590
AR	1,118	39,706	5,087	1,903	NJ	4,067	253,294	44,470	5,285
CA	14,867	864,645	146,454	4,324	NM	728	23,655	2,721	1,496
CO	2,096	112,909	18,243	4,242	NY	8,577	474,337	80,907	4,264
CT	1,672	117,734	22,682	6,659	NC	3,636	156,022	21,231	2,638
DE	378	18,647	2,794	3,564	ND	303	10,735	1,333	2,077
DC	279	16,271	2,839	4,963	OH	5,575	231,057	31,612	2,784
FL	7,499	348,609	56,618	3,543	OK	1,465	54,835	7,150	2,072
GA	3,637	168,486	24,693	3,016	OR	1,562	70,282	9,723	2,842
HI	572	23,929	3,124	2,577	PA	5,806	262,961	39,214	3,193
ID	559	22,572	2,922	2,258	RI	494	23,015	3,316	3,164
IL	5,787	302,994	49,472	3,984	SC	1,802	69,543	8,804	2,194
IN	2,837	119,554	16,416	2,700	SD	355	13,233	1,824	2,415
IA	1,351	54,016	6,896	2,357	TN	2,567	103,066	14,590	2,565
KS	1,223	53,410	7,491	2,787	TX	9,052	417,263	67,590	3,241
KY	1,747	66,933	8,617	2,132	UT	942	40,270	4,964	2,223
LA	1,874	69,184	9,261	2,072	VT	299	12,632	1,705	2,800
ME	606	24,374	3,151	2,471	VA	3,338	171,060	26,051	3,680
MD	2,563	139,963	20,950	3,956	WA	2,773	149,598	25,254	4,285
MA	3,110	202,426	36,438	5,739	WV	750	25,645	3,102	1,716
MI	4,620	217,648	33,783	3,198	WI	2,597	116,346	15,900	2,964
MN	2,386	120,028	17,687	3,596	WY	235	11,020	1,820	3,684
MS	1,173	39,170	4,666	1,640					
MO	2,565	108,519	15,270	2,729	Other[5]	1,474	48,579	7,682	(NA)

NA Not available. [1] Includes returns constructed by Internal Revenue Service for certain self-employment tax returns. [2] Less deficit. [3] Includes additional tax for tax preferences, self-employment tax, tax from investment credit recapture and other income-related taxes. Total is before earned income credit. [4] Based on resident population as of July 1. [5] Includes returns filed from Army Post Office and Fleet Post Office addresses by members of the armed forces stationed overseas; returns by other U.S. citizens abroad; and returns filed by residents of Puerto Rico with income from sources outside of Puerto Rico or with income earned as U.S. government employees.

Source: U.S. Internal Revenue Service, *Statistics of Income Bulletin*, quarterly.

No. 495. Federal Individual Income Tax—Tax Liability and Effective and Marginal Tax Rates for Selected Income Groups: 1990 to 2001

[Refers to income after exclusions. Effective rate represents tax liability divided by stated income. The marginal tax rate is the percentage of the first additional dollar of income which would be paid in income tax. Computations assume the low income allowance, standard deduction, zero bracket amount, or itemized deductions equal to 10 percent of adjusted gross income, whichever is greatest. Excludes self-employment tax]

Adjusted gross income	1990	1995	1997	1998	1999	2000	2001
TAX LIABILITY							
Single person, no dependents:							
$5,000 [1]	-	-314	-332	-341	-347	-353	-364
$10,000 [2]	705	540	480	455	427	391	201
$20,000	2,205	2,040	1,980	1,958	1,943	1,920	1,283
$25,000	2,988	2,790	2,730	2,708	2,693	2,670	2,033
$35,000	5,718	4,973	4,692	4,559	4,479	4,372	3,595
$50,000	9,498	8,865	8,654	8,549	8,483	8,404	7,596
$75,000	16,718	15,418	15,107	14,951	14,852	14,738	13,784
Married couple, two dependents: [3] [4]							
$5,000 [5]	-700	-1,800	-2,000	-2,000	-2,000	-2,000	-2,000
$10,000 [5]	-953	-3,110	-3,556	-3,756	-3,816	-4,000	-4,000
$20,000 [5]	926	-832	-1,414	-1,811	-1,958	-2,553	-3,553
$25,000 [1]	1,703	929	389	-8	-155	-1,500	-2,120
$35,000	3,203	2,768	2,625	2,565	2,520	1,468	570
$50,000	5,960	5,018	4,875	4,815	4,770	3,718	2,820
$75,000	12,386	11,030	10,576	10,371	10,224	9,064	7,895
EFFECTIVE RATE							
Single person, no dependents:							
$5,000 [1]	-	-6.3	-6.6	-6.8	-6.9	-7.1	-7.3
$10,000 [2]	7.1	5.4	4.8	4.6	4.3	3.9	2.0
$20,000	11.0	10.2	9.9	9.8	9.7	9.6	6.4
$25,000	12.0	11.2	10.9	10.8	10.8	10.7	8.1
$35,000	16.3	14.2	13.4	13.0	12.8	12.5	10.3
$50,000	19.0	17.7	17.3	17.1	17.0	16.8	15.2
$75,000	22.3	20.6	20.1	19.9	19.8	19.7	18.4
Married couple, two dependents: [3]							
$5,000 [5]	-14.0	-36.0	-40	-40.0	-40.0	-40.0	-40.0
$10,000 [5]	-9.5	-31.1	-35.6	-37.6	38.2	-40.0	-40.0
$20,000 [5]	4.6	-4.2	-7.1	-9.1	-9.8	-12.8	-17.8
$25,000 [1]	6.8	3.7	1.6	-	-0.6	-6.0	-8.5
$35,000	9.2	7.9	7.5	7.3	7.2	4.2	1.6
$50,000	11.9	10.0	9.8	9.6	9.5	7.4	5.6
$75,000	16.5	14.7	14.1	13.8	13.6	12.1	10.5
MARGINAL TAX RATE							
Single person, no dependents:							
$5,000 [1]	-	-	-	-	-	-	-
$10,000 [2]	15	15	15	23	23	23	18
$20,000	15	15	15	15	15	15	15
$25,000	28	15	15	15	15	15	15
$35,000	28	28	28	28	28	28	28
$50,000	28	28	28	28	28	28	28
$75,000	33	31	31	31	31	31	28
Married couple, two dependents: [3] [4]							
$5,000 [5]	-14	-36	-40	-40	-40	-40	-40
$10,000 [5]	-	-	-	-	-	-40	-40
$20,000 [1]	25	35	36	36	36	21	11
$25,000	15	35	36	36	36	36	21
$35,000	15	15	15	15	15	15	15
$50,000	28	28	15	15	15	15	15
$75,000	28	28	28	28	28	28	28

- Represents zero. [1] Beginning 1999, includes refundable earned income credit. [2] Refundable earned income credit. [3] Only one spouse is assumed to work. [4] Beginning 1998, includes child tax credits. [5] Beginning 1994, includes refundable earned income credit.

Source: U.S. Dept. of the Treasury, Office of Tax Analysis, unpublished data. Internet link <http://www.treas.gov/ota/index.html>.

No. 496. Federal Individual Income Tax—Current Income Equivalent to 1995 Constant Income for Selected Income Groups: 1990 to 2001

[Constant 1995 dollar incomes calculated by using the NIPA Chain-Type Price Index for Person Consumption Expenditures (1996 = 100) 1990, 85.63; 1994, 95.70; 1995, 97.90; 1996, 100.0; 1997, 101.98; 1998, 102.93; 1999, 104.57; 2000, 109.60; and 2001, 111.10]

Adjusted gross income	1990	1995	1997	1998	1999	2000	2001
REAL INCOME EQUIVALENT							
Single person, no dependents:							
$5,000	4,280	4,900	5,100	5,150	5,240	5,380	5,480
$10,000	8,560	9,790	10,200	10,290	10,470	10,750	10,950
$20,000	17,130	19,580	20,400	20,590	20,940	21,500	21,910
$25,000	21,410	24,480	25,500	25,730	26,180	26,880	27,380
$35,000	29,970	34,270	35,690	36,030	36,650	37,630	38,340
$50,000	42,820	48,950	50,990	51,470	52,360	53,760	54,770
$75,000	64,220	73,430	76,490	77,200	78,540	80,640	82,150
Married couple, two dependents: [1]							
$5,000	4,280	4,900	5,100	5,150	5,240	5,380	5,480
$10,000	8,560	9,790	10,200	10,290	10,470	10,750	10,950
$20,000	17,130	19,580	20,400	20,590	20,940	21,500	21,910
$25,000	21,410	24,480	25,500	25,730	26,180	26,880	27,380
$35,000	29,970	34,270	35,690	36,030	36,650	37,630	38,340
$50,000	42,820	48,950	50,990	51,470	52,360	53,760	54,770
$75,000	64,220	73,430	76,490	77,200	78,540	80,640	82,150
EFFECTIVE RATE (percent)							
Single person, no dependents:							
$5,000 [2]	-	-6.4	-6.5	-6.6	-6.6	-6.6	-6.6
$10,000	5.7	5.2	5.0	4.9	4.9	5.0	3.2
$20,000	10.4	10.1	10.0	9.9	9.9	10.0	7.2
$25,000	11.3	11.1	11.0	10.9	11.1	11.0	8.7
$35,000	14.6	13.9	13.7	13.5	13.5	13.6	11.8
$50,000	18.0	17.6	17.5	17.3	17.3	17.4	16.0
$75,000	21.0	20.4	20.3	20.2	20.2	20.2	19.1
Married couple, two dependents: [1]							
$5,000 [3]	-14.0	-36.0	-40.0	-40.0	-40.0	-40.0	-40.0
$10,000 [3]	-11.1	-31.8	-34.9	-36.5	-36.4	-37.3	-37.5
$20,000 [3]	1.2	-5.0	-6.2	-7.8	-9.7	-10.4	-14.1
$25,000	5.4	3.0	2.2	1.0	-2.8	-3.2	-5.0
$35,000	8.2	7.8	7.6	7.5	4.8	4.9	2.8
$50,000	10.2	9.9	9.9	9.8	7.9	8.0	6.4
$75,000	15.1	14.5	14.3	14.2	12.9	13.0	11.8
MARGINAL TAX RATE (percent)							
Single person, no dependents:							
$5,000	-	-	-	-	-	-	-
$10,000	15.0	15.0	15.0	15.0	15.0	15.0	10.0
$20,000	15.0	15.0	15.0	15.0	15.0	15.0	15.0
$25,000	15.0	15.0	15.0	15.0	15.0	15.0	15.0
$35,000	28.0	28.0	28.0	28.0	28.0	28.0	27.5
$50,000	28.0	28.0	28.0	28.0	28.0	28.0	27.5
$75,000	33.0	31.0	31.0	31.0	31.0	31.0	30.5
Married couple, two dependents: [1]							
$5,000 [3]	-14.0	-36.0	-40.0	-40.0	-40.0	-40.0	-40.0
$10,000 [3]	-	-	-	-	-	-	-10.0
$20,000 [3]	25.0	35.2	36.1	36.1	21.1	21.1	21.1
$25,000	15.0	35.2	36.1	36.1	36.1	36.1	21.1
$35,000	15.0	15.0	15.0	15.0	15.0	15.0	15.0
$50,000	15.0	15.0	15.0	15.0	15.0	15.0	15.0
$75,000	28.0	28.0	28.0	28.0	28.0	28.0	27.5

- Represents zero. [1] Only one spouse is assumed to work. [2] Beginning 1994, refundable earned income credit. [3] Refundable earned income credit.

Source: U.S. Dept. of the Treasury, Office of Tax Analysis, unpublished data.

No. 497. Full-Time Federal Civilian Employment—Employees and Average Pay by Pay System: 1990 to 2002

[As of March 31. (2,036 represents 2,036,000). Excludes employees of Congress and federal courts, maritime seamen of Dept. of Commerce, and small number for whom rates were not reported. See text, this section, for explanation of general schedule and wage system]

Pay system	Employees (1,000)				Average pay (dol.)			
	1990	2000	2001	2002	1990	2000	2001	2002
Total, excl. postal	2,036	1,671	1,660	1,681	31,174	50,429	52,911	(NA)
General Schedule	1,506	1,216	1,219	1,238	31,239	49,428	51,733	54,329
Wage System	369	205	199	193	26,565	37,082	38,416	39,892
Other	161	250	242	250	41,149	66,248	70,748	74,771
Postal pay system [1]	753	788	776	(NA)	29,264	(NA)	(NA)	(NA)

NA Not available. [1] Source: Career employees—U.S. Postal Service, *Annual Report of the Postmaster General*. See also <http://www.usps.com/financials/pdf/2001ar.pdf>. Average pay—U.S. Postal Service, *Comprehensive Statement of Postal Operations*, annual.

Source: Except as noted, U.S. Office of Personnel Management, *Pay Structure of the Federal Civil Service*, annual.

Federal Government Finances and Employment

No. 498. Federal Civilian Employment and Annual Payroll by Branch: 1970 to 2002

[Employment in thousands (2,997 represents 2,997,000); payroll in millions of dollars (27,322 represents $27,322,000,000). For fiscal year ending in year shown; see text, Section 8. Includes employees in U.S. territories and foreign countries. Data represent employees in active-duty status, including intermittent employees. Annual employment figures are averages of monthly figures. Excludes Central Intelligence Agency, National Security Agency, and, as of November 1984, the Defense Intelligence Agency, and as of October 1996, the National Imagery and Mapping Agency]

Year	Total	Percent of U.S. employed [1]	Executive Total	Executive Defense	Legislative	Judicial	Payroll Total	Executive Total	Executive Defense	Legislative	Judicial
1970	[2]2,997	3.81	2,961	1,263	29	7	27,322	26,894	11,264	338	89
1971	2,899	3.65	2,861	1,162	31	7	29,475	29,007	11,579	369	98
1972	2,882	3.51	2,842	1,128	32	8	31,626	31,102	12,181	411	112
1973	2,822	3.32	2,780	1,076	33	9	33,240	32,671	12,414	447	121
1974	2,825	3.26	2,781	1,041	35	9	35,661	35,035	12,789	494	132
1975	2,877	3.35	2,830	1,044	37	10	39,126	38,423	13,418	549	154
1976	2,879	3.24	2,831	1,025	38	11	42,259	41,450	14,699	631	179
1977	2,855	3.10	2,803	997	39	12	45,895	44,975	15,696	700	219
1978	2,875	2.99	2,822	987	40	13	49,921	48,899	16,995	771	251
1979	2,897	2.93	2,844	974	40	13	53,590	52,513	18,065	817	260
1980	[2]2,987	3.01	2,933	971	40	14	58,012	56,841	18,795	883	288
1981	2,909	2.90	2,855	986	40	15	63,793	62,510	21,227	922	360
1982	2,871	2.88	2,816	1,019	39	16	65,503	64,125	22,226	980	398
1983	2,878	2.85	2,823	1,033	39	16	69,878	68,420	23,406	1,013	445
1984	2,935	2.80	2,879	1,052	40	17	74,616	73,084	25,253	1,081	451
1985	3,001	2.80	2,944	1,080	39	18	80,599	78,992	28,330	1,098	509
1986	3,047	2.77	2,991	1,089	38	19	82,598	80,941	29,272	1,112	545
1987	3,075	2.73	3,018	1,084	38	19	85,543	83,797	29,786	1,153	593
1988	3,113	2.71	3,054	1,073	38	21	88,841	86,960	29,609	1,226	656
1989	3,133	2.67	3,074	1,067	38	22	92,847	90,870	30,301	1,266	711
1990	[2]3,233	2.72	3,173	1,060	38	23	99,138	97,022	31,990	1,329	787
1991	3,101	2.63	3,038	1,015	38	25	104,273	101,965	32,956	1,434	874
1992	3,106	2.62	3,040	1,004	39	27	108,054	105,402	31,486	1,569	1,083
1993	3,043	2.53	2,976	952	39	28	114,323	111,523	32,755	1,609	1,191
1994	2,993	2.43	2,928	900	37	28	116,138	113,264	32,144	1,613	1,260
1995	2,943	2.36	2,880	852	34	28	118,304	115,328	31,753	1,598	1,379
1996	2,881	2.27	2,819	811	32	29	119,321	116,385	31,569	1,519	1,417
1997	2,816	2.17	2,755	768	31	30	119,603	116,693	31,431	1,515	1,396
1998	2,783	2.12	2,721	730	31	31	121,964	118,800	30,315	1,517	1,647
1999	2,789	2.09	2,726	703	30	32	124,990	121,732	30,141	1,560	1,699
2000	[2]2,879	2.10	2,816	681	31	32	130,832	127,472	29,607	1,619	1,741
2001	2,704	1.97	2,641	672	30	33	131,964	128,502	28,594	1,682	1,780
2002	2,699	1.98	2,635	671	31	34	136,611	132,893	28,845	1,781	1,938

[1] Civilian only. See Table 587. [2] Includes temporary census workers.

Source: U.S. Office of Personnel Management, *Federal Civilian Workforce Statistics—Employment and Trends*, bimonthly; and unpublished data.

No. 499. Paid Civilian Employment in the Federal Government by State: 2000

[As of December 31. (2,674 represents 2,674,000). Excludes Central Intelligence Agency, Defense Intelligence Agency, seasonal and on-call employees, and National Security Agency]

State	Total (1,000)	Percent Defense	Percent change, 1998–2000	State	Total (1,000)	Percent Defense	Percent change, 1998–2000
United States [1]	2,674	23.2	-3.0	Missouri	54	16.9	-5.3
Alabama	48	42.0	-7.7	Montana	11	9.8	-
Alaska	14	30.8	-	Nebraska	15	20.9	-
Arizona	43	18.4	-	Nevada	13	14.8	-
Arkansas	20	17.7	-4.8	New Hampshire	8	12.4	-
California	248	24.0	-6.4	New Jersey	62	22.4	-4.6
Colorado	51	20.4	-5.6	New Mexico	25	26.2	-3.8
Connecticut	21	11.8	-8.7	New York	134	8.3	-3.6
Delaware	5	25.4	-	North Carolina	57	29.0	-
District of Columbia	181	6.9	-	North Dakota	8	21.0	-
Florida	113	23.2	-2.6	Ohio	84	27.2	-3.4
Georgia	89	34.8	1.1	Oklahoma	43	48.8	-
Hawaii	23	70.3	-4.2	Oregon	29	10.3	-3.3
Idaho	11	12.6	-	Pennsylvania	107	23.6	-5.3
Illinois	94	13.3	-4.1	Rhode Island	10	40.4	-9.1
Indiana	37	24.1	-2.6	South Carolina	26	34.5	-3.7
Iowa	18	7.8	-10.0	South Dakota	9	11.9	-10.0
Kansas	25	21.3	-	Tennessee	50	14.0	-3.8
Kentucky	30	22.0	-3.2	Texas	162	23.1	-7.4
Louisiana	33	23.0	-5.7	Utah	30	46.1	7.1
Maine	13	41.5	-	Vermont	6	9.1	-
Maryland	130	24.2	-0.8	Virginia	145	54.8	-1.4
Massachusetts	53	12.7	-5.4	Washington	62	34.6	-1.6
Michigan	58	13.3	-1.7	West Virginia	18	9.2	-
Minnesota	34	7.0	-2.9	Wisconsin	30	9.5	-3.2
Mississippi	24	37.9	-4.0	Wyoming	6	15.2	-

- Represents zero. [1] Includes employees outside the United States not shown separately.

Source: U.S. Office of Personnel Management, *Biennial Report of Employment by Geographic Area, 2000*.

336 Federal Government Finances and Employment

No. 500. Federal Civilian Employment by Branch and Agency: 1990 to 2002

[For fiscal year ending in year shown; excludes Central Intelligence Agency, National Security Agency; and, as of November 1984, the Defense Intelligence Agency; and, as of October 1996, the National Imagery and Mapping Agency]

Agency	1990	1995	2001	2002	Percent change 1990-1995	Percent change 1995-2002
Total, all agencies	3,128,267	2,920,277	2,709,956	2,715,487	-6.6	-7.0
Legislative Branch, total	37,495	33,367	30,439	30,886	-11.0	-7.4
Judicial Branch	23,605	28,993	33,810	34,699	22.8	19.7
Executive Branch, total	3,067,167	2,857,917	2,645,707	2,649,902	-6.8	-7.3
Executive Departments	2,065,542	1,782,834	1,603,426	1,645,361	-13.7	-7.7
State	25,288	24,859	28,122	29,078	-1.7	17.0
Treasury	158,655	155,951	148,186	147,159	-1.7	-5.6
Defense	1,034,152	832,352	671,591	670,166	-19.5	-19.5
Justice	83,932	103,262	127,783	131,378	23.0	27.2
Interior	77,679	76,439	75,846	72,929	-1.6	-4.6
Agriculture	122,594	113,321	108,540	112,278	-7.6	-0.9
Commerce	69,920	36,803	40,289	37,744	-47.4	2.6
Labor	17,727	16,204	16,376	16,302	-8.6	0.6
Health & Human Services	123,959	59,788	64,343	66,837	-51.8	11.8
Housing & Urban Development	13,596	11,822	10,178	10,470	-13.0	-11.4
Transportation [1]	67,364	63,552	65,542	102,826	-5.7	61.8
Energy	17,731	19,589	16,054	16,098	10.5	-17.8
Education	4,771	4,988	4,683	4,647	4.5	-6.8
Veterans Affairs [2]	248,174	263,904	225,893	222,138	6.3	-15.8
Independent agencies	999,894	1,073,510	1,040,657	1,002,846	7.4	-6.6
Board of Governors Federal Reserve System	1,525	1,704	1,680	1,731	11.7	1.6
Commodity Futures Trading Commission	542	544	551	527	0.4	-3.1
Consumer Product Safety Commission	520	486	479	473	-6.5	-2.7
Environmental Protection Agency	17,123	17,910	18,095	18,169	4.6	1.4
Equal Employment Opportunity Commission	2,880	2,796	2,910	2,774	-2.9	-0.8
Federal Communications Commission	1,778	2,116	2,004	2,060	19.0	-2.6
Federal Deposit Insurance Corporation	17,641	14,765	6,402	5,958	-16.3	-59.6
Federal Emergency Management Agency	3,137	5,256	6,147	5,601	67.5	6.6
Federal Trade Commission	988	996	1,052	1,082	0.8	8.6
General Services Administration	20,277	16,500	14,016	14,359	-18.6	-13.0
National Archives & Records Administration	3,120	2,833	2,878	3,019	-9.2	6.6
National Aeronautics & Space Administration	24,872	21,635	18,918	18,826	-13.0	-13.0
National Credit Union Administration	900	912	1,010	958	1.3	5.0
National Labor Relations Board	2,263	2,050	2,110	1,959	-9.4	-4.4
National Science Foundation	1,318	1,292	1,287	1,332	-2.0	3.1
Nuclear Regulatory Commission	3,353	3,212	2,871	2,974	-4.2	-7.4
Office of Personnel Management	6,636	4,354	3,349	3,427	-34.4	-21.3
Peace Corps	1,178	1,179	1,019	1,072	0.1	-9.1
Securities & Exchange Commission	2,302	2,852	3,049	3,027	23.9	6.1
Small Business Administration	5,128	5,085	4,219	3,823	-0.8	-24.8
Smithsonian Institution	5,092	5,444	4,981	5,048	6.9	-7.3
Social Security Administration	(X)	66,850	65,351	64,617	(X)	-3.3
Tennessee Valley Authority	28,392	16,545	13,430	13,444	-41.7	-18.7
U.S. Information Agency	8,555	7,480	2,372	(X)	-12.6	(X)
U.S. Postal Service	816,886	845,393	847,821	811,643	3.5	-4.0

X Not applicable. [1] Beginning 2001, includes the Transportation Security Administration created within the Department of Transportation. [2] Formerly Veterans Administration.
Source: U.S. Office of Personnel Management, *Federal Civilian Workforce Statistics— Employment and Trends*, bimonthly.

No. 501. Federal Employment Trends—Individual Characteristics: 1990 to 2002

[In percents, except as indicated. Covers only federal civilian nonpostal employees]

Characteristics	1990	1995	1996	1997	1998	1999	2000	2001	2002
Average age (years) [1]	42.3	44.3	44.8	45.2	45.6	45.9	46.3	46.5	46.5
Average length of service (years) [1]	13.4	15.5	15.9	16.3	16.6	16.9	17.1	17.1	16.8
Retirement eligible:[2]									
Civil Service Retirement System	8	10	11	12	13	15	17	19	23
Federal Employees Retirement System	3	5	6	7	8	10	11	10	11
College-conferred [3]	35	39	39	40	40	40	41	41	41
Gender:									
Men	57	56	56	56	56	55	55	55	55
Women	43	44	44	44	44	45	45	45	45
Race and national origin:									
Total minorities	27.4	28.9	29.1	29.4	29.7	30.0	30.4	30.6	30.8
Black	16.7	16.8	16.7	16.7	16.7	17.0	17.1	17.1	17
Hispanic	5.4	5.9	6.1	6.2	6.4	6.5	6.6	6.7	6.9
Asian/Pacific Islander	3.5	4.2	4.3	4.4	4.5	4.5	4.5	4.6	4.7
American Indian/Alaska native	1.8	2.0	2.0	2.1	2.1	2.2	2.2	2.2	2.2
Disabled	7.0	7.0	7.0	7.0	7.0	7.0	7.0	7.0	7.0
Veterans preference	30.0	26.0	26.0	25.0	25.0	25.0	24.0	24.0	23.0
Vietnam Era veterans	17.0	17.0	17.0	15.0	14.0	14.0	14.0	13.0	13.0
Retired military	4.9	4.2	4.3	4.2	3.9	3.9	3.9	4.2	4.4
Retired officers	0.5	0.5	0.5	0.5	0.5	0.5	0.5	0.6	0.7

NA Not available. [1] Represents full-time permanent employees. [2] Represents full-time permanent employees under the Civil Service Retirement System (excluding hires since January 1984), and the Federal Employees Retirement System (since January 1984). [3] Bachelor's degree or higher.
Source: U.S. Office of Personnel Management, Office of Workforce Information, *The Fact Book, Federal Civilian Workforce Statistics*, annual. See also <http://www.opm.gov/feddata/02factbk.pdf> (released June 2002).

Federal Government Finances and Employment 337

No. 502. Federal Executive Branch (Nonpostal) Employment by Race and National Origin: 1990 to 2002

[As of Sept. 30. Covers total employment for only Executive Branch agencies participating in OPMs Central Personnel Data File (CPDF). For information on the CPDF, see <http://www.opm.gov/feddata/acpdf.pdf>]

Pay system	1990	1995	2000	2001	2002
All personnel	2,150,359	1,960,577	1,755,689	1,764,083	1,813,047
White, non-Hispanic	1,562,846	1,394,690	1,224,836	1,226,113	1,255,941
General schedule and related	1,218,188	1,101,108	961,261	968,938	973,957
Grades 1-4 ($13,870 - $24,833)	132,028	79,195	55,067	57,368	55,005
Grades 5-8 ($21,370 - $38,108)	337,453	288,755	239,128	239,253	237,807
Grades 9-12 ($32,380 - $61,040)	510,261	465,908	404,649	403,556	405,583
Grades 13-15 ($55,837 - $100,897)	238,446	267,250	262,417	268,761	275,562
Total executives/senior pay levels [1]	9,337	13,307	14,332	14,565	15,428
Wage pay system	244,220	186,184	146,075	142,428	138,785
Other pay systems	91,101	94,091	103,168	100,182	127,771
Black	356,867	327,302	298,701	299,203	306,128
General schedule and related	272,657	258,586	241,135	243,689	243,884
Grades 1-4 ($13,870 - $24,833)	65,077	41,381	26,895	25,873	23,841
Grades 5-8 ($21,370 - $38,108)	114,993	112,962	99,937	100,079	97,731
Grades 9-12 ($32,380 - $61,040)	74,985	79,795	82,809	84,342	86,619
Grades 13-15 ($55,837 - $100,897)	17,602	24,448	31,494	33,395	35,693
Total executives/senior pay levels [1]	479	942	1,180	1,124	1,207
Wage pay system	72,755	55,637	42,590	40,619	39,354
Other pay systems	10,976	12,137	13,796	13,771	21,683
Hispanic	115,170	115,964	115,247	118,272	124,868
General schedule and related	83,218	86,762	89,911	93,360	96,333
Grades 1-4 ($13,870 - $24,833)	15,738	11,081	8,526	8,764	8,314
Grades 5-8 ($21,370 - $38,108)	28,727	31,152	31,703	33,148	34,201
Grades 9-12 ($32,380 - $61,040)	31,615	34,056	36,813	37,820	39,310
Grades 13-15 ($55,837 - $100,897)	7,138	10,473	12,869	13,628	14,508
Total executives/senior pay levels [1]	154	382	547	511	594
Wage pay system	26,947	22,128	16,926	16,526	16,017
Other pay systems	4,851	6,692	7,863	7,875	11,924
American Indian, Alaska Natives, Asians, and Pacific	115,476	122,621	116,905	120,495	126,110
General schedule and related	81,499	86,768	86,074	89,018	92,402
Grades 1-4 ($13,870 - $24,833)	15,286	11,854	9,340	9,556	9,568
Grades 5-8 ($21,370 - $38,108)	24,960	26,580	25,691	26,608	27,479
Grades 9-12 ($32,380 - $61,040)	31,346	33,810	33,167	33,751	35,054
Grades 13-15 ($55,837 - $100,897)	9,907	14,524	17,876	19,103	20,301
Total executives/senior pay levels [1]	148	331	504	555	626
Wage pay system	24,927	21,553	17,613	17,453	17,439
Other pay systems	8,902	13,969	12,714	13,469	15,643

[1] General schedule pay rates and Senior Pay Levels effective as of January 1999.

Source: Office of Personnel Management, Central Personnel Data File.

No. 503. Federal General Schedule Employee Pay Increases: 1980 to 2002

[Percent change from prior year shown, except 1980, change from 1979. Represents legislated pay increases. For some years data based on range for details see source]

Date	Pay increase	Date	Pay increase	Date	Pay increase
1980	9.1	1989	4.1	1997	2.3
1981	4.8	1990	3.6	1998	2.3
1982	4.0	1991	4.1	1999	3.1
1984	4.0	1992	4.2	2000	3.8
1985	3.5	1993	3.7	2001	2.7
1986	-	1994	-	2002	3.6
1987	3.0	1995	2.0		
1988	2.0	1996	2.0		

- Represents zero.
Source: U.S. Office of Personnel Management, *Pay Structure of the Federal Civil Service*, annual.

No. 504. Turnover Data for the Executive Branch—All Areas: 1990 to 2002

[Turnover data exclude Legislative and Judicial Branches, U.S. Postal Service, Postal Rate Commission]

Year	Accessions Total	Accessions New hires	Separations Total	Separations Quits	Total employment Average	Total employment Change from prior year	Total employment Percent change
1990 [1]	819,554	716,066	799,237	165,099	2,348,458	114,477	5.1
1991	495,123	351,112	515,673	134,175	2,224,389	-124,069	-5.3
1992	430,021	290,883	446,126	129,167	2,238,635	14,246	0.6
1993	382,399	253,374	423,830	127,140	2,189,416	-49,219	-2.2
1994	317,509	219,026	398,134	111,096	2,114,387	-75,029	-3.4
1995	345,166	222,025	457,246	91,909	2,037,890	-76,542	-3.6
1996	266,473	199,463	356,566	80,922	1,960,892	-76,953	-3.8
1997	283,517	208,725	333,431	81,574	1,895,295	-65,597	-3.3
1998	320,830	242,637	321,292	84,124	1,855,112	-40,183	-2.1
1999	423,500	346,988	372,778	129,196	1,846,170	-8,942	-0.5
2000 [1]	1,168,783	1,092,888	1,027,653	801,684	1,946,684	100,514	5.4
2001	308,877	233,034	301,659	82,495	1,783,239	-163,445	-8.4
2002	316,941	242,410	280,714	55,167	1,805,627	22,388	1.3

[1] Includes hiring for census enumerators.
Source: U.S. Office of Personnel Management, *Federal Civilian Workforce Statistics—Employment and Trends*, bimonthly. Also in *The Fact Book, Federal Civilian Workforce Statistics*, annual. See also <http://www.opm.gov/feddata/02factbk.pdf> (released June 2002).

338 Federal Government Finances and Employment

No. 505. Accessions to and Separations From Employment in the Federal Government: 2001 and 2002

[As of September 30. Turnover data exclude Legislative and Judicial branches branches, U.S. Postal Service, Postal Rate Commission]

Agency	Accessions Number 2001	Accessions Number 2002	Accessions Rate 2001	Accessions Rate 2002	Separations Number 2001	Separations Number 2002	Separations Rate 2001	Separations Rate 2002
Total, all agencies	518,104	457,647	19.5	17.3	508,495	445,541	19.2	16.8
Legislative Branch, total [1]	1,214	1,349	9.2	10.1	1,937	1,665	14.6	12.5
General Accounting Office	237	255	7.5	7.8	461	485	14.6	14.9
Government Printing Office	163	265	5.3	8.9	314	274	10.2	9.2
Library of Congress	280	368	6.5	8.5	552	334	12.8	7.8
Judicial Branch	-	-	(X)	(X)	-	-	(X)	(X)
Executive Branch, total	516,890	456,402	19.6	17.3	506,558	443,876	19.2	16.8
Executive Office of the President	706	440	44.5	26.1	760	314	47.9	18.6
Executive Departments	286,314	298,478	18.0	18.5	281,489	263,923	17.7	16.4
State	3,945	4,443	14.1	15.5	3,395	3,142	12.1	10.9
Treasury	50,679	5,587	33.2	33.0	46,343	50,082	30.3	32.0
Defense	96,062	103,288	14.3	15.4	106,933	105,644	15.9	15.7
Justice	10,866	13,488	8.6	10.4	7,601	8,388	6.0	6.5
Interior	20,834	2,054	29.0	28.4	14,799	9,015	20.6	12.2
Agriculture [2]	32,087	32,778	31.5	30.9	28,251	31,281	27.8	29.5
Commerce [2]	12,176	5,750	29.7	15.0	25,128	9,318	61.3	24.2
Labor	2,112	1,569	13.1	9.6	1,787	1,666	11.1	10.2
Health & Human Services [3]	11,691	14,084	18.4	21.4	9,048	8,504	14.2	12.9
Housing & Urban Development	807	1,200	7.9	11.7	958	1,003	9.4	9.8
Transportation	5,465	25,080	8.5	34.3	4,234	4,632	6.6	6.3
Energy	1,717	1,394	10.9	8.7	1,272	1,328	8.1	8.3
Education	690	482	14.7	10.3	486	154	10.4	3.3
Veterans Affairs [4]	37,183	28,875	16.7	12.9	31,252	30,042	14.0	13.5
Independent agencies [1]	229,870	157,484	21.9	15.4	224,309	179,629	21.4	17.6
Board of Governors, Federal Reserve System	233	229	14.1	13.4	196	178	11.8	10.4
Environmental Protection Agency	1,635	1,456	9.0	8.1	1,552	1,254	8.6	7.0
Equal Employment Opportunity Comm	289	57	10.4	2.0	146	67	5.3	2.4
Federal Deposit Insurance Corporation	310	262	4.7	4.2	794	686	12.1	11.1
Fed Emergency Management Agency	1,665	1,413	31.2	25.3	1,916	1,829	35.9	32.7
General Services Administration	961	1,532	6.9	10.9	1,022	1,928	7.3	13.7
National Aeronautics & Space Admin	1,829	1,303	9.7	6.9	1,627	1,398	8.6	7.4
National Archives & Records Admin	649	714	22.9	23.7	365	447	12.9	14.9
Nuclear Regulatory Commission	265	352	9.2	12.1	250	231	8.7	7.9
Office of Personnel Management	617	523	18.5	15.6	654	362	19.6	10.8
Panama Canal Comm	-	-	-	-	1	1	19.2	20.8
Railroad Retirement Board	48	47	4.1	4.0	57	54	4.9	4.6
Securities and Exchange Commission	535	252	17.9	8.2	331	69	11.1	2.6
Small Business Administration	1,193	617	28.8	15.3	1,197	1,111	28.9	27.6
Smithsonian Institution	556	695	11.0	13.9	675	703	13.4	14.1
Tennessee Valley Authority	1,018	815	7.7	6.0	715	759	5.4	5.6
U.S. Information Agency	117	167	4.9	7.0	263	137	11.0	5.7
U.S. International Dev Coop Agency	(X)	192	(X)	8.2	(X)	175	(X)	5.6
U.S. Postal Service	208,002	139,453	24.2	16.8	204,886	163,152	23.9	19.7

- Represents or rounds to zero. X Not applicable. [1] Includes other branches, or other agencies, not shown separately. [2] 2000 includes census enumerators for the decennial census. [3] Sizable changes due to the Social Security Administration which was separated from the Department of Health and Human Services to become an independent agency effective April 1995. [4] Formerly Veterans Administration.

Source: U.S. Office of Personnel Management, *Federal Civilian Workforce Statistics— Employment and Trends*, bimonthly.

No. 506. Federal Agencies Employing 500 or More Full-Time Officers With Authority to Carry Firearms and Make Arrests—Number of Officers: 1996 to 2002

[As of June]

Selected agency	1996	1998	2000	2002
All agencies [1]	74,493	83,143	88,496	93,446
Immigration and Naturalization Service	12,403	16,552	17,654	19,101
Federal Bureau of Prisons	11,329	12,587	13,557	14,305
Federal Bureau of Investigation	9,749	10,539	10,522	11,634
U.S. Customs Service	10,389	11,285	11,523	11,248
Drug Enforcement Administration	3,185	3,587	4,039	4,256
U.S. Secret Service	2,777	2,490	3,599	4,050
Administrative Office of the U.S. Courts	2,946	3,305	4,161	4,020
U.S. Postal Inspection Service	3,576	3,490	3,412	3,135
U.S. Marshals Service	3,371	3,011	2,726	2,855
Internal Revenue Service	2,650	2,705	2,735	2,646
National Park Service	1,869	1,723	1,967	2,335
Bureau of Alcohol, Tobacco and Firearms	2,148	2,197	2,188	2,139
U.S. Capitol Police	1,031	1,055	1,199	1,225
U.S. Fish and Wildlife Service	869	831	888	772
GSA - Federal Protective Services	643	900	803	744
U.S. Forest Service	619	601	586	658

[1] Includes agencies not shown separately.

Source: U.S. Bureau of Justice Statistics, *Federal Law Enforcement Officers, 1996, 1998, 2000* and *2002* reports. See also <http://www.ojp.usdoj.gov/bjs/pub/pdf/fleo02.pdf> (issued August 2003).

Federal Government Finances and Employment

No. 507. Federal Land and Buildings Owned and Leased: 1990 to 2002

[For fiscal years ending in years shown; see text, Section 8. Covers federal real property throughout the world, except as noted. Cost of land figures represent total cost of property owned in year shown. For further details see source. For data on federal land by state, see Tables 360 and 508]

Item	Unit	1990	1995	1998	1999	2000	2002
Federally owned:							
Land, worldwide	1,000 acres	650,014	549,670	655,042	630,648	635,824	675,864
United States	1,000 acres	649,802	549,474	654,885	630,266	635,355	674,100
Buildings [1]	1,000	(NA)	(NA)	(NA)	(NA)	435	446
United States	1,000	446	424	420	419	430	441
Buildings floor area [1]	Mil. sq/ft	(NA)	(NA)	(NA)	(NA)	3,003	3,009
United States	Mil. sq/ft	2,859	2,793	2,911	2,875	2,968	2,975
Costs	Mil. dol	187,865	199,387	244,273	238,327	260,069	334,708
Land	Mil. dol	(NA)	18,972	26,450	17,257	21,008	53,930
Buildings	Mil. dol	(NA)	113,018	130,858	132,981	139,291	174,929
Structures and facilities	Mil. dol	(NA)	67,398	86,965	88,090	99,770	105,849
Federally leased:							
Land, worldwide	1,000 acres	994	1,385	1,306	1,400	1,670	894
United States	1,000 acres	938	1,351	1,272	1,342	1,611	842
Buildings [1]	1,000	(NA)	(NA)	(NA)	(NA)	84	57
United States	1,000	47	78	76	77	73	46
Buildings floor area [1]	Mil. sq/ft	(NA)	(NA)	(NA)	(NA)	347	374
United States	Mil. sq/ft	234	275	276	301	313	339
Annual rental	Mil. dol	2,590	3,633	3,628	3,998	3,394	5,111
United States	Mil. dol	2,125	3,174	3,226	3,590	2,931	4,588

NA Not available. [1] Excludes data for Dept. of Defense military functions outside of the United States.

Source: U.S. General Services Administration, *Summary Report on Real Property Owned by the United States Throughout the World*, annual; and *Summary Report of Real Property Leased by the United States Throughout the World, 2002*. See also <http://www.gsa.gov/>.

No. 508. Federally-Owned Property in the United States by State: 2002

[As of September 30. For data on federal land by state, see Table 360]

State	Installations [1]	Buildings	Floor area (mil. sq. ft)	Costs [2] (mil. dol.)	State	Installations [1]	Buildings	Floor area (mil. sq. ft)	Costs [2] (mil. dol.)
U.S.	32,019	441,213	2,973.7	331,578	MO	841	6,567	52.3	6,822
AL	519	8,382	53.6	16,518	MT	744	7,320	15.2	2,525
AK	1,182	8,481	53.1	5,763	NE	538	3,216	18.7	1,415
AZ	621	14,443	53.6	5,148	NV	299	7,959	32.0	2,942
AR	517	5,929	26.5	2,760	NH	174	657	6.3	708
CA	2,170	63,404	407.1	33,735	NJ	476	5,999	55.9	3,675
CO	806	9,287	57.7	5,751	NM	515	13,932	59.6	36,391
CT	235	2,304	18.2	1,125	NY	1,261	11,284	113.0	9,342
DE	60	949	7.5	500	NC	604	15,872	89.3	6,551
DC	119	1,391	67.4	4,476	ND	768	4,104	21.4	2,313
FL	1,215	15,321	116.0	9,524	OH	916	6,019	73.1	5,427
GA	699	13,228	111.9	8,140	OK	499	9,242	56.8	8,487
HI	280	15,468	78.2	5,026	OR	619	7,081	23.1	7,571
ID	414	6,780	19.2	3,975	PA	1,052	7,706	75.7	6,814
IL	1,118	7,708	85.6	7,959	RI	122	1,401	13.6	777
IN	545	5,020	32.8	2,307	SC	363	9,566	60.4	7,311
IA	545	2,320	13.2	1,223	SD	515	3,301	18.2	1,826
KS	487	6,164	43.5	3,340	TN	694	8,452	73.4	18,467
KY	427	7,235	55.4	4,295	TX	2,098	24,244	197.6	19,982
LA	555	6,586	48.1	5,529	UT	445	7,101	37.7	2,716
ME	293	2,089	10.8	931	VT	104	458	2.6	286
MD	434	10,599	109.1	8,885	VA	674	17,812	155.5	10,268
MA	483	4,418	38.2	2,952	WA	682	16,873	84.5	12,949
MI	861	5,456	29.1	2,015	WV	313	1,534	13.2	3,981
MN	630	2,977	22.0	1,828	WI	569	5,003	22.8	1,410
MS	454	5,299	32.5	5,752	WY	465	7,272	11.0	1,165

[1] An installation may consist of land, buildings, other structures and facilities, or combinations of them. Examples of installations are a national forest, national park, a hydroelectric project, a single office or warehouse building, and an unimproved site. [2] Covers cost of land, buildings, and structures and facilities. All properties are reported at actual or estimated cost without considering depreciation, obsolescence, or economic changes in value.

Source: U.S. General Services Administration, *Summary Report of Real Property Owned by the United States Throughout the World, 2002*. See also <http://www.gsa.gov/>.

Section 10
National Defense and Veterans Affairs

This section presents data on national defense and its human and financial costs; active and reserve military personnel; ships, equipment, and aircraft; and federally sponsored programs and benefits for veterans. The principal sources of these data are the annual *Selected Manpower Statistics* and the *Atlas/Data Abstract for the United States and Selected Areas* issued by the Office of the Secretary of Defense; *Annual Report of Secretary of Veterans Affairs, Department of Veterans Affairs,* and *The Budget of the United States Government,* Office of Management and Budget. For more data on expenditures, personnel, and ships, see Section 30.

Department of Defense (DOD)—The Department of Defense is responsible for providing the military forces of the United States. It includes the Office of the Secretary of Defense, the Joint Chiefs of Staff, the Army, the Navy, the Air Force, and the defense agencies. The President serves as Commander in Chief of the Armed Forces; from him, the authority flows to the Secretary of Defense and through the Joint Chiefs of Staff to the commanders of unified and specified commands (e.g., U.S. Strategic Command).

Reserve components—Reserve personnel of the Armed Forces consist of the Army National Guard, Army Reserve, Naval Reserve, Marine Corps Reserve, Air National Guard, Air Force Reserve, and Coast Guard Reserve. They provide trained personnel available for active duty in the Armed Forces in time of war or national emergency and at such other times as authorized by law.

The National Guard has dual federal-state responsibilities and uses jointly provided equipment, facilities, and budget support. The President is empowered to mobilize the National Guard and to use such of the Armed Forces as he considers necessary to enforce federal authority in any state.

The ready reserve includes selected reservists who are intended to assist active forces in a war and the individual ready reserve who, in a major war, would be used to fill out active and reserve units and later would be a source of combat replacements; a portion of the ready reserve serves in an active status. The standby reserve cannot be called to active duty unless the Congress gives explicit approval. The retired reserve represents a low potential for mobilization.

Department of Veterans Affairs (VA)—The Department of Veterans Affairs administers laws authorizing benefits for eligible former and present members of the Armed Forces and for the beneficiaries of deceased members. Veterans benefits available under various acts of Congress include compensation for service-connected disability or death; pensions for nonservice-connected disability or death; vocational rehabilitation, education, and training; home loan insurance; life insurance; health care; special housing and automobiles or other conveyances for certain disabled veterans; burial and plot allowances; and educational assistance to families of deceased or totally disabled veterans, servicemen missing in action, or prisoners of war. Since these benefits are legislated by Congress, the dates they were enacted and the dates they apply to veterans may be different from the actual dates the conflicts occurred.

VA estimates of veterans cover all persons with active duty service during periods of war or armed conflict and until 1982 include those living outside the United States.

No. 509. National Defense Outlays and Veterans Benefits: 1960 to 2004

[For year ending September 30. Includes outlays of Department of Defense, Department of Veterans Affairs, and other agencies for activities primarily related to national defense and veterans programs. For explanation of average annual percent change, see Guide to Tabular Presentation. Minus sign (-) indicates decline]

Year	National defense and veterans outlays				Annual percent change [1]			Defense outlays, percent of—	
	Defense outlays			Veterans outlays (bil. dol.)	Total outlays	Defense outlays	Veterans outlays	Federal outlays	Gross domestic product [2]
	Total outlays (bil. dol.)	Current dollars (bil. dol.)	Constant (1996) dollars (bil. dol.)						
1960	53.5	48.1	280.3	5.4	2.5	2.4	3.1	52.2	9.3
1965	56.3	50.6	267.7	5.7	-6.8	-7.6	0.7	42.8	7.4
1970	90.4	81.7	336.6	8.7	0.3	-1.0	13.6	41.8	8.1
1975	103.1	86.5	239.5	16.6	11.2	9.0	24.0	26.0	5.5
1980	155.1	134.0	244.7	21.1	13.9	15.2	6.3	22.7	4.9
1985	279.0	252.7	329.9	26.3	10.3	11.1	2.7	26.7	6.1
1990	328.4	299.3	354.3	29.1	-1.6	-1.4	-3.2	23.9	5.2
1991	304.6	273.3	309.3	31.3	-7.2	-8.7	7.6	20.6	4.6
1992	332.4	298.4	327.0	34.1	12.0	12.4	8.0	21.6	4.8
1993	326.8	291.1	314.1	35.7	-1.9	-2.4	4.6	20.7	4.4
1994	319.2	281.6	297.9	37.6	-2.3	-3.2	5.4	19.3	4.1
1995	310.0	272.1	281.8	37.9	-2.9	-3.4	0.8	17.9	3.7
1996	302.7	265.8	265.8	37.0	-2.3	-2.3	-2.4	17.0	3.5
1997	309.8	270.5	265.3	39.3	2.3	1.8	6.3	16.9	3.3
1998	310.2	268.5	259.9	41.8	0.1	-0.8	6.3	16.2	3.1
1999	320.2	274.9	260.5	43.2	3.2	2.4	3.4	16.1	3.0
2000	341.6	294.5	270.9	47.1	6.7	7.1	9.0	16.5	3.0
2001	350.5	305.5	275.9	45.0	2.6	3.7	-4.3	16.4	3.0
2002	399.5	348.6	307.6	51.0	14.0	14.1	13.2	17.3	3.4
2003, est	433.4	376.3	327.4	57.1	8.5	8.0	11.9	17.6	3.5
2004, est	452.4	390.4	335.5	62.0	4.4	3.8	8.7	17.5	3.5

[1] Change from prior year shown; for 1960, change from 1955. [2] Represents fiscal year GDP; for definition, see text, Section 13.

No. 510. Federal Budget Outlays for Defense Functions: 1980 to 2003

[In billions of dollars (134.0 represents $134,000,000,000), except percent. For year ending September 30. Minus sign (-) indicates decline]

Defense function	1980	1990	1995	1996	1997	1998	1999	2000	2001	2002	2003, est.
Total	134.0	299.3	272.1	265.8	270.5	268.5	274.9	294.5	305.5	348.6	376.3
Percent change [1]	15.2	-1.4	-3.4	-2.3	1.8	-0.8	2.4	7.1	3.7	14.1	8.0
Defense Dept., military	130.9	289.8	259.4	253.2	258.3	256.1	261.4	281.2	291.0	332.0	358.2
Military personnel	40.9	75.6	70.8	66.7	69.7	69.0	69.5	76.0	74.0	86.8	92.7
Operation, maintenance	44.8	88.3	91.1	88.8	92.5	93.5	96.4	105.9	112.0	130.0	136.3
Procurement	29.0	81.0	55.0	48.9	47.7	48.2	48.8	51.7	55.0	62.5	63.2
Research and development	13.1	37.5	34.6	36.5	37.0	37.4	37.4	37.6	40.5	44.4	52.8
Military construction	2.5	5.1	6.8	6.7	6.2	6.0	5.5	5.1	5.0	5.1	6.0
Family housing	1.7	3.5	3.6	3.8	4.0	3.9	3.7	3.4	3.5	3.7	4.2
Other [2]	-1.1	-1.2	-2.4	1.8	1.2	-1.9	0.1	1.6	1.1	-0.5	3.0
Atomic energy activities [3]	2.9	9.0	11.8	11.6	11.3	11.3	12.4	11.9	13.0	14.9	16.3
Defense-related activities [4]	0.2	0.6	0.8	0.9	0.9	1.1	1.1	1.2	1.5	1.7	1.8

[1] Change from immediate prior year. [2] Revolving and management funds, trust funds, special foreign currency program, allowances, and offsetting receipts. [3] Defense activities only. [4] Includes civil defense activities.

No. 511. National Defense—Budget Authority and Outlays: 1980 to 2003

[In billions of dollars (143.9 represents $143,900,000,000). For year ending September 30]

Item	1980	1990	1995	1997	1998	1999	2000	2001	2002	2003, est.
Defense (Budget authority) [1]	143.9	303.3	266.4	270.4	271.3	292.3	304.1	335.5	362.1	382.7
Department of Defense—Military	140.7	293.0	255.7	258.0	258.6	278.6	290.5	319.5	345.0	364.0
Atomic energy defense activities [1]	3.0	9.7	10.1	11.4	11.7	12.6	12.4	14.4	15.3	16.6
Defense-related activities	0.2	0.6	0.6	1.0	1.0	1.1	1.2	1.6	1.8	2.1
Defense (Outlays) [1]	134.0	299.3	272.1	270.5	268.5	274.9	294.5	305.5	348.6	376.3
Department of Defense—Military	130.9	289.8	259.4	258.3	256.1	261.4	281.2	291.0	332.0	358.2
Atomic energy defense activities [1]	2.9	9.0	11.8	11.3	11.3	12.4	12.2	13.0	14.9	16.3
Defense-related activities	0.2	0.6	0.8	0.9	1.1	1.1	1.1	1.5	1.7	1.8

[1] Includes defense budget authority, balances, and outlays by other departments.

Source of Tables 509-511: U.S. Office of Management and Budget, Budget of the U.S. Government, *Historical Tables*, annual.

No. 512. Military Prime Contract Awards to All Businesses by Program: 1990 to 2002

[In billions of dollars (144.7 represents $144,700,000,000). Net values for year ending September 30. Includes all new prime contracts; debit or credit changes in contracts are also included. Actions cover official awards, amendments, or other changes in prime contracts to obtain military supplies, services, or construction. Excludes term contracts and contracts which do not obligate a firm total dollar amount or fixed quantity, but includes job orders, task orders, and delivery orders against such contracts]

DOD procurement program	1990	1995	1996	1997	1998	1999	2000	2001	2002
Total	144.7	131.4	132.2	128.4	128.8	135.2	143.0	154.1	180.6
Intragovernmental [1]	10.0	12.3	13.0	11.5	9.9	11.6	14.8	13.4	17.0
For work outside the U.S.	7.1	5.6	6.4	6.4	5.6	7.4	7.5	7.1	9.3
Educ. and nonprofit institutions	3.5	3.3	3.3	3.6	3.5	3.9	4.3	4.5	5.5
With business firms for work in the U.S. [2]	123.8	110.0	109.5	106.9	109.7	112.2	116.4	129.2	148.8
Major hard goods	79.1	56.0	55.1	52.5	56.0	57.5	59.8	67.9	76.1
Aircraft	24.0	18.8	20.3	18.4	20.8	23.3	28.8	30.5	30.6
Electronics and communication equip.	18.5	12.3	11.5	12.1	10.7	10.7	9.5	10.9	13.0
Missiles and space systems	17.1	10.6	10.2	9.5	9.9	9.5	8.2	8.2	11.2
Ships	10.3	9.1	7.1	6.8	8.6	7.8	8.3	12.0	11.4
Tanks, ammo., and weapons	9.2	5.3	5.9	5.7	6.0	6.2	5.0	6.3	9.8
Services	14.6	18.6	19.2	20.2	21.2	23.7	24.0	25.9	33.2

[1] Covers only purchases from other federal agencies and reimbursable purchases on behalf of foreign governments.
[2] Includes Department of Defense. Includes other business not shown separately. Contracts awarded for work in U.S. possessions, and other areas subject to complete sovereignty of United States; contracts in a classified location; and any intragovernmental contracts entered into overseas.

Source: U.S. Dept. of Defense, *Prime Contract Awards*, semiannual.

No. 513. Department of Defense Contract Awards, Payroll, and Civilian and Military Personnel—States: 2001

[For years ending Sept. 30 (158,737 represents $158,737,000,000). Contracts refer to awards made in year specified; expenditures relating to awards may extend over several years. Civilian employees include United States citizen and foreign national direct hire civilians subject to Office of Management and Budget (OMB) ceiling controls and civilian personnel involved in civil functions in the United States. Excludes indirect hire civilians and those direct hire civilian not subject to OMB ceiling controls. Military personnel include active duty personnel based ashore. Excludes personnel temporarily shore-based in a transient status, or afloat. Payroll outlays include the gross earnings of civilian and active duty military personnel for services rendered to the government and for cash allowances for benefits. Excludes employer's share of employee benefits, accrued military retirement benefits and most permanent change of station costs]

State	Contract awards [1] (mil. dol.)	Payroll (mil. dol.)	Civilian (1,000)	Military (1,000)	State	Contract awards [1] (mil. dol.)	Payroll (mil. dol.)	Civilian (1,000)	Military (1,000)
U.S.	158,737	114,950	628	1,045	MO	5,756	1,750	9.3	16.1
AL	4,672	2,714	20.5	11.4	MT	129	322	1.2	3.5
AK	911	1,044	4.2	15.9	NE	306	730	3.4	7.8
AZ	6,685	2,188	8.3	22.4	NV	359	905	2.1	8.5
AR	833	849	3.7	4.9	NH	606	292	1.1	0.3
CA	23,816	12,390	58.1	123.9	NJ	3,452	1,580	13.9	6.3
CO	2,624	2,686	10.2	29.7	NM	823	1,161	6.7	11.3
CT	5,639	581	2.5	4.2	NY	4,435	2,075	11.2	20.9
DE	135	371	1.4	3.9	NC	1,520	5,163	16.4	94.3
DC	2,420	1,676	15.6	12.8	ND	207	390	1.6	7.5
FL	7,073	7,546	27.1	55.8	OH	3,444	2,469	22.1	6.9
GA	5,814	5,495	31.2	64.4	OK	1,573	2,553	22.0	23.7
HI	1,433	2,842	16.5	34.6	OR	404	642	3.1	0.7
ID	161	425	1.5	4.3	PA	4,571	2,489	24.9	3.1
IL	2,006	2,438	12.8	25.0	RI	365	573	4.3	3.0
IN	1,860	1,052	8.7	1.0	SC	1,138	2,635	9.4	37.9
IA	552	331	1.5	0.4	SD	191	276	1.2	3.4
KS	1,223	1,244	5.6	15.8	TN	1,305	1,282	5.5	2.6
KY	2,268	2,034	8.3	34.1	TX	13,700	9,414	37.2	115.1
LA	1,683	1,531	7.4	16.5	UT	1,509	1,263	14.7	5.4
ME	1,108	659	5.8	2.7	VT	384	128	0.6	0.1
MD	6,505	4,220	32.1	30.9	VA	18,128	13,039	77.1	90.9
MA	4,929	942	6.8	2.4	WA	2,789	4,382	23.3	38.5
MI	2,180	1,012	8.0	1.2	WV	170	335	1.8	0.6
MN	1,529	526	2.6	0.7	WI	1,065	532	3.1	0.5
MS	2,272	1,518	9.3	14.0	WY	79	256	1.0	3.3

[1] Military awards for supplies, services, and construction. Net value of contracts of over $25,000 for work in each state and DC. Figures reflect impact of prime contracting on state distribution of defense work. Often the state in which a prime contractor is located in is not the state where the subcontracted work is done. See also headnote, Table 512. Undistributed civilians and military personnel, their payrolls, and prime contract awards for performance in classified locations are excluded.

Source: U.S. Dept. of Defense, *Atlas/Data Abstract for the United States and Selected Areas*, annual.

No. 514. U.S. Military Sales and Assistance to Foreign Governments: 1990 to 2001

[In millions of dollars, (16,614 represents $16,614,000,000). For year ending September 30. Department of Defense (DOD) sales deliveries cover deliveries against sales orders authorized under Arms Export Control Act, as well as earlier and applicable legislation. For details regarding individual programs, see source]

Item	1990	1994	1995	1996	1997	1998	1999	2000	2001
Military sales agreements	16,614	12,745	8,410	9,487	8,609	9,201	11,898	11,693	13,162
Military constr. sales agrmts	636	57	25	135	30	430	286	287	123
Military sales deliveries [1]	8,065	9,605	12,015	11,622	15,707	13,290	17,107	10,683	12,399
Military sales financing	4,758	3,917	3,712	3,836	3,530	3,420	3,370	4,333	3,535
Military assistance programs [2]	137	321	117	330	72	95	268	85	41
Military assist. program delivery [3]	27	5	13	27	113	82	12	12	21
IMET program/deliveries [3]	43	22	26	39	43	50	50	50	58

[1] Includes military construction sales deliveries. [2] Also includes Military Assistance Service Funded (MASF) program data, Section 506(a) drawdown authority, and MAP Merger Funds. [3] Includes Military Assistance Service Funded (MASF) program data and Section 506(a) drawdown authority.

No. 515. U.S. Military Sales Deliveries by Major Selected Country: 1990 to 2001

[In millions of dollars (8,065 represents $8,065,000,000). For year ending September 30. Represents Department of Defense military sales]

Country	1990	1994	1995	1996	1997	1998	1999	2000	2001
Total[1]	8,065	9,336	11,797	11,480	15,609	12,908	16,919	10,500	12,155
Australia	384	349	303	228	196	208	269	331	248
Belgium	150	13	8	157	107	194	250	58	170
China	455	845	1,335	833	2,394	1,424	2,522	798	1,176
Egypt	368	889	1,479	1,083	897	571	450	805	882
Germany	366	152	257	377	211	190	251	132	332
Greece	114	235	220	210	717	400	533	316	466
Israel	146	409	327	386	497	1,203	1,224	571	760
Italy	61	181	54	77	51	43	106	41	99
Japan	272	779	693	753	492	409	485	524	503
Korea, South	328	379	442	340	478	836	590	1,457	750
Kuwait	52	215	472	745	1,213	323	318	349	571
Netherlands	397	140	153	392	168	345	321	161	416
Saudi Arabia	874	1,895	3,568	2,838	4,641	3,802	4,697	2,061	2,031
Singapore	44	87	59	80	133	232	560	139	245
Turkey	761	931	368	481	1,153	532	910	217	479

[1] Includes countries not shown.

Source of Tables 514 and 515: U.S. Defense Security Cooperation Agency, *Foreign Military Sales, Foreign Military Construction Sales,* and *Military Assistance Facts,* annual.

No. 516. Military and Civilian Personnel and Expenditures: 1990 to 2002

[For years ending September 30. For definitions, see headnote, Table 513]

Item	1990	1995	1999	2000	2001	2002
Personnel, total [1] (1,000)	3,693	3,391	2,863	2,791	2,781	2,811
Active duty military	1,185	1,085	1,003	984	991	1,045
Civilian	931	768	634	634	628	628
Reserve and National Guard	1,577	1,538	1,226	1,173	1,163	1,138
Expenditures, total (mil. dol.) [2]	209,904	209,695	218,861	229,072	243,778	276,281
Prime contract awards [3] (mil. dol.)	121,254	109,005	114,875	123,295	135,225	158,737
Grants	(NA)	(NA)	2,175	2,330	2,540	3,594

NA Not available. [1] Includes those based ashore and excludes those temporarily shore-based, in a transient status, or afloat. [2] Includes expenditures not shown separately. [3] Represents contract awards over $25,000.

Source: U.S. Dept. of Defense, *Atlas/Data Abstract for the United States and Selected Areas,* annual.

No. 517. Department of Defense Manpower: 1950 to 2002

[In thousands (1,459 represents 1,459,000. For the year ending September 30. Includes National Guard, Reserve, and retired regular personnel on extended or continuous active duty. Excludes Coast Guard. Other officer candidates are included under enlisted personnel]

Year	Total [1] [2]	Army Total [2]	Army White	Army Black	Army Officers	Army Enlisted	Navy [3] Total [2]	Navy White	Navy Black	Navy Officers	Navy Enlisted	Marine Corps Total [2]	MC White	MC Black	MC Officers	MC Enlisted	Air Force Total [2]	AF White	AF Black	AF Officers	AF Enlisted
1950	1,459	593	(NA)	(NA)	73	519	381	(NA)	(NA)	45	333	74	(NA)	(NA)	7	67	411	(NA)	(NA)	57	354
1955	2,935	1,109	(NA)	(NA)	122	986	661	(NA)	(NA)	75	583	205	(NA)	(NA)	18	187	960	(NA)	(NA)	137	823
1960	2,475	873	(NA)	(NA)	101	770	617	(NA)	(NA)	70	545	171	(NA)	(NA)	16	154	815	(NA)	(NA)	130	683
1965	2,654	969	(NA)	(NA)	112	855	670	(NA)	(NA)	78	588	190	(NA)	(NA)	17	173	825	(NA)	(NA)	132	690
1970	3,065	1,323	(NA)	(NA)	167	1,153	691	(NA)	(NA)	81	606	260	(NA)	(NA)	25	235	791	(NA)	(NA)	130	657
1971	2,713	1,124	(NA)	(NA)	149	972	622	(NA)	(NA)	75	542	212	(NA)	(NA)	22	191	755	(NA)	(NA)	126	625
1972	2,322	811	(NA)	(NA)	121	687	587	(NA)	(NA)	73	511	198	(NA)	(NA)	20	178	726	(NA)	(NA)	122	600
1973	2,252	801	(NA)	(NA)	116	682	564	(NA)	(NA)	71	490	196	(NA)	(NA)	19	177	691	(NA)	(NA)	115	572
1974	2,162	783	(NA)	(NA)	106	674	546	(NA)	(NA)	67	475	189	(NA)	(NA)	19	170	644	(NA)	(NA)	110	529
1975	2,128	784	(NA)	(NA)	103	678	535	(NA)	(NA)	66	466	196	(NA)	(NA)	19	177	613	(NA)	(NA)	105	503
1976	2,082	779	(NA)	(NA)	99	678	525	(NA)	(NA)	64	458	192	(NA)	(NA)	19	174	585	(NA)	(NA)	100	481
1977	2,075	782	(NA)	(NA)	98	680	530	(NA)	(NA)	63	462	192	(NA)	(NA)	19	173	571	(NA)	(NA)	96	470
1978	2,062	772	(NA)	(NA)	98	670	530	(NA)	(NA)	63	463	191	(NA)	(NA)	18	172	570	(NA)	(NA)	95	470
1979	2,027	759	(NA)	(NA)	97	657	523	(NA)	(NA)	62	457	185	(NA)	(NA)	18	167	560	(NA)	(NA)	96	459
1980	2,051	777	503	229	99	674	527	436	55	63	460	189	142	39	18	170	558	460	80	98	456
1981	2,083	781	502	230	102	675	540	443	58	65	470	191	145	39	18	172	570	468	83	99	467
1982	2,109	780	504	220	103	673	553	450	62	67	481	192	149	38	19	173	583	476	87	102	476
1983	2,123	780	512	220	106	669	558	462	66	68	485	194	152	37	20	174	592	483	88	105	483
1984	2,138	780	520	215	108	668	565	455	67	69	491	196	153	36	20	176	597	486	89	106	486
1985	2,151	781	523	211	110	667	571	459	70	71	495	198	152	37	20	178	602	488	90	108	489
1986	2,169	781	524	210	110	667	581	464	75	72	504	200	151	38	20	179	608	491	92	109	495
1987	2,174	781	519	212	108	668	587	467	81	72	510	200	150	38	20	179	607	489	92	107	495
1988	2,138	772	507	213	107	660	593	466	85	72	516	197	147	38	20	177	576	462	88	105	467
1989	2,130	770	497	218	107	658	593	461	91	72	516	197	146	38	20	177	571	458	87	104	463
1990	2,044	732	466	213	104	624	579	446	93	72	503	197	145	38	20	177	535	428	82	100	431
1991	1,986	711	452	204	104	603	570	439	92	71	495	194	144	36	20	174	510	409	77	97	409
1992	1,807	610	388	173	95	511	542	415	88	69	468	185	138	32	19	165	470	377	70	90	376
1993	1,705	572	365	158	88	480	510	390	84	66	439	178	134	30	18	160	444	357	65	84	356
1994	1,610	541	344	147	85	453	469	355	78	62	403	174	131	28	18	156	426	341	62	81	341
1995	1,518	509	322	137	83	422	435	326	75	59	372	175	130	28	18	157	400	318	58	78	318
1996	1,472	491	(NA)	(NA)	81	407	417	(NA)	(NA)	57	355	175	(NA)	(NA)	18	157	389	(NA)	(NA)	76	309
1997	1,439	492	(NA)	(NA)	79	408	396	(NA)	(NA)	56	335	174	(NA)	(NA)	18	156	377	(NA)	(NA)	74	299
1998	1,407	484	(NA)	(NA)	78	401	382	(NA)	(NA)	55	323	174	(NA)	(NA)	18	155	368	(NA)	(NA)	72	292
1999	1,386	479	(NA)	(NA)	77	398	373	(NA)	(NA)	54	315	173	(NA)	(NA)	18	155	361	(NA)	(NA)	70	286
2000	1,384	482	(NA)	(NA)	77	401	373	(NA)	(NA)	54	315	173	(NA)	(NA)	18	155	356	(NA)	(NA)	69	282
2001	1,385	481	(NA)	(NA)	76	400	378	(NA)	(NA)	54	320	173	(NA)	(NA)	18	155	354	(NA)	(NA)	69	280
2002	1,414	487	(NA)	(NA)	78	404	385	(NA)	(NA)	55	326	174	(NA)	(NA)	18	155	368	(NA)	(NA)	72	292

NA Not available. [1] Beginning 1980, excludes Navy Reserve personnel on active duty for Training and Administration of Reserves (TARS). Prior to 1980, includes Navy Reserve personnel on active duty for (TARS). [2] Includes cadets, midshipmen, and other not shown separately. [3]

Source: U.S. Dept. of Defense, *Selected Manpower Statistics*, annual.

National Defense and Veterans Affairs 345

U.S. Census Bureau, Statistical Abstract of the United States: 2003

No. 518. Active Duty Military and Civilian Personnel in Installations: 2002

[As of September 30]

State	Military personnel Total [1]	Army	Navy/ Marine Corps	Air Force	Civilian personnel Total [1]	Army	Navy/ Marine Corps	Air Force
United States	**1,045,067**	**383,112**	**355,866**	**306,089**	**628,049**	**213,618**	**177,695**	**151,041**
Alabama	11,354	6,259	643	4,452	20,474	16,607	33	2,357
Alaska	15,906	6,630	140	9,136	4,204	2,215	18	1,708
Arizona	22,448	5,174	5,415	11,859	8,290	3,627	453	3,289
Arkansas	4,855	251	39	4,565	3,686	2,689	5	881
California	123,948	7,932	96,047	19,969	58,076	6,738	33,163	9,934
Colorado	29,733	14,951	908	13,874	10,183	2,682	48	4,965
Connecticut	4,239	22	4,179	38	2,497	460	1,082	263
Delaware	3,899	8	17	3,874	1,429	248	-	1,107
District of Columbia	12,767	5,239	4,425	3,103	15,640	4,566	9,905	876
Florida	55,815	3,098	27,570	25,147	27,144	3,019	12,661	8,632
Georgia	64,392	49,474	4,814	10,104	31,167	11,180	3,883	13,800
Hawaii	34,608	15,985	14,334	4,289	16,508	4,441	8,925	2,075
Idaho	4,251	40	68	4,143	1,472	695	51	681
Illinois	25,036	688	18,627	5,721	12,780	6,400	1,745	3,129
Indiana	1,041	524	386	131	8,719	1,517	3,146	1,049
Iowa	447	274	126	47	1,546	964	5	524
Kansas	15,819	12,665	154	3,000	5,603	4,176	3	1,039
Kentucky	34,081	33,578	279	224	8,348	6,893	192	234
Louisiana	16,541	8,840	1,774	5,927	7,440	3,995	1,319	1,703
Maine	2,689	248	2,389	52	5,791	321	4,879	269
Maryland	30,928	7,140	15,853	7,935	32,090	12,275	15,524	2,128
Massachusetts	2,427	255	515	1,657	6,829	2,381	264	2,986
Michigan	1,173	489	551	133	8,038	5,042	25	1,164
Minnesota	702	308	301	93	2,576	1,494	22	807
Mississippi	14,005	449	5,610	7,946	9,289	3,656	2,535	2,806
Missouri	16,119	9,807	2,254	4,058	9,330	5,828	250	1,208
Montana	3,512	22	19	3,471	1,187	475	-	667
Nebraska	7,793	78	535	7,180	3,365	1,391	17	1,574
Nevada	8,461	93	1,054	7,314	2,072	351	317	1,220
New Hampshire	326	8	261	57	1,051	569	39	284
New Jersey	6,306	821	740	4,745	13,943	9,466	2,105	1,513
New Mexico	11,254	299	223	10,732	6,704	2,902	39	3,273
New York	20,882	17,630	2,819	433	11,220	6,994	154	2,470
North Carolina	94,296	41,120	43,522	9,654	16,444	5,994	7,281	1,225
North Dakota	7,465	19	8	7,438	1,621	452	2	1,081
Ohio	6,899	582	538	5,779	22,080	1,356	47	12,200
Oklahoma	23,664	13,365	1,422	8,877	21,972	4,265	92	16,129
Oregon	705	229	401	75	3,121	2,229	22	839
Pennsylvania	3,098	1,214	1,617	267	24,920	8,186	8,124	1,532
Rhode Island	2,974	108	2,790	76	4,346	276	3,745	230
South Carolina	37,943	10,389	18,279	9,275	9,370	2,739	3,625	1,731
South Dakota	3,350	41	5	3,304	1,219	493	1	671
Tennessee	2,554	370	1,946	238	5,496	2,655	1,077	915
Texas	115,100	61,083	7,800	46,217	37,238	17,289	1,569	14,347
Utah	5,447	320	162	4,965	14,725	2,151	29	11,270
Vermont	61	21	25	15	567	294	2	233
Virginia	90,851	24,916	52,120	13,815	77,119	19,815	34,492	4,082
Washington	38,521	19,555	11,692	7,274	23,259	5,641	14,699	1,866
West Virginia	558	202	309	47	1,783	1,264	70	427
Wisconsin	532	295	160	77	3,074	2,059	11	893
Wyoming	3,292	4	1	3,287	1,004	203	-	755

- Represents zero.   [1] Includes other DOD organizations not shown separately.

Source: U.S. Dept. of Defense, *Selected Manpower Statistics,* annual.

No. 519. Military Personnel on Active Duty by Location: 1980 to 2002

[In thousands (2,051 represents 2,051,000). As of September 30]

Location	1980	1985	1990	1995	1997	1998	1999	2000	2001	2002
Total	2,051	2,151	2,044	1,518	1,439	1,407	1,386	1,384	1,385	1412
Shore-based [1]	1,840	1,920	1,794	1,351	1,294	1,267	1,241	1,237	1,244	1262
Afloat [2]	211	231	252	167	145	140	145	147	141	150
United States [3]	1,562	1,636	1,437	1,280	1,211	1,147	1,133	1,127	1,130	1182
Foreign countries	488	516	609	238	227	260	253	258	255	230

[1] Includes Navy personnel temporarily on shore. [2] Includes Marine Corps. [3] Includes outlying areas.
Source: U.S. Dept. of Defense, *Selected Manpower Statistics*, annual.

No. 520. U.S. Military Personnel on Active Duty in Selected Foreign Countries: 2001

[As of September 30]

Country	2001	Country	2001	Country	2001
In foreign countries [1]	254,788	El Salvador	26	New Zealand	6
Ashore	211,947	France	71	Norway	83
Afloat	42,841	Germany	70,998	Oman	673
Argentina	22	Greece	506	Pakistan	21
Australia	803	Greenland	153	Panama	20
Austria	24	Haiti	13	Peru	43
Bahamas, The	64	Honduras	394	Philippines	35
Bahrain	2,065	Hungary	29	Portugal	1,005
Belgium	1,578	Iceland	1,743	Qatar	116
Bolivia	25	India	18	Russia	20
Bosnia and Herzegovina	3,116	Indonesia	43	Saudi Arabia	4,805
Brazil	39	Israel	35	Serbia and Montenegro	5,679
Canada	163	Italy	11,704	Singapore	160
Chile	337	Jamaica	12	South Africa	31
China	57	Japan	40,217	Spain	1,990
Colombia	63	Jordan	18	Switzerland	18
Croatia	1	Kenya	62	Thailand	113
Cuba (Guantanamo)	557	Korea, South	37,605	Tunisia	15
Cyprus	30	Kuwait	4,208	Turkey	2,153
Denmark	28	Macedonia, The Former Yugoslav Republic of	351	Ukraine	10
Diego Garcia [2]	590			United Arab Emirates	204
Ecuador	22	Mexico	27	United Kingdom	11,318
Egypt	500	Netherlands	676	Venezuela	31

[1] Includes areas not shown separately. [2] British Indian Ocean Territory.
Source: U.S. Dept. of Defense, *Selected Manpower Statistics*, annual. <http://www.dior.whs.mil/mmid/military/miltop.htm>.

No. 521. Coast Guard Personnel on Active Duty: 1970 to 2001

[As of September 30]

Year	Total	Officers	Cadets	Enlisted	Year	Total	Officers	Cadets	Enlisted
1970	38,012	5,512	976	31,524	1994	37,472	7,401	881	29,002
1975	36,788	5,630	1,177	29,981	1995	36,731	7,295	841	28,401
1980	39,100	6,465	874	31,761	1996	35,229	7,106	802	27,129
1985	38,615	6,584	727	31,146	1997	34,890	6,939	805	26,945
1990	36,939	6,713	927	29,136	1998	35,293	6,962	777	27,363
1991	38,444	7,095	900	30,285	1999	35,534	6,942	835	27,593
1992	39,424	7,348	919	30,918	2000	35,952	6,968	856	27,964
1993	39,239	7,471	907	30,699	2001	36,137	7,033	890	28,046

Source: U.S. Dept. of Transportation, *Annual Report of the Secretary of Transportation*.

No. 522. U.S. Active Duty Military Deaths by Manner of Death: 1980 to 2002

Manner of death	1980-2002	1980	1990	1994	1995	1996	1997	1998	1999	2000	2001	2002
Deaths, total	35,583	2,391	1,526	1,109	1,055	1,008	864	815	761	774	890	1,007
Accident	20,848	1,577	864	548	572	518	463	420	411	400	422	538
Illness	6,451	401	275	217	167	180	177	156	126	124	175	178
Homicide	1,922	161	71	86	59	65	43	28	34	31	42	46
Self-inflicted	4,929	236	250	231	242	210	159	155	110	142	118	130
Pending/undetermined	781	15	42	8	9	14	22	53	80	60	78	98
Hostile deaths	652	1	24	19	6	21	-	3	-	17	55	17
Deaths per 100,000 of personnel strength	(X)	116.6	74.7	68.9	69.5	68.5	60.1	57.9	54.9	53.9	57.9	64.4
Nonhostile deaths [1]	(X)	116.5	73.5	67.7	69.1	67.1	60.1	57.7	54.9	52.7	54.3	63.3
Accidents	(X)	76.9	42.3	34.0	37.7	35.2	32.2	29.9	29.7	27.8	27.5	34.4
Illnesses	(X)	19.6	13.5	13.5	11.0	12.2	12.3	11.1	9.1	8.6	11.4	11.4
Homicides	(X)	7.9	3.5	5.3	3.9	4.4	3.0	2.0	2.5	2.2	2.7	2.9
Self-inflicted	(X)	11.5	12.2	14.3	15.9	14.3	11.1	11.0	7.9	9.9	7.7	8.3

- Represents zero. X Not applicable. [1] Includes other items not shown separately.
Source: U.S. Department of Defense, DOD Worldwide U.S. Active Duty Military Personnel. <www.dior.whs.mil/mmid/casualty/castop.htm>.

National Defense and Veterans Affairs

No. 523. Armed Forces Personnel—Summary of Major Conflicts

[For Revolutionary War, number of personnel serving not known, but estimates range from 184,000 to 250,000; for War of 1812, 286,730 served; for Mexican War, 78,718 served. Dates of the major conflicts may differ from those specified in various laws providing benefits for veterans]

Item	Unit	Civil War [1]	World War I	World War II	Korean conflict	Vietnam conflict	Persian Gulf War
Personnel serving [2]	1,000	2,213	4,735	[3]16,113	[4]5,720	[5]8,744	2,233
Average duration of service	Months	20	12	33	19	23	(NA)
Service abroad: Personnel serving	Percent	(NA)	[6]53	73	[7]56	(NA)	(NA)
Average duration [8]	Months	(NA)	6	16	13	(NA)	(NA)
Casualties: [9] Battle deaths [2]	1,000	140	53	292	34	[10]47	(Z)
Other deaths	1,000	224	63	114	3	11	(Z)
Wounds not mortal [2]	1,000	282	204	671	103	[10]153	(Z)
Draftees: Classified	1,000	777	24,234	36,677	9,123	[5]75,717	(X)
Examined	1,000	522	3,764	17,955	3,685	[5]8,611	(X)
Rejected	1,000	160	803	6,420	1,189	[5]3,880	(X)
Inducted	1,000	46	2,820	10,022	1,560	[5]1,759	(X)

NA Not available. X Not applicable. Z Fewer than 500. [1] Union forces only. Estimates of the number serving in Confederate forces range from 600,000 to 1.5 million. [2] Source: U.S. Department of Defense, *Selected Manpower Statistics*, annual. [3] Covers Dec. 1, 1941, to Dec. 31, 1946. [4] Covers June 25, 1950, to July 27, 1953. [5] Covers Aug. 4, 1964, to Jan. 27, 1973. [6] Army and Marines only. [7] Excludes Navy. Covers July 1950 through Jan. 1955. Far East area only. [8] During hostilities only. [9] For periods covered, see footnotes 3, 4, and 5. [10] Covers Jan. 1, 1961, to Jan. 27, 1973. Includes known military service personnel who have died from combat related wounds.

Source: Except as noted, the President's Commission on Veterans' Pensions, *Veterans' Benefits in the United States*, Vol. I, 1956; and U.S. Dept. of Defense, unpublished data.

No. 524. Military Personnel on Active Duty by Rank or Grade: 1990 to 2002

[In thousands (2,043.7 represents 2,043,700). As of Sept. 30]

Rank/grade	1990	1995	1998	1999	2000	2001	2002
Total [1]	2,043.7	1,518.2	1,406.8	1,385.7	1,384.3	1,385.1	1,411.6
Recruit—E-1	97.6	63.4	73.6	81.2	80.0	72.5	64.7
Private—E-2	140.3	99.7	99.0	93.9	99.0	92.4	91.8
Pvt. 1st class—E-3	280.1	197.1	194.7	190.5	196.3	210.4	219.6
Corporal—E-4	427.8	317.2	262.9	262.9	251.0	240.1	248.1
Sergeant—E-5	361.5	261.4	239.9	229.5	229.5	239.7	242.5
Staff Sgt.—E-6	239.1	180.5	163.7	162.9	164.9	164.9	170.0
Sgt. 1st class—E-7	134.1	109.3	100.4	97.1	97.7	98.4	101.9
Master Sgt.—E-8	38.0	28.8	26.6	25.8	26.0	26.7	27.0
Sgt. Major—E-9	15.3	11.1	10.5	10.4	10.2	10.4	10.6
Warrant Officer—W-1	3.2	2.0	2.1	2.2	2.1	2.2	2.3
Chief Warrant—W-4	3.0	2.2	2.0	2.1	2.0	1.9	2.0
2d Lt.—O-1	31.9	25.6	23.8	24.9	26.4	28.1	29.0
1st Lt.—O-2	37.9	26.1	26.2	25.4	24.7	25.7	28.1
Captain—O-3	106.6	84.3	73.8	69.8	68.1	66.0	66.5
Major—O-4	53.2	43.9	43.3	43.5	43.2	43.1	43.6
Lt. Colonel—O-5	32.3	28.7	28.6	28.0	27.5	27.2	28.2
Colonel—O-6	14.0	11.7	11.3	11.3	11.3	11.2	11.4
Brig. General—O-7	0.5	0.4	0.4	0.4	0.4	0.4	0.4
Major General—O-8	0.4	0.3	0.3	0.3	0.3	0.3	0.3
Lt. General—O-9	0.1	0.1	0.1	0.1	0.1	0.1	0.1
General—O-10	(Z)	(Z)	(Z)	(Z)	(Z)	(Z)	(Z)

Z Fewer than 50. [1] Includes cadets and midshipmen and warrant officers, W-2 and W-3.

Source: U.S. Dept. of Defense, *Selected Manpower Statistics*, annual.

No. 525. Military Reserve Personnel: 1990 to 2002

[As of September 30. The Ready Reserve includes the Selected Reserve which is scheduled to augment active forces during times of war or national emergency, and the Individual Ready Reserve which, during times of war or national emergency, would be used to fill out Active, Guard, and Reserve units and which would also be a source for casualty replacements; Ready Reservists serve in an active status (except for the Inactive National Guard - a very small pool within the Army National Guard). The Standby Reserve cannot be called to active duty except in situations where those members are the only available assets with specific required specialties. The Retired Reserve is categorized into three groups, based on age and length of retirement, prioritized for mobilization purposes]

Reserve status and branch of service	1990	1995	1998	1999	2000	2001	2002
Total reserves [1]	1,688,674	1,674,164	1,382,348	1,316,984	1,276,843	1,249,043	1,222,337
Ready reserve	1,658,707	1,648,388	1,353,428	1,288,844	1,251,452	1,224,121	1,199,321
Standby reserve	29,967	25,776	28,920	28,140	25,391	24,922	23,016
Retired reserve	462,371	505,905	562,088	564,358	573,305	580,785	590,018

[1] Less retired reserves.

Source: U.S. Dept. of Defense, *Official Guard and Reserve Manpower Strengths and Statistics*, quarterly.

No. 526. Ready Reserve Personnel Profile—Race and Sex: 1990 to 2002

[In thousands (1,658.7 represents 1,658,700). As of September 30]

Year	Total	Race					Sex			
		White	Black	Asian	American Indian	Hispanic	Officer Male	Officer Female	Enlisted Male	Enlisted Female
1990	1,658.7	1,304.6	272.3	14.9	7.8	83.1	226.8	40.5	1,204.7	186.7
1991	1,776.3	1,393.6	291.1	18.2	9.3	89.6	231.9	43.0	1,299.7	201.8
1992	1,876.4	1,459.5	309.7	20.2	9.3	95.4	232.7	44.7	1,382.4	216.6
1993	1,858.1	1,440.7	310.5	21.3	9.2	98.2	232.5	46.3	1,365.6	213.7
1994	1,795.8	1,380.9	298.3	22.4	9.0	99.1	223.9	46.2	1,315.8	210.0
1995	1,648.4	1,267.7	274.5	22.0	8.8	96.2	209.9	44.7	1,196.8	196.9
1996	1,536.6	1,179.0	249.8	21.5	8.6	93.1	196.9	43.6	1,108.8	187.4
1997	1,451.0	1,113.7	230.6	21.7	8.4	91.5	188.7	43.2	1,037.6	181.5
1998	1,353.4	1,033.9	210.4	21.7	7.8	88.2	175.9	40.3	964.1	173.1
1999	1,288.8	980.0	202.6	22.6	7.6	88.9	166.2	38.4	911.2	173.1
2000	1,251.5	942.2	199.6	26.7	8.4	91.8	159.4	36.9	879.9	175.3
2001	1,224.1	912.7	198.4	27.9	8.5	94.3	158.0	36.6	852.2	177.3
2002	1,199.3	891.3	193.2	27.9	8.8	96.0	152.1	35.6	835.2	176.4

Source: U.S. Dept. of Defense, *Official Guard and Reserve Manpower Strengths and Statistics*, annual.

No. 527. National Guard—Summary: 1980 to 2000

[As of September 30]

Item	Unit	1980	1985	1990	1995	1996	1997	1998	1999	2000
Army National Guard:										
Units	Number	3,379	4,353	4,055	5,872	5,643	5,500	5,415	5,360	5,300
Personnel [1]	1,000	368	438	444	375	373	370	362	357	353
Females	1,000	17	23	31	31	31	34	36	38	38
Funds obligated [2]	Bil. dol.	1.8	4.4	5.2	6.0	5.9	5.7	6.0	6.5	6.9
Value of equipment	Bil. dol.	7.6	18.8	29.0	33.0	33.0	33.0	33.0	34.0	35.0
Air National Guard:										
Units	Number	1,054	1,184	1,339	1,604	1,588	(NA)	1,541	1,541	1,550
Personnel [1]	1,000	96	109	118	110	110	108	108	107	106
Females	1,000	8	12	(NA)	16	16	16	17	17	(NA)
Funds obligated [2]	Bil. dol.	1.7	2.8	3.2	4.2	4.6	4.5	4.4	4.8	5.6
Value of equipment (est.) [3]	Bil. dol.	5.2	21.4	26.4	38.3	40.1	42.0	41.0	43.0	44.0

NA Not available. [1] Officers and enlisted personnel. [2] Federal funds; includes personnel, operations, maintenance, and military construction. [3] Beginning 1985, increase due to repricing of aircraft to current year dollars to reflect true replacement value. Beginning 1994 includes value of aircraft and support equipment.

Source: National Guard Bureau, *Annual Review of the Chief, National Guard Bureau*; and unpublished data.

National Defense and Veterans Affairs

No. 528. Summary of U.S. Military Force Structure: 1993 to 2001

Item	1993	1994	1995	1996	1997	1998	1999	2000	2001
DEPARTMENT OF DEFENSE (DOD) STRATEGIC FORCES [1]									
Land-based ICBMs: [2]									
Minuteman II (1 warhead each) plus Minuteman III (3 warheads each)	737	625	535	530	530	500	500	500	500
Peacekeeper (10 warheads each)	50	50	50	50	50	50	50	50	50
Heavy bombers (PAI): [3]									
B-52	84	64	74	56	56	56	56	56	56
B-1 [4]	84	84	60	60	60	70	74	80	82
B-2	-	3	6	9	10	12	13	16	16
Submarine-launched ballistic missiles: [2]									
Poseidon (C-3) and Trident (C-4) missiles on pre-Ohio-class submarines	96	48	-	-	-	-	-	-	-
Trident (C-4 and D-5) missiles on Ohio-class submarines	312	336	360	384	408	432	432	432	432
DOD AIRLIFT AND SEALIFT FORCES									
Intertheater Airlift (PMAI): [5]									
C-5	109	107	104	104	104	104	104	104	104
C-141	214	214	199	187	163	143	136	104	88
KC-10 [6]	57	54	54	54	54	54	54	54	54
C-17	2	9	17	22	24	30	37	46	58
Intratheater Airlift (PMAI): [5]									
C-130 [7]	380	424	428	432	430	425	425	425	418
Sealift ships (Active): [8]									
Tankers	20	18	18	12	13	10	10	10	10
Cargo	40	51	51	49	48	43	49	52	57
Sealift ships, reserve:									
RRF [9]	97	93	77	82	87	88	87	87	72
SPECIAL OPERATIONS FORCES									
Army:									
Special forces groups, (Active)	5	5	5	5	5	5	5	5	5
Special forces groups, (National Guard)	2	2	2	2	2	2	2	2	2
Special forces groups, (Reserve)	2	-	-	-	-	-	-	-	(NA)
Psychological operations groups (Active)	1	1	1	1	1	1	1	1	1
Special operations aviation regiments	1	1	1	1	1	1	1	1	1
Ranger regiments	1	1	1	1	1	1	1	1	1
Civil affairs battalions (Active)	1	1	1	1	1	1	1	1	1
Civil affairs brigades (Reserve)	9	9	9	9	9	8	8	8	8
Civil affairs commands (Reserve)	3	3	3	3	3	4	4	4	4
Air Force:									
Special operations wings/groups:									
Active	3	3	3	3	3	3	3	3	3
National Guard	1	1	1	1	1	1	1	1	1
Special operations wing (Reserve)	1	1	1	1	1	1	1	1	1
Special tactics groups	1	1	1	1	1	1	1	1	1
Naval:									
Special boat squadrons	2	2	2	2	2	2	2	2	2

- Represents or rounds to zero. NA Not available. [1] Force levels shown are for the ends of the fiscal years in question. The actual force levels for FY 2000 and FY 2001 will depend on future decisions. [2] Number of operational missiles. Not in maintenance or overhaul status. [3] PAI=Primary aircraft inventory. PAI excludes backup and attrition reserve aircrafts as well as aircraft in depot maintenance. Total inventory counts will be higher than the PAI figures given here. [4] B-1 are accountable under START I but will not be accountable under START II. [5] PMAI = Primary mission aircraft inventory for active and reserve components. The numbers shown reflect only combat support and industrial funded PMAI aircraft and not developments/test or training aircraft. [6] Includes 37 KC-10s allocated to an airlift code. [7] Does not include Department of the Navy aircraft. [8] Includes fast sea lift (FSS), afloat prepositioning, and common-user (charter) ships, plus (through FY 1998) aviation support ships. For FY 1999 on, includes LMSR and ready reserve force (RRF) ships tendered to the Military sealift command (MSC). FSS and LMSR vessels are maintained in a reserve, 4-day ready status. [9] The RRF includes vessels assigned to 4-, 5-, 10-, or 20-day reactivation readiness groups. The ship counts shown exclude RRF vessels tendered to the MSC. Inventory figures for FY 1999, FY 2000, and FY 2001 include aviation support ships.

Source: U.S. Dept. of Defense, *Annual Report to the President and the Congress*.

No. 529. Veterans by Sex, Period of Service, and by State: 2002

[In thousands (25,346 represents 25,346,000). As of September 30. Estimated starting with veteran's place of residence as of April 1, 2000, based on 2000 census of population data, extended to later years on the basis of estimates of veteran interstate migration, separations from the Armed Forces, and mortality; not directly comparable with earlier estimates previously published by the VA. Also excludes a small number of National Guard personnel or reservists who incurred service-connected disabilities while on an initial tour of active duty for training only. Veterans who served both in wartime and peacetime are only counted as serving in wartime]

State	Total veterans [1] Both sexes	Male	Female	World War II	Korean conflict	Vietnam era	Persian Gulf War	Peace-time
United States	25,346	23,706	1,640	4,724	3,680	8,206	3,543	6,385
Alabama	436	406	30	69	66	144	75	110
Alaska	68	61	7	5	5	28	15	19
Arizona	564	523	41	113	92	178	79	138
Arkansas	277	259	17	49	40	90	42	71
California	2,392	2,232	160	475	365	799	286	601
Colorado	438	403	35	61	55	158	79	111
Connecticut	289	274	15	68	46	89	23	72
Delaware	82	77	5	14	12	27	11	23
District of Columbia	41	37	4	8	6	12	5	11
Florida	1,846	1,719	128	439	311	539	244	442
Georgia	753	690	62	92	89	257	154	202
Hawaii	116	107	9	19	17	42	18	29
Idaho	137	128	9	23	18	44	25	33
Illinois	945	894	52	191	138	291	119	231
Indiana	566	535	31	97	77	179	72	155
Iowa	281	268	14	56	44	90	34	66
Kansas	257	242	16	49	36	85	39	60
Kentucky	371	350	21	62	52	122	55	94
Louisiana	379	353	27	66	52	120	67	92
Maine	148	139	9	26	22	50	18	39
Maryland	495	455	41	81	65	162	76	137
Massachusetts	524	495	29	123	84	156	44	133
Michigan	865	819	46	162	120	275	104	223
Minnesota	447	424	22	79	64	149	47	118
Mississippi	245	228	17	41	37	77	45	61
Missouri	571	538	33	103	85	184	76	145
Montana	106	99	7	18	14	36	16	26
Nebraska	168	157	11	30	26	55	26	38
Nevada	241	224	17	37	37	86	32	65
New Hampshire	133	125	8	22	19	46	15	37
New Jersey	628	598	30	150	102	185	51	157
New Mexico	187	172	15	31	27	66	29	46
New York	1,254	1,186	68	284	196	361	125	316
North Carolina	779	721	58	120	106	254	140	200
North Dakota	59	55	4	10	8	20	9	14
Ohio	1,086	1,026	61	208	150	337	137	283
Oklahoma	365	343	23	62	52	128	58	85
Oregon	376	351	25	70	51	128	48	95
Pennsylvania	1,210	1,147	63	280	187	357	120	301
Rhode Island	96	91	5	23	15	30	9	24
South Carolina	415	385	30	61	57	143	77	105
South Dakota	78	73	5	13	12	25	13	18
Tennessee	550	515	35	84	75	188	85	144
Texas	1,701	1,577	124	267	224	593	311	410
Utah	159	150	9	30	23	51	26	37
Vermont	60	57	4	11	9	20	6	17
Virginia	764	693	70	105	98	276	162	190
Washington	649	601	48	100	83	236	103	169
West Virginia	195	185	10	36	30	65	25	47
Wisconsin	495	468	27	91	71	154	57	134
Wyoming	57	53	4	9	7	20	10	13

[1] Veterans serving in more than one period of service are counted only once in the total.

No. 530. Veterans Living by Age and by Service: 2002

[In thousands (25,618 represents 25,618,000). As of September 30. Includes Puerto Rico. See headnote, Table 529]

Age	Total veterans	Wartime veterans Total [1]	Persian Gulf War	Vietnam era	Korean conflict	World War II	Peacetime veterans
Total	25,618	19,157	3,573	8,293	3,733	4,762	6,461
Under 35 years old	2,213	2,050	2,050	-	-	-	163
35-39 years old	1,457	568	568	-	-	-	889
40-44 years old	1,833	369	368	-	-	-	1,465
45-49 years old	2,029	1,210	285	1,016	-	-	819
50-54 years old	2,637	2,517	198	2,474	-	-	120
55-59 years old	3,321	3,105	80	3,096	-	-	217
60-64 years old	2,344	1,094	21	1,072	22	-	1,249
65 years old and over	9,784	8,245	5	636	3,710	4,762	1,539
Female, total	1,655	1,084	556	266	87	210	571

- Represents or rounds to zero.   [1] Veterans who served in more than one wartime period are counted only once.

Source of Tables 529 and 530: U.S. Dept. of Veterans Affairs, Office of Policy, Planning and Preparedness, <http://www.va.gov/vetdata/demographics>.

No. 531. Disabled Veterans Receiving Compensation by Period of Service: 1980 to 2002

[In thousands (2,274 represents 2,274,000), except as indicated. For year ending September 30. Represents veterans receiving compensation for service-connected disabilities]

Period of service	1980	1990	1995	1996	1997	1998	1999	2000	2001	2002
Disabled, all periods	2,274	2,184	2,236	2,253	2,263	2,277	2,294	2,308	2,321	2,398
Peacetime	262	444	514	529	539	550	561	567	569	575
World War I [1]	30	3	1	(Z)	(Z)	(Z)	(Z)	(Z)	(Z)	(Z)
World War II	1,193	876	692	655	616	578	541	505	470	440
Korea	236	209	191	187	182	179	175	171	166	165
Vietnam	553	652	705	714	724	729	736	741	750	799
Persian Gulf	(X)	(X)	134	168	202	241	282	325	366	419
Compensation (mil. dol.)	6,104	9,284	11,644	11,072	13,004	13,791	14,542	15,489	16,529	18,547

X Not applicable. Z Less than 500. [1] Includes Spanish-American War and Mexican Border service.

Source: U.S. Dept. of Veterans Affairs, *Annual Report of the Secretary of Veterans Affairs through 1998*; Annual Accountability Report, 1999-2002, and unpublished data. See also <www.va.gov/vetdata/programstatistics/index.htm>.

No. 532. Veterans Benefits—Expenditures by Program: 1980 to 2002

[In millions of dollars (23,187 represents $23,187,000,000). For year ending September 30. Beginning with fiscal year 1990, data are for outlays]

Program	1980	1990	1995	1997	1998	1999	2000	2001	2002
Total	23,187	28,998	37,775	39,277	41,776	43,166	47,087	45,037	50,881
Medical programs	6,042	11,582	16,255	16,900	17,575	18,223	19,637	21,330	23,049
Construction	300	661	641	597	515	521	466	421	449
General operating expenses	605	811	954	1,063	989	1,016	1,222	1,318
Compensation and pension	11,044	14,674	17,765	19,284	20,289	21,024	21,963	23,198	25,408
Vocational rehabilitation and education	2,350	452	1,127	1,287	1,310	1,605	2,053	1,786	2,170
All other [1]	2,846	818	1,034	145	1,209	804	1,952	-2,921	-1,511

[1] Includes insurance, indemnities and miscellaneous funds and expenditures. (Excludes expenditures from personal funds of patients.)

Source: U.S. Dept. of Veterans Affairs, *Expenditure and Workload Data*, annual.

No. 533. Veterans Compensation and Pension Benefits—Number on Rolls by Period of Service and Status: 1980 to 2002

[As of Sept. 30. Living refers to veterans receiving compensation for disability incurred or aggravated while on active duty and war veterans receiving pension and benefits for nonservice connected disabilities. Deceased refers to deceased veterans whose dependents were receiving pensions and compensation benefits]

Period of service and veteran status	1980	1990	1995	1998	1999	2000	2001	2002
Total	4,646	3,584	3,330	3,263	3,252	3,236	3,218	3,285
Living veterans	3,195	2,746	2,669	2,668	2,673	2,672	2,669	2,745
Service connected	2,273	2,184	2,236	2,277	2,294	2,308	2,321	2,398
Nonservice connected	922	562	433	391	379	364	348	347
Deceased veterans	1,451	838	662	595	579	564	549	540
Service connected	358	320	307	303	304	307	307	310
Nonservice connected	1,093	518	355	291	274	257	241	230
Prior to World War I	14	4	2	1	1	1	1	1
Living	(Z)	(Z)	(Z)	(Z)	(Z)	(Z)	(Z)	(Z)
World War I	692	198	89	51	42	34	28	23
Living	198	18	3	1	(Z)	(Z)	(Z)	(Z)
World War II	2,520	1,723	1,307	1,097	1,031	968	906	856
Living	1,849	1,294	961	785	730	676	624	583
Korean conflict [1]	446	390	368	342	333	323	313	308
Living	317	305	290	271	264	255	246	243
Peacetime	312	495	559	592	602	607	608	613
Living	262	444	514	550	561	567	569	575
Vietnam era [2]	662	774	868	932	953	969	987	1,052
Living	569	685	766	819	835	848	862	922
Persian Gulf War [3]	(X)	(X)	138	247	290	334	376	431
Living	(X)	(X)	134	242	283	326	368	421

X Not applicable. Z Fewer than 500. [1] Service during period June 27, 1950, to Jan. 31, 1955. [2] Service from Aug. 5, 1964, to May 7, 1975. [3] Service from August 2, 1990, to the present.

Source: U.S. Dept. of Veterans Affairs, *Annual Report of the Secretary of Veterans Affairs to 1998; Annual Accountability Report 1992-2002*, and unpublished data. See also <www.va.gov/vetdata/index.htm>.

Section 11
Social Insurance and Human Services

This section presents data related to governmental expenditures for social insurance and human services; governmental programs for old-age, survivors, disability, and health insurance (OASDHI); governmental employee retirement; private pension plans; government unemployment and temporary disability insurance; federal supplemental security income payments and aid to the needy; child and other welfare services; and federal food programs. Also included here are selected data on workers compensation and vocational rehabilitation, child support, child care, charity contributions, and philanthropic trusts and foundations.

The principal source for these data is the Social Security Administration's *Annual Statistical Supplement to the Social Security Bulletin* which presents current data on many of the programs.

Social insurance under the Social Security Act—Programs established by the Social Security Act provide protection against wage loss resulting from retirement, prolonged disability, death, or unemployment, and protection against the cost of medical care during old age and disability. The federal OASDI program provides monthly benefits to retired or disabled insured workers and their dependents and to survivors of insured workers. To be eligible, a worker must have had a specified period of employment in which OASDI taxes were paid. The age of eligibility for full retirement benefits has been 65 years old for many years. However, for persons born in 1938 or later that age will gradually increase until it reaches age 67 for those born after 1959. Reduced benefits may be obtained as early as age 62. The worker's spouse is under the same limitations. Survivor benefits are payable to dependents of deceased insured workers. Disability benefits are payable to an insured worker under full retirement age with a prolonged disability and to the disabled worker's dependents on the same basis as dependents of retired workers. Disability benefits are provided at age 50 to the disabled widow or widower of a deceased worker who was fully insured at the time of death. Disabled children, aged 18 or older, of retired, disabled, or deceased workers are also eligible for benefits. A lump sum benefit is generally payable on the death of an insured worker to a spouse or minor children. For information on the medicare program, see Section 3, Health and Nutrition.

Retirement, survivors, disability, and hospital insurance benefits are funded by a payroll tax on annual earnings (up to a maximum of earnings set by law) of workers, employers, and the self-employed. The maximum taxable earnings are adjusted annually to reflect increasing wage levels (see Table 541). Effective January 1994, there is no dollar limit on wages and self-employment income subject to the hospital insurance tax. Tax receipts and benefit payments are administered through federal trust funds. Special benefits for uninsured persons; hospital benefits for persons aged 65 and over with specified amounts of social security coverage less than that required for cash benefit eligibility; and that part of the cost of supplementary medical insurance not financed by contributions from participants are financed from federal general revenues.

Unemployment insurance is presently administered by the U.S. Employment and Training Administration and each state's employment security agency. By agreement with the U.S. Secretary of Labor, state agencies also administer unemployment compensation for eligible ex-military personnel and federal employees. Under state unemployment insurance laws, benefits related to the individual's past earnings are paid to unemployed eligible workers. State laws vary concerning the length of time benefits are paid and their amount. In most states, benefits are payable for 26 weeks and, during periods of high unemployment, extended benefits are payable under a federal-state program to those who have exhausted their regular state benefits. Some states also supplement the basic benefit with allowances for dependents.

Unemployment insurance is funded by a federal unemployment tax levied on the taxable payrolls of most employers. Taxable payroll under the federal act and 12 state laws is the first $7,000 in wages paid each worker during a year. Forty-one states have taxable payrolls above $7,000. Employers are allowed a percentage credit of taxable payroll for contributions paid to states under state unemployment insurance laws. The remaining percent of the federal tax finances administrative costs, the federal share of extended benefits, and advances to states. About 97 percent of wage and salary workers are covered by unemployment insurance.

Retirement programs for government employees—The Civil Service Retirement System (CSRS) and the Federal Employees' Retirement System (FERS) are the two major programs providing age and service, disability, and survivor annuities for federal civilian employees. In general, employees hired after December 31, 1983, are covered under FERS and the social security program (OASDHI), and employees on staff prior to that date are members of CSRS and are covered under medicare. CSRS employees were offered the option of transferring to FERS during 1987 and 1998. There are separate retirement systems for the uniformed services (supplementing OASDHI) and for certain special groups of federal employees. State and local government employees are covered for the most part by state and local retirement systems similar to the federal CSRS. In many jurisdictions these benefits supplement OASDHI coverage.

Workers' compensation—All states provide protection against work-connected injuries and deaths, although some states exclude certain workers (e.g., domestic workers). Federal laws cover federal employees, private employees in the District of Columbia, and longshoremen and harbor workers. In addition, the Department of Labor administers "black lung"

benefits programs for coal miners disabled by pneumoconiosis and for specified dependents and survivors. Specified occupational diseases are compensable to some extent. In most states, benefits are related to the worker's salary. The benefits may or may not be augmented by dependents' allowances or automatically adjusted to prevailing wage levels.

Income support—Income support programs are designed to provide benefits for persons with limited income and resources. The Supplemental Security Income (SSI) program and Temporary Assistance for Needy Families (TANF) program are the major programs providing monthly payments. In addition, a number of programs provide money payments or in-kind benefits for special needs or purposes. Several programs offer food and nutritional services. Also, various federal-state programs provide energy assistance, public housing, and subsidized housing to individuals and families with low incomes. General assistance may also be available at the state or local level.

The SSI program, administered by the Social Security Administration, provides income support to persons aged 65 or older and blind or disabled adults and children. Eligibility requirements and federal payment standards are nationally uniform. Most states supplement the basic SSI payment for all or selected categories of persons.

The Personal Responsibility and Work Opportunity Reconciliation Act of 1996 contained provisions that replaced the Aid to Families With Dependent Children (AFDC), Job Opportunities and Basic Skills (JOBS), and Emergency Assistance programs with the Temporary Assistance for Needy Families block grant program. This law contains strong work requirements, comprehensive child support enforcement, support for families moving from welfare to work, and other features. The TANF became effective as soon as each state submitted a complete plan implementing TANF, but no later than July 1, 1997. The AFDC program provided cash assistance based on need, income, resources, and family size.

Federal food stamp program—Under the food stamp program, single persons and those living in households meeting nationwide standards for income and assets may receive coupons redeemable for food at most retail food stores or provides benefits through electronic benefit transfer. The monthly amount of benefits or allotments a unit receives is determined by household size and income. Households without income receive the determined monthly cost of a nutritionally adequate diet for their household size. This amount is updated to account for food price increases. Households with income receive the difference between the amount of a nutritionally adequate diet and 30 percent of their income, after certain allowable deductions.

To qualify for the program, a household must have less than $2,000 in disposable assets ($3,000 if one member is aged 60 or older), gross income below 130 percent of the official poverty guidelines for the household size, and net income below 100 percent of the poverty guidelines. Households with a person aged 60 or older or a disabled person receiving SSI, social security, state general assistance, or veterans' disability benefits may have gross income exceeding 130 percent of the poverty guidelines. All households in which all members receive TANF or SSI are categorically eligible for food stamps without meeting these income or resource criteria. Households are certified for varying lengths of time, depending on their income sources and individual circumstances.

Health and welfare services—Programs providing health and welfare services are aided through federal grants to states for child welfare services, vocational rehabilitation, activities for the aged, maternal and child health services, maternity and infant care projects, comprehensive health services, and a variety of public health activities. For information about the medicaid program, see Section 3, Health and Nutrition.

Noncash benefits—The U.S. Census Bureau annually collects data on the characteristics of recipients of noncash (in-kind) benefits to supplement the collection of annual money income data in the Current Population Survey (see text, Section 1, Population, and Section 14, Prices). Noncash benefits are those benefits received in a form other than money which serve to enhance or improve the economic well-being of the recipient. As for money income, the data for noncash benefits are for the calendar year prior to the date of the interview. The major categories of noncash benefits covered are public transfers (e.g., food stamps, school lunch, public housing, and medicaid) and employer or union-provided benefits to employees.

Statistical reliability—For discussion of statistical collection, estimation, and sampling procedures and measures of statistical reliability applicable to HHS and Census Bureau data, see Appendix III.

No. 534. Government Transfer Payments to Individuals—Summary: 1970 to 2001

[In billions of dollars (69.3 represents $69,300,000,000)]

Year	Total	Retirement & disability insurance benefits	Medical payments	Income maintenance benefits	Unemployment insurance benefits	Veterans benefits	Federal education & training assistance payments [1]	Other [2]
1970	69.3	34.3	13.0	9.9	4.2	7.5	0.4	0.1
1980	262.7	128.8	62.0	34.3	18.7	14.7	4.1	0.2
1985	394.7	197.2	114.6	44.4	15.9	16.6	5.5	0.6
1990	561.4	263.9	189.1	63.5	18.2	17.7	7.3	1.8
1991	635.7	285.7	223.5	72.5	26.9	18.1	7.3	1.8
1992	714.8	304.7	257.3	84.6	39.7	18.6	8.0	2.0
1993	760.6	320.8	284.7	90.3	34.9	19.4	9.1	1.4
1994	792.8	334.8	308.3	95.6	24.1	19.7	8.6	1.8
1995	841.0	350.0	337.5	100.4	21.9	20.5	9.0	1.6
1996	883.0	364.6	361.3	102.5	22.5	21.4	8.6	2.1
1997	914.9	379.4	379.6	100.3	20.3	22.2	11.5	1.7
1998	935.1	392.0	386.3	100.7	19.9	23.2	11.2	1.9
1999	965.5	402.9	399.8	104.5	20.7	24.1	11.4	2.1
2000	1014.2	425.1	423.2	106.5	21.1	24.9	11.0	2.4
2001	1111.8	449.9	475.8	110.9	32.4	26.5	13.1	3.2

[1] See footnote 9, Table 535. [2] See footnote 10, Table 535.

No. 535. Government Transfer Payments to Individuals by Type: 1990 to 2001

[In millions of dollars (561,399 represents $561,399,000,000)]

Item	1990	1995	1997	1998	1999	2000	2001
Total	561,399	841,041	914,942	935,058	965,463	1,014,230	1,111,824
Retirement & disability insurance benefit payments	263,854	350,027	379,415	391,987	402,862	425,052	449,899
Old age, survivors, & disability insurance	244,135	327,667	356,602	369,347	379,895	401,367	425,167
Railroad retirement and disability	7,221	8,028	8,193	8,225	8,203	8,265	8,413
Worker's compensation payments (federal & state)	8,618	10,530	10,606	10,344	10,429	10,799	11,159
Other government disability insurance & retirement [1]	3,880	3,802	4,014	4,071	4,335	4,621	5,160
Medical payments	189,099	337,532	379,557	386,273	399,838	423,244	475,838
Medicare	107,929	180,283	209,198	208,755	208,102	215,843	239,114
Public assistance medical care [2]	78,176	155,017	168,288	175,475	189,729	205,384	234,693
Military medical insurance [3]	2,994	2,232	2,071	2,043	2,007	2,017	2,031
Income maintenance benefit payments	63,481	100,444	100,288	100,694	104,511	106,532	110,901
Supplemental Security Income (SSI)	16,670	27,726	29,154	30,322	31,023	31,675	33,161
Family assistance [4]	19,187	22,637	17,717	17,026	17,683	18,277	19,212
Food stamps	14,741	22,447	18,732	16,465	15,472	14,897	16,006
Other income maintenance [5]	12,883	27,634	34,685	36,881	40,333	41,683	42,522
Unemployment insurance benefit payments	18,208	21,864	20,299	19,859	20,711	21,057	32,408
State unemployment insurance compensation	17,644	20,975	19,469	19,154	19,976	20,194	31,532
Unemployment compensation for federal civilian employees	215	339	281	236	206	226	245
Unemployment compensation for railroad employees	89	62	72	61	65	81	98
Unemployment compensation for veterans	144	320	259	211	201	182	217
Other unemployment compensation [6]	116	168	218	197	263	374	316
Veterans benefit payments	17,687	20,545	22,233	23,168	24,051	24,934	26,467
Veterans pension and disability	15,550	17,565	19,061	20,049	20,904	21,895	23,261
Veterans readjustment [7]	257	1,086	1,234	1,220	1,323	1,323	1,504
Veterans life insurance benefits	1,868	1,883	1,929	1,891	1,815	1,706	1,692
Other assistance to veterans [8]	12	11	9	8	9	10	10
Federal education & training assistance payments [9]	7,300	9,007	11,481	11,189	11,368	10,985	13,141
Other payments to individuals [10]	1,770	1,622	1,669	1,888	2,122	2,426	3,170

[1] Consists largely of temporary disability payments, pension benefit guaranty payments, and black lung payments. [2] Consists of medicaid and other medical vendor payments. [3] Consists of payments made under the TriCare Management Program (formerly called CHAMPUS) for the medical care of dependents of active duty military personnel and of retired military personnel and their dependents at nonmilitary medical facilities. [4] Through 1995, consists of emergency assistance and aid to families with dependent children. Beginning with 1998, consists of benefits— generally known as temporary assistance for needy families— provided under the Personal Responsibility and Work Opportunity Reconciliation Act of 1996. For 1996-97, consists of payments under all three of these programs. [5] Consists largely of general assistance, expenditures for food under the supplemental program for women, infants, and children; refugee assistance; foster home care and adoption assistance; earned income tax credits; and energy assistance. [6] Consists of trade readjustment allowance payments, Redwood Park benefit payments, public service employment benefit payments, and transitional benefit payments. [7] Consists largely of veterans' readjustment benefit payments, educational assistance to spouses and children of disabled or deceased veterans, payments to paraplegics, and payments for autos and conveyances for disabled veterans. [8] Consists largely of State and local government payments to veterans. [9] Excludes veterans. Consists largely of federal fellowship payments (National Science Foundation fellowships and traineeships, subsistence payments to state maritime academy cadets, and other federal fellowships), interest subsidy on higher education loans, basic educational opportunity grants, and Job Corps payments. [10] Consists largely of Bureau of Indian Affairs payments, education exchange payments, Alaska Permanent Fund dividend payments, compensation of survivors of public safety officers, compensation of victims of crime, disaster relief payments, compensation for Japanese internment, and other special payments to individuals.

Source of Tables 534 and 535: U.S. Bureau of Economic Analysis, "Regional Accounts Data, Annual State Personal Income"; <http://www.bea.doc.gov/bea/regional/spi/>; (accessed 8 May 2003).

No. 536. Government Transfer Payments to Individuals by State: 1995 to 2001

[In millions of dollars (841,041 represents $841,041,000,000)]

State	1995, total	2000, total	2001 Total	Retirement & disability insurance benefits	Medical payments	Income maintenance benefits	Unemployment insurance benefits	Veterans benefits	Federal education & training assistance payments [1]	Other [2]
U.S.	841,041	1,014,230	1,111,824	449,899	475,838	110,901	32,408	26,467	13,141	3,170
AL	13,395	16,709	18,060	7,680	7,207	1,942	332	606	268	25
AK	1,860	2,914	3,043	524	853	310	111	95	15	1,134
AZ	12,653	15,821	17,971	8,108	6,999	1,519	300	602	287	157
AR	8,063	9,855	10,890	4,680	4,208	1,083	314	440	151	15
CA	96,576	113,753	127,064	44,924	54,521	19,941	3,491	2,242	1,697	247
CO	9,273	11,046	12,117	5,182	4,919	1,020	313	467	179	37
CT	12,470	14,299	15,161	6,223	6,848	1,272	497	210	94	17
DE	2,148	2,727	2,968	1,401	1,151	224	91	72	26	4
DC	2,318	2,674	2,772	635	1,532	411	76	63	49	7
FL	52,572	64,402	70,126	31,316	29,731	5,181	1,042	2,044	721	91
GA	19,042	23,508	25,952	10,496	10,651	2,916	636	886	327	41
HI	3,480	3,897	4,171	1,779	1,440	615	149	138	43	7
ID	2,836	3,705	4,137	1,983	1,461	299	166	141	76	11
IL	36,032	41,455	44,571	19,092	17,926	4,410	1,927	626	510	80
IN	16,191	20,281	22,300	10,220	8,976	1,782	600	405	290	28
IA	8,215	9,826	10,555	5,315	3,803	725	316	222	158	17
KS	7,298	8,813	9,559	4,520	3,718	674	249	244	136	18
KY	12,503	15,754	17,014	7,064	6,913	1,879	456	448	236	18
LA	15,257	16,900	19,466	6,417	9,727	2,316	237	480	266	22
ME	4,203	5,174	5,621	2,266	2,367	575	113	239	53	8
MD	13,513	16,647	18,105	7,523	7,833	1,619	445	455	201	30
MA	23,068	26,912	29,475	10,362	14,510	2,351	1,364	602	255	29
MI	29,984	36,281	40,430	17,180	16,678	3,912	1,623	593	394	49
MN	13,241	15,773	17,623	7,428	7,484	1,400	666	405	208	32
MS	8,648	10,758	12,015	4,498	5,219	1,512	194	356	213	23
MO	17,029	21,192	23,268	9,785	10,289	1,898	479	527	259	31
MT	2,636	3,112	3,335	1,627	1,160	269	83	127	55	15
NE	4,425	5,566	6,086	2,839	2,465	401	88	202	83	8
NV	4,217	5,466	6,218	2,952	2,247	429	298	219	50	23
NH	3,461	3,905	4,254	2,001	1,738	258	65	148	39	6
NJ	27,593	32,273	35,350	15,092	15,499	2,337	1,589	507	285	41
NM	4,586	5,918	6,585	2,556	2,611	808	107	291	116	96
NY	82,755	96,094	102,526	32,441	52,432	12,548	2,676	1,181	1,144	103
NC	21,054	27,403	30,598	12,706	12,821	2,752	982	946	347	43
ND	1,940	2,415	2,531	1,231	960	168	37	65	44	26
OH	36,753	42,683	46,365	20,917	18,811	4,013	1,232	874	459	58
OK	9,937	11,965	13,182	5,725	5,198	1,191	201	640	199	28
OR	9,529	12,107	13,573	6,317	4,870	1,106	673	419	158	30
PA	45,821	55,341	59,432	24,512	26,316	4,747	2,254	1,032	512	59
RI	4,027	4,810	5,356	1,983	2,507	493	189	114	60	10
SC	10,621	13,821	15,361	6,613	6,107	1,524	400	505	186	27
SD	2,061	2,493	2,685	1,215	1,039	205	23	104	46	53
TN	17,338	22,259	24,293	9,406	11,172	2,187	612	636	245	34
TX	49,155	60,815	66,744	25,129	29,636	6,987	1,667	2,199	985	140
UT	3,892	4,926	5,416	2,508	1,973	412	183	140	152	48
VT	1,743	2,180	2,385	994	989	243	65	63	28	3
VA	15,539	19,380	21,681	10,167	8,194	1,770	381	861	275	33
WA	16,608	20,346	22,862	9,918	8,612	1,814	1,417	804	240	57
WV	7,426	8,659	9,255	4,550	3,285	867	147	290	105	11
WI	14,829	17,720	19,698	9,029	7,711	1,473	821	437	192	35
WY	1,225	1,496	1,620	874	521	112	29	55	24	4

[1] Excludes veterans. Consists largely of federal fellowship payments (National Science Foundation, fellowships and traineeships, subsistence payments to State maritime academy cadets, and other federal fellowships), interest subsidy on higher education loans, basic educational opportunity grants, and Job Corps payments.   [2] Consists largely of Bureau of Indian Affairs payments, education exchange payments, Alaska Permanent Fund dividend payments, compensation of survivors of public safety officers, compensation of victims of crime, disaster relief payments, compensation for Japanese internment, and other special payments to individuals.

Source: U.S. Bureau of Economic Analysis, "Regional Accounts Data, Annual State Personal Income"; <http://www.bea.doc.gov/bea/regional/spi/>; (accessed 8 May 2003).

No. 537. Number of Persons With Income by Specified Sources of Income: 2001

[In thousands (200,814 represents 200,814,000). Persons 15 years old and over as of March 2002. Based on Current Population Survey; see text, Sections 1 and 13, and Appendix III]

Source of income	Total persons with income	Under 65 years old	65 years old and over	White	Black	Hispanic origin [1]
Total	200,814	167,904	32,910	167,958	22,358	21,457
Earnings	151,441	145,959	5,482	126,057	17,016	17,910
Wages and salary	143,022	138,339	4,683	118,620	16,486	17,193
Nonfarm self-employment	11,564	10,807	757	10,088	857	983
Farm self-employment	2,498	2,241	256	2,251	153	176
Unemployment compensation	7,374	7,199	175	6,043	940	848
Workers compensation	2,135	1,978	157	1,788	261	218
Social security, railroad retirement	39,699	9,276	30,423	34,839	3,720	2,276
Supplemental security income (SSI)	5,002	3,793	1,210	3,339	1,344	706
Public assistance	2,225	2,141	84	1,338	695	423
TANF/Welfare (AFDC) only [2]	1,507	1,471	37	883	476	292
Other assistance only	625	578	48	415	174	113
Both	93	93	-	41	44	18
Veterans payments	2,523	1,400	1,123	2,102	320	108
Survivors benefits	2,737	970	1,767	2,468	211	85
Company or union	1,183	279	904	1,075	95	36
Disability benefits	1,583	1,373	210	1,259	264	153
Company or union	422	380	42	361	51	33
Pensions	14,937	4,686	10,251	13,438	1,171	453
Company or union	10,808	3,252	7,556	9,786	819	342
Federal government	1,721	530	1,190	1,452	206	68
Military retirement	1,118	601	517	960	111	54
State or local government	3,434	1,311	2,123	3,079	278	115
Property income [3]	107,806	88,073	19,733	96,048	6,653	5,748
Interest	102,473	83,709	18,765	91,407	6,221	5,399
Dividends	36,013	29,521	6,492	32,934	1,496	1,138
Rents, royalties, estates or trusts	11,236	8,481	2,755	10,262	498	529
Education	7,798	7,763	34	6,028	1,166	683
Pell grant only	1,564	1,548	16	1,084	372	198
Other government only	1,203	1,195	7	931	175	133
Scholarships only	2,167	2,167	-	1,721	255	146
Child support	5,607	5,589	18	4,383	1,020	559
Alimony	453	421	32	417	30	25
Financial assistance	2,093	1,932	161	1,623	254	177
Other income	1,199	957	242	977	120	49
Combinations of income types:						
Government transfer payments	57,986	26,464	31,522	48,707	7,040	4,393
Public assistance or SSI	6,892	5,627	1,265	4,460	1,950	1,087

- Represents or rounds to zero. [1] Persons of Hispanic origin may be of any race. [2] TANF-Temporary Assistance for Needy Families program; AFDC=Aid to Families with Dependent Children program. [3] Includes estates and trusts reported as survivor benefits.

Source: U.S. Census Bureau, "Table PINC-09. Source of Income in 2001—Number With Income and Mean Income of Specified Type in 2000 of People 15 Years Old and Over, by Race, Hispanic Origin, and Sex"; published 10 March 2002; <http://ferret.bls.census.gov/macro/032002/perinc/toc.htm>.

No. 538. Households Receiving Means-Tested Noncash Benefits: 1980 to 2001

[In thousands (82,368 represents 82,368,000), except percent. Households as of March of following year. Covers civilian noninstitutional population, including persons in the Armed Forces living off post or with their families on post. A means-tested benefit program requires that the household's income and/or assets fall below specified guidelines in order to qualify for benefits. There are general trends toward underestimation of noncash beneficiaries. Households are classified according to poverty status of family or nonfamily householder; for explanation of poverty level, see text, Section 13. Data for 1980 and 1990 based on 1980 census population controls; beginning 1995, based on 1990 census population controls. Based on Current Population Survey; see text, Section 1, and Appendix III]

Type of benefit received	1980	1990	1995	2000	2001 Total	Below poverty level Number	Percent of total	Above poverty level
Total households	82,368	94,312	99,627	106,418	109,297	12,754	100	96,543
Receiving at least one noncash benefit	14,266	16,098	21,148	20,131	21,870	7,524	59	14,346
Not receiving cash public assistance	7,860	8,819	13,335	14,465	16,234	4,720	37	11,514
Receiving cash public assistance [1]	6,407	7,279	7,813	5,667	5,636	2,803	22	2,833
Total households receiving—								
Food stamps	6,769	7,163	8,388	5,563	5,905	3,761	29	2,144
School lunch	5,532	6,252	8,607	7,185	7,942	2,975	23	4,967
Public housing	2,777	4,339	4,846	4,689	5,006	2,585	20	2,421
Medicaid	8,287	10,321	14,111	14,328	15,832	5,865	46	9,967

[1] Households receiving money from aid to families with dependent children program (beginning 2000, temporary assistance for needy families program), supplemental security income program or other public assistance programs.

Source: U.S. Census Bureau, "Table NC1. Means-Tested Noncash Benefits Received by Households, by Selected Household Characteristics, Race and Hispanic Origin, and Poverty Status: 2001"; published 10 December 2002; <http://ferret.bls.census.gov/macro/032002/noncash/nc1000.htm> and Current Population Reports, P-60 reports.

No. 539. Government Expenditures for Income-Tested Benefits by Type of Benefit: 1980 to 2000

[In millions of dollars (105,312 represents $105,312,000,000). For years ending September 30. Programs covered provide cash, goods, or services to persons who make no payment and render no service in return. In case of many programs, including family cash welfare, food and housing programs and some educational programs, some recipients must work or study. Most of the programs base eligibility on individual, household, or family income, but some use group or area income tests; and a few offer help on the basis of presumed need. Constant dollar figures are based on the Consumer Price Index for all Urban Consumers]

Level of government and year	Total spending Current dollars	Total spending Constant (2000) dollars	Medical benefits	Cash aid	Food benefits	Housing benefits	Education benefits	Jobs/training	Services	Energy aid
TOTAL						Constant (2000) dollars				
1980	105,312	224,866	69,606	61,332	28,924	21,869	11,052	18,589	9,818	3,675
1985	144,291	231,158	79,204	60,294	32,666	24,207	15,972	6,370	8,773	3,672
1990	213,055	282,815	115,250	72,019	33,326	23,926	19,102	5,631	11,267	2,294
1993	314,451	374,152	170,155	89,003	43,237	32,672	17,941	6,346	12,889	1,909
1994	352,487	408,624	187,153	100,067	43,909	34,142	18,015	6,393	16,633	2,311
1995	371,109	418,484	196,922	103,291	43,558	35,764	18,146	6,132	12,775	1,896
1996	375,310	411,725	195,199	101,426	42,876	35,656	17,967	5,138	12,090	1,373
1997	384,465	410,821	198,815	99,463	39,908	35,561	18,737	4,246	12,587	1,502
1998	394,687	414,944	203,549	96,269	36,906	34,681	19,052	5,142	17,939	1,405
1999	408,405	421,379	213,619	96,576	35,718	29,848	19,058	5,831	19,291	1,439
2000	436,985	436,985	225,858	91,703	34,347	34,906	20,385	7,347	20,724	1,715
FEDERAL										
1980	80,679	172,268	41,421	40,522	27,948	21,869	10,441	18,416	7,975	3,675
1985	106,061	169,912	44,664	39,227	31,018	24,207	15,245	6,240	5,689	3,622
1990	151,990	201,756	66,671	48,378	31,687	23,926	18,267	5,277	5,421	2,129
1993	225,768	268,632	101,200	63,479	41,374	31,089	17,030	5,677	6,958	1,825
1994	250,066	289,891	108,609	73,494	41,857	32,270	16,968	5,635	8,836	2,222
1995	262,899	296,460	114,359	76,804	41,494	33,142	17,069	5,217	6,779	1,805
1996	268,097	294,110	114,009	76,773	40,770	32,958	16,919	4,432	6,924	1,293
1997	274,153	292,947	115,176	76,687	37,799	32,937	17,641	4,056	7,130	1,434
1998	280,138	294,516	116,604	76,726	34,869	31,939	17,857	4,390	10,848	1,322
1999	291,022	300,267	123,476	76,726	33,618	29,848	17,830	4,994	12,490	1,351
2000	306,520	306,520	131,468	72,516	32,182	29,261	19,043	6,219	14,201	1,630
STATE AND LOCAL										
1980	24,633	52,598	28,185	20,810	976	-	611	173	1,843	-
1985	38,230	61,246	34,540	21,067	1,648	-	727	130	3,084	50
1990	61,065	81,059	48,579	23,641	1,639	1,583	835	354	5,846	165
1993	88,683	105,520	68,955	25,524	1,863	1,872	911	669	5,931	84
1994	102,421	118,733	78,544	26,573	2,052	2,622	1,047	758	7,797	89
1995	108,210	122,024	82,563	26,697	2,064	2,698	1,077	915	5,996	91
1996	107,213	117,615	81,190	24,622	2,106	2,624	1,048	706	5,166	80
1997	110,312	117,874	83,639	22,690	2,109	2,624	1,096	190	5,457	68
1998	114,549	120,428	86,945	19,582	2,037	2,742	1,195	752	7,091	83
1999	117,383	121,112	90,143	19,850	2,100	(NA)	1,228	902	6,801	88
2000	130,465	130,465	94,390	19,187	2,165	5,645	1,342	1,128	6,523	85

- Represents or rounds to zero. NA Not available.

Source: Library of Congress, Congressional Research Service, "Cash and Noncash Benefits for Persons With Limited Income: Eligibility Rules, Recipient and Expenditure Data, FY1998-FY2000"; CRS Report RL 31228; November 19, 2001.

No. 540. Cash and Noncash Benefits for Persons With Limited Income: 1999 and 2000

[For years ending September 30, except as noted (408,405 represents $408,405,000,000). Programs covered provide cash, goods, or services to persons who make no payment and render no service in return. In case of many programs, including family cash welfare, food and housing programs, job and training programs and some educational programs, some recipients must work or study. Most of the programs base eligibility on individual, household, or family income, but some use group or area income tests; and a few offer help on the basis of presumed need]

Program	Average monthly recipients (1,000) 1999	2000	Expenditures (mil. dol.) Total 1999	2000	Federal 1999	2000	State and local 1999	2000
Total.	(X)	(X)	408,405	436,985	291,022	306,520	117,383	130,465
Medical care [1]	(X)	(X)	207,042	225,858	119,674	131,468	87,368	94,390
Medicaid [2] [3]	42,020	(NA)	190,443	207,195	107,819	117,684	82,624	89,511
Veterans [4] [5]	114	123	6,781	7,420	6,781	7,420	-	-
General assistance [5]	(NA)	(NA)	4,052	3,898	-	-	4,052	3,898
State children's health insurance program	1,980	3,300	1,182	2,474	922	1,929	260	545
Indian health services [2] [3]	1,500	1,500	2,240	2,391	2,240	2,391	-	-
Maternal and child health services	27,097	(NA)	1,131	1,144	699	708	432	436
Consolidated health centers [2]	9,150	9,600	925	1,018	925	1,018	-	-
Cash aid [1]	(X)	(X)	93,603	91,703	74,364	72,516	19,239	19,187
Supplemental security income [3] [6]	6,595	6,609	34,838	35,066	30,616	30,718	4,222	4,348
Temporary assistance for needy families (TANF) [7]	7,203	6,035	15,741	14,490	7,882	6,852	7,859	7,638
Earned income tax credit (refunded portion) [8]	57,300	55,320	27,344	25,800	27,344	25,800	-	-
Foster care	302	312	7,585	7,941	4,012	4,237	3,573	3,704
General assistance [6]	(NA)	(NA)	2,867	2,649	-	-	2,867	2,649
Pensions for needy veterans [9] [10]	671	635	3,084	2,953	3,084	2,953	-	-
Food benefits [1]	(X)	(X)	34,618	34,347	32,583	32,182	2,035	2,165
Food stamps [3] [11]	19,300	18,200	20,984	20,341	19,022	18,255	1,962	2,086
School lunch program [12] [13]	15,382	15,389	5,507	5,629	5,507	5,629	(NA)	(NA)
Women, infants and children [3] [14]	7,300	7,200	3,927	3,944	3,927	3,944	-	-
Child and adult care food program [15]	1,900	1,900	1,468	1,557	1,468	1,557	-	-
School breakfast [12]	6,275	6,339	1,299	1,349	1,299	1,349	-	-
Housing benefits [1]	(X)	(X)	28,929	34,906	28,929	29,261	(NA)	5,645
Low-income housing asst. (Sec. 8) [16]	2,985	3,196	15,652	15,972	15,652	15,972	-	-
Low-rent public housing [16] [17]	1,274	1,267	5,956	6,526	5,956	6,526	(NA)	(NA)
Rural housing loans [18] [19]	54	46	3,944	3,291	3,944	3,291	-	-
Home investment partnerships [3] [19] [20]	76	86	1,600	7,275	1,600	1,636	(NA)	5,639
Education aid [1]	(X)	(X)	18,471	20,385	17,281	19,043	1,190	1,342
Pell grants [21] [22]	3,838	3,810	7,345	7,704	7,345	7,704	-	-
Head Start [21]	826	858	5,823	6,583	4,658	5,266	1,165	1,317
Stafford loans [21]	5,388	5,354	2,673	3,332	2,673	3,332	-	-
Federal Work-Study Program [21] [22]	892	930	830	870	830	870	-	-
Services [1]	(X)	(X)	18,697	20,724	12,105	14,201	6,592	6,523
Social services (Title 20) [23]	(NA)	(NA)	6,149	5,623	3,171	2,854	2,978	2,769
Child care for TANF recipients and ex-recipients [24]	(NA)	(NA)	1,139	2,308	604	1,411	535	897
Child care and development block grant [25]	1,875	1,800	6,236	6,934	4,640	5,059	1,596	1,875
TANF services	(NA)	(NA)	3,095	3,687	1,612	2,705	1,483	982
Jobs and training [1]	(X)	(X)	5,651	7,348	4,777	6,219	874	1,128
TANF work activities	(X)	(X)	1,654	2,272	1,125	1,515	529	757
Training for disadvantaged adults and youth [26]	513	(NA)	1,084	1,950	1,084	1,950	-	-
Job Corps	71	70	1,307	1,357	1,307	1,357	-	-
Energy assistance [1]	(X)	(X)	1,394	1,715	1,309	1,630	85	85
Low-income energy assistance [3] [27]	4,400	4,100	1,176	1,495	1,176	1,495	(NA)	(NA)

- Represents zero. NA Not available. X Not applicable. [1] Includes other programs not shown separately. [2] Recipient data represent unduplicated annual number. [3] Expenditures include administrative expenses. [4] Medical care for veterans with a nonservice-connected disability. [5] Estimated expenditures. [6] Includes state-administered SSI supplements. [7] Excludes data for child support operations. [8] Estimated recipients. [9] Estimated recipients as of September. [10] Includes dependents and survivors. [11] Includes Puerto Rico's nutritional assistance program. [12] Free and reduced-price segments. [13] Includes estimate of commodity assistance. [14] Special supplemental food program for women, infants and children. [15] Recipient data are numbers of children receiving free or reduced price meals and snacks in child care centers and estimates of children in family day care homes with incomes below 185 percent of poverty. [16] Recipient data represent units eligible for payment at end of year. [17] Includes operating subsidies, capital grants, and HUD-administered Indian housing. [18] Recipient data represent total families or dwelling units during year. [19] Expenditure data represent amounts obligated. [20] Recipient data are housing units provided or rehabilitated. [21] Recipient data are total numbers for the school year ending in year shown. [22] Expenditure data are appropriations available for school year ending the fiscal year named. [23] Nonfederal expenditure data are rough estimates. [24] P.L. 104-193, which created TANF, established a mandatory block grant for TANF-related child care. [25] Recipient data are estimated number of children served. [26] Recipient data are total number of participants. [27] Households served during the year with heating and winter crisis aid. Federal funds include amounts transferred to other programs serving the needy.

Source: Library of Congress, Congressional Research Service, "Cash and Noncash Benefits for Persons With Limited Income: Eligibility Rules, Recipient and Expenditure Data, FY1998-FY2000"; CRS Report RL31228; November 19, 2001.

No. 541. Social Security—Covered Employment, Earnings, and Contribution Rates: 1980 to 2002

[140.4 represents 140,400,000. Includes Puerto Rico, Virgin Islands, American Samoa, and Guam. Represents all reported employment. Data are estimated. OASDHI=Old-age, survivors, disability, and health insurance; SMI=Supplementary medical insurance]

Item	Unit	1980	1990	1995	1996	1997	1998	1999	2000	2001	2002
Workers with insured status [1]	Million	140.4	164.0	173.2	175.3	177.8	180.2	182.7	185.1	187.5	189.9
Male	Million	76.6	86.5	90.2	91.1	92.1	93.1	94.1	95.2	96.3	97.3
Female	Million	63.8	77.5	83.0	84.2	85.7	87.1	88.6	89.9	91.3	92.6
Under 25 years old	Million	25.7	21.3	18.8	18.8	19.1	19.6	20.2	20.7	21.2	21.6
25 to 34 years old	Million	36.5	41.6	39.4	38.9	38.2	37.5	36.9	36.5	36.3	36.2
35 to 44 years old	Million	23.0	36.4	40.6	41.2	41.8	42.2	42.5	42.5	42.2	41.8
45 to 54 years old	Million	18.6	22.8	29.5	30.8	31.9	33.1	34.4	35.8	36.9	37.7
55 to 59 years old	Million	9.3	8.7	9.7	10.2	10.7	11.3	11.8	12.2	13.0	13.9
60 to 64 years old	Million	8.2	8.8	8.5	8.5	8.8	8.9	9.2	9.4	9.8	10.3
65 to 69 years old	Million	7.0	8.2	8.1	8.1	8.0	7.9	7.9	7.9	8.0	8.1
70 years old and over	Million	12.1	16.3	18.5	18.8	19.3	19.6	19.8	20.1	20.3	20.4
Workers reported with—											
Taxable earnings [2]	Million	113	134	141	143	146	149	151	154	154	153
Maximum earnings [2]	Million	10	8	8	9	9	9	9	10	9	8
Earnings in covered employment [2]	Bil. dol	1,329	2,704	3,359	3,566	3,847	4,143	4,448	4,784	4,874	4,950
Reported taxable [2]	Bil. dol	1,178	2,359	2,920	3,074	3,285	3,522	3,750	3,987	4,143	4,227
Percent of total	Percent	88.6	87.2	86.9	86.2	85.4	85.0	84.3	83.4	85	85.4
Average per worker:											
Total earnings [2]	Dollars	11,761	20,227	23,818	24,869	26,324	27,814	29,402	31,159	31,702	32,396
Taxable earnings [2]	Dollars	10,430	17,642	20,703	21,432	22,483	23,644	24,784	25,972	26,945	27,665
Annual maximum taxable earnings [3]	Dollars	25,900	51,300	61,200	62,700	65,400	68,400	72,600	76,200	80,400	84,900
Contribution rates for OASDHI: [4]											
Each employer and employee	Percent	6.13	7.65	7.65	7.65	7.65	7.65	7.65	7.65	7.65	7.65
Self-employed [5]	Percent	8.10	15.30	15.30	15.30	15.30	15.30	15.30	15.30	15.30	15.30
SMI, monthly premium [6]	Dollars	9.60	28.60	46.10	42.50	43.80	43.80	45.50	45.50	50.00	54.00

[1] Estimated number fully insured for retirement and/or survivor benefits as of end of year. [2] Includes self-employment. [3] Beginning 1994 upper limit on earnings subject to HI taxes was repealed. [4] As of January 1, 2002, each employee and employer pays 7.65 percent and the self-employed pay 15.3 percent. [5] Self-employed pays 11.8 percent in 1985. The additional amount is supplied from general revenues. Beginning 1990, self-employed pays 15.3 percent, and half of the tax is deductible for income tax purposes and for computing self-employment income subject to social security tax. [6] 1980, as of July 1; beginning 1985, as of January 1. As of January 1, 2002, the monthly premium is $54.00.

Source: U.S. Social Security Administration, Annual Statistical Supplement to the Social Security Bulletin; and unpublished data.

No. 542. Social Security Trust Funds: 1990 to 2002

[In billions of dollars (272.4 represents $272,400,000,000)]

Type of trust fund	1990	1995	1996	1997	1998	1999	2000	2001	2002
Old-age and survivors insurance (OASI):									
Net contribution income [1]	272.4	310.1	328.0	357.4	380.4	407.3	433.0	453.4	468.1
Interest received [2]	16.4	32.8	35.7	39.8	44.5	49.8	57.5	64.7	71.2
Benefit payments [3]	223.0	291.6	302.9	316.3	326.8	334.4	352.7	372.3	388.1
Assets, end of year	214.2	458.5	514.0	589.1	681.6	798.8	931.0	1,071.5	1,217.5
Disability insurance (DI):									
Net contribution income [1]	28.7	54.7	57.7	56.5	59.5	63.9	71.8	75.7	78.2
Interest received [2]	0.9	2.2	3.0	4.0	4.8	5.7	6.9	8.2	9.2
Benefit payments [3]	24.8	40.9	44.2	45.7	48.2	51.4	55.0	59.6	65.7
Assets, end of year	11.1	37.6	52.9	66.4	80.8	97.3	118.5	141.0	160.5

[1] Includes deposits by states and deductions for refund of estimated employee-tax overpayment. Beginning in 1990, includes government contributions on deemed wage credits for military service in 1957 and later. Includes taxation of benefits beginning in 1990. [2] In 1990, includes interest on advance tax transfers. Beginning 1990, includes interest on reimbursement for unnegotiated checks. [3] Includes payments for vocational rehabilitation services furnished to disabled persons receiving benefits because of their disabilities. Beginning in 1990, amounts reflect deductions for unnegotiated benefit checks.

Source: U.S. Social Security Administration, Annual Report of Board of Trustees, OASI, DI, HI, and SMI Trust Funds. Also published in Social Security Bulletin, quarterly.

No. 543. Social Security (OASDI)—Benefits by Type of Beneficiary: 1980 to 2002

[35,585 represents 35,585,000. A person eligible to receive more than one type of benefit is generally classified or counted only once as a retired-worker beneficiary. OASDI=Old-age, survivors, and disability insurance. See also headnote, Table 541 and Appendix III]

Type of beneficiary	1980	1990	1995	1996	1997	1998	1999	2000	2001	2002
Number of benefits [1] (1,000)	35,585	39,832	43,387	43,737	43,971	44,246	44,596	45,415	45,878	46,444
Retired workers [2] (1,000)	19,562	24,838	26,673	26,898	27,275	27,511	27,775	28,499	28,837	29,190
Disabled workers [3] (1,000)	2,859	3,011	4,185	4,386	4,508	4,698	4,879	5,042	5,274	5,544
Wives and husbands [2][4] (1,000)	3,477	3,367	3,290	3,194	3,129	3,054	2,987	2,963	2,899	2,833
Children (1,000)	4,607	3,187	3,734	3,803	3,772	3,769	3,795	3,803	3,839	3,910
Under age 18	3,423	2,497	2,956	3,010	2,970	2,963	2,970	2,976	2,994	3,043
Disabled children [5]	450	600	686	697	705	713	721	729	737	745
Students [6]	733	89	92	96	97	93	104	98	109	123
Of retired workers	639	422	442	443	441	439	442	459	467	477
Of deceased workers	2,610	1,776	1,884	1,898	1,893	1,884	1,885	1,878	1,890	1,908
Of disabled workers	1,358	989	1,409	1,463	1,438	1,446	1,468	1,466	1,482	1,526
Widowed mothers [7] (1,000)	562	304	275	242	230	221	212	203	197	194
Widows and widowers [2][8] (1,000)	4,411	5,111	5,226	5,210	5,053	4,990	4,944	4,901	4,828	4,771
Parents [2] (1,000)	15	6	4	4	4	3	3	3	3	2
Special benefits [9] (1,000)	93	7	1	1	(Z)	(Z)	(Z)	(Z)	(Z)	(Z)
AVERAGE MONTHLY BENEFIT, CURRENT DOLLARS										
Retired workers [2]	341	603	720	745	765	780	804	844	874	895
Retired worker and wife [2]	567	1,027	1,221	1,262	1,295	1,318	1,357	1,420	1,466	1,494
Disabled workers [3]	371	587	682	704	722	733	754	786	814	834
Wives and husbands [2][4]	164	298	354	369	379	386	398	416	430	439
Children of retired workers	140	259	322	337	349	358	373	395	413	426
Children of deceased workers	240	406	469	487	500	510	526	550	571	585
Children of disabled workers	110	164	183	194	201	208	216	228	238	245
Widowed mothers [7]	246	409	478	515	532	545	566	595	621	640
Widows and widowers, nondisabled [2]	311	556	680	699	731	749	775	810	841	861
Parents [2]	276	482	591	614	636	651	674	704	729	753
Special benefits [9]	105	167	192	197	201	204	209	217	224	227
AVERAGE MONTHLY BENEFIT, CONSTANT (2002) DOLLARS [10]										
Retired workers [2]	715	815	849	850	858	861	864	877	895	895
Retired worker and wife [2]	1,189	1,389	1,439	1,439	1,452	1,455	1,459	1,476	1,500	1,494
Disabled workers [3]	778	794	804	803	810	809	810	817	834	834
Wives and husbands [2][4]	344	403	417	421	425	426	428	432	440	439
Children of deceased workers	293	350	379	384	391	396	401	411	422	585
Widowed mothers [7]	503	549	553	555	561	562	565	572	584	640
Widows and widowers, nondisabled [2]	231	222	216	221	225	229	232	237	244	861
Number of benefits awarded (1,000)	4,215	3,717	3,882	3,793	3,866	3,800	3,917	4,290	4,162	4,336
Retired workers [2]	1,620	1,665	1,609	1,581	1,719	1,631	1,690	1,961	1,779	1,813
Disabled workers [3]	389	468	646	624	587	608	620	622	691	750
Wives and husbands [2][4]	469	379	322	302	319	311	322	385	358	363
Children	1,174	695	809	798	757	763	773	777	796	846
Widowed mothers [7]	108	58	52	49	44	42	42	40	41	41
Widows and widowers [2][8]	452	452	445	438	440	444	470	505	496	523
Parents [2]	1	(Z)	(Z)	(Z)	(Z)	(Z)	(Z)	(Z)	(Z)	(Z)
Special benefits [9]	1	(Z)	(Z)	(Z)	(Z)	(Z)	(Z)	(Z)	(Z)	(Z)
BENEFIT PAYMENTS DURING YEAR (bil. dol.)										
Total [11]	120.5	247.8	332.6	347.1	362.0	375.0	385.8	407.6	431.9	453.8
Monthly benefits [12]	120.1	247.6	332.4	346.9	361.8	374.8	385.6	407.4	431.7	453.6
Retired workers [2]	70.4	156.8	205.3	213.4	223.6	232.3	238.5	253.5	269.0	281.6
Disabled workers [3]	12.8	22.1	36.6	39.6	41.1	43.5	46.5	49.8	54.2	59.9
Wives and husbands [2][4]	7.0	14.5	17.9	18.2	18.6	18.9	18.8	19.4	19.9	20.3
Children	10.5	12.0	16.1	17.1	17.6	18.1	18.6	19.3	20.4	21.5
Under age 18	7.4	9.0	11.9	12.6	13.0	13.3	13.6	14.1	14.8	15.7
Disabled children [5]	1.0	2.5	3.6	3.8	4.0	4.2	4.4	4.6	4.8	5.1
Students [6]	2.1	0.5	0.6	0.6	0.6	0.7	0.7	0.7	0.7	0.8
Of retired workers	1.1	1.3	1.7	1.8	1.9	1.9	2.0	2.1	2.3	2.5
Of deceased workers	7.4	8.6	10.7	11.2	11.7	11.9	12.1	12.5	13.1	13.7
Of disabled workers	2.0	2.2	3.7	4.0	4.1	4.2	4.4	4.7	4.9	5.3
Widowed mothers [7]	1.6	1.4	1.6	1.5	1.5	1.4	1.4	1.4	1.4	1.5
Widows and widowers [2][8]	17.6	40.7	54.8	57.0	59.3	60.5	61.8	63.9	66.8	68.8
Parents [2]	0.1	(Z)	(Z)	(Z)	(Z)	(Z)	(Z)	(Z)	(Z)	(Z)
Special benefits [9]	0.1	(Z)	(Z)	(Z)	(Z)	(Z)	(Z)	(Z)	(Z)	(Z)
Lump sum	0.4	0.2	0.2	0.2	0.2	0.2	0.2	0.2	0.2	0.2

Z Fewer than 500 or less than $50 million. [1] Number of benefit payments in current-payment status, i.e., actually being made at a specified time with no deductions or with deductions amounting to less than a month's benefit. [2] 62 years and over. [3] Disabled workers under age 65. [4] Includes wife beneficiaries with entitled children in their care and entitled divorced wives. [5] 18 years old and over. Disability began before age 18. [6] Full-time students aged 18-21 through 1984 and aged 18 and 19 beginning 1985. [7] Includes surviving divorced mothers with entitled children in their care and widowed fathers with entitled children in their care. [8] Includes widows aged 60-61, surviving divorced wives aged 60 and over, disabled widows and widowers aged 50 and over; and widowers aged 60-61. [9] Benefits for persons aged 72 and over not insured under regular or transitional provisions of Social Security Act. [10] Constant dollar figures are based on the consumer price index (CPI-U) for December as published by the U.S. Bureau of Labor Statistics. [11] Represents total disbursements of benefit checks by the U.S. Dept. of the Treasury during the years specified. [12] Distribution by type estimated.

Source: U.S. Social Security Administration, *Annual Statistical Supplement* to the *Social Security Bulletin*; and unpublished data.

No. 544. Social Security—Beneficiaries, Annual Payments, and Average Monthly Benefit, 1990 to 2002, and by State and Other Areas, 2002

[39,832 represents 39,832,000. Number of beneficiaries in current-payment status and average monthly benefit as of December. Data based on 10-percent sample of administrative records. See also headnote, Table 543, and Appendix III]

Year, state, and other area	Number of beneficiaries (1,000) Total	Retired workers and dependents[1]	Survivors	Disabled workers and dependents	Annual payments[2] (mil. dol.) Total	Retired workers and dependents[1]	Survivors	Disabled workers and dependents	Average monthly benefit (dol.) Retired workers[3]	Disabled workers	Widows and widowers[4]
1990	39,832	28,369	7,197	4,266	247,796	172,042	50,951	24,803	603	587	557
1995	43,380	30,139	7,379	5,862	332,581	224,381	67,302	40,898	720	682	680
1999	44,599	31,035	7,038	6,526	385,525	258,885	75,309	51,331	804	755	775
2000	45,417	31,761	6,981	6,675	407,431	274,645	77,848	54,938	845	787	810
2001	45,874	32,046	6,915	6,913	431,737	290,799	81,359	59,579	875	815	841
2002, total[5]	46,453	32,362	6,870	7,220	453,601	303,983	83,973	65,645	895	834	861
United States	45,317	31,654	6,651	7,011	446,364	300,047	82,201	64,116	(NA)	(NA)	(NA)
Alabama	857	528	144	185	7,885	4,695	1,598	1,592	850	(NA)	787
Alaska	59	38	10	11	545	344	106	95	868	818	804
Arizona	835	600	107	127	8,240	5,727	1,323	1,190	910	865	890
Arkansas	529	335	83	111	4,749	2,908	896	945	827	786	768
California	4,304	3,110	588	606	42,331	29,237	7,414	5,679	901	849	894
Colorado	550	389	78	82	5,280	3,550	973	758	873	825	869
Connecticut	581	437	71	74	6,247	4,587	959	702	981	864	956
Delaware	141	100	19	22	1,445	989	247	210	936	865	923
District of Columbia	73	51	12	10	624	416	114	94	758	777	710
Florida	3,278	2,433	413	432	32,019	22,871	5,164	3,984	891	838	888
Georgia	1,147	740	184	224	10,799	6,754	2,045	1,999	866	816	802
Hawaii	193	150	23	21	1,855	1,393	273	189	883	847	827
Idaho	205	146	28	30	1,951	1,340	343	268	873	823	872
Illinois	1,862	1,330	285	248	19,186	13,131	3,728	2,327	935	862	923
Indiana	1,012	704	151	157	10,381	6,984	1,970	1,427	937	841	918
Iowa	542	395	80	68	5,348	3,711	1,029	608	893	805	881
Kansas	442	318	65	59	4,440	3,076	840	524	917	810	915
Kentucky	754	448	126	181	6,930	3,913	1,418	1,599	842	822	779
Louisiana	725	436	152	138	6,581	3,701	1,693	1,187	830	834	790
Maine	258	173	34	51	2,321	1,500	404	416	824	761	818
Maryland	744	531	115	98	7,426	5,063	1,408	955	901	868	873
Massachusetts	1,063	754	135	174	10,538	7,225	1,744	1,568	900	822	893
Michigan	1,677	1,152	257	268	17,636	11,663	3,386	2,587	964	892	924
Minnesota	755	556	105	95	7,412	5,206	1,349	858	890	816	873
Mississippi	531	311	91	129	4,641	2,652	931	1,058	814	779	738
Missouri	1,022	693	150	179	9,866	6,461	1,818	1,587	884	815	859
Montana	162	114	24	24	1,525	1,028	286	212	862	814	856
Nebraska	287	210	41	36	2,773	1,936	522	315	877	787	885
Nevada	314	232	36	46	3,121	2,199	462	460	903	897	904
New Hampshire	208	148	26	34	2,083	1,442	335	306	915	838	912
New Jersey	1,363	1,007	182	175	14,828	10,605	2,474	1,750	989	903	950
New Mexico	290	197	45	47	2,589	1,698	486	404	835	799	800
New York	3,024	2,156	402	466	31,358	21,651	5,216	4,491	949	882	913
North Carolina	1,406	941	194	271	13,284	8,685	2,171	2,428	869	813	797
North Dakota	114	82	20	13	1,056	705	240	110	834	781	828
Ohio	1,930	1,340	320	270	19,349	12,750	4,144	2,455	911	824	894
Oklahoma	606	413	99	94	5,712	3,704	1,156	852	856	817	833
Oregon	588	429	77	81	5,847	4,087	999	761	905	828	906
Pennsylvania	2,377	1,703	359	314	24,235	16,587	4,731	2,917	920	851	905
Rhode Island	191	137	22	32	1,892	1,323	280	289	895	816	901
South Carolina	719	467	107	145	6,763	4,291	1,166	1,307	868	823	791
South Dakota	138	98	22	17	1,242	842	258	142	822	770	818
Tennessee	1,028	664	164	200	9,652	6,035	1,854	1,763	866	801	808
Texas	2,731	1,865	477	389	25,804	16,782	5,598	3,424	871	826	836
Utah	251	183	35	33	2,439	1,719	432	288	900	824	919
Vermont	107	74	14	18	1,022	689	173	160	883	801	862
Virginia	1,072	732	158	182	10,284	6,739	1,883	1,663	875	835	822
Washington	874	634	114	126	8,907	6,212	1,498	1,197	932	847	922
West Virginia	399	236	74	89	3,874	2,136	891	847	882	877	825
Wisconsin	915	674	125	117	9,239	6,543	1,632	1,064	917	828	906
Wyoming	79	58	10	11	777	543	131	103	895	838	888
Puerto Rico	688	380	120	188	4,509	2,235	909	1,365	592	713	528
Guam	12	8	2	2	77	47	19	11	624	741	616
American Samoa	5	2	1	2	32	10	10	12	539	622	473
Virgin Islands	15	11	2	2	118	83	19	16	766	829	671
Northern Mariana Islands	2	1	(Z)	(Z)	9	5	3	1	470	394	388
Abroad	414	306	92	16	2,492	1,556	812	124	523	718	573

NA Not available. Z Fewer than 500. [1] Includes special benefits for persons aged 72 and over not insured under regular or transitional provisions of Social Security Act. [2] Unnegotiated checks not deducted. 1990 and 1995 include lump-sum payments to survivors of deceased workers. [3] Excludes persons with special benefits. [4] Nondisabled only. [5] Includes those with state or area unknown.

Source: U.S. Social Security Administration, *Annual Statistical Supplement to the Social Security Bulletin.*

No. 545. Public Employee Retirement Systems—Participants and Finances: 1980 to 2001

[For fiscal year of retirement system, except data for the Thrift Savings Plan are for calendar year (4,629 represents 4,629,000)]

Retirement plan	Unit	1980	1990	1995	1996	1997	1998	1999	2000	2001, proj.
TOTAL PARTICIPANTS [1]										
Federal retirement systems:										
Defined benefit:										
Civil Service Retirement System	1,000	4,629	4,167	3,731	3,663	3,518	3,423	3,362	(NA)	(NA)
Federal Employees Retirement System [2]	1,000	(X)	1,180	1,512	1,615	1,679	1,757	1,879	(NA)	(NA)
Military Service Retirement System [3]	1,000	3,380	3,763	3,387	3,372	3,367	3,368	3,374	3,397	3,418
Thrift Savings Plan [4]	1,000	(X)	1,625	2,195	2,254	2,303	2,300	2,400	(NA)	2,600
State and local retirement systems [5,6]	1,000	(NA)	16,858	14,734	15,153	15,194	16,215	16,195	16,834	17,021
ACTIVE PARTICIPANTS										
Federal retirement systems:										
Defined benefit:										
Civil Service Retirement System	1,000	2,700	1,826	1,525	1,343	1,189	1,099	1,042	(NA)	(NA)
Federal Employees Retirement System [2]	1,000	(X)	1,136	1,318	1,447	1,497	1,547	1,640	(NA)	(NA)
Military Service Retirement System [3]	1,000	2,050	2,130	1,572	1,525	1,491	1,459	1,438	1,437	1,438
Thrift Savings Plan [4]	1,000	(X)	1,419	1,930	1,987	2,011	1,800	1,900	(NA)	1,900
State and local retirement systems [5,6]	1,000	(NA)	11,345	12,524	13,051	12,817	13,059	13,472	13,917	13,977
ASSETS										
Total	Bil. dol.	258	1,047	1,655	1,854	2,110	2,403	2,644	2,943	2,970
Federal retirement systems	Bil. dol.	73	326	537	581	631	686	738	774	812
Defined benefit	Bil. dol.	73	318	502	534	570	608	643	679	711
Civil Service Retirement System	Bil. dol.	73	220	311	329	344	361	376	390	403
Federal Employees Retirement System [2]	Bil. dol.	(X)	18	60	70	83	97	111	126	141
Military Service Retirement System [3]	Bil. dol.	(7)	80	131	135	143	150	156	163	167
Thrift Savings Plan [4]	Bil. dol.	(X)	8	35	47	61	77	95	98	101
State and local retirement systems [5]	Bil. dol.	185	721	1,118	1,273	1,479	1,717	1,906	2,169	2,158
CONTRIBUTIONS										
Total	Bil. dol.	83	103	127	129	139	137	142	143	146
Federal retirement systems	Bil. dol.	19	61	67	66	73	73	75	78	81
Defined benefit	Bil. dol.	19	59	61	60	66	65	67	69	71
Civil Service Retirement System	Bil. dol.	19	28	31	32	33	33	33	33	34
Federal Employees Retirement System [2]	Bil. dol.	(X)	4	6	6	7	6	8	8	9
Military Service Retirement System [3]	Bil. dol.	(7)	27	24	22	26	26	26	28	28
Thrift Savings Plan [4]	Bil. dol.	(X)	2	6	6	7	8	8	9	10
State and local retirement systems [5]	Bil. dol.	64	42	60	63	66	64	67	65	65
BENEFITS										
Total	Bil. dol.	39	89	125	135	142	152	160	172	185
Federal retirement systems	Bil. dol.	27	53	66	70	73	76	78	81	84
Defined benefit	Bil. dol.	27	53	65	69	72	74	76	78	81
Civil Service Retirement System	Bil. dol.	15	31	37	39	41	42	43	44	46
Federal Employees Retirement System [2]	Bil. dol.	(X)	(Z)	1	1	1	1	1	1	1
Military Service Retirement System [3]	Bil. dol.	12	22	28	29	30	31	32	33	34
Thrift Savings Plan [4]	Bil. dol.	(X)	(Z)	1	1	1	2	2	3	3
State and local retirement systems [5]	Bil. dol.	12	36	59	65	69	76	82	91	101

NA Not available. X Not applicable. Z Less than $500 million. [1] Includes active, separated, vested, retired employees, and survivors. [2] The Federal Employees Retirement System was established June 6, 1986. [3] Includes nondisability and disability retirees, surviving families, and all active personnel with the exception of active reserves. [4] The Thrift Savings Plan (a defined contribution plan) was established April 1, 1987. [5] Excludes state and local plans that are fully supported by employee contributions. [6] Not adjusted for double counting of individuals participating in more than one plan. [7] The Military Retirement System was unfunded until October 1, 1984.

Source: Employee Benefit Research Institute, Washington, DC, EBRI Databook on Employee Benefits, Fourth Edition, and unpublished data (copyright). See also <http://www.ebri.org/>.

No. 546. Federal Civil Service Retirement: 1980 to 2002

[As of Sept. 30 or for year ending Sept. 30 (2,720 represents 2,720,000). Covers both Civil Service Retirement System and Federal Employees Retirement System]

Item	Unit	1980	1990	1995	1997	1998	1999	2000	2001	2002
Employees covered [1]	1,000	2,720	2,945	2,668	2,681	2,658	2,668	2,764	2,655	2,654
Annuitants, total	1,000	1,675	2,143	2,311	2,352	2,369	2,368	2,376	2,383	2,383
Age and service	1,000	905	1,288	1,441	1,474	1,488	1,491	1,501	1,509	1,513
Disability	1,000	343	297	263	257	253	246	242	239	236
Survivors	1,000	427	558	607	621	628	631	633	635	634
Receipts, total [2]	Mil. dol.	24,389	52,689	65,684	70,227	72,156	74,522	75,967	77,949	80,069
Employee contributions	Mil. dol	3,686	4,501	4,498	4,358	4,274	4,381	4,637	4,593	4,475
Federal government contributions	Mil. dol	15,562	27,368	33,130	35,386	36,188	36,561	37,722	38,442	39,692
Disbursements, total [3]	Mil. dol.	14,977	31,416	38,435	41,722	43,058	43,932	45,194	47,356	48,970
Age and service annuitants [4]	Mil. dol	12,639	26,495	32,070	34,697	35,806	36,492	37,546	39,397	40,758
Survivors	Mil. dol	1,912	4,366	5,864	6,518	6,763	6,978	7,210	7,533	7,790
Average monthly benefit:										
Age and service	Dollars	992	1,369	1,643	1,749	1,796	1,830	1,885	1,967	2,031
Disability	Dollars	723	1,008	1,164	1,204	1,216	1,221	1,240	1,269	1,286
Survivors	Dollars	392	653	819	881	905	923	952	992	1,024
Cash and security holdings	Bil. dol.	73.7	238.0	366.2	422.2	451.3	481.3	508.1	542.6	573.7

[1] Excludes employees in leave without pay status. [2] Includes interest on investments. [3] Includes refunds, death claims, and administration. [4] Includes disability annuitants.

Source: U.S. Office of Personnel Management, Civil Service Retirement and Disability Trust Fund Annual Report.

No. 547. State and Local Government Retirement Systems—Beneficiaries and Finances: 1990 to 2001

[In billions of dollars, except as indicated (4,026 represents 4,026,000). For fiscal years closed during the 12 months ending June 30]

Year and level of government	Number of beneficiaries (1,000)	Receipts Total	Employee contributions	Government contributions State	Government contributions Local	Earnings of investments	Benefits and withdrawals Total	Benefits	Withdrawals	Cash and security holdings
1990: All systems	4,026	111.3	13.9	14.0	18.6	64.9	38.4	36.0	2.4	721
State-administered	3,232	89.2	11.6	14.0	11.5	52.0	29.6	27.6	2.0	575
Locally administered	794	22.2	2.2	(Z)	7.0	12.9	8.8	8.4	0.4	145
1995: All systems	4,979	148.8	18.6	16.6	24.4	89.2	61.5	58.8	2.7	1,118
State-administered	4,025	123.3	15.7	16.2	15.4	76.0	48.0	45.8	2.2	914
Locally administered	954	25.5	2.9	0.4	9.0	13.3	13.5	13.0	0.5	204
2000: All systems	6,292	297.0	25.0	17.5	22.6	231.9	95.7	91.3	4.4	2,169
State-administered	4,786	247.4	20.7	17.2	16.7	192.8	76.0	72.2	3.8	1,798
Locally administered	1,506	49.7	4.3	0.4	5.9	39.1	19.8	19.1	0.7	371
2001: All systems	7,322	145.5	26.6	17.3	21.1	80.5	111.0	99.6	4.2	2,166
State-administered	4,931	106.0	22.1	16.8	153.8	51.7	88.7	79.7	3.5	1,790
Locally administered	2,391	39.5	4.5	0.5	5.8	28.7	22.3	20.0	0.7	376

Z Less than $50 million.

Source: U.S. Census Bureau, Through 1995, *Finances of Employee-Retirement Systems of State and Local Governments*, Series GF, No. 2, annual; beginning 1999, "Federal, State, and Local Governments, State and Local Government Public Employee Retirement Systems"; <http://www.census.gov/govs/www/retire.html>.

No. 548. Private Pension Plans—Summary by Type of Plan: 1990 to 1998

[712.3 represents 712,300. "Pension plan" is defined by the Employee Retirement Income Security Act (ERISA) as "any plan, fund, or program which was heretofore or is hereafter established or maintained by an employer or an employee organization, or by both, to the extent that such plan (a) provides retirement income to employees, or (b) results in a deferral of income by employees for periods extending to the termination of covered employment or beyond, regardless of the method of calculating the contributions made to the plan, the method of calculating the benefits under the plan, or the method of distributing benefits from the plan." A defined benefit plan provides a definite benefit formula for calculating benefit amounts - such as a flat amount per year of service or a percentage of salary times years of service. A defined contribution plan is a pension plan in which the contributions are made to an individual account for each employee. The retirement benefit is dependent upon the account balance at retirement. The balance depends upon amounts contributed, investment experience, and, in the case of profit sharing plans, amounts which may be allocated to the account due to forfeitures by terminating employees. Employee Stock Ownership Plans (ESOP) and 401(k) plans (see Table 553) are included among defined contribution plans. Data are based on Form 5500 series reports filed with the Internal Revenue Service]

Item	Unit	Total 1990	Total 1995	Total 1997	Total 1998	Defined contribution plan 1990	Defined contribution plan 1995	Defined contribution plan 1997	Defined contribution plan 1998	Defined benefit plan 1990	Defined benefit plan 1995	Defined benefit plan 1997	Defined benefit plan 1998
Number of plans [1]	1,000	712.3	693.4	720.0	730.0	599.2	623.9	660.5	673.6	113.1	69.5	59.5	56.4
Total participants [2,3]	Mil.	76.9	87.5	95.0	99.5	38.1	47.7	54.6	57.9	38.8	39.7	40.4	41.6
Active participants [2,4]	Mil.	61.8	66.2	70.7	73.3	35.5	42.7	48.0	50.3	26.3	23.5	22.7	23.0
Assets [5]	Mil.	1,674.1	2,723.7	3,553.8	4,021.8	712.2	1,321.7	1,818.2	2,085.3	961.9	1,402.1	1,735.6	1,936.6
Contributions [6]	Bil. dol.	98.8	158.8	177.9	201.9	75.8	117.4	148.1	166.9	23.0	41.4	29.9	35.0
Benefits [7]	Bil. dol.	129.4	183.0	232.5	273.1	63.0	97.9	135.3	161.9	66.4	85.1	97.2	111.2

[1] Excludes all plans covering only one participant.   [2] Includes double counting of workers in more than one plan.   [3] Total participants include active participants, vested separated workers, and retirees.   [4] Any workers currently in employment covered by a plan and who are earning or retaining credited service under a plan. Includes any nonvested former employees who have not yet incurred breaks in service.   [5] Asset amounts shown exclude funds held by life insurance companies under allocated group insurance contracts for payment of retirement benefits. These excluded funds make up roughly 10 to 15 percent of total private fund assets.   [6] Includes both employer and employee contributions.   [7] Benefits paid directly from trust and premium payments made from plan to insurance carriers. Excludes benefits paid directly by insurance carriers.

Source: U.S. Dept. of Labor, Pension and Welfare Benefits Administration, *Private Pension Plan Bulletin*, No. 10, winter 2001, and unpublished data.

No. 549. Percent of Workers Participating in Retirement Benefits by Worker Characteristics: 2000

[Based on National Compensation Survey, a sample survey of 3,168 private industry establishments of all sizes, representing over 107 million workers; see Appendix III. See also Table 648]

Characteristic	Total	Defined benefit	Defined contribution	Characteristic	Total	Defined benefit	Defined contribution
Total	48	19	36	Blue-collar and service employees	39	17	27
Professional, technical, and related employees	66	27	53	Full time [1]	55	22	42
Clerical and sales employees	50	18	40	Part time [1]	18	6	12
				Union [2]	83	69	38
				Nonunion [2]	44	14	36

[1] Employees are classified as working either a full-time or part-time schedule based on the definition used by each establishment.   [2] Union workers are those whose wages are determined through collective bargaining.

Source: U.S. Bureau of Labor Statistics, *News*, USDL 01-473, December 19, 2002.

No. 550. Defined Benefit Retirement Plans—Selected Features: 2000

[In percent, except as indicated (19,225 represents 19,225,000). Covers full-time employees in private industry. Based on National Compensation Survey, a sample survey of 1,436 private industry establishments of all sizes, representing over 107 million workers; see Appendix III. See also Table 648]

Feature	All employees	Professional, technical, and related	Clerical and sales	Blue-collar and service
Full-time employees with defined benefit plan (1,000)	19,225	5,794	5,179	8,252
Plan provisions:				
Benefits based on earnings	61	59	67	60
Early retirement benefits available	77	69	78	81
Availability of lump sum benefits at retirement	43	44	51	37
Benefit formula:				
Percent of terminal earnings	48	47	48	50
Percent of career earnings	13	12	19	10
Dollar amount formula	14	9	9	21
Percent of contribution formula	(Z)	-	-	1
Cash account [1]	23	31	23	18
Other	1	1	2	1
Requirements for normal retirement [2]				
No age requirement	11	15	10	8
Less than 20 years of service	5	11	3	1
30 years of service	6	4	7	7
At age 55	4	5	7	2
At age 60	10	16	7	8
At age 62	21	18	16	26
At age 65	49	41	55	51
Sum of age plus service [3]	3	4	5	2

- Represents no employees in this category or data do not meet publication criteria.   Z Less than 0.5 percent.   [1] Cash balance retirement plans are a defined benefit plan in which an account is maintained for each participant, with employer contributions based on employee earnings, plus interest, being credited to that account. Cash balance plans generally do not have provisions for many of the features found in traditional defined benefit plans. Due to the increase in the incidence of cash balance plans, the prevalence of some defined benefit plan provisions has declined from earlier surveys.   [2] Normal retirement is defined as the point at which the participant could retire and immediately receive all accrued benefits by virtue of service and earnings, without reduction due to age. If a plan had alternative age and service requirements, the earliest age and associated service were tabulated; if one alternative did not specify an age, it was the requirement tabulated. Some age and service requirements are not shown separately.   [3] In some plans, participants must also satisfy a minimum age or service requirement.

Source: U.S. Bureau of Labor Statistics, *National Compensation Survey: Employee Benefits in Private Industry in the United States, 2000*. U.S. Department of Labor Bulletin 2555, January 2003.

No. 551. Pension Plan Coverage of Workers by Selected Characteristics: 2001

[65,445 represents 65,445,000. Covers workers as of March 2001 who had earnings in 2000. Based on Current Population Survey; see text, Section 1, and Appendix III]

Sex and age	Number with coverage (1,000)				Percent of total workers			
	Total [1]	White	Black	Hispanic [2]	Total [1]	White	Black	Hispanic [2]
Total	65,445	55,270	6,951	4,720	43.2	43.8	40.8	26.3
Male	35,916	30,960	3,222	2,634	44.7	45.6	40.8	25.2
Under 65 years old	35,140	30,274	3,166	2,590	45.5	46.5	41.3	25.2
15 to 24 years old	1,732	1,462	191	294	13.5	13.6	13.7	13.1
25 to 44 years old	18,417	15,636	1,807	1,546	48.4	49.3	45.3	25.6
45 to 64 years old	14,990	13,176	1,168	750	57.0	58.1	51.4	37.2
65 years old and over	776	687	56	44	24.9	24.8	23.0	28.7
Female	29,529	24,309	3,729	2,085	41.1	41.7	40.9	27.9
Under 65 years old	29,005	23,853	3,673	2,057	42.1	42.5	41.2	27.9
15 to 24 years old	1,403	1,128	205	169	11.9	11.7	13.0	10.9
25 to 44 years old	15,117	12,160	2,105	1,261	45.5	45.9	44.7	30.9
45 to 64 years old	12,485	10,565	1,364	627	52.2	52.6	52.0	36.1
65 years old and over	525	456	56	28	22.0	21.7	25.8	29.0

[1] Includes other races, not shown separately.   [2] Hispanic persons may be of any race.

Source: U.S. Census Bureau, "Table NC8. Pension Plan Coverage of Workers by Selected Characteristics, Gender, Race and Hispanic Origin, and Poverty Status: 2001"; published March 2002; <http://ferret.bls.census.gov/macro/032002/noncash/toc.htm>.

No. 552. U.S. Households Owning IRAs: 2001 and 2002

[41.9 represents 41,900,000. Incidence of IRA ownership is based on an annual tracking survey of 3,000 randomly selected, representative U.S. households conducted in May 2002]

Type of IRA	Millions of U.S. households 2001	Millions of U.S. households 2002 [1]	Percent of U.S. households 2001	Percent of U.S. households 2002 [1]
Any type of IRA [2]	[3]41.9	42.0	[3]39.7	39.5
Traditional IRA	34.1	34.8	32.4	32.7
Roth IRA	11.9	12.9	11.3	12.1
SIMPLE IRA, SEP-IRA, or SAR-SEP IRA	8.1	8.3	7.7	7.8

[1] The number of U.S. households owning IRAs in 2002 is based on the U.S. Census Bureau's most recent estimate of 106.4 million total U.S. households. [2] Excludes ownership of Coverdell Education Savings Accounts, which were referred to as Education IRAs before July 2001. [3] Revised.

Source: Investment Company Institute, Washington, DC, Fundamentals, Investment Company Institute Research in Brief, "IRA Ownership in 2002"; Vol. 11, No. 3, September 2002 <http://www.ici.org> (copyright).

No. 553. 401(k) Plans—Summary: 1985 to 1998

[10,339 represents 10,339,000. A 401(k) plan is a qualified retirement plan that allows participants to have a portion of their compensation (otherwise payable in cash) contributed pretax to a retirement account on their behalf]

Item	1985	1990	1993	1994	1995	1996	1997	1998
Number of plans [1]	29,869	97,614	154,527	174,945	200,813	230,808	265,251	300,593
Active participants [2] (1,000)	10,339	19,548	23,138	26,206	28,061	30,843	33,865	37,114
Assets (bil. dol.)	144	385	616	675	864	1,062	1,264	1,541
Contributions (bil. dol.)	24	49	69	76	87	104	116	135
Benefits (bil. dol.)	16	32	44	51	62	78	93	121
Percentage of all private defined contribution plans:								
Assets	34	54	58	62	65	68	73	74
Contributions	46	65	68	72	74	78	78	81
Benefits	35	51	57	62	64	67	69	75

[1] Excludes single-participant plans. [2] May include some employees who are eligible to participate in the plan but have not elected to join. 401(k) participants may participate in one or more additional plans.

Source: Employee Benefit Research Institute, Washington, DC, EBRI Databook on Employee Benefits, Fourth Edition, and unpublished data (copyright).

No. 554. 401(k) Plans—Selected Features: 2000

[In percent, except as indicated (30,178 represents 30,178,000). Covers full-time employees in private industry. Based on National Compensation Survey, a sample survey of private industry establishments of all sizes, representing millions of workers; see Appendix III. See also Table 648]

Feature	All employees	Professional, technical, and related	Clerical and sales	Blue-collar and service
Full-time employees with 401(k) plan (1,000)	30,178	9,969	9,061	11,147
Transfers/rollovers allowed [1]	70	73	68	69
MAXIMUM PRETAX EMPLOYEE CONTRIBUTIONS [2]				
Percent of employee earnings	84	85	83	85
Specified dollar amount	1	1	1	1
Up to the Internal Revenue Code limit	15	14	16	14
Average maximum pretax contribution as percent of earnings [3]	15.3	15.0	15.1	15.7
INVESTMENT CHOICES				
Employee permitted to choose investments for employee contributions	88	89	88	89
Employee permitted to choose investments for employer contributions	64	65	62	63
Employee not permitted to choose investments	32	32	32	32
Not determinable	4	3	6	4

[1] Participants are allowed to transfer/rollover contributions and earnings from a previous employer's plan. [2] Includes contributions that are not matched by the employer. If maximum contributions vary, such as by length of service, the highest possible contribution was tabulated. [3] The average is presented for all covered workers; averages exclude workers without the plan provision.

Source: U.S. Bureau of Labor Statistics, National Compensation Survey: Employee Benefits in Private Industry in the United States, 2000. See also <http://146.142.4.22/ncs/home.htm>.

Social Insurance and Human Services 367

No. 555. State Unemployment Insurance by State and Other Area: 2002

[10,088 represents 10,088,000. See headnote, Table 556. For state data on insured unemployment, see Table 628]

State and other area	Beneficiaries, first payments (1,000)	Benefits paid (mil. dol.)	Avg. weekly unemployment benefits (dol.)	State and other area	Beneficiaries, first payments (1,000)	Benefits paid (mil. dol.)	Avg. weekly unemployment benefits (dol.)
Total	10,088	41,985	(NA)	MT	26	71	187
				NE	44	124	212
AL	145	309	167	NV	86	343	232
AK	49	108	193	NH	24	117	260
AZ	125	321	176	NJ	349	2,092	331
AR	105	306	223	NM	37	136	207
CA	1,402	6,042	217	NY	618	3,340	275
CO	114	541	313	NC	373	1,096	259
CT	162	712	287	ND	16	47	219
DE	32	118	228	OH	355	1,486	251
DC	18	131	290	OK	70	253	234
FL	358	1,224	225	OR	175	863	277
GA	260	780	239	PA	561	2,639	291
HI	30	161	297	RI	44	204	304
ID	60	181	232	SC	146	424	208
IL	466	2,447	280	SD	12	31	198
IN	199	713	255	TN	220	608	210
IA	111	363	255	TX	544	2,241	259
KS	83	359	276	UT	64	252	275
KY	133	503	246	VT	28	98	250
LA	99	303	197	VA	173	754	311
ME	33	122	224	WA	281	1,562	329
MD	130	500	241	WV	57	165	215
MA	300	1,966	360	WI	330	982	247
MI	472	1,882	276	WY	18	40	232
MN	171	861	318				
MS	77	193	168	PR	116	257	107
MO	185	592	205	VI	3	19	289

NA Not available.

Source: U.S. Employment and Training Administration, *Unemployment Insurance Financial Data Handbook*.

No. 556. State Unemployment Insurance—Summary: 1980 to 2002

[3,356 represents 3,356,000. Includes unemployment compensation for state and local government employees where covered by state law]

Item	Unit	1980	1990	1995	1996	1997	1998	1999	2000	2001	2002
Insured unemployment, avg. weekly	1,000	3,356	2,522	2,572	2,596	2,323	2,222	2,188	2,110	2,974	3,585
Percent of covered employment [1]	Percent	3.9	2.4	2.3	2.3	2.0	1.9	1.8	1.7	2.3	(NA)
Percent of civilian unemployed	Percent	43.9	35.8	34.7	35.9	34.5	35.8	38.0	38.0	45.0	44.0
Unemployment benefits, avg. weekly	Dollars	100	161	187	189	193	200	212	221	238	257
Percent of weekly wage	Percent	36.6	36.0	35.5	34.5	33.5	32.9	33.1	32.9	34.6	(NA)
Weeks compensated	Million	149.0	116.2	118.3	119.0	106.6	101.4	100.6	96.0	136.3	166.3
Beneficiaries, first payments	1,000	9,992	8,629	8,035	7,990	7,325	7,332	6,951	7,033	9,877	10,088
Average duration of benefits [2]	Weeks	14.9	13.4	14.7	14.9	14.6	13.8	14.5	13.7	13.8	16.5
Claimants exhausting benefits	1,000	3,072	2,323	2,662	2,739	2,485	2,266	2,300	2,144	2,827	4,416
Percent of first payment [3]	Percent	33.2	29.4	34.3	33.4	32.8	31.8	31.4	31.8	34.1	42.5
Contributions collected [4]	Bil. dol.	11.4	15.2	22.0	21.6	21.2	19.8	19.2	19.9	19.7	19.7
Benefits paid	Bil. dol.	14.2	18.1	21.2	21.8	19.7	19.4	20.3	20.5	31.6	42.0
Funds available for benefits [5]	Bil. dol.	6.6	37.9	35.4	38.6	43.8	48.0	50.3	54.1	46.6	35.7
Average employer contribution rate [6]	Percent	2.37	1.95	2.44	2.28	2.13	1.92	1.77	1.75	1.71	(NA)

NA Not available. [1] Insured unemployment as percent of average covered employment in preceding year. [2] Weeks compensated divided by first payment. [3] Based on first payments for 12-month period ending June 30. [4] Contributions from employers; also employees in states which tax workers. [5] End of year. Sum of balances in state clearing accounts, benefit-payment accounts, and state accounts in Federal unemployment trust funds. [6] As percent of taxable wages.

Source: U.S. Employment and Training Administration, *Unemployment Insurance Financial Data Handbook*.

No. 557. Persons With Work Disability by Selected Characteristics: 2002

[In thousands, except percent (18,120 represents 18,120,000). As of March. Covers civilian noninstitutional population and members of Armed Forces living off post or with their families on post. Persons are classified as having a work disability if they (1) have a health problem or disability which prevents them from working or which limits the kind or amount of work they can do; (2) have a service-connected disability or ever retired or left a job for health reasons; (3) did not work in survey reference week or previous year because of long-term illness or disability; or (4) are under age 65, and are covered by medicare or receive supplemental security income. Based on Current Population Survey; see text, Section 1, and Appendix III]

Age and participation status in assistance programs	Total [1]	Male	Female	White	Black	Hispanic [2]
Persons with work disability	18,120	8,735	9,385	13,800	3,449	1,884
16 to 24 years old	1,264	630	634	878	330	177
25 to 34 years old	2,284	1,082	1,202	1,683	472	322
35 to 44 years old	3,839	1,855	1,984	2,860	799	396
45 to 54 years old	5,054	2,479	2,575	3,848	965	484
55 to 64 years old	5,678	2,688	2,989	4,530	882	505
Percent work disabled of total population	9.9	9.7	10.1	9.2	15.3	7.9
16 to 24 years old	3.6	3.6	3.6	3.2	6.4	2.9
25 to 34 years old	5.9	5.7	6.2	5.5	9.4	4.6
35 to 44 years old	8.7	8.6	8.8	8.0	14.7	7.3
45 to 54 years old	12.8	12.9	12.7	11.7	21.6	14.3
55 to 64 years old	22.0	21.7	22.1	20.4	35.4	26.0
Percent of work disabled—						
Receiving social security income	32.2	33.3	32.2	33.8	28.0	26.8
Receiving food stamps	16.7	12.9	20.3	13.9	26.9	20.7
Covered by medicaid	66.1	70.3	62.3	69.9	52.2	57.1
Residing in public housing	6.7	5.1	8.2	4.8	14.2	7.8
Residing in subsidized housing	3.5	2.4	4.6	2.9	6.2	4.9

[1] Includes other races not shown separately.   [2] Hispanic persons may be of any race.

Source: U.S. Census Bureau, unpublished data.

No. 558. Vocational Rehabilitation—Summary: 1980 to 1999

[For year ending September 30 (1,076 represents $1,076,000,000). Includes Puerto Rico, Guam, Virgin Islands, American Samoa, Northern Mariana Islands, and the Republic of Palau. State agencies, using matching state and federal funds, provide vocational rehabilitation services to eligible individuals with disabilities to enable them to prepare for and engage in gainful employment. Services may include counseling, guidance and work related placement services, physical and mental restoration, training and rehabilitation technology]

Item	Unit	1980	1985	1990	1994	1995	1996	1997	1998	1999
Federal and state expenditures [1]	Mil. dol.	1,076	1,452	1,910	2,517	2,714	2,844	3,046	3,081	3,138
Federal expenditures	Mil. dol.	817	1,100	1,525	1,891	2,054	2,104	2,164	2,232	2,287
Applicants processed for program eligibility	1,000	717	594	625	675	625	578	617	624	608
Percent accepted into program	Percent	58	60	57	72	76	76	79	75	80
Total persons rehabilitated [2]	1,000	277	228	216	203	210	213	212	224	232
Rehabilitation rate [3]	Percent	64	64	62	49	46	61	61	62	63
Severely disabled persons rehabilitated [2][4]	1,000	143	135	146	149	159	166	168	185	197
Rehabilitation rate [3]	Percent	61	62	62	49	46	60	60	61	62
Percent of total persons rehabilitated	Percent	51	59	68	74	76	78	79	83	85
Persons served, total [5]	1,000	1,095	932	938	1,194	1,250	1,226	1,267	1,211	1,202
Persons served, severely disabled [4][5]	1,000	606	581	640	882	940	951	1,005	988	1,015
Percent of total persons served	Percent	55	62	68	74	75	78	79	82	84

[1] Includes expenditures only under the basic support provisions of the Rehabilitation Act.   [2] Persons successfully placed into gainful employment.   [3] Persons rehabilitated as a percent of all active case closures (whether rehabilitated or not); beginning 1996, as a percent of persons who required services.   [4] An individual with a severe disability is an individual whose severe physical or mental impairment seriously limits one or more functional capacities in terms of an employment outcome, and whose vocational rehabilitation can be expected to require multiple vocational rehabilitation services over an extended period of time.   [5] Includes active cases accepted for rehabilitation services during year plus active cases on hand at beginning of year.

Source: U.S. Dept. of Education, Rehabilitation Services Administration, *Caseload Statistics of State Vocational Rehabilitation Agencies in Fiscal Years*, and *State Vocational Rehabilitation Agency Program Data in Fiscal Years*, both annual.

No. 559. Workers' Compensation Payments: 1980 to 2001

[In billions of dollars, except as indicated (79 represents 79,000,000). See headnote, Table 560]

Item	1980	1990	1994	1995	1996	1997	1998	1999	2000	2001
Workers covered [1] (mil.)	79	106	109	113	115	118	122	124	127	127
Premium amounts paid [2]	22.3	53.1	60.5	57.1	55.3	51.6	51.7	54.0	58.2	62.8
Private carriers [2]	15.7	35.1	34.0	31.6	30.5	30.0	30.4	32.0	35.3	36.8
State funds	3.0	8.0	11.2	10.5	10.2	8.0	7.9	8.0	8.6	11
Federal programs [3]	1.1	2.2	2.5	2.6	2.6	2.0	2.1	2.9	2.2	2.3
Self-insurers	2.4	7.9	12.8	12.5	12.0	11.8	11.3	11.8	12.0	12.7
Annual benefits paid [2]	13.6	38.2	44.6	43.4	41.8	41.4	42.5	44.5	47.0	48.7
By private carriers [2]	7.0	22.2	22.3	21.1	20.4	21.6	23.1	24.6	26.4	26.9
From state funds [4]	4.3	8.8	10.8	11.0	10.6	7.3	7.2	7.3	7.6	8.1
Employers' self-insurance [5]	2.3	7.2	11.5	11.2	10.8	10.6	10.2	10.6	10.8	11.5
Type of benefit:										
Medical/hospitalization	3.9	15.2	17.2	16.7	16.5	17.2	17.9	19.1	20.6	21.9
Compensation payments	9.7	23.1	27.5	26.7	25.3	24.2	24.6	25.4	26.4	26.8
Percent of covered payroll: [1]										
Workers' compensation costs [6] [7]	1.96	2.18	2.05	1.83	1.66	1.49	1.37	1.34	1.34	1.41
Benefits [7]	1.07	1.57	1.51	1.39	1.26	1.14	1.08	1.06	1.03	1.04

[1] Data for years 1980 and 1985 not comparable with later years.   [2] Premium and benefit amounts include estimated payments under insurance policy deductible provisions. Deductible benefits are allocated to private carriers and state funds.   [3] Includes federal employer compensation program only.   [4] Net cash and medical benefits paid by competitive and exclusive state funds and by federal workers' compensation programs, including black lung benefit program.   [5] Cash and medical benefits paid by self-insurers, plus value of medical benefits paid by employers carrying workers' compensation policies that exclude standard medical coverage.   [6] Premiums written by private carriers and state funds and benefits paid by self-insurers increased by 5-10 percent from 1980 to 1990 and by 11 percent for 1994-2000 for administrative costs. Also includes benefits paid and administrative costs of federal system for government employees.   [7] Excludes programs financed from general revenue—black lung benefits and supplemental pensions in some states.

Source: 1980-1990, U.S. Social Security Administration, *Annual Statistical Supplement* to the *Social Security Bulletin*. Beginning 1994, National Academy of Social Insurance, Washington, DC, *Workers' Compensation: Benefits, Coverage, and Costs*, annual.

No. 560. Workers' Compensation Payments by State: 1997 to 2001

[In millions of dollars (42,313 represents $42,313,000,000). Calendar-year data, except fiscal-year data for federal civilian and other programs and for some states with state funds. Payments represent compensation and medical benefits and include insurance losses paid by private insurance carriers (compiled from state workers' compensation agencies and A.M. Best Co); disbursements of state funds (compiled from the A.M. Best Co. and state workers' compensation agencies); and self-insurance payments, based on information from the National Association of Insurance Commissioners and the source's estimates. Includes benefit payments under Longshore and Harbor Workers' Compensation Act for states in which such payments are made]

State	1997	1998	1999	2000	2001	State	1997	1998	1999	2000	2001
Total	42,313	43,355	45,197	47,684	49,354	Montana	143	137	146	170	173
						Nebraska	217	164	198	211	237
Alabama	530	602	551	529	563	Nevada	324	331	384	361	381
Alaska	128	127	130	146	171	New Hampshire	174	170	190	182	215
Arizona	450	433	466	515	393	New Jersey	1,080	1,097	1,152	1,198	1,198
Arkansas	170	171	173	194	201	New Mexico	136	128	136	146	162
California	7,074	7,366	7,852	8,968	9,604	New York	2,620	2,601	2,796	2,909	2,978
Colorado	820	811	739	835	581	North Carolina	687	810	814	853	868
Connecticut	732	715	737	667	661	North Dakota	68	69	70	74	80
Delaware	143	147	133	146	145	Ohio	2,036	2,077	2,039	2,099	2,249
District of Columbia	88	90	90	89	92	Oklahoma	578	536	497	485	497
Florida	2,443	2,538	2,768	2,545	2,639	Oregon	417	431	384	412	456
Georgia	861	889	896	996	1,067	Pennsylvania	2,492	2,418	2,467	2,403	2,440
Hawaii	255	233	222	231	252	Rhode Island	113	109	111	109	115
Idaho	153	164	169	179	197	South Carolina	459	467	512	597	532
Illinois	1,764	1,838	1,953	2,049	2,116	South Dakota	70	67	73	67	75
Indiana	446	481	511	546	528	Tennessee	473	551	586	642	683
Iowa	286	304	309	352	396	Texas	1,477	1,592	1,875	2,005	2,043
Kansas	314	319	326	342	340	Utah	170	189	196	188	209
Kentucky	451	421	478	479	525	Vermont	86	91	106	112	105
Louisiana	440	442	465	494	502	Virginia	562	658	629	681	665
Maine	282	254	266	267	264	Washington	1,218	1,287	1,395	1,528	1,638
Maryland	717	691	714	730	787	West Virginia	614	644	687	690	712
Massachusetts	747	729	733	828	764	Wisconsin	670	704	724	768	922
Michigan	1,332	1,367	1,393	1,474	1,478	Wyoming	70	73	75	83	98
Minnesota	739	737	745	798	908						
Mississippi	231	235	254	269	271	Federal employees	1,901	2,010	2,000	2,119	2,223
Missouri	980	980	1,021	1,085	1,108	Federal total[1]	2,780	2,868	2,862	2,957	3,069

[1] Federal benefits include: those paid under the Federal Employees' Compensation Act for civilian employees; the portion of the Black Lung benefit program that is financed by employers; and a portion of benefits under the Longshore and Harbor Workers' Compensation Act that are not reflected in state data, namely, benefits paid by self-insured employers and by special funds under the LHWCA. See Appendix H of source for more information about federal programs.

Source: National Academy of Social Insurance, Washington, DC, *Workers' Compensation: Benefits, Coverage, and Costs*, annual. Also see <http://www.nasi.org/>.

No. 561. Supplemental Security Income—Recipients and Payments: 1980 to 2001

[As of December, except total payments, calendar year (4,142 represents 4,142,000). See also Appendix III]

Program	Unit	1980	1990	1995	1996	1997	1998	1999	2000	2001
Recipients, total [1]	1,000	4,142	4,817	6,514	6,614	6,495	6,566	6,557	6,602	6,688
Aged	1,000	1,808	1,454	1,446	1,413	1,363	1,332	1,308	1,289	1,264
Blind	1,000	78	84	84	82	81	80	79	79	78
Disabled	1,000	2,256	3,279	4,984	5,119	5,052	5,154	5,169	5,234	5,345
Payments, total [2]	Mil. dol	7,941	16,599	27,628	28,792	29,052	30,216	30,923	31,564	32,165
Aged	Mil. dol	2,734	3,736	4,467	4,507	4,532	4,425	4,712	4,811	4,664
Blind	Mil. dol	190	334	376	372	375	366	391	394	398
Disabled	Mil. dol	5,014	12,521	22,779	23,906	24,006	25,305	25,719	26,198	27,103
Average monthly payment, total [1]	Dollars	168	299	358	363	351	359	368	378	393
Aged	Dollars	128	213	251	261	268	277	289	299	314
Blind	Dollars	213	342	370	379	382	390	401	413	428
Disabled	Dollars	198	337	389	391	373	380	388	397	412

[1] Persons with a federal SSI payment and/or federally administered state supplementation. [2] Includes payments not distributed by reason for eligibility.

Source: U.S. Social Security Administration, *Social Security Bulletin*, quarterly and *Annual Statistical Supplement to the Social Security Bulletin*.

No. 562. Supplemental Security Income (SSI)—Recipients and Payments by State and Other Area: 1995 to 2001

[Recipients as of December; payments for calendar year (6,514 represents 6,514,000). Data cover federal SSI payments and/or federally-administered state supplementation. For explanation of methodology, see Appendix III]

State and other area	Recipients (1,000) 1995	Recipients (1,000) 2000	Payments for year (mil. dol.) 1995	Payments for year (mil. dol.) 2000	Payments for year (mil. dol.) 2001	State and other area	Recipients (1,000) 1995	Recipients (1,000) 2000	Payments for year (mil. dol.) 1995	Payments for year (mil. dol.) 2000	Payments for year (mil. dol.) 2001
Total	6,514	6,602	27,037	30,672	32,166	MO	114	112	431	471	495
						MT	14	14	53	57	61
U.S.	6,513	6,601	27,035	30,669	32,163	NE	21	21	76	85	90
AL	165	159	600	659	698	NV	21	25	79	108	120
AK	7	9	27	37	40	NH	11	12	39	49	52
AZ	73	81	288	355	382	NJ	144	146	594	672	700
AR	94	85	326	333	341	NM	45	47	166	193	205
CA	1,032	1,088	5,391	6,386	6,685	NY	589	617	2,724	3,197	3,320
CO	57	54	217	228	237	NC	191	191	639	732	769
CT	45	49	181	216	227	ND	9	8	29	30	31
DE	11	12	40	50	53	OH	248	240	1,044	1,114	1,162
DC	20	20	83	93	98	OK	74	72	266	302	316
FL	338	377	1,300	1,621	1,724	OR	47	52	183	228	246
GA	199	197	692	785	826	PA	265	284	1,159	1,367	1,464
HI	19	21	82	104	107	RI	24	28	100	130	141
ID	17	18	63	76	81	SC	111	107	384	429	446
IL	267	249	1,160	1,174	1,208	SD	14	13	47	48	51
IN	89	88	348	382	399	TN	180	164	648	664	689
IA	42	40	148	158	167	TX	404	409	1,391	1,575	1,683
KS	38	36	141	151	158	UT	20	20	80	87	93
KY	165	174	635	741	779	VT	13	13	50	51	54
LA	182	166	717	715	741	VA	130	132	471	535	555
ME	31	30	96	116	123	WA	92	101	398	484	521
MD	82	88	332	400	420	WV	68	71	276	318	335
MA	164	168	700	807	833	WI	112	85	487	357	371
MI	210	210	896	988	1,021	WY	6	6	21	23	25
MN	62	64	235	272	289						
MS	141	129	504	512	530	N. Mariana	1	1	2	3	3

Source: U.S. Social Security Administration, *Annual Statistical Supplement* to the *Social Security Bulletin*.

No. 563. Temporary Assistance for Needy Families (TANF)—Families and Recipients: 1980 to 2002

[In thousands (3,712 represents 3,712,000). Average monthly families and recipients for calendar year. Prior to TANF, the cash assistance program to families was called Aid to Families with Dependent Children (1980-1996). Under the new welfare law (Personal Responsibility and Work Opportunity Reconciliation Act of 1996), the program became TANF. See text, this section. Includes Puerto Rico, Guam, and Virgin Islands]

Year	Families	Recipients	Year	Families	Recipients	Year	Families	Recipients
1980	3,712	10,774	1988	3,749	10,915	1996	4,434	12,321
1981	3,835	11,079	1989	3,799	10,993	1997	3,740	10,376
1982	3,542	10,258	1990	4,057	11,695	1998	3,050	8,347
1983	3,686	10,761	1991	4,467	12,930	1999	2,253	6,822
1984	3,714	10,831	1992	4,829	13,773	2000	2,215	5,778
1985	3,701	10,855	1993	5,012	14,205	2001	2,104	5,359
1986	3,763	11,038	1994	5,033	14,161	2002	2,047	5,066
1987	3,776	11,027	1995	4,791	13,418			

Source: U.S. Administration for Children and Families, unpublished data.

No. 564. Temporary Assistance for Needy Families (TANF)—Recipients by State and Other Area: 2000 to 2002

[In thousands (2,215 represents 2,215,000). Average monthly families and recipients for calendar year, except as noted. See headnote, Table 563]

State and other area	Families 2000	Families 2001	Families 2002[1]	Recipients 2000	Recipients 2001	Recipients 2002[1]	State and other area	Families 2000	Families 2001	Families 2002[1]	Recipients 2000	Recipients 2001	Recipients 2002[1]
Total	2,215	2,104	2,047	5,778	5,359	5,066	MT	5	5	6	13	15	17
							NE	9	10	11	24	24	26
U.S.	2,181	2,075	2,022	5,678	5,273	4,991	NV	6	8	12	16	21	28
AL	19	18	18	45	44	42	NH	6	6	6	14	14	15
AK	7	6	6	21	17	17	NJ	50	44	42	125	110	102
AZ	33	35	42	84	85	99	NM	23	18	17	69	51	46
AR	12	12	12	29	28	27	NY	250	218	158	695	580	369
CA	489	465	459	1262	1177	1146	NC	45	43	42	98	93	89
CO	11	11	12	28	28	32	ND	3	3	3	7	8	8
CT	27	26	23	64	59	51	OH	95	84	84	235	195	189
DE	6	5	6	12	12	12	OK	14	14	15	35	35	37
DC	17	16	16	45	43	42	OR	17	17	18	38	38	42
FL	65	58	59	142	123	122	PA	88	82	80	241	214	209
GA	52	51	54	125	121	129	RI	16	15	14	44	41	38
HI	14	13	11	46	39	29	SC	18	20	21	42	48	50
ID	1	1	1	2	2	2	SD	3	3	3	7	6	7
IL	78	58	45	234	169	123	TN	57	60	64	147	158	168
IN	37	43	51	101	121	141	TX	129	130	131	347	344	333
IA	20	20	20	53	55	53	UT	8	7	8	21	19	20
KS	13	13	14	32	34	37	VT	6	5	5	16	14	13
KY	38	36	35	87	81	77	VA	31	29	30	69	65	68
LA	27	25	23	71	64	60	WA	56	54	54	148	141	136
ME	11	10	10	28	26	25	WV	13	15	16	33	41	41
MD	29	28	27	71	68	65	WI	17	18	19	38	41	46
MA	43	43	48	100	101	109	WY	1	1	-	1	1	1
MI	72	72	73	198	198	198							
MN	39	38	36	114	108	95	PR	30	26	22	88	73	63
MS	15	16	18	34	37	42	GU	3	3	3	10	10	11
MO	47	45	44	125	121	116	VI	1	1	1	3	2	2

- Represents zero. [1] January-September period only.

Source: U.S. Administration for Children and Families, unpublished data.

No. 565. Temporary Assistance for Needy Families (TANF)—Expenditures by State: 1999 and 2000

[In millions of dollars (22,585 represents $22,585,000,000), except as indicated. Represents federal and state funds expended in fiscal year]

State	1999, total	2000 Total[1]	2000 Percent federal funds	2000 Expenditures on assistance	State	1999, total	2000 Total[1]	2000 Percent federal funds	2000 Expenditures on assistance
U.S.	22,585	23,590	53	13,323	MO	317	321	54	189
AL	91	93	58	39	MT	41	44	65	24
AK	88	93	46	67	NE	116	77	63	48
AZ	240	265	65	118	NV	65	56	51	23
AR	72	112	79	31	NH	60	73	56	42
CA	6,252	6,228	53	4,761	NJ	450	322	7	226
CO	160	205	42	51	NM	130	149	73	113
CT	385	436	56	171	NY	3,652	3,498	43	2,126
DE	59	55	56	24	NC	394	435	59	140
DC	128	134	42	72	ND	33	33	72	25
FL	484	765	51	265	OH	656	987	60	394
GA	410	383	55	251	OK	151	134	54	85
HI	168	161	52	141	OR	286	256	64	128
ID	27	44	70	4	PA	1,038	891	54	496
IL	840	880	50	280	RI	164	167	51	111
IN	188	342	65	113	SC	107	124	71	29
IA	175	165	63	80	SD	22	21	59	21
KS	176	151	51	174	TN	209	273	68	160
KY	208	205	65	108	TX	591	743	66	315
LA	128	126	55	86	UT	80	91	72	45
ME	109	108	52	94	VT	65	59	54	44
MD	328	333	47	196	VA	258	222	42	100
MA	632	587	39	255	WA	504	531	49	311
MI	1,034	1,198	61	384	WV	58	134	71	72
MN	377	382	50	193	WI	322	419	60	55
MS	44	62	63	37	WY	14	16	30	7

[1] Includes other items not shown separately.

Source: U.S. Administration for Children and Families, *Temporary Assistance for Needy Families (TANF) Program, Annual Report to Congress.*

No. 566. Child Support—Award and Recipiency Status of Custodial Parent: 1999

[In thousands except as noted (13,529 represents 13,529,000). Custodial parents 15 years and older with own children under 21 years of age present from absent parents as of spring 2000. Covers civilian noninstitutional population. Based on Current Population Survey; see text, Section 1, and Appendix III. For definition of mean, see Guide to Tabular Presentation]

Award and recipiency status	All custodial parents Total Number	Percent distribution	Mothers	Fathers	Custodial parents below the poverty level Total Number	Percent distribution	Mothers	Fathers
Total	13,529	(X)	11,499	2,030	3,530	(X)	3,305	225
With child support agreement or award	7,945	(X)	7,150	795	1,803	(X)	1,730	73
Supposed to receive payments in 1999	6,791	100	6,133	658	1,486	100	1,421	65
Actually received payments in 1999	5,005	74	4,578	427	953	64	898	55
Received full amount	3,066	45	2,818	248	476	32	443	33
Received partial payments	1,939	29	1,760	179	477	32	455	22
Did not receive payments in 1999	1,786	26	1,555	231	533	36	523	10
Child support not awarded	5,584	(X)	4,349	1,235	1,727	(X)	1,575	152
MEAN INCOME AND CHILD SUPPORT								
Received child support payments in 1999:								
Mean total money income (dol.)	26,183	(X)	24,983	39,047	7,169	(X)	7,098	(B)
Mean child support received (dol.)	3,787	(X)	3,844	3,175	2,784	(X)	2,788	(B)
Received the full amount due:								
Mean total money income (dol.)	28,277	(X)	27,113	41,480	6,996	(X)	6,927	(B)
Mean child support received (dol.)	4,853	(X)	4,914	4,164	3,999	(X)	4,038	(B)
Received partial payments:								
Mean total money income (dol.)	22,873	(X)	21,573	35,669	7,343	(X)	7,264	(B)
Mean child support received (dol.)	2,100	(X)	2,131	1,802	1,572	(X)	1,572	(B)
Received no payments in 1999:								
Mean total money income (dol.)	23,004	(X)	19,845	44,314	6,230	(X)	6,307	(B)
Without child support agreement or award:								
Mean total money income (dol.)	21,803	(X)	16,762	39,552	5,747	(X)	5,693	6,310

B Base too small to meet statistical standards for reliability. X Not applicable.

Source: U.S. Census Bureau, unpublished data.

No. 567. Child Support Enforcement Program—Caseload and Collections: 1990 to 2002

[For years ending Sept. 30 (12,796 represents 12,796,000). Includes Puerto Rico, Guam, and the Virgin Islands. The child support enforcement program locates absent parents, establishes paternity of children born out-of-wedlock, and establishes and enforces support orders. By law, these services are available to all families that need them. The program is operated at the state and local government level but 68 percent of administrative costs are paid by the federal government. Child support collected for families not receiving Temporary Assistance for Needy Families (TANF) goes to the family to help it remain self-sufficient. Most of the child support collected on behalf of TANF families goes to federal and state governments to offset TANF payments. Some states pass-through a portion of the CS collections to help families become self-sufficient. Based on data reported by state agencies. Minus sign (-) indicates net outlay]

Item	Unit	1990	1995	1997	1998	1999	2000	2001	2002, prel.
Total cases [1]	1,000	12,796	19,162	19,057	19,419	17,330	17,334	17,061	16,061
Paternities established, total [2]	1,000	393	659	814	848	845	867	777	688
Support orders established, total [3]	1,000	1,022	1,051	1,260	1,148	1,220	1,175	1,181	1,220
FINANCES									
Collections, total	Mil. dol.	6,010	10,827	13,364	14,348	15,901	17,854	18,958	20,137
TANF/FC collections [4]	Mil. dol.	1,750	2,689	2,843	2,650	2,482	2,593	2,592	2,893
State share	Mil. dol.	620	939	1,159	1,089	1,048	1,080	1,004	950
Incentive payments to states	Mil. dol.	264	400	410	396	377	353	337	338
Federal share [5]	Mil. dol.	533	822	1,046	961	922	968	895	1,179
Non-TANF collections	Mil. dol.	4,260	8,138	10,521	11,698	13,419	15,261	16,366	17,244
Administrative expenditures, total	Mil. dol.	1,606	3,012	3,428	3,585	4,039	4,526	4,835	5,183
State share	Mil. dol.	545	918	1,100	1,200	1,359	1,519	1,613	1,752
Federal share	Mil. dol.	1,061	2,095	2,328	2,385	2,680	3,006	3,222	3,432
Program savings, total	Mil. dol.	-190	-852	-813	-1,139	-1,692	-2,125	-2,599	-3,053
State share	Mil. dol.	338	421	469	286	66	-87	-272	-463
Federal share	Mil. dol.	-528	-1,273	-1,282	-1,424	-1,758	-2,038	-2,327	-2,590

[1] Passage of PRWORA mandated new categories in 1999 and cases were no longer double counted resulting in a 2 million case reduction. [2] Does not include in-hospital paternities. [3] Through 1990 includes modifications to orders. [4] Collections for current assistance cases where the children are: (1) recipients of TANF under Title IV-A of the Social Security Act or (2) entitled to foster care (FC) maintenance under Title IV-E of the Social Security Act plus collections distributed as assistance reimbursements. Includes medical support and payments to families of current assistance not shown separately. Assistance reimbursements are collections that will be divided between the state and federal governments to reimburse their respective shares of either Title IV-A assistance payments or Title IV-E foster care maintenance payments. [5] Prior to fiscal year 2000, incentives were paid out of the federal share of collections and the net federal share was reported.

Source: U.S. Department of Health and Human Services, Office of Child Support Enforcement, *Annual Report to Congress*.

No. 568. Federal Food Programs: 1990 to 2002

[20.1 represents 20,100,000. For years ending Sept. 30. Program data include Puerto Rico, Virgin Islands, Guam, American Samoa, Northern Marianas, and the former Trust Territory when a federal food program was operated in these areas. Participation data are average monthly figures except as noted. Participants are not reported for the commodity distribution programs. Cost data are direct federal benefits to recipients; they exclude federal administrative payments and applicable state and local contributions. Federal costs for commodities and cash-in-lieu of commodities are shown separately from direct cash benefits for those programs receiving both]

Program	Unit	1990	1995	1997	1998	1999	2000	2001	2002
Food stamp:									
Participants	Million	20.1	26.6	22.9	19.8	18.2	17.2	17.3	19.1
Federal cost	Mil. dol.	14,187	22,765	19,550	16,889	15,755	14,985	15,547	18,243
Monthly average coupon value per recipient	Dollars	58.92	71.26	71.27	71.12	72.21	72.78	74.83	79.60
Nutrition assistance program for Puerto Rico:									
Federal cost	Mil. dol.	937	1,131	1,174	1,204	1,236	1,268	1,296	1,351
National school lunch program (NSLP):									
Free lunches served	Million	1,662	2,090	2,194	2,198	2,207	2,205	2,182	2,278
Reduced-price lunches served	Million	273	309	347	362	392	409	425	441
Children participating [1]	Million	24.1	25.7	26.3	26.6	26.9	27.2	27.5	28.0
Federal cost	Mil. dol.	3,214	4,466	4,934	5,102	5,314	5,493	5,612	6,051
School breakfast (SB):									
Children participating [1]	Million	4.1	6.3	6.9	7.1	7.4	7.6	7.8	8.1
Federal cost	Mil. dol.	596	1,049	1,214	1,272	1,345	1,393	1,450	1,566
Special supplemental food program (WIC): [2]									
Participants	Million	4.5	6.9	7.4	7.4	7.3	7.2	7.3	7.5
Federal cost	Mil. dol.	1,637	2,517	2,815	2,808	2,853	2,852	3,008	3,132
Child and adult care (CAC): [3]									
Participants [4]	Million	1.5	2.4	2.5	2.6	2.7	2.7	2.7	2.9
Federal cost	Mil. dol.	720	1,296	1,393	1,372	1,438	1,501	1,548	1,658
Federal cost of commodities donated to— [5]									
Child nutrition (NSLP, CC, SF [6], and SB) [7]	Mil. dol.	646	733	661	774	754	704	917	864
Emergency feeding [8]	Mil. dol.	286	100	152	190	234	182	333	382

[1] Average monthly participation (excluding summer months of June through August). Includes children in public and private elementary and secondary schools and in residential child care institutes. [2] WIC serves pregnant and postpartum women, infants, and children up to age 5. [3] Program provides year-round subsidies to feed preschool children in child care centers and family day care homes. Certain care centers serving disabled or elderly adults also receive meal subsidies. [4] Average quarterly daily attendance at participating institutions. [5] Includes the federal cost of commodity entitlements, cash-in-lieu of commodities, and bonus foods. [6] Summer Feeding (SF) program provides free meals to children in poor areas during summer months. [7] Includes the value of commodities provided through the national school lunch, school breakfast, child and adult care food, and summer food service programs. [8] Provides free commodities to needy persons for home consumption through food banks, hunger centers, soup kitchens, and similar nonprofit agencies. Includes the emergency food assistance program, the commodity purchases for soup kitchens/food banks program, and commodity disaster relief.

Source: U.S. Dept. of Agriculture, Food and Nutrition Service, "Food and Nutrition Service, Program Data"; <http://www.fns.usda.gov/pd/>; updated monthly.

No. 569. Federal Food Stamp Program by State: 2000 to 2002

[Participation data are average monthly number (17,158 represents 17,158,000). For years ending Sept. 30. Food stamp costs are for benefits only and exclude administrative expenditures]

State	Persons (1,000) 2000	2001	2002	Benefits (mil. dol.) 2000	2001	2002	State	Persons (1,000) 2000	2001	2002	Benefits (mil. dol.) 2000	2001	2002
Total [1]	17,158	17,313	19,100	14,985	15,547	18,243	MS	276	298	325	226	254	298
U.S.	17,120	17,277	19,063	14,928	15,492	18,174	MO	423	454	515	358	395	477
							MT	59	62	63	51	54	58
AL	396	411	444	344	365	417	NE	82	81	88	61	63	74
AK	38	38	46	46	46	59	NV	61	69	97	57	65	96
AZ	259	291	379	240	280	386	NH	36	36	41	28	28	35
AR	247	256	284	206	223	265							
CA	1,832	1,668	1,709	1,639	1,583	1,695	NJ	345	318	320	304	292	314
CO	156	154	178	127	131	165	NM	169	163	170	140	136	154
CT	165	157	169	138	136	146	NY	1,439	1,354	1,347	1,361	1,365	1,479
DE	32	32	40	31	32	39	NC	488	494	574	403	425	536
DC	81	73	74	77	70	76	ND	32	38	37	25	27	31
FL	882	887	990	773	771	878	OH	610	641	735	520	573	726
							OK	253	271	317	208	236	288
GA	559	574	646	489	515	621	OR	234	284	359	198	240	319
HI	118	108	106	166	150	152	PA	777	748	767	656	639	700
ID	58	60	70	46	47	62	RI	74	71	72	59	59	64
IL	779	825	886	777	810	923							
IN	300	347	411	268	317	408	SC	295	316	379	249	269	352
IA	123	126	141	100	107	129	SD	43	45	48	37	39	45
KS	117	124	140	83	92	113	TN	496	522	598	415	454	552
KY	403	413	450	337	350	410	TX	1,333	1,361	1,554	1,215	1,270	1,522
LA	500	518	588	448	483	587	UT	82	80	90	68	67	80
ME	102	104	111	81	86	97	VT	41	39	40	32	31	34
							VA	336	332	354	263	263	304
MD	219	208	228	199	191	215	WA	295	309	350	241	261	318
MA	232	219	243	182	173	209	WV	227	221	236	185	178	198
MI	603	641	750	457	504	645	WI	193	216	262	129	152	197
MN	196	198	217	165	172	201	WY	22	23	24	19	19	22

[1] Includes Guam and the Virgin Islands. Several outlying areas receive nutrition assistance grants in lieu of food stamp assistance (e.g., Puerto Rico, American Samoa and the Northern Marianas).

Source: U.S. Dept. of Agriculture, Food and Nutrition Service. "Food and Nutrition Service, Program Data"; <http://www.fns.usda.gov/pd/>; updated monthly.

No. 570. Selected Characteristics of Food Stamp Households and Participants: 1990 to 2001

[7,803 represent 7,803,000. For years ending September 30. Data for 1990-1992 exclude Guam and the Virgin Islands. Based on a sample of households from the Food Stamp Quality Control System]

Year	Households Total (1,000)	Percent of total With children	Percent of total With elderly [1]	Percent of total With disabled [2]	Participants Total (1,000)	Percent of total Children	Percent of total Elderly [1]
1990	7,803	60.3	18.1	8.9	20,411	49.6	7.7
1992	10,049	62.2	15.4	9.5	25,743	51.9	6.6
1993	10,791	62.1	15.5	10.7	27,595	51.5	6.8
1994	11,091	61.1	15.8	12.5	28,009	51.4	7.0
1995	10,883	59.7	16.0	18.9	26,955	51.5	7.1
1996	10,552	59.5	16.2	20.2	25,926	51.0	7.3
1997	9,452	58.3	17.6	22.3	23,117	51.4	7.9
1998	8,246	58.3	18.2	24.4	19,969	52.8	8.2
1999	7,670	55.7	20.1	26.5	18,149	51.5	9.4
2000	7,335	53.9	21.0	27.5	17,091	51.3	10.0
2001	7,450	53.6	20.4	27.7	17,297	51.1	9.6

[1] Persons 60 years old and over. [2] Beginning 1995, disabled households are defined as households with at least one member under age 65 who received SSI, or at least one member age 18 to 61 who received social security, veterans benefits, or other government benefits as a result of a disability. For years prior to 1995, disabled households are defined as households with SSI but no members over age 59. The substantial increase in the percentage of households with a disabled member between 1994 and 1995 is due in part to the change in the definition of disabled households. Using the previous definition, 13.3 percent of households included a disabled person in fiscal year 1995.

No. 571. Food Stamp Households and Participants—Summary: 2001

[7,450 represents 7,450,000. For year ending September 30. Based on a sample of 46,963 households from the Food Stamp Quality Control System]

Household type and income source	Households Number (1,000)	Households Percent	Age, sex, race, and Hispanic origin	Participants Number (1,000)	Participants Percent
Total	7,450	100.0	Total	17,297	100.0
With children	3,992	53.6	Children	8,841	51.1
Single-parent households	2,690	36.1	Under 5 years old	2,878	16.6
Married-couple households	572	7.7	5 to 17 years old	5,964	34.5
Other	730	9.8	Adults	8,450	48.8
With elderly	1,520	20.4	18 to 35 years old	3,530	20.4
Living alone	1,220	16.4	36 to 59 years old	3,260	18.8
Not living alone	300	4.0	60 years old and over	1,660	9.6
Disabled	2,063	27.7			
Living alone	1,190	16.0	Male	6,949	40.2
Not living alone	873	11.7	Female	10,347	59.8
Earned income	2,009	27.0	White, non-Hispanic	7,088	41.0
Wages and salaries	1,845	24.8	Black, non-Hispanic	6,097	35.2
Unearned income	5,794	77.8	Hispanic	3,171	18.3
TANF [1]	1,723	23.1	Asian	563	3.3
Supplemental Security Income	2,370	31.8	Native American	275	1.6
Social security	1,894	25.4	Other	103	0.6
No income	703	9.4			

[1] Temporary Assistance for Needy Families (TANF) program.

Source of Tables 570 and 571: U.S. Dept. of Agriculture, Food and Nutrition Service, *Characteristics of Food Stamp Households: Fiscal Year 2001*, January 2003.

No. 572. Head Start—Summary: 1980 to 2002

[For years ending September 30 (376 represents 376,000)]

Year	Enrollment (1,000)	Appropriation (mil. dol.)	Age and race	Enrollment, 2002 (percent)	Item	Number
1980	376	735	Under 3 years old	7	Average cost per child:	
1985	452	1,075	3 years old	36	1995	$4,534
1990	541	1,552	4 years old	52	2000	$5,951
1993	714	2,776	5 years old and over	5	2002	$6,934
1994	740	3,326				
1995	751	3,534			Paid staff (1,000):	
1996	752	3,569	White	28	1995	147
1997	794	3,981	Black	33	2000	180
1998	822	4,347	Hispanic	30	2002	198
1999	826	4,658	American Indian	3	Volunteers (1,000):	
2000	858	5,267	Asian	2	1995	1,235
2001	905	6,200	Hawaiian/Pacific		2000	1,252
2002	912	6,537	Islander	1	2002	1,450

Source: U.S. Administration for Children and Families, "Head Start Statistical Fact Sheet"; <http://www2.acf.dhhs.gov/programs/hsb/research/index.htm>.

No. 573. Social Assistance—Taxable Establishments, Receipts, Payroll, and Employees by Kind of Business: 1997

[18,051 represents $18,051,000,000]

Kind of business	NAICS code [1]	All firms Establish- ments (number)	All firms Receipts (mil. dol.)	Employer firms Establish- ments (number)	Employer firms Receipts (mil. dol.)	Annual payroll (mil. dol.)	Paid employ- ees [2] (1,000)
Social assistance	624	583,203	18,051	56,691	12,599	5,766	491.1
Individual & family services	6241	43,070	3,228	9,843	2,636	1,113	68.8
Child & youth services	62411	(NA)	(NA)	1,648	539	210	11.5
Services for elderly & disabled persons	62412	(NA)	(NA)	2,976	807	394	32.2
Other individual & family services	62419	(NA)	(NA)	5,219	1,290	508	25.1
Community/emergency & other relief services	6242	1,682	136	344	112	29	1.6
Community food services	62421	(NA)	(NA)	95	18	4	0.4
Community housing services	62422	(NA)	(NA)	167	74	21	1.0
Emergency & other relief services	62423	(NA)	(NA)	82	20	4	0.2
Vocational rehabilitation services	6243	5,762	1,514	2,549	1,432	676	32.0
Child day care services	6244	532,689	13,172	43,955	8,419	3,948	388.7

NA Not available. [1] North American Industry Classification System, 1997; see text, Section 15. [2] For pay period including March 12.

No. 574. Social Assistance—Tax-Exempt Establishments, Receipts, Payroll, and Employees by Kind of Business: 1997

[44,756 represents $44,756,000,000. Covers establishments with payroll only]

Kind of business	NAICS code [1]	Establishments (number)	Receipts (mil. dol.)	Annual payroll (mil. dol)	Paid employees [2] (1,000)
Social assistance	624	69,737	44,756	18,628	1,253.1
Individual & family services	6241	36,364	26,453	10,781	642.6
Child & youth services	62411	11,086	7,719	3,171	172.0
Services for elderly & disabled persons	62412	9,960	8,217	3,260	226.7
Other individual & family services	62419	15,318	10,516	4,350	243.9
Community/emergency & other relief services	6242	9,606	6,085	1,739	100.8
Community food services	62421	2,988	1,598	324	23.0
Community housing services	62422	4,737	2,954	1,079	60.2
Emergency & other relief services	62423	1,881	1,534	336	17.7
Vocational rehabilitation services	6243	5,668	6,462	3,093	269.7
Child day care services	6244	18,099	5,757	3,015	240.0

[1] North American Industry Classification System, 1997; see text, Section 15. [2] For pay period including March 12.

Source of Tables 573 and 574: U.S. Census Bureau, *1997 Economic Census, Health Care and Social Assistance*, Series EC97S62A-US, issued October 1999 and *Nonemployer Statistics*.

No. 575. Social Assistance Services—Revenue for Employer Firms: 1999 to 2001

[In millions of dollars (66,191 represents $66,191,000,000). Based on the North American Industry Classification System, 1997 (NAICS), see text, Section 15. See Appendix III]

Kind of business	NAICS code	1999, total	2000, total	2001 Total	2001 Taxable firms	2001 Tax-exempt firms
Social assistance	624	66,191	73,754	82,198	18,413	63,785
Individual and family services	6241	33,174	37,277	41,893	4,023	37,869
Child and youth services	62411	8,937	9,993	11,316	851	10,465
Services for elderly and disabled persons	62412	10,259	11,270	12,402	1,174	11,228
Other individual and family services	62419	13,979	16,014	18,175	1,998	16,177
Community, emergency and other relief services	6242	6,981	7,735	8,475	348	8,127
Community food services	62421	1,949	2,193	2,370	173	2,197
Community housing services	62422	3,469	3,855	4,312	153	4,159
Emergency and other relief services	62423	1,563	1,688	1,793	(S)	1,771
Vocational rehabilitation services	6243	9,373	10,558	11,517	2,271	9,245
Child day care services	6244	16,663	18,184	20,314	11,770	8,543

S Figure does not meet publication standards.

Source: U.S. Census Bureau, *Service Annual Survey, 2001*. See also <http://www.census.gov/econ/www/servmenu.html>.

No. 576. Social Assistance—Nonemployer Establishments and Receipts: 1997 to 2000

[Receipts in millions of dollars (5,451 represents $5,451,000,000). Includes only firms subject to federal income tax. Nonemployers are businesses with no paid employees. Based on the North American Industry Classification System, 1997 (NAICS), see text, Section 15]

Kind of business	NAICS code	Establishments 1997	Establishments 1999	Establishments 2000	Receipts 1997	Receipts 1999	Receipts 2000
Social assistance, total	624	526,512	605,113	642,946	5,451	6,793	7,539
Individual & family services	6241	33,227	63,775	72,433	592	949	1,106
Community/emergency & other relief services	6242	1,338	3,333	3,560	24	45	54
Vocational rehabilitation services	6243	3,213	6,731	7,314	82	134	151
Child day care services	6244	488,734	531,274	559,639	4,754	5,665	6,228

Source: U.S. Census Bureau, "Nonemployer Statistics"; published October 2002; <http://www.census.gov/epcd/nonemployer/>.

No. 577. Child Care Arrangements of Preschool Children by Type of Arrangement: 1991 to 2001

[In percent, except as indicated (8,428 represents 8,428,000). Estimates are based on children 3 to 5 years old who have not entered kindergarten. Based on interviews from a sample survey of the civilian, noninstitutional population in households with telephones; see source for details. See also Appendix III]

Characteristic	Number (1,000)	Percent distribution	In relative care	In nonrelative care	In center-based program [2]	With parental care only
1991, total	8,428	100.0	16.9	14.8	52.8	31.0
1995, total	9,232	100.0	19.4	16.9	55.1	25.9
2001, total	8,551	100	22.8	14.1	56.4	26.1
Age:						
3 years old	3,795	44.4	23.6	14.7	42.8	33.8
4 years old	3,861	45.1	22.5	13.6	65.9	20.4
5 years old	896	10.5	20.9	13.1	73.0	18.0
Race-ethnicity:						
White, non-Hispanic	5,313	62.1	19.6	16.5	59.1	25.3
Black, non-Hispanic	1,251	14.6	36.7	8.5	63.1	15.1
Hispanic	1,506	17.6	22.8	11.3	39.9	39.0
Other	482	5.6	22.8	10.8	61.8	23.7
Household income:						
Less than $10,001	951	11.1	37.1	6.2	45.6	30.5
$10,001 to $20,000	1,156	13.5	23.5	10.8	50.6	32.3
$20,001 to $30,000	1,134	13.3	24.3	10.4	49.3	32.4
$30,001 to $40,000	978	11.4	24.5	12.6	48.9	32.2
$40,001 to $50,000	822	9.6	21.9	15.2	42.9	36.4
$50,001 to $75,000	1,724	20.2	20.7	18.6	62.3	20.9
$75,001 or more	1,788	20.9	15.3	18.6	75.1	12.8

[1] Columns do not add to 100.0 because some children participated in more than one type of nonparental arrangement.
[2] Center-based programs include day care centers, head start programs, preschools, prekindergarten, and nursery schools.

Source: U.S. Department of Education, National Center for Education Statistics, Early Childhood Program Participation Survey of the National Household Education Surveys Program (NHES), 2001.

No. 578. Licensed Child Care Centers and Family Child Care Providers by State and Other Area: 2002

[Centers as of February; family child care providers as of August]

State	Licensed child care centers	Licensed family child care providers	State	Licensed child care centers	Licensed family child care providers	State	Licensed child care centers	Licensed family child care providers
US, total	112,574	306,694	KY	2,150	9,234	OK	1,942	4,293
			LA	1,920	8,661	OR	874	5,989
AL	1,400	2,181	ME	848	1,834	PA	3,904	4,900
AK	230	1,819	MD	2,453	10,361	RI	423	1,156
AZ	2,084	4,233	MA	3,246	10,197	SC	1,758	1,859
AR	2,638	1,282	MI	4,873	14,743	SD	227	1,025
CA	14,139	44,197	MN	1,610	14,258	TN	3,351	2,326
CO	2,567	4,853	MS	1,751	883	TX	10,650	14,782
CT	1,632	3,557	MO	1,741	2,175	UT	321	2,068
DE	318	1,707	MT	268	1,525	VT	610	1,320
DC	371	225	NE	815	3,298	VA	2,558	3,701
FL	6,354	7,613	NV	446	598	WA	2,140	7,262
GA	2,580	7,867	NH	792	388	WV	540	5,024
HI	552	501	NJ	4,000	5,100	WI	2,343	8,500
ID	336	1,208	NM	660	7,745	WY	236	514
IL	3,125	10,861	NY	3,681	19,800			
IN	671	4,151	NC	4,000	5,343			
IA	1,512	5,620	ND	116	2,271	PR	490	41
KS	1,353	7,199	OH	3,465	14,487	VI	234	67

Source: Children's Foundation, Washington, DC, *Child Care Center Licensing Study* and *Family Child Care Licensing Study*, annual (copyright).

No. 579. Charity Contributions—Average Dollar Amount: 1991 to 2000

[Estimates cover households' contribution activity (both cash and in-kind) for the year and are based on respondents' replies as to contribution and volunteer activity of household. For 2000, based on a sample survey of 4,216 persons 21 years old and over conducted during the spring of the following year and subject to sampling variability; see source]

Year and age	All contributing households Average amount (dol.)	Percent of household income	Contributors and volunteers Average amount (dol.)	Percent of household income	Household income	All contributing households Average amount (dol.)	Percent of household income	Contributors and volunteers Average amount (dol.)	Percent of household income
1991	899	2.2	1,155	2.6	2000—				
1995	1,017	2.2	1,279	2.6	Under $10,000	296	5.5	382	6.7
					$10,000-$19,999	465	3.3	624	4.4
2000, total	1,623	3.2	2,295	4.0	$20,000-$29,999	916	3.9	1,299	5.5
21-24 years	958	2.3	1,635	3.1	$30,000-$39,999	1,036	3.1	1,408	4.2
25-34 years	1,002	2.3	1,411	3.1	$40,000-$49,999	1,147	2.7	1,638	3.8
35-44 years	1,831	2.8	2,471	3.5	$50,000-$59,999	1,566	3.0	1,989	3.8
45-54 years	1,818	2.9	2,632	3.8	$60,000-$74,999	1,935	3.0	2,483	3.8
55-64 years	1,888	3.3	2,626	4.3	$75,000-$99,999	2,119	2.6	2,530	3.1
65-74 years	1,798	4.5	2,307	5.5	$100,000 and over	3,976	2.7	4,894	3.3
75 years and over	1,628	5.1	2,498	6.5					
					Itemizers [1]	2,288	3.6	2,903	4.3
White	1,693	3.2	2,359	4.0	Claimed charitable deduction	2,733	4.0	3,262	4.6
Black	1,488	3.3	2,300	4.3	Didn't claim charitable deduction	868	2.4	1,207	2.9
Hispanic [2]	1,276	2.5	2,285	3.6	Nonitemizers	954	2.7	1,464	3.6

[1] Persons who itemized their deductions on their 2000 federal tax returns.   [2] Hispanic persons may be of any race.

No. 580. Charity Contributions—Percent of Households Contributing by Dollar Amount, 1991 to 2000, and Type of Charity, 2000

[In percent, except as noted. See headnote, Table 579]

Annual amount of household contributions	All households 1991	1995	2000	Givers 1991	1995	2000	Type of charity	2000 Percentage of households	Average contribution [1] (dol.)
None	27.8	31.5	11.7	(X)	(X)	(X)	Arts, culture, humanities	16.6	234
Givers	72.2	68.5	88.3	100.0	100.0	100.0	Education	29.9	508
$1 to $100	14.9	15.2	14.2	24.9	24.3	17.6	Environment	19.0	195
$101 to $200	8.1	7.2	8.6	13.5	11.6	10.6	Health	38.0	224
$201 to $300	7.3	5.7	5.7	12.2	9.2	7.1	Human services	34.7	338
$301 to $400	3.3	4.7	3.8	5.6	7.5	4.7	International	6.3	254
$401 to $500	3.2	5.2	4.3	5.4	8.3	5.3	Private, community foundations	7.3	238
$501 to $600	2.6	3.0	3.2	4.4	4.7	4.0	Public, societal benefit	11.1	251
$601 to $700	2.5	2.6	3.1	4.2	4.1	3.8	Recreation - adults	5.9	371
$701 to $999	3.4	3.7	6.2	5.7	6.0	7.7	Religion	60.6	1,358
$1,000 or more	14.5	15.2	31.9	24.2	24.3	39.4	Youth development	33.8	254
Not reported	12.4	5.9	7.3	(X)	(X)	(X)			

X Not applicable.   [1] Average contribution per household making a contribution to the specified type of charity.
Source of Tables 579 and 580: Toppe, Chris, Arthur Kirsch, and Westat, Inc., *Giving and Volunteering in the United States: 2001 Edition*. (Copyright and published by INDEPENDENT SECTOR, Washington, DC, 2002).

No. 581. Private Philanthropy Funds by Source and Allocation: 1990 to 2002

[In billions of dollars (101.4 represents $101,400,000,000). Estimates for sources of funds based on U.S. Internal Revenue Service reports of individual charitable deductions and household surveys of giving by Independent Sector and the Center on Philanthropy at Indiana University. For corporate giving, data are corporate charitable deductions from the US Internal Revenue Service and the contributions made by corporate foundations as reported by the Foundation Center. Data about foundation donations are based upon surveys of foundations and data provided by the Foundation Center. Estimates of the allocation of funds were derived from surveys of nonprofits conducted by various sources]

Source and allocation	1990	1992	1993	1994	1995	1996	1997	1998	1999	2000	2001	2002
Total funds	101.4	110.4	116.5	119.2	124.0	138.6	159.4	177.4	201.6	228.3	238.5	240.9
Individuals	81.0	87.7	92.0	92.5	95.4	107.6	124.2	138.4	155.2	175.1	182.5	183.7
Foundations [1]	7.2	8.6	9.5	9.7	10.6	12.0	13.9	17.0	20.5	24.6	27.2	26.9
Corporations	5.5	5.9	6.5	7.0	7.3	7.5	8.6	8.5	10.2	10.7	11.0	12.2
Charitable bequests	7.6	8.2	8.5	10.0	10.7	11.5	12.6	13.6	15.6	17.8	17.7	18.1
Allocation:												
Religion	49.8	51.0	52.9	56.4	58.1	61.9	64.7	68.2	71.2	77.0	80.3	84.3
Health	9.9	10.2	10.8	11.5	12.6	13.9	14.0	16.9	18.0	18.8	19.3	18.9
Education	12.4	14.3	15.4	16.6	17.6	19.2	22.0	25.3	27.5	31.7	31.9	31.6
Human service	11.8	11.6	12.5	11.7	11.7	12.2	12.7	16.1	17.4	18.0	20.7	18.7
Arts, culture and humanities	7.9	9.3	9.6	9.7	10.0	10.9	10.6	10.5	11.1	11.5	12.1	12.2
Public/societal benefit	4.9	5.0	5.4	6.1	7.1	7.6	8.4	10.9	11.0	11.6	11.8	11.6
Environment/wildlife	2.5	2.9	3.0	3.3	3.8	3.8	4.1	5.3	5.8	6.2	6.4	6.6
International	1.3	2.2	2.2	2.4	2.9	2.8	2.6	2.9	3.6	3.7	4.1	4.6
Gifts to foundations [1,2]	3.8	5.0	6.3	6.3	8.5	12.6	14.0	19.9	28.8	24.7	25.7	22
Unallocated [3]	-3.0	-1.2	-1.5	-4.9	-8.2	-6.2	6.3	1.5	7.4	25.2	25.9	30.5

[1] Data are from the Foundation Center.   [2] Estimate for gifts to foundations in 2002 is from *Giving USA*.   [3] Money deducted as a charitable contribution by donors but not allocated to sources. May include gifts to governmental entities, in-kind giving, gifts to new charities.
Source: AAFRC Trust for Philanthropy, Indianapolis, IN, researched and written by the Center on Philanthropy at Indiana University, *Giving USA*, annual (copyright).

378   Social Insurance and Human Services

No. 582. Foundations—Number and Finances: 1980 to 2001

[48.2 represents $48,200,000,000. Covers nongovernmental nonprofit organizations with funds and programs managed by their own trustees or directors, whose goals were to maintain or aid social, educational, religious, or other activities deemed to serve the common good. Excludes organizations that make general appeals to the public for funds, act as trade associations for industrial or other special groups, or do not currently award grants. Constant dollar figures based on Consumer Price Index, all urban consumers, supplied by US Bureau of Labor Statistics. Minus sign (-) indicates decrease]

Year	Number of foundations	Assets Current dollars Amount (bil. dol)	Percent change[1]	Assets Constant (1975) dollars Amount (bil. dol)	Percent change[1]	Total giving[2] Current dollars Amount (bil. dol)	Percent change[1]	Total giving[2] Constant (1975) dollars Amount (bil. dol)	Percent change[1]	Gifts received Current dollars Amount (bil. dol)	Percent change[1]	Gifts received Constant (1978) dollars Amount (bil. dol)	Percent change[1]
1980	22,088	48.2	15.8	31.5	2.0	3.4	20.4	2.2	6.0	2.0	-10.4	1.6	-21.1
1985	25,639	102.1	37.8	51.1	33.1	6.0	19.6	3.0	15.5	4.7	40.8	2.9	35.9
1990	32,401	142.5	3.6	58.7	-1.7	8.7	9.7	3.6	4.1	5.0	-10.0	2.5	-14.6
1992	35,765	176.8	8.5	67.8	5.4	10.2	10.9	3.9	7.6	6.2	13.1	2.9	9.7
1993	37,571	189.2	7.0	70.5	3.9	11.1	8.8	4.1	5.7	7.8	25.6	3.5	22.0
1994	38,807	195.8	3.5	71.1	0.9	11.3	1.6	4.1	-0.9	8.1	4.2	3.6	1.5
1995	40,140	226.7	15.8	80.1	12.6	12.3	8.6	4.3	5.6	10.3	27.0	4.4	23.5
1996	41,588	267.6	18.0	92.2	14.6	13.8	12.9	4.8	9.6	16.0	56.1	6.7	51.7
1997	44,146	329.9	23.3	110.6	19.9	16.0	15.5	5.4	12.8	15.8	-1.2	6.4	-3.4
1998	46,832	385.1	16.7	127.1	14.9	19.5	21.7	6.4	19.8	22.6	42.6	9.0	40.4
1999	50,201	448.6	16.5	144.9	14.0	23.3	19.9	7.5	17.3	32.1	42.1	12.6	39.0
2000	56,582	495.6	10.5	154.9	6.9	27.6	18.2	8.6	14.3	27.6	-13.9	10.5	-16.7
2001	61,810	476.8	-3.8	144.8	-6.5	30.5	10.7	9.3	7.7	28.7	4.1	10.6	1.1

[1] Percent change from immediate preceding year. [2] Includes grants, scholarships, and employee matching gifts.

Source: The Foundation Center, New York, NY, FC Stats; <http://fdncenter.org/fcstats/index.html>; (copyright).

No. 583. Foundations—Number and Finances by Asset Size: 2001

[Figures are for latest year reported by foundations (476,789 represents $476,789,000,000). See headnote, Table 582]

Asset size	Number	Assets (mil. dol.)	Gifts received (mil. dol.)	Expenditures (mil. dol.)	Grants (mil. dol.)	Percent distribution Number	Assets	Gifts received	Expenditures	Grants
Total	61,810	476,789	28,714	37,627	30,502	100.0	100.0	100.0	100.0	100.0
Under $50,000	10,242	174	511	717	662	16.6	(Z)	1.7	1.9	2.2
$50,000-$99,999	4,576	338	179	221	193	7.4	0.1	0.6	0.6	0.6
$100,000-$249,999	8,704	1,454	429	506	441	14.1	0.3	1.5	1.3	1.4
$250,000-$499,999	7,883	2,861	449	553	465	12.8	0.6	1.6	1.5	1.5
$500,000-$999,999	8,482	6,130	749	888	753	13.7	1.3	2.6	2.4	2.5
$1,000,000-$4,999,999	14,046	31,645	3,552	4,002	3,384	22.7	6.6	12.4	10.6	11.1
$5,000,000-$9,999,999	3,277	23,037	1,907	2,215	1,841	5.3	4.8	6.6	5.9	6.0
$10,000,000-$49,999,999	3,475	73,798	5,955	6,665	5,471	5.6	15.5	20.7	17.7	17.9
$50,000,000-$99,999,999	560	39,189	2,795	3,333	2,700	0.9	8.2	9.7	8.9	8.9
$100,000,000-$249,999,999	351	52,652	3,403	3,932	3,184	0.6	11.0	11.8	10.4	10.4
$250,000,000 or more	214	245,510	8,783	14,595	11,408	0.3	51.5	30.6	38.8	37.4

Z Less than 0.05 percent.

Source: The Foundation Center, New York, NY, *Foundation Yearbook*, annual (copyright).

No. 584. Foundations—Grants Reported by Subject Field and Recipient Organization: 2000

[15,015 represents $15,015,000,000. Covers grants of $10,000 or more in size. Based on reports of 1,015 larger U.S. foundations. Grant sample dollar value represented half of all grant dollars awarded by private, corporate, and community foundations. For definition of foundations, see headnote, Table 582]

Subject field	Number of grants Number	Percent distribution	Dollar value Amount (mil. dol.)	Percent distribution	Recipient organization	Number of grants Number	Percent distribution	Dollar value Amount (mil. dol.)	Percent distribution
Total	119,778	100.0	15,015	100.0	Community improvement organizations	6,044	5.0	606	4.0
Arts and culture	17,835	14.9	1,799	12.0	Educational institutions	31,360	26.2	5,562	37.0
Education	24,615	20.6	3,779	25.2	Colleges & universities	14,130	11.8	2,614	17.4
Environment & animals	7,368	6.2	987	6.6	Educational support agencies	7,546	6.3	1,649	11.0
Health	14,517	12.1	3,090	20.6	Schools	7,138	6.0	750	5.0
Human services	29,140	24.3	2,169	14.4	Environmental agencies	4,725	3.9	620	4.1
International affairs, development & peace	3,264	2.7	414	2.8	Hospitals/medical care facilities	4,612	3.9	632	4.2
Public/societal benefit	14,859	12.4	1,692	11.3	Human service agencies	22,694	18.9	1,585	10.6
Science and technology	2,400	2.0	414	2.8	Museums/historical societies	5,018	4.2	622	4.1
Social sciences	1,837	1.5	324	2.2	Public/general health organizations	2,890	2.4	573	3.8
Religion	3,819	3.2	330	2.2					
Other	124	0.1	17	0.1					

Source: The Foundation Center, New York, NY, *Foundation Giving Trends*, annual (copyright). See also <http://www.fdncenter.org/>.

No. 585. Volunteers by Selected Characteristics: 2000

[59,163 represents 59,163,000. Data on volunteers relate to persons who performed unpaid volunteer activities for an organization at any point from September 1, 2001, through the survey period in September 2002. Detail for the above race and Hispanic-origin groups will not sum to totals because data for the "other races" group are not presented and Hispanics are included in both the white and black population groups]

Age, sex, race, and Hispanic origin	Total volunteers Number (1,000)	Percent of population	Median annual hours[1]	Educational attainment, marital status, presence of children, and employment status	Total volunteers Number (1,000)	Percent of population	Median annual hours[1]	Type of main organization	Percent of population involved in activity[2]
								Civic and political[4]	6.1
AGE				**EDUCATIONAL ATTAINMENT**[3]					
Total, 16 yrs. & over	59,163	27.6	52	Less than a high school diploma	2,734	10.1	48		
16 to 24 yrs.	7,860	22.2	40	High school graduate, no college[5]	12,293	21.3	50	Educational or youth service	27.2
16 to 19 yrs.	4,346	26.9	40	Less than a bachelor's degree[6]	14,919	32.9	52		
20 to 24 yrs.	3,515	18.2	36	College graduates	21,357	43.6	60		
25 yrs. and over	51,303	28.7	52					Environmental or animal care	1.6
25 to 34 yrs.	9,279	25.1	34	**MARITAL STATUS**					
35 to 44 yrs.	15,089	34.4	52	Single, never married	12,177	21.2	40		
45 to 54 yrs.	12,296	31.4	53	Married, spouse present	37,823	32.7	53	Hospital or other health	8.6
55 to 64 yrs.	7,146	27.5	60	Other marital status[7]	9,163	22.1	52		
65 yrs. & over	7,492	22.7	96					Public safety	1.4
				PRESENCE OF OWN CHILDREN UNDER 18 YEARS[8]					
SEX				Without own children under 18	35,371	23.7	(NA)	Religious	33.9
Men	24,514	23.8	52	With own children under 18	23,793	36.5	(NA)		
Women	34,649	31.1	50					Social or community service	12.1
				EMPLOYMENT STATUS					
				Civilian labor force	42,396	29.5	48		
RACE AND HISPANIC ORIGIN				Employed	40,379	29.7	48	Sport and hobby[9]	4.0
White	52,164	29.4	52	Full time[10]	31,910	28.5	46		
Black	4,987	19.2	52	Part time[11]	8,469	35.5	52	Other	3.5
Hispanic origin	3,769	15.7	44	Unemployed	2,016	25.3	50		
				Not in the labor force	16,767	23.7	72	Not determined	1.5

NA Not available. [1] For those reporting annual hours. [2] Main organization is defined as the organization for which the volunteer worked the most hours during the year. See headnote for more details. [3] Data refer to persons 25 years and over. [4] Includes professional and/or international. [5] Includes high school diploma or equivalent. [6] Includes the categories, some college, no degree; and associate degree. [7] Includes divorced, separated, and widowed persons. [8] Own children include sons, daughters, stepchildren, and adopted children. Not included are nieces, nephews, grandchildren, and other related and unrelated children. [9] Includes cultural and/or arts. [10] Usually work 35 hours or more a week at all jobs. [11] Usually work less than 35 hours a week at all jobs.

Source: U.S. Bureau of Labor Statistics, News, USDL 02-686, December 18, 2002. <http://www.bls.gov/news.release/volun.nr0.htm>.

No. 586. Community Service Participation of Students in Grades 6 Through 12: 1996 and 1999

[12,627 represents 12,627,000. Based on the National Household Education Survey, a sample survey of approximately 55,000 households with telephones in the civilian, noninstitutional population; for details, see source]

Characteristic	Students participating in community service (1,000) 1996	1999	Percent of students participating in community service 1996	1999	Characteristic	Students participating in community service (1,000) 1996	1999	Percent of students participating in community service 1996	1999
Total[1]	12,627	14,010	49	52	College graduate	2,250	2,648	58	62
Student's grade:					Graduate or professional school	2,653	3,129	64	64
Grades 6 through 8	5,462	5,573	47	48	School type:				
Grades 9 and 10	3,370	3,984	45	50	Public	11,056	12,387	47	50
Grades 11 and 12	3,795	4,448	56	61	Private:				
Sex:					Church-related	1,270	1,244	69	71
Male	5,971	6,490	45	48	Not church-related	301	379	57	68
Female	6,656	7,520	53	57	School size:				
Race/ethnicity:					Under 300 students	1,336	1,681	49	56
White, non-Hispanic	9,113	9,933	53	56	300 to 599 students	3,892	3,806	50	49
Black, non-Hispanic	1,761	1,972	43	48	600 to 999 students	3,111	3,417	48	52
Hispanic	1,246	1,323	38	38	1,000 students or more	4,288	5,106	49	54
Other race-ethnicity	506	781	50	54	School practice:				
Parent's highest level of education:					Requires and arranges service	2,389	2,962	56	60
Less than high school	834	935	34	37	Requires service only	74	162	19	35
High school graduate or equivalent	3,273	3,298	42	46	Arranges service only	9,087	9,953	52	54
Voc/tech education after high school or some college	3,617	4,000	48	50	Neither requires nor arranges service	1,076	933	30	29

[1] Includes students with no grade reported.

Source: U.S. National Center for Education Statistics, Statistics in Brief, November 1999 (NCES 2000-028).

Section 12
Labor Force, Employment, and Earnings

This section presents statistics on the labor force; its distribution by occupation and industry affiliation; and the supply of, demand for, and conditions of labor. The chief source of these data is the Current Population Survey (CPS) conducted by the U.S. Census Bureau for the Bureau of Labor Statistics (BLS). Comprehensive historical and current data are available from the BLS Internet site <http://www.bls.gov/cps/home.htm>. These data are published on a current basis in the BLS monthly publication *Employment and Earnings*. Detailed data on the labor force are also available from the Census Bureaus decennial census of population.

Types of data—Most statistics in this section are obtained by two methods: household interviews or questionnaires and reports of establishment payroll records. Each method provides data that the other cannot suitably supply. Population characteristics, for example, are readily obtainable only from the household survey, while detailed industrial classifications can be readily derived only from establishment records.

Household data are obtained from a monthly sample survey of the population. The CPS is used to gather data for the calendar week including the 12th of the month and provides current comprehensive data on the labor force (see text, Section 1, Population). The CPS provides information on the work status of the population without duplication since each person is classified as employed, unemployed, or not in the labor force. Employed persons holding more than one job are counted only once, according to the job at which they worked the most hours during the survey week.

Monthly, quarterly, and annual data from the CPS are published by the Bureau of Labor Statistics in *Employment and Earnings*. Data presented include national totals of the number of persons in the civilian labor force by sex, race, Hispanic origin, and age; the number employed; hours of work; industry and occupational groups; and the number unemployed, reasons for, and duration of unemployment. Annual data shown in this section are averages of monthly figures for each calendar year, unless otherwise specified. Historical national CPS data are available on the site <http://www.bls.gov/cps/>.

The CPS also produces annual estimates of employment and unemployment for each state, 50 large metropolitan statistical areas, and selected cities. These estimates are published by BLS in its annual *Geographic Profile of Employment and Unemployment*. More detailed geographic data (e.g., for counties and cities) are provided by the decennial population censuses.

Data based on establishment records are compiled by BLS and cooperating state agencies as part of an ongoing Current Employment Statistics program. Survey data, gathered monthly from a sample of employers through electronic interviewing (including touchtone data entry and computer-assisted telephone interviewing) or by mail, fax, or electronic interchange on magnetic tape on computer diskette, are supplemented by data from other government agencies and adjusted at intervals to data from government social insurance program reports. The estimates exclude self-employed persons, private household workers, unpaid family workers, agricultural workers, and the Armed Forces. In March 2002, reporting establishments employed 5 million manufacturing workers (30 percent of the total manufacturing employment at the time), 19 million workers in private nonmanufacturing industries (21 percent of the total in private nonmanufacturing), and 14 million federal, state, and local government employees (64 percent of total government).

The establishment survey counts workers each time they appear on a payroll during the reference period (the payroll period that includes the 12th of the month). Thus, unlike the CPS, a person with two jobs is counted twice. The establishment survey is designed to provide detailed industry information for the nation, states, and metropolitan areas on nonfarm wage and salary employment, average weekly hours, and average hourly and weekly earnings. Establishment survey data also are published in *Employment and Earnings*. Historical national data are available on the site <http://www.bls.gov/ces/>. Historical data for states and metropolitan areas are available on the site <http://www.bls.gov/sae/>.

In June 2003, BLS completed a comprehensive sample redesign of the establishment survey begun in June 2000, changing from a quota-based sample to a probability-based sample. Also in June 2003, all establishment survey employment, hours, and earnings series were converted from being classified by the 1987 Standard Industrial Classification (SIC) system to being classified by the 2002 North American Industry Classification System (NAICS). The NAICS conversion resulted in major definitional changes to many of the previously published SIC-based series. All establishment survey historical time series were reconstructed as part of the NAICS conversion process and all published series have a NAICS-based history extending back to at least 1990. For total nonfarm industries and other high-level aggregates, NAICS history was reconstructed back to the previously existing start date for the series, 1939 in most cases. More information on the sample redesign, the conversion to NAICS, and other changes to the establishment survey implemented in June 2003 appears in "Revisions to the Current Employment Statistics National Estimates Effective May 2003" in the June 2003 issue of *Employment and Earnings,* as well as the Establishment Data portion of the Explanatory Notes and Estimates of Error section of *Employment and Earnings*.

The completion of the sample redesign and the conversion to NAICS for state and metropolitan area establishment survey data was implemented in March 2003 with the release of January 2003 estimates. For a discussion of the changes to the state and area establishment survey data, see "Revisions to the Current Employment Statistics State and Area Estimates Effective January 2003" in the March 2003 issue of *Employment and Earnings*.

Labor force—According to the CPS definitions, the civilian labor force comprises all civilians in the noninstitutional population 16 years and over classified as "employed" or "unemployed" according to the following criteria: Employed civilians comprise (a) all civilians, who, during the reference week, did any work for pay or profit (minimum of an hour's work) or worked 15 hours or more as unpaid workers in a family enterprise and (b) all civilians who were not working but who had jobs or businesses from which they were temporarily absent for noneconomic reasons (illness, weather conditions, vacation, labor-management dispute, etc.) whether they were paid for the time off or were seeking other jobs. Unemployed persons comprise all civilians who had no employment during the reference week, who made specific efforts to find a job within the previous 4 weeks (such as applying directly to an employer or to a public employment service or checking with friends) and who were available for work during that week, except for temporary illness. Persons on layoff from a job and expecting recall also are classified as unemployed. All other civilian persons, 16 years old and over, are classified as "not in the labor force."

Various breaks in the CPS data series have occurred over time due to the introduction of population adjustments and other changes. For details on these breaks in series and the effect that they had on the CPS data, see the section on noncomparability of labor force levels in the Household Data portion of the Explanatory Notes and Estimates of Error section of *Employment and Earnings* available on the site <http://www.bls.gov/cps/cpseetn.pdf>.

In the most recent series break, beginning in January 2003, the CPS reflects the introduction of Census 2000-based population controls. These new population controls substantially increased the size of the civilian noninstitutional population and the civilian labor force. Data from January 2000 through December 2002 were revised to reflect the higher population estimates from Census 2000 and the higher rates of population growth since the census. At the start of the revision period (January 2000), the new population controls raised the civilian noninstitutional population and the civilian labor force by 2.6 and 1.6 million, respectively. By December 2002, the civilian population and labor force were 3.8 and 2.5 million, respectively, higher than originally estimated. The unemployment rate and other ratios were not substantially affected by the population control adjustments. An explanation of the changes and their effects on labor force estimates appears in "Revisions to the Current Population Survey Effective in January 2003" in the February 2003 issue of *Employment and Earnings,* available on the site <http://www.bls.gov/cps/rvcps03.pdf>.

Hours and earnings—Average hourly earnings, based on establishment data, are gross earnings (i.e., earnings before payroll deductions) and include overtime premiums; they exclude irregular bonuses and value of payments in kind. Hours are those for which pay was received. Wages and salaries from the CPS consist of total monies received for work performed by an employee during the income year. It includes wages, salaries, commissions, tips, piece-rate payments, and cash bonuses earned before deductions were made for taxes, bonds, union dues, etc. Persons who worked 35 hours or more are classified as working full time.

Industry and occupational groups—Industry data derived from the CPS for 1983-91 utilize the 1980 census industrial classification developed from the 1972 SIC. CPS data from 1971 to 1982 were based on the 1970 census classification system, which was developed from the 1967 SIC. Most of the industry categories were not affected by the change in classification.

The occupational classification system used in the 1980 census and in the CPS for 1983-91, evolved from the 1980 Standard Occupational Classification (SOC) system, first introduced in 1977. Occupational categories used in the 1980 census classification system are so radically different from the 1970 census system used in the CPS through 1982, that their implementation represented a break in historical data series. In cases where data have not yet been converted to the 1980 classifications and still reflect the 1970 classifications (e.g., Table 643), comparisons between the two systems should not be made.

Beginning in January 1992, the occupational and industrial classification system used in the 1990 census were introduced into the CPS. (These systems were largely based on the 1980 Standard Occupational Classification and the 1987 Standard Industrial Classification Systems, respectively.) For details on the changes over time in the industrial and occupational classification systems used in the CPS, see the section on changes in the occupational and industrial classification systems in the Household Data portion of the Explanatory Notes and Estimates of Error section of *Employment and Earnings* available on the site <http://www.bls.gov/cps/cpseetn.pdf>.

Establishments responding to the establishment survey are classified according to the 2002 North American Industrial Classification System (NAICS). Previously they were classified according to the Standard Industrial Classification Manual (SIC). See text, Section 15, Business Enterprise, for information about the SIC manual and NAICS.

Productivity—BLS publishes data on productivity as measured by output per hour (labor productivity), output per combined unit of labor and capital input (multifactor productivity), and, for manufacturing industries, output per combined unit of capital, labor, energy, materials, and purchased service inputs. Labor productivity and related indexes are published for the business sector as a whole and its major subsectors: nonfarm business, manufacturing, and nonfinancial corporations, and for over 180 four-digit NAICS specific industries. Labor productivity data were converted to a NAICS classification for the SIC classification in September 2003. Data were reconstructed back to 1987. Multifactor productivity and related measures (currently SIC-based) are published for the private business sector and its major subsectors. Productivity indexes that take into account capital, labor, energy, materials, and service inputs are published for the 18 major industry groups that comprise the manufacturing sector, the utility services industry group, for 141 three-digit SIC manufacturing industries, and railroad transportation. The major sector data are published in the BLS quarterly news release, *Productivity and Costs* and in the annual *Multifactor Productivity Trends* release. Industry productivity measures are published annually in the news releases *Productivity and Costs, Manufacturing Industries*, and *Productivity and Costs, Services — Producing and Mining Industries*. Detailed information on methods, limitations, and data sources appears in the BLS *Handbook of Methods*, BLS Bulletin 2490 (1997), Chapters 10 and 11.

Unions—As defined here, unions include traditional labor unions and employee associations similar to labor unions. Data on union membership status provided by BLS are for employed wage and salary workers and relate to their principal job. Earnings by union membership status are usual weekly earnings of full-time wage and salary workers. The information is collected through the Current Population Survey. Collective bargaining settlements data are available for bargaining situations involving 1,000 or more workers in private industry and state and local government.

Work stoppages—Work stoppages include all strikes and lockouts known to BLS that last for at least 1 full day or shift and involve 1,000 or more workers. All stoppages, whether or not authorized by a union, legal or illegal, are counted. Excluded are work slowdowns and instances where employees report to work late or leave early to attend mass meetings or mass rallies.

Seasonal adjustment—Many economic statistics reflect a regularly recurring seasonal movement that can be estimated on the basis of past experience. By eliminating that part of the change which can be ascribed to usual seasonal variation (e.g., climate or school openings and closings), it is possible to observe the cyclical and other nonseasonal movements in the series. However, in evaluating deviations from the seasonal pattern—that is, changes in a seasonally adjusted series—it is important to note that seasonal adjustment is merely an approximation based on past experience. Seasonally adjusted estimates have a broader margin of possible error than the original data on which they are based, since they are subject not only to sampling and other errors, but also are affected by the uncertainties of the adjustment process itself.

Statistical reliability—For discussion of statistical collection, estimation, sampling procedures, and measures of statistical reliability applicable to Census Bureau and BLS data, see Appendix III.

No. 587. Employment Status of the Civilian Population: 1970 to 2002

[In thousands (137,085 represents 137,085,000), except as indicated. Annual averages of monthly figures. For the civilian noninstitutional population 16 years old and over. Based on Current Population Survey; see text, Section 1, and Appendix III]

Year	Civilian noninstitutional population	Civilian labor force Total	Percent of population	Employed	Employment/population ratio [1]	Unemployed Number	Percent of labor force	Not in labor force Number	Percent of population
1970	137,085	82,771	60.4	78,678	57.4	4,093	4.9	54,315	39.6
1980	167,745	106,940	63.8	99,303	59.2	7,637	7.1	60,806	36.2
1981	170,130	108,670	63.9	100,397	59.0	8,273	7.6	61,460	36.1
1982	172,271	110,204	64.0	99,526	57.8	10,678	9.7	62,067	36.0
1983	174,215	111,550	64.0	100,834	57.9	10,717	9.6	62,665	36.0
1984	176,383	113,544	64.4	105,005	59.5	8,539	7.5	62,839	35.6
1985	178,206	115,461	64.8	107,150	60.1	8,312	7.2	62,744	35.2
1986	180,587	117,834	65.3	109,597	60.7	8,237	7.0	62,752	34.7
1987	182,753	119,865	65.6	112,440	61.5	7,425	6.2	62,888	34.4
1988	184,613	121,669	65.9	114,968	62.3	6,701	5.5	62,944	34.1
1989	186,393	123,869	66.5	117,342	63.0	6,528	5.3	62,523	33.5
1990 [2]	189,164	125,840	66.5	118,793	62.8	7,047	5.6	63,324	33.5
1991	190,925	126,346	66.2	117,718	61.7	8,628	6.8	64,578	33.8
1992	192,805	128,105	66.4	118,492	61.5	9,613	7.5	64,700	33.6
1993	194,838	129,200	66.3	120,259	61.7	8,940	6.9	65,638	33.7
1994 [2]	196,814	131,056	66.6	123,060	62.5	7,996	6.1	65,758	33.4
1995	198,584	132,304	66.6	124,900	62.9	7,404	5.6	66,280	33.4
1996	200,591	133,943	66.8	126,708	63.2	7,236	5.4	66,647	33.2
1997 [2]	203,133	136,297	67.1	129,558	63.8	6,739	4.9	66,837	32.9
1998 [2]	205,220	137,673	67.1	131,463	64.1	6,210	4.5	67,547	32.9
1999 [2]	207,753	139,368	67.1	133,488	64.3	5,880	4.2	68,385	32.9
2000 [2]	212,577	142,583	67.1	136,891	64.4	5,692	4.0	69,994	32.9
2001	215,092	143,734	66.8	136,933	63.7	6,801	4.7	71,359	33.2
2002	217,570	144,863	66.6	136,485	62.7	8,378	5.8	72,707	33.4

[1] Civilian employed as a percent of the civilian noninstitutional population.   [2] Data not strictly comparable with data for earlier years. See text, this section, and February 1994, March 1996, February 1997-99, and February 2003 issues of Employment and Earnings.

Source: U.S. Bureau of Labor Statistics, Bulletin 2307; and Employment and Earnings, monthly, January issues and June 2003 issue. See Internet site <http://www.bls.gov/cps/home.htm>.

No. 588. Civilian Labor Force and Participation Rates With Projections: 1980 to 2010

[106.9 represents 106,900,000. For civilian noninstitutional population 16 years old and over. Annual averages of monthly figures. Rates are based on annual average civilian noninstitutional population of each specified group and represent proportion of each specified group in the civilian labor force. Based on Current Population Survey; see text, Section 1, and Appendix III]

Race, sex, and age	Civilian labor force (millions) 1980	1990 [1]	2000 [1]	2001	2002	2010, proj.	Participation rate (percent) 1980	1990 [1]	2000 [1]	2001	2002	2010, proj.
Total [2]	106.9	125.8	142.6	143.7	144.9	157.7	63.8	66.5	67.1	66.8	66.6	67.5
White	93.6	107.4	118.5	119.4	120.2	128.0	64.1	66.9	67.3	67.0	66.8	67.6
Male	54.5	59.6	64.5	65.0	65.3	68.2	78.2	77.1	75.5	75.1	74.8	73.8
Female	39.1	47.8	54.1	54.4	54.8	59.9	51.2	57.4	59.5	59.4	59.3	61.6
Black	10.9	13.7	16.4	16.4	16.6	20.0	61.0	64.0	65.8	65.3	64.8	67.1
Male	5.6	6.8	7.7	7.6	7.8	9.0	70.3	71.0	69.2	68.4	68.4	68.2
Female	5.3	6.9	8.7	8.8	8.8	11.1	53.1	58.3	63.1	62.8	61.8	66.2
Hispanic [3]	6.1	10.7	16.7	17.3	17.9	20.9	64.0	67.4	69.7	69.5	69.1	69.0
Male	3.8	6.5	9.9	10.3	10.6	11.7	81.4	81.4	81.5	81.0	80.2	79.0
Female	2.3	4.2	6.8	7.0	7.3	9.2	47.4	53.1	57.5	57.6	57.6	59.4
Male	61.5	69.0	76.3	76.9	77.5	82.2	77.4	76.4	74.8	74.4	74.1	73.2
16 to 19 years	5.0	4.1	4.3	4.1	3.9	4.7	60.5	55.7	52.8	50.2	47.5	52.3
20 to 24 years	8.6	7.9	7.5	7.6	7.8	8.6	85.9	84.4	82.6	81.6	80.7	81.2
25 to 34 years	17.0	19.9	17.8	17.7	17.6	17.9	95.2	94.1	93.4	92.7	92.4	93.1
35 to 44 years	11.8	17.5	20.1	20.0	19.8	17.8	95.5	94.3	92.7	92.5	92.1	92.3
45 to 54 years	9.9	11.1	16.3	16.8	17.1	18.9	91.2	90.7	88.6	88.5	88.5	87.8
55 to 64 years	7.2	6.6	7.8	8.2	8.8	11.1	72.1	67.8	67.3	68.3	69.2	67.0
65 years and over	1.9	2.0	2.5	2.5	2.5	3.1	19.0	16.3	17.7	17.7	17.9	19.5
Female	45.5	56.8	66.3	66.8	67.4	75.5	51.5	57.5	59.9	59.8	59.6	62.2
16 to 19 years	4.4	3.7	4.0	3.8	3.7	4.6	52.9	51.6	51.2	49.0	47.3	52.2
20 to 24 years	7.3	6.7	6.7	6.9	7.0	8.1	68.9	71.3	73.1	72.7	72.1	75.7
25 to 34 years	12.3	16.1	14.9	14.7	14.6	16.3	65.5	73.5	76.1	75.5	75.1	81.4
35 to 44 years	8.6	14.7	17.5	17.4	17.1	16.2	65.5	76.4	77.2	77.1	76.4	80.0
45 to 54 years	7.0	9.1	14.8	15.2	15.5	17.9	59.9	71.2	76.8	76.4	76.0	80.0
55 to 64 years	4.7	4.9	6.6	6.9	7.6	10.1	41.3	45.2	51.9	53.2	55.2	55.2
65 years and over	1.2	1.5	1.8	1.9	1.9	2.3	8.1	8.6	9.4	9.6	9.8	11.1

[1] See footnote 2, Table 587.   [2] Includes other races, not shown separately.   [3] Persons of Hispanic origin may be of any race.

Source: U.S. Bureau of Labor Statistics, Employment and Earnings, monthly, January issues; Monthly Labor Review, November 2001; and unpublished data. See Internet site <http://www.bls.gov/cps/home.htm>.

No. 589. Employment Status of the Civilian Population: 1970 to 2002

[In thousands (137,085 represents 137,085,000), except as indicated. Annual averages of monthly figures. For the civilian noninstitutional population 16 years old and over. Based on Current Population Survey; see text, Section 1, and Appendix III]

Year, sex, race, and Hispanic origin	Civilian noninstitutional population	Civilian labor force — Total	Percent of population	Employed	Employment/population ratio [1]	Unemployed — Number	Percent of labor force	Not in labor force — Number	Percent of population
Total: [2]									
1970	137,085	82,771	60.4	78,678	57.4	4,093	4.9	54,315	39.6
1980	167,745	106,940	63.8	99,303	59.2	7,637	7.1	60,806	36.2
1990 [3]	189,164	125,840	66.5	118,793	62.8	7,047	5.6	63,324	33.5
1995 [3]	198,584	132,304	66.6	124,900	62.9	7,404	5.6	66,280	33.4
1999 [3]	207,753	139,368	67.1	133,488	64.3	5,880	4.2	68,385	32.9
2000 [3]	212,577	142,583	67.1	136,891	64.4	5,692	4.0	69,994	32.9
2001	215,092	143,734	66.8	136,933	63.7	6,801	4.7	71,359	33.2
2002	217,570	144,863	66.6	136,485	62.7	8,378	5.8	72,707	33.4
Male:									
1970	64,304	51,228	79.7	48,990	76.2	2,238	4.4	13,076	20.3
1980	79,398	61,453	77.4	57,186	72.0	4,267	6.9	17,945	22.6
1990 [3]	90,377	69,011	76.4	65,104	72.0	3,906	5.7	21,367	23.6
1995 [3]	95,178	71,360	75.0	67,377	70.8	3,983	5.6	23,818	25.0
1999 [3]	99,722	74,512	74.7	71,446	71.6	3,066	4.1	25,210	25.3
2000 [3]	101,964	76,280	74.8	73,305	71.9	2,975	3.9	25,684	25.2
2001	103,282	76,886	74.4	73,196	70.9	3,690	4.8	26,396	25.6
2002	104,585	77,500	74.1	72,903	69.7	4,597	5.9	27,085	25.9
Female:									
1970	72,782	31,543	43.3	29,688	40.8	1,855	5.9	41,239	56.7
1980	88,348	45,487	51.5	42,117	47.7	3,370	7.4	42,861	48.5
1990 [3]	98,787	56,829	57.5	53,689	54.3	3,140	5.5	41,957	42.5
1995 [3]	103,406	60,944	58.9	57,523	55.6	3,421	5.6	42,462	41.1
1999 [3]	108,031	64,855	60.0	62,042	57.4	2,814	4.3	43,175	40.0
2000 [3]	110,613	66,303	59.9	63,586	57.5	2,717	4.1	44,310	40.1
2001	111,811	66,848	59.8	63,737	57.0	3,111	4.7	44,962	40.2
2002	112,985	67,363	59.6	63,582	56.3	3,781	5.6	45,621	40.4
White:									
1970	122,174	73,556	60.2	70,217	57.5	3,339	4.5	48,618	39.8
1980	146,122	93,600	64.1	87,715	60.0	5,884	6.3	52,523	35.9
1990 [3]	160,625	107,447	66.9	102,261	63.7	5,186	4.8	53,178	33.1
1995 [3]	166,914	111,950	67.1	106,490	63.8	5,459	4.9	54,965	32.9
1999 [3]	173,085	116,509	67.3	112,235	64.8	4,273	3.7	56,577	32.7
2000 [3]	176,220	118,545	67.3	114,424	64.9	4,121	3.5	57,675	32.7
2001	178,111	119,399	67.0	114,430	64.2	4,969	4.2	58,713	33.0
2002	179,783	120,150	66.8	114,013	63.4	6,137	5.1	59,633	33.2
Black:									
1973	14,917	8,976	60.2	8,128	54.5	846	9.4	5,941	39.8
1980	17,824	10,865	61.0	9,313	52.2	1,553	14.3	6,959	39.0
1990 [3]	21,477	13,740	64.0	12,175	56.7	1,565	11.4	7,737	36.0
1995 [3]	23,246	14,817	63.7	13,279	57.1	1,538	10.4	8,429	36.3
1999 [3]	24,855	16,365	65.8	15,056	60.6	1,309	8.0	8,490	34.2
2000 [3]	24,902	16,397	65.8	15,156	60.9	1,241	7.6	8,505	34.2
2001	25,138	16,421	65.3	15,006	59.7	1,416	8.6	8,717	34.7
2002	25,578	16,565	64.8	14,872	58.1	1,693	10.2	9,013	35.2
Hispanic: [4]									
1980	9,598	6,146	64.0	5,527	57.6	620	10.1	3,451	36.0
1986	12,344	8,076	65.4	7,219	58.5	857	10.6	4,268	34.6
1990 [3]	15,904	10,720	67.4	9,845	61.9	876	8.2	5,184	32.6
1995 [3]	18,629	12,267	65.8	11,127	59.7	1,140	9.3	6,362	34.2
1999 [3]	21,650	14,665	67.7	13,720	63.4	945	6.4	6,985	32.3
2000 [3]	23,938	16,689	69.7	15,735	65.7	954	5.7	7,249	30.3
2001	24,942	17,328	69.5	16,190	64.9	1,138	6.6	7,614	30.5
2002	25,963	17,943	69.1	16,590	63.9	1,353	7.5	8,020	30.9
Mexican:									
1986	7,377	4,941	67.0	4,387	59.5	555	11.2	2,436	33.0
1990 [3]	9,752	6,707	68.8	6,146	63.0	561	8.4	3,045	31.2
1999 [3]	13,582	9,267	68.2	8,656	63.7	611	6.6	4,315	31.8
2000 [3]	15,333	10,783	70.3	10,144	66.2	639	5.9	4,550	29.7
2001	15,909	11,218	70.5	10,471	65.8	747	6.7	4,691	29.5
2002	16,420	11,542	70.3	10,673	65.0	869	7.5	4,878	29.7
Puerto Rican:									
1986	1,494	804	53.8	691	46.3	113	14.0	690	46.2
1990 [3]	1,718	960	55.9	870	50.6	91	9.5	758	44.1
1999 [3]	2,058	1,269	61.6	1,165	56.6	104	8.2	789	38.3
2000 [3]	2,193	1,411	64.3	1,318	60.1	92	6.6	783	35.7
2001	2,367	1,454	61.4	1,341	56.6	114	7.8	913	38.6
2002	2,484	1,546	62.2	1,401	56.4	145	9.4	938	37.8
Cuban:									
1986	842	570	67.7	533	63.3	36	6.4	272	32.3
1990 [3]	918	603	65.7	559	60.9	44	7.2	315	34.3
1999 [3]	1,141	714	62.6	681	59.7	33	4.6	427	37.4
2000 [3]	1,174	740	63.1	707	60.3	33	4.5	434	37.0
2001	1,118	671	60.0	628	56.1	44	6.5	447	40.0
2002	1,141	635	55.6	592	51.9	43	6.7	507	44.4

[1] Civilian employed as a percent of the civilian noninstitutional population. [2] Includes other races, not shown separately. [3] See footnote 2, Table 587. [4] Persons of Hispanic origin may be of any race. Includes persons of other Hispanic origin, not shown separately.

Source: U.S. Bureau of Labor Statistics, Bulletin 2307; and *Employment and Earnings*, monthly, January issues and June 2003 issue. See Internet site <http://www.bls.gov/cps/home.htm>.

No. 590. Civilian Labor Force—Percent Distribution by Sex and Age: 1970 to 2002

[82,771 represents 82,771,000. For civilian noninstitutional population 16 years old and over Annual averages of monthly figures. Based on Current Population Survey; see text, Section 1, and Appendix III]

Year and sex	Civilian labor force (1,000)	16 to 19 years	20 to 24 years	25 to 34 years	35 to 44 years	45 to 54 years	55 to 64 years	65 yrs. and over
Total: 1970	82,771	8.8	12.8	20.6	19.9	20.5	13.6	3.9
1980	106,940	8.8	14.9	27.3	19.1	15.8	11.2	2.9
1990 [1]	125,840	6.2	11.7	28.6	25.5	16.1	9.2	2.7
1995	132,304	5.9	10.3	25.8	27.0	19.1	9.0	2.9
2000 [1]	142,583	5.8	10.0	23.0	26.3	21.8	10.1	3.0
2002	144,863	5.2	10.2	22.2	25.5	22.5	11.3	3.1
Male: 1970	51,228	7.8	11.2	22.1	20.4	20.3	13.9	4.2
1980	61,453	8.1	14.0	27.6	19.3	16.1	11.8	3.1
1990 [1]	69,011	5.9	11.4	28.8	25.3	16.1	9.6	2.9
1995	71,360	5.7	10.3	26.2	26.9	18.8	9.1	3.1
2000 [1]	76,280	5.6	9.9	23.4	26.3	21.3	10.2	3.3
2002	77,500	5.0	10.0	22.7	25.6	22.1	11.3	3.3
Female: 1970	31,543	10.3	15.5	18.1	18.9	20.7	13.2	3.3
1980	45,487	9.6	16.1	26.9	19.0	15.4	10.4	2.6
1990 [1]	56,829	6.5	12.0	28.3	25.8	16.1	8.7	2.6
1995	60,944	6.1	10.4	25.5	27.2	19.4	8.8	2.7
2000 [1]	66,303	6.0	10.2	22.5	26.4	22.3	9.9	2.7
2002	67,363	5.5	10.4	21.7	25.4	22.9	11.2	2.9

[1] See footnote 2, Table 587.

Source: U.S. Bureau of Labor Statistics, Bulletin Bulletin 2307, and *Employment and Earnings*, monthly, January issues and June 2003 issue. See Internet site <http://www.bls.gov/cps/home.htm>.

No. 591. Civilian Labor Force and Participation Rates by Educational Attainment, Sex, Race, and Hispanic Origin: 1992 to 2002

[106,490 represents 106,490,000 Annual averages of monthly figures. For the civilian noninstitutional population 25 years of age and older. See Table 626 for unemployment data. Based on Current Population Survey; see text, Section 1, and Appendix III]

Year, sex, and race	Civilian labor force Total (1,000)	Less than high school diploma	High school graduate, no degree	Less than a bachelor's degree	College graduate	Participation rate [1] Total	Less than high school diploma	High school graduates, no degree	Less than a bachelor's degree	College graduate
Total: [2]										
1992	106,490	12.6	35.6	25.4	26.4	66.5	41.2	66.4	75.3	81.3
1995	110,851	10.8	33.1	27.9	28.1	66.7	39.9	65.4	74.5	81.0
1999 [3]	117,101	10.3	31.9	27.4	30.4	67.4	42.7	64.8	74.1	79.9
2000 [3]	120,061	10.4	31.4	27.7	30.5	67.3	43.5	64.4	73.9	79.4
2001	121,275	10.4	31.0	27.8	30.8	67.3	44.0	64.2	73.7	78.9
2002	122,497	10.3	30.8	27.4	31.4	67.2	44.4	64.2	73.1	78.6
Male:										
1992	58,439	14.1	34.0	24.0	27.9	77.0	54.7	78.3	83.9	86.9
1995	59,986	12.2	32.3	26.1	29.4	76.0	52.1	76.5	82.1	85.8
1999 [3]	62,903	11.7	31.5	25.8	31.1	76.1	54.9	75.6	81.1	84.6
2000 [3]	64,490	11.8	31.1	25.9	31.2	76.1	56.0	75.1	80.9	84.4
2001	65,176	11.8	30.9	25.9	31.5	76.0	56.4	74.5	80.8	84.3
2002	65,861	11.9	30.7	25.5	31.9	75.9	57.2	74.5	80.2	84.0
Female:										
1992	48,051	10.7	37.5	27.1	24.7	57.1	29.5	56.8	67.8	74.8
1995	50,865	9.2	34.2	30.0	26.6	58.3	29.2	56.4	68.1	75.4
1999 [3]	54,198	8.8	32.4	29.3	29.5	59.5	31.9	55.9	68.1	74.8
2000 [3]	55,572	8.8	31.8	29.7	29.7	59.4	32.3	55.5	68.0	74.0
2001	56,099	8.7	31.2	30.0	30.0	59.4	32.7	55.4	67.8	73.1
2002	56,636	8.4	30.9	29.7	31.0	59.4	32.5	55.3	67.2	73.0
White:										
1992	90,627	11.8	35.5	25.5	27.2	66.3	41.1	65.4	74.6	81.0
1995	94,139	10.1	33.0	27.8	29.1	66.7	40.0	64.8	73.8	80.6
1999 [3]	98,025	10.0	31.9	27.2	31.1	67.1	43.1	64.0	73.2	79.6
2000 [3]	99,964	10.1	31.4	27.5	31.0	67.0	44.1	63.6	73.1	79.0
2001	100,854	10.1	31.0	27.7	31.2	67.0	44.6	63.4	72.9	78.6
2002	101,711	10.0	30.8	27.3	31.9	67.0	44.9	63.4	72.5	78.2
Black:										
1992	11,583	18.2	39.5	26.4	15.9	66.7	40.6	72.9	80.9	86.2
1995	12,152	13.9	37.1	30.7	18.3	66.0	36.2	69.7	79.8	85.6
1999 [3]	13,540	12.4	36.5	31.2	19.9	68.5	39.6	70.5	79.3	84.5
2000 [3]	13,582	12.4	36.0	31.2	20.5	68.2	39.3	69.9	79.3	84.4
2001	13,646	12.4	35.5	31.5	20.5	68.0	40.2	68.9	78.7	83.6
2002	13,787	12.5	35.4	31.5	20.5	67.6	40.8	68.4	77.8	82.8
Hispanic: [4]										
1992	8,728	38.9	29.6	20.0	11.5	68.3	56.3	75.5	82.2	83.2
1995	9,599	37.2	29.3	21.7	11.7	67.5	55.3	74.3	79.7	83.1
1999 [3]	11,563	36.5	29.1	21.1	13.2	69.5	58.8	73.8	79.9	83.2
2000 [3]	12,975	36.7	29.3	20.6	13.4	71.5	61.9	75.0	80.8	83.5
2001	13,536	36.7	29.4	20.7	13.2	71.2	61.2	75.2	81.2	82.7
2002	14,162	36.3	29.4	20.3	13.9	71.0	61.3	74.1	80.7	83.2

[1] See headnote, Table 588. [2] Includes other races, not shown separately. [3] See footnote 2, Table 587. [4] Persons of Hispanic origin may be of any race.

Source: U.S. Bureau of Labor Statistics, *Employment and Earnings*, monthly, January issues and June 2003 issue. See Internet site <http://www.bls.gov/cps/home.htm>.

Labor Force, Employment, and Earnings

No. 592. Characteristics of the Civilian Labor Force by State: 2002

[In thousands (144,863 represents 144,863,000), except ratio and rate. For civilian noninstitutional population, 16 years old and over. Annual averages of monthly figures. Because of separate processing and weighting procedures, the totals for the United States may differ from results obtained by aggregating totals for states]

State	Total Number	Total Female	Employed Total	Employed Female	Employed population ratio [1]	Unemployed Total Number	Unemployed Total Female	Rate [2] Total	Rate [2] Male	Rate [2] Female	Participation rate [3] Male	Participation rate [3] Female
United States..	144,863	67,363	136,485	63,582	62.7	8,378	3,781	5.8	5.9	5.6	66.6	59.6
Alabama.........	2,103	999	1,978	938	57.6	124	61	5.9	5.7	6.1	61.3	54.7
Alaska..........	323	148	298	138	66.4	25	10	7.7	8.7	6.5	71.9	66.3
Arizona.........	2,672	1,150	2,507	1,077	62.2	165	73	6.2	6.1	6.3	66.2	57.0
Arkansas	1,285	604	1,216	571	59.0	70	33	5.4	5.4	5.5	62.4	55.4
California.......	17,405	7,832	16,242	7,314	62.3	1,163	518	6.7	6.7	6.6	66.7	58.8
Colorado........	2,437	1,079	2,298	1,016	67.7	140	63	5.7	5.7	5.8	71.8	64.4
Connecticut.....	1,773	852	1,696	819	64.7	77	34	4.3	4.7	3.9	67.6	62.0
Delaware	423	206	405	198	65.1	18	8	4.2	4.4	4.0	68.0	62.5
District of Columbia.	304	152	285	143	61.9	20	9	6.4	6.6	6.2	66.2	61.1
Florida	8,084	3,726	7,642	3,511	59.1	442	215	5.5	5.2	5.8	62.5	55.7
Georgia	4,292	1,990	4,071	1,877	64.3	221	113	5.1	4.7	5.7	67.7	59.8
Hawaii	582	283	557	272	62.7	25	11	4.2	4.7	3.8	65.5	60.8
Idaho...........	684	317	645	299	65.2	40	17	5.8	6.1	5.5	69.2	62.0
Illinois	6,378	3,001	5,963	2,806	62.6	415	194	6.5	6.5	6.5	67.0	60.2
Indiana.........	3,175	1,491	3,012	1,420	64.7	163	70	5.1	5.5	4.7	68.2	61.4
Iowa	1,667	792	1,601	762	70.3	67	30	4.0	4.2	3.8	73.2	67.1
Kansas.........	1,414	672	1,342	643	65.8	72	30	5.1	5.8	4.4	69.3	62.9
Kentucky	1,966	936	1,857	889	58.3	110	47	5.6	6.1	5.0	61.8	55.6
Louisiana	2,006	921	1,883	871	56.4	123	51	6.1	6.7	5.5	60.1	52.1
Maine..........	686	332	656	320	63.5	30	11	4.4	5.3	3.4	66.4	61.6
Maryland	2,898	1,409	2,772	1,347	67.2	126	62	4.4	4.3	4.4	70.2	64.3
Massachusetts...	3,486	1,652	3,301	1,570	65.4	185	82	5.3	5.6	5.0	69.1	62.3
Michigan........	5,001	2,335	4,691	2,202	61.3	310	132	6.2	6.7	5.7	65.4	58.9
Minnesota.......	2,918	1,392	2,790	1,344	72.4	128	48	4.4	5.3	3.4	75.7	71.2
Mississippi	1,298	621	1,210	579	56.6	88	42	6.8	6.9	6.7	60.8	54.0
Missouri........	2,990	1,458	2,825	1,375	65.2	165	83	5.5	5.3	5.7	69.1	63.8
Montana........	464	217	442	209	62.7	21	8	4.6	5.4	3.8	65.7	60.7
Nebraska	959	457	925	442	70.6	34	15	3.6	3.9	3.2	73.2	67.1
Nevada	1,122	485	1060	457	65.6	62	27	5.5	5.4	5.7	69.4	60.9
New Hampshire...	706	330	672	314	68.0	33	15	4.7	4.8	4.6	71.4	65.2
New Jersey......	4,368	2,048	4,113	1,917	62.5	255	131	5.8	5.3	6.4	66.3	59.5
New Mexico.....	878	410	830	390	60.0	48	20	5.4	6.0	4.8	63.5	57.4
New York	9,362	4,420	8,790	4,178	59.3	573	242	6.1	6.7	5.5	63.2	56.6
North Carolina...	4,171	1,959	3,890	1,817	62.1	281	142	6.7	6.3	7.3	66.6	59.9
North Dakota.....	346	166	332	161	67.5	14	6	4.0	4.6	3.4	70.4	65.5
Ohio	5,828	2,772	5,497	2,625	63.2	331	148	5.7	6.0	5.3	67.0	60.7
Oklahoma.......	1,693	782	1,617	751	61.7	76	31	4.5	4.9	4.0	64.6	57.6
Oregon.........	1,834	841	1,695	783	62.4	138	58	7.5	8.1	6.9	67.5	60.6
Pennsylvania....	6,290	2,951	5,934	2,805	61.8	356	147	5.7	6.3	5.0	65.5	58.9
Rhode Island.....	556	267	528	255	62.9	28	12	5.1	5.7	4.4	66.3	59.6
South Carolina...	1,968	944	1,851	884	58.9	117	60	6.0	5.6	6.3	62.6	56.9
South Dakota	421	201	408	195	71.1	13	6	3.1	3.4	2.8	73.4	68.1
Tennessee	2,926	1,367	2,776	1,293	62.4	150	74	5.1	4.9	5.4	65.8	58.3
Texas..........	10,751	4,802	10,070	4,495	63.5	681	307	6.3	6.3	6.4	67.8	58.8
Utah	1,180	523	1,108	489	66.9	72	34	6.1	5.8	6.4	71.3	62.5
Vermont	349	170	336	164	68.6	13	6	3.7	4.1	3.4	71.3	66.5
Virginia.........	3,735	1,774	3,583	1,696	65.7	152	77	4.1	3.8	4.4	68.5	62.3
Washington......	3,097	1,431	2,871	1,333	62.3	226	98	7.3	7.7	6.9	67.2	60.7
West Virginia....	804	367	755	348	52.6	49	20	6.1	6.7	5.4	56.0	48.8
Wisconsin.......	3,028	1,418	2,861	1,356	68.3	167	63	5.5	6.4	4.4	72.3	66.7
Wyoming	270	127	259	121	67.6	11	5	4.2	4.1	4.3	70.5	64.2

[1] Civilian employment as a percent of civilian noninstitutional population. [2] Percent unemployed of the civilian labor force. [3] Percent of civilian noninstitutional population of each specified group in the civilian labor force.

Source: U.S. Bureau of Labor Statistics, Local Area Unemployment Statistics, *Geographic Profile of Employment and Unemployment, 2002*. See Internet site <http://www.bls.gov/gps/>.

No. 593. Civilian Labor Force by Selected Metropolitan Area: 2002

[144,863 represents 144,863,000. For the civilian noninstitutional population 16 years old and over. Annual averages of monthly figures. Data are derived from the Local Area Unemployment Statistics Program. For definition of metropolitan areas, see Appendix II]

Metropolitan areas ranked by labor force size, 2002	Civilian labor force (1,000)	Unemployment rate [1]	Metropolitan areas ranked by labor force size, 2002	Civilian labor force (1,000)	Unemployment rate [1]
U.S. total	144,863	5.8	Las Vegas, NV-AZ MSA	886	5.7
Los Angeles-Long Beach, CA PMSA	4,696	6.8	Columbus, OH MSA	883	4.4
New York, NY PMSA	4,431	7.3	Cincinnati, OH-KY-IN PMSA	867	4.8
Chicago, IL PMSA	4,277	6.7	Sacramento, CA MSA	864	5.2
Washington, DC-MD-VA-WV PMSA	2,823	3.7	Charlotte-Gastonia-Rock Hill, NC-SC MSA	860	6.3
Philadelphia, PA-NJ PMSA	2,649	5.5	Fort Lauderdale, FL PMSA	860	6.0
Atlanta, GA MSA	2,378	5.3	Milwaukee-Waukesha, WI PMSA	817	6.0
Houston, TX PMSA	2,278	5.9	San Antonio, TX MSA	812	5.2
Detroit, MI PMSA	2,220	6.2	Norfolk-Virginia Beach-Newport News, VA-NC MSA	779	4.2
Dallas, TX PMSA	2,039	7.1	Austin-San Marcos, TX MSA	769	5.7
Boston, MA-NH PMSA	1,923	4.8	Salt Lake City-Ogden, UT MSA	747	6.1
Minneapolis-St. Paul, MN-WI MSA	1,833	4.3	Raleigh-Durham-Chapel Hill, NC MSA	700	5.1
Phoenix-Mesa, AZ MSA	1,791	5.7	Nashville, TN MSA	696	4.0
Riverside-San Bernardino, CA PMSA	1,646	5.9	Bergen-Passaic, NJ PMSA	680	5.8
Orange County, CA PMSA	1,560	4.1	Greensboro—Winston-Salem—High Point, NC MSA	678	6.2
Nassau-Suffolk, NY PMSA	1,474	4.3	Middlesex-Somerset-Hunterdon, NJ PMSA	677	5.0
San Diego, CA MSA	1,468	4.3	Providence-Fall River-Warwick, RI-MA MSA	631	5.3
Seattle-Bellevue-Everett, WA PMSA	1,396	6.8	Grand Rapids-Muskegon-Holland, MI MSA	607	6.4
St. Louis, MO-IL MSA	1,380	5.7	Hartford, CT MSA	604	4.5
Baltimore, MD PMSA	1,347	4.8	New Orleans, LA MSA	593	5.4
Tampa-St. Petersburg-Clearwater, FL MSA	1,324	4.6	Jacksonville, FL MSA	591	5.3
Oakland, CA PMSA	1,291	6.1	Memphis, TN-AR-MS MSA	582	5.2
Denver, CO PMSA	1,216	5.9	West Palm Beach-Boca Raton, FL MSA	580	5.9
Pittsburgh, PA MSA	1,211	5.4	Rochester, NY MSA	577	5.9
Miami, FL PMSA	1,121	7.7	Buffalo-Niagara Falls, NY MSA	575	6.1
Cleveland-Lorain-Elyria, OH PMSA	1,113	6.5	Oklahoma City, OK MSA	574	4.1
Portland-Vancouver, OR-WA PMSA	1,092	7.8	Monmouth-Ocean, NJ PMSA	565	5.3
Newark, NJ PMSA	1,061	6.1	Louisville, KY-IN MSA	561	5.2
Kansas City, MO-KS MSA	1,003	5.7	Richmond-Petersburg, VA MSA	540	4.0
San Jose, CA PMSA	958	8.4			
Fort Worth-Arlington, TX PMSA	958	6.1			
Orlando, FL MSA	957	5.3			
San Francisco, CA PMSA	940	5.9			
Indianapolis, IN MSA	893	4.6			

[1] Percent unemployed of the civilian labor force.

Source: U.S. Bureau of Labor Statistics, Local Area Unemployment Statistics program. Local Area Unemployment Statistics program. See Internet site <http://www.bls.gov/lau/>.

No. 594. School Enrollment and Labor Force Status: 1990 and 2002

[In thousands (31,421 represents 31,421,000), except percent. As of October. For the civilian noninstitutional population 16 to 24 years old. Based on Current Population Survey; see text, Section 1, and Appendix III]

Characteristic	Population 1990	Population 2002	Civilian labor force 1990	Civilian labor force 2002	Employed 1990	Employed 2002	Unemployed 1990, total	Unemployed 2002 Total	Unemployed 2002 Rate [1]
Total, 16 to 24 years [2]	31,421	35,498	20,679	22,128	18,317	19,612	3,464	2,515	11.4
Enrolled in school [2]	15,210	19,376	7,301	8,984	6,527	8,088	1,021	895	10.0
16 to 19 years	10,118	12,676	4,244	4,957	3,645	4,339	807	618	12.5
20 to 24 years	5,092	6,699	3,057	4,027	2,882	3,749	214	277	6.9
Sex:									
Male	7,704	9,524	3,635	4,069	3,215	3,640	566	429	10.5
Female	7,507	9,852	3,666	4,914	3,312	4,448	455	466	9.5
College level	8,139	10,213	4,542	5,802	4,231	5,367	364	435	7.5
Full-time	6,810	8,660	3,376	4,490	3,117	4,141	300	349	7.8
Race:									
White	12,308	15,193	6,294	7,510	5,705	6,820	798	690	9.2
Below college	5,535	7,173	2,374	2,776	2,021	2,397	516	379	13.6
College level	6,772	8,020	3,919	4,734	3,685	4,423	282	311	6.6
Black	2,129	2,758	718	923	576	767	189	156	16.9
Below college	1,207	1,478	306	303	212	240	120	63	20.8
College level	922	1,279	411	620	364	527	70	93	15.0
Not enrolled [2]	16,210	16,122	13,379	13,144	11,789	11,524	2,443	1,620	12.3
White	13,317	12,854	11,276	10,683	10,193	9,605	1,803	1,078	10.1
Black	2,441	2,472	1,752	1,842	1,298	1,381	604	461	25.0

[1] Percent unemployed of civilian labor force in each category. [2] Includes other races, not shown separately.

Source: U.S. Bureau of Labor Statistics, Bulletin 2307; *College Enrollment and Work Activity of High School Graduates, News*, USDL 03-330, June 25, 2003; and unpublished data. See Internet site <http://www.bls.gov/bls/newsrels.htm#OEUS>.

Labor Force, Employment, and Earnings 389

No. 595. Labor Force Participation Rates by Marital Status, Sex, and Age: 1970 to 2002

[Annual averages of monthly figures. See Table 592 for definition of participation rate. Based on Current Population Survey; see text, Section 1, and Appendix III]

Marital status and year	Male participation rate							Female participation rate						
	Total	16-19 years	20-24 years	25-34 years	35-44 years	45-64 years	65 and over	Total	16-19 years	20-24 years	25-34 years	35-44 years	45-64 years	65 and over
Single:														
1970	65.5	54.6	73.8	87.9	86.2	75.7	25.2	56.8	44.7	73.0	81.4	78.6	73.0	19.7
1980	72.6	59.9	81.3	89.2	82.2	66.9	16.8	64.4	53.6	75.2	83.3	76.9	65.6	13.9
1985	73.8	56.3	81.5	89.4	84.6	65.5	15.6	66.6	52.3	76.3	82.4	80.8	67.9	9.8
1990 [1]	74.8	55.1	81.6	89.9	84.5	67.3	15.7	66.7	51.7	74.5	80.9	80.8	66.2	12.1
1995	73.7	54.4	80.3	88.7	81.4	67.0	17.9	66.8	52.2	72.9	80.2	79.5	67.3	11.6
1997 [1]	73.1	51.9	80.1	89.0	82.1	68.5	14.8	67.9	51.0	75.1	82.3	80.1	70.8	11.5
1998 [1]	73.3	52.9	79.7	89.1	82.5	70.2	15.2	68.5	52.4	75.3	83.0	80.9	69.9	9.7
1999 [1]	73.4	52.5	79.7	89.5	83.5	70.6	17.3	68.7	51.1	76.1	84.2	80.8	69.6	9.9
2000 [1]	73.6	52.5	80.5	89.4	82.9	69.7	17.3	68.9	51.1	76.1	83.9	80.9	69.9	10.8
2001	72.7	50.0	79.6	89.0	83.2	69.8	15.4	68.1	49.1	75.3	83.2	81.3	69.9	12.1
2002	71.7	47.2	78.7	88.7	83.1	69.6	16.9	67.4	47.3	74.5	83.3	79.9	69.6	14.3
Married: [2]														
1970	86.1	92.3	94.7	98.0	98.1	91.2	29.9	40.5	37.8	47.9	38.8	46.8	44.0	7.3
1980	80.9	91.3	96.9	97.5	97.2	84.3	20.5	49.8	49.3	61.4	58.8	61.8	46.9	7.3
1985	78.7	91.0	95.6	97.4	96.8	81.7	16.8	53.8	49.6	65.7	65.8	68.1	49.4	6.6
1990 [1]	78.6	92.1	95.6	96.9	96.7	82.6	17.5	58.4	49.5	66.1	69.6	74.0	56.5	8.5
1995	77.5	89.2	94.9	96.3	95.4	82.4	18.0	61.0	51.6	64.7	72.0	75.7	62.7	9.1
1997 [1]	77.7	84.6	94.9	96.1	95.7	83.6	18.3	61.6	50.1	66.1	71.9	76.0	64.6	8.9
1998 [1]	77.6	83.8	95.0	96.4	95.8	83.7	17.5	61.2	49.8	66.1	71.6	74.5	64.9	8.9
1999 [1]	77.5	83.2	93.7	96.5	95.9	83.4	18.3	61.2	48.8	64.5	70.9	74.6	65.3	9.6
2000 [1]	77.3	79.5	94.1	96.7	95.8	83.0	19.2	61.1	53.2	63.8	70.3	74.8	65.4	10.1
2001	77.4	77.7	94.2	95.9	95.6	83.7	19.1	61.2	45.1	63.9	69.9	74.5	66.1	10.3
2002	77.4	81.1	93.3	95.7	95.1	83.8	19.4	61.0	49.6	63.4	69.3	73.8	66.5	10.7
Other: [3]														
1970	60.7	(B)	90.4	93.7	91.1	78.5	19.3	40.3	48.6	60.3	64.6	68.8	61.9	10.0
1980	67.5	(B)	92.6	94.1	91.9	73.3	13.7	43.6	50.0	68.4	76.5	77.1	60.2	8.2
1985	68.7	(B)	95.1	93.7	91.8	72.8	11.4	45.1	51.9	66.2	76.9	81.6	61.0	7.5
1990 [1]	68.9	(B)	93.1	93.0	90.7	74.9	12.0	47.2	53.9	65.4	77.0	82.1	65.0	8.4
1995	66.2	(B)	92.7	90.9	88.2	72.4	12.1	47.4	55.8	67.2	77.1	80.7	67.2	8.4
1997 [1]	67.4	60.8	89.9	92.1	89.6	74.7	13.2	48.6	49.7	70.4	80.2	81.9	68.6	8.1
1998 [1]	66.9	66.2	89.1	93.0	89.1	73.7	13.1	48.8	50.4	73.7	81.0	82.8	68.6	8.4
1999 [1]	65.9	(B)	90.2	92.3	88.7	73.4	12.3	49.1	45.3	73.6	82.4	83.4	69.1	8.4
2000 [1]	66.8	60.5	88.1	93.2	89.9	73.9	12.9	49.0	46.0	74.0	83.1	82.9	69.8	8.7
2001	66.0	57.3	85.4	92.4	89.4	73.5	13.9	49.0	47.2	75.5	81.6	82.6	69.3	8.9
2002	65.5	57.5	87.4	91.2	89.6	74.1	13.2	49.2	46.2	74.7	80.7	82.7	69.7	8.9

B Percentage not shown where base is less than 35,000. [1] See footnote 2, Table 587. [2] Spouse present. [3] Widowed, divorced, and married (spouse absent).

Source: U.S. Bureau of Labor Statistics, Bulletins 2217 and 2340; and unpublished data.

No. 596. Marital Status of Women in the Civilian Labor Force: 1970 to 2002

[Annual averages of monthly figures (31,543 represents 31,543,000). For civilian noninstitutional population 16 years old and over. Based on the Current Population Survey; see text, Section 1, and Appendix III]

Year	Female civilian labor force (1,000)				Female participation rate [3]			
	Total	Single	Married [1]	Other [2]	Total	Single	Married [1]	Other [2]
1970	31,543	7,265	18,475	5,804	43.3	56.8	40.5	40.3
1975	37,475	9,125	21,484	6,866	46.3	59.8	44.3	40.1
1980	45,487	11,865	24,980	8,643	51.5	64.4	49.8	43.6
1983	48,503	12,659	26,468	9,376	52.9	65.0	51.8	44.4
1984	49,709	12,867	27,199	9,644	53.6	65.6	52.8	44.7
1985	51,050	13,163	27,894	9,993	54.5	66.6	53.8	45.1
1986	52,413	13,512	28,623	10,277	55.3	67.2	54.9	45.6
1987	53,658	13,885	29,381	10,393	56.0	67.4	55.9	45.7
1988	54,742	14,194	29,921	10,627	56.6	67.7	56.7	46.2
1989	56,030	14,377	30,548	11,104	57.4	68.0	57.8	47.0
1990 [4]	56,829	14,612	30,901	11,315	57.5	66.7	58.4	47.2
1991	57,178	14,681	31,112	11,385	57.4	66.2	58.5	46.8
1992	58,141	14,872	31,700	11,570	57.8	66.2	59.3	47.1
1993	58,795	15,031	31,980	11,784	57.9	66.2	59.4	47.2
1994 [4]	60,239	15,333	32,888	12,018	58.8	66.7	60.7	47.5
1995	60,944	15,467	33,359	12,118	58.9	66.8	61.0	47.4
1996	61,857	15,842	33,618	12,397	59.3	67.1	61.2	48.1
1997 [4]	63,036	16,492	33,802	12,742	59.8	67.9	61.6	48.6
1998 [4]	63,714	17,087	33,857	12,771	59.8	68.5	61.2	48.8
1999 [4]	64,855	17,575	34,372	12,909	60.0	68.7	61.2	49.1
2000 [4]	66,303	17,849	35,146	13,308	59.9	68.9	61.1	49.0
2001	66,848	18,021	35,236	13,592	59.8	68.1	61.2	49.0
2002	67,363	18,203	35,477	13,683	59.6	67.4	61.0	49.2

[1] Husband present. [2] Widowed, divorced, or separated. [3] See footnote 3, Table 592, for definition of participation rate. [4] See footnote 2, Table 587.

Source: U.S. Bureau of Labor Statistics, Bulletin 2307; and unpublished data.

No. 597. Employment Status of Women by Marital Status and Presence and Age of Children: 1970 to 2002

[As of March (7.0 represents 7,000,000). For the civilian noninstitutional persons 16 years and over. Based on the Current Population Survey; see text, Section 1, and Appendix III]

Item	Total Single	Total Married[1]	Total Other[2]	With any children Total Single	With any children Total Married[1]	With any children Total Other[2]	Children 6 to 17 only Single	Children 6 to 17 only Married[1]	Children 6 to 17 only Other[2]	Children under 6 Single	Children under 6 Married[1]	Children under 6 Other[2]
IN LABOR FORCE (mil.)												
1970	7.0	18.4	5.9	(NA)	10.2	1.9	(NA)	6.3	1.3	(NA)	3.9	0.6
1980	11.2	24.9	8.8	0.6	13.7	3.6	0.2	8.4	2.6	0.3	5.2	1.0
1985	12.9	27.7	10.3	1.1	14.9	4.0	0.4	8.5	2.9	0.7	6.4	1.1
1990	14.0	31.0	11.2	1.5	16.5	4.2	0.6	9.3	3.0	0.9	7.2	1.2
1995	15.0	33.6	12.0	2.1	18.0	4.6	0.8	10.2	3.3	1.3	7.8	1.3
1999[3]	17.5	34.3	13.0	3.1	17.9	4.6	1.2	10.6	3.3	1.8	7.2	1.3
2000	17.8	35.0	13.2	3.1	18.2	4.5	1.2	10.8	3.4	1.8	7.3	1.1
2001[3]	17.8	35.7	13.8	3.1	18.7	4.5	1.2	11.2	3.4	1.8	7.4	1.2
2002	18.1	35.6	13.7	3.2	18.3	4.6	1.4	11.1	3.4	1.8	7.2	1.2
PARTICIPATION RATE[4]												
1970	53.0	40.8	39.1	(NA)	39.7	60.7	(NA)	49.2	66.9	(NA)	30.3	52.2
1980	61.5	50.1	44.0	52.0	54.1	69.4	67.6	61.7	74.6	44.1	45.1	60.3
1985	65.2	54.2	45.6	51.6	60.8	71.9	64.1	67.8	77.8	46.5	53.4	59.7
1990	66.4	58.2	46.8	55.2	66.3	74.2	69.7	73.6	79.7	48.7	58.9	63.6
1995	65.5	61.1	47.3	57.5	70.2	75.3	67.0	76.2	79.5	53.0	63.5	66.3
1999[3]	68.1	61.6	49.4	73.4	70.1	80.4	82.6	77.1	81.8	68.1	61.8	77.1
2000	68.6	62.0	50.2	73.9	70.6	82.7	79.7	77.2	85.0	70.5	62.8	76.6
2001[3]	68.2	61.8	50.0	73.5	70.4	83.1	80.8	77.5	85.9	69.2	61.9	75.8
2002	67.1	61.5	49.3	75.3	69.6	82.1	81.7	76.8	83.6	71.0	60.8	77.9
EMPLOYMENT (mil.)												
1970	6.5	17.5	5.6	(NA)	9.6	1.8	(NA)	6.0	1.2	(NA)	3.6	0.6
1980	10.1	23.6	8.2	0.4	12.8	3.3	0.2	8.1	2.4	0.2	4.8	0.9
1985	11.6	26.1	9.4	0.9	13.9	3.5	0.3	8.1	2.6	0.5	5.9	0.9
1990	12.9	29.9	10.5	1.2	15.8	3.8	0.5	8.9	2.7	0.7	6.9	1.1
1995	13.7	32.3	11.3	1.8	17.2	4.2	0.7	9.8	3.1	1.1	7.3	1.2
1999[3]	16.2	33.4	12.3	2.7	17.3	4.3	1.1	10.4	3.1	1.6	7.0	1.1
2000	16.4	34.0	12.7	2.7	17.6	4.3	1.1	10.6	3.2	1.6	7.1	1.1
2001[3]	16.6	34.7	13.2	2.7	18.0	4.3	1.1	10.9	3.2	1.6	7.2	1.1
2002	16.5	34.3	12.9	2.8	17.5	4.3	1.2	10.7	3.2	1.6	6.8	1.1
UNEMPLOYMENT RATE[5]												
1970	7.1	4.8	4.8	(NA)	6.0	7.2	(NA)	4.8	5.9	(NA)	7.9	9.8
1980	10.3	5.3	6.4	23.2	5.9	9.2	15.6	4.4	7.9	29.2	8.3	12.8
1985	10.2	5.7	8.5	23.8	6.6	12.1	15.4	5.5	10.6	28.5	8.0	16.1
1990	8.2	3.5	5.7	18.4	4.2	8.5	14.5	3.8	7.7	20.8	4.8	10.2
1995	8.7	3.9	5.8	16.6	4.3	8.1	11.8	3.6	7.1	19.5	5.3	10.8
1999[3]	7.4	2.8	5.0	11.7	2.9	6.2	8.9	2.4	4.5	13.6	3.7	10.7
2000	7.3	2.7	4.3	11.0	2.9	5.1	8.7	2.6	4.8	12.6	3.5	5.9
2001[3]	7.1	2.9	4.3	12.1	3.4	5.3	10.7	3.0	4.6	13.1	3.9	7.6
2002	8.7	3.7	6.3	12.6	4.1	7.9	11.1	3.5	6.7	13.8	5.1	11.4

NA Not available. [1] Husband present. [2] Widowed, divorced, or separated. [3] See footnote 2, Table 587. [4] Percent of women in each specific category in the labor force. [5] Unemployed as a percent of civilian labor force in specified group.

Source: U.S. Bureau of Labor Statistics, Bulletin 2307; and unpublished data.

No. 598. Labor Force Participation Rates for Wives, Husband Present by Age of Own Youngest Child: 1975 to 2002

[As of March. For civilian noninstitutional population, 16 years old and over. For definition of participation rate, see Table 597. Based on Current Population Survey; see text, Section 1, and Appendix III]

Presence and age of child	Total 1975	Total 1985	Total 2002[1]	White 1975	White 1985	White 2002[1]	Black 1975	Black 1985	Black 2002[1]
Wives, total	44.4	54.2	61.5	43.6	53.3	61.0	54.1	63.8	68.4
No children under 18	43.8	48.2	54.8	43.6	47.5	54.5	47.6	55.2	57.6
With children under 18	44.9	60.8	69.6	43.6	59.9	69.2	58.4	71.7	79.2
Under 6, total	36.7	53.4	60.8	34.7	52.1	60.0	54.9	69.6	75.3
Under 3	32.7	50.5	58.0	30.7	49.4	57.4	50.1	66.2	70.3
1 year or under	30.8	49.4	56.8	29.2	48.6	56.1	50.0	63.7	69.7
2 years	37.1	54.0	62.1	35.1	52.7	61.4	56.4	69.9	74.3
3 to 5 years	42.2	58.4	65.0	40.1	56.6	64.0	61.2	73.8	82.5
3 years	41.2	55.1	61.7	39.0	52.7	60.9	62.7	72.3	78.0
4 years	41.2	59.7	66.8	38.7	58.4	65.9	64.9	70.6	83.7
5 years	44.4	62.1	67.5	43.8	59.9	66.4	56.3	79.1	83.8
6 to 13 years	51.8	68.2	75.3	50.7	67.7	75.0	65.7	73.6	82.1
14 to 17 years	53.5	67.0	80.5	53.4	66.6	80.5	52.3	74.4	82.5

[1] See footnote 2, Table 587.

Source: U.S. Bureau of Labor Statistics, Bulletin 2340; and unpublished data.

No. 599. Families With Own Children—Employment Status of Parents: 1995 and 2002

[In thousands, except percent distribution. Annual average of monthly figures (33,544 represents 33,544,000). For families with own children. Based on the Current Population Survey, see text, Section 1, and Appendix III]

Characteristic	Number 1995	Number 2002	Percent 1995	Percent 2002	Characteristic	Number 1995	Number 2002	Percent 1995	Percent 2002
WITH OWN CHILDREN UNDER 18					Father employed, not mother	2,921	3,229	22.5	23.2
Total families	33,544	35,240	100.0	100.0	Neither parent employed	517	432	4.0	3.1
Parent(s) employed	29,659	31,955	88.4	90.7	Families maintained by women [1]	4,360	4,959	100.0	100.0
No parent employed	3,886	3,285	11.6	9.3	Mother employed	3,142	3,856	72.1	77.8
Married-couple families	24,604	25,191	100.0	100.0	Mother not employed	1,219	1,102	27.9	22.2
Parent(s) employed	23,643	24,372	96.1	96.7	Families maintained by men [1]	908	1,193	100.0	100.0
Mother employed	16,629	16,773	67.6	66.6	Father employed	766	998	84.3	83.7
Both parents employed	15,491	15,439	63.0	61.3	Father not employed	143	194	15.7	16.3
Mother employed, not father	1,137	1,334	4.6	5.3	**WITH OWN CHILDREN UNDER 6**				
Father employed, not mother	7,014	7,599	28.5	30.2	Total families	15,275	15,197	100.0	100.0
Neither parent employed	962	819	3.9	3.3	Parent(s) employed	13,267	13,641	86.9	89.8
Families maintained by women [1]	7,433	8,053	100.0	100.0	No parent employed	2,007	1,557	13.1	10.2
Mother employed	4,755	5,910	64.0	73.4	Married-couple families	11,604	11,300	100.0	100.0
Mother not employed	2,678	2,143	36.0	26.6	Parent(s) employed	11,159	10,913	96.2	96.6
Families maintained by men [1]	1,507	1,995	100.0	100.0	Mother employed	7,066	6,543	60.9	57.9
Father employed	1,261	1,673	83.7	83.9	Both parents employed	6,646	6,053	57.3	53.6
Father not employed	245	323	16.3	16.2	Mother employed, not father	421	490	3.6	4.3
WITH OWN CHILDREN 6 to 17					Father employed, not mother	4,092	4,370	35.3	38.7
Total families	18,270	20,042	100.0	100.0	Neither parent employed	445	388	3.8	3.4
Parent(s) employed	16,391	18,313	89.7	91.4	Families maintained by women [1]	3,073	3,094	100.0	100.0
No parent employed	1,878	1,728	10.3	8.6	Mother employed	1,613	2,054	52.5	66.4
Married-couple families	13,001	13,891	100.0	100.0	Mother not employed	1,460	1,040	47.5	33.6
Parent(s) employed	12,484	13,459	96.0	96.9	Families maintained by men [1]	598	803	100.0	100.0
Mother employed	9,562	10,230	73.6	73.6	Father employed	496	674	82.8	83.9
Both parents employed	8,846	9,386	68.0	67.6	Father not employed	102	129	17.1	16.1
Mother employed, not father	717	844	5.5	6.1					

[1] No spouse present.

Source: U.S. Bureau of Labor Statistics, *Employment Characteristics in Families in 2002, News*, USDL 03-339, July 9, 2003; and earlier issues. See Internet site <http://www.bls.gov/bls/newsrels.htm#OEUS>.

No. 600. Employed Civilians and Weekly Hours: 1980 to 2002

[In thousands (99,303 represents 99,303,000), except as indicated. For civilian noninstitutional population 16 years old and over. Annual averages of monthly figures. Based on Current Population Survey; see text, Section 1, and Appendix III]

Item	1980	1990 [1]	1995	1998 [1]	1999 [1]	2000 [1]	2001	2002
Total employed	99,303	118,793	124,900	131,463	133,488	136,891	136,933	136,485
Age:								
16 to 19 years old	7,710	6,581	6,419	7,051	7,172	7,189	6,740	6,332
20 to 24 years old	14,087	13,401	12,443	12,557	12,891	13,229	13,348	13,351
25 to 34 years old	27,204	33,935	32,356	31,394	30,865	31,549	30,863	30,306
35 to 44 years old	19,523	30,817	34,202	36,278	36,728	36,433	36,049	35,235
45 to 54 years old	16,234	19,525	24,378	27,587	28,635	30,310	31,036	31,281
55 to 64 years old	11,586	11,189	11,445	12,872	13,315	14,002	14,645	15,674
65 years old and over	2,960	3,346	3,666	3,725	3,882	4,179	4,253	4,306
Class of worker:								
Nonagriculture	95,938	115,570	121,460	128,085	130,207	133,509	133,702	133,145
Wage and salary worker	88,525	106,598	112,448	119,019	121,323	124,640	124,920	124,561
Self-employed	7,000	8,719	8,902	8,962	8,790	8,765	8,677	8,490
Unpaid family workers	413	253	110	103	95	104	106	94
Agriculture	3,364	3,223	3,440	3,378	3,281	3,382	3,231	3,340
Wage and salary worker	1,425	1,740	1,814	2,000	1,944	2,096	1,939	2,042
Self-employed	1,642	1,378	1,580	1,341	1,297	1,249	1,264	1,266
Unpaid family workers	297	105	45	38	40	37	28	32
Weekly hours:								
Nonagriculture:								
Wage and salary workers	38.1	39.2	39.2	39.2	39.5	39.7	39.2	39.1
Self-employed	41.2	40.8	39.4	39.6	40.1	40.0	39.5	39.0
Unpaid family workers	34.7	34.0	33.5	34.0	33.4	32.4	30.7	31.6
Agriculture:								
Wage and salary workers	41.6	41.2	41.1	40.6	41.1	41.1	40.7	40.5
Self-employed	49.3	46.8	43.5	43.3	43.3	43.0	43.3	42.2
Unpaid family workers	38.6	38.5	42.0	36.2	36.6	37.5	40.6	38.4

[1] See footnote 2, Table 587.

Source: U.S. Bureau of Labor Statistics, *Employment and Earnings*, monthly, January issues; June 2003 issue; and unpublished data. See Internet site <http://www.bls.gov/cps/home.htm>.

No. 601. Employed Workers Actively Seeking a New Job: 2001

[As of February. In thousands (121,334 represents 121,334,000), except rate. For employed wage and salary workers 16 old and over (except as indicated) responding to the question on actively seeking work in the prior 3 months. Based on the Current Population Survey; see text, Section 1, and Appendix III]

Characteristic	Total employed	Persons responding to search question			Characteristic	Total employed	Persons responding to search question		
		Total	Actively seeking work	Percent			Total	Actively seeking work	Percent
Total................	121,334	118,163	4,937	4.2	Professional specialty....	19,670	19,337	852	4.4
Age:					Technicians and related				
16 to 19 years old......	6,544	6,373	313	4.9	support	4,440	4,332	258	6.0
20 to 24 years old......	12,997	12,632	902	7.1	Sales	13,908	13,545	680	5.0
25 to 34 years old......	28,285	27,472	1,517	5.5	Administrative support,				
35 to 44 years old......	32,887	32,018	1,233	3.9	including clerical......	18,391	17,920	608	3.4
45 to 54 years old......	26,052	25,515	749	2.9	Private household......	592	401	44	11.0
55 to 64 years old......	11,743	11,426	213	1.9	Protective service......	2,436	2,376	79	3.3
65 years old and over ...	2,826	2,728	10	0.4	Service, except private				
Sex: Male..............	62,753	61,106	2,606	4.3	households and				
Female	58,581	57,058	2,332	4.1	protective...........	13,493	13,007	556	4.3
Educational attainment: [1]					Precision production, craft,				
Less than high school diploma	9,515	9,172	233	2.5	and repair	12,770	12,426	395	3.2
High school diploma, no college..............	31,280	30,297	846	2.8	Machine operators, assemblers, and inspectors	6,730	6,613	242	3.7
Some college or associate degree..............	28,984	28,320	1,175	4.1	Transportation and material moving occupations..	5,266	5,109	191	3.7
Bachelor's degree or more...............	32,014	31,370	1,469	4.7	Handlers, equipment cleaners, helpers, and laborers	4,846	4,675	241	5.2
Occupation: Executive, administrative, and managerial....	17,390	17,091	750	4.4	Farming, forestry, and fishing..............	1,402	1,330	41	3.1

[1] Persons 25 years old and over.

Source: U.S. Bureau of Labor Statistics, Current Population Survey, February 2001, unpublished data.

No. 602. Persons at Work by Hours Worked: 2002

[131,091 represents 131,091,000. For civilian noninstitutional population 16 years old and over. Annual averages of monthly figures. Based on Current Population Survey; see text, Section 1, and Appendix III]

Hours of work	Persons at work (1,000)			Percent distribution		
	Total	Agriculture industries	Nonagriculture industries	Total	Agriculture industries	Nonagriculture industries
Total.........................	131,091	3,192	127,899	100.0	100.0	100.0
1 to 34 hours...................	31,174	907	30,267	23.8	28.4	23.7
1 to 4 hours..................	1,336	69	1,267	1.0	2.2	1.0
5 to 14 hours.................	4,870	211	4,659	3.7	6.6	3.6
15 to 29 hours................	15,510	408	15,101	11.8	12.8	11.8
30 to 34 hours................	9,459	219	9,239	7.2	6.9	7.2
35 hours and over	99,917	2,285	97,632	76.2	71.6	76.3
35 to 39 hours................	8,940	177	8,763	6.8	5.5	6.9
40 hours.....................	53,580	949	52,631	40.9	29.7	41.2
41 hours and over.............	37,396	1,159	36,238	28.5	36.3	28.3
41 to 48 hours	13,415	226	13,189	10.2	7.1	10.3
49 to 58 hours	14,053	357	13,695	10.7	11.2	10.7
60 hours and over...........	9,929	575	9,354	7.6	18.0	7.3
Average weekly hours: total at work.........	39.2	41.1	39.1	(X)	(X)	(X)
Persons usually working full time.........	42.9	46.8	42.8	(X)	(X)	(X)

X Not applicable.

Source: U.S. Bureau of Labor Statistics, *Employment and Earnings*, monthly, June 2003 issue. See Internet site <http://www.bls.gov/cps /home.htm>.

No. 603. Persons With a Job, But Not at Work: 1980 to 2002

[In thousands (5,881 represents 5,881,000), except percent. For civilian noninstitutional population 16 years old and over. Annual averages of monthly figures. Based on Current Population Survey; see text, Section 1, and Appendix III]

Reason for not working	1980	1990 [1]	1994 [1]	1995	1996	1997 [1]	1998 [1]	1999 [1]	2000 [1]	2001	2002
All industries, number	5,881	6,160	5,619	5,582	5,768	5,555	5,586	5,407	5,681	5,631	5,394
Percent of employed	5.9	5.2	4.6	4.5	4.6	4.3	4.2	4.1	4.2	4.1	4.0
Reason for not working:											
Vacation.................	3,320	3,529	2,877	2,982	3,085	2,942	3,033	2,899	3,109	3,039	2,929
Illness	1,426	1,341	1,184	1,084	1,090	1,114	1,095	1,096	1,156	1,095	1,072
Bad weather	155	90	165	122	256	146	130	104	89	100	97
Industrial dispute	105	24	15	21	11	20	10	7	14	9	7
All other................	876	1,177	1,378	1,373	1,325	1,334	1,318	1,300	1,313	1,388	1,289

[1] See footnote 2, Table 587.

Source: U.S. Bureau of Labor Statistics, *Employment and Earnings*, monthly, January issues, June 2003 issue; and unpublished data. See Internet site <http://www.bls.gov/cps/home.htm>.

Labor Force, Employment, and Earnings

No. 604. Self-Employed Workers by Industry and Occupation: 1980 to 2002

[In thousands (8,642 represents 8,642,000). For civilian noninstitutional population 16 years old and over. Annual averages of monthly figures. Data from 1990 forward are not fully comparable with data for prior years because of the introduction of the occupational and industrial classification used in the 1990 census. Based on the Current Population Survey; see text, Section 1, and Appendix III]

Item	1980	1990 [1]	1995	1998 [1]	1999 [1]	2000 [1]	2001	2002
Total self-employed	8,642	10,097	10,482	10,303	10,087	10,013	9,941	9,756
Industry:								
Agriculture	1,642	1,378	1,580	1,341	1,297	1,249	1,264	1,266
Nonagriculture	7,000	8,719	8,902	8,962	8,790	8,765	8,677	8,490
Mining	28	24	16	21	16	16	25	13
Construction	1,173	1,457	1,460	1,519	1,545	1,593	1,530	1,483
Manufacturing	358	427	433	428	380	345	360	343
Transportation and public utilities	282	301	396	430	429	405	440	436
Trade	1,899	1,851	1,772	1,640	1,621	1,524	1,491	1,436
Finance, insurance, and real estate	458	630	660	609	661	700	649	649
Services	2,804	4,030	4,166	4,317	4,138	4,182	4,182	4,129
Occupation:								
Managerial and professional specialty	(NA)	3,050	3,147	3,400	3,298	3,150	3,175	3,064
Technical, sales, and administrative support	(NA)	2,240	2,341	2,117	2,111	2,109	1,990	1,927
Service occupations	(NA)	1,207	1,190	1,198	1,136	1,212	1,177	1,245
Precision production, craft, and repair	(NA)	1,675	1,618	1,697	1,665	1,737	1,767	1,686
Operators, fabricators, and laborers	(NA)	567	631	584	607	563	588	586
Farming, forestry, and fishing	(NA)	1,358	1,556	1,307	1,270	1,242	1,245	1,248

NA Not available. [1] See footnote 2, Table 587.
Source: U.S. Bureau of Labor Statistics, Bulletin 2307; *Employment and Earnings*, monthly, June 2003 and January issues; and unpublished data. See Internet site <http://www.bls.gov/cps/home.htm>.

No. 605. Persons Doing Job-Related Work at Home: 2001

[19,759 represents 19,759,000. As of May. For persons at work 16 years and over in nonagricultural industries doing job-related work at home at least once a week as part of their primary job. Based on the Current Population Survey; see text, Section 1, and Appendix III]

Characteristic	Total [1] (1,000)	Rate [2]	Paid [3]	Unpaid	Self-employed [4]	Total [5] (1,000)	Hours vary	Usually less than 8 hours	Usually 35 hours or more
Total [6]	19,759	15.0	17.4	52.0	29.7	3,436	27.4	24.5	15.7
SEX									
Male	10,291	14.8	16.0	50.5	32.6	1,642	30.9	23.3	14.8
Female	9,468	15.2	18.9	53.7	26.5	1,794	24.2	25.7	16.5
RACE AND HISPANIC ORIGIN									
White	17,947	16.3	17.5	51.6	30.0	3,138	27.2	24.4	15.0
Black	1,152	7.6	14.9	57.9	26.0	172	29.7	22.1	28.9
Hispanic origin [7]	937	6.7	20.4	49.2	28.4	191	32.3	15.9	27.6
OCCUPATION									
Managerial and professional	12,628	29.8	14.2	62.8	22.4	1,798	28.0	24.1	13.9
Exec., admin., and managerial	5,262	25.7	16.7	52.5	30.0	880	25.8	24.3	12.9
Professional specialty	7,366	33.5	12.5	70.1	17.0	918	30.1	23.9	14.9
Technical, sales and admin. support	4,669	12.2	24.7	40.2	33.9	1,155	27.3	22.1	16.7
Technicians and related support	305	6.9	36.0	48.4	14.3	110	40.2	24.6	21.2
Sales	3,133	20.0	20.3	40.3	38.9	635	27.8	18.9	13.0
Admin support, inc. clerical	1,231	6.8	33.4	37.8	25.8	411	23.3	26.5	21.0
Service	972	5.3	24.1	18.4	55.1	234	25.6	19.6	33.1
Precision production, craft, and repair	1,050	7.1	15.7	19.4	64.4	165	29.1	47.2	2.7
Operators, fabricators, and laborers	381	2.2	19.4	24.3	49.3	74	(B)	(B)	(B)
Farming, forestry, and fishing	59	8.7	(B)	(B)	(B)	10	(B)	(B)	(B)
INDUSTRY									
Mining	65	11.1	(B)	(B)	(B)	9	(B)	(B)	(B)
Construction	1,134	12.4	11.6	20.5	65.2	131	31.8	36.5	5.1
Manufacturing	1,806	9.3	28.7	54.9	15.7	518	27.0	21.5	12.5
Transportation and public utilities	898	8.9	22.8	49.4	26.0	205	14.1	29.7	25.3
Wholesale trade	1,009	19.4	24.4	47.9	25.6	247	28.1	15.0	12.9
Retail trade	1,529	7.0	12.8	36.4	49.8	196	23.7	32.5	10.3
Finance, insurance, and real estate	1,810	20.8	18.8	48.2	33.0	340	30.7	24.0	9.5
Services	10,926	21.7	14.8	57.2	27.1	1,618	28.0	24.3	19.0
Public administration	581	9.2	29.6	69.8	-	172	33.7	27.1	12.8

- Represents zero. B Base figure too small to meet statistical standards for reliability of a derived figure. [1] Includes unpaid family workers and persons who did not report pay status. [2] Persons working at home as a percent of the total employed. [3] Persons with formal arrangements with their employers to be paid for the work done at home. [4] Includes incorporated and unincorporated self-employed. [5] Includes those not reporting usual number of hours worked. [6] Includes other races, not shown separately. [7] Persons of Hispanic origin may be of any race.
Source: U.S. Bureau of Labor Statistics, *Work at Home in 2001*, News, USDL 02-107, March 1, 2002. See Internet site <http://www.bls.gov/bls/newsrels.htm#OEUS>.

394 Labor Force, Employment, and Earnings

No. 606. Persons on Flexible Schedules: 2001

[In thousands, except percent. (99,631 represents 99,631,000) As of May. For employed full-time wage and salary workers 16 years old and over. Excludes the self-employed. Data relate to the primary job. Based on the Current Population Survey; see text, Section 1, and Appendix III]

Item	Total Total [1]	Total With flexible schedules Number	Total With flexible schedules Percent	Male Total [1]	Male With flexible schedules Number	Male With flexible schedules Percent	Female Total [1]	Female With flexible schedules Number	Female With flexible schedules Percent
Total	99,631	28,724	28.8	56,066	16,792	30.0	43,566	11,931	27.4
AGE									
16 to 19 years old	1,761	339	19.2	988	167	16.9	773	171	22.2
20 to 24 years old	9,343	2,327	24.9	5,219	1,203	23.0	4,124	1,124	27.2
25 to 34 years old	24,552	7,434	30.3	14,058	4,370	31.1	10,494	3,064	29.2
35 to 44 years old	28,702	8,578	29.9	16,522	5,120	31.0	12,180	3,458	28.4
45 to 54 years old	23,946	6,990	29.2	12,902	4,032	31.2	11,044	2,958	26.8
55 to 64 years old	9,971	2,633	26.4	5,531	1,590	28.8	4,440	1,043	23.5
65 years old and over	1,357	423	31.2	847	311	36.7	510	112	22.0
RACE AND HISPANIC ORIGIN									
White	82,205	24,647	30.0	47,498	14,734	31.0	34,707	9,913	28.6
Black	12,390	2,629	21.2	5,776	1,209	20.9	6,614	1,420	21.5
Hispanic origin [2]	11,919	2,356	19.8	7,305	1,344	18.4	4,614	1,011	21.9
OCCUPATION									
Executive, administrative, and managerial	16,279	7,404	45.5	8,748	4,277	48.9	7,531	3,128	41.5
Professional specialty	16,681	5,922	35.5	8,037	3,678	45.8	8,644	2,244	26.0
Technicians and related support	3,757	1,181	31.4	1,863	683	36.7	1,894	498	26.3
Sales	9,852	4,011	40.7	5,424	2,404	44.3	4,428	1,607	36.3
Administrative support, including clerical	13,997	3,426	24.5	3,206	753	23.5	10,791	2,672	24.8
Private household	377	132	35.0	5	3	(B)	371	129	34.8
Protective service	2,144	343	16.0	1,773	291	16.4	371	52	14.0
Service, exc. private household and protective	8,207	1,755	21.4	3,324	698	21.0	4,883	1,057	21.6
Precision production, craft, and repair	12,061	2,209	18.3	11,000	2,026	18.4	1,061	183	17.3
Operators, fabricators, and laborers	14,621	1,999	13.7	11,324	1,689	14.9	3,297	310	9.4
Farming, forestry, fishing	1,653	342	20.7	1,360	291	21.4	293	51	17.5

B Percent not shown where base is less than 75,000. [1] Includes persons who did not provide information on flexible schedules. [2] Persons of Hispanic origin may be of any race.
Source: U.S. Bureau of Labor Statistics, News, Workers on Flexible and Shift Schedules in 2001, USDL 02-225, April 18, 2002. See Internet site <http://www.bls.gov/bls /newsrels.htm#OEUS>.

No. 607. Persons on Shift Schedules: 2001

[In percent, except as indicated. (99,631 represents 99,631,000) As of May. For employed full-time wage and salary workers 16 years old and over. Excludes the self-employed. Data relate to the primary job. Based on the Current Population Survey; see text, Section 1, and Appendix III]

Item	Total workers[1] (1,000)	Regular daytime schedules	Shift workers Total	Evening shift	Night shift	Rotating shift	Split shift	Irregular shift [2]	Other shift
Total	99,631	84.8	14.5	4.8	3.3	2.3	0.4	2.8	0.7
AGE									
16 to 19 years old	1,761	70.2	28.8	13.5	5.4	3.4	0.3	5.3	1.0
20 to 24 years old	9,343	77.8	21.3	8.7	4.7	3.3	0.4	3.5	0.8
25 to 34 years old	24,552	84.9	14.4	4.9	3.3	2.3	0.6	2.4	0.8
35 to 44 years old	28,702	86.2	13.2	3.7	3.3	2.3	0.4	2.8	0.6
45 to 54 years old	23,946	86.3	13.1	4.1	2.9	2.3	0.3	2.6	0.8
55 to 64 years old	9,971	86.3	13.2	4.5	3.1	1.7	0.4	2.8	0.6
65 years old and over	1,357	84.9	15.0	3.9	2.1	1.7	1.3	5.5	0.5
SEX									
Male	56,066	82.9	16.4	5.2	3.6	2.8	0.5	3.3	0.9
Female	43,566	87.3	12.1	4.3	3.0	1.8	0.4	2.1	0.5
RACE AND HISPANIC ORIGIN									
White	82,205	85.8	13.6	4.4	3.0	2.2	0.4	2.8	0.7
Black	12,390	79.3	19.7	7.0	5.0	3.3	0.5	3.2	0.6
Hispanic origin [3]	11,919	84.3	14.8	5.8	3.4	2.0	0.5	2.5	0.5
OCCUPATION									
Executive, administrative, and managerial	16,279	93.9	5.6	1.6	0.7	1.0	0.2	1.8	0.3
Professional specialty	16,681	91.7	7.8	1.7	1.7	1.1	0.3	2.5	0.4
Technicians and related support	3,757	83.9	15.6	3.8	4.2	2.4	0.1	3.8	1.4
Sales	9,852	84.3	15.2	4.1	1.3	3.6	0.3	5.2	0.5
Administrative support, including clerical	13,997	91.1	8.4	3.6	2.4	0.7	0.4	0.9	0.4
Private household	377	82.8	15.6	1.0	0.5	0.7	0.7	9.4	3.3
Protective service	2,144	49.8	49.0	12.4	9.7	12.3	1.1	8.1	5.4
Service, exc. private household and protective	8,207	66.9	32.0	14.5	5.9	3.9	1.3	4.7	1.5
Precision production, craft, and repair	12,061	87.4	12.0	4.0	3.6	2.3	0.3	1.3	0.5
Operators, fabricators, and laborers	14,621	73.6	25.4	8.4	8.0	3.7	0.6	3.8	0.8
Farming, forestry, fishing	1,653	93.5	5.6	2.3	0.8	0.7	0.5	1.0	0.3

[1] Includes persons who did not provide information on usual shift worked. [2] Employer arranged schedule. [3] Persons of Hispanic origin may be of any race.
Source: U.S. Bureau of Labor Statistics, News, Workers on Flexible and Shift Schedules in 2001, USDL 02-225, April 18, 2002. See Internet site <http://www.bls.gov/bls /newsrels.htm#OEUS>.

No. 608. Multiple Jobholders: 2002

[Annual average of monthly figures (7,291 represents 7,291,000). For the civilian noninstitutional population 16 years old and over. Multiple jobholders are employed persons who, either (1) had jobs as wage or salary workers with two employers or more; (2) were self-employed and also held a wage and salary job; or (3) were unpaid family workers on their primary jobs but also held wage and salary job. Based on the Current Population Survey; see text, Section 1, and Appendix III]

Characteristic	Total Number (1,000)	Total Percent of employed	Male Number (1,000)	Male Percent of employed	Female Number (1,000)	Female Percent of employed
Total [1]	7,291	5.3	3,734	5.1	3,557	5.6
Age:						
16 to 19 years old	286	4.5	114	3.6	171	5.4
20 to 24 years old	740	5.5	335	4.8	405	6.4
25 to 54 years old	5,375	5.6	2,815	5.4	2,560	5.7
55 to 64 years old	752	4.8	394	4.7	358	4.9
65 years old and over	139	3.2	76	3.1	63	3.4
Race and Hispanic origin:						
White	6,270	5.5	3,233	5.2	3,037	5.8
Black	709	4.8	343	4.9	366	4.6
Hispanic origin [2]	579	3.5	347	3.5	232	3.4
Marital status:						
Married, spouse present	3,998	5.1	2,362	5.4	1,636	4.8
Widowed, divorced, or separated	1,313	6.1	452	5.1	861	6.7
Single, never married	1,980	5.4	920	4.6	1,060	6.4
Full- or part-time status:						
Primary job full time, secondary job part time	3,937	(X)	2,235	(X)	1,701	(X)
Both jobs part time	1,590	(X)	493	(X)	1,097	(X)
Both jobs full time	276	(X)	186	(X)	90	(X)
Hours vary on primary or secondary job	1,449	(X)	801	(X)	647	(X)

X Not applicable. [1] Includes a small number of persons who work part time on their primary job and full time on their secondary job(s), not shown separately. Includes other races, not shown separately. [2] Persons of Hispanic origin may be of any race.

Source: U.S. Bureau of Labor Statistics, *Employment and Earnings*, June 2003. See Internet site <http://www.bls.gov/cps/home.htm>.

No. 609. Average Number of Jobs Held From Ages 18 to 36: 1978 to 2000

[For persons 35 to 43 in 2000. A job is an uninterrupted period of work with a particular employer. Educational attainment as of 2000. Based on the National Longitudinal Survey of Youth 1979; see source for details]

Sex and educational attainment	Total [1]	18 to 22 years old	22 to 27 years old	28 to 32 years old	33 to 36 years old
Total [2]	9.6	4.4	3.2	2.6	2.0
Less than a high school diploma	9.7	4.0	3.1	2.6	2.0
High school graduates, no college	9.2	4.1	3.0	2.6	2.0
Less than a bachelor's degree	10.0	4.5	3.0	2.7	2.1
Bachelor's degree or more	10.0	5.0	3.5	2.6	1.9
Male	9.9	4.5	3.4	2.8	2.1
Less than a high school diploma	11.1	4.7	3.7	3.0	2.1
High school graduates, no college	9.6	4.4	3.4	2.8	2.0
Less than a bachelor's degree	10.5	4.7	3.5	2.9	2.2
Bachelor's degree or more	9.5	4.6	3.4	2.5	2.0
Female	9.3	4.3	3.0	2.4	1.9
Less than a high school diploma	7.8	3.0	2.3	2.1	1.7
High school graduates, no college	8.7	3.9	3.0	2.4	2.0
Less than a bachelor's degree	9.5	4.4	3.2	2.5	2.0
Bachelor's degree or more	10.6	5.4	3.7	2.6	1.8
White, non-Hispanic	9.8	4.6	3.3	2.6	2.0
Less than a high school diploma	10.3	4.3	3.3	2.7	2.1
High school graduates, no college	9.2	4.3	3.1	2.6	2.0
Less than a bachelor's degree	10.3	4.7	3.5	2.7	2.1
Bachelor's degree or more	10.0	5.1	3.5	2.6	1.9
Black, non-Hispanic	9.1	3.6	3.1	2.7	2.0
Less than a high school diploma	8.3	2.8	2.7	2.5	1.7
High school graduates, no college	9.2	3.5	3.0	2.7	2.1
Less than a bachelor's degree	9.0	3.8	3.1	2.6	2.1
Bachelor's degree or more	10.0	4.4	3.7	2.8	2.2
Hispanic origin	8.9	4.0	3.0	2.5	1.9
Less than a high school diploma	9.2	3.8	2.9	2.4	1.9
High school graduates, no college	8.7	3.9	2.9	2.5	1.9
Less than a bachelor's degree	8.8	4.1	3.0	2.4	1.8
Bachelor's degree or more	9.4	4.3	3.2	2.7	2.0

[1] Jobs held in more than one age category were counted in each category, but only once in the total. [2] Includes other races, not shown separately.

Source: U.S. Bureau of Labor Statistics, Number of Jobs Held, Labor Market Activity, and *Earnings Growth Among Younger Baby Boomers: Results from More Than Two Decades of a Longitudinal Survey*, News, USDL 02-497, August 27, 2002. See Internet site <http://www.bls.gov/nls/home.htm>.

No. 610. Distribution of Workers by Tenure With Current Employer by Selected Characteristic: 2002

[118,424 represents 118,424,000. As of February. For employed wage and salary workers 16 years old and over. Based on the Current Population Survey and subject to sampling error; see source and Appendix III]

Characteristic	Number employed (1,000)	12 months or less	13 to 23 months	2 years	3 to 4 years	5 to 9 years	10 to 14 years	15 to 19 years	20 yrs. or more	Median years [1]
Total [2]	118,424	24.5	8.4	5.8	17.3	17.7	10.4	6.0	9.8	3.7
AGE AND SEX										
16 to 19 years old	5,904	71.5	12.6	7.8	7.5	0.5	-	-	-	0.7
20 years old and over	112,520	22.1	8.2	5.7	17.9	18.6	10.9	6.3	10.3	4.0
20 to 24 years old	12,414	51.4	14.6	9.2	19.2	5.6	(Z)	-	-	1.2
25 to 34 years old	26,959	28.9	11.0	7.5	23.3	22.0	6.5	0.8	(Z)	2.7
35 to 44 years old	31,648	17.9	7.3	5.3	18.4	21.3	14.7	9.3	5.8	4.6
45 to 54 years old	26,422	12.9	5.5	3.7	14.2	18.8	13.8	9.5	21.6	7.6
55 to 64 years old	12,104	10.7	4.6	3.3	12.0	17.1	15.2	9.7	27.4	9.9
65 years old and over	2,973	9.9	4.1	4.5	13.4	19.8	13.9	8.6	25.6	8.7
Male	61,023	23.5	8.1	5.6	17.0	17.7	10.4	6.3	11.3	3.9
16 to 19 years old	2,879	72.2	12.9	7.0	7.4	0.4	-	-	-	0.8
20 years old and over	58,144	21.1	7.9	5.6	17.5	18.6	10.9	6.6	11.8	4.2
20 to 24 years old	6,368	49.4	13.9	9.2	21.0	6.4	0.1	-	-	1.3
25 to 34 years old	14,408	27.2	10.5	7.4	23.2	23.5	7.2	0.9	(Z)	2.9
35 to 44 years old	16,491	16.9	6.8	5.1	17.3	21.4	15.6	10.3	6.6	5.1
45 to 54 years old	13,201	12.1	5.4	3.5	12.7	17.0	13.0	10.1	26.2	9.1
55 to 64 years old	6,118	10.9	4.8	3.3	12.0	15.3	13.4	9.0	31.4	10.2
65 years old and over	1,558	10.0	4.1	5.2	14.1	20.2	12.3	8.3	25.8	8.1
Female	57,401	25.6	8.7	5.9	17.7	17.7	10.4	5.7	8.3	3.4
16 to 19 years old	3,025	71.0	12.3	8.6	7.6	0.5	-	-	-	0.7
20 years old and over	54,376	23.1	8.5	5.8	18.3	18.7	10.9	6.0	8.7	3.7
20 to 24 years old	6,045	53.4	15.4	9.2	17.4	4.6	(Z)	-	-	1.1
25 to 34 years old	12,551	30.8	11.6	7.7	23.4	20.3	5.6	0.6	-	2.5
35 to 44 years old	15,157	19.0	7.8	5.6	19.6	21.2	13.7	8.2	4.8	4.3
45 to 54 years old	13,221	13.8	5.5	4.0	15.7	20.5	14.6	8.9	17.0	6.5
55 to 64 years old	5,986	10.5	4.5	3.3	11.9	19.0	17.0	10.4	23.4	9.6
65 years old and over	1,415	9.8	4.2	3.8	12.6	19.5	15.7	8.9	25.4	9.5
RACE AND HISPANIC ORIGIN										
White	98,670	24.4	8.4	5.6	17.1	17.8	10.5	6.2	10.1	3.7
Male	51,473	23.3	8.0	5.4	16.8	17.8	10.4	6.5	11.9	4.0
Female	47,197	25.5	9.0	5.9	17.3	17.8	10.5	5.9	8.2	3.4
Black	14,143	25.4	7.5	6.6	18.0	17.9	9.6	5.6	9.5	3.5
Male	6,567	24.5	8.2	7.0	16.5	18.2	9.8	6.3	9.4	3.5
Female	7,577	26.3	6.8	6.2	19.2	17.7	9.4	4.9	9.5	3.5
Hispanic origin [3]	13,776	29.4	8.5	7.7	19.2	17.7	8.4	4.0	5.1	2.9
Male	7,807	28.5	7.6	8.2	19.7	17.9	8.6	4.1	5.5	3.0
Female	5,968	30.5	9.7	7.1	18.6	17.5	8.2	3.8	4.5	2.7

- Represents zero.   Z Less than 0.05 percent.   [1] For definition of median, see Guide to Tabular Presentation.   [2] Includes other races, not shown separately.   [3] Persons of Hispanic origin may be of any race.

Source: U. S. Bureau of Labor Statistics, *Employee Tenure in 2002, News*, USDL 02-531, September 19, 2002; and unpublished data. See Internet site <http://www.bls.gov/bls/newsrels.htm#OEUS>.

No. 611. Part-Time Workers by Reason: 2002

[In thousands (31,174 represents 31,174,000), except hours. For persons working 1 to 34 hours per week. For civilian noninstitutional population 16 years old and over. Annual average of monthly figures. Based on the Current Population Survey and subject to sampling error; see text, Section 1, and Appendix III]

Reason	All industries Total	All industries Usually work— Full time	All industries Usually work— Part time	Nonagriculture industries Total	Nonagriculture industries Usually work— Full time	Nonagriculture industries Usually work— Part time
Total working fewer than 35 hours	31,174	9,746	21,429	30,267	9,453	20,814
Economic reasons	4,213	1,627	2,586	4,035	1,535	2,500
Slack work or business conditions	2,788	1,380	1,408	2,671	1,314	1,358
Could find only part-time work	1,124	-	1,124	1,100	-	1,100
Seasonal work	165	112	54	132	89	42
Job started or ended during the week	135	135	-	132	132	-
Noneconomic reasons	26,961	8,119	18,843	26,232	7,918	18,314
Child care problems	777	80	697	765	79	686
Other family or personal obligations	5,766	756	5,010	5,621	739	4,882
Health or medical limitations	746	-	746	716	-	716
In school or training	6,177	88	6,089	6,051	85	5,966
Retired or Social Security limit on earnings	1,911	-	1,911	1,809	-	1,809
Vacation or personal day	3,452	3,452	-	3,388	3,388	-
Holiday, legal, or religious	597	597	-	590	590	-
Weather related curtailment	514	514	-	465	465	-
Other	7,022	2,632	4,390	6,828	2,572	4,256
Average hours per week:						
Economic reasons	23.0	24.1	22.3	23.1	24.2	22.4
Noneconomic reasons	21.4	25.2	19.7	21.4	25.2	19.8

- Represents or rounds to zero.
Source: U.S. Bureau of Labor Statistics, *Employment and Earnings*, monthly, June 2003. See Internet site <http://www.bls.gov/cps/home.htm>.

No. 612. Displaced Workers by Selected Characteristics: 2002

[In percent, except total (3,969 represents 3,969,000). As of February. For persons 20 years old and over with tenure of 3 years or more who lost or left a job between January 1999 and December 2001 because of plant closings or moves, slack work, or the abolishment of their positions. Data revised since originally published. Based on Current Population Survey and subject to sampling error; see source and Appendix III]

Characteristic	Total (1,000)	Employment status			Reason for job loss		
		Employed	Unemployed	Not in the labor force	Plant or company closed down or moved	Slack/ insufficient work	Position or shift abolished
Total [1]	3,969	63.6	21.2	15.2	47.2	25.4	27.3
20 to 24 years old	132	68.7	15.4	15.8	45.4	49.8	4.8
25 to 54 years old	3,117	67.5	21.7	10.8	46.5	25.3	28.2
55 to 64 years old	593	50.9	20.3	28.8	50.7	20.1	29.2
65 years old and over	127	19.8	20.7	59.5	50.9	28.1	21.0
Males	2,186	65.2	22.8	12.0	44.5	27.8	27.7
20 to 24 years old	55	([2])	([2])	([2])	([2])	([2])	([2])
25 to 54 years old	1,740	69.0	22.9	8.1	42.3	28.9	28.7
55 to 64 years old	326	55.0	22.7	22.3	55.6	16.5	27.9
65 years old and over	65	([2])	([2])	([2])	([2])	([2])	([2])
Females	1,783	61.6	19.3	19.1	50.6	22.5	26.9
20 to 24 years old	77	65.8	17.9	16.3	46.2	47.9	5.9
25 to 54 years old	1,377	65.7	20.2	14.2	51.8	20.7	27.5
55 to 64 years old	266	45.8	17.3	36.8	44.8	24.5	30.7
65 years old and over	62	([2])	([2])	([2])	([2])	([2])	([2])
White	3,351	64.7	20.8	14.5	46.9	24.7	28.4
Black	474	57.7	22.3	20.0	49.2	29.5	21.3
Hispanic origin [3]	335	55.0	31.0	14.0	50.1	33.9	16.0

[1] Includes other races, not shown separately. [2] Data not shown where base is less than 75,000. [3] Persons of Hispanic origin may be of any race.

Source: U.S. Bureau of Labor Statistics, *Worker Displacement, 1999-2001, News*, USDL 02-483, August 2, 2002. See Internet site <http://www.bls.gov/bls/newsrels.htm#OEUS>.

No. 613. Labor Force Status of Persons With a Work Disability by Age: 2002

[In percent, except as indicated (22,425 represents 22,425,000). As of March. For civilians 16 to 74 who have a condition which prevents them from working or limits the amount of work they can do. Data from the Current Population Survey and subject to sampling error; see text, Section 1, and Appendix III]

Labor force status	Total	Age					
		16 to 24 years old	25 to 34 years old	35 to 44 years old	45 to 54 years old	55 to 64 years old	65 to 69 years old	70 to 74 years old
Number (1,000)	22,425	1,264	2,284	3,839	5,054	5,678	2,166	2,139
In labor force	24.3	36.3	41.1	33.3	29.2	18.0	7.7	5.4
Employed	21.0	25.5	34.1	28.3	26.3	16.5	6.9	5.2
Full-time	13.4	13.0	21.7	19.8	18.7	9.8	1.8	1.8
Not in labor force	75.7	63.7	58.9	66.7	70.8	82.0	92.3	94.6
Unemployment rate	13.6	29.8	17.1	15.1	10.0	8.0	10.2	4.1

Source: U.S. Census Bureau, "Disability Data from the March Current Population Survey"; <http://www.census.gov/hhes/www/disable/disabcps.html>; (accessed 14 August 2003).

No. 614. Persons Not in the Labor Force: 2002

[In thousands (72,707 represents 72,707,000). Annual average of monthly figures. For the civilian noninstitutional population 16 years old and over. Based on the Current Population Survey; see text, Section 1, and Appendix III]

Status and reason	Total	Age			Sex	
		16 to 24 years old	25 to 54 years old	55 years old and over	Male	Female
Total not in the labor force	72,707	12,976	20,358	39,373	27,085	45,621
Do not want a job now [1]	68,029	11,254	18,286	38,489	24,994	43,035
Want a job now	4,677	1,722	2,071	884	2,091	2,586
In the previous year—						
Did not search for a job	2,673	910	1,112	651	1,135	1,538
Did search for a job [2]	2,004	812	960	233	956	1,048
Not available for work now	565	272	252	41	227	338
Available for work now, not looking for work	1,439	540	708	191	729	710
Reason for not currently looking for work:						
Discouraged over job prospects [3]	369	110	209	51	226	143
Family responsibilities	150	31	99	20	34	116
In school or training	238	195	41	2	126	112
Ill health or disability	107	16	61	30	50	56
Other [4]	575	188	299	88	292	283

[1] Includes some persons who are not asked if they want a job. [2] Persons who had a job in the prior 12 months must have searched since the end of that job. [3] Includes such things as believes no work available, could not find work, lacks necessary schooling or training, employer thinks too young or old, and other types of discrimination. [4] Includes such things as child care and transportation problems.

Source: U.S. Bureau of Labor Statistics, *Employment and Earnings*, monthly, June 2003 issue. See Internet site <http://www.bls.gov/cps/home.htm>.

No. 615. Employed Civilians by Occupation, Sex, Race, and Hispanic Origin: 1983 and 2002

[For civilian noninstitutional population 16 years old and over (100,834 represents 100,834,000). Annual average of monthly figures. Based on Current Population Survey; see text, Section 1, and Appendix III. Persons of Hispanic origin may be of any race. See headnote, Table 604]

Occupation	1983 Total employed (1,000)	1983 Female	1983 Black	1983 Hispanic	2002[1] Total employed (1,000)	2002[1] Female	2002[1] Black	2002[1] Hispanic
Total	100,834	43.7	9.3	5.3	136,485	46.6	10.9	12.2
Managerial and professional specialty[2]	23,592	40.9	5.6	2.6	42,482	50.5	8.0	5.8
Executive, administrative, and managerial[2]	10,772	32.4	4.7	2.8	20,561	45.9	7.6	6.3
Officials and administrators, public	417	38.5	8.3	3.8	720	52.6	13.0	7.6
Financial managers	357	38.6	3.5	3.1	803	50.5	8.4	6.8
Personnel and labor relations managers	106	43.9	4.9	2.6	219	66.0	8.0	5.1
Purchasing managers	82	23.6	5.1	1.4	140	43.3	6.6	4.7
Managers, marketing, advertising and public relations	396	21.8	2.7	1.7	735	38.4	3.7	4.9
Administrators, education and related fields	415	41.4	11.3	2.4	849	64.6	11.3	6.1
Managers, medicine and health	91	57.0	5.0	2.0	828	78.4	9.5	6.2
Managers, properties and real estate	305	42.8	5.5	5.2	618	50.0	7.4	9.8
Management-related occupations	2,966	40.3	5.8	3.5	5,182	58.2	9.0	6.5
Accountants and auditors	1,105	38.7	5.5	3.3	1,702	59.4	9.0	6.0
Professional specialty[2]	12,820	48.1	6.4	2.5	21,921	54.7	8.3	5.3
Architects	103	12.7	1.6	1.5	197	20.1	2.3	5.2
Engineers[2]	1,572	5.8	2.7	2.2	2,028	10.8	4.5	4.0
Aerospace engineers	80	6.9	1.5	2.1	90	8.1	0.9	6.0
Chemical engineers	67	6.1	3.0	1.4	77	16.5	3.1	3.1
Civil engineers	211	4.0	1.9	3.2	267	10.8	5.5	4.0
Electrical and electronic	450	6.1	3.4	3.1	677	10.3	5.9	4.0
Industrial engineers	210	11.0	3.3	2.4	235	17.2	4.4	5.3
Mechanical	259	2.8	3.2	1.1	301	6.9	2.9	2.6
Mathematical and computer scientists[2]	463	29.6	5.4	2.6	2,030	30.8	7.3	5.1
Computer systems analysts, scientists	276	27.8	6.2	2.7	1,742	27.8	6.9	5.2
Operations and systems researchers and analysts	142	31.3	4.9	2.2	238	48.9	10.7	5.6
Natural scientists[2]	357	20.5	2.6	2.1	545	35.1	4.1	2.9
Chemists, except biochemists	98	23.3	4.3	1.2	130	29.8	8.6	3.8
Geologists and geodesists	65	18.0	1.1	2.6	[3]	[3]	[3]	[3]
Biological and life scientists	55	40.8	2.4	1.8	119	44.0	2.3	2.4
Medical scientists	[3]	[3]	[3]	[3]	89	60.4	6.1	3.8
Health diagnosing occupations[2]	735	13.3	2.7	3.3	1,176	29.2	4.7	4.7
Physicians	519	15.8	3.2	4.5	825	30.6	5.0	5.8
Dentists	126	6.7	2.4	1.0	180	19.4	4.0	3.3
Health assessment and treating occupations	1,900	85.8	7.1	2.2	3,267	86.4	9.7	3.7
Registered nurses	1,372	95.8	6.7	1.8	2,311	92.9	10.0	3.3
Pharmacists	158	26.7	3.8	2.6	231	51.7	8.0	2.5
Dietitians	71	90.8	21.0	3.7	74	90.2	18.7	5.0
Therapists[2]	247	76.3	7.6	2.7	562	77.5	8.3	5.5
Respiratory therapists	69	69.4	6.5	3.7	97	58.4	14.1	3.8
Physical therapists	55	77.0	9.7	1.5	167	70.2	4.5	6.9
Speech therapists	51	90.5	1.5	-	117	94.3	4.7	2.8
Physicians' assistants	51	36.3	7.7	4.4	89	59.5	7.4	5.1
Teachers, college and university	606	36.3	4.4	1.8	1,015	42.7	5.4	5.4
Teachers, except college and university[2]	3,365	70.9	9.1	2.7	5,652	75.0	10.1	6.1
Prekindergarten and kindergarten	299	98.2	11.8	3.4	647	97.7	14.7	7.8
Elementary school	1,350	83.3	11.1	3.1	2,341	83.0	11.0	6.4
Secondary school	1,209	51.8	7.2	2.3	1,289	58.1	7.0	5.1
Special education	81	82.2	10.2	2.3	374	85.4	9.9	4.3
Counselors, educational and vocational	184	53.1	13.9	3.2	282	74.3	16.9	6.8
Librarians, archivists, and curators	213	84.4	7.8	1.6	231	78.8	7.0	4.6
Librarians	193	87.3	7.9	1.8	207	81.7	7.8	5.1
Social scientists and urban planners[2]	261	46.8	7.1	2.1	457	59.6	8.3	4.5
Economists	98	37.9	6.3	2.7	123	55.0	6.2	4.6
Psychologists	135	57.1	8.6	1.1	277	65.9	9.5	3.8
Social, recreation, and religious workers[2]	831	43.1	12.1	3.8	1,556	57.3	17.4	7.3
Social workers	407	64.3	18.2	6.3	848	74.0	22.7	8.6
Recreation workers	65	71.9	15.7	2.0	129	74.2	20.5	8.3
Clergy	293	5.6	4.9	1.4	393	14.1	9.8	4.0
Lawyers and judges	651	15.8	2.7	1.0	963	29.3	4.7	3.3
Lawyers	612	15.3	2.6	0.9	929	29.2	4.6	3.1
Writers, artists, entertainers, and athletes[2]	1,544	42.7	4.8	2.9	2,498	49.8	5.7	7.3
Authors	62	46.7	2.1	0.9	139	54.7	2.3	3.8
Technical writers	[3]	[3]	[3]	[3]	68	61.5	5.1	5.2
Designers	393	52.7	3.1	2.7	770	56.4	3.5	8.5
Musicians and composers	155	28.0	7.9	4.4	161	36.4	12.9	5.8
Actors and directors	60	30.8	6.6	3.4	155	38.2	8.4	8.7
Painters, sculptors, craft-artists, and artist printmakers	186	47.4	2.1	2.3	225	47.9	3.4	7.2
Photographers	113	20.7	4.0	3.4	178	33.2	4.1	6.7
Editors and reporters	204	48.4	2.9	2.1	280	48.5	4.7	3.3
Public relations specialists	157	50.1	6.2	1.9	211	68.2	9.2	4.6
Announcers	[3]	[3]	[3]	[3]	52	16.4	11.5	9.8
Athletes	58	17.6	9.4	1.7	95	25.8	11.8	6.8

See footnotes at end of table.

No. 615. Employed Civilians by Occupation, Sex, Race, and Hispanic Origin: 1983 and 2002—Con.

[For civilian noninstitutional population 16 years old and over (100,834 represents 100,834,000). Annual average of monthly figures. Based on Current Population Survey; see text, Section 1, and Appendix III. Persons of Hispanic origin may be of any race. See headnote, Table 604]

Occupation	1983 Total employed (1,000)	1983 Female	1983 Black	1983 Hispanic	2002[1] Total employed (1,000)	2002[1] Female	2002[1] Black	2002[1] Hispanic
Technical, sales, and administrative support	31,265	64.6	7.6	4.3	38,947	63.4	10.8	9.8
Technicians and related support	3,053	48.2	8.2	3.1	4,509	54.1	9.7	7.6
Health technologists and technicians [2]	1,111	84.3	12.7	3.1	1,879	81.5	14.3	8.6
Clinical laboratory technologists and technicians	255	76.2	10.5	2.9	384	76.5	19.4	7.0
Dental hygienists	66	98.6	1.6	-	133	98.1	1.5	2.0
Radiologic technicians	101	71.7	8.6	4.5	182	74.4	5.8	8.6
Licensed practical nurses	443	97.0	17.7	3.1	382	94.9	20.6	5.0
Engineering and related technologists and technicians [2]	822	18.4	6.1	3.5	980	20.8	7.7	7.7
Electrical and electronic technicians	260	12.5	8.2	4.6	433	19.1	9.2	4.9
Drafting occupations	273	17.5	5.5	2.3	247	21.6	4.1	12.3
Surveying and mapping technicians	([3])	([3])	([3])	([3])	65	9.1	0.3	10.2
Science technicians [2]	202	29.1	6.6	2.8	291	47.2	6.5	6.6
Biological technicians	52	37.7	2.9	2.0	131	59.5	3.7	6.1
Chemical technicians	82	26.9	9.5	3.5	64	33.6	11.6	7.3
Technicians, except health, engineering, and science [2]	917	35.3	5.0	2.7	1,359	41.8	5.5	6.2
Airplane pilots and navigators	69	2.1	-	1.6	129	4.2	1.1	0.3
Computer programmers	443	32.5	4.4	2.1	605	25.6	4.0	5.0
Legal assistants	128	74.0	4.3	3.6	401	82.2	7.4	10.7
Sales occupations	11,818	47.5	4.7	3.7	16,254	49.0	8.5	9.6
Supervisors and proprietors	2,958	28.4	3.6	3.4	4,828	39.6	6.4	8.1
Sales representatives, finance and business services [2]	1,853	37.2	2.7	2.2	2,944	44.8	6.8	5.8
Insurance sales	551	25.1	3.8	2.5	612	45.0	6.3	4.6
Real estate sales	570	48.9	1.3	1.5	839	55.1	4.4	5.7
Securities and financial services sales	212	23.6	3.1	1.1	568	28.6	6.4	3.8
Advertising and related sales	124	47.9	4.5	3.3	181	61.8	5.1	6.7
Sales representatives, commodities, except retail	1,442	15.1	2.1	2.2	1,563	25.2	3.1	5.1
Sales workers, retail and personal services	5,511	69.7	6.7	4.8	6,811	62.7	11.9	13.3
Cashiers	2,009	84.4	10.1	5.4	2,942	76.7	15.6	15.4
Sales-related occupations	54	58.7	2.8	1.3	107	71.0	9.0	10.5
Administrative support, including clerical	16,395	79.9	9.6	5.0	18,184	78.5	13.1	10.6
Supervisors	676	53.4	9.3	5.0	717	60.5	15.7	10.8
Computer equipment operators	605	63.9	12.5	6.0	308	47.1	12.0	8.5
Computer operators	597	63.7	12.1	6.0	301	46.9	11.8	8.4
Secretaries, stenographers, and typists [2]	4,861	98.2	7.3	4.5	3,020	97.6	9.9	8.2
Secretaries	3,891	99.0	5.8	4.0	2,302	98.6	8.4	7.9
Typists	906	95.6	13.8	6.4	571	93.9	17.6	10.9
Information clerks	1,174	88.9	8.5	5.5	2,053	89.0	11.7	12.3
Receptionists	602	96.8	7.5	6.6	1,068	97.1	9.2	14.2
Records processing occupations, except financial [2]	866	82.4	13.9	4.8	995	80.5	15.8	10.9
Order clerks	188	78.1	10.6	4.4	289	74.9	20.6	11.2
Personnel clerks, except payroll and time keeping	64	91.1	14.9	4.6	70	79.1	12.1	16.1
Library clerks	147	81.9	15.4	2.5	130	79.2	10.6	6.2
File clerks	287	83.5	16.7	6.1	288	81.5	14.8	14.2
Records clerks	157	82.8	11.6	5.6	206	87.4	15.0	7.7
Financial records processing [2]	2,457	89.4	4.6	3.7	2,205	91.8	8.2	8.1
Bookkeepers, accounting, and auditing clerks	1,970	91.0	4.3	3.3	1,592	92.7	7.1	7.3
Payroll and time keeping clerks	192	82.2	5.9	5.0	175	91.2	9.8	8.5
Billing clerks	146	88.4	6.2	3.9	229	89.7	14.4	9.7
Cost and rate clerks	96	75.6	5.9	5.3	51	81.2	10.8	12.4
Billing, posting, and calculating machine operators	([3])	([3])	([3])	([3])	159	89.8	8.1	12.4
Duplicating, mail and other office machine operators	68	62.6	16.0	6.1	58	55.1	19.2	11.5
Communications equipment operators	256	89.1	17.0	4.4	138	83.6	26.2	11.1
Telephone operators	244	90.4	17.0	4.3	119	85.4	25.9	10.3
Mail and message distributing occupations	799	31.6	18.1	4.5	907	39.7	20.8	8.0
Postal clerks, except mail carriers	248	36.7	26.2	5.2	274	49.5	30.7	5.8
Mail carrier, postal service	259	17.1	12.5	2.7	338	29.9	16.0	5.9
Mail clerks, except postal service	170	50.0	15.8	5.9	165	52.5	21.6	12.6
Messengers	122	26.2	16.7	5.2	130	28.1	11.3	12.1
Material recording, scheduling, and distributing [2,4]	1,562	37.5	10.9	6.6	1,995	45.9	13.7	14.4
Dispatchers	157	67.1	11.4	4.3	258	55.0	14.6	9.9
Production coordinators	182	44.0	6.1	2.2	230	57.4	9.2	7.3
Traffic, shipping, and receiving clerks	421	22.6	9.1	11.1	623	30.9	13.8	21.0
Stock and inventory clerks	532	38.7	13.3	5.5	463	43.9	14.9	12.0
Expediters	112	57.5	8.4	4.3	310	65.7	13.7	13.3
Adjusters and investigators	675	69.9	11.1	5.1	1,929	73.8	16.1	10.3
Insurance adjusters, examiners, and investigators	199	65.0	11.5	3.3	497	71.9	15.8	7.6
Investigators and adjusters, except insurance	301	70.1	11.3	4.8	1,135	74.5	15.0	10.8
Eligibility clerks, social welfare	69	88.7	12.9	9.4	86	87.3	17.0	12.8
Bill and account collectors	106	66.4	8.5	6.5	212	68.5	22.0	13.1
Miscellaneous administrative support [2]	2,397	85.2	12.5	5.9	3,858	84.2	13.8	11.8
General office clerks	648	80.6	12.7	5.2	842	83.3	14.4	10.8
Bank tellers	480	91.0	7.5	4.3	477	87.3	11.9	11.0
Data entry keyers	311	93.6	18.6	5.6	595	81.8	16.1	12.5
Statistical clerks	96	75.7	7.5	3.4	97	85.1	11.2	11.1
Teachers' aides	348	93.7	17.8	12.6	813	91.6	13.2	16.3

See footnotes at end of table.

No. 615. Employed Civilians by Occupation, Sex, Race, and Hispanic Origin: 1983 and 2002—Con.

[For civilian noninstitutional population 16 years old and over (100,834 represents 100,834,000). Annual average of monthly figures. Based on Current Population Survey; see text, Section 1, and Appendix III. Persons of Hispanic origin may be of any race. See headnote, Table 604]

Occupation	1983 Total employed (1,000)	1983 Female	1983 Black	1983 Hispanic	2002[1] Total employed (1,000)	2002[1] Female	2002[1] Black	2002[1] Hispanic
Service occupations	13,857	60.1	16.6	6.8	19,219	59.9	17.6	18.1
Private household[2]	980	96.1	27.8	8.5	746	94.7	12.3	34.4
Child care workers	408	96.9	7.9	3.6	229	97.6	7.7	19.6
Cleaners and servants	512	95.8	42.4	11.8	500	93.7	13.6	40.7
Protective service	1,672	12.8	13.6	4.6	2,596	19.9	19.9	10.7
Supervisors, protective service	127	4.7	7.7	3.1	237	13.3	16.4	11.4
Supervisors, police and detectives	58	4.2	9.3	1.2	126	15.7	17.8	6.9
Firefighting and fire prevention	189	1.0	6.7	4.1	262	4.1	9.5	9.0
Firefighting occupations	170	1.0	7.3	3.8	248	3.4	9.6	9.4
Police and detectives	645	9.4	13.1	4.0	1,076	18.3	17.4	11.4
Police and detectives, public service	412	5.7	9.5	4.4	586	15.5	11.9	11.5
Sheriffs, bailiffs, and other law enforcement officers	87	13.2	11.5	4.0	162	19.3	15.5	12.5
Correctional institution officers	146	17.8	24.0	2.8	328	23.0	28.1	10.6
Guards	711	20.6	17.0	5.6	1,022	27.0	26.0	10.3
Guards and police, except public service	602	13.0	18.9	6.2	885	21.9	28.2	10.7
Service except private household and protective	11,205	64.0	16.0	6.9	15,877	64.9	17.5	18.5
Food preparation and service occupations[2]	4,860	63.3	10.5	6.8	6,614	55.8	11.9	19.8
Bartenders	338	48.4	2.7	4.4	341	55.1	3.2	8.5
Waiters and waitresses	1,357	87.8	4.1	3.6	1,430	74.9	5.8	13.7
Cooks	1,452	50.0	15.8	6.5	2,264	40.3	16.7	27.1
Food counter, fountain, and related occupations	326	76.0	9.1	6.7	398	66.0	12.8	13.1
Kitchen workers, food preparation	138	77.0	13.7	8.1	338	68.5	9.9	15.9
Waiters' and waitresses' assistants	364	38.8	12.6	14.2	696	52.5	8.9	19.7
Health service occupations	1,739	89.2	23.5	4.8	2,817	89.2	30.6	12.7
Dental assistants	154	98.1	6.1	5.7	224	98.0	5.7	14.6
Health aides, except nursing	316	86.8	16.5	4.8	350	78.6	23.8	13.3
Nursing aides, orderlies, and attendants[2]	1,269	88.7	27.3	4.7	2,243	89.9	34.1	12.4
Cleaning and building service occupations[2]	2,736	38.8	24.4	9.2	3,162	45.7	20.3	26.8
Maids and housemen	531	81.2	32.3	10.1	709	82.3	21.4	31.0
Janitors and cleaners	2,031	28.6	22.6	8.9	2,199	36.4	19.6	26.6
Personal service occupations[2]	1,870	79.2	11.1	6.0	3,284	80.7	14.6	12.9
Barbers	92	12.9	8.4	12.1	91	23.4	29.0	15.9
Hairdressers and cosmetologists	622	88.7	7.0	5.7	908	89.7	12.4	10.9
Attendants, amusement and recreation facilities	131	40.2	7.1	4.3	267	40.3	9.8	7.2
Public transportation attendants	63	74.3	11.3	5.9	129	80.0	14.2	10.1
Welfare service aides	77	92.5	24.2	10.5	113	82.8	20.7	16.1
Family child care providers	(NA)	(NA)	(NA)	(NA)	457	99.4	15.6	16.9
Early childhood teachers' assistants	(NA)	(NA)	(NA)	(NA)	536	93.8	17.3	16.5
Precision production, craft, and repair	12,328	8.1	6.8	6.2	14,660	8.2	7.4	17.1
Mechanics and repairers	4,158	3.0	6.8	5.3	4,760	4.5	8.0	12.1
Mechanics and repairers, except supervisors[2]	3,906	2.8	7.0	5.5	4,523	4.4	8.1	12.3
Vehicle and mobile equipment mechanics/repairers[2]	1,683	0.8	6.9	6.0	1,831	1.3	7.0	13.6
Automobile mechanics	800	0.5	7.8	6.0	867	1.4	7.5	16.2
Aircraft engine mechanics	95	2.5	4.0	7.6	126	2.2	7.3	10.6
Electrical and electronic equipment repairers[2]	674	7.4	7.3	4.5	870	12.0	11.2	10.9
Data processing equipment repairers	98	9.3	6.1	4.5	283	16.7	10.5	8.2
Telephone installers and repairers	247	9.9	7.8	3.7	240	15.9	11.7	10.1
Construction trades	4,289	1.8	6.6	6.0	6,304	2.4	6.5	20.6
Construction trades, except supervisors	3,784	1.9	7.1	6.1	5,341	2.4	6.8	22.5
Carpenters	1,160	1.4	5.0	5.0	1,563	1.8	5.6	21.0
Extractive occupations	196	2.3	3.3	6.0	115	1.9	6.5	9.7
Precision production occupations	3,685	21.5	7.3	7.4	3,481	23.8	8.1	17.7
Operators, fabricators, and laborers	16,091	26.6	14.0	8.3	17,697	22.7	15.1	19.6
Machine operators, assemblers, and inspectors[2]	7,744	42.1	14.0	9.4	6,488	35.3	14.9	20.9
Textile, apparel, and furnishings machine operators[2]	1,414	82.1	18.7	12.5	757	67.6	13.8	34.8
Textile sewing machine operators	806	94.0	15.5	14.5	352	77.2	13.4	41.9
Pressing machine operators	141	66.4	27.1	14.2	81	69.5	28.6	42.0
Fabricators, assemblers, and hand working occupations	1,715	33.7	11.3	8.7	1,769	31.7	12.7	18.1
Production inspectors, testers, samplers, and weighers	794	53.8	13.0	7.7	654	49.4	15.7	19.4
Transportation and material moving occupations	4,201	7.8	13.0	5.9	5,814	10.4	16.0	14.2
Motor vehicle operators	2,978	9.2	13.5	6.0	4,482	12.1	16.2	13.8
Trucks drivers	2,195	3.1	12.3	5.7	3,234	4.9	13.2	13.9
Transportation occupations, except motor vehicles	212	2.4	6.7	3.0	169	4.5	9.4	8.1
Material moving equipment operators	1,011	4.8	12.9	6.3	1,163	4.6	16.2	16.8
Industrial truck and tractor operators	369	5.6	19.6	8.2	563	7.1	21.3	22.7
Handlers, equipment cleaners, helpers, and laborers[2]	4,147	16.8	15.1	8.6	5,395	20.9	14.3	23.9
Freight, stock, and material handlers	1,488	15.4	15.3	7.1	1,949	25.4	16.6	15.9
Laborers, except construction	1,024	19.4	16.0	8.6	1,267	21.8	14.3	22.6
Farming, forestry, and fishing	3,700	16.0	7.5	8.2	3,480	20.6	4.9	24.4
Farm operators and managers	1,450	12.1	1.3	0.7	1,168	24.5	1.2	4.2
Other agricultural and related occupations	2,072	19.9	11.7	14.0	2,181	19.2	6.9	36.4
Farm workers	1,149	24.8	11.6	15.9	716	21.0	4.7	45.4
Forestry and logging occupations	126	1.4	12.8	2.1	85	7.3	5.8	8.1
Fishers, hunters, and trappers	53	4.5	1.8	2.5	(³)	(³)	(³)	(³)

- Represents or rounds to zero. NA Not available. [1] See footnote 2, Table 587. [2] Includes other occupations, not shown separately. [3] Level of total employment below 50,000. [4] Includes clerks.

Source: U.S. Bureau of Labor Statistics, *Employment and Earnings*, monthly, June 2003 issue; and unpublished data. See Internet site <http://www.bls.gov/cps/home.htm>

Labor Force, Employment, and Earnings   401

No. 616. Employed Civilians by Occupation—States: 2001

[In thousands. (135,073 represents 135,073,000) Data may not agree with those shown in other tables since data shown here have not been revised using the 2000 Census. Based on the Current Population Survey and subject to sampling error; see text, Section 1, and Appendix III]

State	Total [1]	Managerial and professional specialty — Executive, administrative, and managerial	Managerial and professional specialty — Professional specialty	Technical, sales, and administrative support — Technicians and related support	Technical, sales, and administrative support — Sales	Technical, sales, and administrative support — Administrative support [2]	Service occupations	Operators, fabricators, and laborers — Precision production, craft, and repair	Operators, fabricators, and laborers — Machine operators, assemblers [3]	Operators, fabricators, and laborers — Transportation and material moving	Operators, fabricators, and laborers — Handlers, equipment cleaners, helpers [4]
U.S.	135,073	20,338	21,556	4,497	16,044	18,503	18,359	14,833	6,734	5,638	5,326
AL	2,033	263	297	57	261	279	250	256	143	106	76
AK	302	48	53	10	27	45	43	38	5	13	12
AZ	2,307	355	358	71	302	327	321	272	70	72	101
AR	1,164	151	152	33	137	146	151	135	96	67	56
CA	16,435	2,703	2,770	517	1,981	2,158	2,212	1,678	766	556	645
CO	2,210	390	398	77	282	297	285	230	67	72	76
CT	1,661	291	314	61	210	219	211	174	71	53	39
DE	404	65	65	14	41	69	50	44	16	16	13
DC	260	55	68	13	14	35	40	14	4	8	7
FL	7,309	1,094	1,018	256	1,042	997	1,140	796	220	270	290
GA	3,966	620	600	122	474	608	403	484	200	205	174
HI	577	85	81	16	76	81	116	57	(B)	19	18
ID	648	77	86	21	77	91	93	78	28	30	25
IL	6,006	916	916	190	699	891	779	638	347	293	241
IN	2,970	399	395	78	338	403	356	356	269	155	149
IA	1,535	195	239	52	175	220	185	162	97	67	67
KS	1,322	197	209	49	140	184	191	134	61	57	52
KY	1,860	267	287	60	220	243	225	198	110	105	80
LA	1,928	220	298	80	244	250	298	238	81	101	77
ME	657	87	104	18	76	91	88	87	33	29	23
MD	2,722	521	571	110	278	401	328	253	66	82	78
MA	3,163	532	640	103	350	428	445	308	134	87	101
MI	4,901	662	821	143	567	643	641	576	374	182	200
MN	2,710	437	437	107	307	383	327	295	138	94	75
MS	1,225	143	171	32	136	155	166	163	100	71	56
MO	2,830	382	442	94	331	387	374	324	168	128	127
MT	444	61	61	14	54	52	73	46	13	23	16
NE	899	109	130	29	113	131	117	96	35	36	40
NV	969	141	108	26	125	129	222	102	19	43	40
NH	664	105	109	24	82	87	82	86	32	24	22
NJ	4,004	696	687	157	500	591	546	362	154	161	119
NM	798	111	117	28	101	94	140	99	20	34	28
NY	8,402	1,268	1,487	267	921	1,201	1,404	817	303	336	289
NC	3,773	480	571	125	436	444	498	469	309	181	170
ND	(B)	(B)	(B)	(B)	(B)	(B)	(B)	(B)	(B)	(B)	(B)
OH	5,606	861	845	188	605	784	805	591	345	237	251
OK	1,602	202	227	56	194	233	213	216	71	73	62
OR	1,680	271	270	51	194	213	229	176	75	63	62
PA	5,786	868	946	210	663	818	763	593	307	267	243
RI	480	75	87	16	53	69	68	47	27	16	16
SC	1,843	252	274	68	236	242	235	227	131	76	74
SD	392	50	55	10	44	58	58	38	15	15	13
TN	2,692	381	376	81	327	359	324	323	197	136	141
TX	9,955	1,443	1,474	328	1,262	1,387	1,336	1,196	401	446	388
UT	1,067	164	161	43	126	151	129	128	46	45	45
VT	323	46	60	10	34	42	40	40	18	12	9
VA	3,548	619	660	127	377	467	410	379	150	152	146
WA	2,804	424	479	116	352	354	369	283	113	119	107
WV	792	93	113	38	90	100	123	100	36	51	35
WI	2,854	388	387	82	305	388	371	362	225	118	129
WY	261	35	36	7	28	33	36	37	6	18	10

B Base figure too small to meet statistical standards for reliability of a derived figure. [1] Includes farming, forestry, and fishing not shown separately. [2] Including clerical. [3] Including inspectors. [4] Including laborers.

Source: U.S. Bureau of Labor Statistics, Local Area Unemployment Statistics, *Geographic Profile of Employment and Unemployment, 2001* (published March 03). See Internet site <http://www.bls.gov/gps/>.

No. 617. Employment Projections by Occupation: 2000 and 2010

[In thousands (380 represents 380,000), except percent and rank. Estimates based on the Current Employment Statistics Program; the Occupational Employment Statistics Survey; and the Current Population Survey. See source for methodological assumptions. Occupations based on the 2000 Standard Occupational Classification system]

Occupation	Employment (1,000) 2000	Employment (1,000) 2010	Change 2000-2010 Number (1,000)	Change 2000-2010 Percent	Quartile rank by 2000 median annual earnings [1]	Education and training category
FASTEST GROWING						
Computer software engineers, applications	380	760	380	100	1	Bachelor's degree
Computer support specialists	506	996	490	97	2	Associate degree
Computer software engineers, systems software	317	601	284	90	1	Bachelor's degree
Network and computer systems administrators	229	416	187	82	1	Bachelor's degree
Network systems and data communications analysts	119	211	92	77	1	Bachelor's degree
Desktop publishers	38	63	25	67	2	Postsecondary vocational award
Database administrators	106	176	70	66	1	Bachelor's degree
Personal and home care aides	414	672	258	62	4	Short-term on-the-job training
Computer systems analysts	431	689	258	60	1	Bachelor's degree
Medical assistants	329	516	187	57	3	Moderate-term on-the-job training
Social and human service assistants	271	418	147	54	3	Moderate-term on-the-job training
Physician assistants	58	89	31	53	1	Bachelor's degree
Medical records and health information technicians	136	202	66	49	3	Associate degree
Computer and information systems managers	313	463	150	48	1	Bachelor's or higher degree, plus work experience
Home health aides	615	907	291	47	4	Short-term on-the-job training
Physical therapist aides	36	53	17	46	3	Short-term on-the-job training
Occupational therapist aides	9	12	4	45	3	Short-term on-the-job training
Physical therapist assistants	44	64	20	45	2	Associate degree
Audiologists	13	19	6	45	1	Master's degree
Fitness trainers and aerobics instructors	158	222	64	40	3	Postsecondary vocational award
Computer and information scientists, research	28	39	11	40	1	Doctoral degree
Veterinary assistants and laboratory animal caretakers	55	77	22	40	4	Short-term on-the-job training
Occupational therapist assistants	17	23	7	40	2	Associate degree
Veterinary technologists and technicians	49	69	19	39	3	Associate degree
Speech-language pathologists	88	122	34	39	1	Master's degree
Mental health and substance abuse social workers	83	116	33	39	2	Master's degree
Dental assistants	247	339	92	37	2	Moderate-term on-the-job training
Dental hygienists	147	201	54	37	1	Associate degree
Special education teachers, preschool, kindergarten, and elementary school	234	320	86	37	1	Bachelor's degree
Pharmacy technicians	190	259	69	36	3	Moderate-term on-the-job training
LARGEST JOB GROWTH						
Combined food preparation and serving workers, including fast food	2,206	2,879	673	30	4	Short-term on-the-job training
Customer service representatives	1,946	2,577	631	32	3	Moderate-term on-the-job training
Registered nurses	2,194	2,755	561	26	1	Associate degree
Retail salespersons	4,109	4,619	510	12	4	Short-term on-the-job training
Computer support specialists	506	996	490	97	2	Associate degree
Cashiers, except gaming	3,325	3,799	474	14	4	Short-term on-the-job training
Office clerks, general	2,705	3,135	430	16	3	Short-term on-the-job training
Security guards	1,106	1,497	391	35	4	Short-term on-the-job training
Computer software engineers, applications	380	760	380	100	1	Bachelor's degree
Waiters and waitresses	1,983	2,347	364	18	4	Short-term on-the-job training
General and operations managers	2,398	2,761	363	15	1	Bachelor's or higher degree, plus work experience
Truck drivers, heavy and tractor-trailer	1,749	2,095	346	20	2	Moderate-term on-the-job training
Nursing aides, orderlies, and attendants	1,373	1,697	323	24	3	Short-term on-the-job training
Janitors and cleaners, except maids and housekeeping cleaners	2,348	2,665	317	13	4	Short-term on-the-job training
Postsecondary teachers	1,344	1,659	315	23	1	Doctoral degree
Teacher assistants	1,262	1,562	301	24	4	Short-term on-the-job training
Home health aides	615	907	291	47	4	Short-term on-the-job training
Laborers and freight, stock, and material movers, handlers	2,084	2,373	289	14	3	Short-term on-the-job training
Computer software engineers, systems software	317	601	284	90	1	Bachelor's degree
Landscaping and groundskeeping workers	894	1,154	260	29	4	Short-term on-the-job training
Personal and home care aides	414	672	258	62	4	Short-term on-the-job training
Computer systems analysts	431	689	258	60	1	Bachelor's degree
Receptionists and information clerks	1,078	1,334	256	24	3	Short-term on-the-job training
Truck drivers, light or delivery services	1,117	1,331	215	19	3	Short-term on-the-job training
Packers and packagers, hand	1,091	1,300	210	19	4	Short-term on-the-job training
Elementary school teachers, except special education	1,532	1,734	202	13	1	Bachelor's degree

[1] Quartile ranks based on the Occupational Employment Statistics annual earnings. Ranks: 1 = $39,700 and over; 2 = $25,760 to $39,600; 3 = $18,500 to 25,760; 4 = up to $18,490.

Source: U.S. Bureau of Labor Statistics, *BLS Releases 2000-2010 Employment Projections, News*, USDL 01-443, December 3, 2001. See Internet site <http://www.bls.gov/emp/home.htm>.

No. 618. Occupations of the Employed by Selected Characteristics: 2002

[In thousands (60,301 represents 60,301,000). Annual averages of monthly figures. For civilian noninstitutional population 25 to 64 years old. Based on Current Population Survey; see text, Section 1, and Appendix III]

Sex, race, and educational attainment	Total employed	Managerial/ professional	Tech./ sales/ administrative	Service [1]	Precision production [2]	Operators/ fabricators [3]	Farming, forestry, fishing
Male, total [4]	60,301	19,183	11,349	5,288	11,681	10,807	1,994
Less than a high school diploma	6,769	349	482	968	1,975	2,360	636
High school graduates, no college	18,454	2,165	2,854	1,949	5,321	5,417	747
Less than a bachelor's degree	15,557	3,766	3,840	1,657	3,505	2,411	376
College graduates	19,522	12,903	4,172	714	879	619	235
White	51,058	16,669	9,597	3,964	10,388	8,640	1,800
Less than a high school diploma	5,703	298	398	735	1,758	1,958	557
High school graduates, no college	15,511	1,907	2,425	1,384	4,764	4,362	669
Less than a bachelor's degree	13,172	3,332	3,236	1,298	3,109	1,847	349
College graduates	16,671	11,131	3,538	547	756	474	225
Black	5,755	1,168	1,013	933	856	1,664	121
Less than a high school diploma	720	33	53	155	135	292	52
High school graduates, no college	2,170	169	301	422	391	841	47
Less than a bachelor's degree	1,712	286	408	275	276	446	21
College graduates	1,153	680	250	82	53	85	2
Female, total [4]	52,196	19,567	19,333	8,322	1,052	3,389	532
Less than a high school diploma	4,008	266	866	1,710	177	872	118
High school graduates, no college	15,887	2,558	7,289	3,677	460	1,706	197
Less than a bachelor's degree	15,628	4,766	7,541	2,251	292	644	133
College graduates	16,672	11,977	3,638	684	123	167	84
White	42,590	16,532	16,160	6,039	834	2,522	504
Less than a high school diploma	3,079	209	723	1,230	141	672	104
High school graduates, no college	13,018	2,244	6,280	2,658	373	1,276	188
Less than a bachelor's degree	12,656	4,034	6,165	1,642	227	459	131
College graduates	13,837	10,045	2,992	510	93	115	82
Black	6,631	1,917	2,256	1,720	117	613	10
Less than a high school diploma	656	42	100	373	12	125	4
High school graduates, no college	2,188	237	775	801	51	319	4
Less than a bachelor's degree	2,276	551	1,072	464	43	145	-
College graduates	1,510	1,086	308	81	11	23	1

- Represents or rounds to zero. [1] Includes private household workers. [2] Includes craft and repair. [3] Includes laborers. [4] Includes other races, not shown separately.

Source: U.S. Bureau of Labor Statistics, unpublished data.

No. 619. Employment by Industry: 1980 to 2002

[In thousands (99,303 represents 99,303,000), except percent. See headnote, Table 590. Data for 1990, and also beginning 1995, not strictly comparable with other years due to changes in industrial classification. Based on the Current Population Survey; see text, Section 1, and Appendix III]

Industry	1980	1990 [1]	1995	2000 [1]	2002, total	2002, percent Female	2002, percent Black	2002, percent Hispanic [2]
Total employed	99,303	118,793	124,900	136,891	136,485	46.6	10.9	12.2
Agriculture	3,364	3,223	3,440	3,382	3,340	26.0	3.9	23.3
Mining	979	724	627	524	516	12.2	4.3	8.9
Construction	6,215	7,764	7,668	9,591	9,669	9.3	6.3	18.8
Manufacturing	21,942	21,346	20,493	20,256	18,147	30.7	9.6	13.3
Transportation, communication, and other public utilities	6,525	8,168	8,709	9,846	9,680	28.6	15.3	10.1
Wholesale and retail trade	20,191	24,622	26,071	28,140	28,096	46.7	9.6	13.9
Wholesale trade	3,920	4,669	4,986	5,490	5,082	30.0	7.2	12.7
Retail trade	16,270	19,953	21,086	22,650	23,014	50.4	10.1	14.2
Finance, insurance, real estate	5,993	8,051	7,983	8,828	9,125	57.4	9.2	8.2
Services [3]	28,752	39,267	43,953	50,249	51,727	62.3	12.2	10.4
Business and repair services [3]	3,848	7,485	7,526	9,776	9,447	36.4	11.6	13.9
Advertising	191	277	267	281	272	46.8	5.3	7.3
Services to dwellings and buildings	370	827	829	881	980	53.6	15.5	30.8
Personnel supply services	235	710	853	1,071	983	58.7	19.7	15.5
Computer and data processing	221	805	1,136	2,528	2,094	29.9	6.4	5.5
Detective/protective services	213	378	506	580	729	25.2	27.9	11.3
Automobile services	952	1,457	1,459	1,210	1,232	9.8	6.7	16.6
Personal services [3]	3,839	4,733	4,375	4,599	4,559	70.1	12.9	19.4
Private households	1,257	1,036	971	904	844	90.6	12.8	32.4
Hotels and lodging places	1,149	1,818	1,495	1,631	1,534	57.0	9.5	20.9
Entertainment and recreation	1,047	1,526	2,238	2,595	2,767	42.5	8.5	11.0
Professional and related services [3]	19,853	25,351	29,661	33,123	34,815	70.1	12.6	8.2
Hospitals	4,036	4,700	4,961	5,092	5,340	77.4	16.7	8.0
Health services, except hospitals	3,345	4,673	5,967	6,650	7,313	79.8	15.1	8.8
Elementary, secondary schools	5,550	5,994	6,653	7,696	8,067	76.2	11.6	8.8
Colleges and universities	2,108	2,637	2,768	2,932	3,035	53.9	9.6	6.9
Social services	1,590	2,239	2,979	3,546	3,589	82.3	19.6	11.7
Legal services	776	1,215	1,335	1,373	1,425	55.5	5.7	7.2
Public administration [4]	5,342	5,627	5,957	6,076	6,184	45.2	16.5	8.3

[1] See footnote 2, Table 587. [2] Persons of Hispanic origin may be of any race. [3] Includes industries not shown separately. [4] Includes workers involved in uniquely governmental activities, e.g., judicial and legislative.

Source: U.S. Bureau of Labor Statistics, *Employment and Earnings*, monthly, January issues and June 2003 issue; and unpublished data. See Internet site <http://www.bls.gov/cps/home.htm>.

No. 620. Employment Projections by Industry: 2000 to 2010

[3,887.0 represents 3,887,000. Estimates based on the Current Employment Statistics estimates. See source for methodological assumptions. Minus sign (-) indicates decline]

Industry	1987 SIC code [1]	Employment (1,000) 2000	Employment (1,000) 2010	Change 2000-2010, (1,000)	Average annual rate of change, 2000-2010
LARGEST GROWTH					
Personnel supply services	736	3,887.0	5,800.0	1,913.0	4.1
Computer and data processing services	737	2,094.9	3,900.0	1,805.1	6.4
Retail trade exc eating and drinking places	52-57,59	15,193.5	16,799.9	1,606.4	1.0
Eating and drinking places	58	8,113.7	9,600.0	1,486.3	1.7
Offices of health practitioners	801-804	3,098.8	4,344.0	1,245.2	3.4
State and local government education	(X)	9,471.8	10,548.2	1,076.4	1.1
Miscellaneous business services	732,733,738	2,300.9	3,305.0	1,004.1	3.7
Construction	15,16,17	6,697.5	7,522.3	824.8	1.2
State and local government, n.e.c. [2]	(X)	6,592.2	7,400.0	807.8	1.2
Wholesale trade	50,51	7,023.8	7,800.0	776.2	1.1
Health services, n.e.c. [2]	807-809	1,210.2	1,900.0	689.8	4.6
Amusement and recreation services, n.e.c. [2]	791,799	1,313.6	1,850.0	536.4	3.5
Educational services	82	2,325.1	2,851.8	526.7	2.1
Residential care	836	805.9	1,318.0	512.1	5.0
Hospitals	806	3,990.3	4,500.0	509.7	1.2
Management and public relations	874	1,089.7	1,550.0	460.3	3.6
Nursing and personal care facilities	805	1,795.9	2,190.0	394.1	2.0
Legal services	81	1,009.6	1,350.0	340.4	2.9
Air transportation	45	1,281.3	1,600.0	318.7	2.2
Trucking and courier services except air	421,423	1,649.3	1,962.4	313.1	1.8
MOST RAPID GROWTH					
Computer and data processing services	737	2,094.9	3,900.0	1,805.1	6.4
Residential care	836	805.9	1,318.0	512.1	5.0
Health services, n.e.c. [2]	807-809	1,210.2	1,900.0	689.8	4.6
Cable and pay television services	484	215.8	325.0	109.2	4.2
Personnel supply services	736	3,887.0	5,800.0	1,913.0	4.1
Warehousing and storage	422	206.3	300.0	93.7	3.8
Water and sanitation	494-497	213.9	310.3	96.4	3.8
Miscellaneous business services	732,733,738	2,300.9	3,305.0	1,004.1	3.7
Miscellaneous equipment rental and leasing	735	279.4	397.5	118.1	3.6
Management and public relations	874	1,089.7	1,550.0	460.3	3.6
Child day care services	835	711.9	1,010.0	298.1	3.6
Amusement and recreation services, n.e.c. [2]	791,799	1,313.6	1,850.0	536.4	3.5
Offices of health practitioners	801-804	3,098.8	4,344.0	1,245.2	3.4
Wood buildings and mobile homes, mfg.	245	90.8	127.0	36.2	3.4
Veterinary services	074	240.0	335.9	95.9	3.4
Miscellaneous transportation services	473,474,478	252.8	350.0	97.2	3.3
Landscape and horticultural services	078	808.0	1,093.0	285.0	3.1
Research and testing services	873	642.3	886.0	243.7	3.3
Accounting, auditing, and other services	872,89	720.0	963.0	243.0	3.0
Legal services	81	1,009.6	1,350.0	340.4	2.9
MOST RAPID DECLINE					
Watches, clocks, and parts, mfg.	387	5.3	2.5	-2.8	-7.2
Footwear, except rubber and plastic, mfg.	313,314	30.1	14.2	-15.9	-7.2
Coal mining	12	77.2	54.0	-23.2	-3.5
Metal cans and shipping containers, mfg.	341	35.9	25.6	-10.3	-3.3
Luggage, handbags, and leather products, mfg., n.e.c. [2]	311,315-317,319	41.4	30.0	-11.4	-3.2
Railroad transportation	40	235.5	175.0	-60.5	-2.9
Private households	88	890.0	664.4	-225.6	-2.9
Apparel, mfg.	231-238	417.9	314.9	-103.0	-2.8
Petroleum refining, mfg.	291	84.6	65.0	-19.6	-2.6
Crude petroleum, natural gas, and gas liquids	131-132	129.3	100.0	-29.3	-2.5
Photographic equipment and supplies, mfg.	386	70.2	55.0	-15.2	-2.4
Blast furnaces and basic steel products, mfg.	331	224.5	176.0	-48.5	-2.4
Federal electric utilities	(X)	27.0	21.6	-5.4	-2.2
Dairy products, mfg.	202	145.5	121.1	-24.4	-1.8
Household appliances, mfg.	363	116.2	96.9	-19.3	-1.8
Pipelines, except natural gas	46	13.7	11.5	-2.2	-1.7
Plastics materials and synthetics, mfg.	282	154.3	130.0	-24.3	-1.7
Electrical industrial apparatus, mfg.	362	150.4	127.0	-23.4	-1.7
Service industries for the printing trade, mfg.	279	47.2	40.0	-7.2	-1.6
Tobacco products, mfg.	21	33.9	28.9	-5.0	-1.6

X Not applicable. [1] Based on the 1987 Standard Industrial Classification; see text, this section. [2] N.e.c. means not elsewhere classified.

Source: U.S. Bureau of Labor Statistics, *BLS Releases 2000-2010 Employment Projections, News*, USDL 01-443, December 3, 2001. See Internet site <http://www.bls.gov/emp/home.htm>.

No. 621. Unemployed Workers—Summary: 1980 to 2002

[In thousands (7,637 represents 7,637,000), except as indicated. For civilian noninstitutional population 16 years old and over. Annual averages of monthly figures. For data on unemployment insurance, see Table 556]

Age, sex, race, Hispanic origin	1980	1985	1990 [1]	1995	1999 [1]	2000 [1]	2001	2002
UNEMPLOYED								
Total [2]	7,637	8,312	7,047	7,404	5,880	5,692	6,801	8,378
16 to 19 years old	1,669	1,468	1,212	1,346	1,162	1,081	1,162	1,253
20 to 24 years old	1,835	1,738	1,299	1,244	1,042	1,022	1,209	1,430
25 to 44 years old	2,964	3,681	3,323	3,390	2,432	2,340	2,853	3,581
45 to 64 years old	1,075	1,331	1,109	1,269	1,120	1,117	1,447	1,950
65 years and over	94	93	105	153	124	132	129	163
Male	4,267	4,521	3,906	3,983	3,066	2,975	3,690	4,597
16 to 19 years old	913	806	667	744	633	599	650	700
20 to 24 years old	1,076	944	715	673	562	547	688	792
25 to 44 years old	1,619	1,950	1,803	1,776	1,195	1,159	1,470	1,920
45 to 64 years old	600	766	662	697	606	587	808	1,098
65 years and over	58	55	59	94	70	83	74	87
Female	3,370	3,791	3,140	3,421	2,814	2,717	3,111	3,781
16 to 19 years old	755	661	544	602	529	483	512	553
20 to 24 years old	760	794	584	571	480	475	521	638
25 to 44 years old	1,345	1,732	1,519	1,615	1,238	1,181	1,383	1,661
45 to 64 years old	473	566	447	574	513	529	640	854
65 years and over	36	39	46	60	54	50	55	76
White [3]	5,884	6,191	5,186	5,459	4,273	4,121	4,969	6,137
16 to 19 years old	1,291	1,074	903	952	844	795	845	925
20 to 24 years old	1,364	1,235	899	866	720	682	829	977
Black [3]	1,553	1,864	1,565	1,538	1,309	1,241	1,416	1,693
16 to 19 years old	343	357	268	325	268	230	260	260
20 to 24 years old	426	455	349	311	273	281	307	365
Hispanic [3,4]	620	811	876	1,140	945	954	1,138	1,353
16 to 19 years old	145	141	161	205	196	194	208	221
20 to 24 years old	138	171	167	209	171	190	212	265
Full-time workers	6,269	6,793	5,677	5,909	4,669	4,538	5,546	7,063
Part-time workers	1,369	1,519	1,369	1,495	1,211	1,154	1,254	1,314
UNEMPLOYMENT RATE (percent) [5]								
Total [2]	7.1	7.2	5.6	5.6	4.2	4.0	4.7	5.8
16 to 19 years old	17.8	18.6	15.5	17.3	13.9	13.1	14.7	16.5
20 to 24 years old	11.5	11.1	8.8	9.1	7.5	7.2	8.3	9.7
25 to 44 years old	6.0	6.2	4.9	4.8	3.5	3.3	4.1	5.2
45 to 64 years old	3.7	4.5	3.5	3.4	2.6	2.5	3.1	4.0
65 years and over	3.1	3.2	3.0	4.0	3.1	3.1	2.9	3.7
Male	6.9	7.0	5.7	5.6	4.1	3.9	4.8	5.9
16 to 19 years old	18.3	19.5	16.3	18.4	14.7	14.0	16.0	18.1
20 to 24 years old	12.5	11.4	9.1	9.2	7.7	7.3	9.0	10.2
25 to 44 years old	5.6	5.9	4.8	4.7	3.2	3.1	3.9	5.1
45 to 64 years old	3.5	4.5	3.7	3.5	2.6	2.4	3.2	4.2
65 years and over	3.1	3.1	3.0	4.3	3.0	3.3	3.0	3.4
Female	7.4	7.4	5.5	5.6	4.3	4.1	4.7	5.6
16 to 19 years old	17.2	17.6	14.7	16.1	13.2	12.1	13.4	14.9
20 to 24 years old	10.4	10.7	8.5	9.0	7.2	7.1	7.5	9.1
25 to 44 years old	6.4	6.6	4.9	5.0	3.8	3.6	4.3	5.2
45 to 64 years old	4.0	4.6	3.2	3.3	2.5	2.5	2.9	3.7
65 years and over	3.1	3.3	3.1	3.7	3.2	2.7	2.9	3.9
White [3]	6.3	6.2	4.8	4.9	3.7	3.5	4.2	5.1
16 to 19 years old	15.5	15.7	13.5	14.5	12.0	11.4	12.7	14.5
20 to 24 years old	9.9	9.2	7.3	7.7	6.3	5.9	7.0	8.1
Black [3]	14.3	15.1	11.4	10.4	8.0	7.6	8.6	10.2
16 to 19 years old	38.5	40.2	30.9	35.7	27.9	24.5	29.0	29.8
20 to 24 years old	23.6	24.5	19.9	17.7	14.6	15.0	16.3	19.1
Hispanic [3,4]	10.1	10.5	8.2	9.3	6.4	5.7	6.6	7.5
16 to 19 years old	22.5	24.3	19.5	24.1	18.6	16.6	17.7	20.1
20 to 24 years old	12.1	12.6	9.1	11.5	8.3	7.5	8.1	9.9
Experienced workers [6]	6.9	6.8	5.3	5.4	4.0	3.8	4.6	5.7
Women maintaining families	9.2	10.4	8.3	8.0	6.4	5.9	6.6	8.0
Married men, wife present [2]	4.2	4.3	3.4	3.3	2.2	2.0	2.7	3.6
White	3.9	4.0	3.1	3.0	2.1	1.8	2.5	3.3
Black	7.4	8.0	6.2	5.0	3.8	3.6	4.5	6.0
Percent without work for—								
Fewer than 5 weeks	43.2	42.1	46.3	36.5	43.7	44.9	42.0	34.5
5 to 10 weeks	23.4	22.2	23.5	22.0	21.8	23.0	22.4	20.7
11 to 14 weeks	9.0	8.0	8.5	9.6	9.3	8.9	9.9	10.1
15 to 26 weeks	13.8	12.3	11.7	14.6	12.8	11.8	14.0	16.3
27 weeks and over	10.7	15.4	10.0	17.3	12.3	11.4	11.8	18.3
Unemployment duration, average (weeks)	11.9	15.6	12.0	16.6	13.4	12.6	13.1	16.6

[1] See footnote 2, Table 587. [2] Includes other races, not shown separately. [3] Includes other ages, not shown separately. [4] Persons of Hispanic origin may be of any race. [5] Unemployed as percent of civilian labor force in specified group. [6] Wage and salary workers.

Source: U.S. Bureau of Labor Statistics, *Employment and Earnings*, monthly, January issues; and unpublished data. See Internet site <http://www.bls.gov/cps/>.

No. 622. Job Search Activity Using the Internet: 2001

[For the civilian noninstitutional population 16 years old and over, except as noted. As of September. Refers to use of Internet from any location to search for a job from January to September 2001. Based on the Current Population Survey and subject to sampling error; see text, Section 1, and Appendix III]

Characteristic	Population [1] Total	Total who used Internet for job-searching [2] (1,000)	Per- cent of total	Read online ads or searched on-the- job listings	Research- ed infor- mation on poten- tial em- ployers	Submit- ted a resume or appli- cation	Posted a resume on a site or with a service	Posted a resume on own Web site
Total, 16 years and over [3]	212,357	19,616	9.2	92.0	67.4	49.5	36.7	4.8
Age:								
16 to 24 years old	35,195	4,415	12.5	92.3	63.2	45.9	35.6	4.8
16 to 19 years old	16,206	1,108	6.8	91.5	54.1	34.0	26.3	3.0
20 to 24 years old	18,990	3,308	17.4	92.5	66.2	49.9	38.7	5.4
25 years old and over	177,162	15,201	8.6	91.9	68.7	50.5	37.0	4.8
25 to 34 years old	37,032	6,238	16.8	92.3	70.7	52.9	42.2	5.5
35 to 44 years old	44,318	4,890	11.0	91.9	68.6	50.4	35.4	4.4
45 to 54 years old	38,642	3,051	7.9	91.3	66.2	48.9	32.5	4.3
55 to 64 years old	24,328	877	3.6	89.9	67.4	41.3	26.9	2.7
65 years old and over	32,842	145	0.4	94.1	46.5	43.2	24.6	6.6
Sex:								
Male	102,110	9,700	9.5	91.5	71.5	53.4	40.5	5.9
Female	110,247	9,916	9.0	92.5	63.4	45.6	33.0	3.6
Race and Hispanic origin:								
White	176,220	16,018	9.1	91.9	67.1	48.2	35.1	4.5
Black	25,644	2,396	9.3	92.3	67.1	52.9	41.5	5.5
Hispanic origin [4]	23,288	1,377	5.9	89.2	67.7	47.0	36.6	5.8
Educational attainment:								
Total 25 years old and over	177,162	15,201	8.6	91.9	68.7	50.5	37.0	4.8
Less than high school diploma	27,484	402	1.5	88.8	58.2	38.9	30.3	4.6
High school graduate, no college	57,386	2,812	4.9	90.9	59.2	42.0	31.7	3.3
Some college, no degree	30,641	3,029	9.9	92.2	63.1	48.2	34.7	3.8
Associate degree	14,779	1,667	11.3	93.7	65.4	48.3	34.7	4.7
College degree	46,872	7,291	15.6	91.9	76.0	55.9	40.8	5.7
Advanced degree	16,283	2,390	14.7	91.6	77.8	55.6	39.3	6.4
Occupation [1]	141,447	17,235	12.2	92.2	68.5	50.7	37.4	4.8
Managerial and professional	43,058	7,258	16.9	92.8	74.3	56.0	40.1	5.9
Executive, administrative, managerial	20,851	3,484	16.7	93.4	75.3	58.3	42.1	4.8
Professional specialty	22,206	3,775	17.0	92.4	73.3	53.9	38.2	6.9
Technical, sales, and administrative	40,521	5,809	14.3	92.7	65.7	50.8	38.1	4.3
Technical and related support	4,784	868	18.1	90.1	72.6	54.8	42.4	6.0
Sales	16,709	2,151	12.9	94.5	71.2	54.0	40.5	4.8
Administrative support, inc. clerical	19,028	2,790	14.7	92.1	59.3	47.0	34.9	3.3
Service occupations	19,541	1,477	7.6	90.1	59.4	37.9	29.7	4.0
Precision production, craft, and repair	15,528	1,172	7.5	89.7	65.5	45.3	35.4	2.9
Operators, fabricators, and laborers	19,082	1,361	7.1	91.0	62.6	42.0	32.9	4.4
Farming, forestry, and fishing	3,705	152	4.1	87.5	62.8	37.1	19.9	2.2
Industry [1,5]	141,447	17,235	12.2	92.2	68.5	50.7	37.4	4.8
Private wage and salary workers	106,847	13,819	12.9	92.7	69.7	52.0	38.8	4.7
Agriculture	1,895	123	6.5	89.2	66.7	51.3	27.8	2.5
Nonagriculture	104,951	13,697	13.1	92.7	69.8	52.0	38.9	4.7
Mining	554	52	9.4	98.1	62.3	35.0	11.2	6.1
Construction	7,747	548	7.1	88.3	64.2	44.9	29.2	5.0
Manufacturing	18,412	2,216	12.0	93.2	72.2	53.9	39.8	4.6
Durable goods	11,348	1,454	12.8	92.9	74.4	57.1	41.0	4.8
Nondurable goods	7,064	763	10.8	93.7	68.0	47.7	37.7	4.1
Transportation and public utilities	7,784	1,069	13.7	91.0	70.2	53.2	41.8	6.9
Wholesale trade	4,549	618	13.6	94.7	68.2	55.1	40.4	4.7
Retail trade	22,123	2,348	10.6	93.8	64.1	47.2	36.3	4.7
Finance, insurance, and real estate	7,753	1,307	16.9	92.3	71.6	56.2	42.0	4.7
Services [6]	35,971	5,537	15.4	92.7	71.5	52.6	39.4	4.4
Business, automobile, and repair	8,727	1,739	19.9	94.0	78.6	63.5	49.5	7.0
Personal services, except private households	2,995	324	10.8	91.7	59.8	48.7	35.0	3.6
Entertainment and recreation	2,157	323	15.0	87.7	71.2	45.8	32.8	2.6
Professional services	21,278	3,097	14.6	92.7	68.8	48.4	35.3	3.2
Government workers	19,697	2,524	12.8	90.9	61.4	43.8	29.1	3.9
Federal	3,495	480	13.7	91.7	55.0	46.0	30.7	2.3
State	5,760	891	15.5	90.6	60.8	43.3	28.2	5.1
Local	10,443	1,153	11.0	90.9	64.5	43.2	29.1	3.8
Self-employed	14,778	889	6.0	87.6	69.7	49.4	40.0	9.4

[1] Data for occupation and industry are for the experienced labor force—the sum of the employed and unemployed whose last job was on one of these occupations or industries. [2] Includes other activities, not shown separately. [3] Includes other races, not shown separately. [4] Persons of Hispanic origin may be of any race. [5] Includes unpaid family workers, not shown separately. [6] Includes other industries, not shown separately.

Source: U.S. Bureau of Labor Statistics, *Computer and Internet Use at Work in 2001*, News, USDL 02-601, October 23, 2002. See Internet site <http://www.bls.gov/bls/newsrels.htm#OEUS>.

No. 623. Unemployed Persons by Sex and Reason: 1980 to 2002

[In thousands (4,267 represents 4,267,000). For civilian noninstitutional population 16 years old and over. Annual averages of monthly figures. Based on Current Population Survey; see text, Section 1, and Appendix III]

Sex and reason	1980	1985	1990 [1]	1994 [1]	1995	1996	1997 [1]	1998 [1]	1999 [1]	2000 [1]	2001	2002
Male, total	4,267	4,521	3,906	4,367	3,983	3,880	3,577	3,266	3,066	2,975	3,690	4,597
Job losers [2]	2,649	2,749	2,257	2,416	2,190	2,158	1,902	1,703	1,563	1,516	2,119	2,820
Job leavers	438	409	528	408	407	372	414	368	389	387	422	434
Reentrants	776	876	806	1,265	1,113	1,076	1,004	931	895	854	925	1,068
New entrants	405	487	315	278	273	273	257	264	219	217	223	274
Female, total	3,370	3,791	3,140	3,629	3,421	3,356	3,162	2,944	2,814	2,717	3,111	3,781
Job losers [2]	1,297	1,390	1,130	1,399	1,286	1,212	1,135	1,119	1,059	1,001	1,356	1,787
Job leavers	453	468	513	383	417	402	381	366	394	393	413	432
Reentrants	1,152	1,380	1,124	1,521	1,412	1,435	1,334	1,201	1,111	1,107	1,105	1,300
New entrants	468	552	373	326	306	307	312	257	250	217	237	262

[1] See footnote 2, Table 587. [2] Beginning 1994, persons who completed temporary jobs are identified separately and are included as job losers.

Source: U.S. Bureau of Labor Statistics, *Employment and Earnings*, monthly, January issues; and Bulletin 2307; and unpublished data. See Internet site <http://www.bls.gov/cps/home.htm>

No. 624. Unemployment Rates by Industry, 1980 to 2002, and by Sex, 1980 and 2002

[In percent. For civilian noninstitutional population 16 years old and over. Annual averages of monthly figures. Rate represents unemployment as a percent of labor force in each specified group. Data for 1990 not strictly comparable with other years due to changes in industrial classification]

Industry	1980	1990 [1]	1995	2000 [1]	2001	2002	Male 1980	Male 2002	Female 1980	Female 2002
All unemployed [2]	7.1	5.6	5.6	4.0	4.7	5.8	6.9	5.9	7.4	5.6
Industry: [3]										
Agriculture	11.0	9.8	11.1	7.5	9.5	9.1	9.7	9.0	15.1	9.4
Mining	6.4	4.8	5.2	3.9	4.7	6.2	6.7	6.1	4.5	6.8
Construction	14.1	11.1	11.5	6.3	7.3	9.2	14.6	9.5	8.9	7.3
Manufacturing	8.5	5.8	4.9	3.6	5.2	6.7	7.4	6.0	10.8	8.2
Transportation and public utilities	4.9	3.9	4.5	3.1	4.1	5.5	5.1	5.0	4.4	6.6
Wholesale and retail trade	7.4	6.4	6.5	5.0	5.5	6.8	6.6	6.2	8.3	7.5
Finance, insurance, and real estate	3.4	3.0	3.3	2.3	2.7	3.3	3.2	2.9	3.5	3.5
Services	5.9	5.0	5.4	3.8	4.6	5.5	6.3	6.1	5.8	5.1
Government	4.1	2.7	2.9	2.0	2.1	2.4	3.9	2.5	4.3	2.4

[1] See footnote 2, Table 587. [2] Includes the self-employed, unpaid family workers, and persons with no previous work experience, not shown separately. [3] Covers unemployed wage and salary workers.

Source: U.S. Bureau of Labor Statistics, *Employment and Earnings*, monthly, June 2003; and unpublished data. See Internet site <http://www.bls.gov/cps/home.htm>.

No. 625. Unemployment by Occupation, 1990 to 2002, and by Sex, 2002

[7,047 represents 7,047,000. For civilian noninstitutional population 16 years old and over. Annual averages of monthly data. Rate represents unemployment as a percent of the labor force for each specified group. Based on Current Population Survey; see text, Section 1, and Appendix III. See also headnote, Table 604]

Occupation	Number (1,000) 1990 [1]	Number (1,000) 2000 [1]	Number (1,000) 2002	Unemployment rate 1990 [1]	Unemployment rate 2000 [1]	2002 Total	2002 Male	2002 Female
Total [2]	7,047	5,692	8,378	5.6	4.0	5.8	5.9	5.6
Managerial and professional specialty	666	730	1,357	2.1	1.7	3.1	3.2	3.0
Executive, administrative, and managerial	350	359	717	2.3	1.8	3.4	3.2	3.6
Professional specialty	316	371	640	2.0	1.7	2.8	3.2	2.5
Technical sales, and administrative support	1,641	1,470	2,144	4.3	3.6	5.2	5.0	5.4
Technicians and related support	116	97	175	2.9	2.1	3.7	4.5	3.1
Sales occupations	720	685	1,001	4.8	4.0	5.8	4.7	6.9
Administrative support, including clerical	804	689	968	4.1	3.5	5.1	5.7	4.9
Service occupations	1,139	1,025	1,369	6.6	5.2	6.7	6.8	6.6
Private household	47	58	63	5.6	6.8	7.7	(B)	7.4
Protective service	74	65	102	3.6	2.6	3.8	3.3	5.8
Service except private household and protective	1,018	902	1,205	7.1	5.6	7.1	8.0	6.6
Precision production, craft, and repair	861	560	955	5.9	3.6	6.1	6.0	7.5
Mechanics and repairers	175	130	225	3.8	2.6	4.5	4.5	5.3
Construction trades	483	316	509	8.5	4.8	7.5	7.4	10.9
Other precision production, craft, and repair	202	115	221	4.7	2.8	5.8	5.3	7.5
Operators, fabricators, and laborers	1,714	1,239	1,720	8.7	6.2	8.9	8.3	10.6
Machine operators, assemblers, inspectors	727	461	624	8.1	5.8	8.8	7.5	10.9
Transportation and material moving occupations	329	255	377	6.3	4.3	6.1	6.0	6.8
Handlers, equipment cleaners, helpers, laborers	657	523	719	11.6	8.6	11.8	11.7	12.0
Construction laborers	177	135	178	18.1	11.5	14.1	13.8	21.0
Farming, forestry, and fishing	237	221	275	6.4	6.0	7.3	7.2	7.8

B Base is less than 35,000. [1] See footnote 2, Table 587. [2] Includes persons with no previous work experience and those whose last job was in the Armed Forces.

Source: U.S. Bureau of Labor Statistics, *Employment and Earnings*, monthly, January issues. See Internet site <http://www.bls.gov/cps/home.htm>.

No. 626. Unemployed and Unemployment Rates by Educational Attainment, Sex, Race, and Hispanic Origin: 1992 to 2002

[6,543 represents 6,543,000. Annual averages of monthly figures. For the civilian noninstitutional population 25 years old and over. See Table 591 for civilian labor force and participation rate data. Based on Current Population Survey; see text, Section 1, and Appendix III]

Year, sex, and race	Unemployed (1,000)					Unemployment rate [1]				
	Total	Less than high school diploma	High school graduates, no degree	Less than a bachelor's degree	College graduate	Total	Less than high school diploma	High school graduate, no degree	Less than a bachelor's degree	College graduate
Total: [2]										
1992	6,543	1,533	2,590	1,527	893	6.1	11.5	6.8	5.6	3.2
1995 [3]	4,814	1,076	1,747	1,227	764	4.3	9.0	4.8	4.0	2.4
2000 [3]	3,589	791	1,298	890	610	3.0	6.3	3.4	2.7	1.7
2002	5,695	1,064	1,985	1,523	1,123	4.6	8.4	5.3	4.5	2.9
Male:										
1992	3,767	942	1,462	829	533	6.4	11.4	7.4	5.9	3.3
1995 [3]	2,566	647	924	594	400	4.3	8.8	4.8	3.8	2.3
2000 [3]	1,829	411	682	427	309	2.8	5.4	3.4	2.6	1.5
2002	3,105	613	1,087	770	635	4.7	7.8	5.4	4.6	3.0
Female:										
1992	2,776	591	1,128	697	361	5.8	11.5	6.3	5.4	3.0
1995 [3]	2,248	429	822	633	364	4.4	9.2	4.7	4.1	2.7
2000 [3]	1,760	380	616	463	301	3.2	7.8	3.5	2.8	1.8
2002	2,590	451	898	752	488	4.6	9.5	5.1	4.5	2.8
White:										
1992	4,978	1,145	1,928	1,162	743	5.5	10.7	6.0	5.0	3.0
1995 [3]	3,641	783	1,295	921	642	3.9	8.3	4.2	3.5	2.3
2000 [3]	2,644	564	924	667	489	2.6	5.6	2.9	2.4	1.6
2002	4,235	769	1,454	1,136	876	4.2	7.6	4.6	4.1	2.7
Black:										
1992	1,269	322	565	301	81	11.0	15.3	12.3	9.8	4.4
1995 [3]	902	209	371	251	71	7.4	12.4	8.2	6.7	3.2
2000 [3]	731	179	315	169	68	5.4	10.7	6.4	4.0	2.5
2002	1,068	231	430	289	118	7.7	13.3	8.8	6.7	4.2
Hispanic: [4]										
1992	853	434	235	134	50	9.8	12.8	9.1	7.7	5.0
1995 [3]	725	370	193	123	40	7.6	10.4	6.8	5.9	3.5
2000 [3]	569	297	150	85	38	4.4	6.2	3.9	3.2	2.2
2002	868	397	247	157	67	6.1	7.7	5.9	5.4	3.4

[1] Percent unemployed of the civilian labor force. [2] Includes other races, not shown separately. [3] See footnote 2, Table 587. [4] Persons of Hispanic origin may be of any race.

Source: U.S. Bureau of Labor Statistics, *Employment and Earnings*, monthly, January issues and June 2003 issue. See Internet site <http://www.bls.gov/cps/home.htm>.

No. 627. Unemployed Persons by Reason of Unemployment: 2002

[8,378 represents 8,378,000. Annual averages of monthly data. Based on Current Population Survey; see text, Section 1, and Appendix III]

Age, sex, and reason	Total unemployed (1,000)	Percent distribution by duration				
		Less than 5 weeks	5 to 14 weeks	15 weeks and over		
				Total	15 to 26 weeks	27 weeks or longer
Total 16 years old and over	8,378	34.5	30.8	34.7	16.3	18.3
16 to 19 years old	1,253	46.8	33.5	19.7	11.0	8.7
Total 20 years old and over	7,124	32.4	30.3	37.3	17.3	20.0
Males	3,896	31.9	30.4	37.7	17.2	20.6
Job losers and persons who completed temporary jobs	2,702	31.9	30.4	37.7	18.0	19.7
On temporary layoff	701	48.4	34.8	16.7	10.9	5.8
Not on temporary layoff	2,000	26.1	28.9	45.0	20.4	24.6
Permanent job losers	1,537	23.5	28.6	47.8	21.9	26.0
Persons who completed temporary jobs	464	34.5	29.8	35.7	15.6	20.0
Job leavers	386	35.6	32.1	32.3	14.9	17.4
Reentrants	743	30.3	30.0	39.6	15.8	23.9
New entrants	65	27.4	22.7	49.9	12.9	37.0
Females	3,228	33.0	30.2	36.8	17.4	19.4
Job losers and persons who completed temporary jobs	1,708	31.4	29.3	39.3	19.6	19.7
On temporary layoff	360	54.2	31.3	14.5	9.3	5.2
Not on temporary layoff	1,348	25.3	28.8	45.9	22.3	23.6
Permanent job losers	1,082	23.5	28.2	48.4	23.0	25.4
Persons who completed temporary jobs	265	32.6	31.3	36.1	19.6	16.5
Job leavers	389	41.1	32.8	26.1	13.6	12.5
Reentrants	1,028	33.0	30.9	36.1	15.3	20.9
New entrants	102	29.3	28.3	42.4	17.7	24.7

Source: U.S. Bureau of Labor Statistics, *Employment and Earnings*, June 2003 issue. See Internet site <http://www.bls.gov/cps/home.htm>.

No. 628. Total Unemployed and Insured Unemployed by State: 1980 to 2002

[7,637 represents 7,637,000. For civilian noninstitutional population 16 years old and over. Annual averages of monthly figures. Total unemployment estimates based on the Current Population Survey; see text, Section 1, and Appendix III. U.S. totals derived by independent population controls; therefore state data may not add to U.S. totals]

State	Total unemployed Number (1,000) 1980	1990[2]	2000[2]	2002	Percent[1] 1980	1990[2]	2000[2]	2002	Insured unemployed[3] Number (1,000) 2000	2001	Percent[4] 2000	2001
United States...	7,637	7,047	5,692	8,378	7.1	5.6	4.0	5.8	[5]2,110	[5]2,974	[5]1.7	[5]2.3
Alabama	147	130	97	124	8.8	6.9	4.5	5.9	29.0	38.5	1.6	2.1
Alaska	18	19	21	25	9.7	7.0	6.7	7.7	12.3	12.2	4.9	4.7
Arizona	83	99	98	165	6.7	5.5	4.0	6.2	20.5	32.6	1.0	1.5
Arkansas	76	78	55	70	7.6	7.0	4.4	5.4	23.9	34.7	2.2	3.1
California	790	874	835	1,163	6.8	5.8	4.9	6.7	338.5	435.3	2.4	3.0
Colorado	88	89	65	140	5.9	5.0	2.8	5.7	15.0	27.2	0.7	1.3
Connecticut	94	95	40	77	5.9	5.2	2.2	4.3	28.3	38.3	1.7	2.3
Delaware	22	19	16	18	7.7	5.2	3.9	4.2	5.9	7.3	1.5	1.8
District of Columbia	24	22	18	20	7.3	6.6	5.7	6.4	5.7	6.1	1.3	1.3
Florida	251	390	281	442	5.9	6.0	3.6	5.5	70.8	102.1	1.1	1.5
Georgia	163	182	156	221	6.4	5.5	3.7	5.1	34.5	61.5	0.9	1.6
Hawaii	21	16	25	25	4.9	2.9	4.3	4.2	8.4	11.5	1.7	2.2
Idaho	34	29	32	40	7.9	5.9	4.9	5.8	12.1	16.5	2.3	3.0
Illinois	459	369	281	415	8.3	6.2	4.3	6.5	103.8	150.5	1.8	2.6
Indiana	252	149	100	163	9.6	5.3	3.2	5.1	31.8	55.0	1.1	1.9
Iowa	82	62	41	67	5.8	4.3	2.6	4.0	19.4	28.1	1.4	2.0
Kansas	53	57	52	72	4.5	4.5	3.7	5.1	15.6	21.1	1.2	1.6
Kentucky	133	104	81	110	8.0	5.9	4.1	5.6	25.4	36.5	1.5	2.1
Louisiana	121	117	111	123	6.7	6.3	5.4	6.1	24.0	28.0	1.3	1.5
Maine	39	33	24	30	7.8	5.2	3.5	4.4	8.9	10.9	1.6	1.9
Maryland	140	122	107	126	6.5	4.7	3.8	4.4	28.9	38.8	0.3	1.7
Massachusetts	162	195	88	185	5.6	6.0	2.6	5.3	60.1	89.6	1.9	2.8
Michigan	534	350	183	310	12.4	7.6	3.5	6.2	81.6	135.9	1.8	3.0
Minnesota	125	117	91	128	5.9	4.9	3.3	4.4	31.4	49.5	1.2	1.9
Mississippi	79	90	74	88	7.5	7.6	5.6	6.8	19.7	26.8	1.8	2.4
Missouri	167	151	102	165	7.2	5.8	3.4	5.5	41.8	55.6	1.6	2.1
Montana	23	24	24	21	6.1	6.0	5.0	4.6	7.8	8.7	2.2	2.4
Nebraska	31	18	28	34	4.1	2.2	3.0	3.6	7.3	10.3	0.9	1.2
Nevada	27	33	42	62	6.2	4.9	4.0	5.5	19.5	27.2	2.0	2.7
New Hampshire	22	36	19	33	4.7	5.7	2.8	4.7	3.1	6.4	0.5	1.1
New Jersey	260	206	160	255	7.2	5.1	3.7	5.8	84.8	109.1	2.3	2.9
New Mexico	42	46	42	48	7.5	6.5	5.0	5.4	9.5	11.6	1.4	1.7
New York	597	467	419	573	7.5	5.3	4.6	6.1	146.2	208.5	1.8	2.5
North Carolina	187	144	150	281	6.6	4.2	3.6	6.7	54.3	91.6	1.5	2.4
North Dakota	15	13	11	14	5.0	4.0	3.0	4.0	3.9	4.1	1.3	1.4
Ohio	426	310	233	331	8.4	5.7	4.0	5.7	71.6	113.1	1.3	2.1
Oklahoma	66	86	51	76	4.8	5.7	3.1	4.5	12.2	18.5	0.9	1.3
Oregon	107	83	88	138	8.3	5.6	4.9	7.5	41.2	60.4	2.7	3.8
Pennsylvania	425	315	251	356	7.8	5.4	4.1	5.7	132.4	178.3	2.5	3.3
Rhode Island	34	35	22	28	7.2	6.8	4.1	5.1	12.2	13.9	2.7	3.1
South Carolina	96	83	75	117	6.9	4.8	3.8	6.0	27.1	45.0	1.5	2.5
South Dakota	16	13	9	13	4.9	3.9	2.3	3.1	2.0	2.9	0.6	0.8
Tennessee	152	126	110	150	7.3	5.3	3.9	5.1	42.2	60.4	1.6	2.3
Texas	352	544	441	681	5.2	6.3	4.2	6.3	107.9	152.0	1.2	1.7
Utah	40	35	37	72	6.3	4.3	3.3	6.1	10.5	15.7	1.1	1.6
Vermont	16	15	10	13	6.4	5.0	2.9	3.7	4.8	6.0	1.7	2.1
Virginia	128	141	79	152	5.0	4.3	2.2	4.1	22.2	35.3	0.7	1.1
Washington	156	125	159	226	7.9	4.9	5.2	7.3	70.6	93.5	2.7	3.5
West Virginia	74	64	45	49	9.4	8.4	5.5	6.1	14.1	15.2	2.1	2.3
Wisconsin	167	114	105	167	7.2	4.4	3.6	5.5	53.1	77.4	2.0	2.9
Wyoming	9	13	10	11	4.0	5.5	3.9	4.2	2.9	2.9	1.3	1.3

[1] Total unemployment as percent of civilian labor force. [2] See footnote 2, Table 587. [3] Source: U.S. Employment and Training Administration, *Unemployment Insurance, Financial Handbook*, annual updates. [4] Insured unemployment as percent of average covered employment in the previous year. [5] Includes 49,800 in Puerto Rico and the Virgin Islands in 2000; and 55,400 in 2001.

Source: Except as noted, U.S. Bureau of Labor Statistics, *Geographic Profile of Employment and Unemployment*, annual. See Internet site <http://www.bls.gov/gps/>.

No. 629. Nonfarm Establishments—Employees, Hours, and Earnings by Industry: 1980 to 2002

[Annual averages of monthly data. (90,528 represents 90,528,000). Based on data from establishment reports. Includes all full- and part-time employees who worked during, or received pay for, any part of the pay period reported. Excludes proprietors, the self-employed, farm workers, unpaid family workers, private household workers, and Armed Forces. Establishment data shown here conform to industry definitions in the 2002 North American Industry Classification System (NAICS) and are adjusted to March 2002 employment benchmarks. Based on the Current Employment Statistics Program; see Appendix III]

Item and year	Total nonfarm	Private industry Total [1]	Natural resources and mining	Construction	Manufacturing	Trade, transportation and utilities	Information	Financial activities [2]	Professional and business services [3]	Education and health services [4]	Leisure and hospitality [5]	Government
EMPLOYEES (1,000)												
1980	90,528	74,154	1,077	4,454	18,733	18,413	2,361	5,025	7,544	7,072	6,721	16,375
1985	97,511	80,978	974	4,793	17,819	20,379	2,437	5,815	8,871	8,657	7,869	16,533
1990	109,487	91,072	765	5,263	17,695	22,666	2,688	6,614	10,848	10,984	9,288	18,415
1995	117,298	97,866	641	5,274	17,241	23,834	2,843	6,827	12,844	13,289	10,501	19,432
1997	122,776	103,113	654	5,813	17,419	24,700	3,084	7,178	14,335	14,087	11,018	19,664
1998	125,930	106,021	645	6,149	17,560	25,186	3,218	7,462	15,147	14,446	11,232	19,909
1999	128,993	108,686	598	6,545	17,322	25,771	3,419	7,648	15,957	14,798	11,543	20,307
2000	131,785	110,996	599	6,787	17,263	26,225	3,631	7,687	16,666	15,109	11,862	20,790
2001	131,826	110,707	606	6,826	16,441	25,983	3,629	7,807	16,476	15,645	12,036	21,118
2002	130,376	108,886	581	6,732	15,306	25,493	3,420	7,843	16,010	16,184	11,969	21,489
PERCENT DISTRIBUTION												
1980	100.0	81.9	1.2	4.9	20.7	20.3	2.6	5.6	8.3	7.8	7.4	18.1
1985	100.0	83.0	1.0	4.9	18.3	20.9	2.5	6.0	9.1	8.9	8.1	17.0
1990	100.0	83.2	0.7	4.8	16.2	20.7	2.5	6.0	9.9	10.0	8.5	16.8
1995	100.0	83.4	0.5	4.5	14.7	20.3	2.4	5.8	10.9	11.3	9.0	16.6
1997	100.0	84.0	0.5	4.7	14.2	20.1	2.5	5.8	11.7	11.5	9.0	16.0
1998	100.0	84.2	0.5	4.9	13.9	20.0	2.6	5.9	12.0	11.5	8.9	15.8
1999	100.0	84.3	0.5	5.1	13.4	20.0	2.7	5.9	12.4	11.5	8.9	15.7
2000	100.0	84.2	0.5	5.2	13.1	19.9	2.8	5.8	12.6	11.5	9.0	15.8
2001	100.0	84.0	0.5	5.2	12.5	19.7	2.8	5.9	12.5	11.9	9.1	16.0
2002	100.0	83.5	0.4	5.2	11.7	19.6	2.6	6.0	12.3	12.4	9.2	16.5
WEEKLY EARNINGS [6] (dol.)												
1980	(NA)	240.77	402.75	351.38	283.86	246.40	343.76	209.52	247.65	190.35	105.03	(NA)
1985	(NA)	304.68	529.40	448.85	380.70	295.84	431.07	287.72	317.38	254.56	131.47	(NA)
1990	(NA)	349.29	602.54	513.43	436.16	331.55	479.50	354.65	380.61	319.27	152.47	(NA)
1995	(NA)	399.53	670.32	571.57	509.26	378.79	564.98	436.12	426.44	377.73	171.43	(NA)
1997	(NA)	431.25	720.11	609.48	548.22	407.57	622.40	472.37	465.51	404.65	185.81	(NA)
1998	(NA)	448.04	727.28	629.75	557.12	423.30	646.52	500.95	490.00	418.82	195.82	(NA)
1999	(NA)	462.49	721.74	655.11	573.17	434.31	675.32	517.57	510.99	431.35	202.87	(NA)
2000	(NA)	480.41	734.92	685.78	590.65	449.88	700.89	537.37	535.07	449.29	211.79	(NA)
2001	(NA)	493.20	757.92	695.89	595.19	459.53	731.11	558.02	557.84	473.39	215.19	(NA)
2002	(NA)	506.22	743.11	711.61	618.87	471.09	739.41	575.43	574.59	493.02	221.15	(NA)
WEEKLY HOURS [6]												
1980	(NA)	35.2	44.9	37.5	39.7	35.0	36.3	36.0	34.3	32.1	27.0	(NA)
1985	(NA)	34.9	44.6	38.2	40.5	34.4	36.5	36.1	34.2	31.9	26.4	(NA)
1990	(NA)	34.3	45.0	38.3	40.5	33.7	35.8	35.5	34.2	31.9	26.0	(NA)
1995	(NA)	34.3	45.3	38.8	41.3	34.1	36.0	35.5	34.0	32.0	25.9	(NA)
1997	(NA)	34.5	46.2	38.9	41.7	34.3	36.3	35.7	34.3	32.2	26.0	(NA)
1998	(NA)	34.5	44.9	38.8	41.4	34.2	36.6	36.0	34.3	32.2	26.1	(NA)
1999	(NA)	34.3	44.2	39.0	41.4	33.9	36.7	35.8	34.4	32.1	26.1	(NA)
2000	(NA)	34.3	44.4	39.2	41.3	33.8	36.8	35.9	34.5	32.2	26.1	(NA)
2001	(NA)	34.0	44.6	38.7	40.3	33.5	36.9	35.8	34.2	32.3	25.8	(NA)
2002	(NA)	33.9	43.2	38.4	40.5	33.6	36.5	35.6	34.2	32.4	25.8	(NA)
HOURLY EARNINGS [6] (dol.)												
1980	(NA)	6.84	8.97	9.37	7.15	7.04	9.47	5.82	7.22	5.93	3.89	(NA)
1985	(NA)	8.73	11.87	11.75	9.40	8.60	11.81	7.97	9.28	7.98	4.98	(NA)
1990	(NA)	10.19	13.40	13.42	10.78	9.83	13.40	9.99	11.14	10.00	5.88	(NA)
1995	(NA)	11.64	14.78	14.73	12.34	11.10	15.68	12.28	12.53	11.80	6.62	(NA)
1997	(NA)	12.49	15.57	15.67	13.14	11.90	17.14	13.22	13.57	12.56	7.13	(NA)
1998	(NA)	13.00	16.20	16.23	13.45	12.39	17.67	13.93	14.27	13.00	7.48	(NA)
1999	(NA)	13.47	16.33	16.80	13.85	12.82	18.40	14.47	14.85	13.44	7.76	(NA)
2000	(NA)	14.00	16.55	17.48	14.32	13.31	19.07	14.98	15.52	13.95	8.11	(NA)
2001	(NA)	14.53	17.00	18.00	14.76	13.70	19.80	15.59	16.33	14.64	8.35	(NA)
2002	(NA)	14.95	17.22	18.51	15.29	14.02	20.23	16.17	16.81	15.22	8.57	(NA)

NA Not available. [1] Includes other services industries not shown separately. [2] Finance and insurance; real estate and rental and leasing. [3] Professional, scientific and technical services; management of companies and enterprises; administrative and support and waste management and remediation services. [4] Education services; health care and social assistance. [5] Arts, entertainment and recreation; accommodations and food services. [6] Average hours and earnings of production workers for natural resources and mining, manufacturing, and construction; average hours and earnings of nonsupervisory workers for the service-providing industries.

Source: U.S. Bureau of Labor Statistics, *Employment and Earnings*, monthly, June 2003 issue; and the Current Employment Statistics program Internet site <http://www.bls.gov/ces/home.htm>.

No. 630. Employees in Nonfarm Establishments—States: 2002

[In thousands (130,376 represents 130,376,000). For coverage, see headnote, Table 629. National totals differ from the sum of the state figures because of differing benchmarks among states and differing industrial and geographic stratification. Based on 2002 North American Industry Classification System; see text, this section]

State	Total [1]	Construction	Manufacturing	Trade, transportation, and utilities	Information	Financial activities[2]	Professional and business services[2]	Educational and health services[2]	Leisure and hospitality[2]	Other services	Government
U.S.	130,376	6,732	15,306	25,493	3,420	7,843	16,010	16,184	11,969	5,348	21,489
AL	1,887	100	307	373	34	98	186	183	152	87	354
AK	296	16	11	61	7	14	23	30	29	12	81
AZ	2,265	172	184	442	52	154	315	233	230	86	388
AR	1,148	55	214	242	20	50	101	136	88	41	195
CA	14,477	773	1,641	2,730	498	850	2,126	1,500	1,382	506	2,448
CO	2,184	160	166	413	94	148	290	209	247	86	359
CT	1,668	63	213	310	41	143	202	259	123	63	249
DE	413	[3]24	37	77	8	39	69	49	38	18	56
DC	663	[3]12	3	28	26	31	139	90	48	56	231
FL	7,205	[3]435	408	1,475	177	474	1,223	859	801	311	1,042
GA	3,905	199	472	835	133	213	521	374	338	183	626
HI	556	[3]26	15	107	12	28	67	63	97	24	118
ID	567	36	65	116	9	26	69	60	53	18	112
IL	5,895	276	756	1,197	148	401	786	711	494	255	861
IN	2,891	143	589	582	42	140	250	347	269	108	414
IA	1,447	64	228	305	35	94	106	188	125	57	244
KS	1,338	63	183	268	51	69	127	158	109	53	252
KY	1,786	83	276	371	32	85	155	222	153	76	313
LA	1,900	119	161	384	29	100	182	235	195	71	375
ME	606	29	68	124	12	35	51	105	57	20	103
MD	2,473	[3]168	157	462	53	151	361	331	214	114	461
MA	3,249	140	348	578	99	229	454	567	284	118	430
MI	4,476	201	759	837	75	216	593	532	393	176	685
MN	2,650	123	356	526	67	170	296	355	229	118	404
MS	1,127	55	189	222	16	46	77	112	123	38	241
MO	2,682	135	322	541	71	159	304	349	260	118	420
MT	396	22	20	85	8	19	32	52	51	16	84
NE	906	45	106	196	25	62	91	111	77	34	159
NV	1,050	92	43	191	17	56	114	72	297	30	131
NH	618	28	85	139	13	37	54	92	61	22	88
NJ	3,994	162	369	883	116	277	585	528	309	149	615
NM	766	46	39	136	17	34	89	94	80	28	191
NY	8,440	320	652	1,478	297	705	1,049	1,461	639	346	1,488
NC	3,843	221	642	720	80	189	415	413	327	180	647
ND	330	15	24	72	8	18	24	47	30	15	74
OH	5,446	236	885	1,064	101	308	615	710	487	230	799
OK	1,481	65	152	286	36	84	161	173	127	75	296
OR	1,572	79	202	315	37	94	173	185	150	57	273
PA	5,652	249	762	1,118	130	337	604	967	465	261	741
RI	479	19	62	81	11	33	49	88	48	22	66
SC	1,809	112	292	347	28	90	182	174	187	65	328
SD	378	19	38	77	7	28	25	54	40	16	74
TN	2,666	114	427	575	54	139	307	298	238	101	409
TX	9,427	570	951	1,965	249	581	1,055	1,085	845	356	1,624
UT	1,073	68	114	216	31	63	132	114	101	33	195
VT	300	15	41	59	7	13	20	50	33	10	51
VA	3,495	213	320	637	106	182	547	362	304	178	636
WA	2,657	155	286	511	94	146	290	307	245	98	517
WV	733	34	69	137	13	31	57	107	64	55	143
WI	2,779	123	529	535	51	153	240	357	239	133	415
WY	248	20	10	48	4	10	16	20	30	10	63

[1] Includes natural resources and mining, not shown separately.   [2] See footnotes, Table 629.   [3] Natural resources and mining included with construction.

Source: U.S. Bureau of Labor Statistics, *Employment and Earnings*, monthly, May (state estimates) and June (national estimates) 2003 issues. See also Internet site <http://www.bls.gov/sae/home.htm>. Compiled from data supplied by cooperating state agencies.

No. 631. Nonfarm Industries—Employees and Earnings: 1990 to 2002

[Annual averages of monthly figures (109,487 represents 109,487,000). Covers all full- and part-time employees who worked during, or received pay for, any part of the pay period including the 12th of the month. See also headnote, Table 629]

Industry	2002 NAICS[1] code	All employees (1,000) 1990	1995	2000	2001	2002	Average hourly earnings[2] (dollars) 2000	2001	2002
Total nonfarm	(X)	109,487	117,298	131,785	131,826	130,376	(NA)	(NA)	(NA)
Goods-producing[3]	(X)	23,723	23,156	24,649	23,873	22,619	15.27	15.78	16.33
Service-providing[4]	(X)	85,764	94,142	107,136	107,952	107,757	(NA)	(NA)	(NA)
Total private	(X)	91,072	97,866	110,996	110,707	108,886	14.00	14.53	14.95
Natural resources and mining	(X)	765	641	599	606	581	16.55	17.00	17.22
Mining	21	680	558	520	533	512	16.94	17.33	17.55
Oil and gas extraction	211	190	152	125	124	123	19.43	19.97	19.27
Mining, except oil and gas	212	302	252	225	219	212	18.07	18.22	18.62
Support activities for mining	213	188	154	171	190	177	14.55	15.36	15.58
Construction	23	5,263	5,274	6,787	6,826	6,732	17.48	18.00	18.51
Construction of buildings	236	1,413	1,325	1,633	1,589	1,584	16.74	17.15	17.74
Residential building	2361	673	630	823	781	807	15.18	15.68	16.22
Nonresidential building	2362	741	695	809	808	776	18.18	18.44	19.16
Heavy and civil engineering construction	237	813	775	937	953	930	16.80	17.24	18.00
Highway, street, and bridge construction	2373	289	278	340	346	344	18.17	18.56	19.16
Specialty trade contractors[5]	238	3,037	3,174	4,217	4,284	4,218	17.91	18.47	18.91
Building foundation and exterior contractors	2381	703	711	919	926	915	16.93	17.43	17.78
Building equipment contractors	2382	1,282	1,404	1,897	1,908	1,843	19.52	20.10	20.48
Building finishing contractors	2383	665	642	857	875	880	16.44	17.04	17.72
Manufacturing	31-33	17,695	17,241	17,263	16,441	15,306	14.32	14.76	15.29
Durable goods	(X)	10,736	10,372	10,876	10,335	9,517	14.93	15.38	16.01
Wood products	321	541	574	613	574	557	11.63	11.99	12.33
Nonmetallic mineral products	327	528	513	554	545	519	14.53	14.86	15.39
Cement and concrete products	3273	195	194	234	236	230	14.64	15.13	15.72
Primary metals	331	689	642	622	571	511	16.64	17.06	17.68
Foundries[5]	3315	214	216	217	200	180	14.72	15.25	15.91
Fabricated metal products[5]	332	1,610	1,623	1,753	1,676	1,548	13.77	14.19	14.68
Architectural and structural metals	3323	357	359	428	422	400	13.43	13.81	14.21
Machine shops and threaded products	3327	309	330	365	348	318	14.53	15.07	15.62
Machinery[5]	333	1,408	1,440	1,455	1,368	1,237	15.22	15.49	15.93
Agricultural, construction, and mining machinery	3331	229	215	222	217	201	14.21	14.38	14.51
HVAC & commercial refrigeration equip	3334	165	182	194	184	167	13.10	13.42	13.71
Metalworking machinery	3335	267	273	274	249	217	16.66	16.95	17.39
Computer and electronic products[5]	334	1,903	1,688	1,820	1,749	1,521	14.73	15.42	16.19
Computer and peripheral equipment	3341	367	296	302	286	250	18.39	18.96	19.64
Communications equipment	3342	232	233	248	234	191	14.39	15.04	15.69
Semiconductors and electronic components	3344	574	571	676	645	531	13.46	14.34	15.32
Electronic instruments	3345	626	482	479	475	451	15.83	16.26	16.65
Electrical equipment and appliances	335	633	593	591	557	499	13.23	13.78	13.97
Electrical equipment	3353	244	219	210	197	176	13.28	14.13	14.18
Transportation equipment[5]	336	2,133	1,977	2,056	1,938	1,829	18.89	19.48	20.64
Motor vehicles	3361	271	295	291	279	267	24.45	25.74	27.27
Motor vehicle parts	3363	653	787	840	775	731	17.95	18.22	19.79
Aerospace products and parts	3364	841	514	517	511	468	20.52	21.25	22.06
Furniture and related products	337	601	607	680	642	605	11.72	12.14	12.62
Household and institutional furniture	3371	398	399	440	416	400	11.39	11.81	12.29
Miscellaneous manufacturing	339	690	715	733	715	692	11.93	12.46	12.91
Medical equipment and supplies	3391	288	294	310	311	309	12.70	13.17	13.65
Nondurable goods	(X)	6,959	6,869	6,388	6,107	5,789	13.31	13.75	14.15
Food manufacturing	311	1,507	1,560	1,553	1,551	1,525	11.77	12.18	12.54
Fruit and vegetable preserving and specialty	3114	218	216	197	193	182	11.90	12.32	12.83
Animal slaughtering and processing	3116	427	476	507	516	520	10.27	10.53	10.91
Bakeries and tortilla manufacturing	3118	292	304	306	303	295	11.45	11.90	12.30
Beverages and tobacco products	312	218	203	207	209	205	17.40	17.67	17.68
Beverages	3121	173	164	175	177	172	17.19	17.48	17.38
Textile mills	313	492	469	378	333	293	11.23	11.40	11.73
Textile product mills	314	209	219	216	206	196	10.43	10.60	10.96
Apparel	315	929	814	497	427	358	8.60	8.82	9.10
Cut and sew apparel	3152	776	666	394	335	282	8.40	8.60	8.89
Leather and allied products	316	133	105	69	58	50	10.35	10.69	11.01
Paper and paper products	322	647	640	605	578	550	15.91	16.38	16.89
Pulp, paper, and paperboard mills	3221	238	220	191	179	168	20.62	21.16	21.96
Converted paper products	3222	409	419	413	398	382	13.58	14.07	14.53
Printing and related support activities	323	809	817	807	768	710	14.09	14.48	14.93
Petroleum and coal products	324	153	140	123	121	119	22.80	22.90	23.06
Chemicals	325	1,036	988	980	959	930	17.09	17.57	17.97
Basic chemicals	3251	249	228	188	181	171	21.06	21.43	21.85
Pharmaceuticals and medicines	3254	207	228	274	283	293	17.27	17.77	18.12
Plastics and rubber products	326	826	915	952	897	854	12.69	13.21	13.55
Plastics products	3261	619	703	738	699	668	12.04	12.56	12.84
Rubber products	3262	207	212	214	199	185	14.82	15.38	16.04

See footnotes at end of table.

Labor Force, Employment, and Earnings

No. 631. Nonfarm Industries—Employees and Earnings: 1990 to 2002—Con.

[Annual averages of monthly figures (109,487 represents 109,487,000). Covers all full- and part-time employees who worked during, or received pay for, any part of the pay period including the 12th of the month. See also headnote, Table 629]

Industry	2002 NAICS[1] code	All employees (1,000)					Average hourly earnings [2] (dollars)		
		1990	1995	2000	2001	2002	2000	2001	2002
Trade, transportation, and utilities	(X)	22,666	23,834	26,225	25,983	25,493	13.31	13.70	14.02
Wholesale trade	42	5,268	5,433	5,933	5,773	5,641	16.28	16.77	16.97
Durable goods [5]	423	2,834	2,909	3,251	3,130	3,007	16.71	17.36	17.60
Motor vehicles and parts	4231	309	335	356	347	346	14.27	15.00	15.55
Lumber and construction supplies	4233	181	191	227	221	225	13.61	14.69	15.06
Commercial equipment	4234	597	604	722	696	659	20.29	21.37	21.64
Electric goods	4236	357	361	425	405	367	19.43	19.06	18.87
Hardware and plumbing	4237	216	223	247	241	233	15.07	15.78	16.04
Machinery and supplies	4238	690	680	725	703	676	16.47	16.96	17.41
Nondurable goods [5]	424	1,900	1,969	2,065	2,031	2,015	14.33	14.69	15.05
Paper and paper products	4241	162	168	177	169	160	15.65	15.59	15.69
Druggists' goods	4242	136	146	192	202	213	18.98	18.48	18.07
Grocery and related products	4244	623	654	689	684	676	13.57	14.12	14.60
Electronic markets & agents & brokers	425	535	555	618	611	619	20.79	20.98	20.45
Retail trade	44,45	13,182	13,897	15,280	15,239	15,047	10.86	11.29	11.67
Motor vehicle and parts dealers [5]	441	1,494	1,627	1,847	1,855	1,879	14.94	15.38	15.82
Automobile dealers	4411	983	1,072	1,217	1,225	1,250	16.95	17.29	17.73
Auto parts, accessories, and tire stores	4413	418	459	499	493	487	11.04	11.56	11.77
Furniture and home furnishings stores	442	432	461	544	541	540	12.33	12.59	13.08
Furniture stores	4421	244	255	289	282	281	13.37	13.53	14.23
Home furnishings stores	4422	188	207	254	259	259	11.06	11.48	11.76
Electronics and appliance stores	443	382	449	564	555	529	13.67	14.70	16.22
Building material and garden supply stores	444	891	982	1,142	1,152	1,179	11.25	11.78	12.23
Building material & supplies dealers	4441	753	833	982	997	1,026	11.30	11.87	12.34
Food and beverage stores	445	2,779	2,880	2,993	2,951	2,872	9.76	10.16	10.55
Grocery stores	4451	2,406	2,495	2,582	2,549	2,478	9.71	10.11	10.49
Specialty food stores	4452	232	251	270	261	254	9.97	10.52	10.93
Beer, wine, and liquor stores	4453	141	134	141	140	140	10.40	10.71	11.11
Health and personal care stores	446	792	812	928	952	947	11.68	12.21	12.50
Gasoline stations	447	910	922	936	925	904	8.05	8.27	8.56
Clothing & clothing accessories stores	448	1,313	1,246	1,322	1,321	1,308	9.96	10.29	10.40
Clothing stores	4481	930	892	954	955	957	9.88	10.22	10.20
Shoe stores	4482	216	198	193	191	182	8.96	9.20	9.19
Jewelry, luggage, and leather goods stores	4483	167	157	175	175	169	11.48	11.71	12.34
Sporting goods, hobby, book, and music stores	451	532	606	686	679	660	9.33	9.75	10.05
Sporting goods and musical instrument stores	4511	352	385	437	438	435	9.55	10.10	10.46
Book, periodical, and music stores	4512	180	221	249	242	225	8.91	9.08	9.19
General merchandise stores	452	2,500	2,635	2,820	2,842	2,821	9.22	9.59	9.88
Department stores	4521	1,494	1,630	1,755	1,768	1,710	9.59	10.00	10.20
Miscellaneous store retailers [5]	453	738	841	1,007	993	963	10.20	10.51	10.74
Florists	4531	121	117	130	125	123	8.95	9.14	9.36
Office supplies, stationery, and gift stores	4532	358	391	471	459	435	10.46	10.91	11.24
Nonstore retailers	454	419	435	492	474	447	13.22	13.83	14.13
Electronic shopping and mail-order houses	4541	157	194	257	240	224	13.38	14.36	14.79
Transportation and warehousing	48,49	3,476	3,838	4,410	4,372	4,205	15.05	15.33	15.77
Air transportation	481	529	511	614	615	559	13.57	14.84	15.45
Scheduled air transportation	4811	503	473	570	570	516	13.25	14.41	14.94
Rail transportation	482	272	233	232	227	218	20.55	21.10	20.49
Water transportation	483	57	51	56	54	52	18.07	18.55	19.65
Truck transportation	484	1,122	1,249	1,406	1,387	1,339	15.86	15.32	15.78
General freight trucking	4841	807	901	1,013	992	957	16.37	15.72	16.19
Specialized freight trucking	4842	315	348	393	395	382	14.51	14.29	14.69
Transit & ground passenger transportation	485	274	328	372	375	372	11.88	12.17	12.71
Pipeline transportation	486	60	54	46	45	42	19.86	21.04	21.50
Scenic and sightseeing transportation	487	16	22	28	29	26	12.49	12.78	13.60
Support activities for transportation	488	364	430	537	539	527	14.57	15.56	16.67
Freight transportation arrangement	4885	111	143	178	179	167	13.46	14.57	15.62
Couriers and messengers	492	375	517	605	587	558	13.51	14.01	14.64
Couriers	4921	340	469	546	530	503	13.92	14.46	15.29
Warehousing and storage	493	407	444	514	514	514	14.46	14.85	14.87
Utilities	22	740	666	601	599	600	22.75	23.58	23.94
Power generation and supply	2211	550	486	434	434	436	23.13	23.92	24.56
Natural gas distribution	2212	155	142	121	118	116	23.41	24.37	23.58
Water, sewage and other systems	2213	35	38	46	48	49	16.93	17.72	18.67

See footnotes at end of table.

414 Labor Force, Employment, and Earnings

U.S. Census Bureau, Statistical Abstract of the United States: 2003

No. 631. Nonfarm Industries—Employees and Earnings: 1990 to 2002—Con.

[Annual averages of monthly figures (109,487 represents 109,487,000). Covers all full- and part-time employees who worked during, or received pay for, any part of the pay period including the 12th of the month. See also headnote, Table 629]

Industry	2002 NAICS[1] code	All employees (1,000) 1990	1995	2000	2001	2002	Average hourly earnings [2] (dollars) 2000	2001	2002
Information.	51	2,688	2,843	3,631	3,629	3,420	19.07	19.80	20.23
Publishing industries, except Internet	511	871	911	1,035	1,021	969	20.18	21.56	21.62
Newspaper, book, and directory publishers	5111	773	754	774	752	714	15.06	15.52	15.78
Software publishers	5112	98	157	261	269	256	28.48	30.91	31.14
Motion picture and sound recording industries	512	255	311	383	377	387	21.25	20.70	21.19
Motion picture and video industries	5121	232	284	352	347	360	21.33	20.77	21.39
Broadcasting, except Internet	515	284	298	344	345	334	16.74	17.76	18.57
Radio and television broadcasting	5151	232	234	253	249	241	17.13	18.17	19.02
Cable and other subscription programming	5152	52	64	91	96	93	15.45	16.61	17.43
Internet publishing and broadcasting	516	17	19	51	46	35	24.58	25.61	26.95
Telecommunications [5]	517	980	976	1,263	1,302	1,201	17.81	18.66	19.37
Wired telecommunications carriers	5171	673	611	719	732	662	18.52	19.49	20.82
Wireless telecommunications carriers	5172	36	90	186	201	196	14.41	15.26	15.74
Telecommunications resellers	5173	180	171	214	214	186	19.99	21.08	20.86
Cable and other program distribution	5175	70	87	123	129	128	14.67	15.20	15.72
ISPs, search portals, & data processing	518	252	291	510	494	447	20.57	20.79	20.67
ISPs and web search portals	5181	41	49	194	177	142	25.60	26.46	25.82
Data processing and related services	5182	211	243	316	317	305	16.97	17.27	18.30
Other information services		30	38	46	46	47	10.68	10.95	12.61
Financial activities	(X)	6,614	6,827	7,687	7,807	7,843	14.98	15.59	16.17
Finance and insurance	52	4,979	5,072	5,680	5,773	5,815	15.90	16.59	17.28
Monetary authorities - central bank	521	24	23	23	23	23	15.08	15.99	17.00
Credit intermediation and related activities	522	2,425	2,314	2,548	2,598	2,682	13.14	13.76	14.31
Depository credit intermediation	5221	1,909	1,700	1,681	1,701	1,738	11.97	12.31	12.75
Commercial banking	52211	1,362	1,282	1,251	1,258	1,285	11.83	12.11	12.55
Nondepository credit intermediation	5222	398	467	644	661	690	15.30	16.60	17.53
Activities related to credit intermediation	5223	119	148	222	236	254	15.39	16.21	16.06
Securities, commodity contracts, investments	523	458	562	805	831	801	20.20	21.28	22.49
Securities and commodity contracts brokerage and exchanges	5232	338	414	566	577	539	20.07	21.25	22.09
Other financial investment activities	5239	120	149	239	254	262	20.48	21.36	23.28
Insurance carriers and related activities	524	2,016	2,108	2,221	2,234	2,223	17.37	18.06	18.87
Insurance carriers	5241	1,338	1,396	1,433	1,430	1,402	17.92	18.65	19.54
Insurance agencies, brokerages, and related services	5242	678	713	788	803	821	16.28	16.92	17.61
Funds, trusts, and other financial vehicles	525	56	64	85	88	86	17.66	18.91	19.90
Real estate and rental and leasing	53	1,635	1,755	2,007	2,035	2,028	12.14	12.53	12.79
Real estate	531	1,107	1,179	1,312	1,340	1,348	12.24	12.62	12.87
Lessors of real estate	5311	564	578	607	611	605	11.16	11.79	12.05
Offices of real estate agents and brokers	5312	217	240	281	291	299	12.57	12.63	12.67
Activities related to real estate	5313	327	362	424	438	444	13.60	13.76	14.19
Rental and leasing services [5]	532	514	557	667	666	652	11.69	12.07	12.32
Automotive equipment rental and leasing	5321	163	171	208	208	197	10.70	11.02	11.44
Consumer goods rental	5322	220	251	292	290	290	9.53	10.03	10.32
Lessors of nonfinancial intangible assets	533	14	19	28	29	28	17.68	19.17	19.22
Professional and business services	(X)	10,848	12,844	16,666	16,476	16,010	15.52	16.33	16.81
Professional and technical services	54	4,557	5,101	6,734	6,902	6,715	20.61	21.42	22.00
Legal services	5411	944	959	1,066	1,091	1,112	21.38	22.26	22.52
Accounting and bookkeeping services	5412	664	706	866	872	867	14.42	14.94	15.95
Architectural and engineering services	5413	942	997	1,238	1,275	1,251	20.49	21.06	21.60
Computer systems design and related services	5415	410	611	1,254	1,298	1,163	27.13	28.24	28.97
Management and technical consulting services	5416	324	475	705	746	732	20.86	21.57	22.89
Scientific research and development services	5417	494	472	515	532	537	21.39	22.74	23.51
Advertising and related services	5418	382	396	497	482	442	16.99	17.40	17.59
Other professional and technical services	5419	317	385	462	476	488	13.55	13.88	14.52
Management of companies and enterprises	55	1,667	1,686	1,796	1,779	1,711	15.28	15.77	16.33
Administrative and waste services	56	4,624	6,057	8,136	7,795	7,584	11.66	12.21	12.65
Administrative and support services [5]	561	4,395	5,783	7,823	7,478	7,267	11.49	12.01	12.43
Office administrative services	5611	211	233	264	269	287	14.68	15.17	15.70
Employment services	5613	1,494	2,425	3,817	3,437	3,249	11.83	12.57	13.04
Temporary help services	56132	1,156	1,744	2,636	2,338	2,186	11.79	12.50	12.73
Business support services	5614	505	630	787	780	757	11.08	11.45	11.90
Travel arrangement and reservation services	5615	250	281	299	285	258	12.72	13.18	13.89
Investigation and security services	5616	507	592	689	710	726	9.78	10.13	10.58
Services to buildings and dwellings	5617	1,175	1,302	1,571	1,606	1,597	10.02	10.36	10.69
Waste management and remediation services	562	229	273	313	317	317	15.29	16.16	16.91

See footnotes at end of table.

Labor Force, Employment, and Earnings 415

No. 631. Nonfarm Industries—Employees and Earnings: 1990 to 2002—Con.

[Annual averages of monthly figures (109,487 represents 109,487,000). Covers all full- and part-time employees who worked during, or received pay for, any part of the pay period including the 12th of the month. See also headnote, Table 629]

Industry	2002 NAICS[1] code	All employees (1,000) 1990	1995	2000	2001	2002	Average hourly earnings[2] (dollars) 2000	2001	2002
Education and health services	(X)	10,984	13,289	15,109	15,645	16,184	13.95	14.64	15.22
Educational services	61	1,688	2,010	2,390	2,511	2,651	13.79	14.48	14.67
Elementary and secondary schools	6111	461	571	716	753	785	13.79	14.48	14.67
Junior colleges	6112	44	62	79	84	87	13.79	14.48	14.67
Colleges and universities	6113	939	1,083	1,196	1,258	1,348	13.79	14.48	14.67
Business, computer, and management training	6114	60	62	86	87	83	13.79	14.48	14.67
Technical and trade schools	6115	72	70	91	93	96	13.79	14.49	14.67
Other schools and instruction	6116	96	136	184	194	203	13.79	14.49	14.67
Educational support services	6117	17	26	39	43	49	13.80	14.49	14.67
Health care and social assistance[5]	62	9,296	11,278	12,718	13,134	13,533	13.98	14.67	15.33
Ambulatory health care services[5]	621	2,842	3,768	4,320	4,462	4,633	14.99	15.59	16.27
Offices of physicians	6211	1,278	1,540	1,840	1,911	1,983	15.65	16.26	17.05
Offices of dentists	6212	513	592	688	705	726	15.96	16.74	17.79
Offices of other health practitioners	6213	276	395	438	457	482	14.24	14.85	15.48
Outpatient care centers	6214	261	329	386	400	410	15.29	15.95	16.51
Medical and diagnostic laboratories	6215	129	146	162	170	174	15.74	16.25	17.11
Home health care services	6216	288	622	633	639	675	12.86	13.18	13.37
Hospitals[5]	622	3,513	3,734	3,954	4,051	4,153	16.71	17.72	18.63
General medical & surgical hospitals	6221	3,305	3,520	3,745	3,833	3,926	16.75	17.77	18.70
Psychiatric and substance abuse hospitals	6222	113	101	86	87	90	14.97	15.69	16.19
Nursing and residential care facilities[5]	623	1,856	2,308	2,583	2,676	2,743	10.67	11.20	11.60
Nursing care facilities	6231	1,170	1,413	1,514	1,547	1,574	11.08	11.69	12.13
Residential mental health facilities	6232	269	358	437	461	474	9.96	10.38	10.72
Community care facilities for the elderly	6233	330	414	478	505	530	9.83	10.29	10.69
Social assistance	624	1,085	1,470	1,860	1,946	2,004	9.78	10.17	10.54
Individual and family services	6241	389	527	678	728	767	10.57	10.98	11.43
Emergency and other relief services	6242	67	91	117	124	126	10.95	11.40	11.75
Vocational rehabilitation services	6243	242	295	370	380	376	9.57	9.94	10.34
Child day care services	6244	388	557	696	715	734	8.88	9.23	9.50
Leisure and hospitality	(X)	9,288	10,501	11,862	12,036	11,969	8.11	8.35	8.57
Arts, entertainment, and recreation	71	1,132	1,459	1,788	1,824	1,778	10.68	11.10	11.71
Performing arts and spectator sports	711	273	308	382	382	358	13.11	14.09	15.53
Museums, historical sites, zoos, and parks	712	68	84	110	115	113	12.21	12.61	12.73
Amusements, gambling, and recreation	713	791	1,068	1,296	1,327	1,308	9.86	10.15	10.57
Accommodations and food services	72	8,156	9,042	10,074	10,211	10,191	7.68	7.88	8.04
Accommodations	721	1,616	1,653	1,884	1,852	1,779	9.48	9.76	10.01
Traveler and other longer-term accommodations	7211	1,582	1,617	1,837	1,805	1,738	9.49	9.77	10.01
RV parks and recreational camps	7212	34	35	47	48	42	9.03	9.17	9.76
Food services and drinking places	722	6,540	7,389	8,189	8,359	8,412	7.18	7.38	7.56
Full-service restaurants	7221	3,070	3,468	3,845	3,933	3,990	7.15	7.35	7.57
Limited-service eating places	7222	2,765	3,125	3,462	3,529	3,528	6.85	7.05	7.20
Special food services	7223	392	443	491	501	507	9.45	9.73	9.89
Drinking places, alcoholic beverages	7224	312	353	391	396	387	7.24	7.45	7.52
Other services	81	4,261	4,572	5,168	5,258	5,348	12.73	13.27	13.72
Repair and maintenance	811	1,009	1,079	1,242	1,257	1,241	13.28	13.74	14.13
Automotive repair and maintenance	8111	659	738	888	904	897	12.45	12.94	13.30
Personal and laundry services	812	1,120	1,144	1,243	1,255	1,247	10.18	10.60	11.04
Personal care services	8121	430	445	490	508	523	10.18	10.61	11.18
Death care services	8122	123	123	136	138	139	13.04	13.41	13.70
Dry-cleaning and laundry services	8123	371	376	388	380	366	9.17	9.54	9.85
Dry-cleaning and laundry services, except coin-operated	81232	215	216	211	205	197	8.14	8.39	8.59
Other personal services	8129	196	200	229	229	219	10.52	10.92	11.40
Pet care services, except veterinary	81291	23	26	31	33	35	12.12	12.50	12.49
Membership associations & organizations[5]	813	2,132	2,349	2,683	2,746	2,861	13.66	14.28	14.69
Social advocacy organizations	8133	126	145	143	155	172	12.08	12.66	13.02
Civic and social organizations	8134	377	388	404	413	414	9.85	10.17	10.59
Professional and similar organizations	8139	379	422	473	488	503	15.98	16.47	17.56
Government	92	18,415	19,432	20,790	21,118	21,489	(NA)	(NA)	(NA)
Federal	(X)	3,196	2,949	2,865	2,764	2,767	(NA)	(NA)	(NA)
State government	(X)	4,305	4,635	4,786	4,905	5,006	(NA)	(NA)	(NA)
Local government	(X)	10,914	11,849	13,139	13,449	13,716	(NA)	(NA)	(NA)

NA Not available. X Not applicable. [1] Based on the North American Industry Classification System, 2002 (NAICS). See text, this section. [2] Production workers in the goods-producing industries and nonsupervisory workers in service-producing industries. See footnotes 3 and 4. [3] Natural resources and mining, construction, and manufacturing. [4] Trade, transportation and utilities, information, financial activities, professional and business services, education and health services, leisure and hospitality, other services, and government. [5] Includes other industries not shown separately.

Source: U.S. Bureau of Labor Statistics, *Employment and Earnings*, monthly, June 2003 issue; and the Current Employment Statistics program Internet site <http://www.bls.gov/ces/home.htm>.

No. 632. Annual Indexes of Output Per Hour for Selected NAICS Industries: 1987 to 2001

[For a discussion of productivity measures, see text, this section. Minus sign (-) indicates decrease]

Industry	2002 NAICS code [1]	1987	1990	1995	1999	2000	2001	Average annual percent change [2]
Mining	21	85.2	86.1	101.8	111.1	109.2	107.4	1.7
Oil and gas extraction	211	80.7	78.4	95.5	107.9	114.5	116.6	2.7
Mining, except oil and gas	212	69.5	79.3	94.0	105.9	106.8	109.0	3.3
Nonmetallic mineral mining and quarrying	2123	87.9	92.3	97.3	101.2	96.2	99.4	0.9
Utilities:								
Power generation and supply	2211	64.8	71.2	88.6	104.1	107.0	106.4	3.6
Natural gas distribution	2212	66.7	71.4	89.0	103.1	113.4	110.2	3.6
Manufacturing:								
Fruit and vegetable preserving and specialty	3114	89.3	86.4	97.2	108.5	109.9	117.2	2.0
Dairy products	3115	82.5	90.9	99.0	94.5	96.1	96.3	1.1
Animal slaughtering and processing	3116	98.1	94.6	98.7	100.4	101.9	102.8	0.3
Bakeries and tortilla manufacturing	3118	98.2	92.6	99.7	105.5	105.2	106.2	0.6
Other food products	3119	93.3	92.0	101.2	108.8	110.3	103.4	0.7
Beverages	3121	75.2	86.5	99.6	92.4	90.7	91.8	1.4
Fabric mills	3132	67.6	75.0	95.8	109.8	110.2	109.1	3.5
Textile furnishings mills	3141	91.2	88.1	92.5	101.2	106.6	106.9	1.1
Cut and sew apparel	3152	69.7	70.1	85.5	118.8	127.8	131.8	4.7
Sawmills and wood preservation	3211	77.4	79.2	91.0	105.4	106.5	109.0	2.5
Other wood products	3219	104.7	105.4	100.3	105.3	104.0	104.7	-
Plywood and engineered wood products	3212	99.3	102.3	101.8	99.9	100.6	104.8	0.4
Pulp, paper, and paperboard mills	3221	85.9	88.5	101.9	111.3	115.6	117.2	2.2
Converted paper products	3222	88.6	90.4	97.0	101.5	101.8	100.9	0.9
Printing and related support activities	3231	95.4	96.7	98.8	103.5	105.0	105.7	0.7
Petroleum and coal products	3241	72.1	76.7	90.2	108.0	113.2	112.2	3.2
Basic chemicals	3251	89.8	91.5	92.4	114.8	118.4	111.0	1.5
Resin, rubber, and artificial fibers	3252	76.5	75.7	95.9	108.9	108.1	103.8	2.2
Pharmaceuticals and medicines	3254	86.1	91.4	96.3	94.6	93.4	97.3	0.9
Soap, cleaning compounds, and toiletries	3256	80.9	83.2	93.9	91.2	99.3	102.6	1.7
Other chemical products and preparations	3259	75.5	76.6	94.4	109.2	120.0	111.3	2.8
Plastics products	3261	81.6	84.7	94.4	109.3	111.3	113.1	2.4
Rubber products	3262	77.4	83.0	92.9	101.4	103.8	104.1	2.1
Glass and glass products	3272	82.5	80.0	88.7	108.6	109.8	105.2	1.8
Cement and concrete products	3273	91.9	95.0	98.2	104.3	100.4	97.1	0.4
Other nonmetallic mineral products	3279	83.8	79.8	91.7	95.5	95.6	96.8	1.0
Iron and steel mills and ferroalloy production	3311	63.8	69.6	89.7	106.5	108.5	106.7	3.7
Foundries	3315	81.1	85.1	93.1	104.7	103.8	109.4	2.2
Forging and stamping	3321	85.1	88.6	94.2	110.9	121.3	121.8	2.6
Architectural and structural metals	3323	90.3	87.8	93.8	101.8	101.0	100.7	0.8
Machine shops and threaded products	3327	73.7	78.8	98.8	103.8	107.3	107.4	2.7
Coating, engraving, and heat treating metals	3328	75.9	81.6	102.6	101.3	105.8	104.7	2.3
Other fabricated metal products	3329	91.2	86.6	97.9	100.2	100.7	98.0	0.5
Agriculture, construction, and mining machinery	3331	73.9	82.9	95.7	95.1	101.2	99.5	2.1
Industrial machinery	3332	75.3	80.6	97.9	105.2	129.7	104.6	2.4
Commercial and service industry machinery	3333	84.0	91.6	103.2	111.3	101.6	94.4	0.8
HVAC and commercial refrigeration equipment	3334	83.7	88.6	96.6	110.4	108.3	110.8	2.0
Metalworking machinery	3335	84.6	85.3	98.9	100.4	106.4	102.0	1.3
Other general purpose machinery	3339	84.7	86.0	94.5	105.6	113.0	109.4	1.8
Computer and peripheral equipment	3341	10.5	14.3	51.2	190.3	225.2	237.0	24.9
Communications equipment	3342	38.4	47.3	74.6	134.0	165.5	155.2	10.5
Semiconductors and electronic components	3344	16.5	21.4	63.4	174.5	233.3	231.6	20.8
Electronic instruments	3345	67.7	76.0	96.7	105.0	114.2	116.0	3.9
Electrical equipment	3353	68.2	73.5	98.0	98.8	100.6	100.9	2.8
Other electrical equipment and components	3359	77.4	75.3	92.1	115.1	120.6	113.7	2.8
Motor vehicles	3361	81.4	86.0	88.6	123.2	110.4	108.9	2.1
Motor vehicle bodies and trailers	3362	85.1	75.9	97.2	103.2	98.6	99.4	1.1
Motor vehicle parts	3363	75.3	75.7	92.4	110.5	112.6	114.7	3.1
Aerospace products and parts	3364	84.9	87.7	93.7	118.1	101.0	114.8	2.2
Ship and boat building	3366	95.7	99.7	93.2	112.3	120.1	119.9	1.6
Household and institutional furniture	3371	85.8	87.7	97.0	103.5	102.6	106.1	1.5
Office furniture and fixtures	3372	85.9	80.9	84.5	98.5	100.2	97.1	0.9
Medical equipment and supplies	3391	74.9	81.2	95.0	109.6	114.2	119.0	3.4
Other miscellaneous manufacturing	3399	84.1	96.0	96.0	105.3	113.1	110.9	2.0
Wholesale trade	42	74.3	78.3	93.1	111.6	114.7	116.6	3.3
Durable goods	423	61.8	65.6	88.5	116.6	121.2	119.7	4.8
Nondurable goods	424	94.2	96.7	99.6	104.1	103.5	106.9	0.7
Retail trade	44-45	81.3	83.8	95.0	110.0	114.4	117.4	2.7
Motor vehicle and parts dealers	441	85.9	90.1	97.2	106.4	107.4	109.1	1.7
Automobile dealers	4411	86.9	91.9	97.1	106.4	106.9	108.0	1.6
Other motor vehicle dealers	4412	76.2	72.7	93.0	113.0	108.6	112.4	2.8
Auto parts, accessories, and tire stores	4413	80.6	87.3	99.0	110.0	112.0	109.3	2.2
Furniture and home furnishings stores	442	76.5	81.3	94.4	109.5	115.5	116.5	3.1
Furniture stores	4421	74.6	82.1	92.5	108.2	114.8	119.2	3.4
Home furnishings stores	4422	78.9	79.9	96.6	111.2	116.6	113.5	2.6
Electronics and appliance stores	443	37.3	45.1	88.8	153.6	180.1	202.7	12.9
Building material and garden supply stores	444	78.6	82.3	94.1	112.2	113.1	115.7	2.8

See footnotes at end of table.

No. 632. Annual Indexes of Output Per Hour for Selected NAICS Industries: 1987 to 2001—Con.

[For a discussion of productivity measures, see text, this section. Minus sign (-) indicates decrease]

Industry	2002 NAICS code [1]	1987	1990	1995	1999	2000	2001	Average annual percent change [2]
Building material and supplies dealers	4441	79.1	83.6	95.1	113.5	113.8	115.2	2.7
Lawn and garden equipment and supplies stores	4442	75.4	75.6	87.7	103.7	108.5	119.7	3.4
Food and beverage stores	445	110.7	108.8	103.1	103.6	105.1	107.7	-0.2
Grocery stores	4451	111.4	107.9	103.5	104.3	104.9	107.5	-0.3
Specialty food stores	4452	144.3	141.4	107.3	99.4	105.3	110.8	-1.9
Beer, wine and liquor stores	4453	96.3	100.1	96.2	99.8	111.1	110.4	1.0
Health and personal care stores	446	85.7	92.9	93.1	106.9	111.5	112.4	2.0
Gasoline stations	447	87.8	88.5	101.5	110.6	106.5	110.0	1.6
Clothing and clothing accessories stores	448	67.3	70.2	91.6	112.9	120.3	123.7	4.4
Clothing stores	4481	66.7	69.8	90.7	113.4	120.9	125.3	4.6
Shoe stores	4482	68.1	73.7	93.7	104.9	109.6	115.8	3.9
Jewelry, luggage, and leather goods stores	4483	69.7	68.6	94.1	119.2	128.6	124.1	4.2
Sporting goods, hobby, book, and music stores	451	72.3	81.2	92.7	114.1	120.8	124.4	3.9
Sporting goods and musical instrument stores	4511	71.4	79.6	92.3	119.6	129.2	131.4	4.5
Book, periodical, and music stores	4512	73.8	84.4	93.5	104.1	105.7	110.8	2.9
General merchandise stores	452	73.2	75.3	92.1	113.0	120.1	124.3	3.9
Department stores	4521	87.2	84.1	94.5	104.3	106.5	104.1	1.3
Other general merchandise stores	4529	54.3	61.5	87.5	129.6	146.2	162.6	8.1
Miscellaneous store retailers	453	62.9	68.0	89.5	107.7	109.2	107.7	3.9
Florists	4531	79.3	75.2	83.5	117.3	115.6	121.1	3.1
Office supplies, stationery and gift stores	4532	55.0	62.0	90.9	114.6	122.0	136.1	6.7
Used merchandise stores	4533	79.8	80.8	89.9	105.9	112.6	103.6	1.9
Other miscellaneous store retailers	4539	68.6	75.7	90.6	100.3	97.2	84.4	1.5
Nonstore retailers	454	51.8	55.3	80.1	126.6	155.0	161.8	8.5
Electronic shopping and mail-order houses	4541	36.3	43.5	71.9	141.5	159.8	177.5	12.0
Direct selling establishments	4543	85.3	83.2	98.4	92.2	110.0	105.5	1.5
Transportation and warehousing:								
Air transportation	481	81.1	77.5	95.3	98.2	98.2	91.9	0.9
Line-haul railroads	482111	58.9	69.8	92.0	107.5	115.4	123.1	5.4
General freight trucking, long-distance	48412	79.4	88.5	95.4	102.1	105.2	103.3	1.9
Postal service	491	92.4	96.1	98.3	102.4	104.9	106.1	1.0
Information:								
Newspaper, book, and directory publishers	5111	103.1	97.2	93.3	109.4	110.3	107.6	0.3
Software publishers	5112	14.3	41.3	83.2	115.5	111.1	109.4	15.7
Motion picture and video exhibition	51213	94.1	113.5	101.5	102.0	106.5	104.6	0.8
Radio and television broadcasting	5151	94.9	100.9	106.3	101.8	103.4	98.2	0.2
Wired telecommunications carriers	5171	53.8	65.5	90.6	114.6	122.3	124.3	6.2
Wireless telecommunications carriers	5172	45.7	76.0	98.3	133.9	138.2	171.6	9.9
Finance and insurance:								
Commercial banking	52211	73.8	80.7	95.9	101.5	105.1	102.3	2.4
Real estate and rental leasing:								
Passenger car rental	532111	91.3	89.8	101.1	114.4	113.3	113.4	1.6
Professional and technical services:								
Advertising agencies	54181	73.6	79.8	88.6	111.2	116.7	118.1	3.4
Accommodation and food services:								
Traveler accommodations	7211	111.2	102.8	107.2	102.2	107.1	103.2	-0.5
Food services and drinking places	722	95.9	103.4	100.9	101.7	104.4	104.9	0.6
Full-service restaurants	7221	90.8	99.7	96.9	99.4	101.1	101.1	0.8
Limited-service eating places	7222	95.2	104.0	105.0	103.5	107.0	109.2	1.0
Special food services	7223	105.0	107.2	99.3	106.0	111.7	108.4	0.2
Drinking places, alcoholic beverages	7224	133.4	125.7	104.5	99.4	100.3	98.1	-2.2
Other services:								
Automotive repair and maintenance	8111	87.8	92.8	102.9	106.6	108.1	109.3	1.6
Hair, nail and skin care services	81211	83.0	81.6	92.4	103.7	102.9	107.9	1.9
Drycleaning and laundry services	8123	97.4	95.5	98.9	109.5	114.1	120.7	1.5

- Represents or rounds to zero. [1] North American Industry Classification System, 2002 (NAICS); see text, this section. [2] Average annual percent change, 1987 to 2001, based on compound rate formula.

Source: U.S. Bureau of Labor Statistics, Internet site <http://www.bls.gov/lpc/home.htm>.

No. 633. Productivity and Related Measures: 1980 to 2002

[See text, this section. Minus sign (-) indicates decrease]

Item	1980	1985	1990	1995	1998	1999	2000	2001	2002
INDEXES (1992=100)									
Output per hour, business sector	80.4	88.7	95.2	102.6	110.6	113.5	116.9	118.2	123.8
Nonfarm business	82.0	89.3	95.3	102.8	110.3	112.9	116.2	117.5	123.1
Manufacturing	70.1	82.3	92.9	109.0	123.3	129.7	134.9	136.0	142.1
Output,[1] business sector	69.8	83.1	97.6	111.5	128.5	134.5	140.0	139.8	143.5
Nonfarm business	70.2	83.0	97.8	111.8	128.8	134.8	140.2	140.1	143.9
Manufacturing	75.3	86.0	97.3	113.4	129.8	135.3	138.7	132.0	130.5
Hours,[2] business sector	86.8	93.6	102.6	108.7	116.2	118.5	119.7	118.2	115.9
Nonfarm business	85.6	93.0	102.7	108.8	116.8	119.4	120.6	119.2	116.9
Manufacturing	107.5	104.6	104.8	104.0	105.2	104.4	102.8	97.1	91.8
Compensation per hour,[3] business sector	54.2	72.9	90.7	106.7	119.7	125.2	133.8	137.7	141.1
Nonfarm business	54.6	73.2	90.5	106.6	119.1	124.3	133.0	136.6	139.8
Manufacturing	55.6	75.1	90.8	107.9	117.4	122.1	131.1	133.1	137.5
Real hourly compensation,[3] business sector	89.2	92.5	96.3	99.6	105.0	107.6	111.2	111.4	112.3
Nonfarm business	89.8	92.9	96.2	99.4	104.5	106.8	110.6	110.5	111.3
Manufacturing	91.4	95.3	96.4	100.6	103.0	104.9	109.0	107.7	109.4
Unit labor costs,[4] business sector	67.4	82.1	95.3	104.1	108.2	110.3	114.4	116.5	113.9
Nonfarm business	66.5	82.0	95.0	103.7	108.0	110.1	114.4	116.3	113.6
Manufacturing	79.3	91.3	97.8	99.0	95.2	94.1	97.2	97.9	96.8
ANNUAL PERCENT CHANGE[5]									
Output per hour, business sector	-0.3	2.0	1.3	0.7	2.6	2.6	3.0	1.1	4.8
Nonfarm business	-0.3	1.3	1.1	0.9	2.6	2.4	2.9	1.1	4.8
Manufacturing	0.4	3.6	2.9	3.8	4.9	5.1	4.1	0.8	4.5
Output,[1] business sector	-1.1	4.2	1.5	3.1	4.9	4.7	4.1	-0.2	2.7
Nonfarm business	-1.1	3.9	1.4	3.4	5.0	4.6	4.0	-0.1	2.7
Manufacturing	-4.2	2.8	0.7	4.3	4.7	4.3	2.5	-4.9	-1.1
Hours,[2] business sector	-0.9	2.2	0.2	2.4	2.2	2.0	1.0	-1.3	-2.0
Nonfarm business	-0.8	2.5	0.3	2.4	2.4	2.2	1.0	-1.2	-2.0
Manufacturing	-4.6	-0.7	-2.1	0.4	-0.2	-0.8	-1.5	-5.6	-5.4
Compensation per hour,[3] business sector	10.8	4.9	5.7	2.1	5.5	4.6	6.8	2.9	2.5
Nonfarm business	10.8	4.7	5.5	2.1	5.4	4.4	7.0	2.7	2.4
Manufacturing	12.0	5.5	4.8	2.1	5.3	4.0	7.4	1.5	3.3
Real hourly compensation,[3] business sector	-0.2	1.5	0.7	-0.3	4.0	2.4	3.4	0.2	0.9
Nonfarm business	-0.2	1.3	0.5	-0.3	3.9	2.2	3.5	-0.1	0.8
Manufacturing	0.9	2.1	-0.2	-0.3	3.9	1.8	3.9	-1.2	1.6
Unit labor costs,[4] business sector	11.1	2.9	4.3	1.4	2.8	1.9	3.7	1.8	-2.2
Nonfarm business	11.1	3.3	4.3	1.2	2.7	2.0	3.9	1.6	-2.3
Manufacturing	11.6	1.8	1.9	-1.7	0.4	-1.1	3.2	0.8	-1.2

[1] Refers to gross sectoral product, annual weighted. [2] Hours at work of all persons engaged in the business and nonfarm business sectors (employees, proprietors, and unpaid family workers); employees' and proprietors' hours in manufacturing. [3] Wages and salaries of employees plus employers' contributions for social insurance and private benefit plans. Also includes an estimate of same for self-employed. Real compensation deflated by the consumer price index for all urban consumers; see text, Section 14. [4] Hourly compensation divided by output per hour. [5] All changes are from the immediate prior year.

Source: U.S. Bureau of Labor Statistics, *Productivity and Costs, News,* USDL 03-202, May 1, 2003; and Internet site <http://www.bls.gov/lpc/home.htm>.

No. 634. Employed Persons Using Computers at Work by Sex and Occupation: 2001

[In percent, except as indicated (135,089 represents 135,089,000). As of September. For persons 16 years old and over, except as indicated. Based on the Current Population Survey and subject to sampling error; see Appendix III and source]

Characteristic	Total employed (1,000)	Total using a computer at work (1,000)	Percent of employed	Word processing[1]	Internet or e-mail	Calendar or scheduling	Spreadsheets or databases	Graphics or design	Programming
Total, 16 years and over	135,089	72,277	53.5	67.0	71.8	52.9	62.3	28.8	15.2
Sex: Male	72,306	34,663	47.9	64.3	75.1	55.2	64.9	32.0	20.4
Women	62,784	37,614	59.9	69.4	68.8	50.9	59.9	25.8	10.5
Occupation:									
Managerial and professional	41,936	33,374	79.6	78.3	82.7	60.8	70.3	37.2	18.6
Executive, admin., and managerial	20,279	16,297	80.4	79.0	83.5	65.3	76.9	34.4	16.6
Professional specialty	21,657	17,077	78.9	77.6	81.9	56.5	63.9	39.9	20.5
Technical, sales, and admin. support	38,761	26,056	67.2	62.6	67.3	48.4	59.7	22.5	12.4
Technicians and related support	4,617	3,462	75.0	58.5	70.4	52.3	59.3	29.5	27.0
Sales occupations	15,905	9,173	57.7	59.9	69.3	48.6	60.1	25.6	11.1
Administrative support, incl. clerical	18,238	13,421	73.6	65.6	65.1	47.2	59.6	18.5	9.6
Service occupations	18,279	4,259	23.3	52.6	51.1	45.7	43.8	17.2	8.9
Precision production, craft, and repair	14,850	4,447	29.9	46.5	59.9	45.4	51.7	23.7	17.4
Operators, fabricators, and laborers	17,737	3,465	19.5	35.7	43.1	32.4	41.2	17.1	9.5
Farming, forestry, and fishing	3,527	675	19.1	60.9	67.1	43.7	61.3	21.7	10.6

[1] Or desktop publishing.

Source: U.S. Bureau of Labor Statistics, *Computer and Internet Use at Work, 2001, News,* USDL 02-601, October 23, 2002. See Internet site <http://www.bls.gov/bls/newsrels.htm#OEUS>.

No. 635. Annual Total Compensation and Wages and Salary Accruals Per Full-Time Equivalent Employee by Industry: 1990 to 2001

[In dollars. Wage and salary accruals include executives' compensation, bonuses, tips, and payments-in-kind; total compensation includes in addition to wages and salaries, employer contributions for social insurance, employer contributions to private and welfare funds, director's fees, jury and witness fees, etc. Based on the 1987 Standard Industrial Classification Code (SIC); See text, this section]

Industry	Annual total compensation				Annual wages and salary			
	1990	1995	2000	2001	1990	1995	2000	2001
Domestic industries	31,940	37,742	45,733	47,064	26,259	30,911	38,652	39,667
Private industries	30,822	36,322	44,449	45,671	25,853	30,310	38,343	39,293
Agriculture, forestry, and fishing	18,475	21,022	25,340	27,576	15,996	18,166	22,258	24,219
Mining	45,872	56,523	68,932	71,272	38,024	46,583	58,875	60,871
Construction	33,833	37,285	44,120	45,892	27,871	30,431	37,899	39,385
Manufacturing	36,958	44,713	54,066	54,227	30,054	35,779	45,675	45,580
Transportation	36,459	40,732	46,530	48,104	28,900	32,349	38,429	39,607
Communications	46,281	59,952	75,754	73,826	38,751	48,979	64,057	62,157
Electric, gas, and sanitary services	48,097	59,478	74,189	76,835	39,557	48,751	62,365	64,399
Wholesale trade	37,031	44,508	56,579	57,951	31,499	37,808	48,738	49,701
Retail trade	18,626	21,189	25,315	26,232	15,990	18,246	22,264	23,009
Finance, insurance, and real estate	37,501	49,272	70,219	73,724	31,982	41,661	60,817	63,738
Services	28,807	34,043	41,620	43,166	24,697	29,084	36,396	37,647
Government	37,218	44,951	52,895	54,621	28,176	33,962	40,379	41,700

Source: U.S. Bureau of Economic Analysis, *National Income and Product Accounts, 1929-97*; and *Survey of Current Business*, May 2003. See also <http://www.bea.doc.gov/bea/dn/nipaweb/selecttable.asp?selected=N> (released 30 May 2003).

No. 636. Average Hourly Earnings by Private Industry Group: 1980 to 2002

[In dollars. Average earnings include overtime. Data are for production workers in natural resources and mining, manufacturing, and construction, and nonsupervisory employees in other industries. See headnote, Table 629]

Private industry group	Current dollars					Constant (1982) dollars [1]				
	1980	1990	1995	2000	2002	1980	1990	1995	2000	2002
Total	6.84	10.19	11.64	14.00	14.95	7.99	7.66	7.53	8.03	8.24
Natural resources and mining	8.97	13.40	14.78	16.55	17.22	10.48	10.07	9.56	9.50	9.49
Construction	9.37	13.42	14.73	17.48	18.51	10.95	10.08	9.53	10.03	10.20
Manufacturing	7.15	10.78	12.34	14.32	15.29	8.35	8.10	7.98	8.22	8.42
Trade, transportation and utilities	7.04	9.83	11.10	13.31	14.02	8.22	7.39	7.18	7.64	7.72
Wholesale trade	7.68	11.58	13.34	16.28	16.97	8.97	8.70	8.63	9.34	9.35
Retail trade	5.71	7.71	8.85	10.86	11.67	6.67	5.79	5.72	6.23	6.43
Transportation and warehousing	9.47	12.50	13.18	15.05	15.77	11.06	9.39	8.53	8.63	8.69
Utilities	9.73	16.14	19.19	22.75	23.94	11.37	12.13	12.41	13.05	13.19
Information	9.47	13.40	15.68	19.07	20.23	11.06	10.07	10.14	10.94	11.15
Financial activities [2]	5.82	9.99	12.28	14.98	16.17	6.80	7.51	7.94	8.59	8.91
Professional and business services [2]	7.22	11.14	12.53	15.52	16.81	8.43	8.37	8.10	8.90	9.26
Education and health services [2]	5.93	10.00	11.80	13.95	15.22	6.93	7.51	7.63	8.00	8.39
Leisure and hospitality [2]	3.89	5.88	6.62	8.11	8.57	4.54	4.42	4.28	4.65	4.72
Other services	5.05	9.08	10.51	12.73	13.72	5.90	6.82	6.80	7.30	7.56

[1] Earnings in current dollars divided by the Consumer Price Index (CPI-W) on a 1982 base; see text, Section 14. [2] See footnotes, Table 629.

Source: U.S. Bureau of Labor Statistics, *Employment and Earnings*, monthly, June 2003 issue; and the Current Employment Statistics program Internet site <http://www.bls.gov/ces/home.htm>.

No. 637. Annual Percent Changes in Earnings and Compensation: 1980 to 2002

[Annual percent change from immediate prior year. Minus sign (-) indicates decrease]

Item	1980	1985	1990	1995	1998	1999	2000	2001	2002
Current dollars:									
Hourly earnings, total [1]	8.1	2.9	4.0	2.8	4.1	3.6	3.9	3.8	2.9
Hourly earnings, manufacturing [2]	8.8	3.9	4.2	2.5	2.4	3.0	3.4	3.1	3.6
Compensation per employee-hour [3]	10.7	4.7	5.7	2.1	5.4	4.3	7.0	3.6	2.8
Constant (1982) dollars:									
Hourly earnings, total [1]	-4.9	-0.5	-1.2	-	2.7	1.4	0.4	1.0	1.6
Hourly earnings, manufacturing [2]	-4.1	0.4	-1.0	-0.4	1.0	0.7	-	0.2	2.2
Compensation per employee-hour [3]	-0.3	1.3	0.7	-0.3	3.9	2.2	3.6	0.8	1.2

- Represents or rounds to zero. [1] Production or nonsupervisory workers on private nonfarm payrolls. [2] Production workers. [3] Nonfarm business sector.

Source: U.S. Bureau of Labor Statistics, *News*, USDL 03-411, *Productivity and Costs*, August 7, 2003; and Internet site <http://www.bls.gov/lpc/>.

420 Labor Force, Employment, and Earnings

No. 638. Mean Hourly Earnings and Weekly Hours for Metro and Nonmetro Areas by Selected Characteristics: 2001

[Covers civilian workers in private industry establishments and state and local governments in the 50 states and DC. Excludes private households, federal government and agriculture. Based on establishment survey; see source and Appendix III for details]

Item	Mean hourly earnings (dol.) [1] Total	Metro areas [2]	Nonmetro areas	Mean weekly hours Total	Metro areas [2]	Nonmetro areas
Total	16.23	16.37	(NA)	35.8	35.7	(NA)
Private industry	15.46	15.62	(NA)	35.7	35.6	(NA)
State and local government	20.56	21.32	17.35	36.7	36.7	36.9
WORKER CHARACTERISTIC						
White-collar occupations	19.86	19.96	(NA)	36.0	36.0	(NA)
Professional specialty and technical	26.18	26.58	22.23	35.9	35.8	36.5
Professional	28.21	28.59	24.47	35.8	35.7	36.4
Technical	19.12	19.57	14.91	36.2	36.1	36.6
Executive, administrative, and managerial	28.80	28.95	25.99	40.0	40.1	39.7
Sales	13.74	13.81	11.24	32.7	32.7	32.7
Administrative support	12.80	12.88	11.64	36.4	36.3	37.4
Blue-collar occupations	13.73	13.83	12.80	38.1	38.1	38.6
Precision production, craft, and repair	17.28	17.39	15.79	39.6	39.5	40.0
Machine operators, assemblers, and inspectors	12.29	12.30	12.22	39.2	39.1	39.7
Transportation and material moving	13.53	13.49	14.03	37.2	37.2	36.3
Handlers, equipment cleaners, helpers and laborers	10.37	10.43	9.86	35.6	35.5	36.7
Service occupations	9.86	9.85	(NA)	31.7	31.5	(NA)
Protective service	15.99	16.20	14.48	37.6	37.3	39.5
Food service	7.14	7.05	8.25	29.0	28.8	31.7
Health service	9.93	10.15	8.75	33.6	33.6	33.7
Cleaning and building service	9.77	9.80	9.39	33.3	33.1	36.4
Personal service	9.80	9.85	8.97	29.8	29.7	31.9
Full time	17.13	17.33	14.98	39.6	39.6	39.5
Part time	9.17	9.17	9.12	20.6	20.6	20.8
Union [3]	19.50	19.76	17.15	36.9	36.8	38.1
Nonunion	15.52	15.66	13.78	35.6	35.5	36.6
Time [4]	16.00	16.12	14.64	35.7	35.6	36.8
Incentive [4]	20.38	21.01	12.39	38.1	37.9	40.4
ESTABLISHMENT CHARACTERISTIC						
Goods producing [5]	16.71	17.05	13.93	39.5	39.4	39.9
Service producing [5]	14.96	15.09	11.94	34.3	34.3	34.3
1 to 99 workers [6]	13.80	13.84	12.49	34.8	34.7	35.3
100 to 499 workers	15.77	16.07	(NA)	36.3	36.2	(NA)
500 to 999 workers	17.98	18.38	16.15	37.0	36.9	37.6
1,000 to 2,499 workers	18.82	19.33	(NA)	36.7	36.4	(NA)
2,500 workers or more	22.31	22.32	21.41	37.4	37.3	39.8
GEOGRAPHIC REGION [7]						
New England	17.54	17.69	15.57	35.4	35.4	34.7
Middle Atlantic	18.72	18.77	16.63	34.7	34.6	36.0
East North Central	16.08	16.12	15.68	35.8	35.8	36.5
West North Central	14.99	15.46	12.93	35.4	35.0	36.9
South Atlantic	15.24	15.46	13.34	36.5	36.4	37.5
East South Central	(NA)	(NA)	(NA)	(NA)	(NA)	(NA)
West South Central	15.07	15.12	14.45	36.9	36.9	36.8
Mountain	14.70	14.41	17.56	35.7	35.6	36.9
Pacific	17.64	17.63	(NA)	35.6	35.5	(NA)

NA Not available. [1] Earnings are straight time hourly wages or salary, including incentive pay, cost-of-living adjustments, and hazard pay. Excludes premium pay for overtime, vacations and holidays, nonproduction bonuses and tips. [2] Metropolitan areas defined as of 1994. [3] Workers whose wages are determined through collective bargaining. [4] Time worker wages are based solely on an hourly rate or salary. Incentive workers wages are based at least in part on productivity payments such as piece rates or commissions. [5] For private industry only. [6] Private establishments employing 1 to 99 workers and state and local government establishments employing 50 to 99 workers. [7] Composition of regions: NEW ENGLAND: Maine, New Hampshire, Vermont, Massachusetts, Rhode Island, Connecticut. MIDDLE ATLANTIC: New York, New Jersey, and Pennsylvania. EAST NORTH CENTRAL: Ohio, Indiana, Illinois, Michigan, Wisconsin. WEST NORTH CENTRAL: Minnesota, Iowa, Missouri, North Dakota, South Dakota, Nebraska, and Kansas. SOUTH ATLANTIC: Delaware, Maryland, District of Columbia, Virginia, West Virginia. North Carolina, South Carolina, Georgia, Florida. EAST SOUTH CENTRAL: Kentucky, Tennessee, Alabama, Mississippi. WEST SOUTH CENTRAL: Arkansas, Louisiana, Oklahoma, and Texas. MOUNTAIN: Montana, Idaho, Wyoming, Colorado, New Mexico, Arizona, Utah, Nevada. PACIFIC: Washington, Oregon, California, Alaska, and Hawaii.

Source: U.S. Bureau of Labor Statistics, *National Compensation Survey: Occupational Wages in the United States, 2001*, Bulletin 2552, January 2003. See Internet site <http://www.bls.gov/ncs/home.htm>.

No. 639. Average Annual Pay by State: 2000 and 2001

[2001 data preliminary. In dollars, except percent change. For workers covered by state unemployment insurance laws and for federal civilian workers covered by unemployment compensation for federal employees, approximately 99 percent of wage and salary civilian employment in 2001. Excludes most agricultural workers on small farms, all Armed Forces, elected officials in most states, railroad employees, most domestic workers, most student workers at school, employees of certain nonprofit organizations, and most self-employed individuals. Pay includes bonuses, cash value of meals and lodging, and tips and other gratuities]

State	Average annual pay 2000	2001	Percent change, 2000-01	State	Average annual pay 2000	2001	Percent change, 2000-01
United States	35,320	36,214	2.5	Missouri	31,384	32,422	3.3
Alabama	29,041	30,090	3.6	Montana	24,272	25,194	3.8
Alaska	35,144	36,140	2.8	Nebraska	27,693	28,375	2.5
Arizona	32,610	33,408	2.4	Nevada	32,277	33,122	2.6
Arkansas	26,317	27,258	3.6	New Hampshire	34,736	35,479	2.1
California	41,207	41,358	0.4	New Jersey	43,676	44,285	1.4
Colorado	37,168	37,950	2.1	New Mexico	27,498	28,698	4.4
Connecticut	45,486	46,963	3.2	New York	45,358	46,664	2.9
Delaware	36,535	38,434	5.2	North Carolina	31,068	32,026	3.1
District of Columbia	52,965	56,024	5.8	North Dakota	24,683	25,707	4.1
Florida	30,560	31,551	3.2	Ohio	32,508	33,280	2.4
Georgia	34,214	35,114	2.6	Oklahoma	26,988	28,020	3.8
Hawaii	30,628	31,250	2.0	Oregon	32,776	33,203	1.3
Idaho	27,701	27,765	0.2	Pennsylvania	34,015	34,976	2.8
Illinois	38,045	39,058	2.7	Rhode Island	32,615	33,592	3.0
Indiana	31,030	31,778	2.4	South Carolina	28,179	29,253	3.8
Iowa	27,931	28,840	3.3	South Dakota	24,802	25,600	3.2
Kansas	29,361	30,153	2.7	Tennessee	30,557	31,491	3.1
Kentucky	28,800	30,017	4.2	Texas	34,943	36,039	3.1
Louisiana	27,888	29,134	4.5	Utah	29,229	30,074	2.9
Maine	27,664	28,815	4.2	Vermont	28,914	30,240	4.6
Maryland	36,395	38,237	5.1	Virginia	35,172	36,716	4.4
Massachusetts	44,168	44,976	1.8	Washington	37,099	37,475	1.0
Michigan	37,011	37,387	1.0	West Virginia	26,888	27,982	4.1
Minnesota	35,414	36,585	3.3	Wisconsin	30,694	31,556	2.8
Mississippi	25,208	25,919	2.8	Wyoming	26,836	28,025	4.4

Source: U.S. Bureau of Labor Statistics, *Average Annual Pay by State and Industry, News*, USDL 02-540, September 24, 2002. See Internet site <http://www.bls.gov/cew/home.htm>.

No. 640. Average Annual Pay by Selected Metropolitan Area: 2000 and 2001

[2001 data preliminary. In dollars. Metropolitan areas ranked by average pay 2001. Includes data for metropolitan statistical areas and primary metropolitan statistical areas defined as of June 1999. In the New England areas, the New England County metropolitan area (NECMA) definitions were used. See source for details. See also headnote, Table 639]

Metropolitan area	2000	2001	Metropolitan area	2000	2001
Metropolitan areas	37,017	37,897	Anchorage, AK	36,659	37,826
San Jose, CA	76,252	65,926	Ventura, CA	37,090	37,795
San Francisco, CA	59,288	59,761	Rochester, MN	36,106	37,753
New York, NY	57,213	58,963	Ann Arbor, MI	37,455	37,546
New Haven-Bridgeport-Stamford-Waterbury-Danbury, CT	50,596	52,177	Baltimore, MD	35,577	37,493
Middlesex-Somerset-Hunterdon, NJ	48,987	49,830	Charlotte-Gastonia-Rock Hill, NC-SC	36,103	37,277
Newark, NJ	48,656	47,713	Portland-Vancouver, OR-WA	37,077	37,268
Jersey City, NJ	47,429	47,621	Monmouth-Ocean, NJ	36,404	37,037
Washington, DC-MD-VA-WV	45,374	47,584	Huntsville, AL	35,659	36,709
Oakland, CA	44,207	45,944	Fort Worth-Arlington, TX	34,588	36,382
Boston-Worcester-Lawrence-Lowell-Brockton, MA-NH	45,021	45,768	Santa Rosa, CA	35,742	36,150
Trenton, NJ	44,657	45,746	Springfield, IL	34,563	36,068
Seattle-Bellevue-Everett, WA	45,344	45,326	Cincinnati, OH-KY-IN	35,052	36,042
Bergen-Passaic, NJ	43,879	44,667	Flint, MI	36,327	36,030
Boulder-Longmont, CO	45,564	44,313	Indianapolis, IN	34,906	35,985
Hartford, CT	42,421	43,882	West Palm Beach-Boca Raton, FL	35,233	35,962
Houston, TX	40,996	42,782	Saint Louis, MO-IL	34,909	35,932
Dallas, TX	42,095	42,692	Richmond-Petersburg, VA	34,481	35,872
Chicago, IL	41,527	42,646	Kansas City, MO-KS	34,989	35,795
Detroit, MI	42,321	42,613	Milwaukee-Waukesha, WI	34,605	35,670
Denver, CO	41,401	42,348	Brazoria, TX	34,367	35,655
Wilmington-Newark, DE-MD	39,670	42,190	Cleveland-Lorain-Elyria, OH	34,670	35,513
Los Angeles-Long Beach, CA	39,671	40,907	Phoenix-Mesa, AZ	34,925	35,507
Minneapolis-St. Paul, MN-WI	39,521	40,866	Corvallis, OR	35,355	35,499
Austin-San Marcos, TX	40,998	40,826	Saginaw-Bay City-Midland, MI	35,329	35,470
Atlanta, GA	39,734	40,535	Albany-Schenectady-Troy, NY	33,822	35,359
Orange County, CA	39,243	40,280	Yolo, CA	33,451	35,318
Philadelphia, PA-NJ	39,226	40,222	Bloomington-Normal, IL	34,254	35,106
Nassau-Suffolk, NY	38,958	39,649	Columbus, OH	33,918	35,027
Kokomo, IN	40,281	39,599	Santa Cruz-Watsonville, CA	35,825	35,023
Dutchess County, NY	36,065	38,744	Pittsburgh, PA	33,811	35,021
Raleigh-Durham-Chapel Hill, NC	37,829	38,681	Lansing-East Lansing, MI	33,892	34,749
San Diego, CA	37,546	38,424	Cedar Rapids, IA	34,097	34,672
New London-Norwich, CT	36,757	38,201	Memphis, TN-AR-MS	33,254	34,575
Sacramento, CA	36,595	38,022	Miami, FL	33,333	34,531
			Birmingham, AL	33,283	34,518
			Colorado Springs, CO	33,039	34,381

Source: U.S. Bureau of Labor Statistics, *Average Annual Pay Levels in Metropolitan Areas, News*, USDL 02-625, November 8, 2002. See Internet site <http://www.bls.gov/cew/home.htm>.

422 Labor Force, Employment, and Earnings

No. 641. Full-Time Wage and Salary Workers—Number and Earnings: 1990 to 2002

[In current dollars of usual weekly earnings. Data represent annual averages (85,804 represents 85,804,000). See text, this section, and headnote Table 604, for a discussion of occupational data. Based on Current Population Survey; see text, Section 1, and Appendix III. For definition of median, see Guide to Tabular Presentation]

Characteristic	Number of workers (1,000)				Median weekly earnings (dol.)			
	1990 [1]	1995 [1]	2000 [1,2]	2002	1990 [1]	1995 [1]	2000 [1,2]	2002
All workers [3]	85,804	89,282	99,917	100,204	412	479	576	609
Male	49,564	51,222	56,273	56,431	481	538	646	680
16 to 24 years old	6,824	6,118	6,786	6,320	282	303	376	392
25 years old and over	42,740	45,104	49,487	50,111	512	588	700	732
Female	36,239	38,060	43,644	43,773	346	406	491	530
16 to 24 years old	5,227	4,366	5,147	4,817	254	275	342	366
25 years old and over	31,012	33,695	38,497	38,956	369	428	515	570
White	72,811	74,874	82,475	82,438	424	494	591	624
Male	42,797	43,747	47,578	47,502	494	566	669	702
Female	30,014	31,127	34,897	34,936	353	415	500	549
Black	9,820	10,596	12,556	12,116	329	383	468	498
Male	4,983	5,279	5,989	5,792	361	411	503	523
Female	4,837	5,317	6,568	6,323	308	355	429	474
Hispanic origin [4]	7,812	8,719	11,738	13,168	304	329	396	423
Male	5,000	5,597	7,261	8,298	318	350	414	449
Female	2,812	3,122	4,477	4,870	278	305	364	396
Occupation, male:								
Managerial and professional	12,255	13,684	15,875	16,225	729	829	994	1,058
Exec., admin., managerial	6,389	7,172	8,142	8,432	740	833	1,014	1,081
Professional specialty	5,866	6,512	7,733	7,793	719	827	977	1,037
Technical, sales, and administrative support	9,677	9,894	10,828	10,869	493	556	655	699
Tech. and related support	1,762	1,688	1,882	1,827	567	641	761	841
Sales	4,692	5,000	5,583	5,731	502	579	684	742
Admin. support, incl. clerical	3,224	3,206	3,363	3,312	436	489	563	583
Service	4,602	4,779	5,284	5,554	317	357	414	445
Private household	12	15	20	25	(B)	(B)	(B)	(B)
Protective	1,531	1,691	1,771	1,892	477	552	659	689
Other service	3,059	3,073	3,493	3,637	271	300	357	379
Precision production [5]	10,259	10,046	11,075	10,867	486	534	628	645
Mechanics and repairers	3,687	3,658	4,024	3,881	475	538	649	677
Construction trades	3,650	3,541	4,341	4,440	478	507	599	606
Other	2,922	2,847	2,709	2,543	508	574	651	668
Operators, fabricators and laborers	11,464	11,529	11,837	11,499	375	413	487	511
Machine operators, assemblers, and inspectors	4,594	4,576	4,240	3,876	387	421	495	520
Transportation and material moving	3,752	3,870	4,221	4,284	416	482	558	591
Handlers, equipment cleaners, helpers, and laborers	3,118	3,083	3,376	3,339	306	328	394	411
Farming, forestry, and fishing	1,306	1,290	1,374	1,417	261	294	347	376
Occupation, female:								
Managerial and professional	10,575	12,609	15,580	16,469	510	605	709	756
Exec., admin., managerial	4,758	5,803	7,226	7,633	484	570	686	736
Professional specialty	5,816	6,806	8,354	8,836	534	632	725	773
Technical, sales, and administrative support	16,290	16,004	17,424	16,960	331	383	452	490
Tech. and related support	1,476	1,506	1,769	1,834	417	480	541	591
Sales	3,554	3,862	4,550	4,444	290	330	407	441
Admin. support, incl. clerical	11,260	10,636	11,105	10,683	332	384	449	488
Service	4,577	4,838	5,736	5,988	230	264	316	343
Private household	305	324	348	312	171	193	261	276
Protective	217	266	341	408	405	438	500	501
Other service	4,055	4,249	5,047	5,268	230	264	314	339
Precision production [5]	900	957	1,088	939	316	371	445	479
Mechanics and repairers	139	150	203	194	458	550	627	593
Construction trades	50	66	88	94	393	400	475	553
Other	711	741	796	651	299	346	414	445
Operators, fabricators, and laborers	3,722	3,462	3,574	3,147	261	297	351	385
Machine operators, assemblers, and inspectors	2,878	2,559	2,396	1,965	259	296	355	386
Transportation and material moving	227	261	366	367	314	354	407	449
Handlers, equipment cleaners, helpers, and laborers	616	642	812	814	249	284	320	359
Farming, forestry, and fishing	175	190	242	270	216	249	294	308

B Data not shown where base is less than 50,000. [1] See footnote 2, Table 587. [2] Data do not reflect revisions based on the 2000 Census; data are based on 1990 population controls. [3] Includes other races, not shown separately. [4] Persons of Hispanic origin may be of any race. [5] Includes craft and repair.

Source: U.S. Bureau of Labor Statistics, Bulletin 2307, and *Employment and Earnings*, monthly, January issues and June 2003 issue. See Internet site <http://www.bls.gov/cps/home.htm>.

Labor Force, Employment, and Earnings 423

U.S. Census Bureau, Statistical Abstract of the United States: 2003

No. 642. Workers With Earnings by Occupation of Longest Held Job and Sex: 2001

[Earnings as of March 2001. Covers persons 15 years old and over as of March 2002. (71,232 represents 71,232,000). Based on Current Population Survey; see text, Section 1, and Appendix III. For definition of median, see Guide to Tabular Presentation]

Major occupation of longest job held	All workers Women Number (1,000)	All workers Women Median earnings	All workers Men Number (1,000)	All workers Men Median earnings	Full-time, year-round Women Number (1,000)	Full-time, year-round Women Median earnings	Full-time, year-round Men Number (1,000)	Full-time, year-round Men Median earnings
Total [1]	71,232	20,851	80,209	31,364	41,639	29,215	58,712	38,275
Executive, administrators, & managerial	10,154	35,690	11,779	54,280	7,787	39,217	10,340	57,045
Professional specialty	12,646	34,411	10,426	51,399	7,746	40,930	8,106	57,628
Technical, sales, and administrative support[2]	28,157	20,042	15,351	31,946	16,302	26,629	11,085	40,522
Sales	9,366	13,038	8,846	32,732	4,554	25,677	6,347	41,896
Admin. support, incl. clerical	16,019	21,142	4,400	26,742	9,884	26,355	3,043	32,995
Precision production, craft and repair	1,498	21,695	14,534	31,044	999	26,031	11,232	35,199
Operators, fabricators, and laborers	4,743	16,333	15,743	23,586	2,681	20,800	10,455	29,711
Service workers	13,165	11,045	8,768	16,642	5,732	17,763	5,232	25,004
Private household	813	7,091	48	(B)	231	15,033	19	(B)
Farming, forestry, and fishing	793	7,063	3,032	13,713	331	13,559	1,728	21,016

B Base less than 75,000. [1] Includes people whose longest job was in the Armed Forces. [2] Includes other occupations, not shown separately.

Source: U.S. Census Bureau, Current Population Reports, P60-218 and earlier reports. See Internet site <http://www.census.gov/hhes/www/income01.html>.

No. 643. Employment Cost Index (ECI), Total Compensation by Occupation and Industry: 1982 to 2002

[As of December. The ECI is a measure of the rate of change in employee compensation (wages, salaries, and employer costs for employee benefits). Data are not seasonally adjusted: 1982 and 1985 based on fixed employment counts from 1970 Census of Population; 1990 based on fixed employment counts from the 1980 Census of Population; beginning 1995 based primarily on 1990 Occupational Employment Survey]

Item	Indexes (June 1989=100) 1982	1985	1990	1995	2000	2002	Percent change for 12 months ending Dec.— 1985	1990	1995	2000	2002
Civilian workers [1]	74.8	86.8	107.6	127.2	150.6	162.2	4.3	4.9	2.7	4.1	3.4
Workers, by occupational group:											
White-collar occupations	72.9	85.8	108.3	128.0	152.5	164.3	4.9	5.2	2.9	4.2	3.4
Blue-collar occupations	78.2	88.4	106.5	125.8	146.5	157.5	3.3	4.4	2.5	4.2	3.6
Service occupations	74.3	87.2	108.0	127.4	150.0	162.2	3.9	5.1	2.5	3.6	3.4
Workers, by industry division:											
Manufacturing	76.9	87.8	107.2	128.3	149.3	160.5	3.3	5.1	2.6	4.0	3.8
Nonmanufacturing [2]	73.9	86.4	107.8	126.8	150.7	162.4	4.7	4.9	2.8	4.1	3.3
Service industries	70.5	84.1	110.2	129.4	152.4	163.9	4.7	6.3	2.4	4.0	3.1
Public administration [3]	71.9	85.4	108.7	128.3	148.3	161.7	4.9	5.3	3.3	2.7	4.2
State and local government	70.8	84.6	110.4	129.3	148.9	161.5	5.6	5.8	2.9	3.0	4.1
Workers, by occupational group:											
White-collar occupations	70.4	84.2	110.9	129.1	148.3	160.7	5.8	6.0	2.9	3.0	4.1
Blue-collar workers	73.9	86.7	108.7	128.0	147.2	159.8	5.3	4.8	2.6	3.3	4.3
Workers, by industry division:											
Service industries	70.0	84.0	111.3	129.6	148.9	160.9	5.9	6.3	2.8	3.0	3.9
Schools	69.0	83.6	111.6	129.8	149.0	160.7	6.2	6.0	2.8	3.0	3.8
Elementary and secondary	68.6	83.6	112.1	130.1	148.1	158.8	6.4	6.3	2.8	2.8	3.7
Colleges and universities	(NA)	(NA)	110.2	128.7	151.7	165.8	(NA)	5.3	2.5	3.5	3.9
Services, excluding schools [4]	73.1	85.2	110.2	129.4	148.8	162.8	4.7	6.8	3.0	3.5	4.3
Public administration [3]	71.9	85.4	108.7	128.3	148.3	161.7	4.9	5.3	3.3	2.7	4.2
Private industry workers [5]	75.8	87.3	107.0	126.7	150.9	162.3	3.9	4.6	2.6	4.4	3.2
Workers, by occupational group:											
White-collar occupations	73.7	86.4	107.4	127.6	153.6	165.2	4.9	4.9	2.8	4.6	3.2
Blue-collar occupations	78.4	88.5	106.4	125.6	146.4	157.3	3.1	4.4	2.4	4.2	3.6
Service occupations	76.3	88.4	107.3	125.2	148.1	159.8	3.0	4.7	1.9	3.9	3.2
Workers, by industry division:											
Manufacturing	76.9	87.8	107.2	128.3	149.3	160.5	3.3	5.1	2.6	4.0	3.8
Nonmanufacturing [2]	75.1	87.0	106.9	125.9	151.1	162.5	4.3	4.5	2.7	4.6	3.1
Service industries [2]	(NA)	84.1	109.3	129.4	154.1	165.4	(NA)	6.2	2.2	4.4	2.7
Business services	(NA)	(NA)	107.4	126.3	158.4	167.5	(NA)	6.0	2.7	4.3	0.8
Health services	(NA)	83.7	110.8	132.2	150.6	164.4	(NA)	6.8	2.7	4.4	3.8
Hospitals	(NA)	(NA)	110.7	131.3	151.1	168.1	(NA)	7.0	2.1	4.5	4.9
Workers by bargaining status:											
Union	79.6	90.1	106.2	127.7	146.9	159.5	2.6	4.3	2.8	4.0	4.2
Nonunion	74.3	86.3	107.3	126.5	151.6	162.8	4.6	4.8	2.7	4.4	3.2

NA Not available. [1] Includes private industry and state and local government workers and excludes farm, household, and federal government workers. [2] Includes other industries, not shown separately. [3] Consists of executive, legislative, judicial, administrative, and regulatory activities. [4] Includes library, social, and health services. Formerly called hospitals and other services. [5] Excludes farm and household workers.

Source: U.S. Bureau of Labor Statistics, News, Employment Cost Index, quarterly; and Internet site <http://www.bls.gov/ncs/ect/home.htm>.

No. 644. Federal Minimum Wage Rates: 1950 to 2000

Year	Current dollars	Constant (2000) dollars [1]	Year	Current dollars	Constant (2000) dollars [1]
1950	0.75	5.36	1976	2.30	6.96
1952	0.75	4.87	1977	2.30	6.54
1953	0.75	4.84	1978	2.65	7.00
1954	0.75	4.80	1979	2.90	6.88
1955	0.75	4.82	1980	3.10	6.48
1956	1.00	6.33	1981	3.35	6.35
1957	1.00	6.13	1982	3.35	5.98
1958	1.00	5.96	1983	3.35	5.79
1959	1.00	5.92	1984	3.35	5.55
1960	1.00	5.82	1985	3.35	5.36
1961	1.15	6.62	1986	3.35	5.26
1962	1.15	6.56	1987	3.35	5.08
1963	1.25	7.03	1988	3.35	4.88
1964	1.25	6.94	1989	3.35	4.65
1965	1.25	6.83	1990	3.80	5.01
1966	1.25	6.64	1991	4.25	5.37
1967	1.40	7.22	1992	4.25	5.22
1968	1.60	7.92	1993	4.25	5.06
1969	1.60	7.51	1994	4.25	4.94
1970	1.60	7.10	1995	4.25	4.80
1971	1.60	6.80	1996	4.75	5.21
1972	1.60	6.59	1997	5.15	5.53
1973	1.60	6.21	1998	5.15	5.44
1974	2.00	6.99	1999	5.15	5.32
1975	2.10	6.72	2000	5.15	5.15

[1] Adjusted for inflation using the CPI-U; see text, Section 14.

Source: U.S. Employment Standards Administration, Internet site: <http://www.dol.gov/esa/minwage/chart2.htm> (accessed 30 May 2002).

No. 645. Workers Paid Hourly Rates by Selected Characteristics: 2002

[Data are annual averages (72,720 represents 72,720,000). For employed wage and salary workers. Based on Current Population Survey; see text, Section 1, and Appendix III]

Characteristic	Total paid hourly rates	Number of workers [1] (1,000) At or below $5.15 Total	At $5.15	Below $5.15	Percent of all workers paid hourly rates At or below $5.15 Total	At $5.15	Below $5.15	Median hourly earnings of workers paid hourly rates [2]
Total, 16 years and over [3]	72,720	2,168	570	1,598	3.0	0.8	2.2	10.46
16 to 24 years	16,191	1,158	340	818	7.2	2.1	5.1	7.80
16 to 19 years	5,808	605	226	379	10.4	3.9	6.5	6.90
25 years and over	56,529	1,010	230	780	1.8	0.4	1.4	11.83
Male, 16 years and over	36,135	800	218	582	2.2	0.6	1.6	11.63
16 to 24 years	8,242	453	146	307	5.5	1.8	3.7	8.05
16 to 19 years	2,850	243	97	146	8.4	3.4	5.1	7.02
25 years and over	27,893	347	72	275	1.2	0.3	1.0	13.04
Women, 16 years and over	36,585	1,368	352	1,016	3.7	1.0	2.8	9.89
16 to 24 years	7,949	705	194	511	8.9	2.4	6.4	7.43
16 to 19 years	2,958	361	128	233	12.2	4.3	7.9	6.79
25 years and over	28,636	663	158	505	2.3	0.6	1.8	10.71
White	59,199	1,781	452	1,329	3.0	0.8	2.2	10.71
Black	9,692	276	89	187	2.8	0.9	1.9	9.92
Hispanic origin [4]	11,206	305	110	195	2.7	1.0	1.7	9.20
Full-time workers	55,029	851	169	682	1.5	0.3	1.2	11.63
Part-time workers [5]	17,568	1,309	401	908	7.5	2.3	5.2	7.88
Private sector industries	63,670	2,027	509	1,518	3.2	0.8	2.4	10.19
Goods-producing [6]	17,909	135	46	89	0.8	0.3	0.5	12.08
Service-producing [7]	45,760	1,891	463	1,428	4.1	1.0	3.1	9.80
Public sector	9,050	142	61	81	1.6	0.7	0.9	12.51

[1] Excludes the incorporated self-employed. [2] For definition of median, see Guide to Tabular Presentation. [3] Includes races not shown separately. Also includes a small number of multiple jobholders whose full- part- time status can not be determined for their principal job. [4] Persons of Hispanic origin may be of any race. [5] Working fewer than 35 hours per week. [6] Includes agriculture, mining, construction, and manufacturing. [7] Includes transportation and public utilities; wholesale trade; finance, insurance, and real estate; private households; and other service industries.

Source: U.S. Bureau of Labor Statistics, *Employment and Earnings*, monthly, June 2003 issue. See Internet site <http://www.bls.gov/cps/home.htm>.

No. 646. Employer Costs for Employee Compensation Per Hour Worked: 2003

[In dollars. As of March, for private industry workers. Based on a sample of establishments from the National Compensation Survey; see source for details. See also Appendix III]

Compensation component	Total	Goods producing [1]	Service producing [2]	Manufacturing	Non-manufacturing	Union members	Non-union members	Full-time workers	Part-time workers
Total compensation	22.37	26.25	21.30	26.02	21.71	30.68	21.36	25.37	12.41
Wages and salaries	16.15	17.78	15.70	17.43	15.92	19.95	15.69	18.02	9.96
Total benefits	6.22	8.47	5.60	8.59	5.79	10.72	5.67	7.36	2.45
Paid leave	1.47	1.71	1.40	1.97	1.38	2.19	1.38	1.80	0.38
Vacation	0.74	0.88	0.70	1.00	0.69	1.13	0.69	(NA)	(NA)
Holiday	0.50	0.62	0.47	0.73	0.46	0.71	0.48	(NA)	(NA)
Sick	0.17	0.13	0.18	0.16	0.18	0.25	0.16	(NA)	(NA)
Other	0.06	0.08	0.06	0.10	0.05	0.10	0.05	(NA)	(NA)
Supplemental pay	0.64	1.17	0.50	1.23	0.54	1.11	0.59	0.78	0.20
Premium pay	0.25	0.57	0.16	0.60	0.19	0.70	0.20	(NA)	(NA)
Shift pay	0.06	0.08	0.05	0.11	0.05	0.17	0.05	(NA)	(NA)
Nonproduction bonuses	0.33	0.51	0.28	0.51	0.30	0.24	0.34	(NA)	(NA)
Insurance	1.52	2.15	1.35	2.27	1.39	2.99	1.34	1.85	0.43
Health insurance	1.41	1.98	1.25	2.08	1.29	2.80	1.24	(NA)	(NA)
Retirement and savings	0.67	0.98	0.58	0.86	0.63	1.73	0.54	0.82	0.16
Defined benefit	0.25	0.51	0.18	0.41	0.22	1.24	0.13	(NA)	(NA)
Defined contributions	0.42	0.47	0.40	0.45	0.41	0.49	0.41	(NA)	(NA)
Legally required	1.89	2.40	1.75	2.18	1.84	2.61	1.80	2.07	1.29
Social security	1.35	1.52	1.30	1.51	1.32	1.70	1.31	(NA)	(NA)
Federal unemployment	0.03	0.03	0.03	0.03	0.03	0.03	0.03	(NA)	(NA)
State unemployment	0.11	0.14	0.10	0.13	0.10	0.15	0.10	(NA)	(NA)
Workers compensation	0.40	0.71	0.32	0.51	0.38	0.74	0.36	(NA)	(NA)
Other benefits [3]	0.03	0.06	0.02	0.08	0.02	0.08	0.02	0.04	-

- Represents or rounds to zero. NA Not available. [1] Mining, construction, and manufacturing. [2] Transportation, communications, and public utilities, wholesale and retail trade, finance, insurance, and real estate, and services. [3] Includes severance pay and supplemental unemployment benefits.

Source: U.S. Bureau of Labor Statistics, *Employer Costs for Employee Compensation, News*, USDL 03-297, June 11, 2003. See Internet site <http://www.bls.gov/ncs/ect/home.htm>.

No. 647. Employees With Employer- or Union-Provided Pension Plans or Group Health Plans: 2001

[Total in thousands (151,608 represents 151,608,000). For wage and salary workers 15 years old and over as of March 2002. Based on Current Population Survey; see text, Section 1, and Appendix III. Data based on 1990 population controls]

Occupation	Total (1,000)	Percent— Included in pension plan	Percent— With group health plan	Characteristic	Total (1,000)	Percent— Included in pension plan	Percent— With group health plan
Total	151,608	43.2	53.7	**AGE**			
Executive, admin., managerial	21,951	58.5	68.9	Total	151,608	43.2	53.7
Professional specialty	23,078	60.8	67.3	15 to 24 years	24,593	12.7	21.9
				25 to 44 years old	71,281	47.0	58.5
Technical/related support	4,894	55.3	65.4	45 to 64 years	50,230	54.7	63.7
Sales workers	18,236	32.7	43.8	65 years and over	5,504	23.6	42.6
Admin. support, inc. clerical	20,449	47.3	56.2	**WORK EXPERIENCE**			
				Worked	151,608	43.2	53.7
Precision prod., craft/repair	16,040	41.9	56.1	Full time	122,001	50.1	62.4
				50 weeks or more	100,379	54.5	67.1
Mach. operators, assemblers [1]	7,601	44.3	60.5	27 to 49 weeks	13,177	36.7	49.8
Transportation/material moving	6,397	40.3	55.8	26 weeks or fewer	8,445	19.0	26.2
Handlers, equipment cleaners [2]	6,516	25.5	38.8	Part time	29,607	14.4	17.9
				50 weeks or more	14,094	19.1	22.9
Service workers	21,941	22.8	33.4	27 to 49 weeks	6,187	15.8	19.2
Private households	860	3.5	9.6	26 weeks or fewer	9,326	6.4	9.6
Other	21,080	23.5	34.4	**EMPLOYER SIZE**			
				Under 25 persons	44,717	17.2	29.6
Farming, forestry and fishing	3,853	11.9	22.2	25 to 99 persons	19,311	37.4	54.1
				100 to 499 persons	19,777	50.2	62.9
Armed Forces	653	70.2	36.2	500 to 999 persons	8,467	56.4	65.9
				Over 1,000 persons	59,336	60.4	67.0

[1] Includes inspectors. [2] Includes helpers and laborers.

Source: U.S. Census Bureau, Annual Demographic Survey, March Supplement. See Internet site <http://ferret.bls.census.gov/macro/032002/noncash/toc.htm>.

426 Labor Force, Employment, and Earnings

No. 648. Percent of Workers With Access to Selected Employee Benefits in Private Industry: 1999 and 2000

[Based on National Compensation Survey, a sample survey of private industry establishments of all sizes (1,436 in 2000 and 3,168 in 1999) representing over 107 million workers; see source and Appendix III. See also Tables 155 and 157]

Characteristic	Paid vacation	Paid holidays	Employer assistance for child care	Adoption assistance	Long-term care insurance	Flexible work plans[1]	Nonwage cash payments — Non-production bonus[2]	Severance pay	Subsidized commuting[3]	Educational assistance — Work related	Educational assistance — Nonwork related	Health promotion benefits — Wellness programs	Health promotion benefits — Fitness centers
Total, 1999	79	75	6	6	6	3	42	22	4	(NA)	(NA)	(NA)	(NA)
WORKER CHARACTERISTICS													
Professional, technical, and related	88	89	12	11	11	7	48	36	9	(NA)	(NA)	(NA)	(NA)
Clerical and sales employees	80	77	5	6	7	3	42	24	4	(NA)	(NA)	(NA)	(NA)
Blue-collar and service employees	75	69	4	3	3	1	39	14	3	(NA)	(NA)	(NA)	(NA)
Full time[4]	90	87	6	6	7	4	46	26	5	(NA)	(NA)	(NA)	(NA)
Part time[4]	43	36	6	2	4	1	28	8	3	(NA)	(NA)	(NA)	(NA)
Union[5]	86	82	5	7	3	2	29	28	7	(NA)	(NA)	(NA)	(NA)
Nonunion[5]	78	75	6	5	6	3	43	21	4	(NA)	(NA)	(NA)	(NA)
ESTABLISHMENT CHARACTERISTICS													
Goods producing	84	84	2	7	5	3	47	25	4	(NA)	(NA)	(NA)	(NA)
Service producing	77	73	7	5	6	3	40	21	5	(NA)	(NA)	(NA)	(NA)
1 to 99 workers	73	70	3	1	2	2	46	13	3	(NA)	(NA)	(NA)	(NA)
100 or more workers	86	82	10	11	10	4	37	31	6	(NA)	(NA)	(NA)	(NA)
Total, 2000	80	77	4	5	7	5	48	20	3	38	9	18	9
WORKER CHARACTERISTICS													
Professional, technical, and related	88	85	11	12	14	12	52	35	6	62	19	35	19
Clerical and sales employees	80	80	5	5	7	4	48	24	3	37	8	17	10
Blue-collar and service employees	77	73	2	2	4	1	46	12	2	28	6	11	4
Full time[4]	91	87	5	6	8	5	51	23	3	44	11	21	10
Part time[4]	39	39	3	2	2	2	36	10	1	15	3	7	5
Union[5]	93	89	8	5	15	3	38	31	2	57	18	38	11
Nonunion[5]	79	76	4	5	6	5	49	19	3	36	8	16	9
ESTABLISHMENT CHARACTERISTICS													
Goods producing	89	89	2	6	5	4	51	21	1	45	14	19	10
Service producing	78	74	5	4	8	5	47	20	4	36	8	17	9
1 to 99 workers	73	70	1	1	5	2	49	11	2	26	3	6	4
100 or more workers	89	86	9	9	10	7	46	32	5	52	17	31	16

NA Not available. [1] Arrangements permitting employees to work at home several days of the workweek. [2] A cash payment not directly related to output of the employee or group of employees, such as attendance or profit sharing bonuses. [3] Employers subsidize employees' cost of commuting to and from work via public transportation, company sponsored van pool, discounted subway fares, etc. [4] Employees are classified as working either a full-time or part-time schedule based on the definition used by each establishment. [5] Union workers are those whose wages are determined through collective bargaining.

Source: U.S. Bureau of Labor Statistics, *Employee Benefits in Private Industry*, USDL 01-473, December 19, 2001, and USDL 02-389, July 16, 2002. See Internet site <http://www.bls.gov/ncs/ebs/home.htm>.

Labor Force, Employment, and Earnings   427

U.S. Census Bureau, Statistical Abstract of the United States: 2003

No. 649. Workers Killed or Disabled on the Job: 1970 to 2001

[Data for 2001 are preliminary estimates (13.8 represents 13,800). Excludes homicides and suicides. Estimates based on data from the U.S. National Center for Health Statistics, state vital statistics departments, state industrial commissions and beginning 1995, Bureau of Labor Statistics, Census of Occupational Fatalities. Numbers of workers based on data from the U.S. Bureau of Labor Statistics]

Year	Total Number (1,000)	Total Rate [1]	Manufacturing Number (1,000)	Manufacturing Rate [1]	Nonmanufacturing Number (1,000)	Nonmanufacturing Rate [1]	Disabling injuries [2] (mil.)	Year and industry group	Deaths, 2001 Number	Deaths, 2001 Rate [1]	Disabling injuries 2001 [2] (1,000)
1970	13.8	18	1.7	9	12.1	21	2.2	Total	[3]5,300	3.9	3,900
1975	13.0	15	1.6	9	11.4	17	2.2	Agriculture [4]	700	21.3	130
1980	13.2	13	1.7	8	11.5	15	2.2	Mining and quarrying [5]	180	31.8	20
1985	11.5	11	1.2	6	10.3	12	2.0	Construction	1,210	13.3	470
1990	10.1	9	1.0	5	9.1	9	3.9	Manufacturing	630	3.3	600
1995	5.0	4	0.6	3	4.4	4	3.6	Transportation and			
1997	5.2	4	0.7	3	4.5	4	3.8	utilities	930	11.4	410
1998	5.1	4	0.6	3	4.5	4	3.8	Trade [6]	470	1.7	740
1999	5.2	4	0.6	3	4.6	4	3.8	Services [7]	690	1.4	950
2000	5.0	4	0.6	3	4.4	4	3.9	Government	490	2.4	580
2001	5.3	4	0.6	3	4.7	4	3.9				

[1] Per 100,000 workers. [2] Disabling injury defined as one which results in death, some degree of physical impairment, or renders the person unable to perform regular activities for a full day beyond the day of the injury. Due to change in methodology, data beginning 1990 not comparable with prior years. [3] Includes deaths where industry is not known. [4] Includes forestry and fishing. [5] Includes oil and gas extraction. [6] Includes wholesale and retail trade. [7] Includes finance, insurance, and real estate.

Source: National Safety Council, Itasca, IL, *Accident Facts*, annual through 1998 edition; thereafter, *Injury Facts*, annual, (copyright).

No. 650. Worker Deaths, Injuries, and Production Time Lost: 1995 to 2001

[45.7 represents 45,700. Data may not agree with Table 649 because data here are not revised]

Item	Deaths (1,000) 1995	2000	2001	Disabling injuries [1] (mil.) 1995	2000	2001	Production time lost (mil. days) In the current year 1995	2000	2001	In future years [2] 1995	2000	2001
All accidents	45.7	47.0	48.3	9.9	10.5	10.7	225	240	250	455	460	480
On the job	5.3	5.2	5.3	3.6	3.9	3.9	75	80	85	65	60	65
Off the job	40.4	41.8	43.0	6.3	6.6	6.8	150	160	165	390	400	415
Motor vehicle	22.9	22.8	22.9	1.2	1.2	1.2	(NA)	(NA)	(NA)	(NA)	(NA)	(NA)
Public nonmotor vehicle	7.5	8.3	7.8	2.3	2.8	2.6	(NA)	(NA)	(NA)	(NA)	(NA)	(NA)
Home	10.0	10.7	12.3	2.8	2.6	3.0	(NA)	(NA)	(NA)	(NA)	(NA)	(NA)

NA Not available. [1] See footnote 2, Table 649 for a definition of disabling injuries. [2] Based on an average of 5,850 days lost in future years per fatality and 565 days lost in future years per permanent injury.

Source: National Safety Council, Itasca, IL, *Accident Facts*, annual through 1998 edition; thereafter, *Injury Facts*, annual, (copyright).

No. 651. Industries With the Highest Total Case Incidence Rates for Nonfatal Injuries and Illnesses: 2000 and 2001

[Rates per 100 full-time employees. Industries shown are those with the highest rates for 2001. Rates refer to any occupational injury or illness resulting in (1) lost workday cases, or (2) nonfatal cases without lost workdays. Incidence rates were calculated as: Number of injuries and illnesses divided by total hours worked by all employees during year multiplied by 200,000 as base for 100 full-time equivalent workers (working 40 hours per week, 50 weeks a year)]

Industry	1987 SIC [1] code	2000	2001	Industry	1987 SIC [1] code	2000	2001
Private industry	(X)	6.1	5.7	Public building and related furniture	253	15.8	14.4
Metal sanitary ware	3431	17.5	24.4	Air transportation, scheduled	451	14.7	14.4
Motor vehicles and car bodies	3711	22.7	21.0	Brick and structural clay tile	3251	14.2	14.0
Meat packing plants	2011	24.7	20.0	Steel foundries, n.e.c. [2]	3325	(NA)	14.0
Prefabricated wood buildings	2452	15.3	19.1	Automotive stampings	3465	15.3	14.0
Gray and ductile iron foundries	3321	21.7	18.9	Vitreous plumbing fixtures	3261	11.7	13.9
Secondary nonferrous metals	334	12.8	18.4	Motorcycles, bicycles, and parts	375	11.5	13.9
Truck and bus bodies	3713	19.4	17.9	Architectural metal work	3446	9.5	13.8
Travel trailers and campers	3792	18.1	17.4	Household laundry equipment	3633	(NA)	13.8
Ship building and repairing	3731	22.0	17.2	Concrete block and brick	3271	10.8	13.7
Aluminum die-castings	3363	15.2	16.1	Rubber and plastics footwear	302	(NA)	13.6
Structural wood members, n.e.c. [2]	2439	17.5	15.7	Prefabricated metal buildings	3448	13.2	13.6
Bottled and canned soft drinks	2086	14.4	15.6	Nursing and personal care facilities	805	13.9	13.5
Fabricated structural metal	3441	16.7	15.1	Aluminum foundries	3365	18.3	13.4
Mobile homes	2451	19.7	15.0	Household appliances, n.e.c. [2]	3639	8.7	13.4
Mattresses and bedsprings	2515	13.7	14.7	Fluid milk	2026	13.4	13.3

NA Not available. X Not applicable. [1] 1987 Standard Industrial Classification; see text, this section. [2] N.e.c. means not elsewhere classified.

Source: U.S. Bureau of Labor Statistics, *Occupational Injuries and Illnesses in the United States by Industry*, annual. See Internet site <http://www.bls.gov/iif/home.htm>.

No. 652. Nonfatal Occupational Injury and Illness Incidence Rates: 2000 and 2001

[Rates per 100 full-time employees. Rates refer to any occupational injury or illness resulting in (1) lost workday cases, or (2) nonfatal cases without lost workdays. Incidence rates were calculated as: Number of injuries and illnesses divided by total hours worked by all employees during year multiplied by 200,000 as base for 100 full-time equivalent workers (working 40 hours per week, 50 weeks a year)]

Industry	1987 SIC[1]	2000	2001	Industry	1987 SIC[1]	2000	2001
Private sector[2]	(X)	6.1	5.7	Trucking and warehousing	42	7.9	8.4
Agriculture, forestry, fishing[2]	A	7.1	7.3	Water transportation	44	7.0	6.0
Mining[3]	B	4.7	4.0	Transportation by air	45	13.9	13.3
Metal mining[3]	10	4.9	4.2	Pipelines, except natural gas	46	-	3.4
Coal mining[3]	12	7.5	6.9	Transportation services	47	3.2	3.0
Oil and gas extraction	13	4.2	3.3	Communications	48	2.6	2.9
Nonmetallic minerals, exc. fuels	14	4.3	4.2	Electric, gas, sanitary services	49	6.3	5.7
Construction	C	8.3	7.9	Wholesale and retail trade	F, G	5.9	5.6
General building contractors	15	7.8	6.9	Wholesale trade	F	5.8	5.3
Heavy construction, except building	16	7.6	7.8	Retail trade	G	5.9	5.7
Special trade contractors	17	8.6	8.2	Finance, insurance, real estate	H	1.9	1.8
Manufacturing	D	9.0	8.1	Depository institutions	60	1.4	1.4
Durable goods	(X)	9.8	8.8	Nondepository institutions	61	1.1	1.0
Lumber and wood products	24	12.1	10.6	Security and commodity brokers	62	0.6	0.5
Furniture and fixtures	25	11.2	11.0	Insurance carriers	63	1.9	1.7
Stone, clay, and glass products	32	10.4	10.1	Insurance agents, brokers, and service	64	1.0	0.8
Primary metal industries	33	12.6	10.7	Real estate	65	4.1	4.1
Fabricated metal products	34	11.9	11.1	Holding and other investment offices	67	1.3	1.4
Industrial machinery and equip	35	8.2	7.2	Services[4]	I	4.9	4.6
Electronic/other electric equip	36	5.7	5.0	Hotels and other lodging places	70	6.9	7.2
Transportation equipment	37	13.7	12.6	Personal services	72	3.3	3.1
Instruments/related products	38	4.5	4.0	Business services	73	3.2	2.7
Miscellaneous manufacturing industries	39	7.2	6.4	Auto repair, services, and parking	75	5.0	4.5
Nondurable goods	(X)	7.8	6.8	Miscellaneous repair services	76	4.9	5.4
Food and kindred products	20	12.4	10.9	Motion pictures	78	3.4	2.5
Tobacco products	21	6.2	4.3	Amusement and recreation services	79	6.9	7.1
Textile mill products	22	6.0	5.2	Health services	80	7.4	7.2
Apparel and other textile products	23	6.1	5.0	Legal services	81	0.7	0.8
Paper and allied products	26	6.5	6.0	Educational services	82	3.2	2.9
Printing and publishing	27	5.1	4.6	Social services	83	6.1	5.9
Chemicals and allied products	28	4.2	4.0	Museums, botanical, zoological gardens	84	5.2	6.1
Petroleum and coal products	29	3.7	2.9	Membership organizations	86	3.0	2.8
Rubber and misc. plastics products	30	10.7	8.7	Engineering and management services	87	1.7	1.6
Leather and leather products	31	9.0	8.7				
Transportation/public utilities[3]	E	6.9	6.9				
Railroad transportation[3]	40	3.6	3.4				
Local passenger transit	41	8.0	9.8				

- Represents or rounds to zero.   X Not applicable.   [1] 1987 Standard Industrial Classification; see text, this section.   [2] Excludes farms with fewer than 11 employees.   [3] Data conforming to OSHA definitions for employers in the railroad industry and for mining operators in coal, metal, and nonmetal mining. Independent mining contractors are excluded from the coal, metal, and nonmetal mining industries.   [4] Includes categories not shown separately.

Source: U.S. Bureau of Labor Statistics, *Survey of Occupational Injuries and Illnesses*, annual. See Internet site <http://www.bls.gov/iif/home.htm>.

No. 653. Fatal Work Injuries by Event or Exposure: 2001

[See headnote, Table 654]

Cause	Number of fatalities	Percent distribution	Cause	Number of fatalities	Percent distribution
Total	5,900	100	Contacts with objects and equipment[1]	962	16
			Struck by object[1]	553	9
Transportation accidents[1]	2,517	43	Struck by falling objects	343	6
Highway accidents[1]	1,404	24	Struck by flying object	60	1
Collision between vehicles, mobile equipment	723	12	Caught in or compressed by— Equipment or objects	266	5
Noncollision accidents	339	6	Collapsing materials	122	2
Nonhighway accident (farm, industrial premises)	324	5	Falls	808	14
Aircraft accidents	247	4	Exposure to harmful substances or environments[1]	499	8
Workers struck by a vehicle	383	6	Contact with electric current	285	5
Water vehicle accidents	90	2	Exposure to caustic, noxious or allergenic substances	96	2
Railway accidents	62	1	Oxygen deficiency	83	1
Assaults and violent acts[1]	902	15	Drowning, submersion	59	1
Homicides[1]	639	11			
Shooting	505	9	Fires and explosions	188	3
Stabbing	58	1	Other events and exposures	24	(Z)
Self-inflicted injury	228	4			

Z Less than 0.5 percent.   [1] Includes other causes, not shown separately.

Source: U.S. Bureau of Labor Statistics, *National Census of Fatal Occupational Injuries in 2001, News*, USDL 02-541, September 25, 2002; See Internet site <http://www.bls.gov/iif/home.htm>.

No. 654. Fatal Occupational Injuries by Industry and Event or Exposure: 2001

[For the 50 states and DC. Excludes 2,886 fatalities resulting from the events of September 11, 2001. Based on the censuses of Fatal Occupational Injuries. Due to methodological differences, data differ from those in Table 649. For details, see source]

Industry	1987 SIC[1] code	Fatalities[2]	Trans- portation incidents	Assaults/ violent acts	Contact with objects[3]	Falls	Expo- sure[4]	Rate[5]
Total................	(X)	5,900	43	15	16	14	8	4
Private industry	(X)	5,270	41	15	17	15	9	5
Agriculture, forestry, fishing	A	740	51	7	22	9	9	23
Mining[6]	B	170	29	-	41	6	6	30
Coal mining.................	12	42	21	-	38	-	-	48
Oil and gas extraction	13	98	29	-	43	5	9	28
Construction.................	C	1,225	26	4	18	34	16	13
General building contractors	15	201	19	7	15	47	11	-
Heavy construction, except building...............	16	267	40	2	25	12	18	-
Special trade contractors	17	735	22	3	16	39	16	-
Manufacturing[6]	D	599	30	9	36	8	9	3
Food and kindred products.......	20	57	33	11	28	11	14	4
Lumber and wood products	24	151	26	-	60	6	4	22
Transportation and public utilities[6] ...	E	911	71	8	9	6	5	11
Local passenger transit	41	80	45	49	-	-	-	13
Trucking and warehousing	42	533	78	4	9	5	2	20
Transportation by air	45	85	88	-	6	-	-	10
Electric, gas, sanitary services	49	88	47	-	13	8	19	-
Wholesale trade	F	220	58	9	19	7	5	4
Retail trade[6].................	G	537	25	57	5	7	2	2
Food stores................	54	132	11	82	-	5	-	-
Automotive dealer and service stations	55	83	52	28	-	7	5	-
Eating and drinking places	58	147	16	69	3	5	3	2
Finance, insurance, real estate......	H	86	33	38	-	19	6	1
Services[6]	I	767	38	25	13	12	8	2
Business services.............	73	191	40	23	16	14	7	2
Auto repair, services, and parking...............	75	115	35	23	23	7	-	-
Government...............	J	630	57	20	7	6	7	3

- No data reported or data do not meet publication standards.   X Not applicable.   [1] 1987 Standard Industrial Classification code, see text this section.   [2] Includes 15 fatalities for which there was insufficient information to determine industry classification. Includes fatalities caused by other events and exposures, not shown separately.   [3] Includes equipment.   [4] Exposure to harmful substances or environments.   [5] Rate per 100,000 employed civilians 16 years old and over.   [6] Includes other industries, not shown separately.

Source: U.S. Bureau of Labor Statistics, *National Census of Fatal Occupational Injuries in 2001, News*, USDL 02-541, September 25, 2002; and unpublished data. See Internet site <http://www.bls.gov/iif/>.

No. 655. Work Stoppages: 1960 to 2002

[**896 represents 896,000.** Excludes work stoppages involving fewer than 1,000 workers and lasting less than 1 day. Information is based on reports of labor disputes appearing in daily newspapers, trade journals, and other public sources. The parties to the disputes are contacted by telephone, when necessary, to clarify details of the stoppages]

Year	Number of stop- pages[1]	Workers involved[2] (1,000)	Days idle Number[3] (1,000)	Percent estimated working time[4]	Year	Number of stop- pages[1]	Workers involved[2] (1,000)	Days idle Number[3] (1,000)	Percent estimated working time[4]
1960.....	222	896	13,260	0.09	1985.....	54	324	7,079	0.03
1965.....	268	999	15,140	0.10	1986.....	69	533	11,861	0.05
1969.....	412	1,576	29,397	0.16	1987.....	46	174	[5]4,481	0.02
1970.....	381	2,468	52,761	0.29	1988.....	40	118	[5]4,381	0.02
1971.....	298	2,516	35,538	0.19	1989.....	51	452	16,996	0.07
1972.....	250	975	16,764	0.09	1990.....	44	185	5,926	0.02
1973.....	317	1,400	16,260	0.08	1991.....	40	392	4,584	0.02
1974.....	424	1,796	31,809	0.16	1992.....	35	364	3,989	0.01
1975.....	235	965	17,563	0.09	1993.....	35	182	3,981	0.01
1976.....	231	1,519	23,962	0.12	1994.....	45	322	5,020	0.02
1977.....	298	1,212	21,258	0.10	1995.....	31	192	5,771	0.02
1978.....	219	1,006	23,774	0.11	1996.....	37	273	4,889	0.02
1979.....	235	1,021	20,409	0.09	1997.....	29	339	4,497	0.01
1980.....	187	795	20,844	0.09	1998.....	34	387	5,116	0.02
1981.....	145	729	16,908	0.07	1999.....	17	73	1,996	0.01
1982.....	96	656	9,061	0.04	2000.....	39	394	20,419	0.06
1983.....	81	909	17,461	0.08	2001.....	29	99	1,151	(Z)
1984.....	62	376	8,499	0.04	2002.....	19	46	660	(Z)

Z Less than 0.005 percent.   [1] Beginning in year indicated.   [2] Workers counted more than once if involved in more than one stoppage during the year.   [3] Resulting from all stoppages in effect in a year, including those that began in an earlier year.   [4] Agricultural and government employees are included in the total working time; private household and forestry and fishery employees are excluded.   [5] Revised since originally published.

Source: U.S. Bureau of Labor Statistics, *Major Work Stoppages in 2002, News*, USDL 03-100, March 11, 2003. See Internet site <http://www.bls.gov/cba/>.

No. 656. Labor Union Membership by Sector: 1983 to 2002

[See headnote, Table 658. (17,717.4 represents 17,717,400)]

Sector	1983	1985	1990	1995	1998	1999	2000	2001	2002
TOTAL (1,000)									
Wage and salary workers:									
Union members	17,717.4	16,996.1	16,739.8	16,359.6	16,211.4	16,476.7	16,258.2	16,288.8	15,978.7
Covered by unions	20,532.1	19,358.1	19,057.8	18,346.3	17,918.3	18,182.3	17,944.1	17,878.1	17,501.6
Public sector workers:									
Union members	5,737.2	5,743.1	6,485.0	6,927.4	6,905.3	7,058.1	7,110.5	7,147.5	7,327.2
Covered by unions	7,112.2	6,920.6	7,691.4	7,986.6	7,814.7	7,966.3	7,975.6	7,975.4	8,131.9
Private sector workers:									
Union members	11,980.2	11,253.0	10,254.8	9,432.1	9,306.1	9,418.6	9,147.7	9,141.3	8,651.5
Covered by unions	13,419.9	12,437.5	11,366.4	10,359.8	10,103.6	10,216.0	9,968.5	9,902.7	9,369.7
PERCENT									
Wage and salary workers:									
Union members	20.1	18.0	16.1	14.9	13.9	13.9	13.5	13.5	13.3
Covered by unions	23.3	20.5	18.3	16.7	15.4	15.3	14.9	14.8	14.6
Public sector workers:									
Union members	36.7	35.7	36.5	37.7	37.5	37.3	37.5	37.4	37.8
Covered by unions	45.5	43.1	43.3	43.5	42.5	42.1	42.0	41.7	41.9
Private sector workers:									
Union members	16.5	14.3	11.9	10.3	9.5	9.4	9.0	9.0	8.6
Covered by unions	18.5	15.9	13.2	11.3	10.3	10.2	9.8	9.7	9.3

Source: The Bureau of National Affairs, Inc., Washington, DC, *Union Membership and Earnings Data Book: Compilations from the Current Population Survey (2003 edition)*, (copyright by BNA PLUS); authored by Barry Hirsch of Trinity University, San Antonio, TX and David Macpherson of Florida State University. Internet site <http://www.bna.com/bnaplus/labor/laborrpts.html>.

No. 657. Union Members by Selected Characteristics: 2002

[Annual averages of monthly data (122,009 represents 122,009,000). Covers employed wage and salary workers 16 years old and over. Excludes self-employed workers whose businesses are incorporated although they technically qualify as wage and salary workers. Based on Current Population Survey, see text, Section 1, and Appendix III]

Characteristic	Employed wage and salary workers			Median usual weekly earnings [3] (dol.)			
	Total (1,000)	Percent		Total	Union mem- bers [1]	Repre- sented by unions [2]	Not repre- sented by unions
		Union mem- bers [1]	Repre- sented by unions [2]				
Total [4]	122,009	13.2	14.6	609	740	734	587
16 to 24 years old	19,258	5.1	5.9	381	497	494	374
25 to 34 years old	28,253	11.2	12.5	591	682	670	577
35 to 44 years old	31,296	14.2	15.6	669	759	753	647
45 to 54 years old	27,086	18.5	20.2	707	789	787	675
55 to 64 years old	12,982	17.4	19.0	673	787	784	639
65 years and over	3,133	7.9	9.1	502	592	594	484
Men	63,384	14.7	16.0	680	780	776	652
Women	58,625	11.6	13.0	530	667	662	510
White	**101,082**	**12.8**	**14.1**	**624**	**763**	**757**	**602**
Men	53,305	14.4	15.6	702	804	801	674
Women	47,777	10.9	12.3	549	695	688	521
Black	**14,127**	**16.9**	**18.7**	**498**	**615**	**610**	**477**
Men	6,499	18.2	20.0	523	651	640	502
Women	7,628	15.7	17.7	474	588	588	445
Hispanic [5]	**15,523**	**10.5**	**11.7**	**423**	**623**	**617**	**408**
Men	9,131	11.1	12.2	449	666	655	422
Women	6,392	9.8	11.1	396	558	569	381
Full-time workers	100,204	14.6	16.0	609	740	734	587
Part-time workers	21,573	6.9	7.7	(X)	(X)	(X)	(X)
Managerial and professional specialty	36,969	13.0	15.0	884	890	884	884
Technical sales, and admin. support	35,770	8.9	9.9	550	633	625	536
Service occupations	17,898	12.6	13.8	384	595	585	358
Precision, production, craft, and repair	12,413	20.7	21.6	629	821	814	590
Operators, fabricators, and laborers	16,901	19.1	20.3	482	635	627	445
Farming, forestry, and fishing	2,058	4.3	5.1	363	548	524	357
Private wage and salary workers	102,420	8.5	9.3	591	701	691	581
Agricultural	1,819	2.3	2.6	372	(B)	(B)	371
Mining	458	8.5	10.0	822	(B)	(B)	825
Construction	6,883	17.2	17.8	599	845	836	559
Manufacturing	17,324	14.3	15.1	624	654	653	619
Transportation and public utilities	7,433	23.0	24.3	706	810	805	664
Wholesale and retail trade, total	25,475	4.5	4.9	480	552	540	477
Finance, insurance, and real estate	7,849	1.9	2.5	676	598	601	681
Services	35,179	5.7	6.7	596	650	645	592
Government	19,589	37.5	42.0	708	770	767	640

B Data not shown where base is less than 50,000. X Not applicable. [1] Members of a labor union or an employee association similar to a labor union. [2] Members of a labor union or an employee association similar to a union as well as workers who report no union affiliation but whose jobs are covered by a union or an employee association contract. [3] For full-time employed wage and salary workers. [4] Includes races not shown separately. Also includes a small number of multiple jobholders whose full- and part- time status can not be determined for their principal job. [5] Persons of Hispanic origin may be of any race.

Source: U.S. Bureau of Labor Statistics, *Employment and Earnings*, June 2003. See Internet site <http://www.bls.gov/cps/home.htm>.

Labor Force, Employment, and Earnings

No. 658. Labor Union Membership by State: 1983 and 2002

[Annual averages of monthly figures (17,717.4 represents 17,717,400). For wage and salary workers in agriculture and non-agriculture. Data represent union members by place of residence. Based on the Current Population Survey and subject to sampling error. For methodological details, see source. The 2002 figures are based on publicly released Current Population Survey files. Figures differ slightly from annual figures compiled by the U.S. Bureau of Labor Statistics, which are based on a revised 2002 CPS including new weights from the 2000 census]

State	Union members (1,000) 1983	Union members (1,000) 2002	Workers covered by unions (1,000) 1983	Workers covered by unions (1,000) 2002	Union members 1983	Union members 2002	Covered by unions 1983	Covered by unions 2002	Private sector union members 1983	Private sector union members 2002
United States..	17,717.4	15,978.7	20,532.1	17,501.6	20.1	13.3	23.3	14.6	16.5	8.6
Alabama [1]	228.2	161.4	268.2	188.3	16.9	9.0	19.8	10.5	15.3	6.0
Alaska	41.7	63.6	49.2	69.9	24.9	24.4	29.3	26.8	17.3	12.7
Arizona [1]	125.0	115.5	156.4	136.9	11.4	5.6	14.3	6.6	8.6	3.3
Arkansas [1]	82.2	63.3	103.2	72.4	11.0	6.0	13.8	6.8	10.2	4.0
California	2,118.9	2,578.7	2,505.2	2,760.7	21.9	17.8	25.9	19.1	17.7	10.2
Colorado	177.9	151.6	209.6	173.5	13.6	7.8	16.0	8.9	11.2	5.4
Connecticut	314.0	247.9	345.1	260.2	22.7	16.9	25.0	17.8	16.7	9.8
Delaware	49.2	40.9	54.1	44.4	20.1	11.2	22.1	12.2	15.9	7.4
District of Columbia.	52.4	33.6	69.4	42.9	19.5	14.1	25.9	17.9	15.2	10.0
Florida [1]	393.7	369.8	532.9	484.5	10.2	5.8	13.8	7.6	7.1	2.8
Georgia [1]	267.0	218.1	345.1	253.4	11.9	6.0	15.3	7.0	11.1	3.9
Hawaii	112.6	118.5	124.9	122.4	29.2	24.4	32.4	25.2	21.9	16.9
Idaho [1]	41.3	39.1	53.7	48.5	12.5	7.1	16.2	8.8	10.3	4.9
Illinois	1,063.8	1,035.1	1,205.1	1,082.5	24.2	19.7	27.4	20.6	21.5	15.1
Indiana	503.3	361.6	544.5	393.0	24.9	13.3	27.0	14.5	25.0	10.6
Iowa [1]	185.9	152.6	231.3	187.4	17.2	11.0	21.5	13.6	14.6	7.6
Kansas [1]	125.2	96.4	170.4	115.8	13.7	8.2	18.7	9.8	12.2	6.5
Kentucky	223.7	166.7	259.8	187.0	17.9	10.0	20.8	11.2	18.2	7.6
Louisiana [1]	204.2	140.9	267.8	173.3	13.8	8.4	18.1	10.3	11.0	5.1
Maine	88.0	72.8	100.4	84.1	21.0	13.0	24.0	15.0	14.2	7.2
Maryland	346.5	362.0	423.1	419.9	18.5	14.5	22.6	16.8	14.4	8.6
Massachusetts	603.2	412.1	661.4	447.3	23.7	14.4	26.0	15.6	17.6	7.6
Michigan	1,005.4	896.5	1,084.6	932.0	30.4	21.1	32.8	22.0	25.3	15.7
Minnesota	393.9	415.6	439.4	432.1	23.2	17.5	25.9	18.2	17.1	10.8
Mississippi [1]	79.4	70.6	99.7	85.5	9.9	6.7	12.5	8.1	9.0	6.0
Missouri	374.4	328.7	416.7	361.7	20.8	13.2	23.2	14.5	21.5	11.1
Montana	49.5	51.7	55.5	56.5	18.3	14.1	20.5	15.5	14.8	7.2
Nebraska [1]	80.6	61.6	94.8	85.7	13.6	8.0	16.0	11.1	9.7	4.9
Nevada [1]	90.0	136.5	106.7	149.6	22.4	15.2	26.6	16.7	19.6	12.2
New Hampshire	48.5	57.6	60.8	65.8	11.5	9.8	14.4	11.2	7.5	4.5
New Jersey	822.1	711.2	918.2	747.7	26.9	19.8	30.0	20.8	21.1	11.7
New Mexico	52.6	48.2	70.6	60.5	11.8	6.9	15.8	8.6	10.1	3.5
New York	2,155.6	1,944.7	2,385.9	2,030.4	32.5	25.6	36.0	26.8	24.0	15.8
North Carolina [1]	178.7	112.9	238.1	133.8	7.6	3.4	10.2	4.0	5.4	2.1
North Dakota [1]	28.4	22.3	35.1	26.8	13.2	8.1	16.3	9.7	9.5	4.8
Ohio	1,011.0	835.4	1,125.0	890.7	25.1	16.8	27.9	17.9	22.5	11.6
Oklahoma [2]	131.5	126.6	168.2	149.7	11.5	8.9	14.7	10.6	9.1	5.2
Oregon	222.9	226.3	261.9	239.0	22.3	15.7	26.2	16.6	16.4	9.4
Pennsylvania	1,195.7	824.9	1,350.4	877.7	27.5	15.7	31.1	16.7	23.2	10.0
Rhode Island	85.8	75.6	93.7	78.3	21.5	17.4	23.5	18.0	13.7	9.1
South Carolina [1]	69.6	82.6	100.6	103.2	5.9	5.0	8.6	6.2	3.9	3.7
South Dakota [1]	26.8	18.6	34.8	23.1	11.5	5.5	14.9	6.9	8.0	3.2
Tennessee [1]	252.4	221.4	300.9	256.2	15.1	9.1	18.0	10.5	12.4	6.5
Texas [1]	583.7	458.4	712.8	576.6	9.7	5.2	11.9	6.5	8.1	3.3
Utah [1]	81.6	59.0	100.9	71.6	15.2	6.2	18.9	7.6	11.3	2.9
Vermont	25.9	26.4	31.5	30.4	12.6	9.5	15.3	10.9	6.7	5.0
Virginia [1]	268.3	196.4	346.1	255.0	11.7	6.0	15.1	7.8	10.2	3.5
Washington	419.9	471.8	499.7	509.0	27.1	18.6	32.3	20.1	22.0	13.6
West Virginia	142.7	93.3	160.6	98.4	25.3	13.2	28.5	14.0	26.1	10.5
Wisconsin	465.5	385.2	526.7	405.4	23.8	15.6	26.9	16.4	19.8	9.9
Wyoming [1]	27.1	16.7	31.8	21.2	13.9	7.7	16.2	9.8	10.4	5.5

[1] Right to work state. [2] Passed right to work law in 2001.

Source: The Bureau of National Affairs, Inc., Washington, DC, *Union Membership and Earnings Data Book: Compilations from the Current Population Survey (2003 edition)*, (copyright by BNA PLUS); authored by Barry Hirsch of Trinity University, San Antonio, TX, and David Macpherson of Florida State University. Internet site <http://www.bna.com/bnaplus/labor/laborrpts.html>.

Section 13
Income, Expenditures, and Wealth

This section presents data on gross domestic product (GDP), gross national product (GNP), national and personal income, saving and investment, money income, poverty, and national and personal wealth. The data on income and expenditures measure two aspects of the U.S. economy. One aspect relates to the national income and product accounts (NIPAs), a summation reflecting the entire complex of the nation's economic income and output and the interaction of its major components; the other relates to the distribution of money income to families and individuals or consumer income.

The primary source for data on GDP, GNP, national and personal income, gross saving and investment, and fixed reproducible tangible wealth is the *Survey of Current Business*, published monthly by the Bureau of Economic Analysis (BEA). A comprehensive revision to the NIPAs was released beginning in October 1999. Discussions of the revision appeared in the August, September, October, December 1999, and the April 2000 issues of the *Survey of Current Business*. Summary historical estimates appeared in the August 2000 issue of the *Survey of Current Business*. Detailed historical data will appear in forthcoming *National Income and Product Accounts of the United States, 1929-97* report.

Sources of income distribution data are the decennial censuses of population and the Current Population Survey (CPS), both products of the U.S. Census Bureau (see text, Section 1 and new Section 31). Annual data on income of families, individuals, and households are presented in *Current Population Reports, Consumer Income*, P60 Series, in print, and many data series found on the census Web site at <http://www.census.gov/hhes/www.income.html>. Data from the 2000 census may be found in Tables 680-682, 692, and 697-699.

Data on individuals' saving and assets are published by the Board of Governors of the Federal Reserve System in the quarterly *Flow of Funds Accounts*. The Board also periodically conducts the *Survey of Consumer Finances*, which presents financial information on family assets and net worth. Detailed information on personal wealth is published periodically by the Internal Revenue Service (IRS) in *SOI Bulletin*.

National income and product—Gross domestic product is the total output of goods and services produced by labor and property located in the United States, valued at market prices. GDP can be viewed in terms of the expenditure categories that comprise its major components—purchases of goods and services by consumers and government, gross private domestic investment, and net exports of goods and services. The goods and services included are largely those bought for final use (excluding illegal transactions) in the market economy. A number of inclusions, however, represent imputed values, the most important of which is rental value of owner-occupied housing. GDP, in this broad context, measures the output attributable to the factors of production located in the United States. Gross state product (GSP) is the gross market value of the goods and services attributable to labor and property located in a state. It is the state counterpart of the nation's gross domestic product.

In January 1996, BEA replaced its fixed-weighted index as the featured measure of real GDP with an index based on chain-type annual weights. Changes in this measure of real output and prices are calculated as the average of changes based on weights for the current and preceding years. (Components of real output are weighted by price, and components of prices are weighted by output.) These annual changes are "chained" (multiplied) together to form a time series that allows for the effects of changes in relative prices and changes in the composition of output over time. Quarterly and monthly changes are also based on annual weights. The new output indexes are expressed as 1996=100, and for recent years, in 1996 dollars; the new price indexes are based to 1996=100.

Chained (1996) dollar estimates of most components of GDP are not published for periods prior to 1987, because during periods far from the base period, the levels of the components may provide misleading information about their contributions to an aggregate. Values are published in index form (1996=100) for 1929 to the present to allow users to calculate the percent changes for all components, changes that are accurate for all periods. In addition, the Bureau of Economic Analysis publishes estimates of the contribution of major components to the percent change in GDP for all periods.

Gross national product measures the output attributable to all labor and property supplied by United States residents. GNP differs from "national income" mainly in that GNP includes allowances for depreciation and for indirect business taxes (sales and property taxes); see Table 665.

In December 1991, the Bureau of Economic Analysis began featuring gross domestic product rather than gross national product as the primary measure of U.S. production. GDP is now the standard measure of growth because it is the appropriate measure for much of the short-term monitoring and analysis of the economy. In addition, the use of GDP facilitates comparisons of economic activity in the United States with that in other countries.

National income is the aggregate of labor and property earnings that arises in the current production of goods and services. It is the sum of employee compensation, proprietors' income, rental income of persons, corporate profits, and net interest. It measures the total factor costs of the goods and services produced by the economy. Income is measured before deduction of taxes.

Capital consumption adjustment for corporations and for nonfarm sole proprietorships and partnerships is the difference between capital consumption based on income tax returns and capital consumption measured using empirical evidence on prices of used equipment and structures in resale markets, which have shown that depreciation for most types of assets approximates a geometric pattern. The tax return data are valued at historical costs and reflect changes over time in service lives and depreciation patterns as permitted by tax regulations. *Inventory valuation adjustment* represents the difference between the book value of inventories used up in production and the cost of replacing them.

Personal income is the current income received by persons from all sources minus their personal contributions for social insurance. Classified as "persons" are individuals (including owners of unincorporated firms), nonprofit institutions that primarily serve individuals, private trust funds, and private noninsured welfare funds. Personal income includes transfers (payments not resulting from current production) from government and business such as social security benefits, public assistance, etc., but excludes transfers among persons. Also included are certain nonmonetary types of income—chiefly, estimated net rental value to owner-occupants of their homes and the value of services furnished without payment by financial intermediaries. Capital gains (net losses) are excluded.

Disposable personal income is personal income less personal tax and nontax payments. It is the income available to persons for spending or saving. Personal tax and nontax payments are tax payments (net of refunds) by persons (except personal contributions for social insurance) that are not chargeable to business expense and certain personal payments to general government that are treated like taxes. Personal taxes include income, estate and gift, and personal property taxes and motor vehicle licenses. Nontax payments include passport fees, fines and forfeitures, and donations.

Consumer Expenditure Survey—The Consumer Expenditure Survey program was begun in late 1979. The principal objective of the survey is to collect current consumer expenditure data, which provide a continuous flow of data on the buying habits of American consumers. The data are necessary for future revisions of the Consumer Price Index.

The survey conducted by the Census Bureau for the Bureau of Labor Statistics consists of two components: (1) An interview panel survey in which the expenditures of consumer units are obtained in five interviews conducted every 3 months, and (2) a diary or recordkeeping survey completed by participating households for two consecutive 1-week periods.

Each component of the survey queries an independent sample of consumer units representative of the U.S. total population.

Over 52 weeks of the year, 5,000 consumer units are sampled for the diary survey. Each consumer unit keeps a diary for two 1-week periods yielding approximately 10,000 diaries a year. The interview sample is selected on a rotating panel basis, targeted at 5,000 consumer units per quarter. Data are collected in 88 urban and 16 rural areas of the country that are representative of the U.S. total population. The survey includes students in student housing. Data from the two surveys are combined; integration is necessary to permit analysis of total family expenditures because neither the diary nor quarterly interview survey was designed to collect a complete account of consumer spending.

Distribution of money income to families and individuals—Money income statistics are based on data collected in various field surveys of income conducted since 1936. Since 1947, the Census Bureau has collected the data on an annual basis and published them in *Current Population Reports*, P60 Series. In each of the surveys, field representatives interview samples of the population with respect to income received during the previous year. Money income as defined by the Census Bureau differs from the BEA concept of "personal income."

Data on consumer income collected in the CPS by the Census Bureau cover money income received (exclusive of certain money receipts such as capital gains) before payments for personal income taxes, social security, union dues, medicare deductions, etc. Therefore, money income does not reflect the fact that some families receive part of their income in the form of noncash benefits (see Section 12) such as food stamps, health benefits, and subsidized housing; that some farm families receive noncash benefits in the form of rent-free housing and goods produced and consumed on the farm; or that noncash benefits are also received by some nonfarm residents which often take the form of the use of business transportation and facilities, full or partial payments by business for retirement programs, medical and educational expenses, etc. These elements should be considered when comparing income levels. For data on noncash benefits, see Section 12. None of the aggregate income concepts (GDP, national income, or personal income) is exactly comparable with money income, although personal income is the closest.

In October 1983, the Census Bureau began to collect data under the new Survey of Income and Program Participation (SIPP). The information supplied by this survey is expected to provide better measures of the status and changes in income distribution and poverty of households and persons in the United States. The data collected in SIPP will be used to study federal and state aid programs (such as food stamps, welfare, medicaid, and subsidized housing), to estimate program costs and coverage, and to assess the effects of proposed changes in program eligibility rules or benefit levels. The core questions are repeated at each interview and cover labor force activity, the types and amounts of income received, and participation status in various programs. The core also contains questions covering attendance in postsecondary schools and private health insurance coverage. Various supplements or topical modules covering areas such as educational attainment, assets and liabilities, and pension plan coverage are periodically included.

Poverty—Families and unrelated individuals are classified as being above or below the poverty level using the poverty index originated at the Social Security Administration in 1964 and revised by Federal Interagency Committees in 1969 and 1980.

The poverty index is based solely on money income and does not reflect the fact that many low-income persons receive noncash benefits such as food stamps, medicaid, and public housing. The index is based on the Department of Agriculture's 1961 Economy Food Plan and reflects the different consumption requirements of families based on their size and composition. The poverty thresholds are updated every year to reflect changes in the Consumer Price Index. The following technical changes to the thresholds were made in 1981: (1) distinctions based on sex of householder have been eliminated, (2) separate thresholds for farm families have been dropped, and (3) the matrix has been expanded to families of nine or more persons from the old cut-off of seven or more persons. These changes have been incorporated in the calculation of poverty data beginning with 1981. Besides the Census Bureau Web site at <http://www.census.gov/hhes/www/poverty.html>, information on poverty guidelines and research may be found at the U.S. Department of Human Services Web site at <http://aspe.hhs.gov/poverty/poverty.shtml>.

In the recent past, the Census Bureau has published a number of technical papers that presented experimental poverty estimates based on income definitions that counted the value of selected government noncash benefits. The Census Bureau has also published annual reports on after-tax income. The annual income and poverty reports (P60 Series) have brought together the benefit and tax data that previously appeared in the separate reports. These reports have shown the distribution of income among households and the prevalence of poverty under the official definition of money income and under definitions that add or subtract income components. In addition, in July 1999, the Census Bureau released a report (P60-205) that showed the effect of using experimental poverty following the recommendations of a National Academy of Sciences panel on redefining our nation's poverty measure.

Statistical reliability—For a discussion of statistical collection and estimation, sampling procedures, and measures of statistical reliability pertaining to Census Bureau data, see Appendix III.

Figure 13.1
Consumer Expenditures Per Consumer Unit by Major Types of Expenditures: 2001

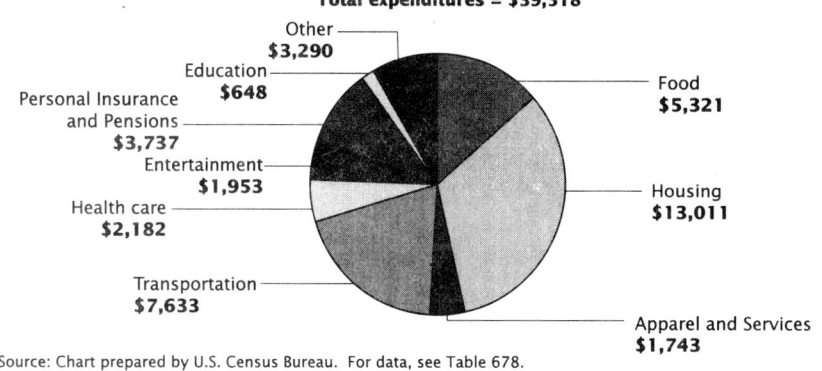

Source: Chart prepared by U.S. Census Bureau. For data, see Table 678.

Figure 13.2
Median Income of Households by Race and Hispanic Origin, in Constant (2001) Dollars: 1990 to 2001

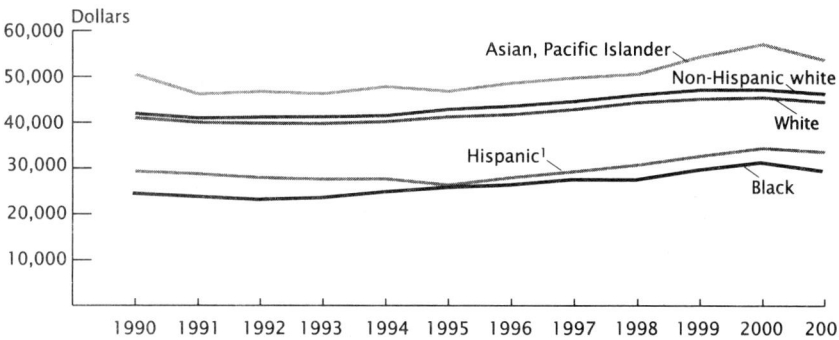

[1] People of Hispanic origin may be of any race.

Source: Chart prepared by U.S. Census Bureau. For data, see Table 684.

Figure 13.3
Percent of Children Below Poverty Level by Race and Hispanic Origin: 1990 to 2001

[1] People of Hispanic origin may be of any race.

Source: Chart prepared by U.S. Census Bureau. For data, see Table 701.

Income, Expenditures, and Wealth 437

U.S. Census Bureau, Statistical Abstract of the United States: 2003

No. 659. Gross Domestic Product in Current and Real (1996) Dollars: 1960 to 2002

[In billions of dollars (527.4 represents $527,400,000,000). For explanation of gross domestic product and chained dollars, see text, this section]

Item	1960	1970	1980	1985	1989	1990	1991	1992	1993	1994	1995	1996	1997	1998	1999	2000	2001	2002
CURRENT DOLLARS																		
Gross domestic product	527.4	1,039.7	2,795.6	4,213.0	5,489.1	5,803.2	5,986.2	6,318.9	6,642.3	7,054.3	7,400.5	7,813.2	8,318.4	8,781.5	9,274.3	9,824.6	10,082.2	10,446.2
Personal consumption expenditures	332.3	648.9	1,762.9	2,712.6	3,596.7	3,831.5	3,971.2	4,209.7	4,454.7	4,716.4	4,969.0	5,237.5	5,529.3	5,856.0	6,246.5	6,683.7	6,987.0	7,303.7
Durable goods	43.3	85.0	214.2	363.3	467.8	467.6	443.0	470.8	513.4	560.8	589.7	616.5	642.5	693.2	755.9	803.9	835.9	871.9
Nondurable goods	152.9	272.0	696.1	928.8	1,165.4	1,246.1	1,278.8	1,322.9	1,375.2	1,438.0	1,497.3	1,574.1	1,641.6	1,708.5	1,830.1	1,972.9	2,041.3	2,115.0
Services	136.1	292.0	852.7	1,420.6	1,963.5	2,117.8	2,249.4	2,415.9	2,566.1	2,717.6	2,882.0	3,047.0	3,245.2	3,454.3	3,660.5	3,906.9	4,109.9	4,316.8
Gross private domestic investment	78.9	152.4	477.9	736.3	872.9	861.7	800.2	866.6	955.1	1,097.1	1,143.8	1,242.7	1,390.5	1,538.7	1,636.7	1,755.4	1,586.0	1,593.2
Fixed investment	75.7	150.4	484.2	714.5	845.2	847.2	800.4	851.6	934.0	1,034.6	1,110.7	1,212.7	1,327.7	1,465.6	1,577.2	1,691.8	1,646.3	1,589.3
Change in business inventories	3.2	2.0	−6.3	21.8	27.7	14.5	−0.2	15.0	21.1	62.6	33.0	30.0	62.9	73.1	59.5	63.6	−60.3	3.9
Net exports of goods and services	2.4	1.2	−14.9	−114.2	−80.7	−71.4	−20.7	−27.9	−60.5	−87.1	−84.3	−89.0	−89.3	−151.7	−249.9	−365.5	−348.9	−423.6
Exports	25.3	57.0	278.9	303.0	509.0	557.2	601.6	636.8	658.0	725.1	818.6	874.2	966.4	964.9	989.3	1,101.1	1,034.1	1,014.9
Imports	22.8	55.8	293.8	417.2	589.7	628.6	622.3	664.6	718.5	812.1	902.8	963.1	1,055.8	1,116.7	1,239.2	1,466.6	1,383.0	1,438.5
Government consumption expenditures and gross investment	113.8	237.1	569.7	878.3	1,100.2	1,181.4	1,235.5	1,270.5	1,293.0	1,327.9	1,372.0	1,421.9	1,487.9	1,538.5	1,641.0	1,751.0	1,858.0	1,972.9
Federal	65.9	116.4	245.3	413.4	482.6	508.4	527.4	534.5	527.3	521.1	521.5	531.6	538.2	539.2	565.0	589.2	628.1	693.7
National defense	55.2	90.9	169.6	312.4	363.2	374.9	384.5	378.5	364.9	355.1	350.6	357.0	352.6	349.1	364.3	374.9	399.9	447.4
State and local	47.9	120.7	324.4	464.9	617.7	673.0	708.1	736.0	765.7	806.8	850.5	890.4	949.7	999.3	1,076.0	1,161.8	1,229.9	1,279.2
CHAINED (1996) DOLLARS																		
Gross domestic product	2,376.7	3,578.0	4,900.9	5,717.1	6,591.8	6,707.9	6,676.4	6,880.0	7,062.6	7,347.7	7,543.8	7,813.2	8,159.5	8,508.9	8,859.0	9,191.4	9,214.5	9,439.9
Personal consumption expenditures	1,510.8	2,317.5	3,193.0	3,820.9	4,393.7	4,474.5	4,466.6	4,594.5	4,748.9	4,928.1	5,075.6	5,237.5	5,423.9	5,683.7	5,964.5	6,223.9	6,377.2	6,576.0
Durable goods	(NA)	(NA)	(NA)	491.7	491.7	487.1	454.9	479.0	518.3	560.8	583.5	616.5	657.3	726.7	812.5	878.9	931.9	999.9
Nondurable goods	(NA)	(NA)	(NA)	(NA)	1,351.0	1,369.6	1,364.0	1,389.7	1,430.3	1,485.1	1,529.0	1,574.1	1,619.9	1,686.4	1,765.1	1,833.8	1,869.8	1,929.5
Services	(NA)	436.2	655.3	863.4	2,546.0	2,616.2	2,651.8	2,729.7	2,802.5	2,886.2	2,963.4	3,047.0	3,147.0	3,273.4	3,395.4	3,524.5	3,594.9	3,675.6
Gross private domestic investment	272.8	(NA)	(NA)	(NA)	936.5	907.3	829.5	899.8	977.9	1,107.0	1,140.6	1,242.7	1,393.3	1,558.0	1,660.5	1,762.9	1,574.6	1,589.6
Fixed investment	(NA)	(NA)	(NA)	(NA)	911.2	894.6	832.5	886.5	958.4	1,045.9	1,109.2	1,212.7	1,328.6	1,480.0	1,595.2	1,691.9	1,627.4	1,577.3
Change in business inventories	(NA)	(NA)	(NA)	(NA)	29.6	16.5	−1.0	17.1	20.0	66.8	30.4	30.0	63.8	76.7	62.8	65.0	−61.4	5.2
Net exports of goods and services	3.2	(NA)	(NA)	(NA)	−79.4	−56.5	−15.8	−19.8	−59.1	−86.5	−78.4	−89.0	−113.3	−221.1	−320.5	−398.8	−415.9	−488.5
Exports	87.5	159.3	(NA)	341.6	529.4	575.7	613.2	651.0	672.7	732.8	808.2	874.2	981.5	1,002.4	1,036.3	1,137.2	1,076.1	1,058.8
Imports	108.0	223.1	(NA)	490.7	608.8	632.2	629.0	670.8	731.8	819.4	886.6	963.1	1,094.8	1,223.5	1,356.8	1,536.0	1,492.0	1,547.4
Government consumption expenditures and gross investment	661.3	931.1	1,020.9	1,190.5	1,343.5	1,387.3	1,403.4	1,410.0	1,398.8	1,400.1	1,406.4	1,421.9	1,455.4	1,483.3	1,540.6	1,582.5	1,640.4	1,712.8
Federal	(NA)	(NA)	(NA)	(NA)	594.7	606.8	604.9	595.1	572.0	551.3	536.5	531.6	529.6	525.4	537.7	544.4	570.6	613.3
National defense	(NA)	(NA)	(NA)	(NA)	443.3	443.2	438.4	417.1	394.7	375.9	361.9	357.0	347.7	341.6	348.8	348.7	366.0	400.0
State and local	(NA)	(NA)	(NA)	(NA)	749.5	781.1	798.9	815.3	827.0	848.9	869.9	890.4	925.8	957.7	1,002.4	1,037.4	1,069.4	1,099.7

NA Not available.

Source: U.S. Bureau of Economic Analysis, *National Income and Product Accounts, 1929-97*; and *Survey of Current Business*, May 2003. See also <http://www.bea.doc.gov/bea/dn/nipaweb/SelectTable.asp?Selected=N> (released as 30 May 2003).

No. 660. Gross Domestic Product in Current and Real (1996) Dollars by Industry: 1990 to 2001

[In billions of dollars (5,803.2 represents $5,803,200,000,000). Data are based on the 1987 SIC. Data include nonfactor charges (capital consumption allowances, indirect business taxes, etc.) as well as factor charges against gross product; corporate profits and capital consumption allowances have been shifted from a company to an establishment basis]

Industry	Current dollars 1990	1995	2000	2001	Chained (1996) dollars 1990	1995	2000	2001
Gross domestic product [1]	5,803.2	7,400.5	9,824.6	10,082.2	6,707.9	7,543.8	9,191.4	9,214.5
Private industries	4,996.7	6,411.1	8,606.9	8,800.8	5,736.8	6,508.7	8,157.8	8,189.4
Agriculture, forestry, and fishing	108.3	109.8	134.3	140.7	118.5	123.1	166.7	163.9
Farms	79.6	73.2	77.8	80.6	84.2	85.5	120.5	114.3
Agricultural services	28.7	36.7	56.5	60.1	34.6	37.6	47.6	49.1
Mining	111.9	95.7	133.1	139.0	105.8	113.0	101.9	106.8
Metal mining	5.2	6.5	5.2	5.7	4.4	5.5	8.0	9.6
Coal mining	11.8	10.7	9.2	10.5	7.5	10.1	11.9	13.9
Oil and gas extraction	87.1	69.3	106.5	110.3	87.5	88.6	70.5	72.9
Nonmetallic minerals, except fuels	7.8	9.1	12.2	12.6	8.1	9.1	12.2	12.4
Construction	248.7	290.3	461.3	480.0	290.7	299.6	378.0	371.9
Manufacturing	1,040.6	1,289.1	1,520.3	1,423.0	1,102.3	1,284.7	1,585.4	1,490.3
Durable goods	586.6	729.8	886.4	812.8	585.1	714.9	1,044.3	990.1
Lumber and wood products	32.2	42.3	42.1	39.2	45.1	41.6	41.8	39.0
Furniture and fixtures	15.6	19.5	26.1	25.0	18.1	20.7	24.1	22.4
Stone, clay, and glass products	25.3	32.4	40.6	36.7	29.4	32.8	37.2	33.9
Primary metal industries	43.2	53.0	50.2	45.1	43.7	49.6	56.1	53.5
Fabricated metal products	69.4	87.2	109.6	100.8	76.1	90.8	102.7	92.3
Industrial machinery	118.2	132.8	173.1	148.2	93.5	124.7	249.2	222.5
Electronic & other electric equipment	105.7	146.9	162.0	143.1	68.6	128.7	311.8	335.2
Motor vehicles and equipment	47.3	98.2	120.4	111.4	68.7	103.2	117.3	108.5
Other transportation equipment	60.5	47.7	66.3	71.4	75.7	49.4	60.5	62.0
Instruments and related products	49.3	47.2	63.5	61.7	68.9	52.6	51.0	46.1
Misc. manufacturing industries	19.8	22.7	32.5	30.2	22.8	23.3	31.3	28.5
Nondurable goods	454.0	559.2	633.9	610.2	520.2	570.3	558.0	518.3
Food and kindred products	96.4	121.1	127.0	123.7	109.5	133.3	111.2	106.5
Tobacco manufactures	11.9	15.1	21.2	21.1	14.5	15.7	6.2	5.0
Textile mill products	22.0	24.8	23.8	22.1	22.8	26.0	23.2	20.7
Apparel and other textile products	25.4	27.3	24.7	23.3	27.3	28.0	23.3	22.3
Paper and allied products	45.0	58.9	60.2	55.9	52.5	52.2	53.1	49.7
Printing and publishing	73.1	80.8	106.5	100.2	102.9	89.2	90.1	80.8
Chemicals and allied products	109.9	150.8	169.0	163.5	131.1	148.0	162.8	157.8
Petroleum and coal products	31.7	29.0	38.5	40.6	22.9	26.9	29.9	24.6
Rubber and misc. plastic products	33.9	46.1	59.3	56.6	34.0	47.0	61.3	57.0
Leather and leather products	4.7	5.3	3.7	3.3	5.2	5.3	3.6	3.1
Transportation and public utilities	490.9	642.6	809.3	819.5	525.0	634.5	781.9	780.5
Transportation	177.4	233.4	313.7	306.1	180.6	225.1	282.5	270.3
Railroad transportation	19.8	23.6	24.8	25.8	18.1	22.7	25.0	25.0
Local & interurban passenger transit	9.1	12.4	18.3	19.1	12.8	13.2	17.2	17.2
Trucking and warehousing	69.4	89.0	123.3	126.0	68.1	86.6	103.4	99.3
Water transportation	10.0	11.6	15.0	15.7	10.2	11.3	13.4	13.3
Transportation by air	45.3	67.7	91.9	80.2	46.9	62.9	84.8	78.3
Pipelines, except natural gas	5.5	5.5	6.3	6.5	5.7	5.0	6.4	6.0
Transportation services	18.2	23.5	34.1	32.9	19.5	23.4	32.4	31.2
Communications	148.1	202.3	279.1	291.5	155.2	202.4	286.7	321.9
Telephone and telegraph	119.4	151.6	208.0	218.5	117.1	147.6	236.7	265.7
Radio and television broadcasting	28.7	50.7	71.1	72.9	37.5	55.2	53.4	60.0
Electric, gas, and sanitary services	165.4	206.9	216.5	221.9	190.0	207.2	213.9	194.3
Wholesale trade	376.1	500.6	696.8	680.7	395.1	483.0	750.2	748.7
Retail trade	507.8	646.8	887.3	931.8	559.5	641.4	909.2	951.2
Finance, insurance, and real estate	1,010.3	1,347.2	1,976.7	2,076.9	1,250.6	1,393.0	1,793.5	1,843.5
Depository institutions	171.3	227.4	361.1	359.8	244.0	242.4	287.4	290.4
Nondepository institutions	23.3	34.1	69.5	88.8	26.3	33.4	79.0	91.9
Security and commodity brokers	42.3	77.7	150.8	175.0	42.0	76.5	216.8	245.1
Insurance carriers	64.6	120.2	182.4	170.1	112.2	129.9	146.0	141.2
Insurance agents, brokers & services	37.7	47.2	61.6	66.5	61.4	49.9	51.9	53.5
Real estate	665.7	832.6	1,123.7	1,171.7	763.4	852.8	1,016.7	1,022.0
Services	1,071.5	1,462.4	2,116.4	2,226.6	1,361.9	1,510.4	1,826.0	1,843.3
Hotels and other lodging places	46.3	61.7	87.4	88.4	55.2	62.7	68.4	65.6
Personal services	38.0	46.7	59.3	62.7	46.4	48.1	52.9	53.3
Business services	203.9	302.0	534.4	544.1	241.3	313.9	460.1	459.4
Auto repair, services, and garages	50.3	65.1	94.9	99.5	61.9	65.9	84.8	87.5
Motion pictures	17.7	22.4	32.5	35.5	21.2	23.6	27.9	29.5
Amusement and recreation services	36.5	53.5	76.6	79.3	45.0	55.6	63.6	62.6
Health services	314.4	433.1	548.5	589.8	423.2	444.3	487.9	501.2
Legal services	82.7	101.1	134.4	145.6	108.8	105.1	116.8	120.2
Educational services	39.6	55.7	77.9	84.4	50.3	58.6	64.1	66.5
Social services & membership organization	30.1	47.4	67.7	74.7	38.0	49.3	56.0	58.4
Other services	149.2	194.4	300.3	320.7	191.3	199.9	263.9	267.1
Government	806.6	989.5	1,217.7	1,281.3	1,008.2	1,017.1	1,088.8	1,107.5
Federal	300.2	342.3	389.5	396.2	384.7	354.3	355.0	350.9
State and local	506.4	647.2	828.2	885.1	624.1	662.9	733.6	756.1

[1] Includes private households and statistical discrepancy, not shown separately.

Source: U.S. Bureau of Economic Analysis, *National Income and Product Accounts, 1929-97*; and Survey of Current Business, November 2002. See also <http://www.bea.doc.gov/bea/ARTICLES/2002/11November/1102GDPbyIndustry.pdf> (released 28 October 2002).

No. 661. Gross Domestic Product in Current and Real (1996) Dollars by Type of Product and Sector: 1990 to 2002

[In billions of dollars (5,803.2 represents $5,803,200,000,000). For explanation of chained dollars, see text, this section]

Type of product and sector	1990	1994	1995	1996	1997	1998	1999	2000	2001	2002
CURRENT DOLLARS										
Gross domestic product	5,803.2	7,054.3	7,400.5	7,813.2	8,318.4	8,781.5	9,274.3	9,824.6	10,082.2	10,446.2
PRODUCT										
Goods	2,266.4	2,680.2	2,798.1	2,951.3	3,145.4	3,305.4	3,473.4	3,651.0	3,593.7	3,694.1
Durable goods	1,002.0	1,197.3	1,273.3	1,351.0	1,469.3	1,569.0	1,649.6	1,735.0	1,611.4	1,644.8
Nondurable goods	1,264.4	1,482.9	1,524.8	1,600.3	1,676.1	1,736.4	1,823.8	1,915.9	1,982.3	2,049.3
Services	3,010.8	3,782.6	3,985.1	4,191.0	4,442.0	4,678.6	4,947.1	5,259.2	5,535.1	5,814.7
Structures	526.0	591.6	617.3	670.9	730.9	797.5	853.8	914.5	953.3	937.5
SECTOR										
Business	4,842.0	5,886.6	6,190.1	6,556.0	7,010.5	7,418.0	7,847.7	8,311.4	8,482.7	8,759.1
Nonfarm	4,762.4	5,803.0	6,116.9	6,463.8	6,922.2	7,337.4	7,772.5	8,233.6	8,402.1	8,680.2
Farm	79.6	83.6	73.2	92.2	88.3	80.6	75.2	77.8	80.6	78.9
Households and institutions	237.9	313.3	330.3	348.6	363.2	383.8	403.1	431.1	459.6	486.1
General government	723.3	854.5	880.1	908.7	944.6	979.8	1,023.5	1,082.1	1,139.8	1,201.1
Federal	259.7	287.4	286.8	292.0	295.4	298.6	307.6	323.4	332.8	355.6
State and local	463.6	567.0	593.3	616.7	649.2	681.2	715.9	758.7	807.0	845.5
CHAINED (1996) DOLLARS										
Gross domestic product	6,707.9	7,347.7	7,543.8	7,813.2	8,159.5	8,508.9	8,859.0	9,191.4	9,214.5	9,439.9
PRODUCT										
Goods	2,404.2	2,708.3	2,813.8	2,951.3	3,145.9	3,332.3	3,510.3	3,674.3	3,589.9	3,710.1
Durable goods	1,007.1	1,179.0	1,264.8	1,351.0	1,491.1	1,634.0	1,756.7	1,870.4	1,754.9	1,822.8
Nondurable goods	1,400.4	1,531.1	1,549.5	1,600.3	1,655.3	1,701.2	1,759.2	1,813.2	1,834.2	1,888.2
Services	3,692.3	4,010.3	4,097.5	4,191.0	4,307.6	4,431.0	4,577.6	4,728.9	4,826.4	4,959.9
Structures	614.8	630.7	632.9	670.9	706.9	748.7	777.2	797.9	797.1	775.0
SECTOR										
Business	5,523.5	6,111.8	6,295.9	6,556.0	6,881.8	7,208.9	7,542.5	7,846.8	7,838.3	8,032.8
Nonfarm	5,440.8	6,013.7	6,210.3	6,463.8	6,778.9	7,107.7	7,434.4	7,729.2	7,724.7	7,917.7
Farm	84.2	100.3	85.5	92.2	103.6	100.3	108.1	120.5	114.7	114.7
Households and institutions	291.5	330.9	341.5	348.6	360.5	371.9	379.2	388.9	398.7	407.7
General government	895.1	905.6	906.7	908.7	917.3	928.8	939.0	958.6	978.5	1,000.9
Federal	331.4	309.9	299.1	292.0	287.9	286.2	285.2	289.4	291.3	297.5
State and local	564.7	596.1	607.7	616.7	629.3	642.5	653.7	669.0	687.0	703.1

Source: U.S. Bureau of Economic Analysis, *National Income and Product Accounts, 1929-97;* and Survey of Current Business, May 2003. See also <http://www.bea.doc.gov/bea/dn/nipaweb/SelectTable.asp?Selected=N> (released as 30 May 2003).

No. 662. GDP Components in Current Dollars—Annual Percent Change: 1990 to 2002

[Change from previous year; for 1990, change from 1989 and for 1994, change from 1993. Minus sign (-) indicates decrease]

Item	1990	1994	1995	1996	1997	1998	1999	2000	2001	2002
Gross domestic product (GDP)	5.7	6.2	4.9	5.6	6.5	5.6	5.6	5.9	2.6	3.6
Personal consumption expenditures	6.5	5.9	5.4	5.4	5.6	5.9	6.7	7.0	4.5	4.5
Durable goods	-	9.2	5.2	4.5	4.2	7.9	9.0	6.4	4	4.3
Nondurable goods	6.9	4.6	4.1	5.1	4.3	4.1	7.1	7.8	3.5	3.6
Services	7.9	5.9	6.0	5.7	6.5	6.4	6.0	6.7	5.2	5.0
Gross private domestic investment	-1.3	14.9	4.2	8.7	11.9	10.7	6.4	7.2	-9.7	0.5
Fixed investment	0.2	10.8	7.4	9.2	9.5	10.4	7.6	7.3	-2.7	-3.5
Nonresidential	2.8	9.7	10.2	9.0	11.1	10.2	6.6	7.9	-5.1	-7.0
Structures	4.7	4.5	9.1	9.9	13.7	10.4	0.5	10.8	3.3	-17.0
Equipment and software	1.9	11.6	10.6	8.7	10.3	10.1	8.7	6.9	-7.8	-3.3
Residential	-6.5	13.6	-0.1	9.7	4.8	11.0	10.8	5.5	4.4	6.1
Exports of goods and services	9.5	10.2	12.9	6.8	10.6	-0.2	2.5	11.3	-6.1	-1.9
Exports of goods	7.2	10.8	14.6	5.9	11.4	-1.1	2.4	12.6	-6.6	-4.1
Exports of services	15.5	8.7	8.9	9.0	8.5	2.2	3.0	8.3	-4.9	3.6
Imports of goods and servics	6.6	13.0	11.2	6.7	9.6	5.8	11.0	18.3	-5.7	4.0
Imports of goods	4.9	14.2	12.0	6.7	9.5	5.1	12.4	18.9	-6.1	2.1
Imports of services	14.6	7.7	7.2	6.6	10.3	9.4	3.9	15.3	-3.4	14.2
Govt. consumption expenditures and gross investment	7.4	2.7	3.3	3.6	4.6	3.4	6.7	6.7	6.1	6.2
Federal	5.4	-1.2	0.1	1.9	1.2	0.2	4.8	4.3	6.6	10.4
National defense	3.2	-2.7	-1.3	1.8	-1.2	-1.0	4.4	2.9	6.7	11.9
Nondefense	12.0	2.2	3.0	2.1	6.3	2.4	5.6	6.8	6.5	7.9
State and local	9.0	5.4	5.4	4.7	6.7	5.2	7.7	8.0	5.9	4.0

- Represents or rounds to zero.

Source: U.S. Bureau of Economic Analysis, *National Income and Product Accounts of the United States, 1929-97,* Volume 1; and Survey of Current Business, May 2003. See also <http://www.bea.doc.gov/bea/dn/nipaweb/SelectTable.asp?Selected=N> (released as 30 May 2003).

No. 663. Gross State Product in Current and Real (1996) Dollars by State: 1990 to 2001

[In billions of dollars (5,706.7 represents $5,706,700,000,000). For definition of gross state product or chained dollars, see text, this section]

State	Current dollars					Chained (1996) dollars [1]				
	1990	1995	1999	2000	2001	1990	1995	1999	2000	2001
United States.....	5,706.7	7,309.5	9,251.5	9,891.2	10,137.2	6,630.7	7,434.0	8,882.6	9,298.2	9,335.4
Alabama............	71.6	95.5	115.1	119.3	121.5	83.2	96.6	110.4	112.3	112.0
Alaska.............	24.8	24.8	25.6	28.1	28.6	27.8	26.4	25.1	24.7	24.5
Arizona............	68.9	104.6	144.6	153.5	160.7	79.0	105.4	141.4	148.8	153.7
Arkansas..........	38.4	53.8	65.0	66.8	67.9	44.1	54.7	63.2	64.0	63.7
California..........	798.9	925.9	1,213.4	1,330.0	1,359.3	927.6	941.9	1,169.8	1,258.4	1,260.0
Colorado...........	74.7	109.0	152.3	169.3	173.8	87.0	111.2	145.5	158.2	159.3
Connecticut........	98.9	118.6	149.0	161.9	166.2	117.3	120.8	142.7	152.0	153.0
Delaware..........	20.3	27.6	34.7	37.2	40.5	25.0	28.2	32.0	33.4	35.7
District of Columbia....	40.4	48.4	55.4	60.0	64.5	50.9	49.7	51.3	54.1	56.1
Florida.............	258.3	344.8	442.6	471.6	491.5	303.7	350.6	420.2	438.6	446.5
Georgia............	141.4	203.5	276.5	295.5	299.9	164.8	206.4	261.5	274.9	273.9
Hawaii.............	32.3	37.2	40.7	42.5	43.7	38.1	37.9	38.0	38.9	38.8
Idaho..............	17.7	27.2	34.6	36.8	36.9	20.0	27.4	34.7	37.1	36.8
Illinois.............	275.8	359.5	440.9	466.3	475.5	317.9	364.1	424.9	441.9	441.8
Indiana............	110.8	148.4	181.3	189.8	189.9	127.0	150.0	175.4	181.5	178.2
Iowa...............	55.8	71.7	85.5	89.7	90.9	63.4	73.1	84.4	87.5	87.0
Kansas............	51.5	64.1	80.2	84.5	87.2	59.8	65.6	77.5	79.9	80.7
Kentucky..........	67.9	91.5	112.4	117.2	120.3	77.5	92.8	106.6	109.5	110.1
Louisiana..........	94.9	112.2	133.9	145.0	148.7	108.0	116.5	129.5	125.7	125.3
Maine..............	23.5	28.0	34.1	36.3	37.4	27.8	28.3	32.4	33.7	34.0
Maryland...........	115.0	139.5	173.8	185.0	195.0	137.1	142.1	164.0	170.7	175.3
Massachusetts.....	160.0	197.5	257.8	283.1	287.8	187.2	200.5	247.4	266.8	265.7
Michigan...........	190.8	254.2	312.1	323.7	320.5	225.1	258.3	299.5	306.4	297.5
Minnesota.........	100.4	131.8	171.5	186.1	188.1	116.6	133.8	165.6	176.8	175.4
Mississippi........	39.2	54.6	64.2	66.2	67.1	44.9	55.4	61.8	62.3	61.5
Missouri...........	104.8	139.5	168.9	177.1	181.5	122.8	141.9	161.4	166.7	167.4
Montana...........	13.4	17.5	20.6	21.7	22.6	15.5	17.9	19.9	20.5	20.7
Nebraska..........	33.5	44.1	53.5	55.6	57.0	38.6	45.2	52.0	53.5	53.6
Nevada............	31.6	49.4	69.5	75.5	79.2	37.1	50.1	64.4	68.2	69.5
New Hampshire....	23.9	32.4	43.4	47.4	47.2	27.3	32.6	42.5	46.1	45.3
New Jersey........	217.0	271.4	332.2	357.5	365.4	253.6	275.0	316.0	332.9	332.9
New Mexico........	27.2	42.2	49.2	52.6	55.4	29.4	42.7	50.3	52.4	54.9
New York..........	502.2	597.6	743.9	798.4	826.5	593.4	609.1	717.7	756.6	766.5
North Carolina.....	141.1	194.6	260.6	272.9	275.6	162.6	197.5	242.9	249.8	246.3
North Dakota.......	11.5	14.5	17.1	18.6	19.0	13.2	15.0	16.8	17.8	17.8
Ohio...............	230.0	295.7	357.4	370.6	373.7	265.9	299.2	345.0	352.7	349.3
Oklahoma..........	57.8	70.0	85.4	90.9	93.9	66.1	71.8	83.0	85.1	85.9
Oregon............	57.8	81.1	110.4	121.4	120.1	66.5	81.3	111.4	124.8	124.8
Pennsylvania......	249.9	318.8	380.2	399.5	408.4	291.5	322.9	362.5	374.0	374.5
Rhode Island.......	21.6	25.7	31.9	36.1	36.9	25.5	26.2	30.1	33.3	33.5
South Carolina.....	66.1	86.9	106.8	112.2	115.2	76.0	87.8	102.4	106.1	106.5
South Dakota......	13.0	18.3	21.7	23.5	24.3	15.1	18.7	21.5	22.9	23.2
Tennessee.........	95.0	136.8	170.8	177.4	182.5	110.5	138.6	162.7	166.6	168.4
Texas..............	388.1	513.9	678.8	738.3	763.9	439.5	527.7	660.5	688.5	698.5
Utah...............	31.4	46.3	62.6	68.4	70.4	36.3	47.0	59.7	63.6	63.9
Vermont............	11.8	14.0	17.2	18.1	19.1	13.4	14.1	16.6	17.4	18.0
Virginia.............	148.2	189.0	241.5	260.8	273.1	174.5	192.5	224.5	236.9	241.5
Washington........	115.5	151.3	208.5	218.1	223.0	136.6	154.0	198.3	202.8	202.5
West Virginia......	28.3	36.3	40.5	40.9	42.4	31.8	36.6	39.1	38.7	39.0
Wisconsin.........	100.4	133.7	164.9	173.0	177.4	115.3	135.2	160.2	166.0	167.3
Wyoming..........	13.4	14.9	17.0	19.1	20.4	14.3	15.6	16.9	17.5	18.3

[1] For chained (1996) dollar estimates, states will not add to U.S. total.

Source: U.S. Bureau of Economic Analysis, Survey of Current Business, June 2003; and Internet site at <http://www.bea.doc.gov/bea/regional/gsp/> and <http://www.bea.doc.gov/bea/newsrel/gsp0503.pdf> (released 22 May 2003).

No. 664. Gross State Product in Chained (1996) Dollars by Industry and State: 2001

[In billions of dollars (9,335.4 represents $9,335,400,000,000). For definition of gross state product or chained dollars, see text, this section. Industries based on 1987 Standard Industrial Classification]

State	Total [1]	Farms, forestry, fisheries [2]	Construction	Manufacturing	Transportation, public utilities	Wholesale trade	Retail trade	Finance, insurance, real estate	Services	Government [3]
United States [4]	9,335.4	163.9	371.9	1,490.3	780.5	748.7	951.2	1,843.6	1,843.3	1,047.4
Alabama	112.0	2.9	4.6	21.9	9.6	8.7	12.8	15.4	18.3	16.6
Alaska	24.5	0.4	1.1	0.9	4.3	0.9	2.0	2.8	3.2	4.8
Arizona	153.7	2.9	7.5	29.4	10.6	11.6	18.0	27.3	28.5	17.4
Arkansas	63.7	2.9	2.6	13.3	6.6	5.0	8.3	7.2	9.6	7.6
California	1,260.0	27.5	44.7	184.0	89.1	98.3	129.7	279.9	270.5	130.6
Colorado	159.3	3.2	9.2	15.3	19.5	11.8	17.3	28.3	34.6	17.7
Connecticut	153.0	1.1	4.6	25.4	9.4	11.0	13.2	46.0	29.6	12.8
Delaware	35.7	0.5	1.2	4.8	1.8	1.7	2.7	14.9	5.2	2.9
District of Columbia	56.1	-	0.4	0.7	3.2	0.8	1.8	9.9	19.7	19.7
Florida	446.5	8.5	20.9	30.3	37.9	41.1	57.2	95.3	104.0	51.4
Georgia	273.9	5.0	11.9	39.9	32.9	29.3	29.0	42.8	50.7	32.0
Hawaii	38.8	0.6	1.5	1.0	3.9	1.8	5.0	8.9	8.1	8.1
Idaho	36.8	2.7	2.0	9.1	2.7	2.5	4.0	3.9	5.5	4.5
Illinois	441.8	4.9	18.3	73.7	38.1	40.8	39.8	93.8	89.6	41.6
Indiana	178.2	3.0	7.7	53.7	13.0	12.8	17.9	23.6	28.4	17.2
Iowa	87.0	4.6	3.1	20.8	7.0	6.9	8.4	12.6	13.4	9.7
Kansas	80.7	3.1	3.1	13.3	10.9	7.2	8.7	10.1	12.9	10.3
Kentucky	110.1	3.1	4.4	27.9	9.2	8.2	11.6	12.2	16.7	14.3
Louisiana	125.3	1.5	5.0	15.3	11.8	8.7	12.8	17.0	20.6	15.0
Maine	34.0	0.7	1.3	5.2	2.3	2.4	4.6	6.2	6.6	4.6
Maryland	175.3	1.9	8.8	14.1	13.6	12.9	17.3	37.1	40.2	29.6
Massachusetts	265.7	1.5	10.5	38.5	15.4	21.4	23.2	66.6	66.3	22.3
Michigan	297.5	3.3	12.4	75.5	19.3	24.9	32.0	43.7	55.2	30.1
Minnesota	175.4	4.0	7.7	31.1	12.7	16.9	18.7	32.1	33.7	17.4
Mississippi	61.5	2.3	2.4	12.0	5.9	4.3	7.5	7.0	9.9	9.9
Missouri	167.4	3.0	7.5	30.2	17.0	14.6	17.9	26.2	32.0	18.5
Montana	20.7	1.1	1.0	1.4	2.3	1.5	2.4	2.8	4.0	3.3
Nebraska	53.6	3.7	2.1	7.4	5.9	4.8	5.1	7.7	9.6	7.0
Nevada	69.5	0.6	5.8	3.0	5.5	4.0	8.7	12.9	19.9	7.1
New Hampshire	45.3	0.4	1.8	9.5	2.6	3.7	5.0	10.3	8.4	3.3
New Jersey	332.9	2.0	12.2	40.3	31.7	37.2	29.6	80.7	69.1	30.8
New Mexico	54.9	1.6	1.9	13.9	3.9	2.4	5.1	6.4	8.4	8.6
New York	766.5	3.9	21.2	76.6	58.2	51.7	57.6	272.0	157.3	69.6
North Carolina	246.3	6.3	10.9	51.6	17.6	18.4	25.6	45.4	39.8	30.9
North Dakota	17.8	1.4	0.7	1.8	1.8	1.8	1.9	2.4	3.0	2.6
Ohio	349.8	4.0	12.8	83.8	24.3	29.2	38.0	57.6	60.9	36.7
Oklahoma	85.9	2.5	3.0	13.6	8.4	6.2	10.0	10.3	14.6	13.6
Oregon	124.8	3.5	4.6	48.0	7.2	9.3	10.3	15.3	18.1	12.6
Pennsylvania	374.5	4.5	14.3	71.2	32.7	27.9	37.8	68.1	80.0	35.6
Rhode Island	33.5	0.2	1.5	4.3	2.2	2.0	3.4	9.5	6.6	3.7
South Carolina	106.5	1.7	5.3	24.0	9.4	7.7	12.5	14.4	16.1	15.4
South Dakota	23.2	2.3	0.7	3.1	1.6	1.9	2.5	4.6	3.5	2.8
Tennessee	168.4	2.2	6.3	34.7	14.3	14.5	20.7	23.9	32.9	18.6
Texas	698.5	11.1	29.3	102.9	79.2	63.4	75.7	101.5	129.9	73.4
Utah	63.9	1.1	3.4	8.0	5.2	4.7	7.1	12.3	12.0	8.9
Vermont	18.0	0.5	0.7	3.7	1.3	1.2	2.0	3.1	3.6	2.2
Virginia	241.5	2.7	10.3	26.0	22.1	16.0	23.2	45.4	53.5	41.7
Washington	202.5	5.4	8.5	26.4	17.4	16.7	22.5	35.8	43.3	26.5
West Virginia	39.0	0.4	1.7	5.1	4.2	2.5	4.4	4.3	6.9	6.1
Wisconsin	167.3	4.4	6.7	45.3	11.3	12.5	16.9	25.3	27.3	17.5
Wyoming	18.3	0.6	0.8	1.4	2.4	0.9	1.5	2.0	2.0	2.4

- Represents zero. [1] Includes mining not shown separately. [2] Includes agricultural services. [3] Includes federal civilian and military and state and local government. [4] States will not add to U.S. total as chained-dollar estimates are usually not additive.

Source: U.S. Bureau of Economic Analysis, Survey of Current Business, June 2003; and Internet site at <http://www.bea.doc.gov/bea/regional/gsp/> and <http://www.bea.doc.gov/bea/newsrel/gsp0503.pdf> (released 22 May 2003).

No. 665. Relation of GDP, GNP, Net National Product, National Income, Personal Income, Disposable Personal Income, and Personal Saving: 1990 to 2002

[In billions of dollars (5,803.2 represents $5,803,200,000,000). For definitions, see text, this section]

Item	1990	1995	1997	1998	1999	2000	2001	2002
Gross domestic product............	5,803.2	7,400.5	8,318.4	8,781.5	9,274.3	9,824.6	10,082.2	10,446.2
Plus: Income receipts from the rest of the world [1]............	188.3	232.3	281.3	286.1	316.9	383.4	316.9	278.0
Less: Income payments to the rest of the world [2]............	159.3	211.9	274.2	289.6	294.1	360.0	295.0	287.6
Equals: Gross national product......	5,832.2	7,420.9	8,325.4	8,778.1	9,297.1	9,848.0	10,104.1	10,436.7
Less: Consumption of fixed capital.....	711.3	911.7	1,013.3	1,072.0	1,145.2	1,228.9	1,329.3	1,393.5
Equals: Net national product [3]......	5,120.9	6,509.1	7,312.1	7,706.1	8,151.9	8,619.1	8,774.8	9,043.2
Less: Indirect business tax and nontax liability...........	447.3	594.6	646.2	681.3	712.9	753.6	774.8	800.4
Plus: Subsidies [4]............	25.3	22.2	19.1	23.5	32.5	34.1	47.3	32.5
Equals: National income [3].........	4,642.1	5,876.7	6,618.4	7,041.4	7,468.7	7,984.4	8,122.0	8,347.9
Less: Corporate profits [5].........	408.6	668.8	833.8	777.4	805.8	788.1	731.6	787.4
Net interest............	452.4	389.8	423.9	511.9	526.6	611.5	649.8	684.2
Contributions for social insurance....	410.1	533.2	587.8	623.3	660.4	701.3	726.1	747.5
Wage accruals less disbursements...	0.1	16.4	-2.9	-0.7	5.2	-	-	-
Plus: Personal interest income........	772.4	792.5	864.0	964.4	969.2	1,077.0	1,091.3	1,078.5
Personal dividend income.........	165.4	254.0	334.9	348.3	328.0	375.7	409.2	433.8
Government transfer payments to persons............	573.1	860.1	934.4	955.0	987.2	1,037.3	1,137.0	1,252.9
Business transfer payments to persons............	21.3	25.8	27.9	28.8	31.3	33.0	33.4	35.1
Equals: Personal income...........	4,903.2	6,200.9	6,937.0	7,426.0	7,786.5	8,406.6	8,685.3	8,929.1
Less: Personal tax and nontax payments.	609.6	778.3	968.8	1,070.4	1,159.1	1,286.4	1,292.1	1,113.6
Equals: Disposable personal income..	4,293.6	5,422.6	5,968.2	6,355.6	6,627.4	7,120.2	7,393.2	7,815.5
Less: Personal outlays............	3,959.3	5,120.2	5,715.3	6,054.1	6,453.3	6,918.6	7,223.5	7,524.5
Equals: Personal saving...........	334.3	302.4	252.9	301.5	174.0	201.5	169.7	291.0

- Represents zero or rounds to zero. [1] Consists largely of receipts by U.S. residents of interest and dividends and reinvested earnings of foreign affiliates of U.S. corporations. [2] Consists largely of payments to foreign residents of interest and dividends and reinvested earnings of U.S. affiliates of foreign corporations. [3] Includes items not shown separately. [4] Less current surplus of government enterprises. [5] With inventory valuation and capital consumption adjustments.

Source: U.S. Bureau of Economic Analysis, *National Income and Product Accounts, 1929-97;* and Survey of Current Business, May 2003. See also <http://www.bea.doc.gov/bea/dn/nipaweb/SelectTable.asp?Selected=N> (released as 30 May 2003).

No. 666. Selected Per Capita Income and Product Measures in Current and Real (1996) Dollars: 1960 to 2002

[In dollars. Based on U.S. Census Bureau estimated population including Armed Forces abroad; based on quarterly averages. For explanation of chained dollars, see text, this section]

Year	Current dollars					Chained (1996) dollars				
	Gross domestic product	Gross national product	Personal income	Disposable personal income	Personal consumption expenditures	Gross domestic product	Gross national product	Disposable personal income	Personal consumption expenditures
1960............	2,918	2,935	2,283	2,026	1,838	13,148	13,232	9,210	8,358
1965............	3,705	3,733	2,868	2,567	2,286	15,583	15,702	10,965	9,764
1970............	5,069	5,101	4,101	3,591	3,164	17,446	17,556	12,823	11,300
1975............	7,571	7,632	6,166	5,470	4,771	18,911	19,065	14,393	12,551
1980............	12,276	12,431	10,205	8,869	7,741	21,521	21,791	16,063	14,021
1981............	13,614	13,765	11,301	9,773	8,453	21,830	22,066	16,265	14,069
1982............	14,035	14,192	11,922	10,364	8,954	21,184	21,418	16,328	14,105
1983............	15,085	15,242	12,576	11,036	9,757	21,902	22,126	16,673	14,741
1984............	16,636	16,786	13,853	12,215	10,569	23,288	23,494	17,799	15,401
1985............	17,664	17,771	14,738	12,941	11,373	23,970	24,112	18,229	16,020
1986............	18,501	18,565	15,425	13,555	12,029	24,565	24,649	18,641	16,541
1987............	19,529	19,585	16,317	14,246	12,787	25,174	25,246	18,870	16,938
1988............	20,845	20,920	17,433	15,312	13,697	25,987	26,080	19,522	17,463
1989............	22,188	22,271	18,593	16,235	14,539	26,646	26,742	19,833	17,760
1990............	23,215	23,330	19,614	17,176	15,327	26,834	26,962	20,058	17,899
1991............	23,637	23,735	20,080	17,669	15,681	26,363	26,469	19,873	17,667
1992............	24,622	24,714	21,004	18,527	16,403	26,809	26,909	20,220	17,903
1993............	25,546	25,640	21,576	18,981	17,133	27,163	27,260	20,235	18,264
1994............	26,803	26,867	22,372	19,626	17,920	27,918	27,981	20,507	18,724
1995............	27,787	27,864	23,283	20,361	18,657	28,325	28,401	20,798	19,058
1996............	28,997	29,064	24,299	21,072	19,438	28,997	29,064	21,072	19,438
1997............	30,505	30,531	25,439	21,887	20,277	29,922	29,954	21,470	19,891
1998............	31,830	31,817	26,917	23,037	21,226	30,842	30,840	22,359	20,601
1999............	33,234	33,315	27,902	23,749	22,384	31,746	31,834	22,678	21,373
2000............	34,823	34,906	29,797	25,237	23,690	32,579	32,667	23,501	22,061
2001............	35,398	35,475	30,494	25,957	24,531	32,352	32,432	23,692	22,390
2002............	36,340	36,307	31,062	27,188	25,408	32,839	32,817	24,479	22,877

Source: U.S. Bureau of Economic Analysis, *National Income and Product Accounts, 1929-97;* and Survey of Current Business, May 2003. See also <http://www.bea.doc.gov/bea/dn/nipaweb/SelectTable.asp?Selected=N> (released as 30 May 2003).

No. 667. Personal Consumption Expenditures in Current and Real (1996) Dollars by Type: 1990 to 2001

[In billions of dollars (3,831.5 represents $3,831,500,000,000). For definition of "chained" dollars, see text, this section]

Expenditure	Current dollars				Chained (1996) dollars			
	1990	1995	2000	2001	1990	1995	2000	2001
Total expenditures [1]	3,831.5	4,969.0	6,683.7	6,987.0	4,474.5	5,075.6	6,223.9	6,377.2
Food and tobacco [1]	677.9	802.5	1,027.2	1,068.7	774.4	825.1	919.4	926.0
Food purchased for off-premise consumption	401.6	459.8	568.6	589.0	452.4	473.7	530.0	533.6
Purchased meals and beverages [2]	227.8	287.5	376.5	393.2	261.8	294.6	339.8	344.0
Tobacco products	41.0	46.7	72.2	76.3	52.0	48.1	42.8	42.1
Clothing, accessories, and jewelry [1]	261.7	317.3	409.8	412.6	258.2	312.9	428.4	435.9
Shoes	31.5	37.1	46.3	47.0	32.0	36.8	48.8	49.9
Clothing	172.4	210.4	267.1	267.9	165.1	207.2	280.3	287.5
Jewelry and watches	30.3	38.1	51.1	51.0	30.1	36.7	58.1	58.0
Personal care	53.7	67.4	87.8	89.1	60.1	68.3	81.7	81.5
Housing [1]	585.6	740.8	960.0	1,014.5	696.2	763.7	851.3	866.0
Owner-occupied nonfarm dwellings-space rent	410.7	529.3	704.9	751.0	488.3	546.1	627.3	643.5
Tenant-occupied nonfarm dwellings-space rent	148.7	177.0	207.8	217.1	174.6	181.6	184.0	184.3
Household operation [1]	433.6	555.0	723.9	747.3	476.8	564.2	712.2	721.8
Furniture [3]	38.4	47.5	64.4	64.0	42.2	48.1	65.0	65.7
Semidurable house furnishings [4]	22.5	29.7	38.3	38.7	21.8	29.0	41.6	43.0
Cleaning and polishing preparations	38.9	47.3	59.3	61.7	42.4	48.5	54.4	54.6
Household utilities	141.1	175.0	209.2	221.7	162.8	180.8	195.0	191.3
Electricity	74.2	91.0	101.5	105.3	83.2	92.5	104.4	101.2
Gas	26.8	31.5	40.8	49.1	29.5	32.8	32.9	33.3
Water and other sanitary services	27.1	38.4	48.8	50.7	37.1	39.8	43.9	44.4
Fuel oil and coal	12.9	14.1	18.1	16.5	13.1	15.7	14.0	12.6
Telephone and telegraph	60.5	87.8	130.6	136.5	62.6	88.1	141.1	151.2
Medical care [1]	619.7	888.6	1,171.1	1,270.2	807.6	907.8	1,062.0	1,110.2
Drug preparations and sundries [5]	65.4	92.1	156.3	176.4	80.3	94.1	140.6	152.3
Physicians	140.4	192.4	244.3	266.7	183.3	193.8	228.0	242.1
Dentists	32.4	46.5	62.7	67.5	44.8	48.7	52.5	54.4
Hospitals and nursing homes [6]	265.0	370.9	471.5	509.6	340.5	381.5	427.4	443.9
Health insurance	37.7	58.0	70.6	75.0	66.0	58.9	63.8	64.5
Medical care [7]	31.7	46.4	63.0	66.8	47.9	47.1	51.4	51.6
Personal business [1]	284.7	406.8	632.5	634.3	363.2	424.4	550.0	550.1
Expense of handling life insurance [8]	55.0	81.8	102.8	103.9	71.2	87.0	82.0	80.3
Legal services	40.9	48.0	65.2	70.4	51.9	49.7	54.4	55.7
Funeral and burial expenses	9.5	13.3	16.4	17.5	12.9	14.0	14.1	14.6
Transportation	455.4	560.3	768.9	794.8	532.2	574.7	726.8	750.4
User-operated transportation [1]	419.0	517.8	711.9	742.0	493.5	532.3	673.9	699.8
New autos	89.7	82.2	105.5	105.9	104.0	83.5	107.0	108.0
Net purchases of used autos	29.3	50.0	59.4	60.6	42.0	51.2	60.4	60.4
Tires, tubes, accessories, etc.	29.9	36.9	45.9	45.8	29.7	36.8	46.7	45.4
Repair, greasing, washing, parking, storage, rental, and leasing	84.9	122.2	175.5	181.6	100.8	124.5	162.1	162.2
Gasoline and oil	107.3	113.3	164.4	162.1	113.1	120.2	135.7	138.8
Purchased local transportation	8.4	10.4	12.7	13.2	10.8	11.4	12.6	12.7
Mass transit systems	5.8	7.1	9.1	9.5	7.4	7.8	9.0	9.1
Taxicab	2.6	3.2	3.6	3.7	3.4	3.6	3.5	3.5
Purchased intercity transportation [1]	28.1	32.1	44.3	39.7	28.1	31.0	40.3	38.0
Railway (commutation)	0.7	0.6	0.8	0.9	0.9	0.7	0.8	0.8
Bus	1.3	1.6	1.5	1.5	1.3	1.6	1.3	1.3
Airline	22.7	25.5	36.7	32.4	22.0	24.3	33.4	31.6
Recreation [1][9]	284.9	401.6	564.7	593.9	292.6	398.7	604.9	644.6
Magazines, newspapers, and sheet music	21.6	26.2	34.2	35.2	27.2	27.2	31.8	32.1
Nondurable toys and sport supplies	32.8	47.2	62.7	66.7	33.7	47.4	74.5	82.6
Video and audio products, including musical instruments and computer goods	52.9	77.0	106.3	105.6	33.0	67.3	185.5	211.5
Computers, peripherals, and software	8.9	21.0	34.5	32.9	2.1	14.6	122.0	152.6
Education and research	83.7	114.5	164.0	174.9	107.6	119.2	141.3	144.9
Higher education	43.8	62.9	83.1	87.6	60.1	65.6	72.2	73.6
Religious and welfare activities	97.1	134.9	190.1	199.6	115.3	138.7	164.9	166.4
Foreign travel and other, net [1]	−6.3	−20.7	−16.1	−12.9	−5.3	−21.4	−7.5	−5.0
Foreign travel by U.S. residents	42.7	54.1	80.9	76.3	51.7	55.3	78.7	73.3
Less: Expenditures in the United States by nonresidents	51.6	75.4	98.3	90.6	60.1	77.4	88.2	80.6

[1] Includes other expenditures not shown separately. [2] Consists of purchases (including tips) of meals and beverages from retail, service, and amusement establishments; hotels; dining and buffet cars; schools; school fraternities; institutions; clubs; and industrial lunch rooms. Includes meals and beverages consumed both on and off-premise. [3] Includes mattresses and bedsprings. [4] Consists largely of textile house furnishings including piece goods allocated to house furnishing use. Also includes lamp shades, brooms, and brushes. [5] Excludes drug preparations and related products dispensed by physicians, hospitals, and other medical services. [6] Consists of (1) current expenditures (including consumption of fixed capital) of nonprofit hospitals and nursing homes and (2) payments by patients to proprietary and government hospitals and nursing homes. [7] Consists of (1) premiums, less benefits and dividends, for health hospitalization and accidental death and dismemberment insurance provided by commercial insurance carriers and (2) administrative expenses (including consumption of fixed capital) of Blue Cross and Blue Shield plans and of other independent prepaid and self-insured health plans. [8] Consists of (1) operating expenses of life insurance carriers and private noninsured pension plans and (2) premiums less benefits and dividends of fraternal benefit societies. Excludes expenses allocated by commercial carriers to accident and health insurance. [9] For additional details, see Table 1233.

Source: U.S. Bureau of Economic Analysis, *National Income and Product Accounts of the United States, 1929-97*; and Survey of Current Business, May 2003. See also <http://www.bea.doc.gov/bea/dn/nipaweb/SelectTable.asp?Selected=N> (released as 30 May 2003).

No. 668. Personal Income and Its Disposition: 1990 to 2002

[In billions of dollars (4,903.2 represents $4,903,200,000,000), except as indicated. For definition of personal income and chained dollars, see text, this section]

Item	1990	1995	1997	1998	1999	2000	2001	2002
Personal income	4,903.2	6,200.9	6,937.0	7,426.0	7,786.5	8,406.6	8,685.3	8,929.1
Wage and salary disbursements	2,754.6	3,424.7	3,888.9	4,192.8	4,470.4	4,836.3	4,950.6	5,003.7
Goods-producing industries [1]	754.4	863.6	975.1	1,038.5	1,088.6	1,163.7	1,142.4	1,117.6
Manufacturing	561.4	647.5	718.4	756.6	782.0	829.4	789.4	759.9
Distributive industries [2]	633.6	782.1	879.6	948.9	1,020.8	1,094.8	1,109.2	1,117.7
Service industries [3]	849.9	1,156.3	1,369.9	1,512.7	1,636.9	1,808.9	1,888.2	1,915.6
Government	516.7	622.7	664.3	692.7	724.2	768.9	810.8	852.8
Other labor income	390.0	497.0	475.4	490.6	510.2	544.2	570.4	610.6
Proprietors' income [4]	381.0	497.7	581.2	623.8	678.4	714.8	727.9	756.5
Rental income of persons [5]	49.1	117.9	128.3	138.6	149.1	146.6	137.9	142.4
Personal dividend income	165.4	254.0	334.9	348.3	328.0	375.7	409.2	433.8
Personal interest income	772.4	792.5	864.0	964.4	969.2	1,077.0	1,091.3	1,078.5
Transfer payments to persons	594.4	885.9	962.2	983.7	1,018.5	1,070.3	1,170.4	1,288.0
Less: Personal contributions for social insurance	203.7	268.8	297.9	316.3	337.4	358.4	372.3	384.5
Less: Personal tax and nontax payments	609.6	778.3	968.8	1,070.4	1,159.1	1,286.4	1,292.1	1,113.6
Equals: Disposable personal income	4,293.6	5,422.6	5,968.2	6,355.6	6,627.4	7,120.2	7,393.2	7,815.5
Less: Personal outlays	3,959.3	5,120.2	5,715.3	6,054.1	6,453.3	6,918.6	7,223.5	7,524.5
Personal consumption expenditures	3,831.5	4,969.0	5,529.3	5,856.0	6,246.5	6,683.7	6,987.0	7,303.7
Interest paid by persons	115.8	134.7	164.8	173.7	179.5	205.4	205.4	188.4
Personal transfer payments to the rest of the world (net)	12.0	16.5	21.2	24.3	27.3	29.5	31.1	32.3
Equals: Personal saving	334.3	302.4	252.9	301.5	174.0	201.5	169.7	291.0
Addenda:								
Disposable personal income:								
Total, billions of chained (1996) dollars	5,014.2	5,539.1	5,854.5	6,168.6	6,328.4	6,630.3	6,748.0	7,036.8
Per capita (dollars):								
Current dollars	17,176	20,361	21,887	23,037	23,749	25,237	25,957	27,188
Chained (1996) dollars	20,058	20,798	21,470	22,359	22,678	23,501	23,692	24,479
Personal saving as percentage of disposable personal income	7.8	5.6	4.2	4.7	2.6	2.8	2.3	3.7

[1] Comprises agriculture, forestry, fishing, mining, construction, and manufacturing. [2] Comprises transportation, communication, public utilities, and trade. [3] Comprises finance, insurance, real estate, services, and rest of world. [4] With capital consumption and inventory valuation adjustments. [5] With capital consumption adjustment.

Source: U.S. Bureau of Economic Analysis, *National Income and Product Accounts, 1929-97*; and Survey of Current Business, May 2003. See also <http://www.bea.doc.gov/bea/dn/nipaweb/SelectTable.asp?Selected=N> (released as 30 May 2003).

No. 669. Gross Saving and Investment: 1990 to 2002

[In billions of dollars (977.7 represents $977,700,000,000)]

Item	1990	1995	1997	1998	1999	2000	2001	2002
Gross saving	977.7	1,257.5	1,502.3	1,647.2	1,704.1	1,807.9	1,662.4	1,572.9
Gross private saving	1,016.2	1,266.0	1,343.7	1,375.0	1,356.1	1,372.1	1,399.3	1,594.8
Personal saving	334.3	302.4	252.9	301.5	174.0	201.5	169.7	291.0
Undistributed corporate profits [1]	102.4	203.6	261.3	189.9	229.6	152.6	122.7	139.9
Undistributed profits	95.3	203.3	220.0	133.6	185.9	146.8	61.2	17.6
Inventory valuation adjustment	-12.9	-18.3	8.4	18.3	-4.2	-15.0	5.0	-6.9
Capital consumption adjustment	19.9	18.6	32.9	38.0	47.9	20.8	56.5	129.1
Corporate consumption of fixed capital	391.1	512.1	581.5	620.2	665.5	721.1	789.1	827.5
Noncorporate consumption of fixed capital	188.4	231.5	250.9	264.2	281.8	296.8	317.7	336.4
Wage accruals less disbursements	-	16.4	-2.9	-0.7	5.2	-	-	-
Gross government saving	-38.6	-8.5	158.6	272.2	348.1	435.8	263.1	-21.9
Federal	-104.3	-108.0	33.4	132.0	203.4	302.8	170.7	-98.0
State and local	65.7	99.4	125.1	140.2	144.7	133.0	92.4	76.1
Gross investment	1,008.2	1,284.0	1,532.1	1,616.2	1,665.4	1,679.4	1,545.1	1,456.2
Gross private domestic investment	861.7	1,143.8	1,390.5	1,538.7	1,636.7	1,755.4	1,586.0	1,593.2
Gross government investment	215.8	238.2	264.6	277.1	304.7	319.8	335.8	351.9
Net foreign investment	-69.2	-98.0	-123.1	-199.7	-276.0	-395.8	-376.7	-488.9
Statistical discrepancy	30.6	26.5	29.7	-31.0	-38.8	-128.5	-117.3	-116.7
Addendum:								
Gross saving as a percentage of gross national product	16.8	16.9	18.0	18.8	18.3	18.4	16.5	15.1

- Represents or rounds to zero. [1] With inventory valuation and capital consumption adjustments.

Source: U.S. Bureau of Economic Analysis, *National Income and Product Accounts, 1929-97*; and Survey of Current Business, May 2003. See also <http://www.bea.doc.gov/bea/dn/nipaweb/SelectTable.asp?Selected=N> (released as 30 May 2003).

No. 670. Personal Income in Current and Constant (1996) Dollars by State: 1980 to 2002

[In billions of dollars (2,313.9 represents $2,313,900,000,000). Represents a measure of income received from all sources during the calendar year by residents of each state. Data exclude federal employees overseas and U.S. residents employed by private U.S. firms on temporary foreign assignment. Totals may differ from those in Tables 665, 666, and 668]

State	Current dollars					Constant (1996) dollars [1]				
	1980	1990	2000	2001	2002, prel.	1980	1990	2000	2001	2002, prel.
United States....	2,313.9	4,885.5	8,398.9	8,677.5	8,922.3	4,191.1	5,705.4	7,820.9	7,920.3	8,033.1
Alabama..........	30.8	64.1	105.5	109.4	112.7	55.8	74.9	98.2	99.8	101.5
Alaska...........	6.0	12.6	18.8	19.7	20.7	10.9	14.7	17.5	17.9	18.6
Arizona...........	26.3	63.3	131.0	137.3	142.9	47.6	73.9	122.0	125.3	128.6
Arkansas.........	17.4	34.2	58.9	61.3	63.7	31.4	39.9	54.9	56.0	57.4
California.........	286.3	655.6	1,100.7	1,129.9	1,158.7	518.5	765.6	1,024.9	1,031.3	1,043.2
Colorado..........	31.4	65.1	143.0	148.2	150.0	57.0	76.0	133.2	135.3	135.0
Connecticut.......	38.7	87.9	141.4	145.5	147.8	70.1	102.7	131.7	132.8	133.1
Delaware.........	6.4	14.5	24.5	25.6	26.5	11.6	16.9	22.8	23.4	23.8
District of Columbia...	7.9	16.1	22.8	23.3	24.0	14.3	18.8	21.3	21.2	21.6
Florida...........	98.9	258.5	455.3	475.6	494.6	179.1	301.9	424.0	434.1	445.3
Georgia..........	46.5	115.4	231.4	239.8	246.7	84.2	134.8	215.5	218.8	222.1
Hawaii...........	11.1	24.9	34.4	35.6	37.3	20.2	29.1	32.0	32.5	33.6
Idaho............	8.3	16.1	31.2	32.4	33.6	15.0	18.7	29.0	29.5	30.3
Illinois...........	126.7	237.6	401.8	413.0	420.9	229.4	277.5	374.2	377.0	379.0
Indiana...........	51.9	97.9	164.5	168.6	173.9	94.0	114.3	153.2	153.9	156.6
Iowa.............	28.2	48.3	77.7	79.8	83.1	51.0	56.4	72.4	72.9	74.8
Kansas...........	23.8	45.1	73.9	76.8	79.1	43.1	52.7	68.8	70.1	71.3
Kentucky.........	30.2	57.2	98.2	101.2	104.7	54.6	66.8	91.5	92.4	94.3
Louisiana.........	37.3	64.2	103.6	109.3	114.1	67.6	75.0	96.5	99.8	102.7
Maine............	9.5	21.5	32.9	34.5	35.9	17.2	25.1	30.6	31.5	32.3
Maryland.........	47.5	110.4	180.9	190.0	198.1	86.0	129.0	168.5	173.4	178.4
Massachusetts.....	61.3	139.8	242.0	248.8	252.3	111.1	163.2	225.3	227.1	227.1
Michigan..........	96.0	177.1	292.8	296.5	304.5	173.8	206.8	272.6	270.6	274.1
Minnesota........	42.2	87.8	159.0	164.8	171.0	76.4	102.5	148.1	150.4	154.0
Mississippi.......	17.9	33.9	59.6	61.9	64.2	32.4	39.6	55.5	56.5	57.8
Missouri..........	46.2	91.0	154.1	159.1	164.1	83.7	106.3	143.5	145.2	147.8
Montana..........	7.2	12.4	20.7	21.8	22.8	13.1	14.5	19.3	19.9	20.5
Nebraska.........	14.6	28.6	47.6	49.6	51.5	26.4	33.4	44.3	45.3	46.3
Nevada...........	9.5	25.2	60.1	63.2	65.6	17.3	29.4	56.0	57.7	59.1
New Hampshire....	9.2	23.0	41.3	42.8	43.8	16.6	26.9	38.4	39.0	39.4
New Jersey.......	86.9	192.1	318.2	328.7	338.9	157.4	224.4	296.3	300.1	305.1
New Mexico.......	11.0	22.7	39.7	42.3	44.4	19.9	26.6	37.0	38.6	40.0
New York.........	194.9	419.7	665.8	684.7	690.5	353.0	490.2	619.9	625.0	621.7
North Carolina.....	48.6	115.6	217.7	224.1	230.6	88.1	135.0	202.7	204.5	207.6
North Dakota......	5.3	10.1	16.0	16.4	17.1	9.6	11.8	14.9	15.0	15.4
Ohio.............	109.1	204.1	319.7	326.9	335.8	197.6	238.4	297.7	298.4	302.4
Oklahoma.........	29.1	51.0	82.9	86.5	89.4	52.8	59.6	77.2	79.0	80.4
Oregon...........	26.9	52.2	95.5	98.0	101.2	48.8	60.9	88.9	89.5	91.1
Pennsylvania......	120.5	235.8	365.6	378.4	391.4	218.2	275.4	340.5	345.3	352.3
Rhode Island......	9.2	20.3	30.7	32.1	33.5	16.7	23.7	28.6	29.3	30.2
South Carolina.....	24.4	56.2	97.4	100.9	104.3	44.2	65.6	90.7	92.1	93.9
South Dakota......	5.6	11.3	19.5	20.1	20.5	10.2	13.2	18.2	18.4	18.4
Tennessee........	38.3	82.3	149.9	154.1	160.4	69.3	96.1	139.6	140.7	144.4
Texas............	142.8	297.6	586.6	608.5	621.8	258.6	347.5	546.2	555.4	559.9
Utah.............	12.5	25.9	52.5	54.8	56.3	22.6	30.3	48.9	50.0	50.7
Vermont..........	4.5	10.2	16.8	17.6	18.2	8.1	11.9	15.6	16.1	16.4
Virginia...........	54.6	127.6	221.8	232.7	240.1	98.9	149.0	206.5	212.4	216.2
Washington.......	45.3	98.1	186.8	191.6	198.3	82.1	114.6	174.0	174.9	178.6
West Virginia......	15.9	26.1	39.4	41.2	42.7	28.9	30.5	36.7	37.6	38.4
Wisconsin.........	47.9	89.0	152.6	157.8	162.8	86.7	104.0	142.1	144.1	146.6
Wyoming.........	5.6	8.2	13.8	14.6	15.2	10.1	9.5	12.9	13.3	13.7

[1] Constant dollar estimates are computed by the U.S. Census Bureau using the national implicit price deflator for personal consumption expenditures from the Bureau of Economic Analysis. Any regional differences in the rate of inflation are not reflected in these constant dollar estimates.

Source: U.S. Bureau of Economic Analysis, Survey of Current Business, May 2003, and unpublished data. See also <http://www.bea.doc.gov/bea/regional/spi/>.

No. 671. Personal Income Per Capita in Current and Constant (1996) Dollars by State: 1990 to 2002

[In dollars, except as indicated. 2002 preliminary. See headnote, Table 670]

State	Current dollars				Constant (1996) dollars [1]				Income rank	
	1990	2000	2001	2002	1990	2000	2001	2002	1990	2002
United States..	19,572	29,760	30,413	30,941	22,856	27,712	27,759	27,857	(X)	(X)
Alabama.........	15,826	23,694	24,477	25,128	18,482	22,064	22,341	22,624	42	43
Alaska	22,712	29,960	31,027	32,151	26,523	27,898	28,320	28,947	6	14
Arizona..........	17,187	25,361	25,878	26,183	20,071	23,616	23,620	23,573	35	38
Arkansas	14,495	22,000	22,750	23,512	16,927	20,486	20,765	21,169	49	49
California	21,882	32,363	32,655	32,996	25,554	30,136	29,806	29,707	8	10
Colorado.........	19,680	33,060	33,455	33,276	22,983	30,785	30,536	29,959	19	9
Connecticut.......	26,712	41,446	42,377	42,706	31,195	38,594	38,679	38,450	1	1
Delaware	21,620	31,092	32,166	32,779	25,248	28,952	29,359	29,512	9	12
District of Columbia .	26,561	39,970	40,539	42,120	31,018	37,219	37,002	37,922	(X)	(X)
Florida	19,832	28,366	29,048	29,596	23,160	26,414	26,513	26,646	17	23
Georgia	17,722	28,103	28,523	28,821	20,696	26,169	26,034	25,949	29	28
Hawaii	22,375	28,354	29,034	30,001	26,130	26,403	26,501	27,011	7	20
Idaho...........	15,858	23,987	24,506	25,057	18,519	22,336	22,368	22,560	41	44
Illinois	20,744	32,297	32,990	33,404	24,225	30,074	30,111	30,075	10	8
Indiana..........	17,616	27,010	27,522	28,240	20,572	25,151	25,120	25,425	30	32
Iowa	17,372	26,540	27,225	28,280	20,287	24,714	24,849	25,461	33	31
Kansas..........	18,177	27,439	28,432	29,141	21,227	25,551	25,951	26,237	23	26
Kentucky	15,478	24,258	24,878	25,579	18,075	22,589	22,707	23,030	44	39
Louisiana	15,215	23,185	24,454	25,446	17,768	21,590	22,320	22,910	45	41
Maine...........	17,473	25,732	26,853	27,744	20,405	23,961	24,510	24,979	31	33
Maryland	23,012	34,060	35,279	36,298	26,874	31,716	32,201	32,680	5	4
Massachusetts.....	23,208	38,034	38,864	39,244	27,103	35,417	35,473	35,333	4	3
Michigan.........	19,020	29,408	29,629	30,296	22,212	27,384	27,044	27,276	20	18
Minnesota........	20,000	32,231	33,059	34,071	23,356	30,013	30,174	30,675	16	7
Mississippi	13,156	20,920	21,653	22,372	15,364	19,480	19,764	20,142	50	50
Missouri	17,743	27,493	28,221	28,936	20,721	25,601	25,758	26,052	28	27
Montana.........	15,516	22,961	24,044	25,020	18,120	21,381	21,946	22,526	43	45
Nebraska	18,077	27,781	28,861	29,771	21,111	25,869	26,343	26,804	25	22
Nevada	20,639	29,794	30,128	30,180	24,103	27,744	27,499	27,172	12	19
New Hampshire....	20,703	33,266	33,969	34,334	24,177	30,977	31,005	30,912	11	6
New Jersey.......	24,748	37,734	38,625	39,453	28,901	35,137	35,255	35,521	2	2
New Mexico	14,944	21,788	23,081	23,941	17,452	20,289	21,067	21,555	47	47
New York	23,292	35,041	35,878	36,043	27,201	32,630	32,747	32,451	3	5
North Carolina.....	17,348	26,939	27,308	27,711	20,259	25,085	24,925	24,949	34	34
North Dakota......	15,872	24,990	25,798	26,982	18,536	23,270	23,547	24,293	40	36
Ohio	18,788	28,130	28,699	29,405	21,941	26,194	26,195	26,474	21	25
Oklahoma........	16,205	24,007	24,945	25,575	18,924	22,355	22,768	23,026	38	40
Oregon..........	18,242	27,836	28,222	28,731	21,303	25,920	25,759	25,867	22	29
Pennsylvania......	19,810	29,759	30,752	31,727	23,134	27,711	28,069	28,565	18	15
Rhode Island......	20,167	29,257	30,256	31,319	23,551	27,244	27,616	28,198	14	16
South Carolina.....	16,040	24,209	24,840	25,400	18,732	22,543	22,673	22,868	39	42
South Dakota	16,227	25,815	26,566	26,894	18,950	24,039	24,248	24,214	37	37
Tennessee	16,808	26,290	26,808	27,671	19,629	24,481	24,469	24,913	36	35
Texas	17,446	27,992	28,472	28,551	20,374	26,066	25,988	25,705	32	30
Utah	14,983	23,410	24,033	24,306	17,497	21,799	21,936	21,883	46	46
Vermont	18,047	27,465	28,756	29,567	21,076	25,575	26,247	26,620	26	24
Virginia..........	20,527	31,210	32,338	32,922	23,972	29,062	29,516	29,641	13	11
Washington.......	20,017	31,605	31,976	32,677	23,376	29,430	29,186	29,420	15	13
West Virginia......	14,579	21,821	22,862	23,688	17,026	20,319	20,867	21,327	48	48
Wisconsin........	18,152	28,389	29,196	29,923	21,198	26,435	26,648	26,941	24	21
Wyoming	17,985	27,941	29,587	30,578	21,003	26,018	27,005	27,530	27	17

X Not applicable. [1] Constant dollar estimates are computed by the U.S. Census Bureau using the national implicit price deflator for personal consumption expenditures from the Bureau of Economic Analysis. Any regional differences in the rate of inflation are not reflected in these constant dollar estimates.

Source: U.S. Bureau of Economic Analysis, Survey of Current Business, May 2003, and unpublished data. See also <http://www.bea.doc.gov/bea/regional/spi/>.

Income, Expenditures, and Wealth

No. 672. Disposable Personal Income Per Capita in Current and Constant (1996) Dollars by State: 1990 to 2002

[In dollars, except percent. 2002 preliminary. Disposable personal income is the income available to persons for spending or saving; it is calculated as personal income less personal tax and nontax payments]

State	Current dollars				Constant (1996) dollars [1]				Percent of U.S. average	
	1990	2000	2001	2002	1990	2000	2001	2002	1990	2002
United States..	17,135	24,908	25,889	27,083	20,011	23,194	23,630	24,384	100.0	100.0
Alabama.........	14,091	20,595	21,547	22,536	16,456	19,178	19,667	20,290	82.2	83.2
Alaska..........	19,931	25,856	27,128	28,741	23,276	24,077	24,761	25,876	116.3	106.1
Arizona.........	15,226	21,446	22,428	23,266	17,781	19,970	20,471	20,947	88.9	85.9
Arkansas.......	12,975	19,280	19,996	21,065	15,152	17,953	18,251	18,966	75.7	77.8
California......	19,021	26,401	27,007	28,384	22,213	24,584	24,650	25,555	111.0	104.8
Colorado........	17,232	27,131	28,284	28,879	20,124	25,264	25,816	26,001	100.6	106.6
Connecticut.....	23,259	32,655	34,195	35,859	27,162	30,408	31,211	32,285	135.7	132.4
Delaware.......	18,598	26,200	27,288	28,492	21,719	24,397	24,907	25,652	108.5	105.2
District of Columbia	22,864	31,578	33,260	35,637	26,701	29,405	30,358	32,085	133.4	131.6
Florida.........	17,711	23,838	25,109	26,244	20,683	22,198	22,918	23,628	103.4	96.9
Georgia........	15,523	23,648	24,463	25,339	18,128	22,021	22,328	22,814	90.6	93.6
Hawaii.........	19,415	24,149	25,302	26,676	22,673	22,487	23,094	24,017	113.3	98.5
Idaho..........	14,064	20,394	21,262	22,340	16,424	18,991	19,407	20,113	82.1	82.5
Illinois.........	18,032	26,860	27,981	29,136	21,058	25,012	25,539	26,232	105.2	107.6
Indiana.........	15,390	23,155	23,839	24,990	17,973	21,562	21,759	22,499	89.8	92.3
Iowa...........	15,288	22,949	23,769	25,222	17,854	21,370	21,695	22,708	89.2	93.1
Kansas.........	16,005	23,461	24,485	25,696	18,691	21,847	22,348	23,135	93.4	94.9
Kentucky.......	13,617	20,729	21,525	22,571	15,902	19,303	19,647	20,321	79.5	83.3
Louisiana.......	13,673	20,393	21,643	22,942	15,968	18,990	19,754	20,655	79.8	84.7
Maine..........	15,408	21,778	23,122	24,443	17,994	20,279	21,104	22,007	89.9	90.3
Maryland.......	19,702	27,906	29,551	31,166	23,008	25,986	26,972	28,060	115.0	115.1
Massachusetts...	19,902	30,587	31,709	33,379	23,242	28,482	28,942	30,052	116.1	123.2
Michigan........	16,587	24,601	25,346	26,615	19,371	22,908	23,134	23,962	96.8	98.3
Minnesota.......	17,318	26,816	27,969	29,473	20,224	24,971	25,528	26,536	101.1	108.8
Mississippi......	11,920	18,655	19,421	20,410	13,920	17,371	17,726	18,376	69.6	75.4
Missouri........	15,603	23,461	24,448	25,647	18,221	21,847	22,315	23,091	91.1	94.7
Montana........	13,778	19,639	21,092	22,365	16,090	18,288	19,252	20,136	80.4	82.6
Nebraska.......	16,061	23,827	25,012	26,364	18,756	22,187	22,829	23,736	93.7	97.3
Nevada........	18,081	25,245	25,887	26,647	21,115	23,508	23,628	23,991	105.5	98.4
New Hampshire..	18,441	28,454	29,218	30,344	21,536	26,496	26,668	27,320	107.6	112.0
New Jersey.....	21,487	30,645	32,237	33,995	25,093	28,536	29,424	30,607	125.4	125.5
New Mexico.....	13,381	19,190	20,252	21,461	15,627	17,869	18,485	19,322	78.1	79.2
New York.......	19,879	28,370	29,614	30,778	23,215	26,418	27,030	27,710	116.0	113.6
North Carolina...	15,241	23,002	23,531	24,394	17,799	21,419	21,478	21,963	88.9	90.1
North Dakota....	14,313	21,993	22,973	24,463	16,715	20,480	20,968	22,025	83.5	90.3
Ohio...........	16,439	23,780	24,562	25,688	19,198	22,144	22,419	23,128	95.9	94.8
Oklahoma.......	14,256	20,591	21,803	22,815	16,648	19,174	19,901	20,541	83.2	84.2
Oregon.........	15,992	23,185	23,933	24,979	18,676	21,590	21,845	22,489	93.3	92.2
Pennsylvania....	17,422	25,164	26,370	27,868	20,346	23,432	24,069	25,090	101.7	102.9
Rhode Island....	17,771	24,966	26,016	27,596	20,753	23,248	23,746	24,846	103.7	101.9
South Carolina...	14,190	20,821	21,724	22,708	16,571	19,388	19,828	20,445	82.8	83.8
South Dakota....	14,837	23,134	23,764	24,463	17,327	21,542	21,690	22,025	86.6	90.3
Tennessee......	15,181	22,987	23,909	25,187	17,729	21,405	21,823	22,674	88.6	93.0
Texas..........	15,589	24,263	24,987	25,678	18,205	22,593	22,807	23,119	91.0	94.8
Utah...........	13,207	20,083	20,706	21,438	15,423	18,701	18,899	19,301	77.1	79.2
Vermont........	15,831	23,011	24,853	26,169	18,488	21,428	22,684	23,561	92.4	96.6
Virginia.........	17,890	25,913	27,196	28,581	20,892	24,130	24,823	25,732	104.4	105.5
Washington.....	17,753	26,291	27,255	28,718	20,732	24,482	24,877	25,856	103.6	106.0
West Virginia....	12,997	19,156	20,220	21,282	15,178	17,838	18,456	19,161	75.9	78.6
Wisconsin.......	15,809	23,878	25,026	26,263	18,462	22,235	22,842	23,645	92.3	97.0
Wyoming.......	16,067	23,300	25,283	26,818	18,763	21,697	23,077	24,145	93.8	99.0

[1] Constant dollar estimates are computed by the Census Bureau using the national implicit price deflator for personal consumption expenditures from the Bureau of Economic Analysis. Any regional differences in the rate of inflation are not reflected in these constant dollar estimates.

Source: U.S. Bureau of Economic Analysis, Survey of Current Business, May 2003, and unpublished data. See also <http://www.bea.doc.gov/bea/regional/spi/>.

No. 673. Personal Income by Selected Large Metropolitan Area: 1999 to 2001

[7,779,521 represents $7,779,521,000,000. Metropolitan areas as defined June 30, 1994. CMSA=Consolidated metropolitan statistical area; MSA=Metropolitan statistical area; NECMA=New England County Metropolitan areas. See Appendix II]

Metropolitan area ranked by 2000 income	Personal income 1999 (mil. dol.)	Personal income 2000 (mil. dol.)	Personal income 2001 (mil. dol.)	Annual percent change, 2000-2001	Per capita personal income 1999 (dol.)	Per capita personal income 2000 (dol.)	Per capita personal income 2001 (dol.)	Percent of national average, 2001
United States	7,779,521	8,398,871	8,677,490	3.32	27,880	29,760	30,413	100.0
New York-No. New Jersey-Long Island, NY-NJ-CT-PA (CMSA)	774,091	846,883	872,675	3.05	36,943	40,046	40,949	134.6
Los Angeles-Riverside-Orange County, CA (CMSA)	450,650	484,858	508,187	4.81	27,842	29,488	30,360	99.8
San Francisco-Oakland-San Jose, CA (CMSA)	283,381	333,236	326,824	-1.92	40,605	47,180	45,778	150.5
Chicago-Gary-Kenosha, IL-IN-WI (CMSA)	298,061	321,557	331,277	3.02	32,771	35,028	35,751	117.6
Washington-Baltimore, DC-MD-VA-WV (CMSA)	264,060	287,952	302,650	5.10	35,119	37,684	38,915	128.0
Boston-Worcester-Lawrence-Lowell-Brockton, MA-NH (NECMA)	211,837	237,575	244,142	2.76	35,178	39,125	39,873	131.1
Philadelphia-Wilmington-Atlantic City, PA-NJ-DE-MD (CMSA)	194,331	209,100	216,243	3.42	31,526	33,750	34,750	114.3
Detroit-Ann Arbor-Flint, MI (CMSA)	169,736	180,724	182,894	1.20	31,182	33,067	33,314	109.5
Dallas-Fort Worth, TX (CMSA)	159,254	175,700	180,072	2.49	31,106	33,412	33,247	109.3
Houston-Galveston-Brazoria, TX (CMSA)	143,594	157,975	167,954	6.32	31,218	33,632	34,916	114.8
Atlanta, GA (MSA)	126,446	139,019	144,477	3.93	31,534	33,507	33,769	111.0
Seattle-Tacoma-Bremerton, WA (CMSA)	121,336	129,721	132,586	2.21	34,428	36,386	36,669	120.6
Minneapolis-St. Paul, MN-WI (MSA)	101,664	110,764	115,330	4.12	34,671	37,152	38,131	125.4
Miami-Fort Lauderdale, FL (CMSA)	100,297	107,399	112,446	4.70	26,289	27,576	28,325	93.1
Denver-Boulder-Greeley, CO (CMSA)	85,768	96,583	100,284	3.83	33,878	37,158	37,607	123.7
San Diego, CA (MSA)	84,585	92,986	97,241	4.58	30,322	32,910	33,883	111.4
Phoenix-Mesa, AZ (MSA)	83,347	91,777	96,047	4.65	26,223	27,991	28,337	93.2
Cleveland-Akron, OH (CMSA)	86,292	90,686	92,446	1.94	29,293	30,773	31,368	103.1
St. Louis, MO-IL (MSA)	77,424	82,714	85,596	3.48	29,838	31,729	32,666	107.4
Pittsburgh, PA (MSA)	68,830	72,987	76,679	5.06	29,092	30,966	32,626	107.3
Portland-Salem, OR-WA (CMSA)	64,163	69,645	71,520	2.69	28,638	30,619	30,822	101.3
Tampa-St. Petersburg-Clearwater, FL (MSA)	64,205	69,119	71,843	3.94	27,101	28,748	29,379	96.6
Cincinnati-Hamilton, OH-KY-IN (CMSA)	57,342	60,627	62,758	3.51	29,124	30,559	31,419	103.3
Kansas City, MO-KS (MSA)	52,969	57,032	58,978	3.41	30,063	32,000	32,693	107.5
Milwaukee-Racine, WI (CMSA)	51,745	54,859	56,513	3.02	30,716	32,436	33,308	109.5
Sacramento-Yolo, CA (CMSA)	49,898	54,257	57,143	5.32	28,235	29,996	30,571	100.5
Indianapolis, IN (MSA)	46,760	50,256	52,244	3.96	29,427	31,155	31,960	105.1
Columbus, OH (MSA)	44,563	47,519	49,093	3.31	29,228	30,737	31,343	103.1
Charlotte-Gastonia-Rock Hill, NC-SC (MSA)	43,384	46,785	48,815	4.34	29,481	30,993	31,526	103.7
West Palm Beach-Boca Raton, FL (MSA)	44,869	47,656	50,676	6.34	40,172	41,945	43,626	143.4
Orlando, FL (MSA)	41,313	44,684	46,064	3.09	25,692	26,974	27,003	88.8
Las Vegas, NV-AZ (MSA)	40,406	43,969	46,155	4.97	26,882	27,777	27,916	91.8
Hartford, CT (NECMA)	39,199	42,490	43,836	3.17	34,345	36,915	37,819	124.4
Norfolk-Virginia Beach-Newport News, VA-NC (MSA)	38,799	41,376	43,516	5.17	24,905	26,288	27,452	90.3
San Antonio, TX (MSA)	39,188	42,152	43,742	3.77	24,920	26,355	26,887	88.4
Austin-San Marcos, TX (MSA)	36,852	40,712	41,673	2.36	30,560	32,185	31,511	103.6
Raleigh-Durham-Chapel Hill, NC (MSA)	35,568	39,128	40,772	4.20	30,613	32,681	32,998	108.5
Nashville, TN (MSA)	36,409	39,065	40,554	3.81	29,973	31,599	32,338	106.3
Greensboro-Winston-Salem-High Point, NC (MSA)	33,981	36,054	36,626	1.59	27,452	28,707	28,774	94.6
Salt Lake City-Ogden, UT (MSA)	32,685	35,039	36,295	3.58	24,748	26,176	26,780	88.1
New Orleans, LA (MSA)	33,672	35,278	37,431	6.10	25,159	26,385	28,048	92.2
Memphis, TN-AR-MS (MSA)	32,011	33,607	35,084	4.39	28,431	29,513	30,559	100.5
Jacksonville, FL (MSA)	29,903	32,189	33,416	3.81	27,475	29,161	29,625	97.4
Buffalo-Niagara Falls, NY (MSA)	30,386	31,895	32,454	1.75	25,902	27,284	27,852	91.6
Richmond-Petersburg, VA (MSA)	29,131	31,331	32,619	4.11	29,513	31,348	32,268	106.1
Rochester, NY (MSA)	30,339	31,715	32,846	3.57	27,675	28,863	29,870	98.2
Louisville, KY-IN (MSA)	29,253	31,202	32,298	3.51	28,677	30,357	31,251	102.8
Grand Rapids-Muskegon-Holland, MI (MSA)	28,993	30,747	31,462	2.33	26,909	28,145	28,471	93.6
Providence-Warwick-Pawtucket, RI (NECMA)	26,040	27,809	29,051	4.47	27,251	28,817	29,824	98.1
Oklahoma City, OK (MSA)	25,953	28,152	29,564	5.02	24,117	25,928	26,970	88.7
Dayton-Springfield, OH (MSA)	26,119	27,251	27,811	2.05	27,402	28,677	29,340	96.5
Birmingham, AL (MSA)	25,654	27,170	28,450	4.71	27,969	29,437	30,620	100.7
Honolulu, HI (MSA)	25,385	26,644	27,511	3.25	28,882	30,420	31,115	102.3
Albany-Schenectady-Troy, NY (MSA)	24,982	26,732	27,956	4.58	28,583	30,503	31,789	104.5
Greenville-Spartanburg-Anderson, SC (MSA)	23,013	24,655	25,239	2.37	24,159	25,534	25,818	84.9
Tulsa, OK (MSA)	22,044	23,738	24,903	4.91	27,604	29,486	30,650	100.8
Omaha, NE-IA (MSA)	21,652	23,174	24,151	4.22	28,030	29,744	30,650	109.3

Source: U.S. Bureau of Economic Analysis, Survey of Current Business, June 2003; press release at <http://www.bea.doc.gov/bea/newsrel/mpi0503.pdf> (released 06 May 2003); and Internet site at <http://www.bea.doc.gov/bea/regional/reis/>. (accessed 14 May 2003).

Income, Expenditures, and Wealth

No. 674. Flow of Funds Accounts—Composition of Individuals' Savings: 1990 to 2002

[In billions of dollars (538.8 represents $538,800,000,000). Combined statement for households, farm business, and nonfarm noncorporate business. Minus sign (-) indicates decrease]

Composition of savings	1990	1995	1996	1997	1998	1999	2000	2001	2002
Increase in financial assets	538.8	534.2	647.8	633.4	946.8	694.0	585.1	730.8	827.1
Foreign deposits	1.4	4.6	12.4	6.5	0.1	5.2	15.0	-5.0	2.2
Checkable deposits and currency	-9.8	-27.1	-53.9	-11.3	6.6	-39.4	-11.0	42.5	58.5
Time and savings deposits	33.6	131.4	156.9	142.6	175.6	101.3	307.1	226.7	306.8
Money market fund shares	27.8	99.6	52.7	83.5	174.5	129.1	122.1	154.1	-35.3
Securities	190.7	21.1	169.9	36.3	132.7	82.8	-449.4	-86.0	100.0
Open market paper	6.2	1.3	6.7	1.5	7.5	4.1	4.9	-19.4	-6.7
U.S. government securities	125.9	5.8	81.6	-112.5	-6.5	165.7	-129.3	-154.7	-104.3
Municipal securities	27.6	-51.0	-31.1	38.5	5.3	24.1	11.1	43.2	110.2
Corporate and foreign bonds	57.1	95.8	87.2	102.0	125.5	22.6	-26.4	76.0	55.2
Corporate equities [1]	-48.6	-96.8	-185.3	-273.9	-280.1	-305.1	-468.2	-231.2	-135.6
Mutual fund shares	22.5	66.0	210.8	280.6	281.0	171.4	158.4	200.1	181.3
Life insurance reserves	26.5	45.8	44.5	59.3	48.0	50.8	50.2	77.2	100.8
Pension fund reserves	207.7	158.8	148.3	201.4	217.4	181.8	209.0	208.4	209.1
Investment in bank personal trusts	32.9	6.4	-5.1	-53.0	-46.1	-8.1	56.6	-59.9	-2.4
Miscellaneous assets	28.1	93.7	122.1	168.1	238.0	190.5	285.6	172.6	87.3
Gross investment in tangible assets	824.0	1,020.2	1,076.9	1,133.0	1,241.0	1,367.0	1,473.6	1,535.4	1,538.4
Minus: Consumption of fixed capital	573.7	701.3	725.4	756.9	790.6	833.5	882.7	934.4	980.9
Equals: Net investment in tangible assets	250.3	318.9	351.5	376.2	450.3	533.4	590.9	601.0	557.5
Net increase in liabilities	234.5	427.9	503.2	575.8	775.1	899.0	927.4	805.8	894.6
Mortgage debt on nonfarm homes	207.1	176.9	240.8	258.1	386.3	422.5	416.4	528.8	722.3
Other mortgage debt [2]	-0.3	5.7	29.1	31.8	86.5	108.5	111.4	118.1	115.7
Consumer credit	11.9	138.9	91.3	57.5	75.0	99.5	139.0	108.8	55.5
Policy loans	4.1	10.5	4.5	3.2	0.1	-5.1	2.8	2.2	2.1
Security credit	-3.7	3.5	15.8	36.8	21.6	75.2	7.2	-38.8	-51.4
Other liabilities [2]	15.4	92.3	121.6	188.4	205.7	198.4	250.6	86.6	50.4
Personal saving with consumer durables [3]	570.1	445.2	519.2	460.2	653.7	364.2	283.6	560.5	522.0
Personal saving, without consumer durable [3]	481.9	308.3	390.8	295.7	447.0	143.1	41.3	290.4	274.0
Personal saving (NIPA, excludes consumer durables) [4]	334.3	302.4	272.1	252.9	301.5	174.1	201.5	169.8	306.7

[1] Only directly held and those in closed-end funds. Other equities are included in mutual funds, life insurance and pension reserves, and bank personal trusts. [2] Includes corporate farms. [3] Flow of Funds measure. [4] National Income and Product Accounts measure.

Source: Board of Governors of the Federal Reserve System, *Flow of Funds Accounts*, quarterly. See also <http://www.federalreserve.gov/releases/Z1/20030306/z1.pdf> (released 06 March 2003).

No. 675. Annual Expenditure Per Child by Husband-Wife Families by Family Income and Expenditure Type: 2001

[In dollars. Expenditures based on data from the 1990-92 Consumer Expenditure Survey updated to 2001 dollars using the Consumer Price Index. Excludes expenses for college. For more on the methodology, see report cited below]

Family income and age of child	Total	Housing	Food	Transportation	Clothing	Health care	Child care and education	Miscellaneous [1]
INCOME: LESS THAN $39,100								
Less than 2 yrs. old	6,490	2,500	910	780	370	460	840	630
3 to 5 yrs. old	6,630	2,470	1,010	750	360	440	950	650
6 to 8 yrs. old	6,710	2,380	1,300	880	400	510	560	680
9 to 11 yrs. old	6,730	2,150	1,560	950	450	560	340	720
12 to 14 yrs. old	7,560	2,400	1,640	1,070	750	560	240	900
15 to 17 yrs. old	7,480	1,940	1,780	1,440	660	600	400	660
INCOME: $39,100-$65,800								
Less than 2 yrs. old	9,030	3,380	1,090	1,160	430	610	1,380	980
3 to 5 yrs. old	9,260	3,350	1,260	1,130	420	580	1,530	990
6 to 8 yrs. old	9,260	3,260	1,600	1,260	470	660	980	1,030
9 to 11 yrs. old	9,190	3,030	1,890	1,330	520	720	640	1,060
12 to 14 yrs. old	9,940	3,280	1,900	1,450	870	720	470	1,250
15 to 17 yrs. old	10,140	2,820	2,110	1,840	780	770	810	1,010
INCOME: MORE THAN $65,800								
Less than 2 yrs. old	13,430	5,370	1,440	1,630	570	700	2,090	1,630
3 to 5 yrs. old	13,720	5,340	1,630	1,600	560	670	2,270	1,650
6 to 8 yrs. old	13,570	5,250	1,970	1,720	610	770	1,560	1,690
9 to 11 yrs. old	13,410	5,020	2,290	1,800	670	820	1,090	1,720
12 to 14 yrs. old	14,260	5,270	2,400	1,920	1,100	830	840	1,900
15 to 17 yrs. old	14,670	4,810	2,530	2,330	1,000	870	1,470	1,660

[1] Expenses include personal care items, entertainment, and reading materials.

Source: Dept. of Agriculture, Center for Nutrition Policy and Promotion, *Expenditures on Children by Families, 2001 Annual Report*. See also <http://www.usda.gov/cnpp/Crc/crc2001.pdf> (released May 2002).

No. 676. Average Annual Expenditures Per Unit by Selected Major Types of Expenditure: 1990 to 2001

[In dollars, except as indicated. Based on Consumer Expenditure Survey. Data are averages for the noninstitutional population. Expenditures reported here are out-of-pocket]

Type	1990	1995	1996	1997	1998	1999	2000	2001
Number of consumer units (1,000)	96,968	103,123	104,212	105,576	107,182	108,465	109,367	110,339
Total expenditures [1]	**$28,381**	**$32,264**	**$33,797**	**$34,819**	**$35,535**	**$36,995**	**$38,045**	**39,518**
Food	4,296	4,505	4,698	4,801	4,810	5,031	5,158	5,321
Food at home [1]	2,485	2,803	2,876	2,880	2,780	2,915	3,021	3,086
Meats, poultry, fish, and eggs	668	752	737	743	723	749	795	828
Dairy products	295	297	312	314	301	322	325	332
Fruits and vegetables	408	457	490	476	472	500	521	522
Other food at home	746	856	889	895	858	896	927	952
Food away from home	1,811	1,702	1,823	1,921	2,030	2,116	2,137	2,235
Alcoholic beverages	293	277	309	309	309	318	372	349
Housing [1]	8,703	10,458	10,747	11,272	11,713	12,057	12,319	13,011
Shelter	4,836	5,928	6,064	6,344	6,680	7,016	7,114	7,602
Fuels, utilities, public services	1,890	2,191	2,347	2,412	2,405	2,377	2,489	2,767
Apparel and services	1,618	1,704	1,752	1,729	1,674	1,743	1,856	1,743
Transportation [1]	5,120	6,014	6,382	6,457	6,616	7,011	7,417	7,633
Vehicle purchase	2,129	2,638	2,815	2,736	2,964	3,305	3,418	3,579
Gasoline and motor oil	1,047	1,006	1,082	1,098	1,017	1,055	1,291	1,279
Other transportation	1,642	2,015	2,058	2,230	2,206	2,254	2,281	2,375
Health care	1,480	1,732	1,770	1,841	1,903	1,959	2,066	2,182
Entertainment	1,422	1,612	1,834	1,813	1,746	1,891	1,863	1,953
Reading	153	162	159	164	161	159	146	141
Tobacco products, smoking supplies	274	269	255	264	273	300	319	308
Personal insurance and pensions	2,592	2,964	3,060	3,223	3,381	3,436	3,365	3,737
Life and other personal insurance	345	373	353	379	398	394	399	410
Pensions and Social Security	2,248	2,591	2,707	2,844	2,982	3,042	2,966	3,326

[1] Includes expenditures not shown separately.

Source: U.S. Bureau of Labor Statistics, *Consumer Expenditures in 2001*; earlier reports. See also <http://www.bls.gov/cex/csxann01.pdf> (released April 2003).

No. 677. Average Annual Expenditures Per Unit by Metropolitan Area: 2000-2001

[In dollars. Metropolitan areas defined June 30, 1983, CMSA=Consolidated Metropolitan Statistical Area; MSA=Metropolitan Statistical Area; PMSA=Primary Metropolitan Statistical Area. See text, Section 1, and Appendix II. See headnote, Table 648]

Metropolitan area	Total expenditures [1]	Food	Housing Total [1]	Shelter	Utility fuels [2]	Transportation Total [1]	Vehicle purchases	Gasoline and motor oil	Health care
Anchorage, AK MSA	$53,618	7,121	17,062	10,467	2,487	9,773	4,115	1,458	2,573
Atlanta, GA MSA	$38,034	4,777	14,223	8,517	3,328	6,577	2,723	1,258	1,943
Baltimore, MD MSA	$37,975	5,309	13,077	7,911	2,665	6,405	2,639	1,268	1,885
Boston-Lawrence-Salem, MA-NH CMSA	$37,740	5,297	13,754	8,889	2,566	6,342	2,332	1,080	1,983
Chicago-Gary-Lake County, IL-IN-WI CMSA	$47,042	5,688	16,937	10,334	3,130	8,189	3,739	1,284	2,136
Cincinnati-Hamilton, OH-KY-IN CMSA	$41,355	5,768	13,201	7,641	2,639	8,166	3,933	1,274	1,931
Cleveland-Akron-Lorain, OH CMSA	$50,135	7,332	15,519	8,661	3,272	10,516	5,623	1,575	2,062
Dallas-Fort Worth, TX CMSA	$44,862	5,499	16,087	10,015	2,518	8,458	3,270	1,279	2,100
Denver-Boulder-Greeley, CO CMSA	$43,343	5,526	14,374	8,018	2,773	8,093	2,639	1,464	1,915
Detroit-Ann Arbor, MI CMSA	$43,024	6,722	13,903	9,460	2,182	6,523	2,329	1,176	2,252
Honolulu, HI MSA	$47,547	6,353	14,591	7,583	3,242	9,566	4,534	1,574	2,455
Houston-Galveston-Brazoria, TX CMSA	$40,520	5,835	12,840	7,209	3,184	7,445	3,055	1,587	2,283
Kansas City, MO-Kansas City, KS CMSA	$39,530	5,469	13,144	7,418	2,899	8,202	3,872	1,264	1,760
Los Angeles-Long Beach, CA PMSA	$45,227	5,737	17,106	10,975	2,500	8,104	3,062	1,525	1,905
Miami-Fort Lauderdale, FL CMSA	$40,760	5,837	14,979	9,155	2,947	7,469	3,133	1,286	1,885
Milwaukee, WI MSA	$40,187	5,201	13,450	8,353	2,392	6,683	3,019	1,200	2,328
Minneapolis-St. Paul, MN-WI MSA	$51,310	5,984	15,826	9,669	2,618	9,176	3,934	1,501	2,254
New York-Northern New Jersey-Long Island, NY-NJ-CT CMSA	$48,237	6,408	17,893	11,624	2,885	7,295	2,776	1,044	2,128
Philadelphia-Wilmington-Trenton, PA-NJ-DE-MD CMSA	$38,523	5,394	13,702	8,079	3,034	6,606	2,652	1,076	1,923
Phoenix-Mesa, AZ MSA	$41,021	5,248	13,361	7,880	2,641	8,910	4,105	1,257	2,051
Pittsburgh-Beaver Valley, PA CMSA	$38,783	5,479	11,406	5,884	2,737	7,715	3,452	1,147	2,151
Portland-Vancouver, OR-WA CMSA	$42,769	5,446	15,060	9,306	2,421	6,917	2,542	1,308	2,143
San Diego, CA MSA	$43,960	4,817	16,472	11,160	2,293	9,161	4,836	1,393	1,771
San Francisco-Oakland-San Jose, CA CMSA	$56,112	6,966	20,877	13,795	2,548	9,492	4,206	1,519	2,170
Seattle-Tacoma, WA CMSA	$47,099	6,237	15,781	10,029	2,497	9,372	4,104	1,476	2,479
St. Louis-East St. Louis-Alton, MO-IL CMSA	$42,076	6,213	12,235	6,702	2,783	8,043	4,051	1,256	2,078
Tampa-St. Petersburg-Clearwater, FL MSA	$37,705	3,960	11,958	6,889	2,759	9,292	5,487	1,220	2,255
Washington, DC-MD-VA MSA	$48,192	5,545	17,973	11,245	2,864	7,647	3,036	1,301	2,285

[1] Includes expenditures not shown separately. [2] Includes public services.

Source: U.S. Bureau of Labor Statistics, *Consumer Expenditures in 2001*; earlier reports. See also <http://www.bls.gov/cex/csxann01.pdf>. (released April 2003).

Income, Expenditures, and Wealth 451

No. 678. Average Annual Expenditures of All Consumer Units by Race, Hispanic Origin, and Age of Householder: 2001

[In dollars. Based on Consumer Expenditure Survey. Data are averages for the noninstitutional population. Expenditures reported here are out-of-pocket]

Item	All consumer units	Black	Hispanic	Under 25 yrs.	25 to 34 yrs.	35 to 44 yrs.	45 to 54 yrs.	55 to 64 yrs.	65 yrs. and over
Expenditures, total	**39,518**	**28,903**	**34,361**	**23,526**	**39,451**	**46,908**	**47,930**	**41,462**	**27,714**
Food	5,321	4,271	5,648	3,724	5,214	6,242	6,451	5,442	3,749
Food at home	3,086	2,804	3,551	1,857	2,936	3,589	3,659	3,238	2,435
Cereals and bakery products	452	402	490	276	419	535	522	463	377
Cereals and cereal products	156	160	188	112	160	188	176	147	122
Bakery products	296	242	302	164	259	348	347	315	255
Meats, poultry, fish, and eggs	828	941	1,098	472	791	948	999	898	641
Beef	248	245	331	147	241	274	308	266	191
Pork	177	229	229	88	167	196	211	205	148
Other meats	102	95	111	60	91	127	124	103	77
Poultry	152	196	206	93	153	181	182	154	108
Fish and seafood	114	132	164	59	107	131	134	134	87
Eggs	35	43	55	25	33	39	40	36	30
Dairy products	332	241	355	194	317	400	388	340	257
Fresh milk and cream	136	98	168	84	137	164	156	126	108
Other dairy products	196	143	186	110	181	236	232	215	148
Fruits and vegetables	522	460	663	295	478	585	607	555	468
Fresh fruits	160	124	218	85	142	178	187	173	151
Fresh vegetables	162	131	231	86	148	176	193	183	141
Processed fruits	116	125	132	78	110	136	128	112	105
Processed vegetables	84	80	82	46	78	95	99	88	72
Other food at home	952	759	946	620	931	1,120	1,142	982	693
Nonalcoholic beverages	256	216	290	168	243	307	319	265	175
Food away from home	2,235	1,467	2,097	1,867	2,277	2,653	2,792	2,204	1,314
Alcoholic beverages	349	156	308	379	393	413	396	322	192
Housing	13,011	10,510	11,747	7,585	13,828	15,870	15,026	12,802	9,354
Shelter	7,602	5,925	7,018	4,862	8,544	9,529	8,824	7,067	4,844
Owned dwellings [1]	4,979	2,981	3,349	778	4,641	6,784	6,498	5,122	3,258
Mortgage interest and charges	2,862	1,880	2,152	434	3,129	4,533	3,935	2,539	849
Property taxes	1,233	703	670	257	833	1,393	1,528	1,434	1,343
Rented dwellings	2,134	2,762	3,503	3,786	3,655	2,261	1,632	1,187	1,201
Other lodging	489	182	167	298	248	484	694	758	386
Utilities, fuels, and public services	2,767	2,955	2,429	1,369	2,606	3,111	3,192	2,998	2,481
Natural gas	411	494	332	142	360	457	466	445	428
Electricity	1,009	1,090	848	483	914	1,145	1,149	1,108	934
Fuel oil and other fuels	112	61	43	22	63	108	135	150	146
Telephone	914	1,024	917	629	1,001	1,035	1,072	926	652
Water and other public services	321	286	290	93	267	366	371	369	321
Household operations	676	417	430	237	775	942	570	491	700
Personal services	291	229	251	140	533	536	141	85	162
Other household expenses	385	189	179	97	242	406	428	406	538
Housekeeping supplies	509	336	432	215	430	576	638	593	430
Household furnishings and equipment [1]	1,458	877	1,437	902	1,473	1,712	1,802	1,653	899
Household textiles	114	67	97	37	90	127	153	149	88
Furniture	372	309	383	253	439	446	451	353	212
Floor coverings	40	30	36	7	22	51	59	49	33
Major appliances	178	118	162	72	200	192	211	192	143
Miscellaneous household equipment	667	315	656	494	655	795	816	789	366
Apparel and services	1,743	1,729	1,857	1,197	1,922	2,110	2,337	1,575	891
Men and boys	423	376	416	293	458	522	597	366	193
Women and girls	677	618	654	395	634	812	930	684	408
Children under 2 years old	81	82	141	103	165	99	66	51	16
Footwear	302	434	406	203	361	377	395	250	143
Other apparel products and services	259	218	241	202	303	301	348	224	131
Transportation	7,633	5,184	7,083	4,834	8,173	9,202	9,355	8,093	4,470
Vehicle purchases (net outlay) [1]	3,579	2,193	3,360	2,463	3,920	4,463	4,319	3,778	1,859
Cars and trucks, new	1,685	821	1,455	710	1,533	2,143	2,013	2,107	1,073
Cars and trucks, used	1,848	1,359	1,880	1,713	2,335	2,259	2,249	1,615	780
Gasoline and motor oil	1,279	968	1,265	867	1,324	1,518	1,586	1,343	783
Other vehicle expenses [1]	2,375	1,766	2,134	1,277	2,563	2,798	2,998	2,473	1,475
Vehicle finance charges	359	302	335	236	471	451	440	364	127
Maintenance and repair	662	443	695	358	605	820	837	677	464
Vehicle insurance	819	643	726	449	822	885	1,032	899	620
Public transportation	400	257	323	226	365	423	452	498	353
Health care [2]	2,182	1,264	1,343	530	1,286	1,879	2,265	2,703	3,493
Entertainment [3]	1,953	988	1,246	1,152	2,001	2,508	2,233	2,337	1,067
Personal care products and services	485	468	467	307	452	525	585	542	396
Reading	141	62	59	60	111	136	172	183	144
Education	648	352	428	1,511	477	669	1,036	438	173
Tobacco products and smoking supplies	308	203	177	265	320	379	374	333	154
Miscellaneous	750	585	457	319	566	740	900	815	891
Cash contributions	1,258	776	727	268	771	1,263	1,575	1,478	1,583
Personal insurance and pensions	3,737	2,356	2,814	1,395	3,938	4,971	5,224	4,401	1,157
Life and other personal insurance	410	310	209	51	239	423	545	653	384
Pensions and Social Security	3,326	2,046	2,605	1,344	3,700	4,548	4,679	3,747	773
Personal taxes [1]	**2,920**	**1,181**	**1,320**	**439**	**2,934**	**3,576**	**4,594**	**3,532**	**1,114**

[1] Includes other expenditures not shown separately. [2] For additional health care expenditures, see Table 138. [3] For additional recreation expenditures, see Section 26.

Source: U.S. Bureau of Labor Statistics, *Consumer Expenditures in 2001*; earlier reports. See also <http://www.bls.gov/cex/csxann01.pdf> (released April 2003).

No. 679. Average Annual Expenditures of All Consumer Units by Region and Size of Unit: 2001

[In dollars. For composition of regions, see map, inside front cover. See headnote, Table 676]

Item	Region				Size of consumer unit				
	North-east	Mid west	South	West	One person	Two per-sons	Three per-sons	Four per-sons	Five or more
Expenditures, total	41,169	39,548	36,285	43,261	23,507	40,359	45,508	54,395	53,805
Food	5,697	5,052	5,153	5,549	2,835	5,291	6,208	7,448	8,194
Food at home	3,399	2,892	2,983	3,183	1,533	2,954	3,696	4,404	5,151
Cereals and bakery products	511	435	431	454	224	420	526	660	800
Cereals and cereal products	179	148	146	162	75	135	186	231	308
Bakery products	332	287	285	292	149	285	340	429	492
Meats, poultry, fish, and eggs	939	720	846	816	369	811	1,040	1,142	1,425
Beef	252	232	257	247	103	251	304	347	428
Pork	181	159	198	161	74	178	228	245	296
Other meats	127	95	99	94	47	95	134	143	173
Poultry	189	124	152	149	68	140	191	207	289
Fish and seafood	154	83	106	123	58	113	141	155	173
Eggs	37	28	35	41	19	33	41	44	65
Dairy products	375	328	301	348	169	304	394	485	573
Fresh milk and cream	140	135	125	150	68	116	162	201	260
Other dairy products	235	193	175	198	101	188	232	284	312
Fruits and vegetables	608	459	482	577	285	512	604	712	834
Fresh fruits	191	147	140	181	91	159	183	212	255
Fresh vegetables	183	134	149	192	86	164	187	214	257
Processed fruits	139	102	108	125	65	107	133	167	193
Processed vegetables	94	77	85	79	43	83	100	120	129
Other food at home	966	951	923	988	486	907	1,132	1,405	1,520
Nonalcoholic beverages	262	261	246	263	134	242	302	379	406
Food away from home	2,299	2,160	2,170	2,366	1,302	2,336	2,512	3,043	3,042
Alcoholic beverages	386	346	298	400	314	400	315	368	309
Housing	14,439	12,458	11,375	15,000	8,371	12,944	14,744	17,914	17,317
Shelter	8,943	7,056	6,101	9,440	5,253	7,463	8,358	10,415	9,851
Owned dwellings	5,789	4,973	3,993	5,872	2,491	4,988	5,737	7,892	7,039
Mortgage interest and charges	2,750	2,742	2,363	3,886	1,175	2,547	3,689	5,019	4,524
Property taxes	2,065	1,290	851	1,072	752	1,328	1,227	1,784	1,590
Maintenance, repair, insurance, other	974	941	778	914	565	1,113	821	1,089	924
Rented dwellings	2,536	1,549	1,754	3,019	2,505	1,834	2,167	1,893	2,249
Other lodging	618	534	353	548	256	640	454	630	563
Utilities, fuels, and public services	2,836	2,823	2,843	2,524	1,799	2,816	3,202	3,530	3,734
Natural gas	498	586	272	373	276	412	461	529	560
Electricity	885	924	1,258	804	642	1,032	1,179	1,273	1,388
Fuel oil and other fuels	319	90	58	46	73	131	106	140	142
Telephone	897	914	924	914	620	905	1,091	1,166	1,194
Water and other public services	237	309	331	388	189	336	365	422	450
Household operations	778	614	619	745	356	474	877	1,356	984
Personal services	305	302	259	319	78	84	497	765	579
Other household expenses	474	312	360	426	278	389	380	591	405
Housekeeping supplies	518	492	494	544	246	556	562	731	719
Household furnishings and equipment	1,365	1,473	1,318	1,748	717	1,636	1,746	1,882	2,029
Household textiles	134	113	100	120	59	138	122	141	146
Furniture	324	349	371	440	161	422	426	574	477
Floor coverings	45	31	30	64	14	49	44	56	63
Major appliances	149	182	161	225	84	219	171	247	238
Small appliances, misc. housewares	79	89	74	111	43	111	79	118	102
Miscellaneous household equipment	634	709	582	787	356	697	902	746	1,003
Apparel and services	2,072	1,695	1,602	1,736	862	1,650	2,013	2,643	2,893
Men and boys	539	429	378	389	197	377	491	694	735
Women and girls	803	703	628	620	342	661	767	985	1,112
Children under 2 years old	95	91	72	74	13	47	140	162	186
Footwear	347	261	291	325	131	302	290	491	545
Other apparel products and services	288	211	233	327	179	263	325	311	314
Transportation	7,194	7,681	7,448	8,258	4,012	7,692	9,348	10,775	11,123
Vehicle purchases (net outlay)	3,131	3,496	3,813	3,676	1,805	3,487	4,325	5,258	5,594
Cars and trucks, new	1,719	1,476	1,785	1,717	832	1,896	1,893	2,376	2,268
Cars and trucks, used	1,396	1,971	1,975	1,902	934	1,556	2,400	2,790	3,275
Gasoline and motor oil	1,086	1,367	1,245	1,408	659	1,301	1,560	1,810	1,872
Other vehicle expenses	2,402	2,464	2,110	2,684	1,275	2,426	3,051	3,256	3,215
Vehicle finance charges	262	373	395	371	142	351	478	552	576
Maintenance and repair	664	626	566	854	419	661	788	867	910
Vehicle insurance	845	803	787	866	442	866	1,059	1,097	1,039
Public transportation	574	353	281	491	273	478	412	450	443
Health care [1]	2,084	2,292	2,194	2,129	1,441	2,827	2,265	2,253	2,150
Entertainment [2]	1,854	2,220	1,652	2,241	1,097	2,051	2,137	2,787	2,718
Personal care products and services	479	482	467	521	297	512	555	614	658
Reading	169	162	101	159	111	168	139	155	131
Education	729	689	483	798	423	476	830	1,059	984
Tobacco products and smoking supplies	304	374	316	230	203	312	397	349	416
Miscellaneous	985	701	605	833	518	744	843	1,156	743
Cash contributions	1,007	1,541	1,206	1,258	1,063	1,429	1,167	1,287	1,399
Personal insurance and pensions	3,770	3,853	3,385	4,149	1,960	3,864	4,547	5,589	4,770
Life and other personal insurance	405	474	418	335	180	482	527	565	477
Pensions and Social Security	3,366	3,379	2,967	3,815	1,779	3,382	4,020	5,024	4,293
Personal taxes	**2,527**	**3,449**	**2,232**	**3,795**	**1,829**	**3,599**	**3,066**	**3,900**	**2,652**

[1] For additional health care expenditures, see Table 138. [2] For additional recreation expenditures, see Section 26.

Source: U.S. Bureau of Labor Statistics, *Consumer Expenditures in 2001*; earlier reports. See also <http://www.bls.gov/cex/csxann01.pdf> (released April 2003).

No. 680. Money Income of Households—Distribution of Income and Median Income by Race and Hispanic Origin: 1999

[In thousands, except as indicated. Households as of April 2000. (105,539 represents 105,539,000). Based on sample data from the 2000 Census of Population and Housing; see text, Section 1, and Appendix III]

Income Interval	All house-holds	White alone	Black or African American alone	American Indian and Alaska Native alone	Asian alone	Native Hawaiian and other Pacific Islander alone	Some other race alone	Two or more races	Hispanic or Latino [1]
All households	105,539	83,698	12,024	770	3,129	100	3,834	1,984	9,273
Under $10,000	10,067	6,584	2,294	128	314	9	469	268	1,150
$10,000 to $14,999	6,657	4,955	1,038	68	143	5	300	148	723
$15,000 to $19,999	6,601	4,974	960	63	143	6	315	141	739
$20,000 to $24,999	6,936	5,303	935	63	153	7	331	145	768
$25,000 to $29,999	6,801	5,259	874	56	146	7	319	140	727
$30,000 to $34,999	6,718	5,281	787	54	157	6	299	134	682
$35,000 to $39,999	6,236	4,953	697	47	149	6	261	122	605
$40,000 to $44,999	5,966	4,794	624	42	154	6	235	111	546
$45,000 to $49,999	5,244	4,249	522	35	136	5	202	95	466
$50,000 to $59,999	9,537	7,834	879	60	267	9	323	165	773
$60,000 to $74,999	11,003	9,161	918	62	349	12	323	180	796
$75,000 to $99,999	10,799	9,121	797	51	396	11	258	164	683
$100,000 to $124,999	5,492	4,695	343	21	247	5	102	78	296
$125,000 to $149,999	2,656	2,285	148	9	136	2	40	36	127
$150,000 to $199,999	2,322	2,023	106	6	128	2	28	29	97
$200,000 and over	2,503	2,227	102	6	111	1	27	28	96
Median income (dollars)	41,994	44,687	29,423	30,599	51,908	42,717	32,694	35,587	33,676
Aggregate household income (mil. dol)	5,978,107	4,996,446	479,476	30,917	211,949	5,318	159,556	94,444	410,310

[1] Persons of Hispanic origin or Latino may be of any race.

Source: U.S. Census Bureau, 2000 Census of Population and Housing, Summary File 3, using American FactFinder, Tables P52, P53, P54, P151A-H, P152A-H, and P153A-H (accessed 05 September 2003).

No. 681. Household Income—Distribution by Income Level and 25 Largest Metropolitan Areas: 1999

[In thousands except percent (1,506 represents 1,506,000). Covers metropolitan statistical area (MSAs) and consolidated metropolitan statistical areas (CMSAs) as defined by the U.S. Office of Management and Budget as of June 30, 1999. For definitions and components of metropolitan areas, see Appendix II]

Metropolitan area based on 2000 population	Number of house-holds (1,000)	Under $15,000	$15,000-$24,999	$25,000-$34,999	$35,000-$49,999	$50,000-$74,999	$75,000-$99,999	$100,000 and over	Median income (dol.)
Atlanta, GA MSA	1,506	10.6	9.5	11.1	16.3	21.9	13.1	17.6	51,948
Boston-Worcester-Lawrence, MA-NH-ME-CT CMSA	2,221	13.2	9.5	9.9	14.3	20.4	13.4	19.3	52,792
Chicago-Gary-Kenosha, IL-IN-WI CMSA	3,303	12.5	9.9	10.8	15.5	21.0	12.8	17.4	51,046
Cincinnati-Hamilton, OH-KY-IN CMSA	768	14.0	12.0	12.5	16.7	20.9	11.3	12.7	44,914
Cleveland-Akron, OH CMSA	1,167	15.3	12.8	12.9	16.7	20.3	10.7	11.2	42,215
Dallas-Fort Worth, TX CMSA	1,908	11.9	11.1	12.6	16.6	20.4	11.7	15.6	47,418
Denver-Boulder-Greeley, CO CMSA	1,004	10.5	9.8	11.9	16.4	21.7	13.0	16.7	51,088
Detroit-Ann Arbor-Flint, MI CMSA	2,083	13.2	11.0	11.2	15.2	20.5	12.8	16.0	49,160
Houston-Galveston-Brazoria, TX CMSA	1,641	14.3	12.0	12.6	15.9	18.9	11.1	15.1	44,761
Kansas City, MO-KS MSA	695	12.3	11.4	13.0	17.3	21.8	11.8	12.5	46,193
Los Angeles-Riverside-Orange County, CA CMSA	5,352	14.8	11.9	11.7	15.2	18.9	11.2	16.2	45,903
Miami-Fort Lauderdale, FL CMSA	1,432	18.8	13.8	13.0	16.0	17.7	9.0	11.7	38,632
Minneapolis-St. Paul, MN-WI MSA	1,137	9.2	9.2	11.0	15.8	23.3	14.6	16.9	54,304
New York-Northern New Jersey-Long Island, NY-NJ-CT-PA CMSA	7,739	15.6	9.8	10.0	13.7	18.4	12.1	20.3	50,795
Philadelphia-Wilmington-Atlantic City, PA-NJ-DE-MD CMSA	2,322	14.5	10.9	11.4	15.4	20.1	12.2	15.5	47,528
Phoenix-Mesa, AZ MSA	1,194	12.4	12.4	13.3	17.6	20.6	11.0	12.9	44,752
Pittsburgh, PA MSA	967	18.2	15.1	13.5	16.6	18.6	8.8	9.2	37,467
Portland-Salem, OR-WA CMSA	867	12.2	11.4	12.9	17.7	22.0	11.5	12.3	46,090
Sacramento-Yolo, CA CMSA	666	13.5	11.5	12.3	16.6	20.6	11.6	14.0	46,106
San Diego, CA MSA	995	12.5	11.8	12.3	16.0	20.1	11.5	15.7	47,067
San Francisco-Oakland-San Jose, CA CMSA	2,559	10.0	7.8	8.7	13.2	19.5	14.0	26.7	62,024
Seattle-Tacoma-Bremerton, WA CMSA	1,393	10.8	10.0	11.6	16.6	22.3	13.3	15.3	50,733
St. Louis, MO-IL MSA	1,013	13.9	12.2	12.8	16.8	21.1	11.1	12.2	44,437
Tampa-St. Petersburg-Clearwater, FL MSA	1,010	16.2	15.4	15.0	17.8	18.1	8.2	9.4	37,406
Washington-Baltimore, DC-MD-VA-WV CMSA	2,874	10.1	8.4	9.9	14.6	21.2	14.2	21.6	57,291

Source: U.S. Census Bureau, "2000 Census of Population and Housing, Profiles of General Demographic Characteristics"; <http://www.census.gov/Press-Release/www/2002/demoprofiles.html>.

No. 682. Household Income—Distribution by Income Level and State: 1999

[Households as of April 2000. (105,539 represents 105,539,000). Based on sample data from the 2000 Census of Population and Housing; see text, Section 1, and Appendix III]

State	Number of households (1,000)	Under $15,000	$15,000-$24,999	$25,000-$34,999	$35,000-$49,999	$50,000-$74,999	$75,000-$99,999	$100,000 and over	Median income (dol.)
U.S.	105,539	16,724	13,537	13,519	17,446	20,541	10,799	12,973	41,994
AL	1,737	391	257	237	287	298	134	133	34,135
AK	222	23	23	25	36	49	30	36	51,571
AZ	1,902	284	264	266	333	365	184	206	40,558
AR	1,043	229	174	157	183	170	67	62	32,182
CA	11,512	1,616	1,318	1,315	1,746	2,203	1,327	1,987	47,493
CO	1,659	197	186	209	282	352	197	236	47,203
CT	1,302	157	126	131	188	265	173	262	53,935
DE	299	36	34	36	51	64	36	42	47,381
DC	249	52	28	31	35	40	22	41	40,127
FL	6,341	1,034	918	901	1,104	1,171	552	661	38,819
GA	3,008	481	369	379	503	593	312	371	42,433
HI	404	51	42	46	63	83	51	67	49,820
ID	470	74	72	70	90	90	39	34	37,572
IL	4,593	636	518	546	745	953	532	663	46,590
IN	2,337	334	315	320	418	500	237	214	41,567
IA	1,150	171	165	169	218	242	101	84	39,469
KS	1,039	155	143	145	188	211	100	96	40,624
KY	1,592	355	245	220	262	275	122	114	33,672
LA	1,657	400	248	223	261	275	127	123	32,566
ME	518	92	77	74	95	100	43	37	37,240
MD	1,982	221	188	212	306	427	269	359	52,868
MA	2,445	352	248	253	355	491	313	432	50,502
MI	3,789	533	469	470	624	779	433	480	44,667
MN	1,896	230	216	234	323	425	229	239	47,111
MS	1,048	261	165	148	171	168	71	63	31,330
MO	2,197	376	320	315	385	416	194	192	37,934
MT	359	72	62	55	65	62	23	20	33,024
NE	667	99	99	98	123	136	58	54	39,250
NV	752	93	93	98	136	163	83	85	44,581
NH	475	51	51	55	82	109	60	65	49,467
NJ	3,066	358	289	305	437	608	414	654	55,146
NM	678	141	107	97	115	112	53	52	34,133
NY	7,061	1,263	823	807	1,047	1,298	746	1,077	43,393
NC	3,133	530	432	436	553	609	279	295	39,184
ND	257	49	41	40	48	48	17	15	34,604
OH	4,447	692	594	603	771	905	445	436	40,956
OK	1,344	278	219	201	230	228	97	89	33,400
OR	1,335	202	179	186	236	269	129	133	40,916
PA	4,779	799	657	634	809	930	457	492	40,106
RI	408	72	51	48	64	82	44	47	42,090
SC	1,534	288	220	214	270	289	130	124	37,082
SD	290	53	47	44	55	54	20	17	35,282
TN	2,234	429	326	320	388	405	180	186	36,360
TX	7,397	1,259	1,004	996	1,219	1,359	706	854	39,927
UT	702	76	83	93	133	158	80	78	45,726
VT	241	35	34	33	45	50	23	21	40,856
VA	2,700	356	309	327	445	549	307	408	46,677
WA	2,272	297	265	285	389	486	264	285	45,776
WV	737	187	128	107	121	111	45	37	29,696
WI	2,086	270	265	276	378	474	226	197	43,791
WY	194	32	29	28	35	39	17	13	37,892

Source: U.S. Census Bureau, "2000 Census of Population and Housing, Profiles of General Demographic Characteristics"; <http://www.census.gov/Press-Release/www/2002/demoprofiles.html>.

No. 683. Money Income of Households—Percent Distribution by Income Level, Race, and Hispanic Origin in Constant (2001) Dollars: 1980 to 2001

[Constant dollars based on CPI-U-RS deflator. **Households as of March of following year.** (82,368 represents 82,368,000). Based on Current Population Survey; see text, Sections 1 and 13, and Appendix III. For data collection changes over time, see <http://www.census.gov/hhes/income/histinc/hstchg.html>. For definition of median, see Guide to Tabular Presentation]

Year	Number of households (1,000)	Under $15,000	$15,000-$24,999	$25,000-$34,999	$35,000-$49,999	$50,000-$74,999	$75,000-$99,999	$100,000 and over	Median income (dollars)
ALL HOUSEHOLDS [1]									
1980	82,368	19.7	15.2	13.9	18.4	19.4	7.8	5.6	36,035
1990	94,312	17.9	13.9	13.3	17.3	18.9	9.4	9.2	39,324
1995	99,627	17.8	14.5	12.9	16.3	18.4	9.8	10.3	39,306
2000 [2]	108,209	15.6	13.0	12.5	15.4	18.6	10.8	14.1	43,162
2001	109,297	15.9	13.3	12.4	15.4	18.4	10.8	13.8	42,228
WHITE									
1980	71,872	17.6	14.8	14.0	18.9	20.4	8.3	6.1	38,017
1990	80,968	15.7	13.8	13.4	17.8	19.7	10.0	9.9	41,016
1995	84,511	15.8	14.2	12.8	16.6	19.1	10.2	11.1	41,255
2000 [2]	90,030	14.2	12.6	12.4	15.5	19.1	11.3	14.9	45,142
2001	90,682	14.3	13.0	12.2	15.5	18.8	11.4	14.8	44,517
BLACK									
1980	8,847	36.9	18.9	13.8	14.2	11.0	3.7	1.5	21,902
1990	10,671	35.1	15.7	13.4	14.6	13.1	4.8	3.4	24,527
1995	11,577	31.6	17.3	14.2	14.2	12.9	6.4	3.4	25,830
2000 [2]	13,174	25.6	16.6	13.9	15.7	14.9	6.8	6.4	30,495
2001	13,315	26.4	16.5	14.3	14.9	15.4	6.8	5.6	29,470
ASIAN AND PACIFIC ISLANDER									
1990	1,958	13.5	11.0	9.9	15.0	21.0	13.9	15.7	50,496
1995	2,777	15.8	10.7	10.8	15.9	19.6	12.0	15.1	46,847
2000 [2]	3,963	11.3	9.4	9.9	13.6	19.3	13.5	23.0	57,313
2001	4,071	12.3	10.0	9.9	14.3	19.0	12.5	21.9	53,635
HISPANIC [3]									
1980	3,906	25.4	20.1	16.2	16.5	14.9	4.4	2.5	27,776
1990	6,220	25.5	18.2	15.1	17.3	14.3	5.5	4.0	29,326
1995	7,939	28.1	19.6	15.1	14.8	13.3	4.9	4.1	26,368
2000 [2]	10,034	18.8	17.2	15.4	17.3	16.9	7.8	6.5	34,093
2001	10,499	18.9	17.5	15.4	17.3	16.5	7.5	7.0	33,565

[1] Includes other races not shown separately. [2] Data reflect implementation of Census 2000-based population controls and a 28,000 household sample expansion to 78,000 households. [3] People of Hispanic origin may be of any race.

No. 684. Money Income of Households—Median Income by Race and Hispanic Origin in Current and Constant (2001) Dollars: 1980 to 2001

[In dollars. See headnote, Table 683]

Year	Median income in current dollars					Median income in constant (2001) dollars				
	All households [1]	White	Black	Asian, Pacific Islander	Hispanic [2]	All households [1]	White	Black	Asian, Pacific Islander	Hispanic [2]
1980	17,710	18,684	10,764	(NA)	13,651	36,035	38,017	21,902	(NA)	27,776
1985	23,618	24,908	14,819	(NA)	17,465	37,059	39,083	23,252	(NA)	27,404
1986	24,897	26,175	15,080	(NA)	18,352	38,365	40,334	23,237	(NA)	28,279
1987	26,061	27,458	15,672	32,226	19,336	38,835	40,917	23,354	48,022	28,814
1988	27,225	28,781	16,407	32,267	20,359	39,144	41,382	23,590	46,394	29,272
1989	28,906	30,406	18,083	36,102	21,921	39,850	41,918	24,929	49,771	30,221
1990	29,943	31,231	18,676	38,450	22,330	39,324	41,016	24,527	50,496	29,326
1991	30,126	31,569	18,807	36,449	22,691	38,183	40,012	23,837	46,197	28,760
1992	30,636	32,209	18,755	37,801	22,597	37,880	39,825	23,190	46,739	27,940
1993	31,241	32,960	19,533	38,347	22,886	37,688	39,762	23,564	46,260	27,609
1994	32,264	34,028	21,027	40,482	23,421	38,119	40,204	24,843	47,829	27,672
1995	34,076	35,766	22,393	40,614	22,860	39,306	41,255	25,830	46,847	26,368
1996	35,492	37,161	23,482	43,276	24,906	39,869	41,743	26,378	48,612	27,977
1997	37,005	38,972	25,050	45,249	26,628	40,699	42,863	27,551	49,766	29,286
1998	38,885	40,912	25,351	46,637	28,330	42,173	44,372	27,495	50,581	30,726
1999 [3]	40,816	42,504	27,910	51,205	30,735	43,355	45,148	29,646	54,391	32,647
2000 [3]	42,151	44,232	30,436	55,525	33,455	43,327	45,467	31,285	57,075	34,389
2000 [4]	41,990	43,916	29,667	55,757	33,168	43,162	45,142	30,495	57,313	34,094
2001	42,228	44,517	29,470	53,635	33,565	42,228	44,517	29,470	53,635	33,565

NA Not available. [1] Includes other races not shown separately. [2] People of Hispanic origin may be of any race. [3] Data based on Census 1990-based population controls and a sample of approximately 50,000 households. [4] Data reflect implementation of Census 2000-based population controls and a 28,000 household sample expansion to 78,000 households.

Source of Tables 683 and 684: U.S. Census Bureau, Current Population Reports, P60-218; and Internet site <http://www.census.gov/hhes/income/histinc/h05.html> (released 30 September 2002).

No. 685. Money Income of Households—Distribution by Income Level and Selected Characteristics: 2001

[109,297 represents 109,297,000. Households as of March of the following year. Based on Current Population Survey; see text, Sections 1 and 13, and Appendix III]

Characteristic	Number of households (1,000)	Under $15,000	$15,000-$24,999	$25,000-$34,999	$35,000-$49,999	$50,000-$74,999	$75,000-$99,999	$100,000 and over	Median income (dollars)
Total [1]	109,297	17,309	14,578	13,590	16,804	20,056	11,837	15,124	42,228
Age of householder:									
15 to 24 years	6,391	1,508	1,285	1,089	1,055	906	302	246	28,196
25 to 34 years	18,988	2,235	2,245	2,551	3,441	4,358	2,189	1,971	45,080
35 to 44 years	24,031	2,193	2,240	2,749	3,857	5,255	3,518	4,219	53,320
45 to 54 years	22,208	2,129	1,914	2,092	3,236	4,674	3,293	4,871	58,045
55 to 64 years	15,203	2,361	1,754	1,747	2,340	2,765	1,626	2,609	45,864
65 years and over	22,476	6,885	5,139	3,361	2,872	2,100	908	1,208	23,118
White	90,682	13,006	11,766	11,108	14,036	17,050	10,314	13,401	44,517
Black	13,315	3,526	2,196	1,901	1,986	2,053	909	744	29,470
Hispanic [2]	10,499	1,987	1,834	1,621	1,812	1,729	787	730	33,565
Region: [3]									
Northeast	21,128	3,391	2,635	2,357	2,937	3,851	2,374	3,581	45,716
Midwest	25,755	3,623	3,462	3,269	4,049	5,134	2,959	3,261	43,834
South	39,151	7,011	5,578	5,085	6,236	6,694	3,898	4,648	38,904
West	23,263	3,283	2,904	2,878	3,582	4,375	2,608	3,634	45,087
Size of household:									
One person	28,775	10,177	5,745	4,133	3,951	2,855	1,029	880	21,761
Two people	36,240	3,840	4,984	4,990	6,061	7,171	3,928	5,264	45,245
Three people	17,742	1,579	1,751	1,939	2,788	3,900	2,617	3,166	54,481
Four people	15,794	988	1,193	1,404	2,273	3,731	2,636	3,571	62,595
Five people	6,948	440	568	745	1,075	1,525	1,108	1,481	59,898
Six people	2,438	192	200	243	402	583	330	491	57,548
Seven or more people	1,360	91	135	138	247	290	188	271	54,560
Type of household:									
Family households	74,329	6,588	8,187	8,726	11,778	15,747	9,954	13,349	52,275
Married-couple	56,747	2,893	4,971	5,820	8,817	13,116	8,799	12,336	60,471
Male householder, wife absent	4,438	512	584	732	851	898	428	430	40,715
Female householder, husband absen.	13,143	3,182	2,631	2,176	2,112	1,735	726	583	28,142
Nonfamily households	34,969	10,721	6,391	4,862	5,025	4,308	1,886	1,775	25,631
Male householder	15,579	3,438	2,459	2,356	2,686	2,400	1,113	1,125	32,312
Female householder	19,390	7,280	3,932	2,506	2,338	1,907	772	650	20,264
Educational attainment of householder: [4]									
Total	102,906	15,801	13,293	12,500	15,749	19,150	11,536	14,878	43,592
Less than 9th grade	6,841	2,853	1,471	908	804	480	188	138	18,120
9th to 12th grade (no diploma)	9,437	3,020	1,934	1,453	1,377	1,043	339	268	23,251
High school graduate	31,360	5,397	5,176	4,616	5,374	5,875	2,763	2,156	36,055
Some college, no degree	18,141	2,146	2,267	2,423	3,044	3,894	2,197	2,170	45,810
Associate degree	8,575	837	815	1,006	1,497	1,973	1,304	1,143	51,162
Bachelor's degree or more	28,552	1,547	1,629	2,095	3,650	5,883	4,742	9,004	72,284
Bachelor's degree	18,359	1,092	1,138	1,495	2,548	4,092	3,033	4,961	67,165
Master's degree	6,974	308	333	446	790	1,387	1,233	2,474	78,902
Professional degree	1,733	82	100	76	165	179	256	873	100,000
Doctorate degree	1,486	62	56	78	147	224	221	696	92,806
Work experience of householder:									
Total	109,297	17,309	14,578	13,590	16,804	20,056	11,837	15,124	42,228
Worked	77,231	5,472	8,047	9,331	13,023	17,210	10,599	13,547	53,002
Worked at full-time jobs	66,589	3,357	6,421	7,976	11,367	15,503	9,687	12,279	55,723
50 weeks or more	56,274	1,758	4,811	6,598	9,658	13,623	8,714	11,111	58,608
27 to 49 weeks	6,844	692	1,013	964	1,205	1,382	734	854	43,558
26 weeks or less	3,471	904	597	416	505	496	240	313	30,239
Worked at part-time jobs	10,643	2,116	1,628	1,353	1,657	1,708	913	1,268	36,726
50 weeks or more	5,621	843	895	742	924	977	490	748	39,961
27 to 49 weeks	2,306	464	328	296	340	377	236	264	37,219
26 weeks or less	2,716	809	403	317	391	351	188	257	29,339
Did not work	32,066	11,836	6,529	4,259	3,781	2,846	1,239	1,577	20,887
Tenure:									
Owner occupied	74,399	8,215	8,249	8,205	11,194	15,229	9,981	13,325	51,597
Renter occupied	33,297	8,645	6,009	5,100	5,384	4,648	1,772	1,741	28,513
Occupier paid no cash rent	1,600	449	321	285	227	181	83	59	26,022

[1] Includes other races not shown separately. [2] People of Hispanic origin may be of any race. [3] For composition of regions, see map inside front cover. [4] People 25 years old and over.

Source: U.S. Census Bureau, Current Population Reports, P60-218; and Internet site <http://ferret.bls.census.gov/macro/032002/hhinc/new01001.htm> (released 23 September 2002).

No. 686. Money Income of Families—Percent Distribution by Income Level, Race, and Hispanic Origin, in Constant (2001) Dollars: 1980 to 2001

[Constant dollars based on CPI-U-RS deflator. Families as of March of following year (60,309 represents 60,309,000). Beginning with 1980, based on householder concept and restricted to primary families. Based on Current Population Survey; see text, Sections 1 and 13, and Appendix III. For data collection changes over time, see <http://www.census.gov/hhes/income/histinc/hstchg.html>. For definition of median, see Guide to Tabular Presentation]

Year	Number of families (1,000)	Under $15,000	$15,000-$24,999	$25,000-$34,999	$35,000-$49,999	$50,000-$74,999	$75,000-$99,999	$100,000 and over	Median income (dollars)
ALL FAMILIES [1]									
1980	60,309	12.0	13.5	14.0	20.3	23.4	9.7	7.0	42,776
1990	66,322	11.7	11.8	12.7	18.2	22.2	11.7	11.7	46,429
1995 [2]	69,597	11.5	12.3	12.6	17.1	21.4	12.0	13.1	46,843
2000 [2]	73,778	9.4	10.9	11.9	15.8	21.1	13.2	17.7	52,148
2001	74,340	9.7	11.3	11.9	15.7	20.8	13.1	17.6	51,407
WHITE									
1980	52,710	9.9	12.8	13.9	20.9	24.6	10.3	7.6	44,569
1990	56,803	9.1	11.4	12.6	18.7	23.2	12.4	12.5	48,480
1995 [2]	58,872	9.4	11.7	12.5	17.3	22.4	12.5	14.2	49,191
2000 [2]	61,330	7.9	10.2	11.6	15.9	21.8	13.9	18.7	54,509
2001	61,647	8.0	10.5	11.6	15.8	21.4	13.8	18.9	54,067
BLACK									
1980	6,317	29.5	19.5	14.6	16.1	13.6	4.8	1.9	25,788
1990	7,471	29.9	15.2	13.5	15.7	15.4	6.0	4.2	28,135
1995 [2]	8,055	26.4	16.8	14.3	15.6	14.7	7.8	4.4	29,956
2000 [2]	8,731	19.7	16.4	14.7	16.1	16.9	8.2	7.9	34,616
2001	8,847	20.9	16.5	14.0	15.2	17.4	8.7	7.2	33,598
ASIAN AND PACIFIC ISLANDER									
1990	1,536	10.1	10.2	9.8	14.5	21.2	16.2	18.1	55,482
1995 [2]	2,125	12.3	9.7	10.0	14.9	21.9	13.6	17.7	53,470
2000 [2]	2,982	7.6	8.2	9.1	13.4	20.1	14.9	26.7	64,365
2001	2,980	7.6	9.8	9.6	13.8	19.7	13.9	25.6	60,158
HISPANIC ORIGIN [3]									
1980	3,235	21.5	20.1	17.0	17.9	16.2	4.6	2.7	29,943
1990	4,981	22.9	18.5	14.9	17.8	15.3	6.1	4.5	30,772
1995 [2]	6,287	24.1	20.5	15.8	15.6	14.0	5.5	4.5	28,341
2000 [2]	8,017	16.7	17.4	15.8	17.5	17.4	8.3	6.9	35,403
2001	8,516	16.8	17.7	16.2	17.3	16.8	8.1	7.3	34,490

[1] Includes other races not shown separately. [2] Data reflect implementation of Census 2000-based population controls and a 28,000 household sample expansion to 78,000 households. [3] People of Hispanic origin may be of any race.

No. 687. Money Income of Families—Median Income by Race and Hispanic Origin in Current and Constant (2001) Dollars: 1980 to 2001

[See headnote, Table 686]

Year	Median income in current dollars					Median income in constant (2001) dollars				
	All families [1]	White	Black	Asian, Pacific Islander	His-panic [2]	All families [1]	White	Black	Asian, Pacific Islander	His-panic [2]
1980	21,023	21,904	12,674	(NA)	14,716	42,776	44,569	25,788	(NA)	29,943
1985	27,735	29,152	16,786	(NA)	19,027	43,518	45,742	26,339	(NA)	29,855
1986	29,458	30,809	17,604	(NA)	19,995	45,393	47,475	27,127	(NA)	30,811
1987	30,970	32,385	18,406	(NA)	20,300	46,151	48,259	27,428	(NA)	30,251
1988	32,191	33,915	19,329	36,560	21,769	46,285	48,763	27,792	52,566	31,300
1989	34,213	35,975	20,209	40,351	23,446	47,166	49,595	27,860	55,628	32,323
1990	35,353	36,915	21,423	42,246	23,431	46,429	48,480	28,135	55,482	30,772
1991	35,939	37,783	21,548	40,974	23,895	45,551	47,888	27,311	51,933	30,286
1992	36,573	38,670	21,103	42,255	23,555	45,221	47,814	26,093	52,246	29,125
1993	36,959	39,300	21,542	44,456	23,654	44,586	47,410	25,987	53,630	28,535
1994	38,782	40,884	24,698	46,122	24,318	45,820	48,304	29,180	54,492	28,731
1995	40,611	42,646	25,970	46,356	24,570	46,843	49,191	29,956	53,470	28,341
1996	42,300	44,756	26,522	49,105	26,179	47,516	50,275	29,792	55,160	29,407
1997	44,568	46,754	28,602	51,850	28,142	49,017	51,421	31,457	57,026	30,951
1998	46,737	49,023	29,404	52,826	29,608	50,689	53,168	31,890	57,293	32,112
1999	48,950	51,224	31,778	56,316	31,663	51,996	54,411	33,755	59,820	33,633
2000 [3]	50,890	53,256	34,192	61,511	35,054	52,310	54,742	35,146	63,228	36,032
2000 [4]	50,732	53,029	33,676	62,617	34,442	52,148	54,509	34,616	64,365	35,403
2001	51,407	54,067	33,598	60,158	34,490	51,407	54,067	33,598	60,158	34,490

NA Not available. [1] Includes other races not shown separately. [2] People of Hispanic origin may be of any race. [3] Data based on Census 1990-based population controls and a sample of approximately 50,000 households. [4] Data reflect implementation of Census 2000-based population controls and a 28,000 household sample expansion to 78,000 households.

Source of Tables 686 and 687: U.S. Census Bureau, Current Population Reports, P60-218; and Internet site <http://www.census.gov/hhes/income/histinc/f05.html> (released 30 September 2002).

No. 688. Share of Aggregate Income Received by Each Fifth and Top 5 Percent of Families: 1980 to 2001

[Families as of March of the following year (60,309 represents 60,309,000). Income in constant 2001 CPI-U-RS adjusted dollars. Based on the Current Population Survey; see text, Sections 1 and 13, and Appendix III. For data collection changes over time, see <http://www.census.gov/hhes/income/histinc/hstchg.html>]

Year	Number of families (1,000)	Income at selected positions (dollars)					Percent distribution of aggregate income						
		Upper limit of each fifth				Top 5 percent	Lowest 5th	Second 5th	Third 5th	Fourth 5th	Highest 5th	Top 5 percent
		Lowest	Second	Third	Fourth							
1980	60,309	21,161	35,628	50,461	70,809	111,910	5.3	11.6	17.6	24.4	41.1	14.6
1985	63,558	20,845	35,910	52,018	75,675	123,902	4.8	11.0	16.9	24.3	43.1	16.1
1986	64,491	21,573	37,137	54,118	77,926	128,515	4.7	10.9	16.9	24.1	43.4	16.5
1987	65,204	21,754	37,526	54,840	79,471	129,569	4.6	10.7	16.8	24.0	43.8	17.2
1988	65,837	21,714	37,645	55,356	80,382	132,280	4.6	10.7	16.7	24.0	44.0	17.2
1989	66,090	22,062	38,601	56,247	82,096	136,431	4.6	10.6	16.5	23.7	44.6	17.9
1990	66,322	22,124	38,143	55,211	80,755	134,426	4.6	10.8	16.6	23.8	44.3	17.4
1991	67,173	21,547	36,897	54,500	79,838	130,325	4.5	10.7	16.6	24.1	44.2	17.1
1992	68,216	20,665	36,690	54,404	79,195	131,079	4.3	10.5	16.5	24.0	44.7	17.6
1993	68,506	20,472	36,191	54,323	80,578	136,539	4.1	9.9	15.7	23.3	47.0	20.3
1994	69,313	21,196	36,980	55,530	82,702	141,829	4.2	10.0	15.7	23.3	46.9	20.1
1995	69,597	21,997	38,047	56,503	83,350	142,633	4.4	10.1	15.8	23.2	46.5	20.0
1996	70,241	22,107	38,546	57,385	84,603	143,784	4.2	10.0	15.8	23.1	46.8	20.3
1997	70,884	22,641	39,594	58,968	87,986	150,765	4.2	9.9	15.7	23.0	47.2	20.7
1998	71,551	23,427	40,879	60,757	90,770	157,477	4.2	9.9	15.7	23.0	47.3	20.7
1999	72,031	24,246	42,064	63,096	93,562	164,686	4.3	9.9	15.6	23.0	47.2	20.3
2000 [1]	72,388	24,670	42,144	63,091	94,259	164,723	4.3	9.8	15.5	22.8	47.4	20.8
2000 [2]	73,778	24,670	41,980	63,037	93,924	164,589	4.3	9.8	15.4	22.7	47.7	21.1
2001	74,340	24,000	41,127	62,500	94,150	164,104	4.2	9.7	15.4	22.9	47.7	21.0

[1] Data based on Census 1990-based population controls and a sample of approximately 50,000 households. [2] Data reflect implementation of Census 2000-based population controls and a 28,000 household sample expansion to 78,000 households.
Source: U.S. Census Bureau, Current Population Reports, P60-218, *Money Income in the United States: 2001*; and Internet sites at <http://www.census.gov/prod/2002pubs/p60-218.pdf> (released 24 September 2002) and <http://www.census.gov/hhes/income/histinc/f01.html> (released 01 October 2002) and <http://www.census.gov/hhes/income/histinc/f02.html> (released 01 October 2002).

No. 689. Money Income of Families—Distribution by Family Characteristics and Income Level: 2001

[74,340 represents 74,340,000. See headnote, Table 686. For composition of regions, see map inside front cover]

Characteristic	Number of families (1,000)	Under $15,000	$15,000 to $24,999	$25,000 to $34,999	$35,000 to $49,999	$50,000 to $74,999	$75,000 to $99,999	$100,000 and over	Median income (dollars)
All families	74,340	7,164	8,403	8,809	11,660	15,429	9,774	13,102	$51,407
Age of householder:									
15 to 24 years old	3,618	949	718	545	607	485	164	151	26,900
25 to 34 years old	13,220	1,685	1,575	1,664	2,158	3,066	1,588	1,483	46,272
35 to 44 years old	18,820	1,461	1,646	1,949	2,904	4,221	2,973	3,666	57,492
45 to 54 years old	16,540	912	1,110	1,282	2,175	3,757	2,890	4,413	68,114
55 to 64 years old	10,501	899	874	1,035	1,694	2,252	1,395	2,352	57,457
65 years old and over	11,641	1,258	2,477	2,334	2,124	1,651	759	1,037	33,816
White	61,647	4,916	6,489	7,167	9,755	13,181	8,507	11,633	54,067
Black	8,847	1,858	1,463	1,242	1,343	1,536	764	639	33,598
Hispanic origin [1]	8,516	1,430	1,502	1,380	1,471	1,427	687	618	34,490
Northeast	14,131	1,288	1,350	1,492	2,018	2,920	1,944	3,121	57,000
Midwest	17,447	1,305	1,861	1,994	2,805	4,036	2,526	2,919	54,096
South	27,021	3,143	3,466	3,373	4,387	5,296	3,257	4,103	46,688
West	15,740	1,430	1,725	1,952	2,453	3,181	2,044	2,959	51,966
Type of family:									
Married-couple families	56,755	2,904	4,989	5,855	8,833	13,116	8,781	12,275	60,335
Male householder, wife absent	4,440	639	648	793	831	796	382	351	36,590
Female householder, husband absent	13,146	3,623	2,764	2,161	1,997	1,517	607	476	25,745
Unrelated subfamilies	474	185	125	77	50	26	5	5	17,707
Education attainment of householder: [2]									
Total	70,722	6,215	7,683	8,265	11,054	14,944	9,609	12,951	52,864
Less than 9th grade	4,306	1,057	1,089	767	696	410	169	118	25,077
9th to 12th grade (no diploma)	6,176	1,214	1,271	1,149	1,108	901	294	241	29,512
High school graduate (includes equivalency)	21,769	2,225	2,985	3,114	4,084	4,987	2,432	1,941	43,870
Some college, no degree	12,627	833	1,213	1,580	2,149	3,099	1,884	1,871	53,809
Associate degree	5,956	312	392	620	1,025	1,517	1,088	1,000	60,033
Bachelor's degree or more	19,887	575	735	1,036	1,992	4,030	3,745	7,780	84,836
Bachelor's degree	12,665	394	516	740	1,443	2,840	2,411	4,321	78,518
Master's degree	4,888	120	144	190	402	917	977	2,138	90,811
Professional degree	1,255	32	41	54	83	132	180	734	100,000
Doctorate degree	1,079	27	33	50	62	144	174	587	100,000

[1] Persons of Hispanic origin may be of any race. [2] Persons 25 years old and over.
Source: U.S. Census Bureau, Current Population Reports, P60-218. See also <http://www.census.gov/prod/2002pubs/p60-218.pdf> (released September 2002) and <http://ferret.bls.census.gov/macro/032002/faminc/new01000.htm> (released 23 September 2002).

Income, Expenditures, and Wealth 459

No. 690. Median Income of Families by Type of Family in Current and Constant (2001) Dollars: 1980 to 2001

[In dollars. See headnote, Table 686. See Appendix III]

	Current dollars					Constant (2001) dollars				
	Married-couple families				Male house-holder, no wife present	Female house-holder, no husband present	Married-couple families				Male house-holder, no wife present	Female house-holder, no husband present
Year	Total	Total	Wife in paid labor force	Wife not in paid labor force			Total	Total	Wife in paid labor force	Wife not in paid labor force	
1980....	21,023	23,141	26,879	18,972	17,519	10,408	42,776	47,086	54,691	38,603	35,646	21,177
1985....	27,735	31,100	36,431	24,556	22,622	13,660	43,518	48,798	57,163	38,530	35,496	21,434
1990....	35,353	39,895	46,777	30,265	29,046	16,932	46,429	52,394	61,432	39,747	38,146	22,237
1995....	40,611	47,062	55,823	32,375	30,358	19,691	46,843	54,284	64,390	37,344	35,017	22,713
1996....	42,300	49,707	58,381	33,748	31,600	19,911	47,516	55,836	65,580	37,910	35,497	22,366
1997....	44,568	51,591	60,669	36,027	32,960	21,023	49,017	56,741	66,726	39,624	36,250	23,122
1998....	46,737	54,180	63,751	37,161	35,681	22,163	50,689	58,761	69,142	40,303	38,698	24,037
1999....	48,950	56,676	66,529	38,626	37,396	23,732	51,996	60,202	70,668	41,029	39,723	25,209
2000 [1]...	50,890	59,184	69,463	39,735	37,529	25,794	52,310	60,836	71,402	40,844	38,576	26,514
2000 [2]...	50,732	59,099	69,235	39,982	37,727	25,716	52,148	60,748	71,167	41,098	38,780	26,434
2001....	51,407	60,335	70,834	40,782	36,590	25,745	51,407	60,335	70,834	40,782	36,590	25,745

[1] Data based on Census 1990-based population controls and a sample of approximately 50,000 households. [2] Data reflect implementation of Census 2000-based population controls and a 28,000 household sample expansion to 78,000 households.

No. 691. Married-Couple Families—Number and Median Income by Work Experience of Husbands and Wives and Presence of Children: 2001

[56,755 represents 56,755,000 as of March 2002. Based on Current Population Survey; see Appendix III]

	Number (1,000)				Median income (dollars)			
			One or more related children under 18 yrs.				One or more related children under 18 yrs.	
Work experience of husband or wife	All married-couple families	No related children	Total	One child	Two children or more	All married-couple families	No related children	Total	One child	Two children or more

Work experience of husband or wife	All married-couple families	No related children	Total	One child	Two children or more	All married-couple families	No related children	Total	One child	Two children or more
All married-couple families..	56,755	29,824	26,931	10,311	16,619	60,335	55,421	65,203	67,527	63,881
Husband worked............	45,207	19,667	25,540	9,613	15,927	68,445	70,857	66,746	70,001	65,134
Wife worked.............	33,739	15,012	18,727	7,520	11,207	73,407	75,769	71,553	74,373	69,605
Wife did not work.........	11,468	4,655	6,813	2,093	4,721	50,926	42,127	50,164	50,469	50,044
Husband year-round, full-time worker................	37,390	15,354	22,036	8,240	13,796	72,025	75,652	69,749	72,267	67,856
Wife worked.............	28,313	12,186	16,127	6,437	9,690	76,461	79,943	74,284	76,755	72,625
Wife did not work.........	9,077	3,168	5,909	1,803	4,106	53,961	55,925	52,383	52,314	52,408
Husband did not work.......	11,547	10,157	1,391	698	692	30,254	30,257	30,213	34,064	26,966
Wife worked.............	3,178	2,382	796	374	423	39,566	40,433	36,758	40,214	32,945
Wife did not work.........	8,369	7,775	595	325	270	27,201	27,524	21,015	24,747	16,617

Source of Tables 690 and 691: U.S. Census Bureau, Current Population Reports, P60-218; and <http://www.census.gov/prod/2002pubs/p60-218.pdf> (released September 2002) and <http://ferret.bls.census.gov/macro/032002/faminc/new04000.htm> (released 23 September 2002).

No. 692. Money Income of Families—Distribution of Income and Median Income by Race and Hispanic Origin: 1999

[In thousands, except as indicated. Families as of April 2000. Based on sample data from the 2000 Census of Population and Housing; see text, Section 1, and Appendix III]

	Race of householder							
Income Interval	All families	White alone	Black or African American alone	American Indian and Alaska Native alone	Asian alone	Native Hawaiian and Other Pacific Islander alone	Some other race alone	Two or more races	Hispanic or Latino [1]
All families	72,262	56,470	8,209	564	2,350	79	3,207	1,382	7,483
Under $10,000.......	4,155	2,241	1,203	75	134	6	359	137	781
$10,000 to $14,999	3,116	1,973	650	46	92	4	260	91	579
$15,000 to $19,999	3,640	2,474	645	46	97	4	277	96	621
$20,000 to $24,999	4,117	2,936	634	46	107	5	291	98	645
$25,000 to $29,999	4,287	3,169	594	42	104	5	275	98	608
$30,000 to $34,999	4,397	3,352	538	40	113	5	255	94	566
$35,000 to $39,999	4,267	3,325	484	35	111	5	220	86	500
$40,000 to $44,999	4,223	3,352	443	32	115	5	197	80	450
$45,000 to $49,999	3,886	3,125	385	28	105	4	169	71	382
$50,000 to $59,999	7,300	5,976	666	48	209	8	268	125	633
$60,000 to $74,999	8,831	7,355	726	50	284	10	266	139	653
$75,000 to $99,999	9,009	7,619	660	42	336	10	212	131	561
$100,000 to $124,999...	4,662	3,992	289	17	214	4	81	63	242
$125,000 to $149,999...	2,274	1,960	125	7	119	2	32	28	104
$150,000 to $199,999...	1,984	1,732	88	5	112	1	22	23	78
$200,000 and over ...	2,113	1,887	78	5	98	1	22	22	80
Median income (dollars) .	50,046	53,356	33,255	33,144	59,324	45,915	32,398	39,432	34,397

[1] Persons of Hispanic origin or Latino may be of any race.
Source: U.S. Census Bureau, 2000 Census of Population and Housing, Summary File 3, using American FactFinder, Tables P76, P77, P78, P154A-H, and P155A-H (accessed 05 September 2003).

No. 693. Money Income of People—Selected Characteristics by Income Level: 2001

[People as of March 2002 (106,910 represents 106,910,000). Covers people 15 years old and over. For definition of median, see Guide to Tabular Presentation. For composition of regions, see map, inside front cover. See Appendix III]

Characteristic	All persons (1,000)	Total (1,000)	Under $5,000 [1]	$5,000 to $9,999	$10,000 to $14,999	$15,000 to $24,999	$25,000 to $34,999	$35,000 to $49,999	$50,000 to $74,999	$75,000 and over	Median income (dollars)
MALE											
Total	106,910	98,873	7,923	8,453	9,290	17,147	15,093	15,802	13,478	11,690	29,101
15 to 24 years old	19,914	14,484	4,937	2,595	1,989	2,732	1,249	652	227	101	9,301
25 to 34 years old	19,234	18,533	766	1,087	1,509	3,703	3,835	3,613	2,607	1,412	30,510
35 to 44 years old	21,822	21,166	663	1,015	1,059	3,061	3,586	4,181	4,004	3,598	38,340
45 to 54 years old	19,332	18,768	601	1,019	1,097	2,227	2,697	3,820	3,710	3,594	41,104
55 to 64 years old	12,373	11,982	543	884	911	1,749	1,793	2,057	1,993	2,051	35,637
65 yr. old and over	14,235	13,941	414	1,853	2,725	3,674	1,932	1,479	936	931	19,688
Northeast	20,584	19,213	1,552	1,635	1,624	3,100	2,817	2,968	2,817	2,701	30,636
Midwest	24,438	23,051	1,788	1,745	2,017	3,946	3,725	4,025	3,298	2,503	30,282
South	37,525	34,368	2,770	3,097	3,517	6,168	5,344	5,490	4,262	3,718	27,345
West	24,364	22,241	1,813	1,975	2,132	3,931	3,207	3,316	3,103	2,765	28,683
Education attainment of householder: [2]											
Total	86,996	84,389	2,986	5,857	7,300	14,413	13,843	15,151	13,249	11,588	32,494
Less than 9th grade	6,200	5,809	356	1,361	1,268	1,596	679	367	122	62	14,594
9th to 12th grade [3]	7,894	7,421	443	1,046	1,196	2,174	1,227	844	347	143	19,434
High school graduate [4]	26,947	25,954	892	1,906	2,636	5,494	5,388	5,063	3,287	1,289	28,343
Some college, no degree	14,661	14,340	522	778	1,004	2,347	2,738	3,112	2,450	1,391	33,777
Associate degree	6,466	6,352	179	201	342	791	1,170	1,567	1,386	718	38,870
Bachelor's degree or more	24,828	24,512	596	564	854	2,009	2,644	4,198	5,661	7,984	54,069
Bachelor's degree	15,925	15,723	408	430	593	1,444	2,004	2,985	3,716	4,143	49,985
Master's degree	5,595	5,522	123	83	151	348	459	840	1,418	2,100	61,960
Professional degree	1,795	1,779	39	23	53	109	98	185	261	1,010	81,602
Doctorate degree	1,514	1,488	26	29	55	107	85	186	265	733	72,642
Tenure:											
Owner occupied	76,943	71,829	5,676	5,151	5,934	11,045	10,512	12,085	11,217	10,209	31,991
Renter occupied	28,489	25,713	2,127	3,167	3,195	5,773	4,327	3,522	2,164	1,438	21,993
Occupier paid no cash rent	1,478	1,332	120	134	160	331	253	195	98	45	22,257
FEMALE											
Total	114,681	101,941	16,452	16,904	13,656	20,076	13,517	10,986	6,819	3,529	16,614
15 to 24 years old	19,535	13,865	5,228	2,874	1,984	2,349	962	331	97	41	7,467
25 to 34 years old	19,436	17,368	2,458	1,758	1,835	3,853	3,178	2,492	1,260	531	21,473
35 to 44 years old	22,461	20,647	2,799	2,055	2,099	4,212	3,460	3,057	1,932	1,034	22,471
45 to 54 years old	20,213	18,713	2,286	1,775	1,875	3,679	2,987	2,947	2,147	1,015	24,135
55 to 64 years old	13,501	12,377	1,955	1,975	1,495	2,347	1,649	1,438	889	629	17,823
65 yr. old and over	19,534	18,969	1,725	6,466	4,368	3,635	1,280	721	494	280	11,313
Northeast	22,434	20,290	3,092	3,376	2,643	3,916	2,620	2,248	1,524	869	17,068
Midwest	26,472	24,354	3,885	3,870	3,277	5,049	3,426	2,593	1,530	720	16,886
South	40,850	35,751	5,882	6,374	4,843	7,059	4,714	3,712	2,142	1,028	15,927
West	24,925	21,546	3,594	3,283	2,892	4,052	2,755	2,434	1,624	913	16,980
Education attainment of householder: [2]											
Total	95,146	88,075	11,224	14,029	11,673	17,729	12,554	10,655	6,723	3,487	18,549
Less than 9th grade	6,370	5,196	980	2,003	1,121	789	162	82	44	15	8,846
9th to 12th grade [3]	8,484	7,376	1,242	2,322	1,562	1,451	478	190	81	50	10,330
High school graduate [4]	31,509	28,945	3,730	5,481	4,662	7,306	4,188	2,356	898	326	15,665
Some college, no degree	16,330	15,420	1,907	1,941	1,915	3,644	2,605	2,014	975	420	20,101
Associate degree	8,585	8,177	899	869	935	1,698	1,494	1,339	684	257	22,638
Bachelor's degree or more	23,868	22,961	2,466	1,413	1,480	2,838	3,627	4,675	4,042	2,420	33,842
Bachelor's degree	16,357	15,660	1,914	1,108	1,137	2,114	2,679	3,093	2,403	1,210	30,973
Master's degree	5,893	5,749	438	251	275	573	803	1,330	1,339	738	40,744
Professional degree	942	899	77	37	37	94	103	128	131	289	46,635
Doctorate degree	676	653	36	17	31	57	40	124	167	185	52,181
Tenure:											
Owner occupied	82,054	73,975	12,287	11,364	9,271	14,005	9,912	8,533	5,625	2,979	17,445
Renter occupied	31,193	26,732	3,901	5,252	4,182	5,826	3,487	2,383	1,166	529	15,039
Occupier paid no cash rent	1,434	1,234	263	287	202	244	119	72	25	20	11,298

[1] Includes persons with income deficit. [2] Persons 25 years and over. [3] No diploma attained. [4] Includes high school equivalency.

Source: U.S. Census Bureau, Current Population Reports, *Money Income in the United States, 2001*, Series P60-218. See also <http://www.census.gov/prod/2002pubs/p60-218.pdf> (released September 2002).

No. 694. Median Income of People With Income in Constant (2001) Dollars by Sex, Race, and Hispanic Origin: 1980 to 2001

[People as of March of following year (78,661 represents 78,661,000). People 15 years old and over. Constant dollars based on CPI-U-RS deflator. Based on the Current Population Survey; see text, Sections 1 and 13, and Appendix III. For data collection changes over time, see <http://www.census.gov/hhes/income/histinc/hstchg.html>]

Item	Male					Female				
	1980	1990	1995	2000 [1]	2001	1980	1990	1995	2000 [1]	2001
NUMBER WITH INCOME (1,000)										
All races	78,661	88,220	92,066	98,504	98,873	80,826	92,245	96,007	101,704	101,941
White	69,420	76,480	79,022	83,372	83,750	70,573	78,566	80,608	84,123	84,207
Black	7,387	8,820	9,339	9,905	9,944	8,596	10,687	11,607	12,461	12,414
Asian and Pacific Islander	(NA)	2,235	3,095	4,303	4,165	(NA)	2,333	3,025	4,192	4,164
Hispanic [2]	3,996	6,767	8,577	11,311	11,766	3,617	5,903	7,478	9,431	9,691
White non-Hispanic	65,564	69,987	70,754	72,530	72,649	67,084	72,939	73,506	75,206	75,117
MEDIAN INCOME IN CONSTANT (2001) DOLLARS										
All races	12,530	20,293	22,562	28,343	29,101	4,920	10,070	12,130	16,063	16,614
White	13,328	21,170	23,895	29,797	30,240	4,947	10,317	12,316	16,079	16,652
Black	8,009	12,868	16,006	21,343	21,466	4,580	8,328	10,961	15,881	16,282
Asian and Pacific Islander	(NA)	19,394	22,162	30,833	31,096	(NA)	11,086	12,862	17,356	18,525
Hispanic [2]	9,659	13,470	14,840	19,498	20,189	4,405	7,532	8,928	12,248	12,583
White non-Hispanic	13,681	21,958	25,481	31,508	31,791	4,980	10,581	12,807	16,665	17,229
White non-Hispanic	13,681	21,958	25,481	32,387	31,791	4,980	10,581	12,807	17,130	17,229

NA Not available. [1] Data reflect implementation of Census 2000-based population controls and a 28,000 household sample expansion to 78,000 households. [2] People of Hispanic origin may be of any race.

No. 695. Average Earnings of Year-Round, Full-Time Workers by Educational Attainment: 2001

[In dollars. For people 18 years old and over as of March 2002]

Sex and age	All workers	Less than 9th grade	High school		College		
			9th to 12th grade (no diploma)	High school graduate (includes equivalency)	Some college, no degree	Associate degree	Bachelor's degree or more
Male, total	51,590	24,271	28,890	37,362	44,377	47,171	80,170
18 to 24 years old	24,315	16,656	20,109	23,416	23,525	28,673	39,390
25 to 34 years old	40,895	24,330	25,705	32,130	38,359	40,823	57,333
35 to 44 years old	56,265	24,802	32,348	39,535	48,305	49,061	87,941
45 to 54 years old	60,331	27,434	32,240	42,064	51,055	50,956	89,739
55 to 64 years old	60,682	24,330	35,951	41,961	51,427	56,882	90,671
65 years old and over	55,244	24,281	28,807	54,640	46,734	40,311	76,746
Female, total	35,348	18,049	24,318	26,660	31,698	34,031	50,220
18 to 24 years old	23,642	14,847	28,807	19,092	21,979	24,376	36,654
25 to 34 years old	34,273	16,862	33,131	25,353	28,784	30,206	44,615
35 to 44 years old	36,395	18,699	20,421	27,248	32,399	34,872	53,252
45 to 54 years old	38,439	18,548	21,586	29,238	34,549	36,399	54,375
55 to 64 years old	36,189	18,287	20,160	27,806	36,077	37,669	53,511
65 years old and over	34,343	18,238	19,742	26,178	58,277	33,735	38,754

No. 696. Per Capita Money Income in Current and Constant (2001) Dollars by Race and Hispanic Origin: 1980 to 2001

[In dollars. Constant dollars based on CPI-U-RS deflator. People as of March of following year. Based on the Current Population Survey; see text, Sections 1 and 13, and Appendix III. For data collection changes over time, see <http://www.census.gov/hhes/income/histinc/hstchg.html>]

Year	Current dollars					Constant (2001) dollars				
	All races [1]	White	Black	Asian, Pacific Islander	His- panic [2]	All races [1]	White	Black	Asian, Pacific Islander	His- panic [2]
1980	7,787	8,233	4,804	(NA)	4,865	15,844	16,752	9,775	(NA)	9,899
1985	11,013	11,671	6,840	(NA)	6,613	17,280	18,313	10,733	(NA)	10,376
1990	14,387	15,265	9,017	(NA)	8,424	18,894	20,047	11,842	(NA)	11,063
1991	14,617	15,510	9,170	(NA)	8,662	18,526	19,658	11,623	(NA)	10,979
1992	14,847	15,785	9,239	(NA)	8,591	18,358	19,517	11,424	(NA)	10,622
1993	15,777	16,800	9,863	15,691	8,830	19,033	20,267	11,898	18,929	10,652
1994	16,555	17,611	10,650	16,902	9,435	19,559	20,807	12,583	19,969	11,147
1995	17,227	18,304	10,982	16,567	9,300	19,871	21,113	12,667	19,109	10,727
1996	18,136	19,181	11,899	17,921	10,048	20,372	21,546	13,366	20,131	11,287
1997	19,241	20,425	12,351	18,226	10,772	21,162	22,464	13,584	20,045	11,847
1998	20,120	21,394	12,957	18,709	11,434	21,821	23,203	14,053	20,291	12,401
1999	21,181	22,375	14,397	21,134	11,621	22,499	23,767	15,293	22,449	12,344
2000 [3]	22,199	23,415	15,198	22,457	12,307	22,819	24,069	15,622	23,084	12,650
2000 [4]	22,346	23,582	14,796	23,350	12,651	22,970	24,240	15,209	24,002	13,004
2001	22,851	24,127	14,953	24,277	13,003	22,851	24,127	14,953	24,277	13,003

NA Not available. [1] Includes other races not shown separately. [2] Persons of Hispanic origin may be of any race. [3] Data based on Census 1990-based population controls and a sample of approximately 50,000 households. [4] Data reflect implementation of Census 2000-based population controls and a 28,000 household sample expansion to 78,000 households.
Source of Tables 694-696: U.S. Census Bureau, Current Population Reports, P60-218, and <http://www.census.gov/hhes/income/histinc/incperdet.html> (released 01 October 2002).

No. 697. People Below Poverty Level by Race, Sex, and Age: 1999

[Persons as of April 2000. Covers persons for whom poverty status was determined. Based on sample data from the 2000 Census of Population and Housing; see text, Section 1, and Appendix III]

Income Interval	All races	White alone	Black or African American alone	American Indian and Alaska Native alone	Asian alone	Native Hawaiian and other Pacific Islander alone	Some other race alone	Two or more races	Hispanic or Latino [1]
NUMBER BELOW POVERTY LEVEL (1,000)									
Total	33,900	18,848	8,146	608	1,257	65	3,688	1,289	7,798
Male	14,925	8,203	3,447	279	598	31	1,766	602	3,699
Female	18,975	10,645	4,699	329	659	34	1,922	687	4,099
Under 5 years old	3,412	1,579	982	69	81	8	489	204	1,030
5 years old	690	317	205	14	18	2	98	35	204
6 to 11 years old	4,149	1,904	1,271	88	120	9	564	192	1,172
12 to 17 years old	3,497	1,669	1,009	79	125	8	461	146	932
18 to 64 years old	18,865	11,007	4,051	327	818	36	1,976	651	4,133
65 years old and over	3,288	2,371	628	31	95	2	100	61	326
65 to 74 years old	1,551	1,040	339	19	56	1	63	34	194
75 years old and over	1,737	1,331	289	12	39	1	37	27	132
PERCENT BELOW POVERTY LEVEL									
Total	12.4	9.1	24.9	25.7	12.6	17.7	24.4	18.2	22.6
Male	11.2	8.1	22.8	24.0	12.5	16.7	22.7	17.1	21.1
Female	13.5	10.1	26.7	27.2	12.7	18.7	26.2	19.3	24.2
Under 5 years old	18.2	12.5	36.7	34.5	12.5	24.7	30.8	21.5	28.8
5 years old	17.6	12.0	35.2	33.6	13.6	24.4	30.6	19.9	28.5
6 to 11 years old	16.9	11.3	33.5	31.7	14.8	23.1	30.3	19.8	28.2
12 to 17 years old	14.8	10.0	29.4	29.0	15.2	20.6	28.2	18.3	26.2
18 to 64 years old	11.1	8.6	20.7	22.6	12.0	15.6	21.3	17.0	19.9
65 years old and over	9.9	8.2	23.5	23.5	12.3	11.5	22.8	16.9	19.6
65 to 74 years old	8.5	6.7	21.4	21.9	11.6	11.7	21.9	15.5	18.4
75 years old and over	11.5	10.0	26.6	26.3	13.7	11.0	24.5	18.9	21.8

[1] Persons of Hispanic origin or Latino may be of any race.
Source: U.S. Census Bureau, 2000 Census of Population and Housing, Summary File 3, using American FactFinder, tables P52, P53, P54, P151A-H, P152A-H, and P153A-H (accessed 05 September 2003).

No. 698. Families and People Below Poverty Level by 25 Largest Metropolitan Areas: 1999

[Number in thousands (72.0 represents 72,000), except percent. Covers metropolitan statistical area (MSAs) and consolidated metropolitan statistical areas (CMSAs) as defined by the U.S. Office of Management and Budget as of June 30, 1999. For definitions and components of metropolitan areas, see Appendix II. For information on poverty, see text, Section 13]

Metropolitan area based on 2000 population	Families Total Number	Families Total Percent	Families with female householder [1] Number	Families with female householder [1] Percent	Persons Total Number	Persons Total Percent	Related children under 18 years old Number	Related children under 18 years old Percent
Atlanta, GA MSA	72.0	6.9	41.0	20.7	379.9	9.4	125.6	11.7
Boston-Worcester-Lawrence, MA-NH-ME-CT CMSA	87.3	6.0	49.7	20.5	482.7	8.6	138.9	10.2
Chicago-Gary-Kenosha, IL-IN-WI CMSA	178.7	7.9	98.1	23.0	943.0	10.5	337.6	14.0
Cincinnati-Hamilton, OH-KY-IN CMSA	36.1	6.9	22.7	25.0	184.3	9.5	62.2	12.1
Cleveland-Akron, OH CMSA	61.8	8.0	39.5	26.1	305.0	10.6	109.5	15.0
Dallas-Fort Worth, TX CMSA	108.2	8.1	48.8	22.2	556.1	10.8	198.8	13.9
Denver-Boulder-Greeley, CO CMSA	36.5	5.6	17.1	18.1	217.2	8.6	64.6	10.0
Detroit-Ann Arbor-Flint, MI CMSA	109.3	7.7	67.6	23.5	571.1	10.6	202.0	14.4
Houston-Galveston-Brazoria, TX CMSA	128.0	10.9	55.0	26.5	628.4	13.7	233.8	17.6
Kansas City, MO-KS MSA	28.7	6.1	16.6	21.1	147.7	8.5	50.5	10.9
Los Angeles-Riverside-Orange County, CA CMSA	461.1	12.2	185.6	26.5	2,510.1	15.6	943.8	20.8
Miami-Fort Lauderdale, FL CMSA	116.1	12.0	54.8	26.1	581.6	15.3	181.7	19.8
Minneapolis-St. Paul, MN-WI MSA	31.7	4.2	17.4	16.5	195.3	6.7	63.7	8.2
New York-Northern New Jersey-Long Island, NY-NJ-CT-PA CMSA	536.7	10.2	291.1	26.3	2,678.8	12.9	880.5	17.2
Philadelphia-Wilmington-Atlantic City, PA-NJ-DE-MD CMSA	124.8	7.9	75.2	23.3	653.8	10.9	215.4	14.0
Phoenix-Mesa, AZ MSA	67.0	8.2	26.0	21.2	383.5	12.0	134.9	15.9
Pittsburgh, PA MSA	49.2	7.8	27.2	25.5	248.6	10.8	74.2	14.4
Portland-Salem, OR-WA CMSA	38.8	6.8	18.4	22.1	222.6	10.0	68.4	12.1
Sacramento-Yolo, CA CMSA	39.2	8.7	18.1	22.2	224.9	12.7	79.6	16.8
San Diego, CA MSA	59.2	8.9	25.8	22.8	338.4	12.4	115.9	16.5
San Francisco-Oakland-San Jose, CA CMSA	95.7	5.7	42.7	16.0	602.7	8.7	162.9	10.1
Seattle-Tacoma-Bremerton, WA CMSA	52.0	5.8	25.9	19.7	297.4	8.5	85.7	10.0
St. Louis, MO-IL MSA	51.0	7.4	32.4	24.3	253.8	9.9	91.7	13.7
Tampa-St. Petersburg-Clearwater, FL MSA	50.2	7.8	24.8	22.5	262.4	11.2	80.2	15.7
Washington-Baltimore, DC-MD-VA-WV CMSA	113.0	5.9	67.7	18.3	613.8	8.3	187.8	10.0

[1] No husband present.
Source: U.S. Census Bureau, "2000 Census of Population and Housing, Profiles of General Demographic Characteristics"; <http://www.census.gov/Press-Release/www/2002/demoprofiles.html>.

No. 699. Families and People Below Poverty Level by State: 1999

[In thousands (6,621 represents 6,621,000), except percent. Families and individuals as of April 2000. Based on sample data from the 2000 Census of Population and Housing; see text, Section 1, and Appendix III. For information about poverty, see text, Section 13]

State	Families Total Number	Families Total Percent	Families with female householder [1] Number	Families with female householder [1] Percent	Persons Total Number	Persons Total Percent	65 years old and over Number	65 years old and over Percent	Related children under 18 years old Number	Related children under 18 years old Percent
U.S.	6,621	9.2	3,316	26.5	33,900	12.4	3,288	9.9	11,386	16.1
AL............	153	12.5	86	35.6	698	16.1	86	15.5	234	21.2
AK............	10	6.7	5	20.0	58	9.4	2	6.8	21	11.2
AZ............	128	9.9	52	25.8	699	13.9	55	8.4	249	18.8
AR............	88	12.0	43	34.7	412	15.8	49	13.8	142	21.4
CA............	846	10.6	350	25.0	4,706	14.2	280	8.1	1,706	19.0
CO	68	6.2	31	20.6	389	9.3	30	7.4	116	10.8
CT............	50	5.6	30	19.6	260	7.9	31	7.0	83	10.0
DE............	13	6.5	8	20.4	70	9.2	8	7.9	23	11.9
DC	19	16.7	14	30.0	110	20.2	11	16.4	34	31.1
FL............	383	9.0	187	25.3	1,953	12.5	247	9.1	608	17.2
GA	210	9.9	120	28.5	1,034	13.0	102	13.5	355	16.7
HI	22	7.6	10	20.6	126	10.7	12	7.4	39	13.5
ID	28	8.3	11	27.7	149	11.8	12	8.3	50	13.8
IL	244	7.8	131	24.1	1,292	10.7	118	8.3	443	14.0
IN	108	6.7	58	23.4	559	9.5	54	7.7	180	11.7
IA............	47	6.0	22	23.4	258	9.1	31	7.7	75	10.5
KS............	47	6.7	22	23.5	258	9.9	27	8.1	80	11.5
KY............	141	12.7	61	33.1	621	15.8	67	14.2	198	20.4
LA............	183	15.8	110	40.6	851	19.6	82	16.7	314	26.3
ME	27	7.8	13	28.1	136	10.9	18	10.2	38	13.0
MD	83	6.1	50	18.4	439	8.5	49	8.5	136	10.3
MA	106	6.7	62	22.1	573	9.3	71	8.9	171	11.6
MI	192	7.4	111	24.0	1,022	10.5	96	8.2	340	13.4
MN	64	5.1	31	19.3	380	7.9	45	8.2	115	9.2
MS	120	16.0	72	40.2	548	19.9	61	18.8	203	26.7
MO	127	8.6	65	26.1	638	11.7	70	9.9	212	15.3
MT	25	10.5	10	33.2	128	14.6	10	9.1	41	18.4
NE............	30	6.7	14	24.0	161	9.7	17	8.0	52	11.8
NV............	38	7.5	17	20.5	206	10.5	15	7.1	67	13.5
NH	14	4.3	7	17.6	79	6.5	10	7.2	22	7.3
NJ............	136	6.3	72	19.4	700	8.5	83	7.8	221	10.8
NM	68	14.5	30	34.1	329	18.4	26	12.8	122	24.6
NY............	536	11.5	295	29.2	2,692	14.6	264	11.3	894	19.6
NC	196	9.0	104	27.4	959	12.3	122	13.2	302	15.7
ND	14	8.3	6	30.6	73	11.9	10	11.1	21	13.5
OH	235	7.8	137	26.3	1,171	10.6	116	8.1	397	14.0
OK	104	11.2	47	32.0	491	14.7	48	11.1	166	19.1
OR	70	7.9	32	25.9	389	11.6	32	7.6	115	14.0
PA............	250	7.8	135	24.9	1,304	11.0	164	9.1	408	14.3
RI	24	8.9	15	29.1	121	11.9	15	10.6	40	16.5
SC............	116	10.7	67	30.6	548	14.1	65	13.9	183	18.5
SD............	18	9.3	8	30.4	96	13.2	11	11.1	33	16.7
TN............	161	10.3	83	29.5	747	13.5	90	13.5	241	17.6
TX............	633	12.0	267	29.5	3,118	15.4	251	12.8	1,162	20.2
UT............	35	6.5	14	22.1	206	9.4	11	5.8	68	9.7
VT............	10	6.3	5	24.1	56	9.4	6	8.5	15	10.7
VA............	130	7.0	71	23.0	657	9.6	72	9.5	202	11.9
WA	111	7.3	52	24.1	612	10.6	48	7.5	194	13.2
WV	70	13.9	27	35.5	316	17.9	32	11.9	94	23.9
WI	78	5.6	42	21.7	452	8.7	49	7.4	144	10.8
WY	11	8.0	5	30.9	55	11.4	5	8.9	17	13.8

[1] No husband present.

Source: U.S. Census Bureau, "2000 Census of Population and Housing, Profiles of General Demographic Characteristics"; <http://www.census.gov/Press-Release/www/2002/demoprofiles.html>.

No. 700. People Below Poverty Level and Below 125 Percent of Poverty Level by Race and Hispanic Origin: 1980 to 2001

[Persons as of March of the following year (29,272 represents 29,272,000). Based on Current Population Survey. See text, this section, Section 1, and Appendix III. For data collection changes over time, see <http://www.census.gov/hhes/income/histinc/hstchg.html>]

Year	Number below poverty level (1,000) All races [1]	White	Black	Asian and Pacific Islander	Hispanic [2]	Percent below poverty level All races [1]	White	Black	Asian and Pacific Islander	Hispanic [2]	Below 125 percent of poverty level Number (1,000)	Percent of total population
1980	29,272	19,699	8,579	(NA)	3,491	13.0	10.2	32.5	(NA)	25.7	40,658	18.1
1981	31,822	21,553	9,173	(NA)	3,713	14.0	11.1	34.2	(NA)	26.5	43,748	19.3
1982	34,398	23,517	9,697	(NA)	4,301	15.0	12.0	35.6	(NA)	29.9	46,520	20.3
1983	35,303	23,984	9,882	(NA)	4,633	15.2	12.1	35.7	(NA)	28.0	47,150	20.3
1984	33,700	22,955	9,490	(NA)	4,806	14.4	11.5	33.8	(NA)	28.4	45,288	19.4
1985	33,064	22,860	8,926	(NA)	5,236	14.0	11.4	31.3	(NA)	29.0	44,166	18.7
1986	32,370	22,183	8,983	(NA)	5,117	13.6	11.0	31.1	(NA)	27.3	43,486	18.2
1987	32,221	21,195	9,520	1,021	5,422	13.4	10.4	32.4	16.1	28.0	43,032	17.9
1988	31,745	20,715	9,356	1,117	5,357	13.0	10.1	31.3	17.3	26.7	42,551	17.5
1989	31,528	20,785	9,302	939	5,430	12.8	10.0	30.7	14.1	26.2	42,653	17.3
1990	33,585	22,326	9,837	858	6,006	13.5	10.7	31.9	12.2	28.1	44,837	18.0
1991	35,708	23,747	10,242	996	6,339	14.2	11.3	32.7	13.8	28.7	47,527	18.9
1992	38,014	25,259	10,827	985	7,592	14.8	11.9	33.4	12.7	29.6	50,592	19.7
1993	39,265	26,226	10,877	1,134	8,126	15.1	12.2	33.1	15.3	30.6	51,801	20.0
1994	38,059	25,379	10,196	974	8,416	14.5	11.7	30.6	14.6	30.7	50,401	19.3
1995	36,425	24,423	9,872	1,411	8,574	13.8	11.2	29.3	14.6	30.3	48,761	18.5
1996	36,529	24,650	9,694	1,454	8,697	13.7	11.2	28.4	14.5	29.4	49,310	18.5
1997	35,574	24,396	9,116	1,468	8,308	13.3	11.0	26.5	14.0	27.1	47,853	17.8
1998	34,476	23,454	9,091	1,360	8,070	12.7	10.5	26.1	12.5	25.6	46,036	17.0
1999 [3]	32,258	21,922	8,360	1,163	7,439	11.8	9.8	23.6	10.7	22.8	44,286	16.2
2000 [3]	31,054	21,242	7,862	1,214	7,153	11.3	9.4	22.0	10.7	21.2	43,377	15.7
2000 [4]	31,581	21,645	7,982	1,258	7,747	11.3	9.5	22.5	9.9	21.5	43,612	15.6
2001	32,907	22,739	8,136	1,275	7,997	11.7	9.9	22.7	10.2	21.4	45,320	16.1

NA Not available. [1] Includes other races not shown separately. [2] Persons of Hispanic origin may be of any race. [3] Data based on Census 1990-based population controls and a sample of approximately 50,000 households. [4] Data reflect implementation of Census 2000-based population controls and a 28,000 household sample expansion to 78,000 households.

Source: U.S. Census Bureau, Current Population Reports, Poverty in the United States, 2001, P60-219. See also <http://www.census.gov/prod/2002pubs/p60-219.pdf> (released September 2002).

No. 701. Children Below Poverty Level by Race and Hispanic Origin: 1980 to 2001

[People as of March of the following year. (11,114 represents 11,114,000). Covers only related children in families under 18 years old. Based on Current Population Survey; see text, this section, and Section 1, and Appendix III. For data collection changes over time, see <http://www.census.gov/hhes/income/histinc/hstchg.html>]

Year	Number below poverty level (1,000) All races [1]	White	Black	Asian and Pacific Islander	Hispanic [2]	Percent below poverty level All races [1]	White	Black	Asian and Pacific Islander	Hispanic [2]
1980	11,114	6,817	3,906	(NA)	1,718	17.9	13.4	42.1	(NA)	33.0
1981	12,068	7,429	4,170	(NA)	1,874	19.5	14.7	44.9	(NA)	35.4
1982	13,139	8,282	4,388	(NA)	2,117	21.3	16.5	47.3	(NA)	38.9
1983	13,427	8,534	4,273	(NA)	2,251	21.8	17.0	46.2	(NA)	37.7
1984	12,929	8,086	4,320	(NA)	2,317	21.0	16.1	46.2	(NA)	38.7
1985	12,483	7,838	4,057	(NA)	2,512	20.1	15.6	43.1	(NA)	39.6
1986	12,257	7,714	4,037	(NA)	2,413	19.8	15.3	42.7	(NA)	37.1
1987	12,275	7,398	4,234	432	2,606	19.7	14.7	44.4	22.7	38.9
1988	11,935	7,095	4,148	458	2,576	19.0	14.0	42.8	23.5	37.3
1989	12,001	7,164	4,257	368	2,496	19.0	14.1	43.2	18.9	35.5
1990	12,715	7,696	4,412	356	2,750	19.9	15.1	44.2	17.0	37.7
1991	13,658	8,316	4,637	348	2,977	21.1	16.1	45.6	17.1	39.8
1992	14,521	8,752	5,015	352	3,440	21.6	16.5	46.3	16.0	39.0
1993	14,961	9,123	5,030	358	3,666	22.0	17.0	45.9	17.6	39.9
1994	14,610	8,826	4,787	308	3,956	21.2	16.3	43.3	17.9	41.1
1995	13,999	8,474	4,644	532	3,938	20.2	15.5	41.5	18.6	39.3
1996	13,764	8,488	4,411	553	4,090	19.8	15.5	39.5	19.1	39.9
1997	13,422	8,441	4,116	608	3,865	19.2	15.4	36.8	19.9	36.4
1998	12,845	7,935	4,073	542	3,670	18.3	14.4	36.4	17.5	33.6
1999 [3]	11,510	7,123	3,644	348	3,382	16.3	12.9	32.7	11.5	29.9
2000 [3]	11,018	6,838	3,417	434	3,173	15.6	12.3	30.4	14.1	27.3
2000 [4]	11,005	6,834	3,495	407	3,342	15.6	12.4	30.9	12.5	27.6
2001	11,175	7,086	3,423	353	3,433	15.6	12.8	30.0	11.1	27.4

NA Not available. [1] Includes other races not shown separately. [2] Persons of Hispanic origin may be of any race. [3] Data based on Census 1990-based population controls and a sample of approximately 50,000 households. [4] Data reflect implementation of Census 2000-based population controls and a 28,000 household sample expansion to 78,000 households.

Source: U.S. Census Bureau, Current Population Reports, Poverty in the United States, 2001, P60-219. See also <http://www.census.gov/prod/2002pubs/p60-219.pdf> (released September 2002).

No. 702. Weighted Average Poverty Thresholds by Size of Family Unit: 1980 to 2001

[In dollars. For information on the official poverty thresholds; see text, this section]

Size of family unit	1980[1]	1990	1995	1996	1997	1998	1999	2000	2001
One person (unrelated individual)	4,190	6,652	7,763	7,995	8,183	8,316	8,501	8,794	9,044
Under 65 years	4,290	6,800	7,929	8,163	8,350	8,480	8,667	8,959	9,214
65 years and over	3,949	6,268	7,309	7,525	7,698	7,818	7,990	8,259	8,494
Two persons	5,363	8,509	9,933	10,233	10,473	10,634	10,869	11,239	11,559
Householder under 65 years	5,537	8,794	10,259	10,564	10,805	10,972	11,214	11,590	11,920
Householder 65 years and over	4,983	7,905	9,219	9,491	9,712	9,862	10,075	10,419	10,715
Three persons	6,565	10,419	12,158	12,516	12,802	13,003	13,290	13,738	14,129
Four persons	8,414	13,359	15,569	16,036	16,400	16,660	17,029	17,603	18,104
Five persons	9,966	15,792	18,408	18,952	19,380	19,680	20,127	20,819	21,411
Six persons	11,269	17,839	20,804	21,389	21,886	22,228	22,727	23,528	24,197
Seven persons	12,761	20,241	23,552	24,268	24,802	25,257	25,912	26,754	27,514
Eight persons	14,199	22,582	26,237	27,091	27,593	28,166	28,967	29,701	30,546
Nine or more persons	16,896	26,848	31,280	31,971	32,566	33,339	34,417	35,060	36,058

[1] Poverty levels for nonfarm families.

Source: U.S. Census Bureau, Current Population Reports, *Poverty in the United States, 2001*, P60-219. See also <http://www.census.gov/prod/2002pubs/p60-219.pdf> (released September 2002).

No. 703. Persons Below Poverty Level by Selected Characteristics: 2001

[People as of March 2002 (32,907 represents 32,907,000). Based on Current Population Survey; see text, this section, Section 1, and Appendix III. For composition of regions, see map, inside front cover]

Characteristic	Number below poverty level (1,000)					Percent below poverty level				
	All races[1]	White	Black	Asian and Pacific Islander	Hispanic[2]	All races[1]	White	Black	Asian and Pacific Islander	Hispanic[2]
Total	32,907	22,739	8,136	1,275	7,997	11.7	9.9	22.7	10.2	21.4
Male	14,327	10,072	3,343	611	3,754	10.4	8.9	20.1	10.1	19.7
Female	18,580	12,667	4,793	664	4,243	12.9	10.9	24.9	10.4	23.2
Under 18 years old	11,733	7,527	3,492	369	3,570	16.3	13.4	30.2	11.5	28.0
18 to 24 years old	4,449	3,044	1,062	260	1,024	16.3	14.1	26.8	18.8	21.0
25 to 34 years old	4,255	2,991	991	182	1,238	11.0	9.7	19.7	8.1	17.7
35 to 44 years old	3,822	2,713	833	166	983	8.6	7.5	15.2	8.0	18.1
45 to 54 years old	2,804	1,949	683	117	443	7.1	5.9	15.3	6.8	13.0
55 to 59 years old	1,274	974	237	42	150	8.7	7.8	16.5	7.6	13.6
60 to 64 years old	1,157	884	212	47	176	10.3	9.1	19.9	12.5	20.9
65 years old and over	3,414	2,656	626	92	413	10.1	8.9	21.9	10.2	21.8
65 to 74 years old	1,664	1,222	355	62	254	9.2	7.8	20.1	11.3	21.6
75 years old and over	1,750	1,434	271	30	159	11.2	10.2	24.8	8.5	22.0
Northeast	5,687	3,827	1,517	297	1,226	10.7	8.7	23.5	12.8	24.7
Midwest	5,966	4,072	1,628	112	465	9.4	7.4	25.0	7.8	16.2
South	13,515	8,470	4,570	231	2,886	13.5	11.0	23.0	9.8	22.2
West	7,739	6,371	421	635	3,419	12.1	12.0	13.7	10.0	20.8
Native	27,698	18,847	7,694	446	4,743	11.1	9.1	23.3	9.5	21.3
Foreign born	5,209	3,891	442	829	3,254	16.1	18.1	15.2	10.7	21.6
Naturalized citizen	1,186	807	111	258	533	9.9	11.2	11.1	7.0	14.1
Not a citizen	4,023	3,084	331	571	2,721	19.7	21.6	17.4	13.9	24.2

[1] Includes other races not shown separately. [2] Persons of Hispanic origin may be of any race.

Source: U.S. Census Bureau, Current Population Reports, *Poverty in the United States, 2001*, P60-219. See also <http://www.census.gov/prod/2002pubs/p60-219.pdf> (released September 2002) and <http://ferret.bls.census.gov/macro/032002/pov/new19007.htm> (released 23 September 2002).

No. 704. Work Experience During 2001 by Poverty Status, Sex, and Age: 2001

[Number in thousands (100,357 represents 100,357,000). Covers only persons 16 years old and over. Based on Current Population Survey; see text, this section, Section 1, and Appendix III]

Sex and age	Worked full-time year-round Number (1,000)	Below poverty level Number (1,000)	Percent	Did not work full-time year-round Number (1,000)	Below poverty level Number (1,000)	Percent	Did not work Number (1,000)	Below poverty level Number (1,000)	Percent
BOTH SEXES									
Total............	100,357	2,567	2.6	50,685	5,964	11.8	66,534	13,715	20.6
16 to 17 years old	112	12	10.4	2,952	226	7.7	5,058	833	16.5
18 to 64 years old	98,110	2,540	2.6	44,364	5,633	12.7	33,211	9,588	28.9
18 to 24 years old....	7,994	407	5.1	12,970	2,055	15.8	6,349	1,986	31.3
25 to 34 years old....	23,674	798	3.4	9,633	1,546	16.0	5,363	1,911	35.6
35 to 54 years old....	54,462	1,138	2.1	16,608	1,686	10.2	12,759	3,801	29.8
55 to 64 years old....	11,980	196	1.6	5,154	345	6.7	8,740	1,889	21.6
65 years old and over...	2,135	15	0.7	3,369	105	3.1	28,265	3,293	11.7
MALE									
Total............	58,715	1,423	2.4	21,256	2,425	11.4	24,885	5,059	20.3
16 to 17 years old	82	10	12.7	1,470	111	7.5	2,602	420	16.2
18 to 64 years old	57,236	1,400	2.4	18,060	2,282	12.6	11,170	3,685	33.0
18 to 24 years old....	4,612	185	4.0	6,323	850	13.4	2,770	824	29.8
25 to 34 years old....	14,033	441	3.1	3,889	572	14.7	1,312	604	46.1
35 to 54 years old....	31,612	656	2.1	5,731	705	12.3	3,811	1,489	39.1
55 to 64 years old....	6,979	118	1.7	2,117	155	7.3	3,276	767	23.4
65 years old and over...	1,397	12	0.9	1,726	32	1.9	11,113	954	8.6
FEMALE									
Total............	41,642	1,144	2.7	29,429	3,538	12.0	41,649	8,656	20.8
16 to 17 years old	30	1	(B)	1,481	115	7.8	2,456	413	16.8
18 to 64 years old	40,874	1,140	2.8	26,304	3,351	12.7	22,041	5,903	26.8
18 to 24 years old....	3,382	223	6.6	6,647	1,205	18.1	3,579	1,162	32.5
25 to 34 years old....	9,641	356	3.7	5,744	974	17.0	4,051	1,307	32.3
35 to 54 years old....	22,850	482	2.1	10,877	982	9.0	8,948	2,313	25.8
55 to 64 years old....	5,001	78	1.6	3,037	190	6.3	5,464	1,122	20.5
65 years old and over...	738	3	0.4	1,643	72	4.4	17,152	2,339	13.6

B Base figure too small to meet statistical standards for reliability of a derived figure.
Source: U.S. Census Bureau, <http://ferret.bls.census.gov/macro/032001/pov/new10001.htm> (released 23 September 2002).

No. 705. Persons Below Poverty Level—Number and Rate by State: 1999 to 2001 Average

[32,426 represents 32,426,000. Based on the Current Population survey; see text, Sections 1 and 13, and Appendix III. The CPS is designed to collect reliable data on income primarily at the national level and secondarily at the regional level. When the income data are tabulated by state, the estimates are considered less reliable and, therefore, particular caution should be used when trying to interpret the results; for additional detail, see source]

State	Number below poverty level (1,000)	Percent below poverty level	State	Number below poverty level (1,000)	Percent below poverty level
United States......	32,426	11.6	Missouri	563	10.2
			Montana	128	14.4
Alabama............	649	14.8	Nebraska............	162	9.7
Alaska	50	7.9	Nevada..............	187	9.0
Arizona.............	667	12.9	New Hampshire	78	6.2
Arkansas............	431	16.3			
California...........	4,449	13.1	New Jersey..........	647	7.7
			New Mexico..........	339	18.8
Colorado............	391	9.0	New York	2,648	14.1
Connecticut.........	251	7.4	North Carolina	1,027	12.9
Delaware...........	66	8.5	North Dakota	77	12.4
District of Columbia....	88	16.1			
Florida	1,923	12	Ohio................	1,211	10.8
			Oklahoma...........	478	14.3
Georgia	1,021	12.6	Oregon.............	403	11.8
Hawaii	126	10.4	Pennsylvania........	1,102	9.2
Idaho	162	12.7	Rhode Island........	103	10.0
Illinois..............	1,257	10.2			
Indiana	473	7.9	South Carolina	496	12.7
			South Dakota........	65	9.0
Iowa................	220	7.7	Tennessee..........	741	13.2
Kansas.............	267	10.1	Texas	3,135	15.2
Kentucky............	491	12.4	Utah................	178	8.0
Louisiana	761	17.5			
Maine...............	131	10.3	Vermont	59	9.8
			Virginia	559	8.0
Maryland............	380	7.3	Washington	604	10.4
Massachusetts.......	639	10.2	West Virginia	275	15.6
Michigan............	957	9.7	Wisconsin	461	8.6
Minnesota	331	6.8	Wyoming............	50	10.3
Mississippi..........	468	16.8			

Source: U.S. Census Bureau, Current Population Reports, *Poverty in the United States, 2001*, P60-219. See also <http://www.census.gov/prod/2002pubs/p60-219.pdf> (released September 2002).

Income, Expenditures, and Wealth 467

No. 706. Families Below Poverty Level and Below 125 Percent of Poverty by Race and Hispanic Origin: 1980 to 2001

[Families as of March of the following year (6,217 represents 6,217,000). Based on Current Population Survey; See text, this section, Section 1, and Appendix III. For data collection changes over time, see <http://www.census.gov/hhes/income/histinc/hstchg.html>]

Year	Number below poverty level (1,000)					Percent below poverty level					Below 125 percent of poverty level	
	All races [1]	White	Black	Asian and Pacific Islander	Hispanic [2]	All races [1]	White	Black	Asian and Pacific Islander	Hispanic [2]	Number (1,000)	Percent
1980	6,217	4,195	1,826	(NA)	751	10.3	8.0	28.9	(NA)	23.2	8,764	14.5
1981	6,851	4,670	1,972	(NA)	792	11.2	8.8	30.8	(NA)	24.0	9,568	15.7
1982	7,512	5,118	2,158	(NA)	916	12.2	9.6	33.0	(NA)	27.2	10,279	16.7
1983	7,647	5,220	2,161	(NA)	981	12.3	9.7	32.3	(NA)	25.9	10,358	16.7
1984	7,277	4,925	2,094	(NA)	991	11.6	9.1	30.9	(NA)	25.2	9,901	15.8
1985	7,223	4,983	1,983	(NA)	1,074	11.4	9.1	28.7	(NA)	25.5	9,753	15.3
1986	7,023	4,811	1,987	(NA)	1,085	10.9	8.6	28.0	(NA)	24.7	9,476	14.7
1987	7,005	4,567	2,117	199	1,168	10.7	8.1	29.4	13.5	25.5	9,338	14.3
1988	6,874	4,471	2,089	201	1,141	10.4	7.9	28.2	13.6	23.7	9,284	14.1
1989	6,784	4,409	2,077	182	1,133	10.3	7.8	27.8	11.9	23.4	9,267	14.0
1990	7,098	4,622	2,193	169	1,244	10.7	8.1	29.3	11.0	25.0	9,564	14.4
1991	7,712	5,022	2,343	210	1,372	11.5	8.8	30.4	13.0	26.5	10,244	15.3
1992	8,144	5,255	2,484	215	1,529	11.9	9.1	31.1	12.2	26.7	10,959	16.1
1993	8,393	5,452	2,499	235	1,625	12.3	9.4	31.3	13.5	27.3	11,203	16.4
1994	8,053	5,312	2,212	208	1,724	11.6	9.1	27.3	13.1	27.8	10,771	15.5
1995	7,532	4,994	2,127	264	1,695	10.8	8.5	26.4	12.4	27.0	10,223	14.7
1996	7,708	5,059	2,206	284	1,748	11.0	8.6	26.1	12.7	26.4	10,476	14.9
1997	7,324	4,990	1,985	244	1,721	10.3	8.4	23.6	10.2	24.7	10,032	14.2
1998	7,186	4,829	1,981	270	1,648	10.0	8.0	23.4	11.0	22.7	9,714	13.6
1999	6,676	4,377	1,898	258	1,525	9.3	7.3	21.9	10.3	20.2	9,320	12.9
2000 [3]	6,222	4,151	1,685	235	1,431	8.6	6.9	19.1	8.8	18.5	8,886	12.3
2000 [4]	6,400	4,333	1,686	233	1,540	8.7	7.1	19.3	7.8	19.2	9,032	12.2
2001	6,813	4,579	1,829	234	1,649	9.2	7.4	20.7	7.8	19.4	9,525	12.8

NA Not available. [1] Includes other races not shown separately. [2] Persons of Hispanic origin may be of any race. [3] Data based on Census 1990-based population controls and a sample of approximately 50,000 households. [4] Data reflect implementation of Census 2000-based population controls and a 28,000 household sample expansion to 78,000 households.

Source: U.S. Census Bureau, Current Population Reports, *Poverty in the United States, 2001*, P60-219. See also <http://www.census.gov/prod/2002pubs/p60-219.pdf> (released September 2002).

No. 707. Families Below Poverty Level by Selected Characteristics: 2001

[Families as of March 2002 (6,813 represents 6,813,000). Based on Current Population Survey; see text, this section, Section 1, and Appendix III]

Characteristic	Number below poverty level (1,000)					Percent below poverty level				
	All races [1]	White	Black	Asian and Pacific Islander	Hispanic [2]	All races [1]	White	Black	Asian and Pacific Islander	Hispanic [2]
Total	6,813	4,579	1,829	234	1,649	9.2	7.4	20.7	7.8	19.4
Age of householder:										
15 to 24 years old	921	520	352	19	204	26.5	20.6	47.8	12.9	26.3
25 to 34 years old	1,868	1,246	540	43	576	14.1	1.9	27.6	6.9	23.5
35 to 44 years old	1,732	1,166	434	74	443	9.2	7.6	18.0	8.9	19.0
45 to 54 years old	889	600	221	48	183	5.4	4.3	12.5	6.6	12.5
55 to 64 years old	735	569	135	21	129	7.0	6.3	14.0	6.0	16.3
65 years old and over	635	456	139	28	105	5.5	4.4	14.2	10.3	15.7
Education of householder: [3]										
No high school diploma	2,128	1,520	509	50	877	20.3	18.0	32.4	16.2	26.8
High school diploma, no college	2,096	1,365	615	67	338	9.6	7.5	22.3	12.9	16.0
Some college, less than bachelor's degree	1,129	768	286	39	149	6.1	5.0	11.8	7.4	10.1
Bachelor's degree or more	506	383	59	59	70	2.5	2.3	4.5	4.0	8.3
Work experience of householder:										
Total [4]	6,176	4,121	1,690	206	1,542	9.9	8.0	21.5	7.6	19.7
Worked during year	3,433	2,324	908	114	916	6.5	5.3	14.3	5.0	14.2
Year-round, full-time	1,267	900	300	45	422	3.2	2.7	6.4	2.5	8.9
Not year-round, full-time	2,166	1,424	608	69	494	16.5	13.3	35.7	12.8	28.8
Did not work	2,744	1,797	782	92	626	28.7	24.0	52.3	43.0	44.4

[1] Includes other races not shown separately. [2] Hispanic persons may be of any race. [3] Householder 25 years old and over. [4] Persons 16-64 years old.

Source: U.S. Census Bureau, Current Population Reports, *Poverty in the United States, 2001*, P60-219. See also <http://www.census.gov/prod/2002pubs/p60-219.pdf> (released September 2002) and <http://ferret.bls.census.gov/macro/032001/pov/new16a000.htm> (released 23 September 2002).

No. 708. Nonfinancial Assets Held by Families by Type of Asset: 2001

[Median value in thousands of dollars. Constant dollar figures are based on consumer price index for all urban consumers published by U.S. Bureau of Labor Statistics. Families include one-person units and, as used in this table, are comparable to the U.S. Census Bureau household concept. For definition of family, see text, Section 1. Based on Survey of Consumer Finance; see Appendix III. For data on financial assets, see Table 1167. For definition of median, see Guide to Tabular Presentation]

Age of family head, and family income	Any asset [1]	Vehicles	Primary residence	Other residential property	Equity in nonresidential property	Business equity	Other	Any nonfinancial asset
PERCENT OF FAMILIES HOLDING ASSET								
All families, total	96.7	84.8	67.7	11.3	8.3	11.8	7.6	90.7
Age of family head:								
Under 35 years old	93.1	78.8	39.9	3.4	2.8	7.0	6.9	83.0
35 to 44 years old	97.4	88.9	67.8	9.2	7.6	14.2	8.0	93.2
45 to 54 years old	98.1	90.5	76.2	14.7	10.0	17.1	7.2	95.2
55 to 64 years old	98.2	90.7	83.2	18.3	12.3	15.6	7.9	95.4
65 to 74 years old	97.1	81.3	82.5	13.7	12.9	11.6	9.7	91.6
75 years old and over	97.8	73.9	76.2	15.2	8.3	2.4	6.2	86.4
Race or ethnicity or respondent:								
White non-Hispanic	99.0	89.1	74.1	12.9	9.6	13.9	9.0	94.7
Non white or Hispanic	89.4	70.9	47.0	6.4	4.1	5.1	2.9	77.9
Tenure:								
Owner occupied	100.0	92.2	100.0	14.9	11.0	15.5	8.7	100.0
Renter occupied or other	89.7	69.3	(X)	3.9	2.6	4.2	5.1	71.3
MEDIAN VALUE [2] ($1,000)								
All families, total	147.4	13.5	122.0	80.0	49.0	100.0	12.0	113.2
Age of family head:								
Under 35 years old	39.4	11.3	95.0	75.0	33.3	50.0	10.0	30.5
35 to 44 years old	157.6	14.8	125.0	75.0	39.5	100.0	9.0	117.8
45 to 54 years old	211.6	15.7	135.0	65.0	56.4	102.0	11.0	140.3
55 to 64 years old	226.3	15.1	130.0	80.0	78.5	100.0	30.0	147.9
65 to 74 years old	214.6	13.6	129.0	145.0	50.0	100.0	20.0	149.2
75 years old and over	169.6	8.8	111.0	80.0	28.0	510.9	15.0	122.6
Race or ethnicity or respondent:								
White non-Hispanic	183.9	14.6	130.0	80.0	50.0	100.0	15.0	131.4
Non white or Hispanic	56.8	10.0	92.0	60.0	22.5	50.0	5.0	58.2
Tenure:								
Owner occupied	240.1	16.2	122.0	80.0	50.0	105.0	15.0	156.9
Renter occupied or other	13.4	7.6	(X)	60.0	32.5	35.0	6.0	8.9

X Not applicable. [1] Financial or nonfinancial. [2] Median value of financial asset for families holding such assets.

No. 709. Family Net Worth—Mean and Median Net Worth in Constant (2001) Dollars by Selected Family Characteristics: 1992 to 2001

[Net worth in thousands of constant (2001) dollars (230.5 represents $230,500). Constant dollar figures are based on consumer price index for all urban consumers published by U.S. Bureau of Labor Statistics. Families include one-person units and as used in this table are comparable to the Census Bureau household concept. Based on Survey of Consumer Finance; see Appendix III. For definition of median, see Guide to Tabular Presentation]

Family characteristic	1992 Mean	1992 Median	1995 Mean	1995 Median	1998 Mean	1998 Median	2001 Mean	2001 Median
All families	230.5	61.3	244.8	66.4	307.4	78.0	395.5	86.1
Age of family head:								
Under 35 years old	56.2	11.4	49.9	13.9	69.5	9.9	90.7	11.6
35 to 44 years old	164.8	55.1	165.9	60.3	213.6	69.0	259.5	77.6
45 to 54 years old	331.7	96.8	342.4	107.5	394.1	114.8	485.6	132.0
55 to 64 years old	418.0	141.1	442.3	133.2	579.3	139.2	727.0	181.5
65 to 74 years old	354.6	121.7	402.9	128.0	507.9	159.5	673.8	176.3
75 years old and over	264.0	107.5	298.5	107.5	338.3	136.7	465.9	151.4
Race or ethnicity or respondent:								
White non-Hispanic	274.8	86.2	289.8	88.5	363.9	103.4	482.9	120.9
Non white or Hispanic	95.8	14.8	89.1	18.3	109.9	17.9	115.3	17.1
Tenure:								
Owner occupied	333.7	122.3	350.8	120.2	439.9	143.8	558.1	171.7
Renter occupied or other	47.8	4.0	50.5	5.6	47.3	4.6	55.0	4.8

Source of Tables 708 and 709: Board of Governors of the Federal Reserve System, *Federal Reserve Bulletin*, January 2003, and unpublished data found at <http://www.federalreserve.gov/pubs/oss/oss2/2001/scf2001home.html>.

Income, Expenditures, and Wealth

No. 710. Household and Nonprofit Organization Sector Balance Sheet: 1980 to 2002

[In billions of dollars (11,011 represents $11,011,000,000,000). As of December 31. For details of financial assets and liabilities, see Table 1149]

Item	1980	1990	1995	1996	1997	1998	1999	2000	2001	2002
Assets	11,011	24,094	32,641	35,507	39,631	43,606	49,163	49,238	48,940	47,905
Tangible assets [1]	4,378	9,255	11,045	11,492	12,142	13,103	14,173	15,484	16,707	17,975
Real estate	3,421	7,382	8,787	9,153	9,722	10,578	11,518	12,667	13,757	14,855
Consumer durable goods	931	1,815	2,176	2,254	2,329	2,427	2,551	2,704	2,830	2,996
Financial assets [1]	6,633	14,839	21,596	24,015	27,489	30,503	34,990	33,753	32,233	29,930
Deposits	1,521	3,259	3,298	3,441	3,622	3,928	4,053	4,401	4,773	5,094
Checkable deposits and currency	220	412	544	471	437	410	330	263	289	335
Time and savings deposits	1,239	2,465	2,281	2,434	2,566	2,733	2,811	3,098	3,305	3,614
Money market fund shares	62	369	450	501	582	747	868	982	1,126	1,090
Credit market instruments [1]	425	1,556	1,944	2,142	2,145	2,264	2,542	2,373	2,307	2,363
U.S. government securities	165	555	927	1,064	987	966	1,195	1,022	856	752
Treasury	160	495	820	872	773	735	844	635	565	582
Savings bonds	73	126	185	187	187	187	186	185	190	195
Corporate equities	875	1,781	4,137	4,861	6,229	7,052	9,053	7,408	6,056	4,187
Mutual fund shares	46	457	1,159	1,512	1,982	2,447	3,181	3,083	2,916	2,627
Pension fund reserves	970	3,376	5,671	6,325	7,323	8,208	9,065	9,069	8,693	8,053
Equity in noncorporate business	2,220	3,179	3,598	3,787	4,053	4,286	4,523	4,753	4,837	5,022
Liabilities	1,453	3,720	5,081	5,446	5,825	6,309	6,888	7,468	8,047	8,761
Credit market instruments	1,402	3,598	4,884	5,224	5,557	6,012	6,510	7,075	7,687	8,444
Home mortgages	932	2,505	3,353	3,578	3,818	4,157	4,531	4,907	5,385	6,054
Consumer credit	355	805	1,123	1,214	1,272	1,347	1,446	1,593	1,702	1,757
Net worth	9,558	20,374	27,560	30,062	33,806	37,297	42,275	41,770	40,893	39,144
Memo:										
Replacement cost value of structures:										
Residential	2,548	4,599	6,012	6,352	6,713	7,159	7,727	8,268	8,753	9,179
Households	2,363	4,337	5,718	6,050	6,396	6,827	7,377	7,900	8,372	8,793
Farm households	112	150	174	179	189	198	211	223	232	234
Nonprofit organizations	73	112	121	124	128	134	139	145	149	152
Nonresidential (nonprofits)	267	475	596	624	665	710	762	817	861	877
Disposable personal income	2,116	4,363	5,505	5,780	6,092	6,467	6,758	7,260	7,391	7,972
Owners' equity in household real estate	2,013	4,070	4,638	4,741	4,964	5,365	5,876	6,544	7,168	7,587

[1] Includes types of assets and/or liabilities not shown separately.
Source: Board of Governors of the Federal Reserve System, *Balance Sheets for the U.S. Economy*, March 6, 2003. See also <http://www.federalreserve.gov/releases/Z1/Current/data.htm> (released 06 March 2003).

No. 711. Net Stock of Fixed Reproducible Tangible Wealth in Current and Real (1996) Dollars: 1980 to 2000

[In billions of dollars (10,297 represents $10,297,000,000,000). As of December 31]

Item	1980	1990	1994	1995	1996	1997	1998	1999	2000
CURRENT DOLLARS									
Net stock	10,297	18,187	22,617	23,701	24,925	26,219	27,856	29,678	31,022
Private	7,213	12,760	15,909	16,723	17,653	18,650	19,880	21,215	22,190
Nonresidential equipment	1,420	2,542	3,183	3,352	3,520	3,712	3,944	4,215	4,335
Information processing and related equipment	225	663	850	906	975	1,036	1,137	1,259	1,288
Industrial equipment	525	893	1,075	1,119	1,157	120	1,241	1,293	1,329
Transportation equipment	306	472	651	690	717	764	816	874	898
Other equipment	319	513	607	637	672	712	749	790	821
Nonresidential structures	2,256	4,081	4,941	5,175	5,487	5,746	6,070	6,480	6,767
Nonresidential buildings, excluding farm	1,169	2,514	3,125	3,286	3,499	3,741	4,012	4,296	4,507
Utilities	695	1,005	1,190	1,229	1,265	1,283	1,322	1,384	1,420
Residential	3,537	6,087	7,723	8,131	8,581	9,124	9,797	10,447	11,012
Housing units	2,898	4,963	6,302	6,625	6,995	7,450	8,016	8,546	9,018
Government	2,151	3,612	4,533	4,725	4,943	5,142	5,425	5,759	6,002
Equipment	300	559	686	692	694	698	718	731	754
Structures	1,952	3,053	3,847	4,033	4,249	4,444	4,708	5,028	5,248
Federal	653	1,087	1,314	1,343	1,367	1,381	1,420	1,454	1,480
Defense	483	743	885	891	893	891	904	911	917
State and local	1,498	2,525	3,219	3,382	3,576	3,760	4,005	4,305	4,522
Consumer durable goods	934	1,815	2,176	2,254	2,329	2,427	2,551	2,704	2,830
Motor vehicles	257	574	647	663	673	703	748	796	849
Furniture and household equipment	459	823	1,011	1,053	1,096	1,142	1,189	1,250	1,285
Other	203	417	519	537	560	583	614	658	696
CHAINED (1996) DOLLARS									
Net stock	14,269	20,650	22,829	23,450	24,126	24,908	25,756	26,649	27,418
Private	9,950	14,562	16,075	16,521	17,010	17,571	18,155	18,772	19,266
Nonresidential equipment	1,855	2,723	3,183	3,354	3,555	3,797	4,045	4,321	4,480
Nonresidential structures	3,177	4,704	5,008	5,094	5,198	5,314	5,435	5,567	5,682
Residential	4,921	7,142	7,884	8,074	8,261	8,474	8,703	8,933	9,162
Government	3,127	4,192	4,585	4,668	4,749	4,835	4,932	5,029	5,125
Consumer durable goods	1,198	1,899	2,170	2,262	2,369	2,508	2,685	2,881	3,082

Source: U.S. Bureau of Economic Analysis, *Fixed Assets and Consumer Durable Goods in the United States, 1925-97*; and *Survey of Current Business*, September 2002.

470   Income, Expenditures, and Wealth

Section 14
Prices

This section presents indexes of producer and consumer prices, actual prices for selected commodities, and energy prices. The primary sources of these data are monthly publications of the Department of Labor, Bureau of Labor Statistics (BLS), which include *Monthly Labor Review, Consumer Price Index, Detailed Report, Producer Price Indexes,* and *U.S. Import and Export Price Indexes.* The Department of Commerce, Bureau of Economic Analysis is the source for gross domestic product measures.

Producer price index (PPI)—This index, dating from 1890, is the oldest continuous statistical series published by BLS. It is designed to measure average changes in prices received by producers of all commodities, at all stages of processing, produced in the United States.

The index has undergone several revisions (see *Monthly Labor Review,* February 1962, April 1978, and August 1988). It is now based on approximately 10,000 individual products and groups of products along with about 100,000 quotations per month. Indexes for the net output of manufacturing and mining industries have been added in recent years. Prices used in constructing the index are collected from sellers and generally apply to the first significant large-volume commercial transaction for each commodity—i.e., the manufacturer's or other producer's selling price or the selling price on an organized exchange or at a central market.

The weights used in the index represent the total net selling value of commodities produced or processed in this country. Values are f.o.b. (free on board) production point and are exclusive of excise taxes. Effective with the release of data for January 1988, many important producer price indexes were changed to a new reference base year, 1982=100, from 1967=100. The reference year of the PPI shipment weights has been taken primarily from the 1987 Census of Manufactures. For further detail regarding the PPI, see the BLS *Handbook of Methods,* Bulletin 2490 (April 1997), Chapter 16. The PPI Web page is <http://stats.bls.gov/ppihome.htm>.

Consumer price indexes (CPI)—The CPI is a measure of the average change in prices over time in a "market basket" of goods and services purchased either by urban wage earners and clerical workers or by all urban consumers. In 1919, BLS began to publish complete indexes at semiannual intervals, using a weighting structure based on data collected in the expenditure survey of wage-earner and clerical-worker families in 1917-19 (BLS Bulletin 357, 1924). The first major revision of the CPI occurred in 1940, with subsequent revisions in 1953, 1964, 1978, 1987, and 1998.

Beginning with the release of data for January 1988 in February 1988, most consumer price indexes shifted to a new reference base year. All indexes previously expressed on a base of 1967=100, or any other base through December 1981, have been rebased to 1982-84=100. The expenditure weights are based upon data tabulated from the Consumer Expenditure Surveys for 1993, 1994, and 1995.

BLS publishes CPIs for two population groups: (1) a CPI for all urban consumers (CPI-U), which covers approximately 80 percent of the total population; and (2) a CPI for urban wage earners and clerical workers (CPI-W), which covers 32 percent of the total population. The CPI-U includes, in addition to wage earners and clerical workers, groups which historically have been excluded from CPI coverage, such as professional, managerial, and technical workers; the self-employed; short-term workers; the unemployed; and retirees and others not in the labor force.

The current CPI is based on prices of food, clothing, shelter, fuels, transportation fares, charges for doctors' and dentists' services, drugs, etc. purchased for day-to-day living. Prices are collected in 87 areas across the country from over 50,000 housing units and 23,000 establishments. Area selection was based on the 1990 census. All taxes directly associated with the purchase and use of items are included in the index. Prices of food, fuels, and a few other items are obtained every month in all 87 locations. Prices of most other commodities and services are collected monthly in the three largest geographic areas and every other month in other areas.

In calculating the index, each item is assigned a weight to account for its relative importance in consumers' budgets. Price changes for the various items in each location are then averaged. Local data are then combined to obtain a U.S. city average. Separate indexes are also published for regions, area size-classes, cross-classifications of regions and size-classes, and for 26 local areas, usually consisting of the Metropolitan Statistical Area (MSA); see Appendix II. Area definitions are those established by the Office of Management and Budget in 1983. Definitions do not include revisions made since 1992. Area indexes do not measure differences in the level of prices among cities; they only measure the average change in prices for each area since the base period. For further detail regarding the CPI, see the BLS *Handbook of Methods*, Bulletin 2490, Chapter 17; the *Consumer Price Index*, and the CPI home page: <http://stats.bls.gov/cpihome.htm>. In January 1983, the method of measuring homeownership costs in the CPI-U was changed to a rental equivalence approach. This treatment calculates homeowner costs of shelter based on the implicit rent owners would pay to rent the homes they own. The rental equivalence approach was introduced into the CPI-W in 1985. The CPI-U was used to prepare the consumer price tables in this section.

Other price indexes—Chain-weighted price indexes, produced by the Bureau of Economic Analysis (BEA), are weighted averages of the detailed price indexes used in the deflation of the goods and services that make up the gross domestic product (GDP) and its major components. Growth rates are constructed for years and quarters using quantity weights for the current and preceding year or quarter; these growth rates are used to move the index for the preceding period forward a year or quarter at a time. The gross domestic purchases chained price index measures the average price of goods and services purchased in the United States. It differs from the GDP chained price index, which measures of the average price of goods produced in the United States, by excluding net exports. All chain-weighted price indexes are expressed in terms of the reference year value 1996=100.

Measures of inflation—Inflation is defined as a time of generally rising prices for goods and factors of production. The Bureau of Labor Statistics samples prices of items in a representative market basket and publishes the result as the CPI. The media invariably announce the inflation rate as the percent change in the CPI from month to month. A much more meaningful indicator of inflation is the percent change from the same month of the prior year. The producer price index measures prices at the producer level only. The PPI shows the same general pattern of inflation as does the CPI but is more volatile. The PPI can be roughly viewed as a leading indicator. It often tends to foreshadow trends that later occur in the CPI.

Other measures of inflation include the gross domestic purchases chain-weighted price index, the index of industrial materials prices; the Dow Jones Commodity Spot Price Index; Futures Price Index; the Employment Cost Index, the Hourly Compensation Index, or the Unit Labor Cost Index as a measure of the change in cost of the labor factor-of-production; and changes in long-term interest rates that are often used to measure changes in the cost of the capital factor of production.

International price indexes—The BLS International Price Program produces export and import price indexes for nonmilitary goods traded between the United States and the rest of the world.

The export price index provides a measure of price change for all products sold by U.S. residents to foreign buyers. The import price index provides a measure of price change for goods purchased from other countries by U.S. residents. The reference period for the indexes is 2000=100, unless otherwise indicated. The product universe for both the import and export indexes includes raw materials, agricultural products, semifinished manufactures, and finished manufactures, including both capital and consumer goods. Price data for these items are collected primarily by mail questionnaire. In nearly all cases, the data are collected directly from the exporter or importer, although in a few cases, prices are obtained from other sources.

To the extent possible, the data gathered refer to prices at the U.S. border for exports and at either the foreign border or the U.S. border for imports. For nearly all products, the prices refer to transactions completed during the first week of the month. Survey respondents are asked to indicate all discounts, allowances, and rebates applicable to the reported prices, so that the price used in the calculation of the indexes is the actual price for which the product was bought or sold.

In addition to general indexes for U.S. exports and imports, indexes are also published for detailed product categories of exports and imports. These categories are defined according to the five-digit level of detail for the Bureau of Economic Analysis End-Use Classification, the three-digit level of detail for the Standard International Trade Classification (SITC), and the four-digit level of detail for the Harmonized System. Aggregate import indexes by country or region of origin are also available.

No. 712. Purchasing Power of the Dollar: 1950 to 2002

[Indexes: PPI, 1982=$1.00; CPI, 1982-84=$1.00. Producer prices prior to 1961, and consumer prices prior to 1964, exclude Alaska and Hawaii. Producer prices based on finished goods index. Obtained by dividing the average price index for the 1982=100, PPI; 1982-84=100, CPI base periods (100.0) by the price index for a given period and expressing the result in dollars and cents. Annual figures are based on average of monthly data]

Year	Producer prices	Consumer prices	Year	Producer prices	Consumer prices
1950	3.546	4.151	1976	1.645	1.757
1951	3.247	3.846	1977	1.546	1.649
1952	3.268	3.765	1978	1.433	1.532
1953	3.300	3.735	1979	1.289	1.380
1954	3.289	3.717	1980	1.136	1.215
			1981	1.041	1.098
1955	3.279	3.732	1982	1.000	1.035
1956	3.195	3.678	1983	0.984	1.003
1957	3.077	3.549	1984	0.964	0.961
1958	3.012	3.457			
1959	3.021	3.427	1985	0.955	0.928
			1986	0.969	0.913
1960	2.994	3.373	1987	0.949	0.880
1961	2.994	3.340	1988	0.926	0.846
1962	2.985	3.304	1989	0.880	0.807
1963	2.994	3.265			
1964	2.985	3.220	1990	0.839	0.766
			1991	0.822	0.734
			1992	0.812	0.713
1965	2.933	3.166	1993	0.802	0.692
1966	2.841	3.080	1994	0.797	0.675
1967	2.809	2.993			
1968	2.732	2.873	1995	0.782	0.656
1969	2.632	2.726	1996	0.762	0.638
			1997	0.759	0.623
1970	2.545	2.574	1998	0.766	0.614
1971	2.469	2.466	1999	0.752	0.600
1972	2.392	2.391			
1973	2.193	2.251	2000	0.725	0.581
1974	1.901	2.029	2001	0.711	0.565
1975	1.718	1.859	2002	0.720	0.556

Source: U.S. Bureau of Labor Statistics. Monthly data in U.S. Bureau of Economic Analysis, Survey of Current Business.

Figure 14.1
Annual Percent Change in Consumer Price Indexes: 1990 to 2002

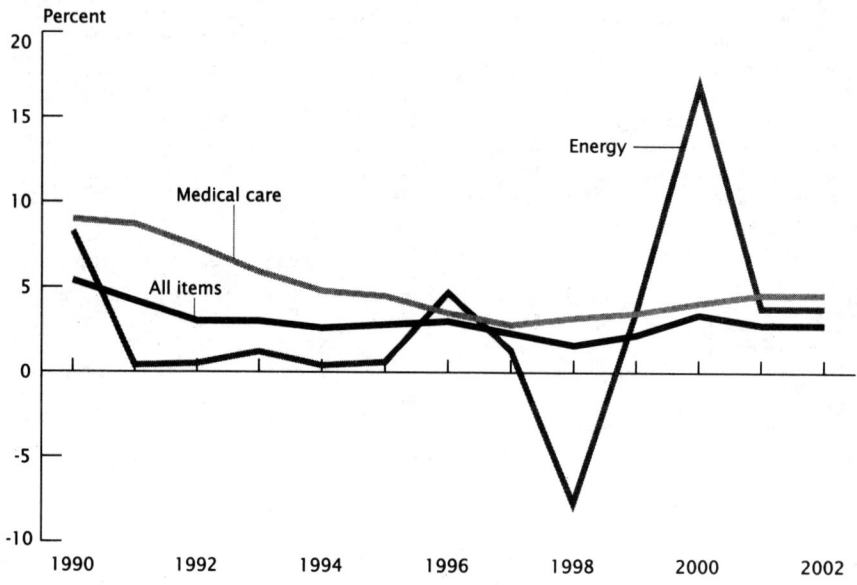

Source: Chart prepared by U.S. Census Bureau. For data, see Table 713.

Figure 14.2
Annual Percent Change in Producer Price Indexes by Stage of Processing: 1990 to 2002

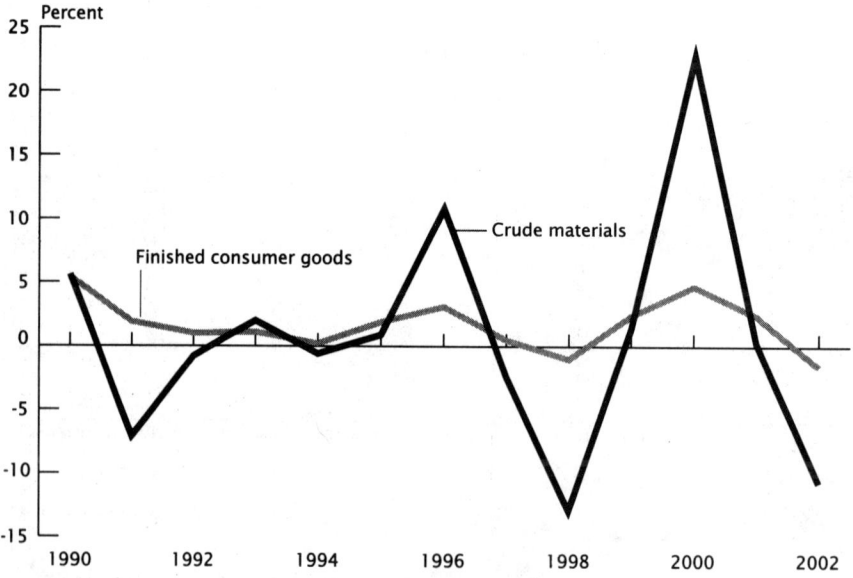

Source: Chart prepared by U.S. Census Bureau. For data, see Table 718.

474 Prices

U.S. Census Bureau, Statistical Abstract of the United States: 2003

No. 713. Consumer Price Indexes (CPI-U) by Major Groups: 1980 to 2002

[1982-84=100, except as indicated. Represents annual averages of monthly figures. Reflects buying patterns of all urban consumers. Minus sign (-) indicates decrease. See text, this section]

Year	All items	Commodities	Services	Food	Energy	All items less food and energy	Food and beverages	Shelter	Transportation	Medical care	Apparel	Education and communication [1]
1980	82.4	86.0	77.9	86.8	86.0	80.8	86.7	81.0	83.1	74.9	90.9	(NA)
1987	113.6	107.7	120.2	113.5	88.6	118.2	113.5	121.3	105.4	130.1	110.6	(NA)
1988	118.3	111.5	125.7	118.2	89.3	123.4	118.2	127.1	108.7	138.6	115.4	(NA)
1989	124.0	116.7	131.9	125.1	94.3	129.0	124.9	132.8	114.1	149.3	118.6	(NA)
1990	130.7	122.8	139.2	132.4	102.1	135.5	132.1	140.0	120.5	162.8	124.1	(NA)
1991	136.2	126.6	146.3	136.3	102.5	142.1	136.8	146.3	123.8	177.0	128.7	(NA)
1992	140.3	129.1	152.0	137.9	103.0	147.3	138.7	151.2	126.5	190.1	131.9	(NA)
1993	144.5	131.5	157.9	140.9	104.2	152.2	141.6	155.7	130.4	201.4	133.7	85.5
1994	148.2	133.8	163.1	144.3	104.6	156.5	144.9	160.5	134.3	211.0	133.4	88.8
1995	152.4	136.4	168.7	148.4	105.2	161.2	148.9	165.7	139.1	220.5	132.0	92.2
1996	156.9	139.9	174.1	153.3	110.1	165.6	153.7	171.0	143.0	228.2	131.7	95.3
1997	160.5	141.8	179.4	157.3	111.5	169.5	157.7	176.3	144.3	234.6	132.9	98.4
1998	163.0	141.9	184.2	160.7	102.9	173.4	161.1	182.1	141.6	242.1	133.0	100.3
1999	166.6	144.4	188.8	164.1	106.6	177.0	164.6	187.3	144.4	250.6	131.3	101.2
2000	172.2	149.2	195.3	167.8	124.6	181.3	168.4	193.4	153.3	260.8	129.6	102.5
2001	177.1	150.7	203.4	173.1	129.3	186.1	173.6	200.6	154.3	272.8	127.3	105.2
2002	179.9	149.7	209.8	176.2	121.7	190.5	176.8	208.1	152.9	285.6	124.0	106.8
PERCENT CHANGE [2]												
1980	13.5	12.3	15.4	8.6	30.9	12.4	8.5	17.6	17.9	11.0	7.1	(NA)
1987	3.6	3.2	4.2	4.1	0.5	4.1	4.0	4.7	3.0	6.6	4.4	(NA)
1988	4.1	3.5	4.6	4.1	0.8	4.4	4.1	4.8	3.1	6.5	4.3	(NA)
1989	4.8	4.7	4.9	5.8	5.6	4.5	5.7	4.5	5.0	7.7	2.8	(NA)
1990	5.4	5.2	5.5	5.8	8.3	5.0	5.8	5.4	5.6	9.0	4.6	(NA)
1991	4.2	3.1	5.1	2.9	0.4	4.9	3.6	4.5	2.7	8.7	3.7	(NA)
1992	3.0	2.0	3.9	1.2	0.5	3.7	1.4	3.3	2.2	7.4	2.5	(NA)
1993	3.0	1.9	3.9	2.2	1.2	3.3	2.1	3.0	3.1	5.9	1.4	(NA)
1994	2.6	1.7	3.3	2.4	0.4	2.8	2.3	3.1	3.0	4.8	-0.2	3.9
1995	2.8	1.9	3.4	2.8	0.6	3.0	2.8	3.2	3.6	4.5	-1.0	3.8
1996	3.0	2.6	3.2	3.3	4.7	2.7	3.2	3.2	2.8	3.5	-0.2	3.4
1997	2.3	1.4	3.0	2.6	1.3	2.4	2.6	3.1	0.9	2.8	0.9	3.3
1998	1.6	0.1	2.7	2.2	-7.7	2.3	2.2	3.3	-1.9	3.2	0.1	1.9
1999	2.2	1.8	2.5	2.1	3.6	2.1	2.2	2.9	2.0	3.5	-1.3	0.9
2000	3.4	3.3	3.4	2.3	16.9	2.4	2.3	3.3	6.2	4.1	-1.3	1.3
2001	2.8	1.0	4.1	3.2	3.8	2.6	3.1	3.7	0.7	4.6	-1.8	2.6
2002	1.6	-0.7	3.1	1.8	-5.9	2.4	1.8	3.7	-0.9	4.7	-2.6	1.5

NA Not available. [1] Dec. 1997=100. [2] Change from immediate prior year. 1980 change from 1979; 1987 change from 1986.

Source: U.S. Bureau of Labor Statistics, *Monthly Labor Review* and *Handbook of Labor Statistics*, periodic.

No. 714. Consumer Price Indexes (CPI-U)—Selected Areas: 2002

[1982-84=100, except as indicated. Represents annual averages of monthly figures. Local area CPI indexes are byproducts of the national CPI program. Each local index has a smaller sample size than the national index and is therefore, subject to substantially more sampling and other measurement error. As a result, local area indexes show greater volatility than the national index, although their long-term trends are similar. Area definitions are those established by the Office of Management and Budget in 1983. For further detail see the U.S. Bureau of Labor Statistics Handbook of Methods, Bulletin 2285, Chapter 19, the Consumer Price Index, and Report 736, the CPI: 1987 Revision. See also text, this section. See Appendix III]

Area	All items	Food and beverages	Food	Housing	Apparel	Transportation	Medical care	Fuel and other utilities
U.S. city average	179.9	176.8	176.2	180.3	124.0	152.9	285.6	143.6
Anchorage, AK MSA	158.2	157.9	158.3	143.5	126.7	151.5	(NA)	162.5
Atlanta, GA MSA	178.2	181.9	187.5	179.7	131.3	139.7	291.0	165.9
Boston, MA MSA	196.5	184.8	185.5	200.3	138.0	149.9	383.4	134.3
Chicago-Gary, IL-IN CMSA	181.2	178.1	177.0	186.7	99.8	148.5	280.8	124.5
Cincinnati-Hamilton, OH-KY-IN CMSA	170.0	162.7	161.0	162.2	119.7	150.0	281.2	127.4
Cleveland-Akron-Lorain, OH CMSA	173.3	180.1	182.5	172.5	117.4	152.6	245.6	135.2
Dallas-Fort Worth, TX CMSA	172.7	176.5	173.3	162.5	123.0	136.2	153.9	267.6
Denver-Boulder-Greely, CO CMSA	184.8	172.0	174.4	184.4	85.0	190.9	332.1	139.7
Detroit-Ann Arbor-Flint, MI CMSA	178.9	171.9	171.4	170.8	125.2	168.3	283.8	144.1
Honolulu, HI MSA	180.3	171.9	171.6	181.2	102.6	170.9	(NA)	142.6
Houston-Galveston-Brazoria, TX CMSA	159.2	164.2	163.7	145.3	135.9	141.5	265.3	114.9
Kansas City, MO-KS CMSA	174.0	174.5	175.8	169.4	113.7	147.8	262.0	147.3
Los Angeles-Anaheim-Riverside, CA CMSA	182.2	184.9	183.1	188.1	109.0	154.5	281.2	187.0
Miami-Fort Lauderdale, FL CMSA	175.5	183.9	184.3	167.8	151.7	157.5	263.4	122.7
Milwaukee, WI PMSA	174.0	176.0	176.9	174.6	110.0	147.7	283.2	129.3
Minneapolis-St. Paul, MN-WI MSA	179.6	188.7	184.9	167.8	131.1	162.1	280.1	130.6
New York-Northern New Jersey-Long Island, NY-NJ-CT CMSA	191.9	180.3	179.0	199.9	115.4	159.8	299.7	122.0
Philadelphia-Wilmington-Trenton, PA-NJ-DE-MD CMSA	184.9	171.8	171.3	188.1	100.7	156.7	326.0	142.6
Pittsburgh, PA MSA	174.0	168.7	167.3	173.6	151.7	137.4	265.6	155.7
Portland, OR MSA	183.8	162.5	162.7	186.3	123.9	164.4	282.8	177.5
San Diego, CA MSA	197.9	184.9	183.0	213.9	127.6	163.0	284.3	151.2
San Francisco-Oakland-San Jose, CA CMSA	193.0	186.2	186.1	221.4	109.0	141.0	265.8	180.1
Seattle-Tacoma, WA CMSA	189.3	185.1	186.2	200.0	128.2	161.3	270.2	158.5
St. Louis-East St. Louis, MO-IL CMSA [1]	169.1	172.0	170.0	161.8	120.5	150.0	279.1	133.5
Tampa-St. Petersburg-Clearwater, FL MSA [1]	153.9	151.4	150.1	149.6	149.3	139.5	215.8	134.3
Washington-Baltimore, DC-MD-VA-WV CMSA [2]	113.0	111.7	111.8	117.3	92.4	105.7	114.9	109.0

NA Not available. [1] 1987=100. [2] 1997=100; except "Apparel and upkeep" and "Transportation," 1996=100.
Source: U.S. Bureau of Labor Statistics, *Monthly Labor Review* and *CPI Detailed Report*, January issues.

No. 715. Consumer Price Indexes for All Urban Consumers (CPI-U) for Selected Items and Groups: 1980 to 2002

[1982-84 = 100 except as noted. Annual averages of monthly figures. See headnote, Table 713]

Item	1980	1990	1995	1997	1998	1999	2000	2001	2002
All Items	82.4	130.7	152.4	160.5	163.0	166.6	172.2	177.1	179.9
Food and beverages	86.7	132.1	148.9	157.7	161.1	164.6	168.4	173.6	176.8
Food	86.8	132.4	148.4	157.3	160.7	164.1	167.8	173.1	176.2
Food at home	88.4	132.3	148.8	158.1	161.1	164.2	167.9	173.4	175.6
Cereals and bakery products	83.9	140.0	167.5	177.6	181.1	185.0	188.3	193.8	198.0
Cereals and cereal products	84.2	141.1	167.1	169.5	171.5	175.0	175.9	178.7	181.8
Cereal	76.3	158.6	192.5	187.5	189.9	195.2	198.0	199.7	203.0
Rice, pasta, and cornmeal	90.9	122.0	140.2	148.8	150.5	151.9	150.7	154.6	155.8
Bakery products	83.8	139.2	167.4	181.1	185.4	189.4	194.1	201.3	206.1
White bread	85.9	136.4	165.5	183.8	187.3	192.5	199.1	208.3	213.4
Cookies, cakes, and cupcakes	81.5	142.7	169.1	179.2	181.2	185.0	187.9	192.0	196.7
Meats, poultry, fish and eggs	92.0	130.0	138.8	148.5	147.3	147.9	154.5	161.3	162.1
Meats	92.7	128.5	135.5	144.4	141.6	142.3	150.7	159.3	160.3
Beef and veal	98.4	128.8	134.9	136.8	136.5	139.2	148.1	160.5	160.6
Uncooked ground beef and related products	104.6	118.1	116.1	116.4	116.1	118.4	125.2	135.5	138.1
Pork	81.9	129.8	134.8	155.9	148.5	145.9	156.5	162.4	161.8
Bacon	73.5	113.4	120.0	164.0	152.0	151.5	177.5	184.6	186.2
Chops	82.9	140.2	144.2	155.2	146.8	143.5	152.2	159.0	156.0
Ham	85.5	132.4	139.6	156.3	150.0	147.0	152.7	157.3	160.0
Poultry	93.7	132.5	143.5	156.6	157.1	157.9	159.8	164.9	167.0
Fish and seafood	87.5	146.7	171.6	177.1	181.7	185.3	190.4	191.1	188.1
Canned fish and seafood	93.7	119.5	125.5	128.4	132.6	131.5	127.4	127.3	130.0
Eggs	88.6	124.1	120.5	140.0	135.4	128.1	131.9	136.4	138.2
Dairy and related products	90.9	126.5	132.8	145.5	150.8	159.6	160.7	167.1	168.1
Fruits and vegetables	82.1	149.0	177.7	187.5	198.2	203.1	204.6	212.2	220.9
Fresh fruits and vegetables	81.8	(NA)	206.0	215.4	231.2	237.2	238.8	247.9	258.4
Fresh fruits	84.8	170.9	219.0	236.3	246.5	266.3	258.3	265.1	270.2
Apples	92.1	147.5	183.5	199.6	202.3	200.1	212.6	213.9	230.7
Bananas	91.5	138.2	153.8	159.6	160.9	159.4	162.5	166.6	166.5
Oranges, tangerines	72.6	160.6	224.5	226.1	251.5	337.0	257.0	271.7	294.6
Fresh vegetables	79.0	151.1	193.1	194.6	215.8	209.3	219.4	230.6	245.4
Potatoes	81.0	162.6	174.7	174.2	185.2	193.1	196.3	202.3	238.5
Lettuce	77.8	150.3	221.2	200.1	229.1	208.3	228.1	233.8	252.1
Tomatoes	81.9	160.8	188.3	213.6	239.2	224.1	234.7	250.0	251.0
Processed fruits and vegetables [1]	(NA)	(NA)	(NA)	(NA)	(NA)	(NA)	105.6	109.0	113.1
Nonalcoholic beverages and beverage materials	91.4	113.5	131.7	133.4	133.0	134.3	137.8	139.2	139.2
Carbonated drinks	86.6	112.1	119.5	118.3	117.5	118.8	123.4	125.4	125.6
Coffee	111.6	117.5	163.1	168.0	163.4	154.8	154.0	146.7	142.6
Food away from home	83.4	(NA)	149.0	157.0	161.1	165.1	169.0	173.9	178.3
Alcoholic beverages	86.4	129.3	153.9	162.8	165.7	169.7	174.7	179.3	183.6
Alcoholic beverages at home	87.3	123.0	143.1	149.5	150.6	153.7	158.1	161.1	164.0
Beer and ale, and other malt beverages	84.8	123.6	143.9	148.2	148.5	151.9	156.8	160.7	164.7
Distilled spirits	89.8	125.7	145.7	150.8	152.7	156.2	162.3	168.0	171.4
Wine	89.5	114.4	133.6	145.5	147.3	149.4	151.6	151.5	152.3
Alcoholic beverages away from home	82.9	144.4	176.5	189.4	195.0	201.0	207.1	215.2	222.5
Housing	81.1	128.5	148.5	156.8	160.4	163.9	169.6	176.4	180.3
Shelter	81.0	140.0	165.7	176.3	182.1	187.3	193.4	200.6	208.1
Owners' equivalent rent of primary residence [2]	(NA)	144.8	171.3	181.9	187.8	192.9	198.7	206.3	214.7
Fuels and utilities	75.4	111.6	123.7	130.8	128.5	128.8	137.9	150.2	143.6
Fuels	74.8	104.5	111.5	117.9	113.7	113.5	122.8	135.4	127.2
Fuel oil and other	86.1	99.3	88.1	99.8	90.0	91.4	129.7	129.3	115.5
Gas (piped) and electricity	71.4	109.3	119.2	125.1	121.2	120.9	128.0	142.4	134.4
Electricity	75.8	117.4	129.6	132.5	127.4	126.5	128.5	137.8	136.2
Utility natural gas service	65.7	97.3	102.9	114.6	112.4	113.0	132.0	158.3	135.3
Water and sewerage maintenance	74.0	150.2	196.5	210.0	217.3	222.0	227.5	234.6	242.5
Garbage and trash collection [3]	(NA)	171.2	241.2	250.5	256.7	263.8	269.8	275.5	283.0

See footnotes at end of table.

No. 715. Consumer Price Indexes for All Urban Consumers (CPI-U) for Selected Items and Groups: 1980 to 2002—Con.

[1982-84 = 100 except as noted. Annual averages of monthly figures. See headnote, Table 713]

Item	1980	1990	1995	1997	1998	1999	2000	2001	2002
Household furnishings and operations	86.3	113.3	123.0	125.4	126.6	126.7	128.2	129.1	128.3
Furniture and bedding	88.0	115.7	130.9	134.5	135.0	134.9	134.4	132.2	129.4
Bedroom furniture	83.5	118.5	136.4	141.5	141.3	141.0	138.4	136.6	135.3
Housekeeping supplies	83.2	125.2	137.1	143.1	145.7	148.1	153.4	158.4	159.8
Apparel	90.9	124.1	132.0	132.9	133.0	131.3	129.6	127.3	124.0
Men's and boy's apparel	89.4	120.4	126.2	130.1	131.8	131.1	129.7	125.7	121.7
Women's and girl's apparel	96.0	122.6	126.9	126.1	126.0	123.3	121.5	119.3	115.8
Infants' and toddlers'	85.5	125.8	127.2	129.0	126.1	129.0	130.6	129.2	126.4
Footwear	91.8	117.4	125.4	127.6	128.0	125.7	123.8	123.0	121.4
Transportation	83.1	120.5	139.1	144.3	141.6	144.4	153.3	154.3	152.9
Private transportation	84.2	118.8	136.3	141.0	137.9	140.5	149.1	150.0	148.8
New vehicles	88.5	121.4	141.0	144.3	143.4	142.9	142.8	142.1	140.0
New cars	88.4	121.0	139.0	141.7	140.7	139.6	139.6	138.9	137.3
New trucks [3]	(NA)	121.6	145.9	151.4	151.1	152.0	151.7	150.7	147.8
Used cars and trucks	62.3	117.6	156.5	151.1	150.6	152.0	155.8	158.7	152.0
Motor fuel	97.4	101.2	100.0	106.2	92.2	100.7	129.3	124.7	116.1
Motor vehicle maintenance and repair	81.5	130.1	154.0	162.7	167.1	171.9	177.3	183.5	190.2
Motor vehicle insurance	82.0	177.9	234.3	251.6	254.3	253.8	256.7	268.1	291.6
Motor vehicle fees [1]	(NA)	(NA)	(NA)	(NA)	102.5	103.8	107.3	109.3	112.5
Public transportation	69.0	142.6	175.9	186.7	190.3	197.7	209.6	210.6	207.4
Airline fares	68.0	148.4	189.7	199.2	205.3	218.8	239.4	239.4	231.6
Medical care	74.9	162.8	220.5	234.6	242.1	250.6	260.8	272.8	285.6
Medical care commodities	75.4	163.4	204.5	215.3	221.8	230.7	238.1	247.6	256.4
Prescription drugs and medical supplies	72.5	181.7	235.0	249.3	258.6	273.4	285.4	300.9	316.5
Nonprescription drugs, and medical supplies [4]	(NA)	120.6	140.5	145.4	147.7	176.7	149.5	150.6	150.4
Medical care services	74.8	162.7	224.2	239.1	246.8	255.1	266.0	278.8	292.9
Professional services	77.9	156.1	201.0	215.4	222.2	229.2	237.7	246.5	253.9
Hospital and related services	69.2	178.0	257.8	278.4	287.5	299.5	317.3	338.3	367.8
Recreation [1]	(NA)	(NA)	(NA)	(NA)	(NA)	102.0	103.3	104.9	106.2
Video and audio [3]	100.7	80.8	73.9	99.4	101.1	100.7	101.0	101.5	102.8
Cable television [3]	(NA)	158.4	200.7	228.7	245.2	254.6	266.8	278.4	295.0
Photography [1]	(NA)	(NA)	(NA)	(NA)	(NA)	99.4	99.2	99.0	97.9
Sporting goods	88.5	114.9	123.5	122.6	121.9	120.3	119.0	118.5	116.4
Other recreational goods [1]	(NA)	(NA)	(NA)	(NA)	97.1	92.3	87.8	84.6	80.5
Pets, pet products and services [1]	(NA)	(NA)	(NA)	(NA)	101.5	103.4	106.1	109.7	113.2
Recreation services [1]	(NA)	(NA)	(NA)	(NA)	102.4	106.9	111.7	116.1	119.6
Recreational reading materials	(NA)	(NA)	(NA)	179.0	184.1	186.1	188.3	191.4	195.8
Tobacco and smoking products	72.0	181.5	225.7	243.7	274.8	355.8	394.9	425.2	461.5
Personal care	81.9	130.4	147.1	152.7	156.7	161.1	165.6	170.5	174.7
Personal care services	83.7	132.8	151.5	162.4	166.0	171.4	178.1	184.3	188.4
Education and communication [1]	(NA)	(NA)	92.2	98.4	100.3	101.2	102.5	105.2	106.8
Education [1]	(NA)	(NA)	(NA)	97.3	102.1	107.0	112.5	118.5	126.0
Educational books and supplies	71.4	171.3	214.4	238.4	250.8	261.7	279.9	295.9	317.6
Tuition/and child care fees and other school fees	71.2	175.7	253.8	280.4	294.2	308.4	324.0	341.1	362.1
College tuition	70.8	175.0	264.8	294.1	306.5	318.7	331.9	348.8	372.6
Communication [1]	(NA)	(NA)	99.0	100.0	97.1	95.9	93.0	93.3	92.3
Postage	76.2	125.1	160.3	160.3	160.3	165.1	165.1	171.5	181.8
Delivery services [1]	(NA)	(NA)	(NA)	100.0	104.2	110.0	114.5	123.0	127.9
Information and information processing [1]	(NA)	(NA)	98.9	100.0	96.9	95.4	92.8	92.3	90.8
Telephone services [1]	(NA)	(NA)	(NA)	(NA)	(NA)	100.1	98.5	99.3	99.7
Telephone services, local charges	72.8	149.3	160.4	163.1	165.7	168.7	175.6	184.8	193.2
Telephone services, long distance charges [1]	(NA)	(NA)	(NA)	100.0	99.9	98.6	97.8	88.8	84.9
Cellular telephone services [1]	(NA)	(NA)	(NA)	100.0	91.7	81.1	76.0	68.1	67.4
Information and information processing other than telephone services [5]	(NA)	(NA)	63.8	50.1	39.9	30.5	25.9	21.3	18.3
Personal computers and peripheral equipment [1]	(NA)	(NA)	(NA)	100.0	64.2	47.2	41.1	29.5	22.2
Computer software and accessories [1]	(NA)	(NA)	(NA)	100.0	90.0	88.2	85.4	79.1	74.0
Computer information processing services [1]	(NA)	(NA)	(NA)	100.0	103.3	96.0	96.4	98.1	98.9
All commodities	86.0	122.8	136.4	141.8	141.9	144.4	149.2	150.7	149.7
All commodities less food	85.7	117.4	129.8	133.4	132.0	134.0	139.2	138.9	136.0
Energy	86.0	102.1	105.2	111.5	102.9	106.6	124.6	129.3	121.7

NA Not available. [1] December 1997=100. [2] December 1982=100. [3] December 1983=100. [4] December 1986=100. [5] December 1988=100.

Source: U.S. Bureau of Labor Statistics, *Monthly Labor Review* and *CPI Detailed Report*, January issues.

No. 716. Cost of Living Index—Selected Metropolitan Areas: Fourth Quarter 2002

[Measures relative price levels for consumer goods and services in participating areas for a midmanagement standard of living. The nationwide average equals 100, and each index is read as a percent of the national average. The index does not measure inflation, but compares prices at a single point in time. Excludes taxes. Metropolitan areas as defined by the Office of Management and Budget. For definitions and components of MSAs, see source for details]

Metropolitan areas (MA)	Composite index (100%)	Grocery items (16%)	Housing (28%)	Utilities (8%)	Transportation (10%)	Health care (5%)	Misc. goods and services (33%)
Anniston, AL MSA	98.2	97.6	91.4	101.8	96.8	83.1	106.1
Birmingham, AL MSA	97.6	107.1	84.4	102.8	97.4	87.1	104.7
Decatur, AL MSA	88.9	91.6	78.6	86.5	101.2	86.5	93.7
Florence, AL MSA	89.9	89.1	78.3	89.1	92.5	83.3	100.7
Huntsville, AL MSA	91.8	96.2	79.0	83.0	100.6	89.3	100.4
Mobile, AL MSA	90.6	91.0	80.7	100.4	94.2	80.0	97.0
Montgomery, AL MSA	92.3	93.2	84.5	102.0	93.8	87.9	96.4
Tuscaloosa, AL MSA	99.3	98.5	97.0	94.3	105.0	82.2	103.8
Anchorage, AK MSA	121.8	129.0	130.7	91.9	110.6	144.4	117.9
Nonmetropolitan areas:							
Fairbanks, AK	127.5	124.0	131.4	154.0	114.3	158.0	118.9
Kodiak, AK	135.4	147.8	133.2	143.0	134.5	140.3	129.1
Flagstaff, AZ-UT MSA	106.7	103.0	118.0	106.1	109.0	108.3	98.2
Las Vegas, NV-AZ MSA:							
Lake Havasu City, AZ	97.3	118.0	84.5	104.3	78.9	102.0	101.3
Phoenix-Mesa, AZ MSA:							
Phoenix, AZ	95.1	102.8	83.8	97.1	103.8	108.4	95.9
Tucson, AZ MSA	96.6	105.7	85.9	111.9	102.6	111.6	93.4
Fayetteville-Springdale-Rogers, AR MSA	91.9	86.6	87.2	90.7	94.8	88.1	98.5
Fort Smith, AR-OK MSA	84.4	86.2	69.6	105.7	86.0	87.4	90.1
Jonesboro, AR MSA	87.7	90.7	82.9	86.2	89.8	81.6	91.1
Fresno, CA MSA	108.8	113.1	106.6	134.0	106.8	105.1	103.7
Los Angeles-Long Beach, CA PMSA	137.8	110.5	207.6	109.3	111.6	112.9	110.3
Riverside-San Bernardino, CA PMSA:							
Riverside City, CA	108.9	112.2	113.7	99.6	108.1	127.6	102.9
Sacramento, CA PMSA	123.8	124.5	145.3	121.7	110.2	142.5	107.1
San Diego, CA MSA	138.2	130.2	195.5	77.5	119.9	135.1	114.1
San Francisco, CA PMSA	182.3	129.7	331.2	109.2	122.1	173.5	118.6
Colorado Springs, CO MSA	97.6	98.9	98.4	89.2	102.5	113.4	94.6
Denver, CO PMSA	105.7	106.8	111.3	81.6	110.9	122.3	102.2
Fort Collins-Loveland, CO MSA:							
Fort Collins, CO	100.2	111.7	102.5	78.0	106.9	111.6	94.3
Grand Junction, CO MSA	101.2	103.4	106.0	78.1	105.2	106.0	99.7
Pueblo, CO MSA	90.2	103.4	80.2	78.4	96.5	95.3	92.4
New Haven-Meriden, CT PMSA	119.4	106.5	140.9	146.1	110.2	140.8	100.6
Washington DC-MD-VA-WV PMSA	137.6	117.9	188.1	113.0	124.8	116.1	117.5
Daytona Beach, FL MSA	98.2	104.3	85.8	104.1	103.0	117.1	100.1
Fort Walton Beach FL, MSA	96.8	101.1	85.6	94.1	99.0	97.0	104.1
Jacksonville, FL MSA	94.3	107.4	82.9	88.0	96.0	82.0	100.4
Orlando, FL MSA	98.0	102.5	86.0	100.2	95.7	101.3	105.8
Panama City, FL MSA	95.8	101.3	81.1	107.5	109.5	90.7	99.4
Pensacola, FL MSA	98.7	102.9	84.6	109.1	101.9	98.6	105.0
Sarasota-Bradenton, FL MSA:							
Sarasota, FL	105.1	106.8	101.1	109.3	111.1	102.4	105.1
Tallahassee, FL MSA	104.8	106.0	100.2	101.1	100.1	114.0	109.0
Tampa-St. Petersburg-Clearwater, FL MSA							
Tampa, FL	95.9	93.6	93.9	104.6	102.2	102.6	93.8
West Palm Beach-Boca Raton, FL MSA	107.8	104.4	107.4	103.1	106.9	99.1	112.5
Albany, GA MSA	89.2	100.6	75.3	94.9	96.3	82.8	92.8
Atlanta, GA MSA:							
Atlanta, GA	98.1	101.9	94.5	92.1	101.8	106.3	98.3
Augusta-Aiken, GA-SC MSA	91.0	104.4	71.9	91.2	99.8	94.3	97.5
Boise City, ID MSA	96.4	87.4	91.3	86.9	101.5	104.9	104.7
Champaign-Urbana, IL MSA	93.4	89.5	87.2	107.2	100.5	97.6	94.5
Peoria-Pekin, IL MSA	92.9	94.5	90.6	92.5	98.0	93.3	92.5
Springfield, IL MSA	98.0	105.6	88.8	85.0	97.3	98.1	105.4
Lafayette, IN MSA	91.9	95.1	86.5	89.6	91.9	95.9	94.9

See footnotes at end of table.

No. 716. Cost of Living Index—Selected Metropolitan Areas: Fourth Quarter 2002—Con.

[See headnote, page 478]

Metropolitan areas (MA)	Composite index (100%)	Grocery items (16%)	Housing (28%)	Utilities (8%)	Transportation (10%)	Health care (5%)	Misc. goods and services (33%)
Lafayette, IN MSA	91.7	90.3	82.7	113.7	95.9	93.9	93.2
South Bend, IN MSA	95.7	88.9	100.8	103.0	94.6	93.1	93.6
Cedar Rapids, IA MSA	92.0	88.6	82.7	106.1	99.3	91.0	96.1
Waterloo-Cedar Falls, IA MSA	94.4	98.5	91.2	97.0	100.6	91.6	93.1
Lawrence, KS MSA	94.1	92.5	85.3	96.9	97.3	93.0	100.8
Wichita, KS MSA	94.7	90.2	80.1	101.8	107.9	98.9	103.1
Cincinnati, OH-KY-IN PMSA:							
Covington, KY	93.5	96.4	85.8	89.9	95.5	90.1	99.5
Clarksville-Hopkinsville, TN-KY MSA	89.0	90.6	78.7	102.0	87.6	86.4	94.6
Lexington, KY MSA	94.2	98.5	93.6	83.8	95.7	97.3	94.3
Louisville, KY-IN MSA	90.9	88.0	83.1	76.7	110.8	83.2	97.5
Baton Rouge, LA MSA	103.9	111.7	94.5	113.3	101.6	109.1	105.6
Lake Charles, LA MSA	96.7	89.0	100.6	97.8	97.1	92.9	97.2
Monroe, LA MSA	97.7	93.4	92.6	101.8	104.1	86.0	102.9
New Orleans, LA MSA	104.3	99.9	110.8	109.2	100.1	90.5	103.2
Shreveport-Bossier City, LA MSA	91.6	86.4	92.9	90.2	94.6	78.9	94.4
Cumberland, MD-WV MSA	93.7	91.9	87.5	107.7	93.2	92.3	96.9
Boston, MA-NH PMSA:							
Boston PMSA (MA Part)	135.5	114.5	178.2	157.9	112.5	135.0	111.0
Grand Rapids-Muskegon-Holland, MI MSA	100.2	112.6	90.4	98.1	111.3	91.3	100.9
Lansing-East Lansing, MI MSA	97.1	105.5	88.8	78.4	98.1	84.6	106.0
Minneapolis-St Paul, MN-WI MSA:							
Minneapolis, MN	110.5	101.8	118.9	113.7	120.3	118.3	102.7
Rochester, MN MSA	101.3	99.6	96.3	111.4	103.6	119.1	100.6
St Cloud, MN MSA	96.5	99.1	88.9	102.4	109.7	98.6	95.9
Hattiesburg, MS MSA	96.8	93.3	87.7	99.7	92.6	88.3	108.1
Jackson, MS MSA	90.4	87.7	84.6	95.7	92.8	80.5	96.2
Columbia, MO MSA	98.1	99.0	92.7	95.5	97.7	92.9	103.9
Joplin, MO MSA	85.3	82.5	80.1	93.3	81.0	92.9	89.4
St Louis, MO-IL MSA	103.5	115.7	96.3	106.9	102.8	99.4	103.6
Springfield, MO MSA	89.2	96.5	79.9	77.5	92.8	96.5	94.4
Billings, MT MSA	97.9	105.3	95.3	82.6	100.3	102.2	98.9
Great Falls, MT MSA	91.7	100.4	81.5	94.9	91.8	87.3	95.9
Missoula, MT MSA	102.3	118.6	102.5	73.2	101.1	90.0	103.5
Lincoln, NE MSA	95.9	92.2	97.4	88.8	99.3	92.2	97.7
Omaha, NE-IA MSA	89.9	93.3	81.1	88.0	100.9	92.5	92.4
Las Vegas, NV-AZ MSA:							
Las Vegas, NV MSA	105.1	113.3	102.6	99.4	109.4	109.0	102.6
Reno, NV MSA	101.1	98.0	99.0	125.6	102.8	107.2	97.1
Albuquerque, NM MSA:							
Albuquerque, NM	99.1	98.9	100.1	97.2	99.2	117.3	96.1
Las Cruces, NM MSA	93.1	94.9	84.2	93.0	89.6	85.0	102.0
Santa Fe, NM MSA:							
Santa Fe, NM	112.5	109.4	137.8	85.8	100.1	108.0	103.4
Buffalo-Niagara Falls, NY MSA	100.2	113.6	91.6	149.7	108.2	90.2	88.0
Glens Falls, NY MSA	101.4	99.8	86.3	130.7	106.1	103.0	106.2
Nassau-Suffolk, NY PMSA	134.3	118.3	174.8	126.0	110.6	139.3	116.3
New York, NY PMSA	216.2	146.2	411.3	158.9	117.5	165.3	136.0
Asheville, NC MSA	96.7	96.9	98.1	95.2	98.2	96.6	95.4
Fayetteville, NC MSA	94.8	107.3	81.7	103.1	94.8	96.7	97.7
Jacksonville, NC MSA	91.6	100.9	80.8	101.5	85.8	97.7	94.7
Raleigh-Durham-Chapel Hill, NC MSA:							
Raleigh, NC	101.0	108.0	96.8	99.5	97.4	102.0	102.4
Wilmington, NC MSA	97.9	98.1	99.5	101.2	88.5	89.3	99.9
Bismarck, ND MSA	94.6	97.7	85.6	82.9	102.6	84.5	102.6
Nonmetropolitan areas:							
Minot, ND	87.6	95.9	79.9	82.7	91.7	70.4	92.5
Akron, OH PMSA	100.8	115.2	93.2	113.8	96.7	95.4	99.2
Cincinnati, OH-KY-IN PMSA:							
Cincinnati, OH	94.6	96.7	85.3	102.1	93.6	96.1	99.8
Cleveland-Lorain-Elyria, OH PMSA	105.0	117.7	95.2	143.1	109.9	105.2	99.3
Dayton-Springfield, OH MSA	96.0	96.5	88.3	103.5	102.4	98.7	98.1
Lima, OH MSA	98.9	106.2	93.0	114.4	100.6	84.9	98.2
Mansfield, OH MSA	92.8	103.4	76.5	117.1	98.5	87.6	94.5
Toledo, OH MSA	98.3	108.1	80.4	126.9	101.3	97.2	101.0
Youngstown-Warren, OH MSA	93.3	104.6	82.1	125.3	91.5	77.1	92.5

See footnotes at end of table.

Prices 479

U.S. Census Bureau, Statistical Abstract of the United States: 2003

No. 716. Cost of Living Index—Selected Metropolitan Areas: Fourth Quarter 2002—Con.

[See headnote, page 478]

Metropolitan areas (MA)	Composite index (100%)	Grocery items (16%)	Housing (28%)	Utilities (8%)	Transportation (10%)	Health care (5%)	Misc. goods and services (33%)
Enid, OK MSA	89.7	92.1	74.2	95.6	94.9	88.3	98.8
Lawton, OK MSA	92.8	100.6	76.9	98.6	100.8	84.3	99.8
Tulsa, OK MSA	91.9	92.4	82.1	83.7	100.2	90.2	99.7
Corvallis, OR MSA	107.3	104.4	110.1	121.4	101.7	123.0	102.3
Portland-Vancouver, OR-WA PMSA	116.4	112.8	131.5	100.1	107.0	119.7	111.5
Salem, OR PMSA	104.1	102.4	97.3	105.3	97.2	118.2	110.5
Philadelphia, PA-NJ PMSA	118.8	119.7	128.9	139.3	112.1	131.6	104.9
Pittsburgh, PA MSA	98.5	103.6	87.7	133.7	112.4	83.5	94.7
Williamsport, PA MSA	101.5	97.3	102.6	111.8	99.9	82.0	103.5
York, PA MSA:							
York County, PA	96.0	90.4	95.9	114.6	96.7	76.3	97.2
Charleston-North Charleston, SC MSA	100.7	98.9	100.9	96.8	99.3	97.7	103.3
Columbia, SC MSA	95.1	99.2	85.4	114.7	88.8	89.7	99.2
Myrtle Beach, SC MSA	99.7	101.3	97.6	107.3	96.2	92.5	101.0
Sumter, SC MSA	92.6	95.5	86.1	89.7	96.8	89.2	96.5
Sioux Falls, SD MSA	95.0	97.4	84.9	108.1	98.5	93.8	98.5
Chattanooga, TN-GA MSA	93.8	99.7	81.7	93.6	99.0	100.9	98.6
Clarksville-Hopkinsville, TN-KY MSA:	88.9	89.0	79.2	85.2	84.8	92.8	98.5
Jackson, TN MSA	90.5	90.8	79.6	90.1	101.0	84.3	97.4
Johnson City-Kingsport-Bristol, TN-VA MSA:							
Johnson City, TN	88.9	88.4	84.0	91.2	83.9	84.7	94.9
Kingsport, TN	87.8	91.7	79.3	70.0	90.6	89.1	96.4
Knoxville, TN MSA	89.1	95.4	78.3	91.8	86.1	88.1	95.7
Memphis, TN-AR-MS MSA	87.1	90.9	78.3	78.5	94.1	90.2	92.3
Abilene, TX MSA	87.2	80.3	76.6	97.7	97.8	88.1	93.6
Amarillo, TX MSA	90.0	88.4	86.3	81.7	94.5	84.3	95.4
Beaumont-Port Arthur, TX MSA	91.9	85.8	77.8	90.5	101.2	103.6	102.4
El Paso, TX MSA	94.0	95.1	79.8	90.9	95.9	110.1	103.1
Fort Worth-Arlington, TX PMSA:							
Houston, TX PMSA:							
Houston, TX PMSA	90.8	82.7	79.6	98.8	106.9	102.8	95.6
Killeen-Temple, TX MSA	93.0	89.5	88.4	84.8	99.2	93.7	98.7
Longview-Marshall, TX MSA	86.8	85.9	78.5	78.2	91.9	95.1	93.5
Lubbock, TX MSA	87.9	87.6	77.9	75.3	95.8	105.3	94.6
Odessa-Midland, TX MSA:							
Odessa, TX	89.0	88.0	76.6	93.3	92.6	91.5	97.4
San Angelo, TX MSA	88.8	88.8	73.1	83.8	98.3	93.3	99.7
San Antonio, TX MSA	91.1	79.9	94.6	79.7	83.7	90.8	98.6
Sherman-Denison, TX MSA	92.3	99.9	80.5	99.3	90.0	98.2	96.7
Tyler, TX MSA	95.1	91.9	92.5	102.9	97.4	106.6	94.5
Victoria, TX MSA	87.4	84.9	76.1	114.9	91.4	84.8	90.7
Waco, TX MSA	89.1	85.4	81.3	104.1	95.8	91.6	91.4
Provo-Orem, UT MSA	94.1	97.8	88.8	87.8	101.9	86.5	97.1
Lynchburg, VA	91.7	92.6	85.6	87.4	91.9	96.1	96.7
Norfolk-Virginia Beach-Newport News VA-NC MSA:							
Hampton Roads/SE Virginia	96.9	96.8	97.7	111.3	98.4	97.3	92.4
Richmond-Petersburg, VA MSA	99.1	104.6	91.4	108.3	101.4	84.1	102.3
Roanoke, VA MSA	92.7	94.3	87.6	91.9	94.5	89.2	96.4
Bellingham, WA MSA	103.6	106.6	102.6	107.4	94.1	110.7	103.9
Olympia, WA PMSA	101.4	113.2	94.3	85.7	104.4	128.7	100.4
Richland-Kennewick-Pasco, WA MSA	100.5	99.5	99.9	97.2	104.6	121.6	97.9
Spokane, WA MSA	100.6	107.1	100.3	96.8	94.3	116.3	98.1
Tacoma, WA MSA	103.7	116.6	95.5	116.2	101.3	129.7	98.2
Yakima, WA MSA	100.6	110.8	92.1	83.2	90.0	117.5	107.6
Huntington-Ashland, WV-KY-OH MSA	91.1	105.7	78.1	84.5	97.3	88.6	95.3
Appleton-Oshkosh-Neenah, WI MSA	93.8	93.2	87.8	99.0	98.6	95.5	96.0
Eau Claire, WI MSA	95.7	94.0	97.0	92.9	101.8	107.6	92.4
Green Bay, WI MSA	94.3	88.5	91.7	97.3	102.6	104.3	94.5
Sheboygan, WI MSA	96.1	93.2	89.3	105.4	103.9	105.2	97.3
Wausau, WI MSA	93.6	89.0	86.8	95.6	98.6	100.6	98.4
Cheyenne, WY MSA	100.2	108.9	96.5	90.5	97.9	100.3	102.2

Source: ACCRA, 4232 King St., Alexandria, VA 22302-1507, *ACCRA Cost of Living Index*, Fourth Quarter 2002 (copyright).

No. 717. Annual Percent Changes From Prior Year in Consumer Prices—United States and OECD Countries: 1990 to 2001

[Covers member countries of Organization for Economic Cooperation (OECD). For consumer price indexes for OECD countries, see Section 30. 1990 change from 1989; 1995 change from 1994]

Country	1990	1995	1996	1997	1998	1999	2000	2001
United States	5.4	2.8	2.9	2.3	1.6	2.2	3.4	2.8
OECD	7.0	5.7	5.4	4.6	4.0	3.4	4.0	3.0
Australia	7.3	4.6	2.6	0.3	0.9	1.5	4.5	3.0
Canada	4.8	2.2	1.6	1.6	1.0	1.7	2.7	4.6
Japan	3.1	-0.1	0.1	1.7	0.7	-0.3	-0.7	-0.2
New Zealand	6.1	3.8	2.3	1.2	1.3	-0.1	2.6	2.7
Austria	3.3	2.2	1.5	1.3	0.9	0.6	2.4	1.7
Belgium	3.4	1.5	2.1	1.6	1.0	1.1	2.5	1.8
Denmark	2.6	2.1	2.1	2.2	1.8	2.5	2.9	2.9
Finland	6.1	0.8	0.6	1.2	1.4	1.2	3.4	1.9
France	3.6	1.8	2.0	1.2	0.8	0.5	1.7	2.6
Greece	20.4	8.9	8.2	5.5	4.8	2.6	3.2	4.4
Ireland	3.3	2.5	1.7	1.4	2.4	1.6	5.6	5.1
Italy [1]	6.5	5.2	4.0	2.0	2.0	1.7	2.5	2.7
Luxembourg	3.3	1.9	1.3	1.4	1.0	1.0	3.2	2.5
Netherlands	2.5	1.9	2.0	2.2	2.0	2.2	2.5	2.7
Norway	4.1	2.4	1.2	2.6	2.3	2.3	3.1	4.8
Portugal [2]	13.4	4.2	3.1	2.3	2.8	2.3	2.9	4.1
Spain	6.7	4.7	3.6	2.0	1.8	2.3	3.4	3.8
Sweden	10.4	2.9	0.8	0.9	0.4	0.3	1.3	3.3
Switzerland	5.4	1.8	0.8	0.5	-	0.8	1.6	1.3
Turkey [2]	60.3	89.1	80.4	85.7	84.6	64.9	54.9	27.0
United Kingdom	9.5	3.4	2.4	3.1	3.4	1.6	2.9	3.2
Germany	2.7	1.7	1.4	1.9	0.9	0.6	1.9	1.3

- Represents zero. [1] Households of wage and salary earners. [2] Excludes rent.

Source: Organization for Economic Cooperation and Development, Paris, France, *Main Economic Indicators*, monthly (copyright).

No. 718. Producer Price Indexes by Stage of Processing: 1980 to 2002

[1982=100, except as indicated. See Appendix III]

Year	Crude materials - Total	Crude materials - Foodstuffs and feedstuffs	Crude materials - Fuel	Crude nonfood materials except fuel	Intermediate materials, supplies, and components	Finished goods - Consumer goods	Finished goods - Capital equipment	Finished consumer foods - Crude	Finished consumer foods - Processed	Finished consumer goods excl. food
1980	95.3	104.6	69.4	91.8	90.3	88.6	85.8	93.9	92.3	87.1
1985	95.8	94.8	102.7	94.3	102.7	103.8	107.5	102.9	104.8	103.3
1987	93.7	96.2	84.1	88.5	101.5	103.6	111.7	107.1	109.6	100.7
1988	96.0	106.1	82.1	85.9	107.1	106.2	114.3	109.8	112.7	103.1
1989	103.1	111.2	85.3	95.8	112.0	112.1	118.8	119.6	118.6	108.9
1990	108.9	113.1	84.8	107.3	114.5	118.2	122.9	123.0	124.4	115.3
1991	101.2	105.5	82.9	97.5	114.4	120.5	126.7	119.3	124.4	118.7
1992	100.4	105.1	84.0	94.2	114.7	121.7	129.1	107.6	124.4	120.8
1993	102.4	108.4	87.1	94.1	116.2	123.0	131.4	114.4	126.5	121.7
1994	101.8	106.5	82.4	97.0	118.5	123.3	134.1	111.3	127.9	121.6
1995	102.7	105.8	72.1	105.8	124.9	125.6	136.7	118.8	129.8	124.0
1996	113.8	121.5	92.6	105.7	125.7	129.5	138.3	129.2	133.8	127.6
1997	111.1	112.2	101.3	103.5	125.6	130.2	138.2	126.6	135.1	128.2
1998	96.8	103.9	86.7	84.5	123.0	128.9	137.6	127.2	134.8	126.4
1999	98.2	98.7	91.2	91.1	123.2	132.0	137.6	125.5	135.9	130.5
2000	120.6	100.2	136.9	118.0	129.2	138.2	138.8	123.5	138.3	138.4
2001	121.0	106.1	151.4	101.5	129.7	141.5	139.7	127.7	142.4	141.4
2002 prel.	108.1	99.5	117.3	100.8	127.8	139.3	139.1	128.3	141.0	138.7
PERCENT CHANGE [1]										
1980	10.9	4.6	21.1	22.0	15.2	14.3	10.7	1.7	6.3	18.5
1985	-7.4	-9.5	-2.3	2.2	-0.4	0.5	2.2	-7.6	-0.1	1.1
1987	6.8	3.2	-8.8	-19.4	2.4	2.2	1.8	1.4	2.0	2.2
1988	2.5	10.3	-2.4	16.4	5.5	2.5	2.3	2.5	2.8	2.4
1989	7.4	4.8	3.9	-2.9	4.6	5.6	3.9	8.9	5.2	5.6
1990	5.6	1.7	-0.6	12.0	2.2	5.4	3.5	2.8	4.9	5.9
1991	-7.1	-6.7	-2.2	-9.1	-0.1	1.9	3.1	-3.0	-	2.9
1992	-0.8	-0.4	1.3	-3.4	0.3	1.0	1.9	-9.8	-	1.8
1993	2.0	3.1	3.7	-0.1	1.3	1.1	1.8	6.3	1.7	0.7
1994	-0.6	-1.8	-5.4	3.1	2.0	0.2	2.1	-2.7	1.1	-0.1
1995	0.9	-0.7	-12.5	9.1	5.4	1.9	1.9	6.7	1.5	2.0
1996	10.8	14.8	28.4	-0.1	0.6	3.1	1.2	8.8	3.1	2.9
1997	-2.4	-7.7	9.4	-2.1	-0.1	0.5	-0.1	-2.0	1.0	0.5
1998	-12.9	-7.4	-14.4	-18.4	-2.1	-1.0	-0.4	0.5	-0.2	-1.4
1999	1.4	-5.0	5.2	7.8	0.2	2.4	0.6	-1.3	0.8	3.2
2000	22.8	1.5	50.1	29.5	4.9	4.7	0.9	-1.6	1.8	6.1
2001	0.3	5.9	10.6	-14.0	0.4	2.4	0.6	3.4	3.0	2.2
2002 prel.	-10.7	-6.2	-22.5	-0.7	-1.5	-1.6	-0.4	0.5	-1.0	-1.9

- Represents or rounds to zero. [1] Change from immediate prior year.

Source: U.S. Bureau of Labor Statistics, *Producer Price Indexes*, monthly and annual.

No. 719. Producer Price Indexes by Stage of Processing: 1990 to 2002

[1982=100, except as indicated. See Appendix III]

Stage of processing	1990	1995	1997	1998	1999	2000	2001	2002 [1]
Finished goods	**119.2**	**127.9**	**131.8**	**130.7**	**133.0**	**138.0**	**140.7**	**138.8**
Finished consumer goods	118.2	125.6	130.2	128.9	132.0	138.2	141.5	139.3
Finished consumer foods	124.4	129.0	134.5	134.3	135.1	137.2	141.3	140.0
Fresh fruits and melons	118.1	85.8	99.4	90.5	103.6	91.4	97.7	91.1
Fresh and dry vegetables	118.1	144.4	123.1	139.5	118.0	126.7	124.7	136.5
Eggs for fresh use (Dec. 1991=100)	(NA)	86.3	97.1	90.1	77.9	84.9	81.8	82.9
Bakery products	141.0	164.3	173.9	175.8	178.0	182.3	187.7	189.8
Milled rice	102.5	113.1	127.3	124.9	121.3	101.2	87.3	80.6
Pasta products (June 1985=100)	114.1	125.0	125.1	122.6	122.1	121.6	122.1	121.7
Beef and veal	116.0	100.9	102.8	99.4	106.3	113.7	120.6	114.7
Pork	119.8	101.5	123.1	96.6	96.0	113.4	120.3	108.5
Processed young chickens	111.0	113.5	118.6	125.2	113.4	110.4	117.2	109.7
Processed turkeys	107.6	104.9	101.0	95.2	94.8	98.7	98.9	95.1
Finfish and shellfish	147.2	170.8	178.1	183.2	190.9	198.1	190.8	191.3
Dairy products	117.2	119.7	128.1	138.2	139.2	133.7	145.2	136.3
Processed fruits and vegetables	124.7	122.4	126.4	125.7	128.1	128.6	129.6	132.5
Confectionery end products	140.0	160.7	168.3	168.7	170.4	170.6	171.4	175.7
Soft drinks	122.3	133.1	133.2	134.8	137.9	144.1	148.2	151.2
Roasted coffee	113.0	146.5	152.9	143.9	134.7	133.5	124.2	121.4
Shortening and cooking oils	123.2	142.5	137.8	143.4	140.4	132.4	132.9	140.9
Finished consumer goods excluding foods	115.3	124.0	128.2	126.4	130.5	138.4	141.4	138.7
Alcoholic beverages	117.2	128.5	135.1	135.2	136.7	140.6	145.4	147.1
Women's apparel	116.1	119.6	120.5	122.3	123.9	124.6	123.7	122.1
Men's and boy's apparel	120.2	130.3	132.7	133.2	133.1	133.2	132.4	129.4
Girls', children's, and infants' apparel	115.3	121.6	122.9	121.8	118.2	117.4	116.6	118.5
Textile house furnishings	109.5	119.5	122.6	123.1	122.7	122.0	122.5	122.2
Footwear	125.6	139.2	143.7	144.7	144.5	144.9	145.8	146.0
Residential electric power (Dec. 1990=100)	(NA)	111.8	112.8	110.7	109.5	110.8	116.6	115.3
Residential gas (Dec. 1990=100)	(NA)	104.4	116.5	114.0	114.3	135.5	158.7	131.8
Gasoline	78.7	63.7	71.9	53.4	64.7	94.6	90.5	83.3
Fuel oil No. 2	73.3	56.6	64.8	48.1	56.1	93.5	84.3	75.0
Pharmaceutical preps, ethical (prescription)	200.8	257.0	273.5	322.9	335.0	344.4	(NA)	(NA)
Pharmaceutical preps, proprietary (overcounter)	156.8	186.5	184.8	184.5	186.0	187.7	(NA)	(NA)
Soaps and synthetic detergents	117.7	122.9	126.4	126.1	126.3	128.2	130.6	130.2
Cosmetics and other toilet preparations	121.6	129.0	130.6	132.9	135.4	137.4	138.5	139.4
Tires, tubes, and tread	96.8	100.2	95.2	94.0	92.9	93.0	94.1	95.2
Sanitary papers and health products	135.3	144.4	147.1	145.1	144.3	146.7	147.3	149.2
Newspaper circulation	144.1	185.6	201.9	202.9	207.1	210.0	219.5	225.4
Periodical circulation	150.3	176.6	188.1	193.8	196.9	198.9	200.7	210.2
Book publishing	153.4	185.0	200.1	205.9	213.0	218.2	225.5	234.8
Household furniture	125.1	141.8	146.2	148.4	150.5	152.7	154.9	157.1
Floor coverings	119.0	123.7	128.0	128.3	127.2	129.6	130.2	130.5
Household appliances	110.8	112.4	110.1	108.9	108.5	107.3	105.3	104.5
Home electronic equipment	82.7	78.9	77.1	75.9	73.7	71.8	70.4	69.1
Household glassware	132.5	153.2	161.3	162.7	163.9	166.0	169.6	170.0
Household flatware	122.1	138.3	138.5	139.2	139.7	142.6	142.8	144.7
Lawn and garden equipment, except tractors	123.0	130.4	132.2	131.7	132.0	132.0	132.8	133.9
Passenger cars	118.3	134.1	133.6	131.9	131.3	132.8	132.0	129.2
Toys, games, and children's vehicles	118.1	124.3	125.2	124.4	123.1	121.9	123.4	124.7
Sporting and athletic goods	112.6	122.0	124.7	126.2	126.2	126.1	126.3	125.2
Tobacco products	221.4	231.3	248.9	283.6	374.0	397.2	441.9	462.1
Mobile homes	117.5	145.6	152.2	154.3	158.4	161.3	164.1	166.5
Jewelry, platinum, and karat gold	122.8	127.8	129.2	128.1	127.1	127.2	128.5	130.0
Costume jewelry and novelties	125.3	135.1	139.9	139.6	140.1	141.6	144.0	144.2
Capital equipment	**122.9**	**136.7**	**138.2**	**137.6**	**137.6**	**138.8**	**139.7**	**139.1**
Agricultural machinery and equipment	121.7	142.9	149.0	150.4	152.1	153.7	156.1	158.1
Construction machinery and equipment	121.6	136.7	142.2	145.2	147.2	148.6	149.1	151.1
Metal cutting machine tools	129.8	148.0	156.0	159.9	160.7	161.9	158.8	152.7
Metal forming machine tools	128.7	145.7	153.9	157.6	159.7	161.8	164.8	166.8
Tools, dies, jigs, fixtures, and industrial molds	117.2	133.8	138.1	138.8	139.8	141.1	141.3	140.6
Pumps, compressors, and equipment	119.2	139.4	146.5	149.0	151.7	154.1	157.6	161.1
Industrial material handling equipment	115.0	125.3	129.7	131.3	132.9	134.7	136.8	136.9

See footnote at end of table.

No. 719. Producer Price Indexes by Stage of Processing: 1990 to 2002—Con.

[1982=100, except as indicated]

Stage of processing	1990	1995	1997	1998	1999	2000	2001	2002 [1]
Capital equipment—Continued								
Electronic computers (Dec. 1990=100)	(NA)	51.8	33.2	24.7	87.2	73.0	56.7	42.9
Textile machinery	128.8	146.7	152.1	152.7	154.2	156.2	158.0	157.0
Paper industries machinery (June 1982=100)	134.8	151.0	157.4	160.3	162.6	164.7	166.8	168.9
Printing trades machinery	124.9	133.6	138.8	141.5	141.0	142.1	143.3	143.7
Transformers and power regulators	120.9	128.9	129.5	131.0	132.6	135.8	134.4	131.7
Communication/related equip. (Dec. 1985=100)	106.1	112.1	114.0	114.0	112.7	110.6	109.5	107.6
X-ray and electromedical equipment	109.8	111.8	107.4	106.7	104.3	101.5	100.2	101.0
Oil field and gas field machinery	102.4	114.1	122.8	125.8	126.5	128.2	134.3	135.8
Mining machinery and equipment	121.0	135.6	140.3	142.2	144.2	146.1	148.5	151.8
Office and store machines and equipment	109.5	111.5	112.4	112.3	112.3	112.7	112.7	112.5
Commercial furniture	133.4	148.2	154.3	155.2	156.6	158.4	160.3	160.5
Light motor trucks	130.0	159.0	158.9	157.5	157.6	157.6	155.0	150.3
Heavy motor trucks	120.3	144.1	140.4	142.1	146.5	148.0	147.7	152.5
Truck trailers	110.8	131.7	130.3	135.0	136.3	139.4	138.8	138.0
Civilian aircraft (Dec. 1985=100)	115.3	141.8	150.0	150.1	151.7	159.6	168.5	171.3
Ships (Dec. 1985=100)	110.1	132.8	143.7	145.7	145.8	146.9	148.9	150.4
Railroad equipment	118.6	134.8	134.7	134.9	135.2	135.7	135.2	134.9
Intermediate materials, supplies, and components	114.5	124.9	125.6	123.0	123.2	129.2	129.7	127.8
Intermediate foods and feeds	113.3	114.8	125.4	116.1	111.1	111.7	115.9	115.6
Flour	103.6	123.0	118.7	109.2	104.3	103.8	109.9	116.8
Refined sugar	122.7	119.3	123.6	119.8	121.0	110.6	109.9	117.8
Confectionery materials	101.2	109.1	105.4	93.8	94.0	94.2	105.8	117.7
Crude vegetable oils	115.8	130.0	116.6	131.1	90.2	73.6	70.1	87.2
Prepared animal feeds	107.4	109.1	132.9	107.9	98.3	102.9	105.1	105.6
Intermediate materials less foods and feeds	120.9	135.2	134.2	133.5	123.9	130.1	130.5	128.5
Synthetic fibers	106.7	109.4	111.1	109.8	103.8	107.2	108.6	106.1
Processed yarns and threads	112.6	112.8	114.0	112.7	108.6	107.9	105.6	102.6
Gray fabrics	117.2	121.2	121.9	121.6	114.4	113.2	114.0	112.6
Leather	177.5	191.4	182.7	178.5	176.3	182.2	200.9	202.3
Liquefied petroleum gas	77.4	65.1	84.5	60.1	73.7	127.1	119.0	103.7
Commercial electric power	115.3	131.7	131.7	130.5	129.1	131.5	139.6	137.5
Industrial electric power	119.6	130.8	130.8	130.0	128.9	131.5	141.1	139.9
Commercial natural gas (Dec. 1990=100)	(NA)	96.5	109.8	106.6	108.1	134.7	168.3	134.6
Industrial natural gas (Dec. 1990=100)	(NA)	90.9	109.3	104.2	103.3	139.0	177.3	136.4
Natural gas to electric utilities (Dec. 1990=100)	(NA)	87.7	96.9	80.5	81.6	120.7	146.5	103.6
Jet fuels	76.0	55.0	62.9	46.0	52.5	88.5	77.4	71.7
No. 2 Diesel fuel	74.1	57.0	64.5	47.3	57.3	93.3	83.4	77.9
Residual fuel	57.7	52.6	59.5	43.8	51.5	84.7	74.6	75.3
Industrial chemicals	113.2	128.4	126.4	121.6	118.9	129.1	128.4	127.5
Prepared paint	124.8	142.1	152.1	155.0	157.4	160.8	164.4	167.1
Paint materials	136.3	139.4	141.5	143.8	144.1	148.5	149.8	166.1
Medicinal and botanical chemicals	102.2	128.3	133.4	135.0	142.2	146.2	141.2	132.5
Fats and oils, inedible	88.1	126.9	132.3	116.9	88.4	70.1	77.6	90.0
Mixed fertilizers	103.3	111.1	113.6	115.3	113.7	112.4	116.6	113.9
Nitrogenates	92.3	129.4	132.3	108.2	94.6	118.2	143.0	105.9
Phosphates	96.5	109.1	110.4	112.5	112.0	96.9	95.2	99.9
Other agricultural chemicals	119.9	144.3	147.8	149.7	144.5	146.1	148.3	148.6
Plastic resins and materials	124.1	143.5	137.3	125.6	125.8	141.6	134.2	130.6
Synthetic rubber	111.9	126.3	119.3	117.2	113.9	119.1	122.9	119.3
Plastic construction products	117.2	133.8	128.2	126.2	128.0	135.8	132.9	136.4
Unsupported plastic film, sheet, and shapes	119.0	135.6	131.7	128.1	127.5	133.2	138.0	136.4
Plastic parts and components for manufacturing	112.9	115.9	117.2	117.1	117.4	117.3	116.9	116.4
Softwood lumber	123.8	178.5	206.5	182.4	196.0	178.6	170.1	170.8
Hardwood lumber	131.0	167.0	174.1	178.7	177.3	185.9	181.3	178.2
Millwork	130.4	163.8	170.9	171.1	174.7	176.4	179.2	179.7
Plywood	114.2	165.3	159.3	157.6	176.4	157.6	154.3	151.7
Woodpile	151.3	183.2	128.6	122.0	119.7	145.3	125.8	116.3
Paper	128.8	159.0	143.9	146.0	141.8	149.8	150.6	144.9
Paperboard	135.7	183.1	144.4	151.7	153.2	176.7	172.1	164.5
Paper boxes and containers	129.9	163.8	144.7	154.7	158.0	172.6	175.2	172.9
Building paper and board	112.2	144.9	129.6	132.8	141.6	138.8	129.3	129.6

See footnotes at end of table.

Prices 483

No. 719. Producer Price Indexes by Stage of Processing: 1990 to 2002—Con.

[1982=100, except as indicated]

Stage of processing	1990	1995	1997	1998	1999	2000	2001	2002 [1]
Intermediate materials less foods and feeds—Continued								
Commercial printing (June 1982=100)	128.0	144.5	148.7	152.1	152.2	155.2	157.6	157.2
Foundry and forge shop products	117.2	129.3	134.1	135.0	135.1	136.5	136.9	136.9
Steel mill products	112.1	120.1	116.4	113.9	105.3	108.4	101.3	104.6
Primary nonferrous metals	133.4	146.8	126.2	106.7	101.5	113.6	105.2	101.0
Aluminum mill shapes	127.9	160.4	147.5	142.1	138.1	149.0	148.7	143.3
Copper and brass mill shapes	174.6	195.2	177.3	153.4	151.2	162.3	155.0	150.4
Nonferrous wire and cable	142.6	151.5	148.1	140.9	135.6	143.7	140.4	134.3
Metal containers	114.0	117.2	108.1	108.7	106.4	106.8	106.3	107.8
Hardware	125.9	141.1	145.6	147.0	148.7	151.2	154.4	156.0
Plumbing fixtures and brass fittings	144.3	166.0	174.5	175.1	176.7	180.4	180.8	181.9
Heating equipment	131.6	147.5	152.4	153.2	154.0	155.6	157.1	157.8
Fabricated structural metal products	121.8	135.1	140.3	142.5	143.3	144.9	144.6	145.0
Fabricated ferrous wire products (June 1982=100)	114.6	125.7	128.0	130.1	130.6	130.0	129.8	129.7
Other miscellaneous metal products	120.7	124.9	126.2	126.2	125.5	126.0	127.0	126.9
Mechanical power transmission equipment	125.3	146.9	154.8	157.7	161.1	163.9	167.0	169.5
Air conditioning and refrigeration equipment	122.1	130.2	132.6	134.6	135.5	135.3	136.0	136.9
Metal valves, excluding fluid power (Dec. 1982=100)	125.3	145.3	153.3	156.6	160.2	162.1	164.7	167.2
Ball and roller bearings	130.6	152.0	162.9	165.2	166.8	168.8	169.5	169.9
Wiring devices	132.2	147.2	154.0	154.2	152.5	152.9	153.5	153.8
Motors, generators, motor generator sets	132.9	143.9	144.7	145.8	145.9	146.2	146.8	146.9
Switchgear and switchboard equipment	124.4	140.3	145.6	148.3	151.0	153.0	156.9	158.4
Electronic components and accessories	118.4	113.6	104.0	100.1	98.2	97.1	93.9	92.6
Internal combustion engines	120.2	135.6	140.1	140.7	143.0	143.8	143.9	144.6
Machine shop products	124.3	131.3	135.2	136.3	136.8	138.0	140.1	140.0
Flat glass	107.5	113.2	108.4	107.2	106.4	109.7	112.0	111.3
Cement	103.7	128.1	139.4	145.7	150.6	150.1	150.2	152.4
Concrete products	113.5	129.4	136.0	140.1	143.7	147.8	151.7	152.7
Asphalt felts and coatings	97.1	100.0	99.9	99.6	99.2	104.1	107.5	111.0
Gypsum products	105.2	154.5	170.8	177.2	208.0	201.4	156.4	168.5
Glass containers	120.4	130.5	125.7	125.9	125.9	127.4	132.9	135.8
Motor vehicle parts	111.2	116.0	115.4	114.6	114.0	113.6	113.3	112.8
Aircraft engines and engine parts (Dec. 1985=100)	113.5	132.8	135.7	136.9	138.5	141.0	145.1	145.7
Aircraft parts and auxiliary equipment, NEC (June 1985=100)	117.7	135.7	141.3	142.6	143.7	145.7	149.2	150.7
Photographic supplies	127.6	126.8	130.0	128.9	128.3	125.2	128.5	121.8
Medical/surgical/personal aid devices	127.3	141.3	143.1	143.3	144.6	146.0	148.3	150.9
Crude materials for further processing	**108.9**	**102.7**	**111.1**	**96.7**	**98.2**	**120.6**	**121.0**	**108.1**
Crude foodstuffs and feedstuffs	113.1	105.8	112.2	103.8	98.7	100.2	106.1	99.5
Wheat	87.6	118.6	108.2	87.8	79.5	80.3	85.5	97.9
Corn	100.9	109.0	110.1	91.7	78.2	76.4	78.8	89.4
Slaughter cattle	122.5	99.5	97.9	92.5	97.6	104.1	108.4	100.8
Slaughter hogs	94.1	70.2	87.0	52.2	53.8	72.7	73.4	55.4
Slaughter broilers/fryers	119.5	129.1	137.2	151.8	134.5	127.6	138.4	125.9
Slaughter turkeys	116.9	120.3	112.9	110.4	120.0	120.7	110.3	104.3
Fluid milk	100.8	93.6	97.5	112.6	106.3	92.0	111.8	90.5
Soybeans	100.8	102.2	131.0	103.4	80.1	83.4	78.6	87.7
Cane sugar, raw	119.2	119.7	116.8	117.2	113.7	101.8	111.4	111.0
Crude nonfood materials	101.5	96.8	106.4	88.3	94.3	130.4	126.8	112.2
Raw cotton	118.2	156.2	116.5	111.0	87.4	95.2	67.2	61.5
Leaf tobacco	95.8	102.5	(NA)	104.6	101.6	(NA)	105.2	(NA)
Cattle hides	217.8	209.9	196.1	153.3	141.9	169.4	(NA)	(NA)
Coal	97.5	95.0	96.3	93.1	90.7	87.9	96.2	99.8
Natural gas	80.4	66.6	101.7	83.7	91.2	155.5	171.8	122.4
Crude petroleum	71.0	51.1	57.5	35.7	50.3	85.2	69.2	67.6
Logs and timber	142.8	220.4	214.4	208.2	202.0	196.4	182.8	180.1
Wastepaper	138.9	371.1	163.3	146.0	183.6	282.5	148.6	173.0
Iron ore	83.3	91.8	96.3	95.5	94.9	94.8	95.6	95.2
Iron and steel scrap	166.0	202.7	188.9	164.9	139.2	142.1	120.0	141.4
Nonferrous metal ores (Dec. 1983=100)	98.3	101.6	82.2	66.9	63.1	68.0	63.7	67.9
Copper base scrap	181.3	193.5	157.7	116.3	108.2	123.7	114.8	111.2
Aluminum base scrap	172.6	209.4	195.1	162.8	161.7	177.0	156.5	157.9
Construction sand, gravel, and crushed stone	125.4	142.3	148.2	152.7	152.2	163.1	168.8	173.0

N.e.c. Not elsewhere classified.   NA Not available.   [1] Preliminary data.

Source: U.S. Bureau of Labor Statistics, *Producer Price Indexes*, monthly and annual.

No. 720. Producer Price Indexes for the Net Output of Selected Industries: 1998 to 2002

[Indexes are based on selling prices reported by establishments of all sizes by probability sampling. Manufacturing industries selected by shipment value. N.e.c.= not elsewhere classified. See text, Section 22. See Appendix III]

Industry	SIC code [1]	Index base [2]	1998	1999	2000	2001	2002 [3]
Iron ores	1011	12/84	94.5	94.0	93.9	95.2	94.2
Copper ores	1021	06/88	76.8	71.3	88.7	81.7	(X)
Lead and zinc ores	1031	12/85	107.0	111.8	118.8	89.2	(X)
Gold ores	1041	06/85	90.0	85.6	84.2	81.5	92.4
Metal mining services	1081	12/85	122.2	120.2	109.0	117.6	115.9
Metal ores, n.e.c.	1099	12/85	89.9	82.9	85.8	77.9	93.0
Bituminous coal and lignite	1211	12/81	93.0	90.6	(X)	(X)	(X)
Anthracite mining	1231	12/79	160.1	158.7	157.3	161.0	163.0
Coal mining services	1241	06/85	108.1	107.7	108.4	117.0	118.4
Crude petroleum and natural gas liquids	1311	06/96	86.1	102.6	174.3	(X)	(X)
Drilling oil and gas wells	1381	12/85	154.6	133.1	138.2	173.9	153.4
Oil and gas exploration services	1382	12/85	114.5	92.7	80.4	72.7	71.0
Oil and gas field services, n.e.c.	1389	12/85	113.6	112.9	123.3	142.4	137.4
Dimension stone	1411	06/85	142.2	145.9	153.4	156.9	163.9
Crushed and broken limestone	1422	12/83	137.4	140.6	145.6	150.9	154.8
Crushed and broken granite, n.e.c.	1423	12/83	166.4	172.5	182.3	188.3	193.1
Crushed and broken stone, n.e.c.	1429	12/83	147.9	149.9	153.1	156.8	160.7
Construction sand and gravel	1442	06/82	163.0	169.0	175.5	181.6	185.8
Industrial sand	1446	06/82	142.2	145.2	148.0	154.3	157.1
Kaolin and ball clay	1455	06/84	115.8	113.3	113.3	119.6	118.8
Clay and related minerals, n.e.c.	1459	06/84	133.4	133.5	135.7	140.3	140.9
Potash, soda, and borate minerals	1474	12/84	118.9	113.6	111.6	110.0	107.8
Chemicals and fertilizer mineral mining, n.e.c.	1479	12/89	93.4	95.0	90.1	85.8	91.5
Nonmetallic minerals (except fuels) services	1481	06/85	104.7	106.5	107.2	109.3	110.5
Miscellaneous nonmetallic minerals	1499	06/85	136.7	138.0	138.7	143.1	143.2
Meat packing plants	2011	12/80	101.4	104.2	113.4	120.3	112.9
Sausage and other prepared meats	2013	12/82	113.3	113.8	121.3	125.8	121.0
Poultry slaughtering and processing	2015	12/81	127.1	119.8	118.3	121.5	115.9
Natural and processed cheese	2022	06/81	126.1	124.3	117.8	129.6	121.6
Dry, condensed, and evaporated milk products	2023	12/83	146.4	142.4	140.9	150.3	140.0
Ice cream and frozen desserts	2024	06/83	142.6	150.0	150.4	157.1	158.8
Fluid milk	2026	12/82	140.4	145.9	141.8	153.6	146.5
Canned specialties	2032	12/82	165.6	168.6	171.5	173.8	174.6
Canned fruits, vegetables, preserves, jams, and jellies	2033	06/81	136.9	138.2	139.1	142.2	143.7
Pickled fruits/veg./veg. sauces/seasonings/salad dressings	2035	06/81	162.2	163.2	163.6	163.1	165.2
Frozen fruits and vegetables	2037	06/81	138.6	141.8	141.0	140.2	144.1
Frozen specialties	2038	12/82	137.0	137.4	136.1	138.8	139.0
Flour and other grain mill products	2041	06/83	103.3	97.1	97.2	101.9	108.0
Cereal breakfast foods	2043	12/83	161.4	159.5	159.6	161.7	163.3
Wet corn milling	2046	06/85	107.1	101.3	102.6	112.3	112.9
Dog and cat food	2047	12/85	132.3	132.2	131.3	134.7	135.7
Prepared animal feeds, n.e.c.	2048	12/80	95.2	86.7	89.0	92.2	95.2
Bread and other bakery products, except cookies and crackers	2051	06/80	201.4	204.5	211.3	221.5	225.0
Cookies and crackers	2052	06/83	170.3	171.0	172.0	173.3	175.0
Candy and other confectionery products, and chewing gum	2064	06/83	146.8	149.4	150.9	152.4	154.4
Soybean oil mill products	2075	12/79	86.7	68.0	69.1	67.3	72.0
Malt beverages	2082	06/82	128.1	131.4	136.1	140.5	142.9
Bottled and canned soft drinks	2086	06/81	142.4	145.7	152.0	156.5	159.5
Flavoring extracts and syrups, n.e.c.	2087	12/85	131.4	133.6	137.3	140.7	142.7
Fresh or frozen packaged fish	2092	12/82	151.7	160.9	171.5	161.7	157.3
Coffee	2095	06/81	153.3	145.8	144.3	136.4	133.7
Potato and corn chips, and similar snacks	2096	06/91	111.1	112.7	116.7	121.8	123.7
Macaroni, spaghetti, and noodles	2098	06/85	122.7	122.3	121.9	122.4	122.0
Food preparations, n.e.c.	2099	12/85	128.5	128.9	129.1	131.0	134.7
Cigarettes	2111	12/82	260.4	356.7	379.2	425.8	445.7
Cigars	2121	12/82	242.7	259.6	268.8	279.1	290.0
Cotton broadwoven fabric	2211	12/80	117.4	114.1	110.6	111.7	108.9
Manmade fiber and silk broadwoven fabric	2221	06/81	114.8	108.6	108.6	108.9	106.4
Narrow fabric mills	2241	06/84	124.3	124.3	125.3	126.2	126.0
Knit outerwear	2253	12/84	118.9	116.4	117.0	116.6	113.6
Carpet and rugs	2273	06/90	106.4	105.6	107.8	108.8	108.9
Spun yarn	2281	12/82	102.5	96.9	95.5	94.0	90.8
Men's and boys' separate trousers and slacks	2325	12/81	136.5	137.0	134.8	135.1	132.8
Women's, misses', and juniors' dresses	2335	12/80	127.0	126.3	125.8	123.6	122.2
Women's, misses', and juniors' outerwear, n.e.c.	2339	06/83	111.2	112.6	113.3	112.1	111.4
House furnishings, n.e.c.	2392	06/83	115.8	118.8	117.7	117.2	116.5
Automotive trimmings, apparel findings, and related products	2396	12/83	124.0	122.6	123.9	124.5	124.8
Logging camps and logging contractors	2411	12/81	188.2	182.8	177.6	167.6	165.2
Sawmills and planing mills	2421	12/80	151.7	157.4	148.0	141.2	139.1
Millwork	2431	06/83	157.2	160.0	161.3	164.8	165.4
Wood kitchen cabinets	2434	06/84	153.1	155.7	159.8	162.6	164.4
Softwood plywood	2436	12/80	142.5	164.7	140.4	135.8	132.0
Mobile homes	2451	06/81	159.9	164.2	167.1	170.0	172.6
Wood household furniture, except upholstered	2511	12/79	195.8	200.5	204.1	207.6	211.4
Upholstered wood household furniture	2512	06/82	140.1	142.0	144.4	146.2	147.7
Nonwood office furniture	2522	12/79	191.6	191.8	193.4	195.3	196.9
Public building and related furniture	2531	12/84	135.9	136.8	138.6	139.1	138.8

See footnotes at end of table.

Prices 485

No. 720. Producer Price Indexes for the Net Output of Selected Industries: 1998 to 2002—Con.

[See headnote, page 485]

Industry	SIC code [1]	Index base [2]	1998	1999	2000	2001	2002 [3]
Paper mills	2621	06/81	144.4	139.7	148.7	150.5	144.2
Paperboard mills	2631	12/82	165.1	167.0	192.4	187.4	179.8
Corrugated and solid fiber boxes	2653	03/80	168.8	175.5	196.8	198.0	193.2
Folding paperboard boxes	2657	12/83	143.6	142.3	145.4	146.9	146.7
Paper coated and laminated, n.e.c.	2672	06/93	109.6	109.8	111.7	112.8	111.9
Plastics, foil and coated paper bags	2673	12/83	156.5	159.0	168.6	169.2	166.9
Sanitary paper products	2676	06/83	146.0	145.1	148.3	148.0	149.7
Newspaper publishing	2711	12/79	328.5	339.3	351.2	367.9	381.6
Periodical publishing	2721	12/79	276.8	284.9	292.6	305.9	320.4
Book publishing	2731	12/80	238.0	247.6	255.0	263.3	273.1
Miscellaneous publishing	2741	06/84	187.8	194.5	201.3	210.0	217.8
Commercial printing, lithographic	2752	06/82	153.3	153.2	156.0	158.1	157.1
Commercial printing, n.e.c.	2759	06/82	160.9	162.6	166.2	168.4	169.8
Manifold business forms	2761	12/83	167.1	170.5	185.7	193.1	199.7
Industrial inorganic chemicals, n.e.c.	2819	12/82	132.3	129.2	132.7	142.6	141.5
Plastic materials and resins	2821	12/80	139.5	142.8	164.3	159.9	149.1
Noncellulosic manmade fibers	2824	06/81	106.6	98.9	101.5	102.8	101.3
Medicinal chemicals and botanical products (in bulk)	2833	06/82	136.3	143.2	147.8	143.3	135.9
Pharmaceutical preparations	2834	06/81	289.9	298.5	306.6	314.5	326.3
In vivo and In vitro diagnostics	2835	03/80	177.8	184.5	189.9	192.0	196.1
Biological products, except diagnostics	2836	06/91	115.8	126.1	127.5	137.5	140.6
Soap and other detergents	2841	06/83	124.8	125.9	127.4	129.6	129.2
Specialty cleaning, polishing and sanitation preparations	2842	06/83	132.6	135.1	138.1	139.9	139.4
Toilet preparations	2844	03/80	171.7	174.8	177.7	179.2	180.4
Paints and allied products	2851	06/83	154.9	157.3	160.5	163.9	166.1
Cyclic (coal tar) crudes and intermediates, organic dyes and pigments	2865	12/82	109.3	110.1	124.3	114.1	114.2
Industrial organic chemicals, n.e.c.	2869	12/82	168.0	169.1	185.5	182.9	179.8
Agricultural chemicals, n.e.c.	2879	06/82	139.4	135.4	136.6	138.0	138.2
Adhesives and sealants	2891	12/83	151.4	151.7	153.6	158.0	158.5
Chemicals and chemical preparations, n.e.c.	2899	06/85	134.3	134.8	135.8	138.0	139.1
Petroleum refining	2911	06/85	62.3	73.6	111.6	103.1	96.3
Tires and inner tubes	3011	06/81	102.2	100.4	100.4	101.5	102.7
Fabricated rubber products, n.e.c.	3069	06/83	132.4	132.2	133.1	134.6	134.9
Unsupported plastic film and sheet	3081	06/93	103.8	103.2	109.0	113.8	112.2
Plastic bottles	3085	06/93	105.5	106.1	110.4	111.3	108.2
Plastic foam products	3086	06/93	108.6	108.6	110.1	110.3	110.5
Custom compounding of purchased plastic resins	3087	06/93	107.4	104.2	111.1	113.5	107.2
Plastic products n.e.c.	3089	06/93	106.3	106.7	108.0	109.3	108.8
Products of purchased glass	3231	06/83	127.5	128.4	131.6	133.7	133.8
Concrete products	3272	12/79	156.7	161.0	166.4	172.3	175.7
Ready-mixed concrete	3273	06/81	142.3	145.6	150.2	153.4	153.0
Blast furnaces and steel mills	3312	06/82	111.4	102.0	104.1	96.9	100.0
Cold finishing of steel shapes - mfpm	3316	06/82	114.7	110.3	113.6	107.5	115.0
Steel pipe and tubes - mfpm	3317	06/82	132.7	127.1	132.1	129.4	132.4
Gray iron foundries	3321	12/80	143.3	144.5	147.1	148.0	148.6
Primary copper	3331	06/80	106.2	102.2	111.6	(NA)	103.8
Secondary nonferrous metals	3341	06/80	85.9	84.8	88.4	85.9	85.1
Rolling, drawing and extruding of copper	3351	12/80	131.9	130.0	137.6	132.2	127.8
Aluminum sheet, plate, foil and welded tube products	3353	06/81	145.5	139.5	150.4	148.2	140.9
Nonferrous wire drawing and insulating	3357	12/82	148.1	143.7	153.2	149.0	144.0
Metal cans	3411	06/81	110.2	107.8	108.1	108.0	109.4
Hardware, n.e.c.	3429	06/85	126.0	127.4	129.7	132.0	133.2
Fabricated structural metal	3441	06/82	136.8	139.1	142.0	140.9	138.5
Metal doors, sash and trim	3442	06/83	152.9	153.6	156.1	158.1	159.2
Fabricated plate work (boiler shops)	3443	03/80	164.7	167.2	168.9	170.4	171.4
Sheet metal work	3444	12/82	139.9	140.1	141.8	141.5	142.8
Bolts, nuts, screws, rivets, and washers	3452	06/82	127.0	126.4	126.5	126.5	127.4
Automotive stampings	3465	12/82	112.1	110.4	110.6	110.1	110.4
Metal stampings, n.e.c.	3469	06/84	128.9	128.6	128.7	129.9	130.6
Metal coating and allied services	3479	12/84	119.1	118.8	119.1	122.5	122.7
Industrial valves	3491	06/91	119.7	122.4	123.9	126.4	128.0
Fabricated metal products, n.e.c.	3499	06/85	131.8	131.8	133.0	133.7	132.5
Turbines and turbine generator sets	3511	06/82	146.9	148.7	149.6	150.8	152.8
Internal combustion engines, n.e.c.	3519	12/82	136.2	138.1	139.0	140.2	141.2
Farm machinery and equipment	3523	12/82	140.4	142.2	143.9	146.4	149.0
Lawn and garden equipment	3524	12/82	124.9	124.5	124.6	125.2	125.9
Construction machinery	3531	12/80	167.8	170.8	172.7	173.5	175.9
Special tools, dies, jigs, fixtures and industrial molds	3544	06/81	144.9	145.8	147.0	146.9	145.7
Special industry machinery, n.e.c.	3559	12/81	166.0	168.2	169.4	170.1	168.4
Pumps and pumping equipment	3561	12/83	153.3	156.2	158.6	162.4	166.1
General industrial machinery, n.e.c.	3569	12/84	151.3	153.8	156.8	159.1	161.5
Electronic computers	3571	12/90	29.1	91.1	80.8	71.3	61.2
Computer storage devices	3572	12/92	45.3	95.0	85.2	78.2	64.4
Computer peripheral equipment, n.e.c.	3577	12/93	84.5	80.1	78.8	78.3	78.6
Refrigeration and heating equipment	3585	12/82	131.3	131.5	130.6	130.6	131.4
Service industry machinery, n.e.c.	3589	06/82	161.7	164.0	165.9	168.5	171.2
Machinery, except electrical, not elsewhere classified	3599	06/84	126.9	127.6	129.8	132.2	132.6
Switchgear and switchboard apparatus	3613	06/83	138.2	141.0	143.3	147.6	149.7
Electric motors and generators	3621	06/83	139.8	139.9	140.4	141.6	142.1
Relays and industrial controls	3625	06/85	140.4	142.8	144.4	148.2	150.2

See footnotes at end of table.

No. 720. Producer Price Indexes for the Net Output of Selected Industries: 1998 to 2002—Con.

[See headnote, page 485]

Industry	SIC code [1]	Index base [2]	1998	1999	2000	2001	2002 [3]
Household audio & video equipment	3651	03/80	79.7	77.8	76.1	74.6	74.0
Telephone & telegraph apparatus	3661	12/85	117.9	115.8	113.1	108.8	104.5
Radio and television broadcast and communication equipment	3663	12/91	105.5	104.1	101.5	101.7	98.3
Printed circuit boards	3672	06/91	93.9	92.2	91.7	91.8	90.4
Semiconductors and related devices	3674	06/81	70.6	97.4	91.1	86.8	83.9
Electronic components, n.e.c.	3679	06/82	114.2	113.8	114.5	109.4	110.2
Electrical equipment for internal combustion engines	3694	12/82	127.9	127.4	127.6	128.1	127.9
Electrical equipment and supplies, not elsewhere classified	3699	12/85	117.5	118.6	118.3	119.0	119.1
Motor vehicles and passenger car bodies	3711	06/82	136.8	137.6	138.7	137.6	134.7
Truck and bus bodies	3713	12/82	155.3	157.0	160.3	163.3	165.6
Motor vehicle parts and accessories	3714	12/82	112.6	112.0	111.6	111.5	111.1
Aircraft	3721	12/85	142.6	144.1	150.5	155.7	158.8
Aircraft engines and engine parts	3724	12/85	135.7	136.8	139.7	144.0	145.8
Aircraft parts and auxiliary equipment, n.e.c.	3728	06/85	140.9	142.2	143.3	146.6	148.1
Ship building and repairing	3731	12/85	134.8	135.4	137.6	140.1	143.9
Railroad equipment	3743	06/84	127.5	128.1	128.6	128.2	127.7
Search, detection, navigation, and guidance systems aeronautical and nautical nav syst	3812	12/91	109.0	109.0	108.7	108.3	110.7
Industrial process control instruments	3823	06/83	149.9	151.0	152.3	154.3	156.7
Electrical measuring and integrating instruments	3825	12/83	135.1	135.5	137.3	138.9	140.2
Laboratory analytical instruments	3826	12/85	118.4	116.9	119.2	121.6	124.0
Surgical and medical instruments and apparatus	3841	06/82	127.9	127.4	127.2	128.7	130.9
Surgical, orthopedic and prosthetic appliances and supplies	3842	06/83	160.5	163.0	166.4	169.8	173.2
Electromedical equipment	3845	06/85	103.8	101.4	98.5	96.6	96.1
Photographic equipment and supplies	3861	12/83	110.0	106.7	106.3	107.5	104.4
Sporting and athletic goods, n.e.c.	3949	12/85	129.1	128.8	127.9	127.8	126.2
Signs and advertising displays	3993	12/85	136.2	139.1	140.7	145.0	146.1
Manufacturing industries, n.e.c.	3999	12/85	125.1	126.1	127.3	128.6	129.9
Railroads, line haul operations	4011	12/84	113.4	113.0	114.5	116.6	119.0
Local trucking without storage	4212	06/93	104.8	106.3	110.0	113.3	115.1
Trucking, except local	4213	06/92	114.1	118.0	123.5	127.0	127.9
Local trucking with storage	4214	06/93	113.0	113.2	114.1	115.7	117.7
Courier services, except by air	4215	12/92	122.2	126.0	130.6	135.4	138.5
Farm product warehousing and storage	4221	12/92	104.1	107.1	110.6	114.2	115.5
Refrigerated warehousing and storage	4222	12/91	105.5	106.4	108.1	109.8	109.8
General warehousing and storage	4225	06/93	107.2	111.5	113.6	117.1	119.1
United States Postal Service	4311	06/89	132.3	135.3	135.2	143.4	150.2
Deep sea foreign transportation of freight	4412	06/88	116.4	134.0	155.8	172.2	184.1
Domestic deep sea transportation of freight	4424	06/88	120.9	124.3	129.8	134.2	139.4
Freight transportation on the Great Lakes-St Lawrence Seaway	4432	12/91	107.4	107.4	107.4	108.2	106.6
Water transportation of freight, n.e.c.	4449	12/90	107.4	111.2	117.9	123.4	120.6
Marine cargo handling	4491	12/91	105.0	106.7	109.1	111.4	110.9
Tugging and towing services	4492	12/92	115.7	119.7	124.2	125.4	127.4
Air transportation, scheduled	4512	12/89	152.6	161.2	186.5	200.6	200.7
Air courier services	4513	12/89	113.2	117.3	128.0	133.6	136.1
Air transportation, nonscheduled	4522	06/92	106.0	109.2	114.7	120.3	122.4
Airports, flying fields, and airport services	4581	06/92	112.5	116.2	121.2	125.6	129.8
Crude petroleum pipelines	4612	06/86	96.8	95.5	101.0	111.1	112.3
Refined petroleum pipelines	4613	06/86	104.8	104.9	105.3	108.5	111.1
Travel agencies	4724	12/89	112.5	112.0	121.8	123.3	114.1
Freight transportation arrangement	4731	12/94	99.8	99.2	100.3	100.3	99.5
Telephone communications, except radiotelephone	4813	06/95	98.5	96.0	93.9	91.3	87.3
Radio broadcasting	4832	06/88	151.2	162.3	170.6	172.3	171.9
Cable and other pay television services	4841	06/93	112.4	116.2	120.9	124.9	128.8
Electric power and natural gas utilities	4981	12/90	110.4	109.5	114.4	123.9	118.4
Scrap and waste materials	5093	12/86	131.7	127.9	152.8	123.9	129.3
Life insurance carriers	6311	12/98	(X)	100.4	99.2	100.1	101.5
Property and casualty insurance	6331	06/98	(X)	100.8	102.0	104.4	108.6
Operators and lessors of nonresidential buildings	6512	12/95	103.1	105.9	109.0	111.6	114.3
Real estate agents and managers	6531	12/95	102.5	104.4	107.8	111.4	113.4
Hotels and motels	7011	06/93	119.8	124.9	128.8	134.6	133.9
Advertising agencies	7311	06/95	105.3	107.4	110.2	116.2	119.0
Building cleaning and maintenance services, n.e.c.	7349	12/94	105.6	108.0	111.3	116.3	117.8
Employment agencies	7361	06/94	106.4	109.9	111.9	114.0	115.3
Help supply services	7363	06/94	109.1	111.1	113.4	114.1	114.7
Prepackaged software	7372	12/97	100.6	100.1	100.8	101.4	97.9
Truck rental and leasing, without drivers	7513	06/91	104.7	104.2	106.8	108.0	107.5
Passenger car rental, without drivers	7514	12/91	132.5	129.4	134.9	133.8	140.7
Offices and clinics of doctors of medicine	8011	12/93	11.2	113.8	115.8	119.1	119.1
Skilled and intermediate care facilities	8053	12/94	119.4	124.1	131.0	139.3	144.7
General medical and surgical hospitals	8062	12/92	114.5	116.6	119.8	123.4	127.6
Psychiatric hospitals	8063	12/92	108.2	109.2	109.1	110.5	113.1
Specialty hospitals, except psychiatric	8069	12/92	117.1	120.0	123.9	126.5	133.4
Medical laboratories	8071	06/94	106.4	105.9	108.0	112.0	113.9
Home health care services	8082	12/96	106.1	107.1	111.1	114.0	116.6
Legal services	8111	12/96	106.2	108.7	112.5	117.9	121.5
Engineering design, analysis, and consulting services	8711	12/96	105.0	107.9	111.1	115.5	121.4
Architectural design, analysis, and consulting services	8712	12/96	105.5	111.8	115.8	117.7	119.6
Accounting, auditing, and bookkeeping services	8721	06/95	108.2	111.9	115.4	117.5	120.1

NA Not available. N.e.c. Not elsewhere classified. X Not applicable. [1] Standard Industrial Classification code. [2] Index base. year equals 100. [3] Preliminary data.

Source: U.S. Bureau of Labor Statistics, *Producer Price Indexes*, monthly.

No. 721. Chain-Type Price Indexes for Personal Consumption Expenditures (PCE): 1980 to 2002

[1996=100. For explanation of "chain-type," see text, Section 13]

Item	1980	1985	1990	1995	2000	2001	2002
Personal consumption expenditures	55.2	71.0	85.6	97.9	107.4	109.6	111.1
Durable goods [1]	76.5	88.6	96.0	101.1	91.5	89.7	87.2
Motor vehicles and parts	61.0	74.2	83.8	98.4	99.5	99.8	98.4
Furniture and household equipment	106.3	116.3	113.6	104.5	81.5	76.9	72.7
Nondurable goods [1]	65.3	77.3	91.0	97.9	107.6	109.2	109.6
Food	60.8	72.9	88.2	97.3	108.7	111.9	114.1
Clothing and shoes	86.5	93.3	103.5	101.4	95.2	93.4	90.8
Gasoline, fuel oil, and other energy goods	90.6	93.3	95.2	93.7	121.9	118.1	110.0
Gasoline and oil	91.4	92.8	94.8	94.2	121.1	116.8	109.1
Fuel oil and coal	87.4	97.6	98.6	89.6	129.1	130.7	117.7
Services [1]	45.9	64.4	81.0	97.3	110.9	114.3	117.4
Housing	47.1	66.7	84.1	97.0	112.8	117.2	121.7
Household operation	56.3	81.8	87.6	98.1	102.2	106.2	105.3
Transportation	51.9	65.5	81.8	98.4	105.9	108.1	110.2
Medical care	37.2	55.9	76.0	97.9	110.2	114.3	117.4
Recreation	53.7	67.9	83.3	96.8	112.8	116.6	120.0
Addenda:							
Energy goods and services	75.5	90.3	92.5	95.6	113.4	116.6	109.4
PCE less food and energy	52.4	69.2	84.7	98.2	106.9	108.8	110.6

[1] Includes other items not shown separately.

Source: U.S. Bureau of Economic Analysis, *The National Income and Product Accounts of the United States*, 1929-97, Vol. 2; and Survey of Current Business, May 2003. See also <http://www.bea.gov/bea/dn/nipaweb/selecttable.asp?selected=N>.

No. 722. Chain-Type Price Indexes for Gross Domestic Product: 1980 to 2002

[1996=100. For explanation of "chain-type," see text, Section 13]

Item	1980	1985	1990	1995	2000	2001	2002
Gross domestic product	57.1	73.7	86.5	98.1	106.9	109.4	110.7
Personal consumption expenditures	55.2	71.0	85.6	97.9	107.4	109.6	111.1
Durable goods	76.5	88.6	96.0	101.1	91.5	89.7	87.2
Nondurable goods	65.3	77.3	91.0	97.9	107.6	109.2	109.6
Services	45.9	64.4	81.0	97.3	110.9	114.3	117.4
Gross private domestic investment	73.0	85.3	95.1	100.3	99.6	100.8	100.2
Fixed investment	71.8	84.5	94.7	100.1	100.0	101.2	100.8
Nonresidential	77.4	89.6	98.2	100.9	95.6	95.7	94.4
Structures	60.0	74.1	85.8	97.4	114.0	119.8	119.0
Equipment/software	86.6	96.3	102.9	102.1	90.1	88.8	87.4
Residential	58.7	72.2	85.5	97.9	114.4	119.1	121.6
Exports of goods and services	83.3	88.7	96.8	101.3	96.8	96.1	95.9
Exports of goods	94.7	95.6	101.4	102.7	94.1	93.4	93.0
Exports of services	58.4	73.4	86.5	98.0	103.9	102.9	103.3
Imports of goods and services	90.5	85.0	99.4	101.8	95.5	92.7	93.0
Imports of goods	95.9	88.8	102.0	102.5	94.6	91.9	90.3
Imports of services	69.0	69.5	88.3	98.3	100.0	97.0	108.5
Government consumption expenditures [1]	55.8	73.8	85.2	97.6	110.7	113.3	115.2
Federal	57.5	75.7	83.8	97.2	108.2	110.1	113.1
National defense	57.9	77.2	84.6	96.9	107.5	109.3	111.9
Nondefense	56.0	71.5	82.0	97.9	109.6	111.6	115.5
State and local	67.1	72.4	87.7	97.7	116.5	120.1	123.5

[1] And gross investment.

Source: U.S. Bureau of Economic Analysis, *The National Income and Product Accounts of the United States, 1929-97*, and Survey of Current Business, May 2003. See also <http://www.bea.gov/bea/dn/nipaweb/selecttable.asp?selected=N>.

No. 723. Commodity Research Bureau Futures Price Index: 1980 to 2002

[1967=100. Index computed daily. Represents unweighted geometric average of commodity futures prices (through 6 months forward) of 17 major commodity futures markets. Represents end of year index]

Item	1980	1985	1990	1994	1995	1996	1997	1998	1999	2000	2001	2002
All commodities	308.5	229.2	222.6	236.6	243.2	239.6	229.1	191.2	205.1	227.8	190.6	234.5
Softs [1]	426.0	398.2	276.0	352.3	354.4	322.2	408.7	344.8	280.9	254.4	252.8	303.7
Industrials	324.6	211.7	245.5	263.6	272.5	266.3	210.9	185.3	192.9	211.0	141.8	176.6
Grains and oilseeds [2]	312.1	198.5	171.2	191.2	218.6	284.7	210.7	172.8	156.6	174.9	159.0	188.2
Energy	(NA)	96.5	246.0	173.8	180.0	224.0	180.4	135.0	221.0	355.8	204.9	320.7
Oilseeds [3]	314.6	245.4	223.6	259.9	277.5	307.9	(³)	(³)	(³)	(³)	(³)	(³)
Livestock and meats	217.4	206.9	226.2	192.3	192.4	241.7	238.1	186.7	239.6	253.6	247.4	251
Metals (precious)	531.4	256.6	257.8	273.9	276.0	271.3	249.3	234.3	253.4	265.7	246.8	289.1

NA Not available. [1] Prior to 1997, reported as Imported. [2] Prior to 1997, reported as Grains. [3] Incorporated into Grains and Oilseeds beginning 1997.

Source: Bride Commodity Research Bureau (CRB), Chicago, IL, *CRB Commodity Index Report*, weekly (copyright).

No. 724. Indexes of Spot Primary Market Prices: 1980 to 2002

[1967=100. Computed weekly for 1980; daily thereafter. Represents unweighted geometric average of price quotations of 23 commodities; much more sensitive to changes in market conditions than is a monthly producer price index]

Items and number of commodities	1980	1985	1990	1995	1996	1997	1998	1999	2000	2001	2002
All commodities (23)	283.5	236.7	258.1	289.1	288.2	271.8	235.2	227.3	224.0	212.1	244.3
Foodstuffs (10)	269.5	235.2	206.4	236.4	231.8	227.3	197.5	178.1	184.7	201.6	238.1
Raw industrials (13)	293.5	237.6	301.2	332.2	334.9	307.5	265.3	268.9	255.8	217.3	248.6
Livestock and products (5).	281.0	271.1	292.7	307.4	363.0	306.1	232.3	265.7	265.5	257.2	317.8
Metals (5)	288.3	207.7	283.2	300.6	289.9	269.8	218.5	261.6	214.0	172.5	184.5
Textiles and fibers (4)	240.4	206.7	257.6	274.3	267.4	261.5	237.5	223.8	245.7	217.4	230.2
Fats and oils (4).	255.9	220.2	188.7	226.7	246.4	257.1	236.0	174.8	163.6	175.8	234.0

Source: Bride Commodity Research Bureau, Chicago, IL, *CRB Commodity Index Report*, weekly (copyright).

No. 725. Average Prices of Selected Fuels and Electricity: 1980 to 2002

[In dollars per unit, except electricity, in cents per kWh. Represents price to end-users, except as noted]

Type	Unit [1]	1980	1990	1995	1996	1997	1998	1999	2000	2001	2002
Crude oil, composite [2]. . .	Barrel	28.07	22.22	17.23	20.71	19.04	12.52	17.51	28.26	22.95	24.09
Motor gasoline: [3]											
Unleaded regular	Gallon.	1.25	1.16	1.15	1.23	1.23	1.06	1.17	1.51	1.46	1.36
Unleaded premium . . .	Gallon.	(NA)	1.35	1.34	1.41	1.42	1.25	1.36	1.69	1.66	1.58
No. 2 heating oil.	Gallon.	0.97	1.06	0.87	0.99	0.98	0.85	0.88	1.31	1.25	1.13
No. 2 diesel fuel.	Gallon.	0.82	0.73	0.56	0.68	0.64	0.49	0.58	0.94	0.84	0.76
Residual fuel oil	Gallon.	0.61	0.44	0.39	0.46	0.42	0.31	0.37	0.60	0.53	0.57
Natural gas, residential . .	1,000 cu/ft. .	3.68	5.80	6.06	6.34	6.94	6.82	6.69	7.76	9.63	7.79
Electricity, residential. . . .	kWh	5.36	7.83	8.40	8.36	8.43	8.26	8.16	8.24	8.62	8.45

NA Not available. [1] See headnote. [2] Refiner acquisition cost. [3] Average, all service.

Source: U.S. Energy Information Administration, *Monthly Energy Review*.

No. 726. Weekly Food Cost by Type of Family: 1990 and 2002

[In dollars. Assumes that food for all meals and snacks is purchased at the store and prepared at home. See source for details on estimation procedures]

Family type	December 1990				December 2002			
	Thrifty plan	Low-cost plan	Moderate-cost plan	Liberal-plan	Thrifty-plan	Low-cost plan	Moderate-cost plan	Liberal-plan
FAMILIES								
Family of two:								
20-50 years.	48.10	60.60	74.70	92.70	63.80	81.40	100.20	124.70
51 years and over	45.60	58.30	71.80	85.80	60.30	78.30	96.70	115.70
Family of four:								
Couple, 20-50 years and children—								
1-2 and 3-5 years.	70.10	87.30	106.60	131.00	92.70	117.00	143.10	176.10
6-8 and 9-11 years	80.10	102.60	128.30	154.40	107.10	138.00	171.80	207.10
INDIVIDUALS [1]								
Child:								
1-2 years	12.70	15.40	18.00	21.80	16.60	20.50	24.10	29.30
3-5 years	13.70	16.80	20.70	24.90	18.10	22.50	27.90	33.40
6-8 years	16.60	22.20	27.90	32.50	22.60	30.00	37.30	43.40
9-11 years	19.80	25.30	32.50	37.60	26.50	34.00	43.40	50.30
Male:								
12-14 years.	20.60	28.60	35.70	42.00	27.50	38.40	47.50	55.90
15-19 years.	21.40	29.60	36.80	42.60	28.50	39.60	49.30	56.90
20-50 years.	22.90	29.30	36.60	44.30	30.50	39.50	49.10	59.50
51 years and over	20.90	27.90	34.30	41.10	27.70	37.60	46.20	55.50
Female:								
12-19 years.	20.80	24.80	30.10	36.30	27.50	33.10	40.10	48.40
20-50 years.	20.80	25.80	31.30	40.00	27.50	34.50	42.00	53.90
51 years and over	20.60	25.10	31.00	36.90	27.10	33.60	41.70	49.70

[1] The costs given are for individuals in four-person families. For individuals in other size families, the following adjustments are suggested: one-person, add 20 percent; two-person, add 10 percent; three-person, add 5 percent; five- or six-person, subtract 5 percent; seven- (or more) person, subtract 10 percent.

Source: U.S. Dept. of Agriculture, *Official USDA Food Plans: Cost of Food at Home at Four Levels*, monthly. See also <http://www.cnpp.USDA.gov/FoodPlans/updates/Fooddec02.pdf>.

No. 727. Food—Retail Prices of Selected Items: 1990 to 2002

Food	1990	1995	1996	1997	1998	1999	2000	2001	2002
Cereals and bakery products:									
Flour, white, all purpose	0.24	0.24	0.29	0.28	0.28	0.27	0.28	0.28	0.29
Rice, white, lg. grain, raw	0.49	0.55	0.55	0.58	0.54	0.50	(NA)	(NA)	0.46
Spaghetti and macaroni	0.85	0.88	0.85	0.88	0.88	0.88	0.88	0.91	0.93
Bread, whole wheat	(NA)	1.15	1.30	1.30	1.32	1.36	1.36	1.46	1.44
Meats, poultry, fish and eggs:									
Ground beef, 100% beef	1.63	1.40	1.42	1.39	1.39	1.53	1.63	1.71	1.69
Ground beef, lean and extra lean	(NA)	2.04	2.05	2.06	2.08	2.15	2.33	2.51	2.62
Sirloin steak, bone-in	3.65	(NA)	(NA)	(NA)	(NA)	(NA)	(NA)	(NA)	(NA)
T-bone steak	5.45	5.92	5.87	6.07	6.40	6.71	6.82	7.31	(NA)
Pork:									
Bacon, sliced	2.28	2.17	2.64	2.61	2.58	2.75	3.03	3.30	3.24
Chops, center cut, bone-in	3.32	3.29	3.44	3.39	3.03	3.21	3.46	3.53	3.32
Sausage	2.42	1.92	2.15	2.08	2.43	2.50	2.75	2.87	(NA)
Poultry:									
Chicken, fresh, whole	0.86	0.94	1.00	1.00	1.06	1.05	1.08	1.11	1.05
Chicken breast, bone-in	2.00	1.95	2.09	1.99	2.11	2.08	2.14	2.11	2.33
Turkey, frozen, whole	0.96	0.99	1.02	0.98	0.95	0.98	0.99	1.00	0.99
Tuna, light, chunk, canned	2.11	2.00	2.03	2.03	2.22	2.03	1.92	1.96	2.03
Eggs, grade A, large, (dozen)	1.00	1.16	1.31	1.17	1.09	0.92	0.96	0.93	1.18
Dairy products:									
Milk, fresh, whole, fortified (1/2 gal.)	1.39	1.48	1.65	1.61	(NA)	(NA)	(NA)	(NA)	(NA)
Butter, salted, grade AA, stick	1.92	1.73	2.17	2.46	3.18	2.27	2.80	3.31	2.84
Ice cream, prepack., bulk,reg.(1/2 gal.)	2.54	2.68	2.94	3.02	3.30	3.40	3.66	3.84	3.76
Fresh fruits and vegetables:									
Apples, red delicious	0.77	0.83	0.89	0.90	0.85	0.92	0.82	0.89	0.99
Bananas	0.43	0.45	0.48	0.46	0.51	0.49	0.49	0.51	0.50
Oranges, navel	0.56	0.64	0.59	0.58	0.61	0.64	0.62	0.71	0.74
Grapefruit	0.56	0.49	0.55	0.53	0.55	0.58	0.58	0.60	0.62
Grapes, thompson seedless	(NA)	1.86	(NA)	2.19	(NA)	2.40	2.36	(NA)	2.27
Lemons	0.97	1.12	1.14	1.06	1.37	1.41	1.11	1.40	1.44
Pears, Anjou	0.79	(NA)	1.06	0.85	0.98	1.03	(NA)	0.98	(NA)
Potatoes, white	0.32	0.38	0.34	0.37	0.38	0.40	0.35	0.41	0.48
Tomatoes, field grown	0.86	1.51	1.21	1.62	1.80	1.41	1.57	1.40	1.66
Cabbage	0.39	0.41	0.40	0.46	0.42	0.42	(NA)	(NA)	(NA)
Carrots, short trimmed and topped	0.44	0.53	0.54	0.50	0.54	0.52	(NA)	(NA)	(NA)
Celery	0.49	0.54	0.44	0.57	0.53	0.56	(NA)	(NA)	(NA)
Cucumbers	0.56	0.53	0.60	0.58	(NA)	0.84	(NA)	(NA)	(NA)
Onions, dry yellow	(NA)	0.41	0.46	0.46	(NA)	(NA)	(NA)	(NA)	(NA)
Peppers, sweet	(NA)	1.32	1.34	1.54	1.46	1.53	(NA)	(NA)	(NA)

NA Not available.

Source: U.S. Bureau of Labor Statistics, *Monthly Labor Review* and *CPI Detailed Report*, January issues.

No. 728. Import Price Indexes—Selected Commodities: 1990 to 2002

[2000 = 100. Indexes are weighted by the 2000 Tariff Schedule of the United States Annotated, a scheme for describing and reporting product composition and value of U.S. imports. Import prices are based on U.S. dollar prices paid by importer. F.o.b. = Free on board; c.i.f. = Cost, insurance, and freight; n.e.s. = Not elsewhere specified]

Commodity	1990	1995 [1]	1997	1998	1999	2000 [1]	2001	2002
All commodities	90.8	101.4	98.8	93.1	92.9	100.2	97.6	94.1
Food and live animals	92.1	108.6	112.5	106.3	101.2	99.0	96.0	94.5
Meat	118.4	100.8	103.6	100.0	96.1	100.8	106.2	104.0
Fish	70.9	92.5	94.3	99.6	94.9	99.3	90.0	79.8
Crustaceans; fresh, chilled, frozen, salted or dried	65.2	91.9	92.0	94.6	88.0	100.9	83.6	70.0
Beverages and tobacco	76.5	88.6	95.5	97.4	98.1	100.4	101.7	103.0
Crude materials	90.4	109.5	106.8	96.2	99.1	99.4	102.8	96.4
Mineral fuels and related products	54.7	61.9	61.6	45.7	54.6	101.3	90.4	86.1
Crude petroleum and petroleum products	54.8	63.0	62.2	43.9	54.6	102.2	89.3	85.9
Natural gas	54.9	49.3	55.1	54.5	51.8	95.2	97.4	83.6
Chemicals and related products	93.7	106.8	102.3	99.3	96.2	99.8	100.5	97.0
Intermediate manufactured products	91.3	102.7	99.5	96.7	94.6	100.4	98.0	92.8
Machinery and transport equipment	100.8	112.4	106.9	102.6	100.9	100.1	98.5	97.1
Computer equipment and office machines	198.5	167.2	135.3	117.2	105.1	99.9	93.6	87.8
Computer equipment	284.6	198.4	160.8	132.3	108.9	100.4	89.3	80.3
Telecommunications [2]	120.9	119.1	110.6	105.9	103.8	100.2	97.2	94.4
Electrical machinery and equipment	111.3	122.9	109.1	102.2	100.1	100.7	98.8	97.1
Road vehicles	82.0	97.3	98.1	98.4	99.6	100.1	99.8	100.2
Miscellaneous manufactured articles	94.7	103.2	103.0	101.4	100.5	99.7	99.8	98.6
Plumbing, heating & lighting fixtures	102.0	107.4	103.0	102.7	99.5	99.2	99.2	98.5
Furniture and parts	96.0	103.1	105.4	102.6	101.1	99.6	98.5	98.8
Articles of apparel and clothing	96.5	99.0	101.5	101.5	100.6	99.6	100.6	99.7
Footwear	96.5	99.3	100.3	100.0	100.0	99.6	100.1	99.2

[1] June 1995 and 2000 may not equal 100 because indexes were reweighted to an "average" trade value in 1995 and 2000.
[2] Includes sound recording and reproducing equipment.

Source: U.S. Bureau of Labor Statistics, *U.S. Import and Export Price Indexes*, monthly.

No. 729. Export Price Indexes—Selected Commodities: 1990 to 2002

[2000=100. Indexes are weighted by 2000 export values according to the Schedule B classification system of the U.S. Census Bureau. Prices used in these indexes were collected from a sample of U.S. manufacturers of exports and are factory transaction prices, except as noted. F.a.s. = free alongside ship. N.e.s. = not elsewhere specified. F.o.b. = free on board]

Commodities	1990	1995	1997	1998	1999	2000 [1]	2001	2002
All commodities	95.1	104.5	103.2	99.9	98.2	100.1	99.4	98.0
Food and live animals	102.4	112.1	113.3	104.6	102.6	100.6	101.1	99.8
Meat	81.4	95.7	91.3	93.7	87.6	104.8	106.1	90.0
Fish	86.8	107.1	88.5	83.8	123.0	100.6	90.8	97.9
Cereals and cereal preparations	126.5	133.2	128.9	115.4	106.0	100.0	102.6	106.5
Wheat	116.9	132.5	126.7	109.6	101.4	99.4	111.3	113.5
Maize	144.0	144.6	133.5	119.5	108.3	101.0	95.9	104.8
Fruits and vegetables	93.2	107.2	113.3	109.8	109.9	97.9	98.6	99.0
Feeding stuff for animals	99.5	104.9	135.7	101.3	92.5	100.4	101.1	101.2
Miscellaneous food products	94.0	94.8	96.9	98.3	100.1	100.0	100.1	100.7
Beverages and tobacco	84.9	98.2	99.1	98.2	99.4	100.0	98.4	98.2
Tobacco and tobacco manufactures	85.0	98.1	98.9	97.8	99.2	99.9	98.2	97.6
Crude materials	96.7	125.4	112.4	98.7	90.2	101.6	92.6	95.3
Oil seeds and oleaginous fruits	116.1	115.6	161.1	122.8	94.8	103.3	95.6	102.9
Cork and wood	76.5	117.5	107.3	94.5	94.4	99.8	92.8	87.1
Pulp and waste paper	70.9	122.2	72.1	70.1	72.3	106.9	80.6	89.3
Textile fibers	118.2	154.3	120.3	114.4	99.1	100.5	90.9	88.6
Metalliferous ores and metal scrap	105.9	132.2	116.4	97.2	89.7	99.2	91.0	99.8
Mineral fuels and related materials	67.2	68.5	74.5	69.3	68.5	97.4	103.2	93.9
Coal, coke and briquettes	109.5	106.4	108.2	106.2	104.3	99.5	106.9	110.9
Crude petroleum and petroleum products	57.5	59.6	68.7	61.4	61.9	96.8	101.8	87.9
Chemicals and related products	90.4	108.4	102.0	97.9	96.4	100.9	96.2	95.8
Organic chemicals	93.9	122.8	97.6	88.7	86.4	102.1	90.6	90.8
Chemical materials and products, n.e.s.	86.4	100.7	104.6	101.2	100.3	99.7	99.1	97.5
Intermediate manufactured products	86.8	100.6	98.1	97.7	96.7	100.2	99.5	98.1
Rubber manufactures	81.4	95.7	99.0	97.7	101.2	100.1	99.8	102.7
Paper and paperboard products	90.8	115.6	93.4	93.7	93.3	100.5	97.4	94.8
Textiles	91.2	102.8	105.0	104.9	100.8	100.2	98.5	100.0
Nonmetallic mineral manufactures	85.8	94.3	98.3	100.6	100.2	100.4	100.8	102.2
Nonferrous metals	87.1	98.2	92.0	86.7	83.7	98.5	98.0	85.3
Manufactures of metals, n.e.s.	81.2	92.3	96.3	98.6	100.2	100.9	101.5	102.5
Machinery and transport equipment [2]	97.9	102.8	103.3	101.4	100.3	100.0	100.3	98.9
Power generating machinery [3]	77.0	88.5	94.4	95.3	97.6	99.7	102.3	104.5
Rotating electric plant and parts thereof, n.e.s.	87.0	97.9	100.5	100.4	100.1	100.1	99.8	107.8
Machinery specialized for particular industries	82.7	94.0	98.0	99.0	99.8	100.2	100.3	101.8
Agricultural machinery and parts [4]	86.0	95.6	98.0	98.3	98.9	99.9	98.9	99.8
Civil engineering and contractors, plant and equip.	81.8	93.6	96.4	98.8	100.4	100.3	100.4	101.6
Metalworking machinery	82.1	92.3	96.3	100.0	100.4	99.3	101.0	99.9
General industrial machines, parts, n.e.s.	82.5	92.0	97.3	98.1	99.2	100.1	101.3	102.3
Computer equipment and office machines	193.2	147.5	123.9	112.0	104.8	99.9	95.6	90.4
Computer equipment	234.5	160.7	125.2	116.9	106.1	99.7	96.0	92.1
Telecommunications [5]	97.3	103.8	103.0	102.1	100.2	100.3	99.8	97.7
Electrical machinery and equipment	112.7	117.2	112.3	107.2	103.1	99.8	98.3	93.9
Electronic valves, diodes, transistors & integr. cir.	135.0	135.1	121.9	112.1	105.0	99.5	95.4	87.5
Road vehicles	88.7	96.1	98.0	98.1	98.6	100.0	100.2	100.3
Miscellaneous manufactured articles	90.5	98.6	100.3	99.4	99.6	99.7	100.1	100.4

[1] June 2000 may not equal 100 because indexes were reweighted to an "average" trade value in 2000. [2] Excludes military and commercial aircraft. [3] Includes equipment. [4] Excludes tractors. [5] Includes sound recording and reproducing equipment.

Source: U.S. Bureau of Labor Statistics, *U.S. Import and Export Price Indexes*, monthly.

No. 730. Refiner/Reseller Sales Price of Gasoline by State: 2001 to 2003

[In cents per gallon. As of March. Represents all refinery and gas plant operators' sales through company-operated retail outlets. Gasoline prices exclude excise taxes]

State	Gasoline excise taxes 2003	Average, all grades 2001	2002	2003	Midgrade 2001	2002	2003	Premium 2001	2002	2003
United States ...	(NA)	102.6	87.5	126.7	109.2	93.2	132.9	117.3	101.1	142.5
Alabama	18.0	100.7	85.0	119.4	107.3	89.0	125.7	116.6	99.1	133.3
Alaska	8.0	137.1	115.2	(NA)	144.6	122.2	(NA)	155.8	127.2	178.5
Arizona	18.0	113.9	88.9	151.8	121.4	96.8	160.8	132.2	102.6	169.9
Arkansas	21.5	96.9	85.5	120.3	102.1	90.4	128.0	110.5	99.7	133.2
California	18.0	120.1	100.3	159.8	123.9	106.7	168.6	133.4	115.2	174.7
Colorado	22.0	107.7	93.2	129.6	115.5	99.8	135.8	123.1	108.9	145.6
Connecticut	25.0	107.0	84.7	125.6	115.0	89.9	131.5	123.8	98.4	140.2
Delaware	23.0	100.5	82.8	121.2	107.8	88.8	128.0	116.3	97.2	137.3
District of Columbia	20.0	(D)	(D)	(D)	(D)	(D)	(NA)	(D)	(D)	(D)
Florida	13.6	98.2	84.1	125.2	104.8	89.7	131.3	112.0	97.6	139.9
Georgia	7.5	95.5	83.9	120.7	100.8	89.2	128.1	109.5	98.4	135.3
Hawaii	16.0	146.3	114.1	156.0	149.9	118.7	151.7	153.8	120.4	169.1
Idaho	25.0	103.4	84.0	127.9	109.8	91.2	135.8	117.8	97.8	141.4
Illinois	19.0	102.4	94.3	126.5	108.8	100.4	134.0	119.3	107.4	142.8
Indiana	18.0	100.5	88.8	123.8	107.2	95.7	131.8	115.3	103.8	139.6
Iowa	20.0	99.0	89.5	120.1	101.9	90.2	123.0	108.7	97.8	132.7
Kansas	23.0	97.1	86.6	119.3	103.6	92.3	126.5	110.7	100.1	135.8
Kentucky	16.4	101.5	88.3	125.2	107.8	94.5	132.3	116.1	104.2	142.3
Louisiana	20.0	98.4	82.8	119.5	105.7	89.1	126.6	115.2	98.3	135.8
Maine	22.0	105.5	87.6	126.8	113.1	94.9	134.9	120.4	102.1	140.2
Maryland	23.5	100.5	84.9	121.8	107.1	89.3	128.1	111.2	95.9	134.9
Massachusetts	21.0	109.0	87.7	128.2	115.8	93.2	134.8	123.2	101.5	143.7
Michigan	19.0	96.6	87.3	124.1	101.6	92.4	129.1	111.4	99.4	136.0
Minnesota	20.0	108.9	97.7	124.4	110.8	98.8	126.2	119.9	108.5	137.0
Mississippi	18.4	104.7	87.1	124.4	110.7	93.7	130.1	119.9	102.6	140.6
Missouri	17.0	99.7	87.9	120.6	106.6	95.0	129.9	115.6	103.5	137.3
Montana	27.0	101.8	91.8	123.4	106.8	97.6	129.6	117.2	102.5	138.4
Nebraska	24.6	100.6	87.7	118.7	105.2	89.5	120.8	109.5	95.4	129.6
Nevada	23.0	126.8	96.4	151.6	138.2	104.9	163.6	141.0	109.6	163.9
New Hampshire	19.5	107.0	88.0	126.7	114.3	96.0	135.3	121.7	102.7	141.7
New Jersey	10.5	106.7	85.0	127.0	112.7	90.5	132.7	120.0	98.6	141.0
New Mexico	18.9	102.6	90.0	126.1	110.2	(NA)	135.9	117.7	105.8	140.3
New York	22.0	101.8	81.5	124.0	108.4	87.6	130.6	115.6	93.9	137.2
North Carolina	23.4	98.1	81.8	120.7	103.7	87.9	127.8	112.1	96.2	136.2
North Dakota	21.0	109.8	94.7	128.3	114.4	97.1	129.0	115.0	98.5	135.3
Ohio	22.0	100.4	90.1	124.1	107.8	97.7	132.4	115.2	107.1	140.9
Oklahoma	17.0	92.0	83.4	115.6	96.9	88.3	121.6	104.3	96.6	128.8
Oregon	24.0	109.4	90.3	144.2	119.7	99.6	154.2	126.2	107.8	162.3
Pennsylvania	25.9	96.1	80.1	118.9	101.6	85.3	125.0	110.6	93.0	133.4
Rhode Island	30.0	102.8	84.3	123.4	110.0	90.6	130.5	116.8	98.2	138.2
South Carolina	16.0	95.4	83.8	120.8	101.7	89.6	127.8	110.7	99.7	137.3
South Dakota	22.0	109.2	94.6	123.0	115.2	96.7	125.8	118.1	107.3	135.1
Tennessee	20.0	96.2	80.8	119.2	102.0	86.7	126.2	108.6	93.9	134.6
Texas	20.0	94.4	83.2	118.4	102.1	89.1	124.9	108.7	97.4	132.3
Utah	24.5	100.0	82.8	124.7	104.2	87.1	129.6	112.9	95.4	138.0
Vermont	20.0	106.8	90.5	128.4	112.8	95.9	134.6	118.2	104.1	141.4
Virginia	17.5	102.0	84.3	122.5	107.7	88.9	128.2	116.2	97.3	137.2
Washington	23.0	111.3	88.8	142.1	119.9	96.9	152.2	129.6	105.2	161.1
West Virginia	25.4	98.5	85.0	125.6	105.0	90.6	132.0	113.0	97.2	139.2
Wisconsin	28.1	100.7	91.0	124.1	103.2	94.5	125.0	113.8	103.0	137.3
Wyoming	14.0	108.4	93.5	131.1	114.8	100.5	138.6	119.7	104.6	144.3

D Withheld to avoid disclosure of individual company data.   NA Not available.

Source: U.S. Energy Information Administration, *Petroleum Marketing Monthly.*

Section 15
Business Enterprise

This section relates to the place and behavior of the business firm and to business initiative in the American economy. It includes data on the number, type, and size of businesses; financial data of domestic and multinational U.S. corporations; business investments, expenditures, and profits; and sales and inventories.

The principal sources of these data are the *Survey of Current Business*, published by the Bureau of Economic Analysis (BEA), the *Federal Reserve Bulletin*, issued by the Board of Governors of the Federal Reserve System, the annual *Statistics of Income (SOI)* reports of the Internal Revenue Service (IRS), and the Census Bureau's Economic Census, *County Business Patterns, Quarterly Financial Report for Manufacturing, Mining, and Trade Corporations (QFR), Surveys of Minority- and Women-Owned Business Enterprises,* and *Annual Capital Expenditures Survey*.

Business firms—A firm is generally defined as a business organization under a single management and may include one or more establishments. The terms firm, business, company, and enterprise are used interchangeably throughout this section. A firm doing business in more than one industry is classified by industry according to the major activity of the firm as a whole.

The IRS concept of a business firm relates primarily to the legal entity used for tax reporting purposes. A sole proprietorship is an unincorporated business owned by one person and may include large enterprises with many employees and hired managers and part-time operators. A partnership is an unincorporated business owned by two or more persons, each of whom has a financial interest in the business. A corporation is a business that is legally incorporated under state laws. While many corporations file consolidated tax returns, most corporate tax returns represent individual corporations, some of which are affiliated through common ownership or control with other corporations filing separate returns.

Economic census—The economic census is the major source of facts about the structure and functioning of the nation's economy. It provides essential information for government, business, industry, and the general public. It furnishes an important part of the framework for such composite measures as the gross domestic product estimates, input/output measures, production and price indexes, and other statistical series that measure short-term changes in economic conditions. The Census Bureau takes the economic census every 5 years, covering years ending in "2" and "7." The economic census forms an integrated program at 5-year intervals since 1967, and before that for 1963, 1958, and 1954. Prior to that time, the individual censuses were taken separately at varying intervals.

The economic census is collected on an establishment basis. A company operating at more than one location is required to file a separate report for each store, factory, shop, or other location. Each establishment is assigned a separate industry classification based on its primary activity and not that of its parent company. Establishments responding to the establishment survey are classified into industries on the basis of their principal product or activity (determined by annual sales volume) in accordance with the *North American Industry Classification System—United States, 1997 manual* (see below).

More detailed information about the scope, coverage, classification system, data items, and publications for each of the economic censuses and related surveys is published in the *Guide to the Economic Censuses and Related Statistics*. More information on the methodology, procedures, and history of the censuses is available in the *History of the 1997 Economic Census* found on the Census Bureau Web site at <http://www.census.gov/prod/ec97/pol00-hec.pdf>.

Data from the 1997 Economic Census were released through the Census Bureau's American FactFinder service, on CD-ROM, and in Adobe Acrobat PDF reports available on the Census Bureau Web site. For more information on these various media of release, see the following page on the Census Bureau Web site <http://www.census.gov/epcd/www/econ97.html>.

North American Industry Classification System (NAICS)—The 1997 Economic Census is the first census to present data based on the new NAICS. Previous census data were based on the Standard Industrial Classification (SIC) system. This new system of industrial classification was developed by experts on classification in government and private industry under the guidance of the Office of Information and Regulatory Affairs, Office of Management and Budget.

There are 20 NAICS sectors, which are subdivided into 96 subsectors (three-digit codes), 313 industry groups (four-digit codes), and, as implemented in the United States, 1,170 industries (five- and six-digit codes). While many of the individual NAICS industries correspond directly to industries as defined under the SIC system, most of the higher level groupings do not.

Most of the 1997 Economic Census data are issued on a NAICS basis as seen in the industry and geographic series from the census. Other related census reports remain on an SIC basis due to use of administrative records and other methodological and data processing issues. Current survey data from the Census Bureau as well as other statistical agencies are converting over time to NAICS after benchmarking to the 1997 Economic Census where appropriate or implementation of data collection on a NAICS basis.

Quarterly Financial Report—The Quarterly Financial Report (QFR) program publishes quarterly aggregate statistics on the financial conditions of U.S. corporations. The QFR requests companies to report estimates from their statements of income and retained earnings, balance sheets, and related financial and operating ratios for domestic operations. The statistical data are classified and aggregated by type of industry and asset size. The QFR sample includes large manufacturing companies, mostly with $250 million or more in assets. It also includes a small sample of manufacturing companies, mostly with assets between $250 thousand and $250 million, and a sample of mining, wholesale, and retail companies, mostly with assets of $50 million or more. The data are published quarterly in the *Quarterly Financial Report for Manufacturing, Mining, and Trade Corporations* and on the Internet at <http://www.census.gov/csd/qfr/>.

No. 731. Number of Returns, Receipts, and Net Income by Type of Business: 1980 to 2000

[8,932 represents 8,932,000. Covers active enterprises only. Figures are estimates based on sample of unaudited tax returns; see Appendix III. Minus sign (-) indicates net loss]

Item	Number of returns (1,000) Nonfarm proprietorships [1]	Number of returns (1,000) Partnerships	Number of returns (1,000) Corporations	Business receipts [2] (bil. dol.) Nonfarm proprietorships [1]	Business receipts [2] (bil. dol.) Partnerships	Business receipts [2] (bil. dol.) Corporations	Net income (less loss) [3] (bil. dol.) Nonfarm proprietorships [1]	Net income (less loss) [3] (bil. dol.) Partnerships	Net income (less loss) [3] (bil. dol.) Corporations
1980	8,932	1,380	2,711	411	286	6,172	55	8	239
1985	11,929	1,714	3,277	540	349	8,050	79	-9	240
1990	14,783	1,554	3,717	731	541	10,914	141	17	371
1991	15,181	1,515	3,803	713	539	10,963	142	21	345
1992	15,495	1,485	3,869	737	571	11,272	154	43	402
1993	15,848	1,468	3,965	757	627	11,814	156	67	498
1994	16,154	1,494	4,342	791	732	12,858	167	82	577
1995	16,424	1,581	4,474	807	854	13,969	169	107	714
1996	16,955	1,654	4,631	843	1,042	14,890	177	145	806
1997	17,176	1,759	4,710	870	1,297	15,890	187	168	915
1998	17,409	1,855	4,849	918	1,534	16,543	202	187	838
1999	17,576	1,937	4,936	969	1,829	18,009	208	228	929
2000	17,905	2,058	5,045	1,021	2,316	19,593	215	269	928

[1] In 1980, represents individually owned businesses, including farms; thereafter, represents only nonfarm proprietors, i.e., business owners. [2] Excludes investment income except for partnerships and corporations in finance, insurance, and real estate before 1998. Beginning 1998, finance and insurance, real estate, and management of companies included investment income for partnerships and corporations. Starting 1985, investment income no longer included for S corporations. [3] Net income (less loss) is defined differently by form of organization, basically as follows: (a) Proprietorships: Total taxable receipts less total business deductions, including cost of sales and operations, depletion, and certain capital expensing, excluding charitable contributions and owners' salaries; (b) Partnerships: Total taxable receipts (including investment income except capital gains) less deductions, including cost of sales and operations and certain payments to partners, excluding charitable contributions, oil and gas depletion, and certain capital expensing; (c) Corporations: Total taxable receipts (including investment income, capital gains, and income from foreign subsidiaries deemed received for tax purposes, except for S corporations beginning 1985) less business deductions, including cost of sales and operations, depletion, certain capital expensing, and officers' compensation excluding S corporation charitable contributions and investment expenses starting 1985; net income is before income tax.

Source: U.S. Internal Revenue Service, *Statistics of Income*, various publications.

No. 732. Number of Returns and Business Receipts by Size of Receipts: 1990 to 2000

[3,717 represents 3,717,000. Covers active enterprises only. Figures are estimates based on sample of unaudited tax returns; see Appendix III]

Size-class of receipts	Returns (1,000) 1990	1995	1998	1999	2000	Business receipts [1] (bil. dol.) 1990	1995	1998	1999	2000
Corporations	3,717	4,474	4,849	4,936	5,045	10,914	13,969	16,543	18,009	19,593
Under $25,000 [2]	879	1,030	1,181	1,189	1,220	5	4	4	4	4
$25,000 to $49,999	252	288	287	297	302	9	11	11	11	10
$50,000 to $99,999	359	447	456	487	477	26	33	34	36	35
$100,000 to $499,999	1,162	1,393	1,481	1,500	1,515	291	350	368	379	397
$500,000 to $999,999	416	513	552	546	582	294	361	389	388	407
$1,000,000 or more	649	803	892	918	946	10,289	13,210	15,738	17,191	18,738
Partnerships	1,554	1,581	1,855	1,937	2,058	541	854	1,534	1,829	2,316
Under $25,000 [2]	963	931	1,038	1,036	1,105	4	4	4	4	5
$25,000 to $49,999	126	133	157	170	183	5	5	6	6	7
$50,000 to $99,999	133	142	157	187	187	10	10	11	14	13
$100,000 to $499,999	222	245	320	338	353	51	56	73	79	82
$500,000 to $999,999	52	59	77	84	92	36	42	54	59	66
$1,000,000 or more	57	69	107	122	137	435	738	1,385	1,667	2,143
Nonfarm proprietorships	14,783	16,424	17,409	17,576	17,905	731	807	918	969	1,021
Under $25,000 [2]	10,196	11,317	11,767	11,821	11,997	69	76	79	80	(NA)
$25,000 to $49,999	1,660	1,983	2,112	2,227	2,247	58	71	75	79	(NA)
$50,000 to $99,999	1,282	1,393	1,590	1,558	1,645	91	99	113	110	(NA)
$100,000 to $499,999	1,444	1,514	1,686	1,702	1,733	296	310	345	349	(NA)
$500,000 to $999,999	143	147	175	182	190	97	100	118	123	(NA)
$1,000,000 or more	57	70	78	86	92	119	151	188	227	(NA)

NA Not available. [1] Excludes investment income except for partnerships and corporations in finance, insurance, and real estate before 1998. Beginning 1998, finance and insurance, real estate, and management of companies included investment income for partnerships and corporations. [2] Includes firms with no receipts.

Source: U.S. Internal Revenue Service, *Statistics of Income Bulletin;* and unpublished data.

Business Enterprise 495

No. 733. Number of Returns, Receipts, and Net Income by Type of Business and Industry: 2000

[17,905 represents 17,905,000. Covers active enterprises only. Figures are estimates based on sample of unaudited tax returns; see Appendix III. Based on the North American Industry Classification System (NAICS), 1997; see text, this section. Minus sign (-) indicates net loss]

Industry	NAICS code	Number of returns (1,000) Non-farm proprietor-ships	Partner-ships	Corporations	Business receipts [1] (bil. dol.) Non-farm proprietor-ships	Partner-ships	Corporations	Net income (less loss) (bil. dol.) Non-farm proprietor-ships	Partner-ships	Corporations
Total [2]	(X)	17,905	2,058	5,045	1,021	2,316	19,593	215	269	928
Agriculture, forestry, fishing, and hunting [3]	11	278	114	141	17	16	106	2	(Z)	1
Mining	21	107	26	33	6	57	141	1	16	10
Utilities	22	14	2	8	(Z)	108	708	(Z)	4	29
Construction	23	2,245	116	598	160	140	1,034	27	10	32
Special trade contractors	235	1,764	43	342	106	22	428	21	2	14
Manufacturing	31-33	352	38	289	28	412	5,259	4	17	272
Wholesale and retail trade [4]	(X)	2,690	148	960	222	493	5,268	15	7	85
Wholesale trade	42	371	31	355	43	238	2,528	5	6	45
Retail trade [5]	44-45	2,318	117	601	180	255	2,738	10	1	40
Motor vehicle and parts dealers	441	123	13	91	31	64	740	1	1	6
Food and beverage stores	445	120	13	87	29	39	435	1	(Z)	7
Gasoline stations	447	30	6	35	26	21	144	(Z)	(Z)	(Z)
Transportation and warehousing	48-49	889	27	160	52	44	506	8	3	8
Information	51	283	27	118	7	139	817	2	-3	6
Broadcasting and telecommunications	513	51	8	30	1	96	460	(Z)	-6	10
Finance and insurance	52	570	252	221	103	280	2,916	14	100	379
Real estate and rental and leasing	53	935	906	532	49	152	205	21	52	6
Professional, scientific, and technical services [5]	54	2,445	136	689	114	194	623	48	43	-8
Legal services	5411	322	32	84	30	79	56	13	29	4
Accounting, tax preparation, bookkeeping, and payroll services	5412	362	15	50	10	38	24	4	7	2
Management, scientific, and technical consulting services	5416	598	26	174	26	25	106	15	4	3
Management of companies and enterprises	55	(NA)	17	48	(NA)	22	693	(NA)	7	78
Administrative and support and waste management and remediation services	56	1,549	38	212	40	40	314	12	2	4
Educational services	61	352	6	37	5	2	22	2	(-Z)	1
Health care and social assistance	62	1,595	44	306	87	73	404	37	10	8
Arts, entertainment and recreation	71	1,076	35	98	21	38	64	5	(Z)	(Z)
Accommodation and food services	72	322	62	258	37	89	347	2	2	10
Accommodation	721	71	22	35	6	48	106	(Z)	2	3
Food services and drinking places	722	252	40	223	31	41	241	2	(Z)	7
Other services [5]	81	1,953	62	316	66	15	164	14	1	5
Auto repair and maintenance	8111	296	21	99	23	7	58	3	(Z)	1
Personal and laundry services	812	1,074	31	129	29	6	68	8	(Z)	2
Religious, grantmaking, civic, professional, and similar organizations	813	267	(Z)	40	3	(Z)	9	1	(Z)	(Z)
Unclassified	(X)	250	3	22	3	(Z)	2	1	(Z)	(Z)

NA Not available. X Not applicable. Z Less than 500 or $500 million. [1] Includes investment income for partnerships and corporations in finance and insurance, real estate, and management of companies industries. Excludes investment income for S corporations. [2] For corporations, includes businesses not allocable to individual industries. [3] For corporations represents agricultural services only. [4] For corporations includes trade business not identified as wholesale or retail. [5] Includes other industries not shown separately.

Source: U.S. Internal Revenue Service, *Statistics of Income,* various publications.

No. 734. Nonfarm Sole Proprietorships—Selected Income and Deduction Items: 1990 to 2000

[In millions of dollars (730,606 represents $730,606,000,000) except as indicated. All figures are estimates based on sample. Tax law changes have affected the comparability of the data over time; see *Statistics of Income* reports for a description. See Appendix III]

Item	1990	1993	1994	1995	1996	1997	1998	1999	2000
Number of returns (1,000)	14,783	15,848	16,154	16,424	16,955	17,176	17,409	17,576	17,905
Businesses with net income (1,000)	11,222	11,872	12,187	12,213	12,524	12,703	13,080	13,159	13,308
Business receipts	730,606	757,215	790,630	807,364	843,234	870,392	918,268	969,347	1,020,957
Income from sales and operations	719,008	746,306	778,494	796,597	831,546	858,453	905,138	955,392	1,007,948
Business deductions [1]	589,250	600,765	623,833	638,127	666,461	683,872	716,157	761,428	806,388
Cost of goods sold/operations [1]	291,010	289,578	301,004	306,959	316,421	319,557	341,133	370,079	387,381
Purchases	210,225	210,260	216,365	219,305	220,029	224,259	231,405	255,539	268,790
Labor costs	22,680	20,685	23,497	24,383	26,002	24,941	27,448	28,723	29,279
Materials and supplies	30,195	32,701	34,304	34,427	40,473	37,552	42,162	41,757	43,196
Advertising	(NA)	(NA)	(NA)	(NA)	(NA)	8,978	9,414	9,454	10,149
Car and truck expenses	21,766	26,714	30,845	32,785	36,700	38,728	39,716	40,787	45,711
Commissions	8,816	8,707	9,029	9,592	10,792	10,986	10,722	11,228	11,621
Depreciation	23,735	24,964	26,158	26,738	27,883	28,625	29,136	30,638	32,196
Pension and profit sharing plans	586	636	605	649	707	728	757	870	893
Insurance	13,358	13,173	13,289	12,978	13,195	13,299	12,938	13,220	13,624
Interest paid	13,312	9,431	9,170	10,057	10,567	10,884	11,159	11,224	12,233
Office expenses	(NA)	(NA)	(NA)	(NA)	(NA)	9,210	9,612	9,921	10,456
Rent paid	23,392	25,008	26,769	27,503	28,516	29,326	30,460	31,418	33,222
Repairs	8,941	9,847	10,385	10,172	10,715	10,897	11,350	11,697	12,281
Salaries and wages (net)	46,998	52,046	53,649	54,471	56,322	57,746	58,865	61,204	63,486
Supplies	(NA)	(NA)	(NA)	(NA)	(NA)	19,546	19,725	21,654	21,794
Taxes paid	10,342	13,062	13,600	13,471	13,736	13,774	13,731	14,000	13,956
Utilities	13,539	16,069	16,918	17,206	18,162	18,575	18,431	18,466	19,382
Net income (less loss) [2]	141,430	156,459	166,799	169,262	176,756	186,644	202,275	207,947	214,715
Net income [2]	161,657	176,983	187,845	191,729	200,124	210,465	226,190	233,405	245,231

NA Not available. [1] Includes other amounts not shown separately. [2] After adjustment for the passive loss carryover from prior years. Therefore, "business receipts" minus "total deductions" do not equal "net income."

Source: U.S. Internal Revenue Service, *Statistics of Income Bulletin*.

No. 735. Partnerships—Selected Income and Balance Sheet Items: 1990 to 2000

[In billions of dollars (1,735 represents $1,735,000,000,000), except as indicated. Covers active partnerships only. All figures are estimates based on samples. See Appendix III]

Item	1990	1993	1994	1995	1996	1997	1998	1999	2000
Number of returns (1,000)	1,554	1,468	1,494	1,581	1,654	1,759	1,855	1,937	2,058
Number with net income (1,000)	854	870	890	955	1,010	1,092	1,171	1,226	1,261
Number of partners (1,000)	17,095	15,627	14,990	15,606	15,662	16,184	15,663	15,924	13,660
Assets [1] [2]	1,735	2,118	2,295	2,719	3,368	4,171	5,127	5,999	6,694
Depreciable assets (net)	681	698	712	767	848	980	1,153	1,314	1,487
Inventories, end of year	57	71	76	88	137	147	176	174	150
Land	215	207	208	221	232	257	291	326	359
Liabilities [1] [2]	1,415	1,620	1,662	1,886	2,235	2,658	3,151	3,453	3,696
Accounts payable	67	80	81	91	121	159	191	244	230
Short-term debt [3]	88	131	126	124	126	127	230	232	252
Long-term debt [4]	498	489	508	544	607	706	884	989	1,132
Nonrecourse loans	470	478	463	466	474	492	523	582	639
Partners' capital accounts [2]	320	499	633	832	1,133	1,513	1,976	2,546	2,999
Receipts [1]	566	656	762	890	1,089	1,354	1,603	1,907	2,405
Business receipts [5]	483	561	732	854	1,042	1,297	1,534	1,829	2,316
Interest received	21	16	19	31	33	41	51	62	82
Deductions [1]	550	589	680	784	943	1,186	1,416	1,679	2,136
Cost of goods sold/operations	243	273	335	395	486	625	737	902	1,226
Salaries and wages	56	65	70	80	94	115	143	170	201
Taxes paid	9	11	12	13	15	18	24	27	31
Interest paid	30	27	36	43	49	60	73	74	93
Depreciation	60	60	22	23	29	38	43	52	59
Net income (less loss)	17	67	82	107	145	168	187	228	269
Net income	116	137	151	179	228	262	298	348	410

[1] Includes items not shown separately. [2] Assets, liabilities, and partners' capital accounts are understated because not all partnerships file complete balance sheets. [3] Mortgages, notes, and bonds payable in less than 1 year. [4] Mortgages, notes, and bonds payable in 1 year or more. [5] Excludes investment income except for partnerships in finance, insurance, and real estate from 1994 to 1997. Beginning 1998, finance and insurance, real estate, and management of companies included investment income for partnerships.

Source: U.S. Internal Revenue Service, *Statistics of Income*, various issues.

No. 736. Partnerships—Selected Items by Industry: 2000

[In millions of dollars (6,694,143 represents $6,694,143,000,000), except as indicated. Covers active partnerships only. Includes partnerships not allocable by industry. Figures are estimates based on samples. Based on the North American Industry Classification System (NAICS), 1997; see text, this section. See Appendix III]

Year	NAICS code	Number of partnerships (1,000) Total	With net income	With net loss	Total assets [1]	Business receipts [2]	Total deductions	Net income less loss	Net income	Net loss
Total	(X)	2,058	1,261	796	6,694,143	2,315,598	2,136,365	268,991	409,973	140,982
Agriculture, forestry, fishing and hunting	11	114	65	49	70,038	16,320	20,944	214	4,668	4,454
Mining	21	26	17	9	115,133	57,347	48,158	15,898	20,474	4,576
Utilities	22	2	1	1	117,373	107,719	106,550	3,608	5,896	2,288
Construction	23	116	75	41	132,074	140,387	134,183	10,320	14,034	3,714
Manufacturing	31-33	38	19	19	307,002	411,568	409,074	17,284	26,947	9,663
Wholesale trade	42	31	17	15	75,538	237,992	235,139	6,492	8,760	2,268
Retail trade	44-45	117	57	60	77,357	255,314	260,083	553	5,612	5,059
Transportation and warehousing	48-49	27	12	15	74,756	43,745	44,645	2,676	5,491	2,815
Information	51	27	9	17	353,350	139,237	153,274	-3,497	20,517	24,014
Finance & insurance	52	252	192	59	2,943,541	279,927	180,270	99,656	115,087	15,431
Real estate & rental & leasing	53	906	557	349	1,844,328	151,799	108,614	51,599	91,407	39,808
Professional, scientific, and technical services	54	136	87	49	93,239	193,999	159,813	42,946	49,517	6,571
Management of companies & enterprises	55	17	8	8	227,691	21,734	14,434	7,300	12,665	5,365
Admin/support waste mgt/ remediation services	56	38	22	15	26,407	40,371	40,311	1,771	2,978	1,207
Educational services	61	6	4	2	3,138	2,033	1,994	75	242	167
Health care and social assistance	62	44	28	16	48,781	73,248	69,205	9,759	12,576	2,817
Arts, entertainment & recreation	71	35	16	19	55,234	38,444	43,759	-303	4,028	4,331
Accommodation & food services	72	62	37	25	117,297	89,092	90,918	1,820	7,499	5,679
Other services	81	62	37	25	11,356	15,046	14,706	824	1,556	732
Nature of business not allocable	(X)	3	1	2	511	277	291	-4	19	23

X Not applicable. [1] Total assets are understated because not all partnerships file complete balance sheets. [2] Finance and insurance, real estate, and management of companies includes investment income for partnerships.

Source: U.S. Internal Revenue Service, Statistics of Income, various issues.

No. 737. Corporate Funds—Sources and Uses: 1990 to 2002

[In billions of dollars (236 represents $236,000,000,000). Covers nonfarm nonfinancial corporate business]

Item	1990	1993	1994	1995	1996	1997	1998	1999	2000	2001	2002
Profits before tax (book)	236	305	381	422	459	494	460	459	436	327	316
-Profit tax accruals	95	105	128	136	150	158	154	166	172	123	128
-Dividends	118	149	158	178	201	216	241	237	258	277	280
+Capital consumption allowance [1]	371	408	445	472	504	540	571	614	633	721	817
=U.S. internal funds, book	393	459	540	579	612	660	636	669	639	648	726
+Foreign earnings retained abroad	51	56	39	59	60	59	63	91	117	124	75
+Inventory valuation adjustment (IVA)	-13	-4	-12	-18	3	8	18	-4	-15	5	-8
=Internal funds + IVA	432	511	567	620	676	728	717	756	741	777	793
Gross investment	377	624	609	674	718	749	780	867	931	801	744
Capital expenditures [2]	436	509	576	639	663	760	826	885	957	794	803
Fixed investment [3]	424	483	526	591	637	694	754	825	894	853	800
Net financial investment	-59	115	34	36	56	-11	-46	-18	-26	7	-59
Net acquisition of financial assets [2]	124	333	275	426	454	272	570	970	1,211	376	240
Checkable deposits and currency	6	20	12	4	39	8	35	60	16	5	-61
Time and savings deposits	-6	16	4	3	(-Z)	20	-7	24	(Z)	22	-6
Money market fund shares	9	-4	3	23	8	20	26	25	47	112	26
Commercial paper	(-Z)	2	-1	1	11	5	3	8	10	-3	(-Z)
U.S. government securities	-20	-1	3	10	-5	-41	-1	-2	2	11	15
Mortgages	-2	-8	4	2	-4	26	-13	-26	2	-3	-3
Consumer credit	3	7	9	-2	-7	1	-4	5	2	-15	-11
Trade receivables	29	51	72	78	88	94	86	200	285	-130	100
Miscellaneous assets [2]	114	237	163	320	314	157	427	661	812	396	188
U.S. direct investment abroad [4]	35	58	79	90	77	84	129	158	147	105	92
Insurance receivables	13	7	6	8	3	2	2	1	(-Z)	10	17
Net increase in liabilities [2]	184	218	242	391	398	283	616	988	1,237	369	299
Net funds raised in markets	71	54	81	169	136	214	193	268	262	206	22
Net new equity issues	-63	21	-45	-58	-47	-77	-216	-110	-118	-47	-40
Credit market instruments [2]	134	33	126	227	183	292	409	378	380	253	62
Commercial paper	10	10	21	18	-1	14	24	37	48	-88	-64
Corporate bonds [4]	47	75	23	91	116	151	235	218	161	341	133
Bank loans n.e.c	3	-8	46	75	40	51	72	61	62	-72	-65
Mortgages	19	-26	2	8	10	32	17	34	40	58	38
Trade payables	28	36	77	81	50	65	58	178	313	-112	93
Miscellaneous liabilities [2]	84	122	83	141	204	-5	360	534	655	272	171
Foreign direct investment in U.S.	59	20	45	54	72	100	144	247	189	67	17

Z Less than $500 million. [1] Consumption of fixed capital plus capital consumption adjustment. [2] Includes other items not shown separately. [3] Nonresidential fixed investment plus residential fixed investment. [4] 1990, corporate bonds include net issues by Netherlands Antillean financial subsidiaries, and U.S. direct investment abroad excludes net inflows from those bond issues.

Source: Board of Governors of the Federal Reserve System, "Federal Reserve Statistical Release, Z.1, Flow of Funds Accounts of the United States"; published: 6 March 2003; <http://www.federalreserve.gov/releases/Z1/20030306/data.htm>.

No. 738. Nonfinancial Corporate Business-Sector Balance Sheet: 1990 to 2002

[In billions of dollars (9,755 represents $9,755,000,000,000). Represents yearend outstandings. Tangible assets stated at either market value or replacement cost]

Item	1990	1995	1996	1997	1998	1999	2000	2001	2002
Assets.	9,755	11,736	12,725	13,681	14,968	16,668	18,555	18,775	19,140
Tangible assets	6,179	6,777	7,267	7,872	8,151	8,574	9,281	9,176	9,388
Real estate [1]	3,385	3,318	3,661	4,101	4,210	4,392	4,805	4,699	4,886
Equipment and software [2]	1,892	2,390	2,515	2,641	2,771	2,924	3,124	3,214	3,213
Inventories [2]	901	1,070	1,091	1,130	1,171	1,258	1,351	1,263	1,289
Financial assets [3]	3,575	4,959	5,458	5,809	6,816	8,094	9,274	9,599	9,752
Money market fund shares	20	60	68	88	114	139	186	298	324
Trade receivables	967	1,185	1,273	1,367	1,453	1,653	1,938	1,808	1,907
Liabilities [3]	4,729	6,010	6,379	6,629	7,458	8,407	9,611	10,085	10,404
Credit market instruments.	2,533	2,909	3,092	3,382	3,791	4,203	4,584	4,838	4,900
Corporate bonds [4]	1,008	1,344	1,460	1,611	1,846	2,064	2,225	2,566	2,699
Bank loans n.e.c.	545	602	642	693	765	825	888	817	751
Other loans and advances	473	454	468	508	562	585	652	664	681
Trade payables	626	878	927	992	1,050	1,228	1,541	1,429	1,523
Net worth (market value).	5,025	5,726	6,346	7,052	7,510	8,261	8,944	8,690	8,736

[1] At market value. [2] At replacement (current) cost. [3] Includes items not shown separately. [4] Through 1992, corporate bonds include net issues by Netherlands Antillean financial subsidiaries.

Source: Board of Governors of the Federal Reserve System, "Federal Reserve Statistical Release, Z.1, Flow of Funds Accounts of the United States"; published: 6 March 2003; <http://www.federalreserve.gov/releases/Z1/20030306/data.htm>.

No. 739. Corporations—Selected Financial Items: 1990 to 2000

[In billions of dollars (18,190 represents $18,190,000,000,000), except as noted. Covers active corporations only. All corporations are required to file returns except those specifically exempt. See source for changes in law affecting comparability of historical data. Based on samples; see Appendix III]

Item	1990	1993	1994	1995	1996	1997	1998	1999	2000
Number of returns (1,000)	3,717	3,965	4,342	4,474	4,631	4,710	4,849	4,936	5,045
Number with net income (1,000)	1,911	2,145	2,392	2,455	2,588	2,647	2,761	2,812	2,819
S Corporation returns [1] (1,000)	1,575	1,902	2,024	2,153	2,304	2,452	2,588	2,726	2,860
Assets [2]	18,190	21,816	23,446	26,014	28,642	33,030	37,347	41,464	47,027
Cash	771	812	853	962	1,097	1,299	1,336	1,597	1,820
Notes and accounts receivable	4,198	4,532	4,768	5,307	5,783	6,632	7,062	7,745	8,754
Inventories.	894	947	1,126	1,045	1,079	1,114	1,139	1,198	1,272
Investments in govt. obligations.	921	1,290	1,309	1,363	1,339	1,343	1,366	1,340	1,236
Mortgage and real estate	1,538	1,627	1,661	1,713	1,825	2,029	2,414	2,555	2,822
Other investments.	4,137	5,701	6,265	7,429	8,657	10,756	13,201	15,799	17,874
Depreciable assets	4,318	4,969	5,284	5,571	5,923	6,208	6,541	6,936	7,292
Depletable assets	129	137	148	154	169	177	193	184	191
Land.	210	230	239	242	254	262	271	286	303
Liabilities [2]	18,190	21,816	23,446	26,014	28,642	33,030	37,347	41,464	47,027
Accounts payable	1,094	1,466	1,606	1,750	1,905	2,111	2,501	2,792	3,758
Short-term debt [3]	1,803	1,569	1,831	2,034	2,328	2,582	3,216	3,658	4,020
Long-term debt [4].	2,665	2,871	3,100	3,335	3,651	4,072	4,813	5,448	6,184
Net worth	4,739	(NA)	7,031	8,132	9,495	11,353	13,108	15,363	17,349
Capital stock	1,585	2,042	2,132	2,194	2,278	2,951	3,244	3,522	3,966
Paid-in or capital surplus	2,814	4,223	4,790	5,446	6,427	7,253	8,610	10,186	12,265
Retained earnings [5].	1,410	1,662	1,698	2,191	2,519	3,113	3,373	3,970	3,627
Receipts [2][6]	11,410	12,270	13,360	14,539	15,526	16,610	17,324	18,892	20,606
Business receipts [6][7].	9,860	10,866	11,884	12,786	13,659	14,461	15,010	16,314	17,637
Interest [8].	977	808	882	1,039	1,082	1,140	1,277	1,354	1,628
Rents and royalties	133	130	132	145	156	176	200	223	254
Deductions [2][6]	11,033	11,765	12,775	13,821	14,728	15,704	16,489	17,967	19,692
Cost of sales and operations [7]	6,611	7,052	7,625	8,206	8,707	9,114	9,362	10,284	11,135
Compensation of officers	205	226	282	304	319	336	357	374	401
Rent paid on business property	185	201	223	232	248	265	308	347	380
Taxes paid.	251	290	322	326	341	350	355	371	390
Interest paid.	825	546	611	744	771	866	967	1,019	1,272
Depreciation	333	364	403	437	474	513	542	584	614
Advertising	126	140	157	163	177	188	198	216	234
Net income (less loss) [6][9]	371	498	577	714	806	915	838	929	928
Net income	553	659	740	881	987	1,118	1,091	1,229	1,337
Deficit.	182	161	162	166	180	202	253	300	409
Income subject to tax	366	437	494	565	640	684	663	694	760
Income tax before credits [10].	119	149	168	194	220	235	231	242	266
Tax credits	32	35	37	42	53	55	50	49	62
Foreign tax credit	25	23	25	30	40	42	37	38	49
Income tax after credits [11]	96	(NA)	136	156	171	184	182	193	204

NA Not available. [1] Represents certain small corporations with up to 75 shareholders (35 for 1990-1996), mostly individuals, electing to be taxed at the shareholder level. [2] Includes items not shown separately. [3] Payable in less than 1 year. [4] Payable in 1 year or more. [5] Appropriated and unappropriated and "adjustments to shareholders' equity" which was formerly included in "retained earnings, appropriated." [6] Receipts, deductions and net income of S corporations are limited to those from trade or business. Those from investments are excluded. [7] Includes gross sales and cost of sales of securities, commodities, and real estate by exchanges, brokers, or dealers selling on their own accounts. Previously, net gain included in total receipts only. Excludes investment income. [8] Includes tax-exempt interest in state and local government obligations. [9] Excludes regulated investment companies. [10] Consists of regular (and alternative tax) only. [11] Includes minimum tax, alternative minimum tax, adjustments for prior year credits, and other income-related taxes.

Source: U.S. Internal Revenue Service, Statistics of Income, Corporation Income Tax Returns, annual.

Business Enterprise 499

No. 740. Corporations by Receipt-Size Class and Industry: 1999 and 2000

[Number of returns in thousands (4,936 represents 4,936,000); receipts and net income in billions of dollars (18,009 represents $18,009,000,000,000). Covers active enterprises only Figures are estimates based on a sample of unaudited tax returns; see Appendix III. Numbers in parentheses represent North American Industry Classification System, 1997 codes, see text, this section]

Industry	1999, total	2000 Total	Under $1 mil.[1]	$1 mil.- $4.9 mil.	$5 mil.- $9.9 mil.	$10 mil.- $49.9 mil.	$50 mil. or more
Total:[2]							
Number of returns[3]	4,936	5,045	4,099	700	115	105	26
Business receipts[3]	18,009	19,593	841	1,497	800	2,123	14,331
Net income (less loss)	929	928	-14	27	16	66	832
Agriculture, forestry, fishing, and hunting (11):							
Number	142	141	126	12	2	1	(Z)
Business receipts[3]	105	106	20	25	12	21	28
Mining (21):							
Number	31	33	27	4	1	1	(Z)
Business receipts[3]	110	141	4	9	4	11	113
Utilities (22):							
Number	7	8	7	1	(Z)	(Z)	(Z)
Business receipts[3]	479	708	1	1	1	3	702
Construction (23):							
Number	580	598	456	110	18	13	2
Business receipts[3]	974	1,034	115	237	124	244	314
Manufacturing (31-33):							
Number	298	289	175	72	17	19	6
Business receipts[3]	4,802	5,259	49	166	121	381	4,542
Wholesale and retail trade (42,44-45):							
Number	948	960	646	222	40	42	10
Business receipts[3]	4,789	5,268	175	487	276	899	3,431
Transportation and warehousing (48-49):							
Number	160	160	130	23	4	3	1
Business receipts[3]	485	506	25	48	31	57	346
Information (51):							
Number	108	118	100	12	4	2	1
Business receipts[3]	761	817	14	28	14	48	713
Finance and insurance (52):							
Number	218	221	184	23	5	7	3
Business receipts[3]	3,008	2,916	29	50	35	140	2,662
Real estate and rental and leasing (53):							
Number	521	532	508	21	2	1	(Z)
Business receipts[3]	185	205	44	42	14	23	82
Professional, scientific, and technical services (54):							
Number	657	689	615	58	9	6	1
Business receipts[3]	576	623	108	119	64	105	227
Management of companies & enterprises (55):							
Number	43	48	41	3	1	2	1
Business receipts[3]	519	693	1	7	10	36	639
Administrative and support and waste management and remediation services (56):							
Number	205	212	182	24	3	2	1
Business receipts[3]	284	314	40	52	24	38	159
Educational services (61):							
Number	35	37	34	2	(Z)	(Z)	(Z)
Business receipts[3]	21	22	5	4	1	4	7
Health care and social services (62):							
Number	303	306	252	45	5	3	1
Business receipts[3]	371	404	73	91	38	59	142
Arts, entertainment, and recreation (71):							
Number	94	98	89	8	1	(Z)	(Z)
Business receipts[3]	71	64	14	15	4	9	22
Accommodation and food services (72):							
Number	252	258	219	34	3	2	(Z)
Business receipts[3]	319	347	60	66	17	29	176
Other services (81):							
Number	306	316	288	26	2	1	(Z)
Business receipts[3]	146	164	62	49	11	15	28

Z Less than 500 returns. [1] Includes businesses without receipts. [2] Includes businesses not allocable to individual industries. [3] Includes investment income for corporations in finance and insurance, real estate, and management of companies industries. Excludes investment income for S corporations (certain small corporations with up to 75 shareholders, mostly individuals, electing to be taxed at the shareholder level).

Source: U.S. Internal Revenue Service, *Statistics of Income*, various publications; and unpublished data.

No. 741. Corporations by Asset-Size Class and Industry: 2000

[In millions of dollars (117,136 represents $117,136,000,000), except number of returns. Covers active corporations only. Excludes corporations not allocable by industry. Numbers in parentheses represent North American Industry Classification System, 1997 codes, see text, this section]

Industry	Total	Under $10 mil.[1]	$10-$24.9 mil.	$25-$49.9 mil.	$50-$99.9 mil.	$100-$249.9 mil.	$250 mil. and over
Agriculture, forestry, fishing, and hunting (11):							
Returns	140,851	139,977	572	159	76	46	19
Total receipts	117,136	78,358	9,327	6,148	6,641	7,897	8,764
Mining (21):							
Returns	32,578	31,499	489	213	113	102	161
Total receipts	158,619	22,109	5,865	5,605	4,434	9,102	111,505
Utilities (22):							
Returns	7,968	7,590	98	48	27	47	158
Total receipts	756,808	26,401	2,034	1,085	1,644	5,240	720,404
Construction (23):							
Returns	597,902	592,610	3,743	862	390	160	137
Total receipts	1,051,896	652,056	109,854	55,187	48,316	34,841	151,642
Manufacturing (31-33):							
Returns	288,506	273,413	7,419	2,976	1,747	1,356	1,595
Total receipts	5,741,290	589,504	199,032	156,460	163,457	261,109	4,371,728
Wholesale and retail trade (42, 44-45):							
Returns	959,575	944,127	9,993	2,702	1,241	796	714
Total receipts	5,397,025	1,809,763	491,552	260,718	222,763	287,879	2,324,349
Transportation and warehousing (48-49):							
Returns	160,437	158,833	926	264	140	150	124
Total receipts	527,167	146,732	26,620	14,267	12,593	26,165	300,790
Information (51):							
Returns	118,073	114,764	1,463	666	391	311	479
Total receipts	967,190	107,341	18,450	15,011	16,954	29,150	780,284
Finance and insurance (52):							
Returns	221,394	203,046	3,561	2,811	2,891	3,452	5,633
Total receipts	2,915,540	285,118	20,878	22,244	32,170	68,493	2,486,637
Real estate and rental and leasing (53):							
Returns	532,426	527,583	3,199	915	378	212	140
Total receipts	235,180	116,989	13,115	9,232	7,469	11,231	77,144
Professional, scientific, and technical services (54):							
Returns	689,412	685,752	1,972	758	427	299	206
Total receipts	658,747	381,606	42,795	31,781	26,409	36,167	139,990
Management of companies & enterprises (55):							
Returns	47,542	41,304	1,138	1,142	1,333	1,455	1,170
Total receipts	693,453	10,861	2,029	3,416	7,931	19,033	650,184
Administrative and support and waste management and remediation services (56):							
Returns	211,993	211,031	487	191	108	83	92
Total receipts	325,400	159,605	19,392	12,154	13,547	24,396	96,306
Educational services (61):							
Returns	36,756	36,614	73	29	16	14	10
Total receipts	25,236	15,537	1,471	1,139	1,344	1,954	3,790
Health care and social assistance (62):							
Returns	306,352	305,395	513	195	106	73	69
Total receipts	417,491	267,107	14,705	11,923	10,013	13,035	100,708
Arts, entertainment, and recreation (71):							
Returns	97,866	97,239	350	132	63	54	28
Total receipts	70,086	38,504	4,208	3,256	4,031	6,940	13,147
Accommodation and food services (72):							
Returns	257,525	256,284	676	226	112	107	120
Total receipts	375,040	162,094	12,986	9,338	8,515	22,291	159,817
Other services (81):							
Returns	316,138	315,662	284	82	59	22	28
Total receipts	170,060	133,873	5,908	2,902	6,539	2,312	18,526

[1] Includes returns with zero assets.

Source: U.S. Internal Revenue Service, *Statistics of Income, Corporation Income Tax Returns*, annual.

No. 742. Economic Census Summary (NAICS Basis): 1997

[178,953 represents 178,953,000,000]

Kind of business	NAICS code [1]	All firms Establish- ments (number)	All firms Sales, receipts or ship- ments (mil. dol.)	Employer firms Establish- ments (number)	Employer firms Sales, receipts or ship- ments (mil. dol.)	Annual payroll (mil. dol.)	Paid employ- ees [2] (1,000)
TAXABLE							
Mining [3]	21	117,240	178,953	25,000	173,989	20,798	509.0
Oil & gas extraction	211	90,006	107,147	8,312	102,837	5,511	110.9
Mining (except oil & gas)	212	13,391	51,585	7,348	51,253	9,422	229.3
Utilities [3]	22	31,406	412,228	15,513	411,713	36,595	702.7
Elec. pwr. generation, transmission & distribution	2211	(NA)	(NA)	7,935	269,095	30,440	564.5
Natural gas distribution	2212	(NA)	(NA)	2,747	136,995	5,110	102.9
Construction	23	2,546,680	945,682	656,448	858,581	174,185	5,664.8
Building, developing, & general contracting	233	611,859	421,524	199,289	386,926	42,546	1,343.0
Heavy construction	234	80,319	132,720	42,557	130,795	30,292	880.4
Special trade contractors	235	1,854,502	391,439	414,602	340,861	101,347	3,441.5
Manufacturing	31-33	666,609	3,854,381	363,753	3,842,061	572,101	16,888.0
Wholesale trade	42	859,328	(NA)	453,470	4,059,658	214,915	5,796.6
Wholesale trade, durable goods	421	526,545	(NA)	290,629	2,179,717	133,237	3,398.3
Wholesale trade, nondurable goods	422	332,783	(NA)	162,841	1,879,940	81,678	2,398.3
Retail trade [3]	44-45	2,949,786	2,530,304	1,118,447	2,460,886	237,196	13,991.1
Motor vehicle & parts dealers	441	240,460	660,682	122,633	645,368	50,239	1,719.0
Bldg material & garden equip. & supp. dealers	444	121,912	229,489	93,117	227,566	25,609	1,117.9
Food & beverage stores	445	239,290	410,287	148,528	401,764	40,581	2,893.1
Health & personal care stores	446	142,491	119,056	82,941	117,701	15,191	903.7
Gasoline stations	447	137,566	199,856	126,889	198,166	11,482	922.1
Clothing & clothing accessories stores	448	251,398	140,565	156,601	136,398	16,597	1,280.2
General merchandise stores	452	56,788	331,453	36,171	330,444	30,871	2,507.5
Nonstore retailers	454	888,564	137,370	44,482	123,107	12,323	506.0
Transportation & warehousing [3][4][5]	48-49	823,908	347,673	178,025	318,245	82,346	2,920.8
Truck transportation	484	426,345	162,104	103,798	141,225	38,471	1,293.8
Information [3]	51	288,500	628,981	114,475	623,214	129,482	3,066.2
Publishing industries	511	79,614	180,434	33,896	179,035	43,358	1,006.2
Broadcasting & telecommunications	513	80,486	347,676	43,480	346,316	63,480	1,434.5
Finance & insurance	52	1,074,360	2,234,737	395,203	2,197,771	264,551	5,835.2
Credit intermediation & related activities	522	330,563	817,504	166,882	808,811	98,723	2,744.9
Security, commodity contracts & like activity	523	242,901	291,425	54,491	274,987	71,281	706.1
Insurance carriers & related activities	524	499,365	1,084,618	172,299	1,072,784	92,230	2,327.3
Real estate & rental & leasing [3]	53	1,684,976	342,621	288,273	240,918	41,591	1,702.4
Real estate	531	1,557,556	252,120	221,650	153,275	27,947	1,117.2
Professional, scientific, & technical services [3]	54	3,265,160	660,707	615,305	579,542	225,376	5,212.7
Legal services	5411	383,682	136,785	173,716	127,052	49,060	1,012.1
Architectural, engineering & related services	5413	(NA)	(NA)	92,710	116,986	46,943	1,038.3
Computer systems design & related services	5415	278,512	115,696	72,278	108,968	42,151	764.7
Management of companies & enterprises	55	(NA)	(NA)	47,319	92,473	154,178	2,617.5
Admin/support waste mgt/remediation services [3]	56	1,168,621	312,912	276,393	295,936	137,337	7,347.4
Administrative & support services	561	1,131,846	272,821	260,025	256,591	128,438	7,066.7
Educational services	61	268,937	17,731	33,783	14,933	4,903	248.7
Health care & social assistance [3]	62	1,698,979	449,806	531,069	418,602	182,256	6,231.8
Ambulatory health care services	621	1,047,100	334,762	440,200	310,012	137,979	3,744.3
Arts, entertainment, & recreation	71	772,981	99,455	79,636	85,088	26,104	1,207.4
Accommodation & food services [3]	72	736,073	359,434	545,068	350,399	97,007	9,451.2
Food services & drinking places [3]	722	630,387	258,040	486,906	251,942	70,334	7,754.6
Full-service restaurants	7221	230,732	114,592	191,245	112,450	34,435	3,641.4
Limited-service eating places	7222	246,138	109,298	214,774	107,788	27,483	3,327.0
Other services (except public administration)	81	2,357,005	206,332	420,950	163,033	48,453	2,493.6
Repair & maintenance	811	800,207	122,886	235,466	105,154	29,875	1,276.4
TAX-EXEMPT							
Professional, scientific, & technical services	54	(NA)	(NA)	5,824	15,709	6,023	148.5
Educational services	61	(NA)	(NA)	7,153	5,506	1,461	72.4
Health care & social assistance	62	(NA)	(NA)	114,784	466,452	195,949	7,329.8
Hospitals	622	(NA)	(NA)	5,340	339,032	141,910	4,421.5
Arts, entertainment, & recreation	71	(NA)	(NA)	19,463	19,627	6,683	380.3
Other services (except public administration)[3]	81	(NA)	(NA)	98,765	102,864	17,068	762.6

NA Not available. [1] North American Industry Classification System, 1997. [2] For pay period including March 12. [3] Includes other kinds of business not shown separately. [4] Data do not include large certificated passenger carriers that report to the Office of Airline Statistics, U.S. Department of Transportation. [5] Railroad transportation and U.S. Postal Service are out of scope for the 1997 Economic Census.

Source: U.S. Census Bureau, 1997 Economic Census, Geographic Area Series, and *Nonemployer Statistics*.

No. 743. Nonemployer Establishments and Receipts by Industry: 1998 to 2000

[**Establishments: 15,709 represents 15,709,000.** Includes only firms subject to federal income tax. Nonemployers are businesses with no paid employees. Based on the North American Industry Classification System (NAICS), 1997; see text, this section]

Kind of business	NAICS code	Establishments (1,000) 1998	1999	2000	Receipts (mil. dol.) 1998	1999	2000
All industries	(X)	15,709	16,153	16,530	643,720	667,220	709,379
Forestry, fishing & hunting, & ag support services	113-115	225	226	223	8,286	8,876	9,196
Mining	21	82	81	86	3,833	3,945	5,227
Utilities	22	15	14	14	504	487	504
Construction	23	1,908	1,986	2,014	94,390	102,909	107,538
Manufacturing	31-33	297	289	285	12,638	12,636	13,022
Wholesale trade	42	400	395	388	31,280	31,434	31,684
Retail trade	44-45	1,762	1,761	1,743	70,971	73,314	73,810
Transportation & warehousing	48-49	662	719	747	31,745	34,994	37,824
Information	51	195	221	238	6,213	7,019	7,620
Finance & insurance	52	708	667	692	38,940	40,288	49,058
Real estate & rental & leasing	53	1,565	1,648	1,696	131,728	125,513	133,398
Professional, scientific, & technical services	54	2,415	2,388	2,420	83,081	85,443	90,272
Admin/support waste mgt/ remediation services	56	925	990	1,032	19,237	21,777	23,754
Educational services	61	244	263	283	3,029	3,360	3,736
Health care & social assistance	62	1,185	1,254	1,317	32,328	34,097	36,550
Arts, entertainment, & recreation	71	713	749	782	15,325	16,656	17,713
Accommodation & food services	72	198	210	218	11,757	12,594	13,418
Other services (except public administration)	81	2,209	2,293	2,350	48,438	51,876	55,056

X Not applicable.

Source: U.S. Census Bureau, "Nonemployer Statistics"; <http://www.census.gov/epcd/nonemployer/>.

No. 744. Establishments, Employees' and Payroll by Employment-Size Class: 1990 to 2001

[**6,176 represents 6,176,000.** Excludes most government employees, railroad employees, self-employed persons. Employees are for the week including March 12. Covers establishments with payroll. An *establishment* is a single physical location where business is conducted or where services or industrial operations are performed. For statement on methodology, see Appendix III]

Employment-size class	Unit	1990	1994	1995	1996	1997	1998	1999	2000	2001
Establishments, total	1,000	6,176	6,509	6,613	6,747	6,895	6,942	7,008	7,070	7,095
Under 20 employees	1,000	5,354	5,662	5,733	5,843	5,968	5,991	6,036	6,069	6,083
20 to 99 employees	1,000	684	704	730	741	767	786	802	826	836
100 to 499 employees	1,000	122	128	135	138	143	147	152	157	157
500 to 999 employees	1,000	10	10	10	11	11	11	12	12	12
1,000 or more employees	1,000	6	6	6	6	6	6	7	7	7
Employees, total	1,000	93,476	96,733	100,335	102,199	105,299	108,118	110,706	114,065	115,061
Under 20 employees	1,000	24,373	25,373	25,785	26,115	26,883	27,131	27,289	27,569	27,681
20 to 99 employees	1,000	27,414	28,138	29,202	29,697	30,631	31,464	32,193	33,147	33,555
100 to 499 employees	1,000	22,926	24,048	25,364	26,086	26,993	27,842	28,707	29,736	29,692
500 to 999 employees	1,000	6,551	6,663	7,021	7,274	7,422	7,689	7,923	8,291	8,357
1,000 or more employees	1,000	12,212	12,513	12,962	13,026	13,370	13,991	14,594	15,322	15,776
Annual payroll, total	Bil. dol.	2,104	2,488	2,666	2,849	3,048	3,309	3,555	3,879	3,989
Under 20 employees	Bil. dol.	485	579	608	647	688	734	773	818	839
20 to 99 employees	Bil. dol.	547	650	696	747	796	866	925	1,006	1,037
100 to 499 employees	Bil. dol.	518	621	675	730	786	858	931	1,031	1,052
500 to 999 employees	Bil. dol.	174	202	219	240	254	277	298	336	342
1,000 or more employees	Bil. dol.	381	436	467	485	524	575	628	690	719

Source: U.S. Census Bureau, "County Business Patterns"; published 2 June 2003; <http://www.census.gov/epcd/cbp/view/cbpview.html>.

No. 745. Establishments, Employees, and Payroll by Employment-Size Class and Industry: 1999 to 2001

[Establishments and employees in thousands (7,008.4 represents 7,008,400); payroll in billions of dollars. See headnote, Table 744. Based on the North American Industry Classification System (NAICS), 1997; see text, this section]

Industry	NAICS code	1999, total	2000, total	2001 Total	Under 20 employees	20 to 99 employees	100 to 499 employees	500 to 999 employees	1,000 or more employees
Establishments, total	(X)	7,008.4	7,070.0	7,095.3	6,083.0	835.8	157.1	12.3	7.0
Agriculture, forestry, fishing & hunting	11	26.9	26.1	26.4	24.8	1.5	0.2	(Z)	(Z)
Mining	21	23.7	23.7	24.3	19.8	3.6	0.7	0.1	(Z)
Utilities	22	16.6	17.3	17.7	12.5	3.8	1.2	0.1	0.1
Construction	23	698.5	709.6	698.9	634.8	56.5	7.2	0.4	0.2
Manufacturing	31-33	360.2	354.5	352.6	236.3	82.7	29.2	3.0	1.4
Wholesale trade	42	450.0	446.2	438.9	373.0	57.1	8.2	0.4	0.1
Retail trade	44-45	1,111.3	1,113.6	1,120.0	971.9	122.7	24.8	0.6	0.1
Transportation and warehousing	48-49	187.3	190.0	190.7	159.7	25.5	4.9	0.3	0.3
Information	51	126.5	133.6	137.3	107.7	22.5	6.1	0.7	0.3
Finance and insurance	52	418.3	423.7	425.0	378.7	38.2	6.6	0.9	0.5
Real estate and rental and leasing	53	298.1	300.2	307.0	291.2	13.9	1.8	0.1	(Z)
Professional, scientific, and technical services	54	704.8	722.7	736.5	677.1	49.7	8.7	0.7	0.3
Management of companies and enterprises	55	46.5	47.4	47.6	31.4	10.8	4.2	0.7	0.4
Admin/support waste mgt/remediation services	56	350.4	351.5	362.7	300.6	45.1	15.0	1.3	0.7
Educational services	61	66.5	68.0	70.9	53.6	13.8	2.8	0.4	0.3
Health care and social assistance	62	649.8	658.6	671.4	570.6	78.5	18.8	1.7	1.8
Arts, entertainment, and recreation	71	102.8	103.8	106.0	88.0	15.2	2.5	0.2	0.1
Accommodation and food services	72	539.6	542.4	548.6	393.8	145.3	8.9	0.3	0.2
Other services [1]	81	717.9	723.3	719.4	670.0	45.2	4.0	0.1	(Z)
Auxiliaries [2]	95	14.6	14.8	14.9	9.3	3.7	1.5	0.3	0.1
Unclassified establishments	99	98.0	99.0	78.6	78.3	0.3	-	-	-
Employees, total	(X)	110,706	114,065	115,061	27,681	33,555	29,692	8,357	15,776
Agriculture, forestry, fishing & hunting	11	192	184	183	(D)	(D)	30	(D)	(D)
Mining	21	457	456	486	92	(D)	149	45	(D)
Utilities	22	667	655	654	66	171	227	92	98
Construction	23	6,202	6,573	6,492	2,478	2,173	1,301	236	304
Manufacturing	31-33	16,660	16,474	15,950	1,382	3,659	5,915	2,045	2,950
Wholesale trade	42	5,972	6,112	6,142	1,846	2,225	1,501	290	281
Retail trade	44-45	14,477	14,841	14,890	5,184	4,905	4,329	368	104
Transportation and warehousing	48-49	3,627	3,790	3,751	667	1,049	899	207	929
Information	51	3,235	3,546	3,755	494	961	1,203	481	615
Finance and insurance	52	5,965	5,963	6,248	1,703	1,489	1,332	625	1,099
Real estate and rental and leasing	53	1,874	1,942	2,014	1,037	521	324	(D)	(D)
Professional, scientific, and technical services	54	6,432	6,816	7,157	2,357	1,954	1,668	440	738
Management of companies and enterprises	55	2,788	2,874	2,879	171	486	912	479	830
Admin/support waste mgt/remediation services	56	8,367	9,138	9,062	1,198	1,977	2,958	879	2,049
Educational services	61	2,432	2,532	2,612	257	582	546	257	971
Health care and social assistance	62	13,865	14,109	14,535	2,961	3,154	3,488	1,192	3,739
Arts, entertainment, and recreation	71	1,640	1,741	1,780	342	636	455	112	235
Accommodation and food services	72	9,638	9,881	9,972	2,370	5,582	1,434	237	349
Other services [1]	81	5,151	5,293	5,370	2,831	1,656	691	87	105
Auxiliaries [2]	95	959	1,001	1,022	59	164	329	200	271
Unclassified establishments	99	106	144	105	(D)	(D)	-	-	-
Annual payroll, total	(X)	3,555	3,879	3,989	839	1,037	1,052	342	719
Agriculture, forestry, fishing & hunting	11	5	5	5	(D)	(D)	1	(D)	(D)
Mining	21	21	22	25	4	(D)	9	2	(D)
Utilities	22	39	41	42	3	10	15	7	7
Construction	23	219	240	247	80	87	57	10	12
Manufacturing	31-33	626	644	618	42	124	217	81	154
Wholesale trade	42	250	270	276	75	96	71	16	16
Retail trade	44-45	282	303	315	101	110	92	8	4
Transportation and warehousing	48-49	117	126	130	20	33	30	7	39
Information	51	170	209	207	25	45	66	27	45
Finance and insurance	52	313	347	374	80	87	86	37	84
Real estate and rental and leasing	53	54	59	64	30	18	12	(D)	(D)
Professional, scientific, and technical services	54	311	362	374	106	110	98	28	33
Management of companies and enterprises	55	192	211	213	14	34	62	34	69
Admin/support waste mgt/remediation services	56	183	210	221	37	52	65	18	49
Educational services	61	57	62	67	6	13	14	5	30
Health care and social assistance	62	409	431	466	109	92	89	38	138
Arts, entertainment, and recreation	71	39	43	46	11	12	15	3	5
Accommodation and food services	72	117	126	129	30	63	22	5	9
Other services [1]	81	102	110	115	57	36	18	2	3
Auxiliaries [2]	95	45	55	53	3	7	16	9	17
Unclassified establishments	99	3	4	2	(D)	(D)	-	-	-

- Represents zero. D Data withheld to avoid disclosure. X Not applicable. Z Less than 50 establishments. [1] Except public administration. [2] Excludes corporate, subsidiary and regional management.

Source: U.S. Census Bureau, "County Business Patterns"; published 2 June 2003; <http://www.census.gov/epcd/cbp/view/cbpview.html>.

No. 746. Major Industries—Employer Firms, Employment, and Annual Payroll by Enterprise Size: 2000

[5,653 represents 5,653,000. A firm is an aggregation of all establishments owned by a parent company (within a geographic location and/or industry) with some annual payroll. A firm may be a single location or it can include multiple locations. Employment is measured in March and payroll is annual leading to some firms with zero employment. Numbers in parentheses represent North American Industry Classification System, 1997 codes, see text, this section]

Industry and data type	Unit	All industries—employment size of enterprise							
		Total	0	1 to 4	5 to 9	10 to 19	20 to 99	100 to 499	Less than 500	More than 500
Total [1]:										
Firms	1,000	5,653	727	2,670	1,021	617	516	84	5,635	17
Employment	1,000	114,065	-	5,593	6,709	8,286	20,277	16,260	57,124	56,941
Annual payroll	Bil. dol	3,879	39	148	174	231	608	528	1,727	2,152
Construction (23):										
Firms	1,000	702	102	338	125	74	55	6	701	1
Employment	1,000	6,573	-	713	821	989	2,077	1,075	5,675	898
Annual payroll	Bil. dol	240	4	19	23	31	78	45	199	41
Manufacturing (31-33):										
Firms	1,000	306	23	94	57	49	64	16	302	5
Employment	1,000	16,474	-	212	378	666	2,647	2,899	6,802	9,672
Annual payroll	Bil. dol	644	2	5	10	20	87	102	226	418
Wholesale trade (42):										
Firms	1,000	354	35	157	65	45	41	8	351	3
Employment	1,000	6,112	-	334	427	600	1,511	1,016	3,887	2,226
Annual payroll	Bil. dol	270	2	12	15	23	60	42	154	116
Retail trade (44-45):										
Firms	1,000	731	79	337	154	88	61	9	729	2
Employment	1,000	14,841	-	746	1,011	1,159	2,280	1,295	6,492	8,349
Annual payroll	Bil. dol	303	3	13	18	23	59	36	151	151
Transportation & warehousing (48-49):										
Firms	1,000	157	23	75	24	16	15	3	156	1
Employment	1,000	3,790	-	147	156	217	582	455	1,556	2,234
Annual payroll	Bil. dol	126	1	3	4	6	16	14	44	82
Information (51):										
Firms	1,000	80	13	32	13	9	9	2	78	1
Employment	1,000	3,546	-	67	83	125	358	363	997	2,549
Annual payroll	Bil. dol	209	2	3	3	5	17	22	52	158
Finance & insurance (52):										
Firms	1,000	227	27	131	33	16	15	4	225	2
Employment	1,000	5,963	-	268	208	211	607	621	1,914	4,049
Annual payroll	Bil. dol	347	2	9	9	11	30	33	93	253
Real estate & rental & leasing (53):										
Firms	1,000	245	35	148	32	15	11	2	243	1
Employment	1,000	1,942	-	281	209	202	379	287	1,358	584
Annual payroll	Bil. dol	59	1	7	5	6	11	9	40	19
Professional, scientific & technical services (54):										
Firms	1,000	670	102	372	98	53	37	6	668	2
Employment	1,000	6,816	-	716	640	706	1,384	963	4,408	2,408
Annual payroll	Bil. dol	362	6	27	25	32	75	58	224	138
Management of companies & enterprises (55):										
Firms	1,000	27	1	4	1	1	5	7	20	7
Employment	1,000	2,874	-	6	4	8	67	222	308	2,566
Annual payroll	Bil. dol	211	1	(Z)	(Z)	1	3	12	17	194
Admin/support waste mgt/ remediation services (56):										
Firms	1,000	299	46	137	49	29	27	8	296	3
Employment	1,000	9,138	-	284	318	392	1,068	1,415	3,477	5,661
Annual payroll	Bil. dol	210	4	7	8	10	27	30	86	125
Health care and social assistance (62):										
Firms	1,000	532	46	229	125	67	49	13	529	3
Employment	1,000	14,109	-	514	820	891	1,931	2,550	6,708	7,401
Annual payroll	Bil. dol	431	3	19	28	32	59	62	203	228
Accommodation & food services (72):										
Firms	1,000	413	56	128	78	68	73	8	411	2
Employment	1,000	9,881	-	296	522	937	2,776	1,423	5,954	3,927
Annual payroll	Bil. dol	126	2	3	5	9	31	17	69	57
Other services (except public administration) (81):										
Firms	1,000	662	57	362	133	64	40	4	660	1
Employment	1,000	5,293	-	768	865	848	1,443	621	4,545	749
Annual payroll	Bil. dol	110	1	13	16	17	29	15	90	19

- Represents zero. Z Less than $500 million. [1] Includes other industries not shown separately.

Source: U.S. Small Business Administration, Office of Advocacy, "Statistics of U.S. Businesses: Firm Size Data provided by U.S. Census Bureau"; published 25 March 2003; <http://www.sbaonline.sba.gov/ADVO/stats/data.html>.

No. 747. Employer Firms, Establishments, Employment, and Annual Payroll by Enterprise Size: 1990 to 2000

[In thousands except as noted (5,074 represents 5,074,000). Firms are an aggregation of all establishments owned by a parent company. Establishments are locations with active payroll in any quarter. Employment is measured in March and payroll is annual leading to some enterprises with zero employment. This table illustrates the changing importance of enterprise sizes over time, not job growth as enterprises can grow or decline and change enterprise size cells over time]

Item	Total	0-4 [1]	5-9	10-19	20-99	100-499	Less than 500	More than 500
Firms:								
1990	5,074	3,021	952	563	454	70	5,060	14
1993	5,194	3,140	962	560	446	72	5,179	15
1994	5,277	3,208	965	563	452	73	5,262	15
1995	5,369	3,250	981	577	470	76	5,354	15
1996	5,478	3,328	996	586	476	76	5,462	16
1997	5,542	3,358	1,007	594	487	80	5,526	16
1998	5,579	3,376	1,012	600	494	80	5,563	16
1999	5,608	3,389	1,013	606	502	81	5,591	17
2000	5,653	3,397	1,021	617	516	84	5,635	17
Establishments:								
1990	6,176	3,032	971	600	590	255	5,448	728
1993	6,401	3,148	981	609	632	285	5,655	746
1994	6,509	3,218	983	609	631	284	5,725	784
1995	6,613	3,260	998	618	639	284	5,799	814
1996	6,738	3,338	1,013	625	636	281	5,893	846
1997	6,895	3,364	1,023	639	683	309	6,018	877
1998	6,942	3,383	1,026	640	675	307	6,030	911
1999	7,008	3,398	1,027	643	671	309	6,048	960
2000	7,070	3,406	1,035	652	674	312	6,080	990
Employment:								
1990	93,469	5,117	6,252	7,543	17,710	13,545	50,167	43,302
1993	94,774	5,258	6,314	7,498	17,421	13,825	50,316	44,458
1994	96,722	5,319	6,333	7,544	17,694	14,118	51,008	45,714
1995	100,315	5,395	6,440	7,734	18,422	14,660	52,653	47,662
1996	102,187	5,486	6,541	7,855	18,643	14,650	53,175	49,013
1997	105,299	5,546	6,610	7,962	19,110	15,317	54,545	50,754
1998	108,118	5,584	6,643	8,048	19,378	15,411	55,064	53,053
1999	110,706	5,606	6,652	8,130	19,703	15,638	55,729	54,977
2000	114,065	5,593	6,709	8,286	20,277	16,260	57,124	56,941
Annual payroll ($bil.):								
1990	2,104	117	114	144	352	279	1,007	1,097
1993	2,363	129	127	159	385	316	1,116	1,247
1994	2,488	135	132	166	408	336	1,176	1,312
1995	2,666	142	137	175	437	361	1,252	1,414
1996	2,849	151	145	185	465	384	1,330	1,518
1997	3,048	158	151	194	495	418	1,416	1,632
1998	3,309	168	160	207	531	446	1,513	1,797
1999	3,555	177	167	218	565	475	1,601	1,954
2000	3,879	186	174	231	608	528	1,727	2,152

[1] Employment is measured in March, thus some firms (start-ups after March, closures before March, and seasonal firms) will have zero employment and some annual payroll.

No. 748. Firm Births and Deaths by Employment Size of Enterprise: 1990 to 2000

[(3,105 represents 3,105,000). Data represent activity from March of the beginning year to March of the ending year. Establishments with no employment in the first quarter of the beginning year were excluded. This table provides the number of births and deaths of initial establishments (based on plant number) as an approximation of firm births and deaths]

Item	Births (initial locations)				Deaths (initial locations)			
	Total	Less than 20	Less than 500	More than 500	Total	Less than 20	Less than 500	More than 500
Firms:								
1990-1991	541,141	515,870	540,889	252	546,518	516,964	546,149	369
1992-1993	564,504	539,601	564,093	411	492,651	466,550	492,266	385
1993-1994	570,587	546,437	570,337	250	503,563	476,667	503,125	438
1994-1995	594,369	568,896	594,119	250	497,246	472,441	496,874	372
1995-1996	597,792	572,442	597,503	289	512,402	485,509	512,024	378
1996-1997	590,644	564,197	590,335	309	530,003	500,014	529,481	522
1997-1998	589,982	564,804	589,706	276	540,601	511,567	540,112	489
1998-1999	579,609	554,288	579,287	322	544,487	514,293	544,040	447
1999-2000	574,300	548,030	574,023	277	542,831	514,242	542,374	457
Employment (1,000):								
1990-1991	3,105	1,713	2,907	198	3,208	1,723	3,044	164
1992-1993	3,438	1,751	3,054	384	2,906	1,516	2,698	209
1993-1994	3,106	1,760	2,890	216	3,077	1,549	2,801	276
1994-1995	3,322	1,836	3,049	273	2,823	1,517	2,634	189
1995-1996	3,256	1,845	3,056	200	3,100	1,560	2,808	291
1996-1997	3,228	1,814	3,030	198	3,275	1,621	2,961	314
1997-1998	3,205	1,812	3,002	203	3,233	1,662	2,992	242
1998-1999	3,225	1,670	2,991	235	3,180	1,645	2,969	210
1999-2000	3,229	1,793	3,031	198	3,177	1,654	2,946	230

Source of Tables 747 and 748: U.S. Small Business Administration, Office of Advocacy, "Statistics of U.S. Businesses: Firm Size Data provided by U.S. Census Bureau"; published 25 March 2003; <http://www.sbaonline.sba.gov/ADVO/stats/data.html>.

No. 749. Employer Firms, Employment, and Payroll by Employment Size of Enterprise and State: 1990 and 2000

[5,073.8 represents 5,073,800. A firm is an aggregation of all establishments owned by a parent company (within a state) with some annual payroll. A firm may be a single location or it can include multiple locations. Employment is measured in March and payroll is annual leading to some firms with zero employment]

State	Employer firms (1,000) 1990 Total	1990 Less than 20 employees	2000 Total	2000 Less than 20 employees	2000 Less than 500 employees	Employment, 2000 (mil.) Total	Less than 20 employees	Less than 500 employees	Annual payroll, 2000 (bil. dol.) Total	Less than 20 employees	Less than 500 employees
U.S.	5,073.8	4,535.6	5,652.5	5,035.0	5,635.4	114.1	20.6	57.1	3,879.4	591.1	1,727.1
AL	71.5	61.7	79.9	68.2	77.6	1.7	0.3	0.8	44.0	6.7	19.6
AK	12.8	11.3	15.9	14.0	15.4	0.2	0.1	0.1	7.6	1.7	4.2
AZ	71.6	61.8	93.0	79.3	90.3	1.9	0.3	0.9	58.2	8.9	25.1
AR	46.0	40.2	52.4	45.4	50.8	1.0	0.2	0.5	24.7	3.9	10.5
CA	628.5	552.8	664.6	581.1	658.9	12.9	2.4	6.8	514.4	80.1	243.4
CO	82.7	72.4	116.2	101.5	113.3	1.9	0.4	1.0	68.2	11.6	30.8
CT	81.1	70.4	78.5	67.2	76.4	1.5	0.3	0.8	67.4	10.2	30.3
DE	16.3	13.6	20.2	16.6	18.9	0.4	0.1	0.2	14.3	1.9	5.2
DC	16.5	12.6	16.3	12.4	15.2	0.4	0.1	0.2	20.0	2.7	9.2
FL	302.8	271.3	354.0	319.3	349.7	6.2	1.2	2.8	177.4	32.2	80.0
GA	128.1	110.5	160.4	138.3	156.5	3.5	0.5	1.5	112.9	16.0	44.8
HI	24.4	20.9	24.3	20.8	23.5	0.4	0.1	0.2	12.3	2.4	6.5
ID	23.0	20.1	32.2	28.0	31.2	0.5	0.1	0.3	12.4	2.5	6.1
IL	230.8	198.8	254.1	218.1	249.6	5.5	0.9	2.7	201.3	28.5	87.9
IN	105.9	90.7	116.3	98.1	113.3	2.7	0.4	1.3	79.0	10.5	34.0
IA	61.4	53.5	65.6	56.2	63.9	1.3	0.2	0.7	33.8	5.0	15.7
KS	55.9	48.3	61.6	52.4	59.6	1.1	0.2	0.6	32.0	5.0	15.1
KY	66.6	57.2	72.3	61.0	70.1	1.5	0.3	0.8	41.2	5.9	18.1
LA	73.2	63.1	81.7	69.5	79.6	1.6	0.3	0.9	43.0	7.1	20.5
ME	30.7	27.2	34.1	30.1	33.3	0.5	0.1	0.3	13.5	2.7	7.4
MD	95.9	81.8	106.0	90.4	103.4	2.1	0.4	1.1	70.9	11.4	34.2
MA	135.6	116.8	148.2	127.8	145.3	3.1	0.5	1.5	131.4	18.1	58.5
MI	175.9	153.0	193.9	167.2	190.7	4.1	0.7	2.1	145.5	20.7	63.1
MN	95.5	82.1	116.2	99.4	113.7	2.4	0.4	1.2	82.5	12.3	37.2
MS	44.5	39.0	48.3	41.5	46.8	1.0	0.2	0.5	22.8	3.6	9.9
MO	109.4	94.8	118.1	101.1	115.2	2.4	0.4	1.2	72.2	10.7	31.9
MT	22.2	19.9	28.0	25.0	27.4	0.3	0.1	0.2	6.8	1.9	4.4
NE	37.6	32.7	41.4	35.5	40.1	0.8	0.1	0.4	20.3	3.2	9.3
NV	26.0	21.8	40.3	33.4	38.5	0.9	0.1	0.4	26.6	4.1	11.8
NH	29.4	25.5	32.1	27.3	31.0	0.5	0.1	0.3	17.8	3.5	9.5
NJ	188.0	165.5	202.2	178.4	199.0	3.5	0.7	1.8	147.1	24.0	65.2
NM	30.7	26.6	35.5	30.1	34.1	0.5	0.1	0.3	14.3	2.8	7.4
NY	412.5	368.1	424.8	379.2	420.5	7.4	1.4	3.8	330.6	49.5	142.3
NC	135.9	119.0	163.6	142.0	160.3	3.4	0.6	1.6	99.7	15.0	42.3
ND	16.6	14.6	17.2	14.7	16.6	0.3	0.1	0.2	6.1	1.3	3.5
OH	200.7	172.7	212.5	180.5	208.7	5.0	0.8	2.4	155.0	21.1	66.8
OK	63.2	55.5	70.2	61.0	68.3	1.2	0.2	0.6	31.7	5.6	15.0
OR	69.9	61.0	85.1	74.2	83.1	1.4	0.3	0.8	43.7	7.5	20.9
PA	233.5	202.8	237.5	204.6	233.6	5.1	0.9	2.6	165.1	23.4	73.0
RI	25.1	21.6	25.2	21.5	24.3	0.4	0.1	0.2	12.6	2.4	6.8
SC	66.1	57.4	78.4	67.2	76.1	1.6	0.3	0.8	43.4	6.7	17.9
SD	18.3	16.0	20.6	17.7	19.9	0.3	0.1	0.2	7.3	1.4	4.0
TN	92.8	79.9	102.4	86.7	99.4	2.4	0.4	1.1	69.4	9.4	28.9
TX	316.9	280.0	369.0	321.3	364.0	8.0	1.3	3.7	269.9	39.0	109.4
UT	30.9	26.2	46.2	39.3	44.5	0.9	0.2	0.4	25.4	4.0	11.3
VT	18.0	16.0	19.1	16.7	18.5	0.3	0.1	0.2	6.9	1.6	4.1
VA	121.3	105.2	139.7	120.3	136.6	2.9	0.5	1.4	97.7	13.9	41.5
WA	113.2	99.3	138.2	120.9	135.6	2.3	0.5	1.3	87.7	13.3	38.8
WV	31.8	27.6	33.5	28.8	32.4	0.6	0.1	0.3	14.0	2.4	6.4
WI	104.3	89.7	115.6	98.2	113.2	2.4	0.4	1.3	72.9	10.9	34.6
WY	13.0	11.4	15.9	13.9	15.4	0.2	0.1	0.1	4.5	1.2	2.8

Source: U.S. Small Business Administration, Office of Advocacy, "Statistics of U.S. Businesses: Firm Size Data provided by U.S. Census Bureau"; published 25 March 2003; <http://www.sbaonline.sba.gov/ADVO/stats/data.html>.

No. 750. U.S. Firms—Ownership by Race and Hispanic Origin: 1997

[20,822 represents 20,822,000. A Hispanic firm may be of any race, and therefore may be included in more than one minority group. See Appendix III]

Group	All firms		Firms with paid employees			
	Firms (1,000)	Sales and receipts (mil. dol.)	Firms (1,000)	Sales and receipts (mil. dol.)	Employees (1,000)	Annual payroll (mil. dol.)
All firms	20,822	18,553,243	5,295	17,907,940	103,360	2,936,493
Black	823	71,215	93	56,378	718	14,322
Hispanic	1,200	186,275	212	158,675	1,389	29,830
Cuban	125	26,492	30	23,873	176	4,163
Mexican, Mexican American, Chicano	472	73,707	91	62,271	695	13,015
Puerto Rican	70	7,461	11	5,814	62	1,497
Spaniard	57	16,923	13	15,264	76	2,046
Hispanic Latin American	287	40,998	43	34,798	239	5,863
Other Spanish/Hispanic/Latino	188	20,694	24	16,654	140	3,247
American Indian and Alaska Native	197	34,344	33	29,226	299	6,624
Asian and Pacific Islander	913	306,933	290	278,294	2,203	46,180
Asian Indian	167	67,503	67	61,760	491	12,586
Chinese	253	106,197	91	98,233	692	12,945
Filipino	85	11,078	15	8,966	110	2,667
Japanese	86	43,741	23	41,295	262	7,107
Korean	136	45,936	50	40,746	334	5,789
Vietnamese	98	9,323	19	6,768	79	1,166
Other Asian	71	19,016	22	16,801	202	3,136
Native Hawaiian	16	2,250	2	1,957	21	498
Other Pacific Islander	4	1,888	1	1,768	13	286
White non-Hispanic	17,317	7,763,011	4,373	7,252,270	54,084	1,395,150
Fifty-percent minority/fifty-percent nonminority	85	37,732	39	34,632	302	8,619
Other [1]	382	10,161,242	(S)	10,104,058	44,458	1,437,195

S Does not meet publication standards. [1] Includes publicly-held corporations, foreign-owned companies, and not-for-profit companies.

Source: U.S. Census Bureau, 1997 Economic Census, Company Statistics Series, *Company Summary 1997*, EC97CS-1; and *Survey of Minority-Owned Business Enterprises—Asians and Pacific Islanders 1997*, EC97CS-5; and *Hispanic 1997*, EC97CS-4.

No. 751. Women-Owned Firms by Industry Division: 1997

[818,669,084 represents $818,669,084,000. Based on the 1987 Standard Industrial Classification code; see text, this section. See Appendix III]

Industry division	All firms		Firms with paid employees			
	Firms [1] (number)	Sales and receipts ($1,000)	Firms [1] (number)	Sales and receipts ($1,000)	Employees (number)	Annual payroll ($1,000)
All Industries	5,417,034	818,669,084	846,780	717,763,965	7,076,081	149,115,699
Agric. services, forestry, and fishing	74,444	5,852,901	16,652	4,599,852	77,370	1,442,618
Mining	20,030	7,186,113	2,180	6,491,900	25,982	873,455
Construction [2]	157,173	67,632,059	65,707	63,738,665	518,142	15,302,000
Manufacturing	121,108	113,722,304	41,141	111,658,770	901,434	24,674,596
Transportation and public utilities	128,999	32,944,160	35,623	30,063,926	321,759	7,803,912
Wholesale trade	125,645	188,488,639	50,459	184,574,784	468,276	14,086,123
Retail trade	919,990	152,041,311	211,583	137,296,015	1,574,747	19,520,353
Finance, insurance, and real estate	479,469	56,021,358	66,375	38,920,419	276,045	7,549,811
Services	2,981,266	186,161,274	355,768	140,255,817	2,908,080	57,808,228
Industries not classified	411,596	8,618,965	3,979	163,817	4,246	54,604

[1] Firms may be classified in more than one industry division. [2] Includes SIC 6552, Subdividers and developers.

Source: U.S. Census Bureau, 1997 Economic Census, Company Statistics Series, *Survey of Women-Owned Business Enterprises, Women-Owned Businesses 1997*, Series EC97CS-2.

No. 752. Hispanic-Owned Firms by Industry Division: 1997

[186,274,582 represents $186,274,582,000. Based on the 1987 Standard Industrial Classification code; see text, this section. See Appendix III]

Industry division	All firms		Firms with paid employees			
	Firms [1] (number)	Sales and receipts ($1,000)	Firms [1] (number)	Sales and receipts ($1,000)	Employees (number)	Annual payroll ($1,000)
All Industries	1,199,896	186,274,582	211,884	158,674,537	1,388,746	29,830,028
Agric. services, forestry, and fishing	40,040	2,279,397	5,925	1,309,733	25,955	416,702
Mining	1,909	429,446	325	367,442	3,569	97,854
Construction [2]	152,573	21,923,384	31,478	19,146,212	168,873	4,218,419
Manufacturing	25,552	28,684,759	10,173	27,719,404	171,738	4,549,598
Transportation and public utilities	84,544	8,293,935	12,735	5,605,332	79,682	1,587,106
Wholesale trade	31,480	40,386,625	14,125	38,746,137	94,281	2,388,988
Retail trade	155,061	32,280,310	48,713	28,599,447	324,474	3,892,182
Finance, insurance, and real estate	56,629	6,644,826	9,944	4,728,312	34,783	949,006
Services	500,449	39,177,767	70,838	30,406,573	463,889	11,297,362
Industries not classified	151,931	6,174,133	7,909	2,045,945	21,502	432,812

[1] Firms may be classified in more than one industry division. [2] Includes SIC 6552, Subdividers and developers.

Source: U.S. Census Bureau, 1997 Economic Census, Company Statistics Series, *Survey of Minority-Owned Business Enterprises, Hispanic 1997*, Series EC97CS-4.

No. 753. Black-Owned Firms by Industry Division: 1997

[71,214,662 represents $71,214,662,000. Based on the 1987 Standard Industrial Classification code; see text, this section. See Appendix III]

Industry division	All firms		Firms with paid employees			
	Firms [1] (number)	Sales and receipts ($1,000)	Firms [1] (number)	Sales and receipts ($1,000)	Employees (number)	Annual payroll ($1,000)
All industries	823,499	71,214,662	93,235	56,377,860	718,341	14,322,312
Agricultural services, forestry, and fishing	12,464	417,169	1,356	259,649	5,457	77,198
Mining	231	21,551	16	12,867	186	5,319
Construction [2]	56,508	7,712,059	12,973	6,587,348	70,928	1,510,252
Manufacturing	10,447	3,682,510	1,931	3,463,861	26,624	652,787
Transportation and public utilities	71,586	6,376,645	6,184	4,252,240	47,289	909,470
Wholesale trade	8,120	5,818,734	2,139	5,573,907	13,746	471,320
Retail trade	87,568	13,803,266	14,074	12,244,399	125,480	1,497,111
Finance, insurance, and real estate	37,934	3,088,582	4,820	2,189,556	18,379	498,318
Services	437,646	25,925,092	43,529	19,503,488	388,398	8,212,775
Industries not classified	101,128	4,369,056	6,347	2,290,545	21,853	487,761

[1] Firms may be classified in more than one industry division. [2] Includes SIC 6552, Subdividers and developers.

Source: U.S. Census Bureau, 1997 Economic Census, Company Statistics Series, *Survey of Minority-Owned Business Enterprises, Black 1997*, Series EC97CS-3.

No. 754. Asian- and Pacific Islander-Owned Firms by Industry Division: 1997

[306,932,982 represents $306,932,982,000. Based on the 1987 Standard Industrial Classification code; see text, this section. See Appendix III]

Industry division	All firms		Firms with paid employees			
	Firms [1] (number)	Sales and receipts ($1,000)	Firms [1] (number)	Sales and receipts ($1,000)	Employees (number)	Annual payroll ($1,000)
All industries	912,960	306,932,982	289,999	278,294,345	2,203,079	46,179,519
Agric. services, forestry, and fishing	12,988	1,140,670	1,927	791,843	11,359	226,707
Mining	660	253,329	87	229,059	1,007	33,447
Construction [2]	27,711	7,485,505	6,398	6,522,807	42,533	1,386,303
Manufacturing	23,242	28,952,417	10,553	28,271,707	238,167	5,513,875
Transportation and public utilities	37,501	5,625,483	5,916	4,427,646	52,441	1,220,240
Wholesale trade	50,400	105,466,223	30,095	102,902,082	211,510	6,128,070
Retail trade	195,691	67,895,241	106,264	62,467,158	644,614	7,497,710
Finance, insurance, and real estate	68,765	11,398,069	9,429	7,585,054	42,243	1,185,688
Services	406,010	67,762,462	107,910	57,153,191	896,731	21,719,605
Industries not classified	90,509	10,953,582	11,937	7,943,797	62,443	1,267,874

[1] Firms may be classified in more than one industry division. [2] Includes SIC 6552, Subdividers and developers.

Source: U.S. Census Bureau, 1997 Economic Census, Company Statistics Series, *Survey of Minority-Owned Business Enterprises, Asians and Pacific Islanders 1997*, Series EC97CS-5.

No. 755. American Indian- and Alaska Native-Owned Firms by Industry Division: 1997

[34,343,907 represents $34,343,907,000. Based on the 1987 Standard Industrial Classification code; see text, this section. See Appendix III]

Industry division	All firms		Firms with paid employees			
	Firms [1] (number)	Sales and receipts ($1,000)	Firms [1] (number)	Sales and receipts ($1,000)	Employees (number)	Annual payroll ($1,000)
All industries	197,300	34,343,907	33,277	29,226,260	298,661	6,624,235
Agric. services, forestry, and fishing	8,942	360,484	797	174,841	2,760	50,041
Mining	947	543,908	199	465,764	2,124	64,737
Construction [2]	27,435	5,384,815	6,012	4,648,924	38,419	1,021,524
Manufacturing	6,717	2,503,417	1,612	2,334,452	21,206	563,454
Transportation and public utilities	6,291	1,620,515	1,118	1,347,949	10,584	276,381
Wholesale trade	4,365	3,155,143	1,145	3,036,534	9,801	260,713
Retail trade	14,768	4,618,484	4,645	4,245,552	31,451	441,783
Finance, insurance, and real estate	4,616	1,190,741	1,004	1,025,527	4,585	133,050
Services	34,144	5,202,704	4,826	4,497,918	66,627	1,541,895
Industries not classified	89,243	9,763,696	12,086	7,448,800	111,103	2,270,656

[1] Firms may be classified in more than one industry division. [2] Includes SIC 6552, Subdividers and developers.

Source: U.S. Census Bureau, 1997 Economic Census, Company Statistics Series, *Survey of Minority-Owned Business Enterprises, American Indians and Alaska Natives 1997*, Series EC97CS-6.

No. 756. Bankruptcy Petitions Filed and Pending by Type and Chapter: 1990 to 2002

[For years ending June 30. Covers only bankruptcy cases filed under the Bankruptcy Reform Act of 1978. *Bankruptcy:* legal recognition that a company or individual is insolvent and must restructure or liquidate. Petitions "filed" means the commencement of a proceeding through the presentation of a petition to the clerk of the court; "pending" is a proceeding in which the administration has not been completed]

Item	1990	1995	1996	1997	1998	1999	2000	2001	2002
Total filed	725,484	858,104	1,042,110	1,316,999	1,429,451	1,391,964	1,276,922	1,386,606	1,505,306
Business [1]	64,688	51,288	52,938	53,993	50,202	39,934	36,910	37,135	39,201
Nonbusiness [2]	660,796	806,816	989,172	1,263,006	1,379,249	1,352,030	1,240,012	1,349,471	1,466,105
Voluntary	723,886	856,991	1,040,915	1,315,782	1,428,550	1,391,130	1,276,146	1,385,840	1,504,500
Involuntary	1,598	1,113	1,195	1,217	901	834	776	766	806
Chapter 7 [3]	505,337	581,390	712,129	917,274	1,015,453	993,414	885,447	972,659	1,053,230
Chapter 9 [4]	7	12	10	9	5	3	8	10	8
Chapter 11 [5]	19,591	13,221	12,859	11,159	9,613	8,684	9,947	10,272	11,401
Chapter 12 [6]	1,351	904	1,063	1,006	845	829	732	206	367
Chapter 13 [7]	199,186	262,551	316,024	387,521	403,501	389,004	380,770	403,418	440,231
Section 304 [8]	12	26	24	29	34	30	18	41	69
Total pending	961,919	1,090,446	1,169,112	1,331,290	1,389,917	1,394,794	1,400,416	1,535,903	1,611,232

[1] Business bankruptcies include those filed under chapters 7, 9, 11, or 12. [2] Bankruptcies include those filed under chapters 7, 11, or 13. [3] Chapter 7, liquidation of nonexempt assets of businesses or individuals. [4] Chapter 9, adjustment of debts of a municipality. [5] Chapter 11, individual or business reorganization. [6] Chapter 12, adjustment of debts of a family farmer with regular income, effective November 26, 1986. [7] Chapter 13, adjustment of debts of an individual with regular income. [8] Chapter 11 U.S.C., Section 304, cases ancillary to foreign proceedings.

Source: Administrative Office of the U.S. Courts, *Statistical Tables for the Federal Judiciary.*

No. 757. Bankruptcy Cases Filed by State: 1995 to 2002

[In thousands (858.1 represents 858,100). For years ending June 30. Covers only bankruptcy cases filed under the Bankruptcy Reform Act of 1978. *Bankruptcy:* legal recognition that a company or individual is insolvent and must restructure or liquidate. Petitions "filed" means the commencement of a proceeding through the presentation of a petition to the clerk of the court]

State	1995	2000	2001	2002	State	1995	2000	2001	2002
Total [1]	858.1	1,276.9	1,386.6	1,505.3	Missouri	15.1	26.3	28.4	31.5
					Montana	2.1	3.3	3.7	4.1
Alabama	24.3	31.4	36.6	39.6	Nebraska	3.4	5.6	6.5	7.3
Alaska	0.9	1.4	1.5	1.4	Nevada	7.3	14.3	16.3	18.6
Arizona	14.8	21.7	22.8	27.3	New Hampshire	3.1	3.9	3.9	3.7
Arkansas	7.9	16.3	19.7	21.8					
California	140.4	160.6	147.9	148.4	New Jersey	25.5	38.7	40.3	40.5
					New Mexico	3.7	7.1	8.0	8.7
Colorado	13.1	15.6	17.4	19.2	New York	48.8	61.7	66.0	67.9
Connecticut	8.5	11.4	11.3	11.2	North Carolina	14.0	25.8	30.7	34.9
Delaware	1.4	4.9	4.0	4.0	North Dakota	1.2	2.0	2.1	2.0
District of Columbia	1.4	2.6	2.5	2.5					
Florida	43.4	74.0	80.4	88.0	Ohio	32.4	53.6	63.6	73.2
					Oklahoma	13.2	19.3	21.9	23.3
Georgia	42.1	57.9	64.9	72.6	Oregon	13.2	18.1	20.9	23.5
Hawaii	1.8	5.0	4.8	4.7	Pennsylvania	22.0	43.8	49.2	52.0
Idaho	3.7	7.3	7.9	8.5	Rhode Island	3.0	4.8	4.8	4.7
Illinois	39.2	62.3	68.2	77.3					
Indiana	22.3	37.5	43.0	50.6	South Carolina	6.9	11.7	13.0	15.1
					South Dakota	1.3	2.1	2.4	2.7
Iowa	5.9	8.2	9.9	11.2	Tennessee	35.5	47.1	55.5	61.5
Kansas	8.5	11.4	12.8	14.0	Texas	43.8	62.9	69.1	77.0
Kentucky	13.0	20.8	24.1	26.3	Utah	6.9	14.4	17.4	20.7
Louisiana	13.4	23.1	25.4	26.5					
Maine	1.9	4.1	4.4	4.4	Vermont	0.9	1.6	1.7	1.7
					Virginia	25.5	37.1	39.2	41.9
Maryland	16.3	31.1	33.7	34.5	Washington	18.6	31.2	34.8	37.3
Massachusetts	14.3	16.7	17.0	16.9	West Virginia	3.8	8.2	9.9	9.7
Michigan	22.7	36.4	41.8	50.2	Wisconsin	11.8	18.0	20.3	23.2
Minnesota	14.1	15.4	16.9	19.1	Wyoming	1.2	2.0	2.4	2.2
Mississippi	10.6	17.9	20.8	22.0					

[1] Includes outlying areas not shown separately.

Source: Administrative Office of the U.S. Courts, unpublished data.

No. 758. Mergers and Acquisitions—Summary: 1990 to 2002

[206 represents $206,000,000,000. Covers transactions valued at $5 million or more. Values based on transactions for which price data revealed. *All activity* includes mergers, acquisitions, acquisitions of partial interest that involve a 40 percent stake in the target or an investment of at least $100 million, divestitures, and leveraged transactions that result in a change in ownership. *Divestiture:* sale of a business, division, or subsidiary by corporate owner to another party. *Leveraged buyout:* acquisition of a business in which buyers use mostly borrowed money to finance purchase price and incorporate debt into capital structure of business after change in ownership]

Item	Unit	1990	1995	1996	1997	1998	1999	2000	2001	2002
All activity:										
Number	Number	4,239	4,981	5,639	8,770	9,634	9,599	11,169	7,713	7,032
Value	Bil. dol.	206	896	1,059	1,610	2,480	3,402	3,440	1,688	1,185
Divestitures:										
Number	Number	1,907	2,227	2,423	3,189	3,304	3,184	3,497	2,816	2,631
Value	Bil. dol.	91	365	319	616	555	678	892	644	473
Leveraged buyouts:										
Number	Number	177	206	169	198	238	344	476	329	303
Value	Bil. dol.	18	24	17	24	27	58	86	60	83
Foreign acquisitions of U.S. companies:										
Number	Number	773	80	73	441	483	560	741	448	336
Value	Bil. dol.	56	4	3	65	233	297	335	125	68
U.S. acquisitions overseas:										
Number	Number	392	317	364	539	746	698	746	470	378
Value	Bil. dol.	21	63	59	88	128	158	136	108	56
U.S. companies acquiring U.S. companies:										
Number	Number	(NA)	2,250	2,670	3,753	3,882	3,353	3,119	2,079	1,994
Value	Bil. dol.	(NA)	462	556	834	1,379	1,259	1,400	638	370

NA Not available.

No. 759. Mergers and Acquisitions by Industry: 2002

[369,648 represents $369,648,000,000. See headnote Table 758]

Industry	U.S. company acquiring U.S. company Number	U.S. company acquiring U.S. company Value (mil. dol.)	Foreign company acquiring U.S. company Number	Foreign company acquiring U.S. company Value (mil. dol.)	U.S. company acquiring foreign company Number	U.S. company acquiring foreign company Value (mil. dol.)
Total activity [1]	1,994	369,648	336	68,035	378	55,739
Advertising services	7	123	3	3,974	-	-
Aerospace and aircraft	6	1,453	4	124	-	-
Agriculture, forestry, and fishing	9	2,476	-	-	1	53
Amusement and recreation services	26	1,668	5	263	1	1,600
Business services	271	23,461	34	6,589	42	3,926
Chemicals	17	3,652	6	687	11	1,237
Commercial banks, bank holding companies	93	8,541	1	213	7	614
Communications equipment	34	2,901	7	140	4	121
Computer and office equipment	18	2,329	4	2,171	5	239
Construction firms	31	3,662	8	276	3	136
Credit institutions	22	5,204	2	15,328	3	1,366
Electric, gas, water distribution	68	15,630	8	630	11	1,435
Electronic and electrical equipment	67	4,285	16	702	28	2,325
Food and kindred products	28	10,608	12	17,161	13	3,498
Health services	65	9,445	4	161	4	355
Holding companies, except banks	6	1,127	-	-	-	-
Hotels and casinos	24	4,149	6	347	-	-
Insurance	44	8,366	2	247	4	1,153
Investment & commodity firms, dealers, exchanges	79	25,075	19	2,107	20	5,535
Machinery	40	7,097	12	466	14	1,274
Measuring, medical, photo equip; clocks	70	4,322	11	821	20	5,531
Metal and metal products	58	6,540	14	760	11	2,137
Mining	17	724	7	511	5	54
Motion picture production and distribution	11	3,954	1	17	4	350
Oil and gas; petroleum refining	98	23,544	16	2,318	12	898
Paper and allied products	16	1,878	4	853	5	751
Personal services	5	797	-	-	2	161
Prepackaged software	126	8,481	21	630	24	1,546
Printing, publishing, and allied services	36	15,120	3	678	3	419
Radio & television broadcasting stations	49	10,303	4	374	6	1,748
Real estate, mortgage bankers and brokers	109	16,958	25	3,247	9	3,887
Retail trade—eating and drinking places	21	3,382	2	188	3	721
Retail trade—general merchandise and apparel	13	2,392	2	91	4	2,105
Rubber & misc. plastic products	19	2,650	6	573	4	197
Real estate, mortgage bankers and brokers	30	8,651	-	-	-	-
Stone, clay, glass and concrete products	8	1,393	6	1,037	5	143
Telecommunications	62	7,358	8	421	14	1,606
Textile and apparel products	16	2,796	5	207	5	272
Transportation and shipping (except air)	42	7,667	4	202	9	387
Transportation equipment	17	17,579	3	166	12	2,653
Wholesale trade—durable goods	20	2,162	7	291	12	926
Wholesale trade—nondurable goods	19	3,192	5	274	5	379
Wood products, furniture, and fixtures	8	697	1	250	2	21

- Represents zero.   [1] Includes other industries not shown separately.

Source of Tables 758 and 759: Thomson Financial, Newark, NJ, Merger & Corporate Transactions Database (copyright).

Business Enterprise   511

No. 760. Small Business Administration Loans to Small Businesses: 1990 to 2002

[576 represents 576,000,000. For year ending September 30. A small business must be independently owned and operated, must not be dominant in its particular industry, and must meet standards set by the Small Business Administration as to its annual receipts or number of employees]

Minority group	Number of loans					Amount (mil. dol.)				
	1990	1995	2000	2001	2002	1990	1995	2000	2001	2002
Total minority loans	2,367	10,877	11,999	11,855	14,300	576	1,838	3,661	3,486	4,250
Percent of all loans	12.0	18.1	24.8	24.6	25.0	(NA)	(NA)	(NA)	(NA)	(NA)
African American	513	2,770	2,120	1,937	2,146	96	293	393	379	422
Asian American	1,075	3,767	5,838	5,720	7,249	317	945	2,397	2,262	2,810
Hispanic American	694	3,940	3,500	3,625	4,270	149	539	768	741	891
Native American	85	400	541	573	635	14	61	102	105	127

NA Not available.

Source: U.S. Small Business Administration, Management Information Summary, unpublished data.

No. 761. Venture Capital Commitments by Source: 1980 to 2002

[In billions of dollars (2.1 represents $2,100,000,000), except as indicated. Venture capital commitment: investment in venture capital partnerships]

Source	1980	1990	1995	1996	1997	1998	1999	2000	2001	2002
Capital commitments, total	2.1	3.5	10.0	12.2	19.0	29.7	62.8	105.8	37.9	7.7
Corporations	0.4	0.3	0.5	2.4	4.8	3.5	8.9	3.9	1.0	0.2
Endowments & foundations	0.3	0.5	2.0	1.5	3.2	1.9	10.8	22.3	8.3	1.6
Individuals & families	0.4	0.4	1.7	0.8	2.4	3.4	6.0	12.5	3.6	0.7
Financial & insurance	0.3	0.4	2.0	0.4	1.2	3.1	9.7	24.7	9.3	2.0
Pension funds	0.7	2.0	3.8	7.1	7.5	17.9	27.3	42.4	15.8	3.2
PERCENT DISTRIBUTION										
Corporations	21	7	5	20	25	12	14	4	3	2
Endowments & foundations	15	14	20	12	17	6	17	21	22	21
Individuals & families	17	12	17	7	12	11	10	12	9	9
Financial & insurance	14	10	20	3	6	10	16	23	24	25
Pension funds	33	56	38	58	39	60	43	40	42	42

Source: Venture Economics Investor Services, Boston, MA, Venture Capital Journal, monthly.

No. 762. Patents and Trademarks: 1980 to 2002

[In thousands (113.0 represents 113,000). Calendar year data. Covers U.S. patents issued to citizens of the United States and residents of foreign countries. For data on foreign countries, see Table 1339]

Type	1980	1985	1990	1995	1998	1999	2000	2001	2002
Patent applications filed	113.0	127.1	176.7	228.8	261.4	289.5	315.8	346.6	357.5
Inventions	104.3	117.0	164.6	212.4	243.0	270.2	295.9	326.5	334.4
Designs	7.8	9.6	11.3	15.4	17.1	17.8	18.3	18.3	20.9
Botanical plants	0.2	0.2	0.4	0.5	0.7	0.9	0.8	0.9	1.1
Reissues	0.6	0.3	0.5	0.6	0.6	0.7	0.8	0.8	1.0
Patents issued	66.2	77.3	99.2	113.8	163.1	169.1	176.0	184.0	184.4
Inventions	61.8	71.7	90.4	101.4	147.5	153.5	157.5	166.0	167.3
Individuals	13.8	12.9	17.3	17.4	22.5	22.8	22.4	21.7	20.5
Corporations:									
United States	27.7	31.2	36.1	44.0	66.1	69.4	70.9	74.3	74.2
Foreign [1]	19.1	26.4	36.0	39.1	57.9	60.3	63.3	69.0	71.8
U.S. Government	1.2	1.1	1.0	1.0	1.0	1.0	0.9	1.0	0.9
Designs	3.9	5.1	8.0	11.7	14.8	14.7	17.4	16.9	15.5
Botanical plants	0.1	0.2	0.3	0.4	0.6	0.4	0.5	0.6	1.1
Reissues	0.3	0.3	0.4	0.3	0.3	0.4	0.5	0.5	0.5
U.S. residents [2]	40.8	43.3	52.8	64.4	90.6	94.0	96.9	98.6	97.1
Foreign country residents [2]	25.4	33.9	46.2	49.4	72.5	75.1	79.1	85.4	87.3
Percent of total	38.4	43.9	46.7	43.4	44.4	44.4	44.9	46.4	47.3
Other published documents [3]	(Z)	(Z)	0.1	0.1	0.1	0.1	0.1	0.1	(Z)
Trademarks:									
Applications filed	46.8	65.1	127.3	188.9	246.6	328.6	296.5	230.9	264.0
Issued	24.7	71.7	60.8	92.5	136.1	191.9	115.2	142.9	176.9
Trademarks	18.9	65.8	53.6	85.6	129.9	184.9	106.4	109.6	146.9
Trademark renewals	5.9	5.9	7.2	6.9	6.2	7.0	8.8	33.3	30.0

Z Less than 50. [1] Includes patents to foreign governments. [2] Includes patents for inventions, designs, botanical plants, and reissues. [3] Includes Defensive Publications, a practice which began in November 1968 and ended in July 1986; and Statutory Invention Registrations, the current practice, which began May 1985. These documents are patent applications, which are published to provide the defensive properties of a patent, but do not have the enforceable rights of a patent.

Source: U.S. Patent and Trademark Office, "Statistical Reports Available For Viewing, Calendar Year Patent Statistics"; published 12 June 2002; <http://www.uspto.gov/web/offices/ac/ido/oeip/taf/reports.htm> and unpublished data.

No. 763. Patents by Industry: 1980 to 2001

[Based on the 1972 Standard Industrial Classification (SIC). Includes all U.S. patents for inventions granted to residents of the United States, its territories, and foreign citizens. Individual industries may not add to total since a patent may be recorded in more than one industry category. Data for all years have been revised to reflect the U.S. Patent Classification System as of December 2001]

Industry	SIC code	1980	1985	1990	1995	2000	2001
Total	(X)	61,819	71,661	90,365	101,419	157,495	166,037
Durable goods:							
Stone, clay, and glass products	32	1,222	1,306	1,639	1,574	2,122	2,414
Primary metals	33, 3462-3	706	780	913	901	979	1,198
Fabricated metal products [1]	34	5,013	5,576	6,786	5,930	8,546	8,384
Machinery, except electrical	35	14,321	16,823	19,193	21,323	35,507	36,983
Electronic and other electric equipment	36, 3825	10,724	13,878	19,060	25,232	44,179	48,298
Transportation equipment	37, 348	3,115	3,751	4,734	4,472	6,731	7,775
Instruments and related products [2]	38	7,452	8,955	12,255	14,387	20,647	20,980
Nondurable goods:							
Food and kindred products	20	484	546	730	601	926	882
Textile mill products	22	420	495	502	609	741	717
Chemicals and allied products	28	9,880	10,275	12,499	13,565	19,435	20,869
Oil and gas extraction, petroleum products	13, 29	595	802	664	643	752	792
Rubber and miscellaneous plastics products	30	2,607	3,038	3,805	3,936	5,035	5,077
Other industries	(X)	5,281	5,437	7,584	8,247	11,894	11,668

X Not applicable. [1] Excludes SIC groups 3462, 3463, and 348. [2] Excludes SIC group 3825.

Source: U.S. Patent and Trademark Office, *Patenting Trends in the United States, State Country Report, 1963-2001*.

No. 764. Patents by State: 2002

[Includes only U.S. patents granted to residents of the United States and territories]

State	Total	Inventions	Designs	Botanical plants	Reissues	State	Total	Inventions	Designs	Botanical plants	Reissues
U.S.[1]	97,083	86,977	9,325	518	263	Missouri	963	838	117	6	2
Alabama	441	398	38	3	2	Montana	152	138	14	-	-
Alaska	50	43	7	-	-	Nebraska	248	212	36	-	-
Arizona	1,699	1,587	107	-	5	Nevada	368	308	60	-	-
Arkansas	213	184	24	4	1	New Hampshire	657	609	46	-	2
California	21,232	18,829	2,080	267	56	New Jersey	4,096	3,762	311	4	19
Colorado	2,130	1,940	182	-	8	New Mexico	388	371	15	-	2
Connecticut	1,991	1,805	173	2	11	New York	7,073	6,360	692	2	19
Delaware	386	355	31	-	-	North Carolina	2,141	1,822	311	5	3
Dist. of Columbia	65	61	4	-	-	North Dakota	86	73	13	-	-
Florida	2,853	2,397	366	82	8	Ohio	3,961	3,329	621	3	8
Georgia	1,532	1,295	223	12	2	Oklahoma	518	466	47	-	5
Hawaii	90	73	10	7	-	Oregon	1,716	1,450	218	44	4
Idaho	1,877	1,828	47	-	2	Pennsylvania	3,641	3,343	276	10	12
Illinois	3,933	3,470	451	2	10	Rhode Island	311	260	50	1	-
Indiana	1,741	1,397	331	9	4	South Carolina	709	599	108	1	1
Iowa	681	630	49	1	1	South Dakota	90	76	14	-	-
Kansas	503	421	82	-	-	Tennessee	1,003	831	166	6	-
Kentucky	496	450	46	-	-	Texas	6,340	6,030	289	5	16
Louisiana	484	445	34	2	3	Utah	747	675	72	-	-
Maine	168	153	14	-	1	Vermont	509	487	22	-	-
Maryland	1,608	1,460	133	8	7	Virginia	1,299	1,160	135	1	3
Massachusetts	3,837	3,608	214	4	11	Washington	2,300	2,099	187	9	5
Michigan	4,231	3,862	348	5	16	West Virginia	166	151	13	1	1
Minnesota	2,976	2,751	213	4	8	Wisconsin	2,118	1,864	244	6	4
Mississippi	180	156	21	2	1	Wyoming	61	48	13	-	-

- Represents zero. [1] Includes U.S. territories not shown separately.

Source: U.S. Patent and Trademark Office, unpublished data.

No. 765. Copyright Registration by Subject Matter: 1990 to 2002

[In thousands (590.7 represents 590,700). For years ending September 30. Comprises claims to copyrights registered for both U.S. and foreign works. Semiconductor chips and renewals are not considered copyright registration claims]

Subject matter	1990	2000	2001	2002	Subject matter	1990	2000	2001	2002
Total copyright claims	590.7	497.6	580.8	501.0	Works of the visual arts [3]	76.7	85.8	99.9	79.9
Monographs [1]	179.7	169.7	212.1	199.2					
Serials	111.5	69.0	62.2	60.8	Semiconductor chip products	1.0	0.7	0.5	0.5
Sound recordings	37.5	34.2	50.3	37.1	Renewals	51.8	16.8	19.7	19.1
Musical works [2]	185.3	138.9	156.3	124.0					

[1] Includes computer software and machine readable works. [2] Includes dramatic works, accompanying music, choreography, pantomimes, motion pictures, and filmstrips. [3] Two-dimensional works of fine and graphic art, including prints and art reproductions; sculptural works; technical drawings and models; photographs; commercial prints and labels; works of applied arts, cartographic works, and multimedia works.

Source: The Library of Congress, Copyright Office, *Annual Report*.

Business Enterprise 513

No. 766. Net Stock of Private Fixed Assets: 1990 to 2001

[In billions of dollars (12,760 represents $12,760,000,000,000). Estimates as of Dec. 31. Net stock estimates are presented in terms of current cost and cover equipment, software, and structures. Based on the 1987 Standard Industrial Classification]

Industry	1990	1995	1998	1999	2000	2001
Fixed private capital	12,760	15,908	18,650	19,880	21,215	22,190
Agriculture, forestry, and fishing	481	551	620	647	674	696
Farms	447	498	554	575	597	616
Housing	161	187	212	226	238	248
Other	285	312	341	349	359	369
Agricultural services, forestry, and fishing	35	53	67	72	76	79
Mining	431	455	530	531	581	610
Metal mining	29	34	36	36	36	35
Coal mining	32	39	44	45	46	47
Oil and gas extraction	350	360	425	424	471	499
Nonmetallic minerals, except fuels	19	21	25	26	28	29
Construction	82	101	126	137	144	146
Manufacturing	1,217	1,457	1,654	1,714	1,777	1,810
Durable goods	636	747	860	893	932	953
Lumber and wood products	25	29	32	33	34	35
Furniture and fixtures	11	13	15	16	17	17
Stone, clay, and glass products	40	44	53	57	61	63
Primary metal industries	116	126	133	135	136	136
Fabricated metal products	70	82	90	92	95	96
Industrial machinery and equipment	110	126	146	153	160	163
Electronic and other electric equipment	92	120	153	160	174	184
Motor vehicles and equipment	64	85	100	103	105	105
Other transportation equipment	51	55	60	63	64	64
Instruments and related products	45	54	62	66	70	72
Miscellaneous manufacturing industries	12	14	15	16	16	16
Nondurable goods	581	711	794	821	846	858
Food and kindred products	119	146	165	173	180	184
Tobacco products	9	9	10	10	10	10
Textile mill products	34	38	40	40	40	40
Apparel and other textile products	11	13	14	15	15	15
Paper and allied products	84	98	107	108	110	110
Printing and publishing	52	59	66	70	73	74
Chemicals and allied products	157	200	228	237	245	250
Petroleum and coal products	75	93	96	97	98	98
Rubber and miscellaneous plastics products	38	52	64	68	72	73
Leather and leather products	3	3	3	3	3	3
Transportation and public utilities	1,855	2,232	2,471	2,578	2,764	2,869
Transportation	582	692	766	777	817	831
Railroad transportation	304	337	347	340	340	329
Local and interurban passenger transit	21	25	28	33	35	37
Trucking and warehousing	71	99	117	122	127	129
Water transportation	35	37	40	40	41	42
Transportation by air	85	115	145	149	171	191
Pipelines, except natural gas	38	44	47	49	50	50
Transportation services	26	34	41	45	52	54
Communications	436	549	653	712	806	860
Telephone and telegraph	377	458	527	573	650	693
Radio and television	59	91	125	139	156	166
Electric, gas, and sanitary services	837	991	1,052	1,089	1,141	1,178
Electric services	609	696	721	741	778	808
Gas services	165	205	231	242	253	256
Sanitary services	63	90	100	105	110	114
Wholesale trade	286	379	464	501	541	561
Retail trade	391	514	618	658	704	734
Finance, insurance, and real estate	7,466	9,481	11,242	12,091	12,906	13,571
Depository institutions	236	268	300	315	328	332
Nondepository institutions	114	166	232	265	289	297
Security and commodity brokers	40	64	86	98	117	127
Insurance carriers	89	139	167	181	195	202
Insurance agents, brokers, and service	8	13	18	19	21	22
Real estate	6,944	8,779	10,362	11,123	11,855	12,481
Owner-occupied housing	4,337	5,718	6,827	7,377	7,900	8,372
Tenant-occupied housing	1,640	1,880	2,153	2,264	2,382	2,469
Other	967	1,182	1,383	1,482	1,573	1,640
Holding and other investment offices	35	52	77	90	102	110
Services	552	739	925	1,024	1,125	1,193
Hotels and other lodging places	105	125	159	172	184	193
Personal services	27	27	29	30	32	32
Business services	99	131	179	216	251	271
Auto repair, services, and parking	62	111	129	137	145	148
Miscellaneous repair services	9	12	14	15	16	17
Motion pictures	16	28	39	41	41	41
Amusement and recreation services	34	47	58	66	77	86
Other services [1]	200	257	318	348	380	404
Health services	98	135	168	183	199	214
Legal services	18	19	22	24	25	26
Educational services	11	14	18	19	21	22
Other	73	90	111	122	135	142

[1] Consists of social services; museums, botanical and zoological gardens, membership organizations; engineering and management services; and services, not elsewhere classified.

Source: U.S. Bureau of Economic Analysis, *Survey of Current Business*, September 2002.

No. 767. Gross Private Domestic Investment in Current and Real (1996) Dollars: 1990 to 2001

[In billions of dollars (861.7 represents $861,700,000,000). Covers equipment, software, and structures]

Item	1990	1995	1996	1997	1998	1999	2000	2001
CURRENT DOLLARS								
Gross private domestic Investment	861.7	1,143.8	1,242.7	1,390.5	1,538.7	1,636.7	1,755.4	1,586.0
Less: Consumption of fixed capital	579.5	743.6	781.9	832.4	884.3	947.3	1,018.0	1,106.8
Equals: Net private domestic investment	282.2	400.1	460.8	558.1	654.4	689.4	737.4	479.2
Fixed investment	847.2	1,110.7	1,212.7	1,327.7	1,465.6	1,577.2	1,691.8	1,646.3
Less: Consumption of fixed capital	579.5	743.6	781.9	832.4	884.3	947.3	1,018.0	1,106.8
Equals: Net fixed investment	267.7	367.1	430.8	495.2	581.3	629.9	673.9	539.5
Nonresidential	630.3	825.1	899.4	999.4	1,101.2	1,173.5	1,265.8	1,201.6
Residential	216.8	285.6	313.3	328.2	364.4	403.7	426.0	444.8
Change in private inventories	14.5	33.0	30.0	62.9	73.1	59.5	63.6	-60.3
CHAINED (1996) DOLLARS								
Gross private domestic Investment	907.3	1,140.6	1,242.7	1,393.3	1,558.0	1,660.5	1,762.9	1,574.6
Less: Consumption of fixed capital	612.6	742.6	781.9	831.8	894.7	962.2	1,024.0	1,110.7
Equals: Net private domestic investment	294.7	398.0	460.8	561.5	663.3	698.4	738.9	463.9
Fixed investment	894.6	1,109.2	1,212.7	1,328.6	1,480.0	1,595.2	1,691.9	1,627.4
Nonresidential	641.7	817.5	899.4	1,009.3	1,135.9	1,228.4	1,324.2	1,255.1
Residential	253.5	291.7	313.3	319.7	345.1	368.3	372.4	373.5
Change in private inventories	16.5	30.4	30.0	63.8	76.7	62.8	65.0	-61.4

Source: U.S. Bureau of Economic Analysis, *National Income and Product Accounts, Volume 1, 1929-97*, and *Survey of Current Business*, May 2003. See also <http://www.bea.gov/bea/dn/nipaweb/selecttable.asp>.

No. 768. Capital Expenditures: 1998 to 2001

[In billions of dollars (971 represents $971,000,000,000)]

Item	All companies 1998	1999	2000	2001	Companies with employees 1998	1999	2000	2001	Companies without employees 1998	1999	2000	2001
Capital expenditures, total	971	1,047	1,161	1,110	896	975	1,090	1,053	74	72	71	57
Structures	329	320	364	362	300	294	338	344	29	26	26	18
New	284	296	329	334	260	276	309	322	24	20	20	12
Used	45	24	35	28	40	18	29	22	4	6	6	6
Equipment[1]	642	727	797	748	596	681	752	709	46	46	45	39
New	606	690	751	709	570	656	718	682	36	33	32	27
Used	36	37	46	39	26	24	34	27	10	13	12	12
Capital leases	17	17	20	16	16	17	19	16	1	1	(Z)	(Z)
Capitalized interest	(NA)	(NA)	(NA)	(NA)	10	10	11	12	(NA)	(NA)	(NA)	(NA)

NA Not available. Z Less than $500 million. [1] Includes software.

No. 769. Capital Expenditures by Industry: 2000 and 2001

[In billions of dollars (1,090 represents $1,090,000,000,000). Covers only companies with employees. Based on the North American Industry Classification System (NAICS), 1997; see text, this section]

Industry	NAICS code	2000	2001	Industry	NAICS code	2000	2001
Total expenditures	(X)	1,090	1,053	Professional, scientific, and technical services	54	34	30
Forestry, fishing, and agricultural services	113-115	1	2	Management of companies and enterprises	55	5	3
Mining	21	43	51	Admin/support waste mgt/ remediation services	56	18	16
Utilities	22	61	83	Educational services	61	18	17
Construction	23	25	25	Health care and social assistance	62	52	53
Manufacturing	31-33	215	192	Arts, entertainment, and recreation	71	19	15
Durable goods	321, 327, 33	134	118	Accommodation and food services	72	26	21
Nondurable goods	31, 322-326	81	74	Other services (except public administration)	81	21	29
Wholesale trade	42	34	30	Structure and equipment expenditures serving multiple industry categories	(X)	2	1
Retail trade	44-45	70	67				
Transportation and warehousing	48-49	60	57				
Information	51	160	146				
Finance and insurance	52	134	131				
Real estate and rental and leasing	53	92	83				

X Not applicable.

Source of Tables 768 and 769: U.S. Census Bureau, *Annual Capital Expenditures, 2001*, Series ACE.

No. 770. Composite Indexes of Leading, Coincident, and Lagging Economic Indicators: 1990 to 2002

Item	Unit	1990	1995	1999	2000	2001	2002
Leading index, composite	1996=100	94.0	97.6	108.6	109.7	108.6	111.0
Average weekly hours, manufacturing	Hours	40.8	41.6	41.7	41.6	40.7	40.8
Average weekly initial claims for unemployment insurance	1,000	385.4	359.1	296.8	299.4	406.8	404.5
Manufacturers' new orders, consumer goods and materials (1996 dol.)	Mil. dol.	128,882	152,881	179,727	178,761	163,052	165,452
Vendor performance, slower deliveries diffusion index	Percent	47.9	52.8	53.3	53.3	48.0	53.2
Manufacturers' new orders, nondefense capital goods (1996 dol.)	Mil. dol.	36,515	40,986	55,171	63,555	52,882	48,304
Building permits, new private housing units	1,000	1,155	1,336	1,664	1,598	1,639	1,717
Stock prices, 500 common stocks	1941-43=10	334.6	541.6	1,326.1	1,426.8	1,192.1	995.6
Money supply, M2 (1996 dol.)	Bil. dol.	3,769	3,642	4,319	4,468	4,762	5,060
Interest rate spread, 10-year Treasury bonds less federal funds	Percent	0.45	0.74	0.67	-0.21	1.13	2.94
Index of consumer expectations	1966:1=100	70.2	83.2	99.3	102.7	82.3	84.6
Coincident index, composite	1996=100	88.6	97.2	111.9	115.7	115.2	115.0
Employees on nonagricultural payrolls	1,000	109,404	117,188	128,904	131,719	131,925	130,776
Personal income less transfer payments (1996 dol.)	Bil. dol.	5,032	5,429	6,462	6,831	6,859	6,880
Industrial production	1997=100	77.6	89.3	110.1	115.3	111.2	110.4
Manufacturing and trade sales (1996 dol.)	Mil. dol.	593,865	699,548	820,869	848,978	842,186	860,131
Lagging index, composite	1996=100	102.0	99.1	103.8	106.6	105.3	100.7
Average duration of unemployment	Weeks	12.0	16.6	13.4	12.7	13.1	16.7
Inventories to sales ratio, manufacturing and trade (1996 dol.)	Ratio	1.47	1.41	1.38	1.41	1.41	1.33
Change in labor cost per unit of output, manufacturing	Percent	1.7	-2.4	-1.4	1.0	0.1	-1.4
Average prime rate	Percent	10.01	8.83	7.99	9.23	6.92	4.68
Commercial and industrial loans outstanding (1996 dol.)	Mil. dol.	609,060	564,576	758,402	850,665	752,862	609,061
Consumer installment credit to personal income ratio	Percent	16.1	16.7	17.6	17.7	18.7	19.1
Change in consumer price index for services	Percent	5.8	3.5	2.6	3.8	3.9	3.2

Source: The Conference Board, New York, NY 10022-6601, Business Cycle Indicators, monthly, <http://www.globalindicators.org/> (copyright).

No. 771. Business Cycle Expansions and Contractions—Months of Duration: 1919 to 2001

[A trough is the low point of a business cycle; a peak is the high point. Contraction, or recession, is the period from peak to subsequent trough; expansion is the period from trough to subsequent peak. Business cycle reference dates are determined by the National Bureau of Economic Research, Inc.]

Business cycle reference date				Contraction (trough from previous peak)	Expansion (trough to peak)	Length of cycle	
Trough		Peak				Trough from previous trough	Peak from previous peak
Month	Year	Month	Year				
March	1919	January	1920	[1]7	10	[2]51	[1]17
July	1921	May	1923	18	22	28	40
July	1924	October	1926	14	27	36	41
November	1927	August	1929	13	21	40	34
March	1933	May	1937	43	50	64	93
June	1938	February	1945	13	80	63	93
October	1945	November	1948	8	37	88	45
October	1949	July	1953	11	45	48	56
May	1954	August	1957	10	39	55	49
April	1958	April	1960	8	24	47	32
February	1961	December	1969	10	106	34	116
November	1970	November	1973	11	36	117	47
March	1975	January	1980	16	58	52	74
July	1980	July	1981	6	12	64	18
November	1982	July	1990	16	92	28	108
March	1991	March	2001	8	120	100	128
Average, all cycles:							
1854 to 1991 (31 cycles)				18	35	53	[3]53
1854 to 1919 (16 cycles)				22	27	48	[4]49
1919 to 1945 (six cycles)				18	35	53	53
1945 to 1991 (nine cycles)				11	50	61	61
Average, peacetime cycles:							
1854 to 1991 (26 cycles)				19	29	48	[5]48
1854 to 1919 (14 cycles)				22	24	46	[6]47
1919 to 1945 (5 cycles)				20	26	46	45
1945 to 1991 (7 cycles)				11	43	53	53

[1] Previous peak: August 1918. [2] Previous trough: December 1914. [3] 30 cycles. [4] 15 cycles. [5] 25 cycles. [6] 13 cycles.

Source: National Bureau of Economic Research, Inc., Cambridge, MA, "Business Cycle Expansions and Contractions"; <http://www.nber.org/cycles.html>; (accessed: 8 May 2003).

No. 772. Industrial Production Indexes by Industry: 1980 to 2002

[Based on the North American Industry Classification System (NAICS), 1997; see text, this section. Minus sign (-) indicates decrease]

Industry	NAICS code	1980	1985	1990	1991	1992	1993	1994	1995	1996	1997	1998	1999	2000	2001	2002	1999-2000	2000-2001	2001-2002
Total index	(X)	63.3	68.6	77.4	76.1	78.2	80.8	85.1	89.2	93.1	100.0	105.6	110.1	115.3	111.2	110.5	4.7	-3.5	-0.7
Manufacturing	(X)	58.7	65.5	75.0	73.5	76.2	78.8	83.6	88.0	92.1	100.0	106.5	111.8	117.4	112.6	111.4	5.0	-4.1	-1.1
Manufacturing (NAICS)	31-33	57.7	64.2	74.0	72.6	75.4	78.1	83.1	87.8	92.1	100.0	106.5	111.9	117.7	112.8	111.7	5.2	-4.1	-1.0
Durable goods	(X)	49.6	55.9	64.6	62.6	65.7	69.3	75.4	82.0	89.1	100.0	110.3	119.3	129.4	122.9	121.1	3…	-5.0	-1.5
Wood products	321	68.1	75.2	86.7	81.2	85.6	86.6	91.8	93.9	97.1	100.0	104.9	108.9	107.4	99.7	100.5	-1.4	-7.2	0.9
Nonmetallic mineral products	327	77.5	77.7	85.1	78.4	81.9	83.7	88.3	90.6	96.8	100.0	104.8	106.2	106.9	106.9	108.0	0.3	0.0	1.0
Primary metals	331	102.6	75.2	85.5	80.3	82.2	86.2	92.6	93.7	95.9	100.0	102.3	101.7	98.8	88.2	85.6	-2.8	-10.8	-3.0
Fabricated metal products	332	75.9	75.2	78.3	74.8	77.0	79.9	87.0	92.2	95.6	100.0	103.0	103.8	108.2	100.5	99.0	4.2	-7.1	-1.5
Machinery	333	89.2	74.6	79.4	74.2	73.7	78.9	86.3	92.3	95.3	100.0	101.9	99.6	106.6	95.1	87.9	7.0	-10.8	-7.5
Computers and electronic products	334	10.1	20.1	28.8	29.9	33.7	37.1	44.1	57.6	73.9	100.0	128.2	166.4	221.1	223.7	220.4	32.9	1.2	-1.5
Electrical equip, appliances, and components	335	75.3	76.9	79.8	75.6	80.2	85.2	91.4	93.5	96.4	100.0	104.0	105.9	111.0	102.3	97.8	4.9	-7.9	-4.4
Motor vehicles and parts	3361-3	45.0	63.0	64.8	61.7	70.3	77.7	89.3	92.0	92.7	100.0	105.1	116.4	116.3	107.6	117.3	-0.1	-7.5	9.0
Aerospace and other misc transportation equipment	3364-9	104.2	101.1	121.6	117.1	108.2	100.9	90.6	86.1	89.7	100.0	115.7	111.5	100.8	98.4	87.6	-9.6	-2.4	-11.0
Furniture and related products	337	65.8	76.2	81.9	75.7	81.6	85.1	88.0	89.5	90.3	100.0	107.1	110.7	113.7	104.9	101.3	2.7	-7.8	-3.4
Miscellaneous products	339	53.4	61.5	79.1	80.7	84.0	88.8	89.4	92.7	97.4	100.0	105.9	108.1	113.2	108.1	109.6	4.7	-3.4	0.2
Nondurable goods	(X)	70.3	77.0	88.2	87.9	90.1	91.3	94.5	96.2	96.5	100.0	101.4	102.2	102.9	99.8	99.5	0.7	-3.0	-0.3
Food, beverage and tobacco products	311,2	77.0	84.0	91.1	91.9	93.1	92.8	95.9	98.6	98.0	100.0	102.8	100.9	101.9	99.8	100.2	1.0	-1.9	0.2
Textile and product mills	313,4	76.1	77.2	85.8	84.7	89.2	92.8	97.8	98.6	94.7	100.0	98.7	99.0	97.0	86.2	82.5	-2.0	-11.2	-4.3
Apparel and leather	315,6	109.5	106.7	98.1	97.7	100.1	102.2	103.4	102.6	100.3	100.0	94.4	90.4	87.3	77.9	72.2	-3.4	-10.7	-7.3
Paper	322	74.6	81.4	92.4	92.3	94.5	96.5	99.7	101.4	98.0	100.0	101.0	102.2	102.5	95.3	94.6	-1.6	-5.3	-0.7
Printing and related support	323	56.8	76.3	92.5	89.7	94.7	94.8	95.9	97.3	98.0	100.0	100.9	101.9	102.5	98.0	97.8	0.6	-4.4	-0.1
Petroleum and coal products	324	92.1	85.9	91.4	90.1	89.7	90.3	92.8	94.5	94.1	100.0	99.9	101.9	103.6	105.0	102.9	-1.9	0.5	1.3
Chemical	325	65.5	70.0	87.0	86.8	88.0	89.0	91.3	92.7	94.6	100.0	101.3	103.8	105.9	105.3	105.1	2.0	-0.6	-0.1
Plastics and rubber products	326	41.4	56.3	71.9	71.3	76.6	82.0	88.9	91.0	94.2	100.0	103.3	108.5	111.3	105.2	106.0	2.5	-5.5	0.8
Other manufacturing (non-NAICS)[1]	1133, 5111	82.0	94.6	99.0	95.1	93.0	93.8	93.1	93.2	92.5	100.0	106.5	109.9	112.4	109.1	105.5	2.2	-2.9	-3.3
Mining	21	106.4	102.6	98.7	96.5	94.4	94.4	96.6	96.4	98.1	100.0	98.2	94.0	96.0	96.6	93.8	2.2	0.6	-2.9
Utilities	2211,2	72.4	75.9	87.1	88.8	88.0	91.5	92.8	96.4	99.7	100.0	101.5	103.9	106.4	105.6	110.2	2.4	-0.8	4.4
Electric pwr generation, transmsn & distribution	2211	67.8	74.8	87.3	88.9	87.6	91.1	92.4	96.2	99.3	100.0	102.9	105.3	107.7	107.1	111.8	2.3	-0.6	4.4
Natural gas distribution	2212	93.0	81.4	86.0	88.3	90.8	94.2	94.9	97.3	102.0	100.0	93.4	96.1	99.1	97.1	97.5	3.1	-2.0	0.4

X Not applicable. [1] Those industries—logging and newspaper, periodical, book, and directory publishing—that have traditionally been considered to be manufacturing.

Source: Board of Governors of the Federal Reserve System, *Federal Reserve Bulletin*, monthly; and *Industrial Production and Capacity Utilization*, Statistical Release G.17, monthly.

Figure 15.1
Total Industrial Production and Capacity: 1980 to 2002

Source: Charts prepared by U.S. Census Bureau. For data, see Tables 772 and 773.

No. 773. Index of Industrial Capacity: 1980 to 2002

[1997 output=100. Annual figures are averages of monthly data. Capacity represents estimated quantity of output relative to output in 1997 which the current stock of plant and equipment was capable of producing]

Year	Index of capacity		Relation of output to capacity (percent)				
				Stage of process			
	Total industry	Manufacturing	Total industry	Crude [1]	Primary and semifinished [2]	Finished [3]	Manufacturing
1980	78.3	74.6	80.9	89.2	78.8	79.7	78.8
1985	86.4	83.4	79.4	83.3	79.9	77.3	78.4
1990	93.9	91.9	82.5	88.9	82.3	80.7	81.6
1991	95.7	93.9	79.6	86.1	79.4	77.9	78.3
1992	97.6	96.0	80.1	85.6	80.8	78.0	79.3
1993	99.6	98.5	81.1	85.4	82.8	78.0	80.0
1994	102.2	101.4	83.3	87.3	86.0	79.0	82.4
1995	106.7	106.4	83.6	88.3	86.3	79.3	82.8
1996	112.9	113.4	82.5	87.8	85.0	78.3	81.2
1997	119.5	120.9	83.7	89.1	85.6	80.1	82.7
1998	127.5	130.0	82.9	86.0	84.0	80.9	81.9
1999	133.7	137.3	82.4	86.3	84.4	79.2	81.4
2000	139.4	144.1	82.7	88.0	84.8	78.9	81.4
2001	143.9	149.1	77.3	84.0	78.6	74.3	75.6
2002	146.0	151.0	75.6	83.2	77.7	71.4	73.8

[1] Crude processing, covers a relatively small portion of total industrial capacity and consists of logging (NAICS 1133), much of mining (excluding stone, sand, and gravel mining and oil and gas drilling, which are NAICS 21231, 21221-2, and 213111) and some basic manufacturing industries, including basic chemicals (NAICS 3251); fertilizers, pesticides, and other agricultural chemicals (NAICS 32531,2); pulp, paper, and paperboard mills (NAICS 3221); and alumina, aluminum, and other nonferrous production and processing mills (NAICS 3313,4). [2] Primary and semifinished processing loosely corresponds to the previously published aggregate, primary processing. Includes utilities and portions of several two-digit SIC industries included in the former advanced processing group. These include printing and related support activities (NAICS 3231); paints and adhesives (NAICS 3255); and newspaper, periodical, book, and directory publishers (NAICS 5111). [3] Finished processing generally corresponds to the previously published aggregate, advanced processing. Includes oil and gas well drilling and carpet and rug mills.

Source: Board of Governors of the Federal Reserve System, *Industrial Production and Capacity Utilization*, G.17 (419), monthly.

No. 774. Manufacturing and Trade—Sales and Inventories: 1993 to 2002

[In billions of dollars (565 represents $565,000,000,000), except ratios. Based on North American Industry Classification System (NAICS), 1997; see text, this section]

Item	1993	1994	1995	1996	1997	1998	1999	2000	2001	2002
Sales, average monthly [1]	565	607	650	682	718	737	781	828	813	821
Manufacturing [2]	249	266	284	294	313	319	329	344	325	321
Retail trade	166	180	189	201	210	220	240	256	263	270
Merchant wholesalers	151	161	176	187	195	198	212	229	226	229
Inventories [3]	864	927	985	1,004	1,044	1,076	1,136	1,198	1,132	1,156
Manufacturing [2]	376	396	421	426	438	443	457	477	439	431
Retail trade	286	312	330	341	351	365	394	418	406	436
Merchant wholesalers	202	219	235	238	255	268	285	302	288	289
Inventory-sales ratios [4]	1.51	1.47	1.49	1.47	1.43	1.44	1.41	1.42	1.44	1.38
Manufacturing [2]	1.51	1.45	1.45	1.44	1.38	1.39	1.36	1.37	1.42	1.34
Retail trade	1.68	1.66	1.72	1.67	1.64	1.62	1.59	1.59	1.58	1.56
Merchant wholesalers	1.31	1.30	1.30	1.28	1.27	1.32	1.31	1.30	1.32	1.25

[1] Averages of monthly not seasonally adjusted figures. [2] Beginning with data for March 2002, the Census Bureau announced that because of data availability, monthly estimates for shipments, order, and inventories would no longer include data on semiconductors. Historical data have been revised to exclude data on semiconductors. [3] Seasonally adjusted end-of-year data. [4] Averages of seasonally adjusted monthly ratios.

Source: U.S. Council of Economic Advisors, *Economic Indicators*, April 2003.

No. 775. Corporate Profits, Taxes, and Dividends: 1990 to 2002

[In billions of dollars (409 represents $409,000,000,000). Covers corporations organized for profit and other entities treated as corporations. Represents profits to U.S. residents, without deduction of depletion charges and exclusive of capital gains and losses; intercorporate dividends from profits of domestic corporations are eliminated; net receipts of dividends, reinvested earnings of incorporated foreign affiliates, and earnings of unincorporated foreign affiliates are added]

Item	1990	1995	1998	1999	2000	2001	2002
Corporate profits with IVA and CCA	409	669	777	806	788	732	787
Corporate profits with IVA	389	650	739	758	767	675	658
Profits before tax	402	668	721	762	782	670	665
Profits tax liability	141	211	239	248	259	199	213
Profits after tax	261	458	482	514	523	471	452
Dividends	166	254	349	328	376	410	434
Undistributed profits	95	203	134	186	147	61	18
Inventory valuation adjustment (IVA)	-13	-18	18	-4	-15	5	-7
Capital consumption adjustment (CCA)	20	19	38	48	21	57	129
Addenda:							
Corporate profits after tax with IVA/CCA [1]	268	458	539	558	529	532	574
Net cash flow with IVA/CCA [1]	494	716	810	895	874	912	967
Undistributed profits with IVA/CCA [1]	102	204	190	230	153	123	140
Consumption of fixed capital	391	512	620	666	721	789	828
Less: Inventory valuation adjustment (IVA)	-13	-18	18	-4	-15	5	-7
Equals: Net cash flow	506	734	792	899	889	907	974

[1] Inventory valuation adjustment/capital consumption adjustment.

Source: U.S. Bureau of Economic Analysis, *National Income and Product Accounts, Volume 1, 1929-97*, and *Survey of Current Business*, monthly. See also <http://www.bea.gov/bea/dn/nipaweb/selecttable.asp>.

No. 776. Corporate Profits Before Taxes by Industry: 1990 to 2001

[In millions of dollars (401,534 represents $401,534,000,000). Profits are without inventory valuation and capital consumption adjustments. Minus sign (-) indicates loss. Based on the 1987 Standard Industrial Classification code. See headnote, Table 775]

Industry	SIC code	1990	1995	1997	1998	1999	2000	2001
Corporate profits before tax	(X)	401,534	668,454	792,396	721,107	762,105	782,293	670,159
Domestic industries	(X)	328,812	576,442	681,706	618,848	641,870	638,957	519,399
Agriculture, forestry, and fishing	A	1,638	1,842	3,059	3,019	4,534	4,785	5,121
Mining	B	2,502	4,517	10,972	2,115	404	11,623	15,766
Construction	C	10,922	17,265	25,696	32,531	38,022	40,815	39,375
Manufacturing	D	113,552	172,518	192,312	153,035	157,686	168,332	84,143
Transportation and public utilities	E	45,931	85,894	83,991	78,867	57,813	37,387	26,210
Transportation	40-47	954	11,613	18,639	21,013	15,628	13,102	652
Communications	48	20,049	33,604	25,570	22,684	6,008	-5,591	-6,046
Electric, gas, and sanitary services	49	24,928	40,677	39,782	35,170	36,177	29,876	31,604
Wholesale trade	F	21,201	35,546	46,315	49,044	55,101	64,549	41,164
Retail trade	G	24,896	47,471	62,648	74,172	77,637	75,773	78,962
Finance, insurance, and real estate	H	88,334	160,062	195,658	174,415	197,925	222,617	211,099
Services	I	19,836	51,327	61,055	51,650	52,748	13,076	17,559
Rest of the world [1]	(X)	72,722	92,012	110,690	102,259	120,235	143,336	150,760

X Not applicable. [1] Consists of receipts by all U.S. residents, including both corporations and persons, of dividends from their incorporated foreign affiliates, their share of reinvested earnings of their incorporated foreign affiliates, and earnings of unincorporated foreign affiliates, net of corresponding payments.

Source: U.S. Bureau of Economic Analysis, *National Income and Product Accounts, Volume 1, 1929-1997*, and *Survey of Current Business*, August 2002. See also <http://www.bea.gov/bea/dn/nipaweb/selecttable.asp>.

No. 777. Corporate Profits With Inventory Valuation and Capital Consumption Adjustments—Financial and Nonfinancial Industries: 1990 to 2002

[In billions of dollars (409 represents $409,000,000,000). Based on the 1987 Standard Industrial Classification code. See headnote, Table 775]

Item	1990	1995	1997	1998	1999	2000	2001	2002
Corporate profits with IVA/CCA [1]	409	669	834	777	806	788	732	787
Domestic industries	336	577	723	675	686	645	581	668
Rest of the world	73	92	111	102	120	143	151	119
Corporate profits with IVA [1]	389	650	801	739	758	767	675	658
Domestic industries	316	558	690	637	638	624	524	539
Financial	92	154	186	158	182	201	191	217
Nonfinancial	224	404	505	479	456	423	334	322
Manufacturing	109	166	195	164	158	160	83	93
Transportation and public utilities	44	86	85	79	57	37	28	17
Wholesale trade	19	29	49	56	54	62	45	47
Retail trade	21	44	64	74	76	73	79	81
Other	31	79	111	106	111	91	99	84
Rest of the world	73	92	111	102	120	143	151	119

[1] Inventory valuation adjustment and capital consumption adjustment.

Source: U.S. Bureau of Economic Analysis, *National Income and Product Accounts, Volume 1, 1929-97*, and *Survey of Current Business*, monthly. See also <http://www.bea.gov/bea/dn/nipaweb/selecttable.asp>.

No. 778. Manufacturing, Mining, and Trade Corporations—Profits and Stockholders' Equity by Industry: 2001 and 2002

[Averages of quarterly figures at annual rates. Manufacturing data exclude estimates for corporations with less than $250,000 in assets at time of sample selection. Based on sample; see source for discussion of methodology. Based on North American Industry Classification System, 1997; see text, this section. Minus sign (-) indicates loss]

Industry	NAICS code	Ratio of profits after taxes to stockholders' equity (percent) 2001	2002	Profits after taxes per dollar of sales (cents) 2001	2002	Ratio of stockholders' equity to debt 2001	2002
Manufacturing	31-33	2.0	8.1	0.8	3.5	1.4	1.4
Nondurable manufacturing	(X)	14.8	15.5	5.6	6.2	1.2	1.2
Food	311	13.9	18.4	3.2	4.7	0.8	0.9
Beverage and tobacco products	312	27.8	36.2	10.2	15.3	0.8	0.8
Textile mills and textile product mills	313, 314	1.3	4.5	0.4	1.3	0.9	1.0
Apparel and leather products	315, 316	17.5	19.2	4.2	5.4	0.9	1.2
Paper	322	1.2	4.0	0.4	1.7	0.8	0.8
Printing and related support activities	323	8.7	18.9	1.8	3.7	0.8	0.8
Petroleum and coal products	324	16.5	8.9	7.4	4.3	2.8	2.2
Chemicals	325	17.0	19.3	8.3	9.1	1.1	1.1
Plastics and rubber products	326	1.8	11.7	0.5	3.4	0.9	0.9
Durable manufacturing	(X)	-7.0	2.5	-3.3	1.1	1.7	1.7
Wood products	321	4.3	8.3	1.0	1.9	1.1	0.9
Nonmetallic mineral products	327	-3.7	-2.7	-1.4	-1.1	1.1	1.0
Primary metals	331	-6.3	-4.0	-2.3	-1.4	1.0	1.0
Fabricated metal products	332	7.6	10.5	2.5	3.5	1.1	1.2
Machinery	333	6.3	-2.9	2.7	-1.5	1.3	1.3
Computer and electronic products	334	-24.4	-4.7	-20.3	-4.3	3.4	3.0
Electrical equipment, appliances, and components	335	16.1	19.6	8.6	10.6	2.6	2.7
Transportation equipment	336	-0.6	6.5	-0.1	1.6	1.2	1.4
Furniture and related products	337	7.9	14.1	2.3	3.8	1.6	1.5
Miscellaneous manufacturing	339	9.2	15.7	4.6	8.4	1.4	1.7
All mining	21	10.0	3.9	8.9	5.2	1.7	1.6
All wholesale trade	42	5.4	10.4	0.8	1.7	1.2	1.4
Durable goods	421	2.0	8.2	0.4	1.6	1.2	1.4
Nondurable goods	422	10.4	13.4	1.2	1.7	1.2	1.3
All retail trade	44-45	10.1	14.2	1.8	2.6	1.2	1.3
Food and beverage stores	445	14.4	16.9	1.8	2.1	0.8	0.8
Clothing and general merchandise stores	448, 452	9.1	12.6	1.9	2.7	1.3	1.3
All other retail trade	(X)	9.4	15.1	1.7	2.8	1.4	1.6

X Not applicable.

Source: U.S. Census Bureau, *Quarterly Financial Report for Manufacturing, Mining, and Trade Corporations.*

No. 779. Gross Product, Employment, and Capital Expenditures of Nonbank U.S. MNCs, U.S. Parents, and Foreign Affiliates: 1989 to 2000

[Gross product and capital expenditures in billions of dollars (1,365 represents $1,365,000,000,000); employees in thousands. See headnote, Table 780. MNC=Multinational company. MOFA=Majority-owned foreign affiliate. Minus sign (-) indicates decrease]

Item	1989	1990	1994	1995	1999[1]	2000[1]	Percent change at annual rates 1989-1999	1994-1999	1999-2000
GROSS PRODUCT									
MNCs worldwide:									
Parents and all affiliates	(NA)	(NA)	(NA)	(NA)	(NA)	(NA)	(NA)	(NA)	(NA)
Parents and MOFAs	1,365	(NA)	1,717	1,831	2,481	2,695	5.7	7.6	8.7
Parents	1,045	(NA)	1,314	1,365	1,914	2,089	5.6	7.8	9.1
Affiliates, total	(NA)	(NA)	(NA)	(NA)	(NA)	(NA)	(NA)	(NA)	(NA)
MOFAs	320	356	404	466	566	606	5.8	7.0	7.0
Other	(NA)	(NA)	(NA)	(NA)	(NA)	(NA)	(NA)	(NA)	(NA)
EMPLOYEES									
MNCs worldwide:									
Parents and all affiliates	25,388	25,264	25,670	25,921	32,227	32,774	1.8	4.7	1.7
Parents and MOFAs	23,879	23,786	24,273	24,500	30,773	31,232	1.9	4.9	1.5
Parents	18,765	18,430	18,565	18,576	23,007	23,167	1.3	4.4	0.7
Affiliates, total	6,622	6,834	7,105	7,345	9,220	9,607	3.0	5.4	4.2
MOFAs	5,114	5,356	5,707	5,924	7,766	8,065	3.9	6.4	3.8
Other	1,508	1,478	1,398	1,421	1,454	1,542	-0.5	0.8	6.0
CAPITAL EXPENDITURES									
MNCs worldwide:									
Parents and all affiliates	277	(NA)	328	(NA)	514	(NA)	6.1	9.4	(NA)
Parents and MOFAs	260	275	303	324	483	520	6.1	9.7	7.6
Parents	202	213	232	248	370	406	5.9	9.8	9.8
Affiliates, total	75	(NA)	96	(NA)	144	(NA)	6.8	8.4	(NA)
MOFAs	59	62	71	76	113	114	6.8	9.7	0.3
Other	16	(NA)	25	(NA)	31	(NA)	6.7	4.5	(NA)

NA Not available. [1] Data for 1999 and 2000 are not strictly comparable with data prior to 1999; see source.

Source: U.S. Bureau of Economic Analysis, *Survey of Current Business,* December 2002.

Business Enterprise 521

No. 780. U.S. Multinational Companies—Selected Characteristics: 2000

[Preliminary. In billions of dollars (12,663 represents $12,663,000,000,000), except as indicated. Consists of nonbank U.S. parent companies and their nonbank foreign affiliates. U.S. parent comprises the domestic operations of a multinational and is a U.S. person that owns or controls directly or indirectly, 10 percent or more of the voting securities of an incorporated foreign business enterprise, or an equivalent interest in an unincorporated foreign business enterprise. A U.S. person can be an incorporated business enterprise. A majority-owned foreign affiliate (MOFA) is a foreign business enterprise in which a U.S. parent company owns or controls 50 percent or more of the voting securities]

Industry [1]	NAICS code	U.S. parents Total assets	U.S. parents Capital expenditures	U.S. parents Gross product	U.S. parents Employment (1,000)	MOFAs Capital expenditures	MOFAs Gross product	MOFAs Employment (1,000)
All industries............	(X)	12,663	406.0	2,089	23,167	113.6	606	8,065
Mining............	21	132	10.5	29	120	19.8	60	137
Utilities............	22	553	25.7	78	348	4.8	11	58
Manufacturing [2]............	31-33	4,057	170.2	1,007	9,237	45.3	317	4,353
Food............	311	163	6.7	51	678	2.6	19	356
Beverages and tobacco products............	312	161	4.2	45	254	1.5	19	161
Petroleum and coal products............	324	420	27.0	120	273	2.3	53	43
Chemicals [2]............	325	591	20.6	143	981	9.5	58	559
Pharmaceuticals and medicines............	3254	249	8.6	66	355	3.4	26	200
Machinery............	333	205	6.2	61	713	1.5	18	344
Computers and electronic products [2]............	334	525	28.3	150	1,251	9.2	42	777
Semiconductors and other electronic components............	3344	156	10.0	54	378	5.6	15	316
Transportation equipment [2]............	336	1,288	44.2	221	2,127	8.6	49	872
Motor vehicles, bodies and trailers, and parts............	3361-3363	801	29.2	134	1,108	8.4	46	832
Wholesale trade............	42	350	16.4	76	822	7.0	87	669
Information [2]............	51	1,325	83.1	304	2,027	11.0	22	333
Broadcasting and telecommunications [2]............	513	984	74.6	209	1,323	9.6	7	126
Telecommunications............	5133	742	67.9	182	975	(D)	8	110
Finance (except depository institutions) and insurance [2]............	52 exc. 521, 522	5,138	25.9	138	1,429	5.4	23	310
Securities, commodity contracts, and other intermediation............	5231	1,783	10.7	75	440	1.3	13	97
Professional, scientific, and technical services [2]............	54	230	15.0	103	1,040	4.2	33	423
Computer systems design and related services............	5415	124	11.6	44	388	2.4	17	172
Other industries [2]............	(X)	877	59.1	355	8,143	16.1	52	1,783
Retail trade............	44-45	337	25.1	147	3,753	3.1	18	553
Transportation and warehousing............	48-49	186	13.1	81	1,007	1.1	6	116

D Data withheld to avoid disclosure. X Not applicable. [1] Represents North American Industry Classification System, 1997, based industry of U.S. parent or industry of foreign affiliate. [2] Includes other industries not shown separately. See text, this section.

Source: U.S. Bureau of Economic Analysis, *Survey of Current Business*, December 2002.

No. 781. U.S. Multinational Companies—Gross Product: 1999 and 2000

[In billions of dollars (2,480.7 represents $2,480,700,000,000). Gross product measures valued added by a firm. See headnote, Table 780. Data are by industry of U.S. parent. Based on the North American Industry Classification System, 1997, (NAICS). See text, this section]

Industry	NAICS code	U.S. multinationals 1999	U.S. multinationals 2000	U.S. parents 1999	U.S. parents 2000	Majority-owned foreign affiliates 1999	Majority-owned foreign affiliates 2000
All industries............	(X)	2,480.7	2,695.3	1,914.3	2,089.4	566.4	605.9
Mining............	21	36.8	50.9	18.7	28.6	18.1	22.3
Utilities............	22	98.3	85.8	90.1	77.8	8.2	8.0
Manufacturing [1]............	31-33	1,308.6	1,415.2	931.2	1,006.6	377.5	408.6
Food............	311	62.5	65.5	48.9	50.8	13.6	14.7
Beverages and tobacco products............	312	74.8	67.0	47.3	45.3	27.5	21.7
Petroleum and coal products............	324	172.7	234.2	82.8	119.9	89.8	114.2
Chemicals [1]............	325	206.0	214.0	134.0	142.7	72.0	71.4
Pharmaceuticals and medicines............	3254	90.0	99.2	56.1	65.8	33.9	33.4
Machinery............	333	69.4	81.6	51.0	60.8	18.4	20.8
Computers and electronic products [1]............	334	143.1	196.4	106.1	149.8	37.0	46.6
Semiconductors and other electronic components............	3344	52.9	69.7	39.1	54.2	13.8	15.5
Transportation equipment [1]............	336	304.2	286.7	236.7	221.4	67.5	65.2
Motor vehicles, bodies and trailers, and parts............	3361-3363	182.5	184.7	132.0	134.4	50.5	50.3
Wholesale trade............	42	110.0	103.4	80.6	76.1	29.4	27.2
Information [1]............	51	270.7	327.5	248.9	303.6	21.8	23.9
Broadcasting and telecommunications [1]............	513	188.1	217.9	180.4	209.2	7.8	8.8
Telecommunications............	5133	155.2	189.2	149.7	182.1	5.5	7.1
Finance (except depository institutions) and insurance [1]............	52 exc. 521, 522	134.2	160.2	109.0	138.5	25.2	21.7
Securities, commodity contracts, and other intermediation............	5231	59.3	84.9	49.1	74.8	10.2	10.2
Professional, scientific, and technical services [1]............	54	135.0	143.0	96.1	103.0	38.9	40.0
Computer systems design and related services............	5415	70.3	73.4	42.2	44.2	28.1	29.2
Other industries [1]............	(X)	387.2	409.3	339.7	355.2	47.4	54.0
Retail trade............	44-45	147.5	165.7	134.6	147.3	13.0	18.4
Transportation and warehousing............	48-49	93.0	88.4	87.1	80.8	5.9	7.6

X Not applicable. [1] Includes other industries not shown separately.

Source: U.S. Bureau of Economic Analysis, *Survey of Current Business*, December 2002

Section 16
Science and Technology

This section presents statistics on scientific, engineering, and technological resources, with emphasis on patterns of research and development (R&D) funding and on scientific, engineering, and technical personnel; education; and employment. Also included are statistics on space program outlays and accomplishments. Principal sources of these data are the National Science Foundation (NSF) and the National Aeronautics and Space Administration (NASA).

NSF gathers data chiefly through recurring surveys. Current NSF publications containing data on funds for research and development and on scientific and engineering personnel include detailed statistical tables; issue briefs; and annual, biennial, triennial, and special reports. Titles or the areas of coverage of these reports include the following: *Science and Engineering Indicators; National Patterns of R&D Resources; Women, Minorities, and Persons with Disabilities in Science and Engineering*—science and technology data presented in chart and tabular form in a pocket-sized publication—*Federal Funds for Research and Development; Federal R&D Funding by Budget Function; Federal Support to Universities, Colleges, and Selected Nonprofit Institutions; Research and Development in Industry;* R&D expenditures and graduate enrollment and support in academic science and engineering; and characteristics of doctoral scientists and engineers and of recent graduates in the United States. Statistical surveys in these areas pose problems of concept and definition and the data should therefore be regarded as broad estimates rather than precise, quantitative statements. See sources for methodological and technical details.

The National Science Board's biennial *Science and Engineering Indicators* contains data and analysis of international and domestic science and technology, including measures of inputs and outputs.

The *Budget of the United States Government,* published by the U.S. Office of Management and Budget, contains summary financial data on federal R&D programs.

Research and development outlays—NSF defines research as "systematic study directed toward fuller scientific knowledge of the subject studied" and development as "the systematic use of scientific knowledge directed toward the production of useful materials, devices, systems, or methods, including design and development of prototypes and processes."

National coverage of R&D expenditures is developed primarily from periodic surveys in four principal economic sectors: (1) *Government,* made up primarily of federal executive agencies; (2) *industry,* consisting of manufacturing and nonmanufacturing firms and the federally funded research and development centers (FFRDCs) they administer; (3) *universities and colleges,* composed of universities, colleges, and their affiliated institutions, agricultural experiment stations, and associated schools of agriculture and of medicine, and FFRDCs administered by educational institutions; and (4) *other nonprofit institutions,* consisting of such organizations as private philanthropic foundations, nonprofit research institutes, voluntary health agencies, and FFRDCs administered by nonprofit organizations.

The R&D funds reported consist of current operating costs, including planning and administration costs, except as otherwise noted. They exclude funds for routine testing, mapping and surveying, collection of general-purpose data, dissemination of scientific information, and training of scientific personnel.

Scientists, engineers, and technicians—Scientists and engineers are defined as persons engaged in scientific and engineering work at a level requiring a knowledge of sciences equivalent at least to that acquired through completion of a 4-year college course. Technicians are defined as persons engaged in technical work at a level requiring knowledge acquired through a technical institute, junior college, or other type of training less extensive than 4-year college training. Craftsmen and skilled workers are excluded.

No. 782. Research and Development (R&D) Expenditures by Source and Objective: 1970 to 2002

[In millions of dollars (26,280 represents $26,280,000,000) except as indicated. For calendar years]

Year	Total	Sources of funds					Objective (percent of total)			Character of work		
		Federal government	Industry	Universities/ colleges	Nonprofit	Nonfederal government [1]	Defense related [2]	Space related [3]	Other	Basic research	Applied research	Development
1970	26,280	14,993	10,449	259	343	237	33	10	57	3,592	5,737	16,950
1971	26,980	15,239	10,824	290	366	262	33	10	57	3,723	5,853	17,404
1972	28,739	16,038	11,715	312	393	282	33	8	59	3,849	6,148	18,742
1973	31,003	16,639	13,299	343	422	302	32	7	61	4,106	6,660	20,237
1974	33,398	17,326	14,885	393	474	320	29	7	64	4,513	7,354	21,532
1975	35,753	18,615	15,824	432	534	348	28	8	64	4,883	8,105	22,765
1976	39,471	20,328	17,702	480	592	369	27	8	65	5,376	8,999	25,096
1977	43,368	22,101	19,642	569	662	394	27	7	66	6,013	9,668	27,687
1978	48,740	24,434	22,457	679	727	443	26	6	68	6,961	10,708	31,070
1979	55,407	27,253	26,097	785	791	482	25	6	69	7,840	12,103	35,463
1980	63,240	30,002	30,929	920	871	519	24	5	71	8,794	13,751	40,695
1981	72,293	33,740	35,948	1,058	967	581	24	5	71	9,828	16,409	46,057
1982	80,808	37,194	40,692	1,207	1,095	621	26	5	69	10,821	18,291	51,696
1983	90,010	41,511	45,264	1,357	1,220	658	28	4	68	12,064	20,406	57,540
1984	102,282	46,508	52,187	1,514	1,351	721	29	3	68	13,483	22,526	66,273
1985	114,692	52,662	57,962	1,743	1,491	834	30	3	67	14,854	25,410	74,428
1986	120,285	54,659	60,991	2,019	1,647	969	31	3	66	17,253	27,257	75,775
1987	126,249	58,498	62,576	2,262	1,849	1,065	32	3	65	18,547	27,852	79,850
1988	133,898	60,148	67,977	2,527	2,081	1,165	30	4	66	19,801	29,528	84,569
1989	141,921	60,495	74,966	2,852	2,333	1,274	28	4	68	21,914	32,280	87,727
1990	151,978	61,596	83,208	3,187	2,589	1,399	25	4	71	23,018	34,907	94,053
1991	160,891	60,799	92,300	3,457	2,852	1,483	22	4	74	27,143	38,648	95,101
1992	165,250	60,815	96,229	3,568	3,113	1,525	22	4	74	27,608	37,915	99,726
1993	165,782	60,581	96,549	3,708	3,387	1,557	21	4	75	28,742	37,297	99,744
1994	169,212	60,787	99,203	3,937	3,664	1,622	20	5	75	29,650	36,623	102,939
1995	183,617	62,965	110,870	4,109	3,924	1,750	19	4	77	29,647	40,856	113,115
1996	197,288	63,341	123,416	4,434	4,238	1,860	18	4	78	32,770	43,160	121,359
1997	212,121	64,548	136,227	4,836	4,589	1,921	17	4	79	36,903	46,547	128,671
1998	226,305	66,340	147,843	5,168	4,984	1,970	16	4	80	35,252	46,364	144,689
1999	243,517	67,015	163,229	5,630	5,549	2,095	15	3	82	38,710	51,864	152,943
2000	264,725	66,371	183,703	6,205	6,204	2,242	13	2	85	42,367	56,511	165,847
2001 [4]	273,565	72,637	184,978	6,819	6,756	2,375	14	2	84	46,723	63,609	163,233
2002 [4]	276,185	78,185	180,769	7,455	7,304	2,472	15	2	83	49,567	64,802	161,816

[1] Nonfederal R&D expenditures to university and college performers. [2] R&D spending by the Department of Defense, including space activities, and a portion of the Department of Energy funds. [3] For the National Aeronautics and Space Administration only. [4] Preliminary.

Source: U.S. National Science Foundation, *National Patterns of R&D Resources*, annual. See also <http://www.nsf.gov/sbe/srs/nsf99335/pdf/nsf99335.pdf> (released June 2003).

No. 783. Performance Sector of R&D Expenditures: 1995 to 2002

[In millions of dollars (183,617 represents $183,617,000,000). For calendar year. FFRDCs are federally funded research and development centers. For most academic institutions and the federal government before 1997 began on July 1 instead of October 1]

Year	Total	Federal government	Industry Total	Industry Funded by Federal government	Industry Funded by Industry [1]	Industry FFRDCs	Universities and colleges Total	U&C Federal government	U&C Nonfederal government [2]	U&C Industry	U&C Universities & colleges	U&C Non-profits	U&C Universities & colleges FFRDCs [3]	Other nonprofit institutions Total	Other Federal government	Other Industry	Other Nonprofits FFRDCs
RESEARCH AND DEVELOPMENT TOTAL																	
1995	183,617	16,904	129,830	21,178	108,652	2,279	22,603	13,582	1,750	1,547	4,109	1,616	5,367	5,827	2,847	671	2,308
1998	226,305	17,362	167,102	22,086	145,016	2,062	26,151	15,147	1,970	1,947	5,168	1,919	5,559	7,225	3,281	880	3,064
1999	243,517	17,851	180,712	20,536	160,176	1,999	28,135	16,223	2,095	2,077	5,630	2,110	5,652	8,175	3,761	975	3,440
2000	264,725	17,917	197,604	17,183	180,421	1,935	30,633	17,681	2,242	2,180	6,205	2,327	5,741	9,429	4,449	1,103	3,877
2001, prel.	273,565	21,048	198,505	16,899	181,606	1,965	33,295	19,332	2,375	2,263	6,819	2,507	5,957	10,667	5,309	1,110	4,248
2002, prel.	276,185	23,788	194,430	17,085	177,345	2,235	36,019	21,066	2,472	2,341	7,455	2,685	6,060	11,620	5,918	1,083	4,619
BASIC RESEARCH																	
1995	29,647	2,689	5,569	190	5,379	575	15,139	9,629	1,069	945	2,509	987	2,702	2,899	1,170	390	1,338
1998	35,252	3,003	5,853	1,002	4,851	564	19,309	11,875	1,331	1,315	3,491	1,296	2,660	3,651	1,461	489	1,701
1999	38,710	3,347	6,571	1,209	5,362	546	20,900	12,773	1,429	1,417	3,841	1,439	2,765	4,185	1,734	541	1,910
2000	42,367	3,765	6,960	943	6,017	529	22,760	13,887	1,536	1,493	4,250	1,594	2,873	4,864	2,099	612	2,153
2001, prel.	46,723	4,317	7,911	754	7,157	537	24,646	15,127	1,619	1,542	4,649	1,709	2,912	5,495	2,520	616	2,359
2002, prel.	49,567	4,617	7,751	762	6,989	611	26,678	16,484	1,685	1,596	5,082	1,830	2,962	6,020	2,854	601	2,565
APPLIED RESEARCH																	
1995	40,856	4,952	26,919	3,164	23,755	459	5,655	2,775	559	494	1,311	516	1,050	1,692	934	170	589
1998	46,364	5,146	32,208	2,632	29,576	241	5,215	2,286	524	518	1,375	511	1,372	2,060	1,060	223	777
1999	51,864	5,530	36,418	3,109	33,309	272	5,843	2,739	546	542	1,467	550	1,251	2,420	1,301	247	872
2000	56,511	6,105	38,818	2,688	36,130	263	6,688	3,342	579	563	1,603	601	1,329	3,099	1,837	279	983
2001, prel.	63,609	7,164	43,486	3,603	39,883	267	7,350	3,706	620	591	1,780	654	1,473	3,567	2,209	281	1,077
2002, prel.	64,802	8,083	42,590	3,643	38,947	304	8,007	4,105	645	611	1,946	701	1,645	3,901	2,456	275	1,171
DEVELOPMENT																	
1995	113,115	9,262	97,342	17,824	79,518	1,246	1,810	1,178	123	108	288	113	1,616	1,236	744	111	381
1998	144,689	9,214	129,041	18,452	110,589	1,257	1,628	985	115	114	302	112	1,527	1,515	760	168	586
1999	152,943	8,974	137,724	16,219	121,505	1,180	1,392	711	120	119	322	121	1,636	1,570	726	187	658
2000	165,847	8,047	151,826	13,552	138,274	1,143	1,186	451	127	124	352	132	1,539	1,466	513	211	742
2001, prel.	163,233	9,567	147,108	12,542	134,566	1,160	1,299	499	136	130	391	144	1,571	1,606	581	212	813
2002, prel.	161,816	11,088	144,088	12,680	131,409	1,320	1,334	477	142	134	427	154	1,452	1,699	608	207	884

[1] For R&D funded by the federal government. FFRDCs are federally funded research and development centers. [2] Includes all nonfederal sources. [3] Includes all R&D expenditures of FFRDCs administered by academic institutions and funded by the federal government.

Source: National Science Foundation. Data derived from: *Research and Development in Industry*, annual; *Academic Research and Development Expenditures*, annual; and *Federal Funds For Research and Development*, annual. Also see <http://www.nsf.gov/sbe/srs/nprdr/start.htm>.

Science and Technology   525

No. 784. National R&D Expenditures as a Percent of Gross Domestic Product by Country: 1985 to 2001

Year	Total R&D						Nondefense R&D [1]					
	United States	Japan	Unified Germany	France	United Kingdom	Italy	United States	Japan	Unified Germany	France	United Kingdom	Italy
1985..	2.72	2.54	2.75	2.22	2.24	1.12	1.9	2.5	2.6	1.8	1.8	1.1
1990..	2.62	2.78	2.75	2.37	2.15	1.29	2.0	2.8	2.6	1.9	1.7	1.3
1995..	2.48	2.69	2.26	2.31	1.95	1.00	2.0	2.7	2.2	2.0	1.7	1.0
1996..	2.53	2.77	2.26	2.30	1.88	1.01	2.1	2.7	2.2	2.0	1.6	1.0
1997..	2.55	2.83	2.29	2.22	1.81	1.05	2.1	2.8	2.2	2.0	1.5	1.1
1998..	2.58	2.94	2.31	2.17	1.80	1.07	2.2	2.9	2.3	2.0	1.5	1.1
1999..	2.63	2.94	2.44	2.19	1.88	1.04	2.2	2.9	2.4	2.0	1.6	1.0
2000..	2.69	2.98	2.48	2.15	1.86	(NA)	2.3	3.0	2.4	(NA)	1.6	(NA)
2001..	2.71	(NA)	2.52	(NA)	(NA)	(NA)	2.3	(NA)	2.5	(NA)	(NA)	(NA)

NA Not available. [1] Estimated.
Source: National Science Foundation, *National Patterns of R&D Resources*, annual; and Organization for Economic Cooperation and Development.

No. 785. Federal Obligations for R&D in Current and Constant (1996) Dollars by Agency: 1980 to 2002

[In millions of dollars (29,830 represents $29,830,000,000). For fiscal years ending in year shown; see text, Section 8. Includes those agencies with obligations of $1 billion or more in 2000]

Agency	Current dollars				Constant (1996) dollars [1]			
	1980	1990	2001, prel.	2002, prel.	1980	1990	2001, prel.	2002, prel.
Obligations, total [2]	29,830	63,559	80,898	80,645	53,278	73,863	73,961	72,191
Dept. of Defense	13,981	37,268	36,334	34,235	24,971	43,310	33,218	30,646
Dept. of Health and Human Services	3,780	8,406	21,355	23,816	6,752	9,769	19,524	21,319
National Aeronautics and Space Administration [3]	3,234	6,533	7,221	7,259	5,776	7,592	6,602	6,498
Dept. of Energy	4,754	5,631	6,712	6,322	8,490	6,544	6,136	5,659
National Science Foundation	882	1,690	3,015	3,017	1,575	1,964	2,756	2,701
Dept. of Agriculture	688	1,108	1,980	1,806	1,228	1,288	1,810	1,617

[1] Based on gross domestic product implicit price deflator. [2] Includes other agencies, not shown separately. [3] Beginning in fiscal year 2000, the National Aeronautics and Space Administration reclassified Space Station as a physical asset and Space Station research as equipment and transferred funding for the program from R&D to R&D plant.
Source: U.S. National Science Foundation, *Federal Funds for Research and Development*, annual. See also <http://www.nsf.gov/>.

No. 786. Federal Obligations for Research in Current and Constant (1996) Dollars by Field of Science: 1980 to 2002

[In millions of dollars (11,597 represents $11,597,000,000). For fiscal years ending in year shown; see text, Section 8. Excludes R&D plant]

Field of science	1980	1985	1990	1995	1998	1999	2000	2001, prel.	2002, prel.
CURRENT DOLLARS									
Research, total	11,597	16,133	21,622	28,434	30,922	33,528	38,471	43,836	45,327
Basic	4,674	7,819	11,286	13,877	15,613	17,444	19,570	22,705	23,399
Applied	6,923	8,315	10,337	14,557	15,309	16,084	18,901	21,131	21,928
Life sciences	4,192	6,363	8,830	11,811	13,558	15,422	17,965	21,118	22,204
Psychology	199	327	449	623	591	633	1,627	1,871	2,075
Physical sciences	2,001	3,046	3,809	4,278	4,210	4,066	4,788	5,163	5,145
Environmental sciences	1,261	1,404	2,174	2,854	3,062	3,095	3,329	3,661	3,644
Mathematics and computer sciences	241	575	841	1,579	1,837	1,981	2,206	2,458	2,618
Engineering	2,830	3,618	4,227	5,708	5,895	6,263	6,346	7,091	7,031
Social sciences	524	460	630	679	806	855	1,050	1,216	1,271
Other sciences, n.e.c. [1]	350	342	664	902	964	1,212	1,160	1,259	1,338
CONSTANT (1996) DOLLARS [2]									
Research, total	20,713	21,953	25,127	29,002	29,908	32,011	35,988	40,077	40,576
Basic	8,348	10,640	13,116	14,154	15,101	16,655	18,307	20,758	20,946
Applied	12,365	11,314	12,013	14,848	14,807	15,356	17,681	19,319	19,629
Life sciences	7,487	8,658	10,261	12,047	13,113	14,724	16,805	19,307	19,876
Psychology	355	445	522	635	572	604	1,522	1,711	1,857
Physical sciences	3,574	4,145	4,426	4,364	4,072	3,882	4,479	4,720	4,606
Environmental sciences	2,252	1,910	2,526	2,911	2,962	2,955	3,114	3,347	3,262
Mathematics and computer sciences	430	782	977	1,611	1,777	1,891	2,064	2,247	2,344
Engineering	5,054	4,923	4,912	5,822	5,702	5,980	5,936	6,483	6,294
Social sciences	936	626	732	693	780	816	982	1,112	1,138
Other sciences, n.e.c. [1]	625	465	772	920	932	1,157	1,085	1,151	1,198

[1] N.e.c. = Not elsewhere classified. [2] Based on gross domestic product implicit price deflator.
Source: U.S. National Science Foundation, *Federal Funds for Research and Development*, annual. Also see <http://128.150.4.107:80/sbe/srs/pubdata.htm>.

No. 787. Federal Budget Authority for R&D in Current and Constant (1996) Dollars by Selected Budget Functions: 1980 to 2003

[In millions of dollars (29,739 represents $29,739,000,000). For fiscal years ending in year shown; see text, Section 8. Excludes R&D plant. Represents budget authority. Functions shown are those for which $1 billion or more was authorized since 1995]

Function	1980	1985	1990	1995	1999	2000	2001	2002, prel.	2003, prel.
CURRENT DOLLARS									
Total [1]	29,739	49,887	63,781	68,791	77,637	78,664	86,756	98,029	107,057
Eight functions, percent of total	96.5	98.3	98.0	97.7	97.6	97.7	97.7	97.9	98.1
National defense	14,946	33,698	39,925	37,204	41,306	42,580	45,713	52,922	58,259
Health	3,694	5,418	8,308	11,407	15,553	17,869	20,758	23,654	26,615
Space research and technology [2]	2,738	2,725	5,765	7,916	8,245	5,363	6,126	6,556	7,435
Energy [3]	3,603	2,389	2,726	2,844	1,131	996	1,314	1,547	1,408
General science [3]	1,233	1,862	2,410	2,794	4,690	4,977	5,468	5,717	5,890
Natural resources and environment	999	1,059	1,386	1,988	1,842	1,999	2,096	2,159	2,136
Transportation	887	1,030	1,045	1,833	1,725	1,636	1,640	1,696	1,554
Agriculture	585	836	950	1,194	1,288	1,426	1,657	1,703	1,703
CONSTANT (1996) DOLLARS [4]									
Total [1]	53,115	67,883	74,121	70,166	74,124	73,587	79,316	87,753	94,116
National defense	26,694	45,854	46,397	37,948	39,437	39,832	41,793	47,374	51,217
Health	6,598	7,372	9,655	11,635	14,849	16,716	18,978	21,174	23,398
Space research and technology [2]	4,890	3,708	6,700	8,074	7,872	5,017	5,601	5,869	6,536
Energy [3]	6,435	3,251	3,168	2,901	1,080	932	1,201	1,385	1,238
General science [3]	2,202	2,534	2,801	2,850	4,478	4,656	4,999	5,118	5,178
Natural resources and environment	1,784	1,441	1,611	2,028	1,759	1,870	1,916	1,933	1,878
Transportation	1,584	1,402	1,214	1,870	1,647	1,530	1,499	1,518	1,366
Agriculture	1,045	1,138	1,104	1,218	1,230	1,334	1,515	1,524	1,497

[1] Includes other functions, not shown separately. [2] In FY 2000, the National Aeronautics and Space Administration reclassified Space Station as a physical asset and Space Station research as equipment and transferred funding for the Space Station program from R&D to R&D plant. [3] Beginning in FY 1998, a number of DOE programs were reclassified from energy (270). [4] Based on gross domestic product implicit price deflator.

Source: U.S. National Science Foundation, *Federal R&D Funding by Budget Function*, annual. For most recent report, see <http://www.nsf.gov/>.

No. 788. R&D Expenditures in Science and Engineering at Universities and Colleges in Current and Constant (1996) Dollars: 1990 to 2001

[In millions of dollars (16,286 represents $16,286,000,000)]

Characteristic	Current dollars				Constant (1996) dollars [1]			
	1990	1995	2000	2001	1990	1995	2000	2001
Total	16,286	22,161	30,042	32,723	18,863	22,604	28,103	29,917
Basic research	10,643	14,802	22,416	24,242	12,327	15,098	20,969	22,163
Applied R&D	5,643	7,359	7,626	8,481	6,536	7,506	7,134	7,754
Source of funds:								
All governments	10,962	15,015	19,704	21,506	12,696	15,315	18,432	19,662
Institutions' own funds	3,006	4,046	5,933	6,553	3,482	4,127	5,550	5,991
Industry	1,127	1,488	2,152	2,234	1,305	1,518	2,013	2,042
Other	1,191	1,613	2,253	2,430	1,379	1,645	2,108	2,222
Fields:								
Physical sciences	1,807	2,254	2,708	2,800	2,093	2,299	2,533	2,560
Environmental sciences	1,069	1,433	1,763	1,827	1,238	1,462	1,649	1,670
Mathematical sciences	222	279	341	357	257	285	319	326
Computer sciences	515	682	875	954	596	696	819	872
Life sciences	8,726	12,185	17,460	19,189	10,107	12,429	16,333	17,543
Psychology	253	370	516	582	293	377	483	532
Social sciences	703	1,018	1,297	1,436	814	1,038	1,213	1,313
Other sciences	336	426	534	579	389	435	500	529
Engineering	2,656	3,515	4,547	4,999	3,076	3,585	4,254	4,570

[1] Based on gross domestic product implicit price deflator.

Source: U.S. National Science Foundation, *Survey of Research and Development Expenditures at Universities and Colleges*, annual. Also see <http://www.nsf.gov/>.

No. 789. Federal Obligations for Science and Engineering to Universities and Colleges in Current and Constant (1996) Dollars: 1990 to 2001

[In millions of dollars (10,471 represents $10,471,000,000) except percent. For fiscal years ending in year shown; see text, Section 8. Minus sign (-) indicates decrease]

Item	Current dollars				Constant (1996) dollars [1]			
	1990	1995	2000	2001	1990	1995	2000	2001
Academic science/engineering obligations	10,471	14,461	19,877	22,488	12,168	14,750	18,601	20,543
Research and development	9,017	12,181	17,290	19,385	10,478	12,424	16,180	17,708
Research and development plant	142	341	240	401	165	348	224	366
Other science/engineering activities	1,312	1,939	2,348	2,703	1,525	1,978	2,197	2,469

[1] Based on gross domestic product implicit price deflator.

Source: U.S. National Science Foundation, *Survey of Federal S&E Support to Universities, Colleges, and Nonprofit Institutions*, annual. Also see <http://www.nsf.gov/>.

No. 790. Federal R&D Obligations to Selected Universities and Colleges: 2000 and 2001

[In millions of dollars (17,289.8 represents $17,289,800,000), except rank. For fiscal years ending in year shown; see text, Section 8. Awards to the administrative offices of university systems are excluded from totals for individual institutions because that allocation of funds is unknown, but those awards are included in "total all institutions"]

Major institution ranked by total 2001 federal R&D obligations	2000	2001	Major institution ranked by total 2001 federal R&D obligations	2000	2001
Total, all institutions [1]	17,289.8	19,384.7	Columbia University—Main Division	282.2	305.8
			University of Pittsburgh	246.2	300.8
Johns Hopkins University	795.5	838.0	University of Colorado	272.3	290.7
University of Washington	396.1	474.5	University of Wisconsin—Madison	263.4	290.2
University of Pennsylvania	348.5	412.0	Yale University	260.0	276.2
University of Michigan	346.7	403.4	Univ. of North Carolina at Chapel Hill	232.7	275.9
University of California—Los Angeles	372.4	363.9	Duke University	232.2	274.1
Stanford University	355.0	351.1	University of Minnesota	276.8	273.1
University of California—San Francisco	289.2	344.9	Cornell University	240.1	271.9
University of California—San Diego	314.4	333.9	Pennsylvania State University	230.1	253.6
Harvard University	299.9	321.7	Massachusetts Institute of Technology	248.9	252.5
Washington University	287.3	314.7	University Southern California	203.9	232.5

[1] Includes other institutions, not shown separately.

Source: U.S. National Science Foundation, *Federal S&E Support to Universities and Colleges and Nonprofit Institutions*, annual.

No. 791. Graduate Science/Engineering Students in Doctorate-Granting Colleges by Characteristic and Field: 1990 to 2001

[In thousands (397.8 represents 397,800). As of fall. Includes outlying areas]

Field of science or engineering	Total 1990	Total 2000	Total 2001	Female 1990	Female 2000	Female 2001	Foreign 2000	Foreign 2001	Part-time 1990	Part-time 2000	Part-time 2001
Total, all surveyed fields	397.8	434.3	452.4	149.7	195.5	204.9	121.3	133.0	123.2	118.6	122.4
Science/engineering	350.5	367.6	384.1	113.4	145.8	153.9	115.9	127.0	100.7	95.0	98.1
Engineering, total	99.9	99.0	103.5	13.6	19.6	21.0	45.5	50.5	35.9	28.1	27.8
Sciences, total	250.7	268.6	280.6	99.8	126.2	133.0	70.4	76.5	64.8	66.9	70.3
Physical sciences	32.5	29.3	30.0	7.6	8.7	9.0	11.4	11.9	3.6	3.2	3.3
Environmental	12.9	12.7	12.6	3.8	5.2	5.3	2.6	2.7	3.0	2.6	2.6
Mathematical sciences	17.3	13.8	15.1	5.3	4.9	5.6	5.7	6.3	4.0	2.7	3.1
Computer sciences	27.7	39.6	43.9	6.4	11.4	12.5	19.2	22.4	12.9	16.4	16.9
Agricultural sciences	10.6	10.9	11.0	3.1	4.6	4.8	2.3	2.4	1.9	2.2	2.3
Biological sciences	46.3	52.5	54.1	21.1	27.5	28.8	11.6	12.1	6.8	7.2	7.4
Psychology	35.8	37.8	39.3	23.6	27.1	28.6	2.0	2.3	10.3	9.5	10.9
Social sciences	67.7	71.9	74.6	29.0	36.9	38.5	15.6	16.4	22.1	23.1	23.9
Health fields, total	47.2	66.7	68.3	36.3	49.7	51.0	5.4	6.0	22.5	23.5	24.3

Source: U.S. National Science Foundation, *Survey of Graduate Science Engineering Students and Postdoctorates*, annual.

No. 792. Doctorates Conferred by Recipients' Characteristics: 1990 and 2001

[In percent, except as indicated]

Characteristic	1990, total	2001 All fields [1]	Engineering	Physical sciences [2]	Earth sciences	Mathematics	Computer sciences	Biological sciences [3]	Agricultural	Social sciences [4]	Psychology
Total conferred (number)	36,068	40,744	5,502	3,358	780	1,006	826	5,678	1,005	3,392	3,433
Male	63.7	55.9	83.0	75.3	68.3	72.6	80.9	55.9	66.1	58.2	33.0
Female	36.3	44.1	16.8	24.5	31.5	27.4	18.8	44.9	33.4	41.6	66.8
Median age [5]	33.9	33.3	31.2	29.9	33.2	30.5	32.0	30.7	34.0	33.9	32.1
CITIZENSHIP [6]											
Total conferred (number)	34,697	38,509	5,207	3,256	716	957	776	5,455	787	3,868	3,165
U.S. citizen	71.8	74.6	41.1	57.1	59.8	48.9	47.0	71.1	51.0	65.3	92.8
Foreign citizen	28.2	25.4	58.9	42.9	40.2	51.1	53.0	28.9	49.0	34.7	7.2
RACE/ETHNICITY [7]											
Total conferred (number)	26,604	28,729	2,435	2,043	464	522	420	4,216	429	2,720	3,013
White [8]	86.5	78.6	71.7	80.6	84.9	81.8	76.0	76.9	86.5	78.2	80.9
Black [8]	3.8	6.0	3.8	2.6	1.1	3.6	3.6	3.2	2.8	6.9	5.8
Asian/Pacific [8]	4.9	7.5	17.3	9.9	7.5	9.2	14.5	13.1	3.7	6.6	4.0
Indian/Alaskan [8]	0.4	0.5	0.3	0.6	-	0.4	0.2	0.4	-	0.7	0.6
Hispanic	3.1	4.4	3.7	3.2	3.2	2.9	1.9	3.9	4.4	4.3	5.8
Other/unknown [9]	1.4	3.0	3.4	3.3	3.4	2.1	3.8	2.9	3.0	2.6	3.2

- Represents zero. [1] Includes other fields, not shown separately. [2] Astronomy, physics, and chemistry. [3] Biochemistry, botany, microbiology, physiology, zoology, and related fields. [4] Anthropology, sociology, political science, economics, international relations and related fields. [5] For definition of median, see Guide to Tabular Presentation. [6] For those with known citizenship. Includes those with temporary visas. [7] Excludes those with temporary visas. [8] Non-Hispanic. [9] For the year 2001, includes Native Hawaiians and other Pacific Islanders, respondents choosing multiple races (excluding those selecting an Hispanic ethnicity), and respondents with unknown race/ethnicity.

Source: U.S. National Science Foundation, *Science and Engineering Doctorate Awards*, annual. See also <http://www.nsf.gov/>.

Figure 16.1
Top 15 Universities - Federal Research and Development Obligations: 2001

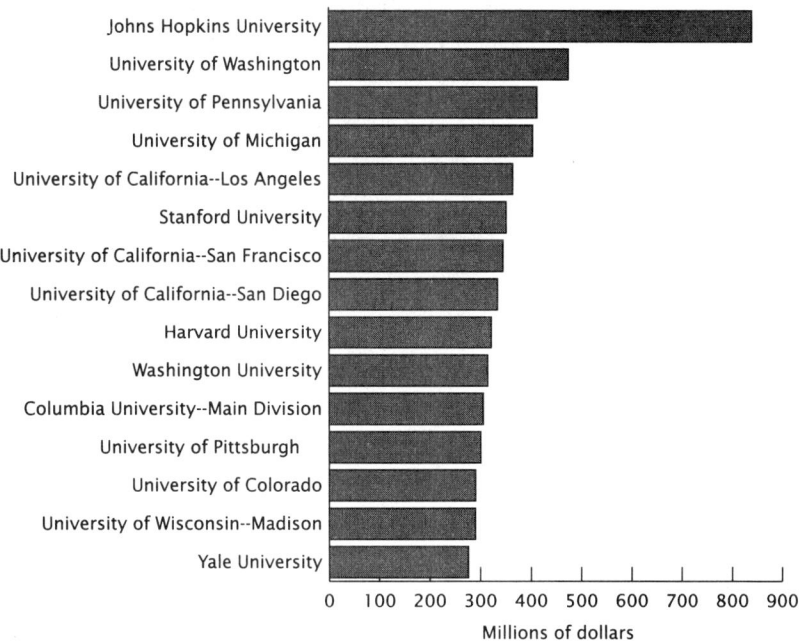

Source: Chart prepared by U.S. Census Bureau. For data, see Table 790.

Figure 16.2
Federal Funding for Research by Field of Science: 2002
Millions of dollars

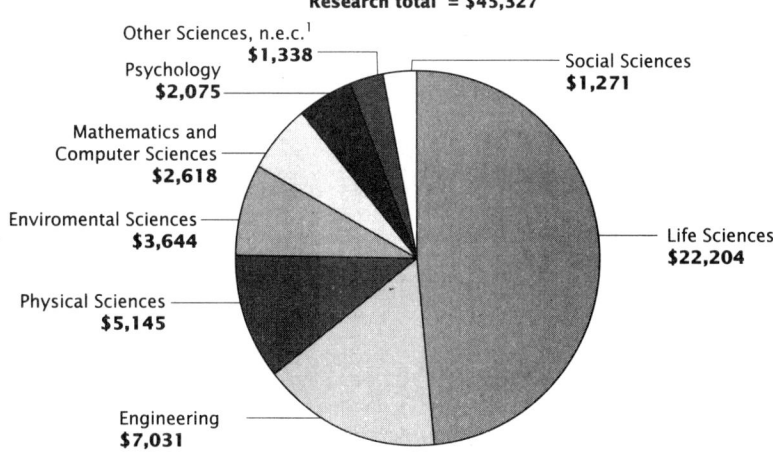

[1] n.e.c = not elsewhere classified.

Source: Chart prepared by U.S. Census Bureau. For data, see Table 786.

Science and Technology 529

No. 793. Funds for Performance of Industrial R&D in Current and Constant (1996) Dollars by Source of Funds and Selected Industries: 1998 to 2001

[In millions of dollars (169,180 represents $169,180,000,000). For calendar years. Covers basic research, applied research, and development. Based on the Survey of Industry Research and Development]

Source of funds and industry	NAICS [1] code	1998	1999	2000	2001
CURRENT DOLLARS					
Total funds	(X)	169,180	182,823	199,539	198,505
Petroleum and coal products	324	1,395	615	(D)	(D)
Chemicals and allied products	325	18,969	20,246	20,918	17,892
Machinery	333	(D)	6,057	6,580	6,404
Navigational, measuring, electromedical, and control instruments	3345	11,232	14,337	15,116	12,947
Electrical equipment, appliances, and components	335	2,280	(D)	(D)	4,980
Motor vehicles, trailers, and parts	3361-3363	(D)	(D)	(D)	(D)
Aerospace products and parts	3364	16,359	14,425	10,319	7,868
All other [2]	(X)	(D)	(D)	(D)	(D)
Company funds	(X)	145,016	160,288	180,421	181,606
Petroleum and coal products	324	1,390	(D)	1,172	1,057
Chemicals	325	18,733	20,051	20,768	17,713
Machinery	333	5,831	5,658	6,539	6,337
Navigational, measuring, electromedical, and control instruments	3345	5,483	8,632	10,114	7,565
Electrical equipment, appliances, and components	335	2,139	3,820	3,390	4,680
Motor vehicles, trailers, and parts	3361-3363	13,781	17,987	18,306	16,089
Aerospace products and parts	3364	6,521	5,309	3,895	4,083
All other [2]	(X)	91,138	(D)	116,237	124,082
CONSTANT (1996) DOLLARS [3]					
Total funds	(X)	163,934	174,383	186,729	181,333
Petroleum and coal products	324	1,352	587	(D)	(D)
Chemicals	325	18,381	19,311	19,575	16,344
Machinery	333	(D)	5,777	6,158	5,850
Navigational, measuring, electromedical, and control instruments	3345	10,884	13,675	14,146	11,827
Electrical equipment, appliances, and components	335	2,209	(D)	(D)	4,549
Motor vehicles, trailers, and parts	3361-3363	(D)	(D)	(D)	(D)
Aerospace products and parts	3364	15,852	13,759	9,657	7,187
All other [2]	(X)	(D)	(D)	(D)	(D)
Company funds	(X)	140,519	152,888	168,839	165,896
Petroleum and coal products	324	1,347	(D)	1,097	966
Chemicals	325	18,152	19,125	19,435	16,181
Machinery	333	5,650	5,397	6,119	5,789
Navigational, measuring, electromedical, and control instruments	3345	5,313	8,233	9,465	6,911
Electrical equipment, appliances, and components	335	2,073	3,644	3,172	4,275
Motor vehicles, trailers, and parts	3361-3363	13,354	17,157	17,131	14,697
Aerospace products and parts	3364	6,319	5,064	3,645	3,730
All other [2]	(X)	88,312	(D)	108,775	113,348

D Figure withheld to avoid disclosure of information pertaining to a specific organization or individual.   X Not applicable.
[1] North American Industry Classification System, 1997; see text, Section 15.   [2] All other manufacturing and nonmanufacturing.
[3] Based on gross domestic product implicit price deflator.

Source: U.S. National Science Foundation, *Research and Development in Industry*, annual.

No. 794. R&D Funds in R&D-Performing Manufacturing Companies by Industry: 1999 to 2001

Industry	NAICS [1] code	Total R&D funds as a percent of net sales 1999	2000	2001	Company R&D funds as a percent of net sales 1999	2000	2001
All industries, total	(X)	3.7	3.8	4.1	3.3	3.4	3.8
All manufacturing industries, total	(X)	3.7	3.6	4.0	3.2	3.3	3.6
Food	311	0.4	(D)	0.5	0.4	0.4	0.5
Paper, printing, and support activities	322, 326	(D)	(D)	(D)	1.4	1.6	2.1
Petroleum and coal products	324	0.4	(D)	(D)	(D)	0.3	0.3
Chemicals	325	5.2	5.9	4.9	5.1	5.9	4.8
Plastic and rubber products	326	1.9	(D)	(D)	1.9	1.8	2.9
Nonmetallic mineral products	327	(D)	1.8	2.4	1.5	1.8	2.3
Primary metals	331	0.4	0.5	0.7	0.4	0.5	0.7
Fabricated metal products	332	1.5	1.4	1.7	1.4	1.4	1.6
Machinery	333	3.5	3.9	4.3	3.3	3.8	4.2
Navigational, measuring, electromedical, and control instruments	3345	15.2	12.0	12.6	9.1	8.0	7.3
Electrical equipment, appliances, and components	335	(D)	(D)	3.1	2.3	2.1	2.9
Motor vehicles, trailers, and parts	3361-3363	(D)	(D)	(D)	2.9	3.2	3.5
Aerospace products and parts	3364	8.8	7.3	5.7	3.2	2.8	3.0
All nonmanufacturing industries, total	(X)	3.7	4.1	4.3	3.2	3.3	4.0
Transportation and warehousing services	48, 49	0.5	(D)	2.5	0.4	0.4	2.4
Software publishing	5112	16.8	20.5	19.4	1.4	1.6	19.3
Architectural, engineering, and related services	5413	10.1	10.8	7.5	(D)	0.3	5.2
Computer systems design and related services	5415	(D)	12.3	17.4	5.1	5.9	16.5
Scientific R&D services	5417	45.3	42.9	47.7	1.9	1.8	36.5
Management of companies and enterprises	55	(D)	4.4	7.8	1.5	1.8	7.8

D Figure withheld to avoid disclosure of information pertaining to a specific organization or individual.   X Not applicable.
[1] North American Industry Classification System, 1997; see text, Section 15.

Source: U.S. National Science Foundation, *Research and Development in Industry*, annual. See also <http://www.nsf.gov/>.

No. 795. R&D Scientists and Engineers—Employment and Cost by Industry: 1999 to 2001

[1,015.7 represents 1,015,700. Data are estimates; on average full-time-equivalent (FTE) basis]

Industry	NAICS [1] code	1999	2000	2001
EMPLOYED SCIENTISTS (1,000)				
Average FTE of scientists and engineers [2] [3]	(X)	1,015.7	1,037.5	1,050.8
Chemicals	325	86.7	82.0	81.4
Machinery	333	74.1	51.9	53.8
Electrical equipment, appliances, and components	335	98.8	23.3	11.4
Motor vehicles, trailers, and parts	3361-3363	69.2	75.4	74.4
Aerospace products and parts	3364	60.9	40.2	22.1
Transportation and warehousing services	48, 49	0.5	1.5	1.3
Software publishing	5112	38.1	79.7	82.2
Architectural, engineering, and related services	5413	16.0	33.0	28.9
Computer systems design and related services	5415	18.4	41.6	54.6
Scientific R&D services	5417	24.0	52.4	58.4
Management of companies and enterprises	55	0.2	0.4	0.9
CONSTANT (1996) DOLLARS [4] ($1,000)				
Cost per scientist or engineer [3] [5]	(X)	171.7	180.0	172.6
Chemicals	325	234.2	238.7	200.8
Machinery	333	113.5	118.8	108.8
Electrical equipment, appliances, and components	335	(D)	(D)	(D)
Motor vehicles, trailers, and parts	3361-3363	(D)	(D)	(D)
Aerospace products and parts	3364	209.8	(D)	326
Transportation and warehousing services	48, 49	494.5	(D)	(D)
Software publishing	5112	146.5	148.4	145.8
Architectural, engineering, and related services	5413	114.9	96.0	107.2
Computer systems design and related services	5415	(D)	116.3	153.1
Scientific R&D services	5417	241.2	230.4	223.0
Management of companies and enterprises	55	(D)	124.4	385.9

D Withheld to avoid disclosure. X Not applicable. [1] North American Industry Classification System, 1997; see text, Section 15. [2] The mean number of FTE R&D scientists and engineers employed in January of the year shown and the following January. [3] Includes industries not shown separately. [4] Based on gross domestic product implicit price deflator. [5] Represents the arithmetic mean of the numbers of R&D scientists and engineers reported in each industry for January in 2 consecutive years divided into total R&D expenditures in each industry.

Source: U.S. National Science Foundation, *Research and Development in Industry*, annual.

No. 796. Civilian Employment of Scientists, Engineers, and Technicians by Occupation and Industry: 2000

[In thousands (6,412.4 represents 6,412,400). Based on sample and subject to sampling error. For details, see source]

Occupation	Total [1]	Mining [2]	Construction	Manufacturing	Transportation [3]	Trade	Fire [4]	Services	Government	Self employed [5]
Scientists, engineers, and technicians, total	6,412.4	38.1	81.6	1,423.1	264.1	377.7	370.2	2,772.7	726.9	343.6
Scientists	922.8	7.4	0.5	108.1	15.2	21.7	43.8	374.0	227.0	118.0
Physical scientists	239.1	7.0	0.2	60.5	5.5	2.3	0.7	82.1	73.8	7.0
Life scientists	184.4	0.2	([6])	21.9	0.2	3.8	0.5	77.1	60.8	12.9
Mathematical scientists	89.4	0.1	([6])	6.9	2.6	1.3	23.0	37.5	17.9	([6])
Social scientists and related occupations	409.9	0.2	0.3	18.8	6.9	14.3	19.5	177.4	74.5	98.1
Computer specialists	2,903.4	4.5	9.5	318.2	115.4	247.3	315.7	1,557.9	179.2	154.3
Engineers [6]	1,465.3	14.5	44.6	642.1	82.4	48.3	8.4	401.2	179.4	42.7
Civil engineers	232.0	0.9	19.1	3.8	2.7	0.2	1.0	120.7	70.0	12.1
Electrical/electronics	287.6	0.4	6.1	139.0	20.4	22.2	0.9	59.1	31.1	8.3
Mechanical engineers	221.4	0.6	5.4	122.3	2.5	8.2	1.0	62.5	11.8	7.1
Engineering and science technicians	1,062.6	9.2	24.6	354.7	50.2	60.3	2.1	396.2	135.5	26.1
Electrical/electronics technicians	232.7	0.8	4.0	101.7	22.1	34.0	0.5	48.3	15.0	6.3
Other engineering technicians	286.6	1.1	5.4	104.1	17.0	16.7	0.6	85.0	52.0	4.6
Drafters	213.1	0.7	15.0	65.5	4.9	5.5	0.5	103.2	6.5	10.0
Life, physical, and social science technicians	330.1	6.7	0.2	83.5	6.1	4.1	0.5	159.7	62.0	5.2
Surveyors [7]	58.3	2.5	2.5	0.1	1.0	0.1	0.4	43.4	5.8	2.5

[1] Includes agriculture, forestry, and fishing not shown separately. [2] Includes oil and gas extraction. [3] Includes communications and public utilities. [4] Finance, insurance, and real estate. [5] Includes secondary jobs. [6] Includes kinds of engineers and technicians not shown separately. [7] Includes cartographers, photogrammetrists, and surveying and mapping technicians.

Source: U.S. Bureau of Labor Statistics, *National Industry-Occupation Employment Matrix* November 2001; and unpublished data. (Data collected biennially.)

Science and Technology 531

No. 797. Space Vehicle Systems—Net Sales and Backlog Orders: 1970 to 2001

[In millions of dollars (1,956 represents $1,956,000,000). Backlog orders as of Dec. 31. Based on data from major companies engaged in manufacture of aerospace products. Includes parts but excludes engines and propulsion units]

Year	Net sales Total	Net sales Military	Net sales Non-military	Backlog orders Total	Backlog orders Military	Backlog orders Non-military	Year	Net sales Total	Net sales Military	Net sales Non-military	Backlog orders Total	Backlog orders Military	Backlog orders Non-military
1970	1,956	1,025	931	1,184	786	398	1996	11,698	5,613	6,085	23,004	9,125	13,879
1975	2,119	1,096	1,023	1,304	1,019	285	1997	13,410	4,916	8,494	23,357	8,790	14,567
1980	3,483	1,461	2,022	1,814	951	863	1998	9,490	4,227	5,264	20,371	7,970	12,402
1985	6,300	4,241	2,059	6,707	4,941	1,766	1999	9,022	5,107	3,915	22,356	10,666	11,690
1990	9,691	6,556	3,135	12,462	8,130	4,332	2000	8,164	3,723	4,441	21,395	8,942	12,453
1995	11,314	4,782	6,532	15,650	5,872	9,778	2001	7,792	4,270	3,522	18,479	8,277	10,202

Source: U.S. Census Bureau, Current Industrial Reports, M336G, *Civil Aircraft and Aircraft Engines*, annual and, beginning 1994, Internet site <http://www.census.gov/industry/1/m336g0113.pdf>.

No. 798. Federal Outlays for General Science, Space, and Other Technology, 1970 to 2002, and Projections, 2003 to 2007, in Current and Constant (1996) Dollars

[In billions of dollars (4.5 represents $4,500,000,000). For fiscal years ending in year shown; see text, Section 8]

Year	Current dollars Total	Current dollars General science/basic research	Current dollars Space and other technologies	Constant (1996) dollars Total	Constant (1996) dollars General science/basic research	Constant (1996) dollars Space and other technologies
1970	4.5	0.9	3.6	18.5	3.9	14.6
1980	5.8	1.4	4.5	11.6	2.7	8.9
1985	8.6	2.0	6.6	12.8	3.0	9.8
1990	14.4	2.8	11.6	18.4	3.6	14.8
1995	16.7	4.1	12.6	17.3	4.3	13.0
1996	16.7	4.0	12.7	16.7	4.0	12.7
1997	17.1	4.1	13.1	16.9	4.0	12.9
1998	18.2	5.3	12.9	17.5	5.1	12.4
1999	18.1	5.6	12.4	17.0	5.3	11.7
2000	18.6	6.2	12.4	17.0	5.6	11.4
2001	19.8	6.5	13.2	17.8	5.9	11.9
2002	20.7	7.2	13.5	18.0	6.3	11.7
2003, proj.	21.6	7.9	13.6	18.6	6.9	11.8
2004, proj.	22.7	8.5	14.3	19.2	7.2	12.1
2005, proj.	23.7	8.9	14.9	19.8	7.4	12.4
2006, proj.	24.7	9.1	15.6	20.2	7.5	12.8
2007, proj.	25.4	9.4	16.0	20.5	7.6	12.9

Source: U.S. Office of Management and Budget, *Budget of the United States, Historical Tables, Fiscal Year 2004*, annual. Also see <http://www.whitehouse.gov/omb/budget/fy2004/pdf/hist.pdf>.

No. 799. U.S. and Worldwide Commercial Space Industry Revenue by Type: 2000 to 2002

[In billions of dollars (35.4 represents $35,400,000,000). For calendar years]

Industry	U.S. 2000	U.S. 2001	U.S. 2002, est.	World 2000	World 2001	World 2002, est.
Revenue, total	35.4	20.8	22.7	73.7	78.6	86.8
Satellite manufacturing [1]	6.0	3.8	4.4	11.5	9.5	12.1
Launch industry	2.7	1.1	1.0	5.3	3.0	3.7
Satellite services [2]	11.8	15.9	17.3	39.2	46.5	49.8
Ground equipment manufacturing [3]	14.9	(NA)	(NA)	17.7	19.6	21.2

NA Not available. [1] Includes revenues from the construction and sale of satellites to both commercial and government. [2] Includes revenues derived from transponder leasing and subscription/retail services such as direct-to-home television and satellite mobile and data communications. [3] Includes revenues from the manufacture of gateways and satellite control stations, satellite news-gathering trucks, very small aperture terminals, direct-to-home television equipment and mobile satellite phones.

Source: Satellite Industry Association/Futron Corporation, Bethesda, MD, *2002-2003 Satellite Industry Indicators Survey* (copyright). Also see <http://www.sia.org/>.

No. 800. National Aeronautics and Space Administration—Budget Authority: 1999 to 2003 and Projections, 2004

[In millions of dollars (13,653.0 represents $13,653,000,000)]

Item	1999	2000	2001	2002	2003	2004
Budget authority, total	13,653.0	13,600.8	14,357.2	15,012.7	15,117.0	15,690.4
Human space flight	5,480.0	5,467.7	7,153.5	6,830.1	6,130.9	5,868.9
International space station	2,299.7	2,323.1	2,127.8	1,721.7	1,492.1	1,195.9
Space flight operations (space shuttle)	2,998.3	2,979.5	3,118.8	3,272.8	3,208.0	3,301.0
Payload utilization and operations	182.0	165.1	(NA)	(NA)	(NA)	(NA)
Payload and elv support	(X)	(X)	90.0	91.3	87.5	91.0
Investments and support	(X)	(X)	1,247.8	1,214.5	1,178.2	1,159.9
Science, aeronautics, and technology	5,653.9	5,580.9	7,076.5	8,047.8	8,844.5	9,679.0
Space science	2,119.2	2,192.8	2,606.6	2,867.1	3,414.3	3,906.9
Earth science	1,413.8	1,443.4	1,762.2	1,625.7	1,628.4	1,620.5
Aerospace technology	1,338.9	1,124.9	2,212.8	2,507.7	2,815.8	3,124.9
Academic programs	138.5	138.8	132.7	227.3	143.7	143.7
Safety, mission assurance, engineering, and advanced concepts	35.6	43.0	47.4	47.6	47.6	47.8
Inspector General	19.6	20.0	22.9	23.7	24.6	25.5

NA Not available. X Not applicable.

Source: U.S. National Aeronautics and Space Administration, <http://ifmp.nasa.gov/codeb/budget2003/2003websites.html> (released February 2002).

No. 801. NASA Space Shuttle Operations Expenditures: 1996 to 2001

[In millions of dollars (2,485.4 represents $2,485,400,000). Data are funding requirements for fiscal years shown]

Operation	1996	1997	1998	1999	2000	2001
Total	2,485.4	2,464.9	2,369.4	2,998.3	2,999.9	3,165.7
Shuttle operations	2,485.4	2,464.9	2,369.4	2,426.7	2,530.9	2,672.8
Orbiter and integration	521.0	492.6	502.9	608.0	746.9	724.5
Propulsion	1,061.5	1,124.7	1,061.8	1,071.2	1,037.6	1,167.4
External tank	327.5	352.4	341.3	363.2	359.2	318.8
Space shuttle main engine	185.0	208.3	204.6	200.0	195.7	263.4
Reusable solid rocket motor	395.7	412.8	380.4	339.0	347.9	377.7
Solid rocket booster	153.3	151.2	135.5	169.0	134.8	125.8
Mission and launch operations	902.9	847.6	804.7	747.5	746.4	780.9
Safety and performance upgrades	(X)	(X)	(X)	571.6	469.0	492.9
Orbiter improvements	(X)	(X)	(X)	234.8	183.7	327.2
Propulsion upgrades	(X)	(X)	(X)	175.7	181.6	60.2
Flight operations and launch site equipment	(X)	(X)	(X)	147.6	92.5	90.0
Construction of facilities	(X)	(X)	(X)	13.5	11.0	15.5

X Not applicable.

Source: U.S. National Aeronautics and Space Administration, *NASA, 1996-97, Pocket Statistics*, annual; thereafter, <http://ifmp.nasa.gov/codeb/budget2003/2003websites.html> (released February 2002).

No. 802. World-Wide Successful Space Launches: 1957 to 2002

[Criterion of success is attainment of Earth orbit or Earth escape]

Country	Total, 1957-02	1957-64	1965-69	1970-74	1975-79	1980-84	1985-89	1990-94	1995-00	2001	2002
Total	32,970	289	586	555	607	605	1,016	466	466	58	62
Soviet Union/Russia [1]	17,100	82	302	405	461	483	617	283	170	23	24
United States	8,658	207	279	139	126	93	250	122	189	21	17
Japan	390	-	-	5	10	12	18	9	7	1	3
ESA [2]	1,284	-	-	-	1	8	87	33	66	8	11
China	570	-	-	2	6	6	35	15	26	1	4
France	60	-	4	3	3	-	-	-	-	-	(NA)
India	72	-	-	-	-	3	-	3	3	2	1
Israel	30	-	-	-	-	-	2	1	1	-	1
Ukraine [1]	42	-	-	-	-	-	-	-	4	2	1
Australia	6	-	1	-	-	-	-	-	-	-	(NA)
United Kingdom	6	-	-	1	-	-	-	-	-	-	(NA)

- Represents zero. NA Not available. [1] Launches conducted by the former Soviet Union are listed separately as Russia or Ukraine. [2] European Space Agency. Includes launches by Arianespace.

Source: Library of Congress, Congressional Research Service, Science Policy Research Division, *Space Activities of the United States, CIS, and Other Launching Countries/Organizations 1957-1999*; thereafter, Resources, Science, and Industry Division, 2002.

Science and Technology 533

No. 803. Space Shuttle Launches—Summary: 1981 to January 2003

Flight number	Mission date	Orbiter name	Crew size (up/down)[1]	Days/hours duration	Flight number	Mission date	Orbiter name	Crew size (up/down)[1]	Days/hours duration
1	04/12/81	Columbia	2	2	58	10/18/93	Columbia	7	14
2	11/12/81	Columbia	2	2	61	12/02/93	Endeavour	7	11
3	03/22/82	Columbia	2	8	60	02/03/94	Discovery	6	8
4	06/27/82	Columbia	2	7	62	03/04/94	Columbia	5	14
5	11/11/82	Columbia	4	5	59	04/09/94	Endeavour	6	11
6	04/04/83	Challenger	4	5	65	07/08/94	Columbia	7	15
7	06/18/83	Challenger	5	6	64	09/09/94	Discovery	6	11
8	08/30/83	Challenger	5	6	68	09/30/94	Endeavour	6	11
9	11/28/83	Columbia	6	10	66	11/03/94	Atlantis	6	11
10	02/03/84	Challenger	5	8	63	02/03/95	Discovery	6	8
11	04/06/84	Challenger	5	7	67	03/02/95	Endeavour	7	17
12	08/30/84	Discovery	6	7	71	06/27/95	Atlantis	7/8	10
13	10/05/84	Challenger	7	8	70	07/13/95	Discovery	5	9
14	11/08/84	Discovery	5	8	69	09/07/95	Endeavour	5	11
15	01/24/85	Discovery	5	4	73	10/20/95	Columbia	7	16
16	04/12/85	Discovery	7	7	74	11/08/95	Atlantis	5	8
17	04/29/85	Challenger	7	7	72	01/11/96	Endeavour	6	9
18	06/17/85	Discovery	7	7	75	02/22/96	Columbia	7	16
19	07/29/85	Challenger	7	8	76	03/22/96	Atlantis	6/5	9
20	08/27/85	Discovery	5	7	77	05/19/96	Endeavour	6	10
21	10/03/85	Atlantis	5	4	78	06/20/96	Columbia	7	17
22	10/30/85	Challenger	8	7	79	09/16/96	Atlantis	6	10
23	11/26/85	Atlantis	7	7	80	11/20/96	Columbia	5	18
24	01/12/86	Columbia	7	6	81	01/12/97	Atlantis	6	10/05
25	01/28/86	Challenger[2]	7	-	82	02/11/97	Discovery	7	10/00
26	09/29/88	Discovery	5	4	83	04/04/97	Columbia	7	03/23
27	12/02/88	Atlantis	5	4	84	05/15/97	Atlantis	7/7	09/05
29	03/13/89	Discovery	5	5	94	07/01/97	Columbia	7	15/07
30	05/04/89	Atlantis	5	4	85	08/07/97	Discovery	5	11/20
28	08/08/89	Columbia	5	5	86	09/25/97	Atlantis	7/7	10/19
34	10/18/89	Atlantis	5	5	87	11/19/97	Columbia	6	15/17
33	11/22/89	Discovery	5	5	89	01/22/98	Endeavor	7/7	08/20
32	01/09/90	Columbia	5	11	90	04/17/98	Columbia	7	15/22
36	02/28/90	Atlantis	5	4	91	06/02/98	Discovery	6/7	09/19
31	04/24/90	Discovery	5	5	95	11/20/98	Discovery	7	08/22
41	10/06/90	Discovery	5	4	88	12/04/98	Endeavor	6	11/19
38	11/15/90	Atlantis	5	5	96	05/27/99	Discovery	7	09/19
35	12/02/90	Columbia	7	9	93	07/23/99	Columbia	5	04/24
37	04/05/91	Atlantis	5	6	103	12/19/99	Atlantis	7	07/23
39	04/28/91	Discovery	7	8	99	02/11/00	Endeavor	6	11/04
40	06/05/91	Columbia	7	9	101	05/19/00	Atlantis	7	09/21
43	08/02/91	Atlantis	5	9	106	09/08/00	Atlantis	7	11/19
48	09/12/91	Discovery	5	5	92	10/11/00	Discovery	7	12/21
44	11/24/91	Atlantis	6	7	98	12/02/00	Endeavor	5	10/20
42	01/22/92	Discovery	7	8	97	02/07/01	Atlantis	5	12/21
45	03/24/92	Atlantis	7	9	102	03/08/01	Discovery	7/7	12/20
49	05/07/92	Endeavour	7	9	100	04/19/01	Endeavor	7	11/20
50	06/25/92	Columbia	7	14	104	07/12/01	Atlantis	5	12/19
46	07/31/92	Atlantis	7	8	105	08/10/01	Discovery	7/7	11/21
47	09/12/92	Endeavour	7	8	108	12/05/01	Endeavor	8/7	10/20
52	10/22/92	Columbia	6	10	109	03/01/02	Columbia	7/7	10/22
53	12/02/92	Discovery	5	7	110	04/08/02	Atlantis	7/7	10/20
54	01/13/93	Endeavour	5	6	111	06/05/02	Endeavour	7/4	13/25
56	04/08/93	Discovery	5	9	112	10/07/02	Atlantis	6/6	10/20
55	04/26/93	Columbia	7	10	113	11/23/02	Endeavour	7/7	13/19
57	06/21/93	Endeavour	6	10	107	01/16/03	Columbia[2]	7	15/22
51	09/12/93	Discovery	5	10					

- Represents zero.   [1] Differences in crew size due to docking with the Mir Space Station.   [2] Loss of vehicle and crew.

Source: U.S. National Aeronautics and Space Administration, Internet site <http://www.ksc.nasa.gov/shuttle/missions/missions.html> (accessed 24 June 2003).

No. 804. Nobel Prize Laureates in Selected Sciences: 1901 to 2002

[Presented by location of award-winning research and by date of award]

Country	1901-2002 Total	Physics	Chemistry	Physiology/ Medicine	1901-1930	1931-1945	1946-1960	1961-1975	1976-1990	1991-2001	2002
Total	487	168	141	178	93	49	74	92	98	73	9
United States	214	72	49	89	6	14	38	41	63	49	5
United Kingdom	75	21	27	27	15	11	14	20	9	4	1
Germany[1]	63	19	29	15	27	11	4	8	7	4	-
France	25	11	7	7	13	2	-	5	2	3	-
Soviet Union	11	8	1	2	2	-	4	3	1	1	-
Japan	8	4	4	-	-	-	1	2	1	2	2
Other countries	91	30	22	39	30	11	13	13	15	3	1

- Represents zero.   [1] Between 1946 and 1991, data are for the former West Germany only.

Source: U.S. National Science Foundation, unpublished data.

Section 17
Agriculture

This section presents statistics on farms and farm operators; land use; farm income, expenditures, and debt; farm output, productivity, and marketings; foreign trade in agricultural products; specific crops; and livestock, poultry, and their products.

The principal sources are the reports issued by the National Agricultural Statistics Service (NASS) and the Economic Research Service (ERS) of the U.S. Department of Agriculture. The information from the 1997 Census of Agriculture is available in printed form in the Volume 1, Geographic Area Series; in electronic format on CD-ROM; and on the Internet site <http://www.nass.usda.gov/census/>. The Department of Agriculture publishes annually *Agricultural Statistics*, a general reference book on agricultural production, supplies, consumption, facilities, costs, and returns. The ERS publishes data on farm assets, debt, and income on the Internet site <http://www.ers.usda.gov/briefing/farmincome/>. Sources of current data on agricultural exports and imports include *Outlook for U.S. Agricultural Trade*, published by the ERS; the ERS Internet site <http://www.ers.usda.gov/briefing/AgTrade>; and the reports of the U.S. Census Bureau, particularly *U.S. Imports of Merchandise on CD-ROM*, and *U.S. Exports of Merchandise on CD-ROM*.

The 45 field offices of the NASS collect data on crops, livestock and products, agricultural prices, farm employment, and other related subjects mainly through sample surveys. Information is obtained on some 75 crops and 50 livestock items as well as scores of items pertaining to agricultural production and marketing. State estimates and supporting information are sent to the Agricultural Statistics Board of NASS, which reviews the estimates and issues reports containing state and national data. Among these reports are annual summaries such as *Crop Production, Crop Values, Agricultural Prices,* and *Livestock Production, Disposition and Income.* For more information about concepts and methods underlying USDA's statistical series, see *Major Statistical Series of the U.S. Department of Agriculture* (Agricultural Handbook No. 671), a 12-volume set of publications.

Farms and farmland—The definitions of a farm have varied through time. Since 1850, when minimum criteria defining a farm for census purposes first were established, the farm definition has changed nine times. The current definition, first used for the 1974 census, is any place from which $1,000 or more of agricultural products were produced and sold, or normally would have been sold, during the census year.

Acreage designated as "land in farms" consists primarily of agricultural land used for crops, pasture, or grazing. It also includes woodland and wasteland not actually under cultivation or used for pasture or grazing, provided it was part of the farm operator's total operation. Land in farms includes acres set aside under annual commodity acreage programs as well as acres in the Conservation Reserve and Wetlands Reserve Programs for places meeting the farm definition. Land in farms is an operating unit concept and includes land owned and operated as well as land rented from others. All grazing land, except land used under government permits on a per-head basis, was included as "land in farms" provided it was part of a farm or ranch.

Since 1945, an evaluation of census coverage has been conducted for each census of agriculture to provide estimates of the completeness of census farm counts. According to coverage evaluation results, the past five censuses of agriculture included an average of 92 percent of U.S. farms and 98 percent of agriculture production. The 1997 coverage evaluation program was designed to measure four components of error in the census farm counts. These components include undercount due to farms not on the mail list; overcount due to farms duplicated or enumerated more than once; undercount due to farms incorrectly classified as nonfarms; and overcount due to nonfarms incorrectly classified as farms. The first component, mail list undercount, is by far the largest component of coverage error. The percentage of farms missed in the census varies considerably by state. In general, farms not on the mail list tended to be small in acreage, production, and sales of agricultural products. For more explanation about mail list compilation and census coverage, see Appendixes A and C, *1997 Census of Agriculture*, Volume 1, reports.

Farm income—The final agricultural sector output comprises cash receipts from farm marketings of crops and livestock, federal government payments made directly to farmers for farm-related activities, rental value of farm homes, value of farm products consumed in farm homes, and other farm-related income such as machine hire and custom work. Farm marketings represent quantities of agricultural products sold by farmers multiplied by prices received per unit of production at the local market. Information on prices received for farm products is generally obtained by the NASS Agricultural Statistics Board from surveys of firms (such as grain elevators, packers, and processors) purchasing agricultural commodities directly from producers. In some cases, the price information is obtained directly from the producers.

Crops—Estimates of crop acreage and production by the NASS are based on current sample survey data obtained from individual producers and objective yield counts, reports of carlot shipments, market records, personal field observations by field statisticians, and reports from other sources. Prices received by farmers are marketing year averages. These averages are based on U.S. monthly prices weighted by monthly marketings during specific periods. U.S. monthly prices are state average prices weighted by marketings during the month. Marketing year average prices do not include allowances for outstanding loans, government purchases, deficiency payments or disaster payments.

All state prices are based on individual state marketing years, while U.S. marketing year averages are based on standard marketing years for each crop. For a listing of the crop marketing years and the participating states in the monthly program, see *Crop Values*. Value of production is computed by multiplying state prices by each state's production. The U.S. value of production is the sum of state values for all states. Value of production figures shown in Tables 834-837, 841, and 842 should not be confused with cash receipts from farm marketings which relate to sales during a calendar year, irrespective of the year of production.

Livestock—Annual inventory numbers of livestock and estimates of livestock, dairy, and poultry production prepared by the Department of Agriculture are based on information from farmers and ranchers obtained by probability survey sampling methods.

Statistical reliability—For a discussion of statistical collection and estimation, sampling procedures, and measures of statistical reliability pertaining to Department of Agriculture data, see Appendix III.

No. 805. Farms—Number and Acreage by Size of Farm: 1987 to 1997

[2,088 represents 2,088,000. See Appendix III]

Size of farm	Number of farms (1,000)			Land in farms (mil. acres)			Cropland harvested (mil. acres)			Percent distribution, 1997		
	1987	1992	1997	1987	1992	1997	1987	1992	1997	Number of farms	All land in farms	Cropland harvested
Total	2,088	1,925	1,912	964.5	945.5	931.8	282.2	295.9	309.4	100.0	100.0	100.0
Under 10 acres	183	166	154	0.7	0.7	0.6	0.2	0.2	0.2	8.1	0.1	0.1
10 to 49 acres	412	388	411	11.1	10.3	11.0	3.9	3.5	3.6	21.5	1.2	1.2
50 to 99 acres	311	283	295	22.5	20.4	21.2	7.9	7.2	7.0	15.4	2.3	2.3
100 to 179 acres	334	301	298	45.3	40.7	40.2	17.1	15.4	14.3	15.6	4.3	4.6
180 to 259 acres	192	172	165	41.5	37.2	35.5	17.2	15.5	14.0	8.6	3.8	4.5
260 to 499 acres	286	255	238	103.0	91.7	85.4	47.3	43.6	39.3	12.4	9.2	12.7
500 to 999 acres	200	186	176	138.5	129.3	122.1	67.4	68.6	65.4	9.2	13.1	21.1
1,000 to 1,999 acres	102	102	101	138.8	139.0	138.8	61.1	69.3	73.8	5.3	14.9	23.9
2,000 acres and over	67	71	75	463.2	476.3	476.9	60.2	72.5	91.8	3.9	51.2	29.7

No. 806. Farms—Number and Acreage by Tenure of Operator: 1987 to 1997

[2,088 represents 2,088,000. *Full owners* own all the land they operate. *Part owners* own a part and rent from others the rest of the land they operate. See Appendix III]

Item and year	Unit	Tenure of operator				Type of organization		
		Total [1]	Full owner	Part owner	Tenant	Individual or family	Partnership	Corporation
NUMBER OF FARMS								
1987	1,000	2,088	1,239	609	240	1,809	200	67
1992	1,000	1,925	1,112	597	217	1,653	187	73
1997	1,000	1,912	1,147	574	191	1,643	169	84
LAND IN FARMS								
1987	Mil. acres	964	318	520	127	628	153	119
1992	Mil. acres	946	296	527	123	604	153	123
1997	Mil. acres	932	316	508	108	585	149	131

[1] Includes other types, not shown separately.

No. 807. Farm Operators—Tenure and Characteristics: 1992 and 1997

[In thousands, except as indicated (1,925 represents 1,925,000). See Appendix III]

Characteristic	All farms		Farms with sales of $10,000 and over		Characteristic	All farms		Farms with sales of $10,000 and over	
	1992	1997	1992	1997		1992	1997	1992	1997
Total operators	1,925	1,912	1,019	949	Full owner	1,112	1,147	422	404
					Part owner	597	574	448	419
White	1,882	1,865	1,003	932	Tenant	217	191	148	126
Black	19	18	5	4	Principal occupation:				
American Indian, Eskimo, and Aleut	8	10	3	4	Farming	1,053	962	754	675
Asian or Pacific Islander	8	9	5	5	Other	872	950	265	274
Other	8	10	3	3	Place of residence: [2]				
					On farm operated	1,379	1,362	736	681
Operators of Hispanic origin [1]	21	28	8	11	Not on farm operated	409	413	215	201
					Years on present farm: [2]				
Female	145	165	50	52	2 years or less	95	93	41	35
					3 to 4 years	133	127	58	46
Under 25 years old	28	21	17	12	5 to 9 years	259	264	121	109
25 to 34 years old	179	128	112	72	10 years or more	1,113	1,114	648	616
35 to 44 years old	382	371	217	200	Days worked off farm: [2]				
45 to 54 years old	429	467	223	232	None	802	755	536	476
55 to 64 years old	430	427	229	212	Less than 100 days	165	165	104	98
65 years old and over	478	497	220	222	100 to 199 days	162	168	76	76
Average age (years)	53.3	54.3	51.9	53.2	200 days or more	666	709	226	229

[1] Operators of Hispanic origin may be of any race. [2] Excludes not reported.

Source of Tables 805-807: U.S. Dept. of Agriculture, National Agricultural Statistics Service, *Census of Agriculture: 1992*, Vol. 1; and *1997*, Vol. 1.

No. 808. Farms—Number and Acreage: 1980 to 2002

[As of June 1 (2,440 represents 2,440,000). Based on 1974 census definition; for definition of farms and farmland, see text of this section. Data for census years (indicated by italics) have been adjusted for underenumeration and are used as reference points along with data from acreage and livestock surveys in estimating data for other years. Minus sign (-) indicates decrease]

Year	Farms Number (1,000)	Annual change[1] (1,000)	Land in farms Total (mil. acres)	Average per farm (acres)	Year	Farms Number (1,000)	Annual change[1] (1,000)	Land in farms Total (mil. acres)	Average per farm (acres)
1980	2,440	3	1,039	426	1997	2,191	-	956	436
1985	2,293	-41	1,012	441	1998	2,191	1	954	435
1990	2,146	-29	987	460	1999	2,192	1	947	432
1992	2,108	-9	979	464	2000	2,172	-20	943	434
1995	2,196	-1	963	438	2001	2,156	-17	941	437
1996	2,191	-6	959	438	2002	2,158	2	941	436

- Represents or rounds to zero. [1] Annual change from immediate preceding year.

No. 809. Farms—Number and Acreage by State: 2000 and 2002

[2,172 represents 2,172,000. See headnote, Table 808]

State	Farms (1,000) 2000	2002	Acreage (mil.) 2000	2002	Acreage per farm 2000	2002	State	Farms (1,000) 2000	2002	Acreage (mil.) 2000	2002	Acreage per farm 2000	2002
U.S.	2,172	2,158	943	941	434	436	Montana	28	28	57	57	2,054	2,025
Alabama	47	47	9	9	191	189	Nebraska	54	52	46	46	859	892
Alaska	1	1	1	1	1,586	1,559	Nevada	3	3	7	7	2,267	2,267
Arizona	8	7	27	27	3,560	3,630	New Hampshire	3	3	(Z)	(Z)	135	132
Arkansas	48	49	15	15	304	301	New Jersey	10	10	1	1	86	85
California	88	84	28	28	318	330	New Mexico	15	15	44	44	2,895	2,933
Colorado	30	30	32	31	1,071	1,043	New York	38	37	8	8	203	205
Connecticut	4	4	(Z)	(Z)	92	92	North Carolina	57	56	9	9	161	163
Delaware	3	2	1	1	223	233	North Dakota	30	30	39	39	1,300	1,313
Florida	44	44	10	10	234	232	Ohio	80	78	15	15	186	188
Georgia	50	50	11	11	222	220	Oklahoma	85	87	34	34	400	391
Hawaii	6	5	1	1	262	272	Oregon	40	41	17	17	430	420
Idaho	25	24	12	12	486	496	Pennsylvania	59	59	8	8	131	131
Illinois	78	76	28	28	355	364	Rhode Island	1	1	(Z)	(Z)	86	86
Indiana	64	63	16	15	242	244	South Carolina	24	25	5	5	200	196
Iowa	95	93	33	33	345	352	South Dakota	33	33	44	44	1,354	1,354
Kansas	64	63	48	47	742	752	Tennessee	90	90	12	12	130	130
Kentucky	90	89	14	14	151	153	Texas	226	230	130	131	575	570
Louisiana	30	29	8	8	275	278	Utah	16	15	12	12	748	773
Maine	7	7	1	1	187	188	Vermont	7	7	1	1	200	203
Maryland	12	12	2	2	169	172	Virginia	49	49	9	9	178	178
Massachusetts	6	6	1	1	93	93	Washington	40	39	16	16	393	403
Michigan	52	52	10	10	200	200	West Virginia	21	21	4	4	176	176
Minnesota	79	79	29	28	362	359	Wisconsin	77	77	16	16	210	206
Mississippi	43	43	11	11	258	256	Wyoming	9	9	35	35	3,761	3,761
Missouri	109	107	30	30	275	279							

Z Less than 500,000 acres.

Source of Tables 808 and 809: U.S. Dept. of Agriculture, National Agricultural Statistics Service, *Farm Numbers, 1975-80; Farms and Land in Farms, Final Estimates by States, 1979-1987; Farms and Land in Farms, Final Estimates, 1988-1992; Farms and Land in Farms, Final Estimates, 1993-1997*; and *Farms and Land In Farms*, February releases.

No. 810. Certified Organic Farmland Acreage and Livestock: 1997 to 2001

Item	Unit	1997	2000	2001	Crop	Certified organic acreage (1,000) 1997	2001
Certified growers	Number	5,021	6,592	6,949	Corn	43	94
					Wheat	126	195
Certified organic acreage, total	1,000	1,347	2,029	2,344	Oats	30	33
					Barley	30	31
Pastureland and rangeland	1,000	496	810	1,040	Rice	11	32
Cropland	1,000	850	1,219	1,305	Millet	12	23
					Buckwheat	8	14
Certified animals:					Soybeans	82	174
Beef cows	Number	4,429	13,829	15,197	Dry beans	5	15
Milk cows	Number	12,897	38,196	48,677	Hay and silage	127	254
Hogs and pigs	Number	482	1,724	3,135	Sunflowers	11	15
Sheep and lambs	Number	705	2,279	4,207	Lettuce	6	16
Layer hens	1,000	538	1,114	1,612	Apples	9	12
Broilers	1,000	38	1,925	3,286	Grapes	19	15
Turkeys	Number	(NA)	9,138	98,653	Cotton	10	11
Unclassified/other	Number	226,105	111,359	17,244	Trees for maple syrup	14	12

NA Not available.

Source: U.S. Dept. of Agriculture, Economic Research Service, *U.S. Organic Farming Emerges in the 1990s: Adoption of Certified Systems*, AIB No. 770, June 2001; *U.S. Organic Farming in 2000-2001: Adoption of Certified Systems*, AIB No. 780, February 2003; and "U.S. Organic Agriculture Data Tables"; <http://www.ers.usda.gov/data/organic>.

No. 811. Gross Farm Product—Summary: 1980 to 2001

[In billions of dollars (142.9 represents $142,900,000,000). For definition of gross product, see text, Section 13. Minus sign (-) indicates decrease]

Item	1980	1990	1993	1994	1995	1996	1997	1998	1999	2000	2001
CURRENT DOLLARS											
Farm output, total	142.9	185.3	187.4	203.3	197.9	222.6	226.3	214.6	207.5	214.3	221.3
Cash receipts from farm marketings	140.3	172.1	182.0	181.0	194.2	201.2	208.6	197.6	191.4	199.4	200.9
Farm housing	5.1	5.1	5.6	5.9	6.0	6.2	6.4	6.7	7.2	7.6	8.0
Farm products consumed on farms	1.2	0.7	0.6	0.6	0.5	0.5	0.5	0.5	0.5	0.6	0.6
Other farm income	2.4	4.9	5.1	5.1	6.3	6.8	7.8	9.0	9.9	8.9	10.3
Change in farm inventories	-6.1	2.4	-5.9	10.8	-9.2	7.9	2.9	0.9	-1.5	-2.2	1.6
Less: Intermediate goods and services purchased [1]	86.8	105.7	113.9	119.8	124.7	130.4	138.1	134.1	132.3	136.5	140.7
Equals: **Gross farm product**	56.1	79.6	73.6	83.6	73.2	92.2	88.3	80.6	75.2	77.8	80.6
Less: Consumption of fixed capital	18.6	22.1	23.5	23.7	24.6	25.4	26.3	27.3	28.9	28.7	29.4
Indirect business tax [2]	3.0	4.3	4.4	4.7	5.0	5.0	5.2	5.2	5.3	5.4	5.6
Plus: Subsidies to operators	1.0	7.5	11.3	6.6	6.1	6.2	6.3	10.4	18.4	19.5	17.7
Equals: **Farm national income**	35.5	60.8	56.9	61.8	49.7	68.1	63.1	58.5	59.3	63.3	63.2
CHAINED (1996) DOLLARS [3]											
Farm output, total	(NA)	200.8	208.3	227.1	217.9	222.6	237.5	238.5	244.1	249.2	246.1
Cash receipts from farm marketings	(NA)	186.3	202.6	202.9	214.7	201.2	218.7	219.8	226.2	233.4	224.4
Farm housing	(NA)	6.9	6.6	6.4	6.3	6.2	6.0	6.0	6.1	6.0	5.9
Farm products consumed on farms	(NA)	0.6	0.6	0.6	0.5	0.5	0.5	0.5	0.5	0.5	0.5
Other farm income	(NA)	5.7	6.0	5.8	7.0	6.8	8.2	9.9	11.8	10.6	12.2
Change in farm inventories	(NA)	2.6	-7.9	13.0	-12.3	7.9	3.2	1.6	-2.0	-2.5	2.0
Less: Intermediate goods and services purchased [1]	(NA)	117.0	122.8	127.7	132.3	130.4	134.4	138.2	137.2	133.3	134.6
Equals: **Gross farm product**	(NA)	84.2	85.8	100.3	85.5	92.2	103.6	100.3	108.1	120.5	114.3

NA Not available. [1] Includes rent paid to nonoperator landlords. [2] Includes nontax liability. [3] See text, Section 13.

Source: U.S. Bureau of Economic Analysis, *National Income and Product Accounts, Volume 1, 1929-97*, and Survey of Current Business, August 2002. See also <http://www.bea.gov/bea/dn/nipaweb/selecttable.asp>.

No. 812. Value Added to Economy by Agricultural Sector: 1980 to 2001

[In billions of dollars (148.0 represents $148,000,000,000). Data are consistent with the net farm income accounts and include income and expenses related to the farm operator dwellings. The concept presented is consistent with that employed by the Organization for Economic Co-Operation and Development]

Item	1980	1990	1993	1994	1995	1996	1997	1998	1999	2000	2001
Final agricultural sector output	148.0	188.8	191.6	208.2	203.5	228.4	230.6	219.7	212.9	218.8	225.8
Final crop output (sales) [1]	64.4	83.3	82.6	100.3	95.7	115.5	112.4	101.7	92.4	95.0	93.9
Final animal output (sales) [1]	70.3	90.2	92.1	89.8	87.8	92.1	94.2	96.5	95.3	99.3	106.3
Services and forestry	13.3	15.3	17.0	18.1	19.9	20.8	21.8	23.8	25.2	24.4	25.6
Machine hire and customwork	0.7	1.8	1.9	2.1	1.9	2.2	2.4	2.2	2.0	2.2	2.0
Forest products sold	1.0	1.9	2.5	2.6	2.8	2.7	2.9	3.1	2.8	2.9	2.8
Other farm income	0.6	4.5	4.6	4.3	5.8	6.2	6.9	8.7	10.2	8.7	10.1
Gross imputed rental value of farm dwellings	11.0	7.2	8.1	9.0	9.4	9.8	9.7	9.9	10.2	10.7	10.6
Less: Intermediate consumption outlays	77.0	92.9	100.7	104.9	109.7	113.2	119.8	117.6	118.6	121.9	127.5
Farm origin [2]	34.9	39.5	41.3	41.3	41.8	42.7	46.9	44.8	45.6	48.1	49.2
Feed purchased	21.0	20.4	21.4	22.6	23.8	25.2	26.3	25.0	24.5	24.5	25.2
Livestock and poultry purchased	10.7	14.6	14.7	13.3	12.5	11.3	13.8	12.6	13.8	16.1	15.7
Manufactured inputs [2]	22.4	22.0	23.1	24.4	26.1	28.6	29.2	28.1	27.1	28.7	29.7
Fertilizers and lime	9.5	8.2	8.4	9.2	10.0	10.9	10.9	10.6	9.9	10.0	10.3
Pesticides	3.5	5.4	6.7	7.2	7.7	8.5	9.0	9.0	8.6	8.5	8.6
Other intermediate expenses [2]	19.7	31.4	36.2	39.2	41.7	41.9	43.7	44.6	45.9	45.1	48.6
Repair and maintenance of capital items	7.1	8.6	9.2	9.1	9.5	10.3	10.4	10.4	10.5	10.8	11.2
Plus: Net government transactions [3]	-2.8	3.1	6.9	1.0	0.1	0.1	0.1	4.9	14.3	15.5	13.2
Direct Government payments	1.3	9.3	13.4	7.9	7.3	7.3	7.5	12.4	21.5	22.9	20.7
Property taxes	3.9	5.9	6.2	6.5	6.7	6.8	6.9	7.0	6.8	6.9	7.0
Equals: **Gross value added**	68.2	98.9	97.8	104.3	93.9	115.3	110.9	107.0	108.6	112.4	111.5
Less: Capital consumption	21.5	18.1	18.3	18.6	19.2	19.4	19.5	19.9	20.1	20.3	20.6
Equals: **Net value added**	46.7	80.8	79.5	85.7	74.8	95.9	91.4	87.2	88.4	92.1	90.9
Less: Employee compensation	8.3	12.5	13.2	13.5	14.3	15.2	15.9	16.8	17.4	17.9	19.0
Less: Net rent received by nonoperator landlords	6.1	10.2	10.9	11.8	10.9	13.0	11.9	11.4	11.3	11.8	12.0
Less: Real estate and nonreal estate interest	16.3	13.4	10.7	11.6	12.6	13.0	13.1	13.4	13.6	14.3	14.1
Equals: **Net farm income**	16.1	44.6	44.7	48.9	36.9	54.8	50.5	45.6	46.2	48.0	45.7

[1] Includes home consumption and value of inventory adjustment. [2] Includes other outlays not shown separately. [3] Direct Government payments minus motor vehicle registration and licensing fees and property taxes.

Source: U.S. Dept. of Agriculture, Economic Research Service, "United States and State Farm Income Data"; <http://www.ers.usda.gov/Data/farmincome/finfidmu.htm>; accessed 1 November 2002.

Agriculture 539

No. 813. Farm Income—Cash Receipts From Farm Marketings: 1995 to 2001

[In millions of dollars (188,049 represents $188,049,000,000). Represents gross receipts from commercial market sales as well as net Commodity Credit Corporation loans. The source estimates and publishes individual cash receipt values only for major commodities and major producing states. The U.S. receipts for individual commodities, computed as the sum of the reported states, may understate the value of sales for some commodities. The degree of underestimation in some of the minor commodities can be substantial]

Commodity	1995	1999	2000	2001	Commodity	1995	1999	2000	2001
Total	188,049	187,481	193,695	202,849	Carrots	545	565	438	577
Livestock and					Corn, sweet	647	680	708	767
products [1]	87,217	95,611	99,559	106,431	Cucumbers	302	367	384	382
Cattle and calves	34,044	36,530	40,711	40,440	Lettuce [1]	2,004	1,435	1,872	1,907
Hogs	10,255	8,622	11,803	12,456	Head	1,447	927	1,202	1,264
Sheep and lambs	566	462	466	394	Onions	706	700	679	777
Dairy products	19,880	23,207	20,608	24,695	Peppers, green	446	484	527	421
Broilers	11,762	15,128	13,989	16,688	Tomatoes	1,584	1,865	1,809	1,665
Chicken eggs	3,893	4,287	4,348	4,445	Fresh	871	952	1,160	1,117
Turkeys	2,769	2,754	2,765	2,729	Processing	713	913	649	548
Horses/mules	662	1,089	1,218	985	Cantaloups	347	390	367	420
Aquaculture [2]	797	827	847	781					
					Fruits/nuts [1]	11,075	11,953	12,626	11,742
					Oranges	1,749	1,452	1,798	1,369
Crops [1]	100,832	91,870	94,136	96,418	Apples	1,558	1,431	1,517	1,370
Rice	1,282	1,500	992	827	Avocados	242	345	353	329
Wheat	9,054	5,426	5,712	5,719	Cherries	212	290	327	326
Barley	825	563	561	529	Grapes [1]	2,045	2,918	3,099	2,924
Corn	18,893	14,663	15,377	17,109	Wine	965	1,556	1,909	1,815
Hay	3,288	3,382	3,845	4,557	Table	367	414	438	435
Sorghum grain	1,377	825	866	905	Raisins	528	677	485	404
Cotton	6,853	4,630	3,840	4,954	Peaches	401	463	489	477
Tobacco	2,548	2,273	2,315	1,880	Strawberries	812	1,134	1,086	1,086
Peanuts	1,014	972	897	1,002	Almonds	881	688	666	732
Soybeans	13,868	11,770	12,394	12,777	Walnuts	328	251	296	342
Sunflower	470	396	305	287					
Vegetables [1]	14,984	15,127	15,600	15,512	Sugarbeets	1,071	1,243	1,113	885
Beans, dry	567	595	414	392	Cane for sugar	893	962	905	918
Potatoes	2,492	2,454	2,368	2,464	Greenhouse/nursery [1]	10,751	13,042	13,741	13,795
Beans, snap	285	396	394	386	Floriculture	3,329	4,097	4,577	4,739
Broccoli	443	518	634	504	Christmas trees	415	448	471	493
Cabbage	260	250	338	375	Mushrooms	758	868	859	834

[1] Includes other commodities not shown separately. [2] See also Table 866.

Source: U.S. Dept. of Agriculture, Economic Research Service, "United States and State Farm Income Data"; <http://www.ers.usda.gov/Data/farmincome/finfidmu.htm>; accessed 6 November 2002.

No. 814. Balance Sheet of the Farming Sector: 1980 to 2001

[In billions of dollars, except as indicated (983 represents $983,000,000,000). As of December 31]

Item	1980	1990	1993	1994	1995	1996	1997	1998	1999	2000	2001
Assets	983	841	909	935	966	1,003	1,051	1,083	1,141	1,206	1,251
Real estate	783	619	678	704	740	770	808	840	889	949	999
Livestock and poultry [1]	61	71	73	68	58	60	67	63	73	77	73
Machinery, motor vehicles [2]	80	86	85	87	88	88	89	90	90	90	91
Crops [3]	33	23	23	23	27	32	33	30	28	28	25
Purchased inputs	(NA)	3	4	5	3	4	5	5	4	5	4
Financial assets	27	38	46	48	49	49	50	55	57	57	59
Claims	983	841	909	935	966	1,003	1,051	1,083	1,141	1,206	1,251
Debt [4]	167	138	142	147	151	156	165	173	176	184	192
Real estate debt	90	75	76	78	79	82	85	90	94	98	103
Non-real estate debt	77	63	66	69	71	74	80	83	82	87	89
Equity	816	703	767	788	815	847	886	910	965	1,022	1,059
FINANCIAL RATIOS (percent)											
Farm debt/equity ratio	20.4	19.6	18.5	18.6	18.5	18.4	18.7	19.0	18.3	18.0	18.1
Farm debt/asset ratio	17.0	16.4	15.6	15.7	15.6	15.6	15.7	16.0	15.5	15.3	15.4
Rate of return on assets from:											
Total	0.9	3.5	6.0	5.2	4.4	6.0	5.7	5.2	5.5	5.3	4.0
Current income [5]	1.2	4.1	3.2	3.8	2.2	4.2	3.0	2.4	1.8	2.0	1.9
Real capital gains [6]	-0.3	-0.6	2.8	1.4	2.2	1.8	2.8	2.8	3.7	3.2	2.2
Rate of return on equity from:											
Total	1.0	3.2	6.1	5.0	4.1	5.9	5.6	4.8	5.3	5.2	3.7
Current income [7]	-0.5	2.9	2.3	3.0	1.1	3.4	2.0	1.4	0.8	1.0	0.9
Real capital gains [8]	1.5	0.2	3.7	2.0	3.0	2.5	3.6	3.5	4.6	4.2	2.9

NA Not available. [1] Excludes horses, mules, and broilers. [2] Include only farm share value for trucks and autos. [3] All non-CCC crops held on farms plus the value above loan rate for crops held under Commodity Credit Corporation. [4] Excludes debt for nonfarm purposes. [5] Returns to farm assets from current income/farm business assets. Measures how efficiently the farm business uses its assets; the per dollar return on farm assets from current income only. [6] Real capital gains on farm business assets/farm business assets. The per dollar return on farm assets from real capital gains. [7] Returns to farm assets from current income minus interest/Farm business equity. Measures the returns to equity capital employed in farm business from current income less interest. [8] Real capital gains on farm business assets/farm business equity. The per dollar return on farm equity from real capital gains.

Source: U.S. Dept. of Agriculture, Economic Research Service, "Farm Business Balance Sheet and Financial Ratios"; published 4 December 2002; <http://www.ers.usda.gov/Data/FarmBalanceSheet/fbsdmu.htm>.

No. 815. Farm Assets, Debt, and Income by State: 2000 and 2001

[Assets and debt, as of December 31 (1,206,477 represents $1,206,477,000,000). Farm income data are after inventory adjustment and include income and expenses related to the farm operator's dwelling]

State	Assets (mil. dol.) 2000	Assets (mil. dol.) 2001	Debt (mil. dol.) 2000	Debt (mil. dol.) 2001	Debt/asset ratio (percent) 2000	Debt/asset ratio (percent) 2001	Final agricultural sector output (mil. dol.) 2000	Final agricultural sector output (mil. dol.) 2001	Net farm income (mil. dol.) 2000	Net farm income (mil. dol.) 2001
United States [1]	1,206,477	1,251,008	184,152	192,027	15.3	15.4	218,811	225,784	48,048	45,741
Alabama	16,678	17,325	2,137	2,256	12.8	13.0	3,845	4,266	1,130	1,581
Alaska	638	675	25	26	3.9	3.8	57	57	15	10
Arizona	35,625	39,413	1,485	1,540	4.2	3.9	2,626	2,815	776	1,004
Arkansas	22,143	22,533	4,468	4,677	20.2	20.8	5,204	5,551	1,483	1,400
California	89,300	91,322	18,641	19,440	20.9	21.3	27,373	27,569	5,562	3,769
Colorado	25,296	25,538	3,824	3,992	15.1	15.6	5,100	5,235	693	990
Connecticut	2,450	2,599	300	324	12.2	12.5	582	558	181	144
Delaware	1,854	1,820	395	418	21.3	23.0	834	938	133	218
Florida	27,249	28,833	4,892	5,109	18.0	17.7	7,070	6,745	2,580	2,166
Georgia	25,202	26,885	3,767	3,973	15.0	14.8	5,783	6,217	1,980	2,299
Hawaii	3,805	4,056	264	275	7.0	6.8	549	546	103	94
Idaho	17,098	17,422	3,107	3,232	18.2	18.6	3,802	4,120	908	1,147
Illinois	76,125	78,738	9,755	10,138	12.8	12.9	7,941	8,154	1,537	1,419
Indiana	41,549	42,556	5,978	6,243	14.4	14.7	5,258	5,713	780	964
Iowa	73,919	75,327	13,646	14,113	18.5	18.7	11,651	11,906	2,427	1,946
Kansas	37,465	37,413	7,375	7,626	19.7	20.4	8,640	9,080	974	958
Kentucky	24,783	25,508	3,539	3,712	14.3	14.6	4,604	4,207	1,731	1,230
Louisiana	11,569	11,742	1,820	1,899	15.7	16.2	1,985	2,036	519	418
Maine	1,835	1,928	397	416	21.6	21.6	558	539	114	82
Maryland	7,706	8,051	1,127	1,204	14.6	15.0	1,739	1,834	450	522
Massachusetts	3,366	3,635	395	420	11.7	11.6	462	442	52	27
Michigan	24,254	25,883	3,169	3,358	13.1	13.0	3,786	3,917	314	191
Minnesota	47,339	48,715	9,297	9,703	19.6	19.9	8,377	8,497	1,302	696
Mississippi	15,954	16,504	3,042	3,158	19.1	19.1	3,314	3,894	786	1,112
Missouri	45,725	49,069	6,296	6,547	13.8	13.3	5,472	5,593	1,001	910
Montana	24,396	24,717	2,781	2,859	11.4	11.6	1,983	1,968	272	304
Nebraska	44,452	44,375	9,617	9,899	21.6	22.3	9,491	10,317	1,357	1,610
Nevada	3,474	3,435	276	293	7.9	8.5	456	466	100	119
New Hampshire	959	1,026	106	115	11.1	11.2	172	177	14	13
New Jersey	5,359	5,751	468	496	8.7	8.6	959	921	246	189
New Mexico	11,485	11,508	1,473	1,548	12.8	13.5	2,197	2,341	541	820
New York	13,672	14,197	2,556	2,699	18.7	19.0	3,379	3,743	594	803
North Carolina	26,800	27,443	3,803	4,054	14.2	14.8	9,490	9,654	3,183	3,201
North Dakota	22,616	23,952	4,082	4,253	18.1	17.8	3,367	3,304	946	587
Ohio	39,515	41,755	4,459	4,714	11.3	11.3	5,420	5,478	1,104	1,049
Oklahoma	26,200	27,363	4,510	4,629	17.2	16.9	4,640	4,639	1,025	922
Oregon	18,956	19,652	2,633	2,732	13.9	13.9	3,686	3,753	378	266
Pennsylvania	23,269	23,840	2,928	3,086	12.6	12.9	4,803	4,883	1,116	969
Rhode Island	343	361	39	42	11.4	11.7	55	54	8	6
South Carolina	8,056	8,490	1,165	1,259	14.5	14.8	1,770	1,979	572	684
South Dakota	24,712	25,701	4,300	4,423	17.4	17.2	4,369	4,321	1,468	1,218
Tennessee	26,784	27,723	2,706	2,857	10.1	10.3	2,677	2,762	538	511
Texas	98,866	103,182	12,353	12,844	12.5	12.5	15,032	15,788	4,023	4,288
Utah	11,515	12,195	887	926	7.7	7.6	1,199	1,317	245	395
Vermont	2,313	2,464	374	400	16.2	16.2	589	610	151	136
Virginia	21,326	22,240	2,147	2,290	10.1	10.3	2,872	2,801	696	600
Washington	20,677	20,499	3,610	3,720	17.5	18.2	5,961	5,788	1,035	621
West Virginia	4,348	4,590	418	437	9.6	9.5	511	519	50	48
Wisconsin	36,597	39,366	6,203	6,500	17.0	16.5	6,067	6,713	716	888
Wyoming	10,838	11,690	1,119	1,151	10.3	9.8	1,055	1,058	141	200

[1] The U.S. total will exceed the sum of the states because data for some states are not included in the state's statistics due to disclosure issues.

Source: U.S. Dept. of Agriculture, Economic Research Service, "Farm Income Summary Totals for 50 States"; published 14 August 2002; <http://www.ers.usda.gov/Data/FarmIncome/50State/50stmenu.htm>; and "Farm Business Balance Sheet and Financial Ratios"; published 4 December 2002; <http://www.ers.usda.gov/Data/FarmBalanceSheet/fbsdmu.htm>.

No. 816. Cash Receipts for Selected Commodities—Leading States: 2001

[40,440 represents $40,440,000,000. See headnote, Table 813]

State	Value of receipts (mil. dol.)	Percent of total receipts	Rank	State	Value of receipts (mil. dol.)	Percent of total receipts	Rank
Cattle and calves	40,440	100.0	(X)	Corn	17,109	100.0	(X)
Texas	6,812	16.8	1	Iowa	3,120	18.2	1
Nebraska	5,067	12.5	2	Illinois	2,972	17.4	2
Kansas	4,915	12.2	3	Nebraska	1,951	11.4	3
Colorado	2,589	6.4	4	Indiana	1,533	9.0	4
Oklahoma	1,865	4.6	5	Minnesota	1,447	8.5	5
Dairy products	24,695	100.0	(X)	Broilers	16,688	100.0	(X)
California	4,630	18.7	1	Georgia	2,432	14.6	1
Wisconsin	3,243	13.1	2	Arkansas	2,238	13.4	2
New York	1,841	7.5	3	Alabama	2,004	12.0	3
Pennsylvania	1,792	7.3	4	North Carolina	1,681	10.1	4
Minnesota	1,297	5.3	5	Mississippi	1,492	8.9	5

X Not applicable.

No. 817. Farm Income—Farm Marketings, 2000 and 2001, and Principal Commodities, 2001 by State

[In millions of dollars (193,695 represents $193,695,000,000). Cattle include calves and greenhouse includes nursery]

State	2000 Total	2000 Crops	2000 Livestock and products	2001 Total	2001 Crops	2001 Livestock and products	State rank for total farm marketings and four principal commodities in order of marketing receipts
U.S.	193,695	94,136	99,559	202,849	96,418	106,431	Cattle, dairy products, corn, broilers
AL	3,205	560	2,646	3,520	705	2,815	23-Broilers, cattle, chicken eggs, greenhouse
AK	52	20	32	52	24	28	49-Greenhouse, potatoes, hay, dairy products
AZ	2,287	1,217	1,070	2,575	1,409	1,166	29-Cattle, lettuce, dairy products, cotton
AR	4,738	1,483	3,255	5,132	1,625	3,507	13-Broilers, cotton, cattle, soybeans
CA	25,683	19,431	6,252	25,892	18,546	7,346	1-Dairy products, greenhouse, grapes, lettuce
CO	4,612	1,281	3,330	4,729	1,354	3,374	16-Cattle, dairy products, corn, hogs
CT	496	328	168	476	299	177	44-Greenhouse, dairy products, chicken eggs, aquaculture
DE	736	179	558	848	186	662	39-Broilers, corn, soybeans, greenhouse
FL	6,777	5,402	1,375	6,416	4,958	1,458	9-Greenhouse, oranges, tomatoes, sugar cane
GA	5,099	1,991	3,107	5,515	1,975	3,540	11-Broilers, cotton, peanuts, chicken eggs
HI	522	430	92	511	419	91	42-Pineapples, greenhouse, sugar cane, macadamia nuts
ID	3,372	1,744	1,628	3,848	1,788	2,060	21-Dairy products, cattle, potatoes, hay
IL	7,127	5,416	1,711	7,547	5,704	1,843	8-Corn, soybeans, hogs, cattle
IN	4,584	2,883	1,701	5,105	3,235	1,870	14-Corn, soybeans, hogs, dairy products
IA	10,804	5,047	5,757	11,550	5,615	5,936	3-Hogs, corn, soybeans, cattle
KS	8,019	2,519	5,500	8,121	2,585	5,536	5-Cattle, wheat, corn, sorghum grain
KY	3,649	1,277	2,372	3,548	1,281	2,268	22-Horses/mules, tobacco, broilers, cattle
LA	1,787	1,135	652	1,817	1,116	701	33-Sugar cane, cotton, cattle, dairy products
ME	502	242	260	485	211	274	43-Dairy products, potatoes, aquaculture, chicken eggs
MD	1,451	615	836	1,596	647	949	36-Broilers, greenhouse, dairy products, corn
MA	388	295	93	367	273	94	47-Greenhouse, dairy products, cranberries, sweet corn
MI	3,322	1,988	1,334	3,469	1,980	1,489	24-Dairy products, greenhouse, corn, soybeans
MN	7,463	3,580	3,883	8,102	3,813	4,288	6-Corn, hogs, dairy products, soybeans
MS	2,727	691	2,036	3,147	871	2,276	26-Broilers, cotton, aquaculture, cattle
MO	4,614	1,933	2,680	4,824	2,145	2,679	15-Cattle, soybeans, corn, hogs
MT	1,844	737	1,106	1,785	657	1,128	34-Cattle, wheat, hay, barley
NE	8,993	3,076	5,917	9,489	3,402	6,086	4-Cattle, corn, soybeans, hogs
NV	387	150	237	425	153	271	45-Cattle, hay, dairy products, greenhouse
NH	151	91	60	155	90	66	48-Greenhouse, dairy products, apples, cattle
NJ	826	635	192	821	617	204	40-Greenhouse, horses/mules, dairy products, blueberries
NM	2,114	500	1,613	2,215	545	1,670	31-Dairy products, cattle, hay, greenhouse
NY	3,122	1,191	1,931	3,420	1,199	2,221	25-Dairy products, greenhouse, cattle, apples
NC	7,340	3,040	4,300	7,731	3,087	4,644	7-Hogs, broilers, greenhouse, tobacco
ND	2,706	2,077	629	2,979	2,259	720	28-Wheat, cattle, soybeans, corn
OH	4,370	2,616	1,754	4,682	2,818	1,864	17-Soybeans, corn, dairy products, greenhouse
OK	4,293	853	3,441	4,027	874	3,153	20-Cattle, hogs, broilers, wheat
OR	3,093	2,264	829	3,123	2,298	825	27-Greenhouse, cattle, dairy products, hay
PA	4,063	1,297	2,766	4,455	1,309	3,146	18-Dairy products, cattle, agaricus mushrooms, greenhouse
RI	46	38	8	47	40	8	50-Greenhouse, dairy products, sweet corn, cattle
SC	1,521	728	793	1,646	764	882	35-Broilers, greenhouse, tobacco, cattle
SD	3,806	1,769	2,037	4,108	1,852	2,255	19-Cattle, corn, soybeans, hogs
TN	1,997	1,007	990	2,161	1,034	1,127	32-Cattle, broilers, dairy products, greenhouse
TX	13,370	4,211	9,159	13,796	4,456	9,339	2-Cattle, greenhouse, broilers, cotton
UT	1,020	248	772	1,116	263	853	37-Cattle, dairy products, hay, hogs
VT	500	69	432	557	67	490	41-Dairy products, cattle, greenhouse, hay
VA	2,285	735	1,549	2,444	771	1,673	30-Broilers, cattle, dairy products, turkeys
WA	5,117	3,408	1,709	5,192	3,464	1,728	12-Dairy products, apples, cattle, potatoes
WV	397	58	339	408	59	348	46-Broilers, cattle, dairy products, turkeys
WI	5,364	1,498	3,866	5,896	1,432	4,464	10-Dairy products, cattle, corn, greenhouse
WY	957	157	800	983	145	837	38-Cattle, hay, hogs, sugar beets

Source of Tables 816 and 817: U.S. Dept. of Agriculture, Economic Research Service, "Farm Income"; published 4 October 2002; <http://www.ers.usda.gov/Data/farmincome/finfidmu.htm>.

No. 818. Indexes of Prices Received and Paid by Farmers: 1990 to 2002

[1990-92=100, except as noted]

Item	1990	2000	2001	2002	Item	1990	2000	2001	2002
Prices received, all products	104	96	102	99	**Prices paid, total** [2]	99	118	122	122
					Production	99	116	120	119
Crops	103	96	99	106	Feed	103	102	109	113
Food grains	100	85	91	104	Livestock & poultry	102	110	111	102
Feed grains and hay	105	86	91	100	Seed	102	124	132	142
Cotton	107	82	64	55	Fertilizer	97	110	123	109
Tobacco	97	107	107	108	Agricultural chemicals	95	120	120	118
Oil-bearing crops	105	85	80	88	Fuels	100	134	119	112
Fruits and nuts	97	99	109	112	Supplies & repairs	96	124	128	131
Commercial vegetables [1]	102	121	126	141	Autos and trucks	97	119	118	116
Potatoes & dry beans	133	93	98	134	Farm machinery	96	139	144	145
All other crops	(NA)	110	112	113	Building materials	99	121	121	122
					Farm services	96	119	121	120
					Rent	(NA)	110	117	119
Livestock and products	105	97	106	91	Interest	107	113	114	109
Meat animals	105	94	97	87	Taxes	95	123	124	126
Dairy products	105	95	115	93	Wage rates	96	140	146	152
Poultry and eggs	105	106	116	97	Parity ratio (1910-14=100) [3]	51	38	40	38

NA Not available. [1] Excludes potatoes and dry beans. [2] Includes production items, interest, taxes, wage rates, and a family living component. The family living component is the Consumer Price Index for all urban consumers from the Bureau of Labor Statistics. See text, Section 14, and Table ???. [3] Ratio of prices received by farmers to prices paid.
Source: U.S. Dept. of Agriculture, National Agricultural Statistics Service, *Agricultural Prices: Annual Summary*.

No. 819. Value of Selected Commodities Produced Under Contracts: 2001

[70,518 represents $70,518,000,000. Marketing contracts refer to verbal or written agreements between a buyer and a grower that set a price and determine an outlet for a specified quantity of a commodity before harvest or before the farmer markets the commodity. Production contracts involve paying the farmer a fee for providing management, labor, facilities, and equipment, while assigning ownership of the product to the contractor. Survey based estimates (see source) exclude Alaska and Hawaii and do not represent official U.S. Dept. of Agriculture estimates of farm sector activity]

Commodity	Value of production under contract (mil. dol.)	Percent of total production [1]	Commodity	Value of production under contract (mil. dol.)	Percent of total production [1]
Total	70,518	36	Sugar beets	548	94
Marketing contracts [2]	39,426	20	Vegetables	[3]3,078	[3]30
Cattle	[3]1,219	[3]3	**Production contracts** [2]	31,092	16
Corn	1,934	13	Poultry and eggs [4]	15,114	81
Cotton	1,621	52	Cattle	[3]6,669	[3]18
Fruits	8,679	56	Hogs	6,092	53
Hogs	[3]812	[3]7	Vegetables	[3]714	[3]7
Soybeans	1,032	9			

[1] Represents percent of value of production under contract as percent of total value of commodity production. [2] Includes other commodities not shown separately. [3] Data have relative standard error between 25 and 49 percent. [4] Data not available to estimate value of production for broilers.
Source: U.S. Dept. of Agriculture, Economic Research Service, Agricultural Resource Management Survey, annual.

No. 820. Civilian Consumer Expenditures for Farm Foods: 1980 to 2001

[In billions of dollars, except percent (264.4 represents $264,400,000,000). Excludes imported and nonfarm foods, such as coffee and seafood, as well as food consumed by the military, or exported]

Item	1980	1990	1993	1994	1995	1996	1997	1998	1999	2000	2001
Consumer expenditures, total	264.4	449.8	489.2	512.2	529.5	546.7	566.5	585.0	625.3	661.1	687.5
Farm value, total	81.7	106.2	109.6	109.6	113.8	122.2	121.9	119.6	122.2	123.3	130.0
Marketing bill, total [1]	182.7	343.6	379.6	402.6	415.7	424.5	444.6	465.4	503.1	537.8	557.5
Percent of total consumer expenditures	69.1	76.4	77.6	78.6	78.5	77.6	78.5	79.6	80.5	81.3	81.1
At-home expenditures [2]	180.1	276.2	294.9	308.7	316.9	328.0	339.2	346.8	370.7	390.2	403.9
Farm value	65.9	80.2	76.4	75.3	76.1	81.6	79.0	77.0	78.7	79.6	83.9
Marketing bill [1]	114.2	196.0	218.5	233.4	240.8	246.4	260.2	269.8	292.0	310.6	320.0
Away-from-home expenditures	84.3	173.6	194.3	203.5	212.6	218.7	227.3	238.2	254.6	270.9	283.6
Farm value	15.8	26.0	33.2	34.3	37.7	40.6	42.9	42.6	43.5	43.7	46.1
Marketing bill [1]	68.5	147.6	161.1	169.2	174.9	178.1	184.4	195.6	211.1	227.2	237.5
Marketing bill cost components:											
Labor cost	81.5	154.0	178.0	186.1	196.6	204.6	216.9	229.9	241.5	252.9	263.8
Packaging materials	21.0	36.5	40.9	43.3	48.2	47.7	48.7	50.4	50.9	53.5	55.0
Rail and truck transport	13.0	19.8	21.2	21.8	22.3	22.9	23.6	24.4	25.2	26.4	27.5
Corporate profits before taxes	9.9	13.2	18.1	20.9	19.5	20.7	22.3	25.5	29.2	31.1	32.0
Fuels and electricity	9.0	15.2	17.2	17.9	18.6	19.6	20.2	20.7	22.0	23.1	24.1
Advertising	7.3	17.1	18.6	19.3	19.8	20.9	22.1	23.4	24.8	26.1	27.5
Depreciation	7.8	16.3	17.2	18.1	18.9	20.1	21.0	21.6	23.0	24.2	24.5
Net interest	3.4	13.5	10.1	11.0	11.6	11.4	12.5	12.9	14.4	16.9	18.6
Net rent	6.8	13.9	17.9	18.9	19.8	21.0	21.8	23.7	25.3	26.7	29.4
Repairs	3.6	6.2	7.2	7.8	7.9	8.5	8.8	9.0	9.6	10.1	10.6
Taxes	8.3	15.7	18.2	18.7	19.1	19.4	19.8	20.9	22.2	23.5	24.1
Other	11.0	22.2	15.0	18.8	13.4	7.7	6.9	3.0	15.0	23.3	20.4

[1] The difference between expenditures for domestic farm-originated food products and the farm value or payment farmers received for the equivalent farm products. [2] Food primarily purchased from retail food stores for use at home.
Source: U.S. Dept. of Agriculture, Economic Research Service, *Food Cost Review, 1950-97*, ERS Agricultural Economic Report No. AER780, June 1999; and "ERS/USDA Briefing Room - Food marketing and price spreads: USDA marketing bill"; <http://www.ers.usda.gov/Briefing/FoodPriceSpreads/bill/>.

Agriculture 543

No. 821. Indexes of Farm Production, Input Use, and Productivity: 1980 to 1999

[1996=100]

Item	1980	1985	1990	1992	1993	1994	1995	1996	1997	1998	1999
Farm output [1]	74	84	89	95	91	101	97	100	104	105	107
Livestock and products [2]	82	84	90	94	95	100	102	100	103	105	108
Meat animals	95	90	93	97	97	103	103	97	103	103	105
Dairy products	83	92	96	98	98	100	101	100	101	102	106
Poultry and eggs	53	59	76	83	87	91	95	100	102	104	109
Cereals	79	102	94	105	79	106	83	100	100	104	100
Forage	95	103	99	99	98	101	101	100	104	103	108
Industrial crops	74	83	85	94	85	106	93	100	110	104	103
Potatoes	61	79	83	89	87	96	90	100	94	95	96
Vegetables and horticulture	53	62	82	87	91	100	96	100	101	102	106
Fruits and nuts	93	88	99	104	110	116	108	109	129	113	123
Other crops	55	70	92	88	79	83	101	100	85	97	84
Farm input [3]	115	104	102	99	99	100	102	100	101	99	100
Farm labor	126	111	105	102	98	99	103	100	101	98	101
Farm real estate	114	110	105	104	102	102	101	100	99	99	98
Durable equipment	186	157	119	113	109	106	103	100	98	98	99
Energy	113	92	94	94	94	97	102	100	102	104	105
Agricultural chemicals [4]	112	90	95	98	94	101	92	100	108	105	104
Other purchased inputs [5]	98	90	96	91	97	98	101	98	99	96	98
Farm output per unit of input	64	81	88	96	91	101	95	100	103	106	107

[1] Annual production available for eventual human use. [2] Includes items not shown separately. [3] Based on physical quantities of resources used in production. [4] Includes fertilizer, lime, and pesticides. [5] Includes purchased services and miscellaneous inputs.

Source: U.S. Dept. of Agriculture, Economic Research Service, unpublished data.

No. 822. Hired Farmworkers—Selected Characteristics: 1990 to 2002

[Annual averages (886 represents 886,000). Data for 1990 are not directly comparable with data for later years. Data are calculated by source using data from the Census Bureau's Current Population Survey earnings microdata file]

Characteristic	1990	1995	1998	1999	2000	2001	2002
Number of workers (1,000)	886	849	875	840	878	745	793
PERCENT DISTRIBUTION							
Total	100.0	100.0	100.0	100.0	100.0	100.0	100.0
Age:							
Less than 25 years old	31.5	30.1	28.4	30.4	26.0	26.2	29.4
25 to 44 years old	47.6	44.2	46.7	44.0	46.9	48.4	43.2
45 to 59 years old	14.4	18.2	17.8	18.8	19.6	19.9	20.4
60 years old and over	6.5	7.5	7.1	6.8	7.5	5.5	7.0
Median age	28.0	32.0	33.0	33.0	35.0	35.0	36.0
Sex:							
Male	82.9	84.5	83.8	80.7	82.1	80.7	78.7
Female	17.1	15.5	16.2	19.3	17.9	19.3	21.3
Racial/ethnic group:							
White	61.0	53.5	52.4	50.1	47.2	49.1	52.2
Hispanic	29.4	41.1	41.8	43.0	46.4	45.7	42.0
Black and other	9.6	5.3	5.8	6.4	6.4	5.2	5.8
Years of school completed:							
0 to 4 years	11.1	14.2	10.9	11.3	13.4	10.6	11.1
5 to 8 years	21.6	22.5	21.1	22.6	21.0	21.2	19.9
9 to 11 years	22.8	22.7	24.9	20.7	21.2	23.3	21.2
12 years [1]	31.4	25.9	26.5	27.1	25.7	27.3	27.6
13 years or more	13.1	14.7	16.6	18.3	18.7	17.6	20.2
Employment status:							
Part-time [2]	21.8	18.3	18.6	20.5	19.3	19.3	17.5
Full-time [2]	78.2	81.7	81.4	79.5	80.7	80.7	82.5
Median weekly earnings (dol.): [3]							
Full-time workers [2]	330	307	318	346	333	350	334
All workers	275	283	287	302	293	305	300

[1] A person received a high school diploma, GED, or equivalent degree. [2] Full-time workers usually work 35 or more hours per week. [3] Median earnings are in 2000 dollars.

Source: U.S. Dept. of Agriculture, Economic Research Service, "Hired Farmworkers' Earnings Increased in 2001 but Still Trail Most Occupations," Rural America, Vol. 17, Issue 3, fall 2002 and unpublished data.

No. 823. Agricultural Exports and Imports—Volume by Principal Commodities: 1990 to 2002

[In thousands of metric tons (2,707 represents 2,707,000)]

Exports	1990	2000	2001	2002	Imports	1990	2000	2001	2002
Animal products [1]	2,707	6,294	6,588	6,646	Fruits, nuts, vegetables	4,696	8,866	9,241	10,237
Wheat and products [2]	28,247	28,412	26,216	24,766	Bananas	3,094	4,031	3,841	3,907
Feed grains and products	61,526	55,602	55,563	54,744	Green coffee	1,174	1,297	1,159	1,163
Rice	2,534	3,241	2,889	3,802	Cocoa and products	716	999	991	916
Feeds and fodders	10,974	13,065	12,587	12,670	Red meat and poultry meat [5]	1,169	1,579	1,635	1,704
Protein meal	5,079	6,462	7,426	6,738					
Oilseeds and products [3]	15,820	28,017	29,974	28,574	Vegetable oils	1,204	1,846	1,898	1,945
Vegetable oils	1,226	2,043	2,193	2,674	Rubber, crude natural	840	1,232	1,002	1,213
Fruits, nuts, vegetables [4]	5,553	7,567	7,520	7,590	Sugar	1,858	1,474	1,356	1,394
Cotton and linters	1,733	1,539	1,894	2,149	Spices	129	211	223	255
Tobacco, unmanufactured	223	180	186	153	Tobacco, unmanufactured	173	216	233	260

[1] Includes meat and products, poultry meats, dairy products, and fats, oils and greases. Excludes live animals, hides, skins, and eggs. [2] Includes flour and bulgur. [3] Includes soybeans, sunflowerseeds, peanuts, cottonseed, safflowerseed, flaxseed, and nondefatted soybean flour. [4] Excludes fruit juices. [5] Excludes horsemeat.

Source: U.S. Dept. of Agriculture, Economic Research Service, *U.S. Agricultural Trade Update*, February 24, 2003; and *Foreign Agricultural Trade of the United States*, calendar year supplements, <http://www.ers.usda.gov/data/fatus/>.

No. 824. Agricultural Exports and Imports—Value: 1980 to 2002

[In billions of dollars, except percent (23.9 represents $23,900,000,000). Includes Puerto Rico. Excludes forest products and distilled liquors; includes crude rubber and similar gums (now mainly plantation products). Includes shipments under foreign aid programs]

Year	Trade balance	Exports, domestic products	Percent of all exports	Imports for consumption	Percent of all imports	Year	Trade balance	Exports, domestic products	Percent of all exports	Imports for consumption	Percent of all imports
1980	23.9	41.2	18	17.4	7	1996	26.9	60.4	10	33.5	4
1990	16.6	39.5	11	22.9	5	1997	21.1	57.2	9	36.1	4
1991	16.5	39.4	10	22.9	5	1998	14.9	51.8	8	36.9	4
1992	18.4	43.2	10	24.8	5	1999	10.7	48.4	8	37.7	4
1993	17.8	42.9	10	25.1	4	2000	12.3	51.2	7	39.0	3
1994	19.2	46.3	10	27.0	4	2001	14.3	53.7	8	39.4	3
1995	26.1	56.3	10	30.3	4	2002	11.1	53.0	8	41.9	4

Source: U.S. Dept. of Agriculture, Economic Research Service, *U.S. Agricultural Trade Update*, February 24, 2003; and *Foreign Agricultural Trade of the United States*, calendar year supplements, <http://www.ers.usda.gov/data/fatus/>.

No. 825. Agricultural Imports—Value by Selected Commodity, 1990 to 2002, and Leading Countries of Origin, 2002

[In millions of dollars (22,918 represents $22,918,000,000)]

Commodity	1990	1995	1999	2000	2001	2002	Leading countries of origin, 2002
Total	22,918	30,255	37,673	38,974	39,366	41,935	Canada, Mexico, Australia
Competitive products	17,344	21,792	29,714	31,213	32,744	34,917	Canada, Mexico, Australia
Cattle, live	978	1,413	1,001	1,152	1,461	1,447	Canada, Mexico, Australia
Beef and veal	1,872	1,447	2,136	2,399	2,712	2,741	Canada, Australia, New Zealand
Pork	938	686	753	997	1,048	1,001	Canada, Denmark, Poland
Dairy products	891	1,118	1,557	1,671	1,789	1,783	New Zealand, Canada, Italy
Fruits and preparations	2,218	2,249	3,540	3,471	3,445	3,839	Mexico, Chile, Costa Rica
Vegetables and preparations	2,317	3,189	4,583	4,740	5,252	5,614	Mexico, Canada, Spain
Wine	917	1,153	2,187	2,207	2,250	2,670	France, Italy, Australia
Malt beverages	923	1,166	1,893	2,179	2,348	2,581	Mexico, Netherlands, Canada
Grains and feeds	1,188	2,312	2,989	3,076	3,320	3,661	Canada, Mexico, Italy
Sugar and related products	1,213	1,335	1,589	1,555	1,600	1,855	Canada, Mexico, Brazil
Oilseeds and products	952	1,746	1,818	1,847	1,630	1,794	Canada, Italy, Malaysia
Noncompetitive products	5,574	8,464	7,959	7,761	6,622	7,018	Indonesia, Canada, Colombia
Coffee and products	1,915	3,263	2,893	2,700	1,677	1,693	Colombia, Brazil, Mexico
Rubber, crude natural	707	1,629	704	842	613	751	Indonesia, Thailand, Malaysia
Cocoa and products	1,072	1,106	1,522	1,404	1,536	1,762	Canada, Cote d'Ivoire, Indonesia
Bananas and plantains	939	1,140	1,209	1,130	1,179	1,175	Ecuador, Costa Rica, Guatemala

Source: U.S. Dept. of Agriculture, Economic Research Service, *U.S. Agricultural Trade Update*, February 24, 2003; and *Foreign Agricultural Trade of the United States*, calendar year supplements, <http://www.ers.usda.gov/data/fatus/>.

No. 826. Imports' Share of Food Consumption by Commodity: 1990 to 2001

[In percent. Import share is the total quantity imported divided by the quantity available for domestic human food consumption. Calculated from supply and utilization balance sheets. A portion of the imports of some commodities is exported plus, some is diverted to such nonfood uses as feed, seed, alcohol and fuel production, and industrial uses. These can overstate the importance of imports]

Commodity	1990	2000	2001	Commodity	1990	2000	2001
Beef	9.7	11.0	11.6	Wine	13.0	21.4	22.6
Pork	5.6	5.2	5.1	Vegetables—fresh, frozen	9.6	14.0	16.6
Dairy products	1.9	2.7	2.8	Cucumbers	33.7	42.4	44.2
Cheese	4.8	4.8	5.1	Onions	10.1	9.3	12.3
Fruits—fresh and frozen	13.2	22.3	23.1	Peppers, bell & chili	19.7	22.2	26.0
Citrus	3.6	11.8	12.5	Potatoes	5.8	6.0	5.0
Noncitrus	16.0	25.3	26.4	Tomatoes	20.5	32.4	35.5
Apples	4.3	7.2	7.0	Vegetables—processed	1.9	1.8	2.0
Grapes	41.1	44.3	44.5	Mushrooms	24.3	36.7	35.3
Melons	15.4	26.2	24.1	Olives	47.0	78.8	60.1
Pears	11.4	21.2	20.6	Vegetable oils	16.5	18.3	15.5
Strawberries	13.0	10.8	11.3	Spices	7.7	14.3	15.4
Fruits—processed	2.6	3.3	3.3	Wheat	4.1	8.7	10.7
Fruit juices	48.6	31.9	31.5	Rice	5.1	9.4	11.0
Orange juice	50.3	20.8	17.4	Barley	7.7	17.0	13.9
Apple juice	57.9	61.6	63.4	Cane and beet sugar	29.9	16.4	15.5
Grape juice	33.6	39.3	41.1	Confectionery products	17.1	28.7	27.3
Tree nuts	35.6	39.3	48.9	Malt beverages	4.5	9.9	10.7

Source: U.S. Dept. of Agriculture, Economic Research Service, "The Import Share of U.S.-Consumed Food Continues to Rise," *Electronic Outlook Report*, FAU-66-01, July 2002 and online at <http://www.ers.usda.gov/data/foodconsumption>.

No. 827. Percent of U.S. Agricultural Commodity Output Exported: 1980 to 2002

[In percent]

Commodity group	1980-84, average	1985-89, average	1990-94, average	1995-99, average	2000	2001	2002, prel.
Total agriculture	29.2	24.6	23.0	22.9	22.4	22.5	21.9
Livestock [1]	2.7	3.5	5.3	9.7	10.4	11.2	10.4
Red meat	1.2	2.0	4.1	7.1	8.2	8.4	8.9
Poultry meat	3.9	3.6	7.4	14.8	15.1	17.0	14.4
Dairy products [2]	8.3	10.4	5.0	4.6	4.1	3.1	3.3
Crops	30.8	26.0	24.2	23.9	23.3	23.3	22.8
Food grains [3]	61.1	53.3	51.0	47.6	45.9	46.7	46.7
Coarse grains [3]	27.4	23.4	21.2	21.5	21.0	20.4	21.3
Oilseeds/meal/oil	32.9	28.3	25.4	26.8	27.2	27.7	24.0
Fruits and nuts [4]	8.7	8.6	12.2	12.9	12.3	13.7	13.9
Vegetables [5]	5.1	4.0	5.7	6.4	6.6	6.7	6.5
Cotton and tobacco	49.0	41.7	40.7	38.1	43.7	57.0	57.6
Other crops [6]	8.2	5.9	7.5	6.9	5.8	5.8	6.2

[1] Excludes hides, animal fats, and live animals. [2] Includes butter, cheese, and nonfat dried milk. [3] Includes corn, barley, sorghum, and oats. [4] Includes fruit juices and wine, whose exports are converted from volume to weight measure using 8.3454 pounds per gallon. [5] Total vegetable production is estimated from U.S. per capita use of major fresh and processing vegetables; includes olives. [6] Estimated from value of exports and farm receipts of sugar, seeds, and nursery crops; not included in total crops export share.

Source: U.S. Dept. of Agriculture, Economic Research Service, USDA's commodity yearbooks, Foreign Agricultural Trade of the U.S., and Production, Supply, and Distribution database.

No. 828. Selected Farm Products—United States and World Production and Exports: 1995 to 2002

[In metric tons, except as indicated (59 represents 59,000,000). Metric ton=1.102 short tons or 0.984 long tons]

Commodity	Unit	United States 1995	United States 2000	United States 2002	World 1995	World 2000	World 2002	U.S. as percent of world 1995	U.S. as percent of world 2000	U.S. as percent of world 2002
PRODUCTION [1]										
Wheat	Million	59	61	44	539	582	564	11.0	10.4	7.8
Corn for grain	Million	188	252	229	515	588	594	36.5	42.8	38.6
Soybeans	Million	59	75	74	125	175	194	47.4	42.9	38.3
Rice, milled	Million	5.6	5.9	6.5	371	398	381	1.5	1.5	1.7
Cotton [2]	Million bales [3]	19.7	17.0	20.3	85.9	87.5	98.4	23.0	19.4	20.6
EXPORTS [4]										
Wheat [5]	Million	33.7	28.9	23.4	99.5	102.8	102.7	33.9	28.1	22.8
Corn	Million	52.7	49.3	40.6	64.9	77.3	74.7	81.1	63.8	54.4
Soybeans	Million	23.1	27.1	27.5	31.9	55.5	63.5	72.4	48.8	43.3
Rice, milled basis	Million	3.1	2.6	3.6	21.0	22.8	27.9	14.8	11.4	12.9
Cotton [2]	Million bales [3]	9.4	6.8	11.0	28.4	27.3	29.0	33.0	24.7	37.9

[1] Production years vary by commodity. In most cases, includes harvests from July 1 of the year shown through June 30 of the following year. [2] For production and trade years ending in year shown. [3] Bales of 480 lb. net weight. [4] Trade years may vary by commodity. Wheat, corn and soybean data are for trade year beginning in year shown. Rice data are for calendar year shown. [5] Includes wheat flour on a grain equivalent.

Source: U.S. Dept. of Agriculture, Foreign Agricultural Service, *Foreign Agricultural Commodity Circular Series*, periodic.

No. 829. Agricultural Exports—Value by Principal Commodities: 1990 to 2002

[In millions of dollars, except percent (39,492 represents $39,492,000,000). Excludes forest products and distilled liquors; includes crude rubber and similar gums (now mainly plantation products). Includes shipments under foreign aid programs]

Commodity	1990	1995	1998	1999	2000	2001	2002	1990 %	2000 %	2002 %
Total agricultural exports [1]	39,492	56,251	51,754	48,378	51,246	53,659	53,005	100.0	100.0	100.0
Grains and feeds [1]	14,409	18,644	14,008	13,995	13,687	13,923	14,435	36.5	26.7	27.2
Feed grains and products	7,150	8,341	5,210	5,747	5,372	5,503	5,863	18.1	10.5	11.1
Corn	6,026	7,304	4,382	4,924	4,469	4,502	4,830	15.3	8.7	9.1
Wheat and products	4,035	5,734	3,905	3,810	3,578	3,560	3,834	10.2	7.0	7.2
Rice	801	996	1,208	942	855	692	768	2.0	1.7	1.4
Oilseeds and products [1]	5,728	8,953	9,495	8,143	8,586	9,219	9,515	14.5	16.8	18.0
Soybeans	3,548	5,400	4,835	4,532	5,258	5,403	5,550	9.0	10.3	10.5
Soybean oilcake and meal	979	986	1,604	1,069	1,169	1,386	1,230	2.5	2.3	2.3
Vegetable oils and waxes	832	1,852	2,272	1,599	1,259	1,250	1,629	2.1	2.5	3.1
Animals and animal products [1]	6,648	10,889	10,567	10,360	11,600	12,431	11,110	16.8	22.6	21.0
Hides and skins, incl. furskins	1,751	1,748	1,259	1,139	1,562	1,963	1,745	4.4	3.0	3.3
Cattle hides	1,369	1,465	993	924	1,227	1,515	1,100	3.5	2.4	2.1
Meats and meat products	2,558	4,522	4,371	4,816	5,276	5,284	5,042	6.5	10.3	9.5
Beef and veal	1,580	2,647	2,326	2,724	2,986	2,632	2,585	4.0	5.8	4.9
Fats, oils, and greases	424	827	647	507	383	334	488	1.1	0.7	0.9
Poultry and poultry products	906	2,345	2,530	2,121	2,232	2,634	2,061	2.3	4.4	3.9
Dairy products	353	795	915	958	1,018	1,130	992	0.9	2.0	1.9
Cotton, excluding linters	2,783	3,681	2,545	954	1,873	2,164	2,015	7.0	3.7	3.8
Tobacco, unmanufactured	1,441	1,400	1,459	1,312	1,204	1,268	1,050	3.6	2.3	2.0
Fruits and preparations	2,379	3,300	3,200	3,267	3,451	3,446	3,467	6.0	6.7	6.5
Fresh fruits	1,486	1,973	1,838	1,820	2,080	2,127	2,133	3.8	4.1	4.0
Vegetables and preparations	2,225	3,637	4,222	4,295	4,457	4,483	4,559	5.6	8.7	8.6
Nuts and preparations	976	1,410	1,360	1,190	1,319	1,292	1,525	2.5	2.6	2.9
Other	2,903	4,337	4,898	4,862	5,069	5,433	5,329	7.4	9.9	10.1

[1] Includes commodities not shown separately.

Source: U.S. Dept. of Agriculture, Economic Research Service, *U.S. Agricultural Trade Update*, February 24, 2003; and *Foreign Agricultural Trade of the United States*, calendar year supplements, <http://www.ers.usda.gov/data/fatus/>.

No. 830. Agricultural Exports—Value by Selected Countries of Destination: 1990 to 2002

[39,492 represents $39,492,000,000. See headnote, Table 829. Totals include transshipments through Canada, but transshipments are not distributed by country prior to 2000]

Country	1990	1995	1998	1999	2000	2001	2002	1990 %	2000 %	2002 %
Total agricultural exports [1]	39,492	56,251	51,754	48,378	51,246	53,659	53,005	100.0	100.0	100.0
Asia [1]	17,625	28,147	20,853	20,109	22,213	22,556	21,870	44.6	43.3	41.3
Japan	8,142	11,160	9,082	8,892	9,290	8,883	8,368	20.6	18.1	15.8
Korea, South	2,650	3,754	2,224	2,448	2,546	2,588	2,674	6.7	5.0	5.0
Taiwan [2]	1,663	2,597	1,794	1,945	1,996	2,009	1,953	4.2	3.9	3.7
China [2]	818	2,633	1,335	854	1,716	1,939	1,960	2.1	3.3	3.7
Hong Kong	704	1,502	1,492	1,209	1,262	1,227	1,091	1.8	2.5	2.1
Indonesia	274	819	454	530	668	907	809	0.7	1.3	1.5
Philippines	381	765	714	783	901	794	776	1.0	1.8	1.5
Israel	304	481	365	423	482	427	464	0.8	0.9	0.9
Turkey	226	515	664	502	658	571	673	0.6	1.3	1.3
Western Europe [1,3]	7,345	8,765	8,151	6,941	6,685	7,042	6,718	18.6	13.0	12.7
European Union [4]	7,061	8,419	7,846	6,413	6,244	6,404	6,145	17.9	12.2	11.6
Belgium-Luxembourg	380	632	636	542	545	624	567	1.0	1.1	1.1
Netherlands	1,586	2,071	1,553	1,533	1,442	1,364	1,173	4.0	2.8	2.2
Germany	1,161	1,212	1,215	923	905	923	970	2.9	1.8	1.8
Spain [5]	931	1,169	1,031	681	609	644	674	2.4	1.2	1.3
United Kingdom	813	1,041	1,245	1,079	1,035	1,062	1,004	2.1	2.0	1.9
Italy	715	700	686	497	551	568	546	1.8	1.1	1.0
France	527	525	486	357	328	386	390	1.3	0.6	0.7
Switzerland	174	211	205	421	352	546	492	0.4	0.7	0.9
Latin America [1]	5,122	8,038	11,375	10,049	10,639	11,740	11,817	13.0	20.8	22.3
Colombia	119	465	576	440	415	452	520	0.3	0.8	1.0
Mexico	2,561	3,538	6,154	5,624	6,410	7,404	7,252	6.5	12.5	13.7
Canada	4,217	5,791	6,993	7,058	7,640	8,121	8,654	10.7	14.9	16.3
Russia	(X)	1,032	835	728	580	917	552	(X)	1.1	1.0
Eastern Europe	531	289	271	170	170	232	213	1.3	0.3	0.4
Africa [1]	1,845	2,818	2,091	2,073	2,308	2,105	2,294	4.7	4.5	4.3
Egypt	687	1,309	904	966	1,050	1,022	860	1.7	2.0	1.6
Oceania	343	507	545	486	489	471	511	0.9	1.0	1.0

X Not applicable. [1] Includes areas not shown separately. [2] See footnote 2, Table 1322. [3] Includes Canary Islands and Madeira Islands. [4] Includes Denmark, Greece, Ireland, and Portugal. Beginning 1995, also includes Austria, Finland, and Sweden. For consistency, data for all years are shown on same basis. [5] Includes Canary Islands and Spanish Africa, not elsewhere classified.

Source: U.S. Dept. of Agriculture, Economic Research Service, *U.S. Agricultural Trade Update*, February 24, 2003; and *Foreign Agricultural Trade of the United States*, calendar year supplements, <http://www.ers.usda.gov/data/fatus/>.

No. 831. Cropland Used for Crops and Acreages of Crops Harvested: 1980 to 2002

[In millions of acres, except as indicated (382 represents 382,000,000)]

Item	1980	1990	1995	1996	1997	1998	1999	2000	2001	2002
Cropland used for crops	382	341	332	346	349	345	344	345	340	340
Index (1977=100)	101	90	88	92	92	91	91	91	90	90
Cropland harvested [1]	342	310	302	314	321	315	316	314	311	307
Crop failure	10	6	8	10	7	10	8	11	10	15
Cultivated summer fallow	30	25	22	22	21	20	20	20	19	19
Cropland idled by all federal programs	(NA)	62	55	34	33	30	30	31	32	34
Acres of crops harvested [2]	352	322	314	326	332	326	327	325	321	317

NA Not available. [1] Land supporting one or more harvested crops. [2] Area in principal crops harvested as reported by Crop Reporting Board plus acreages in fruits, vegetables for sale, tree nuts, and other minor crops.

Source: U.S. Dept. of Agriculture, Economic Research Service, *Major Uses of Land in the United States, 1997*, SB-973, 2001. Also in *Agricultural Statistics*, annual. Beginning 1994 *Agricultural Resources and Environmental Indicators*, periodic, and *AREI Updates: Cropland Use*. See also ERS Briefing Room at <http://www.ers.usda.gov/Briefing/LandUse/majorlandusechapter.htm#trends>.

No. 832. Percent of Corn, Soybean, and Cotton Acreage Planted With Genetically Modified Seed: 2000 and 2003

[In percent. Based on the June Agricultural Survey. Randomly selected farmers across the United States were asked if they planted corn, soybeans, or upland cotton seed that, through biotechnology, is resistant to herbicides, insects, or both. The states published individually below represent 81 percent of all corn planted acres, 89 percent of all soybean planted acres, and 82 percent of all upland cotton planted acres. Conventionally bred herbicide resistant varieties were excluded. Insect resistant varieties include only those containing bacillus thuringiensis (Bt). The acreage estimates are subject to sampling variability because all operations planting biotech varieties are not included in the sample]

State	Corn 2000	Corn 2003	State	Soybeans 2000	Soybeans 2003	State	Cotton 2000	Cotton 2003
US, total	25	40	US, total	54	75	US, total	61	73
IL	17	28	AR	43	84	AR	70	95
IN	11	16	IL	44	77	CA	24	39
IA	30	45	IN	63	88	GA	82	93
KS	33	47	IA	59	84	LA	80	91
MI	12	35	KS	66	87	MS	78	92
MN	37	53	MI	50	73	NC	76	93
MO	28	42	MN	46	79	TX	46	53
NE	34	52	MS	48	89	Other states [1]	74	88
OH	9	9	MO	62	83			
SD	48	75	NE	72	86			
WI	18	32	ND	22	74			
Other states [1]	17	36	OH	48	74			
			SD	68	91			
			WI	51	84			
			Other states [1]	54	76			

[1] Includes all other states in the specified commodity estimating program.

Source: U.S. Dept. of Agriculture, National Agricultural Statistics Service, *Acreage*, annual.

No. 833. Quantity of Pesticides Applied to Selected Crops: 1990 to 2001

[In million pounds of active ingredients, except as indicated (497.7 represents 497,700,000)]

Type of pesticide and commodity	1990	1995	1996	1997	1998	1999	2000	2001
Total	497.7	543.3	575.8	579.3	575.8	553.7	539.4	511.1
Herbicides	344.6	324.9	365.7	362.6	340.3	316.8	308.6	307.5
Insecticides	57.4	69.9	59.2	60.2	52.0	75.4	77.4	62.0
Fungicides	27.8	47.5	46.8	48.5	45.7	42.3	36.6	33.2
Other	67.9	101.0	104.0	108.0	106.4	119.1	116.8	108.3
Corn	240.7	201.3	227.7	227.3	212.4	186.0	176.1	187.3
Cotton	50.9	83.7	65.6	68.4	55.4	90.6	94.5	72.8
Wheat	17.8	21.5	32.9	25.5	23.9	21.4	19.2	18.3
Soybeans	74.4	68.7	78.1	83.5	78.8	77.3	79.1	72.2
Potatoes	43.8	53.1	49.5	59.4	63.6	64.6	61.8	60.5
Other vegetables	39.8	78.0	82.8	73.3	67.8	70.5	70.1	66.5
Citrus fruit	11.0	14.0	14.5	15.0	14.1	13.3	13.0	12.8
Apples	8.3	9.0	9.7	10.6	9.3	7.9	7.6	7.6
Other deciduous fruit	10.9	14.1	14.9	16.4	19.2	22.2	18.1	13.1
POUNDS OF ACTIVE INGREDIENT PER PLANTED ACRE								
Total	2.2	2.4	2.4	2.4	2.3	2.3	2.2	2.2
Herbicides	1.5	1.4	1.5	1.5	1.4	1.3	1.3	1.3
Insecticides	0.3	0.3	0.2	0.2	0.2	0.3	0.3	0.3
Fungicides	0.1	0.2	0.2	0.2	0.2	0.2	0.2	0.1
Other	0.3	0.4	0.4	0.4	0.4	0.5	0.5	0.5

Source: U.S. Dept. of Agriculture, Economic Research Service, *Production Practices for Major Crops in U.S. Agriculture, 1990-97*, Statistical Bulletin No. 969, August 2000, and unpublished data.

No. 834. Principal Crops—Production, Supply, and Disappearance: 1990 to 2002

[67.0 represents 67,000,000. Marketing year beginning January 1 for potatoes, May 1 for hay, June 1 for wheat, August 1 for cotton, September 1 for soybeans and corn. Acreage, production, and yield of all crops periodically revised on basis of census data]

Item	Unit	1990	1995	1998	1999	2000	2001	2002
CORN FOR GRAIN								
Acreage harvested	Million	67.0	65.2	72.6	70.5	72.4	68.8	69.3
Yield per acre	Bushel	119	114	134	134	137	138	130
Production	Mil. bu.	7,934	7,400	9,759	9,431	9,915	9,507	9,008
Farm price [1]	Dol./bu.	2.28	3.24	1.94	1.82	1.85	1.97	2.35
Farm value	Mil. dol.	18,192	24,118	18,922	17,104	18,499	18,888	21,213
Total supply [2]	Mil. bu.	9,282	8,974	11,085	11,232	11,639	11,416	10,619
Total disappearance [3]	Mil. bu.	7,761	8,548	9,298	9,515	9,740	9,820	9,610
Exports	Mil. bu.	1,725	2,228	1,984	1,937	1,941	1,889	1,675
Ending stocks	Mil. bu.	1,521	426	1,787	1,718	1,899	1,596	1,009
SOYBEANS								
Acreage harvested	Million	56.5	61.5	70.4	72.4	72.4	73.0	72.2
Yield per acre	Bushel	34.1	35.3	38.9	36.6	38.1	39.6	37.8
Production	Mil. bu.	1,926	2,174	2,741	2,654	2,758	2,891	2,730
Farm price [1]	Dol./bu.	5.74	6.72	4.93	4.63	4.54	4.38	5.40
Farm value	Mil. dol.	11,042	14,617	13,494	12,205	12,467	12,606	14,755
Total supply [2]	Mil. bu.	2,169	2,514	2,944	3,006	3,052	3,141	2,940
Total disappearance [3]	Mil. bu.	1,840	2,330	2,595	2,716	2,804	2,933	2,795
Exports	Mil. bu.	557	849	805	975	996	1,063	995
Ending stocks	Mil. bu.	329	183	348	290	248	208	145
HAY								
Acreage harvested	Million	61.0	59.8	60.1	63.2	59.9	63.5	64.5
Yield per acre	Sh. tons	2.40	2.58	2.53	2.53	2.54	2.47	2.34
Production	Mil. sh. tons	146	154	152	160	152	157	151
Farm price [4] [5]	Dol./ton	80.60	82.20	84.60	76.90	84.60	96.50	94.00
Farm value	Mil. dol.	10,462	11,042	11,607	11,014	11,417	12,603	12,433
Total supply [2]	Mil. sh. tons	173	175	174	185	181	178	173
Total disappearance [3]	Mil. sh. tons	146	154	149	156	160	155	(NA)
Ending stocks	Mil. sh. tons	27	21	25	29	21	22	(NA)
WHEAT								
Acreage harvested	Million	69.1	61.0	59.0	53.8	53.1	48.6	45.8
Yield per acre	Bushel	39.5	35.8	43.2	42.7	42.0	40.2	35.3
Production	Mil. bu.	2,730	2,183	2,547	2,299	2,232	1,957	1,616
Farm price [1]	Dol./bu.	2.61	4.55	2.65	2.48	2.62	2.78	3.60
Farm value	Mil. dol.	7,184	9,787	6,781	5,594	5,782	5,440	5,863
Total supply [2]	Mil. bu.	3,303	2,757	3,373	3,339	3,272	2,941	2,459
Total disappearance [3]	Mil. bu.	2,435	2,381	2,427	2,390	2,396	2,164	1,994
Exports	Mil. bu.	1,069	1,241	1,046	1,089	1,062	961	875
Ending stocks	Mil. bu.	868	376	946	950	876	777	465
COTTON								
Acreage harvested	Million	11.7	16.0	10.7	13.4	13.1	13.8	12.4
Yield per acre	Pounds	634	537	625	607	632	705	663
Production [6]	Mil. bales [7]	15.5	17.9	13.9	17.0	17.2	20.3	17.1
Farm price [1]	Cents/lb.	68.2	76.5	61.7	46.8	51.6	32.0	43.7
Farm value	Mil. dol.	5,076	6,575	4,120	3,810	4,260	3,122	3,594
Total supply [2]	Mil. bales [7]	18.5	21.0	18.2	21.0	21.1	26.3	24.7
Total disappearance [3]	Mil. bales [7]	16.5	18.3	14.7	17.0	15.6	18.7	18.4
Exports	Mil. bales [7]	7.8	7.7	4.3	6.8	6.7	11.0	10.8
Ending stocks [8]	Mil. bales [7]	2.3	2.6	3.9	3.9	6.0	7.4	6.3
POTATOES								
Acreage harvested	Million	1.4	1.4	1.4	1.3	1.3	1.2	1.3
Yield per acre	Cwt.	293	323	343	359	381	358	363
Production	Mil. cwt.	402	445	476	478	514	438	463
Farm price [1]	Dol./cwt.	6.08	6.77	5.56	5.77	5.08	6.99	6.82
Farm value	Mil. dol.	2,431	2,992	2,635	2,746	2,591	3,058	3,151

NA Not available. [1] Except as noted, marketing year average price. U.S. prices are computed by weighting U.S. monthly prices by estimated monthly marketings and do not include an allowance for outstanding loans and government purchases and payments. [2] Comprises production, imports, and beginning stocks. [3] Includes feed, residual, and other domestic uses not shown separately. [4] Prices are for hay sold baled. [5] Season average prices received by farmers. U.S. prices are computed by weighting state prices by estimated sales. [6] State production figures, which conform with annual ginning enumeration with allowance for cross-state ginnings, rounded to thousands and added for U.S. totals. [7] Bales of 480 pounds, net weight. [8] Stock estimates based on Census Bureau data which results in an unaccounted difference between supply and use estimates and changes in ending stocks.

Source: Production—U.S. Dept. of Agriculture, National Agricultural Statistics Service. In *Crop Production*, annual; and *Crop Values*, annual. Supply and disappearance—U.S. Dept. of Agriculture, Economic Research Service, *Feed Situation*, quarterly; *Fats and Oils Situation*, quarterly; *Wheat Situation*, quarterly; *Cotton and Wool Outlook Statistics*, periodic; and *Agricultural Supply and Demand Estimates*, periodic. Data are also in *Agricultural Statistics*, annual; and *Agricultural Outlook*, monthly.

No. 835. Corn—Acreage, Production, and Value by Leading States: 2000 to 2002

[72,440 represents 72,440,000. One bushel of corn=56 pounds]

State	Acreage harvested (1,000 acres) 2000	2001	2002	Yield per acre (bu.) 2000	2001	2002	Production (mil. bu.) 2000	2001	2002	Price ($/bu.) 2000	2001	2002	Farm value (mil. dol.) 2000	2001	2002
U.S.[1]	72,440	68,808	69,313	137	138	130	9,915	9,507	9,008	1.85	1.97	2.35	18,499	18,888	21,213
IA	12,000	11,400	11,900	144	146	165	1,728	1,664	1,964	1.75	1.90	2.25	3,024	3,162	4,418
IL	11,050	10,850	11,000	151	152	136	1,669	1,649	1,496	1.91	2.04	2.40	3,187	3,364	3,590
MN	6,650	6,200	6,700	145	130	157	964	806	1,052	1.71	1.90	2.15	1,649	1,531	2,262
NE	8,050	7,750	7,350	126	147	128	1,014	1,139	941	1.90	1.94	2.40	1,927	2,210	2,258
IN	5,550	5,670	5,220	146	156	121	810	885	632	1.90	1.98	2.45	1,540	1,751	1,547
WI	2,750	2,600	2,900	132	127	135	363	330	392	1.86	1.97	2.20	675	650	861
SD	3,800	3,400	3,200	112	109	95	426	371	304	1.61	1.75	2.20	685	649	669
KS	3,170	3,050	2,500	130	127	116	412	387	290	2.00	2.03	2.50	824	786	725
MO	2,770	2,600	2,700	143	133	105	396	346	284	1.78	1.96	2.45	705	678	695
OH	3,300	3,170	2,870	147	138	88	485	437	253	1.90	2.00	2.50	922	875	631
MI	1,950	1,900	2,020	124	105	115	242	200	232	1.90	1.97	2.30	459	393	534
TX	1,900	1,420	1,820	124	118	113	236	168	206	2.18	2.29	2.60	514	384	535
ND	930	705	995	112	115	115	104	81	114	1.65	1.87	2.15	172	152	246
CO	1,150	1,070	720	126	140	156	145	150	112	2.08	2.13	2.55	301	319	286
KY	1,230	1,100	1,040	130	142	102	160	156	106	2.07	2.08	2.55	331	325	271
LA	370	307	560	116	148	122	43	45	68	1.75	2.20	2.40	75	100	164
MS	365	385	530	100	130	125	37	50	66	1.91	1.99	2.35	70	100	156
TN	580	620	620	114	132	107	66	82	66	1.96	2.06	2.55	130	169	169
PA	1,080	990	870	127	98	68	137	97	59	2.09	2.33	2.95	287	226	175
NC	640	625	700	116	125	83	74	78	58	2.01	2.36	2.90	149	184	168
NY	450	540	450	98	105	97	44	57	44	2.35	2.51	2.85	104	142	124

[1] Includes other states, not shown separately.

Source: U.S. Dept. of Agriculture, National Agricultural Statistics Service, *Crop Production*, annual; and *Crop Values*, annual.

No. 836. Soybeans—Acreage, Production, and Value by Leading States: 2000 to 2002

[72,408 represents 72,408,000. One bushel of soybeans=60 pounds]

State	Acreage harvested (1,000 acres) 2000	2001	2002	Yield per acre (bu.) 2000	2001	2002	Production (mil. bu.) 2000	2001	2002	Price ($/bu.) 2000	2001	2002	Farm value (mil. dol.) 2000	2001	2002
U.S.[1]	72,408	72,975	72,160	38	40	38	2,758	2,891	2,730	4.54	4.38	5.40	12,467	12,606	14,755
IA	10,680	10,920	10,310	44	44	48	465	480	495	4.49	4.35	5.40	2,086	2,090	2,672
IL	10,450	10,620	10,460	44	45	43	460	478	450	4.62	4.55	5.50	2,124	2,174	2,474
MN	7,150	7,200	7,100	41	37	44	293	266	309	4.38	4.32	5.25	1,284	1,151	1,621
IN	5,480	5,590	5,750	46	49	41	252	274	236	4.61	4.42	5.40	1,162	1,211	1,273
NE	4,575	4,900	4,580	38	46	39	174	223	176	4.44	4.19	5.35	772	934	943
MO	5,000	4,900	5,000	35	38	34	175	186	170	4.55	4.32	5.40	796	804	918
OH	4,440	4,580	4,710	42	41	30	186	188	141	4.63	4.46	5.45	863	837	770
SD	4,370	4,470	4,090	35	32	31	153	143	127	4.27	4.13	5.15	653	591	653
AR	3,150	2,850	2,880	26	32	34	80	91	96	4.73	4.37	5.65	380	399	545
ND	1,850	2,110	2,630	32	34	33	59	71	87	4.23	4.05	5.20	250	286	451
MI	2,030	2,130	2,030	36	30	39	73	64	78	4.54	4.47	5.50	332	286	430
WI	1,500	1,570	1,520	40	37	44	60	58	67	4.45	4.31	5.25	267	250	351
KS	2,500	2,730	2,540	20	32	23	50	87	58	4.50	4.16	5.40	225	363	315
MS	1,580	1,120	1,370	22	33	32	35	37	44	4.71	4.39	5.55	164	162	243

[1] Includes other states, not shown separately.

Source: U.S. Dept. of Agriculture, National Agricultural Statistics Service, *Crop Production*, annual; and *Crop Values*, annual.

No. 837. Wheat—Acreage, Production, and Value by Leading States: 2000 to 2002

[53,133 represents 53,133,000. One bushel of wheat= 60 pounds]

State	Acreage harvested (1,000 acres) 2000	2001	2002	Yield per acre (bu.) 2000	2001	2002	Production (mil. bu.) 2000	2001	2002	Price ($/bu.) 2000	2001	2002	Farm value (mil. dol.) 2000	2001	2002
U.S.[1]	53,133	48,633	45,817	42.0	40.2	35.3	2,232	1,957	1,616	2.62	2.78	3.60	5,782	5,440	5,863
KS	9,400	8,200	8,100	37.0	40.0	33.0	348	328	267	2.65	2.69	3.45	922	882	922
ND	9,413	9,080	7,920	33.7	32.2	27.3	317	292	217	2.71	2.79	4.00	857	813	865
WA	2,420	2,380	2,365	68.1	55.7	54.8	165	133	130	2.70	3.23	4.10	443	428	537
MT	4,920	4,215	4,765	27.5	22.9	23.1	135	97	110	3.02	3.14	4.25	409	304	467
OK	4,200	3,700	3,500	34.0	33.0	28.0	143	122	98	2.57	2.74	3.50	367	335	343
ID	1,300	1,200	1,200	83.4	71.0	73.1	108	85	88	2.63	3.18	3.85	281	270	340
TX	2,200	3,200	2,700	30.0	34.0	29.0	66	109	78	2.52	2.78	3.00	166	302	235
MN	1,971	1,815	1,834	49.0	43.9	33.9	97	80	62	2.89	2.93	4.00	278	233	249

[1] Includes other states, not shown separately.

Source: U.S. Dept. of Agriculture, National Agricultural Statistics Service, *Crop Production*, annual; and *Crop Values*, annual.

No. 838. Floriculture and Nursery Crops—Value of Production, Trade, and Consumption: 1990 to 2002

[In millions of dollars, except as noted (8,677 represents $8,677,000,000). Includes all floriculture and nursery crops except cut Christmas trees, seeds, and food crops grown under cover. Domestic production based on grower wholesale receipts. Domestic consumption equals supply minus exports. Supply equals domestic production plus imports]

Year	Production and trade				Consumption			
	Domestic production	Imports	Supply	Exports	Domestic consumption	Per household (dol.)	Per capita (dol.)	Import share (percent)
1990	8,677	538	9,215	204	9,011	98	36	6.0
1991	9,035	547	9,582	216	9,366	101	37	5.8
1992	9,294	604	9,898	222	9,677	102	38	6.2
1993	9,398	654	10,052	242	9,810	103	38	6.7
1994	9,853	712	10,566	252	10,314	107	39	6.9
1995	10,336	859	11,195	241	10,954	113	41	7.8
1996	10,830	952	11,782	242	11,539	117	43	8.2
1997	11,861	1,004	12,865	283	12,582	126	46	8.0
1998	12,043	1,080	13,124	306	12,818	127	46	8.4
1999	13,042	1,101	14,143	299	13,844	134	50	8.0
2000	13,741	1,160	14,901	279	14,622	139	52	7.9
2001	13,795	1,151	14,946	264	14,681	137	51	7.8
2002	13,829	1,133	14,962	249	14,713	136	51	7.7

Source: U.S. Dept. of Agriculture, Economic Research Service, *Floriculture and Nursery Crops Yearbook.*

No. 839. Fresh Fruits and Vegetables—Supply and Use: 1990 to 2002

[In millions of pounds, except per capita in pounds (7,327 represents 7,327,000,000)]

Year	Utilized production [1]	Imports [2]	Supply, total [1]	Consumption Total	Consumption Per capita	Exports [2]
FRUITS						
Citrus:						
1990	7,327	184	7,510	5,331	21.4	2,179
1995	8,635	449	9,084	6,333	24.1	2,751
2000	8,355	684	9,040	6,602	23.4	2,438
2001	8,331	1,059	9,390	6,923	24.2	2,466
2002	8,573	959	9,532	6,922	23.9	2,610
Noncitrus: [3]						
1990	12,122	7,852	19,974	17,978	70.4	1,995
1995	12,983	9,388	22,371	19,521	74.3	2,850
2000	13,850	11,225	25,074	21,686	76.6	3,389
2001	12,727	10,979	23,706	20,606	71.8	3,101
VEGETABLES & MELONS						
1990	35,341	3,458	39,679	35,364	141.5	2,690
1995	39,507	4,997	45,584	40,279	151.2	3,532
2000	47,270	6,629	55,197	48,928	173.3	4,188
2001	46,742	7,254	55,207	49,011	172.0	4,118
2002	46,180	7,552	55,022	48,837	169.8	4,259
POTATOES						
1990	11,335	684	12,019	11,691	46.8	327
1995	13,020	685	13,704	13,121	49.9	584
2000	13,239	806	14,045	13,368	47.3	677
2001	13,158	671	13,829	13,193	46.3	636
2002	12,693	883	13,576	12,883	44.8	693

[1] Crop-year basis for fruits. [2] Fiscal year for fruits; calendar year for vegetables and potatoes. [3] Includes bananas.

No. 840. Nuts—Supply and Use: 1990 to 2001

[In millions of pounds (shelled) (326.2 represents 326,200,000)]

Year	Beginning stocks	Marketable production [1]	Imports	Supply, total	Consumption	Exports	Ending stocks
1990	326.2	961.5	198.4	1,486.1	609.6	522.6	354.0
1995	334.1	770.1	204.0	1,308.2	512.5	543.8	251.9
1999	223.9	1,295.7	283.4	1,803.0	706.9	730.7	365.6
2000	365.6	1,110.1	280.3	1,756.0	632.1	851.1	272.8
2001	272.8	1,329.0	309.8	1,911.6	838.6	787.8	285.2

[1] Utilized production minus inedibles and noncommercial usage.

Source of Tables 839 and 840: U.S. Dept. of Agriculture, Economic Research Service, *Fruit and Tree Nuts Situation and Outlook Yearbook* and *Vegetables and Specialties Situation and Outlook Yearbook.*

No. 841. Commercial Vegetable and Other Specified Crops—Area, Production, and Value, 2000 to 2002, and Leading Producing States, 2002

[311 represents 311,000. Except as noted, relates to commercial production for fresh market and processing combined. Includes market garden areas but excludes minor producing acreage in minor producing states. Excludes production for home use in farm and nonfarm gardens. Value is for season or crop year and should not be confused with calendar-year income]

Crop	Area [1] (1,000 acres) 2000	2001	2002	Production [2] (1,000 short tons) 2000	2001	2002	Value [3] (mil. dol.) 2000	2001	2002	Leading states in order of production, 2002
Beans, snap	311	292	310	1,128	1,003	1,121	394	390	409	WI, OR, NY [4]
Beans, dry edible	1,608	1,249	1,727	1,320	979	1,499	414	426	520	ND, MI, NE
Broccoli	144	133	126	1,044	964	874	636	501	551	CA, AZ
Cabbage [5]	78	79	77	1,300	1,303	1,221	314	340	301	CA, NY, TX
Cantaloups	99	96	94	1,048	1,136	1,152	367	431	405	CA, AZ, TX
Carrots	123	121	112	2,049	2,025	1,847	437	576	579	CA, MI, GA [5]
Cauliflower	44	44	42	399	351	321	248	199	208	CA, AZ
Celery	26	28	27	921	943	937	341	272	242	CA, MI
Corn, sweet	706	698	669	4,476	4,512	4,406	713	764	741	(NA)
Fresh market	246	252	249	1,320	1,369	1,322	481	535	531	FL, CA, NY
Processed	460	446	420	3,156	3,143	3,084	232	229	210	WA, MN, WI
Cucumbers	158	162	175	1,161	1,120	1,186	383	380	385	MI, NC, FL [4]
Lettuce, head	185	184	184	3,481	3,518	3,386	1,208	1,258	1,456	CA, AZ, CO
Lettuce, leaf	50	53	55	588	591	618	349	324	409	CA, AZ
Lettuce, Romaine	49	55	55	792	774	791	315	298	396	CA, AZ
Mushrooms [6]	151	144	146	427	423	419	829	826	875	PA, CA, FL
Onions	166	162	160	3,586	3,383	3,368	736	698	716	CA, OR, WA
Peppers, green	62	56	56	843	803	808	527	459	499	CA, FL, NJ
Potatoes	1,348	1,222	1,277	25,681	21,894	23,161	2,591	3,058	3,151	ID, WA, WI
Spinach	46	43	44	381	312	362	172	135	179	CA, AZ [5]
Strawberries	48	46	48	951	826	985	1,046	1,070	1,221	CA, FL
Sweet potatoes	95	94	83	690	732	625	211	225	213	NC, CA, MS
Tomatoes	413	399	437	12,741	11,025	13,522	1,809	1,627	1,854	(NA)
Fresh market	123	124	125	1,883	1,776	1,865	1,160	1,080	1,171	FL, CA, OH
Processed	290	275	312	10,858	9,249	11,657	649	547	683	CA, IN, OH
Watermelons	165	161	150	1,881	2,032	1,960	241	275	329	FL, TX, CA

NA Not available. [1] Area of crops for harvest for fresh market, including any partially harvested or not harvested because of low prices or other factors, plus area harvested for processing. [2] Excludes some quantities not marketed. [3] Fresh market vegetables valued at f.o.b. shipping point. Processing vegetables are equivalent returns at packinghouse door. [4] Processed only. [5] Fresh market only. [6] Area is shown in million square feet. All data are for marketing year ending June 30.

Source: U.S. Dept. of Agriculture, National Agricultural Statistics Service, *Vegetables*, annual summary. Also in *Agricultural Statistics*, annual.

No. 842. Fruits and Nuts—Utilized Production and Value, 2000 to 2002, and Leading Producing States, 2002

[5,161 represents 5,161,000]

Fruit or nut	Unit	Utilized production [1] 2000	2001	2002	Farm value (mil. dol.) 2000	2001	2002	Leading states in order of production, 2002
Apples [2]	1,000 tons	5,161	4,607	4,203	1,321	1,453	1,571	WA, NY, MI
Apricots	1,000 tons	88	75	80	32	27	29	CA, WA
Avocados	1,000 tons	239	223	218	331	374	338	CA, FL
Cherries, sweet	1,000 tons	205	220	177	275	271	274	WA, CA, OR
Cherries, tart	1,000 tons	141	154	31	52	57	28	WA, MI, NY
Cranberries	1,000 tons	279	239	284	101	113	185	WI, MA, NJ
Dates (CA)	1,000 tons	17	20	24	21	27	38	CA
Grapefruit	1,000 tons	2,763	2,462	2,427	411	285	286	FL, CA, TX, AZ
Grapes (13 states)	1,000 tons	7,687	6,568	7,362	3,098	2,934	2,853	CA, WA, NY
Lemons	1,000 tons	840	996	828	299	237	341	CA, AZ
Nectarines (CA)	1,000 tons	267	275	299	106	128	115	CA
Olives (CA)	1,000 tons	53	134	103	35	90	61	CA
Oranges	1,000 tons	12,997	12,221	12,543	1,666	1,683	1,834	FL, CA, TX
Papayas	1,000 tons	27	28	23	16	15	12	HI
Peaches	1,000 tons	1,244	1,168	1,236	482	493	504	CA, SC, GA
Pears	1,000 tons	949	964	867	250	254	256	WA, CA, OR
Pineapples	1,000 tons	354	323	320	102	96	101	HI
Plums (CA)	1,000 tons	197	210	201	87	64	78	CA
Prunes (dried basis) (CA)	1,000 tons	201	135	149	155	98	131	CA
Tangerines	1,000 tons	458	373	419	108	97	125	FL, CA
Almonds (shelled basis) (CA)	Mil. lb	703	830	1,060	666	740	1,049	CA
Hazelnuts (in the shell)	1,000 tons	23	50	18	20	35	18	OR
Macadamia nuts	Mil. lb	50	56	52	30	33	29	HI
Pecans (in the shell) (11 states)	Mil. lb	210	339	178	239	201	169	GA, TX, NM
Pistachios	Mil. lb	243	161	300	245	163	333	CA
Walnuts, English (in the shell)	1,000 tons	239	305	282	296	342	(NA)	CA

NA Not available. [1] Excludes quantities not harvested or not marketed. [2] Production in commercial orchards with 100 or more bearing age trees.

Source: U.S. Dept. of Agriculture, National Agricultural Statistics Service, *Noncitrus Fruits and Nuts*, annual; and *Citrus Fruits*, annual.

552 Agriculture

No. 843. Meat Supply and Use: 1980 to 2002

[In millions of pounds (carcass weight equivalent) (**53,151** represents 53,151,000,000). Carcass weight equivalent is the weight of the animal minus entrails, head, hide, and internal organs; includes fat and bone. Covers federal and state inspected, and farm slaughter]

Year and type of meat	Production	Imports	Supply, [1] total	Consumption [2]	Exports	Ending stocks
RED MEAT AND POULTRY						
1980	53,151	2,668	57,036	54,695	1,124	1,217
1990	62,255	3,295	66,673	62,937	2,472	1,263
1995	74,068	2,838	78,636	69,911	6,956	1,768
2000	82,372	4,137	88,481	77,069	9,344	2,069
2001	82,746	4,278	89,093	76,912	10,060	2,120
2002	85,385	4,468	91,973	80,192	9,441	2,339
ALL RED MEATS						
1980	38,978	2,668	42,481	41,170	429	882
1990	38,787	3,295	42,742	40,784	1,250	707
1995	43,675	2,832	47,511	43,967	2,614	929
2000	46,299	4,128	51,341	46,560	3,760	1,021
2001	45,804	4,260	51,085	46,089	3,836	1,160
2002	47,305	4,451	52,916	47,610	4,068	1,238
Beef:						
1980	21,643	2,064	24,166	23,560	173	432
1990	22,743	2,356	25,434	24,031	1,006	397
1995	25,222	2,104	27,874	25,534	1,821	519
2000	26,888	3,032	30,332	27,338	2,468	525
2001	26,212	3,164	29,901	27,026	2,269	606
2002	27,192	3,218	31,016	27,878	2,447	691
Pork:						
1980	16,617	550	17,521	16,838	252	431
1990	15,354	898	16,565	16,031	238	296
1995	17,849	664	18,952	17,768	787	396
2000	18,952	967	20,407	18,643	1,287	478
2001	19,160	951	20,588	18,492	1,560	536
2002	19,685	1,071	21,292	19,145	1,614	533
Veal:						
1980	400	21	432	420	2	9
1990	327	(NA)	331	325	(NA)	6
1995	319	(NA)	326	319	(NA)	7
2000	225	(NA)	230	225	(NA)	5
2001	205	(NA)	210	204	(NA)	6
2002	205	(NA)	211	204	(NA)	7
Lamb and mutton:						
1980	318	33	362	351	1	9
1990	363	41	412	397	6	8
1995	285	64	359	346	6	8
2000	234	130	372	354	5	13
2001	227	146	386	368	7	12
2002	223	162	397	383	7	7
POULTRY, TOTAL						
1980	14,173	-	14,555	13,525	695	334
1990	23,468	-	23,931	22,153	1,222	556
1995	30,393	6	31,125	25,944	4,342	839
2000	36,073	9	37,140	30,508	5,584	1,048
2001	36,942	18	38,008	30,823	6,224	960
2002	38,080	17	39,057	32,582	5,373	1,101
Broilers:						
1980	11,252	-	11,364	10,682	567	115
1990	18,430	-	18,651	17,266	1,143	242
1995	24,827	1	25,286	20,832	3,894	560
2000	30,209	6	31,011	25,295	4,918	798
2001	30,938	14	31,749	25,482	5,555	712
2002	31,895	12	32,619	27,057	4,800	763
Mature chicken:						
1980	551	-	581	507	53	21
1990	523	-	530	496	25	9
1995	496	3	513	406	99	7
2000	531	2	540	311	220	9
2001	515	3	527	337	182	8
2002	547	3	558	418	135	5
Turkeys:						
1980	2,370	-	2,610	2,337	75	198
1990	4,514	-	4,750	4,390	54	306
1995	5,069	2	5,326	4,706	348	271
2000	5,333	1	5,589	4,902	445	241
2001	5,489	1	5,732	5,004	487	241
2002	5,638	1	5,880	5,107	439	333

- Represents zero. NA Not available. [1] Total supply equals production plus imports plus ending stocks of previous year. [2] Includes shipments to territories.

Source: U.S. Department of Agriculture, Economic Research Service, *Food Consumption, Prices, and Expenditures, 1970-2000*; and "Agricultural Outlook: Statistical Indicators"; <http://www.ers.usda.gov/publications/agoutlook/aotables/>.

No. 844. Livestock Inventory and Production: 1990 to 2003

[95.8 represents 95,800,000. Production in live weight; includes animals for slaughter market, younger animals shipped to other states for feeding or breeding purposes, farm slaughter and custom slaughter consumed on farms where produced, minus livestock shipped into states for feeding or breeding with an adjustment for changes in inventory]

Type of livestock	Unit	1990	1995	1996	1997	1998	1999	2000	2001	2002	2003
ALL CATTLE [1]											
Inventory:[2] Number on farms	Mil	95.8	102.8	103.5	101.7	99.7	99.1	98.2	97.3	96.7	96.1
Total value	Bil. dol.	59.0	63.2	52.1	53.4	60.2	58.8	67.1	70.5	72.3	69.8
Value per head	Dol	616	615	503	525	603	594	683	725	747	726
Production: Quantity	Bil. lb	39.2	42.5	40.9	40.9	41.6	42.5	42.8	42.4	42.3	(NA)
Beef, price per 100 lb	Dol	74.60	61.80	58.70	63.10	59.60	63.40	68.60	71.30	66.50	(NA)
Calves, price per 100 lb	Dol	95.60	73.10	58.40	78.90	78.80	87.70	104.00	106.00	96.40	(NA)
Value of production	Bil. dol.	29.3	24.7	22.1	24.8	24.2	26.1	28.4	29.3	26.9	(NA)
HOGS AND PIGS											
Inventory:[3] Number on farms	Mil	53.8	59.7	58.2	56.1	61.2	62.2	59.3	59.1	59.8	58.9
Total value	Bil. dol.	4.3	3.2	4.1	5.3	5.0	2.8	4.3	4.5	4.6	4.2
Value per head	Dol	79.10	53.00	71.00	94.00	82.00	44.00	72.00	77.00	77.00	71.00
Production: Quantity	Bil. lb	21.3	24.4	23.1	24.0	25.7	25.8	25.7	25.9	26.3	(NA)
Price per 100 lb	Dol	53.70	40.50	51.90	52.90	34.40	30.30	42.30	44.30	33.40	(NA)
Value of production	Bil. dol.	11.3	9.8	11.9	12.6	8.7	7.8	10.8	11.4	8.7	(NA)
SHEEP AND LAMBS											
Inventory:[2] Number on farms	Mil	11.4	9.0	8.5	8.0	7.8	7.2	7.0	7.0	6.7	6.4
Total value	Mil. dol	901	663	732	762	798	638	669	694	618	658
Value per head	Dol	79.30	74.70	86.50	96.00	102.00	88.00	95.00	100.00	92.00	104.00
Production: Quantity	Mil. lb	781	602	572	603	555	534	509	496	484	(NA)
Sheep, price per 100 lb	Dol	23.20	28.00	29.90	37.90	30.60	31.10	34.30	34.60	28.20	(NA)
Lambs, price per 100 lb	Dol	55.50	78.20	88.20	90.30	72.30	74.50	79.80	66.90	74.10	(NA)
Value of production	Mil. dol	374	414	441	490	354	349	361	298	313	(NA)

NA Not available. [1] Includes milk cows. [2] As of Jan. 1. [3] As of Dec. 1 of preceding year.
Source: U.S. Dept. of Agriculture, National Agricultural Statistics Service, *Meat Animals—Production, Disposition, and Income*, annual; and annual livestock summaries. Also in *Agricultural Statistics*, annual.

No. 845. Livestock Operations by Size of Herd: 1995 to 2002

[In thousands (1,191 represents 1,191,000). An operation is any place having one or more head on hand at any time during the year]

Size of herd	1995	2000	2002	Size of herd	1995	2000	2002
CATTLE [1]				**MILK COWS** [2]			
Total operations	1,191	1,078	1,033	Total operations	140	105	92
1 to 49 head	746	671	643	1 to 49 head	79	53	44
50 to 99 head	208	186	175	50 to 99 head	39	31	28
100 to 499 head	210	192	187	100 or more head	21	21	20
500 to 999 head	18	19	18				
1,000 head or more	9	10	10	**HOGS AND PIGS**			
				Total operations	168	86	75
BEEF COWS [2]				1 to 99 head	97	48	43
Total operations	898	831	805	100 to 499 head	44	18	13
1 to 49 head	716	654	630	500 to 999 head	15	8	6
50 to 99 head	105	100	99	1,000 to 1,999 head	7	6	5
100 to 499 head	70	71	71	2,000 to 4,999 head	4	5	5
500 head or more	6	6	5	5,000 head or more	1	2	2

[1] Includes calves. [2] Included in operations with cattle.
Source: U.S. Dept. of Agriculture, National Agricultural Statistics Service, *Cattle Final Estimates, 1994-1998*, January 1999; *Cattle*, January 2003; *Milk Cows and Production Final Estimates 1993-1997*, January 1999; *Hogs and Pigs Final Estimates 1993-1997*, December 1998; *Hogs and Pigs*, December 2002; and *Agricultural Statistics*, annual.

No. 846. Hogs and Pigs—Number, Production, and Value by State: 2000 to 2002

[59,138 represents 59,138,000. See headnote, Table 844]

State	Number on farms [1] (1,000)			Quantity produced (mil. lb.)			Value of production (mil. dol.)			Commercial slaughter [2] (mil. lb.)	
	2000	2001	2002	2000	2001	2002	2000	2001	2002	2001	2002
U.S. [3]	59,138	59,804	58,943	25,730	25,884	26,254	10,818	11,430	8,679	25,864	26,561
IA	15,100	15,400	15,300	6,479	6,400	6,681	2,675	2,746	2,023	7,246	7,639
NC	9,300	9,800	9,600	3,708	3,700	3,875	1,648	1,734	1,393	2,502	2,597
MN	5,800	5,800	5,900	2,515	2,774	2,773	1,083	1,231	929	2,208	2,312
IL	4,150	4,250	4,050	1,776	1,826	1,810	762	857	663	2,535	2,495
NE	3,050	2,900	2,900	1,491	1,451	1,496	642	666	552	1,756	1,827
IN	3,350	3,200	3,150	1,388	1,478	1,478	547	617	455	1,693	1,796
MO	2,900	3,000	2,950	1,215	1,188	1,189	504	518	368	([4])	([4])

[1] As of December 1. [2] Includes slaughter in federally inspected and other slaughter plants; excludes animals slaughtered on farms. [3] Includes other states not shown separately. [4] Included in U.S. total. Not printed to avoid disclosing individual operation.
Source: U.S. Dept. of Agriculture, National Agricultural Statistics Service, *Meat Animals-Production, Disposition and Income*, annual; and *Livestock Slaughter*, annual.

No. 847. Cattle and Calves—Number, Production, and Value by State: 2000 to 2003

[97,277 represents 97,277,000. Includes milk cows. See headnote, Table 844]

State	Number on farms [1] (1,000) 2001	2002	2003	Quantity produced (mil. lb.) 2000	2001	2002	Value of production (mil. dol.) 2000	2001	2002	Commercial slaughter [2] (mil. lb.) 2001	2002
U.S. [3]	97,277	96,704	96,106	42,842	42,396	42,250	28,392	29,293	26,915	43,175	35,735
TX	13,700	13,600	14,000	7,469	7,734	7,183	5,039	5,462	4,658	7,516	6,472
NE	6,600	6,400	6,200	4,405	4,335	4,493	2,552	2,711	2,630	9,536	7,862
KS	6,700	6,600	6,350	4,097	3,942	4,067	2,418	2,463	2,364	8,717	7,404
CO	3,150	3,050	2,650	2,121	2,109	2,015	1,337	1,463	1,454	3,243	2,596
OK	5,050	5,200	5,400	1,936	1,825	1,984	1,578	1,475	1,485	39	41
CA	5,150	5,200	5,250	1,923	1,992	1,881	831	945	871	1,348	1,294
IA	3,650	3,550	3,600	1,730	1,616	1,818	1,066	1,132	1,046	964	687
SD	4,050	3,950	3,700	1,627	1,554	1,557	1,269	1,240	1,142	451	184
MO	4,250	4,350	4,500	1,188	1,186	1,186	1,004	997	907	113	90
MN	2,550	2,550	2,470	1,157	1,107	1,163	714	726	691	955	772
ID	1,960	1,990	2,000	975	1,044	1,143	626	702	705	1,052	828

[1] As of January 1. [2] Data cover cattle only. Includes slaughter in federally inspected and other slaughter plants; excludes animals slaughtered on farms. [3] Includes other states not shown separately.

Source: U.S. Dept. of Agriculture, National Agricultural Statistics Service, *Meat Animals-Production, Disposition and Income*, annual; and *Livestock Slaughter*, annual.

No. 848. Milk Cows—Number, Production, and Value by State: 2000 to 2002

[9,206 represents 9,206,000]

State	Number on farms [1] (1,000) 2000	2001	2002	Milk produced on farms (mil. lb.) 2000	2001	2002	Value of production [2] (mil. dol.) 2000	2001	2002
United States [3]	9,206	9,114	9,141	167,559	165,497	169,758	20,771	24,894	20,688
California	1,526	1,589	1,647	32,273	33,217	34,884	3,711	4,630	3,816
Wisconsin	1,344	1,292	1,271	23,259	22,199	22,074	2,721	3,285	2,693
New York	686	672	678	11,921	11,780	12,217	1,562	1,861	1,564
Pennsylvania	617	599	585	11,156	10,849	10,775	1,528	1,801	1,487
Minnesota	534	510	487	9,493	8,812	8,458	1,139	1,313	1,023
Idaho	347	366	388	7,223	7,757	8,155	766	1,047	922
New Mexico	250	268	299	5,236	5,561	6,316	649	823	752
Michigan	300	303	299	5,705	5,870	5,945	736	892	719
Washington	247	247	247	5,593	5,514	5,620	716	827	674

[1] Average number during year. Represents cows and heifers that have calved, kept for milk; excluding heifers not yet fresh. [2] Valued at average returns per 100 pounds of milk in combined marketings of milk and cream. Includes value of milk fed to calves. [3] Includes other states not shown separately.

Source: U.S. Dept. of Agriculture, National Agricultural Statistics Service, *Dairy Products*, annual; and *Milk: Production, Disposition, and Income*, annual.

No. 849. Milk Production and Manufactured Dairy Products: 1980 to 2002

[334 represents 334,000]

Item	Unit	1980	1990	1995	1997	1998	1999	2000	2001	2002
Number of farms with milk cows	1,000	334	193	140	124	117	111	105	98	92
Cows and heifers that have calved, kept for milk	Mil. head	10.8	10.0	9.5	9.3	9.2	9.1	9.2	9.1	9.1
Milk produced on farms	Bil. lb	128	148	155	156	157	163	168	165	170
Production per cow	1,000 lb.	11.9	14.8	16.4	16.9	17.2	17.8	18.2	18.2	18.6
Whole milk sold from farms [1]	Bil. lb	126	146	154	155	156	161	166	164	169
Value of milk produced	Bil. dol.	16.9	20.4	20.1	21.1	24.3	23.4	20.8	24.9	20.7
Gross farm income, dairy products	Bil. dol.	16.7	20.2	19.9	21.0	24.2	23.2	20.6	24.7	20.6
Cash receipts from marketing of milk and cream [1]	Bil. dol.	16.6	20.1	19.9	20.9	24.1	23.2	20.6	24.7	20.5
Number of dairy manufacturing plants	Number	2,257	1,723	1,495	1,384	1,323	1,192	1,163	1,179	1,153
Manufactured dairy products:										
Butter (incl. whey butter)	Mil. lb	1,145	1,302	1,264	1,151	1,168	1,277	1,256	1,232	1,355
Cheese, total [2]	Mil. lb	3,984	6,059	6,917	7,330	7,492	7,941	8,258	8,261	8,599
American (excl. full-skim American)	Mil. lb	2,376	2,894	3,131	3,286	3,315	3,568	3,642	3,544	3,709
Cream and Neufchatel	Mil. lb	229	431	544	615	621	639	687	645	710
All Italian varieties	Mil. lb	983	2,207	2,674	2,881	3,005	3,152	3,289	3,426	3,506
Cottage cheese: Creamed [3]	Mil. lb	825	832	711	706	728	720	735	742	747
Condensed bulk milk	Mil. lb	952	1,426	1,372	1,275	1,263	1,365	1,202	1,110	1,189
Nonfat dry milk [4]	Mil. lb	1,168	902	1,243	1,223	1,140	1,364	1,457	1,419	1,577
Dry whey [5]	Mil. lb	690	1,143	1,147	1,137	1,178	1,147	1,188	1,046	1,116
Yogurt, plain and fruit flavored	Mil. lb	(NA)	(NA)	1,646	1,574	1,639	1,717	1,837	2,003	2,135
Ice cream, regular	Mil. gal	830	824	862	914	935	972	980	970	989
Ice cream, lowfat [6]	Mil. gal	293	352	357	386	407	381	373	380	362

NA Not available. [1] Comprises sales to plants and dealers, and retail sales by farmers direct to consumers. [2] Includes varieties not shown separately. [3] Includes partially creamed (low fat). [4] Includes dry skim milk for animal feed. [5] Includes animal but excludes modified whey production. [6] Includes freezer-made milkshake in most states.

Source: U.S. Dept. of Agriculture, National Agricultural Statistics Service, *Dairy Products*, annual; and *Milk: Production, Disposition, and Income*, annual.

No. 850. Milk Production and Commercial Use: 1980 to 2002

[In billions of pounds milkfat basis (128.4 represents 128,400,000,000)]

Year	Production	Farm use	Commercial Farm marketings	Commercial Beginning stock	Imports	Commercial supply, total	CCC net removals [1]	Commercial Ending stock	Commercial Disappearance	Milk price per 100 lb. [2] (dol.)
1980	128.4	2.3	126.1	5.3	2.1	133.5	8.8	5.6	119.0	13.05
1990	147.7	2.0	145.7	4.1	2.7	152.5	8.5	5.1	138.8	13.68
1995	155.3	1.6	153.7	4.3	2.9	160.9	2.1	4.1	154.7	12.78
1998	157.3	1.4	155.9	4.9	4.6	165.4	0.4	5.3	159.8	15.46
1999	162.7	1.3	161.4	5.3	4.8	171.4	0.3	6.1	164.9	14.38
2000	167.6	1.3	166.2	6.1	4.4	176.8	0.8	6.9	169.1	12.40
2001	165.5	1.3	164.2	6.8	5.7	176.8	0.1	7.0	169.6	15.05
2002	169.8	1.2	168.5	7.0	5.1	180.7	0.3	9.9	170.5	12.12

[1] Removals from commercial supply by Commodity Credit Corporation (CCC). [2] Wholesale price received by farmers for all milk delivered to plants and dealers.

Source: U.S. Dept. of Agriculture, Economic Research Service, "Agricultural Outlook: Statistical Indicators"; <http://www.ers.usda.gov/publications/agoutlook/aotables/>.

No. 851. Broiler, Turkey, and Egg Production: 1990 to 2002

[For year ending November 30 (353 represents 353,000,000)]

Item	Unit	1990	1994	1995	1996	1997	1998	1999	2000	2001	2002
Chickens:[1]											
Number [2]	Million	353	386	388	393	410	425	436	435	442	439
Value per head [2]	Dollars	2.29	2.34	2.41	2.65	2.72	2.69	2.65	2.44	2.42	2.38
Value, total [2]	Mil. dol.	808	902	935	1,039	1,113	1,144	1,155	1,061	1,069	1,045
Number sold [3]	Million	208	197	180	174	191	194	210	218	200	198
Price per lb. [3]	Cents	9.6	7.4	6.5	6.6	7.7	8.1	7.1	5.7	4.5	4.7
Value of sales [3]	Mil. dol.	94	73	60	59	71	76	73	64	46	49
PRODUCTION											
Broilers:[4]											
Number	Million	5,864	7,018	7,326	7,597	7,764	7,934	8,146	8,284	8,389	8,590
Weight	Bil. lb.	25.6	32.5	34.2	36.5	37.5	38.6	40.8	41.6	42.4	44.1
Price per lb	Cents	32.6	35.0	34.4	38.1	37.7	39.3	37.1	33.6	39.3	30.5
Production value	Mil. dol.	8,366	11,372	11,762	13,903	14,159	15,145	15,129	13,989	16,694	13,435
Turkeys:											
Number	Million	282	287	292	303	301	285	270	270	272	272
Weight	Bil. lb.	6.0	6.5	6.8	7.2	7.2	7.1	6.9	6.9	7.2	7.4
Price per lb	Cents	39.6	40.4	41.0	43.3	39.9	38.0	40.8	40.7	39.0	36.5
Production value	Mil. dol.	2,393	2,643	2,769	3,124	2,884	2,679	2,810	2,823	2,790	2,700
Eggs:											
Number	Billion	68.1	73.9	74.8	76.4	77.5	79.8	82.7	84.4	85.7	86.7
Price per dozen	Cents	70.8	61.5	62.5	75.0	70.3	66.8	62.7	61.8	62.2	59.0
Production value	Mil. dol.	4,021	3,790	3,893	4,776	4,540	4,439	4,323	4,345	4,446	4,263

[1] Excludes commercial broilers. [2] As of December 1. [3] Data for 1980 represent number produced and production value. [4] Young chickens of the heavy breeds and other meat-type birds, to be marketed at 2-5 lbs. live weight and from which no pullets are kept for egg production.

Source: U.S. Dept. of Agriculture, National Agricultural Statistics Service, Poultry—Production and Value, annual; Turkeys, annual; and Layers and Egg Production, annual.

No. 852. Broiler and Turkey Production by State: 2000 to 2002

[In millions of pounds, liveweight production (41,625 represents 41,625,000,000)]

State	Broilers 2000	Broilers 2001	Broilers 2002	Turkeys 2000	Turkeys 2001	Turkeys 2002	State	Broilers 2000	Broilers 2001	Broilers 2002	Turkeys 2000	Turkeys 2001	Turkeys 2002
U.S.[1]	41,625	42,446	44,050	6,943	7,155	7,406	MS	3,700	3,827	4,078	(NA)	(NA)	(NA)
AL	5,297	5,139	5,362	(NA)	(NA)	(NA)	MO	1,080	(NA)	(NA)	619	660	783
AR	5,839	5,737	5,813	498	473	522	NC	4,051	4,203	4,411	1,033	1,131	1,160
CA	(NA)	(NA)	(NA)	439	451	439	ND	(NA)	(NA)	(NA)	49	42	50
DE	1,461	1,495	1,544	(Z)	(NA)	(NA)	OH	224	213	215	165	181	207
FL	648	634	631	(NA)	(NA)	(NA)	OK	1,093	1,111	1,141	(NA)	(NA)	(NA)
GA	6,149	6,237	6,453	(NA)	(NA)	(NA)	PA	693	701	706	207	214	234
IL	(NA)	(NA)	(NA)	82	83	90	SC	1,004	1,049	1,080	335	326	369
IN	(NA)	(NA)	(NA)	383	399	403	SD	(NA)	(NA)	(NA)	141	166	159
IA	(NA)	(NA)	(NA)	214	217	211	TN	696	932	895	(NA)	(NA)	(NA)
KY	1,150	1,292	1,404	(NA)	(NA)	(NA)	TX	2,590	2,714	2,882	(NA)	(NA)	(NA)
MD	1,360	1,381	1,377	15	15	14	VA	1,298	1,330	1,301	553	530	446
MI	(NA)	(NA)	(NA)	119	162	180	WV	365	368	359	89	91	80
MN	221	220	230	1,061	1,100	1,148	WI	148	138	145	(NA)	(NA)	(NA)

NA Not available. Z Less than 500,000 pounds. [1] Includes other states not shown separately.

Source: U.S. Dept. of Agriculture, National Agricultural Statistics Service, Poultry—Production and Value, annual; and Turkeys, annual.

Section 18
Natural Resources

This section presents data on the area, ownership, production, trade, reserves, and disposition of natural resources. Natural resources is defined here as including forestry, fisheries, and mining and mineral products.

Forestry—Presents data on the area, ownership, and timber resource of commercial timberland; forestry statistics covering the National Forests and Forest Service cooperative programs; product data for lumber, pulpwood, woodpulp, paper and paperboard, and similar data.

The principal sources of data relating to forests and forest products are *Forest Resources of the United States, 1991; Timber Demand and Technology Assessment, 2001; U.S. Timber Production, Trade, Consumption, and Price Statistics; Land Areas of the National Forest System,* issued annually by the Forest Service of the Department of Agriculture; *Agricultural Statistics* issued by the Department of Agriculture; and reports of the annual survey of manufactures, and the annual *Current Industrial Reports,* issued by the Census Bureau on the Internet and in print in the annual *Manufacturing Profiles.* Additional information is published in the monthly *Survey of Current Business* of the Bureau of Economic Analysis, and the annual *Wood Pulp* and *Fiber Statistics* and *The Statistics of Paper, Paperboard, and Wood Pulp* of the American Forest and Paper Association, Washington, DC.

The completeness and reliability of statistics on forests and forest products vary considerably. The data for forest land area and stand volumes are much more reliable for areas that have been recently surveyed than for those for which only estimates are available. In general, more data are available for lumber and other manufactured products such as particle board and softwood panels, etc., than for the primary forest products such as poles and piling and fuelwood.

Fisheries—The principal source of data relating to fisheries is *Fisheries of the United States,* issued annually by the National Marine Fisheries Service (NMFS), National Oceanic and Atmospheric Administration (NOAA). The NMFS collects and disseminates data on commercial landings of fish and shellfish. Annual reports include quantity and value of commercial landings of fish and shellfish disposition of landings and number and kinds of fishing vessels and fishing gear. Reports for the fish-processing industry include annual output for the wholesaling and fish processing establishments, annual and seasonal employment. The principal source for these data is the annual *Fisheries of the United States.*

Mining and mineral products—Presents data relating to mineral industries and their products, general summary measures of production and employment, and more detailed data on production, prices, imports and exports, consumption, and distribution for specific industries and products. Data on mining and mineral products may also be found in Sections 19, 21, and 28 of this *Abstract;* data on mining employment may be found in Section 12.

Mining comprises the extraction of minerals occurring naturally (coal, ores, crude petroleum, natural gas) and quarrying, well operation, milling, refining and processing, and other preparation customarily done at the mine or well site or as a part of extraction activity. (Mineral preparation plants are usually operated together with mines or quarries.) Exploration for minerals is included as is the development of mineral properties.

The principal governmental sources of these data are the *Minerals Yearbook* and *Mineral Commodity Summaries,* published by the U.S. Geological Survey, Department of the Interior, and various monthly and annual publications of the Energy Information Administration, Department of

Energy. See text, Section 19, for a list of Department of Energy publications. In addition, the Census Bureau conducts a census of mineral industries every 5 years (for 1997 results, see Tables 881 and 882).

Nongovernment sources include the *Annual Statistical Report* of the American Iron and Steel Institute, Washington, DC; *Metals Week* and the monthly *Engineering and Mining Journal,* issued by the McGraw-Hill Publishing Co., New York, NY; *The Iron Age,* issued weekly by the Chilton Co., Philadelphia, PA; and the *Joint Association Survey of the U.S. Oil and Gas Industry,* conducted jointly by the American Petroleum Institute, Independent Petroleum Association of America, and Mid-Continent Oil and Gas Association.

Mineral statistics, with principal emphasis on commodity detail, have been collected by the U.S. Geological Survey and the former Bureau of Mines since 1880. Current data in U.S. Geological Survey publications include quantity and value of nonfuel minerals produced, sold or used by producers, or shipped; quantity of minerals stocked; crude materials treated and prepared minerals recovered; and consumption of mineral raw materials.

Censuses of mineral industries have been conducted by the Census Bureau at various intervals since 1840. Beginning with the 1967 census, legislation provides for a census to be conducted every 5 years for years ending in "2" and "7." The most recent results, published for 1997, are based on the North American Industry Classification System (NAICS). The censuses provide, for the various types of mineral establishments, information on operating costs, capital expenditures, labor, equipment, and energy requirements in relation to their value of shipments and other receipts. Commodity statistics on many manufactured mineral products are also collected by the Census Bureau at monthly, quarterly, or annual intervals and issued in its *Current Industrial Reports* series.

In general, figures shown in the individual commodity tables include data for outlying areas and may therefore not agree with summary tables. Except for crude petroleum and refined products, the export and import figures include foreign trade passing through the customs districts of United States and Puerto Rico but exclude shipments between U.S. territories and the customs districts.

No. 853. Natural Resource-Related Industries—Employees, Annual Payroll, and Establishments by Industry: 1999 to 2001

[Excludes government employees, railroad employees, self-employed persons, etc. See "General Explanation" in source for definitions and statement on reliability of data. An establishment is a single physical location where business is conducted or where services or industrial operations are performed]

Industry	NAICS code[1]	1999			2000			2001							
		Number of employ-ees[2] (1,000)	Annual payroll (bil. dol.)	Average payroll per employee (dol.)	Number of employ-ees[2] (1,000)	Annual payroll (bil. dol.)	Average payroll per employee (dol.)	Number of employ-ees[2] (1,000)	Annual payroll (bil. dol.)	Average payroll per employee (dol.)	Total	Under 20 employ-ees	20 to 99 employ-ees	100 to 499 employ-ees	500 and over employ-ees
											Establishment by employment size-class (1,000)				
Natural resource-related industries, total...	(X)	1,803.0	65.39	36,266	1,791.3	66.58	37,166	1,759.8	69.10	38,718	73,794	47,980	10,973	3,640	289
Percent of all industries...	(X)	1.63	1.19	112.95	1.57	1.72	109.28	1.53	1.73	(X)	1.04	0.79	1.31	2.32	1.50
Forestry, fishing, hunting and agriculture support...	11	192.2	4.81	25,046	183.6	4.68	25,509	183.5	4.79	26,117	26,447	24,813	1,467	159	8
Forestry and logging...	113	83.8	2.26	26,916	83.1	2.26	27,137	78.0	2.16	27,722	12,795	31,445	626	26	-
Timber tract operations...	1131	3.3	0.12	37,422	3.3	0.13	39,563	3.2	0.13	38,399	441	368	29	4	-
Forest nurseries & gathering forest products...	1132	1.4	0.05	35,954	1.7	0.07	39,933	2.0	0.07	34,196	256	227	28	1	-
Logging...	1133	79.2	2.08	26,326	78.1	2.06	26,331	72.7	1.96	27,069	12,098	11,508	569	21	1
Fishing, hunting & trapping...	114	10.0	0.33	33,302	10.0	0.34	34,287	9.9	0.34	34,249	2,636	2,551	72	12	1
Fishing...	1141	7.6	0.26	34,645	7.5	0.27	35,669	7.3	0.26	35,179	2,252	2,183	59	10	-
Hunting & trapping...	1142	2.4	0.07	28,998	2.5	0.08	30,173	2.6	0.08	31,625	384	368	13	2	1
Agriculture & forestry support activities...	115	98.3	2.22	22,613	90.4	2.08	23,043	95.5	2.29	23,960	11,016	10,119	769	121	7
Crop production support activities...	1151	67.4	1.58	23,386	57.6	1.35	23,400	59.6	1.46	24,553	5,464	4,880	491	89	4
Animal production support activities...	1152	16.7	0.33	19,507	18.2	0.38	21,086	20.1	0.45	21,798	3,999	3,820	165	13	1
Forestry support activities...	1153	14.1	0.32	22,603	14.7	0.35	24,067	15.2	0.37	24,587	1,553	1,419	113	19	2
Mining...	21	456.6	20.98	45,935	456.1	22.09	48,432	485.6	25.01	51,516	24,319	9,823	3,628	748	95
Oil & gas extraction...	211	90.0	5.38	59,742	83.0	5.39	64,967	87.9	6.21	70,673	7,691	6,862	687	130	12
Oil & gas extraction...	2111	90.0	5.38	59,742	83.0	5.39	64,967	87.9	6.21	70,673	7,691	6,862	687	130	12
Mining (except oil & gas)...	212	215.9	9.63	44,572	204.3	9.34	45,731	200.7	9.58	47,743	7,323	5,276	1,680	326	41
Coal mining...	2121	76.4	3.70	48,413	70.7	3.54	50,125	71.9	3.78	53,327	1,266	692	392	164	18
Metal ore mining...	2122	39.9	1.84	46,206	34.8	1.72	49,353	32.8	1.65	50,290	484	375	44	44	19
Nonmetallic mineral mining & quarrying...	2123	99.6	4.08	40,972	98.8	4.08	41,313	97.9	4.14	42,791	5,572	4,209	1,244	115	4
Mining support activities...	213	150.7	5.97	39,641	168.8	7.35	43,570	196.8	9.21	46,802	9,305	7,710	1,244	342	42
Mining support activities...	2131	150.7	5.97	39,641	168.8	7.35	43,570	196.8	9.21	46,802	9,305	7,710	1,244	342	42
Timber-related manufacturing...	(X)	1,154.2	39.60	34,309	1,151.6	39.80	34,562	1,090.7	39.30	35,141	23,028	13,344	5,878	2,733	186
Wood product manufacturing...	321	595.2	16.37	27,509	597.7	16.51	27,626	557.5	16.82	28,393	17,289	11,483	4,481	1,311	27
Sawmills & wood preservation...	3211	131.9	3.75	28,431	131.4	3.78	28,798	122.1	3.52	28,811	4,594	3,099	1,203	291	-
Veneer, plywood & engineered wood product manufacturing...	3212	117.5	3.63	30,846	120.6	3.75	31,098	116.4	3.70	31,744	1,944	811	774	348	11
Other wood product manufacturing...	3219	345.7	9.00	26,023	345.8	8.95	25,882	318.8	8.61	27,009	10,751	7,531	2,504	672	44
Paper manufacturing...	322	559.0	23.23	41,549	553.9	23.29	42,046	533.2	22.50	42,196	5,739	1,861	1,397	1,422	159
Pulp, paper & paperboard mills...	3221	185.2	9.74	52,607	177.1	9.48	53,490	170.0	9.20	54,080	606	91	166	234	115
Converted paper product manufacturing...	3222	373.8	13.48	36,071	376.8	13.82	36,666	363.2	13.30	36,632	5,133	1,770	2,131	1,188	44

- Represents zero.   X Not applicable.   [1] North American Industry Classification System, 1997.   [2] Covers full- and part-time employees who are on the payroll in the pay period including March 12.

Source: U.S. Census Bureau, *County Business Patterns: 2000*, Series CBP/00-1. See also <http://www.census.gov/prod/2003pubs/01cbp/cbp01-1.pdf> (issued April 2003).

Natural Resources   559

No. 854. Gross Domestic Product of Natural Resource-Related Industries in Current and Real (1996) Dollars by Industry: 1990 to 2001

[In billions of dollars (5,803.2 represents 5,803,200,000,000). Data are based on the 1987 SIC. Data include nonfactor charges (capital consumption allowances, indirect business taxes, etc.) as well as factor charges against gross product; corporate profits and capital consumption allowances have been shifted from a company to an establishment basis]

Industry	Current dollars				Chained (1996) dollars			
	1990	1995	2000	2001	1990	1995	2000	2001
All industries, total [1]	5,803.2	7,400.5	9,824.6	10,082.2	6,707.9	7,543.8	9,191.4	9,214.5
Industries covered	297.3	306.7	369.7	374.8	321.9	329.9	363.6	359.4
Percent of all industries	5.12	4.14	3.76	3.72	4.80	4.37	3.96	3.90
Agriculture, forestry, and fishing	108.3	109.8	134.3	140.7	118.5	123.1	166.7	163.9
Farms	79.6	73.2	77.8	80.6	84.2	85.5	120.5	114.3
Agricultural services	28.7	36.7	56.5	60.1	34.6	37.6	47.6	49.1
Mining	111.9	95.7	133.1	139.0	105.8	113.0	101.9	106.8
Metal mining	5.2	6.5	5.2	5.7	4.4	5.5	8.0	9.6
Coal mining	11.8	10.7	9.2	10.5	7.5	10.1	11.9	13.9
Oil and gas extraction	87.1	69.3	106.5	110.3	87.5	88.6	70.5	72.9
Nonmetallic minerals, except fuels	7.8	9.1	12.2	12.6	8.1	9.1	12.2	12.4
Timber-related manufacturing	77.2	101.3	102.3	95.1	97.6	93.8	94.9	88.7
Lumber and wood products	32.2	42.3	42.1	39.2	45.1	41.6	41.8	39.0
Paper and allied products	45.0	58.9	60.2	55.9	52.5	52.2	53.1	49.7

[1] For additional industry detail, see Table 660.

Source: U.S. Bureau of Economic Analysis, *National Income and Product Accounts, 1929-97;* and Survey of Current Business, November 2002. See also <http://www.bea.doc.gov/bea/ARTICLES/2002/11November/1102GDPbyIndustry.pdf> (released 28 October 2002).

No. 855. National Forest System Land—State and Other Area: 2002

[In thousands of acres (232,436 represents 232,436,000). As of Sept. 30]

State and other area	Gross area within unit boundaries [1]	National Forest System Land [2]	State and other area	Gross area within unit boundaries [1]	National Forest System Land [2]	State and other area	Gross area within unit boundaries [1]	National Forest System Land [2]
Total	232,436	192,462	KS	116	108	OH	834	234
U.S.	232,380	192,434	KY	2,212	806	OK	772	398
			LA	1,025	604	OR	17,502	15,662
AL	1,288	666	ME	93	53	PA	743	513
AK	24,355	21,982	MD	-	-	RI	-	-
AZ	11,891	11,263	MA	-	-	SC	1,379	620
AR	3,540	2,587	MI	4,894	2,865	SD	2,369	2,013
CA	24,430	20,734	MN	5,467	2,839	TN	1,276	700
CO	16,015	14,485	MS	2,320	1,169	TX	1,998	755
CT	-	-	MO	3,060	1,487	UT	9,209	8,190
DE	-	-	MT	19,110	16,913	VT	817	386
DC	-	-	NE	442	352	VA	3,224	1,661
FL	1,434	1,153	NV	6,275	5,835	WA	10,111	9,261
GA	1,858	867	NH	828	731	WV	1,869	1,034
HI	-	-	NJ	-	-	WI	2,023	1,525
ID	21,652	20,465	NM	10,455	9,417	WY	9,703	9,238
IL	857	293	NY	16	16			
IN	644	200	NC	3,168	1,248	PR	56	28
IA	-	-	ND	1,106	1,106	VI	-	-

- Represents zero or rounds to zero. [1] Comprises all publicly and privately owned land within authorized boundaries of national forests, purchase units, national grasslands, land utilization projects, research and experimental areas, and other areas. [2] Federally owned land within the "gross area within unit boundaries."

Source: U.S. Forest Service, *Land Areas of the National Forest System,* annual.

No. 856. Timber-Based Manufacturing Industries—Employees, Payroll, and Shipments: 2001

[Based on the Annual Survey of Manufactures; for description, see Appendix III]

Selected industries	1997 NAICS code [1]	All employees: Number (1,000)	Payroll Total (mil. dol.)	Payroll Per employee (dol.)	Production workers, total (1,000)	Value added by manufactures Total (mil. dol.)	Value added Per production worker (dol.)	Value of shipments (mil. dol.)
Manufacturing, all industries	31-33	15,879	593,051	37,347	11,235	1,853,929	165,012	3,970,500
Timber-based manufacturing, total	321-322	1,086	37,619	34,636	867	106,166	122,495	243,096
Percent of total manufacturing	(X)	6.84	6.34	(X)	7.71	5.73	(X)	6.12
Wood product manufacturing	321	556	15,431	27,759	459	33,130	72,191	87,250
Sawmills & wood preservation	3211	124	3,481	27,978	106	7,484	70,853	25,924
Sawmills	321113	114	3,169	27,899	97	6,781	69,814	21,694
Wood preservation	321114	11	313	28,805	9	704	82,724	4,231
Veneer, plywood, & engineered wood product	3212	115	3,515	30,463	95	7,586	79,638	19,636
Other wood product	3219	316	8,435	26,685	258	18,060	69,990	41,689
Millwork	32191	146	4,167	28,559	119	9,166	76,752	22,149
Wood container & pallet	32192	49	1,097	22,324	41	2,169	52,756	4,687
All other wood product	32199	121	3,171	26,197	97	6,724	68,974	14,854
Paper	322	530	22,188	41,845	408	73,036	179,108	155,846
Pulp, paper, & paperboard mills	3221	171	9,179	53,783	134	37,279	277,782	71,987
Pulp mills	32211	7	414	57,419	6	1,413	253,647	3,239
Paper mills	32212	115	6,163	53,745	91	24,837	273,804	46,853
Paperboard mills	32213	49	2,601	53,335	38	11,029	290,842	21,896
Converted paper product	3222	360	13,010	36,180	274	35,757	130,703	83,859
Paperboard container	32221	205	7,483	36,502	157	17,534	111,575	45,817
Paper bag & coated & treated paper	32222	71	2,665	37,741	51	8,443	164,924	18,390
Stationery product	32223	45	1,452	32,175	35	3,485	100,021	8,075
Other converted paper product	32229	39	1,410	36,296	30	6,295	207,137	11,576

X Not applicable. [1] North American Industry Classification System, 1997; see text, Section 15.

Source: U.S. Census Bureau, Annual Survey of Manufactures, 2001, Series M01(AS)-1. See also <http://www.census.gov/prod/2003pubs/m01-as1.pdf> (issued January 2003).

No. 857. Timber Products—Production, Foreign Trade, and Consumption by Type of Product: 1990 to 2002

[In millions of cubic feet, roundwood equivalent (15,577 represents 15,577,000,000)]

Type of product	1990	1993	1994	1995	1996	1997	1998	1999	2000	2001	2002
Industrial roundwood:											
Domestic production [1]	15,577	15,011	15,306	15,537	15,413	15,703	15,620	15,632	15,436	14,634	14,902
Softwoods	10,968	10,090	10,268	10,191	10,153	10,180	10,097	10,381	10,201	9,859	10,124
Hardwoods	4,609	4,921	5,038	5,347	5,260	5,523	5,523	5,251	5,235	4,775	4,778
Imports	3,091	3,465	3,632	3,907	3,885	4,008	4,157	4,370	4,529	4,605	4,505
Exports	2,307	2,143	2,139	2,282	2,264	2,290	1,951	1,964	1,996	1,759	1,769
Consumption [2]	16,361	16,334	16,800	17,161	17,034	17,421	17,827	18,038	17,969	17,481	17,637
Softwoods	11,779	11,539	11,906	11,961	11,996	12,072	12,339	12,754	12,659	12,552	12,790
Hardwoods	4,582	4,795	4,894	5,200	5,038	5,349	5,488	5,284	5,310	4,929	4,847
Lumber:											
Domestic production	7,317	6,887	7,052	6,815	6,886	7,103	7,093	7,379	7,199	6,820	7,060
Imports	1,909	2,240	2,395	2,522	2,616	2,619	2,721	2,807	2,845	2,903	3,036
Exports	589	532	512	460	449	452	350	404	428	354	353
Consumption	8,637	8,595	8,935	8,877	9,053	9,270	9,463	9,782	9,616	9,369	9,744
Plywood and veneer:											
Domestic production	1,423	1,293	1,320	1,303	1,281	1,213	1,201	1,208	1,187	1,067	1,074
Imports	97	100	94	107	97	114	131	160	155	173	205
Exports	109	100	86	89	87	103	55	45	42	32	31
Consumption	1,410	1,293	1,328	1,321	1,291	1,224	1,277	1,323	1,300	1,208	1,249
Pulp products:											
Domestic production	5,313	5,423	5,576	6,079	5,908	6,097	6,114	5,813	5,881	5,691	5,708
Imports	1,038	1,065	1,102	1,248	1,144	1,249	1,269	1,355	1,459	1,458	1,180
Exports	646	724	758	905	891	929	818	768	842	801	810
Consumption	5,704	5,764	5,920	6,422	6,161	6,417	6,565	6,400	6,498	6,348	6,078
Logs:											
Imports	4	15	18	13	18	20	30	47	68	70	81
Exports	674	460	429	451	422	384	316	326	331	307	309
Pulpwood chips, exports	288	326	354	377	416	422	412	422	353	265	265
Fuelwood consumption	3,019	3,084	3,134	2,937	2,739	2,542	2,523	2,542	2,561	2,571	2,581

[1] Includes log exports. [2] Includes log imports.

Source: U.S. Forest Service, *U.S. Timber Production, Trade, Consumption, and Price Statistics, 1965-1999*, Research Paper FPL-RP-595; and unpublished data. See also <http://www.fpl.fs.fed.us/documnts/fplrp/fplrp595.pdf>.

No. 858. Selected Timber Products—Imports and Exports: 1990 to 2002

Product	Unit	1990	1995	1996	1997	1998	1999	2000	2001	2002
IMPORTS [1]										
Lumber, total [2]	Mil. bd. ft.	13,063	17,524	18,363	18,237	19,012	19,576	19,906	20,443	21,434
From Canada	Percent	91.3	97.1	97.2	96.3	96.0	93.0	92.0	93.0	90.4
Logs, total	Mil. bd. ft.[3]	23	80	115	128	185	294	435	452	525
From Canada	Percent	84	70	82	83	91	95	96	97	97
Paper and board [4]	1,000 tons	12,195	14,292	13,023	14,525	14,538	16,917	17,555	18,513	19,433
Woodpulp	1,000 tons	4,893	5,969	5,692	6,398	5,984	6,660	7,227	7,348	7,247
Plywood	Mil. sq. ft.[5]	1,687	1,951	1,780	2,111	2,429	2,987	2,917	3,246	3,868
EXPORTS										
Lumber, total [2]	Mil. bd. ft.	4,614	2,958	2,898	2,933	2,189	2,549	2,700	2,190	2,186
To: Canada	Percent	14	22	23	24	26	26	26	26	27
Japan	Percent	28	33	33	27	16	14	12	10	7
Europe	Percent	15	17	17	20	26	21	19	18	16
Logs, total	Mil. bd. ft.[3]	4,213	2,820	2,636	2,398	1,978	2,038	2,068	1,918	1,934
To: Canada	Percent	9	25	20	30	39	39	41	46	50
Japan	Percent	62	61	69	56	51	49	45	39	34
China: Mainland	Percent	9	1	1	1	1	-	-	1	2
Paper and board [4]	1,000 tons	5,163	7,621	9,118	10,368	9,103	9,477	10,003	11,504	11,564
Woodpulp	1,000 tons	5,905	8,261	7,170	6,990	6,025	5,936	6,409	6,167	6,254
Plywood	Mil. sq. ft.[5]	1,766	1,517	1,499	1,802	970	797	754	580	563

- Represents zero. [1] Customs value of imports; see text, Section 28. [2] Includes railroad ties. [3] Log scale. [4] Includes paper and board products. Excludes hardboard. [5] 3/8 inch basis.

Source: U.S. Forest Service, *U.S. Timber Production, Trade, Consumption, and Price Statistics, 1965-1999*, Research Paper FPL-RP-595; and unpublished data. See also <http://www.fpl.fs.fed.us/documnts/fplrp/fplrp595.pdf>.

No. 859. Lumber Consumption by Species Group and End Use: 1995 to 2002

[In million board feet (59.3 represents 59,300,000), except per capita in board feet. Per capita consumption based on estimated resident population as of July 1]

Item	1995	1999	2000	2001	2002	End-use	1995	1999	2000	2001	2002
Total	59.3	68.3	66.1	64.6	67.5	New housing	15.9	22.1	20.6	20.1	20.0
Per capita	225	240	234	227	235	Residential upkeep and improvements	12.4	15.1	16.4	17.0	17.3
Species group:						New nonresidential construction [1]	5.5	5.5	5.6	5.6	5.5
Softwoods	47.6	54.5	54.0	53.7	56.4	Manufacturing	5.5	(NA)	(NA)	(NA)	(NA)
Hardwoods	11.7	13.8	12.2	11.0	11.1	Shipping	7.4	8.2	8.1	8.2	8.0
						Other [2]	6.2	7.3	7.3	7.4	7.5

NA Not available. [1] In addition to new construction, includes railroad ties laid as replacements in existing track and lumber used by railroads for railcar repair. [2] Includes upkeep and improvement of nonresidential buildings and structures; made-at-home projects, such as furniture, boats, and picnic tables; made-on-the-job items such as advertising and display structures; and miscellaneous products and uses.

Source: U.S. Forest Service, *U.S. Timber Production, Trade, Consumption, and Price Statistics, 1965-1999*, Research Paper FPL-RP-595. See also <http://www.fpl.fs.fed.us/documnts/fplrp/fplrp595.pdf>.

No. 860. Selected Timber Products—Producer Price Indexes: 1990 to 2002

[1982=100. For information about producer prices, see text, Section 14]

Product	1990	1995	1996	1997	1998	1999	2000	2001	2002
INDEX									
Lumber and wood products	129.7	178.1	176.1	183.8	179.1	183.6	178.2	174.4	173.3
Lumber	124.6	173.4	179.8	194.5	179.5	188.2	178.8	171.6	170.6
Softwood lumber	123.8	178.5	189.5	206.5	182.7	196.0	178.6	170.1	170.8
Hardwood lumber	131.0	167.0	163.9	174.1	178.7	177.3	185.9	181.3	178.3
Millwork	130.4	163.8	166.6	170.9	171.1	174.7	176.4	179.2	179.8
General millwork	132.0	165.4	167.9	171.1	172.4	175.6	178.0	181.8	183.3
Prefabricated structural members	122.3	163.5	167.5	177.8	170.1	178.1	175.1	173.5	168.5
Plywood	114.2	165.3	156.4	159.3	157.3	176.4	157.6	154.3	151.7
Softwood plywood	119.6	188.1	173.7	175.5	174.9	207.0	173.3	167.8	164.1
Hardwood plywood and related products	102.7	122.2	124.9	127.1	126.9	128.6	130.2	130.4	131.5
Other wood products	114.7	143.7	127.5	128.4	135.2	131.1	130.5	130.5	127.2
Boxes	119.1	145.0	147.1	149.2	150.7	152.3	155.2	154.5	154.3
Pulp, paper, and allied products	141.2	172.2	168.7	167.9	171.7	174.1	183.7	184.8	185.9
Pulp, paper, and prod, ex bldg paper	132.9	163.4	149.7	144.7	147.0	147.9	161.4	157.7	155.3
Woodpulp	151.3	183.2	133.1	128.6	122.6	119.7	145.3	125.8	116.2
Wastepaper	138.9	371.1	141.6	163.3	145.4	183.6	282.5	148.6	173.1
Paper	128.8	159.0	149.4	143.9	145.4	141.8	149.8	150.6	147.7
Writing and printing papers	129.1	158.4	144.6	140.0	139.9	137.8	146.6	146.4	143.8
Newsprint	119.6	161.8	159.5	133.9	143.4	(NA)	127.5	138.6	105.7
Paperboard	135.7	183.1	155.1	144.4	151.6	153.2	176.7	172.1	164.3
Converted paper and paperboard products	135.2	157.0	153.4	148.4	152.2	153.5	162.7	164.5	163.8
Office supplies and accessories	121.4	134.9	132.9	131.0	131.2	129.5	133.8	136.9	135.7
Building paper & building board mill prods	112.2	144.9	137.2	129.6	132.9	141.6	138.8	129.3	129.3

NA Not available.

Source: U.S. Bureau of Labor Statistics, *Producer Price Indexes*, monthly.

No. 861. Selected Species—Stumpage Prices In Current and Constant (1996) Dollars: 1990 to 2002

[In dollars per 1,000 board feet. Stumpage prices are based on sales of sawtimber from National Forests]

Species	1990	1993	1994	1995	1996	1997	1998	1999	2000	2001	2002
CURRENT DOLLARS											
Softwoods:											
Douglas fir [1]	466	318	652	454	436	331	254	315	433	258	185
Southern pine [2]	127	217	266	248	241	307	288	269	258	168	166
Sugar pine [3]	285	598	625	397	318	234	200	229	187	192	209
Ponderosa pine [3,4]	218	535	291	150	274	270	205	181	155	143	118
Western hemlock [5]	203	364	335	297	248	211	161	96	46	34	73
Hardwoods:											
All eastern hardwoods [6]	146	264	352	309	259	287	241	195	341	264	384
Oak, white, red, and black [6]	188	195	317	297	237	265	270	317	258	153	207
Maple, sugar [7]	135	220	313	286	238	357	395	448	314	271	485
CONSTANT (1996) DOLLARS [8]											
Softwoods:											
Douglas fir [1]	428	292	598	417	436	304	233	289	397	237	170
Southern pine [2]	117	199	244	228	241	282	264	247	237	154	153
Sugar pine [3]	262	549	574	364	318	215	183	210	172	176	191
Ponderosa pine [3,4]	200	491	267	138	274	248	188	166	142	131	108
Western hemlock [5]	186	334	307	272	248	194	148	88	42	31	67
Hardwoods:											
All eastern hardwoods [6]	134	242	323	283	259	263	221	179	313	242	353
Oak, white, red, and black [6]	172	179	291	272	237	243	248	291	237	140	190
Maple, sugar [7]	124	202	287	262	238	328	362	411	288	249	445

[1] Western Washington and western Oregon. [2] Southern region. [3] Pacific Southwest region (formerly California region). [4] Includes Jeffrey pine. [5] Pacific Northwest region. [6] Eastern and Southern regions. [7] Eastern region. [8] Deflated by the producer price index, all commodities.

Source: U.S. Forest Service, *Timber Demand and Technology Assessment*, RWU-4851. Also in *Agricultural Statistics*, annual.

No. 862. Paper and Paperboard—Production and New Supply: 1990 to 2001

[In millions of short tons (80.45 represents 80,450,000)]

Item	1990	1994	1995	1996	1997	1998	1999	2000	2001, prel.
Production, total	80.45	90.90	91.33	92.25	96.92	96.40	98.84	96.31	90.73
Paper, total	39.36	43.36	42.87	42.48	44.70	44.76	45.98	45.52	42.10
Paperboard, total	39.32	45.72	46.64	47.95	50.40	49.83	51.04	48.97	46.81
Unbleached kraft	20.36	22.47	22.70	22.23	23.22	23.20	23.11	21.80	20.44
Semichemical	5.64	5.94	5.66	5.62	6.05	5.89	6.01	5.95	5.58
Bleached kraft	4.40	5.03	5.30	5.24	5.55	5.49	5.71	5.44	5.30
Recycled	8.92	12.28	12.98	14.87	15.58	15.25	16.21	15.79	15.50
Wet machine board E	0.15	0.15	0.15	0.10	0.10	0.10	0.10	0.10	0.10
Building paper E	0.81	0.81	0.81	0.79	0.79	0.79	0.79	0.79	0.79
Insulating board E	0.86	0.86	0.86	0.93	0.93	0.93	0.93	0.93	0.93
New supply, all grades, excluding products	87.68	97.45	98.16	98.34	101.27	103.01	107.08	105.38	99.51
Paper, total	49.49	53.08	52.77	50.69	54.15	55.13	57.30	57.22	53.27
Newsprint	13.41	12.89	12.76	11.77	12.61	12.80	13.09	13.01	11.51
Printing/writing papers	25.46	29.44	29.55	28.30	30.75	31.38	32.53	32.99	30.39
Packaging and ind. conv. papers	4.72	4.64	4.24	4.33	4.27	4.29	4.71	4.27	4.31
Tissue	5.90	6.11	6.22	6.29	6.52	6.66	6.98	6.95	7.07
Paperboard, total	36.30	42.44	43.45	43.67	45.13	45.67	47.59	46.02	44.09
Construction and other	1.90	1.94	1.95	1.99	1.99	2.20	2.19	2.14	2.15

Source: American Forest and Paper Association, Washington, DC, *Monthly Statistical Summary of Paper, Paperboard and Woodpulp*.

No. 863. Fishery Products—Domestic Catch, Imports, and Disposition: 1990 to 2001

[Live weight, in millions of pounds (16,349 represents 16,349,000,000). For data on commercial catch for selected countries, see Table 1354, Section 30]

Item	1990	1994	1995	1996	1997	1998	1999	2000	2001
Total	16,349	19,309	16,484	16,474	17,131	16,897	17,378	17,338	18,118
For human food	12,662	13,714	13,584	13,625	13,739	14,175	14,462	14,738	15,306
For industrial use	3,687	5,595	2,900	2,848	3,392	2,722	2,916	2,599	2,812
Domestic catch	9,404	10,461	9,788	9,565	9,845	9,194	9,339	9,068	9,492
For human food	7,041	7,936	7,667	7,476	7,248	7,174	6,832	6,912	7,314
For industrial use	2,363	2,525	2,121	2,090	2,597	2,020	2,507	2,157	2,178
Imports [1]	6,945	8,848	6,696	6,909	7,286	7,703	8,039	8,269	8,626
For human food	5,621	5,778	5,917	6,150	6,491	7,001	7,630	7,827	7,992
For industrial use [2]	1,324	3,070	779	759	795	702	409	442	634
Disposition of domestic catch	9,404	10,461	9,788	9,565	9,846	9,194	9,339	9,069	9,495
Fresh and frozen	6,501	7,475	7,099	7,054	6,877	6,870	6,416	6,657	7,085
Canned	751	622	769	678	648	516	712	530	536
Cured	126	95	90	93	108	129	133	119	123
Reduced to meal, oil, etc.	2,026	2,269	1,830	1,740	2,213	1,679	2,078	1,763	1,748

[1] Excludes imports of edible fishery products consumed in Puerto Rico; includes landings of tuna caught by foreign vessels in American Samoa. [2] Fish meal and sea herring.

No. 864. Fisheries—Quantity and Value of Domestic Catch: 1980 to 2001

Year	Total	For human food	For industrial products [2]	Value (mil. dol.)	Average price per lb. (cents)	Year	Total	For human food	For industrial products [2]	Value (mil. dol.)	Average price per lb. (cents)
1980	6,482	3,654	2,828	2,237	34.5	1991	9,484	7,031	2,453	3,308	34.9
1981	5,977	3,547	2,430	2,388	40.0	1992	9,637	7,618	2,019	3,678	38.2
1982	6,367	3,285	3,082	2,390	37.5	1993	[3]10,467	8,214	2,253	3,471	33.2
1983	6,439	3,238	3,201	2,355	36.6	1994	10,461	7,936	2,525	3,807	36.8
1984	6,438	3,320	3,118	2,350	36.5	1995	9,788	7,667	2,121	3,770	38.5
1985	6,258	3,294	2,964	2,326	37.2	1996	9,565	7,474	2,091	3,487	36.5
1986	6,031	3,393	2,638	2,763	45.8	1997	9,842	7,244	2,598	3,448	35.0
1987	6,896	3,946	2,950	3,115	45.2	1998	9,194	7,173	2,021	3,128	34.0
1988	7,192	4,588	2,604	3,520	48.9	1999	9,339	6,832	2,507	3,467	37.1
1989	8,463	6,204	2,259	3,238	38.3	2000	9,069	6,912	2,157	3,549	39.1
1990	9,404	7,041	2,363	3,522	37.5	2001	9,492	7,314	2,178	3,228	34.0

[1] Live weight. [2] Meal, oil, fish solubles, homogenized condensed fish, shell products, bait, and animal food. [3] Represents record year.

No. 865. Domestic Fish and Shellfish Catch and Value by Major Species Caught: 1990 to 2001

Species	Quantity (1,000 lb.)				Value ($1,000)			
	1990	1995	2000	2001	1990	1995	2000	2001
Total	9,403,571	9,787,554	9,068,985	9,494,863	3,521,995	3,735,615	3,549,481	3,228,285
Fish, total [1]	8,091,068	8,520,086	7,689,661	8,242,490	1,900,097	1,915,642	1,594,815	1,479,988
Cod: Atlantic	95,881	29,631	25,060	33,211	61,329	28,184	26,384	32,086
Pacific	526,396	591,399	530,505	471,711	91,384	109,680	142,330	118,071
Flounder	254,519	423,443	412,723	352,363	112,921	150,239	109,910	105,240
Halibut	70,454	44,796	75,190	77,978	96,700	66,781	143,826	115,169
Herring, sea; Atlantic	113,095	147,181	160,269	209,191	5,746	8,654	9,972	12,717
Herring, sea; Pacific	108,120	117,479	74,835	91,297	32,178	49,245	12,043	13,213
Menhaden	1,962,160	1,846,959	1,760,498	1,741,430	93,896	99,131	112,403	102,690
Pollock, Alaska	3,108,031	2,852,618	2,606,802	3,179,407	268,344	259,614	160,525	230,723
Salmon	733,146	1,020,765	628,638	722,832	612,367	486,107	270,213	208,926
Tuna	62,393	63,864	50,779	51,854	105,040	102,638	95,176	93,497
Whiting (Atlantic, silver)	44,500	33,548	26,855	28,479	11,281	14,632	11,370	13,232
Whiting (Pacific, hake)	21,232	390,302	452,718	379,304	1,229	18,002	18,809	16,147
Shellfish, total [1]	1,312,503	1,267,468	1,379,324	1,249,373	1,621,898	1,819,973	1,954,666	1,748,297
Clams	139,198	134,224	118,482	122,764	130,194	140,414	153,973	161,992
Crabs	499,416	363,639	299,006	272,246	483,837	511,987	405,006	381,667
Lobsters: American	61,017	66,406	83,180	73,637	154,677	214,838	301,300	254,334
Oysters	29,193	40,380	41,146	32,673	93,718	101,574	90,667	80,946
Sea	39,917	18,316	32,747	46,958	153,696	92,826	164,609	175,349
Shrimp	346,494	306,869	332,486	324,481	491,433	570,034	690,453	568,547
Squid, Pacific	36,082	155,280	259,508	191,532	2,636	22,650	27,077	17,834

[1] Includes other types of fish and shellfish, not shown separately.

Source of Tables 863-865: U.S. National Oceanic and Atmospheric Administration, National Marine Fisheries Service, *Fisheries of the United States*, annual. See also <http://www.st.nmfs.gov/st1/fus/fus01/2001-fus.pdf> (released September 2002).

No. 866. U.S. Private Aquaculture—Trout and Catfish Production and Value: 1990 to 2002

[67.8 represents 67,800,000. Periods are from Sept. 1 of the previous year to Aug. 31 of stated year. Data are for foodsize fish, those over 12 inches long]

Item	Unit	1990	1995	1997	1998	1999	2000	2001	2002
TROUT FOODSIZE									
Number sold	Millions	67.8	60.2	59.3	57.6	61.0	58.5	54.5	50.2
Total weight	Mil. lb	56.8	55.6	56.9	57.9	60.2	59.2	56.9	54.5
Total value of sales	Mil. dol.	64.6	60.8	60.7	60.3	64.7	63.7	64.4	58.3
Average price received	Dol./lb	1.14	1.09	1.07	1.04	1.07	1.08	1.13	1.07
Percent sold to processors	Percent	58	68	63	62	68	70	68	68
CATFISH FOODSIZE									
Number sold	Millions	272.9	321.8	391.8	409.8	424.5	420.1	406.9	405.8
Total weight	Mil. lb	392.4	481.5	569.6	601.4	635.2	633.8	647.5	673.7
Total value of sales	Mil. dol.	305.1	378.1	406.8	445.4	464.7	468.8	410.7	378.5
Average price received	Dol./lb	0.78	0.79	0.71	0.74	0.73	0.74	0.63	0.56
Fish sold to processors	Mil. lb	360.4	446.9	524.9	564.4	596.6	593.6	597.1	630.6
Avg. price paid by processors	Cents/lb	75.8	78.6	71.2	74.3	73.7	75.1	64.7	56.8
Processor sales	Mil. lb	183.1	227.0	261.8	281.4	292.7	297.2	296.4	317.6
Avg. price received by processors	Cents/lb	224.1	240.3	226.0	229.0	234.0	236.0	226.0	207.0
Inventory (Jan. 1)	Mil. lb	9.4	10.9	11.9	10.8	12.6	13.6	15.0	12.3

Source: U.S. Dept. of Agriculture, National Agricultural Statistics Service, *Trout Production* released February; *Catfish Production* released February; and *Catfish Processing* released February. Also in *Agricultural Statistics*, annual.

No. 867. Supply of Selected Fishery Items: 1990 to 2001

[In millions of pounds (734 represents 734,000,000). Totals available for U.S. consumption are supply minus exports plus imports. Round weight is the complete or full weight as caught]

Species	Unit	1990	1994	1995	1996	1997	1998	1999	2000	2001
Shrimp	Heads-off weight	734	847	832	842	923	1,002	1,084	1,172	1,312
Tuna, canned	Canned weight	856	850	875	859	829	912	1,020	980	796
Snow crab	Round weight	37	40	42	46	110	254	216	122	170
Clams	Meat weight	152	144	144	134	124	119	125	133	139
Salmon, canned	Canned weight	148	117	147	104	82	83	123	95	108
American lobster	Round weight	95	101	94	97	112	110	122	124	125
Spiny lobster	Round weight	89	76	89	81	76	100	91	99	79
Scallops	Meat weight	74	76	62	71	66	58	64	78	76
Sardines, canned	Canned weight	61	48	44	46	49	50	57	(NA)	(NA)
Oysters	Meat weight	56	50	63	58	58	61	55	71	58
King crab	Round weight	19	12	21	30	45	62	52	41	38
Crab meat, canned	Canned weight	9	9	12	13	15	22	26	29	35

NA Not available.

Source: U.S. National Oceanic and Atmospheric Administration, National Marine Fisheries Service, *Fisheries of the United States*, annual.

No. 868. Canned, Fresh, and Frozen Fishery Products—Production and Value: 1990 to 2001

[Fresh fishery products exclude Alaska and Hawaii. Canned fishery products data are for natural pack only]

Product	Production (mil. lb.)					Value (mil. dol.)				
	1990	1995	1999	2000	2001	1990	1995	1999	2000	2001
Canned, total [1]	1,178	1,927	1,897	1,747	1,664	1,562	1,887	1,861	1,626	1,402
Tuna	581	667	664	671	507	902	939	946	856	658
Salmon	196	244	234	171	212	366	419	393	288	259
Clam products	110	129	123	127	126	76	110	110	120	125
Sardines, Maine	13	14	12	(Z)	(Z)	17	24	20	(Z)	(Z)
Shrimp	1	1	2	2	2	3	7	10	11	10
Crabs	1	(Z)	(Z)	(Z)	(Z)	4	(Z)	(Z)	(Z)	(Z)
Oysters [2]	1	(Z)	(Z)	(Z)	1	1	(Z)	(Z)	1	1
Fish fillets and steaks [3]	441	385	362	368	476	843	841	807	823	915
Cod	65	65	61	56	40	132	152	108	167	123
Flounder	54	35	23	27	31	154	86	67	71	76
Haddock	7	3	5	6	6	24	11	20	24	27
Ocean perch, Atlantic	1	(Z)	1	(Z)	(Z)	1	1	2	1	1
Rockfish	33	25	11	11	9	53	38	23	25	21
Pollock, Atlantic	12	4	2	2	2	21	10	4	4	8
Pollock, Alaska	164	135	144	160	271	174	184	169	178	296
Other	105	118	115	106	117	284	359	414	353	363

Z Less than 500,000 pounds or $500,000. [1] Includes other products, not shown separately. [2] Includes oyster specialties. [3] Fresh and frozen.

Source: U.S. National Oceanic and Atmospheric Administration, National Marine Fisheries Service, *Fisheries of the United States*, annual. See also <http://www.st.nmfs.gov/st1/fus/fus01/2001-fus.pdf> (released September 2002).

Natural Resources 565

No. 869. Mining and Primary Metal Production Indexes: 1990 to 2002

[Index 1997=100]

Industry group	1990	1994	1995	1996	1997	1998	1999	2000	2001	2002
Mining	98.7	96.6	96.4	98.1	100.0	98.2	94.0	96.0	96.6	93.8
Coal	96.4	95.0	94.6	96.9	100.0	101.2	99.4	98.2	100.7	96.3
Oil and gas extraction	102.9	100.8	99.8	99.9	100.0	98.3	96.3	96.5	97.6	97.3
Crude oil and natural gas	104.4	101.4	100.1	99.9	100.0	98.5	96.1	95.9	97.3	97.0
Oil and gas drilling	92.9	83.5	81.3	87.2	100.0	98.3	82.0	110.3	125.0	91.0
Metal mining	84.8	91.9	92.8	94.9	100.0	99.2	90.7	90.3	82.0	74.0
Iron ore	89.2	91.9	98.9	98.1	100.0	99.3	91.3	99.2	72.7	81.8
Nonferrous ores	91.9	100.0	100.4	103.4	100.0	107.5	99.4	94.5	89.3	(NA)
Copper ore	89.4	104.7	104.7	108.7	100.0	105.4	90.7	81.4	76.9	(NA)
Primary metals, manufacturing	85.5	92.6	93.7	95.9	100.0	102.3	101.7	98.8	88.2	85.6
Nonferrous metals	89.4	98.8	98.7	100.8	100.0	109.1	101.4	88.2	90.0	77.3
Copper	60.6	102.6	112.0	95.1	100.0	122.6	107.8	46.7	63.4	50.5
Aluminum	97.6	97.6	93.4	94.9	100.0	104.5	105.0	99.4	86.0	87.3
Iron and steel	85.3	93.3	94.8	97.1	100.0	100.4	100.0	100.3	86.7	88.7

NA Not available.
Source: Board of Governors of the Federal Reserve System, *Federal Reserve Bulletin*, monthly; and *Industrial Production and Capacity Utilization*, Statistical Release G.17, monthly.

No. 870. Mineral Industries—Employment, Hours, and Earnings: 1990 to 2002

[Based on the Current Employment Statistics Program, see Appendix III]

Industry and item	Unit	1990	2000	2002	Industry and item	Unit	1990	2000	2002
All mining:					Avg. weekly hours	Number	44.4	41.3	39.5
All employees	1,000	765	599	581	Avg. weekly earnings	Dollars	591	802	761
Production workers	1,000	538	446	435	Metal mining:				
Avg. weekly hours	Number	45.0	44.4	43.2	All employees	1,000	53	38	29
Avg. weekly earnings	Dollars	603	735	743	Production workers	1,000	42	29	22
Coal mining:					Avg. weekly hours	Number	43	43.4	42.8
All employees	1,000	136	72	75	Avg. weekly earnings	Dollars	646	871	879
Production workers	1,000	110	59	64	Nonmetallic minerals,				
Avg. weekly hours	Number	44.7	45.6	45.4	except fuels:				
Avg. weekly earnings	Dollars	822	945	934	All employees	1,000	113	115	108
Oil and gas extraction:					Production workers	1,000	85	87	80
All employees	1,000	190	125	123	Avg. weekly hours	Number	45.0	46.1	45.2
Production workers	1,000	84	67	69	Avg. weekly earnings	Dollars	532	722	749

Source: U.S. Bureau of Labor Statistics, *Bulletin 2370* and *Employment and Earnings*, March and June issues.

No. 871. Selected Mineral Products—Average Prices: 1980 to 2002

[Excludes Alaska and Hawaii, except as noted]

Year	Copper, electro- lytic (cents per lb.)	Plati- num [1] (dol./ troy oz.)	Gold (dol./ fine oz.)	Silver (dol./ fine oz.)	Lead (cents per lb.)	Tin (New York) (cents per lb.)	Zinc (cents per lb.)	Sulfur, crude [2] (dol./ metric ton)	Bitumi- nous coal [3][4] (dol./ short ton)	Crude petro- leum [3] (dol./ bbl.)	Natural gas [3] (dol./ 1,000 cu. ft.)
1980	101	677	613	20.63	43	846	37	89.06	29.17	21.59	1.59
1981	84	446	460	10.52	37	733	45	111.48	31.51	31.77	1.98
1982	73	327	376	7.95	26	654	39	108.27	32.15	28.52	2.46
1983	77	424	424	11.44	22	655	41	87.24	31.11	26.19	2.59
1984	67	357	361	8.14	26	624	49	94.31	30.63	25.88	2.66
1985	67	291	318	6.14	19	596	40	106.46	30.78	24.09	2.51
1986	66	461	368	5.47	22	383	38	105.22	28.84	12.51	1.94
1987	83	553	478	7.01	36	419	42	89.78	28.19	15.40	1.67
1988	121	523	438	6.53	37	441	60	85.95	27.66	12.58	1.69
1989	131	507	383	5.50	39	520	82	86.62	27.40	15.86	1.69
1990	123	467	385	4.82	46	386	75	80.14	27.43	20.03	1.71
1991	109	371	363	4.04	34	363	53	71.45	27.49	16.54	1.64
1992	107	360	345	3.94	35	402	58	48.14	26.78	15.99	1.74
1993	92	375	361	4.30	32	350	46	31.86	26.15	14.25	2.04
1994	111	411	385	5.29	37	369	49	28.60	25.68	13.19	1.85
1995	138	425	386	5.15	42	416	56	44.46	25.56	14.62	1.55
1996	109	398	389	5.19	49	412	51	34.11	25.17	18.46	2.17
1997	107	397	332	4.89	47	381	65	36.06	24.64	17.23	2.32
1998	79	375	295	5.54	45	373	51	29.14	24.87	10.87	1.96
1999	76	379	280	5.25	44	366	54	37.81	23.92	15.56	2.19
2000	88	549	280	5.00	44	370	56	24.73	24.15	26.72	3.69
2001	77	533	272	4.39	44	315	44	10.11	25.36	21.84	4.02
2002	75	559	305	4.52	44	298	40	25.00	26.35	22.51	2.95

NA Not available. [1] Average annual dealer prices. [2] F.o.b. works. [3] Average value at the point of production or domestic first purchase price. [4] Includes lignite.
Source: Nonfuels, through 1994, U.S. Bureau of Mines, thereafter, U.S. Geological Survey, *Minerals Yearbook* and *Mineral Commodities Summaries*, annual; fuels, U.S. Energy Information Administration, *Annual Energy Review* and most recent year from the *Monthly Energy Review*.

No. 872. Mineral Production: 1990 to 2002

[Data represent production as measured by mine shipments, mine sales or marketable production]

Minerals and metals	Unit	1990	1995	2000	2001	2002, est.
FUEL MINERALS						
Coal, total	Mil. sh. tons	1,029.1	1,033.0	1,073.6	1,127.7	1,093.8
Bituminous	Mil. sh. tons	693.2	613.8	574.3	611.3	565.7
Subbituminous	Mil. sh. tons	244.3	328.0	409.2	434.4	444.7
Lignite	Mil. sh. tons	88.1	86.5	85.6	80.0	82.1
Anthracite	Mil. sh. tons	3.5	4.7	4.6	1.9	1.3
Natural gas (marketed production)	Tril. cu. ft.	18.59	19.51	20	20.63	19.97
Petroleum (crude)	Mil. bbl.[1]	2,686	2,394	2,125	2,118	2,097
Uranium (recoverable content)	Mil. lb.	8.9	6.0	4.0	2.6	(NA)
NONFUEL MINERALS						
Asbestos (sales)	1,000 metric tons	(D)	9	5	5	3
Barite, primary, sold/used by producers	1,000 metric tons	430	543	392	400	400
Boron minerals, sold or used by producers	1,000 metric tons	1,090	1,190	1,070	(NA)	(NA)
Bromine, sold or used by producers	1,000 metric tons	177	218	228	212	225
Cement:						
Portland	Mil. metric tons	67	73	84	(NA)	(NA)
Masonry	Mil. metric tons	3	4	4	(NA)	(NA)
Clays	1,000 metric tons	42,900	43,100	40,800	40,000	40,700
Diatomite	1,000 metric tons	631	722	677	644	700
Feldspar[2]	1,000 metric tons	630	880	790	800	820
Fluorspar, finished shipments	1,000 metric tons	64	51	-	(NA)	(NA)
Garnet (industrial)	1,000 metric tons	47	46	60	53	47
Gypsum, crude	Mil. metric tons	15	17	20	16	16
Helium[3]	Mil. cu. meters	85	101	98	87	85
Lime, sold or used by producers	Mil. metric tons	16	19	20	19	18
Mica, scrap & flake, sold/used by producers	1,000 metric tons	109	108	101	98	84
Peat, sales by producers	1,000 metric tons	721	660	755	870	760
Perlite, processed, sold or used	1,000 metric tons	576	700	672	588	548
Phosphate rock (marketable)	Mil. metric tons	46	44	39	32	36
Potash (K_2O equivalent) sales	1,000 metric tons	1,710	1,480	1,300	1,200	1,200
Pumice & pumicite, producer sales	1,000 metric tons	443	529	697	920	950
Salt, common, sold/used by producers	Mil. metric tons	37	41	46	45	44
Sand & gravel, sold/used by producer	Mil. metric tons	855	935	1,148	1,158	1,158
Construction	Mil. metric tons	829	907	1,120	1,130	1,130
Industrial	Mil. metric tons	26	28	28	28	28
Sodium carbonate (natural) (soda ash)	1,000 metric tons	9,100	10,100	10,200	10,300	10,300
Sodium sulfate (natural)	1,000 metric tons	349	327	491	512	500
Stone[4]	Mil. metric tons	1,110	2,420	2,810	2,820	2,890
Crushed and broken	Mil. metric tons	1,110	1,260	1,560	1,600	1,590
Dimension[5]	1,000 metric tons	1,120	1,160	1,250	1,220	1,300
Sulfur: Total shipments	1,000 metric tons	11,500	12,100	10,300	9,250	9,280
Sulfur: Frasch mines (shipments)	1,000 metric tons	3,680	(D)	10,500	9,100	-
Talc, and pyrophyllite, crude	1,000 metric tons	1,270	1,060	851	853	830
Vermiculite concentrate	1,000 metric tons	209	171	150	(D)	(D)
METALS						
Antimony ore and concentrate	Metric tons	(D)	262	(D)	300	-
Aluminum	1,000 metric tons	4,048	3,375	3,668	2,637	2,700
Bauxite (dried)	1,000 metric tons	(D)	(D)	(NA)	(NA)	(NA)
Copper (recoverable content)	1,000 metric tons	1,590	1,850	1,440	1,340	1,130
Gold (recoverable content)	Metric tons	294	317	353	335	300
Iron ore (gross weight)[6]	Mil. metric tons	57	61	63	46	50
Lead (recoverable content)	1,000 metric tons	484	394	468	466	450
Magnesium metal	1,000 metric tons	139	142	(D)	45	45
Manganiferous ore (gross weight)[7]	1,000 metric ton	(D)	(D)	-	(NA)	(NA)
Mercury[8]	Metric tons	562	(D)	(NA)	(NA)	(NA)
Molybdenum (concentrate)	1,000 metric tons	62	61	41	38	33
Nickel	1,000 metric tons	-	2	-	-	-
Palladium metal	Kilograms	5,930	5,260	10,300	12,100	13,000
Platinum metal	Kilograms	1,810	1,590	3,110	3,610	3,900
Silicon (silicon content)	1,000 metric tons	418	396	367	282	270
Silver (recoverable content)	Metric tons	2,120	1,560	1,860	1,740	1,470
Titanium concentrate: Ilmenite (gross weight)	1,000 metric tons	(D)	(D)	(NA)	(NA)	(NA)
Tungsten ore and concentrate[9]	Metric tons	(D)	(D)	-	(NA)	(NA)
Zinc (recoverable content)	1,000 metric tons	515	614	829	842	740

- Represents zero. D Withheld to avoid disclosing individual company data. NA Not available. [1] 42 gal. bbl.
[2] Beginning 1995, includes aplite. [3] Refined. [4] Excludes abrasive stone, bituminous limestone and sandstone, and ground soapstone, all included elsewhere in table. Includes calcareous marl and slate. [5] Includes Puerto Rico. [6] Represents shipments; includes byproduct ores. [7] 5 to 35 percent manganiferous ore. [8] Covers mercury recovered as a by product of gold ores only. [9] Content of ore and concentrate.

Source: Nonfuels, through 1995, U.S. Bureau of Mines, thereafter, U.S. Geological Survey, *Minerals Yearbook* and *Mineral Commodities Summaries*, annual; fuels, U.S. Energy Information Administration, *Annual Energy Review* and *Uranium Industry Annual*.

No. 873. Nonfuel Mineral Commodities—Summary: 2001

[Preliminary estimates. Average price in dollars per metric tons except as noted]

Mineral	Unit	Production	Exports	Net import reliance [1] (percent)	Consumption, apparent	Average price per unit (dollars)	Employment (number)
Aluminum	1,000 metric tons.	2,700	1,500	39	6,400	[2]65.00	13,700
Antimony (contained)	Metric tons	[3]20,000	7,000	41	18,000	[2]79.00	-
Asbestos	1,000 metric tons.	3	8	100	(NA)	160.00	15
Barite	1,000 metric tons.	400	35	76	1,670	[4]28.80	320
Bauxite and alumina	1,000 metric tons.	(NA)	1,270	100	3,300	[4]21.00	(NA)
Beryllium (contained)	Metric tons	100	60	55	220	[2][6](NA)	(NA)
Bismuth (contained)	Metric tons	-	200	95	(NA)	[2]3.20	-
Boron (B₂O₃ content)	1,000 metric tons.	620	245	([5])	559	[4][7]376.00	1,300
Bromine (contained)	1,000 metric tons.	225	10	-	225	[8][9]99.20	1,700
Cadmium (contained)	Metric tons	[3]700	300	([5])	560	[2][10]0.30	(NA)
Cement	1,000 metric tons.	89,000	900	19	110,000	[4]77.00	18,000
Chromium	1,000 metric tons.	[11]153	10	61	413	[4][12](NA)	(NA)
Clays	1,000 metric tons.	40,700	4,990	([5])	35,900	(NA)	6,550
Cobalt (contained)	Metric tons	[11]2,700	2,100	75	11,800	[2]6.90	(NA)
Copper (Mine, contained)	1,000 metric tons.	1,130	450	37	2,700	75.00	7
Diamond (industrial)	Million carats	318	81	89	432	[14]0.34	(NA)
Diatomite	1,000 metric tons.	700	148	([5])	554	[4]256.00	1,000
Feldspar	1,000 metric tons.	820	8	([5])	817	[4]56.00	400
Fluorspar	1,000 metric tons.	126	25	189	472	(NA)	5
Garnet (industrial)	Metric tons	46,900	10,400	28	58,900	[4]50-2000	220
Germanium (contained)	Kilograms	20,000	(NA)	(NA)	(NA)	(NA)	85
Gold (contained)	Metric tons	300	165	([5])	(NA)	[17]305.00	9,000
Gypsum (crude)	1,000 metric tons.	44,900	380	25	31,800	[4]7.33	5,900
Iodine	Metric tons	1,700	790	76	7,020	[8][21]12.78	30
Iron ore (usable)	Million metric tons.	50	6	11	56	[4][22]23.00	5,000
Iron and steel slag (metal)	1,000 metric tons.	16,500	(Z)	6	19,000	[4]8.10	2,700
Lead (contained)	1,000 metric tons.	1,750	120	18	1,580	[2]44.00	2,820
Lime	1,000 metric tons.	18,400	101	(Z)	18,500	60.60	5,400
Magnesium compounds	1,000 metric tons.	395	65	35	610	(NA)	450
Magnesium metal	1,000 metric tons.	(NA)	27	54	120	(NA)	375
Mercury	Metric tons	[11](NA)	300	(NA)	(NA)	[26]140.00	(NA)
Mica, scrap and flake	1,000 metric tons.	160	11	24	111	[4]100.00	(NA)
Molybdenum (contained)	Metric tons	32,600	23,100	([5])	19,900	[2]8.30	360
Nickel (contained)	Metric tons	-	15,920	43	114,000	[22]3.07	-
Nitrogen (fixed)-ammonia	1,000 metric tons.	9,500	650	29	13,500	[4][28]140.00	1,700
Peat	1,000 metric tons.	760	34	50	1,540	[4]24.60	800
Perlite	1,000 metric tons.	548	45	23	713	[4]33.74	145
Phosphate rock	1,000 metric tons.	35,800	-	6	(NA)	[4]27.69	6,000
Platinum-group metals	Kilograms	16,900	72,326	162	(NA)	[17][29](NA)	1,400
Potash (K₂O equivalent)	1,000 metric tons.	1,200	400	80	5,600	[4][30]155.00	1,185
Pumice and pumicite	1,000 metric tons.	950	30	28	1,320	[4]24.00	100
Salt	1,000 metric tons.	43,900	1,000	18	50,200	[4][31]122.00	4,000
Silicon (contained)	1,000 metric tons.	270	21	47	509	52.00	(NA)
Silver (contained)	Metric tons	1,470	885	61	5,340	[17]4.52	1,100
Sodium carbonate (soda ash)	1,000 metric tons.	10,300	4,100	([5])	6,240	[33]105.00	2,600
Sodium sulfate	1,000 metric tons.	500	100	([5])	440	[34]114.00	225
Stone (crushed)	Million metric tons.	1,590	4	(Z)	1,600	[4]5.72	79,000
Sulfur (all forms)	1,000 metric tons.	9,280	550	15	10,900	[4][35]25.00	2,700
Talc	1,000 metric tons.	830	160	8	900	[4]112.00	530
Thallium (contained)	Kilograms	-	(NA)	100	(NA)	[8]1,250.00	(NA)
Tin (contained)	Metric tons	[11]13,500	3,500	79	54,000	[2]188.00	(NA)
Titanium dioxide	1,000 metric tons.	1,380	470	([5])	1,160	[2][36]1.05	4,500
Tungsten (contained)	Metric tons	4,500	3,590	70	12,900	[37]55.00	(NA)
Vermiculite	1,000 metric tons.	(D)	5	(D)	(D)	143.00	100
Zinc (contained)	1,000 metric tons.	1,080	711	60	1,500	[2]0.40	2,900
Zirconium (Z,02) content	Metric tons	100,000	25,387	(NA)	(D)	[4][39]350.00	(NA)

- Represents or rounds to zero. D Withheld to avoid disclosure. NA Not available. Z Less than half the unit of measure. [1] Calculated as a percent of apparent consumption. [2] Dollars per pound. [3] Refinery production. [4] Dollars per metric ton. [5] Net exporter. [6] Metal, vacuum-cast ingot. [7] Granulated pentahydrate borax in bulk, f.o.b mine. [8] Dollars per kilogram. [9] Bulk, purified bromine. [10] 1- to 5-short ton lots. [11] Secondary production. [12] Turkish, chromite price. [13] Columbite price. [14] Value of imports, dollars per carat. [15] Reported consumption. [16] Zone refined. [17] Dollars per troy ounce. [18] Price of flake imports. [19] Includes employment at calcining plants. [20] 99.97% indium. [21] C.i.f. value, crude, per kilogram. [22] Price of eastern Canadian ore. [23] Delivered, No. 1 Heavy Melting composite price. [24] Year-end price. [25] 46%-48% Mn metallurgical ore, per unit contained Mn, c.i.f. U.S. ports. [26] Dollars per 76-pound flask. [27] London Metal Exchange cash price. [28] F.o.b. gulf coast. [29] Dealer price of platinum. [30] Price of K20, muriate. [31] Vacuum and open pan, bulk, pellets and packaged, f.o.b. mine and plant. [32] Ferrosilicon, 50% Si. [33] Quoted year-end price, dense, bulk, f.o.b. Green River, WY, dollars per short ton. [34] Quoted price, bulk, f.o.b. works East, dollars per short ton. [35] Elemental sulfur, f.o.b. mine and/or plant. [36] Rutile, list, year-end. [37] Dollars per unit W03 (7.93 kilograms of contained tungsten per unit). [38] All forms. [39] Price for imported zircon, f.o.b. U.S. east coast.

Source: U.S. Geological Survey, *Mineral Commodity Summaries*, annual.

No. 874. Value of Domestic Nonfuel Mineral Production by State: 1990 to 2002

[In millions of dollars (33,445 represents 33,445,000,000), except as indicated. For similar data on fuels, see Table 881]

State	1990	1995	1999	2000	2001	2002 Total (mil. dol.)	Rank	Percent of U.S.
United States [1]..	33,445	38,506	39,100	40,100	38,900	38,000	(X)	100.00
Alabama..........	559	706	1,080	1,070	938	968	16	2.55
Alaska...........	577	538	1,090	1,140	1,060	1,030	13	2.72
Arizona..........	3,085	4,190	2,510	2,550	2,110	1,920	5	5.05
Arkansas.........	381	492	518	506	491	543	25	1.43
California........	2,771	2,760	3,200	3,350	3,250	3,440	1	9.07
Colorado.........	377	570	555	566	676	619	23	1.63
Connecticut......	122	93	[3]103	[3]100	104	142	42	0.37
Delaware [2]......	10	9	[3]10	[3]12	13	17,500	49	0.05
Florida...........	1,574	1,540	1,930	1,920	1,750	2,020	4	5.32
Georgia..........	1,504	1,690	1,840	1,660	1,610	1,450	7	3.82
Hawaii...........	106	114	89	91	70	75	45	0.02
Idaho............	375	510	420	398	344	307	35	0.81
Illinois...........	667	828	913	907	911	950	17	2.50
Indiana..........	428	589	717	729	718	740	18	1.95
Iowa.............	310	456	537	510	487	487	26	1.28
Kansas...........	349	498	566	624	640	661	21	1.74
Kentucky.........	359	432	483	497	531	372	32	0.98
Louisiana.........	368	434	374	404	274	294	36	0.77
Maine............	55	68	101	[3]102	91	106	43	0.28
Maryland.........	368	324	336	357	356	375	31	0.99
Massachusetts....	128	190	204	210	209	235	38	0.62
Michigan.........	1,440	1,520	1,660	1,670	1,620	1,580	6	4.16
Minnesota........	1,482	1,530	1,580	1,570	1,440	1,090	11	2.86
Mississippi.......	111	131	190	157	177	176	40	0.46
Missouri.........	1,105	1,140	1,380	1,320	1,340	1,290	8	3.39
Montana.........	573	574	491	582	514	442	30	1.16
Nebraska.........	90	146	163	170	163	89	44	0.23
Nevada..........	2,621	3,060	2,780	[3]2,800	2,930	2,900	2	7.63
New Hampshire...	36	50	[3]64	[3]59	60	68	47	0.18
New Jersey.......	229	243	300	286	348	285	37	0.75
New Mexico......	1,103	1,130	671	812	615	571	24	1.50
New York.........	773	886	935	970	1,050	1,010	15	2.67
North Carolina....	586	735	761	779	744	708	19	1.86
North Dakota.....	25	31	38	42	39	39	48	0.10
Ohio.............	733	891	1,040	1,060	1,070	1,060	12	2.78
Oklahoma........	259	357	475	453	530	462	27	1.22
Oregon..........	205	239	303	[3]439	326	320	34	0.84
Pennsylvania.....	1,031	1,080	[3]1,270	[3]1,250	1,270	1,270	9	3.35
Rhode Island.....	18	31	[3]25	24	28	17	50	0.05
South Carolina....	450	447	574	560	531	460	28	1.21
South Dakota.....	319	332	226	260	255	186	39	0.49
Tennessee........	663	665	710	770	708	629	22	1.66
Texas............	1,459	1,680	1,780	2,050	2,210	2,180	3	5.74
Utah.............	1,335	1,850	1,260	[3]1,420	1,310	1,240	10	3.26
Vermont.........	87	60	[3]83	43	69	71	46	0.19
Virginia..........	507	515	667	692	751	697	20	1.83
Washington.......	483	582	631	691	545	450	29	1.18
West Virginia.....	133	181	180	[3]182	185	173	41	0.45
Wisconsin........	215	416	[3]334	349	368	340	33	0.89
Wyoming.........	911	973	956	922	986	1,010	14	2.67

X Not applicable. [1] Includes undistributed not shown separately. [2] Includes District of Columbia. [3] Partial data only; excludes values withheld to avoid disclosing individual company data.

Source: U.S. Geological Survey, *Minerals Yearbook*, annual, and *Mineral Commodities Summaries*, annual. See also <http://minerals.er.usgs.gov/minerals/pubs/mcs/2003/mcs2003.pdf> (released 31 January 2003).

No. 875. Principal Fuels, Nonmetals, and Metals—World Production and the U.S. Share: 1980 to 2001

Mineral	Unit	World production				Percent U.S. of world			
		1980	1990	1995	2001	1980	1990	1995	2001
Fuels: [1]									
Coal	Mil. sh. ton	4,193	5,386	5,157	5,266	19.8	19.1	20.0	21.3
Petroleum (crude)	Bil. bbl	21.8	22.1	22.8	24.8	14.4	12.2	10.5	8.5
Natural gas (dry, marketable)	Tril. cu. ft	53.5	73.6	78.0	90.72	36.3	24.2	23.9	21.3
Natural gas plant liquids	Bil. bbl	1.3	1.7	2.0	2.4	45.7	33.7	32.1	28.3
Nonmetals:									
Asbestos	1,000 metric tons	4,699	4,003	2,420	2,050	2	(D)	(Z)	(Z)
Barite	1,000 metric tons	7,495	5,633	4,300	6,700	27	8	13	6
Feldspar	1,000 metric tons	3,202	5,456	6,780	9,500	20	12	13	8
Fluorspar	1,000 metric tons	5,006	5,131	4,050	4,530	2	1	1	-
Gypsum	Mil. metric tons	78	100	97	104	14	15	17	16
Mica (incl. scrap)	1,000 metric tons	228	215	253	300	46	51	43	33
Nitrogen, (fixed) – ammonia	Mil. metric tons	74	97	96	106	20	13	14	9
Phosphate rock, gross wt	Mil. metric tons	144	162	130	126	38	29	33	25
Potash (K_2O equivalent)	Mil. metric tons	28	28	25	26	8	6	6	5
Sulfur, elemental	Mil. metric tons	55	58	53	57	22	20	22	16
Metals, mine basis:									
Bauxite	Mil. metric tons	89	109	107	138	2	(D)	(D)	39
Columbian concentrates (Nb content)	1,000 metric tons	15	15	18	26	-	-	-	-
Copper	1,000 metric tons	7,405	9,017	10,100	13,700	16	18	18	10
Gold	Metric tons	1,219	2,133	2,220	2,570	2	14	14	13
Iron ore	Mil. metric tons	891	982	1,027	1,060	8	6	6	4
Lead [2]	1,000 metric tons	3,470	3,353	2,780	3,100	17	15	14	15.0
Mercury	Metric tons	6,806	4,523	3,160	1,400	16	12	(D)	(D)
Molybdenum	1,000 metric tons	111	128	141	130	62	48	43	29
Nickel [2]	1,000 metric tons	779	965	1,030	1,330	2	(Z)	(Z)	(Z)
Silver	1,000 metric tons	11	16	15	19	9	13	10	9
Tantalum concentrates	Metric tons	544	400	362	1,300	-	-	-	-
Titanium concentrates:									
Ilmenite	1,000 metric tons	3,726	4,072	3,970	4,600	14	(D)	(D)	7
Rutile	1,000 metric tons	436	481	416	410	(D)	(D)	(D)	-
Tungsten [2]	1,000 metric tons	52	43	39	44	5	14	-	-
Vanadium [2]	1,000 metric tons	37	31	35	58	12	(D)	(D)	-
Zinc [2]	1,000 metric tons	5,954	7,184	7,240	8,850	6	8	9	10
Metals, smelter basis:									
Aluminum	1,000 metric tons	15,383	19,292	19,900	24,400	30	21	17	11
Cadmium	1,000 metric tons	18	20	19	18	9	8	7	4
Copper	1,000 metric tons	7,649	9,472	10,200	13,700	14	15	16	10
Iron, pig	Mil. metric tons	514	532	533	581	12	9	10	7
Lead [3]	1,000 metric tons	5,430	5,763	5,590	3,100	23	23	25	15
Magnesium [4]	1,000 metric tons	316	354	389	426	49	39	37	(NA)
Raw Steel	Mil. metric tons	717	771	755	851	14	12	13	11
Tin [5]	1,000 metric tons	251	223	201	222	1	-	-	-
Zinc	1,000 metric tons	6,049	7,060	7,550	8,850	6	5	5	10

- Represents or rounds to zero. D Withheld to avoid disclosing company data. NA Not available. Z Less than half the unit of measure. [1] Source: Energy Information Administration, *International Energy Annual*. [2] Content of ore and concentrate. [3] Refinery production. [4] Primary production; no smelter processing necessary. [5] Production from primary sources only.

Source: Nonfuels, through 1990, U.S. Bureau of Mines, thereafter, U.S. Geological Survey, *Minerals Yearbook*, annual, and *Mineral Commodities Summaries*, annual; fuels, U.S. Energy Information Administration, *International Energy Annual*. See also <http://minerals.er.usgs.gov/minerals/pubs/mcs/2003/mcs2003.pdf>.

No. 876. Federal Strategic and Critical Materials Inventory: 1990 to 2001

[As of Dec. 31. Covers strategic and critical materials essential to military and industrial requirements in time of national emergency]

Mineral	Unit	Quantity [1]				Value (mil. dol.) [2]			
		1990	1995	2000	2001	1990	1995	2000	2001
Bauxite [3]	1,000 lg. ton	18,033	16,032	6,267	2,032	888	203	49	22
Chromium [4]	1,000 sh. ton	1,074	1,192	937	902	917	839	606	599
Cobalt	Mil. lb	53	44	23	16	443	1,121	313	187
Diamonds: Stones	Carat 1,000	7,777	5,135	1,509	1,006	267	52	15	10
Industrial, bort	Carat 1,000	17,353	1,967	-	-	16	9	-	-
Lead	1,000 sh. ton	(NA)	465	226	197	(NA)	263	103	86
Manganese [5]	1,000 sh. ton	4,017	2,817	2,146	2,052	962	464	255	249
Palladium	1,000 troy oz	(NA)	1,265	842	523	(NA)	143	326	286
Platinum	1,000 troy oz	453	453	217	108	186	154	84	44
Silver	1,000 troy oz	92,151	46,667	15,942	6,817	374	158	61	25
Tantalum Group	1,000 lb	(NA)	3,031	2,282	2,120	(NA)	127	94	86
Tin	1,000 metric ton	169	130	60	54	962	908	323	282
Titanium	1,000 sh. ton	37	37	30	21	402	221	96	64
Tungsten [6]	Mil. lb	82	82	74	69	253	253	156	140
Zinc	1,000 sh. ton	379	301	151	125	483	281	152	123

- Represents or rounds to zero. NA Not available. [1] Consists of stockpile and nonstockpile grades and reflects uncommitted balances. [2] Market values are estimated trade values of similar materials and not necessarily amounts that would be realized at time of sale. [3] Consists of abrasive grade, metallic grade Jamaica, metallic grade Suriname, and refractory. [4] Consists of ferro-high carbon, ferro-low carbon, ferro-silicon, and metal. [5] Consists of chemical grade, dioxide battery natural, dioxide battery synthetic, electrolytic, ferro-high carbon, ferro-med. carbon, ferro-silicon, and metal. [6] Consists of carbide powder, ferro, metal powder, and ores and concentrates.

Source: U.S. Defense Logistics Agency, *Statistical Supplement, Stockpile Report to the Congress* (AP-3).

No. 877. Net U.S. Imports of Selected Minerals and Metals as Percent of Apparent Consumption: 1980 to 2002

[In percent. Based on net imports which equal the difference between imports and exports plus or minus Government stockpile and industry stock changes]

Minerals in rank of net imports	1980	1990	1995	1997	1998	1999	2000	2001	2002
Bauxite [1]	94	98	99	100	100	100	100	100	100
Columbium	100	100	100	100	100	100	100	100	100
Manganese	98	100	100	100	100	100	100	100	100
Mica (sheet)	100	100	100	100	100	100	100	100	100
Strontium	100	100	100	100	100	100	100	100	100
Vanadium	35	(D)	84	(D)	78	80	(NA)	100	100
Tin	79	71	84	86	85	85	86	88	79
Barite	44	71	65	76	80	67	71	87	76
Potash	65	68	75	80	80	80	70	80	80
Tantalum	90	71	80	75	80	80	80	80	80
Chromium	91	84	80	75	80	80	78	78	63
Cobalt	93	86	79	76	73	73	74	78	75
Zinc [2]	60	41	35	35	35	30	60	60	60
Tungsten	53	81	90	84	77	81	68	59	70
Nickel	76	64	60	56	64	63	58	56	43
Silver	7	(NA)	(NA)	([3])	14	14	52	44	61
Aluminum	([3])	36	23	23	27	30	33	35	39
Copper	16	15	27	13	14	27	37	31	37
Gypsum	35	46	30	28	28	29	22	25	25
Iron and steel	13	13	21	20	27	22	17	15	14
Iron ore	25	3	14	14	12	17	19	15	11
Sulfur	14	21	21	13	18	17	22	12	15
Cadmium	55	([3])	23	16	20	19	6	3	-
Mercury	27	(D)	(NA)	(D)	(NA)	(NA)	(NA)	(NA)	(NA)
Platinum group	87	88	(NA)	(NA)	(NA)	(NA)	(NA)	(NA)	(NA)
Selenium	59	46	31	(D)	(D)	(D)	(NA)	(NA)	(NA)

- Represents zero. D Withheld to avoid disclosure. NA Not available. [1] Includes alumina. [2] Beginning 1990, effect of sharp rise in exports of concentrates. If calculated on a refined zinc-only basis, reliance would be about the same as pre-1990 level; 1990, 64 percent; 1991, 61 percent; 1992, 61 percent; 1993,67 percent; 1994,70 percent; 1995, 71 percent; and 1996 and 1997, 70 percent; 1998, 69 percent; and 1999, 71 percent. [3] Net exports.

Source: Through 1994, U.S. Bureau of Mines; thereafter, U.S. Geological Survey, *Mineral Commodity Summaries;* import and export data from U.S. Census Bureau.

No. 878. Federal Offshore Leasing, Exploration, Production, and Revenue: 1990 to 2002

[See source for explanation of terms and for reliability statement]

Item	Unit	1990	1995	1997	1998	1999	2000	2001	2002
Tracts offered	Number	10,459	10,995	9,870	8,205	7,453	7,992	8,790	8,548
Tracts leased	Number	825	835	1,780	1,157	333	553	942	804
Acres offered	Millions	56.79	59.70	26.24	44.10	40.22	42.89	49.15	45.69
Acres leased	Millions	4.30	4.34	9.62	6.34	1.77	2.92	5.00	4.20
Bonus paid for leased tracts	Bil. dol.	0.6	0.4	(NA)	1.3	0.3	0.3	1.0	0.1
New wells being drilled:									
Active	Number	120	124	186	173	219	224	213	119
Suspended	Number	266	247	244	122	110	146	97	72
Cumulative wells (since 1953):									
Wells completed	Number	13,167	13,475	13,546	13,702	13,676	13,718	13,921	13,282
Wells plugged and abandoned	Number	14,677	18,008	18,728	21,050	22,115	22,814	24,218	25,232
Revenue, total [1]	Bil. dol.	3.4	2.7	5.3	4.3	3.2	5.2	[4]5.8	[5]5.0
Bonuses	Bil. dol.	0.8	0.4	1.4	1.3	0.2	0.4	[4]0.5	[5]0.1
Oil and gas royalties [1]	Bil. dol.	2.6	2.1	3.4	2.7	2.6	4.1	[4]4.8	[5]4.7
Rentals	Bil. dol.	0.09	0.09	0.23	0.26	0.21	0.21	[4]0.13	[5]0.4
Sales value [2]	Bil. dol.	17.0	13.8	22.3	17.6	17.4	27.4	[4]31.4	[5]31.0
Oil	Bil. dol.	7.0	6.3	9.0	6.2	6.5	11.5	[4]11.3	[5]12.1
Natural gas	Bil. dol.	9.5	7.5	13.3	11.4	10.9	15.9	[4]20.1	[5]18.9
Sales volume: [3]									
Oil	Mil. bbls.	324	409	479	477	513	566	[4]463	[5]612
Natural gas	Bil. cu. ft	5,093	4,692	5,077	4,836	4,992	4,723	[4]3,470	[5]4,971

NA Not available. [1] Includes condensate royalties. [2] Production value is value at time of production, not current value. [3] Excludes sales volumes for gas lost, gas plant products or sulfur. [4] Covers January through September 2001 only. [5] Estimated.

Source: U.S. Dept. of the Interior, Minerals Management Service, *Federal Offshore Statistics,* annual.

No. 879. Petroleum Industry—Summary: 1980 to 2001

[Includes all costs incurred for drilling and equipping wells to point of completion as productive wells or abandonment after drilling becomes unproductive. Based on sample of operators of different size drilling establishments]

Item	Unit	1980	1990	1995	1996	1997	1998	1999	2000	2001
Crude oil producing wells (Dec. 31)	1,000	548	602	574	574	573	562	546	534	(NA)
Daily output per well	Bbl.	15.9	12.2	11.4	11.3	11.3	11.1	10.8	10.9	(NA)
Completed wells drilled, total	1,000	57.73	31.56	21.06	22.90	27.47	24.08	18.18	25.14	(NA)
Crude oil	1,000	30.88	12.20	7.63	8.31	10.44	7.06	4.09	4.73	(NA)
Gas	1,000	15.25	11.04	8.35	9.30	11.33	12.11	10.51	15.21	(NA)
Dry	1,000	11.60	8.31	5.08	5.28	5.70	4.91	3.58	5.20	(NA)
Average depth per well [1]	Feet	4,171	4,871	5,596	5,636	5,704	6,213	5,944	5,308	5,184
Average cost per well [1]	$1,000	368	384	513	496	604	769	856	755	943
Average cost per foot [1]	Dollars	77.02	76.07	87.22	88.92	107.83	128.97	152.02	142.16	181.94
Crude oil production, total	Mil. bbl	3,138	2,685	2,394	2,360	2,355	2,282	2,141	2,131	2,123
Value at wells	Bil. dol.	67.7	53.8	35.0	43.6	40.6	24.8	33.3	56.9	46.3
Average price per barrel	Dollars	21.59	20.03	14.62	18.46	17.23	10.87	15.56	26.72	21.84
Lower 48 states	Mil. bbl	2,548	2,037	1,853	1,851	1,882	1,853	1,764	1,775	1,766
Alaska	Mil. bbl	590	647	542	508	473	429	383	354	351
Onshore	Mil. bbl	2,760	2,290	1,838	1,789	1,753	1,664	1,508	1,494	(NA)
Offshore	Mil. bbl	377	395	557	570	602	618	639	635	(NA)
Imports: Crude oil	Mil. bbl	1,921	2,151	2,639	2,740	3,002	3,178	3,187	3,260	3,405
Refined petroleum products	Mil. bbl	601	775	586	719	707	731	775	789	636
Exports: Crude oil	Mil. bbl	104.8	39.8	34.7	40.2	39.4	40.2	43.1	18.3	7.4
Proved reserves	Bil. bbl.	29.8	26.3	22.4	22.0	22.5	21.0	21.8	22.0	22.4
Operable refineries	Number	319	205	175	170	164	163	159	158	(NA)
Capacity (Jan. 1)	Mil. bbl	6,566	5,683	5,632	5,595	5,639	5,734	5,935	6,026	(NA)
Refinery input, total	Mil. bbl	5,117	5,325	5,555	5,654	5,807	5,891	5,877	5,950	(NA)
Crude oil	Mil. bbl	4,920	4,895	5,099	5,179	5,351	5,435	5,402	5,504	(NA)
Natural gas plant liquids	Mil. bbl	168	172	172	164	153	146	135	135	(NA)
Other liquids	Mil. bbl	29	259	285	307	303	310	339	310	(NA)
Refinery output, total	Mil. bbl	5,336	5,574	5,836	5,957	6,117	6,216	6,201	6,296	(NA)
Motor gasoline	Mil. bbl	2,369	2,540	2,723	2,759	2,825	2,880	2,894	2,902	(NA)
Jet fuel	Mil. bbl	365	544	518	555	566	558	573	588	(NA)
Distillate fuel oil	Mil. bbl	971	1,066	1,153	1,212	1,237	1,248	1,241	1,307	(NA)
Residual fuel oil	Mil. bbl	577	347	288	266	259	277	256	259	(NA)
Liquefied petroleum gases	Mil. bbl	120	183	237	241	252	245	248	256	(NA)
Utilization rate	Percent	75.4	87.1	92.0	94.1	95.2	95.6	92.6	92.6	(NA)

NA Not available. [1] Source: American Petroleum Institute, *Joint Association Survey on Drilling Costs*, annual.
Source: Except as noted, U.S. Energy Information Administration, *Annual Energy Review, Petroleum Supply Annual; U.S. Crude Oil, Natural Gas, and Natural Gas Liquids Reserves*; and *Monthly Energy Review*.

No. 880. U.S. Petroleum Balance: 1980 to 2002

[In millions of barrels (6,242 represents 6,242,000,000)]

Item	1980	1990	1995	1997	1998	1999	2000	2001	2002
Petroleum products supplied for domestic use	6,242	6,201	7,087	6,796	6,905	7,125	7,211	7,172	7,213
Production of products	5,765	5,934	6,940	6,671	6,733	6,774	6,903	6,942	6,925
Crude input to refineries	4,934	4,894	5,718	5,351	5,434	5,403	5,514	5,522	5,456
Oil, field production	3,138	2,685	2,406	2,355	2,282	2,147	2,125	2,118	2,097
Alaska	592	647	542	473	429	383	354	351	359
Lower 48 States	2,555	2,037	1,853	1,882	1,853	1,764	1,771	1,766	1,738
Net imports	1,821	2,112	2,604	2,963	3,137	3,144	3,301	3,398	3,333
Imports (gross excluding SPR) [1]	1,910	2,142	2,639	3,002	3,178	3,184	3,317	3,401	3,330
SPR [1] imports	16	10	-	-	-	3	3	4	5,767
Exports	-105	40	35	39	40	43	18	7	3,296
Other sources	33	98	102	34	15	113	82	7	26
Natural gas liquids (NGL), supply	577	574	708	721	717	757	799	801	798
Other liquids	253	465	514	599	582	614	589	619	671
Net imports of refined products	484	326	101	154	225	252	305	303	249
Imports	578	598	407	469	508	537	648	636	581
Exports	94	272	307	315	283	284	343	333	332
Stock withdrawal, refined products	-7	-59	46	-29	-53	98	2	-73	39
TYPE OF PRODUCT SUPPLIED									
Total products supplied for domestic use	6,242	6,201	6,469	6,796	6,905	7,125	7,211	7,172	7,213
Finished motor gasoline	2,407	2,641	2,843	2,926	3,012	3,077	3,101	3,143	3,229
Distillate fuel oil	1,049	1,103	1,170	1,254	1,263	1,304	1,362	1,404	1,378
Residual fuel oil	918	449	311	291	324	303	333	296	255
Liquefied petroleum gases [2]	414	568	693	744	713	801	816	746	789
Other	1,454	1,440	1,452	1,582	1,593	1,639	1,598	1,583	1,561
ENDING STOCKS									
Ending stocks, all oils	1,392	1,621	1,563	1,560	1,647	1,493	1,468	1,586	1,548
Crude oil and lease condensate	358	323	303	305	324	284	286	312	278
Strategic Petroleum Reserve (SPR) [1]	108	586	592	563	571	567	541	550	599
Other	926	712	668	692	752	641	641	724	671

- Represents zero. [1] SPR=Strategic petroleum reserve. For more information, see Table 911. [2] Includes ethane.
Source: U.S. Energy Information Administration, *Petroleum Supply Annual*, Volume 1. See also <http://www.eia.doe.gov/pub/oil_gas/petroleum/data_publications/petroleumsupplyannual/psavolume1/current/pdf/volume1all.pdf> (released June 2003).

572 Natural Resources

No. 881. Crude Petroleum and Natural Gas—Production and Value by Major Producing States: 1990 to 2002

[2,685 mil. bbl. represents 2,685,000,000 bbl. or 18,594 bil. cu. ft. represents 18,594,000,000,000 cu. ft.]

State	Crude petroleum						Natural gas marketed production [1]					
	Quantity (mil. bbl.)			Value (mil. dol.)			Quantity (bil. cu. ft.)			Value (mil. dol.)		
	1990	2000	2001	1990	2000	2001	1990	2000	2001	1990	2000	2001
Total [2]	2,685	2,131	2,123	53,772	56,932	46,246	18,594	20,198	20,656	31,658	74,339	82,980
AL	18	10	9	387	289	216	135	523	522	373	2,087	2,193
AK	658	355	351	10,086	8,439	6,448	403	459	471	554	807	939
AR	10	7	8	222	193	166	175	172	167	360	898	832
CA	322	271	261	5,732	6,729	5,242	363	377	378	857	1,812	2,619
CO	31	18	17	722	533	410	243	753	696	377	2,765	2,820
FL	6	5	4	(NA)	(NA)	(NA)	6	6	6	15	(NA)	(NA)
IL	20	12	10	467	343	240	1	-	-	1	(NA)	(NA)
IN	3	2	2	73	59	47	(Z)	1	1	1	3	3
KS	59	34	34	1,359	970	800	574	526	480	893	1,690	1,758
KY	5	3	3	124	92	67	75	82	82	169	258	391
LA	148	105	105	3,409	3,060	2,564	5,242	5,069	5,249	9,587	18,642	20,964
MI	20	8	7	458	222	167	140	297	275	420	724	953
MS	30	20	20	630	520	413	95	89	108	167	293	422
MT	20	15	16	429	429	369	50	70	81	90	198	254
NE	5	3	3	119	83	69	1	1	1	2	3	3
NM	66	67	68	1,472	1,935	1,613	965	1,687	1,689	1,629	5,790	6,564
NY	(Z)	-	-	9	6	4	25	18	28	55	67	139
ND	39	33	32	849	922	746	52	52	55	93	206	193
OH	8	7	6	196	181	136	155	105	100	393	426	454
OK	117	70	69	2,690	2,035	1,691	2,258	1,613	1,615	3,548	5,857	6,502
PA	2	2	2	54	43	40	178	201	157	417	(NA)	(NA)
TX	674	443	424	15,060	12,681	9,933	6,343	6,205	6,520	9,939	24,384	26,978
UT	23	16	15	524	446	367	146	269	284	249	883	998
WV	2	1	1	43	38	27	178	264	251	568	(NA)	(NA)
WY	103	61	57	2,169	1,633	1,238	736	1,088	1,364	856	3,640	4,757
Federal offshore	296	558	592	6,468	28,420	24,652	(NA)	(NA)	(NA)	(NA)	(NA)	(NA)

NA Not available. Z Less than 500,000 barrels, 500 million cubic feet, or less than $500,000. [1] Excludes nonhydrocarbon gases. [2] Includes other states not shown separately. State production does not include state offshore production. U.S. level totals shown in Tables 879 and 880 may contain revisions not carried to state level.

Source: U.S. Energy Information Administration, *Petroleum Supply Annual*, Vol. 2, and *Petroleum Marketing Annual*; and *Natural Gas Annual*, and *Natural Gas Monthly*.

No. 882. Crude Oil, Natural Gas, and Natural Gas Liquids—Reserves by State: 1990 and 2001

[26,254 mil. bbl. represents 26,254,000,000 bbl. As of December 31. Proved reserves are estimated quantities of the mineral, which geological and engineering data demonstrate with reasonable certainty, to be recoverable in future years from known reservoirs under existing economic and operating conditions. Indicated reserves of crude oil are quantities other than proved reserves, which may become economically recoverable from existing productive reservoirs through the application of improved recovery techniques using current technology. Based on a sample of operators of oil and gas wells]

Area	1990				2001			
	Crude oil		Natural gas (bil. cu. ft.)	Natural gas liquids (mil. bbl.)	Crude oil		Natural gas (bil. cu. ft.)	Natural gas liquids (mil. bbl.)
	Proved (mil. bbl.)	Indicated (mil. bbl.)			Proved (mil. bbl.)	Indicated (mil. bbl.)		
United States [1]	26,254	3,483	169,346	7,586	22,446	(NA)	183,460	7,993
Lower 48 States	19,730	2,514	160,046	7,246	17,595	(NA)	174,660	7,588
Alabama	44	(Z)	[1]4,125	170	42	(NA)	3,915	64
Alaska	6,524	969	9,300	340	4,851	(NA)	8,800	405
Arkansas	60	1	1,731	9	43	(NA)	1,616	5
California	[2]4,658	[2]1,425	[2]3,185	[2]105	3,627	(NA)	2,681	76
Colorado	305	8	4,555	169	196	(NA)	12,527	345
Florida	(NA)	(NA)	(NA)	(NA)	75	(NA)	84	12
Illinois	(NA)	(NA)	(NA)	(NA)	92	(NA)	(NA)	(NA)
Indiana	131	-	(NA)	(NA)	12	(NA)	(NA)	(NA)
Kansas	(NA)	(NA)	(NA)	(NA)	216	(NA)	5,101	302
Kentucky	321	(Z)	9,614	313	17	(NA)	1,860	72
Louisiana	33	-	1,016	25	564	(NA)	9,811	391
Michigan	(NA)	(NA)	(NA)	(NA)	46	(NA)	2,976	43
Mississippi	(NA)	(NA)	(NA)	(NA)	167	(NA)	661	10
Montana	(NA)	(NA)	(NA)	(NA)	260	(NA)	898	5
Nebraska	221	-	899	15	15	(NA)	(NA)	(NA)
New Mexico	(NA)	(NA)	(NA)	(NA)	715	(NA)	17,414	873
New York	687	256	17,260	990	(NA)	(NA)	318	(NA)
North Dakota	285	-	586	60	328	(NA)	443	57
Ohio	65	-	1,214	(NA)	46	(NA)	970	(NA)
Oklahoma	734	37	16,151	657	556	(NA)	13,558	694
Pennsylvania	22	-	1,720	(NA)	10	(NA)	1,775	(NA)
Texas	[2]7,106	618	[2]38,192	2,575	4,944	(NA)	43,527	2,653
Utah	249	44	1,510	([3])	271	(NA)	4,579	([3])
Virginia	(NA)	(NA)	138	(NA)	(NA)	(NA)	1,752	(NA)
West Virginia	31	-	2,207	86	8	(NA)	2,678	106
Wyoming	794	42	9,944	[4]812	489	(NA)	18,398	[4]947
Federal offshore	2,805	49	31,433	619	4,835	(NA)	27,036	1078

- Represents or rounds to zero. NA Not available. Z Less than 500,000 barrels. [1] Includes miscellaneous not shown separately. [2] Excludes Federal offshore. [3] Included with Wyoming. [4] Includes Utah.

Source: Energy Information Administration, *U.S. Crude Oil, Natural Gas, and Natural Gas Liquids Reserves, 2001 Annual Report*, December 2002.

Natural Resources   573

No. 883. World Daily Crude Oil Production by Major Producing Country: 1980 to 2001

[In thousands of barrels per day (59,600 barrels represents 59,600,000 barrels]

Country	1980	1990	1995	1996	1997	1998	1999	2000	2001
World, total [1]	59,600	60,566	62,335	63,711	65,690	66,921	65,848	68,342	68,057
Algeria	1,106	1,175	1,202	1,242	1,277	1,246	1,202	1,254	1,270
Angola	150	475	646	709	714	735	745	746	742
Argentina	491	483	715	756	834	847	802	761	781
Australia	380	575	562	570	588	544	539	722	657
Brazil	182	631	695	795	841	969	1,132	1,269	1,295
Canada	1,435	1,553	1,805	1,837	1,922	1,981	1,907	1,977	2,029
China	2,114	2,774	2,990	3,131	3,200	3,198	3,195	3,249	3,300
Colombia	126	440	585	623	652	733	816	691	602
Egypt	595	873	920	922	856	834	852	748	698
India	182	660	703	651	675	661	653	646	642
Indonesia	1,577	1,462	1,503	1,547	1,520	1,518	1,472	1,423	1,369
Iran	1,662	3,088	3,643	3,686	3,664	3,634	3,557	3,696	3,724
Iraq	2,514	2,040	560	579	1,155	2,150	2,508	2,571	2,432
Kazakhstan	(X)	(X)	362	403	466	476	530	610	704
Kuwait	1,656	1,175	2,057	2,062	2,007	2,085	1,898	2,079	1,998
Libya	1,787	1,375	1,390	1,401	1,446	1,390	1,319	1,410	1,367
Malaysia	283	619	682	695	700	720	693	690	659
Mexico	1,936	2,553	2,618	2,855	3,023	3,070	2,906	3,012	3,157
Nigeria	2,055	1,810	1,993	2,001	2,132	2,153	2,130	2,165	2,256
Norway	528	1,704	2,768	3,104	3,143	3,017	3,018	3,197	3,117
Oman	282	685	851	883	904	900	910	970	960
Qatar	472	406	442	510	550	696	665	737	714
Russia	(X)	(X)	5,995	5,850	5,920	5,854	6,079	6,479	7,049
Saudi Arabia	9,900	6,410	8,231	8,218	8,362	8,389	7,833	8,404	8,031
Syria	164	388	575	582	561	553	538	523	518
United Arab Emirates	1,709	2,117	2,233	2,278	2,316	2,345	2,169	2,368	2,276
United Kingdom	1,622	1,820	2,489	2,568	2,518	2,616	2,684	2,275	2,282
United States	8,597	7,355	6,560	6,465	6,452	6,252	5,881	5,822	5,801
Venezuela	2,168	2,137	2,750	2,938	3,280	3,167	2,826	3,155	2,880
Yemen	(X)	193	345	340	362	388	409	440	438

X Not applicable.   [1] Includes countries not shown separately.

Source: U.S. Energy Information Administration, *International Energy Annual, 2001*. See also <http://tonto.eia.doe.gov/FTPROOT/international/021901.pdf> (issued March 2003).

No. 884. Liquefied Petroleum Gases—Summary: 1980 to 2002

[In millions of 42-gallon barrels (561 barrels represents 561,000,000 barrels). Includes ethane]

Item	1980	1990	1995	1997	1998	1999	2000	2001	2002
Production	561	638	760	799	775	814	845	813	813
At natural gas plants	441	456	521	547	529	564	587	570	568
At refineries	121	182	234	252	246	250	258	243	245
Imports	79	68	53	62	71	66	79	75	67
Refinery input	85	107	105	96	92	87	87	88	90
Exports	9	14	21	18	15	18	27	16	24
Stocks, Dec. 31	116	98	93	89	115	89	83	121	106

Source: U.S. Energy Information Administration, *Petroleum Supply Annual*, Volume 1.

No. 885. Natural Gas Plant Liquids—Production and Value: 1980 to 2002

[Barrels of 42 gallons (576 barrels represents 576,000,000 barrels)]

Item	Unit	1980	1990	1995	1997	1998	1999	2000	2001	2002
Field production [1]	Mil. bbl	576	566	643	663	642	675	699	682	686
Pentanes plus	Mil. bbl	126	112	122	116	113	111	112	112	109
Liquefied petroleum gases	Mil. bbl	441	454	521	547	529	564	587	570	577
Natural gas processed	Tril. cu. ft.	15	15	17	17	17	17	17	17	(NA)

NA Not available.   [1] Includes other finished petroleum products, not shown separately.

Source: U.S. Energy Information Administration, *Petroleum Supply Annual* and *Natural Gas Annual*.

No. 886. Natural Gas—Supply, Consumption, Reserves, and Marketed Production: 1980 to 2000

[182 represents 182,000 wells]

Item	Unit	1980	1990	1994	1995	1996	1997	1998	1999	2000
Producing wells (year-end)	1,000	182	269	292	299	302	311	317	302	306
Production value at wells	Bil. dol	32.1	31.8	36.5	30.2	43.0	46.1	38.2	43.4	73.6
Avg. per 1,000 cu. ft	Dollars	1.59	1.71	1.85	1.55	2.17	2.32	1.96	2.19	3.68
Proved reserves [1]	Tril. cu. ft	199	169	164	165	166	167	164	167	177
Marketed production [2]	**Bil. cu. ft**	**20,180**	**18,594**	**19,710**	**19,506**	**19,812**	**19,866**	**19,961**	**19,805**	**20,002**
Minus: Extraction losses [3]	Bil. cu. ft.	777	784	889	908	958	964	938	973	1,016
Equals: Dry production	Bil. cu. ft.	19,403	17,810	18,821	18,599	18,854	18,902	19,024	18,832	18,987
Plus: Supplemental gas supplies	Bil. cu. ft.	155	123	111	110	109	103	102	99	86
Equals: Dry production with supplemental gas	Bil. cu. ft.	19,558	17,932	18,932	18,709	18,964	19,005	19,126	18,931	19,073
Plus: Withdrawals from storage	Bil. cu. ft.	1,972	1,986	2,579	3,025	2,981	2,894	2,432	2,808	3,550
Plus: Imports [4]	Bil. cu. ft.	985	1,532	2,624	2,841	2,937	2,994	3,152	3,586	3,782
Plus: Balancing item	Bil. cu. ft.	-640	-152	-416	-230	217	61	-334	-897	-827
Equals: Total supply	Bil. cu. ft.	21,875	21,299	23,719	24,345	25,099	24,954	24,376	24,427	25,577
Minus: Exports	Bil. cu. ft.	49	86	162	154	153	157	159	163	244
Minus: Additions to storage [5]	Bil. cu. ft.	1,949	2,499	2,865	2,610	2,979	2,870	2,961	2,636	2,721
Equals: Consumption, total	**Bil. cu. ft**	**19,877**	**18,715**	**20,708**	**21,581**	**21,967**	**21,959**	**21,277**	**21,620**	**22,547**
Lease and plant fuel	Bil. cu. ft.	1,026	1,236	1,124	1,220	1,250	1,203	1,173	1,079	1,130
Pipeline fuel	Bil. cu. ft.	635	660	685	700	711	751	635	645	644
Residential	Bil. cu. ft.	4,752	4,391	4,848	4,850	5,241	4,984	4,520	4,726	4,992
Commercial [6]	Bil. cu. ft.	2,611	2,623	2,895	3,031	3,158	3,215	2,999	3,045	3,218
Industrial	Bil. cu. ft.	7,172	7,018	8,167	8,580	8,870	8,832	8,686	9,006	9,512
Vehicle fuel	Bil. cu. ft.	(NA)	-	2	3	3	4	5	6	8
Electric utilities	Bil. cu. ft.	3,682	2,786	2,987	3,197	2,732	2,968	3,258	3,113	3,043
World production (dry)	Tril. cu. ft	53.5	73.6	76.9	78.0	81.7	81.5	83.0	84.9	88.0
U.S. production (dry)	Tril. cu. ft	19.4	17.8	18.8	18.6	18.9	18.9	19.0	18.8	19.0
Percent U.S. of world	Percent	36.3	24.2	24.5	23.9	23.1	23.2	22.9	22.2	21.6

- Represents zero. NA Not available. [1] Estimated, end of year. Source: U.S. Energy Information Administration, *U.S. Crude Oil, Natural Gas, and Natural Gas Liquids Reserves*, annual. [2] Marketed production includes gross withdrawals from reservoirs less quantities used for reservoir repressuring and quantities vented or flared. For 1980 and thereafter, it excludes the nonhydrocarbon gases subsequently removed. [3] Volumetric reduction in natural gas resulting from the extraction of natural gas constituents at natural gas processing plants. [4] Includes imports of liquefied natural gas. [5] Includes liquefied natural gas (LNG) storage in above ground tanks. [6] Includes deliveries to municipalities and public authorities for institutional heating and other purposes.

Source: Except as noted, U.S. Energy Information Administration, *Annual Energy Review, International Energy Annual, Natural Gas Annual*, Volume I and II, and *Monthly Energy Review*.

No. 887. World Natural Gas Production by Major Producing Country: 1980 to 2001

[In trillion cubic feet (53.35 represents 53,350,000,000,000]

Country	1980	1990	1995	1996	1997	1998	1999	2000	2001
World, total [1]	**53.35**	**73.57**	**77.96**	**81.65**	**81.52**	**83.03**	**84.91**	**88.09**	**90.72**
Russia	(X)	(X)	21.01	21.23	20.17	20.87	20.83	20.63	20.51
United States	19.40	17.81	18.60	18.85	18.90	19.02	18.83	18.99	19.36
Canada	2.76	3.85	5.60	5.71	5.76	5.98	6.26	6.47	6.60
Algeria	0.41	1.79	2.05	2.19	2.43	2.60	2.88	2.94	2.84
Netherlands	3.40	2.69	2.98	3.37	2.99	2.84	2.67	2.56	2.75
Indonesia	0.63	1.53	2.24	2.35	2.37	2.27	2.51	2.36	2.44
Uzbekistan	(X)	(X)	1.70	1.70	1.74	1.94	1.96	1.99	2.23
Iran	0.25	0.84	1.25	1.42	1.66	1.77	2.04	2.13	2.17
Norway	0.92	0.98	1.08	1.45	1.62	1.63	1.76	1.87	1.93
Malaysia	0.06	0.65	1.02	1.23	1.36	1.37	1.42	1.50	1.90
Saudi Arabia	0.33	1.08	1.34	1.46	1.60	1.65	1.63	1.76	1.90
Turkmenistan	(X)	(X)	1.14	1.31	0.90	0.47	0.79	1.64	1.70
United Arab Emirates	0.20	0.78	1.11	1.19	1.28	1.31	1.34	1.36	1.59
Argentina	0.28	0.63	0.88	0.94	0.97	1.04	1.22	1.32	1.31
Mexico	0.90	0.90	0.96	1.06	1.17	1.27	1.29	1.31	1.30
Australia	0.31	0.72	1.03	1.06	1.06	1.10	1.10	1.16	1.17
Qatar	0.18	0.28	0.48	0.48	0.61	0.69	0.78	1.03	1.14
Venezuela	0.52	0.76	0.89	0.96	0.99	1.11	0.95	0.96	1.12
China	0.51	0.51	0.60	0.67	0.75	0.78	0.85	0.96	1.07
Pakistan	0.29	0.48	0.65	0.70	0.70	0.71	0.78	0.86	0.83
India	0.05	0.40	0.63	0.70	0.72	0.76	0.75	0.79	0.80
Germany	0.93	0.72	0.74	0.80	0.79	0.77	0.82	0.78	0.78
Egypt	0.03	0.29	0.44	0.47	0.48	0.49	0.52	0.65	0.75
Thailand	(X)	0.21	0.37	0.43	0.54	0.57	0.63	0.66	0.66
Ukraine	(X)	(X)	0.62	0.64	0.64	0.64	0.63	0.64	0.64
Nigeria	0.04	0.13	0.18	0.19	0.21	0.21	0.25	0.44	0.55
Italy	0.44	0.61	0.72	0.71	0.68	0.67	0.62	0.59	0.55
Trinidad and Tobago	0.08	0.18	0.27	0.30	0.33	0.33	0.41	0.49	0.54
Romania	1.20	1.00	0.68	0.63	0.61	0.52	0.50	0.48	0.51
Oman	0.03	0.10	0.15	0.15	0.18	0.25	0.20	0.32	0.49
Brunei	0.32	0.32	0.33	0.33	0.32	0.32	0.33	0.35	0.37
Kazakhstan	(X)	(X)	0.17	0.15	0.22	0.19	0.16	0.31	0.36
Bangladesh	0.05	0.16	0.26	0.27	0.27	0.29	0.32	0.34	0.35
Kuwait	0.24	0.19	0.21	0.33	0.33	0.29	0.32	0.34	0.34
Bahrain	0.10	0.21	0.23	0.29	0.29	0.30	0.30	0.30	0.31

- Represents zero. X Not applicable. [1] Includes countries not shown separately.
Source: U. S. Energy Information Administration, *International Energy Annual*, 2001. See also <http://tonto.eia.doe.gov/FTPROOT/international/021901.pdf> (issued March 2003).

Natural Resources 575

No. 888. U.S. Coal Supply, Disposition, and Prices: 1997 to 2002

[In millions of short tons (1,089.9 represents 1,089,900,000]

Item	1997	1998	1999	2000	2001	2002
United States, total	1,089.9	1,117.5	1,100.4	1,073.6	1,127.7	1,093.8
Consumption by sector:						
Total	1,030.1	1,038.3	1,045.3	1,084.1	1,060.8	1,071.9
Electric power	922.0	937.8	946.8	985.8	965.1	981.9
Electric utilities	900.4	910.9	894.1	(NA)	(NA)	(NA)
Other power producers [1]	21.6	26.9	52.7	(NA)	(NA)	(NA)
Coke plants	30.2	28.2	28.1	28.9	26.1	22.5
Other industrial plants	71.5	67.4	65.5	65.2	65.3	63.1
Residential/commercial users	6.5	4.9	4.9	4.1	4.4	4.4
Year-end coal stocks:						
Total	140.4	164.6	183.0	140.0	181.9	181.9
Electric power	98.8	120.5	136.0	102.0	138.5	143.0
Coke plants	2.0	2.0	1.9	1.5	1.5	1.2
Other industrial plants	5.6	5.5	5.6	4.6	6.0	5.8
Producers/distributors	34.0	36.5	39.5	31.9	35.9	32.0
U.S. coal trade:						
Net exports	76.1	69.3	49.4	46.0	28.9	22.7
Exports	83.5	78.0	58.5	58.5	48.7	39.6
Steam coal	31.4	31.0	26.3	25.7	23.3	18.1
Metallurgical coal	52.2	47.1	32.1	32.8	25.4	21.5
Imports	7.5	8.7	9.1	12.5	19.8	16.9
Average delivered price (dollars per short ton):						
Electric utilities	26.16	25.64	24.72	24.28	24.68	24.84
Coke plants	47.61	46.06	45.85	44.38	46.42	51.27
Other industrial plants	32.41	32.26	31.59	31.46	32.26	33.39
Average free alongside ship (f.a.s.):						
Exports	40.55	38.89	36.50	34.90	36.97	40.44
Steam coal	32.42	30.24	29.91	29.67	31.88	34.51
Metallurgical coal	45.45	44.58	41.91	38.99	41.63	45.41
Imports	34.32	32.18	30.77	30.10	34.00	35.51

NA Not available. [1] Includes utility coal-fired power plants sold to nonutilities during 1998, 1999, and 2000. Coal consumption by cogenerators are included in the end-use sector.

Source: U.S. Energy Information Administration, *U.S. Coal Supply and Demand: 2002 Review*, annual. See also <http://tonto.eia.doe.gov/FTPROOT/coal/coalpubs.htm>.

No. 889. Coal and Coke—Summary: 1980 to 2000

[830 short tons represents 830,000,000 short tons. Includes coal consumed at mines. Demonstrated coal reserve base for United States on Jan. 1, 1997, was an estimated 508 billion tons. Recoverability varies between 40 and 90 percent for individual deposits; 50 percent or more of overall U.S. coal reserve base is believed to be recoverable]

Item	Unit	1980	1990	1995	1996	1997	1998	1999	2000
COAL									
Coal production, total [1]	Mil. sh. tons	830	1,029	1,033	1,064	1,090	1,118	1,100	1,074
Value	Bil. dol.	20.45	22.39	19.45	19.68	19.77	19.75	19.42	18.02
Anthracite production	Mil. sh. tons	6.1	3.5	4.7	4.8	4.7	5.3	4.8	4.6
Bituminous coal and lignite	Mil. sh. tons	824	1,026	1,028	1,059	1,085	1,112	1,096	1,069
Underground	Mil. sh. tons	337	425	396	410	421	417	392	374
Surface	Mil. sh. tons	487	605	637	654	669	700	709	700
Exports	Mil. sh. tons	92	106	89	90	84	78	59	59
Imports	Mil. sh. tons	1	3	9	9	8	8	9	13
Consumption [2]	Mil. sh. tons	703	896	941	1,006	1,030	1,038	1,045	1,081
Electric power utilities	Mil. sh. tons	569	774	829	875	900	911	894	859
Industrial	Mil. sh. tons	126	115	106	103	102	96	94	94
Number of mines	Number	5,598	3,243	2,104	1,903	1,828	1,726	1,591	707
Daily employment	1,000	225	131	90	83	82	85	79	72
Production, by state:									
Alabama	Mil. sh. tons	26	29	25	25	24	23	20	19
Illinois	Mil. sh. tons	63	60	48	47	41	40	40	33
Indiana	Mil. sh. tons	31	36	26	30	35	37	34	28
Kentucky	Mil. sh. tons	150	173	154	152	156	150	140	131
Montana	Mil. sh. tons	30	38	39	38	41	43	41	38
Ohio	Mil. sh. tons	39	35	26	29	29	28	22	22
Pennsylvania	Mil. sh. tons	93	71	62	68	76	81	76	75
Virginia	Mil. sh. tons	41	47	34	36	36	34	32	33
West Virginia	Mil. sh. tons	122	169	163	170	174	171	158	158
Wyoming	Mil. sh. tons	95	184	264	278	282	314	337	339
Other states	Mil. sh. tons	140	187	192	192	195	196	200	197
World production	Mil. sh. tons	4,200	5,386	5,218	5,265	5,278	5,169	5,053	5,059
Percent U.S. of world	Percent	19.8	19.1	19.8	20.2	20.6	21.6	21.8	21.2
COKE									
Coke production [3]	Mil. sh. tons	46.13	27.62	23.75	23.08	22.12	20.04	20.02	20.81
Imports	Mil. sh. tons	0.66	0.77	3.82	2.54	3.14	3.83	3.22	3.78
Exports	Mil. sh. tons	2.07	0.57	1.36	1.62	1.27	1.13	0.90	1.15
Consumption	Mil. sh. tons	41.28	27.82	25.85	23.97	24.02	23.11	22.42	23.24

[1] Includes bituminous coal, subbituminous coal, lignite, and anthracite. [2] Includes some categories not shown separately. [3] Includes beehive coke.

Source: U.S. Energy Information Administration, *Coal Industry*, annual; *Annual Energy Review*, *International Energy Annual*, and *Quarterly Coal Report*. See also <ftp://ftp.eia.doe.gov/pub/pdf/coal.nuclear/05842000.pdf> (issued June 2002).

No. 890. World Coal Production by Major Producing Country: 1980 to 2001

[In millions of short tons (4,188.6 represents 4,188,600,000]

Country	1980	1990	1995	1996	1997	1998	1999	2000	2001
World, total . . .	**4,188.6**	**5,440.9**	**5,156.89**	**5,193.46**	**5,196.23**	**5,093.28**	**4,987.93**	**4,995.16**	**5,266.01**
China.	663.6	1,190.4	1,536.97	1,545.25	1,507.13	1,428.99	1,364.94	1,314.43	1,459.02
United States	**829.7**	**1,029.1**	**1,032.97**	**1,063.86**	**1,089.93**	**1,117.53**	**1,100.43**	**1,073.61**	**1,121.33**
India	125.9	233.4	297.77	314.85	326.06	322.17	326.83	342.65	338.62
Australia.	116.1	225.8	266.55	272.44	292.08	316.75	320.77	338.19	356.85
South Africa	132.0	247.6	227.30	227.48	244.32	246.92	242.99	248.43	250.28
Russia	(X)	(X)	296.35	304.04	257.89	241.03	259.22	279.18	299.50
Germany [1]	532.2	513.7	274.15	264.99	251.74	233.00	225.97	225.26	225.66
Poland	253.5	237.1	220.17	193.08	221.52	196.17	187.57	178.27	178.94
Korea, North	39.7	99.2	106.92	105.71	104.72	99.48	100.48	105.68	105.27
Ukraine	(X)	(X)	94.60	83.47	84.82	85.07	90.86	90.24	90.06
Kazakhstan.	(X)	(X)	91.88	84.69	80.08	76.91	64.35	79.65	88.52
Canada	40.4	75.4	82.57	83.47	86.82	82.90	79.91	76.24	77.68
Turkey	20.2	52.6	60.71	62.13	66.06	74.28	73.90	69.59	72.57
Indonesia	0.6	11.6	45.66	55.48	60.20	66.49	79.37	84.44	99.64
Czech Republic	(X)	(X)	81.94	84.02	81.04	74.44	65.18	71.83	72.87
Greece.	25.6	57.2	63.56	65.90	64.86	67.11	68.40	70.42	74.49
Colombia	4.5	22.6	28.37	33.14	35.93	37.20	36.11	42.04	47.89
Yugoslavia	(X)	(X)	44.10	42.38	44.82	48.59	36.72	37.85	39.46
United Kingdom	143.8	104.1	52.48	53.50	51.79	44.14	39.86	33.73	34.74
Romania.	38.8	42.1	45.33	46.15	37.27	28.91	25.22	32.28	33.08
Bulgaria	39.6	39.0	33.89	33.72	32.75	34.14	31.22	32.69	31.47
Spain.	40.9	39.6	31.28	30.75	29.16	28.74	26.77	25.87	25.00
Thailand	1.6	13.7	20.31	23.92	25.84	22.04	20.13	19.61	21.61
Hungary	28.3	19.7	16.08	16.74	17.18	17.05	16.82	16.16	15.95
Mexico	4.0	8.6	10.26	11.14	11.48	12.38	11.38	12.50	12.81

X Not applicable. [1] For 1980 and 1990, represents East and West Germany combined.

Source: U.S. Energy Information Administration, *International Energy Annual, 2001*. See also <http://tonto.eia.doe.gov/FTPROOT/international/021901.pdf> (issued March 2003).

No. 891. Demonstrated Coal Reserves by Type of Coal and Major Producing State: 2001

[In millions of short tons. As of January 1. The demonstrated reserve base represents the sum of coal in both measured and indicated resource categories of reliability. Measured resources of coal are estimates that have a high degree of geologic assurance from sample analyes and measurements from closely spaced and geological well known sample sites. Indicated resources are estimates based partly from sample and analyses and measurements and partly from reasonable geologic projections. For more information on the classification of coal resources and related terminology, see report cited below]

State	Total reserves	Type of coal				Method of mining	
		Anthracite	Bituminous	Sub-bituminous	Lignite	Under ground	Surface
United States.	**501,059**	**7,465**	**266,629**	**183,160**	**43,805**	**338,525**	**162,534**
Alabama.	4,389	-	3,306	-	1,083	1,157	3,232
Alaska	6,118	-	698	5,407	14	5,423	695
Colorado.	16,552	26	8,550	3,787	4,190	11,780	4,772
Illinois	104,773	-	104,773	-	-	88,188	16,586
Indiana.	9,738	-	9,738	-	-	8,831	907
Iowa	2,189	-	2,189	-	-	1,732	457
Kentucky	31,053	-	31,053	-	-	17,797	13,257
Kentucky, Eastern	11,326	-	11,326	-	-	1,727	9,598
Kentucky, Western	19,728	-	19,728	-	-	16,069	3,658
Missouri	5,992	-	5,992	-	-	1,479	4,513
Montana.	119,472	-	1,385	102,329	15,758	70,958	48,514
New Mexico	12,324	2	3,658	8,664	-	6,203	6,121
North Dakota.	9,243	-	-	-	9,243	-	9,243
Ohio	23,495	-	23,495	-	-	17,679	5,816
Oklahoma.	1,566	-	1,566	-	-	1,235	331
Pennsylvania.	28,101	7,208	20,893	-	-	23,769	4,332
Anthracite	7,208	7,208	-	-	-	3,847	3,361
Bituminous	20,893	-	20,893	-	-	19,922	971
Texas.	12,672	-	-	-	12,672	-	12,672
Utah	5,639	-	5,638	1	-	5,371	268
Virginia.	1,960	125	1,835	-	-	1,332	628
Washington.	1,368	-	304	1,056	8	1,332	36
West Virginia.	34,244	-	34,244	-	-	30,097	4,147
Wyoming	66,219	-	4,320	61,898	-	42,501	23,718
East of the MS River.	239,379	7,333	230,962	-	1,083	190,116	49,262
West of the MS River	261,680	132	35,666	183,160	42,722	148,409	113,271

- Represents or rounds to zero.

Source: U.S. Energy Information Administration, unpublished data from the Coal Reserves Database.

Natural Resources 577

No. 892. Uranium Concentrate (U$_3$O$_8$) Industry—Summary: 1990 to 2002

[See also Table 920 in Section 19]

Item	Unit	1990	1991	1992	1993	1994	1995	1996	1997	1998	1999	2000	2001	2002
Exploration and development,														
surface drilling	Mil. ft.	1.7	1.8	1.1	1.1	0.7	1.3	3.0	4.9	4.6	2.5	1.0	0.7	(D)
Expenditures	Mil. dol.	17.1	17.8	14.5	11.3	3.7	6.0	10.1	30.4	21.7	9.0	6.7	4.8	0.4
Number of mines operated	Number	39	15	17	12	12	12	13	14	15	14	10	7	6
Underground	Number	27	6	4	-	-	-	1	1	4	3	1	-	-
Openpit	Number	2	2	1	-	-	-	-	-	-	-	-	-	-
In situ leaching	Number	7	6	4	5	5	5	6	7	6	6	4	3	3
Other sources	Number	3	1	8	7	7	7	6	6	5	5	5	4	3
Mine production	1,000 pounds	5,876	5,182	986	2,050	2,526	3,528	4,705	4,710	4,782	4,548	3,123	2,647	2,405
Underground	1,000 pounds	(D)	(D)	(D)	-	-	-	(D)	(D)	(D)	(D)	(D)		
Openpit	1,000 pounds	1,881	2,528	(D)	-	-	-	-	-	-	-	-	-	-
In situ leaching	1,000 pounds	(D)	(D)	(D)	(D)	2,448	3,372	4,379	4,084	3,721	3,830	2,995	(D)	(D)
Other sources	1,000 pounds	3,995	2,654	986	2,050	78	156	326	626	1,062	718	128	(D)	(D)
Uranium concentrate production[1]	1,000 pounds	8,886	7,952	5,645	3,063	3,352	6,043	6,321	5,643	4,705	4,611	3,958	2,639	2,344
Concentrate shipments from mills and plants	1,000 pounds	12,957	8,437	6,853	3,374	6,319	5,500	5,982	5,817	4,863	5,527	3,187	2,203	3,810
Employment	Person-years	1,335	1,016	682	871	980	1,107	1,118	1,097	1,120	848	627	423	426

- Represents zero. D Data withheld to avoid disclosing figures for individual companies. [1] U$_3$O$_8$.

Source: U.S. Department of Energy, *Uranium Industry*, annual. See also <http://www.eia.doe.gov/cneaf/nuclear/uia/uia.pdf> (released May 2003) and <http://www.eia.doe.gov/cneaf/nuclear/uia/contents.html> (released May 2003).

Section 19
Energy and Utilities

This section presents statistics on fuel resources, energy production and consumption, electric energy, hydroelectric power, nuclear power, solar energy, wood energy, and the electric and gas utility industries. The principal sources are the U.S. Department of Energy's Energy Information Administration (EIA), the Edison Electric Institute, Washington, DC, and the American Gas Association, Arlington, VA. The Department of Energy was created in October 1977 and assumed and centralized the responsibilities of all or part of several agencies including the Federal Power Commission (FPC), the U.S. Bureau of Mines, the Federal Energy Administration, and the U.S. Energy Research and Development Administration. For additional data on transportation, see Section 23; on fuels, see Section 18; and on energy-related housing characteristics, see Section 20.

The EIA, in its *Annual Energy Review*, provides statistics and trend data on energy supply, demand, and prices. Information is included on petroleum and natural gas, coal, electricity, hydroelectric power, nuclear power, solar, wood, and geothermal energy. Among its annual reports are *Annual Energy Review, Electric Power Annual, Natural Gas Annual, Petroleum Supply Annual, State Energy Data Report, State Energy Price and Expenditure Report, Financial Statistics of Selected Electric Utilities, Performance Profiles of Major Energy Producers, Annual Energy Outlook*, and *International Energy Annual*. These various publications contain state, national, and international data on production of electricity, net summer capability of generating plants, fuels used in energy production, energy sales and consumption, and hydroelectric power. The EIA also issues the *Monthly Energy Review*, which presents current supply, disposition, and price data and monthly publications on petroleum, coal, natural gas, and electric power. Data on residential energy consumption, expenditures, and conservation activities are available from EIA's Residential Energy Consumption Survey and are published every 4 years.

The Edison Electric Institute's monthly bulletin and annual *Statistical Year Book of the Electric Utility Industry for the Year* contain data on the distribution of electric energy by public utilities; information on the electric power supply, expansion of electric generating facilities, and the manufacture of heavy electric power equipment is presented in the annual *Year-End Summary of the Electric Power Situation in the United States*. The American Gas Association, in its monthly and quarterly bulletins and its yearbook, *Gas Facts*, presents data on gas utilities and financial and operating statistics.

Btu conversion factors—Various energy sources are converted from original units to the thermal equivalent using British thermal units (Btu). A Btu is the amount of energy required to raise the temperature of 1 pound of water 1 degree Fahrenheit (F) at or near 39.2 degrees F. Factors are calculated annually from the latest final annual data available; some are revised as a result. The following list provides conversion factors used in 2001 for production and consumption, in that order, for various fuels: Petroleum, 5.800 and 5.345 mil. Btu per barrel; total coal, 20.443 and 20.655 mil. Btu per short ton; and natural gas (dry), 1,028 Btu per cubic foot for both. The factors for the production of nuclear power and geothermal power were 10,442 and 21,017 Btu per kilowatt-hour, respectively. The fossil fuel steam-electric power plant generation factor of 10,127 Btu per kilowatt-hour was used for hydroelectric power generation and for wood and waste, wind, photovoltaic, and solar thermal energy consumed at electric utilities.

No. 893. Utilities—Establishments, Revenue, Payroll, and Employees by Kind of Business (NAICS Basis): 1997

[411,713 represents $411,713,000,000. See Appendix III]

Kind of business	NAICS code [1]	Establishments (number)	Revenue Total (mil. dol.)	Revenue Per paid employee (dol.)	Annual payroll Total (mil. dol.)	Annual payroll Per paid employee (dol.)	Paid employee for pay period including March 12 (number)
Utilities	22	15,513	411,713	585,899	36,595	52,077	702,703
Electric power generation, transmission, & distribution	2211	7,935	269,095	476,676	30,440	53,921	564,525
Electric power generation	22111	1,745	73,375	493,492	8,369	56,289	148,686
Fossil fuel electric power generation	221112	1,009	48,324	515,374	5,049	53,843	93,765
Nuclear electric power generation	221113	67	13,967	406,231	2,202	64,045	34,381
Other electric power generation	221119	316	8,011	608,723	725	55,069	13,160
Electric power transmission, control & distribution	22112	6,190	195,720	470,663	22,070	53,074	415,839
Electric bulk power transmission & control	221121	120	956	395,361	116	47,852	2,418
Electric power distribution	221122	6,070	194,764	471,103	21,955	53,105	413,421
Other combination utilities	2211223	30	428	630,811	52	76,771	678
Natural gas distribution	2212	2,747	136,995	1,331,629	5,110	49,666	102,878
Natural gas transmission & distribution	2212101	713	18,267	629,034	1,534	52,838	29,039
Natural gas distribution	2212102	1,682	87,105	1,387,135	2,955	47,059	62,795
Mixed, manu., or LP gas pro &/or dist.	2212103	86	(D)	(NA)	(D)	(NA)	([2])
Electric & other serv. combined (natural gas distribution)	2212104	145	28,110	4,193,063	413	61,565	6,704
Gas & other serv. combined (natural gas distribution)	2212105	119	2,853	915,151	149	47,705	3,117
Water, sewage, & other systems	2213	4,831	5,623	159,284	1,045	29,614	35,300
Water supply & irrigation systems	22131	4,052	4,454	159,447	825	29,550	27,933
Sewage treatment facilities	22132	696	596	106,399	139	24,816	5,600
Steam & air-conditioning supply	22133	83	573	324,314	81	45,838	1,767

D Withheld to avoid disclosing data of individual companies; data are included in higher level totals. NA Not available.
[1] North American Industry Classification System, 1997; see text, Section 15. [2] 1,000 to 2,499 employees.

Source: U.S. Census Bureau, *1997 Economic Census, Utilities*, Series EC97T22A-US, issued December 1999.

No. 894. Private Utilities—Employees, Annual Payroll, and Establishments by Industry: 2001

[41,942 represents $41,942,000,000. Excludes government employees, railroad employees, self-employed persons, etc. See "General Explanation" in source for definitions and statement on reliability of data. An *establishment* is a single physical location where business is conducted or where services or industrial operations are performed. See Appendix III]

Year and industry	NAICS code [1]	Number of employees [2]	Annual payroll (mil. dol.)	Average payroll per employee (dol.)	Total	Under 20 employees	20 to 99 employees	100 to 499 employees	500 and over employees
Utilities, total	22	654,484	41,942	64,085	17,702	12,505	3,837	1,168	192
Electric power generation, transmission and distribution	2211	515,988	34,338	66,548	9,207	5,202	2,902	933	170
Electric power generation	22111	139,254	10,188	73,162	2,208	1,305	582	263	58
Hydroelectric power generation	221111	11,650	793	68,028	462	363	71	25	3
Fossil fuel electric power generation	221112	80,674	5,683	70,445	1,301	664	412	211	14
Nuclear electric power generation	221113	33,064	2,791	84,424	72	18	9	11	34
Other electric power generation	221119	13,866	921	66,426	373	260	90	16	7
Electric pwr transmsn, control & distribution	22112	376,734	24,150	64,103	6,999	3,897	2,320	670	112
Electric bulk power transmission & control	221121	6,233	366	58,683	161	103	45	12	1
Electric power distribution	221122	370,501	23,784	64,194	6,838	3,794	2,275	658	111
Natural gas distribution	2212	95,348	6,001	62,939	2,831	2,001	616	194	20
Water, sewage & other systems	2213	43,148	1,603	37,162	5,664	5,302	319	41	2
Water supply & irrigation systems	22131	35,206	1,325	37,634	4,832	4,562	234	34	2
Sewage treatment facilities	22132	6,312	198	31,340	748	688	54	6	-
Steam & air-conditioning supply	22133	1,630	81	49,506	84	52	31	1	-

- Represents zero. [1] North American Industry Classification System, 1997. [2] Covers full- and part-time employees who are on the payroll in the pay period including March 12.

Source: U.S. Census Bureau, *County Business Patterns*, annual. See also <http://www.census.gov/epcd/cbp/view/us01.txt> (issued April 2003).

No. 895. Energy Supply and Disposition by Type of Fuel: 1960 to 2001

[In quadrillion British thermal units (Btu) (42.80 represents 42,800,000,000,000,000 Btu). For Btu conversion factors, see source and text, this section]

Year	Production Total[1]	Crude oil[2]	Natural gas	Coal	Nuclear power[3]	Renewable energy[4] Total[1]	Hydro-electric power	Biofuel[5]	Solar energy	Net imports total[6,7]	Consumption Total[1,8]	Petro-leum[9]	Natural gas[10]	Coal	Nuclear power	Renewable energy[1] total
1960	42.80	14.94	12.66	10.82	(Z)	2.93	1.61	1.32	(NA)	2.74	45.12	19.92	12.39	9.84	(Z)	2.98
1970	63.50	20.40	21.67	14.61	0.24	4.08	2.63	1.43	(NA)	5.72	67.86	29.52	21.80	12.27	0.24	4.10
1971	62.72	20.03	22.28	13.19	0.41	4.27	2.82	1.43	(NA)	7.41	69.31	30.56	22.47	11.60	0.41	4.31
1972	63.92	20.04	22.21	14.09	0.58	4.40	2.86	1.50	(NA)	9.32	72.76	32.95	22.70	12.08	0.58	4.48
1973	63.59	19.49	22.19	13.99	0.91	4.43	2.86	1.53	(NA)	12.68	75.81	34.84	22.51	12.97	0.91	4.58
1974	62.37	18.58	21.21	14.07	1.27	4.77	3.18	1.54	(NA)	12.19	74.08	33.46	21.73	12.66	1.27	4.90
1975	61.36	17.73	19.64	14.99	1.90	4.72	3.16	1.50	(NA)	11.75	72.04	32.73	19.95	12.66	1.90	4.79
1976	61.60	17.26	19.48	15.65	2.11	4.77	2.98	1.71	(NA)	14.65	76.07	35.18	20.35	13.58	2.11	4.86
1977	62.05	17.45	19.57	15.76	2.70	4.25	2.33	1.84	(NA)	18.02	78.12	37.12	19.93	13.92	2.70	4.43
1978	63.14	18.43	19.49	14.91	3.02	5.04	2.94	2.04	(NA)	17.32	77.97	37.12	20.00	13.77	3.02	5.24
1979	65.95	18.10	20.08	17.54	2.78	5.17	2.93	2.15	(NA)	16.75	81.04	37.12	20.67	15.04	2.78	5.38
1980	67.24	18.25	19.91	18.60	2.74	5.49	2.90	2.49	(NA)	12.25	78.44	34.20	20.39	15.42	2.74	5.71
1981	67.01	18.15	19.70	18.38	3.01	5.47	2.76	2.59	(NA)	9.65	76.57	31.93	19.93	15.91	3.01	5.82
1982	66.57	18.31	18.32	18.64	3.13	5.99	3.27	2.62	(NA)	7.46	73.44	30.23	18.51	15.32	3.13	6.29
1983	64.11	18.39	16.59	17.25	3.20	6.49	3.53	2.83	(NA)	8.31	73.32	30.05	17.36	15.89	3.20	6.86
1984	68.83	18.85	18.01	19.72	3.55	6.43	3.39	2.88	(Z)	8.96	76.97	31.05	18.51	17.07	3.55	6.85
1985	67.65	18.99	16.98	19.33	4.08	6.03	2.97	2.86	(Z)	7.87	76.71	30.92	17.83	17.48	4.08	6.46
1986	67.09	18.38	16.54	19.51	4.38	6.13	3.07	2.84	(Z)	10.38	76.97	32.20	16.71	17.26	4.38	6.51
1987	67.61	17.68	17.14	20.14	4.75	5.69	2.64	2.82	(Z)	11.91	79.48	32.87	17.74	18.01	4.75	6.17
1988	68.95	17.28	17.60	20.74	5.59	5.49	2.33	2.94	(Z)	13.15	82.99	34.22	18.55	18.85	5.59	5.82
1989[11]	69.34	16.12	17.85	21.35	5.60	6.27	2.83	3.06	0.06	14.19	84.93	34.21	19.71	19.05	5.60	6.44
1990	70.73	15.57	18.36	22.46	6.10	6.10	3.03	2.66	0.06	14.09	84.57	33.55	19.72	19.16	6.10	6.21
1991	70.33	15.70	18.23	21.59	6.42	6.13	3.00	2.70	0.06	13.34	84.64	32.85	20.15	18.99	6.42	6.28
1992	69.93	15.22	18.38	21.63	6.48	5.91	2.62	2.85	0.06	14.62	86.05	33.53	20.84	19.12	6.48	6.13
1993	68.26	14.49	18.58	20.25	6.41	6.16	2.89	2.80	0.07	17.22	87.78	33.84	21.35	19.84	6.41	6.40
1994	70.68	14.10	19.35	22.11	6.69	6.07	2.68	2.94	0.07	18.65	89.57	34.67	21.84	19.91	6.69	6.40
1995	71.18	13.89	19.10	22.03	7.08	6.67	3.21	3.07	0.07	18.03	91.50	34.55	22.78	20.09	7.08	6.96
1996	72.49	13.72	19.36	22.68	7.09	7.14	3.59	3.13	0.07	19.37	94.52	35.76	23.20	21.00	7.09	7.45
1997	72.39	13.66	19.39	23.21	6.60	7.08	3.64	3.01	0.07	20.94	94.97	36.27	23.33	21.45	6.60	7.32
1998	72.79	13.24	19.61	23.94	7.07	6.56	3.30	2.84	0.07	22.47	95.34	36.93	22.93	21.66	7.07	6.78
1999	71.64	12.45	19.34	23.19	7.61	6.59	3.27	2.87	0.07	23.75	96.97	37.96	23.01	21.62	7.61	6.79
2000	71.06	12.36	19.46	22.62	7.86	6.20	2.81	2.95	0.07	25.21	99.32	38.40	24.04	22.58	7.86	6.47
2001	71.67	12.39	19.84	23.44	8.03	5.52	2.22	2.87	0.06	26.03	96.95	38.23	23.22	21.93	8.03	5.68

NA Not available. Z Less than 50 trillion. [1] Includes types of fuel not shown separately. [2] Includes lease condensate. [3] Data on the generation of electricity in the United States represent net generation, which is gross output of electricity (measured at the generator terminals) minus power plant use. Nuclear electricity generation data are gross outputs of electricity. [4] End-use consumption and electricity net generation. [5] Alcohol is ethanol blended into motor gasoline. [6] Imports minus exports. [7] Net import totals may not equal sum of components due to independent rounding. [8] Alcohol (ethanol blended into motor gasoline) is included in both "Petroleum" and "Alcohol," but is counted only once in total energy consumption. [9] Petroleum products supplied, including natural gas plant liquids and crude oil burned as fuel. [10] Includes supplemental gaseous fuels. [11] There is a discontinuity in this time series between 1989 and 1990 due to the expanded coverage of nonelectric utility use of renewable energy beginning in 1990.

Source: U.S. Energy Information Administration, *Annual Energy Review*, and Internet site <http://www.eia.doe.gov/emeu/aer/overview.html> (released October 2002).

Energy and Utilities 581

Figure 19.1
Energy Production, Trade, and Consumption: 1980 to 2001

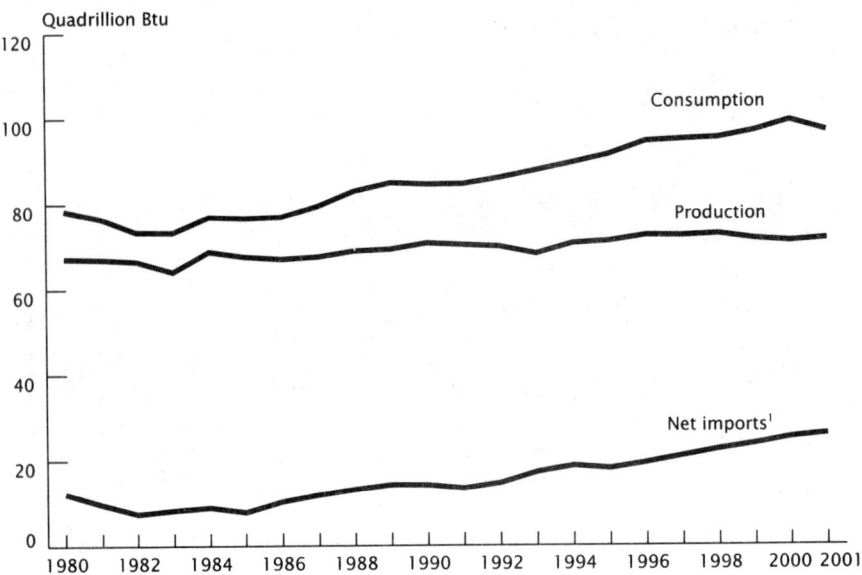

[1] Imports minus exports.
Source: Chart prepared by U.S. Census Bureau. For data, see Table 895.

Figure 19.2
Top Suppliers of U.S. Crude Oil Imports: 2002
(In millions of barrels)   Total imports = 3,336

[1] Imports from the neutral zone between Kuwait and Saudi Arabia are included in Saudi Arabia.
Source: Chart prepared by U.S. Census Bureau. For data, see Table 910.

No. 896. Energy Supply and Disposition by Type of Fuel—Estimates, 2000 and 2001, and Projections, 2005 to 2020

[Quadrillion Btu (72.15 represents 72,150,000,000,000,000) per year. Btu=British thermal unit. Totals may not equal sum of components due to rounding. Projections are "reference" or mid-level forecasts. See report for methodology and assumptions used in generating projections]

Type of fuel	2000	2001	Projections				
			2005	2010	2015	2020
Production, total	72.15	72.81	74.60	79.27	82.25	86.10
Crude oil and lease condensate	12.44	12.29	11.82	11.91	11.11	11.56
Natural gas plant liquids	2.71	2.65	2.95	3.16	3.42	3.59
Natural gas, dry	19.50	19.97	20.68	22.47	24.47	25.75
Coal	22.58	23.97	23.33	25.30	26.37	27.69
Nuclear power	7.87	8.03	8.28	8.36	8.41	8.43
Renewable energy [1]	5.96	5.33	6.71	7.23	7.75	8.28
Other [2]	1.09	0.57	0.83	0.84	0.74	0.80
Imports, total	28.98	30.13	31.94	37.96	43.43	47.76
Crude oil [3]	19.69	20.26	22.34	25.13	26.93	27.61
Petroleum products [4]	4.73	5.04	4.25	6.41	9.59	11.97
Natural gas	3.86	4.10	4.54	5.52	5.94	7.22
Other imports [5]	0.69	0.73	0.81	0.90	0.98	0.96
Exports, total	3.92	3.64	3.64	3.76	3.55	3.49
Petroleum [6]	2.15	2.01	2.05	2.24	2.26	2.34
Natural gas	0.25	0.37	0.59	0.62	0.55	0.41
Coal	1.53	1.27	1.00	0.91	0.74	0.74
Consumption, total	99.38	97.30	103.16	113.26	121.91	130.12
Petroleum products [7]	38.53	38.46	39.79	44.65	48.93	52.60
Natural gas	24.07	23.26	25.24	27.75	30.25	32.96
Coal	22.64	22.02	22.82	24.98	26.30	27.68
Nuclear power	7.87	8.03	8.28	8.36	8.41	8.43
Renewable energy [1] other [8]	6.27	5.54	7.03	7.52	8.02	8.45
Net imports of petroleum	22.28	23.29	24.54	29.31	34.26	37.24
Prices (1999 dollars per unit):						
World oil price (dol. per bbl.) [9]	28.35	22.01	23.27	23.99	24.72	25.48
Gas wellhead price (dol. per mcf.) [10]	3.83	4.12	2.88	3.29	3.55	3.69
Coal minemouth price (dol. per ton)	17.18	17.59	16.50	14.99	14.67	14.38
Average electric price (cents per kWh)	6.9	7.3	6.5	6.4	6.5	6.6

[1] Includes grid-connected electricity from conventional hydroelectric; wood and wood waste; landfill gas; municipal solid waste; other biomass; wind; photovoltaic and solar thermal sources; nonelectric energy from renewable sources, such as active and passive solar systems, and wood; and both the ethanol and gasoline components of E85, but not the ethanol components of blends less than 85 percent. Excludes electricity imports using renewable sources and nonmarketed renewable energy. See Table A18 for selected nonmarketed residential and commercial renewable energy. [2] Includes liquid hydrogen, methanol, supplemental natural gas, and some domestic inputs to refineries. [3] Includes imports of crude oil for the Strategic Petroleum Reserve. [4] Includes imports of finished petroleum products, imports of unfinished oils, alcohols, ethers, and blending components. [5] Includes coal, coal coke (net), and electricity (net). [6] Includes crude oil and petroleum products. [7] Includes natural gas plant liquids, crude oil consumed as a fuel, and nonpetroleum based liquids for blending, such as ethanol. [8] Includes net electricity imports, methanol, and liquid hydrogen. [9] Average refiner acquisition cost for imported crude oil. [10] Represents lower 48 onshore and offshore supplies.

Source: U.S. Energy Information Administration, Annual Energy Outlook, 2003, DOE/EIA-0383(2003). See also <http://www.eia.doe.gov/oiaf/aeo/pdf/appa.pdf> (released 9 January 2003).

No. 897. Energy Consumption by End-Use Sector: 1970 to 2001

[67.86 represents 67,860,000,000,000,000 Btu) Btu=British thermal units. For Btu conversion factors, see source and text, this section. See Appendix III]

Year	Total consumption (quad. Btu)	Residential and commercial [1] (quad. Btu)	Industrial [2] (quad. Btu)	Transportation (quad. Btu)	Percent of total		
					Residential and commercial [1]	Industrial [2]	Transportation
1970	67.86	22.11	29.65	16.10	32.6	43.7	23.7
1975	72.04	24.33	29.46	18.24	33.8	40.9	25.3
1980	78.44	26.53	32.21	19.70	33.8	41.1	25.1
1985	76.70	27.58	29.06	20.07	36.0	37.9	26.2
1990	84.57	30.15	31.90	22.53	35.6	37.7	26.6
1992	86.05	30.85	32.74	22.46	35.9	38.0	26.1
1993	87.78	32.17	32.74	22.88	36.6	37.3	26.1
1994	89.57	32.41	33.67	23.50	36.2	37.6	26.2
1995	91.50	33.50	34.04	23.96	36.6	37.2	26.2
1996	94.52	34.99	35.01	24.51	37.0	37.0	25.9
1997	94.97	34.90	35.25	24.81	36.7	37.1	26.1
1998	95.34	35.14	34.85	25.35	36.9	36.6	26.6
1999	96.97	36.13	34.74	26.09	37.3	35.8	26.9
2000	99.32	37.75	34.86	26.70	38.0	35.1	26.9
2001 [3]	96.95	37.60	32.60	26.75	38.8	33.6	27.6

[1] Commercial sector fuel use, including that at commercial combined-heat-and-power (CHP) and industrial electricity-only plants. [2] Industrial sector fuel use, including that at industrial combined-heat-and-power (CHP) and industrial electricity-only plants. [3] Preliminary.

Source: U.S. Energy Information Administration, Annual Energy Review 2000, DOE/EIA-0384(2001). See also <http://www.eia.doe.gov/emeu/aer/pdf/pages/sec24.pdf> (released October 2002).

No. 898. Energy Consumption—End-Use Sector and Selected Source by State: 2000

[In trillions of Btu (98,216 represents 98,216,000,000,000,000), except as indicated]

State	Total [1]	Per capita [2] (mil. Btu)	End-use sector [3] Residential	Commercial	Industrial [1]	Transportation	Source Petroleum	Natural gas (dry) [4]	Coal	Hydro electric power [5]	Nuclear electric power
United States..	98,216	349	18,178	14,931	38,217	26,889	38,402	23,003	22,580	3,020	7,862
Alabama	1,977	445	339	219	936	483	581	351	900	59	327
Alaska	627	1,001	42	63	310	212	260	334	22	10	-
Arizona	1,216	237	283	263	206	463	506	207	433	89	317
Arkansas	1,084	405	194	126	466	298	394	259	268	24	122
California	8,519	252	1,318	1,189	2,950	3,063	3,558	2,273	70	436	367
Colorado	1,200	279	267	247	316	370	455	349	388	15	-
Connecticut	863	253	243	191	200	230	376	130	36	16	171
Delaware	303	386	54	48	128	73	139	54	50	-	-
District of Columbia	166	291	33	102	3	27	34	34	(Z)	-	-
Florida	3,944	247	989	795	736	1,425	1,971	561	761	1	337
Georgia	2,770	338	589	429	883	869	1,040	408	820	24	339
Hawaii	265	219	24	26	89	127	222	3	18	1	-
Idaho	511	395	95	88	201	127	175	73	14	113	-
Illinois	4,418	356	885	719	1,839	975	1,327	1,043	1,027	2	933
Indiana	2,778	457	463	306	1,342	667	910	591	1,595	6	-
Iowa	1,099	376	213	154	458	274	417	234	446	9	46
Kansas	1,036	385	201	168	384	282	407	324	363	(Z)	95
Kentucky	1,868	462	306	214	903	446	713	234	1,002	24	-
Louisiana	3,965	887	322	238	2,505	900	1,681	1,605	253	5	165
Maine	561	440	92	61	287	122	251	9	10	78	-
Maryland	1,520	287	353	325	436	407	553	217	312	18	144
Massachusetts	1,723	271	418	329	521	455	677	349	115	15	58
Michigan	3,122	314	734	553	1,013	822	1,062	950	779	13	197
Minnesota	1,688	343	346	221	604	517	680	360	374	64	135
Mississippi	1,144	402	206	141	432	365	469	294	148	-	112
Missouri	1,659	297	425	330	343	561	693	290	689	4	104
Montana	595	659	63	54	369	108	168	68	177	98	-
Nebraska	584	341	129	114	166	175	226	125	207	15	90
Nevada	633	317	125	96	207	206	230	188	199	25	-
New Hampshire	329	266	79	59	90	102	181	22	44	25	83
New Jersey	2,707	322	530	506	744	927	1,262	614	115	[6]-1	298
New Mexico	621	341	92	108	192	229	251	227	306	2	-
New York	4,620	244	1,132	1,253	1,252	984	1,699	1,292	331	315	329
North Carolina	2,502	311	567	434	792	709	976	236	786	33	408
North Dakota	365	569	54	43	187	81	120	59	425	23	-
Ohio	4,002	353	844	622	1,541	994	1,331	917	1,438	6	175
Oklahoma	1,401	406	262	195	514	429	522	539	381	22	-
Oregon	1,080	316	225	182	354	319	378	231	39	390	-
Pennsylvania	4,780	389	854	609	2,305	1,012	1,416	728	1,507	19	769
Rhode Island	250	239	66	51	68	66	97	81	(Z)	10	-
South Carolina	1,477	368	285	201	608	383	481	160	432	5	531
South Dakota	246	326	54	40	67	86	119	40	51	59	-
Tennessee	2,026	356	404	316	687	589	720	276	705	58	269
Texas	11,589	556	1,333	1,161	6,483	2,611	5,501	4,253	1,548	12	392
Utah	718	322	125	119	251	223	275	173	403	8	-
Vermont	165	270	44	29	40	52	88	11	(Z)	38	47
Virginia	2,304	325	497	455	658	694	904	282	505	[6]-6	295
Washington	2,174	369	410	321	815	627	868	297	106	795	90
West Virginia	744	411	136	100	321	187	218	154	980	12	-
Wisconsin	1,800	336	369	277	731	423	666	396	499	23	120
Wyoming	417	845	36	44	223	114	158	102	506	10	-

- Represents zero. Z Less than 0.5 trillion Btu. [1] U.S. total energy and U.S. industrial sector include 65.4 trillion Btu of net imports of coal coke that is not allocated to the states. State and U.S. totals include 81.8 trillion Btu of net imports of electricity generated from nonrenewable energy sources. [2] Based on estimated resident population as of July 1. [3] End-use sector data include electricity sales and associated electrical system energy losses. [4] Includes supplemental gaseous fuels. [5] Includes net imports of hydroelectricity. A negative number in this column results from pumped storage for which, overall, more electricity is expended than created to provide electricity during peak demand periods. [6] Minus sign (-) indicates when amount of energy expended exceeds amount of energy consumed.

Source: U.S. Energy Information Administration, *State Energy Data Report, 2000*, annual. See also <http://www.eia.doe.gov/emeu/states/sepsum/html/pdf/sumuseall.pdf> (released May 2003).

No. 899. Renewable Energy Consumption Estimates by Type: 1995 to 2001

[In quadrillion Btu (7.31 represents 7,310,000,000,000,000). Renewable energy is obtained from sources that are essentially inexhaustible unlike fossil fuels of which there is a finite supply]

Source and sector	1995	1996	1997	1998	1999	2000	2001 [1]
Consumption, total	(NA)	(NA)	7.31	6.77	6.78	6.45	5.67
Conventional hydroelectric power [2]	(NA)	(NA)	3.80	3.52	3.47	3.08	2.38
Geothermal energy [3]	(NA)	(NA)	0.33	0.33	0.33	0.32	0.32
Biomass [4]	(NA)	(NA)	3.00	2.82	2.86	2.93	2.85
Solar energy [5]	(NA)	(NA)	0.07	0.07	0.07	0.07	0.06
Wind energy [6]	(NA)	(NA)	0.03	0.03	0.05	0.06	0.06
Residential [7]	0.67	0.67	0.51	0.46	0.49	0.50	0.48
Biomass [4]	0.60	0.60	0.43	0.39	0.41	0.43	0.41
Geothermal [3]	0.01	0.01	0.01	0.01	0.01	0.01	0.01
Solar [5,8]	0.07	0.07	0.07	0.07	0.06	0.06	0.06
Commercial [9]	0.09	0.11	0.11	0.11	0.11	0.11	0.10
Biomass [4]	0.09	0.10	0.11	0.10	0.11	0.10	0.09
Geothermal [3]	0.01	0.01	0.01	0.01	0.01	0.01	0.01
Hydroelectric [2]	(Z)	(Z)	(Z)	(Z)	(Z)	(Z)	(Z)
Industrial [10]	1.91	1.97	1.98	1.84	1.83	1.87	1.82
Biomass [4]	1.85	1.91	1.92	1.78	1.78	1.82	1.77
Geothermal [3]	(Z)	(Z)	(Z)	(Z)	(Z)	(Z)	0.01
Hydroelectric [2]	0.06	0.06	0.06	0.06	0.05	0.04	0.04
Transportation:							
Alcohol fuels [11]	0.11	0.08	0.10	0.11	0.11	0.13	0.13
Electric power [12]	3.89	4.31	4.38	4.03	4.03	3.58	2.99
Electric utilities [13]	3.17	3.55	3.62	3.28	3.12	2.61	2.04
Biomass [4]	0.02	0.02	0.02	0.02	0.02	0.02	0.02
Geothermal [3]	0.10	0.11	0.12	0.11	0.04	(Z)	(Z)
Hydroelectric [2]	3.06	3.42	3.49	3.15	3.07	2.58	2.02
Solar [5]	(Z)	(Z)	(Z)	(Z)	(Z)	(Z)	(Z)
Wind [6]	(Z)	(Z)	(Z)	(Z)	(Z)	(Z)	(Z)

NA Not available. Z Less than 5 trillion Btu. [1] Preliminary [2] Power produced from natural streamflow as regulated by available storage. [3] As used at electric power plants, hot water or steam extracted from geothermal reservoirs in the Earth's crust that is supplied to steam turbines at electric power plants that drive generators to produce electricity. [4] Organic nonfossil material of biological origin constituting a renewable energy source. [5] The radiant energy of the sun, which can be converted into other forms of energy, such as heat or electricity. [6] Energy present in wind motion that can be converted to mechanical energy for driving pumps, mills, and electric power generators. Wind pushes against sails, vanes, or blades radiating from a central rotating shaft. [7] Consists of living quarters for private households, but excludes institutional living quarters. [8] Includes small amounts of distributed solar thermal and photovoltaic energy used in the commercial, industrial, and electric power sectors. other private and public organizations. Includes institutional living quarter and sewage treatment facilities. [9] Consists of service-providing facilities and equipment of businesses, governments, and other private and public organizations. Includes institutional living quarters and sewage treatment facilities. [10] Consists of all facilities and equipment used for producing, processing, or assembling goods. [11] Ethanol primarily derived from corn. [12] Consists of electricity only and combined heat and power plants who sell electricity and heat to the public. [13] A corporation or other legal entity aligned with distribution facilities for delivery of electric energy, primarily for public use.

Source: U.S. Energy Information Administration, Renewable Energy Annual 2001, Series DOE/EIA-0603(2001). See also <http://tonto.eia.doe.gov/FTPROOT/renewables/060301.pdf> (issued November 2002).

No. 900. Energy Expenditures and Average Fuel Prices by Source and Sector: 1970 to 2000

[82,898 represents $82,898,000,000. For definition of Btu, see text, this section. End-use sector and electric utilities exclude expenditures and prices on energy sources such as hydropower, solar, wind, and geothermal. Also excludes expenditures for reported amounts of energy consumed by the energy industry for production, transportation, and processing operations]

Source and sector	1970	1975	1980	1985	1990	1995	1996	1997	1998	1999	2000
EXPENDITURES (mil. dol.)											
Total [1]	82,898	171,802	374,319	437,271	472,214	516,207	562,600	569,011	527,028	560,161	703,188
Natural gas	10,891	20,061	51,061	72,938	64,102	74,150	85,634	91,736	81,628	83,559	115,910
Petroleum products	47,942	103,372	237,628	223,597	235,328	237,110	268,447	267,621	232,367	262,912	362,026
Motor gasoline	31,596	59,446	124,408	118,048	126,558	136,647	148,344	149,668	132,730	149,260	193,999
Coal	4,630	13,021	22,607	29,673	28,637	27,632	28,168	28,276	28,139	27,621	28,728
Electricity sales	23,345	50,680	98,095	149,233	176,737	205,932	211,011	213,645	216,928	216,737	231,653
Residential sector [2]	20,213	36,932	69,438	98,899	109,954	128,330	137,931	138,848	134,977	137,300	155,625
Commercial sector [2]	10,628	22,869	46,932	70,349	78,942	91,644	95,959	100,362	98,298	98,089	113,030
Industrial sector [1]	16,678	41,068	94,268	106,835	102,650	108,484	120,549	120,852	109,104	115,755	152,582
Transportation sector	35,379	70,933	163,680	161,188	180,668	187,749	208,161	208,950	184,649	209,017	(NA)
Motor gasoline	30,525	57,992	121,809	115,205	123,845	134,641	146,106	147,164	130,709	147,592	(NA)
Electric utilities [1,3]	4,316	16,396	37,435	42,507	38,287	34,765	36,635	37,765	37,527	36,490	41,375
AVERAGE FUEL PRICES (dol. per mil. Btu)											
All sectors [1]	1.65	3.33	6.89	8.36	8.25	8.24	8.72	8.78	8.15	8.34	9.85
Residential sector [2]	2.10	3.81	7.46	10.96	11.94	12.60	12.71	13.28	13.46	13.17	14.28
Commercial sector [2]	1.98	4.08	7.85	11.65	11.95	12.69	12.82	13.09	13.08	12.78	13.93
Industrial sector [1]	0.98	2.12	5.15	6.27	5.18	4.32	5.11	4.83	4.24	4.38	5.18
Transportation sector	2.31	4.02	8.61	8.26	8.28	8.09	8.76	8.70	7.48	8.19	
Electric utilities [1,3]	0.32	0.96	1.75	1.85	1.46	1.23	1.28	1.30	1.24	1.22	1.43

NA Not available. [1] There are no direct fuel costs for hydroelectric, geothermal, wind, photovoltaic, or solar thermal energy. [2] There are no direct fuel costs for geothermal, photovoltaic, or solar thermal energy. [3] Net imports of electricity generated from nonrenewable energy sources are included in this total but not in any other columns.

Source: U.S. Energy Information Administration, State Energy Price and Expenditure Report, annual. See also <http://www.eia.doe.gov/emeu/states/sepprices/total/pdf/prus.pdf> (accessed May 2003).

No. 901. Energy Expenditures—End-Use Sector and Selected Source by State: 2000

[In millions of dollars (703,188 represents $703,188,000,000). End-use sector and electric utilities exclude expenditures on energy sources such as hydroelectric, photovoltaic, solar thermal, wind, and geothermal. Also excludes expenditures for reported amounts of energy consumed by the energy industry for production, transportation, and processing operations]

State	Total [1]	End-use sector					Source			
		Residential	Commercial	Industrial	Transportation	Petroleum products	Natural gas	Coal	Electricity sales
U.S.	703,188	155,625	113,030	152,582	281,952	362,026	115,910	28,728	231,653
AL	12,094	2,739	1,574	2,863	4,919	5,787	1,550	1,291	4,592
AK	2,722	354	368	239	1,759	1,992	247	47	532
AZ	10,562	2,520	1,961	1,094	4,987	5,439	1,100	546	4,431
AR	7,326	1,571	784	1,939	3,032	3,809	1,254	383	2,349
CA	71,058	13,305	11,886	13,084	32,784	35,101	13,512	115	22,915
CO	8,690	1,894	1,472	1,189	4,135	4,820	1,458	361	2,508
CT	8,275	2,631	1,699	1,012	2,933	4,314	997	83	2,852
DE	2,072	494	311	454	811	1,121	294	74	682
DC	1,530	312	853	18	347	400	338	(Z)	798
FL	31,178	8,220	5,448	3,098	14,412	17,476	2,803	1,240	13,526
GA	19,782	4,876	3,047	3,412	8,447	9,827	2,479	1,269	7,368
HI	2,634	512	500	525	1,097	1,614	47	31	1,341
ID	3,158	599	427	674	1,457	1,838	324	16	953
IL	30,122	7,248	5,257	6,671	10,947	13,259	6,682	1,226	9,293
IN	17,033	3,321	1,898	4,830	6,984	8,426	3,067	1,889	5,022
IA	8,314	1,807	1,052	2,438	3,017	4,457	1,454	408	2,319
KS	7,392	1,607	1,149	1,983	2,653	3,941	1,359	359	2,242
KY	11,356	1,961	1,201	3,466	4,729	6,495	1,220	1,242	3,248
LA	20,726	2,680	1,856	8,999	7,191	11,753	4,986	327	5,117
ME	3,772	1,029	579	732	1,433	2,426	43	22	1,179
MD	11,796	3,134	2,356	1,437	4,869	5,940	1,731	405	4,089
MA	15,459	4,242	3,032	2,677	5,508	7,439	2,829	244	4,914
MI	22,704	5,194	3,988	4,462	9,061	11,283	3,975	1,049	7,400
MN	12,224	2,684	1,447	2,543	5,549	6,723	1,954	434	3,477
MS	7,462	1,628	990	1,545	3,299	4,091	1,148	225	2,606
MO	13,277	3,271	2,121	1,850	6,035	7,142	1,870	644	4,370
MT	2,852	429	310	901	1,213	1,481	366	279	717
NE	4,323	886	679	861	1,897	2,376	668	123	1,292
NV	4,834	932	631	907	2,364	2,567	951	253	1,692
NH	3,227	919	594	459	1,255	1,906	174	66	1,143
NJ	21,639	4,902	4,247	3,307	9,183	11,403	3,565	161	6,599
NM	4,109	741	731	587	2,050	2,460	571	421	1,219
NY	42,563	12,818	12,854	5,321	11,571	17,030	9,695	487	16,167
NC	19,351	5,009	3,023	3,608	7,712	9,884	1,539	1,142	7,767
ND	2,077	388	263	615	810	1,187	189	430	509
OH	29,645	7,173	4,754	6,675	11,043	13,359	5,544	2,110	10,499
OK	9,337	1,990	1,272	1,916	4,159	4,788	2,344	384	2,897
OR	7,644	1,488	1,033	1,422	3,701	4,129	1,135	41	2,460
PA	30,484	8,076	4,796	6,579	11,033	14,115	4,545	2,001	10,175
RI	2,381	690	480	413	798	1,088	544	(Z)	743
SC	10,176	2,387	1,398	2,318	4,074	4,810	934	613	4,332
SD	1,952	429	264	336	923	1,233	198	54	524
TN	13,792	3,059	2,156	2,618	5,959	6,858	1,505	798	5,313
TX	74,045	11,356	8,257	29,809	24,623	43,536	15,373	1,902	20,328
UT	4,561	799	630	690	2,442	2,725	679	429	1,111
VT	1,629	501	287	186	655	996	57	(Z)	579
VA	16,791	4,237	2,813	2,305	7,437	9,041	1,867	715	5,722
WA	13,180	2,439	1,688	2,378	6,675	7,548	1,476	235	4,131
WV	4,434	947	584	1,063	1,841	2,305	595	1,207	1,395
WI	13,059	2,962	1,795	3,269	5,032	6,878	2,415	537	3,691
WY	2,242	237	235	663	1,107	1,413	260	413	526

Z Less than $500,000.   [1] Includes sources not shown separately. Total expenditures are the sum of purchases for each source (including electricity sales) less electric utility purchases of fuel.

Source: U.S. Energy Information Administration, *State Energy Price and Expenditure Report, 2000*, Series DOE/EIA-0376(00). See also <http://www.eia.doe.gov/emeu/states/sepfuel/html/pdf/fuelte.pdf>.

No. 902. Residential Energy Consumption, Expenditures, and Average Price: 1980 to 1997

[9.32 represents 9,320,000,000,000,000 Btu. For period April to March for 1980-1984; January to December for 1987 to 1997. Excludes Alaska and Hawaii in 1980. Covers occupied units only. Excludes household usage of gasoline for transportation and the use of wood or coal. Based on Residential Energy Consumption Survey; see source. For composition of regions, see inside front cover. Btu=British thermal unit; see text, this section]

Type of fuel	Unit	1980	1984	1987	1990	1993	1997
CONSUMPTION							
Total	Quad. Btu	9.32	9.04	9.13	9.22	10.00	10.25
Avg. per household	Mil. Btu	114	105	101	98	104	102
Natural gas	Quad. Btu	4.97	4.98	4.83	4.86	5.27	5.28
Electricity	Quad. Btu	2.48	2.48	2.76	3.03	3.28	3.54
Fuel oil, kerosene	Quad. Btu	1.52	1.26	1.22	1.04	1.07	1.07
Liquid petroleum gas	Quad. Btu	0.35	0.31	0.32	0.28	0.38	0.36
EXPENDITURES							
Total	Bil. dol.	74.80	97.00	97.70	110.20	123.91	135.79
Avg. per household	Dollars	(NA)	(NA)	1,080	1,172	1,282	1,338
Natural gas	Bil. dol.	19.77	29.78	26.10	27.30	32.04	35.81
Electricity	Bil. dol.	40.81	54.48	61.60	71.50	81.08	88.33
Fuel oil, kerosene	Bil. dol.	12.24	9.60	7.20	8.30	6.98	7.61
Liquid petroleum gas	Bil. dol.	2.80	3.12	2.81	3.14	3.81	4.04
AVERAGE PRICE							
Total	Dol./mil. Btu	8.03	10.73	10.70	11.95	12.39	13.25
Natural gas	Dol./mil. Btu	3.98	5.98	5.40	5.62	6.08	6.78
Electricity	Dol./mil. Btu	16.46	21.97	22.32	23.60	24.72	24.97
Fuel oil, kerosene	Dol./mil. Btu	8.05	7.62	5.90	7.98	6.52	15.56
Liquid petroleum gas	Dol./mil. Btu	8.00	10.06	8.78	11.21	10.03	11.23

NA Not available.

Source: U.S. Energy Information Administration, *Residential Energy Consumption Survey: Consumption and Expenditures*, annual through 1983 beginning 1985, triennial. For 1987 to 1997, *Household Energy Consumption and Expenditures, 1997*. Also see <http://www.eia.doe.gov/residential.html>.

No. 903. Residential Energy Consumption and Expenditures by Type of Fuel and Selected Household Characteristic: 1997

[For period January through December. Quad.=quadrillion (10.25 represents 10,250,000,000,000,000 Btu). See headnote, Table 902]

Characteristic	Consumption (Btu)					Expenditures				
	Total [1] (quad.)	Avg. per house-hold [1] (mil.)	Natural gas (quad.)	Electricity (quad.)	Fuel oil[2] (quad.)	Total [1] (bil. dol.)	Avg. per house-hold [1] (dol.)	Natural gas (bil. dol.)	Electricity (bil. dol.)	Fuel oil[2] (bil. dol.)
Total households	10.25	101	5.28	3.54	1.01	135.8	1,338	35.81	88.33	7.11
Single family	8.46	115	4.46	2.84	0.83	110.0	1,492	29.97	70.33	6.13
Two-to-four unit building	0.51	92	0.34	0.12	0.05	6.2	1,108	2.36	3.47	0.35
Five-or-more unit building	0.77	49	0.32	0.32	0.12	11.9	755	2.46	8.84	0.59
Mobile home	0.50	80	0.16	0.25	(B)	7.6	1,206	1.02	5.68	(B)
Year house built:										
1949 or earlier	3.48	125	2.05	0.74	0.54	39.6	1,420	14.15	20.03	3.77
1950 to 1959	1.33	106	0.77	0.39	0.15	16.8	1,340	5.30	10.14	1.08
1960 to 1969	1.39	96	0.73	0.47	0.14	18.3	1,264	4.88	11.85	0.97
1970 to 1979	1.71	87	0.74	0.80	0.09	25.3	1,291	4.75	19.03	0.63
1980 to 1989	1.41	82	0.56	0.74	0.06	22.5	1,302	3.83	17.62	0.44
1990 to 1997	0.92	95	0.43	0.41	0.03	13.3	1,369	2.91	9.66	0.22
1997 family income:										
Less than $10,000	1.02	76	0.53	0.33	0.11	13.3	2,013	(NA)	(NA)	(NA)
$10,000 to $24,999	2.54	87	1.30	0.89	0.22	33.7	3,478	(NA)	(NA)	(NA)
$25,000 to $49,999	3.19	103	1.65	1.08	0.31	41.6	2,670	(NA)	(NA)	(NA)
$50,000 or more	3.49	125	1.80	1.24	0.37	47.3	3,434	(NA)	(NA)	(NA)

B Base figure too small to meet statistical standards for reliability of a derived figure. NA Not available. [1] Includes liquid petroleum gas, not shown separately. [2] Includes kerosene.

Source: U.S. Energy Information Administration, *Household Energy Consumption and Expenditures*, 1987, 1990, 1993, and 1997. Also see <http://www.eia.doe.gov/emeu/recs/contents.html>.

No. 904. Commercial Buildings—Energy Consumption and Expenditures: 1999

[4,657 represents 4,657,000. Covers buildings using one or more major fuel. Excludes industrial buildings, predominantly residential buildings, and buildings of less than 1,000 sq. ft. Based on a sample survey of building representatives and energy suppliers; therefore, subject to sampling variability. For characteristics of commercial buildings, see Table 982 in Section 20. For composition of regions, see inside front cover]

Building characteristic	All buildings using any major fuel		Consumption (tril. Btu)			Expenditures (mil. dol.)		
	Number (1,000)	Square feet (mil.)	Major fuel, total [1]	Electricity	Natural gas	Major fuel, total [1]	Electricity	Natural gas
All buildings	4,657	67,338	5,733	3,098	2,023	81,552	66,424	10,609
Region:								
Northeast	686	12,360	1,116	543	299	18,996	15,133	1,895
Midwest	1,188	16,761	1,509	662	709	17,258	12,933	3,277
South	1,762	23,485	1,961	1,247	618	27,303	23,275	3,294
West	1,021	14,731	1,147	645	396	17,995	15,083	2,144
Year constructed:								
1919 or before	419	4,034	275	91	120	3,271	2,170	684
1920 to 1945	499	6,445	461	184	195	5,797	4,174	968
1946 to 1959	763	9,127	674	310	256	9,216	6,989	1,390
1960 to 1969	665	10,866	975	468	372	13,237	10,250	1,986
1970 to 1979	774	11,840	1,044	621	326	15,858	13,461	1,726
1980 to 1989	846	13,931	1,214	755	391	18,342	15,777	2,033
1990 to 1999	690	11,094	1,090	669	364	15,832	13,604	1,820
Principal activity within building:								
Education	327	8,651	649	257	227	8,018	5,820	1,111
Food sales	174	994	201	165	31	3,587	3,359	195
Food service	349	1,851	447	216	216	6,380	5,082	1,185
Health care	127	2,918	515	232	217	5,653	4,268	881
Inpatient	11	1,865	427	172	195	4,151	2,948	757
Outpatient	116	1,053	88	60	22	1,503	1,320	124
Lodging	153	4,521	450	196	181	5,716	4,266	943
Mercantile	667	10,398	724	521	186	13,085	11,851	1,126
Retail (other than mall)	534	4,766	344	221	110	5,922	5,166	670
Enclosed and strip malls	133	5,631	380	301	76	7,164	6,685	456
Office	739	12,044	1,089	767	219	17,775	15,683	1,215
Public assembly	305	4,393	359	191	96	5,096	3,983	560
Public order and safety	72	1,168	102	40	33	1,222	805	176
Religious worship	307	3,405	110	42	62	1,494	1,041	409
Service	478	3,388	421	138	260	4,639	3,108	1,371
Warehouse and storage	603	10,477	461	220	230	6,029	4,829	1,124
Other	102	1,222	176	101	45	2,498	2,063	224
Vacant	253	1,908	31	10	19	361	265	89
Square footage:								
1,001 to 5,000	2,348	6,774	772	415	312	12,355	10,262	1,802
5,001 to 10,000	1,110	8,238	608	283	292	9,228	7,146	1,810
10,001 to 25,000	708	11,153	743	370	319	10,873	8,663	1,813
25,001 to 50,000	257	9,311	692	371	234	10,090	8,188	1,274
50,001 to 100,000	145	10,112	865	494	250	12,057	10,023	1,253
100,001 to 200,000	59	8,271	772	451	230	10,344	8,555	1,104
200,001 to 500,000	23	6,851	660	340	237	8,015	6,432	958
500,001 and over	7	6,628	621	373	149	8,592	7,155	594

[1] Includes fuel oil, propane, and purchased steam not shown separately.

Source: U.S. Energy Information Administration, *Commercial Buildings Energy Survey: Consumption and Expenditures, 1999.* See also <http://www.eia.doe.gov/emeu/cbecs/pdf/alltables.pdf> (accessed May 2003).

No. 905. Fossil Fuel Prices in Current and Constant (1996) Dollars by Type of Fuel: 1980 to 2001

[In cents per million British thermal units (Btu), except as indicated. All fuel prices taken as close to the point of production as possible. See text, this section, for explanation of Btu conversions from mineral fuels]

Fuel	1980	1985	1990	1994	1995	1996	1997	1998	1999	2000	2001 [1]
CURRENT DOLLARS											
Composite [2]	2.04	2.51	1.84	1.53	1.47	1.82	1.81	1.41	1.65	2.60	[6]2.56
Crude oil [3]	3.72	4.15	3.45	2.27	2.52	3.18	2.97	1.87	2.68	4.61	3.77
Natural gas [4]	1.45	2.26	1.55	1.67	1.40	1.96	2.10	1.77	1.98	3.33	3.72
Bituminous coal [5]	1.10	1.15	1.00	0.91	0.88	0.87	0.85	0.83	0.79	0.80	[6]0.80
CONSTANT (1996) DOLLARS											
Composite [2]	3.58	3.41	2.13	1.59	1.50	1.82	1.77	1.37	1.58	2.43	[6]2.34
Crude oil [3]	6.52	5.64	3.99	2.37	2.57	3.18	2.91	1.82	2.56	4.30	3.45
Natural gas [4]	2.54	3.06	1.79	1.74	1.43	1.96	2.06	1.71	1.89	3.11	3.40
Bituminous coal [5]	1.93	1.56	1.15	0.94	0.90	0.87	0.84	0.80	0.75	0.74	[6]0.73

[1] Preliminary. [2] Derived by multiplying the price per Btu of each fossil fuel by the total Btu content of the production of each fossil fuel and dividing this accumulated value of total fossil fuel production by the accumulated Btu content of total fossil fuel production. [3] Domestic first purchase prices. [4] Wellhead prices. [5] Includes bituminous coal, subbituminous coal, and lignite. [6] Calculated using the 2000 coal price for the 2001 value.

Source: U.S. Energy Information Administration, *Annual Energy Review.* See also <http://www.eia.doe.gov/emeu/aer/finan.html> (released October 2002).

No. 906. Manufacturing Energy Consumption for all Purposes by Type of Fuel and Major Industry Group: 1998

[In trillions of Btu (23,783 represents 23,783,000,000,000). Estimates represented consumption of energy for all purposes (First Use) represents unduplicated demand for energy by manufacturers. "First Use" is all energy produced offsite, all energy produced onsite, either directly from captive mines and wells or as byproducts from nonenergy materials (such as sawdust from furniture production, hydrogen from electrolysis of brine, nut shells from peanut processing). Based on the Manufacturing Energy Consumption Survey and subject to sampling variability]

Industry	NAICS [1] code	Total	Net elec- tricity [2]	Residual fuel oil	Distil- late fuel oil [3]	Natural gas [4]	LPG and NGL [5]	Coal	Coke and breeze	Other [6]
All industries, total	(X)	23,783	3,035	406	142	7,426	1,882	1,814	461	8,967
Food and kindred products	311	1,044	213	14	16	568	5	129	2	97
Beverage and tobacco products	312	108	24	2	2	45	1	29	-	4
Textile mills	313	256	102	12	4	103	2	20	-	14
Textile product mills	314	50	18	3	(S)	25	(Z)	3	-	(Z)
Apparel	315	48	18	2	1	23	1	1	-	4
Leather and allied products	316	8	3	(Z)	(Z)	4	(Z)	-	-	(Z)
Wood products	321	509	72	1	13	73	4	2	-	343
Paper	322	2,733	240	151	9	586	5	277	-	1,465
Printing and related support	323	98	51	(Z)	(Z)	44	1	(Z)	-	2
Petroleum and coal products	324	7,320	126	72	28	1,007	39	12	-	6,082
Petroleum refineries	324110	7,130	118	70	4	948	33	(Z)	-	5,957
Chemicals [7]	325	6,064	577	98	10	2,709	1,796	300	7	677
Petrochemicals	325110	723	8	-	(Z)	(D)	222	(D)	-	(D)
Other basic organic chemicals	325199	1,740	73	3	(D)	782	639	(D)	-	201
Plastics materials and resins	325211	1,067	66	2	1	259	675	17	(Z)	60
Nitrogenous fertilizers	325311	592	13	-	(Z)	572	(Z)	-	-	6
Plastics and rubber products	326	328	183	5	1	126	5	3	-	5
Nonmetallic mineral products	327	979	134	4	17	444	3	284	11	82
Primary metals [7]	331	2,560	545	30	9	933	3	715	437	82
Iron and steel mills	331111	1,584	158	29	5	494	(Z)	680	388	22
Alumina and aluminum	3313	490	246	(Z)	1	189	1	2	2	49
Primary aluminum	331312	254	196	(Z)	(Z)	(D)	(Z)	(D)	-	41
Fabricated metal products	332	445	176	2	6	241	5	3	3	10
Machinery	333	217	96	1	3	99	3	6	-	7
Computer and electronic products	334	205	137	1	1	64	(Z)	(Z)	-	1
Electrical equipment, appliances, and component	335	143	55	1	1	53	2	1	(Z)	30
Transportation equipment	336	492	195	5	15	212	4	29	1	31
Furniture and related products	337	88	30	(Z)	1	27	1	2	-	28
Miscellaneous	339	89	40	1	2	40	1	(Z)	-	4

- Represents or rounds to zero. D Withheld to avoid disclosing data for individual establishments. S Withheld because Relative Standard Error is greater than 50 percent. X Not applicable. Z Less than 0.5 trillion Btu. [1] North American Industry Classification System, 1997; see text, Section 15. [2] Net electricity is obtained by aggregating purchases, transfers in, and generation from noncombustible renewable resources minus quantities sold and transferred out. Excludes electricity inputs from onsite cogeneration or generation from combustible fuels because that energy has already been included as generating fuel (for example, coal). [3] Includes Nos. 1, 2, and 4 fuel oils and Nos. 1, 2, and 4 diesel fuels. [4] Includes natural gas obtained from utilities, transmission pipelines, and any other supplier such as brokers and producers. [5] Liquid petroleum gas and natural gas liquids. [6] Includes net steam, and other energy that respondents indicated was used to produce heat and power or as feedstock/raw material inputs. [7] Includes types not shown separately.

Source: U.S. Energy Information Administration, <http://www.eia.doe.gov/emeu/mecs/mecs98/datatables/contents.html> (accessed 22 January 2001).

No. 907. Energy Prices: 1980 to 2001

Product	Unit	1980	1990	1995	1996	1997	1998	1999	2000	2001
Crude oil domestic first purchase price:										
Nominal	Dol./bbl	21.6	20.0	14.6	18.5	17.2	10.9	15.6	26.7	21.9
Real [1]	Dol./bbl	37.9	23.2	14.9	18.5	16.9	10.5	14.9	25.0	20.0
Motor gasoline	Cents/gal	122.0	122.0	121.0	129.0	129.0	112.0	122.0	156.0	153.0
Leaded regular	Cents/gal	119.0	115.0	(NA)	(NA)	(NA)	(NA)	(NA)	(NA)	(NA)
Unleaded regular	Cents/gal	125.0	116.0	115.0	123.0	123.0	106.0	117.0	151.0	146.0
Premium	Cents/gal	(NA)	135.0	134.0	141.0	142.0	125.0	136.0	169.0	166.0
Natural gas, residential	Dol/1,000 cu. ft.	3.7	5.8	6.1	6.3	6.9	6.8	6.7	7.8	10.0
Heating oil, residential	Cents/gal	97.4	106.3	86.7	98.9	98.4	85.2	87.6	131.1	124.9
Coal, all	Dol/short tons	24.7	21.8	18.8	18.5	18.1	17.7	16.6	16.8	(NA)
Electricity, total	Cents/kWh	4.7	6.6	6.9	6.9	6.9	6.7	6.7	6.8	7.3
Uranium, domestic purchases	Dol/lb	(NA)	15.7	11.1	13.8	12.9	12.3	11.9	11.5	10.5

NA Not available. [1] In chained (1996) dollars, calculated by using gross domestic product implicit price deflators.

Source: U.S. Energy Information Administration, Annual Energy Review, 2001. Also see <http://www.eia.doe.gov/emeu/aer/contents.html> (released October 2002).

No. 908. Energy Imports and Exports by Type of Fuel: 1980 to 2001

[In quadrillion of Btu (12.25 represents 12,250,000,000,000,000 Btu). For definition of Btu, see text, this section]

Type of fuel	1980	1985	1990	1994	1995	1996	1997	1998	1999	2000	2001 [1]
Net imports, total [2]	12.25	7.87	14.09	18.65	18.03	19.37	20.94	22.47	23.75	25.21	26.03
Coal	-2.39	-2.39	-2.70	-1.66	-2.08	-2.17	-2.01	-1.87	-1.30	-1.21	-0.77
Natural gas (dry)	0.96	0.90	1.46	2.52	2.74	2.85	2.90	3.06	3.50	3.62	3.72
Petroleum [3]	13.50	8.95	15.29	17.26	16.89	18.23	19.64	20.94	21.18	22.38	22.82
Other [4]	0.18	0.41	0.03	0.53	0.47	0.46	0.41	0.35	0.37	0.42	0.25
Imports, total	15.97	12.10	18.95	22.73	22.57	24.01	25.51	26.85	27.54	29.31	29.95
Coal	0.03	0.05	0.07	0.22	0.24	0.20	0.19	0.22	0.23	0.31	0.49
Natural gas (dry)	1.01	0.95	1.55	2.68	2.90	3.00	3.06	3.22	3.66	3.87	4.12
Petroleum [3]	14.66	10.61	17.12	19.24	18.88	20.29	21.74	22.91	23.13	24.53	24.88
Other [4]	0.28	0.49	0.22	0.58	0.55	0.52	0.52	0.50	0.52	0.59	0.45
Exports, total	3.72	4.23	4.87	4.08	4.54	4.64	4.56	4.37	3.80	4.09	3.92
Coal	2.42	2.44	2.77	1.88	2.32	2.37	2.19	2.09	1.53	1.53	1.27
Natural gas (dry)	0.05	0.06	0.09	0.16	0.16	0.16	0.16	0.16	0.16	0.25	0.40
Petroleum [3]	1.16	1.66	1.82	1.99	1.99	2.06	2.10	1.97	1.95	2.15	2.06
Other [4]	0.09	0.08	0.18	0.05	0.07	0.06	0.11	0.15	0.15	0.17	0.20

[1] Preliminary. [2] Net imports equals imports minus exports. Minus sign (-) denotes an excess of exports over imports. [3] Includes imports into the Strategic Petroleum Reserve, which began in 1977. [4] Coal coke and small amounts of electricity transmitted across U.S. borders with Canada and Mexico.

Source: U.S. Energy Information Administration, *Annual Energy Review*. See also <http://www.eia.doe.gov/emeu/aer/pdf/pages/sec1-45.pdf> (released November 2002).

No. 909. U.S. Foreign Trade in Selected Mineral Fuels: 1980 to 2001

[985 represents 985,000,000,000 cu. ft. Minus sign (-) indicates an excess of imports over exports]

Mineral fuel	Unit	1980	1985	1990	1995	1997	1998	1999	2000	2001 [1]
Natural gas:										
Imports [2]	Bil. cu. ft.	985	950	1,532	2,841	2,994	3,152	3,586	3,782	4,029
Exports	Bil. cu. ft.	49	55	86	154	157	159	163	244	394
Net trade	Bil. cu. ft.	-936	-894	-1,447	-2,687	-2,837	-2,993	-3,422	-3,538	-3,635
Crude oil:										
Imports [3]	Mil. bbl.	1,921	1,168	2,151	2,639	3,002	3,178	3,187	3,311	3,338
Exports	Mil. bbl.	105	74	40	35	39	40	43	18	8
Net trade	Mil. bbl.	-1,816	-1,094	-2,112	-2,604	-2,963	-3,138	-3,144	-3,293	-3,330
Petroleum products:										
Imports	Mil. bbl.	601	681	775	586	707	731	775	872	903
Exports	Mil. bbl.	94	211	273	312	327	305	300	361	350
Net trade	Mil. bbl.	-507	-470	-502	-274	-380	-426	-475	-511	-553
Coal:										
Imports	Mil. sh. tons	1.2	2.0	2.7	9.5	7.5	8.7	9.1	12.5	19.8
Exports	Mil. sh. tons	91.7	92.7	105.8	88.5	83.5	78.0	58.5	58.5	48.7
Net trade	Mil. sh. tons	90.5	90.7	103.1	79.0	76.0	69.3	49.4	46.0	28.9

[1] Preliminary. [2] Included in the total, but not shown separately, are liquified natural gas imports from Indonesia in 2000, Malaysia in 1999, and Oman in 2000 and 2001. [3] Beginning 1980, includes strategic petroleum reserve imports.

Source: U.S. Energy Information Administration, *Annual Energy Review*. See also <http://www.eia.doe.gov/eneu/aer/contents.html> (accessed August 4, 2003).

No. 910. Crude Oil Imports Into the U.S. by Country of Origin: 1980 to 2002

[In millions of barrels (1,921 represents 1,921,000,000). Barrels contain 42 gallons]

Country of origin	1980	1985	1990	1995	1996	1997	1998	1999	2000	2001	2002
Total imports	1,921	1,168	2,151	2,639	2,740	3,002	3,178	3,187	3,311	3,405	3,336
OPEC,[1 2 3 4] total	1,410	479	1,283	1,219	1,255	1,378	1,522	1,543	1,659	1,770	1,490
Algeria	166	31	23	10	3	2	4	9	(Z)	4	11
Iraq	10	17	188	-	(Z)	32	123	265	226	290	168
Kuwait [5]	10	1	29	78	86	92	110	90	96	87	79
Saudi Arabia [5]	456	48	436	460	456	472	512	506	556	588	554
United Arab Emirates	63	13	3	2	1	-	1	-	1	8	4
Indonesia	115	107	36	23	16	19	18	26	13	15	18
Nigeria	307	102	286	227	217	251	251	227	319	307	215
Venezuela	57	112	243	420	476	509	503	420	446	471	438
Non-OPEC[6], total	511	689	869	1,419	1,486	1,624	1,656	1,643	1,652	1,635	1,846
Angola	(NA)	(NA)	86	131	126	155	170	130	108	117	117
Canada	73	171	235	380	392	437	462	430	492	495	527
Colombia	(NA)	(NA)	51	76	82	99	127	165	116	95	86
Ecuador [2]	6	20	([2])	35	35	42	36	42	46	41	37
Gabon [3]	9	19	([3])	84	67	84	76	61	52	51	52
Mexico	185	261	251	375	441	496	482	458	479	509	548
Norway	53	11	35	94	107	105	81	96	110	103	127
Trinidad and Tobago	42	36	28	23	21	20	19	15	20	19	25
United Kingdom	63	101	57	124	79	62	59	104	106	89	148

- Represents zero. NA Not available. Z Represents less than half the unit of measure. [1] OPEC (Organization of Petroleum Exporting Countries)includes the Persian Gulf nations shown below, except Bahrain, which is not a member of OPEC, and also includes nations shown under "Other OPEC." [2] Ecuador withdrew from OPEC on Dec. 31, 1992; therefore, it is included under OPEC for the period 1973 to 1992. [3] Gabon withdrew from OPEC on Dec. 31, 1994; therefore, it is included under OPEC for the period 1973 to 1994. [4] Excludes petroleum imported into the United States indirectly from members of the Organization of Petroleum Exporting Countries (OPEC), primarily from Caribbean and West European areas, as petroleum products that were refined from crude oil produced by OPEC. [5] Imports from the Neutral Zone between Kuwait and Saudi Arabia are included in Saudi Arabia. [6] Includes petroleum imported into the United States indirectly from member of OPEC, primarily from Caribbean and West European areas, as petroleum products that were refined from crude oil produced by OPEC.

Source: U.S. Energy Information Administration, *Petroleum Supply Annual*, Vol. I. See also <http://www.eia.doe.gov/pub/oilgas/petroleum/datapublications/petroleumsupplyannual/psavolume1/current/pdf/tables03>.

No. 911. Crude Oil and Refined Products—Summary: 1980 to 2002

[13,481 represents 13,481,000 bbl. Barrels of 42 gallons. Data are averages]

Year	Crude oil (1,000 bbl. per day)					Refined oil products (1,000 bbl. per day)			Total oil imports [2] (1,000 bbl. per day)	Crude oil stocks[3] (mil. bbl.)	
	Input to refineries	Domestic production	Imports			Domestic demand	Imports	Exports		Total	Strategic reserve
			Total [1]	Strategic reserve	Exports						
1980	13,481	8,597	5,263	44	287	17,056	1,646	258	6,909	[4]466	108
1985	12,002	8,971	3,201	118	204	15,726	1,866	577	5,067	814	493
1990	13,409	7,355	5,894	27	109	16,988	2,123	748	8,018	908	586
1992	13,411	7,171	6,083	10	89	17,033	1,805	861	7,888	893	575
1993	13,613	6,847	6,787	15	98	17,237	1,833	904	8,620	922	587
1994	13,866	6,662	7,063	12	99	17,718	1,933	843	8,996	929	592
1995	13,973	6,560	7,230	-	95	17,725	1,605	855	8,835	895	592
1996	14,195	6,465	7,508	-	110	18,309	1,971	871	9,478	850	566
1997	14,662	6,452	8,225	-	108	18,620	1,936	896	10,162	868	563
1998	14,889	6,252	8,706	-	110	18,917	2,002	835	10,708	895	571
1999	14,804	5,881	8,731	8	118	19,519	2,122	822	10,852	852	567
2000	15,067	5,822	9,071	8	50	19,701	2,389	990	11,459	826	541
2001	15,128	5,801	9,328	11	20	19,649	2,543	951	11,871	862	550
2002	14,947	5,746	9,140	16	9	19,761	2,390	975	11,530	877	599

- Represents zero. [1] Includes Strategic Petroleum Reserve. [2] Crude oil (including Strategic Petroleum Reserve imports) plus refined products. [3] End of year. [4] Stocks of Alaskan crude oil in transit are included from January 1985 forward.
Source: U.S. Energy Information Administration, *Monthly Energy Review,* July 2003 issue.

No. 912. Petroleum and Coal Products Corporations—Sales, Net Profit, and Profit Per Dollar of Sales: 1990 to 2002

[318.5 represents $318,500,000,000. Represents SIC group 29 (NAICS group 324). Through 2000 based on Standard Industrial Classification code; beginning 2001 based on North American Industry Classification System, 1997. Profit rates are averages of quarterly figures at annual rates. Beginning 1990, excludes estimates for corporations with less than $250,000 in assets]

Item	Unit	1990	1993	1994	1995	1996	1997	1998	1999	2000	2001	2002
Sales	Bil. dol	318.5	266.1	268.2	283.1	323.5	320.0	250.4	277.0	455.2	472.5	484.9
Net profit:												
Before income taxes	Bil. dol	23.1	14.9	17.2	16.5	32.6	36.8	9.7	20.3	55.5	47.2	24.6
After income taxes	Bil. dol	17.8	13.0	14.9	13.9	26.6	29.4	8.3	17.2	42.6	35.8	20.8
Depreciation[1]	Bil. dol	18.7	17.4	17.1	16.7	16.7	15.9	15.6	14.7	13.5	17.2	17.7
Profits per dollar of sales:												
Before income taxes	Cents	7.3	5.6	6.3	5.8	10.1	11.5	3.5	7.1	12.2	9.7	5.2
After income taxes	Cents	5.6	4.9	5.5	4.9	8.2	9.2	3.1	6.0	9.4	7.4	4.3
Profits on stockholders' equity:												
Before income taxes	Percent	16.4	11.8	13.2	12.6	23.2	23.5	6.0	13.0	29.4	21.8	1.5
After income taxes	Percent	12.7	10.2	11.4	10.6	18.9	18.9	5.2	11.0	22.6	16.5	8.9

[1] Includes depletion and accelerated amortization of emergency facilities.
Source: U.S. Census Bureau, *Quarterly Financial Report for Manufacturing, Mining and Trade Corporations.*

No. 913. Major Petroleum Companies—Financial Summary: 1980 to 2002

[32.9 represents $32,900,000,000. Data represent a composite of approximately 42 major worldwide petroleum companies aggregated on a consolidated total company basis]

Item	1980	1985	1990	1995	1997	1998	1999	2000	2001	2002
FINANCIAL DATA (bil. dol.)										
Net income	32.9	19.4	26.8	24.3	40.0	14.5	35.3	76.4	62.0	44.3
Depreciation, depletion, etc	32.5	53.0	38.7	43.1	46.0	61.0	45.0	53.3	63.4	61.2
Cash flow [1]	65.4	72.4	65.5	67.4	86.0	75.5	75.3	129.7	140.0	118.0
Dividends paid	9.3	12.0	15.9	17.6	20.1	20.9	21.7	23.0	29.7	27.3
Net internal funds available for investment or debt repayment [2]	56.1	60.4	49.6	49.8	65.9	54.6	54.1	106.7	110.4	90.7
Capital and exploratory expenditures	62.1	58.3	59.6	59.8	75.3	83.9	67.7	72.8	99.9	88.7
Long-term capitalization	211.4	272.1	300.0	304.3	372.5	382.0	456.2	516.9	543.8	548.1
Long-term debt	49.8	93.5	90.4	85.4	86.1	103.9	105.4	112.8	143.2	153.5
Preferred stock	2.0	3.3	5.2	5.7	5.1	3.9	4.8	5.4	6.7	2.5
Common stock and retained earnings [3]	159.6	175.3	204.4	213.2	281.3	274.2	346.0	398.7	393.9	392.1
Excess of expenditures over cash income [4]	6.0	-2.1	10.0	10.0	9.4	29.3	13.6	-33.9	-10.5	-2.0
RATIOS [5] (percent)										
Long-term debt to long-term capitalization	23.6	34.4	30.1	28.1	23.1	27.2	23.1	21.8	26.7	28.3
Net income to total average capital	17.0	7.0	9.1	8.1	11.3	3.8	8.9	15.7	12.3	8.7
Net income to average common equity	22.5	10.8	13.5	11.6	15.1	5.2	12.4	20.5	16.3	11.5

[1] Generally represents internally-generated funds from operations. Sum of net income and noncash charges such as depreciation, depletion, and amortization. [2] Cash flow minus dividends paid. [3] Includes common stock, capital surplus, and earned surplus accounts after adjustments. [4] Capital and exploratory expenditures plus dividends paid minus cash flow. [5] Represents approximate year-to-year comparisons because of changes in the makeup of the group due to mergers and other corporate changes.
Source: Carl H. Pforzheimer & Co., New York, NY, *Comparative Oil Company Statements,* annual.

Energy and Utilities   591

No. 914. Electric Power Industry—Sales, Prices, Net Generation, Net Summer Capability, and Consumption of Fuels: 1990 to 2001

[2,827.1 represents 2,827,100,000,000 kWh. Net generation for calendar years; capability as of December 31]

Item	Unit	1990	1995	1998	1999	2000	2001
ELECTRIC POWER INDUSTRY							
Consumption, total	Bil. kWh	2,827.1	3,157.3	3,425.1	3,494.6	3,604.8	3,602.1
Net generation, total	Bil. kWh	3,023.6	3,353.5	3,620.3	3,694.8	3,802.1	3,719.5
Electric utilities	Bil. kWh	2,808.2	2,994.5	3,212.2	3,173.7	3,015.4	2,630.0
Nonutilities	Bil. kWh	87.8	199.7	245.2	356.3	622.2	932.0
Electricity imports	Bil. kWh	18.4	42.9	39.5	42.9	48.9	38.5
Electricity exports	Bil. kWh	16.1	3.6	13.2	14.0	14.8	18.2
Electricity losses and unaccounted for	Bil. kWh	198.8	235.4	221.5	229.1	231.4	137.7
Electric utility retail sales of electricity	Bil. kWh	2,712.6	3,013.3	3,264.2	3,312.1	3,421.4	3,396.8
Direct Use of electricity at nonutilities	Bil. kWh	114.6	144.1	160.9	182.5	183.4	205.4
Electricity retail prices per kWh:							
All sectors, current dollars	Cents	6.57	6.89	6.74	6.66	6.81	7.26
All sectors, real (1996) dollars	Cents	7.59	7.02	6.53	6.36	6.36	6.64
Residential, current dollars	Cents	7.83	8.40	8.26	8.16	8.24	8.57
Residential, real (1996) dollars	Cents	9.05	8.56	8.00	7.80	7.70	7.84
Commercial, current dollars	Cents	7.34	7.69	7.41	7.26	7.43	7.91
Commercial, real (1996) dollars	Cents	8.48	7.84	7.18	6.94	6.94	7.23
Industrial, current dollars	Cents	4.74	4.66	4.48	4.43	4.64	5.07
Industrial, real (1996) dollars	Cents	5.48	4.75	4.34	4.23	4.33	4.64
Other users, current dollars	Cents	6.40	6.88	6.63	6.35	6.56	6.45
Other users, real (1996) dollars	Cents	7.40	7.01	6.42	6.07	6.13	5.90
Net generation, total [1]	Bil. kWh	3,023.6	3,353.5	3,620.3	3,694.8	3,802.1	3,719.5
Coal	Bil. kWh	1,591.1	1,709.4	1,873.5	1,881.1	1,966.3	1,904.0
Petroleum	Bil. kWh	125.2	74.6	128.8	118.1	111.2	126.0
Natural gas	Bil. kWh	368.7	496.1	531.3	556.4	601.1	613.0
Nuclear	Bil. kWh	576.9	673.4	673.7	728.3	753.9	768.8
Hydroelectric pumped storage plants	Bil. kWh	-3.5	-2.7	-4.5	-6.1	-5.5	-8.8
Conventional hydroelectric power plants	Bil. kWh	291.2	310.8	323.3	319.5	275.6	217.5
Geothermal	Bil. kWh	14.9	13.4	14.8	14.8	14.1	13.8
Wood	Bil. kWh	30.0	36.5	36.3	37.0	37.6	36.9
Waste	Bil. kWh	13.1	20.4	22.4	22.6	23.1	22.8
Wind	Bil. kWh	2.3	3.2	3.0	4.5	5.6	5.8
Solar	Bil. kWh	0.4	0.5	0.5	0.5	0.5	0.5
Net summer capability, total [1]	Mil. kW	734.1	769.5	775.9	785.9	812.7	854.7
Coal-fired plants	Mil. kW	307.4	311.4	315.8	315.5	316.0	316.2
Petroleum-fired plants	Mil. kW	49.0	43.7	40.4	35.6	36.0	38.4
Natural gas-fired plants	Mil. kW	56.2	75.4	75.8	73.6	95.7	135.3
Dual-fired plants	Mil. kW	113.6	122.0	130.4	146.0	149.8	147.5
Nuclear electric power plants	Mil. kW	99.6	99.5	97.1	97.4	97.9	98.1
Hydroelectric pumped storage plants	Mil. kW	19.5	21.4	19.5	19.6	19.5	19.5
Conventional hydroelectric power plants	Mil. kW	73.9	78.6	79.2	79.4	79.4	79.4
Geothermal energy plants	Mil. kW	2.7	3.0	2.9	2.8	2.8	2.8
Wood energy plants	Mil. kW	5.5	6.7	6.8	6.8	6.1	6.2
Waste energy plants	Mil. kW	2.5	3.5	3.7	3.7	3.9	3.9
Wind energy plants	Mil. kW	1.8	1.7	1.7	2.3	2.4	4.1
Solar energy plants	Mil. kW	0.3	0.3	0.3	0.4	0.4	0.4
Fuel consumption:							
Coal	Mil. sh. tons	790.2	860.6	946.3	949.8	994.9	975.6
Distillate fuel and kerosene	Mil. bbl	17.9	19.6	25.1	26.0	31.7	32.0
Residual fuel	Mil. bbl	188.3	95.5	172.7	158.2	143.4	163.2
Petroleum coke	Mil. sh. tons	1.8	3.4	4.9	4.6	3.7	4.2
Natural gas	Bil. cu. ft.	3,653	4,738	5,081	5,322	5,691	5,690
ELECTRIC UTILITIES							
Net generation, total [1]	Bil. kWh	2,837.2	3,052.8	3,303.6	3,374.6	3,472.9	3,391.1
Coal	Bil. kWh	1,560.2	1,658.0	1,823.0	1,832.1	1,910.6	1,848.4
Petroleum	Bil. kWh	117.5	62.0	115.7	104.8	98.0	113.0
Natural gas	Bil. kWh	264.6	317.4	335.9	356.6	399.4	411.3
Nuclear	Bil. kWh	576.9	673.4	673.7	728.3	753.9	768.8
Hydroelectric pumped storage plants	Bil. kWh	-3.5	-2.7	-4.5	-6.1	-5.5	-8.8
Conventional hydroelectric power plants	Bil. kWh	288.4	305.4	317.9	314.7	271.3	213.8
Net summer capability, total [1]	Mil. kW	698.6	719.1	721.4	730.0	755.2	790.3
Coal-fired plants	Mil. kW	299.9	301.3	305.9	305.5	305.8	306.0
Petroleum-fired plants	Mil. kW	47.8	42.4	38.8	34.2	34.5	37.0
Natural gas-fired plants	Mil. kW	44.1	55.5	50.3	49.8	67.6	100.3
Dual-fired plants	Mil. kW	106.4	112.1	122.5	135.2	141.8	139.5
Nuclear electric power plants	Mil. kW	99.6	99.5	97.1	97.4	97.9	98.1
Hydroelectric pumped storage plants	Mil. kW	19.5	21.4	19.5	19.6	19.5	19.5
Conventional hydroelectric power plants	Mil. kW	73.3	77.4	78.0	78.3	78.2	78.3
NONUTILITY PLANTS							
Net generation, total [1]	Bil. kWh	122.0	151.0	154.1	156.3	156.7	150.1
Coal	Bil. kWh	19.3	22.4	22.3	21.5	22.1	22.0
Petroleum	Bil. kWh	6.2	6.0	6.2	6.1	5.6	5.9
Natural gas	Bil. kWh	57.1	71.7	77.1	78.8	78.8	73.6
Net summer capability, total [1]	Mil. kW	22.9	25.5	26.0	27.1	27.3	26.6
Coal-fired plants	Mil. kW	4.8	5.0	4.6	4.4	4.6	4.6
Petroleum-fired plants	Mil. kW	0.9	0.8	1.0	0.8	0.8	0.8
Natural gas-fired plants	Mil. kW	8.1	9.5	10.8	11.5	12.5	11.7
Dual-fired plants	Mil. kW	2.2	1.9	1.3	1.6	1.3	1.3

[1] Includes types not shown separately.

Source: U.S. Energy Information Administration, *Electric Power Annual* and *Annual Energy Review*.

No. 915. Electric Utility Industry—Capability, Peak Load, and Capacity Margin: 1980 to 2001

[558,237 represents 558,237,000kW. Excludes Alaska and Hawaii. Capability represents the maximum kilowatt output with all power sources available and with hydraulic equipment under actual water conditions, allowing for maintenance, emergency outages, and system operating requirements. Capacity margin is the difference between capability and peak load]

Year	Capability at the time of— Summer peak load (1,000 kW) Amount	Change from prior year	Capability at the time of— Winter peak load (1,000 kW) Amount	Change from prior year	Noncoincident peak load Summer	Noncoincident peak load Winter	Capacity margin Summer Amount (1,000 kW)	Percent of capability	Capacity margin Winter Amount (1,000 kW)	Percent of capability
1980	558,237	13,731	572,195	17,670	427,058	384,567	131,179	23.5	187,628	32.8
1982	586,142	13,923	598,066	11,497	415,618	373,985	170,524	29.1	224,081	37.5
1983	596,449	10,307	612,453	14,387	447,526	410,779	148,923	25.0	201,674	32.9
1984	604,240	7,791	622,125	9,672	451,150	436,374	153,090	25.3	185,751	29.9
1985	621,597	17,357	636,475	14,350	460,503	423,660	161,094	25.9	212,815	33.4
1986	633,291	11,694	646,721	10,246	476,320	422,857	156,971	24.8	223,864	34.6
1987	648,118	14,827	662,977	16,256	496,185	448,277	151,933	23.4	214,700	32.4
1988	661,580	13,462	676,940	13,963	529,460	466,533	132,120	20.0	210,407	31.1
1989	673,316	11,736	685,249	8,309	523,432	496,378	149,884	22.3	188,871	27.6
1990	685,091	11,775	696,757	11,508	545,537	484,014	139,554	20.4	212,743	30.5
1991	690,915	5,824	703,212	6,455	551,320	485,435	139,595	20.2	217,777	31.0
1992	695,436	4,521	707,752	4,540	548,707	492,983	146,729	21.1	214,769	30.3
1993	694,250	-1,186	711,957	4,205	575,356	521,733	118,894	17.1	190,224	26.7
1994	702,985	8,735	715,090	3,133	585,320	518,253	117,665	16.7	196,837	27.5
1995	714,222	11,237	727,679	12,589	620,249	544,684	93,973	13.2	182,995	25.1
1996	723,571	9,349	740,526	12,847	615,529	545,061	108,042	14.9	195,465	26.4
1997	729,079	5,508	743,774	3,248	631,355	560,228	97,724	13.4	183,546	24.7
1998	724,193	-4,886	735,090	-8,684	660,293	567,558	63,900	8.8	167,532	22.8
1999	733,481	9,288	748,036	12,946	681,449	570,915	52,032	7.1	177,121	23.7
2000	750,771	17,290	767,505	19,469	678,413	588,426	72,358	9.6	179,079	23.3
2001	783,737	32,966	806,598	39,093	687,812	576,312	95,925	12.2	230,286	28.6

Source: Edison Electric Institute, Washington, DC, *Statistical Yearbook of the Electric Utility Industry*, annual.

No. 916. Electric Energy Sales by Class of Service and State: 2001

[In billions of kilowatt-hours (3,369.8 represents 3,369,800,000,000)]

State	Total [1]	Residential	Commercial	Industrial	State	Total [1]	Residential	Commercial	Industrial
United States	3,369.8	1,202.6	1,089.2	964.2	Missouri	73.2	30.2	26.0	15.8
Alabama	79.2	27.8	18.9	31.8	Montana	11.2	3.9	3.6	3.3
Alaska	5.4	1.9	2.3	1.1	Nebraska	24.7	8.6	7.2	7.3
Arizona	62.3	26.2	22.1	11.4	Nevada	28.2	9.6	6.7	11.2
Arkansas	41.7	15.1	9.2	16.7	New Hampshire	10.3	3.8	3.9	2.5
California	235.4	77.3	100.2	46.5	New Jersey	72.3	25.4	34.0	12.4
Colorado	44.2	14.5	17.9	10.9	New Mexico	18.7	5.0	6.8	5.3
Connecticut	30.5	12.0	12.4	5.6	New York	141.4	44.0	59.4	24.7
Delaware	10.7	3.7	3.6	3.2	North Carolina	117.6	46.2	37.7	31.5
District of Columbia	9.4	1.7	7.3	0.3	North Dakota	9.8	3.5	3.1	2.8
Florida	199.7	101.4	74.0	18.8	Ohio	154.5	47.3	39.5	63.8
Georgia	117.8	44.4	37.8	33.9	Oklahoma	49.7	19.8	13.6	13.4
Hawaii	9.8	2.8	3.1	3.8	Oregon	45.9	17.5	14.8	13.1
Idaho	21.1	6.9	6.5	7.3	Pennsylvania	137.9	46.3	44.0	46.4
Illinois	135.7	41.8	43.8	37.9	Rhode Island	7.8	2.7	3.7	1.3
Indiana	97.7	29.4	25.6	42.1	South Carolina	74.8	24.9	17.5	31.5
Iowa	39.2	12.4	8.5	16.2	South Dakota	8.6	3.6	2.9	1.7
Kansas	35.8	12.1	12.8	10.6	Tennessee	95.3	36.9	26.0	31.3
Kentucky	80.0	23.7	14.3	38.7	Texas	316.1	117.3	88.2	95.8
Louisiana	74.7	25.8	17.7	28.6	Utah	23.2	6.7	8.3	7.4
Maine	11.8	4.7	4.5	2.6	Vermont	5.6	2.0	2.0	1.6
Maryland	59.8	24.0	25.4	9.7	Virginia	96.1	37.3	29.0	19.5
Massachusetts	52.7	18.0	25.0	9.0	Washington	79.7	31.6	23.8	20.5
Michigan	102.0	32.3	34.9	33.9	West Virginia	27.7	9.8	6.8	11.0
Minnesota	60.3	19.4	19.8	20.4	Wisconsin	65.2	20.4	18.7	25.3
Mississippi	44.3	16.9	11.4	15.3	Wyoming	13.0	2.1	2.9	7.7

[1] Includes "other service" not shown separately.

Source: U.S. Energy Information Administration, *Electric Sales and Revenue 2001*. Also see <http://www.eia.doe.gov/cneaf/electricity/esr/table1abcd.xls#A105> (issued January 2003).

Energy and Utilities 593

No. 917. Electric Utilities—Net Generation and Net Summer Capability by State: 1995 to 2001

[Capability as of Dec. 31. (2,994.5 represents 2,994,500,000,000). Covers utilities for public use]

State	Net generation (bil. kWh) 1995	1999	2000	2001 Total	2001 Percent from coal	Net summer capability (mil. kW) 1995	1999	2000	2001
United States	2,994.5	3,173.7	3,015.4	2,630.0	59.3	706.1	639.3	604.3	549.9
Alabama	99.6	113.9	118.0	118.7	60.2	20.5	21.5	22.4	22.5
Alaska	4.8	4.6	4.9	5.4	3.6	1.7	1.7	1.8	1.8
Arizona	69.0	83.1	88.2	85.8	46.3	15.2	15.1	15.1	15.3
Arkansas	39.5	44.1	41.5	44.7	55.2	9.6	9.3	9.3	9.6
California	121.9	87.9	85.9	70.1	-	43.3	24.3	24.3	24.4
Colorado	32.7	36.2	40.1	42.0	85.0	6.6	7.3	7.3	7.5
Connecticut	26.9	20.5	17.0	2.8	-	6.7	2.9	2.2	0.2
Delaware	8.3	6.2	4.1	1.9	86.9	2.2	2.3	1.0	0.2
District of Columbia	0.2	0.2	0.1	(NA)	(NA)	0.8	0.8	(NA)	(NA)
Florida	147.2	166.9	169.9	171.0	36.9	35.9	36.5	37.3	38.2
Georgia	102.0	110.5	116.2	110.6	66.4	22.3	23.3	24.9	24.1
Hawaii	6.2	6.5	6.5	6.4	-	1.6	1.6	1.6	1.6
Idaho	10.1	12.5	10.1	6.7	-	2.6	2.6	2.6	2.7
Illinois	145.2	149.8	113.6	29.8	97.6	33.1	17.0	17.5	4.4
Indiana	105.2	114.2	119.7	114.7	98.7	20.7	20.4	20.6	20.6
Iowa	33.5	37.0	39.6	38.8	86.4	8.2	8.4	8.5	8.4
Kansas	38.2	42.0	44.8	44.6	71.2	9.7	10.0	10.1	10.2
Kentucky	86.2	81.7	81.4	83.7	94.9	15.4	14.7	14.8	15.2
Louisiana	65.6	64.8	57.6	50.4	21.7	17.0	16.3	14.3	14.2
Maine	2.7	1.2	(Z)	(Z)	-	2.4	0.1	(Z)	(Z)
Maryland	44.7	49.3	31.8	0.1	-	11.0	11.0	0.8	0.1
Massachusetts	27.0	4.4	1.7	1.6	70.0	9.3	2.2	1.0	1.0
Michigan	92.5	87.9	89.6	97.1	69.0	22.0	22.4	22.8	22.8
Minnesota	42.5	44.2	46.6	44.8	69.3	8.9	9.0	9.1	10.1
Mississippi	26.4	32.2	33.9	47.6	40.4	7.2	6.8	7.1	8.0
Missouri	65.4	73.5	76.3	79.0	82.9	15.7	16.8	17.2	17.7
Montana	25.4	27.6	6.6	4.4	7.0	4.9	3.0	3.0	2.2
Nebraska	25.3	30.0	29.0	30.4	66.4	5.5	5.8	5.9	6.0
Nevada	20.0	26.5	29.3	27.9	63.6	5.6	5.4	5.4	5.4
New Hampshire	13.9	13.9	12.7	13.1	28.3	2.5	2.3	2.3	1.1
New Jersey	27.1	38.9	25.3	1.6	88.3	13.8	12.1	1.2	1.2
New Mexico	29.4	31.7	32.9	32.2	88.2	5.1	5.3	5.3	5.3
New York	101.2	97.0	73.2	58.6	3.6	32.1	17.7	15.8	11.6
North Carolina	96.1	109.9	114.4	109.8	62.6	20.6	21.2	22.0	23.5
North Dakota	28.8	31.3	31.1	30.1	95.5	4.5	4.7	4.7	4.7
Ohio	137.9	140.9	144.4	135.5	87.7	27.4	27.1	26.3	27.1
Oklahoma	48.0	50.3	51.4	50.4	63.8	12.9	12.9	13.4	13.4
Oregon	44.0	51.7	46.1	38.1	11.6	10.4	10.3	10.4	10.4
Pennsylvania	168.9	161.6	97.1	27.6	50.2	33.7	25.3	13.4	5.0
Rhode Island	0.7	(Z)	(Z)	(Z)	-	0.4	(Z)	(Z)	(Z)
South Carolina	78.4	87.3	90.4	86.7	41.9	16.7	17.7	17.7	18.2
South Dakota	8.8	10.6	9.7	7.4	48.8	3.0	2.9	2.8	2.8
Tennessee	82.3	89.7	92.3	92.9	62.6	16.1	17.3	17.9	18.6
Texas	261.7	292.5	297.3	265.0	49.9	64.4	65.3	65.4	38.9
Utah	32.1	36.1	35.8	35.1	94.5	4.8	5.1	5.1	5.1
Vermont	4.8	4.7	5.3	4.7	-	1.1	0.8	0.8	0.3
Virginia	52.7	65.1	65.8	62.1	49.3	14.3	15.3	15.6	15.8
Washington	95.7	112.1	96.2	67.7	-	24.3	25.2	23.8	24.1
West Virginia	77.3	91.7	89.7	51.6	99.0	14.5	14.5	14.5	10.2
Wisconsin	51.0	54.7	55.7	55.0	73.1	11.5	12.1	12.2	12.2
Wyoming	39.7	43.0	44.6	43.8	97.3	6.0	6.0	6.0	6.1

- Represents zero. NA Not available. Z Represents less than 50 million kWh or 50,000 kW.

Source: U.S. Energy Information Administration, *Electric Power Annual 2001* and *Inventory of Electric Utility Power Plants in the United States 2000*. Also see <http://www.eia.doe.gov/fuelelectric.html> (accessed August 4, 2003).

No. 918. Nuclear Power Plants—Number, Capacity, and Generation: 1980 to 2001

[51.8 represents 51,800,000 kW]

Item	1980	1985	1990	1993	1994	1995	1996	1997	1998	1999	2000	2001
Operable generating units [1]	71	96	112	110	109	109	109	107	104	104	104	104
Net summer capability [1] [2] (mil. kW)	51.8	79.4	99.6	99.1	99.1	99.5	100.8	99.7	97.1	97.4	97.9	98.1
Net generation (bil. kWh)	251.1	383.7	576.9	610.3	640.4	673.4	674.7	628.6	673.7	728.3	753.9	768.8
Percent of total electric utility generation	11.0	15.5	19.1	19.1	19.7	20.1	19.6	18.0	18.6	19.7	19.8	20.7
Capacity factor [3]	56.3	58.0	66.0	70.5	73.8	77.4	76.2	71.1	78.2	85.3	88.1	89.4

[1] As of year-end.   [2] Net summer capability is the peak steady hourly output that generating equipment is expected to supply to system load, exclusive of auxiliary and other power plant, as demonstrated by test at the time of summer peak demand.   [3] Weighted average of monthly capacity factors. Monthly factors are derived by dividing actual monthly generation by the maximum possible generation for the month (hours in month times net maximum dependable capacity).

Source: U.S. Energy Information Administration, *Annual Energy Review, 2001*. See also <http://www.eia.doe.gov/emeu/aer/nuclear.html> (accessed August 6, 2003).

No. 919. Nuclear Power Plants—Number of Units, Net Generation, and Net Summer Capability by State: 2001

[768,826 represents 768,826,000,000 kWh]

State	Number of units	Net generation Total (mil. kWh)	Net generation Percent of total[1]	Net summer capability Total (mil. kW)	Net summer capability Percent of total[1]	State	Number of units	Net generation Total (mil. kWh)	Net generation Percent of total[1]	Net summer capability Total (mil. kW)	Net summer capability Percent of total[1]
U.S.	104	768,826	20.6	98.16	11.6	MS	1	9,924	18.8	1.21	10.9
AL	5	30,357	24.2	4.97	20.8	MO	1	8,384	10.5	1.14	6.0
AZ	3	28,724	31.9	3.73	22.3	NE	2	8,726	28.6	1.23	20.5
AR	2	14,781	31.3	1.78	17.6	NH	1	8,693	57.6	1.16	40.8
CA	4	33,220	16.6	4.32	7.9	NJ	4	30,469	51.1	3.27	20.3
CT	2	15,428	50.5	2.61	33.1	NY	6	40,395	28.1	5.05	14.2
FL	5	31,583	16.5	3.90	9.1	NC	5	37,775	32.1	4.73	18.1
GA	4	33,682	28.4	4.02	13.6	OH	2	15,464	10.9	2.11	7.1
IL	11	92,358	51.6	10.96	27.4	PA	9	73,731	37.5	9.13	24.2
IA	1	3,853	9.5	0.52	5.7	SC	7	49,870	55.5	6.45	33.2
KS	1	10,347	23.1	1.17	11.3	TN	3	28,576	29.7	3.37	16.7
LA	2	17,336	19.5	2.07	9.5	TX	4	38,163	10.4	4.74	5.4
MD	2	13,656	27.9	1.68	14.0	VT	1	4,171	76.1	0.51	52.2
MA	1	5,144	13.2	0.67	5.6	VA	4	25,759	34.8	3.47	17.3
MI	4	26,711	23.8	3.93	14.6	WA	1	8,250	9.9	1.11	4.2
MN	3	11,789	24.3	1.65	14.9	WI	3	11,507	19.6	1.51	10.7

[1] For total capability and generation, see Table 917.

Source: U.S. Energy Information Administration, *Electric Power Annual and Electric Power Monthly*, December issues.

No. 920. Uranium Concentrate—Supply, Inventories, and Average Prices: 1980 to 2002

[43.70 represents 43,700,000 lb. Years ending Dec. 31. For additional data on uranium, see Section 18]

Item	Unit	1980	1990	1995	1997	1998	1999	2000	2001	2002
Production	Mil. lb.	43.70	8.89	6.04	5.64	4.71	4.61	3.96	2.64	2.34
Exports	Mil. lb.	5.8	2.0	9.8	17.0	15.1	8.5	13.6	11.7	15.4
Imports	Mil. lb.	3.6	23.7	41.3	43.0	43.7	47.6	44.9	46.7	52.7
Utility purchases from domestic suppliers	Mil. lb.	(NA)	20.5	22.3	19.4	21.6	21.4	24.3	27.5	22.7
Loaded into U.S. nuclear reactors [1]	Mil. lb.	(NA)	(NA)	51.1	48.2	38.2	58.8	51.5	52.7	57.3
Inventories, total	Mil. lb.	(NA)	129.1	72.5	106.2	136.5	127.1	111.3	103.8	101.1
At domestic suppliers	Mil. lb.	(NA)	26.4	13.7	40.4	70.7	68.8	56.5	48.1	47.9
At electric utilities	Mil. lb.	(NA)	102.7	58.7	65.9	65.8	58.3	54.8	55.6	53.3
Average price per pound: Purchased imports	Dollars	(NA)	12.55	10.20	11.81	11.96	11.45	10.68	9.87	10.37
Domestic purchases	Dollars	(NA)	15.70	11.11	12.87	12.31	11.88	11.45	10.45	10.35

NA Not available.   [1] Does not include any fuel rods removed from reactors and later reloaded into the reactor.

Source: Through 2000, U.S. Energy Information Administration, *Annual Energy Review 2001*, thereafter, U.S. Energy Information Administration, *Uranium Industry Annual 2002*. Also see <http://www.eia.doe.gov/emeu/aer/nuclear.html>.

No. 921. Nonutility Electric Power Producers—Summary by Type of Fuel: 1998 to 2000

[98,213 represents 98,213,000 kWh. All data is for 1 megawatt and greater. A nonutility power producer may be a corporation, person, agency, authority, or other legal entity or instrumentality that owns electric generating capacity and is not an electric utility. Nonutility power producers include qualifying cogenerators, qualifying small power producers, and other nonutility generators (including independent power producers) without a designated franchised service area, and which do not file forms listed in the Code of Federal Regulations, Title 18, Part 141]

Type of fuel	Installed capacity [1,2] (1,000 kWh) 1998	1999	2000	Gross generation [3] (Mil. kWh) 1998	1999	2000
All types, total	98,213	160,525	228,594	422,985	544,561	828,325
Coal [4]	17,217	40,580	59,196	70,014	121,072	287,141
Petroleum	2,472	4,161	11,015	19,519	33,087	41,249
Natural gas [5]	39,795	47,516	73,186	227,719	268,237	323,143
Other gas [6]	1,560	1,813	1,723	13,893	14,632	14,620
Dual fired [3]	18,171	41,190	47,534	(X)	(X)	(X)
Hydroelectric pumped storage	-	600	1,453	-	-	1,655
Hydroelectric (conventional)	4,340	5,403	5,761	14,713	20,147	22,644
Geothermal	1,424	2,719	2,683	9,932	13,638	14,461
Solar	864	963	410	529	518	526
Wind	1,711	2,222	2,323	3,053	4,510	5,621
Biomass [7]	10,545	10,510	10,144	59,894	61,211	62,288
Nuclear	-	2,527	12,622	-	3,318	49,959
Other [8]	114	322	545	3,718	4,191	5,017

- Represents or rounds to zero.   X Not applicable.   [1] There is a discontinuity in capacity estimates between 1999 and earlier years due to a change in reporting practices. In 1999 for the first time respondents self identified the facility's primary energy source resulting in a reclassification compared to earlier years in some cases. 1998 and 1999 data in this table have been adjusted accordingly, but data corresponding to this table in previous editions are not comparable.   [2] Petroleum figures are for petroleum only.   [3] Petroleum figures include petroleum, petroleum coke, diesel, kerosene, light oil, liquid butane, liquid propane, oil waste, sludge oil, and tar oil.   [4] Includes coal, anthracite culm, bituminous gob, coke breeze, fine coal, lignite waste, tar coal, and waste coal.   [5] Includes natural gas and waste heat.   [6] Includes butane, propane, and other gas.   [7] Includes black liquor, peat, railroad ties, red liquor, sludge wood, spent sulfite liquor, utility poles, and wood/waste, agricultural byproducts, digester gas, fish oil, liquid acetonitrile waste, landfill gas, medical waste, methane, municipal solid waste, paper pellets, sludge waste, solid byproducts, straw, tires, tall oil, and waste alcohol.   [8] Includes batteries, chemicals, hydrogen, pitch, purchased steam, and sulfer.

Source: Energy Information Administration, *Electric Power Annual*, Vol. II. Also see <http://tonto.eia.doe.gov/FTPROOT/electricity/0348002.pdf>; and *Inventory of Nonutility Electric Power Plants in the United States*, annual. Also see <http://www.ei.doe.gov/cneaf/electricity/ipp/ippsum2.html>.

No. 922. Electric Utilities—Generation, Sales, Revenue, and Customers: 1980 to 2002

[2,290 represents 2,290,000,000,000 kWh. Sales and revenue are to and from ultimate customers]

Class	Unit	1980	1990	1995	1997	1998	1999	2000	2001	2002
Generation [1,2]	Bil. kWh	2,290	3,038	3,353	3,492	3,620	3,695	3,802	3,737	3,839
Sales [3]	Bil. kWh	2,126	2,684	3,007	3,139	3,240	3,236	3,379	3,396	3,471
Residential or domestic	Bil. kWh	734	916	1,042	1,079	1,128	1,141	1,194	1,206	1,267
Percent of total	Percent	34.5	34.1	34.7	34.4	34.8	35.3	35.3	35.5	36.5
Commercial [4]	Bil. kWh	524	739	864	929	969	971	1,037	1,110	1,122
Industrial [5]	Bil. kWh	794	932	1,006	1,028	1,040	1,018	1,041	970	973
Revenue [3]	Bil. dol	95.5	176.5	207.6	215.1	218.4	215.5	226.3	238.7	250.1
Residential or domestic	Bil. dol	37.6	71.7	87.6	90.9	93.2	93.1	97.8	102.1	106.8
Percent of total	Percent	39.4	40.6	42.2	42.2	42.7	43.2	43.2	42.7	42.7
Commercial [4]	Bil. dol	27.4	54.2	66.5	70.5	71.8	70.5	74.6	82.0	89.0
Industrial [5]	Bil. dol	27.3	44.9	46.9	46.7	46.8	45.1	46.9	47.1	47.1
Ultimate customers, Dec. 31 [3]	Million	92.7	110.1	118.3	122.2	124.0	125.2	128.5	130.7	(NA)
Residential or domestic	Million	82.2	97.0	103.9	107.1	108.7	109.8	112.6	114.3	(NA)
Commercial [4]	Million	9.7	12.1	12.9	13.5	13.8	14.0	14.4	14.8	(NA)
Industrial [5]	Million	0.5	0.5	0.6	0.6	0.5	0.5	0.5	0.6	(NA)
Avg. kWh used per customer	1,000	22.9	24.4	25.4	25.7	26.1	25.8	26.3	26.0	(NA)
Residential	1,000	8.9	9.4	10.0	10.1	10.4	10.4	10.6	10.5	(NA)
Commercial	1,000	54.0	61.0	66.7	68.7	70.0	69.5	72.0	75.1	(NA)
Avg. annual bill per customer	Dollar	1,030	1,603	1,755	1,761	1,760	1,720	1,761	1,826	(NA)
Residential	Dollar	457	739	843	849	857	848	868	892	(NA)
Commercial [4]	Dollar	4,059	3,356	3,259	3,123	3,084	3,096	3,001	2,894	(NA)
Avg. revenue per kWh sold	Cents	13.00	19.27	19.91	19.95	19.36	18.89	18.95	19.79	19.74
Residential	Cents	5.12	7.83	8.40	8.43	8.26	8.16	8.19	8.46	8.43
Commercial [4]	Cents	5.22	7.33	7.70	7.58	7.41	7.26	7.20	7.39	7.93
Industrial [5]	Cents	3.44	4.82	4.66	4.54	4.48	4.43	4.51	4.85	4.84

NA Not available.   [1] Source: U.S. Energy Information Administration, *Monthly Energy Review*, monthly. Also see <http://www.eia.doe.gov/emeu/mer/pdf/pages/sec75.pdf>.   [2] "Generation" includes batteries, chemicals, hydrogen, pitch, sulfur, and purchased steam.   [3] Includes other types not shown separately.   [4] Small light and power.   [5] Large light and power.

Source: Except as noted, Edison Electric Institute, Washington, DC, *Statistical Yearbook of the Electric Utility Industry*, annual.

No. 923. Major Investor-Owned Electric Utilities—Balance Sheet and Income Account of Privately Owned Companies: 1995 to 2000

[In millions of dollars (199,967 represents $199,967,000,000). As of Dec. 31. Covers approximately 180 investor-owned electric utilities that during each of the last 3 years met any one or more of the following conditions—1 mil. megawatt-hrs. of total sales; 100 megawatt-hrs. of sales for resale, 500 megawatt-hrs. of gross interchange out, and 500 megawatt-hrs. of wheeling for other]

Item	1995	1996	1997	1998	1999	2000
COMPOSITE INCOME ACCOUNTS						
Operating revenue	199,967	207,459	215,083	218,175	214,160	235,336
Electric	183,655	188,901	195,898	201,970	197,578	214,707
Gas	15,580	17,869	18,663	15,735	16,033	19,948
Other utility	731	689	522	470	550	682
Operating expenses [1]	165,321	173,920	182,796	186,498	182,258	210,324
Electric [1]	150,599	156,938	165,443	171,689	167,266	191,329
Operation	91,881	97,207	104,337	110,759	108,461	132,662
Maintenance	11,767	12,050	12,368	12,486	12,276	12,185
Depreciation [2]	19,885	21,194	23,072	24,122	23,968	23,670
Taxes other than income taxes	13,519	13,569	13,612	12,867	12,336	11,883
Income taxes	11,480	11,195	11,862	13,037	14,843	7,641
Deferred income tax	1,474	1,617	25	-476	-2,216	-945
Investment tax credit (net)	-550	-577	-448	-651	-1,695	-561
Gas	14,073	16,258	16,925	14,396	14,493	18,341
Other utility	649	725	427	413	499	654
Operating income	34,646	33,539	32,286	31,677	31,902	25,012
Electric	33,057	31,963	30,454	30,281	30,311	23,377
Gas	1,507	1,612	1,737	1,339	1,540	1,607
Other utility	82	-36	95	57	51	29
Total income before interest charges	36,457	35,153	34,100	32,788	33,567	28,621
Less: Net interest charges	14,421	13,990	14,086	14,057	13,691	13,781
Interest expense	14,170	13,646	13,768	13,670	13,376	13,666
Less allow. for borrowed funds used during constuction	435	326	331	328	331	397
Other charges, net	687	671	649	715	646	512
Net income before extraordinary charges	22,036	21,162	20,014	18,732	19,876	14,840
Less extraordinary items after taxes	-25	-66	3,151	1,344	2,793	1,567
Equals: Net income	**22,061**	**21,228**	**16,863**	**17,388**	**17,083**	**13,274**
Dividends declared - preferred stock	1,519	1,248	1,005	750	687	568
Earnings available for common stock	20,542	19,980	15,857	16,638	16,396	12,706
Dividends declared - common stock	16,250	16,810	17,756	17,414	18,687	16,677
Additions total earnings	4,282	2,193	-1,960	-199	-2,785	-3,971
COMPOSITE BALANCE SHEET						
Total assets and other debits	**578,934**	**581,991**	**586,241**	**598,856**	**585,827**	**606,372**
Utility plant, net	397,383	396,438	385,258	362,388	344,112	340,897
Electric utility plant, net	366,116	363,854	351,427	327,646	310,317	307,284
Electric utility plant	553,858	569,969	579,042	575,651	567,825	570,320
Construction work in progress	13,523	11,396	11,164	11,886	12,306	14,766
Less accumulated depreciation	201,265	217,510	238,779	259,892	269,813	277,802
Nuclear fuel, net	5,286	5,444	5,219	4,731	4,265	3,974
Other utility plant, net	25,981	27,140	28,613	30,011	29,529	29,639
Other property and investments	27,988	33,120	43,248	48,853	54,546	56,992
Current and accrued assets	44,140	43,515	47,639	54,901	57,324	79,169
Deferred debits	109,423	108,918	110,096	132,714	129,845	129,312
CAPITALIZATION AND LIABILITIES						
Liabilities and other credits	**578,934**	**581,991**	**586,241**	**598,856**	**585,827**	**606,372**
Capitalization	365,775	365,783	369,079	367,052	345,786	341,163
Common stock equity (end of year)	170,497	174,325	174,467	172,239	165,341	160,380
Preferred stock	21,569	18,830	16,080	14,447	12,061	9,893
Long-term debt	173,708	172,627	178,532	180,366	168,384	170,891
Current liabilities and deferred credits	213,159	216,208	217,162	231,803	240,041	265,208

[1] Includes items not shown separately. [2] Includes amortization and depletion.

Source: U.S. Energy Information Administration, *Electric Power Annual*, Vol. II, 2000. Also see <http://www.eia.doe.gov/cneaf/electricity/epav2/backissues.html>.

No. 924. Solar Collector Shipments by Type, End Use, and Market Sector: 1980 to 2001

[Shipments in thousands of square feet (19,398 represents 19,398,000). Solar collector is a device for intercepting sunlight, converting the light to heat, and carrying the heat to where it will be either used or stored. 1985 data are not available]

Year	Number of manufacturers	Total shipments [1,2,3]	Collector type			End use			Market sector		
			Low temperature	Medium temperature, special, other [2]		Pool heating	Hot water	Space heating	Residential	Commercial	Industrial
1980	233	19,398	12,233	7,165		12,029	4,790	1,688	16,077	2,417	488
1986 [4]	98	9,360	3,751	1,111		3,494	1,181	127	4,131	703	13
1990 [4]	51	11,409	3,645	2,527		5,016	1,091	2	5,835	294	22
1995	36	7,666	6,813	840		6,763	755	132	6,966	604	82
1999	29	8,583	8,152	427		8,141	373	42	7,774	785	18
2000	26	8,354	7,948	400		7,863	367	99	7,473	810	57
2001	26	11,189	10,919	268		10,797	274	70	10,125	1,012	17

[1] Includes shipments of high temperature collectors to the government, including some military, but excluding space applications. Also includes end uses such as process heating, utility, and other market sectors not shown separately. [2] Includes imputation of shipment data to account for nonrespondents. [3] Total shipments include all domestic and export shipments and may include imported collectors that subsequently were shipped to domestic or foreign customers. [4] Declines between 1986 and 1990 are primarily due to the expiration of the federal energy tax credit and industry consolidation.

Source: U.S. Energy Information Administration, 1974-1993, *Solar Collector Manufacturing Activity*, annual reports; thereafter, *Renewable Energy Annual*. See also <http://www.eia.doe.gov/cneaf/solar.renewables/page/readata/rea.pdf> (released November 2002).

No. 925. Total Renewable Net Generation by Source and State: 2000

[In millions of kilowatthours (275,573 represents 275,573,000,000). MSW=municipal solid waste]

State	Total [1]	Hydro-electric	MSW/ landfill gas	Other bio-mass [2]	Wood/ wood waste	State	Total [1]	Hydro-electric	MSW/ landfill gas	Other bio-mass [2]	Wood/ wood waste
U.S...	356,480	275,573	20,305	2,828	37,595	MO....	683	600	73	10	(X)
AL....	9,894	5,818	4	25	4,047	MT....	9,670	9,623	(X)	(X)	47
AK....	1,002	1,002	(X)	(X)	(X)	NE....	1,517	1,501	(X)	17	(X)
AZ....	8,359	8,354	(X)	5	(X)	NV....	3,800	2,429	(X)	(X)	(X)
AR....	3,965	2,370	(X)	7	1,587	NH....	2,534	1,427	244	(X)	862
CA....	60,837	38,334	1,938	673	3,574	NJ....	1,378	14	1,350	14	(X)
CO....	1,474	1,454	(X)	19	(X)	NM....	230	221	(X)	8	(X)
CT....	2,679	526	1,957	196	(X)	NY....	27,792	24,910	2,227	4	640
DE....	19	(X)	19	(X)	(X)	NC....	4,911	3,138	98	11	1,664
DC....	(X)	(X)	(X)	(X)	(X)	ND....	2,131	2,123	(X)	8	(X)
FL....	5,777	87	3,037	594	2,059	OH....	1,230	583	27	(X)	621
GA....	5,586	2,481	17	72	3,015	OK....	2,425	2,277	2	(X)	146
HI....	921	103	350	188	(X)	OR....	38,819	38,116	95	(X)	541
ID....	11,450	10,967	(X)	(X)	483	PA....	5,021	2,290	1,954	74	692
IL....	1,052	144	611	297	(X)	RI....	120	5	115	(X)	(X)
IN....	718	588	130	(X)	(X)	SC....	2,953	1,533	63	6	1,351
IA....	1,486	904	71	18	(X)	SD....	5,716	5,716	(X)	(X)	(X)
KS....	15	15	(X)	(X)	(X)	TN....	7,196	6,396	37	2	761
KY....	2,337	2,325	(X)	(X)	12	TX....	2,600	829	60	66	1,152
LA....	3,325	532	(X)	95	2,698	UT....	907	746	9	(X)	(X)
ME....	7,413	3,591	421	160	3,241	VT....	1,581	1,221	(X)	(X)	348
MD....	2,551	1,733	639	(Z)	180	VA....	2,856	712	461	6	1,677
MA....	3,262	1,065	2,050	25	122	WA....	81,754	80,263	205	45	1,241
MI....	4,317	1,428	1,031	68	1,791	WV....	1,165	1,151	-	14	(X)
MN....	2,975	931	790	8	522	WI....	3,139	1,986	220	90	841
MS....	1,680	1,680	(X)	(Z)	(X)	WY....	1,257	1,011	(X)	(X)	(X)

- Represents zero. X Not applicable. Z Less than 500,000 thousand kilowatthours. [1] Includes types not shown separately. [2] Agriculture byproducts/crops, sludge waste, tires and other biomass solids, liquids, and gases.

Source: Energy Information Administration, *Renewable Energy Annual 2001*. Also see <http://www.eia.doe.gov/cneaf/solar.renewables/page/readata/rea.pdf>.

No. 926. Privately Owned Gas Utility Industry—Balance Sheet and Income Account: 1980 to 2001

[In millions of dollars (75,851 represents $75,851,000,000). The gas utility industry consists of pipeline and distribution companies. Excludes operations of companies distributing gas in bottles or tanks]

Item	1980	1990	1995	1996	1997	1998	1999	2000	2001
COMPOSITE BALANCE SHEET									
Assets, total	75,851	121,686	141,965	121,328	134,715	119,715	155,413	165,709	170,898
Total utility plant	67,071	112,863	143,636	135,179	140,268	135,092	166,134	162,206	175,280
Depreciation and amortization	26,162	49,483	62,723	58,815	62,554	61,226	73,823	69,366	74,167
Utility plant (net)	40,909	63,380	80,912	76,364	77,714	73,866	92,311	92,839	101,113
Investment and fund accounts	15,530	23,872	26,489	13,207	22,812	12,337	17,344	10,846	10,674
Current and accrued assets	17,243	23,268	18,564	17,393	19,084	17,348	22,443	35,691	29,053
Deferred debits [1]	2,169	9,576	13,923	11,983	12,844	13,721	20,922	24,279	28,206
Liabilities, total	75,851	121,686	141,965	121,328	134,775	119,715	155,413	165,709	170,898
Capitalization, total	51,382	74,958	90,581	77,440	78,887	71,718	95,244	96,079	106,635
Capital stock	29,315	43,810	54,402	43,555	42,530	37,977	859	760	734
Long-term debts	22,067	31,148	35,548	33,644	35,971	33,386	46,906	48,267	49,145
Current and accrued liabilities	18,119	29,550	28,272	22,098	33,507	26,953	32,683	42,312	35,214
Deferred income taxes [2]	4,149	11,360	14,393	13,326	13,636	13,239	17,120	17,157	20,180
Other liabilities and credits	2,201	5,818	8,715	8,464	8,745	7,806	10,365	10,161	8,869
COMPOSITE INCOME ACCOUNT									
Operating revenues, total	85,918	66,027	58,390	63,600	62,617	57,117	59,142	72,042	78,489
Minus: Operating expenses [3]	81,789	60,137	50,760	56,695	59,375	50,896	38,752	64,988	70,443
Operation and maintenance	74,508	51,627	37,966	43,742	46,070	41,026	41,415	54,602	58,506
Federal, state, and local taxes	4,847	4,957	6,182	6,362	7,182	5,429	5,605	6,163	7,055
Equals: Operating income	4,129	5,890	7,630	6,905	3,242	6,220	20,390	7,053	8,046
Utility operating income	4,471	6,077	7,848	7,013	3,337	6,361	16,614	7,166	8,174
Income before interest charges	6,929	8,081	9,484	8,030	4,193	7,779	17,531	7,589	8,261
Net income	4,194	4,410	5,139	4,797	48	4,379	10,420	4,245	4,003
Dividends	2,564	3,191	4,037	4,138	6,258	2,263	5,595	3,239	3,757

[1] Includes capital stock discount and expense and reacquired securities. [2] Includes reserves for deferred income taxes. [3] Includes expenses not shown separately.

Source: American Gas Association, Arlington, VA, *Gas Facts*, annual (copyright).

No. 927. Gas Utility Industry—Summary: 1980 to 2001

[47,223 represents 47,223,000. Covers natural, manufactured, mixed, and liquid petroleum gas. Based on a questionnaire mailed to all privately and municipally owned gas utilities in United States, except those with annual revenues less than $25,000]

Item	Unit	1980	1990	1995	1997	1998	1999	2000	2001
End users [1]	1,000	47,223	54,261	58,728	59,790	62,421	64,071	64,194	64,792
Residential	1,000	43,489	49,802	53,955	54,993	57,465	58,939	59,129	59,729
Commercial	1,000	3,498	4,246	4,530	4,589	4,755	4,920	4,820	4,869
Industrial and other	1,000	187	166	181	170	164	174	163	172
Sales [2]	Tril. Btu [3]	15,413	9,842	9,221	8,880	8,630	8,889	9,025	8,565
Residential	Tril. Btu	4,826	4,468	4,803	5,013	4,828	4,865	4,948	4,739
Percent of total	Percent	31.3	45.4	52.0	56.3	56.3	54.7	54.8	55.3
Commercial	Tril. Btu	2,453	2,192	2,281	2,234	2,157	2,087	2,118	2,142
Industrial	Tril. Btu	7,957	3,010	1,919	1,511	1,528	1,868	1,361	1,225
Other	Tril. Btu	177	171	218	123	117	69	599	458
Revenues [2]	Mil. dol	48,303	45,153	46,436	51,531	47,930	48,423	59,705	71,730
Residential	Mil. dol	17,432	25,000	28,742	33,175	31,333	31,472	37,522	44,789
Percent of total	Percent	36.1	55.4	61.9	64.2	65.4	65.0	62.8	62.4
Commercial	Mil. dol	8,183	10,604	11,573	12,632	11,523	11,133	13,662	17,831
Industrial	Mil. dol	22,215	8,996	5,571	5,236	4,684	5,547	6,000	6,820
Other	Mil. dol	473	553	549	488	391	272	2,521	2,290
Prices per mil. Btu [3]	Dollars	3.13	4.59	5.05	5.80	5.55	5.45	6.62	8.38
Residential	Dollars	3.61	5.60	6.00	6.62	6.49	6.47	7.58	9.45
Commercial	Dollars	3.34	4.84	5.07	5.65	5.34	5.34	6.45	8.32
Industrial	Dollars	2.79	2.99	2.98	3.53	3.18	3.19	4.41	5.57
Gas mains mileage	1,000	1,052	1,207	1,261	1,251	1,295	1,389	1,380	1,433
Field and gathering	1,000	84	90	60	43	40	40	36	35
Transmission	1,000	266	280	264	251	256	254	246	259
Distribution	1,000	702	837	937	957	999	1,095	1,098	1,139
Construction expenditures [4]	Mil. dol	5,350	7,899	10,760	6,830	10,978	8,320	8,624	9,511
Transmission	Mil. dol	1,583	2,886	3,380	1,319	3,656	1,785	1,590	3,234
Distribution	Mil. dol	1,869	3,714	5,394	4,188	5,035	4,180	5,437	4,520
Production and storage	Mil. dol	1,150	309	367	276	598	161	138	113
General	Mil. dol	352	770	1,441	891	1,389	1,974	1,273	1456
Underground Storage	Mil. dol	396	219	177	156	299	220	185	188

[1] Annual average. [2] Excludes sales for resale. [3] For definition of Btu, see text, this section. [4] Includes general.

Source: American Gas Association, Arlington, VA, *Gas Facts,* annual (copyright).

No. 928. Gas Utility Industry—Customers, Sales, and Revenues by State: 2001

[64,792 represents 64,792,000. See headnote, Table 927. For definition of Btu, see text, this section]

State	Customers [1] (1,000) Total	Resi-dential	Sales [2] (tril. Btu) Total	Resi-dential	Revenues [2] (mil. dol.) Total	Resi-dential	State	Customers [1] (1,000) Total	Resi-dential	Sales [2] (tril. Btu) Total	Resi-dential	Revenues [2] (mil. dol.) Total	Resi-dential
U.S.	64,792	59,729	8,565	4,739	71,730	44,789	MO	1,078	986	143	89	1,360	901
AL	920	846	117	54	1,090	618	MT	255	226	30	20	217	142
AK	107	94	59	17	146	71	NE	537	479	77	44	609	380
AZ	930	875	94	36	747	377	NV	584	551	55	33	455	292
AR	625	553	77	38	631	369	NH	123	103	19	9	205	101
CA	10,037	9,596	718	518	7,095	5,324	NJ	2,814	2,566	515	234	3,622	1,807
CO	1,551	1,411	204	130	1,626	1,084	NM	530	486	58	35	421	267
CT	511	464	91	42	874	515	NY	4,328	3,996	512	326	5,465	3,765
DE	134	123	19	9	162	83	NC	1,004	889	140	62	1,339	732
DC	128	119	17	10	219	138	ND	123	107	22	11	156	81
FL	758	706	69	19	693	288	OH	2,724	2,511	342	246	3,065	2,287
GA	415	378	66	23	520	238	OK	1,016	928	124	70	1,024	648
HI	101	93	9	2	167	41	OR	685	607	91	45	760	416
ID	337	299	39	23	308	193	PA	2,566	2,358	340	222	3,579	2,489
IL	3,847	3,602	532	409	4,658	3,678	RI	250	224	29	9	325	226
IN	1,746	1,595	230	146	2,042	1,364	SC	555	496	92	29	786	337
IA	916	819	122	74	1,110	728	SD	163	143	23	12	185	111
KS	1,708	1,557	189	131	1,690	1,240	TN	1,231	1,094	183	78	1,597	768
KY	1,097	987	139	77	1,217	712	TX	4,026	3,710	873	214	5,286	1,951
LA	974	912	192	46	1,178	446	UT	1,381	1,284	179	115	1,249	863
ME	49	35	10	2	94	21	VT	36	31	8	3	60	29
MD	833	778	87	62	956	709	VA	987	899	134	70	1,358	815
MA	1,663	1,524	216	130	2,350	1,604	WA	1,043	942	149	84	1,358	764
MI	3,230	2,998	474	337	2,591	1,885	WV	402	366	59	33	413	256
MN	1,402	1,276	264	128	2,015	1,112	WI	1,686	1,530	230	130	1,847	1,124
MS	487	435	80	31	644	300	WY	159	142	24	14	167	100

[1] Averages for the year. [2] Excludes sales for resale.

Source: American Gas Association, Arlington, VA, *Gas Facts,* annual (copyright).

Energy and Utilities

No. 929. Public Drinking Water Systems by Size of Community Served and Source of Water: 2002

[As of September. Covers systems that provide water for human consumption through pipes and other constructed conveyances to a least 15 service connection or serve an average of at least 25 persons for at least 60 days a year. Based on reported data in the Safe Drinking Water Information System maintained by the Environmental Protection Agency]

Type of system	Total	500 or fewer persons	501 to 3,300 persons	3,301 to 10,000 persons	10,001 to 100,000 persons	100,000 persons or more	Ground water	Surface water
Total systems	161,316	132,974	19,706	4,799	3,467	370	146,752	14,564
COMMUNITY WATER SYSTEMS [1]								
Number of systems	53,437	30,703	14,331	4,606	3,436	361	41,691	11,746
Percent of systems	100	57	27	9	6	1	78	22
Population served (1,000)	267,723	5,045	20,180	26,717	96,258	119,523	84,025	183,698
Percent of systems	100	2	8	10	36	45	31	69
NONTRANSIENT, NONCOMMUNITY WATER SYSTEM [2]								
Number of systems	18,687	15,887	2,690	93	14	3	17,931	756
Percent of systems	100	85	14	-	-	-	96	4
Population served (1,000)	6,033	2,218	2,643	467	325	380	5,298	735
Percent of systems	100	37	44	8	5	6	88	12
TRANSIENT NONCOMMUNITY WATER SYSTEM [3]								
Number of systems	89,192	86,384	2,685	100	17	6	87,130	2,062
Percent of systems	100	97	3	-	-	-	98	2
Population served (1,000)	22,850	7,338	2,645	538	370	11,958	12,107	10,742
Percent of systems	100	32	12	2	2	52	53	47

- Represents zero. [1] A public water system that suplies water to the same population year-round. [2] A public water system that regularly supplies water to at least 25 of the same people at least 6 months per year, but not year-round. Some examples are schools, factories, and office buildings which have their own water systems. [3] A public water system that provides water in a place such as a gas station or campground where people do not remain for long periods of time.

Source: U.S. Environmental Protection Agency, *Factoids: Drinking Water* and <http://www.epa.gov/safewater/data/pdfs/02factoids.pdf> (accessed May 2003).

No. 930. Water and Sewage Treatment Facilities: 1997

[Based on the North American Industry Classification System, 1997; see Appendix III]

State	Water supply (NAICS 2213101) Number of establishments	Water supply Paid employees	Sewage treatment facilities (NAICS 22132) Number of establishments	Sewage treatment facilities Paid employees	State	Water supply (NAICS 2213101) Number of establishments	Water supply Paid employees	Sewage treatment facilities (NAICS 22132) Number of establishments	Sewage treatment facilities Paid employees
U.S.	3,721	26,597	696	5,600	MO	57	[4]	15	[5]
AL	96	[1]	13	[2]	MT	35	113	6	[3]
AK	6	[3]	(NA)	(NA)	NE	(NA)	(NA)	(NA)	(NA)
AZ	129	1,131	8	40	NV	23	[5]	(NA)	(NA)
AR	140	[4]	9	[5]	NH	10	[2]	(NA)	(NA)
CA	374	2,848	27	116	NJ	49	[6]	24	[4]
CO	71	314	14	51	NM	90	323	(NA)	(NA)
CT	32	[6]	9	[5]	NY	41	[4]	28	[2]
DE	9	[1]	(NA)	(NA)	NC	81	577	18	[5]
DC	(NA)	(NA)	(NA)	(NA)	ND	24	[5]	(NA)	(NA)
FL	129	1,393	88	[4]	OH	60	686	19	[2]
GA	34	130	10	[5]	OK	105	[1]	9	[2]
HI	9	24	13	[2]	OR	63	[2]	7	[5]
ID	35	[2]	6	20	PA	125	2,568	59	[1]
IL	82	[4]	27	[2]	RI	(NA)	(NA)	(NA)	(NA)
IN	114	[6]	30	[2]	SC	48	[1]	12	[5]
IA	25	[2]	7	[5]	SD	29	[2]	(NA)	(NA)
KS	38	[2]	(NA)	(NA)	TN	30	[1]	11	[2]
KY	42	[1]	13	116	TX	601	2,514	38	[4]
LA	192	[4]	21	[2]	UT	23	71	(NA)	(NA)
ME	22	[2]	(NA)	(NA)	VT	7	[5]	(NA)	(NA)
MD	8	[5]	9	107	VA	48	[1]	12	[5]
MA	18	[2]	21	[1]	WA	148	[1]	8	[5]
MI	12	66	10	24	WV	40	523	20	94
MN	6	[5]	13	[5]	WI	(NA)	(NA)	13	47
MS	332	1,001	14	[5]	WY	16	[5]	(NA)	(NA)

NA Not available. [1] 250-499 employees. [2] 100-249. [3] 1-19. [4] 500-999. [5] 20-99. [6] 1000-2499.

Source: U.S. Census Bureau, *1997 Economic Census, Utilities*. See also <http://www.census.gov/epcd/www/97EC22.htm> (accessed May 2002).

Section 20
Construction and Housing

This section presents data on the construction industry and on various indicators of its activity and costs; on housing units and their characteristics and occupants; and on the characteristics and vacancy rates for commercial buildings. This edition contains data from the 2002 American Housing Survey in metropolitan areas.

The principal source of these data is the U.S. Census Bureau, which issues a variety of current publications, as well as data from the decennial census. Current construction statistics compiled by the Census Bureau appear in its *New Residential Construction* and *New Residential Sales* press releases and Web sites <http://www.census.gov/const/www/>. Statistics on expenditures by owners of residential properties are issued quarterly and annually in *Expenditures for Residential Upkeep and Improvements*. *Value of New Construction Put in Place* presents data on all types of construction and includes monthly composite cost indexes. Reports of the censuses of construction industries (see below) are also issued on various topics.

Other Census Bureau publications include the *Current Housing Reports* series, which comprises the quarterly *Housing Vacancies*, the quarterly *Market Absorption of Apartments*, the biennial *American Housing Survey* (formerly *Annual Housing Survey*), and reports of the censuses of housing and of construction industries. *Construction Review*, published quarterly by the International Trade Administration, U.S. Department of Commerce, contains many of the census series and other construction statistics series from the federal government and private agencies.

Other sources include the monthly *Dodge Construction Potentials* of F. W. Dodge Division, McGraw-Hill Information Systems Company, New York, NY, which presents national and state data on construction contracts; the National Association of Home Builders with state-level data on housing starts; the NATIONAL ASSOCIATION OF REALTORS®, which presents data on existing home sales; the Society of Industrial and Office Realtors and Oncor International on commercial office and industrial space; the Bureau of Economic Analysis, which presents data on residential capital and gross housing product; and the U.S. Energy Information Administration, which provides data on commercial buildings through its periodic sample surveys.

Censuses and surveys—Censuses of the construction industry were first conducted by the Census Bureau for 1929, 1935, and 1939; beginning in 1967, a census has been taken every 5 years (through 1997, for years ending in "2" and "7"). The latest complete reports are for 1997. The 1997 census results are part of the 1997 Economic Census. See Table 932. See also text, Section 15, Business Enterprise.

The construction sector of the economic census, covers all employer establishments primarily engaged in (1) building construction by general contractors or operative builders; (2) heavy (nonbuilding) construction by general contractors; and (3) construction by special trade contractors. The 1997 census was conducted in accordance with the 1997 *North American Industry Classification System* (NAICS); the 1992 census was conducted in accordance with the 1987 *Standard Industrial Classification* (SIC). This sector now includes construction management and land subdividers and developers, not included previously. See text, Section 15, Business Enterprise, for general information on the SIC and NAICS.

From 1850 through 1930, the Census Bureau collected some housing data as part of its censuses of population and agriculture. Beginning in 1940, separate censuses of housing have been taken at 10-year intervals. For the 1970 and 1980 censuses, data on year-round housing units were collected and issued on occupancy and structural characteristics, plumbing facilities, value, and rent; for 1990 such characteristics were presented for all housing units.

The American Housing Survey (*Current Housing Reports* Series H-150 and H-170), which began in 1973, provided an annual and ongoing series of data on selected housing and demographic characteristics until 1983. In 1984, the name of the survey was changed from the Annual Housing Survey. Currently, national data are collected every other year, and data for selected metropolitan areas are collected on a rotating basis. All samples represent a cross section of the housing stock in their respective areas. Estimates are subject to both sampling and nonsampling errors; caution should therefore be used in making comparisons between years.

Data on residential mortgages were collected continuously from 1890 to 1970, except 1930, as part of the decennial census by the Census Bureau. Since 1973, mortgage status data, limited to single family homes on less than 10 acres with no business on the property, have been presented in the American Housing Survey. Data on mortgage activity are covered in Section 25, Banking and Finance.

Housing units—In general, a housing unit is a house, an apartment, a group of rooms or a single room occupied or intended for occupancy as separate living quarters; that is, the occupants live separately from any other individual in the building, and there is direct access from the outside or through a common hall. Transient accommodations, barracks for workers, and institutional-type quarters are not counted as housing units.

Statistical reliability—For a discussion of statistical collection and estimation, sampling procedures, and measures of statistical reliability applicable to Census Bureau data, see Appendix III.

No. 931. Construction—Establishments, Employees, and Payroll by Kind of Business (NAICS Basis): 2000 and 2001

[For establishments with payroll. (6,572.8 represents 6,572,800). See Appendix III]

Industry	NAICS code [1]	Establishments 2000	Establishments 2001	Paid employees [2] (1,000) 2000	Paid employees [2] (1,000) 2001	Annual payroll (mil. dol.) 2000	Annual payroll (mil. dol.) 2001
Construction	23	709,590	698,898	6,572.8	6,491.9	239,910.1	247,211.1
Building, developing, & general contracting	233	216,354	215,806	1,604.9	1,616.9	60,798.1	64,956.9
Land subdivision & land development	2331	13,111	13,358	77.9	88.9	3,269.2	3,990.1
Residential building construction	2332	159,550	155,437	781.0	735.3	25,519.7	25,985.7
Single-family housing construction	23321	151,296	146,670	713.3	661.4	23,058.3	23,160.0
Multifamily housing construction	23322	8,254	8,767	67.7	73.9	2,461.3	2,825.8
Nonresidential building construction	2333	43,693	47,011	746.0	792.5	32,009.3	34,980.9
Mfg & industrial building construction	23331	7,039	5,887	164.9	114.0	6,797.3	4,565.6
Commercial & institutional building construction	23332	36,654	41,124	581.2	678.5	25,212.0	30,415.3
Heavy construction	234	39,516	40,476	901.0	901.2	38,628.0	39,801.6
Highway, street, bridge, & tunnel construction	2341	11,795	12,133	304.9	311.0	14,316.1	15,697.5
Highway & street construction	23411	10,889	11,314	265.7	275.1	12,328.6	13,758.5
Bridge & tunnel construction	23412	906	819	39.3	35.8	1,987.5	1,938.9
Other heavy construction	2349	27,721	28,343	596.1	590.1	24,311.9	24,104.0
Water, sewer, & pipeline construction	23491	7,483	9,090	165.8	193.3	7,033.0	8,484.8
Power & communication transmission line construction	23492	3,644	4,065	97.5	114.9	3,815.8	4,382.0
Industrial nonbuilding structure construction	23493	689	647	101.7	105.3	4,137.8	4,036.4
All other heavy construction	23499	15,905	14,541	231.0	176.4	9,325.3	7,200.6
Special trade contractors	235	453,720	442,616	4,066.9	3,973.8	140,484.1	142,452.8
Plumbing, heating, & air-conditioning contractors	2351	90,487	89,550	897.9	898.4	33,406.0	34,507.9
Painting & wall covering contractors	2352	40,973	40,364	221.8	220.4	6,121.4	6,300.6
Electrical contractors	2353	66,802	65,860	815.1	831.8	32,698.0	33,480.1
Masonry, drywall, insulation, & tile contractors	2354	53,625	50,885	565.0	529.5	17,389.8	17,188.6
Masonry & stone contractors	23541	25,030	23,664	197.9	178.8	5,667.8	5,605.9
Drywall, plastering, acoustical, & insulation contractors	23542	21,774	20,337	319.3	300.9	10,224.4	9,973.1
Tile, marble, terrazzo, & mosaic contractors	23543	6,821	6,884	47.8	49.7	1,497.7	1,609.4
Carpentry & floor contractors	2355	58,525	57,441	347.3	337.5	9,963.6	9,951.5
Carpentry contractors	23551	45,028	44,391	269.8	262.9	7,533.3	7,507.0
Floor laying & other floor contractors	23552	13,497	13,050	77.5	74.6	2,430.3	2,444.4
Roofing, siding, & sheet metal contractors	2356	30,966	30,247	260.8	247.4	7,928.8	7,833.9
Concrete contractors	2357	30,238	30,743	292.6	295.2	9,501.2	10,419.0
Water well drilling contractors	2358	3,797	3,722	21.6	22.2	688.5	758.9
Other special trade contractors	2359	78,307	73,804	644.9	590.9	22,786.6	22,012.3
Structural steel erection contractors	23591	5,382	4,782	93.6	81.9	3,585.8	3,260.9
Glass & glazing contractors	23592	5,772	5,531	45.8	47.1	1,570.1	1,756.1
Excavation contractors	23593	27,005	25,409	152.5	144.4	5,253.6	5,482.1
Wrecking & demolition contractors	23594	1,752	1,923	21.9	27.1	808.7	953.0
Building equip & other machinery installation contractors	23595	4,820	4,600	80.9	72.6	3,859.6	3,543.1
All other special trade contractors	23599	33,576	31,559	250.1	217.7	7,708.7	7,016.5

[1] North American Industry Classification System, 1997 code; see text, Section 15. [2] Employees on the payroll for the pay period including March 12.

Source: U.S. Census Bureau, "County Business Patterns"; 2001 data published 10 April 2003; <http://www.census.gov/epcd/cbp view/cbpview.html>.

No. 932. Construction—Establishments, Employees, and Payroll by Kind of Business (NAICS Basis): 1997

[For establishments with payroll (174,185 represents $174,185,000,000). Based on the 1997 Economic Census; See Appendix III]

Kind of business	NAICS code [1]	Number of establishments	Number of employees All	Number of employees Construction workers	Payroll (mil. dol.) All employees	Payroll (mil. dol.) Construction workers	Net value of construction work (mil. dol.)
Construction.............	23	656,448	5,664,853	4,332,737	174,185	119,677	612,209
Building, developing, & general contracting..	233	199,289	1,342,953	885,939	42,546	23,136	198,827
Land subdivision & land development....	2331	8,186	41,827	10,977	1,510	254	10,248
Residential building construction........	2332	146,394	629,887	407,801	16,731	8,762	100,124
Nonresidential building construction.....	2333	44,710	671,239	467,161	24,305	14,119	88,455
Heavy construction................	234	42,557	880,400	710,898	30,292	22,219	105,639
Highway, street, bridge, & tunnel construction.................	2341	12,448	325,743	265,267	11,375	8,474	46,274
Other heavy construction	2349	30,109	554,657	445,630	18,917	13,745	59,365
Special trade contractors.............	235	414,602	3,441,500	2,735,901	101,347	74,322	307,743
Plumbing, heating, & air-conditioning contractors...................	2351	84,876	788,930	599,940	25,720	18,280	78,496
Painting & wall covering contractors.....	2352	37,480	195,331	160,740	4,543	3,431	12,050
Electrical contractors...............	2353	61,414	641,985	510,921	21,680	16,261	61,121
Masonry, drywall, insulation, & tile contractors...................	2354	49,917	470,701	407,700	12,612	10,073	34,843
Carpentry & floor contractors.........	2355	56,936	290,942	228,273	7,163	5,116	24,049
Roofing, siding, & sheet metal contractors.	2356	30,557	253,315	197,294	6,495	4,370	21,976
Concrete contractors...............	2357	30,417	262,256	222,121	6,858	5,298	23,604
Water well drilling contractors.........	2358	3,862	21,214	15,360	576	399	2,132
Other special trade contractors	2359	59,143	516,824	393,552	15,699	11,095	49,472

[1] North American Industry Classification System, 1997; see text, Section 15.

Source: U.S. Census Bureau, 1997 Economic Census, Construction, Series EC97C23S-IS, issued January 2000. See Internet site <http://www.census.gov/epcd/www/econ97.html>.

No. 933. Construction Materials—Producer Price Indexes: 1990 to 2002

[1982=100, except as noted. Data for 2002 are preliminary. For discussion of producer price indexes, see text, Section 14. This index, more formally known as the special commodity grouping index for construction materials, covers materials incorporated as an integral part of a building or normally installed during construction and not readily removable. Excludes consumer durables such as kitchen ranges, refrigerators, etc. This index is not the same as the stage-of-processing index of intermediate materials and components for construction]

Commodity	1990	1995	1996	1997	1998	1999	2000	2001	2002
Construction materials..............	119.6	138.8	139.6	142.1	141.4	142.8	144.1	142.8	144.0
Interior solvent based paint.............	133.0	164.5	175.6	180.5	185.7	188.0	191.1	190.2	190.5
Construction products from plastics.........	117.2	133.8	130.9	128.2	126.2	128.0	135.8	132.9	136.4
Douglas fir, dressed..................	138.4	198.8	227.1	221.3	186.1	212.1	185.2	178.1	178.5
Southern pine, dressed................	111.2	166.9	177.9	201.2	177.3	185.7	161.0	152.5	145.4
Millwork.........................	130.4	163.8	166.6	170.9	171.1	174.7	176.4	179.2	179.7
Softwood plywood...................	119.6	188.1	173.7	175.5	174.9	207.0	173.3	167.8	164.1
Hardwood plywood and related products	102.7	122.2	124.9	127.1	126.9	128.6	130.2	130.4	131.5
Softwood plywood veneer, ex. reinforced/backed ...	142.3	203.5	189.3	201.7	180.1	197.4	182.2	175.5	172.8
Building paper and building board mill products....	112.2	144.9	137.2	129.6	132.9	141.6	138.8	129.3	129.6
Steel pipe and tubes [1].................	102.6	104.4	103.2	106.9	109.4	102.5	106.6	104.0	106.2
Builders hardware...................	133.0	153.2	156.5	158.4	160.8	161.9	163.8	166.4	169.4
Plumbing fixtures and brass fittings..........	144.3	166.0	171.1	174.5	175.1	176.7	180.4	180.8	181.9
Heating equipment...................	131.6	147.5	151.2	152.4	153.3	154.0	155.6	157.1	157.8
Metal doors, sash, and trim..............	131.4	156.5	159.3	161.0	161.3	162.2	165.1	167.1	168.0
Siding, aluminum [2]..................	(NA)	132.4	125.5	132.1	134.5	135.4	142.2	141.5	140.6
Outdoor lighting equipment, including parts [3].....	113.0	120.8	122.9	123.2	122.8	122.3	124.7	125.7	126.1
Commercial fluorescent fixtures [4]...........	113.0	121.0	123.4	122.8	119.0	118.7	117.7	113.6	113.9
Architectural and ornamental metalwork [5]......	118.7	128.0	131.3	133.5	135.4	136.2	139.8	141.7	144.2
Fabricated ferrous wire products [1]..........	114.6	125.7	126.8	128.0	130.1	130.6	130.0	129.8	129.7
Elevators, escalators, and other lifts..........	110.1	113.0	113.7	114.8	116.0	117.5	118.7	119.4	120.0
Stamped metal switch and receptacle box	158.0	183.5	186.3	189.0	191.5	192.8	183.0	195.4	195.4
Concrete ingredients and related products	115.3	134.7	138.8	142.5	147.6	152.1	155.6	159.1	162.5
Concrete products...................	113.5	129.4	133.2	136.0	140.0	143.7	147.8	151.7	152.7
Clay construction products exc. refractories......	129.9	141.3	142.3	143.5	144.9	148.3	152.8	155.7	152.7
Prep. asphalt and tar roofing and siding products...	95.8	97.8	97.4	96.5	95.7	95.2	100.0	103.3	106.7
Gypsum products....................	105.2	154.5	154.0	170.8	177.6	208.0	201.4	156.4	168.5
Insulation materials..................	108.4	118.8	118.9	117.7	119.7	131.7	128.6	127.6	128.4
Paving mixtures and blocks..............	101.2	105.8	107.6	113.2	112.5	112.9	130.4	134.6	136.2

NA Not available. [1] June 1982=100. [2] December 1982=100. [3] June 1985=100. [4] Recessed nonair. [5] December 1983=100.

Source: U.S. Bureau of Labor Statistics, Producer Price Indexes, monthly and annual. See Internet site <http://www.bls.gov/ppi/home.htm>.

No. 934. Price and Cost Indexes for Construction: 1980 to 2002

[1996=100. Excludes Alaska and Hawaii. Indexes of certain of these sources are published on bases different from those shown here]

Name of index	1980	1985	1990	1995	1998	1999	2000	2001	2002
U.S. Census Bureau Composite:									
Fixed-weighted [1]	59.3	71.8	85.5	97.7	106.0	110.3	115.3	120.2	122.7
Implicit price deflator [2]	59.0	71.1	85.0	97.8	106.1	110.4	115.4	119.6	122.6
U.S. Census Bureau houses under construction: [3]									
Fixed-weighted	58.0	69.8	84.6	98.1	105.6	110.4	115.4	121.2	124.4
Price deflator	57.0	68.3	83.4	98.1	105.6	110.4	115.5	121.3	124.4
Federal Highway Administration, composite [4]	79.7	83.6	88.9	99.8	105.2	111.9	119.3	118.7	121.2
Bureau of Reclamation composite [5]	62	75	85	98	105	107	111	112	114
Turner Construction Co.: Building construction [6]	54	74	87	97	109	113	118	121	123
Engineering News-Record: [7]									
Buildings	60.6	75.8	84.4	97.1	105.8	107.9	110.5	111.6	113.1
Construction	57.6	74.6	84.2	97.3	105.3	107.8	110.7	112.7	116.3
Handy-Whitman public utility: [8]									
Buildings	66	76	85	97	104	107	110	114	116
Electric [9]	60	74	86	98	104	105	109	113	116
Gas	60	75	86	99	104	107	111	114	116
Water [10]	64	76	85	98	104	107	112	116	120
C. A. Turner Telephone Plant [11]	79	77	87	96	102	101	103	106	108

[1] Weighted average of the various indexes used to deflate the Construction Put in Place series. In calculating the index, the weights (i.e., the composition of current dollar estimates in 1996 by category) are held constant. [2] Derived ratio of total current to constant dollar Construction Put in Place (multiplied by 100). [3] Excludes value of site. [4] Based on average contract unit bid prices for composite mile (involving specific average amounts of excavation, paving, reinforcing steel, structural steel, and structural concrete). [5] Derived from the four quarterly indexes which are weighted averages of costs of labor, materials, and equipment for the construction of dams and reclamation projects. [6] Based on firm's cost experience with respect to labor rates, materials prices, competitive conditions, efficiency of plant and management, and productivity. [7] Building construction index computed on the basis of a hypothetical unit of construction requiring 6 bbl. of portland cement, 1,088 M bd. ft. of 2"x4" lumber, 2,500 lb. of structural steel, and 68.38 hours of skilled labor. General construction index based on same materials components combined with 200 hours of common labor. [8] Based on data covering public utility construction costs in six geographic regions. Covers skilled and common labor. [9] As derived by U.S. Census Bureau. Covers steam generation plants only. [10] As derived by U.S. Census Bureau. Reflects costs for structures and improvements at water pumping and treatment plants. [11] Computed by the Census Bureau by averaging the weighted component indexes published for six geographic regions.

Source: U.S. Census Bureau, Current Construction Reports, Series C30, *Value of Construction Put in Place*. See Internet site <http://www.census.gov/const/C30/annindex.pdf>. Also in U.S. International Trade Administration, *Construction Review*, quarterly.

No. 935. Value of New Construction Put in Place: 1964 to 2002

[In millions of dollars (75,097 represents $75,097,000,000). Represents value of construction put in place during year; differs from building permit and construction contract data in timing and coverage. Includes installed cost of normal building service equipment and selected types of industrial production equipment (largely site fabricated). Excludes cost of shipbuilding, land, and most types of machinery and equipment. For methodology, see Appendix III]

Year	Current dollars					Constant (1996) dollars				
		Private					Private			
	Total	Total [1]	Residential buildings	Nonresidential buildings	Public	Total	Total [1]	Residential buildings	Nonresidential buildings	Public
1964	75,097	54,893	30,526	17,385	20,203	405,864	300,372	169,635	96,497	105,492
1970	105,890	77,982	35,863	28,171	27,908	429,041	321,940	155,113	115,372	107,101
1975	152,635	109,342	51,581	35,409	43,293	404,132	298,555	149,410	96,407	105,577
1980	273,936	210,290	100,381	72,480	63,646	464,144	364,101	175,822	129,275	100,043
1982	279,332	216,268	84,676	92,690	63,064	423,729	333,894	134,605	145,054	89,835
1983	311,887	248,437	125,833	87,069	63,450	465,073	375,193	195,028	131,289	89,880
1984	370,190	299,952	155,015	107,680	70,238	534,557	437,325	231,396	155,261	97,232
1985	403,416	325,601	160,520	127,466	77,815	567,689	463,854	234,955	178,925	103,835
1986	433,454	348,872	190,677	120,917	84,582	588,804	479,623	266,431	163,740	109,182
1987	446,643	355,994	199,652	123,247	90,648	585,103	470,575	267,063	160,363	114,528
1988	462,012	367,277	204,496	130,854	94,735	583,396	467,599	263,385	164,191	115,797
1989	477,502	379,328	204,255	139,953	98,174	579,583	463,541	252,745	169,173	116,042
1990	476,778	369,300	191,103	143,506	107,478	560,802	436,999	228,943	167,896	123,803
1991	432,592	322,483	166,251	116,570	110,109	503,711	378,245	197,526	135,389	125,467
1992	463,661	347,814	199,393	105,646	115,847	533,322	401,567	232,134	120,921	131,755
1993	491,033	375,073	225,067	107,715	115,960	544,285	415,565	249,763	118,988	128,720
1994	539,193	418,999	258,561	120,193	120,193	574,256	445,414	274,966	127,576	128,842
1995	557,818	427,885	247,351	138,015	129,933	570,188	436,738	251,953	141,218	133,450
1996	615,900	476,638	281,115	155,858	139,263	615,797	476,650	281,207	155,813	139,147
1997	653,429	502,734	289,014	173,875	150,695	632,680	487,197	280,720	167,610	145,483
1998	705,685	551,383	314,607	190,710	154,302	665,156	519,859	297,960	177,644	145,297
1999	766,065	596,331	350,562	193,935	169,732	694,326	540,220	317,236	173,429	154,106
2000	828,768	642,633	374,457	208,241	186,135	718,708	557,186	323,977	178,074	161,523
2001	852,553	652,496	388,324	202,334	200,057	709,233	541,110	318,803	166,852	168,123
2002	860,923	650,495	421,521	167,084	210,428	701,943	528,844	338,852	135,764	173,099

[1] Includes other types of private construction, not shown separately.

Source: U.S. Census Bureau, Current Construction Reports, Series C30, *Value of Construction, Put in Place*, monthly. See Internet site <http://www.census.gov/ftp/pub/const/www/c30index.html>.

No. 936. Value of New Construction Put in Place by Type: 1990 to 2002

[In millions of dollars (476,778 represents $476,778,000,000). Represents value of construction put in place during year; differs from building permit and construction contract data in timing and coverage. Includes installed cost of normal building service equipment and selected types of industrial production equipment (largely site fabricated). Excludes cost of shipbuilding, land, and most types of machinery and equipment. For methodology, see Appendix III]

Type of construction	Current dollars					Constant (1996) dollars				
	1990	1995	2000	2001	2002	1990	1995	2000	2001	2002
Total new construction.	476,778	557,818	828,768	852,553	860,923	560,802	570,188	718,708	709,233	701,943
Private construction	369,300	427,885	642,633	652,496	650,495	436,999	436,738	557,186	541,110	528,844
Residential buildings	191,103	247,351	374,457	388,324	421,521	228,943	251,953	323,977	318,803	338,852
New housing units	132,137	171,404	265,047	279,391	298,450	158,319	174,585	229,324	229,426	239,908
1 unit	112,886	153,515	236,788	249,086	265,889	135,253	156,363	204,867	204,522	213,727
2 or more units	19,250	17,889	28,259	30,305	32,561	23,066	18,222	24,457	24,903	26,182
Improvements	58,966	75,947	109,410	108,933	123,071	70,625	77,368	94,653	89,377	98,944
Nonresidential buildings . . .	143,506	138,015	208,241	202,334	167,084	167,896	141,218	178,074	166,852	135,764
Industrial	33,636	35,498	31,801	29,521	16,580	39,350	36,322	27,194	24,358	13,475
Office	35,055	25,613	55,605	52,260	37,578	41,027	26,218	47,534	43,126	30,536
Hotels, motels.	10,679	7,112	16,293	14,490	10,285	12,497	7,274	13,944	11,950	8,359
Other commercial	40,047	42,654	60,381	60,760	55,879	46,847	43,636	51,635	50,077	45,404
Religious	3,566	4,326	8,019	8,385	8,217	4,169	4,426	6,858	6,908	6,676
Educational	4,616	5,493	11,375	12,591	12,841	5,398	5,621	9,726	10,371	10,434
Hospital and institutional .	10,868	11,248	14,434	14,910	17,434	12,710	11,512	12,342	12,295	14,161
Miscellaneous [1]	5,040	6,071	10,332	9,418	8,269	5,897	6,209	8,842	7,766	6,719
Farm nonresidential	2,801	3,014	5,988	5,135	5,040	3,276	3,084	5,116	4,230	4,095
Public utilities	28,933	36,084	50,994	53,849	54,370	33,505	36,965	47,400	48,752	48,036
Telecommunications	9,803	11,093	18,799	19,569	18,024	11,346	11,556	18,255	18,473	16,757
Other public utilities	19,130	24,991	32,195	34,280	36,346	22,159	25,409	29,145	30,280	31,280
Railroads	2,600	3,509	4,263	4,456	4,864	2,969	3,609	3,782	3,861	4,108
Electric light and power	11,299	14,274	22,038	23,803	24,789	13,083	14,535	20,090	21,120	21,396
Gas	4,820	6,279	4,891	5,078	5,500	5,627	6,329	4,377	4,468	4,747
Petroleum pipelines . .	411	929	1,003	943	1,193	480	936	897	830	1,029
All other private [2]	2,957	3,420	2,954	2,853	2,481	3,379	3,518	2,619	2,473	2,096
Public construction	107,478	129,933	186,135	200,057	210,428	123,803	133,450	161,523	168,123	173,099
Buildings	43,615	57,754	90,005	94,407	102,071	51,117	59,074	77,003	77,774	82,876
Housing and redevelopment	3,808	4,698	4,927	5,096	5,507	4,560	4,786	4,263	4,186	4,427
Industrial	1,434	1,508	1,158	1,556	1,906	1,677	1,544	991	1,282	1,548
Educational	16,055	25,783	45,643	50,035	56,154	18,772	26,374	39,023	41,207	45,623
Hospital	2,860	4,236	4,785	4,243	4,932	3,348	4,335	4,092	3,497	4,006
Other [3]	19,458	21,528	33,494	33,477	33,572	22,760	22,034	28,635	27,602	27,273
Highways and streets	32,105	37,616	52,992	58,942	59,613	35,879	38,952	45,992	49,549	48,677
Military facilities	2,665	3,011	2,441	2,842	2,923	3,050	3,102	2,105	2,365	2,382
Conservation and development	4,686	6,308	6,381	7,269	7,937	5,482	6,443	5,779	6,503	6,938
Sewer systems	10,276	8,420	10,332	10,339	11,072	12,010	8,600	9,363	9,249	9,676
Water supply facilities	4,909	4,709	7,028	8,358	8,528	5,730	4,809	6,247	7,173	7,107
Miscellaneous public [4] . . .	9,223	12,116	16,955	17,899	18,284	10,535	12,468	15,033	15,511	15,443

[1] Includes amusement and recreational buildings, bus and airline terminals, animal hospitals and shelters, etc. [2] Includes privately owned streets and bridges, parking areas, sewer and water facilities, parks and playgrounds, golf courses, airfields, etc. [3] Includes general administrative buildings, prisons, police and fire stations, courthouses, civic centers, passenger terminals, space facilities, postal facilities, etc. [4] Includes open amusement and recreational facilities, power generating facilities, transit systems, airfields, open parking facilities, etc.

Source: U.S. Census Bureau, Current Construction Reports, Series C30, *Value of Construction, Put in Place*, monthly. See Internet site <http://www.census.gov/ftp/pub/const/www/c30index.html>.

No. 937. Value of Private Construction Put in Place: 1993 to 2002

[In millions of dollars (375,073 represents $375,073,000,000). Represents value of construction put in place during year; differs from building permit and construction contract data in timing and coverage. Data are not directly comparable to Tables 935 and 936 due to a new classification system which bases project types on their end usage instead of building/nonbuilding and ownership types. See Appendix III]

Type of construction	1993	1995	1996	1997	1998	1999	2000	2001	2002 [1]
Total construction [2]	375,073	427,885	476,638	502,734	551,383	596,331	642,633	652,496	650,495
Residential	225,067	247,351	281,115	289,014	314,607	350,562	374,457	388,324	421,521
New single family	140,123	153,515	170,790	175,179	199,409	223,837	236,788	249,086	265,889
New multifamily	10,788	17,889	20,324	22,883	24,574	27,434	28,259	30,305	32,561
Improvements	74,156	75,947	90,002	90,951	90,624	99,290	109,410	108,933	123,071
Lodging	4,590	7,131	10,914	12,898	14,818	15,955	16,304	14,519	10,292
Office	[2]19,999	22,996	26,530	32,813	40,394	45,052	52,407	49,745	35,149
General	17,314	20,569	23,216	29,301	37,615	41,745	49,637	47,136	32,184
Financial	2,604	2,339	3,231	3,157	2,636	3,125	2,689	2,586	2,881
Commercial [2]	34,396	44,096	49,381	53,088	55,681	59,376	64,055	63,606	58,231
Automotive [2]	2,077	4,191	5,251	5,736	5,270	5,904	5,967	5,650	5,809
Sales	473	883	1,250	1,743	1,542	1,573	1,629	2,014	2,243
Service/parts	1,099	2,448	2,993	3,213	2,527	3,270	3,009	2,394	2,366
Parking	421	860	1,008	781	1,200	1,062	1,330	1,242	1,201
Food/beverage [2]	6,201	7,169	7,478	8,566	9,118	8,277	8,786	8,765	7,929
Food	2,766	3,062	3,776	4,658	4,665	4,610	4,792	4,300	4,242
Dining/drinking	2,108	3,408	2,958	3,058	3,817	2,874	2,935	3,441	2,919
Fast food	1,243	699	744	850	636	793	1,058	1,024	768
Multiretail [2]	11,483	11,976	13,331	12,157	13,254	15,234	14,911	16,373	15,460
General merchandise	3,787	5,339	5,159	4,083	3,778	4,668	5,100	5,066	5,958
Shopping center	4,942	4,086	5,496	5,694	6,045	7,187	6,803	7,769	6,513
Shopping mall	1,973	2,175	2,189	1,949	2,917	2,873	2,523	2,701	2,122
Other commercial [2]	5,934	8,432	8,202	10,203	11,050	11,179	13,537	11,945	11,971
Drug store	349	536	750	1,007	1,409	1,645	1,682	1,185	1,641
Building supply store	850	1,372	1,201	1,323	1,742	1,588	2,592	3,016	2,499
Other stores	4,264	5,653	5,327	7,090	7,025	6,849	8,136	6,995	7,000
Warehouse	5,181	9,299	11,458	12,563	12,698	13,702	14,822	15,691	11,911
General commercial	5,079	8,944	10,849	11,501	11,732	12,756	13,511	14,440	10,909
Farm	3,392	3,014	3,658	3,815	4,284	5,059	5,988	5,135	5,040
Health care	14,939	15,259	15,420	17,390	17,737	18,388	19,455	19,506	22,157
Hospital	9,754	8,807	8,348	9,968	9,469	9,491	10,183	11,113	13,704
Medical building	2,840	4,064	3,728	4,001	4,070	4,910	5,066	4,638	4,868
Special care	2,345	2,388	3,344	3,421	4,197	3,987	4,206	3,555	3,532
Educational [2]	4,814	5,699	6,985	8,802	9,829	9,756	11,683	12,846	13,036
Preschool	169	326	398	531	619	663	770	874	603
Primary/secondary	725	1,245	1,560	2,032	2,174	2,420	2,948	3,536	3,474
Higher education [2]	3,240	3,055	3,619	4,327	4,945	5,204	6,333	6,597	6,927
Instructional	1,806	1,712	2,028	1,991	2,469	2,258	3,058	3,210	3,575
Dormitory	521	483	573	789	955	1,274	1,356	1,555	1,482
Sports/recreation	220	192	260	475	403	515	645	755	919
Other educational	549	817	1,042	1,714	1,798	1,232	1,318	1,421	1,639
Gallery/museum	357	571	662	1,107	1,127	778	920	990	1,296
Religious [2]	3,894	4,348	4,537	5,782	6,604	7,371	8,030	8,393	8,219
House of worship	2,804	2,951	3,211	3,844	4,549	5,057	5,656	6,040	5,938
Other religious	1,075	1,389	1,318	1,935	2,054	2,314	2,347	2,330	2,279
Auxiliary building	382	619	620	874	992	1,252	1,280	1,247	1,337
Public safety	215	185	321	569	586	465	423	274	246
Amusement and recreation [2]	4,601	5,886	7,016	8,537	8,589	9,550	8,768	7,828	7,402
Theme/amusement park	478	563	727	723	866	919	747	462	218
Sports	534	910	1,193	1,333	1,136	1,495	1,068	1,067	1,350
Fitness	509	637	622	801	889	1,137	1,152	1,294	1,324
Performance/meeting center	274	365	539	628	603	546	732	977	910
Social center	1,488	1,558	1,597	1,979	2,093	2,006	2,368	2,337	2,280
Movie theater/studio	331	848	1,271	2,199	2,441	2,376	1,461	792	574
Transportation [2]	4,680	4,759	5,820	6,208	7,290	6,525	6,879	7,058	7,016
Air	1,026	666	871	901	1,093	1,106	1,804	1,993	1,290
Land	3,509	4,008	4,794	5,183	6,112	5,164	4,907	4,883	5,593
Railroad	3,108	3,509	4,398	4,922	5,736	4,670	4,263	4,456	4,864
Communication	9,751	11,112	11,824	12,452	12,473	18,405	18,799	19,596	18,059
Power	23,554	22,006	17,413	16,362	21,078	21,136	28,008	30,032	31,729
Electricity	16,260	14,274	11,256	11,325	12,381	14,585	22,038	23,803	24,789
Gas	5,645	6,279	4,722	4,006	7,372	4,918	4,891	5,078	5,500
Oil	986	929	1,015	969	1,265	1,489	1,003	943	1,193
Sewage and waste disposal	373	576	637	468	339	516	508	402	255
Water supply	426	670	468	448	543	413	714	563	416
Manufacturing [2]	23,371	35,364	38,101	37,624	40,482	32,631	31,800	29,529	16,606
Food/beverage/tobacco	2,031	4,525	4,294	3,957	3,538	3,383	3,374	3,193	2,087
Textile/apparel/leather & allied	773	824	743	584	712	456	350	240	210
Wood	279	616	689	522	492	427	412	266	330
Paper	1,886	1,448	1,711	1,548	1,232	838	628	990	423
Print/publishing	539	1,197	993	930	1,104	856	719	959	546
Petroleum/coal	2,729	4,741	2,348	1,186	1,064	927	1,069	907	522
Chemical	4,937	5,531	5,445	6,034	8,264	6,181	3,223	3,800	4,078
Plastic/rubber	1,808	1,475	1,632	1,959	2,137	2,222	1,398	1,077	563
Nonmetallic mineral	160	856	1,220	1,004	1,481	1,188	1,603	1,734	402
Primary metal	834	2,533	2,244	2,802	2,603	1,992	1,677	611	229
Fabricated metal	442	808	1,585	2,162	2,036	1,891	1,823	1,128	606
Machinery	352	1,275	1,169	1,106	1,257	966	731	674	580
Computer/electronic/electrical	2,158	6,332	8,945	7,537	7,557	4,415	5,386	4,734	1,313
Transportation equipment	2,289	2,382	2,948	3,453	3,497	3,418	5,347	5,385	2,817
Furniture	121	213	308	167	296	282	348	182	111

[1] Preliminary. [2] Includes other types of construction, not shown separately.

Source: U.S. Census Bureau, "Construction Spending," Internet site <http://www.census.gov/const/www/c30index.html>.

No. 938. Value of State and Local Government Construction Put in Place: 1993 to 2002

[In millions of dollars (101,535 represents $101,535,000,000). See headnote, Table 937]

Type of construction	1993	1995	1996	1997	1998	1999	2000	2001	2002 [1]
Total construction [2]	101,535	114,181	123,938	136,608	139,984	155,706	171,969	184,976	194,115
Residential	3,686	4,043	4,220	4,336	4,340	4,603	4,246	4,568	4,592
Multifamily	3,441	3,976	4,144	4,238	4,242	4,584	4,221	4,498	4,491
Office	3,192	3,914	4,404	4,619	4,605	4,521	6,300	6,793	7,446
Commercial [2]	1,119	1,329	1,724	2,227	1,993	2,519	2,562	3,011	2,789
Automotive	619	965	1,257	1,553	1,603	1,915	1,731	2,341	1,923
Parking	430	794	1,020	1,425	1,549	1,703	1,607	2,323	1,899
Warehouse	252	231	280	295	258	342	468	375	359
Health care	2,676	3,156	3,442	3,501	2,884	3,166	3,973	3,590	4,141
Hospital	1,431	1,960	2,108	2,498	1,980	2,220	2,735	2,593	3,049
Medical building	751	801	937	657	515	494	689	594	582
Special care	495	395	396	345	389	452	549	403	511
Educational [2]	19,227	25,743	28,603	33,758	35,015	41,117	45,713	50,001	56,091
Primary/secondary [2]	12,781	17,545	20,009	23,853	26,064	30,494	32,960	34,718	39,555
Elementary	4,533	5,242	6,301	8,015	9,492	10,314	11,965	13,351	14,224
Middle/junior high	2,789	3,745	3,685	3,988	3,930	5,992	5,688	6,556	7,930
High	3,170	4,833	6,130	6,687	7,627	11,053	13,016	13,325	16,208
Higher education [2]	5,294	6,883	7,311	8,198	7,721	8,914	10,504	12,655	13,507
Instructional	3,311	4,277	4,746	4,459	4,307	5,272	6,175	7,456	7,578
Parking	91	158	169	262	331	369	499	532	411
Administration	107	128	91	189	179	270	287	188	429
Dormitory	346	324	396	388	548	802	1,053	1,354	1,527
Library	252	300	439	695	368	327	301	354	418
Student union/cafeteria	104	238	231	405	318	298	314	585	976
Sports/recreation	474	625	538	873	795	767	944	1,218	1,450
Infrastructure	537	788	585	654	780	701	816	790	502
Other educational	929	1,110	1,121	1,250	1,128	1,372	1,606	2,048	2,482
Library/archive	475	704	853	779	566	945	950	1,585	2,000
Public safety [2]	5,226	5,928	6,718	6,668	7,575	7,858	8,204	7,404	6,929
Correctional	4,459	4,854	5,586	5,701	6,588	6,575	6,658	5,987	5,292
Detention	3,964	4,049	4,749	4,786	5,618	5,338	5,470	4,701	3,989
Police/sheriff	495	804	837	916	970	1,237	1,188	1,286	1,304
Other public safety	705	1,025	1,126	967	988	1,284	1,546	1,417	1,637
Fire/rescue	496	652	831	773	795	1,095	1,397	1,212	1,431
Amusement and recreation [2]	4,943	6,142	6,056	6,857	7,666	9,159	10,638	11,166	10,735
Sports	1,398	1,637	1,477	2,311	3,173	3,402	3,202	3,322	2,984
Performance/meeting center	1,517	1,751	2,127	1,629	1,343	1,572	2,928	3,570	3,464
Convention center	1,158	1,224	1,318	938	835	1,099	1,972	2,767	2,537
Social center	883	772	911	961	947	1,399	1,617	1,738	1,601
Neighborhood center	487	581	612	673	622	1,059	1,243	1,294	1,111
Park/camp	916	1,696	1,430	1,874	2,020	2,584	2,699	2,249	2,257
Transportation	8,803	8,967	9,998	9,708	10,197	11,296	14,337	15,150	16,000
Air [2]	5,088	3,855	4,666	4,852	5,594	5,960	7,404	7,477	7,478
Passenger terminal	1,650	1,209	1,656	2,086	2,196	2,217	3,220	2,659	2,743
Runway	2,503	2,176	2,593	2,260	2,563	3,100	3,550	4,128	4,025
Land [2]	2,952	4,009	4,067	3,642	3,823	4,275	5,688	5,977	6,795
Passenger terminal	526	1,147	1,362	1,237	1,222	1,249	1,375	1,490	1,728
Mass transit	1,273	1,734	1,787	1,607	1,548	1,347	1,635	2,371	3,186
Railroad	327	462	402	401	564	1,033	1,618	1,063	597
Water [2]	764	1,103	1,264	1,214	780	1,061	1,245	1,696	1,727
Dock/marina	524	690	898	729	421	657	946	1,218	1,102
Dry dock/marine terminal	101	204	308	477	352	404	258	453	624
Power	3,159	2,879	2,503	3,101	2,495	3,228	3,894	4,121	4,034
Electrical	2,654	2,231	2,225	2,893	2,052	2,538	3,718	3,868	3,558
Distribution	920	733	656	1,650	1,511	1,494	1,480	1,062	1,666
Highway and street [2]	34,353	37,616	39,500	43,017	44,782	49,174	53,062	59,003	59,856
Pavement	26,503	29,164	30,472	32,416	33,180	36,464	39,034	43,002	43,062
Lighting	543	659	796	812	1,180	910	878	1,283	953
Retaining wall	219	187	176	493	711	816	1,132	652	801
Tunnel	393	346	430	539	862	926	918	1,118	709
Bridge	5,961	6,615	6,682	7,299	7,229	8,479	9,565	11,408	12,565
Toll/weigh	170	152	138	219	247	277	331	109	242
Maintenance building	119	53	159	307	362	354	302	425	315
Rest facility/streetscape	27	167	464	722	838	940	901	1,006	1,208
Sewage and waste disposal [2]	8,875	8,419	9,801	10,515	9,943	10,524	10,330	10,340	11,073
Sewage/dry waste [2]	5,237	4,825	6,420	6,830	6,589	7,082	6,891	6,602	7,222
Plant	2,076	1,641	2,173	1,969	1,925	2,178	2,041	1,756	1,933
Line/pump station	2,612	2,960	4,001	4,639	4,422	4,612	4,667	4,656	5,145
Waste water	3,480	3,522	3,346	3,664	3,317	3,436	3,440	3,738	3,851
Plant	2,714	2,467	2,211	2,680	2,276	2,613	2,381	2,786	3,054
Line/drain	766	1,055	1,135	984	1,041	823	1,059	952	797
Water supply [2]	5,089	4,713	5,618	6,493	6,678	6,967	7,027	8,359	8,528
Plant	1,520	1,204	1,372	1,664	1,912	2,154	2,263	2,972	2,767
Well	118	212	260	179	247	254	279	288	400
Line	2,550	2,516	2,841	3,353	3,106	3,089	3,424	3,870	3,819
Pump station	193	286	437	349	418	571	461	500	629
Reservoir	317	208	409	514	429	409	196	299	337
Tank/tower	262	246	298	433	565	491	404	430	576
Conservation and development [2]	1,052	1,265	1,191	1,503	1,444	1,346	1,313	1,318	1,215
Dam/levee	149	329	349	631	597	525	428	299	330
Breakwater/jetty	320	358	472	360	456	382	379	599	483
Dredging	105	151	83	161	121	177	199	139	101

[1] Preliminary. [2] Includes other types of construction, not shown separately.
Source: U.S. Census Bureau, "Construction Spending," Internet site <http://www.census.gov/const/www/c30index.html>.

No. 939. Construction Contracts—Value of Construction and Floor Space of Buildings by Class of Construction: 1980 to 2002

[151.8 represents $151,800,000,000. Building construction includes new structures and additions; nonbuilding construction includes major alterations to existing structures which affect only valuation, since no additional floor area is created by "alteration"]

Year	Residential buildings Total	Nonresidential buildings Total	Commercial[1]	Manufacturing	Educational[2]	Health	Public buildings	Religious	Social and recreational	Miscellaneous	Nonbuilding construction
VALUE (bil. dol.)											
1980	151.8	60.4	56.9	27.7	9.2	7.4	5.4	1.6	1.2	2.7	1.7	34.5
1985	235.6	102.1	92.1	54.6	8.1	10.0	7.8	3.1	2.0	4.0	2.5	41.4
1990	246.0	100.9	95.4	44.8	8.4	16.6	9.2	5.7	2.2	5.3	3.1	49.7
1993	271.5	123.9	88.8	34.2	9.0	19.3	10.5	3.9	2.4	6.8	2.6	58.9
1994	296.7	133.6	101.5	40.8	11.2	21.0	10.5	6.1	2.5	6.5	3.0	61.6
1995	306.5	127.9	114.2	46.6	13.8	22.9	10.8	6.3	2.8	7.1	3.8	64.4
1996	332.0	146.5	120.5	51.9	13.1	23.0	11.1	6.3	2.9	8.1	4.1	65.1
1997	362.4	153.6	138.9	59.8	14.0	28.4	11.9	7.0	3.8	10.0	4.0	69.8
1998	405.6	179.8	154.5	74.0	12.1	30.1	12.9	6.6	4.3	10.8	3.6	71.3
1999	447.2	195.0	168.7	77.2	11.3	37.1	13.6	8.2	4.5	11.6	5.1	83.5
2000	473.4	208.3	173.6	81.1	8.9	40.9	12.4	7.5	4.6	13.8	4.4	91.4
2001	495.8	219.5	169.1	70.3	8.1	47.0	14.3	7.8	4.8	12.0	4.8	107.2
2002	502.0	247.5	154.3	59.1	5.2	45.3	16.1	7.4	5.1	11.3	4.6	100.2
FLOOR SPACE (mil. sq. ft.)											
1980	3,102	1,839	1,263	738	220	103	55	18	28	49	52	(X)
1985	3,853	2,324	1,529	1,039	165	111	73	28	32	44	38	(X)
1990	3,020	1,817	1,203	694	128	152	69	47	29	51	32	(X)
1993	3,062	2,091	971	481	110	165	75	30	30	51	29	(X)
1994	3,411	2,267	1,144	600	143	172	72	45	30	51	31	(X)
1995	3,454	2,172	1,281	700	163	186	70	40	33	56	33	(X)
1996	3,776	2,479	1,297	723	155	177	77	41	32	60	33	(X)
1997	4,126	2,586	1,540	855	191	204	89	48	42	77	35	(X)
1998	4,812	3,015	1,797	1,107	166	219	96	42	47	85	34	(X)
1999	5,092	3,253	1,839	1,115	141	261	98	49	48	87	39	(X)
2000	4,986	3,113	1,872	1,184	111	273	88	44	49	94	29	(X)
2001	4,827	3,157	1,670	988	93	295	91	44	50	81	27	(X)
2002	4,767	3,340	1,427	802	66	277	97	37	52	71	25	(X)

X Not applicable. [1] Includes nonindustrial warehouses. [2] Includes science.

Source: McGraw-Hill Construction Dodge, a Division of the McGraw-Hill Companies, New York, NY (copyright).

No. 940. Construction Contracts—Value by State: 1990 to 2002

[In millions of dollars (246,022 represents $246,022,000,000). Represents value of construction in states in which work was actually done. See headnote, Table 939]

State	1990	1995	2002 Total[1]	2002 Residential	2002 Nonresidential	State	1990	1995	2002 Total[1]	2002 Residential	2002 Nonresidential
U.S.	246,022	306,527	502,015	247,518	154,255	MO	3,833	6,438	8,638	4,190	2,614
AL	2,939	4,308	7,062	2,685	2,444	MT	332	865	933	351	232
AK	1,919	1,660	2,000	462	754	NE	1,318	1,694	3,336	1,313	1,275
AZ	4,553	8,784	14,427	9,517	3,350	NV	3,334	5,555	8,111	4,466	2,017
AR	1,438	2,903	3,599	1,559	1,041	NH	1,021	1,039	2,423	1,256	839
CA	37,318	29,045	57,545	29,749	16,230	NJ	6,141	6,454	11,407	3,964	4,886
CO	3,235	6,476	12,199	7,259	2,778	NM	1,124	2,108	2,862	1,250	898
CT	3,058	3,124	4,817	2,002	2,087	NY	14,137	13,380	24,330	6,953	10,135
DE	787	871	1,433	749	484	NC	6,614	10,599	17,546	11,009	4,356
DC	795	656	2,461	431	1,663	ND	506	791	994	294	257
FL	16,975	21,453	42,308	25,772	10,477	OH	9,885	12,430	17,242	7,565	5,714
GA	7,120	12,156	19,577	10,734	5,440	OK	2,164	2,968	4,552	2,017	1,654
HI	2,831	2,273	1,749	951	388	OR	3,101	5,451	6,402	3,723	1,742
ID	986	1,864	2,618	1,717	543	PA	10,117	9,348	16,168	5,680	5,513
IL	10,796	11,744	20,729	8,867	7,135	RI	594	465	1,297	411	431
IN	6,350	7,896	11,317	5,904	3,483	SC	3,664	4,580	8,478	4,753	2,121
IA	2,034	2,883	4,801	1,721	1,614	SD	468	706	1,281	516	302
KS	2,193	3,264	4,959	2,085	1,625	TN	4,388	7,167	9,335	5,122	2,783
KY	3,174	4,464	6,828	2,849	2,138	TX	13,197	23,022	41,631	21,503	12,735
LA	3,191	4,354	5,241	2,237	1,755	UT	1,884	4,218	5,189	2,641	1,432
ME	897	1,076	1,825	955	554	VT	515	484	945	406	390
MD	6,056	6,299	8,769	4,192	3,344	VA	7,180	8,794	13,921	7,441	4,288
MA	5,135	7,411	9,932	3,590	4,241	WA	6,185	7,334	10,872	5,817	3,465
MI	7,646	9,947	13,115	6,691	4,144	WV	1,253	1,215	1,872	565	460
MN	4,953	5,607	9,181	5,143	2,413	WI	4,654	5,652	8,908	4,782	2,305
MS	1,569	2,718	3,448	1,364	1,054	WY	462	532	1,071	345	235

[1] Includes nonbuilding construction, not shown separately.

Source: McGraw-Hill Construction Dodge, a Division of the McGraw-Hill Companies, New York, NY, (copyright).

No. 941. New Privately-Owned Housing Units Authorized by State: 2000 and 2002

[1,592.3 represents 1,592,300. Based on about 19,000 places in United States having building permit systems]

State	Housing units (1,000) 2000	Housing units (1,000) 2002 Total	Housing units (1,000) 2002 1 unit	Valuation (mil. dol.) 2000	Valuation (mil. dol.) 2002 Total	Valuation (mil. dol.) 2002 1 unit	State	Housing units (1,000) 2000	Housing units (1,000) 2002 Total	Housing units (1,000) 2002 1 unit	Valuation (mil. dol.) 2000	Valuation (mil. dol.) 2002 Total	Valuation (mil. dol.) 2002 1 unit
U.S.	1,592.3	1,747.7	1,332.6	185,744	219,189	190,433	MO...	24.3	28.3	20.7	2,569	3,187	2,703
AL...	17.4	18.4	15.1	1,718	1,965	1,822	MT...	2.6	3.6	2.1	235	339	253
AK...	2.1	3.0	1.7	333	469	312	NE...	9.1	9.3	7.2	830	1,025	910
AZ...	61.5	66.0	55.8	7,158	8,575	7,939	NV...	32.3	35.6	27.6	3,312	4,120	3,593
AR...	9.2	12.4	8.0	859	1,199	1,016	NH...	6.7	8.7	6.8	937	1,203	1,068
CA...	145.6	159.6	123.0	23,344	26,863	23,588	NJ...	34.6	30.4	22.4	3,376	3,430	2,852
CO...	54.6	47.9	35.0	6,822	6,357	5,416	NM...	8.9	12.1	10.4	1,073	1,445	1,372
CT...	9.4	9.7	8.5	1,425	1,584	1,515	NY...	44.1	49.1	25.6	4,992	5,916	4,070
DE...	4.6	6.3	6.1	414	703	693	NC...	78.4	79.8	66.4	8,643	9,882	9,084
DC...	0.8	1.6	0.4	54	121	48	ND...	2.1	3.3	1.8	190	310	234
FL...	155.3	185.4	128.7	17,462	22,468	17,913	OH...	49.7	51.2	39.8	6,154	6,838	6,213
GA...	91.8	97.5	75.5	8,722	10,046	8,830	OK...	11.1	13.0	11.2	1,204	1,588	1,475
HI...	4.9	5.9	4.6	823	1,121	957	OR...	19.9	22.2	17.4	2,533	3,347	2,962
ID...	10.9	13.5	10.8	1,359	1,626	1,486	PA...	41.1	45.1	38.7	4,616	5,573	5,138
IL...	51.9	61.0	42.5	6,528	8,546	6,879	RI...	2.6	2.8	2.2	296	344	316
IN...	37.9	39.6	30.8	4,414	4,980	4,480	SC...	32.8	34.1	28.6	3,533	4,102	3,723
IA...	12.5	14.8	10.0	1,333	1,693	1,377	SD...	4.2	4.8	3.8	369	464	413
KS...	12.5	13.0	10.3	1,397	1,628	1,461	TN...	32.2	34.3	29.1	3,378	3,961	3,630
KY...	18.5	19.5	16.3	1,767	2,081	1,926	TX...	141.2	165.0	122.6	15,418	17,557	15,497
LA...	14.7	18.4	15.2	1,553	1,942	1,786	UT...	17.6	19.3	15.7	2,138	2,456	2,158
ME...	6.2	7.2	6.4	723	899	838	VT...	2.5	3.1	2.5	319	451	414
MD...	30.4	29.3	24.0	3,232	3,518	3,196	VA...	48.4	59.4	45.7	5,052	6,589	5,893
MA...	18.0	17.5	13.6	2,741	2,788	2,461	WA...	39.0	40.2	30.2	4,426	5,473	4,665
MI...	52.5	50.0	41.7	6,256	6,372	5,789	WV...	3.8	4.9	4.5	360	560	541
MN...	32.8	39.0	28.6	4,204	5,369	4,363	WI...	34.2	38.2	26.0	3,917	4,758	3,925
MS...	11.3	11.3	8.9	918	1,055	949	WY...	1.6	2.0	1.8	314	305	290

Source: U.S. Census Bureau, Construction Reports, Series C40, *Building Permits*, monthly; publication discontinued in 2001. See Internet site <http://www.census.gov/ftp/pub/const/www/newresconstindex.html> and *New Residential Construction*, monthly.

No. 942. New Privately-Owned Housing Units Started—Selected Characteristics: 1970 to 2002

[In thousands (1,434 represents 1,434,000). For composition of regions, see map, inside front cover]

Year	Total units	Structures with— One unit	Structures with— 2 to 4 units	Structures with— 5 or more units	Region Northeast	Region Midwest	Region South	Region West	Units for sale Total	Units for sale Single-family	Units for sale Multi-family
1970	1,434	813	85	536	218	294	612	311	(NA)	(NA)	(NA)
1975	1,160	892	64	204	149	294	442	275	576	531	45
1976	1,538	1,162	86	289	169	400	569	400	768	705	63
1977	1,987	1,451	122	414	202	465	783	538	994	904	90
1978	2,020	1,433	125	462	200	451	824	545	1,032	901	131
1979	1,745	1,194	122	429	178	349	748	470	915	742	173
1980	1,292	852	110	331	125	218	643	306	689	526	163
1981	1,084	705	91	288	117	165	562	240	584	426	158
1982	1,062	663	80	320	117	149	591	205	549	409	140
1983	1,703	1,068	113	522	168	218	935	382	923	713	210
1984	1,750	1,084	121	544	204	243	866	436	934	728	206
1985	1,742	1,072	93	576	252	240	782	468	867	713	154
1986	1,805	1,179	84	542	294	296	733	483	925	782	143
1987	1,621	1,146	65	409	269	298	634	420	862	732	130
1988	1,488	1,081	59	348	235	274	575	404	808	709	99
1989	1,376	1,003	55	318	179	266	536	396	735	648	87
1990	1,193	895	37	260	131	253	479	329	585	529	56
1991	1,014	840	36	138	113	233	414	254	531	490	41
1992	1,200	1,030	31	139	127	288	497	288	659	618	41
1993	1,288	1,126	29	133	126	298	562	302	760	716	44
1994	1,457	1,198	35	224	138	329	639	351	815	763	52
1995	1,354	1,076	34	244	118	290	615	331	763	712	51
1996	1,477	1,161	45	271	132	322	662	361	833	774	59
1997	1,474	1,134	44	296	137	304	670	363	843	784	59
1998	1,617	1,271	43	303	149	331	743	395	941	882	59
1999	1,641	1,302	32	307	156	347	746	392	981	912	69
2000	1,569	1,231	39	299	155	318	714	383	946	871	75
2001	1,603	1,273	37	293	149	330	732	391	990	919	71
2002	1,705	1,359	39	308	158	350	782	416	1,070	999	71

NA Not available.

Source: U.S. Census Bureau, Current Construction Reports, Series C20, *Housing Starts*, monthly; publication discontinued in 2001. See Internet site <http://www.census.gov/const/www/newresconstindex.html> and *New Residential Construction*, monthly.

No. 943. New Privately-Owned Housing Units Started by State: 1997 to 2000

[In thousands of units (1,476 represents 1,476,000)]

State	1997	1998	1999	2000 Total units	2000 Single-family units	State	1997	1998	1999	2000 Total units	2000 Single-family units
U.S.	1,476	1,623	1,660	1,535	1,223	MO	27.9	29.7	29.6	26.0	22.2
AL	21.7	23.7	23.5	21.2	17.7	MT	2.5	2.4	2.5	2.2	1.4
AK	2.5	2.7	2.4	2.1	1.6	NE	9.8	9.8	9.7	8.4	6.2
AZ	58.2	65.2	66.5	60.0	48.2	NV	35.6	36.4	35.1	34.5	25.3
AR	13.0	12.9	13.7	12.5	9.5	NH	5.3	5.7	6.0	6.0	5.6
CA	109.1	123.0	129.9	128.2	99.9	NJ	26.8	29.7	31.9	31.2	25.4
CO	43.8	50.6	49.9	45.9	36.0	NM	10.5	9.4	9.2	8.1	7.2
CT	9.1	11.0	10.6	10.0	8.7	NY	30.5	34.0	36.3	34.9	22.7
DE	4.9	5.5	5.4	5.2	4.8	NC	74.1	81.5	85.8	74.8	59.2
DC	-	0.4	0.7	0.4	0.3	ND	3.2	3.3	3.2	2.7	1.8
FL	135.2	143.9	152.8	148.1	104.9	OH	44.6	47.0	49.8	45.3	37.7
GA	78.6	87.1	88.4	81.5	68.4	OK	13.2	16.3	16.2	15.5	12.4
HI	3.8	3.4	3.7	3.8	3.2	OR	26.6	25.6	24.5	22.2	15.8
ID	10.5	12.0	12.6	11.5	10.1	PA	38.6	40.1	41.1	37.5	32.4
IL	46.5	49.2	52.4	48.1	38.9	RI	2.6	2.7	2.9	2.7	2.5
IN	36.0	40.8	41.8	37.6	32.3	SC	31.2	33.2	35.8	33.9	27.1
IA	11.2	13.7	13.6	13.0	10.7	SD	3.4	3.8	4.1	3.5	2.8
KS	13.6	15.6	16.4	15.2	11.7	TN	37.8	37.4	37.3	33.9	29.9
KY	20.5	23.2	23.2	21.4	17.5	TX	134.0	159.8	155.2	148.4	108.3
LA	16.7	17.8	18.6	15.8	13.4	UT	19.8	21.1	20.5	19.5	16.1
ME	4.6	5.8	5.8	5.8	5.5	VT	1.8	2.2	2.4	2.4	2.1
MD	26.5	31.2	30.3	27.9	23.0	VA	46.9	50.9	53.0	50.2	42.6
MA	16.9	18.2	18.0	17.7	15.5	WA	40.7	44.0	43.7	40.9	28.4
MI	49.0	54.5	55.4	50.9	44.2	WV	5.1	5.1	5.8	5.3	4.1
MN	25.2	30.8	32.9	30.7	26.8	WI	30.7	34.3	35.4	32.0	24.7
MS	12.2	15.0	15.2	12.8	10.1	WY	1.9	2.1	2.0	1.8	1.5

- Represents or rounds to zero.

Source: National Association of Home Builders, Economics Division, Washington, DC. Data provided by the Econometric Forecasting Service.

No. 944. Characteristics of New Privately-Owned One-Family Houses Completed: 1990 to 2002

[Percent distribution (966 represents 966,000). Data are percent distribution of characteristics for all houses completed (includes new houses completed, houses built for sale completed, contractor-built and owner-built houses completed, and houses completed for rent). Percents exclude houses for which characteristics specified were not reported]

Characteristic	1990	1995	2000	2001	2002	Characteristic	1990	1995	2000	2001	2002
Total houses (1,000)	966	1,066	1,242	1,256	1,325	Bedrooms	100	100	100	100	100
						2 or less	15	13	11	11	11
Construction type	100	100	100	100	100	3	57	57	54	52	52
Site built	(NA)	94	94	94	94	4 or more	29	30	35	37	36
Modular	(NA)	3	3	3	3						
Other	(NA)	3	3	2	3	Bathrooms	100	100	100	100	100
						1 1/2 or less	13	11	7	6	6
Exterior wall material	100	100	100	100	100	2	42	41	39	38	39
Brick	18	20	20	20	20	2 1/2 or more	45	48	54	56	55
Wood	39	25	14	11	10						
Stucco	18	16	17	18	19	Heating fuel	100	100	100	100	100
Vinyl siding [1]	(NA)	30	39	39	40	Gas	59	67	70	70	68
Aluminum siding	5	3	1	1	1	Electricity	33	28	27	27	28
Other [1]	20	6	7	10	11	Oil	5	3	3	3	3
						Other	3	1	1	1	1
Floor area	100	100	100	100	100						
Under 1,200 sq. ft	11	10	6	6	5	Heating system	100	100	100	100	100
1,200 to 1,599 sq. ft	22	22	18	18	19	Warm air furnace	65	67	71	71	71
1,600 to 1,999 sq. ft	22	23	23	21	21	Electric heat pump	23	25	23	23	23
2,000 to 2,399 sq. ft	17	17	18	18	18	Other	12	9	6	5	6
2,400 sq. ft. and over	29	28	35	38	37						
Average (sq. ft.)	2,080	2,095	2,266	2,324	2,320	Central air-conditioning	100	100	100	100	100
Median (sq. ft.)	1,905	1,920	2,057	2,103	2,114	With	76	80	85	86	87
						Without	24	20	15	14	13
Number of stories	100	100	100	100	100						
1	46	49	47	46	47	Fireplaces	100	100	100	100	100
2 or more	49	48	52	53	52	No fireplace	34	37	40	42	42
Split level	4	3	1	1	1	1 or more	66	63	60	58	58
Foundation	100	100	100	100	100	Parking facilities	100	100	100	100	100
Full or partial basement	38	39	37	35	34	Garage	82	84	89	89	88
Slab	40	42	46	48	50	Carport	2	2	1	1	1
Crawl space	21	19	17	17	16	No garage or carport	16	14	11	11	10

NA Not available. [1] Prior to 1995 "other" includes vinyl siding.

Source: U.S. Census Bureau and U.S. Dept. of Housing and Urban Development, Current Construction Reports, Series C25, *New One-Family Houses Sold*, monthly, and *Characteristics of New Housing*, annual; publication discontinued in 2001, see Internet site <http://www.census.gov/const/www/charindex.html>.

No. 945. New Privately Owned One-Family Houses Sold by Region and Type of Financing, 1980 to 2002, and by Sales-Price Group, 2002

[In thousands (545 represents 545,000). Based on a national probability sample of monthly interviews with builders or owners of one-family houses for which building permits have been issued or, for nonpermit areas, on which construction has started. For details, see source. For composition of regions, see map inside front cover. See Appendix III]

Year and sales-price group	Total sales	Region				Financing type			
		North-east	Midwest	South	West	Conventional [1]	FHA and VA	Rural Housing Service [2]	Cash
1980	545	50	81	267	145	302	196	14	32
1985	688	112	82	323	170	403	208	11	64
1990	534	71	89	225	149	337	138	10	50
1991	509	57	93	215	144	329	128	9	43
1992	610	65	116	259	170	428	134	7	41
1993	666	60	123	295	188	476	147	6	37
1994	670	61	123	295	191	490	130	9	41
1995	667	55	125	300	187	490	129	9	39
1996	757	74	137	337	209	570	140	9	38
1997	804	78	140	363	223	616	137	6	46
1998	886	81	164	398	243	693	136	9	48
1999	880	76	168	395	242	689	143	6	41
2000	877	71	155	406	244	695	138	4	40
2001	908	66	164	439	239	726	141	2	39
2002	973	65	185	450	273	788	140	4	42
Under $100,000	62	1	10	47	4	(NA)	(NA)	(NA)	(NA)
$100,000 to $149,999	232	8	47	136	41	(NA)	(NA)	(NA)	(NA)
$150,000 to $199,999	237	13	53	117	54	(NA)	(NA)	(NA)	(NA)
$200,000 to $299,999	246	17	48	90	91	(NA)	(NA)	(NA)	(NA)
$300,000 and over	196	26	28	60	83	(NA)	(NA)	(NA)	(NA)

NA Not available. [1] Includes all other types of financing. [2] Prior to 1996, the Farmers Home Administration.
Source: U.S. Census Bureau and U.S. Dept. of Housing and Urban Development, Current Construction Reports, Series C25, Characteristics of New Housing, annual; and New One-Family Houses Sold, monthly; publications discontinued in 2001. See Internet site <http://www.census.gov/const/www/newressalesindex.html> and New Residential Sales, monthly.

No. 946. Median Sales Price of New Privately Owned One-Family Houses Sold by Region: 1980 to 2002

[In dollars. For definition of median, see Guide to Tabular Presentation. See headnote, Table 945]

Year	U.S.	North-east	Mid-west	South	West	Year	U.S.	North-east	Mid-west	South	West
1980	64,600	69,500	63,400	59,600	72,300	1996	140,000	186,000	138,000	126,200	153,900
1985	84,300	103,300	80,300	75,000	92,600	1997	146,000	190,000	149,900	129,600	160,000
1990	122,900	159,000	107,900	99,000	147,500	1998	152,500	200,000	157,500	135,800	163,500
1992	121,500	169,000	115,600	105,500	130,400	1999	161,000	210,500	164,000	145,900	173,700
1993	126,500	162,600	125,000	115,000	135,000	2000	169,000	227,400	169,700	148,000	196,400
1994	130,000	169,000	132,900	116,900	140,400	2001	175,200	246,400	172,600	155,400	213,600
1995	133,900	180,000	134,000	124,500	141,400	2002	187,600	264,300	178,000	163,400	238,500

Source: U.S. Census Bureau and U.S. Dept. of Housing and Urban Development, Current Construction Reports, Series C25, Characteristics of New Housing, annual; and New One-Family Houses Sold, monthly; publications discontinued in 2001. See Internet site <http://www.census.gov/const/www/newressalesindex.html> and New Residential Sales, monthly.

No. 947. New Manufactured (Mobile) Homes Placed for Residential Use and Average Sales Price by Region: 1980 to 2002

[233.7 represents 233,700. A mobile home is a moveable dwelling, 8 feet or more wide and 40 feet or more long, designed to be towed on its own chassis, with transportation gear integral to the unit when it leaves the factory, and without need of permanent foundation. Excluded are travel trailers, motor homes, and modular housing. Data are based on a probability sample and subject to sampling variability; see source. For composition of regions, see map inside front cover]

Year	Units placed (1,000)					Average sales price (dol.)				
	Total	North-east	Mid-west	South	West	U.S.	North-east	Mid-west	South	West
1980	233.7	12.3	32.3	140.3	48.7	19,800	18,500	18,600	18,200	25,400
1985	283.4	20.2	38.6	187.6	36.9	21,800	22,700	21,500	20,400	28,700
1990	195.4	18.8	37.7	108.4	30.6	27,800	30,000	27,000	24,500	39,300
1991	174.3	14.3	35.4	97.6	27.0	27,700	30,400	27,600	24,500	38,600
1992	212.0	15.0	42.2	124.4	30.4	28,400	30,900	28,800	25,400	39,000
1993	242.5	15.4	44.5	146.7	35.9	30,500	32,000	31,400	27,700	40,500
1994	290.9	16.3	53.3	177.7	43.6	32,800	32,900	34,000	30,200	41,900
1995	319.4	15.0	57.5	203.2	43.7	35,300	35,800	35,700	33,300	44,100
1996	337.7	16.2	58.8	218.2	44.4	37,200	37,300	38,000	35,500	45,000
1997	336.3	14.3	55.3	219.4	47.3	39,800	41,300	40,300	38,000	47,300
1998	373.7	14.7	58.3	250.3	50.4	41,600	42,200	42,400	40,100	48,400
1999	338.3	14.1	53.6	227.2	43.5	43,300	44,000	44,400	41,900	49,600
2000	280.9	14.9	48.7	178.7	38.6	46,400	47,000	47,900	44,300	54,100
2001	196.2	12.2	37.6	116.4	30.0	48,900	50,000	49,100	46,500	58,000
2002	171.6	11.8	33.3	99.6	26.9	51,300	52,900	51,700	48,000	62,700

Source: U.S. Census Bureau, Manufactured Housing Statistics ; <http://www.census.gov/const/www/mhsindex.html>.

No. 948. Existing One-Family Homes Sold and Price by Region: 1970 to 2002

[1,612 represents 1,612,000. Includes existing detached single-family homes and townhomes. Based on data (adjusted and aggregated to regional and national totals) reported by participating real estate multiple listing services. For definition of median, see Guide to Tabular Presentation. For composition of regions, see map inside front cover]

Year	Homes sold (1,000)					Median sales price (dol.)				
	Total	North-east	Mid-west	South	West	Total	North-east	Mid-west	South	West
1970	1,612	251	501	568	292	23,000	25,700	20,100	22,200	24,300
1975	2,476	370	701	862	543	35,300	39,300	30,100	34,800	39,600
1980	2,973	403	806	1,092	672	62,200	60,800	51,900	58,300	89,300
1985	3,134	561	806	1,063	704	75,500	88,900	58,900	75,200	95,400
1986	3,474	635	922	1,145	773	80,300	104,800	63,500	78,200	100,900
1987	3,436	618	892	1,163	763	85,600	133,300	66,000	80,400	113,200
1988	3,513	606	865	1,224	817	89,300	143,000	68,400	82,200	124,900
1989 [1]	3,325	490	832	1,185	818	89,500	127,700	71,800	84,400	127,100
1990	3,219	458	809	1,193	759	92,000	126,400	75,300	85,100	129,600
1991	3,186	463	812	1,173	737	97,100	129,100	79,500	88,500	135,300
1992	3,479	521	913	1,242	802	99,700	128,900	83,000	91,500	131,500
1993	3,786	550	967	1,386	882	103,100	129,100	86,000	94,300	132,500
1994	3,916	552	965	1,436	962	107,200	129,100	89,300	95,700	139,400
1995	3,888	547	945	1,433	964	110,500	126,700	94,800	97,700	141,000
1996	4,196	584	986	1,511	1,116	115,800	127,800	101,000	103,400	147,100
1997	4,382	607	1,005	1,595	1,174	121,800	131,800	107,000	109,600	155,200
1998	4,970	662	1,130	1,868	1,309	128,400	135,900	114,300	116,200	164,800
1999	5,205	656	1,148	2,015	1,386	133,300	139,000	119,600	120,300	173,900
2000	5,152	643	1,119	2,015	1,376	139,000	139,400	123,600	128,300	183,000
2001	5,296	638	1,158	2,114	1,386	147,800	146,500	130,200	137,400	194,500
2002	5,566	656	1,217	2,203	1,490	158,100	164,400	135,800	147,500	215,500

[1] Beginning 1989 data not comparable to earlier years due to rebenchmarking.

Source: NATIONAL ASSOCIATION OF REALTORS®, Washington, DC, prior to 1990, *Home Sales*, monthly, and *Home Sales Yearbook: 1990*; (copyright); thereafter, *Real Estate Outlook; Market Trends & Insights*, monthly, (copyright). See Internet site <http://www.realtor.org/research>.

No. 949. Median Sales Price of Existing One-Family Homes by Selected Metropolitan Area: 2000 to 2002

[In thousands of dollars (139.0 represents $139,000). Includes existing detached single-family homes and townhouses. Areas are metropolitan statistical areas defined by Office of Management and Budget as of 1992, except as noted]

Metropolitan area	2000	2001	2002	Metropolitan area	2000	2001	2002
United States, total	139.0	147.8	158.1	NY: New York-North NJ-Long Island, NY	230.2	258.2	309.8
Anaheim-Santa Ana, CA (Orange Co.)[1]	316.2	355.6	412.7	NY: Bergen-Passaic, NJ	261.2	288.8	337.9
Atlanta, GA	131.2	138.8	146.5	NY: Middlesex-Somerset-Hunterdon, NJ	219.7	244.3	284.1
Atlantic City, NJ	121.5	125.7	143.6	NY: Monmouth-Ocean, NJ	179.0	208.6	251.7
Aurora-Elgin, IL	163.0	178.2	193.3	NY: Nassau-Suffolk, NY	214.0	248.4	312.9
Austin-San Marcos, TX	142.8	152.0	156.5	NY: Newark, NJ	242.4	263.1	300.5
Baltimore, MD	153.0	158.2	179.6	Orlando, FL	111.2	124.1	136.6
Birmingham, AL	125.5	133.6	137.4	Philadelphia, PA-NJ	125.2	134.8	146.1
Boston, MA	314.2	356.6	395.9	Phoenix, AZ	134.4	139.4	143.8
Bradenton, FL[2]	127.3	137.8	150.0	Portland, ME	142.0	158.0	180.0
Charleston, SC	137.9	150.8	159.4	Portland, OR	170.1	172.3	180.4
Charlotte-Gastonia-Rock Hill, NC-SC	140.3	145.3	149.1	Providence, RI	137.8	158.0	193.2
Chicago, IL	171.8	198.5	220.9	Raleigh-Durham, NC	158.4	168.2	172.2
Colorado Springs, CO	154.1	173.3	176.9	Reno, NV	157.3	165.1	183.2
Columbus, OH	129.1	135.7	140.3	Richland-Kennewick-Pasco, WA	119.6	(NA)	140.8
Denver, CO	196.8	218.3	228.1	Richmond-Petersburg, VA	129.8	133.3	142.3
Eugene-Springfield, OR	132.8	134.6	143.7	Riverside-San Bernardino, CA[1]	138.6	156.7	176.5
Ft. Lauderdale-Hollywood-Pompano Beach, FL	148.7	168.1	197.0	Sacramento, CA[1]	145.2	173.2	209.5
Greensboro-Winston Salem-High Point, NC	129.3	132.7	135.8	Salt Lake City-Ogden, UT	141.5	147.6	148.8
Hartford, CT	159.9	167.3	175.9	San Diego, CA[1]	269.4	298.6	364.2
Honolulu, HI	295.0	299.9	335.0	San Francisco Bay Area, CA[1]	454.6	475.9	517.1
Kansas City, MO-KS	127.4	135.7	137.4	Sarasota, FL[2]	132.0	(NA)	176.2
Lake County, IL	169.4	178.9	195.8	Seattle, WA	230.1	245.4	254.0
Las Vegas, NV	137.4	149.1	159.8	Springfield, MA	120.4	127.4	139.8
Los Angeles Area, CA[1]	215.9	241.4	286.0	Tacoma, WA	151.1	159.5	170.4
Madison, WI	153.6	162.5	177.0	Tallahassee, FL	122.5	129.7	136.9
Miami-Hialeah, FL	144.6	162.7	189.8	Trenton, NJ	150.9	165.3	179.5
Milwaukee, WI	140.7	149.4	173.8	Tucson, AZ	120.5	128.8	146.4
Minneapolis-St. Paul, MN-WI	151.4	167.4	185.0	Washington, DC-MD-VA	182.6	213.9	250.2
New Haven-Meriden, CT	151.6	168.0	192.3	Wilmington, DE-NJ-MD	127.6	136.5	150.1
				Worcester, MA	131.8	152.6	187.7

NA Not available. [1] California data supplied by the California Association of REALTORS. [2] In 1992, Bradenton and Sarasota were merged and Aurora/Elgin was incorporated into Chicago. The source still collects price data on the previous jurisdictions.

Source: NATIONAL ASSOCIATION OF REALTORS®, Washington, DC, *Real Estate Outlook: Market Trends & Insights*, monthly, (copyright). See Internet site <http://www.realtor.org/research>.

Construction and Housing 613

No. 950. Existing Home Sales by State: 1990 to 2002

[In thousands (3,599 represents 3,599,000). Includes condos and co-ops as well as single-family homes]

State	1990	2000	2001	2002	State	1990	2000	2001	2002
United States	3,599	5,814	6,042	6,387	Missouri	77.1	119.9	122.9	125.4
Alabama	52.0	79.8	85.8	97.9	Montana	13.5	18.5	21.6	24.0
Alaska	12.3	17.7	21.2	21.2	Nebraska	23.6	32.4	32.9	34.3
Arizona	71.8	167.0	185.1	204.3	Nevada	26.9	52.4	63.2	74.5
Arkansas	33.7	57.7	58.8	67.0	New Hampshire	13.5	40.3	39.7	35.8
California	413.1	677.8	622.1	696.0	New Jersey	85.7	135.3	132.3	140.3
Colorado	77.7	147.0	144.5	144.3	New Mexico	24.7	28.7	34.1	37.4
Connecticut	37.4	49.4	49.8	51.5	New York	135.9	179.8	183.1	191.1
Delaware	7.9	8.0	8.6	9.0	North Carolina	98.9	233.5	234.6	247.2
District of Columbia	7.2	13.4	13.3	14.1	North Dakota	8.5	10.4	11.1	11.8
Florida	281.1	529.9	542.8	578.1	Ohio	146.9	192.2	201.2	210.6
Georgia	91.2	152.2	172.2	184.3	Oklahoma	62.2	96.5	109.2	114.0
Hawaii	19.0	21.3	22.7	27.1	Oregon	56.6	59.9	65.8	69.0
Idaho	22.3	28.5	31.3	30.4	Pennsylvania	143.2	169.3	173.1	178.5
Illinois	163.3	241.1	246.8	264.4	Rhode Island	9.6	19.5	20.0	19.5
Indiana	83.6	129.5	138.1	146.1	South Carolina	54.3	107.6	114.1	121.5
Iowa	42.8	54.4	56.9	59.5	South Dakota	10.8	15.4	15.5	18.2
Kansas	36.8	65.8	69.8	75.0	Tennessee	66.2	148.4	156.1	165.4
Kentucky	47.9	75.6	81.4	84.3	Texas	311.8	549.0	569.6	593.1
Louisiana	57.1	89.0	92.8	95.5	Utah	29.4	47.7	52.3	55.0
Maine	17.0	37.6	36.6	39.3	Vermont	7.2	6.7	6.4	7.2
Maryland	67.0	106.7	119.4	124.8	Virginia	89.3	138.9	148.9	160.4
Massachusetts	47.9	88.6	87.6	91.4	Washington	85.9	173.7	175.7	179.7
Michigan	137.6	153.3	157.9	168.6	West Virginia	22.6	22.6	25.6	27.7
Minnesota	68.1	108.0	130.7	137.5	Wisconsin	62.1	97.0	103.8	111.7
Mississippi	28.2	47.6	56.2	59.1	Wyoming	8.5	12.6	14.6	13.9

Source: NATIONAL ASSOCIATION OF REALTORS®, Washington, DC, *Real Estate Outlook: Market Trends & Insights*, monthly (copyright). See Internet site <http://www.realtor.org/research>.

No. 951. Existing Apartment Condos and Co-Ops—Units Sold and Median Sales Price by Region: 1990 to 2002

[348 represents 348,000. For definition of median, see Guide to Tabular Presentation. For composition of regions, see map inside front cover]

Year	Units sold (1,000)					Median sales price (dol.)				
	Total	North-east	Mid-west	South	West	U.S.	North-east	Mid-west	South	West
1990	348	45	42	151	110	85,200	110,200	70,200	66,800	105,200
1993	400	63	53	175	108	84,400	99,200	78,900	69,300	102,700
1994	439	69	54	196	119	87,200	99,500	86,200	69,500	108,800
1995	428	70	53	188	116	87,400	94,800	90,700	70,600	105,300
1996	476	78	58	206	134	90,900	97,500	95,200	73,500	109,900
1997	524	88	64	220	152	95,500	101,100	90,700	76,300	118,300
1998	607	104	75	252	176	100,600	103,400	106,400	80,000	126,400
1999	681	118	81	295	190	108,000	112,500	114,600	84,100	132,100
2000	706	116	82	311	197	111,800	111,200	121,700	87,700	136,800
2001	746	121	88	339	198	123,200	124,200	134,900	97,100	141,900
2002	820	132	97	376	215	137,200	145,200	148,900	115,000	165,700

Source: NATIONAL ASSOCIATION OF REALTORS®, Washington, DC, *Real Estate Outlook: Market Trends & Insights*, monthly (copyright). See Internet site <http://www.realtor.org/research>.

No. 952. New Apartments Completed and Rented in 3 Months by Region: 1990 to 2002

[214.3 represents 214,300. Structures with five or more units, privately financed, nonsubsidized, unfurnished rental apartments. Based on sample and subject to sampling variability; see source for details. For composition of regions, see map, inside front cover]

Year and rent	Number (1,000)					Percent rented in 3 months				
	U.S.	North-east	Mid-west	South	West	U.S.	North-east	Mid-west	South	West
1990	214.3	12.7	44.3	77.2	80.0	67	66	75	64	65
1995	155.0	7.1	31.7	78.5	37.7	73	74	75	72	73
2000	226.2	14.8	39.5	125.9	45.9	72	85	76	67	77
2001	193.1	16.5	31.6	97.4	47.6	64	83	67	60	64
2002, prel.	204.7	19.3	34.6	96.9	53.9	59	49	69	57	58
Less than $550	32.0	0.4	6.5	18.2	7.0	65	23	81	63	60
$550 to $749	59.9	0.7	17.1	33.2	8.9	60	51	68	55	61
$550 to $649	30.7	0.3	10.2	16.0	4.2	60	29	72	53	63
$650 to $749	29.2	0.4	6.9	17.2	4.7	59	66	62	57	60
$750 to $949	37.3	3.2	4.2	19.5	10.3	61	81	63	59	56
$750 to $849	18.7	0.5	2.5	9.4	6.3	59	57	62	59	58
$850 to $949	18.6	2.7	1.7	10.1	4.0	63	86	66	59	54
$950 or more	75.5	15.0	6.6	26.1	27.8	54	43	65	54	58
Median monthly asking rent	905	(¹)	758	833	(¹)	(X)	(X)	(X)	(X)	(X)

X Not applicable. ¹ Over $1,050.

Source: U.S. Census Bureau, Current Housing Reports, Series H130, *Market Absorption of Apartments*, and unpublished data. See Internet site <http://www.census.gov/prod/www/abs/apart.html>.

No. 953. Total Housing Inventory for the United States: 1980 to 2002

[In thousands (87,739 represents 87,739,000), except percent. Based on the Current Population Survey and the Housing Vacancy Survey and subject to sampling error; see source for details and Appendix III]

Item	1980	1985	1990	1995	1997	1998	1999	2000	2001	2002
All housing units	87,739	97,333	106,283	112,655	115,621	117,282	119,044	119,628	121,480	123,318
Vacant	8,101	9,446	12,059	12,669	13,419	13,748	14,116	13,908	14,470	14,779
Year-round vacant	5,996	7,400	9,128	9,570	10,114	10,516	10,848	10,439	10,916	11,272
For rent	1,575	2,221	2,662	2,946	2,978	3,046	3,119	3,024	3,203	3,497
For sale only	734	1,006	1,064	1,022	1,133	1,205	1,184	1,148	1,301	1,277
Rented or sold	623	664	660	810	867	927	956	856	882	877
Held off market	3,064	3,510	4,742	4,793	5,136	5,338	5,589	5,411	5,530	5,621
Occasional use	814	977	1,485	1,667	1,818	1,792	1,948	1,892	1,887	1,902
Usual residence elsewhere	568	659	1,068	801	885	910	965	1,037	1,064	1,035
Other	1,683	1,875	2,189	2,325	2,433	2,636	2,676	2,482	2,579	2,684
Seasonal [1]	2,106	2,046	2,931	3,099	3,305	3,232	3,268	3,469	3,554	3,507
Total occupied	79,638	87,887	94,224	99,985	102,202	103,534	104,928	105,720	107,010	108,539
Owner	52,223	56,152	60,248	64,739	67,143	68,638	70,097	71,250	72,593	73,713
Renter	27,415	31,736	33,976	35,246	35,059	34,896	34,831	34,470	34,417	34,826
PERCENT DISTRIBUTION										
All housing units	100.0	100.0	100.0	100.0	100.0	100.0	100.0	100.0	100.0	100.0
Vacant	9.2	9.7	11.3	11.2	11.6	11.7	11.9	11.6	11.9	12.0
Total occupied	90.8	90.3	88.7	88.8	88.4	88.3	88.1	88.4	88.1	88.0
Owner	59.5	57.7	56.7	57.5	58.1	58.5	58.9	59.6	59.8	59.8
Renter	31.2	32.6	32.0	31.3	30.3	29.8	29.3	28.8	28.3	28.2

[1] Beginning 1990 includes vacant seasonal mobile homes. For years shown, seasonal vacant housing units were underreported prior to 1990.
Source: U.S. Census Bureau, "Housing Vacancies and Home Ownership." See Internet site <http://www.census.gov/hhes/www/hvs.html>.

No. 954. Occupied Housing Inventory by Age of Householder: 1985 to 2002

[In thousands (87,887 represents 87,887,000). Based on the Current Population Survey/Housing Vacancy Survey; See source for details]

Age of householder	1985	1990	1995	1996	1997	1998	1999	2000	2001	2002
Total [1]	87,887	94,224	99,986	100,983	102,201	103,534	104,929	105,719	107,009	108,538
Less than 25 years old	5,483	5,143	5,502	5,467	5,517	5,750	6,000	6,221	6,460	6,715
25 to 29 years old	9,543	9,508	8,662	8,669	8,755	8,666	8,661	8,482	8,358	8,411
30 to 34 years old	10,288	11,213	11,206	10,936	10,622	10,494	10,400	10,219	10,301	10,352
35 to 39 years old	9,615	10,914	11,993	12,083	12,166	12,026	11,950	11,834	11,587	11,356
40 to 44 years old	7,919	9,893	11,151	11,644	11,869	12,141	12,206	12,377	12,504	12,538
45 to 49 years old	6,517	8,038	10,080	10,523	10,532	10,744	10,973	11,164	11,529	11,741
50 to 54 years old	6,157	6,532	7,882	7,981	8,650	9,040	9,412	9,834	10,288	10,407
55 to 59 years old	6,558	6,182	6,355	6,474	6,731	7,051	7,389	7,602	7,827	8,511
60 to 64 years old	6,567	6,446	5,860	5,836	5,947	6,055	6,183	6,215	6,345	6,591
65 to 69 years old	5,976	6,407	6,088	6,099	5,926	5,852	5,845	5,816	5,749	5,815
70 to 74 years old	5,003	5,397	5,693	5,602	5,574	5,583	5,621	5,567	5,496	5,292
75 years old and over	7,517	8,546	9,514	9,669	9,912	10,131	10,289	10,388	10,565	10,809

[1] 1985 total includes ages not reported. Thereafter cases allocated by age.
Source: U.S. Census Bureau, "Housing Vacancies and Home Ownership." See Internet site <http://www.census.gov/hhes/www/hvs.html>.

No. 955. Vacancy Rates for Housing Units—Characteristics: 1990 to 2002

[In percent. Rate is relationship between vacant housing for rent or for sale and the total rental and homeowner supply, which comprises occupied units, units rented or sold and awaiting occupancy, and vacant units available for rent or sale. Based on the Current Population/Housing Vacancy Survey; see source for details. For composition of regions, see map, inside front cover]

Characteristic	Rental units					Homeowner units				
	1990	1995 [1]	2000	2001	2002	1990	1995 [1]	2000	2001	2002
Total units	7.2	7.6	8.0	8.4	9.0	1.7	1.5	1.6	1.8	1.7
Inside MSAs	7.1	7.6	7.7	8.0	8.8	1.7	1.5	1.4	1.6	1.6
Outside MSAs	7.6	7.9	9.5	10.4	10.6	1.8	1.6	2.1	2.3	2.0
Northeast	6.1	7.2	5.6	5.3	5.8	1.6	1.5	1.2	1.2	1.2
Midwest	6.4	7.2	8.8	9.7	10.1	1.3	1.3	1.3	1.7	1.8
South	8.8	8.3	10.5	11.1	11.8	2.1	1.7	1.9	2.1	1.9
West	6.6	7.5	5.8	6.2	6.9	1.8	1.7	1.5	1.6	1.6
Units in structure:										
1 unit	4.0	5.4	7.0	7.9	8.1	1.4	1.4	1.5	1.6	1.6
2 units or more	9.0	9.0	8.7	8.9	9.7	7.1	4.8	4.7	5.7	4.8
5 units or more	9.6	9.5	9.2	9.6	10.5	8.4	5.1	5.8	6.0	5.2
Units with—										
3 rooms or less	10.3	11.4	10.3	10.5	11.1	10.2	9.2	10.4	8.7	9.0
4 rooms	8.0	8.2	8.2	8.8	8.9	3.2	2.8	2.9	3.0	2.6
5 rooms	5.7	5.8	6.9	7.5	8.7	2.0	1.8	2.0	2.1	2.0
6 rooms or more	3.0	3.8	5.2	5.6	6.4	1.1	1.1	1.1	1.2	1.2

[1] Beginning 1995, based on 1990 population census controls.
Source: U.S. Census Bureau, "Housing Vacancies and Home Ownership." See Internet site <http://www.census.gov/hhes/www/hvs.html>.

No. 956. Housing Units and Tenure—States: 2000

[115,905 represents 115,905,000. As of April 1. Based on the 2000 Census of Population and Housing; see text, Section 1, and Appendix III]

State	Housing units Total (1,000)	Occu- pied (1,000)	Vacant Total	Vacant For seasonal use [1]	Vacancy rate Home- owner [2]	Vacancy rate Renter [3]	Owner occupied units Total (1,000)	Owner occupied units Average house- hold size	Renter occupied units Total (1,000)	Renter occupied units Average house- hold size
United States..	115,905	105,480	10,425	3,579	1.7	6.8	69,816	2.69	35,664	2.40
Alabama	1,964	1,737	227	47	2.0	11.8	1,259	2.57	478	2.30
Alaska	261	222	39	21	1.9	7.8	139	2.89	83	2.49
Arizona	2,189	1,901	288	142	2.1	9.2	1,294	2.69	608	2.53
Arkansas	1,173	1,043	130	29	2.5	9.6	724	2.54	319	2.40
California	12,215	11,503	712	237	1.4	3.7	6,546	2.93	4,957	2.79
Colorado	1,808	1,658	150	72	1.4	5.5	1,116	2.64	542	2.30
Connecticut	1,386	1,302	84	23	1.1	5.6	870	2.67	432	2.25
Delaware	343	299	44	26	1.5	8.2	216	2.61	83	2.37
District of Columbia	275	248	27	2	2.9	5.9	101	2.31	147	2.06
Florida	7,303	6,338	965	483	2.2	9.3	4,442	2.49	1,896	2.39
Georgia	3,282	3,006	275	50	1.9	8.2	2,029	2.71	977	2.51
Hawaii	461	403	57	26	1.6	8.2	228	3.07	175	2.71
Idaho	528	470	58	27	2.2	7.6	340	2.75	130	2.52
Illinois	4,886	4,592	294	30	1.5	6.2	3,089	2.76	1,503	2.37
Indiana	2,532	2,336	196	34	1.8	8.8	1,669	2.64	667	2.24
Iowa	1,233	1,149	83	16	1.7	6.8	831	2.57	318	2.15
Kansas	1,131	1,038	93	10	2.0	8.8	719	2.63	319	2.25
Kentucky	1,751	1,591	160	30	1.8	8.7	1,125	2.55	465	2.27
Louisiana	1,847	1,656	191	40	1.6	9.3	1,125	2.70	531	2.44
Maine	652	518	134	101	1.7	7.0	371	2.54	147	2.03
Maryland	2,145	1,981	164	39	1.6	6.1	1,342	2.73	639	2.35
Massachusetts	2,622	2,444	178	94	0.7	3.5	1,508	2.72	936	2.17
Michigan	4,234	3,786	449	234	1.6	6.8	2,793	2.67	993	2.24
Minnesota	2,066	1,895	171	106	0.9	4.1	1,413	2.69	482	2.03
Mississippi	1,162	1,046	116	22	1.6	9.2	757	2.67	289	2.52
Missouri	2,442	2,195	247	66	2.1	9.0	1,542	2.59	652	2.20
Montana	413	359	54	24	2.2	7.6	248	2.55	111	2.22
Nebraska	723	666	56	12	1.8	7.6	449	2.63	217	2.20
Nevada	827	751	76	17	2.6	9.7	457	2.71	294	2.47
New Hampshire	547	475	72	56	1.0	3.5	331	2.70	144	2.14
New Jersey	3,310	3,065	246	109	1.2	4.5	2,011	2.81	1,053	2.43
New Mexico	781	678	103	32	2.2	11.6	474	2.72	204	2.41
New York	7,679	7,057	622	235	1.6	4.6	3,739	2.78	3,318	2.41
North Carolina	3,524	3,132	392	135	2.0	8.8	2,172	2.54	960	2.37
North Dakota	290	257	33	8	2.7	8.2	171	2.60	86	2.02
Ohio	4,783	4,446	337	47	1.6	8.3	3,073	2.62	1,373	2.19
Oklahoma	1,514	1,342	172	32	2.5	10.6	918	2.55	424	2.36
Oregon	1,453	1,334	119	37	2.3	7.3	857	2.59	477	2.36
Pennsylvania	5,250	4,777	473	148	1.6	7.2	3,406	2.62	1,371	2.12
Rhode Island	440	408	31	13	1.0	5.0	245	2.66	163	2.19
South Carolina	1,754	1,534	220	70	1.9	12.0	1,108	2.59	426	2.37
South Dakota	323	290	33	10	1.8	8.0	198	2.64	92	2.22
Tennessee	2,439	2,233	207	37	2.0	8.8	1,561	2.57	672	2.29
Texas	8,158	7,393	764	173	1.8	8.5	4,717	2.87	2,676	2.53
Utah	769	701	67	30	2.1	6.5	502	3.28	200	2.75
Vermont	294	241	54	43	1.4	4.2	170	2.58	71	2.11
Virginia	2,904	2,699	205	55	1.5	5.2	1,838	2.62	861	2.36
Washington	2,451	2,271	180	60	1.8	5.9	1,467	2.65	804	2.32
West Virginia	845	736	108	33	2.2	9.1	554	2.47	183	2.17
Wisconsin	2,321	2,085	237	142	1.2	5.6	1,426	2.66	658	2.15
Wyoming	224	194	30	12	2.1	9.7	136	2.58	58	2.25

[1] For seasonal, recreational or occasional use. [2] Proportion of the homeowner housing inventory which is vacant for sale. [3] Proportion of the rental inventory which is vacant for rent.

Source: U.S. Census Bureau, "2000 Census of Population and Housing, Profiles of General Demographic Characteristics"; <http://www.census.gov/Press-Release/www/2002/demoprofiles.html>.

No. 957. Housing Units and Tenure for Large Cities: 2000

[115,905 represents 115,905,000. As of April 1. For cities with 200,000 or more inhabitants in 2000. Based on the 2000 Census of Population and Housing; see text, Section 1, and Appendix III]

City	Housing units						Housing tenure			
			Vacant		Vacancy rate		Owner occupied units		Renter occupied units	
	Total (1,000)	Occu- pied (1,000)	Total	For sea- sonal use [1]	Home- owner [2]	Renter [3]	Total (1,000)	Average house- hold size	Total (1,000)	Average house- hold size
United States.....	115,905	105,480	10,425	3,579	1.7	6.8	69,816	2.69	35,664	2.40
Albuquerque, NM......	198.5	183.2	15.2	0.8	1.9	11.8	110.6	2.55	72.6	2.16
Anaheim, CA........	99.7	97.0	2.8	0.2	0.9	3.2	48.5	3.24	48.5	3.45
Anchorage, AK	100.4	94.8	5.5	1.1	1.4	5.3	57.0	2.81	37.9	2.46
Arlington, TX........	130.6	124.7	5.9	0.4	1.4	6.1	68.3	2.87	56.4	2.38
Atlanta, GA..........	186.9	168.1	18.8	1.1	4.1	7.2	73.5	2.37	94.7	2.25
Aurora, CO	109.3	105.6	3.6	0.2	1.1	3.5	67.5	2.65	38.1	2.50
Austin, TX..........	276.8	265.6	11.2	1.4	1.0	3.5	119.1	2.65	146.5	2.19
Baltimore, MD	300.5	258.0	42.5	1.4	3.6	7.6	129.9	2.57	128.1	2.27
Boston, MA.........	251.9	239.5	12.4	1.6	1.0	3.0	77.2	2.51	162.3	2.22
Buffalo, NY.........	145.6	122.7	22.9	0.3	4.2	11.1	53.3	2.47	69.4	2.16
Charlotte, NC	230.4	215.4	15.0	0.7	2.2	8.4	123.9	2.56	91.6	2.30
Chicago, IL..........	1,152.9	1,061.9	90.9	4.5	1.7	5.7	464.9	2.90	597.1	2.49
Cincinnati, OH.......	166.0	148.1	17.9	0.6	2.2	9.9	57.7	2.43	90.4	1.97
Cleveland, OH.......	215.9	190.6	25.2	0.8	2.1	10.8	92.5	2.56	98.1	2.32
Colorado Springs, CO...	148.7	141.5	7.2	0.7	1.2	6.2	86.0	2.65	55.5	2.27
Columbus, OH........	327.2	301.5	25.6	1.1	2.0	8.3	148.0	2.48	153.5	2.13
Corpus Christi, TX	107.8	98.8	9.0	1.1	2.0	9.5	58.9	2.89	39.9	2.56
Dallas, TX..........	484.1	451.8	32.3	1.5	1.4	7.0	195.3	2.78	256.5	2.44
Denver, CO	251.4	239.2	12.2	1.4	1.7	4.5	125.5	2.41	113.7	2.10
Detroit, MI..........	375.1	336.4	38.7	0.6	1.6	8.3	184.6	2.84	151.8	2.68
El Paso, TX..........	193.7	182.1	11.6	0.7	1.6	7.9	111.8	3.20	70.3	2.86
Fort Worth, TX........	211.0	195.1	16.0	0.6	1.9	9.1	109.1	2.84	86.0	2.44
Fresno, CA	149.0	140.1	8.9	0.4	1.9	6.4	70.9	2.94	69.2	3.05
Honolulu, HI [4].....	158.7	140.3	18.3	5.2	1.7	10.2	65.9	2.75	74.5	2.40
Houston, TX	782.0	717.9	64.1	4.2	1.6	8.7	328.7	2.84	389.2	2.54
Indianapolis, IN [5]....	352.4	320.1	32.3	1.2	2.0	10.9	187.6	2.53	132.5	2.18
Jacksonville, FL.......	308.8	284.5	24.3	0.9	1.8	9.0	179.7	2.64	104.8	2.34
Kansas City, MO	202.3	184.0	18.4	0.7	1.9	9.6	106.1	2.52	77.9	2.11
Las Vegas, NV	190.7	176.8	14.0	1.8	2.5	8.4	104.5	2.76	72.3	2.52
Lexington-Fayette, KY...	116.2	108.3	7.9	0.9	1.1	8.4	59.9	2.47	48.4	2.07
Long Beach, CA	171.6	163.1	8.5	0.8	2.2	4.2	66.9	2.81	96.2	2.74
Los Angeles, CA	1,337.7	1,275.4	62.3	4.9	1.8	3.5	491.9	2.99	783.5	2.73
Louisville, KY........	121.3	111.4	9.9	0.4	1.8	7.5	58.5	2.33	52.9	2.10
Memphis, TN.........	271.6	250.7	20.8	0.7	2.0	8.4	140.0	2.62	110.7	2.40
Mesa, AZ	175.7	146.6	29.1	18.1	2.4	10.7	97.3	2.74	49.3	2.54
Miami, FL...........	148.4	134.2	14.2	2.9	2.9	6.6	46.8	2.79	87.4	2.52
Milwaukee, WI........	249.2	232.2	17.0	0.5	1.3	6.0	105.2	2.60	127.0	2.42
Minneapolis, MN	168.6	162.4	6.3	0.8	0.7	2.8	83.4	2.43	78.9	2.05
Nashville-Davidson, TN [5].	242.5	227.4	15.0	1.1	2.0	6.5	124.0	2.43	103.4	2.13
New Orleans, LA	215.1	188.3	26.8	2.4	2.2	7.9	87.6	2.60	100.7	2.37
New York, NY	3,200.9	3,021.6	179.3	28.2	1.7	3.2	912.3	2.81	2,109.3	2.50
Newark, NJ..........	100.1	91.4	8.8	0.1	2.0	5.6	21.7	3.22	69.6	2.74
Oakland, CA	157.5	150.8	6.7	0.4	1.0	2.7	62.5	2.76	88.3	2.49
Oklahoma City, OK.....	228.1	204.4	23.7	1.1	2.2	12.3	121.5	2.51	82.9	2.27
Omaha, NE..........	165.7	156.7	9.0	0.5	1.0	7.2	93.4	2.64	63.3	2.10
Philadelphia, PA.......	662.0	590.1	71.9	1.8	1.9	7.0	349.6	2.65	240.4	2.23
Phoenix, AZ	495.8	465.8	30.0	4.5	1.4	7.9	282.7	2.89	183.2	2.63
Pittsburgh, PA	163.4	143.7	19.6	0.9	2.8	8.8	74.9	2.37	68.8	1.95
Portland, OR	237.3	223.7	13.6	1.0	2.3	6.2	124.8	2.47	99.0	2.08
Raleigh, NC	120.7	112.6	8.1	0.4	2.1	8.3	58.1	2.43	54.5	2.15
Riverside, CA	86.0	82.0	4.0	0.2	1.9	4.8	46.5	3.18	35.6	2.81
Sacramento, CA......	164.0	154.6	9.4	0.6	2.0	5.4	77.5	2.65	77.1	2.50
San Antonio, TX.......	433.1	405.5	27.6	2.3	1.4	6.9	235.7	2.95	169.8	2.51
San Diego, CA........	469.7	450.7	19.0	5.1	0.8	3.2	223.3	2.71	227.4	2.52
San Francisco, CA	346.5	329.7	16.8	3.8	0.8	2.5	115.4	2.73	214.3	2.06
San Jose, CA	281.8	276.6	5.2	0.8	0.4	1.8	171.0	3.22	105.6	3.16
Santa Ana, CA.......	74.6	73.0	1.6	0.1	0.8	1.9	36.0	4.54	37.0	4.57
Seattle, WA..........	270.5	258.5	12.0	1.8	1.2	3.5	125.2	2.32	133.3	1.84
St. Louis, MO	176.4	147.1	29.3	0.5	3.5	11.8	68.9	2.49	78.1	2.12
St. Paul, MN	115.7	112.1	3.6	0.4	0.7	2.8	61.5	2.72	50.6	2.15
Tampa, FL	135.8	124.8	11.0	0.8	2.1	7.8	68.6	2.49	56.2	2.20
Toledo, OH	139.9	128.9	10.9	0.4	1.5	8.8	77.1	2.50	51.9	2.19
Tucson, AZ..........	209.6	192.9	16.7	3.5	1.6	8.1	103.1	2.58	89.8	2.24
Tulsa, OK	179.4	165.7	13.7	0.9	1.6	8.7	92.2	2.41	73.5	2.18
Virginia Beach, VA	162.3	154.5	7.8	2.3	1.5	4.0	101.3	2.79	53.1	2.54
Washington, DC.......	274.8	248.3	26.5	2.2	2.9	5.9	101.2	2.31	147.1	2.06
Wichita, KS..........	152.1	139.1	13.0	0.4	2.0	12.0	85.7	2.61	53.4	2.17

[1] For seasonal, recreational or occasional use. [2] Proportion of the homeowner housing inventory which is vacant for sale. [3] Proportion of the rental inventory which is vacant for rent. [4] The population shown in this table is for the census designated place (CDP). [5] Represents the portion of a consolidated city that is not within one or more separately incorporated places.

Source: U.S. Census Bureau, "2000 Census of Population and Housing, Profiles of General Demographic Characteristics"; <http://www.census.gov/Press-Release/www/2002/demoprofiles.html>.

No. 958. Housing Inventory for Selected Metropolitan Areas— Summary Characteristics: 1995 to 2002

[539.4 represents 539,400. Based on the American Housing Survey and subject to sampling error; see Appendix III and source for details. For definition of median, see Guide to Tabular Presentation]

Year and metropolitan area	Total units (1,000)	Percent Owner occu- pied	Percent Renter occu- pied	Percent Vacant and sea- sonal	Percent Single- family	Percent Multi- family	Percent Mobile homes	Owner occupied Median monthly hous- ing costs (dol.)	Owner occupied Median value (dol.)	Renter occu- pied, median monthly housing costs (dol.)
1995										
Charlotte, NC-SC MSA	539.4	62.7	30.6	6.7	68.4	20.8	10.8	532	86,763	489
Chicago, IL Area PMSA	2,987.1	59.6	33.8	6.6	54.7	44.5	0.7	850	136,362	584
Columbus, OH MSA	604.9	57.9	34.0	8.1	75.8	21.4	2.8	654	92,664	484
Denver, CO PMSA	773.9	61.2	32.5	6.2	68.9	28.8	2.2	763	119,694	539
Detroit, MI PMSA	1,802.7	66.3	26.9	6.7	75.0	22.9	2.1	551	89,648	508
Kansas City, MO-KS MSA	715.5	61.9	30.2	7.9	76.2	21.0	2.8	565	78,542	481
Los Angeles-Long Beach, CA PMSA	3,276.0	42.0	48.0	10.0	54.7	44.0	1.3	943	192,803	654
Miami-Fort Lauderdale, FL CMSA	1,483.8	52.1	31.8	16.1	49.9	46.5	3.5	729	97,058	609
New Orleans, LA MSA	547.7	54.6	33.9	11.5	65.2	30.2	4.7	404	75,768	441
New York-Nausau-Suffolk-Orange County, NY PMSA	4,577.3	41.0	50.9	8.1	32.3	67.4	0.3	931	172,651	650
Northern New Jersey PMSA	2,442.2	56.0	34.2	9.8	59.2	40.0	0.8	976	176,713	669
Philadelphia, PA-NJ PMSA	1,986.6	63.7	28.0	8.4	73.1	25.8	1.0	673	112,769	578
Pittsburgh, PA MSA	1,051.7	66.5	25.7	7.8	73.9	21.5	4.7	416	73,383	417
Portland, OR-WA PMSA	702.6	60.3	32.9	6.8	70.2	23.9	5.9	704	127,731	566
San Antonio, TX MSA	538.7	55.4	34.6	10.0	67.0	27.3	5.6	507	62,577	475
1996										
Atlanta, GA MSA	1,421.1	58.6	33.4	8.1	66.9	28.6	4.5	803	105,037	651
Cleveland, OH PMSA	829.6	62.4	30.7	6.9	67.0	31.5	1.5	552	99,283	492
Hartford, CT MSA	480.2	60.5	31.1	8.4	63.0	36.5	0.5	888	139,641	616
Indianapolis, IN MSA	640.8	62.2	30.2	7.6	73.4	22.5	4.0	603	91,213	507
Memphis, TN-AR-MS MSA	442.0	59.3	31.5	9.2	70.0	26.1	3.9	592	76,175	477
Oklahoma City, OK MSA	446.4	57.8	28.7	13.5	72.0	22.1	6.0	461	65,638	434
Sacramento, CA PMSA	625.4	55.1	34.1	10.8	71.2	24.0	4.8	874	140,758	590
St. Louis, MO-IL MSA	1,107.0	64.3	26.5	9.2	71.2	23.6	5.2	557	82,111	462
Seattle-Everett, WA PMSA	965.3	58.3	35.1	6.5	60.4	33.9	5.7	897	164,554	630
1998										
Baltimore, MD MSA	1,028.2	61.7	27.8	10.5	78.8	19.6	1.6	739	127,557	589
Birmingham, AL MSA	394.0	64.1	26.9	9.0	75.9	15.6	8.5	385	87,670	480
Boston, MA-NH CMSA	1,345.9	56.5	37.4	6.1	59.2	39.8	1.0	933	191,179	748
Cincinnati, OH-KY-IN, PMSA	647.5	61.2	30.3	8.5	68.1	28.6	3.3	611	103,553	484
Houston, TX, PMSAs	1,547.3	53.0	36.6	10.4	68.7	26.9	4.4	678	82,543	557
Minneapolis-St. Paul, MN-WI MSA	1,150.3	70.6	26.0	3.3	72.0	25.6	2.4	786	122,624	583
Norfolk-Virginia Beach-Newport News, VA MSA	632.1	55.9	33.3	10.8	73.8	22.2	4.0	729	101,935	582
Oakland, CA, PMSA	895.0	56.8	38.8	4.4	71.8	26.4	1.9	1,086	226,173	775
Providence-Pawtucket-Warwick, RI-MA PMSA	415.4	57.8	33.6	8.6	62.0	36.6	1.4	768	124,005	540
Rochester, NY, MSA	448.5	63.8	27.6	8.6	71.0	24.4	4.6	724	94,468	572
Salt Lake City, UT MSA	444.0	67.9	24.5	7.5	75.0	21.7	3.3	713	141,888	594
San Francisco, CA, PMSA	700.2	46.2	48.5	5.3	57.7	41.4	0.9	1,229	(1)	899
San Jose, CA PMSA	591.0	58.2	37.6	4.2	72.7	23.2	4.1	1,186	(1)	1,038
Tampa-St. Petersburg, FL MSA	1,138.3	58.6	23.6	17.8	62.8	19.6	17.6	541	81,510	565
Washington, DC-MD-VA, MSA	1,817.4	59.3	32.7	8.0	72.4	26.7	0.9	1,104	170,022	746
1999										
Chicago, IL, PMSA	3,060.7	60.7	32.4	7.0	58.5	40.8	0.7	855	147,742	637
Detroit, MI, PMSA	1,876.7	68.0	24.8	7.2	77.8	20.1	2.1	583	124,157	557
Los Angeles-Long Beach, CA PMSA	3,278.5	44.0	49.4	6.6	60.9	37.8	1.3	1,033	199,011	663
New York-Nausau-Suffolk-Orange County, NY PMSA	4,615.9	41.7	52.1	6.2	39.0	60.6	0.4	910	186,164	684
Northern NJ, PMSA	2,502.1	59.7	32.9	7.4	65.4	33.8	0.7	983	181,898	732
Philadelphia, PA, PMSA	2,025.2	65.9	26.7	7.4	80.6	18.7	0.7	660	116,478	642
2002										
Anaheim-Santa Ana, CA PMSA	995.6	60.0	34.2	5.8	74.8	21.6	3.6	1,394	(1)	1,030
Buffalo, NY CMSA	515.5	61.0	28.5	10.5	63.9	34.3	1.7	684	92,434	522
Charlotte, NC-SC MSA	667.8	63.5	25.4	11.1	77.4	13.9	8.8	782	125,551	634
Columbus, OH MSA	682.6	58.8	31.0	10.2	79.2	18.0	2.8	769	135,208	607
New Orleans, LA MSA	1,365.4	57.4	33.0	9.5	72.6	23.2	4.1	1,011	126,492	692
Fort Worth-Arlington, TX PMSA	639.4	61.4	30.2	8.4	77.6	17.9	4.5	809	99,230	642
Kansas City, MO-KS MSA	766.5	63.5	27.4	9.0	83.5	13.8	2.6	745	116,778	605
Miami-Fort Lauderdale, FL CMSA	1,638.7	56.6	31.0	12.5	65.7	31.1	3.2	860	136,773	711
Milwaukee, WI PMSA	626.5	59.3	34.0	6.7	62.9	36.6	0.6	879	143,281	604
Phoenix, AZ MSA	1,340.4	60.5	26.5	13.0	71.7	20.7	7.6	913	140,490	673
Portland, OR-WA PMSA	811.7	61.3	30.8	7.9	71.4	23.8	4.8	1,017	179,311	684
Riverside-San Bernardino-Ontario, CA PMSA	1,229.5	62.3	25.8	11.9	79.8	10.1	10.0	964	164,853	676
San Diego, CA MSA	1,072.0	54.6	38.5	6.8	66.9	28.3	4.7	1,210	297,453	886

[1] More than $300,000.

Source: U.S. Census Bureau, *American Housing Survey for the (name) Metropolitan Area (year)*, Series H-170. See Internet site <http://www.census.gov/hhes/www/housing/ahs/metropolitandata.html>.

618 Construction and Housing

No. 959. Housing Units—Characteristics by Tenure and Region: 2001

[In thousands of units (119,117 represents 119,117,000), except as indicated. As of Oct. 1. Based on the American Housing Survey; see Appendix III. For composition of regions, see map, inside front cover]

Characteristic	Total housing units	Sea- sonal	\multicolumn{8}{c	}{Year-round units}	Vacant
			\multicolumn{7}{c	}{Occupied}		
			Total	Owner	Renter	North- east	Mid- west	South	West	

Characteristic	Total housing units	Sea- sonal	Total	Owner	Renter	North- east	Mid- west	South	West	Vacant
Total units	119,117	3,078	106,261	72,265	33,996	20,321	24,758	38,068	23,115	9,777
Percent distribution	100.0	2.6	89.2	60.7	28.5	17.1	20.8	32.0	19.4	8.2
Units in structure:										
Single family detached	73,427	1,900	67,129	59,239	7,890	11,121	17,307	24,576	14,125	4,399
Single family attached	8,428	167	7,305	3,722	3,583	1,920	1,165	2,583	1,637	956
2 to 4 units	9,354	105	8,200	1,291	6,909	2,544	1,860	1,953	1,843	1,049
5 to 9 units	5,682	62	4,994	503	4,490	942	1,077	1,714	1,261	626
10 to 19 units	5,367	63	4,620	502	4,118	820	884	1,757	1,159	684
20 to 49 units	3,898	65	3,253	391	2,862	936	595	805	917	580
50 or more units	4,084	89	3,543	615	2,927	1,454	654	678	757	453
Mobile home or trailer	8,876	626	7,219	6,001	1,218	584	1,217	4,002	1,416	1,031
Stories in structure:[1]										
One story	(NA)	1,334	34,145	25,665	8,480	1,234	3,934	18,667	10,310	(NA)
2 stories	(NA)	725	34,824	22,418	12,406	6,230	9,817	10,424	8,352	(NA)
3 stories	(NA)	242	22,942	15,403	7,539	8,235	8,415	3,964	2,328	(NA)
4 to 6 stories	(NA)	53	5,208	2,312	2,896	2,973	1,042	672	520	(NA)
7 or more stories	(NA)	99	1,924	466	1,458	1,065	332	338	189	(NA)
Foundation:[2]										
Full or partial basement	(NA)	424	33,092	29,556	3,536	10,996	14,045	5,134	2,919	(NA)
Crawlspace	(NA)	810	18,840	15,574	3,266	787	2,606	9,845	5,601	(NA)
Concrete slab	(NA)	591	21,947	17,434	4,513	1,173	1,704	11,955	7,115	(NA)
Other	(NA)	242	554	396	158	85	117	224	128	(NA)
Year structure built:										
Median year	1970	1970	1970	1971	1967	1954	1964	1975	1973	1970
1980 or later	35,747	841	31,948	23,365	8,583	3,460	6,036	14,806	7,646	2,957
1970 to 1979	23,529	675	20,917	13,868	7,048	2,660	4,468	8,529	5,261	1,936
1960 to 1969	15,894	477	14,396	9,741	4,655	2,558	3,316	5,104	3,418	1,021
1950 to 1959	13,779	366	12,501	9,068	3,433	2,665	3,209	3,855	2,771	912
1940 to 1949	8,284	246	7,278	4,775	2,504	1,694	1,694	2,317	1,574	760
1939 and earlier	21,885	472	19,221	11,448	7,773	7,284	6,035	3,457	2,445	2,190
Main heating equipment:										
Warm-air furnace	71,804	1,272	65,262	47,867	17,395	8,114	19,833	22,510	14,805	5,270
Electric heat pump	12,693	373	11,080	8,099	2,981	293	566	8,917	1,304	1,240
Steam or hot water system	14,420	94	13,441	7,801	5,640	9,661	2,190	732	858	884
Floor, wall, or pipeless furnace	6,133	174	5,343	2,365	2,978	470	515	1,409	2,949	616
Built-in electric units	5,929	269	5,063	2,385	2,678	1,266	1,156	928	1,713	597
Room heaters with flue	1,856	98	1,542	866	676	193	216	787	345	216
Room heaters without flue	1,916	75	1,558	1,019	539	34	32	1,440	52	283
Stoves	1,501	255	1,131	917	214	180	175	396	380	115
Fireplaces	274	37	209	170	39	14	18	71	107	27
Cooking stoves	213	9	193	74	118	44	7	72	69	12
None	1,017	309	401	146	255	10	6	98	287	308
Portable electric heaters	893	58	746	390	356	10	18	560	158	89
Other	467	56	292	163	128	34	24	147	87	119
Kitchen equipment:										
Lacking complete facilities	5,260	570	1,646	380	1,266	455	312	440	439	3,044
With complete facilities	113,857	2,508	104,615	71,885	32,730	19,866	24,446	37,628	22,673	6,733
Kitchen sink	118,085	2,863	105,929	72,176	33,753	20,224	24,696	37,989	23,019	9,293
Refrigerator	116,219	2,764	105,859	72,091	33,768	20,218	24,681	37,942	23,018	7,597
Cooking stove or range	115,374	2,604	105,358	71,863	33,495	20,126	24,585	37,742	22,906	7,412
Burners only, no stove or range	178	4	169	73	96	37	19	73	40	6
Microwave oven only	487	18	399	222	177	72	95	150	82	70
Dishwasher	67,251	1,023	62,352	48,852	13,501	10,321	13,074	23,645	15,312	3,876
Washing machine	90,160	1,213	85,562	68,950	16,612	15,019	20,381	32,157	18,005	3,385
Clothes dryer	87,145	1,378	81,591	66,752	14,840	13,732	20,098	30,547	17,214	4,176
Disposal in kitchen sink	52,671	718	48,604	34,329	14,276	4,661	11,412	16,523	16,009	3,348
Trash compactor	4,483	138	4,010	3,305	706	576	635	1,566	1,234	335
Air conditioning: Central	69,145	917	63,854	48,816	15,038	5,473	15,532	32,535	10,314	4,374
Percent of total units	58.0	29.8	60.1	67.6	44.2	26.9	62.7	85.5	44.6	44.7
One or more room units	29,347	675	26,563	15,519	11,042	9,930	6,749	6,724	3,159	2,110
Source of water:										
Public system or private company	102,924	1,837	92,576	60,126	32,451	17,184	20,769	33,054	21,570	8,510
Percent of total units	86.4	59.7	87.1	83.2	95.5	84.6	83.9	86.8	93.3	87.0
Well serving 1 to 5 units	15,337	972	13,245	11,767	1,478	3,032	3,901	4,833	1,479	1,121
Other	855	270	440	372	68	105	89	181	66	146
Means of sewage disposal:										
Public sewer	92,680	1,232	83,870	52,502	31,368	16,014	19,815	27,940	20,101	7,578
Percent of total units	77.8	40.0	78.9	72.7	92.3	78.8	80.0	73.4	87.0	77.5
Septic tank, cesspool, chemical toilet	25,977	1,570	22,328	19,720	2,608	4,305	4,934	10,084	3,005	2,078
Other	459	276	63	43	20	3	9	43	8	120

NA Not available. [1] Excludes mobile homes. [2] Limited to single-family units.

Source: U.S. Census Bureau, Current Housing Reports, Series H150/01, *American Housing Survey for the United States*. See Internet site <http://www.census.gov/hhes/www/housing/ahs/nationaldata.html>.

Construction and Housing 619

U.S. Census Bureau, Statistical Abstract of the United States: 2003

No. 960. Housing Units by Units in Structure by State: 2000

[In percent, except as indicated (115,905 represents 115,905,000. As of April 1. Based on the 2000 Census of Population and Housing; see text, Section 1, and Appendix III]

State	Total housing units (1,000)	1-unit detached	1-unit attached	2 units	3 or 4 units	5 to 9 units	10 to 19 units	20 or more units	Mobile homes	Boat, RV, van, etc.
U.S.	115,905	60.3	5.6	4.3	4.7	4.7	4.0	8.6	7.6	0.2
AL	1,964	66.2	2.0	2.2	3.3	3.8	2.4	3.6	16.3	0.3
AK	261	58.5	7.0	5.5	7.4	5.7	3.0	5.4	6.8	0.7
AZ	2,189	56.8	6.0	1.5	3.4	3.8	3.7	9.7	13.8	1.3
AR	1,173	69.0	1.8	3.2	3.0	2.7	2.3	2.8	14.9	0.4
CA	12,215	56.4	7.6	2.7	5.7	5.9	5.1	12.0	4.4	0.3
CO	1,808	62.1	6.3	2.1	3.8	4.6	5.6	9.7	5.7	0.2
CT	1,386	58.9	5.1	8.6	9.2	5.5	3.8	7.9	0.8	(Z)
DE	343	55.9	14.1	2.0	2.6	3.7	5.5	4.9	11.2	0.2
DC	275	13.2	26.4	3.0	8.0	7.9	10.3	30.9	0.1	0.1
FL	7,303	52.3	5.9	2.7	4.3	5.0	5.0	12.9	11.6	0.4
GA	3,282	64.2	2.9	2.8	4.0	5.3	3.9	4.7	12.0	0.1
HI	461	52.0	8.3	2.3	4.6	6.7	5.0	20.8	0.2	0.1
ID	528	70.1	2.9	2.8	4.1	2.7	1.8	3.0	12.2	0.5
IL	4,886	57.9	4.8	6.9	6.5	6.2	4.3	10.1	3.2	(Z)
IN	2,532	71.2	2.9	3.4	4.0	4.6	3.2	4.1	6.6	0.1
IA	1,233	74.0	2.3	3.2	3.9	3.7	3.1	4.6	5.3	0.1
KS	1,131	72.4	3.5	3.0	3.6	3.5	3.1	4.4	6.4	0.1
KY	1,751	66.0	2.1	3.2	4.1	4.3	3.1	2.9	14.1	0.1
LA	1,847	64.1	3.8	4.0	4.5	3.1	2.2	4.9	13.0	0.3
ME	652	67.4	2.2	5.6	5.8	4.3	1.7	2.9	9.8	0.3
MD	2,145	51.2	21.0	2.1	2.9	5.6	7.9	7.2	1.9	(Z)
MA	2,622	52.4	4.0	11.6	11.4	6.0	4.3	9.3	0.9	(Z)
MI	4,234	70.6	3.9	3.5	2.8	4.0	3.4	5.1	6.5	0.2
MN	2,066	67.8	5.2	3.0	2.3	2.4	3.8	10.7	4.5	0.3
MS	1,162	68.1	1.7	2.4	3.3	3.4	1.5	2.7	16.6	0.2
MO	2,442	68.8	2.7	3.9	5.1	3.8	3.2	4.1	8.2	0.3
MT	413	67.0	2.7	3.3	4.6	2.9	1.8	3.1	14.3	0.3
NE	723	71.9	2.9	2.6	3.0	3.8	4.5	6.1	5.1	0.1
NV	827	52.3	5.4	1.5	7.3	8.0	5.4	10.0	9.7	0.5
NH	547	62.4	4.4	6.5	6.0	5.0	3.2	5.8	6.5	0.1
NJ	3,310	54.2	8.6	10.0	6.8	4.8	4.9	9.6	1.0	(Z)
NM	781	61.0	4.5	2.0	3.5	2.5	2.3	5.1	18.6	0.6
NY	7,679	41.7	4.9	10.9	7.3	5.3	4.3	22.9	2.7	0.1
NC	3,524	64.4	3.0	2.5	3.2	4.3	3.2	2.9	16.4	0.2
ND	290	62.1	4.1	2.5	4.3	4.2	5.3	8.6	9.0	0.1
OH	4,783	67.4	3.8	5.2	4.8	4.8	3.9	5.5	4.6	0.1
OK	1,514	71.4	2.4	1.9	2.8	3.6	2.7	4.2	10.7	0.4
OR	1,453	62.8	3.3	3.0	4.2	4.3	3.8	7.8	10.3	0.6
PA	5,250	55.9	17.9	5.2	4.6	3.4	2.5	5.4	4.9	0.1
RI	440	54.8	2.9	12.3	12.8	5.2	3.4	7.5	1.0	(Z)
SC	1,754	61.5	2.3	2.5	3.3	4.4	2.4	3.2	20.3	0.1
SD	323	67.4	2.3	2.7	3.7	3.5	3.4	5.6	11.4	0.1
TN	2,439	67.3	2.8	3.4	3.4	4.4	3.1	4.3	11.0	0.2
TX	8,158	63.4	3.1	2.1	3.3	4.4	4.3	10.0	9.0	0.4
UT	769	67.7	4.9	3.8	4.8	3.6	3.9	5.8	5.1	0.3
VT	294	65.6	3.4	7.2	6.4	5.1	1.5	2.8	7.7	0.2
VA	2,904	62.3	9.6	2.1	3.3	5.0	5.3	5.9	6.4	0.1
WA	2,451	62.3	3.1	2.8	3.8	4.6	5.1	9.3	8.5	0.5
WV	845	69.1	1.6	2.6	2.9	2.6	1.5	2.4	16.9	0.4
WI	2,321	66.0	3.4	8.2	3.9	4.6	3.3	6.2	4.4	0.1
WY	224	64.9	3.6	2.5	4.6	3.0	1.9	3.2	15.9	0.4

Z Less than 0.05 percent.

Source: U.S. Census Bureau, "2000 Census of Population and Housing, Profiles of General Demographic Characteristics"; <http://www.census.gov/Press-Release/www/2002/demoprofiles.html>.

No. 961. Housing Units—Size of Units and Lot: 2001

[In thousands (119,117 represents 119,117,000), except as indicated. As of Oct. 1. Based on the American Housing Survey; see Appendix III. For composition of regions, see map inside front cover]

Item	Total housing units	Sea-sonal	Year-round units						
			Occupied						Vacant
			Total	Owner	Renter	North-east	Mid-west	South	West	

Item	Total hous-ing units	Sea-sonal	Total	Owner	Renter	North-east	Mid-west	South	West	Vacant
Total units	119,117	3,078	106,261	72,265	33,996	20,321	24,758	38,068	23,115	9,777
Rooms:										
1 room	622	57	394	16	378	159	55	24	156	171
2 rooms	1,406	161	993	87	906	302	153	201	338	252
3 rooms	10,698	484	8,800	1,029	7,771	2,262	1,774	2,463	2,301	1,413
4 rooms	23,082	1,090	19,003	7,169	11,834	3,429	4,163	7,012	4,398	2,989
5 rooms	27,896	746	24,798	17,180	7,618	3,912	5,888	9,727	5,271	2,353
6 rooms	24,637	299	22,768	19,205	3,563	4,382	5,354	8,705	4,328	1,570
7 rooms	14,710	121	14,032	12,841	1,190	2,655	3,419	5,000	2,957	558
8 rooms or more	16,066	120	15,473	14,737	736	3,220	3,952	4,935	3,365	471
Complete bathrooms:										
No bathrooms	2,227	595	681	288	393	175	125	224	157	950
1 bathroom	48,464	1,484	42,113	18,408	23,705	10,289	10,723	12,883	8,217	4,867
1 and one-half bathrooms	17,756	195	16,548	13,062	3,486	4,019	5,272	4,592	2,665	1,013
2 or more bathrooms	50,670	804	46,920	40,507	6,412	5,838	8,638	20,368	12,076	2,946
Square footage of unit:										
Single detached and mobile homes [1]	82,303	2,526	74,347	65,240	9,107	11,705	18,523	28,578	15,541	5,429
Less than 500	1,198	319	725	445	280	109	113	332	170	155
500 to 749	3,047	556	2,080	1,317	764	281	479	942	378	410
750 to 999	6,875	485	5,542	4,162	1,380	646	1,487	2,332	1,077	848
1,000 to 1,499	20,267	455	18,306	15,488	2,818	2,029	4,286	7,750	4,241	1,506
1,500 to 1,999	18,574	249	17,492	15,799	1,693	2,422	4,096	6,750	4,223	833
2,000 to 2,499	12,293	128	11,699	11,043	656	2,012	3,098	4,183	2,406	466
2,500 to 2,999	6,289	74	5,955	5,685	271	1,141	1,560	2,165	1,091	259
3,000 to 3,999	5,540	76	5,231	5,036	195	1,120	1,444	1,705	962	233
4,000 or more	3,016	24	2,854	2,708	146	736	734	960	424	137
Other [2]	5,204	160	4,463	3,558	905	1,210	1,226	1,459	568	582
Median square footage	1,693	909	1,737	1,798	1,298	1,951	1,779	1,663	1,692	1,336
Lot size:										
Single detached and attached units and mobile homes	88,223	2,554	79,647	67,362	12,285	13,250	19,278	30,582	16,536	6,022
Less than one-eighth acre	12,711	562	10,942	8,282	2,660	2,167	2,580	2,994	3,201	1,207
One-eighth to one-quarter acre	24,365	559	22,041	18,027	4,013	2,748	5,745	7,329	6,218	1,765
One-quarter to one-half acre	17,131	339	15,846	13,980	1,866	2,563	3,870	6,108	3,305	945
One-half up to one acre	11,464	321	10,497	9,200	1,297	2,066	2,258	4,894	1,279	646
1 to 5 acres	15,659	482	14,197	12,483	1,713	2,795	2,949	6,766	1,687	981
5 to 10 acres	2,496	45	2,352	2,157	195	340	683	1,011	318	99
10 acres or more	4,397	246	3,772	3,233	539	572	1,193	1,479	527	380
Median acreage	0.35	0.36	0.36	0.38	0.23	0.42	0.33	0.45	0.23	0.26

[1] Does not include selected vacant units. [2] Represents units not reported or size unknown.

Source: U.S. Census Bureau, Current Housing Reports, Series H150/01, *American Housing Survey for the United States*. See Internet site <http://www.census.gov/hhes/www/housing/ahs/nationaldata.html>.

No. 962. Occupied Housing Units—Tenure by Race of Householder: 1991 to 2001

[In thousands (93,147 represents 93,147,000), except percent. As of fall. Based on the American Housing Survey; see Appendix III]

Race of householder and tenure	1991	1993	1995	1997	1999	2001
ALL RACES [1]						
Occupied units, total	93,147	94,724	97,693	99,487	102,803	106,261
Owner occupied	59,796	61,252	63,544	65,487	68,796	72,265
Percent of occupied	64.2	64.7	65.0	65.8	66.9	68.0
Renter occupied	33,351	33,472	34,150	34,000	34,007	33,996
WHITE						
Occupied units, total	79,140	80,029	81,611	82,154	83,624	85,292
Owner occupied	53,749	54,878	56,507	57,781	60,041	62,465
Percent of occupied	67.9	68.6	69.2	70.3	71.8	73.2
Renter occupied	25,391	25,151	25,104	24,372	23,583	22,826
BLACK						
Occupied units, total	10,832	11,128	11,773	12,085	12,936	13,292
Owner occupied	4,635	4,788	5,137	5,457	6,013	6,318
Percent of occupied	42.8	43.0	43.6	45.2	46.5	47.5
Renter occupied	6,197	6,340	6,637	6,628	6,923	6,974
HISPANIC ORIGIN [2]						
Occupied units, total	6,239	6,614	7,757	8,513	9,041	9,814
Owner occupied	2,423	2,788	3,245	3,646	4,087	4,731
Percent of occupied	38.8	42.2	41.8	42.8	45.2	48.2
Renter occupied	3,816	3,826	4,512	4,867	4,955	5,083

[1] Includes other races, not shown separately. [2] Persons of Hispanic origin may be of any race.

Source: U.S. Census Bureau, Current Housing Reports, Series H150/91, H150/93, H150/95RV, H150/97, H150/99, and H150/01, *American Housing Survey for the United States*. See Internet site <http://www.census.gov/hhes/www/housing/ahs/nationaldata.html>.

Construction and Housing   621

No. 963. Homeownership Rates by Age of Householder and Household Status: 1985 to 2002

[In percent. Represents the proportion of owner households to the total number of occupied households. Based on the Current Population Survey/Housing Vacancy Survey; see source for details and see Appendix III]

Age of householder and household type	1985	1990	1995	1996	1997	1998	1999	2000	2001	2002
United States	63.9	63.9	64.7	65.4	65.7	66.3	66.8	67.4	67.8	67.9
AGE OF HOUSEHOLDER										
Less than 25 years old	17.2	15.7	15.9	18.0	17.7	18.2	19.9	21.7	22.5	23.0
25 to 29 years old	37.7	35.2	34.4	34.7	35.0	36.2	36.5	38.1	38.9	39.0
30 to 34 years old	54.0	51.8	53.1	53.0	52.6	53.6	53.8	54.6	54.8	55.0
35 to 39 years old	65.4	63.0	62.1	62.1	62.6	63.7	64.4	65.0	65.5	65.2
40 to 44 years old	71.4	69.8	68.6	69.0	69.7	70.0	69.9	70.6	70.8	71.7
45 to 49 years old	74.3	73.9	73.7	74.4	74.2	73.9	74.5	74.7	75.4	74.9
50 to 54 years old	77.5	76.8	77.0	77.2	77.7	77.8	77.8	78.5	78.2	77.8
55 to 59 years old	79.2	78.8	78.8	79.4	79.7	79.8	80.7	80.4	81.0	80.8
60 to 64 years old	79.9	79.8	80.3	80.7	80.5	82.1	81.3	80.3	81.8	81.5
65 to 69 years old	79.5	80.0	81.0	82.4	81.9	81.9	82.9	83.0	82.4	82.8
70 to 74 years old	76.8	78.4	80.9	81.4	82.0	82.2	82.8	82.6	82.5	82.5
75 years old and over	69.8	72.3	74.6	75.3	75.8	76.2	77.1	77.7	78.1	78.4
Less than 35 years old	39.9	38.5	38.6	39.1	38.7	39.3	39.7	40.8	41.2	41.3
35 to 44 years old	68.1	66.3	65.2	65.5	66.1	66.9	67.2	67.9	68.2	68.6
45 to 54 years old	75.9	75.2	75.2	75.6	75.8	75.7	76.0	76.5	76.7	76.3
55 to 64 years old	79.5	79.3	79.5	80.0	80.1	80.9	81.0	80.3	81.3	81.1
65 years and over	74.8	76.3	78.1	78.9	79.1	79.3	80.1	80.4	80.3	80.5
TYPE OF HOUSEHOLD										
Family households:										
Married-couple families	78.2	78.1	79.6	80.2	80.8	81.5	81.8	82.4	82.9	83.1
Male householder, no spouse present	57.8	55.2	55.3	55.5	54.0	55.7	56.1	57.5	57.9	58.0
Female householder, no spouse present	45.8	44.0	45.1	46.1	46.1	47.0	48.2	49.1	49.9	49.2
Nonfamily households:										
One-person	45.8	49.0	50.5	51.4	51.8	52.1	52.7	53.6	54.4	54.8
Male householder	38.8	42.4	43.8	44.9	45.2	45.7	46.3	47.4	48.2	48.7
Female householder	51.3	53.6	55.4	56.0	56.7	56.9	57.6	58.1	59.0	59.4
Other:										
Male householder	30.1	31.7	34.2	35.5	35.9	36.7	37.2	38.0	38.6	38.8
Female householder	30.6	32.5	33.0	35.9	39.5	40.3	41.5	40.6	41.0	41.6

Source: U.S. Census Bureau, "Housing Vacancies and Home Ownership." See Internet site <http://www.census.gov/hhes/www/hvs.html>.

No. 964. Homeownership Rates by State: 1985 to 2002

[In percent. See headnote, Table 963]

State	1985	1990	1995	2000	2001	2002	State	1985	1990	1995	2000	2001	2002
United States	63.9	63.9	64.7	67.4	67.8	67.9	Missouri	69.2	64.0	69.4	74.2	74.0	74.6
Alabama	70.4	68.4	70.1	73.2	73.2	73.5	Montana	66.5	69.1	68.7	70.2	68.3	69.3
Alaska	61.2	58.4	60.9	66.4	65.3	67.3	Nebraska	68.5	67.3	67.1	70.2	70.1	68.4
Arizona	64.7	64.5	62.9	68.0	68.1	65.9	Nevada	57.0	55.8	58.6	64.0	64.6	65.5
Arkansas	66.6	67.8	67.2	68.9	71.2	70.2	New Hampshire	65.5	65.0	66.0	69.2	68.4	69.5
California	54.2	53.8	55.4	57.1	58.2	58.0	New Jersey	62.3	65.0	64.9	66.2	66.5	67.2
Colorado	63.6	59.0	64.6	68.3	68.5	69.1	New Mexico	68.2	68.6	67.0	73.7	70.8	70.3
Connecticut	69.0	67.9	68.2	70.0	71.8	71.6	New York	50.3	53.3	52.7	53.4	53.9	55.0
Delaware	70.3	67.7	71.7	72.0	75.4	75.6	North Carolina	68.0	69.0	70.1	71.1	71.3	70.0
Dist. of Columbia	37.4	36.4	39.2	41.9	42.7	44.1	North Dakota	69.9	67.2	67.3	70.7	71.0	69.5
Florida	67.2	65.1	66.6	68.4	69.2	68.7	Ohio	67.9	68.7	67.9	71.3	71.2	72.0
Georgia	62.7	64.3	66.6	69.8	70.1	71.7	Oklahoma	70.5	70.3	69.8	72.7	71.5	69.4
Hawaii	51.0	55.5	50.2	55.2	55.5	57.4	Oregon	61.5	64.4	63.2	65.3	65.8	66.2
Idaho	71.0	69.4	72.0	70.5	71.7	73.0	Pennsylvania	71.6	73.8	71.5	74.7	74.3	74.0
Illinois	60.6	63.0	66.4	67.9	69.4	70.2	Rhode Island	61.4	58.5	57.9	61.5	60.1	59.6
Indiana	67.6	67.0	71.0	74.9	75.3	75.0	South Carolina	72.0	71.4	71.3	76.5	76.1	77.3
Iowa	69.9	70.7	71.4	75.2	76.6	73.9	South Dakota	67.6	66.2	67.5	71.2	71.5	71.5
Kansas	68.3	69.0	67.5	69.3	70.4	70.2	Tennessee	67.6	68.3	67.0	70.9	69.7	70.1
Kentucky	68.5	65.8	71.2	73.4	73.9	73.5	Texas	60.5	59.7	61.4	63.8	63.9	63.8
Louisiana	70.2	67.8	65.3	68.1	67.1	67.1	Utah	71.5	70.1	71.5	72.7	72.4	72.7
Maine	73.7	74.2	76.7	76.5	75.5	73.9	Vermont	69.5	72.6	70.4	68.7	69.8	70.2
Maryland	65.6	64.9	65.8	69.9	70.7	72.0	Virginia	68.5	69.8	68.1	73.9	75.1	74.3
Massachusetts	60.5	58.6	60.2	59.9	60.6	62.7	Washington	66.8	61.8	61.6	63.6	66.4	67.0
Michigan	70.7	72.3	72.2	77.2	77.1	76.0	West Virginia	75.9	72.0	73.1	75.9	76.4	77.0
Minnesota	70.0	68.0	73.3	76.1	76.1	77.3	Wisconsin	63.8	68.3	67.5	71.8	72.3	72.0
Mississippi	69.6	69.4	71.1	75.2	74.5	74.8	Wyoming	73.2	68.9	69.0	71.0	73.5	72.8

Source: U.S. Census Bureau, "Housing Vacancies and Home Ownership." See Internet site <http://www.census.gov/hhes/www/hvs.html>.

No. 965. Occupied Housing Units—Costs by Region: 2001

[As of fall. (72,265 represents 72,265,000). Specified owner-occupied units are limited to one-unit structures on less than 10 acres and no business on property. Specified renter-occupied units exclude one-unit structures on 10 acres or more. See headnote Table 966 for an explanation of housing costs. Based on the American Housing Survey; See Appendix III. For composition of regions, see map inside front cover]

Category	Number (1,000)					Percent distribution				
	Total units	North-east	Mid-west	South	West	Total units	North-east	Mid-west	South	West
OWNER OCCUPIED UNITS										
Total	72,265	12,987	18,049	26,715	14,514	100.0	100.0	100.0	100.0	100.0
Monthly housing costs:										
Less than $300	15,633	1,506	3,739	8,126	2,263	21.6	11.6	20.7	30.4	15.6
$300 to $399	6,850	1,287	1,991	2,338	1,234	9.5	9.9	11.0	8.8	8.5
$400 to $499	5,146	1,138	1,416	1,779	812	7.1	8.8	7.8	6.7	5.6
$500 to $599	4,856	1,054	1,313	1,862	627	6.7	8.1	7.3	7.0	4.3
$600 to $699	4,261	777	1,263	1,600	620	5.9	6.0	7.0	6.0	4.3
$700 to $799	4,110	698	1,235	1,510	667	5.7	5.4	6.8	5.7	4.6
$800 to $999	7,813	1,352	2,110	2,858	1,493	10.8	10.4	11.7	10.7	10.3
$1,000 to $1,249	7,214	1,424	1,798	2,385	1,608	10.0	11.0	10.0	8.9	11.1
$1,250 to $1,499	5,245	1,027	1,203	1,576	1,439	7.3	7.9	6.7	5.9	9.9
$1,500 or more	11,137	2,722	1,982	2,682	3,751	15.4	21.0	11.0	10.0	25.8
Median (dol.)[1]	686	805	645	560	938	(X)	(X)	(X)	(X)	(X)
RENTER OCCUPIED UNITS										
Total	33,996	7,334	6,709	11,353	8,600	100.0	100.0	100.0	100.0	100.0
Monthly housing costs:										
Less than $300	3,370	865	807	1,141	558	9.9	11.8	12.0	10.1	6.5
$300 to $399	2,442	416	613	971	442	7.2	5.7	9.1	8.6	5.1
$400 to $499	3,911	696	1,076	1,458	680	11.5	9.5	16.0	12.8	7.9
$500 to $599	4,686	881	1,147	1,657	1,001	13.8	12.0	17.1	14.6	11.6
$600 to $699	4,559	1,023	878	1,471	1,188	13.4	13.9	13.1	13.0	13.8
$700 to $799	3,682	815	614	1,237	1,017	10.8	11.1	9.2	10.9	11.8
$800 to $999	4,526	1,117	651	1,343	1,416	13.3	15.2	9.7	11.8	16.5
$1,000 to $1,249	2,363	559	276	641	888	7.0	7.6	4.1	5.6	10.3
$1,250 to $1,499	1,046	247	105	202	493	3.1	3.4	1.6	1.8	5.7
$1,500 or more	1,209	336	118	217	538	3.6	4.6	1.8	1.9	6.3
No cash rent	2,201	380	426	1,016	380	6.5	5.2	6.3	8.9	4.4
Median (dol.)[1]	633	661	556	596	724	(X)	(X)	(X)	(X)	(X)

X Not applicable.   [1] For explanation of median, see Guide to Tabular Presentation.

No. 966. Occupied Housing Units—Financial Summary by Selected Characteristics of the Householder: 2001

[In thousands of units (106,261 represents 106,261,000), except as indicated. As of fall. Housing costs include real estate taxes, property insurance, utilities, fuel, water, garbage collection, and mortgage. Based on the American Housing Survey; see Appendix III]

Characteristic	Total occupied units	Tenure		Black		Hispanic origin[1]		Elderly[2]		Households below poverty level	
		Owner	Renter	Owner	Renter	Owner	Renter	Owner	Renter	Owner	Renter
Total units[3]	106,261	72,265	33,996	6,318	6,974	4,731	5,083	17,513	4,299	6,713	7,889
Monthly housing costs:											
Less than $300	19,003	15,633	3,370	1,607	1,082	897	439	7,452	966	2,817	1,908
$300-$399	9,292	6,850	2,442	587	554	312	320	2,987	342	821	807
$400-$499	9,056	5,146	3,911	488	838	302	561	1,733	529	655	1,095
$500-$599	9,542	4,856	4,686	551	1,017	325	784	1,296	461	523	1,057
$600-$699	8,820	4,261	4,559	420	971	300	809	832	403	371	756
$700-$799	7,793	4,110	3,682	437	736	270	693	639	310	296	530
$800-$999	12,339	7,813	4,526	683	843	582	719	889	380	397	503
$1,000 or more	28,215	23,596	4,618	1,546	534	1,745	590	1,686	430	832	485
Median amount (dol.)[4]	658	686	633	587	580	786	644	339	516	356	478
Monthly housing costs as percent of income:[5]											
Less than 5 percent	5,217	4,906	311	329	84	225	27	1,043	39	29	34
5 to 9 percent	12,267	11,131	1,136	912	204	583	133	2,857	86	78	50
10 to 14 percent	15,166	12,316	2,850	995	456	626	387	2,972	182	156	83
15 to 19 percent	14,879	10,913	3,966	842	666	649	487	2,212	231	271	127
20 to 24 percent	12,616	8,544	4,072	719	822	593	596	1,562	314	309	272
25 to 29 percent	9,555	5,932	3,623	528	702	384	588	1,147	411	297	406
30 to 34 percent	6,840	4,181	2,659	414	576	362	443	846	293	275	322
35 to 39 percent	4,758	2,728	2,030	261	424	256	336	706	248	265	350
40 percent or more	19,871	10,057	9,815	1,188	2,242	957	1,741	3,512	1,868	3,540	4,307
Median amount (percent)[4]	21	18	29	20	31	22	32	19	41	62	65
Median monthly costs (dol.):[4]											
Electricity	59	65	44	68	47	65	44	58	38	59	43
Piped gas	55	61	39	68	46	44	33	61	38	60	41
Fuel oil	75	79	60	70	49	70	61	74	63	69	49

[1] Persons of Hispanic origin may be of any race.   [2] Householders 65 years old and over.   [3] Includes units with mortgage payment not reported and no cash rent not shown separately.   [4] For explanation of median, see Guide to Tabular Presentation.   [5] Money income before taxes.

Source of Tables 965 and 966: U.S. Census Bureau, Current Housing Reports, Series H150/01, *American Housing Survey for the United States.* See Internet site <http://www.census.gov/hhes/www/housing/ahs/nationaldata.html>.

Construction and Housing   623

No. 967. Specified Owner-Occupied Housing Units—Value and Costs by State: 2000

[In percent, except as indicated (55,212 represents 55,212,000. As of April 1. Specified owner-occupied units are owner-occupied, one-family, attached and detached houses on less than 10 acres without a business or medical office on the property. Based on the 2000 Census of Population and Housing; see text, Section 1, and Appendix III. For definition of median, see Guide to Tabular Presentation]

State	Total (1,000)	Percent of units with value of— $99,999 or less	$100,000 to $199,999	$200,000 or more	Median value (dol.)	Median selected monthly owner costs[1] (dol.)	Less than 15 percent	15 to 24 percent	25 to 34 percent	35 percent or more
U.S.	55,212	40.3	38.4	21.4	119,600	1,088	36.5	31.4	15.5	15.8
AL	919	61.9	28.8	9.3	85,100	816	43.5	29.1	12.1	13.9
AK	106	22.5	57.9	19.7	144,200	1,315	32.6	33.3	17.4	16.7
AZ	1,032	35.6	45.9	18.5	121,300	1,039	34.8	31.8	16.3	16.2
AR	513	72.3	22.0	5.7	72,800	737	45.3	29.0	11.8	12.7
CA	5,528	11.6	35.5	52.9	211,500	1,478	28.0	28.7	19.3	23.2
CO	903	13.3	52.4	34.3	166,600	1,197	32.2	32.5	18.2	16.6
CT	728	12.5	50.6	36.9	166,900	1,426	31.8	32.9	17.7	17.1
DE	177	28.1	54.0	17.9	130,400	1,101	38.5	32.2	14.8	13.8
DC	76	18.6	43.5	37.8	157,200	1,291	38.2	27.0	14.6	18.6
FL	3,242	46.9	38.5	14.7	105,500	1,004	34.2	30.5	15.8	18.5
GA	1,596	43.7	39.1	17.2	111,200	1,039	36.4	32.5	15.0	15.2
HI	174	6.7	21.7	71.5	272,700	1,571	35.7	23.7	17.9	22.1
ID	255	45.2	43.9	10.9	106,300	887	36.6	32.6	15.6	14.5
IL	2,470	35.7	41.0	23.3	130,800	1,198	36.1	32.4	15.9	14.9
IN	1,379	55.3	36.4	8.3	94,300	869	42.7	32.5	12.9	11.2
IA	665	65.7	28.2	6.1	82,500	829	45.2	32.4	12.2	9.6
KS	582	61.6	29.9	8.4	83,500	888	43.5	32.8	12.5	10.5
KY	806	61.8	30.2	8.1	86,700	816	44.3	30.1	12.3	12.3
LA	865	62.3	29.2	8.5	85,000	816	45.7	27.0	11.4	14.2
ME	255	51.3	38.1	10.7	98,700	923	35.8	33.8	15.2	14.7
MD	1,179	23.1	50.3	26.6	146,000	1,296	32.1	33.7	17.6	16.1
MA	1,188	9.5	46.4	44.1	185,700	1,353	33.4	33.1	16.7	16.2
MI	2,269	41.3	41.6	17.2	115,600	972	41.8	31.5	13.2	12.7
MN	1,117	35.1	49.4	15.5	122,400	1,044	38.7	34.9	14.9	11.1
MS	532	72.5	21.8	5.7	71,400	752	42.4	27.5	12.3	16.0
MO	1,188	58.1	32.0	9.9	89,900	861	43.4	31.6	12.6	11.6
MT	165	50.5	40.2	9.3	99,500	863	38.0	30.9	15.1	15.3
NE	370	61.4	31.7	6.9	88,000	895	42.1	33.1	13.6	10.6
NV	363	15.7	63.7	20.6	142,000	1,190	28.0	32.1	19.2	19.8
NH	249	26.7	54.2	19.1	133,300	1,226	28.8	36.7	18.7	15.3
NJ	1,702	15.2	46.7	38.0	170,800	1,534	27.0	32.6	19.3	20.5
NM	340	45.2	40.3	14.6	108,100	929	40.3	27.9	14.6	16.0
NY	2,690	32.2	35.7	32.1	148,700	1,357	31.5	31.4	16.8	19.6
NC	1,616	45.3	39.7	15.0	108,300	985	37.7	31.5	14.8	15.0
ND	122	73.3	23.5	3.3	74,400	818	44.9	32.5	12.1	9.7
OH	2,613	47.7	40.8	11.4	103,700	963	38.6	33.1	14.5	13.2
OK	699	73.8	21.4	4.9	70,700	764	45.3	29.6	11.9	12.1
OR	654	17.0	56.4	26.6	152,100	1,125	32.2	32.0	17.8	17.5
PA	2,889	52.4	36.2	11.3	97,000	1,010	37.8	31.5	14.8	15.1
RI	202	20.5	61.1	18.3	133,000	1,205	30.2	33.6	18.5	17.1
SC	784	54.1	33.2	12.7	94,900	894	40.9	30.2	13.5	14.3
SD	138	68.9	26.0	5.1	79,600	828	43.4	32.5	13.0	10.4
TN	1,206	55.9	33.0	11.1	93,000	882	40.4	30.4	13.8	14.4
TX	3,850	63.3	26.9	9.8	82,500	986	40.7	31.5	13.2	13.6
UT	427	16.1	60.8	23.1	146,100	1,102	34.9	30.4	18.1	16.2
VT	106	41.0	48.2	10.8	111,500	1,021	30.1	35.6	17.7	16.2
VA	1,511	36.7	40.2	23.1	125,400	1,144	35.5	33.5	16.3	14.1
WA	1,157	15.1	48.5	36.4	168,300	1,268	30.3	31.9	19.1	18.1
WV	393	73.8	21.7	4.6	72,800	713	50.8	25.7	10.4	11.9
WI	1,122	41.9	46.1	12.0	112,200	1,024	36.8	35.1	15.6	12.0
WY	96	53.6	37.2	9.2	96,600	825	45.1	30.3	12.7	11.3

[1] For homes with a mortgage. Includes mortgages, deeds of trust, taxes, utilities, etc.

Source: U.S. Census Bureau, "2000 Census of Population and Housing, Profiles of General Demographic Characteristics"; <http://www.census.gov/Press-Release/www/2002/demoprofiles.html>.

No. 968. Specified Owner-Occupied Housing Units—Value and Costs by the 25 Largest Metropolitan Areas: 2000

[In percent, except as indicated (884.3 represents 884,300). As of April 1. Specified owner-occupied units are owner-occupied, one-family, attached and detached houses on less than 10 acres without a business or medical office on the property. Based on sample data from the 2000 Census of Population and Housing; see text, Section 1, and Appendix III. See headnote Table 971 for information regarding metropolitan areas]

Metropolitan area	Total (1,000)	Percent of units with value of— $99,999 or less	Percent of units with value of— $200,000 or more	Median value (dol.)	Median selected monthly owner costs[1] (dol.)	Less than 15 percent	15 to 24 percent	25 to 34 percent	35 percent or more
Atlanta, GA MSA	884.3	27.9	24.3	135,300	1,165	32.8	34.9	16.3	15.4
Boston-Worcester-Lawrence, MA-NH-ME-CT CMSA	1,067.8	7.4	46.8	192,500	1,415	32.0	34.0	17.3	16.2
Chicago-Gary-Kenosha, IL-IN-WI CMSA	1,717.3	18.4	32.0	159,000	1,347	31.5	33.1	17.8	17.0
Cincinnati-Hamilton, OH-KY-IN CMSA	439.2	38.8	15.5	116,500	1,064	36.3	35.3	15.5	12.4
Cleveland-Akron, OH CMSA	711.1	37.7	15.3	117,900	1,049	35.5	33.2	15.6	15.1
Dallas-Fort Worth, TX CMSA	1,003.7	50.0	14.6	100,000	1,148	35.7	34.9	14.9	13.7
Denver-Boulder-Greeley, CO CMSA	565.3	6.1	39.7	179,500	1,271	30.7	33.4	18.8	16.6
Detroit-Ann Arbor-Flint, MI CMSA	1,305.3	32.4	22.7	132,600	1,076	40.1	31.6	13.7	13.8
Houston-Galveston-Brazoria, TX CMSA	863.4	57.4	12.2	89,700	1,072	39.4	32.6	13.1	13.8
Kansas City, MO-KS MSA	418.0	47.3	12.4	104,700	986	39.5	34.4	13.7	11.8
Los Angeles-Riverside-Orange County, CA CMSA	2,498.4	9.6	51.0	203,300	1,494	26.4	28.3	19.5	25.0
Miami-Fort Lauderdale, FL CMSA	634.5	33.1	18.3	126,100	1,225	24.2	30.0	18.8	25.9
Minneapolis-St. Paul, MN-WI MSA	704.0	18.3	21.2	141,200	1,157	34.2	37.1	16.7	11.8
New York-Northern New Jersey-Long Island, NY-NJ-CT-PA CMSA	3,088.9	7.0	51.0	203,100	1,679	27.8	30.7	18.5	22.3
Philadelphia-Wilmington-Atlantic City, PA-NJ-DE-MD CMSA	1,456.0	37.3	18.2	122,300	1,224	32.3	32.2	16.8	17.8
Phoenix-Mesa, AZ MSA	689.5	30.5	20.5	127,900	1,088	33.0	33.1	17.0	16.2
Pittsburgh, PA MSA	601.3	62.0	8.2	86,100	937	40.2	30.8	13.7	14.4
Portland-Salem, OR-WA CMSA	453.7	8.3	31.8	165,400	1,232	29.0	32.9	19.4	18.2
Sacramento-Yolo, CA CMSA	359.8	14.2	31.2	159,700	1,298	28.7	31.6	19.4	19.7
St. Louis, MO-IL MSA	624.4	50.4	13.5	99,400	953	42.0	32.8	12.9	11.6
San Diego, CA MSA	457.3	3.5	59.8	227,200	1,541	27.7	28.4	19.9	23.2
San Francisco-Oakland-San Jose, CA CMSA	1,258.0	2.7	82.5	353,500	1,822	29.4	28.2	19.5	22.2
Seattle-Tacoma-Bremerton, WA CMSA	719.2	6.2	47.8	195,400	1,399	27.8	32.3	20.3	19.0
Tampa-St. Petersburg-Clearwater, FL MSA	540.9	55.5	11.0	93,800	938	35.1	31.6	15.5	16.9
Washington-Baltimore, DC-MD-VA-WV CMSA	1,621.6	17.4	34.2	161,600	1,382	31.7	34.6	17.7	15.5

[1] For homes with a mortgage. Includes mortgages, deeds of trust, taxes, utilities, etc.

No. 969. Specified Owner-Occupied Housing Units—Value and Costs by the 25 Largest Cities: 2000

[In percent, except as indicated (104.8 represents 104,800). As of April 1. See headnote, Table 968 for coverage]

City	Total (1,000)	$99,999 or less	$100,000 to $199,999	$200,000 or more	Median value (dol.)	Median selected monthly owner costs[1] (dol.)	Less than 15 percent	15 to 24 percent	25 to 34 percent	35 percent or more
Austin, TX	104.8	35.5	40.9	23.6	124,700	1,181	34.3	34.3	16.0	14.8
Baltimore, MD	116.6	83.3	12.5	4.3	69,100	853	35.0	28.0	14.8	20.5
Boston, MA	30.5	5.8	49.5	44.7	190,600	1,370	33.1	30.9	15.0	20.0
Chicago, IL	263.9	31.3	48.3	20.5	132,400	1,216	32.6	28.7	16.2	21.2
Columbus, OH	134.0	49.0	45.3	5.7	101,400	987	30.9	36.3	17.2	15.0
Dallas, TX	173.6	55.2	25.0	19.7	89,800	1,054	38.9	29.3	13.6	16.9
Denver, CO	104.3	10.7	55.6	33.7	165,800	1,134	33.2	29.7	17.2	19.2
Detroit, MI	164.2	84.8	12.9	2.3	63,600	769	41.1	23.9	12.0	20.4
El Paso, TX	102.0	79.9	16.4	3.7	71,300	810	38.4	30.3	14.4	15.7
Houston, TX	295.5	64.4	22.6	13.0	79,300	965	41.7	28.8	12.3	15.6
Indianapolis, IN[2]	172.7	51.7	39.6	8.7	98,200	928	37.6	33.6	14.5	13.5
Jacksonville, FL	157.7	61.3	30.4	8.4	87,800	902	37.2	32.4	14.2	15.2
Los Angeles, CA	412.8	4.6	39.7	55.7	221,600	1,556	27.2	24.8	17.4	29.4
Memphis, TN	130.7	73.2	19.3	7.5	72,800	838	34.0	29.4	15.1	19.8
Milwaukee, WI	82.3	73.0	24.8	2.2	80,400	863	36.7	32.5	15.0	15.0
Nashville-Davidson, TN[2]	109.1	41.2	43.3	15.5	113,300	1,006	35.6	32.1	16.2	15.3
New York, NY	391.4	4.2	40.8	55.0	211,900	1,535	30.4	25.3	15.8	26.8
Philadelphia, PA	315.4	84.9	12.6	2.5	59,700	800	39.2	26.3	12.8	19.4
Phoenix, AZ	250.1	41.9	41.0	17.1	112,600	1,021	30.7	33.6	17.0	17.8
San Antonio, TX	217.3	74.9	20.4	4.7	68,800	881	40.4	30.9	13.8	13.9
San Diego, CA	188.0	4.0	34.6	61.4	233,100	1,526	29.2	28.1	19.1	22.8
San Francisco, CA	79.5	5.6	3.6	90.8	396,400	1,693	36.9	23.7	15.6	22.9
San Jose, CA	146.9	2.1	3.4	94.5	394,000	1,717	27.5	30.1	20.0	21.8
Seattle, WA	102.7	2.5	25.9	71.6	259,600	1,497	32.0	29.0	18.7	19.7
Washington, DC	76.3	18.6	43.5	37.8	157,200	1,291	38.2	27.0	14.6	18.6

[1] Includes mortgages, deeds of trust, taxes, utilities, etc. [2] Represents the portion of a consolidated city that is not within one or more separately incorporated places.

Source of Tables 968 and 969: U.S. Census Bureau, "2000 Census of Population and Housing, Profiles of General Demographic Characteristics"; <http://www.census.gov/Press-Release/www/2002/demoprofiles.html>.

Construction and Housing 625

No. 970. Specified Renter-Occupied Housing Units—Gross Rent by State: 2000

[In percent, except as indicated (35,200 represents 35,200,000. As of April 1. Specified renter-occupied units include all renter-occupied units except 1-unit attached or detached houses on 10 acres or more. Based on the 2000 Census of Population and Housing; see text, Section 1, and Appendix III. For definition of median, see Guide to Tabular Presentation]

State	Total[1] (1,000)	$299 or less	$300 to $499	$500 to $749	$750 to $999	$1,000 or more	Median gross rent (dol.)	Less than 15 percent	15 to 24 percent	25 to 34 percent	35 percent or more
U.S.	35,200	10.4	22.0	33.7	17.2	11.6	602	18.1	27.1	17.8	29.5
AL	469	20.3	34.1	26.3	6.4	2.5	447	19.6	24.0	15.1	27.4
AK	82	4.0	11.7	31.7	22.4	16.9	720	17.3	26.1	17.2	25.4
AZ	605	6.8	20.6	38.8	18.3	10.1	619	15.8	26.9	18.8	30.9
AR	310	16.6	37.1	27.5	5.8	2.0	453	19.4	25.1	15.3	26.7
CA	4,922	4.9	12.6	31.3	23.6	24.5	747	14.6	26.7	19.2	34.1
CO	534	7.2	16.3	35.2	21.4	16.4	671	15.2	28.8	20.4	30.4
CT	429	9.6	12.8	35.6	22.7	15.0	681	18.4	27.5	18.5	29.0
DE	82	10.1	14.3	41.6	19.4	8.8	639	19.5	28.6	17.8	26.7
DC	147	12.8	17.6	34.5	16.8	15.4	618	20.0	26.9	17.8	28.2
FL	1,889	7.2	18.4	38.3	20.8	10.7	641	14.6	26.3	18.6	33.0
GA	964	11.9	20.9	31.2	20.8	9.2	613	18.4	27.4	17.5	28.1
HI	174	6.7	8.6	24.8	22.8	23.8	779	14.2	23.6	17.2	29.1
ID	126	12.7	30.4	34.0	10.9	3.7	515	17.5	27.1	17.6	28.1
IL	1,488	10.6	21.2	36.1	17.5	10.8	605	20.0	28.3	17.1	28.3
IN	654	11.9	31.2	38.4	9.7	3.4	521	21.0	28.3	17.0	26.4
IA	302	17.1	35.8	31.2	7.1	2.6	470	22.4	28.2	16.8	24.8
KS	310	13.9	33.4	31.4	10.3	4.8	498	21.1	29.3	16.7	25.0
KY	449	18.9	36.8	26.2	6.1	2.1	445	20.8	25.5	16.0	25.6
LA	526	17.3	34.4	28.7	7.0	2.9	466	18.6	23.3	14.8	29.8
ME	144	16.2	30.7	32.5	10.0	3.3	497	16.9	28.1	19.2	27.4
MD	632	8.7	14.2	33.6	24.3	14.9	689	18.2	29.3	19.1	27.0
MA	932	13.0	14.1	28.7	21.8	18.8	684	18.9	26.8	19.5	28.6
MI	976	10.8	28.3	38.3	12.5	5.7	546	20.9	27.2	16.8	28.4
MN	471	14.4	23.3	35.6	15.5	7.5	566	18.7	29.5	19.6	27.1
MS	283	21.1	33.3	25.9	6.0	1.9	439	18.9	23.4	14.8	27.6
MO	633	15.1	34.9	31.8	8.6	3.3	484	20.3	28.2	16.8	26.3
MT	105	18.6	36.9	26.4	6.1	2.4	447	18.2	25.6	16.9	28.2
NE	207	14.2	34.6	32.9	8.3	3.8	491	21.4	30.2	17.2	23.5
NV	293	4.1	12.2	40.7	26.7	13.0	699	15.2	28.5	20.2	30.5
NH	141	9.0	15.8	39.9	21.5	9.8	646	18.0	31.7	19.2	25.6
NJ	1,049	7.9	8.6	31.8	29.9	18.6	751	18.5	27.6	18.3	29.9
NM	201	13.4	31.3	28.9	10.8	5.8	503	16.6	24.5	16.8	30.5
NY	3,302	10.2	15.7	32.5	21.2	17.3	672	19.1	24.2	16.9	33.4
NC	944	11.2	26.8	34.7	13.7	5.3	548	19.3	27.2	16.3	26.7
ND	83	22.9	40.7	21.9	3.7	1.7	412	22.7	28.9	15.4	22.6
OH	1,353	12.7	32.0	36.1	10.3	4.0	515	20.5	28.1	17.0	27.4
OK	414	15.2	39.6	27.5	6.4	2.6	456	19.8	26.4	16.0	26.7
OR	468	7.4	18.9	42.4	18.0	9.4	620	14.7	28.0	19.6	32.2
PA	1,349	13.0	28.9	33.7	12.4	6.3	531	19.2	26.6	17.3	28.6
RI	163	15.6	22.6	38.5	12.9	6.5	553	18.7	26.5	19.4	28.9
SC	421	14.1	29.1	33.0	9.7	4.1	510	19.1	26.1	15.4	26.8
SD	88	22.9	35.7	25.3	4.7	2.0	426	20.9	29.2	16.3	22.7
TN	657	15.3	30.0	33.3	10.1	3.7	505	18.9	26.7	17.3	27.2
TX	2,649	9.1	25.1	37.1	15.4	7.9	574	18.8	28.8	17.4	27.1
UT	199	7.7	21.0	42.2	15.3	8.5	597	18.1	28.7	18.8	27.7
VT	67	11.6	25.2	38.1	14.0	5.4	553	15.9	27.7	20.1	29.5
VA	843	9.3	18.9	30.7	20.3	15.0	650	18.2	29.3	18.5	26.3
WA	796	7.3	16.4	36.4	21.6	14.0	663	15.1	28.4	19.8	30.8
WV	176	22.8	38.8	19.7	3.3	1.2	401	18.9	21.3	14.6	28.3
WI	642	10.5	29.5	39.7	12.3	4.3	540	21.1	30.8	17.5	25.4
WY	56	16.4	42.0	23.6	5.5	2.7	437	24.1	26.3	15.2	23.3

[1] Includes units with no cash rent.

Source: U.S. Census Bureau, "2000 Census of Population and Housing, Profiles of General Demographic Characteristics"; <http://www.census.gov/Press-Release/www/2002/demoprofiles.html>.

No. 971. Specified Renter-Occupied Housing Units—Gross Rent by the 25 Largest Metropolitan Areas: 2000

[In percent, except as indicated (501.9 represents 501,900). As of April 1. Specified renter-occupied units include all renter-occupied units except one-unit attached or detached houses on 10 acres or more. Based on sample data from the 2000 Census of Population and Housing; see text, Section 1, and Appendix III. Covers metropolitan statistical areas (MSAs) and consolidated metropolitan statistical areas (CMSAs) as defined by the U.S. Office of Management and Budget as of June 30, 1999. For definitions of metropolitan areas, see Appendix II. For definition of median, see Guide to Tabular Presentation]

Metropolitan area	Total [1] (1,000)	$499 or less	$500 to $749	$750 or more	Median gross rent (dol.)	Less than 15 percent	15 to 24 percent	25 to 34 percent	35 percent or more
Atlanta, GA MSA	501.9	16.3	33.0	48.0	746	17.1	29.9	19.4	28.5
Boston-Worcester-Lawrence, MA-NH-ME-CT CMSA	847.2	23.6	28.3	44.9	720	18.7	27.6	19.6	28.3
Chicago-Gary-Kenosha, IL-IN-WI CMSA	1,145.5	23.5	39.0	34.8	659	19.2	28.7	17.5	29.1
Cincinnati-Hamilton, OH-KY-IN CMSA	250.3	45.4	34.4	16.7	516	21.2	28.9	16.9	27.4
Cleveland-Akron, OH CMSA	360.8	38.9	39.5	17.6	545	18.9	27.6	17.6	29.3
Dallas-Fort Worth, TX CMSA	750.9	21.7	42.9	32.8	649	18.9	32.0	19.0	25.4
Denver-Boulder-Greeley, CO CMSA	334.3	19.2	35.8	42.7	706	15.1	29.3	21.0	30.5
Detroit-Ann Arbor-Flint, MI CMSA	574.0	33.0	39.9	23.4	584	21.2	26.9	16.5	29.0
Houston-Galveston-Brazoria, TX CMSA	643.0	30.6	41.5	24.7	589	20.3	30.0	17.4	26.2
Kansas City, MO-KS MSA	219.9	34.2	39.8	21.9	575	20.2	31.2	17.6	24.7
Los Angeles-Riverside-Orange County, NCA CMSA	2,412.5	16.2	35.0	46.4	733	14.2	26.3	19.1	35.2
Miami-Fort Lauderdale, FL CMSA	526.4	20.8	36.9	39.3	689	12.3	24.1	18.9	37.7
Minneapolis-St. Paul, MN-WI MSA	310.9	24.7	41.7	31.5	641	17.3	30.9	20.3	28.0
New York-Northern New Jersey-Long Island, NY-NJ-CT-PA CMSA	3,627.1	19.8	30.4	47.2	740	19.5	24.9	17.2	32.5
Philadelphia-Wilmington-Atlantic City, PA-NJ-DE-MD CMSA	695.1	24.0	38.9	33.0	651	17.3	26.8	17.7	31.2
Phoenix-Mesa, AZ MSA	381.2	20.4	41.6	34.3	661	15.3	28.2	19.7	30.9
Pittsburgh, PA MSA	275.0	50.3	31.3	12.3	482	20.2	25.7	17.2	28.5
Portland-Salem, OR-WA CMSA	317.1	18.8	45.0	33.4	660	14.8	29.7	20.2	30.9
Sacramento-Yolo, CA CMSA	255.9	20.6	40.6	36.2	673	14.9	27.6	19.1	33.8
St. Louis, MO-IL MSA	287.5	42.7	37.1	15.5	525	20.6	28.4	16.5	27.6
San Diego, CA MSA	441.6	13.0	33.4	49.4	761	12.6	27.0	20.3	34.1
San Francisco-Oakland-San Jose, CA CMSA	1,072.2	11.0	17.2	69.2	968	16.4	28.5	19.7	31.0
Seattle-Tacoma-Bremerton, WA CMSA	514.8	16.9	35.7	44.1	723	14.9	29.8	20.6	29.8
Tampa-St. Petersburg-Clearwater, FL MSA	294.3	27.8	42.6	25.5	608	15.7	28.3	19.0	30.7
Washington-Baltimore, DC-MD-VA-WV CMSA	996.7	19.1	29.9	47.5	744	18.6	30.3	19.2	26.2

[1] Includes units with no cash rent.

No. 972. Specified Renter-Occupied Housing Units—Gross Rent by the 25 Largest Cities: 2000

[In percent, except as indicated (146.1 represents 146,100). As of April 1. See headnote, Table 971 for coverage]

City	Total [1] (1,000)	$299 or less	$300 to $499	$500 to $749	$750 to $999	$1,000 or more	Median gross rent (dol.)	Less than 15 percent	15 to 24 percent	25 to 34 percent	35 percent or more
Austin, TX	146.1	3.2	9.0	41.0	28.9	16.1	724	14.4	28.3	19.4	33.5
Baltimore, MD	127.6	19.3	29.8	34.3	9.7	4.3	498	18.8	23.7	17.9	33.0
Boston, MA	162.1	15.6	8.8	19.2	24.0	30.5	803	17.2	24.2	20.0	32.1
Chicago, IL	596.1	10.1	18.8	39.6	17.4	12.1	616	19.3	27.4	16.9	30.8
Columbus, OH	153.3	8.1	23.5	46.5	14.9	5.3	586	18.3	30.3	18.0	29.0
Dallas, TX	256.1	5.4	19.2	45.3	18.4	10.0	623	18.8	30.6	19.2	26.8
Denver, CO	113.4	9.5	18.1	37.6	19.8	13.0	631	16.5	28.4	20.3	30.6
Detroit, MI	150.8	13.5	37.4	33.8	8.5	2.8	486	21.1	21.2	14.8	33.9
El Paso, TX	70.3	17.3	35.3	30.7	8.3	3.3	474	15.9	25.1	18.9	32.0
Houston, TX	388.6	5.1	27.9	42.0	14.9	7.8	575	19.9	29.5	17.7	27.0
Indianapolis, IN [2]	132.1	7.3	26.9	45.5	13.8	4.2	567	18.6	30.3	17.9	28.5
Jacksonville, FL	104.5	10.3	21.0	40.3	18.5	5.8	598	17.5	30.1	18.8	26.8
Los Angeles, CA	782.2	5.7	15.8	38.4	20.7	17.5	672	14.1	24.4	18.8	37.1
Memphis, TN	110.4	12.9	26.5	40.5	13.0	3.8	548	17.7	26.2	17.7	31.8
Milwaukee, WI	126.7	10.3	32.5	42.4	9.2	3.7	527	18.8	27.6	17.0	32.0
Nashville-Davidson, TN [2]	103.1	11.0	16.6	44.8	17.4	7.3	614	17.1	29.9	20.1	27.8
New York, NY	2,108.5	11.0	12.0	32.2	23.5	19.4	705	20.5	23.5	16.4	33.7
Philadelphia, PA	240.0	10.9	24.8	38.3	14.7	7.5	569	16.1	22.9	15.9	36.0
Phoenix, AZ	183.0	5.3	19.2	44.3	19.5	9.2	622	15.6	28.3	20.3	30.9
San Antonio, TX	169.7	10.7	28.1	37.9	13.3	6.0	549	17.5	29.7	18.3	28.0
San Diego, CA	227.2	4.1	11.0	31.4	23.6	25.9	763	12.8	26.6	20.0	34.4
San Francisco, CA	214.2	7.6	9.1	18.1	19.6	43.6	928	20.9	28.2	18.6	28.2
San Jose, CA	105.4	3.5	4.2	9.2	21.3	59.9	1,123	14.3	28.6	20.9	32.3
Seattle, WA	133.3	8.6	9.7	35.3	24.3	20.2	721	14.6	29.4	21.5	30.6
Washington, DC	146.9	12.8	17.6	34.5	16.8	15.4	618	20.0	26.9	17.8	28.2

[1] Includes units with no cash rent. [2] Represents the portion of a consolidated city that is not within one or more separately incorporated places.

Source of Tables 971 and 972: U.S. Census Bureau, "2000 Census of Population and Housing, Profiles of General Demographic Characteristics"; <http://www.census.gov/Press-Release/www/2002/demoprofiles.html>.

No. 973. Mortgage Characteristics—Owner Occupied Units: 2001

[In thousands (72,265 represents 72,265,000). As of fall. Based on the American Housing Survey; see Appendix III]

Mortgage characteristic	Total owner-occupied units	Housing unit characteristics		Household characteristics				
		New construction [1]	Mobile homes	Black	Hispanic [2]	Elderly [3]	Moved in past year	Below poverty level
ALL OWNERS								
Total [4]	72,265	4,690	6,001	6,318	4,731	17,513	5,723	6,713
Mortgages currently on property:								
None, owned free and clear	25,675	938	3,228	2,113	1,397	12,792	1,103	3,924
Regular and home equity mortgages	44,970	3,647	2,609	4,013	3,241	4,317	4,491	2,569
Regular mortgage only	41,717	3,559	2,450	3,785	3,093	3,490	4,384	2,367
Home equity mortgage only	4,752	233	159	343	201	498	172	196
With regular mortgage, home equity not reported	6,481	314	78	310	278	845	234	243
No regular mortgage, home equity not reported	1,583	103	163	190	91	376	129	213
Number of regular and home equity mortgages: [4]								
1 mortgage	32,721	2,828	2,332	3,165	2,562	3,268	3,786	1,947
2 mortgages	8,470	575	126	487	434	497	446	245
3 mortgages or more	1,008	63	14	86	51	68	35	38
Type of home equity mortgage:								
Regular and home equity lump sum [4]	3,090	174	43	194	121	150	107	75
With home equity line of credit	549	30	4	43	23	45	15	25
No home equity line of credit	2,513	141	38	148	98	104	90	49
Regular no home equity lump sum [4]	38,627	3,385	2,407	3,591	2,972	3,340	4,277	2,292
With home equity line of credit	4,051	250	29	180	177	235	175	107
No home equity line of credit	31,929	2,957	2,257	3,142	2,607	2,646	3,883	1,858
Home equity lump sum no regular [4]	1,661	60	116	149	80	348	65	122
With home equity line of credit	290	5	7	7	10	87	2	31
No home equity line of credit	1,332	55	102	141	70	245	60	88
No regular or home equity lump sum [4]	28,886	1,072	3,435	2,385	1,558	13,675	1,274	4,225
With home equity line of credit	1,592	29	43	80	68	479	42	81
No home equity line of credit	25,712	940	3,230	2,115	1,400	12,820	1,103	3,931
OWNERS WITH ONE OR MORE REGULAR OR LUMP SUM HOME EQUITY MORTGAGES, 2001								
Total [4]	43,378	3,618	2,566	3,934	3,173	3,838	4,449	2,488
Type of primary mortgage:								
FHA	6,110	494	116	1,023	840	339	811	295
VA	2,177	208	70	271	174	145	279	81
Farmers Home Administration	318	36	14	48	23	30	25	43
Other types	31,796	2,694	2,211	2,225	1,919	2,766	3,086	1,646
Mortgage origination:								
Placed new mortgage(s)	42,799	3,599	2,491	3,852	3,089	3,780	4,379	2,431
Primary obtained when property acquired	30,230	3,336	2,121	2,979	2,462	2,181	4,228	1,821
Obtained later	12,569	263	369	872	626	1,599	151	610
Assumed	492	17	74	62	70	53	60	53
Wrap-around	16	2	-	2	2	2	4	-
Combination of the above	72	-	2	18	12	2	7	5
Payment plan of primary mortgage:								
Fixed payment, self amortizing	35,689	3,058	2,169	3,127	2,643	2,776	3,745	1,746
Adjustable rate mortgage	1,964	155	88	163	142	175	148	91
Adjustable term mortgage	504	21	45	41	24	106	42	59
Graduated payment mortgage	382	48	10	46	26	15	46	30
Balloon	357	23	25	18	31	29	44	17
Combination of the above	326	27	26	29	13	42	51	21
Payment plan of secondary mortgage:								
Units with two or more mortgages [4]	5,388	409	115	397	319	253	321	161
Fixed payment, self amortizing	4,501	339	112	343	276	189	274	128
Adjustable rate mortgage	187	8	-	12	4	5	7	5
Adjustable term mortgage	244	18	2	19	11	23	12	10
Graduated payment mortgage	19	-	-	-	3	-	-	-
Balloon	118	16	-	5	5	3	11	-
Other	-	-	-	-	-	-	-	-
Combination of the above	98	9	-	3	4	19	3	3
Reason primary refinanced:								
Units with a refinanced primary mortgage [5]	11,133	303	267	645	581	847	140	342
To get a lower interest rate	8,877	258	154	439	447	646	130	212
To increase payment period	319	8	15	21	11	38	5	25
To reduce payment period	1,318	19	34	78	72	73	17	32
To renew or extend a loan that has fallen due	204	4	13	10	23	17	5	13
To receive cash	1,579	11	66	137	82	164	17	57
Other reason	1,504	43	62	127	82	107	6	62
Cash received in primary mortgage refinance:								
Units receiving refinance cash	1,579	11	66	137	82	164	17	57
Median amount received (dol.)	24,513	-	14,066	24,346	24,224	26,800	-	-

- Represents or rounds to zero. [1] Constructed in the past 4 years. [2] Persons of Hispanic origin may be of any race. [3] 65 years old and over. [4] Includes don't know and not reported. [5] Persons reporting more than one reason are counted once in the total.

Source: U.S. Census Bureau, Current Housing Reports, Series H150/01, *American Housing Survey for the United States*. See Internet site <http://www.census.gov/hhes/www/housing/ahs/nationaldata.html>.

No. 974. Occupied Housing Units—Neighborhood Indicators by Selected Characteristics of the Householder: 2001

[In thousands (106,261 represents 106,261,000). As of fall. Based on the American Housing Survey; see Appendix III]

Characteristic	Total occupied units	Tenure Owner	Tenure Renter	Black Owner	Black Renter	Hispanic origin[1] Owner	Hispanic origin[1] Renter	Elderly[2] Owner	Elderly[2] Renter	Households below poverty level Owner	Households below poverty level Renter
Total units[3]	106,261	72,265	33,996	6,318	6,974	4,731	5,083	17,513	4,299	6,713	7,889
Street noise or traffic present[3]	29,889	17,572	12,318	1,854	2,883	1,194	1,634	4,463	1,460	1,782	3,038
Condition not bothersome	18,064	10,571	7,493	1,070	1,697	666	933	3,106	1,052	1,053	1,865
Condition bothersome	11,757	6,981	4,776	782	1,167	525	698	1,353	405	727	1,164
So bothersome they want to move	4,457	2,235	2,222	306	705	215	332	321	138	242	554
Neighborhood crime present[3]	15,948	8,657	7,291	1,326	2,230	706	1,034	1,734	693	901	1,885
Condition not bothersome	6,675	3,746	2,928	510	843	283	346	859	365	359	690
Condition bothersome	9,215	4,888	4,327	811	1,373	423	685	866	328	534	1,185
So bothersome they want to move	3,934	1,538	2,397	322	863	207	451	211	115	213	744
Odors present[3]	6,462	3,771	2,691	445	757	317	479	785	232	449	762
Condition not bothersome	2,314	1,385	929	130	224	72	147	315	88	139	225
Condition bothersome	4,139	2,386	1,754	316	527	245	329	471	143	310	538
So bothersome they want to move	1,635	723	912	124	358	116	177	129	58	118	308
Other problems:											
Noise	2,652	1,554	1,098	149	267	128	178	347	87	141	286
Litter or housing deterioration	1,980	1,324	656	198	225	160	106	307	58	113	199
Poor city or county services	929	605	332	119	140	71	80	118	23	72	115
People	4,075	2,410	1,665	255	456	221	263	463	145	243	458
With public transportation[3]	58,642	34,434	24,208	3,830	5,546	2,936	4,100	8,328	3,071	2,821	5,649
Household uses it at least weekly	11,609	4,291	7,317	926	2,267	562	1,790	870	938	493	2,269
Household uses it less than weekly	9,366	5,485	3,880	660	905	456	632	1,062	462	414	856
Household does not use	36,699	24,167	12,532	2,203	2,250	1,878	1,636	6,295	1,614	1,855	2,418
No public transportation	44,409	35,683	8,726	2,343	1,267	1,682	870	8,707	1,133	3,639	2,043
Police protection:											
Satisfactory	95,179	64,906	30,273	5,446	5,992	4,096	4,451	15,862	3,960	5,787	6,855
Unsatisfactory	7,594	5,146	2,448	645	703	487	477	1,076	215	664	718
Secured communities[4]:											
Community access secured with walls or fences	7,033	3,097	3,935	196	839	332	776	905	508	285	802
Community access not secured	98,497	68,615	29,882	6,049	6,095	4,365	4,284	16,458	3,760	6,336	7,034
Secured multiunits[4]:											
Multiunit access secured	5,330	886	4,445	49	980	54	560	372	1,060	95	1,066
Multiunit access not secured	19,035	2,365	16,670	216	3,615	219	2,818	685	1,973	195	3,883
Senior citizen communities:											
Households with persons 55 years old and over	39,049	31,419	7,630	2,638	1,393	1,639	907	17,513	4,299	4,465	2,412
Community age restricted[5]	2,195	1,116	1,079	21	159	37	80	884	911	169	431
Community quality:											
Some or all activities present	40,538	26,372	14,166	2,260	3,070	1,554	1,852	6,700	2,182	2,164	3,148
Community center or clubhouse	24,039	14,580	9,459	1,134	2,017	825	1,118	4,242	1,628	1,232	2,005
Golf in the community	11,459	8,820	2,639	440	314	324	273	2,237	325	580	485
Trails in the community	18,496	13,169	5,326	942	843	759	623	2,876	628	923	969
Shuttle bus	10,313	6,330	3,983	530	726	417	537	2,014	978	593	1,064
Day care	17,307	11,545	5,762	1,418	1,634	761	899	2,435	633	916	1,424
Private or restricted beach, park or shoreline	6,700	4,964	1,736	256	319	229	205	1,154	210	376	353
Trash, litter or junk on street:[6]											
None	94,194	65,592	28,602	5,323	5,419	4,073	4,108	16,121	3,861	5,876	6,322
Minor accumulation	6,931	3,422	3,509	557	905	342	680	653	240	407	981
Major accumulation	2,815	1,470	1,345	244	488	181	227	364	98	250	444

[1] Persons of Hispanic origin may be of any race. [2] Householders 65 years old and over. [3] Includes those not reported.
[4] Public access is restricted (walls, gates, private security). Includes high rise apartments, retirement communitites, resorts, etc.
[5] At least one family member must be aged 55 years old or older. [6] Or on any properties within 300 feet.

Source: U.S. Census Bureau, Current Housing Reports, Series H150/01, *American Housing Survey for the United States.* See Internet site <http://www.census.gov/hhes/www/housing/ahs/nationaldata.html>.

No. 975. Heating Equipment and Fuels for Occupied Units: 1993 to 2001

[As of fall (94,724 represents 94,724,000). Based on American Housing Survey. See Appendix III]

Type of equipment or fuel	Number (1,000) 1993	1995	1997	1999	2001	Percent distribution 1993	2001
Occupied units, total.......	94,724	97,692	99,487	102,803	106,261	100.0	100.0
Heating equipment:							
Warm air furnace............	51,248	53,165	58,603	62,018	65,262	54.1	61.4
Heat pumps................	8,422	9,406	11,101	10,992	11,080	8.9	10.4
Steam or hot water..........	13,657	13,669	12,929	13,153	13,441	14.4	12.6
Floor, wall, or pipeless furnace...	4,746	4,963	5,588	5,310	5,343	5.0	5.0
Built-in electric units...........	6,722	7,035	4,531	4,939	5,063	7.1	4.8
Room heaters with flue........	1,766	1,620	1,584	1,624	1,542	1.9	1.5
Room heaters without flue......	1,597	1,642	1,754	1,790	1,558	1.7	1.5
Fireplaces, stoves, portable heaters or other............	5,654	5,150	2,780	2,434	2,571	6.0	2.4
None....................	911	1,043	617	544	401	1.0	0.4
House main heating fuel:							
Utility gas.................	47,669	49,203	51,052	52,366	54,689	50.3	51.5
Fuel oil, kerosene, etc.........	12,189	12,029	10,855	10,750	10,473	12.9	9.9
Electricity.................	25,107	26,771	29,202	31,142	32,590	26.5	30.7
Bottled, tank, or LP gas	3,922	4,251	5,398	5,905	6,079	4.1	5.7
Coal or coke...............	297	210	183	168	128	0.3	0.1
Wood and other fuel	4,630	4,186	2,177	1,927	1,902	4.9	1.8
None....................	911	1,043	620	544	401	1.0	0.4
Cooking fuel:							
Electricity.................	55,887	57,621	58,818	61,315	63,685	59.0	59.9
Gas [1]....................	37,996	39,218	40,083	41,051	42,161	40.1	39.7
Other fuel	479	566	113	69	66	0.5	0.1
None....................	361	287	474	367	349	0.4	0.3

[1] Includes utility, bottled, tank, and LP gas.

Source: U.S. Census Bureau, Current Housing Reports, Series H150/93, H150/95RV, H150/97, H150/99, and H150/01, *American Housing Survey for the United States*. See Internet site <http://www.census.gov/hhes/www/housing/ahs/nationaldata.html>.

No. 976. Occupied Housing Units—Housing Indicators by Selected Characteristics of the Householder: 2001

[In thousands of units (106,261 represents 106,261,000). As of fall. Based on the American Housing Survey; see Appendix III]

Characteristic	Total occupied units	Tenure Owner	Renter	Black Owner	Renter	Hispanic origin [1] Owner	Renter	Elderly [2] Owner	Renter	Households below poverty level Owner	Renter
Total units..........	106,261	72,265	33,996	6,318	6,974	4,731	5,083	17,513	4,299	6,713	7,889
Amenities:											
Porch, deck, balcony or patio.	88,834	65,479	23,354	5,389	4,573	4,132	3,161	15,688	2,549	5,870	4,934
Usable fireplace...........	35,097	31,079	4,018	1,859	548	1,460	447	6,292	311	1,810	456
Separate dining room	50,125	40,568	9,553	3,698	2,157	2,332	1,225	9,153	913	3,171	1,852
With 2 or more living rooms or recreation rooms.......	30,451	28,300	2,151	2,117	292	1,333	146	5,907	234	1,578	293
Garage or carport with home .	64,547	53,778	10,769	3,543	1,404	3,424	1,617	13,307	1,191	4,050	1,805
Cars and trucks available:											
No cars, trucks, or vans	9,342	2,699	6,643	529	2,254	188	1,123	1,741	1,957	902	3,075
Other households without cars....................	11,828	8,273	3,555	478	374	697	633	1,291	198	796	666
1 car with or without trucks or vans.................	51,749	34,657	17,092	2,996	3,329	2,106	2,375	10,408	1,865	3,684	3,374
2 cars	25,866	20,234	5,632	1,743	896	1,324	784	3,385	250	1,057	680
3 or more cars............	7,476	6,401	1,075	572	120	416	168	690	29	275	93
With cars, no trucks or vans..	50,031	31,832	18,199	3,276	3,666	1,789	2,368	9,899	1,880	3,167	3,434
1 truck or van with or without cars....................	33,775	26,617	7,158	1,942	852	1,899	1,236	4,614	357	1,919	1,061
2 or more trucks or vans	13,113	11,116	1,997	572	201	854	356	1,259	106	726	318
Selected deficiencies:											
Signs of rats in last 3 months .	1,021	482	539	47	182	87	154	82	57	78	185
Holes in floors............	1,148	550	598	55	192	76	141	107	36	125	228
Open cracks or holes	5,697	2,896	2,801	372	783	319	495	472	163	434	836
Broken plaster or peeling paint (interior of unit).......	2,707	1,274	1,433	199	442	127	261	203	101	199	413
No electrical wiring.........	72	65	7	15	-	-	-	9	-	25	5
Exposed wiring	535	300	235	22	48	21	39	86	19	47	93
Rooms without electric outlet .	1,308	706	602	76	114	56	86	167	53	115	145
Water leakage [3]..........	9,985	5,649	4,336	641	1,066	372	654	794	300	506	1,037

- Represents zero. [1] Persons of Hispanic origin may be of any race. [2] Householders 65 years old and over. [3] During the 12 months prior to the survey.

Source: U.S. Census Bureau, Current Housing Reports, Series H150/01, *American Housing Survey for the United States*. See Internet site <http://www.census.gov/hhes/www/housing/ahs/nationaldata.html>.

630 Construction and Housing

No. 977. Appliances and Office Equipment Used by Households by Region and Household Income: 2001

[In millions (107.0 represents 107,000,000). Preliminary. Represents appliances possessed and generally used by the household. Based on Residential Energy Consumption Survey; see source. For composition of regions, see map inside front cover]

Type of appliance	Households using appliance	Region				Household income in 2001			
		Northeast	Midwest	South	West	Under $15,000	$15,000-$29,999	$30,000-$49,999	$50,000 and over
Total households.......	107.0	20.3	24.5	38.9	23.3	18.7	22.9	27.1	38.3
Oven [1]	101.7	19.6	23.8	36.2	22.1	18.0	22.0	26.1	35.6
Electric	63.0	9.9	14.0	26.0	13.1	10.1	12.9	16.2	23.8
Natural gas	34.3	8.6	8.7	8.7	8.2	7.1	7.8	8.6	10.9
Self cleaning oven	48.2	10.2	12.3	16.1	9.6	4.1	8.5	12.4	23.2
Range [1]	105.7	20.1	24.1	38.6	22.9	18.5	22.5	26.9	37.7
Electric	64.2	9.9	13.9	27.2	13.2	10.4	13.2	16.5	24.1
Natural gas	36.7	9.0	9.1	9.8	8.8	7.3	8.0	9.0	12.5
Refrigerator.........	106.8	20.2	24.5	38.9	23.2	18.6	22.8	27.1	38.3
Frost free	96.9	18.3	21.7	36.3	20.7	15.5	19.9	25.0	36.5
Freezer	34.2	4.9	9.6	13.6	6.2	4.4	6.9	9.2	13.7
One	30.8	4.5	8.6	12.2	5.6	3.9	6.1	8.4	12.4
Two or more	3.4	0.4	1.0	1.4	0.6	0.4	0.9	0.8	1.3
Most used defrost method:									
Frost free	12.2	1.8	2.8	5.7	1.8	1.3	2.0	3.2	5.7
Manual	22.0	3.1	6.7	7.9	4.4	3.0	4.9	6.0	8.1
Dishwasher...........	56.7	9.2	12.1	22.1	13.2	3.3	9.1	14.9	29.3
Electric coffee maker	65.5	12.4	16.1	23.0	14.0	8.7	12.8	16.7	27.3
Electric toaster oven.......	36.1	8.5	5.5	14.7	7.4	5.1	7.7	8.9	14.3
Microwave oven.........	92.1	15.2	22.3	34.7	19.9	14.0	19.4	23.8	35.0
Air conditioning	80.8	14.2	20.2	36.9	9.6	11.9	16.7	21.0	31.2
Central system	57.3	5.7	14.3	30.3	7.0	6.1	10.7	15.2	25.3
Room	23.5	8.5	5.8	6.6	2.6	5.8	6.0	5.8	5.9
Color TV.............	105.8	20.0	24.4	38.4	22.9	18.1	22.7	26.9	38.0
One	29.3	5.8	6.4	9.8	7.3	8.5	8.6	6.5	5.7
Two	38.4	8.1	8.2	13.7	8.4	6.4	8.5	10.7	12.8
Three	23.3	3.8	5.9	9.2	4.3	2.5	3.8	6.1	10.9
Four................	10.2	1.6	2.7	3.9	2.0	0.6	1.4	2.6	5.7
Five or more	4.5	0.7	1.1	1.8	0.9	(S)	0.4	1.1	2.9
Large screen TV [2]	36.6	7.1	8.1	13.3	8.0	4.7	6.7	9.8	15.3
One	27.3	5.3	5.9	9.7	6.5	3.7	5.1	7.0	11.4
Two	7.9	1.4	1.8	3.3	1.4	0.9	1.5	2.2	3.2
Three or more	1.4	(S)	(S)	(S)	(S)	(S)	(S)	0.5	0.7
Cable/satellite dish-antenna ..	82.2	16.3	19.1	30.2	16.6	12.1	16.2	20.9	33.0
VCR and DVD players	96.1	18.0	22.5	34.6	21.0	13.9	19.8	25.3	37.0
Stereo equipment........	80.3	15.1	18.2	28.5	18.5	10.2	15.4	20.9	33.8
Clothes washer	84.1	14.7	19.8	32.7	16.9	10.7	16.4	22.1	34.9
Clothes dryer [1]	78.8	13.3	19.2	30.3	16.0	8.4	15.0	21.3	34.1
Electric	61.1	9.2	13.4	26.6	11.9	6.9	12.2	16.8	25.1
Natural gas	16.9	4.0	5.4	3.4	4.1	1.4	2.6	4.2	8.7
Water heater [1]	107.0	20.3	24.5	38.9	23.3	18.7	22.9	27.1	38.3
Electric	40.9	4.7	6.4	22.5	7.4	8.3	9.6	10.7	12.4
Natural gas	57.9	10.8	16.9	15.4	14.9	9.3	11.6	14.1	22.9
Personal computers	60.0	10.9	14.1	20.7	14.3	3.7	8.7	16.0	31.6
Access to Internet.......	50.7	9.7	11.8	16.9	12.2	2.8	6.6	13.1	28.3
Cell/mobile telephone	56.8	10.3	12.8	21.4	12.3	4.4	8.6	14.7	29.1

S Figure does not meet publication standards. [1] Includes other types, not shown separately. [2] Determined by respondent.

Source: U.S. Energy Information Administration, "Residential Energy Consumption Survey—Detailed Tables"; <http://www.eia.doe.gov/emeu/recs/recs2001/detailtables.html> (accessed 08 May 2003).

No. 978. Net Stock of Residential Fixed Assets: 1990 to 2001

[In billions of dollars (6,287.4 represents $6,287,400,000,000). End of year estimates]

Item	1990	1994	1995	1996	1997	1998	1999	2000	2001
Total residential fixed assets ..	6,287.4	7,654.5	7,973.1	8,391.5	8,850.1	9,405.1	10,091.6	10,755.2	11,333.0
By type of owner and legal form of organization:									
Private................	6,137.7	7,472.2	7,784.2	8,195.3	8,646.3	9,191.8	9,866.7	10,519.8	11,088.2
Corporate	68.0	76.0	78.2	81.6	86.5	91.8	96.6	102.2	106.4
Noncorporate	6,069.6	7,396.3	7,706.0	8,113.8	8,559.8	9,100.1	9,770.1	10,417.6	10,981.8
Government	149.7	182.3	188.8	196.2	203.8	213.3	224.9	235.4	244.8
Federal	52.5	60.7	62.4	64.5	66.7	69.5	73.1	76.2	79.4
State and local	97.2	121.6	126.5	131.7	137.2	143.8	151.9	159.2	165.4
By tenure group: [1]									
Owner occupied	4,486.9	5,628.7	5,891.6	6,228.8	6,584.7	7,025.1	7,588.0	8,122.8	8,603.8
Farm	150.3	169.6	174.0	178.9	188.7	198.3	211.1	222.7	232.1
Nonfarm	4,336.6	5,459.1	5,717.7	6,049.9	6,396.0	6,826.9	7,376.9	7,900.2	8,371.7
Tenant occupied	1,774.5	1,997.3	2,052.5	2,133.1	2,234.9	2,348.1	2,469.5	2,596.3	2,691.3
Farm	10.9	12.5	12.8	13.2	13.6	14.0	14.8	15.3	15.7
Nonfarm	1,763.6	1,984.8	2,039.7	2,119.9	2,221.4	2,334.1	2,454.8	2,581.0	2,675.6

[1] Excludes stocks of other nonfarm residential assets, which consists primarily of dormitories, and of fraternity and sorority houses.

Source: U.S. Bureau of Economic Analysis, Survey of Current Business, September 2001 issue, and <http://www.bea.doc.gov/bea/dn/faweb/> (accessed 30 April 2003).

Construction and Housing

No. 979. Expenditures by Residential Property Owners for Improvements and Maintenance and Repairs by Type of Property and Activity: 1990 to 2002

[In millions of dollars (115,432 represents $115,432,000,000). Based on personal interviews and mail surveys; see source for details]

Year and type of expenditure	Total	1-unit properties with owner occupant	Other properties	Additions and alterations Total	To structures Additions	To structures Alterations	To property outside of structures	Major replacements	Maintenance and repairs
1990	115,432	63,441	51,991	39,929	9,160	23,510	7,261	19,700	55,800
1992	115,569	72,930	42,639	44,041	7,401	24,870	11,771	20,705	50,821
1993	121,899	77,626	44,273	53,512	16,381	27,657	9,472	22,604	45,785
1994	130,625	85,903	44,722	56,835	12,906	30,395	13,534	26,606	47,185
1995	124,971	79,003	45,968	51,011	11,197	29,288	10,526	26,928	47,032
1996	131,362	84,462	46,900	64,513	17,388	32,889	14,235	26,738	40,108
1997	133,577	90,677	42,900	65,222	14,575	37,126	13,523	27,210	41,145
1998	133,693	96,159	37,534	62,971	11,897	38,787	12,287	28,741	41,980
1999	142,900	95,778	47,122	72,056	16,164	42,058	13,833	28,493	42,352
2000	152,975	100,161	52,814	77,979	18,189	40,384	19,407	32,760	42,236
2001, total [1]	157,765	105,997	51,768	77,560	14,133	47,208	16,218	32,714	47,491
Heating and air conditioning [2]	12,210	7,554	4,655	2,408	(NA)	2,408	(NA)	7,181	2,621
Plumbing	12,823	5,218	7,604	4,597	(NA)	3,827	769	3,465	4,761
Roofing	11,024	6,513	4,510	(NA)	(NA)	(NA)	(NA)	7,090	3,933
Painting	16,679	7,828	8,851	(NA)	(NA)	(NA)	(NA)	(NA)	16,679
2002, total [1]	173,324	116,192	57,132	88,708	20,624	49,566	18,518	37,238	47,379
Heating and air conditioning [2]	11,232	7,163	4,069	2,369	(NA)	2,369	(NA)	6,305	2,558
Plumbing	14,062	5,857	8,205	3,982	(NA)	2,572	1,411	4,470	5,610
Roofing	12,236	7,715	4,521	(NA)	(NA)	(NA)	(NA)	8,936	3,300
Painting	14,685	6,802	7,884	(NA)	(NA)	(NA)	(NA)	(NA)	14,685

NA Not available. [1] Includes types of expenditures not separately specified. [2] Central air-conditioning.
Source: U.S. Census Bureau, Current Construction Reports, Series C50, *Expenditures for Residential Improvement*, quarterly. See Internet site <http://www.census.gov/const/www/c50index.html>.

No. 980. Home Remodeling—Work Done and Amount Spent: 2002

[In thousands, except percent (3,729 represents 3,729,000). As of fall 2002. For work done in the prior 12 months. Based on household survey and subject to sampling error; see source]

Remodeling project	Households with work done [1] Number	Percent of households	Work done by— Household member	Work done by— Outside contractor	Amount spent (dol.) Under $1,000	Amount spent (dol.) $1,000 to $2,999	Amount spent (dol.) Over $3,000
Conversion of garage/attic/basement into living space	3,729	1.8	2,550	753	883	992	1,138
Remodel bathroom	14,776	7.2	9,619	3,292	7,182	2,830	1,831
Remodel kitchen	10,523	5.1	5,992	2,885	3,347	2,060	2,793
Remodel bedroom	7,668	3.7	5,479	1,088	4,344	1,105	573
Remodel/convert room to home office	2,075	1.0	1,648	58	1,006	248	154
Remodel other rooms	8,273	4.0	5,503	1,333	3,810	1,426	1,260
Add bathroom	1,406	0.7	741	386	333	331	305
Add/extend garage	1,663	0.8	792	691	255	117	1,027
Add other rooms - exterior addition	1,822	0.9	824	737	98	154	1,198
Add deck/porch/patio	5,171	2.5	3,072	1,614	1,693	1,450	1,150
Roofing	10,673	5.2	2,354	6,462	2,305	2,456	3,858
Siding - vinyl/metal	3,407	1.7	958	1,770	550	586	1,496
Aluminum windows	1,742	0.9	823	502	553	305	278
Clad-wood/Wood windows	1,216	0.6	412	499	266	315	369
Vinyl windows	4,354	2.1	1,330	2,303	920	1,126	1,316
Ceramic tile floors	7,419	3.6	3,689	2,635	3,634	1,490	873
Hardwood floors	4,365	2.1	1,788	1,615	1,436	917	953
Laminate flooring	3,003	1.5	1,572	932	1,277	838	285
Vinyl flooring	4,474	2.2	2,011	1,539	2,628	562	100
Carpeting	11,019	5.4	2,800	6,376	4,661	2,827	1,175
Kitchen cabinets	5,698	2.8	2,577	1,808	1,565	893	1,446
Kitchen counter tops	5,696	2.8	1,954	2,547	2,368	866	1,077
Skylights	980	0.5	278	512	443	241	87
Exterior doors	6,642	3.2	3,015	2,600	3,852	966	466
Interior doors	4,710	2.3	2,701	1,074	2,937	308	331
Garage doors	4,234	2.1	875	2,258	2,134	930	171
Concrete or masonry work	5,153	2.5	1,708	2,578	1,746	1,285	1,133
Swimming pool—in ground	711	0.4	78	534	59	58	467
Wall paneling	1,314	0.6	855	216	880	121	13
Ceramic wall tile	2,343	1.1	1,298	571	1,400	183	45

[1] Includes no response and amount unknown.
Source: Mediamark Research Inc., New York, NY, *Top-Line Reports*, (copyright), Internet site <http://www.mediamark.com/>.

No. 981. Commercial Office Space—Overview for Selected Market Areas: 2002

[As of mid-October (4,001,982 represents 4,001,982,000.) For the 76 market areas with the highest vacancy rates in 2002. Data based on responses from individuals knowledgeable in the local markets]

Market area	Inventory (1,000 sq. ft.)	Vacant space (1,000 sq. ft.)	Vacancy rate (percent)	Construction (1,000 sq. ft.)	Net absorption [1] (1,000 sq. ft.)
United States, all market areas [2]	4,001,982	601,991	15.0	59,582	-36,501
Akron	4,053	588	14.5	362	-67
Allentown	5,633	1,665	29.6	690	129
Annapolis	3,075	445	14.5	-	-56
Atlanta	147,275	30,764	20.9	2,626	-339
Austin	32,795	4,786	14.6	522	980
Baltimore	49,354	8,380	17.0	290	12
Boston	133,876	25,375	19.0	4,589	-5,474
Bridgeport/Stratford	6,434	1,138	17.7	-	-179
Charleston	5,405	893	16.5	70	191
Charlotte	38,031	5,220	13.7	385	2,301
Chicago	227,327	38,444	16.9	1,359	-5,380
Cincinnati	29,244	4,741	16.2	-	-2,228
Cleveland	37,137	5,571	15.0	526	-520
Columbia	6,155	1,010	16.4	175	-106
Columbus, OH	38,887	5,125	13.2	275	829
Corpus Christi	2,799	380	13.6	-	96
Dallas	206,784	43,442	21.0	562	-4,386
Denver	82,734	14,430	17.4	437	1,008
Des Moines	10,354	1,357	13.1	836	-15
Detroit	92,878	13,627	14.7	1,733	-1,422
El Paso	7,947	1,717	21.6	-	-3,478
Fort Wayne	5,837	852	14.6	-	-148
Fort Worth	20,385	2,716	13.3	-	19
Greensboro, High-Point, Winston-Salem	15,878	2,736	17.2	147	184
Greenville	7,347	1,080	14.7	175	309
Hartford	22,386	4,292	19.2	-	-423
Honolulu	11,725	1,536	13.1	-	61
Houston	115,767	15,216	13.1	-1,355	449
Indianapolis	26,129	4,582	17.5	527	60
Kansas City	43,194	8,732	20.2	1,074	-2,256
Lake Charles	643	142	22.2	-	-65
Lansing	9,161	1,292	14.1	47	751
Las Vegas	20,587	2,787	13.5	1,629	418
Los Angeles-Central	27,507	5,425	19.7	-	-604
Los Angeles-San Fernando Valley	33,597	5,375	16.0	150	-1,028
Los Angeles-South Bay	28,752	5,146	17.9	-	66
Los Angeles-West	32,153	5,356	16.7	-	-279
Louisville	17,257	3,182	18.4	65	213
Madison	9,199	1,249	13.6	311	210
Marin County	6,303	1,019	16.2	89	-
Memphis	26,169	3,513	13.4	180	607
Miami	30,947	6,049	19.5	986	-989
Milwaukee	28,300	3,844	13.6	900	556
Minneapolis/St. Paul	61,677	10,594	17.2	-	-684
Mobile	13,495	2,750	20.4	100	98
Nashua	2,284	506	22.1	12	-98
Nashville	21,185	3,507	16.6	175	931
New Haven	14,700	2,500	17.0	65	425
New Orleans	14,940	2,014	13.5	-	273
Oklahoma City	15,150	2,532	16.7	-	198
Omaha	10,477	1,926	18.4	145	304
Orange County	83,123	14,354	17.3	989	188
Orlando	22,480	3,274	14.6	600	-498
Peoria	2,053	400	19.5	-	-
Philadelphia	109,575	18,133	16.5	1,611	-1,429
Phoenix	30,365	6,176	20.3	374	-865
Pittsburgh	42,990	6,795	15.8	1,014	-315
Raleigh	33,099	5,221	15.8	463	559
Richmond	22,612	3,843	17.0	90	-3,567
Rochester	15,403	2,635	17.1	90	-449
Salt Lake City	13,046	2,313	17.7	-	-16
San Antonio	18,256	2,833	15.5	82	-462
San Francisco	59,352	14,692	24.8	951	-3,873
San Mateo	27,261	5,780	21.2	-	294
Santa Rosa/Sonoma Valley	10,379	1,380	13.3	1,571	802
Shreveport	3,421	477	13.9	-	42
South Bend	2,902	424	14.6	-	16
St. Louis	41,673	8,299	19.9	255	1,672
Tacoma	3,763	580	15.4	-	-
Tampa	42,521	6,878	16.2	-	-451
Toledo	9,350	1,447	15.5	26	87
Tucson	7,053	937	13.3	155	-261
West Palm Beach	21,395	2,868	13.4	88	-202
Westchester	33,254	5,253	15.8	-	-1,404
Wichita	6,191	1,659	26.8	14	-
Wilmington, DE	12,530	2,398	19.1	-	-393

- Represents zero.   [1] Net change in occupied stock.   [2] Includes other market areas, not shown separately.

Source: Society of Industrial and Office REALTORS, Washington DC, *2002 Comparative Statistics of Industrial and Office Real Estate Markets* (copyright).

No. 982. Commercial Buildings—Summary: 1999

[4,675 represents 4,675,000. Excludes buildings 1,000 square feet or smaller. Building type based on predominant activity in which the occupants were engaged. Based on a sample survey of building representatives conducted in 1999, therefore subject to sampling variability]

Characteristic	All buildings (1,000)	Floor-space (mil. sq. ft.)	Mean sq. ft. per building (1,000)	Characteristic	All buildings (1,000)	Floor-space (mil. sq. ft.)	Mean sq. ft. per building (1,000)
All buildings	4,657	67,338	14.5	1980 to 1989	846	13,931	16.5
Building floorspace (sq. ft.):				1990 to 1999	690	11,094	16.1
1,001 to 5,000	2,348	6,774	2.9	Workers (main shift):			
5,001 to 10,000	1,110	8,238	7.4	Fewer than 5	2,376	14,321	6.0
10,001 to 25,000	708	11,153	15.7	5 to 9	807	6,325	7.8
25,001 to 50,000	257	9,311	36.2	10 to 19	683	8,028	11.8
50,001 to 100,000	145	10,112	69.9	20 to 49	487	10,814	22.2
100,001 to 200,000	59	8,271	139.4	50 to 99	174	8,898	51.1
200,001 to 500,000	23	6,851	296.3	100 to 249	90	8,356	92.4
Over 500,000	7	6,628	929.0	250 or more	39	10,595	270.0
Principal activity within building:				Energy sources:[1]			
Education	327	8,651	26.4	Electricity	4,395	65,716	15.0
Food sales	174	994	5.7	Natural gas	2,670	45,525	17.1
Food service	349	1,851	5.3	Fuel oil	434	13,285	30.6
Health care	127	2,918	22.9	District heat	117	5,891	50.2
Inpatient	11	1,865	168.2	District chilled water	50	2,750	55.4
Outpatient	116	1,053	9.1	Propane	451	6,290	14.0
Lodging	153	4,521	29.5	Wood	79	570	7.2
Mercantile	667	10,398	15.6	Heating equipment:[1]			
Retail (other than mall)	534	4,766	8.9	Heat pumps	492	8,923	18.1
Enclosed mall and strip center	133	5,631	42.2	Furnaces	1,460	14,449	9.9
				Individual space heaters	894	17,349	19.4
Office	739	12,044	16.3	District heat	96	5,534	57.7
Public assembly	305	4,393	14.4	Boilers	581	19,522	33.6
Public order and safety	72	1,168	16.2	Packaged heating units	1,347	25,743	19.1
Religious worship	307	3,405	11.1	Other	185	4,073	22.1
Service	478	3,388	7.1	Cooling equipment:[1]			
Warehouse and storage	603	10,477	17.4	Residential-type central A/C	676	8,329	12.3
Other	102	1,222	12.0	Heat pumps	485	9,147	18.8
Vacant	253	1,908	7.6	Individual A/C	799	14,276	17.9
Year constructed:				District chilled water	50	2,750	55.4
1919 or before	419	4,034	9.6	Central chillers	130	12,909	99.7
1920 to 1945	499	6,445	12.9	Packaged A/C units	1,953	36,527	18.7
1946 to 1959	763	9,127	12.0	Swamp coolers	136	2,219	16.3
1960 to 1969	665	10,866	16.3	Other	49	1,312	26.7
1970 to 1979	774	11,840	15.3				

[1] More than one type may apply.
Source: U.S. Energy Information Administration, "1999 Commercial Buildings Energy Consumption Buildings (CBECS) Detailed Tables"; <http://www.eia.doe.gov/emeu/cbecs/detailedtables1999.html> (released August 2002).

No. 983. Office Building Markets—Summary: 2002

[As of end-of-year. In thousands of square feet, except as indicated. (153,384 represents 153,384,000). For top 27 areas in market size. Excludes government owned, and occupied, owner-occupied, and medical office buildings. Minus sign (-) indicates loss. CBD means central business district]

Market area	Total market size	Total market vacancy rate (percent)	Market absorption	CBD market size	Suburban market size	CBD market construction	Suburban market construction	CBD rental rate[1] (dol.)
Atlanta	153,384	21.05	-2,230	46,794	106,590	547	1,058	23.00
Baltimore	56,666	13.71	2,115	13,876	42,790	172	1,056	23.00
Boston	135,257	19.70	-2,819	53,598	81,659	2,752	1374	45.00
Central New Jersey	72,421	12.48	12,349	(X)	72,421	(NA)	975	(NA)
Charlotte	38,194	14.46	614	14,188	24,007	100	380	20.00
Chicago	205,027	15.20	-1,543	125,939	79,087	3,413	-	38.00
Columbus	66,766	13.54	3,055	22,696	44,070	9	138	17.00
Dallas	202,587	25.00	-246	42,910	159,677	-	1,706	20.17
Denver	84,337	22.59	-1,684	23,095	61,242	285	578	21.00
Detroit	73,831	15.84	-1,561	15,807	58,024	1,000	497	27.50
Houston	173,717	13.82	-2	40,898	132,820	1,522	220	25.38
Los Angeles	290,841	12.58	459	32,025	258,816	-	1,460	24.95
Miami	35,197	18.30	-10,005	11,439	23,758	461	521	29.68
Milwaukee	48,176	12.78	111	15,012	33,164	426	143	23.50
Minneapolis	54,326	16.99	-1,507	26,159	28,168	1,138	32	25.51
Northern New Jersey	107,893	11.46	3,566	15,706	92,187	-	809	27.25
Orlando	51,401	12.83	2,325	8,218	43,183	96	747	24.00
Philadelphia	102,064	18.96	11,958	38,511	63,554	-	1,300	24.75
Phoenix	91,949	15.98	589	20,388	71,560	-	593	22.00
Sacramento	54,375	12.23	1,008	5,042	49,333	229	1,285	31.00
San Diego	55,463	12.60	1,607	9,205	46,258	-	1,027	28.00
San Francisco	63,156	20.37	-663	41,439	21,716	-	1,186	31.00
Seattle	41,640	19.04	234	23,387	18,253	845	752	31.11
Silicon Valley	51,982	24.85	-1,461	9,097	42,885	380	2,584	35.40
St. Louis	39,525	16.14	-260	10,264	29,261	-	334	20.00
Tampa/St. Petersburg	76,212	13.40	-317	13,345	62,867	-	415	19.00
Washington, DC	111,119	5.42	2,187	111,119	(X)	5,685	(NA)	45.00

- Represents zero.   NA Not available.   X Not applicable.   [1] Per square foot.
Source: ONCOR International, Houston, TX, Year-End 2002 Market Data Book (copyright).

634   Construction and Housing

Section 21
Manufactures

This section presents summary data for manufacturing as a whole and more detailed information for major industry groups and selected products. The types of measures shown at the different levels include data for establishments, employment and wages, plant and equipment expenditures, value and quantity of production and shipments, value added by manufacture, inventories, and various indicators of financial status.

The principal sources of these data are U.S. Census Bureau reports of the censuses of manufactures conducted every 5 years, the *Annual Survey of Manufactures*, and *Current Industrial Reports*. Reports on current activities of industries or current movements of individual commodities are compiled by such government agencies as the Bureau of Labor Statistics; the Economic Research Service of the Department of Agriculture; the International Trade Administration; and by private research or trade associations such as The Conference Board, Inc., the American Iron and Steel Institute, the Electronic Industries Association, and several others.

Data on financial aspects of manufacturing industries are collected by the Bureau of Economic Analysis (BEA) and the U.S. Census Bureau (see especially tables 997-999). Industry aggregates in the form of balance sheets, profit and loss statements, analyses of sales and expenses, lists of subsidiaries, and types and amounts of security issues are published for leading manufacturing corporations registered with the Securities and Exchange Commission. The BEA issues data on capital in manufacturing industries and capacity utilization rates in manufacturing. See also Section 15, Business Enterprise.

Several private trade associations provide industry coverage for certain sections of the economy. They include the Aluminum Association (Table 1006), American Iron and Steel Institute (Tables 1007 and 1008), Consumer Electronics Association (Tables 1014 and 1015), and the Aerospace Industries Association (Tables 1020 and 1022). Machine tool consumption data (Table 1010) is produced jointly by the Association for Manufacturing Technology and American Machine Tool Distributors Association.

Censuses and annual surveys—The first census of manufactures covered the year 1809. Between 1809 and 1963, a census was conducted at periodic intervals. Since 1967, it has been taken every 5 years (for years ending in "2" and "7"). Results from the 1997 census are presented in this section utilizing the new NAICS (North American Industry Classification System). Data from the 2002 census will be released in 2004 and will appear in the next edition of the *Statistical Abstract*. For additional information see text, Section 15, Business Enterprise, and the Census Bureau Web site at <http://www.census.gov/epcd/www/NAICS.html>. Census data either direct reports or estimates from administrative records, are obtained for every manufacturing plant with one paid employee or more.

The *Annual Survey of Manufactures* (ASM), conducted for the first time in 1949, collects data for the years between censuses for the more general measure of manufacturing activity covered in detail by the censuses. The annual survey data are estimates derived from a scientifically selected sample of establishments. The 1999 annual survey is based on a sample of about 55,000 establishments of an approximate total of 230,000. These establishments represent all manufacturing establishments of multiunit companies and all single-establishment manufacturing companies mailed schedules in the 1997 Census of Manufactures. For the current panel of the ASM sample, all establishments of companies with 1997 shipments in manufacturing in excess of $500 million were included in the survey with certainty. For the remaining portion of the mail survey, the establishment was defined as the sampling unit. For this portion, all establishments with 250 employees or more and establishments with a very large value of shipments also were included. Therefore, of the 58,000 establishments included in the ASM panel, approximately 33,000 are selected with certainty. These establishments account for approximately 80 percent of total value of shipments in the 1992 census. Smaller establishments in the remaining portion of the mail survey were selected by sample.

Establishments and classification—Each of the establishments covered in the 1997 Economic Census—Manufacturing was classified in 1 of 480 industries (473 manufacturing industries and 7 former manufacturing industries) in accordance with the industry definitions in the 1997 NAICS Manual. In the NAICS system, an industry is generally defined as a group of establishments that have similar production processes. To the extent practical, the system uses supply based or production-oriented concepts in defining industries. The resulting group of establishments must be significant in terms of number, value added by manufacture, value of shipments, and number of employees.

Establishments frequently make products classified both in their industry (primary products) and other industries (secondary products). Industry statistics (employment, payroll, value added by manufacture, value of shipments, etc.) reflect the activities of the establishments, which may make both primary and secondary products. Product statistics, however, represent the output of all establishments without regard for the classification of the producing establishment. For this reason, when relating the industry statistics, especially the value of shipments, to the product statistics, the composition of the industry's output should be considered.

The censuses of manufactures for 1947 through 1992 cover operating manufacturing establishments as defined in the Standard Industrial Classification Manual (SIC), issued by the U.S. Office of Management and Budget (see text, Section 12). The Manual is also used for classifying establishments in the annual surveys. The comparability of manufactures data over time is affected by changes in the official definitions of industries as presented in the Manual. It is important to note, therefore, that the 1987 edition of the Manual was used for the 1987 and 1992 censuses; and the 1972 edition of the Manual and the 1977 Supplement were used for the 1972 through 1982 censuses. The Manual defines an industry as a number of establishments producing a single product or a closely related group of products. In the manual, an establishment is classified in a particular industry if its production of a product or product group exceeds in value added its production of any other product group. While some establishments produce only the products of the industry in which they are classified, few within an industry specialize to that extent. The statistics on employment, payrolls, value added, inventories, and expenditures, therefore, reflect both the primary and secondary activities of the establishments in that industry. For this reason, care should be exercised in relating such statistics to the total shipments figures of products primary to the industry.

Establishment—Establishment signifies a single physical plant site or factory. It is not necessarily identical to the business unit or company, which may consist of one or more establishments. A company operating establishments at more than one location is required to submit a separate report for each location. An establishment engaged in distinctly different lines of activity and maintaining separate payroll and inventory records is also required to submit separate reports.

Durable goods—Items with a normal life expectancy of 3 years or more. Automobiles, furniture, household appliances, and mobile homes are common examples.

Nondurable goods—Items which generally last for only a short time (3 years or less). Food, beverages, clothing, shoes, and gasoline are common examples.

Statistical reliability—For a discussion of statistical collection and estimation, sampling procedures, and measures of statistical reliability applicable to Census Bureau data, see Appendix III.

No. 984. Gross Domestic Product in Manufacturing in Current and Real (1996) Dollars by Industry: 1990 to 2001

[In billions of dollars (5,803.2 represents 5,803,200,000,000). Data are based on the 1987 Standard Industrial Classification (SIC). Data include nonfactor charges (capital consumption allowances, indirect business taxes, etc.) as well as factor charges against gross product; corporate profits and capital consumption allowances have been shifted from a company to an establishment basis]

Industry [1]	1990	1995	1996	1997	1998	1999	2000	2001
CURRENT DOLLARS								
Gross domestic product, total [1]	5,803.2	7,400.5	7,813.2	8,318.4	8,781.5	9,274.3	9,824.6	10,082.2
Manufacturing	1,040.6	1,289.1	1,316.0	1,379.6	1,431.5	1,481.3	1,520.3	1,423.0
Durable goods	586.6	729.8	748.4	791.2	830.7	853.8	886.4	812.8
Lumber and wood products	32.2	42.3	39.9	41.2	41.9	44.1	42.1	39.2
Furniture and fixtures	15.6	19.5	20.7	22.7	24.3	25.8	26.1	25.0
Stone, clay, and glass products	25.3	32.4	33.2	37.2	38.7	41.4	40.6	36.7
Primary metal industries	43.2	53.0	50.8	52.6	53.1	50.5	50.2	45.1
Fabricated metal products	69.4	87.2	93.1	97.6	101.7	106.9	109.6	100.8
Industrial machinery	118.2	132.8	136.3	143.2	158.6	152.3	173.1	148.2
Electronic & other electric equipment	105.7	146.9	153.2	165.9	159.2	161.2	162.0	143.1
Motor vehicles and equipment	47.3	98.2	92.2	96.5	111.5	119.4	120.4	111.4
Other transportation equipment	60.5	47.7	51.4	55.5	58.4	65.1	66.3	71.4
Instruments and related products	49.3	47.2	53.7	53.6	57.5	58.2	63.5	61.7
Misc. manufacturing industries	19.8	22.7	23.8	25.2	25.9	28.9	32.5	30.2
Nondurable goods	454.0	559.2	567.6	588.4	600.8	627.5	633.9	610.2
Food and kindred products	96.4	121.1	118.7	123.1	121.8	136.6	127.0	123.7
Tobacco manufactures	11.9	15.1	14.8	15.4	17.3	19.4	21.2	21.1
Textile mill products	22.0	24.8	25.3	25.7	25.8	24.9	23.8	22.1
Apparel and other textile products	25.4	27.3	27.0	26.5	26.0	24.7	24.7	23.3
Paper and allied products	45.0	58.9	55.9	53.8	55.7	56.8	60.2	55.9
Printing and publishing	73.1	80.8	88.2	91.1	95.6	105.4	106.5	100.2
Chemicals and allied products	109.9	150.8	153.6	164.8	164.8	167.3	169.0	163.5
Petroleum and coal products	31.7	29.0	30.2	31.4	32.9	30.4	38.5	40.6
Rubber and misc. plastic products	33.9	46.1	49.7	52.1	56.8	58.7	59.3	56.6
Leather and leather products	4.7	5.3	4.2	4.3	4.1	3.4	3.7	3.3
CHAINED (1996) DOLLARS								
Gross domestic product, total [1]	6,707.9	7,543.8	7,813.2	8,159.5	8,508.9	8,858.9	9,191.4	9,214.5
Manufacturing	1,102.3	1,284.7	1,316.0	1,387.3	1,444.3	1,513.9	1,585.4	1,490.3
Durable goods	585.1	714.9	748.4	813.0	892.9	949.3	1,044.3	990.1
Lumber and wood products	45.1	41.6	39.9	39.5	40.1	40.9	41.8	39.0
Furniture and fixtures	18.1	20.7	20.7	22.1	22.9	23.7	24.1	22.4
Stone, clay, and glass products	29.4	32.8	33.2	36.6	36.6	37.4	37.2	33.9
Primary metal industries	43.7	49.6	50.8	52.7	54.5	57.0	56.1	53.5
Fabricated metal products	76.1	90.8	93.1	96.2	96.5	97.7	102.7	92.3
Industrial machinery	93.5	124.7	136.3	158.4	195.8	206.7	249.2	222.5
Electronic & other electric equipment	68.6	128.7	153.2	182.2	210.8	249.2	311.8	335.2
Motor vehicles and equipment	68.7	103.2	92.2	97.1	111.6	115.0	117.3	108.5
Other transportation equipment	75.7	49.4	51.4	54.8	56.7	61.7	60.5	62.0
Instruments and related products	68.9	52.6	53.7	49.8	49.0	47.6	51.0	46.1
Misc. manufacturing industries	22.8	23.3	23.8	24.8	24.9	27.4	31.3	28.5
Nondurable goods	520.2	570.3	567.6	574.7	555.5	570.8	558.0	518.3
Food and kindred products	109.5	133.3	118.7	118.1	112.1	120.5	111.2	106.5
Tobacco manufactures	14.5	15.7	14.8	13.9	11.9	6.8	6.2	5.0
Textile mill products	22.8	26.0	25.3	25.0	24.1	23.0	23.2	20.7
Apparel and other textile products	27.3	28.0	27.0	26.5	25.2	22.9	23.3	22.3
Paper and allied products	52.5	52.2	55.9	58.3	56.2	56.1	53.1	49.7
Printing and publishing	102.9	89.2	88.2	86.4	85.6	90.4	90.1	80.8
Chemicals and allied products	131.1	148.0	153.6	164.2	155.2	160.6	162.8	157.8
Petroleum and coal products	22.9	26.9	30.2	25.6	26.4	35.3	29.9	24.6
Rubber and misc. plastic products	34.0	47.0	49.7	53.2	55.6	57.6	61.3	57.0
Leather and leather products	5.2	5.3	4.2	4.2	3.8	3.2	3.6	3.1

[1] For additional industry detail, see Table 660.

Source: U.S. Bureau of Economic Analysis, *National Income and Product Accounts, 1929-97;* and Survey of Current Business, November 2002. See also <http://www.bea.doc.gov/bea/ARTICLES/2002/11November/1102GDPbyIndustry.pdf> (released 28 October 2002).

No. 985. Manufacturing—Establishments, Employees, and Annual Payroll by Industry: 2000 and 2001

[114,065 represents 114,065,000. Excludes government employees, railroad employees, self-employed persons, etc. See "General Explanation" in source for definitions and statement on reliability of data. An *establishment* is a single physical location where business is conducted or where services or industrial operations are performed. See Appendix III]

Industry	NAICS code [1]	2000 Establishments, number	2000 Number of employees [2] (1,000)	2000 Annual payroll (mil. dol.)	2001 Establishments, number	2001 Number of employees [2] (1,000)	2001 Annual payroll (mil. dol.)
All industries, total	(X)	7,070,048	114,065	3,879,430	7,095,302	115,061	3,989,086
Manufacturing, total	31-33	354,498	16,474	643,954	352,619	15,950	617,699
Percent of all industries	(X)	5.01	14.44	16.60	4.97	13.86	15.48
Food	311	26,401	1,468	43,773	26,785	1,470	44,085
Beverage & tobacco product	312	2,869	169	7,318	3,212	171	7,258
Textile mills	313	4,449	339	9,491	4,452	308	8,403
Textile product mills	314	6,881	216	5,364	6,966	202	5,059
Apparel manufacturing	315	16,505	510	10,426	16,152	442	9,262
Leather & allied product	316	1,783	69	1,711	1,763	61	1,496
Wood product	321	17,328	598	16,511	17,289	558	15,829
Paper	322	5,790	554	23,291	5,739	533	22,501
Printing & related support activities	323	39,035	813	28,319	37,895	785	27,051
Petroleum & coal products	324	2,210	109	6,386	2,253	104	6,336
Chemical	325	13,426	886	45,610	13,361	870	46,395
Plastics & rubber products	326	16,292	1,057	34,110	15,981	1,003	32,641
Nonmetallic mineral product	327	16,537	524	19,123	16,732	524	19,350
Primary metal	331	6,300	602	25,545	6,684	573	23,642
Fabricated metal product	332	61,144	1,791	64,244	60,791	1,761	61,803
Machinery	333	29,442	1,378	58,387	28,922	1,333	54,714
Computer & electronic product	334	17,148	1,557	90,397	16,764	1,593	84,522
Electrical equip, appliance & component	335	7,041	589	21,853	6,940	575	20,873
Transportation equipment	336	12,766	1,873	88,632	12,627	1,753	83,440
Furniture & related product	337	19,848	640	17,964	20,593	619	17,434
Miscellaneous	339	31,303	732	25,500	30,718	713	25,605

X Not applicable. [1] North American Industry Classification System, 1997; see text, Section 15. [2] Covers full- and part-time employees who are on the payroll in the pay period including March 12.

Source: U.S. Census Bureau, *County Business Patterns*, annual. See also <http://www.census.gov/prod/2003pubs/01cbp/cbp01-1.pdf> (issued April 2003).

No. 986. Manufacturing Establishments, Employees, and Annual Payroll by State: 2001

[15,950 represents 15,950,000. Excludes government employees, railroad employees, self-employed persons, etc. See "General Explanation" in source for definitions and statement on reliability of data. An *establishment* is a single physical location where business is conducted or where services or industrial operations are performed. See Appendix III]

State	Establishments	Number of employees [1] (1,000)	Annual payroll (mil. dol.)	State	Establishments	Number of employees [1] (1,000)	Annual payroll (mil. dol.)
United States	352,619	15,950	617,699	Missouri	7,261	335	11,318
Alabama	5,200	312	10,202	Montana	1,226	21	646
Alaska	503	11	367	Nebraska	1,934	109	3,361
Arizona	4,937	194	7,917	Nevada	1,722	40	1,464
Arkansas	3,226	229	6,462	New Hampshire	2,249	96	3,819
California	49,022	1,741	75,803	New Jersey	10,872	380	17,283
Colorado	5,449	162	6,569	New Mexico	1,585	37	1,299
Connecticut	5,413	233	11,202	New York	21,499	689	27,241
Delaware	694	42	1,745	North Carolina	10,844	691	21,583
District of Columbia	162	3	92	North Dakota	681	24	762
Florida	15,392	413	14,578	Ohio	17,597	936	37,463
Georgia	8,688	492	16,141	Oklahoma	4,025	163	5,509
Hawaii	940	15	463	Oregon	5,587	198	7,981
Idaho	1,729	67	2,138	Pennsylvania	16,796	780	29,312
Illinois	17,134	820	32,832	Rhode Island	2,185	67	2,333
Indiana	9,131	604	23,471	South Carolina	4,430	326	11,289
Iowa	3,721	238	8,355	South Dakota	922	47	1,401
Kansas	3,240	191	7,302	Tennessee	7,013	449	15,237
Kentucky	4,210	280	10,182	Texas	21,370	948	37,288
Louisiana	3,436	159	6,539	Utah	3,001	120	4,241
Maine	1,866	77	2,705	Vermont	1,180	48	1,825
Maryland	3,936	157	6,792	Virginia	5,804	344	12,574
Massachusetts	9,015	390	18,907	Washington	7,565	316	14,458
Michigan	15,431	756	33,634	West Virginia	1,471	72	2,628
Minnesota	8,146	374	14,846	Wisconsin	9,846	544	20,145
Mississippi	2,815	201	5,674	Wyoming	563	9	321

[1] Covers full- and part-time employees who are on the payroll in the pay period including March 12.

Source: U.S. Census Bureau, *County Business Patterns*, annual. See also <http://www.census.gov/prod/2003pubs/01cbp/cbp01-1.pdf> (issued April 2003).

No. 987. Manufactures—Summary by Selected Industry: 2001

[15,879.5 represents 15,879,500. Based on the Annual Survey of Manufactures; see Appendix III]

Industry based on shipments	NAICS code [1]	All employees [2] Number (1,000)	Payroll Total (mil. dol.)	Payroll Per employee (dol.)	Production workers[2] (1,000)	Value added by manufactures [3] (mil. dol.)	Value of shipments [4] (mil. dol.)
Manufacturing, total	31-33	15,879.5	593,051	37,347	11,235.1	1,853,929	3,970,500
Food	311	1,504.7	43,586	28,967	1,145.1	193,224	451,386
Grain and oilseed milling	3112	55.4	2,375	42,848	41.2	18,156	46,176
Fruit and vegetable preserving and specialty food	3114	176.8	5,132	29,027	151.5	27,370	52,262
Dairy product	3115	132.2	4,715	35,676	88.1	20,832	65,512
Meat product	3116	493.4	11,950	24,220	427.3	38,051	125,411
Bakeries and tortilla	3118	323.3	9,186	28,410	197.1	31,885	49,133
Other food	3119	148.0	4,801	32,445	106.7	29,926	51,818
Beverage and tobacco product	312	177.5	7,023	39,562	95.9	77,735	118,786
Beverage	3121	150.8	5,632	37,346	76.3	31,643	65,688
Tobacco	3122	26.7	1,391	52,074	19.6	46,092	53,098
Textile mills	313	293.9	8,040	27,353	247.5	18,842	45,681
Textile product mills	314	209.7	5,051	24,091	170.1	12,852	31,971
Apparel	315	456.5	9,205	20,165	369.3	24,809	54,598
Cut and sew apparel	3152	335.8	6,670	19,865	269.2	19,500	43,563
Leather and allied product	316	61.7	1,483	24,010	49.1	4,178	8,834
Wood product	321	555.9	15,431	27,759	458.9	33,130	87,250
Sawmills and wood preservation	3211	124.4	3,481	27,978	105.6	7,484	25,924
Other wood product	3219	316.1	8,435	26,685	258.0	18,060	41,689
Paper	322	530.2	22,188	41,845	407.8	73,036	155,846
Pulp, paper, and paperboard mills	3221	170.7	9,179	53,783	134.2	37,279	71,987
Converted paper product	3222	359.6	13,010	36,180	273.6	35,757	83,859
Printing and related support activities	323	799.2	27,158	33,980	574.2	60,483	100,792
Printing and related support activities	3231	799.2	27,158	33,980	574.2	60,483	100,792
Petroleum and coal products	324	101.5	5,830	57,465	67.5	47,346	219,075
Petroleum and coal products	3241	101.5	5,830	57,465	67.5	47,346	219,075
Chemical	325	875.0	43,800	50,060	499.2	226,615	438,410
Basic chemical	3251	183.2	10,582	57,754	106.0	37,576	104,430
Resin, syn. rubber, and artif. & syn. fibers	3252	97.6	5,180	53,078	67.3	22,070	60,638
Pharmaceutical and medicine	3254	251.3	13,396	53,308	120.4	91,697	130,021
Soap, cleaning compound, and toilet preparation	3256	120.2	4,708	39,155	74.7	34,814	57,995
Other chemical product	3259	115.5	5,173	44,797	70.2	18,355	38,317
Plastics and rubber products	326	1,028.1	32,539	31,651	810.9	86,558	170,717
Plastics product	3261	834.5	25,588	30,664	657.8	69,475	137,276
Rubber product	3262	193.6	6,951	35,904	153.1	17,083	33,441
Nonmetallic mineral product	327	507.3	18,147	35,771	394.6	53,195	94,861
Cement and concrete product	3273	222.3	7,927	35,653	168.7	23,446	43,852
Primary metal	331	532.8	22,199	41,664	420.2	53,111	138,245
Iron and steel mills and ferroalloy	3311	130.3	6,700	51,421	102.0	14,749	44,896
Alumina and aluminum production and processing	3313	76.4	3,105	40,661	59.4	8,600	28,094
Fabricated metal product	332	1,724.7	59,569	34,539	1,296.0	138,793	253,113
Architectural and structural metals	3323	403.5	13,314	32,996	296.8	30,921	61,666
Machine shops, turned product & screw, nut, bolt	3327	417.6	14,739	35,296	321.6	29,153	44,982
Other fabricated metal product	3329	304.5	11,140	36,581	220.3	28,552	49,741
Machinery	333	1,314.7	52,844	40,194	844.1	131,103	266,553
Agriculture, construction, and mining machinery	3331	185.8	7,271	39,125	127.2	20,929	49,859
Industrial machinery	3332	190.5	8,533	44,786	105.1	17,448	35,211
Metalworking machinery	3335	217.7	9,055	41,601	153.0	16,030	26,684
Engine, turbine, and power transmission equipment	3336	106.8	4,811	45,066	71.1	18,962	37,230
Other general-purpose machinery	3339	328.2	13,056	39,774	198.2	30,065	62,107
Computer and electronic product	334	1,598.8	77,137	48,248	779.9	223,718	429,471
Computer and peripheral equipment	3341	193.1	9,165	47,461	65.2	34,394	89,528
Communications equipment	3342	301.7	17,089	56,636	120.3	50,757	102,004
Semiconductor & other elect. components	3344	566.9	23,944	42,240	355.3	71,289	124,215
Navigational, measuring, medical, control instruments	3345	468.1	24,461	52,254	192.8	60,035	97,169
Electrical equipment, appliance, & component	335	556.6	19,466	34,970	395.7	56,304	114,067
Electrical equipment	3353	186.8	6,660	35,662	124.7	17,340	33,934
Other electrical equipment & component	3359	209.1	7,483	35,779	145.5	22,563	45,336
Transportation equipment	336	1,717.6	80,416	46,818	1,246.5	227,675	602,496
Motor vehicle	3361	214.0	12,647	59,102	186.2	54,173	216,128
Motor vehicle parts	3363	736.0	31,501	42,800	584.6	74,532	186,839
Aerospace product and parts	3364	433.1	24,542	56,660	220.8	71,839	134,867
Furniture and related product	337	608.0	16,950	27,880	481.5	39,849	72,147
Miscellaneous	339	725.1	24,989	34,463	481.2	71,372	116,201
Medical equipment and supplies	3391	305.1	12,171	39,890	190.3	40,157	57,766
Other miscellaneous	3399	420.0	12,818	30,521	290.9	31,215	58,435

[1] North American Industry Classification System, 1997; see text, Section 15. [2] Includes employment and payroll at administrative offices and auxiliary units. All employees represents the average of production workers plus all other employees for the payroll period ended nearest the 12th of March. Production workers represents the average of the employment for the payroll periods ended nearest the 12th of March, May, August, and November. [3] Adjusted value added; takes into account (a) value added by merchandising operations (that is, difference between the sales value and cost of merchandise sold without further manufacture, processing, or assembly), plus (b) net change in finished goods and work-in-process inventories between beginning and end of year. [4] Includes extensive and unmeasurable duplication from shipments between establishments in the same industry classification.

Source: U.S. Census Bureau, Annual Survey of Manufactures, *Statistics for Industry Groups and Industries*, Series M01(AS)-1. See also <http://www.census.gov/prod/2003pubs/m01as-1.pdf> (issued January 2003).

No. 988. Manufactures—Summary by State: 2001

[15,879.5 represents 15,879,500. Sum of state totals may not add to U.S. total because U.S. and state figures were independently derived. See Appendix III]

State	All employees [1] Number (1,000)	All employees [1] Payroll Total (mil. dol.)	All employees [1] Payroll Per employee (dol.)	Production workers [1] Total (1,000)	Production workers [1] Wages (mil. dol.)	Value added by manufactures [2] Total (mil. dol.)	Value added by manufactures [2] Per production worker (dol.)	Value of shipments [3] (mil. dol.)
United States	15,879.5	593,051	37,347	11,235.1	342,990	1,853,929	165,012	3,970,500
Alabama	315.1	9,890	31,391	247.2	6,708	27,844	112,653	67,172
Alaska	12.6	409	32,426	10.1	297	1,182	116,523	3,987
Arizona	186.4	7,367	39,527	114.6	3,146	28,430	248,027	42,168
Arkansas	227.0	6,363	28,037	184.6	4,538	19,868	107,611	46,530
California	1,792.2	72,189	40,279	1,147.6	33,383	219,584	191,347	414,762
Colorado	163.1	6,541	40,112	108.1	3,317	17,799	164,582	35,627
Connecticut	229.8	10,557	45,936	137.2	4,807	27,595	201,099	47,055
Delaware	38.0	1,458	38,402	28.4	928	6,621	232,937	16,664
District of Columbia	1.8	90	50,984	1.3	51	93	69,147	178
Florida	401.3	13,591	33,868	268.1	6,757	39,974	149,095	76,541
Georgia	484.0	15,721	32,483	371.8	10,281	57,578	154,882	127,624
Hawaii	14.4	447	31,108	9.1	225	907	100,159	3,196
Idaho	63.9	2,126	33,281	47.6	1,424	3,670	77,084	15,076
Illinois	811.3	31,498	38,826	559.5	17,577	94,124	168,233	196,449
Indiana	597.7	23,155	38,739	448.7	15,195	72,122	160,749	154,264
Iowa	235.9	8,221	34,854	176.7	5,221	29,636	167,718	65,428
Kansas	193.8	7,093	36,600	140.0	4,366	21,008	150,069	53,031
Kentucky	276.3	10,002	36,196	214.1	6,734	31,722	148,156	84,180
Louisiana	156.9	6,335	40,376	115.9	4,191	22,545	194,532	85,488
Maine	77.7	2,832	36,466	57.7	1,822	7,880	136,654	15,066
Maryland	162.4	6,917	42,601	103.9	3,324	18,757	180,611	36,038
Massachusetts	376.7	16,623	44,128	226.7	7,535	44,447	196,045	79,851
Michigan	749.5	33,028	44,068	563.8	22,179	86,262	153,010	209,046
Minnesota	376.7	14,519	38,549	249.2	7,709	38,545	154,675	82,304
Mississippi	197.8	5,559	28,110	158.3	3,838	15,573	98,400	38,560
Missouri	346.6	12,226	35,269	252.3	7,432	40,284	159,688	89,682
Montana	20.4	619	30,384	15.0	417	2,091	139,673	5,423
Nebraska	105.0	3,348	31,889	82.9	2,282	11,962	144,213	31,133
Nevada	40.4	1,518	37,629	27.6	791	3,844	139,224	7,581
New Hampshire	96.7	3,795	39,234	67.1	2,218	8,621	128,506	16,975
New Jersey	379.5	15,534	40,931	253.5	8,167	50,754	200,228	98,230
New Mexico	32.7	1,147	35,068	23.4	735	6,632	282,930	11,464
New York	707.2	26,380	37,300	482.1	14,217	78,484	162,782	146,455
North Carolina	693.7	21,436	30,902	531.7	13,622	91,184	171,497	167,124
North Dakota	23.4	726	31,063	16.7	439	2,669	159,523	6,517
Ohio	923.5	36,190	39,186	682.1	23,431	107,440	157,514	241,902
Oklahoma	161.7	5,350	33,093	117.7	3,341	18,059	153,390	40,063
Oregon	199.2	7,200	36,148	142.4	4,369	22,027	154,646	43,271
Pennsylvania	768.7	28,512	37,093	544.5	16,896	87,984	161,581	178,613
Rhode Island	70.0	2,396	34,216	46.3	1,260	5,877	126,922	10,958
South Carolina	312.4	10,694	34,236	240.5	6,951	35,017	145,574	78,738
South Dakota	39.6	1,115	28,191	29.4	729	4,558	154,839	11,093
Tennessee	441.4	14,531	32,923	335.0	9,387	46,349	138,337	104,109
Texas	950.4	35,377	37,222	647.8	19,410	120,086	185,381	321,361
Utah	121.8	4,174	34,263	82.2	2,341	11,783	143,270	25,908
Vermont	45.8	1,740	37,963	30.1	849	5,078	168,881	8,926
Virginia	327.4	11,268	34,418	245.9	7,076	53,043	215,686	92,874
Washington	309.2	12,603	40,759	194.6	6,922	38,193	196,236	89,280
West Virginia	67.7	2,519	37,207	50.4	1,643	7,202	142,804	16,201
Wisconsin	544.3	19,817	36,406	396.6	12,302	59,585	150,257	126,542
Wyoming	9.0	305	33,958	6.9	213	1,358	197,002	3,835

[1] Includes employment and payroll at administrative offices and auxiliary units. All employees represents the average of production workers plus all other employees for the payroll period ended nearest the 12th of March. Production workers represents the average of the employment for the payroll periods ended nearest the 12th of March, May, August, and November. [2] Adjusted value added; takes into account (a) value added by merchandising operations (that is, difference between the sales value and cost of merchandise sold without further manufacture, processing, or assembly), plus (b) net change in finished goods and work-in-process inventories between beginning and end of year. [3] Includes extensive and unmeasurable duplication from shipments between establishments in the same industry classification.

Source: U.S. Census Bureau, Annual Survey of Manufactures, *Geographic Area Statistics*, Series M01(AS)-3. See also <http://www.census.gov/prod/2003pubs/m01as-3.pdf> (issued January 2003).

No. 989. Manufacturers' E-Commerce Shipments by Industry: 2000 and 2001

[4,208,582 represents $4,208,582,000,000. Based on the Annual Survey of Manufactures; subject to sampling variability. E-commerce is the value of goods and services sold over computer-mediated networks (open or proprietary)]

Industry	NAICS code [1]	2000 Ship-ments, total (mil. dol.)	2000 E-commerce Ship-ments, total (mil. dol.)	2000 E-commerce Percent of total shipments	2000 E-commerce Percent distribution	2001 Ship-ments, total (mil. dol.)	2001 E-commerce Ship-ments, total (mil. dol.)	2001 E-commerce Percent of total shipments	2001 E-commerce Percent distribution
Manufacturing, total	31-33	4,208,582	755,807	18.0	100.0	3,970,500	725,149	18.3	100.0
Food products	311	435,230	54,837	12.6	7.3	451,386	53,556	11.9	7.4
Beverage and tobacco	312	111,692	42,862	38.4	5.7	118,786	45,665	38.4	6.3
Textile mills	313	52,112	5,214	10.0	0.7	45,681	4,435	9.7	0.6
Textile product mills	314	33,654	5,800	17.2	0.8	31,971	7,409	23.2	1.0
Apparel	315	60,339	12,063	20.0	1.6	54,598	10,652	19.5	1.5
Leather and allied products	316	9,647	2,122	22.0	0.3	8,834	1,438	16.3	0.2
Wood products	321	93,669	5,957	6.4	0.8	87,250	4,919	5.6	0.7
Paper	322	165,297	20,617	12.5	2.7	155,846	20,208	13.0	2.8
Printing and related support activities	323	104,396	5,966	5.7	0.8	100,792	5,885	5.8	0.8
Petroleum and coal products	324	235,134	16,647	7.1	2.2	219,075	16,312	7.4	2.2
Chemicals	325	449,159	52,974	11.8	7.0	438,410	54,515	12.4	7.5
Plastics and rubber products	326	178,236	28,400	15.9	3.8	170,717	27,409	16.1	3.8
Nonmetallic mineral products	327	97,329	8,174	8.4	1.1	94,861	7,895	8.3	1.1
Primary metals	331	156,598	15,403	9.8	2.0	138,245	14,274	10.3	2.0
Fabricated metal products	332	268,212	25,798	9.6	3.4	253,113	24,168	9.5	3.3
Machinery	333	291,548	40,441	13.9	5.4	266,553	35,799	13.4	4.9
Computer and electronic products	334	510,639	77,933	15.3	10.3	429,471	73,232	17.1	10.1
Electrical equipment, appliances, and components	335	125,443	30,003	23.9	4.0	114,067	28,019	24.6	3.9
Transportation equipment	336	639,861	281,396	44.0	37.2	602,496	264,368	43.9	36.5
Furniture and related products	337	75,107	8,400	11.2	1.1	72,147	9,347	13.0	1.3
Miscellaneous	339	115,280	14,800	12.8	2.0	116,201	15,644	13.5	2.2

[1] North American Industry Classification System, 1997; see text, Section 15.

Source: U.S. Census Bureau, Internet site <http://www.census.gov/eos/www/papers/estatstext.pdf> and <http://www.census.gov/eos/www/papers/2001/2001estatstables.pdf> (released 19 March 2003).

No. 990. Manufacturing Employer Costs for Employee Compensation Per Hour Worked: 1990 to 2003

[As of March, for private industry workers. Based on a sample of establishments from the National Compensation Survey, see Appendix III and source for details. See also Table 646, Section 12]

Compensation component	Cost (dol.) 1990	2000	2001	2002	2003	Percent distribution 1990	2000	2001	2002	2003
Total compensation	17.33	23.41	24.30	25.20	26.02	100.0	100.0	100.0	100.0	100.0
Wages and salaries	11.86	16.01	16.66	17.19	17.43	68.4	68.4	68.6	68.2	67.0
Total benefits [1]	5.47	7.40	7.64	8.01	8.59	31.6	31.6	31.4	31.8	33.0
Paid leave	1.31	1.74	1.85	1.91	1.97	7.6	7.4	7.6	7.6	7.6
Vacation	0.67	0.86	0.92	0.97	1.00	3.9	3.7	3.8	3.8	3.8
Holiday	0.48	0.65	0.68	0.70	0.73	2.8	2.8	2.8	2.8	2.8
Sick	0.12	0.13	0.15	0.14	0.16	0.7	0.6	0.6	0.6	0.6
Other	0.05	0.10	0.10	0.10	0.10	0.3	0.4	0.4	0.4	0.4
Supplemental pay	0.65	1.04	1.09	1.13	1.23	3.8	4.4	4.5	4.5	4.7
Premium pay	0.34	0.58	0.58	0.56	0.60	2.0	2.5	2.4	2.2	2.3
Nonproduction bonuses	0.22	0.36	0.41	0.46	0.51	1.3	1.5	1.7	1.8	2.0
Shift pay	0.09	0.10	0.11	0.11	0.11	0.5	0.4	0.5	0.4	0.4
Insurance	1.37	1.85	1.93	2.11	2.27	7.9	7.9	7.9	8.4	8.7
Health insurance	(NA)	1.69	1.75	1.92	2.08	(NA)	7.2	7.2	7.6	8.0
Retirement and savings	0.56	0.75	0.75	0.74	0.86	3.2	3.2	3.1	2.9	3.3
Defined benefit	(NA)	0.34	0.29	0.30	0.41	(NA)	1.5	1.2	1.2	1.6
Defined contributions	(NA)	0.41	0.46	0.44	0.45	(NA)	1.8	1.9	1.7	1.7
Legally required	1.54	1.92	1.95	2.05	2.18	8.9	8.2	8.0	8.1	8.4
Social Security	1.02	1.38	1.42	1.48	1.51	5.9	5.9	5.8	5.9	5.8
Federal unemployment	0.03	0.03	0.03	0.03	0.03	0.2	0.1	0.1	0.1	0.1
State unemployment	0.12	0.11	0.10	0.11	0.13	0.7	0.5	0.4	0.4	0.5
Workers compensation	0.36	0.40	0.40	0.43	0.51	2.1	1.7	1.6	1.7	2.0
Other benefits [1]	0.04	0.09	0.07	0.07	0.08	0.2	0.4	0.3	0.3	0.3

NA Not available. [1] Includes severance pay, and supplemental unemployment benefits.

Source: U.S. Bureau of Labor Statistics, *Employer Costs for Employee Compensation Historical Listing, annual, 1986-2001*, and *Employer Costs for Employee Compensation, March 2003*. See also <ftp://ftp.bls.gov/pub/special.requests/ocwc/ect/ececrlse.pdf> (issued 19 June 2002) and <http://www.bls.gov/news.release/pdf/ecec.pdf> (issued 11 June 2003).

No. 991. Average Hourly Earnings of Production Workers in Manufacturing Industries by State: 2001 and 2002

[In dollars. Based on data on the North American Classification System, 1997; see text, Section 12 and 15]

State	2001	2002	State	2001	2002
United States	14.76	15.29	Missouri	16.11	16.79
Alabama	12.76	13.10	Montana	14.03	14.43
Alaska	11.70	13.24	Nebraska	13.64	14.05
Arizona	13.80	14.16	Nevada	13.79	14.62
Arkansas	12.90	13.30	New Hampshire	13.98	14.20
California	14.69	14.89	New Jersey	14.74	15.20
Colorado	14.72	15.85	New Mexico	13.27	13.43
Connecticut	16.42	17.25	New York	16.24	16.74
Delaware	16.56	16.62	North Carolina	12.81	13.18
District of Columbia [1]	15.14	15.39	North Dakota	12.77	13.17
Florida	12.68	13.30	Ohio	16.79	17.49
Georgia	12.50	13.39	Oklahoma	13.66	14.12
Hawaii	13.18	13.07	Oregon	14.74	15.06
Idaho	13.85	13.80	Pennsylvania	14.37	14.75
Illinois	14.66	14.99	Rhode Island	12.68	12.75
Indiana	16.42	17.16	South Carolina	13.79	14.00
Iowa	14.67	15.31	South Dakota	12.11	12.60
Kansas	15.48	15.98	Tennessee	12.88	13.15
Kentucky	15.44	15.73	Texas	14.04	13.93
Louisiana	16.18	17.03	Utah	13.76	14.12
Maine	14.71	15.55	Vermont	14.18	14.33
Maryland	14.56	15.21	Virginia	14.49	15.25
Massachusetts	15.75	16.25	Washington	17.96	18.15
Michigan	19.45	20.48	West Virginia	14.80	15.40
Minnesota	14.76	15.06	Wisconsin	15.44	15.86
Mississippi	11.93	12.32	Wyoming	17.26	17.73

[1] Washington PMSA (primary metropolitan statistical area).

Source: U.S. Bureau of Labor Statistics, *Employment and Earnings,* May 2003 issue.

No. 992. Manufacturing Full-Time Equivalent Employees and Wages by Industry: 1990 to 2001

[(18,679 represents 18,679,000).]

Industry	SIC[1] code	Full-time equivalent (FTE) employees (1,000)				Wage and salary accruals per FTE worker (dol.)			
		1990	1995	2000	2001	1990	1995	2000	2001
Manufacturing, total	(X)	18,679	18,190	18,159	17,319	30,054	35,779	45,675	45,580
Durable goods	(X)	10,959	10,561	11,004	10,445	31,658	37,660	47,930	47,409
Lumber & wood products	24	725	772	827	783	21,712	25,110	30,005	30,978
Furniture & fixtures	25	493	502	546	510	21,404	25,048	30,694	31,465
Stone, clay, & glass products	32	550	530	571	560	28,342	33,283	40,718	40,900
Primary metal industries	33	749	697	694	640	33,637	40,067	45,493	45,808
Fabricated metal products	34	1,398	1,421	1,523	1,439	28,248	32,927	38,305	39,096
Industrial machinery & equipment	35	2,053	2,051	2,080	1,973	34,030	40,063	54,703	51,717
Electronic, other electric equipment	36	1,664	1,607	1,699	1,604	31,055	38,922	57,307	54,729
Motor vehicles & equipment	371	816	961	1,013	934	38,202	46,658	55,296	54,783
Other transportation equipment	372-9	1,171	809	828	803	37,348	44,611	51,877	54,315
Instruments & related products	38	975	827	831	828	35,896	44,654	58,957	58,347
Misc. manufacturing industries	39	365	384	392	371	24,468	28,219	34,635	36,356
Nondurable goods	(X)	7,720	7,629	7,155	6,874	27,777	33,176	42,207	42,801
Food & kindred products	20	1,596	1,642	1,661	1,659	25,909	30,139	35,990	36,755
Tobacco products	21	50	41	34	33	40,860	53,854	68,265	74,667
Textile mill products	22	682	654	528	467	20,217	23,985	29,394	29,957
Apparel & other textile products	23	1,001	919	597	540	16,174	18,800	25,268	25,944
Paper & allied products	26	687	685	649	622	33,514	39,458	46,462	47,265
Printing & publishing	27	1,474	1,450	1,463	1,419	28,888	34,539	43,254	43,533
Chemicals & allied products	28	1,071	1,027	1,024	1,005	40,949	51,054	68,311	66,825
Petroleum & coal products	29	155	142	125	123	44,974	54,739	64,560	67,618
Rubber & misc. plastics products	30	872	963	1,003	945	25,500	29,867	35,623	36,199
Leather & leather products	31	132	106	71	61	18,189	22,321	29,606	31,459

X Not applicable. [1] Based on the Standard Industrial Classification system, 1987.

Source: U.S. Bureau of Economic Analysis, *National Income and Product Accounts, 1929-97*; and *Survey of Current Business,* November 2002. See also <http://www.bea.doc.gov/bea/ARTICLES/2002/11November/1102GDPbyIndustry.pdf> (issued November 2002).

No. 993. Manufactures' Shipments, Inventories, and New Orders: 1992 to 2002

[In billions of dollars (2,904 represents 2,904,000,000,000), except ratio. Based on a sample survey; for methodology, see publication cited below. These data are now on a NAICS (North American Industry Classification System, 1997) basis and not comparable to previous data, which were based on the Standard Industrial Classification system. See text, Section 15]

Year	Shipments	Inventories (Dec. 31)[1]	Ratio of inventories to shipments [2]	New orders (Dec. 31)	Unfilled orders (Dec. 31)
1992	2,904	370	1.57	(NA)	448
1993	3,020	371	1.51	2,960	422
1994	3,238	391	1.48	3,200	431
1995	3,480	415	1.47	3,427	443
1996	3,597	421	1.44	3,567	485
1997	3,835	433	1.39	3,780	508
1998	3,900	439	1.38	3,808	492
1999	4,032	453	1.38	3,957	501
2000	4,209	470	1.37	4,161	545
2001	3,970	442	1.37	3,875	513
2002	3,892	434	1.37	3,801	481

NA Not available. [1] Inventories are stated at current cost. [2] Ratio based on December seasonally adjusted data.

Source: U.S. Census Bureau, Current Industrial Reports, *Manufacturers' Shipments, Inventories, and Orders: 1992-2002*, Series M3-1(02). See also <http://www.census.gov/prod/2003pubs/m3-02.pdf> (released August 2003).

No. 994. Ratios of Manufacturers' Inventories to Shipments and Unfilled Orders to Shipments by Industry Group: 1996 to 2002

[Based on a sample survey; for methodology, see publication cited below. These data are on a NAICS (North American Industry Classification System, 1997) basis and not comparable to previous data, which were based on the Standard Industrial Classification system. See text, Section 15]

Industry	1996	1997	1998	1999	2000	2001	2002
INVENTORIES TO SHIPMENTS RATIO							
All manufacturing industries	1.44	1.39	1.38	1.38	1.37	1.37	1.37
Durable goods	1.65	1.57	1.56	1.53	1.55	1.57	1.53
Wood products	1.28	1.26	1.26	1.26	1.32	1.34	1.33
Nonmetallic mineral products	1.29	1.25	1.17	1.17	1.23	1.21	1.29
Primary metals	1.65	1.60	1.59	1.69	1.68	1.67	1.67
Fabricated metals	1.68	1.60	1.55	1.56	1.55	1.55	1.51
Machinery	2.12	2.04	2.01	2.05	2.08	2.06	2.04
Computers and electronic products	1.53	1.51	1.41	1.42	1.55	1.59	1.57
Electrical equipment, appliances, and components	1.59	1.51	1.45	1.42	1.44	1.47	1.47
Transportation equipment	1.59	1.44	1.57	1.42	1.34	1.39	1.31
Furniture and related products	1.49	1.43	1.34	1.35	1.35	1.32	1.34
Miscellaneous products	2.02	1.92	1.85	1.89	1.90	1.87	1.83
Nondurable goods	1.17	1.16	1.14	1.18	1.14	1.13	1.18
Food products	0.88	0.85	0.82	0.86	0.88	0.85	0.87
Beverages and tobacco products	1.58	1.71	1.63	1.55	1.51	1.47	1.58
Textile mills	1.45	1.41	1.45	1.52	1.49	1.48	1.38
Textile product mills	1.72	1.76	1.63	1.62	1.76	1.83	1.72
Apparel	1.64	1.71	1.75	1.89	1.89	1.68	1.58
Leather and allied products	2.06	1.99	2.05	2.18	2.13	2.10	1.91
Paper products	1.20	1.21	1.15	1.16	1.11	1.16	1.17
Printing	0.89	0.88	0.80	0.81	0.79	0.77	0.78
Petroleum and coal products	0.88	0.82	0.84	0.90	0.71	0.74	0.90
Basic chemicals	1.35	1.31	1.31	1.38	1.40	1.39	1.44
Plastics and rubber products	1.27	1.22	1.19	1.20	1.21	1.18	1.30
UNFILLED ORDERS TO SHIPMENTS RATIO							
All manufacturing industries	1.63	1.61	1.53	1.51	1.57	1.56	1.50
Durable goods	2.96	2.87	2.67	2.61	2.78	2.86	2.74
Primary metals	1.81	1.94	1.56	1.69	1.45	1.47	2.06
Fabricated metals	1.99	2.08	2.00	2.02	2.02	1.93	5.14
Machinery	2.62	2.60	2.40	2.50	2.51	2.46	3.84
Computers and electronic products	2.65	2.49	2.57	2.93	3.07	3.56	5.69
Electrical equipment, appliances, and components	1.61	1.65	1.56	1.78	1.75	1.54	0.66
Transportation equipment	6.09	5.59	5.00	4.24	4.93	5.03	7.52
Furniture and related products	1.05	1.38	1.19	1.27	1.14	1.09	0.63
Miscellaneous products	0.32	0.37	0.46	0.49	0.62	0.44	0.09

Source: U.S. Census Bureau, Current Industrial Reports, *Manufacturers' Shipments, Inventories, and Orders: 1992-2002*, Series M3-1(02). See also <http://www.census.gov/prod/2003pubs/m3-02.pdf> (released August 2003).

Manufactures 643

No. 995. Value of Manufacturers' Shipments, Inventories, and New Orders by Industry: 1996 to 2002

[In millions of dollars (3,597,188 represents $3,597,188,000,000). Based on a sample survey; for methodology, see publication cited below. These data are on a NAICS (North American Industry Classification System, 1997) basis and not comparable to previous data, which were based on the Standard Industrial Classification system. See text, Section 15]

Industry	1996	1997	1998	1999	2000	2001	2002
SHIPMENTS							
All manufacturing industries	3,597,188	3,834,699	3,899,813	4,031,887	4,208,584	3,970,499	3,891,753
Durable goods	1,978,597	2,147,384	2,231,588	2,326,736	2,373,688	2,174,406	2,131,404
Wood products	81,827	88,470	91,175	97,311	93,669	87,250	87,652
Nonmetallic mineral products	81,308	86,465	92,501	96,153	97,329	94,861	88,222
Primary metals	157,638	168,118	166,109	156,648	156,598	138,246	135,930
Fabricated metals	222,995	242,812	253,720	257,071	268,213	253,113	252,232
Machinery	257,459	270,687	280,651	276,904	291,548	266,554	255,651
Computers and electronic products	399,516	439,380	443,768	467,059	510,639	429,471	392,026
Electrical equipment, appliances, and components	105,283	112,116	116,024	118,313	125,443	114,068	103,673
Transportation equipment	516,030	575,307	612,882	676,328	639,861	602,495	624,129
Furniture and related products	61,156	64,299	69,616	72,659	75,107	72,147	69,999
Miscellaneous products	95,385	99,730	105,142	108,290	115,281	116,201	121,890
Nondurable goods	1,618,591	1,687,315	1,668,225	1,705,151	1,834,896	1,796,093	1,760,349
Food products	404,173	421,737	428,479	426,001	435,229	451,385	450,183
Beverages and tobacco products	94,033	96,971	102,359	106,920	111,692	118,786	109,832
Textile mills	59,796	58,707	57,416	54,306	52,112	45,681	43,170
Textile product mills	28,515	31,052	31,137	32,689	33,654	31,971	34,232
Apparel	64,237	68,018	64,932	62,305	60,339	54,598	53,621
Leather and allied products	10,032	10,877	10,186	9,653	9,647	8,834	10,408
Paper products	152,860	150,296	154,984	156,915	165,298	155,845	151,530
Printing	95,072	97,485	100,297	101,536	104,396	100,792	97,968
Petroleum and coal products	174,181	177,394	137,957	162,620	235,134	219,074	206,879
Basic chemicals	385,919	415,617	416,742	420,321	449,159	438,410	424,143
Plastics and rubber products	149,773	159,161	163,736	171,885	178,236	170,717	178,383
INVENTORIES (Dec. 31)							
All manufacturing industries	420,680	433,451	438,845	452,803	470,084	441,527	433,756
Durable goods	265,170	273,330	282,698	288,362	298,232	275,855	264,446
Wood products	8,879	9,441	9,684	10,289	10,329	9,664	9,566
Nonmetallic mineral products	8,560	8,840	8,877	9,279	9,799	9,440	9,306
Primary metals	21,945	22,728	22,305	22,309	22,199	19,502	19,144
Fabricated metals	30,611	31,776	32,215	32,800	34,085	32,145	31,227
Machinery	43,869	44,490	45,728	46,050	49,151	44,532	42,296
Computers and electronic products	48,997	53,045	50,066	52,838	63,024	54,598	49,287
Electrical equipment, appliances, and components	13,342	13,530	13,503	13,510	14,505	13,488	12,234
Transportation equipment	65,927	66,414	77,014	76,781	69,199	67,188	65,769
Furniture and related products	7,426	7,527	7,599	7,983	8,261	7,765	7,632
Miscellaneous products	15,614	15,539	15,707	16,523	17,680	17,533	17,985
Nondurable goods	155,510	160,121	156,147	164,441	171,852	165,672	169,310
Food products	29,751	30,152	29,419	30,650	31,882	31,865	32,534
Beverages and tobacco products	12,731	14,188	14,294	14,167	14,331	14,855	14,717
Textile mills	6,972	6,640	6,684	6,648	6,243	5,411	4,759
Textile product mills	3,898	4,331	4,024	4,219	4,698	4,648	4,691
Apparel	8,397	9,267	9,114	9,454	9,170	7,363	6,784
Leather and allied products	1,640	1,718	1,667	1,675	1,634	1,479	1,580
Paper products	15,120	15,042	14,688	15,034	15,205	14,950	14,621
Printing	6,529	6,621	6,212	6,394	6,445	6,046	5,985
Petroleum and coal products	12,087	11,492	9,102	11,375	12,840	12,479	14,302
Basic chemicals	42,782	44,691	44,943	47,806	51,623	50,052	50,363
Plastics and rubber products	15,603	15,979	16,000	17,019	17,781	16,524	18,974
NEW ORDERS							
All manufacturing industries	3,567,384	3,779,835	3,808,143	3,957,242	4,161,472	3,875,329	3,800,930
Durable goods	1,948,793	2,092,520	2,139,918	2,252,091	2,326,576	2,079,236	2,040,581
Wood products	81,827	88,470	91,175	97,311	93,669	87,250	87,652
Paper products	81,308	86,465	92,501	96,153	97,329	94,861	88,222
Primary metals	158,066	171,407	160,743	156,968	153,625	136,291	134,089
Fabricated metals	227,447	247,839	253,847	258,116	270,021	248,872	249,408
Machinery	258,405	272,998	278,100	278,277	294,608	260,392	244,559
Computers and electronic products	327,288	363,635	372,433	402,216	436,415	363,049	325,378
Electrical equipment, appliances, and components	104,837	113,411	115,711	120,774	126,196	110,628	103,013
Transportation equipment	552,024	581,780	600,205	660,215	663,226	591,756	617,098
Furniture and related products	61,499	66,256	69,098	73,393	74,532	71,614	68,959
Miscellaneous products	96,092	100,259	106,105	108,668	116,855	114,523	122,203
Nondurable goods	1,618,591	1,687,315	1,668,225	1,705,151	1,834,896	1,796,093	1,760,349

Source: U.S. Census Bureau, Current Industrial Reports, *Manufacturers' Shipments, Inventories, and Orders: 1992-2002*, Series M3-1(02). See also <http://www.census.gov/prod/2003pubs/m3-02.pdf> (released August 2003).

No. 996. Value of Manufactures' Shipments, Inventories, and New Orders by Market Grouping: 1996 to 2002

[In millions of dollars (3,597,188 represents $3,597,188,000,000). Based on a sample survey; for methodology, see publication cited below. These data are on a NAICS (North American Industry Classification System, 1997) basis and not comparable to previous data, which were based on the Standard Industrial Classification system. See text, Section 15]

Market grouping	1996	1997	1998	1999	2000	2001	2002
SHIPMENTS							
All manufacturing industries	3,597,188	3,834,699	3,899,813	4,031,887	4,208,584	3,970,499	3,891,753
Consumer goods	1,304,283	1,369,992	1,364,326	1,438,519	1,514,377	1,493,707	1,472,647
Consumer durable goods	339,730	371,669	385,918	426,337	405,308	380,734	396,590
Consumer nondurable goods	964,553	998,323	978,408	1,012,182	1,109,069	1,112,973	1,076,057
Aircraft and parts	80,582	100,126	116,812	120,242	111,658	118,226	111,726
Defense aircraft and parts	29,693	27,472	26,938	27,719	24,560	27,928	35,127
Nondefense aircraft and parts	50,889	72,654	89,874	92,523	87,098	90,298	76,599
Construction materials and supplies	371,401	399,880	418,756	434,138	444,812	424,517	419,040
Motor vehicles and parts	387,394	421,573	439,590	498,716	471,180	427,175	450,136
Computers and related products	93,926	110,055	114,482	113,162	110,242	89,529	81,449
Information technology industries	311,028	349,846	362,564	374,384	399,751	353,237	319,391
Nondefense capital goods	630,932	702,971	747,046	768,799	808,345	727,980	673,223
Excluding aircraft	605,295	665,074	695,717	713,042	757,617	677,991	634,549
Defense capital goods	73,703	76,261	74,690	70,955	67,051	74,019	79,825
Durables excluding capital goods	1,273,962	1,368,152	1,409,852	1,486,982	1,498,292	1,372,407	1,378,356
INVENTORIES (Dec. 31)							
All manufacturing industries	420,680	433,451	438,845	452,803	470,084	441,527	433,756
Consumer goods	115,751	118,980	116,715	123,218	129,478	126,855	129,445
Consumer durable goods	25,212	25,251	25,137	26,307	27,438	25,704	26,289
Consumer nondurable goods	90,539	93,729	91,578	96,911	102,040	101,151	103,156
Aircraft and parts	35,905	37,509	46,921	42,599	36,091	36,393	34,978
Defense aircraft and parts	8,641	8,380	11,376	11,052	9,423	9,384	9,610
Nondefense aircraft and parts	27,264	29,129	35,545	31,547	26,668	27,009	25,368
Construction materials and supplies	43,275	44,877	45,617	47,510	49,389	46,344	46,196
Motor vehicles and parts	20,744	20,298	20,764	22,102	22,283	19,653	20,256
Computers and related products	8,841	10,289	8,017	7,963	8,350	6,341	5,975
Information technology industries	41,784	46,117	43,592	44,375	50,795	46,650	41,802
Nondefense capital goods	110,904	117,932	122,415	121,653	127,162	119,258	109,106
Excluding aircraft	90,031	95,226	94,045	96,254	106,669	98,483	90,539
Defense capital goods	17,336	14,814	17,775	19,754	17,153	17,677	17,705
Durables excluding capital goods	136,930	140,584	142,508	146,955	153,917	138,920	137,635
NEW ORDERS							
All manufacturing industries	3,567,384	3,779,835	3,808,143	3,957,242	4,161,472	3,875,329	3,800,930
Consumer goods	1,305,517	1,372,919	1,364,268	1,440,903	1,515,799	1,491,143	1,471,270
Consumer durable goods	340,964	374,596	385,860	428,721	406,730	378,170	395,213
Consumer nondurable goods	964,553	998,323	978,408	1,012,182	1,109,069	1,112,973	1,076,057
Aircraft and parts	104,614	109,077	108,004	107,336	130,575	111,432	105,382
Defense aircraft and parts	32,520	23,280	23,854	25,717	31,326	37,311	40,087
Nondefense aircraft and parts	72,094	85,797	84,150	81,619	99,249	74,121	65,295
Construction materials and supplies	373,536	403,860	419,330	435,034	446,792	420,300	418,315
Motor vehicles and parts	385,712	422,427	440,934	499,527	468,470	425,580	450,183
Computers and related products	95,070	107,564	115,806	114,481	107,656	89,320	82,398
Information technology industries	310,074	352,700	365,723	389,160	409,500	350,726	314,473
Nondefense capital goods	648,797	728,362	745,600	772,703	831,335	700,027	647,894
Excluding aircraft	607,174	676,119	698,279	728,089	767,754	665,899	617,878
Defense capital goods	88,471	64,497	64,127	67,900	79,598	83,033	79,264
Durables excluding capital goods	1,211,525	1,299,661	1,330,191	1,411,488	1,415,643	1,296,176	1,313,423

Source: U.S. Census Bureau, Current Industrial Reports, Manufacturers' Shipments, Inventories, and Orders: 1992-2002, Series M3-1(02). See also <http://www.census.gov/prod/2003pubs/m3-02.pdf> (released August 2003).

No. 997. Finances and Profits of Manufacturing Corporations: 1990 to 2002

[In billions of dollars (2,811 represents $2,811,000,000,000). Data exclude estimates for corporations with less than $250,000 in assets at time of sample selection. For 1990-2001, based on Standard Industrial Classification system; thereafter, based on North American Industry Classification System. See Table 778 for individual industry data]

Item	1990	1995	1996	1997	1998	1999	2000	2001 [1]	2001 [2]	2002 [2]
Net sales	2,811	3,528	3,758	3,920	3,949	4,149	4,548	4,308	4,295	4,221
Net operating profit	173	268	277	298	298	317	348	185	186	230
Net profit:										
Before taxes	160	274	307	331	315	355	381	82	83	207
After taxes	112	198	225	245	234	258	275	36	36	146
Cash dividends	62	81	96	108	121	104	132	102	103	103
Net income retained in business	49	117	129	136	114	154	143	-67	-66	43

[1] Based on Standard Industrial Classification system; see text, Section 15. [2] Based on the North American Industry Classification System, 1997; see text, Section 15.

Source: U.S. Census Bureau, *Quarterly Financial Report for Manufacturing, Mining, and Trade Corporations.*

No. 998. Manufacturing Corporations—Number, Assets, and Profits by Asset Size: 1990 to 2002

[Corporations and assets as of end of 4th quarter; profits for entire year (2,629,458 represents $2,629,458,000,000). Through 2000 based on Standard Industrial Classification code; beginning 2001 based on North American Industry Classification System (see footnote 3). For corporations above a certain asset value based on complete canvass. The asset value for complete canvass was raised in 1988 to $50 million and in 1995 to $250 million. Asset sizes less than these values are sampled, except as noted. For details regarding methodology, see Appendix III. Minus sign (-) indicates loss]

Year	Unit	Total	Under $10 mil.[1]	$10-$25 mil.	$25-$50 mil.	$50-$100 mil.	$100-$250 mil.	$250 mil.-$1 bil.	$1 bil. and over
Corporations:									
1990	Number	(NA)	(NA)	(NA)	(NA)	834	774	597	367
1995	Number	(NA)	(NA)	(NA)	(NA)	574	639	727	447
1996	Number	(NA)	(NA)	(NA)	(NA)	532	620	745	484
1997	Number	(NA)	(NA)	(NA)	(NA)	470	615	748	529
1998	Number	(NA)	(NA)	(NA)	(NA)	416	531	753	549
1999	Number	(NA)	(NA)	(NA)	(NA)	438	486	730	601
2000	Number	(NA)	(NA)	(NA)	(NA)	450	499	722	635
2001[3]	Number	(NA)	(NA)	(NA)	(NA)	504	504	735	576
2001[4]	Number	(NA)	(NA)	(NA)	(NA)	(NA)	(NA)	(NA)	(NA)
2002	Number	(NA)	(NA)	(NA)	(NA)	491	519	780	580
Assets:									
1990	Mil. dol	2,629,458	142,498	74,477	55,914	72,554	123,967	287,512	1,872,536
1995	Mil. dol	3,345,229	155,618	87,011	68,538	87,262	159,133	370,263	2,417,403
1996	Mil. dol	3,574,407	163,928	87,096	69,722	93,205	156,702	398,651	2,605,102
1997	Mil. dol	3,746,797	167,921	87,398	76,034	85,186	157,130	397,559	2,775,570
1998	Mil. dol	3,967,309	170,068	87,937	69,627	86,816	148,060	419,153	2,985,647
1999	Mil. dol	4,382,814	170,058	85,200	67,352	97,810	138,143	398,881	3,425,370
2000	Mil. dol	4,852,106	171,666	85,482	72,122	90,866	149,714	389,537	3,892,720
2001[3]	Mil. dol	4,750,401	170,948	84,710	67,977	88,267	135,152	393,861	3,809,487
2001[4]	Mil. dol	4,747,789	169,701	84,664	67,493	88,088	131,617	393,752	3,812,474
2002	Mil. dol	4,826,279	166,749	83,263	62,517	83,437	134,137	412,736	3,883,439
Net profit:[2]									
1990	Mil. dol	110,128	8,527	5,160	2,769	2,661	3,525	7,110	80,377
1995	Mil. dol	198,151	13,224	5,668	3,767	5,771	7,000	16,549	146,172
1996	Mil. dol	224,869	15,802	6,872	4,266	5,664	7,935	16,059	168,271
1997	Mil. dol	244,505	17,948	8,383	4,153	4,675	7,074	18,433	183,836
1998	Mil. dol	234,386	18,350	6,421	3,790	4,681	5,610	14,364	181,170
1999	Mil. dol	257,805	17,398	7,618	3,504	4,798	4,795	12,756	206,934
2000	Mil. dol	275,313	16,578	6,820	3,403	2,742	3,510	15,121	227,136
2001[3]	Mil. dol	35,638	8,411	3,458	-443	519	-3,296	-5,988	32,978
2001[4]	Mil. dol	36,168	8,387	3,366	-408	403	-543	-6,782	31,746
2002	Mil. dol	146,144	10,126	3,017	976	1,798	3,681	1,396	125,153

NA Not available. [1] Excludes estimates for corporations with less than $250,000 in assets at time of sample selection. [2] After taxes. [3] Data reported on a Standard Industrial Classification basis. [4] Beginning 2001, data reported on a NAICS basis.
Source: U.S. Census Bureau, *Quarterly Financial Report for Manufacturing, Mining and Trade Corporations*. See also <http://www.census.gov/prod/2003pubs/qfr02-q4.pdf> (released April 2003).

No. 999. Manufacturing Corporations—Selected Finances: 1980 to 2002

[In billions of dollars (1,913 represents $1,913,000,000,000). Data are not necessarily comparable from year to year due to changes in accounting procedures, industry classifications, sampling procedures, etc.; for detail, see source. For 1980-2001, on Standard Industrial Classification code; beginning 2001 based on North American Industry Classification System (NAICS), 1997. See footnote 5]

	All manufacturing corps.					Durable goods industries					Nondurable goods industries				
		Profits[1]		Stock hold- ers' equi- ty	Debt[2]		Profits[1]		Stock hold- ers' equi- ty	Debt[2]		Profits[1]		Stock hold- ers' equi- ty	Debt[2]
Year	Sales	Before taxes	After taxes			Sales	Before taxes	After taxes			Sales	Before taxes	After taxes		
1980	1,913	146	93	668	292	889	57	36	318	143	1,024	88	57	350	149
1985	2,331	137	88	866	454	1,143	62	39	421	167	1,189	76	49	445	267
1990	2,811	158	110	1,044	782	1,357	57	41	515	328	1,454	101	69	529	453
1991	2,761	99	66	1,064	814	1,304	14	7	507	338	1,457	85	59	557	476
1992[3]	2,890	31	22	1,035	819	1,390	-34	-24	474	333	1,500	65	46	561	485
1993	3,015	118	83	1,040	819	1,490	39	27	483	327	1,525	79	56	557	492
1994	3,256	244	175	1,110	815	1,658	121	87	533	316	1,598	123	88	577	500
1995	3,528	275	198	1,241	862	1,808	131	94	614	333	1,721	144	104	627	529
1996	3,758	307	225	1,348	920	1,942	147	106	674	366	1,816	160	119	674	554
1997	3,922	331	244	1,464	953	2,076	167	121	744	386	1,847	164	123	721	566
1998	3,949	315	234	1,487	1,065	2,169	175	128	794	458	1,781	140	107	694	607
1999	4,149	355	258	1,637	1,199	2,314	199	140	928	551	1,835	157	117	709	648
2000	4,548	381	275	1,892	1,308	2,457	191	132	1,101	610	2,091	190	144	791	698
2001[4]	4,308	82	36	1,827	1,296	2,332	-70	-77	1,049	640	1,976	152	112	779	656
2001[5]	4,295	36	36	1,843	1,287	2,321	-69	-76	1,080	632	1,974	152	112	762	655
2002	4,221	207	146	1,813	1,276	2,268	48	26	1,038	600	1,954	159	120	774	676

[1] Beginning 1998, profits before and after income taxes reflect inclusion of minority stockholders' interest in net income before and after income taxes. [2] Annual data are average debt for the year (using four end-of-quarter figures). [3] Data for 1992 (most significantly 1992:I qtr.) reflect the early adoption of Financial Accounting Standards Board Statement 106 (Employer's Accounting for Post-Retirement Benefits Other Than Pensions) by a large number of companies during the fourth quarter of 1992. Data for 1993: I qtr. also reflect adoption of Statement 106. Corporations must show the cumulative effect of a change in accounting principle in the first quarter of the year in which the change is adopted. [4] Data reported on a Standard Industrial Classification (SIC) basis. [5] Beginning 2001, data reported on a NAICS basis.
Source: U.S. Census Bureau, *Quarterly Financial Report for Manufacturing, Mining and Trade Corporations*. See also <http://www.census.gov/prod/2003pubs/qfr02-q4.pdf> (released April 2003).

No. 1000. Tobacco Products—Summary: 1990 to 2002

[710 represents 710,000,000,000. Production data are for calendar years. Excludes cigars produced in customs bonded manufacturing warehouses]

Item	Unit	1990	1995	1996	1997	1998	1999	2000	2001	2002
PRODUCTION										
Cigarettes, total	Billions	710	747	758	720	680	607	565	562	565
Nonfilter tip	Billions	23	15	14	12	12	8	7	6	6
Filter tip	Billions	687	732	744	708	669	599	558	556	559
Cigars	Billions	1.9	2.1	2.4	2.3	2.8	2.9	3	4	3
Tobacco [1]	Mil. lb.	142	131	131	134	131	133	133	131	133
Smoking	Mil. lb.	16	12	12	11	13	15	14	13	16
Chewing tobacco	Mil. lb.	73	63	61	58	53	51	49	47	45
Snuff	Mil. lb.	53	60	62	64	66	67	70	71	73
EXPORTS										
Cigarettes	Billions	164.3	231.1	243.9	217.0	201.3	151.4	147.9	133.9	127.2
Cigars	Billions	72	94	84	86	93	84	113	124	236
Smoking tobacco	Billions	0.8	0.3	0.7	0.8	1.1	1.6	0.5	11.0	7.6
IMPORTS										
Cigarettes	Billions	1.4	3.0	2.8	3.2	4.3	8.7	11.3	14.7	20.9
Cigars	Billions	111	195	320	448	582	463	497	543	417
Smoking tobacco	Billions	2.9	4.2	4.2	4.3	4.3	4.3	4.2	1.9	0.9
CONSUMPTION										
Consumption per person [2]	Lb. [3]	5.6	4.7	4.7	4.5	4.5	4.3	4.2	4.1	4.2
Cigarettes	1,000	3	3	3	2	2	2	2	2	2
Cigars [4]	Number	13	15	18	18	18	19	19	20	18
EXPENDITURES										
Consumer expenditures, total	Bil. dol.	43.8	48.7	50.4	52.2	57.3	72.1	77.5	82.8	(NA)
Cigarettes	Bil. dol.	41.6	45.8	47.2	48.7	53.2	68.3	72.9	77.8	(NA)
Cigars	Bil. dol.	0.7	1.0	1.0	1.2	1.6	1.8	1.8	2.0	(NA)
Other	Bil. dol.	1.5	2.5	2.2	2.2	2.4	2.7	2.7	2.9	(NA)

NA Not available.

[1] Smoking and chewing tobaccos and snuff output. [2] Based on estimated population 18 years old and over, as of July 1, including Armed Forces abroad. [3] Unstemmed processing weight equivalent. [4] Weighing over 3 pounds per 1,000.
Source: U.S. Dept. of Agriculture, Economic Research Service, *Tobacco Situation and Outlook*, quarterly.

No. 1001. Cotton, Wool, and Manmade Fibers—Consumption by End-Use: 1990 to 2001

[14,011 represents 14,011,000,000. Represents products manufactured by U.S. mills. Excludes glass fiber]

	Cotton		Wool		Manufactured fibers			
					Artificial [1]		Synthetic [2]	
Year	Total (mil. lb.)	Total (mil. lb.)	Percent of end-use	Total (mil. lb.)	Percent of end-use	Total (mil. lb.)	Percent of end-use	Total (mil. lb.)	Percent of end-use
Total:									
1990	14,011	4,699	33.5	185	1.3	9,127	65.1	599	4.3	8,528	60.9
1995	16,815	5,508	32.8	184	1.1	11,123	66.1	540	3.2	10,583	62.9
1998	17,698	5,514	31.2	170	1.0	12,014	67.9	370	2.1	11,526	65.1
1999	17,735	5,328	30.0	135	0.8	12,272	69.2	330	1.9	11,902	67.1
2000	17,148	4,938	28.8	131	0.8	12,080	70.4	303	1.8	11,776	68.7
2001	15,456	4,201	27.2	116	0.8	11,139	72.1	265	1.7	10,874	70.4
Apparel:									
1990	5,204	2,897	55.7	118	2.3	2,189	42.1	287	5.5	1,902	36.5
1995	6,877	3,640	52.9	132	1.9	3,106	45.2	306	4.4	2,800	40.7
1998	6,526	3,329	51.0	113	1.7	3,083	47.3	208	3.2	2,875	44.1
1999	6,417	3,262	50.8	89	1.4	3,065	47.8	172	2.7	2,894	45.1
2000	6,057	3,007	49.6	79	1.3	2,971	49.1	150	2.5	2,822	46.6
2001	5,294	2,515	47.5	73	1.4	2,706	51.1	135	2.6	2,571	48.6
Home textiles:									
1990	2,235	1,325	59.3	14	0.6	896	40.1	104	4.7	792	35.4
1995	2,530	1,487	58.8	12	0.5	1,030	40.7	93	3.7	937	37.0
1998	2,916	1,779	61.0	15	0.5	1,122	38.5	67	2.3	1,056	36.2
1999	2,815	1,656	58.8	15	0.5	1,145	40.7	66	2.3	1,080	38.3
2000	2,727	1,526	56.0	15	0.5	1,186	43.5	65	2.4	1,122	41.1
2001	2,392	1,355	56.6	13	0.5	1,025	42.9	53	2.2	972	40.6
Floor coverings:									
1990	3,075	18	0.6	21	0.7	3,036	98.7	-	-	3,036	98.7
1995	3,731	25	0.7	25	0.7	3,681	98.7	-	-	3,681	98.7
1998	4,123	36	0.9	29	0.7	4,058	98.4	-	-	4,058	98.4
1999	4,247	39	0.9	29	0.7	4,180	98.4	-	-	4,180	98.4
2000	4,107	36	0.9	24	0.6	4,048	98.6	-	-	4,048	98.6
2001	3,849	28	0.7	20	0.5	3,801	98.8	-	-	3,801	98.8
Industrial: [3]									
1990	2,965	313	10.6	10	0.3	2,642	89.1	179	6.0	2,463	83.1
1995	3,677	355	9.7	15	0.4	3,307	89.9	141	3.8	3,165	86.1
1997	3,871	360	9.4	16	0.4	3,495	90.2	113	2.9	3,382	87.3
1998	4,016	371	9.2	13	0.3	3,632	90.4	95	2.4	3,537	88.1
1999	4,227	372	8.8	13	0.3	3,843	90.9	93	2.2	3,750	88.7
2000	4,257	369	8.7	13	0.3	3,875	91.0	89	2.1	3,785	88.9

- Represents or rounds to zero. [1] Rayon and acetate. [2] Nylon, polyester, acrylic, and olefin. [3] Includes consumer-type products.
Source: Fiber Economics Bureau, Inc., Arlington, VA, *Fiber Organon*, monthly (copyright).

No. 1002. Broadwoven and Knit Fabrics—Shipments and Foreign Trade: 2001

[3,100,592 represents 3,100,592,000. Fabric blends as shown in the report are reported based on the chief weight of the fiber; whereas, fabrics blends as shown for imports are based on the chief value of the fiber. Apparent consumption represents new domestic supply and is derived by subtracting exports for the total manufacturers' shipments plus imports]

Product description	Manufacturers' shipments (quantity)	Imports for consumption Quantity	Imports for consumption Value [1] ($1,000)	Percent imports to manufacturers' shipments	Exports of domestic merchandise Quantity	Exports of domestic merchandise Value ($1,000)	Percent exports to manufacturers' shipments
BROADWOVEN FABRICS (quantity 1,000 sq. meters)							
Cotton fabrics [2]	3,100,592	1,478,797	1,631,892	47.7	623,614	1,187,542	20.1
Manmade fiber fabrics	7,855,344	1,056,474	1,209,243	13.4	622,240	1,328,639	7.9
Silk fabrics	(D)	28,736	241,167	(D)	2,391	17,694	(D)
Wool fabrics	44,450	16,451	126,741	37.0	15,048	78,099	33.9
KNIT FABRICS (quantity in 1,000 kilograms)							
Total	576,931	133,455	917,756	23.1	156,972	1,148,391	27.2
Pile fabrics	52,508	30,115	222,661	57.4	43,384	248,595	82.6
Elastic fabric	25,252	17,405	186,256	(S)	20,841	317,358	82.5
Other warp knit fabrics	52,976	12,191	99,966	23.0	15,032	126,763	28.4
Other narrow knit fabrics	12,100	2,984	23,947	24.7	1,319	12,068	10.9
Other knit fabrics	434,097	70,760	384,926	16.3	76,396	443,607	17.6

D Data withheld to avoid disclosing figures for individual companies. S Does not meet publication standards. [1] Dollar value represents the c.i.f. (cost, insurance, and freight) at the first port of entry in the United States plus calculated import duty. [2] Includes all cotton and chiefly cotton mixed with manmade fiber.

Source: U.S. Census Bureau, Current Industrial Reports, Series MQ313 and MA313K, annual. See also <http://www.census.gov/industry/1/mq313t015.pdf> (issued June 2002) and <http://www.census.gov/industry/1/ma313k01.pdf> (issued August 2002).

No. 1003. Footwear—Production, Foreign Trade, and Apparent Consumption: 2002

[Quantity in thousands of pairs (60,327 represents 60,327,000 pairs), value in thousands of dollars (315,587 represents $315,587,000)]

Product description	Manufacturers' shipments (quantity)	Exports of domestic merchandise Quantity	Exports of domestic merchandise Value	Percent exports to domestic production	Imports for consumption Quantity	Imports for consumption Value	Apparent consumption (quantity)	Percent imports to apparent consumption
Total	60,327	26,291	315,587	43.6	1,508,305	13,215,517	1,542,341	97.8
Rubber or plastic uppers and rubber or plastic	2,712	10,170	108,197	375.0	521,015	2,968,166	513,557	101.5
Waterproof	2,464	824	8,686	33.4	11,037	63,139	12,677	87.1
Not waterproof	248	9,346	99,511	3,768.5	509,978	2,905,027	500,880	101.8
Leather uppers	18,248	7,861	157,752	43.1	666,889	9,023,999	677,276	98.5
Athletic	1,576	4,557	82,239	289.1	507,097	5,910,167	504,116	100.6
Leather soles	5,442	1,686	45,288	31.0	43,128	1,139,015	46,884	92.0
Other soles	11,230	1,618	30,225	14.4	116,664	1,974,817	126,276	92.4
Fabric uppers	36,163	8,260	49,638	174.3	320,401	1,223,352	348,304	92.0

Source: U.S. Census Bureau, Current Industrial Reports, Series MA316A, annual. See also <http://www.census.gov/industry/1/ma316a02.pdf> (released June 2003).

No. 1004. Pharmaceutical Preparations—Value of Shipments: 1990 to 2001

[In millions of dollars (33,954 represents $33,954,000,000)]

Product description	Product code	1990	1995	1998	1999	2000	2001
Pharmaceutical preparations, except biologicals	(X)	33,954	48,864	65,712	70,417	79,262	90,674
Affecting neoplasms, endocrine systems, and metabolic disease	3254121000	2,743	4,076	7,633	7,988	9,784	14,427
Acting on the central nervous system and sense organs	3254124000	7,219	9,228	13,605	14,881	18,508	19,737
Acting on the cardiovascular system	3254127000	4,815	5,988	9,368	9,601	8,993	9,700
Acting on the respiratory system	325412A000	3,724	5,196	6,725	8,155	10,179	11,653
Acting on the digestive system	325412D000	4,840	8,593	9,502	8,741	10,046	12,652
Acting on the skin	325412G000	1,558	2,171	2,245	2,798	2,941	2,717
Vitamin, nutrient, and hematinic preps.	325412L000	2,588	4,812	5,851	6,161	5,676	6,072
Affecting parasitic and infective disease	325412P000	5,411	7,196	8,780	9,778	11,037	11,219
Pharmaceutical preps. for veterinary use	325412T000	1,057	1,605	2,003	2,314	2,096	2,499

X Not applicable.

Source: U.S. Census Bureau, 1990, Current Industrial Reports, Series MA28G; thereafter, MA325G(01)-1. See also <http://www.census.gov/industry/1/ma325g01.pdf> (released September 2002).

No. 1005. Inorganic Chemicals and Fertilizers—Production: 1995 to 2001

[17,402 represents 17,402,000]

Product description	Unit	1995	1997	1998	1999	2000	2001
INORGANIC FERTILIZERS							
Ammonia, synthetic anhydrous	1,000 sh. tons	17,402	17,891	18,475	17,337	15,809	12,538
Ammonium nitrate, original solution	1,000 sh. tons	8,489	8,604	9,079	7,630	7,979	6,920
Ammonium sulfate	1,000 sh. tons	2,647	2,711	2,787	2,875	2,808	2,556
Urea (100%)	1,000 sh. tons	8,117	8,190	8,865	8,907	7,682	6,883
Nitric acid (100%)	1,000 sh. tons	8,839	9,433	9,285	8,945	8,708	7,074
Phosphoric acid (100% P2O5)	1,000 sh. tons	13,134	13,159	13,891	13,708	12,492	11,566
Sulfuric acid, gross (100%)	1,000 sh. tons	47,519	47,929	48,513	44,756	43,643	40,793
Superphosphates and other fertilizer materials (100% P2O5)	1,000 sh. tons	10,364	10,473	10,260	9,133	8,899	8,109
INORGANIC CHEMICALS							
Chlorine gas	1,000 metric tons	12,395	12,922	11,650	12,114	14,000	12,694
Sodium hydroxide, total liquid	1,000 metric tons	11,408	11,972	11,886	11,974	11,523	10,650
Potassium hydroxide liquid	1,000 metric tons	(D)	533	450	430	539	512
Finished sodium bicarbonate	1,000 metric tons	520	522	493	505	536	566
Titanium dioxide, composite and pure	1,000 metric tons	1,382	1,477	1,323	1,355	1,547	1,463
Hydrochloric acid	1,000 metric tons	3,904	4,411	4,226	4,191	4,717	4,379
Hydroflouric acid	1,000 metric tons	(D)	(D)	(D)	(NA)	(NA)	(NA)
Aluminum oxide	1,000 metric tons	4,764	5,072	4,537	4,016	(D)	3,156
Aluminum sulfate (commercial)	1,000 metric tons	1,144	1,161	1,058	1,052	1,076	1,137
Sodium chlorate	1,000 metric tons	617	626	707	742	940	873
Sodium phosphate tribasic	1,000 metric tons	21	(D)	19	27	(NA)	(NA)
Sodium phosphate tripoly	1,000 metric tons	(D)	(D)	205	(D)	(D)	(D)
Sodium silicats [1]	1,000 metric tons	1,203	1,214	1,097	992	1,136	1,179
Sodium metasilicates	1,000 metric tons	93	83	70	63	72	(D)
Sodium sulfate	1,000 metric tons	(D)	(D)	571	599	509	565
Calcium phosphorous	1,000 metric tons	1,567	1,486	1,798	1,808	(D)	(D)
Carbon activated [2]	1,000 metric tons	156	173	150	151	166	(S)
Hydrogen peroxide	1,000 metric tons	355	369	324	342	1,083	780
Phosphorous, elemental	1,000 metric tons	(D)	(D)	(D)	(NA)	(NA)	(NA)
Phosphorous, oxychloride and trichlorde	1,000 metric tons	226	298	(D)	163	(D)	(D)

D Withheld to avoid disclosing data for individual companies. NA Not available. [1] Other than metasilicates. [2] Granular and pulverized.

Source: U.S. Census Bureau, Current Industrial Reports, Series MAQ325A, and MA325B, annual. See also <http://www.census.gov/cir/www/325/mq325a.html> (released August 2002) and <http://www.census.gov/industry/1/mq325b015.pdf> (released September 2002).

No. 1006. Aluminum—Supply, Shipments, and Foreign Trade: 1990 to 2002

[In millions of pounds (17,334 represents 17,334,000,000)]

Item	1990	1995	1997	1998	1999	2000	2001	2002
SUPPLY								
Aluminum supply, total	17,334	20,425	21,945	22,970	24,590	23,586	20,071	20,776
Primary production	8,925	7,441	7,944	8,185	8,330	8,087	5,812	5,964
Recovery from scrap	5,276	7,028	7,819	7,589	8,146	7,606	6,572	6,270
Imports of ingot and mill products	3,133	5,956	6,183	7,196	8,113	7,893	7,687	8,542
Aluminum net shipments, total [1]	17,188	21,019	22,513	23,189	24,673	24,496	22,519	23,601
PRODUCT								
Mill products, total	13,013	15,716	16,609	17,019	17,989	17,676	15,467	15,715
Sheet, plate, and foil	9,297	11,168	11,536	11,801	12,437	12,116	10,376	10,573
Rod, bar, and wire	370	534	621	657	670	690	571	591
Electrical conductor	542	566	629	631	676	681	676	705
Extruded shapes and tube	2,546	3,102	3,473	3,559	3,817	3,792	3,482	3,484
Powder and paste	106	108	118	123	130	142	142	142
Forgings and impacts	152	238	232	248	259	255	220	220
Ingot for castings and other [2]	4,175	5,303	5,904	6,170	6,684	6,820	7,052	7,886
MARKET								
Domestic, total	14,637	18,152	19,523	20,358	21,707	21,680	20,531	21,245
Building and construction	2,663	2,679	2,921	3,070	3,237	3,204	3,297	3,447
Transportation	3,205	5,749	6,592	7,162	7,938	7,947	7,035	7,516
Consumer durables	1,122	1,369	1,529	1,599	1,675	1,692	1,502	1,592
Electrical	1,309	1,395	1,532	1,527	1,646	1,704	1,513	1,493
Machinery and equipment	992	1,257	1,381	1,386	1,458	1,496	1,414	1,359
Containers and packaging	4,772	5,088	4,895	5,012	5,106	4,992	4,961	4,979
Other	574	615	673	602	647	645	809	859
Exports	2,551	2,867	2,990	2,831	2,967	2,816	1,988	2,356
FOREIGN TRADE [3]								
Exports	3,753	3,846	3,763	3,743	3,865	4,097	3,712	3,729
Imports	3,718	6,910	7,209	8,342	9,506	9,357	8,853	9,680

[1] Data presented on this report have been adjusted to shipments and inventories plus imports by consumers. [2] Net ingot for foundry castings, export and destructive uses. [3] U.S. imports and exports of aluminum ingot, mill products and scrap.

Source: The Aluminum Association, Inc., Washington, DC, *Aluminum Statistical Review*, annual; and *Aluminum Facts at a Glance*, October 2002.

Manufactures 649

No. 1007. Iron and Steel Industry—Summary: 1990 to 2002

[95.5 represents 95,500,000 tons. For financial data, the universe in 1992 consists of the companies that produced 68 percent of the total reported raw steel production. The financial data represent the operations of the steel segment of the companies. Minus sign (-) indicates net loss]

Item	Unit	1990	1995	1997	1998	1999	2000	2001	2002, prel.
Steel mill products, apparent supply	Mil. tons [1]	95.5	109.6	124.6	131.6	127.9	131.9	116.4	117.0
Net shipments	Mil. tons [1]	85.0	97.5	105.9	102.4	106.2	109.1	98.9	99.2
Exports	Mil. tons [1]	4.3	7.1	6.0	5.5	5.4	6.5	6.1	6.0
Imports	Mil. tons [1]	17.2	24.4	31.2	41.5	31.2	29.4	30.1	32.6
Scrap consumed	Mil. tons [1]	50.1	62.0	64.0	64.0	62.0	65.0	63.0	(NA)
Scrap inventory	Mil. tons [1]	3.6	4.1	5.5	4.5	5.3	5.3	4.9	(NA)
Iron and steel products: Exports	Mil. tons [1]	5.3	8.2	7.4	6.9	6.7	7.7	7.2	7.0
Imports	Mil. tons [1]	21.9	27.3	34.4	45.4	40.2	42.6	34.4	37.3
Capacity by steelmaking process	Mil. net tons.	116.7	112.4	121.4	125.3	128.2	130.3	125.5	113.7
Revenue	Bil. dol	30.9	35.1	36.6	38.1	36.3	38.8	31.0	(NA)
Net income	Bil. dol	0.1	1.5	1.0	1.1	-0.5	-1.1	-3.9	(NA)
Stockholders' equity	Bil. dol	4.3	8.6	9.8	12.5	11.8	9.9	5.5	(NA)
Total assets	Bil. dol	28.3	35.1	38.3	42.2	43.7	43.9	38.1	(NA)
Capital expenditures	Bil. dol	2.6	2.5	2.7	3.1	2.8	2.1	1.1	(NA)
Working capital ratio [2]	Ratio	1.6	1.5	1.6	1.6	1.7	1.7	1.6	(NA)
Inventories	Bil. dol	4.7	5.1	5.8	6.8	6.5	6.8	5.7	(NA)
Average employment	1,000	169.0	122.6	111.8	109.6	102.2	99.5	88.0	(NA)
Hours worked	Million	350.0	269.2	247.2	240.0	222.7	219.7	186.4	(NA)
Index of output, all employees [3]	1987=100	109.7	142.6	155.0	151.0	155.6	160.1	(NA)	(NA)

NA Not available.   [1] In millions of short tons.   [2] Current assets to current liabilities.   [3] Output per hour. Source: U.S. Bureau of Labor Statistics, Internet site <http://www.bls.gov/pc/>.
Source: Except as noted, American Iron and Steel Institute, Washington, DC, *Annual Statistical Report* (copyright).

No. 1008. Steel Products—Net Shipments by Market Classes: 1990 to 2002

[In thousands of short tons (84,981 represents 84,981,000). Comprises carbon, alloy, and stainless steel]

Market class	1990	1995	1997	1998	1999	2000	2001	2002
Net shipments, total [1]	84,981	97,494	105,858	102,420	106,201	109,050	99,448	99,191
Automotive	11,100	14,622	15,251	15,842	16,771	16,063	14,059	12,562
Steel service centers, distributors	21,111	23,751	27,800	27,751	28,089	30,108	27,072	22,828
Construction, incl. maintenance [2]	9,245	14,892	15,885	15,289	18,428	20,290	21,543	15,729
Containers, packaging, shipping	4,474	4,139	4,163	3,829	3,842	3,708	3,232	3,251
Machinery, industrial equipment, tools	2,388	2,310	2,355	2,147	1,722	1,784	1,456	1,137
Steel for converting and processing	9,441	10,440	11,263	9,975	11,309	12,708	10,311	7,201
Rail transportation	1,080	1,373	1,410	1,657	1,031	1,307	981	751
Contractors' products	2,870	(²)	(²)	(²)	(²)	(²)	(²)	(²)
Oil and gas industries	1,892	2,643	3,811	2,649	2,151	2,885	2,953	1,658
Electrical equipment	2,453	2,397	2,434	2,255	2,267	2,055	1,684	1,336
Appliances, utensils, and cutlery	1,540	1,589	1,635	1,729	1,789	1,907	1,820	1,734

[1] Includes nonclassified shipments and other classes not shown separately.   [2] Beginning 1995, contractors' products included with construction.
Source: American Iron and Steel Institute, Washington, DC, *Annual Statistical Report* (copyright).

No. 1009. Metalworking Machinery—Value of Shipments: 1990 to 2002

[In millions of dollars (3,426.1 represents $3,426,100,000)]

Product	NAICS product code	1990	1995	1998	1999	2000	2001	2002
Metalworking machinery	(X)	3,426.1	4,547.1	4,817.1	3,783.3	3,632.4	2,987.6	2,002.1
Metal cutting type [1]	(X)	2,371.3	3,036.6	3,481.8	2,512.6	2,552.4	2,163.7	1,418.7
Boring machines [2]	333512A1	(²)	172.4	73.6	53.8	87.2	124.8	128.3
Drilling machines [2]	333512A1	184.1	78.9	102.9	50.6	23.7	22.6	17.1
Gear cutting machines	33351211	102.7	137.1	197.7	132.0	180.6	137.2	111.0
Grinding and polishing machines	33351220	433.6	549.6	535.5	477.1	454.3	367.7	210.7
Lathes [3]	33351230	355.6	478.0	472.9	297.4	287.0	262.0	132.4
Milling machines [4]	33351240	214.3	194.8	281.1	200.5	150.5	137.8	56.1
Machining centers [5]	33351270	437.0	698.8	897.3	597.9	629.7	435.5	273.6
Station type machines	33351280	502.1	477.0	571.0	407.1	401.8	347.9	169.9
Other metal cutting machine tools [6]	33351290	141.9	246.2	344.6	291.7	332.2	276.4	238.3
Metal forming type	(X)	1,080.2	1,510.5	1,335.3	1,270.7	1,080.0	823.9	583.4
Punching and shearing machines	33351310 pt.	200.1	326.3	254.3	220.0	230.8	155.3	105.9
Bending and forming machines	33351310 pt.	222.9	256.9	262.7	265.8	262.4	202.6	141.3
Presses, except forging	33351330	308.3	379.2	399.5	433.7	303.1	180.3	140.1
Forging machines [7]	33351350 pt.	73.9	(D)	(D)	(D)	(D)	(D)	(D)
Other metal forming [7]	33351350 pt.	275.0	548.1	418.8	351.2	310.7	275.8	187.4

D Data withheld to avoid disclosure.   X Not applicable.   [1] Beginning 1995, data for "All lathes (turning machines)" and "All milling machines," valued at under $3,025 each are included in total "Metal cutting type" for 1995 through 2000.   [2] For 1990, data for "Boring machines" were combined with "Drilling machines" to avoid disclosing individual company data.   [3] Beginning 1995, product code 33351230, "Lathes," excludes the value for product code 3335123031, All lathes valued under $3,025 each.   [4] Beginning 1995, product code 33351240, "Milling machines," excludes the value for product code 3335124001, "All milling machines valued under $3,025 each."   [5] Multifunction numerically controlled machines.   [6] Excludes those designed primarily for home workshops, labs, etc.   [7] For 1995 through 2002, data for "Forging machines" have been combined with "Other metal forming machines" to avoid disclosing individual company data.
Source: U.S. Census Bureau, 1990, Current Industrial Reports, Series MQ35W; and thereafter, MQ333W. See also <http://www.census.gov/industry/1/mq333w025.pdf> (released July 2003).

No. 1010. U.S. Machine Tool Consumption—Gross New Orders and Exports: 2001 and 2002

[Value in millions of dollars (3,025 represents $3,025,000,000)]

Item	2001 Total	2001 Metal cutting machines	2001 Metal forming machines	2001 Other manufacturing technology	2002 Total	2002 Metal cutting machines	2002 Metal forming machines	2002 Other manufacturing technology
New order units, total..	20,594	17,462	1,619	1,511	17,890	14,642	1,686	1,562
Northeast [1]	3,850	3,233	327	290	2,847	2,355	267	225
South [2]	3,208	2,611	313	284	3,197	2,528	347	323
Midwest [3]	6,281	5,294	490	497	5,537	4,398	546	593
Central [4]	4,032	3,416	348	268	3,716	3,090	370	256
West [5]	3,223	2,910	141	172	2,594	2,273	156	165
New order value, total	3,025	2,445	223	357	2,385	1,832	228	325
Northeast [1]	495	405	38	52	350	279	32	39
South [2]	450	337	40	73	410	307	47	57
Midwest [3]	1,192	942	88	162	921	653	94	174
Central [4]	531	444	42	45	443	366	38	39
West [5]	357	318	15	24	262	227	18	17
Export order units [6]	1,518	1,222	137	159	1,205	951	138	116
Export order value [6]	424	309	35	79	267	202	27	38

[1] Covers Maine, New Hampshire, Vermont, New York, Massachusetts, Connecticut, Rhode Island, New Jersey, and Pennsylvania. [2] Covers Delaware, Maryland, Virginia, West Virginia, Kentucky, North Carolina, South Carolina, Tennessee, Mississippi, Alabama, Georgia, and Florida. [3] Covers Wisconsin, Michigan, Ohio, Illinois, and Indiana. [4] Covers Minnesota, North Dakota, South Dakota, Montana, Wyoming, Idaho, Iowa, Nebraska, Kansas, Missouri, Oklahoma, Arkansas, Louisiana, Texas, New Mexico, Colorado, and Utah. [5] Covers Washington, Oregon, California, Nevada, and Arizona. [6] Represents orders placed with U.S. builders.

Source: The Association for Manufacturing Technology, McLean, VA, (copyright); and American Machine Tool Distributors Association, Rockville, MD, *U.S. Machine Tool Consumption Report*, monthly.

No. 1011. Semiconductors, Printed Circuit Boards, and Other Electronic Components—Value of Shipments by Class of Product: 1990 to 2002

[In millions of dollars (56,301 represents $56,301,000,000). N.e.c.=not elsewhere classified]

Class of product	Product code	1990	1995	1999	2000	2001	2002
Total	(X)	56,301	118,906	141,660	164,854	118,868	111,407
Transmittal, industrial, and special-purpose electron tubes (except x-ray)	3344111	1,097	855	673	703	700	594
Electron tubes, receiving type	(X)	24	([1])	([1])	([1])	([1])	([1])
Receiving type electron tubes and cathode ray picture tubes	3344114	1,344	[1]2,907	[1]3,579	[1]3,458	[1]2,847	[1]2,043
Electron tube parts	3344117	143	120	136	144	125	69
Printed circuit boards	3344120	7,175	8,367	9,150	11,892	8,910	6,045
Integrated microcircuits (semiconductor networks)	3344131	16,623	48,438	62,868	73,664	46,337	55,772
Transistors	3344134	682	943	994	1,569	913	747
Diodes and rectifiers	3344137	668	1,067	1,038	621	403	281
Other semiconductor devices	334413A	5,741	12,639	11,745	9,757	7,632	6,805
Capacitors for electronic applications	3344140	1,392	1,785	2,035	2,786	1,734	1,300
Resistors	3344150	800	953	971	982	776	683
Coils, transformers, reactors, and chokes for electronic applications	3344160	976	1,412	1,423	1,719	1,362	1,130
Coaxial connectors	3344171	420	732	631	805	506	366
Cylindrical connectors	3344174	514	553	550	725	688	672
Rack and panel connectors	3344177	500	541	391	532	359	234
Printed circuit connectors	334417A	805	1,026	1,376	1,811	1,147	744
Other connectors including parts	334417D	1,085	1,402	2,041	2,059	2,052	1,288
Filters (except microwave) and piezoelectric devices	3344191	457	729	858	1,168	984	718
Transducers, electrical/electronic input or output	3344194	741	1,111	1,331	1,519	1,331	1,154
Switches, mechanical types for electronic circuitry	3344197	579	666	883	903	828	840
Printed circuit assemblies	334418A	8,269	24,448	30,091	37,273	31,214	23,259
Microwave components and devices	334419A	1,369	1,233	1,622	2,435	1,848	1,599
All other electronic components n.e.c	334419D	4,898	6,978	7,276	8,332	6,173	5,067

X Not applicable. [1] Product codes combined to avoid disclosing figures for individual companies. [2] N.e.c. means not elsewhere classified.

Source: U.S. Census Bureau, 1990, Current Industrial Reports, Series MA36Q; thereafter, MA334Q. See also <http://www.census.gov/industry/1/ma334q02.pdf> (revised 07 August 2003).

No. 1012. Computers and Office and Accounting Machines—Value of Shipments: 1990 to 2002

[In millions of dollars (25,630 represents $25,630,000,000)]

Selected products	1990	1995	1998	1999	2000	2001	2002
Electronic computers [1]	25,630	49,038	56,892	64,696	62,857	48,541	41,818
Host computers (multi-users)	(NA)	(NA)	15,010	21,089	22,877	16,469	14,207
Single user computers	(NA)	(NA)	41,002	42,765	38,981	31,492	26,749
Other computers	(NA)	(NA)	48	(D)	998	581	862
Loaded computer processor boards and board subassemblies [2]	2,247	24,448	26,047	30,091	37,273	31,214	23,259
Computer storage devices & equipment	7,488	7,903	9,319	9,827	8,995	7,319	5,661
Parts for computer storage devices & subassemblies	955	2,236	2,310	2,254	1,692	1,699	1,560
Computer terminals	2,067	1,086	529	541	415	361	286
Computer peripheral equipment, n.e.c.[3]	7,697	12,331	12,145	12,889	12,434	10,637	10,364
Parts for input/output equipment	3,706	2,391	2,630	2,388	2,766	2,360	2,217
Calculating and accounting machines	(D)	1,279	1,061	1,196	1,210	1,191	828
Magnetic and optical recording media	3,695	5,106	4,736	3,907	3,206	2,228	2,325

D Withheld to avoid disclosing data for individual companies. NA Not available. [1] Beginning 1998, computer industry data are not entirely comparable to previous years. [2] These data are collected on two Current Industrial Report forms, MA35R, "Computers and Office and Accounting Machines (Shipments) and MA36Q, Semiconductors, Printed Circuit Boards, And Other Electronic Components. [3] N.e.c. means not elsewhere classified.

Source: U.S. Census Bureau, Current Industrial Reports, Series MA334R. See also <http://www.census.gov/industry/1/ma334r02.pdf> (released August 2003).

No. 1013. Computers and Office and Accounting Machines—Shipments: 2001 and 2002

[Quantity in thousands of units (22,209 represents 22,209,000, value in millions of dollars (48,541 represents $48,541,000,000)]

Product	Number of companies, 2002	Quantity (1,000) 2001	Quantity (1,000) 2002	Value (mil. dol.) 2001	Value (mil. dol.) 2002
Electronic computers (automatic data processors)	125	22,209	19,647	48,541	41,818
Host computers (multi-users):					
Large scale systems and unix servers	13	309	106	4,701	4,036
Medium-scale systems and unix servers	22	323	279	8,301	6,704
PC servers	24	(D)	(D)	(D)	(D)
Other host computers	9	(D)	(D)	(D)	(D)
Single user computers:					
Personal computers	34	14,591	12,920	18,870	16,186
Workstations	38	1,316	1,132	3,381	2,380
Laptops (AC/DC)	9	7	8	21	23
Notebooks, subnotebooks (battery operated)	16	4,249	4,126	8,682	7,850
Personal digital assistants	6	(D)	(D)	(D)	(D)
Other portable computers	7	(D)	(D)	(D)	(D)
Other single user computers	6	184	102	94	55
Other computers	31	106	120	581	862
Computer storage devices and equipment	58	(X)	(X)	7,319	5,661
Parts for computer storage devices and subassemblies	18	(X)	(X)	1,699	1,560
Computer terminals	31	(X)	(X)	361	286
Computer peripheral equipment, n.e.c.[1]	202	(X)	(X)	10,637	10,364
Keyboards	24	(D)	(D)	(D)	(D)
Computer printers:					
Laser	25	3,475	1,270	2,011	1,803
Inkjet	11	7,986	(D)	615	(D)
Calculating and accounting machines	33	(X)	(X)	1,191	828
Printed circuit assemblies	654	(X)	(X)	31,214	23,259
Magnetic and optical recording media	36	(X)	(X)	2,228	2,325

X Not applicable. D Withheld to avoid disclosure of individual companies. [1] N.e.c. = Not elsewhere classified.
Source: U.S. Census Bureau, Current Industrial Reports, Series MA334R. See also <http://www.census.gov/industry/1/ma334r02.pdf> (released August 2003).

No. 1014. Computers and Industrial Electronics—Factory Shipments: 1990 to 2000

[In millions of dollars (50,793 represents $50,793,000,000)]

Item	1990	1995	1997	1998	1999	2000
Computer and peripheral equipment, total	50,793	73,555	76,287	78,356	87,412	84,310
Computers	25,973	49,038	50,250	56,892	64,696	62,072
Peripheral equipment	24,820	24,517	26,037	21,464	22,716	22,238
Industrial electronics, total	26,183	33,732	38,108	36,887	37,734	40,566
Controlling, processing equipment	12,728	16,450	18,212	18,082	18,221	18,597
Testing, measuring equipment	6,859	10,109	11,966	11,213	11,564	14,554
Nuclear electronic equipment	567	501	516	560	538	568
Robots, accessories, and components	275	(NA)	(NA)	(NA)	(NA)	(NA)
Other electronic equipment	5,754	6,672	7,414	7,033	7,412	6,847

NA Not available.
Source: Consumer Electronics Association, Washington, DC, Electronic Market Data Book, annual (copyright).

No. 1015. Consumer Electronics and Electronic Components—Factory Sales by Product Category: 1990 to 2001

[In millions of dollars (43,033 represents $43,033,000,000). Factory sales include imports]

Product category	1990	1995	1997	1998	1999	2000	2001
Total [1]	43,033	67,905	75,356	79,427	85,633	94,924	91,706
Video products:	(NA)	15,376	13,893	14,898	16,671	18,545	17,043
Direct-view color TV	6,197	6,798	6,023	6,122	6,199	6,140	5,130
LCD color TV	50	44	38	39	36	43	42
Analog projection TV	626	1,417	1,361	1,577	1,632	1,481	1,060
TV/VCR combinations	178	723	684	832	1,014	969	790
Monochrome TV	99	34	27	23	20	15	15
LCD Monochrome TV	33	31	30	28	25	21	20
VCR decks	2,439	2,767	2,618	2,409	2,333	1,861	1,058
Camcorders	2,260	2,130	1,894	2,011	2,444	2,838	2,081
Laserdisc players	72	108	25	10	3	3	3
Direct-to-home satellite	421	1,265	726	733	957	1,102	921
Videocassette players	65	59	39	21	15	7	5
Digital versatile disc players (DVD)	(NA)	(NA)	171	421	1,099	1,713	2,697
Home and portable products:	(NA)	6,378	5,911	5,875	6,048	5,924	5,944
Compact audio systems	1,270	1,162	1,417	1,554	1,695	1,778	1,357
Separate audio components	1,935	1,911	1,606	1,448	1,442	1,523	1,357
Home radios	360	284	300	300	348	351	325
Portable audio equipment	1,645	2,506	2,033	2,146	2,086	1,640	1,967
Mobile electronics:	(NA)	11,422	11,311	11,542	12,169	15,433	15,336
Aftermarket autosound equipment	1,192	1,931	1,811	1,899	2,157	2,169	2,135
Factory installed autosound	3,100	3,100	2,710	2,540	2,610	2,700	2,850
Wireless (cellular) telephones	1,133	2,574	5,940	6,000	6,066	8,995	8,651
Pagers	118	300	460	550	660	750	790
Vehicle security	190	142	210	213	205	218	266
Home office products:	(NA)	24,140	31,982	33,455	35,219	36,652	34,281
Cordless telephones	842	1,141	1,672	1,745	1,808	1,307	1,358
Corded telephones	638	557	515	489	471	393	294
Telephone answering devices	827	1,077	1,020	1,104	1,044	984	1,062
Home computers	4,187	12,600	15,950	16,640	16,390	16,400	12,960
Computer printers	(NA)	2,430	3,900	4,188	4,500	5,116	5,245
Modems/fax modems	(NA)	770	1,170	1,305	1,460	1,564	1,564
Computer peripherals	1,980	816	1,212	1,440	1,950	2,150	2,365
Computer software (incl. CDROM)	971	2,500	3,450	3,930	4,480	5,062	5,771
Home fax machines	920	919	1,137	647	455	387	349
Digital cameras	(NA)	(NA)	483	519	1,209	1,823	1,972
Electronic gaming:							
Electronic gaming hardware	975	1,500	1,650	1,980	2,250	2,700	3,250
Electronic gaming software	2,400	3,000	3,900	4,480	5,100	5,850	6,725
Blank media:							
Blank audio cassettes	376	334	281	248	208	162	106
Blank videocassettes	948	708	695	647	590	567	604
Blank computer media	314	373	500	700	900	1,200	1,550
Accessories and batteries:							
Electronic accessories	793	944	964	1,119	1,198	1,281	1,389
Total primary batteries	1,383	2,600	2,869	2,963	3,620	4,860	3,658
Home security systems	(NA)	1,130	1,400	1,520	1,660	1,750	1,820

NA Not available.   [1] Includes categories, not shown separately.
Source: Consumer Electronics Association, Washington, DC, *Electronic Market Data Book*, annual (copyright).

No. 1016. Communication Equipment—Value of Shipments: 1990 to 2001

[In millions of dollars (36,990 represents $36,990,000,000]

Product description	Product code	1990	1995	1998	1999	2000	2001
Total	(X)	36,990	56,362	82,176	89,557	105,403	91,861
Telephone switching and switchboard equipment	3342101	7,537	8,178	12,422	13,742	14,433	11,821
Carrier line equipment and modems	3342104	5,014	5,869	9,379	9,263	14,816	10,839
Other telephone and telegraph equipment and components	3342107	3,181	10,510	19,897	23,268	26,260	26,563
Communication systems and equipment (except broadcast)	3342201	14,768	23,032	31,128	33,281	38,301	30,930
Broadcast, studio, and related electronic equipment	3342203	1,856	2,845	3,603	4,000	3,902	3,488
Intercommunications systems, including inductive paging systems (selective calling)	3342903	346	296	249	401.1	495	474
Alarm systems	3342901	1,027	1,662	2,024	2,218	2,376	3,343
Vehicular and pedestrian traffic control equipment and electrical railway signals and attachments	3342902	471	711	912	952.3	935	878
Electronic teaching machines, teaching aids, trainers and simulators	3333197	1,209	913	713	700.7	814	742
Laser sources [1]	3359997	(NA)	788	(S)	(S)	1,204	1,139
Ultrasonic equipment	335999A	109	172	205	225.7	267	233
Other electronic systems and equipment, n.e.c [2]	335999C	1,473	1,387	1,645	1,515	1,602	1,411

NA Not available.   S Does not meet publication standards.   X Not applicable.   [1] Beginning in 1995, data for laser equipment, instrumentation, and components were eliminated from this survey. Only laser sources are being collected.   [2] N.e.c. = Not elsewhere classified.

Source: U.S. Census Bureau, *Current Industrial Reports*, Series MA334P. See also <http://www.census.gov/industry/1/ma334p01.pdf> (released September 2002).

Manufactures   653

No. 1017. Motor Vehicle Manufactures—Summary by Selected Industry: 2001

[Payroll of 47,955 represents $47,955,000,000. Based on the Annual Survey of Manufactures; see Appendix III]

Industry	NAICS code [1]	All employees [2] Number	Payroll Total (mil. dol.)	Payroll Per employee (dol.)	Production workers [2]	Value of shipments [3] (mil. dol.)
Motor vehicle manufacturing, total	3361-3363	1,073,104	47,955	44,688	867,975	427,176
Motor vehicle, total	3361	213,981	12,647	59,102	186,209	216,128
Automobile & light duty motor vehicle	33611	186,527	11,435	61,304	165,090	203,514
Automobile	336111	91,062	5,388	59,166	78,607	87,046
Light truck & utility vehicle	336112	95,465	6,047	63,343	86,483	116,468
Heavy duty truck	33612	27,454	1,212	44,142	21,119	12,613
Motor vehicle body & trailer	3362	123,120	3,807	30,924	97,153	24,209
Motor vehicle body & trailer	33621	123,120	3,807	30,924	97,153	24,209
Motor vehicle body	336211	41,771	1,325	31,725	30,934	10,535
Truck trailer	336212	26,360	825	31,286	20,830	4,296
Motor home	336213	16,102	502	31,169	13,064	3,345
Travel trailer & camper	336214	38,887	1,156	29,716	32,325	6,034
Motor vehicle parts	3363	736,003	31,501	42,800	584,613	186,839
Motor vehicle gasoline engine & engine parts	33631	88,635	4,288	48,377	73,021	28,202
Carburetor, piston, piston ring, & valve	336311	16,656	745	44,749	13,944	2,907
Gasoline engine & engine parts	336312	71,979	3,543	49,217	59,077	25,294
Motor vehicle electrical & electronic equip.	33632	109,477	4,312	39,391	80,650	23,310
Vehicular lighting equipment	336321	14,665	640	43,665	10,913	2,780
Other motor vehicle electrical & electronic equipment	336322	94,812	3,672	38,730	69,737	20,530
Motor vehicle steering & suspension components, ex. spring	33633	47,015	2,207	46,948	38,239	10,044
Motor vehicle brake system	33634	38,736	1,420	36,660	29,542	10,636
Motor vehicle transmission & power train parts	33635	98,753	5,178	52,435	79,306	31,466
Motor vehicle seating & interior trim	33636	52,670	1,675	31,793	42,269	14,814
Motor vehicle metal stamping	33637	112,488	5,392	47,932	94,033	21,858
Other motor vehicle parts	33639	188,229	7,029	37,341	147,553	46,510

[1] North American Industrial Classification System, 1997; see text, Section 15. [2] Includes employment and payroll at administrative offices and auxiliary units. All employees represents the average of production workers plus all other employees for the payroll period ended nearest the 12th of March. Production workers represents the average of the employment for the payroll periods ended nearest the 12th of March, May, August, and November. [3] Includes extensive and unmeasurable duplication from shipments between establishments in the same industry classification.

Source: U.S. Census Bureau, Annual Survey of Manufactures, *Statistics for Industry Groups and Industries*, Series M01(AS)-1. See also <http://www.census.gov/prod/2003pubs/m01-as1.pdf> (issued January 2003).

No. 1018. Motor Vehicle Manufactures—Employees, Payroll, and Shipments by Major State: 2001

[Payroll of 12,647 represents 12,647,000,000. Industry based on the North American Industrial Classification System (NAICS), 1997; see text, Section 15]

Major State based on employment	Motor vehicle manufacturing (NAICS 3361) Employees, total	Payroll (mil. dol.)	Shipments (mil. dol.)	Motor vehicle body and trailer manufacturing (NAICS 3362) Employees, total	Payroll (mil. dol.)	Shipments (mil. dol.)	Motor vehicle parts manufacturing (NAICS 3363) Employees, total	Payroll (mil. dol.)	Shipments (mil. dol.)
United States	213,981	12,647	216,128	123,120	3,807	24,209	736,003	31,501	186,839
Alabama	(D)	(D)	(D)	3,158	94	754	11,531	565	3,315
Arkansas	(NA)	(NA)	(NA)	1,549	35	281	7,522	173	873
California	7,429	416	2,965	11,287	341	4,693	25,824	771	3,849
Florida	(NA)	(NA)	(NA)	3,793	134	806	4,409	124	625
Georgia	7,620	386	8,130	2,977	80	(S)	9,394	273	2,114
Illinois	8,083	481	7,863	3,719	127	649	28,464	930	5,271
Indiana	11,867	618	10,811	24,414	867	4,845	93,497	4,226	22,712
Iowa	(NA)	(NA)	(NA)	8,000	247	1,403	9,169	307	1,693
Kentucky	18,810	1,287	22,470	(NA)	(NA)	(NA)	27,764	934	7,240
Michigan	42,260	2,722	51,873	3,925	113	599	178,681	9,230	52,242
Mississippi	(NA)	(NA)	(NA)	780	22	109	9,718	296	1,673
Missouri	(D)	(D)	(D)	2,049	52	227	19,520	569	4,030
Nebraska	(NA)	(NA)	(NA)	1,109	29	190	3,609	123	668
New York	(NA)	(NA)	(NA)	1,088	32	768	30,232	1,737	8,703
North Carolina	(D)	(D)	(D)	3,714	141	961	18,661	619	4,512
Ohio	29,972	1,784	32,648	4,387	142	809	96,775	4,881	29,924
Oklahoma	(D)	(D)	(D)	4,086	105	691	5,531	165	1,031
Oregon	1,749	60	781	4,635	113	552	2,525	98	500
Pennsylvania	(D)	(D)	(D)	7,243	191	1,118	15,328	581	3,328
South Carolina	6,210	298	4,501	(S)	(S)	(S)	16,109	557	4,570
Tennessee	14,241	840	7,552	1,818	52	381	32,130	1,065	8,098
Texas	(D)	(D)	(D)	5,963	169	800	16,186	468	3,389
Utah	(NA)	(NA)	(NA)	1,085	27	177	5,341	223	2,387
Virginia	(D)	(D)	(D)	(D)	(D)	(D)	6,747	253	1,718
Wisconsin	(D)	(D)	(D)	5,258	188	909	23,387	970	5,412

D Withheld to avoid disclosing data on individual companies. NA Not available.

Source: U.S. Census Bureau, Annual Survey of Manufactures, *Geographic Area Statistics*, Series M01(AS)-3. See also <http://www.census.gov/prod/2003pubs/m01as-3.pdf> (issued January 2003).

No. 1019. Aerospace—Sales, New Orders, and Backlog: 1990 to 2002

[In billions of dollars (136.6 represents $136,600,000,000), except as indicated. Reported by establishments in which the principal business is the development and/or production of aerospace products]

Item	1990	1995	1998	1999	2000	2001	2002
Net sales	136.6	102.8	119.3	124.2	109.3	117.1	111.3
Percent U.S. government	53.8	50.5	33.5	36.3	37.5	38.6	46.5
Complete aircraft and parts [1]	49.9	42.5	63.6	68.0	57.2	58.7	51.9
Aircraft engines and parts	16.4	12.5	12.8	14.4	12.5	15.9	14.8
Missiles and space vehicles, parts	22.0	18.4	16.1	15.7	15.6	15.5	15.0
Other products, services	48.3	29.4	26.7	26.1	24.0	26.9	29.6
Net, new orders	146.0	109.1	110.0	115.3	140.1	122.2	114.6
Backlog, Dec. 31	250.1	202.6	200.3	188.4	215.0	220.1	222.8

[1] Except engines sold separately.

Source: U.S. Census Bureau, 1990-1997, Current Industrial Reports, Series M37G; thereafter M336G. See also <http://www.census.gov/industry/1/m336g0213.pdf> (released August 2003).

No. 1020. Net Orders for U.S. Civil Jet Transport Aircraft: 1990 to 2002

[1990 data are net new firm orders; beginning 1995, net announced orders. Minus sign (-) indicates net cancellations. In 1997 Boeing acquired McDonnell Douglas]

Type of aircraft and customer	1990	1995	1997	1998	1999	2000	2001	2002
Total number [1]	670	421	501	601	346	585	271	174
U.S. customers	259	138	258	392	192	412	49	89
Foreign customers	411	283	243	209	70	193	130	172
Boeing 737, total	189	189	280	350	258	378	184	117
U.S. customers	38	85	120	207	155	302	51	64
Foreign customers	151	104	160	143	45	86	73	127
Boeing 747, total	153	35	37	-4	22	24	16	17
U.S. customers	24	2	15	1	1	1	7	-
Foreign customers	129	33	22	-5	19	18	13	13
Boeing 757, total	66	-7	45	47	18	43	23	-
U.S. customers	33	-6	25	34	7	38	15	2
Foreign customers	33	-1	20	13	2	14	6	-
Boeing 767, total	60	26	96	40	32	6	32	-2
U.S. customers	23	4	85	31	21	-2	-1	1
Foreign customers	37	22	11	9	1	14	9	12
Boeing 777, total	34	83	46	65	21	113	30	26
U.S. customers	34	-	24	42	8	60	-	-1
Foreign customers	-	83	22	23	8	53	20	27
McDonnell Douglas MD-11, total	52	-6	11	12	-	-	-	-
U.S. customers	16	3	-	3	-	-	-	-
Foreign customers	36	-9	11	9	-	-	-	-
McDonnell Douglas MD-80/90, total	116	51	-14	26	-20	-	-	-
U.S. customers	91	-	-11	24	-	-	-	-
Foreign customers	25	51	-3	2	-20	-	-	-
McDonnell Douglas MD-95, total	-	50	-	65	15	21	-14	16
U.S. customers	-	50	-	50	-	13	-23	23
Foreign customers	-	-	-	15	15	8	9	-7

- Represents zero. [1] Includes types of aircraft not shown separately. Beginning 1999, includes unidentified customers.

Source: Aerospace Industries Association of America, Washington, DC, Research Center, Statistical Series 23, Internet site at <http://www.aia-aerospace.org/stats/aerostats/aerostats.cfm>.

No. 1021. U.S. Aircraft Shipments: 1980 to 2003

[Value in millions of dollars (18,929 represents $18,929,000,000)]

Year	Total Units	Total Value	Large transports Units	Large transports Value	General aviation [1] Units	General aviation [1] Value	Helicopters Units	Helicopters Value	Military Units	Military Value
1980	14,677	18,929	387	9,895	11,877	2,486	1,366	656	1,047	5,892
1985	3,610	27,269	278	8,448	2,029	1,431	384	506	919	16,884
1990	3,321	38,585	521	22,215	1,144	2,007	603	254	1,053	14,109
1991	3,092	44,657	589	26,856	1,021	1,968	571	211	911	15,622
1992	2,585	47,397	567	28,750	941	1,840	324	142	753	16,665
1993	2,585	41,166	408	24,133	964	2,144	258	113	955	14,776
1994	2,309	36,568	309	18,124	928	2,357	308	185	764	15,902
1995	2,436	33,658	256	15,263	1,077	2,842	292	194	811	15,359
1996	2,235	36,247	269	17,564	1,130	3,127	278	193	558	15,363
1997	2,777	42,614	374	25,810	1,569	4,674	346	231	488	11,899
1998	3,560	55,286	559	36,880	2,220	5,874	363	252	418	12,280
1999	3,849	58,128	620	38,475	2,525	7,935	345	200	359	11,518
2000	4,027	51,664	485	31,171	2,816	8,558	493	270	233	11,665
2001	3,809	56,470	526	35,056	2,618	8,517	415	247	250	12,650
2002	3,233	48,613	379	26,000	2,203	7,876	321	157	330	14,580
2003, prel.	2,925	40,535	275	18,300	1,895	6,415	420	290	335	15,530

[1] Excludes off-the-shelf military aircraft.

Source: U.S. Department of Commerce, International Trade Administration, Internet site <http://www.ita.doc.gov/td/aerospace/inform/information.htm>.

No. 1022. Aerospace Industry Sales by Product Group and Customer: 1990 to 2003

[In billions of dollars (134.4 represents $134,400,000,000). Due to reporting practices and tabulating methods, figures may differ from those in Table 1019]

Product group and customer	Current dollars					Constant (1987) dollars [3]				
	1990	2000	2001 [1]	2002 [2]	2003 [2]	1990	2000	2001 [1]	2002 [2]	2003 [2]
Total sales............	134.4	144.7	153.1	148.2	138.4	123.7	108.6	112.0	106.5	98.6
PRODUCT GROUP										
Aircraft, total...............	71.4	82.1	86.3	80.3	70.8	65.7	61.7	63.1	57.7	50.4
Civil [4]................	31.3	48.4	51.3	43.3	31.5	28.8	36.4	37.5	31.2	22.4
Military.................	40.1	33.7	35.0	36.9	39.3	36.9	25.3	25.6	26.6	28
Missiles.................	14.2	9.5	10.4	12.4	12.7	13.1	7.1	7.6	8.9	9.0
Space..................	26.4	30.3	30.9	30.8	31.9	24.4	22.8	22.6	22.2	22.7
Related products and services [5]..	22.4	24.4	25.5	24.7	23.1	20.6	18.3	18.7	17.8	16.4
CUSTOMER GROUP										
Aerospace, total.............	112.0	121.8	127.6	123.5	115.4	103.1	91.5	93.4	88.8	82.2
DOD [6].................	60.5	47.0	49.5	54	58.4	55.7	35.3	36.2	38.8	41.6
NASA [7] and other agencies...	11.1	13.3	14.5	13.5	12.7	10.0	10.0	10.6	9.7	9.0
Other customers [8].........	40.4	61.5	63.7	56.1	44.3	36.5	46.2	46.6	40.3	31.5
Related products and services [5]..	22.4	24.4	25.5	24.7	23.1	20.6	18.3	18.7	17.8	16.4

[1] Preliminary. [2] Estimate. [3] Based on AIA's aerospace composite price deflator. [4] All civil sales of aircraft (domestic and export sales of jet transports, commuters, business, and personal aircraft and helicopters). [5] Electronics, software, and ground support equipment, plus sales of nonaerospace products which are produced by aerospace-manufacturing use technology, processes, and materials derived from aerospace products. [6] Department of Defense. [7] National Aeronautics and Space Administration. [8] Includes civil aircraft sales (see footnote 4), commercial space sales, all exports of military aircraft and missiles and related propulsion and parts.

Source: Aerospace Industries Association of America, Inc., Washington, DC, *2002 Year-end Review and Forecast*; and Internet site <http://www.aia-aerospace.org>.

No. 1023. Major Household Appliances—Value of Shipments: 1990 to 2002

[In millions of dollars (11,670.0 represents $11,670,000,000)]

Product	Product code	1990	1995	1998	1999	2000	2001	2002
Total...................	33522	11,670.0	13,966.2	15,551.4	16,622.3	17,041.0	16,710.6	17,672.8
Electric household ranges, ovens, and surface cooking units, equipment and parts...................	3352211110	1,659.8	1,791.8	2,242.9	2,197.1	2,170.3	2,004.5	1,918.4
Gas household ranges, ovens, and surfacecooking units, equipment and parts...................	3352213000	739.4	654.1	696.7	786.3	779.1	902.0	937.1
Other household ranges, cooking equipment, outdoor cooking equipment incl. parts and accessories....	3352215000	581.1	911.6	1,029.0	1,218.6	1,251.1	1,027.0	1,054.0
Household refrigerators [1] [2].........	3352221000	3,208.1	4,739.4	5,035.6	4,968.8	5,395.8	5,227.1	5,164.3
Food freezers, complete units, for freezing and/or storing frozen food- (household type) [2].............	3352222000	226.6	(D)	(D)	(D)	(D)	(D)	(D)
Parts and attachments for household refrigerators and freezers.........	3352223000	134.0	111.8	89.7	92.4	99.4	63.7	77.9
Household laundry machines and parts.................	3352240000	2,924.5	3,095.4	3,327.3	4,029.7	4,046.6	4,162.0	4,296.4
Water heaters, electric............	3352281000	433.8	513.0	541.3	580.0	572.7	555.7	576.0
Water heaters, except electric.......	3352283000	577.2	681.8	810.7	842.8	843.6	799.3	842.9
Household appliances, n.e.c.[3] and parts...................	3352285000	1,185.5	1,579.2	1,867.9	1,998.8	2,066.1	2,033.1	2,255.0

D Withheld to avoid disclosing data for individual companies. [1] Includes combination refrigerator-freezers. [2] Product code 33522210000 and 3352222000 are combined to avoid disclosing data for individual companies. [3] N.e.c. means not elsewhere classified.

Source: U.S. Census Bureau, 1990, Current Industrial Reports, Series MA36F; thereafter Series MA335F. See also <http://www.census.gov/industry/1/ma335f02.pdf> (released July 2003).

Section 22
Domestic Trade

This section presents statistics relating to the distributive trades, specifically wholesale trade and retail trade. Data shown for the trades are classified by kind of business and cover sales or receipts, establishments, employees, payrolls, and other items. The principal sources of these data are from the Census Bureau and include the *1997 Economic Census* reports, annual survey reports, and the *County Business Patterns* program. These data are supplemented by several tables from trade associations, such as the National Automobile Dealers Association (Table 1034). Several notable research groups are also represented, such as Claritas (Table 1032), National Research Bureau and the International Council of Shopping Centers (Tables 1047 and 1048), Jupiter Media Matrix (Table 1042), and Forrester Research, Inc. (Table 1041).

Data on retail and wholesale trade appear in several other sections. For instance, labor force employment and earnings data appear in Section 12, Labor Force, Employment, and Earnings; gross domestic product of the industry (Table 660) appear in the Section 13, Income, Expenditures, and Wealth; financial data (several tables) from the quarterly *Statistics of Income Bulletin,* published by the Internal Revenue Service, appear in Section 15, Business Enterprise.

Censuses—Censuses of retail trade and wholesale trade have been taken at various intervals since 1929. Beginning with the 1967 census, legislation provides for a census of each area to be conducted every 5 years (for years ending in "2" and "7"). For more information on these censuses, see the *History of the 1997 Economic Census* found at <http://www.census.gov/prod/ec97/pol00-hec.pdf>. The industries covered in the censuses and surveys of business are those classified in 13 sectors defined in the *North American Industry Classification System,* called NAICS (see below). *Retail trade* refers to places of business primarily engaged in retailing merchandise generally in small quantities to the general public; and *wholesale trade,* to establishments primarily engaged in selling goods to other businesses and normally operate from a warehouse or office that have little or no display of merchandise. All Census Bureau tables in this section are utilizing the new NAICS codes, which replaced the Standard Industrial Classification (SIC) system. NAICS makes substantial structural improvements and identifies over 350 new industries. At the same time, it causes breaks in time series far more profound than any prior revision of the previously used SIC system. For information on this system and how it affects the comparability of retail and wholesale statistics historically, see text, Section 15, Business Enterprise, and especially the Census Bureau Web site at <http://www.census.gov/epcd/www/naics.html>. In general, the 1997 Economic Census has two series of publications and documents for these two sectors subject series with reports on such as commodity line sales and establishment and firm sizes and geographic reports with individual reports for each state. For information on these series, see the Census Bureau Web site at <http://www.census.gov/epcd/www/97EC42.htm> and <http://www.census.gov/epcd/www/ 97EC44.htm>.

Current surveys—Current sample surveys conducted by the Census Bureau cover various aspects of the retail and wholesale trade. Its *Monthly Retail Trade and Food Services* contains monthly estimates of sales, inventories, and inventory/sales ratios, purchases, and accounts receivable for the United States, by kind of business. Annual figures on sales, year-end inventories, and inventory/sales ratios, purchases, and accounts receivable, by kind of business, appear in the *Annual Benchmark Report for Retail Trade and Food Services*. Statistics from the Bureau's monthly wholesale trade survey include national estimates of merchant wholesalers' sales, inventories, and inventory/sales ratios by major summary groups "durable and nondurable," and four-digit NAICS industry groups. Merchant wholesalers are those wholesalers who take title to the goods they sell (e.g., jobbers, exporters, importers, industrial distributors). These data, based on reports submitted by a sample of firms, appear in the *Monthly Wholesale Trade Report*. Annual figures on sales, inventory/sales ratios, year-end inventories, and purchases appear in the *Annual Benchmark Report for Wholesale Trade*. The reports just mentioned may appear in print in some cases, but principally are available as documents on the Census Bureau Web site at <http://www.census.gov/econ/www/retmenu.html>.

E-commerce—Electronic commerce (or e-commerce) are sales of goods and services over the Internet and extranet, electronic data interchange (EDI), or other online systems. Payment may or may not be made online. This edition has several tables on e-commerce sales, such as Tables 1044 to 1046 in this section, 989 in Section 21, Manufactures, and 1268 in Section 27, Accommodation, Food Services, and Other Services. Also, there are several private sources for similar data such as Forrester Research Inc., Cambridge MA; BizRate.com, Los Angeles, CA; and Jupiter Media Matrix, New York, NY. These sources show estimated and projected online retail sales by key categories from business to consumers or to other businesses. Their methods of collecting the data vary widely between the sources and consequently these estimates of this activity vary also. Users of these estimates may want to contact the sources for descriptions of their methodology. Methodology for Census Bureau estimates can be found at <www.census.gov/estats>.

Statistical reliability—For a discussion of statistical collection and estimation, sampling procedures, and measures of statistical reliability applicable to Census Bureau data, see Appendix III.

No. 1024. Wholesale and Retail Trade—Establishments, Employees, and Payroll by State: 2000 and 2001

[6,112 represents 6,112,000. Covers establishments with payroll. Employees are for the week including March 12. Excludes most government employees, railroad employees, and self-employed persons. Kind-of-business classification based on North American Industry Classification System (NAICS); see text, Section 15. For statement on methodology, see Appendix III]

State	Wholesale establishments (NAICS 42)						Retail establishments (NAICS 44,45)					
	Number of establishments		Number of employees (1,000)		Annual payroll (mil. dol.)		Number of establishments		Number of employees (1,000)		Annual payroll (mil. dol.)	
	2000	2001	2000	2001	2000	2001	2000	2001	2000	2001	2000	2001
U.S.	446,237	438,924	6,112	6,142	270,122	275,899	1,113,573	1,119,950	14,841	14,890	302,553	314,757
AL	6,132	5,984	82	80	2,892	2,866	19,723	19,654	230	227	4,074	4,193
AK	752	716	7	7	281	292	2,733	2,696	33	33	790	825
AZ	6,731	6,620	86	88	3,627	3,824	16,911	17,182	255	266	5,694	6,080
AR	3,505	3,479	45	44	1,402	1,443	12,211	12,250	135	137	2,268	2,373
CA	58,326	57,975	808	830	40,011	41,903	107,987	109,405	1,491	1,532	36,073	37,999
CO	7,452	7,352	97	99	4,906	5,014	18,748	19,046	252	261	5,883	5,993
CT	5,076	4,979	77	79	4,481	4,493	14,111	14,053	191	187	4,540	4,775
DE	1,009	989	19	24	1,117	1,433	3,742	3,778	52	52	1,048	1,116
DC	372	345	5	6	282	289	1,945	1,903	19	18	431	417
FL	30,671	29,958	315	311	12,536	12,493	67,396	69,077	903	915	18,044	18,942
GA	13,892	13,629	199	202	9,064	9,447	33,788	34,179	464	465	9,365	9,583
HI	1,809	1,803	19	20	627	652	4,924	5,012	63	65	1,313	1,342
ID	2,012	1,958	24	25	845	854	5,871	5,897	70	72	1,347	1,399
IL	21,509	20,975	344	343	16,683	16,482	43,800	43,716	637	609	12,992	13,119
IN	8,642	8,573	120	120	4,607	4,605	24,261	24,274	354	351	6,332	6,468
IA	5,155	5,020	65	65	2,173	2,171	14,382	14,239	184	182	3,169	3,288
KS	4,876	4,811	62	59	2,333	2,283	12,261	12,206	153	152	2,747	2,813
KY	4,939	4,803	74	74	2,536	2,616	16,988	16,852	221	221	3,804	3,934
LA	6,192	6,035	79	78	2,723	2,839	17,755	17,862	232	229	4,032	4,162
ME	1,740	1,723	22	22	744	776	7,015	7,040	77	80	1,436	1,540
MD	6,098	5,967	95	95	4,526	4,543	19,539	19,659	285	285	6,062	6,397
MA	9,735	9,627	156	162	9,114	9,220	25,813	25,539	353	352	7,729	8,408
MI	13,576	13,226	191	189	8,887	8,888	38,862	39,097	545	544	10,667	11,094
MN	9,294	9,159	137	140	6,399	6,705	20,862	21,196	304	316	5,980	6,711
MS	3,116	3,054	40	37	1,222	1,145	12,794	12,649	141	140	2,384	2,467
MO	9,072	8,841	146	141	5,458	5,088	23,911	23,812	318	317	6,258	6,453
MT	1,537	1,523	15	15	433	453	5,101	5,179	52	53	920	969
NE	3,061	2,981	41	39	1,346	1,320	8,248	8,256	110	109	1,895	1,979
NV	2,556	2,512	31	32	1,238	1,311	6,940	7,065	108	112	2,533	2,660
NH	2,105	2,069	25	24	1,184	1,161	6,545	6,570	93	93	1,930	2,054
NJ	17,157	16,791	279	281	14,724	15,163	34,841	35,071	439	434	9,897	10,461
NM	2,162	2,088	22	22	753	750	7,249	7,256	91	89	1,745	1,789
NY	36,606	36,019	422	427	20,941	21,246	75,500	75,910	844	841	18,116	18,937
NC	12,364	12,187	173	172	7,153	7,235	35,785	35,889	450	441	8,739	8,768
ND	1,543	1,518	18	17	532	534	3,435	3,460	42	41	719	754
OH	16,646	16,502	261	263	10,437	10,707	42,708	42,868	644	638	11,903	12,299
OK	5,005	4,868	62	62	2,126	2,194	14,147	14,087	168	169	2,913	3,027
OR	5,836	5,840	79	81	3,266	3,535	14,256	14,246	193	194	4,126	4,165
PA	16,796	16,447	243	244	10,287	10,679	48,518	48,597	668	670	12,556	13,155
RI	1,530	1,504	21	19	768	727	4,342	4,288	53	54	1,149	1,226
SC	5,091	4,991	65	62	2,353	2,266	18,619	18,629	224	219	4,083	4,025
SD	1,390	1,324	16	16	472	478	4,181	4,231	50	50	879	924
TN	8,006	7,823	127	130	4,848	5,173	24,624	24,337	311	310	5,908	6,025
TX	32,631	32,174	458	457	20,176	20,538	74,758	75,834	1,021	1,049	21,846	22,758
UT	3,294	3,310	44	44	1,583	1,670	7,952	8,189	124	126	2,455	2,474
VT	889	876	11	11	401	414	3,974	3,989	38	39	750	801
VA	7,893	7,756	110	111	4,651	4,799	28,794	28,998	399	399	7,949	8,252
WA	9,869	9,771	125	125	5,412	5,518	22,700	22,711	313	317	7,181	7,246
WV	1,869	1,800	22	22	698	698	7,788	7,713	92	88	1,493	1,497
WI	7,928	7,832	119	120	4,636	4,707	21,354	21,465	322	316	5,891	6,078
WY	790	817	7	7	229	260	2,881	2,839	28	29	515	543

Source: U.S. Census Bureau, *County Business Patterns*, annual. See also <http://www.census.gov/prod/2003pubs/01cbp/cbp01-1.pdf> (issued April 2003).

No. 1025. Retail Trade—Establishments, Employees, and Payroll: 2000 and 2001

[1,113.6 represents 1,113,600 except as indicated. Covers establishments with payroll. Employees are for the week including March 12. Most government employees are excluded. For statement on methodology, see Appendix III]

Kind of business	NAICS code [1]	Establishments (1,000) 2000	Establishments (1,000) 2001	Employees (1,000) 2000	Employees (1,000) 2001	Payroll (bil. dol.) 2000	Payroll (bil. dol.) 2001
Retail trade, total	44,45	1,113.6	1,120.0	14,841	14,890	302.6	314.8
Motor vehicle & parts dealers [2]	441	124.5	125.7	1,866	1,850	63.9	66.6
Automobile dealers	4411	50.9	51.6	1,222	1,225	47.8	50.1
New car dealers	44111	26.2	26.4	1,112	1,112	44.8	46.9
Used car dealers	44112	24.7	25.1	110	113	3.1	3.2
Automotive parts, accessories & tire stores	4413	59.1	59.1	517	493	12.2	12.4
Furniture & home furnishing stores	442	64.8	65.7	549	567	13.4	13.6
Electronics & appliance stores	443	45.6	47.7	407	425	11.2	11.5
Appliance, TV & all other electronics stores	44311	29.6	31.6	279	295	6.6	7.2
Computer & software stores	44312	12.9	13.0	106	109	4.2	3.8
Camera & photographic supplies stores	44313	3.1	3.0	22	22	0.4	0.4
Bldg material & garden equip & supp dealers	444	91.9	94.1	1,235	1,249	32.5	34.7
Building material & supplies dealers	4441	70.9	71.8	1,055	1,062	28.4	30.3
Lawn & garden equip & supplies stores	4442	21.0	22.2	180	186	4.0	4.3
Food & beverage stores	445	154.5	156.2	3,004	2,963	48.4	49.3
Grocery stores	4451	98.3	99.3	2,717	2,665	44.0	44.6
Grocery (except convenience) stores	44511	68.8	68.7	2,544	2,487	41.8	42.3
Convenience stores	44512	29.5	30.5	173	178	2.2	2.3
Specialty food stores	4452	27.8	28.2	154	161	2.4	2.5
Meat markets	44521	6.5	6.6	41	42	0.6	0.7
Fish & seafood markets	44522	1.9	1.9	8	9	0.1	0.1
Fruit & vegetable markets	44523	3.2	3.3	18	21	0.3	0.4
Other specialty food stores	44529	16.2	16.2	86	90	1.3	1.3
Beer, wine & liquor stores [3]	4453	28.5	28.6	134	136	2.1	2.1
Health & personal care stores	446	81.2	81.9	914	958	19.3	20.6
Pharmacies & drug stores	44611	40.6	40.0	680	699	14.5	15.4
Cosmetics, beauty supplies & perfume stores	44612	9.6	10.6	61	76	0.8	1.0
Optical goods stores	44613	14.3	14.0	74	75	1.7	1.7
Other health & personal care stores	44619	16.7	17.2	98	109	2.2	2.4
Food (health) supplement stores	446191	8.7	9.0	49	59	0.7	0.8
All other health & personal care stores	446199	8.0	8.2	49	50	1.5	1.6
Gasoline stations	447	119.6	118.8	937	927	13.3	13.4
Gasoline stations with convenience stores	44711	80.5	81.1	653	655	8.9	9.0
Other gasoline stations	44719	39.1	37.7	284	271	4.4	4.4
Clothing & clothing accessories stores	448	150.9	151.7	1,369	1,393	20.2	21.1
Clothing stores	4481	90.0	92.7	1,015	1,033	13.7	14.5
Men's clothing stores	44811	10.7	10.7	85	86	1.6	1.6
Women's clothing stores	44812	35.6	35.5	302	305	3.9	4.0
Children's & infants' clothing stores	44813	5.6	5.7	59	57	0.7	0.7
Family clothing stores	44814	20.6	21.8	453	470	5.9	6.4
Clothing accessories stores	44815	5.7	5.9	28	29	0.4	0.4
Other clothing stores	44819	11.8	12.0	88	87	1.2	1.3
Shoe stores	4482	29.7	28.2	185	188	2.6	2.7
Jewelry, luggage & leather goods stores	4483	31.3	31.8	168	172	3.9	3.9
Jewelry stores	44831	29.3	29.8	156	159	3.6	3.7
Luggage & leather goods stores	44832	2.0	2.0	12	12	0.2	0.2
Sporting goods, hobby, book & music stores	451	65.0	64.5	616	622	8.8	9.2
Sporting goods, hobby, musical instrument stores	4511	43.6	43.2	389	408	6.0	6.3
Book, periodical & music stores	4512	21.4	21.3	228	214	2.8	2.9
Prerecorded tape, CD & record stores	45122	7.7	7.7	76	70	0.9	0.9
General merchandise stores	452	39.6	41.2	2,526	2,526	39.8	42.2
Department stores	4521	10.4	10.4	1,766	1,727	27.2	28.6
Other general merchandise stores	4529	30.8	30.8	760	799	12.6	13.6
Warehouse clubs & superstores	45291	2.0	2.1	478	495	8.7	9.3
All other general merchandise stores	45299	27.2	28.7	283	303	3.8	4.3
Miscellaneous store retailers [2]	453	131.0	129.3	850	842	13.8	13.9
Used merchandise stores	4533	17.5	17.4	114	116	1.6	1.7
Other miscellaneous store retailers	4539	46.4	45.5	264	262	5.4	5.3
Nonstore retailers	454	44.8	42.9	567	566	18.1	18.3
Electronic shopping & mail-order houses	4541	11.8	11.0	277	281	10.4	10.4
Vending machine operators	4542	6.2	6.0	67	64	1.5	1.5
Direct selling establishments	4543	26.8	26.0	223	221	6.1	6.4
Fuel dealers	45431	11.8	11.6	106	105	3.1	3.3
Other direct selling establishments	45439	15.0	14.2	117	116	3.0	3.1

[1] Based on North American Industry Classification System; see text, Section 15. [2] Includes other kinds of business not shown separately. [3] Includes government employees.

Source: U.S. Census Bureau, *County Business Patterns*, annual. See also <http://www.census.gov/prod/2003pubs/01cbp/cbp01-1.pdf> (issued April 2003).

No. 1026. Retail Trade—Establishments, Sales, Payroll, and Employees by Kind of Business: 1997

[2,460,886 represents $2,460,886,000,000. Covers only establishments with payroll. See Appendix III]

Kind of business	NAICS code [1]	Estab- lish- ments (number)	Sales Total (mil. dol.)	Sales Per paid employee (dol.)	Annual payroll Total (mil. dol.)	Annual payroll Per paid employee (dol.)	Paid employee for pay period including March 12 (1,000)
Retail trade	44,45	1,118,447	2,460,886	175,889	237,196	16,953	13,991.1
Motor vehicle & parts dealers [2]	441	122,633	645,368	375,440	50,239	29,226	1,719.0
Automobile dealers	4411	49,237	553,652	486,088	37,400	32,836	1,139.0
New car dealers	44111	25,897	518,972	496,034	35,203	33,647	1,046.2
Used car dealers	44112	23,340	34,680	373,905	2,197	23,691	92.8
Automotive parts, accessories, & tire stores	4413	59,807	62,825	131,653	10,269	21,519	477.2
Automotive parts & accessories stores	44131	42,519	43,166	129,024	6,718	20,081	334.6
Tire dealers	44132	17,288	19,659	137,821	3,551	24,892	142.6
Furniture & home furnishings stores	442	64,725	71,691	148,476	9,959	20,627	482.8
Furniture stores	4421	29,461	40,968	163,026	5,620	22,362	251.3
Home furnishings stores	4422	35,264	30,722	132,685	4,340	18,743	231.5
Electronics & appliance stores	443	43,373	68,561	198,704	7,064	20,473	345.0
Appliance, television, & other electronics stores	44311	28,789	42,251	178,249	4,462	18,826	237.0
Computer & software stores	44312	11,741	24,059	265,839	2,278	25,168	90.5
Camera & photographic supplies stores	44313	2,843	2,252	128,609	324	18,504	17.5
Building material & garden equipment & supplies dealers	444	93,117	227,566	203,564	25,609	22,908	1,117.9
Building material & supplies dealers	4441	71,916	195,888	205,701	22,313	23,431	952.3
Lawn & garden equipment & supplies stores	4442	21,201	31,678	191,273	3,296	19,900	165.6
Food & beverage stores	445	148,528	401,764	138,871	40,581	14,027	2,893.1
Grocery stores	4451	96,542	368,250	139,298	37,426	14,157	2,643.6
Supermarkets & other grocery (except convenience) stores	44511	69,461	351,403	141,141	35,828	14,390	2,489.7
Convenience stores	44512	27,081	16,848	109,481	1,598	10,387	153.9
Specialty food stores	4452	22,373	10,830	91,137	1,456	12,250	118.8
Meat markets	44521	7,214	4,347	109,041	544	13,656	39.9
Fish & seafood markets	44522	1,634	1,038	145,724	102	14,316	7.1
Fruit & vegetable markets	44523	3,179	2,107	122,128	237	13,736	17.3
Other specialty food stores [2]	44529	10,346	3,339	61,152	572	10,483	54.6
Baked goods stores	445291	2,790	890	60,115	191	12,899	14.8
Confectionery & nut stores	445292	3,684	1,228	56,907	191	8,842	21.6
Beer, wine, & liquor stores	4453	29,613	22,684	173,645	1,699	13,008	130.6
Health & personal care stores	446	82,941	117,701	130,244	15,191	16,809	903.7
Pharmacies & drug stores	44611	43,615	98,631	140,150	11,588	16,465	703.8
Cosmetics, beauty supplies, & perfume stores	44612	9,014	4,419	94,977	604	12,973	46.5
Optical goods stores	44613	15,192	6,432	88,052	1,401	19,182	73.0
Other health & personal care stores	44619	15,120	8,219	102,269	1,598	19,888	80.4
Gasoline stations	447	126,889	198,166	214,916	11,482	12,453	922.1
Gasoline stations with convenience stores	44711	81,684	127,609	207,847	7,229	11,774	614.0
Other gasoline stations	44719	45,205	70,557	229,002	4,254	13,805	308.1
Clothing & clothing accessories stores	448	156,601	136,398	106,548	16,597	12,965	1,280.2
Clothing stores	4481	94,740	95,918	103,368	11,225	12,097	927.9
Men's clothing stores	44811	12,143	9,865	118,025	1,325	15,855	83.6
Women's clothing stores	44812	39,672	27,258	89,169	3,366	11,011	305.7
Children's & infant's clothing stores	44813	5,115	4,638	99,699	474	10,198	46.5
Family clothing stores	44814	20,450	44,796	114,197	4,797	12,229	392.3
Clothing accessories stores	44815	5,860	2,132	82,794	314	12,184	25.8
Other clothing stores	44819	11,500	7,229	97,535	949	12,799	74.1
Shoe stores	4482	31,399	20,543	110,565	2,349	12,640	185.8
Jewelry, luggage, & leather goods stores	4483	30,462	19,936	119,795	3,024	18,169	166.4
Jewelry stores	44831	28,336	18,511	119,523	2,836	18,311	154.9
Luggage & leather goods stores	44832	2,126	1,425	123,448	188	16,259	11.5
Sporting goods, hobby, book, & music stores	451	69,149	62,011	110,568	7,113	12,683	560.8
Book, periodical, & music stores	4512	22,834	20,596	104,089	2,295	11,597	197.9
Prerecorded tape, compact disc, & record stores	45122	8,158	7,367	110,575	728	10,927	66.6
General merchandise stores	452	36,171	330,444	131,780	30,871	12,311	2,507.5
Department stores (incl. leased depts) [3]	4521	10,366	223,232	(NA)	(NA)	(NA)	(NA)
Department stores (excl. leased depts)	4521	10,366	220,108	122,584	22,083	12,299	1,795.6
Other general merchandise stores	4529	25,805	110,336	154,975	8,788	12,343	712.0
Miscellaneous store retailers	453	129,838	78,109	103,733	10,165	13,500	753.0
Florists	4531	26,200	6,555	52,359	1,396	11,154	125.2
Office supplies, stationery, & gift stores	4532	44,615	31,573	103,014	3,637	11,868	306.5
Used merchandise stores	4533	17,990	6,044	61,692	1,204	12,286	98.0
Other miscellaneous store retailers	4539	41,033	33,937	151,958	3,928	17,588	223.3
Nonstore retailers	454	44,482	123,107	243,297	12,323	24,355	506.0
Electronic shopping & mail-order houses	4541	10,013	79,018	361,795	5,743	26,297	218.4
Vending machine operators	4542	7,070	6,884	103,763	1,333	20,097	66.3
Direct selling establishments	4543	27,399	37,204	168,161	5,246	23,714	221.2
Fuel dealers	45431	12,532	22,622	217,987	2,755	26,550	103.8
Other direct selling establishments	45439	14,867	14,582	124,140	2,491	21,209	117.5

NA Not available. [1] North American Industry Classification System, 1997; see text, Section 15. [2] Includes other kinds of business only shown separately. [3] Not included in broader kind-of-business totals.

Source: U.S. Census Bureau, 1997 Economic Census, Retail Trade, *Geographic Area*, Series EC97R44A-US(RV); issued March 2000.

Domestic Trade 661

No. 1027. Retail Trade and Food Services—Sales by Kind of Business: 1992 to 2002

[In billions of dollars (2,062.5 represents $2,062,500,000,000)]

Kind of business	NAICS code [1]	1992	1995	1997	1998	1999	2000	2001	2002
Retail and food services sales, total	44, 45, 72	2,062.5	2,502.0	2,778.4	2,917.6	3,164.3	3,378.0	3,471.6	3,580.0
Retail sales, total	44, 45	1,859.1	2,268.3	2,520.3	2,645.0	2,878.4	3,071.7	3,153.3	3,245.4
GAFO, total [2]		536.9	653.0	715.7	762.6	823.1	872.3	893.9	935.2
Motor vehicle and parts dealers	441	427.6	588.0	660.7	699.5	779.8	816.6	840.5	852.7
Automobile and other motor vehicle dealers	4411, 4412	377.2	528.7	596.3	631.9	707.9	742.0	766.8	777.7
Automobile dealers	4411	359.1	502.5	565.5	597.5	669.5	699.3	723.3	732.3
New car dealers	44111	333.8	464.6	519.0	545.1	611.6	638.8	662.2	669.2
Used cars dealers	44112	25.3	37.8	46.5	52.3	57.9	60.5	61.2	63.1
Auto parts, access., and tire stores	4413	50.4	59.3	64.4	67.6	71.9	74.6	73.7	75.0
Furniture, home furnishings, electronics and appliance stores	442, 443	97.8	130.4	144.3	154.6	167.1	178.0	176.7	185.1
Furniture and home furnishings stores	442	55.0	65.5	74.1	78.6	85.2	91.7	91.4	95.0
Furniture stores	4421	31.6	37.0	41.9	44.1	47.0	50.5	50.5	52.6
Home furnishings stores	4422	23.4	28.5	32.1	34.4	38.2	41.1	40.9	42.4
Electronics and appliance stores [3]	443	42.8	64.9	70.2	76.0	81.9	86.4	85.2	90.1
Appl. TV, and other elect. stores	44311	29.0	42.1	43.1	46.3	51.4	56.9	58.5	62.3
Computer and software stores	44312	11.5	20.5	24.8	27.2	27.7	26.4	24.1	25.0
Building mat. garden equip. & supply stores	444	160.2	199.1	229.5	243.5	263.0	276.2	287.4	300.9
Building mat. & supply dealers	4441	135.5	172.3	197.4	210.0	229.3	241.1	251.1	264.8
Food and beverage stores [3]	445	371.5	391.3	410.3	421.6	442.5	460.5	480.5	490.8
Grocery stores	4451	337.9	356.9	373.1	382.4	401.9	416.7	434.4	443.0
Beer, wine and liquor stores	4453	21.8	22.1	24.2	25.7	26.9	29.1	30.4	31.3
Health and personal care stores	446	90.8	102.5	119.1	130.2	143.7	157.0	167.6	180.2
Pharmacies and drug stores	44611	77.8	85.9	98.8	108.3	121.1	130.9	141.5	153.0
Gasoline stations	447	156.6	181.3	199.9	191.7	211.3	246.8	245.4	240.9
Clothing and clothing access, stores [3]	448	120.3	131.6	140.6	149.4	160.0	167.9	167.2	171.9
Clothing stores [3]	4481	85.9	91.4	98.5	104.9	112.4	118.6	119.6	123.6
Men's clothing stores	44811	10.2	9.3	10.1	10.6	10.5	10.8	10.3	9.9
Women's clothing stores	44812	31.8	28.7	27.9	28.7	30.2	32.5	33.1	34.3
Family clothing stores	44814	33.2	40.0	45.3	49.5	53.8	56.4	56.7	59.4
Shoe stores	4482	18.1	19.8	20.8	21.5	22.0	22.1	22.0	21.8
Jewelry stores	44831	15.2	19.2	19.8	21.5	24.1	25.3	24.2	25.1
Sporting goods, hobby, book & music stores [3]	451	49.3	60.9	65.6	69.5	74.0	77.9	79.4	82.0
Sporting goods stores	45111	15.7	20.0	21.3	22.6	24.2	26.0	26.7	28.0
Book stores	451211	8.3	11.2	12.8	13.4	14.5	15.4	15.8	15.8
General merchandise stores	452	248.0	300.6	331.5	351.9	381.5	406.2	430.4	455.7
Department stores (excl. L.D.) [4]	4521	177.1	205.9	220.1	223.7	231.0	233.6	230.2	225.9
Department stores (incl. L.D.) [4]	4521	181.3	210.9	225.1	228.5	236.1	238.7	234.3	230.0
Other general merchandise stores	4529	70.9	94.7	111.3	128.2	150.5	172.6	200.2	229.8
Warehouse clubs and superstores	45291	40.0	65.1	81.9	98.8	119.3	140.2	165.6	193.5
Miscellaneous stores retail	453	55.8	77.2	91.7	99.8	105.8	108.5	105.0	104.5
Nonstore retailers	454	81.3	105.4	127.4	133.3	149.7	176.2	173.3	180.8
Electronic shopping and mail order	4541	35.3	52.7	70.1	79.5	92.6	110.3	109.5	116.7
Fuel dealers	45431	19.3	21.6	22.9	19.7	20.7	27.8	27.2	25.7
Food services and drinking places [3]	722	203.4	233.6	258.0	272.6	285.9	306.3	318.3	334.6
Full service restaurants	7221	86.5	99.4	114.6	119.7	124.9	132.9	138.1	146.1
Limited service eating places	7222	87.4	103.1	109.3	116.8	122.2	131.3	137.7	143.9
Drinking places	7224	12.4	12.5	13.4	14.1	14.8	15.7	15.9	17.4

[1] North American Industry Classification System, 1997; see text, Section 15. [2] GAFO represents store classified in the following NAICS codes: 442,443,448,451,452, and 4532. [3] Includes other kinds of business not shown separately. [4] L.D. represents leased departments.

Source: U.S. Census Bureau, Current Business Reports, *Annual Benchmark Report for Retail Trade and Food Services, January 1992 Through March 2003*, Series BR/01-A.

No. 1028. Retail Trade Corporations—Sales, Net Profit, and Profit Per Dollar of Sales: 2002

[Represents North American Industry Classification System, 1997 (NAICS) groups 44 and 45. Profit rates are averages of quarterly figures at annual rates. Covers corporations with assets of $50,000,000 or more]

Item	Unit	Total retail trade	Food and beverage stores NAICS 445	Clothing and general merchandise stores NAICS 448 and 452	All other retail stores
Sales	Bil. dol.	1,415.5	311.9	586.1	517.5
Net profit:					
Before income taxes	Bil. dol.	58.7	10.3	25.8	22.6
After income taxes	Bil. dol.	37.0	6.6	16.2	14.3
Profits per dollar of sales:					
Before income taxes	Cents	4.2	3.3	4.3	4.4
After income taxes	Cents	2.6	2.1	2.7	2.8
Profits on stockholders' equity:					
Before income taxes	Percent	22.5	26.4	20.2	23.8
After income taxes	Percent	14.2	16.9	12.6	15.1

Source: U.S. Census Bureau, *Quarterly Financial Report for Manufacturing, Mining and Trade Corporations*, annual.

No. 1029. Retail Trade and Food Services—Estimated Per Capita Sales by Selected Kinds of Business: 1992 to 2002

[As of Dec. 31. In dollars. Based on estimated resident population estimates as of July 1. For statement on methodology, see Appendix III]

Kind of business	NAICS code [1]	1992	1994	1995	1996	1997	1998	1999	2000	2001	2002
Retail sales, total	44-45	7,290	8,283	8,631	9,097	9,412	9,787	10,556	11,264	11,052	11,254
Total (Excluding motor vehicle and parts dealers)	44-45 ex 441	5,613	6,170	6,394	6,702	6,945	7,199	7,696	8,270	8,106	8,297
Motor vehicle and parts dealers	441	1,677	2,113	2,237	2,395	2,467	2,588	2,860	2,995	2,946	2,957
Furniture, home furnishings	442	216	241	249	262	277	291	313	336	320	329
Electronics and appliance stores	443	168	221	247	258	262	281	300	317	299	312
Building material and garden equipment and supply stores	444	628	733	757	802	857	901	964	1,013	1,007	1,042
Food and beverage stores	445	1,456	1,480	1,489	1,516	1,532	1,560	1,623	1,689	1,684	1,702
Health and personal care stores	446	356	374	390	415	445	482	527	576	587	625
Gasoline stations	447	614	658	690	734	746	710	775	905	860	835
Clothing and clothing accessories stores	448	472	497	501	516	525	553	587	616	586	596
Sporting goods, hobby, book, and music stores	451	193	221	232	242	245	257	272	286	278	284
General merchandise stores	452	972	1,096	1,144	1,189	1,238	1,302	1,399	1,490	1,508	1,580
Miscellaneous store retailers	453	219	271	294	317	342	369	388	398	368	362
Nonstore retailers	454	319	378	401	451	476	493	549	646	607	627
Food services and drinking places	722	798	867	889	916	964	1,009	1,049	1,123	1,116	1,160

[1] North American Industry Classification System, 1997; see text, Section 15.
Source: U.S. Census Bureau, Current Business Reports, *Annual Benchmark Report for Retail Trade and Food Services: January 1992 Through March 2003, Drinking Places Series*, (BR/01-A) and Population Division, Population Estimates Program.

No. 1030. Retail Trade—Estimated Purchases by Kind of Business: 1992 to 2001

[In billions of dollars. (1,351.1 represents $1,351,100,000,000)]

Kind of business	NAICS code [1]	1992	1995	1996	1997	1998	1999	2000	2001
Total	44,45	1,351.1	1,650.0	1,754.6	1,834.9	1,923.3	2,101.9	2,241.7	2,299.9
Total (excl. motor vehicle and parts dealers)	(X)	1,008.4	1,178.6	1,244.0	1,300.1	1,353.7	1,464.4	1,570.6	1,609.6
Motor vehicle and parts dealers	441	342.6	471.4	510.5	534.8	569.6	637.5	671.2	690.3
Furniture and home furnishings stores	442	32.1	38.3	40.6	43.0	45.2	48.8	52.1	51.2
Electronics and appliance stores	443	30.8	49.0	51.5	52.1	56.6	61.0	63.3	62.2
Building material, garden equipment and supplies dealers	444	115.9	145.2	155.1	169.8	177.9	192.3	197.1	203.4
Food and beverage stores	445	279.2	290.3	298.2	303.6	310.0	323.4	334.2	345.6
Health and personal care stores	446	63.7	72.3	77.3	83.0	90.6	102.0	110.3	119.1
Gasoline stations	447	125.4	140.1	151.2	155.7	149.6	166.4	198.1	196.4
Clothing and clothing accessories stores	448	71.7	78.3	81.1	83.5	87.2	92.6	98.6	96.6
Sporting goods, hobby, book, and music stores	451	31.1	39.2	40.9	41.1	44.4	47.2	49.6	49.1
General merchandise stores	452	182.0	223.1	232.7	243.4	257.0	280.3	299.0	322.1
Miscellaneous store retailers	453	31.5	44.8	48.6	53.1	58.7	62.7	63.7	61.7
Nonstore retailers	454	45.1	58.0	66.9	71.8	76.4	87.7	104.6	102.2
Electronic shopping and mail order	4541	19.3	30.1	35.2	41.2	47.7	57.2	67.9	67.2

X Not applicable. [1] North American Industry Classification System, 1997; see text, Section 15.
Source: U.S. Census Bureau, Current Business Reports, *Annual Benchmark Report for Retail Trade and Food Services, January 1992 Through March 2003*, Series (BR/01-A), and unpublished data.

No. 1031. Retail Trade—Merchandise Inventories and Inventory/Sales Ratio by Kind of Business: 1992 to 2002

[Inventories in billions of dollars (267.9 represents 267,900,000,000). As of Dec. 31. Estimates excludes food services. Includes warehouses. Adjusted for seasonal variations. Sales data also adjusted for holiday and trading-day differences]

Kind of business	NAICS code [1]	Inventories 1992	2000	2001	2002	Inventory/sales ratio 1992	2000	2001	2002
Total	44,45	267.9	417.8	405.6	436.3	1.68	1.62	1.53	1.57
Excluding motor vehicle and parts dealers	44,45 ex 441	196.7	286.0	282.7	289.9	1.61	1.49	1.46	1.43
Motor vehicle and parts dealers	441	71.3	131.8	122.9	146.5	1.92	1.99	1.71	1.95
Furniture, home furnishings, electronics, and appliance stores	442,443	16.5	25.6	24.3	26.5	1.98	1.80	1.58	1.71
Building material and garden equipment and supplies dealers	444	25.3	40.6	40.7	43.3	1.92	1.72	1.70	1.71
Food and beverage stores	445	27.3	32.9	34.2	34.3	0.88	0.84	0.84	0.84
Clothing and clothing accessories stores	448	27.4	36.4	35.2	36.1	2.64	2.58	2.48	2.48
General merchandise stores	452	49.8	65.3	65.2	66.3	2.28	1.87	1.74	1.73
Department stores	4521	38.3	42.9	40.7	37.6	2.50	2.17	2.11	2.06

[1] North American Industry Classification System, 1997; see text, Section 15.
Source: U.S. Census Bureau, Current Business Reports, *Annual Benchmark Report for Retail Trade and Food Services: January 1992 Through March 2003*, Series BR/01-A, and unpublished data.

Domestic Trade

No. 1032. Retail Trade and Food Services—Sales by Type of Store and State: 2001

[In millions of dollars,(3,324,957 represents $3,324,957,000,000) except as indicated. Kind-of-business classification based on North American Industry Classification System (NAICS), 1997; see text, Section 15. Data are estimates]

State	All retail stores [1] (NAICS 44, 45)	Total retail sales + food and drink	Motor vehicle and parts dealers (NAICS 441)	Furniture and home furnishings (NAICS 442)	Electronics and appliances (NAICS 443)	Building material & garden equip. & supp. dealers (NAICS 444)	Food and beverage stores (NAICS 445)	Health and personal care (NAICS 446)
U.S...	3,324,957	3,658,749	961,940	97,673	95,700	285,912	493,963	163,680
AL	45,174	49,494	13,638	1,129	736	4,124	6,215	2,012
AK	7,549	8,427	1,805	117	160	881	1,468	117
AZ	64,152	70,071	19,317	2,055	1,862	4,952	9,399	2,912
AR	27,368	29,653	8,568	568	476	2,507	3,156	944
CA	392,114	436,531	112,317	12,468	18,029	31,932	62,429	19,088
CO	58,342	64,382	16,769	2,206	2,008	5,752	9,160	1,701
CT	46,624	50,728	12,780	1,428	1,420	4,052	7,651	2,657
DE	11,180	12,271	3,171	478	424	1,111	1,562	658
DC	2,540	3,994	138	114	84	198	568	337
FL.....	195,869	213,757	63,565	6,002	5,428	13,999	31,793	10,390
GA	99,789	110,074	30,825	3,386	2,535	10,608	14,638	3,656
HI.....	12,308	14,505	2,289	199	201	580	2,337	884
ID.....	15,563	16,754	4,639	420	393	1,805	2,304	360
IL.....	138,373	154,272	39,602	4,044	3,960	11,768	20,524	8,153
IN.....	73,717	80,757	22,327	1,773	1,671	6,908	8,951	3,706
IA	34,875	37,645	10,763	883	830	4,170	4,840	1,381
KS	34,662	37,358	9,971	972	1,014	2,860	5,029	1,251
KY	41,201	46,131	11,374	844	667	4,090	5,967	2,083
LA	45,044	49,918	13,612	957	747	3,915	6,519	2,141
ME	17,793	19,096	4,536	322	222	1,606	3,624	609
MD	60,240	66,360	16,483	1,906	2,054	4,741	11,253	3,268
MA	81,369	91,407	21,653	2,182	1,757	5,849	13,666	5,182
MI.....	124,085	135,390	38,446	3,407	3,085	9,791	14,390	7,937
MN	73,837	79,832	19,802	2,531	2,615	7,708	8,934	3,181
MS	28,351	30,639	8,559	745	444	2,818	4,185	1,152
MO	67,548	73,955	21,229	1,607	1,490	5,486	8,601	2,684
MT	9,133	10,144	2,485	218	195	1,131	1,672	254
NE	20,214	22,084	5,351	902	422	2,246	2,833	775
NV	26,257	29,439	6,899	766	834	2,264	4,002	1,067
NH	22,720	24,308	7,137	613	754	1,656	3,338	812
NJ.....	104,969	113,988	28,746	3,494	3,444	6,719	17,105	7,655
NM	20,125	22,006	5,342	603	409	1,568	2,736	907
NY	185,761	206,352	43,783	5,689	5,470	13,945	30,224	13,986
NC	93,780	103,573	28,291	3,586	2,190	10,302	13,170	4,060
ND	7,844	8,487	2,100	188	169	1,374	823	358
OH	135,446	148,948	39,924	4,101	4,028	11,788	18,386	8,019
OK	35,455	38,976	11,558	944	961	2,599	4,405	1,459
OR	45,834	50,235	13,243	1,192	1,134	4,734	6,315	1,245
PA	134,331	147,088	39,501	3,127	2,695	10,892	21,354	8,215
RI.....	10,136	11,546	2,654	274	212	610	1,926	917
SC	45,266	49,994	12,825	1,267	787	5,609	6,813	1,889
SD	14,448	15,247	2,758	194	175	1,204	1,314	339
TN	70,106	76,919	20,694	1,910	1,242	5,892	12,115	3,039
TX	262,791	288,536	83,426	7,643	8,247	19,580	34,349	8,904
UT	26,877	28,959	7,551	1,043	856	2,808	4,979	401
VT	7,466	8,091	2,235	157	172	816	1,269	341
VA	81,954	89,613	22,511	2,900	2,895	7,365	11,929	3,466
WA	72,294	80,954	18,276	2,044	2,029	7,203	10,545	3,124
WV	17,415	18,960	4,908	318	224	1,499	2,633	1,218
WI.....	68,292	73,982	19,753	1,641	1,752	7,341	9,579	2,670
WY	6,376	6,917	1,809	116	94	557	988	116

See footnotes at end of table.

No. 1032. Retail Trade and Food Services—Sales by Type of Store and State: 2001—Con.

[See headnote, page 664]

State	Gasoline stations (NAICS 447)	Clothing and clothing accessories (NAICS 448)	Sporting goods, hobby, book & music stores (NAICS 451)	General merchandise (NAICS 452)	Miscellaneous stores (NAICS 453)	Nonstore retailers (NAICS 454)	Food services & drinking places (NAICS 722)
U.S...	261,964	178,525	85,849	441,892	108,738	149,120	333,792
AL	4,541	2,232	769	7,532	1,419	829	4,320
AK	545	335	197	1,441	217	268	878
AZ	5,685	2,221	1,757	8,240	2,727	3,026	5,919
AR	2,811	1,028	486	5,440	869	516	2,285
CA	28,144	23,766	11,890	49,221	12,523	10,307	44,417
CO	4,353	2,519	2,177	7,430	2,235	2,031	6,040
CT	2,959	3,125	1,378	3,624	1,495	4,056	4,104
DE	626	621	371	1,379	388	393	1,091
DC	212	392	181	108	160	47	1,454
FL.....	13,476	10,788	4,416	23,134	6,120	6,758	17,888
GA	9,350	5,029	1,844	12,938	3,015	1,966	10,284
HI.....	915	1,509	399	2,336	563	95	2,198
ID.....	1,288	456	435	2,061	564	840	1,191
IL.....	9,734	8,832	3,384	16,551	3,990	7,830	15,899
IN.....	6,690	2,693	1,386	11,281	2,136	4,194	7,040
IA.....	3,854	1,150	641	4,603	800	962	2,770
KS.....	3,219	1,601	785	6,212	1,058	689	2,696
KY.....	4,414	1,532	746	7,231	1,513	739	4,930
LA.....	4,745	2,070	760	7,626	1,235	717	4,874
ME....	1,475	899	384	1,826	513	1,776	1,303
MD....	4,056	4,030	1,963	6,828	1,888	1,770	6,121
MA....	5,394	6,151	2,724	8,716	2,797	5,298	10,038
MI.....	8,540	5,221	4,101	20,820	5,172	3,176	11,305
MN....	6,108	2,823	2,569	9,076	2,490	6,001	5,994
MS....	3,070	1,021	363	4,721	828	443	2,289
MO....	7,244	2,457	1,361	9,916	2,058	3,415	6,407
MT....	792	268	280	1,381	275	182	1,011
NE....	1,793	820	424	2,751	464	1,432	1,870
NV....	1,919	2,067	671	2,714	1,294	1,758	3,182
NH....	1,461	1,026	657	2,856	646	1,763	1,588
NJ.....	5,856	7,136	3,578	10,563	3,687	6,984	9,019
NM....	1,975	781	505	3,103	1,169	1,026	1,882
NY....	10,704	18,848	6,520	19,884	7,894	8,814	20,591
NC....	7,887	4,317	1,751	11,785	3,754	2,688	9,774
ND....	703	220	216	1,196	215	281	642
OH....	10,558	6,099	2,981	19,912	3,677	5,972	13,502
OK....	3,869	1,031	713	6,110	1,097	708	3,522
OR....	3,072	1,890	1,318	7,897	1,758	2,035	4,401
PA....	9,654	7,557	3,093	15,008	3,492	9,740	12,757
RI.....	771	573	290	916	319	675	1,411
SC	4,354	2,290	737	6,110	1,869	716	4,728
SD	976	302	204	1,228	327	5,427	800
TN	6,240	3,584	1,309	10,678	2,173	1,230	6,813
TX	22,156	12,865	5,783	36,286	7,775	15,777	25,744
UT	2,094	1,081	812	3,738	547	967	2,082
VT	669	299	204	485	221	599	625
VA	7,394	4,615	1,927	11,424	2,179	3,349	7,659
WA....	4,763	3,372	2,524	12,028	2,791	3,596	8,660
WV....	1,935	688	279	2,926	504	283	1,544
WI.....	5,912	2,126	1,471	9,650	1,628	4,768	5,690
WY....	1,009	168	132	967	208	210	542

[1] Includes other types of stores, not shown separately.

Source: Market Statistics, a division of Claritas Inc., Arlington, VA, *The Survey of Buying Power Data Service*, annual (copyright).

No. 1033. Retail Trade—Nonemployer Establishments and Receipts by Kind of Business: 1998 to 2000

[1,762 represents 1,762,000. Includes only firms subject to federal income tax. Nonemployers are businesses with no paid employees. Based on the North American Industry Classification System (NAICS), 1997. See text, Section 15]

Kind of business	NAICS code	Establishments (1,000) 1998	1999	2000	Receipts (mil. dol.) 1998	1999	2000
Retail trade, total	44-45	1,762	1,761	1,743	70,971	73,314	73,810
Motor vehicle & parts dealers [1]	441	119	121	122	16,180	17,184	17,355
Used car dealers	44112	73	74	74	12,525	13,212	13,255
Motorcycle & boat & other MV dealers	44122	20	20	21	1,713	1,874	1,969
Automotive parts, accessories, & tire stores	4413	24	24	25	1,694	1,839	1,872
Furniture & home furnishings stores	442	38	37	37	2,534	2,542	2,574
Furniture stores	4421	14	14	14	1,025	1,026	1,034
Home furnishings stores	4422	24	23	23	1,510	1,516	1,540
Electronics & appliance stores	443	29	30	29	1,716	1,741	1,688
Bldg material & garden equip & supp dealers [1]	444	28	28	28	2,032	2,165	2,182
Building material & supplies dealers	4441	20	20	20	1,578	1,685	1,677
Food & beverage stores	445	87	84	82	8,503	8,465	8,493
Grocery stores	4451	42	40	39	4,706	4,597	4,609
Specialty food stores	4452	35	34	33	2,151	2,141	2,135
Beer, wine, & liquor stores	4453	10	10	10	1,646	1,727	1,749
Health & personal care stores	446	80	89	92	1,607	1,813	1,915
Gasoline stations	447	11	10	10	1,739	1,713	1,721
Clothing & clothing accessories stores [1]	448	89	88	89	4,250	4,389	4,464
Clothing stores	4481	60	60	60	2,580	2,647	2,718
Jewelry stores	44831	23	23	23	1,348	1,406	1,416
Sporting goods, hobby, book, & music stores [1]	451	97	98	96	3,655	3,775	3,761
Sporting goods stores	45111	25	24	23	1,301	1,330	1,340
Book, periodical, & music stores	4512	32	33	32	1,024	1,025	1,007
General merchandise stores	452	24	26	28	1,170	1,250	1,291
Miscellaneous store retailers [1]	453	367	350	339	13,324	13,169	12,963
Gift, novelty, & souvenir stores	45322	71	72	73	2,072	2,130	2,104
Used merchandise stores	4533	84	80	76	2,286	2,243	2,115
Nonstore retailers [1]	454	793	799	792	14,261	15,109	15,401
Electronic shopping & mail-order houses	4541	42	45	49	1,100	1,260	1,391
Direct selling establishments	4543	713	717	708	12,203	12,860	13,047

[1] Includes other kinds of business not shown separately.

Source: U.S. Census Bureau, "Nonemployer Statistics"; published 28 March 2003; <http://www.census.gov/epcd/nonemployer/>.

No. 1034. Franchised New Car Dealerships—Summary: 1980 to 2002

[130.5 represents $130,500,000,000]

Item	Unit	1980	1985	1990	1995	1997	1998	1999	2000	2001	2002
Dealerships [1]	Number	27,900	24,725	24,825	22,800	22,700	22,600	22,400	22,250	21,800	21,725
Sales	Bil. dol.	130.5	251.6	316.0	456.2	507.5	546.3	606.5	650.3	690.4	679.5
New cars sold [2]	1,000	8,979	11,042	9,300	8,635	8,272	8,137	8,699	8,847	8,423	8,103
Used vehicles sold	Millions	9.72	13.30	14.18	18.48	19.19	19.33	20.07	20.45	21.39	19.42
Employment	1,000	745	856	924	996	1,046	1,048	1,081	1,114	1,130	1,130
Annual payroll	Bil. dol.	11.0	20.1	24.0	33.1	37.4	39.8	42.5	46.1	48.0	48.8
Advertising expenses	Bil. dol.	1.2	2.8	3.7	4.6	5.1	5.3	5.6	6.4	6.6	7.5
Dealer pretax profits as a percentage of sales	Percent	0.6	2.2	1.0	1.4	1.4	1.7	1.8	1.6	2.0	1.9
Inventory: [3]											
Domestic: [4]											
Total	1,000	2,112	2,339	2,537	2,974	2,813	2,732	2,901	3,183	2,824	2,727
Days' supply	Days	57	60	73	71	66	63	62	68	63	63
Imported: [4]											
Total	1,000	269	345	707	445	338	350	378	468	508	521
Days' supply	Days	31	30	72	72	54	54	47	50	51	49

[1] At beginning of year. [2] Data provided by "Ward's Automotive Reports." [3] Annual average. Includes light trucks. [4] Classification based on where automobiles are produced (i.e., automobiles manufactured by foreign companies but produced in the U.S. are classified as domestic).

Source: National Automobile Dealers Association, McLean, VA, NADA Data, annual.

666 Domestic Trade

No. 1035. New Motor Vehicle Sales and Expenditures by Model Year: 1990 to 2002

[In thousands of units (14,169 represents 14,169,000), except as indicated. A model year begins on Oct. 1 and ends on Sept. 30. It covers the fourth quarter of one calendar year and the first three quarters of the next calendar year]

Sales and expenditures	1990	1995	1997	1998	1999	2000	2001	2002
New motor vehicle sales	14,169	15,204	15,498	15,963	17,414	17,817	17,472	17,118
New-car sales	9,436	8,687	8,273	8,142	8,697	8,852	8,422	8,082
Domestic	6,790	7,178	6,906	6,764	6,982	6,833	6,323	5,854
Import	2,645	1,510	1,366	1,378	1,715	2,019	2,100	2,228
New-truck sales	4,733	6,517	7,226	7,821	8,717	8,965	9,050	9,036
Light	4,428	6,089	6,797	7,297	8,072	8,387	8,607	8,633
Domestic	3,996	5,694	6,226	6,651	7,310	7,546	7,629	7,572
Import	432	395	571	646	763	841	978	1,061
Other	306	429	429	524	645	578	443	402
Domestic-car production	6,231	6,351	5,927	5,547	5,637	5,540	4,879	5,016
Avg. expenditure per new car [1] (dollar)	14,371	17,959	19,531	20,370	20,673	20,909	21,258	21,440
Domestic (dollar)	13,936	16,864	17,907	18,485	18,639	18,884	19,039	19,126
Import (dollar)	15,510	23,202	27,722	29,615	28,951	27,766	27,941	27,524

[1] BEA estimate based on the manufacturer's suggested retail price.

Source: U.S. Bureau of Economic Analysis, *Survey of Current Business*, February 2002 and unpublished data. Data on unit sales and production are mainly from "Ward's Automotive Reports" published by Ward's Communications, Southfield, MI.

No. 1036. New and Used Car Sales and Leases: 1990 to 2001

[In thousands (46,830 represents 46,830,000, except as indicated)]

Item	1990	1994	1995	1996	1997	1998	1999	2000	2001
Total car sales	46,830	49,131	50,393	49,327	49,512	48,982	49,438	50,466	(NA)
New passenger car sales [1]	9,300	8,990	8,635	8,526	8,272	8,142	8,698	8,846	(NA)
Used passenger car sales [2]	37,530	40,141	41,758	40,801	41,237	40,841	40,739	41,620	42,624
Value of transactions (bil. dol.)	220	291	319	329	336	335	350	357	376
Average price (dol.)	5,857	7,245	7,644	8,073	8,139	8,211	8,587	8,578	8,832
New passenger car leases [3]	534	1,715	1,795	1,806	2,062	2,174	2,271	2,272	(NA)

NA Not available. [1] Includes leased cars. [2] Used car sales include sales from franchised dealers, independent dealers, and casual sales. [3] Consumer leases only.

Source: U.S. Bureau of Transportation Statistics, *National Transportation Statistics 2000*. Data supplied by following sources: New passenger car sales: 1994-98, American Automobile Manufacturers Association, *Motor Vehicle Facts & Figures, 1999*, Southfield, MI; *Ward's Motor Vehicle Facts & Figures, 2002*, Southfield, MI: 2001; Used passenger car sales: ADT Automotive, *2001 Used Car Market Report* Nashville, TN; Leased passenger cars: CNW Marketing/Research, Bandon, OR, personal communication, May 31, 2000, August 13, 2001, and August 26, 2002.

No. 1037. Toy Industry—Retail Sales by Type of Product: 2001 and 2002

[In millions of dollars (34,388 represents $34,388,000,000), except as indicated. Minus sign (-) indicates decrease]

Product	Sales 2001	Sales 2002	Percent change, 2001-2002	Product	Sales 2001	Sales 2002	Percent change, 2001-2002
Total	34,388	30,606	-11	Games/puzzles	2,237	2,094	-6
Video games	9,409	10,326	10	Building/construction	882	751	-15
Traditional toy industry	24,979	20,280	-19	Arts & crafts	2,630	2,183	-17
Infant/preschool	3,154	2,807	-11	Models/accessories	281	253	-10
Dolls	3,061	2,429	-21	Learning/exploration	464	371	-20
Plush	2,031	1,555	-23	Pretend play	479	554	16
Action figure toys	1,618	1,258	-22	Trading cards/accessories	318	285	-10
Vehicles	2,821	2,101	-26	Sports	1,528	987	-35
Ride-ons	773	566	-27	All other toys	2,703	2,086	-23

Source: NPD Group, Inc., Port Washington, NY and Toy Industry Association, Inc., New York, NY, *Toy Industry Fact Book*, annual (copyright).

Domestic Trade 667

U.S. Census Bureau, Statistical Abstract of the United States: 2003

No. 1038. Retail Foodstores—Number and Sales by Type: 1990 to 2001

[282.6 represents 282,600. Beginning with 2001 data based on North American Industry Classification System (NAICS), 1997. All other years based on Standard Industrial Classification (SIC) codes]

Type of foodstore	Number[1] (1,000)					Sales[2] (bil. dol.)					Percent distribution			
											Number		Sales	
	1990	1995	1999	2000	2001	1990	1995	1999	2000	2001	1990	2001	1990	2001
Total	282.6	264.4	247.8	243.8	219.5	368.3	402.5	458.3	483.7	442.0	100.0	100.0	100.0	100.0
Grocery stores	190.3	176.9	165.8	163.2	145.4	348.2	382.2	434.7	458.3	425.4	67.3	66.3	94.5	96.2
Supermarkets[3]	24.5	25.3	24.4	24.6	23.9	261.7	300.4	325.7	337.3	354.5	8.7	10.9	71.1	80.2
Conventional	13.2	12.3	10.3	9.9	8.9	92.3	76.4	63.6	63.4	65.8	4.7	4.0	25.1	14.9
Superstore[4]	5.8	6.8	7.6	7.9	7.9	87.6	116.7	138.9	142.4	152.1	2.1	3.6	23.8	34.4
Warehouse[5]	3.4	2.7	2.4	2.4	2.7	33.1	20.7	20.9	22.0	24.2	1.2	1.2	9.0	5.5
Combination food and drug[6]	1.6	2.7	3.4	3.7	3.9	29.3	59.3	75.5	81.8	83.8	0.6	1.8	8.0	19.0
Superwarehouse[7]	0.3	0.6	0.5	0.5	0.5	12.6	17.8	17.1	17.4	17.7	0.1	0.2	3.4	4.0
Hypermarket[8]	0.1	0.2	0.2	0.2	0.2	6.8	9.5	9.7	10.3	11.0	(Z)	0.1	1.8	2.5
Convenience stores[9]	93.0	86.9	82.9	81.9	56.2	37.0	42.4	47.6	48.5	19.5	32.9	25.6	10.0	4.4
Superette[10]	72.8	64.7	58.5	56.7	65.2	49.5	39.4	61.4	72.5	51.4	25.8	29.7	13.4	11.6
Specialized food stores[11]	92.3	87.5	82.0	80.6	74.1	20.1	20.3	23.6	25.4	16.6	32.7	33.7	5.5	3.8

Z Less than 0.05 percent. [1] Estimated. [2] Includes nonfood items. [3] A grocery store, primarily self-service in operation, providing a full range of departments, and having at least $2.5 million in annual sales in 1985 dollars. [4] Contains greater variety of products than conventional supermarkets, including specialty and service departments, and considerable nonfood (general merchandise) products. [5] Contains limited product variety and fewer services provided, incorporating case lot stocking and shelving practices. [6] Contains a pharmacy, a nonprescription drug department, and a greater variety of health and beauty aids than that carried by conventional supermarkets. [7] A larger warehouse store that offers expanded product variety and often service meat, deli, or seafood departments. [8] A very large store offering a greater variety of general merchandise—like clothes, hardware, and seasonal goods—and personal care products than other grocery stores. [9] A small grocery store selling a limited variety of food and nonfood products, typically open extended hours. [10] A grocery store, primarily self-service in operation, selling a wide variety of food and nonfood products with annual sales below $2.5 million (1985 dollars). [11] Primarily engaged in the retail sale of a single food category such as meat and seafood stores and retail bakeries.
Source: U.S. Dept. of Agriculture, Economic Research Service, *Food Marketing Review*, annual.

No. 1039. Percent of Supermarkets Offering Selected Services and Product Lines: 1990 to 2002

[In percent Based on a sample survey of chain and independent supermarkets and subject to sampling variability; for details, see source]

Service or product line offered	1990	1993	1996	1997	1998	1999	2000	2001	2002
Service delicatessen	73	79	80	81	81	81	81	80	80
Service bakery	60	62	69	69	69	69	71	72	72
Service meat	42	47	74	60	59	60	62	66	66
Service seafood	33	37	46	43	43	45	45	51	43
Specialty cheese department	33	34	31	30	31	32	33	42	36
Salad bar	18	19	27	24	24	24	25	22	22
Automated teller machines (ATMs)	20	38	60	62	62	63	64	65	68
Banking in store	(NA)	(NA)	14	22	21	22	21	20	22
Pharmacy	15	20	26	26	32	30	32	36	34
Warehouse aisle	(NA)	(NA)	10	16	17	17	16	14	14

NA Not available.
Source: Progressive Grocer, New York, NY, *Progressive Grocer 70th Annual Report* (copyright). Used by permission of Progressive Grocer magazine(A VNU company).

No. 1040. Food and Alcoholic Beverage Sales by Sales Outlet: 1990 to 2002

[In billions of dollars (556.6 represents $556,600,000,000)]

Sales outlet	1990	1994	1995	1996	1997	1998	1999	2000	2001	2002
Food sales, total[1]	556.6	635.3	654.7	679.9	705.3	737.2	779.7	825.5	861.7	900.1
Food at home	308.1	344.1	352.7	367.8	377.3	391.6	417.6	439.8	463.6	485.2
Food stores[2]	256.4	274.0	276.1	285.6	289.6	296.1	309.3	326.8	347.1	356.3
Other stores[3]	32.3	47.8	53.1	57.3	61.8	69.7	80.7	84.2	87.7	99.4
Home-delivered, mail order	5.3	8.0	8.6	10.0	10.6	10.6	11.4	12.2	11.8	12.4
Farmers, manufacturers, wholesalers	6.3	7.2	7.8	8.1	8.8	8.6	9.0	9.4	9.6	9.8
Home production and donations	7.7	7.1	7.0	6.8	6.4	6.6	7.2	7.2	7.3	7.3
Food away from home[4]	248.5	291.2	302.0	312.1	328.0	345.6	362.0	385.7	398.1	415.0
Alcoholic beverage sales, total	72.6	78.3	80.5	83.9	86.9	92.5	98.1	102.8	105.9	112.3
Packaged alcoholic beverages	38.0	40.4	41.6	43.7	44.9	48.6	52.1	54.1	55.6	59.2
Liquor stores	18.6	19.0	19.0	20.1	20.9	22.3	23.4	25.3	26.4	27.2
Food stores	10.8	11.8	12.3	13.0	12.8	13.8	14.5	14.9	15.3	16.2
All other	8.6	9.7	10.3	10.6	11.2	12.5	14.2	13.9	13.9	15.8
Alcoholic drinks[5]	34.5	37.9	38.9	40.2	42.0	43.9	46.0	48.8	50.3	53.2
Eating and drinking places[5]	26.6	29.4	30.3	31.6	33.7	35.2	36.8	39.2	40.4	43.2
Hotels and motels	3.8	3.9	3.9	3.9	4.1	4.1	4.4	4.6	4.7	4.7
All other	4.1	4.7	4.7	4.7	4.3	4.5	4.8	5.0	5.2	5.3

[1] Includes taxes and tips. [2] Excludes sales to restaurants and institutions. [3] Includes eating and drinking establishments, trailer parks, commissary stores, and military exchanges. [4] Includes food furnished and donations. [5] Includes tips.
Source: U.S. Department of Agriculture, Economic Research Service, "food cpi, prices, and expenditures: food expenditure tables"; published 2 June 2003; <http://www.ers.usda.gov/briefing/CPIFoodAndExpenditures/Data/>.

No. 1041. U.S. Online Retail E-Commerce Projections: 2001 to 2003

[In millions of dollars (73,926 represents $73,926,000,000), except as indicated]

Online product or service	Projected online sales 2001	Projected online sales 2002	Projected online sales 2003	Percent change 2001-2002	Percent change 2002-2003
Retail trade, total [1]	73,926	110,748	155,833	49.8	40.7
Media	9,807	13,019	16,513	32.8	26.8
Event tickets	933	1,986	3,289	112.9	65.6
Flowers	1,266	1,812	2,384	43.1	31.6
Recreation	4,148	5,916	8,227	42.6	39.1
Apparel	8,915	14,461	22,251	62.2	53.9
Electronics	11,856	18,306	24,119	54.4	31.8
Leisure travel	16,700	21,000	25,200	25.7	20.0
Automobiles	5,315	9,360	15,626	76.1	66.9
Home products	4,659	8,256	12,515	77.2	51.6
Pet supplies	1,523	2,519	2,996	65.4	18.9
Health and beauty	2,656	4,460	6,572	67.9	47.4
Food and beverage	2,455	5,063	10,441	106.2	106.2

[1] Includes items sold to consumers in product categories not shown separately.

Source: Forrester Research, Inc., Cambridge, MA, *Online Retail Ripple Effect* (copyright).

No. 1042. Online Consumer Spending Forecast by Kind of Business: 2001 to 2003

[Forecast data: October 2002. (31.0 represents $31,000,000,000). Figures below reflect a partial revision of the Jupiter Internet Shopping Model;

Category	Online retail spending (bil. dol.) 2001	2002	2003	Percentage of spending online 2001	2002	2003	Number of online buyers (mil.) 2001	2002	2003	Percentage of online buyers that purchase within category 2001	2002
Total	31.0	40.4	51.7	(X)	(X)	(X)	(X)	(X)	(X)	(X)	(X)
PCs	6.9	7.5	8.8	29.6	31.6	35.8	5.4	6.8	8.6	8	8
Peripherals	2.1	2.3	2.5	20.2	21.5	22.8	11.0	13.4	15.9	17	16
Software	2.0	2.6	2.9	25.2	32.3	35.9	21.1	25.3	29.0	31	30
Consumer electronics	1.5	2.0	2.5	3.3	4.3	5.2	5.6	7.8	10.2	8	9
Books	2.3	2.8	3.1	10.2	11.9	13.0	32.1	41.3	50.0	49	51
Music	0.8	0.9	1.3	5.6	6.9	9.5	28.1	35.0	41.0	46	50
Videos	0.6	0.9	1.1	4.7	6.0	7.1	14.1	18.5	23.2	22	23
Movie tickets	0.2	0.3	0.4	2.4	3.3	4.3	5.9	9.0	13.2	8	11
Event tickets	1.6	2.1	2.7	9.1	11.9	14.3	15.0	18.6	22.0	21	21
Over-the-counter drugs	0.1	0.1	0.2	0.3	0.5	1.0	4.6	6.2	9.2	9	11
Nutraceuticals	0.1	0.1	0.3	0.5	0.6	1.4	8.7	11.1	13.5	13	14
Medical supplies and contact lenses	0.1	0.2	0.3	1.0	1.2	2.0	4.5	6.5	8.7	7	8
Personal care	0.1	0.2	0.5	0.3	0.5	1.1	8.4	12.2	15.2	11	13
Apparel	3.3	4.7	6.1	1.7	2.3	2.9	26.9	36.2	45.6	40	43
Footwear	0.5	0.8	1.0	0.9	1.4	1.7	6.9	10.4	14.6	11	13
Jewelry	0.9	1.1	1.3	2.9	3.5	3.9	5.2	6.8	8.9	8	9
Grocery	0.7	1.0	1.6	0.1	0.2	0.3	1.1	1.5	2.3	2	2
Pets	0.1	0.2	0.3	0.7	1.1	1.6	2.7	3.8	5.2	4	4
Toys	1.0	1.2	1.3	3.2	3.7	3.9	18.5	22.8	26.4	28	27
Sporting goods	0.7	0.9	1.2	2.9	3.9	5.1	8.0	11.2	15.2	12	14
Flowers	0.6	0.8	1.0	3.7	4.9	6.0	12.1	16.6	21.1	18	20
Specialty gifts	0.6	0.8	1.0	1.6	2.2	2.8	11.0	14.1	17.3	17	17
Furniture	0.1	0.3	0.4	0.2	0.4	0.6	0.6	1.2	2.5	1	1
Large appliances	0.3	0.5	0.7	1.5	2.3	3.0	0.6	0.9	1.2	1	1
Housewares/small appliances	0.6	1.1	1.9	0.9	1.5	2.6	6.0	8.5	13.9	9	10
Art and collectibles	0.3	0.5	0.6	1.1	1.6	2.2	1.5	2.1	3.0	2	3
Home improvement	0.3	0.6	1.0	0.2	0.4	0.6	3.9	6.3	9.3	6	7
Garden supplies	0.1	0.2	0.3	0.3	0.5	0.7	2.4	3.4	5.6	4	4
Office products	0.6	1.1	1.7	2.0	3.5	5.0	8.9	13.0	17.7	13	16
Auto parts	-	0.1	0.3	0.1	0.3	0.8	0.3	1.0	2.6	-	1
Other	1.8	2.6	3.3	(NA)	(NA)	(NA)	(NA)	(NA)	(NA)	(NA)	(NA)

- Represents or rounds to zero. NA Not available. X Not applicable.

Source: Jupiter Media Metrix, Inc., New York, NY Unpublished data.

No. 1043. Electronic Shopping and Mail-Order Houses—Total and E-Commerce Sales by Merchandise Line: 2001

[109,463 represents $109,463,000,000 in sales. Represents NAICS code 454110. Covers establishments with payroll. Based on 2001 Annual Retail Trade Survey]

Merchandise line	Value of sales Total (mil. dol.)	Value of sales E-commerce (mil. dol.)	E-commerce as percent of total sales	Percent distribution of total sales	Percent distribution of E-commerce sales
Electronic shopping and mail-order houses, total [1]	109,463	25,690	23.5	100.0	100.0
Books and magazines	3,872	1,739	44.9	3.5	6.8
Clothing and clothing accessories (includes footwear)	15,351	3,250	21.2	14.0	12.7
Computer hardware	21,968	5,655	25.7	20.1	22.0
Computer software	3,955	1,203	30.4	3.6	4.7
Drugs, health aids, beauty aids	16,203	950	5.9	14.8	3.7
Electronics and appliances	3,739	1,470	39.3	3.4	5.7
Food, beer and wine	1,832	444	24.2	1.7	1.7
Furniture and home furnishings	6,530	1,658	25.4	6.0	6.5
Music and videos	3,971	1,306	32.9	3.6	5.1
Office equipment and supplies	6,605	1,981	30.0	6.0	7.7
Sporting goods	1,640	464	28.3	1.5	1.8
Toys, hobby goods, and games	3,008	931	31.0	2.7	3.6
Other merchandise [2]	16,710	3,082	18.4	15.3	12.0
Nonmerchandise receipts [3]	4,079	1,557	38.2	3.7	6.1

[1] This industry comprises businesses primarily engaged in retailing all types of merchandise through catalogs, television, and the Internet. Data are preliminary and, therefore, subject to revision. [2] Includes other merchandise such as jewelry, collectibles, souvenirs, auto parts and accessories, hardware, and lawn and garden equipment and supplies. [3] Includes nonmerchandise receipts such as auction commissions, shipping and handling, customer training, customer support, and online advertising.

Source: U.S. Census Bureau, *2002 Annual Retail Trade Survey*, "2002 E-Commerce Multi-Sector Report"; published April 2003 <http://www.census.gov/eos/www/ebusiness614.htm>.

No. 1044. Retail E-Commerce Sales, Number of Orders, and Average Purchase Amount in Key Categories: 2001 and 2002

[261.7 represents 261,700,000). As of fourth quarter. Based on a point-of-sale-survey of online buyers covering approximately 1,000 merchants. Minus sign (-) indicates decrease]

Category	Orders (mil.) 2001	Orders (mil.) 2002	Percent change, 2001-2002	Sales (mil. dol.) [1] 2001	Sales (mil. dol.) [1] 2002	Percent change, 2001-2002	Average purchase amount (dol.) [1] 2001	Average purchase amount (dol.) [1] 2002	Percent change, 2001-2002
Total	261.7	350.6	34.0	35,872	46,890	30.7	137	134	-2.2
Apparel	38.3	48.4	26.5	4,014	4,815	20.0	105	99	-5.7
Computer goods	70.5	91.6	29.9	19,212	25,384	32.1	273	277	1.5
Consumer goods	32.2	49.0	52.0	3,904	5,149	31.9	121	105	-13.2
Entertainment	61.1	83.1	36.1	3,511	4,772	35.9	57	57	-
Food/wine	6.5	8.3	28.8	456	546	19.7	71	66	-7.0
Gifts	23.7	29.9	26.3	1,609	2,103	30.7	68	70	2.9
Home & garden	13.3	15.9	19.1	1,576	1,924	22.1	118	121	2.5
Toys	16.2	24.5	51.5	1,590	2,196	38.1	98	90	-8.2

- Represents zero. [1] Includes shipping and handling charges.

Source: BizRate.Com, Los Angeles, CA, *Consumer Online Report, Fourth Quarter, 2001* (copyright).

No. 1045. Retail Trade Sales—Total and E-Commerce by Kind of Business: 2001

[3,153,315 represents $3,153,315,000,000. Covers retailers with and without payroll. Based on 2001 Annual Retail Trade Survey, See Appendix III]

Kind of business	NAICS code [1]	Value of sales (mil. dol.) Total	Value of sales (mil. dol.) E-commerce	E-commerce as percent of total sales	Percent distribution of E-commerce sales
Retail trade, total	44,45	3,153,315	34,595	1.1	100.0
Motor vehicle and parts dealers	441	840,510	5,393	0.6	15.6
Furniture and home furnishings stores	442	91,428	(S)	(S)	(S)
Electronics and appliance stores	443	85,239	605	0.7	1.7
Building material and garden equipment supplies stores	444	287,360	547	0.2	1.6
Food and beverage stores	445	480,530	(S)	(S)	(S)
Health and personal care stores	446	167,567	(S)	(S)	(S)
Gasoline stations	447	245,404	(Z)	(Z)	(Z)
Clothing and clothing acces. stores	448	167,241	354	0.2	1.0
Sporting goods, hobby, book and music stores	451	79,382	506	0.6	1.5
General merchandise stores	452	430,363	(S)	(S)	(S)
Miscellaneous store retailers	453	104,975	517	0.5	1.5
Nonstore retailers	454	173,316	26,065	15.0	75.3
Electronic shopping and mail-order houses	454110	109,463	25,690	23.5	74.3

S Data do not meet publication standards because of high sampling variability or poor response quality. Unpublished estimates derived from this table by subtraction should be used with caution and not be attributed to the U.S. Census Bureau. For more information on methodology visit <www.census.gov/estats>. Z Less than $500,000 or 0.05 percent. [1] North American Industry Classification System, 1997; see text, Section 15.

Source: U.S. Census Bureau, "E-Stats"; published April 2003; <http://www.census.gov/eos/www/ebusiness614.htm>.

No. 1046. Merchant Wholesale Trade Sales—Total and E-Commerce: 2001

[2,708,666 represents $2,708,666,000,000. Covers only businesses with paid employees. Based on 2001 Annual Trade Survey, see Appendix III]

Kind of business	NAICS code [1]	Value of sales (mil. dol.) Total	Value of sales (mil. dol.) E-commerce	E-commerce as percent of total sales	Percent distribution of E-commerce sales
Merchant wholesale trade, total	42	2,708,666	272,183	10.0	100.0
Durable goods [2]	421	1,350,272	125,207	9.3	46.0
Motor vehicles, parts and supplies	4211	205,577	46,771	22.8	17.2
Furniture and home furnishings	4212	44,390	3,727	8.4	1.4
Professional & commercial equipment & supplies	4214	249,981	30,904	12.4	11.4
Computer, peripheral equipment and software	42143	122,458	15,776	12.9	5.8
Electrical goods	4216	214,312	12,111	5.7	4.4
Hardware, and plumbing and heating equipment and supplies	4217	64,864	6,497	10.0	2.4
Machinery, equipment and supplies	4218	243,312	7,947	3.3	2.9
Miscellaneous durable goods	4219	161,549	14,099	8.7	5.2
Nondurable goods [2]	422	1,358,394	146,976	10.8	54.0
Drugs and druggists' sundries	4222	201,114	96,363	47.9	35.4
Apparel, piece goods and notions	4223	87,362	11,828	13.5	4.3
Groceries and related products	4224	395,590	12,101	3.1	4.4
Farm product raw materials	4225	107,286	3,353	3.1	1.2

[1] North American Industry Classification System, 1997; see text, Section 15. [2] Includes kinds of business not shown separately.

Source: U.S. Census Bureau, 2000 E-Commerce Multi-Sector Report; published April 2003; <http://www.census.gov/eos/www/ebusiness614.htm>.

No. 1047. Shopping Centers—Number, Gross Leasable Area, and Retail Sales by Gross Leasable Area: 1990 to 2002

[4,390 represents 4,390,000,000. As of December 31. A shopping center is a group of architecturally unified commercial establishments built on a site that is planned, developed, owned, and managed as an operating unit related in its location, size, and type of shops to the trade area that the unit serves. The unit provides on-site parking in definite relationship to the types and total size of the stores. The data base attempts to include all centers with three or more stores. Estimates are based on a sample of data available on shopping center properties; for details, contact source]

Year	Total	Less than 100,001	100,001- 200,000	200,001- 400,000	400,001- 800,000	800,001- 1,000,000	More than 1 million
NUMBER							
1990	36,515	23,231	8,756	2,781	1,102	288	357
1995	41,235	26,001	9,974	3,345	1,234	301	380
2000	45,115	28,062	10,958	3,935	1,424	326	410
2001	45,827	28,474	11,100	4,038	1,466	329	420
2002	46,438	28,819	11,220	4,137	1,507	332	424
Percent distribution	100.0	62.1	24.2	8.8	3.2	0.7	0.9
Percent change, 2001-2002	1.3	1.2	1.1	2.5	2.8	0.9	1.0
GROSS LEASABLE AREA							
1990 (mil. sq. ft.)	4,390	1,125	1,197	734	618	259	457
1995 (mil. sq. ft.)	4,967	1,267	1,368	886	689	271	486
2000 (mil. sq. ft.)	5,566	1,383	1,514	1,059	790	294	526
2001 (mil. sq. ft.)	5,679	1,406	1,534	1,091	812	296	539
2002 (mil. sq. ft.)	5,774	1,424	1,552	1,119	836	299	544
Percent distribution	100.0	24.8	27.0	19.2	14.3	5.2	9.5
Percent change, 2001-2002	1.7	1.3	1.1	2.6	2.9	0.9	0.9
RETAIL SALES							
1990 (bil. dol.)	706.4	205.1	179.5	108.0	91.7	45.1	77.0
1995 (bil. dol.)	893.8	259.6	227.1	136.4	115.8	57.0	97.8
2000 (bil. dol.)	1,181.1	342.8	300.0	180.5	152.8	75.2	129.8
2001 (bil. dol.)	1,221.7	354.5	310.3	186.8	158.0	77.8	134.4
2002 (bil. dol.)	1,277.2	370.6	324.4	195.3	165.1	81.3	140.6
Percent distribution	100.0	29.0	25.4	15.3	12.9	6.4	11.0
Percent change, 2001-02	4.5	4.5	4.5	4.6	4.5	4.5	4.6

No. 1048. Shopping Centers—Gross Leasable Area and Retail Sales by State: 2002

[5,774 represents 5,774,000,000. See headnote, Table 1047.]

State	Gross leasable area, (mil. sq. ft.)	Retail sales, (bil. dol.)	Retail sales per sq. ft, (dol.)	Percent change, 2001-2002 Gross leasable area	Percent change, 2001-2002 Retail sales	State	Gross leasable area, (mil. sq. ft.)	Retail sales, (bil. dol.)	Retail sales per sq. ft, (dol.)	Percent change, 2001-2002 Gross leasable area	Percent change, 2001-2002 Retail sales
U.S.	5,774	1,277.2	221	1.7	4.5	MO	122	27.8	228	3.2	4.3
						MT	10	2.5	245	2.6	4.5
AL	81	18.6	230	2.3	3.9	NE	37	7.0	186	-	4.2
AK	8	2.6	344	-	5.7	NV	57	8.4	148	6.6	4.9
AZ	139	30.5	219	3.7	4.7	NH	25	5.9	231	-	6.6
AR	37	8.9	238	-	3.6						
CA	725	153.1	211	1.7	4.5	NJ	181	35.8	198	1.6	5.1
						NM	32	7.7	243	0.5	4.0
CO	112	28.9	258	4.3	5.0	NY	257	54.7	213	1.3	4.4
CT	99	24.0	243	1.0	5.5	NC	189	35.4	188	2.8	4.3
DE	23	5.6	245	-	5.5	ND	10	2.6	262	-	4.5
DC	10	2.1	212	4.2	4.5						
FL	461	118.2	257	1.8	5.1	OH	259	50.7	195	0.8	4.2
						OK	61	15.5	253	0.1	3.4
GA	195	38.4	197	3.0	4.2	OR	61	11.7	194	-	4.9
HI	20	5.7	279	0.8	6.7	PA	259	49.9	193	1.6	4.6
ID	20	4.0	198	-	3.8	RI	21	4.7	227	3.1	4.6
IL	271	52.4	194	1.3	4.8						
IN	127	26.0	205	2.0	4.1	SC	90	19.0	212	2.2	4.1
						SD	7	1.6	225	-	4.2
IA	47	9.2	197	3.8	4.3	TN	138	28.2	204	0.4	4.4
KS	60	14.2	236	0.4	4.2	TX	390	107.0	274	1.4	4.3
KY	69	16.8	242	0.9	4.1	UT	39	7.8	201	-	3.8
LA	88	22.8	258	2.4	4.2						
ME	19	5.4	290	4.2	5.7	VT	9	2.3	256	6.4	5.5
						VA	180	39.6	220	1.4	4.8
MD	132	30.8	232	0.5	4.5	WA	104	22.1	213	1.8	4.7
MA	118	29.3	248	1.6	5.0	WV	23	4.4	194	-	3.5
MI	150	31.0	207	1.8	4.4	WI	79	18.1	229	0.4	4.6
MN	72	17.2	238	1.5	4.6	WY	6	1.6	264	-	3.9
MS	45	9.6	213	0.8	3.3						

- Represents zero.

Source of Tables 1047 and 1048: National Research Bureau, Chicago, IL. Data for 1995-2002 published by International Council of Shopping Centers in *Shopping Centers Today*, April issues (copyright—Trade Dimensions International, Inc.).

No. 1049. Merchant Wholesalers—Summary: 1992 to 2002

[In billions of dollars (1,731.6 represents $1,731,600,000,000) except ratios. Inventories and stock/sales ratios, as of December, seasonally adjusted. Data reflect latest revision. Based on Annual Trade Survey; see Appendix III]

Kind of business	NAICS code [1]	1992	1994	1996	1998	2000	2001	2002
SALES								
Merchant wholesalers	(X)	1,731.6	1,933.6	2,239.8	2,379.8	2,742.6	2,708.7	2,751.0
Durable goods	(X)	832.8	1,004.2	1,156.6	1,265.8	1,422.6	1,350.3	1,338.8
Motor vehicles, parts, and supplies	4211	149.6	163.4	165.7	173.2	199.5	205.6	212.6
Furniture and homefurnishings	4212	28.5	31.3	36.5	40.4	46.7	44.4	42.9
Lumber and construction materials	4213	45.8	56.0	59.1	63.7	70.8	73.6	80.0
Professional and commercial equipment	4214	133.5	165.4	220.2	254.1	269.1	250.0	247.1
Computer, peripheral equipment, and software	42143	(NA)	(NA)	(NA)	150.8	150.4	122.5	115.4
Metals and minerals, except petroleum	4215	76.7	89.1	94.5	97.1	102.6	92.7	89.3
Electrical goods	4216	98.2	141.3	171.5	186.7	240.4	214.3	209.5
Hardware, plumbing and heating equipment	4217	41.3	49.2	54.3	60.4	67.1	64.9	66.0
Machinery, equipment and supplies	4218	147.5	174.4	206.6	242.5	252.3	243.3	224.5
Miscellaneous durable goods	4219	111.5	134.0	148.2	147.7	174.0	161.5	166.8
Nondurable goods	(X)	898.8	929.4	1,083.2	1,114.1	1,320.0	1,358.4	1,412.2
Paper and paper products	4221	48.1	55.4	64.8	69.9	80.0	75.5	73.6
Drugs, proprietaries, and sundries	4222	67.1	76.4	94.3	124.6	168.5	201.1	233.5
Apparel, piece goods, and notions	4223	62.7	68.5	73.1	84.2	88.9	87.4	89.9
Groceries and related products	4224	274.8	289.9	317.8	344.4	382.0	395.6	411.8
Farm-product raw materials	4225	106.2	99.1	137.5	108.0	107.0	107.3	113.3
Chemicals and allied products	4226	39.2	43.3	53.6	55.1	60.5	60.4	61.5
Petroleum and petroleum products	4227	137.5	125.4	143.5	116.4	185.9	180.5	183.7
Beer, wine, and distilled beverages	4228	50.4	52.0	55.9	61.8	71.6	75.3	81.6
Miscellaneous nondurable goods	4229	112.8	119.4	142.5	149.7	175.6	175.4	163.4
INVENTORIES								
Merchant wholesalers	(X)	194.5	219.8	238.8	269.4	302.5	287.6	288.8
Durable goods	(X)	119.8	138.4	153.2	174.6	194.0	175.7	173.8
Motor vehicles, parts, and supplies	4211	21.4	21.5	21.6	22.8	26.0	23.8	25.1
Furniture and homefurnishings	4212	4.2	4.4	4.8	5.1	5.9	5.3	5.2
Lumber and construction materials	4213	4.8	5.4	5.7	5.9	7.1	7.1	7.2
Professional and commercial equipment	4214	16.9	21.0	24.6	26.5	27.4	23.7	23.5
Computer, peripheral equipment, and software	42143	(NA)	(NA)	(NA)	12.4	10.6	7.8	7.5
Metals and minerals, except petroleum	4215	10.3	12.6	12.7	14.3	14.5	12.9	13.6
Electrical goods	4216	14.9	18.5	21.3	23.3	29.1	23.9	23.6
Hardware, plumbing and heating equipment	4217	6.4	7.8	8.6	9.6	10.9	10.4	10.3
Machinery, equipment and supplies	4218	28.0	31.6	37.7	48.2	51.3	48.8	45.7
Miscellaneous durable goods	4219	12.9	15.5	16.3	18.9	21.8	19.8	19.7
Nondurable goods	(X)	74.6	81.4	85.6	94.8	108.5	111.9	115.0
Paper and paper products	4221	4.5	4.9	5.3	6.0	7.0	6.4	6.1
Drugs, proprietaries, and sundries	4222	9.3	10.8	11.9	15.4	22.4	28.1	28.6
Apparel, piece goods, and notions	4223	10.5	12.0	12.0	13.6	12.6	12.4	12.4
Groceries and related products	4224	18.0	17.9	18.2	19.3	21.8	21.4	22.6
Farm-product raw materials	4225	8.1	9.9	9.5	10.1	10.9	10.3	9.7
Chemicals and allied products	4226	3.8	4.6	5.3	5.8	5.9	6.0	6.0
Petroleum and petroleum products	4227	3.9	4.2	4.5	3.4	4.3	4.2	5.0
Beer, wine, and distilled beverages	4228	4.3	4.6	5.1	5.8	6.9	6.7	7.5
Miscellaneous nondurable goods	4229	12.2	12.5	13.9	15.4	16.6	16.2	17.2
STOCK/SALES RATIO								
Merchant wholesalers	(X)	1.34	1.29	1.26	1.34	1.29	1.30	1.24
Durable goods	(X)	1.68	1.55	1.57	1.65	1.66	1.61	1.57
Motor vehicles, parts, and supplies	4211	1.72	1.57	1.56	1.54	1.55	1.39	1.39
Furniture and homefurnishings	4212	1.70	1.55	1.50	1.51	1.52	1.48	1.51
Lumber and construction materials	4213	1.28	1.10	1.13	1.06	1.20	1.09	1.10
Professional and commercial equipment	4214	1.44	1.37	1.33	1.22	1.30	1.17	1.13
Computer, peripheral equipment and software	42143	(NA)	(NA)	(NA)	1.02	0.97	0.82	0.79
Metals and minerals, except petroleum	4215	1.58	1.58	1.59	1.85	1.72	1.84	1.95
Electrical goods	4216	1.72	1.44	1.57	1.50	1.44	1.39	1.38
Hardware, plumbing and heating equipment	4217	1.84	1.76	1.84	1.85	1.93	1.85	1.93
Machinery, equipment and supplies	4218	2.23	2.04	2.09	2.39	2.47	2.54	2.46
Miscellaneous durable goods	4219	1.32	1.30	1.25	1.57	1.51	1.51	1.42
Nondurable goods	(X)	1.01	1.01	0.94	1.00	0.93	1.00	0.93
Paper and paper products	4221	1.11	0.94	0.98	1.00	1.05	1.04	0.98
Drugs, proprietaries, and sundries	4222	1.63	1.66	1.43	1.37	1.47	1.54	1.42
Apparel, piece goods, and notions	4223	1.94	2.16	1.79	2.02	1.63	1.67	1.68
Groceries and related products	4224	0.78	0.71	0.70	0.66	0.66	0.64	0.65
Farm-product raw materials	4225	0.94	1.12	0.86	1.10	1.14	1.26	0.87
Chemicals and allied products	4226	1.13	1.16	1.20	1.28	1.11	1.21	1.18
Petroleum and petroleum products	4227	0.36	0.40	0.35	0.37	0.25	0.33	0.28
Beer, wine, and distilled beverages	4228	1.04	1.03	1.09	1.08	1.14	1.02	1.05
Miscellaneous nondurable goods	4229	1.39	1.19	1.19	1.14	1.09	1.17	1.28

NA Not available.   X Not applicable.   [1] North American Industry Classification System, 1997; see text, Section 15.

Source: U.S. Census Bureau, Current Business Reports, *Annual Benchmark Report for Wholesale Trade, January 1992 through January 2003*, Series BW/01-A.

No. 1050. Wholesale Trade—Establishments, Sales, Payroll, and Employees by Kind of Business: 1997

[4,059,658 represents $4,059,658,000,000. Covers only establishments with payroll]

Kind of business	NAICS code [1]	Establishments (number)	Sales Total (mil. dol.)	Sales Per paid employee (dol.)	Annual payroll Total (mil. dol.)	Annual payroll Per paid employee (dol.)	Paid employees for pay period including March 12 (1,000)
Wholesale trade.................	42	453,470	4,059,658	700,357	214,915	37,076	5,796.6
Wholesale trade, nondurable goods	422	162,841	1,879,940	783,865	81,678	34,057	2,398.3
Paper & paper product wholesalers.........	4221	15,848	117,062	546,128	7,730	36,064	214.4
Drugs & druggists' sundries wholesalers.....	4222	8,053	203,148	1,068,485	8,395	44,154	190.1
Apparel, piece goods & notions wholesalers...	4223	20,707	124,104	597,880	7,760	37,382	207.6
Grocery & related products wholesalers......	4224	41,760	588,970	688,919	26,778	31,322	854.9
Farm-product raw material wholesalers......	4225	10,343	166,786	1,710,260	2,306	23,646	97.5
Chemical & allied products wholesalers......	4226	15,920	128,923	777,735	7,241	43,683	165.8
Petroleum & petroleum products wholesalers..	4227	11,297	267,624	1,941,710	4,480	32,503	137.8
Beer, wine & distilled alcoholic bev., wholesalers........................	4228	4,850	69,703	459,550	5,667	37,363	151.7
Misc. nondurable goods wholesale	4229	34,063	213,619	564,336	11,321	29,909	378.5
Merchant wholesalers....................	(X)	376,330	2,333,131	508,187	158,373	34,496	4,591.1
Manufacturers' sales branches & sales offices..............................	(X)	29,305	1,258,875	1,365,066	45,912	49,785	922.2
Agents, brokers and commission merchants....	(X)	47,835	467,652	1,650,981	10,630	37,529	283.3

X Not applicable. [1] North American Industry Classification System, 1997; see text, Section 15.

Source: U.S. Census Bureau, *1997 Economic Census, Wholesale Trade*, Series EC97W42A-US(RV), issued March 2000.

No. 1051. Wholesale Trade—Establishments, Employees, and Payroll: 2000 and 2001

[446.2 represents 446,200. Covers establishments with payroll. Employees are for the week including March 12. Excludes most government employees, railroad employees, and self-employed persons. Kind-of-business classification based on North American Industry Classification System (NAICS); see text, Section 15. For statement on methodology, see Appendix III]

Kind of business	NAICS code	Establishments (1,000) 2000	Establishments (1,000) 2001	Employees (1,000) 2000	Employees (1,000) 2001	Payroll (bil. dol.) 2000	Payroll (bil. dol.) 2001
Wholesale trade	42	446.2	438.9	6,112	6,142	270.1	275.9
Wholesale trade, durable goods	421	288.6	283.4	3,625	3,633	171.8	173.2
Motor vehicle/motor vehicle pt & supply whsle .	4211	28.4	27.6	402	387	14.1	14.1
Furniture & home furnishing whsle	4212	14.9	14.5	167	166	6.6	6.6
Lumber & other construction materials whsle ..	4213	15.1	15.5	184	185	7.2	7.5
Professional & commercial equip & supp whsle.	4214	44.4	43.1	763	777	44.9	45.1
Metal & mineral (except petroleum) whsle	4215	12.1	11.9	173	166	7.6	7.2
Electrical goods whsle	4216	38.3	37.8	535	559	33.9	34.8
Hardware, & plumbing & heating equip. & sup. whsle	4217	21.4	21.3	249	248	10.4	10.7
Machinery, equipment, & supplies whsle	4218	73.7	72.1	796	797	34.2	34.3
Miscellaneous durable goods whsle	4219	40.2	39.6	355	347	12.9	12.9
Wholesale trade, nondurable goods	422	157.7	155.5	2,487	2,509	98.4	10.3
Paper & paper product whsle	4221	14.9	14.4	232	226	8.9	8.9
Drugs & druggists' sundries whsle	4222	7.4	7.2	210	235	12.0	13.7
Apparel, piece goods & notions whsle.......	4223	20.0	19.5	214	212	8.9	9.0
Grocery & related product whsle	4224	39.7	39.2	875	871	31.6	33.0
Farm product raw material whsle	4225	9.5	9.3	92	91	2.5	2.6
Chemical & allied products whsle..........	4226	15.3	15.8	166	164	8.3	8.3
Petroleum & petroleum products whsle	4227	10.7	10.4	132	129	5.2	5.6
Beer/wine/distilled alcoholic beverage whsle...	4228	4.6	4.6	157	161	6.8	7.1
Miscellaneous nondurable goods whsle......	4229	35.4	35.1	409	420	14.3	14.6

Source: U.S. Census Bureau, *County Business Patterns*, annual. See also <http://www.census.gov/prod/2003pubs/01cbp/cbp01-1.pdf> (issued April 2002).

Section 23
Transportation

This section presents data on civil air transportation, both passenger and cargo, and on water transportation, including inland waterways, oceanborne commerce, the merchant marine, cargo, and vessel tonnages.

This section also presents statistics on revenues, passenger and freight traffic volume, and employment in various revenue-producing modes of the transportation industry, including motor vehicles, trains, and pipelines. Data are also presented on highway mileage and finances, motor vehicle travel, accidents, and registrations; and characteristics of public transit, railroads, and pipelines. Data from the 2001 National Household Travel Survey are also included.

Principal sources of air and water transportation data are the annual *National Transportation Statistics*, issued by the U.S. Bureau of Transportation Statistics; the *Annual Report* issued by the Air Transport Association of America, Washington, DC; and the annual *Waterborne Commerce of the United States* issued by the Corps of Engineers of the Department of the Army. In addition, the U.S. Census Bureau in its commodity transportation survey (part of the census of transportation, taken every 5 years through 1997, for years ending in "2" and "7") provides data on the type, weight, and value of commodities shipped by manufacturing establishments in the United States, by means of transportation, origin, and destination. The latest complete reports for 1997 are part of the 1997 Economic Census. See text, Section 15, Business Enterprise, for a discussion of the 1997 Economic Census.

Additional sources of data on water transportation include *Merchant Fleets of the World*, issued periodically by the U.S. Maritime Administration; *The Bulletin*, issued monthly by the American Bureau of Shipping, New York, NY; and the annual *World Fleet Statistics*.

The principal compiler of data on public roads and on operation of motor vehicles is the U.S. Department of Transportation's (DOT) Federal Highway Administration (FHWA). These data appear in FHWA's annual *Highway Statistics* and other publications.

The U.S. National Highway Traffic Safety Administration issues data on traffic accident deaths and death rates in two annual reports: the *Fact Book* and the *Fatal Accident Reporting System Annual Report*. DOTs Federal Railroad Administration presents data on accidents involving railroads in its annual *Accident/Incident Bulletin*, and the *Rail-Highway Crossing Accident/Incident and Inventory Bulletin*.

The data for the truck transportation component of the 1997 Economic Census are presented in the *Truck Inventory and Use Survey*.

Data are also presented in many nongovernment publications. Among them are the weekly and annual *Cars of Revenue Freight Loaded* and the annual *Yearbook of Railroad Facts*, both published by the Association of American Railroads, Washington, DC; *Transit Fact Book*, containing electric railway and motorbus statistics, published annually by the American Public Transit Association, Washington, DC.; *Accident Facts*, issued by the National Safety Council, Chicago, IL; and *Transportation in America*, issued by the Eno Foundation for Transportation, Westport, Connecticut.

Civil aviation—Federal promotion and regulation of civil aviation have been carried out by the FAA and the Civil Aeronautics Board (CAB). The CAB promoted and regulated the civil air transportation industry within the United States and between the United States and foreign countries. The Board granted licenses to provide air transportation service, approved or disapproved proposed rates and fares, and approved or disapproved proposed agreements and corporate relationships involving air carriers. In December 1984, the CAB ceased to exist as an agency. Some of its functions were transferred to the Department of Transportation (DOT), as outlined below. The responsibility for investigation of aviation accidents resides with the National Transportation Safety Board.

The Office of the Secretary, DOT aviation activities include: negotiation of international air transportation rights, selection of U.S. air carriers to serve capacity controlled international markets, oversight of international rates and fares, maintenance of essential air service to small communities, and consumer affairs. DOT's Bureau of Transportation Statistics (BTS) handles aviation information functions formerly assigned to CAB. Prior to BTS, the Research and Special Programs Administration handled these functions.

The principal activities of the FAA include: the promotion of air safety; controlling the use of navigable airspace; prescribing regulations dealing with the competency of airmen, airworthiness of aircraft and air traffic control; operation of air route traffic control centers, airport traffic control towers, and flight service stations; the design, construction, maintenance, and inspection of navigation, traffic control, and communications equipment; and the development of general aviation.

The CAB published monthly and quarterly financial and traffic statistical data for the certificated route air carriers. BTS continues these publications, including both certificated and noncertificated (commuter) air carriers. The FAA publishes annually data on the use of airway facilities; data related to the location of airmen, aircraft, and airports; the volume of activity in the field of nonair carrier (general aviation) flying; and aircraft production and registration.

General aviation comprises all civil flying (including such commercial operations as small demand air taxis, agriculture application, powerline patrol, etc.) but excludes certificated route air carriers, supplemental operators, large-aircraft commercial operators, and commuter airlines.

Air carriers and service—The CAB previously issued "certificates of public convenience and necessity" under Section 401 of the Federal Aviation Act of 1958 for scheduled and nonscheduled (charter) passenger services and cargo services. It also issued certificates under Section 418 of the Act to cargo air carriers for domestic all-cargo service only. The DOT Office of the Secretary now issues the certificates under a "fit, willing, and able" test of air carrier operations. Carriers operating only a 60-seat-or-less aircraft are given exemption authority to carry passengers, cargo, and mail in scheduled and nonscheduled service under Part 298 of the DOT (formerly CAB) regulations. Exemption authority carriers who offer scheduled passenger service to an essential air service point must meet the "fit, willing, and able" test.

Vessel shipments, entrances, and clearances—Shipments by dry cargo vessels comprise shipments on all types of watercraft, except tanker vessels; shipments by tanker vessels comprise all types of cargo, liquid and dry, carried by tanker vessels.

A vessel is reported as entered only at the first port which it enters in the United States, whether or not cargo is unloaded at that port. A vessel is reported as cleared only at the last port at which clearance is made to a foreign port, whether or not it takes on cargo. Army and Navy vessels entering or clearing without commercial cargo are not included in the figures.

Units of measurement—Cargo (or freight) tonnage and shipping weight both represent the gross weight of the cargo including the weight of containers, wrappings, crates, etc. However, shipping weight excludes lift and cargo vans and similar substantial outer containers. Other tonnage figures generally refer to stowing capacity of vessels, 100 cubic feet being called 1 ton. Gross tonnage comprises the space within the frames and the ceiling of the hull, together with those closed-in spaces above deck available for cargo, stores, passengers, or crew, with certain minor exceptions. Net or registered tonnage is the gross tonnage less the spaces occupied by the propelling machinery, fuel, crew quarters, master's cabin, and navigation spaces. Substantially, it represents space available for cargo and passengers. The net tonnage capacity of a ship may bear little relation to weight of cargo. Deadweight tonnage is the weight in long tons required to depress a vessel from light water line (that is, with only the machinery and equipment on board) to load line. It is, therefore, the weight of the cargo, fuel, etc., which a vessel is designed to carry with safety.

Federal-aid highway systems—The Intermodal Surface Transportation Efficiency Act (ISTEA) of 1991 eliminated the historical Federal-Aid Highway Systems and created the National Highway System (NHS) and other federal-aid highway categories. The final NHS was approved by Congress in December of 1995 under the National Highway System Designation Act.

Functional systems—Roads and streets are assigned to groups according to the character of service intended. The functional systems are (1) arterial highways that generally handle the long trips, (2) collector facilities that collect and disperse traffic between the arterials and the lower systems, and (3) local roads and streets that primarily serve direct access to residential areas, farms, and other local areas.

Regulatory bodies—The ICC, created by the U.S. Congress to regulate transportation in interstate commerce, has jurisdiction over railroads, trucking companies, bus lines, freight forwarders, water carriers, coal slurry pipelines, and transportation brokers. The Federal Energy Regulatory Commission is responsible for setting rates and charges for transportation and sale of natural gas and for establishing rates or charges for transportation.

Motor carriers—For 1960-73, Class I for-hire motor carriers of freight were classified by the ICC as those with $1 million or more of gross annual operating revenue; 1974-79, the class minimum was $3 million. Effective January 1, 1980, Class I carriers are those with $5 million or more in revenue. For 1960-68, Class I motor carriers of passengers were classified by the ICC as those with $200,000 or more of gross annual operating revenue; for 1969-76, as those with revenues of $1 million or more; and since 1977, as those with $3 million or more. Effective January 1, 1988, Class I motor carriers of passengers are those with $5 million or more in operating revenues; Class II less than $5 million in operating revenues.

Railroads—Railroad companies reporting to the ICC are divided into specific groups as follows: (1) Regular line-haul (interstate) railroads (and their nonoperating subsidiaries), (2) switching and terminal railroads, (3) private railroads prior to 1964 (identified by ICC as "circular" because they reported on brief circulars), and (4) unofficial railroads, so designated when their reports are received too late for tabulation. For the most part, the last three groups are not included in the statistics shown here.

For years prior to 1978, Class I railroads were those with annual revenues of $1 million or more for 1950-55; $3 million or more for 1956-64; $5 million or more for 1965-75; and $10 million or more for 1976-77. In 1978, the classification became Class I, those having more than $50 million gross annual operating revenue; Class II, from $10 million to $50 million+; and Class III, less than $10 million. Effective January 1, 1982, the ICC adopted a procedure to adjust the threshold for inflation by restating current revenues in constant 1978 dollars. In 1988, the criteria for Class I and Class II railroads were $92.0 million and $18.4 million, respectively. Also effective January 1, 1982, the ICC adopted a Carrier Classification Index Survey Form for carriers not filing annual report Form R-1 with the commission. Class II and Class III railroads are currently exempted from filing any financial report with the Commission. The form is used for reclassifying carriers.

The Surface Transportation Board (STB) was established pursuant to the ICC Termination Act of 1995, Pub. L. No. 104-88, 109 Stat. 803 (1995) (ICCTA), to assume certain of the regulatory functions that had been administered by the Interstate Commerce Commission. The Board has broad economic regulatory oversight of railroads, addressing such matters as rate reasonableness, car service and interchange, mergers and line acquisitions, line construction, and line abandonments. 49 U.S.C. 10101-11908. Other ICC regulatory functions were either eliminated or transferred to the Federal Highway Administration or the Bureau of Transportation Statistics within DOT.

Class I Railroads are regulated by the STB and subject to the Uniform System of Accounts and required to file annual and periodic reports. Railroads are classified based on their annual operating revenues. The class to which a carrier belongs is determined by comparing its adjusted operating revenues for 3 consecutive years to the following scale: Class I, $250 million or more, Class II $20 million to $250 million, and Class III $0 to 20 million.

Postal Service—The Postal Service provides mail processing and delivery services within the United States. The Postal Reorganization Act of 1970 created the Postal Service, effective July 1971, as an independent establishment of the Federal Executive Branch.

Revenue and cost analysis describes the Postal Service's system of attributing revenues and costs to classes of mail and service. This system draws primarily upon probability sampling techniques to develop estimates of revenues, volumes, and weights, as well as costs by class of mail and special service. The costs attributed to classes of mail and special services are primarily incremental costs which vary in response to changes in volume; they account for roughly 60 percent of the total costs of the Postal Service. The balance represents "institutional costs." Statistics on revenues, volume of mail, and distribution of expenditures are presented in the Postal Service's annual report, *Cost and Revenue Analysis,* and its *Annual Report of the Postmaster General* and its annual *Comprehensive Statement on Postal Operations.*

Statistical reliability—For a discussion of statistical collection and estimation, sampling procedures, and measures of statistical reliability applicable to Census Bureau data, see Appendix III.

No. 1052. Transportation-Related Components of U.S. Gross Domestic Product: 1980 to 2001

[In billions dollars (349.4 represents $349,400,000,000), except percent]

Item	1980	1985	1990	1995	2000	2001
CURRENT DOLLARS						
Total transportation-related final demand	349.4	495.9	617.5	782.0	1,031.8	1,046.9
Total gross domestic product (GDP)	2,795.6	4,213.0	5,803.2	7,400.5	9,824.6	10,082.2
Transportation-related final demand as a percent of GDP	12.5	11.8	10.6	10.6	10.5	10.4
Personal consumption of transportation	238.4	372.9	455.5	560.3	768.8	794.8
Motor vehicles and parts	87.0	175.7	206.4	249.3	336.6	361.3
Gasoline and oil	86.7	97.2	107.3	113.3	164.4	162.1
Transportation services	64.7	100.0	141.8	197.7	267.8	271.4
Gross private domestic investment	52.1	74.0	78.7	130.5	195.0	170.8
Transportation structures	3.7	4.3	3.0	4.4	5.3	5.0
Transportation equipment	48.4	69.7	75.7	126.1	189.7	165.8
Net exports of transportation-related goods and service [1]	-1.1	-34.7	-28.5	-43.3	-108.8	-108.1
Exports (+)	45.7	57.5	106.0	132.9	179.4	174.3
Civilian aircraft, engines, and parts	14.1	13.5	32.2	26.1	48.1	52.6
Automotive vehicles, engines, and parts	17.4	24.9	36.5	61.8	80.4	75.4
Passenger fares	2.6	4.4	15.3	18.9	20.8	18.0
Other transportation	11.6	14.7	22.0	26.1	30.1	28.3
Imports (-)	46.8	92.2	134.5	176.2	288.2	282.4
Civilian aircraft, engines, and parts	3.1	5.3	10.5	10.7	26.4	31.4
Automotive vehicles, engines, and parts	28.3	64.9	88.5	123.8	195.9	189.8
Passenger fares	3.6	6.4	10.5	14.7	24.3	22.4
Other transportation	11.8	15.6	25.0	27.0	41.6	38.8
Government transportation-related purchases	60.0	83.7	111.8	134.5	176.8	189.4
Federal purchases [2]	7.0	10.0	12.9	16.3	19.4	20.9
State and local purchases [2]	48.8	67.5	90.1	109.8	148.4	159.4
Defense-related purchases [3]	4.2	6.2	8.8	8.4	9.0	9.1
Total domestic transportation-related final demand [4]	350.5	530.6	642.4	825.3	1,140.6	1,155.0
Total gross domestic demand (GDD)	2,810.5	4,327.2	5,874.6	7,484.7	10,190.1	10,431.0
Transportation-related final demand as a percent of GDP	12.5	12.3	10.9	11.0	11.2	11.1
CHAINED (1996) DOLLARS						
Total transportation-related final demand	537.7	643.3	719.9	802.8	977.8	984.1
Total gross domestic product (GDP)	4,900.9	5,717.1	6,707.9	7,543.8	9,191.4	9,214.5
Transportation-related final demand as a percent of GDP	11.0	11.3	10.7	10.6	10.6	10.7
Personal consumption of transportation	362.3	494.3	532.6	574.7	727.1	751.8
Motor vehicles and parts	142.7	236.9	246.1	253.4	338.4	361.9
Gasoline and oil	94.9	104.8	113.1	120.2	135.7	138.8
Transportation services	124.7	152.6	173.4	201.0	253.0	251.1
Gross private domestic investment	84.0	99.6	91.1	132.8	191.7	168.6
Transportation structures	6.4	5.7	3.7	4.6	5.1	5.0
Transportation equipment	77.6	93.9	87.4	128.2	186.6	163.6
Net exports of transportation-related goods and service [1]	-5.0	-56.1	-31.3	-43.1	-103.2	-103.5
Exports (+)	76.2	76.0	123.7	135.4	169.5	161.8
Civilian aircraft, engines, and parts	26.9	19.5	40.9	27.2	43.2	44.8
Automotive vehicles, engines, and parts	28.3	30.5	39.8	62.5	78.5	73.4
Passenger fares	4.5	7.1	19.1	18.9	19.8	17.0
Other transportation	16.5	18.9	23.9	26.8	28.0	26.6
Imports (-)	81.2	132.1	155.0	178.5	272.7	265.3
Civilian aircraft, engines, and parts	6.0	7.7	13.5	11.2	23.9	27.3
Automotive vehicles, engines, and parts	52.5	95.8	101.6	124.6	192.5	186.7
Passenger fares	5.5	9.3	12.7	14.9	20.9	17.7
Other transportation	17.2	19.3	27.2	27.8	35.4	33.6
Government transportation-related purchases	96.4	105.5	127.5	138.5	162.2	167.2
Federal purchases [2]	13.3	13.9	16.1	17.2	19.3	20.1
State and local purchases [2]	77.3	83.5	101.1	112.6	134.2	138.4
Defense-related purchases [4]	5.8	8.1	10.3	8.7	8.7	8.7
Total domestic transportation-related final demand [4]	542.5	699.4	751.2	845.9	1,081.0	1,087.6
Total gross domestic demand (GDD)	4,890.9	5,866.2	6,764.9	7,621.8	9,561.2	9,600.7
Transportation-related final demand as a percent of GDP	11.1	11.9	11.1	11.1	11.3	11.3

[1] Sum of exports and imports. [2] Federal purchases and state and local purchases are the sum of consumption expenditures and gross investment. [3] Defense-related purchases are the sum of transportation of material and travel. [4] Sum of total personal consumption of transportation, total gross private domestic investment, net exports of transportation-related goods and services, and total government transportation-related purchases.

Source: U.S. Bureau or Transportation Statistics, *National Transportation Statistics, 2002*. See Internet site <http://www.bts.gov/publications/nts/index.html>.

No. 1053. Transportation Outlays by Type of Transport: 1970 to 2001

[In billions of dollars (97.0 represents $97,000,000,000)]

Type of transport	1970	1980	1985	1990	1995	2000	2001
Private transportation	97.0	305.2	434.7	517.2	629.8	831.3	862.1
Automobiles	95.0	297.1	426.8	507.3	619.4	809.4	835.6
New and used cars	32.0	71.5	137.1	148.1	169.6	205.4	200.6
Other motor vehicles[1]	2.7	11.8	40.8	57.5	80.2	125.9	149.0
Tires, tubes, accessories	7.0	20.6	27.9	32.9	40.6	45.9	45.8
Gasoline and oil	27.4	99.7	111.8	118.0	124.6	164.4	162.1
Tolls	0.8	1.3	1.7	2.5	3.7	4.6	4.9
Insurance less claims	4.4	10.8	11.5	19.9	32.7	30.7	32.1
Interest on debt	4.7	39.1	21.0	28.2	38.0	48.7	51.0
Auto registration fees	1.7	2.9	4.8	6.1	7.0	7.6	7.7
Operators' permit fees	0.2	0.4	0.5	0.6	0.8	0.7	0.8
Repair, greasing, washing, parking, leasing, rentals	14.1	39.1	69.6	93.4	122.2	175.5	181.6
Air	2.0	8.1	7.9	9.9	10.4	21.9	26.5
Aircraft	0.3	2.9	2.3	3.4	4.3	14.3	18.5
Operating costs	1.7	5.2	5.6	6.5	6.1	7.6	8.0
For-hire transportation	14.9	51.0	71.9	99.6	117.6	159.9	148.1
Local	5.0	17.3	25.3	31.6	41.0	52.5	53.4
Bus and transit[2]	1.8	9.3	13.5	16.7	21.6	30.6	30.6
Taxi	1.7	2.8	3.8	4.0	5.0	5.6	5.7
Railroad commutation[2]	0.2	1.5	2.2	2.8	4.5	4.2	4.5
School bus	1.2	3.8	5.7	8.0	9.9	12.1	12.6
Intercity	7.7	28.4	39.5	53.1	57.8	79.9	70.2
Air[3]	6.6	25.1	35.9	49.5	54.0	75.1	64.9
Bus	0.8	1.7	2.0	1.8	1.5	2.0	2.2
Rail[4]	0.3	1.5	1.6	1.7	2.2	2.7	2.9
Water	(Z)	(Z)	0.1	0.1	0.1	0.2	0.1
International	2.2	5.3	7.1	14.9	18.8	27.5	24.5
Air[3]	1.9	5.0	6.6	13.6	16.8	23.0	20.4
Water	0.3	0.3	0.5	1.3	2.0	4.5	4.0
Freight, total	84.0	213.7	273.6	351.0	442.6	575.8	579.6
Highway	62.5	155.3	205.6	270.8	348.1	460.8	467.3
Truck, intercity[5]	33.6	94.6	123.2	162.3	219.6	305.2	309.4
Truck, local[6]	28.8	60.5	82.2	108.4	128.4	155.5	157.7
Bus, intercity	0.1	0.2	0.2	0.1	0.1	0.1	0.1
Rail	11.9	27.9	29.2	30.1	34.6	36.5	36.7
Water	5.3	15.5	18.4	20.1	22.7	28.7	27.6
Oil pipeline	1.4	7.5	8.9	8.5	9.1	9.0	9.1
Air carrier	1.2	4.0	6.8	13.7	18.8	27.6	25.8
Other carriers	0.4	1.1	1.7	4.0	5.0	7.8	7.7
Other shipper costs	1.4	2.4	3.0	3.7	4.4	5.4	5.4

Z Less than $50,000,000. [1] Includes small pickup trucks, vans, recreational vehicles, and mobile homes. [2] Includes federal, state, and local government operating subsidies and capital grants, except 1970 data for railroad commutation. [3] Includes domestic and international air passenger federal excise taxes. [4] Includes federal operating subsidies and capital grants for Amtrak and the Northeast Corridor. [5] Includes freight, mail, express, and where applicable, subsidies and user fees. [6] Excludes use of small trucks/vans used almost exclusively for personal travel.

Source: Eno Transportation Foundation, Inc., Washington, D.C. *Transportation in America*, annual (copyright).

No. 1054. Volume of Domestic Intercity Freight and Passenger Traffic by Type of Transport: 1980 to 2001

[Freight traffic in billion ton-miles (2,487 represents 2,487,000,000,000); passenger traffic in billion passenger-miles. A ton-mile is the movement of 1 ton (2,000 pounds) of freight for the distance of 1 mile. A passenger-mile is the movement of one passenger for the distance of 1 mile. Comprises public and private traffic, both revenue and nonrevenue. ICC = Interstate Commerce Commission]

Type of transport	1980	1985	1990	1994	1995	1996	1997	1998	1999	2000	2001, est.
Freight traffic, total[1]	2,487	2,458	2,896	3,261	3,407	3,516	3,534	3,591	3,686	3,746	3,733
Railroads	932	895	1,091	1,275	1,375	1,426	1,421	1,442	1,499	1,534	1,558
Truck:											
ICC truck	242	250	311	391	401	428	436	459	474	483	471
Non-ICC truck	313	360	424	517	520	544	560	568	585	591	580
Water:											
Rivers/canals	311	306	390	388	406	392	392	392	403	409	400
Great Lakes	96	76	85	87	91	93	95	96	92	97	94
Oil pipelines	588	564	584	591	601	619	617	620	618	617	616
Domestic airways[2]	5	7	10	12	13	14	14	14	15	16	15
Passenger traffic, total	1,468	1,636	1,847	2,065	2,098	2,182	2,247	2,328	2,424	2,494	2,498
Private automobiles[3]	1,210	1,310	1,452	1,625	1,641	1,693	1,740	1,806	1,873	1,911	1,938
Air, private carrier[4]	15	12	13	10	11	12	13	13	14	15	16
Air, public carrier	204	278	346	388	404	435	451	463	488	515	488
Bus	27	24	23	28	28	29	31	32	35	38	42
Railroads[5]	11	11	13	14	14	13	13	14	14	15	15

[1] Includes both for-hire and private carrier freight, mail and express. [2] Includes both scheduled and nonscheduled carriers. [3] Includes small trucks used for travel purposes. [4] General aviation including air taxi and small air commuter. [5] Traffic by other than Amtrak and classified as noncommutation.

Source: Eno Transportation Foundation, Inc., Washington, DC, *Transportation in America*, annual (copyright).

No. 1055. Transportation Revenues by Level of Government and Mode: 1990 to 2001

[In millions of dollars. For fiscal years. Based on reports of various government agencies; for details, see source]

Level of government and source	1990	1995	1997	1998	1999	2000	2001, est.
Total	**69,753**	**93,659**	**100,516**	**111,234**	**126,895**	**(NA)**	**(NA)**
Federal	21,384	30,166	31,440	38,934	51,996	46,756	47,784
State	34,629	44,846	47,729	50,009	51,584	(NA)	(NA)
Local	13,740	18,647	21,348	22,291	23,315	(NA)	(NA)
Highway, total	49,945	66,743	71,814	77,299	88,668	(NA)	(NA)
Federal, total	13,453	19,377	21,314	24,307	33,823	30,347	30,735
Highway Trust Fund—Highway Account	13,453	19,377	21,314	24,307	33,823	30,347	30,735
Excise taxes	12,472	18,829	20,509	23,141	33,821	30,347	(NA)
Motor fuel	10,522	15,743	17,773	19,838	29,782	25,663	(NA)
Gasoline	7,472	10,735	12,483	14,101	20,806	17,579	(NA)
Gasohol	154	492	575	748	1,256	1,093	(NA)
Diesel & special fuels	2,896	4,516	4,715	4,989	7,720	6,991	(NA)
Interest	981	548	805	1,166	2	-	(NA)
State, total [1]	32,644	42,415	45,034	47,214	48,784	(NA)	(NA)
Motor fuel taxes	19,379	25,440	27,214	28,345	29,130	(NA)	(NA)
Motor vehicle license taxes	9,848	12,414	12,840	13,662	14,083	(NA)	(NA)
Local, total	3,848	4,952	5,466	5,779	6,061	(NA)	(NA)
Transit, total	7,193	9,352	11,417	11,872	13,186	(NA)	(NA)
Highway Trust Fund—Transit Account	1,977	2,813	3,996	4,326	5,478	4,625	4,696
State transit charges	1,074	1,257	1,339	1,384	1,404	(NA)	(NA)
Local transit charges	4,142	5,283	6,082	6,162	6,304	(NA)	(NA)
Air, total	10,119	13,954	13,544	18,176	21,079	(NA)	(NA)
Federal Airport and Airway Trust Fund, total [1]	4,945	6,291	4,488	8,654	11,089	10,544	11,285
Passenger ticket	3,219	4,768	3,389	5,455	5,941	5,103	5,273
Passenger flight segment	-	-	-	547	1,339	1,655	1,830
Fuel Tax	141	211	128	659	1,009	887	1,000
International departure/arrival	181	233	194	948	1,484	1,349	1,412
State airport charges	556	695	765	768	744	(NA)	(NA)
Local airport charges	4,617	6,968	8,291	8,754	9,246	(NA)	(NA)
Water, total	2,487	3,567	3,704	3,850	3,923	(NA)	(NA)
Federal water receipts, total	999	1,644	1,605	1,611	1,568	1,175	1,008
State water transportation charges	355	479	590	643	651	(NA)	(NA)
Local water transportation charges	1,133	1,444	1,509	1,597	1,704	(NA)	(NA)
Pipeline, total	10	35	30	29	30	40	46
Pipeline Safety Fund	10	35	30	29	30	40	46
General support, total	-	7	7	8	8	25	14
Emergency Preparedness Fund	-	7	7	8	8	25	14

- Represents zero. NA Not available. [1] Includes other revenue raising instruments, not shown separately.

Source: U.S. Bureau of Transportation Statistics, *Government Transportation Statistics 2001*. See Internet site <http://www.bts.gov/publications/governmenttransportationfinancialstatistics/>.

No. 1056. Employment and Earnings in Transportation and Warehousing by Industry: 1990 to 2002

[3,476 represents 3,476,000. Annual average of monthly figures. Earnings data for rail and water transportation are not available. Based on Current Employment Statistics program; see Appendix III]

Industry	2002 NAICS code [1]	1990	1995	1997	1998	1999	2000	2001	2002
NUMBER (1,000)									
Transportation and warehousing	**48,49**	**3,476**	**3,838**	**4,027**	**4,168**	**4,300**	**4,410**	**4,372**	**4,205**
Air transportation	481	529	511	542	563	586	614	615	559
Rail transportation	482	272	233	221	225	229	232	227	218
Water transportation	483	57	51	51	51	52	56	54	52
Truck transportation	484	1,122	1,249	1,308	1,354	1,392	1,406	1,387	1,339
Transit and ground	485	274	328	350	363	371	372	375	372
Pipeline transportation	486	60	54	50	48	47	46	45	42
Scenic and sightseeing	487	16	22	25	25	26	28	29	26
Support activities	488	364	430	473	497	518	537	539	527
Couriers and messengers	491,2	375	517	546	568	586	605	587	558
Warehousing and storage	493	407	444	462	474	494	514	514	514
AVG. WEEKLY EARNINGS [2](dol.)									
Transportation and warehousing	**48,49**	**472**	**513**	**543**	**547**	**548**	**562**	**563**	**581**
Air transportation	481	497	485	478	482	457	496	536	560
Truck transportation	484	490	554	592	610	626	635	604	627
Transit and ground	485	316	356	374	385	391	400	400	423
Pipeline transportation	486	610	751	775	793	806	826	860	936
Scenic and sightseeing	487	289	303	305	322	340	360	372	361
Support activities	488	437	491	515	525	530	549	578	616
Couriers and messengers	491,2	236	343	395	380	382	384	390	398
Warehousing and storage	493	405	463	498	516	536	558	565	572

[1] North American Industry Classification System, 2002, see text, Sections 12 and 15. [2] For nonsupervisory workers.

Source: U.S. Bureau of Labor Statistics, *Employment and Earnings*, monthly, June 2003 issue. See also Internet site <http://www.bls.gov/ces/>.

No. 1057. Transportation and Warehousing—Establishments, Employees, and Payroll by Kind of Business (NAICS Basis): 2000 and 2001

[3,790.0 represents 3,790,000. For establishments with payroll. See Appendix III. County Business Patterns excludes rail transportation (NAICS 482) and the National Postal Service (NAICS 491)]

Industry	NAICS code [1]	Establishments 2000	Establishments 2001	Paid employees [2] (1,000) 2000	Paid employees [2] (1,000) 2001	Annual payroll (mil. dol.) 2000	Annual payroll (mil. dol.) 2001
Transportation & warehousing	48-49	190,044	190,683	3,790.0	3,750.7	125,592.4	129,506.2
Air transportation	481	5,429	5,451	615.6	609.0	26,569.3	28,780.7
Scheduled air transportation	4811	3,324	3,331	570.9	562.1	24,484.5	26,589.7
Scheduled passenger air transportation	481111	2,740	2,825	536.2	533.5	23,470.7	25,672.1
Scheduled freight air transportation	481112	584	506	34.7	28.6	1,013.8	917.6
Nonscheduled air transportation	4812	2,105	2,120	44.7	46.9	2,084.8	2,190.9
Water transportation	483	1,900	1,871	67.6	70.5	3,003.2	3,342.1
Deep sea, coastal, & Great Lakes water transportation	4831	1,254	1,227	47.8	50.7	2,214.2	2,491.1
Inland water transportation	4832	646	644	19.7	19.7	789.0	850.9
Inland water freight transportation	483211	402	395	16.3	16.0	673.9	729.3
Inland water passenger transportation	483212	244	249	3.5	3.8	115.1	121.6
Truck transportation	484	110,416	109,814	1,415.8	1,397.9	46,451.5	46,080.9
General freight trucking	4841	55,874	56,378	922.7	915.0	31,614.0	31,223.9
General freight trucking, local	48411	20,329	20,726	153.3	149.8	4,529.8	4,434.0
General freight trucking, long distance	48412	35,545	35,652	769.5	765.2	27,084.2	26,789.8
Specialized freight trucking	4842	54,542	53,436	493.1	482.9	14,837.5	14,857.1
Used household & office goods moving	48421	9,147	8,913	128.9	128.2	3,661.4	3,657.9
Specialized freight (except used goods) trucking, local	48422	32,493	32,099	200.4	196.2	5,692.4	5,800.4
Specialized freight (except used goods) trucking, long-distance	48423	12,902	12,424	163.7	158.5	5,483.7	5,398.7
Transit & ground passenger transportation	485	16,383	16,466	386.9	391.6	7,214.7	7,558.7
Urban transit systems	4851	705	715	43.1	42.2	1,295.8	1,345.6
Mixed mode systems	485111	152	164	6.2	5.5	146.9	137.4
Commuter rail	485112	15	15	(D)	(D)	(D)	(D)
Bus and other motor vehicle mode systems	485113	505	496	31.4	31.6	925.1	952.6
Other	485119	33	40	(D)	(D)	(D)	(D)
Interurban & rural bus transportation	4852	444	460	26.8	24.7	709.7	811.0
Taxi & limousine service	4853	6,806	6,842	67.8	69.4	1,244.3	1,257.7
Taxi service	48531	3,116	3,086	30.4	30.3	485.2	488.7
Limousine service	48532	3,690	3,756	37.5	39.2	759.1	769.0
School & employee bus transportation	4854	4,217	4,287	162.9	168.9	2,322.6	2,471.8
Charter bus industry	4855	1,451	1,395	34.1	33.4	668.7	659.5
Other transit & ground passenger transportation	4859	2,760	2,767	52.2	52.9	973.6	1,013.2
Special needs transpiration	485991	1,914	1,887	34.8	35.9	648.9	697.4
Pipeline transportation	486	2,802	2,785	53.0	50.9	3,828.6	3,880.3
Pipeline transportation of crude oil	4861	307	229	6.7	6.0	425.6	430.9
Pipeline transportation of natural gas	4862	1,938	2,017	39.2	38.2	2,961.1	2,981.3
Other pipeline transportation	4869	557	539	7.0	6.7	441.9	468.1
Scenic & sightseeing transportation	487	2,254	2,380	23.6	23.4	583.5	556.8
Scenic & sightseeing transportation, land	4871	454	521	8.7	8.6	192.8	188.1
Scenic & sightseeing transportation, water	4872	1,642	1,699	13.0	12.9	331.2	313.3
Scenic & sightseeing transportation, other	4879	158	160	2.0	1.9	59.5	55.4
Support activities for transportation	488	31,440	31,876	472.4	484.6	16,507.0	17,098.2
Support activities for air transportation	4881	4,368	4,417	126.7	127.6	3,634.0	3,713.4
Airport operations	48811	1,834	1,811	67.9	65.9	1,569.5	1,515.3
Air traffic control	488111	137	151	0.8	0.8	29.9	35.9
Other support activities for air transportation	48819	2,534	2,606	58.8	61.7	2,064.6	2,198.1
Support activities for rail transportation	4882	821	831	21.4	23.0	714.4	739.0
Support activities for water transportation	4883	2,543	2,496	81.6	78.7	3,250.7	3,350.0
Port and harbor operations	48831	196	201	7.4	7.3	265.8	254.9
Marine cargo handling	48832	607	612	53.5	50.3	2,194.7	2,249.5
Navigational services to shipping	48833	863	830	11.8	12.0	478.7	507.8
Other	48839	877	853	8.9	9.2	311.5	337.8
Support activities for road transportation	4884	7,010	7,325	56.2	61.3	1,308.8	1,483.3
Motor vehicle towing	48841	6,078	6,294	41.8	43.7	961.7	1,030.8
Freight transportation arrangement	4885	15,177	15,334	161.7	168.2	6,620.3	6,829.4
Other support activities for transportation	4889	1,521	1,473	24.7	25.9	978.6	983.1
Couriers & messengers	492	12,297	12,855	619.3	577.6	17,399.4	17,815.3
Couriers	4921	6,667	7,105	548.9	513.6	15,890.5	16,455.5
Local messengers & local delivery	4922	5,630	5,750	70.5	64.0	1,508.9	1,359.8
Warehousing & storage	493	7,123	7,185	135.9	145.3	4,035.3	4,393.1

D Figure withheld to avoid disclosure pertaining to individual companies. [1] North American Industry Classification System, 1997; see text, Section 15. [2] For employees on the payroll for the pay period including March 12.

Source: U.S. Census Bureau, "County Business Patterns"; 2001 published 10 April 2003; <http://www.census.gov/epcd/cbp/view/cbpview.html>.

No. 1058. Transportation Accidents, Deaths, and Injuries: 1980 to 2001

[6,216 represents 6,216,000]

Year and casualty	Motor vehicle [1] (1,000)	Rail-road [2]	Air-lines [3]	Commuter air carriers [4]	On demand air carriers [5]	General aviation	Recreational boating [6]	Pipeline [7] Gas	Hazardous liquid	Water-borne [8]	Rail Rapid Transit [9]	Hazardous materials [10]
Accidents:												
1980	6,216	8,205	19	38	171	3,590	5,513	1,524	246	4,624	6,789	15,719
1990	6,471	2,879	24	15	107	2,241	6,411	198	180	3,613	12,178	8,879
1995	6,699	2,459	36	12	75	2,056	8,019	161	188	4,298	14,327	14,742
2000	6,394	2,983	56	12	80	1,835	7,740	234	147	3,791	(NA)	17,583
2001	6,323	2,987	45	7	72	1,723	(NA)	209	129	(NA)	(NA)	17,557
Deaths:												
1980	51.1	584	1	37	105	1,239	1,360	15	4	206	83	19
1990	44.6	599	39	6	51	767	865	6	3	85	117	8
1995	41.8	567	168	9	52	735	829	18	3	51	51	7
2000	41.9	512	92	5	71	593	701	37	1	32	32	15
2001	42.1	548	531	13	60	563	681	7	-	(NA)	(NA)	7
Injuries:												
1980	2,848	58,696	19	14	43	681	2,650	177	15	180	6,801	626
1990	3,231	22,736	29	11	36	409	3,822	69	7	175	10,036	423
1995	3,465	12,546	25	17	14	396	4,141	53	11	145	11,238	400
2000	3,189	10,424	27	7	12	310	4,355	77	4	125	(NA)	248
2001	3,033	9,739	16	4	23	322	(NA)	46	10	(NA)	(NA)	135

- Represents zero. NA Not available. [1] Data on deaths are from U.S. National Highway Traffic Safety Administration and are based on 30 day definition. Includes only police reported crashes. For more detail, see Table 1077. [2] Accidents which result in damages to railroad property. Grade crossing accidents are also included when classified as a train accident. Deaths exclude fatalities in railroad-highway grade crossing accidents. [3] Includes scheduled and nonscheduled (charter) air carriers. Represents serious injuries. [4] All scheduled service. Represents serious injuries. [5] All nonscheduled service. Represents serious injuries. [6] Accidents resulting in death; injury or requiring medical treatment beyond first aid; damages exceeding $500; or a person's disappearance. [7] Beginning 1990, pipeline accidents/incidents are credited to year of occurrence; 1980 data are credited to the year filed. [8] Covers accidents involving commercial vessels which must be reported to U.S. Coast Guard if there is property damage exceeding $25,000; material damage affecting the seaworthiness or efficiency of a vessel; stranding or grounding; loss of life; or injury causing a person's incapacity for more than 3 days. [9] Reporting criteria and source of data changed between 1989 and 1990; these data from 1990 to present are not comparable to earlier years. [10] Accidents, deaths, and injuries involving hazardous materials cover all types of transport.

Source: U.S. Bureau of Transportation Statistics. *National Transportation Statistics*, annual. See Internet site <http://www.bts.gov/publications/nts/index.html>.

No. 1059. U.S. Scheduled Airline Industry—Summary: 1992 to 2002

[For calendar years or Dec. 31 (475.1 represents 475,100,000). For domestic and international operations. Covers carriers certificated under Section 401 of the Federal Aviation Act. Minus sign (-) indicates loss]

Item	Unit	1992	1995	1997	1998	1999	2000	2001[1]	2002[1]
SCHEDULED SERVICE									
Revenue passengers enplaned	Mil.	475.1	547.8	594.7	612.9	636.0	666.2	622.1	611.7
Revenue passenger miles	Bil.	478.6	540.7	603.4	618.1	652.0	692.8	651.7	639.6
Available seat miles	Bil.	752.8	807.1	857.2	874.1	918.4	957.0	930.5	892.7
Revenue passenger load factor	Percent	63.6	67.0	70.4	70.7	71.0	72.4	70.0	71.6
Mean passenger trip length [2]	Miles	1,007	987	1,015	1,008	1,025	1,040	1,048	1,046
Freight and express ton miles	Mil.	11,130	14,578	17,959	18,131	19,317	21,443	20,119	23,160
Aircraft departures	1,000	7,051	8,062	8,127	8,292	8,627	9,035	8,788	9,029
FINANCES									
Total operating revenue [3]	Mil. dol.	78,357	95,117	109,917	113,810	119,455	130,839	115,524	106,788
Passenger revenue	Mil. dol.	59,844	69,835	79,540	81,052	84,383	93,622	80,946	73,277
Freight and express revenue	Mil. dol.	5,916	8,616	10,477	10,697	11,415	12,486	12,066	12,662
Mail revenue	Mil. dol.	1,184	1,266	1,362	1,708	1,739	1,970	1,062	658
Charter revenue	Mil. dol.	2,989	3,742	3,748	4,059	4,284	4,913	4,449	4,430
Total operating expense	Mil. dol.	80,803	89,266	101,375	104,528	111,119	123,840	125,850	115,348
Operating profit	Mil. dol.	-2,446	5,852	8,542	9,283	8,337	6,999	-10,326	-8,560
Interest expense	Mil. dol.	-1,743	-2,426	-1,738	-1,753	-1,833	-2,193	-2,506	-3,261
Net profit	Mil. dol.	-4,787	2,283	5,119	4,847	5,277	2,486	-8,275	-11,285
Revenue per passenger mile	Cents	12.5	12.9	13.2	13.1	12.9	13.5	12.4	11.5
Rate of return on investment	Percent	-9.0	11.9	14.7	12.0	11.1	6.4	-6.5	-8.6
Operating profit margin	Percent	-3.1	6.2	7.8	8.2	7.0	5.3	-8.9	-8.0
Net profit margin	Percent	-6.1	2.4	4.7	4.3	4.4	1.9	-7.2	-10.6
EMPLOYEES [4]									
Total	1,000	540.4	547.0	586.5	621.1	646.4	680.0	672.0	601.4
Pilots and copilots	1,000	51.1	55.4	60.4	64.1	67.2	72.4	73.8	67.5
Other flight personnel	1,000	8.2	8.6	10.7	11.1	12.4	10.8	9.6	7.4
Flight attendants	1,000	86.3	86.7	96.2	97.6	105.6	112.6	111.0	98.1
Mechanics	1,000	58.6	50.5	65.5	69.9	70.3	72.1	70.8	61.6
Aircraft and traffic servicing personnel	1,000	243.1	251.1	269.6	290.1	295.6	311.7	303.9	282.4
All other	1,000	93.2	94.8	84.1	88.3	95.3	100.3	102.9	84.4

[1] Includes cash compensation remitted to carriers under the Air Transportation Safety and System Stabilization Act (P.L. 107-42). [2] For definition of mean, see Guide to Tabular Presentation. [3] Includes other types of revenues, not shown separately. [4] Average number of full time equivalents.

Source: Air Transport Association of America, Washington, DC, *Air Transport Annual Report*.

No. 1060. Airline Cost Indexes: 1980 to 2001

[Covers U.S. major and national service carriers. Major carriers have operating revenues of $1 billion or more; nationals have operating revenues from $75 million to $1 billion]

Index	Index (1982=100)								Percent distribution of total operating expenses [1]			
	1980	1985	1990	1995	1998	1999	2000	2001	1980	1990	1995	2001
Composite index	86.8	102.8	122.6	131.3	134.8	137.2	150.1	154.9	100.0	100.0	100.0	100.0
Labor costs:												
Passenger carriers.	85.8	110.5	121.7	155.7	164.5	166.6	176.3	184.8	35.2	31.6	35.5	36.1
Cargo carriers.	78.3	116.0	148.8	151.7	159.1	164.8	170.1	186.4	27.3	30.0	40.0	29.9
Fuel	89.7	79.6	77.2	55.3	49.4	51.4	78.3	78.5	30.0	17.3	12.0	12.8
Aircraft fleet [2] [3]	88.1	123.7	177.0	222.8	228.2	229.8	252.0	265.2	5.2	7.9	9.7	9.4
Interest [2] [4]	88.1	98.0	96.0	93.5	67.4	68.9	59.9	53.2	3.2	2.6	3.1	2.1
Insurance	80.4	155.3	68.2	111.6	64.5	44.3	41.9	68.6	0.3	0.3	0.8	0.5
Maintenance material.	104.9	119.9	190.5	153.4	201.2	187.0	200.5	182.6	2.5	3.4	2.8	2.7
Landing fee	87.2	99.9	139.0	176.6	177.4	186.8	186.4	198.5	1.7	1.8	2.2	1.9
Traffic commissions [2].	75.4	112.9	169.2	139.4	113.0	97.9	80.4	67.4	4.9	9.4	8.6	3.5
Communication [2]	65.8	96.6	111.2	116.0	119.0	138.1	135.8	149.6	1.1	1.4	1.6	1.6
Advertising and promotion [2] . .	67.1	96.2	97.8	63.6	59.2	59.7	57.0	52.8	1.6	2.0	1.5	1.0
Passenger food [2]	90.6	98.9	128.4	110.9	105.2	106.8	104.9	106.1	2.9	3.5	3.4	2.7
All other	86.3	111.3	130.6	147.6	155.0	158.0	161.3	165.1	11.8	19.1	22.7	27.7

[1] Total operating expenses plus interest on long term debt, less depreciation and amortization. [2] Passenger airlines only.
[3] Includes lease, aircraft and engine rentals, depreciation and amortization. [4] Interest on debt.

Source: Air Transport Association of America, Washington, DC, *Annual Report* ; and unpublished data.

No. 1061. Top 40 Airports in 2002—Passengers Enplaned: 1992 and 2002

[In thousands (454,060 represents 454,060,000), except rank. For calendar year. Airports ranked by total passengers enplaned by large certificated air carriers, 2002]

Airport	1992		2002		Airport	1992		2002	
	Total	Rank	Total	Rank		Total	Rank	Total	Rank
All airports.	454,060	(X)	558,705	(X)	Philadelphia, PA	6,968	23	9,788	19
Total top 40	343,114	(X)	428,111	(X)	Boston, (Logan Intl), MA . . .	9,320	13	9,174	20
Atlanta (Hartsfield Intl), GA. .	19,705	3	34,927	1	Baltimore, MD	3,648	35	8,949	21
Chicago (O'Hare Intl), IL . . .	28,958	1	27,029	2	Chicago, IL (Midway).	1,983	56	7,770	22
Dallas/Ft.Worth Intl, TX	24,671	2	22,759	3	Salt Lake City, UT.	6,096	25	7,718	23
Los Angeles Intl, CA	18,395	4	19,397	4	Pittsburgh, PA	8,582	18	7,688	24
Denver Intl, CO	13,595	6	16,077	5	Miami/Ft. Lauderdale, FL . . .	3,499	38	7,676	25
Phoenix Sky Harbor Intl, AZ .	10,787	7	15,952	6	Miami Intl, FL.	9,076	15	7,444	26
Las Vegas (McCarran Intl)					Tampa, FL.	4,398	30	7,317	27
NV.	9,347	12	15,581	7	New York,(JFK), NY	8,468	20	7,293	28
Minneapolis-St. Paul Intl,					Honolulu, HI.	8,742	17	7,169	29
MN.	10,055	11	14,639	8	San Diego (Intl-Lindbergh),				
Detroit (Wayne County), MI .	10,425	10	13,939	9	CA	5,657	26	7,114	30
Houston International, TX. . .	8,358	21	13,343	10	Oakland Metro Intl, CA	3,104	42	5,977	31
Seattle-Tacoma Intl, WA. . . .	8,572	19	12,222	11	Portland, OR	3,588	36	5,795	32
Orlando Intl, FL	8,765	16	12,133	12	Washington (Reagan				
St Louis (Lambert-St.					National), DC	6,837	24	5,715	33
Louis Muni), MO	10,436	9	11,748	13	Kansas City, MO.	3,515	37	5,105	34
San Francisco Intl, CA.	14,208	5	11,253	14	San Jose Int'l, CA.	3,137	41	5,028	35
Newark, NJ	10,479	8	11,138	15	Cleveland (Hopkins Intl), OH.	3,785	34	5,003	36
Charlotte (Douglas Muni),					Washington (Dulles Intl), DC .	4,479	28	4,978	37
NC	8,239	22	10,147	16	Memphis, TN	3,339	39	4,702	38
New York (LaGuardia), NY . .	9,252	14	9,889	17	New Orleans, LA	3,252	40	4,548	39
Cincinatti, OH.	4,916	27	9,882	18	Sacramento, CA.	2,489	49	4,107	40

X Not applicable.
Source: U.S. Bureau of Transportation Statistics, Office of Airline Information, BTS Form 41, Schedule T-3, unpublished data.

No. 1062. Domestic Airline Markets: 2002

[In thousands (3,158 represents 3,158,000). For calendar year. Data are for the 25 top markets and include all commercial airports in each metro area. Data do not include connecting passengers]

Market	Passengers	Market	Passengers
New York to—from Ft. Lauderdale	3,158	Chicago to—from Las Vegas	1,421
New York to—from Chicago	2,707	New York to—from West Palm Beach. . . .	1,410
New York to—from Orlando	2,646	New York to—from San Juan	1,393
New York to—from Los Angeles	2,401	New York to—from Miami.	1,345
New York to—from Atlanta	2,215	Los Angeles to—from Las Vegas	1,330
Honolulu to—from Kahului, Maui	2,019	New York to—from Tampa	1,272
New York to—from Boston	1,637	Honolulu to—from Kona, Hawaii	1,263
New York to—from Washington	1,627	Los Angeles to—from Oakland	1,241
Chicago to—from Los Angeles	1,521	Chicago to—from Orlando	1,210
Dallas/Ft. Worth to—from Houston	1,520	New York to—from Dallas/Ft. Worth	1,209
New York to—from San Francisco	1,500	Chicago to—from Phoenix	1,124
New York to—from Las Vegas.	1,472	Honolulu to—from Hilo, Hawaii	1,103
Honolulu to—from Lihue, Kauai.	1,430		

Source: Air Transport Association of America, Washington, DC, *Annual Report*.

No. 1063. Worldwide Airline Fatalities: 1987 to 2002

[For scheduled air transport operations]

Year	Fatal accidents	Passenger deaths	Death rate [1]	Death rate [2]	Year	Fatal accidents	Passenger deaths	Death rate [1]	Death rate [2]
1987	25	900	0.09	0.06	1995	25	711	0.05	0.03
1988	29	742	0.07	0.04	1996	24	1,146	0.07	0.05
1989	29	879	0.08	0.05	1997	26	929	0.06	0.04
1990	27	544	0.05	0.03	1998	20	904	0.05	0.03
1991	29	638	0.06	0.03	1999	21	499	0.03	0.02
1992	28	1,076	0.09	0.06	2000	18	755	0.04	0.03
1993	33	864	0.07	0.04	2001	13	577	0.03	0.02
1994	27	1,171	0.09	0.06	2002	14	791	0.04	0.03

[1] Rate per 100 million passenger miles flown.   [2] Rate per 100 million passenger kilometers flown.

Source: International Civil Aviation Organization, Montreal, Canada, *Civil Aviation Statistics of the World*, annual.

No. 1064. Airline Passenger Screening Results: 1980 to 2000

[Calendar year data (585 represents 585,000,000)]

Item	1980	1985	1990	1995	1997	1998	1999	2000
Persons screened (mil.)	585	993	1,145	1,263	1,660	1,903	1,754	1,812
WEAPONS DETECTED								
Firearms, total	1,914	2,913	2,549	2,390	2,067	1,515	1,552	1,937
Handguns	1,878	2,823	2,490	2,230	1,905	1,401	1,421	1,643
Long guns	36	90	59	160	162	114	131	294
Other/other dangerous articles	108	74	304	(X)	(X)	(X)	(X)	(X)
Explosive/incendiary devices	8	12	15	(X)	(X)	(X)	(X)	(X)
Persons arrested:								
Carrying firearms/explosives	1,031	1,310	1,336	1,194	924	660	633	600
Giving false information	32	42	18	68	72	86	58	61
Bomb threats received:								
Against airports	1,179	477	448	346	(NA)	(NA)	(NA)	(NA)
Against aircraft	268	153	338	327	(NA)	(NA)	(NA)	(NA)

NA Not available.   X Not applicable.

Source: U.S. Bureau of Transportation Statistics, *National Transportation Statistics, 2002*. See Internet site <http://www.bts.gov/publications/nts/index.html>.

No. 1065. Aircraft Accidents: 1982 to 2002

[For years ending December 31]

Item	Unit	1982	1985	1990	1995	2000	2001	2002, prel.
Air carrier accidents, all services [1]	Number	18	21	24	36	56	45	41
Fatal accidents	Number	5	7	6	3	3	6	-
Fatalities [2]	Number	235	526	39	168	92	531	-
Aboard	Number	223	525	12	162	92	525	-
Rates per 100,000 flight hours:								
Accidents	Rate	0.241	0.241	0.198	0.267	0.306	0.231	0.228
Fatal accidents	Rate	0.057	0.080	0.049	0.022	0.016	0.011	-
Commuter air carrier accidents [3]	Number	26	18	15	12	12	7	8
Fatal accidents	Number	5	7	3	2	1	2	-
Fatalities	Number	14	37	6	9	5	13	-
Aboard	Number	14	36	4	9	5	13	-
Rates per 100,000 flight hours:								
Accidents	Rate	2.000	1.036	0.641	0.457	3.247	2.33	2.595
Fatal accidents	Rate	0.385	0.403	0.128	0.076	0.271	0.666	-
On-demand air taxi accidents [4]	Number	132	157	107	75	80	72	58
Fatal accidents	Number	31	35	29	24	22	18	17
Fatalities	Number	72	76	51	52	71	60	33
Aboard	Number	72	75	49	52	68	59	33
Rates per 100,000 flight hours:								
Accidents	Rate	4.39	6.11	4.76	3.02	2.25	2.27	1.90
Fatal accidents	Rate	1.03	1.36	1.29	0.97	0.62	0.57	0.56
General aviation accidents [5]	Number	3,233	2,739	2,241	2,056	1,837	1,726	1,714
Fatal accidents	Number	591	498	443	413	344	325	343
Fatalities	Number	1,187	956	767	735	595	562	576
Aboard	Number	1,170	945	762	728	584	558	570
Rates per 100,000 flight hours:								
Accidents	Rate	10.90	9.63	7.85	8.21	6.30	6.28	6.56
Fatal accidents	Rate	1.99	1.73	1.55	1.63	1.16	1.18	1.30

- Represents zero.   [1] U.S. air carriers operating under 14 CFR 121. Beginning 1999, includes aircraft with 10 or more seats, previously operating under 14 CFR 135.   [2] Other than persons aboard aircraft who were killed, fatalities resulting from the September 11, 2001 terrorist acts are excluded.   [3] All scheduled service of U.S. air carriers operating under 14 CFR 135. Beginning 1999, only aircraft with fewer than 10 seats.   [4] All nonscheduled service of U.S. air carriers operating under 14 CFR 135.   [5] U.S. civil registered aircraft not operated under 14 CFR 121 or 135.

Source: U.S. National Transportation Safety Board, "Aviation Accident Statistics," Internet site - http://www.ntsb.gov/aviation/stats.htm > (accessed 28 May 2002).

No. 1066. On-Time Flight Arrivals and Departures at Major U.S. Airports: 2002

[In percent. Quarterly, based on gate arrival and departure times for domestic scheduled operations of U.S. major airlines. All U.S. airlines with 1 percent or more of total U.S. domestic scheduled airline passenger revenues are required to report on-time data. A flight is considered on time if it operated less than 15 minutes after the scheduled time shown in the carrier's computerized reservation system. Cancelled and diverted flights are considered late. See source for data on individual airlines]

Airport	On-time arrivals				On-time departures			
	1st qtr.	2d qtr.	3d qtr.	4th qtr.	1st qtr.	2d qtr.	3d qtr.	4th qtr.
Total, all airports	79.8	81.5	78.8	82.7	83.2	85.0	81.4	85.5
Total major airports	78.8	80.4	77.7	82.3	82.8	84.7	81.2	85.6
Atlanta, Hartsfield International	75.3	77.0	78.6	75.4	79.5	84.9	82.8	82.0
Baltimore/Washington International	82.2	82.3	76.5	84.8	81.4	79.4	74.1	82.1
Boston, Logan International	83.1	83.0	78.2	82.3	85.2	84.4	81.0	83.7
Charlotte Douglas	82.5	83.7	84.4	85.7	82.8	82.7	82.7	87.2
Chicago Midway	82.9	83.2	78.2	84.1	77.2	74.5	65.8	78.2
Chicago, O'Hare	76.4	79.1	73.1	81.5	80.0	82.8	75.5	84.3
Cincinnati International	78.5	79.1	80.7	85.2	84.8	85.9	84.8	87.0
Dallas/Ft. Worth Regional	81.8	83.2	82.5	85.7	82.2	84.1	82.8	87.0
Denver International	81.6	85.9	83.9	89.6	84.3	89.9	84.3	91.3
Detroit, Metro Wayne	79.2	83.5	79.4	85.8	72.4	79.1	75.8	84.5
Fort Lauderdale	76.8	80.9	74.7	81.7	83.5	86.2	82.2	86.5
Houston George Bush	86.2	87.3	82.0	81.3	90.0	91.3	86.9	88.0
Las Vegas, McCarran International	77.8	79.5	80.7	81.9	80.0	81.7	79.5	82.8
Los Angeles International	81.9	81.7	83.0	82.8	84.7	85.7	83.1	86.1
Miami International	79.8	84.5	77.1	82.3	85.0	87.7	80.3	87.4
Minneapolis/St. Paul International	81.3	82.6	79.0	85.4	81.7	84.8	79.5	88.0
Newark International	82.0	82.1	78.0	80.1	87.7	88.7	84.8	86.6
New York, Kennedy International	80.3	78.6	71.0	80.4	81.5	85.3	78.0	84.0
New York, LaGuardia	81.6	74.3	74.5	79.2	87.0	83.6	81.6	85.0
Orlando International	81.1	83.4	77.6	84.5	86.8	88.4	83.0	88.9
Philadelphia International	74.9	75.8	75.2	82.2	79.1	79.2	78.9	83.2
Phoenix, Sky Harbor International	82.7	84.2	82.7	81.1	81.5	83.4	79.1	81.0
Pittsburgh, Greater International	82.8	82.8	82.3	87.1	86.0	85.3	84.7	88.4
Portland International	78.1	83.6	79.4	83.9	83.9	88.2	82.7	86.3
Ronald Reagan National	84.8	82.1	79.6	86.0	89.9	87.4	85.9	89.1
St. Louis, Lambert	82.6	83.1	81.4	86.5	85.2	85.4	82.7	89.3
Salt Lake City International	76.9	82.9	82.8	86.0	82.7	88.0	87.1	89.7
San Diego International, Lindbergh	80.6	82.4	83.7	81.6	83.8	85.0	83.4	84.6
San Francisco International	74.2	75.9	78.6	79.1	85.3	88.6	86.8	86.7
Seattle-Tacoma International	74.0	80.4	77.0	80.7	80.3	85.1	80.2	84.5
Tampa International	78.3	83.7	77.8	83.6	83.9	87.4	82.1	87.7
Washington/Dulles	81.9	84.5	79.9	86.7	87.1	88.2	84.0	88.8

Source: U.S. Department of Transportation, Aviation Consumer Protection Division, *Air Travel Consumer Report*, monthly. See Internet site <http://airconsumer.ost.dot.gov>.

No. 1067. Consumer Complaints Against U.S. Airlines: 1990 to 2002

[Calendar year data. Represents complaints filed by consumers to the U.S. Department of Transportation, Aviation Consumer Protection Division, regarding service problems with air carrier personnel. See source for data on individual airlines]

Complaint category	1990	1995	1996	1997	1998	1999	2000	2001	2002
Total	7,703	4,629	5,782	6,394	7,980	17,345	20,564	14,076	7,698
Flight problems [1]	3,034	1,133	1,628	1,699	2,270	6,449	8,698	5,048	1,808
Customer service [2]	758	667	999	1,418	1,716	3,657	4,074	2,531	1,481
Baggage	1,329	628	882	826	1,105	2,351	2,753	1,965	1,081
Ticketing/boarding [3]	624	666	857	904	805	1,329	1,405	1,310	897
Refunds	701	576	521	531	601	935	803	942	736
Fares [4]	312	185	180	195	276	584	708	568	436
Disability [5]	(NA)	(NA)	(NA)	(NA)	331	520	612	457	420
Oversales [6]	399	263	353	414	387	673	759	539	363
Discrimination [7]	(NA)	(NA)	(NA)	(NA)	(NA)	(NA)	(NA)	164	174
Advertising	96	66	61	57	39	57	42	42	43
Tours	29	18	16	13	23	28	25	11	([8])
Animals	(NA)	(NA)	(NA)	(NA)	(NA)	(NA)	1	6	-
Smoking	74	15	13	5	([9])	([9])	([9])	([9])	([9])
Credit	5	4	3	1	([9])	([9])	([9])	([9])	([9])
Other	342	408	269	331	427	762	684	493	259

- Represents zero. NA Not available. [1] Cancellations, delays, etc. from schedule. [2] Unhelpful employees, inadequate meals or cabin service, treatment of delayed passengers. [3] Errors in reservations and ticketing; problems in making reservations and obtaining tickets. [4] Incorrect or incomplete information about fares, discount fare conditions, and availability, etc. [5] Prior to 1998, included in ticketing/boarding. [6] All bumping problems, whether or not airline complied with DOT regulations. [7] Allegations of discrimination by airlines due to factors other than disability, such as race, religion, national origin or sex. [8] Included in "Other" beginning 2002. [9] Included in "Other" beginning 1998.

Source: U.S. Department of Transportation, Aviation Consumer Protection Division, *Air Travel Consumer Report*, monthly. See Internet site <http://airconsumer.ost.dot.gov>.

No. 1068. Commuter/Regional Airline Operations—Summary: 1980 to 2001

[Calendar year data (14.8 represents 14,800,000). Commuter/regional airlines operate primarily aircraft of predominately 75 passengers or less and 18,000 pounds of payload capacity serving short haul and small community markets. Represents operations within all North America by U.S. Regional Carriers. Averages are means. For definition of mean, see Guide to Tabular Presentation]

Item	Unit	1980	1985	1990	1995	1998	1999	2000	2001
Passenger carriers operating	Number	214	179	150	124	97	97	94	91
Passengers enplaned	Millions	14.8	[1]26.0	42.1	57.2	71.1	78.1	84.6	82.8
Average passengers enplaned per carrier	1,000	69.2	152.4	277.5	461.4	733.0	804.7	830.4	910.2
Revenue passenger miles (RPM)	Billions	1.92	[1]4.41	7.61	12.75	17.42	20.81	25.27	25.74
Average RPMs per carrier	Millions	8.97	[1]24.64	50.75	102.80	179.64	214.49	268.83	282.83
Airports served	Number	732	854	811	780	773	734	729	726
Average trip length	Miles	129	173	183	223	245	267	299	311
Passenger aircraft operated	Number	1,339	1,745	1,917	2,138	2,150	2,187	2,271	2,323
Average seating capacity (seats)	Number	13.9	19.2	22.1	24.6	27.7	29.8	31.7	33.5
Fleet flying hours [2]	1,000	1,740	2,854	3,447	4,659	4,631	5,058	5,362	5,161
Average annual utilization per aircraft	Hours	1,299	1,635	1,798	2,179	2,154	2,313	2,368	2,222

[1] Adjusted to exclude a merger in 1986. [2] Prior to 1995, utilization results reflected airborne rather than block hours.

Source: Regional Airline Association and AvStat Associates, Washington, DC, *Annual Report of the Regional Airline Industry* (copyright).

No. 1069. Airports, Aircraft, and Airmen: 1980 to 2001

[As of Dec. 31 or for years ending Dec. 31]

Item	1980	1985	1990	1995	1998	1999	2000	2001
Airports, total [1]	15,161	16,319	17,490	18,224	18,770	19,098	19,281	19,306
Public	4,814	5,858	5,589	5,415	5,352	5,324	5,317	5,315
Percent—With lighted runways	66.2	68.1	71.4	74.3	74.8	76.1	75.9	75.9
With paved runways	72.3	66.7	70.7	73.3	74.2	74.2	74.3	74.3
Private	10,347	10,461	11,901	12,809	13,418	13,774	13,964	13,990
Percent—With lighted runways	15.2	9.1	7.0	6.4	6.3	6.7	7.2	7.3
With paved runways	13.3	17.4	31.5	33.0	33.2	31.8	32.0	32.0
Certificated [2]	730	700	680	667	660	655	651	635
Civil	(X)	(X)	(X)	572	566	565	563	562
Civil military	(X)	(X)	(X)	95	94	90	88	73
General aviation	14,431	15,619	16,810	17,557	18,110	18,443	18,630	18,760
Active air carrier fleet [3]	3,808	4,678	6,083	7,411	8,111	8,228	7,935	(NA)
Fixed wing	3,803	4,673	6,072	7,293	7,994	8,106	7,898	(NA)
Helicopter	2	5	11	118	117	122	37	(NA)
General aviation fleet [4]	211,043	196,500	198,000	188,089	204,710	219,464	217,533	(NA)
Fixed-wing	200,097	184,700	184,500	162,342	175,203	184,724	183,277	(NA)
Turbojet	2,992	4,100	4,100	4,559	6,066	7,120	7,001	(NA)
Turboprop	4,090	5,000	5,300	4,995	6,174	5,680	5,763	(NA)
Piston	193,014	175,600	175,200	152,788	162,963	171,924	170,513	(NA)
Rotocraft	6,001	6,000	6,900	5,830	7,425	7,448	7,150	(NA)
Other	4,945	5,800	6,600	4,741	5,580	6,766	6,701	(NA)
Gliders	(NA)	(NA)	(NA)	2,182	2,105	2,041	2,041	(NA)
Lighter than air	(NA)	(NA)	(NA)	2,559	3,475	4,725	4,660	(NA)
Experimental	(NA)	(NA)	(NA)	15,176	16,503	20,528	20,406	(NA)
Airman certificates held: [5]								
Pilot, total	827,071	709,540	702,659	639,184	618,298	635,472	625,581	612,274
Women	52,902	43,082	40,515	38,032	35,762	37,373	36,757	34,257
Student	199,833	146,652	128,663	101,279	97,736	97,359	93,064	86,731
Recreational	(NA)	(NA)	87	232	305	343	340	316
Airplane:								
Private	357,479	311,086	299,111	261,399	247,226	258,749	251,561	243,823
Commercial	183,442	151,632	149,666	133,980	122,053	124,261	121,858	120,502
Air transport	69,569	82,740	107,732	123,877	134,612	137,642	141,596	144,702
Rotocraft only [6]	6,030	8,123	9,567	7,183	6,964	7,728	7,775	7,727
Glider only	7,039	8,168	7,833	11,234	9,402	9,390	9,387	8,473
Flight instructor certificates	60,440	58,940	63,775	77,613	79,171	79,694	80,931	82,875
Instrument ratings	260,462	258,559	297,073	298,798	300,183	308,951	311,944	315,276
Nonpilot [7]	368,356	395,139	492,237	651,341	549,588	538,264	547,453	513,100
Mechanic	250,157	274,100	344,282	405,294	336,670	340,402	344,434	310,850
Repairmen	(NA)	(NA)	(NA)	61,233	52,909	35,989	38,208	40,085
Parachute rigger	9,547	9,395	10,094	11,824	10,459	10,447	10,477	7,927
Ground instructor	61,550	58,214	66,882	96,165	70,334	71,238	72,326	72,261
Dispatcher	6,799	8,511	11,002	15,642	14,804	15,655	16,340	16,070
Flight navigator	1,936	1,542	1,290	916	712	642	570	509
Flight engineer	38,367	43,377	58,687	60,267	63,700	63,891	65,098	65,398

NA Not available. X Not applicable. [1] Existing airports, heliports, seaplane bases, etc. recorded with FAA. Includes military airports with joint civil and military use. Includes U.S. outlying areas. Airport-type definitions: Public—publicly owned and under control of a public agency; private—owned by a private individual or corporation. May or may not be open for public use. [2] Certificated airports serve air-carriers with aircraft seating more that 30 passengers. [3] Air-carrier aircraft are aircraft carrying passengers or cargo for hire under 14 CFR 121 (large aircraft—more than 30 seats) and 14 CFR 135 (small aircraft— 30 seats or fewer). [4] Beginning 1995 excludes commuters. [5] Source: U.S. Federal Aviation Administration. See Internet site <http://api.hq.faa.gov/civilair/index.htm> for data beginning 1990 (accessed 19 June 2002). Prior years in the *Statistical Handbook of Aviation*, annual. [6] Data for 1980 and 1985 are for helicopters only. [7] All certificates on record. No medical examination required.

Source: Except as noted, U.S. Bureau of Transportation Statistics, *National Transportation Statistics, 2002*. See Internet site <http://www.bts.gov/publications/nts/index.html>.

Transportation 687

No. 1070. Freight Carried on Major U.S. Waterways: 1980 to 2001

[In millions of tons (4.0 represents 4,000,000)]

Item	1980	1985	1990	1995	1997	1998	1999	2000	2001
Atlantic intracoastal waterway	4.0	3.1	4.2	3.5	3.6	3.8	3.4	3.1	2.5
Great Lakes	183.5	148.1	167.1	177.7	188.6	192.2	182.9	187.5	171.4
Gulf intracoastal waterway	94.5	102.5	115.5	117.9	118.1	113.8	109.6	113.6	112.2
Mississippi River system [1]	584.2	527.8	659.6	710.1	707.1	708.3	716.9	715.5	714.8
Mississippi River mainstem	441.5	384.0	475.6	520.2	504.7	504.4	512.3	515.6	504.2
Ohio River system [2]	179.3	203.9	260.0	267.6	274.9	278.8	277.9	274.4	281.8
Columbia River	49.2	42.4	51.4	57.1	52.7	49.1	50.7	55.2	50.3
Snake River	5.1	3.5	4.8	6.8	6.1	5.8	5.8	6.7	5.6

[1] Main channels and all tributaries of the Mississippi, Illinois, Missouri, and Ohio Rivers. [2] Main channels and all navigable tributaries and embayments of the Ohio, Tennessee, and Cumberland Rivers.

Source: U.S. Army Corps of Engineers, *Waterborne Commerce of the United States*, annual.

No. 1071. Waterborne Commerce by Type of Commodity: 1990 to 2001

[In millions of short tons (2,163.9 represents 2,163,900,000). Domestic trade includes all commercial movements between United States ports and on inland rivers, Great Lakes, canals, and connecting channels of the United States, Puerto Rico, and Virgin Islands]

Commodity	1990	1995	2000	2001 Total	2001 Domestic	2001 Foreign imports	2001 Foreign exports
Total [1]	2,163.9	2,240.4	2,424.6	2,386.8	1,042.5	945.1	399.0
Coal	339.9	324.5	297.0	303.3	227.7	19.9	55.8
Petroleum and petroleum products	923.2	907.1	1,044.0	1,048.6	369.7	620.6	58.3
Crude petroleum	485.7	504.6	571.4	573.6	86.0	486.2	1.3
Petroleum products [1]	437.5	402.5	472.4	475.0	283.8	134.3	57.0
Gasoline	116.9	114.4	125.2	127.7	93.1	27.7	6.9
Distillate fuel oil	77.4	76.7	91.7	91.1	65.6	20.6	5.0
Residual fuel oil	145.2	111.9	131.6	133.7	78.7	40.9	14.0
Chemicals and related products	123.8	153.7	172.4	169.7	71.1	43.8	54.7
Fertilizers	32.2	35.7	35.1	39.0	14.2	11.3	13.6
Other chemicals and related products	91.6	118.0	137.3	130.6	56.9	32.6	41.2
Crude material, inedible [1]	374.7	381.7	380.3	354.0	213.7	95.0	45.3
Forest products, wood and chips	55.7	47.2	33.1	27.1	10.2	6.1	10.7
Pulp and waste paper	11.8	14.9	13.6	13.8	0.2	1.2	12.5
Soil, sand, gravel, rock, and stone	144.2	152.5	165.0	162.6	129.3	29.8	3.5
Limestone	43.1	54.0	67.4	68.9	56.0	10.4	2.4
Phosphate rock	14.6	10.7	3.4	1.7	1.7	-	-
Sand & gravel	62.9	77.0	79.0	77.5	68.5	8.1	0.9
Iron ore and scrap	101.7	104.9	97.9	76.8	54.0	13.4	9.3
Marine shells	2.1	0.5	0.3	0.3	0.2	-	-
Nonferrous ores and scrap	31.2	27.9	29.2	25.7	6.2	17.1	2.4
Sulphur, clay and salt	8.2	23.4	11.3	10.3	1.5	3.9	4.9
Slag	2.3	1.9	4.0	4.4	1.7	2.6	0.1
Other nonmetal minerals	17.5	8.4	25.9	33.1	10.5	20.9	1.8
Primary manufactured goods [1]	76.0	106.3	153.0	137.1	40.3	82.9	13.9
Papers products	10.7	13.1	12.1	11.9	0.4	5.4	6.1
Lime, cement and glass	28.3	33.9	55.9	52.1	19.9	31.0	1.3
Primary iron and steel products	25.1	44.1	57.1	46.6	13.9	31.6	1.0
Primary nonferrous metal products	8.9	12.3	25.5	23.8	6.1	12.6	5.1
Primary wood products	3.0	2.9	2.5	2.7	0.1	2.3	0.3
Food and farm products [1]	267.5	303.2	283.3	281.9	96.5	30.8	154.6
Fish	3.2	3.6	2.4	2.4	0.1	1.3	1.0
Grain [1]	157.3	167.9	145.2	140.7	54.8	1.6	84.3
Corn	96.1	105.0	88.2	87.9	39.0	0.1	48.8
Wheat	44.5	48.5	43.4	40.3	12.1	0.2	28.0
Oilseeds	36.0	46.1	57.6	61.5	25.2	0.6	35.6
Soybeans	32.2	42.0	47.3	49.4	20.0	-	29.4
Vegetables products	6.7	9.0	8.9	8.8	1.2	3.5	3.9
Processed grain and animal feed	28.2	33.0	23.1	22.4	7.7	1.0	13.9
Other agricultural products	36.3	43.5	46.1	46.1	7.3	23.0	15.8
All manufacturing equip, machinery and products	42.2	57.0	83.6	80.3	19.9	47.7	12.8
Waste and scrap, nec.	13.2	5.4	4.3	3.5	3.5	-	-
Unknown or not elsewhere classified	3.4	1.6	6.8	8.2	0.1	4.4	3.7

- Represents or rounds to zero. [1] Includes categories not shown separately.

Source: U.S. Army Corps of Engineers, *Waterborne Commerce of the United States*, annual.

No. 1072. Cargo-Carrying U.S.-Flag Fleet by Area of Operation: 2002

[Tons in thousands of metric tons (30,282 represents 30,282,000. As of January 1. One ton equals 100 cubic feet of space. Represents active vessels]

Area of operation	Total fleet Number	Total fleet Tons	Liquid carriers Number	Liquid carriers Tons	Dry bulk carriers Number	Dry bulk carriers Tons	Containerships Number	Containerships Tons	Other freighters [1] Number	Other freighters [1] Tons
VESSELS OF 1,000 GROSS TONS AND OVER										
Grand total	3,166	30,282	1,954	16,888	627	5,132	117	3,206	468	5,056
Foreign waterborne trade [2]	347	6,672	73	1,642	169	1,659	61	2,373	44	998
Domestic trade	2,639	20,053	1,853	14,362	458	3,473	51	747	277	1,471
Coastal	953	13,190	511	9,935	209	1,387	51	747	182	1,121
Inland waterway	1,634	5,297	1,339	4,410	206	572	-	-	89	315
Great Lakes	52	1,566	3	17	43	1,514	-	-	6	35
Government	180	3,557	28	884	-	-	5	86	147	2,587
Total self-propelled	489	17,567	137	8,393	60	2,363	90	3,050	202	3,761
Foreign waterborne trade [2]	150	5,662	24	1,332	22	979	61	2,373	43	978
Domestic trade	159	8,348	85	6,177	38	1,384	24	591	12	196
Coastal	121	6,976	85	6,177	1	33	24	591	11	175
Inland waterway	-	-	-	-	-	-	-	-	-	-
Great Lakes	38	1,372	-	-	37	1,351	-	-	1	21
Government	180	3,557	28	884	-	-	5	86	147	2,587
Total non-self-propelled [3]	2,677	12,715	1,817	8,495	567	2,769	27	156	266	1,295
Foreign waterborne trade [2]	197	1,010	49	310	147	680	-	-	1	20
Domestic trade	2,480	11,705	1,768	8,185	420	2,089	27	156	265	1,275
Coastal	832	6,214	426	3,758	208	1,354	27	156	171	946
Inland waterway	1,634	5,297	1,339	4,410	206	572	-	-	89	315
Great Lakes	14	194	3	17	6	163	-	-	5	14
VESSELS LESS THAN 1,000 GROSS TONS										
Grand total	27,552	40,938	1,767	2,689	21,705	34,449	-	-	4,080	3,800
Foreign waterborne trade [2]	101	51	6	4	95	47	-	-	-	-
Domestic trade	27,451	40,887	1,761	2,685	21,610	34,402	-	-	4,080	3,800
Coastal	1,847	1,432	110	117	380	549	-	-	1,357	766
Inland waterway	25,493	39,301	1,647	2,565	21,211	33,828	-	-	2,635	2,908
Great Lakes	111	154	4	3	19	25	-	-	88	126
Total self-propelled	111	55	20	14	3	2	-	-	88	39
Domestic trade	111	55	20	14	3	2	-	-	88	39
Coastal	75	31	17	10	-	-	-	-	58	21
Inland waterway	27	21	1	3	-	-	-	-	26	18
Great Lakes	9	3	2	1	3	2	-	-	4	-
Total non-self-propelled	27,441	40,883	1,747	2,675	21,702	34,447	-	-	3,992	3,761
Foreign waterborne trade [2]	101	51	6	4	95	47	-	-	-	-
Domestic trade	27,340	40,832	1,741	2,671	21,607	34,400	-	-	3,992	3,761
Coastal	1,772	1,401	93	107	380	549	-	-	1,299	745
Inland waterway	25,466	39,280	1,646	2,562	21,211	33,828	-	-	2,609	2,890
Great Lakes	102	151	2	2	16	23	-	-	84	126

- Represents zero. [1] Includes general cargo, ro-ro (roll-on, roll-off), multipurpose, lighter aboard ship (LASH) vessels, and deck barges. Excludes offshore supply vessels. [2] Includes U.S./Canada TransLakes. [3] Includes Integrated Tug Barge (ITB) Units.

Source: U.S. Maritime Administration, Office of Statistical & Economic Analysis; adapted from Corps of Engineers, Lloyds Maritime Information Service, U.S. Coast Guard and Customs Service data.

No. 1073. Jobs on U.S. Deep Sea Commercial Fleet and Typical Basic Monthly Wage for Able-Bodied Seamen: 1980 to 2002

[Employment in thousands (19.6 represents 19,600)]

Year	Employment [1]	Year	Employment [1]	Year	East coast wage rate [2]	West coast wage rate [2]	Year	East coast wage rate [2]	West coast wage rate [2]
1980.....	19.6	1997.....	8.6	1980.....	967	1,414	1997.....	2,094	2,879
1985.....	13.1	1998.....	7.9	1985.....	1,419	2,029	1998.....	2,178	2,994
1990.....	11.1	1999.....	7.3	1990.....	1,505	2,218	1999.....	2,265	3,114
1994.....	9.1	2000.....	6.6	1994.....	1,790	2,536	2000.....	2,453	3,114
1995.....	7.9	2001.....	(NA)	1995.....	1,918	2,637	2001.....	(NA)	(NA)
1996.....	7.5	2002.....	8.5	1996.....	2,014	2,769	2002.....	(NA)	(NA)

NA Not available. [1] As of Sept. 30, except 2002 as of December. Estimates of personnel employed on merchant ships, 1,000 gross tons and over. Excludes vessels on inland waterways, Great Lakes, and those owned by, or operated for, U.S. Army and Navy, and special types such as cable ships, tugs, etc. [2] As of January. Basic monthly wage, over and above subsistence (board and room); excludes overtime and fringe pay benefits. West coast incorporates extra pay for Saturdays and Sundays at sea into base wages but east coast does not.

Source: U.S. Maritime Administration, Office of Sealift Support.

No. 1074. Selected U.S. Ports by Tons of Traffic: 2001

[In thousands of short tons, except rank (16,769 represents 16,079,000). For calendar year. Represents tons of cargo shipped from or received by the specified port. Excludes cargo carried on general ferries; coal and petroleum products loaded from shore facilities directly onto bunkers of vessels for fuel; and amounts of less than 100 tons of government owned equipment in support of Corps projects]

Port name	Rank	Total	Foreign Total	Foreign Inbound	Foreign Outbound	Domestic
Anacortes, WA............................	41	16,769	2,010	1,076	934	14,759
Ashtabula, OH............................	50	10,934	5,814	797	5,016	5,120
Baltimore, MD............................	19	42,072	25,350	18,268	7,082	16,722
Baton Rouge, LA..........................	10	61,415	20,651	14,219	6,432	40,765
Beaumont, TX............................	5	79,131	61,984	56,720	5,263	17,147
Boston, MA...............................	33	20,581	12,430	11,791	639	8,151
Charleston, SC...........................	27	23,250	17,127	11,116	6,011	6,123
Chicago, IL..............................	29	21,976	2,623	2,055	568	19,353
Cincinnati, OH...........................	43	14,099	-	-	-	14,099
Cleveland, OH...........................	48	11,938	2,734	2,430	304	9,204
Conneaut, OH...........................	52	10,485	6,645	180	6,466	3,840
Corpus Christi, TX.......................	6	77,576	53,921	44,987	8,934	23,654
Detroit, MI...............................	39	16,991	4,727	4,465	261	12,264
Duluth-Superior, MN and WI.............	20	39,811	13,276	746	12,529	26,535
Freeport, TX.............................	24	30,143	24,894	22,645	2,249	5,249
Honolulu, HI.............................	42	16,562	4,790	4,270	520	11,772
Houston, TX.............................	2	185,050	120,593	85,485	35,108	64,457
Huntington - Tristate, WV, OH, KY........	7	76,670	-	-	-	76,670
Indiana Harbor, IN.......................	45	13,579	743	743	-	12,837
Jacksonville, FL..........................	38	17,809	8,943	8,047	897	8,866
Lake Charles, LA.........................	13	52,845	31,920	27,743	4,177	20,925
Long Beach, CA..........................	8	67,644	51,561	37,740	13,821	16,083
Los Angeles, CA..........................	14	51,396	44,966	30,317	14,649	6,430
Louisville, KY............................	55	9,087	-	-	-	9,087
Marcus Hook, PA.........................	37	19,124	8,246	8,231	15	10,878
Memphis, TN.............................	40	16,907	-	-	-	16,907
Mobile, AL...............................	16	48,116	27,981	17,723	10,258	20,135
New Haven, CT...........................	53	9,876	3,123	3,091	32	6,753
New Orleans, LA..........................	4	85,628	50,297	27,074	23,222	35,332
New York, NY and NJ.....................	3	137,484	67,267	59,226	8,041	70,218
Newport News, VA.......................	44	13,860	6,678	1,581	5,098	7,182
Norfolk Harbor, VA.......................	21	37,310	26,978	7,306	19,672	10,332
Oakland, CA..............................	47	12,273	10,717	3,850	6,868	1,555
Pascagoula, MS..........................	25	29,549	18,486	15,290	3,196	11,063
Paulsboro, NJ............................	31	21,261	12,919	12,811	107	8,342
Philadelphia, PA..........................	17	46,372	32,943	32,420	523	13,429
Pittsburgh, PA............................	12	53,009	-	-	-	53,009
Plaquemines, LA, Port of.................	11	60,694	23,354	14,931	8,423	37,340
Port Arthur, TX...........................	28	22,802	15,130	12,531	2,599	7,672
Port Everglades, FL......................	30	21,915	9,618	7,430	2,188	12,297
Portland, ME.............................	26	28,492	26,449	26,249	200	2,043
Portland, OR.............................	23	31,339	17,012	4,149	12,863	14,328
Presque Isle, MI..........................	54	9,475	1,841	62	1,779	7,634
Richmond, CA............................	32	21,220	9,993	8,871	1,122	11,227
San Juan, PR.............................	46	12,805	5,213	4,757	455	7,592
Savannah, GA............................	36	19,392	16,931	9,648	7,283	2,461
Seattle, WA...............................	34	20,546	14,921	7,696	7,225	5,626
South Louisiana, LA, Port of.............	1	212,565	95,681	32,540	63,140	116,884
St. Louis, MO and IL......................	22	34,432	-	-	-	34,432
Tacoma, WA..............................	35	20,523	12,376	3,993	8,383	8,147
Tampa, FL................................	18	45,794	17,445	8,956	8,489	28,349
Texas City, TX............................	9	62,270	44,130	40,304	3,826	18,141
Toledo, OH...............................	51	10,535	6,004	1,378	4,626	4,531
Two Harbors, MN.........................	49	11,875	-	-	-	11,875
Valdez, AK................................	15	50,977	3	-	3	50,975

- Represents zero.
Source: U.S. Army Corps of Engineers, *Waterborne Commerce of the United States*, 2001. See Internet site <http://www.iwr.usace.army.mil /ndc/>.

No. 1075. Highway Mileage—Urban and Rural by Ownership: 1980 to 2001

[In thousands (3,955 represents 3,955,000). As of Dec. 31. Includes Puerto Rico beginning 1997]

Type and control	1980	1985	1990	1995	1997	1998	1999	2000	2001
Total mileage [1]	[2]3,955	3,862	3,880	3,912	3,959	3,920	3,932	3,951	3,963
Urban mileage [3]	624	691	757	819	843	849	853	859	884
Under state control	79	111	96	112	114	111	111	112	110
Under local control	543	578	661	706	728	736	740	746	771
Rural mileage	[2]3,331	3,171	3,123	3,093	3,116	3,072	3,079	3,092	3,079
Under state control	702	773	703	691	695	663	663	664	665
Under local control	2,270	2,173	2,242	2,231	2,254	2,291	2,299	2,311	2,295
Under federal control	262	225	178	170	167	118	117	117	119

[1] Beginning 1985, includes only public road mileage as defined 23 USC 402. [2] Includes 98,000 miles of nonpublic road mileage previously contained in other rural categories. [3] Includes a small amount of road owned by the federal government, such as roads in federal parks that are not part of a state or local highway system.

Source: U.S. Federal Highway Administration, *Highway Statistics*, annual. See Internet site <http://www.fhwa.dot.gov/policy/ohpi/hss/hsspubs.htm>.

No. 1076. Highway Mileage—Functional Systems and Urban/Rural: 2001

[As of Dec. 31. Excludes Puerto Rico. For definition of functional systems see text, this section]

State	Total	Interstate	Other freeways and expressways	Arterial	Collector	Local	Urban	Rural
U.S	3,948,335	46,467	9,126	379,790	793,374	2,719,578	877,004	3,071,331
AL	94,439	906	21	8,815	20,523	64,174	20,705	73,734
AK	13,630	1,083	-	1,511	2,736	8,300	1,814	11,816
AZ	55,245	1,168	143	4,716	8,515	40,703	18,005	37,240
AR	98,133	656	86	6,830	20,114	70,447	10,797	87,336
CA	168,771	2,455	1,372	26,862	32,318	105,764	85,485	83,286
CO	85,853	954	225	8,209	16,588	59,877	14,764	71,089
CT	20,908	346	197	2,841	3,011	14,513	11,836	9,072
DE	5,814	41	14	625	939	4,195	2,004	3,810
DC	1,533	15	21	264	152	1,081	1,533	-
FL	117,302	1,472	455	12,169	14,220	88,986	67,889	49,413
GA	115,533	1,245	120	13,137	23,279	77,752	28,153	87,380
HI	4,277	55	34	753	820	2,615	2,102	2,175
ID	46,308	611	-	3,796	9,840	32,061	4,194	42,114
IL	138,359	2,169	88	13,990	21,629	100,483	36,747	101,612
IN	94,037	1,169	136	7,959	22,662	62,111	20,175	73,862
IA	113,439	782	-	9,553	31,546	71,558	9,928	103,511
KS	134,726	874	133	9,191	33,350	91,178	10,426	124,300
KY	78,912	762	90	5,527	17,601	54,932	11,807	67,105
LA	60,829	894	48	5,300	12,543	42,044	13,939	46,890
ME	22,671	367	18	2,291	5,973	14,022	2,630	20,041
MD	30,623	481	234	3,573	5,022	21,313	14,506	16,117
MA	35,410	566	211	5,620	5,489	23,524	23,153	12,257
MI	121,789	1,241	222	12,261	25,722	82,343	30,101	91,688
MN	132,279	912	150	12,770	29,565	88,882	16,217	116,062
MS	73,700	685	41	7,107	15,517	50,350	8,104	65,596
MO	124,325	1,180	319	9,403	24,978	88,445	17,614	106,711
MT	69,503	1,191	-	6,010	16,380	45,922	2,603	66,900
NE	92,765	482	17	7,903	20,787	63,576	5,198	87,567
NV	38,656	560	50	2,867	5,222	29,957	5,666	32,990
NH	15,508	224	40	1,552	2,722	10,970	2,996	12,512
NJ	36,175	431	313	5,358	4,554	25,519	24,203	11,972
NM	59,884	1,000	11	4,574	6,936	47,363	5,964	53,920
NY	112,960	1,674	793	13,505	20,559	76,429	41,121	71,839
NC	101,195	1,025	280	8,936	17,792	73,162	23,783	77,412
ND	86,590	572	-	5,872	11,569	68,577	1,834	84,756
OH	117,268	1,573	394	10,636	22,112	82,553	33,602	83,666
OK	112,696	930	144	7,860	25,376	78,386	13,367	99,329
OR	66,784	727	55	6,688	17,336	41,978	11,164	55,620
PA	119,986	1,758	490	13,160	19,788	84,790	34,526	85,460
RI	6,051	70	69	845	856	4,211	4,718	1,333
SC	66,167	829	71	6,864	13,378	45,025	10,667	55,500
SD	83,560	678	-	6,299	19,280	57,303	2,106	81,454
TN	87,825	1,073	121	8,740	18,079	59,812	17,852	69,973
TX	300,767	3,234	1,129	28,343	63,134	204,927	82,231	218,536
UT	42,207	938	8	3,337	7,824	30,100	7,778	34,429
VT	14,289	320	19	1,298	3,123	9,529	1,383	12,906
VA	70,717	1,118	224	8,176	14,116	47,083	19,063	51,654
WA	80,984	764	314	7,293	16,798	55,815	18,190	62,794
WV	36,997	549	9	3,237	8,783	24,419	3,119	33,878
WI	112,664	745	194	11,693	21,527	78,505	16,776	95,888
WY	27,292	913	3	3,671	10,691	12,014	2,466	24,826

- Represents zero.

Source: U.S. Federal Highway Administration, *Highway Statistics*, annual. See Internet site <http://www.fhwa.dot.gov/policy/ohpi/hss/hsspubs.htm>.

No. 1077. Commodity Shipments—Value, Tons, and Ton-Miles: 1993 and 1997

[Based on the 1997 Economic Census; see Appendix III]

Mode of transportation	Value (mil. dol.) 1993	Value (mil. dol.) 1997	Tons (1,000) 1993	Tons (1,000) 1997	Ton-miles (mil.) 1993	Ton-miles (mil.) 1997
All modes	5,846,334	6,943,988	9,688,493	11,089,733	2,420,915	2,661,363
Single modes	4,941,452	5,719,558	8,922,286	10,436,538	2,136,873	2,383,473
Truck [1]	4,403,494	4,981,531	6,385,915	7,700,675	869,536	1,023,506
For-hire truck	2,625,093	2,901,345	2,808,279	3,402,605	629,000	741,117
Private truck	1,755,837	2,036,528	3,543,513	4,137,294	235,897	268,592
Rail	247,394	319,629	1,544,148	1,549,817	942,561	1,022,547
Water	61,628	75,840	505,440	563,369	271,998	261,747
Shallow draft	40,707	53,897	362,454	414,758	164,371	189,284
Great Lakes	(S)	1,504	33,041	38,421	12,395	13,415
Deep draft	19,749	20,439	109,945	110,191	95,232	59,047
Air (includes truck and air)	139,086	229,062	3,139	4,475	4,009	6,233
Pipeline [2]	89,849	113,497	483,645	618,202	(S)	(S)
Multiple modes	662,603	945,874	225,676	216,673	191,461	204,514
Parcel, U.S. Postal Service or courier	563,277	855,897	18,892	23,689	13,151	17,994
Truck and rail	83,082	75,695	40,624	54,246	37,675	55,561
Truck and water	9,392	8,241	67,995	33,215	40,610	34,767
Rail and water	3,636	1,771	79,222	79,275	70,219	77,590
Other multiple modes	3,216	4,269	18,943	26,248	(S)	18,603
Other and unknown modes	242,279	278,555	540,530	436,521	92,581	73,376

S Data do not meet publication standards due to high sampling variability or other reasons. [1] Truck as a single mode includes shipments that went by private truck only, for hire truck only, or a combination of private truck and for-hire truck. [2] Commodity Flow Survey data exclude most shipments of crude oil.

Source: U.S. Bureau of Transportation Statistics and U.S. Census Bureau, 1997 Economic Census, *Transportation, 1997 Commodity Flow Survey*, Series EC97TCF-US, issued December 1999. See Internet site <http://www.census.gov/econ/www/cfsnew.html>.

No. 1078. Hazardous Material Shipment Characteristics: 1997

[466,407 represents $466,407,000,000. Based on the 1997 Economic Census; see Appendix III]

Item	Value Amount (mil. dol.)	Value Percent	Tons Number (1,000)	Tons Percent	Ton-miles Number (mil.)	Ton-miles Percent	Average miles per shipment
MODE OF TRANSPORTATION							
All modes	466,407	100.0	1,565,196	100.0	263,809	100.0	113
Single modes	452,727	97.1	1,541,716	98.5	258,912	98.1	95
Truck [1]	298,173	63.9	869,796	55.6	74,939	28.4	73
For-hire truck	134,308	28.8	336,363	21.5	45,234	17.1	260
Private truck	160,693	34.5	522,666	33.4	28,847	10.9	35
Rail	33,340	7.1	96,626	6.2	74,711	28.3	853
Water	26,951	5.8	143,152	9.1	68,212	25.9	(S)
Air (includes truck and air)	8,558	1.8	66	-	95	-	1,462
Pipeline [2]	85,706	18.4	432,075	27.6	(S)	(S)	(S)
Multiple modes	5,735	1.2	6,022	0.4	3,061	1.2	645
Parcel, U.S. Postal Service or courier	2,874	0.6	143	-	78	-	697
Other multiple modes	2,861	0.6	5,879	0.4	2,982	1.1	(S)
Other and unknown modes	7,945	1.7	17,459	1.1	1,837	0.7	38
HAZARDOUS CLASS AND DESCRIPTION							
Total	466,407	100.0	1,565,196	100.0	263,809	100.0	113
Class 1, explosives	4,342	0.9	1,517	0.1	(S)	(S)	549
Class 2, gases	40,884	8.8	115,021	7.3	21,842	8.3	66
Class 3, flammable liquids	335,619	72.0	1,264,281	80.8	159,979	60.6	73
Class 4, flammable solids	3,898	0.8	11,804	0.8	9,618	3.6	838
Class 5, oxidizers and organic peroxides	4,485	1.0	9,239	0.6	4,471	1.7	193
Class 6, toxic (poison)	10,086	2.2	6,366	0.4	2,824	1.1	402
Class 7, radioactive materials	2,722	0.6	87	-	48	-	445
Class 8, corrosive materials	40,423	8.7	91,564	5.9	41,161	15.6	201
Class 9, misc. dangerous goods	23,946	5.1	65,317	4.2	22,727	8.6	323

- Represents or rounds to zero. S Data do not meet publication standards because of high sampling variability or other reasons. [1] "Truck" as a single mode includes shipments which went by private truck only, for-hire truck only or a combination of private truck and for-hire truck. [2] Commodity Flow Survey data exclude most shipments of crude oil.

Source: U.S. Bureau of Transportation Statistics and U.S. Census Bureau, 1997 Economic Census, *Transportation, 1997 Commodity Flow Survey, Hazardous Materials*, Series EC97TCF-US(HM)RV, issued April 2000. See Internet site <http://www.census.gov/econ/www/cfsnew.html>.

No. 1079. Bridge Inventory—Total and Deficient, 1996 to 2002, and by State, 2002

[Based on the National Bridge Inventory program]

State and year	Number of bridges	Deficient and obsolete					
		Total number	Percent	Structurally deficient [1]		Functionally obsolete [2]	
				Number	Percent	Number	Percent
1996, total	581,862	182,726	31.4	101,518	17.4	81,208	14.0
1997, total	582,751	175,885	30.2	98,475	16.9	77,410	13.3
1998, total	582,984	172,582	29.6	93,076	16.0	79,506	13.6
1999, total	585,542	170,050	29.0	88,150	15.1	81,900	14.0
2000, total	587,755	167,993	28.6	87,106	14.8	80,887	13.8
2001, total	590,066	165,099	28.0	83,630	14.2	81,469	13.8
U.S. total, 2002	**591,220**	**163,010**	**27.6**	**81,437**	**13.8**	**81,573**	**13.8**
Alabama	15,697	4,887	31.1	2,611	16.6	2,276	14.5
Alaska	1,437	427	29.7	176	12.2	251	17.5
Arizona	7,055	750	10.6	187	2.7	563	8.0
Arkansas	12,438	3,383	27.2	1,399	11.2	1,984	16.0
California	23,754	6,764	28.5	2,757	11.6	4,007	16.9
Colorado	8,105	1,450	17.9	597	7.4	853	10.5
Connecticut	4,173	1,316	31.5	342	8.2	974	23.3
Delaware	835	135	16.2	51	6.1	84	10.1
District of Columbia	244	166	68.0	21	8.6	145	59.4
Florida	11,376	2,135	18.8	302	2.7	1,833	16.1
Georgia	14,456	3,307	22.9	1,475	10.2	1,832	12.7
Hawaii	1,089	522	47.9	171	15.7	351	32.2
Idaho	4,090	759	18.6	321	7.8	438	10.7
Illinois	25,610	4,648	18.1	2,609	10.2	2,039	8.0
Indiana	18,087	4,172	23.1	2,197	12.1	1,975	10.9
Iowa	24,955	7,027	28.2	5,069	20.3	1,958	7.8
Kansas	25,618	6,376	24.9	3,453	13.5	2,923	11.4
Kentucky	13,461	3,997	29.7	1,170	8.7	2,827	21.0
Louisiana	13,399	4,487	33.5	2,321	17.3	2,166	16.2
Maine	2,363	845	35.8	348	14.7	497	21.0
Maryland	4,950	1,433	28.9	429	8.7	1,004	20.3
Massachusetts	4,925	2,505	50.9	645	13.1	1,860	37.8
Michigan	10,799	3,318	30.7	1,990	18.4	1,328	12.3
Minnesota	12,845	1,783	13.9	1,208	9.4	575	4.5
Mississippi	16,809	4,986	29.7	3,652	21.7	1,334	7.9
Missouri	23,495	8,578	36.5	5,479	23.3	3,099	13.2
Montana	4,986	1,092	21.9	557	11.2	535	10.7
Nebraska	15,462	4,189	27.1	2,570	16.6	1,619	10.5
Nevada	1,562	223	14.3	68	4.4	155	9.9
New Hampshire	2,355	792	33.6	374	15.9	418	17.7
New Jersey	6,375	2,336	36.6	906	14.2	1,430	22.4
New Mexico	3,800	727	19.1	379	10.0	348	9.2
New York	17,389	6,501	37.4	2,252	13.0	4,249	24.4
North Carolina	17,116	5,252	30.7	2,465	14.4	2,787	16.3
North Dakota	4,517	1,119	24.8	859	19.0	260	5.8
Ohio	27,988	7,072	25.3	3,273	11.7	3,799	13.6
Oklahoma	22,989	9,228	40.1	7,684	33.4	1,544	6.7
Oregon	7,352	1,730	23.5	474	6.4	1,256	17.1
Pennsylvania	22,153	9,407	42.5	5,484	24.8	3,923	17.7
Rhode Island	749	394	52.6	187	25.0	207	27.6
South Carolina	9,091	2,079	22.9	1,234	13.6	845	9.3
South Dakota	5,979	1,690	28.3	1,106	18.5	584	9.8
Tennessee	19,467	4,606	23.7	1,707	8.8	2,899	14.9
Texas	48,202	10,506	21.8	2,978	6.2	7,528	15.6
Utah	2,781	546	19.6	253	9.1	293	10.5
Vermont	2,716	959	35.3	461	17.0	498	18.3
Virginia	12,932	3,420	26.4	1,175	9.1	2,245	17.4
Washington	7,624	2,027	26.6	479	6.3	1,548	20.3
West Virginia	6,821	2,646	38.8	1,125	16.5	1,521	22.3
Wisconsin	13,563	2,601	19.2	1,713	12.6	888	6.5
Wyoming	3,077	662	21.5	432	14.0	230	7.5
Puerto Rico	2,109	1,050	49.8	262	12.4	788	37.4

[1] Bridges are structurally deficient if they have been restricted to light vehicles, require immediate rehabilitation to remain open, or are closed. [2] Bridges are functionally obsolete if they have deck geometry, load caring capacity, clearance or approach roadway alignment that no longer meet the criteria for the system of which the bridge is a part.

Source: U.S. Federal Highway Administration, Office of Bridge Technology, Internet site <http://www.fhwa.dot.gov/bridge/britab.htm>.

No. 1080. Funding for Highways and Disposition of Highway-User Revenue: 1990 to 2001

[In millions of dollars (75,444 represents $75,444,000,0000. Data compiled from reports of state and local authorities]

Type	1990	1995	1996	1997	1998	1999	2000	2001
Total receipts	75,444	96,269	102,771	107,421	111,581	121,650	131,115	132,324
Current income	69,880	87,620	94,972	98,667	102,533	110,376	119,815	119,659
Highway user revenues	44,346	59,331	64,052	66,266	68,951	74,222	81,335	77,719
Other taxes and fees	19,827	21,732	23,830	25,424	25,395	29,380	31,137	34,190
Investment income, other receipts	5,707	6,557	7,090	6,977	8,187	6,774	7,342	7,749
Bond issue proceeds [1]	5,564	8,649	7,799	8,754	9,048	11,274	11,301	12,665
Funds from (+) or to (-) reserves	-36	-2,791	-4,689	-5,468	-3,606	-5,639	-8,418	-2,423
Total funds available	75,408	93,478	98,082	101,953	107,975	116,011	122,697	129,900
Total disbursements	75,408	93,478	98,082	101,953	107,975	116,011	122,697	129,900
Current disbursements	72,457	88,994	93,492	97,320	102,828	111,097	117,592	124,815
Capital outlay	35,151	44,228	46,810	48,360	52,308	57,227	61,323	65,968
Maintenance and traffic services	20,365	24,319	25,564	26,777	28,173	29,997	30,636	31,677
Administration and research	6,501	8,419	8,445	8,256	8,523	9,130	10,020	10,423
Law enforcement and safety	7,235	8,218	8,897	9,761	9,445	10,393	11,031	11,977
Interest on debt	3,205	3,810	3,776	4,166	4,379	4,350	4,583	4,770
Bond retirement [1]	2,951	4,484	4,590	4,633	5,147	4,914	5,105	5,086

[1] Excludes issue and redemption of short-term notes or refunding bonds.
Source: U.S. Federal Highway Administration, *Highway Statistics*, annual. See Internet site <http://www.fhwa.dot.gov/policy/ohpi/hss/hsspubs.htm>.

No. 1081. Federal Aid to State and Local Governments for Highway Trust Fund and Federal Transit Administration (FTA) by State: 2002

[Year ending Sept. 30. (29,444 represents $29,444,000,000)]

State	Highway trust fund Total (mil. dol.)	Per capita (dol.)[1]	FTA Total (mil. dol.)	Per capita (dol.)[1]	State	Highway trust fund Total (mil. dol.)	Per capita (dol.)[1]	FTA Total (mil. dol.)	Per capita (dol.)[1]	State	Highway trust fund Total (mil. dol.)	Per capita (dol.)[1]	FTA Total (mil. dol.)	Per capita (dol.)[1]
U.S.[2]	29,444	100.6	5,223	17.8	IA	333	113.3	22	7.5	NC	959	115.2	42	5.0
U.S.[3]	28,539	99.0	5,024	17.4	KS	360	132.5	18	6.7	ND	216	340.4	4	6.6
					KY	524	127.9	22	5.3	OH	901	78.9	137	12.0
AL	673	150.1	25	5.7	LA	448	99.9	36	8.1	OK	347	99.3	20	5.8
AK	328	509.5	12	18.9	ME	162	125.0	8	6.0	OR	272	77.4	122	34.8
AZ	481	88.1	61	11.1	MD	572	104.8	105	19.3	PA	1,345	109.1	269	21.8
AR	395	145.7	10	3.5	MA	505	78.6	131	20.3	RI	171	160.2	26	24.5
CA	2,628	74.8	1,008	28.7	MI	823	81.9	89	8.9	SC	411	100.0	14	3.3
CO	342	76.0	91	20.3	MN	384	76.4	108	21.5	SD	199	261.1	5	6.2
CT	493	142.6	79	22.8	MS	385	134.2	5	1.9	TN	521	89.9	39	6.6
DE	120	148.5	3	3.8	MO	727	128.1	36	6.3	TX	2,209	101.4	271	12.4
DC	150	262.6	260	454.7	MT	295	324.2	5	5.6	UT	239	103.2	55	23.8
FL	1,496	89.5	135	8.0	NE	193	111.9	10	5.8	VT	134	216.8	3	5.6
GA	873	102.0	96	11.3	NV	161	74.3	16	7.3	VA	882	121.0	66	9.1
HI	122	98.2	33	26.7	NH	141	110.8	8	6.2	WA	548	90.4	106	17.5
ID	206	153.5	7	4.9	NJ	710	82.7	291	33.8	WV	318	176.5	8	4.5
IL	889	70.5	259	20.5	NM	302	162.8	8	4.3	WI	587	107.8	36	6.7
IN	560	90.9	29	4.8	NY	1,274	66.5	773	40.3	WY	224	448.4	2	4.1

[1] Based on estimated resident population as of July 1. [2] Includes outlying areas and undistributed funds not shown separately. [3] For the 50 states and DC.
Source: U.S. Census Bureau, *Federal Aid to States for Fiscal Year, 2002*. See Internet site <http://www.census.gov/prod/2003pubs/fas02.pdf> (issued May 2003).

No. 1082. State Motor Fuel Tax Receipts, 2000 and 2001, and Gasoline Tax Rates, 2001

[580 represents $580,000,000]

State	Net receipts (mil. dol.) 2000	2001	Tax rate,[1] 2001	State	Net receipts (mil. dol.) 2000	2001	Tax rate,[1] 2001	State	Net receipts (mil. dol.) 2000	2001	Tax rate,[1] 2001
AL	580	559	18.00	KY	440	465	16.40	ND	101	98	21.00
AK	29	28	8.00	LA	543	545	20.00	OH	1,495	1,490	22.00
AZ	574	585	18.00	ME	178	167	22.00	OK	414	401	17.00
AR	399	412	21.70	MD	646	683	23.50	OR	393	394	24.00
CA	3,043	3,147	18.00	MA	653	661	21.00	PA	1,696	1,726	26.00
CO	521	542	22.00	MI	1,067	1,068	19.00	RI	134	134	29.00
CT	499	407	25.00	MN	607	619	20.00	SC	463	456	16.00
DE	104	99	23.00	MS	392	375	18.40	SD	119	125	22.00
DC	32	29	20.00	MO	671	661	17.00	TN	717	705	20.00
FL	1,603	1,682	13.60	MT	197	176	27.00	TX	2,720	2,784	20.00
GA	431	446	7.50	NE	307	297	24.50	UT	327	311	24.50
HI	69	71	16.00	NV	307	375	24.75	VT	88	87	20.00
ID	207	226	25.00	NH	138	142	19.50	VA	778	814	17.50
IL	1,236	1,217	19.00	NJ	525	534	10.50	WA	737	739	23.00
IN	744	740	15.00	NM	239	236	18.50	WV	295	297	25.65
IA	397	396	20.00	NY	1,406	1,454	22.00	WI	809	827	27.30
KS	358	357	21.00	NC	1,042	1,185	24.10	WY	101	96	14.00

[1] Cents per gallon. In effect Dec. 31.
Source: U.S. Federal Highway Administration, *Highway Statistics*, annual. See Internet site <http://www.fhwa.dot.gov/policy/ohpi/hss/hsspubs.htm>.

No. 1083. Public Highway Debt—State and Local Governments: 1980 to 2001

[In millions of dollars (2,381 represents $2,381,000,000). Long-term obligations. Data are for varying calendar and fiscal years. Excludes duplicated and interunit obligations]

Item	1980	1985	1990	1995	1997	1998	1999	2000	2001
Total debt issued	2,381	8,194	5,708	11,305	12,347	16,412	12,822	14,513	(NA)
State	1,160	5,397	3,147	4,718	8,174	9,789	9,554	9,067	11,012
Local [1]	1,221	2,797	2,561	6,587	4,173	6,623	3,268	5,446	(NA)
Total debt redeemed	1,987	5,294	3,120	5,634	7,043	11,735	5,808	8,623	(NA)
State	1,114	3,835	1,648	2,939	4,228	6,466	3,609	3,897	4,660
Local [1]	873	1,459	1,472	2,695	2,815	5,269	2,199	4,726	(NA)
Total debt outstanding [2]	27,616	32,690	46,586	68,733	77,501	82,599	89,778	96,383	(NA)
State	20,210	21,277	28,362	39,228	45,666	49,182	55,646	61,434	66,256
Local [1]	7,406	11,413	18,224	29,505	31,835	33,417	34,132	34,949	(NA)

NA Not available. [1] Local data estimated. [2] End-of-year.

Source: U.S. Federal Highway Administration, *Highway Statistics,* annual. See Internet site <http://www.fhwa.dot.gov/policy/ohpi/hss/hsspubs.htm>.

No. 1084. State Disbursements for Highways by State: 1995 to 2001

[In millions of dollars (67,615 represents $67,615,000,000). Comprises disbursements from current revenues or loans for construction, maintenance, interest and principal payments on highway bonds, transfers to local units, and miscellaneous. Includes transactions by state toll authorities. Excludes amounts allocated for collection expenses and nonhighway purposes, and bonds redeemed by refunding]

State	1995	1996	1997	1998	1999	2000	2001
United States	67,615	71,736	73,994	80,518	83,675	89,832	94,513
Alabama	1,002	1,064	1,019	1,053	1,085	1,246	1,433
Alaska	438	453	435	404	416	501	482
Arizona	1,199	1,532	1,359	1,430	1,860	2,040	2,149
Arkansas	666	755	832	815	736	817	976
California	5,966	5,831	6,219	6,574	6,876	6,750	6,795
Colorado	922	922	887	1,166	1,260	1,392	1,616
Connecticut	1,153	1,202	1,173	1,427	1,094	1,304	1,236
Delaware	441	452	449	647	507	595	647
District of Columbia	140	163	151	259	242	244	406
Florida	3,421	3,472	3,734	4,024	3,992	4,208	4,348
Georgia	1,437	1,675	1,372	1,613	1,763	1,567	1,748
Hawaii	360	405	387	326	355	272	263
Idaho	350	369	403	414	445	492	480
Illinois	3,006	3,097	2,992	3,306	2,957	3,447	3,788
Indiana	1,433	1,444	1,636	1,652	1,522	1,932	3,202
Iowa	1,078	1,128	1,173	1,177	1,253	1,494	1,388
Kansas	1,019	1,162	1,087	1,306	1,155	1,206	1,271
Kentucky	1,397	1,372	1,331	1,481	1,578	1,651	1,612
Louisiana	1,198	1,417	1,189	1,400	1,237	1,301	1,154
Maine	379	509	474	485	458	488	505
Maryland	1,289	1,449	1,489	1,492	1,554	1,599	1,673
Massachusetts	2,501	2,545	3,287	3,351	4,407	3,524	3,965
Michigan	1,974	1,966	2,100	2,745	2,629	2,748	2,920
Minnesota	1,210	1,374	1,450	1,377	1,534	1,692	1,683
Mississippi	662	826	809	843	968	1,039	911
Missouri	1,313	1,402	1,492	1,438	1,600	1,818	2,044
Montana	388	377	379	378	434	474	469
Nebraska	578	595	611	589	681	745	661
Nevada	484	468	431	446	557	651	668
New Hampshire	328	346	360	371	416	387	445
New Jersey	2,102	2,928	2,247	2,513	2,905	4,503	4,276
New Mexico	535	532	546	570	753	1,162	1,119
New York	4,584	4,424	4,778	6,051	5,347	5,307	5,301
North Carolina	1,871	1,939	2,099	2,352	2,441	2,621	2,868
North Dakota	270	266	326	306	413	385	358
Ohio	2,637	2,709	2,940	3,327	3,158	3,351	3,493
Oklahoma	828	918	867	944	1,322	1,417	1,443
Oregon	888	995	992	1,051	1,009	1,010	984
Pennsylvania	3,153	3,118	3,764	3,902	4,143	4,517	4,875
Rhode Island	290	297	225	339	316	256	380
South Carolina	668	678	741	766	885	970	1,104
South Dakota	286	289	349	305	371	466	463
Tennessee	1,230	1,283	1,351	1,420	1,398	1,440	1,563
Texas	3,593	4,312	4,253	4,295	4,840	5,665	5,716
Utah	431	457	802	1,129	1,072	1,072	941
Vermont	194	192	213	222	252	287	297
Virginia	2,107	2,321	2,358	2,619	2,771	2,678	2,909
Washington	1,909	1,766	1,851	1,805	1,780	1,871	2,042
West Virginia	781	935	940	893	930	1,170	1,289
Wisconsin	1,252	1,324	1,354	1,398	1,614	1,663	1,793
Wyoming	272	283	284	321	386	396	360

Source: U.S. Federal Highway Administration, *Highway Statistics,* annual. See Internet site <http://www.fhwa.dot.gov/policy/ohpi/hss/hsspubs.htm>.

No. 1085. State Motor Vehicle Registrations: 1980 to 2001

[In thousands (155,796 represents 155,796,000). Compiled principally from information obtained from state authorities, but it was necessary to draw on other sources and to make numerous estimates in order to complete series. See also Table 1088 excludes motorcycles]

Item	1980	1990	1995	1998	1999	2000	2001
All motor vehicles	155,796	188,798	201,530	211,617	216,309	221,475	230,428
Private and commercial	153,265	185,541	197,941	207,841	212,474	217,567	226,646
Publicly owned	2,531	3,257	3,589	3,776	3,834	3,908	3,782
Automobiles [1]	121,601	133,700	128,387	131,839	132,432	133,621	137,633
Private and commercial	120,743	132,164	126,900	130,500	131,077	132,247	136,341
Publicly owned	857	1,536	1,487	1,339	1,355	1,374	1,293
Buses	529	627	686	716	729	746	750
Private and commercial	254	275	288	302	307	314	318
Publicly owned	275	351	398	413	422	432	432
Trucks [1]	33,667	54,470	72,458	79,062	83,148	87,108	92,045
Private and commercial	32,268	53,101	70,754	77,039	81,091	85,005	89,988
Publicly owned	1,399	1,369	1,704	2,024	2,057	2,103	2,058

[1] Trucks include pickups, panels and delivery vans. Beginning 1990, personal passenger vans, passenger minivans and utility-type vehicles are no longer included in automobiles but are included in trucks.

Source: U.S. Federal Highway Administration, *Highway Statistics*, annual. See Internet site <http://www.fhwa.dot.gov/policy/ohpi/hss/hsspubs.htm>.

No. 1086. Alternative Fueled Vehicles in Use by Fuel Type: 2000 to 2002

[363,313 represents 363,313,000]

Fuel type	Alternative fueled vehicles			Fuel consumption (1,000 gasoline-equivalent gallons)		
	2000	2001	2002	2000	2001	2002
Total	455,906	490,019	518,919	363,313	385,421	394,438
Liquified petroleum gases (LPG)	272,193	276,597	281,286	247,062	251,353	255,515
Compressed natural gas (CNG)	100,738	113,835	126,341	98,351	111,797	113,554
Liquified natural gas (LNG)	2,090	2,576	3,187	7,121	8,786	10,504
M85 (Mixture: 85% methanol + 15% gasoline)	10,426	7,827	5,873	585	440	330
Neat methanol (M100)	-	-	-	437	406	-
E85 (Mixture: 85% ethanol + 15% gasoline)	58,621	71,336	82,477	7,074	8,736	10,075
E95 (Mixture: 95% ethanol + 5% gasoline)	4	-	-	13	-	-
Electricity	11,834	17,848	19,755	2,670	3,903	4,460

- Represents zero.

Source: Energy Information Administration, *Alternatives to Traditional Transportation Fuels*. See Internet site <http://www.eia.doe.gov/fuelalternate.html> (released September 2002).

No. 1087. Number of Households Leasing Vehicles and Number of Vehicles Leased Per Household: 1992 to 2001

[Based on the Survey of Consumer Finances; see Appendix III]

Item	Share of households leasing a vehicle for personal use (percent)				Average number of leased vehicles, among households having such vehicles			
	1992	1995	1998	2001	1992	1995	1998	2001
All households	2.9	4.5	6.4	5.8	1.1	1.1	1.2	1.2
Household income:								
Less than $10,000	(Z)	(Z)	(Z)	(Z)	(Z)	(Z)	1.1	(Z)
$10,000 to $24,999	(Z)	1.3	4.1	1.8	(Z)	1.0	1.1	1.1
$25,000 to $49,999	3.1	3.2	4.6	5.3	1.1	1.0	1.1	1.0
$50,000 to $99,999	3.7	9.2	9.2	7.6	1.1	1.1	1.2	1.2
$100,000 and over	9.5	12.6	13.8	12.9	1.1	1.3	1.3	1.3
Age of household head:								
Less than 35 years	3.2	4.8	8.2	7.3	1.0	1.0	1.1	1.1
35 to 44 years	4.3	5.4	8.3	5.9	1.1	1.1	1.1	1.2
45 to 54 years	3.2	7.9	7.6	6.1	1.2	1.2	1.3	1.2
55 to 64 years	3.2	4.1	4.4	5.5	1.2	1.2	1.1	1.1
65 to 74 years	1.0	1.3	2.9	6.3	1.0	1.1	1.2	1.1
75 years and over	(Z)	0.5	1.9	1.6	(Z)	1.0	1.0	1.0
Race/ethnicity of respondent:								
White non-Hispanic	3.1	4.4	6.3	6.3	1.1	1.1	1.1	1.2
Non-White and Hispanic	2.3	4.9	6.5	4.2	1.1	1.1	1.3	1.1
Work status of household head:								
Work for someone else	3.4	6.0	8.1	6.2	1.1	1.1	1.2	1.2
Self employed	7.2	5.2	9.0	9.4	1.1	1.3	1.1	1.3
Retired	0.7	1.4	1.5	3.1	1.3	1.0	1.2	1.1
Other not working	(Z)	2.6	(Z)	(Z)	(Z)	1.0	(Z)	(Z)
Homeownership status:								
Owner	3.5	5.8	7.2	6.2	1.1	1.2	1.2	1.2
Renter or other	1.8	2.3	4.8	5.0	1.1	1.1	1.1	1.1
Net worth percentile:								
Bottom 25 percent	2.1	2.7	4.9	3.9	1.1	1.1	1.1	1.2
25 to 49.9 percent	1.6	4.2	5.4	4.4	1.0	1.0	1.1	1.1
50 to 74.9 percent	2.9	4.3	7.1	6.3	1.1	1.1	1.2	1.3
75 to 89.9 percent	3.7	6.2	7.0	7.6	1.0	1.2	1.2	1.2
Top 10 percent	6.5	8.2	9.9	10.2	1.2	1.3	1.2	1.2

Z Ten or fewer observations.

Source: Board of Governors of the Federal Reserve System, unpublished data. See Internet site <http://www.federalreserve.gov/pubs/oss/oss2/2001/scf2001home.html>.

No. 1088. State Motor Vehicle Registrations, 1980 to 2001, and Licensed Drivers and Motorcycle Registrations by State: 2001

[In thousands (155,796 represents 155,796,000). Motor vehicle registrations cover publicly, privately, and commercially owned vehicles. For uniformity, data have been adjusted to a calendar-year basis as registration years in states differ; figures represent net numbers where possible, excluding re-registrations and nonresident registrations. See also Table 1085]

State	Motor vehicle registrations [1]							2001		2001
	1980	1985	1990	1995	1999	2000	Total	Automobiles (incl. taxis)	Motorcycle registration (incl. official) [2]	Licensed drivers
U.S.	155,796	171,689	188,798	201,530	216,309	221,475	230,428	137,633	4,862	191,276
AL	2,938	3,383	3,744	3,553	3,957	3,960	4,235	1,765	55	3,560
AK	262	353	477	542	571	594	598	242	17	472
AZ	1,917	2,235	2,825	2,873	3,606	3,795	3,967	2,264	191	3,550
AR	1,574	1,384	1,448	1,613	1,818	1,840	1,864	974	29	1,962
CA	16,873	18,899	21,926	22,432	26,362	27,698	28,780	17,919	473	21,624
CO	2,342	2,759	3,155	2,812	3,858	3,626	4,649	2,368	195	3,288
CT	2,147	2,465	2,623	2,622	2,766	2,853	2,917	2,051	52	2,650
DE	397	465	526	592	616	630	653	410	13	564
DC	268	306	262	243	235	242	249	204	1	328
FL	7,614	9,865	10,950	10,369	11,390	11,781	14,340	8,938	299	12,743
GA	3,818	4,580	5,489	6,120	6,973	7,155	7,305	4,085	91	5,834
HI	570	651	771	802	718	738	868	529	21	788
ID	834	854	1,054	1,043	1,130	1,178	1,324	578	39	897
IL	7,477	7,527	7,873	8,973	9,355	8,973	9,861	6,425	257	7,810
IN	3,826	3,824	4,366	5,072	5,495	5,571	5,625	3,229	127	4,117
IA	2,329	2,696	2,632	2,814	3,050	3,106	3,318	1,870	138	1,979
KS	2,007	2,148	2,012	2,085	2,224	2,296	2,331	842	51	1,871
KY	2,593	2,615	2,909	2,631	2,662	2,826	3,626	2,123	46	2,757
LA	2,779	3,012	2,995	3,286	3,505	3,557	3,609	1,994	50	2,718
ME	724	840	977	967	915	1,024	1,018	618	33	943
MD	2,803	3,276	3,607	3,654	3,896	3,848	3,939	2,596	55	3,452
MA	3,749	3,738	3,726	4,502	5,333	5,265	5,198	3,531	115	4,611
MI	6,488	6,727	7,209	7,674	8,290	8,436	8,454	4,903	198	6,977
MN	3,091	3,385	3,508	3,882	4,010	4,630	4,554	2,565	152	2,961
MS	1,577	1,746	1,875	2,144	2,317	2,289	1,954	1,147	27	1,859
MO	3,271	3,558	3,905	4,255	4,404	4,580	4,208	2,491	64	3,862
MT	680	652	783	968	998	1,026	1,033	460	26	683
NE	1,254	1,258	1,384	1,467	1,570	1,619	1,633	834	23	1,267
NV	655	709	853	1,047	1,162	1,220	1,280	679	32	1,421
NH	704	974	946	1,122	1,051	1,052	1,100	684	53	942
NJ	4,761	5,164	5,652	5,906	6,103	6,390	6,580	4,518	125	5,715
NM	1,068	1,226	1,301	1,484	1,576	1,529	1,428	671	28	1,232
NY	8,002	9,042	10,196	10,274	10,756	10,235	10,196	7,597	118	11,015
NC	4,532	4,501	5,162	5,682	5,690	6,223	6,180	3,714	86	5,885
ND	627	655	630	695	704	694	708	348	18	456
OH	7,771	8,102	8,410	9,810	10,236	10,467	10,555	6,666	268	7,736
OK	2,583	2,911	2,649	2,856	2,931	3,014	3,281	1,749	77	2,172
OR	2,081	2,204	2,445	2,785	3,013	3,022	3,039	1,559	72	2,534
PA	6,926	7,209	7,971	8,481	9,009	9,260	9,631	6,231	237	8,226
RI	623	610	672	699	747	760	764	536	21	660
SC	1,996	2,222	2,521	2,833	3,026	3,095	3,143	1,919	56	2,850
SD	601	657	704	709	782	793	803	389	31	545
TN	3,271	3,754	4,444	5,400	4,427	4,820	5,139	3,012	84	4,188
TX	10,475	12,444	12,800	13,682	14,069	14,070	14,359	7,724	210	13,046
UT	992	1,099	1,206	1,447	1,577	1,628	1,752	924	39	1,496
VT	347	398	462	492	518	515	534	302	24	515
VA	3,626	4,253	4,938	5,613	5,871	6,046	6,171	3,976	65	4,921
WA	3,225	3,526	4,257	4,503	4,862	5,116	5,179	2,903	123	4,238
WV	1,320	1,143	1,225	1,425	1,379	1,442	1,452	787	27	1,317
WI	2,941	3,187	3,815	3,993	4,266	4,366	4,473	2,579	209	3,667
WY	467	500	528	601	528	586	573	211	21	371

[1] Automobiles, trucks, and buses. Excludes vehicles owned by military services.   [2] Private and commercial.

Source: U.S. Federal Highway Administration, *Highway Statistics*, annual; and *Selected Highway Statistics and Charts*, annual. See Internet site <http://www.fhwa.dot.gov/policy/ohpi/hss/hsspubs.htm>.

Transportation   697

No. 1089. Roadway Congestion: 2000

[15,375 represents 15,375,000 Various federal, state, and local information sources were used to develop the data base with the primary source being the Federal Highway Administration's Highway Performance Monitoring System. Areas shown are rated the top 70 in annual per person hours of delay]

Urbanized areas	Freeway daily vehicle miles of travel		Annual person hours of delay		Annual congestion cost		
	Total miles (1,000)	Per lane-mile of freeway	Total hours (1,000)	Per person	Per person (dol.)	Delay and fuel cost (mil. dol.)	Fuel wasted (gal. per person)
Total, average	15,375	16,035	47,595	27	505	900	43
Albany-Schenectady-Troy NY	5,500	10,000	2,980	6	115	60	10
Albuquerque NM	3,770	16,045	12,240	21	380	225	32
Atlanta GA	42,940	18,550	97,245	33	635	1,885	56
Austin TX	8,800	15,305	20,640	28	550	400	48
Bakersfield CA	1,930	10,160	1,585	4	60	25	7
Baltimore MD	22,660	15,365	44,385	20	395	860	35
Beaumont TX	1,560	11,555	850	6	105	15	7
Birmingham AL	8,685	12,865	9,610	14	285	190	25
Boston MA	22,890	17,610	84,845	28	525	1,595	45
Boulder CO	490	9,800	510	5	45	5	3
Buffalo-Niagara Falls NY	6,365	10,025	5,560	5	95	105	8
Charleston SC	2,815	11,980	5,625	12	220	100	20
Charlotte NC	7,640	15,915	13,950	22	410	265	37
Chicago IL-Northwestern IN	48,400	18,160	221,300	27	505	4,095	43
Cincinnati OH-KY	15,745	16,150	25,385	20	395	505	34
Cleveland OH	17,285	13,505	15,965	8	165	315	15
Colorado Springs CO	2,515	10,935	5,880	13	235	110	19
Columbus OH	11,850	13,940	17,790	17	330	345	30
Dallas-Fort Worth TX	48,700	15,460	141,125	37	695	2,640	60
Denver CO	16,905	16,335	66,165	35	640	1,225	55
Detroit MI	31,125	17,150	101,340	25	475	1,905	41
El Paso TX-NM	3,975	14,195	6,360	10	185	120	15
Eugene-Springfield OR	1,335	12,135	1,445	7	115	25	9
Fort Myers-Cape Coral FL	400	8,890	2,115	7	105	30	14
Fresno CA	2,550	12,750	6,145	11	215	120	18
Ft. Lauderdale-Hollywood-Pompano Beach FL	12,750	17,585	44,445	28	520	810	44
Hartford-Middletown CT	8,405	13,450	6,805	11	215	140	19
Honolulu HI	5,625	14,065	7,690	11	225	155	19
Houston TX	37,900	15,315	120,945	36	675	2,285	59
Indianapolis IN	11,260	15,530	20,630	20	385	395	34
Jacksonville FL	9,835	13,565	12,585	15	285	245	24
Kansas City MO-KS	19,310	11,160	12,395	9	175	245	16
Las Vegas NV	6,850	16,505	21,650	18	345	415	28
Los Angeles CA	126,495	23,425	791,970	62	1,155	14,635	94
Louisville KY-IN	10,040	14,985	17,855	21	400	335	37
Memphis TN-AR-MS	6,890	13,645	15,460	16	290	285	26
Miami-Hialeah FL	13,585	18,115	74,850	33	600	1,365	51
Milwaukee WI	9,700	15,770	20,360	15	285	390	25
Minneapolis-St. Paul MN	27,095	17,150	63,135	26	495	1,220	44
Nashville TN	10,000	13,160	14,170	20	395	275	34
New Orleans LA	5,615	13,530	11,425	10	195	215	17
New York NY-Northeastern NJ	101,295	15,350	400,115	23	450	7,660	39
Norfolk-Newport News-Virginia Beach VA	11,270	12,880	17,420	12	230	345	20
Oklahoma City OK	8,930	12,070	6,260	6	115	125	10
Omaha NE-IA	3,300	11,000	7,070	11	200	125	18
Orlando FL	9,430	12,920	37,385	31	575	690	48
Pensacola FL	1,130	10,275	3,430	11	165	50	16
Philadelphia PA-NJ	25,445	14,625	70,630	15	290	1,325	25
Phoenix AZ	19,425	18,860	72,590	28	525	1,360	44
Pittsburgh PA	11,130	9,355	12,510	7	130	235	11
Portland-Vancouver OR-WA	12,595	17,865	34,360	23	445	670	38
Providence-Pawtucket RI-MA	8,465	13,125	17,130	19	365	335	32
Richmond VA	7,000	11,025	6,495	10	195	125	17
Sacramento CA	12,170	17,765	27,140	19	385	540	33
Salem OR	1,190	11,900	1,340	7	130	25	10
Salt Lake City UT	6,415	12,830	8,410	9	190	170	17
San Antonio TX	15,775	14,810	25,505	20	380	475	34
San Bernardino-Riverside CA	16,600	18,865	41,825	30	575	810	48
San Diego CA	33,745	18,800	65,305	24	480	1,295	41
San Francisco-Oakland CA	47,980	20,550	167,200	41	795	3,210	67
San Jose CA	16,530	18,680	55,920	33	635	1,065	53
Seattle-Everett WA	22,455	17,475	67,550	34	660	1,315	56
Spokane WA	1,500	11,110	1,760	5	90	30	9
St. Louis MO-IL	25,740	14,460	41,690	20	395	805	35
Tacoma WA	5,305	17,685	8,470	14	280	170	23
Tampa-St. Petersburg-Clearwater FL	8,460	13,115	41,285	21	380	745	32
Tucson AZ	2,150	11,620	7,680	11	220	150	18
Tulsa OK	6,270	11,720	6,965	9	170	135	14
Washington DC-MD-VA	34,535	18,320	123,190	35	655	2,325	56
West Palm Beach-Boca Raton-Delray Beach FL	8,365	16,400	21,010	20	385	395	33

Source: Texas Transportation Institute, College Station, Texas; *2002 Urban Mobility Study* (issued June 2002). (Copyright). See <http://mobility.tamu.edu/ums/>.

No. 1090. Commuting to Work by State: 2000

[In percent, except as indicated (128,279 represents 128,279,000). **As of April 1.** For workers 16 years old and over. Based on sample data from the 2000 Census of Population and Housing; see text Section 1, and Appendix III]

State	Total workers (1,000)	Percent of workers who—						Mean travel time to work (min.)
		Commuted by car, truck, or van		Used public transportation [1]	Walked	Used other means	Worked at home	
		Drove alone	Car-pooled					
U.S.	128,279	75.7	12.2	4.7	2.9	1.2	3.3	25.5
AL.	1,900	83.0	12.3	0.5	1.3	0.8	2.1	24.8
AK.	291	66.5	15.5	1.8	7.3	4.8	4.1	19.6
AZ.	2,210	74.1	15.4	1.9	2.6	2.3	3.7	24.9
AR.	1,160	79.9	14.1	0.4	1.9	1.0	2.6	21.9
CA.	14,525	71.8	14.5	5.1	2.9	1.9	3.8	27.7
CO	2,192	75.1	12.2	3.2	3.0	1.5	4.9	24.3
CT.	1,641	80.0	9.4	4.0	2.7	0.7	3.1	24.4
DE.	373	79.2	11.5	2.8	2.6	1.0	3.0	24.0
DC	261	38.4	11.0	33.2	11.8	1.9	3.8	29.7
FL.	6,910	78.8	12.9	1.9	1.7	1.7	3.0	26.2
GA.	3,833	77.5	14.5	2.3	1.7	1.1	2.8	27.7
HI.	563	63.9	19.0	6.3	4.8	2.4	3.6	26.1
ID.	595	77.0	12.3	1.1	3.5	1.4	4.7	20.0
IL.	5,746	73.2	10.9	8.7	3.1	1.0	3.1	28.0
IN.	2,911	81.8	11.0	1.0	2.4	0.9	2.9	22.6
IA.	1,470	78.6	10.8	1.0	4.0	0.9	4.7	18.5
KS.	1,311	81.5	10.6	0.5	2.5	0.9	4.0	19.0
KY.	1,782	80.2	12.6	1.2	2.4	0.9	2.7	23.5
LA.	1,831	78.1	13.6	2.4	2.2	1.6	2.1	25.7
ME	615	78.6	11.3	0.8	4.0	0.9	4.4	22.7
MD	2,592	73.7	12.4	7.2	2.5	0.8	3.3	31.2
MA	3,103	73.8	9.0	8.7	4.3	1.0	3.1	27.0
MI.	4,540	83.2	9.7	1.3	2.2	0.7	2.8	24.1
MN	2,542	77.6	10.4	3.2	3.3	0.9	4.6	21.9
MS	1,164	79.4	15.2	0.6	1.9	1.0	1.9	24.6
MO	2,629	80.5	11.6	1.5	2.1	0.8	3.5	23.8
MT	422	73.9	11.9	0.7	5.5	1.7	6.4	17.7
NE.	873	80.0	10.5	0.7	3.2	0.9	4.6	18.0
NV.	923	74.5	14.7	3.9	2.7	1.6	2.6	23.3
NH	639	81.8	9.8	0.7	2.9	0.8	4.0	25.3
NJ.	3,876	73.0	10.6	9.6	3.1	0.9	2.7	30.0
NM	759	75.8	14.8	0.8	2.8	1.6	4.2	21.9
NY.	8,212	56.3	9.2	24.4	6.2	0.8	3.0	31.7
NC	3,838	79.4	14.0	0.9	1.9	1.1	2.7	24.0
ND	319	77.7	10.0	0.4	5.0	0.8	6.0	15.8
OH	5,308	82.8	9.3	2.1	2.4	0.7	2.8	22.9
OK	1,540	80.0	13.2	0.5	2.1	1.1	3.1	21.7
OR	1,601	73.2	12.2	4.2	3.6	1.9	5.0	22.2
PA.	5,556	76.5	10.4	5.2	4.1	0.8	3.0	25.2
RI	491	80.1	10.4	2.5	3.8	1.0	2.2	22.5
SC.	1,823	79.4	14.0	0.8	2.3	1.3	2.1	24.3
SD.	373	77.3	10.4	0.5	4.5	0.8	6.5	16.6
TN.	2,618	81.7	12.5	0.8	1.5	0.8	2.6	24.5
TX.	9,158	77.7	14.5	1.9	1.9	1.3	2.8	25.4
UT.	1,033	75.5	14.1	2.2	2.8	1.2	4.2	21.3
VT.	312	75.2	11.9	0.7	5.6	0.9	5.7	21.6
VA.	3,482	77.1	12.7	3.6	2.3	1.2	3.2	27.0
WA	2,785	73.3	12.8	4.9	3.2	1.4	4.3	25.5
WV	718	80.3	12.7	0.8	2.9	0.9	2.4	26.2
WI.	2,691	79.5	9.9	2.0	3.7	0.9	3.9	20.8
WY	240	75.4	13.2	1.4	4.4	1.3	4.3	17.8

[1] Including taxicabs.

Source: U.S. Census Bureau, "2000 Census of Population and Housing, Profiles of General Demographic Characteristics"; <http://www.census.gov/Press-Release/www/2002/demoprofiles.html>.

No. 1091. Commuting to Work—25 Largest Metropolitan Areas: 2000

[In percent, except as indicated (2,060.6 represents 2,060,600). As of April 1. For workers 16 years old and over. Based on sample data from the 2000 Census of Population and Housing; see text Section 1, and Appendix III. Covers metropolitan statistical areas (MSAs) and consolidated metropolitan statistical areas (CMSAs) as defined by the U.S. Office of Management and Budget as of June 30, 1999. For definitions of metropolitan areas see Appendix II. For definition of median, see Guide to Tabular Presentation]

Metropolitan area	Total workers (1,000)	Drove alone	Car-pooled	Used public transportation [1]	Walked	Used other means	Worked at home	Mean travel time to work (min.)
Atlanta, GA MSA	2,060.6	77.0	13.6	3.7	1.3	1.0	3.5	31.2
Boston-Worcester-Lawrence, MA-NH-ME-CT CMSA	2,898.7	73.9	8.8	9.0	4.1	1.0	3.2	27.8
Chicago-Gary-Kenosha, IL-IN-WI CMSA	4,218.1	70.5	11.0	11.5	3.1	1.0	2.9	31.0
Cincinnati-Hamilton, OH-KY-IN CMSA	951.7	81.4	10.0	2.9	2.3	0.6	2.7	24.3
Cleveland-Akron, OH CMSA	1,375.8	82.3	8.7	3.4	2.1	0.7	2.7	24.0
Dallas-Fort Worth, TX CMSA	2,527.6	78.8	14.0	1.8	1.5	1.0	3.0	27.5
Denver-Boulder-Greeley, CO CMSA	1,346.0	75.6	11.5	4.3	2.4	1.4	4.7	25.9
Detroit-Ann Arbor-Flint, MI CMSA	2,482.5	84.2	9.3	1.8	1.8	0.7	2.3	26.1
Houston-Galveston-Brazoria, TX CMSA	2,081.6	77.0	14.2	3.3	1.6	1.3	2.5	28.8
Kansas City, MO-KS MSA	881.3	82.8	10.4	1.3	1.4	0.7	3.4	22.9
Los Angeles-Riverside-Orange County, CA CMSA	6,767.6	72.4	15.2	4.7	2.6	1.6	3.6	29.1
Miami-Fort Lauderdale, FL CMSA	1,642.9	76.6	13.4	3.9	1.8	1.5	2.8	28.9
Minneapolis-St. Paul, MN-WI MSA	1,595.6	78.3	10.0	4.5	2.4	0.9	3.8	23.7
New York-Northern New Jersey-Long Island, NY-NJ-CT-PA CMSA	9,319.2	56.3	9.4	24.9	5.6	0.9	3.0	34.0
Philadelphia-Wilmington-Atlantic City, PA-NJ-DE-MD CMSA	2,815.4	73.3	10.3	8.7	3.9	1.0	2.8	27.9
Phoenix-Mesa, AZ MSA	1,466.4	74.6	15.3	2.0	2.1	2.2	3.7	26.1
Pittsburgh, PA MSA	1,057.4	77.4	9.7	6.2	3.6	0.7	2.4	25.3
Portland-Salem, OR-WA CMSA	1,105.1	73.1	12.1	5.7	3.0	1.5	4.6	24.4
Sacramento-Yolo, CA CMSA	800.0	75.3	13.5	2.7	2.2	2.2	4.0	25.6
St. Louis, MO-IL MSA	1,239.0	82.6	9.9	2.4	1.6	0.6	2.8	25.5
San Diego, CA MSA	1,299.5	73.9	13.0	3.4	3.4	1.9	4.4	25.3
San Francisco-Oakland-San Jose, CA CMSA	3,432.2	68.1	12.9	9.5	3.3	2.2	4.1	29.3
Seattle-Tacoma-Bremerton, WA CMSA	1,776.2	71.6	12.8	6.8	3.2	1.4	4.2	27.7
Tampa-St. Petersburg-Clearwater, FL MSA	1,064.0	79.7	12.4	1.4	1.7	1.7	3.1	25.6
Washington-Baltimore, DC-MD-VA-WV CMSA	3,839.1	70.4	12.8	9.4	3.0	0.9	3.5	31.7

[1] Includes taxicabs.

Source: U.S. Census Bureau, "2000 Census of Population and Housing, Profiles of General Demographic Characteristics"; <http://www.census.gov/Press-Release/www/2002/demoprofiles.html>.

No. 1092. Commuting to Work—25 Largest Cities: 2000

[In percent, except as indicated (353.1 represents 353,100). As of April 1. For workers 16 years old and over. Based on sample data from the 2000 Census of Population and Housing; see text Section 1, and Appendix III]

City	Total workers (1,000)	Drove alone	Car-pooled	Used public transportation [1]	Walked	Used other means	Worked at home	Mean travel time to work (min.)
Austin, TX	353.1	73.6	13.9	4.5	2.5	2.1	3.4	22.4
Baltimore, MD	249.4	54.7	15.2	19.5	7.1	1.1	2.3	31.1
Boston, MA	278.5	41.5	9.2	32.3	13.0	1.6	2.4	28.8
Chicago, IL	1,192.1	50.1	14.5	26.1	5.7	1.3	2.4	35.2
Columbus, OH	367.4	79.0	10.8	3.9	3.2	0.8	2.3	21.9
Dallas, TX	537.0	70.8	17.8	5.5	1.9	1.2	2.8	26.9
Denver, CO	278.7	68.3	13.5	8.4	4.3	1.8	3.7	24.5
Detroit, MI	319.4	68.6	17.1	8.7	2.8	1.1	1.8	28.4
El Paso, TX	208.1	76.5	15.8	2.3	2.0	1.2	2.2	22.4
Houston, TX	841.7	71.8	15.9	5.9	2.3	1.7	2.3	27.4
Indianapolis, IN [2]	385.2	80.0	12.3	2.4	2.0	0.8	2.5	22.7
Jacksonville, FL	350.5	79.2	13.4	2.1	1.8	1.6	1.9	25.2
Los Angeles, CA	1,494.9	65.7	14.7	10.2	3.6	1.6	4.1	29.6
Memphis, TN	274.9	76.6	15.7	3.0	1.9	1.0	1.7	23.0
Milwaukee, WI	249.9	68.8	13.6	10.3	4.7	0.9	1.7	22.5
Nashville-Davidson, TN [2]	274.0	78.5	13.5	1.8	2.4	0.9	3.0	23.3
New York, NY	3,192.1	24.9	8.0	52.8	10.4	1.0	2.9	40.0
Philadelphia, PA	569.8	49.2	12.8	25.4	9.1	1.6	1.9	32.0
Phoenix, AZ	599.6	71.7	17.4	3.3	2.2	2.2	3.3	26.1
San Antonio, TX	491.4	75.6	15.2	3.8	2.2	1.1	2.2	23.8
San Diego, CA	580.3	74.0	12.2	4.2	3.6	2.0	4.0	23.2
San Francisco, CA	418.6	40.5	10.8	31.1	9.4	3.6	4.6	30.7
San Jose, CA	428.0	76.4	14.1	4.1	1.4	1.5	2.5	27.8
Seattle, WA	316.5	56.5	11.2	17.6	7.4	2.7	4.6	24.8
Washington, DC	260.9	38.4	11.0	33.2	11.8	1.9	3.8	29.7

[1] Includes taxicabs. [2] Represents the portion of a consolidated city that is not within one or more separately incorporated places.

Source: U.S. Census Bureau, "2000 Census of Population and Housing, Profiles of General Demographic Characteristics"; <http://www.census.gov/Press-Release/www/2002/demoprofiles.html>.

No. 1093. Summary of Travel Trends: 1977 to 2001

[108,826 represents 108,826,000,000. Data obtained by collecting information on all trips taken by the respondent on a specific day (known as travel day), combined with longer trips taken over a 2-week period (known as travel period). For compatibility with previous survey data, all data are based only on trips taken during travel day. Be aware that terminology changes from survey to survey. See source for details. 1995 and 2001 not comparable directly with prior years due to methodology changes]

Characteristics	Unit	1977	1983	1990	1995	2001
Vehicle trips	Millions	108,826	126,874	158,927	229,745	234,994
Vehicle miles of travel (VMT)	Millions	907,603	1,002,139	1,409,600	2,068,368	2,281,863
Person trips	Millions	211,778	224,385	249,562	378,930	410,969
Person miles of travel	Millions	1,879,215	1,946,662	2,315,300	3,411,122	4,026,158
Average annual VMT per household [1]	Miles	12,036	11,739	15,100	20,895	21,252
To or from to work	Miles	3,815	3,538	4,853	6,492	5,783
Shopping	Miles	1,336	1,567	1,743	2,807	2,993
Other family or personal business	Miles	1,444	1,816	3,014	4,307	4,080
Social and recreational	Miles	3,286	3,534	4,060	4,764	5,102
Average annual vehicle trips per household [1]	Number	1,442	1,486	1,702	2,321	2,188
To or from to work	Number	423	414	448	553	479
Shopping	Number	268	297	345	501	456
Other family or personal business	Number	215	272	411	626	555
Social and recreational	Number	320	335	349	427	441
Average vehicle trip length [1]	Miles	8.35	7.90	8.98	9.06	9.82
To or from to work	Miles	9.02	8.55	10.97	11.80	12.19
Shopping	Miles	4.99	5.28	5.10	5.64	6.61
Other family or personal business	Miles	6.72	6.68	7.43	6.93	7.43
Social and recreational	Miles	10.27	10.55	11.80	11.24	9.40
Average vehicle occupancy [1]	Persons	1.9	1.7	1.6	1.6	1.6
To or from to work	Persons	1.3	1.3	1.1	1.1	1.1
Shopping	Persons	2.1	1.8	1.7	1.7	1.8
Other family or personal business	Persons	2.0	1.8	1.8	1.8	1.8
Social and recreational	Persons	2.4	2.1	2.1	2.0	2.1
Workers by usual mode to work	Percent	100.0	100.0	100.0	100.0	100.0
Auto	Percent	93.0	92.4	87.8	91.0	92.7
Public transit	Percent	4.7	5.8	5.3	5.1	4.0
Other	Percent	2.3	1.8	6.9	3.9	3.3

[1] Includes other purposes not shown separately.

Source: 1995 and prior years—U.S. Federal Highway Administration, Summary of Travel Trends, 1995 National Personal Transportation Survey, December 1999; 2001—U.S. Federal Highway Administration and the U.S. Bureau of Transportation Statistics, 2001 National Household Travel Survey. See Internet site <http://nhts.ornl.gov>.

No. 1094. Urban Travel by Sex of Traveler and Purpose of Trip: 2001

[In percent, except as indicated. For trips of 75 miles or less. For the civilian noninstitutional population. Based on telephone survey of persons in urbanized households taken between March 2001 and May 2002. Data relate to trips on one travel day. For details, see source. Information on the 2001 National Household Travel Survey (NHTS) and a copy of the source article are at Internet site <http://nhts.ornl.gov/2001/index.shtml>]

Mode of transportation	Total person urban trips	Sex of traveler - Male	Sex of traveler - Female	Work and work related	Shopping and services	Social and recreation	School and church
Total trips [1] (bil.)	287.7	139.8	147.9	50.3	62.4	144.4	27.9
PERCENT DISTRIBUTION	100.0	100.0	100.0	100.0	100.0	100.0	100.0
Auto, total	85.8	85.6	86.0	92.1	91.5	84.1	72.9
SOV [2]	37.6	40.8	34.5	75.4	38.4	27.6	17.1
HOV [3]	48.2	44.7	51.5	16.8	53.2	56.6	55.9
Transit, total	1.7	1.7	1.8	3.7	1.4	1.0	2.2
Bus and light rail [4]	1.2	1.1	1.3	2.1	1.2	0.7	1.8
Metro/subway/heavy rail [5]	0.4	0.4	0.4	1.1	0.1	0.3	0.4
Commuter rail [6]	0.1	0.2	0.1	0.5	(Z)	(Z)	(Z)
Nonmotorized, total	10.5	10.6	10.5	3.9	6.8	14.0	11.2
Walk	9.6	9.3	9.9	3.4	6.5	12.7	10.5
Bicycle	0.9	1.2	0.5	0.5	0.3	1.3	0.7
School bus	1.4	1.6	1.3	0.1	(Z)	0.2	13.6
Taxicab	0.1	0.1	0.1	0.1	0.1	0.1	0.1
Other	0.4	0.5	0.3	0.1	0.2	0.1	0.1

Z Less than 0.05 percent. [1] Includes trips for other purposes, not shown separately. [2] SOV (single occupancy vehicle) includes vehicles with drivers and no passengers. [3] HOV (high occupancy vehicle) includes vehicles with two or more occupants. [4] Light rail also includes conventional streetcars. [5] Metro/subway/heavy rail includes elevated rail and rail rapid transit. [6] Commuter rail includes suburban/regional rail systems and short-distance service provided by Amtrak.

Source: The Eno Foundation, Washington DC, Transportation Quarterly, Vol. 57, No.3, Summer 2003, *Socioeconomics of Urban Travel: Evidence from the 2001 NHTS*, by John Pucher and John Renne, Rutgers University, New Brunswick, NJ; and unpublished data.

No. 1095. Motor Vehicle Distance Traveled by Type of Vehicle: 1970 to 2001

[1,110 represents 1,110,000,000,000. Travel estimates based on automatic traffic recorder data. Speed trend data for 1970 were collected by several state highway agencies, normally during summer months; beginning 1980 all states have monitored speeds at locations on several highways of the Highway Systems Monitoring Program]

Year	Vehicle-miles of travel (bil.)					Avg. miles per vehicle (1,000)				
		Passenger cars					Passenger cars			
	Total [1]	Cars [1]	Buses [2]	Vans, pickups, SUVs	Trucks [3]	Total [1]	Cars [1]	Buses [2]	Vans, pickups, SUVs	Trucks [3]
1970	1,110	920	4.5	123	62	10.0	10.0	12.0	8.7	13.6
1975	1,328	1,040	6.1	201	81	9.6	9.3	13.1	9.8	15.2
1980	1,527	1,122	6.1	291	108	9.5	8.8	11.5	10.4	18.7
1981	1,555	1,144	6.2	296	109	9.5	8.9	11.5	10.2	19.0
1982	1,595	1,172	5.8	306	111	9.6	9.1	10.4	10.3	19.9
1983	1,653	1,204	5.2	328	116	9.8	9.1	8.9	10.5	21.1
1984	1,720	1,236	4.6	358	122	10.0	9.2	8.0	11.2	22.6
1985	1,775	1,256	4.5	391	124	10.0	9.4	7.5	10.5	20.6
1986	1,835	1,280	4.7	424	127	10.1	9.5	7.9	10.8	22.1
1987	1,921	1,325	5.3	457	134	10.5	9.7	8.9	11.1	23.3
1988	2,026	1,380	5.5	502	138	10.7	10.0	8.9	11.5	22.5
1989	2,096	1,412	5.7	536	143	10.9	10.2	9.1	11.7	22.9
1990	2,144	1,418	5.7	575	146	11.1	10.3	9.1	11.9	23.6
1991	2,172	1,367	5.8	649	150	11.3	10.3	9.1	12.2	24.2
1992	2,247	1,381	5.8	707	153	11.6	10.6	9.0	12.4	25.4
1993	2,296	1,385	6.1	746	160	11.6	10.5	9.4	12.4	26.3
1994	2,358	1,416	6.4	765	170	11.7	10.8	9.6	12.2	25.8
1995	2,423	1,438	6.4	790	178	11.8	11.2	9.4	12.0	26.5
1996	2,486	1,470	6.6	817	183	11.8	11.3	9.4	11.8	26.1
1997	2,562	1,503	6.8	851	191	12.1	11.6	9.8	12.1	27.0
1998	2,632	1,550	7.0	868	196	12.2	11.8	9.8	12.2	25.4
1999	2,691	1,569	7.7	901	203	12.2	11.9	10.5	12.0	26.0
2000	2,747	1,600	7.6	923	206	12.2	11.9	10.2	11.7	25.7
2001	2,782	1,619	7.0	938	208	11.8	11.8	9.3	11.1	26.4

[1] Motorcycles included in cars through 1994; thereafter in total, not shown separately. [2] Includes school buses. [3] Includes combinations.

Source: U.S. Federal Highway Administration, *Highway Statistics*, annual. See Internet site <http://www.fhwa.dot.gov/policy/ohpi/hss/hsspubs.htm>.

No. 1096. Domestic Motor Fuel Consumption by Type of Vehicle: 1970 to 2001

[92.3 represents 92,300,000,000. Comprises all fuel types used for propulsion of vehicles under state motor fuels laws. Excludes federal purchases for military use. Minus sign (-) indicates decrease]

Year	Annual fuel consumption (bil. gal)						Average miles per gallon				
	All vehicles [1]	Avg. annual percent change [2]	Cars [1]	Buses [3]	Vans, pickups, SUVs	Trucks [4]	All vehicles [1]	Cars [1]	Buses [3]	Vans, pickups, SUVs	Trucks [4]
1970	92.3	4.8	67.8	0.8	12.3	11.3	12.0	13.5	5.5	10.0	5.5
1975	109.0	2.5	74.3	1.1	19.1	14.6	12.2	14.0	5.8	10.5	5.6
1980	115.0	-5.9	70.2	1.0	23.8	20.0	13.3	16.0	6.0	12.2	5.4
1981	114.5	-0.4	69.3	1.1	23.7	20.4	13.6	16.5	5.9	12.5	5.3
1982	113.4	-1.0	69.3	1.0	22.7	20.4	14.1	16.9	5.9	13.5	5.5
1983	116.1	2.4	70.5	0.9	23.9	20.8	14.2	17.1	5.9	13.7	5.6
1984	118.7	2.2	70.8	0.8	25.6	21.4	14.5	17.4	5.7	14.0	5.7
1985	121.3	2.2	71.7	0.8	27.4	21.4	14.6	17.5	5.4	14.3	5.8
1986	125.2	3.2	73.4	0.9	29.1	21.9	14.7	17.4	5.3	14.6	5.8
1987	127.5	1.8	73.5	0.9	30.6	22.5	15.1	18.0	5.8	14.9	5.9
1988	130.1	2.0	73.5	0.9	32.7	22.9	15.6	18.8	5.8	15.4	6.0
1989	131.9	1.4	74.1	0.9	33.3	23.5	15.9	18.0	6.0	16.1	6.1
1990	130.8	-0.8	69.8	0.9	35.6	24.5	16.4	20.3	6.4	16.1	6.0
1991	128.6	-1.7	64.5	0.9	38.2	25.0	16.9	21.2	6.7	17.0	6.0
1992	132.9	3.3	65.6	0.9	40.9	25.5	16.9	21.0	6.6	17.3	6.0
1993	137.3	3.3	67.2	0.9	42.9	26.2	16.7	20.6	6.6	17.4	6.1
1994	140.8	2.5	68.1	1.0	44.1	27.7	16.7	20.8	6.6	17.3	6.1
1995	143.8	2.1	68.1	1.0	45.6	29.0	16.8	21.1	6.6	17.3	6.1
1996	147.4	2.5	69.2	1.0	47.4	29.6	16.9	21.2	6.6	17.2	6.2
1997	150.4	2.0	69.9	1.0	49.4	29.9	17.0	21.5	6.7	17.2	6.4
1998	155.4	3.3	71.7	1.1	50.5	32.0	16.9	21.6	6.7	17.2	6.1
1999	161.4	3.9	73.2	1.1	52.8	33.9	16.7	21.4	6.7	17.0	6.0
2000	162.5	0.7	73.1	1.1	52.9	35.2	16.9	21.9	6.8	17.4	5.8
2001	163.0	0.3	73.3	1.0	52.9	35.3	17.1	22.1	6.9	17.6	5.9

[1] Motorcycles included in cars through 1994; thereafter in total, not shown separately. [2] Change from immediate prior year. [3] Includes school buses. [4] Includes combinations.

Source: U.S. Federal Highway Administration, *Highway Statistics*, annual. See Internet site <http://www.fhwa.dot.gov/policy/ohpi/hss/hsspubs.htm>.

No. 1097. Motor Vehicle Accidents—Number and Deaths: 1980 to 2001

[17.9 represents 17,900,000]

Item	Unit	1980	1985	1990	1995	1997	1998	1999	2000	2001
ACCIDENTS										
Motor vehicle accidents [1]	Million	17.9	19.3	11.5	10.7	13.8	12.7	11.4	13.4	12.5
Vehicles involved:										
Cars	Million	22.8	25.6	14.3	12.3	16.0	13.8	11.6	15.9	13.6
Trucks	Million	5.5	6.1	4.4	4.5	7.7	7.3	6.2	8.8	7.4
Motorcycles	1,000	560	480	180	152	138	100	70	130	119
DEATHS										
Motor vehicle deaths within 1 yr. [2]	1,000	53.2	45.9	46.8	43.4	43.5	43.5	43.0	43.0	42.9
Noncollision accidents	1,000	14.7	12.6	4.9	4.4	4.4	4.2	4.3	4.6	5.1
Collision accidents:										
With other motor vehicles	1,000	23.0	19.9	19.9	19.0	19.9	18.5	18.8	20.6	18.4
With pedestrians	1,000	9.7	8.5	7.3	6.4	5.9	5.9	5.8	5.3	5.8
With fixed objects	1,000	3.7	3.2	13.1	12.1	12.0	12.0	11.1	11.2	12.3
Deaths within 30 days [3]	1,000	51.1	43.8	44.6	41.8	42.0	41.5	41.7	41.9	42.1
Occupants	1,000	41.9	36.0	37.1	35.3	35.7	35.4	35.9	36.3	36.4
Passenger cars	1,000	27.4	23.2	24.1	22.4	22.2	21.2	20.9	20.7	20.2
Light trucks	1,000	7.5	6.7	8.6	9.6	10.2	10.7	11.3	11.5	11.7
Large trucks	1,000	1.3	1.0	0.7	0.6	0.7	0.7	0.8	0.8	0.7
Motorcycles [4]	1,000	5.1	4.6	3.2	2.2	2.1	2.3	2.5	2.9	3.2
Buses	1,000	(Z)	0.1	(Z)	(Z)	(Z)	(Z)	0.1	(Z)	(Z)
Other/unknown	1,000	0.5	0.5	0.5	0.4	0.4	0.4	0.4	0.5	0.6
Nonoccupants	1,000	9.2	7.8	7.5	6.5	6.3	6.1	5.8	5.6	5.7
Pedestrians	1,000	8.1	6.8	6.5	5.6	5.3	5.2	4.9	4.8	4.9
Pedicyclist	1,000	1.0	0.9	0.9	0.8	0.8	0.8	0.8	0.7	0.7
Other/unknown	1,000	0.1	0.1	0.1	0.1	0.2	0.1	0.1	0.1	0.1
Traffic death rates: [3] [5]										
Per 100 million vehicle miles	Rate	3.3	2.5	2.1	1.7	1.6	1.6	1.6	1.5	1.5
Per 100,000 licensed drivers	Rate	35.2	27.9	26.7	23.7	23.0	22.4	22.3	22.0	22.0
Per 100,000 registered vehicles	Rate	34.8	26.4	24.2	21.2	20.6	20.0	19.6	19.3	19.0
Per 100,000 resident population	Rate	22.5	18.4	17.9	15.9	15.7	15.4	15.3	14.9	14.8

Z Fewer than 50. [1] Covers only accidents occurring on the road. [2] Deaths that occur within 1 year of accident. Includes collision categories not shown separately. [3] Within 30 days of accident. Source: U.S. National Highway Traffic Safety Administration, *Traffic Safety Facts*, annual; and unpublished data. See Internet site <http://www.nhtsa.dot.gov/people/Crash/Index.html>. [4] Includes motorized cycles. [5] Based on 30-day definition of traffic deaths.

Source: Except as noted, National Safety Council, Itasca, IL, *Injury Facts*, annual (copyright). See Internet site <http://www.nsc.org/>.

No. 1098. Traffic Fatalities by State: 1980 to 2001

[For deaths within 30 days of the accident]

State	1980	1990	2000	2001	Fatality rate [1] 1980	Fatality rate [1] 2001	State	1980	1990	2000	2001	Fatality rate [1] 1980	Fatality rate [1] 2001
U.S. [1]	51,091	44,599	41,945	42,116	3.3	1.5	MO	1,175	1,097	1,157	1,098	3.4	1.6
							MT	325	212	237	230	4.9	2.3
AL	940	1,121	996	994	3.2	1.8	NE	396	262	276	246	3.5	1.4
AK	88	98	106	85	3.3	1.8	NV	346	343	323	313	5.7	1.7
AZ	947	869	1,036	1,048	5.3	2.1	NH	194	158	126	142	3.0	1.2
AR	588	604	652	611	3.6	2.1	NJ	1,120	886	731	747	2.2	1.1
CA	5,496	5,192	3,753	3,956	3.5	1.3	NM	606	499	432	463	5.4	2.0
CO	709	544	681	736	3.2	1.7	NY	2,610	2,217	1,460	1,548	3.4	1.2
CT	575	385	341	312	3.0	1.0	NC	1,503	1,385	1,557	1,530	3.6	1.7
DE	153	138	123	136	3.6	1.6	ND	151	112	86	105	2.9	1.5
DC	41	48	48	68	1.2	1.8	OH	2,033	1,638	1,366	1,378	2.8	1.3
FL	2,825	2,891	2,999	3,011	3.6	1.9	OK	959	641	650	676	3.5	1.6
GA	1,508	1,562	1,541	1,615	3.5	1.5	OR	646	579	451	488	3.4	1.4
HI	186	177	132	140	3.3	1.6	PA	2,089	1,646	1,520	1,530	2.9	1.5
ID	331	244	276	259	4.8	1.8	RI	129	84	80	81	2.4	1.0
IL	1,975	1,589	1,418	1,414	3.0	1.4	SC	852	979	1,065	1,059	3.8	2.3
IN	1,166	1,049	886	909	3.0	1.3	SD	228	153	173	171	3.7	2.0
IA	626	465	445	447	3.3	1.5	TN	1,153	1,177	1,307	1,251	3.4	1.8
KS	595	444	461	494	3.4	1.8	TX	4,366	3,250	3,779	3,724	3.8	1.7
KY	820	849	820	845	3.2	1.8	UT	334	272	373	292	3.1	1.2
LA	1,219	959	938	954	5.0	2.3	VT	137	90	76	92	3.7	1.0
ME	265	213	169	192	3.5	1.3	VA	1,045	1,079	929	935	2.7	1.3
MD	756	707	588	660	2.6	1.3	WA	971	825	631	649	3.4	1.2
MA	881	605	433	477	2.5	0.9	WV	523	481	411	376	4.9	1.9
MI	1,750	1,571	1,382	1,328	2.8	1.3	WI	972	769	799	763	3.1	1.3
MN	848	566	625	568	3.0	1.1	WY	245	125	152	186	4.9	2.2
MS	695	750	949	784	4.2	2.2							

[1] Deaths per 100 million vehicle miles traveled.

Source: U.S. National Highway Safety Traffic Administration, *Traffic Safety Facts*, annual. See Internet site <http://www.nhtsa.dot.gov/people/Crash/Index.html>.

No. 1099. Fatal Motor Vehicle Accidents—National Summary: 1990 to 2001

[Based on data from the Fatality Analysis Reporting System (FARS). FARS gathers data on accidents that result in loss of human life. FARS is operated and maintained by National Highway Traffic Safety Administration's (NHTSA) National Center for Statistics and Analysis (NCSA). FARS data are gathered on motor vehicle accidents that occurred on a roadway customarily open to the public, resulting in the death of a person within 30 days of the accident. Collection of these data depend on the use of police, hospital, medical examiner/coroner, and Emergency Medical Services reports; state vehicle registration, driver licensing, and highway department files; and vital statistics documents and death certificates. See source for further detail]

Item	1990	1995	1996	1997	1998	1999	2000	2001
Fatal crashes, total	39,836	37,241	37,494	37,324	37,107	37,140	37,526	37,795
One vehicle involved	23,445	21,250	21,134	20,807	20,900	20,911	21,117	21,477
Two or more vehicles involved	16,391	15,991	16,360	16,517	16,207	16,229	16,409	16,318
Persons killed in fatal crashes	44,599	41,817	42,065	42,013	41,501	41,717	41,945	42,116
Occupants	37,134	35,291	35,695	35,725	35,382	35,875	36,348	36,386
Drivers	25,750	24,390	24,534	24,667	24,743	25,257	25,567	25,840
Passengers	11,276	10,782	11,058	10,944	10,530	10,521	10,695	10,441
Other	108	119	103	114	109	97	86	105
Nonmotorists	7,465	6,526	6,370	6,288	6,119	5,842	5,597	5,730
Pedestrians	6,482	5,584	5,449	5,321	5,228	4,939	4,763	4,882
Pedalcyclists	859	833	765	814	760	754	693	728
Other	124	109	156	153	131	149	141	120
Occupants killed by vehicle type:								
Passenger cars	24,092	22,423	22,505	22,199	21,194	20,862	20,699	20,233
Minicompact (95 inches)	3,556	2,207	2,037	1,763	1,480	1,224	1,113	881
Subcompact (95 to 99 inches)	4,753	4,584	4,581	4,457	4,034	3,663	3,660	3,536
Compact (100 to 104 inches)	5,310	6,899	7,288	7,195	6,804	6,942	7,022	6,718
Intermediate (105 to 109) inches	4,849	4,666	4,670	4,794	4,617	4,721	5,204	5,401
Full size (110 to 114) inches	2,386	2,116	2,147	2,242	2,014	2,179	2,287	2,304
Largest (115 inches and over)	2,249	1,297	1,270	1,239	1,092	708	897	864
Unknown	989	654	512	509	1,153	1,425	516	529
Motorcycles	3,129	2,114	2,046	2,028	2,186	2,374	2,783	3,064
Other motorized cycles	115	113	115	88	108	109	114	117
Light Trucks	8,601	9,568	9,932	10,249	10,705	11,265	11,526	11,677
Pickup	5,979	5,938	5,904	5,887	5,921	6,127	6,003	6,116
Utility	1,214	1,935	2,147	2,380	2,713	3,026	3,358	3,515
Van	1,154	1,639	1,832	1,914	2,042	2,088	2,129	2,011
Other	254	56	49	68	29	24	36	35
Medium trucks	134	96	87	122	99	90	106	81
Heavy trucks	571	552	534	601	643	669	648	616
Buses	32	33	21	18	38	59	22	34
Other vehicles	296	307	340	343	336	355	401	403
Unknown	164	85	115	77	73	92	49	161
Persons involved in fatal crashes	107,777	102,102	103,347	102,197	101,100	100,666	100,716	100,968
Occupants	99,297	94,621	96,159	95,050	94,241	93,959	94,325	94,526
Drivers	58,893	56,164	57,001	56,688	56,604	56,502	57,280	57,480
Passengers	40,229	38,252	38,913	38,184	37,448	37,280	36,889	36,812
Other	175	205	245	178	189	177	156	234
Nonoccupants	8,480	7,481	7,188	7,147	6,859	6,707	6,391	6,442
Vehicle miles traveled (VMT) (100 mil)	21,444	24,227	24,858	25,617	26,315	26,911	27,469	27,815
Licensed drivers (1,000)	167,015	176,628	179,539	182,709	184,861	187,170	190,625	191,276
Registered vehicles (1,000)	184,275	197,065	201,631	203,568	208,076	212,685	217,028	221,230
Percent distribution of fatal accidents by the highest blood alcohol concentration (BAC) in accident:								
0.00 percent	49.5	57.7	57.9	60.3	59.8	60.2	58.7	58.8
0.01 to 0.07 percent	6.5	5.7	5.7	5.3	5.8	5.5	5.9	5.9
0.08 percent and over	44.0	36.7	36.4	34.3	34.4	34.3	35.4	35.4
Fatalities per 100,000 population:								
Under 5 years old	4.9	4.3	4.6	4.1	4.0	3.9	3.7	(NA)
5 years to 15 years old	6.4	6.0	5.7	5.6	5.2	5.1	4.7	(NA)
16 years to 24 years old	35.2	30.7	30.7	29.3	28.5	28.9	28.5	(NA)
25 years to 44 years old	19.7	17.2	16.9	16.6	16.4	16.4	16.1	(NA)
45 years to 64 years old	14.9	13.6	13.8	14.2	14.0	13.8	13.8	(NA)
65 years to 79 years old	18.8	18.5	18.7	19.2	18.7	18.3	17.1	(NA)
80 years old and over	26.8	28.0	27.8	29.2	28.4	27.3	25.0	(NA)
Fatalities per 100 million VMT [1]	2.1	1.7	1.7	1.6	1.6	1.6	1.5	1.5
Fatalities per 100,000 licensed drivers	26.7	23.7	23.4	23.0	22.4	22.3	22.0	22.0
Licensed driver per person	0.7	0.7	0.7	0.7	0.7	0.7	0.7	0.7
VMT [1] per registered vehicle	11,637	12,294	12,329	12,584	12,647	12,653	12,657	12,573
Fatalities per 100,000 registered vehicles	24.2	21.2	20.9	20.6	20.0	19.6	19.3	19.0
Fatal crashes per 100 million VMT [1]	1.9	1.5	1.5	1.5	1.4	1.4	1.4	1.4
Involved vehicles per fatal crash	1.5	1.5	1.5	1.5	1.5	1.5	1.5	1.5
Fatalities per fatal crash	1.1	1.1	1.1	1.1	1.1	1.1	1.1	1.1
Average occupants per fatal crash	2.5	2.5	2.6	2.5	2.5	2.5	2.5	2.5
Fatalities per 100,000 population	17.9	15.9	15.9	15.7	15.4	15.3	14.9	14.8

NA Not available. [1] VMT = Vehicle miles of travel.

Source: U.S. National Highway Traffic Safety Administration, *Fatality Analysis Reporting System*, annual. See Internet site <http://www.nhtsa.dot.gov/people/Crash/Index.html>.

No. 1100. Motor Vehicle Occupants and Nonoccupants Killed and Injured: 1985 to 2001

[For deaths within 30 days of the accident. (3,416 represents 3,416,000)]

Year	Total	Occupants Total	Passenger cars	Light trucks[1]	Large trucks[1]	Motor-cycles[2]	Buses	Other/unknown	Nonoccupants Total	Pedestrian	Pedal-cyclist	Other/unknown
KILLED												
1985	43,825	36,043	23,212	6,689	977	4,564	57	544	7,782	6,808	890	84
1986	46,087	38,234	24,944	7,317	926	4,566	39	442	7,853	6,779	941	133
1987	46,390	38,565	25,132	8,058	852	4,036	51	436	7,825	6,745	948	132
1988	47,087	39,170	25,808	8,306	911	3,662	54	429	7,917	6,870	911	136
1989	45,582	38,087	25,063	8,551	858	3,141	50	424	7,495	6,556	832	107
1990	44,599	37,134	24,092	8,601	705	3,244	32	460	7,465	6,482	859	124
1991	41,508	34,740	22,385	8,391	661	2,806	31	466	6,768	5,801	843	124
1992	39,250	32,880	21,387	8,098	585	2,395	28	387	6,370	5,549	723	98
1993	40,150	33,574	21,566	8,511	605	2,449	18	425	6,576	5,649	816	111
1994	40,716	34,318	21,997	8,904	670	2,320	18	409	6,398	5,489	802	107
1995[3]	41,817	35,291	22,423	9,568	648	2,227	33	392	6,526	5,584	833	109
1996	42,065	35,695	22,505	9,932	621	2,161	21	455	6,368	5,449	765	154
1997	42,013	35,725	22,199	10,249	723	2,116	18	420	6,288	5,321	814	153
1998	41,501	35,382	21,194	10,705	742	2,294	38	409	6,119	5,228	760	131
1999	41,717	35,875	20,862	11,265	759	2,483	59	447	5,842	4,939	754	149
2000	41,945	36,348	20,699	11,526	754	2,897	22	450	5,597	4,763	693	141
2001	42,116	36,386	20,233	11,677	704	3,181	34	557	5,730	4,882	728	120
INJURED (1,000)												
1988	3,416	3,224	2,585	478	37	105	15	4	192	110	75	8
1989	3,284	3,088	2,431	511	43	83	15	5	196	112	73	11
1990	3,231	3,044	2,376	505	42	84	33	4	187	105	75	7
1991	3,097	2,931	2,235	563	28	80	21	4	166	88	67	11
1992	3,070	2,908	2,232	545	34	65	20	12	162	89	63	10
1993	3,149	2,978	2,265	601	32	59	17	4	171	94	68	9
1994	3,266	3,102	2,364	631	30	57	16	4	164	92	62	9
1995	3,465	3,303	2,469	722	30	57	19	4	162	86	67	10
1996	3,483	3,332	2,458	761	33	55	20	4	151	82	58	11
1997	3,348	3,201	2,341	755	31	53	17	6	146	77	58	11
1998	3,192	3,061	2,201	763	29	49	16	4	131	69	53	8
1999	3,236	3,097	2,138	847	33	50	22	7	140	85	51	3
2000	3,189	3,055	2,052	887	31	58	18	10	134	78	51	5
2001	3,033	2,901	1,927	861	29	60	15	9	131	78	45	8

[1] See footnotes 2 and 3 in Table 1101. [2] Includes motorized cycles. [3] Includes two fatalities of unknown type.

Source: U.S. National Highway Traffic Safety Administration, *Traffic Safety Facts, 2001*; and unpublished data. See Internet site <http://www.nhtsa.dot.gov/people/Crash/Index.html>.

No. 1101. Vehicles Involved in Crashes by Vehicle Type, Rollover Occurrence, and Crash Severity: 2001

[Numbers in thousands (11,127.0 represents 11,127,000]

Vehicle type	Total Number	Total Percent	Rollover Yes Number	Rollover Yes Percent	Rollover No Number	Rollover No Percent
Total[1]	11,127.0	100.0	296.0	2.7	10,831.0	97.3
Passenger cars	6,705.0	100.0	120.0	1.8	6,585.0	98.2
Light trucks:[2]						
Pick-up	1,792.0	100.0	72.0	4.0	1,720.0	96.0
Utility	1,208.0	100.0	67.0	5.5	1,141.0	94.5
Van	857.0	100.0	16.0	1.8	841.0	98.2
Other	61.0	100.0	1.0	1.3	61.0	98.7
Large truck[3]	429.0	100.0	18.0	4.2	411.0	95.8
Bus	54.0	100.0	(Z)	0.2	54.0	99.8
Other/unknown	20.0	100.0	2.0	11.7	18.0	88.3
Fatal crashes	54.6	100.0	10.6	19.5	43.9	80.5
Passenger cars	27.4	100.0	4.3	15.7	23.1	84.3
Light trucks:[2]						
Pick-up	11.0	100.0	2.8	25.1	8.2	74.9
Utility	5.9	100.0	2.1	35.2	3.8	64.8
Van	3.7	100.0	0.7	19.2	3.0	80.8
Other	0.1	100.0	0.0	13.8	0.1	86.2
Large truck[3]	4.8	100.0	0.6	13.0	4.2	87.0
Bus	0.3	100.0	(Z)	3.1	0.3	96.9
Other/unknown	1.3	100.0	0.2	11.3	1.2	88.7

Z Less than 500. [1] Includes injury and property damage only crashes, not shown separately. [2] Trucks of 10,000 pounds gross vehicle weight rating or less. [3] Trucks over 10,000 pounds gross vehicle weight rating.

Source: U.S. National Highway Safety Traffic Administration, *Traffic Safety Facts, 2001*. See Internet site <http://www.nhtsa.dot.gov/people/Crash/Index.html>.

No. 1102. Speeding-Related Traffic Fatalities by Road Type and Speed Limit: 2001

[Speeding consists of exceeding the posted speed limit or driving too fast for the road conditions or any speed related violation charged (Racing, driving above speed limit, speed greater than reasonable, exceeding special speed limit]

State	Traffic fatalities, total	Interstate Total [1]	Interstate Over 55 mph	Interstate At or under 55 mph	Noninterstate 55 mph	Noninterstate 50 mph	Noninterstate 45 mph	Noninterstate 40 mph	Noninterstate 35 mph	Noninterstate Under 35 mph
United States........	42,116	12,850	1,287	377	3,352	541	1,442	878	1,329	1,329
Alabama............	994	351	48	2	97	8	111	22	28	19
Alaska.............	85	35	12	6	6	3	6	-	1	-
Arizona.............	1,048	383	58	13	37	25	71	51	30	35
Arkansas...........	611	143	13	3	76	1	10	3	15	16
California...........	3,956	1,443	225	14	357	63	132	99	170	139
Colorado............	736	341	24	22	48	13	51	38	47	44
Connecticut.........	312	143	8	11	9	9	18	10	17	59
Delaware............	136	37	5	1	5	14	-	3	5	3
District of Columbia.....	68	19	-	1	-	1	4	5	1	6
Florida..............	3,011	529	41	1	38	7	46	22	27	26
Georgia.............	1,615	341	33	12	96	5	39	15	39	27
Hawaii..............	140	38	-	4	3	-	7	-	16	8
Idaho...............	259	84	13	1	13	13	10	-	9	6
Illinois..............	1,414	537	44	55	194	10	51	55	72	54
Indiana.............	909	229	18	14	74	14	21	27	24	31
Iowa................	447	63	5	2	32	2	1	2	4	11
Kansas.............	494	150	8	2	57	6	10	9	5	22
Kentucky............	845	156	14	7	95	2	10	-	13	7
Louisiana...........	954	127	14	4	61	5	13	3	15	8
Maine...............	192	73	3	1	5	9	28	5	10	9
Maryland............	660	230	13	10	23	33	16	37	37	32
Massachusetts.......	477	144	14	6	-	8	8	12	11	59
Michigan............	1,328	307	24	7	148	8	18	13	21	48
Minnesota...........	568	153	13	14	69	9	-	5	5	26
Mississippi..........	784	149	19	2	38	7	43	4	13	9
Missouri............	1,098	444	46	14	135	10	21	28	40	57
Montana............	230	99	22	-	3	-	8	-	5	4
Nebraska...........	246	66	9	1	3	19	6	6	3	11
Nevada.............	313	121	23	1	8	2	22	1	20	8
New Hampshire.....	142	29	1	1	6	4	-	5	6	5
New Jersey.........	747	75	3	4	4	21	7	10	4	18
New Mexico.........	463	154	17	4	27	3	17	9	18	23
New York............	1,548	486	7	25	183	14	27	29	31	75
North Carolina......	1,530	574	25	12	333	14	112	2	53	7
North Dakota........	105	59	5	1	35	2	4	1	-	1
Ohio................	1,378	242	21	4	6	-	-	-	7	8
Oklahoma...........	676	286	35	3	42	11	61	19	24	9
Oregon..............	488	130	6	3	73	6	5	7	9	16
Pennsylvania........	1,530	551	24	20	145	9	101	73	112	53
Rhode Island........	81	50	2	4	1	5	-	4	13	21
South Carolina......	1,059	490	41	6	153	13	91	25	72	34
South Dakota........	171	59	4	-	20	6	5	2	5	3
Tennessee...........	1,251	288	21	6	84	7	52	33	25	44
Texas...............	3,724	1,416	184	36	178	53	93	114	117	128
Utah................	292	83	21	2	6	7	5	9	7	7
Vermont............	92	49	3	1	1	23	1	10	5	3
Virginia.............	935	224	27	10	106	4	32	6	20	16
Washington.........	649	237	34	2	18	32	12	30	62	25
West Virginia........	376	97	7	1	40	-	13	6	18	10
Wisconsin...........	763	258	12	1	151	1	22	5	18	37
Wyoming............	186	78	18	-	10	-	1	4	-	2

- Represents zero. [1] Includes fatalities that occurred on roads for which the speed limit was unknown.

Source: U.S. National Highway Traffic Safety Administration, *Traffic Safety Facts, Speeding*, annual; and unpublished data. See Internet site <http://www.nhtsa.dot.gov/people/Crash/Index.html>.

No. 1103. Traffic Fatalities by State and Highest Blood Alcohol Concentration (BAC) in the Crash: 2001

[BAC means blood alcohol concentration; g/dl means grams per deciliter]

State	Traffic fatalities, total	No alcohol (BAC=0.00 g/dl) Number	No alcohol Percent	Any alcohol (BAC=0.01 g/dl) or more Number	Any alcohol Percent	Low alcohol (BAC=0.01-0.07 g/dl) Number	Low alcohol Percent	High alcohol (BAC=0.08 g/dl or more) Number	High alcohol Percent
United States	42,116	24,668	59	17,448	41	2,515	6	14,933	35
Alabama	994	618	62	376	38	39	4	336	34
Alaska	85	42	50	43	50	4	4	39	46
Arizona	1,048	560	53	488	47	64	6	424	40
Arkansas	611	418	68	193	32	44	7	150	25
California	3,956	2,387	60	1,569	40	292	7	1,277	32
Colorado	736	408	55	328	45	50	7	278	38
Connecticut	312	154	49	158	51	19	6	139	45
Delaware	136	71	52	65	48	8	6	58	42
District of Columbia	68	30	45	38	55	5	8	32	48
Florida	3,011	1,748	58	1,264	42	175	6	1,088	36
Georgia	1,615	1,058	65	557	35	91	6	466	29
Hawaii	140	80	57	60	43	9	7	51	36
Idaho	259	162	63	97	37	11	4	85	33
Illinois	1,414	794	56	620	44	86	6	535	38
Indiana	909	572	63	337	37	54	6	283	31
Iowa	447	292	65	155	35	29	6	126	28
Kansas	494	300	61	194	39	25	5	169	34
Kentucky	845	598	71	247	29	35	4	213	25
Louisiana	954	509	53	445	47	62	6	383	40
Maine	192	127	66	65	34	5	3	60	31
Maryland	660	370	56	290	44	51	8	239	36
Massachusetts	477	244	51	234	49	28	6	206	43
Michigan	1,328	810	61	518	39	77	6	441	33
Minnesota	568	342	60	226	40	30	5	196	34
Mississippi	784	502	64	282	36	29	4	253	32
Missouri	1,098	575	52	523	48	82	7	441	40
Montana	230	126	55	104	45	8	4	96	42
Nebraska	246	150	61	96	39	17	7	79	32
Nevada	313	180	58	133	42	21	7	112	36
New Hampshire	142	73	51	70	49	15	10	55	39
New Jersey	747	450	60	297	40	53	7	244	33
New Mexico	463	249	54	214	46	35	7	179	39
New York	1,548	1,050	68	498	32	94	6	404	26
North Carolina	1,530	997	65	533	35	77	5	456	30
North Dakota	105	52	50	53	50	8	8	44	42
Ohio	1,378	774	56	604	44	89	6	515	37
Oklahoma	676	410	61	266	39	33	5	233	34
Oregon	488	298	61	190	39	34	7	157	32
Pennsylvania	1,530	867	57	663	43	83	5	580	38
Rhode Island	81	32	40	49	60	9	11	40	49
South Carolina	1,059	467	44	592	56	73	7	519	49
South Dakota	171	87	51	84	49	9	5	75	44
Tennessee	1,251	714	57	537	43	75	6	462	37
Texas	3,724	1,935	52	1,789	48	205	5	1,584	43
Utah	292	224	77	68	23	12	4	56	19
Vermont	92	57	62	35	38	2	2	33	35
Virginia	935	595	64	340	36	54	6	287	31
Washington	649	368	57	281	43	42	6	239	37
West Virginia	376	241	64	135	36	16	4	119	32
Wisconsin	763	399	52	364	48	39	5	325	43
Wyoming	186	105	56	81	44	11	6	71	38

Source: U.S. National Highway Traffic Safety Administration, *Traffic Safety Facts*, annual; and unpublished data. See Internet site <http://www.nhtsa.dot.gov/people/Crash/Index.html>.

No. 1104. Fatalities by Highest Blood Alcohol Concentration in the Crash: 1985 to 2001

[BAC means blood alcohol concentration; g/dl means grams per deciliter]

Item	1985	1990	1995	1997	1998	1999	2000	2001
Total fatalities	43,825	44,599	41,817	42,013	41,501	41,717	41,945	42,116
Fatalities in alcohol-related crashes	23,167	22,587	17,732	16,711	16,673	16,572	17,380	17,448
Percent	52.9	50.6	42.4	39.8	40.2	39.7	41.4	41.4
BAC = 0.01-0.07 g/dl:								
Number	3,081	2,980	2,490	2,290	2,465	2,321	2,511	2,515
Percent	7.0	6.7	6.0	5.4	5.9	5.6	6.0	6.0
BAC = 0.08 g/dl or more:								
Number	20,086	19,607	15,242	14,421	14,207	14,250	14,870	14,933
Percent	45.8	44.0	36.5	34.3	34.2	34.2	35.5	35.5
Fatalities with BAC = 0.00 g/dl:								
Number	20,659	22,012	24,085	25,302	24,828	25,145	24,565	24,668
Percent	47.1	49.4	57.6	60.2	59.8	60.3	58.6	58.6

Source: U.S. National Highway Traffic Safety Administration, *Traffic Safety Facts*, annual; and unpublished data. See Internet site <http://www.nhtsa.dot.gov/people/Crash/Index.html>.

No. 1105. Crashes by Crash Severity: 1990 to 2001

[6,471 represents 6,471,000. A crash is a police-reported event that produces injury and/or property damage, involves a vehicle in transport and occurs on a trafficway or while the vehicle is in motion after running off the trafficway]

Item	1990	1994	1995	1996	1997	1998	1999	2000	2001
Crashes (1,000)	6,471	6,496	6,699	6,770	6,624	6,335	6,279	6,394	6,323
Fatal	39.8	36.3	37.2	37.5	37.3	37.1	37.1	37.5	37.8
Nonfatal injury	2,122	2,123	2,217	2,238	2,149	2,029	2,054	2,070	2,003
Property damage only	4,309	4,336	4,446	4,494	4,438	4,269	4,188	4,286	4,282
Percent of total crashes:									
Fatal	0.6	0.6	0.6	0.6	0.6	0.6	0.6	0.6	0.6
Nonfatal injury	32.8	32.7	33.1	33.1	32.4	32.0	32.7	32.4	31.7
Property damage only	66.6	66.8	66.4	66.4	67.0	67.4	66.7	67.0	67.7

Source: U.S. National Highway Safety Traffic Administration, *Traffic Safety Facts*, annual. See Internet site <http://www.nhtsa.dot.gov/people/Crash/Index.html>.

No. 1106. Alcohol Involvement for Drivers in Fatal Crashes: 1991 and 2001

[BAC = blood alcohol concentration]

Drivers involved in fatal crashes	1991 Number of drivers	1991 Percentage with BAC of 0.08% or greater	2001 Number of drivers	2001 Percentage with BAC of 0.08% or greater
Total drivers [1]	54,391	27	57,480	21
Drivers by age group:				
16 to 20 years old	8,002	23	7,963	18
21 to 24 years old	6,748	38	6,016	33
25 to 34 years old	14,151	36	11,534	28
35 to 44 years old	9,482	28	11,201	25
45 to 64 years old	9,153	17	13,005	17
65 years old and over	5,471	7	6,421	6
Drivers by sex:				
Male	40,731	30	41,711	24
Female	12,825	16	14,867	13
Drivers by vehicle type:				
Passenger cars	31,102	27	27,287	23
Light trucks	14,702	30	20,595	23
Large trucks	4,291	3	4,749	1
Motorcycles	2,816	44	3,245	29

[1] Includes age, sex, and types of vehicles unknown.

Source: U.S. National Highway Safety Traffic Administration, *Traffic Safety Facts, 2001*. See Internet site <http://www.nhtsa.dot.gov/people/Crash/Index.html>.

No. 1107. Licensed Drivers and Number in Accidents by Age: 2001

[193,300 represents 193,300,000]

Age group	Licensed drivers Number (1,000)	Licensed drivers Percent	Drivers in accidents Fatal Number	Drivers in accidents Fatal Percent	Drivers in accidents All Number (1,000)	Drivers in accidents All Percent	Accidents per number of drivers Fatal [1]	Accidents per number of drivers All [2]
Total	193,300	100.0	55,700	100.0	21,300	100.0	29	11
Under 16 years old	57	(Z)	300	0.5	90	0.4	([3])	([3])
16 years old	1,506	0.8	900	1.6	510	2.4	60	34
17 years old	2,331	1.2	1,300	2.3	660	3.1	56	28
18 years old	2,850	1.5	1,800	3.2	810	3.8	63	28
19 years old	3,212	1.7	2,100	3.8	780	3.7	65	24
19 years old and under	9,956	5.2	6,400	11.5	2,850	13.4	64	29
20 years old	3,253	1.7	1,700	3.1	720	3.4	52	22
21 years old	3,396	1.8	1,900	3.4	670	3.1	56	20
22 years old	3,227	1.7	1,600	2.9	610	2.9	50	19
23 years old	3,235	1.7	1,500	2.7	570	2.7	46	18
24 years old	3,275	1.7	1,300	2.3	530	2.5	40	16
20 to 24 years old	16,386	8.5	8,000	14.4	3,100	14.6	49	19
25 to 34 years old	34,967	18.1	11,500	20.6	4,670	21.9	33	13
35 to 44 years old	42,732	22.1	10,900	19.6	4,350	20.4	26	10
45 to 54 years old	37,823	19.6	8,500	15.3	3,160	14.8	22	8
55 to 64 years old	23,481	12.1	4,600	8.3	1,620	7.6	20	7
65 to 74 years old	16,030	8.3	2,900	5.2	890	4.2	18	6
75 years old and over	11,925	6.2	2,900	5.2	660	3.1	24	6

Z Less than 0.05. [1] Per 100,000 licensed drivers. [2] Per 100 licensed drivers. [3] Rates for drivers under age 16 are substantially overstated due to the high proportion of unlicensed drivers involved.

Source: National Safety Council, Itasca, IL, *Injury Facts, 2002*, (copyright). See Internet site <http://www.nsc.org/>.

No. 1108. Passenger Transit Industry—Summary: 1980 to 2001

[6,510 represents $6,510,000,000. Includes Puerto Rico. Includes aggregate information for all transit systems in the United States. Excludes nontransit services such as taxicab, school bus, unregulated jitney, sightseeing bus, intercity bus, and special application mass transportation systems (e.g., amusement parks, airports, island, and urban park ferries). Includes active vehicles only]

Item	Unit	1980	1985	1990	1995	1999	2000	2001
Operating systems	Number	1,044	4,972	5,078	5,973	6,000	6,000	6,000
Motor bus systems	Number	1,040	2,631	2,688	2,250	2,262	2,262	2,264
Passenger vehicles, active [1]	Number	75,388	94,368	92,961	115,874	128,516	131,493	134,271
Motor bus	Number	59,411	64,258	58,714	67,107	74,228	75,013	76,075
Trolley bus	Number	823	676	832	885	859	951	600
Heavy rail	Number	9,641	9,326	10,419	10,157	10,306	10,591	10,718
Light rail	Number	1,013	717	913	999	1,297	1,577	1,366
Commuter rail	Number	4,500	4,035	4,415	4,565	4,883	5,073	5,124
Demand response	Number	(NA)	14,490	16,471	29,352	31,884	33,080	34,661
Operating funding, total	Mil. dol	6,510	12,195	16,053	18,241	22,220	24,243	25,288
Passenger funding	Mil. dol	2,557	4,575	5,891	6,801	8,282	8,746	8,891
Other operating funding [2]	Mil. dol	248	702	895	2,812	3,648	4,217	3,580
Operating assistance	Mil. dol	3,705	6,918	9,267	8,628	10,290	11,280	12,817
Federal	Mil. dol	1,094	940	970	817	872	994	1,130
Local [3]	Mil. dol	2,611	5,979	5,327	3,981	4,540	5,319	5,986
State [3]	Mil. dol	(NA)	(NA)	2,970	3,830	4,878	4,967	5,701
Total expense	Mil. dol	6,711	14,077	17,979	21,540	25,538	28,194	29,279
Operating expense	Mil. dol	6,247	12,381	15,742	17,849	20,512	22,646	23,517
Reconciling expense	Mil. dol	464	1,696	2,237	3,691	5,025	5,548	5,762
Capital and planning grants, federal [4]	Mil. dol	2,787	2,559	2,428	5,534	5,395	7,366	6,795
Capital expenditures	Million	(NA)	(NA)	(NA)	7,230	8,975	9,587	11,419
Vehicle-miles operated	Million	2,287	2,791	3,242	3,550	3,972	4,081	4,196
Motor bus	Million	1,677	1,863	2,130	2,184	2,276	2,315	2,377
Trolley bus	Million	13	16	14	14	14	14	13
Heavy rail	Million	385	451	537	537	578	595	608
Light rail	Million	18	17	24	35	49	53	54
Commuter rail	Million	179	183	213	238	266	271	277
Demand response	Million	(NA)	247	306	507	718	759	789
Other	Million	15	15	18	37	71	74	78
Passengers carried	Million	8,567	8,636	8,799	7,763	9,168	9,363	9,653
Motor bus	Million	5,837	5,675	5,677	4,848	5,648	5,678	5,849
Trolley bus	Million	142	142	126	119	120	122	119
Heavy rail	Million	2,108	2,290	2,346	2,033	2,521	2,632	2,728
Light rail	Million	133	132	175	251	292	320	336
Commuter rail	Million	280	275	328	344	396	413	419
Demand response	Million	(NA)	59	68	88	100	105	105
Other	Million	67	63	79	80	91	93	97
Avg. funding per passenger	Cents	29.8	53.0	66.9	87.6	90.3	93.4	92.1
Employees, number (avg.) [5]	1,000	187	270	273	311	350	360	371
Payroll, employee	Mil. dol	3,281	5,843	7,226	8,213	9,495	10,400	10,627
Fringe benefits, employee	Mil. dol	1,353	2,868	3,986	4,484	5,052	5,413	5,706

NA Not available. [1] Includes other categories, not shown separately. [2] Beginning 1995, includes taxes levied directly by transit agency and other dedicated funds, formerly included in Local. [3] Includes other operating revenue, nonoperating revenue, and auxiliary income. Data for 1985 are state and local combined. [4] 1980, capital grants only. [5] Through 1990, represents employee equivalents of 2,080 hours = one employee; beginning 1995, equals actual employees.

Source: American Public Transportation Association, Washington, DC, *Public Transportation Fact Book*, annual. See Internet site <http://www.apta.com/>.

No. 1109. Class I Intercity Motor Carriers of Passengers: 1990 to 2001

[943 represents $943,000,000. For carriers whose adjusted annual gross operating revenues are $5 million or more. Intercity carriers have intercity revenues which are 50 percent or more of their total operating revenues. Minus sign (-) indicated deficit]

Item	Unit	1990	1993	1994	1995	1996	1997	1998	1999	2000	2001
Number of intercity carriers [1]	Number	21	21	20	20	17	17	15	14	12	12
Operating revenue	Mil. dol.	943	928	870	917	912	1,000	999	1,014	1,088	1,076
Intercity regular route	Mil. dol.	739	747	718	767	771	834	860	864	920	917
Other	Mil. dol.	204	182	152	150	141	165	139	150	168	158
Operating expenses	Mil. dol.	1,026	880	919	899	878	948	947	1,014	1,035	1,039
Operating income	Mil. dol.	-83	48	-48	18	33	52	52	0.2	53	36
Revenue passengers	Million	44	40	41	43	37	52	47	43	33	32
Intercity regular route passengers	Million	37	35	36	38	34	41	37	33	31	30
Other passengers	Million	7	5	4	5	4	12	10	10	2	2
Average fare, intercity regular route	Dol.	20.22	21.32	19.77	20.10	22.85	20.57	23.14	26.16	29.46	30.27

[1] Excludes carriers preponderantly in local or suburban service and carriers engaged in transportation of both property and passengers.

Source: U.S. Bureau of Transportation Statistics, *Selected Earnings Data, Class I Motor Carriers of Passengers. Carriers of Passengers, 1988-1997, 1998, 1999, 2000* and *2001*. See Internet site <http://www.bts.gov/mcs/prod.html>.

No. 1110. Truck Transportation, Couriers and Messengers, and Warehousing and Storage—Estimated Revenue: 2000 and 2001

[In millions of dollars (237,251 represents $237,251,000,000), except percent. For taxable and tax-exempt employer firms. Estimates have been adjusted to the results of the 1997 Economic Census. Based on the North American Industry Classification System; see text, Section 15. Minus sign (-) indicates decrease]

Kind of business	NAICS code [1]	2000	2001	Percent change, 2000-2001
Selected transportation industries	48, 49	237,251	234,436	-1.2
Truck transportation	484	171,691	167,800	-2.3
General freight trucking	4841	109,347	107,386	-1.8
General freight trucking, local	48411	15,152	14,956	-1.3
General freight trucking, long-distance	48412	94,195	92,429	-1.9
General freight trucking, long-distance, truckload	484121	61,932	62,601	1.1
General freight trucking, long-distance, less than truckload	484122	32,263	29,828	-7.5
Specialized freight trucking	4842	62,344	60,414	-3.1
Used household and office goods moving	48421	15,875	14,578	-8.2
Specialized freight (except used goods) trucking, local	48422	25,332	25,360	0.1
Specialized freight (except used goods) trucking, long-distance	48423	21,138	20,476	-3.1
Couriers and messengers	492	52,773	53,363	1.1
Couriers	4921	48,293	49,114	1.7
Local messengers and local delivery	4922	4,480	4,248	-5.2
Warehousing and storage	493	12,787	13,273	3.8
General warehousing and storage	49311	7,004	7,429	6.1
Refrigerated warehousing and storage	49312	2,426	2,336	-3.7
Farm product warehousing and storage	49313	647	688	6.4
Other warehousing and storage	49319	2,710	2,819	4.0

[1] Based on the North American Industry Classification System, 1997; see text, Section 15.

Source: U.S. Census Bureau, 2001 Service Annual Survey, *Truck Transportation, Messenger Services and Warehousing.* Internet site <http://www.census.gov/econ/www/tasmenu.html> (published 15 January 03).

No. 1111. Truck Transportation—Summary: 2000 and 2001

[In millions of dollars (171,691 represents $171,691,000,000), except as indicated. For taxable and tax-exempt employer firms. Covers NAICS 484. Estimates have been adjusted to the results of the 1997 Economic Census. Based on the North American Industry Classification System, 1997; see text, Section 15. Minus sign (-) indicates decrease]

Item	2000	2001	Percent change, 2000-2001
Total operating revenue	171,691	167,800	-2.3
Total motor carrier revenue	160,290	157,215	-1.9
Local trucking [1]	51,860	52,216	0.7
Long-distance trucking [1]	108,430	104,999	-3.2
Size of shipments:			
Less-than-truckload	48,157	47,034	-2.3
Truckload	112,132	110,182	-1.7
Commodities handled:			
Agricultural and fish products	12,064	11,783	-2.3
Grains, alcohol, and tobacco products	5,717	6,388	11.7
Stone, nonmetallic minerals, and metallic ores	10,293	10,642	3.4
Coal and petroleum products	5,915	6,082	2.8
Pharmaceutical and chemical products	9,330	8,483	-9.1
Wood products, textiles, and leathers	16,126	16,456	2.0
Base metal and machinery	12,527	12,409	-0.9
Electronic, motorized vehicles, and precision instruments	9,896	9,933	0.4
Used household and office goods	10,297	9,677	-6.0
New furniture and miscellaneous manufactured products	15,529	15,777	1.6
Other goods	52,596	49,586	-5.7
Hazardous materials	9,969	9,680	-2.9
Origin and destination of shipments:			
U.S. to U.S.	154,270	151,895	-1.5
U.S. to Canada	1,749	1,594	-8.8
U.S. to Mexico	1,284	1,155	-10.1
Canada to U.S.	1,222	1,055	-13.7
Mexico to U.S.	1,118	982	-12.2
All other destinations	646	535	-17.3
Inventory of revenue generating equipment (1,000):			
Trucks	211	212	0.5
Owned	178	180	1.1
Leased	33	32	-3.0
Truck-tractors	938	958	2.1
Owned	793	816	2.9
Leased	145	143	-1.4
Trailers	1,931	1,999	3.5
Owned	1,605	1,675	4.4
Leased	326	324	-0.6
Highway miles traveled (mil.):			
Total	86,576	86,668	0.1
By loaded or partially loaded vehicles	68,672	68,887	0.3
By empty vehicles	17,905	17,781	-0.7

[1] Local trucking is the carrying of goods within a single metro area and its adjacent nonurban areas; long-distance trucking is the carrying of goods between metro areas.

Source: U.S. Census Bureau, 2001 Service Annual Survey, *Truck Transportation, Messenger Services and Warehousing.* Internet site <http://www.census.gov/econ/www/tasmenu.html> (published 15 January 03).

No. 1112. Railroads, Class I—Summary: 1990 to 2001

[As of Dec. 31, or calendar year data, except as noted (216 represents 216,000). Compiled from annual reports of class I railroads only except where noted. Minus sign (-) indicates deficit]

Item	Unit	1990	1994	1995	1996	1997	1998	1999	2000	2001
Class I line-hauling companies [1]	Number.	14	13	11	10	9	9	9	8	8
Employees [2]	1,000	216	190	188	182	178	178	178	168	162
Compensation	Mil. dol	8,654	8,874	9,070	9,202	9,235	9,938	9,603	9,623	9,430
Average per hour	Dollars	15.8	18.5	19.0	20.1	20.3	21.3	21.0	21.5	22.1
Average per year	Dollars	39,987	46,714	48,188	50,611	51,882	55,764	54,082	57,157	58,153
Mileage:										
Railroad line owned [3]	1,000	146	138	137	136	133	132	122	121	119
Railroad track owned [4]	1,000	244	232	228	228	225	224	207	205	204
Equipment:										
Locomotives in service	Number.	18,835	18,505	18,812	19,269	19,684	20,261	20,256	20,028	19,745
Average horsepower	1,000 lb.	2,665	2,832	2,927	2,985	3,060	3,126	3,200	3,261	3,275
Cars in service:										
Freight train [5]	1,000	1,212	1,192	1,219	1,241	1,270	1316	1,369	1,381	1,314
Freight cars [6]	1,000	659	591	583	571	568	576	579	560	500
Income and expenses:										
Operating revenues	Mil. dol	28,370	30,809	32,279	32,693	33,118	33,151	33,521	34,102	34,576
Operating expenses	Mil. dol	24,652	25,511	27,897	26,331	27,291	27,916	28,011	29,040	29,164
Net revenue from operations	Mil. dol	3,718	5,298	4,383	6,361	5,827	5,235	5,510	5,062	5,412
Income before fixed charges	Mil. dol	4,627	6,184	5,016	7,055	6,168	5,803	6,001	5,361	5,517
Provision for taxes [7]	Mil. dol	1,088	1,455	1,556	2,056	1,886	1,573	1,664	1,430	1,614
Ordinary income	Mil. dol	1,961	3,315	2,439	3,885	3,156	2,807	2,976	2,501	2,740
Net income	Mil. dol	1,977	3,298	2,324	3,885	3,156	2,807	2,971	2,500	2,740
Net railway operating income	Mil. dol	2,648	3,392	2,858	4,338	3,984	3,698	4,047	3,924	4,111
Total taxes [8]	Mil. dol	3,780	4,512	4,075	4,669	4,514	4,411	4,459	4,379	4,673
Indus. return on net investment	Percent.	8.1	9.4	7.0	9.4	7.6	7	6.9	6.5	6.9
Gross capital expenditures	Mil. dol	3,591	5,035	5,720	6,550	6,737	7,357	6,193	5,290	5,113
Equipment	Mil. dol	996	1,734	2,343	2,202	2,146	2,321	2,183	1,508	1,013
Roadway and structures	Mil. dol	2,644	3,152	3,651	3,899	4,121	4,875	4,446	4,549	4,421
Other	Mil. dol	-49	150	-275	449	471	161	-436	-767	-321
Balance sheet:										
Total property investment	Mil. dol	70,348	78,384	86,186	90,046	96,058	102,171	103,424	106,136	108,588
Accrued depreciation and amortization	Mil. dol	22,222	24,200	23,439	23,932	21,862	23,338	23,177	23,989	24,635
Net investment	Mil. dol	48,126	54,184	62,746	66,113	74,196	78,832	80,247	82,147	83,953
Shareholder's equity	Mil. dol	23,662	27,389	31,419	32,255	34,996	32,976	30,478	32,401	34,822
Net working capital	Mil. dol	-3,505	-3,059	-2,634	-2,942	-3,434	-4,443	-4,834	-5,783	-6,282
Cash dividends	Mil. dol	2,074	1,698	1,518	3,937	995	1,521	2,084	819	2,120
AMTRAK passenger traffic:										
Passenger revenue	Mil. dol	941.9	717.9	734.1	756.2	792.1	821.5	1,067.8	1,201.6	1,299.9
Revenue passengers carried	1,000	22,382	21,239	20,349	19,700	20,200	21,248	21,544	22,985	23,444
Revenue passenger miles	Million.	6,125	5,869	5,401	5,066	5,166	5,325	5,289	5,574	5,571
Averages:										
Revenue per passenger	Dollars	42.1	33.8	36.1	38.4	39.2	38.7	49.6	52.3	55.4
Revenue per passenger mile	Cents	15.4	12.2	13.6	14.9	15.3	15.4	20.2	21.6	23.3
Freight service:										
Freight revenue	Mil. dol	24,471	29,931	31,356	31,889	32,322	32,247	32,680	33,083	33,533
Per ton-mile	Cents	2.7	2.5	2.4	2.4	2.4	2.3	2.3	2.3	2.2
Per ton originated	Dollar	19.3	20.4	20.2	19.8	20.4	19.6	19.0	19.0	19.3
Revenue-tons originated	Million.	1,425	1,470	1,550	1,611	1,585	1,649	1,717	1,738	1,742
Revenue-tons carried	Million.	2,024	2,185	2,322	2,229	2,114	2,158	2,155	2,179	2,187
Tons carried one mile	Billion.	1,034	1,201	1,306	1,356	1,349	1,377	1,433	1,466	1,495
Average miles of road operated	1,000	133	123	125	127	122	120	121	121	121
Revenue ton-miles per mile of road	1,000	7,763	9,735	10,439	10,704	11,087	11,491	11,848	12,156	12,358
Revenue per ton-mile	Cents	3	2	2	2	2	2	2	2	2
Train miles	Million.	380	441	458	469	475	475	490	504	500
Net ton-miles per train-mile [9]	Number.	2,755	2,746	2,870	2,912	2,861	2,923	2,947	2,923	3,005
Net ton-miles per loaded car-mile [9]	Number.	69.1	72.2	73.6	75.0	74.0	73.2	73.8	73.1	72.4
Train-miles per train-hour	Miles	23.7	22.4	21.8	22.0	19.2	19	20	21	21
Haul per ton, U.S. as a system	Miles	726	817	843	842	851	835	835	843	858
Accidents/incidents: [10]										
Casualties—all railroads:										
Persons killed	Number.	1,297	1,226	1,146	1,039	1,063	1,008	932	937	971
Persons injured	Number.	25,143	16,812	14,440	12,558	11,767	11,459	11,700	11,643	10,985
Class I railroads:										
Persons killed	Number.	1,166	1,080	994	896	895	900	808	778	805
Persons injured	Number.	19,284	11,348	9,571	7,839	7,439	7,532	7,805	7,655	7,232

[1] See text, this section, for definition of Class I. [2] Average midmonth count. [3] Represents the aggregate length of roadway of all line-haul railroads. Excludes yard tracks, sidings, and parallel lines. (Includes estimate for class II and III railroads). [4] Includes multiple main tracks, yard tracks, and sidings owned by both line-haul and switching and terminal. (Includes estimate for Class II and III railroads). [5] Includes cars owned by all railroads, private car companies, and shippers. [6] Class I railroads only. [7] Includes state income taxes. [8] Includes payroll, income, and other taxes. [9] Revenue and nonrevenue freight. [10] Source: Federal Railroad Admin., *Accident Bulletin,* annual. Includes highway grade crossing casualties. See Internet site <http://www.fra.dot.gov/site/>.

Source: Except as noted, Association of American Railroads, Washington, DC, *Railroad Facts, Statistics of Railroads of Class I,* annual, and *Analysis of Class I Railroads,* annual. See Internet site <http://www.aar.org/AboutTheIndustry/AboutTheIndustry.asp>.

Transportation 711

No. 1113. Railroads, Class I Cars of Revenue Freight Loaded, 1970 to 2002, and by Commodity Group, 2001 and 2002

[In thousands (27,160 represents 27,160,000). Figures are 52-week totals]

Year	Carloads [1]	Commodity group	Carloads 2001 [3]	Carloads 2002 [3]	Commodity group	Carloads 2001 [3]	Carloads 2002 [3]
1970	27,160	Coal	6,982	6,734	Metals and products	594	607
1980	22,598	Metallic ores	229	265	Stone, clay, and glass products	483	491
1990	16,177	Chemicals, allied products	1,405	1,440	Crushed stone, gravel, sand	879	863
1994	16,763	Grain	1,117	1,079	Nonmetallic minerals	360	375
1995	16,763	Motor vehicles and equipment	1,201	1,245	Waste and scrap materials	434	443
1996 [2]	16,521	Pulp, paper, allied products	427	425	Lumber, wood products	267	277
1997 [2]	16,568	Primary forest products	213	189	Coke	193	184
1998 [2]	16,914	Food and kindred products	444	439	Petroleum products	294	291
1999 [2]	16,407	Grain mill products	468	476	All other carloads	296	279
2000 [3]	16,354						
2001 [3]	16,286						
2002 [3]	16,100						

[1] Beginning 1990 excludes intermodal. [2] Excludes 2 Class I railroads. [3] Excludes 3 Class I railroads. 2002 data preliminary.

Source: Association of American Railroads, Washington, DC, *Weekly Railroad Traffic*, annual. See Internet site <http://www.aar.org/AboutTheIndustry/AboutTheIndustry.asp>.

No. 1114. Railroads, Class I Line-Haul-Revenue Freight Originated by Commodity Group: 1990 to 2001

[21,401 represents 21,401,000]

Commodity group	1990	1994	1995	1996	1997	1998	1999	2000	2001
Carloads (1,000) [1]	21,401	23,179	23,726	24,159	25,016	25,705	27,096	27,763	27,205
Farm products	1,689	1,459	1,692	1,530	1,408	1,404	1,477	1,437	1,461
Metallic ores	508	440	463	443	327	311	295	322	251
Coal	5,912	5,681	6,095	6,746	6,703	7,027	6,965	6,954	7,295
Nonmetallic minerals	1,202	1,138	1,159	1,176	1,160	1,256	1,306	1,309	1,280
Food and kindred products	1,307	1,381	1,377	1,302	1,295	1,282	1,354	1,377	1,446
Lumber and wood products	780	771	719	682	669	645	673	648	603
Pulp, paper, allied products	611	651	628	589	582	547	612	633	601
Chemicals, allied products	1,531	1,695	1,642	1,639	1,674	1,653	1,814	1,820	1,777
Petroleum and coal products	573	602	596	567	534	510	543	565	547
Stone, clay, and glass products	539	512	516	491	485	475	538	541	528
Primary metal products	477	579	575	597	604	644	682	723	642
Fabricated metal products	31	37	32	29	29	27	27	30	51
Machinery, exc. electrical	39	40	41	40	43	37	34	35	46
Transportation equipment	1,091	1,448	1,473	1,442	1,485	1,671	1,896	1,984	1,777
Waste and scrap materials	439	604	623	605	608	581	624	619	591
Tons (mil.) [1]	1,425	1,470	1,550	1,611	1,585	1,649	1,717	1,738	1,742
Farm products	147	131	154	142	126	129	139	136	137
Metallic ores	47	40	44	42	32	31	29	32	25
Coal	579	574	627	705	705	749	751	758	801
Nonmetallic minerals	109	106	110	113	109	120	125	126	123
Food and kindred products	81	88	91	87	86	87	92	94	98
Lumber and wood products	53	54	51	49	48	47	50	49	46
Pulp, paper, allied products	33	37	36	33	32	31	35	36	34
Chemicals, allied products	126	142	138	139	140	139	154	155	150
Petroleum and coal products	40	43	43	42	39	38	40	42	42
Stone, clay, and glass products	44	42	43	42	41	41	47	48	46
Primary metal products	38	47	47	49	50	53	56	60	53
Fabricated metal products	1	1	1	1	1	1	1	1	1
Machinery, exc. electrical	1	1	1	1	1	1	1	1	1
Transportation equipment	23	30	30	29	31	36	40	42	37
Waste and scrap materials	28	37	38	38	37	36	40	40	37
Gross revenue (mil. dol.) [1]	29,775	32,424	33,782	34,310	34,964	34,898	35,441	36,331	36,063
Farm products	2,422	2,407	3,020	2,807	2,645	2,529	2,720	2,673	2,741
Metallic ores	408	378	394	382	399	373	336	338	288
Coal	6,954	7,021	7,356	7,706	7,698	7,997	7,739	7,794	8,181
Nonmetallic minerals	885	862	875	895	899	920	955	969	945
Food and kindred products	2,188	2,427	2,464	2,378	2,385	2,378	2,400	2,424	2,579
Lumber and wood products	1,390	1,421	1,385	1,409	1,471	1,487	1,528	1,524	1,519
Pulp, paper, allied products	1,486	1,510	1,543	1,485	1,507	1,472	1,457	1,526	1,457
Chemicals, allied products	3,933	4,520	4,553	4,660	4,764	4,610	4,616	4,636	4,504
Petroleum and coal products	918	967	997	1,013	1,028	991	980	1,010	1,014
Stone, clay, and glass products	931	1,009	1,044	1,033	1,063	1,056	1,089	1,113	1,090
Primary metal products	979	1,114	1,199	1,254	1,294	1,304	1,289	1,371	1,292
Fabricated metal products	42	50	44	41	41	37	38	48	65
Machinery, exc. electrical	67	65	69	70	73	64	55	61	73
Transportation equipment	3,100	3,257	3,269	3,390	3,462	3,339	3,582	3,843	3,590
Waste and scrap materials	504	655	685	702	711	693	689	706	685

[1] Includes commodity groups and small packaged freight shipments, not shown separately.

Source: Association of American Railroads, Washington, DC, *Freight Commodity Statistics*, annual. See Internet site <http://www.aar.org/AboutTheIndustry/AboutTheIndustry.asp>.

No. 1115. Railroad Freight—Producer Price Indexes: 1990 to 2002

[Dec. 1984=100. Reflects prices for shipping a fixed set of commodities under specified and unchanging conditions]

Commodity	1990	1995	1997	1998	1999	2000	2001	2002, prel.
Railroad line-haul operating	107.5	111.7	112.1	113.4	113.0	114.5	116.6	119.0
Coal	104.2	107.3	107.0	108.7	107.3	108.7	110.6	110.0
Farm products	110.4	115.6	120.4	123.9	121.7	123.1	124.5	125.5
Food products	105.4	111.2	107.6	107.4	99.7	100.4	102.8	103.1
Metallic ores	106.5	101.9	103.4	104.4	103.8	105.9	107.0	107.1
Chemicals and allied products	111.7	120.0	119.6	120.1	119.1	121.3	122.3	126.4
Nonmetallic minerals	111.7	119.5	120.6	121.5	121.7	122.1	123.0	124.6
Lumber and wood products	107.5	110.0	111.0	110.3	109.8	109.0	112.2	120.4
Transportation equipment	107.5	112.8	113.2	113.4	113.3	112.6	118.7	130.6
Pulp, paper, and allied products	108.0	108.7	111.2	113.7	115.5	119.0	122.4	122.4
Primary metal products	113.1	115.6	114.0	116.1	118.4	124.1	128.8	132.2
Stone, clay, glass, and concrete products	114.1	121.4	119.8	121.8	122.6	128.7	129.0	124.4
Petroleum and coal products	109.2	114.3	120.5	122.5	123.0	124.6	126.8	127.5

Source: U.S. Bureau of Labor Statistics, *Producer Price Indexes*, monthly and annual. See Internet site <http://www.bls.gov/ppi/>.

No. 1116. Petroleum Pipeline Companies—Characteristics: 1980 to 2001

[173 represents 173,000. Covers pipeline companies operating in interstate commerce and subject to jurisdiction of the Federal Energy Regulatory Commission]

Item	Unit	1980	1985	1990	1995	1997	1998	1999	2000	2001
Miles of pipeline, total	1,000	173	171	168	177	160	157	154	152	164
Gathering lines	1,000	36	35	32	35	31	21	20	18	19
Trunk lines	1,000	136	136	136	142	130	136	134	134	145
Total deliveries	Mil. bbl	10,600	10,745	11,378	12,862	12,481	12,914	13,317	14,450	13,352
Crude oil	Mil. bbl	6,405	6,239	6,563	6,952	6,795	7,639	7,551	6,923	7,082
Products	Mil. bbl	4,195	4,506	4,816	5,910	5,686	5,275	5,766	7,527	6,270
Total trunk line traffic	Bil. bbl-miles	3,405	3,342	3,500	3,619	3,683	3,442	3,738	3,508	3,505
Crude oil	Bil. bbl-miles	1,948	1,842	1,891	1,899	1,901	1,747	1,815	1,602	1,566
Products	Bil. bbl-miles	1,458	1,500	1,609	1,720	1,782	1,696	1,923	1,906	1,939
Carrier property value	Mil. dol	19,752	21,605	25,828	27,460	30,655	30,181	33,780	29,648	32,148
Operating revenues	Mil. dol	6,356	7,461	7,149	7,711	7,215	6,890	7,220	7,483	7,730
Net income	Mil. dol	1,912	2,431	2,340	2,670	2,255	2,051	2,928	2,705	3,007

Source: PennWell Publishing Co., Houston, Texas, *Oil & Gas Journal*, annual (copyright).

No. 1117. U.S. Postal Service Rates for Letters and Post Cards: 1958 to 2002

[Domestic airmail letters discontinued in 1973 at 13 cents per ounce; superseded by express mail. Prior to February 3, 1991, international airmail rates were based on international zones which have been discontinued. Rates exclude Canada and Mexico]

Domestic mail date rate of change	Surface mail — Letters Each ounce	Surface mail — Letters First ounce	Surface mail — Letters Each added ounce	Post cards	Express mail [1]	International air mail date of rate change	Letters First 1/2 ounce	Letters Second 1/2 ounce	Letters Each added 1/2 ounce	Post cards	Aero-grammes
1958 (Aug. 1)	$0.04	(X)	(X)	$0.03	(X)	1961 (July 1)	(X)	(X)	(X)	$0.11	$0.11
1963 (Jan. 7)	$0.05	(X)	(X)	$0.04	(X)	1967 (May 1)	(X)	(X)	(X)	$0.13	$0.13
1968 (Jan. 7)	$0.06	(X)	(X)	$0.05	(X)	1971 (July 1)	(X)	(X)	(X)	$0.13	$0.13
1971 (May 16)	$0.08	(X)	(X)	$0.06	(X)	1974 (Mar. 2)	(X)	(X)	(X)	$0.18	$0.18
1974 (Mar. 2)	$0.10	(X)	(X)	$0.08	(X)	1976 (Jan. 3)	(X)	(X)	(X)	$0.21	$0.22
1975 (Sept. 14)	(X)	$0.10	$0.09	$0.07	(X)	1981 (Jan. 1)	(X)	(X)	(X)	$0.28	$0.30
1975 (Dec. 31)	[2](X)	[2]$0.13	[2]$0.11	[2]$0.09	(X)	1985 (Feb. 17)	(X)	(X)	(X)	$0.33	$0.36
1978 (May 29)	(X)	$0.15	$0.13	$0.10	(X)	1988 (Apr. 17)	(X)	(X)	(X)	$0.36	$0.39
1981 (Mar. 22)	(X)	$0.18	$0.17	$0.12	(X)	1991 (Feb. 3)	$0.50	$0.45	[3]$0.39	$0.40	$0.45
1981 (Nov. 1)	(X)	$0.20	$0.17	$0.13	$9.35	1995 (July 9)	$0.60	[3]$0.40	(X)	$0.40	$0.45
1985 (Feb.17)	(X)	$0.22	$0.17	$0.14	$10.75	1999 (Jan. 10)	$0.60	[3]$0.40	(X)	$0.50	$0.50
1988 (Apr. 3)	(X)	$0.25	$0.20	$0.15	[4]$12.00	2001 (Jan. 7)	[3,5]$0.80	[3,5]$1.70	(X)	$0.70	$0.70
1991 (Jan. 1)	(X)	$0.29	$0.23	$0.19	[4]$13.95	2002 (June 30)	[3]$0.80	[3]$1.70	(X)	$0.70	$0.70
1995 (Jan. 1)	(X)	$0.32	$0.23	$0.20	[4]$15.00						
1999 (Jan. 10)	(X)	$0.33	$0.22	$0.20	[4]$15.75						
2001 (Jan. 7)	(X)	$0.34	$0.21	$0.20	[4]$16.00						
2002 (June 30)	(X)	$0.37	$0.23	$0.23	[4]$17.85						

X Not applicable. [1] Post Office to addressee rates. Rates shown are for weights up to 2 pounds, all zones. Beginning Feb. 17, 1985, for weights between 2 and 5 lbs, $12.85 is charged. Prior to Nov. 1, 1981, rate varied by weight and distances. Over 5 pounds still varies by distance. [2] As of October 11, 1975, surface mail service upgraded to level of airmail. [3] Up to the limit of 64 ounces. [4] Over 8 ounces and up to 2 pounds. [5] The rate increments changed to 1 oz.

Source: U.S. Postal Service, "United States Domestic Postage Rate: Recent History," and unpublished data. See Internet site <http://www.usps.com/common/category/postage.htm>.

No. 1118. U.S. Postal Service—Summary: 1980 to 2002

[106,311 represents 106,311,000,000. For years ending September 30. Includes Puerto Rico and all outlying areas. See text, this section]

Item	1980	1990	1995	1999	2000	2001	2002
Offices, stations, and branches	39,486	40,067	39,149	38,169	38,060	38,123	37,683
Number of post offices	30,326	28,959	28,392	27,893	27,876	27,876	27,791
Number of stations and branches	9,160	11,108	10,757	10,276	10,184	10,247	9,892
Pieces of mail handled (mil.)	106,311	166,301	180,734	201,644	207,882	207,463	202,822
Domestic [1]	105,348	165,503	179,933	200,613	206,782	206,381	201,918
First class [2]	60,276	89,270	96,296	101,937	103,526	103,656	102,379
Express mail	17	59	57	69	71	69	61
Priority mail	248	518	869	1,190	1,223	1,118	998
Periodicals (formerly 2d class)	10,220	10,680	10,194	10,274	10,365	10,077	9,690
Standard A (formerly 3d class)	30,381	63,725	71,112	85,662	90,057	89,938	87,231
Standard B (formerly 4th class)	633	663	936	1,043	1,128	1,093	1,075
Mailgram	39	14	5	4	4	3	3
U.S. Postal Service	(NA)	538	412	382	363	381	425
Free for the blind	28	35	52	53	47	45	57
International surface	450	166	106	103	79	60	39
International air	513	632	696	928	1,021	1,022	865
Employees, total (1,000)	667	843	875	906	901	891	854
Career	643	761	753	798	788	776	753
Headquarters	3	2	2	2	2	2	2
Headquarters support	(NA)	6	4	4	6	6	4
Inspection Service	5	4	4	4	4	4	4
Inspector General	(X)	(X)	(X)	(Z)	1	1	1
Field career	635	747	745	786	775	764	743
Postmasters	29	27	27	26	26	26	26
Supervisors/managers	36	43	35	39	39	39	38
Professional, administrative, and technical	5	10	11	11	10	10	10
Clerks	263	290	274	292	282	270	257
Mail handlers	37	51	57	62	61	60	59
City carriers	187	236	240	242	241	240	234
Motor vehicle operators	6	7	8	9	9	9	9
Rural carriers	33	42	46	55	57	60	61
Special delivery messengers	3	2	2	(X)	(X)	(X)	(X)
Building and equipment maintenance	27	33	38	42	42	43	42
Vehicle maintenance	5	5	5	6	6	6	6
Other [3]	4	1	2	2	2	1	1
Noncareer	25	83	122	108	114	115	101
Casuals	5	27	26	25	30	30	19
Transitional	(X)	(X)	32	12	13	14	13
Rural substitutes	20	43	50	57	58	58	56
Relief/Leave replacements	(X)	12	13	12	12	12	12
Nonbargaining temporary	(X)	(Z)	1	1	1	1	1
Compensation and employee benefits (mil. dol.)	16,541	34,214	41,931	47,333	49,532	51,351	51,557
Avg. salary per employee (dol.) [4]	24,799	37,570	45,001	48,111	50,103	54,481	54,225
Pieces of mail per employee, (1,000)	159	197	207	223	231	233	237
Total revenue (mil. dol.) [5]	19,253	40,074	54,509	62,755	64,540	65,834	66,463
Operating postal revenue	17,143	39,201	54,176	62,655	64,476	65,766	66,411
Mail revenue [6]	16,377	37,892	52,490	60,418	62,284	63,425	63,761
First class mail	10,146	24,023	31,955	34,933	35,516	35,876	36,483
Priority mail [7]	612	1,555	3,075	4,533	4,837	4,916	4,723
Express mail [8]	184	630	711	942	996	996	911
Mailgram	15	8	2	2	2	1	1
Periodicals (formerly 2d class)	863	1,509	1,972	2,115	2,171	2,205	2,165
Standard mail A (formerly 3d class)	2,412	8,082	11,792	14,436	15,193	15,705	15,819
Standard mail B (formerly 4th class)	805	919	1,525	1,829	1,912	1,994	2,080
International surface	154	222	205	194	180	178	150
International air	442	941	1,254	1,434	1,477	1,554	1,429
Service revenue	765	1,310	1,687	2,237	2,191	2,341	2,655
Registry [9]	157	174	118	95	98	98	87
Certified [9]	120	310	560	377	385	495	606
Insurance [9]	55	47	52	92	109	123	135
Collection-on-delivery	21	26	21	20	22	15	14
Special delivery [10]	73	6	3	(X)	(X)	(X)	(X)
Money orders	95	155	196	228	235	225	239
Other [9]	244	592	737	1,425	1,342	1,384	1,574
Operating expenses (mil. dol.) [11]	19,413	40,490	50,730	60,642	62,992	65,640	65,234

NA Not available. X Not applicable. Z Fewer than 500. [1] Data for 1980 includes penalty and franked mail, not shown separately. [2] Items mailed at 1st class rates and weighing 11 ounces or less. [3] Includes discontinued operations, area offices, and nurses. [4] For career bargaining unit employees. Includes fringe benefits. [5] Net revenues after refunds of postage. Includes operating reimbursements, stamped envelope purchases, indemnity claims, and miscellaneous revenue and expenditure offsets. Shown in year which gave rise to the earnings. [6] For 1980, includes penalty and franked mail, not shown separately. Later years have that mail distributed into the appropriate class. [7] Provides 2 to 3 day delivery service. [8] Overnight delivery of packages weighing up to 70 pounds. [9] Beginning 1998, return receipt revenue broken out from registry, certified, and insurance and included in "other." [10] Special delivery discontinued June 8, 1997. [11] Shown in year in which obligation was incurred.

Source: U.S. Postal Service, *Annual Report of the Postmaster General* and *Comprehensive Statement on Postal Operations*, annual; and unpublished data.

Section 24
Information and Communications

This section presents statistics on the various information and communications media: publishing, including newspapers, periodicals, books, and software; motion pictures, sound recordings, broadcasting, and telecommunications; and information services, such as libraries. Statistics on computer use and Internet access are also included. Data on the usage, finances, and operations of the Postal Service previously shown in this section are now presented in Section 23, Transportation.

Information industry—The U.S. Census Bureau's *Service Annual Survey, Information Services Sector,* provides estimates of operating revenue of taxable firms and revenues and expenses of firms exempt from federal taxes for industries in the information sector of the economy. Similar estimates were previously issued in the *Annual Survey of Communications Services.* Data beginning 1998 are based on the North American Industry Classification System (NAICS) and the information sector is a newly created economic sector. It comprises establishments engaged in the following processes: (a) producing and distributing information and cultural products, (b) providing the means to transmit or distribute these products as well as data or communications, and (c) processing data. It includes establishments previously classified in the Standard Industrial Classification (SIC) in manufacturing (publishing); transportation, communications, and utilities (telecommunications and broadcasting); and services (software publishing, motion picture production, data processing, online information services, and libraries).

This new sector is comprised of industries which existed previously, were revised from previous industry definitions, or are completely new industries. Among those which existed previously are newspaper publishers, motion picture and video production, and online information services. Revised industries include book publishers and libraries and archives. Newly created industries include database and directory publishers, record production, music publishers, sound recording studios, cable networks, wired telecommunications carriers, paging, and satellite telecommunications. The following URL contains detailed information about NAICS and provides a comparison of the SIC and NAICS <http://www.census.gov/epcd/www/naics.html>. See also the text in Section 15, Business Enterprise.

Beginning 2001, the Service Annual Survey estimates reflect the introduction of the provisional North American Product Classification System (NAPCS) for the information sector. Data for prior years are not comparable. See <http://www.census.gov/eos/www/napcs/napcs.htm>.

The 1997 Economic Census was the first economic census to cover the new information sector of the economy. The census, conducted every 5-years, for the years ending "2" and "7," provides information on the number of establishments, receipts, payroll, and paid employees for the United States and various geographic levels.

The Federal Communications Commission (FCC), established in 1934, regulates wire and radio communications. Only the largest carriers and holding companies file annual financial reports which are publically available. The FCC has jurisdiction over interstate and foreign communication services but not over intrastate or local services. The gross operating revenues of the telephone carriers reporting publically available data annually to the FCC, however, are estimated to cover about 90 percent of the revenues of all U.S. telephone companies. Data are not comparable with Census Bureau *Annual Survey* because of coverage and different accounting practices for those telephone companies which report to the FCC.

Reports filed by the broadcasting industry cover all radio and television stations operating in the United States. The private radio services represent the largest and most diverse group of licensees regulated by the FCC. These services provide voice, data communications, point-to-point, and point-to-multipoint radio communications for fixed and mobile communicators. Major users of these services are small businesses, the aviation industry, the maritime trades, the land transportation industry, the manufacturing industry, state and local public safety and governmental authorities, emergency medical service providers, amateur radio operators, and personal radio operations (CB and the General Mobile Radio Service). The FCC also licenses entities as private and common carriers. Private and common carriers provide fixed and land mobile communications service on a for-profit basis. Principal sources of wire, radio, and television data are the FCC's *Annual Report* and its annual *Statistics of Communications Common Carriers*.

Statistics on publishing are available from the Census Bureau, as well as from various private agencies. Editor & Publisher Co., New York, NY, presents annual data on the number and circulation of daily and Sunday newspapers in its *International Year Book*. Data on book production and prices are available from Information Today, Medford, NJ. The Book Industry Study Group, New York, NY, collects data on books sold and domestic consumer expenditures. Book purchasing data are from Ipsos, NPD, Inc., Rosemont, IL. Data on academic and public libraries are collected by the U.S. National Center for Education Statistics. Public library data are also gathered by Information Today, Medford, NJ, and the National Commission on Libraries and Information Science, Washington, DC.

Advertising—Data on advertising previously shown in this section are now presented in Section 27, Accommodation, Food Services, and Other Services.

Statistical reliability—For a discussion of statistical collection and estimation, sampling procedures, and measures of statistical reliability applicable to Census Bureau data, see Appendix III.

No. 1119. Information Industries—Establishments, Receipts, Payroll, and Employees by Kind of Business (NAICS Basis): 1997

[623,214 represents $623,214,000,000. For establishments with payroll. Based on the 1997 Economic Census; see Appendix III]

Industry	NAICS code [1]	Establishments (number)	Receipts Total (mil. dol.)	Receipts Per paid employee (dol.)	Annual payroll Total (mil. dol.)	Annual payroll Per paid employee (dol.)	Paid employee for pay period including March 12 (1,000)
Information industries	51	114,475	623,214	203,255	129,482	42,229	3,066.2
Publishing industries	511	33,896	179,035	177,930	43,358	43,090	1,006.2
Newspaper, periodical, book, & database publishers [2]	5111	21,806	117,336	158,598	24,971	33,753	739.8
Newspaper publishers	51111	8,758	41,601	103,137	11,789	29,228	403.4
Periodical publishers	51112	6,298	29,885	217,265	5,993	43,571	137.6
Book publishers	51113	2,684	22,648	251,933	3,643	40,522	89.9
Database & directory publishers	51114	1,458	12,258	284,312	1,655	38,384	43.1
Software publishers	5112	12,090	61,699	231,622	18,387	69,025	266.4
Motion picture & sound recording industries	512	22,204	55,926	202,643	9,392	34,032	276.0
Motion picture & video industries	5121	19,269	44,786	175,998	8,280	32,540	254.5
Sound recording industries	5122	2,935	11,140	517,797	1,112	51,671	21.5
Broadcasting & telecommunications	513	43,480	346,316	241,427	63,480	44,253	1,434.5
Radio & television broadcasting	5131	8,789	40,425	161,885	9,869	39,521	249.7
Radio broadcasting	51311	6,894	10,648	84,060	3,604	28,455	126.7
Television broadcasting	51312	1,895	29,777	242,007	6,264	50,913	123.0
Cable networks & program distribution	5132	4,679	45,390	260,324	6,151	35,280	174.4
Telecommunications [2]	5133	30,012	260,501	257,822	47,460	46,972	1,010.4
Wired telecommunications carriers	51331	20,815	208,791	256,051	39,565	48,520	815.4
Wireless telecommunications carriers (except satellite)	51332	6,386	37,889	258,977	5,839	39,913	146.3
Information services & data processing services	514	14,895	41,937	119,986	13,252	37,915	349.5
Information services [2]	5141	7,307	11,101	127,202	3,478	39,854	87.3
Libraries & archives	51412	2,298	861	39,055	373	16,928	22.0
Other information services	51419	4,482	8,837	158,544	2,639	47,351	55.7
Online information services	514191	4,165	8,043	161,061	2,356	47,181	49.9
Data processing services	5142	7,588	30,837	117,585	9,774	37,269	262.3

[1] North American Industry Classification System, 1997; see text, this section, and Section 15.   [2] Includes other industries, not shown separately.

Source: U.S. Census Bureau, 1997 Economic Census, *Information*, Series EC97S51A-US, issued October 1999. See Internet site <http://www.census.gov/epcd/www/97EC51.htm>.

No. 1120. Information Sector Services—Estimated Revenue: 1999 to 2001

[In millions of dollars (774,394 represents $774,394,000,000), except percent. For taxable and tax-exempt employer and nonemployer firms. Except as indicated, estimates adjusted to the results of the 1997 Economic Census]

Industry	NAICS code [1]	1999	2000	2001	Percent change, 2000-01
Information industries	51	774,394	853,285	878,302	2.9
Publishing industries	511	220,631	235,193	235,073	-0.1
Newspaper, periodical, book, database, and other publishers [2]	5111	139,145	146,575	143,825	-1.9
Newspaper publishers	51111	48,603	51,711	47,470	-8.2
Periodical publishers	51112	38,370	40,314	39,772	-1.3
Book publishers	51113	24,356	25,481	26,362	3.5
Database and directory publishers	51114	15,526	16,757	17,576	4.9
Software publishers	5112	81,486	88,618	91,249	3.0
Motion picture and sound recording industries	512	65,051	68,160	69,366	1.8
Motion picture and video	5121	52,850	55,339	57,189	3.3
Sound recording [2]	5122	12,201	12,821	12,177	-5.0
Broadcasting and telecommunications	513	426,756	471,278	489,184	3.8
Radio and television broadcasting	5131	47,593	52,992	47,380	-10.6
Radio broadcasting	51311	13,208	15,001	13,911	-7.3
Television broadcasting	51312	34,386	37,991	33,468	-11.9
Cable networks and program distribution [2]	5132	60,059	68,110	74,631	9.6
Telecommunications [3]	5133	319,102	350,176	367,173	4.9
Wired telecommunications carriers	51331	247,828	266,018	264,374	-0.6
Wireless telecommunications carriers (except satellite) [2]	51332	53,771	64,612	83,225	28.8
Information services and data processing services	514	61,958	78,653	84,680	7.7
Information services [3]	5141	23,995	35,813	36,829	2.8
Libraries and archives	51412	1,133	1,289	1,253	-2.8
Other information services	51419	20,967	32,452	33,533	3.3
Online information services	514191	18,795	27,515	29,710	8.0
Data processing services	5142	37,963	42,841	47,851	11.7

[1] Based on the North American Industry Classification System, 1997; see text, this section, and Section 15.   [2] Estimates not adjusted to the 1997 Economic Census.   [3] Includes other industries, not shown separately.

Source: U.S. Census Bureau, 2001 Service Annual Survey, *Information Sector Services*. See <http://www.census.gov/econ/www/servmenu.html> (released February 2003).

No. 1121. Information Industries—Establishments, Payroll, and Employees: 2000 and 2001

[For establishments with payroll (3,545.7 represents 3,545,700). Excludes most government employees, railroad employees and self-employed persons]

Industry	NAICS code [1]	Establishment 2000	Establishment 2001	Paid employees [2] (1,000) 2000	Paid employees [2] (1,000) 2001	Annual payroll (mil. dol.) 2000	Annual payroll (mil. dol.) 2001
Information industries............	51	133,590	137,293	3,545.7	3,754.7	209,394	207,124
Publishing industries..................	511	32,545	32,111	1,080.7	1,100.9	75,348	68,981
Newspaper, periodical, book, & database publishers.....................	5111	21,946	21,758	749.2	747.1	31,258	32,026
Newspaper publishers..............	51111	8,586	8,540	412.6	414.0	14,216	14,747
Periodical publishers..............	51112	6,252	6,248	135.6	133.2	7,676	7,544
Book publishers..................	51113	2,661	2,698	87.2	89.7	4,310	4,803
Database & directory publishers........	51114	1,370	1,394	46.2	45.1	2,418	2,328
Other publishers....................	51119	3,077	2,878	67.5	65.6	2,637	2,604
Greeting card publishers...........	511191	112	102	17.8	17.4	631	688
All other publishers..............	511199	2,965	2,776	49.7	48.2	2,006	1,916
Software publishers.................	5112	10,599	10,353	331.5	353.3	44,090	36,955
Motion picture & sound recording industries...	512	22,899	22,782	304.2	297.1	11,736	11,986
Motion picture & video industries.........	5121	19,730	19,532	276.6	270.1	9,806	10,156
Motion picture & video production.......	51211	10,018	10,595	84.5	96.9	5,723	6,816
Motion picture & video distribution......	51212	678	537	13.9	5.9	1,119	307
Motion picture & video exhibition.......	51213	5,884	5,353	144.0	132.7	1,130	1,189
Motion picture theaters (except drive-ins).....................	512131	5,593	5,050	142.3	130.9	1,107	1,162
Drive-in motion picture theaters.......	512132	291	303	1.7	1.7	23	26
Post production & other motion picture & video industries.................	51219	3,150	3,047	34.2	34.7	1,834	1,846
Teleproduction & other postproduction services......................	512191	2,816	2,702	29.7	30.2	1,591	1,589
Other motion picture & video industries.....................	512199	334	345	4.5	4.6	243	257
Sound recording industries.............	5122	3,169	3,250	27.6	27.0	1,930	1,830
Record production.................	51221	276	270	1.1	1.2	55	73
Integrated record production/distribution...	51222	310	305	9.0	8.8	1,100	1,043
Music publishers..................	51223	670	645	5.1	5.1	283	277
Sound recording studios.............	51224	1,516	1,621	8.1	8.4	327	313
Other sound recording industries.......	51229	397	409	4.3	3.5	166	123
Broadcasting & telecommunications........	513	54,971	59,675	1,631.8	1,777.0	88,766	93,960
Radio & television broadcasting.........	5131	8,492	9,234	253.6	269.4	12,292	12,740
Radio broadcasting................	51311	6,442	7,297	121.5	142.7	4,841	5,381
Radio networks.................	513111	334	359	9.3	12.2	516	375
Radio stations..................	513112	6,108	6,938	112.1	130.5	4,325	5,006
Television broadcasting.............	51312	2,050	1,937	132.2	126.7	7,451	7,359
Cable networks & program distribution.....	5132	5,270	6,692	212.7	245.4	10,084	11,730
Cable networks..................	51321	689	887	39.1	41.0	2,654	2,964
Cable & other program distribution......	51322	4,581	5,805	173.6	204.4	7,430	8,767
Telecommunications.................	5133	41,209	43,749	1,165.5	1,262.2	66,389	69,490
Wired telecommunications carriers.......	51331	26,223	27,509	870.2	905.5	49,010	50,210
Wireless telecommunications carriers (except satellite).................	51332	10,424	11,610	202.5	256.6	11,027	13,368
Paging......................	513321	4,098	3,900	72.4	72.5	3,396	3,488
Cellular & other wireless telecommunications.............	513322	6,326	7,710	130.1	184.1	7,631	9,880
Telecommunications resellers...........	51333	2,458	2,475	54.6	59.9	3,342	3,218
Satellite telecommunications..........	51334	728	737	21.3	21.3	1,680	1,492
Other telecommunications...........	51339	1,379	1,418	16.9	18.9	1,330	1,202
Information services & data processing services.............................	514	23,175	22,725	529.0	579.6	33,544	32,197
Information services.................	5141	14,139	13,437	232.5	262.1	19,023	16,709
News syndicates.................	51411	567	540	11.3	12.2	648	680
Libraries & archives..............	51412	2,754	2,725	33.8	36.1	679	920
Other information services..........	51419	10,818	10,172	187.4	213.7	17,696	15,109
Online information services........	514191	10,257	9,608	177.3	202.1	15,690	14,410
All other information services.......	514199	561	564	10.1	11.6	2,006	700
Data processing services.............	5142	9,036	9,288	296.6	317.5	14,521	15,488

[1] North American Industry Classification System, 1997; see text, this section, and Section 15. [2] For employees on the payroll for the pay period including March 12.

Source: U.S. Census Bureau, "County Business Patterns"; 2001 data published 10 April 2003; <http://www.census.gov/epcd/cbp/view/cbpview.html>.

No. 1122. Gross Domestic Income in Information Technologies (IT) Industries: 1992 to 2000

[In millions of dollars (353,202 represents $353,202,000,000), except as noted]

Industry	NAICS [1] code	1992	1995	1998	1999	2000 est.
Total IT-producing industries	(X)	353,202	470,912	646,930	718,151	796,567
Percent share of the economy	(X)	5.6	6.4	7.3	7.7	8.0
Hardware	(X)	110,050	155,409	210,914	225,368	251,655
Computers and equipment, calc. machines	[2]	24,102	31,036	39,211	38,583	46,223
Computers and equipment wholesale sales	421430pt.,3pt.	39,743	51,114	75,084	81,016	87,676
Computer and equipment retail sales	443120pt.	1,915	2,861	3,407	3,676	3,985
Electron tubes	334411	1,053	1,206	1,316	1,349	1,525
Printed circuit boards	334412	3,556	4,406	5,527	5,908	5,985
Semiconductors	334413	18,308	40,836	57,055	64,072	72,293
Passive electronic components	334414,5,6,8pt.,9	13,494	15,310	12,072	12,881	14,503
Industrial instruments for measurement	334513	2,552	2,526	4,874	5,010	5,156
Instruments for measuring electricity	334514pt.,334515	3,493	3,981	8,383	8,659	9,212
Laboratory analytical instruments	334516	1,835	2,134	3,986	4,213	5,098
Software and services [3]	(X)	75,490	111,350	185,609	213,986	245,656
Computer programming services	541511	18,624	26,119	47,796	55,013	62,715
Prepackaged software	511210,334611	14,554	22,768	34,497	40,016	46,419
Computer integrated system design	541512	11,814	13,599	24,691	28,420	32,598
Computer processing, data preparation	514210	12,554	21,844	28,062	32,300	37,048
Information retrieval services	514191,8	2,879	3,910	8,977	10,333	11,852
Computer services management	541513	1,910	2,090	2,942	3,386	3,884
Computer rental and leasing	532420	1,528	1,880	2,944	3,389	3,887
Computer maintenance and repair	811212	4,989	6,949	10,029	11,544	13,241
Computer related services, n.e.c.[4]	541519	4,406	9,305	21,261	24,471	28,081
Communications hardware [3]	(X)	23,970	30,775	46,709	51,431	61,464
Telephone equipment, exc. ext. modems	334210,334418pt.	10,251	12,139	21,807	24,968	29,712
Radio & TV communications equipment	334220, 334290	10,134	14,310	20,642	22,252	26,524
Communications services	(X)	143,692	173,378	203,698	227,366	237,792
Telephone and telegraph communications	[5]	128,700	151,600	173,900	195,100	204,075
Cable and other pay TV services	513210,20	14,992	21,778	29,798	32,266	33,718

X Not applicable. [1] North American Industry Classification System, 1997; see text, Section 15. [2] NAICS 334111,2,3,9, 334418pt., 333311pt.,3pt. [3] Includes other industries, not shown separately. [4] N.e.c means not elsewhere classified. [5] NAICS 513310,21,22,30,40,90.

No. 1123. Information Technologies (IT)—Employment and Wages: 1995 to 2000

[97,885 represents 97,885,000]

Industry	1987 SIC [1] code	Employment (1,000) 1995	1999	2000	Annual wages per worker (dol.) 1995	1999	2000
Total private	(X)	97,885	108,709	111,079	27,200	32,900	35,000
Total IT-producing industries	(X)	4,004.2	5,256.0	5,596.6	46,900	65,600	73,800
Hardware	(X)	1,475.3	1,707.2	1,748.7	46,300	65,900	77,200
Electronic computers	3571	190.0	195.7	198.0	59,600	98,000	124,300
Computers and equipment wholesalers	5045pt	285.1	392.0	387.7	54,300	80,400	88,200
Computers and equipment retailers	5734pt	93.7	136.8	142.5	33,700	43,300	47,900
Computer storage devices & peripheral equipment	3572,7	104.5	114.8	107.3	46,500	65,600	84,200
Computer terminals, office & accounting, machines	3575,8,9	57.7	57.0	56.1	46,600	64,300	67,600
Electron tubes	3671	24.0	20.7	20.1	41,900	48,400	59,900
Semiconductors	3674	235.2	272.1	293.9	53,800	74,900	93,500
Printed circuit boards, electronic capacitors	3672,5-8	187.0	195.6	210.5	28,300	35,100	39,800
Electronic components, n.e.c.[2]	3679	134.6	152.4	157.7	32,900	41,800	45,900
Industrial instruments for measurement	3823	64.2	69.9	72.6	38,400	48,500	54,300
Instruments for measuring electricity	3825	71.2	68.3	69.6	51,600	70,600	82,500
Analytical instruments	3826	28.1	31.9	32.7	44,200	58,700	75,400
Software/services [3]	(X)	1,109.6	1,903.2	2,122.8	50,700	72,200	80,900
Computer programming services	7371	245.3	454.7	518.7	52,700	69,000	81,800
Prepackaged software	7372	180.8	270.1	299.9	63,700	115,400	117,400
Computer integrated systems design	7373	129.9	210.7	223.5	54,700	69,400	78,700
Computer processing & data preparation	7374	223.1	276.1	284.8	39,700	49,200	52,300
Information retrieval services	7375	56.9	158.4	243.0	42,200	73,200	89,500
Computer maintenance & repair	7378	48.6	58.2	53.7	37,800	42,700	44,800
Computer services management, rental & leasing	7376,7,9	205.3	447.2	471.3	51,800	68,400	74,900
Communications equipment [3]	(X)	337.3	334.5	341.5	43,200	59,200	68,300
Telephone and telegraph equipment	3661	111.7	120.9	126.7	49,900	70,700	80,500
Radio and TV communications equipment, n.e.c.[2]	3663,9	153.2	147.6	149.5	42,700	57,200	68,200
Communication services	(X)	1,081.9	1,311.1	1,383.6	45,100	57,300	60,100
Telephone communications	481	899.7	1,078.7	1,133.9	46,800	58,800	62,100
Telephone & telegraph communications	482,489	26.7	33.2	33.9	48,500	71,200	76,500
Cable & other pay TV services	4841	155.5	199.2	215.8	34,600	47,000	47,200

X Not applicable. [1] 1987 Standard Industrial Classification code. See text, Section 12. [2] N.e.c. means not elsewhere classified. [3] Includes other industries, not shown separately.

Source of tables 1122 and 1123: U.S. Department of Commerce, Economics and Statistics Administration, *The Digital Economy 2002*, March 2002. See Internet site <http://www.esa.doc.gov/pdf/DE2002r1.pdf>.

Information and Communications 719

No. 1124. Communications Industry—Finances: 1998 to 2001

[In millions of dollars (198,877 represents $198,877,000,000). Covers 353 publicly reporting media and communications companies with revenues of over $1 million in 12 media and communication industry segments. Minus sign (-) indicates loss]

Industry	Revenue 1998	Revenue 1999	Revenue 2000	Revenue 2001	Operating income 1998	Operating income 1999	Operating income 2000	Operating income 2001
Total	198,877	221,199	255,246	261,655	25,884	25,705	19,716	15,758
Advertising, marketing services and specialty media [1]	27,247	32,119	36,797	38,110	3,553	3,693	3,536	3,912
Marketing services holding companies	16,278	18,896	20,771	22,781	1,950	2,276	2,643	2,760
Telephone directory publishing	4,305	4,411	4,751	4,482	1,113	1,180	1,344	1,356
Specialty media	2,632	2,922	3,310	3,463	310	367	456	421
E-marketers	1,161	1,871	2,619	1,851	-127	-367	-1,394	-699
Broadcast television	24,026	25,623	30,414	29,820	4,609	5,078	6,330	5,085
Television network companies	18,855	19,989	23,997	24,201	2,979	3,515	4,500	4,003
Television station broadcasters	5,171	5,634	6,418	5,619	1,630	1,563	1,830	1,081
Cable and satellite television	29,033	34,210	44,567	51,984	2,650	1,715	-1,672	-1,125
Cable and satellite providers	19,022	23,055	31,650	37,851	944	226	-1,715	-3,780
Cable and satellite networks	10,011	11,155	12,918	14,133	1,706	1,488	43	2,655
Radio broadcasting	3,500	4,595	6,876	6,766	822	1,136	999	699
Entertainment	44,029	46,532	47,362	44,093	3,996	3,775	1,726	1,530
Filmed entertainment	27,106	27,053	26,950	27,208	2,038	1,850	1,151	1,142
Recorded music	9,544	10,672	11,433	9,208	606	432	29	-341
Interactive entertainment	7,379	8,806	8,978	7,677	1,353	1,493	546	729
Consumer Internet	4,527	6,834	11,301	12,326	-341	-1,037	960	-38
Internet service providers	3,995	5,650	8,873	10,352	-53	-340	2,111	2,983
Newspaper publishing	22,135	23,904	24,900	23,728	4,547	5,268	5,318	3,946
Consumer book publishing	3,952	4,067	4,197	4,552	186	278	471	483
Consumer magazine publishing	7,311	7,113	7,245	7,460	938	1,024	56	-205
Business-to-business communications	2,094	2,251	2,443	2,186	310	308	410	172
Professional, educational and training media	9,675	11,059	12,792	12,289	959	1,122	1,187	992
Professional and educational media	6,460	7,132	8,155	6,768	690	876	1,093	731
Adult education/corporate training	3,215	3,928	4,637	5,521	269	246	94	261
Business information services [1]	21,347	22,891	26,354	28,341	3,654	3,346	396	308
Financial information	13,461	13,755	14,900	15,699	2,687	2,596	2,349	2,456
Healthcare information	3,256	3,945	4,571	4,701	341	195	-2,245	-2,116

[1] Includes other industries, not shown separately.

No. 1125. Media Usage and Consumer Spending: 1998 to 2006

[Estimates of time spent were derived using rating data for television, cable and satellite television, and radio; survey research and consumer purchase data (units, admissions, access) for books, home video, Internet, interactive TV, magazines, movies in theaters, newspapers, recorded music, and video games. Adults 18 and older were the basis for estimates for television, cable & satellite television, daily newspapers, consumer books, consumer magazines, home video, and interactive TV. Persons 12 and older were the basis for estimates for radio, recorded music, movies in theaters, video games, and consumer Internet]

Item	1998	1999	2000	2001	2002, proj.	2003, proj.	2004, proj.	2005, proj.	2006, proj.
HOURS PER PERSON PER YEAR									
Total	3,347	3,469	3,519	3,570	3,623	3,661	3,715	3,750	3,785
Television	1,551	1,588	1,640	1,661	1,661	1,656	1,669	1,672	1,679
Broadcast TV	884	867	865	815	810	798	796	790	787
Network stations [1]	710	706	805	753	749	736	735	729	726
Independent stations [1]	174	162	61	62	61	61	61	61	61
Cable & satellite TV	667	720	774	846	851	858	873	881	892
Basic cable and satellite TV [1]	565	617	638	692	698	706	720	729	726
Premium cable and satellite TV [1]	101	103	137	154	153	152	153	152	166
Radio	936	967	964	983	1,001	1,014	1,032	1,049	1,062
Box office [2]	13	13	12	13	13	13	14	14	14
Home video [2]	36	39	46	56	77	96	109	120	126
Interactive TV [3]	-	2	2	2	2	3	3	5	6
Recorded music	283	290	264	238	228	219	211	203	195
Video games	43	61	75	78	84	90	95	101	106
Consumer Internet	54	82	106	134	157	174	189	199	213
Daily newspapers	185	183	179	177	175	173	172	170	169
Consumer books	120	121	111	109	107	106	105	104	103
Consumer magazines	125	124	121	119	117	116	115	113	112
CONSUMER SPENDING PER PERSON PER YEAR (dol.)									
Total	570.29	622.32	645.10	683.33	727.90	774.52	815.59	852.93	885.31
Television	167.38	181.71	194.63	210.58	225.34	241.30	255.18	269.18	282.17
Broadcast TV	-	-	-	-	-	-	-	-	-
Cable and satellite TV	167.38	181.71	194.63	210.58	225.34	241.30	255.18	269.18	282.17
Basic cable and satellite networks	125.77	135.61	146.73	158.94	168.75	178.64	187.65	195.62	202.64
Premium cable & satellite services	41.61	46.10	47.90	51.64	56.58	62.66	67.54	73.56	79.53
Radio	-	-	-	-	-	-	-	-	-
Box office [2]	31.23	33.11	33.40	36.57	39.79	41.86	44.33	45.82	48.88
Home video [2]	92.58	97.33	102.46	109.60	119.23	127.80	135.84	141.35	141.84
Interactive TV [3]	-	2.22	2.86	5.02	6.63	8.09	9.50	11.28	12.85
Recorded music	61.67	65.13	62.80	60.57	58.81	57.27	55.82	54.30	52.70
Video games	18.49	24.45	25.93	27.96	30.46	33.60	35.87	38.38	40.92
Consumer Internet	27.63	41.77	50.63	62.08	75.10	88.96	100.99	111.76	122.32
Newspapers	53.37	53.83	53.39	54.12	54.70	55.68	56.24	56.57	57.36
Consumer books	84.16	89.04	87.34	86.13	87.02	88.95	90.68	92.37	93.75
Consumer magazines	46.45	46.15	44.87	43.57	44.07	44.60	45.10	46.26	47.42

- Represents zero. [1] UPN, WB, and PAX affiliates included in independent stations and pay-per-view included basic cable from 1998 to 1999. UPN, WB, and PAX affiliates moved to network-affiliated stations and pay-per-view moved to premium services in 2000. [2] Playback of prerecorded tapes only. [3] Video-on-demand (VOD) only. Personal video recorders (PVRs) included in total TV.

Source for Tables 1124 and 1125: Veronis Suhler Stevenson, New York, NY, *Communications Industry Report Forecast*, annual (copyright) and *Communications Industry Forecast*, annual (copyright).

No. 1126. Utilization of Selected Media: 1970 to 2001

[62.0 represents 62,000,000]

Item	Unit	1970	1980	1990	1995	1996	1997	1998	1999	2000	2001
Households with—											
Telephone service [1]	Percent	87.0	93.0	93.3	93.9	93.8	93.9	94.1	94.0	94.6	94.6
Radio [2]	Millions	62.0	78.6	94.4	98.0	98.0	98.0	(NA)	(NA)	(NA)	(NA)
Percent of total households	Percent	98.6	99.0	99.0	99.0	99.0	99.0	99.0	99.0	99.0	99.0
Average number of sets	Number	5.1	5.5	5.6	5.6	5.6	5.6	5.6	5.6	5.6	5.6
Television [3]	Millions	59	76	92	95	96	97	98	99	101	102
Percent of total households	Percent	95.3	97.9	98.2	98.3	98.3	98.4	98.3	98.2	98.2	98.2
Television sets in homes	Millions	81	128	193	217	223	229	235	240	245	248
Average number of sets per home	Number	1.4	1.7	2.1	2.3	2.3	2.4	2.4	2.4	2.4	2.4
Color set households	Millions	21	63	90	94	95	97	98	99	101	102
Cable television [4]	Millions	4	15	52	60	63	64	66	67	69	69
Percent of TV households	Percent	6.7	19.9	56.4	63.4	65.3	66.5	67.2	67.5	68.0	68.0
VCRs [4]	Millions	(NA)	1	63	77	79	82	83	84	86	88
Percent of TV households	Percent	(NA)	1.1	68.6	81.0	82.2	84.2	84.6	84.6	85.1	86.2
Commercial radio stations: [2]											
AM	Number	4,323	4,589	4,987	4,909	4,857	4,762	4,793	4,783	4,685	4,727
FM	Number	2,196	3,282	4,392	5,296	5,419	5,542	5,662	5,766	5,892	6,051
Television stations: [5] Total	Number	862	1,011	1,442	1,532	1,533	1,564	1,589	1,615	1,663	1,686
Commercial	Number	677	734	1,092	1,161	1,174	1,195	1,221	1,243	1,288	1,309
VHF	Number	501	516	547	562	554	555	561	561	567	572
UHF	Number	176	218	545	599	620	640	660	682	721	737
Cable television:											
Systems [6]	Number	2,490	4,225	9,575	11,218	11,119	10,950	10,845	10,700	10,243	9,926
Households served [7]	Millions	4.5	17.7	54.9	63.0	64.6	65.9	67.0	68.5	69.3	73.0
Daily newspaper circulation [8]	Millions	62.1	62.2	62.3	58.2	57.0	56.7	56.2	56.0	55.8	55.6

NA Not available. [1] For occupied housing units. 1970 and 1980 as of April 1; all other years as of March. Source: U.S. Census Bureau, 1970 and 1980 Census of Housing, Vol. 1; thereafter Federal Communications Commission, Trends in Telephone Service, annual. [2] 1980-1995 as of December 31, except as noted. Source: M Street Corp. as reported by Radio Advertising Bureau New York, NY, through 1990, Radio Facts, annual, (copyright); beginning 1995, Radio Marketing Guide and Fact Book for Advertisers, annual, (copyright). Number of stations on the air compiled from Federal Communications Commission reports. Beginning 1996, Federal Communications Commission, unpublished data as of Sept. 30. [3] 1970, as of September of prior year; all other years as of January of year shown. Excludes Alaska and Hawaii. Source: Television Bureau of Advertising, Inc., Trends in Television, annual (copyright). [4] As of February. Excludes Alaska and Hawaii. Source: See footnote 3. [5] Source: Beginning 1997, Federal Communications Commission, unpublished data. See Internet site <http://www.fcc.gov/mb/audiol/totals.html>, 1997 and 1998 as of December; beginning 1999, as of September. For prior years data, see footnote 3. [6] As of January 1. Source: Warren Communications News, Washington DC, Television and Cable Factbook (copyright). [7] Source: Nielsen Media Research, New York, NY, Nielsen Station Index, November estimates (copyright). [8] As of September 30. Source: Editor & Publisher, Co., New York, NY, Editor & Publisher International Year Book, annual (copyright).
Source: Compiled from sources mentioned in footnotes.

No. 1127. Multimedia Audiences—Summary: 2002

[In percent, except total (203,836 represents 203,836,000). As of spring. For persons 18 years old and over. Represents the percent of persons participating during the prior week, except as indicated. Based on sample and subject to sampling error; see source for details]

Item	Total population (1,000)	Television viewing	Television prime time viewing	Cable viewing [1]	Radio listening	Newspaper reading	Accessed Internet [2]
Total	203,836	94.3	83.1	76.5	83.9	80.0	57.8
18 to 24 years old	26,865	92.6	75.8	73.6	90.6	75.1	69.7
25 to 34 years old	37,787	93.5	82.2	74.2	90.2	76.8	69.4
35 to 44 years old	44,988	93.9	82.9	78.1	90.0	82.3	66.1
45 to 54 years old	37,479	94.1	83.6	79.0	87.2	82.8	65.3
55 to 64 years old	23,719	94.9	86.3	79.6	79.8	82.1	49.9
65 years old and over	32,997	96.8	87.7	74.0	61.9	79.7	20.7
Male	97,691	94.5	83.1	77.2	85.7	80.0	59.2
Female	106,145	94.2	83.2	75.8	82.2	80.0	56.5
White	169,680	94.1	83.2	77.7	84.2	80.0	59.7
Black	24,452	96.0	84.6	71.6	85.7	82.8	42.3
Asian	6,030	93.0	78.7	66.7	73.3	71.9	67.2
Other	3,675	96.4	77.8	67.0	75.2	72.3	59.3
Spanish speaking	24,128	96.1	85.1	64.5	87.2	66.7	44.3
Not high school graduate	34,243	94.4	82.4	62.9	73.9	63.1	19.0
High school graduate	66,300	94.9	84.3	77.5	82.5	79.9	44.7
Attended college	55,432	94.5	82.9	80.3	87.8	83.2	72.5
College graduate	47,861	93.1	82.2	80.3	88.2	88.4	86.7
Employed:							
Full time	111,801	93.5	82.4	79.2	90.9	82.2	70.3
Part time	19,402	94.1	79.9	76.5	88.2	82.0	65.4
Not employed	72,634	95.6	85.2	72.3	71.9	76.1	36.5
Household income:							
Less than $10,000	12,463	93.6	83.2	55.9	69.2	66.8	19.5
$10,000 to $19,999	22,354	94.6	82.9	62.3	72.2	69.4	24.4
$20,000 to $29,999	24,287	94.6	83.9	67.8	77.9	73.5	35.0
$30,000 to $34,999	11,616	94.9	84.4	72.2	82.7	77.0	43.3
$35,000 to $39,999	11,365	94.3	84.5	74.2	84.5	78.9	48.1
$40,000 to $49,999	20,910	94.2	83.8	77.2	86.0	79.7	56.8
$50,000 or more	100,840	94.2	82.5	84.8	89.3	86.0	78.4

[1] In the past 7 days. [2] In the last 30 days.
Source: Mediamark Research Inc., New York, NY, Multimedia Audiences, spring 2002 (copyright).

No. 1128. Newspapers and Periodicals—Number by Type: 1980 to 2002

[Data refer to year of compilation of the directory cited as the source, i.e., generally to year preceding year shown. Data for 1995 and prior years include Canada and Mexico]

Type	1980	1985	1990	1995	1997	1998	1999	2000	2001	2002
Newspapers [1]	9,620	9,134	11,471	12,246	10,042	10,504	10,530	10,696	10,739	10,855
Semiweekly	537	517	579	705	558	557	560	558	573	555
Weekly	7,159	6,811	8,420	9,011	7,191	7,267	7,471	7,594	7,622	7,440
Daily	1,744	1,701	1,788	1,710	1,582	1,461	1,647	1,661	1,656	1,507
Periodicals [1]	10,236	11,090	11,092	11,179	8,530	12,448	11,751	13,019	13,878	13,846
Weekly	1,716	1,367	553	513	350	382	366	402	407	393
Monthly	3,985	4,088	4,239	4,067	3,067	3,378	3,204	3,572	3,636	3,605
Bimonthly	1,114	1,361	2,087	2,568	1,943	2,184	2,034	2,294	2,358	2,328
Quarterly	1,444	1,759	2,758	3,621	2,893	3,386	3,158	3,578	3,814	3,826

[1] Includes other items not shown separately.

Source: Gale Group, Farmington Hills, MI, *Gale Directory of Publications and Broadcast Media*, annual (copyright).

No. 1129. Newspaper, Periodical, Database, and Directory Publishers—Estimated Revenue, Printing Expenses, and Inventories: 1999 to 2001

[In millions of dollars (48,414 represents $48,414,000,000). For taxable and tax-exempt employer firms. Estimates have not been adjusted to the results of the 1997 Economic Census. Based on the North American Industry Classification System, 1997; see text, this section, and Section 15]

Item	Newspaper publishers (NAICS 51111) 1999	2000	2001	Periodical publishers (NAICS 51112) 1999	2000	2001	Database and directory publishers (NAICS 51114) 1999	2000	2001
Revenue [1]	48,414	51,507	47,277	37,901	39,834	39,266	15,433	16,657	17,469
Print	(NA)	(NA)	42,367	(NA)	(NA)	31,714	(NA)	(NA)	11,730
Subscription and sales	(NA)	(NA)	9,394	(NA)	(NA)	13,816	(NA)	(NA)	594
Advertising	(NA)	(NA)	32,973	(NA)	(NA)	17,898	(NA)	(NA)	11,136
Internet	(NA)	(NA)	433	(NA)	(NA)	1,150	(NA)	(NA)	1,010
Subscription and sales	(NA)	(NA)	(S)	(NA)	(NA)	856	(NA)	(NA)	603
Advertising	(NA)	(NA)	324	(NA)	(NA)	293	(NA)	(NA)	407
Contract printing	(NA)	(NA)	1,788	(NA)	(NA)	934	(NA)	(NA)	144
Distribution of flyers, inserts, etc.	(NA)	(NA)	977	(NA)	(NA)	110	(NA)	(NA)	(NA)
Graphic design services	(NA)	(NA)	42	(NA)	(NA)	44	(NA)	(NA)	(NA)
Sales or licensing of rights of content	(NA)	(NA)	75	(NA)	(NA)	231	(NA)	(NA)	121
Rental or sales of mailing lists	(NA)	(NA)	14	(NA)	(NA)	161	(NA)	(NA)	1,253
Publishing services for others	(NA)	(NA)	12	(NA)	(NA)	369	(NA)	(NA)	31
Expenses: Purchased printing	3,427	3,352	3,121	4,287	4,981	4,426	1,198	1,112	1,238
Inventories at end of year	737	786	748	1,258	1,340	1,185	408	398	376
Finished goods and work-in-process	43	51	63	377	879	773	383	370	355
Materials, supplies, fuel, etc.	694	736	685	381	462	413	(S)	(S)	22

NA Not available.   S Data do not meet publication standards.   [1] Includes other sources of revenue, not shown separately.

Source: U.S. Census Bureau, 2001 Service Annual Survey, *Information Sector Services* and prior issues. See Internet site <http://www.census.gov/econ/www/servmenu.html> (released February 2003).

No. 1130. Daily and Sunday Newspapers—Number and Circulation: 1970 to 2002

[Number of newspapers as of February 1 the following year. Circulation figures as of September 30 of year shown (62.1 represents 62,100,000). For English language newspapers only]

Type	1970	1975	1980	1985	1990	1995	1997	1998	1999	2000	2001	2002
NUMBER												
Daily: Total [1]	1,748	1,756	1,745	1,676	1,611	1,533	1,509	1,489	1,483	1,480	1,468	1,457
Morning	334	339	387	482	559	656	705	721	736	766	776	777
Evening	1,429	1,436	1,388	1,220	1,084	891	816	781	760	727	704	692
Sunday	586	639	736	798	863	888	903	898	905	917	913	913
CIRCULATION (mil.)												
Daily: Total [1]	62.1	60.7	62.2	62.8	62.3	58.2	56.7	56.2	56.0	55.8	55.6	55.2
Morning	25.9	25.5	29.4	36.4	41.3	44.3	45.4	45.6	46.0	46.8	46.8	46.6
Evening	36.2	35.2	32.8	26.4	21.0	13.9	11.3	10.5	10.0	9.0	8.8	8.6
Sunday	49.2	51.1	54.7	58.8	62.6	61.5	60.5	60.1	59.9	59.4	59.1	58.8
PER CAPITA CIRCULATION [2]												
Daily: Total [1]	0.30	0.28	0.27	0.26	0.25	0.22	0.21	0.20	0.20	0.20	0.19	0.19
Morning	0.13	0.12	0.13	0.15	0.17	0.17	0.17	0.17	0.16	0.17	0.16	0.16
Evening	0.18	0.16	0.14	0.11	0.08	0.05	0.04	0.04	0.04	0.03	0.03	0.03
Sunday	0.24	0.24	0.24	0.25	0.25	0.23	0.22	0.22	0.21	0.21	0.21	0.20

[1] All-day newspapers are counted in both morning and evening columns but only once in total. Circulation is divided equally between morning and evening.   [2] Based on U.S. Census Bureau estimated resident population as of July 1, except 2000, enumerated resident population as of April 1.

Source: Editor & Publisher Co., New York, NY, *Editor & Publisher International Year Book*, annual (copyright).

No. 1135. American Book Title Production: 1999 and 2000

[Data compiled from R.R. Bowker's Books in Print database. Includes the output of small presses and self publishers]

Subject	Total 1999	Total 2000, prel.	Hardcover 1999	Hardcover 2000, prel.	Mass market[1] 1999	Mass market[1] 2000, prel.	Trade[2] 1999	Trade[2] 2000, prel.
Total.................	119,357	96,080	53,109	44,695	8,281	6,114	57,967	45,271
Agriculture...............	1,037	881	504	457	10	8	523	416
Art.......................	4,795	3,896	2,293	2,010	22	15	2,480	1,871
Biography.................	4,051	2,898	2,227	1,569	111	59	1,713	1,270
Business.................	3,789	2,761	1,408	1,305	14	20	2,367	1,436
Education.................	3,408	2,639	1,175	877	44	14	2,189	1,748
Fiction...................	12,372	11,808	3,992	3,532	4,217	3,468	4,163	4,808
General works.............	1,456	878	732	396	42	14	682	468
History...................	7,486	6,948	3,841	3,906	35	32	3,610	3,010
Home economics...........	2,564	1,982	1,160	872	55	33	1,349	1,077
Juvenile.................	9,438	6,708	5,469	4,007	2,653	1,843	1,316	858
Language.................	2,565	2,132	1,035	1,029	48	25	1,482	1,078
Law.......................	3,078	2,299	1,406	1,129	6	2	1,666	1,168
Literature.................	3,646	2,803	2,068	1,501	137	43	1,441	1,259
Medicine.................	6,153	4,817	2,758	2,190	114	88	3,281	2,539
Music....................	1,593	987	550	446	25	11	1,018	530
Philosophy, psychology....	5,861	4,317	2,415	1,885	216	83	3,230	2,349
Poetry and drama........	2,455	1,860	936	550	50	35	1,469	1,275
Religion.................	6,044	5,086	2,446	2,191	136	85	3,462	2,810
Science.................	7,862	7,140	4,658	4,426	89	62	3,115	2,652
Sociology, economics.....	14,579	12,039	6,855	6,209	119	75	7,605	5,755
Sports, recreation........	3,252	2,695	1,143	1,041	95	66	2,014	1,588
Technology...............	8,896	6,449	3,436	2,698	24	13	5,436	3,738
Travel...................	2,977	2,057	602	469	19	20	2,356	1,568

[1] "Pocket-sized" books sold primarily through magazine and news outlets, supermarkets, variety stores, etc. [2] All paperbound books, except mass market.

Source: Information Today, Inc., Medford, NJ, The Bowker Annual Library and Book Trade Almanac, 2001. (Copyright 2001 by Information Today, Inc.)

No. 1136. Average Per Volume Book Prices: 1999 and 2000

[In dollars. Data compiled from R.R. Bowker's Books in Print database. Includes the output of small presses and self publishers]

Subject	Hardcover 1999	Hardcover 2000	Mass market[1] 1999	Mass market[1] 2000	Trade[2] 1999	Trade[2] 2000
Total.....................	62.32	60.80	5.64	5.76	32.93	29.48
Agriculture...............	55.40	67.24	6.42	7.86	39.26	45.68
Art.......................	59.31	48.35	6.95	7.84	26.54	25.83
Biography.................	45.20	45.41	6.37	6.18	19.99	18.91
Business.................	131.50	134.26	7.61	8.16	48.85	50.82
Education.................	59.75	57.75	7.39	7.25	29.18	27.60
Fiction...................	27.95	25.33	5.58	5.81	16.09	15.75
General works.............	153.98	137.29	7.01	6.95	40.76	41.44
History...................	52.25	51.46	6.65	6.79	26.05	26.49
Home economics...........	38.52	40.16	6.99	7.04	19.32	18.89
Juvenile.................	23.06	19.91	5.12	5.18	19.47	17.52
Language.................	55.92	56.01	7.13	6.94	30.17	26.58
Law.......................	100.13	100.35	6.66	6.99	49.52	49.21
Literature.................	73.92	56.84	6.49	7.26	20.52	20.47
Medicine.................	90.03	82.25	6.32	5.62	44.41	34.36
Music....................	55.55	50.63	6.64	8.65	21.71	23.94
Philosophy, psychology....	54.01	50.53	7.20	7.53	23.49	20.97
Poetry and drama........	46.11	36.98	6.26	5.61	16.04	16.19
Religion.................	44.68	41.89	7.48	8.20	20.40	18.38
Science.................	94.55	85.77	6.34	5.80	49.33	38.62
Sociology, economics.....	62.24	64.67	6.53	6.87	39.20	38.30
Sports, recreation........	38.45	37.75	6.73	6.31	22.62	20.99
Technology...............	100.53	93.86	6.89	6.60	59.82	51.40
Travel...................	40.31	40.17	8.35	8.29	21.56	19.24

[1] "Pocket-sized" books sold primarily through magazine and news outlets, supermarkets, variety stores, etc. [2] All paperbound books, except mass market.

Source: Information Today, Inc., Medford, NJ, The Bowker Annual Library and Book Trade Almanac, 2001. (Copyright 2001 by Information Today, Inc.)

No. 1137. Book Publishers—Estimated Revenue, Printing Expenses, and Inventories: 1998 to 2001

[In millions of dollars (22,480 represents $22,480,000,000). For taxable and tax-exempt employer firms. For NAICS 51113. Estimates have not been adjusted to the results of the 1997 Economic Census. Based on the North American Industry Classification System, 1997; see text, this section, and Section 15]

Item	1998	1999	2000	2001
Revenue, total	22,480	24,129	25,236	26,096
Books, print, total	(NA)	(NA)	(NA)	21,310
Books, Internet, total	(NA)	(NA)	(NA)	1,503
Books, other media, total	(NA)	(NA)	(NA)	829
Sale or licensing of rights to content	(NA)	(NA)	(NA)	303
Contract printing services	(NA)	(NA)	(NA)	188
Fulfillment services	(NA)	(NA)	(NA)	143
Rental or sale of mailing lists	(NA)	(NA)	(NA)	(S)
Publishing services for others	(NA)	(NA)	(NA)	39
Other services revenue	(NA)	(NA)	(NA)	1,772
Expenses: Purchased printing	3,908	4,104	4,229	4,212
Inventories at end of year	2,737	2,984	3,463	4,092
Finished goods and work-in-process	2,510	2,723	3,200	3,889
Materials, supplies, fuel, etc.	227	261	263	203

NA Not available.   S Data do not meet publication standards.
Source: U.S. Census Bureau, 2001 Service Annual Survey, *Information Sector Services*, and prior issues. See Internet site <http://www.census.gov/econ/www/servmenu.html> (released February 2003).

No. 1138. Book Purchasing for Adults: 1991 and 2002

[In percent. Excludes all children's books and books purchased for children under age 14. Based on an ongoing survey of 12,000 households conducted over 12 months ending in December of year shown. For details, see source]

Characteristic	Total 1991	Total 2002	Mass market[1] 1991	Mass market[1] 2002	Trade[2] 1991	Trade[2] 2002	Hardcover 1991	Hardcover 2002	Audio[3] 2002
Total	100.0	100.0	100.0	100.0	100.0	100.0	100.0	100.0	100.0
Age of purchaser:									
Under 25 years old	4.4	5.6	3.8	4.4	5.2	8.0	4.4	4.0	3.5
25 to 34 years old	18.7	13.4	14.0	11.5	25.5	15.8	19.6	12.7	8.8
35 to 44 years old	23.7	17.8	22.7	15.1	25.1	20.5	23.7	21.9	18.6
45 to 54 years old	22.4	24.1	26.0	23.4	18.5	23.9	20.6	25.1	29.8
55 to 64 years old	15.6	21.7	15.8	24.1	13.9	18.8	17.2	19.4	24.2
65 years old and over	15.2	17.4	17.7	21.5	11.8	13.0	14.5	16.9	15.1
Education of household head:									
Not a high school graduate	8.2	7.0	11.6	9.4	5.0	5.2	5.9	5.6	8.4
High school graduate	53.5	54.7	61.2	59.0	44.4	50.7	49.9	54.4	60.8
College graduate	19.0	21.4	15.1	18.6	23.9	23.2	20.3	22.5	18.7
Post college	19.3	16.9	12.1	13.0	26.7	20.9	23.9	17.5	12.1
Occupation of household head:									
Professional/managerial	39.2	35.9	32.0	27.9	47.9	42.8	42.1	39.8	32.2
Sales/service	7.7	8.8	6.6	8.1	8.2	9.3	9.2	10.6	7.8
Blue collar	23.2	18.9	27.0	19.2	19.6	18.2	20.6	18.7	24.0
Retired/unemployed	25.9	34.0	30.4	43.1	20.2	26.5	24.3	28.9	32.3
Other	4.0	2.4	4.0	1.7	4.1	3.2	3.8	2.0	3.7
Household income:									
Under $30,000	41.8	25.7	46.1	30.8	36.8	23.3	39.4	22.8	25.2
$30,000 to 49,999	30.6	21.9	30.2	22.8	31.3	21.6	30.6	21.2	24.2
$50,000 to 74,999	20.1	19.3	18.6	17.5	22.0	19.6	20.6	20.2	19.4
$75,000 and over	7.5	33.1	5.1	28.9	9.9	35.5	9.4	35.8	31.2
Household size:									
One member	20.8	16.6	17.7	16.6	24.1	16.7	22.8	15.4	16.7
Two members	40.4	44.6	42.3	47.0	38.0	41.9	39.7	43.5	43.9
Three or more members	38.8	38.8	40.0	36.4	37.9	41.4	37.5	41.1	39.4
Age of intended reader:									
Under 25 years old	7.4	7.9	5.2	5.5	10.2	12.2	7.7	6.2	5.7
25 to 34 years old	18.6	14.1	14.1	12.0	24.6	16.9	19.8	13.5	9.2
35 to 44 years old	22.9	17.2	22.3	14.6	23.9	19.1	22.7	21.6	17.9
45 to 54 years old	20.8	22.9	24.9	22.6	16.5	22.3	18.5	23.8	28.3
55 to 64 years old	14.9	20.6	15.9	23.4	12.8	17.2	15.7	18.5	22.7
65 years old and over	15.4	17.3	17.6	21.9	12.0	12.3	15.6	16.4	16.2
Category of book:									
Popular fiction	54.9	58.5	93.0	96.0	14.9	23.9	31.8	48.8	76.0
General nonfiction	10.3	7.9	3.6	1.6	15.6	10.6	16.5	11.8	7.5
Cooking/crafts	10.8	8.6	0.4	0.2	20.6	15.9	18.2	12.0	0.4
Other	24.0	25.0	3.0	2.2	48.9	49.6	33.5	27.4	16.1
Where purchased (channel):									
Book stores[4]	57.3	42.6	48.4	37.8	73.7	50.6	54.7	39.6	26.5
Mass merchandisers	4.7	5.8	8.7	11.8	1.0	2.0	1.6	3.0	9.5
Book clubs	16.6	19.3	17.8	22.1	9.5	13.3	22.6	22.8	24.0
Online retailer/Internet	(NA)	8.1	(NA)	4.7	(NA)	9.9	(NA)	9.2	8.4
Other[5]	21.4	24.2	25.1	23.6	15.8	24.2	21.1	25.4	31.6

NA Not available.   [1] "Pocket size" books sold primarily through magazine and news outlets, supermarkets, variety stores, etc.   [2] All paperbound books, except mass market.   [3] Audio and digital books were added to questionnaire in January 2001. Sample size for digital book purchasing (i.e. eBooks) was too small to show detailed breaks.   [4] Includes independent, chain and used bookstores.   [5] Includes mail order, price clubs, discount stores, food/drug stores, multimedia, and other outlets.
Source: Ipsos-NPD, Inc., Rosemont IL., *Ipsos BookTrends*, a service mark of Ipsos-NPD, Inc. (copyright).

No. 1131. Daily Newspapers—Number and Circulation by Size of City: 1980 to 2002

[Number of newspapers as of February 1 the following year. Circulation as of September 30 (29,413 represents 29,413,000). For English language newspapers only. See Table 29 for number of cities by population size. All-day newspapers are counted in both morning and evening columns; circulation is divided equally between morning and evening]

Type of daily and population-size class	Number 1980	1990	1995	2000	2002	Net paid circulation (1,000) 1980	1990	1995	2000	2002
Morning dailies, total	387	559	656	766	776	29,413	41,311	44,310	46,772	46,617
In cities of—										
1,000,001 or more	20	18	25	26	26	8,795	6,508	10,173	10,820	10,613
500,001 to 1,000,000	27	22	22	25	31	5,705	4,804	5,587	5,412	6,727
100,001 to 500,000	99	138	153	163	162	8,996	20,051	17,214	17,469	16,512
50,001 to 100,000	75	100	138	162	159	2,973	4,373	5,602	5,887	5,576
25,001 to 50,000	64	102	115	141	148	1,701	3,209	3,150	3,899	3,764
Less than 25,000	102	179	203	249	250	1,243	2,365	2,584	3,285	3,424
Evening dailies, total	1,388	1,084	891	727	704	32,788	21,017	13,883	9,000	8,569
In cities of—										
1,000,001 or more	11	7	3	1	1	2,984	1,423	390	1	1
500,001 to 1,000,000	23	12	7	3	6	4,101	1,350	1,017	519	833
100,001 to 500,000	123	71	45	32	28	8,178	4,687	2,529	1,603	1,366
50,001 to 100,000	156	94	72	54	51	4,896	2,941	2,029	1,332	1,181
25,001 to 50,000	246	204	158	124	123	5,106	4,278	2,819	1,898	1,790
Less than 25,000	829	696	606	513	495	7,523	6,338	5,099	3,648	3,398

Source: Editor & Publisher Co., New York, NY, *Editor & Publisher International Year Book*, annual (copyright).

No. 1132. Daily and Sunday Newspapers—Number and Circulation, 1991 to 2001, and by State, 2002

[Number of newspapers as of February 1 the following year. Circulation as of September 30 (60,687 represents 60,687,000). For English language newspapers only. California, New York, Massachusetts, and Virginia Sunday newspapers include national circulation]

State	Daily Number	Circulation[1] Net paid (1,000)	Per capita[2]	Sunday Number	Net paid circulation (1,000)	State	Daily Number	Circulation[1] Net paid (1,000)	Per capita[2]	Sunday Number	Net paid circulation (1,000)
Total, 1991	1,586	60,687	0.24	875	62,068	Maine	7	230	0.18	4	193
Total, 1992	1,570	60,164	0.23	891	62,160	Maryland	13	596	0.11	9	917
Total, 1993	1,556	59,812	0.23	884	62,566	Massachusetts	32	1,610	0.25	16	1,548
Total, 1994	1,548	59,305	0.23	886	62,294	Michigan	48	1,704	0.17	27	1,935
Total, 1995	1,533	58,193	0.22	888	61,529	Minnesota	25	835	0.17	14	1,127
Total, 1996	1,520	56,983	0.21	890	60,798	Mississippi	23	369	0.13	18	374
Total, 1997	1,509	56,728	0.21	903	60,484	Missouri	43	944	0.17	23	1,173
Total, 1998	1,489	56,182	0.20	898	60,066	Montana	11	184	0.20	7	185
Total, 1999	1,483	55,979	0.20	905	59,894	Nebraska	17	407	0.24	6	389
Total, 2000	1,480	55,773	0.20	917	59,421	Nevada	8	299	0.14	4	325
Total, 2001	1,468	55,578	0.19	913	59,090	New Hampshire	11	221	0.17	8	230
Total, 2002	**1,457**	**55,186**	**0.19**	**913**	**58,780**	New Jersey	18	1,328	0.15	15	1,637
Alabama	24	633	0.14	20	709	New Mexico	18	281	0.15	13	287
Alaska	7	108	0.17	5	125	New York	59	6,610	0.35	37	5,481
Arizona	16	790	0.14	11	892	North Carolina	47	1,325	0.16	39	1,463
Arkansas	28	471	0.17	16	538	North Dakota	10	163	0.26	7	167
California	91	5,930	0.17	61	6,669	Ohio	84	2,354	0.21	42	2,645
Colorado	29	1,037	0.23	15	1,188	Oklahoma	43	618	0.18	36	768
Connecticut	17	701	0.20	13	785	Oregon	19	669	0.19	11	717
Delaware	2	138	0.17	2	160	Pennsylvania	82	2,686	0.22	41	3,074
District of Columbia	2	848	1.49	2	1,095	Rhode Island	6	220	0.21	3	264
						South Carolina	16	621	0.15	14	716
Florida	40	3,005	0.18	36	3,800	South Dakota	11	156	0.20	4	136
Georgia	33	983	0.11	28	1,274	Tennessee	25	840	0.14	17	1,018
Hawaii	6	269	0.22	6	305	Texas	84	2,866	0.13	81	3,789
Idaho	12	206	0.15	8	228	Utah	6	327	0.14	6	357
Illinois	66	2,353	0.19	30	2,455	Vermont	8	121	0.20	3	96
Indiana	68	1,282	0.21	25	1,255	Virginia	25	3,132	0.43	17	1,161
Iowa	37	601	0.20	12	621	Washington	23	1,083	0.18	17	1,233
Kansas	43	416	0.15	14	374	West Virginia	21	351	0.19	12	354
Kentucky	23	594	0.15	14	630	Wisconsin	35	881	0.16	18	1,070
Louisiana	26	704	0.16	21	777	Wyoming	9	86	0.17	5	70

[1] Circulation figures based on the principal community served by a newspaper which is not necessarily the same location as the publisher's office. [2] Per capita based on estimated resident population as of July 1, except 2000, enumerated resident population as of April 1.

Source: Editor & Publisher Co., New York, NY, *Editor & Publisher International Year Book*, annual (copyright).

No. 1133. Periodicals—Average Retail Prices: 1999 to 2003

[In dollars]

Subject	1999	2000	2001	2002	2003
Agriculture	469.90	509.65	536.65	578.14	630.29
Anthropology	259.21	273.84	269.51	329.79	353.44
Art and architecture	98.24	101.02	104.29	105.74	121.64
Astronomy	1,074.54	1,094.78	1,155.22	1,290.83	1,357.23
Biology	902.43	973.36	1,031.12	1,097.09	1,175.68
Botany	710.92	763.92	794.60	834.40	900.62
Business and economics	408.35	457.56	501.79	551.37	590.84
Chemistry	1,682.94	1,825.68	1,986.00	2,185.76	2,403.06
Education	207.79	230.20	254.71	278.50	305.73
Engineering and technology	981.19	1,071.02	1,166.22	1,263.49	1,359.52
Food science	650.23	708.06	767.16	799.16	829.44
General science	697.93	773.15	852.43	929.86	992.52
General works	85.69	88.11	88.99	95.26	105.34
Geography	566.11	636.44	686.60	775.62	819.45
Geology	778.55	840.59	898.94	972.52	1,037.93
Health sciences	626.44	677.78	730.52	783.34	849.62
History	101.72	107.60	113.76	120.24	137.34
Language and literature	92.31	96.37	101.72	110.28	124.47
Law	140.06	148.08	159.51	175.66	198.22
Library and information science	222.15	233.88	249.86	266.69	296.25
Math and computer science	890.12	965.98	1,039.88	1,119.75	1,151.71
Military and naval science	282.33	308.11	360.56	354.20	396.85
Music	87.33	89.01	91.49	94.29	104.04
Philosophy and religion	123.27	131.48	136.78	148.64	169.89
Physics	1,747.89	1,877.86	2,016.08	2,194.09	2,357.86
Political science	208.07	229.01	257.31	287.96	315.00
Psychology	275.93	303.44	330.60	362.54	396.04
Recreation	103.33	110.85	122.33	139.84	170.47
Sociology	252.82	278.20	306.86	336.56	365.66
Technology	874.66	951.13	1,030.11	1,122.85	1,200.22
Zoology	751.64	822.40	891.33	967.58	1,019.57

Source: Library Journal, New York, NY, *Library Journal*, April 15, 2002. (Copyright 2003, used with permission of Library Journal, a publication of Reed Business Information, a division of Reed Elsevier).

No. 1134. Quantity of Books Sold and Value of U.S. Domestic Consumer Expenditures: 1998 to 2002

[2,414 represents 2,414,000,000. Includes all titles released by publishers in the United States and imports which appear under the imprints of American publishers. Multivolume sets, such as encyclopedias, are counted as one unit]

Type of publication	Net publishers shipments [1] (mil.)					Domestic consumer expenditures [2] (mil. dol.)				
	1998	1999	2000	2001	2002	1998	1999	2000	2001	2002
Total	2,414	2,505	2,493	2,411	2,394	28,816	33,605	34,514	34,466	36,569
Trade	860	935	904	846	818	10,350	11,921	11,469	11,171	12,154
Adult	497	529	457	442	437	7,791	8,882	7,994	7,988	8,942
Hardback	241	260	227	215	212	4,435	5,218	4,666	4,563	5,102
Paperback	256	269	230	227	225	3,357	3,665	3,329	3,425	3,840
Juvenile	364	406	447	404	381	2,558	3,038	3,476	3,229	3,212
Hardback	198	213	230	172	153	1,552	1,814	2,050	1,585	1,612
Paperback	166	193	217	232	228	1,007	1,224	1,425	1,644	1,600
Mass market paperbacks- rack sized	484	485	471	455	453	2,348	2,518	2,644	2,623	2,930
Bookclubs	142	146	143	144	143	1,935	2,036	2,067	2,135	2,342
Hardback	46	48	47	47	47	1,545	1,623	1,649	1,703	1,867
Paperback	95	98	96	96	97	391	413	416	432	474
Mail order publications	78	66	65	52	48	487	495	517	424	400
Religious	171	174	171	174	174	2,037	2,221	2,276	2,383	2,305
Hardback	64	65	64	66	65	1,295	1,410	1,440	1,509	1,460
Paperback	106	108	107	108	109	742	810	836	874	845
Professional	170	178	187	168	167	4,751	5,297	5,753	5,315	5,767
Hardback	66	69	72	65	65	3,406	3,797	4,128	3,811	4,133
Paperback	104	109	115	103	103	1,345	1,501	1,624	1,505	1,634
University press	30	32	31	30	29	485	531	531	522	524
Hardback	9	10	10	9	9	234	256	267	262	262
Paperback	21	22	22	21	20	251	274	264	260	261
Elhi text	302	305	334	349	363	3,736	3,859	4,373	4,714	4,478
Hardback	115	116	127	133	139	2,033	2,103	2,382	2,563	2,434
Paperback	187	189	206	216	224	1,703	1,756	1,991	2,151	2,044
College text	176	184	186	194	198	3,365	3,773	3,905	4,187	4,706
Hardback	79	82	83	87	89	2,252	2,524	2,609	2,823	3,173
Paperback	97	102	103	107	109	1,113	1,250	1,296	1,363	1,533
Subscription reference	1	1	1	1	1	929	955	980	992	965

[1] Net, after returns. [2] Revised since originally published.

Source: Book Industry Study Group, Inc., New York, NY, *Book Industry Trends, 2003*, annual (copyright).

724 Information and Communications

No. 1139. Software Publishers—Estimated Revenue, Expenses, and Inventories: 1998 to 2001

[In millions of dollars (72,098 represents $72,098,000,000). For taxable and tax-exempt employer firms. Covers NAICS 5112. Estimates have been adjusted to the results of the 1997 Economic Census. Based on the North American Industry Classification System, 1997; see text, this section, and Section 15]

Item	1998	1999	2000	2001
Revenue	72,098	80,959	88,042	90,622
System software publishing, total	(NA)	(NA)	(NA)	29,367
Operating system software	(NA)	(NA)	(NA)	9,464
Network software	(NA)	(NA)	(NA)	6,514
Database management software	(NA)	(NA)	(NA)	8,083
Development tools and programming languages software	(NA)	(NA)	(NA)	3,827
Other systems software	(NA)	(NA)	(NA)	1,478
Application software publishing, total	(NA)	(NA)	(NA)	39,173
General business productivity and home use applications	(NA)	(NA)	(NA)	17,022
Cross-industry application software	(NA)	(NA)	(NA)	12,542
Vertical market application software	(NA)	(NA)	(NA)	8,250
Utilities software	(NA)	(NA)	(NA)	969
Other application software	(NA)	(NA)	(NA)	391
Custom application design and development services	(NA)	(NA)	(NA)	(S)
Customization and integration of packaged software	(NA)	(NA)	(NA)	3,786
Information technology consulting services	(NA)	(NA)	(NA)	6,420
Application service provisioning	(NA)	(NA)	(NA)	(S)
Business process management services	(NA)	(NA)	(NA)	(S)
Resale of computer hardware and software	(NA)	(NA)	(NA)	(S)
Information technology related training services	(NA)	(NA)	(NA)	1,104
Other services revenue	(NA)	(NA)	(NA)	8,537
Expenses: Selected purchases, total	4,751	5,460	6,060	5,903
Purchased printing	627	693	769	719
Purchased software reproduction	2,136	2,413	2,777	2,610
Purchased programming services	1,987	2,354	2,514	2,574
Inventories at end of year	784	863	1,020	1,112
Finished goods and work-in-process	665	697	864	967
Materials, supplies, fuel, etc.	119	167	157	145

NA Not available. S Data do not meet publication standards.

Source: U.S. Census Bureau, 2001 Service Annual Survey, *Information Sector Services,* and prior issues. See Internet site <http://www.census.gov/econ/www/servmenu.html> (released February 2003).

No. 1140. Motion Picture and Sound Recording Industries—Estimated Revenue and Inventories: 1998 to 2001

[In millions of dollars (58,759 represents $58,759,000,000), except percent. For taxable and tax-exempt employer firms. For NAICS 512. Except where indicated, estimates have been adjusted to results of the 1997 Economic Census. Based on the North American Industry Classification System, 1997; see text, this section, and Section 15. Minus sign (-) indicates decrease]

Item	1998	1999	2000	2001	Percent change, 2000-01
Motion picture and recording industries (NAICS 512):					
Operating revenue	58,759	63,091	66,107	67,240	1.7
Total inventories	14,370	15,407	15,796	15,762	-0.2
Finished goods and work-in-process	14,208	15,230	15,593	15,543	-0.3
Materials, supplies, fuel, etc.	163	177	203	219	8.2
Motion picture and video (NAICS 5121):					
Operating revenue	48,002	51,227	53,660	55,445	3.3
Total inventories	14,053	15,101	15,437	15,371	-0.4
Finished goods and work-in-process	13,942	14,983	15,308	15,231	-0.5
Materials, supplies, fuel, etc.	112	118	130	(S)	(S)
Sound recording (NAICS 5122): [1]					
Operating revenue	10,758	11,864	12,447	11,795	-5.2
Total inventories	317	306	359	391	9.2
Finished goods and work-in-process	266	248	286	313	9.5
Materials, supplies, fuel, etc.	51	58	73	79	7.9

S Data do note meet publication standards.   [1] Estimates not adjusted to the results of the 1997 Economic Census.

Source: U.S. Census Bureau, 2001 Service Annual Survey, *Information Sector Services.* See Internet site <http://www.census.gov/econ/www/servmenu.html> (released February 2003).

Information and Communications

No. 1141. Recording Media—Manufacturers' Shipments and Value: 1982 to 2002

[577.4 represents 577,400,000. Based on reports of RIAA member companies who distributed about 84 percent of the prerecorded music in 2002. These data are supplemented by other sources. Minus sign (-) indicates returns greater than shipments]

Medium	1982	1985	1990	1995	1998	1999	2000	2001	2002
UNIT SHIPMENTS [1] (mil.)									
Total [2]	577.4	653.0	865.7	1,112.7	1,123.9	1,160.6	1,079.2	968.5	859.7
CDs	(X)	22.6	286.5	722.9	847.0	938.9	942.5	881.9	803.3
CD singles	(X)	(X)	1.1	21.5	56.0	55.9	34.2	17.3	4.5
Cassettes	182.3	339.1	442.2	272.6	158.5	123.6	76.0	45.0	31.1
Cassette singles	(X)	(X)	87.4	70.7	26.4	14.2	1.3	-1.5	-0.5
Albums—LPs and EPs	243.9	167.0	11.7	2.2	3.4	2.9	2.2	2.3	1.7
Vinyl singles	137.2	120.7	27.6	10.2	5.4	5.3	4.8	5.5	4.4
Music video	(X)	(X)	9.2	12.6	27.2	19.8	18.2	17.7	14.7
DVD video	(X)	(X)	(X)	(X)	0.5	2.5	3.3	7.9	10.7
DVD audio	(X)	(X)	(X)	(X)	(X)	(X)	(X)	0.3	0.4
VALUE (mil. dol.)									
Total [2]	3,641.6	4,378.8	7,541.1	12,320.3	13,711.2	14,584.7	14,323.7	13,740.9	12,614.2
CD's	(X)	389.5	3,451.6	9,377.4	11,416.0	12,816.3	13,214.5	12,909.4	12,044.1
CD singles	(X)	(X)	6.0	110.9	213.2	222.4	142.7	79.4	19.6
Cassettes	1,384.5	2,411.5	3,472.4	2,303.6	1,419.9	1,061.6	626.0	363.4	209.8
Cassette singles	(X)	(X)	257.9	236.3	94.4	48.0	4.6	-5.3	-1.6
Albums—LPs and EPs	1,925.1	1,280.5	86.5	25.1	34.0	31.8	27.7	27.4	20.5
Vinyl singles	283.0	281.0	94.4	46.7	25.7	27.9	26.3	31.4	24.9
Music video	(X)	(X)	172.3	220.3	508.0	376.7	281.9	329.2	288.4
DVD video	(X)	(X)	(X)	(X)	12.2	66.3	80.3	190.7	236.3
DVD audio	(X)	(X)	(X)	(X)	(X)	(X)	(X)	6.0	8.5

X Not applicable. [1] Net units, after returns. [2] Includes discontinued media.

Source: Recording Industry Association of America, Washington, DC, *2002 Yearend Statistics* and earlier issues (copyright). See Internet site <http://www.riaa.com> (accessed 20 June 2003).

No. 1142. Profile of Consumer Expenditures for Sound Recordings: 1990 to 2002

[In percent, except total value (7,541.1 represents $7,541,100,000). Based on monthly telephone surveys of the population 10 years old and over]

Item	1990	1995	1997	1998	1999	2000	2001	2002
Total value (mil. dol.)	7,541.1	12,320.3	12,236.8	13,711.2	14,584.5	14,323.0	13,740.9	12,614.2
PERCENT DISTRIBUTION [1]								
Age: 10 to 14 years	7.6	8.0	8.9	9.1	8.5	8.9	8.5	8.9
15 to 19 years	18.3	17.1	16.8	15.8	12.6	12.9	13.0	13.3
20 to 24 years	16.5	15.3	13.8	12.2	12.6	12.5	12.2	11.5
25 to 29 years	14.6	12.3	11.7	11.4	10.5	10.6	10.9	9.4
30 to 34 years	13.2	12.1	11.0	11.4	10.1	9.8	10.3	10.8
35 to 39 years	10.2	10.8	11.6	12.6	10.4	10.6	10.2	9.8
40 to 44 years	7.8	7.5	8.8	8.3	9.3	9.6	10.3	9.9
45 years and over	11.1	16.1	16.5	18.1	24.7	23.8	23.7	25.5
Sex: Male	54.4	53.0	48.6	48.7	50.3	50.6	48.8	49.4
Female	45.6	47.0	51.4	51.3	49.7	49.4	51.2	50.6
Sales outlet:								
Record store	69.8	52.0	51.8	50.8	44.5	42.4	42.5	36.8
Other store	18.5	28.2	31.9	34.4	38.3	40.8	42.4	50.7
Music club	8.9	14.3	11.6	9.0	7.9	7.6	6.1	4.0
Ad or 800 number	2.5	4.0	2.7	2.9	2.5	2.4	3.0	2.0
Internet [2]	(NA)	(NA)	0.3	1.1	2.4	3.2	2.9	3.4
Music type: [3]								
Rock	36.1	33.5	32.5	25.7	25.2	24.8	24.4	24.7
Pop	13.7	10.1	9.4	10.0	10.3	11.0	12.1	9.0
Rap/Hip Hop	8.5	6.7	10.1	9.7	10.8	12.9	11.4	13.8
R&B/Urban	11.6	11.3	11.2	12.8	10.5	9.7	10.6	11.2
Country	9.6	16.7	14.4	14.1	10.8	10.7	10.5	10.7
Religious	2.5	3.1	4.5	6.3	5.1	4.8	6.7	6.7
Jazz	4.8	3.0	2.8	1.9	3.0	2.9	3.4	3.2
Classical	3.1	2.9	2.8	3.3	3.5	2.7	3.2	3.1
Soundtracks	0.8	0.9	1.2	1.7	0.8	0.7	1.4	1.1
New age	1.1	0.7	0.8	0.6	0.5	0.5	1.0	0.5
Oldies	0.8	1.0	0.8	0.7	0.7	0.9	0.8	0.9
Children's	0.5	0.5	0.9	0.4	0.4	0.6	0.5	0.4
Other	5.6	7.0	5.7	7.9	9.1	8.3	7.9	8.1
Media type: CDs	31.1	65.0	70.2	74.8	83.2	89.3	89.2	90.5
Cassettes	54.7	25.1	18.2	14.8	8.0	4.9	3.4	2.4
Singles (all types)	8.7	7.5	9.3	6.8	5.4	2.5	2.4	1.9
Music video [4]	(NA)	0.9	0.6	1.0	0.9	0.8	1.1	0.7
DVD audio	(NA)	(NA)	(NA)	(NA)	(NA)	(NA)	1.1	1.3
Digital download	(NA)	(NA)	(NA)	(NA)	(NA)	(NA)	0.2	0.5
Vinyl LPs	4.7	0.5	0.7	0.7	0.5	0.5	0.6	0.7

NA Not available. [1] Percent distributions exclude nonresponses and responses of don't know. [2] Excludes record club purchases over the Internet. [3] As classified by respondent. [4] Beginning 2001 includes video DVDs.

Source: Recording Industry Association of America, Inc., Washington, DC, *2002 Consumer Profile* and earlier issues (copyright). See Internet site <http://www.riaa.com> (accessed 20 June 2003).

No. 1143. Radio and Television Broadcasting—Estimated Revenue and Expenses: 1999 to 2001

[In millions of dollars (47,292 represents $47,292,000,000). For taxable and tax-exempt employer firms. Covers NAICS 5131. Estimates have been adjusted to the results of the 1997 Economic Census. Based on the North American Industry Classification System, 1997; see text, this section, and Section 15]

Item	Total (NAICS 5131) 1999	2000	2001	Radio broadcasting (NAICS 51311) 1999	2000	2001	TV broadcasting (NAICS 51312) 1999	2000	2001
Operating revenue	47,292	52,668	47,077	13,030	14,811	13,728	34,262	37,858	33,349
Station time sales	(NA)	(NA)	28,817	(NA)	(NA)	11,489	(NA)	(NA)	17,328
Network compensation	(NA)	(NA)	514	(NA)	(NA)	90	(NA)	(NA)	424
National/regional advertising	(NA)	(NA)	9,500	(NA)	(NA)	2,537	(NA)	(NA)	6,963
Local advertising revenue	(NA)	(NA)	18,804	(NA)	(NA)	8,862	(NA)	(NA)	9,942
Network time sales	(NA)	(NA)	14,097	(NA)	(NA)	1,096	(NA)	(NA)	13,001
Program rights	(NA)	(NA)	19	(NA)	(NA)	13	(NA)	(NA)	(S)
Production and post-production services	(NA)	(NA)	57	(NA)	(NA)	(S)	(NA)	(NA)	(S)
Public and noncommercial programming rights	(NA)	(NA)	(S)	(NA)	(NA)	(S)	(NA)	(NA)	(S)
Other operating services revenue	(NA)	(NA)	2,336	(NA)	(NA)	604	(NA)	(NA)	1,732
Expenses	37,551	40,366	39,090	10,308	11,406	11,242	27,243	28,960	27,848
Annual payroll	10,814	11,280	11,021	4,165	4,458	4,476	6,649	6,821	6,545
Employer contributions to Social Security and other supplemental benefits	1,427	1,535	1,566	503	590	566	924	945	999
Broadcast rights and music license fees	11,438	12,754	11,441	626	713	728	10,811	12,041	10,713
Depreciation	3,411	3,648	3,989	1,579	1,638	1,572	1,832	2,010	2,416
Lease and rental	616	655	731	268	294	386	349	362	346
Purchased repairs	266	276	264	86	91	94	180	185	170
Purchased communications and utilities	601	634	629	258	273	274	343	361	356
Purchased advertising	1,458	1,534	1,436	393	455	523	1,066	1,079	913
Other operating expenses (including network compensation fees)	7,521	8,052	8,013	2,431	2,896	2,623	5,090	5157	5,390

NA Not available. S Does not meet publication standards.

Source: U.S. Census Bureau, 2001 Service Annual Survey, *Information Sector Services* and prior issues. See Internet site <http://www.census.gov/econ/www/servmenu.html> (released February 2003).

No. 1144. Cable and Pay TV—Summary: 1975 to 2002

[9,800 represents 9,800,000. Cable TV for calendar year. Pay TV as of Dec. 31 of year shown]

Year	Cable TV Avg. basic subscribers (1,000)	Avg. monthly basic rate (dol.)	Revenue [1] (mil. dol.) Total	Basic	Pay TV Units [2] (1,000) Total pay [3]	Pay cable	Noncable delivered premium	Monthly rate (dol.) All pay weighted average [3]	Pay cable	Noncable delivered premium
1975	9,800	6.50	804	764	194	194	(NA)	(NA)	7.85	(NA)
1980	17,500	7.69	2,609	1,615	8,581	7,336	(NA)	8.91	8.62	(NA)
1982	25,250	8.30	5,032	2,515	19,395	17,007	(NA)	9.49	9.30	(NA)
1983	29,430	8.61	6,485	3,041	24,515	22,818	(NA)	9.82	9.70	(NA)
1984	32,800	8.98	7,738	3,534	28,815	27,754	(NA)	10.03	9.96	(NA)
1985	35,440	9.73	8,831	4,138	29,885	29,418	(NA)	10.29	10.25	(NA)
1986	38,170	10.67	9,955	4,887	31,033	30,668	(NA)	10.35	10.31	(NA)
1987	41,160	12.18	11,563	6,016	33,528	33,232	(NA)	10.25	10.23	(NA)
1988	44,160	13.86	13,409	7,345	37,085	36,777	(NA)	10.24	10.17	(NA)
1989	47,500	15.21	15,378	8,670	39,055	38,916	(NA)	10.25	10.20	(NA)
1990	50,520	16.78	17,582	10,174	39,902	39,751	(NA)	10.35	10.30	(NA)
1991	52,570	18.10	19,426	11,418	39,983	36,569	(NA)	10.35	10.27	(NA)
1992	54,300	19.08	21,079	12,433	40,893	36,879	(NA)	10.29	10.17	(NA)
1993	56,200	[4]19.39	22,809	13,528	42,010	37,113	(NA)	9.27	9.11	(NA)
1994	58,450	21.62	23,160	15,164	47,478	42,528	4,950	8.64	8.83	6.99
1995	60,900	23.07	24,945	16,763	55,723	46,798	8,925	8.29	8.54	6.99
1996	62,300	24.41	27,312	18,249	63,705	49,728	13,977	8.05	8.35	6.99
1997	63,600	26.48	30,085	20,213	72,785	51,933	20,852	7.91	8.29	6.99
1998	64,650	27.81	32,377	21,574	80,605	55,280	25,325	7.82	8.20	6.99
1999	65,500	28.92	34,866	22,732	88,455	59,005	29,450	7.69	8.04	6.99
2000	66,250	30.37	37,876	24,142	102,590	65,918	36,672	7.64	8.00	6.99
2001	66,900	32.87	43,128	26,390	115,325	75,433	39,892	7.65	7.96	7.06
2002, est.	66,898	34.71	48,701	27,867	118,575	77,292	41,283	7.67	8.00	7.06

NA Not available. [1] Includes installation revenue, subscriber revenue, and nonsubscriber revenue; excludes telephony and high-speed access. [2] Individual program services sold to subscribers. [3] Includes multipoint distribution service (MDS), satellite TV (STV), multipoint multichannel distribution service (MMDS), satellite master antenna TV (SMATV), C-band satellite, and DBS satellite. Includes average pay unit price based on data for major premium pay movie services. [4] Weighted average representing 8 months of unregulated basic rate and 4 months of FCC rolled-back rate.

Source: Kagan World Media, a Media Central/Primedia Company. From the *Broadband Cable Financial Databook 2002* (copyright); and *The Pay TV Newsletter*, June 28, 2002, and July 31, 2002, and various other publications.

No. 1145. Cable Networks and Program Distribution Services—Estimated Revenue and Expenses: 1998 to 2001

[In millions of dollars (52,310 represents $52,310,000,000). For taxable and tax-exempt employer firms. Covers NAICS 5132. Estimates have not been adjusted to the results of the 1997 Economic Census. Based on the North American Industry Classification System, 1997; see text, this section, and Section 15]

Item	1998	1999	2000	2001
Operating revenue	52,310	59,895	67,930	74,419
Air time (advertising)	(NA)	(NA)	(NA)	12,225
Special programming service	(NA)	(NA)	(NA)	12,466
Basic programming service	(NA)	(NA)	(NA)	32,148
Premium cable programming packages	(NA)	(NA)	(NA)	5,215
Pay-per-view service	(NA)	(NA)	(NA)	1,927
Program distribution installation services	(NA)	(NA)	(NA)	512
Program distribution equipment sales and rentals	(NA)	(NA)	(NA)	1,779
Other program distribution related services	(NA)	(NA)	(NA)	2,350
Internet access services	(NA)	(NA)	(NA)	2,127
Basic fixed local telephony	(NA)	(NA)	(NA)	1,031
Basic fixed long-distance	(NA)	(NA)	(NA)	128
Other communication services	(NA)	(NA)	(NA)	400
Other operating revenue	(NA)	(NA)	(NA)	2,111
Operating expenses	45,231	52,952	62,039	70,820
Annual payroll	7,138	8,388	9,696	10,642
Employer contributions to social security and other supplemental benefits	1,443	1,666	1,929	2,019
Program and production costs	14,601	16,525	19,077	22,173
Depreciation	9,425	11,498	13,965	16,870
Lease and rental	760	878	1,005	1,058
Purchased repairs	662	721	684	761
Purchased communications and utilities	736	840	921	812
Purchased advertising	1,590	1,836	2251	2,318
Other operating expenses	8,876	10,600	12,510	14,168

NA Not available.
Source: U.S. Census Bureau, 2001 Service Annual Survey, *Information Sector Services* and prior issues. See Internet site <http://www.census.gov/econ/www/servmenu.html> (released February 2003).

No. 1146. Telecommunications—Estimated Revenue and Expenses: 1999 to 2001

[In millions of dollars (318,097 represents $318,097,000,000), except percent. For taxable and tax-exempt employer firms. Except for NAICS 51332, wireless telecommunications carriers (except satellite), estimates have been adjusted to the results of the 1997 Economic Census. Based on the North American Industry Classification System, 1997; see text, this section, and Section 15. Minus sign (-) indicates decrease. See Table 1147 for wireless telecommunications carriers, NAICS 51332]

Item	Telecommunucations (NAICS 5133) 1999	2000	2001	Wired telecommunications carriers (NAICS 51331) 1999	2000	2001
Operating revenue	318,097	349,109	366,042	247,532	265,704	264,062
Fixed total	(NA)	(NA)	192,499	(NA)	(NA)	182,419
Fixed local	(NA)	(NA)	89,180	(NA)	(NA)	87,813
Basic service	(NA)	(NA)	73,776	(NA)	(NA)	72,581
Fixed long-distance	(NA)	(NA)	78,438	(NA)	(NA)	74,114
Outbound service	(NA)	(NA)	67,658	(NA)	(NA)	64,171
Fixed all distance	(NA)	(NA)	5,306	(NA)	(NA)	5,030
Dedicated network services	(NA)	(NA)	11,736	(NA)	(NA)	8,371
Data transmission services	(NA)	(NA)	7,840	(NA)	(NA)	7,091
Mobile total	(NA)	(NA)	75,972	(NA)	(NA)	833
Mobile telephony services	(NA)	(NA)	70,741	(NA)	(NA)	(NA)
Local access and use	(NA)	(NA)	51,126	(NA)	(NA)	(NA)
Messaging services	(NA)	(NA)	5,039	(NA)	(NA)	(NA)
Mobile dispatch services	(NA)	(NA)	193	(NA)	(NA)	(NA)
Carrier services	(NA)	(NA)	58,328	(NA)	(NA)	52,205
Network access	(NA)	(NA)	52,633	(NA)	(NA)	50,096
Other telecommunications services	(NA)	(NA)	9,086	(NA)	(NA)	6,750
Other services revenue [1]	(NA)	(NA)	30,157	(NA)	(NA)	21,856
Telecommunications network installation services	(NA)	(NA)	2,355	(NA)	(NA)	2,035
Telecommunications equipment sales	(NA)	(NA)	7,463	(NA)	(NA)	1,902
Sales of directory advertising space	(NA)	(NA)	1,301	(NA)	(NA)	1,104
Other revenue	(NA)	(NA)	17,821	(NA)	(NA)	15,772
Operating expenses	266,792	306,706	328,520	200,833	230,098	232,941
Annual payroll	54,447	65,306	66,740	43,193	52,517	51,316
Employer contributions to social security and other supplemental benefits	12,415	14,119	15,486	10,106	11,414	12,511
Access charges	37,581	40,530	41,528	31,657	32,891	32,318
Depreciation	49,929	59,725	70,035	38,120	44,075	48,976
Lease and rental	6,349	8,010	9,037	3,368	4,476	5,005
Purchased repairs	3,581	4,477	5,002	2,830	3,504	3,872
Purchased communications and utilities	14,330	15,890	16,586	12,437	12,929	13,061
Purchased advertising	7,122	8,499	8,836	4,532	4,909	4,390
Universal service, contributions, and other similar charges	5,527	5,658	5,381	5,017	5,037	4,650
Other operating expenses	75,602	84,492	89,890	49,665	58,344	56,842

NA Not available. [1] Includes other revenue sources, not shown separately.
Source: U.S. Census Bureau, 2001 Service Annual Survey, *Information Sector Services* and prior issues. See Internet site <http://www.census.gov/econ/www/servmenu.html> (released February 2003).

No. 1151. Information Services and Data Processing Services—Estimated Revenue: 1998 to 2001

[In millions of dollars (46,994 represents $46,994,000,000), except percent. For taxable and tax-exempt employer firms. Covers NAICS 514. Except where indicated, estimates adjusted to results of the 1997 Economic Census. Based on the North American Industry Classification System, 1997; see text, this section, and Section 15. Minus sign (-) indicates decrease]

Item	1998	1999	2000	2001
Total revenue	46,994	60,105	76,524	82,316
News syndicates (NAICS 51411):				
Revenue	1,586	1,823	1,986	1,960
Fees from supplying information	(NA)	(NA)	(NA)	1,871
Other services revenue	(NA)	(NA)	(NA)	89
Libraries and archives (NAICS 51412):				
Revenue	954	1,018	1,151	1,118
Subsidies, contributions, gifts, and grants	(NA)	(NA)	(NA)	821
Fees from educational workshops and seminars	(NA)	(NA)	(NA)	(S)
Fees and dues from providing access to collections	(NA)	(NA)	(NA)	41
Sales of books and other educational materials	(NA)	(NA)	(NA)	(S)
Other services revenue	(NA)	(NA)	(NA)	248
Online information services (NAICS 514191):				
Revenue	10,882	18,012	26,577	28,623
Internet access services	(NA)	(NA)	(NA)	15,563
Advertising	(NA)	(NA)	(NA)	3,867
Web site hosting	(NA)	(NA)	(NA)	994
Internet backbone services	(NA)	(NA)	(NA)	(S)
Internet telecommunications services	(NA)	(NA)	(NA)	295
Information technology consulting services	(NA)	(NA)	(NA)	320
Information technology design and development	(NA)	(NA)	(NA)	212
Application service provisioning	(NA)	(NA)	(NA)	(S)
Business process management	(NA)	(NA)	(NA)	272
Video and audio streaming services	(NA)	(NA)	(NA)	(S)
Other services revenue	(NA)	(NA)	(NA)	3,320
All other information services (NAICS 514199): [1]				
Revenue	985	2,109	4,861	3,768
Advertising	(NA)	(NA)	(NA)	1,778
Information search services	(NA)	(NA)	(NA)	803
Stock photo services	(NA)	(NA)	(NA)	810
Data processing services (NAICS 5142):				
Revenue	32,588	37,143	41,950	46,848
Business process management	(NA)	(NA)	(NA)	14,709
Information and document transformation	(NA)	(NA)	(NA)	1,204
Information technology design and development	(NA)	(NA)	(NA)	14,305
Data storage services	(NA)	(NA)	(NA)	113
Data management services	(NA)	(NA)	(NA)	3,832
Collocation services	(NA)	(NA)	(NA)	(S)
Information technology consulting services	(NA)	(NA)	(NA)	2,282
Web site hosting	(NA)	(NA)	(NA)	1,204
Software publishing	(NA)	(NA)	(NA)	599
Rental and leasing of computer hardware	(NA)	(NA)	(NA)	(S)
Application service provisioning	(NA)	(NA)	(NA)	837
Video and audio streaming services	(NA)	(NA)	(NA)	45
Other services revenue	(NA)	(NA)	(NA)	7,375

NA Not available. S Data do not meet publication standards. [1] Includes other sources of revenue, not shown separately. Estimates have not been adjusted to the results of the 1997 Economic Census.

Source: U.S. Census Bureau, 2001 Service Annual Survey, *Information Sector Services*, and prior issues. See Internet site <http://www.census.gov/econ/www/servmenu.html> (released February 2003).

No. 1152. Academic Libraries—Summary: 1998

[For fiscal year. For 2- and 4-year degree granting institutions. Based on survey; see source for details]

Item	Number of libraries	Circulation (1,000) General	Circulation (1,000) Reserve	Paper volumes held (1,000)[1]	Staff[2] Total	Staff[2] Librarians (percent)	Expenditures Total (mil. dol.)	Expenditures Salary[3] (percent)	Percent with access from within library to— Electronic catalog	Percent with access from within library to— Internet
Total	3,658	175,409	40,658	878,906	96,709	25.7	4,593	50.4	84.2	94.6
Control:										
Public	1,583	116,158	25,267	521,817	58,314	25.0	2,780	52.4	95.7	97.5
Private	2,075	59,251	15,391	357,090	38,395	26.6	1,813	47.4	75.0	92.3
Level:[4]										
4-year degree and above[5]	2,220	150,575	34,453	821,965	82,533	25.4	4,072	48.5	86.7	95.4
Doctor's	570	105,614	22,469	569,295	54,478	24.5	2,924	47.1	94.8	97.3
Master's	944	33,869	8,747	186,922	20,547	27.2	868	52.4	87.9	95.7
Bachelor's	703	11,083	3,236	65,645	7,499	27.0	280	51.0	78.3	93.5
Less than 4-year	1,438	24,834	6,205	56,941	14,176	27.4	520	65.4	80.1	93.3
Enrollment:[2]										
Less than 1,500	2,041	24,946	6,173	117,188	14,949	29.3	567	52.0	73.0	91.4
1,500 to 4,999	1,053	33,992	9,259	172,047	22,221	27.2	947	52.8	96.4	98.7
5,000 or more	564	116,472	25,226	589,671	59,539	24.2	3,078	49.3	99.1	98.0

[1] At end-of-year. [2] Full-time equivalent. [3] Salary and wages. [4] Level of highest degree offered. [5] Includes three institutions granting "other" degrees, not shown separately.

Source: U.S. National Center for Education Statistics, *Academic Libraries, 1998*, NCES 2001-341, July 2001.

No. 1153. Libraries—Number by Type: 1980 to 2000

Type	1980	1985	1990	2000	Type	1980	1985	1990	2000
Total [1]	31,564	32,323	34,613	37,024	Junior college... Colleges,	1,191	1,188	1,233	1,283
United States...	28,638	29,843	30,761	32,914	universities....	3,400	3,846	3,360	3,494
Public	8,717	8,849	9,060	9,480	Departmental	1,489	1,824	1,454	1,454
Public branches...	5,936	6,330	5,833	6,957	Law,				
Special [2]	7,649	7,530	9,051	9,948	medicine,				
Medicine	1,674	1,667	1,861	1,955	religious..	269	531	501	418
Religious	913	839	946	1,015	Government.....	1,260	1,574	1,735	1,411
Law [3]	417	435	647	1,172	Armed Forces....	485	526	489	341
Academic	4,591	5,034	4,593	4,777	Outlying areas..	113	114	110	(NA)

NA Not available. [1] Includes Canadian libraries, and libraries in regions administered by the United States, not shown separately. Data are exclusive of elementary and secondary school libraries. Law libraries with fewer than 10,000 volumes are included only if they specialize in a particular field. [2] Includes other types of special libraries, not shown separately. Increase between 1985 and 1990 is due mainly to revised criteria for identifying special libraries and improved methods of counting. [3] Increase in 2000 due to increased effort in identifying special libraries.

Source: Information Today, Inc., Medford, NJ, *The Bowker Annual Library and Book Trade Almanac* and *American Library Directory*, annual. (Copyright 2001 by Information Today, Inc.)

No. 1154. Public Libraries by Selected Characteristics: 2001

[8,223 represents $8,223,000,000. Based on survey of public libraries. Data are for public libraries in the 50 states and the District of Columbia. The response rates for these items are between 96 and 97 percent]

Population of service area	Number of—		Operating income—			Paid staff [3]		Libraries with Internet access
	Public libraries	Stationary outlets [1]	Total (mil. dol.) [2]	State government	Local government	Total	Librarians with ALA-MLS [4]	
Total	9,129	16,421	8,223	12.7	77.3	133,456	30,094	8,785
1,000,000 or more	24	977	1,223	9.2	78.7	16,608	4,757	24
500,000 to 999,000	52	1,104	1,305	16.0	75.3	18,313	4,630	52
250,000 to 499,999	95	1,099	946	13.1	79.0	14,794	3,695	95
100,000 to 249,999	327	1,992	1,322	11.9	80.0	22,117	4,878	327
50,000 to 99,999	541	1,642	1,061	15.2	76.2	17,729	3,968	538
25,000 to 49,999	913	1,706	985	13.4	77.4	16,789	3,840	909
10,000 to 24,999	1,767	2,273	866	11.8	76.1	15,488	3,120	1,757
5,000 to 9,999	1,443	1,597	297	11.2	74.4	6,110	861	1,425
2,500 to 4,999	1,305	1,354	123	7.7	74.2	2,808	229	1,272
1,000 to 2,499	1,621	1,631	74	6.0	67.0	2,003	94	1,548
Fewer than 1,000	1,041	1,046	21	7.6	66.0	697	22	838

[1] The sum of central and branches libraries. The total number of central libraries was 8,971; the total of branch libraries was 7,450. [2] Includes income from the federal government (0.6%) and other sources (9.4%), not shown separately. [3] Full-time equivalents. [4] Librarians with master's degrees from a graduate library education program accredited by the American Library Association (ALA). Total librarians, including those without ALA-MLS, were 44,428.

Source: U.S. National Center for Education Statistics, *Public Libraries in the United States: 2001*, NCES 2003-399, June 2003.

No. 1155. Public Library Use of the Internet: 2002

[In percent, except number of outlets. As of spring. Based on sample survey; see source for details]

Item	Metropolitan status [1]				Poverty status [2]		
	Total	Urban	Suburban	Rural	Less than 20 percent	20 to 40 percent	More than 40 percent
All libraries outlets [3]	16,004	2,742	4,764	8,498	12,847	2,832	325
Connected to the Internet	98.7	100.0	99.7	97.8	99.0	97.4	100.0
Connected with public access	95.3	100.0	95.3	93.7	94.4	98.9	100.0
Average number of workstations	10.8	20.6	11.9	6.7	9.8	15.1	10.6
Speed of access: [4]							
56kpbs dial-up	6.5	-	2.8	11.0	7.7	2.2	-
56kpbs direct connect	14.8	6.6	10.6	20.1	14.3	15.8	23.7
64kpbs to 1.5mbps	16.6	11.9	19.7	16.5	16.8	16.7	7.2
1.5mbps (T1) or greater	49.1	77.2	59.3	33.2	48.0	53.9	47.2
Public access database subscription services available on—							
All workstations	65.0	75.5	61.7	63.3	64.5	69.0	53.2
Some workstations	25.6	21.8	31.0	23.8	25.5	24.4	36.2
No workstations	9.4	2.7	7.3	12.9	10.0	6.6	10.6
Database subscription services offered remotely to off-site users	44.3	61.9	41.2	40.0	44.7	43.1	42.5
Public access Internet content filtering/blocking on—							
All workstations	24.4	38.9	19.5	22.1	21.6	36.9	23.2
Some workstations	17.5	18.1	23.8	13.7	18.5	12.7	23.2
No workstations	58.1	43.0	56.7	64.2	59.9	50.4	53.6

- Represents or rounds to zero. [1] Urban = inside central city; Suburban = in metro area, outside of a central city; Rural = outside a metro area. [2] Determined by the 1990 poverty status of the service area of the outlet. [3] Central libraries and branches; excludes bookmobiles. [4] Less than 56kbps accounts for 1.7 percent of public libraries connected to the Internet. "Don't know" responses are 10.5 percent total.

Source: National Commission on Libraries and Information Science, Washington, DC, *Public Libraries and the Internet 2002: Summary Findings and Data Tables*, September 2002, by John Carlo Bartot and Charles R. McClure, Florida State University, Tallahassee, FL.

No. 1147. Wireless Telecommunications Carriers (Except Satellite)—Estimated Revenue and Expenses: 1998 to 2001

[In millions of dollars (42,363 represents $42,363,000,000). For taxable and tax-exempt employer firms. For NAICS 51332. Estimates have not been adjusted to the results of the 1997 Economic Census. Based on the North American Industry Classification System, 1997; see text, this section, and Section 15. See Table 1146 for telecommunications total and wired carriers (NAICS 5133 and 51331)]

Item	1998	1999	2000	2001
Operating revenue	42,363	53,485	64,309	82,870
Mobile total	(NA)	(NA)	(NA)	73,420
Mobile telephony services	(NA)	(NA)	(NA)	68,801
Local access and use	(NA)	(NA)	(NA)	50,850
Mobile value-added services	(NA)	(NA)	(NA)	2,299
Mobile long distance	(NA)	(NA)	(NA)	5,053
Mobile all distance	(NA)	(NA)	(NA)	8,288
Dedicated network services	(NA)	(NA)	(NA)	(S)
Other mobile telephony revenue	(NA)	(NA)	(NA)	2,312
Messaging services	(NA)	(NA)	(NA)	4,428
Mobile dispatch services	(NA)	(NA)	(NA)	191
Carrier services	(NA)	(NA)	(NA)	2,802
Network access	(NA)	(NA)	(NA)	1,141
Other carrier services	(NA)	(NA)	(NA)	1,662
Other telecommunications services	(NA)	(NA)	(NA)	1,458
Other services revenue	(NA)	(NA)	(NA)	5,190
Operating expenses	39,720	50,381	59,214	77,838
Annual payroll	6,722	8,259	9,224	11,679
Employer contributions to social security and other supplemental benefits	1,490	1,787	2,095	2,258
Access charges	2,233	3,371	5,038	6,735
Depreciation	8,743	10,376	13,275	18,528
Lease and rental	1,923	2,328	2,793	3,434
Purchased repairs	719	660	846	985
Purchased communications and utilities	1,051	1,311	1,757	2,039
Purchased advertising	2,467	2,343	3,330	4,188
Universal service, contributions, and other similar charges	325	441	526	623
Other operating expenses	14,047	19,505	20,329	27,368

NA Not available. S Data do not meet publication standards.

Source: U.S. Census Bureau, 2001 Service Annual Survey, *Information Sector Services* and prior issues. See Internet site <http://www.census.gov/econ/www/servmenu.html> (released February 2003).

No. 1148. Telecommunications Industry—Carriers and Revenue: 1995 to 2002

[Revenue in millions of dollars (190,076 represents $190,076,000,000). Data based on carrier filings to the FCC. Because of reporting changes, data beginning 1999 are not strictly comparable with previous years; see source for details]

Category	Carriers 1995	1999	2000	2001	2002	Telecommunications revenue 1995	1999	2000	2001	2002
Total [1]	3,058	4,822	4,850	5,679	5,364	190,076	268,505	292,762	301,799	294,367
Local service providers	1,675	2,589	2,617	2,990	2,905	103,792	119,938	128,075	133,502	128,231
Incumbent local exchange carriers (ILECs)	1,347	1,335	1,327	1,329	1,337	102,820	112,216	116,158	117,885	109,517
Pay telephone providers	271	758	683	936	761	349	1,213	972	836	201
Competitors of ILECs	57	496	607	725	807	623	6,508	10,945	14,781	18,512
CAPs and CLECs [2]	57	349	485	532	609	623	5,652	9,814	12,998	16,603
Local resellers	([3])	87	82	134	133	([3])	511	879	1,393	1,488
Other local exchange carriers	([3])	60	40	59	65	([3])	171	11	329	356
Private carriers	([3])	([3])	([3])	([3])	([3])	([3])	87	39	15	27
Shared tenant service providers	([3])	([3])	([3])	([3])	([3])	([3])	87	202	46	39
Wireless service providers [4]	930	1,495	1,451	1,761	1,387	18,627	50,152	63,280	74,596	83,952
Telephony [5]	792	806	810	858	433	17,208	46,513	59,823	71,887	81,948
Paging service providers	138	427	418	576	194	([3])	3,232	3,102	2,197	1,215
Toll service providers	453	738	782	928	1,072	76,447	98,414	101,407	93,702	82,184
Interexchange carriers	130	204	202	229	261	70,938	87,570	87,311	81,272	69,905
Operator service providers	25	21	21	22	23	500	337	635	611	564
Prepaid service providers	8	21	24	32	37	16	866	727	133	72
Satellite service carriers	([3])	21	24	31	34	([3])	280	336	373	381
Toll resellers	260	454	482	576	625	4,220	9,211	10,641	8,797	9,073
Other toll carriers	30	17	29	38	92	773	150	1,758	2,516	2,189

[1] Revenue data include adjustments, not shown separately. For 1995, revenue data include some nontelecommunications revenue, formerly reported as local exchange wireless revenue. [2] Competitive access providers (CAPs) and competitive local exchange carriers (CLECs). [3] Data not available separately. [4] Includes specialized mobile radio services and other services, not shown separately. [5] Cellular service, personal communications service, and specialized mobile radio.

Source: U.S. Federal Communications Commission, *Trends in Telephone Service*, annual.

Information and Communications

No. 1149. Telephone Systems—Summary: 1985 to 2001

[112 represents 112,000,000. Covers principal carriers filing annual reports with Federal Communications Commission]

Item	Unit	1985	1990	1995	1996	1997	1998	1999	2000	2001 [1]
LOCAL EXCHANGE CARRIERS [2]										
Carriers [3]	Number	55	51	53	51	51	52	52	52	30
Access lines	Millions	112	130	166	178	194	205	228	245	253
Business access lines	Millions	31	36	46	49	53	57	57	58	54
Residential access lines	Millions	79	89	101	104	108	110	115	115	112
Other access lines (public, mobile, special)	Millions	2	6	19	25	33	38	55	72	87
Number of local calls (originating)	Billions	365	402	484	504	522	544	554	537	515
Number of toll calls (originating)	Billions	(NA)	63	94	95	101	97	102	106	98
Gross book cost of plant	Bil. dol.	191	240	284	296	309	325	342	362	360
Depreciation and amortization reserves	Bil. dol.	49	89	127	138	149	163	176	190	194
Net plant	Bil. dol.	142	151	157	158	160	161	166	172	166
Total assets	Bil. dol.	162	180	197	198	198	200	204	214	208
Total stockholders equity	Bil. dol.	63	74	72	74	72	70	67	72	66
Operating revenues	Bil. dol.	73	84	96	101	103	108	113	117	109
Local revenues	Bil. dol.	32	37	46	50	52	55	58	60	55
Operating expenses [4]	Bil. dol.	48	62	72	74	75	78	79	81	77
Net operating income [5]	Bil. dol.	13	14	14	16	16	18	20	20	19
Net income	Bil. dol.	9	11	11	13	12	12	13	15	11
Employees	(1,000)	(NA)	569	447	437	435	436	436	434	386
Compensation of employees	Bil. dol.	(NA)	23	21	23	22	23	24	24	23
Average monthly residential local telephone rate [6]	Dollars	(NA)	19.24	20.01	19.95	19.88	19.76	19.93	20.78	21.84
Average monthly single-line business telephone rate [6]	Dollars	(NA)	41.21	41.80	41.81	41.67	41.29	41.21	41.80	42.18
LONG DISTANCE CARRIERS										
Number of carriers with presubscribed lines	Number	(NA)	325	583	621	(NA)	(NA)	(NA)	(NA)	(NA)
Number of presubscribed lines	Millions	(NA)	132	153	159	(NA)	(NA)	(NA)	(NA)	(NA)
Total toll service revenues	Bil. dol.	43	52	74	82	89	94	99	101	91
Interstate switched access minutes	Bil. min.	167	307	432	468	497	519	553	568	540
INTERNATIONAL TELEPHONE SERVICE [7]										
Number of U.S. billed calls	Millions	425	984	2,830	3,520	4,259	4,477	5,305	5,742	6,265
Number of U.S. billed minutes	Millions	3,446	8,030	15,889	19,325	22,753	24,250	28,515	30,135	33,287
U.S. billed revenues	Mil. dol.	3,487	8,059	14,335	14,598	15,662	14,726	14,980	14,909	11,386
U.S. carrier revenue net of settlements with foreign carriers	Mil. dol.	2,332	5,188	9,397	8,939	10,232	10,242	10,379	10,982	8,040
Revenue from private-line service	Mil. dol.	172	201	514	661	851	921	1,216	1,480	1,417
Revenue from resale service	Mil. dol.	(NA)	167	1,756	3,637	4,112	4,798	4,528	7,600	5,414

NA Not available. [1] Beginning 2001, detailed financial data only filed by regional Bell operating companies. Access lines and calls reported by 50 reporting companies. [2] Gross operating revenues, gross plant, and total assets of reporting carriers estimated at more than 90 percent of total industry. New accounting rules became effective in 1990; prior years may not be directly comparable on a one-to-one basis. Includes Virgin Islands, and prior to 1995, Puerto Rico. [3] The reporting threshold for carriers is $100 million in annual operating revenue. [4] Excludes taxes. [5] After tax deductions. [6] Based on surveys conducted by FCC. [7] Beginning 1995, data are for all U.S. points, and include calls to and from Alaska, Hawaii, Puerto Rico, Guam, the U.S. Virgin Islands, and offshore U.S. points. Beginning 1995, carriers first started reporting traffic to and from Canada and Mexico. Data for Canada and Mexico in prior years are staff estimates.

Source: U.S. Federal Communications Commission, *Statistics of Communications Common Carriers*, annual; *Trends in Telephone Service*, annual; and *Trends in the International Telecommunications Industry*, annual.

No. 1150. Cellular Telecommunications Industry: 1990 to 2002

[Calendar year data, except as noted (5,283 represents 5,283,000). Based on a survey mailed to all cellular, personal communications services, and enhanced special mobile radio (ESMR) systems. For 2002 data, the universe was 2,481 systems and the response rate was 87 percent. The number of operational systems beginning 2000 differs from that reported for previous periods as a result of the consolidated operation of ESMR systems in a broader service area instead of by a city-to-city basis]

Item	Unit	1990	1995	1997	1998	1999	2000	2001	2002
Systems	Number	751	1,627	2,228	3,073	3,518	2,440	2,587	2,481
Subscribers	1,000	5,283	33,786	55,312	69,209	86,047	109,478	128,375	140,766
Cell sites [1]	Number	5,616	22,663	51,600	65,887	81,698	104,288	127,540	139,338
Employees	Number	21,382	68,165	109,387	134,754	155,817	184,449	203,580	192,410
Service revenue	Mil. dol.	4,548	19,081	27,486	33,133	40,018	52,466	65,016	76,508
Roamer revenue [2]	Mil. dol.	456	2,542	2,974	3,501	4,085	3,883	3,936	3,896
Capital investment	Mil. dol.	6,282	24,080	46,058	60,543	71,265	89,624	105,030	126,922
Average monthly bill [3]	Dollars	80.90	51.00	42.78	39.43	41.24	45.27	47.37	48.40
Average length of call [3]	Minutes	2.20	2.15	2.31	2.39	2.38	2.56	2.74	2.73

[1] The basic geographic unit of a wireless PCS or cellular system. A city or county is divided into smaller "cells," each of which is equipped with a low-powered radio transmitter/receiver. The cells can vary in size depending upon terrain, capacity demands, etc. By controlling the transmission power, the radio frequencies assigned to one cell can be limited to the boundaries of that cell. When a wireless PCS or cellular phone moves from one cell toward another, a computer at the Switching Office monitors the movement and at the proper time, transfers or hands off the phone call to the new cell and another radio frequency. [2] Service revenue generated by subscribers' calls outside of their system areas. [3] As of December 31.

Source: Cellular Telecommunications & Internet Association, Washington, DC, *Semiannual Wireless Survey* (copyright).

No. 1156. Internet Access and Usage and Online Service Usage: 2003

[For persons 18 years old and over (206,900 represents 206,900,000). As of spring. Based on sample and subject to sampling error; see source for details]

Item	Total adults	Any online/ Internet usage	Have Internet access				Used the Internet in the last 30 days			Used any online service in the past 30 days
			Home or work or other	Home only	Work only		Home or work or other	Home only	Work only	
Total adults (1,000)............	206,900	126,979	162,408	124,466	70,555		123,734	104,280	59,498	114,615
PERCENT DISTRIBUTION										
Age:										
18 to 34 years old............	31.5	37.8	34.3	33.0	34.3		38.2	35.8	34.2	38.1
35 to 54 years old............	40.3	45.5	43.4	46.5	53.9		45.4	46.9	54.6	45.5
55 years old and over.........	28.2	16.7	22.3	20.5	11.8		16.4	17.4	11.2	16.4
Sex:										
Male..........................	48.0	48.8	48.5	49.1	50.3		48.6	49.1	50.6	48.5
Female........................	52.0	51.2	51.5	50.9	49.7		51.4	50.9	49.4	51.5
Household size:										
1 to 2 persons................	47.7	41.6	43.9	40.0	42.7		41.7	40.5	43.4	41.1
3 to 4 persons................	37.1	43.1	40.6	43.6	44.0		43.1	44.2	44.1	43.3
5 or more persons.............	15.1	15.3	15.5	16.3	13.3		15.1	15.3	12.5	15.6
Any child in household........	41.1	45.9	44.0	46.5	46.6		45.8	46.6	46.5	46.2
Marital status:										
Single........................	24.3	26.7	25.1	23.0	23.3		26.9	24.7	23.0	27.3
Married.......................	56.9	60.9	59.5	64.5	64.3		60.8	64.0	65.0	60.4
Other.........................	18.8	12.4	15.3	12.5	12.4		12.3	11.2	12.0	12.3
Educational attainment:										
Graduated college plus.........	24.0	35.0	29.2	33.9	45.4		35.5	37.6	49.8	34.4
Attended college..............	27.1	33.7	30.9	32.2	31.9		34.0	33.7	31.4	34.3
Did not attend college........	48.9	31.3	39.9	33.9	22.7		30.5	28.7	18.7	31.2
Employed full time............	53.5	64.1	59.3	61.1	87.9		64.4	63.1	89.1	64.1
Employed part time............	10.5	12.3	11.7	12.0	11.8		12.3	12.6	10.5	12.2
Occupation:										
Professional..................	10.4	15.8	13.0	14.6	24.9		16.2	16.6	26.4	15.5
Exec./manager/administrator...	9.8	14.1	11.9	13.8	22.7		14.3	14.8	25.2	13.9
Clerical/sales/technical......	18.2	24.3	21.3	22.1	32.7		24.5	23.5	32.9	24.6
Precision/crafts/repair.......	6.8	6.5	6.9	6.9	6.6		6.4	6.3	5.4	6.5
Household income:										
Less than $50,000.............	49.3	33.4	40.0	31.4	22.6		33.2	29.4	20.0	33.1
$50,000 to $74,999............	20.6	24.2	23.4	25.0	24.7		24.1	24.5	24.0	24.3
$75,000 to $149,999...........	23.6	32.9	28.5	33.8	40.4		33.1	35.4	42.6	33.1
$150,000 or more..............	6.5	9.5	8.0	9.9	12.4		9.7	10.7	13.3	9.5

Source: Mediamark Research Inc., New York, NY, CyberStats, spring 2003 (copyright). Internet site <http://www.mriplus.com/pocketpiece.html> (accessed 30 July 2003).

No. 1157. Programs for Adults in Public Library Outlets: 2000

[In percent. For activities offered during a typical week during the prior year. Represents programs for which the outlet provided funding, materials, or staff to support the program or the library system ran the program within or on behalf of of the outlet. Based on the Fast Response Survey System and subject to sampling error; see source for details]

Program and group	All outlets	Number of visits per week			Metropolitan status [1]		
		Less than 300	300 to 1,400	1,500 or more	Urban	Suburban	Rural
GENERAL PROGRAMS							
Computer/Internet instruction............	56	36	59	77	68	59	49
Book/film discussions or presentations.....	43	22	45	69	56	50	34
Cultural performances [2]................	41	11	48	71	60	51	28
Recreational activities [2]..............	39	24	40	59	52	50	29
Parenting skills........................	20	6	22	38	28	24	15
Financial planning/investment information...	18	4	19	38	30	26	11
Employment/career guidance..............	17	8	20	24	31	18	12
College/continuing education guidance.....	15	9	18	18	21	14	13
Citizenship preparation.................	5	5	4	5	7	6	3
PROGRAMS FOR SPECIFIC GROUPS							
Senior citizens.........................	24	12	25	38	35	29	18
Parents.................................	24	10	27	38	32	31	17
Limited English speaking and/or recent immigrants...........................	9	1	11	19	20	11	5
Adults with physical disabilities.......	6	4	7	9	7	5	6
Adults with learning disabilities........	5	2	6	6	8	3	5

[1] Urban = inside central city; Suburban = In metro area, outside of a central city; Rural = outside a metro area. [2] Such as crafts and hobbies.

Source: U.S. National Center for Education Statistics, Fast Response Survey System, Programs for Adults in Public Library Outlets, NCES 2003-010, November 2002.

No. 1158. Households With Computers and Internet Access by Selected Characteristic: 2001

[In percent. Based on the Current Population Survey and subject to sampling error; for details see source. See also text, Section 1, and Appendix III]

Characteristic	Households with computers				Households with Internet access			
	Total	Rural [1]	Urban [1]	Central city [1]	Total	Rural [1]	Urban [1]	Central city [1]
All households	56.5	55.6	56.7	51.5	50.5	48.7	51.1	45.7
Age of householder:								
Under 25 years old	51.1	41.3	53.0	50.9	44.7	33.5	46.7	45.3
25 to 34 years old	62.5	61.5	62.8	57.5	57.3	55.4	58.8	53.9
35 to 44 years old	69.9	71.2	69.4	62.1	62.6	62.3	63.4	54.3
45 to 54 years old	66.9	68.0	66.4	59.9	60.9	61.1	61.3	53.4
55 years old or over	39.1	38.0	39.5	35.5	33.9	32.1	35.0	29.9
Householder race/ethnicity:								
White [2]	61.1	58.0	62.4	60.0	55.4	51.0	56.8	54.8
Black [2]	37.1	31.5	37.7	33.9	30.8	24.4	30.9	27.4
American, Indian, Eskimo, Aleut [2]	44.7	37.6	49.5	[3]49.5	38.7	31.4	41.5	44.1
Asian or Pacific Islander [2]	72.7	[3]69.4	72.8	67.4	68.1	68.2	64.1	[3]63.1
Hispanic	40.0	36.6	40.3	38.1	32.0	29.9	32.6	29.8
Household type:								
Married couple with children under 18	78.9	78.6	79.0	72.4	71.6	69.7	73.6	64.6
Male householder with children under 18	55.1	53.6	55.6	51.8	44.9	39.9	47.2	44.3
Female householder with children under 18	49.2	51.0	48.9	41.6	40.0	40.9	42.3	33.5
Family households without children	58.8	55.0	60.4	55.2	53.2	48.9	55.3	49.7
Nonfamily households	39.2	31.6	40.9	41.4	35.0	26.9	36.2	37.0
Education of householder:								
Elementary	16.0	13.4	17.1	16.9	11.2	10.4	11.6	11.5
Some high school	28.2	27.6	28.4	25.5	22.7	22.4	22.6	19.8
High school graduate or GED	46.5	50.0	45.0	39.0	39.8	42.1	39.3	32.5
Some college	64.5	68.5	63.2	58.4	57.7	60.2	57.3	52.0
Bachelor's degree or more	79.8	81.1	79.5	76.7	75.2	75.1	75.0	72.0
Household income:								
Under $5,000	25.9	17.9	28.2	24.5	20.5	12.5	23.0	20.2
$5,000 to $9,999	19.2	16.4	20.1	20.6	14.4	11.0	15.5	14.5
$10,000 to $14,999	25.7	24.3	26.3	24.3	19.4	18.1	20.7	19.3
$15,000 to $19,999	31.8	29.4	32.6	33.9	23.6	21.0	25.3	24.6
$20,000 to $24,999	40.1	40.0	40.1	36.4	31.8	31.7	32.4	28.7
$25,000 to $34,999	49.7	49.4	49.9	49.9	42.2	40.5	43.7	41.3
$35,000 to $49,999	64.3	64.7	64.2	64.4	56.4	55.0	57.5	56.2
$50,000 to $74,999	77.7	78.1	77.6	75.8	71.4	70.6	71.7	70.5
$75,000 and over	89.0	89.0	88.9	86.4	85.4	84.8	85.5	83.8

[1] See text, Section 1, and Appendix II. [2] Non-Hispanic. [3] Figure does not meet standards of reliability or precision.

Source: U.S. Dept. of Commerce, National Telecommunications and Information Administration, *A Nation Online: How Americans Are Expanding Their Use of the Internet*, February 2002. Internet site <http://www.ntia.doc.gov/ntiahome/dn/index.html> (accessed 18 June 2003).

No. 1159. Households With Computers and Internet Access: 1998 and 2001

[In percent. Based on survey and subject to sampling error; for details, see source]

State	1998 Computers	1998 Internet access	2001 Computers	2001 Internet access	State	1998 Computers	1998 Internet access	2001 Computers	2001 Internet access
U.S.	42.1	26.2	56.5	50.5	MO	41.8	24.3	55.3	49.9
AL	34.3	21.6	43.7	37.6	MT	40.9	21.5	56.0	47.5
AK	62.4	44.1	68.7	64.1	NE	42.9	22.9	55.6	45.5
AZ	44.3	29.3	59.4	51.9	NV	41.6	26.5	58.2	52.5
AR	29.8	14.7	46.8	36.9	NH	54.2	37.1	55.0	50.2
CA	47.5	30.7	61.5	55.3	NJ	48.1	31.3	61.2	57.2
CO	55.3	34.5	64.7	58.5	NM	42.2	25.8	67.7	61.6
CT	43.8	31.8	58.7	55.0	NY	37.3	23.7	50.6	43.1
DE	40.5	25.1	58.4	52.5	NC	35.0	19.9	50.1	44.5
DC	41.4	24.2	49.3	41.4	ND	40.2	20.6	53.0	46.5
FL	39.5	27.8	55.9	52.8	OH	40.7	24.6	57.6	50.9
GA	35.8	23.9	52.4	46.7	OK	37.8	20.4	49.9	43.8
HI	42.3	27.9	63.1	55.2	OR	51.3	32.7	65.8	58.2
ID	50.0	27.4	62.8	52.7	PA	39.3	24.9	53.5	48.7
IL	42.7	26.5	53.0	46.9	RI	41.0	27.1	58.6	53.1
IN	43.5	26.1	53.2	47.3	SC	35.7	21.4	52.2	45.0
IA	41.4	21.8	59.4	51.0	SD	41.6	23.9	55.3	47.6
KS	43.7	25.7	57.5	50.9	TN	37.5	21.3	51.3	44.8
KY	35.9	21.1	49.8	44.2	TX	40.9	24.5	53.7	47.7
LA	31.1	17.8	45.7	40.2	UT	60.1	35.8	67.7	54.1
ME	43.4	26.0	62.8	53.3	VT	48.7	31.8	60.4	53.4
MD	46.3	31.0	64.1	57.8	VA	46.4	27.9	58.8	54.9
MA	43.4	28.1	59.1	54.7	WA	56.3	36.6	66.5	60.4
MI	44.0	25.4	58.3	51.2	WV	28.3	17.6	48.0	40.7
MN	47.6	29.0	64.6	55.6	WI	43.0	25.1	56.4	50.2
MS	25.7	13.6	41.9	36.1	WY	46.1	22.7	58.1	51.0

Source: U.S. Department of Commerce, National Telecommunications and Information Administration, *Falling through the Net: Defining the Digital Divide*, July 1999 and *A Nation Online: How Americans Are Expanding Their Use of the Internet*, February 2002. Internet site <http://www.ntia.doc.gov/ntiahome/dn/index.html> (accessed 18 June 2003).

Section 25
Banking, Finance, and Insurance

This section presents data on the nation's finances, various types of financial institutions, money and credit, securities, insurance, and real estate. The primary sources of these data are publications of several departments of the federal government, especially the Treasury Department, and independent agencies such as the Federal Deposit Insurance Corporation, the Federal Reserve System, and the Securities and Exchange Commission. National data on insurance are available primarily from private organizations, such as the American Council of Life Insurers, and the Insurance Information Institute.

Flow of funds—The flow of funds accounts of the Federal Reserve System bring together statistics on all of the major forms of financial instruments to present an economy-wide view of asset and liability relationships. In flow form, the accounts relate borrowing and lending to one another and to the nonfinancial activities that generate income and production. Each claim outstanding is included simultaneously as an asset of the lender and as a liability of the debtor. The accounts also indicate the balance between asset totals and liability totals over the economy as a whole. Several publications of the Board of Governors of the Federal Reserve System contain information on the flow of funds accounts: Summary data on flows and outstandings, in the *Federal Reserve Bulletin*, and *Flow of Funds Accounts of the United States* (quarterly); and concepts and organization of the accounts, in *Guide to the Flow of Funds Accounts* (2000). Data are also available at the Boards Web site <http://www.federalreserve.gov/releases/>.

Survey of Consumer Finances (SCF)—The Federal Reserve Board in cooperation with the Department of the Treasury sponsors this survey, which is conducted every 3 years to provide detailed information on the finances of U.S. families. Among the topics covered are the balance sheet, pension, income, and other demographic characteristics of U.S. families. The survey also gathers information on the use of financial institutions. Since 1992, data for the SCF have been collected by the National Organization for Social Science and Survey Research at the University of Chicago. Data from the survey are published periodically in the *Federal Reserve Bulletin*. The latest survey is available in the January 2003 issue of the Bulletin. More data and information on the survey are available at the following Web site of the Federal Reserve Board, <http://www.federalreserve.gov/pubs/oss/oss2/scfindex.html>.

Banking system—Banks in this country are organized under the laws of both the states and the federal government and are regulated by several bank supervisory agencies. National banks are supervised by the Comptroller of the Currency. *Reports of Condition* have been collected from national banks since 1863. Summaries of these reports are published in the Comptroller's *Annual Report*, which also presents data on the structure of the national banking system.

The Federal Reserve System was established in 1913 to exercise central banking functions, some of which are shared with the U.S. Treasury. It includes national banks and such state banks that voluntarily join the system. Statements of state bank members are consolidated by the Board of Governors of the Federal Reserve System with data for national banks collected by the Comptroller of the Currency into totals for all member banks of the system. Balance sheet data for member banks and other commercial banks are published quarterly in the *Federal Reserve Bulletin*. The Federal Deposit Insurance Corporation (FDIC), established in 1933, insures each depositor up to $100,000. Major item balance sheet and income data for all insured financial institutions are published in the *FDIC Quarterly Banking*

Profile. This publication is also available on the Internet at the following address: <http://www.fdic.gov>. Balance sheet and income data for individual institutions are also available at this site in the Institution Directory (ID) system.

Credit unions—Federally chartered credit unions are under the supervision of the National Credit Union Administration. State-chartered credit unions are supervised by the respective state supervisory authorities. The administration publishes comprehensive program and statistical information on all federal and federally insured state credit unions in the *Annual Report of the National Credit Union Administration.* Deposit insurance (up to $100,000 per account) is provided to members of all federal and those state credit unions that are federally-insured by the National Credit Union Share Insurance Fund which was established in 1970. Deposit insurance for state chartered credit unions is also available in some states under private or state-administered insurance programs.

Other credit agencies—Insurance companies, finance companies dealing primarily in installment sales financing, and personal loan companies represent important sources of funds for the credit market. Statistics on loans, investments, cash, etc., of life insurance companies are published principally by the American Council of Life Insurers in its *Life Insurers Fact Book*. Consumer credit data are published currently in the *Federal Reserve Bulletin*.

Government corporations and credit agencies make available credit of specified types or to specified groups of private borrowers, either by lending directly or by insuring or guaranteeing loans made by private lending institutions. Data on operations of government credit agencies, along with other government corporations, are available in reports of individual agencies; data on their debt outstanding are published in the *Federal Reserve Bulletin*.

Securities—The Securities and Exchange Commission (SEC) was established in 1934 to protect the interests of the public and investors against malpractices in the securities and financial markets and to provide the fullest possible disclosure of information regarding securities to the investing public. Statistical data are published in the *SEC Annual Report*.

Data on the securities industry and securities transactions are also available from a number of private sources. The Securities Industry Association, New York, NY, (<http://www.sia.com/>), publishes the SIA Annual Report and the periodic *Securities Industry Trends*. The Investment Company Institute, Washington, DC, (<http://www.ici.org/>) publishes a reference book, research newsletters, and a variety of research reports that examine the industry, its shareholders, or industry issues. The annual *Mutual Fund Fact Book* is a guide to trends and statistics observed in the investment company industry. *Fundamentals* is a newsletter summarizing the findings of major Institute research projects. Institute research reports provide a detailed examination of shareholder demographics and other aspects of fund ownership.

Among the many sources of data on stock and bond prices and sales are the New York Stock Exchange, New York, NY, (<http://www.nyse.com/>); NASDAQ, Washington, DC, (<http://www.nasdaq.com/>); Global Financial Data, Los Angeles, CA, <http://www.globalfindata.com/>; Dow-Jones & Company, Inc., New York, NY, (<http://www.dj.com/>); and the Bond Market Association, New York, NY, (<http://www.bondmarkets.com/>).

Insurance—Insuring companies, which are regulated by the various states or the District of Columbia, are classified as either life or property. Both life and property insurance companies may underwrite health insurance. Insuring companies, other than those classified as life, are permitted to underwrite one or more property lines provided they are so licensed and have the necessary capital or surplus.

There are a number of published sources for statistics on the various classes of insurance—life, health, fire, marine, and casualty. Organizations representing certain classes of insurers publish reports for these classes. The American Council of Life Insurers publishes statistics on life insurance purchases, ownership, benefit payments, and assets in its *Life Insurers Fact Book*.

No. 1164. Flow of Funds Accounts—Credit Market Debt Outstanding: 1990 to 2002

[In billions of dollars (13,755 represents $13,755,000,000,000). As of Dec. 31]

Item	1990	1994	1995	1996	1997	1998	1999	2000	2001	2002
Credit market debt...	13,755	17,183	18,414	19,777	21,260	23,437	25,602	27,349	29,394	31,702
U.S. government	2,498	3,492	3,637	3,782	3,805	3,752	3,681	3,385	3,380	3,637
Nonfederal domestic nonfinancial	8,352	9,493	10,045	10,624	11,390	12,488	13,626	14,782	15,914	17,020
Households [1]	3,598	4,547	4,884	5,224	5,557	6,012	6,510	7,075	7,687	8,444
Corporations	2,533	2,682	2,909	3,092	3,382	3,791	4,203	4,584	4,838	4,900
Nonfarm noncorporate business	1,093	1,016	1,062	1,129	1,224	1,384	1,566	1,750	1,907	2,039
Farm business	135	142	145	150	156	164	169	180	188	196
State and local government	992	1,106	1,045	1,029	1,071	1,138	1,177	1,192	1,295	1,442
Rest of the world	289	375	454	542	608	651	677	742	705	727
Financial sectors	2,616	3,822	4,279	4,829	5,458	6,545	7,619	8,439	9,395	10,318
Commercial banking	198	228	251	264	309	382	449	509	562	610
Savings institutions	140	112	115	141	160	212	260	288	295	281
Credit unions	-	-	-	-	1	1	3	3	5	7
Life insurance companies	-	1	1	2	2	2	3	2	3	5
Government-sponsored enterprises [2]	399	701	807	897	995	1,274	1,592	1,826	2,114	2,346
Federally-related mortgage pools	1,020	1,472	1,570	1,711	1,826	2,018	2,292	2,492	2,830	3,158
Asset-backed securities issuers	271	570	713	863	1,077	1,398	1,610	1,812	2,130	2,393
Finance companies	374	434	484	534	568	625	696	777	777	820
Mortgage companies	25	19	17	21	16	18	18	18	19	19
Real estate investment trusts	28	40	45	56	96	159	165	168	170	189
Security brokers and dealers	15	34	29	27	35	43	25	41	42	41
Funding corporations	147	211	249	312	373	413	504	504	448	447

- Represents or rounds to zero. [1] Includes nonprofit organizations. [2] U.S. government.

Source: Board of Governors of the Federal Reserve System, "Federal Reserve Statistical Release, Z.1, Flow of Funds Accounts of the United States"; published: 6 March 2003; <http://www.federalreserve.gov/releases/Z1/20030306/data.htm>.

No. 1165. Flow of Funds Accounts—Business Credit Market Debt Outstanding by Type of Instrument: 1990 to 2002

[In billions of dollars (2,533 represents $2,533,000,000,000). As of Dec. 31. N.e.c.=Not elsewhere classified]

Item	1990	1994	1995	1996	1997	1998	1999	2000	2001	2002
NONFARM NONFINANCIAL CORPORATE										
Total	2,533	2,682	2,909	3,092	3,382	3,791	4,203	4,584	4,838	4,900
Commercial paper	117	139	157	156	169	193	230	278	190	126
Municipal securities [1]	115	132	135	138	142	148	153	154	158	161
Corporate bonds [2]	1,008	1,253	1,344	1,460	1,611	1,846	2,064	2,225	2,566	2,699
Bank loans, n.e.c.	545	527	602	642	693	765	825	888	817	751
Other loans and advances	473	421	454	468	508	562	585	652	664	681
Savings institutions	17	5	6	8	9	12	15	20	21	23
Finance companies	241	247	271	274	274	307	356	413	402	410
U.S. government	9	8	10	9	8	8	8	8	7	7
Acceptance liabilities to banks	29	15	14	13	11	7	4	4	4	4
Rest of the world	172	122	122	126	143	142	120	117	116	126
Asset-backed securities issuers	4	24	30	38	62	86	83	91	113	111
Mortgages	275	210	217	228	260	277	346	386	444	482
Percent of total credit market debt:										
Short-term debt [3]	45	41	42	41	40	40	39	40	35	32
Long-term debt [4]	55	59	58	59	60	60	61	60	65	68
NONFARM NONCORPORATE										
Total	1,093	1,016	1,062	1,129	1,224	1,384	1,566	1,750	1,907	2,039
Bank loans, n.e.c.	136	154	165	194	237	266	296	326	332	319
Other loans and advances	94	85	92	93	96	109	117	128	128	131
Mortgages	863	777	805	843	891	1,009	1,153	1,296	1,446	1,589
Percent of total credit market debt:										
Short-term debt [3]	21	23	24	25	27	27	26	26	24	22
Long-term debt [4]	79	77	76	75	73	73	74	74	76	78

[1] Industrial revenue bonds. Issued by state and local governments to finance private investment and secured in interest and principal by the industrial user of the funds. [2] Through 1992:Q4, includes net issues by Netherlands Antillean financial subsidiaries. [3] Bank loans, n.e.c. plus other loans and advances. For corporate debt also includes commercial paper. [4] Mortgages. For corporate debt also includes municipal securities and corporate bonds.

Source: Board of Governors of the Federal Reserve System, "Federal Reserve Statistical Release, Z.1, Flow of Funds Accounts of the United States"; published: 6 March 2003; <http://www.federalreserve.gov/releases/Z1/20030306/data.htm>.

No. 1166. Flow of Funds Accounts—Assets of Households: 1990 to 2002

[As of December 31 (14,839 represents $14,839,000,000,000). Includes nonprofit organizations]

Type of instrument	Total (bil. dol.) 1990	1995	1998	1999	2000	2001	2002	Percent distribution 1990	2000	2002
Total financial assets	14,839	21,596	30,503	34,990	33,753	32,233	29,930	100.0	100.0	100.0
Deposits	3,259	3,298	3,928	4,053	4,401	4,773	5,094	22.0	13.0	17.0
Foreign deposits	13	23	38	44	59	54	56	0.1	0.2	0.2
Checkable deposits and currency	412	544	410	330	263	289	335	2.8	0.8	1.1
Time and savings deposits	2,465	2,281	2,733	2,811	3,098	3,305	3,614	16.6	9.2	12.1
Money market fund shares	369	450	747	868	982	1,126	1,090	2.5	2.9	3.6
Credit market instruments	1,556	1,944	2,264	2,542	2,373	2,307	2,363	10.5	7.0	7.9
Open-market paper	63	48	64	68	73	53	47	0.4	0.2	0.2
U.S. government securities	555	927	966	1,195	1,022	856	752	3.7	3.0	2.5
Treasury issues	495	820	735	844	635	565	582	3.3	1.9	1.9
Agency issues	60	107	232	352	388	290	170	0.4	1.1	0.6
Municipal securities	575	433	428	452	464	507	617	3.9	1.4	2.1
Corporate and foreign bonds	219	426	695	717	702	778	834	1.5	2.1	2.8
Mortgages	144	109	110	110	112	113	114	1.0	0.3	0.4
Corporate equities [1]	1,781	4,137	7,052	9,053	7,408	6,056	4,187	12.0	21.9	14.0
Mutual fund shares	457	1,159	2,447	3,181	3,083	2,916	2,627	3.1	9.1	8.8
Security credit	62	128	277	324	412	454	402	0.4	1.2	1.3
Life insurance reserves	392	566	718	784	819	880	958	2.6	2.4	3.2
Pension fund reserves	3,376	5,671	8,208	9,065	9,069	8,693	8,053	22.8	26.9	26.9
Investment in bank personal trusts	552	803	1,001	1,130	1,096	961	841	3.7	3.2	2.8
Equity in noncorporate business	3,179	3,598	4,286	4,523	4,753	4,837	5,022	21.4	14.1	16.8
Miscellaneous assets	224	292	321	334	339	355	383	1.5	1.0	1.3

[1] Only those directly held and those in closed-end and exchange-traded funds. Other equities are included in mutual funds, life insurance and pension reserves, and bank personal trusts.

Source: Board of Governors of the Federal Reserve System, "Federal Reserve Statistical Release, Z.1, Flow of Funds Accounts of the United States"; published: 6 March 2003; <http://www.federalreserve.gov/releases/Z1/20030306/data.htm>.

No. 1167. Financial Assets Held by Families by Type of Asset: 1995 to 2001

[Median value in thousands of constant 2001 dollars (18.0 represents $18,000). All dollar figures are adjusted to 2001 dollars using the "current methods" version of the consumer price index for all urban consumers published by U.S. Bureau of Labor Statistics. Families include one-person units; for definition of family, see text, Section 1. Based on Survey of Consumer Finance; see Appendix III]

Age of family head and family income	Any financial asset [1]	Transaction accounts [2]	Certificates of deposit	Savings bonds	Stocks [3]	Mutual funds [4]	Retirement accounts [5]	Life insurance [6]	Other managed [7]
PERCENT OF FAMILIES OWNING ASSET									
1995, total	91.0	87.0	14.3	22.8	15.2	12.3	45.2	32.0	3.9
1998, total	92.9	90.5	15.3	19.3	19.2	16.5	48.8	29.6	5.9
2001, total	93.1	90.9	15.7	16.7	21.3	17.7	52.2	28.0	6.6
Under 35 years old	89.2	86.0	6.3	12.7	17.4	11.5	45.1	15.0	2.1
35 to 44 years old	93.3	90.7	9.8	22.6	21.6	17.5	61.4	27.0	3.1
45 to 54 years old	94.4	92.2	15.2	21.0	22.0	20.2	63.4	31.1	6.4
55 to 64 years old	94.8	93.6	14.4	14.3	26.7	21.3	59.1	35.7	13.0
65 to 74 years old	94.6	93.8	29.7	11.3	20.5	19.9	44.0	36.7	11.8
75 years old and over	95.1	93.7	36.5	12.5	21.8	19.5	25.7	33.3	11.2
Percentiles of income: [8]									
Less than 20 ($10,300)	74.8	70.9	10.0	3.8	3.8	3.6	13.2	13.8	2.2
20-39.9 ($24,400)	93.0	89.4	14.7	11.0	11.2	9.5	33.3	24.7	3.3
40-59.9 ($39,900)	98.3	96.1	17.4	14.1	16.4	15.7	52.8	25.6	5.4
60-79.9 ($64,800)	99.6	98.8	16.0	24.4	26.2	20.6	75.7	35.7	8.5
80-89.9 ($98,700)	99.8	99.7	18.3	30.3	37.0	29.0	83.7	38.6	10.7
90-100 ($302,700)	99.7	99.2	22.0	29.7	60.6	48.8	88.3	41.8	16.7
MEDIAN VALUE [9]									
1995, total	18.0	2.5	11.6	1.2	10.4	23.1	19.6	5.8	34.7
1998, total	24.5	3.3	16.3	1.1	19.0	27.2	26.1	7.9	34.3
2001, total	28.0	4.0	15.0	1.0	20.0	35.0	29.0	10.0	70.0
Under 35 years old	6.3	1.8	4.0	0.3	5.7	9.0	6.6	10.0	40.0
35 to 44 years old	26.9	3.4	6.0	1.0	15.0	17.5	28.5	9.0	50.0
45 to 54 years old	45.7	4.6	12.0	1.0	15.0	38.5	48.0	11.0	60.0
55 to 64 years old	56.6	5.5	19.0	2.5	37.5	60.0	55.0	10.0	55.0
65 to 74 years old	51.4	8.0	20.0	2.0	85.0	70.0	60.0	8.8	120.0
75 years old and over	40.0	7.3	25.0	3.0	60.0	70.0	46.0	7.0	100.0

[1] Includes other types of financial assets, not shown separately. [2] Checking, savings, and money market deposit accounts, money market mutual funds, and call accounts at brokerages. [3] Covers only those stocks that are directly held by families outside mutual funds, retirement accounts and other managed assets. [4] Excludes money market mutual funds and funds held through retirement accounts or other managed assets. [5] The tax-deferred retirement accounts consist of IRAs, Keogh accounts, and certain employer-sponsored accounts. Employer-sponsored accounts include 401(k), 403(b), and thrift saving accounts from current or past jobs; other current job plans from which loans or withdrawals can be made; and accounts from past jobs from which the family expects to receive the account balance in the future. [6] Cash value. [7] Includes personal annuities and trusts with an equity interest and managed investment accounts. [8] Value in parentheses represent median income for that percentile group. Percentile: A value on a scale of zero to 100 that indicates the percent of a distribution that is equal to or below it. For example, a family with income in the 80th percentile has income equal to or better than 80 percent of all other families. [9] Median value of financial asset for families holding such assets.

Source: Board of Governors of the Federal Reserve System, Federal Reserve Bulletin, January 2003, and unpublished revisions.

No. 1160. Gross Domestic Product in Finance, Insurance, and Real Estate in Current and Real (1996) Dollars: 1990 to 2001

[In **billions of dollars, except percent (1,010.3 represents $1,010,300,000,000)**. For definition of gross domestic product, see text, Section 13. Based on 1987 Standard Industrial Classification; see text, Section 15]

Industry	Current dollars				Chained (**1996**) dollars [1]			
	1990	1995	2000	2001	1990	1995	2000	2001
Finance, insurance, real estate, total	**1,010.3**	**1,347.2**	**1,976.7**	**2,076.9**	**1,250.6**	**1,393.0**	**1,793.5**	**1,843.5**
Percent of gross domestic product	17.4	18.2	20.1	20.6	18.6	18.5	19.5	20.0
Depository institutions	171.3	227.4	361.1	359.8	244.0	242.4	287.4	290.4
Nondepository institutions	23.3	34.1	69.5	88.8	26.3	33.4	79.0	91.9
Security and commodity brokers	42.3	77.7	150.8	175.0	42.0	76.5	216.8	245.1
Insurance carriers	64.6	120.2	182.4	170.1	112.2	129.9	146.0	141.2
Insurance agents, brokers, and service	37.7	47.2	61.6	66.5	61.4	49.9	51.9	53.5
Real estate	665.7	832.6	1,123.7	1,171.7	763.4	852.8	1,016.7	1,022.0
Nonfarm housing services	488.3	628.9	811.4	845.1	580.1	648.0	722.9	725.6
Other real estate	177.3	203.7	312.3	326.6	182.9	204.9	295.5	298.2
Holding and other investment offices	5.5	8.0	27.7	45.0	10.2	9.9	13.7	22.7

[1] See text, Section 13.

Source: U.S. Bureau of Economic Analysis, *National Income and Product Accounts, 1929-97*; and *Survey of Current Business*, November 2002. See also <http://www.bea.doc.gov/bea/articles/2002/11november/1102GDPIindustry.pdf>.

No. 1161. Finance and Insurance—Establishments, Employees, and Payroll: 2000 and 2001

[**423.7 represents 423,700.** Covers establishments with payroll. Employees are for the week including March 12. Most government employees are excluded. For statement on methodology, see Appendix III]

Kind of business	NAICS code [1]	Establishments (1,000)		Employees (1,000)		Payroll (bil. dol.)	
		2000	2001	2000	2001	2000	2001
Finance & insurance, total	52	**423.7**	**425.0**	**5,963.4**	**6,248.4**	**346.8**	**373.6**
Monetary authorities—central bank	521	0.1	0.1	22.3	23.6	1.1	1.2
Credit intermediation & related activities	522	176.3	180.8	2,753.2	2,917.6	116.1	130.4
Depository credit intermediation [2]	5221	105.6	107.2	1,934.7	2,062.5	78.5	85.3
Commercial banking	52211	73.9	75.8	1,492.8	1,603.2	63.6	69.2
Savings institutions	52212	15.9	15.7	243.6	253.1	9.2	9.8
Credit unions	52213	15.6	15.5	192.3	200.4	5.4	6.0
Nondepository credit intermediation	5222	49.3	49.8	620.9	646.4	29.6	35.2
Credit card issuing	52221	0.8	0.8	68.0	72.1	2.5	3.2
Sales financing	52222	7.4	7.5	154.1	160.5	8.8	9.4
Other nondepository credit intermediation [2]	52229	41.1	41.5	398.8	413.7	18.2	22.6
Consumer lending	522291	13.1	13.4	93.3	95.5	3.8	4.1
Real estate credit	522292	19.8	19.8	237.7	251.5	10.8	14.8
Activities related to credit intermediation [2]	5223	21.4	23.7	197.6	208.7	7.9	9.9
Mortgage & nonmortgage brokers	52231	11.0	12.2	66.5	70.3	2.7	4.0
Security, commodity contracts & like activity	523	72.9	76.9	866.2	947.1	119.5	125.0
Scrty & comdty contracts intermed & brokerage [2]	5231	38.1	39.6	539.0	575.3	80.2	84.7
Investment banking & securities dealing	52311	6.3	7.0	138.5	172.7	31.2	35.2
Securities brokerage	52312	29.5	30.3	377.7	381.1	47.0	47.5
Securities & commodity exchanges	5232	(Z)	0.1	6.8	6.5	0.5	0.6
Other financial investment activities [2]	5239	34.8	37.2	320.4	365.2	38.8	39.8
Portfolio management	52392	11.6	11.3	156.2	171.5	24.9	23.7
Investment advice	52393	12.8	16.0	66.2	83.4	6.9	8.3
Insurance carriers & related activities	524	172.2	164.8	2,290.2	2,326.1	108.1	114.8
Insurance carriers [2]	5241	37.4	30.9	1,489.2	1,505.0	74.7	78.5
Direct life/health/medical insurance carriers	52411	13.9	13.5	813.4	821.9	40.0	41.8
Direct life insurance carriers	524113	10.7	10.6	491.1	500.0	25.7	26.9
Direct health & medical insurance carriers	524114	3.1	3.0	322.3	321.8	14.3	15.0
Other direct insurance carriers [2]	52412	23.0	16.8	660.4	668.6	33.5	35.4
Direct property & casualty insurance carriers	524126	19.8	12.2	609.4	592.6	31.1	31.3
Direct title insurance carriers	524127	3.0	4.3	47.5	72.0	2.2	3.9
Agencies & other insurance related activities [2]	5242	134.8	134.0	801.0	821.1	33.3	36.3
Insurance agencies & brokerages	52421	121.5	120.9	596.2	613.0	24.7	27.1
Other insurance related activities [2]	52429	13.3	13.1	204.8	208.1	8.6	9.1
Insurance & pension funds, third party admin	524292	6.2	5.9	123.1	118.9	5.1	5.1
Funds, trusts, & other financial vehicles (part)	525	2.3	2.4	31.5	34.0	2.1	2.1

Z Less than 500. [1] North American Industry Classification System; see text, Section 15. [2] Includes industries not shown separately.

Source: U.S. Census Bureau, *County Business Patterns*, annual, <http://www.census.gov/prod/2003pubs/01cbp/cbp01-1.pdf>, (issued April 2003).

No. 1162. Flow of Funds Accounts—Financial Assets of Financial and Nonfinancial Institutions by Holder Sector: 1990 to 2002

[In billions of dollars (36,344 represents $36,344,000,000,000). As of Dec. 31]

Sector	1990	1994	1995	1996	1997	1998	1999	2000	2001	2002
All sectors	36,344	47,581	53,731	59,698	67,587	76,233	87,078	89,751	90,768	89,832
Households [1]	14,839	19,005	21,596	24,015	27,489	30,503	34,990	33,753	32,233	29,930
Nonfinancial business	3,979	5,009	5,568	6,162	6,644	7,869	9,337	10,763	11,233	11,509
Farm business	47	59	61	61	62	64	65	65	67	71
Nonfarm noncorporate	356	473	548	643	774	989	1,178	1,424	1,567	1,686
Nonfinancial corporations	3,575	4,477	4,959	5,458	5,809	6,816	8,094	9,274	9,599	9,752
State and local government	963	1,026	994	1,008	1,033	1,180	1,258	1,296	1,350	1,432
U.S. government	442	440	441	441	438	443	557	506	607	606
Monetary authorities	342	452	472	495	534	567	697	636	683	754
Commercial banking	3,337	4,160	4,494	4,710	5,175	5,629	5,982	6,469	6,831	7,357
U.S.-chartered commercial banks	2,644	3,123	3,322	3,445	3,742	4,081	4,431	4,774	5,015	5,426
Foreign banking offices in U.S.	367	590	666	715	811	806	751	789	794	817
Bank holding companies	298	414	467	511	575	686	741	842	942	1,025
Banks in U.S.-affiliated areas	28	33	39	40	46	56	59	63	80	89
Savings institutions	1,323	1,009	1,013	1,032	1,029	1,089	1,150	1,218	1,299	1,358
Credit unions	217	294	311	330	354	391	415	441	506	563
Bank personal trusts, estates	522	670	775	842	918	976	1,104	1,068	929	808
Life insurance	1,351	1,863	2,064	2,246	2,515	2,770	3,068	3,136	3,225	3,366
Other insurance	533	678	740	770	843	876	875	866	863	912
Private pension funds	1,634	2,460	2,923	3,251	3,747	4,178	4,630	4,515	4,171	3,686
State and local govt. retirement funds	801	1,088	1,303	1,495	1,817	2,054	2,227	2,290	2,180	1,968
Money market funds	493	600	741	887	1,043	1,330	1,579	1,812	2,241	2,224
Mutual funds	608	1,477	1,853	2,342	2,989	3,613	4,538	4,435	4,135	3,635
Closed-end funds	53	118	131	142	143	146	147	136	138	148
Exchange-traded funds	-	(Z)	1	2	7	16	34	66	83	102
U.S. govt.-sponsored enterprises	478	782	897	989	1,099	1,404	1,721	1,969	2,301	2,548
Federally-related mortgage pools	1,020	1,472	1,570	1,711	1,826	2,018	2,292	2,492	2,830	3,158
Asset-backed securities issuers	270	568	709	855	1,066	1,385	1,601	1,805	2,123	2,388
Finance companies	547	600	672	717	764	853	1,003	1,138	1,156	1,189
Mortgage companies	49	36	33	41	32	35	36	36	37	39
Real estate investment trusts	28	31	33	38	64	71	68	62	70	94
Security brokers and dealers	262	455	568	636	779	921	1,001	1,221	1,466	1,359
Funding corporations	251	380	394	499	613	717	967	1,107	1,119	1,135
Rest of the world	1,998	2,910	3,435	4,042	4,627	5,200	5,800	6,516	6,960	7,566

- Represents zero.   Z Less than $500 million.   [1] Includes nonprofit organizations.

Source: Board of Governors of the Federal Reserve System, "Federal Reserve Statistical Release, Z.1, Flow of Funds Accounts of the United States"; published: 6 March 2003; <http://www.federalreserve.gov/releases/Z1/20030306/data.htm>.

No. 1163. Flow of Funds Accounts—Financial Assets and Liabilities of Foreign Sector: 1990 to 2002

[In billions of dollars (1,998 represents $1,998,000,000,000). As of Dec. 31]

Type of instrument	1990	1994	1995	1996	1997	1998	1999	2000	2001	2002
Total financial assets [1]	1,998	2,910	3,435	4,042	4,627	5,200	5,800	6,516	6,960	7,566
Net interbank assets	53	218	229	177	173	146	140	161	112	106
U.S. checkable deposits and currency	107	180	194	214	244	258	298	290	314	337
U.S. time deposits	49	56	50	61	74	87	102	103	86	95
Security RPs [2]	20	47	68	71	91	72	80	91	151	185
Credit market instruments	889	1,216	1,493	1,840	2,098	2,278	2,355	2,621	2,354	3,371
Open market paper	11	25	43	58	78	115	102	112	118	133
U.S. government securities	488	758	966	1,222	1,375	1,413	1,381	1,471	1,594	1,820
Official holdings	291	407	507	631	648	670	694	750	799	879
Treasury	286	397	490	606	615	623	618	625	651	696
Agency	5	10	18	25	33	47	76	125	148	183
Private holdings	197	351	459	591	727	743	687	721	796	941
Treasury	152	236	330	441	551	562	463	401	389	443
Agency	45	115	129	150	176	181	224	320	407	498
U.S. corporate bonds [3]	217	311	361	433	502	608	752	921	1,126	1,293
Loans to U.S. corporate business	172	122	122	126	143	142	120	117	116	126
U.S. corporate equities	244	398	550	672	953	1,250	1,612	1,626	1,534	1,351
Trade receivables	45	52	53	58	59	53	47	47	44	48
Miscellaneous assets	591	743	799	950	937	1,056	1,167	1,577	1,765	2,073
Foreign direct investment in U.S [4]	505	618	680	746	824	920	1,101	1,375	1,499	1,545
Other	86	125	119	204	113	136	66	202	266	527
Total liabilities [1]	1,389	1,743	2,012	2,317	2,562	2,788	3,108	3,479	3,628	4,104
U.S. official foreign exchange and net IMF position	61	53	64	54	49	60	50	46	47	56
U.S. private deposits	298	374	419	522	618	642	704	825	909	955
Credit market instruments [1]	289	375	454	542	608	651	677	742	705	727
Commercial paper	75	43	56	67	65	73	89	121	107	143
Bonds	115	242	299	366	428	463	477	501	488	472
Bank loans n.e.c. [5]	19	26	35	44	52	59	59	71	63	69
Miscellaneous liabilities [1]	713	901	1,030	1,156	1,238	1,390	1,628	1,817	1,920	2,326
U.S. direct investment abroad [3,4]	629	787	886	990	1,068	1,196	1,377	1,515	1,623	1,738

[1] Includes other items not shown separately.   [2] Repurchase agreements.   [3] Through 1992, corporate bonds include net issues by Netherlands Antillean financial subsidiaries; U.S. direct investment abroad excludes net inflows from those bond issues.   [4] Direct investment is valued on a current-cost basis.   [5] Not elsewhere classified.

Source: Board of Governors of the Federal Reserve System, "Federal Reserve Statistical Release, Z.1, Flow of Funds Accounts of the United States"; published: 6 March 2003; <http://www.federalreserve.gov/releases/Z1/20030306/data.htm>.

No. 1168. Flow of Funds Accounts—Liabilities of Households: 1990 to 2002

[As of December 31 (3,720 represents $3,720,000,000,000). Includes nonprofit organizations. See Appendix III]

Type of instrument	Total (bil. dol.) 1990	1995	1998	1999	2000	2001	2002	Percent distribution 1990	2000	2002
Total liabilities	3,720	5,081	6,309	6,888	7,468	8,047	8,761	100.0	100.0	100.0
Credit market instruments	3,598	4,884	6,012	6,510	7,075	7,687	8,444	96.7	94.7	96.4
Home mortgages [1]	2,505	3,353	4,157	4,531	4,907	5,385	6,054	67.3	65.7	69.1
Consumer credit	805	1,123	1,347	1,446	1,593	1,702	1,757	21.6	21.3	20.1
Municipal securities	87	98	127	137	143	157	170	2.3	1.9	1.9
Bank loans, n.e.c.[2]	18	57	73	66	72	55	42	0.5	1.0	0.5
Other loans	101	160	204	219	246	263	278	2.7	3.3	3.2
Commercial mortgages	83	92	105	111	114	125	143	2.2	1.5	1.6
Security credit	39	79	153	228	235	196	145	1.0	3.1	1.7
Trade payables	67	101	127	131	139	145	152	1.8	1.9	1.7
Unpaid life insurance premiums [3]	16	18	17	19	20	19	20	0.4	0.3	0.2

[1] Includes loans made under home equity lines of credit and home equity loans secured by junior liens.   [2] Not elsewhere classified.   [3] Includes deferred premiums.

Source: Board of Governors of the Federal Reserve System, "Federal Reserve Statistical Release, Z.1, Flow of Funds Accounts of the United States"; published: 6 March 2003; <http://www.federalreserve.gov/releases/Z1/20030306/data.htm>.

No. 1169. Financial Debt Held by Families by Type of Debt: 1995 to 2001

[Median debt in thousands of constant 2001 dollars (25.0 represents $25,000). See headnote, Table 1167]

Age of family head and family income	Any debt	Home-secured debt [1]	Other residential property	Installment	Credit card balances [2]	Other lines of credit	Other debt [3]
PERCENT OF FAMILIES HOLDING DEBTS							
1995, total	74.5	41.0	4.9	45.9	47.3	1.9	8.5
1998, total	74.1	43.1	5.1	43.7	44.1	2.3	8.8
2001, total	**75.1**	**44.6**	**4.7**	**45.2**	**44.4**	**1.5**	**7.2**
Under 35 years old	82.7	35.7	2.7	63.8	49.6	1.7	8.8
35 to 44 years old	88.6	59.6	4.9	57.1	54.1	1.7	8.0
45 to 54 years old	84.6	59.8	6.5	45.9	50.4	1.5	7.4
55 to 64 years old	75.4	49.0	8.0	39.3	41.6	3.1	7.4
65 to 74 years old	56.8	32.0	3.4	21.1	30.0	(B)	5.0
75 years old and over	29.2	9.5	2.0	9.5	18.4	(B)	3.6
Percentiles of income: [4]							
Less than 20 ($10,300)	49.3	13.8	(B)	25.5	30.3	1.3	5.9
20-39.9 ($24,400)	70.2	27.0	1.8	43.2	44.5	1.5	5.6
40-59.9 ($39,900)	82.1	44.4	3.2	51.9	52.8	1.5	7.7
60-79.9 ($64,800)	85.6	61.8	5.4	56.7	52.6	1.5	7.7
80-89.9 ($98,700)	91.4	76.9	10.3	55.7	50.3	2.6	9.3
90-100 ($302,700)	85.3	75.4	14.9	41.2	33.1	1.4	8.8
MEDIAN DEBT [5]							
1995, total	25.0	59.1	34.7	7.0	1.7	4.0	2.3
1998, total	35.4	67.5	43.5	9.5	1.9	2.7	3.3
2001, total	**38.8**	**70.0**	**40.0**	**9.7**	**1.9**	**3.9**	**3.0**
Under 35 years old	24.9	77.0	52.0	9.5	2.0	0.5	2.0
35 to 44 years old	61.5	80.0	45.5	11.1	2.0	0.7	3.1
45 to 54 years old	54.3	75.0	33.5	9.6	2.3	5.3	5.0
55 to 64 years old	34.6	55.0	40.0	9.0	1.9	20.5	5.0
65 to 74 years old	13.1	39.0	77.0	7.0	1.0	(B)	2.5
75 years old and over	5.0	44.8	42.0	5.8	0.7	(B)	2.5

B Base figure too small.   [1] First and second mortgages and home equity loans and lines of credit secured by the primary residence.   [2] Families that had an outstanding balance on any of their credit cards after paying their most recent bills.   [3] Includes loans on insurance policies, loans against pension accounts, borrowing on margin accounts and unclassified loans.   [4] Value in parentheses represent median income for that percentile group. See footnote 8, Table 1167.   [5] Median amount of financial debt for families holding such debts.

No. 1170. Percent Distribution of Amount of Debt Held by Families: 1998 and 2001

[See headnote, Table 1167]

Type of debt	1998	2001	Purpose of debt	1998	2001	Type of lending institution	1998	2001
Total	100.0	100.0	**Total**	100.0	100.0	**Total**	100.0	100.0
Home-secured debt	71.3	75.1	Home purchase	67.7	70.7	Commercial bank	32.8	34.1
Installment loans	13.0	12.3	Home improvement	2.1	1.9	Savings and loan	9.7	6.1
Credit card balances	3.9	3.4	Investment, excluding			Credit union	4.2	5.5
Other lines of credit	0.3	0.5	real estate	3.3	2.8	Finance or loan company	4.2	4.3
Other residential property	7.7	6.4	Vehicles	7.6	7.8	Brokerage	3.8	3.1
Other debt	3.7	2.3	Goods and services	6.1	5.7	Real estate lender	35.5	38.0
			Other residential property	7.9	6.6	Individual lender	3.3	2.0
			Education	3.4	3.1	Other nonfinancial	1.3	1.4
			Other loans	1.9	1.4	Government	0.6	1.1
						Credit and store cards	3.9	3.7
						Other loans	0.7	0.8

Source of Tables 1169 and 1170: Board of Governors of the Federal Reserve System, *Federal Reserve Bulletin*, January 2003, and unpublished revisions.

No. 1171. Ratios of Debt Payments to Family Income: 1995 to 2001

[In percent. All dollar figures are adjusted to 2001 dollars using the "current methods" version of the consumer price index for all urban consumers published by U.S. Bureau of Labor Statistics. Families include one-person units; for definition of family, see text, Section 1. Based on Survey of Consumer Finance; see Appendix III. For definition of median, see Guide to Tabular Presentation]

Age of family head and family income (constant (2001) dollars)	Ratio of debt payments to family income							Percent of debtors with—					
	Aggregate			Median			Ratios above 40 percent			Any payment 60 days or more past due		
	1995	1998	2001	1995	1998	2001	1995	1998	2001	1995	1998	2001
All families	13.6	14.4	12.5	15.6	18.1	16.0	10.6	12.8	11.0	7.1	8.1	7.0
Under 35 years old	17.1	16.6	16.6	16.2	18.3	16.7	11.4	11.8	10.8	8.7	11.1	11.9
35 to 44 years old	16.7	17.1	14.7	17.6	19.6	17.3	9.3	11.8	9.4	7.7	8.4	5.9
45 to 54 years old	14.7	15.9	12.4	16.1	18.0	16.8	10.6	11.5	10.9	7.4	7.4	6.2
55 to 64 years old	11.5	13.0	10.7	13.9	17.0	13.8	14.4	13.9	12.2	3.2	7.5	7.1
65 to 74 years old	6.9	8.5	8.8	11.1	14.9	15.1	7.8	17.5	13.9	5.3	3.1	1.5
75 years old and over	2.4	3.9	3.7	2.0	9.0	7.0	7.4	20.9	14.3	5.4	1.1	0.8
Percentiles of income:[1]												
Less than 20	18.0	17.9	15.3	12.1	26.4	17.2	26.2	28.2	27.0	10.2	12.9	13.4
20-39.9	16.1	15.7	15.1	16.1	17.8	15.9	16.0	17.2	16.0	10.1	12.3	11.7
40-59.9	14.9	17.8	16.5	15.1	19.0	16.9	8.1	15.3	11.7	8.7	10.0	7.9
60-79.9	17.4	18.5	16.3	18.3	19.2	17.9	7.1	8.6	5.6	6.6	5.9	4.0
80-89.9	16.2	16.4	16.5	16.5	17.4	17.0	4.6	3.4	3.5	2.8	3.9	2.6
90-100	9.3	10.2	8.0	12.2	13.5	11.1	2.0	2.6	2.0	1.0	1.6	1.3

[1] See footnote 8, Table 1167.

Source: Board of Governors of the Federal Reserve System, *Federal Reserve Bulletin*, January 2003, and unpublished revisions.

No. 1172. Household Debt-Service Payments as a Percentage of Disposable Personal Income: 1980 to 2002

[In percent. As of end of year. Seasonally adjusted. The household debt-service burden is an estimate of the ratio of debt payments to disposable personal income. Debt payments consist of the estimated required payments on outstanding mortgage and consumer debt]

Year	Total	Consumer	Mortgage	Year	Total	Consumer	Mortgage	Year	Total	Consumer	Mortgage
1980	12.52	7.96	4.56	1988	13.42	7.58	5.84	1996	13.27	7.44	5.83
1981	12.47	7.60	4.87	1989	13.65	7.58	6.07	1997	13.39	7.50	5.89
1982	12.47	7.45	5.02	1990	13.35	7.10	6.25	1998	13.40	7.59	5.82
1983	12.48	7.46	5.03	1991	12.71	6.51	6.20	1999	13.71	7.72	5.99
1984	12.96	7.80	5.16	1992	11.83	5.97	5.86	2000	13.93	7.80	6.12
1985	13.90	8.29	5.61	1993	11.79	6.09	5.69	2001	14.41	8.05	6.36
1986	14.34	8.48	5.85	1994	12.19	6.48	5.71	2002	14.03	7.70	6.33
1987	13.74	7.91	5.83	1995	12.87	7.04	5.83				

Source: Board of Governors of the Federal Reserve System, "Household Debt Service Burden"; <http://www.federalreserve.gov/releases/housedebt/default.htm>.

No. 1173. Selected Financial Institutions—Number and Assets by Asset Size: 2002

[As of December (7,075.8 represents $7,075,800,000,000). FDIC=Federal Deposit Insurance Corporation]

Asset size	Number of institutions			Assets (bil. dol.)		
	F.D.I.C.-insured		Credit unions[1]	F.D.I.C.-insured		Credit unions[1]
	Commercial banks	Savings institutions		Commercial banks[2]	Savings institutions	
Total	7,887	1,467	9,688	7,075.8	1,359.4	557.1
Less than $5.0 million	22	10	3,430	(NA)	(NA)	6.7
$5.0 million to $9.9 million	92	22	1,539	(NA)	(NA)	11.2
$10.0 million to $24.9 million	651	59	1,812	12.1	1.0	29.4
$25.0 million to $49.9 million	1,373	153	1,110	51.6	5.7	39.6
$50.0 million to $99.9 million	2,027	268	751	146.5	19.6	52.8
$100.0 million to $499.9 million	2,949	666	842	616.4	158.6	177.4
$500.0 million to $999.9 million	368	138	133	253.4	96.8	89.7
$1.0 billion to $2.9 billion	221	87	62	367.9	138.7	93.5
$3.0 billion or more	184	64	9	5,627.1	938.5	56.8
	Percent distribution					
Total	100.0	100.0	100.0	100.0	100.0	100.0
Less than $5.0 million	0.3	0.7	35.4	(NA)	(NA)	1.2
$5.0 million to $9.9 million	1.2	1.5	15.9	(NA)	(NA)	2.0
$10.0 million to $24.9 million	8.3	4.0	18.7	0.2	0.1	5.3
$25.0 million to $49.9 million	17.4	10.4	11.5	0.7	0.4	7.1
$50.0 million to $99.9 million	25.7	18.3	7.8	2.1	1.4	9.5
$100.0 million to $499.9 million	37.4	45.4	8.7	8.7	11.7	31.8
$500.0 million to $999.9 million	4.7	9.4	1.4	3.6	7.1	16.1
$1.0 billion to $2.9 billion	2.8	5.9	0.6	5.2	10.2	16.8
$3.0 billion or more	2.3	4.4	0.1	79.5	69.1	10.2

NA Not available. [1] Source: National Credit Union Administration, *National Credit Union Administration Yearend Statistics 2002*. Excludes nonfederally insured state chartered credit unions and federally insured corporate credit unions. [2] Includes foreign branches of U.S. banks.

Source: Except as noted, U.S. Federal Deposit Insurance Corporation, *Statistics on Banking, 2002*.

No. 1174. FDIC-Insured Financial Institutions—Number, Assets, and Liabilities: 1990 to 2002

[In billions of dollars, except as indicated (4,649 represents $4,649,000,000,000). As of Dec. 31. 2002 data preliminary. Includes outlying areas. Except as noted, includes foreign branches of U.S. banks]

Item	1990	1995	1996	1997	1998	1999	2000	2001	2002
All banking offices	84,353	81,350	82,578	83,641	84,587	86,040	85,952	86,506	87,075
Commercial bank offices, total [1]	62,723	65,888	66,811	68,810	70,052	71,534	71,911	72,458	73,380
Number of main offices	12,376	9,971	9,553	9,165	8,793	8,597	8,331	8,095	7,903
Number of branches	50,347	55,917	57,258	59,645	61,259	62,937	63,580	64,363	65,477
Savings institutions offices, total	21,630	15,462	15,767	14,831	14,535	14,506	14,041	14,048	13,695
Number of main offices	2,815	2,030	1,926	1,780	1,690	1,642	1,589	1,534	1,467
Number of branches	18,815	13,432	13,841	13,051	12,845	12,864	12,452	12,514	12,228
Number of financial institutions reporting	15,158	11,970	11,453	10,923	10,464	10,222	9,905	9,613	9,354
Assets, total [2]	**4,649**	**5,338**	**5,607**	**6,045**	**6,531**	**6,884**	**7,462**	**7,868**	**8,435**
Net loans and leases	2,867	3,198	3,439	3,611	3,896	4,187	4,576	4,687	4,972
Real estate loans	1,586	1,690	1,776	1,877	1,990	2,181	2,396	2,561	2,850
1-4 family residential mortgages	859	1,006	1,054	1,110	1,170	1,251	1,340	1,380	1,513
Commercial real estate	328	349	366	389	418	471	525	570	628
Construction and development	171	90	102	108	130	165	197	232	245
Home equity loans [3]	86	98	104	116	113	121	151	184	256
Commercial and industrial loans	646	674	724	811	920	996	1,086	1,020	954
Loans to individuals	451	576	607	613	624	618	672	701	772
Credit cards and related plans	142	224	242	246	242	227	266	250	292
Farm loans	33	40	41	45	47	46	49	48	47
Other loans and leases	245	294	367	332	385	416	448	440	437
Less: Reserve for losses	65	60	61	62	64	66	71	80	85
Less: Unearned income	29	15	16	5	4	4	3	3	4
Securities	890	1,099	1,063	1,121	1,249	1,338	1,361	1,465	1,633
Domestic office assets	4,259	4,753	4,935	5,297	5,807	6,144	6,702	7,119	7,684
Foreign office assets	390	585	672	748	724	740	760	749	752
Liabilities and capital, total	**4,649**	**5,338**	**5,607**	**6,045**	**6,531**	**6,884**	**7,462**	**7,868**	**8,435**
Noninterest-bearing deposits	511	641	695	710	761	745	802	927	999
Interest-bearing deposits	3,127	3,129	3,230	3,416	3,625	3,793	4,113	4,262	4,570
Other borrowed funds	569	849	917	1,043	1,171	1,376	1,467	1,496	1,570
Subordinated debt	28	46	54	65	76	79	90	99	99
Other liabilities	128	238	250	304	341	315	356	377	422
Equity capital	286	436	461	507	557	575	634	707	776
Domestic office deposits	3,344	3,315	3,451	3,600	3,814	3,882	4,208	4,560	4,910
Foreign office deposits	293	454	474	526	572	656	707	630	658
Estimated insured deposits [4]	2,629	2,662	2,689	2,745	2,849	2,868	3,054	3,210	3,386

[1] Includes insured branches of foreign banks that file a Call Report. [2] Includes other items not shown separately. [3] For one- to four-family residential properties. [4] Excludes foreign office deposits which are uninsured.

No. 1175. FDIC-Insured Financial Institutions—Income and Selected Measures of Financial Condition: 1990 to 2002

[In billions of dollars, except as indicated (437.7 represents $437,700,000,000). 2002 data preliminary. Includes outlying areas. Includes foreign branches of U.S. banks]

Item	1990	1995	1996	1997	1998	1999	2000	2001	2002
Interest income	437.7	373.4	385.0	408.7	433.1	441.5	512.2	486.8	429.8
Interest expense	295.9	190.7	192.2	205.6	221.2	218.0	276.5	235.0	152.8
Net interest income	141.8	182.7	192.9	203.1	211.9	223.5	235.7	251.8	277.0
Provisions for loan losses	41.4	14.7	18.8	22.0	24.0	23.4	32.0	46.3	51.4
Noninterest income	62.2	89.5	101.0	111.5	132.9	154.2	164.8	168.8	182.5
Percent of net operating revenue [1]	30.5	32.9	34.4	35.4	38.5	40.8	41.1	40.1	39.7
Noninterest expense	144.2	171.6	186.4	191.1	217.7	228.2	241.6	251.1	262.8
Income taxes	9.1	30.3	31.1	36.7	37.2	45.5	43.7	44.0	52.1
Net income	11.3	56.4	59.3	67.9	72.0	82.4	81.7	87.2	105.4
PERFORMANCE RATIOS									
Return on assets [2] (percent)	0.24	1.10	1.10	1.18	1.16	1.25	1.14	1.14	1.31
Return on equity [3] (percent)	3.95	13.63	13.31	14.03	13.49	14.71	13.55	12.99	14.17
Net interest margin [4] (percent)	3.47	4.05	4.06	4.04	3.91	3.90	3.78	3.78	3.96
Net charge-offs [5]	34.8	14.4	17.6	19.9	22.2	21.6	26.3	38.9	46.9
Net charge-offs to loans and leases, total (percent)	1.19	0.46	0.53	0.57	0.59	0.53	0.59	0.83	1.00
Net charge-off rate, credit card loans (percent)	3.39	3.39	4.33	5.11	5.17	4.40	4.37	5.15	6.37
CONDITION RATIOS									
Equity capital to assets (percent)	6.16	8.16	8.22	8.39	8.52	8.35	8.49	8.99	9.21
Noncurrent assets plus other real estate owned to assets [6] (percent)	3.16	0.92	0.81	0.71	0.66	0.63	0.71	0.88	0.90
Percentage of banks losing money	16.5	3.1	5.6	4.7	6.0	7.6	7.5	8.2	6.3
Number of problem institutions	1,492	193	117	92	84	79	94	114	136
Assets of problem institutions	640	31	12	6	11	10	24	40	39
Number of failed/assisted institutions	169	6	6	1	3	8	7	4	11

[1] Net operating revenue equals net interest income plus noninterest income. [2] Net income (including securities transactions and nonrecurring items) as a percentage of average total assets. [3] Net income as a percentage of average total equity capital. [4] Interest income less interest expense as a percentage of average earning assets (i.e. the profit margin a bank earns on its loans and investments). [5] Total loans and leases charged off (removed from balance sheet because of uncollectibility), less amounts recovered on loans and leases previously charged off. [6] Noncurrent assets: the sum of loans, leases, debt securities and other assets that are 90 days or more past due, or in nonaccrual status. Other real estate owned: Primarily foreclosed property.

Source of Tables 1174 and 1175: U.S. Federal Deposit Insurance Corporation, *Annual Report; Statistics on Banking*, annual; *FDIC Quarterly Banking Profile*; and *FDIC Quarterly Banking Profile Graph Book*.

No. 1176. FDIC-Insured Financial Institutions by Asset Size: 2002

[In percent, except as indicated. Preliminary. See headnote, Table 1175]

Item	Total	Less than $100 million	$100 million to $1 billion	$1 billion to $10 billion	Greater than $10 billion
COMMERCIAL BANKS					
Number of institutions reporting............	7,887	4,169	3,313	325	80
Assets, total (bil. dol.)...................	7,076	211	869	937	5,058
Deposits (bil. dol.)....................	4,690	178	707	640	3,165
Net income (bil. dol.)...................	90	2	10	14	64
Return on assets.......................	1.33	1.01	1.26	1.52	1.32
Return on equity.......................	14.51	9.04	12.79	14.85	15.05
Equity capital to assets.................	9.16	11.12	9.88	10.34	8.73
Noncurrent assets plus other real estate owned to assets......................	0.94	0.86	0.76	0.72	1.01
Net charge-offs to loans and leases.........	1.12	0.35	0.44	0.88	1.32
Percentage of banks losing money..........	6.4	9.8	2.6	2.5	2.5
SAVINGS INSTITUTIONS					
Number of institutions reporting............	1,467	512	804	125	26
Assets, total (bil. dol.)...................	1,359	27	255	342	736
Deposits (bil. dol.)....................	879	21	194	223	441
Net income (bil. dol.)...................	15.2	0.2	2.1	3.9	8.9
Return on assets.......................	1.16	0.88	0.84	1.23	1.26
Return on equity.......................	12.37	6.94	7.08	13.40	14.15
Equity capital to assets.................	9.46	12.59	10.67	9.28	9.02
Noncurrent assets plus other real estate owned to assets......................	0.69	0.80	0.65	0.63	0.74
Net charge-offs to loans and leases.........	0.29	0.14	0.29	0.14	0.35
Percentage of banks losing money..........	6.7	12.3	3.9	3.2	3.9

Source: U.S. Federal Deposit Insurance Corporation, *Annual Report; Statistics on Banking*, annual; and *FDIC Quarterly Banking Profile*. <http://www.fdic.gov/bank/index.html>.

No. 1177. Retail Fees and Services of Depository Institutions: 2001 and 2002

[In dollars, except as noted. As of June. For most services, fees are reported in terms of (1) the proportion of those institutions offering a service that charge for the service and (2) the average fee charged by the institutions that charge for the service. Based on a random sample of depository institutions belonging to the Bank Insurance Fund, whose members are predominantly commercial banks, or the Savings Association Insurance Fund, whose members are predominantly savings and loans associations]

Type of account or service	2001	2002	Type of account or service	2001	2002
NONINTEREST CHECKING ACCOUNT			AUTOMATED TELLER MACHINES (ATMs)		
Percent offering..................	96.7	96.1	Percent offering.................	90.9	93.4
Single-balance, single-fee account: [1]			Annual fee:		
Percent offering................	29.6	32.3	Percent charging...............	10.7	10.3
Monthly fee (low balance).........	7.12	7.35	Average.....................	10.35	11.65
Minimum balance to avoid fee.....	527	591	Fees for customer withdrawals on us: [4]		
Fee-only account: [2]			Percent charging...............	3.6	2.7
Percent offering................	37.7	39.9	Average.....................	0.81	0.56
Monthly fee...................	4.74	5.27	Fees for customer withdrawals on others: [4]		
NOW ACCOUNTS [3]			Percent charging...............	78.5	69.0
Percent offering..................	96.2	95.6	Average.....................	1.17	1.14
Single-fee account: [1]			Surcharge: [5]		
Percent offering................	49.5	40.9	Percent charging...............	88.5	89.4
Monthly fee (low balance).........	8.15	8.71	Average.....................	1.32	1.36
Minimum balance to avoid fee.....	1,132	1,091			

[1] A monthly fee for balances below the minimum, no monthly fee for balances above the minimum, and no other charges.
[2] A monthly fee, no minimum balance to eliminate the fee, and a charge per check in some cases. [3] NOW (negotiable order of withdrawal) accounts are checking accounts that pay interest and often have fee structures that differ from those of noninterest checking accounts. [4] An institution's "customer" is one who has an account at the institution. A customer's ATM transactions in which the machine used is that of the customer's institution are called "on us"; a customer's transactions in which the machine used is that of another institution are called "on others." [5] An ATM surcharge is a fee imposed by the ATM's institution, typically on every transaction by the machine's noncustomer users.
Source: Board of Governors of the Federal Reserve System, *Annual Report to the Congress on Retail Fees and Services of Depository Institutions*, June 2003.

No. 1178. U.S. Banking Offices of Foreign Banks—Summary: 1990 to 2002

[In billions of dollars, except as indicated (791 represents $791,000,000,000). As of December. Data cover foreign-bank branches and agencies in the 50 states and the District of Columbia, New York investment companies (through September 1996) and U.S. commercial banks of which more than 25 percent is owned by foreign banks, and International Banking Facilities. Foreign banks are those owned by institutions located outside of the United States and its affiliated insular areas]

Item	1990	1995	1997	1998	1999	2000	2001	2002	Share [1] 1990	1995	2000	2002
Assets...............	791	984	1,126	1,118	1,228	1,299	1,385	1,338	21.4	21.7	19.9	18.3
Loans, total...........	398	461	495	494	499	531	523	471	18.0	17.3	13.7	11.4
Business............	193	249	282	280	279	296	271	238	30.8	35.1	27.1	24.8
Deposits.............	384	523	603	558	697	709	743	665	14.5	17.6	17.6	14.8

[1] Percent of "domestically owned" commercial banks plus U.S. offices of foreign banks.
Source: Board of Governors of the Federal Reserve System, "Share Data for U.S. Offices of Foreign Banks"; published 17 June 2003; <http://www.federalreserve.gov/releases/Iba/Share/SHRTBL1.html>.

No. 1183. Characteristics of Conventional First Mortgage Loans for Purchase of Single-Family Homes: 1990 to 2002

[In percent, except as indicated (154.1 represents $154,100). Annual averages. Covers fully amortized conventional mortgage loans used to purchase single-family nonfarm homes. Excludes refinancing loans, nonamortized and balloon loans, loans insured by the Federal Housing Administration, and loans guaranteed by the Veterans Administration. Based on a sample of mortgage lenders, including savings and loans associations, savings banks, commercial banks, and mortgage companies]

Loan characteristics	New homes						Previously occupied homes					
	1990	1995	1999	2000	2001	2002	1990	1995	1999	2000	2001	2002
Contract interest rate,[1]												
all loans	9.7	7.7	6.9	7.4	6.9	6.3	9.8	7.7	7.2	7.9	7.0	6.3
Fixed-rate loans	10.1	8.0	7.3	8.0	7.0	6.6	10.1	8.0	7.3	8.2	7.0	6.6
Adjustable-rate loans [2]	8.9	7.2	6.3	6.5	6.4	5.6	8.9	7.0	6.5	7.2	6.3	5.6
Initial fees, charges [3]	1.98	1.20	0.76	0.69	0.67	0.61	1.74	0.93	0.73	0.66	0.51	0.44
Effective interest rate,[4]												
all loans	10.1	7.9	7.0	7.5	7.0	6.4	10.1	7.8	7.3	8.1	7.0	6.5
Fixed-rate loans	10.4	8.2	7.4	8.2	7.1	6.7	10.4	8.2	7.4	8.3	7.1	6.7
Adjustable-rate loans [2]	9.2	7.4	6.3	6.5	6.4	5.6	9.2	7.1	6.6	7.2	6.4	5.7
Term to maturity (years)	27.3	27.7	28.8	29.2	28.8	28.9	27.0	27.4	28.1	28.6	27.5	27.1
Purchase price ($1,000)	154.1	175.4	210.7	234.9	244.8	261.7	140.3	137.3	179.3	191.8	211.5	227.5
Loan to price ratio	74.9	78.6	78.8	77.4	77.3	77.7	74.9	80.1	78.4	77.9	76.0	74.8
Percent of number of loans with adjustable rates	31	37	35	40	18	27	27	31	18	21	11	16

[1] Initial interest rate paid by the borrower as specified in the loan contract. [2] Loans with a contractual provision for periodic adjustments in the contract interest rate. [3] Includes all fees, commissions, discounts and "points" paid by the borrower, or seller, in order to obtain the loan. Excludes those charges for mortgage, credit, life or property insurance; for property transfer; and for title search and insurance. [4] Contract interest rate plus fees and charges amortized over a 10-year period.

Source: U.S. Federal Housing Finance Board, *Rates & Terms on Conventional Home Mortgages, Annual Summary.*

No. 1184. Mortgage Delinquency and Foreclosure Rates: 1990 to 2002

[In percent. Covers one- to four-family residential nonfarm mortgage loans]

Item	1990	1995	1996	1997	1998	1999	2000	2001	2002
Delinquency rates: [1]									
Total	4.7	4.3	4.3	4.3	4.4	4.0	4.0	4.6	4.7
Conventional loans	3.0	2.8	2.8	2.8	2.9	2.5	2.5	3.0	3.1
VA loans	6.4	6.4	6.7	6.9	7.1	6.8	6.8	7.7	7.9
FHA loans	6.7	7.6	8.0	8.1	8.5	8.6	9.1	10.8	11.5
Foreclosure rates: [2]									
Total	0.9	0.9	1.0	1.1	1.1	1.0	0.9	1.0	1.2
Conventional loans	0.7	0.7	0.7	0.8	0.7	0.6	0.6	0.8	0.9
VA loans	1.2	1.3	1.6	1.8	1.9	1.7	1.2	1.3	1.6
FHA loans	1.3	1.3	1.8	2.1	2.4	2.0	1.7	2.2	2.8

[1] Number of loans delinquent 30 days or more as percentage of mortgage loans serviced in survey. Annual average of quarterly figures. [2] Percentage of loans in the foreclosure process at yearend, not seasonally adjusted.

Source: Mortgage Bankers Association of America, Washington, DC, *National Delinquency Survey,* quarterly.

No. 1185. Insured Commercial Banks—Delinquency Rates on Loans: 1990 to 2002

[In percent. Annual averages of quarterly figures, not seasonally adjusted. Delinquent loans are those past due 30 days or more and still accruing interest as well as those in nonaccrual status. They are measured as a percentage of end-of-period loans]

Type of loan	1990	1995	1996	1997	1998	1999	2000	2001	2002
Total loans	**5.33**	**2.48**	**2.40**	**2.27**	**2.18**	**2.13**	**2.18**	**2.61**	**2.69**
Real estate	6.10	2.94	2.67	2.37	2.16	1.93	1.89	2.13	1.99
Residential [1]	(NA)	2.20	2.31	2.31	2.16	2.08	2.11	2.29	2.11
Commercial [2]	(NA)	3.94	3.13	2.39	2.04	1.69	1.49	1.79	1.71
Consumer	3.83	3.08	3.52	3.72	3.73	3.61	3.55	3.68	3.51
Credit cards	(NA)	3.73	4.34	4.69	4.70	4.54	4.50	4.86	4.87
Other	(NA)	2.67	2.98	3.08	3.13	3.09	2.98	3.05	2.80
Leases	1.97	0.79	1.06	1.08	1.04	1.28	1.59	2.09	2.23
Commercial and industrial	5.34	1.95	1.88	1.66	1.68	1.91	2.22	3.08	3.84
Agricultural	3.84	2.50	3.00	2.64	2.73	3.00	2.54	2.63	2.51

NA Not available. [1] Residential real estate loans include loans secured by one- to four-family properties, including home equity lines of credit. [2] Commercial real estate loans include construction and land development loans, loans secured by multifamily residences, and loans secured by nonfarm, nonresidential real estate.

Source: Federal Financial Institutions Examination Council (FFIEC), *Consolidated Reports of Condition and Income* (1990-2000: FFIEC 031 through 034; beginning 2001: FFIEC 031 & 041).

No. 1186. Percent of U.S. Households That Use Selected Payment Instruments: 1995 and 2001

[In percent. Based on Survey of Consumer Finance conducted by the Board of Governors of the Federal Reserve System; see Appendix III]

Age and education	Any of these instruments 1995	Any of these instruments 2001	ATM[1] 1995	ATM[1] 2001	Debit card 1995	Debit card 2001	Direct deposit 1995	Direct deposit 2001	Automatic bill paying 1995	Automatic bill paying 2001	Smart card[1] 1995	Smart card[1] 2001
All households	76.5	88.4	61.2	69.8	17.6	47.0	46.8	67.3	21.8	40.3	1.2	2.9
Under 30 years old	75.2	83.0	71.1	78.1	24.5	60.6	31.1	48.8	17.9	32.1	1.8	2.6
30 to 60 years old	77.4	89.3	67.2	76.8	19.7	53.4	42.9	64.8	24.5	44.1	1.5	3.3
61 years old and over	75.2	89.2	43.1	48.9	9.6	24.6	63.2	83.2	18.2	35.9	0.3	2.1
No college degree	69.8	84.7	52.8	63.7	14.3	42.3	40.4	61.8	18.2	33.7	0.8	2.4
College degree	91.5	95.6	80.1	81.6	25.2	56.2	61.0	78.0	30.1	53.2	2.1	3.8

[1] The questions on ATMs and smart cards asked whether any member of the household had an ATM card or a smart card, not whether the member used it. The other questions asked about usage.

Source: Mester, Loretta J., "Changes in the Use of Electronic Means of Payment: 1995-2001," forthcoming in *Business Review*, Third Quarter 2003, published by Federal Reserve Bank of Philadelphia.

No. 1187. Consumer Payment Systems by Method of Payment, 2000 and 2002, and Projections, 2005

[112.3 represents 112,300,000,000]

Method of payment	Transactions Number (bil.) 2000	2002	2005, proj.	Percent distribution 2000	2005, proj.	Volume Amount (bil. dol.) 2000	2002	2005, proj.	Percent distribution 2000	2005, proj.
Total	112.3	120.7	132.4	100.0	100.0	5,183	5,660	6,465	100.0	100.0
Paper	80.2	80.7	76.0	71.5	57.4	3,371	3,439	3,180	65.0	49.2
Direct check payments[1]	30.2	29.5	28.2	26.9	21.3	2,276	2,206	2,081	43.9	32.2
Cash	48.8	49.9	46.4	43.5	35.0	978	1,103	947	18.9	14.6
Money orders	0.9	1.0	1.1	0.8	0.9	82	94	114	1.6	1.8
Travelers cheques	0.2	0.2	0.2	0.2	0.1	13	12	12	0.3	0.2
Official checks[2]	0.1	0.1	0.1	0.1	0.1	22	23	26	0.4	0.4
Cards	30.0	37.0	50.2	26.7	37.9	1,593	1,904	2,570	30.7	39.7
Credit cards[3]	19.9	21.2	24.4	17.7	18.5	1,238	1,361	1,683	23.9	26.0
Debit cards[4]	8.3	13.3	22.7	7.4	17.1	309	477	801	6.0	12.4
Stored value cards[5]	1.3	1.8	2.0	1.1	1.5	31	48	59	0.6	0.9
EBT cards and food stamps[6]	0.6	0.7	1.0	0.5	0.8	15	18	27	0.3	0.4
Electronic	2.1	2.9	6.3	1.8	4.7	219	317	715	4.2	11.1
Preauthorized payments[7]	1.5	2.0	3.2	1.4	2.5	166	229	379	3.2	5.9
Remote payments[8]	0.5	0.9	3.0	0.5	2.3	53	88	337	1.0	5.2

[1] Excludes consumer check repayments and prepayments involving other payment systems as well as all commercial and government checks. [2] Official checks include cashier's checks, teller checks, and certified checks purchased from financial institutions. Excludes those purchased by businesses. [3] Credit cards include general purpose cards usable at all kinds of merchants and proprietary cards usable only at selected outlets. Includes some purchases on personal cards for government, commercial, and business-related spending. Cash advances are excluded. [4] Debit cards include general purpose cards carrying the Visa or MasterCard brand, electronic funds transfer (EFT) brands of regional EFT systems, proprietary commercial cards issued by private firms to drivers in the long-haul trucking and business aviation industry, and proprietary consumer cards issued by supermarkets. Cash withdrawals at ATMs and cash back over the counter are excluded. [5] Stored value cards are used primarily for gift certificates and telephone calls. [6] Electronic benefits transfer cards are replacements for paper scrip food stamps. [7] Preauthorized payments are handled electronically "end-to-end" through an automated clearing house. [8] Remote payments are made using a telephone or a computer and include point-of-sale check conversions and utility-bill payments made at ATMs, self-service clerk-assisted electronic banking machines kiosks and clerk-assisted machines at supermarkets.

Source: HSN Consultants Inc., Oxnard, CA, *The Nilson Report*, twice-monthly. (Copyright used by permission.)

No. 1188. Debit Cards—Holders, Number, Transactions, and Volume, 2000 and 2002, and Projections, 2005

[168 represents 168,000,000]

Type of debit card	Cardholders (mil.) 2002	2005, proj.	Number of cards (mil.) 2000	2002	2005, proj.	Number of transactions (mil.) 2000	2002	2005, proj.	Volume (bil. dol.) 2000	2002	2005, proj.
Total[1]	168	181	235	260	283	9,834	15,585	25,550	448	700	1,137
Bank[2]	150	156	137	175	205	6,797	10,332	14,093	327	496	712
EFT systems[3]	167	180	223	249	271	2,979	5,235	11,439	119	203	425
Other[4]	11	11	11	11	11	59	18	19	1	1	1

[1] Cardholders may hold more than one type of card. Bank cards and EFT cards are the same pieces of plastic that carry multiple brands. The total card figure shown does not include any duplication. [2] Visa Check Card and MasterCard MasterMoney. [3] Cards issued by financial institution members of regional and national switches. EFT=Electronic funds transfer. [4] Commercial fuel cards issued by private-label firms plus retail cards such as those issued by supermarkets and oil companies.

Source: HSN Consultants Inc., Oxnard, CA, *The Nilson Report*, twice-monthly. (Copyright used by permission.)

No. 1179. FDIC-Insured Financial Institutions—Number and Assets by State: 2002

[In billions of dollars, except as indicated (8,436.0 represents $8,436,000,000,000). As of Dec. 31. Information is obtained primarily from the Federal Financial Institutions Examination Council (FFIEC) Call Reports and the Office of Thrift Supervision's Thrift Financial Reports. Data are based on the location of each reporting institution's main office. Reported data may include assets located outside of the reporting institution's home state]

State	Number of institutions	Total	Less than $1 bil.	$1 bil. to $10 bil.	Greater than $10 bil.	State	Number of institutions	Total	Less than $1 bil.	$1 bil. to $10 bil.	Greater than $10 bil.
Total	9,354	8,436.0	1,362.7	1,278.9	5,794.4	NV	36	40.5	5.3	35.2	-
AL	163	203.6	22.4	5.5	175.7	NH	32	29.4	6.6	8.0	14.8
AK	8	7.2	1.6	5.6	-	NJ	150	137.6	33.1	64.4	40.0
AZ	46	48.9	5.8	5.5	37.6	NM	60	18.8	8.7	10.2	-
AR	177	35.4	26.8	8.6	-	NY	211	1,620.0	40.3	115.2	1,464.5
CA	325	853.1	64.2	120.4	668.4	NC	108	1,006.8	24.2	5.9	976.7
CO	179	50.3	26.9	6.5	17.0	ND	107	19.5	9.8	9.7	-
CT	67	54.4	14.9	13.9	25.6	OH	315	599.5	44.9	37.9	516.7
DE	35	193.6	5.4	26.3	161.9	OK	280	56.3	26.4	29.8	-
DC	5	0.7	0.7	-	-	OR	37	20.8	6.4	14.4	-
FL	301	99.9	51.9	48.0	-	PA	283	285.5	65.4	59.0	161.1
GA	341	192.3	49.3	27.8	115.1	RI	14	200.8	2.3	19.1	179.4
HI	9	30.4	1.6	28.8	-	SC	102	36.8	14.9	21.9	-
ID	20	4.2	4.2	-	-	SD	97	74.4	11.6	15.6	47.2
IL	787	518.5	115.4	56.9	346.1	TN	213	115.5	35.5	1.5	78.4
IN	211	129.3	36.6	45.3	47.3	TX	715	216.9	85.8	75.7	55.4
IA	433	55.1	42.2	12.9	-	UT	60	138.2	10.3	12.5	115.4
KS	380	51.4	34.5	16.9	-	VT	20	7.2	4.2	3.1	-
KY	248	55.1	31.4	23.7	-	VA	146	151.3	33.3	23.8	94.2
LA	172	50.1	22.4	10.3	17.3	WA	102	72.2	20.8	24.7	26.7
ME	39	36.1	11.4	1.4	23.4	WV	76	20.3	9.3	10.9	-
MD	129	58.6	26.3	16.3	15.9	WI	314	103.1	41.9	23.1	38.2
MA	214	202.0	52.4	47.1	102.4	WY	50	7.4	5.2	2.2	-
MI	180	166.4	33.4	22.3	110.7						
MN	487	111.2	42.4	3.6	65.2	AS	1	0.1	0.1	-	-
MS	105	38.2	14.1	14.0	10.2	GU	3	0.9	0.9	-	-
MO	382	80.3	45.8	23.4	11.2	FM	1	0.1	0.1	-	-
MT	84	14.3	9.1	5.1	-	PR	11	67.0	0.7	44.9	21.5
NE	281	48.2	21.1	14.0	13.1	VI	2	0.1	0.1	-	-

- Represents zero.

Source: U.S. Federal Deposit Insurance Corporation, Statistics on Banking, annual. <http://www.fdic.gov/bank/index.html>.

No. 1180. FDIC-Insured Financial Institutions—Number of Offices and Deposits by State: 2002

[As of June 30 (4,605.5 represents $4,605,500,000,000). Includes insured U.S. branches of foreign banks. The term "offices" includes both main offices and branches. "Banking office" is defined to include all offices and facilities that actually hold deposits, and does not include loan production offices, computer centers, and other nondeposit installations, such as automated teller machines (ATMs). Several institutions have designated home offices that do not accept deposits; these have been included to provide a more complete listing of all offices. The figures for each geographical area only include deposits of offices located within that area. Based on the Summary of Deposits survey]

State and other area	Number of offices	Total deposits (bil. dol.)	State and other area	Number of offices	Total deposits (bil. dol.)	State and other area	Number of offices	Total deposits (bil. dol.)
Total	86,497	4,605.5	KY	1,690	52.9	OR	994	33.5
U.S.	85,890	4,563.8	LA	1,504	49.8	PA	4,588	188.3
			ME	507	14.8	RI	225	15.7
AL	1,422	55.5	MD	1,684	70.7	SC	1,262	42.5
AK	129	5.0	MA	2,045	153.3	SD	437	14.6
AZ	960	48.8	MI	2,910	126.6	TN	2,008	77.2
AR	1,265	35.7	MN	1,668	77.7	TX	4,980	256.6
CA	6,269	533.8	MS	1,100	31.3	UT	577	84.2
CO	1,291	55.3	MO	2,107	81.8	VT	263	8.4
CT	1,160	64.1	MT	354	10.5	VA	2,430	117.7
DE	241	85.3	NE	950	29.3	WA	1,736	70.6
DC	193	13.4	NV	435	27.4	WV	634	22.0
FL	4,626	242.8	NH	414	29.4	WI	2,172	83.6
GA	2,441	109.3	NJ	3,039	181.0	WY	195	8.0
HI	297	19.3	NM	480	15.5			
ID	462	11.8	NY	4,526	516.0	AS	5	0.1
IL	4,103	266.3	NC	2,480	121.0	GU	37	1.3
IN	2,209	75.5	ND	412	11.6	FM	9	0.1
IA	1,496	47.5	OH	3,882	186.7	PR	534	38.9
KS	1,447	43.0	OK	1,191	40.9	VI	22	1.3

Source: U.S. Federal Deposit Insurance Corporation, Bank and Thrift Branch Office Data Book, annual.

Banking, Finance, and Insurance 747

No. 1181. Federal and State-Chartered Credit Unions—Summary: 1990 to 2002

[Except as noted, as of December 31 (36,241 represents 36,241,000). Federal data include District of Columbia, Puerto Rico, Guam, and Virgin Islands. Excludes state-insured, privately-insured, and noninsured state-chartered credit unions and corporate central credit unions which have mainly other credit unions as members]

Year	Operating credit unions Federal	Operating credit unions State	Number of failed institutions [1]	Members (1,000) Federal	Members (1,000) State	Assets (mil. dol.) Federal	Assets (mil. dol.) State	Loans outstanding (mil. dol.) Federal	Loans outstanding (mil. dol.) State	Savings (mil. dol.) Federal	Savings (mil. dol.) State
1990	8,511	4,349	164	36,241	19,454	130,073	68,133	83,029	44,102	117,892	62,082
1995	7,329	4,358	26	42,163	24,927	193,781	112,860	120,514	71,606	170,300	99,838
1996	7,152	4,240	19	43,546	25,652	206,695	120,193	134,127	79,661	180,969	105,743
1997	6,981	4,257	16	43,491	27,921	215,104	136,074	140,104	92,117	187,822	119,359
1998	6,814	4,181	17	43,865	29,674	231,890	156,811	144,849	100,890	202,651	137,348
1999	6,566	4,062	23	44,076	31,308	239,316	172,086	155,578	116,366	207,614	149,305
2000	6,336	3,980	29	43,883	33,705	242,881	195,363	163,851	137,485	210,188	169,053
2001	6,118	3,866	22	43,817	35,560	270,123	231,432	170,326	152,112	235,201	201,923
2002	5,953	3,735	15	44,600	36,300	301,238	255,837	181,768	160,881	261,819	222,372

[1] 1990 for year ending September 30; 1995 reflects 15-month period from October 1994 through December 1995; beginning 1996 reflects calendar year. A failed institution is defined as a credit union which has ceased operation because it was involuntarily liquidated or merged with assistance from the National Credit Union Share Insurance Fund.

Source: National Credit Union Administration, *Annual Report of the National Credit Union Administration*, and unpublished data.

No. 1182. Mortgage Debt Outstanding by Type of Property and Holder: 1990 to 2002

[In billions of dollars (3,805 represents $3,805,000,000,000). As of Dec. 31. Includes Puerto Rico and Guam]

Type of property and holder	1990	1993	1994	1995	1996	1997	1998	1999	2000	2001	2002
Mortgage debt, total	3,805	4,207	4,380	4,575	4,864	5,202	5,715	6,320	6,894	7,598	8,476
Residential nonfarm	2,908	3,388	3,571	3,754	4,008	4,280	4,697	5,160	5,614	6,191	6,956
One- to four-family homes	2,620	3,119	3,301	3,478	3,720	3,979	4,366	4,791	5,209	5,738	6,460
Savings institutions	488	470	478	482	514	521	534	548	594	621	631
Mortgage pools or trusts [1]	1,046	1,518	1,656	1,768	1,935	2,099	2,375	2,690	2,925	3,340	3,759
Government National Mortgage Association	392	405	441	461	494	523	522	565	593	569	512
Federal Home Loan Mortgage Corp.	308	443	488	512	552	577	643	745	817	941	1,073
Federal National Mortgage Assoc	291	487	521	570	633	688	804	925	1,016	1,238	1,479
Private mortgage conduits [2]	55	184	206	224	256	311	405	455	500	591	695
Commercial banks	430	532	590	647	678	746	797	880	966	1,024	1,222
Individuals and others [3]	377	361	341	343	367	393	435	459	496	507	555
Federal and related agencies [4]	153	230	228	229	220	213	218	208	223	242	287
Federal National Mortgage Assoc	94	151	159	164	155	150	148	141	144	155	171
Life insurance companies	13	9	9	9	7	7	7	6	5	5	5
Five or more units	288	269	269	275	288	301	331	369	405	453	497
Nonfarm, nonresidential	818	738	726	737	769	832	922	1,058	1,171	1,290	1,395
Farm	79	81	83	85	87	90	97	103	109	116	125
TYPE OF HOLDER											
Savings institutions	641	598	596	597	628	632	644	668	723	758	781
Commercial banks	849	948	1,013	1,090	1,145	1,245	1,337	1,495	1,660	1,790	2,059
Life insurance companies	268	224	216	213	208	207	214	231	236	243	247
Individuals and others [3]	562	532	515	520	550	600	648	658	700	715	769
Mortgage pools or trusts [1]	1,085	1,579	1,724	1,848	2,037	2,233	2,581	2,948	3,231	3,715	4,183
Government National Mortgage Assoc.	404	414	451	472	506	537	537	582	612	591	538
Federal Home Loan Mortgage Corp	316	447	491	515	554	579	646	749	822	948	1,082
Federal National Mortgage Association	300	496	530	583	651	710	835	961	1,058	1,290	1,538
Farmers Home Administration	(Z)	(Z)	(Z)	(Z)	(Z)	(Z)	-	-	-	-	-
Private mortgage conduits	66	222	252	277	326	407	563	655	740	885	1,025
Federal and related agencies [4]	239	326	316	308	294	285	292	320	344	377	437
Federal National Mortgage Association	105	166	174	178	168	160	156	149	156	170	191
Farmers Home Administration	41	41	42	42	42	41	41	74	73	72	72
Federal Land Banks	29	28	29	28	30	31	33	34	36	41	46
Federal Home Loan Mortgage Corp	22	47	42	44	47	48	57	57	59	63	64
Federal Housing and Veterans Admin	9	12	11	10	6	4	4	4	4	3	4
Government National Mortgage Assoc.	(Z)	(Z)	(Z)	(Z)	(Z)	(Z)	(Z)	(Z)	(Z)	(Z)	(Z)
Federal Deposit Insurance Corp	-	14	8	4	2	(Z)	(Z)	(Z)	(Z)	(Z)	(Z)
Resolution Trust Corporation	33	17	10	2	(X)	(X)	(X)	(X)	(X)	(X)	(X)
Federal Home Loan Bank	-	-	-	-	-	-	1	2	16	28	61

- Represents zero. X Not applicable. Z Less than $500 million. [1] Outstanding principal balances of mortgage pools backing securities insured or guaranteed by the agency indicated. Includes other pools not shown separately. [2] Includes securitized home equity loans. [3] Includes mortgage companies, real estate investment trusts, state and local retirement funds, noninsured pension funds, state and local credit agencies, credit unions, and finance companies. [4] Includes other agencies not shown separately.

Source: Board of Governors of the Federal Reserve System, *Federal Reserve Bulletin*, monthly.

No. 1189. Consumer Credit Outstanding and Finance Rates: 1990 to 2002

[In billions of dollars, except percent (789.1 represents $789,100,000,000). Covers most short- and intermediate-term credit extended to individuals, excluding loans secured by real estate. Estimated amounts of seasonally adjusted credit outstanding as of end of year; finance rates, annual averages]

Type of credit	1990	1994	1995	1996	1997	1998	1999	2000	2001	2002
Total	789.1	960.4	1,095.8	1,185.1	1,243.0	1,317.0	1,415.5	1,560.2	1,666.9	1,725.7
Revolving	238.6	365.6	443.1	498.9	531.0	562.5	598.0	668.0	701.4	712.9
Nonrevolving [1]	550.5	594.9	652.7	686.1	712.0	754.5	817.5	892.1	965.5	1,012.8
FINANCE RATES (percent)										
Commercial banks:										
New automobiles (48 months)	11.78	8.12	9.57	9.05	9.02	8.72	8.44	9.34	8.50	6.71
Other consumer goods (24 months)	15.46	13.19	13.94	13.54	13.90	13.74	13.39	13.90	13.22	11.59
Credit-card plans	18.17	16.04	15.90	15.63	15.77	15.71	15.21	15.71	14.89	13.42
Finance companies:										
New automobiles	12.54	9.79	11.19	9.83	7.12	6.30	6.66	6.61	5.65	4.29
Used automobiles	15.99	13.49	14.48	13.53	13.27	12.64	12.60	13.55	12.18	10.73

[1] Comprises automobile loans and all other loans not included in revolving credit, such as loans for mobile homes, education, boats, trailers, or vacations. These loans may be secured or unsecured.

Source: Board of Governors of the Federal Reserve System, *Federal Reserve Bulletin*, monthly.

No. 1190. Credit Cards—Holders, Number, Spending, and Debt, 2000 and 2002, and Projections, 2005

[159 represents 159,000,000]

Type of credit card	Cardholders (mil.) 2000	2002	2005, proj.	Number of cards (mil.) 2000	2002	2005, proj.	Credit card spending (bil. dol.) 2000	2002	2005, proj.	Credit card debt outstanding (bil. dol.) 2000	2002	2005, proj.
Total [1]	159	163	173	1,425	1,452	1,430	1,458	1,638	2,022	680	764	922
Bank [2]	107	112	120	455	525	580	938	1,095	1,359	480	560	683
Phone	125	126	128	181	182	184	21	20	22	3	2	3
Store	114	115	118	597	547	464	120	127	147	92	91	97
Oil company	76	75	73	98	97	90	50	54	71	5	5	7
Other [3]	7	7	7	94	100	111	330	342	423	101	105	133

[1] Cardholders may hold more than one type of card. [2] Visa and MasterCard credit cards. Excludes debit cards. [3] Includes UATP, automobile rental, and miscellaneous cards. Except for cardholders, also includes Discover, American Express, and Diners Club.

Source: HSN Consultants Inc., Oxnard, CA, *The Nilson Report*, twice-monthly. (Copyright used by permission.)

No. 1191. Usage of General Purpose Credit Cards by Families: 1992 to 2001

[General purpose credit cards include Mastercard, Visa, Optima, and Discover cards. Excludes cards used only for business purposes. All dollar figures are given in constant 2001 dollars based on consumer price index data as published by U.S. Bureau of Labor Statistics. Families include one-person units; for definition of family, see text, Section 1. Based on Survey of Consumer Finance; see Appendix III. For definition of median, see Guide to Tabular Presentation]

Age of family head and family income	Percent having a general purpose credit card	Median number of cards	Median new charges on last month's bills (dol.)	Percent having a balance after last month's bills	Median balance [1] (dol.)	Almost always pay off the balance	Sometimes pay off the balance	Hardly ever pay off the balance
1992, total	62.4	2	100	52.6	1,200	53.0	19.6	27.4
1995, total	66.5	2	200	56.0	1,700	52.4	20.1	27.5
1998, total	67.5	2	200	54.7	2,000	53.8	19.3	26.9
2001, total	72.7	2	200	53.7	1,800	55.3	19.1	25.6
Under 35 years old	64.2	2	100	68.2	1,800	40.6	24.1	35.4
35 to 44 years old	76.9	2	200	62.9	2,000	47.0	22.8	30.2
45 to 54 years old	80.0	2	200	57.3	2,000	54.3	19.3	26.4
55 to 64 years old	76.0	2	300	48.2	2,000	59.8	17.8	22.3
65 to 74 years old	76.5	2	200	30.0	1,100	75.8	11.0	13.2
75 years old and over	59.7	2	200	24.2	700	81.2	9.3	9.4
Less than $10,000	28.5	1	-	67.4	1,000	45.3	23.0	31.7
$10,000 to $24,999	56.1	2	100	57.0	1,000	49.5	19.9	30.6
$25,000 to $49,999	76.1	2	100	61.3	1,700	46.7	19.7	33.6
$50,000 to $99,999	87.9	2	200	53.9	2,000	55.2	20.8	24.0
$100,000 and more	95.8	2	1,000	36.1	3,000	75.2	13.9	10.9

- Represents zero. [1] Among families having a balance.

Source: Board of Governors of the Federal Reserve System, unpublished data.

No. 1192. Money Stock: 1980 to 2002

[In billions of dollars (408 represents $408,000,000,000). As of December. Seasonally adjusted averages of daily figures]

Item	1980	1985	1986	1987	1988	1989	1990	1991	1992	1993	1994	1995	1996	1997	1998	1999	2000	2001	2002
M1, total	**408**	**619**	**724**	**749**	**786**	**792**	**824**	**896**	**1,024**	**1,129**	**1,150**	**1,127**	**1,078**	**1,071**	**1,095**	**1,122**	**1,085**	**1,173**	**1,211**
Currency [1]	115	168	180	197	212	222	246	267	292	322	354	372	394	425	460	518	531	581	627
Travelers checks [2]	3	5	5	6	6	6	7	7	8	7	8	8	8	8	8	8	8	8	8
Demand deposits [3]	261	267	303	287	287	279	277	290	340	385	384	389	400	393	377	352	307	326	296
Other checkable deposits [4]	28	180	236	260	281	285	294	332	384	415	404	357	276	246	250	244	239	259	280
M2, total	**1,600**	**2,495**	**2,732**	**2,831**	**2,994**	**3,158**	**3,277**	**3,377**	**3,431**	**3,483**	**3,496**	**3,640**	**3,814**	**4,030**	**4,382**	**4,648**	**4,927**	**5,441**	**5,796**
M1	408	619	724	749	786	792	824	896	1,024	1,129	1,150	1,127	1,078	1,071	1,095	1,122	1,085	1,173	1,211
Non-M1 components in M2	1,192	1,876	2,008	2,082	2,208	2,366	2,453	2,480	2,407	2,354	2,346	2,513	2,736	2,958	3,287	3,526	3,842	4,267	4,586
Money market funds, retail	64	175	209	223	245	321	357	371	352	352	380	448	515	590	732	833	925	991	944
Savings deposits (including MMDAs [5])	400	815	941	937	926	894	923	1,044	1,187	1,219	1,150	1,134	1,274	1,401	1,603	1,738	1,874	2,303	2,758
Commercial banks	186	457	534	535	542	541	581	664	754	785	753	775	906	1,023	1,188	1,289	1,422	1,734	2,047
Thrift institutions	215	359	407	403	384	353	342	379	433	434	397	359	368	378	415	450	452	569	710
Small time deposits [6]	729	886	858	921	1,037	1,151	1,173	1,066	868	782	816	931	947	968	951	955	1,043	973	884
Commercial banks	286	386	369	392	451	534	611	602	508	468	503	575	593	625	626	635	699	634	584
Thrift institutions	442	499	489	529	586	618	563	463	360	314	314	357	354	343	326	320	344	339	300
M3, total	**1,996**	**3,208**	**3,499**	**3,686**	**3,928**	**4,076**	**4,152**	**4,205**	**4,216**	**4,277**	**4,360**	**4,625**	**4,970**	**5,444**	**6,032**	**6,529**	**7,090**	**7,994**	**8,511**
M2	1,600	2,495	2,732	2,831	2,994	3,158	3,277	3,377	3,431	3,483	3,496	3,640	3,814	4,030	4,382	4,648	4,927	5,441	5,796
Non-M2 components in M3	396	713	767	855	934	918	875	828	785	794	864	985	1,156	1,415	1,651	1,881	2,164	2,553	2,715
Large time deposits [7]	260	422	419	462	512	528	480	415	350	332	370	428	509	618	669	741	820	786	800
Commercial banks [8]	215	270	269	299	338	366	358	331	283	270	305	354	431	533	581	650	717	671	683
Thrift institutions	45	152	150	163	175	161	121	83	67	62	65	74	78	85	88	91	103	115	117
Repurchase agreements [9]	58	121	146	178	197	169	151	131	142	173	196	199	210	254	293	336	363	375	469
Eurodollars [9]	61	104	116	121	132	109	103	92	80	73	86	94	115	147	149	169	192	202	213
Money market funds, institution only	16	65	86	94	112	112	140	190	213	217	211	264	322	395	539	634	788	1,190	1,233

[1] Currency outside U.S. Treasury, Federal Reserve Banks and the vaults of depository institutions. [2] Outstanding amount of nonbank issuers. [3] At commercial banks and foreign-related institutions. [4] Consists of negotiable order of withdrawal (NOW) and automatic transfer service (ATS) accounts at all depository institutions, credit union share draft balances, and demand deposits at thrift institutions. [5] Money market deposit accounts (MMDA). [6] Issued in amounts of less than $100,000. [7] Issued in amounts of $100,000 or more. Excludes those booked at international banking facilities. [8] Excludes retail repurchase agreements. Excludes individual retirement accounts (IRAs) and Keogh accounts. [9] Issued in amounts of $100,000 or more. Excludes those booked at international banking facilities. [8] Excludes those held by money market mutual funds, depository institutions, U.S. Government, foreign banks and official institutions. [9] Excludes those held by depository institutions and money market mutual funds.

Source: Board of Governors of the Federal Reserve System, Federal Reserve Bulletin, monthly, and Money Stock Measures, Federal Reserve Statistical Release H.6, weekly.

752 Banking, Finance, and Insurance

U.S. Census Bureau, Statistical Abstract of the United States: 2003

No. 1193. Money Market Interest Rates and Mortgage Rates: 1980 to 2002

[Percent per year. Annual averages of monthly data, except as indicated]

Type	1980	1985	1990	1991	1992	1993	1994	1995	1996	1997	1998	1999	2000	2001	2002
Federal funds, effective rate	13.35	8.10	8.10	5.69	3.52	3.02	4.21	5.83	5.30	5.46	5.35	4.97	6.24	3.88	1.67
Prime rate charged by banks	15.26	9.93	10.01	8.46	6.25	6.00	7.15	8.83	8.27	8.44	8.35	8.00	9.23	6.91	4.67
Discount rate	11.77	7.69	6.98	5.45	3.25	3.00	3.60	5.21	5.02	5.00	4.92	4.62	5.73	3.40	1.17
Eurodollar deposits, 3-month	14.00	8.27	8.16	5.86	3.70	3.18	4.63	5.93	5.38	5.61	5.45	5.31	6.45	3.70	1.73
Large negotiable CDs:															
3-month, secondary market	13.02	8.04	8.15	5.83	3.68	3.17	4.63	5.92	5.39	5.62	5.47	5.33	6.46	3.71	1.73
6-month, secondary market	12.94	8.24	8.17	5.91	3.76	3.28	4.96	5.98	5.47	5.73	5.44	5.46	6.59	3.66	1.81
Taxable money market funds [2]	12.68	7.71	7.82	5.71	3.36	2.70	3.75	5.48	4.95	5.10	5.04	4.64	5.89	3.67	1.29
Tax-exempt money market funds [2]	(NA)	4.90	5.45	4.13	2.58	1.97	2.38	3.39	2.99	3.14	2.94	2.72	3.54	2.24	0.94
Certificates of deposit (CDs): [3]															
6-month	(NA)	8.05	7.79	5.80	3.51	2.88	3.42	4.92	4.68	4.86	4.58	4.27	5.09	3.43	1.67
1-year	(NA)	8.53	7.92	6.03	3.78	3.16	4.01	5.39	4.95	5.15	4.81	4.56	5.46	3.60	1.98
2½-year	(NA)	9.32	7.96	6.46	4.56	3.80	4.58	5.69	5.14	5.40	4.93	4.74	5.64	3.97	2.74
5-year	(NA)	9.99	8.06	7.02	5.76	4.98	5.42	6.00	6.46	5.66	5.08	4.93	5.97	4.58	3.96
U.S. government securities:															
Secondary market: [4]															
3-month Treasury bill	11.39	7.47	7.50	5.38	3.43	3.00	4.25	5.49	5.01	5.06	4.78	4.64	5.82	3.40	1.61
6-month Treasury bill	11.32	7.65	7.46	5.44	3.54	3.12	4.64	5.56	5.08	5.18	4.83	4.75	5.90	3.34	1.68
Auction average: [5]															
3-month Treasury bill	11.51	7.48	7.51	5.42	3.45	3.02	4.29	5.51	5.02	5.07	4.81	4.66	5.85	3.45	1.62
Home mortgages:															
New-home mortgage yields [6]	12.66	11.55	10.05	9.32	8.24	7.20	7.49	7.87	7.80	7.71	7.07	7.04	7.52	7.00	6.43
Conventional, 15 yr. fixed [3]	(NA)	11.48	9.73	8.76	7.80	6.65	7.77	7.39	7.28	7.16	6.58	7.09	7.76	6.53	6.02
Conventional, 30 yr. fixed [3]	(NA)	11.85	9.97	9.09	8.27	7.17	8.28	7.86	7.76	7.57	6.92	7.46	8.08	7.01	6.56

NA Not available. [1] Rate for the Federal Reserve Bank of New York. [2] 12 month return for period ending December 31. Source: iMoneyNet, Inc., Westborough, MA, *Money Market Insight*, monthly, <http://www.imoneynet.com> (copyright). [3] Annual averages. Source: Bankrate, Inc., North Palm Beach, FL, *Bank Rate Monitor*, weekly (copyright). [4] Averages based on daily closing bid yields in secondary market, bank discount basis. [5] Averages computed on an issue-date basis; bank discount basis. Source: U.S. Council of Economic Advisors, *Economic Indicators*, monthly. [6] Effective rate (in the primary market) on conventional mortgages, reflecting fees and charges as well as contract rate and assumed, on the average, repayment at end of ten years. Source: U.S. Federal Housing Finance Board, *Rates & Terms on Conventional Home Mortgages, Annual Summary*.

Source: Except as noted, Board of Governors of the Federal Reserve System, *Federal Reserve Bulletin*, monthly.

No. 1194. Bond Yields: 1980 to 2002

[Percent per year. Annual averages of daily figures, except as indicated]

Type	1980	1985	1990	1995	1996	1997	1998	1999	2000	2001	2002
U.S. Treasury, constant maturities: [1] [2]											
1-year	12.00	8.42	7.89	5.94	5.52	5.63	5.05	5.08	6.11	3.49	2.00
2-year	11.73	9.27	8.16	6.15	5.84	5.99	5.13	5.43	6.26	3.83	2.64
3-year	11.51	9.64	8.26	6.25	5.99	6.10	5.14	5.49	6.22	4.09	3.10
5-year	11.45	10.12	8.37	6.38	6.18	6.22	5.15	5.55	6.16	4.56	3.82
7-year	11.40	10.50	8.52	6.50	6.34	6.33	5.28	5.79	6.20	4.88	4.30
10-year	11.43	10.62	8.55	6.57	6.44	6.35	5.26	5.65	6.03	5.02	4.61
20-year	(NA)	(NA)	(NA)	6.95	6.83	6.69	5.72	6.20	6.23	5.63	5.43
State and local govt. bonds, Aaa	7.84	8.60	6.96	5.79	5.52	5.32	4.93	5.29	5.58	5.01	4.87
State and local govt. bonds, Baa	8.99	9.59	7.30	6.05	5.79	5.50	5.14	5.70	6.19	5.75	5.64
Municipal (Bond Buyer, 20 bonds)	8.55	9.11	7.27	5.95	5.76	5.52	5.09	5.43	5.71	5.15	5.04
High-grade municipal bonds (Standard & Poor's) [3]	8.51	9.18	7.25	5.95	5.75	5.55	5.12	5.43	5.77	5.19	5.05
Corporate Aaa seasoned [4]	11.94	11.37	9.32	7.59	7.37	7.26	6.53	7.05	7.62	7.08	6.49
Corporate Baa seasoned [4]	13.67	12.72	10.36	8.20	8.05	7.87	7.22	7.88	8.37	7.95	7.80
Corporate seasoned, all industries [4]	12.75	12.05	9.77	7.84	7.67	7.53	6.87	7.45	7.98	7.49	7.10

NA Not available. [1] Yields on the more actively traded issues adjusted to constant maturities by the U.S. Treasury.
[2] Through September 1996, yields are based on closing bid prices quoted by at least five dealers. Beginning October 1996, yields are based on closing indicative prices quoted by secondary market participants. [3] Source: U.S. Council of Economic Advisors, *Economic Indicators*, monthly. [4] Source: Moody's Investors Service, New York, NY.
Source: Except as noted, Board of Governors of the Federal Reserve System, *Federal Reserve Bulletin*, monthly.

No. 1195. Volume of Debt Markets by Type of Security: 1990 to 2002

[In billions of dollars (2,907 represents $2,907,000,000,000). Covers debt markets as represented by the source]

Type of security	1990	1995	1998	1999	2000	2001	2002
NEW ISSUE VOLUME							
Total	2,907	6,868	10,760	11,415	12,745	16,487	16,872
U.S. Treasury securities [1]	1,531	2,331	1,969	2,028	2,038	2,743	3,812
Federal agency debt	637	3,531	6,348	7,077	8,746	10,496	9,236
Municipal	163	198	321	264	241	343	431
Mortgage-backed securities [2]	378	348	1,167	1,047	709	1,672	2,313
Asset-backed securities [3]	50	143	343	359	387	426	485
Corporate debt [4]	149	317	612	639	625	807	594
DAILY TRADING VOLUME							
Total	111.2	246.3	352.8	316.5	357.7	508.8	613.4
U.S. Treasury securities [1] [5]	111.2	193.2	226.6	186.5	206.6	297.9	366.4
Federal agency debt [5]	(NA)	23.7	47.6	54.6	72.8	90.2	81.8
Municipal [6]	(NA)	(NA)	7.7	8.3	8.8	8.8	10.7
Mortgage-backed securities [2] [5]	(NA)	29.4	70.9	67.1	69.5	112.0	154.5
VOLUME OF SECURITIES OUTSTANDING							
Total	7,745	11,229	14,447	16,026	17,056	18,588	20,155
U.S. Treasury securities [1]	2,196	3,307	3,356	3,281	2,967	2,968	3,205
Federal agency debt [7]	435	845	1,297	1,617	1,852	2,143	2,359
Municipal	1,184	1,294	1,464	1,533	1,568	1,685	1,795
Mortgage-backed securities [2]	1,333	2,352	2,955	3,334	3,565	4,126	4,705
Asset-backed securities [3] [7]	90	316	732	901	1,072	1,281	1,543
Money market instruments [8]	1,157	1,177	1,978	2,339	2,661	2,567	2,551
Corporate debt [4] [7]	1,350	1,938	2,666	3,023	3,372	3,818	3,997

NA Not available. [1] Marketable public debt. [2] Includes only Government National Mortgage Association (GNMA), Federal National Mortgage Association (FNMA), Federal Home Loan Mortgage Corporation (FHLMC) mortgage-backed securities (MBS) and collateralized mortgage obligations (CMOs) and private-label MBS/CMOs. [3] Excludes mortgage-backed assets. [4] Includes nonconvertible corporate debt, Yankee bonds, and MTNs (Medium-Term Notes), but excludes all issues with maturities of one year or less, agency debt, and all CDs. [5] Primary dealer transactions. [6] Beginning September 1998 includes customer-to-dealer and dealer-to-dealer transactions. [7] The Bond Market Association estimates. [8] Commercial paper, bankers acceptances, and large time deposits.
Source: The Bond Market Association, New York, NY. Copyright. Based on data supplied by Board of Governors of the Federal Reserve System, U.S. Dept. of Treasury, Thompson Financial Securities Data Company, Inside MBS & ABS, FHLMC, FNMA, GNMA, Federal Home Loan Banks, Student Loan Marketing Association, Federal Farm Credit Banks, Tennessee Valley Authority, and Municipal Securities Rulemaking Board.

No. 1196. Commercial Paper Outstanding by Type of Company: 1990 to 2002

[In billions of dollars (563 represents $563,000,000,000). As of December 31. Seasonally adjusted. Commercial paper is an unsecured promissory note having a fixed maturity of no more than 270 days]

Type of company	1990	1993	1994	1995	1996	1997	1998	1999	2000	2001	2002
All issuers	563	555	595	675	775	967	1,163	1,403	1,615	1,439	1,322
Financial companies [1]	415	399	431	487	591	766	936	1,124	1,272	1,214	1,168
Dealer-placed paper [2]	215	219	223	276	361	513	614	787	973	989	950
Directly-placed paper [3]	200	180	208	211	230	253	322	337	299	225	218
Nonfinancial companies [4]	148	156	165	188	185	201	227	279	343	225	154

[1] Institutions engaged primarily in commercial, savings, and mortgage banking; sales, personal, and mortgage financing; factoring, finance leasing, and other business lending; insurance underwriting; and other investment activities. [2] Includes all financial company paper sold by dealers in the open market. [3] As reported by financial companies that place their paper directly with investors. [4] Includes public utilities and firms engaged primarily in such activities as communications, construction, manufacturing, mining, wholesale and retail trade, transportation, and services.
Source: Board of Governors of the Federal Reserve System, *Federal Reserve Bulletin*, monthly.

No. 1197. Total Returns of Stocks, Bonds, and Treasury Bills: 1950 to 2002

[In percent. Average annual percent change. Stock return data are based on the Standard & Poor's 500 index. Minus sign (-) indicates loss]

Period	Stocks				Treasury bills, total return	Bonds (10-year), total return
	Total return	Capital gains	Dividends and reinvestment	Total return after inflation		
1950 to 1959	19.25	13.58	4.99	16.65	2.02	0.69
1960 to 1969	7.78	4.39	3.25	5.14	4.06	2.35
1970 to 1979	5.88	1.60	4.20	-1.38	6.48	5.94
1980 to 1989	17.55	12.59	4.40	11.85	9.13	13.01
1990 to 1999	18.21	15.31	2.51	14.85	4.95	8.02
2000 to 2002	-14.55	-15.71	1.38	-16.58	3.62	12.51

Source: Global Financial Data, Los Angeles, CA, "GFD Guide to Total Returns"; <http://www.globalfindata.com/articles/totalreturnworksheet.xls>; and unpublished data. (copyright).

No. 1198. Equities, Corporate Bonds, and Municipal Securities—Holdings and Net Purchases by Type of Investor: 1990 to 2002

[In billions of dollars (3,543 represents $3,543,000,000,000). Holdings as of Dec. 31. Minus sign (-) indicates net sales]

Type of investor	Holdings					Net purchases				
	1990	1995	2000	2001	2002	1990	1995	2000	2001	2002
EQUITIES [1]										
Total [2]	3,543	8,475	17,612	15,246	11,734	-45.7	-3.9	1.1	100.5	46.4
Household sector [3]	1,781	4,137	7,408	6,056	4,187	-48.6	-96.8	-468.2	-231.2	-135.6
Rest of the world [4]	244	550	1,626	1,534	1,351	-16.0	16.5	193.5	121.4	54.4
Bank personal trusts and estates	190	225	357	281	217	0.5	1.6	-2.5	-32.5	-1.7
Life insurance companies	82	315	941	855	757	-5.7	18.6	105.9	70.3	56.0
Other insurance companies	80	134	194	174	156	-7.0	-0.6	0.7	-0.3	1.2
Private pension funds	606	1,289	2,195	1,926	1,515	0.9	-69.5	-49.9	-33.3	-53.8
State and local retirement funds	285	679	1,335	1,222	1,012	22.5	18.2	-18.4	22.3	29.5
Mutual funds	233	1,025	3,227	2,836	2,184	14.4	87.4	189.1	109.7	31.1
CORPORATE & FOREIGN BONDS										
Total [2]	1,706	2,848	5,023	5,692	6,208	123.4	344.1	384.4	669.5	515.5
Household sector [3]	219	426	702	778	834	57.1	95.8	-26.4	76.0	55.2
Rest of the world [4]	217	361	921	1,126	1,293	5.3	50.1	168.4	205.7	166.9
Commercial banking	89	111	279	376	380	4.6	8.4	58.1	97.8	3.7
Life insurance companies	567	870	1,222	1,342	1,486	56.5	90.7	49.0	120.2	143.9
Other insurance companies	89	123	188	196	208	10.4	12.7	6.4	8.9	11.6
Private pension funds	158	242	321	331	339	19.9	13.4	18.8	9.8	8.5
State and local retirement funds	142	189	340	351	359	-10.5	10.1	29.7	11.4	7.7
Money market mutual funds	2	22	162	163	171	-1.7	6.4	38.2	1.1	7.7
Mutual funds	59	196	362	420	471	4.7	23.3	-6.2	58.1	50.9
Government-sponsored enterprises	-	31	117	133	148	-	10.3	25.8	15.5	14.8
Brokers and dealers	29	76	113	161	192	-4.0	12.0	19.3	48.6	30.3
MUNICIPAL SECURITIES [5]										
Total [2]	1,184	1,268	1,481	1,600	1,763	49.3	-57.6	23.6	119.2	163.0
Household sector [3]	575	433	464	507	617	27.6	-51.6	11.3	43.0	110.0
Other insurance companies	137	161	184	174	183	1.8	7.0	-14.9	-10.3	9.6
Money market mutual funds	84	128	245	281	283	13.9	14.3	34.3	36.2	1.8
Mutual funds	113	210	230	253	278	13.9	3.2	-8.9	23.0	25.0

- Represents or rounds to zero. [1] Excludes mutual fund shares. [2] Includes other types not shown separately. [3] Includes nonprofit organizations. [4] Holdings and net purchases of U.S. issues by foreign residents. [5] Includes loans.

Source: Board of Governors of the Federal Reserve System, "Federal Reserve Statistical Release, Z.1, Flow of Funds Accounts of the United States"; published: 6 March 2003; <http://www.federalreserve.gov/releases/Z1/20030306/data.htm>.

No. 1199. New Security Issues of Corporations by Type of Offering: 2000 to 2002

[In billions of dollars (942.2 represents $942,200,000,000). Represents gross proceed of issues maturing in more than one year. Figures are the principal amount or the number of units multiplied by the offering price. Excludes secondary offerings, employee stock plans, investment companies other than closed-end, intracorporate transactions, and Yankee bonds. Stock data include ownership securities issued by limited partnerships]

Type of offering	2000	2001	2002	Type of offering	2000	2001	2002
Total [1]	942.2	1,382.0	1,262.6	Stocks, total	311.9	230.6	170.7
Bonds, total	807.3	1,253.4	1,152.2	Public	134.9	128.6	110.4
Sold in the United States	684.5	1,197.1	1,065.9	Nonfinancial	118.4	77.6	62.1
Sold abroad	122.8	56.4	86.2	Financial	16.5	51.0	48.3
Nonfinancial	242.2	445.9	267.2	Private placement	177.0	102.1	60.2
Financial	565.1	807.5	885.0				

[1] Excludes private placements of stocks.

Source: Board of Governors of the Federal Reserve System, *Federal Reserve Bulletin*, monthly.

Banking, Finance, and Insurance 755

No. 1200. Purchases and Sales by U.S. Investors of Foreign Bonds and Stocks, 1990 to 2002, and by Selected Country, 2002

[In billions of dollars (31.2 represents $31,200,000,000). Covers transactions in all types of long-term foreign securities as reported by banks, brokers, and other entities in the United States. Data cover new issues of securities, transactions in outstanding issues, and redemptions of securities. Includes transactions executed in the United States for the account of foreigners and transactions executed abroad for the account of reporting institutions and their domestic customers. Data by country show the country of domicile of the foreign buyers and sellers of the securities; in the case of outstanding issues, this may differ from the country of the original issuer. The term "foreigner" covers all institutions and individuals domiciled outside the United States, including U.S. citizens domiciled abroad, and the foreign branches, subsidiaries and other affiliates abroad of U.S. banks and businesses; the central governments, central banks, and other official institutions of foreign countries; and international and regional organizations. "Foreigner" also includes persons in the United States to the extent that they are known by reporting institutions to be acting on behalf of foreigners. Minus sign (-) indicates net sales by U.S. investors or a net inflow of capital into the United States]

Year and country	Net purchases			Total transactions [1]			Bonds		Stocks	
	Total	Bonds	Stocks	Total	Bonds	Stocks	Purchases	Sales	Purchases	Sales
1990	31.2	21.9	9.2	907	652	255	337	315	132	123
1991	46.8	14.8	32.0	949	675	273	345	330	153	121
1992	47.9	15.6	32.3	1,375	1,043	332	529	514	182	150
1993	143.1	80.4	62.7	2,126	1,572	554	826	746	308	245
1994	57.3	9.2	48.1	2,526	1,706	820	858	848	434	386
1995	98.7	48.4	50.3	2,569	1,827	741	938	890	396	346
1996	110.6	51.4	59.3	3,239	2,279	960	1,165	1,114	510	450
1997	89.1	48.1	40.9	4,505	2,952	1,553	1,500	1,452	797	756
1998	11.1	17.3	-6.2	4,527	2,674	1,853	1,346	1,328	923	930
1999	-10.0	5.7	-15.6	3,941	1,602	2,339	804	798	1,162	1,177
2000	17.1	4.1	13.1	5,539	1,922	3,617	963	959	1,815	1,802
2001	19.6	-30.5	50.1	5,135	2,290	2,845	1,130	1,160	1,448	1,398
2002, total [2]	-26.8	-28.4	1.6	5,248	2,726	2,522	1,349	1,377	1,262	1,260
United Kingdom	-5.5	-12.1	6.6	2,368	1,312	1,056	650	662	531	525
Japan	9.1	8.0	1.1	480	198	283	103	95	142	141
Cayman Islands	-3.0	-4.2	1.2	441	211	230	103	108	116	115
Bermuda	(Z)	-0.7	0.8	358	262	96	131	131	48	48
Canada	-4.8	-0.8	-4.0	245	120	124	60	60	60	64
Germany	1.0	2.4	-1.4	170	113	57	58	55	28	29
Hong Kong	-3.5	-2.3	-1.2	118	24	95	11	13	47	48
France	3.1	2.7	0.3	114	54	60	29	26	30	30
Bahamas, The	1.6	0.7	0.9	91	56	35	28	28	18	17
Brazil	-0.6	-1.6	1.0	65	46	19	22	24	10	9
Netherlands	-4.6	-1.5	-3.1	60	18	42	8	10	20	23
Switzerland	2.2	-1.2	3.4	59	14	45	6	7	24	21
Singapore	-2.8	-2.3	-0.6	58	24	34	11	13	17	17
Australia	-0.4	-0.5	(Z)	50	15	35	7	8	17	17
Netherlands Antilles	-1.4	(Z)	-1.4	50	17	33	8	8	16	17
Ireland	-3.8	-3.6	-0.2	43	20	24	8	12	12	12

Z Less than $50 million. [1] Total purchases plus total sales. [2] Includes other countries, not shown separately.

Source: U.S. Dept. of Treasury, *Treasury Bulletin*, quarterly.

No. 1201. U.S. Holdings of Foreign Stocks and Bonds by Country: 2000 to 2002

[In billions of dollars (1,852.9 represents $1,852,900,000,000)]

Country	Stocks			Country	Bonds		
	2000	2001	2002		2000	2001	2002
Total holdings	1,852.9	1,612.7	1,345.2	Total holdings	532.5	502.1	501.8
Western Europe [1]	1,118.4	934.2	777.5	Western Europe [1]	236.8	231.2	226.9
United Kingdom	411.7	350.0	299.2	United Kingdom	72.6	72.2	65.5
Finland	52.7	51.3	42.4	France	21.5	24.3	28.7
France	137.2	112.2	93.9	Germany	48.5	43.5	49.1
Germany	76.7	72.2	58.1	Italy	13.5	12.5	12.6
Ireland	31.3	28.4	22.9	Netherlands	25.6	27.9	26.4
Italy	42.5	33.7	27.4	Sweden	9.8	8.8	9.5
Netherlands	147.9	112.8	89.7	Canada	104.0	104.6	111.0
Spain	38.4	32.5	26.7	Japan	23.2	24.7	34.5
Sweden	36.0	24.3	19.3	Latin America [1]	67.1	50.0	49.0
Switzerland	94.9	75.6	65.3	Argentina	12.0	3.4	1.4
Canada	108.6	89.6	69.7	Brazil	12.4	11.0	10.1
Japan	197.8	170.7	140.5	Mexico	26.5	21.2	22.7
Latin America [1]	66.6	59.3	53.2	Other Western Hemisphere [1]	26.6	30.1	26.9
Argentina	3.7	0.7	0.6	Cayman Islands	16.8	21.9	19.0
Brazil	24.2	21.8	20.0	Other countries [1]	62.2	50.6	43.1
Mexico	28.0	26.3	23.8	Australia	13.7	14.2	14.7
Other Western Hemisphere [1]	170.7	172.4	148.6	Korea, South	7.5	4.7	8.0
Bermuda	108.1	118.9	98.3	International organizations	12.6	10.9	10.4
Netherlands Antilles	23.1	14.5	10.7				
Other countries [1]	190.8	186.5	155.7				
Australia	43.4	37.1	30.4				
Hong Kong	34.3	30.2	23.8				
Singapore	24.9	21.4	16.9				

[1] Includes other countries not shown separately.

Source: U.S. Bureau of Economic Analysis, *Survey of Current Business*, July 2003.

No. 1202. Foreign Purchases and Sales of U.S. Securities by Type of Security, 1990 to 2002, and by Selected Country, 2002

[In billions of dollars (18.7 represents $18,700,000,000). Covers transactions in all types of long-term domestic securities by foreigners as reported by banks, brokers, and other entities in the United States (except nonmarketable U.S. Treasury notes, foreign series; and nonmarketable U.S. Treasury bonds and notes, foreign currency series). See headnote, Table 1200. Minus sign (-) indicates net sales by foreigners or a net outflow of capital from the United States]

	Net purchases					Total transactions [4]				
Year and country	Total	Treasury bonds and notes [1]	U.S. govt. corporations [2] bonds	Corporate bonds [3]	Corporate rate stocks	Total	Treasury bonds and notes [1]	U.S. govt. corporations [2] bonds	Corporate bonds [3]	Corporate rate stocks
1990	16.7	17.9	6.3	9.7	-15.1	4,204	3,620	104	117	362
1991	58.1	19.9	10.2	16.9	11.1	4,706	4,016	124	155	411
1992	73.2	39.3	18.3	20.8	-5.1	5,282	4,444	204	187	448
1993	111.1	23.6	35.4	30.6	21.6	6,314	5,195	263	239	618
1994	140.4	78.8	21.7	38.0	1.9	6,562	5,343	297	222	699
1995	231.9	134.1	28.7	57.9	11.2	7,243	5,828	222	278	915
1996	370.2	232.2	41.7	83.7	12.5	8,965	7,134	241	422	1,169
1997	388.0	184.2	49.9	84.4	69.6	12,759	9,546	469	617	2,126
1998	277.8	49.0	56.8	121.9	50.0	14,989	10,259	992	641	3,097
1999	350.2	-10.0	92.2	160.4	107.5	14,617	8,586	880	577	4,574
2000	457.8	-54.0	152.8	184.1	174.9	16,910	7,795	1,305	775	7,036
2001	520.8	18.5	164.0	222.0	116.4	20,003	10,517	2,239	1,260	5,986
2002, total [5]	548.9	121.7	195.5	182.3	49.4	25,710	14,632	3,262	1,460	6,356
United Kingdom	186.0	61.0	33.1	76.7	15.2	6,954	4,905	342	616	1,091
Cayman Islands	47.1	9.2	22.6	23.1	-7.8	5,200	1,853	1,732	321	1,294
Bermuda	8.8	1.6	5.2	11.2	-9.2	2,159	764	199	95	1,102
Canada	1.2	-5.2	-1.5	0.4	7.4	1,364	937	63	30	334
Japan	91.5	30.7	37.6	10.9	12.3	1,211	863	191	39	119
France	5.6	-0.3	1.2	2.6	2.1	1,068	572	18	20	457
Netherlands Antilles	1.2	-0.8	1.9	0.7	-0.5	689	390	17	10	272
Netherlands	-12.9	-17.0	-2.0	1.6	4.5	670	511	68	11	80
Germany	1.1	-3.9	3.2	2.0	-0.1	503	350	22	22	109
Ireland	8.5	0.6	0.7	5.1	2.1	474	303	22	25	123
Bahamas, The	18.3	16.0	1.5	0.7	0.1	455	306	10	36	104
Hong Kong	9.2	-9.1	12.6	3.9	1.8	294	197	63	13	21
Switzerland	10.7	-0.5	3.6	4.9	2.7	284	116	28	18	121
Singapore	9.1	-2.6	2.2	1.3	8.2	253	123	27	21	81
Italy	1.3	-0.3	-0.2	0.2	1.5	201	112	8	4	77

[1] Marketable bonds and notes. [2] Includes federally-sponsored agencies. [3] Includes transactions in directly placed issues abroad by U.S. corporations and issues of states and municipalities. [4] Total purchases plus total sales. [5] Includes other countries, not shown separately.

Source: U.S. Dept. of Treasury, *Treasury Bulletin*, quarterly.

No. 1203. Foreign Holdings of U.S. Securities by Country: 2000 to 2002

[In billions of dollars (1,026.1 represents $1,026,100,000,000). Covers only private holdings of U.S. securities, except as noted]

Country	U.S. Treasury securities [1]			Country	Corporate and agency bonds			Corporate stocks		
	2000	2001	2002		2000	2001	2002	2000	2001	2002
Total holdings [2]	1,026.1	1,039.7	1,214.2	Total holdings	1,076.0	1,391.6	1,690.3	1,547.7	1,464.1	1,170.8
Japan	325.6	329.7	386.7	Western Europe [2]	710.6	910.5	1,058.9	1,016.2	969.5	770.1
China [3]	62.3	81.9	109.3	United Kingdom	517.2	691.0	807.6	381.0	368.9	295.6
Hong Kong	39.8	49.5	51.6	France	11.2	15.8	19.5	47.0	46.1	37.1
Germany	50.7	50.3	48.4	Germany	42.7	51.8	57.0	111.0	104.8	79.6
United Kingdom	36.5	7.6	47.5	Italy	4.0	2.2	2.5	39.8	36.5	29.1
Korea, South	29.7	33.3	45.0	Netherlands	20.5	19.7	19.5	97.4	95.6	77.8
Taiwan [3]	34.5	37.0	37.4	Canada	24.1	25.2	22.8	156.6	147.9	123.9
Cayman Islands	8.0	19.4	31.6	Japan	100.5	120.3	163.4	134.4	123.4	106.2
Mexico	15.6	19.8	24.0	Latin America	18.7	25.2	34.7	28.7	32.4	25.5
Italy	21.5	19.9	20.6	Other Western Hemisphere	172.7	231.3	303.0	125.1	102.3	62.1
				Other countries	49.4	79.1	107.5	86.7	88.6	83.0

[1] Includes foreign official holdings. [2] Includes other countries not shown separately. [3] With the establishment of diplomatic relations with China on January 1, 1979, the U.S. government recognized the People's Republic of China as the sole legal government of China and acknowledged the Chinese position that there is only one China and that Taiwan is part of China.

Source: U.S. Bureau of Economic Analysis, *Survey of Current Business*, July 2003.

No. 1204. Stock Prices and Yields: 1990 to 2002

[Closing values as of end of December, except as noted]

Index	1990	1995	1998	1999	2000	2001	2002
STOCK PRICES							
Standard & Poor's indices: [1]							
S&P 500 composite (1941-43=10)	330.2	615.9	1,229.2	1,469.3	1,320.3	1,148.1	879.8
S&P 400 MidCap Index (1982=100)	100.0	217.8	392.3	444.7	516.7	508.3	429.8
S&P 600 Small Cap Index (Dec. 31, 1993=100)	(NA)	121.1	177.4	197.8	219.6	232.2	196.6
S&P 500/Barra Value Index (Dec. 31, 1974=35)	177.7	325.1	551.6	610.6	636.2	552.0	428.0
S&P 500/Barra Growth Index (Dec. 31, 1974=35)	159.9	302.0	697.3	887.3	687.6	594.6	448.8
Russell indices: [2]							
Russell 1000 (Dec. 31, 1986=130)	171.2	328.9	642.9	768.0	700.1	604.9	466.2
Russell 2000 (Dec. 31, 1986=135)	132.2	316.0	422.0	504.8	483.5	488.5	383.1
Russell 3000 (Dec. 31, 1986=140)	180.9	351.9	664.3	793.3	725.8	634.2	489.5
N.Y. Stock Exchange common stock index							
Composite (Dec. 31, 2002=5000)	1,908.5	3,484.2	6,299.9	6,876.1	6,945.6	6,236.4	5,000.0
Yearly high	2,126.7	3,501.7	6,352.2	7,011.7	7,164.6	7,048.1	6,445.0
Yearly low	1,715.1	2,651.2	5,045.8	6,092.3	6,094.9	5,331.4	4,452.5
Industrial (Dec. 31, 1965=50)	223.6	413.3	743.7	828.2	803.3	735.7	584.0
Transportation (Dec. 31, 1965=50)	141.5	302.0	482.4	466.7	462.8	438.8	395.8
Utility (Dec. 31, 1965=100)	182.6	252.9	445.9	511.2	440.5	329.8	233.1
Finance (Dec. 31, 1965=50)	122.1	274.3	521.4	516.6	647.0	593.7	510.5
American Stock Exchange Composite Index							
(Dec. 29, 1995=550)	(NA)	550.0	689.0	877.0	897.8	847.6	824.4
NASDAQ composite index (Feb. 5, 1971=100)	373.8	1,052.1	2,192.7	4,069.3	2,470.5	1,950.4	1,335.5
Nasdaq-100 (Jan. 31, 1985=125)	200.5	576.2	1,836.0	3,708.0	2,341.7	1,577.1	984.4
Industrial (Feb. 5, 1971=100)	406.1	964.7	1,304.3	2,239.0	1,483.0	1,389.2	1,029.7
Banks (Feb. 5, 1971=100)	254.9	1,009.4	1,838.0	1,691.3	1,939.5	2,134.9	2,231.3
Dow-Jones and Co., Inc.:							
Composite (65 stocks)	920.6	1,693.2	2,870.8	3,214.4	3,317.4	2,892.2	2,375.0
Industrial (30 stocks)	2,633.7	5,117.1	9,181.4	11,497.1	10,786.9	10,021.5	8,341.6
Transportation (20 stocks)	910.2	1,981.0	3,149.3	2,977.2	2,946.6	2,640.0	2,310.0
Utility (15 stocks)	209.7	225.4	312.3	283.4	412.2	293.9	215.2
Wilshire 5000 Total Market Index [3]							
(Dec. 31, 1980=1404.596)	3,101.4	6,057.2	11,317.6	13,812.7	12,175.9	10,818.6	8,343.2
COMMON STOCK YIELDS (percent)							
Standard & Poor's composite index (500 stocks): [4]							
Dividend-price ratio [5]	3.61	2.56	1.49	1.25	1.15	1.32	1.61
Earnings-price ratio [6]	6.47	6.09	3.46	3.17	3.63	2.95	2.92

NA Not available. [1] Standard & Poor's Indices are market-value weighted and are chosen for market size, liquidity, and industry group representation. The S&P 500 index represents the 500 largest publicly traded companies. The S&P MidCap Index tracks mid-cap companies. The S&P SmallCap Index consists of 600 domestic small-cap stocks. [2] The Russell 1000 and 3000 indices show respectively the 1000 and 3000 largest capitalization stocks in the United States. The Russell 2000 index shows the 2000 largest capitalization stocks in the United States after the first 1000. [3] The Wilshire 5000 Total Market Index measures the performance of all U.S. headquartered equity securities with readily available prices. [4] Source: U.S. Council of Economic Advisors, *Economic Report of the President*, annual. [5] Aggregate cash dividends (based on latest known annual rate) divided by aggregate market value based on Wednesday closing prices. Averages of monthly figures. [6] Averages of quarterly ratios which are ratio of earnings (after taxes) for 4 quarters ending with particular quarter to price index for last day of that quarter.

Source: Except as noted, Global Financial Data, Los Angeles, CA, <http://www.globalfindata.com/trial/index2.html>; (copyright).

No. 1205. Dow-Jones U.S. Equity Market Index by Industry: 1995 to 2002

[As of end of year]

Industry	1995	1997	1998	1999	2000	2001	2002
U.S. Equity Market Index, total	147.49	228.67	281.61	341.57	306.88	266.71	204.51
Basic materials	139.19	167.34	150.23	187.16	154.49	153.22	136.97
Consumer, cyclical	140.43	210.75	282.76	341.88	277.68	278.19	209.66
Consumer, noncyclical	134.27	213.66	246.00	244.64	215.56	217.96	204.19
Energy	134.70	200.81	186.15	219.71	272.96	236.74	200.29
Financial	176.95	337.27	356.05	354.55	440.91	404.50	346.36
Healthcare	127.76	201.53	277.52	263.62	360.18	310.76	242.87
Industrial	156.26	224.43	245.89	308.19	276.11	245.14	179.78
Technology	229.07	381.45	648.08	1,188.60	749.01	535.89	327.84
Telecommunications	154.78	205.40	305.76	356.97	210.38	180.62	115.04
Utilities	109.20	130.82	141.84	118.12	177.80	127.04	95.75

Source: Dow Jones & Company, Inc., New York, NY, *Dow Jones Indexes* (copyright).

No. 1206. NASDAQ—Securities Listed and Volume of Trading: 1990 to 2002

Item	Unit	1990	1994	1995	1996	1997	1998	1999	2000	2001	2002
Member firms	Number	5,827	5,426	5,451	5,553	5,597	5,592	5,482	5,579	5,499	5,392
Branch offices	Number	24,457	57,105	58,119	60,151	62,966	70,752	80,035	82,126	88,168	91,473
Companies listed	Number	4,132	4,902	5,112	5,556	5,487	5,068	4,829	4,734	4,109	3,663
Shares traded	Billion	33.4	74.4	101.2	138.1	163.9	202.0	272.6	442.8	471.2	441.7
Average daily volume	Million	132	295	401	544	648	802	1,082	1,757	1,907	1,753
Value of shares traded	Bil. dol.	452	1,449	2,398	3,302	4,482	5,759	11,013	20,395	10,935	7,254

Source: National Association of Securities Dealers, Washington, DC, *NASD Annual Report* (copyright).

758 Banking, Finance, and Insurance

No. 1207. Sales of Stocks on Registered Exchanges: 1990 to 2002

[1,752 represents $1,752,000,000,000. Excludes over-the-counter trading]

Exchange	Unit	1990	1994	1995	1996	1997	1998	1999	2000	2001	2002
Market value of all sales, all exchanges [1,2]	Bil. dol	1,752	2,966	3,690	4,735	6,879	8,698	11,220	14,552	13,315	13,662
New York	Bil. dol	1,394	2,483	3,078	4,013	5,848	7,275	9,087	11,217	10,738	10,793
American	Bil. dol	65	83	105	131	204	355	543	915	884	681
Chicago	Bil. dol	74	98	114	136	213	326	540	1,038	702	526
CBOE [3]	Bil. dol	81	87	107	130	179	214	271	330	197	157
Pacific	Bil. dol	53	70	94	108	151	182	255	248	96	98
Philadelphia	Bil. dol	41	51	59	68	89	97	103	165	130	86
STOCKS [4]											
Shares sold, all exchanges [2]	Billion	53.3	90.5	106.4	125.7	159.7	206.4	244.1	317.7	371.1	480.2
New York	Billion	43.8	76.7	90.1	108.2	138.8	178.9	207.7	265.7	313.4	376.7
American	Billion	3.1	4.3	4.8	5.3	6.2	7.6	8.7	11.9	15.3	16.1
Chicago	Billion	2.5	3.5	3.9	4.2	6.0	9.5	14.4	24.1	27.3	24.0
Pacific	Billion	1.7	2.1	2.7	3.0	3.2	4.0	4.9	4.1	1.5	3.0
Market value, all exchanges [2]	Bil. dol	1,612	2,817	3,507	4,511	6,559	8,307	10,680	13,691	12,721	13,210
New York	Bil. dol	1,390	2,482	3,076	4,011	5,847	7,274	9,087	11,216	10,737	10,730
American	Bil. dol	36	56	73	86	139	280	446	758	807	635
Chicago	Bil. dol	74	98	114	136	213	326	540	1,038	702	526
Pacific	Bil. dol	45	59	79	92	123	148	206	163	46	76

[1] Includes market value of stocks, rights, warrants, and options trading. [2] Includes other registered exchanges, not shown separately. [3] Chicago Board Options Exchange, Inc. [4] Includes voting trust certificates, American Depository Receipts, and certificate of deposit for stocks.

Source: U.S. Securities and Exchange Commission, *Annual Report*.

No. 1208. Volume of Trading on New York Stock Exchange: 1990 to 2002

[39,946 represents 39,946,000,000. Round lot: A unit of trading or a multiple thereof. On the NYSE the unit of trading is generally 100 shares in stocks. For some inactive stocks, the unit of trading is 10 shares. Odd lot: An amount of stock less than the established 100-share unit or 10-share unit of trading]

Item	Unit	1990	1995	1996	1997	1998	1999	2000	2001	2002
Shares traded	Million	39,946	87,873	105,477	134,404	171,188	206,299	265,499	311,290	366,102
Round lots	Million	39,665	87,218	104,636	133,312	169,745	203,914	262,478	307,509	363,135
Average daily shares	Million	157	346	412	527	674	809	1,042	1,240	1,441
High day	Million	292	653	681	1,201	1,216	1,350	1,560	2,368	2,813
Low day	Million	57	118	130	155	247	312	403	414	462
Odd lots	Million	282	656	841	1,091	1,443	2,384	3,021	3,781	2,967
Value of shares traded	Bil. dol	1,336	3,110	4,102	5,833	7,395	9,073	11,205	10,645	10,492
Round lots	Bil. dol	1,325	3,083	4,064	5,778	7,318	8,945	11,060	10,489	10,278
Odd lots	Bil. dol	11	27	38	56	77	128	145	155	213
Bond volume [1]	Mil. dol	10,893	6,979	5,529	5,046	3,838	3,221	2,328	2,668	3,625
Daily average	Mil. dol	43.1	27.7	21.8	19.9	15.2	12.8	9.2	10.8	14.4

[1] Par value.

Source: New York Stock Exchange, Inc., New York, NY, *Fact Book*, annual (copyright).

No. 1209. Securities Listed on New York Stock Exchange: 1990 to 2002

[As of December 31, except cash dividends are for calendar year (1,689 represents $1,689,000,000,000)]

Item	Unit	1990	1993	1994	1995	1996	1997	1998	1999	2000	2001	2002
BONDS												
Number of issuers	Number	743	574	583	564	563	533	474	416	392	369	343
Number of issues	Number	2,912	2,103	2,141	2,097	2,064	1,965	1,858	1,736	1,627	1,447	1,323
Face value	Bil. dol	1,689	2,342	2,526	2,773	2,845	2,625	2,554	2,402	2,125	1,654	1,378
STOCKS												
Companies	Number	1,774	2,361	2,570	2,675	2,907	3,047	3,114	3,025	2,862	2,798	2,783
Number of issues	Number	2,284	2,904	3,060	3,126	3,285	3,358	3,382	3,286	3,072	2,984	2,959
Shares listed	Billion	90.7	131.1	142.3	154.7	176.9	207.1	239.3	280.9	313.9	341.5	349.9
Market value	Bil. dol	2,820	4,541	4,448	6,013	7,300	9,413	10,864	12,296	12,372	11,714	9,603
Average price	Dollars	31.08	34.65	31.26	38.86	41.26	45.45	45.40	43.77	42.14	34.11	28.39
Cash dividends on common stock [1]	Bil. dol	103.2	120.2	130.0	147.0	150.6	159.4	179.0	174.7	165.6	186.0	(NA)

NA Not available. [1] Estimate based on average annual yield of the NYSE composite index.

Source: New York Stock Exchange, Inc., New York, NY, *Fact Book*, annual (copyright).

Banking, Finance, and Insurance

No. 1210. Stock Ownership by Age of Head of Family and Family Income: 1995 to 2001

[Median value in thousands of constant 2001 dollars (16.9 represents $16,900). Constant dollar figures are based on consumer price index data published by U.S. Bureau of Labor Statistics. Families include one-person units; for definition of family, see text, Section 1. Based on Survey of Consumer Finance; see Appendix III. For definition of median, see Guide to Tabular Presentation]

Age of family head and family income (constant (2001) dollars)	Families having direct or indirect stock holdings [1] (percent) 1995	1998	2001	Median value among families with holdings 1995	1998	2001	Stock holdings' share of group's financial assets (percent) 1995	1998	2001
All families	40.4	48.9	51.9	16.9	27.2	34.3	39.9	53.9	56.0
Under 35 years old	36.6	40.8	48.9	5.9	7.6	7.0	27.2	44.8	52.6
35 to 44 years old	46.4	56.7	59.5	11.6	21.8	27.5	39.5	54.6	57.3
45 to 54 years old	48.9	58.6	59.2	30.0	41.4	50.0	42.6	55.7	59.1
55 to 64 years old	40.0	55.9	57.1	35.8	51.2	81.2	44.2	58.4	56.1
65 to 74 years old	34.4	42.7	39.2	39.3	61.0	150.0	35.8	51.3	55.1
75 years old and over	27.9	29.4	34.2	23.1	65.3	120.0	39.8	48.7	51.4
Percentiles of income: [2]									
Less than 20 ($10,300)	6.5	10.0	12.4	4.3	5.4	7.0	14.2	20.4	36.9
20-39.9 ($24,400)	24.7	30.8	33.5	7.3	10.9	7.5	26.7	29.7	34.9
40-59.9 ($39,900)	41.5	50.2	52.1	7.2	13.1	15.0	28.4	37.9	46.4
60-79.9 ($64,800)	54.3	69.3	75.7	14.6	20.4	28.5	35.6	45.7	51.7
80-89.9 ($98,700)	69.7	77.9	82.0	28.9	49.0	64.6	41.3	50.4	57.4
90-100 ($302,700)	80.0	90.4	89.6	69.3	146.5	247.7	45.4	62.5	60.4

[1] Indirect holdings are those in mutual funds, retirement accounts, and other managed assets. [2] See footnote 8, Table 1167.
Source: Board of Governors of the Federal Reserve System, *Federal Reserve Bulletin*, January 2003, and unpublished data.

No. 1211. Household Ownership of Equities: 2002

[52.7 represents 52,700,000. Based on a national probability sample of 4,009 household financial decisionmakers. Further questions about equity ownership were asked of those 1,986 decisionmakers who indicated they owned equities]

Type of holding	Households owning equities Number (mil.)	Percent of all households	Number of individual investors (mil.)
Any type of equity (net) [1]	52.7	49.5	84.3
Any equity inside employer-sponsored retirement plans	36.2	34.0	57.9
Any equity outside employer-sponsored retirement plans	35.9	33.7	57.4
Individual stock (net) [1]	25.4	23.9	38.1
Individual stock inside employer-sponsored retirement plans	8.8	8.3	12.3
Individual stock outside employer-sponsored retirement plans	21.0	19.7	31.5
Stock mutual funds (net) [1]	47.0	44.2	70.5
Stock mutual funds inside employer-sponsored retirement plans	33.2	31.2	46.5
Stock mutual funds outside employer-sponsored retirement plans	28.7	27.0	43.1

[1] Multiple responses included.

No. 1212. Characteristics of Equity Owners: 2002

[In percent, except as indicated. See headnote, Table 1211. For definition of median, see Guide to Tabular Presentation]

Item	Total	Age 18 to 34 years old	35 to 44 years old	45 to 54 years old	55 to 64 years old	65 years old and over	Household income Less than $50,000	$50,000 to $99,999	$100,000 and over
Median age of owner (years)	47	29	40	50	59	73	46	44	47
Median household income (dol.)	62,500	60,000	70,000	68,000	62,500	45,000	34,000	70,000	125,000
Median household financial assets [1] (dol.)	100,000	32,500	99,100	136,800	274,300	415,100	37,500	100,000	421,500
Equity investments owned:									
Individual stock (net) [2]	49	41	49	50	50	56	39	48	64
Inside retirement plans [3]	17	18	21	18	16	6	11	18	22
Outside retirement plans [3]	41	33	40	42	44	50	31	40	57
Stock mutual funds (net) [2]	89	85	90	93	93	83	88	90	91
Inside retirement plans [3]	66	67	76	77	61	28	57	73	73
Outside retirement plans [3]	56	47	54	52	67	67	50	50	67
Nonequity investments owned: [2]									
Savings accounts, MMDAs, or CDs [4]	86	88	87	84	82	86	78	89	87
Bond investments (net) [2]	36	28	31	35	44	48	26	35	43
Individual bonds	17	13	15	16	21	28	13	15	21
Bond mutual funds	26	19	23	25	31	34	17	25	31
Fixed or variable annuities	23	13	19	25	31	33	21	23	24
Hybrid mutual funds	52	43	51	55	60	52	43	51	61
Money market mutual funds	35	27	35	35	43	36	25	33	44
Investment real estate	24	15	20	29	32	30	17	22	40
Have retirement plan coverage [3]	79	81	87	84	78	58	75	87	83
Have Individual Retirement Account (IRA)	57	46	56	62	66	55	43	58	72

[1] Includes assets in employer-sponsored retirement plans but excludes value of primary residence. [2] Multiple responses included. [3] Employer-sponsored. [4] MMDA=money market deposit account; CD=certificate of deposit.
Source of Tables 1211 and 1212: Investment Company Institute, Washington, DC, and Securities Industry Association, New York, NY, *Equity Ownership in America, Fall 2002* (copyright).

No. 1213. Households Owning Mutual Funds by Age and Income: 2000 and 2002

[In percent. Includes money market, stock, bond and hybrid, variable annuity, IRA, Keogh, and employer-sponsored retirement plan fund owners. In 2002, an estimated 54,200,000 households own mutual funds. Based on a sample survey of 3,000 households; for details, see source]

Age of household head and household income	Percent distribution, 2002	As percent of all households 2000	As percent of all households 2002	Age of household head and household income	Percent distribution, 2002	As percent of all households 2000	As percent of all households 2002
Total	100	49	50	Less than $25,000	7	17	14
Less than 25 years old	3	23	27	$25,000 to $34,999	10	37	36
25 to 34 years old	17	49	48	$35,000 to $49,999	17	49	48
35 to 44 years old	25	58	57	$50,000 to $74,999	30	66	67
45 to 54 years old	24	59	59	$75,000 to $99,999	16	77	79
55 to 64 years old	15	54	55	$100,000 and over	20	79	82
65 years old and over	16	32	37				

Source: Investment Company Institute, Washington, DC, *Fundamentals, Investment Company Institute Research in Brief*, Vol. 9, No. 4, August 2000, and Vol. 11, No. 5, October 2002 (copyright).

No. 1214. Characteristics of Mutual Fund Owners: 2001

[In percent, except as indicated. Mutual fund ownership includes holdings of money market, stock, bond, and hybrid mutual funds; and funds owned through variable annuities, Individual Retirement Accounts (IRAs), Keoghs, and employer-sponsored retirement plans. Based on a national probability sample of 2,592 primary financial decisionmakers in households with mutual fund investments. For definition of median, see Guide to Tabular Presentation]

Characteristic	Total	Age Under 40 years old	Age 40 to 64 years old	Age 65 years old and over	Household income Less than $50,000	Household income $50,000 to $100,000	Household income Over $100,000
Median age (years)	46	33	49	72	43	45	46
Median household income (dol.)	62,100	60,000	70,000	50,000	32,500	65,000	130,000
Median household financial assets [1] (dol.)	100,000	50,000	150,000	243,000	40,000	100,000	300,000
Own an IRA	60	59	60	58	51	60	66
Household has a defined contribution retirement plan(s), net [2]	81	87	84	58	75	88	86
401(k) plan	64	75	67	20	55	68	72
403(b) plan	11	12	11	10	9	12	13
State, local, or federal government plan	35	31	36	42	34	38	38
Median mutual fund assets (dol.)	40,000	20,000	60,000	59,500	17,500	44,800	120,000
Median number of mutual funds owned	4	4	4	3	3	4	6
Own: [2]							
Equity funds	88	90	89	80	86	87	96
Bond funds	37	31	39	41	31	34	44
Hybrid funds	34	33	34	34	33	32	43
Money market mutual funds	48	41	52	50	44	44	53
Own mutual funds bought: [2]							
Outside employer-sponsored retirement plan(s)	69	59	71	89	60	60	75
Inside employer-sponsored retirement plan(s)	62	71	66	24	57	69	76

[1] Includes assets in employer-sponsored retirement plans but excludes value of primary residence.   [2] Multiple responses included.
Source: Investment Company Institute, Washington, DC, *2001 Profile of Mutual Fund Shareholders*, 2001 (copyright).

No. 1215. Mutual Funds—Summary: 1990 to 2002

[Number of funds and assets as of December 31 (1,065 represents $1,065,000,000,000). A mutual fund is an open-end investment company that continuously issues and redeems shares that represent an interest in a pool of financial assets. Excludes data for funds that invest in other mutual funds. Minus sign (-) indicates net redemptions]

Type of fund	Unit	1990	1995	1996	1997	1998	1999	2000	2001	2002
Number of funds, total	Number	3,079	5,725	6,248	6,684	7,314	7,791	8,155	8,307	8,256
Equity funds	Number	1,099	2,139	2,570	2,951	3,513	3,952	4,385	4,717	4,756
Hybrid funds	Number	193	412	466	501	525	532	523	484	475
Bond funds	Number	1,046	2,177	2,224	2,219	2,250	2,262	2,208	2,091	2,036
Money market funds, taxable [1]	Number	506	674	666	682	685	702	703	689	679
Money market funds, tax-exempt [2]	Number	235	323	322	331	341	343	336	326	310
Assets, total	Bil. dol.	1,065	2,811	3,526	4,468	5,525	6,846	6,965	6,975	6,392
Equity funds	Bil. dol.	240	1,249	1,726	2,368	2,978	4,042	3,962	3,418	2,667
Hybrid funds	Bil. dol.	36	210	253	317	365	379	346	346	327
Bond funds	Bil. dol.	291	599	645	724	831	813	811	925	1,125
Money market funds, taxable [1]	Bil. dol.	415	630	762	898	1,163	1,409	1,607	2,013	1,997
Money market funds, tax-exempt [2]	Bil. dol.	84	123	140	161	189	204	238	272	275
Equity, hybrid and bond funds:										
Sales	Bil. dol.	149	475	681	869	1,058	1,274	1,630	1,383	1,435
Redemptions	Bil. dol.	98	313	397	541	748	1,021	1,330	1,177	1,228
Net sales	Bil. dol.	51	163	283	328	310	252	300	206	207
Money market funds, taxable: [1]										
Sales	Bil. dol.	1,219	2,729	3,524	4,395	5,534	7,083	8,691	10,701	11,011
Redemptions	Bil. dol.	1,183	2,617	3,415	4,265	5,289	6,866	8,499	10,314	11,075
Net sales	Bil. dol.	36	112	108	129	244	217	192	387	-64
Money market funds, tax-exempt: [2]										
Sales	Bil. dol.	197	396	467	536	639	687	788	783	750
Redemptions	Bil. dol.	190	385	453	518	612	675	757	751	736
Net sales	Bil. dol.	7	11	13	18	27	12	31	31	14

[1] Funds invest in short-term, high-grade securities sold in the money market.   [2] Funds invest in municipal securities with relatively short maturities.
Source: Investment Company Institute, Washington, DC, *Mutual Fund Fact Book*, annual (copyright).

No. 1216. Mutual Fund Shares—Holdings and Net Purchases by Type of Investor: 1990 to 2002

[In billions of dollars (608 represents $608,000,000,000). Holdings as of Dec. 31. Minus sign (-) indicates net sales]

Type of investor	Holdings					Net purchases				
	1990	1995	2000	2001	2002	1990	1995	2000	2001	2002
Total	608	1,853	4,435	4,135	3,635	53.7	147.4	235.0	201.4	182.2
Households, nonprofit organizations	457	1,159	3,083	2,916	2,627	22.5	66.0	158.4	200.1	181.3
Nonfinancial corporate business	10	46	129	108	78	-1.0	4.6	12.9	-5.2	-5.2
State and local governments	5	35	26	32	26	3.3	5.9	0.8	5.1	-5.5
Commercial banking	2	2	15	21	20	-0.3	0.3	2.5	7.8	1.7
Credit unions	1	3	2	4	4	0.2	0.2	-0.3	1.5	-0.2
Bank personal trusts and estates	63	254	397	359	303	9.7	11.9	48.5	-6.1	-0.4
Life insurance companies	31	28	48	44	38	12.6	13.5	11.0	2.0	2.0
Private pension funds	40	327	734	652	540	6.6	45.0	1.2	-3.8	8.6

Source: Board of Governors of the Federal Reserve System, "Federal Reserve Statistical Release, Z.1, Flow of Funds Accounts of the United States"; published: 6 March 2003; <http://www.federalreserve.gov/releases/Z1/20030306/data.htm>.

No. 1217. Mutual Fund Retirement Assets: 1990 to 2002

[In billions of dollars, except percent (207 represents $207,000,000,000). Based on data from the Institute's Annual Questionnaire for Retirement Statistics. The 2002 survey gathered data from 12,760 mutual fund share classes representing approximately 81 percent of mutual fund industry assets. Assets were estimated for all nonreporting funds. Estimates of retirement assets in street name and omnibus accounts were derived from data reported on the Annual Questionnaire for Retirement Statistics and the Annual Institutional Survey]

Type of account	1990	1995	1997	1998	1999	2000	2001	2002
Mutual fund retirement assets	207	914	1,522	1,925	2,499	2,456	2,332	2,082
Percent of total retirement assets	5	13	17	19	22	21	21	21
Individual retirement accounts (IRAs)	140	475	775	976	1,264	1,247	1,189	1,068
Employer-sponsored defined contribution retirement plans	67	439	747	949	1,234	1,209	1,142	1,014
401(k) plans [1]	35	266	471	605	793	799	770	686
Percent of total 401(k) assets	9	31	37	39	44	45	45	45
403(b) plans [2]	15	119	184	227	283	258	231	194
457 plans [3]	2	8	16	23	38	37	36	30
Other defined contribution plans [4]	15	46	77	93	121	115	106	104
Percent of all mutual funds:								
Mutual fund retirement assets	19	33	34	35	36	35	33	33
Individual retirement accounts (IRAs)	13	17	17	18	18	18	17	17
Employer-sponsored retirement plans	6	16	17	17	18	17	16	16

[1] See headnote, Table 553. Predominantly 401(k) assets, but may also include some profit-sharing plan assets that do not have a 401(k) feature. [2] Section 403(b) of the Internal Revenue Code permits employees of certain charitable organizations, nonprofit hospitals, universities, and public schools to establish tax-sheltered retirement programs. These plans may invest in either annuity contracts or mutual fund shares. [3] These plans are deferred compensation arrangements for government employees and employees of certain tax-exempt organizations. [4] Includes Keoghs; target benefit plans; thrift savings plans, stock bonus plans, and money purchase plans without a 401(k) feature; and all other defined contribution plans not specified elsewhere.

Source: Investment Company Institute, Washington, DC, *Fundamentals, Investment Company Institute Research in Brief*, "Mutual Funds and the Retirement Market in 2002"; Vol. 12, No. 1, June 2003 <http://www.ici.org> (copyright).

No. 1218. Individual Retirement Accounts (IRA) Plans—Value by Institution: 1990 to 2002

[As of December 31 (637 represents $637,000,000,000). Estimated]

Institution	Amount (bil. dol.)									Percent distribution		
	1990	1995	1996	1997	1998	1999	2000	2001	2002	1990	2000	2002
Total IRA assets	637	1,288	1,467	1,728	2,150	2,651	2,629	2,540	2,333	100	100	100
Bank and thrift deposits [1]	266	261	258	254	249	244	252	255	263	42	10	11
Life insurance companies [2]	40	81	92	135	156	201	202	210	208	6	8	9
Mutual funds	140	475	596	775	976	1,264	1,247	1,189	1,068	22	47	46
Securities held in brokerage accounts [3]	190	472	520	564	769	942	929	886	794	30	35	34

[1] Includes Keogh deposits. [2] Annuities held by IRAs, excluding variable annuity mutual fund IRA assets. [3] Excludes mutual fund assets held through brokerage accounts, which are included in mutual funds.

Source: Investment Company Institute, Washington, DC, *Fundamentals, Investment Company Institute Research in Brief*, "Mutual Funds and the Retirement Market in 2002"; Vol. 12, No. 1, June 2003 <http://www.ici.org> (copyright).

No. 1219. Assets of Private and Public Pension Funds by Type of Fund: 1990 to 2002

[In billions of dollars (3,005 represents $3,005,000,000,000). As of end of year. Except for corporate equities, represents book value. Excludes social security trust funds and U.S. government pension funds; see Tables 542 and 546]

Type of pension fund	1990	1995	1996	1997	1998	1999	2000	2001	2002
Total, all types	3,005	5,107	5,700	6,650	7,480	8,288	8,261	7,816	7,135
Private funds	2,204	3,804	4,205	4,833	5,426	6,061	5,972	5,636	5,167
Insured [1]	570	881	954	1,086	1,248	1,431	1,456	1,465	1,481
Noninsured [2] [3]	1,634	2,923	3,251	3,747	4,178	4,630	4,515	4,171	3,686
Credit market instruments [3]	472	631	627	675	651	668	702	722	753
U.S. government securities [3]	263	356	343	355	307	319	334	341	349
Agency	133	214	204	211	195	209	225	237	238
Corporate and foreign bonds	158	242	245	279	300	302	321	331	339
Corporate equities	606	1,289	1,464	1,696	1,991	2,326	2,195	1,926	1,515
Mutual fund shares	40	327	412	570	668	754	734	652	540
Unallocated insurance contracts [4]	215	332	361	382	385	393	378	369	366
State and local pension funds [3]	801	1,303	1,495	1,817	2,054	2,227	2,290	2,180	1,968
Credit market instruments [3]	402	530	565	632	705	751	806	788	792
U.S. government securities	231	291	308	340	360	376	399	366	357
Corporate and foreign bonds	142	189	211	245	280	310	340	351	359
Corporate equities	285	679	828	1,085	1,234	1,343	1,335	1,222	1,012

[1] Annuity reserves held by life insurance companies, excluding unallocated contracts held by private pension funds.
[2] Private defined benefit plans and defined contribution plans (including 401(k) type plans). Also includes Federal Employees Retirement System (FERS) Thrift Savings Plan. [3] Includes other types of assets not shown separately. [4] Assets held at life insurance companies (e.g., guaranteed investment contracts (GICs), variable annuities).

Source: Board of Governors of the Federal Reserve System, "Federal Reserve Statistical Release, Z.1, Flow of Funds Accounts of the United States"; published: 6 March 2003; <http://www.federalreserve.gov/releases/Z1/20030306/data.htm>.

No. 1220. Annual Revenues of Selected Securities Industries: 1998 to 2001

[In millions of dollars (242,845 represents $242,845,000,000). Covers taxable employer firms only. Based on the North American Industry Classification System (NAICS); see text, Section 15. Based on Service Annual Survey; see Appendix III]

Kind of business	NAICS code	1998	1999	2000	2001
Total	523x	242,845	288,575	338,071	293,981
Securities and commodity contracts intermediation and brokerage	5231	164,559	197,017	232,798	195,667
Investment banking & securities dealing	52311	88,871	107,180	119,730	102,118
Securities brokerage	52312	71,242	85,282	108,404	88,778
Commodity contracts dealing	52313	1,632	1,807	1,920	1,980
Commodity contracts brokerage	52314	2,814	2,748	2,744	2,791
Other financial investment activities [1]	5239x	78,286	91,558	105,273	98,314
Portfolio management	52392	66,143	76,275	88,012	82,759
Investment advice	52393	12,142	15,283	17,261	15,555

[1] Excludes NAICS 52391 (miscellaneous intermediation) and NAICS 52399 (all other financial investment activities).

Source: U.S. Census Bureau, Service Annual Survey: 2001.

No. 1221. Securities Industry—Financial Summary: 1990 to 2001

[In billions of dollars (71.4 represents $71,400,000,000)]

Type	1990	1994	1995	1996	1997	1998	1999	2000	2001
Number of firms	(NA)	7,632	7,722	7,774	7,796	7,685	7,461	7,258	7,002
Revenues, total	71.4	112.8	143.4	172.4	207.2	235.0	266.8	349.5	280.1
Commissions	12.0	19.8	23.2	27.9	32.7	36.7	45.9	54.1	44.8
Trading/investment gains	15.7	20.2	29.0	30.8	36.0	32.8	55.5	70.8	39.0
Underwriting profits	3.7	6.8	8.9	12.6	14.6	16.2	17.8	18.7	16.9
Margin interest	3.2	4.7	6.5	7.4	10.6	12.7	15.2	24.5	13.9
Mutual fund sales	3.2	6.9	7.4	10.1	12.4	14.8	16.7	19.4	16.4
Other	33.4	54.3	68.5	83.7	101.0	121.7	115.7	161.9	149.1
Expenses, total	70.6	109.3	132.1	155.4	187.3	217.8	237.7	310.4	260.7
Interest expense	28.1	40.3	56.9	64.7	80.7	98.1	87.5	131.9	98.9
Compensation	22.9	37.6	41.5	51.0	58.6	65.0	81.7	95.2	83.5
Commissions/clearance paid	3.0	5.4	5.7	7.4	8.9	10.3	13.5	15.5	14.0
Other	16.6	26.1	28.0	32.3	39.2	44.3	55.0	67.8	64.2
Net income, pretax	0.8	3.5	11.3	17.0	20.0	17.2	29.1	39.1	19.4
Pretax profit margin (percent)	(NA)	3.1	7.9	9.8	9.6	7.3	10.9	11.2	6.9
Pretax return on equity (percent)	(NA)	6.5	20.1	27.3	27.1	19.4	27.8	31.1	13.8
Assets	(NA)	1,252	1,494	1,748	2,079	2,187	2,537	2,866	3,371
Liabilities	(NA)	1,198	1,435	1,682	1,997	2,092	2,423	2,728	3,227
Ownership equity	(NA)	54	59	66	82	95	114	138	144

NA Not available.

Source: U.S. Securities and Exchange Commission, Annual Report.

No. 1222. Life Insurance in Force and Purchases in the United States—Summary: 1990 to 2001

[As of December 31 or calendar year, as applicable (389 represents 389,000,000). Covers life insurance with life insurance companies only. Represents all life insurance in force on lives of U.S. residents whether issued by U.S. or foreign companies. For definition of household, see text, Section 1]

Year	Number of policies, total (mil.)	Life insurance in force Value (bil. dol.) Total [1]	Ordinary [2]	Group	Average amount per insured household ($1,000)	Number of policies purchased [3] (1,000) Total [1]	Ordinary [2]	Group	Amount purchased [3] (bil. dol.) Total [1]	Ordinary [2]	Group
1990	389	9,393	5,367	3,754	124.5	28,791	14,066	14,592	1,529	1,070	459
1993	363	11,105	6,428	4,456	143.1	31,238	13,574	17,574	1,678	1,101	577
1994	390	11,057	6,407	4,442	146.3	32,225	13,675	18,390	1,611	1,051	560
1995	393	11,638	6,816	4,603	148.9	31,999	12,466	19,404	1,543	1,005	538
1996	355	12,704	7,408	5,068	157.3	30,783	11,926	18,761	1,704	1,089	615
1997	351	13,364	7,855	5,279	167.6	31,708	11,667	19,973	1,893	1,204	689
1998	358	14,471	8,506	5,735	178.6	31,891	11,522	20,332	2,065	1,325	740
1999	367	15,496	9,172	6,110	189.8	38,584	11,673	26,912	2,367	1,400	967
2000	369	15,953	9,376	6,376	196.2	34,882	13,345	21,537	2,515	1,594	921
2001	377	16,290	9,346	6,765	194.1	40,095	14,059	26,036	2,773	1,600	1,172

[1] Includes other types of policy not shown separately. [2] Beginning 1999 industrial policies are included in ordinary. [3] Excludes revivals, increases, dividend additions, and reinsurance acquired. Includes long-term credit insurance (life insurance on loans of more than 10 years' duration).
Source: American Council of Life Insurers, Washington, DC, *Life Insurers Fact Book*, annual (copyright).

No. 1223. U.S. Life Insurance Companies—Summary: 1990 to 2001

[As of December 31 or calendar year, as applicable (402.2 represents $402,200,000,000). Covers domestic and foreign business of U.S. companies. Beginning 1994 includes annual statement data for companies that primarily are health insurance companies]

Item	Unit	1990	1993	1994	1995	1996	1997	1998	1999	2000	2001
U.S. companies [1]	Number	2,195	1,844	2,136	2,079	1,679	1,620	1,563	1,470	1,280	1,225
Income	Bil. dol.	402.2	466.4	492.6	528.1	561.1	610.6	663.4	726.9	811.4	724.4
Life insurance premiums	Bil. dol.	76.7	94.4	98.9	102.8	107.6	115.0	119.9	120.3	130.6	125.3
Annuity considerations	Bil. dol.	129.1	156.4	153.0	158.4	178.4	197.5	229.5	270.2	306.7	251.3
Health insurance premiums	Bil. dol.	58.3	68.7	86.2	90.0	92.2	92.7	94.9	100.0	105.6	103.4
Investment and other	Bil. dol.	138.2	146.8	154.5	176.9	182.9	205.3	219.1	236.4	268.5	244.4
Payments to life insurance beneficiaries	Bil. dol.	24.6	28.8	32.6	34.5	36.3	37.5	40.1	41.4	44.1	46.5
Payments under life insurance and annuity contracts	Bil. dol.	63.8	71.2	168.2	193.1	210.7	239.1	261.8	313.9	333.4	258.3
Surrender values under life insurance [2]	Bil. dol.	18.0	16.9	18.0	19.5	24.5	24.0	26.8	32.8	27.4	30.7
Surrender values under annuity policies [2]	Bil. dol.	(NA)	(NA)	92.8	105.4	115.7	140.8	154.5	198.3	214.0	151.3
Policy dividends	Bil. dol.	12.0	12.7	15.9	17.8	18.1	18.0	18.9	19.1	20.3	20.0
Annuity payments	Bil. dol.	32.6	40.3	40.4	48.5	51.1	55.1	60.4	62.5	70.5	55.2
Matured endowments	Bil. dol.	0.7	0.6	0.6	1.0	0.7	0.6	0.6	0.6	0.5	0.5
Other payments	Bil. dol.	0.6	0.6	0.5	0.9	0.6	0.6	0.6	0.6	0.6	0.6
Health insurance benefit payments	Bil. dol.	40.0	46.0	60.1	64.7	66.7	67.4	70.0	74.5	79.7	77.2
BALANCE SHEET											
Assets	Bil. dol.	1,408	1,839	1,942	2,144	2,328	2,579	2,827	3,071	3,182	3,269
Government securities	Bil. dol.	211	384	396	409	411	391	379	362	364	377
Corporate securities	Bil. dol.	711	982	1,072	1,241	1,416	1,658	1,896	2,180	2,238	2,263
Percent of total assets	Percent	50.5	53.4	55.2	57.9	60.8	64.3	67.1	71.0	70.3	69.2
Bonds	Bil. dol.	583	730	791	869	962	1,060	1,140	1,190	1,241	1,354
Stocks	Bil. dol.	128	252	282	372	454	598	758	990	997	909
Mortgages	Bil. dol.	270	229	215	212	212	210	216	230	237	244
Real estate	Bil. dol.	43	54	54	52	50	46	41	38	36	32
Policy loans	Bil. dol.	63	78	85	96	102	105	105	99	102	104
Other	Bil. dol.	110	112	120	133	137	169	187	163	205	248
Interest earned on assets [3]	Percent	8.89	7.52	7.14	7.34	7.25	7.35	6.95	6.71	7.05	6.31
Obligations and surplus funds [4]	Bil. dol.	1,408	1,839	1,942	2,144	2,328	2,579	2,827	3,071	3,182	3,269
Policy reserves [5]	Bil. dol.	1,197	1,550	1,644	1,812	1,966	2,165	2,377	2,610	2,712	2,446
Annuities [6]	Bil. dol.	798	1,041	1,095	1,213	1,312	1,455	1,608	1,781	1,841	1,516
Group	Bil. dol.	516	602	612	619	690	762	845	907	960	571
Individual	Bil. dol.	282	439	482	594	622	693	763	874	881	945
Supplementary contracts [7]	Bil. dol.	17	21	23	25	28	28	31	32	34	13
Life insurance	Bil. dol.	349	436	468	511	556	606	656	705	742	816
Health insurance	Bil. dol.	33	51	58	63	70	75	82	92	96	101
Asset valuation reserve	Bil. dol.	15	25	25	30	33	36	38	40	38	31
Capital and surplus	Bil. dol.	91	128	137	151	147	160	173	181	188	191

NA Not available. [1] Beginning 1994 includes life insurance companies that sell accident and health insurance. [2] Beginning with 1994, "surrender values" include annuity withdrawals of funds, which were not included in prior years. [3] Net rate. [4] Includes other obligations not shown separately. [5] Includes the business of health insurance departments of life companies. [6] Beginning 2001, excludes reserves for guaranteed interest contracts (GICs). [7] Through 2000 includes reserves for contracts with and without life contingencies; 2001 includes only reserves for contracts with life contingencies.
Source: American Council of Life Insurers, Washington, DC, *Life Insurers Fact Book*, annual (copyright).

No. 1224. Property and Casualty Insurance—Summary: 1990 to 2001

[In billions of dollars (217.8 represents $217,800,000,000). Minus sign (-) indicates loss]

Item	1990	1995	1996	1997	1998	1999	2000	2001
Premiums, net written	217.8	259.8	268.6	276.4	281.5	286.9	299.6	323.4
Automobile, private [1]	78.4	102.0	107.7	113.6	117.3	118.6	119.6	127.8
Automobile, commercial [1]	17.0	17.2	17.6	18.0	18.1	18.1	19.5	21.7
Liability other than auto	22.1	23.4	24.5	25.0	24.2	23.9	25.5	28.0
Fire and allied lines	7.1	9.4	9.9	8.4	8.4	8.1	8.3	9.9
Homeowners' multiple peril	18.6	24.0	25.4	26.9	29.0	30.6	32.4	35.1
Commercial multiple peril	17.7	18.8	18.9	19.0	19.0	18.9	19.8	22.2
Workers' compensation	31.0	26.2	25.1	24.1	23.2	22.2	24.8	26.0
Marine, inland and ocean	5.7	7.1	7.5	7.6	7.6	7.7	8.1	8.5
Accident and health	5.0	7.8	7.8	8.3	9.8	11.1	13.3	14.4
Other lines	15.2	23.9	24.2	25.5	24.9	27.7	28.3	29.8
Losses and expenses	234.7	268.4	277.1	272.6	289.7	302.6	321.4	361.6
Underwriting gain/loss	-20.9	-17.7	-16.7	-5.8	-16.8	-23.1	-31.2	-52.6
Net investment income	32.9	36.8	38.0	41.5	39.9	38.9	40.7	37.8
Operating earnings after taxes	9.0	20.6	24.4	36.8	30.8	21.9	20.6	-7.0
Assets	556.3	765.2	802.3	870.1	907.8	918.3	912.0	952.6
Policyholders' surplus	138.4	230.0	255.5	308.5	333.3	334.3	317.4	289.6

[1] Includes premiums for automobile liability and physical damage.

Source: Insurance Information Institute, New York, NY, *The Fact Book, Property/Casualty Insurance Facts*, annual (copyright).

No. 1225. Automobile Insurance—Average Expenditures Per Insured Vehicle by State: 1995 to 2001

[In dollars. Average expenditure equals total premiums written divided by liability car-years. A car-year is equal to 365 days of insured coverage for a single vehicle. The average expenditures for automobile insurance in a state are affected by a number of factors, including the underlying rate structure, the coverages purchased, the deductibles and limits selected, the types of vehicles insured, and the distribution of driver characteristics]

State	1995	2000	2001	State	1995	2000	2001	State	1995	2000	2001
U.S.	667	687	718	KS	474	540	556	ND	381	477	498
				KY	555	616	645	OH	531	579	614
AL	549	594	605	LA	788	806	839	OK	526	603	622
AK	730	770	826	ME	472	528	545	OR	565	625	643
AZ	727	792	822	MD	732	757	784	PA	667	699	726
AR	500	606	621	MA	898	946	936	RI	870	825	880
CA	794	661	689	MI	645	702	735	SC	582	620	617
CO	722	755	808	MN	628	696	735	SD	428	482	510
CT	881	871	912	MS	579	654	638	TN	519	592	611
DE	784	849	851	MO	573	612	634	TX	711	678	735
DC	959	996	1,012	MT	468	530	572	UT	547	620	640
FL	739	746	788	NE	452	533	554	VT	512	568	603
GA	597	674	703	NV	759	829	851	VA	553	576	610
HI	963	702	705	NH	609	665	686	WA	650	722	750
ID	447	505	523	NJ	1,013	977	1,028	WV	646	680	707
IL	612	652	683	NM	639	674	662	WI	506	545	573
IN	542	570	615	NY	906	939	1,015	WY	433	496	528
IA	429	479	513	NC	501	564	565				

Source: National Association of Insurance Commissioners (NAIC), Kansas City, MO, *State Average Expenditures and Premiums for Personal Automobile Insurance*, annual (copyright). Reprinted with permission of the NAIC. Further reprint or distribution strictly prohibited without prior written permission of the NAIC.

No. 1226. Average Premiums for Renters and Homeowners Insurance by State: 1999

[In dollars. Average premium equals premiums divided by exposure per house-years. A house-year is equal to 365 days of insured coverage for a single dwelling and is the standard measurement for homeowners insurance]

State	Renters [1]	Home owners [2]	State	Renters [1]	Home owners [2]	State	Renters [1]	Home owners [2]
U.S.	171	487	KS	162	576	ND	100	403
			KY	137	394	OH	138	314
AL	159	457	LA	241	714	OK	203	594
AK	160	601	ME	116	336	OR	150	334
AZ	194	418	MD	133	372	PA	134	403
AR	189	501	MA	182	526	RI	169	520
CA	262	578	MI	153	417	SC	171	505
CO	168	559	MN	125	390	SD	106	378
CT	182	546	MS	224	594	TN	187	474
DE	136	317	MO	156	441	TX [3]	228	861
DC	160	617	MT	132	429	UT	142	369
FL	222	657	NE	124	467	VT	123	414
GA	203	448	NV	232	474	VA	133	345
HI	201	606	NH	136	410	WA	155	413
ID	137	319	NJ	167	497	WV	134	388
IL	157	387	NM	197	451	WI	105	266
IN	143	373	NY	197	533	WY	154	491
IA	124	347	NC	167	427			

[1] Based on the HO-4 renters insurance policy for tenants. Includes broad named-peril coverage for the personal property of tenants. [2] Based on the HO-3 homeowner package policy for owner-occupied dwellings, 1-4 family units. Provides "all risks" coverage (except those specifically excluded in the policy) on buildings, broad named-peril coverage on personal property, and is the most common package written. [3] The Texas Insurance Commissioner promulgates residential policy forms which are similar but not identical to the standard forms. Insurers can use State-promulgated or standard forms.

Source: National Association of Insurance Commissioners (NAIC), Kansas City, MO, *Dwelling Fire, Homeowners Owner-Occupied, and Homeowners Tenant and Condominium/Cooperative Unit Owners Insurance* (copyright). Reprinted with permission of the NAIC. Further reprint or distribution strictly prohibited without prior written permission of the NAIC.

No. 1227. Real Estate, Rental, and Leasing—Nonemployer Establishments and Receipts by Kind of Business: 1998 to 2000

[1,565 represents 1,565,000. Includes only firms subject to federal income tax. Nonemployers are businesses with no paid employees. Based on the North American Industry Classification System (NAICS), see text, Section 15]

Kind of business	NAICS code	Establishments (1,000) 1998	1999	2000	Receipts (mil. dol.) 1998	1999	2000
Real estate & rental & leasing, total	53	1,565	1,648	1,696	131,728	125,513	133,398
Real estate	531	1,492	1,569	1,616	126,566	120,409	127,862
Lessors of real estate	5311	710	683	714	88,023	81,152	86,934
Offices of real estate agents & brokers	5312	496	524	522	20,265	22,066	22,623
Activities related to real estate	5313	286	362	380	18,278	17,191	18,305
Rental & leasing services	532	72	78	79	5,071	5,013	5,440
Automotive equipment rental & leasing	5321	17	18	19	1,002	962	995
Consumer goods rental [1]	5322	16	17	17	754	748	766
Video tape & disk rental	53223	7	6	6	299	278	268
General rental centers	5323	2	2	3	176	203	252
Commercial/industrial equip rental & leasing	5324	37	40	41	3,139	3,100	3,426
Lessors of other nonfinancial intangible assets	533	1	1	1	91	90	96

[1] Includes other kinds of business not shown separately.

Source: U.S. Census Bureau, "Nonemployer Statistics"; published August 2002; <http://www.census.gov/epcd/nonemployer/>.

No. 1228. Real Estate, Rental, and Leasing—Establishments, Employees, and Payroll: 2000 and 2001

[300.2 represents 300,200. Covers establishments with payroll. Employees are for the week including March 12. Most government employees are excluded. For statement on methodology, see Appendix III]

Kind of business	NAICS code [1]	Establishments (1,000) 2000	2001	Employees (1,000) 2000	2001	Payroll (bil. dol.) 2000	2001
Real estate & rental & leasing, total	53	300.2	307.0	1,942	2,014	59.2	64.0
Real estate	531	234.9	241.1	1,280	1,335	40.4	44.4
Lessors of real estate	5311	108.2	108.0	501	513	12.5	13.9
Offices of real estate agents & brokers	5312	65.1	68.9	271	284	10.6	11.1
Activities related to real estate	5313	61.6	64.2	507	538	17.3	19.5
Rental & leasing services	532	63.2	63.8	636	653	17.2	18.0
Automotive equipment rental & leasing	5321	11.1	12.1	182	189	5.1	5.3
Passenger car rental & leasing	53211	5.2	5.5	129	136	3.4	3.6
Truck, utility trailer & RV rental & leasing	53212	5.8	6.6	53	53	1.7	1.8
Consumer goods rental [2]	5322	33.1	32.3	255	256	4.2	4.4
Video tape & disc rental	53223	19.6	18.6	152	150	1.6	1.6
General rental centers	5323	6.4	6.4	42	41	1.2	1.2
Commercial/industrial equip rental & leasing	5324	12.6	13.0	157	166	6.7	7.0
Lessors of other nonfinancial intangible assets	533	2.1	2.1	26	26	1.6	1.6

[1] North American Industry Classification System; see text, Section 15. [2] Includes other kinds of businesses not shown separately.

Source: U.S. Census Bureau, County Business Patterns, annual; <http://www.census.gov/prod/2003pubs/01cbp/cbp01-1.pdf> (issued April 2003).

No. 1229. Rental and Leasing Services—Revenue by Kind of Business: 1999 to 2001

[In millions of dollars (98,173 represents $98,173,000,000). Based on the North American Industry Classification System (NAICS); see text, Section 15. Estimates have been adjusted using the results of the 1997 Economic Census. Based on Service Annual Survey; see Appendix III]

Kind of business	NAICS code	Employer and nonemployer firms 1999	2000	2001	Employer firms 1999	2000	2001
Rental & leasing services	532	98,173	106,287	104,091	93,158	100,847	98,508
Automotive equipment rental & leasing	5321	35,094	37,496	36,338	34,132	36,501	35,367
Passenger car rental & leasing	53211	22,705	24,357	23,829	22,137	23,769	23,288
Truck, utility trailer, & RV rental & leasing	53212	12,389	13,139	12,509	11,994	12,732	12,079
Consumer goods rental [1]	5322	17,658	18,320	18,367	16,910	17,554	17,561
Video tape & disc rental	53223	8,712	8,968	8,584	8,434	8,700	8,312
General rental centers	5323	5,107	5,504	5,050	4,904	5,252	4,819
Commercial/industrial equip rental & leasing	5324	40,313	44,967	44,336	37,213	41,541	40,761

[1] Includes other kinds of businesses not shown separately.

Source: U.S. Census Bureau, Service Annual Survey: 2001.

Section 26
Arts, Entertainment, and Recreation

This section presents data on the arts, entertainment, and recreation economic sector of the economy, and personal recreational activities, the arts and humanities, and domestic and foreign travel.

Arts, Entertainment, and Recreation Industry—The U.S. Census Bureau's *Service Annual Survey, Arts, Entertainment, and Recreation Sector*, provides estimates of operation revenue of taxable firms and revenues and expenses of firms exempt from federal taxes for industries in this sector of the economy. Data beginning 1998 are based on the North American Industry Classification System (NAICS). Most establishments were previously classified in the Standard Industrial Classification (SIC) in services, some in retail trade.

This new sector is comprised of industries which existed previously, were revised from previous industry definitions, or are completely new industries. Among those which existed previously are amusement and theme parks. Revised industries include museums. New industries include theater companies and dinner theaters. The following URL contains detailed information about NAICS and provides a comparison of the SIC and NAICS <http://www.census.gov/epcd/www/naics.html>. See also the text in Section 15, Business Enterprise.

The 1997 Economic Census was the first economic census to cover the new Information Sector of the economy. The Census, conducted every 5-years, for the years ending "2" and "7," provides information on the number of establishments, receipts, payroll and paid employees for the U.S. and various geographic levels.

Recreation and leisure activities—Data on the participation in various recreation and leisure time activities are based on several sample surveys. Data on participation in fishing, hunting, and other forms of wildlife-associated recreation are published periodically by the U.S. Department of Interior, Fish and Wildlife Service. The most recent data are from the 2001 survey. Data on participation in various sports recreation activities are published by the National Sporting Goods Association. Mediamark, Inc. also conducts periodic surveys on sports and leisure activities, as well as other topics.

Parks and recreation—The Department of the Interior has responsibility for administering the national parks. The National Park Service publishes information on visits to national park areas in its annual report, *National Park Statistical Abstract*. *The National Parks: Index (year)* is a biannual report which contains brief descriptions, with acreages, of each area administered by the service, plus certain "related" areas. The annual *Federal Recreation Fee Report* summarizes the prior year's recreation fee receipts and recreation visitation statistics for seven federal land managing agencies. Statistics for state parks are compiled by the National Association of State Park Directors, which issues its *Annual Information Exchange*.

Travel—Statistics on arrivals to the United States are reported by the International Trade Administration (ITA). Statistics on departures from the United States include the Department of Transportation's *International Air Travel Statistics* and other sources. Data on domestic travel, business receipts and employment of the travel industry, and travel expenditures are published by the U.S. Travel Data Center, which is the research department of the Travel Industry Association and the national nonprofit center for travel and tourism research located in Washington, DC. Other data on household transportation characteristics are in Section 23, Transportation.

Statistical reliability—For a discussion of statistical collection and estimation, sampling procedures, and measures of statistical reliability applicable to Census Bureau data, see Appendix III.

No. 1230. Arts, Entertainment and Recreation Services—Estimated Revenue: 2000 and 2001

[In millions of dollars (122,117 represents $122,117,000,000), except percent. For taxable and tax-exempt employer firms. Except as indicated, estimates adjusted to the results of the 1997 Economic Census. Minus sign (-) indicates decrease. See Appendix III]

Industry	NAICS code [1]	Total 2000	Total 2001	Percent change, 2000-2001	Taxable 2000	Taxable 2001	Percent change, 2000-2001
Arts, entertainment, and recreation	71	122,117	128,904	5.6	99,565	105,730	6.2
Performing arts, spectator sports	711	43,792	46,391	5.9	38,273	40,522	5.9
Performing arts companies [2]	7111	9,199	9,252	0.6	5,508	5,389	-2.2
Spectator sports	7112	17,449	18,416	5.5	17,449	18,416	5.5
Sports teams and clubs	711211	10,404	11,104	6.7	10,404	11,104	6.7
Racetracks	711212	5,235	5,337	1.9	5,235	5,337	1.9
Other spectator sports	711219	1,809	1,975	9.2	1,809	1,975	9.2
Promoters of performing arts, sports and similar events	7113	7,434	8,131	9.4	5,606	6,125	9.2
Agents and managers for artists, athletes, entertainers and other public figures	7114	3,249	3,468	6.7	3,249	3,468	6.7
Independent artists, writers, and performers	7115	6,461	7,125	10.3	6,461	7,125	10.3
Museums, historical sites, and similar institutions	712	8,239	8,173	-0.8	836	844	1.0
Amusement, gambling, and recreation industries	713	70,086	74,341	6.1	60,455	64,363	6.5
Amusement parks and arcades	7131	9,295	9,664	4.0	9,295	9,664	4.0
Amusement and theme parks	71311	8,155	8,542	4.8	8,155	8,542	4.8
Amusement arcades	71312	1,141	1,122	-1.6	1,141	1,122	-1.6
Gambling industries	7132	18,807	21,510	14.4	18,807	21,510	14.4
Casinos (except casino hotels)	71321	13,105	15,230	16.2	13,105	15,230	16.2
Other gambling industries	71329	5,702	6,280	10.1	5,702	6,280	10.1
Other amusement and recreation industries	7139	41,984	43,167	2.8	32,353	33,189	2.6
Golf courses and country clubs	71391	15,935	16,090	1.0	9,769	9,745	-0.2
Skiing facilities	71392	1,489	1,569	5.4	1,489	1,569	5.4
Marinas [3]	71393	3,254	3,264	0.3	3,254	3,264	0.3
Fitness and recreational sports centers	71394	12,603	13,617	8.1	9,864	10,770	9.2
Bowling centers	71395	2,977	3,106	4.3	2,977	3,106	4.3
All other amusement and recreation	71399	5,726	5,520	-3.6	5,000	4,735	-5.3

[1] Based on the North American Industry Classification System; see text, this section, and Section 15.   [2] Estimates for NAICS 71113 and 71119 not adjusted to the 1997 Economic Census.   [3] Estimates not adjusted to the 1997 Economic Census.

Source: U.S. Census Bureau, *2001 Service Annual Survey, Information Sector Services.* See <http://www.census.gov/econ/www/servmenu.html> (releasd 2 December 2002).

No. 1231. Arts, Entertainment, and Recreation—Nonemployer Establishments and Receipts by Kind of Business (NAICS Basis): 1998 to 2000

[713.1 represents 713,100. Includes only firms subject to federal income tax. Nonemployers are businesses with no paid employees]

Kind of business	NAICS code [1]	Establishments (1,000) 1998	1999	2000	Receipts (mil. dol.) 1998	1999	2000
Arts, entertainment, and recreation	71	713.1	748.7	781.7	15,324.6	16,656.4	17,713.4
Performing arts, spectator sports, and related industries	711	571.1	611.2	645.4	11,002.1	12,178.3	13,008.4
Performing arts companies	7111	15.3	17.5	19.3	439.8	501.6	575.9
Spectator sports	7112	64.4	65.8	67.3	1,382.5	1,398.1	1,480.7
Promoters of performing arts, sports, and similar events	7113	18.5	21.1	23.1	714.7	830.6	850.6
Agents/managers for artists, athletes, and other public figures	7114	21.8	25.0	27.1	677.9	776.4	856.8
Independent artists, writers and performers	7115	451.1	481.8	508.6	7,787.2	8,671.6	9,244.4
Museums, historical sites, and similar institutions	712	2.7	3.3	3.6	42.1	47.0	51.5
Amusement, gambling, and recreation industries	713	139.3	134.2	132.7	4,280.4	4,431.2	4,653.5
Amusement parks and arcades	7131	6.6	5.6	5.4	413.3	324.7	291.4
Gambling industries	7132	4.1	5.6	5.9	318.3	475.2	532.1
Other amusement and recreation services	7139	128.5	123.0	121.3	3,548.8	3,631.2	3,829.9

[1] Based on the North American Industry Classification System (NAICS), see text, Section 15.
Source: U.S. Census Bureau, "Nonemployer Statistics"; published October 2002; and previous reports. See Internet site <http://www.census.gov/epcd/nonemployer/>.

No. 1232. Arts, Entertainment, and Recreation—Establishments, Payroll, and Employees by Kind of Business (NAICS Basis): 2000 and 2001

[For establishments with payroll (1,741.5 represents 1,741,500). See Appendix III]

Industry	NAICS code [1]	Establishments 2000	2001	Paid employees [2] (1,000) 2000	2001	Annual payroll (mil. dol.) 2000	2001
Arts, entertainment, & recreation, total	71	103,816	105,961	1,741.5	1,780.4	43,204	46,133
Performing arts, spectator sports	711	33,859	34,840	351.9	361.7	19,090	20,393
Performing arts companies	7111	9,253	9,327	126.4	127.8	3,251	3,344
Theater companies & dinner theaters	71111	3,367	3,354	63.4	66.4	1,469	1,517
Dance companies	71112	584	604	10.7	10.9	216	218
Musical groups & artists	71113	4,497	4,562	44.0	43.0	1,341	1,349
Other performing arts companies	71119	805	807	8.3	7.5	226	260
Spectator sports	7112	4,461	4,584	100.2	104.4	9,215	9,955
Sports teams & clubs	711211	684	735	36.3	40.1	7,587	8,268
Racetracks	711212	899	881	45.8	45.2	994	989
Other spectator sports	711219	2,878	2,968	18.1	19.1	633	697
Promoters of performing arts, sports, and similar events	7113	4,394	4,456	71.8	73.9	1,917	2,010
Promoters of performing arts, sports, and similar events with facilities	71131	1,107	1,184	44.3	48.3	787	942
Promoters of performing arts, sports, and similar events without facilities	71132	3,287	3,272	27.6	25.6	1,130	1,068
Agents/managers for artists, athletes, and other public figures	7114	3,048	3,107	16.0	16.2	1,117	1,139
Independent artists, writers, & performers	7115	12,703	13,366	37.5	39.4	3,589	3,946
Museums, historical sites, & similar institutions	712	5,777	6,032	110.4	113.5	2,549	2,781
Museums	71211	3,988	4,140	75.4	76.8	1,765	1,907
Historical sites	71212	892	893	8.3	8.4	143	154
Zoos & botanical gardens	71213	414	459	20.5	21.8	509	558
Nature parks & other similar institutions	71219	483	540	6.2	6.5	133	162
Amusement, gambling, & recreation industries	713	64,180	65,089	1,279.2	1,305.1	21,564	22,958
Amusement parks & arcades	7131	2,879	2,783	124.0	119.3	2,277	2,314
Amusement & theme parks	71311	716	700	102.8	98.8	2,011	2,044
Amusement arcades	71312	2,163	2,083	21.3	20.5	266	270
Gambling industries	7132	2,191	2,175	202.6	215.6	4,757	5,400
Casinos (except casino hotels)	71321	537	562	150.2	156.2	3,592	4,007
Other gambling industries	71329	1,654	1,613	52.4	59.5	1,165	1,392
Other amusement & recreation services	7139	59,110	60,131	952.6	970.1	14,531	15,244
Golf courses & country clubs	71391	11,885	11,861	297.9	295.1	6,243	6,472
Skiing facilities	71392	389	404	56.9	63.9	452	495
Marinas	71393	4,126	4,121	24.8	24.7	640	675
Fitness & recreational sports centers	71394	23,003	24,068	382.8	399.4	4,499	4,844
Bowling centers	71395	5,234	5,059	87.9	84.6	888	889
All other amusement & recreation industries	71399	14,473	14,618	102.4	102.5	1,808	1,870

[1] North American Industry Classification System code; see text, this section, and Section 15. [2] For employees on the payroll for the period including March 12.
Source: U.S. Census Bureau, "County Business Patterns"; 2001 data published April 2003; <http://www.census.gov/prod/www/abs/cbptotal.html>.

No. 1233. Expenditures Per Consumer Unit for Entertainment and Reading: 1990 to 2001

[Data are annual averages. In dollars, except as indicated. Based on Consumer Expenditure Survey; see text, Section 13, for description of survey. See also headnote, Table 678. For composition of regions, see map, inside front cover]

Year and characteristic	Entertainment and reading Total	Entertainment and reading Percent of total expenditures	Entertainment Total	Entertainment Fees and admissions	Entertainment Television, radios, and sound equipment	Entertainment Other equipment and services [1]	Reading
1990	1,575	5.6	1,422	371	454	597	153
1991	1,635	5.5	1,472	378	468	627	163
1992	1,662	5.6	1,500	379	492	629	162
1993	1,792	5.8	1,626	414	590	621	166
1994	1,732	5.5	1,567	439	533	595	165
1995	1,775	5.5	1,612	433	542	637	163
1996	1,993	5.9	1,834	459	561	814	159
1997	1,977	5.7	1,813	471	577	766	164
1998	1,907	5.4	1,746	449	535	762	161
1999	2,050	5.5	1,891	459	608	824	159
2000	2,009	5.3	1,863	515	622	727	146
2001, total	2,094	5.3	1,953	526	660	767	141
Age of reference person:							
Under 25 years old	1,212	5.2	1,152	289	506	356	60
25 to 34 years old	2,112	5.4	2,001	492	698	810	111
35 to 44 years old	2,644	5.6	2,508	707	787	1,014	136
45 to 54 years old	2,405	5.0	2,233	635	781	817	172
55 to 64 years old	2,520	6.1	2,337	588	642	1,107	183
65 to 74 years old	1,455	4.5	1,296	379	500	417	159
75 years old and over	950	4.1	822	207	361	254	128
Origin of reference person:							
Hispanic	1,305	3.8	1,246	277	593	376	59
Non-Hispanic	2,170	5.4	2,021	550	666	805	149
Race of reference person:							
White and other	2,237	5.5	2,085	573	671	841	152
Black	1,050	3.6	988	188	575	225	62
Region of residence:							
Northeast	2,023	4.9	1,854	561	681	611	169
Midwest	2,382	6.0	2,220	587	680	953	162
South	1,753	4.8	1,652	410	614	628	101
West	2,400	5.5	2,241	620	693	928	159

[1] Other equipment and services includes pets, toys, and playground equipment; sports, exercise, and photographic equipment; and recreational vehicles.

Source: U.S. Bureau of Labor Statistics, *Consumer Expenditure Survey*, annual.

No. 1234. Personal Consumption Expenditures for Recreation: 1990 to 2001

[In billions of dollars (284.9 represents $284,900,000,000), except percent. Represents market value of purchases of goods and services by individuals and nonprofit institutions]

Type of product or service	1990	1995	1997	1998	1999	2000	2001
Total recreation expenditures	284.9	401.6	456.6	489.1	526.5	564.7	593.9
Percent of total personal consumption [1]	7.4	8.1	8.3	8.4	8.4	8.4	8.5
Books and maps	16.2	23.1	26.3	28.2	30.8	33.2	35.1
Magazines, newspapers, and sheet music	21.6	26.2	29.1	31.0	32.5	34.2	35.2
Nondurable toys and sport supplies	32.8	47.2	53.2	56.5	60.4	62.7	66.7
Wheel goods, sports and photographic equipment [2]	29.7	38.5	42.8	46.2	50.4	55.3	60.8
Video and audio products, computer equipment, and musical instruments	52.9	77.0	83.7	90.3	98.1	106.3	105.6
Video and audio goods, including musical instruments	43.9	55.9	57.9	61.6	66.7	71.8	72.7
Computers, peripherals, and software	8.9	21.0	25.9	28.7	31.4	34.5	32.9
Radio and television repair	3.7	3.6	4.0	4.1	4.1	4.1	4.2
Flowers, seeds, and potted plants	10.9	13.8	15.3	15.9	16.7	17.5	18.5
Admissions to specified spectator amusements	14.8	19.2	22.1	23.4	25.0	27.1	29.4
Motion picture theaters	5.1	5.5	6.3	6.9	7.6	7.8	8.7
Legitimate theaters and opera, and entertainments of nonprofit institutions [3]	5.2	7.6	8.6	8.7	8.9	9.9	10.6
Spectator sports [4]	4.5	6.1	7.1	7.7	8.5	9.5	10.1
Clubs and fraternal organizations except insurance [5]	8.7	12.7	14.6	14.9	15.9	16.7	17.3
Commercial participant amusements [6]	24.6	43.9	52.8	57.3	63.0	68.4	73.3
Pari-mutuel net receipts	3.5	3.5	3.6	4.3	4.5	4.7	4.8
Other [7]	65.4	93.1	109.1	117.0	125.1	134.4	142.9

[1] See Table 667. [2] Includes boats and pleasure aircraft. [3] Except athletic. [4] Consists of admissions to professional and amateur athletic events and to racetracks, including horse, dog, and auto. [5] Consists of dues and fees excluding insurance premiums. [6] Consists of billiard parlors; bowling alleys; dancing, riding, shooting, skating, and swimming places; amusement devices and parks; golf courses; sightseeing buses and guides; private flying operations; casino gambling; and other commercial participant amusements. [7] Consists of net receipts of lotteries and expenditures for purchases of pets and pet care services, cable TV, film processing, photographic studios, sporting and recreation camps, video cassette rentals, and recreational services, not elsewhere classified.

Source: U.S. Department of Commerce, Bureau of Economic Analysis, *National Income and Product Accounts, Volume 1, 1929-97*, and *Survey of Current Business*, May 2003. See also <http://www.bea.gov/bea/dn/nipaweb/selecttable.asp> (released as of 30 May 2003)

No. 1235. Performing Arts—Selected Data: 1985 to 2001

[Sales, receipts and expenditures in millions of dollars (209 represents $209,000,000). For season ending in year shown, except as indicated]

Item	1985	1990	1994	1995	1996	1997	1998	1999	2000	2001
Legitimate theater: [1]										
Broadway shows:										
New productions	33	40	39	33	38	37	33	39	37	28
Attendance (mil.)	7.3	8.0	8.1	9.0	9.5	10.6	11.5	11.7	11.4	11.9
Playing weeks [2,3]	1,078	1,070	1,066	1,120	1,146	1,349	1,442	1,441	1,464	1,484
Gross ticket sales	209	282	356	406	436	499	558	588	603	666
Broadway road tours:										
Attendance (mil.)	8.2	11.1	16.0	15.6	18.1	17.6	15.2	14.6	11.7	11.0
Playing weeks	993	944	1,249	1,242	1,345	1,334	1,127	1,082	888	823
Gross ticket sales	226	367	705	701	796	782	721	707	572	541
Nonprofit professional theatres: [4]										
Companies reporting	217	185	231	215	228	197	189	313	262	363
Gross income	234.7	307.6	455.1	444.4	450.7	565.0	570.0	740.0	791.0	961.1
Earned income	146.1	188.4	277.4	281.2	274.0	349.9	342.0	442.0	466.0	554.5
Contributed income	88.6	119.2	177.7	163.1	176.7	215.1	228.0	298.0	325.0	406.6
Gross expenses	239.3	306.3	460.2	444.9	439.5	526.6	518.5	701.0	708.0	923.6
Productions	2,710	2,265	2,929	2,646	3,074	2,295	2,135	3,921	3,241	4,787
Performances	52,341	46,131	59,542	56,608	56,954	51,453	46,628	64,556	66,123	81,828
Total attendance (mil.)	14.2	15.2	20.7	18.6	17.1	17.2	14.6	18.0	22.0	21.1
OPERA America professional										
Member companies: [5]										
Number of companies reporting [6]	97	98	86	88	83	91	89	95	98	96
Expenses [6]	216.4	321.2	404.9	435.0	466.7	534.1	556.3	591.1	636.7	685.1
Performances [7]	1,909	2,336	1,982	2,251	2,019	2,137	2,222	2,200	2,153	2,031
Total attendance (mil.) [7,8]	6.7	7.5	6.0	6.5	6.5	6.9	6.6	6.6	6.7	6.5
Main season attendance (mil.) [7,9]	3.3	4.1	3.7	3.9	3.9	4.0	3.7	4.0	4.3	4.2
Symphony orchestras: [10]										
Concerts	19,573	18,931	17,795	29,328	28,887	26,906	31,766	31,549	33,154	36,437
Attendance (mil.)	24.0	24.7	24.4	30.9	31.1	31.9	32.2	30.8	31.7	31.5
Gross revenue	252.4	377.5	442.5	536.2	558.9	575.5	627.6	671.8	734.0	774.7
Operating expenses	426.1	621.7	710.0	858.8	892.4	937.1	1,012.0	1,088.0	1,126.3	1,285.9
Support	188.1	257.8	293.1	351.0	382.8	401.1	459.7	486.0	521.0	559.6

[1] Source: The League of American Theaters and Producers, Inc, New York, NY. For season ending in year shown. [2] All shows (new productions and holdovers from previous seasons). [3] Eight performances constitute one playing week. [4] Source: Theatre Communications Group, New York, NY. For years ending on or prior to Aug. 31. [5] Source: OPERA America, Washington, DC. For years ending on or prior to Aug 31. [6] United States companies. [7] Prior to 1993 and for 1999, United States and Canadian companies; 1993 to 1998, U.S. companies only. [8] Includes educational performances, outreach, etc. [9] For paid performances. [10] Source: American Symphony Orchestra League, Inc., New York, NY. For years ending Aug. 31. Prior to 1995 represents 254 U.S. orchestras; beginning 1995, represents all U.S. orchestras, excluding college/university and youth orchestras. Also, beginning 1995, data based on 1,200 orchestras.

Source: Compiled from sources listed in footnotes.

Arts, Entertainment, and Recreation 771

No. 1236. Arts and Humanities—Selected Federal Aid Programs: 1980 to 2001

[In millions of dollars (188.1 represents $188,100,000), except as indicated. For fiscal year ending September 30]

Type of fund and program	1980	1990	1995	1996	1997	1998	1999	2000	2001
National Endowment for the Arts:									
Funds available [1]	188.1	170.8	152.1	86.9	98.4	85.3	85.0	85.2	94.0
Program appropriation	97.0	124.3	109.0	63.5	65.8	64.3	66.0	66.0	86.7
Matching funds [2]	42.9	32.4	28.5	17.2	16.8	16.8	14.5	13.0	-
Grants awarded (number)	5,505	4,475	3,685	1,751	1,098	1,459	1,675	1,882	2,093
Funds obligated [3][4]	166.4	157.6	147.9	75.3	94.4	82.3	82.6	83.5	92.5
Partnership agreements	22.1	26.1	39.2	25.9	30.0	33.4	33.8	33.4	36.1
Music	13.6	16.5	10.9	5.4	(X)	(X)	(X)	(X)	(X)
Museums	11.2	12.1	9.0	3.8	(X)	(X)	(X)	(X)	(X)
Theater	8.4	10.6	7.3	5.2	(X)	(X)	(X)	(X)	(X)
Dance	8.0	9.6	7.1	4.2	(X)	(X)	(X)	(X)	(X)
Media arts	8.4	13.9	8.9	3.0	(X)	(X)	(X)	(X)	(X)
Challenge [5]	50.8	19.7	21.1	4.0	(X)	(X)	(X)	(X)	(X)
Visual arts	7.3	5.9	4.4	1.2	(X)	(X)	(X)	(X)	(X)
Other	36.6	43.1	40.0	22.6	(X)	(X)	(X)	(X)	(X)
National Endowment for the Humanities:									
Funds available [1]	186.2	140.6	152.3	93.9	94.8	94.0	95.5	102.6	106.8
Program appropriation	100.3	114.2	125.7	77.2	80.0	80.0	80.0	82.7	86.4
Matching funds [2]	38.4	26.3	25.7	15.9	13.9	13.9	13.9	15.1	15.6
Grants awarded (number)	2,917	2,195	1,871	815	900	852	874	1,230	1,290
Funds obligated [3]	185.5	141.0	151.8	93.4	94.8	92.7	92.1	100.0	105.7
Education programs	18.3	16.3	19.2	13.5	10.5	10.8	10.3	13.0	12.1
State programs	26.0	29.6	32.0	29.0	29.5	29.1	29.3	30.6	32.1
Research grants	32.0	22.5	22.2	5.1	8.5	7.7	6.6	6.9	7.0
Fellowship program	18.0	15.3	16.5	5.1	5.6	5.7	5.6	6.1	7.0
Challenge [5]	53.5	14.6	13.8	9.9	9.9	9.9	9.9	10.8	11.9
Public programs	25.1	25.4	25.8	12.5	12.6	11.1	12.2	11.8	16.3
Preservation and access	(X)	17.5	22.2	18.3	18.2	18.4	18.2	20.7	19.2

-Represents zero. X Not applicable. [1] Includes other funds, shown separately. Excludes administrative funds. [2] Represents federal funds obligated only upon receipt or certification by Endowment of matching nonfederal gifts. [3] Includes obligations for new grants, supplemental awards on previous years' grants, and program contracts. [4] Beginning with 1997 data, the grantmaking structure changed from discipline-based categories to thematic ones. [5] Program designed to stimulate new sources and higher levels of giving to institutions for the purpose of guaranteeing long-term stability and financial independence. Program usually requires a match of at least 3 private dollars to each federal dollar. Funds for challenge grants are not allocated by program area because they are awarded on a grant-by-grant basis.

Source: U.S. National Endowment for the Arts, *Annual Report;* and U.S. National Endowment for the Humanities, *Annual Report.*

No. 1237. Attendance Rates for Various Arts Activities: 2002

[In percent. For persons 18 years old and over. Represents attendance at least once in the prior 12 months. Excludes elementary and high school performances. Based on the 2002 household survey Public Participation in the Arts. Data are subject to sampling error; see source. See also Tables 1239 and 1240]

Item	Jazz performance	Classical music performance	Opera	Musical play	Non-musical play	Ballet	Art museum	Historic parks	Arts/ craft fairs
Total	11	12	3	17	12	4	27	32	33
Sex:									
Male	11	10	3	14	10	3	25	31	27
Female	11	13	4	20	14	5	28	33	39
Race:									
Hispanic	6	6	2	7	6	2	16	17	20
White	11	14	4	20	14	5	30	36	38
African American	13	5	1	10	7	2	15	18	10
Other	7	10	3	12	10	2	33	30	26
Age:									
18 to 24 years old	11	8	2	15	11	3	24	28	29
25 to 34 years old	11	9	3	15	11	4	27	33	34
35 to 44 years old	13	11	3	19	13	5	27	36	37
45 to 54 years old	14	15	4	19	15	5	33	38	39
55 to 64 years old	9	16	4	20	14	3	28	32	35
65 to 74 years old	8	13	4	17	13	3	23	24	31
75 years old and older	4	10	2	10	5	2	13	13	16
Education:									
Grade school	1	2	-	2	1	-	5	6	8
Some high school	3	2	1	4	4	1	8	11	14
High school graduate	5	5	1	9	6	1	14	20	26
Some college	12	12	3	19	13	4	29	37	38
College graduate	19	22	6	30	23	7	47	51	49
Graduate school	24	34	11	38	32	13	59	57	52

- Represents or rounds to zero.

Source: U.S. National Endowment for the Arts, 2003. *Survey of Public Participation in the Arts, 2002.*

No. 1238. Public School Supplemental Arts Education Programs by School Characteristic: 1998-99

[In percent. For activities during 1998-99 school year. Based on survey of school principals, during the 1999-2000 school year. For details, see source]

School characteristic	Public elementary schools				Public secondary schools			
	Field trips to arts performances	Field trips to art galleries or museums	Visiting artist(s)	Artist(s) in-residence	Field trips to arts performances	Field trips to art galleries or museums	Visiting artist(s)	Artist(s) in-residence
All schools	77	65	38	22	69	68	34	18
Enrollment size: [1]								
Less than 300	67	60	32	18	(NA)	(NA)	(NA)	(NA)
300 to 599	79	65	40	21	(NA)	(NA)	(NA)	(NA)
600 or more	86	70	41	28	(NA)	(NA)	(NA)	(NA)
Less than 400	(NA)	(NA)	(NA)	(NA)	65	64	33	15
400 to 999	(NA)	(NA)	(NA)	(NA)	69	64	32	21
1,000 or more	(NA)	(NA)	(NA)	(NA)	77	82	38	18
Region: [2]								
Northeast	79	73	47	31	78	80	37	33
Southeast	82	57	37	17	67	63	33	14
Central	74	61	35	23	71	67	34	16
West	77	67	34	19	64	68	33	15
Percent minority enrollment:								
5 percent or less	70	58	33	17	71	72	32	20
6 to 20 percent	79	69	39	25	71	67	38	18
21 to 50 percent	87	64	40	22	64	70	36	19
More than 50 percent	75	68	38	24	72	66	28	15
Percent of students eligible for free or reduced-price lunch:								
Less than 35 percent	79	71	41	26	74	74	34	19
35 to 49 percent	82	62	34	17	67	62	36	26
50 to 74 percent	79	56	40	20	61	60	34	15
75 percent or more	72	65	35	21	63	68	28	14

NA Not available. [1] As of October 1, 1999. [2] For composition of regions, see map, inside front cover.

Source: U.S. National Center for Education Statistics, *Arts Education in Public Elementary and Secondary Schools: 1999-2000*, NCES 2002-131.

No. 1239. Participation in Various Leisure Activities: 2002

[In percent, except as indicated (205.9 represents 205,900,000). Covers activities engaged in at least once in the prior 12 months. See headnote, Table 1237. See also Table 1240]

Item	Adult population (mil.)	Attendance at—			Participation in—			
		Movies	Sports events	Amusement park	Exercise program	Playing sports	Charity work	Home improvement/ repair	Gardening
Total	205.9	60	35	42	55	30	29	42	47
Sex:									
Male	98.7	60	41	40	55	39	26	46	37
Female	107.2	61	29	43	55	23	32	39	57
Race:									
Hispanic	22.7	53	26	39	40	22	15	28	35
White	150.1	63	38	43	59	33	33	48	52
African American	23.7	49	27	37	46	23	23	26	30
Other	9.5	58	22	44	50	27	23	34	41
Age:									
18 to 24 years old	26.8	83	46	58	61	49	25	21	21
25 to 34 years old	36.9	73	42	56	60	40	26	41	41
35 to 44 years old	44.2	68	42	53	60	37	33	53	52
45 to 54 years old	39.0	60	36	37	59	29	33	55	55
55 to 64 years old	25.9	47	26	27	48	16	28	45	57
65 to 74 years old	17.6	32	20	18	47	14	29	38	57
75 years old and over	15.5	20	11	10	31	6	21	22	48
Education:									
Grade school	11.6	20	9	17	21	7	8	20	33
Some high school	20.1	39	17	31	33	17	13	25	31
High school graduate	63.8	52	28	38	46	23	20	36	44
Some college	56.9	69	40	49	62	35	33	47	50
College graduate	36.1	77	51	50	73	45	43	56	56
Graduate school	17.4	78	48	44	77	44	53	62	63
Income:									
$9,999 or less	14.4	39	17	30	37	15	16	20	32
$10,000 to $19,999	22.7	42	20	31	42	19	19	24	39
$20,000 to $29,999	25.0	48	23	35	45	21	21	28	41
$30,000 to $39,999	24.2	58	30	39	53	27	27	42	47
$40,000 to $49,999	17.6	63	35	43	55	29	29	46	49
$50,000 to $74,999	34.7	69	45	50	63	36	35	54	54
$75,000 or More	45.8	79	53	54	73	48	42	61	56
Not Reported	21.5	51	28	31	45	23	23	34	43

Source: U.S. National Endowment for the Arts. *Survey of Public Participation in the Arts 2002.*

No. 1240. Participation in Various Arts Activities: 2002

[In percent. Covers activities engaged in at least once in the prior 12 months. See headnote in Tables 1237 and 1239]

Item	Playing classical music	Other dancing[1]	Drawing	Pottery work[2]	Weaving	Photography[3]	Creative writing	Buying art work	Singing in groups
Total	2	4	9	7	16	12	7	30	5
Sex:									
Male	2	3	6	5	2	11	6	30	4
Female	2	5	11	9	29	12	8	29	6
Race:									
Hispanic	1	4	7	5	13	7	4	38	3
White	2	4	9	8	18	13	8	29	5
African American	-	4	6	4	9	8	7	36	9
Other	2	6	7	7	15	12	5	26	4
Age:									
18 to 24 years old	3	6	15	9	10	13	13	41	5
25 to 34 years old	1	5	10	8	13	12	8	39	4
35 to 44 years old	2	4	8	7	15	14	7	31	5
45 to 54 years old	3	4	8	8	19	12	7	28	5
55 to 64 years old	2	3	7	6	19	11	5	26	6
65 to 74 years old	1	4	5	5	21	8	4	24	5
75 years old and older	1	3	3	2	18	4	4	11	4
Education:									
Grade school	-	1	2	2	12	2	2	23	1
Some high school	-	4	5	4	11	5	3	24	3
High school graduate	1	3	6	6	15	8	4	23	3
Some college	2	6	12	9	18	13	9	28	6
College graduate	4	5	11	8	17	17	11	31	6
Graduate school	5	6	11	7	18	20	13	34	7
Income:									
$9,999 or less	2	3	7	7	16	7	8	23	3
$10,000 to $19,999	1	3	7	6	18	7	6	22	5
$20,000 to $29,999	1	5	7	6	16	7	6	27	4
$30,000 to $39,999	2	5	10	7	17	11	8	27	6
$40,000 to $49,999	3	4	9	7	18	14	7	24	5
$50,000 to $74,999	3	5	8	8	17	13	7	31	6
$75,000 or More	2	4	11	8	15	17	9	34	5
Not Reported	1	5	7	5	12	9	6	26	4

-Represents or rounds to zero. [1] Dancing other than ballet (e.g. folk and tap). [2] Includes ceramics, jewelry, leatherwork, and metalwork. [3] Includes making movies or video as an artistic activity.

Source: U.S. National Endowment for the Arts. *Survey of Public Participation in the Arts 2002*, 2003

No. 1241. Retail Sales and Household Participation in Lawn and Garden Activities: 1998 to 2002

[For calendar year. (30,188 represents $30,188,000,000). Based on national household sample survey conducted by the Gallup Organization. Subject to sampling variability; see source]

Activity	Retail sales (mil. dol.) 1998	1999	2000	2001	2002	Percent households engaged in activity 1998	1999	2000	2001	2002
Total	30,188	33,519	33,404	37,734	39,635	65	64	72	80	79
Lawn care	8,543	8,986	9,794	12,672	11,963	47	43	50	56	55
Indoor houseplants	1,159	1,270	1,332	1,784	2,128	29	32	39	46	44
Flower gardening	3,965	3,976	4,167	3,926	3,131	39	45	45	43	41
Insect control	1,671	1,214	1,232	2,058	2,281	22	23	27	33	32
Shrub care	1,635	1,376	1,429	1,298	1,072	25	29	31	30	27
Vegetable gardening	2,006	2,595	2,169	1,535	1,270	24	29	27	25	25
Tree care	1,733	1,732	1,872	2,121	2,790	18	20	23	25	26
Landscaping	6,435	8,585	6,809	6,310	8,854	22	25	30	37	34
Flower bulbs	579	657	912	1,188	1,191	21	23	28	31	29
Fruit trees	301	264	284	748	695	10	13	13	15	12
Container gardening	783	1,020	1,257	1,202	1,362	11	15	18	22	23
Raising transplants[1]	160	302	334	291	262	7	12	11	12	12
Herb gardening	146	185	204	413	444	7	11	12	14	15
Growing berries	82	87	147	227	171	5	7	8	8	7
Ornamental gardening	333	464	519	756	580	5	6	8	9	8
Water gardening	659	806	943	1,205	1,441	4	7	10	13	14

[1] Starting plants in advance of planting in ground.

Source: The National Gardening Association, Burlington, VT, *National Gardening Survey*, annual (copyright).

No. 1242. Household Pet Ownership: 2001

[Based on a sample survey of 80,000 households in 2001; for details, see source]

Item	Unit	Dog	Cat	Pet bird	Horse
Percent of households owning companion pets [1]	Percent	36.1	31.6	4.6	1.7
Average number owned	Number	1.6	2.1	2.1	3.0
Households obtaining veterinary care [2]	Percent	85.0	66.8	12.9	56.7
Average visits per household per year	Number	2.8	1.9	0.3	2.2
PERCENT OF HOUSEHOLDS OWNING PETS					
Annual household income:					
Under $20,000	Percent	29.7	28.1	5.1	1.0
$20,000 to $34,999	Percent	33.9	30.9	4.5	1.3
$35,000 to $54,999	Percent	37.9	32.2	4.8	2.0
$55,000 to $84,999	Percent	40.5	34.3	4.4	2.1
$85,000 and over	Percent	39.7	33.7	4.2	2.1
Household size: [1]					
One person	Percent	20.8	23.5	2.8	0.7
Two persons	Percent	34.3	31.3	4.0	1.6
Three persons	Percent	46.2	37.4	5.9	2.2
Four persons	Percent	50.6	38.2	6.3	2.3
Five or more persons	Percent	53.0	39.7	8.3	3.2

[1] As of December 31, 2001. [2] During 2001.
Source: American Veterinary Medical Association, Schaumburg, IL, *U.S. Pet Ownership and Demographics Sourcebook, 2002* (copyright).

No. 1243. Adult Attendance at Sports Events: 2002

[In thousands (8,827 represents 8,827,000), except percent. For fall 2002. Based on survey and subject to sampling error; see source]

Event	Attend one or more times a month Number	Percent	Attend less than once a month Number	Percent	Event	Attend one or more times a month Number	Percent	Attend less than once a month Number	Percent
Baseball	8,827	4.3	17,873	8.7	Golf	1,899	0.9	4,397	2.2
Basketball:					High school sports	11,662	5.7	8,335	4.1
College games	4,138	2.0	6,396	3.1	Horse racing:				
Professional games	3,588	1.8	8,779	4.3	Flats, runners	979	0.5	3,381	1.7
Bowling	1,604	0.8	2,733	1.3	Trotters/harness	446	0.2	2,374	1.2
Boxing	1,482	0.7	2,449	1.2	Ice hockey	2,307	1.1	7,357	3.6
Equestrian events	514	0.3	2,880	1.4	Motorcycle racing	913	0.5	2,971	1.5
Figure skating	621	0.3	2,770	1.4	Pro beach volleyball	397	0.2	2,061	1.0
Fishing tournaments	819	0.4	2,416	1.2	Rodeo	1,193	0.6	3,890	1.9
Football:					Soccer	2,740	1.3	3,570	1.7
College games	6,225	3.0	8,073	3.9	Tennis	1,060	0.5	3,071	1.5
Monday night professional games	1,917	0.9	3,494	1.7	Truck and tractor pull/mud racing	851	0.4	3,289	1.6
Weekend professional games	3,541	1.7	8,282	4.0	Wrestling—professional	1,282	0.6	3,098	1.5

Source: Mediamark Research, Inc., New York, NY *Top-line Reports* (copyright). Internet site <http://www.mediamark.com/mri/docs/TopLineReports.html>.

No. 1244. Adult Participation in Selected Leisure Activities by Frequency: 2002

[In thousands (30,254 represents 30,254,000), except percent. For fall 2002. Based on sample and subject to sampling error; see source]

Activity	Participated in the last 12 months Number	Percent	Two or more times a week Number	Percent	Once a week Number	Percent	Two to three times a month Number	Percent	Once a month Number	Percent
Attend music performances [1]	30,254	14.8	452	0.2	585	0.3	1,517	0.7	3,464	1.7
Baking	36,551	17.8	7,098	3.5	6,393	3.1	7,459	3.6	5,154	2.5
Barbecueing	66,686	32.5	10,094	4.9	10,005	4.9	16,031	7.8	9,298	4.5
Board games	33,582	16.4	2,730	1.3	2,978	1.5	5,990	2.9	5,671	2.8
Cooking for fun	33,746	16.5	11,522	5.6	5,351	2.6	4,809	2.4	3,664	1.8
Crossword puzzles	32,178	15.7	13,771	6.7	4,237	2.1	3,216	1.6	2,021	1.0
Dining out	103,148	50.3	21,358	10.4	24,671	12.0	24,215	11.8	12,307	6.0
Entertain friends or relatives at home	80,642	39.3	7,010	3.4	9,926	4.8	19,324	9.4	16,433	8.0
Go to bars/night clubs	43,415	21.2	3,288	1.6	5,075	2.5	7,212	3.5	7,372	3.6
Go to beach	51,413	25.1	3,385	1.7	2,457	1.2	4,812	2.4	4,845	2.4
Go to live theater	31,530	15.4	148	0.1	324	0.2	1,379	0.7	3,408	1.7
Play cards	43,246	21.1	5,612	2.7	5,221	2.6	6,382	3.1	6,324	3.1
Reading books	81,538	39.8	44,462	21.7	8,174	4.0	7,067	3.5	5,643	2.8
Surf the Net	55,361	27.0	34,302	16.7	6,981	3.4	4,754	2.3	1,687	0.8

[1] Excluding country and rock.
Source: Mediamark Research, Inc., New York, NY, *Top-line Reports* (copyright). Internet site <http://www.mediamark.com/mri/docs/TopLineReports.html>.

No. 1245. Selected Spectator Sports: 1985 to 2001

[47,742 represents 47,742,000]

Sport	Unit	1985	1990	1995	1997	1998	1999	2000	2001
Baseball, major leagues: [1]									
Attendance	1,000	47,742	55,512	51,288	64,921	71,930	71,558	74,339	73,881
Regular season	1,000	46,824	54,824	50,469	63,168	70,372	70,139	72,748	72,267
National League	1,000	22,292	24,492	25,110	31,885	38,424	38,323	39,851	39,558
American League	1,000	24,532	30,332	25,359	31,283	31,948	31,817	32,898	32,709
Playoffs [2]	1,000	591	479	533	1,349	1,314	1,202	1,314	1,247
World Series	1,000	327	209	286	404	243	216	277	366
Players' salaries: [3]									
Average	$1,000	371	598	1,111	1,337	1,399	1,607	1,896	2,139
Basketball: [4] [5]									
NCAA—Men's college:									
Teams	Number	753	767	868	865	895	926	932	937
Attendance	1,000	26,584	28,741	28,548	27,738	28,032	28,505	29,025	28,949
NCAA—Women's college:									
Teams	Number	746	782	864	879	911	940	956	958
Attendance	1,000	2,072	2,777	4,962	6,734	7,387	8,010	8,698	8,825
Pro: [6]									
Teams	Number	23	27	27	29	29	29	29	29
Attendance, total [7]	1,000	11,534	18,586	19,883	21,677	21,801	13,450	21,503	21,436
Regular season	1,000	10,506	17,369	18,516	20,305	20,373	12,135	20,059	19,956
Average per game	Number	11,141	15,690	16,727	17,077	17,135	16,738	16,870	16,784
Playoffs	1,000	985	1,203	1,347	1,352	1,409	1,315	1,427	1,460
Average	Number	14,479	16,704	18,457	18,774	19,851	19,926	19,202	20,565
All-Star game	1,000	43.1	14.8	18.8	20.6	18.3	(X)	18.3	20.4
Players' salaries:									
Average	$1,000	325	750	1,900	2,200	3,000	3,000	3,600	(NA)
Football:									
NCAA College: [5]									
Teams	Number	509	533	565	581	595	601	606	608
Attendance	1,000	34,952	35,330	35,638	36,858	37,491	39,483	39,059	40,481
National Football League: [8]									
Teams	Number	28	28	30	31	31	32	31	31
Attendance, total [9]	1,000	14,058	17,666	19,203	19,050	19,742	20,763	20,954	20,590
Regular season	1,000	13,345	13,960	15,044	14,967	15,365	16,207	16,387	16,166
Average per game	Number	59,567	62,321	62,682	62,364	64,020	65,349	66,078	65,187
Postseason games [10]	1,000	711	848	(NA)	(NA)	823	794	809	767
Players' salaries: [11]									
Average	$1,000	217	354	584	585	655	708	787	986
Median base salary	$1,000	160	275	301	302	326	400	441	501
National Hockey League: [12]									
Regular season attendance	1,000	11,634	12,580	9,234	17,641	17,265	17,152	18,800	20,373
Playoffs attendance	1,000	1,108	1,356	1,329	1,495	1,507	1,472	1,525	1,584
Horseracing: [13] [14]									
Racing days	Number	13,745	13,841	13,243	11,958	11,380	11,398	11,348	(NA)
Attendance	1,000	73,346	63,803	38,934	41,846	37,728	(NA)	(NA)	(NA)
Pari-mutuel turnover	Mil. dol	12,222	7,162	14,592	15,220	15,561	15,828	16,040	(NA)
Revenue to government	Mil. dol	625	624	456	422	432	392	368	(NA)
Greyhound: [13]									
Total performances	Number	9,590	14,915	16,110	14,557	14,943	14,455	14,403	(NA)
Attendance	1,000	23,853	28,660	(NA)	14,306	(NA)	(NA)	(NA)	(NA)
Pari-mutuel turnover	Mil. dol	2,702	3,422	2,730	2,291	2,237	2,130	2,054	(NA)
Revenue to government	Mil. dol	201	235	157	114	109	101	98	(NA)
Jai alai: [13]									
Total performances	Number	2,736	3,620	2,748	2,648	2,600	2,119	2,034	(NA)
Games played	Number	32,260	(NA)	37,052	(NA)	37,175	28,706	27,461	(NA)
Attendance	1,000	4,722	5,329	3,208	2,125	(NA)	(NA)	(NA)	(NA)
Total handle	Mil. dol	664	546	296	251	153	119	1,959	(NA)
Revenue to government	Mil. dol	50	39	13	10	9	5	4	(NA)
Professional rodeo: [15]									
Rodeos	Number	617	754	739	729	703	700	688	668
Performances	Number	1,887	2,159	2,217	2,213	2,125	2,128	2,081	2,015
Members	Number	5,239	5,693	6,894	7,178	7,301	7,403	6,255	5,913
Permit-holders (rookies)	Number	2,534	3,290	3,835	4,197	4,117	3,511	3,249	2,544
Total prize money	Mil. dol	15.1	18.2	24.5	28.0	29.9	31.1	32.3	33.1

NA Not available. X Not applicable. [1] Source: Major League Baseball (previously, The National League of Professional Baseball Clubs), New York, NY, *National League Green Book;* and The American League of Professional Baseball Clubs, New York, NY, *American League Red Book.* [2] Beginning 1997, two rounds of playoffs were played. Prior years had one round. [3] Source: Major League Baseball Players Association, New York, NY. [4] Season ending in year shown. [5] Source: National Collegiate Athletic Assn., Indianapolis, IN (copyright). For women's attendance total, excludes double-headers with men's teams. [6] Source: National Basketball Assn., New York, NY. For season ending in year shown. [7] Includes All-Star game, not shown separately. [8] Source: National Football League, New York, NY. [9] Beginning 1987 includes preseason attendance, not shown separately. [10] Includes Pro Bowl, a nonchampionship game and Super Bowl. [11] Source: National Football League Players Association, Washington, DC. [12] For season ending in year shown. Source: National Hockey League, Montreal, Quebec. [13] Source: Association of Racing Commissioners International, Inc., Lexington, KY. [14] Includes thoroughbred, harness, quarter horse, and fairs. [15] Source: Professional Rodeo Cowboys Association, Colorado Springs, CO, *Official Professional Rodeo Media Guide,* annual (copyright).

Source: Compiled from sources listed in footnotes.

No. 1246. Selected Recreational Activities: 1985 to 2001

[41 represents 41,000,000]

Activity	Unit	1985	1990	1995	1997	1998	1999	2000	2001
Softball, amateur: [1]									
Total participants [2]	Million	41	41	42	41	40	35	31	31
Youth participants	1,000	712	1,100	1,350	1,440	1,400	1,411	1,370	1,355
Adult teams [3]	1,000	152	188	187	178	166	163	155	149
Youth teams [3]	1,000	31	46	74	80	81	83	81	80
Golfers (one round or more) [4] [5]	1,000	17,520	27,800	25,000	26,474	26,427	26,446	26,738	27,600
Golf rounds played [4] [5]	1,000	414,777	502,000	490,200	547,200	528,500	564,100	587,100	552,000
Golf facilities [4]	Number	12,346	12,846	14,074	14,602	14,900	15,195	15,489	15,689
Classification:									
Private	Number	4,861	4,810	4,324	4,257	4,251	4,285	4,290	4,313
Daily fee	Number	5,573	6,024	7,491	7,984	8,247	8,470	8,761	8,972
Municipal	Number	1,912	2,012	2,259	2,361	2,402	2,440	2,438	2,404
Tennis: [6]									
Players	1,000	13,000	21,000	17,820	19,500	(NA)	20,000	22,900	22,000
Courts	1,000	220	220	240	245	(NA)	(NA)	(NA)	(NA)
Indoor	1,000	14	14	15	15	(NA)	(NA)	(NA)	(NA)
Tenpin bowling: [7]									
Participants, total	Million	67.0	71.0	79.0	91.0	91.0	91.0	53.8	55.4
Male	Million	32.0	35.4	36.3	41.8	41.8	41.8	27.9	28.2
Female	Million	35.0	35.6	42.6	49.2	49.2	49.2	26.9	27.2
Establishments	Number	8,275	7,611	7,049	6,688	6,398	6,398	6,247	6,022
Lanes	1,000	155	148	139	133	128	128	125	123
Membership, total [8]	1,000	8,064	6,588	4,925	4,405	4,156	4,156	3,756	3,553
American Bowling Congress	1,000	3,657	3,036	2,370	2,135	2,027	2,027	1,866	1,767
Women's Bowling Congress	1,000	3,714	2,859	2,036	1,798	1,678	1,678	1,481	1,373
Young American Bowling Alliance [9]	1,000	693	693	519	472	451	451	409	413
Motion picture screens [10]	1,000	21	24	28	32	35	38	38	37
Indoor	1,000	18	23	27	31	34	37	37	37
Drive-in	1,000	3	1	1	1	1	1	1	1
Receipts, box office	Mil. dol.	3,749	5,022	5,494	6,366	6,949	7,448	7,661	8,413
Admission, average price	Dollars	3.55	4.23	4.35	4.59	4.69	5.08	5.39	5.66
Attendance	Million	1,056	1,189	1,263	1,388	1,481	1,465	1,421	1,487
Boating: [11]									
Recreational boats owned	1,000	13,778	15,987	15,375	16,230	16,657	16,791	17,032	17,192
Retail expenditures on boating [12]	Mil. dol.	13,284	13,731	17,226	19,344	19,001	21,736	27,843	28,521
Retail units purchased:									
Total all boats [13]	1,000	675	525	664	610	576	585	577	882
Outboard boats	1,000	305	227	231	200	214	230	241	218
Inboard boats	1,000	17	15	12	12	18	19	24	22
Sterndrive boats	1,000	115	97	94	92	78	80	78	72
Jet boats	1,000	(NA)	(NA)	15	12	10	8	7	6
Personal watercraft	1,000	(NA)	(NA)	200	176	130	106	92	81
Sailboats	1,000	38	21	14	14	19	21	22	20
Canoes	1,000	79	75	98	104	108	121	112	106
Kayaks [14]	1,000	(NA)	(NA)	(NA)	(NA)	(NA)	(NA)	(NA)	357
Inflatable boats	1,000	34	27	(NA)	(NA)	(NA)	(NA)	(NA)	(NA)
Sailboard	1,000	50	42	(NA)	(NA)	(NA)	(NA)	(NA)	(NA)
Boat trailers	1,000	192	165	207	181	174	168	159	136
Outboard motors	1,000	392	352	317	302	314	332	349	299
Sterndrive and inboard engines	1,000	155	134	120	116	105	109	110	104

NA Not available. [1] Source: Amateur Softball Association, Oklahoma City, OK. [2] Amateur Softball Association teams and other amateur softball teams. [3] Amateur Softball Association teams only. [4] Source: National Golf Foundation, Jupiter, FL. [5] Prior to 1990, for persons 5 years of age and over; thereafter for persons 12 years of age and over. [6] Source: Tennis Industry Association, Hilton Head, SC. Players for persons 12 years old and over who played at least once. [7] For season ending in year shown. Persons 5 years old and over. Source: Bowling Headquarters, Greendale, WI. [8] Membership totals are for U.S., Canada and for U.S. military personnel worldwide. [9] Prior to 1985, represents American Jr. Bowling Congress and ABC/WIBC Collegiate Division. [10] Source: Motion Picture Association of America, Inc., Encino, CA. 1975 figures represent theaters. [11] Source: National Marine Manufacturers Association, Chicago, IL. (copyright). [12] Represents estimated expenditures for new and used boats, motors and engines, accessories, safety equipment, fuel, insurance, docking, maintenance, launching, storage, repairs, and other expenses. [13] 1985 through 1990 includes other boats, not shown separately. [14] Kayak category added in 2001.

Source: Compiled from sources listed in footnotes.

No. 1247. Participation in Selected Sports Activities: 2001

[In thousands (251,239 represents 251,239,000), except rank. For persons 7 years of age or older. Except as indicated, a participant plays a sport more than once in the year]

Activity	All persons Number	Rank	Sex Male	Sex Female	Age 7-11 years	Age 12-17 years	Age 18-24 years	Age 25-34 years	Age 35-44 years	Age 45-54 years	Age 55-64 years	Age 65 years and over	Household income (dol.) Under 15,000	15,000-24,999	25,000-34,999	35,000-49,999	50,000-74,999	75,000 and over
Total	251,239	(X)	122,222	129,016	20,262	23,782	27,188	37,063	44,692	38,640	24,549	35,062	32,344	27,625	33,015	44,321	53,001	60,932
SERIES I SPORTS [1]																		
Number participated in— [2]																		
Aerobic exercising [3]	24,251	13	6,499	17,752	769	1,755	4,262	6,347	5,208	3,326	1,447	1,137	1,956	1,667	2,444	3,866	5,265	9,052
Backpacking	14,509	17	8,775	5,734	1,959	1,824	2,298	3,273	3,146	1,328	483	198	1,562	1,281	2,136	2,840	3,503	3,187
Badminton	5,194	27	2,183	3,011	1,028	1,211	657	624	1,101	311	80	183	641	409	654	797	1,265	1,428
Baseball	14,868	16	11,550	3,318	4,654	4,095	1,535	1,627	1,490	838	287	342	1,190	814	1,772	2,948	3,929	4,214
Basketball	28,104	9	19,009	9,095	6,356	7,818	3,955	4,397	3,616	1,278	422	261	2,854	2,264	3,625	5,036	6,329	7,996
Bicycle riding [2]	39,004	7	21,826	17,178	9,753	7,255	2,833	5,447	6,833	3,468	1,759	1,656	2,954	3,182	4,927	6,759	9,270	11,912
Billiards	32,718	8	19,924	12,795	1,517	3,505	7,083	9,010	6,806	3,099	878	820	3,365	3,206	4,484	6,165	7,698	7,800
Bowling	40,302	5	21,223	19,079	5,330	5,893	6,806	8,597	7,205	3,649	1,265	1,558	3,779	3,759	4,516	7,965	9,551	10,732
Calisthenics [2]	10,942	23	5,199	5,743	1,393	2,293	1,483	2,052	1,906	879	339	597	905	700	1,349	1,909	2,270	3,809
Camping [4]	45,534	3	24,153	21,381	5,984	6,458	5,141	7,713	10,380	5,953	2,284	1,621	3,739	4,188	5,754	8,917	12,287	10,648
Exercise walking [2]	71,219	1	26,403	44,816	2,417	3,550	6,936	12,332	14,692	13,616	8,237	9,438	8,046	6,445	8,568	11,971	15,906	20,282
Exercising with equipment [2]	43,028	4	20,513	22,514	752	3,592	6,539	9,357	9,378	6,667	3,600	3,141	2,482	2,859	4,243	7,257	10,552	15,634
Fishing—fresh water	39,077	6	27,152	11,925	5,124	4,480	4,265	7,057	7,881	5,343	2,924	2,004	3,714	4,190	5,343	7,933	9,802	8,095
Fishing—salt water	11,268	21	8,194	3,074	1,176	1,067	978	1,967	2,643	1,854	876	706	703	724	1,388	2,037	2,713	3,703
Football—tackle	8,631	25	7,856	775	1,460	3,593	1,651	680	566	295	169	218	973	711	1,312	1,602	2,100	1,933
Football—touch	8,900	24	7,073	1,827	1,938	2,614	1,685	1,194	930	345	81	111	889	839	1,189	1,463	2,232	2,289
Golf	26,637	10	21,340	5,297	1,011	2,264	3,022	5,197	5,906	4,754	2,033	2,450	1,126	1,357	2,629	4,051	6,881	10,594
Hiking	26,101	11	13,709	12,392	2,577	3,008	3,094	5,050	6,007	3,682	1,444	1,239	2,302	2,442	2,682	4,057	6,456	8,161
Hunting with firearms	19,173	15	16,729	2,444	1,086	1,896	2,838	3,686	4,339	2,836	1,621	870	1,370	2,447	3,037	3,940	4,613	3,766
Martial arts	5,132	28	3,276	1,857	1,558	975	910	626	744	192	100	27	756	473	617	721	1,243	1,322
Racquetball	3,385	29	2,368	1,017	94	264	855	983	605	397	98	88	378	231	307	640	467	1,361
Running/jogging [2]	24,537	12	13,426	11,111	1,607	4,446	4,725	5,614	4,372	2,456	768	550	1,725	2,179	2,408	4,001	5,341	8,883
Soccer	13,886	18	8,036	5,850	5,867	1,811	1,312	1,115	972	447	146	196	939	742	1,631	2,143	3,623	4,808
Softball [2]	13,213	19	6,772	6,441	2,486	2,286	1,788	2,925	2,384	795	246	303	974	923	1,651	2,754	3,683	3,228
Swimming [2]	54,788	2	25,216	29,572	9,283	8,933	6,393	7,549	9,934	6,446	2,892	3,357	3,646	4,971	6,369	9,445	13,620	16,736
Table tennis	8,370	26	5,085	3,285	1,045	1,694	1,463	1,126	1,580	887	276	299	846	502	736	1,170	2,107	3,008
Tennis	10,911	23	5,389	5,523	728	1,963	1,487	2,256	2,157	1,217	535	569	699	799	907	1,467	2,396	4,644
Volleyball	12,027	20	5,551	6,476	1,309	3,319	2,254	2,074	2,045	653	212	160	1,292	1,054	1,295	2,211	2,664	3,511
Weightlifting	21,229	14	14,076	7,153	378	3,459	4,557	5,448	4,204	2,145	686	353	1,405	1,478	2,312	3,894	4,950	7,191

See footnotes at end of table.

778 Arts, Entertainment, and Recreation

U.S. Census Bureau, Statistical Abstract of the United States: 2003

Participation in Various Sports Activities: 2001

[In thousands (251,238 represents 251,238,000), except rank. For persons 7 years old and over. Based on a sampling of 15,000 households.]

Activity	All persons Number	Rank	Sex Male	Sex Female	Age 7-11 years	Age 12-17 years	Age 18-24 years	Age 25-34 years	Age 35-44 years	Age 45-54 years	Age 55-64 years	Age 65 years and over	Household income (dol.) Under 15,000	15,000-24,999	25,000-34,999	35,000-49,999	50,000-74,999	75,000 and over
Total	251,238	(X)	122,221	129,017	20,262	23,783	27,187	37,061	44,692	38,642	24,550	35,061	30,972	28,295	32,776	44,957	54,061	60,177
SERIES II SPORTS[5]																		
Number participating in—																		
Archery (target)	4,706	20	3,616	1,090	552	889	520	895	855	331	173	93	395	373	621	972	1,010	1,336
Boating, motor/power	22,613	2	13,124	9,489	1,934	2,415	2,893	3,918	4,946	3,579	1,794	1,134	1,025	1,371	2,564	3,855	5,801	7,997
Canoeing	6,808	11	3,835	2,973	798	1,128	858	1,211	1,404	904	329	175	401	533	797	1,214	1,727	2,135
Dart throwing	16,932	8	10,643	6,290	1,185	2,211	3,179	4,734	3,534	1,415	464	210	1,701	1,662	2,983	3,321	3,478	3,787
Hunting with bow and arrow	4,723	19	4,328	395	117	495	550	1,174	1,258	599	328	202	350	400	646	1,166	1,215	947
Ice hockey	2,193	26	1,774	418	384	441	338	498	328	96	26	81	108	170	141	385	535	854
Ice/figure skating	5,344	17	2,007	3,337	1,528	1,321	574	716	673	322	95	116	194	189	669	817	1,564	1,911
Kayaking/rafting	3,530	21	1,935	1,594	428	544	475	609	813	403	152	105	183	219	559	521	762	1,286
Mountain biking-off road	6,301	12	4,319	1,982	530	1,195	824	1,812	1,189	479	145	126	714	682	733	1,223	1,314	1,636
Mountain biking-on road	14,037	6	7,720	6,317	1,957	1,835	1,963	3,568	2,913	1,172	456	174	1,286	912	1,718	2,810	3,498	3,814
Muzzleloading	2,976	22	2,686	290	33	236	392	554	787	496	325	154	207	324	430	727	620	668
Paintball games	5,556	15	4,741	816	568	2,018	1,404	851	423	203	65	24	382	360	623	1,254	1,360	1,576
Roller hockey	2,235	25	1,883	352	831	689	172	172	145	80	70	75	117	88	191	199	650	990
Roller skating/in-line wheels	19,225	3	9,135	10,090	7,108	5,059	1,870	2,475	2,005	400	170	137	1,284	1,252	2,035	3,553	5,195	5,906
Roller skating/traditional 2x2 wheel	7,651	10	3,145	4,506	3,123	1,413	502	1,020	985	366	137	105	822	679	1,178	1,375	2,116	1,482
Sailing	2,696	23	1,545	1,151	104	282	377	409	580	535	207	202	98	97	189	333	667	1,313
Scooter riding	12,675	4	7,122	5,553	7,427	3,425	222	608	526	222	110	136	698	865	1,282	2,447	3,570	3,813
Scuba (open water)	2,131	27	1,473	661	-	106	544	546	450	336	114	37	41	216	136	220	572	948
Skateboarding	9,623	8	7,702	1,921	4,512	3,961	491	256	194	63	61	83	722	643	973	1,897	2,452	2,936
Skiing—alpine	7,660	9	4,615	3,045	614	1,453	1,173	1,588	1,524	907	275	126	194	237	649	1,008	1,847	3,726
Skiing—cross country	2,337	24	1,168	1,169	222	186	360	346	553	399	166	104	115	131	242	282	603	965
Snorkeling	5,970	13	3,314	2,656	368	615	896	1,410	1,344	774	402	161	200	261	383	999	1,357	2,770
Snowboarding	5,343	18	3,867	1,476	960	1,640	1,410	824	247	147	110	4	394	460	636	725	1,447	1,680
Step aerobics	5,733	14	512	5,221	45	182	847	1,662	1,396	854	359	389	358	450	711	866	1,276	2,073
Target shooting	15,913	5	12,573	3,340	1,058	2,081	2,232	3,283	3,334	2,314	1,069	542	1,061	1,517	2,434	3,285	3,635	3,980
Water skiing	5,458	16	3,147	2,311	549	1,075	889	1,242	1,162	368	107	66	142	277	476	820	1,496	2,246
Wind surfing	449	28	244	205	-	60	131	53	56	4	17	36	72	12	18	97	213
Work-out at club	26,476	1	12,531	13,945	362	1,251	5,316	6,754	5,774	3,749	1,761	1,508	1,165	1,578	2,855	4,339	6,208	10,331

- Represents or rounds to zero. X Not applicable. [1] Based on a sampling of 15,000 households. [2] Participant engaged in activity at least six times in the year. [3] Includes wilderness camping. [4] Vacation/overnight. [5] Based on a sampling of 20,000 households.

Source: National Sporting Goods Association, Mt. Prospect, IL, *Sports Participation in 2001: Series I and Series II* (copyright).

No. 1248. High School Students Engaged in Organized Physical Activity by Sex, Race, and Hispanic Origin: 2001

[In percent. For students in grades 9 to 12. Based on the Youth Risk Behavior Survey, a school-based survey and subject to sampling error; for details see source]

Characteristic	Enrolled in physical education class			Played on a sports team
	Total	Attended daily	Exercised 20 minutes or more per class [1]	
All students	51.7	32.2	83.4	55.2
Male	55.6	36.3	87.7	60.9
Grade 9	74.0	48.2	85.0	63.5
Grade 10	58.4	37.4	87.7	61.6
Grade 11	46.7	30.0	90.6	61.5
Grade 12	36.9	26.1	91.2	55.9
Female	48.0	28.4	78.8	49.9
Grade 9	73.4	49.3	78.9	56.7
Grade 10	49.9	26.1	80.3	50.8
Grade 11	31.6	15.6	79.1	47.7
Grade 12	26.0	14.7	75.0	41.4
White, non-Hispanic	48.3	29.5	85.2	57.4
Male	52.0	33.8	90.3	61.7
Female	44.9	25.6	79.7	53.3
Black, non-Hispanic	60.5	40.8	76.4	52.7
Male	67.4	46.3	81.0	64.4
Female	54.0	35.6	71.0	41.6
Hispanic	58.4	38.7	81.9	48.8
Male	61.6	41.9	84.6	57.8
Female	55.3	35.7	79.2	40.1

[1] For students enrolled in physical education classes.

Source: U.S. Centers for Disease Control and Prevention, Atlanta, GA, *Youth Risk Behavior Surveillance—United States, 2001, Morbidity and Mortality Weekly Report*, Vol. 51, No. SS-4, June 28, 2002.

No. 1249. Participation in High School Athletic Programs by Sex: 1972 to 2002

[Data based on number of state associations reporting and may underrepresent the number of schools with and participants in athletic programs]

Year	Participants [1]		Sex and sport	Most popular sports, 2001-2002 [2]	
	Males	Females		Schools	Participants
1972-73	3,770,621	817,073	**MALES**		
1973-74	4,070,125	1,300,169			
1975-76	4,109,021	1,645,039	Football (11-player)	13,509	1,023,712
1977-78	4,367,442	2,083,040	Basketball	17,135	540,597
1978-79	3,709,512	1,854,400	Track & field (outdoor)	15,261	494,022
1979-80	3,517,829	1,750,264	Baseball	14,924	451,674
1980-81	3,503,124	1,853,789	Soccer	9,903	339,101
1981-82	3,409,081	1,810,671	Wrestling	9,578	244,637
1982-83	3,355,558	1,779,972	Cross country	12,456	190,993
1983-84	3,303,599	1,747,346	Golf	13,031	163,299
1984-85	3,354,284	1,757,884	Tennis	9,365	139,483
			Swimming & diving	5,540	90,698
1985-86	3,344,275	1,807,121			
1986-87	3,364,082	1,836,356	**FEMALE**		
1987-88	3,425,777	1,849,684			
1988-89	3,416,844	1,839,352	Basketball	16,851	456,169
1989-90	3,398,192	1,858,659	Track & field (outdoor)	15,151	415,677
1990-91	3,406,355	1,892,316	Volleyball	14,083	395,124
1991-92	3,429,853	1,940,801	Softball (fast pitch)	13,807	355,960
1992-93	3,416,389	1,997,489	Soccer	9,186	295,265
1993-94	3,472,967	2,130,315	Cross country	11,976	160,178
1994-95	3,536,359	2,240,461	Tennis	9,378	160,114
1995-96	3,634,052	2,367,936	Swimming & diving	5,935	141,218
1996-97	3,706,225	2,474,043	Competitive spirit squads	4,245	94,635
1997-98	3,763,120	2,570,333	Field hockey	1,646	60,737
1998-99	3,832,352	2,652,726			
1999-00	3,861,749	2,675,874			
2000-01	3,921,069	2,784,154			
2001-02	3,960,517	2,806,998			

[1] A participant is counted in the number of sports participated in.   [2] Ten most popular sports for each sex in terms of number of participants.

Source: National Federation of State High School Associations, Indianapolis, IN, *The 2001-2002 High School Athletics Participation Survey* (copyright).

No. 1250. Participation in NCAA Sports: 2001-2002

Sport	Males Teams	Males Athletes	Males Average squad	Females Teams	Females Athletes	Females Average squad
Total [1]	8,151	212,140	(X)	8,920	155,513	(X)
Baseball	866	26,343	30.4	(X)	(X)	(X)
Basketball	990	15,883	16.0	1,017	14,524	14.3
Bowling [2]	2	7	3.5	39	325	8.3
Cross country	858	10,840	12.6	928	12,008	12.9
Equestrian [2]	8	87	10.9	46	1,031	22.4
Fencing [3]	38	586	15.4	46	633	13.8
Field hockey	(X)	(X)	(X)	252	5,296	21.0
Football	617	58,090	94.1	(X)	(X)	(X)
Golf	754	7,631	10.1	451	3,447	7.6
Gymnastics	23	371	16.1	89	1,440	16.2
Ice hockey [4]	134	3,708	27.7	69	1,433	20.8
Lacrosse	211	6,551	31.0	249	5,326	21.4
Rifle [3]	43	227	5.3	46	240	5.2
Rowing [5]	57	1,557	27.3	140	6,191	44.2
Sailing [2]	24	285	11.9	(X)	(X)	(X)
Skiing [3]	41	539	13.1	45	496	11.0
Soccer	734	18,559	25.3	868	19,467	22.4
Softball	(X)	(X)	(X)	895	15,514	17.3
Squash [2]	22	306	13.9	27	380	14.1
Swimming/diving	388	7,307	18.8	478	10,279	21.5
Synchronized swimming [4]	(X)	(X)	(X)	9	101	11.2
Tennis	770	7,441	9.7	898	8,378	9.3
Track, indoor	553	17,483	31.6	595	16,334	27.5
Track, outdoor	657	20,382	31.0	697	18,433	26.4
Volleyball	81	1,115	13.8	974	13,107	13.5
Water polo	48	891	18.6	55	1,055	19.2
Wrestling	231	5,943	25.7	(X)	(X)	(X)

X Not applicable. [1] Includes other sports, not shown separately. [2] Sport recognized by the NCAA but does not have an NCAA championship. [3] Co-ed championship sport. [4] Sport recognized by the NCAA but does not have an NCAA championship for women. [5] Sport recognized by the NCAA but does not have an NCAA championship for men.
Source: The National Collegiate Athletic Association (NCAA), Indianapolis, IN, *2001-02 Participation Study* (copyright).

No. 1251. Participants in Wildlife Related Recreation Activities: 2001

[Preliminary. In thousands (37,805 represents 37,805,000). For persons 16 years old and over engaging in activity at least once in 2001. Based on survey and subject to sampling error; see source for details]

Participant	Number	Days of participation	Trips	Participant	Number	Days of participation
Total sportsmen [1]	37,805	785,762	636,787	Wildlife watchers [1]	66,105	(X)
Total anglers	34,071	557,394	436,662	Nonresidential [2]	21,823	372,006
Freshwater	28,439	466,984	365,076	Observe wildlife	20,080	295,345
Excluding Great Lakes	27,913	443,247	349,188	Photograph wildlife	9,427	76,324
Great Lakes	1,847	23,138	15,888	Feed wildlife	7,077	103,307
Saltwater	9,051	90,838	71,586	Residential [3]	62,928	(X)
Total hunters	13,034	228,368	200,125	Observe wildlife	42,111	(X)
Big game	10,911	153,191	114,445	Photograph wildlife	13,937	(X)
Small game	5,434	60,142	46,450	Feed wildlife	53,988	(X)
Migratory birds	2,956	29,310	24,155	Visit public parks	10,981	(X)
Other animals	1,047	19,207	15,074	Maintain plantings or natural areas	13,072	(X)

X Not applicable. [1] Detail does not add to total due to multiple responses and nonresponse. [2] Persons taking a trip of at least 1 mile for activity. [3] Activity within 1 mile of home.

No. 1252. Expenditures for Wildlife Related Recreation Activities: 2001

[Preliminary. See headnote, Table 1251. (35,632 represents $35,632,000,000)]

Type of expenditure	Fishing Expenditures (mil. dol.)	Fishing Spenders Number (1,000)	Fishing Percent of anglers	Hunting Expenditures (mil. dol.)	Hunting Spenders Number (1,000)	Hunting Percent of hunters	Wildlife watching Expenditures (mil. dol.)	Wildlife watching Spenders Number (1,000)	Wildlife watching Percent of watchers
Total [1]	35,632	31,950	94	20,611	12,585	97	38,414	52,083	79
Food and lodging	5,881	25,603	75	2,450	10,073	77	4,819	15,365	70
Food	4,141	25,406	75	1,980	10,057	77	2,836	15,263	70
Lodging	1,740	6,473	19	470	1,701	13	1,983	5,648	26
Transportation	3,516	25,146	74	1,789	10,502	81	2,596	17,091	78
Public	400	1,254	4	186	452	3	702	1,986	9
Private	3,115	24,816	73	1,603	10,421	80	1,893	16,495	76
Other trip-related costs	5,259	25,658	75	1,013	3,479	27	748	6,350	29
Sport specific equipment [2]	4,618	21,228	62	4,562	9,516	73	7,354	45,802	69
Auxiliary equipment [3]	721	4,347	13	1,203	4,584	35	717	3,807	6
Special equipment [4]	11,625	2,319	7	4,597	573	4	15,469	1,410	2
Other expenditures [5]	4,013	(NA)	(NA)	4,997	(NA)	(NA)	6,712	(NA)	(NA)

NA Not available. [1] Total not adjusted for multiple responses or nonresponse. [2] Items owned primarily for each specific activity, such as rods and reels for fishing and guns and rifles for hunting. [3] Equipment such as camping gear owned for wildlife-associated recreation. [4] "Big ticket" equipment such as campers and boats owned for wildlife-associated recreation. [5] Books, magazines, membership dues and contributions, land leasing and ownership, licenses and plantings.
Source of Tables 1251 and 1252: U.S. Fish and Wildlife Service, *2001 National Survey of Fishing, Hunting, and Wildlife Associated Recreation*, May 2002.

No. 1253. Sporting Goods Sales by Product Category: 1990 to 2002

[In millions of dollars (50,725 represents $50,725,000,000), except percent. Based on a sample survey of consumer purchases of 80,000 households, (100,000 beginning 1995), except recreational transport, which was provided by industry associations. Excludes Alaska and Hawaii. Minus sign (-) indicates decrease]

Selected product category	1990	1995	1996	1997	1998	1999	2000	2001	2002, proj.
Sales, all products	50,725	59,794	62,818	67,333	69,848	71,161	74,442	73,485	75,356
Annual percent change [1]	(NA)	6.5	5.1	7.2	3.7	1.9	4.6	-1.3	2.5
Percent of retail sales	(NA)	2.6	2.6	2.7	2.6	2.5	2.4	2.3	2.3
Athletic and sport clothing	10,130	10,311	11,127	12,035	12,844	10,307	11,030	11,068	11,367
Athletic and sport footwear [2]	11,654	11,415	12,815	13,319	13,068	12,546	13,026	13,275	13,460
Aerobic shoes	611	372	401	380	334	275	292	281	275
Basketball shoes	918	999	1,192	1,134	1,000	821	786	761	792
Cross training shoes	679	1,191	1,417	1,450	1,402	1,364	1,528	1,476	1,490
Golf shoes	226	225	231	239	220	208	226	223	222
Gym shoes, sneakers	2,536	1,741	1,996	1,980	2,010	1,936	1,871	2,004	2,064
Jogging and running shoes	1,110	1,043	1,132	1,482	1,469	1,502	1,638	1,670	1,637
Tennis shoes	740	480	541	545	515	505	533	505	495
Walking shoes	2,950	2,841	3,079	3,236	3,192	3,099	3,317	3,280	3,346
Athletic and sport equipment [2]	14,439	18,809	18,988	19,033	19,192	20,343	21,608	21,510	21,895
Archery	265	287	276	270	255	262	259	270	270
Baseball and softball	217	251	277	290	304	329	319	316	319
Billiards and pool	192	304	271	242	347	354	516	508	513
Camping	1,072	1,205	1,127	1,153	1,204	1,265	1,354	1,370	1,424
Exercise equipment	1,824	2,960	3,232	2,968	3,233	3,396	3,610	3,842	4,043
Fishing tackle	1,910	2,010	1,970	1,891	1,903	1,917	2,030	2,070	2,112
Golf	2,514	3,194	3,560	3,703	3,658	3,567	3,805	3,874	3,797
Hunting and firearms	2,202	3,003	2,521	2,562	2,200	2,437	2,274	2,206	2,184
In-line skating and wheel sports	150	646	590	562	509	473	1,074	(NA)	(NA)
Optics	438	655	673	690	710	718	729	767	790
Skin diving and scuba	294	328	340	332	345	363	355	348	359
Skiing, alpine	475	562	707	723	718	648	495	476	509
Tennis	333	297	296	319	318	338	383	371	382
Recreational transport	14,502	19,259	19,888	22,946	24,743	27,965	28,779	27,632	28,634
Bicycles and supplies	2,423	3,390	3,187	4,860	4,957	4,770	5,131	4,725	4,749
Pleasure boats	7,644	9,064	9,399	10,208	10,539	11,962	13,224	13,524	13,795
Recreational vehicles	4,113	5,895	6,327	6,904	8,364	10,413	9,529	8,598	9,282
Snowmobiles	322	910	974	975	883	820	894	784	808

NA Not available. [1] Represents change from immediate prior year. [2] Includes other products not shown separately.

Source: National Sporting Goods Association, Mt. Prospect, IL, *The Sporting Goods Market in 2002*; and prior issues (copyright).

No. 1254. Consumer Purchases of Sporting Goods by Consumer Characteristics: 2001

[In percent. Based on sample survey of consumer purchases of 100,000 households. Excludes Alaska and Hawaii]

		Footwear					Equipment				
Characteristic	Total house-holds	Aero-bic shoes	Gym shoes/ sneak-ers	Jog-ging/ run-ning shoes	Skate-board-ing shoes	Walk-ing shoes	Fish-ing tackle	Camp-ing equip-ment	Exer-cise equip-ment	Hunt-ing equip-ment	Golf equip-ment
Total	100	100	100	100	100	100	100	100	100	100	100
Age of user:											
Under 14 years old	20	6	43	13	41	5	5	17	1	2	3
14 to 17 years old	6	7	13	11	35	3	3	9	2	4	5
18 to 24 years old	10	13	7	10	16	4	8	10	5	4	6
25 to 34 years old	14	17	10	17	3	8	22	22	22	24	22
35 to 44 years old	16	23	10	20	3	14	22	18	32	22	19
45 to 64 years old	22	25	13	25	2	41	31	16	29	36	31
65 years old and over	13	9	4	4	-	24	2	1	7	5	11
Multiple ages	-	-	-	-	-	-	7	7	2	3	3
Sex of user:											
Male	49	11	49	53	83	36	80	57	39	90	80
Female	51	89	51	47	17	64	12	31	52	8	17
Both sexes	-	-	-	-	-	-	5	14	9	2	3
Education of household head:											
Less than high school	8	4	6	3	6	5	10	5	3	10	2
High school	23	17	24	16	20	23	27	20	22	18	9
Some college	36	38	37	31	43	36	40	38	33	46	33
College graduate	33	40	34	50	31	36	23	37	42	26	56
Annual household income:											
Under $15,000	15	7	10	4	3	10	10	10	3	5	1
$15,000 to $24,999	14	7	12	7	11	11	11	10	9	14	4
$25,000 to $34,999	13	9	12	9	10	11	11	10	10	12	8
$35,000 to $49,999	15	17	15	15	17	16	14	15	15	18	9
$50,000 to $74,999	19	21	23	23	31	21	26	26	24	20	25
$75,000 to $99,999	12	21	14	21	12	17	12	14	22	17	21
$100,000 and over	12	17	13	22	17	15	16	15	17	14	32

- Represents or rounds to zero.

Source: National Sporting Goods Association, Mt. Prospect, IL, *The Sporting Goods Market in 2001* (copyright).

No. 1255. National Park System—Summary: 1990 to 2001

[For year ending September 30, except as noted. (986.1 represents $986,100,000). Includes data for five areas in Puerto Rico and Virgin Islands, one area in American Samoa, and one area in Guam]

Item	1990	1995	1996	1997	1998	1999	2000	2001
Finances (mil. dol.): [1]								
Expenditures reported	986.1	1,445.0	1,391.0	1,473.0	1,604.0	1,530.0	1,833.0	1,985.0
Salaries and wages	459.1	633.0	650.0	683.0	721.0	733.0	799.0	840.0
Improvements, maintenance	160.0	234.0	234.0	246.0	255.0	289.0	299.0	305.0
Construction	108.5	192.0	168.0	188.0	191.0	62.0	215.0	199.0
Other	258.5	386.0	339.0	356.0	437.0	446.0	520.0	641.0
Funds available	1,505.5	2,225.0	2,116.0	2,301.0	2,658.0	2,972.0	3,316.0	3,642.0
Appropriations	1,052.5	1,325.0	1,346.0	1,625.0	1,765.0	1,867.0	1,881.0	2,241.0
Other [2]	453.0	900.0	770.0	676.0	893.0	1,105.0	1,435.0	1,401.0
Revenue from operations	78.6	106.3	133.2	174.8	202.8	215.3	233.8	246.1
Recreation visits (millions): [3]								
All areas	258.7	269.6	265.8	275.3	286.7	287.1	285.9	279.9
National parks [4]	57.7	64.8	63.1	65.3	64.5	64.3	66.1	64.1
National monuments	23.9	23.5	23.6	24.1	23.6	24.3	23.8	21.8
National historical, commemorative, archaeological [5]	57.5	56.9	59.0	63.0	74.2	72.6	72.2	66.7
National parkways	29.1	31.3	30.9	31.6	32.8	34.6	34.0	34.4
National recreation areas [4]	47.2	53.7	52.6	51.6	53.0	52.8	50.0	48.3
National seashores and lakeshores	23.3	22.5	20.3	22.4	22.6	22.7	22.5	22.2
National Capital Parks	7.5	5.5	6.1	5.1	4.2	3.9	5.4	4.6
Recreation overnight stays (millions)	17.6	16.8	16.6	15.8	15.6	15.9	15.4	15.3
In commercial lodgings	3.9	3.8	3.7	3.6	3.6	3.7	3.7	3.6
In Park Service campgrounds	7.9	7.1	6.5	6.3	6.1	6.2	5.9	5.7
In backcountry	1.7	2.2	2.1	2.2	2.1	2.0	1.9	2.0
Other	4.2	3.7	3.7	3.8	3.9	4.1	3.8	3.9
Land (1,000 acres): [6]								
Total	76,362	77,355	77,458	77,457	77,654	78,166	78,153	78,943
Parks	46,089	49,307	49,315	49,384	49,416	49,859	49,785	49,862
Recreation areas	3,344	3,353	3,353	3,329	3,361	3,404	3,388	3,388
Other	26,929	24,695	24,790	24,744	24,877	24,903	24,980	25,693
Acquisition, net	21	27	98	61	95	44	222	20

[1] Financial data are those associated with the National Park System. Certain other functions of the National Park Service (principally the activities absorbed from the former Heritage Conservation and Recreation Service in 1981) are excluded. [2] Includes funds carried over from prior years. [3] For calendar year. Includes other areas, not shown separately. [4] For 1990, combined data for North Cascades National Park and two adjacent National Recreation Areas are included in National Parks total. [5] Includes military areas. [6] Federal land only, as of Dec. 31. Federal land acreages, in addition to National Park Service administered lands, also include lands within national park system area boundaries but under the administration of other agencies. Year-to-year changes in the federal lands figures include changes in the acreages of these other lands and hence often differ from "net acquisition."

Source: U.S. National Park Service, Visits, *National Park Statistical Abstract*, annual; and unpublished data. Other data are unpublished.

No. 1256. State Parks and Recreation Areas by State: 2002

[For year ending June 30 (13,162 represents 13,162,000). Data are shown as reported by state park directors. In some states, park agency has under its control forests, fish and wildlife areas, and/or other areas. In other states, agency is responsible for state parks only]

State	Acreage (1,000)	Visitors (1,000)[1]	Revenue Total ($1,000)	Percent of operating expenditures	State	Acreage (1,000)	Visitors (1,000)[1]	Revenue Total ($1,000)	Percent of operating expenditures
United States	13,162	758,216	667,715	35.4	Missouri	139	17,760	4,555	15.1
					Montana	66	1,219	1,255	20.8
Alabama	50	5,163	24,095	78.5	Nebraska	134	9,802	11,652	59.1
Alaska	3,326	4,283	1,949	34.7	Nevada	133	3,286	2,177	25.5
Arizona	59	2,410	3,017	17.7	New Hampshire	85	6,779	7,595	100.0
Arkansas	51	8,218	12,837	42.2	New Jersey	377	15,040	3,133	8.5
California	1,457	85,665	71,380	21.4	New Mexico	91	3,923	4,318	25.6
Colorado	365	11,098	17,371	64.6	New York	1,159	56,864	47,522	29.2
Connecticut	200	9,001	3,741	38.5	North Carolina	168	12,758	3,703	11.9
Delaware	22	3,207	8,575	46.2	North Dakota	17	1,097	1,103	41.7
Florida	592	17,735	31,925	45.4	Ohio	205	57,246	29,030	44.4
Georgia	81	14,623	27,415	46.4	Oklahoma	72	14,057	24,008	53.4
Hawaii	28	6,340	1,642	23.5	Oregon	95	39,439	15,425	42.2
Idaho	45	2,497	3,427	16.7	Pennsylvania	289	36,627	16,925	21.2
Illinois	306	43,623	6,988	12.6	Rhode Island	9	7,270	3,839	67.1
Indiana	179	16,879	33,514	78.7	South Carolina	80	8,151	16,537	69.0
Iowa	63	15,439	3,386	33.4	South Dakota	105	8,822	7,624	63.6
Kansas	32	7,991	5,000	69.3	Tennessee	144	26,275	31,824	49.6
Kentucky	44	7,873	55,457	66.6	Texas	668	17,090	14,860	25.6
Louisiana	38	2,008	253	1.4	Utah	115	5,941	8,213	36.5
Maine	97	2,554	2,214	30.6	Vermont	69	994	5,827	93.1
Maryland	266	10,340	14,299	31.4	Virginia	62	6,856	5,207	28.8
Massachusetts	294	11,884	2,904	9.1	Washington	262	48,864	10,229	23.6
Michigan	285	25,297	27,654	51.4	West Virginia	196	7,318	19,214	63.3
Minnesota	267	8,076	7,549	24.9	Wisconsin	133	15,528	8,498	43.3
Mississippi	24	4,225	6,645	43.5	Wyoming	119	2,784	1,269	23.1

[1] Includes overnight visitors.

Source: National Association of State Park Directors, Tucson, AZ, *2003 Annual Information Exchange*.

Arts, Entertainment, and Recreation 783

No. 1257. Domestic Overnight Travel by U.S. Resident Households—Summary: 1996 to 2002

[In millions (453.0 represents 453,000,000), except party size. See headnote, Table 1258]

Type of overnight trip	1996	1997	1998	1999	2000	2001	2002
All overnight travel:							
Household trips [1]	453.0	458.6	468.1	464.3	466.2	472.2	471.2
Person-trips	791.6	819.8	824.8	823.0	837.5	854.5	866.0
Party size	1.9	1.9	1.9	2.0	2.0	2.0	2.1
Overnight auto travel: [2]							
Household trips	310.0	312.6	319.2	312.8	314.0	322.8	331.1
Person-trips	597.6	618.2	620.2	613.9	625.0	642.7	665.5
Party size	2.2	2.2	2.2	2.2	2.2	2.2	2.3
Overnight air travel:							
Household trips	114.6	116.2	120.6	123.1	123.4	120.0	110.5
Person-trips	155.2	160.5	165.5	169.8	171.7	169.6	157.3
Party size	1.4	1.4	1.5	1.5	1.5	1.5	1.5
Overnight business travel:							
Household trips	137.5	136.5	141.5	141.7	137.1	132.7	126.9
Person-trips	178.5	181.0	185.4	184.0	181.3	176.3	170.5
Party size	1.4	1.4	1.4	1.4	1.4	1.4	1.4
Overnight leisure travel:							
Household trips	304.1	310.2	315.0	311.0	316.5	327.4	331.9
Person-trips	590.8	616.2	617.3	617.3	632.4	654.7	670.5
Party size	2.2	2.2	2.2	2.2	2.2	2.3	2.3

[1] Includes other trips (e.g. medical, funerals, weddings), not shown separately. [2] Includes trips taken by auto, truck, rental car, or recreational vehicle as the primary mode of transportation.
Source: Travel Industry Association of America, Washington, DC, *TravelScope*, annual (copyright).

No. 1258. Characteristics of Domestic Overnight Leisure Trips by U.S. Resident Households: 1997 to 2002

[In millions (310.2 represents 310,200,000). Represents household trips to destinations 50 miles or more, one-way, away from home and including one or more overnights. Based on a monthly mail panel survey of 25,000 U.S. households. For details, see source.]

Overnight leisure trip characteristics	Unit	1997	1998	1999	2000	2001	2002
Total overnight leisure trips	Millions	310.2	315.0	311	316.5	327.4	331.9
Average household members on trip	Number	2.2	2.2	2.2	2.2	2.3	2.3
Average nights per trip	Number	4.2	4.2	4.2	4.2	4.2	4.2
Traveled primarily by auto/truck/RV rental car	Percent	77	75	74	74	74	75
Traveled primarily by air	Percent	18	17	18	18	18	17
Used a rental car while on trip [1]	Percent	5	5	5	5	5	5
Stayed in a hotel/motel/B&B while on trip	Percent	40	41	42	43	42	43
Household income:							
Less than $50,000	Percent	(NA)	(NA)	(NA)	48	44	(NA)
$50,000 or more	Percent	(NA)	(NA)	(NA)	52	56	(NA)

NA Not available. [1] As a secondary mode of transportation.
Source: Travel Industry Association of America, Washington, DC, *TravelScope*, annual (copyright). <http://www.tia.org/home.asp>.

No. 1259. Domestic Travel Expenditures by State: 2000

[490,263 represents $490,263,000,000. Represents U.S. spending on domestic overnight trips and day trips of 50 miles or more, one way, away from home. Excludes spending by foreign visitors and by U.S. residents in U.S. territories and abroad. Includes travelers' expenditures in Indian casino gaming]

State	Total (mil. dol.)	Share of total (percent)	Rank	State	Total (mil. dol.)	Share of total (percent)	Rank	State	Total (mil. dol.)	Share of total (percent)	Rank
U.S., total	490,263	100.0	(X)	KY	5,206	1.1	29	OH	12,952	2.6	11
AL	5,205	1.1	30	LA	8,503	1.7	19	OK	3,848	0.8	34
AK	1,381	0.3	49	ME	1,928	0.4	43	OR	5,544	1.1	28
AZ	8,869	1.8	18	MD	8,399	1.7	20	PA	14,726	3.0	8
AR	3,794	0.8	37	MA	11,133	2.3	14	RI	1,427	0.3	46
CA	63,790	13.0	1	MI	12,063	2.5	13	SC	6,982	1.4	24
CO	9,320	1.9	17	MN	7,793	1.6	23	SD	1,402	0.3	47
CT	6,780	1.4	26	MS	4,995	1.0	31	TN	9,867	2.0	15
DE	1,051	0.2	51	MO	9,619	2.0	16	TX	32,307	6.6	3
DC	4,439	0.9	32	MT	1,963	0.4	42	UT	3,831	0.8	35
FL	41,692	8.5	2	NE	2,654	0.5	39	VT	1,389	0.3	48
GA	14,269	2.9	9	NV	19,581	4.0	6	VA	13,294	2.7	10
HI	7,810	1.6	22	NH	2,502	0.5	40	WA	8,093	1.7	21
ID	2,198	0.4	41	NJ	14,756	3.0	7	WV	1,721	0.4	44
IL	21,931	4.5	5	NM	3,795	0.8	36	WI	6,793	1.4	25
IN	6,464	1.3	27	NY	29,296	6.0	4	WY	1,554	0.3	45
IA	4,367	0.9	33	NC	12,249	2.5	12				
KS	3,582	0.7	38	ND	1,155	0.2	50				

X Not applicable.
Source: Travel Industry Association of America, Washington, DC, *Impact of Travel on State Economies, 2000* (copyright).

No. 1260. International Travelers and Expenditures: 1990 to 2001

[47,880 represents $47,880,000,000. For coverage, see Table 1261. Some traveler data revised since originally issued]

Year	Travel and passenger fare (mil. dol.) Payments by U.S. travelers Total [1]	Expenditures abroad	Receipts from foreign visitors Total [1]	Travel receipts	U.S. net travel and passenger payments (mil. dol.)	U.S. travelers to foreign countries (1,000)	International visitors to the U.S. (1,000)
1990	47,880	37,349	58,305	43,007	10,425	44,623	39,363
1993	52,123	40,713	74,403	57,875	22,280	44,411	45,779
1994	56,844	43,782	75,414	58,417	18,570	46,450	44,753
1995	59,579	44,916	82,304	63,395	22,725	50,835	43,318
1996	63,887	48,078	90,231	69,809	26,344	52,311	46,489
1997	70,189	52,051	94,294	73,426	24,105	52,944	47,752
1998	76,480	56,509	91,384	71,286	14,904	56,288	46,396
1999	80,180	58,865	94,516	74,731	14,336	57,598	48,492
2000	89,094	64,788	103,027	82,267	13,933	60,891	50,945
2001	82,535	60,117	91,126	73,119	8,591	57,963	44,898

[1] Includes passenger fares not shown separately.

Source: U.S. Dept. of Commerce, International Trade Administration, Tourism Industries. Internet site <http://www.tinet.ita.doc.gov>.

No. 1261. Foreign Travel: 1990 to 2001

[In thousands (44,623 represents 44,623,000). U.S. travelers cover residents of the United States, its territories and possessions. Foreign travelers to the U.S. include travelers for business and pleasure, international travelers in transit through the United States, and students; excludes travel by international personnel and international businessmen employed in the United States]

Item and area	1990	1995	1996	1997	1998	1999	2000	2001
U.S. travelers to foreign countries	44,623	50,835	52,311	52,944	56,288	57,598	60,891	57,963
Canada	12,252	13,005	12,909	13,401	14,880	15,276	15,188	15,561
Mexico	16,381	18,771	19,616	17,909	18,338	17,743	18,849	17,153
Total overseas	15,990	19,059	19,786	21,634	23,069	24,579	26,853	25,249
Europe	8,043	8,596	8,706	9,800	11,143	11,577	13,373	11,438
Foreign travelers to the U.S.	39,363	43,318	46,489	47,752	46,396	48,492	50,945	44,898
Canada	17,263	14,662	15,301	15,127	13,422	14,110	14,648	13,507
Mexico	7,041	8,016	8,530	8,431	9,276	9,915	10,322	9,558
Total overseas	15,059	20,639	22,658	24,194	23,698	24,466	25,975	21,833
Europe	6,659	8,793	9,727	10,390	10,675	11,243	11,597	9,496
South America	1,328	2,449	2,461	2,831	2,957	2,733	2,941	2,531
Central America	412	509	524	564	697	731	822	771
Caribbean	1,137	1,044	1,133	1,189	1,161	1,258	1,331	1,202
Far East	4,360	6,616	7,500	7,756	6,724	6,935	7,554	6,316
Middle East	365	454	480	552	587	625	702	644
Oceania	662	588	629	680	639	667	731	586
Africa	137	186	205	234	258	274	295	287

Source: U.S. Dept. of Commerce, International Trade Administration, Tourism Industries. Internet site <http://www.tinet.ita.doc.gov>.

No. 1262. Top States and Cities Visited by Overseas Travelers: 2000 and 2001

[25,975 represents 25,975,000. Includes travelers for business and pleasure, international travelers in transit through the United States, and students; excludes travel by international personnel and international businessmen employed in the United States]

State	Overseas visitors (1,000) 2000	2001	Market share (percent) 2000	2001	City	Overseas visitors (1,000) 2000	2001	Market share (percent) 2000	2001
Total overseas travelers [1]	25,975	21,833	100.0	100.0	New York City, NY	5,714	4,803	22.0	22.0
California	6,364	4,847	24.5	22.2	Los Angeles, CA	3,533	2,816	13.6	12.9
Florida	6,026	5,262	23.2	24.1	Orlando, FL	3,013	2,467	11.6	11.3
New York	5,922	5,043	22.8	23.1	Miami, FL	2,935	2,554	11.3	11.7
Hawaiian Islands	2,727	2,205	10.5	10.1	San Francisco, CA	2,831	1,965	10.9	9.0
Nevada	2,364	1,572	9.1	7.2	Las Vegas, NV	2,260	1,506	8.7	6.9
Massachusetts	1,429	1,179	5.5	5.4	Oahu/Honolulu, HI	2,234	1,747	8.6	8.0
Illinois	1,377	1,113	5.3	5.1	Washington, DC	1,481	1,201	5.7	5.5
Guam	1,325	1,113	5.1	5.1	Chicago, IL	1,351	1,070	5.2	4.9
Texas	1,169	939	4.5	4.3	Boston, MA	1,325	1,070	5.1	4.9
New Jersey	909	808	3.5	3.7	San Diego, CA	701	589	2.7	2.7
Arizona	883	633	3.4	2.9	Atlanta, GA	701	699	2.7	3.2
Georgia	805	786	3.1	3.6	Tampa/St. Petersburg, FL	519	502	2.0	2.3
Pennsylvania	649	699	2.5	3.2	San Jose, CA	494	415	1.9	1.9
Colorado	519	437	2.0	2.0	Anaheim, CA	494	393	1.9	1.8
Michigan	494	437	1.9	2.0	Dallas/Ft. Worth, TX	494	349	1.9	1.6
Washington	468	393	1.8	1.8	Ft. Lauderdale, FL	468	415	1.8	1.9
Utah	416	284	1.6	1.3	Houston, TX	442	415	1.7	1.9
North Carolina	416	306	1.6	1.4	Maui, HI	442	284	1.7	1.3
Louisiana	390	437	1.5	2.0	Seattle, WA	416	349	1.6	1.6
Ohio	390	393	1.5	1.8	Philadelphia, PA	390	415	1.5	1.9
Virginia	364	327	1.4	1.5	New Orleans, LA	364	393	1.4	1.8
Minnesota	364	284	1.4	1.3	Detroit, MI	338	284	1.3	1.3

[1] Includes other states and cities, not shown separately.

Source: U.S. Dept. of Commerce, International Trade Administration, Internet site <http://www.tinet.ita.doc.gov>.

No. 1263. Impact of International Travel on States' Economies: 2000

[Preliminary. (79,265.9 represents $79,265,900,000)]

State	Travel expenditures (mil. dol.)	Travel generated payroll (mil. dol.)	Travel generated employment (1,000)	Travel generated tax receipts (mil. dol.)	State	Travel expenditures (mil. dol.)	Travel generated payroll (mil. dol.)	Travel generated employment (1,000)	Travel generated tax receipts (mil. dol.)
U.S., total...	79,265.9	21,628.8	1,003.8	13,665.5	MO	177.7	49.0	2.6	32.9
AL	90.2	21.0	1.4	12.3	MT	101.4	24.3	2.0	13.8
AK	162.9	67.4	3.0	32.0	NE	63.7	17.7	1.2	11.2
AZ	1,746.9	494.9	25.4	288.2	NV	2,865.2	915.4	41.9	393.3
AR	50.3	13.2	0.9	7.6	NH	122.0	28.8	1.7	14.8
CA	15,079.7	3,999.0	179.1	2,417.1	NJ	933.0	252.6	10.8	188.3
CO	877.5	293.9	14.6	204.2	NM	114.9	27.4	1.9	16.0
CT	211.8	46.9	2.1	34.0	NY	10,271.5	2,793.5	108.1	2,164.9
DE	90.8	21.6	1.2	15.4	NC	584.3	185.3	9.2	107.6
DC	1,961.0	431.8	16.6	288.5	ND	46.4	12.2	1.0	10.7
FL	18,171.9	4,767.7	235.9	2,899.3	OH	620.9	176.5	9.6	121.6
GA	1,246.6	475.1	19.3	318.2	OK	90.1	34.5	1.7	16.0
HI	7,436.1	1,773.4	78.1	1,053.7	OR	371.5	104.5	6.2	61.6
ID	113.6	28.6	1.9	21.1	PA	1,246.2	364.8	17.7	227.4
IL	1,796.4	490.6	22.5	354.2	RI	119.4	26.1	1.5	15.8
IN	244.0	75.6	4.1	45.1	SC	491.8	124.2	7.7	76.3
IA	143.3	35.5	2.5	21.7	SD	40.1	10.7	0.9	5.6
KS	104.9	25.2	1.7	15.8	TN	442.2	197.3	7.7	105.2
KY	130.6	55.2	2.7	28.3	TX	3,751.3	1,162.0	54.3	705.2
LA	514.9	118.4	7.1	72.7	UT	381.1	130.2	8.0	76.5
ME	193.6	44.9	3.2	26.4	VT	144.5	35.5	2.2	20.5
MD	447.3	130.1	5.7	91.3	VA	500.8	151.7	8.1	82.1
MA	2,178.3	564.4	25.1	359.5	WA	909.3	249.4	12.3	172.7
MI	764.7	205.4	11.2	141.5	WV	32.2	8.0	0.5	5.0
MN	620.6	231.0	10.7	195.6	WI	334.4	90.2	6.0	57.9
MS	57.2	26.4	1.4	9.5	WY	75.1	19.7	1.6	9.3

Source: Travel Industry Association of America, Washington, DC, Impact of Travel on State Economies, 2000 (copyright).

No. 1264. Foreign Visitors for Pleasure Admitted by Country of Last Residence: 1990 to 2001

[In thousands (13,418 represents 13,418,000). For years ending September 30. Represents non-U.S. citizens admitted to the country for a temporary period of time (also known as nonimmigrants)]

Country	1990	1995	2000	2001	Country	1990	1995	2000	2001
All countries[1]	13,418	17,612	30,511	29,420	United Arab Emirates	7	14	36	36
					Africa [1]	105	137	327	332
Europe [1]	5,383	7,012	11,806	10,854	South Africa	26	59	114	107
United Kingdom	1,899	2,342	4,671	4,580	Egypt	16	16	44	46
Germany [2]	969	1,550	1,925	1,541	Nigeria	11	10	27	34
France	566	738	1,113	1,017	Oceania [1]	562	478	748	700
Italy	308	427	626	572	Australia	380	327	535	487
Netherlands	214	308	559	477	New Zealand [4]	153	115	170	162
Switzerland	236	321	400	358	North America [1]	2,463	2,240	6,501	6,691
Spain	183	248	370	345	Canada	119	127	277	292
Ireland	81	126	325	327	Mexico	1,061	893	3,972	4,154
Sweden	230	142	321	274	Caribbean [1]	963	831	1,404	1,350
Belgium	95	153	254	213	Bahamas, The	332	234	377	364
Austria	87	146	182	144	Jamaica	132	130	240	238
Denmark	75	78	150	141	Dominican Republic	137	138	195	194
Norway	80	71	144	137	Trinidad and Tobago	81	64	133	135
Poland	55	36	116	114	Haiti	57	43	72	68
Finland	83	47	95	82	Barbados	34	36	57	53
Portugal	30	40	86	81	Cayman Islands	31	31	53	52
Russia	(X)	33	74	72	Netherlands Antilles	31	32	43	37
Greece	43	44	60	57	British Virgin Islands	8	9	31	31
Hungary	15	29	58	51	Aruba	10	19	24	23
Czech Republic	(X)	12	44	42	Central America [1]	320	387	792	837
Iceland	10	14	27	24	Guatemala	91	99	177	195
Asia [1]	3,830	5,666	7,853	7,642	El Salvador	46	63	175	211
Japan	2,846	3,986	4,946	4,757	Costa Rica	62	91	172	165
China [3]	187	378	656	596	Panama	43	54	106	98
Korea	120	427	606	623	Honduras	52	37	87	92
Israel	128	160	319	334	Nicaragua	13	28	47	45
India	75	75	253	253	South America [1]	1,016	1,978	2,867	2,831
Hong Kong	111	162	195	183	Brazil	300	710	706	664
Philippines	76	85	163	181	Venezuela	199	400	570	594
Singapore	32	61	131	120	Argentina	136	320	515	503
Turkey	20	27	93	83	Colombia	122	174	411	400
Thailand	25	59	76	72	Chile	54	117	194	173
Saudi Arabia	33	45	67	66	Peru	97	98	190	197
Malaysia	27	40	64	64	Ecuador	57	77	122	149
Indonesia	28	44	62	61	Uruguay	16	37	66	68
Pakistan	27	27	47	59	Bolivia	14	16	48	39

X Not applicable. [1] Includes other countries and countries unknown, not shown separately. [2] Data for 1990 are for former West Germany. [3] Includes People's Republic of China and Taiwan. [4] Prior to fiscal year 1995, data for Niue are included in New Zealand.

Source: U.S. Bureau of Citizenship and Immigration Services, Statistical Yearbook, annual. See also <http://www.bcis.gov/graphics/shared/aboutus/statistics/yearbook2001.pdf>.

Section 27
Accommodation, Food Services, and Other Services

This section presents statistics relating to services other than those covered in the previous few sections (22 to 26) on domestic trade, transportation, communications, financial services, and recreation services. Data shown for the services are classified by kind of business and cover sales or receipts, establishments, employees, payrolls, and other items. The principal sources of these data are from the Census Bureau and include the *1997 Economic Census* reports, annual surveys, and the *County Business Patterns* program. These data are supplemented by data from several sources such as the National Restaurant Association on food and drink sales (Table 1271), the American Hotel & Motel Association on lodging (Table 1269), and McCann-Erickson, Inc. and Publishers Information Bureau on advertising (Tables 1274 and 1275, respectively).

Data on these services also appear in several other sections. For instance, labor force employment and earnings data appear in Section 12, Labor Force; gross domestic product of the industry (Table 660) appear in Section 13, Income, Expenditures, and Wealth; and financial data (several tables) from the quarterly *Statistics of Income Bulletin,* published by the Internal Revenue Service, appear in Section 15, Business Enterprise.

Censuses—Limited coverage of the services industries started in 1933. Beginning with the 1967 census, legislation provides for a census of each area to be conducted every 5 years (for years ending in "2" and "7"). For more information on the most current census, see the *History of the 1997 Economic Census* found at <http://www.census.gov/prod/ec97/pol00-hec.pdf>. The industries covered in the censuses and surveys of business are those classified in 13 sectors defined in the *North American Industry Classification System,* called NAICS (see below). All Census Bureau tables in this section are utilizing the new NAICS codes, which replaced the Standard Industrial Classification (SIC) system. NAICS makes substantial structural improvements and identifies over 350 new industries. At the same time, it causes breaks in time series far more profound than any prior revision of the previously used SIC system. For information on this system and how it affects the comparability of statistics historically, see text, Section 15, Business Enterprise, and especially the Census Web site at <http://www.census.gov/epcd/www/naics.html>.

The *Accommodation and Food Services sector* (NAICS sector 72) comprises establishments providing customers with lodging and/or prepared meals, snacks, and beverages for immediate consumption. The *Other Services (Except Public Administration) sector* (NAICS sector 81) covers establishments with payroll engaged in providing services not specifically provided for elsewhere in the NAICS. Establishments in this sector are primarily engaged in activities such as repair and maintenance of equipment and machinery, personal and laundry services, and religious, grantmaking, civic, professional, and similar organizations. Establishments providing death care services, pet care services, photofinishing services, temporary parking services, and dating services are also included. Private households that employ workers on or about the premises in activities primarily concerned with the operation of the household are included in this sector but are not included in the scope of the census. In general, the 1997 Economic Census has two series of publications and documents for these two sectors: 1) subject series with reports on such as commodity line sales and establishment and firm sizes and 2) geographic reports with individual reports for each state. For information on these series, see the Census Web site at <http://www.census.gov/epcd/www/97EC72.htm> and <http://www.census.gov/epcd/www/97EC81.htm>.

Current surveys—The Service Annual Survey provides annual estimates of nationwide receipts for selected personal, business, leasing and repair, amusement and entertainment, social and health, and other professional service industries in the United States. For selected accommodation, social, health, and other professional service industries, separate estimates are developed for receipts of taxable firms and revenue and expenses for firms and organizations exempt from federal income taxes. Several service sectors from this survey are covered in other sections of this publication. The estimates for tax exempt firms in these industries are derived from a sample of employer firms only. Estimates obtained from annual and monthly surveys are based on sample data and are not expected to agree exactly with results that would be obtained from a complete census of all establishments. Data include estimates for sampling units not reporting.

Statistical reliability—For a discussion of statistical collection and estimation, sampling procedures, and measures of statistical reliability applicable to Census Bureau data, see Appendix III.

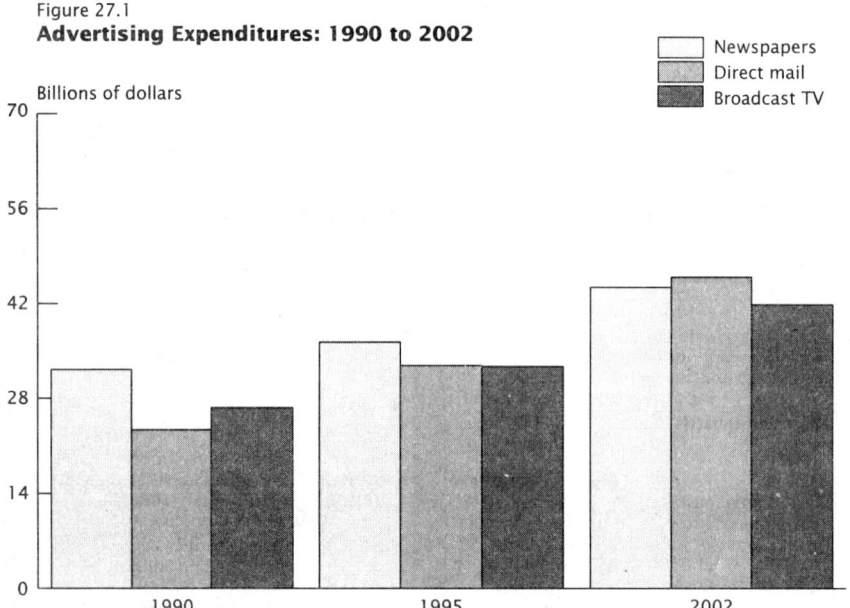

Figure 27.1
Advertising Expenditures: 1990 to 2002

Source: Chart prepared by U.S. Census Bureau. For data, see Table 1274.

No. 1265. Service-Related Industries—Establishments, Employees, and Payroll by Industry: 2000 and 2001

[7,070 represents 7,070,000. Covers establishments with payroll. Employees are for the week including March 12. Excludes most government employees, railroad employees, and self-employed persons. Kind-of-business classification based on North American Industry Classification System, 1997 (NAICS); see text, Section 15. For statement on methodology, see Appendix III]

Kind of business	NAICS code	Establishments (1,000) 2000	Establishments (1,000) 2001	Employees (1,000) [1] 2000	Employees (1,000) [1] 2001	Payroll (bil. dol.) 2000	Payroll (bil. dol.) 2001
All industries, total	(X)	7,070	7,095	114,065	115,061	3,879	3,989
Service-related industries, total	(X)	3,842	4,386	61,662	62,887	1,740	2,032
Transportation & warehousing	48-49	190	191	3,790	3,751	126	130
Air transportation	481	5	5	616	609	27	29
Water transportation	483	2	2	68	70	3	3
Truck transportation	484	110	110	1,416	1,398	46	46
Transit & ground passenger transportation	485	16	16	387	392	7	8
Pipeline transportation	486	3	3	53	51	4	4
Scenic & sightseeing transportation	487	2	2	24	23	1	557
Transportation support activities	488	31	32	472	485	17	17
Couriers & messengers	492	12	13	619	578	17	18
Warehousing & storage	493	7	7	136	145	4	4
Information	51	134	137	3,546	3,755	209	207
Publishing industries	511	33	32	1,081	1,101	75	69
Motion picture & sound recording industries	512	23	23	304	297	12	12
Broadcasting & telecommunications	513	55	60	1,632	1,777	89	94
Information & data processing services	514	23	23	529	580	34	32
Real estate & rental & leasing	53	300	307	1,942	2,014	59	64
Real estate	531	235	241	1,280	1,335	40	44
Rental & leasing services	532	63	64	636	653	17	18
Lessors of other nonfinancial intangible asset	533	2	2	26	26	2	2
Professional, scientific, & technical services	54	723	736	6,816	7,157	362	374
Professional, scientific, & technical services	541	723	736	6,816	7,157	362	374
Legal services	5411	177	177	1,089	1,110	62	67
Accounting/tax prep/bookkeep/payroll services	5412	100	102	1,164	1,191	38	38
Architectural, engineering & related services	5413	102	104	1,213	1,286	65	69
Specialized design services	5414	28	29	140	148	6	6
Computer systems design & related services	5415	100	101	1,171	1,255	85	85
Management, sci. & tech. consulting services	5416	97	108	712	806	44	47
Scientific R&D services	5417	13	14	359	387	25	25
Advertising & related services	5418	40	39	472	464	23	22
Other professional/scientific/technical services	5419	65	64	496	509	14	15
Management of companies & enterprises	55	47	48	2,874	2,879	211	213
Admin/support waste mgt/remediation services	56	352	363	9,138	9,062	210	221
Administrative & support services [2]	561	336	346	8,847	8,761	200	210
Employment services	5613	42	45	4,573	4,364	98	101
Temporary help services	56132	28	30	3,013	2,676	59	57
Business support services	5614	35	34	702	711	17	18
Travel arrangement & reservation services	5615	33	32	308	313	10	10
Waste management & remediation services	562	16	17	291	301	11	11
Educational services	61	68	71	2,532	2,612	62	67
Health care & social assistance	62	659	671	14,109	14,535	431	466
Ambulatory health care services	621	459	467	4,566	4,737	180	195
Hospitals	622	7	7	5,015	5,085	170	181
Nursing & residential care facilities	623	63	65	2,592	2,671	50	55
Social assistance	624	129	132	1,936	2,042	31	35
Arts, entertainment, & recreation	71	104	106	1,741	1,780	43	46
Perform arts, spectator sports, and related ind [2]	711	34	35	352	362	19	20
Performing arts companies	7111	9	9	126	128	3	3
Spectator sports	7112	4	5	100	104	9	10
Museums, historical sites, & like institutions	712	6	6	110	114	3	3
Amusement, gambling, & recreation industries [2]	713	64	65	1,279	1,305	22	23
Gambling industries	7132	2	2	203	216	5	5
Accommodation & food services	72	542	549	9,881	9,972	126	129
Accommodation [2]	721	60	60	1,768	1,753	35	34
Traveler accommodation	7211	50	50	1,714	1,698	34	33
RV parks & recreational camps	7212	7	7	38	39	1	901
Food services & drinking places	722	483	488	8,113	8,220	91	95
Full-service restaurants	7221	192	193	3,897	3,963	47	49
Limited-service eating places	7222	211	216	3,385	3,407	33	35
Special food services	7223	29	29	502	514	7	8
Drinking places (alcoholic beverages)	7224	51	50	329	335	3	3
Other services (except public administration)	81	723	719	5,293	5,370	110	115
Repair & maintenance [2]	811	233	231	1,334	1,343	37	38
Automotive R&M	8111	164	164	856	871	21	21
Electronic & precision equipment R&M	8112	15	15	144	141	7	6
Personal and laundry services	812	199	197	1,293	1,312	23	24
Religious/grantmaking/prof/like organizations	813	291	292	2,666	2,716	50	53

X Not applicable. [1] Includes employees on the payroll for the pay period including March 12. [2] Includes other kinds of business not shown separately.

Source: U.S. Census Bureau, County Business Patterns, annual. See also <http://www.census.gov/epcd/cbp/view/cbpview.html>.

No. 1266. Service-Related Industries—Establishments, Employees, and Annual Payroll by State: 2001

[374,709,080 represents 374,409,080,000. Covers establishments with payroll. Employees are for the week including March 12. Excludes most government employees, railroad employees, and self-employed persons. Kind-of-business classification based on North American Industry Classification System, 1997 (NAICS); see text, Section 15. For statement on methodology, see Appendix III]

State	Professional, scientific, & technical services (NAICS 54)			Admin/support waste mgt/remediation services (NAICS 56)			Accommodation and food services (NAICS 72)		
	Establishments	Employees[1]	Annual payroll (1,000 dol.)	Establishments	Employees[1]	Annual payroll (1,000 dol.)	Establishments	Employees[1]	Annual payroll (1,000 dol.)
United States..	736,454	7,156,579	374,409,080	362,665	9,061,987	221,385,956	548,569	9,972,301	128,649,922
Alabama	8,375	76,061	3,334,028	4,089	123,738	2,454,774	6,870	127,776	1,304,633
Alaska	1,651	11,404	588,333	965	11,258	365,267	1,793	21,926	402,301
Arizona	12,785	117,366	4,729,182	7,141	189,748	4,135,469	9,429	205,693	2,540,445
Arkansas	4,872	31,999	1,082,341	2,274	63,007	1,053,946	4,464	76,932	748,423
California	96,210	1,177,669	65,613,606	42,499	1,108,895	29,507,772	64,337	1,137,789	16,119,057
Colorado	18,201	149,387	8,198,312	7,579	185,708	5,237,450	10,311	206,313	2,673,618
Connecticut	10,174	95,724	5,900,336	5,598	104,122	2,869,296	6,755	95,378	1,437,101
Delaware	2,223	19,564	1,114,496	1,225	30,194	713,008	1,608	27,263	378,750
District of Columbia	4,249	80,331	6,334,238	1,094	31,489	963,847	1,692	44,054	913,132
Florida	52,752	371,157	17,142,317	28,023	1,043,426	24,169,798	28,978	613,432	8,065,587
Georgia	22,446	205,699	10,806,397	10,880	334,934	8,538,482	15,047	303,213	3,631,958
Hawaii	2,838	19,500	852,402	1,751	34,208	751,384	3,036	85,949	1,648,747
Idaho	3,074	29,655	1,112,024	1,718	30,140	580,241	2,888	44,741	444,164
Illinois	35,518	353,262	20,607,684	16,192	476,766	11,507,622	23,573	416,554	5,245,707
Indiana	11,462	91,045	3,421,507	6,928	146,328	3,170,650	11,577	221,665	2,349,436
Iowa	5,601	38,349	1,314,886	3,341	62,223	1,231,595	6,436	102,977	1,003,054
Kansas	6,492	52,362	2,152,937	3,421	65,681	1,416,480	5,551	96,466	960,196
Kentucky	7,271	56,400	1,930,604	3,702	74,841	1,398,158	6,609	137,195	1,518,009
Louisiana	10,280	79,445	3,005,486	4,351	105,432	2,135,350	7,294	164,550	1,981,242
Maine	3,160	22,612	900,725	1,793	27,438	620,884	3,624	44,004	606,124
Maryland	17,030	207,526	11,103,513	7,527	165,733	4,190,891	9,099	168,647	2,225,229
Massachusetts	21,182	257,577	17,195,835	9,561	211,977	6,559,907	14,578	236,346	3,610,981
Michigan	21,522	212,598	10,174,034	12,274	298,865	7,868,602	18,793	329,888	3,647,178
Minnesota	15,077	123,646	6,395,833	6,994	145,826	3,595,188	9,947	194,845	2,270,143
Mississippi	4,180	28,387	1,012,486	2,163	48,137	790,952	4,127	98,228	1,233,085
Missouri	12,273	121,844	5,768,099	6,817	151,422	3,367,258	10,927	210,613	2,400,977
Montana	2,707	16,191	500,952	1,289	12,340	211,374	3,148	39,599	398,472
Nebraska	3,719	35,738	1,471,557	2,427	51,261	1,166,660	3,918	61,095	590,672
Nevada	5,858	42,395	1,948,112	3,316	67,938	1,718,061	3,982	267,436	6,161,122
New Hampshire	3,779	26,701	1,338,803	1,948	41,320	1,079,160	3,062	47,926	656,091
New Jersey	30,489	282,874	16,720,205	13,535	312,917	8,089,023	16,725	253,626	4,388,690
New Mexico	4,217	30,545	1,259,843	1,837	35,462	776,046	3,641	69,852	767,717
New York	53,393	554,444	34,403,364	23,188	493,679	14,524,839	38,526	511,955	8,243,386
North Carolina	18,150	158,447	7,072,529	10,571	233,720	4,858,832	15,234	281,651	3,155,774
North Dakota	1,271	9,200	279,339	787	10,912	217,052	1,723	26,361	241,049
Ohio	23,921	236,447	10,357,324	13,931	340,181	7,034,161	22,352	416,681	4,385,546
Oklahoma	8,074	53,702	2,084,032	3,870	90,510	1,767,527	6,444	109,271	1,102,456
Oregon	9,694	69,510	3,096,272	4,653	81,322	1,813,015	8,408	126,746	1,559,433
Pennsylvania	27,210	302,487	16,003,065	14,071	294,291	6,933,411	24,144	367,312	4,237,861
Rhode Island	2,795	19,490	834,791	1,678	27,119	678,086	2,604	36,976	483,796
South Carolina	8,039	65,784	2,709,892	4,862	138,534	2,691,051	7,887	154,358	1,751,199
South Dakota	1,526	8,108	252,229	881	10,393	171,126	2,213	31,020	303,361
Tennessee	9,954	96,986	3,997,260	6,302	180,803	3,940,517	9,736	198,727	2,306,052
Texas	49,728	479,969	25,726,093	23,388	775,682	20,496,765	35,508	717,945	8,765,822
Utah	5,731	58,516	2,297,077	2,970	78,145	1,656,982	4,028	81,135	863,074
Vermont	1,957	11,533	463,806	910	8,246	189,987	1,865	28,533	350,726
Virginia	21,733	305,927	17,790,511	9,507	226,279	5,484,917	12,900	251,664	3,087,098
Washington	16,331	141,642	7,309,247	8,153	125,282	3,561,751	13,258	203,038	2,682,071
West Virginia	2,893	20,679	629,289	1,428	29,927	580,063	3,231	52,958	557,600
Wisconsin	10,848	92,118	3,863,327	6,521	117,893	2,442,282	12,958	199,482	1,969,379
Wyoming	1,539	6,577	208,520	742	6,295	108,997	1,731	24,517	282,198

[1] Includes employees on the payroll for the pay period including March 12.

Source: U.S. Census Bureau, *County Business Patterns*, annual. See also <http://www.census.gov/epcd/cbp/view/cbpview.html>.

No. 1267. Service-Related Industries—Nonemployer Establishments and Receipts by Kind of Business: 1998 to 2000

[2,415 represents 2,415,000. Includes only firms subject to federal income tax. Nonemployers are businesses with no paid employees. Based on the North American Industry Classification System, 1997 (NAICS), see text, Section 15]

Kind of business	NAICS code	Establishments (1,000) 1998	1999	2000	Receipts (mil. dol.) 1998	1999	2000
Professional, scientific & technical services	54	2,415	2,388	2,420	83,081	85,443	90,272
Management, sci. & tech. consulting services	5416	427	392	383	16,367	16,350	17,123
Admin/support waste mgt/remediation services	56	925	990	1,032	19,237	21,777	23,754
Administrative & support services	561	908	974	1,017	18,407	20,919	22,858
Accommodation & food services	72	198	210	218	11,757	12,594	13,418
Accommodation	721	48	50	51	3,142	3,310	3,528
Food services & drinking places	722	151	160	167	8,615	9,284	9,890
Other services (except public administration) [1]	81	2,209	2,293	2,350	48,438	51,876	55,056
Repair & maintenance [1]	811	599	619	624	19,044	20,245	21,139
Automotive R&M	8111	266	265	263	10,634	11,091	11,492
Personal & household goods R&M	8114	239	257	264	5,261	5,775	6,109
Personal & laundry services	812	1,451	1,512	1,562	27,037	29,226	31,459
Personal care services	8121	549	574	598	9,726	10,670	11,631

[1] Includes other kinds of business not shown separately.
Source: U.S. Census Bureau, "Nonemployer Statistics"; published August 2003; <http://www.census.gov/epcd/nonemployer/>.

No. 1268. Selected Service Industries—E-Commerce Revenue: 2000 and 2001

[37,312 represents $37,312,000,000. Includes data only for businesses with paid employees, except for accommodation and food services, which also includes businesses with and without paid employees. Except as noted, based on the Service Annual Survey.

Kind of business	NAICS code [1]	E-commerce revenue (mil. dol.) 2000	2001	E-commerce as percent of total revenue, 2001	E-commerce revenue, percent distribution, 2001
Selected service industries, total	(X)	37,312	37,261	0.8	100
Selected transportation and warehousing [2]	48-49	3,691	3,930	1.7	10.5
Information [3]	51	9,305	10,438	1.2	28
Publishing industries	511	4,748	4,941	2.1	13.3
Online information services	51419	1,997	1,850	5.7	5
Selected finance [4]	52	5,976	3,754	1.3	10.1
Securities and commodity contracts intermediation and brokerage	5231	5,664	3,570	1.8	9.6
Rental and leasing services	532	(S)	(S)	(S)	(S)
Selected professional, scientific, and technical services [5]	54	5,550	5,309	0.6	14.2
Computer systems design and related services	5415	3,541	3,609	2.1	9.7
Selected administrative and support and waste management and remediation services [6]	56	9,680	9,599	2.3	25.8
Health care and social assistance services	62	(S)	(S)	(S)	(S)
Arts, entertainment, and recreation services	71	(S)	(S)	(S)	(S)
Accommodation and food services [7]	72	(S)	(S)	(S)	(S)
Selected other services [8]	81	554	656	0.2	1.8

S Data do not meet publication standards because of high sampling variability or poor response quality. X Not applicable.
[1] North American Industry Classification System; see text Section 15. [2] Excludes NAICS 481 (air transportation), 482 (rail transportation), 483 (water transportation), 485 (transit and ground passenger transportation), 487 (scenic and sightseeing transportation), 488 (support activities for transportation) and 491 (postal service). [3] Includes other industries not listed separately. [4] Excludes NAICS 521 (monetary authorities-central bank), 522 (credit intermediation and related activities), 5232 (securities and commodity exchanges), NAICS 52391 (miscellaneous intermediation), 52399 (all other financial investment activities), 524 (insurance carriers and related activities) and 525 (funds and trusts). [5] Excludes NAICS 54112 (offices of notaries) and 54132 (landscape architectural services). [6] Excludes NAICS 56173 (landscaping services). [7] Based on Annual Retail Trade Survey. [8] Excludes NAICS 81311 (religious organizations), 81393 (labor and similar organizations), 81394 (political organizations) and 814 (private households).
Source: U.S. Census Bureau, "E-Stats"; published 19 March 2003; <http://www.census.gov/eos/www/ebusiness614.htm>.

No. 1269. Lodging Industry Summary: 1990 to 2001

Year	Average occupancy rate (percent)	Average room rate (dol.)	Room size of property	2001 Establishments	Rooms (mil.)	Item	2001 Business traveler	Leisure traveler
1990	63.3	57.96	Total	41,393	4.2	Typical night:		
1993	63.6	60.53				Made reservations (percent)	92	83
1994	65.2	62.86	Percent:			Amount paid	$95.00	$87.00
1995	65.5	66.65	Under 75 rooms	52.1	22.8	Length of stay (percent):		
1996	65.2	70.93	75-149 rooms	33.4	35.3			
1997	64.5	75.31	150-299 rooms	10.6	21.0	One night	42	47
1998	64.0	78.62	300-500 rooms	2.6	9.7	Two nights	25	27
1999	63.2	81.33	Over 500 rooms	1.2	11.2	Three or more	33	26
2000	63.7	85.89						
2001	60.3	88.27						

Source: American Hotel & Motel Association, Washington, DC, Lodging Industry Profile (copyright).

No. 1270. Accommodation and Food Services—Establishments, Employees, and Payroll by Kind of Business: 2000 and 2001

[9,880.9 represents 9,880,900. Covers establishments with payroll. Employees are for the week including March 12. Excludes most government employees, railroad employees, and self-employed persons. Kind-of-business classification based on North American Industry Classification System, 1997 (NAICS); see text, Section 15. For statement on methodology, see Appendix III]

Kind of business	NAICS code	Establishments (number) 2000	2001	Employees (1,000) 2000	2001	Payroll (mil. dol.) 2000	2001
Accommodation & food services, total	72	542,411	548,569	9,880.9	9,972.3	125,582	128,650
Accommodation	721	59,851	60,196	1,767.8	1,752.8	34,708	34,096
Traveler accommodation	7211	49,736	50,206	1,714.1	1,698.2	33,661	32,986
Hotels (exc. casino hotels) & motels	72111	45,554	45,972	1,378.8	1,377.2	25,181	24,807
Casino hotels	72112	288	304	311.6	296.8	8,143	7,837
Other traveler accommodation	72119	3,894	3,930	23.7	24.3	337	342
Bed & breakfast inns	721191	2,999	3,042	19.0	19.7	254	265
All other traveler accommodation	721199	895	888	4.6	4.7	83	77
RV parks & recreational camps	7212	6,975	7,000	38.1	38.8	843	901
RV parks & campgrounds	721211	3,691	3,750	17.7	17.8	334	351
Recreational/vacation camps (exc. campgrounds)	721214	3,284	3,250	20.4	21.0	509	550
Rooming & boarding houses	7213	3,140	2,990	15.6	15.6	204	209
Food services & drinking places	722	482,560	488,373	8,113.1	8,219.5	90,874	94,554
Full-service restaurants	7221	192,342	193,262	3,897.1	3,963.3	46,707	48,702
Limited-service eating places	7222	210,895	215,793	3,385.5	3,407.3	33,454	34,789
Limited-service restaurants	722211	170,565	173,753	2,967.9	2,997.2	28,852	30,134
Cafeterias	722212	4,199	4,464	69.9	69.5	875	890
Snack & nonalcoholic beverage bars	722213	36,131	37,576	347.7	340.6	3,728	3,765
Special food services	7223	28,745	29,345	501.9	513.8	7,367	7,576
Food service contractors	72231	16,894	17,330	377.5	384.6	5,632	5,771
Caterers	72232	8,714	9,058	108.6	113.5	1,470	1,543
Mobile food services	72233	3,137	2,957	15.8	15.7	265	262
Drinking places (alcoholic beverages)	7224	50,578	49,973	328.6	335.2	3,345	3,486

Source: U.S. Census Bureau, *County Business Patterns*, annual. See also <http://www.census.gov/epcd/cbp/view/cbpview.html>.

No. 1271. Commercial and Noncommercial Groups—Food and Drink Establishments and Sales: 1990 to 2003

[Sales in millions of dollars (238,149 represents $238,149,000,000). Excludes military. Data refer to sales to consumers of food and alcoholic beverages. Sales are estimated. For details, see source]

Type of group	Establishments, 2000	Sales (mil. dol.) 1990	1995	1999	2000	2001	2002	2003[1]
Total	868,581	238,149	294,631	358,017	377,652	391,083	406,334	424,554
Commercial restaurant services [2][3]	685,932	211,606	265,910	326,567	345,345	358,212	373,632	391,477
Eating places [2]	444,830	155,552	198,293	245,786	259,743	271,324	283,594	297,004
Full-service restaurants	205,838	77,811	96,396	125,430	133,834	140,393	146,149	153,164
Limited-service restaurants [4]	183,223	69,798	92,901	103,026	107,147	111,112	116,113	120,874
Snack and nonalcoholic beverage bars	45,179	([5])	([5])	11,548	12,867	13,877	15,350	16,914
Bars and taverns [6]	51,303	9,533	9,948	11,912	12,412	12,810	13,270	13,722
Managed services [2]	19,430	14,149	18,186	23,382	24,841	25,772	26,841	28,525
Manufacturing and industrial plants	(NA)	3,856	4,814	5,984	6,223	6,283	6,185	6,441
Colleges and universities	(NA)	2,788	3,989	5,443	5,879	6,308	6,762	7,233
Lodging places	13,276	13,568	15,561	18,032	19,438	18,124	18,458	19,259
Retail hosts [2][7]	133,526	9,513	12,589	13,996	14,869	15,756	16,443	17,343
Department store restaurants	4,111	876	1,038	873	903	(NA)	(NA)	(NA)
Grocery store restaurants [7]	60,541	5,432	6,624	6,823	7,116	(NA)	(NA)	(NA)
Gasoline service stations	52,441	1,718	2,520	4,289	4,693	(NA)	(NA)	(NA)
Recreation and sports	15,485	2,871	3,866	4,623	4,772	4,921	5,105	5,310
Noncommercial restaurant services [2]	182,649	26,543	28,722	31,450	32,307	32,871	32,702	33,077
Employee restaurant services	4,049	1,864	1,364	1,036	986	921	826	790
Industrial, commercial organizations	1,812	1,603	1,129	775	717	(NA)	(NA)	(NA)
Educational restaurant services	102,087	7,671	9,059	9,831	9,977	10,121	9,990	10,010
Elementary and secondary schools	97,925	3,700	4,533	4,993	5,039	5,115	4,974	4,959
Hospitals	5,791	8,968	9,219	9,734	9,982	10,096	10,006	9,926
Miscellaneous [3]	33,966	2,892	3,673	4,630	4,898	5,068	5,096	5,322
Clubs	10,514	1,993	2,278	2,971	3,164	(NA)	(NA)	(NA)

NA Not available. [1] Projection. [2] Includes other types of groups, not shown separately. [3] Data for establishments with payroll. [4] Fast-food restaurants. [5] Snack and nonalcoholic beverage bars included in limited service restaurants. [6] For establishments serving food. [7] Includes a portion of delicatessen sales in grocery stores.

Source: National Restaurant Association, Washington, DC, *Restaurant Numbers: 25 Year History, 1970-1995*, 1998; *Restaurant Industry in Review*, annual; and *National Restaurant Association Restaurant Industry Forecast*, December 2002 (copyright).

No. 1272. Professional, Scientific, and Technical Services—Estimated Revenue for Employer and Nonemployer Firms: 1998 to 2001

[745,427 represents 745,427,000,000. Estimates are based on data from the 2001 Service Annual Survey and administrative data. Estimates for 2000 are revised to reflect the latest administrative data for nonemployers. Except where indicated, estimates have been adjusted using the results of the 1997 Economic Census]

Kind of business	NAICS code	Estimated revenue for employer and nonemployer firms				Estimated revenue for taxable employer firms			
		1998	1999	2000	2001	1998	1999	2000	2001
Professional, scientific, and technical services (except notaries and landscape architectural services)	54	745,427	812,941	895,736	937,176	646,167	710,038	787,406	824,057
Legal services (except notaries)	5411	148,406	157,373	164,190	175,383	136,228	144,369	150,699	160,907
Offices of lawyers	54111	142,495	151,304	158,247	168,821	130,749	138,787	145,261	154,956
Other legal services [1]	54119	5,912	6,069	6,944	6,562	5,479	5,581	5,438	5,952
Accounting, tax preparation, bookkeeping, and payroll services	5412	67,002	72,264	80,066	85,072	61,864	66,783	74,229	78,987
Architectural, eng., & related services (exc. landscape architectural services)	5413	137,989	148,240	166,709	174,949	131,220	141,191	159,105	166,993
Architectural services	54131	22,827	24,411	27,174	29,004	20,691	22,207	24,867	26,554
Engineering services	54133	99,920	108,675	123,463	127,852	96,390	104,997	119,441	123,666
Specialized design services	5414	19,206	20,786	23,120	23,027	15,512	16,478	18,276	18,181
Interior design services	54141	6,904	7,401	8,104	8,243	5,232	5,452	5,911	5,997
Computer systems design and services	5415	139,723	163,682	185,208	184,240	131,481	154,414	175,495	174,574
Management, scientific, and technical consulting services	5416	89,268	96,530	105,663	116,216	72,902	79,973	88,540	98,079
Management consulting services	54161	74,293	80,987	88,327	96,743	61,361	67,905	74,797	82,498
Environmental consulting services [2]	54162	6,783	7,350	8,076	8,977	5,776	6,332	7,022	7,822
Other scientific and technical consulting services	54169	8,192	8,193	9,260	10,496	5,765	5,737	6,721	7,759
Scientific research & development serv.	5417	41,695	45,739	51,428	57,473	25,508	28,743	33,221	38,796
Research & develop. in physical, engineering, and life sciences	54171	38,325	42,077	47,411	53,111	24,237	27,300	31,657	37,091
Research and development in social sciences and humanities	54172	3,370	3,662	4,017	4,362	1,271	1,443	1,564	1,704
Advertising and related services [3]	5418	60,467	65,605	73,593	71,994	55,404	60,436	68,267	66,963
Advertising agencies	54181	19,776	22,419	26,350	26,054	18,634	21,253	25,149	24,780
Public relations agencies	54182	6,364	7,026	8,693	8,238	5,419	6,061	7,699	7,290
Display advertising	54185	5,598	6,244	6,701	6,571	5,320	5,960	6,409	6,291
Direct mail advertising	54186	9,581	9,929	10,359	10,721	9,078	9,415	9,830	10,198
Other professional, scientific, & tech. services (exc. veterinary services) [3]	5419	41,672	42,722	45,759	48,823	16,049	17,650	19,574	20,576
Mrktng. research & pub. opinion polling	54191	8,457	9,609	10,366	10,136	7,878	8,974	9,667	9,444
Photographic services	54192	7,859	8,001	8,560	8,705	5,822	5,883	6,322	6,463

[1] Estimates for NAICS 541191 (title abstract and settlement offices), not shown separately, have not been adjusted using the results of the 1997 Economic Census. [2] Estimates have not been adjusted using the results of the 1997 Economic Census. [3] Includes services not listed separately.
Source: U.S. Census Bureau, "Service Annual Survey 2001"; published February 2003; <http://www.census.gov/svsd/www/sas01rpt.pdf>.

No. 1273. Computer Systems Design and Related Services—Estimated Revenue for Employer Firms: 2001

[174,574 represent 174,574,000,000. Estimates are based on data from the 2001 Service Annual Survey and administrative data. Except where indicated, estimates have been adjusted using the results of the 1997 Economic Census]

Kind of business	2001	Kind of business	2001
Computer systems design and related services (NAICS 5415), total revenue	**174,574**	Network design and development services	1,116
Information tech. design & development total	89,810	Information technical infrastructure (computer) and network management services	3,309
Custom application design and development	44,984	Information technology technical support services	3,778
Computer system design, development, and integration services	36,826	Information technology consulting services	5,308
Network design and development services	7,999	Software publishing	2,852
Information technical infrastructure (computer) and network management services	23,626	Information technology related training services	801
Information technology technical support services	13,615	Resale of computer hardware and software	1,934
Information technology consulting services	12,341	Other services revenue	2,995
Software publishing	7,375	**Computer systems design services (NAICS 541512), total revenue**	**82,441**
Data storage services	1,023	Information tech. design & development, total	45,575
Data management services	2,310	Custom application design and development	11,073
Information technology related training services	2,565	Computer systems design, development, and integration services	28,225
Internet access services	452	Network design and development services	6,277
Web site hosting services	1,060	Information technology infrastructure (computer) and network management services	5,049
Application service provisioning	1,916	Information technology technical support services	7,084
Business process management services	2,222	Information technology consulting services	4,489
Resale of computer hardware and software	7,156	Software publishing	3,568
Other services revenue	8,968	Data storage services	851
Custom computer programming services (NAICS 541511), total revenue	**63,354**	Data management services	1,534
Information tech. design & development, total	40,478	Information technology related training services	1,254
Custom application design and development	32,058	Internet access services	395
Computer systems design, development, and integration services	7,304	Rental and leasing of computer hardware	102
		Resale of computer hardware and software	4,383

Source: U.S. Census Bureau, "Service Annual Survey 2001"; published February 2003; <http://www.census.gov/svsd/www/sas01rpt.pdf>.

Accommodation, Food Services, and Other Services

No. 1274. Advertising—Estimated Expenditures by Medium: 1990 to 2002

[In millions of dollars (129,968 represents $129,968,000,000). See source for definitions of types of advertising]

Medium	1990	1995	1996	1997	1998	1999	2000	2001	2002
Total	129,968	165,147	178,113	191,307	206,697	222,308	247,472	231,287	237,425
National	73,638	96,933	105,054	112,809	122,271	132,170	151,664	141,797	145,615
Local	56,330	68,214	73,059	78,498	84,426	90,138	95,808	89,490	91,810
Newspapers	32,281	36,317	38,402	41,670	44,292	46,648	49,050	44,255	44,380
National	3,867	3,996	4,400	5,016	5,402	6,358	7,229	6,615	6,680
Local	28,414	32,321	34,002	36,654	38,890	40,290	41,821	37,640	37,700
Magazines	6,803	8,580	9,010	9,821	10,518	11,433	12,370	11,095	10,990
Broadcast TV	26,616	32,720	36,046	36,893	39,173	40,011	44,802	38,881	41,830
Four TV networks	9,863	11,600	13,081	13,020	13,736	13,961	15,888	14,300	15,300
Syndication	1,109	2,016	2,218	2,438	2,609	2,870	3,108	3,102	3,135
Spot (National)	7,788	9,119	9,803	9,999	10,659	10,500	12,264	9,223	10,335
Spot (Local)	7,856	9,985	10,944	11,436	12,169	12,680	13,542	12,256	13,060
Cable TV	2,631	6,166	7,778	8,750	10,340	12,570	15,455	15,536	15,810
Cable TV networks	2,000	4,500	5,695	6,450	7,640	9,405	11,765	11,883	11,890
Spot (Local)	631	1,666	2,083	2,300	2,700	3,165	3,690	3,653	3,920
Radio	8,726	11,338	12,269	13,491	15,073	17,215	19,295	17,861	18,940
Network	482	480	523	560	622	684	780	711	780
Spot (National)	1,635	1,959	2,135	2,455	2,823	3,275	3,668	2,956	3,250
Local (Local)	6,609	8,899	9,611	10,476	11,628	13,256	14,847	14,194	14,910
Yellow Pages	8,926	10,236	10,849	11,423	11,990	12,652	13,228	13,592	13,720
National	1,132	1,410	1,555	1,711	1,870	1,986	2,093	2,087	2,100
Local	7,794	8,826	9,294	9,712	10,120	10,666	11,135	11,505	11,620
Direct mail	23,370	32,866	34,509	36,890	39,620	41,403	44,591	44,725	45,860
Business papers	2,875	3,559	3,808	4,109	4,232	4,274	4,915	4,468	4,245
Out of home [1]	1,084	1,263	1,339	1,455	1,576	1,725	5,176	5,134	5,365
National	640	701	743	795	845	925	2,068	2,051	2,140
Local	444	562	596	660	731	800	3,108	3,083	3,225
Internet	(NA)	(NA)	(NA)	800	1,383	2,832	6,507	5,752	5,465
Miscellaneous [2]	16,656	22,102	24,103	26,005	28,500	31,545	32,083	29,988	30,820
National	12,074	16,147	17,574	18,745	20,312	22,264	24,418	22,829	23,445
Local	4,582	5,955	6,529	7,260	8,188	9,281	7,665	7,159	7,375

NA Not available. [1] Prior to 2000, represents only "outdoor" billboards. Beginning 2000 includes other forms of outdoor advertising (i.e. transportation vehicles, bus shelters, telephone kiosks, etc.) previously covered under "Miscellaneous."
[2] Beginning 2000, part of miscellaneous now included under "Out of home" advertising. See footnote 1.

Source: McCann-Erickson, Inc., New York, NY. Compiled for Crain Communications, Inc. in *Advertising Age* (copyright).

No. 1275. Magazine Advertising Revenue by Category: 1999 to 2002

[15,508 represents $15,508,000,000. Represents the volume of advertising in the consumer magazines belonging to the Publishers Information Bureau]

Category	Pages 1999	Pages 2000	Pages 2002	Volume (mil. dol.) 1999	Volume (mil. dol.) 2000	Volume (mil. dol.) 2002
Total [1]	255,146	269,016	225,620	15,508	17,052	16,689
Automotive	24,753	22,295	20,290	1,844	1,730	1,793
Automotive accessories and equipment	24,502	22,012	20,062	1,833	1,711	1,773
Technology [1]	22,009	26,536	13,850	1,385	1,736	1,093
Telecommunications	4,734	4,812	2,362	312	311	195
Computers and software	13,252	17,156	7,827	894	1,205	701
Home furnishings and supplies [1]	17,273	16,611	15,845	1,185	1,197	1,359
Household furnishings and accessories	4,709	4,597	3,794	283	272	271
Audio and video equipment and supplies	5,057	4,507	4,317	277	284	345
Toiletries and cosmetics [1]	15,857	15,741	16,683	1,143	1,218	1,510
Cosmetics and beauty aids [2]	8,484	8,781	9,021	578	640	797
Personal hygiene and health [2]	3,238	2,818	2,769	287	271	295
Hair products and accessories [2]	2,589	2,837	3,411	185	217	299
Direct response companies	22,163	19,554	18,506	1,121	1,034	1,135
Apparel and accessories [1]	24,776	26,576	22,657	1,120	1,295	1,265
Ready-to-wear	12,771	13,648	10,152	499	586	518
Footwear	3,349	4,058	3,950	158	218	206
Jewelry and watches	4,214	5,021	4,576	210	282	286
Financial, insurance and real estate	16,253	16,976	11,604	1,023	1,154	939
Financial	12,557	13,453	8,328	757	894	666
Insurance and real estate	3,697	3,524	3,276	266	260	273
Food and food products [1]	9,894	10,693	10,947	1,003	1,140	1,332
Prepared foods	1,919	1,961	2,103	194	212	267
Dairy, produce, meat and bakery goods	2,809	2,858	3,200	288	315	397
Beverages	1,854	1,981	1,758	166	197	192
Drugs and remedies	11,759	12,470	13,757	977	1,121	1,405
Medicines and proprietary remedies	10,272	10,506	11,807	850	965	1,224
Media and advertising	11,418	15,328	11,777	846	1,145	1,022
Retail stores	15,798	19,263	13,957	826	1,056	864
Retail stores [3]	12,786	15,869	10,798	671	863	662
Public transportation, hotels, and resorts	15,231	15,421	13,856	705	743	696
Cigarettes, tobacco and accessories	6,034	4,677	1,987	481	388	215
Beer, wine and liquor	4,565	5,016	4,749	299	360	404
Liquor	3,600	3,874	3,436	235	286	302
Miscellaneous services and amusements	5,424	5,803	4,895	277	310	294
Sporting goods	10,503	13,752	13,668	240	263	260

[1] Includes other categories, not shown separately. [2] Women's, men's, and unisex. [3] Includes apparel, business, drugs and toiletries, and food and beverage.
Source: Publishers Information Bureau, Inc., New York, NY, as compiled by Competitive Media Reporting.

No. 1276. Administrative and Support and Waste Management and Remediation Services—Estimated Revenue: 1999 to 2001

[In millions of dollars (374,765 represents $374,765,000,000), except percent. For taxable and tax-exempt employer firms. Except as indicated, estimates adjusted to the results of the 1997 Economic Census. Based on the Service Annual Survey; see Appendix III]

Kind of business	NAICS code [1]	1999	2000	2001	Percent change, 2000-2001
Admin/support waste mgt/remediation services	56	374,765	411,236	411,947	0.2
Administrative & support services	561	327,714	362,457	363,817	0.2
Office administrative services	5611	41,322	48,732	54,729	12.3
Facilities support services	56121	8,055	9,109	8,746	-4.0
Employment services [2]	5613	114,361	125,618	114,304	-9.0
Temporary help services	56132	71,504	74,492	64,438	-13.5
Employee leasing services	56133	35,964	42,855	40,981	-4.4
Business support services [2]	5614	43,281	47,543	51,058	7.4
Telephone call centers	56142	14,817	16,115	16,647	3.3
Business service centers	56143	9,602	10,303	10,459	1.5
Travel arrangement & reservation services [2]	5615	24,996	26,306	26,054	-1.0
Travel agencies	56151	10,770	10,766	9,383	-12.8
Other travel arrangement & reservation services	56159	11,152	12,485	13,829	10.8
Investigation and security services	5616	24,410	25,978	27,057	4.2
Investigation, guard, & armored car services	56161	14,281	14,910	14,798	-0.8
Security guards & patrol services	561612	10,316	10,735	10,449	-2.7
Security systems services	56162	10,130	11,068	12,258	10.8
Services to buildings & dwellings	5617	36,949	41,065	43,744	6.5
Janitorial services	56172	26,712	30,097	32,089	6.6
Other support services	5619	34,341	38,107	38,125	(Z)
Convention & trade show organizers	56192	7,779	9,383	9,329	-0.6
Waste management & remediation services	562	47,052	48,779	48,131	-1.3
Waste collection	5621	25,295	26,823	26,012	-3.0
Waste treatment & disposal [3]	5622	11,101	11,689	11,517	-1.5
Remediation & other waste management services	5629	10,655	10,267	10,602	3.3

Z Less than 0.05 percent. [1] North American Industry Classification System, 1997; see text, Section 15. [2] Includes other kinds of business not shown separately. [3] Estimates have not been adjusted to the results of the 1997 Economic Census.

Source: U.S. Census Bureau, "Service Annual Survey 2001"; published February 2003; <http://www.census.gov/svsd/www/sas01rpt.pdf>.

No. 1277. Other Services—Estimated Revenue for Employer and Nonemployer Firms: 1999 to 2001

[In millions of dollars (353,370 represents $353,370,000,000), except percent. Except where indicated, results have been adjusted to the results of the 1997 Economic Census. Based on the Service Annual Survey. See text, this section, and Appendix III.]

Kind of business	NAICS code [1]	1999	2000	2001	Percent change, 2000-2001
Other services (except public administration, religious, labor, and political organizations, and private households)	81	353,370	374,348	379,473	1.4
Repair & maintenance	811	139,734	146,172	152,593	4.4
Automotive R&M	8111	81,588	85,796	89,965	4.9
Automotive mechanical & electrical R&M	81111	42,648	44,607	47,063	5.5
Automotive body/paint/interior & glass repair	81112	26,988	28,580	29,231	2.3
Other automotive R&M	81119	11,953	12,608	13,671	8.4
Electronic and precision equipment R&M [2]	8112	18,745	18,776	19,125	1.9
Commercial equipment (exc. auto. elec.) R&M	8113	21,305	22,898	24,451	6.8
Personal and household goods R&M	8114	18,096	18,703	19,052	1.9
Home/garden equipment & appliance R&M	81141	6,476	6,537	6,653	1.8
Reupholstery & furniture repair	81142	2,320	2,410	2,393	-0.7
Footwear & leather goods repair	81143	396	384	379	-1.5
Other personal & household goods R&M	81149	8,904	9,371	9,628	2.7
Personal & laundry services	812	94,009	99,709	102,423	2.7
Personal care services	8121	26,605	28,772	30,084	4.6
Hair, nail, & skin care services	81211	22,716	24,568	25,335	3.1
Other personal care services	81219	3,889	4,204	4,749	13.0
Death care services	8122	13,957	13,903	14,425	3.7
Funeral homes	81221	10,998	10,993	11,623	5.7
Cemeteries & crematories	81222	2,959	2,910	2,802	-3.7
Drycleaning & laundry services	8123	21,668	22,732	23,266	2.3
Coin-operated laundries & drycleaners	81231	3,908	4,303	4,433	3.0
Drycleaning and laundry services, (exc. coin-op)	81232	8,756	9,043	9,004	-0.4
Linen & uniform supply	81233	9,004	9,385	9,829	4.7
Other personal services	8129	31,779	34,302	34,648	1.0
Religious/grantmaking/prof/like organizations (except religious, labor, and political organizations) [3]	813	119,627	128,467	124,457	-3.1

[1] North American Industry Classification System, 1997; see text, Section 15. [2] Estimates for NAICS 811219 (other electronics and precision equipment repair and maintenance) have not been adjusted to the results of the 1997 Economic Census. [3] Estimates for NAICS 813211 (grantmaking foundations) have not been adjusted to the results of the 1997 Economic Census.

Source: U.S. Census Bureau, "Service Annual Survey 2001"; published February 2003; <http://www.census.gov/svsd/www/sas01rpt.pdf>.

Accommodation, Food Services, and Other Services

No. 1278. Religious, Grantmaking, Civic, and Professional Service Firms—Revenue and Expenses for Tax-Exempt Employer Firms: 1999 to 2001

[In millions of dollars (119,627 represents $119,627,000,000), except as indicated. Based on the Service Annual Survey; subject to sampling variability. See text, this section, and Appendix III]

Kind of business	NAICS code [1]	Revenue 1999	Revenue 2000	Revenue 2001	Percent change, 2000-2001	Expenses, 2001
Religious/grantmaking/prof/like organizations (except religious, labor, and political organizations)	813	119,627	128,467	124,457	-3.1	110,371
Grantmaking and giving services [2]	8132	57,667	63,057	55,978	-11.2	45,663
Social advocacy organizations	8133	9,882	10,438	10,871	4.1	10,424
Civic & social organizations	8134	11,408	12,175	12,526	2.9	11,969
Business, professional, and other organizations (except labor and political organizations)	8139	40,670	42,798	45,083	5.3	42,314

[1] North American Industry Classification System, 1997; see text, Section 15. [2] Estimates for NAICS 813211 (grantmaking foundations) have not been adjusted to the results of the 1997 Economic Census.

Source: U.S. Census Bureau, "Service Annual Survey 2001"; published February 2003; <http://www.census.gov/svsd/www/sas01rpt.pdf>.

No. 1279. National Nonprofit Associations—Number by Type: 1980 to 2002

[Data compiled during last few months of year previous to year shown and the beginning months of year shown]

Type	1980	1985	1990	1995	1996	1997	1998	1999	2000	2001	2002
Total	14,726	19,121	22,289	22,663	23,004	22,901	22,049	22,474	21,840	22,449	22,141
Trade, business, commercial	3,118	3,719	3,918	3,757	3,784	3,755	3,714	3,815	3,880	3,922	3,883
Agriculture and environment	677	882	940	1,122	1,128	1,124	1,107	1,113	1,103	1,120	1,125
Legal, governmental, public admin., military	529	658	792	776	777	780	755	778	790	807	814
Scientific, engineering, tech	1,039	1,270	1,417	1,355	1,372	1,381	1,306	1,332	1,302	1,317	1,309
Educational	[1]2,376	2,822	1,291	1,290	1,308	1,310	1,274	1,321	1,297	1,346	1,307
Cultural	([1])	([1])	1,886	1,918	1,925	1,918	1,841	1,876	1,786	1,812	1,766
Social welfare	994	1,450	1,705	1,885	1,928	1,934	1,896	1,913	1,829	1,925	1,917
Health, medical	1,413	1,886	2,227	2,348	2,418	2,453	2,383	2,481	2,495	2,574	2,601
Public affairs	1,068	1,935	2,249	2,148	2,160	2,113	1,855	1,877	1,776	1,857	1,808
Fraternal, nationality, ethnic	435	492	573	552	552	541	542	552	525	537	529
Religious	797	953	1,172	1,230	1,240	1,230	1,156	1,151	1,123	1,160	1,154
Veteran, hereditary, patriotic	208	281	462	686	738	745	861	877	835	834	785
Hobby, avocational	910	1,311	1,475	1,549	1,568	1,548	1,468	1,463	1,330	1,408	1,380
Athletic sports	504	737	840	838	845	836	765	782	717	762	730
Labor unions	235	252	253	245	247	245	235	235	232	233	218
Chambers of Commerce [2]	105	142	168	168	168	162	129	146	143	142	141
Greek and non-Greek letter societies	318	331	340	336	338	335	313	313	296	312	301
Fan clubs	(NA)	(NA)	581	460	507	491	449	449	381	381	373

NA Not available. [1] Data for cultural associations included with educational associations. [2] National and binational. Includes trade and tourism organizations.

Source: Gale Group, Farmington Hills, MI. Compiled from *Encyclopedia of Associations*, annual (copyright).

Section 28
Foreign Commerce and Aid

This section presents data on the flow of goods, services, and capital between the United States and other countries; changes in official reserve assets of the United States; international investments; and foreign assistance programs.

The Bureau of Economic Analysis publishes current figures on U.S. international transactions and the U.S. international investment position in its monthly *Survey of Current Business*. Statistics for the foreign aid programs are presented by the Agency for International Development (AID) in its annual *U.S. Overseas Loans and Grants and Assistance from International Organizations* and by the Department of Agriculture in its *Foreign Agricultural Trade of the United States*.

The principal source of merchandise import and export data is the U.S. Census Bureau. Current data are presented monthly in *U.S. International Trade in Goods and Services* report Series FT 900. The *Guide to Foreign Trade Statistics*, found on the Census Bureau Web site at <http://www.census.gov/foreign-trade/guide/index.html>, lists the Bureau's monthly and annual products and services in this field. In addition, the International Trade Administration and the Bureau of Economic Analysis present summary as well as selected commodity and country data for U.S. foreign trade in the *U.S. Foreign Trade Highlights* and the *Survey of Current Business*, respectively. The merchandise trade data in the latter source include balance of payments adjustments to the Census Bureau data. The Treasury Department's *Monthly Treasury Statement of Receipts and Outlays of the United States Government* contains information on import duties. The International Trade Commission, U.S. Department of Agriculture, U.S. Department of Energy, and the U.S. Geological Survey release various reports and specialized products on U.S. trade.

International accounts—The international transactions tables (Nos. 1281 to 1283) show, for given time periods, the transfer of goods, services, grants, and financial assets and liabilities between the United States and the rest of the world. The international investment position table (No. 1283) presents, for specific dates, the value of U.S. investments abroad and of foreign investments in the United States. The movement of foreign and U.S. capital as presented in the balance of payments is not the only factor affecting the total value of foreign investments. Among the other factors are changes in the valuation of assets or liabilities, including changes in prices of securities, defaults, expropriations, and write-offs.

Direct investment abroad means the ownership or control, directly or indirectly, by one person of 10 percent or more of the voting securities of an incorporated business enterprise or an equivalent interest in an unincorporated business enterprise. Direct investment position is the value of U.S. parents claims on the equity of and receivables due from foreign affiliates, less foreign affiliates receivables due from their U.S. parent's. Income consists of parents shares in the earnings of their affiliates' plus net interest received by parents' on intercompany accounts, less withholding taxes on dividends and interest.

Foreign aid—Foreign assistance is divided into three major categories—grants (military supplies and services and other grants), credits, and other assistance (through net accumulation of foreign currency claims from the sale of agricultural commodities). *Grants* are transfers for which no payment is expected (other than a limited percentage of the foreign currency "counterpart" funds generated by the grant), or which at most involve an obligation on the part of the receiver to extend aid to the United States or other countries to achieve a common objective. *Credits* are loan disbursements or transfers under other agreements which give rise to specific obligations to repay, over a period of years, usually with interest. All known returns to the U.S. government stemming from grants and credits (reverse grants, returns of grants, and payments of principal) are taken into account in net grants and net credits, but no allowance is made for interest or commissions. *Other assistance* represents the transfer of U.S. farm products in exchange for foreign currencies (plus, since enactment of Public Law 87-128, currency claims from principal and interest collected on credits extended under the farm products program), less the government's disbursements of the currencies as grants, credits, or for purchases. The net acquisition of currencies represents net transfers of resources to foreign countries under the agricultural programs, in addition to those classified as grants or credits.

The basic instrument for extending military aid to friendly nations has been the Mutual Defense Assistance Program authorized by the Congress in 1949. Prior to 1952, economic and technical aid was authorized in the Foreign Assistance Act of 1948, the 1950 Act for International Development, and other legislation which set up programs for specific countries. In 1952, these economic, technical, and military aid programs were combine under the Mutual Security Act, which in turn was followed by the Foreign Assistance Act passed in 1961. Appropriations to provide military assistance were also made in the Department of Defense Appropriation Act (rather than the Foreign Assistance Appropriation Act) beginning in 1966 for certain countries in Southeast Asia and in other legislation concerning program for specific countries (such as Israel). Figures on activity under the Foreign Assistance Act as reported in the *Foreign Grants and Credits* series differ from data published by AID or its immediate predecessors, due largely to differences in reporting, timing, and treatment of particular items.

Exports—The Census Bureau compiles export data primarily from Shipper's Export Declarations required to be filed with customs officials for shipments leaving the United States. They include U.S. exports under mutual security programs and exclude shipments to U.S. Armed Forces for their own use.

The value reported in the export statistics is generally equivalent to a free alongside ship (f.a.s.) value at the U.S. port of export, based on the transaction price, including inland freight, insurance, and other charges incurred in placing the merchandise alongside the carrier at the U.S. port of exportation. This value, as defined, excludes the cost of loading merchandise aboard the exporting carrier and also excludes freight, insurance, and any other charges or transportation and other costs beyond the U.S. port of exportation. The country of destination is defined as the country of ultimate destination or country where the merchandise is to be consumed, further processed, or manufactured, as known to the shipper at the time of exportation. When ultimate destination is not known, the shipment is statistically credited to the last country to which the shipper knows the merchandise will be shipped in the same form as exported.

Effective January 1990, the United States began substituting Canadian import statistics for U.S. exports to Canada. As a result of the data exchange between the United States and Canada, the United States has adopted the Canadian import exemption level for its export statistics based on shipments to Canada.

Data are estimated for shipments valued under $2,501 to all countries, except Canada, using factors based on the ratios of low-valued shipments to individual country totals.

Prior to 1989, exports were based on Schedule B, Statistical Classification of Domestic and Foreign Commodities Exported from the United States. These statistics were retabulated and published using Schedule E, Standard International Trade Classification, Revision 2. Beginning in 1989, Schedule B classifications were based on the Harmonized System and made to coincide with the Standard International Trade Classification, Revision 3. This revision will affect the comparability of most export series beginning with the 1989 data for commodities.

Imports—The Census Bureau compiles import data from various customs forms required to be filed with customs officials. Data on import values are presented on two valuations bases in this section: The c.i.f. (cost, insurance, and freight) and the customs import value (as appraised by the U.S. Customs Service in accordance with legal requirements of the Tariff Act of 1930, as amended). This latter valuation, primarily used for collection of import duties, frequently does not reflect the actual transaction value. Country of origin is defined as country where the merchandise was grown, mined, or manufactured. If country of origin is unknown, country of shipment is reported.

Imports are classified either as "General imports" or "Imports for consumption." *General imports* are a combination of entries for immediate consumption, entries into customs bonded warehouses, and entries into U.S. Foreign Trade Zones, thus generally reflecting total arrivals of merchandise. *Imports for consumption* are a combination of entries for immediate consumption, withdrawals from warehouses for consumption, and entries of merchandise into U.S. customs territory from U.S. Foreign Trade Zones, thus generally reflecting the total of the commodities entered into U.S. consumption channels.

Prior to 1989, imports were based on the Tariff Schedule of the United States Annotated. The statistics were retabulated and published using Schedule A, Standard International Trade Classification, Revision 2. Beginning in 1989, the statistics are based on the Harmonized Tariff Schedule of the United States, which coincides with the Standard International Trade Classification, Revision 3. This revision will affect the comparability of most import series beginning with the 1989 data.

Area coverage—Except as noted, the geographic area covered by the export and import trade statistics is the United States Customs area (includes the 50 states, the District of Columbia, and Puerto Rico), the U.S. Virgin Islands (effective January 1981), and U.S. Foreign Trade Zones (effective July 1982). Data for selected tables and total values for 1980 have been revised to reflect the U.S. Virgin Islands' trade with foreign countries, where possible.

Statistical reliability—For a discussion of statistical collection and estimation, sampling procedures, and measures of statistical reliability applicable to Census Bureau data, see Appendix III.

Figure 28.1
U.S. International Transaction Balances: 1990 to 2002

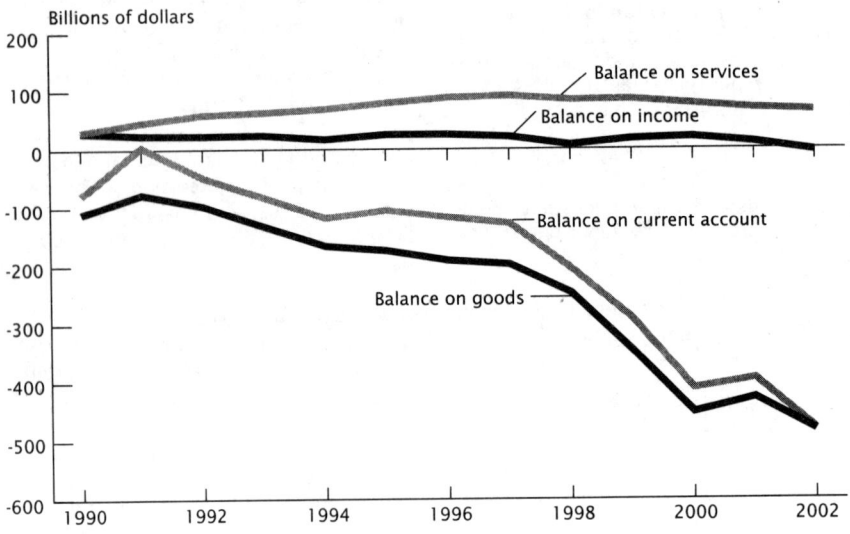

Source: Chart prepared by U.S. Census Bureau. For data, see Table 1280.

Figure 28.2
Top Purchasers of U.S. Exports and Suppliers of U.S. General Imports: 2001

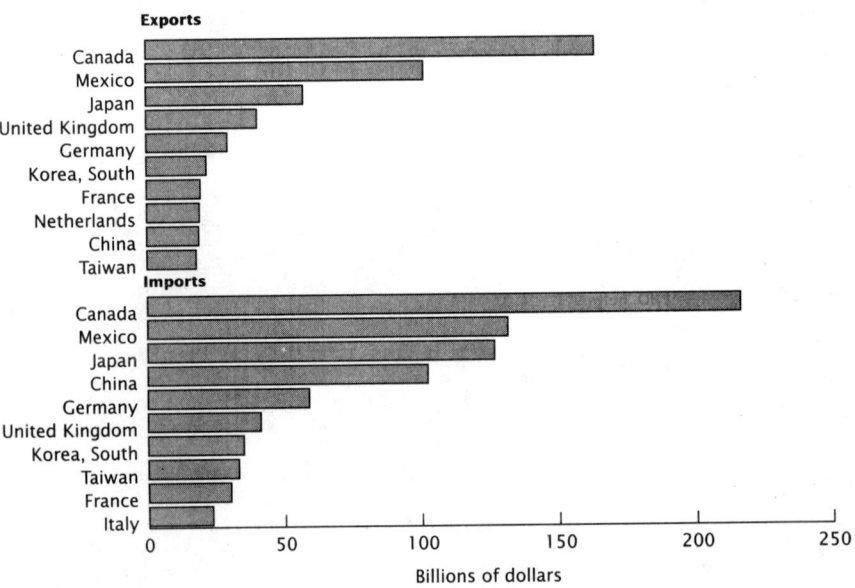

Source: Chart prepared by U.S. Census Bureau. For data, see Table 1300.

800 Foreign Commerce and Aid

U.S. Census Bureau, Statistical Abstract of the United States: 2003

No. 1280. U.S. International Transactions by Type of Transaction: 1990 to 2002

[In millions of dollars (706,975 represents $706,975,000,000). Minus sign (-) indicates debits]

Type of transaction	1990	1993	1994	1995	1996	1997	1998	1999	2000	2001	2002
Exports of goods and services and income receipts	**706,975**	**776,921**	**868,460**	**1,005,645**	**1,077,148**	**1,194,899**	**1,191,206**	**1,255,671**	**1,416,915**	**1,284,942**	**1,229,649**
Exports of goods and services	535,233	642,376	702,622	793,725	850,877	933,873	932,558	965,473	1,070,054	1,007,580	974,107
Goods, balance of payments basis [1]	387,401	456,943	502,859	575,204	612,113	678,366	670,416	683,965	771,994	718,712	681,874
Services [2]	147,832	185,433	199,763	218,521	238,764	255,507	262,142	281,508	298,060	288,868	292,233
Transfers under U.S. military agency sales contracts [3]	9,932	13,471	12,787	14,643	16,446	16,675	17,405	15,928	13,790	12,539	11,943
Travel	43,007	57,875	58,417	63,395	69,809	73,426	71,325	74,801	82,400	71,893	66,547
Passenger fares	15,298	16,528	16,997	18,909	20,422	20,868	20,098	19,785	20,687	17,326	17,046
Other transportation	22,042	21,958	23,754	26,081	26,074	27,006	25,604	26,916	29,803	28,442	29,166
Royalties and license fees [5]	16,634	21,695	26,712	30,289	32,470	33,228	35,626	39,670	43,233	41,098	44,142
Other private services [4,5]	40,251	53,023	60,209	64,386	72,615	83,349	91,158	103,523	107,361	116,139	122,594
U.S. government miscellaneous services	668	883	887	818	928	955	926	885	786	831	795
Income receipts	171,742	134,545	165,838	211,920	226,271	261,026	258,648	290,198	346,861	277,362	255,542
Income receipts on U.S.-owned assets abroad	170,570	132,725	163,895	209,741	224,090	258,756	256,211	287,450	343,928	274,272	252,379
Direct investment receipts	65,973	67,246	77,344	95,260	102,505	115,323	103,963	131,626	151,839	124,333	142,933
Other private receipts	94,072	60,353	82,423	109,768	116,994	139,874	148,647	152,627	188,243	146,378	106,143
U.S. government receipts	10,525	5,126	4,128	4,713	4,591	3,559	3,601	3,197	3,846	3,561	3,303
Compensation of employees	1,172	1,820	1,943	2,179	2,181	2,270	2,437	2,748	2,933	3,090	3,163
Imports of goods and services and income payments	**-759,287**	**-821,797**	**-948,555**	**-1,075,674**	**-1,155,489**	**-1,281,291**	**-1,347,462**	**-1,499,762**	**-1,772,694**	**-1,632,072**	**-1,651,657**
Imports of goods and services	-616,094	-711,542	-799,811	-888,794	-953,746	-1,040,920	-1,095,711	-1,226,674	-1,445,438	-1,365,399	-1,392,145
Goods, balance of payments basis [1]	-498,435	-589,394	-668,690	-749,374	-803,113	-876,485	-917,112	-1,029,987	-1,224,417	-1,145,927	-1,164,746
Services [2]	-117,659	-122,148	-131,121	-139,420	-150,633	-164,435	-178,599	-196,687	-221,021	-219,472	-227,399
Direct defense expenditures	-17,531	-12,086	-10,217	-10,043	-11,061	-11,707	-12,185	-13,335	-13,473	-14,975	-19,245
Travel	-37,349	-40,713	-43,782	-44,916	-48,078	-52,051	-56,483	-58,963	-64,705	-60,200	-58,044
Passenger fares	-10,531	-11,410	-13,062	-14,663	-15,809	-18,138	-19,971	-21,315	-24,274	-22,633	-19,969
Other transportation	-24,966	-24,524	-26,019	-27,034	-27,403	-28,959	-30,363	-34,139	-41,425	-38,682	-38,527
Royalties and license fees [5]	-3,135	-5,032	-5,852	-6,919	-7,837	-9,161	-11,235	-13,107	-16,468	-16,713	-19,258
Other private services [4,5]	-22,229	-26,129	-29,629	-33,222	-37,758	-41,657	-45,513	-53,007	-57,793	-63,387	-69,436
U.S. government miscellaneous services	-1,919	-2,255	-2,560	-2,623	-2,687	-2,762	-2,849	-2,821	-2,883	-2,882	-2,920
Income payments	-143,192	-110,255	-148,744	-186,880	-201,743	-240,371	-251,751	-273,088	-327,256	-266,673	-259,512
Income payments on foreign-owned assets in the U.S.	-139,728	-105,123	-142,792	-180,617	-195,443	-233,705	-244,757	-265,133	-319,737	-258,571	-251,108
Direct investment payments	-3,450	-7,943	-22,150	-30,318	-33,093	-42,950	-38,418	-53,437	-56,910	-17,848	-49,458
Other private payments	-95,508	-57,804	-76,450	-96,490	-97,079	-112,117	-127,052	-137,149	-179,854	-160,042	-127,735
U.S. government payments	-40,770	-39,376	-44,192	-53,809	-65,271	-78,638	-79,287	-74,547	-82,973	-80,681	-73,915
Compensation of employees	-3,464	-5,132	-5,952	-6,263	-6,300	-6,666	-6,994	-7,955	-7,519	-8,102	-8,404
Unilateral current transfers, net	**-26,654**	**-37,113**	**-37,583**	**-35,188**	**-38,862**	**-41,292**	**-48,435**	**-46,755**	**-55,679**	**-46,615**	**-58,853**
U.S. Government grants [3]	-10,359	-17,036	-14,978	-11,190	-15,401	-12,472	-13,270	-13,774	-16,714	-11,517	-17,097
U.S. Government pensions and other transfers	-3,224	-4,104	-4,556	-3,451	-4,466	-4,191	-4,305	-4,406	-4,705	-5,798	-5,125
Private remittances and other transfers [6]	-13,070	-15,973	-18,049	-20,547	-18,995	-24,629	-30,860	-28,575	-34,260	-29,300	-36,631

See footnotes at end of table.

No. 1280. U.S. International Transactions by Type of Transaction: 1990 to 2002—Con.

[See headnote, page 801]

Type of transaction	1990	1993	1994	1995	1996	1997	1998	1999	2000	2001	2002
Capital account transactions, net.	-6,579	-1,299	-1,723	-927	-654	-1,044	-740	-4,843	-799	-1,062	-1,285
U.S. assets abroad, net (increase/financial outflow (-)).	-81,234	-200,552	-176,056	-352,376	-413,923	-487,599	-347,829	-503,640	-569,798	-349,939	-178,985
U.S. official reserve assets, net.	-2,158	-1,379	5,346	-9,742	6,668	-1,010	-6,783	8,747	-290	-4,911	-3,681
Gold	-	-	-	-	-	-	-	-	-	-	-
Special drawing rights	-192	-537	-441	-808	370	-350	-147	10	-722	-630	-475
Reserve position in the International Monetary Fund	731	-44	494	-2,466	-1,280	-3,575	-5,119	5,484	2,308	-3,600	-2,632
Foreign currencies	-2,697	-797	5,293	-6,468	7,578	2,915	-1,517	3,253	-1,876	-681	-574
U.S. govt. assets, other than official reserve assets, net.	2,317	-351	-390	-984	-989	68	-422	2,750	-941	-486	-32
U.S. credits and other long-term assets [8]	-8,410	-6,311	-5,383	-4,859	-5,025	-5,417	-4,678	-6,175	-5,182	-4,431	-5,611
Repayments on U.S. credits and other long-term assets [8]	10,856	6,270	5,088	4,125	3,930	5,438	4,111	9,559	4,265	3,873	5,684
U.S. foreign currency holdings and U.S. short-term assets, net.	-130	-310	-95	-250	106	47	145	-634	-24	72	-105
U.S. private assets, net.	-81,393	-198,822	-181,012	-341,650	-419,602	-486,657	-340,624	-515,137	-568,567	-344,542	-175,272
Direct investments abroad.	-37,183	-83,950	-80,167	-98,750	-91,885	-104,803	-142,644	-224,934	-159,212	-119,963	-137,836
Foreign securities	-28,765	-146,253	-60,309	-122,506	-149,829	-118,976	-124,204	-116,236	-121,908	-84,637	15,801
U.S. claims on unaffiliated foreigners reported by U.S. nonbanking concerns.	-27,824	766	-36,336	-45,286	-86,333	-121,760	-38,204	-97,704	-138,790	-4,997	-31,880
U.S. claims reported by U.S. banks, n.i.e.	12,379	30,615	-4,200	-75,108	-91,555	-141,118	-35,572	-76,263	-148,657	-134,945	-21,357
Foreign assets in the U.S., net (increase/financial inflow (+)).	141,571	282,040	305,989	438,562	551,096	706,809	423,569	740,210	1,026,139	765,531	706,983
Foreign official assets in the U.S., net.	33,910	71,753	39,583	109,880	126,724	19,036	-19,903	43,543	37,724	5,104	94,860
Other foreign assets in the U.S., net.	107,661	210,287	266,406	328,682	424,372	687,773	443,472	696,667	988,415	760,427	612,123
Direct investments in U.S	48,494	51,362	46,121	57,776	86,502	105,603	179,045	289,444	321,274	151,581	39,633
U.S. Treasury securities	-2,534	24,381	34,274	91,544	147,022	130,435	28,581	-44,497	-76,949	-7,438	96,217
U.S. securities other than U.S. Treasury securities.	1,592	80,092	56,971	77,249	103,272	161,409	156,315	298,834	455,318	406,633	291,492
U.S. currency flows	18,800	18,900	23,400	12,300	17,362	24,782	16,622	22,407	1,129	23,783	21,513
U.S. liabilities to unaffiliated foreigners reported by U.S. nonbanking concerns.	45,133	10,489	1,302	59,637	53,736	116,518	23,140	76,247	170,672	67,489	72,142
U.S. liabilities reported by U.S. banks, n.i.e.	-3,824	25,063	104,338	30,176	16,478	149,026	39,769	54,232	116,917	118,379	91,126
Statistical discrepancy.	25,208	1,799	-10,532	19,958	-19,316	-90,482	129,691	59,119	-44,084	-20,785	-45,852
Balance on goods	-111,034	-132,451	-165,831	-174,170	-191,000	-198,119	-246,696	-346,022	-452,423	-427,215	-482,872
Balance on services	30,173	63,285	68,642	79,101	88,131	91,072	83,543	84,821	77,039	69,396	64,834
Balance on income.	28,550	24,290	17,094	25,040	24,528	20,655	6,897	17,110	19,605	10,689	-3,970
Balance on current account [9]	-78,965	-81,989	-117,678	-105,217	-117,203	-127,684	-204,691	-290,846	-411,458	-393,745	-480,861

- Represents or rounds to zero. [1] Excludes exports of goods under U.S. military agency sales contracts identified in census export documents, excludes imports of goods under direct defense expenditures identified in census import documents, and reflects various other adjustments (for valuation, coverage, and timing) of census statistics to balance of payments basis. [2] Includes some goods: Mainly military equipment included in "Transfers under U.S. military agency sales contracts"; major equipment, other materials, supplies, and petroleum products purchased abroad by U.S. military agencies included in "Direct defense expenditures" under "Imports," and fuels purchased by airline and steamship operators included in "Other transportation" under "Exports" and "Imports." [3] Includes transfers of goods and services under U.S. military grant programs. [4] Break in series. See Technical Notes in the June 1989, June 1990, 1992, 1993, 1995, and July 1996-99 issues of the survey. [5] These lines are presented on a gross basis. Exports exclude U.S. parents' payments to foreign affiliates and include U.S. affiliates' receipts from foreign parents. Imports include U.S. parents' payments to foreign affiliates and exclude U.S. affiliates' receipts from foreign parents. [6] The "other transfers" component includes taxes paid by U.S. private residents to foreign governments and taxes paid by private nonresidents to the U.S. government. [7] At the present time, all U.S. Treasury-owned gold is held in the United States. [8] Includes sales of foreign obligations to foreigners. [9] Conceptually, "Balance on current account" is equal to "net foreign investment" in the national income and product accounts (NIPAs). However, the foreign transactions account in the NIPAs (a) includes adjustments for the different geographical treatment of transactions with U.S. territories and Puerto Rico, and (c) includes services furnished without payment by financial pension plans except life insurance carriers and private noninsured pension plans.

Source: U.S. Bureau of Economic Analysis, *Survey of Current Business*, July 2003, and <http://www.bea.doc.gov/bea/international/bpweb/list.cfm?anon=153&registered=0> (released 19 June 2003).

802 Foreign Commerce and Aid

U.S. Census Bureau, Statistical Abstract of the United States: 2003

No. 1281. U.S. Balances on International Transactions by Area and Selected Country: 2001 and 2002

[In millions of dollars (-427,215 represents -$427,215,000,000). Minus sign (-) indicates debits]

Area or country	2001, balance on— Goods[1]	Services	Income	Current account	2002, balance on— Goods[1]	Services	Income	Current account
All areas	-427,215	69,396	10,689	-393,745	-482,872	64,834	-3,970	-480,861
Western Europe	-69,610	9,061	-5,648	-60,057	-92,532	12,077	-16,356	-95,055
European Economic[2]	-63,703	9,329	-6,854	-54,691	-85,029	12,167	-15,559	-86,298
Belgium-Luxembourg	3,384	962	-2,428	1,770	3,524	1,801	255	5,456
France	-10,655	215	-1,829	-12,507	-9,404	938	-1,118	-9,734
Germany	-29,672	-1,975	11,639	-17,486	-36,453	-3,822	4,493	-34,970
Italy	-14,051	-793	2,166	-12,934	-14,388	-2	2,043	-12,499
Netherlands	9,872	1,072	9,411	20,039	8,310	1,365	9,971	19,514
United Kingdom	-1,281	3,962	-31,184	-25,033	-8,376	4,893	-35,649	-37,574
Eastern Europe	-7,537	1,971	-771	-9,954	-8,517	1,675	-1,145	-12,401
Canada	-55,478	6,816	21,416	-28,089	-50,866	5,796	15,259	-30,401
Latin America, other Western Hemisphere	-40,637	16,160	3,342	-41,095	-57,070	12,400	-4,291	-72,259
Mexico	-31,024	4,431	-1,324	-34,314	-38,220	4,670	-1,945	-42,113
Venezuela	-9,650	2,813	-327	-7,325	-11,127	2,429	-250	-9,102
Japan[3]	-70,605	12,520	-18,470	-76,680	-71,764	11,455	-20,247	-80,064
Other Asia and Africa	-187,482	19,049	-5,938	-193,824	-208,437	16,190	5,125	-212,513
Australia	4,134	1,278	1,279	6,263	6,314	2,296	2,687	11,059
South Africa	-1,479	370	148	-1,371	-1,520	307	287	-1,159
International and unallocated	(NA)	2,541	15,479	9,691	(NA)	2,945	14,998	10,773

NA Not available. [1] Adjusted to balance of payments basis; excludes exports under U.S. military sales contracts and imports under direct defense expenditures. [2] Includes Denmark, Greece, Ireland, Spain, Portugal, European Atomic Energy Community, European Coal and Steel Community, and European Investment Bank, not shown separately. [3] Includes Ryukyu Islands.
Source: U.S. Bureau of Economic Analysis, Survey of Current Business, July 2003 and <http://www.bea.doc.gov/bea/international/bpweb/list.cfm?anon=153&registered=0> (released 19 June 2003).

No. 1282. Private International Service Transactions by Type of Service and Country: 1990 to 2002

[In millions of dollars (137,232 represents $137,232,000,000). For all transactions, see Table 1280]

Type of service and country	Exports 1990	2000	2001	2002	Imports 1990	2000	2001	2002
Total private services	137,232	283,484	275,498	279,495	98,210	204,665	201,615	205,234
TYPE								
Travel	43,007	82,400	71,893	66,547	37,349	64,705	60,200	58,044
Passenger fares	15,298	20,687	17,926	17,046	10,531	24,274	22,633	19,969
Other transportation	22,042	29,803	28,442	29,166	24,966	41,425	38,682	38,527
Freight	8,379	12,547	11,731	12,330	15,046	27,388	25,736	25,973
Port services	13,662	17,256	16,711	16,836	9,920	14,037	12,946	12,554
Royalties and license fees	16,634	43,233	41,098	44,142	3,135	16,468	16,713	19,258
Other private services	40,251	107,361	116,139	122,594	22,229	57,793	63,387	69,436
Affiliated services	13,622	35,857	39,760	43,500	9,117	28,776	30,053	32,367
Unaffiliated services	26,629	71,504	76,379	79,094	13,111	29,017	33,334	37,069
Education	5,126	10,348	11,478	12,759	658	2,034	2,269	2,466
Financial services	4,417	15,522	15,228	15,859	2,475	4,564	4,049	3,665
Insurance, net	230	2,486	2,399	2,839	1,910	7,598	11,613	15,348
Telecommunications	2,735	3,883	4,504	4,137	5,583	5,428	4,756	4,180
Business, professional, and technical services	7,752	25,318	28,611	28,799	2,093	8,769	10,034	10,732
AREA AND COUNTRY								
Canada	15,684	24,400	24,544	24,296	9,130	17,565	17,599	18,413
Europe	48,192	107,676	104,933	110,299	39,815	88,809	88,574	89,923
Belgium-Luxembourg	1,763	3,285	3,360	4,235	1,022	2,376	2,249	2,177
France	5,542	10,508	10,115	10,740	4,169	10,544	9,891	9,654
Germany	7,364	16,105	15,146	16,057	6,819	12,264	12,554	14,703
Italy	3,279	5,431	5,146	5,386	3,469	5,036	5,198	4,615
Netherlands	3,269	7,048	6,981	7,219	1,935	5,592	6,194	6,038
United Kingdom	12,989	31,738	30,887	31,818	11,564	27,643	26,658	26,586
Latin America and other Western Hemisphere	21,957	54,256	54,364	52,303	18,643	36,701	38,301	39,593
Mexico	8,590	14,301	15,152	15,904	6,731	10,772	10,543	11,066
Venezuela	1,273	3,305	3,483	2,883	659	610	658	454
Australia	3,260	5,540	4,871	5,202	2,290	3,480	3,653	2,935
Japan	21,159	33,145	30,054	29,685	10,529	17,329	16,556	17,312
Int'l organizations and unallocated	6,077	6,387	5,908	6,491	2,646	3,928	3,364	3,545

Source: U.S. Bureau of Economic Analysis, Survey of Current Business, October 2002 and July 2003.

No. 1283. International Investment Position by Type of Investment: 1990 to 2001

[In millions of dollars (-245,347 represents -$245,347,000,000). Estimates for end of year; subject to considerable error due to nature of basic data. Unless otherwise specified, types below refer to current-cost method. For information on current-cost method and market value, see article cited]

Type of investment	1990	1995	1997	1998	1999	2000	2001
U.S. net international investment position:							
Current cost	-245,347	-495,966	-833,158	-918,319	-784,094	-1,350,791	-1,948,134
Market value	-164,495	-343,340	-835,208	-1,094,156	-1,053,554	-1,583,153	-2,309,117
U.S.-owned assets abroad:							
Current cost	2,178,978	3,451,983	4,567,906	5,091,058	5,959,014	6,191,934	6,196,139
Market value	2,294,085	3,930,269	5,379,128	6,174,452	7,386,970	7,350,862	6,862,943
U.S. official reserve assets	174,664	176,061	134,836	146,006	136,418	128,400	129,961
Gold	102,406	101,279	75,929	75,291	75,950	71,799	72,328
Special drawing rights	10,989	11,037	10,027	10,603	10,336	10,539	10,783
Reserve position in IMF	9,076	14,649	18,071	24,111	17,950	14,824	17,869
Foreign currencies	52,193	49,096	30,809	36,001	32,182	31,238	28,981
U.S. Government assets, other	84,344	85,064	86,198	86,768	84,224	85,164	85,650
U.S. loans and other long-term assets	83,716	82,802	84,130	84,850	81,654	82,570	83,128
Repayable in dollars	82,602	82,358	83,780	84,528	81,364	82,289	82,850
Other	1,114	444	350	322	290	281	278
U.S. foreign currency holdings and short-term assets	628	2,262	2,068	1,918	2,570	2,594	2,522
U.S. private assets:							
Current cost	1,919,970	3,190,858	4,346,872	4,858,284	5,738,372	5,978,370	5,980,528
Market value	2,035,077	3,669,144	5,158,094	5,941,678	7,166,328	7,137,298	6,647,332
Direct investments abroad:							
Current cost	616,655	885,506	1,068,063	1,196,207	1,377,263	1,515,279	1,623,122
Market value	731,762	1,363,792	1,879,285	2,279,601	2,805,219	2,674,207	2,289,926
Foreign securities	342,313	1,169,636	1,751,183	2,052,929	2,583,326	2,389,427	2,110,520
Bonds	144,717	392,827	543,396	576,745	556,688	557,019	545,782
Corporate stocks	197,596	776,809	1,207,787	1,476,184	2,026,638	1,832,408	1,564,738
U.S. claims on unaffiliated foreigners [1]	265,315	367,567	545,524	588,322	677,498	821,564	830,111
U.S. claims reported by U.S. banks [2]	695,687	768,149	982,102	1,020,826	1,100,285	1,252,100	1,416,775
Foreign-owned assets in the U.S.:							
Current cost	2,424,325	3,947,949	5,401,064	6,009,377	6,743,108	7,542,725	8,144,273
Market value	2,458,580	4,273,609	6,214,336	7,268,608	8,440,524	8,934,015	9,172,060
Foreign official assets in the U.S.	373,293	682,873	873,716	896,174	945,594	1,008,890	1,021,738
U.S. Government securities	291,228	507,460	648,188	669,768	693,781	749,904	798,844
U.S. Treasury securities	285,911	489,952	615,076	622,921	617,680	625,161	650,703
Other	5,317	17,508	33,112	46,847	76,101	124,743	148,141
Other U.S. government liabilities	17,243	23,573	21,712	18,386	15,647	13,739	11,857
U.S. liabilities reported by U.S. banks	39,880	107,394	135,384	125,883	138,847	153,403	123,125
Other foreign official assets	24,942	44,446	68,432	82,137	97,319	91,844	87,912
Other foreign assets in the U.S:							
Current cost	2,051,032	3,265,076	4,527,348	5,113,203	5,797,514	6,533,835	7,122,535
Market value	2,085,287	3,590,736	5,340,620	6,372,434	7,494,930	7,925,125	8,150,322
Direct investments:							
Current cost	505,346	680,066	824,136	919,804	1,100,777	1,374,752	1,498,924
Market value	539,601	1,005,726	1,637,408	2,179,035	2,798,193	2,766,042	2,526,711
U.S. Treasury securities	152,452	330,210	550,613	562,036	462,761	400,966	388,774
U.S. currency	85,933	169,484	211,628	228,250	250,657	251,786	275,569
U.S. securities other than U.S. Treasury securities	460,644	969,849	1,512,725	1,903,443	2,351,291	2,623,628	2,856,654
Corporate and other bonds	238,903	459,080	618,837	724,619	825,175	1,075,988	1,392,620
Corporate stocks	221,741	510,769	893,888	1,178,824	1,526,116	1,547,640	1,464,034
U.S. liabilities to unaffiliated foreigners [1]	213,406	300,424	459,407	485,675	564,873	729,340	804,417
U.S. liabilities reported by U.S. banks [2]	633,251	815,043	968,839	1,013,995	1,067,155	1,153,363	1,298,197

[1] Reported by U.S. nonbanking concerns.   [2] Not included elsewhere.

Source: U.S. Bureau of Economic Analysis, *Survey of Current Business*, July 2002.

No. 1284. U.S. Reserve Assets: 1990 to 2002

[In billions of dollars (83.3 represents $83,300,000,000). As of end of year, except as indicated]

Type	1990	1995	1996	1997	1998	1999	2000	2001	2002
Total	83.3	85.8	75.1	70.0	81.8	71.5	67.6	68.7	79.0
Gold stock	11.1	11.1	11.0	11.0	11.0	11.0	11.0	11.0	11.0
Special drawing rights	11.0	11.0	10.3	10.0	10.6	10.3	10.5	10.8	12.2
Foreign currencies	52.2	49.1	38.3	30.8	36.0	32.2	31.2	29.0	33.8
Reserve position in IMF [1]	9.1	14.6	15.4	18.1	24.1	18.0	14.8	17.9	22.0

[1] International Monetary Fund.

Source: Board of Governors of the Federal Reserve System, *Federal Reserve Bulletin*, monthly; and Department of the Treasury, *Treasury Bulletin*, monthly.

No. 1285. Foreign Direct Investment Position in the United States on a Historical-Cost Basis by Industry and Selected Country: 1990 to 2002

[In millions of dollars (394,911 represents $394,911,000,000)]

Country	1990	1995	2000	2001	2002 Total [1]	2002 Manufacturing	2002 Wholesale	2002 Information
All countries	394,911	535,553	1,256,867	1,355,114	1,347,994	470,893	188,819	185,408
Canada	29,544	45,618	114,309	102,127	92,041	23,343	1,969	3,880
Europe	247,320	332,374	887,014	1,005,606	1,006,530	383,544	120,727	165,305
Austria	625	1,553	3,007	2,878	3,439	1,541	192	-2
Belgium	3,900	4,397	14,787	16,796	9,608	2,843	1,242	(D)
Denmark	819	3,444	4,025	1,736	1,924	2,259	(D)	-1
Finland	1,504	2,710	8,875	7,615	7,212	4,447	(D)	318
France	18,650	36,167	125,740	148,282	170,619	70,169	12,623	30,799
Germany	28,232	46,017	122,412	164,017	137,036	51,190	8,952	28,997
Ireland	1,340	4,749	25,523	24,958	26,179	2,657	5,006	645
Italy	1,524	3,062	6,576	6,629	6,695	1,508	827	25
Luxembourg	2,195	5,756	58,930	34,111	34,349	12,926	1,156	5,523
Netherlands	64,671	65,116	138,894	157,596	154,753	59,640	6,557	5,634
Norway	773	2,172	2,665	2,570	3,416	2,208	415	(D)
Spain	792	3,237	5,068	4,640	4,739	1,588	128	(D)
Sweden	5,484	9,584	21,991	22,011	21,989	8,979	4,117	94
Switzerland	17,674	27,458	64,719	118,447	113,232	77,630	4,117	11,339
United Kingdom	98,676	116,272	277,613	269,321	283,317	74,243	73,742	71,830
Latin America and other Western Hemisphere	20,168	27,873	53,691	54,082	52,291	5,405	8,391	-704
South and Central America	6,140	8,067	13,384	16,338	16,917	-1,607	5,474	(D)
Mexico	575	1,850	7,462	7,336	7,857	788	1,440	(D)
Panama	4,188	4,939	3,819	4,391	5,668	-2,672	26	-7
Other Western Hemisphere	14,028	19,806	40,307	37,744	35,374	7,012	2,918	(D)
Bahamas	1,535	1,286	1,254	1,153	1,332	213	637	1
Netherlands Antilles	12,974	8,044	3,807	4,255	4,680	565	373	(D)
United Kingdom Islands, Caribbean	-2,979	7,207	15,191	26,200	25,502	4,377	1,671	247
Africa	505	1,113	2,700	2,397	2,344	661	364	(D)
Middle East	4,425	5,801	6,506	6,145	6,766	836	2,554	(D)
Israel	640	1,883	3,012	2,945	3,205	858	139	339
Kuwait	1,805	2,525	908	964	989	2	(Z)	-
Saudi Arabia	1,811	1,211	(D)	(D)	(D)	-17	(D)	-
Asia and Pacific	92,948	122,774	192,647	184,757	188,023	57,105	54,814	16,408
Australia	6,542	10,356	18,775	22,289	24,470	3,457	45	(D)
Hong Kong	1,511	1,511	1,493	1,542	2,189	588	438	202
Japan	83,091	104,997	159,690	150,008	152,032	49,833	52,383	(D)
Singapore	1,289	1,637	5,087	3,490	2,902	1,703	52	36
Taiwan	836	2,142	3,174	2,537	2,311	1,015	348	34

- Represents or rounds to zero. D Suppressed to avoid disclosure of data of individual companies. Z Less than $500,000. [1] Includes other industries not shown separately.
Source: U.S. Bureau of Economic Analysis, *Survey of Current Business*, September 2002.

No. 1286. U.S. Affiliates of Foreign Companies—Assets, Sales, Employment, Land, Exports, and Imports: 2000

[A U.S. affiliate is a U.S. business enterprise in which one foreign owner (individual, branch, partnership, association, trust, corporation, or government) has a direct or indirect voting interest of 10 percent or more. Estimates cover the universe of nonbank affiliates. These data are now on a NAICS (North American Industry Classification System, 1997) basis and not comparable to previous data, which were based on the Standard Industrial Classification system]

Industry	Total assets (mil. dol.)	Sales (mil. dol.)[1]	Employment (1,000)[2]	Employee compensation (mil. dol.)	Gross book value (mil. dol.) P & E[3]	Gross book value Land	Merchandise exports[4] (mil. dol.)	Merchandise imports[4] (mil. dol.)
All industries	4,847,267	2,334,692	6,429.2	329,686	1,176,129	54,136	165,321	366,647
Manufacturing[5]	1,108,046	979,597	2,658.3	152,332	507,657	16,569	101,248	149,875
Petroleum and coal products	60,570	108,263	28.8	2,311	44,925	1,182	1,381	12,096
Chemicals	257,094	160,496	386.8	28,085	115,618	3,145	15,528	16,388
Computers and electronic products	173,303	129,225	337.4	23,465	45,576	935	19,329	37,731
Transportation equipment	199,695	205,220	390.8	21,906	86,404	866	30,731	46,806
Wholesale trade[5]	407,715	637,978	574.4	36,404	182,941	4,792	57,844	207,041
Motor vehicles and motor vehicle parts and supplies	91,594	123,174	57.5	4,453	42,448	783	2,931	75,208
Petroleum and petroleum products	109,166	170,369	67.7	4,414	(D)	(D)	11,856	24,187
Retail trade	74,259	114,977	674.4	16,005	36,256	2,455	1,535	(D)
Information	318,489	121,684	408.9	26,441	105,989	1,110	709	240
Finance (except depository institutions) and insurance	2,472,481	243,237	291.8	36,492	57,144	1,312	(Z)	5
Real estate and rental and leasing	122,797	25,691	49.5	2,855	98,483	15,498	(D)	649
Professional, scientific, and technical services	51,405	32,241	148.9	9,401	12,406	230	366	336
Other industries	292,075	179,186	1,623.1	49,756	175,252	12,171	(D)	(D)

D Withheld to avoid disclosure of data of individual companies. Z Less than $500,000. [1] Excludes returns, discounts, allowances, and sales and excise taxes. [2] Average number of full-time and part-time employees. [3] Plant and equipment (P & E). Includes mineral rights and minor amounts of property other than land. [4] F.a.s. value at port of exportation. [5] includes industries not shown separately.
Source: U.S. Bureau of Economic Analysis, *Survey of Current Business*, August 2002; and *Foreign Direct Investment in the United States, Operations of U.S. Affiliates of Foreign Companies, Preliminary 2000 Estimates.*

Foreign Commerce and Aid   805

No. 1287. Foreign Direct Investment in the United States—Gross Book Value and Employment of U.S. Affiliates of Foreign Companies by State: 1990 to 2000

[578,355 represents $578,355,000,000. A U.S. affiliate is a U.S. business enterprise in which one foreign owner (individual, branch, partnership, association, trust corporation, or government) has a direct or indirect voting interest of 10 percent or more. Estimates cover the universe of nonbank U.S. affiliates]

State and other area	Gross book value of property, plant, and equipment (mil. dol.) 1990	1995	1999	2000, prel.	Total employment 1990 (1,000)	1995 (1,000)	1999 (1,000)	2000, prel. Total (1,000)	Percent of all businesses
Total	578,355	769,491	1,075,364	1,176,129	4,734.5	4,941.8	6,027.6	6429.2	(X)
United States	552,902	733,089	981,405	1,071,711	4,704.4	4,898.9	6,002.7	6403.8	5.6
Alabama	7,300	10,598	17,758	17,208	55.7	60.6	80.6	76.8	4.7
Alaska	19,435	25,558	28,205	28,992	13.2	9.8	10.7	11.6	5.4
Arizona	7,234	6,699	10,597	10,692	57.1	51.9	70.7	75.2	3.8
Arkansas	2,344	3,666	4,540	4,603	29.2	32.1	38.1	40.4	4.1
California	75,768	96,576	111,629	120,949	555.9	548.6	641.4	737.6	5.7
Colorado	6,544	8,602	10,352	15,133	56.3	72.2	92.5	101.0	5.2
Connecticut	5,357	8,466	11,297	13,217	75.9	73.3	103.4	116.0	7.6
Delaware	5,818	2,919	5,552	6,603	43.1	15.8	28.0	33.4	8.9
District of Columbia	3,869	4,983	3,859	4,263	11.4	13.4	15.6	17.1	3.7
Florida	18,659	24,865	36,263	38,281	205.7	210.0	286.5	306.9	4.8
Georgia	16,729	22,432	27,378	29,739	161.0	180.1	215.7	223.9	6.5
Hawaii	11,830	15,972	11,460	10,696	53.0	48.9	44.3	43.3	9.5
Idaho	776	1,026	2,253	2,624	11.7	11.3	18.4	14.2	3.0
Illinois	23,420	34,305	44,988	46,416	245.8	237.0	285.8	317.1	5.9
Indiana	13,426	18,782	29,378	30,095	126.9	136.9	164.9	165.9	6.2
Iowa	2,712	4,527	7,432	7,259	32.8	35.8	40.6	40.3	3.2
Kansas	5,134	3,233	7,151	8,893	29.6	34.0	54.9	60.6	5.3
Kentucky	9,229	15,136	18,021	21,933	65.7	83.4	97.0	104.1	6.7
Louisiana	17,432	20,543	31,868	31,050	61.4	51.0	62.7	61.1	3.8
Maine	2,080	3,885	4,404	5,000	26.6	29.1	32.8	33.4	6.5
Maryland	5,713	9,197	11,277	13,052	79.6	95.0	98.3	110.4	5.3
Massachusetts	8,890	12,707	17,344	23,151	131.2	141.5	194.6	223.2	7.4
Michigan	12,012	21,370	41,561	39,090	139.6	170.3	247.4	246.5	6.0
Minnesota	11,972	8,688	11,413	13,174	89.8	79.8	91.1	103.1	4.3
Mississippi	2,989	3,055	4,417	4,043	23.6	22.6	25.3	23.9	2.5
Missouri	5,757	8,327	15,360	15,500	73.7	79.3	101.0	105.1	4.4
Montana	2,181	1,938	2,488	3,066	5.1	4.4	13.7	6.8	2.1
Nebraska	776	1,320	2,649	2,730	14.9	15.7	25.2	21.8	2.8
Nevada	5,450	8,242	10,217	10,457	22.7	25.0	34.0	35.7	3.8
New Hampshire	1,446	2,212	2,852	5,104	25.9	30.0	35.9	45.9	8.3
New Jersey	18,608	26,175	34,855	36,734	227.0	205.2	246.6	269.1	7.7
New Mexico	4,312	4,363	5,534	6,076	17.4	16.2	16.4	16.3	2.8
New York	36,424	52,992	61,900	71,657	347.5	343.8	410.3	471.6	6.4
North Carolina	15,234	21,475	28,932	29,777	181.0	225.3	261.8	261.6	7.7
North Dakota	1,251	915	1,819	1,817	3.1	3.2	7.7	8.6	3.2
Ohio	20,549	29,932	38,622	37,597	219.1	222.1	263.7	259.4	5.2
Oklahoma	6,049	5,448	6,834	7,822	43.6	34.2	44.0	41.8	3.4
Oregon	3,427	5,807	9,479	13,153	39.1	49.7	58.8	62.3	4.5
Pennsylvania	16,587	24,432	33,742	34,170	221.6	231.6	261.5	280.8	5.5
Rhode Island	1,120	2,240	2,505	3,418	13.3	16.2	21.6	24.4	5.7
South Carolina	10,067	13,438	21,680	23,666	104.7	111.6	137.0	137.6	8.7
South Dakota	553	665	932	1,023	4.5	4.6	6.5	6.9	2.2
Tennessee	10,280	14,227	19,331	20,314	116.9	136.3	151.7	148.6	6.2
Texas	57,079	68,142	96,570	110,853	299.5	326.4	416.0	437.9	5.4
Utah	3,918	5,612	9,336	14,308	21.0	28.6	35.2	37.4	4.0
Vermont	631	1,037	1,296	2,138	7.7	10.4	11.6	11.6	4.4
Virginia	10,702	15,129	21,491	23,241	113.3	141.4	171.1	179.2	6.1
Washington	7,985	11,462	19,001	22,100	77.5	83.0	96.4	104.2	4.5
West Virginia	7,975	7,809	7,288	6,973	34.9	31.9	27.6	27.6	4.8
Wisconsin	5,088	7,415	10,900	13,771	81.4	71.5	99.4	106.8	4.3
Wyoming	2,782	4,544	5,396	8,089	5.8	6.9	6.7	7.8	4.2
Puerto Rico	1,499	2,174	2,157	2,194	16.1	27.4	16.7	17.9	(NA)
Other territories and offshore	18,484	17,798	29,121	33,981	9.0	13.1	7.9	7.1	(NA)
Foreign	5,470	16,430	1,635	2,329	5.0	2.4	0.3	0.5	(NA)
Unspecified [1]	(NA)	(NA)	61,046	65,914	(NA)	(NA)	(NA)	(NA)	(NA)

NA Not available.   X Not applicable.   [1] Covers property, plant, and equipment not located in a particular state, including aircraft, railroad rolling stock, satellites, undersea cable, and trucks engaged in interstate transportation.

Source: U.S. Bureau of Economic Analysis, *Survey of Current Business*, August 2002 issue, and *Foreign Direct Investment in the United States, Operations of U.S. Affiliates of Foreign Companies*, annual.

No. 1288. U.S. Businesses Acquired or Established by Foreign Direct Investors—Investment Outlays by Industry of U.S. Business Enterprise and Country of Ultimate Beneficial Owner: 1990 to 2002

[In millions of dollars (65,932 represents $65,932,000,000). Foreign direct investment is the ownership or control directly or indirectly, by one foreign individual branch, partnership, association, trust, corporation, or government of 10 percent or more of the voting securities of a U.S. business enterprise or an equivalent interest in an unincorporated one. Data represent number and full cost of acquisitions of existing U.S. business enterprises, including business segments or operating units of existing U.S. business enterprises and establishments of new enterprises. Investments may be made by the foreign direct investor itself, or indirectly by an existing U.S. affiliate of the foreign direct investor. Covers investments in U.S. business enterprises with assets of over $1 million, or ownership of 200 acres of U.S. land]

Industry and country	1990	1995	1997	1998	1999	2000	2001	2002, prel.
Total	65,932	57,195	69,708	215,256	274,956	335,629	147,109	52,558
By type of investment:								
U.S. businesses acquired	(NA)	47,179	60,733	182,357	265,127	322,703	138,091	42,773
U.S. businesses established	(NA)	10,016	8,974	32,899	9,829	12,926	9,017	9,785
By type of investor:								
Foreign direct investors	(NA)	11,927	13,899	120,828	120,878	105,151	23,134	14,512
U.S. affiliates	(NA)	45,268	55,809	94,428	154,078	230,478	123,975	38,045
INDUSTRY								
Manufacturing	(NA)	(NA)	(NA)	149,243	73,122	143,285	37,592	17,259
Wholesale trade	(NA)	(NA)	(NA)	3,321	(D)	8,561	3,982	381
Retail trade	(NA)	(NA)	(NA)	1,153	3,458	1,672	1,913	433
Information	(NA)	(NA)	(NA)	13,399	90,855	67,932	27,599	14,235
Depository institutions	(NA)	(NA)	(NA)	1,563	(D)	2,636	5,709	705
Finance, (except depository institutions) and insurance	(NA)	(NA)	(NA)	21,057	46,380	44,420	40,780	3,241
Real estate and rental and leasing	(NA)	(NA)	(NA)	6,299	5,206	4,526	3,572	4,573
Professional, scientific, and technical services	(NA)	(NA)	(NA)	4,289	9,366	32,332	7,044	4,424
Other industries	(NA)	(NA)	(NA)	14,932	32,680	30,264	18,917	7,306
COUNTRY [1]								
Canada	3,430	8,029	11,755	22,635	9,271	28,346	16,646	3,533
Europe	36,011	38,195	44,014	170,173	196,288	249,167	78,328	39,374
France	10,217	1,129	2,578	14,493	23,750	26,149	5,772	15,566
Germany	2,363	13,117	6,464	39,873	21,514	18,452	12,733	2,194
Netherlands	2,247	1,061	10,244	19,009	22,265	47,686	14,879	3,181
Switzerland	3,905	7,533	6,745	4,525	7,512	22,789	16,468	2,756
United Kingdom	13,096	9,094	11,834	84,995	109,226	110,208	17,095	12,956
Other Europe	4,183	6,261	6,149	7,278	12,021	23,883	11,381	2,721
Latin America and other Western Hemisphere	796	1,550	924	11,354	33,046	15,400	15,274	3,021
South and Central America	399	1,283	166	920	1,622	5,334	431	407
Other Western Hemisphere	397	267	758	10,433	31,424	10,066	14,843	2,613
Africa	(D)	(D)	(D)	212	(D)	(D)	(D)	565
Middle East	472	447	847	2,810	848	947	(D)	283
Asia and Pacific	23,170	8,688	11,786	7,329	15,100	40,282	11,383	5,352
Australia	1,412	2,270	7,600	(D)	(D)	(D)	4,869	1,654
Japan	19,933	3,602	2,326	4,862	11,696	26,044	5,345	3,429
Other Asia and Pacific	1,825	2,816	1,860	(D)	(D)	(D)	1,169	269

D Suppressed to avoid disclosure of data of individual companies. NA Not available. [1] For investments in which more than one investor participated, each investor and each investor's outlays are classified by country of each ultimate beneficial owner.
Source: U.S. Bureau of Economic Analysis, *Survey of Current Business*, June 2003, and previous June issues.

No. 1289. U.S. Direct Investment Position Abroad, Capital Outflows, and Income by Industry of Foreign Affiliates: 2000 to 2002

[In millions of dollars (1,316,247 represents $1,316,247,000,000). See headnote, Table 1290]

Industry	Direct investment position on a historical-cost basis			Capital outflows (inflows (-))			Income		
	2000	2001	2002	2000	2001	2002	2000	2001	2002
All industries, total	1,316,247	1,383,225	1,520,965	142,627	103,767	119,742	133,692	107,060	123,889
Mining	72,111	78,319	80,976	2,174	12,823	9,011	13,164	10,011	10,165
Utilities	21,964	23,214	20,932	2,466	2,436	-3,301	1,610	1,574	1,552
Manufacturing	343,899	365,924	392,553	43,002	29,899	29,510	42,230	32,234	31,279
Food	23,497	24,681	28,240	2,014	2,274	3,893	2,681	2,626	3,440
Chemicals	75,807	93,779	99,371	3,812	8,270	10,116	11,552	10,313	12,065
Primary and fabricated metals	21,644	22,699	24,359	1,233	1,251	1,814	1,536	1,379	973
Machinery	22,229	21,292	22,025	2,659	-845	161	2,257	1,261	1,412
Computer and electronic products	59,909	65,559	69,208	17,303	8,659	992	8,860	5,868	3,764
Electrical equipment, appliances, and components	1,079	478	397	10,005	10,118	10,166	2,100	1,115	100
Transportation equipment	49,887	44,210	48,378	7,814	2,809	3,238	4,107	1,921	1,477
Wholesale trade	93,936	102,322	114,895	11,938	9,096	7,182	14,198	13,002	13,229
Information	52,345	50,492	53,841	16,531	3,519	1,533	-964	-3,491	237
Depository institutions	40,152	52,681	52,935	-1,274	9,715	-1,185	2,191	2,662	2,270
Finance and insurance	217,086	225,556	244,480	21,659	5,807	25,775	15,210	8,430	14,005
Professional, scientific, and technical	32,868	34,704	38,307	5,441	3,442	2,448	3,548	2,084	2,968
Other industries	441,886	450,013	522,047	40,690	27,030	48,769	42,504	40,555	48,184

Source: U.S. Bureau of Economic Analysis, *Survey of Current Business*, July 2003 issue.

Foreign Commerce and Aid   807

No. 1290. U.S. Direct Investment Position Abroad on a Historical-Cost Basis by Country: 1990 to 2002

[In millions of dollars (430,521 represents 430,521,000,000). U.S. direct investment abroad is the ownership or control by one U.S. person of 10 percent or more of the voting securities of an incorporated foreign business enterprise or an equivalent interest in a unincorporated foreign business enterprise. Negative position can occur when a U.S. parent company's liabilities to the foreign affiliate are greater than its equity in, and loans to the foreign affiliate]

Country	1990	1995	1997	1998	1999	2000	2001	2002
All countries	430,521	699,015	871,316	1,000,703	1,215,960	1,316,247	1,383,225	1,520,965
Canada	69,508	83,498	96,626	98,200	119,590	132,472	141,789	152,522
Europe	214,739	344,596	425,139	518,433	627,754	687,320	716,901	796,913
Austria	1,113	2,829	2,646	3,856	3,848	2,872	3,629	3,988
Belgium	9,464	18,706	17,337	17,899	21,756	17,973	19,395	24,122
Denmark	1,726	2,161	2,385	2,764	3,846	5,270	4,615	7,688
Finland	544	965	1,311	1,628	1,379	1,342	1,421	1,397
France	19,164	33,358	36,630	42,328	43,120	42,628	40,839	43,978
Germany	27,609	44,242	40,726	47,685	53,399	55,508	65,800	64,739
Greece	282	533	634	648	760	795	842	1,056
Ireland	5,894	7,996	11,339	21,825	25,157	35,903	35,712	41,636
Italy	14,063	17,096	15,547	15,548	17,889	23,484	25,015	28,499
Luxembourg	1,697	5,929	10,258	14,571	22,148	27,849	29,940	35,727
Netherlands	19,120	42,113	68,619	89,978	121,315	115,429	126,076	145,474
Norway	4,209	4,741	6,633	6,897	5,944	4,379	5,659	7,348
Portugal	897	1,413	1,399	1,360	2,188	2,664	2,852	3,394
Spain	7,868	10,856	11,541	14,221	19,970	21,236	20,514	23,884
Sweden	1,787	6,816	3,542	5,237	10,624	25,959	17,356	18,999
Switzerland	25,099	31,125	30,634	38,225	40,532	55,377	60,675	70,051
Turkey	522	973	1,033	1,014	1,792	1,826	1,698	1,888
United Kingdom	72,707	106,332	154,462	183,035	216,638	230,762	238,773	255,391
Latin America and other Western Hemisphere	71,413	131,377	180,818	196,755	253,928	266,576	282,328	272,363
South America	22,933	49,170	69,507	72,593	83,477	84,220	82,799	74,694
Argentina	2,531	7,660	10,980	12,327	18,865	17,488	15,799	11,303
Brazil	14,384	25,002	35,778	37,195	37,184	36,717	35,523	31,715
Chile	1,896	6,216	9,148	9,029	10,177	10,052	12,026	11,625
Colombia	1,677	3,506	4,097	3,749	3,775	3,693	3,603	3,735
Ecuador	280	889	838	904	1,116	832	480	1,082
Peru	599	1,335	2,147	2,148	3,148	3,130	3,127	3,237
Venezuela	1,087	3,634	5,339	5,912	7,385	10,531	10,632	10,819
Other	479	928	1,182	1,329	1,828	1,778	1,608	1,177
Central America	20,415	33,493	48,549	56,035	73,761	73,841	84,659	81,199
Costa Rica	251	921	1,529	2,074	1,493	1,716	1,677	1,602
Honduras	262	68	183	111	347	399	242	184
Mexico	10,313	16,873	24,050	26,657	37,151	39,352	56,554	58,074
Panama	9,289	15,123	22,016	25,924	33,493	30,758	25,170	20,003
Other	299	506	771	1,269	1,277	1,618	1,015	1,336
Other Western Hemisphere	28,065	48,714	62,761	68,127	96,690	108,515	114,870	116,470
Barbados	252	698	787	929	3,030	2,141	1,435	1,487
Bermuda	20,169	28,374	38,071	41,908	50,847	60,114	66,144	68,856
Dominican Republic	529	330	488	645	968	1,143	1,233	1,123
Africa	3,650	6,017	11,330	14,061	13,118	11,891	13,411	15,066
Egypt	1,231	1,093	1,603	1,963	2,210	1,998	2,537	2,959
Nigeria	-401	629	1,396	1,686	233	470	788	1,761
South Africa	775	1,422	2,499	2,344	3,474	3,562	3,088	3,428
Other	2,045	2,873	5,833	8,068	7,202	5,861	6,998	6,919
Middle East	3,959	7,198	8,836	10,739	10,950	10,863	12,351	14,154
Israel	746	1,831	2,071	2,837	4,777	3,735	4,864	5,207
Saudi Arabia	1,899	2,741	3,821	4,672	3,336	3,661	3,527	3,687
United Arab Emirates	409	500	567	674	540	683	847	1,398
Other	905	2,126	2,377	2,556	2,298	2,784	3,113	3,862
Asia and Pacific	64,716	122,712	144,815	159,678	190,621	207,125	216,445	269,947
Australia	15,110	24,328	28,404	31,483	35,386	34,838	32,574	36,337
China	354	2,765	5,150	6,350	9,401	11,140	11,387	10,294
Hong Kong	6,055	11,768	17,315	17,548	22,759	27,447	32,089	35,764
India	372	1,105	1,563	1,592	2,390	2,379	2,775	3,678
Indonesia	3,207	6,777	6,729	8,104	8,402	8,904	8,227	7,546
Japan	22,599	37,309	33,854	41,423	55,120	57,091	58,233	65,676
Korea, South	2,695	5,557	6,467	7,365	7,474	8,968	10,524	12,192
Malaysia	1,466	4,237	6,530	5,629	6,222	7,910	7,748	8,576
New Zealand	3,156	4,601	7,160	6,021	4,852	4,271	4,395	4,383
Philippines	1,355	2,719	3,219	3,931	3,517	3,638	3,279	4,097
Singapore	3,975	12,140	18,026	17,550	20,665	24,133	26,749	61,361
Taiwan	2,226	4,293	5,007	6,295	6,744	7,836	9,109	10,091
Thailand	1,790	4,283	4,332	5,209	5,500	5,824	6,444	6,883
Other	356	830	1,058	1,177	2,190	2,746	2,911	3,068

Source: U.S. Bureau of Economic Analysis, *Survey of Current Business*, July 2003, and earlier issues.

No. 1291. U.S. Government Foreign Grants and Credits by Type and Country: 1990 to 2002

[In millions of dollars (14,396 represents $14,396,000,000). See text, this section. Negative figures (-) occur when the total of grant returns, principal repayments, and/or foreign currencies disbursed by the U.S. Government exceeds new grants and new credits utilized and/or acquisitions of foreign currencies through new sales of farm products]

Country	1990	1995	1997	1998	1999	2000	2001	2002
Total, net	14,396	12,666	12,833	14,029	18,559	17,858	12,601	17,212
Investment in financial institutions	1,304	1,517	1,588	1,580	1,451	1,500	1,704	1,485
Western Europe	-103	177	390	317	431	183	220	104
Austria	-10	-1	-1	(Z)	-	-	-	-
Belgium and Luxembourg	-9	-	-	-	-	-	-	-
Denmark	-	-	-	-	-	-	-	-
Finland	-8	-1	-1	(Z)	-	-	-	-
France	-15	-	(Z)	-	-	-	-	-
Germany	-338	(Z)	-	-	-	-	-	-1
Iceland	(Z)	-	-	-	-	-	-	-
Ireland	2	-	39	8	-	-	-	-
Italy	-30	(Z)	-	-	-	-	-	(Z)
Netherlands	-	-	-	-	-	-	-	-
Norway	-	-	-	-	-	-	-	-
Portugal	56	-16	-	26	4	-79	-28	-27
Spain	-122	-59	-37	-37	-28	-19	-19	-19
Sweden	-	-	-	-	-	-	-	-
United Kingdom	-111	-120	-127	-130	-136	-135	-56	-66
Yugoslavia [1]	-39	(X)	(X)	-1	-	1	-	-51
Former Yugoslavia [1]:								
Bosnia and Hercegovina	(X)	94	311	236	188	52	115	64
Croatia	(X)	9	-7	-11	1	3	18	36
Macedonia	(X)	1	18	7	20	50	29	15
Slovenia	(X)	-24	-15	-15	2	2	2	7
Former Yugoslavia - Regional [3]	(X)	(Z)	-8	8	21	74	87	128
Other [2] and unspecified [3]	520	293	220	229	355	234	72	17
Eastern Europe	973	1,979	1,410	1,790	2,152	1,810	1,300	1,464
Albania	-	15	11	16	4	26	38	40
Bulgaria	-	6	14	14	26	46	54	34
Czechoslovakia	(Z)	-2	-11	-	-	1	-	-
Czech Republic	(X)	3	5	5	-8	11	11	23
Estonia	(X)	2	4	6	4	6	3	-2
Hungary	1	36	-16	13	13	12	8	16
Latvia	(X)	2	4	8	9	6	1	11
Lithuania	(X)	28	23	15	4	-16	(Z)	3
Poland	912	6	29	38	24	40	-1	16
Romania	79	9	5	28	10	38	43	48
Slovakia	-	2	11	6	8	7	10	10
Soviet Union	-30	(X)	(X)	-	-	-	-	-
Newly Independent States:								
Armenia	(X)	102	26	39	35	20	52	54
Azerbaijan	(X)	19	4	6	6	8	15	32
Belarus	(X)	50	19	3	6	1	4	2
Georgia	(X)	89	38	28	23	36	49	97
Kazakhstan	(X)	17	52	70	45	42	58	52
Kyrgyzstan	(X)	33	26	30	15	15	32	36
Moldova	(X)	19	8	5	32	32	60	28
Russia	(X)	465	361	444	968	797	280	266
Tajikistan	(X)	34	27	30	6	8	34	18
Turkmenistan	(X)	16	1	3	3	4	8	6
Ukraine	(X)	171	97	172	318	138	195	118
Uzbekistan	(X)	1	2	7	19	22	41	39
Former Soviet Union - Regional [3]	(X)	613	582	603	506	501	295	510
Other [2] and unspecified [3]	11	241	85	200	61	29	10	7
Near East and South Asia	6,656	3,025	4,675	5,045	4,378	7,658	2,520	5,656
Afghanistan	57	10	17	-	2	5	6	140
Bangladesh	181	87	42	24	65	43	89	45
Cyprus	16	6	10	14	-	-	-	-
Egypt	4,976	1,639	1,375	2,018	2,093	3,091	1,296	1,689
Greece	282	261	-210	-240	-145	-169	-153	-218
India	13	48	238	167	-79	-64	-56	-122
Iran	-	-	-	-	-	-	-	-
Iraq [4]	-7	128	11	-	-	(Z)	1	(Z)
Israel	4,380	420	2,896	2,842	2,221	3,932	589	3,061
Jordan	155	129	279	217	186	317	298	483
Kuwait	-2,506	-	-	-	-	-	-	-
Lebanon	9	5	3	2	9	22	60	28
Nepal	20	20	24	20	19	15	27	28
Oman	4	4	26	20	-6	-6	-10	-8
Pakistan	531	-187	-62	-82	79	366	170	445
Saudi Arabia	-1,614	-	-	-	-	-	-	-
Sri Lanka	72	27	7	1	-6	-15	-6	-10
Syria	(Z)	-	-	-	-	-	-	-
Turkey	367	147	-129	-159	-259	-86	-5	-138
United Arab Emirates	-361	-	-	-	-	-	-	-
Yemen (Sanaa)	(X)	(X)	(X)	-	-	-	-	-
Yemen	43	3	12	5	10	16	7	5
UNRWA [5]	7	103	59	78	93	97	77	71
West Bank-Gaza	1	58	53	80	88	64	115	143
Other and unspecified [3]	29	118	25	39	10	30	15	14

See footnotes at end of table.

No. 1291. U.S. Government Foreign Grants and Credits by Type and Country: 1990 to 2002—Con.

[In millions of dollars. See headnote, p. 809]

Country	1990	1995	1997	1998	1999	2000	2001	2002
Africa	1,883	2,217	1,354	1,366	841	1,042	1,562	2,015
Algeria	59	755	93	45	-46	-53	182	-73
Angola	-15	37	41	38	21	31	43	87
Benin	5	14	23	14	23	22	38	23
Botswana	17	18	9	5	3	1	1	12
Burkina	15	23	15	17	9	7	9	12
Burundi	18	39	4	9	6	3	6	3
Cameroon	42	4	(Z)	6	2	1	3	6
Cape Verde	8	11	11	6	1	1	2	2
Chad	24	14	6	3	2	2	7	3
Congo (Kinshasa)	242	1	(Z)	1	2	9	16	33
Cote d'Ivoire	18	16	16	8	11	9	2	32
Eritrea	-	9	17	21	7	48	45	36
Ethiopia	57	127	77	162	44	142	98	87
Ghana	14	63	55	40	38	40	86	48
Guinea	16	28	28	18	22	19	45	41
Kenya	115	35	27	37	31	44	108	50
Lesotho	16	13	5	3	1	1	1	1
Liberia	32	67	28	19	26	19	19	10
Madagascar	34	33	35	44	30	21	63	36
Malawi	35	64	30	23	30	45	41	46
Mali	31	31	11	36	36	50	9	49
Mauritania	13	2	5	4	2	2	5	4
Morocco	96	-48	-42	-48	-28	-9	-29	760
Mozambique	83	115	79	81	74	119	133	105
Niger	34	31	11	13	7	5	5	9
Nigeria	156	1	-10	-4	-38	-17	17	45
Rwanda	13	138	88	32	29	26	57	32
Senegal	61	24	36	18	26	27	51	42
Sierra Leone	2	11	18	14	5	10	11	29
Somalia	80	26	10	4	12	7	1	6
South Africa	20	112	113	90	91	68	119	98
Sudan	150	11	24	28	16	17	13	11
Swaziland	14	13	12	14	-	-	-	-
Tanzania	51	19	18	27	22	15	50	44
Togo	10	3	1	2	2	2	2	4
Tunisia	44	-4	-6	-19	-22	-19	-18	-12
Uganda	43	56	56	19	51	92	55	71
Zambia	63	27	47	14	27	44	42	34
Zimbabwe	10	29	21	47	18	23	24	21
Other and unspecified [3]	157	246	343	475	248	168	200	168
Far East and Pacific	39	753	137	759	1,145	550	628	141
Australia	-34	-	-	-	-	-	-	-
Burma	1	-2	-2	-2	-	-	1	4
Cambodia	5	39	28	35	16	23	42	35
China	71	136	227	248	293	167	132	45
Hong Kong	-8	73	44	17	-17	-15	-24	-20
Indonesia	46	25	-48	24	483	270	488	221
Japan and Ryukyu Islands	-635	(Z)	-	-	-	-	1	-
Korea, Republic of	-192	-49	-51	-52	330	-132	-215	-134
Laos	(Z)	3	4	5	4	5	6	7
Malaysia	-1	(Z)	1	2	-	134	184	11
Mongolia	-	11	13	23	14	9	18	20
New Zealand	-2	-	-	-	-	-	-	-
Pacific Islands, Trust Territory of the [6]	220	209	140	175	145	145	206	193
Philippines	557	56	-46	297	-34	20	-17	-46
Singapore	(Z)	1	-	-	-	-	-	-
Taiwan	-7	-5	-1	-1	-1	-1	-1	-1
Thailand	-19	205	-285	-63	-120	-102	-118	-27
Vietnam	1	(Z)	49	-9	-6	1	10	7
Other and unspecified [3]	38	51	63	58	36	26	12	16
Western Hemisphere	2,025	485	663	1,033	5,120	1,140	1,380	704
Argentina	64	-26	-82	-84	-96	-73	-55	4
Bolivia	114	101	122	97	104	136	189	152
Brazil	261	-204	-31	90	38	195	119	106
Canada	-41	-	-	-	-	-	-	-
Chile	-32	-24	-2	5	-8	-22	-19	-19
Colombia	-30	5	27	43	173	33	71	76
Costa Rica	108	-28	-30	-27	-37	-34	-31	-27
Dominican Republic	28	-15	-29	-14	-13	-58	-41	-65
Ecuador	61	5	6	3	14	14	38	75
El Salvador	303	119	92	41	38	27	78	45

See footnotes at end of table.

No. 1291. U.S. Government Foreign Grants and Credits by Type and Country: 1990 to 2002—Con.

[In millions of dollars. See headnote, p. 809]

Country	1990	1995	1997	1998	1999	2000	2001	2002
Western Hemisphere—Continued:								
Guatemala	98	39	37	36	45	49	106	54
Guyana	42	10	12	12	5	5	9	4
Haiti	54	156	93	88	86	63	106	66
Honduras	226	77	29	31	82	100	258	85
Jamaica	108	30	-30	-21	-24	-34	-21	-15
Mexico	140	-198	-75	-127	-118	-123	14	-13
Nicaragua	105	41	44	50	53	53	152	60
Panama [7]	102	8	-15	-20	4,100	-13	-9	(Z)
Paraguay	(Z)	1	3	2	6	4	9	9
Peru	93	151	134	113	101	87	133	109
Trinidad and Tobago	5	-14	5	205	-39	-19	-21	-26
Uruguay	-3	1	2	1	2	-2	(Z)	-2
Venezuela	-18	-2	3	5	4	133	2	-8
Other [8] and unspecified [3]	236	251	351	505	605	652	292	40
Other international organizations and unspecified areas [3]	1,619	2,513	2,616	2,138	3,141	3,942	3,191	5,447

- Represents zero or rounds to zero.   X Not applicable.   Z Less than $500,000.   [1] Includes European Atomic Energy Community, European Coal and Steel Community, European Payments Union, European Productivity Agency, North Atlantic Treaty Organization, and Organization for European Economic Cooperation.   [2] In 1992, some successor countries assumed portions of outstanding credits of the former Yugoslavia (assignment of the remaining portions is pending). Subsequent negative totals reflect payments to the United States on these assumed credits which were greater than the extension of new credits and grants to these countries.   [3] In recent years, significant amounts of foreign assistance has been reported on a regional, inter-regional, and worldwide basis. Country totals in this table may understate actual assistance to many countries.   [4] Foreign assistance to Iraq in 1994-96 was direct humanitarian assistance to ethnic minorities of Northern Iraq after the conflict in the Persian Gulf.   [5] United Nations Relief and Works Agency for Palestine refugees.   [6] Excludes transactions with Commonwealth of the Northern Mariana Islands after October 1986; includes transactions with Federated States of Micronesia, Republic of the Marshall Islands, and Republic of Palau.   [7] Includes transfer of Panama Canal to the Republic of Panama on December 1999.   [8] Includes Andean Development Corporation, Caribbean Development Bank, Central American Bank for Economic Integration, Eastern Caribbean Central Bank, Inter-American Institute of Agricultural Science, Organizations of American States, and Pan American Health Organization.

Source: U.S. Bureau of Economic Analysis, press releases, and unpublished data.

No. 1292. U.S. Foreign Economic and Military Aid Programs: 1980 to 2000

[In millions of dollars (9,695 represents $9,695,000,000). For years ending September 30. Economic aid shown here represents U.S. economic aid—not just aid under the Foreign Assistance Act. Major components in recent years include AID, Food for Peace, Peace Corps, and paid-in subscriptions to international financial institutions, such as IBRD, and IDB. Annual figures are gross unadjusted program figures]

Year and region	Total economic and military aid	Economic aid Total	Economic aid Loans	Economic aid Grants	Military aid Total	Military aid Loans	Military aid Grants
1980	9,695	7,573	1,993	5,580	2,122	1,450	672
1981	10,550	7,305	1,460	5,845	3,245	2,546	699
1982	12,324	8,129	1,454	6,675	4,195	3,084	1,111
1983	14,202	8,603	1,619	6,984	5,599	3,932	1,667
1984	15,524	9,038	1,621	7,417	6,486	4,401	2,085
1985	18,128	12,327	1,579	10,748	5,801	2,365	3,436
1986	16,739	10,900	1,330	9,570	5,839	1,980	3,859
1987	14,488	9,386	1,138	8,248	5,102	953	4,149
1988	13,792	8,961	852	8,109	4,831	763	4,068
1989	14,688	9,860	694	9,166	4,828	410	4,418
1990	15,727	10,834	756	10,078	4,893	404	4,489
1991	16,663	11,904	354	11,550	4,760	428	4,332
1992	15,589	11,242	494	10,748	4,347	345	4,002
1993	28,196	24,054	462	23,593	4,143	855	3,288
1994	15,870	11,940	887	11,053	3,931	770	3,161
1995	15,108	11,295	190	11,105	3,813	558	3,255
1996	13,559	9,589	329	9,260	3,970	544	3,426
1997	13,037	9,171	218	8,953	3,866	298	3,568
1998	13,907	10,318	271	10,047	3,589	100	3,489
1999	15,987	12,308	408	11,899	3,679	152	3,527
2000, total	16,943	11,740	304	11,436	5,204	-	5,204
Near East	6,860	2,180	10	2,170	4,680	-	4,680
Sub Saharan Africa	1,553	1,499	9	1,490	54	-	54
Latin America	1,977	1,960	23	1,937	17	-	17
Asia	862	845	45	800	18	-	18
Eastern Europe	9	9	-	9	1	-	1
Western Europe	1,141	1,124	212	911	17	-	17
Eurasia	899	748	5	744	150	-	150
Oceania and other	3	3	-	-	3	-	3
Nonregional	3,639	3,375	-	3,375	263	-	263

- Represents zero.

Source: U.S. Agency for International Development, *U.S. Overseas Loans and Grants and Assistance from International Organizations,* annual.

No. 1293. U.S. Foreign Economic and Military Aid by Major Recipient Country: 1996 to 2000

[In millions of dollars (13,559.8 represents $13,559,800,000), except as indicated. For years ending Sept. 30]

Recipient country	1996	1997	1998	1999	2000 Total (mil. dol.)	Rank	Military aid (mil. dol.)	Economic aid (mil. dol.)
Total [1]	13,559.8	13,034.7	13,907.0	15,986.5	16,948.9	(X)	5,203.8	11,745.0
Afghanistan	15.2	28.3	-	19.2	30.1	55	-	30.1
Albania	21.8	8.4	34.3	53.8	65.0	28	2.2	62.8
Angola	83.5	49.4	62.8	48.5	92.3	17	-	92.3
Armenia	70.7	16.8	74.3	74.3	93.0	16	-	93.0
Azerbaijan	5.6	2.1	24.7	28.9	48.9	37	-	48.9
Bangladesh	55.5	78.2	97.7	190.6	71.9	25	0.5	71.5
Benin	16.7	17.3	22.8	29.0	21.1	64	0.4	20.7
Bolivia	90.6	131.7	109.5	135.7	232.4	7	0.5	231.9
Bosnia Hercegovina	245.6	184.1	283.5	189.6	149.4	13	51.9	97.5
Brazil	5.2	7.8	17.1	15.8	17.9	71	0.2	17.7
Bulgaria	33.3	12.4	48.2	36.7	44.3	41	5.8	38.5
Burkina Faso	13.4	13.1	16.1	17.3	16.0	73	-	16.0
Cambodia	28.9	36.5	-	14.6	24.0	61	-	24.0
Colombia	16.9	35.1	61.8	212.8	1,027.0	3	0.9	1,026.1
Congo (Kinshasa)	1.3	-	-	19.1	22.4	63	-	22.4
Croatia	15.8	2.6	17.8	16.3	54.4	33	4.5	49.9
Dominican Republic	14.3	15.1	18.3	33.7	18.4	70	0.9	17.5
East Timor	(X)	(X)	(X)	-	35.4	48	8.5	26.9
Ecuador	14.1	15.5	15.3	26.9	61.6	30	0.5	61.1
Egypt	2,125.3	2,111.7	2,129.4	2,161.3	2,042.4	2	1,301.0	741.4
El Salvador	79.0	31.6	40.7	49.4	34.0	51	0.5	33.5
Eritrea	13.8	25.0	18.5	11.2	25.7	59	-	25.7
Ethiopia	111.1	79.5	114.1	126.6	241.0	6	0.2	240.8
Georgia	20.3	2.0	81.2	101.3	105.0	15	3.4	101.6
Ghana	43.8	47.5	48.9	74.8	62.5	29	0.5	62.0
Guatemala	37.3	61.6	82.7	101.7	66.5	27	0.2	66.2
Guinea	15.7	31.7	45.9	27.5	32.4	53	0.2	32.3
Haiti	99.5	101.7	103.0	94.6	86.2	19	4.3	81.9
Honduras	26.3	29.0	21.6	105.6	38.4	47	0.5	37.8
India	157.5	126.0	126.9	172.8	168.6	12	0.5	168.1
Indonesia	34.0	34.9	99.2	205.1	201.2	8	-	201.2
Israel	3,000.0	3,000.0	3,000.0	2,940.0	4,069.1	1	3,120.0	949.1
Jamaica	32.6	24.1	15.9	21.7	19.4	66	1.0	18.5
Jordan	133.7	184.4	139.6	290.1	473.2	4	226.4	246.9
Kazakhstan	30.1	10.1	31.0	49.0	51.6	36	2.1	49.6
Kenya	16.4	29.2	67.4	78.8	79.8	21	0.4	79.4
Korea, South	6.3	50.2	70.4	156.6	79.4	22	-	79.4
Kyrgyzstan	17.3	5.5	18.5	42.8	38.7	46	1.4	37.3
Lebanon	1.5	11.6	15.0	13.8	27.5	57	0.6	26.9
Liberia	57.9	37.3	42.5	24.5	13.1	75	-	13.1
Macedonia, The Former Yugoslav Republic of	9.9	1.6	50.6	43.0	56.7	31	0.5	56.2
Madagascar	19.8	18.8	28.2	24.6	27.1	58	0.2	26.9
Malawi	31.5	37.3	39.5	29.0	44.4	40	0.3	44.0
Mali	31.1	38.5	46.8	40.8	42.9	42	0.3	42.7
Mexico	26.3	11.6	24.8	20.3	24.2	60	0.9	23.3
Moldova	32.0	4.8	31.3	48.8	45.3	38	1.7	43.5
Mongolia	5.1	11.0	13.0	14.5	18.9	69	0.5	18.4
Morocco	16.7	19.7	21.3	18.1	41.5	44	2.4	39.1
Mozambique	59.5	55.2	72.4	78.6	82.2	20	0.2	82.0
Namibia	7.0	10.5	11.9	11.6	15.0	74	0.2	14.9
Nepal	15.8	19.6	29.8	19.6	18.9	68	0.2	18.7
Nicaragua	27.3	26.9	54.4	65.8	32.2	54	0.2	32.0
Nigeria	1.8	1.3	9.6	23.7	89.1	18	10.5	78.5
Peru	103.7	126.7	168.5	196.8	191.0	10	0.5	190.5
Philippines	58.3	41.7	69.6	69.1	78.2	23	4.9	73.3
Poland	51.0	33.4	163.0	30.7	19.2	67	9.7	9.5
Romania	29.8	4.9	51.3	64.9	44.9	39	7.1	37.8
Russia	178.8	65.8	138.2	689.1	439.7	5	0.7	438.9
Rwanda	120.8	87.2	40.7	47.7	35.2	50	0.2	35.0
Senegal	20.4	21.7	22.8	30.2	29.1	56	0.8	28.3
Sierra Leone	28.3	16.5	32.6	17.4	25.7	59	-	25.7
South Africa	117.2	80.1	76.0	58.8	52.6	35	0.9	51.7
Sudan	23.5	27.2	64.1	84.2	42.8	43	-	42.8
Tajikistan	3.4	10.6	11.6	25.8	21.1	64	-	21.1
Tanzania	11.9	12.2	36.4	66.3	40.9	45	0.2	40.7
Uganda	39.7	65.3	85.3	73.1	75.2	24	0.2	75.0
Ukraine	121.8	50.7	164.7	227.9	178.3	11	4.6	173.7
Uzbekistan	11.2	4.7	15.1	34.7	33.8	52	2.3	31.5
West Bank/Gaza	63.4	67.0	60.7	79.6	121.4	14	-	121.4
Yemen, Republic of	1.4	8.4	60.5	23.0	55.2	32	0.1	55.0
Yugoslavia (Kosovo)	(X)	(X)	(X)	57.6	195.6	9	33.4	162.3
Yugoslavia (Montenegro)	(X)	(X)	(X)	1.7	71.3	26	-	71.3
Yugoslavia (Serbia)	-	-	9.9	-	22.8	62	-	22.8
Yugoslavia (Serbia/Montenegro)	(X)	(X)	(X)	45.2	54.3	34	-	54.3
Zambia	11.1	16.3	33.5	30.9	35.3	49	0.1	35.2
Zimbabwe	19.7	11.5	21.3	12.3	16.2	72	0.3	15.9

- Represents zero or rounds to zero. X Not applicable. [1] Includes countries not shown separately.

Source: U.S. Agency for International Development, *U.S. Overseas Loans and Grants*, annual.

No. 1294. U.S. International Trade in Goods and Services: 1995 to 2002

[In millions of dollars (-95,069 represents $-95,609,000,000). Data presented on a balance of payments basis and will not agree with the following merchandise trade Tables 1295 to 1304]

Category	1995	1996	1997	1998	1999	2000	2001	2002
TRADE BALANCE								
Total	-95,069	-102,869	-107,047	-163,153	-261,201	-375,384	-357,819	-418,038
Goods	-174,170	-191,000	-198,119	-246,696	-346,022	-452,423	-427,215	-482,872
Services	79,101	88,131	91,072	83,543	84,821	77,039	69,396	64,834
Travel	18,479	21,731	21,375	14,842	15,838	17,695	11,693	8,503
Passenger fares	4,246	4,613	2,730	127	-1,530	-3,587	-4,707	-2,923
Other transportation	-953	-1,329	-1,953	-4,759	-7,223	-11,622	-10,240	-9,361
Royalties, license fees	23,370	24,633	24,067	24,391	26,563	26,765	24,385	24,884
Other private services	31,164	34,857	41,692	45,645	50,516	49,568	52,752	53,158
Other [1]	4,600	5,385	4,968	5,220	2,593	317	-2,436	-7,302
U.S. govt. miscellaneous services	-1,805	-1,759	-1,807	-1,923	-1,936	-2,097	-2,051	-2,125
EXPORTS								
Total	793,725	850,877	933,873	932,558	965,473	1,070,054	1,007,580	974,107
Goods	575,204	612,113	678,366	670,416	683,965	771,994	718,712	681,874
Services	218,521	238,764	255,507	262,142	281,508	298,060	288,868	292,233
Travel	63,395	69,809	73,426	71,325	74,801	82,400	71,893	66,547
Passenger fares	18,909	20,422	20,868	20,098	19,785	20,687	17,926	17,046
Other transportation	26,081	26,074	27,006	25,604	26,916	29,803	28,442	29,166
Royalties, license fees	30,289	32,470	33,228	35,626	39,670	43,233	41,098	44,142
Other private services	64,386	72,615	83,349	91,158	103,523	107,361	116,139	122,594
Other [1]	14,643	16,446	16,675	17,405	15,928	13,790	12,539	11,943
U.S. govt. miscellaneous services	818	928	955	926	885	786	831	795
IMPORTS								
Total	888,794	953,746	1,040,920	1,095,711	1,226,674	1,445,438	1,365,399	1,392,145
Goods	749,374	803,113	876,485	917,112	1,029,987	1,224,417	1,145,927	1,164,746
Services	139,420	150,633	164,435	178,599	196,687	221,021	219,472	227,399
Travel	44,916	48,078	52,051	56,483	58,963	64,705	60,200	58,044
Passenger fares	14,663	15,809	18,138	19,971	21,315	24,274	22,633	19,969
Other transportation	27,034	27,403	28,959	30,363	34,139	41,425	38,682	38,527
Royalties, license fees	6,919	7,837	9,161	11,235	13,107	16,468	16,713	19,258
Other private services	33,222	37,758	41,657	45,513	53,007	57,793	63,387	69,436
Other [1]	10,043	11,061	11,707	12,185	13,335	13,472	14,975	19,245
U.S. govt. miscellaneous services	2,623	2,687	2,762	2,849	2,821	2,883	2,882	2,920

[1] Represents transfers under U.S. military sales contracts for exports and direct defense expenditures for imports.
Source: U.S. Census Bureau, *U.S. International Trade in Goods and Services, Annual Revision for 2002*, Series FT-900(03.) See also <http://www.census.gov/foreign-trade/Press-Release/2002pr/FinalRevisions2002/02final.pdf> (released 13 June 2003).

No. 1295. U.S. Exports, General Imports, and Trade Balance in Goods: 1980 to 2002

[In billions of dollars (225.7 represents $225,700,000,000). Domestic and foreign exports, are f.a.s. value basis; general imports are on customs value basis]

Year	Total goods [1]			Manufactured goods [2][3]			Agricultural products [4]			Mineral fuels [3][5]		
	Exports	Imports	Balance	Exports	Imports	Balance	Exports	Imports	Balance	Exports	Imports	Balance
1980	225.7	245.3	-19.6	160.7	133.0	27.7	41.8	17.4	24.3	8.2	78.9	-70.7
1981	238.7	261.0	-22.3	171.7	149.8	22.0	43.8	17.2	26.6	10.3	81.2	-70.9
1982	216.4	244.0	-27.6	155.3	151.7	3.6	37.0	15.7	21.3	12.8	65.3	-52.5
1983	205.6	258.0	-52.4	148.5	171.2	-22.7	36.5	16.5	19.9	9.8	57.8	-48.0
1983	205.6	258.0	-52.4	148.7	170.9	-22.2	36.1	16.0	20.2	9.8	57.8	-48.0
1984	224.0	330.7	-106.7	164.1	230.9	-66.8	37.9	19.3	18.6	9.7	60.8	-51.1
1985	218.8	336.5	-117.7	168.0	257.5	-89.5	29.3	19.5	9.8	10.3	53.7	-43.4
1986	227.2	365.4	-138.2	179.8	296.7	-116.8	26.3	20.9	5.4	8.4	37.2	-28.8
1987	254.1	406.2	-152.1	199.9	324.4	-124.6	28.7	20.3	8.4	8.0	44.1	-36.1
1988	322.4	441.0	-118.6	255.6	361.4	-105.7	37.1	20.7	16.4	8.5	41.0	-32.5
1989	363.8	473.2	-109.4	287.0	379.4	-92.4	41.6	21.1	20.5	9.9	52.6	-42.7
1990	393.6	495.3	-101.7	315.4	388.8	-73.5	39.6	22.3	17.2	12.4	64.7	-52.3
1991	421.7	488.5	-66.8	345.1	392.4	-47.3	39.4	22.1	17.2	12.3	54.1	-41.8
1992	448.2	532.7	-84.5	368.5	434.3	-65.9	43.1	23.4	19.8	11.3	55.3	-43.9
1993	465.1	580.7	-115.6	388.7	479.9	-91.2	42.8	23.6	19.2	9.9	55.9	-46.0
1994	512.6	663.3	-150.7	431.1	557.3	-126.3	45.9	26.0	20.0	9.0	56.4	-47.4
1995	584.7	743.4	-158.7	486.7	629.7	-143.0	56.0	29.3	26.8	10.5	59.1	-48.6
1996	625.1	795.3	-170.2	524.7	658.8	-134.1	60.6	32.6	28.1	12.4	78.1	-65.7
1997	689.2	870.7	-181.5	592.5	728.9	-136.4	57.1	35.2	21.9	13.0	78.3	-65.3
1998	682.1	911.9	-229.8	596.6	790.8	-194.2	52.0	35.7	16.3	10.4	57.3	-47.0
1999	698.0	1,024.6	-328.8	611.6	882.7	-271.1	48.2	36.7	11.5	9.9	75.2	-65.3
2000	781.9	1,218.0	-436.1	691.5	1,012.7	-321.3	53.0	39.2	13.8	13.4	135.4	-122.0
2001	729.1	1,141.0	-411.9	640.2	950.7	-310.4	55.2	39.5	15.7	12.7	121.9	-109.2
2002	693.5	1,163.6	-470.1	606.6	975.4	-368.8	54.7	42.0	12.7	11.7	117.1	-105.4

[1] Includes nonmonetary gold, military grant aid, special category shipments, trade between the U.S. Virgin Islands and foreign countries and undocumented exports to Canada. Adjustments were also made for carryover. Import values are based on transaction prices whenever possible. [2] Manufactured goods include commodity sections 5-9 under Schedules A and E for 1980-1982 and SITC Rev. 3 for 1983-forward. Manufactures include undocumented exports to Canada, nonmonetary gold (excluding gold ore, scrap, and base bullion), and special category shipments. [3] Data for 1980 exclude trade between the U.S. Virgin Islands and foreign countries. Census data concordances link the 1980-92 trade figures into time series that are as consistent as possible. Import values are for Customs value; these values are based on transaction prices while maintaining a data series as consistent as possible over time. 1991 Imports include revisions for passenger cars, trucks, petroleum and petroleum products not included elsewhere. [4] Agricultural products for 1983-forward utilize the latest census definition that excludes manufactured goods that were previously classified as manufactured agricultural products. [5] Mineral fuels include commodity Section 3 under SITC Rev. 2 for 1980-1982 and SITC Rev. 3 for 1983-forward.
Source: U.S. International Trade Administration, through 1996, *U.S. Foreign Trade Highlights*, annual; and thereafter, <http://www.ita.doc.gov/td/industry/otea/usfth/aggregate/H02t03.pdf> (released 02 February 2003).

Foreign Commerce and Aid 813

No. 1296. U.S. Exports and Imports for Consumption of Merchandise by Customs District: 1990 to 2002

[In billions of dollars (393.0 represents $393,000,000,000). Exports are f.a.s. (free alongside ship) value all years; imports are on customs value basis]

Customs district	Exports					Imports for consumption				
	1990	1995	2000	2001	2002	1990	1995	2000	2001	2002
Total [1]	393.0	584.7	780.0	731.0	693.1	490.6	738.6	1,205.6	1,132.6	1,152.5
Anchorage, AK	3.7	5.9	5.9	7.7	7.3	0.7	5.7	13.4	11.5	11.3
Baltimore, MD	6.7	9.0	6.2	5.7	5.1	11.2	14.4	18.6	18.4	19.5
Boston	5.6	4.6	7.0	7.0	6.8	12.2	13.4	18.7	16.8	15.4
Buffalo, NY	15.8	30.5	38.2	31.1	25.7	19.2	29.1	38.4	34.7	34.3
Charleston, SC [2]	6.7	10.1	12.6	13.5	11.9	6.8	10.4	16.9	17.2	17.5
Chicago, IL	10.2	18.4	21.7	21.5	19.6	18.3	31.3	51.1	49.1	53.0
Cleveland, OH	4.0	7.8	22.7	18.0	16.5	11.3	21.7	36.5	35.2	33.3
Dallas/Fort Worth, TX	3.4	4.4	11.5	10.2	11.5	4.8	8.8	18.8	19.7	19.2
Detroit, MI	35.6	56.8	79.4	77.2	86.2	37.8	64.7	97.6	91.3	93.7
Duluth, MN	0.8	1.4	1.5	1.3	1.6	3.9	6.0	7.0	6.4	6.6
El Paso, TX	3.9	7.9	18.0	16.3	16.5	5.0	12.9	24.1	23.9	24.7
Great Falls, MT	2.4	3.0	5.0	6.1	4.6	4.7	6.9	14.3	17.6	14.8
Honolulu, HI	0.5	1.1	0.7	0.6	2.7	2.1	2.7	2.9	2.3	2.1
Houston/Galveston, TX	17.6	27.4	29.7	29.5	29.5	21.6	23.4	40.9	39.3	39.9
Laredo, TX	15.2	24.3	57.7	52.1	48.9	10.0	24.7	62.7	62.3	64.6
Los Angeles, CA	42.1	67.0	77.6	69.1	63.3	64.1	96.3	150.1	141.7	149.5
Miami, FL	11.2	22.7	31.0	29.9	26.3	7.1	11.9	23.3	22.5	22.4
Milwaukee, WI	0.1	0.1	0.1	0.2	0.2	1.1	1.5	1.5	1.3	1.4
Minneapolis, MN	0.9	1.3	1.4	1.4	1.5	2.0	2.8	4.3	3.8	4.4
Mobile, AL [2]	1.9	3.4	4.0	4.8	4.3	3.4	3.9	7.9	7.3	8.1
New Orleans, LA	18.0	28.4	35.9	33.1	32.7	24.1	34.4	54.0	47.8	51.0
New York, NY	50.9	61.4	79.5	76.2	68.4	68.0	87.6	145.6	137.8	140.7
Nogales, AZ	2.1	4.0	7.3	6.2	5.3	4.2	7.7	14.1	12.9	11.7
Norfolk, VA [2]	11.7	14.4	12.4	12.4	11.9	7.4	8.6	13.6	12.8	15.0
Ogdensburg, NY	7.9	9.2	12.4	11.6	10.5	9.8	14.4	23.7	22.0	21.0
Pembina, ND	3.4	5.5	8.7	8.2	7.8	4.1	7.2	11.0	10.3	9.7
Philadelphia, PA	4.0	6.7	6.0	8.0	7.1	18.3	18.3	28.3	28.1	27.3
Port Arthur, TX	0.9	1.3	1.2	1.0	1.1	3.2	4.8	10.9	9.0	10.9
Portland, ME	1.7	2.1	2.6	2.3	2.4	4.3	4.4	8.7	9.2	8.2
Portland, OR	5.8	10.2	7.2	6.1	6.0	5.6	7.9	12.5	12.4	12.7
Providence, RI	(Z)	0.1	(Z)	(Z)	(Z)	1.3	0.9	1.3	1.4	1.5
San Diego, CA	3.4	6.1	12.7	12.3	12.9	4.3	8.9	22.2	21.2	22.9
San Francisco, CA	23.1	43.7	58.3	45.8	35.1	28.0	58.8	68.6	49.1	44.3
San Juan, PR	2.5	2.6	4.8	5.8	5.7	5.4	6.8	11.8	12.9	14.8
Savannah, GA	7.4	10.9	15.9	15.5	15.7	9.8	14.7	26.1	25.2	29.5
Seattle, WA	32.6	31.4	40.4	41.4	39.9	20.9	24.1	40.5	38.0	35.9
St. Albans, VT	4.0	4.4	4.5	3.1	3.0	5.2	7.4	9.4	9.2	8.4
St. Louis, MO	0.3	0.3	1.3	0.8	0.8	3.0	4.4	7.9	7.1	6.6
Tampa, FL	4.3	6.7	4.8	4.7	5.8	7.0	9.2	14.7	13.4	14.1
Virgin Islands of the U.S.	0.2	0.2	0.3	0.3	0.4	2.1	2.1	4.8	3.9	3.6
Washington, DC	1.1	2.3	2.8	3.0	2.5	0.8	1.2	2.6	2.3	2.3
Wilmington, NC	3.0	4.4	2.5	2.3	1.7	3.3	7.4	10.6	10.8	11.9

Z Less than $50 million. [1] Totals shown for exports reflect the value of estimated parcel post and Special Category shipments, and beginning 1990, adjustments for undocumented exports to Canada which are not distributed by customs district. The value of bituminous coal exported through Norfolk, VA; Charleston, SC; and Mobile, AL is reflected in the total but not distributed by district. [2] Excludes exports of bituminous coal, which are included in the "Total" line.

Source: U.S. Census Bureau, 1990, *U.S. Merchandise Trade: Selected Highlights*, Series FT 920, monthly; beginning 1995, *U.S. Export History* and *U.S. Import History* on compact disc.

No. 1297. Export and Import Unit Value Indexes—Selected Countries: 1998 to 2002

[Indexes in U.S. dollars, 1995=100. A unit value is an implicit price derived from value and quantity data]

Country	Export unit value					Import unit value				
	1998	1999	2000	2001	2002	1998	1999	2000	2001	2002
United States	95.9	94.7	96.2	95.4	94.5	92.6	93.4	99.4	95.9	93.5
Australia	86.7	82.7	86.0	84.4	(NA)	86.8	87.2	85.3	72.0	(NA)
Belgium	87.9	83.6	79.6	78.8	82.3	87.4	84.5	82.6	82.1	84.3
Canada	92.3	93.0	100.6	96.5	96.2	96.0	95.7	98.0	93.9	96.5
Denmark	85.8	83.1	78.4	(NA)	(NA)	86.6	82.8	77.0	(NA)	(NA)
France	85.9	81.6	63.0	61.3	61.8	86.4	82.4	67.1	64.0	63.5
Germany	79.5	75.1	67.3	66.6	68.3	80.1	75.4	72.4	70.3	70.3
Greece	87.8	92.1	74.8	78.4	84.0	85.8	89.9	69.2	73.5	77.6
Ireland	91.7	91.8	83.5	82.0	86.1	90.3	88.3	82.9	82.9	85.1
Italy	99.3	94.6	86.3	87.3	90.2	92.6	87.6	86.4	85.7	86.9
Japan	80.5	83.3	87.3	81.7	77.8	83.0	83.3	92.1	85.8	81.5
Korea	61.0	61.6	61.8	53.7	51.4	76.4	74.7	85.6	77.9	74.9
Norway	81.9	89.2	114.4	106.6	108.3	84.0	75.2	69.0	67.7	70.3
Singapore	81.1	80.2	83.4	77.2	75.5	80.9	81.2	87.0	84.0	83.5
Spain	87.1	82.6	75.8	75.6	79.7	84.8	81.0	79.1	76.4	77.8
Switzerland	84.5	82.7	76.0	77.6	(NA)	82.4	78.0	73.5	74.7	(NA)
United Kingdom	95.1	92.1	89.2	85.0	88.4	92.1	88.9	86.5	82.0	82.9

NA Not available.

Source: International Monetary Fund, Washington, DC, *International Financial Statistics*, monthly, (copyright).

No. 1298. U.S. Exports by State of Origin: 2000 to 2002

[In millions of dollars (782,429 represents $782,429,000,000). Exports are on a f.a.s. value basis. Exports are based on origin of movement]

State and other area	2000	2001	2002 Total	2002 Rank	State and other area	2000	2001	2002 Total	2002 Rank
Total	782,429	730,897	693,517	(X)	Montana	541	489	386	50
					Nebraska	2,511	2,702	2,528	34
United States	712,055	678,756	648,800	(X)	Nevada	1,482	1,423	1,177	44
Alabama	7,317	7,570	8,267	25	New Hampshire	2,373	2,401	1,863	42
Alaska	2,464	2,418	2,516	36					
Arizona	14,334	12,513	11,871	16	New Jersey	18,638	18,946	17,002	10
Arkansas	2,599	2,911	2,804	33	New Mexico	2,391	1,405	1,196	43
California	119,640	106,777	92,214	2	New York	42,846	42,172	36,977	3
Colorado	6,593	6,125	5,522	27	North Carolina	17,946	16,799	14,719	14
Connecticut	8,047	8,610	8,313	24	North Dakota	626	806	859	46
Delaware	2,197	1,985	2,004	39	Ohio	26,322	27,095	27,723	6
District of Columbia	1,003	1,034	1,066	(X)	Oklahoma	3,072	2,661	2,444	37
Florida	26,543	27,185	24,544	8	Oregon	11,441	8,900	10,086	22
					Pennsylvania	18,792	17,433	15,768	12
Georgia	14,925	14,644	14,413	15	Rhode Island	1,186	1,269	1,121	45
Hawaii	387	370	514	49					
Idaho	3,559	2,122	1,967	41	South Carolina	8,565	9,956	9,656	23
Illinois	31,438	30,434	25,686	7	South Dakota	679	595	597	47
Indiana	15,386	14,365	14,923	13	Tennessee	11,592	11,320	11,621	17
Iowa	4,466	4,660	4,755	29	Texas	103,866	94,995	95,396	1
Kansas	5,145	5,005	4,988	28	Utah	3,221	3,506	4,543	30
Kentucky	9,612	9,048	10,607	20	Vermont	4,097	2,830	2,521	35
Louisiana	16,814	16,589	17,567	9	Virginia	11,698	11,631	10,796	18
Maine	1,779	1,813	1,973	40	Washington	32,215	34,929	34,627	4
					West Virginia	2,219	2,241	2,237	38
Maryland	4,593	4,975	4,474	31	Wisconsin	10,508	10,489	10,684	19
Massachusetts	20,514	17,490	16,708	11	Wyoming	503	503	553	48
Michigan	33,845	32,366	33,775	5					
Minnesota	10,303	10,524	10,402	21	Puerto Rico	9,735	10,573	9,732	(X)
Mississippi	2,726	3,557	3,058	32	Virgin Islands	174	187	258	(X)
Missouri	6,497	6,173	6,791	26	Other [1]	60,464	41,377	34,727	(X)

X Not applicable. [1] Includes unreported, not specified, special category, estimated shipments, re-exports, and any timing adjustments.

Source: U.S. Census Bureau, *U.S. International Trade in Goods and Services*, Series FT-900, December issues. For most recent release, see <http://www.census.gov/foreign-trade/Press-Release/2002pr/12/ft900.pdf> (released 20 February 2003).

No. 1299. U.S. Agriculture Exports by State: 1997 to 2001

[In millions of dollars (57,269 represents $57,269,000,000). Fiscal years]

State	1997	1998	1999	2000	2001	State	1997	1998	1999	2000	2001
U.S.	57,269	53,653	49,043	50,744	52,735	MT	441	422	393	388	321
						NE	3,255	2,814	2,804	2,980	2,915
AL	544	466	374	390	408	NV	5	5	4	17	17
AK	(Z)	(Z)	(Z)	(Z)	1	NH	131	129	127	130	134
AZ	456	444	389	439	448	NJ	222	193	181	184	234
AR	1,832	1,733	1,301	1,371	1,385						
CA	8,265	8,007	7,366	7,982	8,698	NM	83	98	75	105	84
CO	848	785	807	919	869	NY	424	402	407	432	456
CT	82	97	95	110	78	NC	1,556	1,467	1,215	1,194	1,389
DE	152	131	106	107	139	ND	1,437	1,243	1,239	996	1,203
FL	1,309	1,131	1,097	1,222	1,242	OH	1,229	1,302	1,082	993	1,135
GA	1,340	1,166	909	1,005	1,107	OK	410	450	462	442	540
						OR	720	659	645	618	681
HI	132	128	132	147	163	PA	668	596	584	614	732
ID	832	803	773	808	820	RI	2	1	1	1	1
IL	3,627	3,151	2,812	2,876	3,057	SC	358	318	240	237	317
IN	1,725	1,606	1,415	1,410	1,546						
IA	4,058	3,569	3,231	3,327	3,259	SD	1,245	1,098	1,104	1,092	1,106
KS	2,892	2,954	3,024	3,243	3,099	TN	664	580	463	462	549
KY	1,084	926	860	790	1,010	TX	3,330	3,376	2,791	3,407	3,333
LA	863	750	565	686	765	UT	153	137	147	184	198
ME	35	38	37	57	60	VT	11	10	10	12	2
MD	285	230	180	188	246	VA	532	451	387	417	450
						WA	1,930	1,705	1,820	1,666	1,938
MA	88	90	72	83	28	WV	32	28	20	23	36
MI	836	884	744	816	776	WI	1,184	1,203	1,190	1,268	1,307
MN	2,607	2,289	2,207	2,204	2,299	WY	40	44	32	49	53
MS	870	826	549	620	620						
MO	1,448	1,328	1,024	990	1,151	Unallocated	1,000	1,392	1,547	1,045	328

Z Less than $500,000.

Source: U.S. Dept. of Agriculture, Economic Research Service, *Foreign Agricultural Trade of the United States (FATUS)*, annual. See also <http://www.ers.usda.gov/publications/fau/july02/fau6602/fau6602.pdf> (revised August 2002).

Foreign Commerce and Aid

No. 1300. U.S. Exports, Imports, and Merchandise Trade Balance by Country: 1998 to 2002

[In millions of dollars (682,137.7 represents $682,137,700,000). Includes silver ore and bullion. Country totals include exports of special category commodities, if any. Data include nonmonetary gold and includes trade of Virgin Islands with foreign countries. Minus sign (-) denotes an excess of imports over exports]

Country	Exports, domestic and foreign					General imports					Merchandise trade balance				
	1998	1999	2000	2001	2002	1998	1999	2000	2001	2002	1998	1999	2000	2001	2002
Total [1]	682,137.7	695,797.2	781,917.7	729,100.3	693,103.2	911,896.1	1,024,618.2	1,218,022.0	1,140,999.4	1,161,366.0	-229,758.4	-328,821.0	-436,104.3	-411,899.1	-468,262.8
Afghanistan	7.0	18.0	8.2	5.8	80.0	16.7	9.3	0.8	0.8	3.3	-9.7	8.8	7.4	5.0	76.7
Albania	14.9	24.8	20.9	15.5	14.8	12.4	9.0	7.8	7.3	5.8	2.5	15.8	13.1	8.2	9.0
Algeria	651.4	458.8	861.8	1,037.8	984.4	1,638.0	1,824.4	2,724.3	2,701.9	2,360.2	-986.6	-1,365.5	-1,862.5	-1,664.1	-1,375.8
Andorra	22.4	7.8	10.2	8.2	11.0	0.1	0.1	0.3	0.2	0.8	22.3	7.7	9.9	8.0	10.2
Angola	354.7	252.0	225.3	275.9	374.0	2,240.9	2,418.3	3,555.3	3,095.9	3,122.7	-1,886.2	-2,166.3	-3,330.0	-2,820.0	-2,748.7
Anguilla	16.7	22.2	29.9	20.1	19.9	2.1	2.3	1.7	1.8	1.0	14.6	19.9	28.2	18.3	18.9
Antigua and Barbuda	96.7	95.2	138.0	54.9	81.4	1.9	1.8	2.3	3.7	3.5	94.8	93.4	135.7	51.2	77.9
Argentina	5,885.8	4,949.9	4,695.6	3,920.2	1,585.4	2,230.9	2,598.3	3,099.5	3,013.4	3,187.3	3,654.9	2,351.5	1,596.1	906.8	-1,601.9
Armenia	51.4	51.2	55.6	49.9	111.8	16.7	15.3	23.0	32.9	30.7	34.7	35.9	32.6	17.0	81.1
Aruba	351.2	307.2	291.4	276.5	464.6	469.5	674.8	1,535.5	1,034.0	773.7	-118.3	-367.6	-1,244.1	-757.5	-309.1
Australia	11,917.6	11,818.4	12,482.3	10,930.5	13,085.0	5,386.8	5,280.1	6,438.1	6,477.9	6,478.8	6,530.8	6,538.2	6,044.2	4,452.6	6,606.2
Austria	2,142.9	2,588.2	2,591.5	2,604.7	2,427.4	2,561.0	2,909.3	3,226.6	3,968.5	3,814.9	-418.1	-321.1	-635.1	-1,363.8	-1,387.5
Azerbaijan	123.1	54.8	209.6	64.3	69.6	4.9	26.3	20.9	20.6	34.4	118.2	28.6	188.7	43.7	35.2
Bahamas, The	815.6	842.0	1,069.3	1,026.3	975.3	142.4	195.3	275.0	313.9	449.7	673.2	646.7	794.3	712.4	525.6
Bahrain	294.6	347.8	449.0	432.7	419.3	155.5	225.4	337.6	424.1	394.9	139.1	122.3	111.4	8.6	24.4
Bangladesh	318.4	274.2	239.1	306.9	269.1	1,845.9	1,918.2	2,417.6	2,359.0	2,134.2	-1,527.5	-1,644.0	-2,178.5	-2,052.1	-1,865.1
Barbados	281.4	304.9	306.9	286.6	267.6	34.5	58.9	38.6	39.5	34.4	246.9	246.0	268.3	247.1	233.2
Belarus	30.4	26.1	31.1	34.9	19.1	105.4	93.6	104.0	108.2	125.5	-75.0	-67.6	-72.9	-73.3	-106.4
Belgium	13,917.8	12,381.4	13,925.7	13,502.3	13,325.8	8,440.0	9,196.1	9,929.3	10,158.4	9,806.8	5,477.8	3,185.4	3,996.4	3,343.9	3,519.0
Belize	120.2	135.8	208.4	173.2	137.7	65.9	80.6	93.6	97.4	77.7	54.3	55.2	114.8	75.8	60.0
Benin	43.6	31.4	26.4	32.2	35.2	3.6	17.8	2.4	1.3	0.7	40.0	13.5	24.0	30.9	34.5
Bermuda	400.3	343.8	428.5	371.0	415.1	11.5	24.6	39.0	65.6	22.9	388.8	319.2	389.5	305.4	392.2
Bolivia	416.6	298.3	253.0	215.9	192.1	223.6	223.7	184.8	166.4	160.4	193.0	74.6	68.2	49.5	31.7
Bosnia and Herzegovina	40.0	43.7	44.1	43.1	31.7	7.4	14.7	17.8	11.9	15.5	32.6	28.8	26.3	31.2	16.2
Brazil	15,142.0	13,202.6	15,320.9	15,879.5	12,376.0	10,101.9	11,313.8	13,852.5	14,466.4	15,780.6	5,040.1	1,888.8	1,468.4	1,413.1	-3,404.6
Brunei	122.8	66.7	156.3	104.0	46.3	211.2	388.7	383.8	398.9	287.1	-88.4	-322.0	-227.5	-294.9	-240.8
Bulgaria	112.4	102.8	114.0	108.4	101.4	219.1	198.8	235.6	337.0	339.7	-106.7	-96.0	-121.6	-228.6	-238.3
Burkina Faso	16.1	10.9	15.9	4.4	18.8	0.6	2.8	2.5	5.0	2.9	15.5	8.1	13.4	-0.6	15.9
Burma	31.9	8.6	17.1	11.4	10.1	163.7	232.1	470.7	469.9	356.4	-131.8	-223.5	-453.6	-458.5	-346.3
Cameroon	75.1	37.0	59.3	184.0	155.8	53.3	77.4	155.1	101.6	172.1	21.8	-40.4	-95.8	82.4	-16.3
Canada	156,603.4	166,600.0	178,941.0	163,424.1	160,922.6	173,256.1	198,711.1	230,838.3	216,267.8	209,087.6	-16,652.7	-32,111.1	-51,897.3	-52,843.7	-48,165.0
Cayman Islands	421.9	368.8	354.5	261.8	231.6	18.1	9.4	6.6	6.8	8.8	403.8	359.4	347.9	255.0	222.8
Chad	3.5	2.7	10.8	137.0	127.3	7.5	6.9	4.6	5.7	5.7	-4.0	-4.3	6.2	131.3	121.6
Chile	3,979.3	3,078.5	3,460.3	3,118.4	2,609.0	2,452.5	2,953.1	3,269.0	3,495.3	3,784.5	1,526.8	125.2	191.3	-376.9	-1,175.5
China	14,241.3	13,111.0	16,185.3	19,182.3	22,127.8	71,168.7	81,788.2	100,018.4	102,278.3	125,192.5	-56,927.4	-68,677.2	-83,833.1	-83,096.0	-103,064.7
Colombia	4,816.0	3,559.5	3,671.2	3,583.1	3,582.5	4,656.2	6,259.0	6,968.1	5,710.3	5,604.3	159.8	-2,699.4	-3,296.9	-2,127.2	-2,021.8
Congo (Brazzaville)	92.0	47.0	81.7	90.0	52.4	315.4	414.6	473.8	473.8	182.1	-223.4	-367.6	-450.0	-383.8	-129.7
Congo (Kinshasa)	34.1	21.0	10.0	18.6	28.1	171.1	229.0	214.8	154.0	204.1	-137.0	-207.9	-204.8	-135.4	-176.0
Costa Rica	2,296.5	2,380.6	2,460.4	2,502.3	3,116.5	2,744.9	3,967.8	3,538.7	2,886.1	3,141.8	-448.4	-1,587.2	-1,078.3	-383.8	-25.3
Cote d'Ivoire	151.4	151.4	94.8	96.8	76.2	425.9	425.9	383.9	333.1	376.4	-274.5	-274.5	-289.1	-236.3	-300.2
Croatia	96.8	107.5	89.9	109.8	78.1	72.6	110.0	141.0	139.0	145.6	24.2	-2.5	-51.1	-29.2	-67.5
Cyprus	161.9	191.7	190.1	267.9	193.4	31.8	31.4	23.4	35.1	25.6	130.1	160.2	166.7	232.8	167.8
Czech Republic	569.0	609.7	735.8	706.1	653.7	673.4	753.6	1,070.2	1,116.2	1,233.4	-104.4	-143.9	-334.4	-410.1	-579.7

See footnotes at end of table.

816 Foreign Commerce and Aid

U.S. Census Bureau, Statistical Abstract of the United States: 2003

Country	Exports, domestic and foreign						General imports						Merchandise trade balance					
	1998	1999	2000	2001	2002		1998	1999	2000	2001	2002		1998	1999	2000	2001	2002	
Denmark	1,874.3	1,725.6	1,506.8	1,609.2	1,495.9		2,395.0	2,818.7	2,965.0	3,406.7	3,237.3		-520.7	-1,093.1	-1,458.2	-1,797.5	-1,741.4	
Djibouti	20.4	26.4	16.8	18.6	58.6		0.5	0.1	0.4	1.0	1.9		19.9	26.3	16.4	17.6	56.7	
Dominica	52.1	38.6	37.5	30.7	45.0		6.4	19.1	6.9	5.3	4.7		45.7	19.5	30.6	25.4	40.3	
Dominican Republic	3,943.8	4,100.4	4,472.8	4,397.6	4,250.1		4,441.2	4,286.7	4,383.3	4,183.4	4,168.9		-497.4	-186.3	-1,200.0	214.2	81.2	
Ecuador	1,683.1	909.9	1,037.8	1,412.1	1,605.7		1,752.1	1,821.3	2,237.8	2,009.7	2,143.4		-69.0	-911.4	89.5	-597.6	-537.7	
Egypt	3,058.6	3,000.8	3,333.9	3,564.4	2,868.4		660.3	617.6	887.7	882.0	1,356.0		2,398.3	2,383.2	2,446.2	2,682.4	1,512.4	
El Salvador	1,513.5	1,519.1	1,780.2	1,759.5	1,664.1		1,437.9	1,605.0	1,932.9	1,880.2	1,982.3		75.6	-85.9	-152.7	-120.7	-318.2	
Estonia	87.4	162.9	88.0	57.7	81.5		125.4	237.0	572.9	241.1	163.6		-38.0	-74.0	-484.9	-183.4	-82.1	
Ethiopia	88.9	163.5	165.3	61.1	60.5		52.3	30.2	28.7	29.1	25.7		36.6	133.3	136.6	32.0	34.8	
Fiji	74.2	126.4	23.0	19.4	16.9		101.1	99.8	146.8	182.3	156.3		-26.9	26.6	-123.8	-162.9	-139.4	
Finland	1,914.8	1,668.8	1,570.9	1,554.0	1,534.9		2,595.6	2,907.7	3,250.8	3,393.8	3,447.0		-680.8	-1,238.9	-1,679.9	-1,839.8	-1,912.1	
France	17,728.7	18,877.4	20,361.5	19,864.5	19,016.2		24,015.9	25,708.6	29,800.1	30,408.2	28,240.1		-6,287.2	-6,831.2	-9,438.6	-10,543.7	-9,223.9	
French Guiana	246.5	194.2	17.0	129.9	249.7		3.2	4.2	43.9	0.4	7.5		243.3	190.0	14.7	129.5	242.2	
French Polynesia	99.7	93.5	93.9	83.0	78.9		32.7	42.7	43.9	48.0	44.1		67.0	50.9	50.0	35.0	34.8	
Gabon	61.6	45.4	63.5	73.0	65.5		1,258.8	1,543.2	2,196.5	1,659.7	1,587.5		-1,197.2	-1,497.8	-2,133.0	-1,586.7	-1,522.0	
Gambia, The	9.3	9.6	9.1	8.4	9.6		2.0	0.2	0.4	0.5	0.3		7.3	9.4	8.7	7.9	9.3	
Georgia	136.5	83.5	109.5	105.9	98.8		14.2	18.3	31.9	30.7	17.5		122.3	65.3	77.6	75.2	81.3	
Germany	26,657.4	26,800.2	29,448.4	29,995.3	26,629.6		49,842.0	55,228.4	58,512.8	59,076.7	62,505.7		-23,184.6	-28,428.2	-29,064.4	-29,081.4	-35,876.1	
Ghana	225.1	232.7	191.2	199.6	192.6		143.2	208.6	204.5	186.9	116.3		81.9	24.1	-13.3	12.7	76.3	
Gibraltar	8.8	4.1	15.1	10.4	25.7		6.0	9.5	1.4	2.6	1.1		2.8	-5.5	13.7	7.8	24.6	
Greece	1,355.2	995.1	1,221.8	1,293.6	1,151.8		466.7	563.1	591.4	505.2	546.2		888.5	432.3	630.4	788.4	605.6	
Greenland	6.1	3.1	1.1	4.7	4.0		7.3	13.3	15.7	28.8	22.6		-1.2	-10.1	-14.6	-24.1	-18.6	
Grenada	56.4	66.2	79.5	59.8	56.4		12.1	19.8	27.1	24.1	6.9		44.3	46.4	52.4	35.8	49.5	
Guadeloupe	64.0	85.9	85.9	50.9	39.7		2.8	2.8	9.6	10.6	10.5		61.7	60.4	76.3	48.2	29.2	
Guatemala	1,937.8	1,811.9	1,900.7	1,869.6	2,044.4		2,071.6	2,265.2	2,607.4	2,588.6	2,796.4		-133.8	-453.2	-706.7	-719.0	-752.0	
Guinea	65.4	54.6	68.0	73.3	62.9		115.3	116.9	88.4	87.8	71.6		-49.9	-62.4	-20.4	-14.5	-8.7	
Guyana	145.6	145.1	159.2	141.3	128.2		137.0	120.5	139.9	140.3	115.6		8.6	24.5	19.3	1.0	12.6	
Haiti	548.6	613.8	576.6	573.2	573.2		271.8	301.1	296.9	263.1	255.0		276.8	312.7	279.7	287.3	318.2	
Honduras	2,317.5	2,369.8	2,584.0	2,415.9	2,571.1		2,544.4	2,713.3	3,090.2	3,126.5	3,261.3		-226.9	-343.5	-506.2	-710.6	-690.2	
Hong Kong	12,925.3	12,651.8	14,582.0	14,027.5	12,594.4		10,538.2	10,527.9	11,449.0	9,646.3	9,328.2		2,387.1	2,123.9	3,133.0	4,381.3	3,266.2	
Hungary	482.6	504.1	569.1	685.5	687.9		1,566.5	1,892.6	2,715.2	2,964.6	2,637.4		-1,083.9	-1,388.5	-2,146.1	-2,279.1	-1,949.5	
Iceland	236.5	297.6	255.6	225.4	219.0		267.9	303.7	259.8	232.5	296.9		-31.4	-6.0	-4.2	-7.1	-77.9	
India	3,564.4	3,687.8	3,667.2	3,757.0	4,101.1		8,237.2	9,070.8	10,686.6	9,737.2	11,818.3		-4,672.8	-5,383.0	-7,019.4	-5,980.2	-7,717.2	
Indonesia	2,298.9	2,038.3	2,401.9	2,520.6	2,555.3		9,340.6	9,525.4	10,367.0	10,103.6	9,643.3		-7,041.7	-7,487.0	-7,965.1	-7,583.0	-7,087.5	
Iran	-	-	16.8	8.1	31.8		-	-	168.8	143.4	156.3		-	45.7	-152.0	-135.3	-124.5	
Iraq	106.4	9.5	10.4	46.2	31.6		1,183.2	4,226.4	6,065.9	5,820.3	3,548.2		-1,076.8	-4,216.7	-6,055.5	-5,774.1	-3,516.6	
Ireland	5,646.8	6,383.6	7,713.5	7,144.0	6,745.1		8,400.9	10,994.3	16,463.6	18,499.3	22,437.7		-2,754.1	-4,610.7	-8,750.1	-11,355.3	-15,692.6	
Israel	6,983.3	7,690.8	7,745.9	7,475.3	7,026.7		8,640.4	9,864.3	12,964.4	11,959.0	12,415.7		-1,657.1	-2,173.5	-5,218.5	-4,483.7	-5,389.0	
Italy	8,990.8	10,090.6	11,060.3	9,915.6	10,056.8		20,959.1	22,356.5	25,042.7	23,789.9	24,220.3		-11,968.3	-12,265.9	-13,982.4	-13,874.3	-14,163.5	
Jamaica	1,304.2	1,292.9	1,375.8	1,405.5	1,420.2		755.0	678.1	648.2	460.6	396.3		549.2	614.8	727.6	944.9	1,023.9	
Japan	57,831.0	57,465.7	64,924.4	57,451.6	51,449.3		121,845.0	130,863.9	146,479.4	126,473.3	121,428.7		-64,014.0	-73,398.2	-81,555.0	-69,021.7	-69,979.4	
Jordan	352.9	275.6	316.7	339.0	404.4		16.4	30.9	73.3	229.1	412.3		336.5	244.7	243.4	109.9	-7.9	
Kazakhstan	103.1	179.5	124.2	160.3	604.6		168.7	229.1	429.0	351.8	334.6		-65.6	-49.6	-304.8	-191.5	270.0	
Kenya	198.9	189.2	237.6	577.7	271.2		98.5	106.3	110.1	128.3	188.6		100.4	82.8	127.5	449.4	82.6	

See footnotes at end of table.

Foreign Commerce and Aid 817

U.S. Census Bureau, Statistical Abstract of the United States: 2003

No. 1300. U.S. Exports, Imports, and Merchandise Trade Balance by Country: 1998 to 2002—Con.

[See headnote, page 816]

Country	Exports, domestic and foreign					General imports					Merchandise trade balance				
	1998	1999	2000	2001	2002	1998	1999	2000	2001	2002	1998	1999	2000	2001	2002
Korea, South	16,485.5	22,958.4	27,830.0	22,180.6	22,575.8	23,941.8	31,178.6	40,307.7	35,181.4	35,571.8	-7,456.3	-8,220.2	-12,477.7	-13,000.8	-12,996.0
Kuwait	1,524.1	864.4	787.0	902.4	1,014.7	1,266.0	1,439.2	2,781.2	1,990.7	1,940.4	258.1	-574.9	-1,994.2	-1,088.3	-925.7
Kyrgyzstan	20.6	22.8	22.8	27.7	31.1	0.3	0.5	1.9	3.3	4.8	20.3	22.3	20.9	24.4	26.3
Latvia	186.8	218.2	133.6	110.5	90.8	114.7	228.8	287.7	144.5	197.0	72.1	-10.6	-154.1	-34.0	-106.2
Lebanon	513.8	356.5	354.7	418.2	317.4	82.5	51.4	76.8	89.6	61.7	431.3	305.1	277.9	328.6	255.7
Lesotho	1.4	0.7	0.9	0.8	2.0	100.0	110.8	140.3	215.3	321.7	-98.6	-110.1	-139.4	-214.5	-319.7
Liberia	50.1	44.7	43.1	36.8	27.7	25.1	30.3	45.4	42.6	45.8	25.0	14.4	-2.3	-5.8	-18.1
Liechtenstein	7.3	9.1	13.9	27.1	14.5	242.6	276.8	278.2	224.2	237.7	-235.3	-267.8	-264.3	-217.1	-223.2
Lithuania	62.2	66.0	59.4	99.8	102.8	80.9	96.8	135.0	164.2	299.6	-18.7	-30.8	-75.6	-64.4	-196.8
Luxembourg	605.8	983.4	397.4	548.6	480.1	373.1	313.9	331.6	305.6	300.0	232.7	669.5	65.8	243.0	180.1
Macau	40.7	41.9	70.5	70.1	79.0	1,108.6	1,124.4	1,266.3	1,225.1	1,231.7	-1,067.9	-1,082.5	-1,195.8	-1,155.0	-1,152.7
Macedonia, the Former Yugoslav Republic of	14.8	56.2	68.5	32.9	18.6	175.4	136.5	151.8	111.6	73.2	-160.6	-80.3	-83.3	-78.7	-54.6
Madagascar	14.9	105.8	15.4	21.0	15.4	71.4	80.3	157.8	271.6	215.8	-56.5	25.5	-142.4	-250.6	-200.4
Malawi	14.5	7.4	13.7	12.8	30.1	60.4	72.5	55.4	77.9	70.8	-45.9	-65.1	-41.7	-65.1	-40.7
Malaysia	8,957.0	9,060.0	10,937.5	9,357.7	10,343.7	19,000.0	21,424.3	25,568.2	22,340.3	24,008.9	-10,043.0	-12,364.3	-14,630.7	-12,982.6	-13,665.2
Maldives	4.8	8.5	6.1	6.4	4.1	32.9	54.9	94.1	97.7	113.6	-28.1	-46.4	-88.0	-91.3	-109.5
Mali	25.3	29.8	2.6	32.7	11.2	3.4	9.0	9.8	6.1	2.6	21.9	20.8	-7.2	26.6	8.6
Malta	267.0	190.4	334.7	258.9	210.1	340.3	325.0	482.4	368.9	309.9	-73.3	-134.6	-147.7	-110.0	-99.8
Marshall Islands	25.0	35.8	60.2	26.5	28.7	3.8	9.8	5.0	5.5	9.4	21.2	26.0	55.2	21.0	19.3
Martinique	26.4	34.9	21.6	25.4	23.7	1.0	0.8	1.7	0.6	0.7	25.4	34.1	19.9	22.6	23.0
Mauritania	19.5	25.2	16.2	25.4	22.9	0.4	0.8	0.4	0.3	0.9	19.1	24.4	15.8	25.1	22.0
Mauritius	23.2	39.0	39.0	29.0	27.5	271.6	259.3	285.9	277.9	280.6	-248.4	-220.3	-262.0	-248.9	-253.1
Mexico	78,772.5	86,908.9	111,349.0	101,296.5	97,470.3	94,629.0	109,720.6	135,926.4	131,337.9	134,615.8	-15,856.5	-22,811.6	-24,577.4	-30,041.4	-37,145.5
Micronesia, Federated States of	31.0	25.0	29.1	30.0	27.2	12.6	10.1	13.7	20.8	15.2	18.4	14.9	15.4	9.2	12.0
Moldova	20.6	10.6	27.3	35.5	30.7	109.3	87.1	105.4	68.3	39.1	-88.7	-76.6	-78.1	-32.8	-8.4
Monaco	6.4	12.6	28.2	15.0	11.4	25.7	14.3	22.9	15.0	15.1	-19.3	-1.7	5.3	.	-3.7
Mongolia	20.3	10.1	17.7	12.1	66.3	41.8	60.8	116.7	143.8	161.7	-21.5	-50.7	-99.0	-131.7	-95.4
Morocco	561.4	565.8	523.2	282.2	565.4	343.0	386.4	440.8	434.6	392.4	218.4	179.5	82.4	-152.4	173.0
Mozambique	45.7	34.8	57.8	28.4	94.6	25.8	10.3	24.4	7.1	8.5	19.9	24.5	32.6	21.3	86.1
Namibia	51.2	195.6	80.4	255.6	57.8	51.8	29.7	45.0	37.3	57.4	-0.6	165.9	35.4	218.3	0.4
Netherlands	18,977.7	19,436.6	21,836.0	19,484.7	18,310.7	7,599.3	8,475.0	9,670.6	9,515.3	9,848.5	11,378.4	10,961.6	12,165.4	9,969.4	8,462.2
Netherlands Antilles	750.7	597.4	673.9	816.4	741.4	308.2	384.3	718.7	484.6	361.7	442.5	213.1	-44.8	331.8	379.7
New Caledonia	19.2	41.7	19.3	25.1	36.6	21.7	8.6	31.4	14.6	9.6	-2.5	33.0	-12.1	10.5	27.0
New Zealand	1,886.5	1,923.4	1,970.3	2,110.5	1,813.1	1,644.6	1,748.2	2,080.2	2,199.2	2,281.6	241.9	175.2	-109.9	-88.7	-468.5
Nicaragua	336.5	373.7	380.1	443.1	437.0	452.7	495.2	588.5	603.6	679.6	-116.2	-121.5	-208.4	-160.5	-242.6
Niger	18.2	18.5	36.5	63.4	40.9	1.7	12.1	7.0	4.6	0.9	16.5	6.4	29.5	58.8	40.0
Nigeria	816.8	627.8	721.8	1,547.2	1,057.8	4,194.0	4,385.1	10,537.6	8,774.8	5,945.4	-3,377.2	-3,757.3	-9,815.8	-7,819.7	-4,887.6
Norway	1,709.3	1,439.4	1,547.2	1,834.7	1,406.5	2,871.6	4,042.6	5,706.1	5,202.8	5,842.6	-1,162.3	-2,603.2	-4,158.9	-3,368.1	-4,436.1
Oman	302.7	188.2	199.8	306.2	356.0	216.8	219.5	257.5	420.1	400.6	85.9	-31.3	-57.7	-113.9	-44.6
Pakistan	720.4	496.7	462.2	541.3	693.4	1,691.7	1,740.7	2,166.8	2,249.4	2,305.0	-971.3	-1,244.0	-1,704.6	-1,708.1	-1,611.6
Panama	1,753.0	1,742.3	1,612.4	1,330.5	1,406.7	312.3	364.8	307.0	290.7	302.6	1,440.7	1,377.5	1,305.4	1,039.8	1,104.1
Papua New Guinea	65.3	37.1	23.0	22.2	23.0	129.6	144.5	34.5	39.3	90.2	-64.3	-107.3	-11.5	-17.1	-67.0
Paraguay	785.9	514.7	445.8	388.8	432.9	33.5	48.1	40.9	32.6	43.7	752.4	466.6	404.9	356.2	389.2
Peru	2,062.6	1,696.5	1,659.9	1,564.3	1,562.5	1,975.5	1,928.4	1,994.9	1,843.8	1,939.3	87.1	-231.9	-335.0	-279.5	-376.8
Philippines	6,736.6	7,222.1	8,799.2	7,660.0	7,276.0	11,947.3	12,352.8	13,934.7	11,325.4	10,979.9	-5,210.7	-5,130.6	-5,135.5	-3,665.4	-3,703.9

See footnotes at end of table.

818   Foreign Commerce and Aid

U.S. Census Bureau, Statistical Abstract of the United States: 2003

Country	Exports, domestic and foreign						General imports						Merchandise trade balance					
	1998	1999	2000	2001	2002		1998	1999	2000	2001	2002		1998	1999	2000	2001	2002
Poland	882.0	826.2	757.2	787.7	686.3		783.7	816.2	1,041.3	952.6	1,108.5		98.3	10.0	-284.1	-164.9	-422.2
Portugal	888.3	1,091.8	984.2	1,239.7	861.3		1,265.3	1,355.8	1,578.5	1,555.4	1,672.6		-377.0	-264.0	-594.3	-315.7	-811.3
Qatar	354.4	145.5	191.1	335.9	313.9		220.4	272.2	485.6	502.2	484.7		134.0	-126.7	-294.5	-166.3	-170.8
Romania	336.6	176.0	232.7	374.5	248.2		393.3	442.4	472.8	519.9	695.1		-56.7	-266.4	-240.1	-145.4	-446.9
Russia	3,552.6	2,059.8	2,092.4	2,716.1	2,397.0		5,747.2	5,920.8	7,658.7	6,264.4	6,870.2		-2,194.6	-3,861.0	-5,566.3	-3,548.3	-4,473.2
Saint Lucia	92.4	98.1	107.4	86.7	99.5		22.4	28.0	22.3	28.9	19.2		70.0	70.1	85.1	57.8	80.3
Saint Vincent and the Grenadines	274.2	92.1	37.9	38.8	40.4		4.8	8.2	8.9	22.5	16.5		269.4	83.8	29.0	16.3	23.9
Samoa	10.4	12.4	64.0	69.9	7.6		6.8	5.3	5.5	7.3	6.4		3.6	7.0	58.5	62.6	1.2
Saudi Arabia	10,519.8	7,911.9	6,234.1	5,957.5	4,780.7		6,241.3	8,253.5	14,364.7	13,272.2	13,149.9		4,278.5	-341.6	-8,130.6	-7,314.7	-8,369.2
Senegal	59.1	63.4	81.7	79.5	74.6		5.2	9.2	4.2	103.8	3.6		53.9	54.3	77.5	-24.3	71.0
Singapore	15,693.6	16,247.3	17,806.3	17,651.7	16,217.9		18,355.7	18,191.4	19,178.3	15,000.0	14,802.2		-2,662.1	-1,944.1	-1,372.0	2,651.7	1,415.7
Slovakia	110.6	127.2	110.1	69.8	92.7		165.7	169.3	240.8	237.6	260.3		-55.1	-42.1	-130.7	-167.8	-167.6
Somalia	2.7	2.8	4.9	6.6	6.2		0.6	0.2	0.5	0.3	0.3		2.1	2.6	4.4	6.3	5.9
South Africa	3,628.0	2,585.5	3,089.5	2,959.6	2,525.5		3,049.1	3,194.4	4,210.1	4,432.6	4,034.1		578.9	-609.0	-1,120.6	-1,473.0	-1,508.6
Spain	5,453.6	6,133.4	6,322.3	5,756.0	5,297.9		4,780.2	5,059.2	5,713.3	5,197.3	5,733.0		673.4	1,074.2	609.0	558.7	-435.1
Sri Lanka	190.4	167.1	204.7	183.0	171.9		1,766.5	1,742.2	2,001.9	1,984.2	1,810.4		-1,576.1	-1,575.1	-1,797.2	-1,801.2	-1,638.5
Sudan	6.8	8.8	17.4	17.0	10.8		3.1	0.1	1.8	3.4	1.4		3.7	8.8	15.6	13.6	9.4
Suriname	187.2	143.8	143.2	155.3	124.8		106.1	122.9	135.2	142.9	132.7		81.1	20.9	-1.0	12.4	-7.9
Sweden	3,822.1	4,250.5	4,553.7	3,541.0	3,153.0		7,848.0	8,102.7	9,597.1	8,908.5	9,216.3		-4,025.9	-3,852.2	-5,043.4	-5,367.5	-6,063.3
Switzerland	7,247.4	8,371.3	9,953.6	9,807.3	7,782.5		8,690.3	9,538.6	10,159.9	9,669.6	9,382.0		-1,442.9	-178.2	-206.3	-137.8	-1,599.5
Syria	161.4	173.1	226.0	69.8	274.1		94.9	100.7	158.6	158.5	160.8		115.5	67.4	72.9	113.3
Taiwan	18,164.5	19,131.4	24,405.9	18,121.6	18,381.8		33,124.8	35,204.4	40,502.8	33,374.5	32,147.9		-14,960.3	-16,073.1	-16,096.9	-15,252.9	-13,766.1
Tajikistan	12.2	0.7	12.1	28.6	3.1		32.6	22.7	9.0	5.2	1.1		-20.4	-8.9	3.1	23.4	32.0
Tanzania	66.9	68.4	44.7	64.0	62.7		31.5	35.4	32.2	27.9	24.8		35.4	33.0	12.5	36.1	37.9
Thailand	5,228.6	4,984.6	6,617.5	5,999.4	4,860.2		13,436.4	14,329.9	16,385.3	14,727.2	14,792.9		-8,197.8	-9,345.3	-9,767.8	-8,737.8	-9,932.7
Togo	25.4	25.7	10.6	16.3	13.8		2.2	3.2	6.0	12.6	2.7		23.2	22.5	4.6	3.7	11.1
Trinidad and Tobago	983.1	785.3	1,099.6	1,087.1	1,020.2		976.9	1,286.7	2,228.8	2,380.0	2,440.3		6.2	-501.4	-1,129.2	-1,292.9	-1,420.1
Tunisia	195.6	280.2	288.9	276.0	194.8		61.5	74.6	93.9	121.7	93.2		134.1	205.6	195.0	154.3	101.6
Turkey	3,505.5	3,217.1	3,720.1	3,094.7	3,113.0		2,542.7	2,629.4	3,041.5	3,054.8	3,516.0		962.8	587.7	678.6	39.9	-403.0
Turkmenistan	28.0	18.4	84.4	248.4	47.1		2.8	8.5	28.0	45.5	59.6		25.2	9.9	56.4	202.9	-12.5
Turks and Caicos Islands	63.8	94.8	88.6	31.7	53.6		4.6	6.3	5.9	8.1	5.1		59.2	88.5	82.7	69.0	48.5
Uganda	23.8	25.0	28.2	17.1	47.1		15.1	20.3	29.1	17.7	15.3		14.7	4.7	-0.9	14.0	8.7
Ukraine	367.5	204.6	191.0	200.1	254.8		531.4	528.9	872.2	673.6	362.4		-163.9	-324.3	-681.2	-473.5	-107.6
United Arab Emirates	2,365.9	2,707.8	2,284.7	2,637.9	3,593.2		659.9	714.3	971.8	1,194.2	922.9		1,706.0	1,993.5	1,312.9	1,443.7	2,670.3
United Kingdom	39,058.2	38,407.1	41,570.4	40,714.2	33,204.7		34,838.2	39,237.2	41,368.8	41,368.8	40,744.9		4,220.0	-830.1	-1,774.7	-654.5	-7,540.2
Uruguay	591.3	494.5	536.9	406.3	208.6		255.7	198.6	313.0	227.7	193.2		335.6	295.9	223.9	178.6	15.4
Uzbekistan	147.3	339.0	157.7	144.9	138.5		34.1	25.6	41.2	53.5	77.1		113.2	313.4	116.5	91.4	61.4
Venezuela	6,515.8	5,353.5	5,549.9	5,642.1	4,429.7		9,181.4	11,334.5	18,623.2	15,250.5	15,093.5		-2,665.6	-5,981.0	-13,073.3	-9,608.4	-10,663.8
Vietnam	274.1	291.5	367.6	460.3	580.2		554.1	608.3	821.4	1,052.9	2,394.7		-280.0	-316.8	-453.8	-592.6	-1,814.5
Virgin Islands, British	62.6	60.1	63.4	74.7	67.4		7.5	22.3	30.9	11.9	40.5		55.1	37.8	32.5	62.8	26.9
Yemen	177.7	157.0	189.4	185.4	366.1		37.6	23.6	255.6	202.4	246.3		140.1	133.4	-66.2	-17.0	119.8
Yugoslavia, Fed. Rep. of	74.4	58.6	29.9	66.2	78.1		12.6	4.5	2.3	6.1	9.6		61.8	54.1	27.6	60.1	68.5
Zambia	21.7	19.8	19.1	31.2	35.7		47.3	37.7	17.7	15.6	7.9		-25.6	-17.8	1.4	15.6	27.8
Zimbabwe	93.1	60.9	52.4	31.2	49.3		127.2	132.8	112.4	90.8	102.8		-34.1	-71.9	-60.0	-59.6	-53.5

- Represents or rounds to zero. X Not applicable. [1] Includes timing adjustment and other countries, not shown separately.

Source: U.S. Census Bureau, *U.S. International Trade in Goods and Services*, Series FT-900(03), and previous final reports. See also <http://www.census.gov/foreign-trade/Press-Release/2002pr/FinalRevisions2002/02final.pdf> (released 13 June 2003).

Foreign Commerce and Aid   819

U.S. Census Bureau, Statistical Abstract of the United States: 2003

No. 1301. U.S. Exports and General Imports by Selected SITC Commodity Groups: 1999 to 2002

[In millions of dollars (695,797 represents $695,797,000,000). SITC=Standard International Trade Classification. N.e.s.=Not elsewhere specified]

Selected commodities	Exports [1]				General imports [2]			
	1999	2000	2001	2002	1999	2000	2001	2002
Total...................	695,797	781,918	729,100	693,103	1,024,618	1,218,022	1,140,999	1,161,366
Agricultural commodities........	47,091	51,296	53,705	53,115	36,681	39,186	39,544	42,012
Animal feeds...............	3,372	3,780	4,221	3,824	564	597	574	605
Coffee.....................	9	9	16	8	2,534	2,350	1,357	1,369
Corn.....................	5,126	4,695	4,755	5,108	156	160	135	137
Cotton, raw and linters..........	968	1,893	2,174	2,031	148	28	27	25
Hides and skins..............	1,020	1,426	1,813	1,594	100	109	100	84
Meat and preparations..........	6,506	7,004	7,231	6,356	3,259	3,841	4,254	4,269
Soybeans..................	4,569	5,284	5,429	5,734	29	31	31	28
Sugar....................	4	4	3	13	557	461	480	495
Tobacco, unmanufactured........	1,312	1,204	1,269	1,050	753	569	710	701
Vegetables and fruits...........	7,152	7,477	7,415	7,607	9,259	9,286	9,517	10,194
Wheat....................	3,578	3,374	3,375	3,630	273	229	282	266
Manufactured goods...........	565,490	625,894	577,714	544,913	882,013	1,012,855	950,679	974,576
ADP equipment, office machinery..	40,787	46,595	39,240	30,368	84,430	92,133	75,859	76,877
Airplane parts................	12,141	15,062	15,735	14,309	5,827	5,572	6,287	4,986
Airplanes..................	32,665	24,777	26,961	27,115	9,222	12,412	14,884	12,329
Alcoholic bev, distilled.........	432	424	489	505	2,618	2,946	3,063	3,273
Aluminum..................	3,564	3,780	3,253	2,947	6,269	6,949	6,406	6,757
Artwork/antiques..............	1,148	1,387	1,637	977	4,890	5,864	5,458	5,194
Basketware, etc..............	2,872	3,309	3,579	3,842	4,378	4,840	5,591	6,564
Chemicals, cosmetics..........	4,853	5,292	5,825	5,870	3,148	3,539	3,750	4,195
Chemicals, dyeing............	3,620	4,089	3,782	3,860	2,633	2,667	2,478	2,357
Chemicals, fertilizers...........	2,921	2,249	2,077	2,106	1,501	1,684	1,890	1,619
Chemicals, inorganic...........	4,632	5,359	5,578	5,464	5,167	6,108	6,153	6,018
Chemicals, medicinal...........	11,203	12,893	15,031	15,732	13,497	14,685	18,628	24,748
Chemicals, n.e.s..............	11,068	12,264	12,382	12,348	5,084	5,725	5,927	6,168
Chemicals, organic............	15,376	17,990	16,424	16,406	21,896	28,578	29,712	30,366
Chemicals, plastics............	16,832	19,519	18,485	19,380	9,279	10,647	10,401	10,760
Cigarettes..................	3,226	3,304	2,118	1,466	151	258	238	316
Clothing...................	7,962	8,191	6,510	5,485	56,412	64,296	63,856	63,803
Cork, wood, lumber............	4,253	4,320	3,533	3,364	8,925	8,227	7,968	7,872
Crude fertilizers..............	1,536	1,724	1,654	1,520	1,268	1,401	1,318	1,275
Electrical machinery...........	75,249	89,917	72,055	66,948	88,620	108,747	84,670	81,158
Fish and preparations..........	2,742	2,806	3,069	2,976	8,910	9,907	9,742	10,000
Footwear...................	694	663	639	518	14,064	14,842	15,234	15,387
Furniture and parts............	4,343	4,744	4,255	3,814	16,181	18,923	18,610	21,577
Gem diamonds...............	312	1,289	1,714	1,182	9,885	12,068	10,616	12,088
General industrial machinery.....	29,882	33,094	32,153	30,075	31,467	34,667	33,264	35,200
Gold, nonmonetary............	5,226	5,898	4,872	3,244	3,032	2,657	2,079	2,428
Iron and steel mill products......	4,989	5,715	5,482	5,252	13,369	15,807	12,449	12,951
Lighting, plumbing............	1,298	1,384	1,321	1,333	4,330	5,104	4,895	5,566
Metal manufactures, n.e.s........	11,185	13,453	11,365	11,170	14,414	16,204	15,510	16,681
Metal ores; scrap.............	3,484	4,234	4,420	4,626	3,647	3,817	3,237	3,101
Metalworking machinery.........	5,268	6,191	4,703	4,140	6,782	7,726	6,587	5,104
Optical goods................	2,231	3,246	3,036	2,132	3,077	4,019	3,455	2,836
Paper and paperboard..........	9,863	10,640	10,042	9,551	13,400	15,185	14,815	14,435
Photographic equipment.........	3,624	4,236	3,281	3,529	6,111	6,896	5,596	5,325
Plastic articles, n.e.s...........	6,362	7,607	7,065	6,820	7,013	8,034	8,257	9,138
Platinum...................	503	888	962	723	3,613	5,566	5,240	2,830
Power generating machinery......	30,894	32,743	33,577	32,430	31,551	33,773	36,118	33,922
Printed materials..............	4,581	4,776	4,746	4,429	3,323	3,680	3,721	3,960
Pulp and waste paper..........	3,528	4,576	3,690	3,842	2,597	3,381	2,630	2,363
Records/magnetic media........	5,802	5,395	4,611	4,414	4,703	5,172	4,883	5,279
Rubber articles, n.e.s...........	1,401	1,673	1,569	1,423	1,791	1,962	1,979	2,139
Rubber tires and tubes.........	2,400	2,379	2,287	2,232	4,638	4,785	4,209	4,765
Scientific instruments...........	25,644	30,984	29,123	27,087	17,658	22,007	21,356	20,884
Ships, boats................	1,632	1,070	1,801	1,200	1,127	1,178	1,209	1,325
Silver and bullion.............	214	227	234	262	630	775	530	687
Spacecraft..................	641	158	201	509	245	217	71	310
Specialized industrial machinery...	24,941	30,959	25,747	23,532	21,596	22,711	19,554	18,401
Television, VCR, etc...........	24,404	27,921	24,230	19,374	50,936	70,468	62,836	66,212
Textile yarn, fabric............	9,245	10,534	10,074	10,263	13,578	15,171	14,616	16,097
Toys/games/sporting goods.......	3,315	3,609	3,217	2,985	18,987	20,011	20,901	22,067
Travel goods................	329	351	308	277	4,148	4,430	4,300	4,402
Vehicles...................	54,299	57,421	54,347	57,698	145,927	161,544	157,400	168,073
Watches/clocks/parts...........	334	348	277	236	3,258	3,481	3,048	3,203
Wood manufactures............	1,739	1,842	1,568	1,564	7,089	7,228	6,998	7,853
Mineral fuel [3].................	9,880	13,179	12,494	11,541	75,803	135,367	121,923	115,748
Coal.....................	2,268	2,162	1,915	1,673	665	805	1,022	966
Crude oil..................	772	463	187	92	50,890	89,876	74,293	79,252
Petroleum preparations..........	3,414	5,746	5,034	6,009	14,183	25,673	24,620	20,748
Natural gas................	218	411	536	995	6,669	12,594	15,417	10,974
Reexports...................	50,969	68,203	64,780	63,792	(X)	(X)	(X)	(X)

X Not applicable. [1] F.a.s. basis. Exports by commodity are only for domestic exports. [2] Customs value basis. [3] Includes other mineral fuels not shown separately.

Source: U.S. Census Bureau, *U.S. International Trade in Goods and Services,* Series FT-900(03), and previous final reports. See also <http://www.census.gov/foreign-trade/Press-Release/2002pr/FinalRevisions2002/02final.pdf> (released 13 June 2003).

No. 1302. United States Total and Aerospace Foreign Trade: 1980 to 2002

[In millions of dollars (245,262 represents $245,262,000,000), except percent. Data are reported as exports of domestic merchandise, including Department of Defense shipments and undocumented exports to Canada, f.a.s. (free alongside ship) basis, and imports for consumption, customs value basis. Minus sign (-) indicates deficit]

Year	Merchandise trade			Aerospace trade						
	Trade balance	Imports	Exports	Trade balance	Imports	Total Exports	Percent of U.S. exports	Civil Total	Trans-ports	Military
1980	-19,696	245,262	225,566	11,952	3,554	15,506	6.9	13,248	6,727	2,258
1981	-22,267	260,982	238,715	13,134	4,500	17,634	7.4	13,312	7,180	4,322
1982	-27,510	243,952	216,442	11,035	4,568	15,603	7.2	9,608	3,834	5,995
1983	-52,409	258,048	205,639	12,619	3,446	16,065	7.8	10,595	4,683	5,470
1984	-106,703	330,678	223,976	10,082	4,926	15,008	6.7	9,659	3,195	5,350
1985	-117,712	336,526	218,815	12,593	6,132	18,725	8.6	12,942	5,518	5,783
1986	-138,279	365,438	227,159	11,826	7,902	19,728	8.7	14,851	6,276	4,875
1987	-152,119	406,241	254,122	14,575	7,905	22,480	8.8	15,768	6,377	6,714
1988	-118,526	440,952	322,426	17,860	9,087	26,947	8.4	20,298	8,766	6,651
1989	-109,399	473,211	363,812	22,083	10,028	32,111	8.8	25,619	12,313	6,492
1990	-101,718	495,311	393,592	27,282	11,801	39,083	9.9	31,517	16,691	7,566
1991	-66,723	488,453	421,730	30,785	13,003	43,788	10.4	35,548	20,881	8,239
1992	-84,501	532,665	448,164	31,356	13,662	45,018	10.0	36,906	22,379	8,111
1993	-115,568	580,659	465,091	27,235	12,183	39,418	8.5	31,823	18,146	7,596
1994	-150,630	663,256	512,626	25,010	12,363	37,373	7.3	30,050	15,931	7,322
1995	-158,801	743,543	584,742	21,561	11,509	33,071	5.7	25,079	10,606	7,991
1996	-170,214	795,289	625,075	26,602	13,668	40,270	6.4	29,477	13,624	10,792
1997	-180,522	869,704	689,182	32,239	18,134	50,374	7.3	40,075	21,028	10,299
1998	-229,758	911,896	682,138	40,960	23,110	64,071	9.4	51,999	29,168	12,072
1999	-328,821	1,024,618	695,797	37,381	25,063	62,444	9.0	50,624	25,694	11,820
2000	-436,104	1,218,022	781,918	26,734	27,944	54,679	7.0	45,566	19,615	9,113
2001	-411,899	1,140,999	729,100	26,035	32,473	58,508	8.0	49,371	22,151	9,137
2002	-470,260	1,163,561	693,302	29,534	27,242	56,775	8.2	47,348	21,661	9,427

Source: Aerospace Industries Association of America, Washington, DC, *Aerospace Facts and Figures*, annual.

No. 1303. U.S. Exporting Companies Profile by Company Type and Employment-Size Class: 1992 and 2000

[Data are based on economic census and survey data on file at the Census Bureau, administrative records from other government agencies, and documents filed for export clearances]

Company type and employment-size-class	Number of exporters		Known export value [1] (mil. dol.)		Percent of—			
					Number of exporters		Known export value	
	1992	2000	1992	2000	1992	2000	1992	2000
All companies, total	112,854	246,452	348,960	668,310	100.0	100.0	100.0	100.0
No employees	15,534	74,772	9,178	47,024	13.8	30.3	2.6	7.0
1 to 19 employees	51,186	96,268	29,397	45,272	45.4	39.1	8.4	6.8
20 to 49 employees	18,501	31,362	17,005	21,262	16.4	12.7	4.9	3.2
50 to 99 employees	10,505	16,988	13,840	19,711	9.3	6.9	4.0	2.9
100 to 249 employees	8,679	13,685	18,371	32,192	7.7	5.6	5.3	4.8
250 to 499 employees	3,621	5,454	15,055	27,397	3.2	2.2	4.3	4.1
500 or more employees	4,828	7,923	246,114	475,453	4.3	3.2	70.5	71.1
Manufacturers	(NA)	69,253	(NA)	471,692	(NA)	28.1	(NA)	70.6
No employees	(NA)	12,668	(NA)	15,541	(NA)	5.1	(NA)	2.3
1 to 19 employees	(NA)	19,719	(NA)	4,420	(NA)	8.0	(NA)	0.7
20 to 49 employees	(NA)	13,876	(NA)	6,309	(NA)	5.6	(NA)	0.9
50 to 99 employees	(NA)	8,968	(NA)	7,704	(NA)	3.6	(NA)	1.2
100 to 249 employees	(NA)	7,554	(NA)	15,996	(NA)	3.1	(NA)	2.4
250 to 499 employees	(NA)	2,948	(NA)	16,843	(NA)	1.2	(NA)	2.5
500 or more employees	(NA)	3,520	(NA)	404,879	(NA)	1.4	(NA)	60.6
Wholesalers	(NA)	72,323	(NA)	96,628	(NA)	29.3	(NA)	14.5
No employees	(NA)	16,727	(NA)	9,381	(NA)	6.8	(NA)	1.4
1 to 19 employees	(NA)	39,383	(NA)	24,325	(NA)	16.0	(NA)	3.6
20 to 49 employees	(NA)	8,814	(NA)	7,539	(NA)	3.6	(NA)	1.1
50 to 99 employees	(NA)	3,569	(NA)	6,787	(NA)	1.4	(NA)	1.0
100 to 249 employees	(NA)	2,330	(NA)	9,236	(NA)	0.9	(NA)	1.4
250 to 499 employees	(NA)	751	(NA)	4,618	(NA)	0.3	(NA)	0.7
500 or more employees	(NA)	749	(NA)	34,743	(NA)	0.3	(NA)	5.2
Other companies	(NA)	90,331	(NA)	85,426	(NA)	36.7	(NA)	12.8
No employees	(NA)	35,397	(NA)	17,663	(NA)	14.4	(NA)	2.6
1 to 19 employees	(NA)	35,360	(NA)	15,005	(NA)	14.3	(NA)	2.2
20 to 49 employees	(NA)	7,455	(NA)	5,880	(NA)	3.0	(NA)	0.9
50 to 99 employees	(NA)	3,729	(NA)	4,659	(NA)	1.5	(NA)	0.7
100 to 249 employees	(NA)	3,329	(NA)	5,610	(NA)	1.4	(NA)	0.8
250 to 499 employees	(NA)	1,606	(NA)	5,328	(NA)	0.7	(NA)	0.8
500 or more employees	(NA)	3,455	(NA)	31,282	(NA)	1.4	(NA)	4.7
Unclassified companies	(NA)	14,545	(NA)	14,564	(NA)	5.9	(NA)	2.2

NA Not available. [1] Known value is defined as the value of exports by known exporters, i.e., those export transactions that could be matched to specific companies. Export values are on f.a.s. or "free alongside ship basis." Total export value was $251 billion in 1987 and $448 billion in 1992.

Source: U.S. Census Bureau, *A Profile of U.S. Exporting Companies, 1992* and *2000-2001*. See also <http://www.census.gov/foreign-trade/aip/edbrel-0001.pdf> (released 20 February 2003).

Foreign Commerce and Aid 821

No. 1304. Domestic Exports and Imports for Consumption of Merchandise by Selected NAICS Product Category: 2000 to 2002

[In millions of dollars (712,285 represents $712,285,000,000). Includes nonmonetary gold. NAICS=North American Industry Classification System; see text, this section]

Product category	2000	2001	2002
Domestic exports, total	712,285	666,021	629,599
Agricultural, forestry and fishery products	29,153	29,666	30,068
Agricultural products, total	23,596	24,068	24,827
Livestock and livestock products	1,255	1,309	1,020
Forestry products, not elsewhere specified	1,644	1,436	1,419
Fish, fresh or chilled; and other marine products	2,658	2,854	2,802
Mining, total	6,187	5,403	5,585
Oil and gas	1,706	1,261	1,725
Minerals and ores	4,481	4,141	3,860
Manufacturing, total	644,440	597,101	562,834
Food and kindred products	24,966	26,486	25,175
Beverages and tobacco products	5,568	4,334	3,559
Textiles and fabrics	7,010	7,098	7,397
Textile mill products	2,236	1,991	1,875
Apparel and accessories	8,104	6,469	5,462
Leather and allied products	2,322	2,285	2,049
Wood products	4,854	3,944	3,777
Paper products	15,539	14,045	13,640
Printed, publishing & similar products	4,869	4,867	4,509
Petroleum and coal products	8,862	8,214	7,897
Chemicals	77,649	76,837	78,049
Plastics and rubber products	16,970	15,745	15,383
Nonmetallic mineral products	7,830	7,378	6,025
Primary metal products	20,126	18,150	15,371
Fabricated metal products	21,737	19,547	18,893
Machinery, except electrical	85,038	76,572	70,178
Computers and electronic products	161,449	134,263	116,243
Electrical equipment, appliances and components	25,401	22,764	20,587
Transportation equipment	121,701	122,877	123,970
Furniture and fixtures	2,882	2,419	2,158
Miscellaneous manufactured commodities	19,327	20,815	20,640
Special classification provisions	32,505	33,852	31,112
Waste & scrap	4,948	4,738	5,081
Used or second-hand merchandise	1,950	2,169	1,562
Goods returned or reimported	333	310	241
Special classification provision, not elsewhere specified	25,274	26,635	24,228
Imports for consumption, total	1,205,339	1,132,635	1,154,811
Agricultural, forestry and fishery products	24,378	23,598	24,327
Agricultural products, total	11,771	11,290	11,773
Livestock and livestock products	3,085	3,445	3,455
Forestry products, not elsewhere specified	1,409	1,158	1,288
Fish, fresh or chilled; and other marine products	8,113	7,706	7,811
Mining, total	79,841	76,243	76,288
Oil and gas	76,166	72,690	72,830
Minerals and ores	3,675	3,553	3,458
Manufacturing, total	1,040,329	972,669	995,103
Food and kindred products	18,944	19,646	21,110
Beverages and tobacco products	8,350	8,723	9,772
Textiles and fabrics	7,042	6,336	6,778
Textile mill products	7,347	7,580	8,643
Apparel and accessories	62,928	62,429	62,313
Leather and allied products	21,463	21,865	22,104
Wood products	15,388	14,968	15,720
Paper products	19,080	18,170	17,528
Printed, publishing & similar products	4,197	4,143	4,432
Petroleum and coal products	40,156	35,222	31,976
Chemicals	76,606	80,681	87,311
Plastics and rubber products	17,362	16,887	18,554
Nonmetallic mineral products	14,740	13,552	13,547
Primary metal products	43,833	36,350	34,356
Fabricated metal products	27,974	26,386	28,607
Machinery, except electrical	79,366	72,124	68,645
Computers and electronic products	250,694	204,950	205,564
Electrical equipment, appliances and components	39,567	38,949	39,707
Transportation equipment	213,110	212,013	219,186
Furniture and fixtures	15,607	15,266	17,492
Miscellaneous manufactured commodities	56,577	56,427	61,759
Special classification provisions	60,791	60,125	59,093
Waste & scrap	1,875	1,590	1,613
Used or second-hand merchandise	6,345	5,902	5,668
Goods returned or reimported	33,851	34,682	34,981
Special classification provision, not elsewhere specified	18,720	17,951	16,831

Source: U.S. Census Bureau, *U.S. International Trade in Goods and Services*, Series FT-900, December issues. For most recent, see <http://www.census.gov/foreign-trade/Press-Release/2002pr/12/ft900.pdf> (released 20 February 2003).

Section 29
Puerto Rico and the Island Areas

This section presents summary economic and social statistics for Puerto Rico, the U.S. Virgin Islands, Guam, American Samoa, and the Northern Mariana Islands. Primary sources are the decennial censuses of population and housing, county business patterns, and the censuses of agriculture, business, manufactures, and construction (taken every 5 years) conducted by the U.S. Census Bureau; the annual *Vital Statistics of the United States*, issued by the National Center for Health Statistics; and the annual *Income and Product* of the Puerto Rico Planning Board, San Juan.

Jurisdiction—The United States gained jurisdiction over these areas as follows: The islands of *Puerto Rico* and *Guam*, surrendered by Spain to the United States in December 1898, were ceded to the United States by the Treaty of Paris, ratified in 1899. Puerto Rico became a commonwealth on July 25, 1952, thereby achieving a high degree of local autonomy under its own constitution. The *U.S. Virgin Islands*, comprising 50 islands and cays, was purchased by the United States from Denmark in 1917. *American Samoa*, a group of seven islands, was acquired by the United States in accordance with a convention among the United States, Great Britain, and Germany, ratified in 1900 (Swains Island was annexed in 1925). By an agreement approved by the Security Council and the United States, the Northern Mariana Islands, previously under Japanese mandate, was administered by the United States between 1947 and 1986 under the United Nations trusteeship system. The Northern Mariana Islands became a commonwealth in 1986.

Censuses—Because characteristics of the Puerto Rico and the Island Areas differ, the presentation of census data for them is not uniform. The 1960 Census of Population covered all of the places listed above except the Commonwealth of the Northern Mariana Islands (their census was conducted in April 1958 by the Office of the High Commissioner), while the 1960 Census of Housing also excluded American Samoa. The 1970, 1980, 1990, and 2000 Censuses of Population and Housing covered all five areas. The 1959, 1969, and 1978 Censuses of Agriculture covered Puerto Rico, American Samoa, Guam, and the Virgin Islands; the 1964, 1974, and 1982 censuses covered the same areas except American Samoa; and the 1969, 1978, 1987, 1992, and 1997 censuses included the Commonwealth of the Northern Mariana Islands. Beginning in 1967, Congress authorized the economic censuses, to be taken at 5-year intervals, for years ending in "2" and "7." Prior economic censuses were conducted in Puerto Rico for 1949, 1954, 1958, and 1963 and in Guam and the U.S. Virgin Islands for 1958 and 1963. In 1967, the census of construction industries was added for the first time in Puerto Rico; in 1972, the U.S. Virgin Islands and Guam were covered. For 1982, 1987, 1992, and 1997 the economic censuses covered the Commonwealth of the Northern Mariana Islands.

Information in other sections—In addition to the statistics presented in this section, other data are included as integral parts of many tables showing distribution by states in various sections of the *Abstract*. See "Puerto Rico and the Island Areas" in the Index. For definition and explanation of terms used, see Section 1, Population; Section 4, Education; Section 17, Agriculture; Section 20, Construction and Housing; Section 21, Manufactures; and Section 22, Domestic Trade.

Figure 29.1
Selected Island Areas of the United States

824 Puerto Rico and the Island Areas

U.S. Census Bureau, Statistical Abstract of the United States: 2003

No. 1305. Estimated Resident Population With Projections: 1970 to 2010

[In thousands (2,722 represents 2,722,000). Population as of July 1. Population data generally are de-facto figures for the present territory. Data for 1990 to 2000 are adjusted to the 2000 Census of Population for Puerto Rico only. See text, Section 30, for general comments regarding the data. For details of methodology, coverage, and reliability, see source]

Area	1970	1980	1990	1995	1998	1999	2000	2001	2002	2010, proj.
Puerto Rico	2,722	3,210	3,537	3,683	3,781	3,800	3,816	3,838	3,859	4,001
American Samoa	27	32	47	57	62	64	57	58	58	57
Guam	86	107	134	144	149	152	155	158	161	181
Virgin Islands	63	98	104	114	118	120	109	109	109	108
Northern Mariana Islands	12	17	44	58	67	69	69	72	74	91

Source: U.S. Census Bureau, International Data Base. See Internet site <http://census.gov/ipc/www/idbnew.html>.

No. 1306. Vital Statistics—Specified Areas: 1980 to 2001

[Births, deaths, and infant deaths by place of residence. Rates for 1960, 1970, 1980, 1990 and 2000 based on population enumerated as of **April 1;** for other years, on population estimated as of **July 1**]

Area and year	Births Number	Births Rate [1]	Deaths Number	Deaths Rate [1]	Infant deaths Number	Infant deaths Rate [2]
Puerto Rico:						
1980	72,986	22.8	20,413	6.4	1,351	18.5
1990	66,417	18.8	25,957	7.3	888	13.4
1995	63,425	17.0	30,032	8.1	804	12.7
2000	59,333	15.2	28,369	7.2	574	9.7
2001 [3]	55,866	14.2	29,082	7.6	517	9.3
Guam:						
1980	2,945	27.8	393	3.7	43	14.6
1990	3,839	28.6	520	3.9	31	8.1
1995	4,180	29.0	592	4.1	38	9.4
2000	3,766	24.4	648	4.2	22	5.8
2001 [3]	3,564	22.6	663	4.2	35	9.8
Virgin Islands:						
1980	2,504	25.9	504	5.2	61	24.4
1990	2,267	21.8	480	4.6	33	14.6
1995	2,063	18.1	664	5.8	34	16.6
2000	1,564	12.9	641	5.3	21	13.4
2001 [3]	1,669	13.7	605	5.6	13	(NA)
American Samoa:						
1997	1,634	27.1	257	4.3	17	(B)
2001 [3]	1,655	24.7	239	4.2	14	(NA)
Northern Marianas:						
1998	1,462	21.9	162	2.4	13	(B)
2001 [3]	1,449	19.4	148	2.1	11	(NA)

B Base figure too small to meet statistical standards of reliability. NA Not available. [1] Per 1,000 population. [2] Per 1,000 live births. [3] Mortality data for 2001 is preliminary.
Source: U.S. National Center for Health Statistics, *Vital Statistics of the United States*, annual; and *National Vital Statistics Reports (NSVR)* and unpublished data.

No. 1307. Population Characteristics by Area: 2000

[As of April 1. Based on the Census of Population; see Appendix III. See Table 359 for land area. For definition of median, see Guide to Tabular Presentation]

Item	United States	Puerto Rico	Virgin Islands	Guam	American Samoa	Northern Mariana Islands
Total resident population	281,421,906	3,808,610	108,612	154,805	57,291	69,221
Percent increase, 1990-2000	13.2	8.1	6.7	16.3	22.5	59.7
Male	138,053,563	1,833,577	51,864	79,181	29,264	31,984
Female	143,368,343	1,975,033	56,748	75,624	28,027	37,237
Males per 100 females	96.3	92.8	91.4	104.7	104.4	85.9
Median age (years)	35.3	32.1	33.4	27.4	21.3	28.7
Marital status, persons 15 years and over	221,148,671	2,903,329	80,207	107,649	35,079	53,632
Never married	59,913,370	813,784	32,764	37,711	12,741	22,462
Now married, excludes separated	120,231,273	1,509,403	31,223	57,505	19,519	28,224
Separated	4,769,220	104,897	2,639	1,453	437	916
Widowed	14,674,500	197,123	4,078	4,253	1,570	1,121
Divorced	21,560,308	278,122	9,503	6,727	812	909
Households and families:						
Households	105,480,101	1,261,325	40,648	38,769	9,349	14,055
Family households (families) [1]	71,787,347	1,004,080	26,636	32,367	8,706	9,407
With own children under 18 years	34,588,368	486,409	14,107	19,678	6,297	6,569
Married-couple family	54,493,232	682,804	13,498	22,693	6,596	6,445
With own children under 18 years	24,835,505	337,190	5,905	13,964	5,261	4,526
Female household, no husband present	12,900,103	268,476	10,132	6,284	1,398	1,663
With own children under 18 years	7,561,874	131,584	6,450	3,753	640	1,106
Nonfamily households	33,692,754	257,245	14,012	6,402	643	4,648
Average household size	2.59	2.98	2.64	3.89	6.05	3.66
Average family size	3.14	3.41	3.34	4.27	6.24	4.16

[1] Includes other family types, not shown separately.
Source: U.S. Census Bureau, United States and Puerto Rico: DP-1, "Profile of General Demographic Characteristics: 2000 (area)" and DP-2, "Profile of Selected Social Characteristics: 2000 (area)"; Virgin Islands, Guam, and Northern Mariana Islands: "Population and Housing Profile: 2000 (area)". See Internet sites <http://www.census.gov/population/www/cen2000/islandareas.html> and <http://www.census.gov/census2000/states/pr.html>.

No. 1308. Puerto Rico—General Demographic Characteristics: 1990 and 2000

[As of April 1. Based on the Census of Population and Housing; see Appendix III]

Characteristic	1990, number	2000 Number	2000 Percent	Characteristic	1990, number	2000 Number	2000 Percent
SEX AND AGE				**HOUSEHOLD TYPE**			
Total population	3,522,037	3,808,610	100.0	Total households	1,054,924	1,261,325	100.0
Male	1,705,642	1,833,577	48.1	Family households (families)[2]	886,339	1,004,080	79.6
Female	1,816,395	1,975,033	51.9	With own children under 18 years[2]	487,058	486,409	38.6
Under 5 years	302,173	295,406	7.8	Married-couple family	634,872	682,804	54.1
5 to 9 years	316,473	305,162	8.0	With own children under 18 years	363,989	337,190	26.7
10 to 14 years	339,573	305,800	8.0	Female householder, no husband present	205,508	268,476	21.3
15 to 19 years	326,717	313,436	8.2	With own children under 18 years	105,085	131,584	10.4
20 to 24 years	287,227	301,191	7.9	Nonfamily households	168,585	257,245	20.4
25 to 34 years	524,849	534,332	14.0	Householder living alone	155,151	232,560	18.4
35 to 44 years	462,479	515,663	13.5	Householder 65 years and over	66,187	92,673	7.3
45 to 54 years	355,858	463,036	12.2	Average household size	3.31	2.98	(X)
55 to 59 years	140,952	188,883	5.0	Average family size	3.69	3.41	(X)
60 to 64 years	124,852	160,564	4.2	**HOUSING OCCUPANCY**			
65 to 74 years	199,397	240,951	6.3	Total housing units	1,188,985	1,418,476	100.0
75 to 84 years	108,822	136,480	3.6	Occupied housing units	1,054,924	1,261,325	88.9
85 years and over	32,665	47,706	1.3	Vacant housing units	134,061	157,151	11.1
Median age (years)	28.4	32.1	(X)	For seasonal, recreational, or occasional use	21,413	32,041	2.3
18 years and over	2,367,510	2,716,509	71.3	Homeowner vacancy rate (percent)	1.7	1.7	(X)
Male	1,118,038	1,274,998	33.5	Rental vacancy rate (percent)	7.3	7.4	(X)
Female	1,249,472	1,441,511	37.8	**HOUSING TENURE**			
65 years and over	340,884	425,137	11.2	Occupied housing units	1,054,924	1,261,325	100.0
Male	156,226	186,203	4.9	Owner-occupied	760,233	919,769	72.9
Female	184,658	238,934	6.3	Renter-occupied	294,691	341,556	27.1
RELATIONSHIP				Average household size of owner-occupied units	3.36	3.00	(X)
Total population	3,522,037	3,808,610	100.0	Average household size of renter-occupied units	3.17	2.94	(X)
In households	3,487,667	3,761,836	98.8				
Householder	1,054,924	1,261,325	33.1				
Spouse	634,872	682,804	17.9				
Child	1,475,741	1,431,769	37.6				
Own child under 18 years	1,013,894	936,719	24.6				
Other relatives	270,181	305,075	8.0				
Under 18 years	128,384	139,420	3.7				
Nonrelatives	51,949	80,863	2.1				
Unmarried partner [1]	22,200	40,238	1.1				
In group quarters	34,370	46,774	1.2				

X Not applicable. [1] 1990 are sample data on unmarried partner households. [2] Includes male family householder, no wife present, not shown separately.

Source: U.S. Census Bureau, "Puerto Rico's Census 2000 Demographic Profile." Internet site <http://www.census.gov/Press-Release/www/2001/tables/redistr.html#demoprofile> (released 03 July 2001).

No. 1309. Puerto Rico, Guam, Virgin Islands, American Samoa, and Northern Mariana Islands—Population: 1990 and 2000

[As of April 1. Minus sign (-) indicates decrease]

Area	1990	2000	Percent change, 1990 to 2000	Area	1990	2000	Percent change, 1990 to 2000
PUERTO RICO				Arecibo zona urbana	49,545	49,318	-0.5
Municipio:				Fajardo zona urbana	31,659	33,286	5.1
San Juan	437,745	434,374	-0.8	Levittown comunidad zona urbana	30,807	30,140	-2.2
Bayamon	220,262	224,044	1.7	Catano zona urbana	34,587	30,071	-13.1
Ponce	187,749	186,475	-0.7	**GUAM**			
Carolina	177,806	186,076	4.7				
Caguas	133,447	140,502	5.3	Dedido District	31,728	42,980	35.5
Arecibo	93,385	100,131	7.2	Yigo District	14,213	19,474	37.0
Guaynabo	92,886	100,053	7.7	Mangilao District	10,483	13,313	27.0
Mayaguez	100,371	98,434	-1.9	**U.S. VIRGIN ISLANDS**			
Toa Baja	89,454	94,085	5.2				
Trujillo Alto	61,120	75,728	23.9	St. Croix Island	50,139	53,234	6.2
Aguadilla	59,335	64,685	9.0	St Thomas Island	48,166	51,181	6.3
Toa Alta	44,101	63,929	45.0	Charlotte Amalie subdistrict	20,589	18,914	-8.1
Vega Baja	55,997	61,929	10.6	St John Island	3,504	4,197	19.8
Humacao	55,203	59,035	6.9	**AMERICAN SAMOA**			
Rio Grande	45,648	52,362	14.7				
Place:				Eastern District	21,175	23,441	10.7
San Juan zona urbana	426,832	421,958	-1.1	Ma'oputasi County	10,640	11,695	9.9
Bayamon zona urbana	202,103	203,499	0.7	Western District	23,868	32,435	35.9
Carolina zona urbana	162,404	168,164	3.5	Tualauta County	14,724	22,025	49.6
Ponce zona urbana	159,151	155,038	-2.6	**NORTHERN MARIANA ISLANDS**			
Caguas zona urbana	92,429	88,680	-4.1				
Guaynabo zona urbana	73,385	78,806	7.4	Saipan Municipality	38,896	62,392	60.4
Mayaguez zona urbana	83,010	78,647	-5.3				
Trujillo Alto zona urbana	44,336	50,841	14.7				

Source: U.S. Census Bureau, Internet releases (03 July 2001) <http://www.census.gov/Press-Release/www/2001/tables/redistpr.html#demoprofile>; <http://www.census.gov/Press-Release/www/2001/tables/redistgu.html>; <http://www.census.gov/Press-Release/www/2001/tables/redistvi.html>; <http://www.census.gov/Press-Release/www/2001/tables/redistas.html>; <http://www.census.gov/Press-Release/www/2001/tables/redistnmi.html>.

No. 1310. Selected Social and Economic Characteristics by Area: 2000

[As of April 1. Based on the Census of Population and Housing; see Appendix III]

Characteristic	United States	Puerto Rico	Virgin Islands	Guam	American Samoa	Northern Mariana Islands
EDUCATIONAL ATTAINMENT						
Persons 25 years and over	182,211,639	2,288,326	65,603	83,281	25,380	42,123
Less than 9th grade	13,755,477	581,225	12,133	7,843	3,120	5,794
9th to 12th grade, no diploma	21,960,148	335,179	13,743	11,862	5,476	7,181
High school graduate	52,168,981	509,856	17,044	26,544	9,983	14,986
Some college or associate degree	49,864,428	443,813	11,694	20,398	4,928	7,634
Bachelor's degree or higher	44,462,605	418,253	10,989	16,634	1,873	6,528
EMPLOYMENT STATUS						
Persons, 16 years old and over	217,168,077	2,842,876	78,265	105,014	33,945	52,898
In labor force	138,820,935	1,156,532	51,042	68,894	17,664	44,471
Percent of total	63.9	40.7	65.2	65.6	52.0	84.1
Armed forces	1,152,137	4,669	109	4,442	37	6
Civilian labor force	137,668,798	1,151,863	50,933	64,452	17,627	44,465
Employed	129,721,512	930,865	46,565	57,053	16,718	42,753
Unemployed	7,947,286	220,998	4,368	7,399	909	1,712
Percent of civilian labor force	5.8	19.2	8.6	11.5	5.2	3.9
Not in labor force	78,347,142	1,686,344	27,223	36,120	16,281	8,427
FAMILY INCOME IN 1999						
Families	72,261,780	1,008,555	26,636	32,367	8,706	9,407
Less than $10,000	4,155,386	316,675	5,584	3,955	2,107	1,553
$10,000 to $14,999	3,115,586	150,199	2,142	1,734	1,449	1,162
$15,000 to $24,999	7,757,397	202,824	4,203	3,923	1,995	1,864
$25,000 to $34,999	8,684,429	123,810	3,529	4,082	1,146	1,280
$35,000 to $49,999	12,377,108	101,047	4,011	5,400	969	1,301
$50,000 to $74,999	16,130,100	64,839	3,782	6,267	677	1,191
$75,000 or more	20,041,774	49,161	3,385	7,006	363	1,056
Median family income (dollars)	50,046	16,543	28,553	41,229	18,357	25,853
RESIDENCE IN 1995						
Persons 5 years and over	262,375,152	3,515,228	100,059	138,020	49,471	63,429
Same house	142,027,478	2,560,034	61,879	73,120	37,103	23,989
Different house in this area	112,851,828	820,514	27,688	40,945	5,763	15,576
Outside area	7,495,846	134,680	10,492	23,955	6,605	23,864
LANGUAGE SPOKEN AT HOME						
Persons 5 years and over	262,375,152	3,515,228	100,059	138,020	49,471	63,429
Speak only English at home	215,423,557	506,661	74,740	52,831	1,440	6,819

Source: U.S. Census Bureau, United States and Puerto Rico: DP-1, "Profile of General Demographic Characteristics: 2000 (area)" and DP-2, "Profile of Selected Social Characteristics: 2000 (area)"; Virgin Islands, Guam, and Northern Mariana Islands: "Population and Housing Profile: 2000 (area)." See Internet sites <http://www.census.gov/population/www/cen2000/islandareas.html> and <http://www.census.gov/census2000/states/pr.html>.

No. 1311. Federal Direct Payments: 2002

[In thousands of dollars (5,281,765 represents $5,281,765,000). For fiscal years ending September 30]

Selected program payments	Puerto Rico	Guam	Virgin Islands	American Samoa	Northern Mariana Islands
Direct payments to individuals for retirement and disability [1]	5,281,765	198,143	138,036	39,395	20,995
Social security:					
Retirement insurance	2,140,073	61,279	77,965	9,692	4,910
Survivors insurance	951,565	25,533	21,093	10,405	4,206
Disability insurance	1,469,432	12,798	16,587	10,215	1,140
Federal retirement and disability:					
Civilian [2]	201,060	59,290	15,019	1,556	4,827
Military	88,265	29,137	4,548	3,290	1,497
Veterans benefits:					
Service connected disability	232,426	7,392	1,412	3,309	462
Other	172,984	1,777	618	885	69
Other direct payments [1]	2,657,610	78,121	89,694	2,303	3,206
Medicare:					
Hospital insurance	541,283	772	13,569	-	-
Supplemental medical insurance	874,790	535	9,610	-	-
Food stamp payments [3]	-	51,816	17,431	-	-
Housing assistance	104,286	2,459	20,222	-	-
Agriculture assistance	29,331	19	4,115	-	9
Federal employees life and health insurance	65,913	14,168	-	-	-
Other	704,589	8,353	7,327	2,303	3,198

- Represents zero or rounds to zero. [1] Includes other payments, not shown separately. [2] Includes retirement and disability payments to former U.S. Postal Service employees. [3] Food stamp program in Puerto Rico was replaced by the Nutrition Assistance Grant Program in 1982.

Source: U.S. Census Bureau, Consolidated Federal Funds Report for Fiscal Year, 2002 (issued May 2003). See also <http://www.census.gov/govs/www/cffr02.html>.

No. 1312. Public Elementary and Secondary Schools by Area: 2001

[For school year ending in year shown, unless otherwise indicated. (2,257,837 represents $2,257,837,000)]

Item	Puerto Rico	Guam	Virgin Islands	American Samoa	Item	Puerto Rico	Guam	Virgin Islands	American Samoa
Enrollment, fall	604,177	31,992	18,780	15,897	School staff	51,247	3,210	(NA)	1,316
Elementary (kindergarten-grade 8)	438,053	23,133	13,421	11,911	Teachers	42,906	1,918	(NA)	914
					Student support staff	3,854	53	(NA)	73
Secondary (grades 9-12 and post graduates)	166,124	8,859	5,359	3,986	Other support services staff	18,082	140	(NA)	172
Staff, fall	75,254	3,765	(NA)	1,686	Current expenditures [1]				
School district staff	2,071	362	(NA)	125	($1,000)	2,257,837	(NA)	125,252	40,642

NA Not available   [1] Public elementary and secondary day schools.

Source: U.S. National Center for Education Statistics, *Digest of Education Statistics*, annual; and unpublished data. See Internet site <http://nces.ed.gov/edstats>.

No. 1313. Puerto Rico—Summary: 1980 to 2002

[3,184.0 represents 3,184,000]

Item	Unit	1980	1990	1995	1998	1999	2000	2001	2002
POPULATION									
Total [1]	1,000	3,184.0	3,512.4	3,641.1	3,770.3	3,790.6	3,808.0	3,827.9	3,851.5
Persons per family	Number	4.3	3.7	3.5	3.4	3.4	3.4	3.4	3.4
EDUCATION [2]									
Enrollment, total	1,000	941.4	953.0	932.7	936.9	907.1	918.8	999.1	(NA)
Public (except public colleges or universities)	1,000	716.1	651.2	621.4	617.2	613.9	612.3	610.8	603.5
Private schools	1,000	95.2	145.8	145.9	144.1	118.7	183.7	197.5	272.9
College and university	1,000	130.1	156.0	165.4	175.6	174.5	174.6	190.8	(NA)
Expenses	Mil. dol.	825.0	1,686.4	2,555.8	3,748.7	3,950.6	4,254.1	4,646.6	4,532.9
As percent of GNP	Percent	7.5	7.8	9.0	10.7	10.3	10.3	10.1	10.0
Public	Mil. dol.	612.2	1,054.2	1,689.4	2,857.9	2,970.0	3,160.4	3,298.9	3,328.6
Private	Mil. dol.	212.8	644.2	866.4	890.8	980.6	1,093.7	1,165.7	1,204.3
LABOR FORCE [3]									
Total [4]	1,000	907	1,124	1,219	1,317	1,310	1,303	1,293	1,330
Employed [5]	1,000	753	963	1,051	1,137	1,147	1,159	1,158	1,170
Agriculture [6]	1,000	38	36	34	31	27	24	22	23
Manufacturing	1,000	143	168	172	161	159	159	159	139
Trade	1,000	138	185	211	236	229	239	242	240
Government	1,000	184	222	232	244	246	249	251	261
Unemployed	1,000	154	161	168	179	163	143	135	160
Unemployment rate [7]	Rate	17.0	14.0	14.0	13.6	12.5	11.0	10.5	12.0
Compensation of employees	Mil. dol.	7,200	13,639	17,773	21,156	22,098	23,504	24,432	25,111
Average compensation	Dollar	9,563	14,854	16,911	18,607	19,266	20,280	21,098	21,462
Salary and wages	Mil. dol.	7,200	13,639	17,773	21,156	22,098	23,504	24,432	25,111
INCOME [8]									
Personal income:									
Current dollars	Mil. dol.	11,002	21,105	27,378	34,340	36,614	38,856	41,411	42,630
Constant (1954) dollars	Mil. dol.	3,985	5,551	6,547	7,806	8,250	8,491	8,790	8,981
Disposable personal income:									
Current dollars	Mil. dol.	10,403	19,914	25,591	32,066	34,042	36,239	38,736	39,843
Constant (1954) dollars	Mil. dol.	3,768	5,238	6,119	7,289	7,671	7,919	8,223	8,393
Average family income:									
Current dollars	Dollar	14,858	22,232	26,316	30,968	32,842	34,693	36,782	37,633
Constant (1954) dollars	Dollar	5,381	5,847	6,293	7,040	7,400	7,581	7,808	7,928
BANKING [9]									
Assets	Mil. dol.	10,223	27,902	39,859	46,088	53,338	58,813	55,701	66,294
TOURISM [8]									
Number of visitors	1,000	2,140	3,426	4,087	4,671	4,221	4,566	4,908	4,364
Visitor expenditures	Mil. dol.	619	1,366	1,828	2,233	2,138	2,388	2,728	2,486
Average per visitor	Dollar	289	399	447	478	507	523	556	570
Net income from tourism	Mil. dol.	202	383	499	598	577	615	663	645

NA Not available.   [1] 1980, and 1990 enumerated as of April 1; all other years estimated as of July 1.   [2] Enrollment for the first school month. Expenses for school year ending in year shown. "Public" includes: Public preschool, public elementary, public intermediate, public high school, public post-high school, public technological, public adult education, public vocational education, and public special education. "College and university" includes both public and private colleges and universities.   [3] Annual average of monthly figures. For fiscal years.   [4] For population 16 years old and over.   [5] Includes other employment not shown separately.   [6] Includes forestry and fisheries.   [7] Percent unemployed of the labor force.   [8] For fiscal years.   [9] As of June 30. Does not include federal savings banks and international banking entities.

Source: Puerto Rico Planning Board, San Juan, PR, *Income and Product* annual; and *Socioeconomics Statistics*, annual.

No. 1314. Puerto Rico—Gross Product and Net Income: 1990 to 2002

[In millions of dollars (21,619 represents $21,619,000,000). For fiscal years ending June 30. Data for 2002 are preliminary]

Item	1990	1995	1998	1999	2000	2001	2002
Gross product	21,619	28,452	35,111	38,281	41,419	44,173	45,189
Agriculture	434	318	437	336	529	453	424
Manufacturing	12,126	17,867	22,994	23,312	24,079	28,806	29,991
Contract construction and mining [1]	720	1,006	1,482	1,668	1,875	1,800	1,842
Transportation & other public services [2]	2,468	3,276	3,978	4,032	4,237	4,688	5,078
Trade	4,728	5,989	7,287	8,112	8,340	8,656	8,718
Finance, insurance, real estate	3,896	5,730	7,672	8,183	9,977	11,116	11,288
Services	3,015	4,724	5,723	6,140	6,603	6,976	7,163
Government	3,337	4,440	5,251	5,530	5,478	5,992	6,295
Commonwealth	2,884	3,793	4,462	4,693	4,601	5,084	5,356
Municipalities	453	647	789	836	877	908	939
Rest of the world	-8,985	-14,195	-18,976	-19,560	-20,283	-25,139	-25,926
Statistical discrepancy	-121	-703	-739	529	585	824	317
Net income	17,941	23,653	28,824	29,908	32,610	34,476	35,602
Agriculture	486	442	594	619	669	613	599
Manufacturing	11,277	16,685	21,529	21,662	22,348	27,013	28,088
Mining	26	30	35	34	41	45	42
Contract construction	679	903	1,313	1,474	1,691	1,577	1,596
Transportation and other public services [2]	1,778	2,360	2,784	2,632	2,968	3,207	3,510
Trade	3,420	4,108	5,060	5,462	5,752	6,002	6,032
Finance, insurance, and real estate	3,280	4,735	6,251	6,743	8,264	9,165	9,240
Services	2,643	4,146	4,983	5,313	5,682	6,002	6,126
Commonwealth government [3]	3,337	4,440	5,251	5,530	5,478	5,992	6,295
Rest of the world	-8,985	-14,195	-18,976	-19,560	-20,283	-25,139	-25,926

[1] Mining includes only quarries. [2] Includes other public utilities, and radio and television broadcasting. [3] Includes public enterprises not elsewhere classified.

No. 1315. Puerto Rico—Transfer Payments: 1990 to 2002

[In millions of dollars (4,871 represents $4,871,000,000). Data represent transfer payments between federal and state governments and other nonresidents. See headnote, Table 1314]

Item	1990	1995	1998	1999	2000	2001	2002
Total receipts	4,871	6,236	7,758	8,627	8,659	9,501	9,824
Federal government	4,649	5,912	7,364	8,057	7,966	8,712	9,047
Transfers to individuals [1]	4,577	5,838	7,175	7,866	7,868	8,606	8,922
Veterans benefits	349	440	495	479	491	490	519
Medicare	368	661	1,117	1,112	1,196	1,262	1,433
Old age, disability, survivors (social security)	2,055	2,912	3,472	3,556	3,863	4,336	4,643
Nutritional assistance	880	1,063	1,109	1,088	1,193	1,208	1,194
Industry subsidies	72	74	189	191	98	106	124
U.S. state governments	18	18	18	17	15	11	17
Other nonresidents	205	307	376	553	679	778	760
Total payments	1,801	2,301	2,551	2,565	2,763	2,900	2,988
Federal government	1,756	2,132	2,496	2,499	2,693	2,845	2,884
Transfers from individuals	817	1,052	1,231	1,237	1,326	1,408	1,444
Contribution to Medicare	97	162	173	182	191	205	227
Employee contribution for social security	720	888	1,056	1,053	1,133	1,200	1,215
Transfers from industries	16	49	45	47	51	52	59
Unemployment insurance	247	184	217	216	234	233	228
Employer contribution for social security	675	847	1,003	999	1,081	1,152	1,153
Other nonresidents [2]	45	164	55	66	70	55	104
Net balance	3,070	3,935	5,207	6,062	5,897	6,602	6,835
Federal government	2,893	3,780	4,868	5,558	5,273	5,868	6,162
U.S. state governments	16	13	14	12	10	6	-32
Other nonresidents	162	143	325	492	614	728	705

[1] Includes other receipts and payments not shown separately. [2] Includes U.S. state governments.

Source of Tables 1314 and 1315: Puerto Rico Planning Board, San Juan, PR, *Economic Report of the Governor*, annual.

No. 1316. Puerto Rico—Merchandise Imports and Exports: 1980 to 2002

[In millions of dollars (9,018 represents $9,018,000,000). Imports are imports for consumption; see text, Section 28]

Item	1980	1985	1990	1994	1995	1996	1997	1998	1999	2000	2001	2002
Imports	9,018	10,162	16,200	17,152	18,969	19,422	21,928	21,706	26,697	27,199	27,642	30,511
From U.S.	5,345	6,130	10,792	11,455	12,213	12,220	13,904	13,318	15,949	15,171	14,718	15,675
From other	3,673	4,032	5,408	5,697	6,756	7,202	8,024	8,388	10,748	12,027	12,924	14,836
Exports	6,576	11,087	20,402	22,711	23,573	22,379	26,653	31,501	37,779	43,191	46,806	50,641
To U.S.	5,643	9,873	17,915	20,098	20,986	19,907	25,045	28,109	33,173	38,335	40,981	44,907
To other	933	1,214	2,487	2,613	2,587	2,472	1,608	3,392	4,606	4,856	5,825	5,734

Source: U.S. Census Bureau, *Foreign Commerce and Navigation of the United States*, annual; *U.S. Trade with Puerto Rico and U.S. Possessions, FT895*; and, through 1985, *Highlights of U.S. Export and Import Trade, FT990*; thereafter, FT920 supplement.

No. 1317. Puerto Rico—Economic Summary by Industry: 2001

[13,700.7 represents 13,700,700,000. Covers establishments with payroll. Employees are for the pay period including March 12. See headnote Table 744. Based on the County Business Patterns. This annual series is used as a benchmark for statistical series, surveys, and databases between economic censuses. For a description of County Business Patterns; see Appendix III]

Industry	1987 SIC code [1]	Total number of establishments	Number of employees	Annual payroll (mil. dol.)
Total industry	(X)	44,372	723,998	13,700.7
Construction industries [2]	C	2,261	64,369	970.8
General contractors and operative builders	15	848	33,800	497.6
Manufacturing [2]	D	1,938	135,857	3,542.4
Food and kindred products	20	278	15,091	326.6
Tobacco products	21	4	1,423	37.7
Textile mill products	22	23	1,843	21.3
Apparel and other textile products	23	187	13,221	162.3
Lumber & wood products	24	90	1,555	15.4
Furniture and fixtures	25	128	1,639	22.5
Paper and allied products	26	40	2,019	46.3
Printing and publishing	27	190	5,520	154.9
Chemicals and allied products	28	169	34,920	1,390.3
Petroleum and coal products	29	28	1,345	46.7
Rubber and misc. plastic products	30	62	3,906	80.0
Leather and leather products	31	17	2,296	32.0
Stone, clay, and glass products	32	150	4,734	109.7
Fabricated metal products	34	212	6,521	117.7
Industrial machinery and equip	35	80	6,065	172.1
Electronic and other electronic equip	36	76	17,068	396.4
Transportation equipment	37	26	1,118	20.5
Instruments and related products	38	66	13,025	316.0
Miscellaneous manufacturing products	39	60	1,613	28.5
Wholesale trade [2]	F	2,674	41,454	1,107.7
Durable goods	50	1,490	19,376	523.7
Nondurable goods	51	1,166	21,322	555.6
Retail trade [2]	G	14,529	172,619	2,104.3
Building materials, garden supplies	52	956	8,136	108.9
General merchandise stores	53	464	23,030	285.9
Food stores	54	1,921	28,526	295.5
Automotive dealers and service stations	55, ex. 5	2,215	13,371	240.6
Gasoline service stations	554	1,037	5,326	52.2
Apparel and accessory stores	56	1,870	17,300	183.3
Furniture and home furnishings	57	1,096	8,046	125.2
Eating and drinking places	58	3,226	45,142	420.1
Drug stores & proprietary stores	591	768	8,990	148.9
Miscellaneous retail	59, ex. 5	1,932	10,871	148.3
Service industries [2]	I	15,913	223,149	3,685.5
Arrangement of passenger transportation	472	309	1,904	24.6
Hotels, paradores & motels	701	234	14,044	249.6
Personal services	72	959	5,327	66.1
Business services	73	2,040	61,539	891.4
Auto repair, services, and parking	75	1,208	6,169	88.6
Miscellaneous repair services	76	479	3,655	62.4
Motion pictures	78	179	1,867	24.3
Amusement and recreation services	79	357	3,565	52.7
Dental laboratories	80	5,108	53,122	914.7
Legal services	81	1,358	6,008	143.6
Engineering and management services	87, ex. 8	1,240	14,707	340.5

X Not applicable. [1] 1987 Standard Industrial Classification (SIC) code; see text, Section 12. [2] Includes other industries not shown separately.

Source: U.S. Census Bureau, *The Commonwealth—Employees, Payroll, and Establishments by Industry: 2001*. See Internet site <http://www.census.gov/epcd/cbp/view/cbpview.html>.

No. 1318. Guam, Virgin Islands, and Northern Mariana Islands—Economic Summary: 1997

[Sales and payroll in millions of dollars (4,640 represents $4,640,000,000). Based on the 1997 Economic Census; see Appendix III]

Item	Guam	Virgin Islands	Northern Mariana Islands	Item	Guam	Virgin Islands	Northern Mariana Islands
Total: Establishments	2,707	2,032	1,232	Wholesale trade:			
Sales	4,640	2,296	2,083	Establishments	270	115	87
Annual payroll	750	382	323	Sales	941	252	223
Paid employees [1]	42,477	21,216	28,906	Annual payroll	77	27	9
Construction: Establishments	354	203	85	Paid employees [1]	3,393	1,144	745
Sales	506	185	88	Retail trade:			
Annual payroll	139	52	21	Establishments	1,091	973	519
Paid employees [1]	7,094	2,623	2,302	Sales	1,840	1,058	570
Manufacturing:				Annual payroll	221	136	54
Establishments	60	74	84	Paid employees [1]	15,334	8,966	4,811
Sales	165	146	762	Services: Establishments	932	667	457
Annual payroll	33	28	147	Sales	1,188	655	440
Paid employees [1]	1,320	1,194	13,715	Annual payroll	280	139	91
				Paid employees [1]	15,336	7,289	7,333

[1] For pay period including March 12.
Source: U.S. Census Bureau, *1997 Economic Census of Puerto Rico and the Island Areas*, OA97-E-5 to OA97-E-7. See Internet site <http://www.census.gov/csd/ia/index.html>.

Section 30
Comparative International Statistics

This section presents statistics for the world as a whole and for many countries on a comparative basis with the United States. Data are shown for population, births and deaths, social and industrial indicators, finances, agriculture, communication, and military affairs.

Statistics of the individual nations may be found primarily in official national publications, generally in the form of yearbooks, issued by most of the nations at various intervals in their own national languages and expressed in their own or customary units of measure. (For a listing of selected publications, see Guide to Sources.) For handier reference, especially for international comparisons, the United Nations Statistics Division compiles data as submitted by member countries and issues a number of international summary publications, generally in English and French. Among these are the *Statistical Yearbook*; the *Demographic Yearbook*; *International Trade Statistics Yearbook*; *National Accounts Statistics: Main Aggregates and Detailed Tables*; *Population and Vital Statistics Reports* (quarterly); the *Monthly Bulletin of Statistics*; and the *Energy Statistics Yearbook*. Specialized agencies of the United Nations also issue international summary publications on agricultural, labor, health, and education statistics. Among these are the *Production Yearbook* and *Trade Yearbook* issued by the Food and Agriculture Organization, the *Yearbook of Labour Statistics* issued by the International Labour Office, *World Health Statistics* issued by the World Health Organization, and the *Statistical Yearbook* issued by the Educational, Scientific, and Cultural Organization.

The U.S. Census Bureau presents estimates and projections of basic demographic measures for countries and regions of the world in the *World Population Reports* (WP) series. The *International Population Reports* (Series IPC), and *International Briefs* (Series IB) also present population figures for many foreign countries. Detailed population statistics are also available from the Census Bureau's International Data Base (http://www.census.gov/ipc/www/idbnew.html>.

The International Monetary Fund (IMF) and the Organization for Economic Cooperation and Development (OECD) also compile data on international statistics. The IMF publishes a series of reports relating to financial data. These include *International Financial Statistics*, *Direction of Trade*, and *Balance of Payments Yearbook*, published in English, French, and Spanish. The OECD publishes a vast number of statistical publications in various fields such as economics, health, and education. Among these are *OECD in Figures*, *Main Economic Indicators*, *Economic Outlook*, *National Accounts*, *Labour Force Statistics*, *OECD Health Data*, and *Education at a Glance*.

Statistical coverage, country names, and classifications—Problems of space and availability of data limit the number of countries and the extent of statistical coverage shown. The list of countries included and the spelling of country names are based almost entirely on the list of sovereign nations, dependencies, and areas of special sovereignty provided by the U.S. Department of State.

In recent years, several important changes took place in the status of the world's nations. In 1990, a unified Germany was formed from the Federal Republic of Germany (West) and the German Democratic Republic (East). The Republic of Yemen was formed by union of the Yemen Arab Republic and the People's Democratic Republic of Yemen. Also in 1990, Namibia, once a United Nations mandate, realized its independence from South Africa.

In 1991, the Soviet Union broke up into 15 independent countries: Armenia, Azerbaijan, Belarus, Estonia, Georgia, Kazakhstan, Kyrgyzstan, Latvia, Lithuania, Moldova, Russia, Tajikistan, Turkmenistan, Ukraine, and Uzbekistan.

Following the breakup of the Socialist Federal Republic of Yugoslavia in 1992, the United States recognized Bosnia and Herzegovina, Croatia, Slovenia, and The Former Yugoslav Republic of Macedonia as independent countries.

On January 1, 1993, Czechoslovakia was succeeded by two independent countries: the Czech Republic and Slovakia. Eritrea announced its independence from Ethiopia in April 1993 and was subsequently recognized as an independent nation by the United States.

The population estimates and projections used in Tables 1319, 1320, 1322, 1323, and 1326 were prepared by the Census Bureau. For each country, the data on population, by age and sex, fertility, mortality, and international migration were evaluated and, where necessary, adjusted for inconsistencies and errors in the data. In most instances, comprehensive projections were made by the component method, resulting in distributions of the population by age and sex and requiring an assessment of probable future trends of fertility, mortality, and international migration.

Economic associations—The Organization for European Economic Co-Operation (OEEC), a regional grouping of Western European countries established in 1948 for the purpose of harmonizing national economic policies and conditions, was succeeded on September 30, 1961, by the Organization for Economic Cooperation and Development (OECD). The member nations of the OECD are Australia, Austria, Belgium, Canada, Czech Republic, Denmark, Finland, France, Germany, Greece, Hungary, Iceland, Ireland, Italy, Japan, Luxembourg, Mexico, the Netherlands, New Zealand, Norway, Poland, Portugal, Slovakia, South Korea, Spain, Sweden, Switzerland, Turkey, the United Kingdom, and the United States.

Quality and comparability of the data—The quality and comparability of the data presented here are affected by a number of factors:

(1) The year for which data are presented may not be the same for all subjects for a particular country or for a given subject for different countries, though the data shown are the most recent available. All such variations have been noted. The data shown are for calendar years except as otherwise specified.

(2) The bases, methods of estimating, methods of data collection, extent of coverage, precision of definition, scope of territory, and margins of error may vary for different items within a particular country, and for like items for different countries. Footnotes and headnotes to the tables give a few of the major time-periods and coverage qualifications attached to the figures; considerably more detail is presented in the source publications. Many of the measures shown are, at best, merely rough indicators of magnitude.

(3) Figures shown in this section for the United States may not always agree with figures shown in the preceding sections. Disagreements may be attributable to the use of differing original sources, a difference in the definition of geographic limits (the 50 states, conterminous United States only, or the United States including certain outlying areas and possessions), or to possible adjustments made in the United States figures by other sources in order to make them more comparable with figures from other countries.

International comparisons of national accounts data—In order to compare national accounts data for different countries, it is necessary to convert each country's data into a common unit of currency, usually the U.S. dollar. The market exchange rates, which are often used in converting national currencies, do not necessarily reflect the relative purchasing power in the various countries. It is necessary that the goods and services produced in different countries be valued consistently if the differences observed are meant to reflect real differences in the volumes of goods and services produced. The use of purchasing power parities (see Table 1334) instead of exchange rates is intended to achieve this objective.

The method used to present the data shown in Table 1334 is to construct volume measures directly by revaluing the goods and services sold in different countries at a common set of international prices. By dividing the ratio of the gross domestic products of two countries expressed in their own national currencies by the corresponding ratio calculated at constant international prices, it is possible to derive the implied purchasing power parity (PPP) between the two currencies concerned. PPPs show how many units of currency are needed in one country to buy the same amount of goods and services that one unit of currency will buy in the other country. For further information, see *National Accounts, Main Aggregates, Volume I,* issued annually by the Organization for Economic Cooperation and Development, Paris, France.

International Standard Industrial Classification—The original version of the International Standard Industrial Classification of All Economic Activities (ISIC) was adopted in 1948. Wide use has been made both nationally and internationally in classifying data according to kind of economic activity in the fields of production, employment, national income, and other economic statistics. A number of countries have utilized the ISIC as the basis for devising their industrial classification scheme.

Substantial comparability has been attained between the industrial classifications of many other countries, including the United States and the ISIC by ensuring, as far as practicable, that the categories at detailed levels of classification in national schemes fitted into only one category of the ISIC. The United Nations, the International Labour Organization, the Food and Agriculture Organization, and other international bodies have utilized the ISIC in publishing and analyzing statistical data. Revisions of the ISIC were issued in 1958, 1968, and 1989.

International maps—A series of regional world maps is provided on pages 834-840. References are included in Table 1322 for easy location of individual countries on the maps. The Robinson map projection is used for this series of maps. A map projection is used to portray all or part of the round Earth on a flat surface, but this cannot be done without some distortion. For the Robinson projection, distortion is very low along the Equator and within 45 degrees of the center but is greatest near the poles. For additional information on map projections and maps, please contact the Earth Science Information Center, U.S. Geological Survey, 507 National Center, Reston, VA 22092.

World

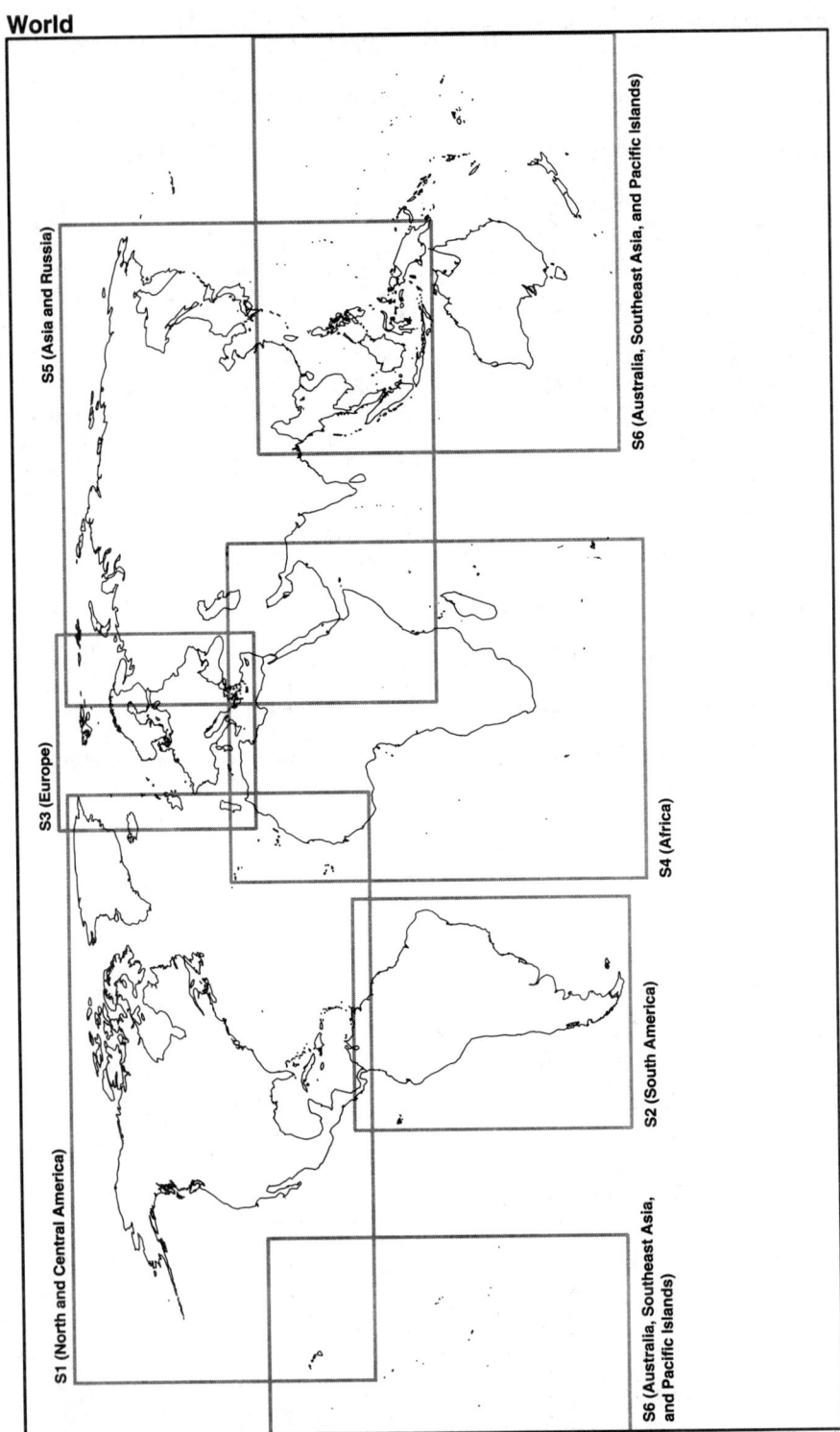

834 Comparative International Statistics

U.S. Census Bureau, Statistical Abstract of the United States: 2003

S1 (North and Central America)

Comparative International Statistics 835

S2 (South America)

836 Comparative International Statistics

U.S. Census Bureau, Statistical Abstract of the United States: 2003

S3 (Europe)

Map of Europe showing:

- Norway (part) (Svalbard)
- Arctic Ocean
- Iceland
- Denmark (part) (Faroe Islands)
- Finland
- Norway (part)
- Sweden
- Estonia
- United Kingdom (part) (Isle of Man)
- Latvia
- Russia (part)
- Lithuania
- Ireland
- Denmark (part)
- Netherlands (part)
- United Kingdom (part)
- Belarus
- United Kingdom (part) (Guernsey)
- Germany
- Poland
- United Kingdom (part) (Jersey)
- Luxembourg
- Belgium
- Czech Republic
- Moldova
- Ukraine
- France (part)
- Switzerland
- Slovakia
- Atlantic Ocean
- Austria
- Liechtenstein
- Slovenia
- Hungary
- Romania
- San Marino
- Croatia
- Bosnia & Herzegovina
- Black Sea
- Andorra
- Serbia
- Montenegro
- Spain
- Monaco
- Italy (part)
- Bulgaria
- France (part) (Corsica)
- Albania
- Portugal (part)
- Spain (parts) (Balearic Is.)
- Italy (part) (Sardinia)
- Italy (part) (Sicily)
- The Former Yugoslav Republic of Macedonia
- Greece
- Malta
- Mediterranean Sea

S4 (Africa)

S5 (Asia and Russia)

Comparative International Statistics 839

U.S. Census Bureau, Statistical Abstract of the United States: 2003

S6 (Australia, Southeast Asia, and Pacific Islands)

No. 1319. Total World Population: 1980 to 2050

[As of midyear (4,454 represents 4,454,000,000)]

Year	Population (mil.)	Average annual [1] Growth rate (percent)	Average annual [1] Population change (mil.)	Year	Population (mil.)	Average annual [1] Growth rate (percent)	Average annual [1] Population change (mil.)
1980	4,454	1.69	75.9	2015	7,172	0.98	70.4
1985	4,850	1.68	82.3	2020	7,516	0.87	66.0
1990	5,276	1.58	83.9	2025	7,836	0.77	60.6
1995	5,686	1.38	79.2	2030	8,130	0.69	56.0
2002	6,229	1.18	73.8	2035	8,401	0.61	51.6
2003	6,302	1.16	73.4	2040	8,651	0.55	47.3
2005	6,449	1.12	72.7	2045	8,879	0.48	43.0
2010	6,812	1.06	72.4	2050	9,084	(NA)	(NA)

NA Not available. [1] Represents change from year shown to immediate succeeding year.

Source: U.S. Census Bureau, "Total Midyear Population for the World: 1950-2050," updated 17 July 2003; <http://www.census.gov/ipc/www/worldpop.html>.

No. 1320. Population by Continent: 1980 to 2050

[In millions, except percent (4,454 represents 4,454,000,000)]

Year	World	Africa	North America	South America	Asia	Europe	Oceania
1980	4,454	473	372	242	2,651	694	23
1990	5,276	627	425	297	3,180	721	27
2000	6,079	804	487	350	3,679	729	31
2010	6,812	979	541	396	4,132	729	35
2020	7,516	1,156	595	435	4,567	725	38
2030	8,130	1,349	647	468	4,915	710	41
2040	8,651	1,560	695	489	5,175	688	43
2050	9,084	1,793	737	501	5,351	658	45
PERCENT DISTRIBUTION							
1980	100.0	10.6	8.4	5.4	59.5	15.6	0.5
2000	100.0	13.2	8.0	5.8	60.5	12.0	0.5
2050	100.0	19.7	8.1	5.5	58.9	7.2	0.5

Source: U.S. Census Bureau, "International Data Base" (as of July 2003); <http://www.census.gov/ipc/www/idbagg.html>.

No. 1321. World Summary: 1980 to 2002

[4.8 represents 4,800,000. See text of this section for general comments concerning quality of the data]

Item	Unit	1980	1985	1990	1995	1998	1999	2000	2001	2002
Agriculture, forestry, fishing:										
Coffee	Mil. metric tons	4.8	5.8	6.1	5.5	6.6	6.7	7.4	7.2	(NA)
Cotton (lint)	Mil. metric tons	13.9	17.3	18.4	20.3	18.2	18.2	18.7	21.0	(NA)
Tobacco	Mil. metric tons	5.3	7.1	7.1	6.3	6.9	7.0	6.7	6.3	(NA)
Roundwood	Mil. cubic meters	2,920	3,167	3,382	3,243	2,909	3,026	3,081	3,060	(NA)
Fish catches	Mil. metric tons	72.3	87.2	99.0	116.4	117.7	126.2	(NA)	(NA)	(NA)
Textile fiber production, total: [1]	Billion pounds	66.5	78.6	87.2	95.8	101.5	105.0	109.7	113.2	(NA)
Rayon and acetate	Billion pounds	7.1	6.5	6.1	5.3	4.9	4.6	4.9	4.6	(NA)
Noncellulosic fibers	Billion pounds	23.1	27.5	32.8	40.5	51.3	54.0	57.6	56.8	(NA)
Cotton	Billion pounds	30.4	38.4	41.8	44.8	40.9	42.0	42.6	47.2	42.2
Wool, clean	Billion pounds	3.7	3.8	4.4	3.3	3.1	3.0	3.0	2.9	2.9
Silk	Billion pounds	0.1	0.2	0.1	0.2	0.2	0.2	0.2	0.2	(NA)
Flax	Billion pounds	1.4	1.6	1.6	1.6	0.9	1.1	1.3	1.4	(NA)
Hemp [2]	Billion pounds	0.6	0.5	0.4	0.1	0.2	0.1	0.1	0.1	(NA)
Industrial production:										
Wine	Mil. hectoliters	352.1	309.5	279.6	241.9	266.2	287.3	295.2	277.7	(NA)
Sugar	Mil. metric tons	79.0	90.8	111.2	118.5	128.2	133.7	130.5	131.8	(NA)
Wheat flour	Mil. metric tons	229.7	267.9	241.2	240.7	245.7	249.1	(NA)	(NA)	(NA)
Pig iron and ferroalloys [3]	Mil. metric tons	542	507	517	533	539	543	573	(NA)	(NA)
Crude steel [4]	Mil. metric tons	699	685	773	734	725	769	792	(NA)	(NA)
Sawnwood [5]	Mil. cubic meters	451	468	505	426	416	428	425	415	(NA)
Woodpulp [6]	Mil. metric tons	125.8	141.8	155.1	161.7	159.9	163.5	170.7	163.6	(NA)
Newsprint	Mil. metric tons	25.4	28.3	30.1	35.9	36.2	38	39.3	38	(NA)
Merchant vessels, launched	Mil. gross tons	13.9	17.3	14.8	23.0	23.0	(NA)	25.2	28.7	(NA)
External trade:										
Imports, c.i.f.	Bil. U.S. dollars	2,045	1,998	3,557	5,084	5,295	5,511	6,204	5,981	(NA)
Exports, f.o.b.	Bil. U.S. dollars	2,001	1,921	3,438	5,045	5,422	6,048	5,814	(NA)	(NA)
Civil aviation, kilometers flown [7]	Millions	(NA)	(NA)	(NA)	19,470	22,430	23,672	(NA)	(NA)	(NA)

NA Not available. [1] Source: U.S. Dept. of Agriculture, Economic Research Service, *Cotton and Wool Situation and Outlook Yearbook*. Data from International Wool Textile Organization. [2] Beginning 1998 not comparable with earlier years. [3] Pig iron (foundry and steel making) plus other ferro alloys (spiegeleisen and ferro-manganese). [4] Castings and ingots. [5] Broadleaved and coniferous. [6] Mechanical plus dissolving grades plus sulphate and soda plus sulphate and semi-chemical. [7] Scheduled services of members of International Civil Aviation Organization.

Source: Except as noted, Statistical Division of the United Nations, New York, NY, *Monthly Bulletin of Statistics*, (copyright).

Comparative International Statistics

No. 1322. Population by Country: 1990 to 2010

[5,275,139 represents 5,275,139,000. Population data generally are de facto figures for the present territory. Population estimates were derived from information available as of spring 2001. East Timor became independent of Indonesia, but population data will not be available until the next update of the International Data Base. See text of this section for general comments concerning the data. For details of methodology, coverage, and reliability, see coverage, and reliability, see source. Minus sign (-) indicates decrease]

Country or area	Map reference	Mid-year population (1,000) 1990	2001	2002	2010, proj.	Population rank, 2002	Annual rate of growth,[1] 2000-2010 (percent)	Population per sq. mile, 2002	Area (sq. mile)
World	S0	5,275,139	6,153,427	6,227,689	6,811,080	(X)	1.1	123	50,574,664
Afghanistan	S5	14,750	26,813	27,756	33,864	39	2.7	111	250,000
Albania	S3	3,251	3,490	3,509	3,660	128	0.5	332	10,579
Algeria	S4	25,341	31,736	32,278	36,589	34	1.6	35	919,591
Andorra	S3	53	68	68	74	203	1.0	393	174
Angola	S4	8,049	10,342	10,554	12,250	73	1.9	22	481,351
Antigua and Barbuda	S1	63	67	67	71	204	0.6	397	170
Argentina	S2	33,022	37,917	38,331	41,405	31	1.0	36	1,056,637
Armenia	S5	3,366	3,336	3,330	3,365	130	0.1	289	11,506
Australia	S6	17,022	19,358	19,547	20,925	52	0.9	7	2,941,285
Austria	S3	7,723	8,132	8,148	8,214	87	0.1	255	31,942
Azerbaijan	S5	7,200	7,771	7,798	8,221	88	0.6	233	33,436
Bahamas, The	S1	257	293	295	311	176	0.7	76	3,888
Bahrain	S4	500	645	656	737	162	1.5	2,746	239
Bangladesh	S5	109,897	132,975	135,657	159,765	8	2.0	2,624	51,703
Barbados	S1	263	275	276	283	178	0.3	1,664	166
Belarus	S3	10,215	10,350	10,335	10,294	74	-0.1	129	80,154
Belgium	S3	9,969	10,292	10,312	10,423	75	0.2	883	11,672
Belize	S1	191	253	260	312	179	2.3	30	8,803
Benin	S4	4,662	6,630	6,835	8,504	95	2.8	160	42,710
Bhutan	S5	1,598	2,049	2,094	2,476	142	2.1	115	18,147
Bolivia	S2	6,574	8,300	8,445	9,499	86	1.5	20	418,683
Bosnia and Herzegovina	S3	4,424	3,922	3,964	4,103	120	0.7	201	19,741
Botswana	S4	1,312	1,581	1,579	1,420	147	-1.1	7	226,012
Brazil	S2	151,084	177,753	179,914	195,580	5	1.1	55	3,265,061
Brunei	S6	258	344	351	408	174	1.9	172	2,035
Bulgaria	S3	8,894	7,738	7,662	7,149	91	-0.9	180	42,683
Burkina Faso	S4	9,090	12,549	12,887	15,748	65	2.5	122	105,714
Burma	S5	38,526	42,035	42,282	43,721	27	0.5	166	253,954
Burundi	S4	5,285	5,838	5,965	7,296	100	2.4	602	9,903
Cambodia	S5	9,271	12,660	12,890	14,902	64	1.8	189	68,154
Cameroon	S4	11,685	15,110	15,428	17,938	61	1.9	85	181,251
Canada	S1	27,791	31,593	31,902	34,253	35	0.9	9	3,560,219
Cape Verde	S1	349	405	409	431	172	0.7	263	1,556
Central African Republic	S4	2,803	3,562	3,623	4,073	126	1.5	15	240,533
Chad	S4	6,030	8,693	8,971	11,302	82	2.9	18	486,178
Chile	S2	13,128	15,328	15,499	16,727	60	1.0	54	289,112
China[2]	S5	1,138,895	1,271,085	1,279,161	1,342,783	1	0.6	355	3,600,930
Colombia	S2	32,859	40,349	41,008	46,109	28	1.5	102	401,042
Comoros	S4	429	596	614	773	163	2.9	733	838
Congo (Brazzaville)[3]	S4	2,240	2,860	2,908	3,209	133	1.3	22	131,853
Congo (Kinshasa)[3]	S4	37,969	53,455	55,042	69,577	23	2.9	63	875,521
Costa Rica	S2	3,027	3,773	3,835	4,306	124	1.5	196	19,560
Cote d'Ivoire	S4	11,901	16,234	16,598	19,485	57	2.1	135	122,780
Croatia	S3	4,508	4,334	4,391	4,505	118	0.5	201	21,829
Cuba	S1	10,545	11,182	11,227	11,507	69	0.3	262	42,803
Cyprus	S5	681	763	767	801	159	0.5	215	3,568
Czech Republic	S3	10,310	10,262	10,256	10,202	77	-0.1	338	30,365
Denmark	S3	5,141	5,356	5,375	5,516	105	0.3	329	16,359
Djibouti	S4	366	438	447	526	167	2.0	53	8,486
Dominica	S1	73	71	70	70	202	-0.2	242	290
Dominican Republic	S1	7,076	8,475	8,596	9,521	85	1.3	460	18,680
Ecuador	S2	10,317	13,184	13,447	15,518	63	1.8	126	106,888
Egypt	S4	56,694	71,902	73,313	84,348	15	1.8	191	384,344
El Salvador	S1	5,100	6,238	6,354	7,293	98	1.7	794	8,000
Equatorial Guinea	S4	368	486	498	604	164	2.4	46	10,830
Eritrea	S4	2,944	4,249	4,306	5,128	119	1.9	92	46,842
Estonia	S3	1,573	1,423	1,416	1,372	149	-0.4	81	17,413
Ethiopia	S4	47,958	63,959	65,254	75,066	18	1.8	151	432,310
Fiji	S6	738	844	856	958	157	1.4	121	7,054
Finland	S3	4,986	5,180	5,193	5,255	109	0.2	44	117,942
France	S3	56,735	59,658	59,925	61,638	20	0.4	284	210,668
Gabon	S4	938	1,255	1,288	1,562	151	2.5	13	99,486
Gambia, The	S4	962	1,411	1,456	1,833	148	2.9	377	3,861
Georgia	S5	5,457	4,989	4,961	4,815	112	-0.4	184	26,911
Germany	S3	79,380	82,281	82,351	82,283	13	(Z)	609	135,236
Ghana	S4	15,400	19,843	20,163	22,230	50	1.3	227	88,811
Greece	S3	10,130	10,582	10,604	10,750	72	0.2	210	50,502
Grenada	S2	92	89	89	91	197	0.2	682	131
Guatemala	S1	9,654	13,179	13,542	16,589	62	2.6	323	41,865
Guinea	S4	6,280	8,717	8,816	10,800	84	2.2	93	94,927
Guinea-Bissau	S4	996	1,306	1,333	1,566	150	2.0	123	10,811
Guyana	S2	742	698	700	732	161	0.5	9	76,004
Haiti	S1	6,075	7,288	7,405	8,555	92	1.8	696	10,641
Honduras	S1	4,757	6,358	6,514	7,686	97	2.1	151	43,201
Hungary	S3	10,372	10,109	10,083	9,880	80	-0.3	283	35,653
Iceland	S1	255	278	279	289	177	0.4	7	38,707
India	S5	841,655	1,018,504	1,034,173	1,155,011	2	1.4	901	1,147,950
Indonesia	S6	188,005	227,741	231,326	258,825	4	1.4	331	699,548
Iran	S5	57,551	66,791	67,538	73,661	16	1.1	107	631,660

See footnotes at end of table.

No. 1322. Population by Country: 1990 to 2010—Con.
[See headnote, page 842]

Country or area	Map reference	Mid-year population (1,000) 1990	2001	2002	2010, proj.	Population rank, 2002	Annual rate of growth,[1] 2000-2010 (percent)	Population per sq. mile, 2002	Area (sq. mile)
Iraq	S5	18,135	23,332	24,002	29,672	44	2.7	143	167,556
Ireland	S3	3,508	3,835	3,879	4,250	122	1.1	146	26,598
Israel	S4	4,512	5,938	6,030	6,645	99	1.3	768	7,849
Italy	S3	56,743	57,845	57,927	58,091	22	0.1	510	113,521
Jamaica	S1	2,463	2,666	2,680	2,851	136	0.7	641	4,181
Japan	S5	123,537	126,892	127,066	127,195	10	(Z)	834	152,411
Jordan	S4	3,262	5,153	5,307	6,486	107	2.6	150	35,344
Kazakhstan	S5	16,708	16,731	16,742	17,276	56	0.3	16	1,049,150
Kenya	S4	23,934	30,777	31,223	33,654	36	1.0	142	219,788
Kiribati	S6	71	94	96	115	195	2.3	348	277
Korea, North	S5	20,019	21,940	22,215	23,802	49	0.9	478	46,490
Korea, South	S5	42,869	47,619	47,963	50,180	25	0.6	1,265	37,911
Kuwait	S5	2,142	2,042	2,112	2,788	141	3.5	307	6,880
Kyrgyzstan	S5	4,390	4,753	4,822	5,444	113	1.5	63	76,641
Laos	S5	4,210	5,636	5,778	6,994	102	2.4	65	89,112
Latvia	S3	2,672	2,385	2,367	2,252	139	-0.7	95	24,903
Lebanon	S4	3,147	3,628	3,678	4,056	125	1.3	931	3,950
Lesotho	S4	1,693	1,853	1,858	1,862	146	0.1	159	11,718
Liberia	S4	2,189	3,206	3,262	3,935	131	2.2	88	37,189
Libya	S4	4,140	5,241	5,369	6,447	106	2.3	8	679,359
Liechtenstein	S3	29	33	33	35	213	0.8	528	62
Lithuania	S5	3,702	3,611	3,601	3,560	127	-0.2	143	25,174
Luxembourg	S3	383	445	451	498	166	1.3	452	998
Macedonia, The Former Yugoslav Republic of	S3	1,893	2,046	2,055	2,115	143	0.4	207	9,928
Madagascar	S4	11,522	15,983	16,473	20,993	58	3.0	73	224,533
Malawi	S4	9,215	11,134	11,393	13,416	67	2.1	314	36,324
Malaysia	S5	17,504	22,229	22,662	26,144	46	1.8	179	126,853
Maldives	S5	216	311	320	400	175	2.8	2,764	116
Mali	S4	8,228	10,980	11,300	14,012	68	2.7	24	471,042
Malta	S4	359	395	397	420	173	0.7	3,207	124
Marshall Islands	S6	46	54	55	66	209	2.2	789	70
Mauritania	S4	1,984	2,747	2,829	3,561	134	2.9	7	397,838
Mauritius	S4	1,074	1,190	1,200	1,280	153	0.8	1,681	714
Mexico	S1	84,914	101,247	102,480	112,469	11	1.2	138	742,486
Micronesia, Federated States of	S6	109	108	108	107	193	-0.1	399	271
Moldova	S5	4,398	4,432	4,435	4,535	117	0.2	341	13,012
Monaco	S3	30	32	32	33	214	0.4	41,423	1
Mongolia	S5	2,216	2,637	2,674	3,004	137	1.4	4	604,247
Morocco	S4	24,686	30,645	31,168	35,301	37	1.6	181	172,317
Mozambique	S4	12,649	17,997	18,296	19,721	54	1.1	60	302,737
Namibia	S4	1,409	1,863	1,897	2,036	145	1.1	6	317,873
Nauru	S6	9	12	12	14	223	1.9	1,521	8
Nepal	S5	19,325	25,284	25,874	30,758	40	2.2	490	52,819
Netherlands	S3	14,952	16,017	16,123	16,783	59	0.5	1,230	13,104
New Zealand	S6	3,360	3,864	3,908	4,228	121	1.0	38	103,734
Nicaragua	S2	3,643	4,918	5,024	5,839	111	1.9	108	46,430
Niger	S4	7,630	10,465	10,760	13,220	70	2.6	22	489,073
Nigeria	S4	92,566	127,120	130,500	156,787	9	2.4	371	351,649
Norway	S3	4,242	4,515	4,536	4,676	115	0.4	38	118,865
Oman	S5	1,773	2,622	2,713	3,523	135	3.3	33	82,031
Pakistan	S5	113,975	144,617	147,663	171,373	6	1.9	491	300,664
Palau	S6	15	19	19	22	219	1.4	110	177
Panama	S2	2,388	2,879	2,920	3,220	132	1.3	100	29,340
Papua New Guinea	S6	3,825	5,049	5,172	6,171	110	2.3	30	174,405
Paraguay	S2	4,236	5,734	5,884	7,162	101	2.5	38	153,398
Peru	S2	21,989	27,484	27,950	31,471	38	1.5	57	494,208
Philippines	S6	64,318	81,370	82,995	95,868	12	1.8	721	115,124
Poland	S3	38,119	38,634	38,625	38,691	30	(Z)	329	117,571
Portugal	S3	9,923	10,066	10,084	10,183	79	0.1	285	35,382
Qatar	S5	481	769	793	970	158	2.6	187	4,247
Romania	S5	22,866	22,428	22,404	22,181	48	-0.1	252	88,934
Russia	S5	148,082	145,470	144,979	142,328	7	-0.3	22	6,592,817
Rwanda	S4	6,962	7,532	7,668	8,821	90	1.7	796	9,633
Saint Kitts and Nevis	S1	41	39	39	40	212	0.4	279	139
Saint Lucia	S1	140	158	160	177	190	1.3	679	236
Saint Vincent and the Grenadines	S1	107	116	116	119	191	0.3	889	131
Samoa	S0	170	179	179	176	186	-0.2	162	1,100
San Marino	S3	23	27	28	31	215	1.3	1,197	23
Sao Tome and Principe	S4	119	165	170	219	188	3.1	460	371
Saudi Arabia	S4	15,847	22,757	23,513	30,546	45	3.3	28	829,996
Senegal	S4	7,362	10,046	10,311	12,534	76	2.5	139	74,131
Serbia and Montenegro	S3	9,766	10,678	10,658	10668	71	(Z)	270	39,435
Seychelles	S4	73	80	80	83	198	0.4	455	176
Sierra Leone	S4	4,226	5,388	5,565	6,688	103	2.5	201	27,653
Singapore	S6	3,016	4,300	4,453	5,776	116	3.3	18,482	241
Slovakia	S3	5,263	5,405	5,410	5,470	104	0.1	287	18,842
Slovenia	S3	1,896	1,930	1,933	1,947	144	0.1	247	7,819
Solomon Islands	S6	335	480	495	610	165	2.7	47	10,633
Somalia	S4	6,675	7,489	7,753	9,922	89	3.1	32	242,216
South Africa	S4	37,191	42,573	42,716	40,608	26	-0.4	91	471,444
Spain	S3	39,351	40,087	40,153	40,549	29	0.1	208	192,819

See footnotes at end of table.

Comparative International Statistics 843

U.S. Census Bureau, Statistical Abstract of the United States: 2003

No. 1322. Population by Country: 1990 to 2010—Con.

[See headnote, page 842]

Country or area	Map reference	Mid-year population (1,000) 1990	2001	2002	2010, proj.	Population rank, 2002	Annual rate of growth,[1] 2000-2010 (percent)	Population per sq. mile, 2002	Area (sq. mile)
Sri Lanka	S5	18,304	19,409	19,577	20,832	51	0.8	783	24,996
Sudan	S4	26,627	36,080	37,090	45,485	32	2.6	40	917,375
Suriname	S2	395	432	434	441	170	0.3	7	62,344
Swaziland	S4	885	1,136	1,150	1,170	154	0.4	173	6,641
Sweden	S3	8,601	8,940	8,954	9,074	83	0.2	56	158,927
Switzerland	S3	6,837	7,311	7,362	7,623	93	0.5	479	15,355
Syria	S4	12,436	16,729	17,156	20,606	55	2.3	241	71,062
Tajikistan	S5	5,332	6,579	6,720	8,007	96	2.2	122	55,251
Tanzania	S4	25,651	34,583	35,302	41,197	33	2.0	103	342,100
Thailand	S5	55,250	63,007	63,645	68,058	19	0.9	322	197,595
Togo	S4	3,705	5,167	5,299	6,256	108	2.2	252	21,000
Tonga	S0	92	104	106	123	194	1.8	383	277
Trinidad and Tobago	S2	1,198	1,118	1,112	1,042	155	-0.8	561	1,981
Tunisia	S4	8,207	9,705	9,816	10,661	81	1.1	164	59,985
Turkey	S5	56,085	66,494	67,309	73,322	17	1.1	226	297,591
Turkmenistan	S5	3,668	4,603	4,689	5,431	114	1.8	25	188,456
Tuvalu	S6	9	11	11	13	224	1.5	1,110	10
Uganda	S4	17,242	24,170	24,889	31,570	42	3.0	323	77,108
Ukraine	S5	51,658	48,760	48,396	46,193	24	-0.6	208	233,089
United Arab Emirates	S5	1,951	2,407	2,446	2,763	138	1.5	76	32,278
United Kingdom	S3	57,493	59,723	59,912	61,285	21	0.3	642	93,278
United States	S1	250,132	285,024	287,676	309,163	3	0.9	81	3,539,227
Uruguay	S2	3,106	3,360	3,387	3,600	129	0.8	51	67,035
Uzbekistan	S5	20,624	25,155	25,563	29,280	41	1.7	148	172,741
Vanuatu	S6	154	193	196	221	184	1.5	34	5,699
Venezuela	S2	19,325	23,917	24,288	27,134	43	1.4	71	340,560
Vietnam	S5	66,637	79,544	80,577	89,223	14	1.3	641	125,622
Yemen	S5	12,416	18,078	18,701	24,637	53	3.4	92	203,849
Zambia	S4	7,876	9,986	10,149	11,286	78	1.4	35	285,992
Zimbabwe	S4	10,154	12,332	12,463	12,926	66	0.6	83	149,293
OTHER									
Taiwan [2]	S5	20,279	22,304	22,454	23,562	47	0.6	1,803	12,456
AREAS OF SPECIAL SOVEREIGNTY AND DEPENDENCIES									
American Samoa	S0	47	58	58	57	207	(Z)	751	77
Anguilla	S1	8	12	12	14	222	1.8	354	35
Aruba	S1	67	70	70	73	201	0.5	945	75
Bermuda	S1	58	63	64	67	206	0.7	3,383	19
Cayman Islands	S1	26	40	41	50	211	2.7	406	100
Cook Islands	S0	18	21	21	22	218	0.9	224	93
Faroe Islands	S3	47	46	46	48	210	0.6	85	541
French Guiana	S2	116	178	182	214	185	2.1	5	34,421
French Polynesia	S0	202	254	258	291	180	1.5	182	1,413
Gaza Strip [4]	S4	643	1,178	1,226	1,651	152	3.8	8,334	147
Gibraltar	S3	29	28	28	28	216	0.2	11,963	2
Greenland	S1	56	56	56	56	208	(Z)	(Z)	131,931
Guadeloupe	S1	378	431	436	468	169	0.9	641	680
Guam	S6	134	158	161	181	189	1.5	771	209
Guernsey	S3	63	64	65	66	205	0.3	862	75
Hong Kong	S5	5,688	7,211	7,303	7,981	94	1.1	19,126	382
Jersey	S3	84	89	90	92	196	0.3	1,987	45
Macau	S6	352	434	438	468	168	0.8	70,868	6
Man, Isle of	S3	69	73	74	77	200	0.5	325	227
Martinique	S1	374	418	422	448	171	0.8	1,033	409
Mayotte	S4	90	163	171	231	187	3.9	1,177	145
Montserrat	S1	11	8	8	10	225	4.3	219	39
Netherlands Antilles	S2	189	212	214	228	182	0.8	577	371
New Caledonia	S6	168	205	208	230	183	1.3	29	7,243
Northern Mariana Islands	S6	44	72	74	91	199	2.6	402	184
Puerto Rico	S1	3,537	3,838	3,859	4,001	123	0.5	1,116	3,459
Reunion	S4	597	733	744	829	160	1.4	771	965
Saint Helena	S4	7	7	7	8	226	0.6	46	158
Saint Pierre and Miquelon	S1	6	7	7	7	227	0.2	75	93
Turks and Caicos Islands	S1	12	18	19	24	220	3.0	113	166
Virgin Islands	S1	104	109	109	108	192	-0.1	805	135
Virgin Islands, British	S1	16	21	21	25	217	2.0	367	58
Wallis and Futuna	S6	14	15	16	17	221	0.9	147	106
West Bank [4]	S4	1,255	2,091	2,164	2,765	140	3.1	993	2,178
Western Sahara	S4	191	251	256	301	181	2.1	2	102,703

X Not applicable. Z Less than one person per square mile or less than 0.05 percent. [1] Computed by the exponential method. For explanation of average annual percent change, see Guide to Tabular Presentation. [2] With the establishment of diplomatic relations with China on January 1, 1979, the U.S. government recognized the People's Republic of China as the sole legal government of China and acknowledged the Chinese position that there is only one China and that Taiwan is part of China. [3] "Congo" is the official short-form name for both the Republic of Congo and the Democratic Republic of the Congo. To distinguish one from the other the U.S. Dept. of State adds the capital in parentheses. This practice is unofficial and provisional. [4] The Gaza Strip and West Bank are Israeli occupied with interim status subject to Israeli/Palestinian negotiations. The final status is to be determined.

Source: U.S. Census Bureau, "International Data Base" (as of August 2002); <http://www.census.gov/ipc/www/idbnew.html>.

No. 1323. Age Distribution by Country: 2002 and 2010

[In percent. Covers countries with 5 million or more population in 2002]

Country or area	2002 Under 15 years old	2002 65 years old and over	2010, proj. Under 15 years old	2010, proj. 65 years old and over	Country or area	2002 Under 15 years old	2002 65 years old and over	2010, proj. Under 15 years old	2010, proj. 65 years old and over
World	**29.0**	**7.1**	**26.5**	**7.7**	Korea, South	20.9	7.6	18.3	9.9
Afghanistan	42.0	2.8	40.5	3.0	Laos	42.5	3.3	40.5	3.1
Algeria	33.5	4.1	28.5	4.4	Libya	34.9	4.0	32.9	4.4
Angola	43.5	2.8	43.1	2.8	Madagascar	45.0	3.2	44.5	2.9
Argentina	26.5	10.4	24.1	11.0	Malawi	46.7	2.7	46.9	2.8
Australia	20.4	12.6	18.7	13.9	Malaysia	34.1	4.3	31.0	5.1
Austria	16.4	15.6	14.3	18.1	Mali	47.2	3.0	46.4	2.8
Azerbaijan	28.3	7.4	24.5	6.9	Mexico	32.6	5.2	28.7	6.4
Bangladesh	34.9	3.3	33.8	3.7	Morocco	33.8	4.7	29.6	5.2
Belarus	17.3	14.1	15.6	13.6	Mozambique	43.9	2.7	41.3	3.1
Belgium	17.3	17.1	16.0	17.8	Nepal	40.0	3.5	37.3	3.9
Benin	47.1	2.3	45.2	2.4	Netherlands	18.5	13.7	17.2	15.2
Bolivia	37.8	4.5	32.1	4.9	Nicaragua	38.3	3.0	33.2	3.4
Brazil	27.7	5.5	24.0	6.8	Niger	47.8	2.2	46.1	2.2
Bulgaria	15.0	16.9	13.8	17.9	Nigeria	43.7	2.8	42.5	3.0
Burkina Faso	46.1	2.9	45.6	2.8	Pakistan	39.9	4.1	34.6	4.4
Burma	28.6	4.8	25.4	5.3	Papua New Guinea	38.6	3.7	36.6	4.1
Burundi	47.1	2.8	44.7	2.5	Paraguay	38.7	4.7	36.5	5.1
Cambodia	40.4	3.0	33.1	3.1	Peru	34.0	4.9	29.4	5.8
Cameroon	42.6	3.2	40.5	3.4	Philippines	36.6	3.8	33.2	4.4
Canada	18.7	12.9	16.7	14.2	Poland	17.9	12.6	15.7	13.1
Chad	47.8	2.8	47.4	2.7	Portugal	16.9	15.8	16.6	16.9
Chile	26.8	7.5	22.7	9.3	Romania	17.3	13.9	15.5	14.7
China [1]	23.8	7.3	19.6	8.3	Russia	16.7	13.2	15.3	13.1
Colombia	31.6	4.8	28.5	5.7	Rwanda	42.7	2.8	43.0	2.5
Congo (Kinshasa) [2]	48.3	2.5	47.2	2.4	Saudi Arabia	42.4	2.8	41.8	3.7
Cote d'Ivoire	45.6	2.2	43.9	2.4	Senegal	44.1	3.1	40.8	3.0
Cuba	21.0	9.7	18.2	11.7	Serbia and Montenegro	19.5	15.1	18.4	15.4
Czech Republic	15.7	13.9	13.5	15.9	Sierra Leone	44.8	3.2	43.8	3.4
Denmark	18.8	14.8	17.9	16.6	Slovakia	18.4	11.6	15.7	12.6
Dominican Republic	34.0	5.1	31.1	6.0	Somalia	44.7	2.7	45.0	2.5
Ecuador	35.3	4.4	31.5	5.0	South Africa	30.6	4.9	26.7	6.3
Egypt	34.3	4.2	31.0	4.9	Spain	14.4	17.5	14.5	18.4
El Salvador	37.4	5.1	35.0	5.4	Sri Lanka	25.6	6.8	22.6	8.2
Ethiopia	44.9	2.8	43.4	2.9	Sudan	44.2	2.2	40.7	2.7
Finland	17.9	15.3	16.2	17.2	Sweden	18.1	17.2	15.5	19.3
France	18.7	16.2	18.0	16.7	Switzerland	17.1	15.2	15.4	16.6
Germany	15.2	17.3	13.5	20.4	Syria	39.2	3.2	35.5	3.4
Ghana	39.7	3.5	32.7	4.0	Taiwan [1]	20.4	9.1	18.4	10.4
Greece	14.6	18.1	14.2	19.4	Tajikistan	40.4	4.7	36.9	4.1
Guatemala	43.1	3.3	41.2	3.4	Tanzania	44.5	2.6	42.9	2.7
Guinea	44.5	3.2	44.1	3.2	Thailand	24.3	6.8	22.4	8.5
Haiti	43.2	3.7	39.7	3.7	Togo	45.1	2.5	40.2	2.9
Honduras	41.9	3.6	38.6	4.0	Tunisia	27.8	6.3	22.8	7.1
Hungary	16.5	14.7	14.8	16.0	Turkey	27.8	6.3	23.5	7.3
India	32.7	4.7	29.2	5.3	Uganda	51.0	2.4	49.0	2.2
Indonesia	29.9	4.8	27.6	5.8	Ukraine	16.8	14.5	15.4	14.8
Iran	30.8	4.7	23.5	5.0	United Kingdom	18.5	15.6	16.5	16.4
Iraq	41.1	3.0	38.5	3.0	**United States**	**21.1**	**12.4**	**20.0**	**13.0**
Israel	27.1	9.9	25.4	10.0	Uzbekistan	35.5	4.7	31.7	4.3
Italy	14.1	18.5	13.4	20.3	Venezuela	31.6	4.8	26.6	5.7
Japan	14.5	18.2	14.1	22.1	Vietnam	30.9	5.6	26.0	5.6
Jordan	36.6	3.4	30.5	4.3	Yemen	47.0	2.9	46.1	2.5
Kazakhstan	26.0	7.5	24.2	7.5	Zambia	46.6	2.7	44.4	2.8
Kenya	42.0	2.8	36.5	3.2	Zimbabwe	40.0	3.5	38.7	4.1
Korea, North	25.2	6.9	22.2	9.5					

[1] See footnote 2, Table 1322. [2] See footnote 3, Table 1322.

Source: U.S. Census Bureau, "International Data Base" (as of 17 July 2003); <http://www.census.gov/ipc/www/idbnew.html>.

No. 1324. Foreign or Foreign-Born Population and Labor Force in Selected OECD Countries: 1990 and 2000

[In Australia, Canada, and the United States the data refer to people present in the country who are foreign born. In the European countries and Japan they generally refer to foreigners and represent the nationalities of residents]

Country	Foreign population [1] Number (1,000) 1990	2000	Percent of total population 1990	2000	Foreign labor force [2] Number (1,000) 1990	2000	Percent of total labor force 1990	2000
United States [3]	(NA)	28,400	(NA)	10.4	11,565	17,400	9.4	12.4
Australia [3]	(NA)	4,517	(NA)	23.6	(NA)	2,365	25.7	24.5
Austria	456	758	5.9	9.3	230	346	7.4	10.5
Belgium	905	862	9.1	8.4	289	(NA)	7.1	(NA)
Canada [3]	(NA)	(NA)	(NA)	(NA)	(NA)	(NA)	(NA)	(NA)
Denmark	161	259	3.1	4.8	69	97	2.4	3.4
France	3,597	(NA)	6.3	(NA)	1,550	1,578	6.2	6.0
Germany	5,343	7,297	8.4	8.9	(NA)	3,546	(NA)	8.8
Italy	781	1,388	1.4	2.4	(NA)	851	(NA)	3.6
Japan	1,075	1,686	0.9	1.3	(NA)	155	(NA)	0.2
Luxembourg	113	165	29.4	37.3	85	153	45.2	57.3
Netherlands	692	668	4.6	4.2	197	(NA)	3.1	(NA)
Spain	279	896	0.7	2.2	85	(NA)	0.6	(NA)
Sweden	484	477	5.6	5.4	246	222	5.4	5.0
Switzerland	1,100	1,384	16.3	19.3	670	717	18.9	18.3
United Kingdom	1,723	2,342	3.2	4.0	882	1,229	3.3	4.4

NA Not available. [1] Data are from population registers except for France (census), the United Kingdom (labor force survey), Japan and Switzerland (register of foreigners), and Italy and Spain (residence permits). [2] Includes unemployed except for Italy, Luxembourg, Netherlands, and United Kingdom. Data for Austria, Germany, and Luxembourg are from social security registers, and for Denmark, from the register of population. Data for Italy, Spain, and Switzerland are from residence or work permits. Figures for Japan and Netherlands are estimates. Data for other countries are from labor force surveys. [3] Census data from Current Population Survey.

Source: Organization for Economic Cooperation and Development, Paris, France, Trends in International Migration (2002 Editions) (copyright).

No. 1325. Medical Doctors and Inpatient Care—Selected Countries: 1990 to 2001

Country	Medical doctors per 1,000 population 1990	2000	2001	Inpatient care Acute care beds per 1,000 population 1990	2000	2001	Average length of stay (days) 1990	2000	2001
United States	2.4	(NA)	(NA)	3.7	2.9	2.9	9.1	6.8	6.7
Australia	2.2	2.4	2.5	(NA)	3.8	(NA)	(NA)	15.9	(NA)
Austria	2.2	3.1	3.2	7.0	6.2	6.2	12.8	8.6	(NA)
Belgium	3.3	3.9	(NA)	4.9	(NA)	(NA)	13.8	(NA)	(NA)
Canada	2.1	2.1	2.1	4.0	3.2	(NA)	13.0	(NA)	(NA)
Czech Republic	2.7	3.4	3.4	8.5	6.6	6.5	15.4	11.4	11.3
Denmark	3.1	3.4	3.4	4.1	(NA)	(NA)	8.2	6.0	5.9
Finland	2.4	3.1	3.1	4.3	2.4	2.4	18.2	10.3	10.6
France	3.1	3.3	3.3	8.5	6.7	(NA)	15.1	13.1	(NA)
Germany	(NA)	3.3	3.3	7.5	6.4	6.3	17.2	11.9	11.6
Greece	3.4	4.5	4.4	4.0	(NA)	(NA)	9.9	(NA)	(NA)
Hungary	2.9	(NA)	2.9	7.1	6.3	6.0	12.6	9.7	8.7
Iceland	2.8	3.4	3.5	4.3	(NA)	(NA)	18.3	(NA)	(NA)
Ireland	(NA)	2.2	2.4	3.3	3.0	3.0	7.9	7.4	7.5
Italy	(NA)	4.1	4.3	6.2	4.3	(NA)	11.7	7.7	(NA)
Japan	1.7	1.9	(NA)	(NA)	(NA)	(NA)	50.5	(NA)	(NA)
Korea, South	0.8	1.3	1.4	2.7	5.2	5.2	13.0	14.0	13.0
Luxembourg	2.0	2.5	2.5	7.0	6.7	6.6	17.6	(NA)	(NA)
Mexico	(NA)	1.4	1.5	(NA)	1.0	1.0	4.4	4.3	4.2
Netherlands	2.5	3.2	3.3	4.3	3.5	3.3	34.1	33.4	33.0
New Zealand	1.9	2.2	(NA)	8.0	(NA)	(NA)	9.4	7.7	7.7
Norway	(NA)	2.9	3.0	3.8	3.1	3.1	(NA)	8.9	8.7
Poland	2.1	2.2	2.2	6.3	5.1	5.0	12.5	8.9	8.4
Portugal	2.8	3.2	3.2	3.4	(NA)	(NA)	10.8	(NA)	(NA)
Slovak Republic	(NA)	3.7	3.6	(NA)	5.9	5.6	(NA)	10.4	10.1
Spain	(NA)	3.3	3.1	3.3	(NA)	(NA)	12.2	(NA)	(NA)
Sweden	2.9	3.0	(NA)	4.1	2.4	(NA)	18.0	6.4	6.4
Switzerland	3.0	3.5	3.5	6.5	4.1	3.9	(NA)	12.8	12.7
Turkey	0.9	1.3	1.3	2.0	2.2	2.1	6.9	5.9	5.8
United Kingdom	1.5	2.0	(NA)	(NA)	3.9	3.9	15.6	(NA)	(NA)

NA Not available.

Source: Organization for Economic Cooperation and Development, Paris, France, OECD Health Data 2003 (copyright).

846 Comparative International Statistics

No. 1326. Vital Statistics by Country: 2002 and 2010

[Covers countries with 10 million or more population in 2002]

Country or area	Crude birth rate [1] 2002	2010, proj.	Crude death rate [2] 2002	2010, proj.	Expectation of life at birth (years) 2002	2010, proj.	Infant mortality rate [3] 2002	2010, proj.	Total fertility rate per woman [4] 2002	2010, proj.
United States	14.2	14.2	8.6	8.3	76.9	78.4	6.9	6.2	2.06	2.11
Afghanistan	41.0	37.3	17.4	15.2	46.6	49.6	144.8	126.5	5.72	5.09
Algeria	22.3	19.9	5.2	4.9	70.2	72.5	39.2	28.9	2.63	2.17
Angola	46.0	42.4	25.8	26.8	37.1	35.0	195.2	183.6	6.43	5.94
Argentina	17.7	15.8	7.6	7.5	75.3	76.9	16.7	13.1	2.33	2.03
Australia	12.7	11.7	7.3	7.7	80.0	81.0	4.9	4.4	1.77	1.75
Bangladesh	29.7	27.8	8.7	7.7	61.0	63.9	67.9	54.3	3.19	3.04
Belarus	9.9	12.1	14.0	13.5	68.3	70.6	14.1	11.5	1.31	1.57
Belgium	10.9	10.1	10.2	10.5	78.1	79.4	4.9	4.4	1.64	1.65
Brazil	18.1	15.5	6.1	6.3	70.8	73.0	32.9	24.9	2.05	1.81
Burkina Faso	45.1	42.4	18.8	18.6	44.7	43.6	100.9	92.1	6.39	5.92
Burma	19.6	16.9	12.2	12.0	55.6	57.7	72.0	59.7	2.23	1.86
Cambodia	27.5	26.6	9.4	8.5	57.4	60.6	78.3	61.9	3.65	3.10
Cameroon	35.9	32.5	15.3	15.5	48.1	47.9	71.1	62.7	4.72	4.08
Canada	11.1	10.7	7.5	8.0	79.7	80.7	5.0	4.5	1.60	1.62
Chile	16.5	14.5	5.6	6.0	76.1	77.7	9.1	7.4	2.13	1.90
China [5]	13.1	13.9	6.7	7.1	72.0	74.0	26.3	19.0	1.69	1.80
Colombia	22.0	19.3	5.7	5.6	70.9	73.1	23.2	17.8	2.64	2.44
Congo (Kinshasa) [6]	45.6	42.4	15.1	13.4	48.7	50.5	98.5	83.2	6.77	6.11
Cote d'Ivoire	40.4	36.8	18.4	19.0	42.8	41.7	99.6	88.4	5.61	4.79
Cuba	12.6	11.3	7.2	7.4	76.6	78.1	6.7	5.8	1.66	1.67
Czech Republic	9.1	8.8	10.6	10.8	75.3	77.0	4.1	3.8	1.16	1.25
Ecuador	25.5	21.8	5.4	5.0	71.6	73.8	33.0	25.3	3.05	2.62
Egypt	24.9	21.3	5.4	5.2	70.1	72.4	36.7	26.7	3.10	2.61
Ethiopia	40.4	35.6	20.0	20.7	41.6	40.1	104.3	94.9	5.67	4.76
France	12.7	11.5	9.1	9.4	79.1	80.3	4.4	4.0	1.86	1.83
Germany	8.8	8.2	10.3	11.0	78.3	79.4	4.3	4.0	1.36	1.42
Ghana	26.8	21.4	10.4	11.5	56.8	55.6	53.8	47.6	3.47	2.54
Greece	9.7	9.3	10.0	10.6	78.6	79.8	5.9	5.1	1.31	1.37
Guatemala	35.5	32.0	6.8	6.6	65.3	65.9	39.0	31.4	4.73	4.19
India	23.8	20.7	8.6	7.9	63.3	66.1	61.3	48.5	2.98	2.55
Indonesia	21.9	18.7	6.3	6.3	68.6	71.1	39.4	30.0	2.54	2.28
Iran	17.4	17.5	5.6	5.6	69.0	71.4	45.5	35.6	2.06	1.76
Iraq	34.2	29.4	6.0	4.9	67.4	70.3	57.6	42.2	4.63	3.76
Italy	9.3	8.0	10.0	10.8	79.3	80.3	6.3	5.4	1.25	1.32
Japan	9.6	8.7	8.4	10.0	80.8	81.6	3.3	3.2	1.37	1.42
Kazakhstan	17.8	20.9	10.7	10.4	63.4	65.7	59.0	52.5	2.12	2.38
Kenya	29.8	23.6	15.7	18.3	45.5	43.7	64.1	58.0	3.62	2.63
Korea, North	18.7	13.8	6.9	7.5	70.5	72.7	26.5	20.5	2.30	1.90
Korea, South	12.9	11.0	5.9	6.8	75.1	76.8	7.4	6.5	1.55	1.58
Madagascar	42.4	40.5	12.2	10.1	55.7	58.9	81.9	68.7	5.77	5.47
Malawi	45.0	41.9	22.3	23.1	38.5	36.9	106.1	97.9	6.16	5.66
Malaysia	24.2	22.1	5.2	5.1	71.4	73.6	19.7	15.0	3.18	2.92
Mali	48.3	44.0	19.3	18.8	45.6	44.3	120.4	110.1	6.73	6.06
Mexico	22.3	19.4	4.7	4.8	74.4	76.3	23.3	17.8	2.58	2.31
Morocco	23.7	20.6	5.9	5.4	69.7	72.1	46.5	34.7	2.97	2.46
Mozambique	37.8	32.9	22.2	29.1	39.2	32.4	138.5	133.0	4.95	4.29
Nepal	32.9	28.8	10.0	8.7	58.6	61.7	72.4	58.7	4.48	3.73
Netherlands	12.0	10.3	8.7	8.8	78.4	79.6	5.3	4.7	1.66	1.66
Niger	50.2	45.3	21.9	21.0	42.2	41.4	124.6	117.1	7.00	6.28
Nigeria	39.2	35.3	13.6	15.7	51.5	47.3	72.2	65.8	5.49	4.79
Pakistan	30.4	24.9	9.0	7.5	61.8	64.8	78.5	63.3	4.25	3.16
Peru	23.4	19.8	5.7	5.6	70.6	72.9	38.2	29.3	2.89	2.41
Philippines	26.8	23.2	5.7	5.2	69.0	71.4	25.8	20.2	3.35	2.89
Poland	10.3	10.9	10.0	10.3	73.7	75.6	9.2	7.6	1.37	1.42
Portugal	11.5	10.4	10.2	10.6	76.1	77.7	5.8	5.1	1.48	1.52
Romania	10.7	10.4	11.6	11.9	70.6	72.7	28.9	22.1	1.34	1.40
Russia	9.7	12.1	13.9	14.5	67.5	68.8	19.8	17.7	1.30	1.56
Saudi Arabia	37.3	37.1	5.9	5.4	68.4	70.9	49.6	37.4	6.21	5.74
Senegal	36.8	32.8	11.0	9.8	56.2	58.2	58.6	50.4	5.03	4.29
Serbia and Montenegro	12.8	12.1	10.6	11.1	73.7	75.6	17.3	13.7	1.78	1.71
South Africa	19.4	16.4	16.6	30.1	48.8	36.5	59.5	65.1	2.30	1.96
Spain	10.0	9.5	9.4	10.1	79.1	80.2	4.6	4.2	1.25	1.32
Sri Lanka	16.4	14.8	6.5	6.6	72.4	74.4	15.7	12.5	1.93	1.78
Sudan	37.2	33.8	9.8	8.3	57.3	60.5	67.1	55.2	5.22	4.21
Syria	30.1	25.2	5.1	4.6	69.1	71.5	32.7	25.0	3.84	3.02
Taiwan [5]	12.8	12.0	6.1	6.9	76.7	78.1	6.8	5.9	1.56	1.59
Tanzania	40.0	35.7	17.3	17.1	44.7	44.6	105.3	92.3	5.33	4.62
Thailand	16.7	14.2	6.8	7.3	71.1	73.0	22.5	17.4	1.92	1.83
Turkey	18.0	15.6	6.0	6.1	71.5	73.7	45.8	34.3	2.07	1.82
Uganda	46.9	45.0	17.3	15.2	44.5	46.8	89.7	76.6	6.80	6.12
Ukraine	9.6	11.6	16.4	15.7	66.3	68.5	21.1	17.5	1.32	1.58
United Kingdom	11.1	10.7	10.2	10.0	78.0	79.2	5.3	4.8	1.66	1.66
Uzbekistan	26.1	26.1	8.0	7.4	63.9	66.2	71.7	65.6	3.03	2.80
Venezuela	20.2	17.8	4.9	5.0	73.6	75.5	24.6	18.9	2.41	2.13
Vietnam	19.6	18.7	6.2	6.0	69.7	72.1	31.8	24.7	2.26	2.10
Yemen	43.3	41.8	9.3	7.4	60.6	63.6	66.8	53.4	6.90	6.23
Zambia	40.1	35.9	24.3	25.4	35.3	34.4	100.2	92.3	5.35	4.53
Zimbabwe	30.7	27.8	20.8	27.4	40.2	34.6	65.9	69.0	3.72	3.26

[1] Number of births during 1 year per 1,000 persons (based on midyear population). [2] Number of deaths during 1 year per 1,000 persons (based on midyear population). [3] Number of deaths of children under 1 year of age per 1,000 live births in a calendar year. [4] Average number of children that would be born if all women lived to the end of their childbearing years and, at each year of age, they experienced the birth rates occurring in the specified year. [5] See footnote 2, Table 1322. [6] See footnote 3, Table 1322.

Source: U.S. Census Bureau, "International Data Base" (as of 17 July 2003); <http://www.census.gov/ipc/www/idbnew.html>.

No. 1327. Health Expenditures as Percent of GDP by Country: 1980 to 2001

[In percent. G.D.P.=gross domestic product; for explanation, see text, Section 13]

Country	Total health expenditures					Public health expenditures				
	1980	1990	1999	2000	2001	1980	1990	1999	2000	2001
United States	8.7	11.9	13.0	13.1	13.9	3.6	4.7	5.7	5.8	6.2
Australia	7.0	7.8	8.7	8.9	(NA)	4.4	5.2	6.0	6.1	(NA)
Austria	7.6	7.1	7.8	7.7	7.7	5.2	5.2	5.4	5.4	5.3
Belgium	6.4	7.4	8.5	8.6	9.0	(NA)	(NA)	6.2	6.2	6.4
Canada	7.1	9.0	9.1	9.2	9.7	5.4	6.7	6.4	6.5	6.9
Czech Republic	(NA)	5.0	7.1	7.1	7.3	(NA)	4.9	6.5	6.5	6.7
Denmark	9.1	8.5	8.5	8.3	8.6	8.0	7.0	7.0	6.9	7.1
Finland	6.4	7.8	6.9	6.7	7.0	5.0	6.3	5.2	5.0	5.3
France	(NA)	8.6	9.3	9.3	9.5	(NA)	6.6	7.1	7.1	7.2
Germany [1]	8.7	8.5	10.6	10.6	10.7	6.8	6.5	8.0	7.9	8.0
Greece	6.6	7.4	9.6	9.4	9.4	3.7	4.0	5.1	5.3	5.2
Hungary	(NA)	(NA)	6.8	6.7	6.8	(NA)	(NA)	5.3	5.1	5.1
Iceland	6.2	8.0	9.5	9.3	9.2	5.5	6.9	8.0	7.8	7.6
Ireland	8.4	6.1	6.2	6.4	6.5	6.8	4.4	4.6	4.7	4.9
Italy	(NA)	8.0	7.8	8.2	8.4	(NA)	6.4	5.6	6.0	6.3
Japan	6.4	5.9	7.5	7.6	(NA)	4.6	4.6	5.8	6.0	(NA)
Korea, South	(NA)	4.8	5.6	5.9	(NA)	(NA)	1.7	2.4	2.6	(NA)
Luxembourg	5.9	6.1	6.1	5.6	(NA)	5.5	5.7	5.4	4.9	(NA)
Mexico	(NA)	4.5	5.5	5.6	6.6	(NA)	2.0	2.7	2.7	3.0
Netherlands	7.5	8.0	8.7	8.6	8.9	5.2	5.4	5.5	5.5	5.7
New Zealand	5.9	6.9	7.9	8.0	8.1	5.2	5.7	6.1	6.2	6.2
Norway	6.9	7.7	8.5	7.6	8.0	5.9	6.4	7.3	6.5	6.8
Poland	(NA)	5.3	6.2	6.0	6.3	(NA)	4.8	4.4	4.2	4.6
Portugal	5.6	6.2	8.7	9.0	9.2	3.6	4.1	5.9	6.2	6.3
Slovak Republic	(NA)	(NA)	5.8	5.7	5.7	(NA)	(NA)	5.2	5.1	5.1
Spain	5.4	6.7	7.5	7.5	7.5	4.3	5.3	5.4	5.3	5.4
Sweden	8.8	8.2	8.4	8.4	8.7	8.2	7.4	7.2	7.1	7.4
Switzerland	7.6	8.5	10.7	10.7	10.9	(NA)	4.5	5.9	5.9	(NA)
Turkey	3.3	3.6	(NA)	(NA)	(NA)	0.9	2.2	(NA)	(NA)	(NA)
United Kingdom	5.6	6.0	7.2	7.3	7.6	5.0	5.0	5.8	5.9	6.2

NA Not available. [1] Data prior to 1991 are for former West Germany.
Source: Organization for Economic Cooperation and Development, Paris, France, *OECD Health Data 2003*, 2nd ed. (copyright).

No. 1328. Average Temperatures and Precipitation—Selected International Cities

[In degrees Fahrenheit, except as noted. Data are generally based on a standard 30-year period; for details, see source. For data on U.S. cities, see Tables 389-392]

City	January					July				
	Average high	Average low	Warmest	Coldest	Average precipitation (inches)	Average high	Average low	Warmest	Coldest	Average precipitation (inches)
Amsterdam, Netherlands	41	34	57	3	3.1	69	55	90	39	2.9
Athens, Greece	55	44	70	28	1.9	89	73	108	61	0.2
Baghdad, Iraq	58	38	75	25	1.1	110	78	122	61	-
Bangkok, Thailand	89	71	95	54	0.4	90	78	99	72	6.2
Beijing, China	34	17	54	1	0.2	86	72	104	63	8.8
Berlin, Germany	35	26	58	-11	(NA)	73	56	95	41	(NA)
Bogota, Colombia	66	43	84	27	1.9	64	47	82	32	1.8
Brasilia, Brazil	81	64	95	54	(NA)	79	52	97	37	(NA)
Buenos Aires, Argentina	85	64	104	44	4.2	58	41	88	23	2.3
Cairo, Egypt	65	49	86	32	0.2	93	72	108	63	-
Frankfurt, Germany	38	30	56	-4	1.8	75	57	97	38	2.4
Geneva, Switzerland	39	29	57	-2	2.2	77	56	96	41	2.8
Hong Kong, China	67	58	79	43	1.1	89	81	97	70	14.3
Istanbul, Turkey	46	37	64	16	3.7	82	66	100	50	0.7
Jakarta, Indonesia	83	75	92	72	(NA)	88	74	92	67	(NA)
Kabul, Afghanistan	36	23	64	-4	1.3	88	67	102	49	0.2
Karachi, Pakistan	76	55	93	39	0.3	89	83	109	68	3.5
Lagos, Nigeria	82	79	93	64	(NA)	79	76	88	70	(NA)
London, England	45	36	61	15	2.4	72	56	93	45	1.8
Madrid, Spain	51	32	68	14	1.8	90	61	104	46	0.4
Manila, Philippines	86	71	95	61	0.8	88	76	99	70	15.9
Mexico City, Mexico	70	45	86	26	0.3	74	56	86	37	5.1
Montreal, Canada	21	7	52	-31	2.8	79	61	93	43	3.4
Moscow, Russia	21	11	46	-33	1.4	71	55	95	41	3.2
Nairobi, Kenya	77	58	88	45	1.8	71	54	85	43	0.5
New Delhi, India	68	48	85	32	0.9	93	81	111	70	7.9
Paris, France	43	34	59	1	(NA)	75	58	95	41	(NA)
Rio De Janeiro, Brazil	91	74	109	64	5.3	81	64	102	52	1.8
Rome, Italy	55	39	64	19	3.2	83	66	100	55	0.6
Seoul, Korea	33	21	55	-1	(NA)	82	71	97	55	(NA)
Singapore, Singapore	85	73	100	66	9.4	86	76	99	70	5.9
Sydney, Australia	79	65	109	49	4.0	62	44	80	32	2.5
Tel Aviv, Israel	62	46	84	32	(NA)	87	69	100	50	(NA)
Tokyo, Japan	48	35	66	25	2.0	82	71	95	55	5.3
Toronto, Canada	28	15	59	-24	1.9	79	60	99	45	2.8

- Represents zero. NA Not available.
Source: U.S. National Oceanic and Atmospheric Administration, *Climates of the World*.

No. 1329. Selected Environmental Data—OECD Countries

[Figures are for 1998 or the latest available year. Varying definitions and survey methods can limit the comparability across countries]

Country	Air pollutant emissions per capita			Waste generated			
	Sulfur oxides (kilograms)	Nitrogen oxides (kilograms)	Carbon dioxide [1] (tons)	Municipal [2] (kilograms per capita)	Nuclear [3] Amount (tons)	Per unit of energy (tons per Mtoe [4])	Per 1,000 persons (kilograms)
United States	63	84	21	760	1,900	0.9	7.1
Australia	96	135	17	690	-	-	-
Austria	5	23	8	560	-	-	-
Belgium	20	36	12	550	165	1.3	16.2
Canada	82	67	17	350	1,515	5.0	50.0
Czech Republic	26	39	12	330	43	1.1	4.2
Denmark	5	39	9	660	-	-	-
Finland	15	46	11	460	72	2.2	14.0
France	14	28	6	510	1,165	4.5	19.8
Germany	10	20	10	[5]540	450	1.3	5.5
Greece	51	36	8	430	-	-	-
Hungary	59	22	6	450	80	1.9	7.9
Iceland	33	92	8	700	-	-	-
Ireland	42	32	11	560	-	-	-
Italy	16	26	7	500	-	-	-
Japan	7	13	9	410	897	1.9	7.1
Korea, South	25	23	10	360	370	2.7	8.0
Luxembourg	7	39	18	640	-	-	-
Mexico	12	12	4	320	22	0.1	0.2
Netherlands	6	27	11	610	12	0.2	0.8
New Zealand	12	53	8	[6]380	-	-	-
Norway	6	54	8	620	-	-	-
Poland	39	22	8	290	(NA)	(NA)	(NA)
Portugal	38	37	6	450	-	-	-
Spain	40	33	7	660	97	1.2	2.5
Sweden	8	30	5	450	238	4.7	26.9
Switzerland	4	15	6	650	64	2.4	9.0
Turkey	33	14	3	390	-	-	-
United Kingdom	20	27	9	560	865	3.4	14.6

- Represents zero.   NA Not available.   [1] Carbon dioxide from energy use only. Excludes international marine bunkers.   [2] Municipal waste is that which is collected and treated by or for municipalities: household waste and bulky waste as well as comparable waste from small communities or industrial enterprises; and market and garden residue.   [3] Wastes from spent fuel arising in nuclear power plants, measured in terms of heavy metal.   [4] Mtoe=million tons of oil equivalent (primary energy supply).   [5] Includes separate collection by private sector.   [6] Household waste only.

Source: Organization for Economic Cooperation and Development, Paris, France, *OECD Environmental Data Compendium*, 2002 (copyright).

No. 1330. Carbon Dioxide Emissions From Consumption of Fossil Fuels by Country 1990 to 2001, and Projections, 2005 and 2010

[In million metric tons of carbon (5,873 represents 5,873,000,000). Includes carbon dioxide emissions from the consumption of petroleum, natural gas, and coal, and the flaring of natural gas]

Country	1990	1995	1997	1998	1999	2000	2001, prel.	2005	2010
World, total	5,873	6,086	6,282	6,259	6,324	6,471	6,568	7,015	7,835
Australia	72	80	90	90	96	96	99	(NA)	(NA)
Brazil	63	82	87	88	93	95	96	108	139
Canada	128	135	146	145	153	160	156	158	165
China [1]	617	788	824	805	791	780	832	889	1,131
France	102	101	104	110	110	109	108	116	120
Germany	(X)	239	239	235	226	226	223	246	252
India	156	226	230	234	236	251	251	300	351
Indonesia	41	58	67	64	71	75	87	(NA)	(NA)
Iran	56	71	79	83	85	88	90	(NA)	(NA)
Italy	112	118	113	115	118	121	122	131	137
Japan	269	298	309	300	305	310	316	324	330
Korea, South	61	109	118	101	104	116	121	128	144
Mexico	84	87	95	104	104	102	96	124	145
Netherlands	58	61	64	62	59	62	68	66	67
Poland	89	83	91	85	82	82	79	(NA)	(NA)
Russia	(X)	445	395	396	415	428	440	(NA)	(NA)
Saudi Arabia	59	69	72	70	78	81	85	(NA)	(NA)
South Africa	81	94	104	99	102	103	105	(NA)	(NA)
Spain	62	67	73	74	80	84	83	(NA)	(NA)
Taiwan [1]	32	51	57	63	61	69	71	(NA)	(NA)
Thailand	23	43	46	46	46	46	48	(NA)	(NA)
Turkey	35	41	49	50	49	50	50	57	66
Ukraine	(X)	122	102	100	102	98	97	(NA)	(NA)
United Kingdom	164	153	153	148	149	152	154	168	177
United States	1,355	1,443	1,513	1,519	1,537	1,585	1,565	1,690	1,809

NA Not available.   X Not applicable.   [1] See footnote 2, Table 1322.

Source: U.S. Energy Information Administration, *International Energy Annual, 2001*, and *International Energy Outlook, 2002*.

No. 1331. Educational Attainment by Country: 2000

[Percent distribution. Persons 25 to 64 years old]

Country	Total	Preprimary and primary education	Lower secondary education	Upper secondary education	Post-secondary nontertiary education [1]	Non-university tertiary education [2]	University education
United States	100	5	8	50	([3])	9	28
Australia	100	([4])	[4]41	30	([3])	10	19
Austria [5]	100	([4])	[4]24	55	7	7	7
Belgium [5]	100	20	22	30	1	15	12
Canada	100	6	12	28	12	21	20
Czech Republic	100	([4])	[4]14	75	([3])	([6])	11
Denmark	100	(Z)	7 20	[7]52	2	19	8
Finland	100	([4])	[4]26	42	([3])	17	15
France	100	18	18	41	(Z)	11	12
Germany	100	2	16	55	5	10	13
Greece	100	39	10	28	5	5	12
Hungary	100	3	27	51	5	(Z)	14
Iceland	100	2	34	29	10	6	19
Ireland	100	25	18	22	([8])	22	14
Italy	100	22	33	33	2	([6])	10
Japan	100	([4])	[4]17	49	(NA)	15	19
Korea, South	100	17	15	44	(X)	7	17
Mexico	100	55	23	7	(X)	2	13
Netherlands [5]	100	13	22	37	4	3	21
New Zealand	100	([4])	[4]24	40	7	15	14
Norway [5]	100	1	14	54	3	3	26
Poland	100	([4])	[4]19	66	3	([6])	12
Portugal	100	68	12	11	([3])	2	7
Spain	100	35	25	17	([9])	7	17
Sweden	100	9	10	49	([9])	15	17
Switzerland	100	3	9	55	7	10	16
Turkey	100	66	9	16	(X)	([6])	9
United Kingdom	100	([4])	[4]17	57	(NA)	8	18

NA Not available.   X Not applicable.   Z Less than 0.5 percent.   [1] This level straddles the boundary between upper secondary and postsecondary education from an international point of view, even though it might clearly be considered upper secondary or postsecondary in a national context. Although the content may not be significantly more advanced than upper secondary programs, it serves to broaden the knowledge of participants who have already gained an upper secondary qualification.   [2] These programs focus on practical, technical, or occupational skills for direct entry into the labor market, although some theoretical foundations may be covered. They have a minimum duration of 2 years full-time equivalent at the tertiary level.   [3] Postsecondary nontertiary included in upper secondary.   [4] Preprimary and primary education included in lower secondary.   [5] Data for 2000.   [6] Nonuniversity tertiary included in university.   [7] Part of upper secondary included in lower secondary.   [8] Postsecondary nontertiary included in upper secondary and nonuniversity tertiary.   [9] Postsecondary nontertiary included in nonuniversity tertiary.

Source: Organization for Economic Cooperation and Development, Paris, France, Education at a Glance, annual, (copyright).

No. 1332. Participation in Job-Related Continuing Education and Training by Country

[Percentage of the employed population 25 to 64 years old. Data refer to all job-related education and training organized, financed, or sponsored by authorities, provided by employers, or self-financed. Job-related continuing education and training refers to all organized, systematic education and training activities in which people take part in order to obtain knowledge and/or learn new skills for a current or a future job, to increase earnings, improve job and/or career opportunities in current or other fields, and generally to improve their opportunities for advancement and promotion. Data are based on International Adult Literacy Survey 1994-1998 and national household surveys on adult education and training]

Country	Time period	Total	Male	Female
United States [1]	2001	40	39	41
Australia	1996-97	47	46	50
Canada	1997	28	26	30
Czech Republic	1998-99	27	31	23
Denmark	1998-99	55	52	58
Finland [1]	2000	43	41	45
Germany [1]	2000	29	34	23
Hungary	1998-99	20	17	23
Ireland	1995-96	24	21	29
Italy	1998-99	25	25	25
Netherlands	1994-95	33	35	29
New Zealand	1995-96	47	46	47
Norway	1998-99	51	49	54
Poland	1994-95	17	16	17
Switzerland	1998-99	37	39	35
United Kingdom	1995-96	52	51	53

[1] Includes the unemployed population.

Source: Organization for Economic Cooperation and Development, Paris, France, Education at a Glance, 2002 (copyright).

No. 1333. Gross National Income by Country: 1990 and 2001

[61 represents $61,000,000,000. GNI (gross national product, or GNP, in the terminology of the 1968 United Nations System of National Accounts) measures the total domestic and foreign value added claimed by residents. GNI comprises GDP plus net receipts of primary income (compensation of employees and property income) from nonresident sources]

Country	Gross national product [1] Total (bil. dol.) 1990	2001	Per capita (dol.) 1990	2001	GNP on purchasing power parity basis [2] Total (bil. dol.) 1990	2001	Per capita (dol.) 1990	2001
Algeria	61	51	2,440	1,650	124	182	4,980	5,910
Angola	8	7	800	500	17	23	1,770	1,690
Argentina	104	260	3,200	6,940	228	412	7,020	10,980
Australia	302	386	17,720	19,900	267	478	15,670	24,630
Bangladesh	31	49	280	360	105	213	950	1,600
Belarus	(NA)	13	(NA)	1,290	68	76	6,680	7,630
Belgium	184	245	18,460	23,850	177	269	17,760	26,150
Brazil	411	529	2,780	3,070	761	1,219	5,140	7,070
Bulgaria	20	13	2,260	1,650	51	54	5,860	6,740
Burkina Faso	3	3	290	220	6	13	730	1,120
Cambodia	1	3	140	270	10	22	1,120	1,790
Cameroon	11	9	960	580	16	24	1,420	1,580
Canada	551	682	19,840	21,930	508	825	18,270	26,530
Chile	29	71	2,190	4,590	58	136	4,450	8,840
China [3]	368	1,131	320	890	1,478	5,027	1,300	3,950
Colombia	41	82	1,180	1,890	182	292	5,220	6,790
Congo (Kinshasa) [4]	8	4	230	80	50	33	1,360	630
Cote d'Ivoire	9	10	780	630	15	23	1,260	1,400
Czech Republic	(NA)	54	(NA)	5,310	116	146	11,170	14,320
Ecuador	10	14	950	1,080	25	38	2,440	2,960
Egypt	42	100	810	1,530	122	232	2,320	3,560
Ethiopia	8	7	160	100	28	53	550	800
France [5]	1,142	1,381	19,660	22,730	961	1,425	16,950	24,080
Germany	1,612	1,940	20,290	23,560	1,443	2,078	18,170	25,240
Ghana	6	6	390	290	22	43	1,480	2,170
Greece	79	121	7,770	11,430	117	186	11,520	17,520
Guatemala	8	20	970	1,680	28	51	3,160	4,380
Hong Kong	72	170	12,680	25,330	92	172	16,210	25,560
Hungary	30	49	2,880	4,830	90	122	8,680	11,990
India	331	477	390	460	1,345	2,913	1,580	2,820
Indonesia	111	145	620	690	313	591	1,760	2,830
Iran	141	109	2,590	1,680	201	383	3,700	5,940
Iraq	39	(NA)	2,170	(NA)	(NA)	(NA)	(NA)	(NA)
Italy	988	1,124	17,420	19,390	988	1,422	17,410	24,530
Japan	3,348	4,523	27,100	35,610	2,344	3,246	18,980	25,550
Kazakhstan	(NA)	20	(NA)	1,350	96	92	5,890	6,150
Kenya	9	11	380	350	21	30	880	970
Korea, South	246	448	5,740	9,460	315	713	7,340	15,060
Madagascar	3	4	240	260	9	13	740	820
Malawi	2	2	200	160	4	6	410	560
Malaysia	43	79	2,380	3,330	78	188	4,310	7,910
Mali	2	3	270	230	5	9	550	770
Mexico	236	550	2,830	5,530	483	820	5,810	8,240
Morocco	25	35	1,030	1,190	63	102	2,640	3,500
Mozambique	2	4	170	210	8	19	570	1,050
Nepal	4	6	220	250	15	32	850	1,360
Netherlands	280	390	18,720	24,330	270	439	18,050	27,390
Niger	2	2	310	180	6	10	820	880
Nigeria	26	37	270	290	63	102	650	790
Pakistan	43	60	390	420	144	263	1,330	1,860
Peru	17	52	780	1,980	66	118	3,040	4,470
Philippines	45	81	740	1,030	192	319	3,150	4,070
Poland	(NA)	164	(NA)	4,230	207	362	5,430	9,370
Portugal	64	109	6,450	10,900	110	178	11,120	17,710
Romania	(NA)	39	(NA)	1,720	122	130	5,250	5,780
Russia	(NA)	253	(NA)	1,750	1,184	995	7,990	6,880
Saudi Arabia	105	181	6,620	8,460	186	284	11,790	13,290
Senegal	5	5	720	490	8	14	1,100	1,480
Serbia and Montenegro	(NA)	10	(NA)	930	(NA)	(NA)	(NA)	(NA)
Singapore	36	89	11,740	21,500	37	94	12,270	22,850
South Africa	102	122	2,890	2,820	321	472	9,110	10,910
Spain	454	588	11,680	14,300	506	816	13,020	19,860
Sri Lanka	8	16	490	880	31	61	1,890	3,260
Sudan	14	11	580	340	25	56	1,000	1,750
Sweden	219	226	25,540	25,400	145	212	16,940	23,800
Switzerland	225	277	33,510	38,330	168	224	24,990	30,970
Syria	11	17	940	1,040	25	52	2,100	3,160
Tanzania	5	9	190	270	10	18	410	520
Thailand	84	118	1,520	1,940	200	381	3,600	6,230
Turkey	127	167	2,270	2,530	242	386	4,320	5,830
Uganda	6	6	340	260	14	33	850	1,460
Ukraine	83	35	1,600	720	366	210	7,050	4,270
United Kingdom	932	1,477	16,190	25,120	922	1,431	16,020	24,340
United States	**5,846**	**9,781**	**23,440**	**34,280**	**5,847**	**9,781**	**23,440**	**34,280**
Uzbekistan	(NA)	14	(NA)	550	49	60	2,380	2,410
Venezuela	52	117	2,650	4,760	91	138	4,660	5,590
Vietnam	9	33	130	410	61	164	930	2,070
Yemen	(NA)	8	(NA)	450	6	13	520	730
Zimbabwe	9	6	880	480	22	28	2,150	2,220

NA Not available. [1] Gross national income calculated using the World Bank Atlas method; for details, see source. [2] See footnote 2, Table 1334. [3] See footnote 2, Table 1322. [4] See footnote 3, Table 1322. [5] GNI and GNI per capita estimates include the French overseas departments of French Guiana, Guadeloupe, Martinique, and Reunion.

Source: The World Bank, Washington, DC, *World Development Indicators CD-ROM*, annual (copyright).

No. 1334. Gross Domestic Product (GDP) by Country: 1995 to 2001

[23,674 represents $23,674,000,000,000. Except as noted, based on the System of National Accounts, 1993; for details, see source]

Country	Current price levels and exchange rates (bil. dol.) 1995	1998	1999	2000	2001	Constant (1995) price levels and exchange rates (bil. dol.) 1995	1998	1999	2000	2001	GDP per capita, 2001 based on current Exchange rates	PPPs[2]
OECD, total [3,4]	23,674	23,602	24,879	25,221	24,793	23,674	25,717	26,478	27,406	27,579	23,083	25,168
OECD Europe [3,4]	9,253	9,171	9,175	8,507	8,479	9,253	9,938	10,196	10,551	10,686	18,428	22,773
European Union [4]	8,622	8,550	8,565	7,892	7,909	8,622	9,240	9,498	9,825	9,969	20,844	25,532
Australia	373	372	406	388	369	373	426	443	450	468	18,940	27,417
Austria	235	212	210	191	190	235	253	260	269	271	23,313	28,224
Belgium	277	250	251	228	228	277	296	305	317	319	22,132	27,699
Canada	582	607	650	707	695	582	641	676	707	717	22,343	28,923
Czech Republic	52	57	55	51	57	52	53	54	55	57	5,529	15,028
Denmark	180	172	174	160	162	180	195	200	206	207	30,155	29,679
Finland [5]	129	129	128	121	122	129	151	157	166	167	23,454	26,538
France	1,553	1,452	1,444	1,305	1,310	1,553	1,655	1,708	1,772	1,805	21,505	26,179
Germany	2,458	2,145	2,108	1,870	1,853	2,458	2,561	2,613	2,688	2,703	22,509	26,321
Greece	118	122	126	113	117	118	129	134	139	145	10,695	16,249
Hungary	45	47	48	47	52	45	50	52	54	57	5,079	13,432
Iceland	7	8	9	9	8	7	8	8	9	9	27,051	29,281
Ireland	67	87	96	95	102	67	87	96	106	112	26,590	30,002
Italy	1,097	1,197	1,181	1,073	1,089	1,097	1,152	1,170	1,204	1,225	18,795	26,165
Japan	5,292	3,941	4,494	4,765	4,141	5,292	5,513	5,550	5,681	5,648	32,556	26,416
Korea, South	489	317	406	462	422	489	512	568	620	639	8,917	15,904
Luxembourg	18	19	20	19	19	18	22	23	25	25	43,430	48,530
Mexico	286	421	481	580	617	286	338	350	373	372	6,227	9,146
Netherlands	415	394	399	371	384	415	463	482	498	504	23,938	29,248
New Zealand [6]	61	54	56	51	51	61	64	67	69	71	13,128	21,218
Norway	148	150	158	167	168	148	168	172	176	178	37,232	36,474
Poland	127	159	155	158	176	127	151	157	163	165	4,561	9,934
Portugal	107	112	115	106	110	107	121	125	129	131	10,914	17,987
Slovakia	19	22	20	20	21	19	22	23	23	24	3,804	12,036
Spain	584	588	602	561	583	584	650	677	705	724	14,482	21,393
Sweden [6]	248	248	252	240	219	248	267	279	292	294	24,600	25,972
Switzerland	307	262	259	240	246	307	321	326	336	339	33,998	29,919
Turkey	169	200	185	199	148	169	201	191	206	190	2,157	5,830
United Kingdom	1,135	1,423	1,460	1,438	1,422	1,135	1,240	1,270	1,309	1,335	24,187	26,226
United States	7,338	8,720	9,213	9,762	10,020	7,338	8,286	8,629	8,955	8,978	35,045	35,045

[1] Based on constant (1995) price data converted to U.S. dollars using 1995 exchange rates. [2] The goods and services produced in different countries should be valued consistently if the differences observed are meant to reflect real differences in the volumes of goods and services produced. The use of purchasing power parities (PPP) instead of exchange rates is intended to achieve this objective. PPPs show how many units of currency are needed in one country to buy the same amount of goods and services which one unit of currency will buy in the other country. See text of this section. [3] Excluding Czech Republic, Hungary, Poland, and Slovakia. [4] European Union: Austria, Belgium, Denmark, Finland, France, Germany, Greece, Ireland, Italy, Luxembourg, Netherlands, Portugal, Spain, Sweden, and United Kingdom. OECD Europe: Austria, Belgium, Denmark, Finland, France, Germany, Greece, Iceland, Ireland, Italy, Luxembourg, Netherlands, Norway, Portugal, Spain, Sweden, Switzerland, Turkey, and United Kingdom. [5] Includes overseas departments. [6] Based on System of National Accounts, 1968.

Source: Organization for Economic Cooperation and Development, Paris, France, "National Accounts of OECD Countries," annual, Vol. 1; published July 2003.

No. 1335. Selected International Economic Indicators by Country: 1980 to 2002

[Data cover gross domestic product (GDP) at market prices. Gross fixed capital formation covers private and government sectors except military. Savings data are calculated by deducting outlays—such as personal consumption expenditures, interest paid, and transfer payments to foreigners—from disposable personal income]

Year	United States	France	Germany	Italy	Netherlands	United Kingdom	Japan	Canada
Ratio of gross fixed capital formation to GDP (current prices):								
1980	20.0	23.8	22.6	25.2	22.7	18.7	31.8	23.1
1985	19.4	20.3	19.5	21.8	20.9	18.1	27.8	20.2
1990	17.2	22.6	20.9	21.5	22.5	20.5	32.2	21.3
1995	17.5	18.8	22.4	18.3	20.3	16.3	27.7	17.6
2000	19.9	20.2	21.6	19.8	22.5	16.7	26.2	19.3
2001	19.1	20.1	20.1	19.8	21.9	16.5	25.6	19.9
2002	18.0	19.5	18.4	19.7	21.0	16.1	24.1	19.7
Ratio of savings to disposable personal income:								
1980	10.2	17.2	13.4	27.9	7.8	12.4	19.9	15.6
1985	9.2	14.1	12.1	30.7	5.6	9.8	16.5	15.8
1990	7.8	13.1	13.9	27.8	11.6	8.0	14.0	13.0
1995	5.6	16.0	11.2	22.5	14.9	10.0	11.9	9.2
2000	2.8	15.7	9.8	14.5	6.7	4.3	9.8	4.6
2001	2.3	16.2	10.1	15.4	9.6	5.7	6.9	4.5
2002	3.7	16.7	10.4	16.0	10.7	4.7	5.8	4.2

Source: U.S. Dept. of Commerce, International Trade Administration, Office of Trade and Economic Analysis, based on official statistics of listed countries.

No. 1336. International Economic Composite Indexes by Country: 1980 to 2002

[Average annual percent change from previous year; derived from indexes with base 1990=100. The coincident index changes are for calendar years and the leading index changes are for years ending June 30 because they lead the coincident indexes by about 6 months, on average. The G-7 countries are United States, Canada, France, Germany, Italy, United Kingdom, and Japan. Minus sign (-) indicates decrease]

Country	1980	1985	1990	1994	1995	1996	1997	1998	1999	2000	2001	2002
LEADING INDEX												
Total, 13 countries	1.8	2.4	2.5	3.3	6.5	1.0	3.3	1.8	0.4	6.2	-0.6	-4.3
12 countries, excluding U.S.	6.9	5.0	4.6	2.8	6.8	1.7	3.0	1.2	0.2	7.4	1.8	-3.0
G-7 countries	1.8	2.0	2.5	3.1	6.4	0.9	3.2	1.8	0.1	5.9	-0.8	-4.9
North America	-4.3	-1.1	-1.1	4.5	6.0	-0.1	3.7	3.1	0.9	4.3	-4.2	-6.3
United States	-4.8	-1.5	-1.2	4.4	5.8	-0.2	3.7	2.9	0.6	4.1	-4.8	-6.7
Canada	4.3	5.0	-0.9	7.3	7.4	1.3	4.4	6.0	4.0	6.8	3.7	-1.7
Four European countries	3.2	3.4	1.9	4.1	6.3	0.2	1.2	5.8	1.3	3.5	0.3	-4.8
France	2.5	1.9	0.9	4.5	4.1	-0.2	2.3	4.7	0.8	1.0	-5.1	-8.5
Germany	3.5	3.5	4.4	2.6	6.9	-0.7	1.8	6.4	1.5	3.4	1.3	-3.6
Italy	4.8	6.1	0.5	7.3	10.4	1.0	-2.1	9.5	0.6	7.3	3.0	-3.8
United Kingdom	2.2	3.0	-0.3	3.9	4.5	1.8	1.6	2.9	2.2	3.8	0.6	-1.4
Seven Pacific region countries	11.7	6.9	7.6	1.0	7.4	3.2	4.6	-3.4	-1.2	11.5	3.5	-1.7
Australia	0.8	7.1	-1.5	6.0	6.4	1.0	2.1	4.5	4.6	8.1	-0.8	1.1
Taiwan [1]	2.6	5.5	5.4	6.9	7.0	2.2	8.1	7.3	3.6	8.0	0.4	2.7
Thailand	2.2	5.3	12.4	10.7	9.2	5.3	0.5	-2.4	1.9	9.7	3.9	7.6
Japan	13.5	7.3	8.3	-0.5	7.3	3.3	4.8	-4.8	-2.6	11.8	4.3	-3.1
Korea, South	0.6	6.0	6.5	11.1	10.5	6.1	4.7	1.3	8.8	15.9	2.5	6.2
Malaysia	5.5	-3.1	1.3	6.1	4.6	-1.0	1.8	-5.9	-7.4	10.4	-5.0	-0.2
New Zealand	2.3	3.2	0.7	6.4	1.4	1.6	2.9	0.9	1.7	1.6	0.1	2.7
COINCIDENT INDEX												
Total, 13 countries	2.9	4.8	5.0	-0.1	3.5	1.5	2.7	2.9	1.3	4.6	3.1	-2.5
12 countries, excluding U.S.	4.7	3.4	7.1	-1.8	2.3	1.1	1.9	1.0	-0.5	4.5	4.1	-1.6
G-7 countries	2.8	4.8	5.0	-0.4	3.2	1.2	2.7	2.9	1.5	4.4	2.9	-2.9
North America	-0.3	7.9	1.2	4.0	6.3	2.4	4.3	6.3	5.1	5.5	-1.1	-3.9
United States	-0.9	7.7	1.1	4.1	6.1	2.5	4.5	6.1	4.9	5.1	0.8	-4.2
Canada	7.1	9.6	1.5	3.9	9.6	0.2	3.0	9.1	7.2	10.2	3.6	-0.5
Four European countries	3.0	1.6	6.0	-3.1	3.3	1.8	1.6	5.6	5.4	8.8	8.4	2.2
France	-1.0	-4.1	8.3	-4.2	5.1	1.5	0.3	7.5	8.1	12.1	11.4	2.0
Germany	3.9	2.5	5.6	-3.2	3.0	0.5	-0.3	2.9	5.4	8.1	6.0	-0.4
Italy	10.0	6.6	7.2	-7.6	-0.4	2.8	3.8	7.7	5.6	12.3	15.0	7.7
United Kingdom	2.3	3.2	3.1	2.8	5.0	3.8	4.6	6.6	2.4	3.5	3.4	2.5
Seven Pacific region countries	6.3	4.4	8.4	-1.2	1.2	0.6	2.1	-2.8	-5.5	0.5	0.3	-5.2
Australia	2.9	7.8	6.0	5.0	10.0	6.0	2.3	6.2	7.6	7.0	2.3	6.2
Taiwan [1]	9.0	6.4	6.9	6.6	6.3	2.4	3.7	7.4	3.3	5.6	1.3	-2.8
Thailand	5.2	3.7	12.0	9.1	9.9	8.0	2.1	-5.7	1.3	14.4	7.6	7.5
Japan	6.9	4.3	8.6	-2.5	-0.1	-0.4	1.8	-3.4	-6.8	-2.0	-0.7	-7.4
Korea, South	-0.4	7.6	9.4	7.7	8.5	7.5	5.9	-4.1	-5.1	18.3	7.4	7.0
Malaysia	-1.0	-5.1	2.5	3.8	4.4	2.5	-0.2	-5.8	-11.2	3.8	-1.0	-10.5
New Zealand	1.7	9.5	-5.2	18.2	18.7	11.8	4.5	-3.2	-	11.1	7.0	8.2

- Represents or rounds to zero. [1] See footnote 2, Table 1322.

Source: Foundation for International Business and Economic Research, New York, NY, *International Economic Indicators*, monthly.

Comparative International Statistics 853

No. 1337. Index of Industrial Production by Country: 1980 to 2002

[Annual averages of monthly data. Industrial production index measures output in the manufacturing, mining, and electric, gas and water utilities industries. Minus sign (-) indicates decrease]

Country	Index (1995=100)								Annual percent change				
	1980	1985	1990	1998	1999	2000	2001	2002	1997-98	1998-99	1999-00	2000-01	2001-02
OECD, total.....	(NA)	(NA)	(NA)	110.6	114.4	121.2	118.2	118.1	2.2	3.4	5.9	-2.5	-0.1
Australia.........	70.1	77.8	92.9	107.7	112.5	116.8	116.7	120.8	2.1	4.5	3.8	-0.1	3.5
Austria..........	70.2	76.6	92.3	116.2	123.2	134.1	135.2	135.4	8.6	6.0	8.8	0.8	0.1
Belgium [1].......	83.4	86.8	99.3	108.8	109.7	115.6	111.8	113.6	3.4	0.8	5.4	-3.3	1.6
Canada .... [1]	71.8	83.0	88.4	108.3	116.7	122.9	118.7	120.7	0.9	7.8	5.3	-3.4	1.7
Czech Republic [1]...	(X)	(X)	144.9	108.3	104.8	110.5	117.7	128.8	1.7	-3.2	5.4	6.5	9.4
Denmark.........	63.0	77.0	86.0	110.0	113.0	120.0	122.0	122.0	1.0	2.7	6.2	1.7	-
Finland..........	66.4	76.7	86.9	122.5	129.0	144.3	143.1	145.5	8.1	5.3	11.9	-0.8	1.7
France..........	89.5	89.5	100.4	110.0	112.4	116.3	117.3	116.2	5.7	2.2	3.5	0.9	-0.9
Germany	85.6	88.3	103.2	108.5	110.4	117.2	117.8	116.2	4.2	1.8	6.2	0.5	-1.4
Greece..........	92.6	99.2	101.9	109.8	114.1	114.7	116.3	116.8	7.1	3.9	0.5	(NA)	0.4
Hungary [1].......	116.7	128.1	113.8	129.1	142.4	168.3	174.3	178.8	12.5	10.3	18.2	3.6	2.6
Ireland..........	34.2	43.9	63.2	142.3	174.6	201.5	222.1	239.5	14.3	22.7	15.4	10.2	7.8
Italy............	77.2	73.9	93.2	102.9	102.9	107.5	106.2	104.8	1.1	-	4.5	-1.2	-1.3
Japan [1]........	69.9	82.8	103.2	99.0	99.8	105.4	97.8	96.4	-6.6	0.8	5.6	-7.2	-1.4
Korea, South [1].....	22.0	36.2	66.4	106.2	131.9	154.0	156.0	167.4	-7.2	24.2	16.8	1.3	7.3
Luxembourg	71.0	79.8	97.1	105.8	118.0	123.0	125.2	126.4	-0.1	11.5	4.2	1.8	1.0
Mexico [2]........	80.3	85.0	95.7	127.9	133.3	141.3	136.4	136.4	6.3	4.2	6.0	-3.5	-
Netherlands	78.7	83.1	90.6	105.1	106.8	110.6	112.1	109.8	-1.3	1.6	3.6	1.4	-2.1
New Zealand.....	74.0	85.0	87.0	105.0	101.0	105.0	105.0	109.0	-	-3.8	4.0	-	3.8
Norway..........	50.6	61.5	78.6	108.4	108.1	111.2	111.0	110.6	-0.6	-0.3	2.9	-0.2	-0.4
Poland..........	(X)	107.3	87.7	127.4	133.5	143.5	144.1	146.1	4.7	4.8	7.5	0.4	1.4
Portugal.........	62.1	71.7	97.0	114.1	117.6	115.3	118.8	118.3	5.6	3.1	-2.0	3.0	-0.4
Spain...........	80.1	82.7	96.6	111.4	114.2	119.2	117.5	117.8	5.5	2.5	4.4	-1.4	0.3
Sweden [3,4].....	73.0	80.5	88.0	112.1	115.6	122.2	120.9	120.5	4.2	3.1	5.7	-1.1	-0.3
Switzerland......	77.0	80.0	96.0	108.0	112.0	122.0	121.0	115.0	2.9	3.7	8.9	-0.8	-5.0
Turkey	38.2	57.2	81.3	120.5	116.0	124.0	113.2	123.8	1.3	-3.7	6.9	-8.7	9.4
United Kingdom...	76.8	83.0	94.1	102.8	104.1	105.9	103.5	100.0	0.7	1.3	1.7	-2.3	-3.4
United States.....	69.6	76.9	86.4	117.2	121.9	129.1	124.6	123.6	5.8	4.0	5.9	-3.5	-0.8

- Represents or rounds to zero.   NA Not available.   X Not applicable.   [1] Not adjusted for unequal number of working days in the month.   [2] Including construction.   [3] Mining and manufacturing.   [4] Annual figures correspond to official annual figures and differ from the average of the monthly figures.

Source: Organization for Economic Cooperation and Development, Paris, France, *Main Economic Indicators*, monthly (copyright).

No. 1338. Labor Productivity and Hours Worked by Country: 1990 to 2002

[Annual percent change for period shown. Data are derived from an annual database supported by the source. The Groningen Growth and Development Centre at the University of Groningen, Netherlands maintains the database. For OECD countries and Eastern Europe, estimates are based on gross domestic product per hour worked, converted at purchasing power parities for 1999. Hence, estimates expressed in U.S. dollars at the price level of 1999 are corrected for differences in relative price levels. Minus sign (-) indicates decrease]

Country	Labor productivity		Total hours worked	
	1990-1995	1995-2002	1990-1995	1995-2002
OECD, total [1]...................	1.7	1.8	0.3	0.8
OECD, excl. United States [1]...........	1.9	1.7	-0.1	0.6
European Union [2].................	2.5	1.3	-0.8	1.0
Australia.......................	2.2	2.2	1.0	1.4
Austria........................	1.8	2.4	0.3	-0.3
Belgium	2.4	2.2	-0.7	0.1
Canada	1.6	1.5	0.1	2.0
Czech Republic..................	-0.6	2.6	-0.3	-1.0
Denmark.......................	2.4	1.6	-0.4	0.6
Finland........................	2.8	2.6	-3.4	1.3
France........................	1.4	1.6	-0.4	0.7
Germany	3.5	1.7	-1.4	-0.2
Greece........................	0.6	3.2	0.7	0.4
Hungary	3.0	2.6	-5.2	1.2
Ireland........................	3.6	5.1	1.1	3.1
Italy..........................	2.3	0.7	-1.0	0.9
Japan	1.8	1.8	-0.4	-0.9
Mexico........................	-1.1	2.2	2.7	1.8
Netherlands	1.1	0.5	1.0	2.2
New Zealand....................	1.0	0.6	2.1	1.9
Norway........................	3.4	1.8	0.3	1.0
Poland........................	4.9	4.8	-2.6	-0.8
Portugal.......................	3.5	1.7	-1.8	1.3
South Korea	5.1	4.0	2.2	0.8
Spain.........................	2.3	-0.4	-0.7	3.8
Sweden	1.9	1.7	-1.3	0.8
Switzerland.....................	0.6	1.2	-0.6	0.2
Turkey	1.7	2.1	1.5	0.1
United Kingdom..................	2.6	1.5	-0.9	1.1
United States...................	1.1	1.9	1.2	1.4

[1] Excludes Luxembourg.   [2] European Union: Austria, Belgium, Denmark, Finland, France, Germany, Greece, Ireland, Italy, Netherlands, Portugal, Spain, Sweden, and United Kingdom.

Source: The Conference Board, New York, NY, *Performance 2002: Productivity, Employment, and Income in the World's Economies*, by Robert H. McGuckin and Bart van Ark, 2003 (copyright).

No. 1339. Patents by Country: 2001

[Includes only U.S. patents granted to residents of areas outside of the United States and its territories]

Country	Total [1]	Inventions	Designs	Country	Total [1]	Inventions	Designs
Total............	85,383	78,431	6,526	Sweden	1,933	1,741	185
				Switzerland	1,557	1,420	133
Japan............	34,890	33,223	1,546	Netherlands.......	1,494	1,332	101
Germany..........	11,892	11,259	588	Israel	1,031	970	45
Taiwan [2]........	6,544	5,371	1,168	Australia..........	1,030	875	126
France	4,456	4,041	396	Belgium	796	718	72
United Kingdom	4,355	3,965	370	Finland...........	769	732	37
Canada...........	4,063	3,606	439	Austria	632	589	41
Korea, South	3,763	3,538	216	Denmark..........	556	479	54
Italy	1,978	1,709	254	Other countries	3,644	2,863	755

[1] Includes patents for botanical plants and reissues.   [2] See footnote 2, Table 1322.

Source: U.S. Patent and Trademark Office, Technology Assessment and Forecast Database.

No. 1340. Annual Percent Changes in Consumer Prices by Country: 1995 to 2002

[Change from previous year. See text of this section for general comments concerning the data. For additional qualifications of the data for individual countries, see source. Minus sign (-) indicates decrease]

Country	1995	1999	2000	2001	2002	Country	1995	1999	2000	2001	2002
United States	2.8	2.2	3.4	2.8	1.6	Japan..............	-0.1	-0.3	-0.7	-0.7	-0.9
						Kenya..............	0.8	5.7	10.0	5.7	2.0
Argentina	3.4	-1.2	-0.9	-1.1	25.9	Korea, South	4.5	0.8	2.2	4.1	2.8
Australia	4.6	1.5	4.5	4.4	3.0	Malaysia	5.3	2.7	1.5	1.4	1.8
Austria	2.3	0.6	2.4	2.7	1.8	Mexico	35.0	16.6	9.5	6.4	5.0
Bangladesh	5.8	8.9	3.9	1.1	6.8	Netherlands.........	1.9	2.2	2.5	4.5	3.5
Belgium	1.5	1.1	2.5	2.5	1.6	Nigeria	72.8	4.8	14.5	13.0	12.9
Bolivia	10.2	2.2	4.6	1.6	0.9	Norway	2.5	2.3	3.1	3.0	1.3
Brazil	66.0	4.9	7.0	6.8	8.4	Pakistan	12.3	4.1	4.4	3.1	3.3
Canada..............	2.2	1.7	2.7	2.5	2.2	Peru................	11.1	3.5	3.8	2.0	0.2
Chile	8.2	3.3	3.8	3.6	2.5	Philippines...........	8.0	6.7	4.4	6.1	3.1
Colombia............	21.0	10.9	9.2	8.0	6.3	Portugal	4.1	2.3	2.8	4.4	3.5
Egypt	15.7	3.1	2.7	2.3	2.7	Romania	32.2	45.8	45.7	34.5	22.5
France	1.8	0.5	1.7	1.6	1.9	Russia	197.4	85.7	20.8	21.5	15.8
Germany............	1.8	0.6	1.9	2.5	1.3	South Africa.........	8.6	5.3	5.3	4.8	8.9
Ghana	59.5	12.4	25.2	32.9	14.8	Spain	4.7	2.3	3.4	3.6	3.1
Greece	8.9	2.6	3.1	3.4	3.6	Sri Lanka	7.7	4.7	6.2	14.2	9.6
Guatemala	8.4	4.9	6.0	7.6	8.0	Sweden	2.5	0.5	0.9	2.4	2.2
India................	10.2	4.7	4.0	3.7	4.4	Switzerland	1.8	0.7	1.6	1.0	0.6
Indonesia	9.4	20.3	4.5	12.0	11.5	Thailand	5.8	0.3	1.5	1.7	0.6
Iran	49.6	20.1	14.5	11.3	14.3	Turkey	88.1	64.9	54.9	54.4	45.0
Israel	10.0	5.2	1.1	1.1	5.6	United Kingdom	3.4	1.6	2.9	1.8	1.6
Italy	5.2	1.7	2.5	2.8	2.5	Venezuela...........	59.9	23.6	16.2	12.5	22.4

Source: International Monetary Fund, Washington, DC, *International Financial Statistics*, monthly (copyright).

No. 1341. Comparative Price Levels—Selected OECD Countries: 2003

[**As of May**. Example of data: An item that costs $1.00 in the United States would cost $1.42 (U.S. dollars) in Japan]

Country	United States (U.S. dollar)	Canada (Canadian dollar)	Mexico (Mexican peso)	Japan (yen)	France (euro)	Germany (euro)	Italy (euro)	United Kingdom (pound)
United States	100	109	140	71	91	94	102	91
Australia [1].........	92	101	130	65	84	87	94	84
Austria	105	114	147	74	95	99	107	95
Canada	92	100	129	65	84	87	94	83
Denmark..........	134	145	187	94	122	126	137	121
Finland............	125	136	175	88	114	118	128	113
France	110	120	154	78	100	104	112	100
Germany	106	115	149	75	97	100	108	96
Hungary	59	64	83	42	54	56	61	54
Ireland	126	137	176	89	114	118	128	114
Italy	98	106	137	69	89	92	100	89
Japan	142	154	198	100	129	133	145	128
Korea, South......	69	75	96	48	62	65	70	62
Mexico	71	78	100	50	65	67	73	65
Netherlands	113	123	158	80	102	106	115	102
New Zealand [1].....	85	92	119	60	77	80	87	77
Norway............	145	157	203	102	132	136	148	131
Poland............	56	61	79	40	51	53	57	51
Portugal	83	90	116	58	75	78	85	75
Spain.............	93	102	131	66	85	88	95	85
Sweden	127	138	178	90	116	120	130	115
Switzerland	144	156	201	101	131	135	147	130
Turkey	63	68	88	44	57	59	64	57
United Kingdom	110	120	155	78	100	104	113	100

[1] Estimates based on quarterly consumer prices.

Source: Organization for Economic Cooperation and Development, Paris, France, *Main Economic Indicators*, May 2003 (copyright).

Comparative International Statistics   855

No. 1342. Gross Public Debt, Expenditures, and Receipts by Country: 1990 to 2002

[Percent of nominal gross domestic product. 2002 data estimated. Expenditures cover current outlays plus net capital outlays. Receipts cover current receipts but exclude capital receipts. Nontax current receipts include operating surpluses of public enterprises, property income, fees, charges, fines, etc]

Country	Gross debt 1990	Gross debt 1995	Gross debt 2002	Expenditures 1990	Expenditures 1995	Expenditures 2002	Receipts 1990	Receipts 1995	Receipts 2002
United States [1]	49.9	58.9	44.2	36.5	36.4	35.6	32.1	33.3	32.2
Australia	10.7	27.3	6.0	36.0	38.8	36.0	34.2	35.0	35.9
Austria	37.5	50.5	49.8	53.1	57.3	51.9	50.6	52.0	51.3
Belgium [2]	116.8	123.2	95.8	53.4	52.8	50.2	46.6	48.5	50.2
Canada [2]	43.4	68.0	40.4	48.8	48.5	40.6	42.9	43.1	41.9
Czech Republic	(X)	(NA)	(NA)	(X)	60.4	45.3	(X)	48.0	40.8
Denmark	19.0	26.7	6.3	57.0	60.3	55.3	56.0	58.0	57.1
Finland	-35.4	-12.5	-44.5	48.8	59.4	49.2	53.9	55.5	54.0
France	17.5	38.9	39.7	50.7	55.2	54.0	48.6	49.7	50.9
Germany [3]	21.0	39.6	47.2	44.5	49.4	48.6	42.5	46.1	45.0
Greece	89.0	108.7	(NA)	50.5	49.4	46.3	34.7	39.3	45.1
Hungary	(NA)	(NA)	(NA)	(NA)	56.9	52.2	(NA)	49.3	43.8
Iceland	19.4	40.5	24.1	42.5	43.8	44.6	39.2	40.8	44.9
Ireland	92.4	80.0	(NA)	43.2	41.5	34.4	40.4	39.4	34.1
Italy	84.5	109.7	96.7	54.3	53.4	47.7	42.6	45.8	45.2
Japan [4]	24.8	24.8	71.7	32.1	36.1	38.6	34.1	31.4	31.4
Korea, South	-17.2	-18.0	-35.8	19.5	20.6	24.6	23.0	24.8	30.5
Netherlands	35.6	53.2	41.0	54.8	51.4	47.3	49.5	47.3	46.2
New Zealand	(NA)	35.5	19.5	(NA)	38.4	36.5	(NA)	41.3	37.8
Norway	-41.6	-32.6	-85.2	54.1	51.6	46.7	56.5	55.0	59.5
Portugal	(NA)	64.2	(NA)	42.1	45.0	46.1	35.5	39.6	43.5
Spain	31.8	49.2	39.0	43.4	45.0	39.8	39.6	38.4	39.8
Sweden	-7.6	25.2	-4.1	59.4	67.6	58.3	63.1	60.2	59.3
United Kingdom	15.1	36.9	28.7	42.2	44.6	40.9	40.7	38.9	39.6

NA Not available. X Not applicable. [1] Includes funded part of central government employee pension liabilities amounting to 8.3 percent of GDP in 1999. Expenditures data includes outlays net of surpluses of public enterprises. Receipts exclude the operating surpluses of public enterprises. [2] Includes funded government employee pension liabilities amounting to 19 percent of GDP in 1999. This overstates the Canadian debt position relative to countries that have large unfunded liabilities for such pensions which are not counted in those countries' debt figures. [3] Debt data include accounts of the Inherited Debt Fund from 1995 on. The 1995 outlays are net of the debt taken on this year from the Inherited Debt Funds. [4] Debt data include debt of the Japan Railway Settlement Corporation and the National Forest Special Account from 1998 on. The 1998 expenditures would have risen by 5.4 percentage points of GDP if account were taken of the assumption by the central government of the debt of these two entities. Receipts data includes deferred tax payments on postal savings accounts in 2002.

Source: Organization for Economic Cooperation and Development, Paris, France, OECD Economic Outlook, December 2002 (copyright).

No. 1343. Percent Distribution of Tax Receipts by Country: 1980 to 2000

Country	Total [1]	Income and profits taxes [2] Total [3]	Individual	Corporate	Social security contributions Total [4]	Employees	Employers	Taxes on goods and services [5] Total [3]	General consumption taxes [6]	Taxes on specific goods, services [7]
United States: 1980	100.0	49.8	39.1	10.8	21.9	9.2	11.9	17.6	7.0	8.3
1990	100.0	45.4	37.7	7.7	25.9	11.0	13.4	17.3	8.0	7.1
2000	100.0	50.9	42.4	8.5	23.3	10.2	11.9	15.7	7.5	6.3
Canada: 1980	100.0	46.6	34.1	11.6	10.5	3.7	6.6	32.6	11.5	13.0
1990	100.0	48.6	40.8	7.0	12.1	4.4	7.6	25.9	14.1	10.3
2000	100.0	49.0	36.8	11.1	14.3	5.7	8.2	24.4	14.4	8.5
France: 1980	100.0	16.8	11.6	5.1	42.7	11.1	28.4	30.4	21.1	8.4
1990	100.0	17.2	11.8	5.3	44.1	13.2	27.2	28.4	18.8	8.7
2000 [2]	100.0	25.0	18.0	7.0	36.1	8.9	24.9	25.8	16.9	8.2
Germany: 1980 [8]	100.0	35.1	29.6	5.5	34.3	15.3	18.4	27.1	16.6	9.3
1990	100.0	32.4	27.6	4.8	37.5	16.2	19.1	26.7	16.6	9.2
2000	100.0	30.1	25.3	4.8	39.0	17.2	19.2	28.1	18.4	8.8
Italy: 1980	100.0	31.1	23.1	7.8	38.0	6.9	28.4	26.5	15.6	9.7
1990	100.0	36.5	26.3	10.0	32.9	6.3	23.6	28.0	14.7	10.6
2000	100.0	33.2	25.7	7.5	28.5	5.4	19.8	28.4	15.8	10.0
Japan: 1980	100.0	46.1	24.3	21.8	29.1	10.2	14.8	16.3	-	14.1
1990	100.0	48.5	26.8	21.6	29.0	11.0	15.0	13.2	4.3	7.3
2000	100.0	34.1	20.6	13.5	36.5	14.2	18.6	18.9	8.9	7.8
Netherlands: 1980	100.0	32.8	26.3	6.6	38.1	15.7	17.8	25.2	15.8	7.3
1990	100.0	32.2	24.7	7.5	37.4	23.1	7.5	26.4	16.5	7.5
2000	100.0	25.0	14.9	10.1	38.9	19.5	11.4	29.0	17.3	8.8
Sweden: 1980	100.0	43.5	41.0	2.5	28.8	0.1	27.6	24.0	13.4	9.2
1990	100.0	41.6	38.5	3.1	27.2	0.1	26.0	25.0	14.9	9.2
2000	100.0	43.2	35.6	7.5	28.1	5.5	22.0	20.7	13.4	6.7
United Kingdom: 1980	100.0	37.8	29.4	8.4	16.7	6.4	10.1	29.2	14.7	13.3
1990	100.0	38.3	27.1	11.2	16.7	6.5	9.7	30.5	16.4	12.4
2000	100.0	39.0	29.2	9.8	16.4	6.7	9.4	32.3	18.4	12.4

- Represents zero. [1] Includes property taxes, employer payroll taxes other than social security contributions, and miscellaneous taxes, not shown separately. [2] Includes taxes on capital gains. [3] Includes other taxes not shown separately. [4] Includes contributions of self-employed not shown separately. [5] Taxes on the production, sales, transfer, leasing, and delivery of goods and services and rendering of services. [6] Primary value-added and sales taxes. [7] For example, excise taxes on alcohol, tobacco, and gasoline. [8] Data are for former West Germany.

Source: Organization for Economic Cooperation and Development, Paris, France, Revenue Statistics of OECD Member Countries, annual (copyright).

No. 1344. Household Tax Burden by Country: 2002

[Percent of gross earnings equivalent to the average production worker. The tax burden reflects income tax plus employee contributions less cash benefits]

Country	Single person without children	One earner family with two children	Country	Single person without children	One earner family with two children
Australia	23.6	14.7	Korea	8.7	8.1
Austria	28.6	9.0	Luxembourg	22.1	-3.6
Belgium	41.4	21.6	Mexico	3.6	3.6
Canada	25.7	15.1	Netherlands	28.7	17.2
Czech Republic	23.7	3.7	Norway	28.8	17.9
Denmark	43.1	30.5	Poland	31.0	25.0
Finland	31.7	23.2	Portugal	16.5	5.2
France	26.5	14.2	Slovak Republic	19.3	3.1
Germany	41.2	18.6	Spain	19.2	10.4
Greece	16.5	17.0	Sweden	30.4	21.0
Hungary	29.1	7.8	Switzerland	21.5	8.6
Ireland	16.4	-0.8	Turkey	30.0	30.0
Italy	28.1	12.2	United Kingdom	23.3	10.8
Japan	16.2	11.9	United States	24.3	11.3

Source: Organization for Economic Cooperation and Development, Paris, France, *Taxing Wages, 2001-2002*, (copyright).

No. 1345. Income Tax and Social Security Contributions as Percent of Labor Costs: 2000

[Data are for single individual at the income level of the average production worker]

Country	Labor costs [1] (dol.)	Total [2]	Income tax	Social security contributions Employee	Employer [3]
Belgium	42,216	56	21	11	25
Germany	38,945	52	18	17	17
Switzerland	36,194	29	9	10	10
Italy	33,340	47	14	7	25
Netherlands	36,017	45	7	25	14
Denmark	32,789	44	32	12	-
Canada	32,246	31	19	6	6
Norway	28,231	37	19	7	11
United States	33,283	31	17	7	7
Luxembourg	32,429	35	11	12	12
Austria	31,025	45	7	14	24
Sweden	31,678	50	19	5	25
Australia	31,731	23	23	-	-
Finland	31,215	47	21	6	21
United Kingdom	30,924	30	14	7	9
France	29,421	48	9	9	29
Japan	31,141	24	6	9	9
Ireland	26,234	29	14	5	11
Spain	24,655	38	9	5	23
Korea, South	33,730	17	2	6	8
Greece	18,852	36	2	12	22
Turkey	24,185	40	12	12	16
Czech Republic	17,832	43	8	9	26
Poland	14,100	43	5	21	17
Hungary	12,400	52	14	9	29
Mexico	9,291	15	1	1	13

- Represents or rounds to zero. [1] Adjusted for purchasing power parities, see text of this section. Labor costs include gross wages plus employers compulsory social security contributions. [2] Due to rounding total may differ one percentage point from aggregate columns for income tax and social security contributions. [3] Includes reported payroll taxes.
Source: Organization for Economic Cooperation and Development, Paris, France, *Taxing Wages, 2000-2001* (copyright).

No. 1346. Age of Withdrawal From Labor Force and Retirement Duration: 1999

[This table shows the median age at which people completely withdraw from the labor force. For example, half of Canadian men leave the labor force at age 62.4 or before and live another 18.2 years without working. A quarter of Canadian men leave the labor force before the age of 57.8 and another quarter after the age of 66.5.]

Country	A quarter of the population Withdraws earlier than age Men / Women	Never withdraws or later than age Men / Women	Median age of withdrawal Men / Women	Duration of complete retirement Men / Women
Nine-country average	58.1 / 57.2	67.0 / 65.1	62.3 / 61.1	17.8 / 23.0
Canada	57.8 / 56.8	66.5 / 65.2	62.4 / 60.8	18.2 / 23.5
Finland	56.0 / 56.8	63.0 / 62.5	59.6 / 59.8	18.9 / 23.7
Germany [1]	57.4 / 57.8	63.9 / 62.4	60.3 / 60.1	18.8 / 23.2
Italy	54.5 / 53.4	63.4 / 61.9	58.8 / 57.9	20.7 / 26.2
Japan	62.7 / 59.1	77.7 / 73.2	68.5 / 64.7	14.9 / 22.3
Netherlands [1]	57.8 / 56.9	64.1 / 62.4	60.4 / 59.8	18.2 / 23.2
Sweden	59.9 / 59.1	66.7 / 65.3	63.7 / 62.7	17.5 / 22.0
United Kingdom	57.8 / 57.2	66.5 / 64.5	62.6 / 60.4	16.8 / 22.3
United States	59.4 / 59.0	71.4 / 68.8	64.6 / 63.4	16.3 / 20.4

[1] 1998 data.
Source: Organization for Economic Cooperation and Development, Paris, France, *Ageing and Income, 2001* (copyright).

No. 1347. Civilian Labor Force, Employment, and Unemployment by Country: 1980 to 2002

[106,940 represents 106,940,000. Data based on U.S. labor force definitions (see source) except that minimum age for population base varies as follows: United States, Canada, France, Sweden, and United Kingdom, 16 years; Australia, Japan, Netherlands, Germany, and Italy (beginning 1995), 15 years; and Italy (1980 and 1990) 14 years]

Year	United States	Canada	Australia	Japan	France	Germany[1]	Italy	Netherlands	Sweden	United Kingdom
Civilian labor force (1,000):										
1980	106,940	11,707	6,693	55,740	22,930	27,260	21,120	5,870	4,312	26,520
1990	[2]125,840	14,044	8,440	63,050	24,290	29,410	[2]22,670	[2]6,660	[2]4,597	28,730
1995	[2]132,304	14,517	8,995	65,990	24,750	38,980	22,460	7,200	4,460	28,040
2000	[2]142,583	15,789	9,678	66,990	26,050	39,750	23,340	8,130	4,489	28,780
2001	143,734	16,027	9,817	66,870	26,340	39,780	23,540	8,290	4,530	28,870
2002	144,863	16,475	9,964	[3]66,240	(NA)	(NA)	23,750	(NA)	[3]4,542	(NA)
Labor force participation rate:[4]										
1980	63.8	64.9	62.1	62.6	57.5	54.7	48.2	55.4	66.9	62.5
1990	[2]66.5	67.3	64.7	62.6	56.0	55.3	47.2	56.3	67.4	64.1
1995	[2]66.6	64.9	64.6	62.9	55.4	57.1	47.1	58.7	64.1	62.3
2000	[2]67.1	65.9	64.7	62.0	56.5	57.4	48.1	64.4	63.8	62.8
2001	66.8	66.0	64.7	61.6	56.8	57.2	48.3	65.4	63.7	62.7
2002	66.6	66.8	[3]64.7	[3]60.8	(NA)	(NA)	48.6	(NA)	[3]63.6	(NA)
Civilian employment (1,000):										
1980	99,303	10,857	6,284	54,600	21,440	26,490	20,200	5,520	4,226	24,670
1990	[2]118,793	12,961	7,877	61,710	22,080	27,950	21,080	6,270	4,513	26,740
1995	[2]124,900	13,271	8,256	63,890	21,950	35,780	19,820	6,730	4,056	25,600
2000	[2]136,891	14,827	9,068	63,790	23,670	36,540	20,840	7,900	4,229	27,200
2001	136,933	14,997	9,157	63,470	24,100	36,590	21,270	8,090	4,303	27,400
2002	136,485	15,325	9,334	[3]62,650	(NA)	(NA)	21,580	(NA)	[3]4,308	(NA)
Employment-population ratio:[5]										
1980	59.2	60.2	58.3	61.3	53.8	53.1	46.1	52.1	65.6	58.1
1990	[2]62.8	62.2	60.4	61.3	50.9	52.6	43.9	53.0	66.1	59.6
1995	[2]62.9	59.4	59.2	60.9	49.1	52.4	41.5	54.9	58.3	56.9
2000	[2]64.4	62.1	60.6	59.0	51.4	52.7	42.9	62.6	60.1	59.4
2001	63.7	61.9	60.4	58.4	51.9	52.6	43.6	63.9	60.5	59.5
2002	62.7	62.4	[3]60.6	[3]57.5	(NA)	(NA)	44.1	(NA)	[3]60.3	(NA)
Unemployment rate:										
1980	7.1	7.3	6.1	2.0	6.5	2.8	4.4	6.0	2.0	7.0
1990	[2]5.6	7.7	6.7	2.1	9.1	5.0	7.0	5.9	1.8	6.9
1995	5.6	8.6	8.2	3.2	11.3	8.2	11.8	6.7	9.1	8.7
2000	[2]4.0	6.1	6.3	4.8	9.1	8.1	10.7	2.7	5.8	5.5
2001	4.7	6.4	6.7	5.1	8.5	8.0	9.6	2.4	5.0	5.1
2002	5.8	7.0	6.3	[3]5.4	[3]8.8	[3]8.4	9.1	(NA)	[3]5.2	[3]5.2
Under 25 years old	12.0	12.8	12.6	[3]10.0	(NA)	(NA)	(NA)	(NA)	(NA)	(NA)
Teenagers[6]	16.5	17.0	16.7	[3]13.0	(NA)	(NA)	(NA)	(NA)	(NA)	(NA)
20 to 24 years old	9.7	10.3	9.7	[3]9.3	(NA)	(NA)	(NA)	(NA)	(NA)	(NA)
25 years old and over	4.6	5.9	4.8	[3]4.9	(NA)	(NA)	(NA)	(NA)	(NA)	(NA)

NA Not available. [1] Unified Germany for 1991 onward. Prior to 1991, data relate to the former West Germany. [2] Break in series. Data not comparable with prior years. [3] Preliminary. [4] Civilian labor force as a percent of the civilian working age population. Germany and Japan include the institutionalized population as part of the working age population. [5] Civilian employment as a percent of the civilian working age population. Germany and Japan include the institutionalized population as part of the working age population. [6] 16-to 19-year-olds in the United States, Canada, France, Sweden, and the United Kingdom; 15-to 19-year-olds in Australia, Japan, Germany, and Italy.
Source: U.S. Bureau of Labor Statistics, *Comparative Civilian Labor Force Statistics, Ten Countries, 1959-2002*, April 2003, and *Monthly Labor Review*.

No. 1348. Percent of Persons 15 to 24 Years Old Not in Education or at Work by Age Group and Sex: 2001

[Represents those persons not in education and either unemployed or not in the labor force]

Country	15 to 19 years old			20 to 24 years old		
	Total	Male	Female	Total	Male	Female
Australia	7.6	7.9	7.2	13.9	11.4	16.5
Belgium	6.3	6.0	6.5	13.0	10.9	15.2
Canada	5.9	6.7	5.0	14.3	14.4	14.2
Czech Republic	6.9	6.4	7.3	18.0	12.7	23.7
Denmark	3.7	4.7	2.7	6.5	3.8	9.3
Finland	8.0	12.0	3.7	14.4	16.0	12.9
France	3.4	3.4	3.5	13.4	10.9	15.8
Germany	5.1	4.9	5.3	16.4	14.3	18.7
Greece	7.5	5.6	9.6	23.3	17.7	28.4
Hungary	8.4	8.8	7.9	20.2	15.6	24.5
Italy	12.2	11.8	12.5	25.6	23.9	27.3
Luxembourg	1.8	1.6	2.0	9.0	7.2	10.8
Mexico	17.9	7.2	28.3	27.1	5.6	46.1
Netherlands[1]	3.8	4.1	3.4	8.1	5.1	11.2
Poland	5.8	6.3	5.3	27.1	25.6	28.5
Portugal	7.7	5.5	10.0	10.7	8.3	13.0
Spain	9.0	8.6	9.5	14.3	10.7	17.9
Sweden	5.2	6.4	3.7	10.2	10.2	10.1
Switzerland	6.2	5.7	6.7	8.4	6.9	-
United States[1]	7.0	6.8	8.9	14.4	10.5	19.0

- Represents zero. [1] Data for 2000.
Source: Organization for Economic Cooperation and Development, Paris, France, *Education at a Glance 2002* (copyright).

No. 1349. Unemployment Rates by Country: 1995 to 2002

[Annual averages. The standardized unemployment rates shown here are calculated as the number of unemployed persons as a percentage of the civilian labor force. The unemployed are persons of working age who, in the reference period, are without work, available for work and have taken specific steps to find work]

Country	1995	2000	2001	2002	Country	1995	2000	2001	2002
OECD, total	7.5	6.3	6.5	6.9	Ireland	12.3	4.3	3.9	4.4
European Union [1]	10.7	7.8	7.4	7.6	Italy	11.9	10.4	9.4	9.0
					Japan	3.1	4.7	5.0	5.4
United States	5.6	4.0	4.7	5.8	Korea, South	(NA)	4.3	3.9	(NA)
Australia	8.6	6.3	6.7	6.3	Luxembourg	2.9	2.3	2.0	2.4
Austria	3.9	3.7	3.6	4.3	Netherlands	6.9	2.8	2.4	2.7
Belgium	9.9	6.9	6.7	7.3	New Zealand	6.3	6.0	5.3	5.2
Canada	9.5	6.8	7.2	7.7	Norway	5.0	3.4	3.6	3.9
Czech Republic	(NA)	8.7	8.0	7.3	Poland	(NA)	16.4	18.5	19.9
Denmark	7.2	4.4	4.3	4.5	Portugal	7.3	4.1	4.1	5.1
Finland	16.2	9.7	9.1	9.1	Spain	22.9	11.3	10.6	11.4
France	11.7	9.3	8.5	8.7	Sweden	8.8	5.6	4.9	4.9
Germany	8.2	7.8	7.8	8.2	Switzerland	3.5	2.6	2.5	(NA)
Hungary	(NA)	6.3	5.6	5.6	United Kingdom	8.7	5.4	5.0	5.1

NA Not available. [1] See footnote 4, Table 1334.

Source: Organization for Economic Cooperation and Development, Paris, France, *Main Economic Indicators*, April 2003 and earlier releases.

No. 1350. Female Labor Force Participation Rates by Country: 1980 to 2000

[In percent. Female labor force of all ages divided by female population 15-64 years old]

Country	1980	1990	1995	2000	Country	1980	1990	1995	2000
Australia	52.7	62.1	64.8	66.4	Korea, South	(NA)	51.2	53.2	54.3
Austria	48.7	55.4	62.3	62.2	Luxembourg	39.9	50.7	58.0	68.8
Belgium	47.0	52.4	56.1	59.2	Mexico	33.7	(NA)	40.1	42.4
Canada	57.8	67.6	67.6	70.4	Netherlands	35.5	[1]53.1	[1]59.0	65.2
Czech Republic	(X)	69.1	[1]65.4	64.3	New Zealand	44.6	[1]63.0	63.3	67.6
Denmark	(NA)	78.5	73.6	75.9	Norway	62.3	71.2	72.4	76.3
Finland	70.1	73.8	70.3	72.2	Poland	(NA)	(NA)	61.1	59.7
France	54.4	57.8	59.4	62.0	Portugal	54.3	62.9	62.4	67.2
Germany [2]	52.8	56.7	61.7	64.0	Slovak Republic	(NA)	(NA)	(NA)	63.0
Greece	33.0	43.6	45.9	50.2	Spain	32.2	41.2	45.1	50.7
Hungary	(NA)	(NA)	50.5	52.5	Sweden	74.1	[1]80.4	76.1	75.0
Iceland	(NA)	65.6	81.9	82.8	Switzerland	54.1	65.7	[1]67.8	70.6
Ireland	36.3	43.8	47.8	56.2	Turkey	(NA)	36.7	34.2	26.9
Italy	39.6	45.9	[1]43.3	46.8	United Kingdom	58.3	66.5	66.6	67.8
Japan	54.8	60.3	62.2	64.2	United States	59.7	[1]68.5	70.7	71.7

NA Not available. X Not applicable. [1] Break in series. Data not comparable with prior years. [2] Prior to 1991 data are for former West Germany.

Source: Organization for Economic Cooperation and Development, Paris, France, *OECD in Figures*, annual (copyright).

No. 1351. Civilian Employment-Population Ratio: 1980 to 2002

[Civilian employment as a percent of the civilian working age population. See headnote, Table 1347]

Country	Women 1980	Women 1990	Women 1995	Women 2001	Women 2002	Men 1980	Men 1990	Men 1995	Men 2001	Men 2002
United States	47.7	[1]54.3	55.6	57.0	56.3	72.0	[1]72.0	70.8	70.9	69.7
Canada	46.8	54.1	52.8	56.2	56.9	74.0	70.6	66.2	67.9	68.2
Australia	41.9	49.6	50.5	52.8	[2]53.1	75.1	71.4	68.2	68.0	[2]68.2
Japan	45.7	48.0	47.7	46.2	[2]45.4	77.9	75.4	75.0	71.5	[2]70.4
France	40.3	41.5	41.6	45.0	(NA)	68.9	61.3	57.6	59.6	(NA)
Germany [3]	38.9	40.9	42.7	44.8	(NA)	69.6	65.6	63.1	61.1	(NA)
Italy	27.9	29.2	28.0	31.6	32.2	66.0	62.0	60.0	65.5	57.2
Netherlands	31.0	39.4	44.1	54.0	(NA)	74.1	67.0	65.9	74.0	(NA)
Sweden	58.0	61.8	54.7	56.8	[2]56.8	73.6	70.6	62.1	64.5	[2]64.0
United Kingdom	44.8	49.8	49.8	52.7	(NA)	72.8	70.3	64.6	66.8	(NA)

NA Not available. [1] Break in series. Data not comparable with previous years. [2] Preliminary. [3] Unified Germany for 1991 onward. Prior to 1991, data relate to the former West Germany.

Source: U.S. Bureau of Labor Statistics, *Comparative Civilian Labor Force Statistics, Ten Countries, 1959-2002*, April 2003, and *Monthly Labor Review*. Also see <http://stats.bls.gov/fls/flslforc.pdf>.

No. 1352. Civilian Employment by Industry and Country: 1990 and 2002

[118,793 represents 118,793,000. Data based on U.S. labor force definitions except that minimum age for population base varies as follows: United States, Canada, France, Sweden, and United Kingdom, 16 years; Australia, Germany, Italy, Japan, 15 years; and Italy (1990), 14 years. Industries based on International Standard Industrial Classification; see text of this section]

Industry	United States	Canada	Australia	Japan	France	Germany [1]	Italy	Sweden	United Kingdom
TOTAL EMPLOYMENT (1,000)									
1990, total	[2]118,793	13,084	7,877	61,710	22,081	27,952	21,080	4,501	26,818
Agriculture, forestry, fishing [3]	[2]3,394	559	441	4,270	1,262	965	1,879	178	573
Industry [4]	[2]29,834	3,063	1,879	20,890	6,344	10,875	6,842	1,268	[5]8,128
Manufacturing	[2]21,346	2,053	1,184	15,010	(NA)	8,839	4,755	943	[5]5,971
Services [6]	[2]85,565	9,462	5,557	36,550	14,475	16,112	12,355	3,056	18,117
2002, total	136,485	15,412	9,334	[7]62,650	(NA)	(NA)	(NA)	(NA)	(NA)
Agriculture, forestry, fishing [3]	3,479	433	406	[7]2,800	(NA)	(NA)	(NA)	(NA)	(NA)
Industry [4]	28,332	3,378	1,919	[7]18,360	(NA)	(NA)	(NA)	(NA)	(NA)
Manufacturing	18,147	2,326	1,123	[7]12,180	(NA)	(NA)	(NA)	(NA)	(NA)
Services [6]	104,674	11,601	7,010	[7]41,490	(NA)	(NA)	(NA)	(NA)	(NA)
PERCENT DISTRIBUTION									
1990, total	[2]100.0	100.0	100.0	100.0	100.0	100.0	100.0	100.0	100.0
Agriculture, forestry, fishing [3]	[2]2.9	4.3	5.6	6.9	5.7	3.5	8.9	4.0	2.1
Industry [4]	[2]25.1	23.4	23.9	33.9	29.0	38.9	32.5	28.2	30.3
Manufacturing	[2]18.0	15.7	15.0	24.3	(NA)	31.6	22.6	20.9	[5]22.3
Services [6]	[2]72.0	72.3	70.5	59.2	65.3	57.6	58.6	67.9	67.6
2002, total	100.0	100.0	100.0	100.0	(NA)	(NA)	(NA)	(NA)	(NA)
Agriculture, forestry, fishing [3]	2.5	2.8	4.3	[7]4.5	(NA)	(NA)	(NA)	(NA)	(NA)
Industry [4]	20.8	21.9	20.6	[7]29.3	(NA)	(NA)	(NA)	(NA)	(NA)
Manufacturing	13.3	15.1	12.0	[7]19.4	(NA)	(NA)	(NA)	(NA)	(NA)
Services [6]	76.7	75.3	75.1	[7]66.2	(NA)	(NA)	(NA)	(NA)	(NA)

NA Not available. [1] Data for 1990 are for former West Germany (prior to unification); later data are for unified Germany. [2] Break in series. [3] Includes hunting. [4] Includes mining and construction. [5] Includes mining. [6] Transportation, communication, public utilities, trade, finance, public administration, private household services, and miscellaneous services. [7] Preliminary.

Source: U.S. Bureau of Labor Statistics, *Comparative Civilian Labor Force Statistics, Ten Countries, 1959-2002*, April 2003 and unpublished data.

No. 1353. World Food Production by Commodity: 1990 to 2002

[In millions of metric tons (1,768.8 represents 1,768,800,000)]

Commodity	1990	1995	1996	1997	1998	1999	2000	2001	2002
Grains, total	1,768.8	1,712.2	1,870.9	1,880.8	1,872.7	1,871.6	1,839.8	1,859.7	1,863.7
Wheat	588.0	538.4	582.0	610.2	589.7	586.2	583.9	579.6	580.7
Coarse grains	828.7	802.9	908.5	883.8	888.9	876.1	858.1	882.8	902.7
Corn	482.5	517.2	592.0	574.9	605.8	607.3	588.3	598.7	594.0
Rice, milled	352.0	370.9	380.4	386.8	394.1	409.3	397.8	397.3	380.3
Oils	58.1	73.1	73.7	75.2	80.5	86.0	89.5	91.4	92.2
Soybeans	104.1	124.9	132.2	158.1	159.8	159.9	175.1	184.3	194.0
Rapeseed	25.1	34.4	31.5	33.2	35.9	42.5	37.6	36.1	32.0
Pulses [1]	58.3	55.6	54.0	55.0	56.3	57.2	54.9	52.5	54.2
Vegetables and melons [1]	462.1	560.5	594.0	609.6	634.7	683.4	733.9	753.3	772.7
Fruits [1]	351.6	406.5	425.2	440.9	432.7	457.0	468.3	468.3	471.4
Nuts [1]	4.7	5.6	6.1	6.4	6.4	6.7	7.0	7.0	7.4
Beef and pork	117.2	124.2	117.9	123.3	128.2	131.4	131.4	132.0	135.7
Poultry	37.4	40.6	43.5	43.0	44.8	48.1	50.6	52.5	54.1
Milk	441.3	(NA)	(NA)	370.1	373.7	378.1	382.4	384.4	389.8

[1] Data from Food and Agriculture Organization of the United Nations, Rome, Italy.

Source: U.S. Dept. of Agriculture, Economic Research Service, *Agricultural Outlook*, monthly.

No. 1354. Fisheries—Commercial Catch by Country: 1990 to 2000

[In thousands of metric tons, live weight (97,854 represents 97,854,000). Catch of fish, crustaceans, mollusks (including weight of shells). Does not include marine mammals and aquatic plants]

Country	1990	1995	1999	2000	Country	1990	1995	1999	2000
World [1]	97,854	116,042	126,651	130,434	Thailand	2,786	3,573	3,621	3,631
China [2]	12,095	28,418	40,030	41,568	Norway	1,745	2,803	3,096	3,191
Japan	10,354	6,787	5,961	5,752	Korea, South	1,745	2,688	2,423	2,146
India	3,794	4,906	5,592	5,689	Philippines	2,210	2,222	2,201	2,281
United States	5,868	5,638	5,228	5,174	Iceland	1,508	1,616	1,740	1,986
Russia	7,808	4,374	4,210	4,048	Vietnam	960	1,394	1,853	1,952
Indonesia	3,044	4,139	4,736	4,929	Denmark	1,518	2,044	1,448	1,578
Peru	6,875	8,943	8,437	10,662	Bangladesh	848	1,173	1,579	1,661
Chile	5,195	7,591	5,325	4,692	Spain	1,380	1,391	1,511	1,289
					Mexico	1,401	1,355	1,251	1,368

[1] Includes other countries, not shown separately.   [2] See footnote 2, Table 1322.

Source: U.S. National Oceanic and Atmospheric Administration, National Marine Fisheries Service, *Fisheries of the United States*, annual. Data from Food and Agriculture Organization of the United Nations, Rome, Italy.

No. 1355. Meat Production by Type and Country: 2000 to 2001

[In thousands of metric tons (48,983 represents 48,983,000). Carcass weight basis for beef, veal, and pork. Excludes offals and rabbit]

Country	Beef and veal 2000	2001, prel.	Country	Pork [1] 2000	2001, prel.	Country	Poultry meat 2000	2001, prel.
World [2]	49,983	48,889	World [2]	81,386	83,155	World [2]	45,800	47,618
United States	12,196	11,890	China [3]	40,314	41,845	United States	13,703	14,033
European Union	7,462	6,896	European Union	17,585	17,419	European Union	6,654	6,822
Brazil	6,520	6,895	United States	8,597	8,691	Brazil	5,980	6,567
China [3]	5,328	5,488	Brazil	2,010	2,230	China [3]	5,050	5,200
Argentina	2,880	2,680	Canada	1,638	1,729	Mexico	1,936	2,067
Australia	1,988	2,052	Russia	1,500	1,560	India	1,080	1,250
Mexico	1,900	1,925	Poland	1,620	1,547	Thailand	1,070	1,230
India	1,700	1,770	Japan	1,269	1,245	Japan	1,091	1,074
Russia	1,840	1,760	Korea, South	1,004	1,077	Canada	877	927
Canada	1,246	1,250	Mexico	1,035	1,065	Argentina	870	870

[1] Includes edible pork fat, but excludes lard and inedible greases (except United States).   [2] Includes other countries, not shown separately.   [3] See footnote 2, Table 1322.

Source: U.S. Dept. of Agriculture, National Agricultural Statistics Service, *Agricultural Statistics*, annual.

No. 1356. Meat Consumption by Type and Country: 2001 to 2002

[In thousand metric tons (12,351 represents 12,351,000). Carcass weight basis for beef, veal, and pork. Broiler (chicken 16 week-old) weight based on ready to cook equivalent]

Country	Beef and veal 2001 [1]	2002 [1]	Country	Pork 2001 [1]	2002 [1]	Country	Poultry meat 2001 [1]	2002 [1]
United States	12,351	12,739	China [2]	41,764	42,835	United States	11,557	12,273
European Union [3]	6,459	7,422	European Union [3]	16,239	16,315	China [2]	9,262	9,555
Brazil	6,191	6,437	United States	8,388	8,684	European Union [3]	6,522	6,410
China [2]	5,448	5,586	Russian	2,119	2,429	Brazil	5,326	5,767
Russia	2,404	2,465	Japan	2,268	2,362	Mexico	2,308	2,452
Mexico	2,341	2,421	Brazil	1,919	1,975	Japan	1,797	1,809
Argentina	2,515	2,370	Poland	1,487	1,580	Russia	1,588	1,697
India	1,400	1,410	Mexico	1,305	1,345	Canada	927	944
Japan	1,371	1,297	South Korea	1,159	1,206	Thailand	805	915
Canada	968	991	Philippines	1,073	1,105	South Korea	494	525
Australia	654	714	Canada	1,087	1,087	Poland	448	483
Colombia	672	693	Taiwan	976	932	Hong Kong [2]	291	255

[1] Preliminary data.   [2] Hong Kong & China data series has been revised to more accurately reflect actual demand and not just transshipments.   [3] See footnote 3, Table 1334.

Source: U.S. Department of Agriculture, Foreign Agricultural Service, *Livestock and Poultry: World Markets and Trade*, annual. Also see <http://www.fas.usda.gov/dlp/circular/2003/03-03LP/toc.htm>.

No. 1357. World Crop Production Summary: 2001 to 2003

[In millions of metric tons, (581.08 represents $581,080,000), except as indicated]

Commodity	Unit	World	North America			Europe			Asia				South America		Selected other		
			United States	Canada	Mexico	European Union	Oth. W. Europe	Eastern Europe	China	India	Indonesia	Pakistan	Argentina	Brazil	Australia	South Africa	Turkey
Wheat:																	
2001-2002	Mil. metric tons	581.08	53.26	20.57	3.27	91.20	0.77	34.92	93.87	69.68	-	19.02	15.50	3.25	24.85	2.49	15.50
2002-2003 prel.	Mil. metric tons	563.04	43.99	15.69	3.18	103.32	0.89	30.56	90.29	71.81	-	18.23	12.30	2.94	9.39	2.32	16.80
Coarse grains:																	
2001-2002	Mil. metric tons	892.31	261.86	22.60	27.17	106.67	1.54	51.02	122.27	34.68	6.00	1.83	18.72	36.80	12.56	10.45	9.52
2002-2003 prel.	Mil. metric tons	867.95	245.04	19.59	25.77	106.13	1.69	50.31	129.15	25.66	6.10	1.85	19.44	46.95	5.30	9.61	10.12
Rice (Milled):[1]																	
2001-2002	Mil. metric tons	398.61	6.74	-	0.19	1.62	(Z)	0.04	124.31	93.08	33.09	3.88	0.41	7.12	0.91	-	0.23
2002-2003 prel.	Mil. metric tons	379.64	6.51	-	0.10	1.71	(Z)	0.04	122.18	75.70	33.20	4.23	0.41	7.25	0.28	-	0.23
Total grains[1]:																	
2001-2002	Mil. metric tons	1,872.01	321.86	43.17	30.62	199.49	2.31	85.98	340.45	197.44	39.09	24.73	34.63	47.17	38.33	12.94	25.25
2002-2003 prel.	Mil. metric tons	1,810.62	295.54	35.28	29.05	211.16	2.58	80.90	341.62	173.17	39.30	24.30	32.15	57.13	14.96	11.93	27.15
Oilseeds[2]:																	
2001-2002	Mil. metric tons	324.45	89.83	6.66	0.35	13.88	0.05	5.38	52.19	24.05	1.93	3.99	34.31	44.98	2.97	1.31	1.90
2002-2003 prel.	Mil. metric tons	327.85	83.25	6.08	0.29	13.54	0.07	5.55	52.67	18.83	1.83	3.80	39.52	54.14	1.32	0.95	2.32
Cotton:																	
2001-2002	Mil. 480 lb. bales	98.46	20.30	-	0.43	2.58	-	0.03	24.40	12.30	0.06	8.30	0.30	3.52	3.20	0.08	3.98
2002-2003 prel.	Mil. 480 lb. bales	87.99	17.21	-	0.19	2.16	-	0.03	22.60	10.60	0.04	7.80	0.29	3.80	1.70	0.07	4.13

- Indicates no reported or insignificant production. Z Less than 5,000 metric tons. [1] Includes wheat, coarse grains, and rice (milled) shown above. [2] Includes soybean, cottonseed, peanut (inshell), sunflowerseed, rapeseed for individual countries. Copra and palm kernel are added to world totals.

Source: U.S. Department of Agriculture, Foreign Agricultural Service, World Agricultural Production, August 2003. Also see <http://www.fas.usda.gov/waparc.html>.

No. 1358. Wheat, Rice, and Corn—Exports and Imports of Leading Countries: 1995 to 2002

[In thousands of metric tons (33,778 represents 33,778,000). Wheat data are for trade year beginning in July of year shown; rice data are for calendar year; corn data are for trade year beginning in October of year shown. Countries listed are the ten leading exporters or importers in 2002]

Leading exporters	Exports 1995	Exports 2000	Exports 2002	Leading importers	Imports 1995	Imports 2000	Imports 2002
WHEAT				**WHEAT**			
United States	33,778	28,904	23,814	European Union [1]	2,545	3,159	10,500
European Union [1]	13,242	15,225	15,500	Brazil	5,809	7,201	7,200
Russia	206	696	10,000	Egypt	5,932	6,050	6,200
Ukraine	1,343	78	8,500	Japan	6,101	5,885	5,800
Argentina	4,483	11,272	8,100	Algeria	3,782	5,600	4,800
Canada	16,342	17,316	8,000	Indonesia	3,632	4,069	4,000
Australia	13,311	15,930	7,000	Korea	2,554	3,127	3,800
Kazakhstan	4,279	3,668	5,000	Philippines	1,980	3,050	3,300
India	1,500	1,569	5,000	Mexico	1,581	3,066	3,300
China [2]	496	623	1,500	Morocco	2,336	3,632	3,000
RICE				**RICE**			
Thailand	5,281	7,521	7,750	Indonesia	1,081	1,500	3,250
Vietnam	3,040	3,528	4,250	Nigeria	300	1,250	1,822
India	3,700	1,685	4,250	Iran	1,574	765	1,500
United States	2,694	2,590	3,349	Iraq	234	959	1,100
China [2]	265	1,847	2,250	Philippines	975	1,410	1,000
Pakistan	1,632	2,429	1,000	Saudi Arabia	618	992	900
Burma	265	670	1,000	European Union [1]	819	926	900
Uruguay	600	736	625	Senegal	500	502	816
Egypt	338	705	400	South Africa	448	523	800
Australia	550	617	350	Brazil	770	654	725
CORN				**CORN**			
United States	56,589	49,313	44,452	Japan	15,976	16,340	16,000
China [2]	168	7,276	12,000	Korea	8,963	8,743	9,000
Argentina	7,494	9,676	10,000	Mexico	6,433	5,928	6,500
Brazil	267	6,261	2,000	Egypt	2,257	5,268	5,200
Hungary	120	730	1,800	Taiwan [2]	5,734	4,924	4,500
South Africa	2,650	1,281	1,200	Canada	823	2,746	4,000
Ukraine	58	397	600	European Union [1]	8,972	5,714	5,000
Canada	604	122	400	Malaysia	2,309	2,588	2,400
Serbia	280	50	300	Colombia	1,430	1,857	1,900
Paraguay	124	465	300	Algeria	488	1,600	1,650

[1] See footnote 3, Table 1334. [2] See footnote 2, Table 1322.
Source: U.S. Department of Agriculture, Economic Research Service, unpublished data from the PS&D (Production, supply and distribution) database.

No. 1359. Unmanufactured Tobacco and Cigarettes—Selected Countries: 1995 to 2002

[5,546 represents 5,546,000. Tobacco is on dry weight basis]

Country	Unmanufactured tobacco (1,000 metric tons) 1995	2000	2002	Country	Cigarettes (bil. pieces) 1995	2000	2002
PRODUCTION				**PRODUCTION**			
World, total	5,546	6,097	6,048	World, total	5,599	5,469	5,464
China [1]	2,083	2,295	2,366	China [1]	1,735	1,699	1,710
India	528	599	592	United States	746	595	580
Brazil	324	493	551	Russia	141	341	375
United States	513	408	363	Japan	263	258	241
Indonesia	(NA)	37	145	Indonesia	186	232	230
EXPORTS				Germany	221	207	218
World, total	1,767	1,962	2,098	Turkey	100	128	129
Brazil	256	342	476				
United States	209	180	153	**EXPORTS**			
China [1]	(NA)	113	141	World, total	987	907	929
Malawi	99	101	124	United States	231	148	136
India	(NA)	123	120	Germany	85	91	110
IMPORTS				Netherlands	82	102	110
World, total	1,781	2,011	2,472	United Kingdom	85	111	102
China [1]	(NA)	57	388	Singapore	50	59	59
Russia	148	285	308	Hong Kong	74	28	29
Germany	210	263	257	Japan	(NA)	14	25
United States	199	197	264	Switzerland	(NA)	23	23
United Kingdom	141	108	119	**IMPORTS**			
CONSUMPTION				World, total	668	618	624
World, total	6,305	5,135	6,594	Japan	72	83	83
China [1]	2,209	1,235	2,773	France	51	68	64
India	464	474	481	Singapore	38	49	49
United States	699	499	463	Germany	(NA)	34	40
Russia	142	301	309	Hong Kong	59	24	22
Germany	(NA)	175	180	Taiwan [1]	(NA)	20	21
				Korea, South	(NA)	9	20

NA Not available. [1] See footnote 2, Table 1322.
Source: U.S. Dept. of Agriculture, Foreign Agricultural Service, *Tobacco: World Markets and Trade*, April 2003.

No. 1360. Wood Products—Production, Exports, and Consumption for Selected Countries: 1990 to 2002

[In thousand cubic meters (5,830 represents 5,830,000)]

Country	Production 1990	Production 2001	Production 2002	Exports 1990	Exports 2001	Exports 2002	Consumption 1990	Consumption 2001	Consumption 2002
SOFTWOOD LOGS									
Australia	5,830	12,873	16,477	-	752	900	5,830	12,122	15,578
Canada	122,000	152,600	168,000	800	2,929	4,200	125,289	154,402	167,800
China [1]	69,080	27,281	27,335	8	1	(NA)	72,836	36,422	39,645
Finland	19,600	26,000	26,000	161	431	500	19,734	31,505	31,500
France	14,189	18,000	(NA)	477	800	400	13,969	17,320	(NA)
Germany [2]	(NA)	17,000	18,000	1,947	3,200	3,500	(NA)	16,800	17,500
Japan	16,775	14,000	(NA)	11	2	(NA)	33,446	24,139	24,098
New Zealand	8,361	16,000	16,000	2,931	6,975	6,975	5,435	9,029	(NA)
Russia	(NA)	64,000	66,000	(NA)	20,000	21,500	(NA)	44,000	44,500
Sweden	24,700	30,200	30,000	336	1,699	2,000	24,787	39,737	37,000
SOFTWOOD LUMBER									
Canada	53,777	64,797	69,000	37,008	48,714	43,900	17,767	16,630	25,600
China [1]	17,650	3,397	(NA)	15	132	(NA)	17,733	5,167	5,510
Finland	7,400	12,700	13,000	4,152	8,200	8,500	3,261	3,400	(NA)
Germany [2]	12,145	14,600	14,600	839	3,300	3,500	15,551	15,600	15,600
Japan	26,551	14,570	14,300	7	2	(NA)	33,854	22,593	22,295
Russia	(NA)	14,000	14,100	(NA)	4,350	4,400	(NA)	9,650	9,700
Sweden	11,785	15,606	16,000	6,500	10,941	11,300	5,431	4,000	(NA)
TEMPERATE HARDWOOD LOGS									
China [1]	42,340	13,850	14,127	83	17	12	42,286	18,823	19,703
France	10,157	7,876	7,000	1,655	2,053	958	8,621	6,096	6,266
Russia	(NA)	23,000	23,500	(NA)	9,200	9,600	(NA)	13,800	13,900
TEMPERATE HARDWOOD LUMBER									
China [1]	10,819	2,561	3,059	65	346	350	10,755	4,913	5,622
France	3,303	2,395	2,320	646	546	540	2,767	2,116	1,979
Russia	(NA)	4,650	4,700	(NA)	360	380	(NA)	4,290	4,320
TROPICAL HARDWOOD LOGS									
Brazil	33,000	28,270	28,835	(NA)	13	14	33,146	28,257	28,821
Indonesia	27,000	26,500	26,500	-	-	(NA)	27,068	26,500	26,500
Malaysia	39,655	18,922	19,500	20,378	5,040	4,300	19,286	14,576	15,500
TROPICAL HARDWOOD LUMBER									
Brazil	8,500	14,800	15,300	525	316	370	8,252	14,532	14,963
Indonesia	9,000	6,400	6,500	561	(NA)	(NA)	8,439	6,400	6,500
Malaysia	8,780	4,823	5,000	5,247	2,356	2,500	3,568	2,926	4,000

- Represents zero. NA Not available. [1] See footnote 2, Table 1322. [2] Data for 1990 do not include East Germany.

Source: U.S. Dept. of Agriculture, Foreign Agricultural Service, *Wood Products: International Trade and Foreign Markets, Biennial Production, Consumption, and Trade Edition*, Circular Series WP-1-01, March 2001, year 1990; thereafter Production, Supply & Distribution Online <http://www.fas.usda.gov/psd/completetables/FO-table2-40.htm> (published June 2003).

No. 1361. World Production of Major Mineral Commodities: 1990 to 2001

[5,386 represents 5,386,000,000]

Commodity	Unit	1990	1995	2000	2001, prel.	Leading producers, 2000
MINERAL FUELS						
Coal	Mil. short tons	5,386	5,157	4,995	5,266	China, United States, Afghanistan
Dry natural gas	Tril. cu. ft.	73.6	78.0	88.1	90.7	Russia, United States, Canada
Natural gas plant liquids [1]	Mil. barrels [2]	1,691	2,005	2,295	2,409	United States, Canada, Saudi Arabia
Petroleum, crude	Mil. barrels [2]	22,107	22,752	24,945	24,841	Saudi Arabia, Russia, United States
NONMETALLIC MINERALS						
Cement, hydraulic	Mil. metric tons	1,160	1,444	1,600	1,700	China, India, United States (inc. Puerto Rico)
Diamond, gem and industrial	Mil. carats	111	113	(NA)	(NA)	(NA)
Nitrogen in ammonia	Mil. metric tons	97.5	100.0	109.0	106.0	China, India, United States
Phosphate rock	Mil. metric tons	162	130	133	126	United States, Morocco and Western Sahara, China
Potash, marketable	Mil. metric tons	27.5	24.6	25.3	26.4	Canada, Russia, Belarus
Salt	Mil. metric tons	183	192	214	225	Canada, China, Germany
Sulfur, elemental basis	Mil. metric tons	57.8	53.2	57.2	57.3	Canada, United States, Russia
METALS						
Aluminum [3]	Mil. metric tons	19.3	19.7	24.0	24.4	Russia, China, United States
Bauxite, gross weight	Mil. metric tons	113.0	112.0	135.0	138.0	Australia, Guinea, Brazil
Chromite, gross weight [1]	1,000 metric tons	13,200	14,300	14,400	12,100	South Africa, Kazakhstan, India
Copper, metal content [4]	1,000 metric tons	8,950	10,100	13,200	13,700	Chile, United States, Indonesia
Gold, metal content	Metric tons	2,180	2,210	2,550	2,570	South Africa, United States, Australia
Iron ore, gross weight [5]	Mil. metric tons	983	1,031	1,060	1,060	China, Brazil, Australia
Lead, metal content [4]	1,000 metric tons	3,370	2,820	3,100	3,100	Australia, China, United States
Nickel, metal content [4]	1,000 metric tons	974	1,030	1,250	1,330	Russia, Australia, Canada
Tin, metal content [4]	1,000 metric tons	221	193	238	222	China, Indonesia, Peru
Zinc, metal content [4]	1,000 metric tons	7,150	7,280	8,730	8,850	China, Australia, Peru

NA Not available. [1] Excludes China. [2] 42-gallon barrels. [3] Unalloyed ingot metal. [4] Mine output. [5] Includes iron ore concentrates and iron ore agglomerates.

Source: Mineral fuels, U.S. Energy Information Administration, *International Energy Annual*; nonmetallic minerals and metals, 1990, U.S. Bureau of Mines, thereafter, U.S. Geological Survey, *Minerals Yearbook*; Annual Reports; and *Mineral Commodity Summaries, 2002*.

No. 1362. World Primary Energy Production by Region and Type: 1980 to 2001

[In quadrillion Btu (286.4 represents 286,400,000,000,000,000). Btu=British thermal units. For Btu conversion factors, see source]

Region and type	1980	1985	1990	1995	1996	1997	1998	1999	2000	2001 [1]
World total [2]	289.3	309.1	352.2	365.9	375.1	382.3	385.7	385.5	396.0	403.4
North America	83.3	87.6	91.8	96.1	98.5	99.0	99.6	98.4	98.6	99.4
United States	67.3	67.7	70.7	71.2	72.5	72.4	72.8	71.6	71.1	71.6
Central and South America	12.1	13.7	16.8	21.2	22.6	24.2	24.9	24.6	26.1	25.6
Western Europe	30.7	37.4	38.5	41.7	44.0	44.1	43.9	44.2	44.3	44.7
Eastern Europe and former U.S.S.R.	67.8	77.1	81.9	60.0	60.1	58.3	57.7	59.6	62.2	64.7
Middle East	42.3	25.8	41.0	48.0	49.0	51.3	54.5	53.3	57.0	56.3
Africa	17.4	18.4	21.6	24.2	24.7	26.2	26.3	26.6	27.8	28.0
Far East and Oceania	35.9	49.1	60.6	74.8	76.2	79.2	78.8	78.8	79.9	84.8
Crude oil	133.2	121.2	136.4	141.5	145.0	149.0	151.9	149.7	155.9	155.3
Natural gas	52.7	61.4	75.9	80.3	84.0	83.9	85.6	87.5	90.8	93.5
Coal	74.5	85.8	91.9	90.6	91.1	94.0	92.4	91.2	91.2	96.0
Hydroelectric power	18.1	20.6	22.6	25.6	26.1	26.6	26.6	26.9	27.3	26.7
Nuclear electric power	7.6	15.4	20.4	23.2	24.1	23.8	24.3	25.1	25.5	26.5
Geothermal, solar, wind, wood, and waste	0.4	0.6	1.7	2.3	2.3	2.5	2.6	2.8	3.0	3.1

[1] Preliminary. [2] Includes geothermal, solar, and wood and waste energy produced in the United States and not used for generating electricity, not shown separately by type.

No. 1363. World Primary Energy Consumption by Region and Type: 1980 to 2001

[In quadrillion Btu (284.9 represents 284,900,000,000,000,000). Btu=British thermal units. For Btu conversion factors, see source]

Region and type	1980	1985	1990	1995	1996	1997	1998	1999	2000	2001 [1]
World total [2]	284.9	310.6	348.4	368.3	377.9	382.0	383.1	389.6	398.9	403.9
North America	91.7	91.1	100.6	108.6	112.2	113.0	113.3	115.8	118.7	115.6
United States	78.5	76.7	84.6	91.5	94.5	95.0	95.3	97.0	99.3	97.1
Central and South America	11.5	12.3	14.4	17.5	18.5	19.4	20.1	20.4	21.0	20.9
Western Europe	58.7	60.0	64.0	66.7	68.5	68.9	70.3	70.4	71.5	72.8
Eastern Europe and former U.S.S.R.	61.4	70.7	74.2	53.3	52.5	49.8	48.8	49.5	50.5	51.5
Middle East	5.9	8.6	11.1	13.9	14.6	15.4	16.2	16.6	17.3	17.9
Africa	6.8	8.5	9.3	10.6	10.9	11.4	11.3	11.6	12.0	12.5
Far East and Oceania	49.0	59.6	74.8	97.6	100.8	104.1	103.0	105.4	108.0	112.8
Petroleum	130.9	123.1	134.9	142.6	145.8	148.4	150.2	153.4	155.9	156.5
Natural gas	54.2	63.7	74.5	81.0	84.6	84.5	85.5	87.7	91.4	93.1
Coal	71.6	84.2	90.0	91.2	92.7	93.8	91.7	91.5	93.7	95.9
Hydroelectric power	18.3	21.0	22.7	25.9	26.4	26.8	26.9	27.1	27.5	26.9
Nuclear electric power	7.6	15.4	20.4	23.2	24.1	23.8	24.3	25.1	25.5	26.5
Geothermal, solar, wind, wood, and waste	0.3	0.5	1.7	2.3	2.3	2.5	2.6	2.8	3.0	3.1

[1] Preliminary. [2] See footnote 2, Table 1362.

Source of Tables 1362 and 1363: U.S. Energy Information Administration, *International Energy Annual, 2001*. Also see <http://tonto.eia.doe.gov/FTPROOT/international/021901.pdf>.

No. 1364. World Energy Consumption by Region and Energy Source, 1990 to 2001, and Projections, 2005 to 2020

[In quadrillion Btu (348.4 represents 348,400,000,000,000,000). Btu=British thermal units. For Btu conversion factors, see source. Energy totals include net imports of coal coke and electricity generated from biomass in the United States. Totals may not equal sum of components due to independent rounding. The electricity portion of the national consumption values consists of generation for domestic use plus an adjustment for electricity trade based on a fuel's share of total generation in the exporting country]

Region and energy source	1990	2000	2001 [1]	Projections 2005	2010	2015	2020
World, total	348.4	398.9	403.9	433.3	480.6	531.7	583.0
North America	100.6	118.7	115.6	124.6	137.2	148.7	159.4
United States	84.6	99.3	97.0	103.2	113.3	121.9	130.1
Western Europe	59.9	66.8	68.2	69.1	72.1	74.7	77.3
Industrialized Asia	22.3	27.5	27.7	28.8	30.8	32.8	34.4
Eastern Europe and former Soviet Union	76.3	52.2	53.3	61.1	65.9	71.6	76.7
Developing Asia	52.5	80.5	85.0	92.5	110.1	130.5	151.9
Middle East	13.1	20.3	20.8	21.4	25.0	28.3	32.0
Africa	9.3	11.9	12.4	13.3	14.4	16.1	18.0
Central and South America	14.4	21.0	20.9	22.7	25.2	29.0	33.4
Oil	135.1	155.9	156.5	164.2	181.7	200.1	219.2
Natural gas	75.0	91.4	93.1	103.0	117.5	137.3	158.5
Coal	91.6	93.6	95.9	100.7	110.9	119.6	128.1
Nuclear	20.3	25.5	26.4	27.8	29.1	30.3	29.9
Other	26.4	32.8	32.2	37.6	41.5	44.5	47.3

[1] Preliminary.

Source: 1990, 2000, 2001: U.S. Energy Information Administration (EIA), International *Energy Annual 2001*; Projections: *International Energy Outlook 2003*. Also see <http://www.eia.doe.gov/bookshelf/internat.html>.

Comparative International Statistics 865

No. 1365. Energy Consumption and Production by Country: 1995 and 2001

[368.3 represents 368,300,000,000,000,000. See text of this section for general comments about the data. For data qualifications for countries, see source]

Country	Primary energy consumed Total (quad. Btu) 1995	2001 prel.	Primary energy consumed Per capita (mil. Btu) 1995	2001, prel.	Dry natural gas production (tril. cu. ft) 1995	2001, prel.	Crude petroleum production (1,000 barrels per day) 1995	2001, prel.	Coal production (mil. short tons) 1995	2001, prel.
World	368.3	403.9	65	66	78.0	90.7	62,335	68,057	5,157	5,266
United States	91.5	97.1	348	342	18.6	19.4	6,560	5,801	1,033	1,121
Algeria	1.3	1.3	46	41	2.1	2.8	1,202	1,270	(Z)	(Z)
Argentina	2.3	2.7	67	71	0.9	1.3	715	781	(Z)	(Z)
Australia	4.1	5.0	226	255	1.0	1.2	562	657	267	357
Austria	1.3	1.4	159	176	0.1	0.1	23	19	1	1
Bahrain	0.3	0.4	500	600	0.2	0.3	41	35	(NA)	(NA)
Bangladesh	0.4	0.5	3	4	0.3	0.4	1	3	(NA)	(NA)
Belarus	1.1	1.2	103	121	(Z)	(Z)	38	37	(NA)	(NA)
Belgium	2.4	2.8	233	270	-	-	(NA)	(NA)	1	(Z)
Brazil	7.3	8.8	47	51	0.2	0.2	695	1,295	5	5
Bulgaria	1.0	0.9	118	118	(Z)	(Z)	1	1	34	31
Burma	(NA)	(NA)	(NA)	(NA)	0.1	0.3	10	14	(Z)	1
Canada	11.8	12.5	400	403	5.6	6.6	1,805	2,029	83	78
Chile	0.8	1.1	54	69	0.1	(Z)	11	7	1	1
China [1]	35.2	39.7	29	31	0.6	1.1	2,990	3,300	1,537	1,459
Colombia	1.1	1.1	29	26	0.2	0.2	585	602	28	48
Congo (Kinshasa) [2]	(NA)	(NA)	(NA)	(NA)	(NA)	(NA)	30	24	(Z)	(Z)
Cuba	0.4	0.4	38	35	(Z)	(Z)	26	50	(NA)	(NA)
Czech Republic	1.7	1.5	163	149	(Z)	(Z)	3	7	82	73
Denmark	0.9	0.9	168	169	0.2	0.3	186	346	(NA)	(NA)
Ecuador	(NA)	(NA)	(NA)	(NA)	(Z)	(Z)	392	412	(NA)	(NA)
Egypt	1.6	2.1	27	31	0.4	0.8	920	698	-	(NA)
Finland	1.1	1.3	219	256	(NA)	(NA)	(NA)	(NA)	(NA)	(NA)
France	9.5	10.5	164	178	0.1	0.1	50	28	11	3
Germany	14.3	14.4	175	174	0.7	0.8	59	65	274	226
Greece	1.1	1.4	107	131	(Z)	(Z)	9	5	64	74
Hong Kong	0.7	0.9	107	129	(NA)	(NA)	(NA)	(NA)	(NA)	(NA)
Hungary	1.1	1.1	104	110	0.2	0.1	35	27	16	16
India	11.1	12.8	12	13	0.6	0.8	703	642	298	339
Indonesia	3.3	4.6	17	22	2.2	2.4	1,503	1,369	46	100
Iran	3.8	5.2	64	80	1.3	2.2	3,643	3,724	1	2
Iraq	1.1	1.1	56	46	0.1	0.1	560	2,432	(NA)	(NA)
Ireland	0.5	0.6	125	159	0.1	(Z)	(NA)	(NA)	(Z)	(NA)
Israel	0.6	0.8	110	122	(Z)	(Z)	(Z)	(Z)	(NA)	(NA)
Italy	7.6	8.1	132	140	0.7	0.6	93	78	(Z)	(Z)
Japan	20.8	21.9	166	172	0.1	0.1	11	6	7	4
Korea, North	3.0	2.8	137	127	(NA)	(NA)	(NA)	(NA)	107	105
Korea, South	6.6	8.1	147	170	(NA)	(NA)	(NA)	(NA)	6	4
Kuwait	0.6	0.9	328	467	0.2	0.3	2,057	1,998	(NA)	(NA)
Libya	0.6	0.7	118	120	0.2	0.2	1,390	1,367	(NA)	(NA)
Malaysia	1.5	2.3	71	96	1.0	1.9	682	659	(Z)	(Z)
Mexico	5.3	6.0	58	59	1.0	1.3	2,618	3,157	10	13
Morocco	0.4	0.5	14	16	(Z)	(Z)	(Z)	(Z)	1	(Z)
Netherlands	3.7	4.2	239	264	3.0	2.8	66	26	(NA)	(NA)
New Zealand	0.9	0.8	235	218	0.2	0.2	32	33	4	4
Nigeria	0.8	0.9	8	8	0.2	0.6	1,993	2,256	(Z)	(Z)
Norway	1.7	1.9	397	424	1.1	1.9	2,768	3,117	(Z)	2
Pakistan	1.6	1.9	12	13	0.7	0.8	57	60	3	4
Peru	(NA)	(NA)	(NA)	(NA)	(Z)	(Z)	130	93	(Z)	(Z)
Philippines	1.0	1.3	14	16	(Z)	(Z)	3	8	1	1
Poland	3.7	3.5	96	92	0.2	0.2	5	17	220	179
Portugal	0.9	1.1	86	109	(NA)	(NA)	(NA)	(NA)	-	-
Romania	2.0	1.6	89	73	0.7	0.5	135	119	45	33
Russia	28.2	28.2	191	195	21.0	20.5	5,995	7,049	296	300
Saudi Arabia	3.9	4.9	225	233	1.3	1.9	8,231	8,031	(NA)	(NA)
Serbia and Montenegro	0.5	0.6	44	59	(Z)	(Z)	22	15	44	39
South Africa	4.1	4.6	102	104	0.1	0.1	-	26	227	250
Spain	4.5	5.7	114	142	(Z)	(Z)	13	7	31	25
Sweden	2.3	2.2	265	251	(NA)	(NA)	(Z)	-	-	-
Switzerland	1.2	1.3	166	180	-	-	(NA)	(NA)	(NA)	(NA)
Syria	0.7	0.9	46	51	0.1	0.2	575	518	(NA)	(NA)
Taiwan [1]	2.9	4.1	137	182	(Z)	(Z)	1	1	(Z)	-
Thailand	2.3	2.9	38	46	0.4	0.7	51	114	20	22
Trinidad and Tobago	(NA)	(NA)	(NA)	(NA)	0.3	0.5	131	113	(NA)	(NA)
Tunisia	(NA)	(NA)	(NA)	(NA)	(Z)	0.1	89	70	(NA)	(NA)
Turkey	2.5	2.9	41	42	(Z)	(Z)	67	48	61	73
Ukraine	7.2	6.1	139	124	0.6	0.6	65	76	95	90
United Arab Emirates	1.6	2.1	693	777	1.1	1.6	2,233	2,276	(NA)	(NA)
United Kingdom	9.6	9.8	164	165	2.7	3.7	2,489	2,282	52	35
Venezuela	2.5	3.0	113	120	0.9	1.1	2,750	2,880	4	8
Vietnam	0.5	0.8	7	10	(Z)	0.1	173	357	9	11

- Represents zero. NA Not available. Z Less than 50 billion cubic feet, 500 barrels per day, or 500,000 short tons.
[1] See footnote 2, Table 1322. [2] See footnote 3, Table 1322.

Source: U.S. Energy Information Administration, *International Energy Annual*.

No. 1366. Net Electricity Generation by Type and Country: 2000

[14,617.0 represents 14,617,000,000,000]

Country	Total [1] (bil. kWh)	Thermal [2]	Hydro	Nuclear	Country	Total [1] (bil. kWh)	Thermal [2]	Hydro	Nuclear
World, total	14,617.0	63.8	18.0	16.7	Korea, South	273.6	60.6	1.5	37.8
Argentina	85.2	59.3	33.6	7.0	Malaysia	65.4	89.4	10.6	-
Australia	200.3	90.9	8.3	-	Mexico	193.9	75.9	16.9	4.0
Austria	58.8	26.4	70.7	-	Netherlands	84.3	89.6	0.1	4.4
Belgium	78.2	39.4	0.6	58.4	New Zealand	37.8	25.1	64.6	-
Brazil	339.5	6.1	88.9	1.4	Norway	140.9	0.3	99.5	-
Bulgaria	39.0	47.7	7.9	44.4	Pakistan	63.4	72.6	26.8	0.6
Canada	587.1	26.6	60.4	11.7	Paraguay	53.0	-	99.8	-
China [3]	1,287.5	81.5	17.1	1.2	Poland	135.2	98.1	1.6	-
Colombia	42.9	24.7	74.1	-	Romania	49.6	60.1	29.4	10.5
Czech Republic	69.4	78.0	2.4	18.6	Russia	835.4	66.1	18.9	14.7
Denmark	34.1	82.4	-	-	Saudi Arabia	120.7	100.0	-	-
Egypt	71.7	80.8	19.2	-	Serbia and Montenegro	30.6	61.1	63.6	-
Finland	66.8	33.7	21.7	31.9	South Africa	196.2	92.7	0.7	6.6
France	511.1	9.2	13.0	77.2	Spain	210.3	55.3	13.4	28.0
Germany	536.2	62.5	4.0	30.1	Sweden	141.4	3.5	55.3	38.3
Greece	50.4	91.7	7.3	-	Switzerland	62.7	1.6	58.2	37.8
Hungary	33.4	59.0	0.6	40.4	Taiwan [3]	149.8	69.5	5.8	24.7
India	512.0	82.5	14.4	2.8	Thailand	91.5	91.9	6.6	-
Indonesia	87.6	86.8	10.3	-	Turkey	119.0	74.0	25.7	-
Iran	114.3	96.9	3.1	-	Ukraine	160.1	48.5	7.1	44.4
Italy	256.0	80.0	17.1	-	United Kingdom	351.9	73.9	1.4	23.2
Japan	1,015.0	60.7	8.5	28.9	United States	3,802.1	70.8	7.1	19.8
Kazakhstan	48.9	84.7	15.3	-	Uzbekistan	44.3	86.9	13.1	-
Korea, North	30.8	31.5	68.5	-	Venezuela	83.2	25.2	74.8	-

- Represents zero. [1] Includes geothermal, solar, wind, and wood and waste generation, not shown separately. [2] Electricity generated from coal, oil, and gas. [3] See footnote 2, Table 1322.

Source: U.S. Energy Information Administration, *International Energy Annual 2001*.

No. 1367. Commercial Nuclear Power Generation by Country: 1990 to 2002

[Generation for calendar years; other data as of December (1,743.9 represents 1,743,900,000,000)]

Country	Reactors 1990	1995	2001	2002	Gross electricity generated (bil. kWh) 1990	1995	2001	2002	Gross capacity (1,000 kW) 1990	1995	2001	2002
Total	368	423	427	436	1,743.9	2,271.7	2,602.8	2,666.7	301,745	358,414	370,366	380,261
United States	112	109	104	104	606.4	705.7	794.5	811.9	105,998	105,810	103,759	104,209
Argentina	2	2	2	2	7.0	7.0	7.1	5.8	1,005	1,005	1,005	1,005
Armenia	(NA)	1	1	1	(NA)	0.3	(NA)	2.2	(NA)	408	408	408
Belgium	7	7	7	7	42.7	41.3	46.3	47.3	5,740	5,911	5,995	6,050
Brazil	1	1	2	2	2.0	2.5	14.3	13.8	657	657	2,007	2,007
Bulgaria	(NA)	6	6	6	(NA)	17.1	(NA)	(NA)	(NA)	3,760	(NA)	(NA)
Canada	19	22	21	21	74.0	100.2	77.5	75.9	13,855	16,699	15,795	15,795
China [1]	(NA)	(NA)	2	2	(NA)	(NA)	14.9	14.7	(NA)	(NA)	1,968	1,968
Czech Republic	(NA)	(NA)	4	4	(NA)	(NA)	13.6	13.3	(NA)	(NA)	1,760	1,760
Finland	4	4	4	4	18.9	18.9	22.8	22.3	2,400	2,400	2,760	2,760
France	58	56	57	59	314.1	377.2	409.4	434.7	58,862	60,674	62,920	66,042
Germany	22	21	19	19	147.2	154.1	171.3	164.8	23,973	24,035	22,365	22,365
Great Britain	42	34	31	25	68.8	82.7	90.5	89.6	15,274	14,022	14,612	14,240
Hungary	4	4	4	4	13.6	14.0	14.1	13.9	1,760	1,840	1,866	1,866
India	6	10	14	14	6.0	7.6	19.2	19.5	1,330	2,270	2,720	2,720
Italy	2	(NA)	(NA)	(NA)	(NA)	(NA)	(NA)	(NA)	1,132	(NA)	(NA)	(NA)
Japan	40	50	52	53	191.9	286.0	319.3	313.5	31,645	41,356	45,082	45,907
Korea, South	9	10	16	18	52.8	63.9	112.1	116.5	7,616	8,615	13,768	15,768
Lithuania	(NA)	2	2	2	(NA)	9.6	11.4	13.2	(NA)	3,000	3,000	3,000
Mexico	1	2	2	2	2.1	7.9	8.7	9.7	675	1,350	1,350	1,350
Netherlands	2	2	1	1	3.4	4.0	3.9	3.9	540	540	480	480
Pakistan	1	1	2	2	0.4	0.5	2.2	1.9	137	137	462	462
Romania	(NA)	(NA)	1	1	(NA)	(NA)	5.4	5.5	(NA)	(NA)	706	706
Russia	(NA)	29	30	30	(NA)	98.7	134.5	139.7	(NA)	21,266	22,266	22,266
Slovakia	(NA)	(NA)	6	6	(NA)	(NA)	17.1	18.2	(NA)	(NA)	2,640	2,640
Slovenia	1	1	1	1	4.6	4.7	5.3	5.5	664	664	707	707
South Africa	2	2	2	2	8.9	11.9	11.3	12.6	1,930	1,930	1,930	1,930
Spain	10	9	9	9	54.3	55.4	63.7	63.0	7,984	7,400	7,815	7,870
Sweden	12	12	11	11	68.2	69.9	72.2	68.5	10,344	10,442	9,844	9,844
Switzerland	5	5	5	5	23.6	24.8	26.7	27.1	3,079	3,200	3,352	3,352
Taiwan [1]	6	6	6	6	32.9	35.3	35.5	39.5	5,146	5,144	5,144	5,144
Ukraine	(NA)	15	13	13	(NA)	70.5	76.2	77.9	(NA)	13,880	11,880	11,880

- Represents zero. NA Not available. [1] See footnote 2, Table 1322.

Source: McGraw-Hill, Inc., New York, NY, *Nucleonics Week*, March issues (copyright).

Comparative International Statistics 867

No. 1368. Selected Indexes of Manufacturing Activity by Country: 1980 to 2002

[1992=100. Data relate to employees (wage and salary earners) in Belgium and Italy, and to all employed persons (employees, self-employed workers, and unpaid family workers) in the other countries. Minus sign (-) indicates decrease. For explanation of average annual percent change, see Guide to Tabular Presentation]

Index	United States	Canada	Japan	Belgium	France	Germany	Italy	Netherlands	Norway	Sweden	United Kingdom
Output per hour:											
1980	70.5	72.9	63.2	65.4	61.5	(NA)	74.2	69.1	77.9	73.1	54.3
1990	96.9	93.4	94.4	96.8	93.8	(NA)	95.8	98.7	98.1	94.6	89.2
1995	113.8	112.4	111.0	113.2	113.8	112.3	108.0	117.3	100.7	124.5	106.4
2000	142.1	118.4	135.9	133.2	143.4	126.7	112.7	132.7	106.6	181.0	120.1
2001	142.7	116.1	133.8	134.9	149.3	128.4	114.6	132.3	108.9	182.6	123.2
2002	151.9	117.9	140.7	143.4	153.3	131.4	113.0	133.1	110.9	196.5	123.7
Average annual percent change:											
1995-2000	4.5	1.1	4.1	3.3	4.7	2.4	0.9	2.5	1.1	7.8	2.5
2000-2001	0.4	-2.0	-1.6	1.2	4.1	1.4	1.7	-0.3	2.2	0.9	2.6
2001-2002	6.4	1.5	5.2	6.3	2.7	2.3	-1.4	0.5	1.8	7.6	0.4
Compensation per hour, national currency basis: [1]											
1980	55.6	47.6	58.5	52.5	41.3	(NA)	30.4	60.5	39.0	37.3	32.1
1990	90.8	88.3	90.6	90.1	90.9	(NA)	87.6	89.8	92.3	87.8	82.9
1995	107.9	106.0	108.3	109.2	110.0	117.6	111.3	112.1	109.2	106.8	109.4
2000	131.1	113.9	113.7	120.5	120.8	137.2	127.8	132.0	140.5	133.2	137.6
2001	134.3	117.8	114.5	126.7	126.9	141.4	132.4	138.9	148.2	139.8	143.8
2002	141.0	123.2	112.7	135.0	130.9	144.5	135.6	146.0	157.2	145.1	148.6
Average annual percent change:											
1995-2000	4.0	1.4	1.0	2.0	1.9	3.1	2.8	3.3	5.2	4.8	4.7
2000-2001	2.4	3.5	0.7	5.2	5.0	3.1	3.6	5.2	5.5	3.4	4.6
2001-2002	5.0	4.6	-1.6	6.5	3.2	2.2	2.5	5.1	6.0	3.7	3.3
Real hourly compensation: [1,2]											
1980	91.4	91.6	75.3	86.5	80.6	(NA)	85.3	82.2	86.0	87.7	66.7
1990	96.4	94.7	95.1	95.2	96.3	(NA)	98.0	95.6	97.7	97.6	91.0
1995	100.7	101.7	106.3	102.3	104.2	107.8	97.4	104.2	102.7	97.8	101.7
2000	109.0	99.9	109.9	103.9	107.7	118.1	99.1	110.2	118.0	119.1	111.9
2001	108.6	100.8	111.5	106.7	111.3	119.3	99.9	111.0	120.8	120.4	115.0
2002	112.3	103.3	110.7	111.8	112.6	120.4	99.9	112.6	126.5	122.2	116.8
Average annual percent change:											
1995-2000	1.6	-0.4	0.7	0.3	0.7	1.8	0.3	1.1	2.8	4.0	1.9
2000-2001	-0.4	0.9	1.5	2.7	3.3	1.0	0.8	0.7	2.4	1.1	2.8
2001-2002	3.4	2.5	-0.7	4.8	1.2	0.9	-	1.4	4.7	1.5	1.6
Unit labor costs, national currency:											
1980	78.8	65.2	92.6	80.3	67.2	(NA)	41.0	87.6	50.0	51.0	59.0
1990	93.7	94.6	95.9	93.0	96.9	(NA)	91.5	91.1	94.2	92.9	92.9
1995	94.8	94.3	97.6	96.4	96.7	104.7	103.0	95.6	108.4	85.8	102.8
2000	92.3	96.1	83.6	90.4	84.3	108.3	113.4	99.5	131.9	74.7	114.5
2001	94.1	101.5	85.6	93.9	85.0	110.1	115.5	105.0	136.1	76.6	116.7
2002	92.8	104.6	80.1	94.1	85.4	110.0	120.1	109.7	141.8	73.8	120.1
Average annual percent change:											
1995-2000	-0.5	0.4	-3.0	-1.3	-2.7	0.7	1.9	0.8	4.0	-2.7	2.2
2000-2001	2.0	5.5	2.4	3.9	0.9	1.7	1.9	5.5	3.2	2.5	1.9
2001-2002	-1.3	3.1	-6.4	0.2	0.4	-0.1	4.0	4.5	4.2	-3.6	2.9
Unit labor costs, U.S. dollar basis: [3]											
1980	78.8	67.4	51.8	88.3	84.2	(NA)	59.0	77.5	62.9	70.2	77.7
1990	93.7	98.0	83.9	89.5	94.2	(NA)	94.1	87.9	93.6	91.3	93.8
1995	94.8	83.0	131.6	105.2	102.6	114.2	77.9	104.8	106.4	70.0	91.9
2000	92.3	78.2	98.4	66.5	62.8	79.8	66.6	73.3	93.0	47.5	98.3
2001	94.1	79.2	89.3	67.0	61.4	78.7	65.8	75.0	94.0	43.1	95.1
2002	92.8	80.5	81.1	70.9	65.1	83.0	72.2	82.8	110.3	44.2	102.1
Average annual percent change:											
1995-2000	-0.5	-1.2	-5.7	-8.8	-9.4	-6.9	-3.1	-6.9	-2.7	-7.5	1.3
2000-2001	2.0	1.2	-9.2	0.7	-2.2	-1.4	-1.2	2.3	1.1	-9.1	-3.2
2001-2002	-1.3	1.6	-9.2	5.8	6.1	5.5	9.8	10.4	17.4	2.5	7.4
Employment:											
1980	111.6	115.1	88.9	119.3	124.7	(NA)	122.6	107.4	134.2	130.9	151.4
1990	105.4	113.2	97.5	102.5	105.2	(NA)	104.6	100.0	105.2	117.2	115.4
1995	102.5	104.8	90.1	91.9	92.8	86.2	95.6	92.1	107.0	98.0	99.3
2000	101.8	121.2	81.7	88.6	91.3	82.7	96.9	93.1	107.5	98.0	93.9
2001	97.0	120.7	79.6	88.7	92.3	83.0	96.9	92.6	106.0	97.0	89.8
2002	90.4	121.5	74.5	85.9	90.7	81.3	97.9	90.6	104.8	94.3	85.2
Average annual percent change:											
1995-2000	-0.1	3.0	-1.9	-0.7	-0.3	-0.8	0.3	0.2	0.1	-	-1.1
2000-2001	-4.7	-0.4	-2.6	0.1	1.1	0.4	-	-0.5	-1.4	-1.0	-4.4
2001-2002	-6.8	0.7	-6.4	-3.1	-1.7	-2.1	1.0	-2.2	-1.1	-2.8	-5.1
Aggregate hours:											
1980	107.5	114.6	95.6	119.7	132.7	(NA)	113.8	111.2	134.7	124.0	160.5
1990	104.8	113.5	102.9	104.3	105.7	(NA)	103.7	100.3	103.4	116.4	118.1
1995	104.0	106.4	89.1	92.0	92.2	84.8	99.3	92.3	106.6	105.9	101.2
2000	102.8	125.6	80.3	91.6	86.7	78.8	100.8	92.5	105.9	105.6	94.4
2001	96.3	123.9	77.7	90.7	85.8	78.2	100.0	91.9	104.1	103.1	89.8
2002	89.5	125.2	72.7	85.7	83.6	76.1	100.7	89.9	101.6	98.6	85.9
Average annual percent change:											
1995-2000	-0.2	3.4	-2.0	-0.1	-1.2	-1.5	0.3	-	-0.1	-0.1	-1.4
2000-2001	-6.4	-1.4	-3.4	-1.0	-1.1	-0.8	-0.9	-0.6	-1.7	-2.4	-4.8
2001-2002	-7.0	1.1	-6.4	-5.5	-2.6	-2.6	0.7	-2.2	-2.4	-4.4	-4.4

- Represents or rounds to zero.   NA Not available.   [1] Compensation includes, but real hourly compensation excludes, adjustments for payroll and employment taxes that are not payments to employees, but are labor costs to employers.   [2] Index of hourly compensation divided by the index of consumer prices to adjust for changes in purchasing power.   [3] Indexes in national currency adjusted for changes in prevailing exchange rates.

Source: U.S. Bureau of Labor Statistics, *International Comparisons of Manufacturing Productivity and Unit Labor Cost Trends*, September 9, 2003.

868   Comparative International Statistics

No. 1369. Indexes of Hourly Compensation Costs for Production Workers in Manufacturing by Country: 1980 to 2001

[United States=100. Compensation costs include pay for time worked, other direct pay (including holiday and vacation pay, bonuses, other direct payments, and the cost of pay in kind), employer expenditures for legally required insurance programs and contractual and private benefit plans, and for some countries, other labor taxes. Data adjusted for exchange rates. Area averages are trade-weighted to account for difference in countries' relative importance to U.S. trade in manufactured goods. The trade weights used are the sum of U.S. imports of manufactured products for consumption (customs value) and U.S. exports of domestic manufactured products (f.a.s. value) in 1992; see source for detail]

Area or country	1980	1985	1990	1995	2000	2001	Area or country	1980	1985	1990	1995	2000	2001
United States	100	100	100	100	100	100	Austria [7]	90	58	119	147	99	96
Total [1]	66	51	80	89	72	68	Belgium	133	69	129	161	110	104
OECD [2]	72	55	86	95	77	72	Denmark	110	63	121	145	109	108
Europe	99	61	115	127	94	90	Finland [8]	84	63	143	142	99	98
Asian newly industrial-izing economies [3]	12	13	25	38	36	34	France	91	58	104	113	79	78
							Germany [7,9]	124	73	146	184	122	117
Canada	88	84	107	94	81	77	Greece	38	28	45	53	(NA)	(NA)
Mexico	22	12	11	10	11	12	Ireland	61	46	79	80	63	65
Australia [4]	86	63	89	91	73	65	Italy	83	59	117	94	71	68
Hong Kong [5]	15	13	22	29	29	29	Luxembourg	117	58	108	136	90	86
Israel	38	31	57	61	65	67	Netherlands	122	67	121	140	97	95
Japan	56	49	86	139	112	96	Norway	117	80	144	142	114	114
Korea, South	10	10	25	42	43	40	Portugal	21	12	25	31	24	(NA)
New Zealand	53	34	55	58	41	38	Spain	60	36	76	75	55	54
Singapore	15	19	25	43	38	38	Sweden	127	74	140	125	102	90
Sri Lanka	2	2	2	3	2	(NA)	Switzerland	112	74	140	170	108	108
Taiwan [6]	10	12	26	34	30	28	United Kingdom	77	48	85	80	83	79

NA Not available. [1] The 28 foreign economies shown below. [2] Organization for Economic Cooperation and Development; see text of this section. [3] Hong Kong, South Korea, Singapore, and Taiwan. [4] Includes nonproduction workers, except in managerial, executive, professional, and higher supervisory positions. [5] Average of selected manufacturing industries. [6] See footnote 2, Table 1322. [7] Excludes workers in establishments considered handicraft manufactures (including all printing and publishing and miscellaneous manufacturing in Austria). [8] Includes workers in mining and electrical power plants. [9] Former West Germany.

Source: U.S. Bureau of Labor Statistics, News Release USDL 01-311, September 27, 2002. Also see <ftp://ftp.bls.gov/pub/special.requests/ForeignLabor/supptab.txt>.

No. 1370. Motor Vehicle Transportation Indicators for Selected Countries: 2000

[133,621 represents 133,621,000]

Item	United States [1]	Canada	France	Germany	Japan	Mexico	Sweden	United Kingdom
NUMBER [2] (1,000)								
Automobiles [3,4]	133,621	13,887	28,060	42,324	52,437	10,443	3,999	22,115
Motorcycles [3,4]	4,304	334	(NA)	4,560	13,974	270	276	684
Buses	747	68	80	84,687	235	112	14	80
Trucks, SUVs, and Vans	87,108	3,626	5,673	4,382	18,226	4,932	374	3,089
Per 1,000 persons:								
Automobiles [3,4]	474.8	439.6	471.2	509.7	413.6	102.5	450.6	370.8
Motorcycles [3,4]	15.3	10.6	(NA)	54.9	110.2	2.7	31.1	11.5
Buses	2.7	2.2	1.3	1.0	1.9	1.1	1.6	1.3
Trucks, SUVs, and Vans	309.5	114.8	95.3	52.8	143.8	48.4	42.2	51.8
ROADS [5]								
Total kilometers (1,000)	6,359	902	894	656	1,162	330	212	372
Kilometers per 1,000 persons	22.59	28.55	15.01	7.90	9.17	3.23	23.93	6.57
Kilometers per square kilometer	0.69	0.10	1.64	1.88	3.10	0.17	0.52	1.54
VEHICLE KILOMETERS OF TRAVEL [6]								
Automobiles (bil.)	2,579	(NA)	402	528	502	(NA)	57	380
Motorcycles (bil.)	17	(NA)	4	15	(NA)	(NA)	1	5
Buses (bil.)	12	(NA)	2	4	7	(NA)	1	5
Trucks (bil.) [7]	1,819	(NA)	115	58	257	(NA)	12	77
AVERAGE VEHICLE KILOMETERS PER VEHICLE [6]								
Automobiles	19,099	(NA)	14,629	12,475	8,032	(NA)	14,611	17,187
Motorcycles	4,063	(NA)	1,723	3,377	(NA)	(NA)	2,378	6,725
Buses	16,793	(NA)	30,000	43,690	28,032	(NA)	79,470	62,500
Trucks [7]	21,877	(NA)	20,035	13,192	12,859	(NA)	32,548	25,025

NA Not available. [1] Does not include Puerto Rico. [2] Data for UK and Canada are for 1998. Data for Germany are for 1999. [3] Includes mopeds. [4] Data for Germany and Sweden are from 1998; data for Mexico are from 1996. [5] Data for Japan, France, Germany, UK, and Mexico are from 1999; data for Canada are from 1995. [6] Data for Japan, France, and UK are from 1999. Data for Germany are from 1998. [7] U.S. data are light two-axle four-tire trucks such as vans, sport utility vehicles, pickup trucks, heavy single-unit trucks, and combination trucks. Non-U.S. data does not include travel by combination trucks.

Source: U.S. Federal Highway Administration, Highway Statistics, 2001. Also see <http://www.fhwa.dot.gov/ohim/hs01/in3.htm>.

Comparative International Statistics 869

No. 1371. Key Global Telecom Indicators for the World Telecommunication Service Sector: 1995 to 2002

[In billions U.S. dollars (779 represents $779,000,000,000), except where noted. All data were converted by annual average exchange rates. Country fiscal year data was aggregated to obtain calendar year estimates]

Indicators	1995	1996	1997	1998	1999	2000	2001	2002, prel.
Telecom market total revenue	779	885	946	1,015	1,123	1,210	1,232	1,295
Telecom telephone services revenue [1]	428	444	437	456	476	477	472	465
Other statistics								
Main telephone lines [2]	689	738	792	846	905	983	1,053	1,129
Mobile cellular subscribers [2]	91	145	215	318	490	740	955	1,155
International telephone traffic minutes [3]	63	71	79	89	100	118	127	135
Personal computers [2]	235	275	325	375	435	500	555	615
Internet users [2]	40	74	117	183	277	399	502	580

[1] Revenue from installation, subscription and local, trunk and international call charges for fixed telephone service. [2] Data are in millions. [3] From 1995 including traffic between countries of former Soviet Union.

Source: International Telecommunication Union, Geneva Switzerland, 2003; <http://www.itu.int/ITU-D/ict/statistics/atglance/KeyTelecom99.html>.

No. 1372. Telephones and Computers by Country: 2001

[Rates per 1,000 persons. See text of this section for general comments about the data. For data qualifications for countries, see source]

Country	Telephone main lines	Cellular phone subscribers	Personal computers [1]	Country	Telephone main lines	Cellular phone subscribers	Personal computers [1]
Algeria	61	3	7	Japan	586	588	349
Argentina	224	193	91	Korea, South	486	621	481
Australia	519	576	516	Kuwait	208	386	120
Austria	468	817	335	Lebanon	221	239	60
Belgium	498	746	233	Malaysia	198	314	126
Brazil	218	167	63	Mexico	137	217	69
Bulgaria	359	191	(NA)	Morocco	41	164	14
Canada	676	362	460	Netherlands	621	767	428
Chile	233	342	107	New Zealand	477	599	393
China [2]	137	110	19	Norway	720	815	508
Colombia	171	76	42	Pakistan	23	6	4
Cuba	51	1	20	Panama	130	164	38
Czech Republic	378	680	146	Peru	78	59	48
Denmark	720	738	540	Philippines	42	150	22
Dominican Republic	110	147	(NA)	Poland	295	260	85
Ecuador	104	67	23	Portugal	427	774	117
Egypt	104	43	16	Puerto Rico	346	316	(NA)
Finland	548	804	424	Romania	184	172	36
France	574	605	337	Russia	243	38	50
Germany	634	682	382	Saudi Arabia	145	113	63
Ghana	12	9	3	Singapore	471	724	508
Greece	529	751	81	South Africa	111	242	70
Guatemala	65	97	13	Spain	434	734	168
Honduras	47	36	12	Sweden	739	790	561
Hungary	375	498	100	Switzerland	743	728	538
India	38	6	6	Syria	103	12	16
Indonesia	35	31	11	Taiwan [2]	573	969	253
Iran	169	32	70	Thailand	99	123	28
Iraq	29	-	(NA)	Turkey	285	295	41
Ireland	485	774	391	United Kingdom	588	770	366
Israel	466	907	246	**United States**	**667**	**451**	**625**
Italy	472	883	195	Uruguay	283	155	110
Jamaica	205	244	50	Venezuela	109	264	53

- Represents or rounds to zero. NA Not available. [1] In many countries mainframe computers are used extensively, and thousands of users can be connected to a single mainframe computer; thus the number of PCs understates the total use of computers. [2] See footnote 2, Table 1322.

Source: International Telecommunications Union, Geneva, Switzerland, *World Telecommunication Indicators,* (copyright).

No. 1373. Dow-Jones World Stock Index by Country and Industry: 1995 to 2002

[Index figures shown are as of December 31. Based on share prices denominated in U.S. dollars. Stocks in countries that impose significant restrictions on foreign ownership are included in the world index in the same proportion that shares are available to foreign investors]

Country and industry	1995	2000	2001	2002	Country and industry	1995	2000	2001	2002
World, total	132.4	210.9	175.7	171.7	Asia/Pacific	118.5	93.0	73.2	66.5
Americas	145.3	299.1	259.5	199.8	Australia	132.9	156.2	154.1	149.4
United States	147.5	306.9	266.7	204.5	Hong Kong	201.9	245.6	195.2	156.3
Canada	112.9	225.4	180.1	157.5	Indonesia	174.7	31.2	25.4	33.1
Mexico	79.0	132.2	157.4	133.5	Japan	111.1	88.3	62.3	56.5
Europe	131.0	241.1	189.2	152.6	Malaysia	224.3	88.5	91.6	86.1
Austria	103.5	86.1	86.2	104.4	New Zealand	178.8	96.7	102.7	119.8
Belgium	144.0	196.7	170.5	154.3	Singapore	187.8	135.3	108.4	97.7
Denmark	113.0	243.9	187.3	160.1	Thailand	196.6	27.2	28.4	33.5
Finland	267.1	1,536.0	955.0	671.5					
France	117.9	252.6	193.4	153.8	Basic materials	128.1	117.7	109.8	107.6
Germany	133.9	218.8	165.8	112.1	Consumer, cyclical	131.7	188.0	171.4	136.9
Ireland	155.6	312.0	301.0	236.7	Consumer, noncyclical	125.5	180.8	173.2	166
Italy	80.3	192.0	137.8	123.6	Energy	132.7	230.7	206.4	187.3
Netherlands	176.0	335.3	257.2	199.5	Financial	134.9	207.1	175.5	147.7
Norway	129.8	167.4	125.0	110.8	Healthcare	133.3	329.8	281.7	224.6
Spain	111.2	193.3	167.3	142.6	Industrial	124.0	167.1	138.5	106.6
Sweden	157.0	338.9	236.1	163.3	Technology	188.1	552.4	377.3	229.6
Switzerland	225.7	415.5	293.9	259.1	Telecommunications	146.8	273.3	208.6	147.9
United Kingdom	122.5	199.8	166.7	137.9	Utilities	118.8	156.0	123.3	101.9

Source: Dow Jones & Company, Inc., New York, NY, *Dow Jones Indexes*, (copyright).

No. 1374. Foreign Stock Market Activity—Morgan Stanley Capital International Indexes: 1995 to 2002

[Index figures shown are as of December 31. January 1, 1970=100, except as noted. Based on share prices denominated in U.S. dollars. EM=Emerging Markets]

Index and country	1995	2001	2002	2001	2002	Index and country	1995	2001	2002	2001	2002
ALL COUNTRY (AC) INDEXES						Sweden	1,796	3,047	2,088	-28.2	-31.5
						Switzerland	1,569	2,104	1,873	-21.9	-11.0
AC World index	182.0	240.0	190.8	-17.3	-20.5	United Kingdom	716.4	962.0	791.1	-16.1	-17.8
AC World index except USA	153.8	152.9	127.6	-21.0	-16.5	Hong Kong	4,818	4,314	3,424	-21.2	-20.6
AC Asia Pacific	124.5	70.0	63.1	-21.8	-9.8	Japan	3,348	1,789	1,593	-29.9	-11.0
AC Europe	201.9	297.2	238.1	-21.1	-19.9	Singapore	2,735	1,560	1,356	-25.0	-13.1
European Union	189.2	284.5	224.1	-21.3	-21.2						
						EMERGING MARKETS					
DEVELOPED MARKETS						EM Far East index	263.7	140.0	130.0	9.5	-7.1
						India [5]	98.8	90.3	95.6	-21.2	5.9
World index [2]	734.0	1,004	792.2	-17.8	-21.1	Indonesia	508.2	69.4	95.8	-10.9	38.1
EAFE index [3]	1,136	1,155	952.7	-22.6	-17.5	Korea, South	173.8	114.4	123.4	46.0	7.4
Europe index	733.4	1,086	867.4	-21.2	-20.1	Malaysia	347.0	164.3	160.0	2.3	-2.7
Pacific index	2,362	1,352	1,211	-26.2	-10.4	Pakistan [5]	91.5	29.0	64.4	-35.0	122.4
Far East index	3,384	1,833	1,615	-29.1	-11.9	Philippines	442.5	117.8	81.9	-19.7	-30.5
						Sri Lanka [5]	105.6	49.4	64.1	36.1	29.8
United States	581.1	1,085	824.6	-13.2	-24.0	Taiwan [6]	227.9	208.6	155.6	8.8	-25.4
Canada	403.9	654.2	560.1	-21.4	-14.4	Thailand	523.3	60.6	75.4	2.9	24.3
Australia	304.2	315.8	303.9	-0.6	-3.8						
New Zealand [4]	114.2	59.6	71.5	5.6	20.0	EM Latin America	781.8	876.2	658.9	-4.3	-24.8
						Argentina	1,239	959.6	470.3	-22.2	-51.0
Austria	890.4	655.6	749.8	-7.4	14.4	Brazil	578.1	597.1	395.4	-21.8	-33.8
Belgium	897.0	1,063	880.5	-13.0	-17.2	Chile	902.8	568.7	445.5	-6.0	-21.7
Denmark	1,124	1,850	1,535	-15.9	-17.0	Colombia [5]	110.2	57.7	68.3	37.1	18.3
Finland [4]	128.8	561.7	386.3	-39.1	-31.2	Mexico	744.5	1,698	1,443	15.9	-15.0
France	672.1	1,160	902.1	-23.2	-22.2	Peru [5]	221.3	144.1	182.7	15.3	26.8
Germany	818.1	1,099	724.9	-23.5	-34.1	Venezuela	75.4	95.4	77.7	-10.0	-18.6
Greece [4]	238.2	326.6	234.6	31.4	-28.2						
Ireland [4]	215.7	295.6	212.7	-4.1	-28.1	Czech Republic	(NA)	76.6	107.9	-4.2	40.9
Italy	208.6	322.4	290.2	-27.9	-10.0	Hungary	(NA)	209.1	269.5	-10.5	28.9
Luxembourg	(NA)	265.4	(NA)	-46.0	(NA)	Jordan	96.1	71.1	72.9	29.0	2.5
Netherlands	1,192	1,665	1,290	-23.5	-22.5	Poland	(NA)	355.8	354.0	-28.7	-0.5
Norway	1,023	1,018	926.2	-13.8	-9.0	Russia	(NA)	237.8	270.7	53.2	13.9
Portugal [4]	68.4	98.4	83.2	-23.0	-15.5	South Africa	(NA)	125.6	154.9	-20.3	23.3
Spain	162.3	302.7	251.6	-12.8	-16.9	Turkey	103.1	164.1	104.2	-33.7	-36.5

NA Not available. [1] Percent change during calendar year (e.g. December 31, 2001, through December 31, 2002). Adjusted for foreign exchange fluctuations relative to U.S. dollar. [2] Includes South African gold mines quoted in London. [3] Europe, Australasia, Far East Index. Comprises all European and Far East countries listed under developed markets plus Australia, Malaysia, and New Zealand. [4] January 1, 1988=100. [5] December 1992=100. [6] See footnote 2, Table 1322.

Source: Morgan Stanley Capital International, New York, NY, <http://www.msci.com/equity/index.html> (copyright). This information may not be reproduced or redisseminated in any form without prior written permission from Morgan Stanley Capital International. This information is provided on an "as is" basis. Neither Morgan Stanley or any other party makes any representation or warranty of any kind either express or implied, with respect to this information (or the results to be obtained by the use thereof) and Morgan Stanley expressly disclaims any and all warranties of originality, accuracy, completeness, merchantability, and fitness for any particular purpose. The user of this information assumes the entire risk of any use made of the information. In no event shall Morgan Stanley or any other part be liable to the user for any direct or indirect damages, including without limitation, any lost profits, lost savings, or any other incidental or consequential damages arising out of use of this information.

No. 1375. Foreign Stock Market Indices: 1980 to 2002

[As of year end. The DAX index is a total return index which includes dividends, whereas the other foreign indices are price indices which exclude dividends]

Year	London FTSE 100	Tokyo Nikkei 225	Hong Kong Hang Seng	Germany DAX-30	Paris CAC-40	Dow Jones Europe STOXX 50
1980	647	7,116	1,477	481	(X)	(X)
1985	1,413	13,113	1,752	1,366	(X)	(X)
1990	2,144	23,849	3,025	1,398	1,518	835
1991	2,493	22,984	4,297	1,578	1,766	1,000
1992	2,847	16,925	5,512	1,545	1,858	1,058
1993	3,418	17,417	11,888	2,267	2,268	1,429
1994	3,066	19,723	8,191	2,107	1,881	1,299
1995	3,689	19,868	10,073	2,254	1,872	1,538
1996	4,119	19,361	13,452	2,889	2,316	1,850
1997	5,136	15,259	10,723	4,250	2,999	2,634
1998	5,883	13,842	9,507	5,002	3,943	3,320
1999	6,930	18,934	16,962	6,958	5,958	4,742
2000	6,223	13,786	15,096	6,434	5,926	4,557
2001	5,217	10,543	11,397	5,160	4,625	3,707
2002	3,940	8,579	9,321	2,893	3,064	2,408

X Not applicable.

Source: Global Financial Data, Los Angeles, CA.

No. 1376. United States and Foreign Stock Markets—Market Capitalization and Value of Shares Traded: 1990 to 2001

[In billions of U.S. dollars (3,059.4 represents $3,059,400,000,000). Market capitalization is the market value of all domestic listed companies at the end of the year. The market value of a company is the share price times the number of shares outstanding. Value of shares traded is the annual total turnover of listed company shares]

Country	Market capitalization				Value of shares traded			
	1990	1995	2000	2001	1990	1995	2000	2001
United States	3,059.4	6,857.6	15,104.0	13,983.9	1,751.3	5,108.6	31,862.5	23,030.5
Argentina	3.3	37.8	166.1	192.5	0.9	4.6	6.0	6.6
Australia	107.6	245.2	372.8	374.3	40.1	98.7	226.3	240.0
Austria	11.5	32.5	29.9	25.2	18.6	25.8	9.4	7.7
Belgium	65.4	105.0	182.5	1,843.5	6.4	15.2	38.0	3,172.6
Brazil	16.4	147.6	226.2	186.2	5.6	79.2	101.3	57.9
Canada	241.9	366.3	841.4	615.3	71.3	183.7	634.7	446.3
Chile	13.6	73.9	60.4	56.7	0.8	11.1	6.1	4.1
China [1]	(NA)	42.1	581.0	524.0	(NA)	49.8	721.5	718.2
Denmark	39.1	56.2	107.7	85.2	11.1	25.9	91.6	91.8
Egypt	1.8	8.1	28.7	24.2	0.1	0.7	11.1	6.9
Finland	22.7	44.1	293.6	190.5	3.9	19.0	206.6	29.8
France	314.4	522.1	1,446.6	1,843.5	116.9	364.6	1,083.3	3,172.6
Germany	355.1	577.4	1,270.2	1,071.8	501.8	573.5	1,069.1	1,434.5
Greece	15.2	17.1	110.8	84.2	3.9	6.1	95.1	37.3
Hong Kong	83.4	303.7	623.4	506.1	34.6	106.9	377.9	196.4
India	38.6	127.2	148.1	110.4	21.9	13.7	509.8	249.3
Indonesia	8.1	66.6	26.8	23.0	4.0	14.4	14.3	23.3
Iran	(NA)	6.6	34.0	9.7	(NA)	0.7	5.0	1.1
Ireland	(NA)	25.8	81.9	78.7	(NA)	13.2	14.4	23.6
Israel	3.3	36.4	64.1	57.6	5.5	9.2	23.4	15.0
Italy	148.8	209.5	768.4	672.1	42.6	86.9	778.4	546.4
Japan	2,917.7	3,667.3	3,157.2	3,910.0	1,602.4	1,231.6	2,693.9	1,696.7
Korea, South	110.6	182.0	171.6	232.1	75.9	185.2	1,067.7	694.2
Luxembourg	10.5	30.4	34.0	22.7	0.1	0.2	1.2	0.7
Malaysia	48.6	222.7	116.9	119.0	10.9	76.8	58.5	23.6
Mexico	32.7	90.7	125.2	126.6	12.2	34.4	45.3	60.4
Morocco	1.0	6.0	10.9	9.1	0.1	2.4	1.1	1.2
Netherlands	119.8	356.5	640.5	1,843.5	40.2	248.6	677.2	3,172.6
New Zealand	8.8	32.0	18.6	17.8	1.9	8.4	10.8	8.4
Norway	26.1	44.6	65.0	69.1	14.0	24.4	60.1	52.4
Philippines	5.9	58.9	51.6	21.3	1.2	14.7	8.2	3.0
Poland	(NA)	4.6	31.3	25.9	(NA)	2.8	14.6	10.6
Portugal	9.2	18.4	60.7	60.7	1.7	4.2	54.4	34.8
Russia	(NA)	15.9	38.9	76.2	(NA)	0.5	20.3	22.9
Saudi Arabia	(NA)	40.9	67.2	73.2	(NA)	6.2	17.3	22.3
Singapore	34.3	148.0	152.8	117.1	20.3	60.5	91.5	63.0
Sweden	97.9	178.0	328.3	232.6	17.6	93.2	390.0	294.9
Switzerland	160.0	433.6	792.3	521.2	(NA)	310.9	609.1	576.9
Taiwan [1]	100.7	187.2	247.6	293.5	715.0	383.1	983.5	524.4
Thailand	23.9	141.5	29.5	36.3	22.9	57.0	23.3	31.1
Turkey	19.1	20.8	69.7	47.7	5.8	51.4	179.2	64.7
United Kingdom	848.9	1,407.7	2,580.0	2,149.5	278.7	510.1	1,835.3	4,594.1

NA Not available.   [1] See footnote 2, Table 1322.

Source: Standard and Poor's, New York, NY, *Standard & Poor's Emerging Stock Markets Factbook 2002* (copyright).

No. 1377. Foreign Exchange Rates: 2002

[Foreign currency units per U.S. dollar. Rates shown include market, official, principal, and secondary rates, as published by the International Monetary Fund in *International Financial Statistics*]

Country	Currency	2002	Country	Currency	2002
Afghanistan [1]	Afghanis	3,000.00	Laos	Kip	10,056.3
Albania	Leks	140.15	Latvia	Lats	0.62
Algeria	Algerian Dinar	79.68	Lebanon	Lebanese Pounds	1,507.50
Antigua and Barbuda	E.Caribbean Dollar	2.70	Lesotho	Maloti	10.54
Argentina	Argentine Pesos	3.06	Liberia	Liberian Dollar	61.75
Armenia	Dram	573.35	Libya [1]	Libyan Dinars	1.21
Aruba	Aruban Florins	1.79	Lithuania	Litai	3.68
Australia	Australian Dollar	1.68	Luxembourg [2]	Euro	(NA)
Austria [2]	Euro	(NA)	Macedonia, The Former		
Bahamas, The	Bahamian Dollar	1.00	Yugoslav Republic of	Denar	64.35
Bahrain	Bahrain Dinars	0.38	Madagascar	Malagasy Francs	6,832.00
Bangladesh	Taka	57.89	Malaysia	Ringgit	3.80
Barbados	Barbados Dollar	2.00	Mali	Cfa Francs	696.99
Belarus	Belarusian Rubel	1,790.92	Malta	Maltese Liri	0.43
Belgium [2]	Euro	(NA)	Mauritania	Ouguiyas	255.63
Belize	Belize Dollar	2.00	Mauritius	Mauritian Rupees	29.96
Benin	Cfa Francs	696.99	Mexico	Mexican Pesos	9.66
Bolivia	Bolivianos	7.17	Moldova	Lei	13.57
Botswana	Pula	6.33	Mongolia	Togrogs	1,110.31
Brazil	Reais	2.92	Morocco	Dirhams	11.02
Bulgaria	Leva	2.08	Mozambique	Meticais	23,678.0
Burkina Faso	Cfa Francs	696.99	Namibia	Namibia Dollar	10.54
Burma [1]	Kyat	6.64	Nepal	Nepalese Rupees	77.88
Cambodia	Riels	3,912.10	Netherlands [2]	Euro	(NA)
Cameroon	Cfa Francs	696.99	Netherlands Antilles	Euro	(NA)
Canada	Canadian Dollar	1.57	New Zealand	New Zealand Dollar	2.15
Central African Republic	Cfa Francs	696.99	Nicaragua	Cordobas	14.25
Chad	Cfa Francs	696.99	Niger	Cfa Francs	696.99
Chile	Chilean Pesos	688.94	Nigeria	Naira	120.58
China [3]	Yuan	8.28	Norway	Norwegian Kroner	7.98
Colombia	Colombian Pesos	2,504.24	Oman	Rials Omani	0.38
Comoros	Comorian Francs	522.74	Pakistan	Pakistan Rupees	59.72
Congo (Brazzaville) [4]	Cfa Francs	696.99	Panama	Balboas	1.00
Costa Rica	Colones	359.82	Papua New Guinea	Kina	3.89
Cote d'Ivoire	Cfa Francs	696.99	Paraguay	Guaranies	5,716.30
Croatia	Kuna	7.87	Peru	Nuevos Soles	3.52
Cyprus	Cyprus Pounds	0.61	Philippines	Philippine Pesos	51.60
Czech Republic	Koruny	32.74	Poland	Zlotys	4.08
Denmark	Kroner	7.90	Portugal [2]	Euro	(NA)
Djibouti	Djibouti Francs	177.72	Qatar	Qatar Riyals	3.64
Dominica	E.Caribbean Dollar	2.70	Romania	Lei	33,055.4
Dominican Republic	Dominican Pesos	18.61	Russia	Russian Rubles	31.35
Ecuador	U.S. Dollar	25,000.0	Rwanda	Rwanda Francs	475.37
Egypt	Egyptian Pounds	4.50	Saint Kitts and Nevis	E.Caribbean Dollar	2.70
El Salvador	Colones	8.75	Saint Lucia	E.Caribbean Dollar	2.70
Equatorial Guinea	Cfa Francs	696.99	Saint Vincent and the		
Estonia	Krooni	16.61	Grenadines	E.Caribbean Dollar	2.70
Ethiopia [1]	Birr	8.57	Saudi Arabia	Saudi A. Riyals	3.75
Euro area (EMU-11) [2]	Euro	1.06	Senegal	Cfa Francs	696.99
Fiji	Fiji Dollar	2.19	Sierra Leone	Leones	2,099.03
Finland [2]	Euro	(NA)	Singapore	Singapore Dollar	1.79
France [2]	Euro	(NA)	Slovakia	Koruny	45.33
Gabon	Cfa Francs	696.99	Slovenia	Tolars	240.25
Georgia	Lari	2.20	South Africa	Rand	10.54
Germany [2]	Euro	(NA)	Spain [2]	Euro	(NA)
Greece	Euro	(NA)	Sri Lanka	Sri Lanka Rupees	95.66
Guatemala	Quetzales	7.82	Sudan	Sudanese Dinars	263.31
Guyana	Guyana Dollar	190.70	Suriname [1]	Suriname Guilders	2,346.75
Haiti	Gourdes	29.25	Swaziland	Emalangeni	10.48
Honduras	Lempiras	16.43	Sweden	Swedish Kronor	9.74
Hong Kong	Hong Kong Dollar	7.80	Switzerland	Swiss Francs	1.56
Hungary	Forint	257.89	Syria	Syrian Pounds	11.23
Iceland	Kronur	91.66	Tanzania	Tanzania Shilling	966.58
India	Indian Rupees	48.61	Thailand	Baht	42.96
Indonesia	Rupiah	9,311.20	Togo	Cfa Francs	696.99
Iran	Rials	6,906.96	Trinidad and Tobago	Tt Dollars	6.25
Iraq	Dinars	0.31	Tunisia	Tunisian Dinars	1.42
Ireland [2]	Euro	(NA)	Turkey	Liras	1,507,226
Israel	New Sheqalim	4.74	Uganda	Uganda Shilling	1,797.60
Italy [2]	Euro	(NA)	Ukraine	Hryvnias	5.33
Jamaica	Jamaica Dollars	48.42	United Arab Emirates	Dirhams	3.67
Japan	Yen	125.39	United Kingdom	Pounds Sterling	0.67
Jordan	Jordinian Dinars	0.71	Uruguay	Uruguayan Pesos	21.26
Kazakhstan	Tenge	153.28	Vanuatu	Vatu	139.20
Kenya	Kenya Shillings	78.75	Venezuela	Bolivares	1,160.95
Korea, South	Won	1,251.09	Yemen	Rials	175.63
Kuwait	Kuwaiti Dinars	0.30	Zambia	Zambian Kwacha	4,398.60
Kyrgyzstan	Soms	46.94	Zimbabwe	Zimbabwe Dollar	55.05

NA Not available. [1] End-of year values were used if annual averages were unavailable. Some values were estimated using partial year data. [2] The euro became the official currency of the 11 euro area (EMU) nations. [3] See footnote 2, Table 1322. [4] See footnote 3, Table 1322.

Source: U.S. Dept. of Commerce, International Trade Administration, "Foreign Exchange Rates, 1994-02"; accessed September 2003. Also see <http://www.ita.doc.gov/td/industry/otea/usfth/aggregate/H02T34.html>.

No. 1378. Reserve Assets and International Transaction Balances by Country: 1995 to 2002

[In millions of U.S. dollars (74,780 represents $74,780,000,000). Assets include holdings of convertible foreign currencies, special drawing rights, and reserve position in International Monetary Fund and exclude gold holdings. Minus sign (-) indicates debits]

Country	Total reserve assets 1995	2001	2002 Total	2002 Currency holdings[1]	Current account balance 1995	2001	2002	Merchandise trade balance 1995	2001	2002
United States......	74,780	57,630	67,960	33,820	-109,890	-393,740	-480,860	-172,330	-424,110	-479,380
Algeria...........	2,005	18,081	23,238	23,108	(NA)	(NA)	(NA)	(NA)	(NA)	(NA)
Argentina.........	14,288	14,553	10,489	10,395	-5,210	-4,554	(NA)	2,358	7,451	(NA)
Australia..........	11,896	17,955	20,689	18,618	-19,323	-8,678	-17,879	-4,223	1,874	-5,428
Austria...........	18,730	12,509	9,683	8,540	-5,448	-3,621	838	-6,656	-1,269	3,572
Bangladesh	2,340	1,275	1,683	1,681	-824	-535	(NA)	(NA)	-2,049	(NA)
Belgium [2]........	16,177	11,266	11,855	8,909	14,232	9,392	11,515	(NA)	3,707	8,118
Brazil............	49,708	35,739	37,683	37,409	-18,136	-23,215	-7,696	-3,157	2,650	13,143
Burma...........	561	401	470	470	-259	-306	(NA)	(NA)	-269	(NA)
Cameroon	4	332	630	628	90	(NA)	(NA)	(NA)	(NA)	(NA)
Canada...........	15,049	33,962	36,984	32,685	-4,328	17,422	14,909	25,855	45,864	36,838
Chile	14,140	14,379	15,341	14,814	-1,350	-1,241	(NA)	(NA)	2,094	(NA)
China [3]	75,377	215,605	291,128	286,407	1,618	17,401	35,422	18,050	34,017	44,167
Colombia	8,349	10,154	10,732	10,190	-4,596	-1,215	-1,578	-2,545	520	228
Congo (Brazzaville) [4] .	59	69	32	28	(NA)	-28	-35	(NA)	1,374	1,598
Cote d'Ivoire	529	1,019	1,863	1,862	-492	-60	767	1,376	1,528	2,735
Denmark	11,016	17,110	26,986	25,901	1,855	4,051	4,918	6,528	6,780	8,360
Ecuador..........	1,628	840	715	689	-994	-800	-1,222	-66	-462	-1,004
Egypt	16,181	12,926	13,242	13,151	-254	-388	470	-7,597	-6,935	-5,747
Finland	10,038	7,983	9,285	8,437	5,231	8,642	9,890	12,437	12,659	13,146
France...........	26,853	31,749	28,365	21,965	10,840	23,120	25,740	11,000	2,840	8,990
Germany	85,005	51,309	51,171	42,495	-18,930	2,440	46,590	65,110	88,510	122,180
Ghana...........	698	298	540	536	-145	(NA)	(NA)	(NA)	(NA)	(NA)
Greece	14,780	5,154	8,083	7,629	-2,864	-9,400	-10,405	-14,425	-19,087	-21,452
Hungary..........	11,974	10,727	10,348	9,721	-2,530	-1,097	-2,644	-2,433	-2,018	-2,119
India	17,922	45,870	67,665	66,994	-5,563	(NA)	(NA)	-6,719	(NA)	(NA)
Indonesia.........	13,708	27,246	30,969	30,753	-6,431	6,899	7,451	6,533	22,695	23,212
Ireland...........	8,630	5,587	5,415	4,879	1,721	-690	-925	13,557	27,263	34,898
Israel............	8,119	23,379	24,083	23,665	-4,994	-1,730	-2,135	-7,261	-3,549	-3,757
Italy.............	34,905	24,419	28,603	24,588	25,076	-652	-6,741	38,729	15,540	16,533
Japan	183,250	395,155	461,186	451,458	111,040	87,800	112,450	131,790	70,210	93,830
Kenya	353	1,065	1,068	1,050	-400	-318	(NA)	(NA)	-1,282	(NA)
Korea, South	32,678	102,753	121,345	120,811	-8,507	8,239	6,092	-4,444	13,492	14,180
Kuwait...........	3,561	9,897	9,208	8,357	5,016	8,562	(NA)	(NA)	9,238	(NA)
Malaysia	23,774	30,474	34,222	33,280	-8,644	7,287	(NA)	(NA)	18,383	(NA)
Mexico...........	16,847	44,741	50,594	49,895	-1,576	-18,033	-14,069	7,089	-9,955	-7,995
Morocco..........	3,601	8,474	10,133	9,915	-1,296	1,606	1,488	-2,482	-3,022	-3,036
Nepal	586	1,038	1,018	1,010	-356	-339	(NA)	(NA)	-765	(NA)
Netherlands	33,714	9,034	9,563	6,017	25,759	8,144	9,866	23,812	20,913	25,754
Nigeria...........	1,443	10,457	7,331	7,331	-2,578	(NA)	(NA)	(NA)	(NA)	(NA)
Norway	22,518	15,488	20,682	19,374	4,854	26,530	25,148	8,571	26,446	24,371
Pakistan..........	1,733	3,640	8,078	8,076	-3,349	1,880	(NA)	(NA)	-608	(NA)
Peru	8,222	8,618	9,339	9,338	-4,125	-1,098	(NA)	(NA)	-92	(NA)
Philippines	6,372	13,442	13,144	13,015	-1,980	4,150	(NA)	(NA)	2,763	(NA)
Poland...........	14,774	25,648	28,650	27,959	854	-5,357	(NA)	(NA)	-7,660	(NA)
Portugal..........	15,850	9,667	11,179	10,656	-132	-10,404	-9,120	-8,910	-13,301	-12,411
Romania	1,579	5,442	7,211	7,209	-1,780	-2,229	-1,573	-1,577	-2,969	-2,613
Saudi Arabia......	8,622	17,596	20,610	16,715	-5,325	9,366	11,696	24,390	39,418	42,037
Singapore	68,695	75,375	82,021	81,367	14,900	17,884	(NA)	(NA)	12,872	(NA)
South Africa......	2,820	6,045	5,904	5,601	-2,205	-296	290	2,667	4,860	4,372
Spain	34,485	29,582	34,536	32,590	792	-16,404	-15,942	-18,415	-32,539	-33,098
Sri Lanka.........	2,088	1,287	1,631	1,564	-770	-265	(NA)	(NA)	-554	(NA)
Sudan...........	163	118	441	441	-500	-618	-960	-510	304	-204
Sweden	24,051	13,977	17,127	15,520	4,940	6,696	(NA)	(NA)	13,832	(NA)
Switzerland.......	36,413	32,006	40,155	38,164	21,804	22,624	(NA)	(NA)	1,564	(NA)
Syria	(NA)	(NA)	(NA)	(NA)	263	(NA)	(NA)	(NA)	(NA)	(NA)
Thailand..........	35,982	32,355	38,046	38,042	-13,554	6,221	7,650	-7,968	8,582	9,775
Trinidad and Tobago..	358	1,907	2,028	1,924	294	(NA)	(NA)	(NA)	(NA)	(NA)
Turkey...........	12,442	18,879	27,069	26,884	-2,338	3,396	-1,789	-13,212	-4,537	-8,635
United Kingdom....	42,020	37,280	39,360	32,790	-14,290	-17,890	-14,410	19,010	-48,200	-53,050
Venezuela	6,283	9,239	8,487	8,038	2,014	3,931	(NA)	(NA)	9,335	(NA)

NA Not available. [1] Holdings of convertible foreign currencies. [2] Balance of payments current account and trade balance data prior to 2002 is for Belgium-Luxembourg. Thereafter, data is for Belgium only. [3] See footnote 2, Table 1322. [4] See footnote 3, Table 1322.

Source: International Monetary Fund, Washington, DC, *International Financial Statistics*, monthly, (copyright).

No. 1379. Foreign Trade—Destination of Exports and Source of Imports for Selected Countries: 2001

[In billions of dollars (1,132.5 represents $1,132,500,000,000), except as indicated]

Country	United States Imports	United States Exports	Canada Imports	Canada Exports	Australia Imports	Australia Exports	Japan Imports	Japan Exports	France Imports	France Exports	Germany Imports	Germany Exports	Italy Imports	Italy Exports	United Kingdom Imports	United Kingdom Exports
World [1]	1,132.5	731.0	221.3	259.6	60.9	63.3	348.6	402.6	304.2	299.8	486.3	572.0	241.2	250.1	337.8	282.1
Canada	216.8	163.7	-	-	0.9	0.9	7.7	6.6	1.9	2.7	2.9	4.6	1.4	2.4	5.5	4.7
Mexico	130.5	101.5	4.6	1.7	0.3	0.2	2.0	4.1	0.6	1.3	1.4	4.7	0.3	1.8	1.0	1.0
United States	-	-	140.9	226.3	11.1	6.2	63.6	122.3	27.2	26.5	39.8	59.7	11.8	24.2	45.1	42.9
Australia	6.3	10.9	1.0	0.7	-	-	14.4	7.7	0.8	1.0	1.0	3.2	1.4	1.4	2.6	3.3
Japan	126.1	57.6	9.5	5.3	7.9	12.2	-	-	10.2	5.0	20.4	11.4	5.8	4.3	13.5	5.3
Korea	34.9	22.2	3.0	1.3	2.4	4.9	17.2	25.3	2.1	2.2	4.3	4.0	2.2	1.9	4.1	1.9
Czech Republic	1.1	0.7	0.1	(Z)	(Z)	0.1	0.2	0.3	1.4	2.0	12.9	12.9	1.3	2.0	1.6	1.6
Hungary	3.0	0.7	0.1	0.1	(Z)	(Z)	0.4	0.7	1.8	1.7	10.7	9.3	1.8	2.8	1.0	0.9
Norway	5.2	1.8	2.3	0.6	0.1	0.1	1.0	0.7	6.5	1.1	6.6	4.3	0.8	1.0	8.5	0.9
Poland	1.0	0.8	0.2	0.1	(Z)	(Z)	0.1	0.3	2.0	3.2	11.9	13.4	2.0	3.9	1.7	2.7
Switzerland	9.7	9.8	0.9	0.2	0.7	(Z)	3.3	2.0	7.1	10.1	17.3	23.9	9.0	9.1	7.0	1.9
Russia	6.2	2.7	0.2	0.2	(Z)	0.1	3.8	0.7	4.7	2.1	8.7	9.1	4.8	3.3	3.0	5.4
Algeria	2.6	1.0	0.7	0.2	(Z)	(Z)	0.1	0.2	2.8	3.1	0.8	1.3	1.1	1.4	0.3	1.3
Egypt	0.9	3.8	(Z)	0.1	(Z)	0.4	0.3	0.6	0.2	0.9	0.3	0.9	1.0	1.0	0.6	0.2
Nigeria	8.9	1.0	0.3	0.1	(Z)	(Z)	0.3	0.4	1.1	0.7	0.6	0.9	0.4	0.5	0.1	0.7
South Africa	4.4	3.0	0.3	0.2	0.4	0.7	2.8	1.5	0.9	1.0	2.9	3.9	1.9	1.0	4.3	2.2
Columbia	5.6	3.6	0.3	0.2	(Z)	(Z)	0.3	0.6	0.2	0.3	0.5	0.5	0.3	0.8	0.5	0.2
Brazil	14.4	15.9	1.0	0.6	0.1	0.2	2.5	2.5	2.4	2.6	3.7	5.0	2.1	2.4	1.9	1.2
Argentina	3.0	3.9	0.3	0.1	0.2	0.1	0.4	0.9	0.5	0.7	0.8	1.0	0.9	0.8	0.3	0.4
Israel	12.0	7.5	0.4	0.2	0.7	0.2	0.8	0.5	0.9	1.3	1.8	2.3	0.8	1.7	1.4	2.0
Saudi Arabia	12.4	6.0	0.5	0.3	(Z)	0.1	12.3	3.6	2.3	1.4	0.8	2.7	2.0	1.6	1.4	2.2
Iran	0.1	(Z)	(Z)	(Z)	(Z)	0.4	5.0	0.8	0.7	1.1	0.4	1.7	2.2	1.1	(Z)	0.6
Pakistan	2.2	0.7	0.2	0.4	(Z)	0.2	2.2	0.5	0.4	0.3	0.5	0.5	0.3	0.3	0.6	0.3
India	9.7	3.8	0.7	0.3	0.4	1.3	10.4	1.9	1.7	0.9	2.2	2.0	1.5	0.9	2.7	2.6
Thailand	14.7	6.0	1.1	0.2	1.4	1.3	12.8	11.9	1.8	0.8	2.3	2.1	0.6	0.6	2.4	0.9
Malaysia	22.2	9.4	1.2	0.2	2.0	1.7	14.8	11.0	1.2	0.9	3.2	2.2	0.6	1.0	2.9	0.9
Indonesia	9.9	2.5	0.6	0.3	2.0	1.7	14.8	6.4	1.0	0.5	2.1	1.7	0.9	0.5	1.7	0.4
China [2]	102.1	19.2	8.2	2.7	5.3	3.9	57.8	30.9	10.0	3.0	17.7	10.7	6.9	3.0	8.6	2.5
European Union [1]	218.9	159.4	24.8	11.8	13.7	7.6	44.5	64.4	180.8	183.1	242.5	307.6	135.1	133.2	162.9	154.9
Denmark	3.4	1.6	0.5	0.3	0.3	0.1	2.1	0.6	2.2	2.2	7.6	11.4	1.7	1.9	3.9	3.2
Sweden	8.8	3.5	1.1	0.2	0.8	0.1	2.2	1.4	4.0	4.5	8.0	11.4	3.2	2.3	6.6	5.6
United Kingdom	41.1	40.8	7.5	3.3	3.2	2.7	6.0	12.1	22.8	29.5	32.8	46.4	12.2	16.7	-	-
Austria	3.9	2.6	0.7	0.2	0.3	(Z)	0.9	0.9	3.0	3.0	18.2	29.3	5.8	5.3	2.7	1.7
Belgium-Luxembourg	10.3	14.1	3.6	1.3	1.3	0.5	1.5	4.8	21.2	22.7	25.1	30.7	11.3	7.9	16.5	13.8
France	30.0	20.1	5.1	1.4	3.4	0.6	6.2	6.3	-	-	44.3	61.3	26.9	30.3	26.9	27.0
Germany	58.9	30.1	4.5	1.9	4.0	0.7	12.4	15.6	50.7	43.0	-	-	42.7	36.1	40.7	33.2
Finland	3.4	1.6	0.4	0.2	0.4	0.2	0.9	1.0	2.3	1.7	5.8	5.9	1.6	1.2	4.2	2.3
Ireland	18.6	7.1	0.9	0.2	0.7	0.7	3.6	1.3	5.5	2.6	14.1	3.4	3.3	1.4	13.4	20.2
Italy	23.7	9.9	2.6	1.0	1.8	1.1	5.4	4.8	27.2	26.3	31.3	41.4	-	-	14.3	11.8
Netherlands	9.4	19.5	0.9	1.0	0.5	0.8	1.9	11.5	14.4	12.0	35.6	34.0	13.9	6.6	21.3	20.5
Spain	5.2	5.8	0.6	0.6	0.4	0.4	1.9	2.7	20.7	28.9	13.5	24.5	10.1	15.3	9.7	11.7

- Represents zero. Z Less than 50,000,000. [1] Includes other countries not shown separately. [2] See footnote 2, Table 1322.

Source: Organization for Economic Cooperation and Development, Paris, France, OECD International Trade by Commodities Statistics, 2001.

Comparative International Statistics 875

No. 1380. International Tourism Arrivals, Expenditures, and Receipts—Leading Countries: 1990 to 2001

[Expenditures in billions of dollars; receipts in millions of dollars; arrivals in thousands of visitors (457,298 represents 457,298,000). Receipts are dollars spent by foreign tourists. Excludes international transport receipts]

Country	Arrivals 1990	Arrivals 1995	Arrivals 1998	Arrivals 1999	Arrivals 2000	Arrivals 2001	Expenditures 2000	Expenditures 2001	Receipts 1990	Receipts 1995	Receipts 1998	Receipts 1999	Receipts 2000	Receipts 2001
World, total[1]	457,298	551,724	628,765	652,315	696,758	692,583	(NA)	(NA)	263,364	405,251	443,982	457,217	477,031	463,572
United States	39,362	43,318	46,404	48,497	50,945	45,490	64.5	58.9	43,007	63,395	71,286	74,731	82,042	72,295
Spain	34,085	34,920	43,396	46,776	47,898	49,519	5.6	(NA)	18,593	25,388	29,839	32,497	31,454	32,873
France	52,497	60,033	70,040	73,042	75,580	76,506	17.8	17.7	20,184	27,527	29,931	31,507	30,754	29,979
Italy	26,679	31,052	34,933	36,516	41,181	39,055	15.7	14.2	16,458	28,729	29,866	28,359	27,500	25,787
Ireland	3,666	4,818	6,064	6,403	6,749	6,448	3.0	(NA)	1,883	2,691	3,247	3,320	3,387	3,547
United Kingdom	18,013	23,537	25,744	25,396	25,211	22,833	36.3	36.5	13,762	18,554	20,978	20,223	19,544	16,283
Germany	17,045	14,847	16,511	17,116	18,983	17,861	47.6	46.2	14,288	18,135	16,766	18,116	18,483	17,225
Austria	19,011	17,173	17,352	17,467	17,982	18,180	8.5	8.9	13,417	12,927	11,276	11,035	9,931	10,118
Canada	15,209	16,932	18,828	19,367	19,663	19,697	12.1	11.6	6,339	7,882	9,396	10,171	10,704	10,774
Greece	8,873	10,130	10,916	12,164	13,096	(NA)	4.6	(NA)	2,587	4,136	6,188	8,783	9,219	7,625
Australia	2,215	3,726	4,167	4,459	4,946	4,817	5.7	(NA)	4,088	7,857	7,335	8,027	8,452	7,618
Switzerland	13,200	11,500	10,900	10,700	11,000	10,700	6.2	6.6	7,411	9,365	7,973	7,769	7,500	(NA)
Russia	(NA)	10,290	15,805	18,496	21,169	(NA)	(NA)	(NA)	(NA)	4,312	6,508	7,510	(NA)	(NA)
Poland	20,510	19,215	18,780	17,950	17,400	15,000	3.6	(NA)	358	6,614	7,946	6,100	6,100	4,815
Hungary	(NA)	19,620	16,812	14,102	15,571	15,340	1.1	(NA)	824	2,640	3,514	3,407	3,438	3,933
Czech Republic	(NA)	3,381	5,482	5,610	4,666	5,194	1.3	(NA)	419	2,875	3,719	3,035	2,869	2,979
Ukraine	7,049	3,716	6,208	4,232	4,406	5,791	(NA)	(NA)	(NA)	3,865	3,317	2,124	2,207	2,725
Croatia	1,091	1,485	4,499	3,805	5,831	6,544	0.6	(NA)	1,704	1,349	3,311	2,493	2,758	3,335
Brazil	1,091	1,991	4,818	5,107	5,313	4,773	3.9	(NA)	1,444	2,097	3,678	3,994	4,228	3,701
Mexico	17,176	20,241	19,392	19,043	20,641	19,811	5.5	11.6	5,467	6,179	7,493	7,223	8,295	8,401
Netherlands	5,795	6,574	9,312	9,874	10,003	9,500	12.2	12.0	4,155	6,562	6,850	6,996	7,217	6,722
Belgium	(NA)	5,560	6,179	6,369	6,457	6,452	9.4	9.8	3,721	4,677	4,623	6,472	6,588	6,917
China[2]	(NA)	20,034	25,073	27,047	31,229	33,167	13.1	(NA)	2,218	8,733	12,602	14,099	16,224	17,792
Hong Kong	6,581	10,200	10,160	11,328	13,059	13,725	12.5	12.5	5,032	9,604	7,496	7,210	7,886	8,241
Macau	2,513	4,202	4,517	5,050	5,197	5,842	(NA)	(NA)	1,473	3,233	2,648	2,598	3,205	3,745
Korea, South	2,959	3,753	4,250	4,660	5,322	5,147	6.2	6.9	3,559	5,587	5,934	6,802	6,811	6,283
Thailand	5,299	6,952	7,843	8,651	9,579	10,133	2.1	(NA)	4,326	7,664	5,934	6,734	7,146	6,731
Malaysia	7,446	7,469	5,551	7,931	10,222	12,775	5.0	(NA)	1,667	3,900	2,456	3,540	4,936	(NA)
Singapore	4,842	6,422	5,631	6,258	6,917	6,726	1.1	(NA)	4,937	8,390	5,402	5,859	6,018	3,800
Egypt	2,411	2,871	3,213	4,490	5,116	4,357	1.7	(NA)	1,100	2,684	2,565	3,903	4,345	3,745
Turkey	4,799	7,083	8,960	6,893	9,586	10,783	2.2	(NA)	3,225	4,957	7,809	5,203	7,636	8,932
Portugal	8,020	9,511	11,295	11,632	12,097	12,167	3.2	(NA)	3,555	4,339	5,302	5,261	5,257	5,479
Indonesia	2,178	4,324	4,606	4,728	5,064	5,154	2.0	(NA)	2,105	5,229	4,331	4,710	5,749	5,411
South Africa	1,029	4,684	5,898	6,026	6,001	5,908	0.3	(NA)	992	2,126	2,717	2,637	2,707	(NA)
Tunisia	3,204	4,120	4,718	4,832	5,057	5,387	0.3	(NA)	948	1,393	1,557	1,560	1,496	1,605

NA Not available. [1] Includes other countries not shown separately. [2] See footnote 2, Table 1322.

Source: World Tourism Organization, Madrid, Spain, *Yearbook of Tourism Statistics, 2002* (copyright).

No. 1381. Net Flow of Financial Resources to Developing Countries and Multilateral Organizations: 1995 to 2001

[165,182 represents $165,182,000,000. Net flow covers loans, grants, and grant-like flows minus amortization on loans. Military flows are excluded. Developing countries cover countries designated by Development Assistance Committee as developing. GNP=gross national product]

Type of aid and country	Amount (mil. dol.)					Percent of GNP	
	1995	1998	1999	2000	2001	2000	2001
Total net flows	165,182	182,407	193,740	133,788	108,193	0.56	0.46
Official Development Assistance [1]	58,926	52,084	56,378	(NA)	(NA)	(X)	(X)
Other Official Flows [2]	9,872	13,491	15,477	(NA)	(NA)	(X)	(X)
Private flows at market terms [3]	90,411	111,223	110,404	(NA)	(NA)	(X)	(X)
Net grants by nongovernment organizations	5,973	5,609	6,684	(NA)	(NA)	(X)	(X)
United States	46,984	48,421	50,138	25,252	38,618	0.25	0.38
Australia	2,536	1,745	1,279	1,491	1,183	0.40	0.34
Austria	906	889	1,963	1,067	882	0.57	0.48
Belgium	-234	7,725	5,528	2,281	304	1.00	0.13
Canada	5,724	9,227	6,992	6,483	1,538	0.95	0.22
Denmark	1,799	1,806	1,992	2,176	2,645	1.39	1.67
Finland	604	1,633	858	1,087	1,317	0.91	1.09
France	12,477	8,402	9,160	5,557	16,327	0.43	1.24
Germany	21,197	22,436	20,006	12,331	5,872	0.66	0.32
Greece	-	189	195	229	202	0.20	0.17
Ireland	247	333	251	741	735	0.93	0.85
Italy	2,800	13,171	11,337	10,846	-189	1.01	-0.02
Japan	42,295	17,902	20,794	11,264	14,608	0.23	0.35
Luxembourg	72	118	124	129	146	0.75	0.85
Netherlands	6,795	12,752	7,985	6,947	-3,432	1.85	-0.89
New Zealand	166	154	163	142	139	0.32	0.32
Norway	1,670	1,983	2,060	1,437	1,485	0.91	0.91
Portugal	395	2,015	2,457	4,622	1,775	4.45	1.66
Spain	2,025	11,841	29,029	23,471	11,523	4.25	2.01
Sweden	2,224	2,847	2,892	3,952	3,077	1.76	1.49
Switzerland	1,118	4,683	3,241	2,054	-158	0.80	-0.06
United Kingdom	13,382	12,136	15,299	10,230	9,597	0.72	0.67

- Represents zero.   NA Not available.   X Not applicable.   [1] Grants or loans to countries and territories on Part I of the DAC List of Aid Recipients (developing countries) which are: (a) undertaken by the official sector; (b) with promotion of economic development and welfare as the main objective; (c) at concessional financial terms (if a loan, having a grant element of at least 25 per cent). Technical cooperation is included in aid.   [2] Transactions by the official sector with countries on the List of Aid Recipients which do not meet the conditions for eligibility as Official Development Assistance or Official Aid, either because they are not primarily aimed at development, or because they have a grant element of less than 25 per cent.   [3] Consists of flows at market terms financed out of private sector resources (i.e. changes in holdings of private long term assets held by residents of the reporting country) and private grants (i.e. grants by nongovernment organizations, net of subsidies received from the official sector).

Source: Organization for Economic Cooperation and Development, Paris, France, *Annual Reports of the Development Assistance Committee* (copyright).

No. 1382. External Debt by Country: 1990 to 2001

[In millions of dollars (28,149 represents $28,149,000,000). Total external debt is debt owed to nonresidents repayable in foreign currency, goods or services. Total external debt is the sum of public, publicly guaranteed, and private nonguaranteed long-term debt, use of IMF credit, and short-term debt. Short-term debt includes all debt having an original maturity of 1 year or less and interest in arrears on long-term debt]

Country	1990	1995	2000	2001	Country	1990	1995	2000	2001
Algeria	28,149	33,042	25,273	22,503	Malaysia	15,328	34,343	41,797	43,351
Angola	8,594	11,502	9,309	9,600	Mexico	104,442	166,637	158,479	158,290
Argentina	62,233	98,802	145,879	136,709	Morocco	24,458	22,665	17,945	16,963
Bangladesh	12,439	15,924	15,679	15,216	Nigeria	33,439	34,093	31,355	31,119
Brazil	119,964	160,505	238,797	226,362	Pakistan	20,663	30,229	32,791	32,020
Bulgaria	10,890	10,291	10,143	9,615	Panama	6,507	6,108	7,046	8,245
Cameroon	6,676	9,385	9,243	8,338	Peru	20,064	30,852	28,703	27,512
Chile	19,226	22,038	36,997	38,360	Philippines	30,580	37,831	50,382	52,356
China [1]	55,301	118,090	145,706	170,110	Poland	49,364	44,263	63,259	62,393
Colombia	17,222	25,048	33,934	36,699	Romania	1,140	6,784	10,177	11,653
Congo (Kinshasa) [2]	10,259	13,239	11,692	11,392	Russia	59,340	122,050	160,100	152,649
Cote d'Ivoire	17,251	18,899	12,138	11,582	Serbia and Montenegro	17,792	11,137	11,725	11,740
Croatia	(NA)	3,830	10,519	10,742	Slovakia	2,008	5,744	12,109	11,121
Czech Republic	6,383	16,218	21,609	21,691	South Africa	(NA)	25,358	24,861	24,050
Ecuador	12,107	13,994	13,252	13,910	Sri Lanka	5,863	8,369	9,019	8,529
Egypt	33,017	33,337	29,027	29,234	Sudan	14,762	17,603	15,741	15,348
Ghana	3,881	5,936	6,658	6,759	Syria	17,259	21,415	21,657	21,305
Hungary	21,202	31,649	29,511	30,289	Tanzania	6,456	7,412	7,386	6,676
India	83,628	94,464	99,098	97,320	Thailand	28,095	100,039	79,695	67,384
Indonesia	69,872	124,398	144,057	135,704	Tunisia	7,690	10,820	10,610	10,884
Iran	9,021	21,879	7,982	7,483	Turkey	49,424	73,781	118,285	115,118
Jordan	8,333	7,659	7,366	7,480	Ukraine	(NA)	8,429	12,190	12,811
Kazakhstan	(NA)	3,750	11,805	14,372	Uruguay	4,415	5,318	8,196	9,706
Korea, South	34,968	85,810	128,396	110,109	Venezuela	33,171	35,538	37,838	34,660
Lebanon	1,779	2,966	9,856	12,450	Vietnam	23,270	25,427	12,835	12,578

NA Not available.   [1] See footnote 2, Table 1322.   [2] See footnote 3, Table 1322.

Source: The World Bank, Washington, DC, *2003 World Development Indicators CD-ROM* (copyright).

No. 1383. Military Expenditures and Armed Forces Personnel by Country: 1990 and 1999

[Military expenditures in millions of dollars, except as indicated (306,000 represents $306,000,000,000). Personnel data as of July. For most countries, data for expenditures and for gross national product (GNP) were based on local currencies which were deflated to constant 1999 local currency values before conversion to U.S. dollar equivalents. In general, the rates used for conversion are the 1999 average par/market exchange rates as supplied by the World Bank. Armed Forces refer to active-duty military personnel, including paramilitary forces where those forces resemble regular units in their organization, equipment, training, or mission. Reserve forces are not included]

Country	Current dollars 1990	Current dollars 1999	Constant (1999) dollars 1990	Constant (1999) dollars 1999 Total	Constant (1999) dollars 1999 Percent of GNP	Constant (1999) dollars 1999 Per capita (dollars)	Armed Forces Number (1,000) 1990	Armed Forces Number (1,000) 1999	Per 1,000 population 1990	Per 1,000 population 1999
United States	306,000	281,000	370,000	281,000	3.0	1,030	2,180	1,490	8.7	5.4
Algeria	654	1,830	791	1,830	4.0	60	126	120	5.0	3.9
Angola	1,560	[1]2,460	1,880	[1]2,460	[1]21.2	[1]248	115	100	13.6	10.1
Argentina	2,690	4,300	3,260	4,300	1.6	118	85	73	2.6	2.0
Australia	5,100	7,060	6,160	7,060	1.8	372	68	55	4.0	2.9
Bangladesh	293	624	354	624	1.3	5	103	[1]110	0.9	[1]0.9
Belgium	4,130	3,600	4,990	3,600	1.4	352	106	42	10.6	4.1
Brazil	6,210	9,920	7,510	9,920	1.9	58	295	300	2.0	1.8
Bulgaria	(NA)	1,240	(NA)	1,240	3.0	158	129	70	14.4	8.9
Burma	(NA)	4,650	(NA)	4,650	7.8	112	230	345	5.6	8.3
Canada	7,750	8,320	9,370	8,320	1.4	269	87	60	3.3	1.9
Chile	[1]946	1,990	[1]1,140	1,990	3.0	133	95	88	7.2	5.9
China [2]	47,800	88,900	57,700	88,900	2.3	71	3,500	2,400	3.1	1.9
Colombia	1,190	2,670	1,430	2,670	3.2	68	110	155	3.3	4.0
Congo (Kinshasa) [3]	(NA)	[1]5,150	(NA)	[1]5,150	[1]14.4	102	55	55	1.5	1.1
Croatia	(NA)	2,090	(NA)	2,090	6.4	491	(NA)	60	(NA)	14.1
Cuba	1,380	[1]630	1,670	[1]630	1.9	[1]57	297	50	28.1	4.5
Czech Republic	(X)	3,000	(X)	3,000	2.3	292	(X)	54	(X)	5.3
Egypt	1,610	2,390	1,940	2,390	2.7	36	434	430	7.7	6.4
France	36,000	38,900	43,500	38,900	2.7	658	550	421	9.7	7.1
Germany [4]	37,200	32,600	45,000	32,600	1.6	395	545	331	6.9	4.0
Greece	3,830	6,060	4,630	6,060	4.7	573	201	204	19.9	19.3
Hungary	1,970	1,880	2,380	1,880	1.7	185	94	51	9.1	5.0
India	6,170	11,300	7,460	11,300	2.5	11	1,260	1,300	1.5	1.3
Indonesia	1,160	1,450	1,400	1,450	1.1	7	283	296	1.5	1.3
Iran	8,260	6,880	9,990	6,880	2.9	106	440	460	7.7	[1]7.1
Iraq	12,000	1,250	14,500	1,250	5.5	57	1,390	420	75.4	19.1
Israel	6,850	8,700	8,290	8,700	8.8	1,510	190	173	42.1	30.1
Italy	18,200	23,700	22,000	23,700	2.0	412	493	391	8.5	6.8
Japan	31,100	43,200	37,500	43,200	1.0	342	250	240	2.0	1.9
Jordan	416	725	503	725	9.2	150	100	102	30.5	21.1
Kenya	206	[1]200	248	[1]200	[1]1.9	[1]7	20	24	0.8	0.8
Korea, North	5,940	4,260	7,180	4,260	18.8	199	1,200	1,000	56.0	46.8
Korea, South	8,430	11,600	10,200	11,600	2.9	246	650	665	15.2	14.1
Kuwait	[1]12,900	2,690	[1]15,600	2,690	7.7	1,410	7	21	3.3	11.0
Libya	(NA)	(NA)	(NA)	(NA)	(NA)	(NA)	86	[1]85	19.7	[1]17.0
Malaysia	921	1,660	1,110	1,660	2.3	78	130	95	7.4	4.4
Mexico	1,430	2,700	1,730	2,700	0.6	27	175	255	2.1	2.6
Netherlands	6,410	7,030	7,750	7,030	1.8	445	104	54	7.0	3.4
New Zealand	695	587	841	587	1.2	156	11	10	3.3	2.6
Nigeria	1,150	1,560	1,390	1,560	[1]1.6	[1]13	94	77	1.1	0.6
Pakistan	2,450	[1]3,520	2,960	[1]3,520	[1]5.9	[1]25	550	590	4.8	4.3
Peru	660	1,200	798	1,200	2.4	45	125	115	5.7	4.3
Philippines	1,070	1,110	1,300	1,110	1.4	14	109	107	1.7	1.3
Poland	[1]8,760	6,690	[1]10,600	6,690	2.1	173	313	187	8.2	4.8
Romania	4,870	2,190	5,890	2,190	1.6	97	126	170	5.5	7.6
Russia	(X)	35,000	(X)	35,000	5.6	239	(X)	900	(X)	6.1
Saudi Arabia	[1]23,200	21,200	[1]28,000	21,200	14.9	996	146	190	9.2	8.9
Serbia and Montenegro	[1]3,700	[1]1,030	[1]4,480	[1]1,030	5.0	103	180	105	7.6	10.5
Singapore	1,850	4,400	2,230	4,400	4.8	1,100	56	60	18.4	15.0
Slovakia	(X)	1,010	(X)	1,010	1.8	187	(X)	36	(X)	6.7
Slovenia	(X)	436	(X)	436	1.4	227	(X)	10	(X)	5.2
South Africa	[1]3,690	1,960	[1]4,460	1,960	1.5	45	85	68	2.3	1.6
Spain	7,090	7,560	8,580	7,560	1.3	192	263	155	6.8	3.9
Sri Lanka	(NA)	729	(NA)	729	4.7	38	22	110	1.3	5.8
Sweden	4,360	5,330	5,270	5,330	2.3	601	65	52	7.6	5.9
Syria	(NA)	4,450	(NA)	4,450	7.0	280	408	310	32.3	19.5
Taiwan [2]	6,720	15,200	8,130	15,200	5.2	690	370	370	18.2	16.8
Tanzania	83	122	100	122	1.4	4	40	35	1.6	1.0
Thailand	1,690	2,040	2,040	2,040	1.7	34	283	300	5.1	4.9
Turkey	4,090	9,950	4,950	9,950	5.3	154	769	789	13.7	12.2
Ukraine	(X)	5,110	(X)	5,110	3.0	103	(X)	340	(X)	6.9
United Kingdom	39,700	36,500	48,000	36,500	2.5	615	308	218	5.4	3.7
Vietnam	5,170	(NA)	6,250	(NA)	(NA)	(NA)	1,050	485	15.9	6.2

NA Not available. X Not applicable. [1] Data probably omit a major share of total military expenditures, probably including most arms acquisitions. [2] See footnote 2, Table 1322. [3] See footnote 3, Table 1322. [4] Data for 1990 are for former West Germany (prior to unification); data for 1999 are for unified Germany.

Source: U.S. Dept. of State, Bureau of Verification and Compliance, *World Military Expenditures and Arms Transfers*, annual.

Section 31
Congressional District Profiles

This section presents selected population and housing items from the 108th Congressional District Summary Files of the 2000 Census of Population and Housing. Statistics are presented for all states and the District of Columbia for the newly defined boundaries of the 108th Congress. More information and maps for each congressional district are available through American FactFinder at the following Census Web page: <http://www.census.gov/PressRelease/www/2003/108th.html>.

Statistical reliability—For a discussion of statistical collection and estimation, sampling procedures, and measures of statistical reliability applicable to Census Bureau data, see Appendix III.

No. 1384. Congressional District Profiles—108th Congress: 2000

[Data in these profiles provide summaries from Census 2000 for the newly defined boundaries of the 108th Congress. See Appendix III for comments on methodology. Maps for each congressional district are available at source listed at bottom of table]

State and district	Total population (number)	Age Under 18 years	Age 65 years and over	Race White alone	Black or African American alone	American Indian and Alaska native alone	Asian alone	Native Hawaiian and Other Pacific Islander alone	Two or more races	Hispanic or Latino origin[1]	Foreign born	Average population per household	High school graduate or higher, percent of population 25 yrs. and over	Management, professional and related occupations	Manufacturing industries	Median household income in 1999 (dol.)	Percent of population below poverty level in 1999[2]	Percent owner occupied	Median value[3] (dol.)
AL........	4,447,100	25.3	13.0	71.1	26.0	0.5	0.7	.	1.0	1.7	2.0	2.49	75.3	29.5	18.4	34,135	16.1	72.5	85,100
1st...	635,300	26.7	13.0	68.5	28.1	1.0	1.0	.	1.0	1.2	2.0	2.57	77.0	28.2	15.5	34,739	16.9	73.1	85,300
2d...	635,300	25.6	13.3	67.7	29.6	0.4	0.6	.	1.0	1.5	1.7	2.48	74.3	28.9	15.4	32,460	17.2	71.7	79,100
3d...	635,300	24.6	12.9	65.5	32.4	0.3	0.6	.	0.8	1.2	1.5	2.47	71.9	26.9	22.1	30,806	18.8	71.0	76,400
4th...	635,300	24.2	14.6	91.5	5.2	0.4	0.2	.	1.0	3.0	2.2	2.49	68.9	23.2	26.5	31,344	14.7	78.1	75,000
5th...	635,300	24.9	12.3	77.8	17.0	1.0	1.0	.	1.6	2.0	2.6	2.46	78.5	33.3	22.9	38,054	12.5	72.5	90,500
6th...	635,300	24.5	12.3	89.7	7.7	0.3	0.9	.	0.8	1.6	2.3	2.50	82.9	38.5	11.3	46,946	8.1	78.0	129,100
7th...	635,300	26.4	13.0	36.0	62.0	0.2	0.6	.	0.7	1.3	1.5	2.49	73.2	25.4	15.0	26,672	24.7	62.8	68,100
AK........	626,932	30.4	5.7	69.3	3.5	15.6	4.0	0.5	5.4	4.1	5.9	2.74	88.3	34.4	3.3	51,571	9.4	62.5	144,200
At large..	626,932	30.4	5.7	69.3	3.5	15.6	4.0	0.5	5.4	4.1	5.9	2.74	88.3	34.4	3.3	51,571	9.4	62.5	144,200
AZ........	5,130,632	26.6	13.0	75.5	3.1	5.0	1.8	0.1	2.9	25.3	12.8	2.64	81.0	32.7	10.2	40,558	13.9	68.0	121,300
1st...	641,329	28.2	13.7	65.8	1.3	22.6	0.5	0.1	2.2	16.4	4.9	2.74	77.3	28.5	6.2	32,979	20.3	71.5	103,500
2d...	641,329	24.0	20.5	85.5	2.2	1.3	1.7	0.1	2.3	7.4	7.4	2.50	84.1	30.0	8.9	42,432	8.9	79.3	118,000
3d...	641,329	25.0	10.3	85.7	2.4	1.3	2.1	0.1	2.5	14.1	11.0	2.50	87.8	37.4	8.6	48,108	8.7	66.5	140,400
4th...	641,329	32.9	6.7	54.2	7.9	3.2	1.4	0.2	4.2	58.0	29.7	3.18	63.1	18.3	12.2	30,624	25.6	50.7	80,300
5th...	641,329	22.6	12.4	83.0	2.8	2.1	3.4	0.2	2.7	13.3	10.7	2.42	91.7	42.4	12.2	51,780	8.4	63.0	160,500
6th...	641,329	27.9	11.5	84.2	2.1	1.0	1.8	0.1	2.5	17.2	9.8	2.72	85.4	33.8	15.2	47,976	7.7	77.4	135,200
7th...	641,329	29.7	11.3	61.9	3.0	6.4	1.4	0.2	3.5	50.6	20.1	2.88	68.0	25.1	8.9	30,828	21.8	66.1	85,800
8th...	641,329	22.9	16.8	83.7	3.1	1.0	2.1	0.1	3.0	18.2	8.8	2.36	88.5	38.8	8.7	40,656	10.5	67.1	124,600
AR........	2,673,400	25.4	14.0	80.0	15.7	0.7	0.8	0.1	1.3	3.2	2.8	2.49	75.3	27.7	19.4	32,182	15.8	69.4	72,800
1st...	668,360	25.7	15.1	81.0	16.7	0.4	0.3	.	1.0	1.6	1.0	2.50	70.4	24.9	21.7	28,940	18.5	69.6	63,600
2d...	666,058	25.2	12.2	76.6	19.5	0.5	0.9	.	1.3	2.4	2.6	2.46	81.3	32.3	12.2	37,221	12.7	67.1	83,800
3d...	672,756	25.8	13.1	90.1	2.0	1.3	1.4	0.2	1.9	6.3	5.3	2.54	76.8	27.9	21.8	33,915	13.7	68.7	82,800
4th...	666,226	25.2	15.6	72.1	24.5	0.5	0.4	.	1.1	2.7	2.1	2.48	72.7	25.1	22.5	29,675	18.5	72.2	59,300
CA........	33,871,648	27.3	10.6	59.5	6.7	1.0	10.9	0.3	4.7	32.4	26.2	2.87	76.8	36.0	13.1	47,493	14.2	56.9	211,500
1st...	639,087	24.5	13.2	78.7	1.4	2.9	3.9	0.2	4.0	17.9	13.1	2.56	81.0	34.5	9.6	38,918	15.3	60.7	182,600
2d...	639,087	26.4	14.5	81.6	1.2	2.2	3.6	0.1	4.7	14.0	7.8	2.59	79.4	29.6	7.8	33,559	17.0	63.1	120,600
3d...	639,088	25.6	12.3	79.2	4.5	1.0	6.0	0.1	4.7	10.7	10.6	2.61	88.3	38.4	7.4	51,313	8.5	68.6	162,500
4th...	639,088	26.6	13.8	88.6	1.2	1.4	2.4	0.2	3.2	8.9	6.3	2.59	88.1	36.5	8.8	49,387	8.7	73.2	191,500
5th...	639,088	28.3	10.8	50.9	14.8	1.3	15.1	0.9	6.7	20.8	20.5	2.64	77.8	33.1	6.8	36,719	19.7	49.6	120,300
6th...	639,087	22.7	12.8	82.4	2.1	0.9	3.8	0.2	3.9	14.5	15.2	2.49	87.7	41.9	9.4	59,115	7.7	63.3	352,800
7th...	639,088	27.4	9.8	51.8	17.1	0.8	13.5	0.6	5.9	21.4	21.1	2.85	81.4	31.8	9.2	52,778	10.0	64.0	190,100

See footnotes at end of table.

No. 1384. Congressional District Profiles—108th Congress: 2000—Con.

[Data in these profiles provide summaries from Census 2000 for the newly defined boundaries of the 108th Congress. See Appendix III for comments on methodology. Maps for each congressional district are available at source listed at bottom of table]

State and district	Total population (number)	Age Under 18 years	Age 65 years and over	Race White alone	Race Black or African American alone	Race American Indian and Alaska native alone	Race Asian alone	Race Native Hawaiian and Other Pacific Islander alone	Race Two or more races	Hispanic or Latino origin[1]	Foreign born	Average population per household	High school graduate or higher, percent of population 25 yrs. and over	Percent of employed civilians, 16 yrs. and over Management, professional, and related occupations	Percent of employed civilians, 16 yrs. and over Manufacturing industries	Median household income in 1999 (dol.)	Percent of population below poverty level in 1999[2]	Occupied housing units Percent owner occupied	Occupied housing units Median value[3] (dol.)
CA—Con.																			
8th	639,088	14.3	13.0	49.4	8.8	0.5	28.9	0.6	4.4	15.7	36.7	2.25	79.8	47.4	6.6	52,322	12.2	30.2	367,300
9th	639,088	23.1	10.8	42.2	26.4	0.6	15.5	0.5	5.2	18.7	24.4	2.52	79.6	44.4	8.4	44,314	16.9	45.6	286,300
10th	639,088	26.6	11.8	72.2	5.8	0.6	9.3	0.4	5.4	15.0	15.9	2.70	89.3	41.7	8.9	65,245	6.3	69.8	274,300
11th	639,088	28.7	9.8	72.2	3.5	0.8	8.9	0.3	5.0	19.7	14.7	2.84	83.8	39.7	12.7	61,996	8.8	68.9	254,500
12th	639,088	20.7	13.9	55.5	2.6	0.4	28.1	0.9	5.1	15.7	34.3	2.67	87.3	44.2	8.9	70,307	5.4	62.3	443,400
13th	639,088	25.4	10.4	47.5	6.5	0.7	28.4	0.9	6.4	21.1	33.7	2.91	82.9	39.2	19.9	62,415	7.1	60.7	295,000
14th	639,088	22.5	11.6	67.4	3.1	0.5	16.1	0.7	3.8	15.7	28.2	2.59	88.5	57.2	20.6	77,985	6.4	58.5	626,500
15th	639,088	24.2	9.5	54.7	2.5	0.6	29.4	0.7	4.6	17.5	33.8	2.82	86.8	50.0	29.4	74,947	6.6	58.0	432,400
16th	639,088	27.3	8.0	45.8	3.6	0.9	23.6	0.3	5.2	37.6	37.0	3.38	76.3	36.3	26.7	67,689	9.8	64.1	376,700
17th	639,088	27.3	10.0	60.9	2.8	1.1	5.1	0.3	4.9	42.9	26.1	2.82	73.8	36.3	8.2	49,234	13.3	55.5	298,100
18th	639,088	33.5	9.6	53.3	5.9	1.4	9.2	0.3	6.1	41.9	24.2	3.22	72.3	31.9	13.9	34,211	22.7	56.9	108,100
19th	639,088	28.4	11.8	70.7	3.6	1.5	4.5	0.3	4.6	28.2	14.5	2.82	76.8	32.3	9.8	41,225	14.8	64.4	131,900
20th	639,088	34.9	7.4	40.0	7.6	1.8	5.8	0.1	4.6	63.1	28.9	3.61	50.2	17.7	8.8	26,800	32.2	50.0	79,600
21st	639,088	32.4	10.3	60.7	2.3	1.6	5.0	0.2	4.6	20.7	19.7	3.14	67.8	28.1	8.8	36,047	20.7	61.7	105,400
22d	639,088	28.6	11.0	75.3	3.5	1.3	3.0	0.1	4.0	21.0	9.2	2.73	79.9	32.0	7.0	41,801	13.7	65.2	115,100
23d	639,088	25.2	11.8	65.3	2.2	1.2	5.0	0.2	4.3	43.4	24.6	2.91	74.9	31.9	10.4	44,874	15.7	53.8	248,600
24th	639,088	27.7	11.3	79.1	1.8	0.9	4.5	0.1	3.7	21.7	15.1	2.86	85.9	40.1	13.1	61,453	7.2	71.0	256,400
25th	639,088	32.2	8.0	68.7	8.2	1.3	3.9	0.2	4.7	22.3	15.2	3.01	80.8	33.3	12.0	49,002	12.6	70.0	147,600
26th	639,088	27.1	10.9	64.2	4.6	0.6	15.3	0.1	4.4	24.4	22.2	2.89	85.8	42.0	12.3	58,968	8.4	68.7	238,300
27th	639,088	25.5	10.7	62.0	4.7	0.7	10.6	0.1	5.4	36.5	35.8	2.83	76.3	35.8	12.0	46,781	13.4	54.1	211,300
28th	639,087	28.6	8.6	53.3	4.4	0.8	6.0	0.2	5.6	55.6	44.0	3.06	63.0	32.3	14.0	40,439	19.1	43.9	195,400
29th	639,088	23.0	13.2	51.0	6.1	0.5	23.9	0.1	6.5	26.1	43.8	2.69	78.4	42.1	10.6	43,895	14.5	44.1	270,000
30th	639,088	17.0	14.7	68.1	2.7	0.3	8.9	0.1	3.9	8.3	26.4	2.12	92.5	58.2	6.5	60,713	9.0	47.7	490,000
31st	639,087	30.0	7.3	34.2	4.7	1.1	14.0	0.1	5.8	70.2	41.7	3.70	47.5	20.1	19.1	26,093	30.1	23.0	173,300
32d	639,087	31.0	9.1	32.5	2.8	1.2	18.7	0.1	4.5	62.3	37.5	3.29	59.1	23.2	20.3	41,394	18.0	55.9	169,500
33d	639,088	24.4	10.3	31.5	30.5	0.7	12.2	0.1	5.1	34.6	37.2	2.55	71.5	35.3	8.5	31,655	23.5	30.5	228,200
34th	639,088	32.5	7.6	41.6	4.8	1.1	5.6	0.2	4.8	77.2	47.2	3.55	17.6	17.6	25.5	29,863	26.0	30.6	178,300
35th	639,088	32.9	7.7	26.0	34.7	0.7	5.7	0.4	4.5	47.4	32.6	3.19	60.7	24.1	16.2	32,156	26.4	39.4	169,800
36th	639,087	22.9	10.3	61.3	4.2	0.7	13.6	0.5	5.0	30.3	28.3	2.49	81.9	44.3	13.8	51,633	12.7	44.8	320,200
37th	639,088	32.9	8.0	30.2	25.2	0.8	11.2	1.4	5.0	43.2	31.7	3.25	63.5	25.9	17.1	34,006	25.2	44.1	163,200
38th	639,088	31.8	9.1	32.2	3.9	1.2	10.4	0.2	4.9	70.6	38.3	3.79	58.4	22.5	21.3	42,488	16.3	62.5	162,500
39th	639,088	32.5	8.2	45.0	6.4	1.0	9.7	0.4	4.7	61.2	35.4	3.64	62.9	25.4	20.7	45,307	15.7	59.5	184,600
40th	639,088	26.9	10.6	62.9	2.4	0.7	9.7	0.2	4.3	29.6	28.3	3.04	79.9	34.9	17.5	54,356	10.2	60.0	238,700
41st	639,087	28.5	13.5	73.7	5.5	1.5	3.7	0.2	4.5	23.4	11.6	2.74	80.2	31.4	7.7	38,721	15.2	66.8	119,100
42d	639,088	28.2	8.3	66.1	3.0	0.5	16.0	0.2	4.1	23.8	22.7	3.04	87.5	43.5	15.3	70,463	6.0	76.5	262,500

See footnotes at end of table.

No. 1384. Congressional District Profiles—108th Congress: 2000—Con.

[Data in these profiles provide summaries from Census 2000 for the newly defined boundaries of the 108th Congress. See Appendix III for comments on methodology. Maps for each congressional district are available at source listed at bottom of table]

State and district	Total population (number)	Age Under 18 years	Age 65 years and over	White alone	Black or African American alone	American Indian and Alaska native alone	Asian alone	Native Hawaiian and Other Pacific Islander alone	Two or more races	Hispanic or Latino origin[1]	Foreign born	Average population per household	High school graduate or higher, percent of population 25 yrs. and over	Management, professional, and related occupations	Manufacturing industries	Median household income in 1999 (dol.)	Percent of population below poverty level in 1999[2]	Percent owner occupied	Median value[3] (dol.)
CA.—Con.																			
43d	639,087	36.6	6.3	43.9	12.8	1.3	3.2	0.4	5.3	58.3	26.5	3.61	61.7	19.2	17.0	37,390	20.7	59.9	118,200
44th	639,088	30.6	8.4	65.1	5.7	1.0	4.9	0.3	4.6	35.0	19.0	3.12	77.2	31.9	14.8	51,578	12.1	65.8	175,300
45th	639,088	29.1	15.7	65.6	6.6	1.0	3.0	0.2	3.9	38.0	20.5	2.85	74.3	26.5	7.9	40,468	15.0	69.2	138,400
46th	639,088	22.0	12.9	70.8	1.5	0.6	15.5	0.3	3.9	16.9	23.8	2.60	86.7	44.1	15.2	61,567	7.8	61.6	305,000
47th	639,087	33.2	6.5	43.3	1.8	1.1	14.0	0.4	4.7	65.3	50.7	4.20	50.4	17.2	24.3	41,618	19.1	47.6	183,600
48th	639,087	23.3	11.8	75.3	1.5	0.4	12.8	0.2	3.8	14.7	22.5	2.54	91.8	50.1	13.3	69,663	6.3	65.1	338,100
49th	639,087	29.1	12.6	70.0	5.3	1.4	3.6	0.6	4.4	29.5	17.5	2.95	80.1	30.9	13.9	46,445	11.9	66.8	187,600
50th	639,087	25.3	12.3	74.2	1.9	0.6	10.4	0.3	4.0	18.8	14.7	2.72	87.1	45.2	13.5	59,813	6.3	65.9	282,000
51st	639,087	30.7	9.9	43.5	9.8	1.0	12.7	0.6	5.2	53.3	32.7	3.33	69.0	26.4	10.3	39,243	8.1	56.7	158,500
52d	639,087	26.6	11.1	79.7	3.8	0.9	5.5	0.4	4.5	13.7	12.5	2.71	88.5	38.8	9.9	52,940	8.1	63.8	232,300
53d	639,087	20.8	9.9	63.1	7.5	0.8	8.5	0.4	5.0	29.4	24.1	2.35	80.1	38.6	8.1	36,637	20.2	34.4	218,700
CO	4,301,261	25.6	9.7	82.8	3.8	1.0	2.2	0.1	2.8	17.1	8.6	2.53	86.9	37.4	9.1	47,203	9.3	67.3	166,600
1st	614,465	21.9	11.3	67.1	10.4	1.3	2.8	0.1	3.7	30.0	16.8	2.26	79.6	37.7	6.5	39,658	13.7	52.1	164,800
2d	614,465	24.8	6.6	86.3	1.0	0.8	3.2	0.1	2.5	14.7	9.1	2.59	89.7	39.9	11.1	55,204	7.4	69.1	196,900
3d	614,467	25.1	13.3	86.3	0.8	1.9	0.5	0.1	2.5	21.5	4.2	2.48	83.8	30.2	5.6	35,970	12.8	70.4	116,000
4th	614,466	26.1	10.4	87.0	0.8	0.8	1.1	0.2	2.3	17.0	7.0	2.61	85.3	35.2	13.9	43,389	10.9	68.0	151,800
5th	614,467	26.7	9.3	82.6	6.0	1.0	2.7	0.2	3.6	11.1	5.9	2.58	90.2	36.2	10.4	45,454	8.3	66.5	145,100
6th	614,466	29.4	6.6	91.1	1.9	0.5	2.7	0.1	3.0	5.8	5.7	2.76	95.6	48.0	7.6	73,393	2.7	84.9	214,200
7th	614,465	25.2	10.2	79.0	6.0	1.0	2.9	0.1	3.3	19.6	11.6	2.51	84.6	32.6	8.5	46,149	8.9	63.2	161,200
CT	3,405,565	24.7	13.8	81.6	9.1	0.3	2.4	-	2.2	9.4	10.9	2.53	84.0	39.1	14.8	53,935	7.9	66.8	166,900
1st	681,113	24.5	14.8	75.2	13.1	0.2	2.5	-	2.4	11.4	11.8	2.46	82.2	38.0	14.1	50,227	9.6	63.6	145,100
2d	681,113	24.2	12.4	90.5	3.5	0.5	1.7	-	1.9	4.3	5.1	2.53	86.7	37.4	15.2	54,498	5.8	72.0	147,000
3d	681,113	23.7	14.7	79.8	11.9	0.2	2.5	-	2.0	8.0	9.3	2.47	83.6	37.5	15.1	49,752	8.8	63.5	155,000
4th	681,113	26.0	13.4	77.6	11.4	0.2	3.3	-	2.5	12.8	17.2	2.67	84.6	45.3	11.9	66,598	7.4	67.8	347,200
5th	681,113	25.2	13.8	85.1	5.6	0.2	2.1	-	2.2	10.5	10.9	2.55	82.9	37.7	17.7	53,118	7.7	67.6	167,000
DC	572,059	20.1	12.2	30.8	60.0	0.3	2.7	0.1	2.4	7.9	12.9	2.16	77.8	51.1	1.5	40,127	20.2	40.8	157,200
At large	572,059	20.1	12.2	30.8	60.0	0.3	2.7	0.1	2.4	7.9	12.9	2.16	77.8	51.1	1.5	40,127	20.2	40.8	157,200
DE	783,600	24.8	13.0	74.6	19.2	0.3	2.1	-	1.7	4.8	5.7	2.54	82.6	35.3	13.2	47,381	9.2	72.3	130,400
At large	783,600	24.8	13.0	74.6	19.2	0.3	2.1	-	1.7	4.8	5.7	2.54	82.6	35.3	13.2	47,381	9.2	72.3	130,400

See footnotes at end of table.

No. 1384. Congressional District Profiles—108th Congress: 2000—Con.

[Data in these profiles provide summaries from Census 2000 for the newly defined boundaries of the 108th Congress. See Appendix III for comments on methodology. Maps for each congressional district are available at source listed at bottom of table]

State and district	Total population (number)	Age Under 18 years	Age 65 years and over	White alone	Black or African American alone	American Indian and Alaska native alone	Asian alone	Native Hawaiian and Other Pacific Islander alone	Two or more races	Hispanic or Latino origin[1]	Foreign born	Average population per household	High school graduate or higher, percent of population 25 yrs. and over	Management, professional and related occupations	Manufacturing industries	Median household income in 1999 (dol.)	Percent of population below poverty level in 1999[2]	Percent owner occupied	Median value[3] (dol.)
FL........	15,982,378	22.8	17.6	78.0	14.6	0.3	1.7	0.1	2.4	16.8	16.7	2.46	79.9	31.5	7.3	38,819	12.5	70.1	105,500
1st......	639,295	24.4	12.7	79.7	14.1	0.9	1.3	.	2.3	3.0	3.9	2.49	82.5	29.8	6.8	36,738	13.1	70.6	91,200
2d.......	639,295	22.8	12.0	73.4	22.3	0.5	1.3	.	1.5	3.3	3.7	2.42	80.1	34.8	5.2	34,718	16.5	68.4	95,600
3d.......	639,295	28.3	10.8	42.4	49.9	0.3	1.7	.	2.7	8.0	8.8	2.63	71.3	22.6	7.8	29,785	21.5	55.7	69,300
4th......	639,295	24.4	11.0	80.4	13.7	0.4	2.5	0.1	1.8	4.2	5.8	2.49	84.7	34.5	7.4	43,947	9.1	69.3	104,200
5th......	639,295	20.3	25.6	91.4	4.7	0.4	0.8	.	1.8	5.6	5.3	2.37	78.8	26.8	6.6	34,815	10.6	85.2	94,800
6th......	639,295	22.9	15.5	82.1	12.0	0.4	2.3	.	1.8	5.2	5.6	2.48	82.8	33.1	6.9	36,846	13.4	72.9	93,300
7th......	639,295	22.1	18.2	85.8	5.3	0.4	3.0	.	1.5	6.9	7.1	2.41	84.5	33.4	6.9	40,525	10.1	74.1	106,400
8th......	639,295	23.3	13.8	80.6	7.7	0.4	1.4	.	2.8	17.6	12.0	2.48	83.7	34.1	6.9	41,568	9.4	66.3	107,900
9th......	639,295	21.9	20.5	85.8	3.7	0.3	1.8	0.1	1.5	7.9	9.6	2.36	83.6	36.7	7.6	40,742	8.6	76.3	107,000
10th.....	639,296	18.0	23.3	90.9	3.7	0.3	2.3	.	1.8	4.4	8.5	2.12	83.4	33.9	10.7	37,168	8.9	71.7	94,400
11th.....	639,295	25.2	12.1	61.7	28.1	0.4	2.3	0.1	2.9	20.0	12.8	2.42	76.5	36.7	7.6	33,559	17.5	55.5	81,000
12th.....	639,295	25.2	17.2	78.1	13.3	0.4	1.1	0.1	1.9	12.0	7.7	2.56	76.3	30.0	8.8	37,769	12.4	72.6	87,600
13th.....	639,295	18.0	28.5	90.5	4.5	0.3	0.8	.	1.2	7.7	9.5	2.21	83.8	27.3	8.0	40,187	9.4	77.5	119,400
14th.....	639,295	18.3	27.4	89.6	5.3	0.2	0.8	.	1.5	9.0	10.0	2.26	84.2	30.2	4.4	42,541	8.8	77.3	128,000
15th.....	639,295	22.1	20.2	84.8	5.7	0.4	1.0	.	1.5	11.3	9.1	2.40	83.8	29.6	10.3	39,397	9.8	73.2	99,200
16th.....	639,295	21.1	15.5	87.9	6.0	0.4	0.8	0.1	1.5	10.1	10.1	2.39	81.0	30.7	5.8	39,408	10.0	81.6	103,500
17th.....	639,296	29.3	10.8	33.9	56.9	0.2	1.0	.	4.7	21.2	34.1	2.93	66.5	29.5	6.2	30,426	23.3	57.4	89,600
18th.....	639,295	19.3	17.9	73.2	7.2	0.2	1.0	.	3.2	62.7	54.0	2.45	67.1	32.3	5.7	32,298	19.3	47.9	161,500
19th.....	639,295	18.9	29.7	86.6	6.3	0.3	2.0	0.1	2.1	12.7	18.0	2.23	85.7	34.3	6.2	42,237	7.7	79.1	134,300
20th.....	639,295	21.3	17.4	83.5	8.3	0.2	1.8	0.1	2.3	20.6	26.7	2.30	85.3	38.2	6.1	44,034	7.7	70.0	138,600
21st.....	639,295	24.4	12.9	82.1	7.6	0.2	1.8	.	3.5	69.7	56.6	2.99	68.8	31.2	9.7	41,426	9.6	61.9	139,800
22d......	639,295	18.9	20.8	80.3	4.0	0.2	1.7	.	1.8	16.7	16.7	2.21	88.6	39.6	6.6	51,200	13.0	74.4	165,200
23d......	639,295	28.2	12.1	37.5	52.0	0.3	1.3	0.1	4.9	13.7	26.9	2.75	66.5	21.6	7.1	31,309	21.9	56.5	85,400
24th.....	639,295	23.1	14.7	86.2	6.5	0.3	2.1	0.1	2.0	9.8	7.9	2.51	86.4	35.5	8.2	43,954	7.9	74.3	105,800
25th.....	639,295	28.7	8.6	76.3	10.8	0.2	1.6	.	3.9	62.4	46.6	3.21	72.4	29.5	5.5	44,489	13.7	72.7	126,200
GA........	8,186,453	26.5	9.6	65.1	28.7	0.3	2.1	0.1	1.4	5.3	7.1	2.65	78.6	32.7	14.8	42,433	13.0	67.5	111,200
1st......	629,761	27.5	10.6	72.6	22.7	0.3	0.9	0.1	1.3	4.1	3.5	2.64	77.2	28.4	15.6	36,158	14.8	71.4	89,400
2d.......	629,735	27.7	11.9	51.5	44.8	0.3	0.6	0.1	1.0	3.5	2.7	2.62	70.3	25.9	17.2	29,354	22.5	62.5	71,200
3d.......	629,748	26.2	12.2	57.1	40.0	0.2	0.6	.	0.8	2.6	2.2	2.58	70.6	25.2	16.4	31,433	19.9	69.0	71,000
4th......	629,690	24.9	7.7	35.8	53.5	0.2	4.3	0.1	2.2	8.5	16.2	2.63	85.4	35.8	8.3	49,307	10.5	57.7	135,000
5th......	629,727	21.8	8.8	37.0	56.1	0.2	2.2	.	1.5	6.1	9.2	2.63	80.8	41.2	7.4	39,725	19.7	42.1	132,700
6th......	629,725	27.6	6.8	85.6	5.6	0.2	4.0	.	1.5	4.5	9.6	2.73	93.9	50.1	10.1	75,611	3.7	79.1	185,100
7th......	629,706	29.4	6.0	85.2	7.1	0.3	3.8	.	1.4	5.4	8.7	2.92	86.8	39.5	12.6	63,455	4.5	84.9	143,600
8th......	629,700	27.3	9.4	84.0	12.6	0.3	1.3	.	1.0	2.1	3.2	2.75	83.0	33.1	15.2	52,406	6.3	80.7	120,300

See footnotes at end of table.

No. 1384. Congressional District Profiles—108th Congress: 2000—Con.

[Data in these profiles provide summaries from Census 2000 for the newly defined boundaries of the 108th Congress. See Appendix III for comments on methodology. Maps for each congressional district are available at source listed at bottom of table]

State and district	Total population (number)	Age Under 18 years	Age 65 years and over	Race White alone	Race Black or African American alone	Race American Indian and Alaska native alone	Race Asian alone	Race Native Hawaiian and Other Pacific Islander alone	Race Two or more races	Hispanic or Latino origin[1]	Foreign born	Average population per household	High school graduate or higher, percent of population 25 yrs. and over	Percent of employed civilians, 16 yrs. and over Management, professional, and related occupations	Percent of employed civilians, 16 yrs. and over Manufacturing industries	Median household income in 1999 (dol.)	Percent of population below poverty level in 1999	Occupied housing units Percent owner occupied	Occupied housing units Median value[3] (dol.)
GA—Con.																			
9th	629,762	25.8	12.2	82.5	13.7	0.3	1.2	0.1	1.1	2.6	3.1	2.62	75.4	28.6	19.3	39,987	11.2	76.9	103,200
10th	629,702	26.3	10.5	89.7	3.4	0.3	0.7	0.1	1.2	9.4	7.8	2.73	71.4	25.9	27.3	42,037	10.3	76.4	108,200
11th	629,730	26.1	10.9	64.8	28.5	0.3	1.3	0.1	1.6	7.2	7.9	2.62	72.6	26.1	19.0	37,582	13.8	64.1	89,300
12th	629,735	25.3	10.7	53.1	42.6	0.2	1.4	0.1	1.3	2.9	3.7	2.55	74.9	28.6	14.1	31,108	21.7	58.4	80,900
13th	629,732	28.4	6.9	47.0	41.1	0.3	5.1	0.1	2.1	10.2	13.8	2.80	77.8	26.6	12.3	43,429	11.2	59.2	99,800
HI																			
1st	1,211,537	24.4	13.3	24.3	1.8	0.3	41.6	9.4	21.4	7.2	17.5	2.92	84.6	32.2	3.5	49,820	10.7	56.5	272,700
2d	606,718	21.8	15.1	18.8	2.0	0.2	54.3	6.8	16.9	5.4	22.9	2.80	84.1	34.0	4.0	50,798	9.7	53.1	328,900
	604,819	27.1	11.4	29.8	1.6	0.4	28.8	11.9	26.0	9.0	12.2	3.04	85.1	30.4	3.1	48,686	11.7	60.2	227,600
IA																			
1st	2,926,324	25.1	14.9	93.9	2.1	0.3	1.3	-	1.1	2.8	3.1	2.46	86.1	31.3	17.0	39,469	9.1	72.3	82,500
2d	585,302	25.3	14.5	93.1	3.8	0.2	0.9	-	1.2	2.0	3.2	2.48	85.6	29.7	18.8	38,727	10.1	72.6	82,500
3d	585,241	24.2	13.3	93.7	2.0	0.2	1.5	-	1.2	2.7	3.2	2.42	87.5	32.8	18.8	40,121	9.9	70.8	89,500
4th	585,305	25.6	13.3	91.6	3.2	0.4	1.9	-	1.3	3.3	4.3	2.46	87.2	33.4	13.8	43,176	9.0	71.5	93,100
5th	585,171	24.4	16.4	95.8	0.8	0.2	1.1	-	0.8	2.5	2.8	2.43	86.7	32.0	16.4	38,242	8.9	73.3	75,200
		25.8	17.1	95.5	0.7	0.5	0.9	-	0.9	3.6	3.0	2.48	83.6	28.3	17.3	36,773	8.9	73.6	71,900
ID																			
1st	1,293,953	28.5	11.3	91.6	0.4	1.4	0.9	0.1	2.0	7.9	5.0	2.69	84.7	31.4	13.1	37,572	11.8	72.4	106,300
2d	648,774	28.1	11.6	91.6	0.3	1.4	0.9	0.1	2.0	6.8	4.3	2.67	84.3	30.5	14.4	38,364	11.0	75.7	113,500
	645,179	28.9	11.0	90.4	0.5	1.4	0.9	0.1	2.0	8.9	5.6	2.71	85.2	32.3	11.9	36,934	12.6	69.0	97,700
IL																			
1st	12,419,293	26.1	12.1	73.5	15.1	0.2	3.4	-	1.9	12.3	12.3	2.63	81.4	34.2	16.0	46,590	10.7	67.3	130,800
2d	653,647	28.4	12.7	29.5	65.5	0.2	1.4	-	1.4	4.8	5.1	2.75	77.5	30.3	9.6	37,222	19.7	54.5	118,900
3d	653,647	29.5	11.6	29.7	62.4	0.2	0.6	-	1.8	10.4	6.4	2.84	79.3	29.6	11.4	41,330	15.2	66.2	96,700
4th	653,647	25.7	14.5	77.9	5.9	0.3	2.9	0.1	2.7	21.3	19.0	2.73	77.3	28.6	15.2	48,048	8.3	72.6	145,600
5th	653,647	31.9	6.1	46.5	4.3	0.7	1.8	-	4.5	23.0	40.6	3.37	51.7	19.7	24.7	35,935	20.2	39.2	124,000
6th	653,647	19.8	11.8	77.5	2.3	0.3	6.5	-	3.5	74.5	29.3	2.42	79.3	38.2	14.2	48,531	8.5	49.7	173,800
7th	653,647	26.7	10.4	82.3	2.7	0.3	8.1	0.1	2.0	12.5	18.8	2.76	86.7	38.2	16.8	62,640	4.3	75.8	181,700
8th	653,647	28.2	9.6	29.8	62.0	0.2	3.9	-	1.5	5.8	7.9	2.50	76.1	42.2	9.7	62,762	24.0	41.8	144,900
9th	653,647	28.2	8.2	84.4	3.3	0.2	5.7	-	1.8	10.8	13.8	2.77	88.0	37.8	20.1	40,361	4.4	77.6	170,400
10th	653,647	20.6	15.5	68.5	10.9	0.2	12.4	0.1	3.3	11.5	30.7	2.35	84.0	42.6	11.4	46,531	11.0	54.7	222,100
11th	653,647	27.1	12.2	81.2	5.4	0.2	5.9	-	1.7	12.3	18.4	2.75	88.7	47.3	16.5	71,663	4.8	78.7	268,100
12th	653,647	26.8	11.9	87.0	7.8	0.3	0.8	-	1.3	6.7	4.2	2.66	84.0	28.4	15.7	47,800	8.4	74.7	117,600
13th	653,647	25.1	14.5	80.6	16.4	0.3	0.8	-	1.2	1.8	1.8	2.47	79.5	28.4	13.1	35,198	15.0	69.4	67,300
	653,647	28.3	8.8	84.9	5.0	0.1	6.6	-	1.5	5.5	11.1	2.78	91.9	45.6	13.7	71,686	2.9	80.6	203,000

See footnotes at end of table.

No. 1384. Congressional District Profiles—108th Congress: 2000—Con.

[Data in these profiles provide summaries from Census 2000 for the newly defined boundaries of the 108th Congress. See Appendix III for comments on methodology. Maps for each congressional district are available at source listed at bottom of table]

State and district	Total population (number)	Age Under 18 years	Age 65 years and over	White alone	Black or African American alone	American Indian and Alaska native alone	Asian alone	Native Hawaiian and Other Pacific Islander alone	Two or more races	Hispanic or Latino origin[1]	Foreign born	Average population per household	High school graduate or higher, percent of population 25 yrs. and over	Management, professional, and related occupations	Manufacturing industries	Median household income in 1999 (dol.)	Percent of population below poverty level in 1999[2]	Percent owner occupied	Median value[3] (dol.)
IL—Con.																			
14th	653,647	28.7	9.1	83.4	4.7	0.3	1.8	-	1.9	18.5	12.7	2.88	82.1	32.5	19.8	56,314	7.0	74.8	150,000
15th	653,647	23.5	13.9	89.5	5.7	0.2	2.3	-	1.2	2.2	3.5	2.41	84.8	33.0	15.8	38,583	11.7	68.8	79,200
16th	653,647	27.6	12.1	88.9	5.4	0.2	1.3	-	1.4	6.5	5.6	2.64	84.2	31.0	25.0	48,960	7.3	75.5	112,900
17th	653,647	24.0	16.2	89.0	7.2	0.2	0.6	-	1.3	3.7	1.4	2.40	81.3	26.4	17.6	35,066	12.5	71.0	66,100
18th	653,647	24.4	15.1	90.8	6.5	0.2	0.9	-	1.2	1.5	2.0	2.44	84.5	32.6	15.9	41,934	8.9	73.5	85,000
19th	653,647	24.3	15.4	94.6	3.5	0.2	0.5	-	0.8	1.1	1.1	2.47	81.5	30.5	15.4	38,955	9.1	78.1	76,100
IN	**6,080,485**	**25.9**	**12.4**	**87.5**	**8.4**	**0.3**	**1.0**	-	**1.2**	**3.5**	**3.1**	**2.53**	**82.1**	**28.7**	**22.9**	**41,567**	**9.5**	**71.4**	**94,300**
1st	675,562	26.6	12.6	75.0	18.4	0.3	0.8	-	1.7	10.0	4.6	2.64	82.3	26.8	19.7	44,087	10.5	71.0	102,800
2d	675,766	26.1	13.3	86.4	8.2	0.3	0.8	-	1.1	5.0	4.2	2.54	80.3	26.6	28.2	40,381	9.5	72.8	85,700
3d	675,457	28.2	11.4	89.4	5.6	0.3	1.0	-	1.4	4.5	3.7	2.63	82.1	27.3	32.4	44,013	9.5	75.0	93,600
4th	675,617	25.7	11.1	94.8	1.3	0.2	1.5	-	0.9	2.6	3.3	2.57	85.6	31.1	20.0	45,947	8.0	73.5	112,600
5th	675,577	26.8	11.1	94.1	2.6	0.2	1.0	-	1.1	1.6	2.6	2.56	88.4	37.0	21.4	52,800	5.2	76.0	122,000
6th	675,669	25.1	14.0	94.0	3.8	0.3	0.5	-	1.0	1.3	1.6	2.50	80.6	25.7	26.4	39,002	9.7	74.3	83,200
7th	675,674	25.8	11.1	64.8	29.5	0.3	1.3	-	1.8	4.4	4.7	2.37	79.5	29.5	13.6	36,522	13.5	55.8	87,900
8th	675,564	24.3	14.4	94.2	3.7	0.2	0.6	-	0.9	0.9	1.2	2.46	81.3	26.6	19.2	36,732	10.7	74.0	77,900
9th	675,599	24.2	12.1	94.6	2.3	0.2	0.9	-	1.0	1.5	2.1	2.49	80.1	26.9	24.6	39,011	10.5	71.7	92,600
KS	**2,688,418**	**26.5**	**13.3**	**86.1**	**5.7**	**0.9**	**1.7**	-	**2.1**	**7.0**	**5.0**	**2.51**	**86.0**	**33.9**	**15.0**	**40,624**	**9.9**	**69.2**	**83,500**
1st	672,091	26.5	16.4	89.0	2.1	0.5	1.0	-	1.7	10.9	6.2	2.49	82.3	29.4	13.8	34,869	11.0	71.4	63,100
2d	672,102	25.3	13.5	89.3	5.1	1.3	1.0	-	2.1	3.8	2.3	2.49	86.9	32.3	12.3	37,855	9.5	69.0	74,900
3d	672,124	26.6	10.1	82.7	8.9	0.7	2.6	0.1	2.0	6.8	6.5	2.55	89.9	41.5	10.4	51,118	7.8	67.7	131,600
4th	672,101	27.7	13.0	83.6	6.9	1.2	2.4	-	2.6	6.6	5.0	2.52	85.0	31.5	24.1	40,917	9.6	68.8	76,800
KY	**4,041,769**	**24.6**	**12.5**	**90.1**	**7.3**	**0.2**	**0.7**	-	**1.1**	**1.5**	**2.0**	**2.47**	**74.1**	**28.7**	**17.6**	**33,672**	**15.8**	**70.8**	**86,700**
1st	673,629	24.1	14.6	90.4	7.3	0.3	0.4	-	1.0	1.5	1.2	2.44	71.3	24.2	22.7	30,360	16.5	74.0	66,900
2d	673,224	24.2	11.6	91.4	5.7	0.2	0.7	0.1	1.2	1.7	2.1	2.56	75.5	25.2	21.8	35,724	13.3	73.5	85,900
3d	674,032	24.1	13.7	77.0	19.3	0.2	1.4	0.1	1.2	1.8	3.5	2.36	82.1	33.4	13.3	39,468	12.4	64.7	104,500
4th	673,588	25.9	11.6	95.8	2.3	0.2	0.5	-	0.8	1.1	1.4	2.56	77.4	29.1	16.8	40,150	11.4	73.5	96,100
5th	673,670	24.6	12.4	97.6	1.1	0.2	0.2	-	0.7	0.7	0.6	2.50	59.2	24.5	13.3	21,915	28.1	76.3	58,300
6th	673,626	23.2	11.0	88.3	8.3	0.2	1.2	-	1.2	2.1	3.2	2.41	79.1	33.4	17.0	37,544	13.2	63.2	97,200
LA	**4,468,976**	**27.3**	**11.6**	**63.9**	**32.5**	**0.6**	**1.2**	-	**1.1**	**2.4**	**2.6**	**2.62**	**74.8**	**29.9**	**10.1**	**32,566**	**19.6**	**67.9**	**85,000**
1st	638,355	24.9	12.7	82.6	12.9	0.3	1.5	-	1.3	4.7	4.7	2.50	82.4	37.2	8.0	40,948	12.1	70.2	123,800
2d	638,562	28.3	10.3	30.2	64.1	0.3	2.7	-	1.4	3.8	4.8	2.63	72.1	29.2	7.0	27,514	26.8	50.5	80,100

See footnotes at end of table.

Congressional District Profiles 885

No. 1384. Congressional District Profiles—108th Congress: 2000—Con.

[Data in these profiles provide summaries from Census 2000 for the newly defined boundaries of the 108th Congress. See Appendix III for comments on methodology. Maps for each congressional district are available at source listed at bottom of table]

State and district	Total population (number)	Age Under 18 years	Age 65 years and over	Race White alone	Black or African American alone	American Indian and Alaska native alone	Asian alone	Native Hawaiian and Other Pacific Islander alone	Two or more races	Hispanic or Latino origin[1]	Foreign born	Average population per household	High school graduate or higher, percent of population 25 yrs. and over	Percent of employed civilians, 16 yrs. and over Management, professional, and related occupations	Manufacturing industries	Median household income in 1999 (dol.)	Percent of population below poverty level in 1999[2]	Occupied housing units Percent owner occupied	Median value[3] (dol.)
LA—Con.																			
3d	638,322	28.8	10.7	70.9	24.7	1.6	1.0	-	1.1	2.1	1.8	2.81	68.9	23.8	13.1	34,463	18.6	77.4	81,700
4th	638,466	27.1	12.9	63.0	33.5	0.8	0.7	-	1.3	2.0	1.6	2.56	76.5	27.2	12.0	31,085	20.0	68.5	71,400
5th	638,517	27.0	13.1	64.1	33.9	0.4	0.5	-	0.7	1.3	1.0	2.59	70.5	28.0	10.5	27,453	23.6	70.3	65,500
6th	638,324	26.8	9.6	63.7	33.3	0.2	1.4	0.1	0.8	1.6	2.8	2.62	80.3	33.3	11.3	37,931	16.6	68.7	98,100
7th	638,430	28.1	11.7	72.8	25.0	0.3	0.7	-	0.8	1.4	1.5	2.63	72.3	28.7	9.3	31,453	19.9	70.3	78,100
ME	1,274,923	23.6	14.4	96.9	0.5	0.6	0.7	-	1.0	0.7	2.9	2.39	85.4	31.5	14.2	37,240	10.9	71.6	98,700
1st	666,936	23.8	14.0	96.8	0.7	0.3	0.9	*	1.0	0.8	3.0	2.40	87.9	34.6	13.1	41,585	8.8	70.4	119,000
2d	607,987	23.4	14.8	97.1	0.4	0.9	0.5	*	1.0	0.7	2.7	2.39	82.5	28.0	15.6	32,678	13.2	72.8	80,800
MD	5,296,486	25.6	11.3	64.0	27.9	0.3	4.0	*	2.0	4.3	9.8	2.61	83.8	41.3	7.3	52,868	8.5	67.7	146,000
1st	662,062	25.1	13.5	85.5	11.2	0.2	1.4	*	1.1	1.6	3.2	2.60	84.2	37.0	11.1	51,918	7.3	78.6	148,900
2d	662,060	25.7	12.3	67.3	27.3	0.3	2.5	0.1	1.8	2.2	5.4	2.51	79.8	31.8	10.3	44,309	9.8	62.3	110,500
3d	662,060	23.0	12.6	57.3	16.3	0.3	3.2	*	1.8	2.9	8.1	2.42	84.1	44.8	7.3	52,906	7.7	67.6	134,600
4th	662,062	28.4	7.3	30.3	57.3	0.3	5.7	0.1	2.7	7.5	15.6	2.78	86.3	42.6	3.8	57,727	7.3	62.9	154,500
5th	662,062	26.3	8.7	62.0	30.3	0.4	3.7	0.1	2.2	3.5	8.3	2.75	87.7	41.4	4.3	62,661	5.6	74.8	158,100
6th	662,060	25.9	12.0	92.3	4.9	0.2	1.0	*	1.0	1.4	2.6	2.65	83.8	35.5	10.6	50,957	6.7	75.5	144,900
7th	662,060	26.1	11.7	34.9	59.1	0.3	3.6	*	1.5	1.7	2.9	2.56	76.2	40.4	7.0	38,885	17.6	55.5	104,300
8th	662,060	24.4	12.4	62.6	16.7	0.3	10.9	0.1	3.6	13.7	29.2	2.61	88.4	55.6	3.9	68,306	6.2	65.3	229,000
MA	6,349,097	23.6	13.5	84.5	5.4	0.2	3.8	*	2.3	6.8	12.2	2.51	84.8	41.1	12.8	50,502	9.3	61.7	185,700
1st	634,479	24.2	14.0	91.4	1.9	0.2	1.7	*	1.7	6.3	5.5	2.47	84.4	34.8	17.0	42,570	10.5	65.5	127,200
2d	634,444	25.6	13.7	85.6	5.9	0.2	1.3	0.1	1.9	9.2	6.1	2.53	81.9	34.2	16.9	44,336	10.8	65.8	132,900
3d	634,585	25.5	12.9	88.9	2.8	0.2	3.2	*	2.0	6.0	9.2	2.56	82.4	39.6	17.4	50,223	8.9	62.9	168,800
4th	634,624	24.0	13.7	89.4	2.2	0.2	3.2	*	2.0	3.3	10.8	2.53	82.1	43.5	12.7	53,169	8.4	65.1	187,900
5th	635,326	27.3	11.1	83.5	2.3	0.2	5.3	*	2.3	11.6	12.9	2.72	83.6	42.5	20.2	56,217	8.9	67.2	206,900
6th	636,554	24.2	14.4	91.4	1.2	0.2	2.5	*	1.5	4.4	8.9	2.55	88.4	42.4	13.5	57,826	6.3	68.9	239,800
7th	634,287	20.5	15.5	86.1	3.5	0.2	5.7	*	2.3	4.8	16.6	2.41	87.5	46.8	9.3	56,110	6.7	57.1	251,600
8th	634,835	18.5	9.3	54.8	23.2	0.4	8.2	0.1	4.9	15.9	28.1	2.31	78.4	46.9	6.6	39,300	19.9	28.3	200,900
9th	634,062	23.8	14.1	81.2	8.5	0.2	3.7	*	2.8	4.6	13.4	2.57	86.9	41.3	8.7	55,407	7.5	64.4	200,600
10th	635,901	22.7	16.8	93.0	1.6	0.3	2.7	*	1.4	1.3	6.5	2.45	90.8	38.3	6.6	51,928	5.9	73.6	194,600
MI	9,938,444	26.1	12.3	80.2	14.2	0.6	1.8	*	1.9	3.3	5.3	2.56	83.4	31.5	22.5	44,667	10.5	73.8	115,600
1st	662,563	23.1	17.0	94.3	1.1	2.4	0.4	*	1.5	0.9	1.4	2.39	83.0	26.3	15.0	34,076	11.2	80.1	79,600
2d	662,563	27.6	12.3	89.8	4.5	0.7	1.0	*	1.6	5.2	3.2	2.65	83.6	27.3	28.4	42,589	8.9	80.0	107,900

See footnotes at end of table.

No. 1384. Congressional District Profiles—108th Congress: 2000—Con.

[Data in these profiles provide summaries from Census 2000 for the newly defined boundaries of the 108th Congress. See Appendix III for comments on methodology. Maps for each congressional district are available at source listed at bottom of table]

State and district	Total population (number)	Age: Under 18 years	Age: 65 years and over	Race: White alone	Race: Black or African American alone	Race: American Indian and Alaska native alone	Race: Asian alone	Race: Native Hawaiian and Other Pacific Islander alone	Two or more races	Hispanic or Latino origin[1]	Foreign born	Average population per household	High school graduate or higher, percent of population 25 yrs. and over	Management, professional, and related occupations	Manufacturing industries	Median household income in 1999 (dol.)	Percent of population below poverty level in 1999[2]	Percent owner occupied	Median value[3] (dol.)
MI—Con.																			
3d	662,563	28.1	10.5	84.7	8.1	0.5	1.6	-	2.0	6.2	5.8	2.65	84.5	30.4	24.3	45,936	8.6	72.5	112,800
4th	662,563	24.6	13.6	94.2	2.1	0.9	0.8	-	1.3	2.4	2.0	2.52	84.5	28.4	19.9	39,020	10.5	77.7	95,900
5th	662,563	27.3	12.3	76.7	18.6	0.5	0.7	-	2.1	3.6	1.9	2.54	82.0	26.3	22.8	39,675	13.7	73.8	87,200
6th	662,563	25.9	12.5	86.0	8.9	0.5	1.1	-	1.9	3.8	3.8	2.53	83.5	29.0	26.4	40,943	11.4	72.9	98,100
7th	662,563	26.0	12.5	90.1	5.7	0.4	0.8	-	1.7	3.2	2.1	2.56	85.3	29.2	24.6	45,181	7.9	76.8	103,400
8th	662,563	26.3	8.8	89.5	4.9	0.5	1.9	-	1.9	3.5	4.2	2.62	89.5	36.2	18.0	52,510	8.4	75.2	144,600
9th	662,563	24.4	12.4	83.1	8.1	0.4	4.8	-	1.8	3.0	11.7	2.47	90.1	48.7	21.1	65,358	5.4	74.3	198,000
10th	662,562	26.6	11.1	94.9	1.5	0.4	1.2	-	1.4	2.1	5.5	2.67	84.6	30.3	27.9	52,690	6.0	82.1	152,000
11th	662,563	25.4	11.6	90.9	3.7	0.3	3.0	-	1.5	2.0	6.7	2.54	88.0	37.5	24.3	59,177	4.3	78.5	153,700
12th	662,563	22.7	15.7	82.6	12.0	0.3	2.3	-	2.2	1.5	9.8	2.39	81.4	31.2	23.3	46,784	7.3	73.0	121,400
13th	662,563	30.1	11.5	31.8	60.8	0.4	1.2	-	2.3	7.2	5.9	2.70	69.4	24.8	19.2	31,165	24.4	55.7	71,600
14th	662,563	29.0	12.3	33.0	61.4	0.3	1.2	-	3.5	1.8	7.9	2.69	75.6	25.2	20.1	36,099	19.7	64.9	84,500
15th	662,563	24.6	10.0	80.9	11.8	0.4	3.8	-	2.3	2.8	7.2	2.52	84.7	34.9	20.9	48,963	10.3	68.3	130,500
MN	4,919,479	26.2	12.1	89.4	3.5	1.1	2.9	-	1.7	2.9	5.3	2.52	87.9	35.8	16.3	47,111	7.9	74.6	122,400
1st	614,935	25.5	15.1	94.6	1.0	0.2	1.7	-	1.0	3.0	3.8	2.49	85.1	32.9	19.9	40,941	8.5	76.8	89,300
2d	614,934	29.8	7.5	93.2	1.6	0.4	2.3	-	1.4	2.6	4.2	2.77	91.6	37.2	16.7	61,344	3.9	82.2	149,900
3d	614,935	26.6	10.2	89.5	3.8	0.4	4.0	-	1.6	1.8	6.8	2.56	94.0	43.2	16.2	63,816	3.5	77.4	159,000
4th	614,935	25.8	11.7	79.9	6.7	0.8	7.6	0.1	2.7	5.2	9.5	2.46	88.1	39.1	14.3	46,811	9.6	65.3	127,800
5th	614,935	21.5	11.7	73.5	12.9	1.6	5.2	0.1	3.6	6.0	12.4	2.25	87.0	39.7	12.4	41,569	12.7	57.2	121,300
6th	614,935	29.2	7.6	95.6	1.0	0.4	1.4	-	1.1	1.3	2.4	2.80	90.6	33.4	19.5	56,862	4.7	82.8	137,500
7th	614,935	26.1	16.9	94.3	0.4	2.5	0.5	0.1	1.0	2.6	2.0	2.49	82.1	30.4	17.5	36,453	10.3	77.8	77,100
8th	614,935	24.8	15.8	95.1	0.5	2.6	0.4	-	1.1	0.8	1.5	2.45	85.2	28.6	13.2	37,911	10.4	80.2	87,100
MS	2,844,658	27.3	12.1	61.4	36.3	0.4	0.7	-	0.7	1.4	1.4	2.63	72.9	27.4	18.3	31,330	19.9	72.3	71,400
1st	711,160	26.6	12.4	71.9	26.3	0.2	0.4	-	0.6	1.4	1.2	2.59	70.4	24.0	27.5	32,535	16.4	75.1	74,000
2d	711,164	29.4	11.4	35.0	63.5	0.2	0.4	-	0.6	1.2	0.9	2.76	68.6	27.2	15.5	26,894	27.3	65.7	58,700
3d	711,115	26.4	12.8	64.2	33.3	0.9	0.6	-	0.6	1.4	1.4	2.56	74.8	31.3	15.5	31,907	19.2	75.7	74,900
4th	711,219	26.6	11.7	74.4	22.3	0.4	1.2	-	1.0	1.8	2.2	2.61	77.4	27.0	14.6	33,023	16.9	72.4	78,000
MO	5,595,211	25.5	13.5	84.9	11.2	0.4	1.1	-	1.5	2.1	2.7	2.48	81.3	31.5	14.8	37,934	11.7	70.3	89,900
1st	621,690	26.5	13.8	46.5	49.8	0.2	1.5	0.1	1.4	1.3	3.2	2.44	80.0	32.7	13.0	36,314	15.8	62.1	73,200
2d	621,690	27.3	11.3	94.2	2.2	0.2	2.0	-	1.0	1.4	3.5	2.65	90.8	42.2	14.5	61,416	3.6	81.5	147,900
3d	621,690	24.7	13.0	86.7	9.2	0.3	1.7	-	1.5	1.8	4.5	2.42	80.4	32.6	13.8	41,091	10.1	69.0	97,500
4th	621,690	25.5	14.4	93.3	3.2	0.6	0.6	0.1	1.5	1.9	1.8	2.50	79.6	26.9	16.2	34,541	12.1	73.5	80,200

See footnotes at end of table.

No. 1384. Congressional District Profiles—108th Congress: 2000—Con.

[Data in these profiles provide summaries from Census 2000 for the newly defined boundaries of the 108th Congress. See Appendix III for comments on methodology. Maps for each congressional district are available at source listed at bottom of table]

State and district	Total population (number)	Age Under 18 years	Age 65 years and over	Percent of total population - Race - White alone	Black or African American alone	American Indian and Alaska native alone	Asian alone	Native Hawaiian and Other Pacific Islander alone	Two or more races	Hispanic or Latino origin	Foreign born	Average population per household	High school graduate or higher, percent of population 25 yrs. and over	Percent of employed civilians, 16 yrs. and over - Management, professional, and related occupations	Manufacturing industries	Median household income in 1999 (dol.)	Percent of population below poverty level in 1999	Occupied housing units - Percent owner occupied	Median value[3] (dol.)
MO—Con.																			
5th	621,691	25.6	13.0	68.8	24.4	0.5	1.3	0.2	2.3	5.6	4.5	2.40	82.8	32.7	11.0	38,311	12.4	62.4	83,100
6th	621,690	25.4	13.2	93.8	2.8	0.4	0.8	0.1	1.4	2.4	1.9	2.49	85.7	31.7	13.6	41,225	8.7	72.0	92,100
7th	621,690	24.5	13.9	94.1	1.3	1.0	0.7	0.1	1.7	2.6	2.1	2.44	81.7	27.6	16.1	32,929	13.0	68.8	83,200
8th	621,690	25.1	15.8	93.1	4.4	0.6	0.4	-	1.2	1.0	1.1	2.46	70.4	24.7	18.8	27,865	18.2	72.0	64,100
9th	621,690	25.1	13.0	93.3	3.9	0.3	0.9	-	1.2	1.1	1.8	2.50	80.5	30.1	16.7	36,693	11.8	72.6	87,800
MT																			
At large	902,195	25.5	13.4	90.6	0.3	6.2	0.5	0.1	1.7	2.0	1.8	2.45	87.2	33.1	6.0	33,024	14.6	69.1	99,500
	902,195	25.5	13.4	90.6	0.3	6.2	0.5	0.1	1.7	2.0	1.8	2.45	87.2	33.1	6.0	33,024	14.6	69.1	99,500
NE	1,711,263	26.3	13.6	89.6	4.0	0.9	1.3	-	1.4	5.5	4.4	2.49	86.6	33.0	12.2	39,250	9.7	67.4	88,000
1st	570,325	25.3	13.4	92.1	1.4	1.3	1.5	-	1.4	4.2	4.4	2.48	86.8	32.1	14.6	40,021	9.2	67.4	92,100
2d	570,421	27.4	10.1	82.3	10.3	0.6	1.8	0.1	1.9	6.3	5.5	2.53	88.4	36.5	9.2	45,235	8.8	63.8	103,300
3d	570,517	26.2	17.2	94.4	0.3	0.8	0.5	-	1.0	6.0	3.2	2.46	84.7	30.2	12.9	33,866	11.1	71.0	66,700
NV	1,998,257	25.6	11.0	75.2	6.8	1.3	4.5	0.4	3.8	19.7	15.8	2.62	80.7	25.7	4.9	44,581	10.5	60.9	142,000
1st	666,088	26.6	10.0	65.9	12.2	0.8	4.7	0.5	4.5	28.2	22.2	2.68	74.3	21.3	3.3	39,480	13.9	51.8	126,000
2d	666,087	25.9	11.3	81.9	2.5	2.4	2.9	0.3	3.1	15.3	12.2	2.56	82.8	27.8	7.4	43,879	10.1	63.6	147,300
3d	666,082	24.3	11.6	77.7	5.6	0.7	6.0	0.4	3.9	15.6	14.1	2.61	84.6	27.6	4.0	50,749	7.5	66.9	150,500
NH	1,235,786	25.0	12.0	96.0	0.7	0.2	1.3	-	1.1	1.7	4.4	2.53	87.4	35.8	18.1	49,467	6.5	69.7	133,300
1st	617,575	25.0	11.7	96.1	0.8	0.2	1.2	-	1.1	1.6	4.4	2.53	87.5	35.2	17.2	50,135	5.8	68.5	139,000
2d	618,211	25.1	12.3	96.0	0.7	0.3	1.4	-	1.1	1.7	4.4	2.53	87.3	36.4	19.0	48,762	6.4	70.8	127,000
NJ	8,414,350	24.8	13.2	72.6	13.6	0.2	5.7	-	2.5	13.3	17.5	2.68	82.1	38.0	12.0	55,146	8.5	65.6	170,800
1st	647,258	26.5	12.0	74.0	17.0	0.2	2.7	-	1.8	8.2	5.4	2.68	80.2	32.8	11.2	47,473	9.9	70.0	108,600
2d	647,257	24.1	14.1	75.7	14.4	0.4	2.4	-	2.1	10.3	7.1	2.61	77.6	27.9	9.3	44,173	10.3	71.1	116,000
3d	647,257	24.0	17.0	85.6	4.8	0.2	2.8	-	1.6	3.8	6.5	2.60	86.3	38.1	8.9	55,282	5.1	82.5	137,300
4th	647,258	25.1	16.3	85.3	7.8	0.2	2.3	-	1.7	7.6	9.4	2.63	83.8	36.4	9.7	54,073	6.6	77.7	145,800
5th	647,258	26.1	13.3	89.3	1.5	0.2	6.6	-	1.3	4.5	12.9	2.78	90.1	44.0	11.9	72,781	3.6	81.6	238,400
6th	647,257	23.8	11.7	67.5	16.8	0.2	8.4	-	2.6	11.7	19.2	2.69	83.4	37.4	11.3	55,681	9.1	61.3	164,000
7th	647,257	24.8	13.1	83.4	4.6	0.1	8.2	-	1.6	6.9	16.4	2.72	89.1	47.5	14.2	74,823	3.4	78.6	224,300
8th	647,258	25.1	13.4	63.5	13.4	0.3	5.3	-	3.8	25.8	26.1	2.81	76.8	35.5	15.6	51,954	10.7	56.7	200,700
9th	647,257	21.3	14.8	63.1	7.1	0.2	10.8	0.1	3.5	18.8	32.4	2.55	80.6	36.0	12.2	52,437	7.6	52.8	198,100
10th	647,258	27.1	10.9	28.4	57.7	0.3	3.6	-	3.9	15.0	22.7	2.76	72.7	27.7	11.7	38,177	17.5	38.6	144,000
11th	647,258	25.1	11.9	87.5	2.8	0.1	6.4	-	1.5	6.8	14.7	2.72	90.9	48.6	14.4	79,009	3.5	77.9	256,900

See footnotes at end of table.

U.S. Census Bureau, Statistical Abstract of the United States: 2003

No. 1384. Congressional District Profiles—108th Congress: 2000—Con.

[Data in these profiles provide summaries from Census 2000 for the newly defined boundaries of the 108th Congress. See Appendix III for comments on methodology. Maps for each congressional district are available at source listed at bottom of table]

State and district	Total population (number)	Age Under 18 years	Age 65 years and over	Race White alone	Race Black or African American alone	Race American Indian and Alaska native alone	Race Asian alone	Race Native Hawaiian and Other Pacific Islander alone	Race Two or more races	Hispanic or Latino origin[1]	Foreign born	Average population per household	High school graduate or higher, percent of population 25 yrs. and over	Percent of employed civilians, 16 yrs. and over Management, professional, and related occupations	Percent of employed civilians, 16 yrs. and over Manufacturing industries	Median household income in 1999 (dol.)	Percent of population below poverty level in 1999[2]	Occupied housing units Percent owner occupied	Occupied housing units Median value[3] (dol.)
NJ—Con.																			
12th	647,258	24.9	12.7	75.4	11.7	0.1	9.1	–	1.8	5.5	15.6	2.67	88.8	48.8	10.9	69,668	5.2	75.1	206,000
13th	647,258	23.5	10.8	56.1	12.8	0.5	5.6	0.1	5.8	47.6	39.6	2.68	64.6	28.2	14.0	37,129	18.0	28.8	140,100
NM	**1,819,046**	**28.0**	**11.7**	**66.8**	**1.9**	**9.5**	**1.1**	**0.1**	**3.6**	**42.1**	**8.2**	**2.63**	**78.9**	**34.0**	**6.5**	**34,133**	**18.4**	**70.0**	**108,100**
1st	606,400	25.8	11.4	71.1	2.6	3.5	1.8	0.1	4.2	42.6	8.6	2.50	83.9	37.3	7.8	38,413	14.0	65.4	127,100
2d	606,406	28.9	13.0	68.8	1.8	5.5	0.6	0.1	3.3	47.3	11.2	2.70	73.1	28.9	6.4	29,269	22.4	72.0	76,900
3d	606,240	29.2	10.7	60.4	1.2	19.6	0.8	0.1	3.4	36.3	4.9	2.70	79.3	34.9	5.1	35,058	19.0	72.9	114,100
NY	**18,976,457**	**24.7**	**12.9**	**67.9**	**15.9**	**0.4**	**5.5**	**–**	**3.1**	**15.1**	**20.4**	**2.61**	**79.1**	**36.7**	**10.0**	**43,393**	**14.6**	**53.0**	**148,700**
1st	654,360	25.6	12.1	89.3	4.3	0.3	2.4	–	1.7	7.5	9.0	2.84	87.2	36.0	7.8	61,884	6.0	79.4	176,700
2d	654,360	26.7	11.6	78.4	10.4	0.1	3.0	–	2.4	13.9	14.0	3.12	85.6	37.3	11.1	71,147	5.9	81.7	204,200
3d	654,361	24.4	14.6	91.2	1.9	0.1	3.0	–	1.5	6.9	11.2	2.87	88.5	38.6	7.4	70,561	4.3	81.7	224,500
4th	654,360	25.1	14.4	68.9	18.2	0.2	4.5	–	2.8	13.6	21.7	3.03	83.3	37.6	6.4	66,799	6.4	77.3	224,700
5th	654,361	21.8	14.7	55.7	8.8	0.3	24.6	0.1	3.9	23.5	45.6	2.82	77.9	36.9	8.0	51,156	12.1	53.2	341,000
6th	654,361	27.0	10.7	18.9	53.9	0.7	9.0	–	7.7	16.9	39.5	3.14	73.0	27.2	6.0	43,546	14.5	52.6	180,000
7th	654,360	23.6	12.8	45.1	18.7	0.6	12.9	0.1	5.6	39.5	38.8	2.69	71.6	27.9	7.7	36,990	15.7	32.3	204,900
8th	654,360	17.9	13.8	74.6	6.1	0.2	11.1	–	3.3	11.7	33.2	2.08	81.8	55.0	5.5	47,061	17.7	26.2	260,000
9th	654,361	21.1	16.8	71.0	4.4	0.2	14.6	0.1	2.4	13.6	40.1	2.53	80.7	39.0	7.0	45,426	18.7	46.2	246,000
10th	654,361	30.3	9.6	21.0	63.0	0.4	2.7	0.1	4.0	17.2	28.3	2.83	67.6	31.0	6.5	30,212	29.0	28.6	193,900
11th	654,361	27.1	9.3	24.9	61.2	0.2	4.2	–	4.1	12.1	41.7	2.71	72.2	35.1	5.5	34,082	23.2	21.6	214,800
12th	654,361	25.7	9.4	39.5	10.9	0.4	16.0	–	5.9	48.5	41.5	2.87	56.4	25.9	4.8	29,195	28.3	18.7	189,700
13th	654,361	23.7	13.3	76.8	6.9	0.7	9.2	0.1	3.1	11.0	23.9	2.67	79.4	34.9	13.3	50,092	11.9	54.0	217,800
14th	654,361	13.3	13.3	73.1	5.2	0.2	11.4	–	4.3	14.0	31.9	1.88	86.6	57.7	5.1	57,152	12.4	25.8	252,500
15th	654,361	24.0	10.7	28.2	34.6	0.2	2.9	–	5.9	47.9	33.6	2.49	63.1	38.1	5.9	27,934	30.5	10.1	314,700
16th	654,360	34.5	6.7	20.4	36.0	0.9	1.2	0.1	6.6	62.8	30.2	3.01	50.5	18.2	8.1	19,311	42.2	7.2	155,600
17th	654,361	26.6	12.7	48.9	32.3	0.4	4.6	0.1	4.2	20.4	22.8	2.71	77.7	37.8	6.6	44,868	16.0	41.1	230,600
18th	654,360	24.7	14.3	74.9	10.0	0.2	5.3	–	2.9	16.2	22.8	2.70	84.3	47.5	6.6	68,887	7.8	63.7	346,500
19th	654,361	27.0	10.9	88.1	5.4	0.2	2.2	–	1.7	7.7	9.4	2.79	86.4	40.6	9.3	64,337	6.4	75.2	188,800
20th	654,361	24.4	13.7	94.7	2.5	0.2	0.8	–	1.1	2.2	3.7	2.50	84.4	35.7	11.5	44,239	7.9	73.8	110,600
21st	654,361	23.3	15.5	87.0	7.8	0.3	2.1	–	1.7	3.2	5.3	2.35	84.1	37.8	8.4	40,254	11.2	60.8	100,500
22d	654,361	23.8	13.6	83.7	8.2	0.3	2.6	–	2.3	7.8	8.1	2.47	81.4	35.0	11.8	38,586	14.3	61.2	98,500
23d	654,361	25.1	12.4	93.8	2.7	0.5	0.6	–	1.0	1.7	2.8	2.54	79.6	28.4	14.2	35,434	13.5	71.0	71,900
24th	654,361	24.4	15.1	93.4	3.4	0.9	0.9	–	1.3	2.3	3.6	2.46	80.9	32.5	15.4	36,082	12.6	69.7	75,300
25th	654,361	25.9	13.8	87.7	7.3	0.2	1.8	–	1.9	2.3	5.3	2.49	85.8	37.7	16.5	43,188	10.4	69.1	89,000
26th	654,361	24.6	14.1	93.3	3.2	0.3	1.5	–	1.0	1.9	4.5	2.56	85.7	35.6	19.1	46,653	6.9	75.0	97,600

See footnotes at end of table.

No. 1384. Congressional District Profiles—108th Congress: 2000—Con.

[Data in these profiles provide summaries from Census 2000 for the newly defined boundaries of the 108th Congress. See Appendix III for comments on methodology. Maps for each congressional district are available at source listed at bottom of table]

State and district	Total population (number)	Age Under 18 years	Age 65 years and over	Race White alone	Race Black or African American alone	Race American Indian and Alaska native alone	Race Asian alone	Race Native Hawaiian and Other Pacific Islander alone	Race Two or more races	Hispanic or Latino origin[1]	Foreign born	Average population per household	High school graduate or higher, percent of population 25 yrs. and over	Management, professional, and related occupations	Manufacturing industries	Median household income in 1999 (dol.)	Percent of population below poverty level in 1999[2]	Percent owner occupied	Median value[3] (dol.)
NY—Con.																			
27th	654,361	24.0	15.8	90.8	4.2	0.8	0.7	.	1.4	4.6	3.6	2.42	81.3	30.8	16.6	36,884	12.0	66.1	84,500
28th	654,360	26.0	14.2	63.9	29.2	0.5	1.5	.	2.2	5.5	5.4	2.37	79.2	31.9	17.3	31,751	18.7	55.4	76,900
29th	654,361	25.1	14.1	93.4	2.7	0.5	1.8	.	1.1	1.4	4.2	2.52	85.6	36.8	20.0	41,875	9.9	74.0	87,700
NC	**8,049,313**	**24.4**	**12.0**	**72.1**	**21.6**	**1.2**	**1.4**	.	**1.3**	**4.7**	**5.3**	**2.49**	**78.1**	**31.2**	**19.7**	**39,184**	**12.3**	**69.4**	**108,300**
1st	619,178	26.0	14.1	45.4	50.7	0.7	0.5	.	1.0	3.1	2.6	2.52	69.2	23.3	21.4	28,410	21.1	63.4	73,500
2d	619,178	25.5	9.9	61.8	30.4	0.6	0.9	.	1.7	7.9	6.2	2.60	76.3	27.5	18.5	46,813	14.3	66.5	96,400
3d	619,178	23.8	11.6	77.9	16.8	0.4	0.9	.	1.5	4.4	3.5	2.49	81.4	30.5	12.2	37,510	12.4	70.9	100,700
4th	619,178	24.6	8.1	71.0	20.7	0.3	3.9	.	1.6	5.0	9.5	2.50	88.4	51.1	11.9	53,847	9.5	64.1	167,300
5th	619,178	23.1	13.5	89.5	6.8	0.2	0.8	0.1	0.9	3.6	3.7	2.43	76.4	30.0	24.5	39,710	9.5	76.8	109,800
6th	619,178	23.9	13.7	87.2	8.7	0.4	0.5	.	0.9	3.9	4.2	2.48	79.1	30.4	25.5	33,998	8.2	76.7	117,200
7th	619,178	24.5	12.7	64.4	23.2	8.6	1.0	.	1.1	3.6	3.7	2.49	75.6	26.9	16.0	43,503	16.7	73.1	98,900
8th	619,178	26.1	10.6	64.7	26.9	1.8	0.5	0.1	1.8	3.9	6.8	2.58	77.5	27.8	20.0	38,390	12.4	66.2	93,200
9th	619,178	25.3	10.0	84.7	6.5	0.3	1.7	0.1	1.1	6.6	5.8	2.51	86.3	40.4	15.0	55,059	6.2	72.9	146,200
10th	619,178	24.3	13.0	86.6	9.3	0.3	0.3	.	0.9	3.5	3.7	2.51	71.9	23.0	34.9	37,649	10.6	75.2	93,500
11th	619,178	21.3	17.8	91.2	4.6	1.6	0.5	.	1.0	2.6	3.2	2.33	78.5	28.3	19.5	34,720	12.0	75.4	107,700
12th	619,177	25.6	10.8	47.2	45.0	0.4	2.1	.	1.6	7.1	8.1	2.52	74.7	25.7	19.3	35,775	15.9	56.8	93,000
13th	619,178	23.1	10.8	65.9	27.1	0.4	2.0	.	1.6	6.0	8.4	2.42	80.4	34.7	17.6	41,060	11.6	62.4	117,500
ND	**642,200**	**25.0**	**14.7**	**92.4**	**0.6**	**4.9**	**0.6**	.	**1.2**	**1.2**	**1.9**	**2.41**	**83.9**	**33.3**	**7.1**	**34,604**	**11.9**	**66.6**	**74,400**
At large	642,200	25.0	14.7	92.4	0.6	4.9	0.6	.	1.2	1.2	1.9	2.41	83.9	33.3	7.1	34,604	11.9	66.6	74,400
OH	**11,353,140**	**25.4**	**13.3**	**85.0**	**11.5**	**0.2**	**1.2**	.	**1.4**	**1.9**	**3.0**	**2.49**	**83.0**	**31.0**	**20.0**	**40,956**	**10.6**	**69.1**	**103,700**
1st	630,730	26.4	13.0	69.1	27.5	0.2	1.3	.	1.4	1.1	2.9	2.42	80.1	31.8	14.6	37,414	13.9	57.6	100,000
2d	630,730	26.2	12.3	92.3	4.7	0.3	1.3	.	1.0	1.0	2.6	2.51	83.3	37.4	18.0	46,813	8.4	71.5	124,000
3d	630,730	25.0	13.6	80.1	17.0	0.2	1.1	.	1.3	1.1	2.1	2.42	83.8	33.5	19.2	41,591	10.2	67.4	102,800
4th	630,730	25.9	13.6	92.4	5.2	0.3	0.6	.	1.1	1.4	1.4	2.54	82.4	24.6	29.9	40,100	9.4	73.8	88,300
5th	630,730	26.3	13.1	95.5	1.1	0.2	1.0	.	1.1	1.2	1.3	2.46	81.2	26.2	31.9	32,888	7.6	76.5	92,800
6th	630,730	23.0	15.4	95.8	2.4	0.3	0.1	.	0.9	3.8	1.7	2.58	84.2	29.9	18.0	43,248	14.0	75.1	78,400
7th	630,730	25.4	11.9	89.3	7.5	0.2	1.0	.	1.5	0.8	1.2	2.56	81.2	29.9	16.4	43,753	8.8	71.2	103,600
8th	630,730	26.3	11.8	92.4	4.4	0.2	1.2	.	0.9	1.1	2.0	2.58	83.5	30.0	24.4	40,265	8.8	68.3	105,500
9th	630,730	25.7	13.6	81.5	13.7	0.3	1.0	.	1.2	4.0	2.2	2.46	83.3	29.2	20.0	40,265	12.0	68.3	97,900
10th	630,730	23.4	16.2	89.5	4.4	0.2	1.7	.	2.0	5.0	7.1	2.36	82.7	32.6	17.2	31,841	19.5	54.3	116,000
11th	630,730	26.3	15.4	39.7	55.9	0.2	1.6	.	1.6	2.3	5.3	2.36	78.2	34.2	14.9	31,998	19.5	54.3	92,300
12th	630,730	27.2	9.7	72.9	21.9	0.2	2.1	.	2.0	1.7	4.8	2.49	87.5	38.9	11.2	47,289	10.0	62.5	131,800

See footnotes at end of table.

No. 1384. Congressional District Profiles—108th Congress: 2000—Con.

[Data in these profiles provide summaries from Census 2000 for the newly defined boundaries of the 108th Congress. See Appendix III for comments on methodology. Maps for each congressional district are available at source listed at bottom of table]

State and district	Total population (number)	Age Under 18 years	Age 65 years and over	Race White alone	Black or African American alone	American Indian and Alaska native alone	Asian alone	Native Hawaiian and Other Pacific Islander alone	Two or more races	Hispanic or Latino origin[1]	Foreign born	Average population per household	High school graduate or higher, percent of population 25 yrs. and over	Percent of employed civilians, 16 yrs. and over Management, professional, and related occupations	Manufacturing industries	Median household income in 1999 (dol.)	Percent of population below poverty level in 1999[2]	Occupied housing units Percent owner occupied	Median value[3] (dol.)
OH—Con.																			
13th	630,730	25.8	13.5	83.2	12.3	0.2	1.2	-	1.7	3.5	3.6	2.53	84.6	31.6	20.6	44,524	9.4	72.7	117,700
14th	630,730	26.0	13.4	94.8	2.5	0.1	1.1	-	0.9	1.3	3.7	2.61	87.2	35.4	23.0	51,304	5.7	79.6	142,300
15th	630,730	23.4	10.0	86.3	7.3	0.3	3.3	-	1.9	2.3	5.7	2.37	85.5	37.7	10.3	43,885	10.8	59.1	119,500
16th	630,730	25.7	14.0	92.9	4.8	0.2	0.6	-	1.4	0.9	1.8	2.55	83.9	29.0	24.0	41,801	8.3	73.6	108,600
17th	630,730	23.9	14.8	85.3	11.8	0.2	0.7	-	1.4	1.6	2.3	2.45	82.2	25.2	23.0	36,705	12.3	70.0	85,800
18th	630,730	26.0	13.7	96.3	1.9	0.2	0.3	-	1.0	0.6	0.8	2.56	77.5	23.4	24.5	34,462	12.6	74.3	83,800
OK	3,450,654	25.9	13.2	76.3	7.6	7.9	1.4	0.1	4.5	5.2	3.8	2.49	80.6	30.3	12.5	33,400	14.7	68.4	70,700
1st	690,131	26.4	12.1	76.1	9.4	5.9	1.4	0.1	4.6	5.3	4.7	2.46	84.7	33.5	12.4	38,610	11.3	64.8	85,800
2d	690,131	25.2	15.2	71.1	4.1	17.1	0.3	-	6.5	2.4	1.4	2.52	73.8	25.5	17.1	27,885	18.5	74.3	56,400
3d	690,131	26.5	14.2	83.0	3.8	6.2	0.8	0.1	3.5	5.2	2.8	2.51	80.5	29.3	11.8	32,098	15.0	72.5	60,800
4th	690,131	25.8	12.1	79.7	6.7	5.7	1.7	0.1	4.1	4.8	3.5	2.53	82.5	30.6	11.5	35,510	13.1	69.7	73,200
5th	690,131	25.6	12.5	70.9	13.7	4.7	2.6	0.1	4.0	8.3	6.8	2.42	81.5	31.8	10.5	33,893	15.8	61.2	73,600
OR	3,421,399	24.7	12.8	86.6	1.6	1.3	3.0	0.2	3.1	8.0	8.5	2.51	85.1	33.1	14.4	40,916	11.6	64.3	152,100
1st	684,280	25.3	10.1	84.9	1.2	0.8	5.1	0.2	3.0	9.4	11.7	2.49	88.4	39.1	18.3	48,464	8.7	59.7	180,800
2d	684,280	25.5	15.1	89.1	0.4	2.1	0.8	0.2	2.5	8.8	5.2	2.52	82.7	29.2	11.9	35,600	13.0	68.2	121,900
3d	684,279	24.0	15.1	79.8	5.3	1.0	5.4	0.3	4.0	7.6	12.2	2.50	84.5	31.6	13.4	42,063	11.7	61.3	156,300
4th	684,280	24.3	15.1	91.7	0.5	1.4	1.5	0.3	3.2	4.2	4.2	2.44	84.9	30.5	15.2	35,796	13.7	65.6	132,200
5th	684,280	25.6	12.7	87.1	0.7	1.3	1.9	0.3	2.9	10.3	9.0	2.58	85.1	34.1	12.6	44,409	10.9	66.6	163,800
PA	12,281,054	23.8	15.6	85.4	10.0	0.1	1.8	-	1.2	3.2	4.1	2.48	81.9	32.6	16.0	40,106	11.0	71.3	97,000
1st	646,331	28.4	12.0	37.2	45.8	0.3	4.8	0.1	2.7	15.0	9.2	2.63	66.8	27.2	10.0	28,295	26.9	60.3	51,400
2d	646,361	24.1	13.8	30.8	61.3	0.2	4.4	-	2.0	3.0	7.2	2.37	74.3	37.8	6.7	30,626	23.8	53.4	58,300
3d	646,364	24.3	15.4	94.4	3.5	0.1	0.5	-	0.7	1.3	1.9	2.49	82.7	26.0	22.7	35,876	11.6	73.5	83,100
4th	646,476	23.9	17.2	94.5	3.4	0.1	1.1	-	0.6	0.6	2.3	2.45	87.1	36.2	13.9	43,628	7.5	78.6	99,400
5th	646,371	23.6	15.4	96.5	1.3	0.2	1.1	-	0.6	0.8	1.9	2.42	82.1	28.0	21.8	33,320	13.5	72.9	73,900
6th	646,483	24.6	13.8	88.2	6.8	0.1	2.0	-	1.3	3.5	5.0	2.54	85.8	40.9	17.1	55,615	5.9	74.2	142,400
7th	646,530	23.9	15.4	88.9	5.5	0.1	3.7	-	1.0	2.8	6.9	2.53	89.0	43.3	10.8	56,154	5.4	77.5	148,300
8th	646,340	25.5	12.6	92.1	3.5	0.1	2.4	-	1.0	2.3	6.0	2.69	88.3	38.2	15.2	59,184	4.5	76.6	158,300
9th	645,612	23.5	15.9	96.9	1.6	0.1	0.4	-	0.6	0.9	1.0	2.50	78.9	25.0	18.3	34,850	11.1	75.7	83,000
10th	646,537	23.5	16.6	96.3	1.9	0.2	0.5	-	0.7	1.4	1.9	2.47	81.6	28.1	18.8	35,984	10.3	70.3	91,400
11th	646,209	22.2	17.9	94.4	2.6	0.1	0.7	-	1.0	2.5	2.8	2.42	80.4	26.4	17.2	34,979	11.3	73.4	90,100
12th	646,079	21.3	19.1	95.3	3.3	0.1	0.3	-	0.8	0.6	1.0	2.38	80.1	25.7	15.2	30,614	13.6	73.4	68,400
13th	646,167	20.9	17.2	87.1	6.1	0.1	4.1	-	1.2	3.1	9.6	2.51	83.3	38.1	13.6	49,311	7.1	72.3	122,400
14th	646,196	20.9	18.0	73.5	22.6	0.2	1.7	-	1.5	1.1	3.9	2.21	82.3	32.7	7.5	30,140	17.1	58.0	61,300

See footnotes at end of table.

No. 1384. Congressional District Profiles—108th Congress: 2000—Con.

[Data in these profiles provide summaries from Census 2000 for the newly defined boundaries of the 108th Congress. See Appendix III for comments on methodology. Maps for each congressional district are available at source listed at bottom of table]

State and district	Total population (number)	Age Under 18 years	Age 65 years and over	Race White alone	Black or African American alone	American Indian and Alaska native alone	Asian alone	Native Hawaiian and Other Pacific Islander alone	Two or more races	Hispanic or Latino origin	Foreign born	Average population per household	High school graduate or higher, percent of population 25 yrs. and over	Management, professional, and related occupations	Manufacturing industries	Median household income in 1999 (dol.)	Percent of population below poverty level in 1999[2]	Percent owner occupied	Median value[3] (dol.)
PA—Con.																			
15th	646,495	24.0	15.5	89.5	3.1	0.2	1.7	-	1.6	7.9	5.2	2.52	81.2	32.5	20.8	45,419	8.2	71.6	119,600
16th	646,156	26.9	13.2	87.7	4.4	0.2	1.4	-	1.5	9.2	4.5	2.67	77.6	30.0	21.2	45,941	9.5	69.5	124,000
17th	646,465	23.3	16.0	88.7	7.5	0.1	1.1	-	1.1	3.2	2.6	2.43	80.0	29.1	18.8	40,334	8.4	72.6	94,100
18th	646,817	22.3	17.6	95.8	2.0	0.1	1.3	-	0.7	0.6	2.8	2.42	88.5	38.0	12.2	44,864	6.3	77.2	101,800
19th	647,065	23.7	14.1	93.4	3.1	0.2	1.1	-	1.1	2.7	2.7	2.49	82.4	30.1	19.7	45,363	6.8	74.9	103,600
RI	1,048,319	23.6	14.5	85.0	4.5	0.5	2.3	-	2.7	8.7	11.4	2.47	78.0	33.9	16.4	42,090	11.9	60.0	133,000
1st	524,157	22.7	15.4	85.7	4.4	0.3	1.9	-	2.9	7.5	12.3	2.41	76.3	34.5	16.8	40,616	11.9	55.7	136,500
2nd	524,162	24.5	13.7	84.3	4.5	0.6	2.6	-	2.5	9.8	10.5	2.54	79.6	33.4	16.1	44,129	11.9	64.6	129,700
SC	4,012,012	25.2	12.1	67.2	29.5	0.3	0.9	0.1	1.0	2.4	2.9	2.53	76.3	29.1	19.4	37,082	14.1	72.2	94,900
1st	668,668	24.1	11.8	74.8	21.1	0.4	1.3	0.1	1.3	2.5	3.8	2.48	83.8	32.0	9.1	40,713	11.5	69.4	120,800
2d	668,668	25.3	11.2	69.5	26.4	0.3	1.2	-	1.2	3.3	3.8	2.52	83.6	35.9	10.9	42,915	11.0	73.4	113,900
3d	668,669	24.3	13.4	76.9	20.6	0.2	0.6	-	0.8	1.9	2.2	2.50	76.8	26.6	27.2	36,092	13.3	75.5	86,900
4th	668,669	24.7	12.2	76.2	19.8	0.2	1.4	-	1.1	3.2	4.2	2.49	76.4	30.1	24.5	39,417	11.4	70.1	99,500
5th	668,668	26.3	11.9	64.9	32.3	0.6	0.5	-	0.8	1.8	1.8	2.59	71.0	24.4	26.7	35,416	15.2	74.6	83,200
6th	668,670	26.3	12.0	40.8	57.0	0.3	0.5	-	0.8	1.5	1.7	2.60	69.6	24.2	18.6	28,967	22.4	70.2	73,000
SD	754,844	26.8	14.3	88.7	0.6	8.3	0.6	-	1.3	1.4	1.8	2.50	84.6	32.6	11.1	35,282	13.2	68.2	79,600
At large	754,844	26.8	14.3	88.7	0.6	8.3	0.6	-	1.3	1.4	1.8	2.50	84.6	32.6	11.1	35,282	13.2	68.2	79,600
TN	5,689,283	24.6	12.4	80.2	16.4	0.3	1.0	-	1.1	2.2	2.8	2.48	75.9	29.5	18.9	36,360	13.5	69.9	93,000
1st	632,143	22.0	14.5	95.8	2.2	0.2	0.4	-	0.8	1.5	1.6	2.38	71.8	25.4	23.8	31,228	14.8	74.2	86,900
2d	632,144	22.7	13.2	90.7	6.3	0.3	1.0	-	1.1	1.3	2.1	2.38	79.2	32.4	15.9	36,796	12.2	70.9	97,300
3d	632,143	23.6	13.6	85.9	11.1	0.3	0.9	-	1.1	1.6	2.3	2.44	75.2	29.1	21.2	35,434	13.4	70.5	90,300
4th	632,143	24.2	14.5	93.3	4.5	0.3	0.3	-	0.9	1.6	1.3	2.49	69.0	23.0	26.8	31,645	15.2	76.7	78,400
5th	632,143	22.9	10.8	70.0	23.6	0.3	2.0	-	1.8	4.2	6.2	2.35	80.9	35.6	10.3	40,419	12.2	58.1	115,600
6th	632,143	25.5	10.9	90.3	6.4	0.3	0.9	-	1.0	2.6	2.8	2.59	84.7	26.9	23.0	39,721	11.1	73.3	102,900
7th	632,143	27.2	9.8	84.6	11.5	0.3	1.5	-	1.2	2.2	3.1	2.68	83.7	37.2	24.4	50,090	8.0	79.3	137,900
8th	632,139	25.9	13.2	75.2	22.4	0.3	0.5	-	0.9	1.6	1.5	2.53	71.8	23.8	24.4	33,001	15.0	70.3	74,100
9th	632,143	27.5	10.7	36.1	59.7	0.2	1.5	-	1.0	3.0	4.1	2.52	77.3	30.5	10.4	33,806	19.4	56.9	77,600
TX	20,851,820	28.2	9.9	71.0	11.5	0.6	2.7	0.1	2.5	32.0	13.9	2.74	75.7	33.3	11.8	39,927	15.4	63.8	82,500
1st	651,619	25.5	15.0	77.8	16.3	0.6	0.4	-	1.3	7.4	4.2	2.54	74.8	26.0	16.2	31,894	16.8	73.9	62,000
2d	651,619	25.6	13.5	79.8	13.9	0.5	0.4	-	1.3	8.8	4.0	2.63	72.5	24.3	14.7	32,986	15.9	77.7	62,700

See footnotes at end of table.

No. 1384. Congressional District Profiles—108th Congress: 2000—Con.

[Data in these profiles provide summaries from Census 2000 for the newly defined boundaries of the 108th Congress. See Appendix III for comments on methodology. Maps for each congressional district are available at source listed at bottom of table]

State and district	Total population (number)	Age Under 18 years	Age 65 years and over	Race White alone	Race Black or African American alone	Race American Indian and Alaska native alone	Race Asian alone	Race Native Hawaiian and Other Pacific Islander alone	Race Two or more races	Hispanic or Latino origin [1]	Foreign born	Average population per household	High school graduate or higher, percent of population 25 yrs. and over	Percent of employed civilians, 16 yrs. and over Management, professional, and related occupations	Percent of employed civilians, 16 yrs. and over Manufacturing industries	Median household income in 1999 (dol.)	Percent of population below poverty level in 1999 [2]	Occupied housing units Percent owner occupied	Occupied housing units Median value [3] (dol.)
TX—Con.																			
3d	651,620	29.0	5.7	76.7	6.7	0.5	7.5	0.1	2.3	14.4	15.6	2.75	88.7	47.8	14.7	65,546	5.7	68.9	134,600
4th	651,620	26.7	13.7	80.8	11.7	0.7	0.6	-	1.6	9.4	5.5	2.61	78.6	29.7	15.5	38,677	12.5	72.2	79,400
5th	651,620	26.9	11.5	70.9	15.9	0.6	1.8	.	2.1	17.7	10.2	2.63	75.5	29.4	10.4	39,227	12.3	65.7	81,700
6th	651,620	29.3	9.0	78.5	10.3	0.5	2.6	0.1	2.1	13.5	7.9	2.82	82.6	33.6	16.7	49,763	8.2	74.3	90,700
7th	651,620	26.3	7.6	63.1	11.6	0.4	10.9	0.1	3.9	25.9	28.5	2.54	84.1	42.6	9.8	48,561	10.6	49.5	109,400
8th	651,619	29.3	7.3	84.6	5.3	0.4	3.0	-	1.9	13.0	10.1	2.81	87.1	40.3	12.1	60,198	6.7	74.4	118,400
9th	651,619	26.4	11.2	67.6	21.1	0.4	4.4	0.1	3.1	14.4	7.9	2.58	80.9	34.2	13.9	41,416	13.6	65.7	77,900
10th	651,619	23.0	6.6	63.1	11.2	0.6	4.4	0.1	1.9	33.0	16.7	2.44	81.5	39.7	12.6	41,374	14.8	45.7	112,400
11th	651,619	27.3	11.3	70.9	15.7	0.6	1.6	-	3.1	16.4	6.3	2.65	80.4	30.5	12.1	36,378	14.8	61.4	75,100
12th	651,619	27.2	13.7	81.1	4.6	0.8	2.3	0.1	2.7	19.9	6.3	2.57	79.6	32.0	14.4	44,624	9.8	65.3	85,600
13th	651,619	27.2	10.2	79.3	5.7	0.8	1.1	0.3	2.2	21.6	10.7	2.65	75.8	28.7	14.4	33,361	14.4	68.4	58,800
14th	651,619	27.3	12.9	75.2	7.9	0.8	0.8	0.1	2.3	32.0	6.4	2.57	72.9	27.3	11.1	35,966	15.0	71.0	70,200
15th	651,619	32.8	10.5	77.7	1.5	0.8	0.7	-	2.3	78.3	6.3	3.32	58.1	28.0	13.8	27,530	30.5	70.8	55,400
16th	651,619	31.6	10.0	73.9	3.2	0.8	1.0	0.1	3.2	77.7	27.0	3.15	66.4	28.0	7.8	31,245	23.6	62.8	70,000
17th	651,619	25.6	15.1	84.6	3.9	0.6	0.6	-	1.9	19.6	4.4	2.53	75.4	28.9	14.2	31,725	15.1	70.7	55,900
18th	651,619	27.2	9.6	37.1	42.5	0.4	2.9	0.1	2.5	32.6	18.5	2.72	65.6	28.3	10.2	32,413	23.7	51.1	63,400
19th	651,619	28.4	11.8	75.1	5.8	0.7	0.8	-	2.2	34.1	7.1	2.64	73.1	30.6	7.0	32,409	17.5	66.7	57,800
20th	651,619	28.8	10.0	66.1	5.6	1.0	1.4	0.1	4.0	68.2	13.3	2.82	70.3	26.8	6.8	31,801	20.3	52.7	59,400
21st	651,619	24.9	13.7	88.2	2.1	0.5	2.0	0.1	2.0	17.2	6.4	2.50	89.5	45.5	6.8	52,751	7.0	73.3	135,200
22d	651,619	30.1	6.8	79.7	10.2	0.4	4.4	.	2.4	19.7	12.9	2.98	85.5	42.6	15.0	62,678	6.6	79.2	111,200
23d	651,619	32.2	9.2	79.7	1.5	0.4	1.1	-	2.6	66.8	19.4	3.14	67.2	35.0	6.6	36,158	22.1	72.2	84,700
24th	651,619	29.9	7.9	51.6	22.0	0.4	3.1	-	3.1	38.0	21.6	2.87	68.0	26.5	14.9	36,962	17.2	52.9	69,600
25th	651,619	28.7	6.8	53.0	23.0	0.4	4.0	0.1	3.1	34.3	24.8	2.68	74.3	34.6	9.9	38,048	16.3	46.5	82,600
26th	651,619	27.9	5.2	83.4	5.1	0.4	4.0	0.2	1.7	11.0	9.2	2.65	90.7	43.0	11.1	61,287	5.7	64.5	140,100
27th	651,619	31.2	11.2	67.2	2.3	0.6	0.7	0.1	2.7	71.6	16.6	3.09	64.1	28.7	8.5	30,431	26.5	64.2	60,800
28th	651,620	32.5	10.6	57.0	7.8	0.5	1.0	0.1	3.0	69.6	15.7	3.14	61.1	22.1	7.5	29,127	26.7	71.9	49,800
29th	651,619	33.2	6.2	52.0	14.9	0.6	2.2	0.1	3.6	62.2	31.4	3.30	52.3	16.7	13.0	32,128	21.5	53.0	56,400
30th	651,620	29.4	8.0	38.9	40.8	0.4	3.1	0.1	2.4	31.1	19.5	2.85	66.9	25.6	11.5	35,612	19.1	49.6	71,400
31st	651,620	28.1	7.3	78.0	9.2	0.5	2.3	0.1	2.1	16.9	8.8	2.76	84.5	40.1	14.2	35,252	11.3	69.1	111,300
32d	651,619	23.3	8.4	69.4	9.3	0.5	6.3	-	2.8	27.4	25.6	2.37	82.1	43.4	10.3	48,848	11.3	42.9	166,400
UT	2,233,169	32.2	8.5	89.2	0.8	1.3	1.7	0.7	2.1	9.0	7.1	3.13	87.7	32.5	12.1	45,726	9.4	71.5	146,100
1st	744,389	32.3	8.5	88.0	1.2	0.9	1.7	0.6	2.3	11.1	7.8	3.07	86.7	31.3	15.5	45,058	9.5	70.7	137,800
2d	744,390	29.7	10.9	90.8	0.6	2.3	1.6	0.3	1.9	5.9	5.8	2.89	89.4	36.0	8.2	45,583	9.0	70.6	164,500
3d	744,390	34.5	6.2	88.9	0.5	0.8	1.8	1.1	2.2	10.0	7.7	3.48	86.9	30.1	12.7	46,568	9.7	73.5	140,700

See footnotes at end of table.

No. 1384. Congressional District Profiles—108th Congress: 2000—Con.

[Data in these profiles provide summaries from Census 2000 for the newly defined boundaries of the 108th Congress. See Appendix III for comments on methodology. Maps for each congressional district are available at source listed at bottom of table]

State and district	Total population (number)	Age: Under 18 years	Age: 65 years and over	Race: White alone	Race: Black or African American alone	Race: American Indian and Alaska native alone	Race: Asian alone	Race: Native Hawaiian and Other Pacific Islander alone	Two or more races	Hispanic or Latino origin	Foreign born	Average population per household	High school graduate or higher, percent of population 25 yrs. and over	Management, professional and related occupations	Manufacturing industries	Median household income in 1999 (dol.)	Percent of population below poverty level in 1999[2]	Occupied housing units: Percent owner occupied	Occupied housing units: Median value[3] (dol.)
VT............	608,827	24.2	12.7	96.8	0.5	0.4	0.9	-	1.2	0.9	3.8	2.44	86.4	36.3	15.1	40,856	9.4	70.6	111,500
At large.....	608,827	24.2	12.7	96.8	0.5	0.4	0.9	-	1.2	0.9	3.8	2.44	86.4	36.3	15.1	40,856	9.4	70.6	111,500
VA............	7,078,515	24.6	11.2	72.3	19.6	0.3	3.7	0.1	2.0	4.7	8.1	2.54	81.5	38.2	11.3	46,677	9.6	68.1	125,400
1st...........	643,514	26.4	11.3	76.1	18.6	0.4	1.7	0.1	2.0	3.0	4.0	2.63	84.6	36.7	9.0	50,257	6.7	72.7	131,400
2d............	643,510	25.6	9.4	69.2	21.8	0.4	4.1	0.1	2.6	4.4	6.2	2.62	87.5	34.0	7.9	44,193	8.7	63.4	113,900
3d............	643,476	25.8	11.6	38.6	56.4	0.5	1.4	0.1	2.9	2.6	3.2	2.46	75.1	27.8	13.0	32,238	18.9	52.2	83,600
4th...........	643,477	26.7	10.7	62.9	33.3	0.3	1.4	-	1.9	2.0	2.8	2.66	78.5	31.4	15.2	45,249	9.5	73.5	105,700
5th...........	643,497	24.8	14.8	73.2	24.1	0.2	1.0	-	1.3	1.6	3.5	2.42	72.4	29.3	20.8	35,739	13.2	72.4	92,900
6th...........	643,504	22.4	15.0	85.9	11.0	0.2	1.0	-	1.0	2.0	3.0	2.40	77.6	29.3	18.0	37,773	11.0	69.2	99,500
7th...........	643,499	25.0	12.1	79.1	16.2	0.3	2.3	-	1.2	2.0	4.8	2.50	84.9	39.8	9.8	50,990	6.1	72.8	128,800
8th...........	643,503	19.7	8.9	64.5	13.7	0.3	9.5	0.1	4.4	16.4	27.9	2.29	87.1	55.9	2.9	63,430	7.5	50.1	227,500
9th...........	643,503	22.0	14.5	94.0	3.9	0.3	0.8	-	0.8	1.1	1.6	2.38	68.7	26.2	21.9	29,783	16.2	74.2	75,700
10th..........	643,512	28.2	7.4	80.6	6.9	0.3	6.6	0.1	2.5	7.1	13.6	2.80	88.2	48.2	7.2	71,560	4.4	75.3	189,900
11th..........	643,509	27.0	7.5	71.4	10.3	0.3	10.9	0.1	3.4	9.1	13.6	2.87	91.7	52.1	3.8	80,397	3.8	76.7	210,300
WA............	5,894,121	25.7	11.2	81.8	3.2	1.6	5.5	0.4	3.6	7.5	10.4	2.53	87.1	35.6	12.5	45,776	10.6	64.6	168,300
1st...........	654,904	25.5	9.5	83.8	1.8	0.9	7.9	0.3	3.5	4.3	12.0	2.57	92.8	42.5	13.1	58,565	5.6	67.9	229,300
2d............	654,903	26.4	11.5	88.0	1.1	2.0	2.8	0.2	2.9	5.8	7.9	2.59	87.3	30.9	16.0	45,441	10.0	67.2	170,900
3d............	654,898	27.1	11.4	89.8	1.1	1.2	2.6	0.2	2.9	4.6	6.6	2.59	86.4	30.1	14.5	44,426	10.5	68.0	147,400
4th...........	654,901	30.4	11.2	75.7	0.9	1.1	1.7	0.1	3.0	26.4	14.4	2.82	75.2	30.1	9.8	37,764	16.2	66.0	119,200
5th...........	654,904	25.5	12.9	89.7	1.3	2.2	1.3	0.2	2.0	5.1	4.1	2.48	87.1	29.5	11.2	35,720	14.4	66.0	110,800
6th...........	654,902	25.0	13.9	79.8	5.7	2.4	4.5	0.7	4.8	5.8	7.6	2.45	85.8	33.5	9.3	39,205	13.2	63.5	133,300
7th...........	654,904	17.0	11.8	69.3	8.4	1.1	13.3	0.6	4.6	4.0	17.2	2.15	88.5	46.3	9.1	45,864	11.5	50.6	242,800
8th...........	654,905	27.8	8.8	84.1	2.0	0.9	7.9	0.3	3.2	5.8	11.6	2.70	92.1	41.7	15.5	63,854	5.1	75.6	237,700
9th...........	654,902	26.4	9.9	76.0	6.5	1.3	7.2	1.0	5.0	6.7	11.4	2.56	87.4	30.6	13.6	46,495	9.2	59.5	160,500
WV............	1,808,344	22.3	15.3	95.0	3.2	0.2	0.5	-	0.9	0.7	1.1	2.40	75.2	27.9	11.9	29,696	17.9	75.2	72,800
1st...........	602,545	21.8	15.8	96.4	1.8	0.2	0.7	-	0.8	0.7	1.4	2.38	79.4	28.4	13.7	30,303	17.0	74.0	71,000
2d............	602,243	23.1	14.6	94.4	3.6	0.2	0.5	-	1.0	0.8	1.1	2.42	76.9	29.1	13.1	33,198	14.8	75.5	83,900
3d............	603,556	21.9	15.6	94.4	4.1	0.2	0.4	-	0.8	0.6	0.7	2.39	69.4	25.9	8.3	25,630	21.9	76.0	63,300
WI............	5,363,675	25.5	13.1	88.9	5.7	0.9	1.7	-	1.2	3.6	3.6	2.50	85.1	31.3	22.2	43,791	8.7	68.4	112,200
1st...........	670,458	26.1	12.4	90.1	4.7	0.3	1.0	-	1.4	5.7	4.2	2.57	85.4	31.0	25.6	50,372	6.3	70.8	127,100
2d............	670,457	23.5	10.9	90.6	3.6	0.4	2.4	-	1.6	3.4	5.0	2.42	89.1	37.9	15.5	46,979	8.7	62.3	134,600
3d............	670,462	25.3	13.4	96.6	0.5	0.6	1.2	-	0.8	0.9	1.5	2.53	85.5	29.6	18.7	40,006	9.8	72.1	91,400

See footnotes at end of table.

894 Congressional District Profiles

U.S. Census Bureau, Statistical Abstract of the United States: 2003

No. 1384. Congressional District Profiles—108th Congress: 2000—Con.

[Data in these profiles provide summaries from Census 2000 for the newly defined boundaries of the 108th Congress. See Appendix III for comments on methodology. Maps for each congressional district are available at source listed at bottom of table]

State and district	Total population (number)	Age Under 18 years	Age 65 years and over	Race White alone	Race Black or African American alone	Race American Indian and Alaska native alone	Race Asian alone	Race Native Hawaiian and Other Pacific Islander alone	Two or more races	Hispanic or Latino origin[1]	Foreign born	Average population per household	High school graduate or higher, percent of population 25 yrs. and over	Management, professional, and related occupations	Manufacturing industries	Median household income in 1999 (dol.)	Percent of population below poverty level in 1999[2]	Percent owner occupied	Median value[3] (dol.)
WI—Con.																			
4th	670,458	28.0	11.4	54.8	33.4	0.9	2.7	-	2.6	11.2	7.3	2.47	75.8	27.5	19.2	33,121	19.8	46.6	84,200
5th	670,458	25.3	13.7	95.3	1.3	0.2	1.5	-	0.9	2.2	3.9	2.52	90.9	40.9	21.8	58,594	3.4	73.4	161,700
6th	670,440	24.8	14.3	95.3	1.1	0.4	1.5	-	0.8	2.3	2.5	2.49	84.0	26.4	31.2	44,242	6.1	73.3	99,100
7th	670,462	25.3	15.2	95.6	0.3	1.5	1.5	-	0.8	0.9	1.8	2.49	83.8	27.3	22.3	39,026	8.6	76.1	86,100
8th	670,480	25.8	13.5	93.2	0.6	2.7	1.4	-	1.0	2.2	2.6	2.51	85.3	28.6	23.5	43,274	6.8	73.3	103,600
WY																			
At large	493,782	26.1	11.7	92.1	0.8	2.3	0.6	0.1	1.8	6.4	2.3	2.48	87.9	30.0	4.9	37,892	11.4	70.0	96,600
	493,782	26.1	11.7	92.1	0.8	2.3	0.6	0.1	1.8	6.4	2.3	2.48	87.9	30.0	4.9	37,892	11.4	70.0	96,600

- Represents or rounds to zero.   [1] Persons of Hispanic origin may be of any race.   [2] Percent of population for whom poverty status is determined.   [3] Specified owner-occupied housing units.

Source: U.S. Census Bureau, 108th Congressional District Summary Files, <http://www.census.gov/Press-Release/www/2003/108th.html>.

Appendix I
Guide to—Sources of Statistics, State Statistical Abstracts, and Foreign Statistical Abstracts

Alphabetically arranged, this guide contains references to the important primary sources of statistical information for the United States published since 1990. Secondary sources have been included if the information contained in them is presented in a particularly convenient form or if primary sources are not readily available. Nonrecurrent publications presenting compilations or estimates for years later than 1990 or types of data not available in regular series are also included. Much data are also available in press releases.

Much valuable information may also be found in state reports, foreign statistical abstracts, which are included at the end of this appendix and in reports for particular commodities, industries, or similar segments of our economic and social structures, many of which are not included here.

Publications listed under each subject are divided into two main groups: "U.S. Government" and "Nongovernment." The location of the publisher of each report is given except for federal agencies located in Washington, DC. Most federal publications may be purchased from the Superintendent of Documents, U.S. Government Printing Office, Washington, DC 20402, tel. 202-512-1800, (Web site <http://www.access.gpo.gov> or from Government Printing Office bookstores in certain major cities. In some cases, federal publications may be obtained from the issuing agency.

U.S. GOVERNMENT

Administrative Office of the United States Courts
http://www.uscourts.gov
Calendar Year Reports on Authorized Wiretaps. (State and Federal.)
Federal Court Management Statistics. Annual.
Federal Judicial Caseload Statistics. Annual.
Judicial Business of the United States Courts.
Statistical Tables for the Federal Judiciary. Semiannual.

Agency for International Development
http://www.usaid.gov
U.S. Overseas Loans and Grants and Assistance From International Organizations. Annual.

Army, Corps of Engineers
http://www.usace.army.mil
Waterborne Commerce of the United States (in five parts). Annual.

Board of Governors of the Federal Reserve System
http://www.federalreserve.gov
Annual Statistical Digest.
Domestic Offices, Commercial Bank Assets and Liabilities Consolidated Report of Condition. Quarterly.

Board of Governors of the Federal Reserve System —Con.
Federal Reserve Banks. Monthly review published by each Bank with special reference to its own Federal Reserve District.
Federal Reserve Bulletin. Monthly. (Also monthly releases on industrial production indexes.)
Flow of Funds Accounts of the United States: Flows and Outstandings. Z.1(780). Quarterly.
Industrial Production and Capacity Utilization G.17. Monthly.
Money Stock and Debt Measures. H.6. Weekly.

Bureau of Alcohol, Tobacco, and Firearms
http://www.atf.treas.gov
Alcohol and Tobacco Summary Statistics. Annual.

Bureau of Economic Analysis
http://www.bea.doc.gov
National Income and Product Accounts of the United States, 1929-1997: Statistical Tables, early 2001.
Survey of Current Business. Monthly. (March, June, September, and December issues contain data on U.S. international

Bureau of Economic Analysis —Con.
transactions. Articles on foreign direct investment in the United States, U.S. direct investment abroad, and other topics appear periodically in other issues.)

U.S. Direct Investment Abroad: 1994 Benchmark Survey, 1998.

U.S. Direct Investment Abroad: Operations of U.S. Parent Companies and their Foreign Affiliates. Preliminary, 1997. Estimates, 1999

Bureau of Justice Statistics
http://www.ojp.usdoj.gov

ADAM 1999 Annual Report on Drug Use Among Adult and Juvenile Arrestees. July 2000.

Age Patterns in Violent Victimizations, 1976-2000. February 2002

Alcohol and Crime: An Analysis of National Data on the Prevalence of Alcohol Involvement in Crime. April 1998.

Background Checks for Firearm Transfers, 2001. September 2002.

Campus Law Enforcement Agencies, 1995. December 1996.

Capital Punishment, 2001. Annual.

Carjackings in the United States, 1992-96. March 1999.

Census of State and Local Law Enforcement Agencies, 2000. October 2003.

Characteristics of Adults on Probation, 1995, December 1997.

Characteristics of Drivers Stopped by Police, 1999. March 2002.

Child Victimizers: Violent Offenders and Their Victims. March 1996.

Civil Rights Complaints in U.S. District Courts, 2000. July 2002.

Civil Trial Cases and Verdicts in Large Counties, 1996. September 1999.

Correctional Populations in the United States, 1997. Annual.

Crimes Against Persons Age 65 or Older, 1992-97. January 2000.

Criminal Victimization 2001: Changes 2000-01 With Trends, 1993-01. September 2002.

Federal Criminal Case Processing, 2001: With Trends 1982-01. January 2003.

Federal Law Enforcement Officers, 2000. July 2001.

Federal Tort Trials and Verdicts, 1996-97. March 1999.

Felony Defendants in Large Urban Counties, 1998. November 2001. Biennial.

Felony Sentences in State Courts, June 2003. Biennial.

Firearm Injury From Crime: Firearms, Crime, and Criminal Justice. April 1996.

Firearm Use by Offenders. November 2001.

HIV in Prisons, 2000. October 2002.

Bureau of Justice Statistics —Con.
Incarcerated Parents and Their Children. August 2000.

Indicators of School Crime and Safety. November 2002. Annual.

Indigent Defense Services in Large Counties, 1999. November 2000.

Intimate Partner Violence, 1993-2001. February 2003.

Jails in Indian Country, 2001. May 2002.

Justice Expenditure and Employment in the United States, 1999. February 2002.

Lifetime Likelihood of Going to State or Federal Prison. March 1997.

Local Police Departments, 2000. January 2003.

Medical Problems of Inmates, 1997. January 2001.

National Corrections Reporting Program. June 2003. Annual.

Presale Handgun Checks, the Brady Interim Period, 1994-98. June 1999.

Prior Abuse Reported by Inmates and Probationers. April 1999.

Prison and Jail Inmates, 1995, 1996. April 1999. Annual.

Prisoners, July 2003. Annual.

Profile of State Prisoners Under Age 18, 1985-97. February 2000.

Prosecutors in State Courts, 2001. May 2002.

Rape and Sexual Assault: Reporting to Police and Medical Attention, 1992-2000. August 2002.

Sex Offenses and Offenders: An Analysis of Data on Rape and Sexual Assault. February 1997.

Sheriffs' Department, 1997. 2000. Quadrenniel.

Sourcebook of Criminal Justice Statistics. CD-ROM. 2001, most recent. Annual.

State Court Sentencing of Convicted Felons. February 2000. Through 2000, biennial. Thereafter, electronic only.

Substance Abuse and Treatment of State and Federal Prisoners, 1997. December 1998.

Survey of DNA Crime Laboratories, 2001. January 2002.

Survey of State Criminal History Information Systems, 2001. Biennial.

Survey of State Procedures Related to Firearm Sales, 2002. April 2003. Annual.

Time Served in Prison by Federal Offenders. 1986-97. June 1999.

Traffic Stop Data Collection Policies for State Police, 2001. December 2001.

Urban, Suburban, and Rural Victimization, 1993-98. October 2000.

Veterans in Prison or Jail. January 2000.

Violence-Related Injuries Treated in Hospital Emergency Departments. August 1997.

Bureau of Labor Statistics
http://www.bls.gov
- College Enrollment and Work Activity of High School Graduates. Annual.
- Comparative Labor Force Statistics, Ten Countries. Annual.
- Compensation and Working Conditions. Quarterly. 1996-2001, prints. Thereafter, electronic only.
- Consumer Expenditure Survey, Integrated Diary and Interview Survey data.
- Consumer Prices: Energy and Food. Monthly.
- CPI Detailed Report. Monthly.
- Employee Benefits in Medium and Large Firms. Biennial.
- Employee Benefits in Small Private Establishments. Biennial.
- Employee Benefits in State and Local Governments. Biennial.
- Employer Costs for Employee Compensation. Annual.
- Employment and Earnings. Monthly.
- Employment and Wages. Annual.
- Employment Characteristics of Families. Annual.
- Employment Cost Index. Quarterly.
- Employment Cost Indexes and Levels. Annual.
- Employment Outlook: 1994-2005. (Bulletin 2472)
- The Employment Situation. Monthly.
- Geographic Profile of Employment and Unemployment. Annual.
- International Comparisons of Hourly Compensation Costs for Production Workers in Manufacturing. Annual.
- International Comparisons of Manufacturing Productivity and Unit Labor Cost Trends. Annual.
- Monthly Labor Review.
- Occupational Injuries and Illnesses in the United States by Industry. Annual.
- Occupational Projections and Training Data. Biennial.
- Producer Price Indexes. Detailed report. Monthly, with annual supplement.
- Productivity Measures for Selected Industries and Government Services. Annual.
- Real Earnings. Monthly.
- Regional and State Employment and Unemployment. Monthly.
- Relative Importance of Components in the Consumer Price Indexes. Annual.
- Metropolitan Area Employment and Unemployment. Monthly.
- Union Members. Annual.
- U.S. Import and Export Price Indexes. Monthly.
- Usual Weekly Earnings of Wage and Salary Workers. Quarterly.
- Work Experience of the Population. Annual.

Bureau of Land Management
http://www.blm.gov
- Public Land Statistics. Annual.

Census Bureau
http://www.census.gov
- Major reports, such as the Census of Population, which consist of many volumes, are listed by their general, all-inclusive titles. In most cases, separate reports of the most recent censuses are available for each state, subject, industry, etc.
- 1997 Economic Census.
- Comparative Statistics.
- Bridge Between NAICS and SIC.
- Business Expenses.
- Nonemployer Statistics.
- Minority- and Women-Owned Business Enterprises.
- Annual Benchmark Report for Retail Trade.
- Annual Benchmark Report for Wholesale Trade and Food Services.
- Annual Survey of Manufactures. (1994, most recent.)
- Census of Governments. Quinquennial.
- Compendium of Public Employment. Series GC, Vol. 3.
- Employee-Retirement Systems of State and Local Governments. Series GC, Vol. 4.
- Employment of Major Local Governments. Series GC, Vol. 3.
- Finances of County Governments. Series GC, Vol. 4.
- Government Organization. Series GC, Vol. 1.
- Public Education Finances. Series GC, Vol. 4.
- Census of Housing. Decennial. (2000, most recent.)
- Census of Population. Decennial. (2000, most recent.)
- CFFR Consolidated Federal Funds Report. Annual.
  - Volume I County Areas
  - Volume II Subcounty Areas
- County Business Patterns. Annual.
- Current Construction Reports: New Residential Construction and New Residential Sales: Press Releases and Web Sites. Value of Construction Put in Place, C30 (monthly with occasional historical supplement); Residential Improvements and Repairs, C50 (quarterly and annual).
- Current Housing Reports: Housing Vacancies, H111 (quarterly and annual); Who Can Afford to Buy a House, H121 (biennial) Market Absorption of Apartments, H130 (quarterly and annual); Characteristics of Apartments Completed, H131 (annual); American Housing Survey for the United States, H150 (biennial); American Housing Survey for Selected Metropolitan Areas, H170; Survey for Selected Metropolitan Areas, H171.
- Current Population Reports. (Series P20.)

Census Bureau —Con.
Consumer Income and Poverty, P60 and Household Economic Studies, P70.
Economic Census. Quinquennial.
Economic Census of Outlying Areas. Quinquennial.
FAS Federal Aid to States for Fiscal Year. Annual.
International Briefs. (Series IB.)
International Population Reports. (Series IPC.)
Manufacturing Profiles. (Series MP-1.) Annual. 1994-1998.
Manufacturers' Shipments, Inventories, and Orders. Monthly.
Manufacturers' Shipments, Inventories, and Orders: 1995-2001.
Population Profile of the United States. (Biennial Series P23.)
Quarterly Financial Report for Manufacturing, Mining, and Trade Corporations.
Service Annual Survey Report.
Summary of U.S. International Trade in Goods and Services: includes cumulative data. (FT 900.)
Survey of Plant Capacity Utilization. (Current Industrial Reports MQ-C1.)
U.S. Trade with Puerto Rico and U.S. Possessions. Monthly and Annual. (FT 895.)
Vehicle Inventory and Use Survey. Quinquennial.
World Population Profile: 1998 (Series WP.)

Centers for Disease Control and Prevention, Atlanta, GA
http://www.cdc.gov
Morbidity and Mortality Weekly Report. Annual.

Centers for Medicare and Medicaid Services
http://www.cms.hhs.gov/researcher/default.asp (CMS)
Health Care Financing Review. Medicare and Medicaid Statistical Supplement. Annual.
Health Care Financing Research Reports. Occasional.
Health Care Financing Review. Quarterly.

Coast Guard (See Department of Homeland Security)

Comptroller of the Currency
http://www.occ.treas.gov
Quarterly Journal.

Congressional Clerk of the House
http://clerkweb.house.gov
Statistics of the Presidential and Congressional Election Years. Biennial.

Council of Economic Advisers
http://www.whitehouse.gov
Economic Indicators. Monthly.
Economic Report of the President. Annual.

Council on Environmental Quality
http://www.whitehouse.gov/ceq
Environmental Quality. Annual.

Department of Agriculture
http://www.usda.gov
Agricultural Chemical Usage. Field crops, vegetables (fruits and vegetables alternate years), restricted use pesticides. Chemical application rates and acres treated, selected states and U.S. Annual.
Agricultural Income and Finance. Situation and Outlook Report. Quarterly.
Agricultural Outlook. 11 issues per year.
Agricultural Price Reports. Reports on prices received for farm commodities, prices paid for farm supplies, indexes and parity ratios. Monthly and annual.
Agriculture and Trade Reports (five per year).
  Western Europe
  China
  Developing Economies
  Pacific Rim
  USSR
CATFISH. Catfish and Trout Production. Annual.
Census of Agriculture. Quinquennial. (1997, most recent.)
Cotton Ginnings and Winter Wheat Seedings.
Crop Production Reports. Acreage, yield, and production of various commodities. Monthly and annual.
Crop Values Report. Price and value of various commodities. Annual.
Dairy Product Prices. U.S. cheddar cheese, butter, nonfat dry milk, and dry whey prices and sales volumes. Regional cheddar cheese prices and sales volumes. Weekly.
Farm Labor. Quarterly.
Farmline. 11 issues per year.
Farm Numbers, Value. Farm numbers and land in farms, agricultural cash rents, agricultural land values, foreign ownership of U.S. Agricultural Land (ERS). Annual.
Financial Characteristics of U.S. (Agriculture Information Bulletin. No. 569.) Annual.
Food Consumption, Prices, and Expenditures, 1970-97. (Statistical Bulletin No. 928.) Revised annually.
Food Marketing Review, (Agricultural Economic Report No. 743). Revised annually.
Food Review. Quarterly.
Food Spending in American Households. (Statistical Bulletin No. 824.) Annual.
Foreign Agricultural Trade of the United States (FATUS). Bimonthly with annual supplements on calendar year and fiscal year trade statistics.

Department of Agriculture —Con.

Fruit and Vegetable Reports. Acreage, yield, production, value, and utilization of various fruits and vegetables. Periodic.

Geographic Area Series (Internet, CD-ROM, Print), Volume 1

Journal of Agricultural Economics Research. Quarterly.

Livestock Reports. Cattle, Cattle on Feed, Hogs and Pigs. Sheep, Goats, Wool, and Mohair. Monthly, Quarterly, and Annual.

Milk and Dairy Products Reports. Milk cows, milk production, and dairy products. Monthly and Annual.

Winter Wheat Seedings.

Department of Agriculture, Food and Nutrition Service

http://www.fns.usda.gov

Annual Historical Review:

Food and Consumer Service Programs.

Department of Agriculture, National Resource and Conservation Service

http://www.nrcs.usda.gov

National Resources Inventory. Periodic.

Other Reports. Reports on varied items including cold storage, catfish, cherries, cranberries, trout, farm employment and wages, farm production expenditures, mink, mushrooms, and floriculture crops. Monthly and annual.

Poultry and Egg Reports. Reports covering eggs, chickens, turkeys, hatcheries, egg products, and poultry slaughter. Weekly, monthly, annual.

Rural Conditions and Trends. Quarterly.

Rural Development Perspectives. Three issues per year.

Situation and Outlook Reports. Issued for agricultural exports, cotton and wool, dairy, feed, fruit and tree nuts, agricultural resources, livestock and poultry, oil crops, rice, aquaculture, sugar and sweeteners, tobacco, vegetables, wheat, and world agriculture. Periodic.

Stock Reports. Stocks of grain, hops, peanuts, potatoes, rice, and soybeans. Quarterly, annual, periodic.

Usual planting and harvesting dates. Dates for major field crops. Periodic.

Weekly Weather and Crop Bulletin. Report summarizing weather and its effect on crops the previous week. Weekly.

Department of Defense

http://www.defenselink.mil

Foreign Military Sales and Military Assistance Facts. Annual.

Department of Education

http://www.ed.gov

Rehabilitation Services Administration

http://www.ed.gov

Annual Report.

Department of Health and Human Services

http://www.os.hhs.gov

Annual Report.

Department of Homeland Security (DHS)

Bureau of Citizenship and Immigration Services

Coast Guard

http://www.uscg.mil

Annual Report of the Secretary of Transportation.

Marine Casualty Statistics. Annual.

Polluting Incidents in and Around U.S. Waters. Annual.

Office of Immigration Statistics

http://www.immigration.gov

Yearbook of Immigration Statistics. Annual. (Formerly entitled Statistical Yearbook of the Immigration and Naturalization Service).

Department of Housing and Urban Development

http://www.hud.gov

Survey of Mortgage Lending Activity. Monthly and quarterly press releases.

Department of Labor

http://www.dol.gov

Annual Report of the Secretary.

Department of State

http://www.state.gov

United States Contribution to International Organizations. Issued in the House Documents series. Annual.

Department of State, Bureau of Consular Affairs

http://travel.state.gov

Report of the Visa Office. Annual. (Dept. of State Pub. 8810.)

Summary of Passport Statistics. Annual.

Department of Transportation

http://www.faa.gov

Airport Activity Statistics of Certified Route Air Carriers. Annual.

Condition and Performance Report. 1999. Biennial.

National Transportation Statistics, 1998.

Report of Passenger Travel Between the United States and Foreign Countries. Annual, semiannual, quarterly. Monthly.

Transportation Safety Information Report. Quarterly.

U.S. International Air Travel Statistics. Annual.

Wage Statistics of Class I Railroads in the United States. Annual. (Statement No. 300.)

Department of the Treasury
http://www.irs.ustreas.gov
Active Foreign Credits of the United States Government. Quarterly.
Consolidated Financial Statements of the United States Go ernment. (Prototype.)
Daily Treasury Statement.
Monthly Statement of the Public Debt of the United States.
Monthly Treasury Statement of Receipts and Outlays of the United States Government.
Statement of United States Currency and Coin. Monthly.
Treasury Bulletin. Quarterly.
United States Government Annual Report and Appendix.

Department of Veterans Affairs
http://www.va.gov
Annual Report of The Secretary of Veterans Affairs.
Disability Compensation, Pension, and Death Pension Data. Annual.
Government Life Insurance Programs for Veterans and Members of the Service. Annual.
Selected Compensation and Pension Data by State of Residence. Annual.
Veterans Affairs Annual Accountability Report.

Drug Enforcement Administration
http://www.whitehousedrugpolicy.gov
Drug Abuse and Law Enforcement Statistics. Irregular.

Employment and Training Administration
http://www.doleta.gov
Employment and Training Report of the President. Annual.
Unemployment Insurance Claims. Weekly.

Energy Information Administration
http://www.eia.doe.gov
Annual Energy Outlook. 2003.
Annual Energy Review. 2001.
Annual Coal Report. 2001. Annual.
Cost and Quality of Fuels for Electric Utility Plants. Annual.
Electric Power. Annual. 2001
Electric Power. Monthly.
Emmissions of Greenhouse Gases in the U.S. 2001. Annual
Foreign Direct Investment in U.S. Energy. 2001. (Web only).
International Energy. Annual.
International Energy Outlook.
Monthly Energy Review.
Natural Gas. 2001. Annual.
Natural Gas. Monthly.
Performance Profiles of Major Energy Producers. Annual.
Petroleum Marketing. 2001. Annual.
Petroleum Marketing. Monthly.

Energy Information Administration —Con.
Petroleum Supply. 2001 Volume 1. Annual.
Petroleum Supply. 2001 Volume 2. Annual. (Web only).
Petroleum Supply Monthly.
Quarterly Coal Report.
Renewable Energy Annual.
Residential Energy Consumption Survey: Housing Characteristics. Quadrennial.
Short-Term Energy Outlook. Monthly. (Web only)
Uranium Industry. 2000. Annual.
U.S. Crude Oil, Natural Gas, and Natural Gas Liquids Reserves. 2001. Annual.
Weekly Coal Production. (Electronic Only)

Environmental Protection Agency
http://www.epa.gov
Air Quality Data. Annual.
Cost of Clean Water. Annual.
Drinking Water Infrastructure Needs Survey. Second Report to Congress (EPA 816-R-01-004, February 2001).
Federal Certification Test Results for Motor Vehicles. Annual.
Municipal Water Facilities Inventory. Quinquennial.
National Air Quality and Emissions Trends Report. 1999. Annual
Needs Survey, Conveyance and Treatment of Municipal Wastewater Summaries of Technical Data. Biennial.
Pesticides Monitoring Journal. Quarterly.
Radiation Data and Reports. Monthly.
Sewage Facility Construction. Annual.
Summary of Water Enforcement Actions Pursued by EPA since December 3, 1970. (Updated continuously)
Toxics Release Inventory (EPA 260-R-01-001). Annual (Most Recent 1999).
Water Quality Report to Congress, 1998. Biennial.

Export-Import Bank of the United States
http://www.exim.gov
Annual Report.
Report to the U.S. Congress on Export Credit Competition and the Export-Import Bank of the United States. Annual.

Farm Credit Administration.
http://www.fca.gov
Annual Report on the Work of the Cooperative Farm Credit System.
Loans and Discounts of Farm Credit Banks and Associations. Annual.
Production Credit Association: Summary of Operations. Annual.
Report to the Federal Land Bank Associations. Annual.

Federal Bureau of Investigation
http://www.fbi.gov
Bomb Summary. Annual.

Federal Bureau of Investigation —Con.
Crime in the United States. Annual.
Hate Crime Statistics. Annual.
Law Enforcement Officers Killed and Assaulted. Annual.

Federal Communications Commission
http://www.fcc.gov
Annual Report.
Statistics of Communications Common Carriers. Annual.

Federal Deposit Insurance Corporation
http://www.fdic.gov
Annual Report.
Data Book-Operating Banks and Branches. Annual.
Quarterly Banking Profile.
Quarterly Banking Review.
Statistics on Banking. Annual, and Historical 1934-1996, Volume I.
Trust Assets of Insured Commercial Banks. Annual.

Federal Highway Administration
http://www.fhwa.dot.gov
Highway Statistics. Annual.

Federal Railroad Administration
http://www.fra.dot.gov
Accident/Incident Bulletin. Summary, statistics, and analysis of accidents on railroads in the United States. Annual.
Rail-Highway Crossing Accident/Incident and Inventory Bulletin. Annual.

Forest Service
http://www.fs.fed.us
An Analysis of the Timber Situation in the United States. 1996-2050.
Land Areas of the National Forest System. Annual.
The 1993 RPA Timber Assessment Update. Forthcoming.
U.S. Timber Production, Trade, Consumption, and Price Statistics. 2001.

Fish and Wildlife Service
http://endangered.fws.gov
Federal Aid in Fish and Wildlife Restoration. Annual.
1996 National Survey of Fishing, Hunting, and Wildlife Associated Recreation.

General Services Administration
http://www.gsa.gov
Inventory Report on Real Property Leased to the United States Throughout the World. Annual.
Inventory Report on Real Property Owned by the United States Throughout the World. Annual.

Geological Survey
http://ask.usgs.gov
A Statistical Summary of Data from the U.S. Geological Survey's National Water Quality Networks. (Open-File Report 83-533.)
Mineral Commodity Summaries. Annual.
Mineral Industry Surveys. (Monthly, quarterly, or annual report.)
Minerals Yearbook. (Monthly, quarterly, or annual report.)

Immigration and Naturalization Service (See Department of Homeland Security.

International Trade Administration
http://www.ita.doc.gov
U.S. Foreign Trade Highlights. (Print discontinued 1997.) Available electronically at http://www.ita.doc.gov/td/industry/otea/usfth/
U.S. Industry and Trade Outlook. (Discontinued, 2000, most recent.)

International Trade Commission
http://www.usitc.gov
Synthetic Organic Chemicals, U.S. Production and Sales. Annual.

Internal Revenue Service
http://www.irs.ustreas.gov
Corporation Income Tax Returns. Annual.
Individual Income Tax Returns. Annual.
IRS Data Book.
Statistics of Income Bulletin. Quarterly.
Statistics of Income Division. (Annual report on Corporation Income Tax Returns. Periodic compendiums on Studies of International Income and Taxes.)

Library of Congress
http://www.loc.gov
Annual Report.

Maritime Administration
http://www.marad.dot.gov
Annual Report.
Cargo-Carrying U.S. Flag Fleet by Area of Operation. (Semiannual)
Merchant Fleet Ocean-Going Vessels 1,000 Gross Tons and Over. Quarterly.
Seafaring Wage Rates. Biennial.

Mine Safety and Health Administration
http://www.msha.gov
Informational Reports by Mining Industry: Coal; Metallic Minerals; Nonmetallic Minerals (except stone and coal); Stone, Sand, and Gravel. Annual.
Mine Injuries and Worktime. (Some preliminary data.) Quarterly.

National Aeronautics and Space Administration
http://ifmp.nasa.gov
Annual Procurement Report.
The Civil Service Work Force.

National Center for Education Statistics
http://nces.ed.gov
College and University Library Survey.
The Condition of Education. Annual.
Digest of Education Statistics. Annual.
Earned Degrees Conferred. Annual.
Faculty Salaries, Tenure, and Benefits. Annual.
Fall Enrollment in Degree-Granting Institutions. Annual.
Fall Staff in Postsecondary Institutions. Biennial.
Financial Statistics of Higher Education.
National Assessment of Educational Progress.
Private School Survey. Biennial.
Projections of Education Statistics. Annual.
Revenues and Expenditures for Public Elementary and Secondary Education. Annual.
School and Staffing Survey. Quadrennial.
Statistics of Public Elementary and Secondary School Systems. Fall. Annual.

National Center for Health Statistics
http://www.cdc.gov/nchs/
Ambulatory Care Visits to Physician Offices, Hospital Outpatient Departments and Emergency Departments. Annual.
Health: United States. Annual. (DHHS Pub. No. PHS year-1232.)
National Hospital Discharge Survey: Annual Summary. Annual.
National Vital Statistics Reports (NVRS) Monthly.
Vital and Health Statistics. (A series of statistical reports covering health-related topics.)
  Series 10: Health Interview Survey Statistics.
    Attention Deficit Disorder and Learning Disability.
    Current Estimates from the Health Interview Survey. Annual.
    Injury and Poisoning Episodes and Condition.
    Summary Health Statistics for U.S. Adults. Annual.
    Summary Health Statistics for U.S. Children. Annual
  Series 11: Health and Nutrition Examination Survey Statistics. Irregular.
  Series 13: Data From National Health Care Survey.

National Center for Health Statistics —Con.
  Series 14: Data on Health Resources: Manpower and Facilities
  Series 20: Mortality Data. Irregular.
  Series 21: Natality, Marriage, and Divorce Data. Irregular.
  Series 23: Data From the National Survey of Family Growth.
Vital Statistics of the United States. Annual.
  Volume I, Natality
  Volume II, Mortality
  Volume III, Marriage and Divorce

National Credit Union Administration
http://www.ncua.gov
Annual Report.
Midyear Statistics.
Yearend Statistics.

National Guard Bureau
http://www.ngb.dtic.mil
Annual Review of the Chief.

The National Library of Medicine (for clinical medical reports)
http://www.nlm.nih.gov
Annual Report.

National Oceanic and Atmospheric Administration
http://www.lib.noaa.gov
Climates of the World, HCS 6-4. Monthly and annual.
Climatological Data. Issued in sections for states and outlying areas. Monthly with annual summary.
Climatography of the United States, No. 20, Supplement No. 1, Freeze/Frost Data.
Comparative Climatic Data. Annual.
Daily Normals of Temp, Precip, HDD, & CDD/Clim 84. Periodic.
General Summary of Tornadoes. Annual.
Hourly Precipitation Data. Monthly with annual summary; for each state.
Local Climatological Data. Monthly with annual summary; for major cities.
Monthly Climatic Data for the World. Monthly.
Monthly Normals of Temp, Precip, HDD, & CDD/Clim 84. Periodic.
Our Living Oceans. Periodic.
Storm Data. Monthly.
Weekly Weather and Crop Bulletin. National summary.

National Park Service
http://www.nps.gov
Federal Recreation Fee Report. Annual.
National Park Statistical Abstract. Annual.

National Science Foundation
http://www.nsf.gov
Academic Research and Development Expenditures. Detailed Statistical Tables. Annual
Academic Science and Engineering: Graduate Enrollment and Support: Detailed Statistical Tables. Annual
Characteristics of Doctoral Scientists and Engineers in the United States. Detailed Statistical Tables. Biennial.
Characteristics of Recent Science/Engineering Graduates. Detailed Statistical Tables. Biennial.
Federal Funds for Research and Development. Detailed Statistical Tables. Annual.
Federal R&D Funding by Budget Function. Report. Annual.
Federal Science and Engineering Support to Universities, Colleges, and Nonprofit Institutions. Detailed Statistical Tables. Annual.
Federal Support to Universities, Colleges, and Nonprofit Institutions. Detailed Statistical Tables. Annual.
Graduate Students and Postdoctorates in Science and Engineering. Annual.
Immigrant Scientists, Engineers and Technicians. Detailed Statistical Tables. Annual.
International Science and Technology Data Update. Report. Annual.
National Patterns of R&D Resources. Report. Annual.
Planned R&D Expenditures of Major U.S. Firms. Special Report. (NSF 91-306.)
Research and Development in Industry. Detailed Statistical Tables. Annual.
Science and Engineering Degrees. Annual.
Science and Engineering Degrees, by Race/Ethnicity of Recipients. Detailed Statistical Tables. Annual.
Science and Engineering Doctorates Awards. Detailed Statistical Tables. Annual.
Science and Engineering Indicators. Report. Biennial.
Science and Engineering Personnel: A National Overview. Report. Biennial.
Science and Engineering Profiles. Annual.
Science and Technology Pocket Data Book. Report. Annual.
Science Resources Studies. Data Brief. Frequent.
Scientific and Engineering Research Facilities at Universities and Colleges. Report. Biennial.
Scientists, Engineers, and Technicians in Manufacturing Industries. Detailed Statistical Tables. Triennial.
Scientists, Engineers, and Technicians in Nonmanufacturing Industries. Detailed Statistical Tables. Triennial.

National Science Foundation —Con.
Scientists, Engineers, and Technicians in Trade and Regulated Industries. Detailed Statistical Tables. Triennial.
Survey of Direct U.S. Private Capital Investment in Research and Development Facilities in Japan. Report. (NSH 91-312.)
U.S. Scientists and Engineers. Detailed Statistical Tables. Biennial.
Women, Minorities, and Persons with Disabilities. Report. Biennial
Woman, Minorities in Science and Engineering. Report. Biennial.

National Transportation Safety Board
http://www.ntsb.gov
Accidents; Air Carriers. Annual.
Accidents; General Aviation. Annual.

Office of Management and Budget
http://www.whitehouse.gov/omb
The Budget of the United States Government. Annual.

Office of Personnel Management
http://www.opm.gov
Civil Service Retirement and Disability Fund. Report. Annual.
Demographic Profile of the Federal Workforce. Biennial. (Even years.)
Employment and Trends. Bimonthly. (Odd months.)
Employment by Geographic Area. Biennial. (Even years.)
The Fact Book. Annual.
Occupations of Federal White-Collar and Blue-Collar Workers. Biennial. (Odd years.)
Pay Structure of the Federal Civil Service. Annual.
Statistical Abstract for the Federal Employee Benefit Programs. Annual.
Work Years and Personnel Costs. Annual.

Office of Thrift Supervision
http://www.ots.treas.gov
Annual Report.

Patent and Trademark Office
http://www.uspto.gov
Commissioner of Patents and Trademarks Annual Report.
Technology Assessment and Forecast Reports
"All Technologies." Annual.
"Patenting Trends in the United States." Annual.
"State Country." Annual.

Railroad Retirement Board, Chicago, IL
http://www.rrb.gov
Annual Report.
Monthly Benefit Statistics.
Statistical Supplement to the Annual Report.

Rehabilitation Services Administration. Annual Report.
Caseload Statistics of State Vocational Rehabilitation Agencies in Fiscal Year. Annual.

Securities and Exchange Commission
http://www.sec.gov
Annual Report.

Small Business Administration
http://www.sbaonline.sba.gov
Annual Report.
Handbook of Small Business Data.
The State of Small Business.

Social Security Administration
http://www.ssa.gov
Income of the Population 55 and over, 1994, 1996, 1998, 2000.

Social Security Administration —Con.
Social Security Beneficiaries by State and County Data. Annual.
Annual Statistical Supplement to the Social Security Bulletin Annual. (Data on Social Security Benefits, Supplemental Security Income, Medicare, Medicaid, Temporary Assistance to Needy Families, Food Stamps, Low Income Home Energy Assistance, Black Lung benefits, Workers Compensation, and other programs.)
Social Security Programs in the United States, 1999.
State Assistance Programs for SSI Recipients. Annual.
Supplemental Security Income, State and County Data. Annual.

NONGOVERNMENT

AAFRC Trust For Philanthropy, Indianapolis, IN
http://www.aafrc.org
Giving USA. Annual.

Aerospace Industries Association, Washington, DC
http://www.aia-aerospace.org
Aerospace Facts and Figures. Annual.
Aerospace Industry Year-End Review and Forecast. Annual.
Commercial Helicopter Shipments. Quarterly.
Employment in the Aerospace Industry. Monthly, Tabulated Quarterly.
Exports of Aerospace Products. Quarterly.
Imports of Aerospace Products. Quarterly.
Manufacturing Production, Capacity, and Utilization in Aerospace and Aircraft and parts. Monthly, Tabulated Quarterly.
Orders, Shipments, Backlog and inventories for Aircraft, Missiles, & Parts. Monthly, Tabulated Quarterly.

Air Transport Association of America, Inc., Washington, DC
http://www.airlines.org
Air Transport Association, Annual Report.

The Alan Guttmacher Institute, New York, NY
http://www.guttmacher.org
Perspectives on Sexual and Reproductive Health. Bimonthly.

American Bureau of Metal Statistics, Inc., Secaucus, NJ
http://www.abms.com
Nonferrous Metal Yearbook.

American Council on Education, Washington, DC
http://www.acenet.edu
A Fact Book on Higher Education. Quarterly.
National Norms for Entering College Freshmen. Annual.

American Council of Life Insurance, Washington, DC
http://www.acli.com
Life Insurance Fact Book. Biennial. (Odd years)

American Dental Association, Chicago, IL
http://www.ada.org
Dental Statistics Handbook. Triennial.
Dental Students' Register. Annual.
Distribution of Dentists in the United States by Region and State. Triennial.
Survey of Dental Practice. Annual.

American Forest & Paper Association, Washington, DC
http://www.afandpa.org
Annual Statistical Summary of Recovered Paper Utilization.
Statistical Roundup.
Statistics of Paper, Paperboard, and Wood Pulp. Annual.
U.S. Wood Pulp Data Report. Annual.
U.S. Forest Facts and Figures.

American Frozen Food Institute, Burlingame, CA
http://www.affi.com
Frozen Food Pack Statistics. Annual.

American Gas Association, Arlington, VA
http://www.aga.org
Gas Facts. Annual.

American Iron and Steel Institute, Washington, DC
http://www.steel.org
Annual Statistical Report.

American Jewish Committee, New York, NY
http://www.ajc.org
American Jewish Year Book.

American Medical Association, Chicago, IL
http://www.ama-assn.org
Physician Characteristics and Distribution in the U.S. Annual.
Physician Marketplace Statistics. Annual.
Physician Socioeconomic Statistics. 1991-2000.
Socioeconomic Characteristics of Medical Practice. 1997/98.
U.S. Medical Licensure Statistics, and License Requirements. Annual.

American Metal Market, New York, NY
http://www.amm.com
Metal Statistics. Annual.

American Osteopathic Association, Chicago, IL
http://www.aoa-net.org
Yearbook and Directory of Osteopathic Physicians. Annual.

American Petroleum Institute, Washington, DC
http://www.api.org
American Petroleum Institute, Independent Petroleum Association of America, and Mid-Continent Oil and Gas Association
The Basic Petroleum Data Book. Annual.
Petroleum Industry Environmental Report. Annual.
Quarterly Well Completion Report.

American Public Transportation Association, Washington, DC
http://www.apta.com
Public Transportation Fact Book. Annual.

Association of American Railroads, Washington, DC
http://www.aar.org
Analysis of Class I Railroads. Annual.
Cars of Revenue Freight Loaded. Weekly with annual summary.
Freight Commodity Statistics, Class I Railroads in the United States. Annual.
Yearbook of Railroad Facts.

Association of Racing Commissioners International, Inc., Lexington, KY
http://www.arci.com
Statistical Reports on Greyhound Racing in the United States. Annual.
Statistical Reports on Horse Racing in the United States. Annual.
Statistical Reports on Jai Alai in the United States. Annual.

Book Industry Study Group, Inc., New York, NY
http://www.bisg.org
Book Industry Trends. Annual.

Book Industry Study Group, Inc., New York, NY —Con.
Consumer Research Study on Book Purchasing. Annual.

Boy Scouts of America, Irving, TX
http://www.bsa.scouting.org
Annual Report.

The Bureau of National Affairs, Inc., Washington, DC
http://www.bna.com
Basic Patterns in Union Contracts. Annual.
BNA's Employment Outlook. Quarterly.
BNA's Job Absence and Turnover. Quarterly.
Briefing Sessions on Employee Relations Workbook. Annual.
Calendar of Negotiations. Annual.
Directory of U.S. Labor Organizations. Annual.
National Labor Relations Board Election Statistics. Annual.
NLRB Representation and Decertification Elections Statistics. Quarterly.
PPF Survey (Personnel Policies Forum.) Three times a year.

Carl H. Pforzheimer & Co., New York, NY (No Web site)
Comparative Oil Company Statistics, 1999. Annual.

Chronicle of Higher Education, Inc., Washington, DC
http://chronicle.com
Almanac. Annual.

College Entrance Examination Board, Princeton, NJ
http://www.collegeboard.com
National Report on College-Bound Seniors. Annual.

Commodity Research Bureau, a Bridge Information Systems Inc., Chicago, IL.
http://www.crbindex.com
The Blue Line. Daily
Bridge News Summaries. Daily
Commodity Year Book Update Disk. (Three editions annually.)
CRB Commodity Index Report. Weekly.
CRB Commodity Year Book. Annual.
CRB Futures Perspective. Weekly.
CRB Infotech. CD
Electronic Futures Trend Analyzer. Daily.
Final Markets. End of day.
Futures Market Service. Weekly.
Futures Market Service Fundamental & Technical Commentary. Daily and weekly.
Price Service. Daily

The Conference Board, New York, NY
http://www.conference-board.com
The Conference Board Economic Times. Monthly.

Congressional Quarterly Inc., Washington, DC
http://www.cq.com
America Votes. A handbook of contemporary American election statistics, compiled and edited by Richard M. Scammon, Alice V. McGillivray and Rhodes Cook. Biennial.

Consumer Electronics, Arlington, VA
http://www.eia.org
Electronic Market Data Book. Annual.
Electronic Market Trends. Monthly.
Electronics Foreign Trade. Monthly.

The Council of State Governments, Lexington, KY
http://www.statesnews.org
The Book of the States. Annual.
State Administrative Officials Classified by Function. Annual.
State Elective Officials and the Legislatures. Annual.
State Legislative Leadership, Committees, and Staff. Annual.

Credit Union National Association, Inc., Madison, WI
http://www.cuna.org
The Credit Union Ranking Report. Annual.
Credit Union Services Profile. Annual.
Operating Ratios and Spreads. Semiannual.

Dodge, F.W., National Information Services Division, McGraw-Hill Information Systems Co., New York, NY
http://www.fwdodge.com
Dodge Construction Potentials. Monthly.

Dow Jones & Co., New York, NY.
http://www.dj.com
Wall Street Journal.
Daily except Saturdays, Sundays, and holidays.

Edison Electric Institute, Washington, DC
http://www.eei.org
Statistical Yearbook of the Electric Utility Industry. Annual.

Editor & Publisher Co., New York, NY
http://www.editorandpublisher.com
Editor & Publisher. Weekly.
International Year Book. Annual.
Market Guide. Annual.

ENO Transportation Foundation, Leesburg, VA
http://www.enotrans.com
Transportation in America. Midyear, Annually with Periodic Supplements.

Euromonitor, London, England
http://www.euromonitor.com
Consumer Asia. Annual.
Consumer China. Annual.
Consumer Eastern Europe. Annual.
Consumer Europe. Annual.

Euromonitor, London, England —Con.
Consumer International. Annual.
Consumer Latin America. Annual.
European Marketing Data and Statistics. Annual.
International Marketing Data and Statistics. Annual.
Latin America Marketing Data and Statistic. Annual.
World Consumer Expenditure Patterns. Annual.
World Consumer Income Patterns. Annual.
World Economic Factbook. Annual.
World Retail Data and Statistics. Annual

Federal National Mortgage Association, Washington, DC
http://www.fanniemae.com
Annual Report.

Food and Agriculture Organization of the United Nations, Rome, Italy
http://www.fao.org
Fertilizer Yearbook.
Production Yearbook.
Trade Yearbook.
Yearbook of Fishery Statistics.
Yearbook of Forest Products.

The Foundation Center, New York, NY
http://www.fdncenter.org
Foundation Giving Trends. Annual.
Foundation Yearbook. Annual.

Gale Group Inc., Farmington Hills, MI
http://www.galegroup.com
Gale Directory of Publications and Broadcast Media. 1999.

General Aviation Manufacturers Association, Washington, DC
http://www.generalaviation.org
Shipment Report. Quarterly and Annual.
Statistical Databook. Annual.

Girl Scouts of the U.S.A., New York, NY
www.gsusa.org
Annual Report.

Health Forum, L.L.C., American Hospital Association, Company, Chicago, IL.
http://www.healthforum.com
Annual Report.

Health Insurance Association of America, Washington, DC
http://www.hiaa.org
Source Book of Health Insurance Data. Annual.

Independent Petroleum Association of America, Washington, DC
http://www.ipaa.org
Domestic Oil and Gas Trends. Monthly.
Oil & Natural Gas Production in Your State. Annual.
U.S. Petroleum Statistics. Annual.

Information Today, Inc., Medford, NJ
http://www.infotoday.com
American Library Directory. Annual.
Bowker Annual Library and Book Trade Almanac.

Institute for Criminal Justice Ethics, New York, NY
http://www.lib.jjay.cuny.edu/cje/html/institute.html
Criminal Justice Ethics. Semiannual.

Insurance Information Institute, New York, NY
http://www.iii.org
Insurance Facts. Annual.

Inter-American Development Bank, Washington, DC
http://www.iadb.org
Annual Report.
Economic and Social Progress in Latin America. Annual Survey.

International City Management Association, Washington, DC
http://www.icma.org
Compensation: An Annual Report on Local Government Executive Salaries and Fringe Benefits.
Municipal Year Book. Annual.

International Labour Office, Geneva, Switzerland
http://www.ilo.org
Yearbook of Labour Statistics.

International Monetary Fund, Washington, DC
http://www.imf.org
Annual Report.
Balance of Payments Statistics. Monthly with annual yearbook.
Direction of Trade Statistics. Monthly with annual yearbook.
Government Finance Statistics Yearbook.
International Financial Statistics. Monthly with annual yearbook.

Investment Company Institute, Washington, DC
http://www.ici.org
Mutual Fund Fact Book. Annual.

Jane's Information Group, Coulsdon, UK and Alexandria, VA
http://www.janes.com
Jane's Air-Launched Weapons. (Binder-4 monthly update.)
Jane's All the World's Aircraft. Annual.
Jane's Armour and Artillery. Annual.
Jane's Avionics. Annual.
Jane's Fighting Ships. Annual.
Jane's Infantry Weapons. Annual.
Jane's Merchant Ships. Annual.
Jane's Military Communications. Annual.

Jane's Information Group, Coulsdon, UK and Alexandria, VA —Con.
Jane's Military Logistics. Annual.
Jane's Military Training Systems. Annual.
Jane's NATO Handbook. Annual.
Jane's Spaceflight Directory. Annual.

Joint Center for Political and Economic Studies, Washington, DC
http://www.jointcenter.org
Black Elected Officials: A National Roster. Annual.

McGraw-Hill Informations Service Co., Washington, DC
http://www.fwdodge.com
Electrical world Directory of Electric Utilities. Annual.
Engineering and Mining Journal. Monthly.
Keystone Coal Industry Manual. Annual.

Moody's Investors Service, New York, NY
http://www.moodys.com

National Academy of Sciences, Washington, DC
http://www.pnas.org
Science, Engineering, and Humanities Doctorates in the United States. Biennial.
Summary Report. Doctorate Recipients from United States Universities. Annual.

National Association of Home Builders, Washington, DC
http://www.nahb.org
Housing Economics. Monthly
Housing Market Statistics. Monthly.

National Association of Latino Elected and Appointed Officials, Washington, DC
http://www.naleo.org
National Roster of Hispanic Elected Officials. Annual.

National Association of Realtors. Washington, DC
http://nar.realtor.com
Real Estate Outlook: Market Trends & Insights. Monthly.

National Association of State Budget Officers, Washington, DC
http://www.nasbo.org
"State Expenditure Report". Annual.
Fiscal Survey of the States. Semiannual.

National Association of State Park Directors, Tuscon, AZ
http://www.naspd.org
Annual Information Exchange.

National Catholic Educational Association, Washington, DC
http://www.ncea.org
Catholic Schools in America. Annual.
United States Catholic Elementary and Secondary Schools. Staffing and Enrollment. Annual.

National Catholic Educational Association, Washington, DC —Con.
- U.S. Catholic Elementary Schools and their Finances. Biennial.
- U.S. Catholic Secondary Schools and their Finances. Biennial.

National Center for State Courts, Williamsburg, VA
- http://www.ncsc.dni.us
- State Court Caseload Statistics. Annual.

National Council of the Churches of Christ in the U.S.A., New York, NY
- http://www.ncccusa.org
- Yearbook of American and Canadian Churches. Annual.

National Council of Savings Institutions, Washington, DC
- http://www.bankmag.com
- Fact Book of National Council of Savings Institutions. Annual.

National Education Association, Washington, DC
- http://www.nea.org
- Estimates of School Statistics. Annual.
- Rankings of the States. Annual.
- Status of the American Public School Teacher, 1995-96. Quinquennial.

National Fire Protection Association, Quincy, MA
- http://www.nfpa.org
- NFPA Journal. Bimonthly.

National Golf Foundation, Jupiter, FL
- http://www.ngf.org
- Americans' Attitudes on Golf (in their communities).
- Commercial Golf Range Participation and Supply in the U.S.
- Commercial Golf Ranges in the U.S.
- Directory of Executive and Par-3 Golf Courses in U.S.
- Directory of Golf: The People and Businesses in Golf. Annual.
- Directory of U.S. Golf Courses.
- Directory of U.S. Golf Practice Ranges and Learning Centers.
- Directory of Golf Retailers: Off-Course Golf Retail Stores in U.S.
- Golf Consumer Potential.
- Golf Consumer Spending in the U.S.
- Golf Facilities in Canada.
- Golf Facilities in the U.S. - 1998.
- Golf Facility Employee Compensation tudy.
- Golf Participation in Canada.
- Golf Participation in U.S. - 1998.
- Golf Travel Market Report for the U.S.
- High-Interest Women Golfers—Target Marketing for Success.

National Golf Foundation, Jupiter, FL —Con.
- Hot Spots for Golf Course Construction Activity in the USA.
- NGF's *Infosearch: Accessing the World's Largest Golf Business Library.*
- Operating and Financial Performance Profiles of Golf Facilities in the U.S.
- Senior Golfer Profile.
- Trends in the Golf Industry. Annually.
- Women in Golf—1991-1996

National Marine Manufacturers Association, Chicago, IL.
- http://www.nmma.org
- Boating. (A Statistical Report on America's Top Family Sport.) Annual.
- State Boat Registration. Annual.

National Restaurant Association, Washington, DC
- http://www.restaurant.org
- Compensation for Salaried Personnel in Restaurants. 2001.
- Ethnic Cuisines II. 2000.
- Holiday Dining. 2001.
- Meal Consumption Behavior. 2001.
- Quick-Service Restaurant Trends. Annual.
- Restaurant Economic Trends. Monthly.
- Restaurant Industry Employee Profile. Annual.
- Restaurant Industry Forecast. Annual.
- Restaurant Industry in Review. Annual.
- Restaurant Industry Operations Report. Annual.
- Restaurant Industry Pocket Factbook. Annual.
- Restaurant Industry 2010. 1999.
- Restaurant Numbers: 25-Year History, 1970-95. 1998.
- Restaurant Spending. Annual. Restaurants USA. Monthly.
- Tableservice Restaurant Trends. Annual
- Takeout Foods: A Consumer Study of Carryout and Delivery. 1998
- The Economic Impact of the Nation's Eating and Drinking Places. Annual.

National Safety Council
- http://www.nsc.org
- Injury Facts. Annual

National Sporting Goods Association, Mt. Prospect, IL
- http://www.nsga.org
- Fitness in America, 2001.
- The Sporting Goods Market in 2003. Annual.
- Sports Participation in 2002. Annual.
- Sports Equipment Purchases in 2002. Annual

New York Stock Exchange, Inc., New York, NY
http://www.nyse.com
Fact Book. Annual.

Organization for Economic Cooperation and Development, Paris, France
http://www.oecd.org
Annual Oil Market Report.
Basic Science and Technology Statistics, 2000 Edition on CD-Rom. Annual
Bank Profitability: Financial Statements of Banks. 2000. Annual
Central Government Debt: Statistical Yearbook. 2000. Annual
Coal Information. Annual.
Education at a Glance: OECD Indicators 2001. Annual
Energy Balances of OECD Countries. 1998-1999. 2001 Edition. Annual.
Energy Prices and Taxes. Quarterly.
Energy Statistics of OECD Countries. 1998-1999. 2001 Edition. Annual.
External Debt Statistics: The Debt of Developing Countries and Countries in Transition. Annual.
Financial Market Trends. Triennial.
Food Consumption Statistics. Irregular.
Geographical Distribution of Financial Flows to Developing Countries.
Geographical Distribution of Financial Flows to Aid Recipients. 2001. Annual
Historical Statistics of Foreign Trade Series A. Annual.
Indicators of Industrial Activity. Quarterly.
International Development Statistics CD-ROM and Online Database. 2001. Annual
International Trade by Commodities. Series C. Annual.
Iron and Steel Industry in 1999. 2001 Edition. Annual.
Labour Force Statistics. Annual.
Latest Information on National Accounts of Developing Countries. Annual.
Main Economic Indicators. Monthly.
Main Science and Technology Indicators. Biennial.
Maritime Transport. Annual.
Meat Balances in OECD Countries. Annual.
Milk and Milk Products Balances in OECD Countries. Annual.
Monthly Statistics of International Trade. Series A. Monthly.
National Accounts of OECD Countries. Annual.
  Vol. I: Main Aggregates.
  Vol. II: Detailed Tables.
OECD Agricultural Outlook. 2001-2006. 2001 Edition. Annual
OECD Economic Outlook. Bi-annual. Historical Statistics. Annual.

Organization for Economic Cooperation and Development, Paris, France —Con.
OECD Economic Studies. Annual for member countries.
OECD Economic Surveys. Annual.
OECD Employment Outlook. Annual.
OECD Environmental Outlook 2000. Annual.
OECD Financial Statistics. Annual (three vols.) and monthly supplements.
OECD Health Data. 2001. Annual.
OECD Health Systems: Facts and Trends.
OECD Historical Statistics. (2000 Edition). Annual.
OECD Indicators of Industrial Activity. Quarterly.
OECD Main Economic Indicators. Monthly.
OECD Microtables on Foreign Trade by Commodities covering Series B (individual reporting countries) and Series C (total reporting countries). Annual from 1977.
OECD Observer. Bimonthly.
Oil and Gas Information. Annual.
Oil, Gas, Coal, and Electricity Quarterly Statistics. Quarterly.
The Pulp and Paper Industry. Annual.
Quarterly Labor Force Statistics.
Quarterly National Accounts.
Quarterly Oil Statistics and Energy Balances.
Revenue Statistics of OECD Member Countries. Annual.
Review of Fisheries in OECD Member Countries. Annual.
Statistical Report on Road Accidents. 1997-1998. Annual.
Statistical Trends in Transport (ECMT).
Statistics of Area Production and Field of Crop Products in OECD Member Countries.
Structural Statistics for Industry and Services: Core Data. Annual.
Taxing Wages. 2000. Annual
Statistics of Foreign Trade:
  Monthly Statistics of Foreign Trade. (Series A.)
  Foreign Trade by Commodities. (Series C.) Annual.
Tourism Policy and International Tourism in OECD Member Countries. Annual.
Uranium Resources Production and Demand. Biennial.
World Energy Statistics and Balances.

Pan American Health Organization, Washington, DC
http://www.paho.org
Health Conditions in the Americas. Quadrennial.

PennWell Publishing Co., Tulsa, OK
http://www.pennwell.com
Offshore. Monthly.
Oil and Gas Journal. Weekly.

Population Association of America, Washington, DC
http://www.popassoc.org
Demography. Quarterly.

Puerto Rico Planning Board, San Juan, PR
http://http://www.jp.gobierno.pr
Balance of Payments—Puerto Rico. Annual.
Economic Activity Index. Monthly.
Economic Indicators. Monthly.
Economic Projections. Annual.
Economic Report to the Governor. Annual.
External Trade Statistics-Puerto Rico. Annual.
Income and Product. Annual.
Input-Output—Puerto Rico. Every 5 years.
Statistical Appendix to the Economic Report to the Government. Annual.

Radio Advertising Bureau, New York, NY
http://www.rab.com
Radio Facts. Annual.

Reed Business Information Unit, New York, NY
http://www.cahners.com
Library Journal. Semimonthly.
Publishers Weekly.
School Library Journal. Monthly.

Regional Airline Association, Washington, DC
http://www.raa.org
Annual Report.
Broadcasting Magazine. Weekly.

Research Associates of Washington, Arlington, VA
http://www.rschassoc.com
Inflation Measures for Schools, Colleges, and Libraries. Periodic.

Securities Industry Association, New York, NY
http://www.sia.com
Foreign Activity Report. Quarterly.
Securities Industry Trends. Periodic.
SIA Securities Industry Fact Book. Annual.

Standard and Poor's Corporation, New York, NY
http://www.standardandpoors.com
Analyst's Handbook. Annual with monthly cumulative supplements.
Corporation Records. Six basic volumes; News Supplements, daily; Dividend Record, daily, and cumulative monthly and annual.
Daily Stock Price Records. Quarterly.
Security Owner's Stock Guide. Monthly.
Statistical Service. (Security Price Index Record; business and financial basic statistics with monthly supplement.)

United Nations Educational, Scientific and Cultural Organization, Paris, France
http://www.unesco.org
Statistical Yearbook.

United Nations Statistics Division, New York, NY
http://www.un.org
Compendium of Human Settlements Statistics. (Series N.)
Demographic Yearbook. (Series R.)
Energy Balances and Electricity Profiles. (Series W.)
Energy Statistics Yearbook. (Series J.)
Industrial Statistics Yearbook: (Series P.)
  Commodity Production Statistics.
International Trade Statistics Yearbook. (Series G.)
Monthly Bulletin of Statistics. (Series Q.)
National Accounts Statistics: (Series X, Annually.)
  Main Aggregates and Detailed Tables.
  Analysis of Main Aggregates.
Population and Vital Statistics Report. (Series A, Quarterly.)
Social Statistics and Indicators: (Series K, Occasional.)
  The World's Women: Trends and Statistics.
  Women's Indicators and Statistics Database (CD and diskette only.)
Statistical Yearbook. (Series; also available in CD-ROM, Series S/CD)
World Statistics Pocketbook. (Series V, Annually.)

United States League of Savings Institutions, Chicago, IL
http://www.westernleague.org
Savings Institutions Sourcebook. Annual.

United States Telephone Association, Washington, DC
http://www.usta.org
Statistics of the Local Exchange Carriers. Annual.

United Way of America, Alexandria, VA
http://www.unitedway.org
Annual Directory.

University of Michigan, Center for Political Studies, Institute for Social Research, Ann Arbor, MI
http://www.umich.edu
National Election Studies Cumulative Datafile. Biennial.

Warren Communications News, Washington, DC
http://www.law.emory.edu
Cable Action Update. Weekly.
Cable and Station Coverage Atlas. Annual.

Warren Communications News, Washington, DC —Con.
Television Action Update. Weekly.
Television and Cable Factbook. Annual.
TV Station & Cable Ownership Directory. Semiannual.

World Almanac, New York, NY
http://www.worldalmanac.com
The World Almanac and Book of Facts. Annual.

The World Bank, Washington, DC
http://www.worldbank.org

The World Bank, Washington, DC —Con.
Global Development Finance, 2003. Annual.
The Little Data Book
World Bank Atlas, 2003. Annual
World Development Indicators, 2003. Annual

World Health Organization, Geneva, Switzerland
http://www.who.int
Epidemiological and Vital Statistics Report. Monthly.
World Health Statistics. Quarterly and annual.

Guide to State Statistical Abstracts

This bibliography includes the most recent statistical abstracts for states published since 1995 plus those that will be issued in late 2002. For some states, a near equivalent has been listed in substitution for, or in addition to, a statistical abstract. All sources contain statistical tables on a variety of subjects for the state as a whole, its component parts, or both. The page counts given for publications are approximate. Internet sites also contain statistical data.

Alabama

University of Alabama, Center for Business and Economic Research, Box 870221, Tuscaloosa 35487-0221. 205-348-6191. Fax: 907-269-8125. Internet site <http://cber.cba.ua.edu/>

Economic Abstract of Alabama. 2000. 534 pp.

Alabama Economic Outlook, 2002. Revised annually.

Alaska

Community and Economic Development, Division of Community Advocacy, 550 W. 7th Avenue, Suite 1770, Anchorage, Alaska 99501-3510. 907-269-8110. Fax: 907-269-8125. Internet site <http://www.dced.state.ak.us/cbd/AEIS/AEISHome.htm/>

The Alaska Economy Performance Report. 1996. Online.

Arizona

University of Arizona, Economic and Business Research, Eller College of Business and Public Administration, McClelland Hall 103, P.O. Box 210108, Tucson 85721-0108. 520-621-2523. Fax: 520-621-2150. Internet site <http://www.ebr.eller.arizona.edu/>

Arizona Statistical Abstract, 2003, 692 pp.

Arizona's Economy. 16-20 pp. Quarterly newsletter.

Arizona Economic Indicators 52 pp. Biennial.

Arkansas

University of Arkansas at Little Rock, Institute for Economic Advancement, Economic Research, 2801 South University, Little Rock 72204. 501-569-8551. Internet site <http://www.aiea.ualr.edu/>

Arkansas State and County Economic Data, 2003. 16 pp. Revised annually.

Arkansas Personal Income Handbook, 2003. 98 pp.

University of Arkansas at Little Rock, Institute for Economic Advancement, Census State Data Center, 2801 South University, Reynolds Bldg., Rm: 407, Little Rock 72204. 501-5698533. Internet site <http://www.aiea.ualr.edu/>

Arkansas Statistical Abstract, 2000. 740 pp. Revised biennially.

California

Department of Finance, 915 L Street, 8th Floor, Sacramento 95814. 916-322-2263. Internet site <http://www.dof.ca.gov/html/fsdata/stat-abs/sahome.htm>

California Statistical Abstract. Annual.

Colorado

University of Colorado, Boulder 80309-0184. 303-492-8227. Internet site <http://www.colorado.edu/libraries/govpubs/online.htm/>

Colorado by the Numbers. Online only.

Connecticut

Connecticut Department of Economic & Community Development, 505 Hudson St., Hartford 06106. 1-860-270-8000. Internet site <http://www.ct.gov/ecd/>

Connecticut Town Profiles, 2002-2003.

Delaware

Delaware Economic Development Office, 99 Kings Highway, Dover 19901. 302-739-4271. Fax: 302-739-2027. Internet site <http://www.state.de.us/dedo/>

Delaware Statistical Overview, 2002. 160 pp.

District of Columbia

Office of Planning, Data Management Division, 801 North Capitol St., N.E. Washington 20002. 202-442-7603

Office of Policy and Legislative Affairs, Executive Office of the Mayor, John A. Wilson Bldg., Suite 511, 1350 Pennsylvania Ave., NW, Washington 20004. 202-727-6979.

Indices—A Statistical Index to DC Services, Dec. 1997-98. 273 pp.

Florida

University of Florida, Bureau of Economic and Business Research, P.O. Box 117145, 221 Matherly Hall, Gainesville 32611-7145. 352-392-0171, ext. 212. Internet site <http://www.bebr.ufl.edu/> and <http://info@bebr.ufl.edu/>

Florida Statistical Abstract, 2002. 36th ed. 846 pp. Annual. Also available on CD-ROM.

Florida County Perspective, 2002. One profile for each county. Annual. Also available on CD-ROM.

Florida County Rankings, 2002. 9th edition. 121 pp. Annual. Also available on CD-ROM.

Florida—Con.
Florida and the Nation, 2003. 7th edition. 229 pp. Annual. Also available on CD-ROM.

Georgia
University of Georgia, Selig Center for Economic Growth, Terry College of Business, Athens 30602-6269. 706-542-4085. Internet site <http://www.selig.uga.edu/>
Georgia Statistical Abstract, 2000-01. 500 pp.
Georgia Statistical Abstract, 2002-03. 500 pp.

University of Georgia, Center for Agribusiness and Economic Development, Lumpkin House, Athens 30602. 706-542-8938 or 706-542-0760. Fax 706-542-8934. Internet sites <http://www.georgiastats.uga.edu/> and <http://www.agecon.uga.edu/countyguide/>
The Georgia County Guide, 2003. 22nd edition. 200 pp. Annual.

Hawaii
Hawaii State Department of Business, and Economic Development & Tourism, Research and Economic Analysis Division, Statistics and Data Support Branch P.O. Box 2359, Honolulu 96804. Inquiries 808-586-2424; Copies 808-586-2423. Internet site <http://www.hawaii.gov/dbedt/db01/index.html/>
The State of Hawaii Data Book 2001: A Statistical Abstract. 700 pp.

Idaho
Department of Commerce, 700 West State St., P.O. Box 83720, Boise 83720-0093. 208-334-2470. Internet site <http://www.idoc.state.id.us/data/community/>
County Profiles of Idaho, 2003.
Idaho Community Profiles, 2003.
Profile of Rural Idaho, 1999.

Illinois
University of Illinois, Bureau of Economic and Business Research, 430 Wohlers Hall, 1206 South 6th Street, Champaign 61820. 217-333-2330. Internet site <http://www.cba.uiuc.edu/research/>
Illinois Statistical Abstract. 2000. 15th edition. 759 pp. Online only.

Indiana
Indiana University, Indiana Business Research Center, Kelly School of Business, Ste 3110, 1275 E. 10th Street, Bloomington 47405. 812-855-5507. Internet site <http://www.ibrc.indiana.edu/>

Kansas
University of Kansas, Policy Research Institute, 607 Blake Hall, Lawrence 66044-3177. 785-864-3701. Internet site <http://www.pri.ku.edu/>.
Kansas Statistical Abstract, 2001. 35th ed. 480 pp.

Kansas—Con.
Kansas Statistical Abstract, 2001. 36th ed. 480 pp.
Kansas Statistical Abstract, 2002. 37th ed. 538 pp.

Kentucky
Kentucky Cabinet for Economic Development, Division of Research, 500 Mero Street, Capital Plaza Tower, Frankfort 40601. 502-564-4886. Internet site <http://www.edc.state.ky.us/kyedc/edevlinks.asp/>
Kentucky Deskbook of Economic Statistics. 34th ed. 1998. Online only.

Louisiana
University of New Orleans, Division of Business and Economic Research, New Orleans 70148. 504-280-6240. Internet site <http://leap.nlu.edu/STAAB.HTM/>.
Statistical Abstract of Louisiana. 10th ed. 1997.

Maine
Maine State Planning Office, Station #38, Augusta 04333. 207-287-2989. Internet site <http://www.state.me.us/spo/economics/economics>

Maryland
RESI, Towson University 8000 York Road, Towson 212520001. 410-704-7374. Fax: 410-704-4115. Internet site <http://www.resiusa.org/>.
Maryland Statistical Abstract. 2003. 352 pp.

Massachusetts
Massachusetts Institute for Social and Economic Research, University of Massachusetts, 128 Thompson Hall, 200 Hicks Way, Amherst 01003-9277. 413-545-3460. Fax 413-545-3686. Internet site <http://www.umass.edu/miser/>.

Minnesota
Minnesota Department of Employment and Economic Development, Analysis and Evaluation Office, 500 Metro Square Building, 121 East 7th Place, St. Paul 55101-2146. 651-297-2335. Internet site <http://www.deed.state.mn.us/>.
Compare Minnesota: Profiles of Minnesota's Economy and Population, 2002-2003.

State Demographic Center, Department of Administration, Centennial Bldg., 658 Cedar Street, St. Paul 55155. 651-296-2557. Internet site <http://www.demography.state.mn.us/>

Mississippi
Mississippi State University, College of Business and Industry, Division of Research, P.O. Box 5288 Mississippi State 39762. 662-325-3817. Fax 662-325-8686.
Mississippi Statistical Abstract. 2002. 660 pp.

Missouri
University of Missouri, Economic and Policy Analysis Research Center, 10 Professional Bldg., Columbia 65211. 573-882-4805. Internet site <http://econ.missouri.edu/eparc/>.
Statistical Abstract for Missouri, 2001. 423 pp. Biennial.

Montana
Census and Economic Information Center, Montana Department of Commerce, 301 S. Park, P.O. Box 200505, Helena 59620. 406-841-2740. Internet site <http://ceic.commerce.state.mt.us/>

Nebraska
Nebraska Department of Economic Development, Box 94666, Lincoln 68509-4666. 402-471-3111. Fax 402-471-3778. Internet site <http://info.neded.org/>.
Nebraska Data Book, 2000. 300 pp. Available only on Internet.

Nevada
Department of Administration, Budget and Planning Division, 209 East Musser Street, Suite 200, Carson City 89701. 775-684-0222. Internet site <http://www.budget.state.nv.us/>
Nevada Statistical Abstract. 2001. 50 pp.
Biennial Report 2001-2002.

New Hampshire
NH Office of State Planning and Energy Programs, 57 Regional Drive, Concord 03301. 603-271-2155. Fax 603-271-1728. Internet site <http://www.state.nh.us/osp/sdc/sdc.html/>. Online only.

New Jersey
New Jersey State Data Center, NJ Department of Labor, P.O. Box 388, Trenton 08625-0388. 609-984-2595. Internet site <http://www.state.nj.us/labor/lra/njsdc.html/>.
Labor Market Information. Internet only.

New Mexico
University of New Mexico, Bureau of Business and Economic Research, 1920 Lomas N.E. Albuquerque 87131-6021. 505-277-6626. Fax 505-277-2773. Internet site <http://www.unm.edu/bber/>.
New Mexico Business, Current Economic Report. Monthly.
FOR-UNM Bulletin. Quarterly.

New York
Nelson A. Rockefeller Institute of Government, 411 State Street, Albany 12203-1003. 518-443-5522. Internet site <http:// www.rockinst.org/>
New York State Statistical Yearbook, 2002. 27th ed. 620 pp.

North Carolina
Office of Governor, Office of State Budget and Management, Management Section, Data Services Unit, 20321 Mail Service Center, Raleigh 27699-0321. 919-733-7061. Fax 919-7153562. Internet site <http://www.osbm.state.nc.us/>.

North Dakota
North Dakota Department of Commerce, P.O. Box 2057, 1600 E. Century Avenue, Suite 2, Bismarck 58502-2057. 701-328-5300. Internet site <http://www.ndcommerce.com/>
North Dakota Economic Roadmap 2002. Job Service North Dakota. 135 pp.

Ohio
Office of Strategic Research, Ohio Department of Development, 27th Floor, 77 S. High Street, Columbus 43215-6130. 614-466-2116 or 1-800-848-1300, ext. 6-2116. Fax 614-466-9697. Internet site <http://www.odod.state.oh.us/research>
Research products and services. Updated continuously.
Ohio County Profiles; Ohio County Indicators. Updated periodically.

Oklahoma
University of Oklahoma, Center for Economic and Management Research, Michael F. Price College of Business, 307 West Brooks Street, Norman 73019. 405-325-2931. Fax 405-3257688. Internet site <http://cemr.ou.edu/>
Statistical Abstract of Oklahoma, 2001. Annual. 401 pp.

Oregon
Secretary of State, Archives Division, Archives Bldg., 800 Summer Street, NE Salem 97310. 503-373-0701. Internet site <http://www.sos.state.or.us/>
Oregon Blue Book. 2003-2004. Biennial. 469 pp.

Pennsylvania
Pennsylvania State Data Center, Institute of State and Regional Affairs, Penn State Harrisburg, 777 West Harrisburg Pike, Middletown Pennsylvania 17057-4898. 717-948-6310. Internet site <http://pasdc.hbg.psu.edu/pasdc/>
Pennsylvania Statistical Abstract, 2003. 306 pp.

Rhode Island
Rhode Island Economic Development Corporation, 1 West Exchange Street, Providence 02903. 401-222-2601. Fax 401-2222102. Internet site <http://www.riedc.com/>
Annual Trends and Time Series of Key Statistics, 2002. 12 pp. Excel spreadsheets.

South Carolina
Budget and Control Board, Office of Research and Statistics, 1919 Blanding Street, Columbia 29201. 803-734-3780. Internet site <http://www.ors.state.sc.us/> Fax 803-898-9972.
South Carolina Statistical Abstract: 2001-2002. 423 pp.

South Dakota
South Dakota State Data Center, Business Research Bureau, The University of South Dakota, 414 E. Clark Street, Vermillion 57069. 605-677-5287. Fax 605-677-5427. Internet site <http://www.usd.edu/brbinfo/>
2002 South Dakota Community Abstracts. 400 pp.

Tennessee
University of Tennessee, Center for Business and Economic Research, College of Business Administration, 100 Glocker Bldg., Knoxville 37996-4170. 865-974-5441. Internet site <http://cber.bus.utk.edu/tnsdc/sdcmain.htm./>
Tennessee Statistical Abstract, 2003. 18th ed. 800 pp. Biennial.

Texas
Dallas Morning News, Communications Center, P.O. Box 655237, Dallas 75265-5237. 214-977-8261. Internet site <http://www.texasalmanac.com/rankprofile.html>
Texas Almanac, 2004-2005. 672 pp.

Utah
University of Utah, Bureau of Economic and Business Research, David Eccles School of Business 1645 East Campus Center Drive, Salt Lake City 84112-9302. 801-581-6333. Internet site <http://www.business.utah.edu/bebr/>
Statistical Abstract of Utah. 1996. Centennial. Last in paper format—Online only.
Utah Foundation, 4141 Highland Drive, Suite 102, Salt Lake City 84124. 801-288-1838. Fax 801-263-6492. Internet site <http://www.utahfoundation.org/>
Statistical Review of Government in Utah. 1999. Online only.

Vermont
Labor Market Information, Department of Employment and Training, 5 Green Mountain Drive, P.O. Box 488, Montpelier 05601-0488. 802-828-4202. Internet site <http://www.vtlmi.info/>
Economic and Demographic Profiles. Annual. 62 pp.

Virginia
Weldon Cooper Center, 918 Emmet Street North, Charlottesville 22903-4832. 434-982-5522. Internet site <http://www.ccps.virginia.edu/demographics/>
Virginia Statistical Abstract, 2000. Online only.

Washington
Washington State Office of Financial Management, Forecasting Division P.O. Box 43113 Olympia 98504-3113. 360-902-0599. Fax 360-664-8941. Internet site <http://www.ofm.wa.gov/>
Washington State Data Book, 2001. 309 pp.

West Virginia
West Virginia University, College of Business and Economics, Bureau of Business and Economic Research, P.O. Box 6025, Morgantown 26506-6025. 304-293-7835. Internet site <http://www.bber.wvu.edu/>
2003 County Profiles.
West Virginia Economic Outlook, 2003.
West Virginia Research League, Inc., P.O. Box 11176, Charleston 25339. 304-766-9495. Internet site <http://www.wvrl.org/>
The 2001 Statistical Handbook. Annual.

Wisconsin
Wisconsin Legislative Reference Bureau, P.O. Box 2037, Madison 53701-2037. 608-266-0342 Internet site <http://www.legis.state.wi.us/lrb/bb/>
2003-2004 State of Wisconsin Blue Book. Biennial.

Wyoming
Department of Administration and Information, Division of Economic Analysis, 1807 Capitol Avenue, Suite 206, Cheyenne 82002-0060. 307-777-7504. Internet site <http://eadiv.state.Wy.us/>
The Equality State Almanac 2000. 8th ed. 134 pp.

Guide to Foreign Statistical Abstracts

This bibliography presents recent statistical abstracts for member nations of the Organization for Economic Cooperation and Development and Russia. All sources contain statistical tables on a variety of subjects for the individual countries. Many of the following publications provide text in English as well as in the national language(s). For further information on these publications, contact the named statistical agency which is responsible for editing the publication.

Australia
Australian Bureau of Statistics, Canberra. <http://www.abs.gov.au>
Year Book Australia. Annual. 2003. 974 pp. (In English.)

Austria
Statistik Austria, A-1033 Wien. <http://www.statistik.at/index.shtml>
Statistisches Jahrbuch Osterreichs. Annual. 2003. 620 pp. With CD-ROM. (In German.) With English translations of table headings.

Belgium
Institut National de Statistique, Rue de Louvain; 44-1000 Bruxelles. <http://statbel.fgov.be/info/linksen.asp>
Annuaire statistique de la Belgique. Annual. 1995. 820 pp. (In French.)

Canada
Statistics Canada, Ottawa, Ontario, KIA OT6. <http://www.statcan.ca/start.html>
Canada Yearbook: A review of economic, social and political developments in Canada. 2001. 563 pp. Irregular. (In English.)

Czech Republic
Czech Statistical Office, Sokolovska 142, 186 04 Praha 8; <http://www.czso.cz/>
Statisticka Rocenka Ceske Rpubliky. 2002. 795 pp. (In English and Czech.)

Denmark
Danmarks Statistik, Sejrogade 11, 2100 Kobenhavn O. <http://www.dst.dk/665>
Statistisk ARBOG. 2003. Annual. 600 pp. (Printed version - In Danish only.)

Finland
Statistics Finland, Helsinki. <http://www.stat.fi/tk/tilastotietoaen.html>
Statistical Yearbook of Finland. Annual. 2002. 703 pp. With CD-ROM. (In English, Finnish, and Swedish.)

France
Institut National de la Statistique et des Etudes Economiques, Paris 18, Bld. Adolphe Pinard, 75675 Paris (Cedex 14). <http://www.insee.fr/fr/home/homepage.asp>
Annuaire Statistique de la France. Annual. 2003. 586 pp. (In French.)

Germany
Statistische Bundesamt, D-65180 Wiesbaden. <http://www.destatis.de>
Statistisches Jahrbuch fur die Bundesrepublic Deutschland. Annual. 2002. 714 pp. (In German.)
Statistisches Jahrbuch fur das Ausland. 2002. 368 pp.

Greece
National Statistical Service of Greece, Athens. <http://www.statistics.gr/>
Concise Statistical Yearbook, 2001. 279 pp. Plus 13 pages of graphs. (In English and Greek.)
Statistical Yearbook of Greece. Annual. 2001. 569 pp. Plus 12 pages of graphs. (In English and Greek.)

Hungary
Hungarian Central Statistical Office, 1024 Budapest. <http://www.ksh.hu>
Statistical Yearbook of Hungary, 2001. 647 pp. (In English and Hungarian.)

Iceland
Hagstofa Islands/Statistics Iceland. <http://www.hagstofa.is/template41.asp?PageID=251>
Statistical Yearbook of Iceland. 2002. With CD-ROM. Irregular. 336 pp. (In English and Icelandic.)

Ireland
Central Statistics Office, Skehard Road, Cork. <http://www.cso.ie>
Statistical Yearbook of Ireland. Annual. 2002. 423 pp. (In English.)

Italy
ISTAT (Istituto Centrale di Statistica); <http://www.istat.it> Via Cesare Balbo 16 Roma.
Annuario Statistico Italiano. Annual. 2001. With CD-ROM. 714 pp. (In Italian.)

Japan
Statistics Bureau, Ministry of Public Management, Home Affairs Posts and Telecommunications, Japan. <http://www.stat.go.jp/english/data/index.htm>
Japan Statistical Yearbook. Annual. 2003. 920 pp. (In English and Japanese.)

Korea, South
National Statistical Office, Government Complex, #920 Dunsan-dong Seo-gu Daejeon 302-701. <http://www.nso.go.kr/>
Korea Statistical Yearbook. Annual. 2002. 777 pp. (In Korean and English.)

Luxembourg
STATEC (Service Central de la Statistique et des Etudes), P.O. Box 304, L-2013, Luxembourg. <http://statec.gouvernement.lu/>
Annuaire Statistique. Annual. 2002. (In French.) (Alphabetical numbering system.)

Mexico
Instituto Nacional de Estadistica Geografia e Informatica, Av. Heroe Nacozari Num. 2301 Sur Fracc. Jardines del Parque, CP 20270 Aguascalientes, Ags. <http://www.inegi.gob.mx/difusion/ingles/fiest.html>
Anuario estadistico de los Estados Unidos Mexicanos. Annual. 2002. 727 pp. Also on disc. (In Spanish.)
Agenda Estadistica 2001. 149 pp.

Netherlands
Statistics Netherlands, R L Vellekoop. Prinses Beatrixiaan 428, 2273 X Z Voorburg. <http://www.cbs.nl/en/>
Statistical Yearbook 2003 of the Netherlands. 551 pp. (In English.)
Statistisch Jaarboek 2003. 561 pp. With CD-ROM.

New Zealand
Department of Statistics, Wellington. <http://www.stats.govt.nz/>
New Zealand Official Yearbook. Annual. 2002. 627 pp. (In English.)

Norway
Statistics Norway, Oslo/Kongsvinger. <http://www.ssb.no/english/subjects/>
Statistical Yearbook. Annual. 2002. 537 pp. (In English.)

Poland
Central Statistical Office al. Niepodleglosci 208, 00-925 Warsaw. <http://www.stat.gov.pl/english/index.htm>
Concise Statistical Yearbook. 2003. (In Polish and English.)
Statistical Yearbook of the Republic of Poland. 2002. (In Polish and English.)

Portugal
INE (Instituto Nacional de Estatistica.) <http://www.ine.pt/indexeng.htm> Avenida Antonio Jose de Almeida P-1000-043 Lisboa.
Anuario Estatistico de Portugal. 2002. (In Portuguese and English.)

Russia
State Committee of Statistics of Russia, Moscow. <http://www.gks.ru/eng/>
Statistical Yea' book. 2002. 690 pp. (In Russian.)

Slovakia
Statistical Office of the Slovak Republic, Bradacova 7, 852 86 Bratislava. <http://www.statistics.sk/webdata/english/index2a.htm>
Statisticka Rocenka Slovensak. 2000. 719 pp. Plus 16 pages of graphs. (In English and Slovak.)

Spain
INE (Instituto Nacional de Estadistica); Paseo de la Castellana, 183, Madrid 16. <http://www.ine.es/welcoing.htm>
Espana Anuaria Estadistico. Annual. 2002-2003. 768 pp. 16 pages of graphs. (In Spanish.)

Sweden
Statistics Sweden, S-11581 Stockholm. <http://www.scb.se/indexeng.asp>
Statistisk Arsbok for Sverige. Annual. 2003. 718 pp. (In English and Swedish.)

Switzerland
Bundesamt fur Statistik, Hallwylstrasse 15, CH-3003, Bern
Statistisches Jahrbuch der Schweiz. Annual. 2003. 912 pp. With CD-ROM. (In French and German.)

Turkey
State Institute of Statistics, Prime Ministry, 114 Necatibey Caddesi, Bakanliklar, Yenisehir, Ankara
Statistical Yearbook of Turkey. 1999. 721 pp. (In English and Turkish.)
Turkey in Statistics. 1999. 144 pp. (In English only.)

United Kingdom
The Stationary Office; P.O. Box 29, Norwich, NR3 1GN. <http://www.statistics.gov.uk/>
Annual Abstract of Statistics. Annual. 2002. 429 pp. (In English.)

Appendix II
Metropolitan and Micropolitan Statistical Areas: Concepts, Components, and Population

The United States Office of Management and Budget (OMB) defines metropolitan and micropolitan statistical areas according to published standards that are applied to Census Bureau data. The general concept of a metropolitan or micropolitan statistical area is that of a core area containing a substantial population nucleus, together with adjacent communities having a high degree of economic and social integration with that core. Currently defined metropolitan and micropolitan statistical areas are based on application of 2000 standards (which appeared in the Federal Register on December 27, 2000) to 2000 decennial census data. Current metropolitan and micropolitan statistical area definitions were announced by OMB effective June 6, 2003.

Standard definitions of metropolitan areas were first issued in 1949 by the then Bureau of the Budget (predecessor of OMB), under the designation "standard metropolitan area" (SMA). The term was changed to "standard metropolitan statistical area" (SMSA) in 1959 and to "metropolitan statistical area" (MSA) in 1983. The term "metropolitan area" (MA) was adopted in 1990 and referred collectively to metropolitan statistical areas (MSAs), consolidated metropolitan statistical areas (CMSAs), and primary metropolitan statistical areas (PMSAs). The term "core based statistical area" (CBSA) became effective in 2000 and refers collectively to metropolitan and micropolitan statistical areas.

OMB has been responsible for the official metropolitan areas since they were first defined, except for the period 1977 to 1981, when they were the responsibility of the Office of Federal Statistical Policy and Standards, Department of Commerce. The standards for defining metropolitan areas were modified in 1958, 1971, 1975, 1980, 1990, and 2000.

Defining Metropolitan and Micropolitan Statistical Areas—The 2000 standards provide that each CBSA must contain at least 1 urban area of 10,000 or more population. Each metropolitan statistical area must have at least 1 urbanized area of 50,000 or more inhabitants. Each micropolitan statistical area must have at least 1 urban cluster of at least 10,000 but less than 50,000 population.

Under the standards, the county (or counties) in which at least 50 percent of the population resides within urban areas of 10,000 or more population, or that contain at least 5,000 people residing within a single urban area of 10,000 or more population, is identified as a "central county" (counties). Additional "outlying counties" are included in the CBSA if they meet specified requirements of commuting to or from the central counties. Counties or equivalent entities form the geographic "building blocks" for metropolitan and micropolitan statistical areas throughout the United States and Puerto Rico.

If specified criteria are met, a metropolitan statistical area containing a single core with a population of 2.5 million or more may be subdivided to form smaller groupings of counties referred to as "metropolitan divisions."

As of June 6, 2003, there are 362 metropolitan statistical areas and 560 micropolitan statistical areas in the United States. In addition, there are eight metropolitan statistical areas and five micropolitan statistical areas in Puerto Rico.

Principal Cities and Metropolitan and Micropolitan Statistical Area Titles—The largest city in each metropolitan or micropolitan statistical area is designated a "principal city." Additional cities qualify if specified requirements are met concerning population size and employment. The title of each metropolitan or micropolitan statistical area consists of the names of up to three of its principal cities and the name of each state into which the metropolitan or micropolitan statistical area extends. Titles of metropolitan divisions also typically are based on principal city names but in certain cases consist of county names.

Text continued on page 924.

Figure A1
Metropolitan and Micropolitan Statistical Areas of the United States
As defined by the U.S. Office of Management and Budget, June 6, 2003

Note: Under the 1990 standards, metropolitan areas were defined using counties, except in New England where minor civil divisions (MCDs) were used. Under the 2000 standards, metropolitan and micropolitan statistical areas are defined using counties nationwide. For New England, the 2000 standards also identify a complementary set of areas—New England city and town areas (NECTAs)—defined using MCDs.

Figure A2
Metropolitan Areas of the United States
Metropolitan Statistical Areas (MSAs) and Consolidated Metropolitan Statistical Areas (CMSAs) defined by the U.S. Office of Management and Budget, June 30, 1999

Note: Under the 1990 standards, metropolitan areas were defined using counties, except in New England where minor civil divisions (MCDs) were used. Under the 2000 standards, metropolitan and micropolitan statistical areas are defined using counties nationwide. For New England, the 2000 standards also identify a complementary set of areas—New England city and town areas (NECTAs)—defined using MCDs.

Appendix II 921

U.S. Census Bureau, Statistical Abstract of the United States: 2003

Figure A3
Metropolitan and Micropolitan New England City and Town Areas (NECTAs)
As defined by the U.S. Office of Management and Budget, June 6, 2003

Note: Under the 1990 standards, metropolitan areas were defined using counties, except in New England where minor civil divisions (MCDs) were used. Under the 2000 standards, metropolitan and micropolitan statistical areas are defined using counties nationwide. For New England, the 2000 standards also identify a complementary set of areas—New England city and town areas (NECTAs)—defined using MCDs.

Figure A4
New England Metropolitan Areas
Metropolitan Statistical Areas (MSAs) and Consolidated Metropolitan Statistical Areas (CMSAs) defined by the U.S. Office of Management and Budget, June 30, 1999

Note: Under the 1990 standards, metropolitan areas were defined using counties, except in New England where minor civil divisions (MCDs) were used. Under the 2000 standards, metropolitan and micropolitan statistical areas are defined using counties nationwide. For New England, the 2000 standards also identify a complementary set of areas—New England city and town areas (NECTAs) —defined using MCDs.

U.S. Census Bureau, Statistical Abstract of the United States: 2003

Defining New England City and Town Areas—In view of the importance of cities and town in New England, the 2000 standards also provide for a set of geographic areas that are defined using cities and towns in the six New England states. The New England city and town areas (NECTAs) are defined using the same criteria as metropolitan and micropolitan statistical areas and are identified as either metropolitan or micropolitan, based, respectively, on the presence of either an urbanized area of 50,000 or more population or an urban cluster of at least 10,000 but less than 50,000 population. If the specified criteria are met, a NECTA containing a single core with a population of at least 2.5 million may be subdivided to form smaller groupings of cities and towns referred to as New England city and town area divisions.

Changes in Definitions Over Time—Changes in the definitions of these statistical areas since the 1950 census have consisted chiefly of (1) the recognition of new areas as they reached the minimum required city or urbanized area population and (2) the addition of counties (or cities and towns in New England) to existing areas as new decennial census data showed them to qualify.

In some instances, formerly separate areas have been merged, components of an area have been transferred from one area to another, or components have been dropped from an area. The large majority of changes have taken place on the basis of decennial census data. However, Census Bureau data serve as the basis for intercensal updates in specified circumstances.

Because of these historical changes in geographic definitions, users must be cautious in comparing data for these statistical areas from different dates. For some purposes, comparisons of data for areas as defined at given dates may be appropriate; for other purposes, it may be preferable to maintain consistent area definitions. Historical metropolitan area definitions are available for 1999, 1993, 1990, 1983, 1981, 1973, 1970, 1963, 1960, and 1950.

Excluding Table 26 in the Population section and the tables that follow in this Appendix, the tables presenting data for metropolitan areas in this edition of the *Statistical Abstract* are based on the 1999 or earlier metropolitan area definitions. For a list of component counties according to the 1999 definition see Appendix II in the 2002 edition of the *Statistical Abstract* or <http://www.census.gov/population/www/estimates/pastmetro.html>.

Table A. Metropolitan Statistical Areas and Components as of June 6, 2003

[Population as of July 2002. 159 represents 159,000. All metropolitan areas are arranged alphabetically]

Metropolitan statistical area / Metropolitan division / Component county	Population, 2002 (1,000)	Metropolitan statistical area / Metropolitan division / Component county	Population, 2002 (1,000)	Metropolitan statistical area / Metropolitan division / Component county	Population, 2002 (1,000)
Abilene, TX	159	Henderson County, NC	93	**Barnstable Town, MA**	229
Callahan County, TX	13	Madison County, NC	20	Barnstable County, MA	229
Jones County, TX	20	**Athens-Clarke County, GA**	171	**Baton Rouge, LA**	717
Taylor County, TX	126	Clarke County, GA	104	Ascension Parish, LA	82
Akron, OH	700	Madison County, GA	27	East Baton Rouge Parish, LA	412
Portage County, OH	154	Oconee County, GA	27	East Feliciana Parish, LA	21
Summit County, OH	546	Oglethorpe County, GA	13	Iberville Parish, LA	33
Albany, GA	160	**Atlanta-Sandy Springs-Marietta, GA**	4,529	Livingston Parish, LA	99
Baker County, GA	4	Barrow County, GA	51	Pointe Coupee Parish, LA	23
Dougherty County, GA	96	Bartow County, GA	83	St. Helena Parish, LA	10
Lee County, GA	27	Butts County, GA	21	West Baton Rouge Parish, LA	22
Terrell County, GA	11	Carroll County, GA	95	West Feliciana Parish, LA	15
Worth County, GA	22	Cherokee County, GA	159		
Albany-Schenectady-Troy, NY	836	Clayton County, GA	253	**Battle Creek, MI**	138
Albany County, NY	296	Cobb County, GA	651	Calhoun County, MI	138
Rensselaer County, NY	153	Coweta County, GA	98	**Bay City, MI**	110
Saratoga County, NY	207	Dawson County, GA	18	Bay County, MI	110
Schenectady County, NY	147	DeKalb County, GA	677	**Beaumont-Port Arthur, TX**	382
Schoharie County, NY	32	Douglas County, GA	99	Hardin County, TX	49
Albuquerque, NM	754	Fayette County, GA	97	Jefferson County, TX	249
Bernalillo County, NM	574	Forsyth County, GA	117	Orange County, TX	84
Sandoval County, NM	96	Fulton County, GA	825	**Bellingham, WA**	174
Torrance County, NM	17	Gwinnett County, GA	651	Whatcom County, WA	174
Valencia County, NM	68	Haralson County, GA	27	**Bend, OR**	125
Alexandria, LA	146	Heard County, GA	11	Deschutes County, OR	125
Grant Parish, LA	19	Henry County, GA	140	**Billings, MT**	141
Rapides Parish, LA	127	Jasper County, GA	12	Carbon County, MT	10
Allentown-Bethlehem-Easton, PA-NJ	758	Lamar County, GA	16	Yellowstone County, MT	132
Warren County, NJ	108	Meriwether County, GA	23	**Binghamton, NY**	252
Carbon County, PA	60	Newton County, GA	72	Broome County, NY	200
Lehigh County, PA	318	Paulding County, GA	94	Tioga County, NY	52
Northampton County, PA	273	Pickens County, GA	26	**Birmingham-Hoover, AL**	1,068
		Pike County, GA	15	Bibb County, AL	22
Altoona, PA	128	Rockdale County, GA	74	Blount County, AL	53
Blair County, PA	128	Spalding County, GA	59	Chilton County, AL	41
Amarillo, TX	232	Walton County, GA	67	Jefferson County, AL	661
Armstrong County, TX	2	**Atlantic City, NJ**	259	St. Clair County, AL	67
Carson County, TX	7	Atlantic County, NJ	259	Shelby County, AL	154
Potter County, TX	116	**Auburn-Opelika, AL**	118	Walker County, AL	71
Randall County, TX	107	Lee County, AL	118	**Bismarck, ND**	96
Ames, IA	81	**Augusta-Richmond County, GA-SC**	507	Burleigh County, ND	71
Story County, IA	81	Burke County, GA	23	Morton County, ND	25
Anchorage, AK	334	Columbia County, GA	95	**Blacksburg-Christiansburg-Radford, VA**	153
Anchorage Borough, AK	269	McDuffie County, GA	21	Giles County, VA	17
Matanuska-Susitna Borough, AK	65	Richmond County, GA	198	Montgomery County, VA	85
Anderson, IN	132	Aiken County, SC	145	Pulaski County, VA	35
Madison County, IN	132	Edgefield County, SC	25	Radford city, VA	16
Anderson, SC	171	**Austin-Round Rock, TX**	1,349	**Bloomington, IN**	177
Anderson County, SC	171	Bastrop County, TX	64	Greene County, IN	33
Ann Arbor, MI	334	Caldwell County, TX	35	Monroe County, IN	121
Washtenaw County, MI	334	Hays County, TX	110	Owen County, IN	23
Anniston-Oxford, AL	112	Travis County, TX	851	**Bloomington-Normal, IL**	154
Calhoun County, AL	112	Williamson County, TX	290	McLean County, IL	154
Appleton, WI	209	**Bakersfield, CA**	694	**Boise City-Nampa, ID**	498
Calumet County, WI	42	Kern County, CA	694	Ada County, ID	320
Outagamie County, WI	166	**Baltimore-Towson, MD**	2,602	Boise County, ID	7
Asheville, NC	379	Anne Arundel County, MD	503	Canyon County, ID	145
Buncombe County, NC	211	Baltimore County, MD	770	Gem County, ID	15
Haywood County, NC	55	Carroll County, MD	159	Owyhee County, ID	11
		Harford County, MD	228		
		Howard County, MD	260		
		Queen Anne's County, MD	43		
		Baltimore city, MD	639		
		Bangor, ME	146		
		Penobscot County, ME	146		

Appendix II 925

U.S. Census Bureau, Statistical Abstract of the United States: 2003

Metropolitan statistical area / Metropolitan division / Component county	Population, 2002 (1,000)
Boston-Cambridge-Quincy, MA-NH	4,446
Boston-Quincy, MA	1,832
Norfolk County, MA	656
Plymouth County, MA	486
Suffolk County, MA	690
Cambridge-Newton-Framingham, MA	1,474
Middlesex County, MA	1,474
Essex County, MA	736
Essex County, MA	736
Rockingham County-Strafford County, NH	404
Rockingham County, NH	288
Strafford County, NH	116
Boulder, CO	279
Boulder County, CO	279
Bowling Green, KY	107
Edmonson County, KY	12
Warren County, KY	95
Bremerton-Silverdale, WA	236
Kitsap County, WA	236
Bridgeport-Stamford-Norwalk, CT	896
Fairfield County, CT	896
Bristol, VA	68
Washington County, VA	51
Bristol city, VA	17
Brownsville-Harlingen, TX	354
Cameron County, TX	354
Brunswick, GA	95
Brantley County, GA	15
Glynn County, GA	69
McIntosh County, GA	11
Buffalo-Cheektowaga-Tonawanda, NY	1,163
Erie County, NY	945
Niagara County, NY	218
Burlington, NC	136
Alamance County, NC	136
Burlington-South Burlington, VT	203
Chittenden County, VT	149
Franklin County, VT	47
Grand Isle County, VT	7
Canton-Massillon, OH	407
Carroll County, OH	29
Stark County, OH	378
Cape Coral-Fort Myers, FL	476
Lee County, FL	476
Carson City, NV	54
Carson City, NV	54
Casper, WY	67
Natrona County, WY	67
Cedar Rapids, IA	241
Benton County, IA	26
Jones County, IA	20
Linn County, IA	195
Champaign-Urbana, IL	214
Champaign County, IL	183
Ford County, IL	14
Piatt County, IL	16
Charleston, WV	306
Boone County, WV	26
Clay County, WV	10
Kanawha County, WV	196
Lincoln County, WV	22
Putnam County, WV	52

Metropolitan statistical area / Metropolitan division / Component county	Population, 2002 (1,000)
Charleston-North Charleston, SC	563
Berkeley County, SC	145
Charleston County, SC	317
Dorchester County, SC	101
Charlotte-Gastonia-Concord, NC-SC	1,410
Anson County, NC	25
Cabarrus County, NC	140
Gaston County, NC	193
Mecklenburg County, NC	738
Union County, NC	140
York County, SC	174
Charlottesville, VA	179
Albemarle County, VA	82
Fluvanna County, VA	22
Greene County, VA	16
Nelson County, VA	15
Charlottesville city, VA	44
Chattanooga, TN-GA	483
Catoosa County, GA	56
Dade County, GA	16
Walker County, GA	62
Hamilton County, TN	309
Marion County, TN	28
Sequatchie County, TN	12
Cheyenne, WY	83
Laramie County, WY	83
Chicago-Naperville-Joliet, IL-IN-WI	9,286
Chicago-Naperville-Joliet, IL	7,774
Cook County, IL	5,378
DeKalb County, IL	92
DuPage County, IL	925
Grundy County, IL	39
Kane County, IL	443
Kendall County, IL	61
McHenry County, IL	278
Will County, IL	560
Gary, IN	683
Jasper County, IN	31
Lake County, IN	487
Newton County, IN	14
Porter County, IN	150
Lake County-Kenosha County, IL-WI	829
Lake County, IL	675
Kenosha County, WI	154
Chico, CA	209
Butte County, CA	209
Cincinnati-Middletown, OH-KY-IN	2,041
Dearborn County, IN	47
Franklin County, IN	23
Ohio County, IN	6
Boone County, KY	93
Bracken County, KY	8
Campbell County, KY	89
Gallatin County, KY	8
Grant County, KY	24
Kenton County, KY	152
Pendleton County, KY	15
Brown County, OH	43
Butler County, OH	341
Clermont County, OH	183
Hamilton County, OH	834
Warren County, OH	175
Clarksville, TN-KY	235
Christian County, KY	71
Trigg County, KY	13
Montgomery County, TN	138
Stewart County, TN	13
Cleveland, TN	106
Bradley County, TN	90
Polk County, TN	16

Metropolitan statistical area / Metropolitan division / Component county	Population, 2002 (1,000)
Cleveland-Elyria-Mentor, OH	2,148
Cuyahoga County, OH	1,379
Geauga County, OH	93
Lake County, OH	229
Lorain County, OH	288
Medina County, OH	158
Coeur d'Alene, ID	114
Kootenai County, ID	114
College Station-Bryan, TX	189
Brazos County, TX	156
Burleson County, TX	17
Robertson County, TX	16
Colorado Springs, CO	565
El Paso County, CO	544
Teller County, CO	22
Columbia, MO	149
Boone County, MO	139
Howard County, MO	10
Columbia, SC	664
Calhoun County, SC	15
Fairfield County, SC	24
Kershaw County, SC	54
Lexington County, SC	223
Richland County, SC	329
Saluda County, SC	19
Columbus, GA-AL	283
Russell County, AL	49
Chattahoochee County, GA	15
Harris County, GA	25
Marion County, GA	7
Muscogee County, GA	186
Columbus, IN	72
Bartholomew County, IN	72
Columbus, OH	1,660
Delaware County, OH	125
Fairfield County, OH	129
Franklin County, OH	1,087
Licking County, OH	149
Madison County, OH	40
Morrow County, OH	33
Pickaway County, OH	53
Union County, OH	43
Corpus Christi, TX	405
Aransas County, TX	23
Nueces County, TX	315
San Patricio County, TX	67
Corvallis, OR	79
Benton County, OR	79
Cumberland, MD-WV	101
Allegany County, MD	74
Mineral County, WV	27
Dallas-Fort Worth-Arlington, TX	5,484
Dallas-Plano-Irving, TX	3,673
Collin County, TX	567
Dallas County, TX	2,284
Delta County, TX	5
Denton County, TX	488
Ellis County, TX	120
Hunt County, TX	79
Kaufman County, TX	78
Rockwall County, TX	51
Fort Worth-Arlington, TX	1,811
Johnson County, TX	136
Parker County, TX	95
Tarrant County, TX	1,527
Wise County, TX	53
Dalton, GA	126
Murray County, GA	39
Whitfield County, GA	87

Metropolitan statistical area / Metropolitan division / Component county	Population, 2002 (1,000)	Metropolitan statistical area / Metropolitan division / Component county	Population, 2002 (1,000)	Metropolitan statistical area / Metropolitan division / Component county	Population, 2002 (1,000)
Danville, IL	83	**Eau Claire, WI**	150	**Fort Walton Beach-Crestview-Destin, FL**	176
Vermilion County, IL	83	Chippewa County, WI	56	Okaloosa County, FL	176
Danville, VA	109	Eau Claire County, WI	94	**Fort Wayne, IN**	397
Pittsylvania County, VA	62	**El Centro, CA**	146	Allen County, IN	338
Danville city, VA	48	Imperial County, CA	146	Wells County, IN	28
Davenport-Moline-Rock Island, IA-IL	375	**Elizabethtown, KY**	109	Whitley County, IN	31
Henry County, IL	51	Hardin County, KY	96	**Fresno, CA**	835
Mercer County, IL	17	Larue County, KY	13	Fresno County, CA	835
Rock Island County, IL	148	**Elkhart-Goshen, IN**	186	**Gadsden, AL**	103
Scott County, IA	159	Elkhart County, IN	186	Etowah County, AL	103
Dayton, OH	847	**Elmira, NY**	91	**Gainesville, FL**	237
Greene County, OH	150	Chemung County, NY	91	Alachua County, FL	222
Miami County, OH	100	**El Paso, TX**	698	Gilchrist County, FL	15
Montgomery County, OH	554	El Paso County, TX	698	**Gainesville, GA**	152
Preble County, OH	43	**Erie, PA**	280	Hall County, GA	152
Decatur, AL	146	Erie County, PA	280	**Glens Falls, NY**	125
Lawrence County, AL	35	**Eugene-Springfield, OR**	327	Warren County, NY	64
Morgan County, AL	112	Lane County, OR	327	Washington County, NY	61
Decatur, IL	112	**Evansville, IN-KY**	344	**Goldsboro, NC**	113
Macon County, IL	112	Gibson County, IN	33	Wayne County, NC	113
Deltona-Daytona Beach-Ormond Beach, FL	459	Posey County, IN	27	**Grand Forks, ND-MN**	96
Volusia County, FL	459	Vanderburgh County, IN	172	Polk County, MN	31
Denver-Aurora, CO	2,281	Warrick County, IN	54	Grand Forks County, ND	65
Adams County, CO	374	Henderson County, KY	45	**Grand Junction, CO**	121
Arapahoe County, CO	510	Webster County, KY	14	Mesa County, CO	121
Broomfield County, CO	41	**Fairbanks, AK**	85	**Grand Rapids-Wyoming, MI**	758
Clear Creek County, CO	9	Fairbanks North Star Borough, AK	85	Barry County, MI	58
Denver County, CO	560	**Fargo, ND-MN**	177	Ionia County, MI	63
Douglas County, CO	211	Clay County, MN	52	Kent County, MI	588
Elbert County, CO	22	Cass County, ND	125	Newaygo County, MI	49
Gilpin County, CO	5	**Farmington, NM**	120	**Great Falls, MT**	79
Jefferson County, CO	532	San Juan County, NM	120	Cascade County, MT	79
Park County, CO	16	**Fayetteville, NC**	339	**Greeley, CO**	205
Des Moines, IA	497	Cumberland County, NC	303	Weld County, CO	205
Dallas County, IA	44	Hoke County, NC	36	**Green Bay, WI**	289
Guthrie County, IA	11	**Fayetteville-Springdale-Rogers, AR-MO**	368	Brown County, WI	232
Madison County, IA	14	Benton County, AR	166	Kewaunee County, WI	20
Polk County, IA	386	Madison County, AR	14	Oconto County, WI	37
Warren County, IA	42	Washington County, AR	167	**Greensboro-High Point, NC**	658
Detroit-Warren-Livonia, MI	4,484	McDonald County, MO	22	Guilford County, NC	431
Detroit-Livonia-Dearborn, MI	2,046	**Flagstaff, AZ**	120	Randolph County, NC	134
Wayne County, MI	2,046	Coconino County, AZ	120	Rockingham County, NC	93
Warren-Farmington Hills-Troy, MI	2,439	**Flint, MI**	441	**Greenville, NC**	157
Lapeer County, MI	91	Genesee County, MI	441	Greene County, NC	19
Livingston County, MI	169	**Florence, AL**	142	Pitt County, NC	137
Macomb County, MI	809	Colbert County, AL	55	**Greenville, SC**	575
Oakland County, MI	1,203	Lauderdale County, AL	87	Greenville County, SC	391
St. Clair County, MI	168	**Florence, SC**	195	Laurens County, SC	71
Dothan, AL	132	Darlington County, SC	68	Pickens County, SC	113
Geneva County, AL	25	Florence County, SC	127	**Gulfport-Biloxi, MS**	250
Henry County, AL	16	**Fond du Lac, WI**	98	Hancock County, MS	45
Houston County, AL	90	Fond du Lac County, WI	98	Harrison County, MS	191
Dover, DE	131	**Fort Collins-Loveland, CO**	265	Stone County, MS	14
Kent County, DE	131	Larimer County, CO	265	**Hagerstown-Martinsburg, MD-WV**	231
Dubuque, IA	89	**Fort Smith, AR-OK**	278	Washington County, MD	134
Dubuque County, IA	89	Crawford County, AR	55	Berkeley County, WV	81
Duluth, MN-WI	276	Franklin County, AR	18	Morgan County, WV	15
Carlton County, MN	33	Sebastian County, AR	117	**Hanford-Corcoran, CA**	135
St. Louis County, MN	200	Le Flore County, OK	48	Kings County, CA	135
Douglas County, WI	44	Sequoyah County, OK	40		
Durham, NC	445				
Chatham County, NC	54				
Durham County, NC	234				
Orange County, NC	120				
Person County, NC	37				

Appendix II 927

U.S. Census Bureau, Statistical Abstract of the United States: 2003

Metropolitan statistical area / Metropolitan division / Component county	Population, 2002 (1,000)	Metropolitan statistical area / Metropolitan division / Component county	Population, 2002 (1,000)	Metropolitan statistical area / Metropolitan division / Component county	Population, 2002 (1,000)
Harrisburg-Carlisle, PA	515	**Iowa City, IA**	135	**Killeen-Temple-Fort Hood, TX**	338
Cumberland County, PA.	218	Johnson County, IA	114	Bell County, TX	245
Dauphin County, PA.	253	Washington County, IA.	21	Coryell County, TX.	74
Perry County, PA	44	**Ithaca, NY**	99	Lampasas County, TX	19
Harrisonburg, VA	110	Tompkins County, NY.	99	**Kingsport-Bristol, TN-VA.**	231
Rockingham County, VA.	69	**Jackson, MI**	161	Hawkins County, TN	55
Harrisonburg city, VA	41	Jackson County, MI.	161	Sullivan County, TN	153
Hartford-West Hartford-East Hartford, CT	1,168	**Jackson, MS**	506	Scott County, VA	23
Hartford County, CT.	867	Copiah County, MS	29	**Kingston, NY**	180
Middlesex County, CT	160	Hinds County, MS	250	Ulster County, NY	180
Tolland County, CT	141	Madison County, MS	78	**Knoxville, TN**	630
		Rankin County, MS	122	Anderson County, TN.	72
Hattiesburg, MS	127	Simpson County, MS	28	Blount County, TN	110
Forrest County, MS	73	**Jackson, TN**	109	Knox County, TN.	389
Lamar County, MS.	41	Chester County, TN	16	Loudon County, TN	41
Perry County, MS	12	Madison County, TN	93	Union County, TN	19
Hickory-Morganton-Lenoir, NC	349	**Jacksonville, FL**	1,178	**Kokomo, IN**	101
Alexander County, NC	34	Baker County, FL	23	Howard County, IN	85
Burke County, NC	90	Clay County, FL	152	Tipton County, IN.	17
Caldwell County, NC	79	Duval County, FL.	806	**La Crosse, WI-MN**	128
Catawba County, NC.	147	Nassau County, FL	61	Houston County, MN	20
		St. Johns County, FL.	136	La Crosse County, WI	108
Hinesville-Fort Stewart, GA	73	**Jacksonville, NC**	149		
Liberty County, GA	62	Onslow County, NC	149	**Lafayette, IN**	181
Long County, GA.	11			Benton County, IN	9
Holland-Grand Haven, MI	246	**Janesville, WI**	154	Carroll County, IN	20
Ottawa County, MI.	246	Rock County, WI	154	Tippecanoe County, IN.	152
Honolulu, HI	896	**Jefferson City, MO**	142	**Lafayette, LA**	243
Honolulu County, HI.	896	Callaway County, MO.	42	Lafayette Parish, LA	193
		Cole County, MO.	72	St. Martin Parish, LA	50
Hot Springs, AR	90	Moniteau County, MO	15		
Garland County, AR.	90	Osage County, MO	13	**Lake Charles, LA**	193
Houma-Bayou Cane-Thibodaux, LA	197	**Johnson City, TN**	184	Calcasieu Parish, LA	183
Lafourche Parish, LA	91	Carter County, TN	57	Cameron Parish, LA	10
Terrebonne Parish, LA.	106	Unicoi County, TN	18	**Lakeland-Winter Haven, FL**	499
		Washington County, TN.	109	Polk County, FL.	499
Houston-Baytown-Sugar Land, TX	4,986	**Johnstown, PA**	150	**Lancaster, PA**	479
Austin County, TX	25	Cambria County, PA.	150	Lancaster County, PA.	479
Brazoria County, TX.	257	**Jonesboro, AR**	109	**Lansing-East Lansing, MI**	454
Chambers County, TX	27	Craighead County, AR	84	Clinton County, MI	67
Fort Bend County, TX	400	Poinsett County, AR.	25	Eaton County, MI.	106
Galveston County, TX	261			Ingham County, MI	281
Harris County, TX	3,557	**Joplin, MO**	160		
Liberty County, TX.	74	Jasper County, MO	107	**Laredo, TX**	208
Montgomery County, TX.	328	Newton County, MO.	53	Webb County, TX	208
San Jacinto County, TX	23	**Kalamazoo-Portage, MI**	319	**Las Cruces, NM**	179
Waller County, TX	34	Kalamazoo County, MI.	241	Dona Ana County, NM	179
Huntington-Ashland, WV-KY-OH	286	Van Buren County, MI	77	**Las Vegas-Paradise, NV**	1,522
Boyd County, KY	50	**Kankakee-Bradley, IL**	105	Clark County, NV.	1,522
Greenup County, KY	37	Kankakee County, IL	105	**Lawrence, KS**	102
Lawrence County, OH	62	**Kansas City, MO-KS**	1,889	Douglas County, KS.	102
Cabell County, WV	95	Franklin County, KS.	25	**Lawton, OK**	113
Wayne County, WV	42	Johnson County, KS	477	Comanche County, OK.	113
Huntsville, AL	354	Leavenworth County, KS	71	**Lebanon, PA**	121
Limestone County, AL	68	Linn County, KS	10	Lebanon County, PA	121
Madison County, AL.	286	Miami County, KS	29		
		Wyandotte County, KS.	158	**Lewiston, ID-WA**	58
Idaho Falls, ID	105	Bates County, MO	17	Nez Perce County, ID	37
Bonneville County, ID.	85	Caldwell County, MO	9	Asotin County, WA.	20
Jefferson County, ID	20	Cass County, MO	87		
		Clay County, MO	191	**Lewiston-Auburn, ME**	105
Indianapolis, IN	1,575	Clinton County, MO.	20	Androscoggin County, ME.	105
Boone County, IN	48	Jackson County, MO	661		
Brown County, IN	15	Lafayette County, MO	33	**Lexington-Fayette, KY**	416
Hamilton County, IN.	206	Platte County, MO	78	Bourbon County, KY	20
Hancock County, IN.	58	Ray County, MO	24	Clark County, KY.	34
Hendricks County, IN.	114			Fayette County, KY	264
Johnson County, IN	122	**Kennewick-Richland-Pasco, WA**	203	Jessamine County, KY	41
Marion County, IN	863	Benton County, WA	150	Scott County, KY.	35
Morgan County, IN.	68	Franklin County, WA	53	Woodford County, KY.	23
Putnam County, IN	36				
Shelby County, IN	44				

Metropolitan statistical area Metropolitan division Component county	Population, 2002 (1,000)	Metropolitan statistical area Metropolitan division Component county	Population, 2002 (1,000)	Metropolitan statistical area Metropolitan division Component county	Population, 2002 (1,000)
Lima, OH	108	**McAllen-Edinburg-Pharr,**		**Morgantown, WV**	112
Allen County, OH	108	**TX**	614	Monongalia County, WV	83
Lincoln, NE	274	Hidalgo County, TX	614	Preston County, WV	29
Lancaster County, NE	258	**Medford, OR**	186	**Morristown, TN**	126
Seward County, NE	17	Jackson County, OR	186	Grainger County, TN	21
Little Rock-North Little		**Memphis, TN-MS-AR**	1,231	Hamblen County, TN	59
Rock, AR	623	Crittenden County, AR	51	Jefferson County, TN	46
Faulkner County, AR	90	DeSoto County, MS	118	**Mount Vernon-Anacortes,**	
Grant County, AR	17	Marshall County, MS	35	**WA**	107
Lonoke County, AR	55	Tate County, MS	26	Skagit County, WA	107
Perry County, AR	10	Tunica County, MS	10		
Pulaski County, AR	364	Fayette County, TN	31	**Muncie, IN**	118
Saline County, AR	86	Shelby County, TN	906	Delaware County, IN	118
		Tipton County, TN	53	**Muskegon-Norton Shores,**	
Logan, UT-ID	105			**MI**	172
Franklin County, ID	12	**Merced, CA**	225	Muskegon County, MI	172
Cache County, UT	94	Merced County, CA	225		
				Myrtle Beach-Conway-North	
Longview, TX	197	**Miami-Fort Lauderdale-**		**Myrtle Beach, SC**	206
Gregg County, TX	113	**Miami Beach, FL**	5,232	Horry County, SC	206
Rusk County, TX	48	**Fort Lauderdale-**			
Upshur County, TX	36	**Pompano Beach-**		**Napa, CA**	130
		Deerfield Beach, FL	1,709	Napa County, CA	130
Longview-Kelso, WA	95	Broward County, FL	1,709		
Cowlitz County, WA	95	**Miami-Miami Beach-**		**Naples-Marco Island, FL**	277
		Kendall, FL	2,333	Collier County, FL	277
Los Angeles-Long Beach-		Miami-Dade County, FL	2,333		
Santa Ana, CA	12,745	**West Palm Beach-Boca**		**Nashville-Davidson-**	
Los Angeles-Long		**Raton-Boynton Beach,**		**Murfreesboro, TN**	1,353
Beach-Glendale, CA	9,807	**FL**	1,190	Cannon County, TN	13
Los Angeles County, CA	9,807	Palm Beach County, FL	1,190	Cheatham County, TN	37
Santa Ana-Anaheim-				Davidson County, TN	571
Irvine, CA	2,939	**Michigan City-La Porte, IN**	110	Dickson County, TN	44
Orange County, CA	2,939	La Porte County, IN	110	Hickman County, TN	23
				Macon County, TN	21
Louisville, KY-IN	1,183	**Midland, TX**	118	Robertson County, TN	57
Clark County, IN	98	Midland County, TX	118	Rutherford County, TN	195
Floyd County, IN	72			Smith County, TN	18
Harrison County, IN	35	**Milwaukee-Waukesha-West**		Sumner County, TN	136
Washington County, IN	28	**Allis, WI**	1,513	Trousdale County, TN	7
Bullitt County, KY	64	Milwaukee County, WI	937	Williamson County, TN	137
Henry County, KY	15	Ozaukee County, WI	84	Wilson County, TN	93
Jefferson County, KY	698	Washington County, WI	121		
Meade County, KY	27	Waukesha County, WI	371	**New Haven-Milford, CT**	836
Nelson County, KY	39			New Haven County, CT	836
Oldham County, KY	49	**Minneapolis-St. Paul-**			
Shelby County, KY	35	**Bloomington, MN-WI**	3,055	**New Orleans-Metairie-**	
Spencer County, KY	14	Anoka County, MN	310	**Kenner, LA**	1,315
Trimble County, KY	9	Carver County, MN	76	Jefferson Parish, LA	453
		Chisago County, MN	45	Orleans Parish, LA	474
Lubbock, TX	254	Dakota County, MN	369	Plaquemines Parish, LA	27
Crosby County, TX	7	Hennepin County, MN	1,122	St. Bernard Parish, LA	66
Lubbock County, TX	248	Isanti County, MN	34	St. Charles Parish, LA	49
		Ramsey County, MN	511	St. John the Baptist	
Lynchburg, VA	230	Scott County, MN	104	Parish, LA	45
Amherst County, VA	32	Sherburne County, MN	71	St. Tammany Parish, LA	201
Appomattox County, VA	14	Washington County, MN	210		
Bedford County, VA	62	Wright County, MN	98	**New York-Newark-Edison,**	
Campbell County, VA	51	Pierce County, WI	37	**NY-NJ-PA**	18,603
Bedford city, VA	6	St. Croix County, WI	68	**Edison, NJ**	2,252
Lynchburg city, VA	65			Middlesex County, NJ	776
		Missoula, MT	98	Monmouth County, NJ	630
Macon, GA	225	Missoula County, MT	98	Ocean County, NJ	537
Bibb County, GA	155			Somerset County, NJ	310
Crawford County, GA	13	**Mobile, AL**	400	**Newark-Union, NJ-PA**	2,132
Jones County, GA	24	Mobile County, AL	400	Essex County, NJ	798
Monroe County, GA	23			Hunterdon County, NJ	126
Twiggs County, GA	11	**Modesto, CA**	482	Morris County, NJ	479
		Stanislaus County, CA	482	Sussex County, NJ	149
Madera, CA	130			Union County, NJ	531
Madera County, CA	130	**Monroe, LA**	170	Pike County, PA	50
		Ouachita Parish, LA	147	**New York-Wayne-White**	
Madison, WI	520	Union Parish, LA	23	**Plains, NY-NJ**	11,415
Columbia County, WI	53			Bergen County, NJ	895
Dane County, WI	443	**Monroe, MI**	149	Hudson County, NJ	611
Iowa County, WI	23	Monroe County, MI	149	Passaic County, NJ	497
				Bronx County, NY	1,354
Manchester-Nashua, NH	392	**Montgomery, AL**	351	Kings County, NY	2,488
Hillsborough County,		Autauga County, AL	46	New York County, NY	1,547
NH	392	Elmore County, AL	69	Putnam County, NY	98
		Lowndes County, AL	14	Queens County, NY	2,238
Mansfield, OH	128	Montgomery County, AL	223		
Richland County, OH	128				

Appendix II 929

Metropolitan statistical area / Metropolitan division / Component county	Population, 2002 (1,000)	Metropolitan statistical area / Metropolitan division / Component county	Population, 2002 (1,000)	Metropolitan statistical area / Metropolitan division / Component county	Population, 2002 (1,000)
Richmond County, NY	457	Pascagoula, MS	153	Prescott, AZ	179
Rockland County, NY	292	George County, MS	20	Yavapai County, AZ	179
Westchester County, NY	937	Jackson County, MS	133	**Providence-New Bedford-**	
Suffolk County-Nassau County, NY	**2,804**	**Pensacola-Ferry Pass-Brent, FL**	**424**	**Fall River, RI-MA**	**1,613**
Nassau County, NY	1,345	Escambia County, FL	297	Bristol County, MA	543
Suffolk County, NY	1,459	Santa Rosa County, FL	127	Bristol County, RI	51
Niles-Benton Harbor, MI	**162**	**Peoria, IL**	**366**	Kent County, RI	170
Berrien County, MI	162	Marshall County, IL	13	Newport County, RI	86
Norwich-New London, CT	**263**	Peoria County, IL	182	Providence County, RI	635
New London County, CT	263	Stark County, IL	6	Washington County, RI	127
		Tazewell County, IL	128	**Provo-Orem, UT**	**396**
Ocala, FL	**273**	Woodford County, IL	36	Juab County, UT	9
Marion County, FL	273	**Philadelphia-Camden-Wilmington, PA-NJ-DE-MD**	**5,752**	Utah County, UT	388
Ocean City, NJ	**102**	**Camden, NJ**	**1,212**	**Pueblo, CO**	**147**
Cape May County, NJ	102	Burlington County, NJ	438	Pueblo County, CO	147
Odessa, TX	**122**	Camden County, NJ	512	**Punta Gorda, FL**	**149**
Ector County, TX	122	Gloucester County, NJ	262	Charlotte County, FL	149
Ogden-Clearfield, UT	**461**	**Philadelphia, PA**	**3,873**	**Racine, WI**	**191**
Davis County, UT	249	Bucks County, PA	610	Racine County, WI	191
Morgan County, UT	7	Chester County, PA	450	**Raleigh-Cary, NC**	**859**
Weber County, UT	204	Delaware County, PA	553	Franklin County, NC	50
Oklahoma City, OK	**1,121**	Montgomery County, PA	767	Johnston County, NC	133
Canadian County, OK	91	Philadelphia County, PA	1,492	Wake County, NC	676
Cleveland County, OK	216	**Wilmington, DE-MD-NJ**	**667**	**Rapid City, SD**	**115**
Grady County, OK	47	New Castle County, DE	512	Meade County, SD	24
Lincoln County, OK	32	Cecil County, MD	90	Pennington County, SD	91
Logan County, OK	35	Salem County, NJ	64	**Reading, PA**	**382**
McClain County, OK	28	**Phoenix-Mesa-Scottsdale, AZ**	**3,500**	Berks County, PA	382
Oklahoma County, OK	672	Maricopa County, AZ	3,304	**Redding, CA**	**172**
Olympia, WA	**218**	Pinal County, AZ	196	Shasta County, CA	172
Thurston County, WA	218	**Pine Bluff, AR**	**106**	**Reno-Sparks, NV**	**366**
Omaha-Council Bluffs, NE-IA	**784**	Cleveland County, AR	9	Storey County, NV	3
Harrison County, IA	16	Jefferson County, AR	83	Washoe County, NV	362
Mills County, IA	15	Lincoln County, AR	14	**Richmond, VA**	**1,126**
Pottawattamie County, IA	88	**Pittsburgh, PA**	**2,418**	Amelia County, VA	12
Cass County, NE	25	Allegheny County, PA	1,270	Caroline County, VA	23
Douglas County, NE	473	Armstrong County, PA	72	Charles City County, VA	7
Sarpy County, NE	129	Beaver County, PA	179	Chesterfield County, VA	271
Saunders County, NE	20	Butler County, PA	178	Cumberland County, VA	9
Washington County, NE	19	Fayette County, PA	147	Dinwiddie County, VA	25
Orlando, FL	**1,752**	Washington County, PA	204	Goochland County, VA	18
Lake County, FL	234	Westmoreland County, PA	368	Hanover County, VA	92
Orange County, FL	946	**Pittsfield, MA**	**133**	Henrico County, VA	268
Osceola County, FL	190	Berkshire County, MA	133	King and Queen County, VA	7
Seminole County, FL	382	**Pocatello, ID**	**83**	King William County, VA	14
Oshkosh-Neenah, WI	**158**	Bannock County, ID	76	Louisa County, VA	27
Winnebago County, WI	158	Power County, ID	7	New Kent County, VA	14
Owensboro, KY	**110**	**Portland-South Portland, ME**	**501**	Powhatan County, VA	24
Daviess County, KY	92	Cumberland County, ME	269	Prince George County, VA	34
Hancock County, KY	9	Sagadahoc County, ME	36	Sussex County, VA	12
McLean County, KY	10	York County, ME	195	Colonial Heights city, VA	17
Oxnard-Thousand Oaks-Ventura, CA	**784**	**Portland-Vancouver-Beaverton, OR-WA**	**2,016**	Hopewell city, VA	23
Ventura County, CA	784	Clackamas County, OR	352	Petersburg city, VA	33
Palm Bay-Melbourne-Titusville, FL	**496**	Columbia County, OR	45	Richmond city, VA	197
Brevard County, FL	496	Multnomah County, OR	678	**Riverside-San Bernardino-Ontario, CA**	**3,515**
Panama City-Lynn Haven, FL	**152**	Washington County, OR	473	Riverside County, CA	1,699
Bay County, FL	152	Yamhill County, OR	88	San Bernardino County, CA	1,816
Parkersburg-Marietta, WV-OH	**163**	Clark County, WA	370	**Roanoke, VA**	**289**
Washington County, OH	63	Skamania County, WA	10	Botetourt County, VA	31
Pleasants County, WV	8	**Port St. Lucie-Fort Pierce, FL**	**338**	Craig County, VA	5
Wirt County, WV	6	Martin County, FL	132	Franklin County, VA	48
Wood County, WV	87	St. Lucie County, FL	205	Roanoke County, VA	86
		Poughkeepsie-Newburgh-Middletown, NY	**645**	Roanoke city, VA	94
		Dutchess County, NY	288	Salem city, VA	25
		Orange County, NY	357	**Rochester, MN**	**169**
				Dodge County, MN	19
				Olmsted County, MN	129
				Wabasha County, MN	22

Metropolitan statistical area / Metropolitan division / Component county	Population, 2002 (1,000)	Metropolitan statistical area / Metropolitan division / Component county	Population, 2002 (1,000)	Metropolitan statistical area / Metropolitan division / Component county	Population, 2002 (1,000)
Rochester, NY	**1,043**	Kendall County, TX	25	**Sioux City, IA-NE-SD**	**143**
Livingston County, NY	65	Medina County, TX	41	Woodbury County, IA	103
Monroe County, NY	738	Wilson County, TX	35	Dakota County, NE	20
Ontario County, NY	102			Dixon County, NE	6
Orleans County, NY	44	**San Diego-Carlsbad-San**		Union County, SD	13
Wayne County, NY	94	**Marcos, CA**	**2,907**		
		San Diego County, CA	2,907	**Sioux Falls, SD**	**195**
Rockford, IL	**327**			Lincoln County, SD	28
Boone County, IL	45	**Sandusky, OH**	**79**	McCook County, SD	6
Winnebago County, IL	283	Erie County, OH	79	Minnehaha County, SD	153
				Turner County, SD	9
Rocky Mount, NC	**144**	**San Francisco-Oakland-**			
Edgecombe County, NC	55	**Fremont, CA**	**4,180**	**South Bend-Mishawaka,**	
Nash County, NC	89	Oakland-Fremont-		**IN-MI**	**318**
		Hayward, CA	2,465	St. Joseph County, IN	267
Rome, GA	**93**	Alameda County, CA	1,472	Cass County, MI	51
Floyd County, GA	93	Contra Costa County,			
		CA	992	**Spartanburg, SC**	**259**
Sacramento—Arden-		San Francisco-San		Spartanburg County, SC	259
Arcade—Roseville, CA	**1,930**	Mateo-Redwood City,			
El Dorado County, CA	166	CA	1,715	**Spokane, WA**	**428**
Placer County, CA	279	Marin County, CA	248	Spokane County, WA	428
Sacramento County, CA	1,305	San Francisco County,			
Yolo County, CA	181	CA	764	**Springfield, IL**	**203**
		San Mateo County, CA	703	Menard County, IL	13
Saginaw-Saginaw Township				Sangamon County, IL	191
North, MI	**210**	**San Jose-Sunnyvale-Santa**			
Saginaw County, MI	210	**Clara, CA**	**1,739**	**Springfield, MA**	**684**
		San Benito County, CA	56	Franklin County, MA	72
St. Cloud, MN	**172**	Santa Clara County, CA	1,684	Hampden County, MA	459
Benton County, MN	36			Hampshire County, MA	153
Stearns County, MN	136	**San Luis Obispo-Paso**			
		Robles, CA	**253**	**Springfield, MO**	**379**
St. George, UT	**99**	San Luis Obispo County,		Christian County, MO	59
Washington County, UT	99	CA	253	Dallas County, MO	16
				Greene County, MO	243
St. Joseph, MO-KS	**122**	**Santa Barbara-Santa Maria-**		Polk County, MO	28
Doniphan County, KS	8	**Goleta, CA**	**403**	Webster County, MO	33
Andrew County, MO	17	Santa Barbara County,			
Buchanan County, MO	85	CA	403	**Springfield, OH**	**143**
DeKalb County, MO	12			Clark County, OH	143
		Santa Cruz-Watsonville, CA	**254**		
St. Louis, MO-IL	**2,729**	Santa Cruz County, CA	254	**State College, PA**	**139**
Bond County, IL	18			Centre County, PA	139
Calhoun County, IL	5	**Santa Fe, NM**	**135**		
Clinton County, IL	36	Santa Fe County, NM	135	**Stockton, CA**	**614**
Jersey County, IL	22			San Joaquin County,	
Macoupin County, IL	49	**Santa Rosa-Petaluma, CA**	**468**	CA	614
Madison County, IL	261	Sonoma County, CA	468		
Monroe County, IL	29			**Sumter, SC**	**105**
St. Clair County, IL	258	**Sarasota-Bradenton-Venice,**		Sumter County, SC	105
Franklin County, MO	96	**FL**	**620**		
Jefferson County, MO	204	Manatee County, FL	281	**Syracuse, NY**	**653**
Lincoln County, MO	42	Sarasota County, FL	340	Madison County, NY	70
St. Charles County, MO	303			Onondaga County, NY	461
St. Louis County, MO	1,018	**Savannah, GA**	**300**	Oswego County, NY	123
Warren County, MO	26	Bryan County, GA	25		
Washington County, MO	24	Chatham County, GA	234	**Tallahassee, FL**	**328**
St. Louis city, MO	338	Effingham County, GA	41	Gadsden County, FL	45
				Jefferson County, FL	14
Salem, OR	**358**	**Scranton—Wilkes-Barre,**		Leon County, FL	244
Marion County, OR	293	**PA**	**553**	Wakulla County, FL	25
Polk County, OR	65	Lackawanna County, PA	211		
		Luzerne County, PA	315	**Tampa-St. Petersburg-**	
Salinas, CA	**413**	Wyoming County, PA	28	**Clearwater, FL**	**2,490**
Monterey County, CA	413			Hernando County, FL	138
		Seattle-Tacoma-Bellevue,		Hillsborough County, FL	1,054
Salisbury, MD	**112**	**WA**	**3,126**	Pasco County, FL	371
Somerset County, MD	26	Seattle-Bellevue-Everett,		Pinellas County, FL	927
Wicomico County, MD	86	WA	2,394		
		King County, WA	1,760	**Terre Haute, IN**	**170**
Salt Lake City, UT	**997**	Snohomish County, WA	634	Clay County, IN	26
Salt Lake County, UT	919	Tacoma, WA	732	Sullivan County, IN	22
Summit County, UT	32	Pierce County, WA	732	Vermillion County, IN	16
Tooele County, UT	46			Vigo County, IN	105
		Sheboygan, WI	**112**		
San Angelo, TX	**105**	Sheboygan County, WI	112	**Texarkana, TX-Texarkana,**	
Irion County, TX	2			**AR**	**131**
Tom Green County, TX	103	**Sherman-Denison, TX**	**114**	Miller County, AR	41
		Grayson County, TX	114	Bowie County, TX	90
San Antonio, TX	**1,787**				
Atascosa County, TX	41	**Shreveport-Bossier City,**		**Toledo, OH**	**660**
Bandera County, TX	19	**LA**	**378**	Fulton County, OH	43
Bexar County, TX	1,446	Bossier Parish, LA	101	Lucas County, OH	454
Comal County, TX	85	Caddo Parish, LA	251	Ottawa County, OH	41
Guadalupe County, TX	94	De Soto Parish, LA	26	Wood County, OH	122

Appendix II 931

U.S. Census Bureau, Statistical Abstract of the United States: 2003

Metropolitan statistical area / Metropolitan division / Component county	Population, 2002 (1,000)
Topeka, KS	226
Jackson County, KS	13
Jefferson County, KS	19
Osage County, KS	17
Shawnee County, KS	171
Wabaunsee County, KS	7
Trenton-Ewing, NJ	359
Mercer County, NJ	359
Tucson, AZ	881
Pima County, AZ	881
Tulsa, OK	878
Creek County, OK	69
Okmulgee County, OK	40
Osage County, OK	45
Pawnee County, OK	17
Rogers County, OK	76
Tulsa County, OK	571
Wagoner County, OK	60
Tuscaloosa, AL	194
Greene County, AL	10
Hale County, AL	17
Tuscaloosa County, AL	167
Tyler, TX	181
Smith County, TX	181
Utica-Rome, NY	299
Herkimer County, NY	64
Oneida County, NY	235
Valdosta, GA	121
Brooks County, GA	16
Echols County, GA	4
Lanier County, GA	7
Lowndes County, GA	94
Vallejo-Fairfield, CA	411
Solano County, CA	411
Vero Beach, FL	118
Indian River County, FL	118
Victoria, TX	113
Calhoun County, TX	21
Goliad County, TX	7
Victoria County, TX	85
Vineland-Millville-Bridgeton, NJ	148
Cumberland County, NJ	148
Virginia Beach-Norfolk-Newport News, VA-NC	1,613
Currituck County, NC	20
Gloucester County, VA	36
Isle of Wight County, VA	31
James City County, VA	51
Mathews County, VA	9
Surry County, VA	7

Metropolitan statistical area / Metropolitan division / Component county	Population, 2002 (1,000)
York County, VA	60
Chesapeake city, VA	207
Hampton city, VA	146
Newport News city, VA	180
Norfolk city, VA	239
Poquoson city, VA	12
Portsmouth city, VA	100
Suffolk city, VA	70
Virginia Beach city, VA	434
Williamsburg city, VA	12
Visalia-Porterville, CA	382
Tulare County, CA	382
Waco, TX	218
McLennan County, TX	218
Warner Robins, GA	117
Houston County, GA	117
Washington-Arlington-Alexandria, DC-VA-MD-WV	5,026
Bethesda-Frederick-Gaithersburg, MD	1,119
Frederick County, MD	209
Montgomery County, MD	910
Washington-Arlington-Alexandria, DC-VA-MD-WV	3,907
District of Columbia, DC	571
Calvert County, MD	81
Charles County, MD	129
Prince George's County, MD	833
Arlington County, VA	190
Clarke County, VA	13
Fairfax County, VA	998
Fauquier County, VA	59
Loudoun County, VA	204
Prince William County, VA	312
Spotsylvania County, VA	103
Stafford County, VA	105
Warren County, VA	33
Alexandria city, VA	131
Fairfax city, VA	22
Falls Church city, VA	11
Fredericksburg city, VA	20
Manassas city, VA	37
Manassas Park city, VA	11
Jefferson County, WV	45
Waterloo-Cedar Falls, IA	163
Black Hawk County, IA	127
Bremer County, IA	23
Grundy County, IA	12
Wausau, WI	127
Marathon County, WI	127
Weirton-Steubenville, WV-OH	130
Jefferson County, OH	72

Metropolitan statistical area / Metropolitan division / Component county	Population, 2002 (1,000)
Brooke County, WV	25
Hancock County, WV	32
Wenatchee, WA	100
Chelan County, WA	67
Douglas County, WA	33
Wheeling, WV-OH	150
Belmont County, OH	69
Marshall County, WV	35
Ohio County, WV	46
Wichita, KS	581
Butler County, KS	61
Harvey County, KS	33
Sedgwick County, KS	462
Sumner County, KS	26
Wichita Falls, TX	150
Archer County, TX	9
Clay County, TX	11
Wichita County, TX	130
Williamsport, PA	119
Lycoming County, PA	119
Wilmington, NC	287
Brunswick County, NC	79
New Hanover County, NC	166
Pender County, NC	43
Winchester, VA-WV	108
Frederick County, VA	63
Winchester city, VA	24
Hampshire County, WV	21
Winston-Salem, NC	434
Davie County, NC	37
Forsyth County, NC	315
Stokes County, NC	45
Yadkin County, NC	37
Worcester, MA	770
Worcester County, MA	770
Yakima, WA	225
Yakima County, WA	225
York-Hanover, PA	389
York County, PA	389
Youngstown-Warren-Boardman, OH-PA	596
Mahoning County, OH	253
Trumbull County, OH	224
Mercer County, PA	120
Yuba City-Marysville, CA	145
Sutter County, CA	83
Yuba County, CA	62
Yuma, AZ	167
Yuma County, AZ	167

Source: U.S. Census Bureau, unpublished data.

Table B. Micropolitan Statistical Areas and Components as of June 6, 2003

[Population as of July 2002. 54 represents 54,000. All micropolitan areas are arranged alphabetically]

Micropolitan statistical area Component county	Population, 2002 (1,000)	Micropolitan statistical area Component county	Population, 2002 (1,000)	Micropolitan statistical area Component county	Population, 2002 (1,000)
Abbeville, LA	54	Atchison, KS	17	Big Rapids, MI	41
Vermilion Parish, LA	54	Atchison County, KS	17	Mecosta County, MI	41
Aberdeen, SD	39	Athens, OH	63	Big Spring, TX	33
Brown County, SD	35	Athens County, OH	63	Howard County, TX	33
Edmunds County, SD	4	Athens, TN	50	Bishop, CA	18
Aberdeen, WA	68	McMinn County, TN	50	Inyo County, CA	18
Grays Harbor County, WA	68	Athens, TX	76	Blackfoot, ID	42
Ada, OK	35	Henderson County, TX	76	Bingham County, ID	42
Pontotoc County, OK	35	Auburn, IN	41	Bloomsburg-Berwick, PA	82
Adrian, MI	100	De Kalb County, IN	41	Columbia County, PA	64
Lenawee County, MI	100	Auburn, NY	82	Montour County, PA	18
Alamogordo, NM	62	Cayuga County, NY	82	Bluefield, WV-VA	106
Otero County, NM	62	Augusta-Waterville, ME	118	Tazewell County, VA	44
Albany-Lebanon, OR	105	Kennebec County, ME	118	Mercer County, WV	62
Linn County, OR	105	Austin, MN	39	Blytheville, AR	50
Albemarle, NC	59	Mower County, MN	39	Mississippi County, AR	50
Stanly County, NC	59	Bainbridge, GA	28	Bogalusa, LA	44
Albert Lea, MN	32	Decatur County, GA	28	Washington Parish, LA	44
Freeborn County, MN	32	Baraboo, WI	56	Boone, IA	26
Albertville, AL	84	Sauk County, WI	56	Boone County, IA	26
Marshall County, AL	84	Barre, VT	59	Boone, NC	43
Alexandria, MN	34	Washington County, VT	59	Watauga County, NC	43
Douglas County, MN	34	Bartlesville, OK	49	Borger, TX	23
Alice, TX	40	Washington County, OK	49	Hutchinson County, TX	23
Jim Wells County, TX	40	Bastrop, LA	30	Bozeman, MT	71
Allegan, MI	109	Morehouse Parish, LA	30	Gallatin County, MT	71
Allegan County, MI	109	Batavia, NY	60	Bradford, PA	45
Alma, MI	42	Genesee County, NY	60	McKean County, PA	45
Gratiot County, MI	42	Batesville, AR	34	Brainerd, MN	85
Alpena, MI	31	Independence County, AR	34	Cass County, MN	28
Alpena County, MI	31	Bay City, TX	38	Crow Wing County, MN	57
Altus, OK	27	Matagorda County, TX	38	Branson, MO	70
Jackson County, OK	27	Beatrice, NE	23	Stone County, MO	29
Americus, GA	37	Gage County, NE	23	Taney County, MO	41
Schley County, GA	4	Beaver Dam, WI	87	Brenham, TX	31
Sumter County, GA	33	Dodge County, WI	87	Washington County, TX	31
Amsterdam, NY	49	Beckley, WV	79	Brevard, NC	29
Montgomery County, NY	49	Raleigh County, WV	79	Transylvania County, NC	29
Andrews, TX	13	Bedford, IN	46	Brigham City, UT	44
Andrews County, TX	13	Lawrence County, IN	46	Box Elder County, UT	44
Angola, IN	33	Beeville, TX	32	Brookhaven, MS	33
Steuben County, IN	33	Bee County, TX	32	Lincoln County, MS	33
Arcadia, FL	33	Bellefontaine, OH	46	Brookings, OR	21
DeSoto County, FL	33	Logan County, OH	46	Curry County, OR	21
Ardmore, OK	55	Bemidji, MN	41	Brookings, SD	28
Carter County, OK	46	Beltrami County, MN	41	Brookings County, SD	28
Love County, OK	9	Bennettsville, SC	29	Brownsville, TN	20
Arkadelphia, AR	24	Marlboro County, SC	29	Haywood County, TN	20
Clark County, AR	24	Bennington, VT	37	Brownwood, TX	38
Ashland, OH	53	Bennington County, VT	37	Brown County, TX	38
Ashland County, OH	53	Berlin, NH-VT	40	Bucyrus, OH	46
Ashtabula, OH	103	Coos County, NH	33	Crawford County, OH	46
Ashtabula County, OH	103	Essex County, VT	7	Burley, ID	41
Astoria, OR	36			Cassia County, ID	22
Clatsop County, OR	36			Minidoka County, ID	19

Appendix II 933

U.S. Census Bureau, Statistical Abstract of the United States: 2003

Micropolitan statistical area / Component county	Population, 2002 (1,000)	Micropolitan statistical area / Component county	Population, 2002 (1,000)	Micropolitan statistical area / Component county	Population, 2002 (1,000)
Burlington, IA-IL	50	**Clearlake, CA**	62	**Daphne-Fairhope, AL**	148
Henderson County, IL	8	Lake County, CA	62	Baldwin County, AL	148
Des Moines County, IA	41				
		Cleveland, MS	40	**Decatur, IN**	34
Butte-Silver Bow, MT	33	Bolivar County, MS	40	Adams County, IN	34
Silver Bow County, MT	33				
		Clewiston, FL	37	**Defiance, OH**	39
Cadillac, MI	46	Hendry County, FL	37	Defiance County, OH	39
Missaukee County, MI	15				
Wexford County, MI	31	**Clinton, IA**	50	**Del Rio, TX**	46
		Clinton County, IA	50	Val Verde County, TX	46
Calhoun, GA	47				
Gordon County, GA	47	**Clovis, NM**	45	**Deming, NM**	25
		Curry County, NM	45	Luna County, NM	25
Cambridge, MD	30				
Dorchester County, MD	30	**Coffeyville, KS**	35	**De Ridder, LA**	33
		Montgomery County, KS	35	Beauregard Parish, LA	33
Cambridge, OH	41				
Guernsey County, OH	41	**Coldwater, MI**	46	**Dickinson, ND**	23
		Branch County, MI	46	Billings County, ND	1
Camden, AR	34			Stark County, ND	22
Calhoun County, AR	6	**Columbia, TN**	72		
Ouachita County, AR	28	Maury County, TN	72	**Dillon, SC**	31
				Dillon County, SC	31
Campbellsville, KY	23	**Columbus, MS**	61		
Taylor County, KY	23	Lowndes County, MS	61	**Dixon, IL**	36
				Lee County, IL	36
Canon City, CO	47	**Columbus, NE**	31		
Fremont County, CO	47	Platte County, NE	31	**Dodge City, KS**	33
				Ford County, KS	33
Canton, IL	38	**Concord, NH**	141		
Fulton County, IL	38	Merrimack County, NH	141	**Douglas, GA**	46
				Atkinson County, GA	8
Cape Girardeau-Jackson, MO-IL	91	**Connersville, IN**	25	Coffee County, GA	38
Alexander County, IL	9	Fayette County, IN	25		
Bollinger County, MO	12	**Cookeville, TN**	96	**Dublin, GA**	55
Cape Girardeau County, MO	70	Jackson County, TN	11	Johnson County, GA	9
		Overton County, TN	20	Laurens County, GA	46
Carbondale, IL	60	Putnam County, TN	64	**DuBois, PA**	83
Jackson County, IL	60			Clearfield County, PA	83
		Coos Bay, OR	63		
Carlsbad-Artesia, NM	51	Coos County, OR	63	**Dumas, TX**	20
Eddy County, NM	51			Moore County, TX	20
		Corbin, KY	37		
Cedar City, UT	35	Whitley County, KY	37	**Duncan, OK**	43
Iron County, UT	35			Stephens County, OK	43
		Cordele, GA	22		
Cedartown, GA	39	Crisp County, GA	22	**Dunn, NC**	97
Polk County, GA	39			Harnett County, NC	97
		Corinth, MS	35		
Celina, OH	41	Alcorn County, MS	35	**Durango, CO**	46
Mercer County, OH	41			La Plata County, CO	46
		Cornelia, GA	38		
Central City, KY	32	Habersham County, GA	38	**Durant, OK**	37
Muhlenberg County, KY	32			Bryan County, OK	37
		Corning, NY	99		
Centralia, IL	41	Steuben County, NY	99	**Dyersburg, TN**	37
Marion County, IL	41			Dyer County, TN	37
		Corsicana, TX	47		
Centralia, WA	70	Navarro County, TX	47	**Eagle Pass, TX**	49
Lewis County, WA	70			Maverick County, TX	49
		Cortland, NY	49		
Chambersburg, PA	132	Cortland County, NY	49	**East Liverpool-Salem, OH**	112
Franklin County, PA	132			Columbiana County, OH	112
		Coshocton, OH	37		
Charleston-Mattoon, IL	64	Coshocton County, OH	37	**Easton, MD**	34
Coles County, IL	53			Talbot County, MD	34
Cumberland County, IL	11	**Crawfordsville, IN**	38		
		Montgomery County, IN	38	**East Stroudsburg, PA**	149
Chester, SC	34			Monroe County, PA	149
Chester County, SC	34	**Crescent City North, CA**	27		
		Del Norte County, CA	27	**Edwards, CO**	53
Chillicothe, OH	74			Eagle County, CO	45
Ross County, OH	74	**Crossville, TN**	49	Lake County, CO	8
		Cumberland County, TN	49		
City of The Dalles, OR	24			**Effingham, IL**	34
Wasco County, OR	24	**Crowley, LA**	59	Effingham County, IL	34
		Acadia Parish, LA	59		
Clarksburg, WV	91			**El Campo, TX**	41
Doddridge County, WV	7	**Cullman, AL**	78	Wharton County, TX	41
Harrison County, WV	68	Cullman County, AL	78		
Taylor County, WV	16			**El Dorado, AR**	45
		Danville, KY	52	Union County, AR	45
Clarksdale, MS	30	Boyle County, KY	28		
Coahoma County, MS	30	Lincoln County, KY	24		

934 Appendix II

U.S. Census Bureau, Statistical Abstract of the United States: 2003

Micropolitan statistical area / Component county	Population, 2002 (1,000)	Micropolitan statistical area / Component county	Population, 2002 (1,000)	Micropolitan statistical area / Component county	Population, 2002 (1,000)
Elizabeth City, NC	54	**Freeport, IL**	48	**Hammond, LA**	103
Camden County, NC	7	Stephenson County, IL	48	Tangipahoa Parish, LA	103
Pasquotank County, NC	35	**Fremont, NE**	36	**Hannibal, MO**	38
Perquimans County, NC	11	Dodge County, NE	36	Marion County, MO	28
Elko, NV	46	**Fremont, OH**	62	Ralls County, MO	10
Elko County, NV	45	Sandusky County, OH	62	**Harriman, TN**	52
Eureka County, NV	2	**Gaffney, SC**	54	Roane County, TN	52
Ellensburg, WA	34	Cherokee County, SC	54	**Harrisburg, IL**	26
Kittitas County, WA	34	**Gainesville, TX**	38	Saline County, IL	26
Emporia, KS	39	Cooke County, TX	38	**Harrison, AR**	43
Chase County, KS	3	**Galesburg, IL**	73	Boone County, AR	35
Lyon County, KS	36	Knox County, IL	55	Newton County, AR	9
Enid, OK	57	Warren County, IL	18	**Hastings, NE**	38
Garfield County, OK	57	**Gallup, NM**	74	Adams County, NE	31
Enterprise-Ozark, AL	93	McKinley County, NM	74	Clay County, NE	7
Coffee County, AL	44	**Garden City, KS**	40	**Havre, MT**	16
Dale County, AL	49	Finney County, KS	40	Hill County, MT	16
Escanaba, MI	38	**Gardnerville Ranchos, NV**	43	**Hays, KS**	27
Delta County, MI	38	Douglas County, NV	43	Ellis County, KS	27
Espanola, NM	41	**Georgetown, SC**	58	**Helena, MT**	67
Rio Arriba County, NM	41	Georgetown County, SC	58	Jefferson County, MT	10
Eureka-Arcata-Fortuna, CA	127	**Gettysburg, PA**	94	Lewis and Clark County, MT	57
Humboldt County, CA	127	Adams County, PA	94	**Henderson, NC**	44
Evanston, WY	20	**Gillette, WY**	36	Vance County, NC	44
Uinta County, WY	20	Campbell County, WY	36	**Hereford, TX**	18
Fairmont, MN	21	**Glasgow, KY**	49	Deaf Smith County, TX	18
Martin County, MN	21	Barren County, KY	39	**Hilo, HI**	155
Fairmont, WV	56	Metcalfe County, KY	10	Hawaii County, HI	155
Marion County, WV	56	**Gloversville, NY**	55	**Hilton Head Island-Beaufort, SC**	149
Fallon, NV	24	Fulton County, NY	55	Beaufort County, SC	128
Churchill County, NV	24	**Granbury, TX**	51	Jasper County, SC	21
Faribault-Northfield, MN	59	Hood County, TX	44	**Hobbs, NM**	56
Rice County, MN	59	Somervell County, TX	7	Lea County, NM	56
Farmington, MO	57	**Grand Island, NE**	68	**Homosassa Springs, FL**	124
St. Francois County, MO	57	Hall County, NE	54	Citrus County, FL	124
Fergus Falls, MN	58	Howard County, NE	6	**Hood River, OR**	21
Otter Tail County, MN	58	Merrick County, NE	8	Hood River County, OR	21
Findlay, OH	72	**Grants, NM**	26	**Hope, AR**	33
Hancock County, OH	72	Cibola County, NM	26	Hempstead County, AR	23
Fitzgerald, GA	27	**Grants Pass, OR**	77	Nevada County, AR	10
Ben Hill County, GA	17	Josephine County, OR	77	**Houghton, MI**	38
Irwin County, GA	10	**Great Bend, KS**	28	Houghton County, MI	36
Forest City, NC	63	Barton County, KS	28	Keweenaw County, MI	2
Rutherford County, NC	63	**Greeneville, TN**	64	**Hudson, NY**	64
Forrest City, AR	29	Greene County, TN	64	Columbia County, NY	64
St. Francis County, AR	29	**Greensburg, IN**	25	**Huntingdon, PA**	46
Fort Dodge, IA	40	Decatur County, IN	25	Huntingdon County, PA	46
Webster County, IA	40	**Greenville, MS**	61	**Huntington, IN**	38
Fort Leonard Wood, MO	43	Washington County, MS	61	Huntington County, IN	38
Pulaski County, MO	43	**Greenville, OH**	53	**Huntsville, TX**	62
Fort Morgan, CO	28	Darke County, OH	53	Walker County, TX	62
Morgan County, CO	28	**Greenwood, MS**	48	**Huron, SD**	17
Fort Polk South, LA	51	Carroll County, MS	11	Beadle County, SD	17
Vernon Parish, LA	51	Leflore County, MS	37	**Hutchinson, KS**	64
Fort Valley, GA	24	**Greenwood, SC**	67	Reno County, KS	64
Peach County, GA	24	Greenwood County, SC	67	**Hutchinson, MN**	35
Frankfort, IN	34	**Grenada, MS**	23	McLeod County, MN	35
Clinton County, IN	34	Grenada County, MS	23	**Indiana, PA**	89
Frankfort, KY	68	**Guymon, OK**	20	Indiana County, PA	89
Anderson County, KY	20	Texas County, OK	20		
Franklin County, KY	48				

Appendix II 935

Micropolitan statistical area Component county	Population, 2002 (1,000)	Micropolitan statistical area Component county	Population, 2002 (1,000)	Micropolitan statistical area Component county	Population, 2002 (1,000)
Indianola, MS	34	**Kirksville, MO**	29	**Lock Haven, PA**	38
Sunflower County, MS	34	Adair County, MO	25	Clinton County, PA	38
		Schuyler County, MO	4		
Iron Mountain, MI-WI	32			**Logansport, IN**	41
Dickinson County, MI	27	**Klamath Falls, OR**	64	Cass County, IN	41
Florence County, WI	5	Klamath County, OR	64		
				London, KY	54
Jackson, WY-ID	25	**Kodiak, AK**	14	Laurel County, KY	54
Teton County, ID	7	Kodiak Island Borough, AK	14		
Teton County, WY	19			**Los Alamos, NM**	18
		Laconia, NH	59	Los Alamos County, NM	18
Jacksonville, IL	42	Belknap County, NH	59		
Morgan County, IL	36			**Lufkin, TX**	81
Scott County, IL	5	**La Follette, TN**	40	Angelina County, TX	81
		Campbell County, TN	40		
Jacksonville, TX	47			**Lumberton, NC**	125
Cherokee County, TX	47	**La Grande, OR**	24	Robeson County, NC	125
		Union County, OR	24		
Jamestown, ND	21			**Macomb, IL**	33
Stutsman County, ND	21	**LaGrange, GA**	60	McDonough County, IL	33
		Troup County, GA	60		
Jamestown-Dunkirk-				**Madison, IN**	32
Fredonia, NY	138	**Lake City, FL**	58	Jefferson County, IN	32
Chautauqua County, NY	138	Columbia County, FL	58		
				Madisonville, KY	47
		Lake Havasu City-Kingman,		Hopkins County, KY	47
Jasper, IN	53	**AZ**	166		
Dubois County, IN	40	Mohave County, AZ	166	**Magnolia, AR**	25
Pike County, IN	13			Columbia County, AR	25
		Lamesa, TX	15		
Jennings, LA	31	Dawson County, TX	15	**Malone, NY**	51
Jefferson Davis Parish, LA	31			Franklin County, NY	51
		Lancaster, SC	62		
		Lancaster County, SC	62	**Manhattan, KS**	106
Jesup, GA	27			Geary County, KS	26
Wayne County, GA	27	**Laramie, WY**	32	Pottawatomie County, KS	18
		Albany County, WY	32	Riley County, KS	61
Juneau, AK	31				
Juneau Borough, AK	31	**Las Vegas, NM**	30	**Manitowoc, WI**	82
		San Miguel County, NM	30	Manitowoc County, WI	82
Kahului-Wailuku, HI	134				
Maui County, HI	134	**Laurel, MS**	83	**Mankato-North Mankato,**	
		Jasper County, MS	18	**MN**	87
Kalispell, MT	77	Jones County, MS	65	Blue Earth County, MN	57
Flathead County, MT	77			Nicollet County, MN	30
		Laurinburg, NC	36		
Kapaa, HI	60	Scotland County, NC	36	**Marinette, WI-MI**	69
Kauai County, HI	60			Menominee County, MI	25
		Lawrenceburg, TN	40	Marinette County, WI	43
Kearney, NE	50	Lawrence County, TN	40		
Buffalo County, NE	43			**Marion, IN**	72
Kearney County, NE	7	**Lebanon, MO**	33	Grant County, IN	72
		Laclede County, MO	33		
Keene, NH	75			**Marion, OH**	66
Cheshire County, NH	75	**Lebanon, NH-VT**	170	Marion County, OH	66
		Grafton County, NH	83		
Kendallville, IN	47	Orange County, VT	29	**Marion-Herrin, IL**	62
Noble County, IN	47	Windsor County, VT	58	Williamson County, IL	62
Kennett, MO	33	**Levelland, TX**	23	**Marquette, MI**	64
Dunklin County, MO	33	Hockley County, TX	23	Marquette County, MI	64
Keokuk-Fort Madison,		**Lewisburg, PA**	42	**Marshall, MN**	25
IA-MO	44	Union County, PA	42	Lyon County, MN	25
Lee County, IA	37				
Clark County, MO	7	**Lewistown, PA**	46	**Marshall, MO**	23
		Mifflin County, PA	46	Saline County, MO	23
Kerrville, TX	45				
Kerr County, TX	45	**Lexington, NE**	27	**Marshall, TX**	63
		Dawson County, NE	25	Harrison County, TX	63
Ketchikan, AK	14	Gosper County, NE	2		
Ketchikan Gateway				**Marshalltown, IA**	39
Borough, AK	14	**Lexington Park, MD**	90	Marshall County, IA	39
		St. Mary's County, MD	90		
Key West-Marathon, FL	79			**Martinsville, VA**	73
Monroe County, FL	79	**Lexington-Thomasville, NC**	151	Henry County, VA	57
		Davidson County, NC	151	Martinsville city, VA	15
Kill Devil Hills, NC	32				
Dare County, NC	32	**Liberal, KS**	23	**Maryville, MO**	22
		Seward County, KS	23	Nodaway County, MO	22
Kingsville, TX	32				
Kenedy County, TX	(Z)	**Lincoln, IL**	31	**Mason City, IA**	53
Kleberg County, TX	31	Logan County, IL	31	Cerro Gordo County, IA	45
				Worth County, IA	8
Kinston, NC	59	**Lincolnton, NC**	67		
Lenoir County, NC	59	Lincoln County, NC	67	**Mayfield, KY**	37
				Graves County, KY	37

Micropolitan statistical area Component county	Population, 2002 (1,000)	Micropolitan statistical area Component county	Population, 2002 (1,000)	Micropolitan statistical area Component county	Population, 2002 (1,000)
Maysville, KY	31	**Mountain Home, AR**	39	**North Platte, NE**	36
Lewis County, KY	14	Baxter County, AR	39	Lincoln County, NE	34
Mason County, KY	17			Logan County, NE	1
		Mountain Home, ID	29	McPherson County, NE	1
McAlester, OK	44	Elmore County, ID	29		
Pittsburg County, OK	44			**North Vernon, IN**	28
		Mount Airy, NC	72	Jennings County, IN	28
McComb, MS	52	Surry County, NC	72		
Amite County, MS	13			**North Wilkesboro, NC**	67
Pike County, MS	39	**Mount Pleasant, MI**	65	Wilkes County, NC	67
		Isabella County, MI	65		
McMinnville, TN	39			**Norwalk, OH**	60
Warren County, TN	39	**Mount Pleasant, TX**	28	Huron County, OH	60
		Titus County, TX	28		
McPherson, KS	29			**Oak Harbor, WA**	75
McPherson County, KS	29	**Mount Sterling, KY**	41	Island County, WA	75
		Bath County, KY	11		
Meadville, PA	90	Menifee County, KY	7	**Oak Hill, WV**	47
Crawford County, PA	90	Montgomery County, KY	23	Fayette County, WV	47
Menomonie, WI	41	**Mount Vernon, IL**	49	**Ocean Pines, MD**	49
Dunn County, WI	41	Hamilton County, IL	8	Worcester County, MD	49
		Jefferson County, IL	40		
Meridian, MS	106			**Ogdensburg-Massena, NY**	111
Clarke County, MS	18	**Mount Vernon, OH**	56	St. Lawrence County, NY	111
Kemper County, MS	11	Knox County, OH	56		
Lauderdale County, MS	78			**Oil City, PA**	57
		Murray, KY	34	Venango County, PA	57
Merrill, WI	30	Calloway County, KY	34		
Lincoln County, WI	30			**Okeechobee, FL**	37
		Muscatine, IA	54	Okeechobee County, FL	37
Mexico, MO	26	Louisa County, IA	12		
Audrain County, MO	26	Muscatine County, IA	42	**Olean, NY**	83
				Cattaraugus County, NY	83
Miami, OK	33	**Muskogee, OK**	70		
Ottawa County, OK	33	Muskogee County, OK	70	**Oneonta, NY**	62
				Otsego County, NY	62
Middlesborough, KY	30	**Nacogdoches, TX**	60		
Bell County, KY	30	Nacogdoches County, TX	60	**Ontario, OR-ID**	52
				Payette County, ID	21
Midland, MI	84	**Natchez, MS-LA**	54	Malheur County, OR	31
Midland County, MI	84	Concordia Parish, LA	20		
		Adams County, MS	34	**Opelousas-Eunice, LA**	88
Milledgeville, GA	55			St. Landry Parish, LA	88
Baldwin County, GA	45	**Natchitoches, LA**	39		
Hancock County, GA	10	Natchitoches Parish, LA	39	**Orangeburg, SC**	91
				Orangeburg County, SC	91
Minden, LA	42	**New Bern, NC**	115		
Webster Parish, LA	42	Craven County, NC	92	**Oskaloosa, IA**	22
		Jones County, NC	10	Mahaska County, IA	22
Mineral Wells, TX	27	Pamlico County, NC	13		
Palo Pinto County, TX	27			**Ottawa-Streator, IL**	153
		Newberry, SC	37	Bureau County, IL	35
Minot, ND	65	Newberry County, SC	37	La Salle County, IL	112
McHenry County, ND	6			Putnam County, IL	6
Renville County, ND	3	**New Castle, IN**	48		
Ward County, ND	57	Henry County, IN	48	**Ottumwa, IA**	36
				Wapello County, IA	36
Mitchell, SD	22	**New Castle, PA**	94		
Davison County, SD	19	Lawrence County, PA	94	**Owatonna, MN**	34
Hanson County, SD	3			Steele County, MN	34
		New Iberia, LA	74		
Moberly, MO	25	Iberia Parish, LA	74	**Owosso, MI**	72
Randolph County, MO	25			Shiawassee County, MI	72
		New Philadelphia-Dover, OH	91		
Monroe, WI	34	Tuscarawas County, OH	91	**Oxford, MS**	40
Green County, WI	34			Lafayette County, MS	40
		Newport, TN	34		
Montrose, CO	35	Cocke County, TN	34	**Paducah, KY-IL**	98
Montrose County, CO	35			Massac County, IL	15
		Newton, IA	37	Ballard County, KY	8
Morehead City, NC	60	Jasper County, IA	37	Livingston County, KY	10
Carteret County, NC	60			McCracken County, KY	65
		New Ulm, MN	27		
Morgan City, LA	52	Brown County, MN	27	**Pahrump, NV**	34
St. Mary Parish, LA	52			Nye County, NV	34
		Nogales, AZ	40		
Moscow, ID	35	Santa Cruz County, AZ	40	**Palatka, FL**	71
Latah County, ID	35			Putnam County, FL	71
		Norfolk, NE	50		
Moses Lake, WA	78	Madison County, NE	36	**Palestine, TX**	55
Grant County, WA	78	Pierce County, NE	8	Anderson County, TX	55
		Stanton County, NE	7		
Moultrie, GA	43			**Palm Coast, FL**	57
Colquitt County, GA	43			Flagler County, FL	57

Appendix II   937

Micropolitan statistical area Component county	Population, 2002 (1,000)	Micropolitan statistical area Component county	Population, 2002 (1,000)	Micropolitan statistical area Component county	Population, 2002 (1,000)
Pampa, TX	23	**Price, UT**	20	**St. Marys, PA**	34
Gray County, TX	22	Carbon County, UT	20	Elk County, PA	34
Roberts County, TX	1	**Prineville, OR**	20	**Salina, KS**	60
Paragould, AR	38	Crook County, OR	20	Ottawa County, KS	6
Greene County, AR	38	**Pullman, WA**	41	Saline County, KS	54
Paris, TN	31	Whitman County, WA	41	**Salisbury, NC**	133
Henry County, TN	31	**Quincy, IL-MO**	78	Rowan County, NC	133
Paris, TX	49	Adams County, IL	68	**Sanford, NC**	50
Lamar County, TX	49	Lewis County, MO	10	Lee County, NC	50
Parsons, KS	22	**Raymondville, TX**	20	**Sault Ste. Marie, MI**	39
Labette County, KS	22	Willacy County, TX	20	Chippewa County, MI	39
Payson, AZ	52	**Red Bluff, CA**	57	**Sayre, PA**	63
Gila County, AZ	52	Tehama County, CA	57	Bradford County, PA	63
Pecos, TX	12	**Red Wing, MN**	45	**Scottsbluff, NE**	38
Reeves County, TX	12	Goodhue County, MN	45	Banner County, NE	1
Pendleton-Hermiston, OR	83	**Rexburg, ID**	40	Scotts Bluff County, NE	37
Morrow County, OR	12	Fremont County, ID	12	**Scottsboro, AL**	54
Umatilla County, OR	71	Madison County, ID	28	Jackson County, AL	54
Peru, IN	36	**Richmond, IN**	71	**Scottsburg, IN**	23
Miami County, IN	36	Wayne County, IN	71	Scott County, IN	23
Phoenix Lake-Cedar Ridge, CA	56	**Richmond, KY**	90	**Seaford, DE**	164
Tuolumne County, CA	56	Madison County, KY	73	Sussex County, DE	164
Picayune, MS	50	Rockcastle County, KY	17	**Searcy, AR**	69
Pearl River County, MS	50	**Rio Grande City, TX**	57	White County, AR	69
Pierre, SD	20	Starr County, TX	57	**Sebring, FL**	90
Hughes County, SD	17	**Riverton, WY**	36	Highlands County, FL	90
Stanley County, SD	3	Fremont County, WY	36	**Sedalia, MO**	40
Pierre Part, LA	23	**Roanoke Rapids, NC**	78	Pettis County, MO	40
Assumption Parish, LA	23	Halifax County, NC	57	**Selinsgrove, PA**	38
Pittsburg, KS	38	Northampton County, NC	22	Snyder County, PA	38
Crawford County, KS	38	**Rochelle, IL**	52	**Selma, AL**	46
Plainview, TX	36	Ogle County, IL	52	Dallas County, AL	46
Hale County, TX	36	**Rockingham, NC**	47	**Seneca, SC**	68
Platteville, WI	49	Richmond County, NC	47	Oconee County, SC	68
Grant County, WI	49	**Rockland, ME**	40	**Seneca Falls, NY**	35
Plattsburgh, NY	81	Knox County, ME	40	Seneca County, NY	35
Clinton County, NY	81	**Rock Springs, WY**	37	**Sevierville, TN**	74
Plymouth, IN	46	Sweetwater County, WY	37	Sevier County, TN	74
Marshall County, IN	46	**Rolla, MO**	41	**Seymour, IN**	42
Point Pleasant, WV-OH	57	Phelps County, MO	41	Jackson County, IN	42
Gallia County, OH	31	**Roseburg, OR**	101	**Shawnee, OK**	67
Mason County, WV	26	Douglas County, OR	101	Pottawatomie County, OK	67
Ponca City, OK	48	**Roswell, NM**	60	**Shelby, NC**	98
Kay County, OK	48	Chaves County, NM	60	Cleveland County, NC	98
Pontiac, IL	40	**Russellville, AR**	77	**Shelbyville, TN**	39
Livingston County, IL	40	Pope County, AR	55	Bedford County, TN	39
Poplar Bluff, MO	41	Yell County, AR	21	**Shelton, WA**	51
Butler County, MO	41	**Ruston, LA**	58	Mason County, WA	51
Portales, NM	18	Jackson Parish, LA	15	**Sheridan, WY**	27
Roosevelt County, NM	18	Lincoln Parish, LA	42	Sheridan County, WY	27
Port Angeles, WA	66	**Rutland, VT**	63	**Sidney, OH**	49
Clallam County, WA	66	Rutland County, VT	63	Shelby County, OH	49
Portsmouth, OH	78	**Safford, AZ**	41	**Sierra Vista-Douglas, AZ**	120
Scioto County, OH	78	Graham County, AZ	33	Cochise County, AZ	120
Pottsville, PA	149	Greenlee County, AZ	8	**Sikeston, MO**	40
Schuylkill County, PA	149	**St. Marys, GA**	45	Scott County, MO	40
		Camden County, GA	45		

Micropolitan statistical area Component county	Population, 2002 (1,000)	Micropolitan statistical area Component county	Population, 2002 (1,000)	Micropolitan statistical area Component county	Population, 2002 (1,000)
Silver City, NM	30	Taos, NM	31	Vernal, UT	26
Grant County, NM	30	Taos County, NM	31	Uintah County, UT	26
Silverthorne, CO	25	Taylorville, IL	35	Vernon, TX	14
Summit County, CO	25	Christian County, IL	35	Wilbarger County, TX	14
Snyder, TX	16	The Villages, FL	58	Vicksburg, MS	49
Scurry County, TX	16	Sumter County, FL	58	Warren County, MS	49
Somerset, KY	57	Thomaston, GA	28	Vincennes, IN	39
Pulaski County, KY	57	Upson County, GA	28	Knox County, IN	39
Somerset, PA	79	Thomasville, GA	43	Wabash, IN	35
Somerset County, PA	79	Thomas County, GA	43	Wabash County, IN	35
Southern Pines, NC	78	Tiffin-Fostoria, OH	58	Wahpeton, ND-MN	25
Moore County, NC	78	Seneca County, OH	58	Wilkin County, MN	7
Spearfish, SD	22	Tifton, GA	39	Richland County, ND	18
Lawrence County, SD	22	Tift County, GA	39	Walla Walla, WA	56
Spencer, IA	17	Toccoa, GA	26	Walla Walla County, WA	56
Clay County, IA	17	Stephens County, GA	26	Walterboro, SC	39
Spirit Lake, IA	17	Torrington, CT	187	Colleton County, SC	39
Dickinson County, IA	17	Litchfield County, CT	187	Wapakoneta, OH	46
Starkville, MS	43	Traverse City, MI	137	Auglaize County, OH	46
Oktibbeha County, MS	43	Benzie County, MI	17	Warren, PA	43
Statesboro, GA	57	Grand Traverse County, MI	81	Warren County, PA	43
Bulloch County, GA	57	Kalkaska County, MI	17	Warrensburg, MO	50
Statesville-Mooresville, NC	130	Leelanau County, MI	22	Johnson County, MO	50
Iredell County, NC	130	Troy, AL	30	Warsaw, IN	75
Staunton-Waynesboro, VA	111	Pike County, AL	30	Kosciusko County, IN	75
Augusta County, VA	67	Truckee-Grass Valley, CA	95	Washington, IN	30
Staunton city, VA	24	Nevada County, CA	95	Daviess County, IN	30
Waynesboro city, VA	20	Tullahoma, TN	95	Washington, NC	46
Stephenville, TX	33	Coffee County, TN	49	Beaufort County, NC	46
Erath County, TX	33	Franklin County, TN	40	Washington, OH	28
Sterling, CO	21	Moore County, TN	6	Fayette County, OH	28
Logan County, CO	21	Tupelo, MS	127	Watertown, SD	31
Sterling, IL	60	Itawamba County, MS	23	Codington County, SD	26
Whiteside County, IL	60	Lee County, MS	77	Hamlin County, SD	6
Stevens Point, WI	67	Pontotoc County, MS	27	Watertown-Fort Atkinson, WI	75
Portage County, WI	67	Tuskegee, AL	24	Jefferson County, WI	75
Stillwater, OK	70	Macon County, AL	24	Watertown-Fort Drum, NY	108
Payne County, OK	70	Twin Falls, ID	84	Jefferson County, NY	108
Storm Lake, IA	20	Jerome County, ID	19	Wauchula, FL	27
Buena Vista County, IA	20	Twin Falls County, ID	65	Hardee County, FL	27
Sturgis, MI	62	Ukiah, CA	87	Waycross, GA	52
St. Joseph County, MI	62	Mendocino County, CA	87	Pierce County, GA	16
Sulphur Springs, TX	32	Union, SC	29	Ware County, GA	36
Hopkins County, TX	32	Union County, SC	29	West Helena, AR	25
Summerville, GA	26	Union City, TN-KY	40	Phillips County, AR	25
Chattooga County, GA	26	Fulton County, KY	8	West Plains, MO	37
Sunbury, PA	93	Obion County, TN	32	Howell County, MO	37
Northumberland County, PA	93	Urbana, OH	39	Whitewater, WI	97
Sweetwater, TX	15	Champaign County, OH	39	Walworth County, WI	97
Nolan County, TX	15	Uvalde, TX	27	Willimantic, CT	111
Tahlequah, OK	43	Uvalde County, TX	27	Windham County, CT	111
Cherokee County, OK	43	Valley, AL	36	Williston, ND	20
Talladega-Sylacauga, AL	81	Chambers County, AL	36	Williams County, ND	20
Talladega County, AL	81	Van Wert, OH	29	Willmar, MN	41
Tallulah, LA	13	Van Wert County, OH	29	Kandiyohi County, MN	41
Madison Parish, LA	13	Vermillion, SD	13		
		Clay County, SD	13		

Micropolitan statistical area Component county	Population, 2002 (1,000)	Micropolitan statistical area Component county	Population, 2002 (1,000)	Micropolitan statistical area Component county	Population, 2002 (1,000)
Wilmington, OH	41	**Wisconsin Rapids-**		**Worthington, MN**	20
Clinton County, OH	41	**Marshfield, WI**	75	Nobles County, MN	20
Wilson, NC	75	Wood County, WI	75	**Yankton, SD**	21
Wilson County, NC	75	**Woodward, OK**	18	Yankton County, SD	21
Winfield, KS	36	Woodward County, OK	18	**Yazoo City, MS**	28
Cowley County, KS	36			Yazoo County, MS	28
Winona, MN	49	**Wooster, OH**	113	**Zanesville, OH**	85
Winona County, MN	49	Wayne County, OH	113	Muskingum County, OH	85

Z Less than 500.

Source: U.S. Census Bureau, unpublished data.

Appendix III
Limitations of the Data

Introduction—The data presented in this *Statistical Abstract* came from many sources. The sources include not only federal statistical bureaus and other organizations that collect and issue statistics as their principal activity, but also governmental administrative and regulatory agencies, private research bodies, trade associations, insurance companies, health associations, and private organizations such as the National Education Association and philanthropic foundations. Consequently, the data vary considerably as to reference periods, definitions of terms and, for ongoing series, the number and frequency of time periods for which data are available.

The statistics presented were obtained and tabulated by various means. Some statistics are based on complete enumerations or censuses, while others are based on samples. Some information is extracted from records kept for administrative or regulatory purposes (school enrollment, hospital records, securities registration, financial accounts, social security records, income tax returns, etc.), while other information is obtained explicitly for statistical purposes through interviews or by mail. The estimation procedures used vary from highly sophisticated scientific techniques, to crude "informed guesses."

Each set of data relates to a group of individuals or units of interest referred to as the *target universe* or *target population*, or simply as the *universe* or *population*. Prior to data collection the target universe should be clearly defined. For example, if data are to be collected for the universe of households in the United States, it is necessary to define a "household." The target universe may not be completely tractable. Cost and other considerations may restrict data collection to a *survey universe* based on some available list, such list may be it of date. This list is called a *survey frame* or *sampling frame*.

The data in many tables are based on data obtained for all population units, *a census*, or on data obtained for only a portion, or *sample*, of the population units. When the data presented are based on a sample, the sample is usually a scientifically selected *probability sample*. This is a sample selected from a list or sampling frame in such a way that every possible sample has a known chance of selection and usually each unit selected can be assigned a number, greater than zero and less than or equal to one, representing its likelihood or probability of selection.

For large-scale sample surveys, the probability sample of units is often selected as a multistage sample. The first stage of a multistage sample is the selection of a probability sample of large groups of population members, referred to as primary sampling units (PSUs). For example, in a national multistage household sample, PSUs are often counties or groups of counties. The second stage of a multistage sample is the selection, within each PSU selected at the first stage, of smaller groups of population units, referred to as secondary sampling units. In subsequent stages of selection, smaller and smaller nested groups are chosen until the ultimate sample of population units is obtained. To qualify a multistage sample as a probability sample, all stages of sampling must be carried out using probability sampling methods.

Prior to selection at each stage of a multistage (or a single stage) sample, a list of the sampling units or sampling frame for that stage must be obtained. For example, for the first stage of selection of a national household sample, a list of the counties and county groups that form the PSUs must be obtained. For the final stage of selection, lists of households, and sometimes persons within the households, have to be compiled in the field. For surveys of economic entities and for the economic censuses the Census Bureau generally uses a frame constructed from the Bureau's Business Register. The Business Register contains all establishments with payroll in the United States, including small single establishment firms as well as large multiestablishment firms.

Wherever the quantities in a table refer to an entire universe, but are constructed from data collected in a sample survey, the table quantities are referred to as *sample estimates*. In constructing a sample estimate, an attempt is made to come as close as is feasible to the corresponding universe quantity that would be obtained from a complete census of the universe. Estimates based on a sample will, however, generally differ from the hypothetical census figures. Two classifications of errors are associated with estimates based on sample surveys: (1) *sampling error* the error arising from the use of a sample, rather than a census, to estimate population quantities and (2) *nonsampling error* those errors arising from nonsampling sources. As discussed below, the magnitude of the sampling error for an estimate can usually be estimated from the sample data. However, the magnitude of the nonsampling error for an estimate can rarely be estimated. Consequently, actual error in an estimate exceeds the error that can be estimated.

The particular sample used in a survey is only one of a large number of possible samples of the same size which could have been selected using the same sampling procedure. Estimates derived from the different samples would, in general, differ from each other. The *standard error* (SE) is a measure of the variation among the estimates derived from all possible samples. The standard error is the most commonly used measure of the sampling error of an estimate. Valid estimates of the standard errors of survey estimates can usually be calculated from the data collected in a probability sample. For convenience, the standard error is sometimes expressed as a percent of the estimate and is called the relative standard error or *coefficient of variation* (CV). For example, an estimate of 200 units with an estimated standard error of 10 units has an estimated CV of 5 percent.

A sample estimate and an estimate of its standard error or CV can be used to construct interval estimates that have a prescribed confidence that the interval includes the average of the estimates derived from all possible samples with a known probability. To illustrate, if all possible samples were selected under essentially the same general conditions, and using the same sample design, and if an estimate and its estimated standard error were calculated from each sample, then: (1) Approximately 68 percent of the intervals from one standard error below the estimate to one standard error above the estimate would include the average estimate derived from all possible samples; (2) approximately 90 percent of the intervals from 1.6 standard errors below the estimate to 1.6 standard errors above the estimate would include the average estimate derived from all possible samples; and (3) approximately 95 percent of the intervals from two standard errors below the estimate to two standard errors above the estimate would include the average estimate derived from all possible samples.

Thus, for a particular sample, one can say with the appropriate level of confidence (e.g., 90 percent or 95 percent) that the average of all possible samples is included in the constructed interval. Example of a confidence interval: An estimate is 200 units with a standard error of 10 units. An approximately 90-percent confidence interval (plus or minus 1.6 standard errors) is from 184 to 216.

All surveys and censuses are subject to nonsampling errors. Nonsampling errors are of two kinds *random* and *nonrandom*. Random nonsampling errors arise because of the varying interpretation of questions (by respondents or interviewers) and varying actions of coders, keyers, and other processors. Some randomness is also introduced when respondents must estimate. Nonrandom nonsampling errors result from total nonresponse (no usable data obtained for a sampled unit), partial or item nonresponse (only a portion of a response may be usable), inability or unwillingness on the part of respondents to provide correct information, difficulty interpreting questions, mistakes in recording or keying data, errors of collection or processing, and coverage problems (overcoverage and undercoverage of the target universe). Random nonresponse errors usually, but not always, result in an understatement of sampling errors and thus an overstatement of the precision of survey estimates. Estimating the magnitude of nonsampling errors would require special experiments or access to independent data and, consequently, the magnitudes are seldom available.

Nearly all types of nonsampling errors that affect surveys also occur in complete censuses. Since surveys can be conducted on a smaller scale than censuses, nonsampling errors can presumably be controlled more tightly. Relatively more funds and effort can perhaps be expended toward eliciting responses, detecting and correcting response error, and reducing processing errors. As a result, survey results can sometimes be more accurate than census results.

To compensate for suspected nonrandom errors, adjustments of the sample estimates are often made. For example, adjustments are frequently made for nonresponse, both total and partial. Adjustments made for either type of nonresponse are often referred to as *imputations*. Imputation for total nonresponse is usually made by substituting for the questionnaire responses of the nonrespondents the "average" questionnaire responses of the respondents. These imputations usually are made separately within various groups of sample members, formed by attempting to place respondents and nonrespondents together that have "similar" design or ancillary characteristics. Imputation for item nonresponse is usually made by substituting for a missing item the response to that item of a respondent having characteristics that are "similar" to those of the nonrespondent.

For an estimate calculated from a sample survey, the *total error* in the estimate is composed of the sampling error, which can usually be estimated from the sample, and the nonsampling error, which usually cannot be estimated from the sample. The total error present in a population quantity obtained from a complete census is composed of only nonsampling errors. Ideally, estimates of the total error associated with data given in the *Statistical Abstract* tables should be given. However, because of the unavailability of estimates of nonsampling errors, only estimates of the levels of sampling errors, in terms of estimated standard errors or coefficients of variation, are available. To obtain estimates of the estimated standard errors from the sample of interest, obtain a copy of the referenced report, which appears at the end of each table.

Source of Additional Material: The Federal Committee on Statistical Methodology (FCSM) is an interagency committee dedicated to improving the quality of federal statistics. <http://fcsm.ssd.census.gov/>

Principal data bases—Beginning below are brief descriptions of 46 of the sample surveys and censuses that provide a substantial portion of the data contained in this *Abstract*.

U.S. DEPARTMENT OF AGRICULTURE, National Agriculture Statistics Service
Basic Area Frame Sample

Universe, Frequency, and Types of Data: June agricultural survey collects data on planted acreage and livestock inventories. The survey also serves to measure list incompleteness and is subsampled for multiple frame surveys.

Type of Data Collection Operation: Stratified probability sample of about 11,000 land area units of about 1 sq. mile (range from 0.1 sq. mile in cities to several sq. miles in open grazing areas). Sample includes 42,000 parcels of agricultural land. About 20 percent of the sample replaced annually.

Data Collection and Imputation Procedures: Data collection is by personal enumeration. Imputation is based on enumerator observation or data reported by respondents having similar agricultural characteristics.

Estimates of Sampling Error: Estimated CVs range from 1 percent to 2 percent for regional estimates to 3 percent to 6 percent for state estimates of major crop acres and livestock inventories.

Other (nonsampling) Errors: Minimized through rigid quality controls on the collection process and careful review of all reported data.

Sources of Additional Material: U.S. Department of Agriculture, *National Agricultural Statistics Service: The Fact Finders of Agriculture,* September 1994.

Multiple Frame Surveys

Universe, Frequency, and Types of Data: Surveys of U.S. farm operators to obtain data on major livestock inventories, selected crop acreage and production, grain stocks, and farm labor characteristics; farm economic data and chemical use data.

Type of Data Collection Operation: Primary frame is obtained from general or special purpose lists, supplemented by a probability sample of land areas used to estimate for list incompleteness.

Data Collection and Imputation Procedures: Mail, telephone, or personal interviews used for initial data collection. Mail nonrespondent followup by phone and personal interviews. Imputation based on average of respondents.

Estimates of Sampling Error: Estimated CV for number of hired farm workers is about 3 percent. Estimated CVs range from 1 percent to 2 percent for regional estimates to 3 percent to 6 percent for state estimates of livestock inventories and crop acreage.

Other (nonsampling) Errors: In addition to above, replicated sampling procedures used to monitor effects of changes in survey procedures.

Sources of Additional Material: U.S. Department of Agriculture, *National Agricultural Statistics Service: The Fact Finders of Agriculture,* September 1994.

Objective Yield Surveys

Universe, Frequency, and Types of Data: Surveys for data on corn, cotton, potatoes, soybeans, and wheat to forecast and estimate yields.

Type of Data Collection Operation: Random location of plots in probability sample. Corn, cotton, soybeans, spring wheat, and durum wheat selected in June from Basic Area Frame Sample (see above). Winter wheat and potatoes selected from March and June multiple frame surveys, respectively.

Data Collection and Imputation Procedures: Enumerators count and measure plant characteristics in sample fields. Production measured from plots at harvest. Harvest loss measured from post harvest gleanings.

Estimates of Sampling Error: CVs for national estimates of production are about 2-3 percent.

Other (nonsampling) Errors: In addition to above, replicated sampling procedures used to monitor effects of changes in survey procedures.

Sources of Additional Material: U.S. Department of Agriculture, *National Agricultural Statistics Service: The Fact Finders of Agriculture,* September 1994.

U.S. CENSUS BUREAU

County Business Patterns

Universe, Frequency, and Types of Data: Annual tabulation of basic data items extracted from the Business Register, a file of all known single and multiestablishment companies maintained and updated by the Census Bureau. Data include number of establishments, number of employees, first quarter and annual payrolls, and number of establishments by employment size class. Data are excluded for self-employed persons, domestic service workers, railroad employees, agricultural production workers, and most government employees.

Type of Data Collection Operation: The annual Company Organization Survey provides individual establishment data for multi establishment companies. Data for single establishment companies are obtained from various Census Bureau programs, such as the Annual Survey of Manufactures and Current Business Surveys, as well as from administrative records of the Internal Revenue Service and the Social Security Administration.

Estimates of Sampling Error: Not applicable.

Other (nonsampling) Error: Response rates of greater than 85 percent for the 2000 Company Organization Survey.

1997 Economic Census—Manufacturing Sector

Universe, Frequency, and Types of Data: Conducted every 5 years to obtain information on labor, materials, capital input and output characteristics, plant location, and legal form of organization for all plants in the United States with one or more paid employees. Universe was 36,000 manufacturing establishments in 1997.

Type of Data Collection Operation: Complete enumeration of data items obtained from 200,000 firms. Administrative records from Internal Revenue Service (IRS) and Social Security Administration (SSA) are used for 166,000 smaller single-location firms, which were determined by various cutoffs based on size and industry.

Data Collection and Imputation Procedures: Four mail and telephone follow-ups for larger nonrespondents. Data for small single-location firms (generally those with fewer than 10 employees) not mailed census questionnaires were estimated from administrative records of IRS and SSA. Data for nonrespondents were imputed from related responses or administrative records from IRS and SSA. Approximately 9 percent of total value of shipments was represented by fully imputed records in 1997.

Estimates of Sampling Error: Not applicable.

Other (nonsampling) Errors: Based on evaluation studies, estimates of nonsampling errors for 1972 were about 1.3 percent for estimated total payroll; 2 percent for total employment; and 1 percent for value of shipments. Estimates for later years are not available.

Sources of Additional Material: U.S. Census Bureau, 1997 Economic Census - Manufacturing Sector, Industry Series, Geographic Area Series, Subject Series, and Summary Series.

Foreign Trade—Export Statistics

Universe, Frequency, and Types of Data: The export declarations collected by U.S. Bureau of Customs and Border Protection are processed each month to obtain data on the movement of U.S. merchandise exports to foreign countries. Data obtained include value, quantity, and shipping weight of exports by commodity, country of destination, district of exportation, and mode of transportation.

Type of Data Collection Operation: Shippers Export Declarations (paper and electronic) are generally required to be filed for the exportation of merchandise valued over $2,500. U.S. Bureau of Customs and Boarder Protection officials collect and transmit the documents to the Census Bureau on a flow basis for data compilation. Data for shipments valued under $2,501 are estimated, based on established percentages of individual country totals.

Data Collection and Imputation Procedures: Statistical copies of Shippers Export Declarations are received on a daily basis from ports throughout the country and subjected to a monthly processing cycle. They are fully processed to the extent they reflect items valued over $2,500. Estimates for shipments valued at $2,500 or less are made, based on established percentages of individual country totals.

Estimates of Sampling Error: Not applicable.

Other (nonsampling) Errors: The goods data are a complete enumeration of documents collected by the U.S. Bureau of Customs and Boarder Protection and are not subject to sampling errors; but they are subject to several types of nonsampling errors. Quality assurance procedures are performed at every stage of collection, processing and tabulation; however the data are still subject to several types of nonsampling errors. The most significant of these include reporting errors, undocumented shipments, timeliness, data capture errors, and errors in the estimation of low-valued transactions.

Sources of Additional Material: U.S. Census Bureau, *U.S. International Trade in Goods and Services*, FT 900, *U.S. Imports of Merchandise*, and *U.S. Exports of Merchandise*.
<http://www.census.gov/foreign-trade/guide/sec2.html>

Foreign Trade—Import Statistics

Universe, Frequency, and Types of Data: The import entry documents collected by U.S. Bureau of Customs and Boarder Protection are processed each month to obtain data on the movement of merchandise imported into the United States. Data obtained include value, quantity, and shipping weight by commodity, country of origin, district of entry, and mode of transportation.

Type of Data Collection Operation: Import entry documents, either paper or electronic, are required to be filed for the importation of goods into the United States valued over $2,000 or for articles which must be reported on formal entries. U.S. Bureau of Customs and Boarder Protection officials collect and transmit statistical copies of the documents to the Census Bureau on a flow basis for data compilation. Estimates for shipments valued under $2,001 and not reported on formal entries are based on estimated established percentages for individual country totals.

Data Collection and Imputation Procedures: Statistical copies of import entry documents, received on a daily basis from ports of entry throughout the country, are subjected to a monthly processing cycle. They are fully processed to the extent they reflect items valued at $2,001 and over or items which must be reported on formal entries.

Estimates of Sampling Error: Not applicable.

Other (nonsampling) Errors: The goods data are a complete enumeration of documents collected by the U.S. Bureau of Customs and Boarder Protection and are not subject to sampling errors, but they are subject to several types of nonsampling errors. Quality assurance procedures are performed at every stage of collection, processing and tabulation; however the data are still subject to several types of nonsampling errors. The most significant of these include reporting errors, undocumented shipments, timeliness, data capture errors, and errors in the estimation of low-valued transactions.

Sources of Additional Material: U.S. Census Bureau, *U.S. International Trade in Goods and Services,* FT 900, *U.S. Imports of Merchandise,* and *U.S. Exports of Merchandise.* <http://www.census.gov/foreigntrade/guide/sec2.html>

Census of Governments

Universe, Frequency, and Types of Data: Survey of all governmental units in the United States conducted every 5 years to obtain data on government revenue, expenditures, debt, assets, employment and employee retirement systems, property values, public school systems, and number, size, and structure of governments.

Type of Data Collection Operation: Complete census. List of units derived through classification of government units recently authorized in each state and identification, counting, and classification of existing local governments and public school systems.

Data Collection and Imputation Procedures: Data collected through field and office compilation of financial data from official records and reports for states and large local governments; mail canvass of selected data items, like state tax revenue and employee retirement systems; and collection of local government statistics through central collection arrangements with state governments.

Estimates of Sampling Error: Not applicable.

Other (nonsampling) Errors: Some nonsampling errors may arise due to possible inaccuracies in classification, response, and processing.

Sources of Additional Material: Publications <http://www.census.gov/prod/www/abs/govern.html>: U.S. Census Bureau, *Public Employment in 1992,* GE 92, No. 1, *Governmental Finances in 1991-1992,* GF 92, No. 5, and *Census of Governments, 1997 and 2002,* various reports. Web site references: Census of Governments <http://www.census.gov/govs/www/cog2002.html> and <http://www.census.gov/govs/www/cog.html>. Employment—state and local site: <http://www.census.gov/govs/www/apes.html>. Finance—state and local site: <http://www.census.gov/govs/www/financegen.html>.

Annual Surveys of State and Local Government

Universe, Frequency, and Types of Data: Sample survey conducted annually to obtain data on revenue, expenditure, debt, and employment of state and local governments. Universe is all governmental units in the United States (about 87,500).

Type of Data Collection Operation: Sample survey includes all state governments, county governments with 100,000+ population, municipalities with 75,000+ population, townships with 50,000+ population, all school districts with 10,000+ enrollment in March 2000, and other governments meeting certain criteria; probability sample for remaining units.

Data Collection and Imputation Procedures: Field and office compilation of data from official records and reports for states and large local governments; central collection of local governmental financial data through cooperative agreements with a number of state governments; mail canvass of other units with mail and telephone follow-ups of nonrespondents. Data for nonresponses are imputed from previous year data or obtained from secondary sources, if available.

Estimates of Sampling Error: State and local government totals are generally subject to sampling variability of less than 3 percent.

Other (nonsampling) Errors: Nonresponse rate is less than 15 percent for local governments. Other possible errors may result from undetected inaccuracies in classification, response, and processing.

Sources of Additional Material: Publications <http://www.census.gov/prod/www/abs/govern.html>: U.S. Census Bureau, *Public Employment in 1992*, GE 92, No. 1, *Governmental Finances in 1991-1992*, GF 92, No. 5, and *Census of Governments, 1997 and 2002*, various reports. Web site references: Census of Governments <http://www.census.gov/gov/govs/www/cog202.html> and <http://www.census.gov/govs/www/cog.html>. Employment—state and local site: <http://www.census.gov/govs/www/apes.html>. Finance—state and local site: <http://www.census.gov/govs/www/financegen.html> and <http://www.census.gov/govs/www/statetechdoc.html>.

American Housing Survey

Universe, Frequency, and Types of Data: Conducted nationally in the fall in odd numbered years to obtain data on the approximately 116 million occupied or vacant housing units in the United States (group quarters are excluded). Data include characteristics of occupied housing units, vacant units, new housing and mobile home units, financial characteristics, recent mover households, housing and neighborhood quality indicators, and energy characteristics.

Type of Data Collection Operation: The national sample was a multistage probability sample with about 53,000 units eligible for interview in 2001. Sample units, selected within 394 PSUs, were surveyed over a 4-month period.

Data Collection and Imputation Procedures: For 2001, the survey was conducted by personal interviews. The interviewers obtained the information from the occupants or, if the unit was vacant, from informed persons such as landlords, rental agents, or knowledgeable neighbors.

Estimates of Sampling Error: For the national sample, illustrations of the SE of the estimates are provided in the Appendix D of the 2001 report. As an example, the estimated CV is about 0.2 percent for the estimated percentage of owner occupied units with two persons.

Other (nonsampling) Errors: Response rate was about 93 percent. Nonsampling errors may result from incorrect or incomplete responses, errors in coding and recording, and processing errors. For the 2001 national sample, approximately 1.9 percent of the total housing inventory was not adequately represented by the AHS sample.

Sources of Additional Material: U.S. Census Bureau, *Current Housing Reports,* Series H150 and H-170, *American Housing Survey.* <http://www.census.gov/hhes/www/ahs.html>.

Monthly Survey of Construction

Universe, Frequency, and Types of Data: Survey conducted monthly of newly constructed housing units (excluding mobile homes). Data are collected on the start, completion, and sale of housing. (Annual figures are aggregates of monthly estimates.)

Type of Data Collection Operation: Probability sample of housing units obtained from building permits selected from 19,000 places. For nonpermit places, multistage probability sample of new housing units selected in 169 PSUs. In those areas, all roads are canvassed in selected enumeration districts.

Data Collection and Imputation Procedures: Data are obtained by telephone inquiry and field visit.

Estimates of Sampling Error: Estimated CV of 3 percent to 4 percent for estimates of national totals, but may be higher than 20 percent for estimated totals of more detailed characteristics, such as housing units in multiunit structures.

Other (nonsampling) Errors: Response rate is over 90 percent for most items. Nonsampling errors are attributed to definitional problems, differences in interpretation of questions, incorrect reporting, inability to obtain information about all cases in the sample, and processing errors.

Sources of Additional Material: All data are available on the Internet at <http://www.census.gov/const/www/newsresconstindex.html>. Further documentation of the survey is also available at that site.

Value of Construction Put in Place

Universe, Frequency, and Types of Data: Survey conducted monthly on total value of all construction put in place in the current month, both public and private projects. Construction values include costs of materials and labor, contractors profits, overhead costs, cost of architectural and engineering work, and miscellaneous project costs. (Annual figures are aggregates of monthly estimates.)

Type of Data Collection Operation: Varies by type of activity: Total cost of private one-family houses started each month is distributed into value put in place using fixed patterns of monthly construction progress; using a multistage probability sample, data for private multifamily housing are obtained by mail from owners of multiunit projects. Data for residential additions and alterations are obtained in a quarterly survey measuring expenditures; monthly estimates are interpolated from quarterly data. Estimates of value of private nonresidential construction, and state and local government construction are obtained by mail from owners (or agents) for a probability sample of projects. Estimates of farm nonresidential construction expenditures are based on U.S. Department of Agriculture annual estimates of construction; public utility estimates are obtained from reports submitted to federal regulatory agencies and from private utility companies; estimates of federal construction are based on monthly data supplied by federal agencies.

Data Collection and Imputation Procedures: See "Type of Data Collection" Operation. Imputation accounts for approximately 25 percent of estimated value of construction each month.

Estimates of Sampling Error: CV estimates for private nonresidential construction range from 3 percent for estimated value of industrial buildings to 9 percent for religious buildings. CV is approximately 2 percent for total new private nonresidential buildings.

Other (nonsampling) Errors: For directly measured data series based on samples, some nonsampling errors may arise from processing errors, imputations, and misunderstanding of questions. Indirect data series are dependent on the validity of the underlying assumptions and procedures.

Sources of Additional Material: U.S. Census Bureau, Construction Reports, Series C30, Value of Construction Put in Place.

Annual Survey of Manufactures

Universe, Frequency, and Types of Data: The Annual Survey of Manufactures (ASM) is conducted annually, except for years ending in 2 and 7 for all manufacturing establishments having one or more paid employees. The purpose of the ASM is to provide key intercensal measures of manufacturing activity, products, and location for the public and private sectors. The ASM provides statistics on employment, payroll, worker hours, payroll supplements, cost of materials, value added by manufacturing, capital expenditures, inventories, and energy consumption. It also provides estimates of value of shipments for 1,800 classes of manufactured products.

Type of Data Collection Operation: The ASM includes approximately 55,000 establishments selected from the census universe of 366,000 manufacturing establishments. Some 25,000 large establishments are selected with certainty, and some 30,000 other establishments are selected with probability proportional to a composite measure of establishment size. The survey is updated from two sources; Internal Revenue Service administrative records are used to include new single-unit manufacturers and the Company Organization Survey identifies new establishments of multiunit forms.

Data Collection and Imputation Procedures: Survey is conducted by mail with phone and mail follow-ups of nonrespondents. Imputation (for all nonresponse items) is based on previous year reports, or for new establishments in survey, on industry averages.

Estimates of Sampling Error: Estimated standard errors for number of employees, new expenditure, and for value added totals are given in annual publications. For U.S. level industry statistics, most estimated standard errors are 2 percent or less, but vary considerably for detailed characteristics.

Other (nonsampling) Errors: Response rate is about 85 percent. Nonsampling errors include those due to collection, reporting, and transcription errors, many of which are corrected through computer and clerical checks.

Sources of Additional Material: U.S. Census Bureau, Annual Survey of Manufactures, and Technical Paper 24. <http://www.census.gov/econ/www/mancen.html>.

Census of Population

Universe, Frequency, and Types of Data: Complete count of U.S. population conducted every 10 years since 1790. Data obtained on number and characteristics of people in the U.S.

Type of Data Collection Operation: In 1980, 1990, and 2000 complete census for some items age, sex, race, and relationship to householder. In 1980, approximately 19 percent of the housing units were included in the sample; in 1990 and 2000, approximately 17 percent.

Data Collection and Imputation Procedures: In 1980, 1990, and 2000, mail questionnaires were used extensively with personal interviews in the remainder. Extensive telephone and personal followup for nonrespondents was done in the censuses. Imputations were made for missing characteristics.

Estimates of Sampling Error: Sampling errors for data are estimated for all items collected by sample and vary by characteristic and geographic area. The CVs for national and state estimates are generally very small.

Other (nonsampling) Errors: Since 1950, evaluation programs have been conducted to provide information on the magnitude of some sources of nonsampling errors such as response bias and undercoverage in each census. Results from the evaluation program for the 1990 census indicate that the estimated net under coverage amounted to about 1.5 percent of the total resident population. For Census 2000, the evaluation program indicates a net overcount of 0.5 percent of the resident population.

Sources of Additional Material: U.S. Census Bureau, The Coverage of Population in the 1980 Census, PHC80-E4; *Content Reinterview Study: Accuracy of Data for Selected Population and Housing Characteristics as Measured by Reinterview,* PHC80-E2; *1980 Census of Population,* Vol. 1, (PC80-1), Appendixes B, C, and D; *1990 Census of Population and Housing, Content Reinterview Study,* CPH-E-1, *1990 Census of Population and Housing, Effectiveness of Quality Assurance,* CPH-E-2, *1990 Census of Population and Housing, Programs to Improve Coverage,* CPH-E-3. For 2000 census see <http://www.census.gov/pred/www>.

Current Population Survey (CPS)

Universe, Frequency, and Types of Data: Nationwide monthly sample survey of civilian noninstitutional population, 15 years old or over, to obtain data on employment, unemployment, and a number of other characteristics.

Type of Data Collection Operation: Multi-stage probability sample of about 50,000 households in 754 PSUs in 1996 expanded to about 60,000 households in July 2001. Oversampling in some states and the largest MSAs to improve reliability for those areas of employment data on annual average basis. A continual sample rotation system is used. Households are in sample 4 months, out for 8 months, and in for 4 more. Month-to-month overlap is 75 percent; year-to-year overlap is 50 percent.

Data Collection and Imputation Procedures: For first and fifth months that a household is in sample, personal interviews; other months, approximately, 85 percent of the data collected by phone. Imputation is done for both item and total nonresponse. Adjustment for total nonresponse is done by a predefined cluster of units, by MSA size and residence; for item nonresponse imputation varies by subject matter.

Estimates of Sampling Error: Estimated CVs on national annual averages for labor force, total employment, and nonagricultural employment, 0.2 percent; for total unemployment and agricultural employment, 1.0 percent to 2.5 percent. The estimated CVs for family income and poverty rate for all persons in 1986 are 0.5 percent and 1.5 percent, respectively. CVs for subnational areas, such as states, would be larger and would vary by area.

Other (nonsampling) Errors: Estimates of response bias on unemployment are not available, but estimates of unemployment are usually 5 percent to 9 percent lower than estimates from reinterviews. Six to 7.0 percent of sample households unavailable for interviews.

Sources of Additional Material: U.S. Census Bureau and Bureau of Labor Statistics, *Current Population Survey; Design and Methodology,* (Tech. Paper 63), available on Internet <http://www.census.gov/prod/2002pubs/tp63rv.pdf>; Source and Accuracy of Estimates for *Poverty in the United States,* available on Internet <http://www.census.gov/hhes/poverty/poverty02/pov02src.pdf> and Bureau of Labor Statistics, *Employment and Earnings,* monthly, Explanatory Notes and Estimates of Error, Household Data and *BLS Handbook of Methods,* Chapter 1, available on the Internet at <http://www.bls.gov/opub/hom/homch1a.htm>.

Surveys of Minority- and Women-Owned Business Enterprises (SMOBE/SWOBE)

Universe, Frequency, and Types of Data: The surveys provide basic economic data on businesses owned by Blacks, Hispanics, Asians, Pacific Islanders, Alaska Natives, American Indians, and Women. All firms operating during 1997, except those classified as agricultural, are represented. The lists of all firms (or sample frames) are compiled from a combination of business tax returns and data collected on other economic census reports. The published data include the number of firms, gross receipts, number of paid employees, and annual payroll. The data are presented by geographic area, industry, size of firm, and legal form of organization of firm.

Type of Data Collection Operation: The surveys are based on a stratified probability sample of approximately 2.5 million firms from a universe of approximately 20.8 million firms. There were approximately 5.3 million firms with paid employees and 15.5 million firms with no paid employees. The data are based on the entire firm rather than on individual locations of a firm.

Data Collection and Imputation Procedures: Data were collected through a mailout/mailback operation. Compensation for missing data is addressed through reweighting, edit correction, and standard statistical imputation methods.

Estimates of Sampling Error: Variability in the estimates is due to the sample selection and estimation for items collected by SMOBE/SWOBE. CVs are applicable to only published cells in which sample cases are tabulated. The CVs for number of firms and receipts at the national level range from 1 to 4 percent.

Other (nonsampling) Error: Nonsampling errors are attributed to many sources: inability to obtain information for all cases in the universe, adjustments to the weights of respondents to compensate for nonrespondents, imputation for missing data, data errors and biases, mistakes in recording or keying data, errors in collection or processing, and coverage problems.

Sources of Additional Materials: U.S. Census Bureau, *Guide to the 1997 Economic Census and Related Statistics.*

1997 Economic Census (Geographic Area Series and Subject Series Reports) (for NAICS sectors 22, 42, 4445, 48-49, and 51-81)

Universe, Frequency, and Types of Data: Conducted every 5 years to obtain data on number of establishments, number of employees, total payroll size, total sales, and other industry specific statistics. In 1997, the universe was all employer and nonemployer establishments primarily engaged in wholesale, retail, utilities, finance & insurance, real estate, transportation & warehousing, and other service industries.

Type of Data Collection Operation: All large employer firms were surveyed (i.e. all employer firms above the payroll size cutoff established to separate large from small employers) plus a 5 percent to 25 percent sample of the small employer firms. Firms with no employees were not required to file a census return.

Data Collection and Imputation Procedures: Mail questionnaires were used with both mail and telephone follow-ups for nonrespondents. Data for nonrespondents and for small employer firms not mailed a questionnaire were obtained from administrative records of the IRS and Social Security Administration or imputed. Nonemployer data were obtained exclusively from IRS 1997 income tax returns.

Estimates of Sampling Error: Not applicable for basic data such as sales, revenue, payroll, etc.

Other (nonsampling) Errors: Trade area level unit response rates in 1997 ranged from 85 percent to 99 percent. Item response rates ranged from 60 percent to 90 percent with lower rates for the more detailed questions. Nonsampling errors may occur during the collection, reporting, and keying of data, and industry misclassification.

Sources of Additional Material: U.S. Census Bureau, *1997 Economic Census: Geographic Area Series and Subject Series Reports* (by NAICS sector), Appendix C, and <www.census.gov/con97.html>.

Service Annual Survey

Universe, Frequency, and Types of Data: The U.S. Census Bureau conducts the Service Annual Survey to provide national estimates of revenues, expenses, and e-commerce revenues for taxable and tax-exempt firms classified in selected service industries. Estimates are summarized by industry classification based on the *1997 North American Industry Classification System (NAICS).* Industries covered by the Service Annual Survey include all or part of the following NAICS sectors: Transportation and Warehousing (NAICS 48-49); Information (NAICS 51); Finance and Insurance (NAICS 52); Real Estate and Rental and Leasing (NAICS 53); Professional, Scientific, and Technical Services (NAICS 54); Administrative and Support and Waste Management and Remediation Services

(NAICS 56); Health Care and Social Assistance (NAICS 62); Arts, Entertainment, and Recreation (NAICS 71); and Other Services, except Public Administration (NAICS 81). Data items collected include total revenue, revenue from e-commerce transactions; and for selected industries, revenue from detailed service products, total expenses, and expenses by major type, revenue from exported services, and inventories. Questionnaires are mailed in January and request annual data for the prior year. Estimates are published approximately 12 months after the initial survey mailing.

Type of Data Collection Operation: The *Service Annual Survey* estimates are developed using data from a probability sample and administrative records. *Service Annual Survey* questionnaires are mailed to a probability sample that is periodically reselected from a universe of firms located in the United States and having paid employees. The sample includes firms of all sizes and covers both taxable firms and firms exempt from federal income taxes. Updates to the sample are made on a quarterly basis to account for new businesses. Firms without paid employees or nonemployers are included in the estimates through imputation and/or administrative records data provided by other federal agencies. Links to additional information about confidentiality protection, sampling error, nonsampling error, sample design, definitions, and copies of the questionnaires may be found on the Internet at <www.census.gov/econ/www/servmenu.html>.

Estimates of Sampling Error: Coefficients of variation for the 2001 Service Annual Survey estimates range from 0.7 percent to 2.1 percent for total revenue estimates computed at the NAICS sector (2-digit NAICS code) level. Sampling errors for more detailed industries are shown in the corresponding publications. Links to additional information regarding sampling error may be found at: <www.census.gov/svsd/www/cv.html>.

Other (nonsampling) Errors: Data are imputed for unit nonresponse, item nonresponse, and for reported data that fails edits. The percent of imputed data for total revenue for the 2001 *Service Annual Survey* is approximately 12 percent.

Sources of Additional Material: U.S. Census Bureau, Current Business Reports, Service Annual Survey, Census Bureau Web site: <http://www.census.gov/econ/www/servmenu.html>.

Wholesale Trade Survey

Universe, Frequency, and Types of Data: Provides monthly estimates of wholesale sales and end of month inventories.

Type of Data Collection Operation: Probability sample of all firms from a list frame and additionally, for retail and service an area frame. The list frame is the Bureaus Standard Statistical Establishment List (SSEL) updated quarterly for recent birth Employer Identification (EI) Numbers issued by the Internal Revenue Service and assigned a kind of business code by the Social Security Administration. The largest firms are included monthly.

Data Collection and Imputation Procedures: Data are collected by mail questionnaire with telephone followups for nonrespondents. Imputation made for each nonresponse item and each item failing edit checks.

Estimates of Sampling Error: For the 2001 monthly surveys median CVs are about 0.6 percent for estimated total retail sales, 1.3 for wholesale sales, 1.6 for wholesale inventories. For dollar volume of receipts, CVs from the Service Annual Survey vary by kind of business and range between 1.5 percent to 15.0 percent. Sampling errors are shown in monthly publications.

Other (nonsampling) Errors: Imputation rates are about 18 percent to 23 percent for monthly retail sales, 30 percent for wholesale sales, about 32 percent for monthly wholesale inventories, and 14 percent for the Service Annual Survey.

Sources of Additional Material: U.S. Census Bureau, *Current Business Reports, Monthly Retail Trade, Monthly Wholesale Trade,* and *Service Annual Survey.*

Monthly Retail Trade and Food Service Survey

Universe, Frequency, and Types of Data: Provides monthly estimates of retail and food service sales by kind of business and end of month inventories of retail stores.

Type of Data Collection Operation: Probability sample of all firms from a list frame. The list frame is the Bureaus Standard Statistical Establishment List (SSEL) updated quarterly for recent birth Employer Identification (EI) Numbers issued by the Internal Revenue Service and assigned a kind of business code by the Social Security Administration. The largest firms are included monthly; a sample of others is included every month also.

Data Collection and Imputation Procedures: Data are collected by mail questionnaire with telephone followups for nonrespondents. Imputation made for each nonresponse item and each item failing edit checks.

Estimates of Sampling Error: For the 2003 monthly surveys, CVs are about 0.5 percent for estimated total retail sales and 0.99 percent for estimated total retail inventories. Sampling errors are shown in monthly publications.

Other (nonsampling) Errors: Imputation rates are about 20 percent for monthly retail and food service sales, and 28 percent for monthly retail inventories.

Sources of Additional Material: U.S. Census Bureau, *Current Business Reports, Monthly Retail Trade.*

Nonemployer Statistics

Universe, Frequency, and Types of Data: Nonemployer statistics are an annual tabulation of economic data by industry for active businesses without paid employees that are subject to federal income tax. Data showing the number of establishments and receipts by industry are available for the U.S., states, counties, and metropolitan areas. Most types of businesses covered by the Census Bureaus economic statistics programs are included in the nonemployer statistics. Tax-exempt and agricultural-production businesses are excluded from nonemployer statistics.

Type of Data Collection Operation: The universe of nonemployer establishments is created annually as a byproduct of the Census Bureaus Business Register processing for employer establishments. If a business is active but without paid employees, then it becomes part of the potential nonemployer universe. Industry classification and receipts are available for each potential nonemployer business. These data are obtained primarily from the annual business income tax returns of the Internal Revenue Service (IRS). The potential nonemployer universe undergoes a series of complex processing, editing, and analytical review procedures at the Census Bureau to distinguish nonemployers from employers, and to correct and complete data items used in creating the data tables.

Estimates of Sampling Error: Not applicable.

Other (nonsampling) Errors: The data are subject to nonsampling errors, such as errors of self-classification by industry on tax forms, as well as errors of response, keying, nonreporting, and coverage.

Sources of Additional Material: U. S. Census Bureau, Nonemployer Statistics: 2000 (Introduction; Coverage and Methodology). See also <http://www.census.gov/epcd/nonemployer/view/cov&meth.htm>.

U.S. DEPARTMENT OF EDUCATION, National Center for Education Statistics

Higher Education General Information Survey (HEGIS), Degrees and Other Formal Awards Conferred. Beginning 1986, Integrated Postsecondary Education Data Survey (IPEDS)

Universe, Frequency, and Types of Data: Annual survey of all institutions and branches listed in the *Education Directory, Colleges and Universities* to obtain data on earned degrees and other formal awards, conferred by field of study, level of degree, sex, and by racial/ethnic characteristics (every other year prior to 1989, then annually).

Type of Data Collection Operation: Complete census.

Data Collection and Imputation Procedures: Survey package is usually mailed in the spring with surveys due at varying dates in the summer and fall; mail and phone followup procedures for nonrespondents. Missing data are imputed by using data of similar institutions.

Estimates of Sampling Error: Not applicable.

Other (nonsampling) Errors: For 2000-2001, approximately 92.3 percent response rate for degree-granting institutions.

Sources of Additional Material: <http://www.nces.ed.gov/ipeds/>

Higher Education General Information Survey (HEGIS), Fall Enrollment in Institutions of Higher Education; beginning 1986, Integrated Postsecondary Education Data Survey (IPEDS), Completions Fall Enrollment

Universe, Frequency, and Types of Data: Annual survey of all institutions and branches listed in the *Directory* to obtain data on total enrollment by sex, level of enrollment, type of program, racial/ethnic characteristics (every other year prior to 1989, then annually) and attendance status of student, and on first-time students.

Type of Data Collection Operation: Complete census.

Data Collection and Imputation Procedures: Survey package is usually mailed in the spring with surveys due at varying dates in the summer and fall; mail and phone followup procedures for nonrespondents. Missing data are imputed by using data of similar institutions.

Estimates of Sampling Error: Not applicable.

Other (nonsampling) Errors: For degree-granting institutions approximately 97.2 percent response rate in fall 2000.

Sources of Additional Material: U.S. Department of Education, National Center for Education Statistics, *Fall Enrollment in Higher Education*, annual. <http://www.nces.ed.gov/ipeds/>

Higher Education General Information Survey (HEGIS), Financial Statistics of Institutions of Higher Education; beginning 1986, Integrated Postsecondary Education Data Survey (IPEDS), Finance

Universe, Frequency, and Types of Data: Annual survey of all institutions and branches listed in the *Education Directory, Colleges and Universities* to obtain data on financial status and operations, including current funds revenues, current funds expenditures, and physical plant assets.

Type of Data Collection Operation: Complete census.

Data Collection and Imputation Procedures: Survey package is usually mailed in the spring with surveys due at varying dates in the summer and fall; mail and phone followup procedures for nonrespondents. Missing data are imputed by using data of similar institutions.

Estimates of Sampling Error: Not applicable.

Other (nonsampling) Errors: For 2000, 96.7 percent for degree-granting institutions.

Sources of Additional Material: U.S. Department of Education, National Center for Education Statistics, *Financial Statistics*. <http://www.neces.ed.gov/ipeds/>

National Postsecondary Student Aid Study

Universe, Frequency, and Types of Data: NPSAS is a comprehensive nationwide study conducted every 3 to 4 years by NCES. It was first administered in 1986-87. The purpose of the study is to produce reliable national estimates of how students and their families pay for postsecondary education. Information has been gathered on more than 55,000 students in each study cycle.

Type of Data Collection Operation: The design for the NPSAS sample involves selecting a nationally representative sample of postsecondary education institutions and students within those institutions. NPSAS data come from multiple sources, including institutional records, government databases, and student telephone interviews.

Data Collection and Imputation Procedures: NPSAS:2000 involved a multi-stage effort to collect information related to student aid. An initial NPSAS: 2000 data collection stage collected electronic student aid report information directly from the U.S. Department of Education Central Processing System for federal financial aid applications. The second stage involved abstracting information from the students records at the school from which he/she was sampled, using a computer-assisted data entry system. In the third stage, interviews were conducted with sampled students, primarily using a computer-assisted telephone interviewing (CATI) procedure. Computer-assisted personal interviewing procedures, using field interviewers, were also used for the first time on a NPSAS study, to help reduce the level of nonresponse to CATI. Over the course of data collection, some data were obtained from the Department of Educations National Student Loan Data System (NSLDS), the ACT and the Educational Testing Service. The additional data sources provided a way to check or confirm information obtained from student records or the interview and include other data. After the editing process (which included logical imputations), the remaining missing values for 23 analysis variables were imputed statistically. Most of the variables were imputed using a weighted hot deck procedure.

Estimates of Sampling Error: Estimates vary by characteristic and variable.

Other (nonsampling) Errors: There is nearly complete coverage of the institutions in the target population. Student coverage, however, is dependent upon enrollment lists provided by the institutions. For the 1999-2000 NPSAS, the overall weighted study response rate was 89 percent. There is also error due to unit and item nonresponse, as well as measurement error. Possible sources of measurement error include: incorrect reporting, variation in question delivery or interpretation, and mistakes in data entry.

Sources of Additional Material: U.S. Department of Education, National Center for Education Statistics. *National Postsecondary Student Aid Study, 1999-2000* (NPSAS: 2000), *Methodology Report, NCES 2002152,* by John A. Riccobono, Melissa B. Cominole, Peter H. Siegel, Timothy J. Gabel, Michael W. Link, and Lutz K. Berkner. Project officer, Andrew G. Malizio. Washington, DC: 2001. U.S. Department of Education. National Center for Education Statistics. *NCES Handbook of Survey Methods, NCES 2003603,* by Lori Thurgood, Elizabeth Walter, George Carter, Susan Henn, Gary Huang, Daniel Nooter, Wray Smith, R. William Cash, and Sameena Salvucci. Project Officers, Marilyn Seastrom, Tai Phan, and Michael Cohen. Washington, DC: 2003.

National Household Education Surveys Program

Universe, Frequency, and Types of Data: The National Household Education Surveys Program (NHES) is a system of telephone surveys of the noninstitutionalized civilian population of the United States. Surveys in NHES have varying universes of interest depending on the particular survey. Specific topics covered by each survey are at the NHES Web site <http://neces.ed .gov/nhes>. A list of the surveys fielded as part of NHES, each universe, and the years they were fielded is provided below. (1) Adult Education Interviews were conducted with a representative sample of civilian, noninstitutionalized persons age 16 and older who were not enrolled in grade 12 or below (1991, 1995, 1999, 2001, 2003). (2) Before- and After-School Programs and Activities Interviews were conducted with parents of a representative sample of students in grades K8 (1999, 2001). (3) Civic Involvement

Interviews were conducted with a representative sample of parents, youth, and adults (1996, 1999). (4) Early Childhood Program Participation Interviews were conducted with parents of a representative sample of children from birth through grade 3, with the specific age groups varying by survey year (1991, 1995, 1999, 2001). (5) Household and Library Use Interviews were conducted with a representative sample of U.S. households (1996). (6) Parent and Family Involvement in Education Interviews were conducted with parents of a representative sample of children age three through grade 12 or in grades K-12 depending on the survey year.(1996, 1999, 2003). (7) School Readiness Interviews were conducted with parents of a representative sample of 3- to 7-year-old children (1993, 1999). (8) School Safety and Discipline Interviews were conducted with a representative sample of students in grades 6-12, their parents, and the parents of a representative sample of students in grades 3-5 (1993).

Type of Data Collection Operation: NHES uses telephone interviews to collect data.

Data Collection and Imputation Procedures: Telephone numbers are selected using random digit-dialing techniques. Approximately 45,000 to 64,000 households are contacted in order to identify persons eligible for the surveys. Data are collected using computer-assisted telephone interviewing (CATI) procedures. Missing data are imputed using hot-deck imputation procedures.

Estimates of Sampling Error: Unweighted sample sizes range between 2,500 and 21,000. The average root design effects of the surveys in NHES range from 1.1 to 4.5.

Other (nonsampling) Errors: Because of unit nonresponse and because the samples are drawn from households with telephone instead of all households, nonresponse and/or coverage bias may exist for some estimates. However, both sources of potential bias are adjusted for in the weighting process. Analyses of both potential sources of bias in the NHES collections have been studied and no significant bias has been detected.

Sources of Additional Material: Please see the NHES Web site at <http://nces.ed.gov/nhes>.

U.S. ENERGY INFORMATION ADMINISTRATION
Residential Energy Consumption Survey

Universe, Frequency, and Types of Data: Quadriennial survey of households and their fuel suppliers. Data are obtained on energy-related household characteristics, housing unit characteristics, use of fuels, and energy consumption and expenditures by fuel type.

Type of Data Collection Operation: Probability sample in 116 PSUs. The 1997 survey resulted in 5,900 completed interviews. The 2001 survey resulted in 5,318 completed interviews. For responding units, fuel consumption and expenditure data obtained from fuel suppliers to those households.

Data Collection and Imputation Procedures: Personal interviews. Extensive followup of nonrespondents including mail questionnaires for some households. Adjustments for nonrespondents were made in weighting for respondents. Most item nonresponses were imputed.

Estimates of Sampling Error: Estimated CVs for household averages (1997 survey): for consumption, 1.3 percent; for expenditures, 1.0 percent; for various fuels, values ranged from 2.0 percent; for electricity to 7.0 percent for LPG.

Other (nonsampling) Errors: Household response rate of 81.0 percent for 1997 survey and 76.7 for 2001 survey. Nonconsumption data were mostly imputed for mail respondents (2.5 percent of eligible units in 1997 and 3.9 percent in 2001). Usable responses from fuel suppliers for various fuels ranged from 80.7 percent for electricity to 56.6 percent for fuel oil for the 1997 survey.

Sources of Additional Material: U.S. Energy Information Administration, *A Look at Residential Energy Consumption in 1997*. The Web page for the Residential Energy Consumption Survey is at: <http://www.eia.doe.gov/emeu/recs>.

U.S. NATIONAL CENTER FOR HEALTH STATISTICS (NCHS)

National Vital Statistics System

Universe, Frequency, and Types of Data: Annual data on births and deaths in the United States.

Type of Data Collection Operation: Mortality data based on complete file of death records, except 1972, based on 50 percent sample. Natality statistics 1951-71, based on 50 percent sample of birth certificates, except a 20 percent to 50 percent in 1967, received by NCHS. Beginning 1972, data from some states received through Vital Statistics Cooperative Program (VSCP) and complete file used; data from other states based on 50 percent sample. Beginning 1986, all reporting areas participated in the VSCP.

Data Collection and Imputation Procedures: Reports based on records from registration offices of all states, District of Columbia, New York City, Puerto Rico, Virgin Islands, Guam, American Samoa, and Northern Marianas.

Estimates of Sampling Error: For recent years, CVs for births are small due to large portion of total file in sample (except for very small estimated totals).

Other (nonsampling) Errors: Data on births and deaths believed to be at least 99 percent complete.

Sources of Additional Material: U.S. National Center for Health Statistics, *Vital Statistics of the United States*, Vol. I and Vol. II, annual, and *National Vital Statistics Report.* NCHS Web site at <http://www.cdc.gov/nchs/nvss.htm>.

National Health Interview Survey (NHIS)

Universe, Frequency, and Types of Data: Continuous data collection covering the civilian noninstitutional population to obtain information on personal and demographic characteristics, illnesses, injuries, impairments, and other health topics.

Type of Data Collection Operation: Multi-stage probability sample of 49,000 households (in 198 PSUs) from 1985 to 1994; 43,000 households (358 design PSUs) from 1995 on, selected in groups of about four adjacent households.

Data Collection and Imputation Procedures: Some missing data items (e.g., race, ethnicity) are imputed using a hot deck imputation value. Unit nonresponse is compensated for by an adjustment to the survey weights.

Estimates of Sampling Error: Estimates of standard error (SE): For 1999 medically attended injury episodes rates in the past 12 months by falling for: females 37.66 (1.94), and males 29.69 (1.82) per 1,000 population; for 1999 injury episodes rates during the past 12 months inside the home - 20.38 (1.08) per 1,000 population.

Other (nonsampling) Errors: The response rate was 93.8 percent in 1996; in 1999, the total household response rate was 87.6 percent, with the final family response rate of 86.1 percent, and the final sample adult response rate of 69.6 percent; in 2000, the total household response rate was 88.9 percent, with the final family response rate of 87.3 percent, and the final sample adult response rate was 72.1 percent for the NHIS. 2001 household final response rate was 88.9 percent, with the family/person final response rate of 87.6 percent and the final sample adult response rate was 73.8 percent. (Note: The NHIS sample redesign was conducted in 1995, and the NHIS questionnaire was redesigned in 1997.)

Sources of Additional Material: U.S. National Center for Health Statistics, Summary Health Statistics for U.S. Children: National Health Interview Survey, 1999, Vital and Health Statistics, Series 10 #203; U.S. National Center for Health Statistics, Summary Health Statistics for the U.S. Population: National Health Interview Survey, 1999, Vital and Health Statistics, Series 10 #211; U.S. National Center for Health Statistics, Summary Health Statistics for U.S. Adults: National Health Interview Survey, 1999, Vital and Health Statistics, Series 10 #212; U.S. National Center for Health Statistics, Design and Estimation for the National Health Interview Survey, 1995-2004, Vital and Health Statistics, Series 2

#130; U.S. National Center for Health Statistics, Summary Health Statistics Technical Report: National Health Interview Survey, 1997-2003, Vital and Statistics, Series 2 #134 (in preparation).

U.S. BUREAU OF JUSTICE STATISTICS (BJS)

National Crime Victimization Survey

Universe, Frequency, and Types of Data: Monthly survey of individuals and households in the United States to obtain data on criminal victimization of those units for compilation of annual estimates.

Type of Data Collection Operation: National probability sample survey of about 50,000 interviewed households in 376 PSUs selected from a list of addresses from the 1980 census, supplemented by new construction permits and an area sample where permits are not required.

Data Collection and Imputation Procedures: Interviews are conducted every 6 months for 3 years for each household in the sample; 8,300 households are interviewed monthly. Personal interviews are used in the first interview; the intervening interviews are conducted by telephone whenever possible.

Estimates of Sampling Error: CVs averaged over the period 1998-2001 are: 3.7 percent for personal crimes (includes all crimes of violence plus purse snatching crimes), 3.8 percent for crimes of violence; 12.1 percent for estimate of rape/sexual assault counts; 7.9 percent for robbery counts; 4.1 percent for assault counts; 11.2 percent for purse snatching (it refers to purse snatching and pocket picking); 2.5 percent for property crimes; 3.8 percent for burglary counts; 2.7 percent for theft (of property); and 5.2 percent for motor vehicle theft counts.

Other (nonsampling) Errors: Respondent recall errors which may include reporting incidents for other than the reference period, interviewer coding and processing errors, and possible mistaken reporting or classifying of events. Adjustment is made for a household noninterview rate of about 7 percent and for a within-household noninterview rate of 10 percent.

Sources of Additional Material: U.S. Bureau of Justice Statistics, *Criminal Victimization in the United States,* annual.

U.S. FEDERAL BUREAU OF INVESTIGATION

Uniform Crime Reporting (UCR) Program

Universe, Frequency, and Types of Data: Monthly reports on the number of criminal offenses that become known to law enforcement agencies. Data are collected on crimes cleared by arrest, by age, sex, and race of offender, and on assaults on law enforcement officers.

Type of Data Collection Operation: Crime statistics are based on reports of crime data submitted either directly to the FBI by contributing law enforcement agencies or through cooperating state UCR programs.

Data Collection and Imputation Procedures: States with UCR programs collect data directly from individual law enforcement agencies and forward reports, prepared in accordance with UCR standards, to the FBI. Accuracy and consistency edits are performed by the FBI.

Estimates of Sampling Error: Not applicable.

Other (nonsampling) Errors: Coverage of 90 percent of the population (92 percent in MSAs, 79 percent in "other cities", and 79 percent in rural areas) by UCR program, though varying number of agencies report.

Sources of Additional Material: U.S. Federal Bureau of Investigation, *Crime in the United States,* annual, *Hate Crime Statistics,* annual, *Law Enforcement Officers Killed & Assaulted,* annual, <http://www.fbi.gov/ucr.htm>.

U.S. BUREAU OF LABOR STATISTICS

U.S. Census Bureau, Current Population Survey (CPS)

Universe, Frequency, and Types of Data: Nationwide monthly sample survey of civilian noninstitutional population, 15 years old or over, to obtain data on employment, unemployment, and a number of other characteristics.

Type of Data Collection Operation: Multistage probability sample of about 50,000 households in 754 PSUs in 1996, expanded to about 60,000 households in July 2001. Oversampling in some states and the largest MSAs to improve reliability for those areas of employment data on annual average basis. A continual sample rotation system is used. Households are in sample 4 months, out for 8 months, and in for 4 more. Month-to-month overlap is 75 percent; year-to-year overlap is 50 percent.

Data Collection and Imputation Procedures: For first and fifth months that a household is in sample, personal interviews; other months, approximately, 85 percent of the data collected by phone. Imputation is done for both item and total nonresponse. Adjustment for total nonresponse is done by a predefined cluster of units, by MSA size and residence; for item nonresponse imputation varies by subject matter.

Estimates of Sampling Error: Estimated CVs on national annual averages for labor force, total employment, and nonagricultural employment, 0.2 percent; for total unemployment and agricultural employment, 1.0 percent to 2.5 percent. The estimated CVs for family income and poverty rate for all persons in 1986 are 0.5 percent and 1.5 percent, respectively. CVs for subnational areas, such as states, would be larger and would vary by area.

Other (nonsampling) Errors: Estimates of response bias on unemployment are not available, but estimates of unemployment are usually 5 percent to 9 percent lower than estimates from reinterviews. About 7.5 percent of sample households unavailable for interviews.

Sources of Additional Material: U.S. Census Bureau and Bureau of Labor Statistics, *Current Population Survey; Design and Methodology,* (Tech. Paper 63), available on Internet <http://www.census.gov/prod/2002pubs/tp63rv.pdf>; Source and Accuracy of Estimates for *Poverty in the United States,* available on Internet <http://www.census.gov/hhes/poverty/poverty02/pov02src.pdf> and Bureau of Labor Statistics, *Employment and Earnings,* monthly, Explanatory Notes and Estimates of Error, Household Data and *BLS Handbook of Methods,* Chapter 1, available on the Internet at <http://www.bls.gov/opub/hom/homch1a.htm>.

Consumer Price Index (CPI)

Universe, Frequency, and Types of Data: Monthly survey of price changes of all types of consumer goods and services purchased by urban wage earners and clerical workers prior to 1978, and urban consumers thereafter. Both indexes continue to be published.

Type of Data Collection Operation: Prior to 1978, and since 1998, sample of various consumer items in 87 urban areas; from 1978-1997, in 85 PSUs, except from January 1987 through March 1988, when 91 areas were sampled.

Data Collection and Imputation Procedures: Prices of consumer items are obtained from about 50,000 housing units, and 23,000 other reporters in 87 areas. Prices of food, fuel, and a few other items are obtained monthly; prices of most other commodities and services are collected every month in the three largest geographic areas and every other month in others.

Estimates of Sampling Error: Estimates of standard errors are available.

Other (nonsampling) Errors: Errors result from inaccurate reporting, difficulties in defining concepts and their operational implementation, and introduction of product quality changes and new products.

Sources of Additional Material: U.S. Bureau of Labor Statistics, Internet site <http://stats.bls.gov/cpi> and *BLS Handbook of Methods,* Chapter 17, Bulletin 2490.

Producer Price Index (PPI)

Universe, Frequency, and Types of Data: Monthly survey of producing companies to determine price changes of all commodities produced in the United States for sale in commercial transactions. Data on agriculture, forestry, fishing, manufacturing, mining, gas, electricity, public utilities, and a few services.

Type of Data Collection Operation: Probability sample of approximately 30,000 establishments that result in about 100,000 price quotations per month.

Data Collection and Imputation Procedures: Data are collected by mail and facsimile. If transaction prices are not supplied, list prices are used. Some prices are obtained from trade publications, organized exchanges, and government agencies. To calculate index, price changes are multiplied by their relative weights taken from 1997 shipment values from the census of manufactures.

Estimates of Sampling Error: Not applicable.

Other (nonsampling) Errors: Not available at present.

Sources of Additional Material: U.S. Bureau of Labor Statistics, BLS Handbook of Methods, Chapter 14, Bulletin 2490. U.S. Bureau of Labor Statistics Internet sites <http://stats.bls.gov/ppi>.

Current Employment Statistic (CES) Program

Universe, Frequency, and Types of Data: Monthly survey drawn from a sampling frame of over 8 million Unemployment Insurance tax accounts in order obtain data by industry on employment, hours, and earnings.

Type of Data Collection Operation: In 2003, the CES sample included about 160,000 businesses and government agencies, which represent approximately 400,000 individual worksites.

Data Collection and Imputation Procedures: Each month, the state agencies cooperating with BLS, as well as BLS Data Collection Centers, collect data through various automated collection modes and mail. BLS-Washington staff prepares national estimates of employment, hours, and earnings while states use the data to develop state and area estimates.

Estimates of Sampling Errors: The relative standard error for total nonfarm employment is 0.2 percent.

Other (nonsampling) Errors): Estimates of employment adjusted annually to reflect complete universe. Average adjustment is 0.3 percent over the last decade, ranging from zero to 0.7 percent.

Sources of Additional: U.S. Bureau of Labor Statistics, Employment and Earnings, monthly, Explanatory Notes and Estimates of Errors, Tables 2-A through 2-F.

National Compensation Survey

Universe, Frequency, and Types of Data: Nationwide sample survey of establishments of all employment size classes, stratified by geographic area, in private industry and state and local government. Data collected include wages and salaries, and employer costs of employee benefits. Data produced include percent changes in the cost of employment cited in the Employment Cost Index (ECI) and costs per hour worked for individual benefits cited in the Employer Costs for Employee Compensation (ECEC). The survey provides data by ownership (Private industry and state and local government), industry sector, major industry divisions, major occupational groups, bargaining status, metropolitan area status, and census region. ECEC also provides data by establishment size class.

Type of Data Collection Operation: Probability proportionate to size sample of establishments. The sample is replaced on a continual basis. Establishments are in the survey for approximately 5 years, with some establishments replaced each quarter.

Data Collection and Imputation Procedures: For the initial visit, data are primarily collected in a personal visit to the establishment. Quarterly updates are obtained primarily by mail, fax, and telephone. Imputation is done for individual benefits.

Estimates of Sampling Error: Because standard errors vary from quarter to quarter, the ECI uses a 5-year moving average of standard errors to evaluate published series. These standard errors are available at <http://www.bls.gov/ncs/ect/home.htm>.

Other (nonsampling) Errors: Nonsampling errors have a number of potential sources. The primary sources are (1) survey nonresponse and (2) data collection and processing errors. Nonsampling errors are not measured. Procedures have been implemented for reducing nonsampling errors, primarily through quality assurance programs. These programs include the use of data collection reinterviews, observed interviews, computer edits of the data, and systematic professional review of the reports on which the data are recorded. The programs also serve as a training device to provide feedback to the field economists, or data collectors, on errors. And, they provide information on the sources of error which can be remedied by improved collection instructions or computer processing edits. Extensive training of field economists is also conducted to maintain high standards in data collection.

Sources of Additional Material: Bureau of Labor Statistics, *BLS Handbook of Methods*, Chapter 8 (Bulletin 2490) and <http://www.bls.gov/ncs>.

Consumer Expenditure Survey (CES)

Universe, Frequency and Types of Data: Consists of two continuous components: a quarterly interview survey and a weekly diary or recordkeeping survey. They are nationwide surveys that collect data on consumer expenditures, income, characteristics, and assets and liabilities. Samples are national probability samples of households that are representative of the civilian noninstitutional population. The surveys have been ongoing since 1980.

Type of Data Collection Operation: The Interview Survey is a panel rotation survey. Each panel is interviewed for five quarters and then dropped from the survey. About 7,500 consumer units are interviewed each quarter. The Diary Survey sample is new each year and consists of about 7,500 consumer units. Data are collected on an ongoing basis in 105 PSUs since 1996.

Data Collection and Imputation Procedures: For the Interview Survey, data are collected by personal interview with each consumer unit interviewed once per quarter for five consecutive quarters. Designed to collect information that respondents can recall for 3 months or longer, such as large or recurring expenditures. For the Diary Survey, respondents record all their expenditures in a self-reporting diary for two consecutive 1-week periods. Designed to pick up items difficult to recall over a long period, such as detailed food expenditures. Missing or invalid attributes or expenditures are imputed. Income, assets, and liabilities are not imputed. The U.S. Census Bureau collects the data for the Bureau of Labor Statistics.

Estimates of Sampling Error: Standard error tables are available since 2000.

Other (nonsampling) Errors: Includes incorrect information given by respondents, data processing errors, interviewer errors, and so on. They occur regardless of whether data are collected from a sample or from the entire population.

Sources of Additional Material: Bureau of Labor Statistics, Internet site <http://www.bls.gov/cex> and *BLS Handbook of Methods*, Chapter 16, Bulletin 2490.

BOARD OF GOVERNORS OF THE FEDERAL RESERVE SYSTEM

Survey of Consumer Finances

Universe, Frequency, and Types of Data: Periodic sample survey of families. In this survey a given household is divided into a primary economic unit and other economic units. The primary economic unity, which may be a single individual, is generally chosen as the unit that contains the person who either holds the title to the home or is the first person listed on the lease. The primary unit is used as the reference family. The survey collects detailed data on the composition of family balance sheets, the terms of loans, and relationships with financial institutions. It also gathered information on the employment history and pension rights of the survey respondent and the spouse or partner of the respondent.

Type of Data Collection Operation: The survey employs a two-part strategy for sampling families. Some families were selected by standard multistage area probability sampling methods applied to all 50 states. The remaining families in the survey were selected using statistical records derived from tax returns, under the strict rules governing confidentiality and the rights of potential respondents to refuse participation.

Data Collection and Imputation Procedures: NORC at the University of Chicago has collected data for the survey since 1992. Since 1995, the survey has used computer-assisted personal interviewing. Adjustments for nonresponse are made through multiple imputation of unanswered questions and through weighting adjustments based on data used in the sample design for families that refused participation.

Estimates of Sampling Error: Because of the complex design of the survey, the estimation of potential sampling errors is not straightforward. A replicate-based procedure is available.

Other (nonsampling) Errors: The survey aims to complete 4,500 interviews, with about two-thirds of that number deriving from the area-probability sample. The response rate is typically about 70 percent for the area-probability sample and about 35 percent over all strata in the tax-data sample. Proper training and monitoring of interviewers, careful design of questionnaires, and systematic editing of the resulting data were used to control inaccurate survey responses.

Sources of Additional Material: Board of Governors of the Federal Reserve System, *Recent Changes in U.S. Family Finances: Evidence from the 1998 and 2001 Survey of Consumer Finances, Federal Reserve Bulletin,* January 2003.

U.S. INTERNAL REVENUE SERVICE

Statistics of Income, Individual Income Tax Returns

Universe, Frequency, and Types of Data: Annual study of unaudited individual income tax returns, Forms 1040, 1040A, and 1040EZ, filed by U.S. citizens and residents. Data provided on various financial characteristics by size of adjusted gross income, marital status, and by taxable and nontaxable returns. Data by state, based on 100 percent file, also include returns from 1040NR, filed by nonresident aliens plus certain self employment tax returns.

Type of Data Collection Operation: Annual 2000 stratified probability sample of approximately 196,000 returns broken into sample strata based on the larger of total income or total loss amounts as well as the size of business plus farm receipts. Sampling rates for sample strata varied from 0.05 percent to 100 percent.

Data Collection and Imputation Procedures: Computer selection of sample of tax return records. Data adjusted during editing for incorrect, missing, or inconsistent entries to ensure consistency with other entries on return.

Estimates of Sampling Error: Estimated CVs for tax year 2000: Adjusted gross income less deficit 0.11 percent; salaries and wages 0.21 percent; and tax exempt interest received 1.65 percent. (State data not subject to sampling error.)

Other (nonsampling) Errors: Processing errors and errors arising from the use of tolerance checks for the data.

Sources of Additional Material: U.S. Internal Revenue Service, *Statistics of Income, Individual Income Tax Returns,* annual. For background information for individual tax statistics: <http://www.irs.gov/taxstats/article/0,,id=96571,00.html>

Statistics of Income, Sole Proprietorship Returns and Statistics of Income Bulletin

Universe, Frequency, and Types of Data: Annual study of unaudited income tax returns of nonfarm sole proprietorships, Form 1040 with business schedules. Data provided on various financial characteristics by industry.

Type of Data Collection Operation: Stratified probability sample of approximately 56,000 sole proprietorships for tax year 2000. The sample is classified based on presence or absence of certain business schedules; the larger of total income or loss; and size of business plus farm receipts. Sampling rates vary from 0.05 percent to 100 percent.

Data Collection and Imputation Procedures: Computer selection of sample of tax return records. Data adjusted during editing for incorrect, missing, or inconsistent entries to ensure consistency with other entries on return.

Estimates of Sampling Error: Estimated CVs for tax year 2000 are available. For sole proprietorships, business receipts, 0.69 percent; net income, (less loss), 0.94 percent; depreciation 1.40 percent.

Other (nonsampling) Errors: Processing errors and errors arising from the use of tolerance checks for the data.

Sources of Additional Material: U.S. Internal Revenue Service, *Statistics of Income, Sole Proprietorship Returns* (for years through 1980) and *Statistics of Income Bulletin,* Vol. 22, No. 1 (summer 2002).

Statistics of Income, Partnership Returns and Statistics of Income Bulletin

Universe, Frequency, and Types of Data: Annual study of unaudited income tax returns of partnerships, Form 1065. Data provided on various financial characteristics by industry.

Type of Data Collection Operation: Stratified probability sample of approximately 36,000 partnership returns from a population of 2.2 million filed during calendar year 2000. The sample is classified based on combinations of gross receipts, net income or loss, and total assets, and on industry. Sampling rates vary from 0.09 percent to 100 percent.

Data Collection and Imputation Procedures: Computer selection of sample of tax return records. Data are adjusted during editing for incorrect, missing, or inconsistent entries to ensure consistency with other entries on return. Data not available due to regulations are not imputed.

Estimates of Sampling Error: Estimated CVs for tax year 2000 (latest available): For number of partnerships, 0.3 percent; business receipts, 0.4 percent; net income, 0.5 percent; net loss, 1.9 percent.

Other (nonsampling) Errors: Processing errors and errors arising from the use of tolerance checks for the data.

Sources of Additional Material: U.S. Internal Revenue Service, *Statistics of Income, Partnership Returns and Statistics of Income Bulletin,* Vol. 22, No. 2 (fall 2002).

Corporation Income Tax Returns

Universe, Frequency, and Types of Data: Annual study of unaudited corporation income tax returns, Forms 1120, 1120-A, 1120-F, 1120-L, 1120-PC, 1120-REIT, 1120-RIC, and 1120S, filed by corporations or businesses legally defined as corporations. Data provided on various financial characteristics by industry and size of total assets, and business receipts.

Type of Data Collection Operation: Stratified probability sample of approximately 145,500 returns for tax year 2000, allocated to sample classes which are based on type of return, size of total assets, size of net income or deficit, and selected business activity. Sampling rates for sample classes varied from 0.25 percent to 100 percent.

Data Collection and Imputation Procedures: Computer selection of sample of tax return records. Data adjusted during editing for incorrect, missing, or inconsistent entries to ensure consistency with other entries on return and to comply with statistical definitions.

Estimates of Sampling Error: Estimated CVs for tax year 2000: Returns with assets over $250 million are self-representing. For other returns grouped by assets, CVs ranged from 0.04 percent to 2.88 percent; for amount of net income CV is 0.14 percent.

Other (nonsampling) Errors: Nonsampling errors include coverage errors, processing errors, and response errors.

Sources of Additional Material: U.S. Internal Revenue Service, *Statistics of Income, Corporation Income Tax Returns,* annual. For background information for corporation tax statistics: <http://www.irs.gov/taxstats/article/0,,id=96246,00.html>.

U.S. SOCIAL SECURITY ADMINISTRATION

Benefit Data

Universe, Frequency, and Types of Data: All persons receiving monthly benefits under Title II of Social Security Act. Data on number and amount of benefits paid by type and state.

Type of Data Collection Operation: Data based on administrative records. Data based on 100 percent files, as well as 10 percent and 1 percent sample files.

Data Collection and Imputation Procedures: Records used consist of actions pursuant to applications dated by subsequent post-entitlement actions.

Estimates of Sampling Error: Varies by size of estimate and sample file size.

Other (nonsampling) Errors: Processing errors, which are believed to be small.

Sources of Additional Material: U.S. Social Security Administration, *Annual Statistical Supplement to the Social Security Bulletin.*

Supplemental Security Income (SSI) Program

Universe, Frequency, and Types of Data: All eligible aged, blind, or disabled persons receiving SSI benefit payments under SSI program. Data include number of persons receiving federally administered SSI, amounts paid, and state administered supplementation.

Type of Data Collection Operation: Data based on administrative records.

Data Collection and Imputation Procedures: Data adjusted to reflect returned checks and overpayment refunds. For federally administered payments, actual adjusted amounts are used.

Estimates of Sampling Error: Not applicable.

Other (nonsampling) Errors: Processing errors, which are believed to be small.

Sources of Additional Material: U.S. Social Security Administration, *Annual Statistical Supplement to the Social Security Bulletin.*

National Highway Traffic Safety Administration (NHTSA)

Fatality Analysis Reporting System (FARS)

Universe, Frequency, and Types of Data: Census of all motor vehicle traffic crashes involving at least one person killed as a result of the crash. The crash must be reported to the state and the death of the involved person must be within thirty days of the crash date. These fatal crashes occur throughout the United States (includes the District of Columbia), Puerto Rico, Virgin Islands, and American Pacific Territories.

Type of Data Collection Operation: Each state provides an analyst(s) who extracts data from the official documents and enters it into a standardized database.

Data Collection and Imputation Procedures: Detailed data describing the characteristics of the fatal crash, the vehicles and persons involved are obtained from police crash reports, driver and vehicle registration records, autopsy reports, highway department, etc. Computerized edit checks monitor that accuracy and completeness of the data. The FARS incorporates a sophisticated mathematical multiple imputation model to impute missing blood alcohol concentration (BAC) in the database for drivers and pedestrians only.

Estimates of Sampling Error: Since this is census data, there are no sampling errors.

Other (nonsampling) Errors: Data on the fatal motor vehicle traffic crashes is more than 97 percent complete.

Sources of Additional Material: The FARS *Coding and Validation Manual,* ANSI D16.1, *Manual on Classification of Motor Vehicle Traffic Accidents* (sixth edition).

Appendix IV
Weights and Measures

[For assistance on metric usage, call or write the National Institute of Standards and Technology, Metric Program, 100 Bureau Drive, Stop 2000, Gaithersburg, MD 20899-2000 (301-975-3690) Internet site <http://www.nist.gov/> E-mail: metricprenist.gov]

Symbol	When you know conventional	Multiply by	To find metric	Symbol
in	inch	2.54	centimeter	cm
ft	foot	30.48	centimeter	cm
yd	yard	0.91	meter	m
mi	mile	1.61	kilometer	km
in^2	square inch	6.45	square centimeter	cm^2
ft^2	square foot	0.09	square meter	m^2
yd^2	square yard	0.84	square meter	m^2
mi^2	square mile	2.59	square kilometer	km^2
	acre	0.41	hectare	ha
oz	ounce [1]	28.35	gram	g
lb	pound [1]	.45	kilograms	kg
oz (troy)	ounce [2]	31.10	gram	g
	short ton (2,000 lb)	0.91	metric ton	t
	long ton (2,240 lb)	1.02	metric ton	t
fl oz	fluid ounce	29.57	milliliter	mL
c	cup	0.24	liter	L
pt	pint	0.47	liter	L
qt	quart	0.95	liter	L
gal	gallon	3.78	liter	L
ft^3	cubic foot	0.03	cubic meter	m^3
yd^3	cubic yard	0.76	cubic meter	m^3
F	degrees Fahrenheit (subtract 32)	0.55	degrees Celsius	C

Symbol	When you know metric	Multiply by	To find conventional	Symbol
cm	centimeter	0.39	inch	in
cm	centimeter	0.03	foot	ft
m	meter	1.09	yard	yd
km	kilometer	0.62	mile	mi
cm^2	square centimeter	0.15	square inch	in^2
m^2	square meter	10.76	square foot	ft^2
m^2	square meter	1.20	square yard	yd^2
km^2	square kilometer	0.39	square mile	mi^2
ha	hectare	2.47	acre	
g	gram	.035	ounce [1]	oz
kg	kilogram	2.21	pounds [1]	lb
g	gram	.032	ounce [2]	oz (troy)
t	metric ton	1.10	short ton (2,000 lb)	
t	metric ton	0.98	long ton (2,240 lb)	
mL	milliliter	0.03	fluid ounce	fl oz
L	liter	4.24	cup	c
L	liter	2.13	pint (liquid)	pt
L	liter	1.05	quart (liquid)	qt
L	liter	0.26	gallon	gal
m^3	cubic meter	35.32	cubic foot	ft^3
m^3	cubic meter	1.32	cubic yard	yd^3
C	degrees Celsius (after multiplying, add 32)	1.80	degrees Fahrenheit	F

[1] For weighing ordinary commodities.   [2] For weighing precious metals, jewels, etc.

Appendix V
Tables Deleted From the 2002 Edition of the Statistical Abstract

2002
number

Sec. 1. POPULATION

10	Resident Population—Selected Characteristics, 1950 to 1990, and Projections, 2005 to 2050
11	Resident Population by Sex and Age Group: 1990 to 2001
28	Number and Population of Metropolitan Areas by Population Size of Area in 2000: 2000
32	Households—Cities with 350,000 or More Population: 2000
36	Demographic and Economic Profiles of Selected Racial and Hispanic Origin Populations

Sec. 2. VITAL STATISTICS

83	Number of Pregnancies, Live Births, and Induced Abortions by Age and Race of Woman: 1980 to 1996
85	Live Births—Mothers Who Smoked During Pregnancy: 1999
87	Live Births to Mothers with Selected Complications of Labor and/or Delivery and Rates by Age of Mother: 1999

Sec. 3. HEALTH AND NUTRITION

130	Medicaid—Selected Utilization Measures: 1980 to 1998
141	Health Care Firms—Establishments, Receipts, Payroll, and Employees by Kind of Business (NAICS Basis): 1997

Sec. 4. EDUCATION

214	Public Schools Reporting Criminal Incidents to the Police: 1996-97
227	Employed Students by Selected Characteristic: 1998-99
265	Undergraduates in Postsecondary Institutions Owning Credit Cards and Balance Due: 1999-2000

Sec. 5. LAW ENFORCEMENT, COURTS, AND PRISONS

309	U.S. Population Who Had Contact With Police by Age and Reason for Contact: 1999
310	Drivers Stopped by Police by Sex, Race, and Ethnicity by Age and Cause: 1999
311	Justifiable Homicide by Police and Police Officers Murdered by Felons: 1980 to 1998
325	State Prisons Expenditures by State: 1996

Sec. 9. FEDERAL GOVERNMENT FINANCES AND EMPLOYMENT

455	Federal Trust Fund Receipts, Outlays, and Balances: 1999 to 2001
462	Per Capita Federal Balance of Payments by State: 1990 to 1999

Sec. 10. NATIONAL DEFENSE AND VETERANS AFFAIRS

499	Enlisted Military Personnel Accessions by Branch: 1990 to 1997

Sec. 11. SOCIAL INSURANCE AND HUMAN SERVICES

558	Percent of Adult Population Doing Volunteer Work: 2000

2002
number

Sec. 12. LABOR FORCE, EMPLOYMENT, AND EARNINGS

594	Computer and Internet Access and Internet Job Searching by Labor Force Status and Race: 1998 and 2000
601	Nonfarm Establishments—Employees, Hours, and Earnings by Industry: 1980 to 2001
602	Employees in Nonfarm Establishments—States: 1990 to 2001
603	Nonfarm Industries—Employees and Earnings: 1990 to 2001
604	Annual Indexes of Output Per Hour for Selected Three-Digit SIC Industries: 1990 to 2000
606	Computer Use at Work by Occupation: 2001
608	Average Hourly and Weekly Earnings by Private Industry Group: 1980 to 2001

Sec. 13. INCOME, EXPENDITURES, AND WEALTH

655	Money Income of Households—Median Income and Income Level by Household Type: 2000
656	Median Income of Households in Constant (2000) Dollars by State: 3-Year Averages for 1990 to 2000
661	Money Income of Families—Work Experience by Income Level: 2000

Sec. 15. BUSINESS ENTERPRISE

712	Comparative Statistics for the United States (1987 SIC Basis): 1992 and 1997
751	Nonbank U.S. Multinational Companies—U.S. Parents and Affiliates by Industry: 1999

Sec. 16. SCIENCE AND TECHNOLOGY

755	Performance Sector of R&D Expenditures by State: 1998
761	Percentage of U.S. Scientific and Technical Articles Which Are Coauthored and Internationally Coauthored: 1989 to 1999
762	Citations on U.S. Patents to the U.S. Scientific and Technical Literature by Cited Field: 1990 to 2000
763	Percentage of Citations to Foreign Articles in U.S. Scientific and Technical Public Publications: 1990 to 1999
770	Science and Engineering Degree Recipients in 1995 and 1996

Sec. 17. AGRICULTURE

784	Farms—Number, Acreage, and Value by Type of Organization: 1992 and 1997
785	Corporate Farms—Characteristics by Type: 1997
786	Farms—Number, Acreage, and Value of Sales by Size of Sales: 1997
787	Farms—Number, Acreage, and Value by State: 1992 and 1997

Sec. 18. NATURAL RESOURCES

834	National Forest System—Summary: 1980 to 1998
836	Forest and Timberland Area, Sawtimber, and Stock: 1987 to 1996
850	Mining Industries—Employees, Payroll, and Shipments: 1997
851	Mining Summary by State: 1997

Sec. 19. ENERGY AND UTILITIES

902	Water Power—Developed and Undeveloped Capacity by Division: 1980 to 2001

2002 number	
	Sec. 21. **MANUFACTURES**
968	U.S. Exports of Manufactures—Origin of World Exports of Manufacture by Major Product and Country: 1991 to 1999
975	Glass Containers, Clay Construction Products, and Refractories— Quantity and Value of Shipments: 1990 to 2000
978	Raw Steel, Pig Iron, and Ferroalloys Production: 1990 to 2001
982	Selected Types of Construction Machinery—Value of Shipments: 1990 to 2000
983	Mining and Mineral Processing Equipment—Shipments: 1999 and 2000
984	Engines, Refrigeration and Heating Equipment, and Pumps and Compressors—Shipments: 1995 to 2000
991	Selected Instruments and Related Products—Value of Shipments: 1990 to 2000
	Sec. 22. **DOMESTIC TRADE**
1007	Retail Trade—Establishments and Sales by Merchandise Lines: 1997
1014	Food Sales by Nontraditional Retailers: 1997
	Sec. 23. **TRANSPORTATION**
1032	Transportation and Warehousing—Establishments, Revenue, Payroll, by Kind of Business (NAICS Basis): 1997
1046	Federal Expenditures for Civil Functions of the Corps of Engineers, United States Army: 1970 to 1999
1051	Merchant Fleets of the World: 2001
1067	Travel in the United States by Selected Trip Characteristics: 1995
1073	Large Truck Involvement in Fatal Crashes by State: 2000
1084	Bus Profile: 1990 to 2000
1085	Truck Profile: 1990 to 2000
1086	Trucks by Use, Body Type, Miles, and Acquisition: 1992 and 1997
	Sec. 24. **COMMUNICATIONS**
1134	Computers and Internet Use by Individuals: 1997 and 2001
	Sec. 25. **BANKING, FINANCE, AND INSURANCE**
1138	Finance and Insurance—Establishments, Revenue, Payroll, and Employees by Kind of Business: 1997
1154	Claims of U.S. Banking Organizations on Foreign Counterparties by Type of Claim: 2001
1156	Insured Savings Institutions—Financial Summary: 1990 to 2001
1196	Revenues of Selected Securities Industries by Source of Revenues: 1998 to 2000
1204	Real Estate, Rental, and Leasing—Establishments, Revenue, Payroll, and Employees by Kind of Business: 1997
	Sec. 26. **ARTS, ENTERTAINMENT, AND RECREATION**
1208	Arts, Entertainment, and Recreation—Establishments, Receipts, Payroll, and Employees by Kind of Business (NAICS Basis): 1997

2002
number

Sec. 27. ACCOMMODATION, FOOD SERVICES, AND OTHER SERVICES

1251 Professional, Scientific, & Technical Services (Taxable)—Establishments, Receipts, Payroll, and Employees by Kind of Business: 1997
1252 Professional, Scientific, and Technical Services (Tax-Exempt)— Establishments, Revenue, Payroll, and Employees by Kind of Business: 1997
1255 Administrative and Support and Waste Management and Remediation Services—Establishments, Receipts, Payroll, and Employees by Kind of Business: 1997
1257 Other Services—Establishments, Receipts, Payroll, and Employees by Kind of Business: 1997
1259 Other Services (Tax-Exempt)—Establishments, Revenue, Payroll, and Employees by Kind of Business: 1997

Sec. 28. FOREIGN COMMERCE AND AID

1275 U.S. Foreign Military Aid by Major Recipient Country: 1997 to 2000

Sec. 29. OUTLYING AREAS

1299 Puerto Rico—Agricultural Summary: 1993 and 1998
1300 Puerto Rico—Farms and Market Value of Products Sold: 1998
1301 Puerto Rico—Economic Census of Manufactures by Industry: 1997
1302 Puerto Rico—Economic Summary by Industry: 1992 and 1997

Sec. 30. COMPARATIVE INTERNATIONAL STATISTICS

1342 Wheat, Rice, and Corn Production by Country: 1995 to 2001
1356 Information and Communication Technology (ICT) Sector— Employment by Country: 1997
1357 Information and Communication Technology (ICT)Sector— Foreign Trade by Country: 1998
1370 Military Budget by Country: 2001
1371 Military Manpower Fit for Military Service by Country: 2001

Sec. 31. 2000 CENSUS DATA SAMPLER

1373 Profile of Selected Social Characteristics—United States: 2000
1374 Profile of Selected Economic Characteristics—United States Summary: 2000
1375 Profile of Selected Housing Characteristics—United States Summary: 2000
1376 Educational Attainment by State: 2000
1381 Nativity and Place of Birth of Resident Population by State: 2000
1391 Occupation of Employed Civilians by State: 2000

Appendix VI
New Tables

Table number		Page number
	Sec. 1. POPULATION	1
7	Estimated Unauthorized Immigrants by Selected States and Countries of Origin: 2000	10
27	Metropolitan Areas With 600,000 or More Inhabitants in 2000—Selected Racial Groups: 2000	32
28	Metropolitan Areas With 600,000 or More Inhabitants in 2000—Hispanic and Non-Hispanic Groups: 2000	33
38	Persons 65 Years Old and Over—Grandparents, Disability Status, and Language Spoken at Home: 2000	42
40	Selected Characteristics of the White and Black Populations: 2000	44
41	American Indian and Alaska Native Population by Tribe: 2000	45
42	Population Living on Selected Reservations and Trust Lands: 2000	45
43	Selected Characteristics of the American Indian, Alaska Native, Asian, and Native Hawaiian and Other Pacific Islander Populations: 2000	46
45	Selected Native Hawaiian Home Lands: 2000	47
47	Selected Characteristics of the Hispanic or Latino Populations: 2000	49
56	Language Spoken at Home by Nativity: 2000	56
57	Languages Spoken at Home by Age Group and Language: 2000	56
79	Self-Described Religious Identification of Adult Population: 1990 and 2001	67
	Sec. 2. VITAL STATISTICS	69
111	Death Rates by Hispanic Origin, Age, and Sex: 1985 to 2000	88
	Sec. 3. HEALTH AND NUTRITION	101
143	Medicare—Estimated Benefit Payments by State: 2001	110
154	People Without Health Insurance for the Entire Year by Selected Characteristics: 2000 and 2001	115
156	Outpatient Prescription Drug Benefits—Selected Features: 2000	115
	Sec. 4. EDUCATION	145
233	Students Reporting Being Threatened or Injured With a Weapon on School Property: 1993 to 2001	156
241	Public Elementary and Secondary Schools and Enrollment—States: 2000-01	161
245	Public School Districts With Alternative Schools or Programs for at-Risk Students: 2000-2001	164
287	Average Total Price of Attendance of Undergraduate Education: 1999-2000	186
290	State Appropriations for Public Colleges: 2001	188
291	Average Amount of Aid Received by Undergraduates Receiving Aid: 1999-2000	188
	Sec. 5. LAW ENFORCEMENT, COURTS, AND PRISONS	195
311	Murder Victims of September 11, 2001, Terrorist Attacks by Race, Sex, and Location	202
312	Homicide Trends: 1976 to 2000	203
315	Reporting Rape and Sexual Assault to Police and Medical Attention: 1992 to 2000	204
317	Violent Victimizations Reported to the Police: 1992 to 2000	205
335	Casework Loads in DNA Laboratories: 1997 and 2000	212
346	Characteristics of Missing Children: 1999	218

Table number		Page number
	Sec. 6. **GEOGRAPHY AND ENVIRONMENT**.	223
382	Pollution Abatement Capital Expenditures and Operating Costs by Media and Industry: 1999.	238
383	Pollution Abatement Capital Expenditures and Operating Costs by Media and State: 1999	238
	Sec. 9. **FEDERAL GOVERNMENT FINANCES AND EMPLOYMENT**	319
480	Department of Homeland Security—Budget: 2002 to 2004	325
	Sec. 11. **SOCIAL INSURANCE AND HUMAN SERVICES**	353
550	Defined Benefit Retirement Plans—Selected Features: 2000	366
552	U.S. Households Owning IRAs: 2001 and 2002	367
554	401(k) Plans—Selected Features: 2000	367
585	Volunteers by Selected Characteristics: 2000	380
	Sec. 12. **LABOR FORCE, EMPLOYMENT AND EARNINGS**	381
616	Employed Civilians by Occupation—States: 2001	402
622	Job Search Activity Using the Internet	407
629	Nonfarm Establishments—Employees, Hours, and Earnings by Industry: 1980 to 2002	411
630	Employees in Nonfarm Establishments—States: 2002	412
631	Nonfarm Industries—Employees and Earnings: 1990 to 2002	413
634	Employed Persons Using Computers at Work by Sex and Occupation: 2001	419
	Sec. 13. **INCOME, EXPENDITURES, AND WEALTH**	433
680	Money Income of Households—Distribution of Income and Median Income by Race and Hispanic Origin: 1999	454
692	Money Income of Families—Distribution of Income and Median Income by Race and Hispanic Origin: 1999	460
	Sec. 15. **BUSINESS ENTERPRISE**.	493
749	Employer Firms, Employment, and Payroll by Employment Size of Enterprise and State: 1990 and 2000	507
	Sec. 16. **SCIENCE AND TECHNOLOGY**	523
799	U.S. and Worldwide Commercial Space Industry Revenue by Type: 2000 to 2002.	532
	Sec. 17. **AGRICULTURE**	535
827	Percent of U.S. Agricultural Commodity Output Exported: 1980 to 2002	546
	Sec. 18. **NATURAL RESOURCES**	557
888	U.S. Coal Supply, Disposition, and Prices: 1997 to 2002	576
	Sec. 19. **ENERGY AND UTILITIES**.	579
902	Residential Energy Consumption, Expenditures, and Average Price: 1980 to 1997.	587
903	Residential Energy Consumption and Expenditures by Type of Fuel and Selected Household Characteristics: 1997	587
904	Commercial Buildings—Energy Consumption and Expenditures: 1999	588
907	Energy Prices: 1980 to 2001.	589

Table number		Page number
	Sec. 20. **CONSTRUCTION AND HOUSING**	601
958	Housing Inventory for Selected Metropolitan Areas—Summary Characteristics: 1995 to 2002	618
	Sec. 22. **DOMESTIC TRADE**	657
1028	Retail Trade Corporations—Sales, Net Profit, and Profit Per Dollar of Sales: 2002	662
	Sec. 23. **TRANSPORTATION**	675
1055	Transportation Revenues by Level of Government and Mode: 1990 to 2001	681
1074	Selected U.S. Ports by Tons of Traffic: 2001	690
1094	Urban Travel by Sex of Traveler and Purpose of Trip: 2001	701
1101	Vehicles Involved in Crashes by Vehicle Type, Rollover Occurrence, and Crash Severity: 2001	705
	Sec. 24. **COMMUNICATIONS**	715
1157	Programs for Adults in Library Outlets: 2000	735
	Sec. 25. **BANKING, FINANCE, AND INSURANCE**	737
1165	Flow of Funds Accounts—Business Credit Market Debt Outstanding by Type of Instrument: 1990 to 2002	741
1168	Flow of Funds Accounts—Liabilities of Households: 1990 to 2002	743
1170	Percent Distribution of Amount of Debt Held by Families: 1998 to 2001	743
1171	Ratios of Debt Payments to Family Income: 1995 to 2001	744
1179	FDIC-Insured Financial Institutions—Number and Assets by State: 2002	747
1180	FDIC-Insured Financial Institutions—Number of Offices and Deposits by State: 2002	747
	Sec. 27. **ACCOMMODATION, FOOD SERVICES, AND OTHER SERVICES**	787
1272	Professional, Scientific, and Technical Services—Estimated Revenue for Employer and Nonemployer Firms: 1998 to 2001	793
1273	Computer Systems Design and Related Services—Estimated Revenue for Employer Firms: 2001	793
	Sec. 29. **PUERTO RICO AND THE ISLAND AREAS**	823
1317	Puerto Rico—Economic Summary by Industry: 2001	830
	Sec. 30. **COMPARATIVE INTERNATIONAL STATISTICS**	831
1344	Household Tax Burden by Country: 2002	857
1357	World Crop Production Summary: 2001 to 2003	862
1383	Military Expenditures and Armed Forces Personnel by Country: 1990 and 1999	878
	Sec. 31. **CONGRESSIONAL DISTRICT PROFILES**	879
1384	Congressional District Profiles—108th Congress: 2000	880

Index

A

	Table
Abortions	102, 103, 104
Abrasives, stone	871
Accidents and fatalities	187, 1058, 1097, 1098, 1105, 1112
Age of driver	1107
Aircraft	1058, 1063, 1065
Alcohol involvement	1103, 1104, 1106
Costs	189
Deaths and death rates	115, 117, 118, 119, 1097, 1098, 1112
Infants	83, 113, 114
Fires	358
Industrial	649, 650, 651, 652
Injuries	187, 188
Motor vehicles	115, 118, 1058, 1097, 1098, 1099, 1100, 1101, 1102, 1105, 1370
Motorcycle	1097
Police officers assaulted, killed	336
Railroad	1112
Transportation	1058
Vehicle rollovers	1101
Work fatalities	654
Work time lost	650
Accommodation and food services industry:	
Capital	769
Earnings	631, 742, 745, 746, 1265, 1266, 1270
Electronic commerce	1268
Employees	631, 742, 1265, 1266, 1270
Establishments	742, 743, 746, 1265, 1266, 1267, 1270
Finances	733, 736
Nonemployers	743, 1267
Productivity	632
Sales	733, 736, 740, 741, 742, 743, 1267, 1270
Accountants and auditors	615
Accounting, tax preparation, bookkeeping, and payroll services:	
Earnings	631, 1265
Employees	631, 1265
Establishments	1265
Finances	733
Receipts	733
Acquired immuno-deficiency syndrome (AIDS)	179, 190, 192, 193, 194
Acquisition of territory by the U.S.	360
Activities of daily living (ADLs)	185, 196
Activity limitation caused by chronic conditions	195, 196
Actors	615
Administrative & support & waste management & remediation services industry:	
Capital	769
Earnings	631, 742, 745, 746, 1265, 1266
Electronic commerce	1268
Employees	631, 742, 745, 746, 1265, 1266
Establishments	742, 743, 745, 1265, 1266, 1267
Finance	733, 736
Nonemployers	743, 1267

	Table
Administrative & support & waste management & remediation services industry: —Con.	
Sales, shipments, receipts	733, 736, 740, 741, 742, 743, 1267, 1276, 1277
Adult education	304
Advertising and related services:	
Earnings	631
Employees	631, 619
Establishments	1265
Finances	1274, 1275
Mergers and acquisitions	759
Productivity	632
Receipts	759
Aerobics	1247, 1254
Aeronautics, civil. See Air transportation.	
Aerospace industry:	
Earnings	631, 987
Employees	631, 987, 1069
Foreign trade	1302
Industrial production	772
Productivity	632
New orders, backlog	1019
Research and development	793, 794
Sales	1019, 1022
Shipments	987, 1019, 1020, 1021, 1022
Afghanistan. See Foreign countries.	
Africa. See Foreign countries.	
African American. See Black population.	
Age of population. See Population.	
Aggravated assault	305, 306, 307, 308
Agricultural loans. See Farm mortgage loans.	
Agricultural products. See Farms and individual products.	
Agricultural sciences:	
Degrees conferred	300, 301, 302, 792
Agricultural services:	
Employees	619
Agriculture (see also Farms and Farmers and farm workers):	
Employees	615
Federal aid to state and local governments	438
Foreign trade	824, 825, 827, 829, 830
Value added	812
Agriculture, forestry, and fishing industry:	
Capital	769
Earnings	635, 745, 751, 853
Employees	619, 745, 751, 853
Establishments	745, 853
Finances	731, 733, 736
Gross domestic product	854
Mergers and acquisitions	759
Minority-owned businesses	752, 753, 754, 755
Occupational safety	649, 652, 654
Profits	731, 776
Sales, shipments, receipts	731, 733, 736, 740, 741, 751, 776
Women-owned businesses	751
Agriculture, construction, and mining machinery manufacturing	631, 632, 987

NOTE: Index citations refer to **table** numbers, not page numbers.

Table

Aid to families with dependent children
 (See Temporary assistance for needy
 families program)
AIDS (acquired immuno-deficiency
 syndrome) 179, 190, 192, 193, 194
Air conditioning:
 Homes with 959, 977
Air Force, Department of, personnel .. 517, 518
Air pollution:
 Air pollution control equipment 384
 Emissions 371, 372, 373, 374, 378,
  379, 1329
 Expenditures 382, 383
 Greenhouse gases 374
 Industry 382, 384
 State 383
Air transportation:
 Accidents and deaths 1058, 1063, 1065
 Airline markets 1062
 Airport summary 1061, 1066
  Flight on-time performance 1066
 Bomb threats 1064
 Civil aviation 1069, 1321
 Consumer complaints 1067
 Cost indexes 1060
 Employees 1059
 Federal outlays 475
 Finances 1059
 Freight 1054, 1059
 Manufacturing orders booked/announced . 1020
 Passenger outlays 1053
 Passenger screening 1064
 Price indexes 715
 Regional airlines 1068
 Traffic carried 1054, 1059, 1068
Air transportation industry:
 Earnings 631, 1056, 1057, 1265
 Employees 631, 1056, 1057, 1265
 Establishments 1057, 1265
 Finances 1059, 1060
 Occupational safety 652
 Productivity 632
 Profits 1059
 Revenues 1055, 1059
Aircraft manufacturing. See Aerospace
 industry.
Airline operations (see also Air
 transportation) 1059, 1062
Airmail service 1117
Airplanes 1301
Airports or airfields 1069
 Federal aid to state and local government ...
  438
 Serving regional airlines 1068
 Traffic 1061, 1066
Alaska Native. See American Indian, Alaska
 Native population
Alcoholic beverages (see also Liquors and
 beverages):
 Advertising 1275
 Alcoholism treatment 176, 200
 Consumer expenditures . 676, 678, 679, 1040
 Consumption 201, 216
  "Binge" use 201, 202
 Foreign trade 1301
 Price indexes 715
 Sales 1043
Alcohol involvement in fatal crashes . 1103, 1104,
 1106
Alcohol treatment 176, 200

Table

Aleut population. See American Indian, Alaska
 Native population.
Algeria. See Foreign countries.
Aliens deported 327
Alimony 537
Almonds 813, 857
Altitudes, geographical 363
Aluminum:
 Consumption 872
 Employment 872
 Foreign trade 872, 877, 1301
 Prices 872
 Production 1006
 Recycling 376
 World production 875
Ambulatory health care services industry:
 Earnings 158, 631, 742
 Employees 631, 742
 Establishments 742
 Finances 733
 Sales, receipts 733, 742
American College Testing Program 265
American Indian, Alaska Native
 population 13, 15, 16, 21, 792, 807
 Age and/or sex 13, 14, 16
 Business owners 750, 755
 Charter schools 239
 Cities 31, 32
 College enrollment 278
  Disability 285
  Distance education 286
 Commuting to work 43
 Congressional districts 1384
 Crime 325
 Degrees conferred 299
 Disability status 43
 Educational attainment 43
 Farm operators 807
 Food stamp participants 571
 Foreign born 43
 Health care visits to professionals . 165, 167
 Hospital visits 167, 175
 Immunization of children 191
 Income 680, 692
 Metropolitan areas 27
 Mobility status 43
 Nativity 43
 Nurses 161
 Occupation 43
 Poverty 697
 Projections 15
 Reservation and Trust Lands population . 42
 States 21
 Tribes 41
American Samoa. See Island areas of the U.S.
American sign language 283
American Stock Exchange 1207
 Composite index 1204
AMTRAK 1112
Amusement and recreation services.
 See Arts, entertainment and recreation.
Amusement, gambling, and recreation
 industry:
 Earnings 631, 1231
 Employees 631, 1231
 Establishments 1231, 1232
 Nonemployers establishments 1232
 Receipts, revenue 1230
Amusement parks 1230, 1231, 1232, 1239

NOTE: Index citations refer to **table** numbers, not page numbers.

Index 975

U.S. Census Bureau, Statistical Abstract of the United States: 2003

Table	Table
Analgesics 201	Arizona. See State data.
Ancestry 55	Arkansas. See State data.
Anchovies 865	Armed Forces ... 517, 519, 520, 521, 523, 524, 527
Andorra. See Foreign countries.	
Anemias, deaths 115	Foreign countries 519, 1383
Anesthesiologists 162	Armenia. See Foreign countries.
Angiocardiography 178	Army personnel 517
Angola. See Foreign countries.	Arrests (see also Law enforcement) ... 325, 326, 328, 329
Anguilla. See Foreign countries.	
Animal oils and fats. See Oils, animal.	Arsenic 872
Animal slaughtering and processing industry 631, 632	Arson 325, 358
	Arteriography 178
Animals, domestic (see also individual classes):	Arteriosclerosis, deaths 115, 118, 119
	Arts education 1238
Inventory and production 844	Arts, entertainment, and recreation:
Annuities. See Pensions and retirement benefits.	Capital 769
	Earnings 631, 742, 745, 746, 1231
Antigua and Barbuda. See Foreign countries.	Employees .. 620, 631, 742, 745, 746, 1231
Antimony 872, 877	Establishments 742, 743, 745, 1231
Apparel manufacturing:	Finances 733, 736, 1230, 1231
Capital 766	Gross domestic product 660
Earnings 631, 985, 987, 992	Mergers and acquisitions 759
Electronic commerce 989	Nonemployers 743, 1232
Employees 620, 631, 985, 987, 992	Occupational safety 652
Energy consumption 906	Receipts, revenue . 733, 736, 740, 741, 742, 743, 1230, 1232
Establishments 987	
Finances 778	Arts and humanities:
Foreign trade 1304	Aid to 1236
Gross domestic product 660, 984	Arts education in schools 1238
Industrial production index 772	Attendance 1235, 1237
Mergers and acquisitions 759	Charitable contributions 580
Occupational safety 652	Federal aid 1236
Pollution abatement 382	Grants, foundations 584
Productivity 632	Philanthropy 581
Profits 778	Public confidence 416
Shipments 987, 989	Artwork 1240
Toxic chemical releases 379	Aruba. See Foreign countries.
Apparel goods:	Asbestos 338, 384, 872, 875, 877
Advertising 1275	Asia. See Foreign countries.
Consumer expenditures . 676, 677, 678, 679	Asian and Pacific Islander population ... 13, 14, 15, 16, 21, 23, 44, 54, 792, 807
Foreign trade 1301	
Prices 713, 715, 721	Births 84, 91
Sales 1043	Business owners 750, 754
Apples . 215, 715, 727, 810, 813, 826, 833, 842	Cities 31, 32
Appliances, household:	College enrollment 278
Consumer expenditures 678, 679	College costs 287
Homes with 977	Disability 285
Price indexes 715	Distance education 286
Sales and shipments 1023, 1043	Computer use 260, 1158
Appliances (household) manufacturing:	Congress, members of 408
Capital 766	Crime 333
Employees 620	Educational attainment 227, 228
Inventories 995	Families 44
Shipments 995	Food stamp participants 571
Apricots 842	Foreign-born population 226
Aquaculture 813, 866	Health insurance coverage 154
Archery 1247, 1253	Hospital visits 167, 175
Architectural services. See Engineering and architectural services.	Housing tenure 44
	Immunization of children 191
Area of:	Income 680, 692, 696
Foreign countries 1322	Overweight 209
Forest land 855	Poverty 697
Island areas of the U.S. 359	Projections 15
Parks 1255, 1256	School enrollment 226, 247, 282, 285
States 359	Charter schools 239
United States 1, 359, 1322	States 21
Cities 31	Asian Indian population 23, 750, 1158
Water 1, 359, 365	Asian population 13, 14, 32, 84, 792, 807
World 1322	Commuting to work 43
Argentina. See Foreign countries.	

NOTE: Index citations refer to **table** numbers, not page numbers.

976 Index

U.S. Census Bureau, Statistical Abstract of the United States: 2003

	Table
Asian population —Con.	
Congressional districts	1384
Disability status	43
Educational attainment	43
Foreign born	43
Health care visits to professionals	165
Metropolitan areas	27
Mobility status	43
Nativity	43
Nurses	161
Occupation	43
Asparagus	215
Asphalt	871, 933
Assault	305, 306, 307, 308, 321, 322, 323
Asset-backed securities	1162, 1164, 1195
Assets, personal	708, 709, 710, 1167
Associations, national, nonprofit	1278, 1279
Asthma	115, 117, 119, 168, 176
Atherosclerosis, deaths	115, 118
Athletic goods. See Sporting and athletic goods.	
Athletes	615
Atomic energy defense activities, expenditures	510
Attention deficit disorder	168
Audio equipment	1015
Auditing. See Accounting, tax preparation, bookkeeping, and payroll services.	
Australia. See Foreign countries.	
Austria. See Foreign countries.	
Authors	615
ATMs (automated teller machines)	1039, 1177, 1186
Automatic bill paying	1186
Automobile loans	1189
Automobile rentals and leasing. See Rental and leasing services.	
Automobiles (see also Motor vehicles):	
Advertising	1275
Expenditure per new car	1035
Foreign countries	1370
Foreign trade	1301
Imports	1035
Insurance	1225
Leases	1036
Price indexes	715
Production	1035
Sales	1026, 1035, 1036
Automobile dealers:	
Earnings	631, 1024, 1025, 1026
Employees	631, 1024, 1025, 1026
Establishments	1024, 1025, 1026
Inventories	1031
Productivity	632
Sales	1026, 1027
Automotive equipment rental and leasing	631, 632
Automotive products. See Motor vehicles, tires and tubes, etc.	
Automotive repair and maintenance service:	
Earnings	631
Employees	619, 620
Establishments	1265, 1267
Mergers and acquisitions	759
Nonemployers	1267
Productivity	632
Receipts/revenue	1267, 1277
Avocados	813, 842
Azerbaijan. See Foreign countries.	

	Table
B	
Backpacking	1247
Bacon	715, 727
Badminton	1247
Bahamas, The. See Foreign countries.	
Bahrain. See Foreign countries.	
Bakeries and tortilla manufacturing	631, 632, 987
Bakery products	678, 679, 715
Balance of payments	1280, 1281, 1294
Balance sheet	483, 738, 739
Ballet	1236
Bananas	215, 715, 727, 823, 825
Bangladesh. See Foreign countries.	
Bankruptcies	756, 757
Banks, commercial:	
ATM's	1177
Checking accounts	1177
Consumer credit finance rates	1189
Credit cards	1174, 1185, 1190
Debit cards	1188
Delinquency rates, repossessions, loans	1185
Deposits	1174, 1178
Earnings	631, 1161
Employees	631, 1161
Establishments	1161, 1173, 1174
Federal Reserve Banks	1174
Finances	1162, 1164, 1173, 1174, 1175, 1176, 1178, 1179, 1180, 1182, 1192, 1216
Flow of funds	1162, 1164, 1216
Foreign banking offices in United States	1178
Gross domestic product	1160
Home equity loans	1174
Individual Retirement Accounts, 401(k) plans	1218
Insured banks	1173, 1179
Loans to families	1170
Mergers and acquisitions	759
Occupational safety	652
Productivity	632
Profits	1175, 1176
Robbery	318
State data	1179, 1180
Stock and bond prices and yields	1204
Barbados. See Foreign countries.	
Barbecuing	1244
Barber shops	1277
Barite	871, 872, 875
Barium	813, 877
Barley	810, 826
Bars. See Food services.	
Base, military closings	518
Baseball	1243, 1245, 1247, 1249, 1250, 1253
Basketball	1243, 1245, 1247, 1249, 1250, 1253
Bauxite	871, 875
Consumption	872
Employment	872
Foreign trade	872
Prices	872
Production	875
Strategic and critical materials inventory	876
World production	875, 1361
Beans	215, 810, 813, 818, 841
Beauty shops	1277
Price indexes	715

NOTE: Index citations refer to **table** numbers, not page numbers.

Table

Beef (see also Meat and meat products):
    Consumer expenditures 676, 678, 679
    Consumption 214, 826, 843, 1356
        Foreign countries 1356
    Foreign trade 825, 826, 843
    Price indexes 715
    Prices 715, 727
    Production 843
        Foreign countries 1355
    Supply 843
Beer. See Malt beverages.
Beer, wine, and liquor stores:
    Earnings 631, 1025, 1026
    Employees 631, 1025, 1026
    Establishments 1025, 1026, 1033
    Nonemployers 1033
    Productivity 632
    Sales 1026, 1027, 1033, 1040
Belarus. See Foreign countries.
Belgium. See Foreign countries.
Belize. See Foreign countries.
Benin. See Foreign countries.
Bermuda. See Foreign countries.
Beryllium 872
Beverages and tobacco product manufacturing:
    Capital 766
    Earnings 631, 985, 987
    Employees 631, 985, 987
    Finances 778
    Industrial production index 772
    Multinational companies 780, 781
    Pollution abatement 382
    Productivity 632
    Profits 778
    Shipments 987, 994, 995
Beverages (see also Alcoholic beverages):
    Advertising expenditures 1275
    Consumption 216
    Price indexes 715
Bhutan. See Foreign countries.
Bicycles 318, 1247, 1253, 1254
Billiards 1247
Biological sciences:
    Degrees conferred 792
    Employment 615
Bird ownership 1242
Birth and birth rates .. 4, 83, 84, 85, 87, 88, 90,
                  91, 92, 93, 94, 95, 96, 99, 100
    American Indian, Eskimo, and Aleut
      population 84
    Asian and Pacific Islander population 84
    Births to mothers who smoked 97
    Births to single or unmarried women 84,
                                92, 99
    Births to teenage mothers 86
    Birth weight 84, 94, 95
    Black population 84, 85, 87, 95, 99
    Cesarean section deliveries 96, 178
    Characteristics of mother ... 85, 96, 99, 100
    Delivery procedures 178
    First births 98, 99, 100
    Foreign countries 1326
    Hispanic population 84, 87
    Island areas of the U.S. 1306
    Low birthweight by smoking status 97
    Prenatal care 84, 95
    Projections 89
    Race 85, 87, 90, 92
    States 19, 87, 94

Table

Birth control 101
Birth weights 84, 94, 95
Bismuth 872
Black lung benefit program 560
Black population 15, 16, 21, 54
    Abortions 102, 103
    Activity limitation 195, 196
    Adult education 304
    Age and/or sex 11, 14, 16, 39
    AIDS 192, 193
    Birth and birth rates 84, 85, 87, 90, 91,
                                  95, 99
        Births to teenage mothers 91
        Births to unmarried women 92
    Business owners 750, 753
    Cancer 117, 118, 206
    Charity contributions 579
    Child care 577
    Children under 18 years old 11, 16, 39
        Literacy activities 235, 238
        Poverty 701, 703
        School readiness 235, 238
    Cigarette smoking 203
    Cities 32
    Community service (students) 586
    Commuting to work 40
    Computer use 260, 1158
    Congress, members of 408
    Congressional districts 1384
    Consumer expenditures 678, 679
    Contraceptive use 101
    Crime (arrests) 324, 325
    Criminal victimizations 232, 233, 324
    Deaths and death rates . 108, 113, 114, 117,
                                  118, 193
    Disabled persons 40, 285, 557
    Educational attainment 40
    Elderly 11, 39, 703
    Elected officials 408, 417
    Elections, voter registrations and
      turnout 419
    Families, characteristics 70, 71, 72, 73
    Farm operators, workers 807, 822
    Fertility, fertility rate 88, 89
    Food stamp participants 571
    Foreign-born population 40, 226
    Health care, visits to professionals . 165, 167
    Health insurance coverage ... 145, 152, 154
    High school graduates and dropouts 272
    Home health and hospice care 182
    Homeschooled 243
    Homicides 313
    Hospital use 167, 175
    Households, characteristics .. 67, 71, 72, 73
    Housing 962, 966, 974, 976
    Immunization of children 191
    Income .. 39, 537, 683, 684, 685, 686, 687,
                            688, 689, 693
    Infant deaths 113, 114
    Internet access 260, 1127, 1158
    Jail inmates 347
    Job search 622
    Labor force 588, 589, 591
        Displaced workers 612
        Earnings 641

NOTE: Index citations refer to **table** numbers, not page numbers.

Table	Table
Black population —Con. 　Employed . 589, 605, 606, 607, 608, 609, 　　　　　　　　　　　　　615, 618, 619 　　Employment status .... 589 　　　Educational attainment ..... 591, 626 　　　High school graduates and dropouts, 　　　　employment status .... 273 　　　School enrollment, persons 15 to 　　　　21 years old .... 594 　　　Unemployed .... 621, 626 　　Job search .... 622 　　Persons working at home .... 605 　Language proficiency .... 236 　Life expectancy .... 105, 106, 107 　Living arrangements .... 64 　Marital status .... 44, 61 　Media users .... 1127 　Metropolitan areas .... 27 　Minimum wage workers .... 645 　Mobility status .... 40 　Nativity .... 40 　Nurses .... 161, 532 　Occupation .... 40, 615, 618 　Overweight .... 209 　Pension plan coverage .... 551 　Physical activity .... 210 　Poverty .... 39, 700, 701, 703, 707 　Prisoners .... 351 　Projections .... 15 　Property owners .... 966, 973, 976 　Recreation activities ...... 1237, 1239, 1240 　School dropouts, high school ...... 271, 273 　Schools and education: 　　Adult education .... 304 　　American College Testing Program .. 265 　　Attainment .... 227, 228, 229 　　Enrollment .... 222, 226, 247, 282 　　　Charter schools .... 239 　　　College costs .... 287 　　　College enrollment .... 278, 279, 280 　　　Disability .... 285 　　　Distance education .... 286 　　　Preprimary enrollment .... 237 　　Higher education institutions: 　　　Degrees conferred .... 792 　　　Enrollment .... 226, 278, 279, 280 　　High school dropouts ..... 270, 271, 273 　　High school graduates .... 273 　　Homeschooled .... 243 　　Scholastic Assessment Test .... 264 　　Sports participation .... 1248 　　Teachers .... 249, 263, 615 　Senior citizen communities .... 974 　States .... 21 　Suicides ...... 115, 116, 117, 118, 119, 123 　Union membership .... 657 　Volunteers .... 585 　Voter registration and turnout .... 419 Blast furnace and basic steel products. See 　Iron and steel products. Blind persons .... 561 　Medicaid payments and recipients ...... 146 Blood alcohol concentration . 1103, 1104, 1106 Blue collar workers .... 469, 638, 643 Bluefish .... 865 Board and care homes .... 184 Boating, canoeing, etc. .... 1246, 1247, 1253 　Accidents 1058	Bolivia. See Foreign countries. Bolts, nuts, etc. See Iron and steel products. Bonds: 　Credit outstanding .... 1165 　Foreign .... 1201, 1202 　Holdings by sector .... 1163, 1164, 1166, 　　　　　　　　　　　　1198, 1201, 1203 　Life insurance companies .... 1198, 1223 　New issues .... 1199 　Ownership by equity holders .... 1212 　Prices, yields, sales, and issues .. 486, 1194, 　　　　　　　　1197, 1200, 1202, 1209 　Rating .... 451, 452 　U.S. savings .... 486, 1167 Bookkeeping. See Accounting, tax preparation, 　bookkeeping, and payroll services. Book, periodical and music stores .... 631, 632, 　　　　　　　　　　　　　　　　1026, 1027 Book publishing industry .... 1137 Books (see also Information industry, 　Publishing industry, and Libraries): 　Prices .... 1136 　Production .... 1135 　Reading .... 1125 　Sales .... 1041, 1043, 1124, 1134, 1138 Boots. See Footwear. Border Patrol activities .... 327 Boron .... 871, 872 Bosnia and Herzegovina. See Foreign countries. Botswana. See Foreign countries. Botulism .... 190 Bowling .... 1246, 1247, 1253 Bowling center industry .... 1230, 1231 Boxing .... 1243 Brazil. See Foreign countries. Bread .... 715, 727 Bridge inventory .... 1079 British Virgin Islands. See Foreign countries. Broadcasting and telecommunications industry: 　Earnings .... 631, 742, 1119, 1121 　Employees .... 631, 742, 1119, 1121 　Establishments .... 742, 1119, 1121 　Finances .... 1143, 1145, 1146, 1147 　Multinational companies .... 780, 781 　Receipts, revenue .. 742, 1119, 1120, 1143, 　　　　　　　　　　　1145, 1146, 1147 　World .... 1371 Broadway and off-Broadway shows .... 1235 Broccoli .... 215, 813, 841 Broilers (see also Poultry) .. 810, 813, 816, 843, 　　　　　　　　　　　　　　　　851, 852 Bromine .... 872 Bronchitis, emphysema, etc. .... 115, 117, 118, 　　　　　　　　　　　　　119, 168, 169 Brunei. See Foreign countries. Buckwheat, organic acreage .... 810 Buddhist population. See Religion. Budget, Federal: 　Outlays .... 475, 476, 477, 478, 479 　Receipts .... 475, 481 　Revenue losses (tax expenditures) ...... 482 　Tax expenditures .... 482 　Taxes .... 481 Building contractors, general: 　Earnings .... 631, 742, 931, 932 　Employees .... 631, 742, 931, 932 　Establishments .... 742, 931, 932 　Occupational safety .... 652 　Receipts .... 742 　Value of work 932

NOTE: Index citations refer to **table** numbers, not page numbers.

Index　979

Table

Building materials, and garden supplies, retail stores:
  Earnings 631, 742, 1025, 1026
  Electronic commerce 1045
  Employees 631, 742, 1025, 1026
  Establishments 742, 1025, 1026, 1033
  Inventories 1031
  Nonemployers 1033
  Productivity 632
  Purchases 1030
  Sales .. 742, 1026, 1027, 1029, 1032, 1033
Building permits. See Construction industry, and Housing and housing units.
Buildings (see also Construction industry, and Housing and housing units):
  Characteristics 982
  Construction value . 935, 936, 937, 938, 939
  Correctional facilities 348
  Energy consumption and expenditures . 904
  Federal 507, 508
  Fires and property loss 357
  Floorspace 507, 508, 904, 982
  Office vacancy rate 981, 983
  Principal activity 904, 982
Bulgaria. See Foreign countries.
Burglary 305, 306, 307, 308, 318, 324, 325
Burkina Faso. See Foreign countries.
Burma. See Foreign countries.
Burundi. See Foreign countries.
Buses and bus transportation (see also Passenger transit and Motor vehicles):
  Finances 1109
  Foreign countries 1370
  Passenger traffic and outlays ... 1053, 1054
  Receipts 1109
Business enterprise (see also individual types of business and industry):
  American Indian and Alaska Native owned businesses 750
  Asian and Pacific Islander owned businesses 750
  Bankruptcies filed 756, 757
  Black owned businesses 750
  Capital, fixed by industry 766
  Corporations:
    Philanthropy 581
    Profits and sales 734
  Corporations, partnerships, and proprietorships . 731, 733, 734, 735, 736, 740, 741
  Cycles 771
  Divestitures 758
  Economic indicators 770
  Employees 744, 747, 749, 779
  Establishments 742, 744, 745, 747
  Expenditures, research and development . 923
  Failures and starts 748
  Finances 731, 734, 735, 738, 777, 778, 780, 781, 998, 999
  Firms 747, 749
  Flow of funds 1162
  Foreign investment in the U.S. . 1285, 1286, 1287, 1288
  Hispanic owned businesses 750
  Leading indicators 770
  Leveraged buy-outs 758
  Loans to minority-operated small businesses 760
  Mergers and acquisitions 758, 759
  Multinational companies 779, 780
  Patents 762, 763, 764, 1339

Table

Business enterprise (see also individual types of business and industry): —Con.
  Payroll 744, 747, 749
  Profits 775, 776, 777, 778, 998, 999
  Sales, shipments, receipts ... 993, 995, 996, 999
  Small business 747, 748, 749, 760
  Venture capital 761
  Women owned businesses 750
Business management, degrees conferred . 300, 301, 302
  Salary offers 297
Business services (see individual types of service):
  Capital 766
  Earnings 631
  Employees 619, 620, 631
  Gross domestic product 660, 1001
  Mergers and acquisitions 759
  Multinational companies 781
  Occupational safety 652
  Receipts 1124
Butter 214, 849
Butterfish 865

C

Cabbage 813, 841
Cable and other pay television services 715, 1114, 1126
  Advertising expenditures 1274
  Price indexes 715
  Viewing 1125, 1127
Cable TV industry:
  Earnings 631, 1123
  Employees 620, 631, 1123, 1145
  Finances 1124, 1145
  Gross domestic product 1122
  Receipts 1124, 1145
Cadmium 872, 875, 877
Cafeterias. See Eating and drinking places.
Calcium, dietary 212, 213
Calcium chloride 871
California. See State data.
Calisthenics 1247
Calves 813, 843, 844, 847
Cambodia. See Foreign countries.
Cambodian population 23
Cameroon. See Foreign countries.
Campaigns, fund raising ... 423, 424, 425, 426, 427, 428, 429, 430
Camping 1247, 1253, 1254
Canada. See Foreign countries.
Cancer (malignancies) . 115, 117, 119, 125, 168, 176, 182, 206, 207
  Deaths 118, 119, 120, 193, 207
Cantaloupe 841
Capacity utilization, index 773
Cape Verde. See Foreign countries.
Capital (see individual industries):
  Banking 1174, 1175
  Expenditures . 382, 383, 767, 768, 769, 987
  New security issues 1199
  Pollution abatement 382, 383
  Residential 978
  Stocks 766, 993
  Utilities 923, 926, 1149
Capital equipment, producer price indexes . 719
Capital punishment 354, 355
Carbon dioxide emissions 374, 1330

NOTE: Index citations refer to **table** numbers, not page numbers.

980 Index

U.S. Census Bureau, Statistical Abstract of the United States: 2003

	Table
Carbon dioxide (natural), production and value	871
Cardiac catheterization	178
Cardiovascular disease. See Heart disease.	
Cargo tonnage. See Tonnage U.S. Flag fleet.	
Carrots	215, 813, 841
Cars. See automobiles	
Cash usage	1187
Cassettes	1141
Casualties, military conflicts	523
Casualty insurance	1224
Catalog and mail order sales	1027, 1030, 1033, 1043, 1045
Catfish	866
Catholic population. See Religion.	
CAT scan	178
Cat ownership	1242
Cattle:	
Farm marketings, sales	813, 816, 819
Imports	825
Number on farms	844, 845, 847
Organic	810
Prices	844
Production	844, 847
Slaughter	847
Value on farms	844
Cauliflower	215, 841
Cayman Islands. See Foreign countries.	
Celery	215, 841
Cellular telephones (See also Telephone carriers)	977, 1371
Cement (see also Nonmetallic mineral product manufacturing)	871, 947
Capital	766
Consumption	872
Earnings	631
Employment	631, 872
Foreign trade	872
Price indexes	878
Prices	872
Production and value	871
Productivity	632
World production	1361
Central African Republic. See Foreign countries.	
Central America. See Foreign countries.	
Central and South American population (Hispanic origin)	46, 47, 84
Cereal and bakery products:	
Advertising	1118
Expenditures, prices	676, 678, 679, 715, 820
Foreign trade	1301
Cerebrovascular diseases, deaths	115, 117, 118, 119, 169, 176, 1212
Certificates of deposit	1167, 1193
Cesarean section deliveries	96, 178
Cesium	872
CFC (Chloroflurocarbon) gases	374
Chad. See Foreign countries.	
Charitable contributions (see also Philanthropy)	490, 492, 580, 581
Charter schools	239
Checking accounts	1167, 1177, 1187
Cheese (see also Dairy products)	213, 214, 727, 826, 849
Chemical products	1301
Producer price indexes	715
Production	1004
Toxic chemical releases	378, 379, 380

	Table
Chemicals manufacturing (see also individual chemicals):	
Capital	382, 766
Earnings	631, 985, 987, 992
Electronic commerce	989
Employees	631, 985, 987, 992
Energy consumption	906
Establishments	985
Finances	778
Foreign trade	1304
Gross domestic product	660, 984
Industrial production index	772
Inventories	994, 995
Mergers and acquisitions	759
Multinational companies	780, 781
Occupational safety	652
Patents	763
Pollution abatement	382
Productivity	632
Profits	777, 778
Research and development	793, 794
Shipments	987, 994, 995
Toxic chemical releases	379
Chemistry (see also Physical sciences):	
Employment	615
Nobel prize laureates	804
Salary offers	297
Cherries	813, 842
Chicken pox	190
Chickens. See Poultry.	
Child abuse	344, 345
Child care	577, 578, 715, 974
Expenditures for	675
Child day care services:	
Earnings	573, 574, 631
Employees	573, 574, 620, 631
Establishments	573, 574
Finances	573, 574, 575
Child support	537, 566, 567
Children (see also Population and Vital statistics):	
Activity limitation	195
Age and/or sex	11, 12, 16
Aid, social welfare programs	540
AIDS	192, 193
Alcohol use	201
Child abuse	344, 345
Child case workers	617, 620
Child day care	577, 578, 715
Child support	537, 566, 567
Cigarette smoking	201
College dormitories	77
College enrollment	276
Community service	586
Computer use	256, 258, 260
Congenital abnormalities	176
Correctional institutions	77
Cost of raising	675
Crime, arrests	322, 326
Deaths and death rates	113, 114, 117, 118, 193
Disability status	261
Drug use	201
Families with	65, 70, 71, 72, 73, 74
Food insecurity	211
Food stamp program	570, 571
Foreign born population	54
Foster care	540
Fractures	176

NOTE: Index citations refer to **table** numbers, not page numbers.

Index 981

U.S. Census Bureau, Statistical Abstract of the United States: 2003

Table	Table

Children (see also Population and Vital statistics): —Con.
  Group quarters population 77
  Head start program 572
  Health insurance coverage .. 145, 148, 152, 154, 540
  High school dropouts 270, 271
  High school graduates 240, 269, 275
  Hispanic origin population 13, 16, 191
  Homeschooled 243
  Hospital use 77, 168, 169, 175, 176
  Hunger 211
  Immigrants 6
  Immunization against diseases 191
  Income, families with children 689
  Injuries 187
  Internet access 260
  Juvenile delinquency institutions 77, 342
  Labor force (16 to 19 years old), ... 588
    Employed 600, 601, 608, 610
    Employment status 594
    Minimum wage workers 645
    Multiple job holders 608
    Participation rates 595
    Sex 588, 590
    Unemployed 621, 627
  Language proficiency 236
  Literacy activities 235, 238
  Literacy skills 235, 238
  Missing children 346
  Mobility status 34
  Mothers in the labor force, by age of children 597
  Music purchases 1142
  Parental involvement 234
  Physician visits 165, 167, 168
  Pneumonia 176
  Poverty 701, 703, 698, 699
  Projections 12
  Respiratory infection, acute 176
  School crimes 232, 233
  School enrollment . 217, 219, 221, 222, 223, 224, 225, 240, 244, 246
    Homeschooled 243
    Parental involvement 234
    Preprimary school enrollment 237
    Projections 217
  School readiness 238
  Social Security beneficiaries and payments 543
  Suicides 117
Chile. See Foreign countries.
China. See Foreign countries.
Chinese population 23, 750
Chiropractors' offices 158
Chloroflurocarbon (CFCs) gases 374
Chocolate. See Cocoa and Confectionery products.
Cholelithiasis, deaths 115
Cholera 190
Cholesterol 213
Christian population. See Religion.
Christmas trees 813
Chromite 1361
Chromium 872, 876, 877
Churches (see also Religion):
  Attendance 80
  Construction value 936, 939
	Churches (see also Religion): —Con.
	  Grants, foundations 584
	  Number and membership 80
	  Volunteers 585
	Cigar usage 201
	Cigarettes (see also Tobacco products):
	  Advertising 1275
	  Consumption 1000
	  Foreign trade 1301, 1359
	  Production 1000, 1359
	  Smokers and use 201, 202, 203, 204
	Circuit boards 1011, 1012, 1013
	Circulation of newspapers and periodicals . 1126, 1128, 1130, 1131
	  Foreign countries 1372
	Cirrhosis of liver, deaths 115, 117, 118
	Cities (see also Metropolitan areas):
	  American Indian population 32
	  Asian population 32
	  Black population 32
	  Climate . 389, 390, 391, 392, 393, 394, 395
	    Foreign cities 1328
	  Commuting to work 1092
	  Crime 306, 308
	  Debt 464
	  Disability population 199
	  Drug use 328
	  Employees, earnings, payrolls 473
	  Foreign born 50
	  Foreign travel to 1262
	  Finances of city governments 463, 464
	  Governmental units 431, 433
	  Hawaiian population 32
	  Hispanic population 33
	  Housing 957, 969, 972
	  Language spoken at home 60
	  Office vacancy rates 983
	  Officials elected 417
	  Population 29, 31, 32, 33
	  Property tax rates 460
	  Taxes paid, by family income level 459
	Citrus fruits:
	  Consumption 215, 216, 826, 839
	  Foreign trade 826, 839
	  Pesticide usage 833
	  Production 839, 842
	Civil aviation. See Air transportation.
	Civil cases, U.S. District Courts 338
	Civil service employees. See Government.
	Clams 865, 867, 868
	Clergymen 81
	  Employment 615
	Climate, selected cities 389, 390, 391, 392, 393, 394, 395, 1328
	  Precipitation 392, 393, 394, 1328
	  Temperature . 388, 389, 390, 391, 395, 1328
	Clocks and watches 1301
	Clothing and accessory stores, retail:
	  Earnings 631, 742, 1025, 1026
	  Electronic commerce 1045
	  Employees 631, 742, 1025, 1026
	  Establishments 742, 1025, 1026, 1033
	  Finances 778
	  Inventories 1031
	  Nonemployers 1033
	  Productivity 632
	  Profits 778
	  Purchases 1030

NOTE: Index citations refer to **table** numbers, not page numbers.

Table	Table

Clothing and accessory stores, retail: —Con.
  Sales .. 742, 1026, 1027, 1029, 1032, 1033
Coal (see also Petroleum and coal products and Coal mining):
  Car loadings 1113, 1114
  Consumption ... 895, 896, 898, 1363, 1364
    Electric utilities 914, 917
  Expenditures 900, 901
  Foreign trade 889, 896, 908, 909, 1301
  Prices 719, 873, 889, 907, 923
  Production 871, 889, 895, 896, 1117
    World production 875, 890, 1361, 1362, 1365
  Reserves 891, 892
Coal mining:
  Capital 766, 870
  Earnings 853, 870
  Employment 708, 853, 870, 889
  Establishments 853, 870
  Mines 889
  Occupational safety 652
  Output 869, 871, 895, 898
  Productivity 889
  Shipments 870
  Supply 888
  Value added 870
Coast Guard personnel 521
Coastal population 24
Cobalt 876, 877
Cocaine (see also Drugs (illegal)), arrests and use 201, 329, 330
Cocoa 214, 823, 825, 1301
Cod 865, 868
Coffee:
  Consumption 214, 216
  Foreign trade 823, 825, 1301
  Price indexes 715
  Prices 715, 727
  World production 1321
Cogeneration of electricity 921
Coke. See Coal.
College:
  Aid received 291
  Costs 287
  Price index 715
  State appropriations 290
  Tuition 292
Colleges and universities. See Education, higher education institutions.
Colombia. See Foreign countries.
Colorado. See State data.
Columbium-tantalum 872, 875, 877
Commerce:
  Domestic, by rail 1113
  Domestic, by water 1070, 1071
  Foreign. See Foreign trade.
Commerce and housing credit 476, 479
Commercial buildings:
  Characteristics 982
  Construction value 936, 939
  Cost of construction 934
  Crime incidents 323
  Energy characteristics 982
  Floor space 939, 982
  Inventory 982
  Vacancy rates 981, 983
Commercial paper 1165, 1196
Commodities. See individual types of commodities.
Commodity flow 1077

Communicable diseases 190
Communications, degrees conferred 300, 301, 302
Communications equipment manufacturing:
  Capital 766
  Earnings 631, 985, 987
  Employees 631, 985, 987
  Establishments 985
  Inventories 995
  Mergers and acquisitions 759
  Productivity 632
  Shipments 987, 995, 1016
Communications industry. See Information industry.
Community care facilities for the elderly industry 158
Community development, federal outlays .. 479
Community food, housing services ... 573, 574, 575
Community service 585, 586
Commuting to work 40, 43, 648, 1090, 1091, 1092
Comoros. See Foreign countries.
Compact disks (CD-ROM) 1015, 1141
Computer:
  Advertising expenditures 1275
  Foreign trade 1301
  Sales 1015, 1041, 1042, 1043
  Use 256, 258, 259, 260, 622, 634, 977, 1127, 1156, 1158, 1159, 1239, 1371, 1372
Computer programming and data processing services:
  Earnings 631, 1123
  Employees 620, 631, 1123
  Gross domestic product 1122
Computer specialists:
  Degrees conferred 300, 301, 302, 792
  Labor force 617
    Salary offers 297
Computer systems design:
  Earnings 742, 1265
  Employees 742, 1265
  Establishments 742, 1265
  Multinational companies 780, 781
  Receipts 742, 1273
Computers and electronic product manufacturing:
  Capital 382
  Earnings 631, 985, 987, 1123
  Electronic commerce 989
  Employees 631, 985, 987, 1123
  Establishments 985
  Finances 778
  Gross domestic product 1122
  Industrial production index 772
  Inventories 994, 995
  Mergers and acquisitions 759
  Multinational companies 781
  Pollution abatement 382
  Productivity 632
  Profits 778
  Shipments . 987, 989, 994, 995, 1012, 1013, 1014
Computerized axial tomography (CAT scan) . 178
Concerts, symphony orchestras 1235
Condensed and evaporated milk 214, 849
Condominiums 942, 951
Confectionery products 826
Congo (Brazzaville). See Foreign countries.

NOTE: Index citations refer to **table** numbers, not page numbers.

Index   983

U.S. Census Bureau, Statistical Abstract of the United States: 2003

Congo (Kinshasa). See Foreign countries
Congestion on road 1089
Congress, U.S.:
  Asian, Pacific Islander members 408
  Bills, acts, resolutions 409, 410
  Black members 408
  Campaign finances 423, 424, 429, 430
  Composition 405, 406
  Congressional apportionment 402
  Congressional districts:
    Candidates, votes cast 403
    Characteristics 1384
  Hispanic members 408
  Members, characteristics 408
  Public confidence 416
  Representatives, vote cast ... 403, 404, 422
  Senators, vote cast 401
  Seniority 408
  Time in session 409
  Women members 408
Connecticut. See State data.
Construction industry (see also Building materials and Highways):
  Building authorized 941
  Building permits, value 941
  Capital 766, 769
  Construction contracts 939, 940
  Cost 934
  Earnings 629, 631, 635, 636, 742, 745, 746, 751, 931, 932, 1318
  Employees 605, 619, 624, 629, 630, 631, 653, 742, 745, 746, 751, 783, 931, 932, 1318,
  Establishments ... 742, 743, 745, 931, 932, 1318
  Finances 733, 736, 1314
  Gross domestic product 660, 664, 1314
  Hours 629
  Mergers and acquisitions 759
  Minority-owned businesses . 752, 753, 754, 755
  Industry 742, 932
  Nonemployers 743
  Occupational safety 649, 652, 654
  Producer price indexes .....:............ 933
  Profits 731, 776
  Residential 941, 942, 943, 944
  Shipments, receipts 731, 733, 736, 740, 741, 742, 743, 751, 1318
  Unions 657
  Value, work 932, 935, 936, 937, 938
  Women-owned businesses 751
Construction machinery, manufacturing:
  Earnings 631, 987
  Employees 631, 987
  Inventories 995
  Productivity 632
  Shipments 995
Construction materials. See Building materials.
Consumer:
  Consumer complaints against airlines . 1067
  Consumer goods 719
  Credit . 1164, 1168, 1169, 1172, 1188, 1189
    Delinquency rates 1185
  Electronics 1014, 1015, 1041
  Expenditures ...., 676, 677
    Books 1134
    Communications 1125
    Entertainment 1233

Consumer: —Con.
  Food ...., 676, 677, 820
  Housing ...., 676, 677
  Medical care .. 129, 130, 132, 133, 138, 676, 677, 679
  Metropolitan areas 677
  Reading material 1138, 1233
  Sporting goods 1253
Consumer payment systems 1187
Consumer price indexes 712, 713, 714, 715
  By commodity group 713, 715
  Foreign countries 717, 1340
  Medical care 137, 713, 715
  Purchasing power of the dollar 712
  Year-to-year changes 637
Consumption. See individual commodities.
Contraception use 101
Convenience stores 1026, 1038
Cook Islands. See Foreign countries.
Cookies 715
Cooking oils consumption 214
Copper:
  Consumption 872
  Foreign trade 872, 877
  Prices 872, 873
  Production and value 871
    World production 875, 1361
Copyrights registration 765
Corn:
  Acreage 834, 835
    Genetically modified seed plantings . 832
    Organic 810
  Consumption 214, 215
  Farm marketings, sales 813, 816, 819
  Foreign trade ... 828, 829, 834, 1301, 1358
  Pesticide usage 833
  Prices 834, 835
  Production 828, 834, 835, 841
    World production 828, 1353
  Supply and disappearance 834
Coronary procedures 178
Corporate business sector 737, 738
  Political action committees ... 425, 426, 427
Corporations:
  Capital 739
  Credit market debt outstanding 1165
  Dividend payments 775
  Finances . 731, 732, 733, 734, 735, 736, 737, 738, 739, 740, 741, 1162, 1164, 1216
  Manufacturing 998
  Nonfinancial 737, 738
  Philanthropy 581
  Profits .. 731, 775, 776, 777, 778, 997, 998
  Public confidence 416
  Receipts 731
  Sales 736, 740, 741, 997
  Stocks and bonds 1194, 1195
  Taxes:
    Corporate income tax 775
    Returns 731, 732, 739
Correctional institutions (see also Prisons and prisoners):
  Employment 615, 617
  Expenditures 454, 455
  Facilities 348
  Prisoners 77, 78, 348, 349
Cosmetics, perfume, etc.:
  Advertising expenditures 1275
  Foreign trade 1301

NOTE: Index citations refer to **table** numbers, not page numbers.

Costa Rica. See Foreign countries.	
Cost-of-living indexes	716
Cote d'Ivoire. See Foreign countries.	
Cotton:	
Acreage	834, 835
Genetically modified seed plantings	832
Organic	810
Consumption	1001
Farm marketings, sales	813, 817, 819
Foreign trade	823, 828, 829, 834, 1001, 1301
Pesticide usage	833
Prices	818, 834, 835
Production	821, 828, 834, 835
World	828, 1321, 1357
Supply and disappearance	834
County governments	431, 432, 433
Debt	466
Elected officials	417, 418
Employees, earnings, payroll	474
Finances of county government	465, 466
Couriers and messengers:	
Earnings	631, 1056, 1057
Employees	631, 1056, 1057
Establishments	1057
Revenue	1110
Courts	337, 338
District courts, U.S.	338, 339
Juvenile court cases handled	342
Public officials, prosecutions	340
Sentencing	339
Supreme Court, U.S.	337
Cows (see also Dairy products)	845, 848, 849
Crabs	865, 867, 868
Crack cocaine	201
Cranberries	842
Credit cards	1039, 1169, 1170, 1185, 1187, 1189, 1190, 1191
Credit intermediation industry	
Earnings	742, 1161
Employees	742, 1161
Establishments	742, 1161
Receipts	742
Credit markets	1164, 1189
Federal participation	484
Credit unions:	
Earnings	1161
Employees	1161
Establishments	1161, 1173, 1181
Finances	1162, 1173, 1181, 1189, 1216
Individual Retirement Accounts	1218
Crew	1250
Crime (see also Criminal victimization and Law enforcement):	
Assault	305, 306, 307, 308
Average value lost	318
Burglary	305, 306, 307, 308, 318, 324
Child abuse and neglect	344, 345
DNA crime laboratories	335
Drug abuse violations	329, 339
Hate crimes	319, 320
Homicides, race and sex	313
Larceny-theft	305, 306, 307, 308, 318
Motor vehicle theft	305, 306, 307, 308, 309, 318, 324
Murder, murder circumstances	305, 306, 307, 308, 309, 316
Place and time of occurrence	324
Police officers assaulted, killed	336

Crime (see also Criminal victimization and Law enforcement): —Con.	
Property crime	305, 306, 307, 308
Rape, forcible	305, 306, 307, 308, 314
Robbery	305, 306, 307, 308, 318
Shoplifting	318
Students and schools	232, 233
Violent crime	305, 306, 307, 308, 309, 316
Workplace	653, 654
Criminal victimization	232, 233, 317, 321, 322, 323, 324
Households	324
Place of occurrence	324
Violent	323, 316
Weapons involved	321, 323, 324
Workplace	653, 654
Croaker	865
Croatia. See Foreign countries.	
Crops (see also Farms and individual crops):	
Acreage	831, 834
Farm marketings, sales	812, 813, 817
Foreign trade	827, 829, 834
Prices	818, 834
Production	821, 834
Productivity	831
Supply and disappearance	834
Cross country (running)	1249, 1250
Crossword puzzles	1244
Crude materials:	
Producer price indexes	718, 719
Production	911, 1321
Crude oil (see also Petroleum and products):	
Foreign trade	879, 896, 909, 910, 911
Prices	871, 879, 905
Production	878, 879
World production	883
Cryptosporidiosis	190
Cuba. See Foreign countries.	
Cuban population	22, 23, 28, 33, 46
Business owners	750
Commuting to work	47
Disability status	47
Educational attainment	47, 227
Foreign born	47
Labor force	589
Mobility status	47
Nativity	47
Occupation	47
Cucumbers	215, 813, 826, 841
Currency:	
Foreign exchange rate	1377
Personal saving component	668
Supply	1192
Customs outlays	479
Customs regions, imports and exports	1297
Cyclones	386
Cyprus. See Foreign countries.	
Czech Republic. See Foreign countries.	

D

Dairy products (see also individual products):	
Calcium source	213
Cholesterol source	213
Consumer expenditures	676, 679
Consumption	214, 216, 826
Farm marketings, sales	813, 826, 849
Foreign trade	825, 826, 827, 1301
Iron source	213

NOTE: Index citations refer to **table** numbers, not page numbers.

	Table
Dairy products (see also individual products): —Con.	
Manufacture	849
Prices	818
Production	821, 849
Dairy products manufacturing	632, 987
Dance	1237, 1240
Dart throwing	1247
Data processing services. See Computer programming and data processing services.	
Dates	842
Day care. See Child day care services.	
Death care services	631, 1277
Death penalty	354, 355
Deaths and death rates (see also Accidents and fatalities):	
Age and sex	107, 108, 109, 110, 117, 120, 125
AIDS	115, 193
Black population	113, 117, 193
Cancer	115, 117, 119, 125
Cause	115, 116, 117, 118, 119, 120, 121, 122, 193, 1058, 1112
Fetal and neonatal	113
Foreign countries	1326
Heart disease	115, 117, 118, 119, 120, 125
Industrial	649, 650
Infant	113, 114
Injuries	125
Island areas of the U.S.	1306
Maternal	113
Military deaths	522
Race	107, 108, 113, 114, 117, 120
States	19
Suicide	115, 117, 118, 119, 123
Summary	83
Traffic fatalities	1058, 1097, 1098, 1099, 1100, 1102, 1103, 1104
Weather related	387
Workers deaths	650
Debit cards	1186, 1187, 1188
Debt (see also Loans and mortgages):	
City	461, 464
Consumer	1172, 1189
County governments	466
Farm	814, 815
Federal government	475, 485, 492
Foreign countries	1382
Households	1164, 1169
Local governments	439, 442, 443, 449, 450, 458
State and local government	442, 449
Highways	1083
State government	431, 448, 449, 454, 455, 456
Deductions (taxes)	490, 492, 579
Defense, Department of (see also Army, Navy, and Air Force):	
Budget authority, outlays	476, 477, 479, 509
Contract awards, by states	513
Employees, civilian	513, 517
Expenditures	509, 510, 511, 513
Health and medical care	128, 129, 131
Funds available and outlays	511
Military bases	518
Military personnel	517, 519, 523, 524, 525
Military retirees	517
Property, real and personal	507

	Table
Degrees conferred (see also individual field)	298, 299, 300, 301, 302, 303, 792
Salary offers	297
Delaware. See State data.	
Delinquency. See Juveniles.	
Denmark. See Foreign countries.	
Dentists	160, 615
Charges and expenditures for	129, 130, 133, 137
Dental schools, students, and graduates	164, 303
Medicaid payments, recipients	146
Offices	158, 159
Deoxyribonucleic acid (DNA) crime laboratories	335
Department stores:	
Earnings	631, 1025, 1026, 1029
Employees	631, 1025, 1026, 1029
Establishments	1025, 1026, 1029
Inventories	1031
Productivity	632
Sales	1026, 1027, 1029, 1031, 1032, 1271
Deposits. See banks.	
Dermatologists	162
Diabetes	115, 117, 118, 119, 168, 176
Diagnostic health procedures	178
Diamonds	872, 1361
Foreign trade	1301
World production	1361
Diatomite	871, 872
Dietitians and therapists	615
Diphtheria	191
Direct deposit	1186
Direct mail advertising expenditures	1274
Disability	188
American Indian, Alaska Native population	43
Asian population	43
Beneficiaries	537, 543
Benefits paid	542, 543
Blacks	40
Children	197, 198, 199, 204
Cities	199
Elderly	38, 197, 198, 199
Food stamp participants	570, 571
Government transfer payments	534, 535, 536
Labor force status	613
Medicaid payments and or recipients	146, 557
Metropolitan areas	198
Native Hawaiian, Other Pacific Islander population	43
Payments	542
Persons with disability	38, 197, 198, 199, 557
Poverty	706
Public assistance recipients and/or payments	557, 561
Social Security recipients	543, 544
States	197
Students with disabilities	261, 285
Supplemental Security Income recipients and payments	561
Veterans receiving compensation	531, 533
Vocational rehabilitation	558
Disability Insurance Trust Fund (Social Security)	542
Disasters (tornadoes, floods, etc.)	386

NOTE: Index citations refer to **table** numbers, not page numbers.

Table	
Discount rates, Federal Reserve Bank of New York	1193
Diseases (see also specific diseases and Deaths and death rates)	176, 190, 206
Deaths from	115, 117, 118, 119, 120, 193
Dishwashers	977
Diskettes	1012, 1014, 1015
Disposable personal income (see also Income and National income)	666, 672, 1172
Distance education	286
District Courts, U.S.	338, 339
District of Columbia. See State data.	
Dividends:	
Corporation	775
Individual income tax returns	493
National and/or personal income components	668
Persons receiving income	537
Railroad stock	1112
Divorce. See Marriage and divorce and Marital status.	
Djibouti. See Foreign countries.	
DNA crime laboratories	335
Doctors, M.D.'s. See Physicians.	
Dogs	1242, 1245
Domestic service employees	615
Dominica. See Foreign countries.	
Dominican Republic. See Foreign countries.	
Dormitories, college	77, 78
Dow-Jones stock indices	1204, 1205
Drinking places. See Food services and drinking places.	
Driving (see also Motor vehicles and transportation):	
Crashes	1101, 1105
Fatal accidents	1058, 1099
Intoxicated	325, 361, 1106
Licensed drivers	1088
Traffic offense	325
Drug stores and proprietary stores. See Pharmacies and drug stores.	
Drugs (illegal):	
Arrests	325, 327, 329
Court cases	339
Drug abuse treatment	200
Enforcement activities	327, 330, 1288
Juveniles	342, 343
Usage	201, 202, 328, 329
Drugs and medicines (see also Pharmaceutical and medicine manufacturing):	
Advertising expenditures	1275
Consumer price indexes	137, 715
Drug abuse treatment	200
Expenditures for	127, 129, 130, 131, 133, 136, 138
Foreign trade	1301
Medicaid payments	146
Outpatient prescription benefits	156
Price indexes	137, 715
Retail sales	135, 1043
Drunk driving, arrests	325
Drycleaning and laundry services:	
Earnings	631, 1265
Employees	631, 1265
Establishments	1265
Productivity	632
Receipts	1277
Dryers, clothes	977
Dwellings. See Housing and housing units and Households or families.	

E

Table	
Earnings:	
Agriculture, forestry, fisheries	745
Airlines	1059
College faculty	294
College graduates, starting salaries	297
Construction industry	745, 746
Educational attainment	230, 695
Employment covered by social insurance	541, 556, 559
Family type	537
Foreign born population	54
Government employees:	
Federal	467, 468, 497, 498
State and local	467, 468, 472
Income tax returns (reported totals)	490, 491, 492, 493
Industry	635, 637, 745, 746
Manufacturing	745, 746, 985, 987, 991
Metropolitan areas	640
Mineral industries	870
Minimum wage workers	644, 645
Mining industry	745
Minority-owned businesses	750, 753, 754, 755
Municipal employees	473
Occupations	638, 641, 642
Personal income	668, 670, 671, 672, 673
Physicians	166
Private employer firms	746, 747, 749
Railroads	1112
Retail trade	745, 746
School teachers	240, 249, 250, 263
Seamen	1073
States	639
Telephone systems, employees	1148, 1149
Transportation	745, 746
Union members	638, 657
Wholesale trade	745, 746
Women-owned businesses	750, 751
Earth sciences, degrees conferred	792
Eating and drinking places. See Food services and drinking places.	
E-commerce. See Electronic commerce.	
E coli 0157:H7	190
Economic assistance, foreign	1292
Economic growth rates	662, 1335
Economic indicators	770, 771, 1336
Foreign countries	1335, 1336
Economists, labor force	615
Ecuador. See Foreign countries.	
Education:	
Adult education	304
Advanced placement exams	267
Alternative school	241, 245
American College Testing (ACT) Program	265
Arts education	1238
Attainment	37, 39, 227, 228, 229, 231
American Indian, Alaska Native population	43
Asian population	43
Asian and Pacific Islander population	227, 228
Black population	39, 40, 227, 228, 229, 271, 272
Cigarette smoking	203
Congressional districts	1384

NOTE: Index citations refer to **table** numbers, not page numbers.

Education: —Con.
  Elderly 37, 54
  Foreign born 51, 54
  Foreign countries 1331
  General Education Development
    certificates (GED's) 274
  Hispanic origin population . 39, 46, 227,
    228, 229, 271, 279
  Income 685, 689
  Internet access 1127, 1156, 1158
  Island area of the U.S. 1310
  Labor force status 591, 601, 626
  Media users 1127
  Native Hawaiian, Other Pacific Islander
    population 43
  Occupation 618
  Poverty 706
  Race 39, 44, 272
  Recreation activities 1254
  States 231
  Women 228, 229
  Catholic schools 262
  Charitable contributions 580
  Charter schools 239
  Community service (students) 586
  Computer use in schools 256, 258, 259
  Construction, value 937, 938
  Continuing education 1332
  Credit card use 233
  Crime incidents 232, 323
  Degrees conferred 298, 299, 300, 301,
    302, 303
    Non-resident aliens 299
    Salary offers 297
  Dental schools, students, graduates 164
  Disabled students 261, 285
  Distance education 286
  Employment, state and local
    government 471
  Employment status of high school
    graduates and dropouts 273
  Enrollment .. 217, 219, 221, 222, 223, 224,
    225, 237, 240, 242, 244, 246, 247,
    276, 277, 279, 282
    Catholic schools 262
    Foreign-born students 226
    Homeschooled 243
    Island areas of U.S. 1312, 1313
    Preprimary schools 223, 237
    States 244, 279
  Expenditure (see also Finances):
    Assistance for persons with limited
      income 539, 540
    City government 464
    County government 466
    Local government 458
    Private 218
    State and local government ... 442, 454,
      456
  Federal aid .. 220, 289, 433, 476, 534, 535,
    536, 785
  Federal assistance to families 537
  Foreign language enrollment 268, 283
  General Education Development (GEDs) . 274
  Grants to institutions from foundations . 584
  Handicapped students 261
  Higher education institutions:
    Aid received 291

Education: —Con.
  Beginning salary offers, college
    graduates 297
  Charges for room and board 292
  Costs 287
  Degrees conferred .. 219, 298, 299, 300,
    301, 302, 303, 792
    Non-resident aliens 299
  Dormitories 77, 78
  Enrollment 217, 219, 223, 224, 225,
    276, 277, 278, 279, 281
    College freshmen 284
    Disabled 285
    Distance education 286
    Foreign-born students 226
    Foreign languages 283
    Foreign students 278, 281
    Projections 217, 219
    States 279
    U.S. service schools 279
  Expenditures 218, 293
    Price indexes 288
    Scientific purposes, by type 788
  Faculty 277, 294, 295, 296
  Finances 218, 219, 277, 290
  Financial aid 289
  Libraries 1153, 1154
  Number 277, 279
  Price indexes 288
  Tuition and fees 292
  State appropriations 290
  Voluntary financial support 293
  High school dropouts ... 231, 271, 272, 273
  Homeschooled 243
  Internet access 256, 257, 258, 259
  Island areas of the U.S. 1312, 1313
  Loans and grants, federal government .. 289
  Medical schools, students, graduates ... 164
  Montessori schools 262
  National Assessment of Educational
    Progress Tests (NAEP) 266
  Nursing programs, students, graduates . 164
  Optometry schools, students, graduates . 164
  Parental involvement 234
  Pharmacy schools, students, graduates .. 164
  Philanthropy 580, 581, 584
  Price indexes 715
  Private elementary and secondary schools:
    Computer use 257, 258
    Elementary and secondary 217, 218,
      223, 225, 248, 262
    Expenditures 218
    Internet access 257, 258
    Teachers 262, 263
  Public elementary and secondary schools:
    Alternative education 241, 245
    Charter schools 239
    Computer use 256, 258, 259
    Crimes against students 232
    Enrollment 217, 219, 223, 225, 240,
      244, 246
    Projections 217, 219
    Size 242
    States 244
    Finances 218, 219, 254, 255
    High school graduates 219, 269
    Internet access 256
    Number 242

NOTE: Index citations refer to **table** numbers, not page numbers.

Table

Education: —Con.
  Personnel 252
    Salaries 251
    Price indexes 253
    Special education programs 241, 261
    Teachers 219, 240, 249, 250, 252
      Projections 219
    Vocational education 241
  Scholastic Assessment Test 264
  School activities 234
  School districts 432
  School years completed. See Education attainment.
  Special education programs 261, 262
  State data:
    Elementary and secondary . 244, 250, 255, 269
    Higher education 279, 290
  Teachers:
    Catholic schools 262
    Elementary and secondary . 240, 248, 250
    Employment projections 219, 617
    Higher education 277, 294
    Internet use 259
  Tests:
    Advanced placement exams 267
    American College Testing (ACT) Program 265
    National Assessment of Educational Progress (NAEP) Tests 266
    Scholastic Assessment Tests (SAT) ... 264
  Vocational education 241
  Volunteers 585
Educational expense indexes 715
Educational services:
  Advertising expenditures 1275
  Capital 769
  Earnings 631, 742, 745
  Employees 631, 742, 745
  Establishments 742, 743, 745
  Finances 733, 736
  Gross domestic product 660
  Industry 742
  Nonemployers 743
  Occupational safety 652
  Receipts 733, 736, 740, 741, 742, 743
Education and health services:
  Earnings 629, 631, 636
  Employees 629, 630, 631
  Hours 629
Eggs (see also Poultry):
  Cholesterol source 213
  Consumption 214
  Farm marketings, sales 813
  Iron (dietary), source 213
  Prices 715, 727, 851
  Production 821, 851
Egypt. See Foreign countries.
Elderly (see also Population):
  Activity limitation 195, 196
  Adult education 304
  Age and/or sex 11, 12, 13, 16, 37
  AIDS 192
  Assets 709, 1167
  Black population 16, 39, 37
  Book purchasing 1138
  Cancer 117, 118, 176
  Cerebrovascular disease 118, 176

Table

Elderly (see also Population): —Con.
  Charitable contributions 579
  Children under 18 years old living with elderly parents 85
  Cigarette smoking 203
  Community care facilities 158
  Computer use 1127, 1156
  Congressional districts 1384
  Correctional institutions 77
  Deaths and death rates 118, 120
  Dentists, visits to 165
  Disability population 38, 197, 198, 199
  Education, attainment 37, 229
  Elections, voter registration and turnout . 419
  Food stamps, programs 540, 570, 571
  Foreign-born population 54
  Group quarters population 77
  Health care expenditures 138, 152
  Health insurance coverage ... 145, 152, 154
  Heart disease 117, 120, 176
  Height distribution 208
  Hispanic origin population 13, 16, 46
  Home health and hospice care 182, 183
  Homeownership 954, 963, 966, 973, 974, 976
  Homes for the aged 180
  Hospital use 77, 168, 169, 175, 176
  Households 67, 68, 75
  Income 537
  Internet access 622, 1127, 1158
  Job search 622
  Labor force 588, 590, 595, 621
    Disabled 613
    Displaced workers 612
    Employed . 600, 601, 606, 607, 608, 610
    Participation rates 588, 595
    Reason not in 614
    Tenure with employer 610
    Unemployed 621
  Library programs 1157
  Living arrangements 37, 64
  Marital status 37, 63
  Media users 1127
  Medicaid payments and recipients . 145, 146, 147
  Medicare program 139, 140, 142
  Mobility status 34
  Mutual fund owners 1213, 1214
  Nurses 161
  Nursing homes 77, 180, 185
  Overweight 209
  Persons living alone (one-person households) 37, 76
  Physical activity 210
  Physician visits 165, 167, 168
  Pneumonia 117, 118, 176
  Poverty 37, 703, 699
  Projections 12
  Property owners 963, 966, 973, 976
  Public assistance 537
  Recreation activities . 1233, 1237, 1239, 1240, 1247, 1254
  Senior citizens communities 974
  Social Security beneficiaries, payments . 543
  States 20
  Stock ownership 1210, 1212
  Suicide 117
  TV viewing 1127

NOTE: Index citations refer to **table** numbers, not page numbers.

Index 989

Table	Table

Elderly (see also Population): —Con.
    Victimization 322
    Volunteer work 585
    Voter registration and turnout 419
Elections:
    Black elected officials 417
    Campaign finances . 423, 424, 425, 427, 428, 429, 430
    Congressional 401, 403, 404
    Gubernatorial 411, 412
    Hispanic origin officials 418
    Political action committees (PAC) 425, 426, 427
    Political party identification 421
    Presidential .. 396, 397, 398, 399, 400, 427
    State legislatures 413, 414
    Voter registration 419, 420, 421, 422
    Voter turnout 419, 420, 422
    Votes cast 398, 399, 401, 403, 404, 420
    Voting-age population 419, 420, 422
    Women in public office 415
Electric light and power industry (see also Utilities and Electricity):
    Capital expenditures 382, 767
    Construction costs 934, 936
    Customers 922, 927
    Emissions 373, 374
    Finances 923
    General capability 914, 915
    General capacity, installed 917
    Industrial production index 772
    Multinational companies 781
    Ownership, class of 914
    Peak load 915
    Pollution abatement 382
    Water use 368
Electricity (see also Electric light and power industry):
    Capability 914, 915, 921
    Commercial buildings 904, 982
    Consumption . 902, 903, 904, 914, 916, 922
    Expenditures ......, 679, 900, 901, 902, 908
    Foreign countries 1366, 1367
    Hydroelectric power 895, 898, 914, 925
    Nonutility producers 921
    Nuclear 895, 898, 914, 918, 919, 1131, 1366, 1367
    Price indexes 715, 721
    Prices 907, 914
    Production 914, 917, 921
        World production 1366
    Residential 885, 902, 903, 922
    Sales 916, 922
Electrical equipment and manufacturing (See also Computer and electronic products manufacturing):
    Capital 382, 766
    Earnings 631, 985, 987, 992, 1123
    Electronic commerce 989
    Employees .. 631, 985, 987, 988, 992, 1123
    Energy consumption 906
    Establishments 985
    Finances 776, 778
    Foreign trade 1304
    Gross domestic product 660, 1122
    Industrial production index 772
    Inventories 994, 995
    Mergers and acquisitions 759
    Multinational companies 781

Electrical equipment and manufacturing (See also Computer and electronic products manufacturing): —Con.
    Occupational safety 652
    Pollution abatement 382
    Productivity 632
    Profits 777, 778
    Research and development 793, 794
    Shipments 987, 989, 994, 995
    Toxic chemical releases 379
    Value added 995
Electronic commerce (e-commerce):
    Business sales 1041
    Consumer sales 1041, 1042
    Manufacturing 989
    Retail trade 1043, 1044, 1045
    Services 1268
    Wholesale 1046
Electronic funds transfer payment 1187
Electronic goods:
    Sales, shipments, receipts . 1011, 1014, 1015, 1043
    Foreign trade 1301
Electronic instruments manufacturing . 631, 632
Electronic shopping and mail order houses . 631, 632, 1026, 1027
Electronics and appliance stores:
    Earnings 631, 1025, 1026
    Electronic commerce 1045
    Employees 631, 1025, 1026
    Establishments 1025, 1026, 1033
    Nonemployers 1033
    Productivity 632
    Purchases 1030
    Sales 1026, 1027, 1029, 1033, 1045
El Salvador. See Foreign countries.
Emergency medicine, departments ... 162, 167, 169
Emphysema 117, 176
Employee benefits 648, 155, 157, 647
    Government employees 469, 470
Employees. See Business enterprise and individual industries.
Employee turnover 504
Employment service industry 631
Endangered species 385
Energy (see also Electric light and power industry and various fuel types):
    Air pollutant emissions 374
        Foreign countries 1329, 1330
    Assistance for persons with limited income 539, 540
    Commercial buildings 902, 982
    Consumption . 895, 897, 898, 899, 902, 903, 1363
        Characteristic of household 902, 903
        End-use sector 897, 898
        Foreign countries 1363, 1365
        Renewable sources 899, 925
        Source 895
    End-use sector 897, 898, 901, 906
    Expenditures 900, 901, 902, 903, 904
        Commercial 900, 901, 952
        Residential 900, 901, 903
        Type of structure 902, 903
    Federal outlays 479
    Price indexes:
        Consumer 713, 714, 715

NOTE: Index citations refer to **table** numbers, not page numbers.

	Table
Energy (see also Electric light and power industry and various fuel types):—Con.	
Export	729
Import	728
Producer	719, 720
Prices	905, 907
Solar collectors, manufacturer's shipments	924
Engineering and architectural services:	
Earnings	631, 742, 1265
Employees	631, 742, 1265
Establishments	742, 1265
Receipts	742
Engineers and scientists (see also individual fields):	
Degrees conferred	300, 301, 302, 792
Employment	615, 796
Research and development	788
Salary offers	297
Entertainment (see also Arts, entertainment, and recreation):	
Consumer price indexes	715
Personal expenditures	667, 678, 679, 715, 1233
Environment (see also pollution)	
Environmental industry, agencies	384
Wetlands	364
Volunteers	585
Environmental Protection Agency:	
Employment	500
Waste treatment facilities, Federal aid to state and local governments	439
Equatorial Guinea. See Foreign countries	
Eritrea. See Foreign countries.	
Eskimo population	44
Establishments. See Business enterprise and individual industries.	
Estate and gift taxes	481, 489
Estonia. See Foreign countries.	
Ethane	884
Ethiopia. See Foreign countries.	
Europe. See Foreign countries.	
European Union. See foreign countries.	
Evaporated and condensed milk	214, 849
Excise taxes	481, 488, 489
Executions	354, 355
Executive Office of the President (federal)	498, 500
Exercise equipment	1234, 1253, 1254
Expectation of life (average lifetime)	105, 106, 107
Foreign countries	1326
Projections	105
Expenditures. See individual subjects.	
Expenditures of state and local government. See individual governmental units.	
Expenditures of U.S. Government	434, 435, 436, 437, 438, 439, 443, 444, 445, 479, 1081, 1291, 1292, 1293
Aid to the arts and humanities	1236
Aid to Island areas	439, 1311
Aid to state and local government	437, 438, 439
By function	438
Highway trust fund	439, 1081
Atomic energy defense activities	510
Budget outlays	475, 476, 477, 479
By function	479, 539, 540
By source of funds	481
Capital outlay	444, 445

	Table
Expenditures of U.S. Government —Con.	
Contract awards	512, 513
Education. See federal aid to education.	
Food programs, federal	539, 540
Health	131, 539, 540
Hospitals	170
Justice	341
Land and buildings	507
Military personnel	516, 524
National defense	509, 510, 511
Outlays, by agency	478
Outlays, by function	479
Payments for public assistance	539, 540, 555
Payrolls	467, 468, 497, 498, 499, 503
Public debt	475
Public roads	439, 1081
Research and development	782, 783, 784, 785, 787
Schools	220
Science/space	799
Space programs	798, 801, 802
Veterans benefits. See Veterans affairs.	
Vocational rehabilitation	558
Explosive material shipments	1078
Exports. See Foreign trade.	
Express mail	1117, 1118
Eye care price indexes	715
Eyeglasses and contact lenses	129, 130, 133

F

	Table
Fabricated metal product manufacturing:	
Capital	382, 766, 1290
Earnings	631, 985, 987, 992
Electronic commerce	989
Employees	631, 985, 987, 992
Energy consumption	906
Establishments	985
Finance	778, 1007
Foreign trade	1007, 1304
Gross domestic product	660, 984
Industrial production index	772
Occupational safety	652
Pollution abatement	382
Productivity	632
Profits	777, 778
Shipments	987, 989, 994, 995
Toxic chemical releases	379
Fabrics. See Textile mill products.	
Families. See Households.	
Farm mortgage loans	527, 1182
Farmers and farm workers:	
Employment	615, 822
Indexes of farm inputs	821
Unemployment	625
Farms:	
Acreage	805, 806, 808, 809, 810
Cropland	810, 831
Crops harvested (see also individual crops)	831, 834, 835, 841, 1360
Agrichemicals	818, 821
Agricultural products:	
Exports	1295
Foreign countries, production	1355, 1357
Prices. See Prices received by farmers.	
Railroad car loadings	1113, 1114
Waterborne commerce	1071
World production	1321, 1353, 1355, 1357

NOTE: Index citations refer to **table** numbers, not page numbers.

Table

Farms: —Con.
  Assets and liabilities 814, 815, 1162
  Capital stocks, farm housing 978
  Construction value, farm nonresidential . 936
  Contracts 819
  Corporate 806
  Crops (see also individual crops):
    Acreage 831, 834
    Fruits and nuts 842
    Income 813, 817
    Production 819, 821, 828, 831, 834
      World 1321, 1355, 1357
    Vegetables 841
  Debt 814, 815
    Mortgages outstanding 1182
  Expenses 812
  Farm products sold, marketing receipts . 811, 812, 813, 816, 817, 819
  Government payments to farmers . 811, 812, 817
  Gross farm product 660, 811
  Housing, rental value 811, 812
  Income 811, 812, 813, 815, 817
  Individual or family 806
  Input indexes 821
  Inventories, change in 811
  Labor expenses 812, 818
  Labor inputs 821, 822
  Machinery and motor vehicles . 812, 814, 821
  Mortgage loans 1182
  National income, origin in 811
  Number of farms 805, 806, 808, 809
  Operator characteristics 807
  Organic acreage, livestock 810
  Parity ratio 818
  Partnerships 806
  Prices:
    Crops 818, 834
    Livestock and products 818, 844
  Real estate, input indexes 821
  Taxes 811, 818
  Tenure of operator 806, 807
  Value:
    Farm land and buildings 814
    Farm products sold, marketing receipts 811, 812, 813, 817, 819
Faroe Islands. See Foreign countries.
Fatalities. See Accidents and fatalities.
Fat, nutrient for consumption 212
Fats. See Lard, Margarine, and Oils.
Federal agency debt 1195
Federal aid to education 220, 438, 439, 442
  Elementary and secondary education ... 220
  Higher education institutions 220, 277
  Research and development .. 783, 789, 790
  Science and engineering 788, 789
Federal aid to state and local government . 437, 438, 439, 442
Federal budget. See Expenditures of U.S. Government.
Federal debt 485
Federal employees retirement trust fund. See Government.
Federal funds, summary distribution by state 487
Federal government. See Government.
Federal Government finances. See Receipts and Expenditures of U.S. Government.

Table

Federal Housing Administration, mortgage loans 1182, 1184
Federal National Mortgage Association loans 1182
Federal real property 360
Federated States of Micronesia. See Foreign countries.
Feed. See Grain.
Feldspar 871, 872, 875
Female householder. See Households or families.
Female population. See Women.
Fencing 1250
Fertility rate 88, 89
Fertilizers:
  Farm expenditures for 812
  Foreign trade 1301
  Prices 818
  Shipments 1007
Fetal deaths 113
Fibers 1001
Fiber, dietary 212
Fiji. See Foreign countries.
Filberts 842
Field hockey 1249, 1250
Figure skating 1243, 1247
Filipino population 23, 750
Filling stations. See Gasoline service stations.
Finance 674, 1162, 1164, 1166
  Consumer installment credit 1189
  Corporate funds 737
Finance, insurance, and real estate industry:
  Capital 767, 769, 1199
  Earnings 629, 631, 635, 636, 742, 745, 746, 751, 1161
  Employees 601, 605, 619, 629, 630, 631, 742, 745, 746, 751, 783, 1161
  Establishments 742, 743, 745, 1161
  Finances 731, 733, 736, 1162, 1173, 1189, 1314
  Foreign investments in U.S. 1285, 1286
  Gross domestic product 660, 664, 1160, 1314
  Industry 742
  Mergers and acquisitions 759
  Minority-owned businesses . 752, 753, 754, 755
  Multinational companies 780, 781
  Nonemployers 743
  Profits 731, 776
  Sales or receipts .. 733, 736, 740, 741, 742, 743, 751
  Union membership 657
  Women-owned businesses 751
Financial institution. See Banks, commercial; Credit unions; and Savings institutions.
Finished consumer goods, producer price indexes 719
Finland. See Foreign countries.
Firearms 333, 1064, 1253, 1254
  Deaths 333
Fire departments. See Public safety.
Fire insurance 1224
Fires and property loss 356, 357, 358
  Accidental deaths 358
Firms. See Business enterprise, and individual types of business and industry.
Fish (see also individual species):
  Aquaculture 813, 866
  Canning and preserving 868

NOTE: Index citations refer to **table** numbers, not page numbers.

Fish (see also individual species): —Con.
  Catch, quantity and value ... 863, 864, 865, 1354
  Cholesterol source 213
  Consumer expenditures 676, 678, 679
  Consumption 214
  Foreign trade 863, 1304
  Iron (dietary), source 213
  Prices 715, 864
  Production and value, processed products 866, 868
  Supply 863
Fishing, commercial:
  Catch, quantity, value . 863, 864, 865, 1354
  Foreign trade 1355
  Products 863, 868
Fishing and hunting ... 1247, 1251, 1252, 1253
Flax production 1321
Floods 386, 387
Floriculture 813, 838
Florida. See State data.
Florists:
  Earnings 631, 1025
  Employees 631, 1025, 1026
  Establishments 1025, 1026
  Productivity 632
  Sales 1026
Flounder 865, 868
Flour, consumption (see also Grain) 214
Flowers 838, 1241
Flu 115, 117
Fluorspar 871, 872, 875
Food (see also individual commodities and industry data below):
  Car loadings 1114
  Commercial vegetables 841
  Consumption 214, 215, 216, 826
  Expenditures 676, 678, 820, 1040
  Fish products 676
  Food costs 716, 726, 727
  Hunger, insecurity 211
  Prices (see also individual commodities). 713, 715, 721, 726, 727
  Sales 1043
  World production 1353, 1355
Food and beverage stores:
  Earnings 631, 742, 1024, 1025, 1026
  Electronic commerce 1045
  Employees 631, 742, 1024, 1025, 1026
  Establishments . 742, 1024, 1025, 1026, 1033, 1038
  Finances 733, 778
  Inventories 1031
  Nonemployers 1033
  Productivity 632
  Profits 778
  Purchases 1030
  Sales ... 733, 742, 1024, 1027, 1029, 1031, 1032, 1033, 1038, 1040
    Prescription drugs 135
Food insecurity 211
Food manufacturing:
  Capital 379, 382, 766
  Earnings 631, 985, 987, 992
  Employees 631, 985, 987, 992
  Energy consumption 906
  Establishments 985
  Finances 778
  Foreign trade 1304

Food manufacturing: —Con.
  Gross domestic product 660, 984
  Industrial production index 772
  Mergers and acquisitions 759
  Multinational companies 780, 781
  Occupational safety 651, 652
  Patents 763
  Pollution abatement 382
  Profits 777, 778
  Research and development 794
  Sales or shipments 987, 989, 994, 995
  Toxic chemical releases 379
Food services and drinking places:
  Earnings 631, 742, 1265
  Employees 631, 742, 1265
  Establishments 742, 1024, 1265
  Finances 733
  Mergers and acquisitions 759
  Productivity 632
  Sales 733, 742, 1027, 1040
Food stamps, programs 535, 538, 539, 540, 568, 569, 570, 571, 1187
Football 1243, 1245, 1249, 1250
Footwear:
  Consumer expenditures 678, 679
  Foreign trade 1003, 1301
  Sales or shipments 1003
Foreign aid or assistance 1291, 1293, 1381
Foreign born population . 44, 48, 51, 52, 53, 54
  Age 51, 54
  American Indian, Alaska Native population 43
  Asian population 43
  Black population 40
  Cities 50
  Educational attainment 51, 54
  Earnings 54
  Foreign countries 1324
  Households 54
  Housing tenure 54
  Income 51, 54
  Language spoken at home 56
  Marital status 54
  Metropolitan areas 49
  Native Hawaiian, Other Pacific Islander population 43
  Poverty status 54
  States 48
Foreign companies, U.S. affiliates .. 1286, 1287, 1288
Foreign countries:
  Agricultural trade 830, 1299
  Aid to developing countries 1291, 1292, 1293, 1381
  Air pollution emissions 1329
  Area 1322
  Armed Forces personnel 1383
  Balance of payments 1378
  Births and birth rates 1326
  Carbon dioxide emissions 1330
  Cigarettes 1359
  Coal production . 889, 890, 1362, 1363, 1364, 1365
  College students enrolled in U.S. 281
  Communications 1371, 1372
  Consumer price index 717, 1340
  Crude oil 909, 910
  Death and death rates 1326, 1370

NOTE: Index citations refer to **table** numbers, not page numbers.

Index 993

U.S. Census Bureau, Statistical Abstract of the United States: 2003

Table

Foreign countries: —Con.
- Debt 1382
- Economic indicators 1335, 1336
- Education 1331, 1332
- Electricity generation 1366
- Employment and labor force ... 1336, 1347, 1348, 1349, 1350, 1351, 1352
- Energy production, consumption, and prices 1362, 1363, 1364, 1365
- Exchange rates 1377
- Export and imports 1298, 1358, 1379
- Financial assets, liabilities (flow of funds) 1163
- Fish catches 1354
- Food consumption 1356
- Forest products 1360
- Geothermal energy 1362, 1363
- Government finances 1342, 1343
- Gross domestic product 1334, 1335
- Gross national product 1333
- Health care expenditures 1327
- Hydroelectric power 1362, 1363, 1366
- Immigrant population 1324
- Immigration to U.S. 8, 9, 10
- Income tax 1345
- Inpatient care 1325
- International transactions, balances .. 1281, 1282
- Investment in U.S. .. 1202, 1203, 1283, 1285, 1286, 1287, 1288
- Labor costs 1345, 1368, 1369
- Labor force 1324, 1346, 1347, 1350
- Labor productivity 1338
- Lumber 1360
- Manufacturing 1369
  - Productivity 1368
- Meat 1355, 1356
- Military expenditures 1383
- Military personnel 1383
- Military personnel, U.S. on active duty .. 519
- Military sales 515
- Motor vehicles 1370
- Municipal waste 1329
- Natural gas .. 887, 1362, 1363, 1364, 1365
- Nobel prize laureates 804
- Nuclear power generation . 1362, 1363, 1364, 1366, 1367
- Nuclear waste 1329
- Patents 1339
- Petroleum production 883, 1362, 1363, 1364, 1365
- Physicians 1325
- Population 1322, 1323, 1324
- Precipitation (cities) 1328
- Prices 727, 1340, 1341
- Production:
  - Crops 1357
  - Indexes 1337
  - Meat 1355
  - Minerals 875, 1365
- Rainfall (cities) 1328
- Refugees admitted to U.S. 9
- Research and development expenditures . 784
- Reserve assets 1378
- Retirement 1346
- Roads 1370
- Sales and assistance by U.S. government 514, 515

Table

Foreign countries: —Con.
- Securities .. 1200, 1201, 1202, 1203, 1373, 1374, 1376
- Social security contributions 1345
- Space launches 800
- Tax burden 1344
- Taxes (revenue) 1342, 1343
- Telecommunication services 1371
- Temperature (cities) 1328
- Tobacco 1359
- Trade with United States ... 829, 1282, 1300
- Travelers and expenditures 1260, 1261
- U.S. investment abroad .. 1200, 1201, 1290
- Visitors from 1264
- Vital statistics 1326
- Weather 1328
- Foreign currency holdings 1378
- Foreign exchange rates 1377
- Foreign grants and credits, U.S. government 1291
- Foreign investments .. 1163, 1202, 1285, 1286, 1287, 1289
- Foreign languages:
  - Degrees conferred 300, 301, 302
  - Persons speaking 58, 59, 60, 236
  - Students enrolled 268, 283
- Foreign military sales trust fund 471
- Foreign sales and assistance by U.S. government 1292, 1293
  - Economic assistance 1293
  - Military sales and assistance 514, 1293
- Foreign-stock population 53
- Foreign students, college 281
- Foreign trade (see also Foreign aid, Foreign countries, and individual commodities) . 1295, 1296, 1297, 1298, 1299, 1300, 1304
  - Aerospace products 1301, 1302
  - Agricultural products .. 823, 824, 825, 826, 827, 829, 830, 839, 840, 1295, 1299
  - Aircraft and aircraft parts 1020, 1301
  - Automobiles 1301
  - Balance of trade ... 1280, 1281, 1295, 1300
  - Coal 889, 909
  - Companies exporting 1303
  - Countries 1300, 1379
  - Crude oil 878, 909, 910, 911
  - Customs and districts 1297
  - Fish products 863
  - Indexes, unit value 1298
  - Industry 1304
  - International transactions balances, U.S. .. 1280, 1281, 1282, 1294
  - Mineral imports 877
  - Services 1280, 1282
  - Timber products 858, 1301
  - U.S. affiliates of foreign companies 1286
  - World summary, external trade 1321
- Forest products (see also individual products):
  - Car loadings 1113, 1114
  - Consumption 857
  - Foreign countries 1360
  - Foreign trade 857, 858
  - Producer prices 719, 720, 860
  - Sales 812
  - Shipments 1077
- Forests:
  - Land, acreage, and ownership 362
  - National 855

NOTE: Index citations refer to **table** numbers, not page numbers.

994 Index

U.S. Census Bureau, Statistical Abstract of the United States: 2003

Table	Table
Forgery and counterfeiting (arrests) 325	Furniture and home furnishing stores: —Con.
Foster care 540	Purchases 1030
Foundations, philanthropic . 581, 582, 583, 584	Sales . 1026, 1027, 1029, 1031, 1033, 1043
Foundries 631, 632	Futures price indexes, selected
401(k) plans 549, 553, 554, 1217	commodities 723
France. See Foreign countries.	
Franchised establishments 1034	**G**
Freezers, home 977	Gabon. See Foreign countries.
Freight traffic. See Air transportation,	Gallbladder disorders, deaths 115
Railroads, Rivers, and Waterways.	Gallium 872
French Guiana. See Foreign countries.	Gambia, The. See Foreign countries.
French Polynesia. See Foreign countries.	Gambling, arrests 325
Fruits:	Garages. See Gasoline service stations, and
Consumer expenditures 676, 678, 679	Automobile repair and maintenance service.
Consumption 215, 826, 839	Garden activities and equipment 1241
Farm marketings and sales 813, 819	Garden supplies. See Building materials and
Foreign trade . 823, 826, 827, 829, 839, 1301	garden supplies.
Iron (dietary), source 213	Garnet (abrasive) production and value 871
Pesticide usage 833	Garnet (industrial) 872
Prices 715, 727, 729, 818	Gas (see also Petroleum, and Gas utility
Production 839, 842, 1353	industry):
Fruit and vegetable preserving	Liquefied petroleum gases 884
manufacturing 631, 632, 987	Natural 870, 871, 886
Fuel (see also individual types, and energy):	Consumption .. 886, 895, 898, 902, 903
Commercial building use 903, 904, 982	Energy expenditures 900, 901
Consumer expenditures 678, 679	Foreign trade 896, 908, 909, 1304
Consumption:	Offshore lease revenues 880
Airplanes, aviation, certificated route	Prices 873, 895
carriers 1069	Production and value 871, 880, 886,
Motor vehicles 1096	895, 1362
Utilities 914	Foreign countries 1361, 1365
Electricity generated by 914, 917	Indexes 869
Prices .. 713, 715, 719, 720, 725, 728, 729,	Reserves 886
730, 818, 900, 905, 907	Residential 902, 903, 928
Retail 725	World production 887
Production and value 871, 875, 895	Natural gas plant liquids 881
Residential use 899, 900, 928	Price indexes 715
World production 875	Gas and electric utilities. See Utilities.
Funds, trusts and other financial assets 631,	Gas utility industry (see also Utilities):
1161	Accidents and deaths 1058
Funeral service and crematories. See Death	Capital expenditures 767
care services.	Construction expenditures 927
Furniture 678, 679, 715, 721, 1301	Customers 927, 928
Furniture and related product manufacturing:	End users 927
Capital 382, 766	Finances 926
Earnings 631, 965, 987, 992	Mains, mileage 927
Electronic commerce 989	Prices 927
Employees 631, 985, 987, 992	Revenues 894, 926, 927, 928
Energy consumption 906	Sales 927, 928
Establishments 985	Gasoline (see also motor fuel):
Finances 778	Blending components 879
Foreign trade 1304	Excise taxes 730, 1082
Industrial production index 772	Finished motor gasoline 879
Gross domestic product 660	Prices 907, 730
Mergers and acquisitions 759	Supply 721
Occupational safety 652	Gasoline stations, retail:
Pollution abatement 382	Earnings 631, 742, 1025, 1026
Productivity 632	Electronic commerce 1045
Profits 778	Employees 631, 742, 1025, 1026
Shipments 987, 989, 994, 995	Establishments 742, 1025, 1026, 1033
Toxic chemical releases 379	Finances 733
Furniture and home furnishing stores:	Nonemployers 1033
Earnings 631, 992, 1025, 1026	Productivity 632
Electronic commerce 1045	Purchases 1030
Employees 631, 992, 1025, 1026	Sales 733, 742, 1027, 1029, 1032,
Establishments 1025, 1026, 1033	1033, 1271
Inventories 1031	Gastroenterology 162
Nonemployers 1033	Gaza Strip. See Foreign countries.
Productivity 632	Gem stones 871, 872

NOTE: Index citations refer to **table** numbers, not page numbers.

Index 995

U.S. Census Bureau, Statistical Abstract of the United States: 2003

General merchandise stores:
  Earnings 631, 742, 1025, 1026
  Electronic commerce 1045
  Employees 631, 742, 1025, 1026
  Establishments 742, 1025, 1026, 1033
  Finances 778
  Inventories 1031
  Mergers and acquisitions 759
  Nonemployers 1033
  Productivity 632
  Profits 778
  Purchases 1030
  Sales .. 742, 1026, 1027, 1029, 1030, 1032,
                                1033, 1045, 1271
Genetically modified seed plantings 832
Geography and cartography. See Land.
Georgia. See Foreign countries.
Georgia, state of. See State data.
Geothermal energy 895, 899, 1362, 1363
Germanium 872
Germany. See Foreign countries.
Germany DAX-30 stock market index 1375
Ghana. See Foreign countries.
Gibraltar. See Foreign countries.
Gift, novelty, and souvenir stores .. 1025, 1026
Gift and estate taxes 443, 489
Gold:
  Consumption 872
  Employment 870, 872
  Foreign trade 872, 1301
  Prices 872, 873
  Production and value 871, 872
     World production 875, 1361
  Reserve assets 1284
Golf 974, 1243, 1246, 1247, 1249, 1250,
                                      1253, 1254
Golf courses, industry 1230, 1231
Gonorrhea 190
Government (see also Expenditures of U.S.
 government, and Receipts, and individual
 governmental units):
  Buildings 507, 508
  Capital stock 711
  Construction value of buildings 936
  Earnings 472, 629, 630, 635
  Employees 502, 629, 630, 783
     Benefits 469
     City government 473
     County government 474
     Federal, civilian 467, 500, 501, 506
        Accessions and separations . 503, 505
        Pay increases 503
        Salaries 497
     Law enforcement 506
     Local government .. 334, 467, 468, 471,
                                             472
     Retirement systems . 537, 545, 546, 547
     State government .. 334, 467, 468, 471,
                                             472
     States 471, 472, 499
  Employment cost index 643
  Expenditures:
     Capital outlay 444, 445
     City government 464, 469
     Consumption 434, 435, 436
     County government 465, 466, 469
     Federal .. 443, 444, 445, 475, 477, 479,
                                       481, 482

Government (see also Expenditures of U.S.
 government, and Receipts, and individual
 governmental units): —Con.
  Aid to state and local
    government ... 437, 438, 439, 472,
                                            1081
     Capital outlay 444, 445
     Public assistance programs . 539, 540
     Local government 443, 458
     State and local government ... 440, 441,
                              442, 443, 444, 445, 539
     State government .. 443, 444, 445, 453,
                                       454, 456
     Transfer payments 534, 535, 536
  Federally owned land 360, 507, 508
  Flow of funds 1162, 1164, 1166
  Gross domestic product 440, 441, 664
  Highways .. 1075, 1080, 1081, 1082, 1083,
                                           1084
  Hospitals 170
  Insurance. See Social insurance.
  Land. See Public lands.
  Local government:
     Cities:
        Employees, earnings, payroll 473
        Finances 463, 464
     Counties:
        Employees, earnings, payroll 474
        Finances 465, 466
     Earnings 472
     Employees 334, 467, 468, 471, 472
     Number, by type 431, 432
     Payroll 467, 468, 471
     Population, by size-group 433
  Number of units, by type of
    government 431, 432
  Occupational safety 649, 654
  Payrolls 467, 468, 473, 474
  Purchases of goods and services 440,
                                       659, 662
  Salaries and wages (see also Income, and
   individual industries):
     Federal 487, 497
     National income component 440,
                                       441, 635
     State and local government
       employees 472
  Securities 450, 1193, 1194, 1202
  State and local governments 454, 467,
                                  468, 471, 472
     Benefits 469
     Bond ratings 451, 452
     Employees 348, 467, 468, 471, 472
     Federal aid 437, 438, 439, 1081
     Finances 439, 440, 441, 442, 443,
                                  444, 445, 449
     Payroll 467, 468, 472
     State government 453, 455, 456
     Strategic and critical materials,
       summary 834
Government National Mortgage Association
  loans 1182
Governors, number and vote cast 411, 412
Graduates:
  College 298, 301, 302, 303
  High school 219, 269, 272, 273
Grain (see also individual classes):
  Car loadings 1113

NOTE: Index citations refer to **table** numbers, not page numbers.

996 Index

U.S. Census Bureau, Statistical Abstract of the United States: 2003

	Table
Grain (see also individual classes): —Con.	
Consumption	214
Farm marketings, sales	813
Foreign trade	823, 825, 827, 829
Iron (dietary), source	213
Prices	818
Production	821, 1353, 1357
Grandparents	38
Grants, by foundations	584
Grapefruit	215, 813, 842
Grapes	215, 810, 813, 826, 842
Graphite	872
Grazing:	
National forests, livestock, and receipts	855
Public lands, leases	507
Great Britain. See Foreign countries.	
Great Lakes:	
Area	365
Commerce	1070
Water quality	345
Greece. See Foreign countries.	
Greenhouse and nursery crops	813, 838
Greenhouse gases	374
Greenland. See Foreign countries.	
Grenada. See Foreign countries.	
Grocery stores (See also Food and beverage stores):	
Earnings	631, 1025, 1026
Employees	631, 1025, 1026
Establishments	1027, 1033, 1038
Nonemployers	1033
Productivity	632
Sales	1032, 1033, 1038
Services, products offered	1039
Gross domestic product:	
Components, annual growth rates	440, 441, 659, 661, 662, 1052, 1122
Foreign countries	1334, 1335
Implicit price deflators for	659
Per capita	666
Relation to national and personal income	665
State	663, 664
Gross national product	666
Foreign countries	1333
National defense outlays	509
Gross private domestic investment	659, 662, 722, 756
Ground water used	367
Group health insurance plans	150
Group quarters population	78
Guadeloupe. See Foreign countries.	
Guam. See Island areas of the U.S.	
Guamanian population	23
Guatemala. See Foreign countries.	
Guernsey. See Foreign countries.	
Guinea. See Foreign countries.	
Guinea-Bissau. See Foreign countries.	
Guns. See Firearms.	
Guyana. See Foreign countries.	
Gymnastics	1250
Gypsum and gypsum products	871, 872, 875, 877, 933

H

	Table
Haddock	865, 868
Haemophilus influenza	190
Haiti. See Foreign countries.	
Hake, pacific whiting, imports	865
Halibut	865

	Table
Hallucinogenic drugs	201
Ham price indexes	715
Ham prices	727
Handguns	309, 332, 1064
Handicapped (See Disability)	
Hawaii. See State data.	
Hawaiian population. See Native Hawaiian and Other Pacific Islander population.	
Hay	810, 813, 821, 834
Hazardous waste/materials:	
Abatement expenditures	383
Superfund sites	381
Transportation	1058, 1078
Type of material	1078
Waste management	384
Hazelnuts (filberts)	842
Head start program	572
Health and education service industries	629
Health and Human Services, Department of	785
Health and personal care stores:	
Earnings	631, 742, 1025, 1026
Electronic commerce	1045
Employees	631, 742, 1025, 1026
Establishments	742, 1025, 1026, 1033
Nonemployers	1033
Productivity	632
Purchases	1030
Sales	742, 1026, 1027, 1029, 1031, 1033, 1045
Health care and social assistance industry:	
Earnings	742, 1265
Electronic commerce	1268
Employees	742, 1265
Establishments	742, 743, 1265
Nonemployers	743
Receipts	742, 743
Health clubs	1247
Health insurance (see also Health services, Insurance carriers, Medicaid, and Medicare):	
Coverage	150, 152, 153, 154, 155, 157
Enrollment and payments	142, 147
Expenditures	127, 128, 129, 130, 132, 133, 134, 138, 155, 159
Premiums and expenses	155, 157
Premiums and policy reserves, life insurance companies	1223
State Children's Health Insurance program	148, 540
Health insurance industry, employees	160
Health Maintenance Organizations	150, 151, 155
Health sciences, degrees conferred	164, 300, 301, 302, 303
Health services:	
Buildings and floor space	982
Charitable contributions	580
Construction, value	937, 938
Coverage	139, 142, 145, 147, 152, 533
Employment benefits	155
Expenditures	136
Federal government	127, 128, 131, 134, 438, 539, 540
Private expenditures	127, 128, 129, 130, 132, 133, 134, 138, 678
Public expenditures	127, 128, 129, 130, 131, 132, 133, 134, 539, 540
State and local government	127, 134, 442, 539, 540
City government	464

NOTE: Index citations refer to **table** numbers, not page numbers.

Index 997

U.S. Census Bureau, Statistical Abstract of the United States: 2003

Health services: —Con.
        County government 466
        State government 453, 454, 456
Federal outlays for 128, 131, 134, 438
Foreign countries 1327
Government employment and payrolls . 468
Hospitals 170, 171, 172, 173, 174, 176
Industry:
    Capital expenditures 767, 769
    Earnings 631, 745, 746
    Employees 160, 631, 745, 746
    Establishments 745
    Finances 733, 736
    Gross domestic product 660
    Mergers and acquisitions 759
    Occupational safety 652
    Sales or receipts 733, 736, 740, 741
Medicaid . 134, 145, 146, 147, 152, 438, 540
Medicare 128, 131, 134, 139, 142, 542
Mental health facilities 186
Nursing homes 129, 130, 133, 180
Occupations 162, 163, 615, 617
Philanthropy 133, 581
Price indexes 137, 715
Veterans health care 128, 131
Volunteers 585
Hearing impaired 185
Heart disease ... 115, 117, 119, 120, 168, 176, 182
    Deaths 115, 117, 119, 120
Heat pumps 959
Heating and plumbing equipment 924, 944, 959, 979
HVAC and commercial refrigeration equipment manufacturing 631, 632
Heating oil 725, 879, 880, 924
Heights, average, by age and sex 208
Helium 871
Hepatitis 190
Hernia and intestinal obstruction 115, 178
Heroin 201, 329, 330
Herring, sea 865
Hides and skins (see also Leather and leather products), foreign trade 829, 1301
Highways:
    Accidents 1105
    Bridge inventory 1079
    Construction costs 934
        Value of new construction . 936, 937, 938
    Debt, state and local government 1083
    Employees, government 468, 471
    Expenditures:
        City government 464
        County government 466
        Local government 458
        State and local government ... 439, 443, 444, 445
        State government 454, 456
        U.S. government 1081
        Aid to state and local governments 438
        Highway trust fund 439, 1081
    Federal-aid systems 1075, 1076, 1081
    Highway trust funds 1055
    Mileage 1075, 1076
    Motor fuel consumption 1096
    Motor fuel tax 1082
    Type and control 1075, 1076

Highways: —Con.
    Types of roads traveled 1076
Hiking 1247
Hindu population. See Religion.
Hispanic origin population .. 15, 16, 21, 22, 23, 54
    Activity limitation 195, 196
    Adult education 304
    Age and/or sex 14, 13, 46
    AIDS 192, 193
    Births and birth rates 84, 87, 99
    Business owners 750, 752
    Charity contributions 579
    Child care 577
    Children under 18 years old 16
        Literacy activities 235, 238
    Cities 33
    College enrollment 278
    Community service (students) 586
    Commuting to work 47
    Computer use 260, 1158
    Congress, members of 408
    Congressional districts 1384
    Criminal victimization rates . 232, 233, 322, 324
    Death rates 109, 111
    Degrees conferred 229, 293, 801
    Disability status 47, 285, 557
    Distance education 286
    Educational attainment ... 46, 47, 227, 228, 229
    Elderly 13, 703
    Elected officials 408, 418
    Elections, voter registration and turnout . 419
    Families, characteristics .. 46, 70, 71, 72, 73
    Farm operators, workers 807, 822
    Food stamp participants 571
    Foreign-born populations 47, 226
    Health insurance coverage ... 145, 152, 154
    High school dropouts 270, 271, 272
    Homeschooled 243
    Household or family characteristics . 46, 62, 73
    Housing 46, 962, 966, 973, 976
    Immunization of children 191
    Income:
        Family 686, 687, 689, 692
        Household 683, 684, 685
        Persons 677, 680, 683
    Internet access 260
    Jail inmates 347
    Job search 622
    Labor force and employment 588
        Displaced workers 612
        Earnings 641
        Employed . 46, 589, 605, 606, 607, 608, 609, 615, 619
        By industry, occupation 615, 619
        Minimum wage workers 645
        Job search 622
        Persons working at home 605
        Unemployed 46, 589, 621
        Union membership 657
    Language proficiency 236
    Living arrangements 64
    Marital status 61
    Media users 1127
    Metropolitan areas 28

NOTE: Index citations refer to **table** numbers, not page numbers.

Table

Hispanic origin population —Con.
  Mobility status 47
  Nativity 47
  Nurses 161, 615
  Occupation 47, 615
  Overweight 209
  Pension plan coverage 551
  Physical activity 210
  Poverty .. 46, 145, 697, 700, 701, 703, 707
  Projections 15, 16
  School enrollment . 222, 226, 247, 272, 278,
                                                 282
    Adult education 304
    Charter schools 239
    Homeschooled 243
    Preprimary school 237
  Senior citizen communities 974
  Sports participation 1248
  States 21, 22
  Teachers 249, 263
  Union membership 657
  Volunteers 585
  Voter registration and turnout 419
HIV infection (see also AIDS) . 116, 118, 119, 124
Hmong population 23
Hockey 1245, 1249, 1250
Hogs 810, 813, 819, 843, 844, 845, 846
Home economics, degrees conferred . 300, 301,
                                                 302
Home equity loans/lines of credit ... 973, 1169,
                                                 1174
Home furnishings stores . 631, 632, 1026, 1027
Home furnishings. See Appliances.
Home health care 141, 181, 182, 183
Home health care services:
  Earnings 631
  Employees 631
  Expenditures 129, 130, 131, 133
  Finances 158
Homeland Security, Department of 480
Home remodeling 980, 1170
Homeowners insurance 1224, 1226
Homes. See Housing and housing units.
Homeschooling 243
Homicides . 115, 118, 119, 305, 306, 307, 308,
                           309, 310, 311, 312, 313
Honduras. See Foreign countries.
Hong Kong. See Foreign countries.
Hong Kong Hong Seng stock market index . 1375
Horses:
  Ownership 1242
  Racing 1243, 1245
  Riding 1243
Horses and mules 813
Hospices 141, 181, 182
Hospitals:
  Average daily room charge 171
  Beds 170, 172
  Charges and personal expenditure for . 129,
                 130, 131, 132, 133, 134, 146
  Construction 936, 939
  Consumer price index 137
  Cost to hospital per patient 171
  Diagnostic procedures 178
  Discharges from 174, 176, 179
  Earnings 631, 742
  Emergency departments 167, 169
  Employees ... 160, 170, 471, 619, 631, 742
  Establishments 170, 172, 742

Table

Hospitals: —Con.
  Finances 158, 159, 170, 1271
  Grants, foundations 584
  Medicare program 139, 140, 144
  Mental hospitals 170, 173, 186
  National expenditures . 127, 128, 129, 130,
                           132, 133, 134, 136
  Outpatient visits ... 167, 168, 170, 172, 173
  Patients 170, 172
  Public expenditures 128, 129, 130, 132,
                                     133, 134
    City governments 464
    County governments 466
    State governments 454
  Receipts 158, 159, 742
  States 172
  Surgery 178
    Organ transplants 177
  Use, admissions, and patient days . 170, 172,
                                    173, 174, 176
  Veterans, expenditures and patients 186
Hotels and other lodging places (see also
  Accommodation and food services):
  Buildings and floor space 982
  Earnings 631, 1270
  Employees 631, 1270
  Establishments 1269, 1270
  Gross domestic product 660
  Mergers and acquisitions 759
  New construction 936, 937
  Occupancy rate 1269
  Occupational safety 652
  Productivity 632
  Receipts 1040, 1271
  Travel summary 1269
House of Representatives .. 403, 404, 405, 406,
                                 407, 408, 409
Household workers. See Domestic service.
Households or families (see also Housing
  and housing units and income) 64, 65, 66,
                              67, 70, 72, 74, 1166
  Age of householder 67, 73, 685, 1167,
                                  1169, 1171, 1213
  Asian and Pacific Islander population 44
  Assets . 710, 1162, 1166, 1167, 1198, 1216
  Automobiles, ownership 976, 977
  Balance sheet 710
  Black population . 39, 67, 70, 71, 72, 75, 683,
                     684, 685, 686, 687, 688, 689
  Book purchasing 1138
  Characteristics 65, 67, 70, 71, 72, 74
  Children under 18 years . 65, 70, 71, 72, 73,
                                   74, 675, 689
  Computer use . 260, 977, 1127, 1156, 1158,
                                            1159
  Consumer expenditures . 676, 677, 678, 679
  Criminal victimization 324
  Debt ... 710, 1168, 1169, 1170, 1171, 1172
  Educational attainment 685
  Elderly 685
  Employment of parents 599
  Female householder . 65, 66, 67, 68, 70, 72,
                                     73, 74, 75, 76
  Finances, financial services . 1162, 1164, 1166,
       1167, 1168, 1170, 1171, 1198, 1213, 1216
  Flow of funds 1162, 1164, 1166, 1168
  Food insecurity 211
  Food stamp program 570, 571

NOTE: Index citations refer to **table** numbers, not page numbers.

Index   999

Households or families (see also Housing and housing units and income) —Con.
  Foreign born population 54
  Hispanic origin population .. 46, 62, 67, 70, 71, 73
  Hunger 211
  Income . 683, 684, 685, 686, 687, 688, 689, 690, 691, 1167, 1169, 1171, 1213
  Individual retirement accounts (IRAs) ... 552
  Internet access . 260, 977, 1125, 1127, 1158, 1159
  Interracial married couples 62
  Living arrangements 37, 64
  Marital status of householder 73, 76
  Media users 1127
  Mobility status 35
  Mutual fund ownership 1213
  Net worth 708, 710
  Persons living alone (one-person households) 64, 65, 66, 67, 75, 76
  Poverty 44, 707
    Asian and Pacific Islander population . 44
    Black population 707
    Hispanic origin population 707
  Public assistance to families 538, 540
  Race 39, 44, 73, 689
  Region of householder 68, 689
  Size 54, 66, 67, 72
  States 68
  Stock ownership 1210
  Taxes paid 684
  Telephones 1126
  Types:
    Male householder 65, 73, 74
    Married couples with or without own children . 62, 65, 66, 67, 71, 72, 73, 74
    Non-family 65, 66, 75, 76
    One-person households . 65, 66, 67, 75, 76
  Unmarried partners 69
  Wealth 708, 709
Housekeeping supplies expenditures . 678, 679
Housing and household operations, price indexes 715, 721
Housing and housing units (see also Households or families):
  Age of housing stocks 959
  Amenities 976
  Appliances 977
  Building permit value 941
  Capital 978
  City data 957, 969, 972
  Condominiums 942, 951
  Congressional districts 1384
  Construction:
    Apartments completed and rented .. 952
    Cost indexes 934
    New units 941, 942, 943
    Value 935, 936, 939
  Consumer expenditures . 676, 677, 678, 679
  Consumer price indexes 713, 715
  Costs 958, 966
  Deficiencies 976
  Elderly 963, 966, 976
  Energy:
    Characteristics 944
    Consumption 897, 898, 902, 903
    Expenditures 900, 901, 902, 903

Housing and housing units (see also Households or families): —Con.
  Fires and property loss 357
  Floorspace 944
  Government expenditures ... 442, 443, 454, 464, 479
  Heating equipment used . 944, 959, 963, 975
  Kitchen equipment 959
  Loans and mortgages . 944, 945, 973, 1182, 1183, 1184
    Federal Housing Administration (FHA) 944, 945, 973
    Veterans Administration (VA) .. 944, 945, 973
  Lot size 961
  Maintenance and repair expenditures .. 678, 679, 979
  Metropolitan area data .. 949, 958, 968, 971
  Mobile homes 186, 947, 958, 959, 960
  Neighborhood indicators 974
  New privately owned homes, characteristics 944
  Ownership (see tenure)
  Plumbing 963
  Prices, or costs ... 934, 946, 947, 948, 949, 951, 965, 966
  Public housing, low rent units 538
    Federal aid to state and local governments 438, 439
    Government expenditures 539, 540
  Remodeling 980
  Rent, rental value 965, 966
  Rooms 961
  Sales 945, 948, 950
  Senior citizen communities 974
  Square footage 961
  State data 964
  Structural type 942, 955, 959, 960, 979
  Tenure 34, 39, 46, 54, 685, 953, 954, 956, 957, 958, 959, 962, 963, 964, 965, 966, 1220, 1384
  Vacancies 953, 955, 956, 957, 958
  Value 710, 965, 967, 968, 969, 1384
  Year built 903, 955, 963
Housing and Urban Development, Dept. of:
  Employment 500
  Federal aid to state and local governments 438, 439
Housing assistance 538, 539, 540
Human immunodeficiency virus (HIV) infection (see also AIDS) 118, 119
Hungary. See Foreign countries.
Hunger 211
Hunting and fishing ... 1247, 1251, 1252, 1253
Hurricanes 386, 387
Hydroelectric power 899, 925
  Capacity 914, 925
  Consumption 898, 899, 895, 1363
  Net generation 925
  Production 895, 914, 1362, 1366
Hypertension 168
Hysterectomy 178

I

Ice cream 214, 727, 849
Ice hockey 1243, 1247, 1250
Ice skating 1247
Iceland. See Foreign countries.

NOTE: Index citations refer to **table** numbers, not page numbers.

	Table		Table

Idaho. See State data.
Illegal immigration. See Immigrants.
Illinois. See State data.
Immigrants (see also Foreign-born
  population) 5, 6, 8, 9, 10
  By area of residence 10
  By class of admission 6
  By country of birth 8, 9, 10
  Foreign countries 1324
  Refugees 6, 9
  Unauthorized 7
Immunization of children 191
Imports. See Foreign trade.
Income (see also Poverty, Consumer
  expenditures, and Earnings):
  Adult education 304
  Aggregate income 680, 688
  American Indian 680, 692
  Asian and Pacific Islander population 44,
    680, 684, 692
  Black population ... 39, 537, 680, 686, 687,
    688, 689, 692, 694, 707
  Corporate 731, 733, 739, 740
  Disposable personal 666, 668, 672
  Distribution . 680, 683, 685, 686, 688, 689,
    692, 693
  Energy consumption 903
  Families 37, 39, 46, 686, 687, 688, 689,
    690, 691, 692
    Computer use 260
    Congressional districts 1384
    Island areas 1313
    Type of family . 686, 687, 688, 689, 690,
      691
  Farm 811, 815, 817
  Foreign born 51, 54
  Hispanic origin population 46, 537, 683,
    684, 685, 696
  Household ... 670, 680, 681, 682, 683, 684,
    685, 692, 694
    Age 685, 695
    Black population 680, 683, 684, 685,
      692
    Book purchasing 1138
    Computer use 1156, 1158
    Educational attainment 685
    Elderly 685
    Hispanic origin population . 680, 683, 684,
      685, 692
    Homeschooling 243
    Mobility status 35
    Native Hawaiian and Other Pacific
      Islander 680, 692
    Recreation activities, physical activity . 210,
      1247, 1254
    Stock, mutual fund ownership . 1210, 1212,
      1214
    Taxes 1343, 1345
    Tenure 685
  National income ... 659, 661, 662, 665, 666
    By type of income 665
    Originating in farming 811
  Per capita 666, 696
  Personal 660, 668, 670, 671
  Persons 54, 693, 694, 696
    Educational attainment 693, 695
    Source of income 537
  Savings 669, 674
  Sports participation, goods 1247, 1254

Income security outlays 476
Income tax (see also Tax receipts):
  Average tax by income level 488
  Corporation 488, 489, 739
  Deductions 490, 492, 579
  Foreign countries 1345
  State collections 455
Index numbers. See individual subjects.
India. See Foreign countries.
Indiana. See State data.
Indian, American population. See American
  Indian, Alaska Native population.
Indian, Asian population. See Asian Indian
  population.
Indium 872, 1167
Individual retirement accounts (IRAs) . 552, 1212,
  1214, 1217, 1218
Indonesia. See Foreign countries.
Industrial and commercial enterprises,
  failures 744
Industrial minerals 871
Industrial production indexes 772
  Foreign countries 1337
Industry. See Corporations and individual
  industries.
Infant deaths (see also Deaths and death
  rates) 83, 113, 114
Island areas of the U.S. 1306
Inflation. See Prices, consumer, and Consumer
  price indexes.
Information industry:
  Capital 767, 769
  Earnings . 629, 631, 635, 636, 668, 742, 745,
    746, 1119, 1121, 1123, 1265
  Electronic commerce 1268
  Employees .. 629, 630, 631, 742, 745, 746,
    1119, 1121, 1123, 1265
  Establishments .. 742, 743, 745, 985, 1119,
    1121, 1123, 1265
  Finances 733, 736
  Foreign countries 1372
  Gross domestic product 1122
  Hours 629
  Multinational companies 780, 781
  Nonemployers 743
  Occupational safety 652
  Productivity 632
  Profits 731, 776
  Shipments, revenue 731, 733, 736, 740,
    741, 742, 743, 1119, 1120, 1124, 1129, 1137,
    1139, 1140, 1151
Infrastructure expenditures. See government.
Influenza 115, 117
Inhalants, persons using 201
Injuries (see also Accidents and Occupational
  safety) . 125, 169, 176, 182, 187, 1058, 1112
  Associated with consumer products 188
  Costs 189
  Crime victimization 321, 322, 323, 324
  Industrial 649, 650, 651, 652
  Work time lost 650
Inmates (see also Correctional institutions) . 347,
  351
Installment loans (see also Loans and
  mortgages) 1169, 1189
Institutional care facilities (see also Hospitals
  and Nursing and related care facilities) .. 173,
  180
Institutional population 78
  Mentally ill, retarded 186

NOTE: Index citations refer to **table** numbers, not page numbers.

Table	**Table**

Institutional population —Con.
  Prisoners 349, 351
Institutions. See Hospitals and other individual facilities.
Institutions of higher education. See Education.
Instrumental activities of daily living (IADLs) . 185
Instruments and related products, manufacturing:
  Capital 766
  Earnings 631, 992
  Employees 631, 992
  Foreign trade 1304
  Gross domestic product 660, 984
  Mergers and acquisitions 759
  Occupational safety 652
  Patents 763
  Productivity 632
  Profits..................................... 778
  Toxic chemical releases 379
Insurance. See individual forms of insurance.
Insurance agents, brokers, and service:
  Earnings 1161
  Employees 1161
  Establishments 1161, 1174
  Finances 1198, 1224
  Foreign investments in the U.S. 1288
  Gross domestic product 660, 1160
  Mergers and acquisitions 759
  Occupational safety 652
Insurance carriers:
  Earnings 631, 742, 1161
  Employees 631, 742, 1161
  Establishments 742, 1161
  Finances 1162, 1224
  Gross domestic product 660, 1160
  Occupational safety 652
  Profits.................................... 1224
  Receipts 742
Insurance, government. See Social insurance.
Insurance, medical care 128, 132, 133, 137
Interactive digital media 1124
Inter-American Development Bank 1291
Intercity traffic 1054, 1109
Interest:
  Payments, federal government 476, 479
  Persons receiving income 537
  Receipts, by source:
    Individual income tax returns .. 490, 493
    National and personal income component 668
Interest rates 1193
  Mortgages 1183, 1193
Intermediate goods, price indexes, producer 719
Internal revenue collections (see also Tax receipts) 489
Internal waterways, traffic 1070
International affairs:
  Balance of trade 1295
  Commerce .. 1295, 1296, 1297, 1300, 1316
  Federal outlays 479
  Foreign exchange rates 1377
  Foreign investments in U.S. 1202, 1203, 1285
  International transactions, U.S. .. 1280, 1281, 1282, 1284
  U.S. government aid 1291, 1292, 1293
  U.S. investments .. 1200, 1201, 1280, 1290

International Bank for Reconstruction and Development 1291
International Development Association ... 1291
International Finance Corporation 1291
International investment position, U.S. ... 1280, 1283, 1290
International mail (U.S. postal) 1117
Internet access/use .. 256, 257, 259, 622, 977, 1125, 1127, 1138, 1142, 1155, 1156, 1158, 1159, 1244, 1371
Internet publishing and broadcasting 631
Interracial married couples 62
Intracity transportation price indexes 715
Inventories (see also Stocks, commodity) .. 993, 994, 995, 996, 1031, 1034, 1049
  Business (GDP) 659
Investments (see also Capital stock and Securities):
  Foreign, in U.S. ... 1202, 1203, 1280, 1283, 1285, 1287, 1288, 1289
  Private domestic, gross 659, 669
  U.S. government obligations 1174
  U.S. international . 1200, 1201, 1280, 1283, 1290
  Venture capital 761
Iowa. See State data.
Iran. See Foreign countries.
Iraq. See Foreign countries.
Ireland (Eire). See Foreign countries.
Iron (see also Steel):
  Foreign trade 877, 948, 1301
  Mining industry 870
    Productivity 945
  Prices 873
  Production -................... 871, 875, 948
  World production 875, 1361
Iron (nutritional), available for human consumption 212, 213
Iron and steel mills (see also Primary metal manufacturing):
  Capital 766, 1007
  Earnings 631, 985, 987
  Electronic commerce 989
  Employees 631, 985, 987, 1007
  Establishments 985
  Foreign trade 1007
  Occupational safety 652
  Productivity 632
  Shipments 987, 989, 1007
Iron and steel products 875, 889, 1008
  Production and value 871
  Scrap 872
Irrigation 367, 368
Islamic population. See Religion.
Island areas of the U.S.:
  Aid by U.S. government 1311
  Area 359, 1307
  Banks and banking 1313
  Births and deaths 1306
  Business, summary 1318
  Climate (Puerto Rico) ... 390, 391, 392, 393, 394, 395
  Commerce 1316
  Education 1313
    Attainment 1310
    Enrollment 1312
  Employees 1317, 1318
  Establishments 1317, 1318
  Federal payments 1311

NOTE: Index citations refer to **table** numbers, not page numbers.

Table	Table
Island areas of the U.S.: —Con.	Labor force, employment, and earnings (see also individual industries or occupations): —Con.
Finances 1314, 1315	Work time lost 650
Foreign investment 1287	Average pay, States 639
Foreign trade 1316	Commuting to work 1090, 1091, 1092
Geography 359	Metro areas 640
Gross product 1314	City government 473
Hospital facilities 172	Civilian labor force:
Income 1310, 1313	Adult education 304
Industry 1317, 1318	Asian and Pacific Islander population . 44
Labor force and employment ... 1310, 1313	Black population . 39, 588, 589, 591, 594, 605, 606, 607, 615, 626
Language spoken 1310	
Marital status 1307	Displaced workers 591, 612, 626
Marriage and divorce 1306	Educational attainment ... 591, 618, 626
Mobility 1310	Employed . 587, 589, 592, 593, 594, 597, 599, 601, 602, 605, 606, 607, 608, 609, 611, 617, 618, 619, 620
Payroll by industry 1317, 1318	
Population and/or area ... 359, 1305, 1307, 1308, 1309, 1313, 1322	
	Female ... 589, 590, 591, 592, 594, 595, 596, 597, 598, 605, 606, 607, 626
Public aid 562	
Public libraries 1153	Age of children 597
Sales, shipments, receipts 1318	Marital status 595, 596, 597
Social insurance 544	Multiple job holders 608
Tourism 1313	Foreign-born population 54
Unemployment insurance 555	High school graduates, dropouts 273
Vital statistics 1306	Hispanic origin population . 46, 588, 589, 605, 606, 607, 615, 619
Isle of Man. See Foreign countries.	
Israel. See Foreign countries.	Home-based work 605
Italy. See Foreign countries.	Metropolitan areas 593
Itemized deductions (taxes) 490, 492, 579	Minimum wage workers 645
	Multiple job holders 608
J	Not at work 603
Jails 347, 350	Part-time 611
Jamaica. See Foreign countries.	Participation rates .. 588, 589, 591, 592, 595, 596, 597, 598
Japan. See Foreign countries.	
Japanese population 23, 750	Selected countries 1347, 1350
Jazz 1142, 1237	Wives, by age of youngest child . 598
Jersey. See Foreign countries.	Projections 588, 617, 620
Jewelry luggage and leather goods stores . 631, 632, 1026	Race .. 39, 44, 588, 589, 591, 594, 605, 606, 607, 615, 626
Jewelry sales 1027	Reason not in 614
Jewish population. See Religion.	School enrollment, persons 16 to 24 years old 594
Job Corps 540	
Jogging 1247, 1253, 1254	Self-employed workers 604
Jordan. See Foreign countries.	States 592
Judicial service (Federal):	Unemployed .. 587, 589, 592, 593, 594, 597, 621, 623, 624, 625, 626, 627, 628
Employees and payrolls 498	
Federal outlays 479	Women who gave birth in previous year 99, 100
Juices 216	
Juveniles:	Computer use 1127
Arrest 326	Disabled persons 557, 613
Court cases 342	Displaced workers 612
	Earnings 635, 637, 639, 640, 641, 642
K	Educational attainment 229, 591, 626
Kansas. See State data.	Elderly 37, 588, 590, 595, 600, 621
Kazakhstan. See Foreign countries.	Employee benefits 155, 548, 647, 648
Kentucky. See State data.	Government employees 469
Kenya. See Foreign countries.	Employee training 1332
Keogh plans 492, 1167	Employees 629, 630, 631
Kidney disease and infections, deaths 115	States 630
Kiribati. See Foreign countries.	Employment cost, cost index 643, 1345, 1368, 1369
Korea. See Foreign countries.	
Korean population 23, 750	Employment projections 617, 620
Kuwait. See Foreign countries.	Employment taxes and contributions ... 481
Kyrgyzstan. See Foreign countries.	Female . 589, 590, 591, 592, 594, 595, 596, 597, 598, 615, 618, 619, 623, 624, 626, 627, 641, 642
L	
Laboratories, medical and dental 158	
Labor force, employment, and earnings (see also individual industries or occupations):	Flexible schedules 606
Accidents and fatalities 649, 650, 651, 652, 653, 654	

NOTE: Index citations refer to **table** numbers, not page numbers.

Table

Labor force, employment, and earnings (see also individual industries or occupations): —Con.
    Foreign countries . 1338, 1346, 1347, 1349, 1350, 1351, 1352
    Foreign-owned firms 1286, 1287
    Government. See government.
    High school graduates and dropouts 273
    Hispanic origin population 46, 588, 589, 619, 621
    Hours 1338, 1368
    Indexes of compensation 633, 1369
    Internet access 1127
    Job search 622
    Metropolitan areas 593, 640
    Minimum wage workers 644, 645
    Mobility status 34
    Occupational groups. See Occupations and individual occupations.
    Occupational safety 649, 650, 651, 652, 653, 654
    Persons working at home 605
    Poverty status 704
    Production workers 987, 988
    Productivity 633, 1338, 1368
    Self-employed 604
    Shift work 607
    Social insurance coverage 541
    State data 592, 616, 628, 639
    Tenure with employer 610
    Unemployed workers (see also Unemployment):
        Age 594, 621
        Asian and Pacific Islander population . 44
        Black population . 39, 589, 594, 621, 626
        Educational attainment 229, 626
        Foreign-born population 54
        Foreign countries 1347, 1349
        High school graduates and dropouts . 273
        Hispanic origin population . 46, 588, 621
        Industry 624
        Occupation 625
        Race 39, 589, 594, 621, 626
        Reason 623, 627
        Sex . 589, 592, 594, 597, 621, 623, 624, 626, 627
        States 592, 628
    Union membership 656, 657, 658
    Work stoppages 655
    Youth employment programs 540
Labor organizations or unions:
    Employee benefit costs 646
    Membership 656, 657, 658
    Political action committees (PAC) . 425, 426, 427
    Public confidence 416
Labor strikes 655
Lacrosse 1250
Lakes 365, 369
Lamb and mutton (see also Meat and meat products) 214, 843
Lambs. See Sheep and lambs.
Land (see also Farms and Public lands):
    Area:
        Cities 31
        Coastal 24
        Foreign countries 1322
        Island areas 359, 1307
        National parks 1255

Table

Land (see also Farms and Public lands): —Con.
        States 359
        United States 1, 359
    Farmland 805, 806, 808, 809
    Federal land 360, 507
    Foreign investors 1286, 1287
    Forest, area and ownership 356
    Parks 1255, 1256
    Use 361, 362
Landfills (see also Solid waste) .. 374, 375, 925, 1329
Languages spoken at home . 38, 56, 57, 58, 59, 60, 236
Laos. See Foreign countries.
Laotian population 23
Larceny, larceny-theft . 305, 306, 307, 308, 318, 321, 324
Lard 214
Latex. See Rubber.
Latvia. See Foreign countries.
Laundry, cleaning, and garment services. See Dry-cleaning and laundry services.
Law degrees conferred 300, 301, 302, 303
Law enforcement (see also Courts, crime, and correctional institutions):
    Arrests 325, 328, 329
    Drug enforcement 328, 329, 330
    Employees 468, 506
    Expenditures 442, 443, 454, 456
    Handgun checks 332
    Police officers 334, 336, 468, 506, 615
    Wiretaps 331
    Workplace violence 653, 654
Lawn care 1241
Lawyers (see also Legal services) 615
Lead 872
    Air quality 371, 372, 373
    Consumption 872
    Employment 872
    Foreign trade 872
    Prices 872, 873
    Production and value 871
    World production 875, 1361
Leather and allied product, manufacturing (see also Hides and skins, and Footwear):
    Capital 766
    Earnings 631, 985, 987, 992
    Electronic commerce 989
    Employees 631, 985, 987, 992
    Energy consumption 906
    Establishments 985
    Foreign trade 1304
    Gross domestic product 660, 984
    Industrial production index 772
    Occupational safety 651, 652
    Pollution abatement 382
    Shipments 987, 989, 995
    Toxic chemical releases 379
Lebanon. See Foreign countries.
Legal assistants 615
Legal, governmental, public administrative associations 307
Legal services:
    Earnings 631, 742, 1265
    Employees 617, 619, 631, 742, 1265
    Establishments 742, 1265
    Finances 733
    Gross domestic product 660
    Occupational safety 652

NOTE: Index citations refer to **table** numbers, not page numbers.

Table	Table
Legal services: —Con.	Livestock and livestock products (see also
Receipts 733, 742	Animals, domestic, and individual classes): —Con.
Legionellosis 190	Prices 818, 844
Legislatures, State party composition . 413, 414	Production 821, 843, 844, 847
Leisure and hospitality industry:	Purchases 812
Earnings 629, 631, 636	Supply 843
Employees 629, 630, 631	Value on farms 844
Hours 629	Living cost. See Consumer price indexes and
Leisure activities. See Recreation.	Prices.
Lemons 842	Loans and mortgages (see also Debt):
Leprosy 190	Automobile loans 1189
Lesotho. See Foreign countries.	Banks, commercial 1174, 1185
Letters (postal) 1117, 1118	Commercial paper 1196
Lettuce 215, 727, 810, 813, 841	Consumer credit .. 1168, 1169, 1170, 1172,
Leveraged buy-outs 758	1174, 1185, 1188, 1189
Liberia. See Foreign countries.	Credit market, flow of funds 1164, 1168
Libraries and librarians . 1152, 1153, 1154, 1155	Credit unions 1157
Adult programs 1157	Delinquency rates 1184, 1185
Degrees conferred 300, 301, 302	Direct loans 484
Employees 615	Farm. See Farm mortgage loans.
Grants, foundations 584	Federal Housing Administration (FHA) . 1184
Internet use 1155	Foreclosure rates 1184
Public employment 460	Guaranteed loans 484
Revenue 1151	Home mortgage/equity loans . 710, 973, 1169,
Libya. See Foreign countries.	1172, 1182, 1185
Licenses, permits, etc.:	Installment loans 1169
Public lands 507	Interest rates 1183, 1193
Taxes 454	Life insurance 1223
Liechtenstein. See Foreign countries.	Minority-operated small businesses 760
Life expectancy 105, 106, 107	Mortgage-backed securities 1195
Foreign countries 1326	Mortgage pools 1164
Projections 105	Mortgages ... 710, 1164, 1166, 1168, 1169,
Life insurance 1222, 1223	1170, 1182
Capital 1223	Personal loans 1189
Cash value 1167	Savings institutions 1165, 1181
Consumer expenditures 676, 678	Veterans Administration (VA) 1184
Establishments 1223	Lobsters 865, 867
Finances 1162, 1182, 1198, 1216, 1223	Local and suburban transit. See Passenger
Flow of funds 1198, 1216	transit industry.
In force 1222	Local government. See individual governmental
Individual Retirement Accounts 1218	units and State and local government.
Mortgage loans outstanding 1182	Locomotives (railroad) 1112
Purchases, policies 1166, 1222	Lodging industries. See Hotels and other
Reserves 1166, 1223	lodging places.
Sales 1222, 1223	London FTSE 100 stock market index 1375
Life sciences 792	Long term care insurance 648
Degrees conferred 300, 301, 302	Lotteries 461, 462
Employment 796	Louisiana. See State data.
Life years lost 125	Low birth weight 84, 91, 94, 97
Light and power. See Electric light and power	LSD usage 201
industry.	Lumber (see also Forest products and wood
Lightning 386	products manufacturing):
Lime 871, 872	Consumption 857, 859
Liquefied petroleum gases, consumption ... 884	Foreign countries 1360
Liquor stores, retail. See Beer, wine, and	Foreign trade 857, 858
liquor stores.	Prices 860
Liquors and beverages:	Production 857
Alcoholism treatment 200	Railroad car loadings 1113, 1114
Consumption 201, 216	Waterborne commerce 1071
Government revenues 442, 454, 455	Luxembourg. See Foreign countries.
Literacy activities 235, 238	Lyme disease 190
Lithuania. See Foreign countries.	
Livestock and livestock products (see also	**M**
Animals, domestic, and individual classes):	
Commodity futures trading 723	Macadamia nuts 842
Consumption 214, 843	Macau. See Foreign countries.
Farm marketings, sales 812, 813, 817	Macedonia, the Former Yugoslav Republic of.
Farm output and marketing indexes ... 821	See Foreign countries.
Foreign trade . 823, 825, 827, 829, 843, 1304	Machine tools 1010, 1049
Number and value on farms 844, 847	Machinery manufacturing:
	Capital 382, 766

NOTE: Index citations refer to **table** numbers, not page numbers.

Index 1005

U.S. Census Bureau, Statistical Abstract of the United States: 2003

Table

Machinery manufacturing: —Con.
    Earnings 631, 985, 987, 1123
    Employees 631, 985, 987, 1123
    Energy consumption 906
    Establishments 985
    Finances 778
    Foreign trade 1304
    Gross domestic product 660, 984, 1122
    Industrial production index 772
    Inventories 995
    Mergers and acquisitions 759
    Multinational companies 780, 781
    Occupational safety 651
    Patents 763
    Pollution abatement 382
    Productivity 632
    Profits 777, 778
    Research and development 793, 794
    Shipments 987, 989, 994, 995
    Toxic chemical releases 379
Mackerel, Pacific 868
Madagascar. See Foreign countries.
Magazines:
    Advertising expenditures 1274
    Prices 1133
    Reading 1125
    Receipts 1124
Magnesium 871, 875
Mail 1117, 1118
Mail order houses (including electronic shopping):
    Earnings 631, 1025, 1026
    Employees 631, 1025, 1026
    Establishments 1025, 1026, 1033
    Productivity 632
    Purchases 1030
    Sales 1027, 1033, 1043, 1045
Maine. See State data.
Malaria 190
Malawi. See Foreign countries.
Malaysia. See Foreign countries.
Maldives. See Foreign countries.
Male householder. See Households or families.
Mali. See Foreign countries.
Malt beverages (see also Beverages) .. 216, 825, 826
    Advertising 1275
    Beer 216, 715
Malta. See Foreign countries.
Mammography testing 205
Managed care, health plans 141, 149
Management of companies and enterprises:
    Capital 769
    Earnings 631, 745
    Employees 631, 745
    Establishments 745
    Finances 733, 736, 740
    Receipts 733, 736, 740, 741
Managers. See Proprietors, etc.
Manganese 870, 876, 877
Manganiferous ore 871
Manmade fibers and fabrics (see also Foreign trade and specific items) 1001
Manufactured products (see also individual products):
    Production indexes 772
Manufacturers' excise taxes 489
Manufacturing industry (see also individual industries):
    Capital 767, 769, 999, 1199

Table

Manufacturing industry (see also individual industries): —Con.
    Earnings . 629, 631, 635, 636, 742, 745, 746, 751, 987, 991, 1318
    Economic indicators 770
    Electronic commerce 989
    Employees .. 605, 619, 629, 630, 631, 731, 742, 745, 746, 751, 988, 1318
    Energy consumption 906
    Establishments ... 742, 743, 745, 987, 991, 1318
    Finances 733, 736, 778, 998, 999, 1314
    Foreign countries 1368, 1369
    Foreign investments in U.S. 1285
    Form of organization 987
    Gross domestic product . 660, 664, 984, 1314
    Hours 629
    Industrial production index 772
    Inventories 994, 995
    Investment abroad 1290
    Island areas of the United States . 1317, 1318
    Minority-owned businesses . 752, 753, 754, 755
    Multinational companies 780, 781
    Nonemployers 743
    Occupational safety 649, 652, 654
    Productivity 632, 633, 773
        Foreign countries 1368
    Profits 731, 777, 778, 999
    Sales, shipments, receipts ... 731, 733, 736, 740, 741, 742, 743, 751, 787, 987, 991, 993, 994, 995, 999
    State data 986, 988, 991
    Toxic chemical releases 379
    Union membership 657
    Value added 991
    Women-owned businesses 751
Maple syrup, organic tree acreage 810
Margarine 214, 727
Marihuana (see also Drugs (illegal)):
    Arrests, seizures 329, 330
    Use 201, 202
Marine Corps 517, 518
Marital status of population 61, 63
    Black population 61
    By presence of children 65
    Computer use 1156
    Couples with or without own household . 62, 66
    Elderly 37, 63
    Employed persons 600
    Female householder 73
    Foreign born population 54
    Hispanic origin population 61
    Householder status 73
    Internet access 1156
    Island areas 1307
    Labor force participation rates 595, 596, 597, 598
    Male householder 73
    Nonfamily householder 75
    Unmarried partners 69
    Women in the labor force 596, 597
    Work schedules 608
Marriage and divorce (see also Marital status) 83, 126
    Island areas of the U.S. 1306
Married couples. See Households or families.

NOTE: Index citations refer to **table** numbers, not page numbers.

Married persons. See Marital status.
Marshall Islands. See Foreign countries.
Martial arts 1247
Martinique. See Foreign countries.
Maryland. See State data.
Massachusetts. See State data.
Maternal and child health service,
 expenditures for 128
Mathematics:
 Degrees conferred 300, 301, 302, 792
 Employment 796
 Salary offers 297
Mauritania. See Foreign countries.
Mauritius. See Foreign countries.
Mayotte. See Foreign countries.
Measles 190, 191
Measuring, analyzing, and controlling
 instruments. See Instruments and related
 products, manufacturing.
Meat and meat products (see also Food
 manufacturing and individual meats):
 Cholesterol, source 213
 Consumer expenditures 676, 678, 679
 Consumption 214, 826, 844
 Expenditures 820
  Food at home 676
 Foreign trade . 823, 826, 827, 829, 843, 1301
 Iron (dietary), source 213
 Price indexes 715, 727
 Production 843, 1353, 1355
 Supply 843
Media (see also individual medium) . 416, 1125,
  1126, 1127
Medicaid:
 Coverage, recipients ... 145, 146, 147, 149,
  152, 538, 540
 Expenditures 134, 147, 159, 535, 540
 Nursing homes 146, 184, 185
 State data 147, 149
Medical care (see also Health services):
 Budget outlays 476
 Expenditures for .. 128, 129, 130, 131, 132,
  133, 534, 535, 536, 539, 540, 676, 678, 679
 Insurance benefits 128, 132
 Price indexes, consumer 137, 713, 715
  Fixed-weighted 721
 Products and shipments 996
Medical equipment and supplies
 manufacturing 631, 632, 987
Medical research 128
Medical schools 164, 303
 Foreign graduates 162
 Number, students, graduates 164, 303
Medical sciences, employment 615, 617
Medical services. See Health services.
Medicare:
 Ambulatory care visits 167
 Benefit payments, expenditures .. 128, 134,
  140, 142, 143, 144, 159, 535
 Contributions 144
 Enrollees 139
 Hospital visits 167
 Nursing homes 184, 185
 State data 142, 143
 Trust funds 144
 Utilization and charges 142
Medicines. See Drugs and medicines, and
 Pharmaceutical and medicine manufacturing.
Melons 215, 813, 821, 826, 841
Membership organizations:
 Earnings 631

Membership organizations: —Con.
 Employees 631
 Establishments 1265
 Revenue 1277, 1278
Members of Congress. See Congress, U.S.
Menhaden 865
Meningitis 115, 190
Mental hospitals 170, 173, 186
Merchandise. See Foreign trade and General
 merchandise stores.
Merchant vessels:
 Employment and wage scale 1073
 World 1321
Mercury 871, 872, 875, 877
Mergers and acquisitions 758, 759
Metals . 870, 871, 872, 873, 874, 875, 877, 1114
 Foreign trade 1301, 1304
 Production and value 871
  Indexes of production 869
 Railroad, car loadings of 1113, 1114
 Spot market price indexes 724
 Strategic and critical materials 876
 World production 875, 1321, 1361
Metal ore mining industry:
 Capital 766, 870
 Earnings 870
 Employees 620, 774, 870
 Establishments 870
 Occupational safety 652
 Production indexes 869
 Shipments 870
 Value added 870
Metalworking manufacturing 631, 632, 987
Methamphetamine, illegal use 201
Methane gases 374
Metropolitan areas:
 Airline markets 1062
 American Indian, Alaska Native
  population 27
 Asian population 27
 Black population 27
 Civilian labor force 593
 Commuting to work 1091
 Consumer expenditures 677
 Consumer price index 716
 Disability population 198
 Earnings 640
 Foreign born 49
 Hispanic population 28
 Households 26
 Housing 658, 969, 971
 Housing prices 949
 Income 673, 681
 Language spoken at home 59
 Native Hawaiian, Other Pacific Islander
  population 27
 Population 25, 26, 27
 Poverty 698
Mexican origin population ... 22, 23, 28, 33, 46
 Births and birth rates 87
 Business owners 750
 Commuting to work 47
 Disability status 47
 Educational attainment 47, 227
 Foreign born 47
 Labor force 589
 Nativity 47
 Occupation 47

NOTE: Index citations refer to **table** numbers, not page numbers.

Index 1007

U.S. Census Bureau, Statistical Abstract of the United States: 2003

Table

Mexico. See Foreign countries.
Mica 871, 875, 877
   Foreign trade (sheet) 877
   Production and value 871
   World production 875
Mica, scrap and flake 872
Michigan. See State data.
Microcomputers (see Computers)
Migration 18, 34, 36
Military bases 518
Military outlays 476
Military sciences, degrees conferred 300, 301, 302
Military services:
   Basic pay 524
   Casualties 523
   Contract awards 512, 513, 516
   Construction, value of buildings 936
   Expenditures 509, 510, 511, 516
   Foreign countries 1383
   Military force structure 528
   National Guard 527
   Pay grades 524
   Payroll 513, 516
   Personnel 513, 516, 520
      By war 523
      Rank 524
      Foreign countries 519, 1383
   Reserves, by branch 525
   Sex and age 526
   Retirees 517, 537, 545
   Retirement system 545
Milk, cream and other dairy products:
   Calcium, source 213
   Cholesterol, source 213
   Consumption 214, 850
   Prices 727
   Production 848, 849, 850, 1353
   Sales 849
Millet, organic acreage 810
Milo. See Sorghum for grain.
Mineral fuels 871
Mineral leases, public 516
Minerals and mineral products (see also Mining and individual minerals):
   Foreign trade 877
      Waterborne commerce 1071
   Imports as percent of consumption 877
   Price indexes 728, 729
   Prices 873
   Production and value ... 869, 871, 874, 875
      Foreign countries 1365
   Strategic and critical materials 876
   World production 875, 1361
Mining industry (see also Minerals and mineral products and individual minerals):
   Capital 382, 766
      Expenditures 769, 870
   Earnings . 631, 635, 742, 745, 751, 853, 870
   Employees .. 605, 619, 631, 742, 745, 751, 853, 870
   Establishments 742, 743, 745, 853, 870
   Finances 733, 736, 778, 1314
   Foreign investments in the U.S. 1287
   Gross domestic product 660, 1314
   Industrial production index 772
   Mergers and acquisitions 759
   Minority-owned businesses . 752, 753, 754, 755

Table

Mining industry (see also Minerals and mineral products and individual minerals): —Con.
   Multinational companies 780, 781
   Nonemployers 743
   Occupational safety 649, 652, 654
   Pollution abatement 382
   Productivity 632
   Profits 731, 778
   Receipts 731, 733, 736, 740, 741, 742, 743, 870
   Union membership 657
   Value added 870
   Women-owned businesses 751
Mining machinery, manufacturing 631, 987
Minnesota. See State data.
Mississippi. See State data.
Mississippi River traffic 1070
Missouri. See State data.
Mobile homes 947, 958, 959, 960
Mobility status of population . 34, 35, 36, 40, 43
Moldova. See Foreign countries.
Molybdenum 871, 872, 875
Monaco. See Foreign countries.
Monetary system and banks, flow of funds . 1162
Money market accounts, funds 1162, 1166, 1195
   Families using 1166, 1167, 1212, 1214
Money market rates 1193
Money orders 1118, 1187
Money supply (stock) 1192
Mongolia. See Foreign countries.
Monitors 1021
Montana. See State data.
Montenegro. See Foreign countries.
Montserrat. See Foreign countries.
Morocco. See Foreign countries.
Mortality costs 125
Mortgage pools and trusts ... 1162, 1164, 1182
Mortgages. See Loans and mortgages.
Motion picture and sound recording industry:
   Earnings 631, 1119, 1121
   Employees 631, 1119, 1121
   Establishments 1119, 1121
   Gross domestic product 660
   Inventory 1140
   Mergers and acquisitions 759
   Productivity 631
   Receipts, revenue . 1119, 1120, 1124, 1140
Motor freight transportation and warehousing. See Trucking and warehousing.
Motor fuel taxes 454, 1082, 1096
Motor vehicle and parts dealers, retail:
   Earnings 631, 742, 1025, 1026, 1034
   Electronic commerce 1045
   Employees 631, 742, 1025, 1026, 1034
   Establishments . 742, 1024, 1025, 1026, 1033, 1034
   Finances 733, 1034
   Franchises 1034
   Inventories 1031, 1034
   Nonemployers 1033
   Productivity 632
   Profits 1034
   Purchases 1030
   Sales ... 733, 742, 1024, 1026, 1027, 1029, 1032, 1033, 1034, 1045
Motor vehicles:
   Accidents/deaths .. 119, 1058, 1097, 1099, 1105
   Air pollutant emissions 373

NOTE: Index citations refer to **table** numbers, not page numbers.

| Table |

Motor vehicles: —Con.
   Alternative fueled vehicles in use 1086
   Common carriers 1054, 1108, 1109
   Consumer expenditures . 676, 677, 678, 679
   Crashes 1101
   Drivers licenses 1088
   Expenditure per new car 1035
   Foreign trade 1301
   Fuel consumed 1096
   Fuel prices 907
   Imports 1035
   Insurance 1224
   Leases 1036
   Miles of travel 1088
   Ownership 976, 977
   Passenger outlays 1053
   Price indexes, consumer 715
      Fixed-weighted 721
   Production 1035
   Railroad car loadings 1113
   Registrations 1085, 1088
   Sales 1035, 1036
   Service and repair shops. See Automotive
     repair and maintenance service.
   Taxes, licenses and motor fuel 454
   Theft 305, 306, 307, 318, 324, 325
   Traffic fatalities ... 1097, 1098, 1099, 1100,
                    1102, 1103, 1104
   Trucks 1095, 1096
Motor vehicle manufacturing:
   Capital 766
   Earnings 631, 992
   Employees 631, 992, 1017, 1018
   Foreign trade 1304
   Gross domestic product 660, 984
   Industrial production index 772
   Inventories 995
   Multinational companies 780, 781
   Occupational safety 652
   Productivity 632
   Research and development 793, 794
   Sales, shipments, receipts .. 987, 996, 1008,
                    1017, 1018, 1321
     State data 1018
Motorcycles 1088, 1097, 1301
   Accidents and deaths 1097
   Foreign trade 1301
   Racing 1243
Mountain biking 1247
Movie theaters 1125, 1239, 1246
Mozambique. See Foreign countries.
Mullet, catch 865
Multinational companies 780, 781
Multiple births 93
Multiple jobholders 608
Mumps 190, 191
Municipal and State bonds .. 1165, 1166, 1168,
                    1194, 1195, 1204
Municipal waste 375, 376
   Foreign countries 1329
Municipalities. See Cities and Metropolitan
   areas.
Murders . 305, 306, 307, 308, 309, 310, 313, 325
Museums 1236, 1237
Museums, botanical, zoological gardens.
   See Museums, historical sites.
Museums, historical sites:
   Earnings 631
   Employees 620, 631, 1231

| Table |

Museums, historical sites: —Con.
   Establishments 1231
   Federal aid 1236
   Finances 1231, 1236
   Nonemployers 1232
   Occupational safety 652
   Receipts, revenue 1230, 1232
Mushrooms 813, 826, 841
Music:
   Listening and expenditures 1041, 1125,
                    1142, 1237, 1240
   Industry receipts 1124, 1141
Musicians and composers 615
Muslim population. See Religion.
Mutton (see also Meat and meat products) . 214,
                             843
Mutual funds .. 1162, 1166, 1167, 1198, 1211,
      1212, 1213, 1214, 1215, 1216, 1217,
                        1218, 1221

N

Namibia. See Foreign countries.
National Aeronautics and Space
   Administration 785
   Budget 801
   Expenditures, research and
     development 782
       Space program 801, 802
   Space launches 800, 803
National Association of Securities Dealers
   (NASDAQ) 1206
   Stock indices 1204
NCAA sports participation 1250
National debt. See Debt.
National defense (see also individual military
   services):
   Contract awards and payrolls 513
   Expenditures, world 1383
   Federal employment and payrolls 468
   Federal outlays 475, 479, 510
   Military forces 519, 521
      Foreign countries 1383
   Ready reserves 526
   Outlays 509
National forests. See Forests.
National Guard 527
National health expenditures 128, 129, 130
National income (see also Gross domestic
   product) 666
Native Hawaiian and Other Pacific
   Islander 13, 14, 23, 32
   Births 84
   College costs 287
   Commuting to work 43
   Congressional districts 1384
   Disability status 43, 285
   Distance education 286
   Educational attainment 43
   Foreign born 43
   Head Start 572
   Income 680, 692
   Metropolitan areas 27
   Minority businesses 750
   Mobility status 43
   Nativity 43
   Nurses 161
   Occupation 43
   Poverty 697
Native Hawaiian Home Lands 45

NOTE: Index citations refer to **table** numbers, not page numbers.

	Table
Natural gas:	
Consumption	895, 896, 898, 902, 903, 904, 1363, 1364
Expenditures	900, 901, 902, 903, 904
Foreign trade	896, 908, 909, 1301
Prices	715, 719, 873, 886, 905, 907
Production	881, 895, 896
World	875, 886, 887, 1321, 1361, 1362, 1365
Reserves	882
Natural gas distribution industry	631, 632
Natural gas plant liquids	881
Prediction	881
Reserves	882
Supply	879
Value	881
Natural resources:	
Federal outlays	479
Governmental finances	443
Aid to State and local governments	438
Government employment and payrolls	468
Governmental revenue	443
State and local governments	442
State governments	453, 454
Natural resource industry	629, 636
Nauru. See Foreign countries.	
Navy	517, 518
Nebraska. See State data.	
Nectarines	215, 842
Neonatal deaths (see also Deaths and death rates)	113
Nepal. See Foreign countries.	
Netherlands. See Foreign countries.	
Netherlands Antilles. See Foreign countries.	
Neurologists	162
Nevada. See State data.	
New Caledonia. See Foreign countries.	
New Hampshire. See State data.	
New Jersey. See State data.	
New Mexico. See State data.	
New York. See State data.	
New York Stock Exchange	1204, 1207
Stock indices	1204
New Zealand. See Foreign countries.	
Newspapers (See also Publishing industry):	
Advertising expenditures	1274
Expenditures, consumer	1125, 1234
Frequency of publication	1128
Number and circulation	1126, 1130, 1131
Public confidence in media	416
Reading	1125, 1127
Receipts	1124
Newspaper, book and directory publishers:	
Earnings	631, 1119, 1121
Employees	631, 1119, 1121
Establishments	1119, 1121
Finances	1129
Inventory	1129
Revenue	1119, 1120, 1129
Newsprint	862
Producer prices	860
World production	1321
Nicaragua. See Foreign countries.	
Nickel	871, 875, 877, 1301
Consumption	872
Employment	872
Foreign trade	872, 877, 1301
Prices	872

	Table
Nickel —Con.	
Production and value	871, 872, 875
World production	875, 1361
Niger. See Foreign countries.	
Nigeria. See Foreign countries.	
Nitrogen in ammonia, world production	872, 875, 1361
Nobel prize laureates	804
Nonemployer establishments	576, 743, 1033, 1227, 1232, 1267
Nonfinancial corporations. See Corporations.	
Nonmetallic mineral mining and quarrying, except fuels:	
Capital	766, 870
Earnings	870
Employees	870
Establishments	870
Finances	778
Gross domestic product	660, 854
Industrial production index	772
Occupational safety	652
Productivity	632
Shipments, receipts	870
Value added	870
Nonmetallic mineral product manufacturing (see also Metals and metal products):	
Earnings	631, 985, 987, 992
Electronic commerce	989
Employees	631, 985, 987, 992
Energy consumption	906
Establishments	985
Foreign trade	1304
Gross domestic product	660
Occupational safety	651, 652
Patents	763
Pollution abatement	382
Productivity	632
Profits	778
Sales, shipments, receipts	987, 989, 994, 995
Stone, clay, and glass	1113, 1114
Toxic chemical releases	379
North Carolina. See State data.	
North Dakota. See State data.	
Northern Mariana Islands. See Island areas of the U.S.	
North Korea. See Foreign countries.	
Norway. See Foreign countries.	
Nuclear power	920
Capability	914, 919, 1367
Commercial generation, by country	1367
Consumption	895, 896, 898, 1363, 1364
Production	914, 918, 919, 1362, 1366, 1367
Reactors	919, 1367
State data	918
Waste discharged fuel	920, 1329
Nursery and greenhouse products	813, 838
Nursing personnel	161, 163
Employment	615
Projections	617
Nursing and residential care facilities:	
Earnings	631
Employees	160, 184, 620, 631
Establishments	180, 184
Expenditures	127, 129, 130, 131, 136
Consumer	129, 130
Receipts	158, 159
Residents	77, 78, 184, 185
Nursing programs, students, and graduates	164

NOTE: Index citations refer to **table** numbers, not page numbers.

| Table | | Table |

Nutrition:
    Consumption of major commodities ... 214, 215, 216
    Nutrients and nutritional intake 212
Nutritional deficiencies, deaths 115
Nuts:
    Cash receipts, marketing 813, 816
    Consumption 826, 840
    Foreign trade 827, 829, 840
    Production 821, 840, 1353

O

Oats, organic acreage 810
Obstetricians (See also Physicians) 162
Occupational safety 651, 652
Occupations (see also individual occupations):
    Adult education 304
    American Indian, Alaska Native population 43
    Asian population 43
    Black population 40, 615, 618
    Computer use 634
    Earnings 638, 641, 642
    Employment 605, 606, 607, 615, 616, 617, 618, 625
        Black population 615, 618
        Employee benefits 648
        Flexible schedules 606
        Hispanic origin population 615
        Home-based work 605
        Projections 617
        Race 615
        Sex 615, 618, 619
        Shift work 607
        State data 616
    Employment cost index 643
    Hispanic origin population 615
    Job search 622
    Labor union membership 657
    Mobility status 34
    Native Hawaiian, Other Pacific Islander population 43
    Pension plan/health plan coverage 647
    Sex and educational attainment 618
    White-collar and blue-collar workers 643
Ocean perch, Atlantic 865
Office buildings (see also Commercial buildings) 936, 982
    Construction 936, 981
    Vacancy rates 981, 983
Office equipment. See Computer and office equipment.
Office supplies, stationary and gift stores . 631, 632, 1026
Offshore leases 880
Ohio. See State data.
Oil. See Petroleum and products.
Oil and gas extraction industry:
    Capital 382, 766, 870
    Earnings 631, 742, 870
    Employees 631, 742, 870
    Establishments 742, 870
    Gross domestic product 660, 854
    Mergers and acquisitions 759
    Multinational companies 781
    Occupational safety 652
    Output 869
    Patents 763
    Pollution abatement 382

Oil and gas extraction industry: —Con.
    Production indexes 869
    Productivity 632
    Shipments, receipts 742, 870
    Value added 870
Oil crops 813, 818, 821, 823, 825
Oilseeds, world production 1357
Oil spills 370
Oils:
    Animal (oils and fats) 214, 829
    Animal and vegetable, foreign trade ... 828, 829
    Vegetable:
        Foreign trade . 823, 826, 827, 828, 829, 1301
        Production, consumption, and stocks . 214, 826, 828, 1353
Oklahoma. See State data.
Old-age pensions. See Pensions.
Old-age, survivors, disability, and health insurance. See Social insurance.
Olives 826, 842
Oman. See Foreign countries.
Onions 215, 727, 813, 826, 841
Opera 1235, 1237
Operations performed, medical 178
Ophthalmologists 162
Optical goods 129, 130
Optometrists 129, 130, 158
Optometry schools, students, graduates ... 164
Oranges 215, 813, 826, 842
Oregon. See State data.
Ores, crude. (see also individual ores):
    World production 875
Organ transplants 177
Organic farmland, livestock 810
Orphans 6
Osteopaths (see also Physicians) 162
Otolaryngology 162
Outdoor recreation activities (see also Recreation and specific forms of recreation) 1239, 1247, 1251, 1252
Outlays, Federal budget ... 475, 476, 477, 478, 479
Outpatient care centers industry 158
Outpatient hospital visits 170, 172
Overweight 209
Oysters 865, 867, 868

P

Pacific Islander population 21, 23, 32
Pagers 1015
Pain relievers, illegal use 201
Pakistan. See Foreign countries.
Pakistani population 23
Palau. See Foreign countries.
Panama. See Foreign countries.
Papayas 842
Paper, manufacturing:
    Capital 382, 766
    Earnings 631, 985, 987, 992
    Electronic commerce 989
    Employees 631, 985, 987, 992
    Energy consumption 906
    Establishments 985
    Finances 778
    Foreign trade 1304
    Gross domestic product 660, 854, 984
    Industrial production index 772

NOTE: Index citations refer to **table** numbers, not page numbers.

Index 1011

Table	Table
Paper, manufacturing: —Con.	Perch 868, 984
Mergers and acquisitions 759	Performing arts 1232, 1235, 1244
Occupational safety 652	Performing arts, spectator sports industry:
Output 862	Earnings 631, 1231
Pollution abatement 382	Employees 631, 1231
Productivity 632	Establishments 1231
Profits 778	Nonemployers 1232
Research and development 794	Receipts, revenue 1230, 1232
Sales, shipments, receipts ... 842, 987, 989, 994, 995	Periodical prices. (See also Information industry and Publishing industry) 1133
Toxic chemical releases 379	Periodical publishing 1129
Paper and paperboard products:	Perlite 871, 872
Foreign trade 1301	Personal computers. See Computers.
Producer prices 860	Personal consumption expenditures .. 659, 662, 666, 721, 722, 1234
Production 862	Chain-type price indexes 721
Railroad car loadings 1113, 1114	Recreation 1234
Recycling 376	Personal care price indexes 715
Papua New Guinea. See Foreign countries.	Personal health care:
Paraguay. See Foreign countries.	Expenditures 129, 130, 132, 133
Paris CAC-40 stock market index 1375	Practices 201, 203
Parks 1255, 1256	Personal income 668, 670, 671, 672, 673
Finances 1255, 1256	Personal savings 669, 674
Government employment and payrolls . 468	Personal and laundry services (formerly personal supply services):
National 1255	Earnings 631, 1265
State 1256	Employees 619, 620, 631, 1265, 1277
Parolees (see also Correctional institutions, and Prisons and prisoners) 350	Establishments 1265
Parties, political. See Political parties.	Finances 733
Partnerships, establishments and finances . 731, 732, 733, 735, 736	Occupational safety 652
Passenger transit industry (see also Passengers):	Productivity 632
Earnings 631	Receipts 733, 1277
Employees 632	Pertussis 190
Occupational safety 652	Peru. See Foreign countries.
Passengers (see also Passenger transit industry and various transportation modes):	Pesticides 812, 833
Arriving from overseas ... 1260, 1261, 1262	Pet ownership 1242
Carrier operation, summary 1059, 1108, 1109, 1112	Petroleum and coal product manufacturing:
	Capital 382, 766
Air 1059, 1068	Earnings 631, 985, 992
Rail 1112	Employees 620, 631, 985, 992
Outlays, by type of transport 1053	Energy consumption 906
Passenger traffic, volume 1054	Establishments 985
Railroads 1112	Finances 778, 913
Patents and trademarks ... 762, 763, 764, 1339	Foreign investments in U.S. 1285, 1286, 1288
Pathologists 162	Foreign trade 1304
Payrolls. Earnings and individual industries.	Gross domestic product 660, 984
PCP usage 201	Industrial production index 772
Peaches 215, 813, 842	Mergers and acquisitions 759
Peanuts 214, 813	Multinational companies 780
Peanut butter 727	Occupational safety 652
Pears 215, 727, 826, 842	Pollution abatement 382
Peas 841	Productivity 632
Peat 871, 872	Profits 777, 778, 912, 913
Pecans 813, 842	Research and development 793, 794
Pediatricians (see also Physicians) 162, 166	Sales, shipments 870, 994, 995
Pennsylvania. See State data.	Toxic chemical releases 379
Pensions and retirement benefits (see also Social insurance):	Petroleum products:
Expenditures 545, 553, 676	Consumption 877, 895, 896, 898, 1363, 1364
Families receiving 537, 552	Foreign trade . 877, 878, 896, 908, 909, 910, 911, 912, 1295, 1304
Funds (flow of funds) 1162, 1166, 1219	Lease revenues 880
Government employees . 537, 545, 546, 547	Oil spills 370
Plans 550, 553, 554	Prices 873, 905, 907
Railroad 537	Production .. 871, 873, 875, 878, 880, 883, 887, 895, 896
Retirement and pension plans 545, 548, 549, 553, 647, 1198, 1216, 1217, 1218	World 875, 883, 1361, 1362, 1365
Veterans 529, 537	Railroad, car loadings of 1113, 1114
Peppers 727, 813, 826, 841	

NOTE: Index citations refer to **table** numbers, not page numbers.

Table	Table
Petroleum products: —Con.	Pipelines, transportation industry: —Con.
Refineries 878	Employees 631, 1056, 1057
Reserves 878, 882	Establishments 1057
Stocks 911	Finances 1116
Strategic reserve 911	Occupational safety 652
Value 879, 881	Output 1116
Wells 878, 879	Pistachios 842
Drilling costs 879	Pistols. See Firearms.
Leases and production 880	Plague 190
Pharmaceutical and medicine manufacturing:	Plants 838, 1241
Earnings 631, 985, 987	Plastic and rubber products manufacturing:
Employees 631, 801, 803, 985, 987	Capital 382, 766
Mergers and acquisitions 759	Earnings 631, 985, 987, 992
Multinational companies 781	Electronic commerce 989
Productivity 632	Employees 605, 631, 985, 987, 992
Shipments 987, 1005	Energy consumption 906
Pharmacies and drug stores:	Establishments 985
Earnings 1025, 1026, 1029	Finances 778
Employees 1025, 1026, 1029	Foreign trade ....,.... 1304
Establishments 1025, 1026, 1029	Gross domestic product 660, 984
Sales 1026, 1027, 1029	Industrial production index 772
Pharmacists 615	Inventories 995
Pharmacy schools, students, graduates 164	Mergers and acquisitions 759
Philanthropy 579, 580, 581, 583, 584	Occupational safety 651, 652
Philippines. See Foreign countries.	Patents 763
Phonograph records and tapes 1141	Pollution abatement 382
Phosphate rock:	Productivity 632
Consumption 872	Profits 778
Employment 872	Sales, shipments, receipts ... 987, 989, 994, 995
Foreign trade 872	Toxic chemical releases 379
Prices 872	Plastic surgeons 162
Production and value 871	Plastics 1301
World production 875, 1361	Platinum-group metals 872
Photographic equipment and supplies 1301	Consumption 872
Physical activity 210	Employment 872
Physical sciences:	Foreign trade 872, 877
Degrees conferred 300, 301, 302, 792	Prices 872, 873
Employees 615, 617, 796	Production ...... r......................... 872
Physicians 160, 162, 163, 165	Strategic and critical materials 876
Degrees conferred 303	Plumbing 979
Earnings 166	Plums and prunes 215, 842
Employment 162, 163, 615	Plural births 93
Expenditures for .. 127, 129, 130, 131, 132, 133, 134, 136	Plywood:
	Consumption 857
Foreign countries 1325	Foreign trade 857, 858
Foreign medical school graduates 162	Output 857
Medical schools, students and	Producer price indexes 860
graduates 164, 303	Pneumonia 115, 117, 118, 169, 176
Offices 158, 159	Poland. See Foreign countries.
Patient care activities 166	Police. See Law enforcement and Public safety.
Price index 137	Poliomyelitis 191
Specialty and professional activity 162	Political action committees (PAC) 425, 426, 427, 430
State data 163	
Type of practice 162	Political parties, organizations:
Visits to 165, 167, 168	Campaign finances 423, 428, 429, 430
Physics (see also Physical sciences):	Political action committees (PAC) ... 427, 430
Nobel prize laureates 804	
Salary offers 297	Congress, composition of 405, 406
Physiology, Nobel prize laureates 804	Congressional districts 403
Pig iron. See Iron.	Governors, by party affiliation 411
Piggyback, railroad carloads 1067	Public confidence 416
Pigs. See Hogs.	State legislatures, composition of . 413, 414
Pilchard. See Sardines.	Volunteers 585
Pineapples 215, 842	Voter identification 421
Pipe (smoking), usage 201	Votes ... 396, 398, 399, 400, 401, 404, 412
Pipeline, freight and mileage 1116	Pollock 865, 868
Pipelines, transportation industry:	Pollution:
Capital 766, 1116	Abatement expenditures 382, 383
Earnings 631, 1056, 1057	

NOTE: Index citations refer to **table** numbers, not page numbers.

Index 1013

U.S. Census Bureau, Statistical Abstract of the United States: 2003

	Table		Table
Pollution: —Con.		Population (see also Vital statistics): —Con.	
Air	371, 372, 373, 382, 383	States	21
Hazardous waste sites	381	Resident	1, 2, 3, 4, 11, 20, 24
Industry	384	Rural	30
Motor vehicle emissions	373	Sex	11, 12, 54
Oil spills	368, 370	States	17, 18, 19, 20, 21, 25
Toxic releases	378, 379, 380	American Indian, Alaska Native population	21
Wastewater treatment	930	Asian	21
Water	370, 382	Black population	21
Poor persons. See Income and Poverty.		Density	18
Population (see also Vital statistics):		Hispanic origin population	22
Age:		Native Hawaiian, Other Pacific Islander	21
American Indian, Alaska Native population	13, 14, 16	Race	21
Asian population	13, 14, 16	Voting age	419, 422
Black population	11, 13, 14, 16, 39	Total, including Armed Forces overseas	2
Distribution	11, 12, 13, 16, 20, 54	Townships and special districts	433
Foreign born	51	Urban	30
Hispanic origin population	13, 14, 16, 46	World	1319, 1322, 1323
Island areas	1307, 1308	Pork (see also Meat and meat products):	
Native Hawaiian, Other Pacific Islander	13, 14	Consumption	214, 826, 843
Race	11, 13, 14, 16, 39, 44	Foreign trade	825, 826, 843
School enrollment	219, 222	Production	843, 844, 1355
Sex	11, 12, 23	Supply	843
Voting-age population	419, 422	Pork chops	727
American Indian, Eskimo, Aleut. See American Indian, Alaska Native population.		Portland cement	871
Ancestry	55	Ports, U.S.	1074
Asian, Pacific Islander population. See Asian, Pacific Islander population.		Portugal. See Foreign countries.	
Black. See Black population.		Postal rates	1117
Cities	29, 31, 32, 33	Postal Service	1118, 1128
Civilian	2	Productivity	632
Coastal	24	Potash (potassium salts)	871, 872, 875
Components of change	4, 19	Potassium, foreign trade	877
Congressional districts	1384	Potatoes:	
Continents	1320	Acreage	834, 841
Density	1, 17	Consumption	215, 826, 839
Foreign countries	1322	Farm marketings, sales	813
Elderly	11, 13, 20, 37, 76	Foreign trade	839
Ethnic origin	55	Pesticide usage	833
Fertility	88	Prices	727, 818, 834
Foreign born	48, 49, 52, 54, 1409	Production	834, 839, 841
Students	226	World production	1321
Foreign countries	1322, 1323	Poultry (see also Eggs):	
Group quarters	78	Cholesterol source	213
Hispanic origin. See Hispanic origin population.		Consumer expenditures	678, 679
Households and/or families. See Households or families.		Consumption	214, 843
		Farm marketings, sales	813, 816
Immigrants	5, 6, 8, 9, 10	Foreign trade	827, 829, 843
Island areas of the U.S.	1305, 1307, 1308, 1309, 1313	Iron (dietary), source	213
Labor force. See Labor force, employment and earnings.		Number on farms	851
		Organic	810
Marital status. See Marital status of population.		Prices	727, 818, 851
		Production and sales	819, 821, 843, 851, 852, 1353
Metropolitan areas	25, 26	Foreign countries	1355
Migration	34, 35	Value	851
Mobility	34, 35	Poverty:	
Native Hawaiian, Other Pacific Islander population. See Native Hawaiian, Other Pacific Islander population.		Children	701, 703, 698, 699
		Families	706, 707, 698, 699
		Black population	39, 707
Nativity	48, 49, 54, 1409	Educational attainment	707
Place of birth	48, 49, 1409	Elderly	689
Projections	3, 4, 12, 15	Hispanic origin population	46, 707
Race	12, 13, 15	Housing	933
		Labor force	704, 707
		State	699

NOTE: Index citations refer to **table** numbers, not page numbers.

	Table
Poverty: —Con.	
Foreign born	54
Persons	697, 698, 699
Age	703, 704
American Indian, Alaska Native	697
Asian and Pacific Islander population	700, 701
Asian population	697
Black population	39, 688, 697, 700, 701, 703, 706
Children	701, 703
Congressional districts	1384
Elderly	37, 703
Hispanic origin population	46, 688, 697, 700, 701, 703
Native Hawaiian and Other Pacific Islander	697
State	705
Threshold	702, 699
Power (see also Electric light and power industry):	
Electric	914, 915, 916, 917, 919, 922, 923
Hydro	914
Nuclear	914, 1367
Prices	725, 900
Water	368, 925
Power generation and supply industry	631, 632
Power plants. See Electric light and power industry.	
Precipitation, selected cities	392, 393, 394, 1328
Pregnancies	97, 168
Smoking during pregnancy	97
Teen pregnancies	84, 85, 86, 91, 92, 94
Prenatal care	84, 91, 95
Prescription drugs	127, 129, 130, 131, 132, 133, 135, 136, 137, 156, 715
President, U.S., elections for	396, 397, 398, 399, 400, 422
Campaign finances	424, 427, 428
Prices (see also individual commodities):	
Bonds	1204, 1209
Books and periodicals	1133, 1136
Electricity	725, 900
Energy	905, 907
Fish, by species	864
Food	726, 727
Foreign countries	717, 1340, 1341
Housing	946, 947, 948, 949, 951
Indexes:	
Airline cost	1060
Construction materials	933
Consumer price	713, 715, 1340
Foreign countries	1340
Medical care	137
Metropolitan areas	714, 716
Exports	729
Imports	723, 728
Producer prices	718
Construction materials	933
Railroad freight	1115
Stage-of-processing	718
Timber	860
Purchasing power of the dollar	712
Received by farmers	818
School expenditures	253
Spot market price	724
Lumber and stumpage	861

	Table
Prices (see also individual commodities): —Con.	
Mineral products (see also individual minerals)	873
Received by farmers:	
Crops	834
Indexes	818
Livestock and products, poultry	844, 851
Stocks	1204, 1209
Primaries, Presidential preference	428
Primary metal manufacturing:	
Capital	382, 766
Earnings	631, 985, 987, 992
Electronic commerce	989
Employees	631, 985, 987, 992
Energy consumption	906
Establishments	985
Finance	778, 1007
Foreign trade	1007, 1304
Gross domestic product	660, 984
Industrial production index	772
Mergers and acquisitions	759
Occupational safety	652
Patents	763
Pollution abatement	382
Productivity	632
Profits	777, 778
Research and development	794
Shipments	987, 989, 994, 995, 1008, 1009
Toxic chemical releases	379
Printing and related support activities. See Publishing industry.	
Prisons and prisoners (see also Correctional institutions)	348, 349, 351, 352, 353, 354, 355, 356
Death sentence	352, 353, 354, 355
Executions	354, 355
Expenditures	454, 456
Inmate characteristics	348
Sentence, by offense	339
Probation	350
Producer price indexes	718, 719, 720
Construction materials	933
Railroad freight	1115
Stage-of-processing	718
Timber	860
Productivity (see also individual industries):	
Capacity utilization	773
Farm output	821, 831
Labor	633, 1338, 1368, 1369
Mining industries	889
Professional and business services:	
Earnings	629, 631, 636
Employees	629, 630, 631
Hours	629
Professional scientific and technical services:	
Capital	769
Earnings	631, 742, 745, 746, 1266, 1272
Employees	631, 742, 745, 746, 1266
Establishments	742, 743, 745, 1266, 1267
Finances	733, 736
Multinational companies	780
Nonemployers	743, 1267
Sales, receipts	733, 736, 740, 741, 742, 743, 1267
Profits	739, 1034, 1175, 1176, 1221, 1224
Corporations	669, 731, 775, 776, 777, 778, 997
Partnerships and proprietorships	731, 734, 735

NOTE: Index citations refer to **table** numbers, not page numbers.

Index 1015

U.S. Census Bureau, Statistical Abstract of the United States: 2003

	Table
Projections:	
Births	89, 1326
College enrollment	217, 219
Deaths	1326
Degrees conferred	219
Employment	617, 620
Energy	896
Health expenditures	127, 129, 132
High school graduates	219
Labor force	588, 617, 620
Life expectancy	105, 1326
Population	3, 12, 15, 1322
School enrollment	217, 219
Teachers	219, 617
Property and casualty insurance	1224
Fire losses	356, 357, 358
Property tax	443, 454
Rates, selected cities	460
State and local government	442
Proprietors' income	668
Proprietorships	731, 733, 734
Prostitution and commercialized vice, arrests	325
Protective service workers. See Public safety.	
Protein available for consumption	212
Protestants. See Religion.	
Prunes and plums	215, 842
Psychiatric care and institutions. See Mental hospitals.	
Psychology:	
Degrees conferred	300, 301, 302, 792
Employment	615
Research, U.S. government obligations for	786
Psychotherapeutic drugs, nonmedical use	201
Public administration. See Government.	
Public aid, assistance	539, 562
Benefits paid	562
Federal aid to State and local governments	438, 439
Federal expenditures	128, 131, 142, 146, 147, 538, 539, 540, 563, 564
Health expenditures	128, 131, 142, 146, 147, 538, 539, 540
Recipients	537, 538, 540, 562, 563, 564
Public domain. See Public lands.	
Public housing	439, 538, 539, 540
Public lands (see also Forests):	
Area	360, 362, 507
Cost and usage	507
Leases, permits, licenses	507, 880
National forests	855
National park system	1255
Ownership	507
Recreation	1255
Public officials, prosecutions	340
Public roads. See Highways.	
Public safety (see also Law enforcement):	
Employment	615
City government	473
Fire protection	468
Police protection and correction	468, 471
Expenditures	334
City government	464
Construction, value	937, 938
Local government	458
State and local government	442
State government	454

	Table
Public safety (see also Law enforcement): —Con.	
Volunteers	585
Public schools. See Education.	
Public transportation indexes	715
Publishing. See Books, Newspapers and Printing.	
Books	1134, 1135, 1138
Newspapers	1128, 1130, 1131, 1132
Periodicals	1133
Publishing industries:	
Capital	382
Earnings	631, 742, 1119, 1121
Employees	631, 742, 1119, 1121
Establishments	742, 1119, 1121
Finances	778
Industrial production index	772
Pollution abatement	382
Profit	778
Receipts, revenue	742, 1119, 1120, 1129, 1137, 1139
Puerto Rico. See Island areas of the U.S.	
Puerto Rican population (see also Hispanic origin population)	22, 23, 28, 33, 46
Business owners	718, 750
Commuting to work	47
Disability status	47
Educational attainment	47, 209, 228
Foreign born	47
Labor force	562, 589
Mobility status	47
Nativity	47
Occupation	47
Population	23, 24, 35, 40, 1291, 1304, 1308, 1309
Pulmonary diseases	115, 117, 119, 176, 190
Pulpwood	857, 858
Pulses	215, 1353
Pumice and pumicite	871, 872
Purchasing power of the dollar	712
Pyrites	871

Q

Qatar. See Foreign countries.
Quarries. See Mining industries.
Quicksilver (mercury) 871

R

Rabies	190
Racetrack operations	1245
Racquetball	1247
Radioactive material shipments	1078
Radiologists	162
Radio broadcasting industry:	
Earnings	631, 1121
Employees	631, 1121, 1143
Establishments	1119, 1121
Finances	1124, 1143
Mergers and acquisitions	759
Productivity	632
Revenue	1120, 1124, 1143
Radio broadcasting stations:	
Advertising expenditures	1274
Public confidence in media	416
Stations	1126
Radios:	
Audience characteristics	1125, 1127
Households with	1126
Listening	1125
Railroad employees retirement funds	535

NOTE: Index citations refer to **table** numbers, not page numbers.

	Table
Railroads:	
AMTRAK	1112
Carloadings, by commodity	1113, 1114
Construction value	936
Earnings	631, 1112
Employees	631, 1056, 1112
Equipment in service	1112
Finances	766, 1112, 1194
Freight price indexes	1115
Freight traffic	1054, 1112, 1113, 1114
Mileage owned and operated	1112
Occupational safety	1058, 1112
Passenger traffic and revenue	1054, 1112
Piggyback	1113, 1114
Productivity	632, 1112
Rainfall, selected cities	392, 393, 1328
Raisins	813
Rankings:	
Airport traffic	1061
Cities:	
Population	29, 31
Residential property tax	460
Countries:	
Consumption of beef, pork, poultry	1356
Exports and imports of wheat, rice, corn	1358
Population	1322
Exports	1298
Federal R&D obligations to higher education	790
Hazardous waste sites	380
Sports participation	1247
State:	
Domestic travel expenditures	1259
Farm marketings	817
Foreign trade	1296
Government finances	455
Personal income per capita	671
Disposable	672
Population	18
Public elementary/secondary school finances	255
Rape, forcible	305, 306, 307, 308, 314, 315, 321, 322, 323, 324
Rapeseed	1353
Rare-earth minerals	872
Raw materials. See Crude materials.	
Reading (see also Books and Libraries)	678, 679, 1233, 1237, 1244
Consumer price indexes	715
Real estate and rental and leasing industry:	
Capital	769
Earnings	631, 742, 745, 746, 1228
Employees	615, 631, 742, 745, 746, 1228
Establishments	742, 743, 745, 1227, 1228
Finances	733, 736
Gross domestic product	660, 1160
Mergers and acquisitions	759
Nonemployers	743, 1227
Receipts	733, 736, 740, 741, 742, 743, 1227, 1228
Receipts (see also individual industries and Tax receipts):	
Corporations, partnerships, and proprietorships	731, 732, 733, 734, 735, 736, 739, 740, 741
International transportation	1280
Minority-owned businesses	750, 752, 753, 754, 755, 766

	Table
Receipts (see also individual industries and Tax receipts): —Con.	
Revenue:	
Local governments	443, 457
City governments	463, 464
County governments	465
State and local governments combined	441, 442, 448
State governments	443, 453, 454, 455
Tax collections	455
United States Government	434, 443, 475, 481, 489
Women-owned businesses	750, 751, 766
Recreation (see also Arts, entertainment, and recreation and Sports):	
Activities	210, 1125, 1235, 1237, 1239, 1240, 1241, 1244, 1245, 1246, 1247, 1255, 1256
Building construction, value	939
Consumer expenditures	1125, 1134, 1233, 1234, 1253, 1254
Consumer price indexes	715
Employment and expenditures, government	479
City governments	468
County governments	465
Parks:	
Government expenditures	442, 444
National	1255
Visits	1255, 1256
Performing arts	1235
Spectator sports	1245
Travel	1257, 1258, 1259, 1260, 1261
Volunteers	585
RV parks and recreational camps	631
Recreational vehicles	1246, 1253
Recycling waste	375, 376, 377, 378
Refrigerators and refrigeration equipment	1023
Refugees	6, 9
Refuse collection	377, 715
Religion	79, 80, 81, 82
Charitable contributions	580
Church/synagogue attendance	80
Philanthropy	581, 584
Religious, grantmaking, civic, professional organizations:	
Employees	1265
Establishments	1265
Revenues	1277
Volunteers	585
Religious identification	79, 80
Rental and leasing services	1228, 1229, 1265, 1268
Renters insurance	1226
Rents	715, 970, 971, 972
Repair services. See Automobile repair and maintenance service.	
Representatives, U.S. See Congress, U.S.	
Research and development:	
Employment	795
Expenditures:	
By country	784
College and universities	783, 788
Federal	782, 783, 784, 785, 787, 789, 790
Industry	783
National defense	510, 782
Services	1265

NOTE: Index citations refer to **table** numbers, not page numbers.

Residential buildings. See Construction industry, and Housing and housing units.
Residential capital 978
Restaurants. See Food services and drinking places.
Retail trade:
　Capital expenditures 767, 769
　Earnings . 631, 635, 636, 742, 745, 746, 751, 1024, 1318
　Electronic commerce 1041, 1042
　Employees .. 605, 619, 624, 631, 742, 745, 746, 751, 1024, 1317, 1318
　Establishments . 742, 743, 745, 1024, 1033, 1317, 1318
　Finances ... 731, 733, 736, 778, 1189, 1314
　Foreign investments in the U.S. . 1286, 1288
　Gross domestic product 660, 664, 1314
　Industry 742, 1026
　Inventories 774, 1031
　Mergers and acquisitions 759
　Minority-owned businesses . 752, 753, 754, 755
　Multinational companies 780, 781
　Nonemployers 743, 1033
　Occupational safety 652
　Productivity 632
　Profits 778
　Sales, receipts . 733, 736, 740, 741, 742, 743, 751, 1024, 1027, 1028, 1030, 1031, 1032, 1033, 1041, 1042, 1044, 1318
　Women-owned businesses 751
Retirement age 1346
Retirement systems:
　Benefits paid 545
　Civil service 545, 546, 1219
　Defined benefit retirement plans 550
　Federal other than civil service ... 545, 1219
　Government transfer payments ... 534, 535, 536
　Old-age, survivors, disability, and health insurance. See Social insurance.
　Pension plans 545, 548, 553, 1219
　Public employees 545
　Railroad 1219
　Social security trust funds 542
　State and local government . 442, 472, 1219
Reunion. See Foreign countries.
Revolvers. See Firearms.
Rhode Island. See State data.
Rice:
　Acreage, organic 810
　Consumption 214, 826
　Farm marketings, sales 813
　Foreign trade 823, 826, 828, 829, 1301
　Production 828
　　World 828, 1353
Rifle (NCAA) 1250
Rivers, canals, harbors, etc.:
　Commerce, domestic and foreign 1070
　Drainage area and flow 366
　Length of principal rivers 366
　Water quality 369
Roads, public. See Highways.
Roadway congestion 1089
Robbery ... 305, 306, 307, 308, 318, 321, 322, 323
Rockfish 865, 868
Rodeos 1243, 1245
Roller skating 1247

Romania. See Foreign countries.
Rowing 1250
Rubber, crude natural 823, 825
Rubber and misc. plastics manufacturing. See Plastics and rubber products manufacturing.
Rubber products 1301
Rubella 190, 191
Rugs 188, 1001
Running/jogging 1247
Rural population. 30
Russell stock indices 1204
Russia. See Foreign countries.
Rwanda. See Foreign countries.

S

Sablefish 865
Safflower 813
Sailing 1247
Saint Kitts and Nevis. See Foreign countries.
Saint Lucia. See Foreign countries.
Saint Vincent and the Grenadines. See Foreign countries.
Salad and cooking oils, consumption 214
Salaries and wages. See Earnings.
Sales. See individual commodities and industries.
Salesworkers 615, 616, 625
Salmon 865
　Canned 867, 868
Salmonellosis 190
Salt (common), production/value 871, 1361
Samoa, American. See Island areas of the U.S.
Samoan population 23
Sand and gravel industry (see also Mining industry) 870, 871, 872
Sanitation. See Health and Sewage treatment.
San Marino. See Foreign countries.
Sao Tome and Principe. See Foreign countries.
Sardines 868
Saudi Arabia. See Foreign countries.
Sausages 727
Savings:
　Credit unions 1181
　Deposits 674, 1166
　Gross savings, sources and uses 669
　Personal 668, 669
Savings banks. See Savings institutions.
Savings bonds 486, 1167
Savings institutions:
　Earnings 1161
　Employees 1161
　Establishments 1161, 1174, 1173
　Finances ... 1162, 1164, 1173, 1176, 1182, 1192
　Individual Retirement Accounts 1218
　Mergers and acquisitions 759
Saw logs 857, 860
Scallops 865, 867
Scenic and sightseeing transportation industry:
　Earnings 631, 1056, 1057
　Employees 631, 1056, 1057
　Establishments 1057
Scholastic Assessment Test (SAT) 264
Schools (see also Education):
　Activities for parents 234
　Alternative 241, 245
　Boards, elected officials 417, 418
　Charter schools 239
　Crimes 232, 243
　Districts 240, 432
　Internet access 256, 258, 259

NOTE: Index citations refer to **table** numbers, not page numbers.

Table

Schools (see also Education): —Con.
    Lunch programs 538, 540, 568, 569
    Number 242, 262, 277, 279
    Special education 241
    Vocational 241
Scientific instruments. See Instruments.
Scientific research. See Research and development.
Scientists and engineers (see also individual fields):
    Degrees conferred 300, 301, 302, 792
    Employment . 615, 617, 786, 789, 790, 796
    By industrial sector 796
Scrap metal. See individual commodities.
Scuba diving 1247, 1253
Scup, catch 865
Sea bass 865
Seafoods 866
Sea trout 865
Securities:
    Foreign holdings .. 1163, 1203, 1280, 1283, 1376
    Foreign purchases and sales ... 1200, 1202, 1373, 1374, 1376
    Government . 450, 1163, 1195, 1202, 1203
    Held by life insurance 1223
    Holdings of banks 1174
    Holdings of individuals and businesses . 1166
    New issues 1195, 1199
    Prices, indexes, yields and issues . 1194, 1204, 1205, 1206, 1209, 1374
    Sales, stocks and bonds . 1195, 1200, 1202, 1206, 1373, 1374, 1376
    Savings of individuals 669, 674
    State and local government 431, 1195
Security and commodity brokers:
    Earnings 631, 742, 1161
    Employees 631, 742, 1161
    Establishments 742, 1161
    Finances 1162, 1220, 1221
    Gross domestic product 660, 1160
    Mergers and acquisitions 759
    Multinational companies 780, 781
    Occupational safety 652
    Profits 1221
    Receipts 742
Sedatives, persons using 201
Seeds 821
Selenium 877
Selenium, dietary 212
Semiconductors (see also Computer and electronic product components) 1011
Senators, U.S. 401, 405, 406, 407, 408
Senegal. See Foreign countries.
Septicemia 115
Serbia and Montenegro. See Foreign countries.
Service industries (see also specific sectors):
    Capital 766
    Earnings 631, 635, 636, 751, 1318
    Employees .. 160, 605, 619, 624, 630, 631, 635, 751, 774, 783, 1317, 1318
    Establishments 731, 1317, 1318
    Finances 1314
    Foreign trade 1280, 1282, 1294
    Gross domestic product 660, 664, 1314
    Industry 742, 1278
    Minority-owned businesses . 752, 753, 754, 755
    Multinational companies 780, 781

Table

Service industries (see also specific sectors): —Con.
    Occupational safety 649, 652, 654
    Productivity 632
    Profits 731, 776
    Sales or receipts 731, 751, 1318
    Women-owned businesses 751
Service occupations:
    Benefits 647
    Earnings 641, 642
    Employment 615, 617
        By sex and educational attainment .. 618
        Projections 617
        States 616
    Unemployment 625
    Union membership 657
Service stations. See Gasoline service stations.
Service workers. See Service industries and Service occupations.
Sewage treatment systems 439, 930
    Construction 439, 936
    Employment 468
    Expenditures 442
    Residences 959, 963
Sexual assault (see Rape and assault).
Seychelles. See Foreign countries.
Sheep and lambs 810, 813, 843, 844
Shellfish:
    Canned, quantity and value 868
    Catch, quantity and value 865
    Consumption 214
Shelter (see also Housing and housing units), consumer price indexes 713, 715
Shigellosis 190
Ship and boat building and repairing:
    Earnings 988
    Productivity 632
Shipments, manufacturers' (see also individual products or industries) ... 987, 988, 995, 996
Shipping. See Merchant vessels and Tonnage, U.S. Flag Fleet.
Ships, U.S. Flag fleet 1072
Shoes. See Footwear.
Shoe stores 631, 632, 1026, 1027
Shoplifting 318
Shopping centers 1047, 1048
Shortening 214
Shrimp 865, 867, 868
Sickness. See Illness.
Sierra Leone. See Foreign countries.
Silicon 872
Silk production 1321
Silver 871, 875, 877, 878
    Consumption 872
    Employment 872
    Foreign trade 872, 877
    Prices 872, 873
    Production and value 871, 875, 878
    Strategic and critical material 876
    World production 875
Silverware. See Jewelry.
Singapore. See Foreign countries.
Single persons. See Marital status.
Sinusitis 168
Skate boarding 1247
Skiing 1247, 1250, 1253
Skins. See Hides, etc.
Skilled nursing facilities, services 141, 180
Slaughtering and meat-packing industry. See Meat and meat products.
Slovakia. See Foreign countries.

NOTE: Index citations refer to **table** numbers, not page numbers.

Slovenia. See Foreign countries.
Small business:
  Budget outlays 475
  Employees 746, 747, 748, 749
  Firms 746, 747, 748, 749
  Loans 760
  Payroll 746, 747, 748, 749
Smart card 1186
Smoking 97, 201, 203, 204
Snapper 865
Snorkeling 1247
Snow and ice pellets, selected cities 394
Snowboarding 1247
Snowmobiles 1253
Soccer 1243, 1247, 1249, 1250
Social assistance industry:
  Earnings 573, 574, 631
  Employees 573, 574, 631
  Establishments 573, 574, 576
  Nonemployers 576
  Receipts 573, 574, 575, 576
Social insurance (see also Medicare,
    Retirement systems, and Social Security):
  Employment covered 541
  Expenditures 534, 535, 536
  Government insurance trust funds 443
    Federal receipts and expenditures .. 542
    State and local receipts,
      expenditures 442, 454, 547
  Government transfer payments ... 534, 535,
                                                                536
  Individual programs:
    Beneficiaries and benefits 543, 544
    Coverage 541, 547
    Federal retirement insurance . 546, 1219
      Civil service 546
    Old-age, survivors, disability, and
        health insurance:
      Contributions 542
      Coverage, workers, and earnings . 541
      Payments 535, 542, 543, 544
      Tax collections 489
      Trust funds 542
    Railroad insurance 535, 1219
    State and local public retirement
        systems 547
      Trust funds 1219
    Unemployment insurance (federal and
        state) 534, 535, 536, 555, 556
    Workers' compensation .. 128, 131, 535, 559,
                                                                560
Social sciences:
  Degrees conferred 300, 301, 302, 792
  Employment 615, 796
  Salary offers 297
Social Security (Old-age survivors, disability,
    and health insurance) (see also Social
    insurance):
  Beneficiaries and payments 543, 544
  Contributions, rates 542
    Foreign countries 1345
  Coverage, workers and earnings 541
  Families receiving 537
  Food stamp participants 571
  Outlays 476
  Payments 535, 543, 544
  Trust funds 542
Social services:
  Capital expenditures 767

Social services: —Con.
  Employees 573, 619
  Gross domestic product 660
  Occupational safety 652
Social welfare (see also individual programs):
  Charitable contributions 580
  Employees (State and local government) . 471
  Expenditures:
    City government 464
    County government 466
    State and local government 442
    State government 454, 456
  Volunteers 585
Sodium, dietary 212
Sodium carbonate 871, 872
Sodium sulfate 871, 872
Soft drinks (see also Beverages) 216
Softball 1247, 1249, 1250
Software publishing industry 1015
  Earnings 631, 1119, 1121
  Employees 631, 1119, 1121
  Establishments 1119, 1121
  Finances 1139
  Inventory 1139
  Productivity 632
  Revenue 1119, 1120, 1139
Software sales 1015
Solar energy 899, 921, 924
Solid waste:
  Abatement expenditures 382
  Disposal 375, 376, 445
  Industry 384
  Landfills 375
  Recycling 376, 377
Solomon Islands. See Foreign countries.
Somalia. See Foreign countries.
South Africa. See Foreign countries.
South Carolina. See State data.
South Dakota. See State data.
South Korea. See Foreign countries.
Soybeans:
  Acreage 834, 836
    Genetically modified seed plantings . 832
    Organic 810
  Farm marketings, sales 813, 819
  Foreign trade 828, 829, 834, 1301
  Pesticide usage 833
  Prices 834, 836
  Production 828, 834, 836
    World production 828, 1353
  Supply and disappearance 834
Space expenditures, private 797
Space program:
  Finances 798, 799, 801, 802
  Launches 800
  NASA 801
  Space shuttle 802, 803
  Vehicle systems 798, 1301
Space research and technology, Federal outlays .
                                          479, 798, 801, 802, 1022
Spain. See Foreign countries.
Speeding 1102
Spices, imports 823, 826
Spinach 841
Sporting and athletic goods (see also Sports
    and Retail trade) 1253, 1254, 1301
  Advertising 1275
  Consumer price indexes 715
  Retail stores 1027

NOTE: Index citations refer to **table** numbers, not page numbers.

1020   Index

U.S. Census Bureau, Statistical Abstract of the United States: 2003

Table

Sporting and athletic goods (see also Sports and Retail trade) —Con.
  Sales 444
Sporting goods, hobby, book, and music stores:
  Earnings 631, 1025, 1026
  Electronic commerce 1045
  Employees 631, 1025, 1026
  Establishments 1025, 1026, 1033
  Nonemployers 1033
  Purchases 1030
  Productivity 632
  Sales . 1026, 1027, 1029, 1031, 1033, 1045
Sports ... 1243, 1244, 1246, 1247, 1248, 1249, 1250
  Expenditures 1234, 1253
  NCAA 1250
  Volunteers 585
Sports associations 85
Sports industry 1230, 1231
Spot market price index 724
Squash (NCAA) 1250
Squid 865, 868
Sri Lanka. See Foreign countries.
Stamps, postage, receipts from 1118
Standard & Poor's stock indices 1204
State and local governments, combined data (see also individual governmental units):
  Component of gross domestic product . 440, 441
  Debt 442, 448, 449
    Highways 1083
  Employees 348, 467, 468, 471, 472
    Benefits 469
  Expenditures (see also Finances) .. 441, 442, 443, 444, 445, 448
    By type 443, 444
    Capital outlay 444, 445
    Construction, value 938
    Hospitals and medical care 131, 170, 448
  Federal aid 437, 438, 439, 477
    By function 438, 440, 441
  Finances 443
    Intergovernmental 438, 442, 446
  Flow of funds 1162, 1164
  Hospitals 170, 171
  Number of units 431
  Payrolls 467, 468
  Purchases of goods and services . 440, 441, 659, 661
  Receipts 441
    By source 443
  Retirement systems . 545, 547, 1162, 1198, 1219
  Securities issued 450
  Women holding public office 415
State Children's Health Insurance program . 148, 540
State data:
  Abortions 104
  Agriculture:
    Farms 809
    Income, farm 815, 816, 817
  AIDS 194
  Alcohol use 202
  Altitudes 363
  American Indian, Alaska Native population 21

Table

State data: —Con.
  Ancestry 55
  Apparel and accessory stores, sales ... 1032
  Area 359
  Asian population 21
  Assets and liabilities, farm 815
  Automotive dealers 1024, 1032
  Automobile insurance expenditures ... 1225
  Bankruptcies 757
  Births and birth rates 19
    Birth weight 94
    Births to single or unmarried women . 94
  Black elected officials 417
  Black population 21
  Blood alcohol concentration (BAC) 1103
  Building materials and garden supplies, sales 1032
  Building permits 941
  Cancer 207
  Capital punishment 355
  Child abuse cases 345
  Cigarette smoking 202, 204
  Civilian labor force 592
  Climate 390, 391, 392, 393, 394, 395
  Coal and coke production 889, 892
  Commuting to work 1090
  Computer use 1159
  Congress, U.S., composition 406
  Congressional apportionment 402
  Construction contracts 940
  Corrections 447, 471
  Crime rates 307
  Crops, principal 825, 831, 835, 842
  Deaths and death rates .. 19, 112, 114, 119
    Infant 114
  Defense contracts 513
  Department stores, sales 1032
  Disabled population 197
  Domestic travel expenditures 1259
  Drivers licenses 1088
  Drug use 202
  Earnings 639, 986, 1024
  Eating and drinking places, sales . 1024, 1032
  Elections . 398, 399, 401, 404, 406, 412, 413, 420, 422
    Voter registration 420
  Electrical power 916, 917
  Elevations 363
  Employees .. 471, 472, 499, 630, 749, 986, 1018, 1024
  Energy consumption 898
  Energy expenditures 901
  Energy, renewable 925
  Establishments 986, 1024
  Farms 809
    Assets and liabilities 815
    Income 815, 816, 817
  Federal funds 487
  Financial institutions 1179, 1180
  Fire protection 458, 471
  Food stamp program 569
  Food stores 1024, 1032
  Foreign born 48
  Foreign investment in the U.S. 1287
  Foreign trade 1298, 1299
  Foreign travel to 1262
  Foundations 582
  Fuel production 879

NOTE: Index citations refer to **table** numbers, not page numbers.

State data: —Con.	Table	State data: —Con.	Table
Furniture, home furnishing stores	1032	Police protection	456, 458, 471
Gas utility industry	928	Pollution abatement	382
Gasoline prices	730	Population	17, 18, 19, 20, 21, 25
Gasoline service stations	1032	Age distribution	20
Gasoline tax rates	1082	American Indian Alaska Native	21
General merchandise stores, sales	1032	Asian	21
Government finances:		Black	21
Federal aid to State and local governments	439	Components of change	19
Federal (income tax collections)	494	Density	18
State and local governments	380, 446, 447	Group quarters population	78
		Hispanic origin population	22
State governments	453, 454, 455, 456	Metropolitan areas	25
Tax collections	461	Native Hawaiian, Other Pacific Islander	21
Transfer payments	536	Poultry	852
Governors, vote cast	412	Poverty	673, 699
Gross State product	663, 664	Prescription drug expenditures	136
Group quarters population	78	President, vote cast	396, 398
Hazardous waste sites	380	Prisons and prisoners	325
Health care expenditures	136	Public aid	562
Health insurance coverage	148, 153	Public road and street mileage	1088
Health maintenance organizations (HMO)	151	Recreational areas	1256
Highway funds	1084	Representatives, U.S. vote cast for	403
Highway mileage	1076	Retail trade, sales	1024, 1032
Highway trust fund	1081	Roads and highways	1076, 1081, 1084
Hispanic elected officials	418	Rural population	30
Hispanic population	22	Sales	1024, 1032, 1048
Hospitals	136, 172, 447, 471	Schools and education:	
Households or families	68	Colleges, number	279
Housing	941, 943, 950, 956, 960, 964, 967, 970	Educational attainment	231
		Elementary/secondary teachers, public	250
Sold	950	Enrollment:	
Immigrants admitted	10	Elementary and secondary	241, 244
Income	682, 815	Higher education	279
Disposable personal	670, 672	Finances:	
Personal	670, 671	Elementary and secondary, public	255
Internet access	1159	High school graduates, public	269
Land	360	Higher education appropriations	290
Federal	507	Teachers	250
Language spoken at home	58	Senators, vote cast for	401
Legislatures, composition	413, 414	Services industry	1266
Livestock	847, 848	Shopping centers	1048
Local government units	432	Small businesses	749
Lotteries, revenue from	461	Social Security program	142, 544
Manufactures, summary statistics	991	Supplemental Security Income	562
Marriage and divorce	126	Taxation	455, 461, 494
Medicaid	147	Temperatures (highs and lows)	388
Medicare	142	Temporary assistance for needy families program	564, 565
Metropolitan area population	25		
Migration	18, 36	Toxic chemical releases	380
Milk production	848	Traffic fatalities	1098, 1103
Mining, mineral production value	874	Travel expenditures	1259, 1263
Motorcycles	1088	Unemployment	592, 628
Motor fuel tax	1082	Unemployment insurance	536, 556
Motor vehicle dealers	1024, 1032	Union membership	658
Motor vehicle manufacturing	1018	Urban population	30
Motor vehicle registrations	1088	Vehicle miles of travel	1088
National forests	855	Veterans, number and expenditures	529, 536
Native Hawaiian, Other Pacific Islander population	21		
		Voter registration	420
Newspapers, number and circulation	1132	Voter turnout	422
Nurses	163	Votes cast	398, 399, 401, 412, 422
Nursing home care expenditures	136	Voting age population	420, 422
Occupations	616	Water, sewage, and other services	930
Parks	1255, 1256	Women holding public office	415
Patents	764		
Physicians, physician services	136, 163		

NOTE: Index citations refer to **table** numbers, not page numbers.

	Table
State government (see also State and local governments):	
Debt 449, 454, 456	
Public highways 1083	
Employees and payrolls . 467, 468, 471, 472	
Finances . 441, 443, 445, 453, 454, 455, 456	
Revenue from lotteries 461, 462	
Tax collections 455, 461	
Highway funds, disbursements of 1084	
Park systems 1256	
Public confidence 416	
Receipts, highways 1080	
Taxes 455,	
State highways. See Highways.	
State park systems 1256	
Statehood, admission to 359	
Steak 727	
Steam engines and turbines, electric, locomotive (railroad) 1112	
Steel (see also Iron and steel) . 875, 1007, 1008	
Scrap 1007	
World production 875, 1321	
Steel works and rolling mills. See Iron and steel.	
Stimulants, persons using 201	
Stock exchanges:	
Prices 1204, 1209	
Volume of trading . 1206, 1207, 1208, 1209	
Stockholders' equity, profit rates on 1175	
Stockpiles, government, strategic and critical materials 876	
Stocks:	
Corporate, flow of funds 1162, 1198	
Foreign 1201, 1202	
Foreign market indices 1375	
Holdings by sector . 1163, 1167, 1198, 1201, 1203	
Life insurance 1198, 1223	
New issues 1199	
Ownership 1210, 1211, 1212	
Prices, yield, sales, issues, etc. . 1194, 1197, 1204, 1207, 1373, 1374, 1376	
Stone 871	
Stone, clay, and glass products 1113, 1114	
Stone, clay, and concrete products manufacturing. See Nonmetallic mineral product manufacturing.	
Stone (crushed) 872	
Stoves or ranges 1023	
Strategic and critical materials 876	
Strategic petroleum reserves 879	
Strawberries 813, 826, 841	
Strokes (see also Cerebrovascular diseases) . 115, 117, 119, 176	
Strontium, foreign trade 877	
Students. See Education, enrollment.	
Subways and urban railways 1108	
Sudan. See Foreign countries.	
Sugar and sugar cane (see also Food and kindred products):	
Beet 813, 819	
Consumption 214, 826	
Farm marketings 813	
Foreign trade 823, 825, 826, 1301	
Prices 727	
Production 821	
World 1321	
Suicides 115, 117, 118, 119	
Sulfur:	
Consumption 872	
Employment 872	

	Table
Sulfur: —Con.	
Foreign trade 872, 877	
Prices 872, 873	
Production and value 871, 875	
World production 1361	
Sunflowers 810, 813	
Supermarkets. See Grocery stores.	
Supplemental Security Income .. 535, 537, 540, 561, 562, 571	
States 562	
Supreme Court, U.S. 337	
Surgeons (See also Physicians) 166	
Surgical procedures 178	
Organ transplants, facilities 177	
Suriname. See Foreign countries.	
Swaziland. See Foreign countries.	
Sweden. See Foreign countries.	
Sweet potatoes 215, 841	
Swimming 1247, 1249, 1250	
Swine. See Hogs.	
Switzerland. See Foreign countries.	
Swordfish, imports 865	
Symphony orchestras 1235	
Synagogues. See Religion.	
Syphilis 190, 194	
Syria. See Foreign countries.	

T

Taiwan. See Foreign countries.	
Tajikistan. See Foreign countries.	
Talc, pyrophyllite, and soapstone 871	
Tangerines 842	
Tantalum 877	
Tanzania. See Foreign countries.	
Target shooting 1247	
Tariff. See Customs receipts.	
Taxes:	
Corporate 732, 739, 775	
Deductions 490, 492, 579	
Partnerships 735	
Proprietorships 734	
Tax burden, expenditures, revenue loss estimates 482, 1374	
Tax receipts:	
Foreign countries 1342, 1343	
Governmental revenue, by type of tax .. 443	
Motor-fuel taxes and motor-vehicle fees . 1082	
National (internal revenue) 443, 489	
Adjusted gross income 491	
By type of tax 443	
Collections by source 489	
Corporation income tax:	
Federal budget receipts 481	
Internal revenue collections . 488, 489	
Tax liabilities 739	
Tax returns filed 488, 739	
Employment taxes 481, 488, 489	
Estate and gift taxes 481, 488, 489	
Excise taxes 481, 488, 489	
Individual income tax 443, 455, 481, 488, 489, 490, 491, 492, 493, 494	
Average tax by income level 491	
Rates 495, 496	
Property tax:	
City government 463	
Rates, selected cities 460	
State and local government 442, 443	
State and local government:	
By households 459	
By type of tax 442, 443, 454	

NOTE: Index citations refer to **table** numbers, not page numbers.

	Table
Tax receipts: —Con.	
City government	460, 463
County government	465
State government	454, 455, 456
Local government	457
Tea	216
Teachers:	
Catholic schools	262
Degrees conferred	300, 301, 302
Employment	240, 248, 277, 295, 296, 615
Projections	219, 617
Private schools	262, 263
Public schools	219, 240, 250
Experience, and degrees held	249, 263
Higher education institutions	277, 294
Number	219, 240, 248, 249, 250
Salaries	240, 250
States	250
Technicians	615, 616
Teenagers:	
Abortions	103
AIDS	192
Alcohol use	201
Births/birth rates	85, 86, 89, 91, 92, 94, 98
Child abuse	344
Cigarette smoking	201
Computer use	256, 260, 289, 622
Cost of raising	675
Crimes, arrests	232, 233, 322, 326
Homicide rates	305, 306, 307, 313
Deaths and death rates	117
Disabled	285
Distance education	286
Drug use	201
Education:	
College costs	287
College freshmen, characteristics	284
Enrollment	217, 219, 221, 222, 223, 224, 240, 244, 246, 247, 262, 275, 276, 282
Projections	217, 219
High school dropouts	270, 271
High school graduates	240, 269, 275
School crimes	232, 233
Test scores	264, 265, 266, 267
Health insurance coverage	152
Hispanic origin population	16
Job search	622
Juvenile delinquency	342, 343
Labor force	588
Employed	600, 601, 606, 607, 608, 610
Enrollment status	594, 1348
Minimum wage workers	645
Multiple job holders	608
Participation rates	595
Sex	588, 590
Unemployed	621, 627
Life expectancy	107
Marital status	63
Mobility status	34
Music purchases	1142
Population	11
Foreign born	54
Hispanic origin	16, 46
Projections	12
Race	13, 16
Sports activity participation	1247, 1248, 1249

	Table
Teenagers: —Con.	
Sporting goods purchasers	1254
Suicides	117
Victimization	322
Telecommunications	1016, 1148, 1275, 1301, 1371
Telecommunications indicators (Global)	1371
Telecommunications industry:	
Earnings	631, 1119, 1121
Employees	631, 1119, 1121
Establishments	1119, 1121
Finances	1119, 1120, 1146, 1147, 1148
Productivity	632
Telegraph and other communications	1148, 1149
Telephone carriers	1148
Cellular	1150, 1372
Telephone communication:	
Earnings	631, 1148, 1149
Employees	631, 1149, 1150
Finances	1149, 1150
Price indexes	715
Productivity	632
Receipts	1149
Telephones (see also Telegraph, etc.):	
Access lines	1149, 1371
Calls	1149, 1371
Consumer price index	713
Consumer expenditures	678, 679
Households with service	963, 1126, 1159
Number	1149
Foreign countries	1372
Sales or shipments	1015, 1016
Television broadcasting (see also Cable and other pay TV services):	
Advertising expenditures	1274
Mergers and acquisitions	759
Public confidence in media	416
Television broadcasting industry:	
Earnings	631, 1119, 1121, 1123
Employees	631, 1119, 1121, 1123
Finances	1119, 1120, 1121, 1124, 1143, 1145
Gross domestic product	660, 1122
Productivity	632
Televisions:	
Consumer expenditures	1233, 1234
Households with	1126
Injuries associated	188
Sales or shipments	1015
Viewing	1125, 1127
Temperature:	
Cities	390, 391, 392, 395
Foreign cities	1328
States (highs and lows)	388
Temporary assistance for needy families program	535, 537, 540, 563, 564, 565, 567, 571
Tennessee. See State data.	
Tennis	1243, 1246, 1247, 1249, 1250, 1253
Tenure. See Housing and housing units and Farms.	
Tetanus	190
Texas. See State data.	
Textile mills and product manufacturing:	
Capital	382, 766
Earnings	631, 985, 987, 992
Electronic commerce	987, 989
Employees	631, 985, 987, 992
Energy consumption	906

NOTE: Index citations refer to **table** numbers, not page numbers.

Table	Table
Textile mills and product manufacturing: —Con.	Tobacco manufacturing (see also Beverage and tobacco product manufacturing): —Con.
Establishments 985	Price indexes 715
Finances 778	Shipments 994, 995
Foreign trade 1304	Toxic chemical releases 379
Gross domestic product 660, 984	Togo. See Foreign countries.
Industrial production index 772	Tokyo Nikkei 225 stock market index 1375
Inventories 995	Tomatoes 215, 727, 813, 826, 841
Mergers and acquisitions 759	Tonga. See Foreign countries.
Occupational safety 652	Tonnage, U.S. Flag fleet 1072
Patents 763	Tools. See Machine tools.
Pollution abatement 382	Tornadoes 386
Productivity 632	Tourism, foreign (see also Travel) .. 1260, 1261,
Profits 778	1262, 1264
Shipments 987, 989, 994, 995	Townships and special districts 431, 432
Toxic chemical releases 379	Toxic material shipment 1078
Textile mill products:	Toxic-shock syndrome 190
End-use 1001	Toys and sporting goods:
Foreign trade 1002, 1301, 1304	Consumer expenditures 1234
Production 1002	Foreign trade 1301
World 1321	Price indexes 715
Thai population 23	Sales 1037
Thailand. See Foreign countries.	Track 1249, 1250
Theaters:	Trade (business). See Commerce, Foreign trade, Retail trade, and Wholesale trade.
Attendance and receipts 1235, 1244	Trade, transportation and utilities:
Federal aid 1236	Earnings 629, 631, 636
Personal expenditures 1133	Employees 629, 630, 631
Theft. See Crime and criminals.	Hours 629
Theology, degrees conferred 303	Traffic fatalities 1058, 1097, 1098, 1099,
Thread. See Yarn, thread, etc.	1100, 1102, 1103, 1104
Thrift Savings Plan 545	Tranquilizers 201
Timber (see also Lumber and wood products):	Transit and ground transportation industry.
Consumption 857	See Passenger transit industry and subways.
Foreign trade 857, 858	Earnings 631, 1056, 1057
Producer prices 860, 861	Employees 631, 1056, 1057
Production 857	Establishments 1057
World (roundwood) 1321	Transportation (see also Motor vehicles, and individual modes):
Roundwood products 857	Accidents 1058, 1063, 1065
Tin:	Carriers of passengers .. 1054, 1059, 1108,
Foreign trade 877	1109, 1112
Prices 873	Carriers of property 1054, 1113, 1114
Production 875	Commodity flow 1077
World 1361	Commuting to work 1090, 1091, 1092
Strategic and critical materials 876	Construction, value 937, 938
Tires and tubes 1301	Consumer complaints 1067
Titanium:	Consumer expenditures . 676, 677, 678, 679
Production 871, 875, 885	Consumer price indexes 713, 715
Strategic and critical material 876	Motor fuel 715
World production 875	New cars, and new trucks 715
Tobacco (see also Tobacco products, manufacturing, and Cigarettes):	Cost indexes 1098
Consumer expenditures ... 676, 678, 679	Airlines 1060
Consumption and use . 201, 203, 204, 1000	Railroad 1115
During pregnancy 97	Energy consumption 897, 898, 900, 901
Farm marketings, sales 813	Expenditures 667, 1053
Foreign countries 1359	Federal government:
Foreign trade 823, 828, 1301, 1359	Aid to State and local governments . 438
Prices 715, 818	Outlays 476, 479, 787
Production 821, 1321, 1359	Foreign countries 1370
Taxes 454, 489	Freight 1053
Tobacco manufacturing (see also Beverage and tobacco product manufacturing):	Government employees and payrolls ... 468
Capital 766	Government finances .. 442, 443, 445, 455,
Earnings 992	456, 479, 1055
Employees 992	Metropolitan areas 1062, 1091
Energy consumption 906	Occupations 615, 625, 641, 642, 1059
Foreign trade 1304	Outlays, by type of transport 1053
Gross domestic product 660	Port traffic 1074
Inventories 995	Securities 1204
Occupational safety 652	

NOTE: Index citations refer to **table** numbers, not page numbers.

Index 1025

Transportation (see also Motor vehicles, and individual modes): —Con.	
Stock and bond prices and yields	1204
Travel trends	1093
Travel volume	1054, 1059, 1068
Transportation and warehousing:	
Capital	382, 766, 769
Earnings	631, 636, 742, 745, 746, 1056, 1057
Employees	605, 631, 742, 745, 746, 1056, 1057
Establishments	742, 743, 745, 1057
Finances	733, 736
Multinational companies	780, 781
Nonemployers	743
Occupational safety	652
Pollution abatement	382
Productivity	632
Revenue	1110
Sales, receipts	733, 736, 740, 741, 742, 743
Transportation equipment manufacturing (see also Motor vehicle and Aerospace):	
Capital	766
Earnings	631, 985, 987, 992
Electronic commerce	989
Employees	631, 985, 987, 992
Energy consumption	906
Establishments	985
Finances	778
Foreign trade	1295, 1304
Inventories	995
Mergers and acquisitions	759
Multinational companies	780, 781
Occupational safety	651, 652
Producer prices	720, 721
Productivity	632
Profits	778
Research and development	793, 794
Shipments	987, 989, 994, 995
Toxic chemical releases	379
Transportation, communications, and public utilities industry (see also Energy and utilities, Information, and Transportation and warehousing):	
Capital	766, 767
Construction	936
Cost indexes	934
Earnings	635, 751
Employees	619, 751
Gross domestic product	660, 664
Mergers and acquisitions	759
Minority-owned businesses	752, 753, 754, 755
Multinational companies	781
Occupational safety	649, 652, 654
Profits	731, 776
Union membership	657
Women-owned businesses	751
Transportation support services industry	1056, 1057
Travel:	
Accidents	1058
Air carriers	1063, 1065
Business, pleasure travelers	1257, 1258
Domestic expenditures by state	1259
Foreign	1260, 1261, 1262
Highway mileage	1075, 1076
Household trips	1257, 1258
International expenditures	1260

Travel: —Con.	
States	1263
Passengers	1059, 1068, 1260, 1261
Person trips	1093, 1094, 1256, 1257
Recreation	1257, 1258
Services	1294
Tourists	1260, 1261, 1262, 1380
Urban	1094
Volume	1054, 1059, 1068, 1321
Travel accommodations industry	631, 632
Travel arrangement industry	631
Travel in the United States	1093
Travelers checks	1187, 1192
Treasury bonds:	
Foreign purchases and sales, holdings	1202, 1203
Sales, prices, and yields	1194, 1195
Trichinosis	190
Trinidad and Tobago. See Foreign countries.	
Tripoli	871
Trips. See Travel.	
Truck and tractor pull	1243
Truck transportation industry:	
Earnings	631, 1056, 1057
Employees	631, 1056, 1057
Establishments	1057
Commodities handled	1111
Finances	1111
Productivity	632
Trucks:	
Factory sales (trucks and buses)	1035
Foreign countries	1370
Imports	1035
Motor-fuel consumption	1096
Registration (trucks and buses)	1088
Tuberculosis	190, 194
Deaths	115
Hospitals	170
Tuition	292
Consumer price indexes	715
Tuna	865, 868
Catch	865
Prices	727
Supply	867
Tungsten:	
Foreign trade	877
Production and value	871
Strategic and critical material	876
World production	875
Tunisia. See Foreign countries.	
Turbines. See Steam engines.	
Turkey. See Foreign countries.	
Turkeys	727, 810, 813, 843, 852
Turkmenistan. See Foreign countries.	
Turks and Caicos Islands. See Foreign countries.	
Tuvalu. See Foreign countries.	
Typhoid fever	190
Typhus fever	190
U	
Uganda. See Foreign countries.	
Ukraine. See Foreign countries.	
Ulcer of stomach and duodenum, deaths	115
Ultrasound, diagnostic	178
Unemployment. See Labor force, unemployed workers.	
Unemployment insurance:	
Beneficiaries	537, 555, 556
Coverage, workers and earnings	556
Governmental finances	442, 454, 481

NOTE: Index citations refer to **table** numbers, not page numbers.

Table	Table
Unemployment insurance: —Con.	Venereal diseases (see also AIDS) 190
Payments 534, 535, 536, 555, 556	Venezuela. See Foreign countries.
Union membership 656, 657, 658	Venture capital 761
Employee benefits 648	Vermiculite 871
United Arab Emirates. See Foreign countries.	Vermont. See State data.
United Kingdom. See Foreign countries.	Vessels. See Ships.
United States securities (see also Debt):	Veterans Affairs, Dept. of:
Foreign purchases and sales, holdings . 1202, 1203	Budget outlays 476
Held by banks 1174	Expenditures . 128, 532, 533, 534, 535, 536
Holdings by households 1166	Hospital, medical care 128
Prices, sales, and yields 1194	Home loans 1182, 1184
Taxable yields 1193	Land and buildings 507
Universities. See Education, higher education institutions.	Veterans:
Unmarried-partner households 69	Number 529, 530
Uranium (see also Nuclear power) 871, 892, 907, 920	Pensions and other benefits:
	Disability, service-connected compensation 531
Urban population 30	Disbursements 509, 533, 535
Uruguay. See Foreign countries.	Federal aid to state and local governments 438
Utah. See State data.	Health expenditures 128, 131
Utilities (formally Electric, gas, and sanitary services). See also Gas utility industry and Electric light power industry:	Veterans or dependents receiving .. 531, 533, 537
Capital 769	Vetoed bills, Congressional 410
Earnings 631, 636, 742, 745, 746, 894	VCR's 1015, 1126
Electric supply systems and generating plants, states 917	Video games 1037, 1041, 1125
	Vietnam. See Foreign countries.
Employees 631, 742, 745, 746, 894	Vietnamese population 23, 750
Establishments 742, 743, 745, 894	Violent crime. See Crime.
Finances 733, 736, 1194, 1204	Virgin Islands. See Island areas of the U.S.
Gross domestic product 660	Virginia. See State data.
Industrial production index 772	Visual arts 1240
Industry 742, 893, 894	Visual impairment 185
Mergers and acquisitions 759	Vital statistics (see also Births and Deaths):
Multinational companies 780, 781	Fertility and fertility rate 88
Nonemployers 743	Foreign countries 1326
Occupational safety 652	Island areas 1306
Productivity 632	Life expectancy 105, 106, 107
Sales, shipments, receipts ... 733, 736, 740, 741, 742, 743	Marriage and divorce 83, 126
	Rates, summary 83
Urban transit systems industry 1057	World 1326
Uzbekistan. See Foreign countries.	Vitamins 212
	Vocational education 438
V	Vocational rehabilitation 558
	Medical payments 128
Vacancy rates:	Service industry 573, 574, 575
Housing 953, 955, 956, 957	Volleyball 1243, 1247, 1249, 1250
Office buildings 981, 983	Volunteer workers 585, 1239
Value added (see also individual manufacturing and mining industries):	Voter registration 419, 420
States 991	Voter turnout 419, 420, 422
Vanadium 871, 875, 877	Votes:
Vanuatu. See Foreign countries.	Congressional 401, 403, 404, 422
Veal (see also Beef and Meat and meat products) 214, 843, 1356	Gubernatorial 412
	Presidential .. 396, 397, 398, 399, 400, 422
Vegetable oils. See Oils.	Voting-age population 419, 420, 422
Vegetables (see also individual commodities):	
Acreage 841	**W**
Calcium source 213	
Consumer expenditures 678, 679	Wage earners. See Labor force, employment, and earnings, and individual industries.
Consumption 215, 826, 839	Wages and wage rates. See Earnings.
Farm marketings, sales 813, 819	Wallis and Futuna. See Foreign countries.
Foreign trade . 823, 825, 826, 827, 829, 839, 1301	Walnuts 813, 842
	Warehouses (see Trucking and warehousing) 982
Gardens 1241	Warehousing and storage industry:
Iron (dietary) source 213	Earnings 631, 1056, 1057
Pesticide usage 833	Employees 631, 1056, 1057
Prices 715, 720, 818	Establishments 1057
Production 821, 839, 841, 1353	Revenue 1110
Vehicles. See Motor vehicles, Tractors, etc.	Wars, U.S. troops and casualties 523

NOTE: Index citations refer to **table** numbers, not page numbers.

Index 1027

U.S. Census Bureau, Statistical Abstract of the United States: 2003

Washing machines, homes with 977
Washington. See State data.
Wastepaper 860
Wastewater treatment 894, 930
Watches. See Clocks and watches, etc.
Water (see also Water transportation industry
    and wastewater treatment):
    Area 1, 359
    Consumption 367, 368
    Freight 1054, 1070, 1071
    Pollution:
        Abatement expenditures 382
        Oil spills 370
        Rivers and streams 370
        Toxic releases 378
    Power 368, 914, 925
    Public supply . 367, 368, 894, 929, 959, 963
Water heater 1023
Watermelons 841
Water polo 1250
Water skiing 1247
Water transportation industry:
    Earnings 631, 1057
    Employees 631, 1056, 1057
    Establishments 1057
    Foreign trade 1071
    Freight 1053, 1054, 1070, 1071
    Occupational safety 652, 1058
    Outlays 479
    Revenue ....
Water utility 893, 894, 929
Water, sewage and other systems 631, 930
Waterways 1070
Wealth:
    Business 711
    Families 708, 709
    Government 711
    Households 711
Weather 387, 390, 391, 392, 393, 394, 395
    Foreign countries 1328
Welfare services. See Social welfare; Public
    aid, assistance; and individual programs.
West Bank. See Foreign countries.
West Virginia. See State data.
Western Sahara. See Foreign countries.
Western Samoa. See Foreign countries.
Wetlands 364
Wheat:
    Acreage 834, 837
        Organic 810
    Farm marketings, sales 813
    Farm prices 834, 837
    Foreign trade 823, 826, 828, 829, 834,
                                        1301, 1358
    Pesticide usage 833
    Production 828, 834, 837
        World production 1353
    Supply and disappearance 834
Wheat flour 214, 1321
Wheelchair usage 185
White-collar workers:
    Earnings 638
    Employment cost index 643
    State and local government workers 469
Whiting, quantity and value of catch 865
Wholesale trade:
    Capital expenditures 767, 769
    Companies exporting 1303
    Earnings 631, 635, 636, 742, 745, 746,
                                        751, 1318

Wholesale trade: —Con.
    Employees .. 605, 619, 631, 742, 745, 746,
                                        751, 1317, 1318
    Establishments . 742, 743, 745, 1317, 1318
    Finances 733, 736, 778
    Foreign investments in U.S. 1286
    Gross domestic product 660, 664
    Industry 742, 1050
    Inventories 1049
    Mergers and acquisitions 759
    Minority-owned businesses . 752, 753, 754,
                                                755
    Multinational companies 780, 781
    Nonemployers 743
    Occupational safety 652
    Productivity 632
    Profits 731, 778
    Sales, receipts . 731, 733, 736, 740, 741, 742,
                            743, 751, 1041, 1049, 1318
    Women-owned businesses 751
Whooping cough 190
Wildlife:
    Endangered species 385
    Related recreation activities 1251, 1252
Wilshire equity index 1204
Wind:
    Energy source 899
    Selected cities 395
    Solar energy 899
    Velocity 899
Wind surfing 1247
Wines (see also Alcoholic beverages) . 216, 825,
                                        826, 1321
Wiretaps 331
Wisconsin. See State data.
Women:
    Abortions 102, 103, 104
    Activity limitation 195, 196
    Adult education 304
    Advanced placement exams 267
    Age 11, 12
    AIDS 192, 193
    Births and birth rates . 83, 84, 85, 90, 92, 95,
                            96, 99, 100, 1026
        Births to single women ... 91, 92, 94, 99
        Cesarean section deliveries 96, 178
        Characteristics, selected 85, 99, 100
        First births 99
    Business owners 750, 751, 766
    Cancer 206
    Child day care 577
    Child support 566
    Cigarette smoking 97, 203, 204
    Community service (students) 586
    Computer use 634, 1127, 1156
    Contraceptive use 101
    Correctional institutions 77
    Criminal victimization .. 232, 233, 316, 322
    Deaths and death rates . 108, 117, 120, 193
    Delivery procedures, births 96, 178
    Education:
        Adult education 304, 1332
        American College Testing program .. 265
        Attainment 227, 229, 272, 273, 275
            Labor force status 273
        College costs 287
        College dormitories 77

NOTE: Index citations refer to **table** numbers, not page numbers.

	Table

Women: —Con.
    College enrollment . 219, 224, 275, 276, 277, 278, 791
        By age 276
        By State 279
        Disabled 285
        Distance education 286
    Degrees conferred .. 298, 300, 301, 302, 303, 792
    Enrollment by level 224, 247, 282
    High school dropouts 270, 272, 273
    Teachers 249, 263, 295, 615
    SAT tests 264
Elections, voter registration and turnout . 419
Farmworkers 822
Fertility, fertility rate 88, 89
Food stamp participants 571
Group quarters population 77
Gynecological services 168, 178
Health insurance coverage 152, 154
Height distribution 208
Hispanic origin population 13
Home health and hospice care 182
Homicides 313
Hospital use ... 77, 168, 169, 174, 176, 178
Householders 65, 66, 67, 71, 72, 74, 75
Illness/injury 187
Income 693, 694, 695
Injuries 187
Internet access 622, 1127, 1156
Job search 622
Juvenile institutions 77
Labor force and employment:
    Age 588, 590
    Computer use 634
    Displaced workers 612
    Earnings 641, 642
    Educational attainment .. 591, 609, 618, 626
    Employed . 589, 592, 594, 597, 601, 603, 605, 606, 607, 608, 610, 615, 618, 619
    Foreign countries 1348, 1350, 1351
    Industry 619
    Marital status 595, 596, 597, 598
    Occupation 615, 613, 641, 642
    Participation rates .. 588, 589, 591, 592, 595, 596, 597, 598
    Persons working at home 605
    Projections 588
    Reason not in 614
    School enrollment 594
    Self-employed 604
    States 592
    Tenure with employer 610
    Unemployed .. 589, 592, 594, 597, 621, 623, 624, 625, 626, 627
    Union membership 657
Life expectancy 105, 106, 107
Mammography 205
Marital status 61, 62, 63
Marriage and divorce 126
Military quarters 77
Music purchases 1142
Nursing home residents 77, 185
Overweight 209
Pension plan coverage 551
Persons living alone (one-person households) 76

	Table

Women: —Con.
    Physical activity 210
    Physicians 162
        Visits to 165, 167, 168
    Pilots 1069
    Population 11
    Property owners 963
    Rape 305, 306, 307, 308, 314, 325
    Recreational activities ... 1237, 1239, 1240, 1247, 1254
    Social Security beneficiaries and payments 543
    Sports participation in school .. 1248, 1249, 1250
    Surgical procedures 178
    Travel 1094
    Unemployment ... 589, 592, 594, 597, 621, 623, 624, 625, 626, 627
        Age 621
        Reason 623, 627
    Union membership 657
    Unmarried-partner households 69
    Volunteers 585
    Voter registration and turnout 419
Wood and wood products. See Lumber and wood products.
Wood products manufacturing:
    Capital 766
    Earnings 631, 985, 987, 992, 1287
    Electronic commerce 989
    Employees 631, 985, 987, 992, 1287
    Energy consumption 906
    Establishments 985, 1287
    Finances 778
    Foreign trade 1304
    Gross domestic product 660, 854, 984
    Industrial production index 772
    Mergers and acquisitions 759
    Occupational safety 651, 652
    Prices 860
    Profits 778
    Productivity 632
    Railroad car loadings 1113, 1114
    Renewable energy 925
    Shipments 987, 989
    Toxic chemical releases 379
Woodpulp (see also Paper and paper products):
    Consumption/output 1321
    Foreign trade 858
    Producer price indexes 860
    Production 1321
Wool production 1321
Work stoppages 655
Workplace violence 649, 653, 654
Workers. See Employment and labor force.
Workers' compensation program . 128, 159, 535, 537, 559, 560
Workstations. See Computer.
World summary statistics 889, 1321
    Comparative data (area, population, etc.) 1322, 1323
    Energy 1362, 1363
    Farm commodities 828, 1353, 1357
    Mineral production 886, 889
    Population .. 1319, 1320, 1321, 1322, 1323
    Telecommunication service sector 1371
Wrestling 1243, 1249, 1250
Wyoming. See State data.

NOTE: Index citations refer to **table** numbers, not page numbers.

Table

Y

Yemen. See Foreign countries.
Yogurt consumption/production 214, 849
Youth employment programs 540
Yugoslavia. See Foreign countries.

Z

Zambia. See Foreign countries.
Zimbabwe. See Foreign countries.

Table

Zinc 1301
   Foreign trade 877, 1301
   Mining industry 870
   Prices 873
   Production and value (mine and
     smelter) 871, 875
     World 875, 1361
   Strategic and critical materials 876

NOTE: Index citations refer to **table** numbers, not page numbers.